The Bill James Handbook 2021

Baseball Info Solutions

www.baseballinfosolutions.com

Published by ACTA Sports

A Division of ACTA Publications

Front Cover Photo by Jerome Miron, USA TODAY Sports
Back Cover Photo by USA TODAY Sports

First Edition: November 2020

Published by:
ACTA Sports, a division of ACTA Publications
4848 North Clark Street
Chicago, IL 60640
(800) 397-2282
www.actasports.com www.actapublications.com

ISBN: 978-0-87946-691-6
ISSN: 1940-8668

Printed in the United States of America by McNaughton & Gunn

Dedication

This book is dedicated to all of those deemed an "essential worker" during the pandemic. I have witnessed ordinary people perform extraordinary actions over these past months. Thank you for your personal sacrifices.

In addition, on a personal level, to my wife Debbie, my sister Suzy and to my mother, for always being so supportive of my career that I have been able to achieve my dreams. I am a lucky man to have such a wonderful family.

And finally, to all of the staff at Sports Info Solutions that works tirelessly across a multitude of responsibilities to bring you this annual book, it is such an honor to work with each of you.

Rob Dougherty

Table of Contents

Introduction

It was a rare rainy stretch in Phoenix this past March. Was this a harbinger of things to come? For baseball fans, it was a typical spring. It involved driving to various spring training complexes, watching games in the stands, and eating out at restaurants where the concept of wearing a mask had yet to be considered.

Then things changed.

On March 12, Major League Baseball cancelled the remaining Spring Training games and delayed the start of the regular season for *at least* two weeks. By March 16, it was delayed indefinitely. The Covid-19 pandemic storm cast its shadow on baseball.

It was impossible not to wonder what would unfold…would there be a season and what would it look like? Conversations with the publisher in late spring and early summer focused upon what would fill the many pages of the *2021 Bill James Handbook* if there was no 2020 MLB season. For example, one potential idea was to have 30 accomplished baseball writers each pick one team and write about the season that never was, culminating in a World Series victory for that team. Hopefully, we never need to use that as a fallback for actual live baseball.

As many adjusted to the remote-work shift in business, communication often involved sincere exchanges of concern for each other, their family and their co-workers. At Sports Info Solutions, our regular company-wide meetings always started with our top priority: *Protect the health of our employees and their families*.

We saw the NCAA season stop without a College World Series, along with the cancellation of the Little League World Series. We experienced a complete cancellation of the Minor League Baseball season. We watched international baseball from Korea and Japan to fill that gaping hole in our summer sports programming schedule.

Finally, in July, the MLB shortened season began. A 60-game sprint without fans in the seats and with several rule changes. The three-batter minimum for pitchers had already been approved earlier in the offseason although changes to restrictions on position players pitching had been delayed. New temporary rules included: the universal designated hitter; a runner placed on second base to begin extra innings; weather-affected games were suspended and continued on a future date; unsportsmanlike conduct for failure to adhere to social distancing guidelines; and pitchers were allowed to carry a small wet rag in their back pocket.

Plus, an expansion of the postseason eligible teams to 16, which created a best-of-three wild card round for fans that provided live playoff baseball for several days from lunch until after midnight on the east coast.

Except for the postseason, the following pages will provide you with an analysis of how this unique 2020 season played out. The register section is smaller with the absence of a minor league season, but that gave us the opportunity to add in some players that may have not made it into the *Handbook* under typical statistical years.

Our batter and pitcher projections in last year's book were generated long before a shortened season could have been envisioned, and Bill James discusses the difference between predictions and projections along with his new 2021 projections.

Bill's Hall of Fame Monitor provides insight into the impact of the shortened season on current players' chances to reach the Hall. Has this past season caused your favorite current player more harm or less harm to their Hall consideration than you anticipated?

Also, in this year's *Handbook*, you'll discover what percentage of major league teams from 1900 thru 2014 had a Hall of Famer on their roster, and we also have Bill's reevaluation of the Career Target system.

Most importantly, we were able to produce this annual book through the storm of 2020. Getting the chance to watch Autumn baseball, and hopefully a World Series, seemed more like wishful thinking five months ago than reality. Now it is time for the sun to come out and shine on America's pastime.

Rob Dougherty
October 5, 2020
Coplay, PA

Single Game Batter Game Scores

Bill James

Many years ago I invented something called a Pitcher Game Score. It's just a fun thing, as opposed to a serious analytical tool, although it does have some analytical uses, but basically, it's just something that is fun to have. It's been a fairly popular stat. ESPN carries Game Scores in their Box Scores, so a lot of people know them.

For decades, I have wanted to have a system of Game Scores for hitters. Sometime in the last year, I finally made it work. There were two keys to making it work. One was that I had to invent a way to estimate a batter's Runs Created in one game. The other was that I had to abandon some of the organizing concepts of the Pitcher's Game Score, keeping others, because in some ways what I was doing with pitchers just absolutely doesn't work with hitters. I was slow to accept that I had to give up some of the parameters.

A hitter's Game Score is like a pitcher's Game Score in these ways: that it operates on a 0-to-100 scale, that an occasional game escapes the 0-to-100 confines, but not very often (less than one-tenth of one percent), and that a high score represents a great game for a hitter and a low score a terrible game. But it is UNLIKE the pitcher's Game Score in that (a) it is not actually an integer, although I will often state it as an integer, (b) that it is not centered at 50, but rather at 25, and (c) that it draws from everything the batter does in the game, rather than simply the Box Score line summary. On point c, if two pitchers have a Box Score Line of 9 6 2 2 4 11 (9 innings, 6 hits, 2 runs, 2 earned runs, 4 walks, 11 strikeouts). . .if two pitchers both have that Game Line, they will both score at 74, even if one of them gave up two solo homers but got three ground ball double plays while the other one gave up six singles and threw a Wild Pitch. Nothing contributes to the pitcher's Game Score except what is in the Box Score Line.

But that's not workable for a hitter. A pitcher in a game like that probably faced between 35 and 40 hitters. A batter in a game typically bats 4 times—3 to 5, but most often 4. It's a totally different thing. Pitchers' games can be centered around 50 and represented by a Normal Distribution Curve because there are enough "trials" involved for things to have found a resting point. Batters' games are not like that. In four at bats, the most common thing is one hit. But if one hit was 50, because 50 is average, what would a 4-hit game be, or a 5-hit game, or a 4-homer game? The 4-hit game would have to be 200, maybe; the 4-homer game would have to score like the National Debt.

Here is a point which is, when it has been pointed out to you, seems obvious—but which I had somehow failed to notice in 60 years as a fanatic baseball fan. A hitter—even a great hitter—contributes most of his value to his team in a very limited number of games. An MVP does not make meaningful contributions to victory (with his bat) in 100 games a year, or anything like that number. An MVP usually creates over half of the runs that he creates in the season in about 25 games.

Here is one way to look at it, which may be misleading, but at least what I am telling you is true. Take any great season that you can find, and sort out the best games of the season. Remember the year that Mark McGwire hit 70 Home Runs? He created about 169 runs that year, which is a HUGE number—about 40 to 60 more than your typical MVP.

But he created MOST of those runs—most, meaning over half—in just 27 games. In his best 27 games of the season, McGwire hit .660 with 38 homers and a slugging percentage of 1.967. He created about 86 runs in those 27 games. The rest of the season, he hit .217.

OK, it's a little misleading, because McGwire created 83 runs in the rest of his games, and that's still a lot of runs. He had many quite good games outside of his best 27. Let's give him 50 games, rather than 27. In his best 50 games of the 1998 season, McGwire hit .549 with 59 homers, 103 RBI. But he played 155 games that year. In the other 105 games, he hit .168 with 11 homers, 11 doubles and no triples.

In 2/3 of his games, McGwire was a useless player, well below replacement level—and he was having one of the greatest seasons in major league history. Is this because he was a Home Run hitter, useless when he didn't hit a Home Run?

Let's look at the other side. In 2004, Ichiro Suzuki had 262 hits, the most base hits anyone has ever had in a season.

Like McGwire, Ichiro in 2004 created over one-half of his runs in, as it happened, 27 games.   In his best 27 games of the season, Ichiro hit .707 with 4 triples, 6 homers, 21 RBI, 14-for-15 stealing bases.

But in the OTHER 134 games of the season, Ichiro scored only 56 runs and drove in only 39 runs. His average was OK, yes, but this is 83% of the games of a guy who had 262 hits. In 83% of his games, he wasn't really doing anything other than chipping an occasional single.   And in his WORST 100 games of the historic season, he hit .229 with a .535 OPS and 8-for-17 base stealing:

G	AB	R	H	2B	3B	HR	RBI	BB	SB	CS	AVG	OBP	SLG
134	571	56	168	16	1	2	39	41	22	10	.294	.342	.336
100	420	27	96	4	1	2	25	29	8	9	.229	.278	.257

The 134 games there are the games other than his 27 best games. Dick Allen in 1972 won an MVP, creating over half of his runs in 26 games. But that was a lot; in 1968 he had created over half of his runs in just 16 games, in 1969 18 games, and in 1970, 17 games. The number was up in 1972 because he was having his MVP season. The number of games required to account for half of your Runs Created always goes up when you have your best seasons. Reggie Jackson's data is similar to Allen's. Reggie created over half of his runs in 1970 in 17 games; in 1972, 18 games. In his MVP season, 1973, it was 23 games. His career high was 24.

Mark Belanger played in 145 games in 1968, and created over half of his runs in 9 games.   In 1972, playing in 113 games, he created over half of his runs in just 5 games. Those numbers are unusual, but the number is almost always between 10 and 20%.   In my Game Logs, which involve almost 3,000 player/seasons, the MOST games that any player required to account for over half of his Runs Created was 31, by Tony Phillips in 1993. Phillips hit .313 that season, and led the league in walks, with 132.

That's why it is impossible to have batters' Game Scores centered at 50 on a zero-to-100 scale. In a 150-game season, a hitter—any hitter—does most of his damage in 40 games or less, and is merely voting "present" the rest of the time.

The formula for Game Scores by a hitter is really simple. It is his Runs Created in the game, times 10, plus his RBI in the game, times 5, plus his Runs Scored in the Game, times 5, plus 15. The +15 is there to re-center the Games Scores from 10 (average) to 25, and I moved the center up because otherwise there would be a lot of games that have Negative Game Scores. I liked the 0-to-100 framework of Pitcher's Game Scores, and I was trying to keep that. It is a simple formula, but since it uses Runs Created in the game, the number goes up or down anytime the batter does anything—a walk, a strikeout, a stolen base or caught stealing, a sacrifice hit or sacrifice fly. No matter what a batter does in an at bat, it affects his Game Score.

For the last couple of years I have been building up a file of Game Logs by hitters. It's really just something I like to do, as opposed to being work-oriented or goal-oriented. I have about 200 players in the data, including 40 Hall of Famers, but I have avoided doing the top-level guys, the Babe Ruths and Mickey Mantles and Mike Trouts and Mike Schmidts, because a project like that breaks down if you do all the most interesting guys first and are stuck with running numbers for Cesar Geronimo and Johnny Temple.

Anyway, I currently have 343,582 Game Lines in my file; it will be 100,000 more than that by the time you read this, but of the 343,582, there is one game which has a negative score, and there are 216 games which have scores higher than 100. The one game with a sub-zero score is the game in which Joe Torre grounded into four double plays.

If a player has a Game Score higher than 100, I call that a Super-Game. One game in 1600 (in my data) is a Super-Game; it would be less than that if I had more ordinary players in the data and fewer stars, but one in 1600 is about one game per team season, or about one game for a pretty good hitter in a career. Many very good hitters never had a Super Game, among them Yogi Berra, Tony Perez, Ichiro Suzuki, Lou Brock, Luis Aparicio, Norm Cash, Cecil Cooper, George Scott, Dusty Baker, Rusty Staub, Keith Hernandez, Thurman Munson, Joe Torre and Bill Madlock. Harmon Killebrew and Dick Allen had one each. Reggie had three in the regular season, plus one in the World Series. The leaders in Super-Games, in my data, are two Pirates, Ralph Kiner and Willie Stargell, who had 8 Super-Games each. Ryne Sandberg had 7. Carlton Fisk, Jim Rice and Earl Averill had 6, and Mark McGwire and Hank Greenberg had 5 apiece.

The formula for the Game Score is really simple, but it relies on having a number for the player's Runs Created in the game. The hard part of creating the Game Score was figuring out how to estimate the player's Runs Created in the game in such a manner that, if you added up his one-game runs created for every game all season, it would match (or almost match) our estimate, here in this book, of his Runs Created for the season. The formula for single-game Runs Created by a hitter is in the Glossary, if you want to see it.

Accepting that it is more of a toy than a tool, there are a lot of things you can do with Game Scores. I like to find the best game of each player's career, and send out a tweet on the anniversary of that game. It's just a way of pushing to the surface for a moment the memory of Bob Allison or Gary Gaetti or whoever, giving the reader an opportunity to smile at a moment from long ago if he chooses to do so. Very often somebody responds, "Oh, I was AT that game. I remember that so well." Game Scores make it really easy to identify the craziest Hot Streaks and worst slumps of a season. You can find any player's best Hot Streak or Worst Slump by just getting running totals for the last 10 games, 15 games, whatever. (The greatest Hot Streak in my data is Hank Greenberg in September, 1940. Carried over into the World Series.) You can find any player's best "season", meaning their best 162 consecutive games. You can find the best hitter from any game—which generally you can find without a formula, of course, but it organizes the process in case two guys are about even. Once you have the best hitter from each game, you can ask, "OK, when Mike Trout was the best hitter for the Angels in this game, what was their won-lost record? When Anthony Rendon was their best hitter, what was their won-lost record?"

Maybe it will catch on, maybe it won't, who knows? Maybe, 40 years from now, ESPN will have a line in each box score: Best game by a hitter: Manuel Margot (53). Maybe Baseball Reference will add a tag for each hitter: 10 Best Games (Log). I've enjoyed creating it, and I've enjoyed playing around with it, and if you get something out of it, good for you.

Projecting Injury Risk

John Shirley

Injuries can derail any team's season, or at least make it that much harder for a team to reach the postseason, no matter how promising the pre-season outlook. Teams such as the Astros and Braves had to overcome major injuries to ace starters Justin Verlander and Mike Soroka, respectively, to make postseason runs this year. The Nationals were not as lucky, unable to match their 2019 success after losing Stephen Strasburg early in the season. The Yankees have also had to overcome a rash of injuries in both 2019 and 2020 to make the postseason, after being preseason favorites each year.

For some players with long injury histories, such as Strasburg, these setbacks are less surprising when they happen. In general though, most injuries are unforeseen and cause teams stress in attempting to reshuffle lineups on the fly. Predicting injuries with any level of accuracy could save teams from some of this stress and potentially reshape rosters and lineups.

Any attempt at predicting injuries, as with any projection system, will never be an exact science. Injuries are relatively rare events, and some are the result of truly random events on the field. Even with that knowledge, we can still do our best to attempt to model a relationship between what we know about each player's past performance, injury history, and playing style and his risk of being injured during a given season.

Some work in this area has already been done by Sig Mejdal and presented in previous *Bill James Handbook*s. This earlier research was completed using an injury database collected by David Neft and documented in *The Sports Encyclopedia: Baseball*. This database cataloged injuries only if they caused a player to miss at least 30 days.

Our analysis here will differ in data source, as we use our own injury database collected by in-house Video Scouts and reviewed by our Injury Coordinator for accuracy of diagnosis. This allows us to use more in-depth injury data, as we catalog every injury that occurs both in-season and in the offseason. This includes injuries as minor as getting hit by a pitch, or a foul tip, all the way to the most severe season-ending events. While this limits our dataset to the last five seasons, we were able to use data from 2016 through 2019 to build a robust model.

To build our predictions, we used a machine learning model to calculate the probability of individual players having at least one stint on the IL during a given season. We built two models, one isolating pitchers and one including only position players. This was done so we could include position-specific metrics within each model.

The main inputs for both models are metrics measuring each player's age, body type, injury history, previous season usage, and playing style. Both models were trained on a random selection of player seasons from 2016-2019 and tested on an out-of-sample portion of player seasons from the same time period. We decided to leave out any data from 2020, as it would skew the predictions due to the shortened season.

The models showed the following levels of accuracy among different predicted injury rate buckets from the out-of-sample test data.

Predicted Pitcher Injuries, 2016–2019

Predicted Injury Probability	Number of Players	Actually Injured	Percentage Injured
50% and up	42	20	47.6%
25–49%	140	44	31.4%
0–24%	125	22	17.6%

Predicted Hitter Injuries, 2016–2019

Predicted Injury Probability	Number of Players	Actually Injured	Percentage Injured
50% and up	13	7	53.8%
25–49%	56	14	25.0%
0–24%	190	31	16.3%

The results of both models provided us with some insight into which inputs known before the season have the most impact on injuries.

Some of the most interesting inputs that impacted the hitters model included sprint speed, Body Mass Index (BMI), and "descriptive defense" metrics such as how often the player threw on the move or was the responsible fielder on a difficult play in previous seasons. When combined with inputs like age, games played, and injury history, we were able to get a good sense of who is most likely to be injured.

Within the pitchers model, we found that many of the most impactful inputs had to do with throwing hard. Average velocity of all pitches, average fastball velocity, and fastball usage are weighted heavily by the model along with age, career games played, number of pitches thrown the previous season, and number of injury events during the previous season.

These models are a first step towards more accurately predicting injury risk, and we will be continuing this research in the offseason. That said, we wanted to give readers a first glimpse at what we are working on and the current results. With that in mind, let's now look at a few cases in which our current models predicted a high likelihood of injury during the 2020 season. It is important to remember that these predictions are based on a full 162-game season. The fact that there were only 60 games played this year no doubt had an effect on the model's accuracy in 2020.

Among the top 10 pitchers with the highest likelihood of an IL stint in 2020, an astounding seven of them did in fact land on the IL, even during the shortened season. Some notable hits for the model were Cole Hamels, Cam Bedrosian, and Andrew Miller, who all suffered from arm-related injuries. A few of the top misses include Lucas Giolito and Julio Teheran, who both made it through the season injury free, despite the model predicting them as high risk.

Over the shortened season, our hitters model saw only three of its top 10 likeliest players actually make IL stints. However, if we include players ranked 11th–13th, the model was correct for five of the top 13 players.

Notable hits for the model include Scott Kingery, Miguel Rojas, and David Dahl. The top miss was Freddie Freeman, who played in all 60 games after being projected as the second-most-likely player to land on the IL.

Now that we have looked back at individual cases from the 2020 season, let's take a look ahead and see who our models predict having a high risk of injury for the 2021 season.

Pitchers with the Highest Predicted Injury Risk Entering 2021

Rank	Pitcher
1	Walker Buehler
2	Chris Bassitt
3	Keynan Middleton
4	German Márquez
5	Sam Coonrod
6	Lucas Giolito
7	Mike Clevinger
8	Austin Davis
9	Zack Littell
10	Lance McCullers Jr.

Hitters with the Highest Predicted Injury Risk Entering 2021

Rank	Hitter
1	Josh Bell
2	Miguel Rojas
3	David Dahl
4	Danny Santana
5	Austin Riley
6	Kiké Hernández
7	Cedric Mullins II
8	Manuel Margot
9	Travis Shaw
10	Didi Gregorius

Hall of Famers By Team

Bill James

Will the team that you root for have an eventual Hall of Famer on their roster in 2021? It is extremely likely—at least 3-to-1 likely, probably 4-to-1 likely—that the answer to that question is "Yes".   Most major league teams do have a Hall of Famer on their roster—not necessarily a Hall of Famer in his prime, not even necessarily a player who is there the whole season, but a Hall of Famer. 73% of all teams do, and the 73% figure is actually extremely conservative, as we will see shortly.

The 73% figure is based on the years 1900 to 2014. I started the study in 1900 because 19th century baseball wasn't actually major league baseball, and ended it in 2014 because if you played in 2015, you're not eligible to be in the Hall of Fame yet.   I didn't count as relevant to the study Hall of Fame managers who also played, like Whitey Herzog, Tony LaRussa, Casey Stengel and Dick Williams, but I did count those few Hall of Fame managers who were quite outstanding players and whose selection announcements embrace both their playing and managing careers, like Joe Torre and Red Schoendienst.

There were 2,400 major league teams in those 115 years, of which 1,765 had a Hall of Famer who played for them. That's 73.5%. That number is artificially low, because the players from the last three decades are still filing in to Cooperstown; even the players from the 1970s are still filing into Cooperstown. Ted Simmons, a 1970s star, was just elected last year. There have always been players selected decades after their careers, and we have to expect that this will continue, which will eventually drive the 1900 to 2014 percentage, I would expect, over 80%. This is a decade-by-decade chart:

From	To	Teams	W/HOF	Pct
1900	1909	152	131	86.2%
1910	1919	176	152	86.4%
1920	1929	160	146	91.3%
1930	1939	160	150	93.8%
1940	1949	160	132	82.5%
1950	1959	160	134	83.8%
1960	1969	198	156	78.8%
1970	1979	246	187	76.0%
1980	1989	260	206	79.2%
1990	1999	278	199	71.6%
2000	2009	300	145	48.3%
2010	2014	150	27	18.0%
1900	2014	2400	1765	73.5%

If that is not self-explanatory, from 1900 to 1909 there were 152 major league team/seasons, of which 131 included a Hall of Famer. That's 86.2%. If that's still not clear, call Joe Buck on the telephone, and Joe will come to your house and explain it to you. I haven't asked him, but I'm sure he would be happy to do that. If you're lucky, he'll bring A-Rod.

In the 1930s, 94% of teams had a Hall of Famer on their roster. There were only ten teams during the 1930s which did NOT have one, and only one team from the years 1930 to 1934; the 1931 Red Sox did not have a Hall of Famer on their roster, but every other team in those years did. The 1932 White Sox finished 49-102, but they had three Hall of Famers on their roster (Luke Appling, Ted Lyons and Red Faber.) At least 80% of teams have a Hall of Famer on their roster in the first six decades of the study, and the 1960s, 1970s and 1980s will eventually move over that mark. The 1960s are at 79%, but there are still many 1960s players who might eventually make the Hall of Fame—Jim Kaat, Tommy John, Mickey Lolich, Dick Allen, Curt Flood, Bill White, Pete Rose, Bill Freehan, Minnie Minoso, Roger Maris, Frank Howard, Luis Tiant, Vada Pinson, Don Newcombe, Rocky Colavito, Maury Wills and Tony Oliva, to name a few. If just one of those guys eventually gets in, depending on what teams he played for, the 1960s percentage will go over 80%.

So let's say that 80% of teams have an eventual Hall of Famer on their roster, which I think is a true statement. The percentage swelled in the 1920s/1930s for two reasons. One is that prior to 1980 sportswriters and baseball people looked at batting stats without context. If 25 players in a league hit .330 with 100 RBI each, they didn't figure it was a hitter's league; they took it as evidence that there were a lot of great hitters in that league. The other reason is that the Hall of Fame in the late 1960s unwisely handed the power to elect new Hall of Famers to a cabal of 1920s/1930s baseball stars, who gleefully inducted an unconscionable number of their old teammates.

This article is not about the timeline of the Hall of Fame, however; it is about <u>teams</u> and the Hall of Fame. Here's a fun one, warning you in advance that this is deceptively stated: What franchise had the highest percentage of seasons with at least one Hall of Famer, and which franchise had the lowest? The answers are, the Washington Senators, and the Washington Senators. The first Senators franchise (1901-1960), the team which fled to Minnesota in 1961, had a Hall of Famer on their roster for 53 of their 60 seasons, or 88%, the highest percentage of any franchise, if looked at in exactly the right way. The second Washington Senators team (1961-1971) was there for eleven years and never put a Hall of Famer in the lineup.

Of course, there are a million ways to break down the data and make those statements not true; for example, you can include the first Senators team as a part of the Minnesota franchise and the second one as part of the Texas Rangers, so then you get different data, and if you want to you can make the Braves into the Boston Braves, the Milwaukee Braves, the Atlanta Braves, and the Complete Braves collector set; if you do that then the Milwaukee Braves not only had a Hall of Famer on the roster every year, they actually had at least three Hall of Famers on the roster every year except 1953; in 1953 they only had two. Beating that one, the New York Giants had a Hall of Famer on their roster every year from 1900 to 1957, all 58 years. Also, the statement about the Senators is only true if you include all years 1900 to 2019 or 2020; if you do that it drives the Braves percentage down so that the Senators move into first place, but if you don't do that the Braves are actually the franchise with the highest percentage of years covered, 91%. Ignoring the short-term franchises and without getting into stupid stuff like counting the Rays as two franchises (Rays and Devil Rays) and the Marlins as two franchises (Florida and Miami). . .without getting into that kind of mischief, here is a summary of the franchises, and the percentage of years each one has had a Hall of Fame inductee, up to 2014:

City	Team	Lg	Years	Years	W/HOF	Percentage
New York	Giants	NL	1900 to 1957	58	58	100.0%
Milwaukee	Braves	NL	1953 to 1965	13	13	100.0%
Atlanta	Braves	NL	1966 to 2014	49	46	93.9%
All	Braves	NL	1900 to 2014	115	105	91.3%
New York	Yankees	AL	1903 to 2014	112	102	91.1%
Chicago	White Sox	AL	1901 to 2014	114	103	90.4%
Washington	Senators-1	AL	1901 to 1960	60	53	88.3%
Brooklyn	Dodgers	NL	1900 to 1957	58	51	87.9%
Boston	Red Sox	AL	1901 to 2014	114	100	87.7%
Boston	Braves	NL	1900 to 1952	53	46	86.8%
Detroit	Tigers	AL	1901 to 2014	114	97	85.1%
St. Louis	Cardinals	NL	1900 to 2014	115	97	84.3%
Montreal	Expos	NL	1969 to 2004	36	30	83.3%
St. Louis	Browns	AL	1902 to 1953	52	42	80.8%
Baltimore	Orioles	AL	1954 to 2014	61	48	78.7%
San Diego	Padres	NL	1969 to 2014	46	36	78.3%
All	Dodgers	NL	1900 to 2014	115	89	77.4%
Chicago	Cubs	NL	1900 to 2014	115	88	76.5%
Cincinnati	Reds	NL	1900 to 2014	115	88	76.5%
All	Giants	NL	1900 to 2014	114	84	73.7%
Cleveland	Indians	AL	1901 to 2014	114	83	72.8%
Houston	Astros	Both	1962 to 2014	53	38	71.7%
Pittsburgh	Pirates	NL	1900 to 1914	115	82	71.3%
Philadelphia	Phillies	NL	1900 to 1914	115	79	68.7%
Philadelphia	A's	AL	1901 to 1954	54	37	68.5%
Los Angeles	Dodgers	NL	1958 to 2014	57	38	66.7%
Minnesota	Twins	AL	1961 to 2014	54	35	64.8%
New York	Mets	NL	1962 to 2014	53	34	64.2%
All 3	A's	AL	1901 to 2014	114	72	63.2%
Oakland	A's	AL	1968 to 2014	47	30	60.5%
Seattle	Mariners	AL	1977 to 2014	38	22	57.9%
Texas	Rangers	AL	1972 to 2014	43	24	55.8%
Los Angeles	Angels	AL	1961 to 2014	54	30	55.6%
Milwaukee	Brewers	Both	1970 to 2014	45	23	51.1%
Arizona	D'backs	NL	1998 to 2014	17	8	47.1%
San Francisco	Giants	NL	1958 to 2014	56	26	46.4%
Kansas City	Royals	AL	1969 to 2014	46	21	45.7%
Colorado	Rockies	NL	1993 to 2014	22	10	45.5%
Toronto	Blue Jays	AL	1977 to 2014	38	17	44.7%

City	Team	Lg	Years	Years	W/HOF	Percentage
Kansas City	A's	AL	1955 to 1967	13	5	38.5%
Miami	Marlins	NL	1993 to 2014	22	6	27.3%
Washington	Nationals	NL	2005 to 2014	10	2	20.0%
Tampa Bay	Rays	AL	1998 to 2014	17	2	11.8%
Washington	Senators-2	AL	1961 to 1971	11	0	0.0%

At the end of this article we will relate the success of the franchise to the number of Hall of Famers, but a few other things to explain first. I counted Hall of Fame seasons for each player in three groups:

1) Prime season,

2) Not a prime season or an injury season, and

3) Limited appearance.

"Limited appearance" means that he played in less than one-fourth of the team's games or, if a pitcher, carried less than one-fourth of a full workload. For a prime season, I used a generous definition of a prime season; if one might reasonably say that this was a prime season, then it counts. Vladimir Guerrero in 2010 hit .300 with 29 homers, 115 RBI. Vladimir was 35 years old then and those numbers are not his best seasons; in his best seasons he regularly hit .320+ with 38 to 44 home runs. Still, .300 with 115 RBI is a pretty good hitter. The Rangers made the World Series in part because of Vladimir's bat, and I think you can reasonably say that that's a prime season, so I counted it as a prime season. There's a certain amount of judgment in what is and what isn't a prime season; take it for whatever you think it is worth.

Anyway, I weighted the seasons at 3 for a prime season, 2 for a non-prime season, and 1 for a brief appearance, and scored each team's Hall of Fame "weight" in each year, thus identifying the teams which had the greatest collections of Hall of Famers, and also things like teams which had a lot of Hall of Famers but didn't do anything, and teams which did very well with zero or very little help from the Glory Hounds. The highest density of Hall of Famers ever was the 1932 Yankees, who had 9 Hall of Famers and 25 "points" in this system. They had seven Hall of Famers in their prime (Ruth, Gehrig, Dickey, Lazzeri, Combs, Ruffing and Gomez) plus two who were post-prime (Joe Sewell and Herb

Pennock.) That fact is pretty well known, so we won't dwell on it, but since not all eras are equal in terms of the Hall of Fame mass, I tried to identify the greatest concentrations of Hall of Famers by decade:

In the first decade of the study (1900-1909), the most impressive collection of Hall of Famers is either the 1900 St. Louis Cardinals or the 1904 New York Giants. 1900 was a funny season in which there were only eight major league teams, so the Hall of Famers were packed like sardines. The Cardinals and Braves had five Hall of Famers each, but the Cardinals had three in their prime (Cy Young, Bobby Wallace and Jesse Burkett), so I counted them as the leaders. The 1904 Giants had six Hall of Famers, but three of them just made token appearances.

For the second decade (1910-1919), the most impressive concentration of Hall of Famers is the 1912 Philadelphia A's, who had six Hall of Famers worth 15 points. They had four Hall of Famers in their prime (Chief Bender, Eddie Plank, Eddie Colins and Home Run Baker), plus the 18-year-old Herb Pennock pitched 17 games, 50 innings for them, and Stan Coveleski got into a few games.

The Yankee team mentioned before represents both the 1920s, with the 1928 Yankees, and the 1930s, with the 1931-1932 Yankees (the 1931 team also had nine Hall of Famers.) Then the Cleveland Indians from the late 1940s/early 1950s represent both the 1940s and the 1950s; their peak collection was 1949, when they had seven Hall of Famers representing 17 points. They had three Hall of Famers in their prime (Bob Feller, Bob Lemon and Larry Doby), plus three who were post-prime (Lou Boudreau, Joe Gordon and Satchel Paige), plus Early Wynn, who didn't have what you could reasonably consider to be a prime season. For that matter, it is stretching it to consider Bob Feller's 1949 season to be a prime season, but Feller was still in the rotation and had very good seasons in 1950 and 1951, so I included it.

From the 1960s, the greatest collection of Hall of Famers is the 1963-1966 Giants, with Willie Mays, Willie McCovey, Orlando Cepeda, Juan Marichal and Gaylord Perry, joined by Duke Snider in 1964 and Warren Spahn in 1965. From the 1970s, the winner is the 1971 Cardinals, who had five Hall of Fame players, all in their prime: Lou Brock, Bob Gibson, Steve Carlton, Joe Torre and Ted Simmons. From the 1980s, the leaders are the 1982 Milwaukee Brewers, who had five Hall of Famers, four of them in their prime (Robin Yount, Paul

Molitor, Rollie Fingers and Ted Simmons, plus Don Sutton, who joined them late in the year.)   The leaders both from the 1990s and the 2000s are the Atlanta Braves, with the three pitchers and Chipper. For the last decade, the early leaders are the Yankees, with Rivera and Jeter; the 2012 Phillies also have two Hall of Famers, although both were post-prime (Jim Thome and Roy Halladay.)

This chart gives the number of Hall of Famers by season:

	0	1	2	3	4	5	6	7	8	9	Decade Total
190-	31	30	29	30	34	33	36	33	31	32	319
191-	30	26	31	30	33	35	35	32	27	28	307
192-	29	34	38	40	47	51	52	52	52	53	448
193-	54	48	54	52	50	44	41	42	39	38	462
194-	33	40	34	22	17	16	30	35	30	29	286
195-	29	29	29	30	31	34	36	33	32	33	316
196-	34	35	37	37	35	38	40	38	41	40	375
197-	39	40	40	39	38	38	37	38	37	39	385
198-	39	41	42	40	38	36	37	37	38	35	383
199-	33	37	41	41	36	35	36	34	32	29	354
200-	26	28	25	24	24	20	18	18	17	12	212
201-	9	7	5	3	1	0	0	0	0	0	25

There have been 3,872 seasons of Hall of Fame play from 1900 to 1914, or 34 Hall of Famers per season; however, there are 126 cases in which a Hall of Fame player has played for two teams in a season, so if you add it up team-by-team, you don't get 3,872, you get 3,998.   Of those 3,998 seasons, 2,040 were in the National League, 1,948 in the American League, and 10 were in the Federal League. The National League has a 5% advantage in the number of Hall of Fame seasons.

Tracking that over time, the American League attracted more than half of the National League's stars in its early seasons. In 1902, the American League's second season, they had 20 Hall of Fame players, whereas the National League had only 16. (There were only 29 Hall of Famers that season, but seven of them jumped leagues in mid-season.) The American League generally had a small advantage in Hall of Fame players from 1902 to 1919. From 1920 until 1936, although the American League was probably the stronger league and probably had more legitimate stars, the National League has a few more Hall of Famers because

Frankie Frisch was in the National League. Frisch led the collection of old players who threw open the doors and invited a bunch of their aging and departed teammates to join the party; those were all National League unworthies—George Kelly, Jesse Haines, Jim Bottomley, Freddie Lindstrom, Chick Hafey, Dave Bancroft, Travis Jackson, Ross Youngs. Because of them, the NL holds a 31-24 advantage in Hall of Famers in 1932 and 27-19 in 1935, smaller advantages in the other seasons. For more than 20 years after that the numbers between the two leagues are almost even, and then in the late 1950s the National League started to pull ahead. Well. . .really, they STARTED to pull ahead in 1958-1961, when the Giants and the Cubs were coming up with a Hall of Famer a year, Cepeda-McCovey-Marichal for the Giants and Williams-Santo-Brock for the Cubs. The National League held a 19-16 edge in Hall of Famers in 1959, and then the gap exploded: 21-13 in 1960, 22-13 in 1961, 23-14 in 1962, 24-13 in 1963, and 27-9(!!) in 1964. In 1964 the National League had 27 Hall of Famers; the American League had 9—by far the largest gap between the league in baseball history (other than the surrounding seasons, which have splits almost as large.)

Actually it is 26 to 9; the 27 to 9 number double-counts Lou Brock, who was traded in mid-season. All of those numbers double-count players who played for two teams in a season. The larger point is that I don't think anyone believes that that gap is not legitimate. You would have a hard time naming American League players from that era who should be in the Hall of Fame; you could name Elston Howard and Tony Oliva, but the National League could answer them with Curt Flood and Dick Allen. Almost everyone who comments on the talent gap in that era traces it back to the color line; the American League was slower to integrate. While that is not inaccurate, it is also not a complete explanation. Of the 26 National League Hall of Famers in 1964, twelve were white players. The National League simply had many more franchises with strong scouting and player development operations. Four National League teams in that era—the Giants, Cubs, Dodgers and Pirates—all had extremely strong player development programs; three others were sort of in that group (the Reds, Cardinals and Phillies). The American League had only one comparable program, the Orioles, and maybe two with the Twins.

The Astros also should be mentioned; the Astros did a remarkable job in their first years, producing Joe Morgan and a host of good players/not quite Hall of Famers (Jimmy Wynn, Rusty Staub, Larry Dierker), and then the KC A's started producing stars in the mid-1960s (Catfish Hunter, Reggie Jackson, Bert Campaneris, Sal Bando.) Both the Astros and the A's built their systems by attracting away the key development people from the Orioles.

I never really understood what had happened there until I worked for the Red Sox, starting in 2002. The Red Sox realized that we were in a brutal division, and we had do everything we could to stay even. When the Red Sox started to pull ahead of the Yankees, the Yankees doubled down, and Toronto and Baltimore put the pedal to the metal to try to keep up. Within a few years the American League, and that division in particular, had pulled absurdly far ahead of the National League, so much so that the best National League teams would have struggled to play .500 ball in the American League East. I had thought, before coming into the game, that that was impossible. I reasoned that the National League teams and the American League teams all drafted and signed players together, sent them through minor league systems together, all fed from the same fields and drank from the same streams. How was it possible for one league to get to be significantly stronger than the other? But watching it happen from the inside, it looked a lot different. It's like a footrace; when the lead guy breaks out fast, everybody has to try to keep up. You match your effort to what is required of you. We all do.

Anyway, the Hall of Fame gap between the leagues continued until the late 1970s. In 1965 the count was still 28-12; in 1970, still 28-12, and in 1975, still 22-17. The American League caught up in 1980 and pulled ahead in 1981.

Since I was working on the problem of Hall of Famers by team, I got interested in the question of one-team stars. People will say that back in the day, star players stayed with their teams for their entire careers, whereas now they hop around like frogs on vodka. The problem is, people said the same thing back in the day. I remember people saying that in 1965.

There have been 53 Hall of Famers since 1900 who were one-team players. (If there had been a 19th century/20th century star who played his entire career with one team, I would have counted him, but there was no such player.) This is a chart of the number of one-team Hall of Famers, by season, compared to the total number of Hall of Fame seasons:

	0	1	2	3	4	5	6	7	8	9	Decade Total	Decade Total	Pct
190-	0	0	1	1	1	1	1	2	2	2	11	319	3%
191-	2	1	1	1	2	2	2	3	3	3	20	307	7%
192-	4	4	5	8	10	10	11	10	11	11	84	448	19%
193-	12	12	12	12	11	11	12	11	10	11	114	462	25%
194-	11	14	13	6	3	3	12	11	11	11	95	286	33%
195-	12	11	9	12	13	15	17	14	13	12	128	316	41%
196-	12	11	12	12	11	12	12	12	10	10	114	375	30%
197-	9	9	9	8	10	9	8	9	8	8	87	385	23%
198-	8	9	10	9	9	8	9	10	11	11	94	383	25%
199-	9	10	10	11	9	11	10	9	9	9	97	354	27%
200-	9	9	7	7	7	5	4	4	3	3	58	212	27%
201-	3	3	3	2	1	0	0	0	0	0	12	25	48%

The 53 one-team Hall of Famers in the study account for 914 seasons of play, with the peak number being 17 in 1956. I'll list the 17 one-team Hall of Famers from 1956: Bob Feller, Phil Rizzuto, Pee Wee Reese, Bob Lemon, Jackie Robinson, Roy Campanella, Stan Musial, Ted Williams, Whitey Ford, Mickey Mantle, Ernie Banks, Al Kaline, Roberto Clemente, Bill Mazeroski, Don Drysdale, Sandy Koufax and Brooks Robinson.

The first one-team Hall of Famer of the 20th century (there were a couple in the 19th century). . .the first of the 20th century was Addie Joss, who died before he could get old and get fobbed off on some non-competitive team, which was what was normally happened to aging stars in that era. The phenomenon of a player completing his career with his first team didn't really start to happen until the early 1920s, and it started mostly with players who played for the New York Giants. The Giants of the 1920s had five one-team Hall of Famers—Ross Youngs (who also died before he could get pushed out the door), Travis Jackson, Bill Terry, Carl Hubbell and Mel Ott. With a nod to the White Sox, who also kept three stars for their entire careers (the three mentioned before in regard to 1932), the one-team Hall of Fame phenomenon is largely contained to the three New York City teams, the Giants, Dodgers and Yankees. Of the first 32 one-team Hall of Famers, 17 of them played for one of those three teams.

Apart from the overlap of generations in the mid-1950s, the number of one-team Hall of Famers has not really changed since the 1920s, and probably has not gone up or down significantly to the present time. The number of one-team Hall of Famers active was 9, 10, or 11 in 1924, 1925, 1926, 1927, 1928, 1929, 1934, 1935, 1937, 1938, 1939, 1940, 1947, 1948, 1949, 1951, 1961, 1964, 1968, 1969, 1970, 1971, 1972, 1974, 1975, 1977, 1981, 1982, 1983, 1984, 1986, 1987, 1988, 1989, 1990, 1991, 1992, 1993, 1994, 1995, 1996, 1997, 1998, 1999, 2000, and 2001. One-team Hall of Famers account for 914 of the 3,872 Hall of Fame seasons, or 24%.

OK, my last study of this subject has to do with teams which may be over-represented or under-represented in the Hall of Fame. When I have studied this before, many years ago, I looked at individual players, focusing particularly on marginal players who were or were not selected for the Hall of Fame. What I did this time was to look at (A) the success of every team, and (B) the number of Hall of Fame players on each team.

Actually, I looked at each team over a five-year window. In other words, the data for the Baltimore Orioles in 1966 actually includes the Orioles of 1964, 1965, 1966, 1967 and 1968, but with the 1966 data more than double-weighted. I did that because (a) one does not earn a Hall of Fame induction based on one good season; it's a multi-year thing, and (b) there are an awful lot of teams with one Hall of Famer or two or zero, so if you just use one-year data you have a humongous number of ties. Also, for this study, I did not use teams since the year 2000, as the Hall of Fame selections from the 21st century are just getting underway.

For one season, the most over-represented team in the Hall of Fame is the 1992 Seattle Mariners. The Mariners had three Hall of Famers, two of them in their prime. Edgar Martinez won the batting championship, hitting .343 with 46 doubles, 18 homers. Ken Griffey Jr. drove in 103 runs, hit over .300 and won a Gold Glove; I don't know if he actually won a Gold Glove and I'm not going to check, I'm just assuming that he probably won a Gold Glove. I didn't count Randy Johnson as being in his prime, but he was in the rotation all year and struck out 241 batters, so I suppose you could count that as a prime season if you wanted to.

In spite of having three Hall of Famers kicking some butt, the Mariners lost 98 games. Of relevance to the study, they had all three of those players all five years, 1990 to 1994, and they never really did anything; their best record in that period was 83-79. Over a five-year period but with the emphasis on 1992, they had more Hall of Fame weight than any other team in baseball, but they just did not finish the team.

Another contender for the Hall of Fame underachiever of all time award is the Cubs of the Ryne Sandberg/Lee Smith era. They had those two Hall of Famers throughout that era, plus they had other guys. In 1981 they had two Hall of Fame relievers, Smith and Sutter. They had Ferguson Jenkins in 1982-83; he was post-prime, but he was still damned good in 1982. They had Dennis Eckersley for parts of three seasons. In 1986 they came up with Greg Maddux. In 1987 they signed Andre Dawson. In 1988 they had Goose Gossage; yeah, he was post-prime, but he pitched until 1994.

The Cubs did win their division in 1984, but they had a losing record every other year from 1978 to 1988. You have Ryne Sandberg, Lee Smith, Bruce Sutter, Andre Dawson and Greg Maddux, you would think you could put enough talent around them to finish over .500 once in a while.

The one-year team most UNDER-represented in the Hall of Fame is the 1990 Pittsburgh Pirates. The Pirates won 95 games that year, 98 in 1991, 96 in 1992. They haven't had a Hall of Famer on their roster since Willie Stargell retired. Has something to do with that steroid issue, of course. I'm not commenting on the right and wrong of it; just noting that the team's performance is very good for a team with no Hall of Famers.

Equally under-represented, or nearly so, are the 1987-1989 Blue Jays. The Blue Jays finally reached the top of the hill in 1992-1993, you might remember, by bringing in mass quantities of Hall of Famers: Roberto Alomar, Jack Morris, Paul Molitor, Dave Winfield, Rickey Henderson. This rather obscures the fact that they were a really good team for a long time before they brought in the mercenary soldiers. They won 89 games in 1983, then 89, 99, 86, 96, 87, 89, 86 and 91. Their only Hall of Famer during that period was a 3-game cameo by a 48-year-old pitcher. Contrast that with the Cubs of the same era.

Another team which had a lot more success than Hall of Fame recognition is the Dodgers of a slightly earlier era. The Dodgers won a World Series in 1981 and had good seasons in '82, '83 and '85, but never had a Hall of Famer between 1980, when Don Sutton left the team after the season, until 1988, when Sutton returned to finish his career.

But seeing all of these 1980s teams on the list, I realize now that I have a flaw in my method. I ranked all teams each season based on (a) performance, and (b) Hall of Fame recognition, and then recorded the distance between them.   But since there are 16 teams in 1960 and 30 teams in 2000, this means that teams in 1960 can be +15 to -15 in a season, whereas teams in 2000 can be +29 to -29.

Oh well, there goes the Nobel Prize. We can still identify the most over- and under-represented teams of each era:

Over-Represented:
Mid-teens Pittsburgh Pirates
Early 1920s Chicago White Sox
Early 1930s Cincinnati Reds
Early 1940s New York Giants
Early 1960s Cubs
Late 1970s Expos and Padres

Under-Represented:
Cubs and New York Giants of the teens
Early 1920s St. Louis Browns
1939-1943 Cincinnati Reds
Mid-1960s Twins
Late 1960s Tigers
1970s Yankees

Since most of us are fans of a team, rather than fans of a team in an era, I would guess there would be more interest in the total scores for a team, rather than one-year scores. There are six teams which have had significantly more Hall of Fame recognition than on-field success. Those are:

City	Team	Years	Total
San Diego	Padres	1969-2000	+306
Atlanta	Braves	1900-2000	+246
Chicago	Cubs	1900-2000	+203
Seattle	Mariners	1977-2000	+189
Chicago	White Sox	1901-2000	+131
Montreal	Expos	1969-2000	+130

I'll talk about the Padres in a moment. The Braves were +11 for their years in Boston (1900 to 1952) and were +36 for their Milwaukee sojourn, making them +47 at that time. They are +199 since they moved to Atlanta in 1966. They have had a lot of success there, but even more Hall of Fame recognition. They have had 91 player/seasons of Hall of Fame service (1966 to 2000), and only 4 seasons of that is token appearances. It is mostly prime seasons. I still think that Dale Murphy is deserving of Hall of Fame recognition, but really, it's somebody else's turn; the Braves are ahead of schedule.

The Cubs were way BEHIND schedule in 1950; through 1950 they were -128 in terms of Hall of Fame recognition vs. performance. You probably know; the Cubs had a lot of good teams in there, winning ten National League pennants between 1900 and 1945. Their fair share would have been six. Despite this, their teams got far less Hall of Fame recognition than the Cardinals or Giants, so they were -128 in 1950.

They caught up a little bit during the 1950s, when Ernie Banks was in their lineup every game, but the team wasn't really winning a whole lot. In 1960 they had four Hall of Famers on their roster; in 1961 they had five—and those were still bad teams. (Ernie Banks, Ron Santo, Billy Williams, Richie Ashburn and Lou Brock. Brock was just a token appearance in '61, but he was in their lineup in '62 and '63; not in his prime, but in the lineup.) In 1966 they added Ferguson Jenkins. That's a LOT of Hall of Fame roster space for a team that did not win a pennant, and has as many bad years as good ones. By 1960 they were +15; by 1970 they had crept up to +38, meaning 38 more "points" of Hall of Fame recognition than performance. Then they had the Ryne Sandberg/Lee Smith teams that I talked about earlier, and their Hall of Fame recognition by the end of the century was well ahead of their on-field supremacy.

The White Sox have had consistently generous results in Hall of Fame voting throughout their history, which, in their case, is not TOO difficult to trace to individual players. Harold Baines was a controversial Hall of Fame selection (duh), but Baines had more WAR and more Win Shares than Ray Schalk, longtime White Sox catcher. Of six pitchers who are in the Hall of Fame and spent five or more seasons with the White Sox—Ted Lyons, Red Faber, Hoyt Wilhelm, Ed Walsh, Early Wynn and Goose Gossage—not one is a really obvious Hall of Fame selection. There's no Lefty Grove here, or Bob Gibson or Walter Johnson or Pete Alexander or Bob Feller or Warren Spahn or Mariano Rivera or Steve Carlton or Tom Seaver, although both Seaver and Carlton pitched for the White Sox in 1986, but not in a manner that would put anyone in the Hall of Fame.

The Expos are kind of the opposite; their Hall of Famers are pretty obvious Hall of Famers—Tim Raines, Andre Dawson, and Gary Carter—but, while the Expos had all three of them at the same time, they made the post-season only once. The Expos also housed Tony Pérez on their roster, and Randy Johnson, and Larry Walker, and Vladimir Guerrero, and Lee Smith for one dismal season, and Pedro Martínez for four seasons during which he emerged as *Pedro Martínez*, but still...their won-lost records do not match up to that quite impressive stretch of Hall of Fame talent. Do they? I don't see how anyone could argue that they do.

On the other end of the scale, the teams which have NOT done well as well in terms of Hall of Fame recognition as they have in terms of wins and losses, we have the following:

City	Team	Years	Total
Los Angeles	Dodgers	1900-2000	-320
Cincinnati	Reds	1900-2000	-297
Kansas City	Royals	1969-2000	-199
San Francisco	Giants	1900-2000	-186
New York	Yankees	1903-2000	-179
Toronto	Blue Jays	1977-2000	-170

That's a surprising list; one would not think of the Dodgers and the Yankees as being teams which have done poorly in Hall of Fame representation. But, since the Padres and Royals are both 1969 expansion teams, let us compare the two teams (1969 to 2000) in (1) on-field performance, and (2) Hall of Fame Recognition.

	Royals (1969-2000)	Padres (1969-2000)
World Series Wins	1	0
World Series Appearances	2	2
Division Championships	6	3
100-Win Seasons	1	0
90-Win Seasons	8	3
Winning Seasons	16	9
Regular Season Wins	2548	2315
Regular Season Winning Percentage	.505	.458
Post Season Wins	18	7
100-Loss Seasons	None	5

It is really not a close call as to which franchise was more successful over their first 32 seasons. But now let us compare them in terms of Hall of Famers on the roster:

	Royals (1969-2000)	Padres (1969-2000)
Hall of Fame Players	4	10
Prime Seasons by Hall of Fame Players	12	40
Total seasons by Hall of Fame Players	24	86

The Royals' Hall of Fame players are George Brett, Gaylord Perry, Harmon Killebrew and Orlando Cepeda—and Perry, Killebrew and Cepeda were all *seriously* washed up by the time they came to KC. The Padres Hall of Fame players are Dave Winfield, Willie McCovey, Rollie Fingers, Gaylord Perry, Ozzie Smith, Tony Gwynn, Goose Gossage, Roberto Alomar and Trevor Hoffman.

The Royals' prime seasons by Hall of Fame players are George Brett, 12. The Padres' prime seasons by Hall of Fame players are Tony Gwynn, 15, Trevor Hoffman, 7 (by the year 2000), Rollie Fingers, 5, Dave Winfield, 4, Ozzie Smith, 4, Goose Gossage, 2, Roberto Alomar, 2, and Gaylord Perry, 1.

I hope you understand what I am saying. I am not saying that any particular Padre player does not belong in the Hall of Fame, or that any particular Royals' player does. I am saying that (1) one might reasonably expect that, over time, Hall of Fame recognition would match up with team success at some level, and (2) comparing these two teams, this is manifestly not true.

The Dodgers, now. The Dodgers while they were in Brooklyn basically matched their on-field success and their Hall of Fame recognition. Through 1957 they are +27 points, which, spread over 58 seasons, is almost nothing. This continued to be true through the 1960s, the Drysdale/Koufax seasons. Through 1969, Drysdale's last season, the franchise was +12—over 70 years.

Since 1970 and up to 2000, their Hall of Fame recognition has lagged far, far behind the team's on-field accomplishments. You can't really blame the Hall of Fame voters, or blame the selectors. What has actually happened is that the Dodgers have had a tremendous number of players who were really, really good, but maybe probably not QUITE Hall of Fame good. If you look at the 1981 World Championship team, you could make that statement about all four starting pitchers (Fernando Valenzuela, Jerry Reuss, Burt Hooton and Bob Welch) and all four regular infielders (Garvey, Lopes, Cey and Russell). They were all *good*, but none of them was quite *great*. The same thing with two of their outfielders, Dusty Baker and Pedro Guerrero, and two reserve outfielders on that team, Rick Monday and Reggie Smith; they all had really good careers, but not one of them had a really great career. The only two Hall of Fame talents produced by the Dodger system since 1966 are Pedro Martinez and Mike Piazza, both of whom made their major league debuts in September, 1992, and both of whom got away from the Dodgers relatively early in their careers. In spite of that, the Dodgers have had a lot of good years.

And the pattern for the Dodgers' eternal nemesis, the New York/San Francisco Giants, is exactly the same. While the Giants were in New York, overall, the team's Hall of Fame recognition basically matched their Hall of Fame success, the Giants being just +4 over 58 years through 1957. Through 1970, through Willie Mays' San Francisco seasons, this continued to be true. The Giants had a huge load of Hall of Famers in the early 1960s, but they also won 90+ games every year like clockwork. Through 1972, the Giants are +/- zero, exactly even.

From 1973 to 2000 the Giants were not tremendously successful, but they weren't terrible, either; in that period they had 13 winning seasons, most of those at least ten games over .500. The Giants have not had a prime season by a Hall of Fame player since Gaylord Perry in 1971. Since 1974 they have had only ten seasons by Hall of Fame players, almost all of those tail-end-of-career seasons.

Were it not for the success of the Padres in earning Hall of Fame recognition, one might argue that there is some sort of anti-California unintentional bias at work here. Night games on the coast; nobody sees them. But the Padres kind of kick that argument in the head.

The Cincinnati Reds are the answer to the Chicago White Sox; they have just generally done poorly in Hall of Fame selections from 1900 until now. By 1920 the franchise was -66; by 1940, -97. By 1960 they were -202. By 1980 they were -258. By 2000 they were -297. Ted Kluszewski and Vada Pinson just didn't QUITE make the Hall of Fame. Pete Rose's blundering criminality contributes to the negative score. The Milt Pappas trade didn't help.

And then, the Yankees. This is the most surprising finding of the study. An earlier study that I did argued that the Yankees (and New York teams in general) had been blessed in Hall of Fame selections. That study compared marginal players who were or were not selected to the Hall of Fame, balancing the scales by individual players. This study, of course, approaches the issue in an entirely different way.

And looked at in this way, the Yankees have always been a little bit behind. By 1920, when they acquired the Bambino, they were -24. By 1940, the middle of DiMaggio's career, they were -26. Yes, they had a tremendous number of Hall of Famers in those years—but they _won_, dammit. If you win, you're supposed to have Hall of Famers. By 1960, the middle of Mickey Mantle's career, they were minus 43.

But what really drags them down is the 1970s and 1980s. From 1970 to 2000, the Yankees had 25 winning seasons, won 90 or more games 12 times, won 100 or more games four times, and won I-don't-know-how-many World Championships.

But many of the guys in there who could be in the Hall of Fame, aren't. Ron Guidry isn't. Don Mattingly isn't. Thurman the Nasty isn't. Graig Nettles isn't. Willie Randolph isn't. Roy White and Bobby Murcer, OK, they're not Hall of Famers, but they were really good players.

The Yankees, of course, have significant Hall of Fame participation in those years. They had 55 seasons of Hall of Fame play in there, including 32 prime seasons by Hall of Famers (Dave Winfield, 8, Goose Gossage, 5, Derek Jeter, 5, Mariano Rivera, 5, Reggie Jackson, 4, Rickey Henderson, 3, Catfish Hunter, 1, and Wade Boggs, 1.) Those aren't bad numbers, 55 and 32. The San Diego Padres' counts are 86 and 40.   It doesn't balance.

By my math. If you don't like my math, do your own. It's not like I'm a Yankee fan or something. Thanks for reading.

Hall of Fame Monitor

Bill James

For any active player who hopes to become a Hall of Famer, the 2020 season was a roadblock. Nobody got 200 hits, nobody played in the All Star game, nobody drove in 100 runs or hit 40 homers or broke any big records. Even those things that *were* done, like the batting championships that were won and the awards that will be awarded, have been damaged or devalued by the shortened season. For any player who is in position to make the Hall of Fame but still has work to do, the pandemic of 2020 was a wasted year with the clock running. There very probably are a couple of players who will not make the Hall of Fame because the 2020 season took away a season that they did not have to spare.

Forty years ago, before there were any analytical statistics to summarize the value of the things a player had done (stats like WAR and Win Shares), players were evaluated largely by how often they met standards of excellence. A player made progress toward the Hall of Fame, in that environment, by doing things like hitting .300, winning a batting title, hitting 40 homers, leading the league in homers, driving in 100 runs, scoring 100 runs, getting 200 hits in a season, making the All Star team, winning a Gold Glove, and a few other distinguishing accomplishments.

Many years ago, I studied who got into the Hall of Fame based on which of those accomplishments a player had and how many of them. I tried to assess the "Hall of Fame value" of each accomplishment, and thus tried to ascertain where each player stood in relationship to the Hall of Fame. Over the years we have modified that system to include recognition for success in baseball as measured by modern methods; however, the system has generally been accurate at projecting who will go into the Hall of Fame.

Accurate, but not perfect. The system is set with 100 points as the Hall of Fame breakpoint. If you have more than 100 points, generally speaking, you're a Hall Famer; less than 100, you're not. The system suggests that there are nine active players who have Hall of Fame resumes sufficient to pretty much ensure their enshrinement at Cooperstown. Six of those are unproblematic; that is, most of you would agree that those players are headed for the Hall. Those six are Mike Trout, Clayton Kershaw, Max Scherzer, Miguel Cabrera, Justin Verlander and Albert Pujols.

The other three are problematic. Robinson Canó has 132 points, José Altuve 107, and Ryan Braun 100. While these players have many Hall of Fame type accomplishments among them, there are issues which have come up in their careers which will damage their cases when the time comes.

Beyond those nine, there are three other classes of players that we should discuss. There are players whose accomplishments do not yet guarantee their acceptance as Hall of Famers, but who have good resumes and are still building them. That group includes Mookie Betts, Nolan Arenado, Corey Kluber, Zack Greinke, Joey Votto, Jon Lester, and Yadier Molina. In our view, those players have not yet clinched a plaque on the wall. Craig Kimbrel also falls mathematically into that group, although in his case I lack confidence that the process is working correctly.

A second group of candidates is young players who are still substantially short of a Hall of Fame resume, but who are in good position early in their careers. That group includes Francisco Lindor, Bryce Harper, Manny Machado, Xander Bogaerts, Christian Yelich, and Kris Bryant.

And then there is a third group of players who you can't really say aren't Hall of Famers; they might be, might not. Que sera sera. Cody Bellinger, Alex Bregman, Gerrit Cole, Freddie Freeman, Paul Goldschmidt, Jacob deGrom and many more. That's why we publish these lists, not to decide for you whether a player should be in or out, but simply to help you organize your thinking about the issue. Analytical methods are not supposed to make decisions for us; they are supposed to help us think more clearly, by pointing out to us things—and people—that we might not have thought about.

Thank you for reading.

Bill James

Hall of Fame Monitor

Player	Age	2020	Career
Rafael Devers	**23**	**0**	**18**
Ozzie Albies	23	0	14
Cody Bellinger	**24**	**0**	**33**
Roberto Osuna	**25**	**0**	**24**
Carlos Correa	25	0	18
Andrew Benintendi	25	0	12
Francisco Lindor	**26**	**0**	**42**
Alex Bregman	26	0	27
Edwin Diaz	26	0	24
Corey Seager	26	0	23
Rougned Odor	26	0	12
Joey Gallo	26	0	11
Ketel Marte	26	0	11
Mookie Betts	**27**	**0**	**77**
Bryce Harper	27	0	68
Manny Machado	27	0	45
Xander Bogaerts	27	0	45
Jose Ramirez	27	1	36
Javier Baez	27	0	28
Trevor Story	27	2	24
Blake Snell	27	0	23
Aaron Nola	27	0	17
Matt Chapman	27	0	16
Trea Turner	27	1	13
Tim Anderson	27	1	11
Josh Bell	27	0	11
Kyle Freeland	27	1	10
Gary Sanchez	27	0	10
Mike Trout	**28**	**0**	**127**
Christian Yelich	28	0	46
Kris Bryant	28	0	42
Aaron Judge	28	0	24
Eugenio Suarez	28	0	20
Nicholas Castellanos	28	0	20
Carlos Martinez	28	0	17
Eddie Rosario	28	0	14
Jonathan Schoop	28	0	14
Jorge Soler	28	0	14
Joc Pederson	28	0	11
Willson Contreras	28	0	11
Corey Knebel	28	0	10
Michael Wacha	28	0	10
Nolan Arenado	**29**	**0**	**93**
Gerrit Cole	29	0	45
Marcell Ozuna	29	4	29
Trevor Bauer	29	4	23
J.T. Realmuto	29	0	17
Ken Giles	29	0	17
Alex Wood	29	0	16
Julio Teheran	29	0	15
Ender Inciarte	29	0	14
Marcus Semien	29	0	14
Jonathan Villar	29	0	13
Chris Devenski	29	0	12
Max Muncy	29	0	11
Hansel Robles	29	0	10
Jake Lamb	29	0	10
Joe Panik	29	0	10
Mike Clevinger	29	0	10
Wil Myers	29	0	10
Jose Altuve	**30**	**0**	**107**
Madison Bumgarner	30	0	67
Freddie Freeman	30	1	62
Giancarlo Stanton	30	0	60
Anthony Rizzo	30	0	57

Player	Age	2020	Career
Salvador Perez	30	0	50
Anthony Rendon	30	0	41
Jeurys Familia	30	0	36
Eric Hosmer	30	0	35
Jean Segura	30	0	28
Kelvin Herrera	30	0	27
George Springer	30	0	26
Starlin Castro	30	0	24
Trevor Rosenthal	30	0	24
Brad Hand	30	4	21
Andrelton Simmons	30	0	18
Jason Heyward	30	0	18
Kyle Hendricks	30	0	16
Patrick Corbin	30	0	16
Jackie Bradley Jr.	30	0	14
Raisel Iglesias	30	0	13
Sonny Gray	30	0	13
Travis Shaw	30	0	11
Will Smith	30	0	11
Matt Barnes	30	0	10
Mike Montgomery	30	0	10
DJ LeMahieu	**31**	**2**	**48**
Rick Porcello	31	0	43
Stephen Strasburg	31	0	35
Elvis Andrus	31	0	29
Whit Merrifield	31	0	28
Alex Colome	31	2	23
Mike Moustakas	31	0	20
Jose Quintana	31	0	19
Starling Marte	31	0	19
Corey Dickerson	31	0	15
Liam Hendriks	31	3	14
Eduardo Escobar	31	0	12
Shane Greene	31	0	12
Yasmani Grandal	31	0	12
Hector Neris	31	0	11
Marwin Gonzalez	31	0	11
Clayton Kershaw	**32**	**0**	**145**
Craig Kimbrel	32	0	99
Kenley Jansen	32	0	73
Paul Goldschmidt	32	0	73
J.D. Martinez	32	0	58
Aroldis Chapman	32	0	51
Jacob deGrom	32	4	49
Justin Upton	32	0	39
Dee Gordon	32	0	36
Dallas Keuchel	32	0	35
Zack Britton	32	0	35
Khris Davis	32	0	33
Blake Treinen	32	0	20
Hector Rondon	32	0	18
Bryan Shaw	32	0	17
Brandon Belt	32	0	16
Dellin Betances	32	0	16
Mike Minor	32	0	16
Trevor Cahill	32	0	16
Brad Boxberger	32	0	15
Kenta Maeda	32	0	14
David Peralta	32	0	13
Joe Kelly	32	0	13
Kyle Seager	32	0	13
Wilson Ramos	32	0	13
Jeremy Jeffress	32	0	11
Tommy Pham	32	0	11
Pedro Baez	32	0	10
Charlie Blackmon	**33**	**0**	**55**
Jose Abreu	33	3	54
Andrew McCutchen	33	0	52
Lance Lynn	33	2	36

Player	Age	2020	Career
Jay Bruce	33	0	33
Brian Dozier	33	0	32
Michael Brantley	33	0	32
Brandon Crawford	33	0	31
Pablo Sandoval	33	0	26
Yu Darvish	33	4	25
Jason Kipnis	33	0	24
Carlos Carrasco	33	0	20
Derek Holland	33	0	19
Kirby Yates	33	0	19
AJ Ramos	33	0	18
Josh Reddick	33	0	14
Justin Smoak	33	0	14
Wade Miley	33	0	14
Tanner Roark	33	0	13
Daniel Hudson	33	0	12
Hyun-Jin Ryu	33	0	12
Jake McGee	33	0	12
Alex Avila	33	0	11
Ivan Nova	33	0	11
Sean Doolittle	33	0	11
Tommy Hunter	33	0	11
Corey Kluber	**34**	**0**	**77**
Josh Donaldson	34	0	53
Evan Longoria	34	0	50
Johnny Cueto	34	0	47
Greg Holland	34	0	45
Chris Davis	34	0	44
Jake Arrieta	34	0	40
Wade Davis	34	0	37
Matt Carpenter	34	0	34
Gio Gonzalez	34	0	32
Carlos Santana	34	0	30
Lorenzo Cain	34	0	28
Asdrubal Cabrera	34	0	24
Jordan Zimmermann	34	0	24
Yoenis Cespedes	34	0	24
Dexter Fowler	34	0	22
Steve Cishek	34	0	22
Jonathan Lucroy	34	0	21
Todd Frazier	34	0	17
Matt Wieters	34	0	15
Jared Hughes	34	0	14
Homer Bailey	34	0	12
Mitch Moreland	34	0	11
Adam Ottavino	34	0	10
Brad Brach	34	0	10
Max Scherzer	**35**	**0**	**125**
Matt Kemp	35	0	50
Mark Melancon	35	0	47
Daniel Murphy	35	0	38
Ian Kennedy	35	0	33
Tony Watson	35	0	30
Jeff Samardzija	35	0	25
Tyler Clippard	35	0	25
Andrew Miller	35	0	24
Justin Turner	35	0	17
Pedro Strop	35	0	17
Will Harris	35	0	15
Jon Jay	35	0	13
Brandon Kintzler	35	1	12
Yusmeiro Petit	35	0	11
Ryan Braun	**36**	**0**	**100**
Zack Greinke	36	0	89
Joey Votto	36	0	87
Jon Lester	36	0	81
Cole Hamels	36	0	56
Nick Markakis	36	0	39
Alex Gordon	36	0	34
Joakim Soria	36	0	34
Brett Gardner	36	0	21

Player	Age	2020	Career
Anibal Sanchez	36	0	19
Charlie Morton	36	0	16
Edinson Volquez	36	0	16
Yuli Gurriel	36	0	16
Howie Kendrick	36	0	12
Kurt Suzuki	36	0	11
Miguel Cabrera	**37**	**0**	**190**
Justin Verlander	37	0	166
Robinson Cano	37	0	132
Yadier Molina	37	0	83
Edwin Encarnacion	37	0	65
Sergio Romo	37	0	39
Hunter Pence	37	0	34
Shin-Soo Choo	37	0	29
Darren O'Day	37	0	21
J.A. Happ	37	0	21
Adam Wainwright	**38**	**0**	**75**
Oliver Perez	38	0	16
Nelson Cruz	**39**	**0**	**81**
Albert Pujols	**40**	**0**	**243**

Hall of Fame Value

Mark Simon

Let's talk about the Hall of Fame candidacy of Freddie Freeman for a minute.

Freeman did his best to make the most of a bad situation this year, finishing with 17 Win Shares (most in MLB) and 2.9 Wins Above Replacement according to Baseball-Reference (tied for second among position players), adding 28.6 to his Hall of Fame Value total.

A brief reminder on how Hall of Fame Value works: It's the sum of a players Win Shares and 4 times his WAR. This was introduced in the 2019 Handbook by Bill James, who indicated that a Hall of Fame Value of 500 merited Hall of Fame induction.

Freeman is a likable player, one whose super-friendly dugout hugs were curtailed this season by coronavirus. Freeman himself battled and overcame the virus prior to the start of the season.

He's also in position to surpass the magic 500 number with 100 more points. First base can be a tough position, but consider how closely Freeman's career has statistically paralleled Hall of Fame first baseman Eddie Murray and you'll see a candidacy that is gaining strength.

Through Age-30 Season

	BA	OBP	SLG	OPS+
Freddie Freeman	.295	.383	.509	139
Eddie Murray	.299	.375	.505	143

Age through June 30 of that season

As for current Cooperstown candidates, there are 11 candidates on this year's Hall of Fame ballot who clear the 500 threshold. All 11 of those are holdover candidates from last year's ballot. If you're new to this, the one that might most surprise you is Bobby Abreu (596.1), who ranks fifth and is ahead of such notables as Curt Schilling, Jeff Kent, Sammy Sosa, and Andruw Jones.

As I noted here last year, Abreu hit .291/.395/.475 with 2,470 hits, 288 home runs and 400 stolen bases in an 18-year career. He just surpassed the 5% vote needed to stay on the Hall of Fame ballot, receiving 22 votes (5.5%).

One player whose candidacy is boosted by Hall of Fame Value is third baseman Scott Rolen (584.7). Rolen has some voting momentum—his vote percentage doubled from 17% to 35% on the last two ballots.

Among the new candidates on the ballot, outfielder Torii Hunter has the best case, but comes up a little short (477.3). Hunter hit 353 home runs, won nine Gold Glove Awards, was honored with the Branch Rickey Award for community service, and was nicknamed "Spiderman" for his wall-scaling ability.

But Hunter is hurt by his career OPS being only 10% above league average, when adjusting for ballpark and the era in which he played.

Pitching-wise, it's a similar sentiment for 214-game winner Mark Buehrle, who pitched two no-hitters, including a perfect game, and won a World Series with the 2005 White Sox. His Hall of Fame value of 457.3 is just below fellow lefty Andy Pettitte (465). Both were very good pitchers but don't make the Hall of Fame Value cut.

Body by Jake

Mets pitcher Jacob deGrom is going to make for an interesting Hall of Fame case. DeGrom's MLB career didn't start until he was 26, giving him a late start on some of the typical accomplishments of a Hall-of-Fame–caliber pitcher. He's almost the same age as Clayton Kershaw but has about half of Kershaw's Hall of Fame value.

DeGrom's last three seasons, at ages 30 to 32, have been remarkable. He's pitched to a 2.10 ERA and averaged 11.6 strikeouts per 9 innings. His 47 Win Shares and 20 Pitching WAR are the most of any pitcher in that time.

Hall of Fame Values by Age Group

Player	Age	2020 Season			Career		
		Win Shares	WAR	HoF Value	Win Shares	WAR	HoF Value
Soto, Juan	**21**	**14**	**2.1**	**22.2**	**53**	**9.5**	**90.9**
Tatis Jr., Fernando	21	12	2.5	22.2	30	6.7	56.7
Acuna Jr., Ronald	**22**	**9**	**2.0**	**17.2**	**56**	**11.9**	**103.6**
Albies, Ozzie	**23**	**5**	**0.6**	**7.2**	**60**	**11.6**	**106.2**
Torres, Gleyber	23	3	-0.2	2.1	50	6.4	75.7
Devers, Rafael	23	6	0.4	7.6	46	6.6	72.2
Bellinger, Cody	**24**	**9**	**1.4**	**14.7**	**82**	**19.0**	**157.8**
Adames, Willy	24	9	1.6	15.5	32	7.2	60.8
Flaherty, Jack	24	2	-0.3	0.7	28	7.7	59.0
Keller, Brad	24	5	1.7	11.8	26	8.1	58.2
Correa, Carlos	**25**	**6**	**1.5**	**12.0**	**101**	**24.1**	**197.5**
Marquez, German	25	6	1.7	12.8	47	14.1	103.3
Benintendi, Andrew	25	0	-0.2	-1.0	62	9.2	98.8
Osuna, Roberto	25	1	0.3	2.3	62	8.8	97.4
Moncada, Yoan	25	6	0.5	7.9	48	8.1	80.5
Bieber, Shane	25	11	3.2	24.0	37	8.8	72.3
Margot, Manuel	25	4	0.8	7.2	37	7.2	65.9
Laureano, Ramon	25	7	1.3	12.0	33	7.1	61.6
Mazara, Nomar	25	3	-0.3	1.9	55	1.5	60.8
Happ, Ian	25	9	1.1	13.4	40	4.6	58.2
Ohtani, Shohei	25	1	-0.6	-1.4	33	5.8	56.3
Lowe, Brandon	25	11	2.1	19.5	31	5.6	53.2
Arcia, Orlando	25	5	0.0	4.9	44	2.3	53.2
Giolito, Lucas	25	5	0.8	8.1	25	6.3	50.0
Lindor, Francisco	**26**	**6**	**0.8**	**9.2**	**117**	**29.6**	**235.4**
Bregman, Alex	26	6	0.8	9.2	106	22.8	197.1
Seager, Corey	26	9	1.9	16.5	99	18.8	174.3
Marte, Ketel	26	5	1.3	10.2	72	16.2	136.6
Olson, Matt	26	8	1.1	12.3	57	13.3	110.3
Odor, Rougned	26	3	-0.8	-0.1	82	6.3	107.2
Polanco, Jorge	26	6	0.0	6.0	67	9.0	103.0
DeJong, Paul	26	6	0.2	6.6	55	11.8	102.2
Gallo, Joey	26	6	1.2	11.0	48	9.8	87.2
Buxton, Byron	26	5	1.9	12.6	38	11.8	85.4
Swanson, Dansby	26	10	2.6	20.5	54	6.9	81.6
Berrios, Jose	26	4	0.7	6.9	39	8.2	71.8
Hader, Josh	26	4	0.4	5.6	40	7.0	68.0
Diaz, Edwin	26	4	1.3	9.2	43	6.2	67.7
Fletcher, David	26	7	1.6	13.2	33	8.4	66.4
McCullers Jr., Lance	26	2	0.6	4.2	28	6.9	55.5
Bader, Harrison	26	4	0.8	7.4	28	6.6	54.3
Betts, Mookie	**27**	**13**	**3.4**	**26.5**	**160**	**45.2**	**340.9**
Machado, Manny	27	10	2.8	21.3	169	39.3	326.4
Harper, Bryce	27	9	1.6	15.6	188	33.5	322.0
Ramirez, Jose	27	11	2.1	19.6	119	27.3	228.4
Bogaerts, Xander	27	6	1.4	11.4	123	22.5	212.9
Story, Trevor	27	7	2.1	15.5	81	19.6	159.4
Turner, Trea	27	13	2.1	21.2	91	15.8	154.0
Chapman, Matt	27	5	1.0	9.2	66	21.2	150.9
Baez, Javier	27	3	0.6	5.6	78	18.0	150.0
Nola, Aaron	27	4	2.2	12.9	59	22.1	147.3
Conforto, Michael	27	8	2.0	16.0	83	14.5	140.9
Sanchez, Gary	27	2	-0.5	-0.1	52	10.7	113.8
Anderson, Tim	27	7	2.2	15.8	56	12.7	106.6
Kepler, Max	27	6	0.8	9.1	58	12.1	106.3
Sano, Miguel	27	4	-0.2	3.1	66	7.5	95.9
Snell, Blake	27	4	1.1	8.4	43	11.9	90.7
Freeland, Kyle	27	5	2.2	13.8	37	12.9	88.7
Anderson, Brian	27	12	1.7	18.8	54	8.6	88.4
Davies, Zach	27	6	1.6	12.6	41	9.7	79.6
Schwarber, Kyle	27	6	-0.2	5.3	59	4.8	79.2
Hoskins, Rhys	27	6	0.7	8.8	56	5.3	77.1
Franco, Maikel	27	8	0.9	11.7	65	2.5	75.0
Bell, Josh	27	2	-0.7	-0.7	60	3.6	74.5
Nimmo, Brandon	27	6	1.5	12.2	44	7.6	74.2
Castillo, Luis	27	6	0.9	9.8	34	9.3	71.2

Hall of Fame Values by Age Group

Player	Age	2020 Season			Career		
		Win Shares	WAR	HoF Value	Win Shares	WAR	HoF Value
DeShields, Delino	27	3	-0.2	2.3	47	5.5	69.1
Bundy, Dylan	27	5	1.8	12.1	32	8.7	67.0
Santana, Domingo	27	1	-0.4	-0.5	50	3.7	65.0
Fulmer, Michael	27	0	-0.8	-3.2	28	8.5	62.0
Smith, Mallex	27	0	-0.5	-2.1	38	5.6	60.2
Bradley, Archie	27	4	0.5	6.1	38	5.5	60.0
Walker, Taijuan	27	4	1.3	9.2	31	7.1	59.5
Profar, Jurickson	27	6	1.1	10.6	44	3.7	58.8
Rodon, Carlos	27	0	-0.3	-1.4	27	6.3	52.2
Alfaro, Jorge	27	4	-0.4	2.2	31	2.9	51.1
Trout, Mike	**28**	**10**	**1.6**	**16.3**	**309**	**74.0**	**605.1**
Yelich, Christian	28	4	0.1	4.5	160	33.3	293.1
Bryant, Kris	28	3	0.3	4.0	129	25.4	230.7
Suarez, Eugenio	28	6	0.4	7.6	99	15.1	159.2
Judge, Aaron	28	4	1.0	8.0	68	20.1	148.4
Schoop, Jonathan	28	6	0.9	9.8	82	14.6	140.4
Contreras, Willson	28	9	0.8	12.0	62	12.5	132.2
Castellanos, Nick	28	3	-0.2	2.3	104	6.9	131.5
Martinez, Carlos	28	0	-1.1	-4.6	66	14.0	121.9
Rosario, Eddie	28	9	0.9	12.4	73	11.7	120.0
Pederson, Joc	28	3	-0.4	1.3	72	10.1	112.4
Grichuk, Randal	28	8	0.1	8.5	62	10.1	102.2
Hernandez, Kike	28	4	0.9	7.5	54	10.7	96.7
Sanchez, Yolmer	28	1	0.3	2.2	56	7.8	87.2
Polanco, Gregory	28	1	-1.2	-3.7	66	4.9	85.5
Ray, Robbie	28	1	-0.2	0.3	46	8.7	81.0
Gray, Jon	28	1	-0.2	0.1	40	10.0	80.1
Flores, Wilmer	28	5	1.0	9.2	66	3.0	78.1
McNeil, Jeff	28	6	1.3	11.2	41	9.2	77.8
Frazier, Adam	28	3	0.3	4.4	48	7.3	77.3
Wacha, Michael	28	0	-0.2	-0.9	45	7.0	73.1
Narvaez, Omar	28	4	-0.3	2.6	38	5.2	70.3
Manaea, Sean	28	2	0.3	3.0	30	8.9	65.7
Soler, Jorge	28	4	0.1	4.4	49	4.0	64.9
Renfroe, Hunter	28	2	-0.1	1.4	36	6.1	60.3
Gonzales, Marco	28	5	1.5	10.9	29	7.5	58.9
Lorenzen, Michael	28	3	0.2	4.0	34	6.2	58.8
Claudio, Alex	28	1	0.1	1.4	29	6.0	53.1
Owings, Chris	28	1	0.1	1.5	42	2.6	52.3
Urshela, Gio	28	8	1.9	15.4	33	4.6	51.5
Arenado, Nolan	**29**	**2**	**1.4**	**7.7**	**153**	**41.3**	**318.1**
Realmuto, J.T.	29	6	1.2	10.7	102	19.1	212.2
Ozuna, Marcell	29	13	2.3	22.3	127	21.3	212.1
Semien, Marcus	29	8	0.4	9.5	116	22.1	204.2
Cole, Gerrit	29	6	2.2	14.6	93	25.9	196.5
Wong, Kolten	29	8	1.2	12.7	96	17.0	163.9
Inciarte, Ender	29	1	-0.7	-2.0	86	18.4	159.6
Teheran, Julio	29	0	-1.0	-4.0	75	19.3	152.2
Bauer, Trevor	29	10	2.7	20.9	75	18.0	147.2
Myers, Wil	29	10	1.6	16.6	97	11.0	141.1
Villar, Jonathan	29	2	-0.3	0.8	80	11.7	126.7
Taylor, Chris	29	9	1.8	16.4	69	12.9	120.4
Piscotty, Stephen	29	4	-0.2	3.3	72	8.0	104.0
Clevinger, Mike	29	4	1.1	8.3	48	13.5	102.1
Garcia, Avisail	29	3	-0.5	1.1	75	6.6	101.3
Panik, Joe	29	3	-0.4	1.3	75	6.1	99.3
Zunino, Mike	29	2	-0.2	1.3	54	6.5	96.1
Barnhart, Tucker	29	5	0.8	8.2	54	6.5	95.6
Gausman, Kevin	29	4	1.3	9.1	47	11.5	93.2
Wood, Alex	29	0	-0.4	-1.6	48	11.0	92.0
Hamilton, Billy	29	1	0.1	1.3	53	9.3	90.2
Muncy, Max	29	5	0.2	5.6	51	9.7	90.0
Giles, Ken	29	0	-0.2	-0.6	52	7.8	83.0
Marisnick, Jake	29	1	0.2	1.6	38	10.6	80.5
Lamb, Jake	29	3	-0.6	0.6	54	6.1	78.6
Perez, Martin	29	3	1.0	7.2	42	6.6	68.3
Vazquez, Christian	29	5	0.7	7.8	42	3.7	67.7
Diaz, Aledmys	29	1	0.1	1.5	42	5.9	65.7
Garver, Mitch	29	1	-0.1	0.7	31	5.0	60.5
Rogers, Taylor	29	2	-0.7	-0.6	34	5.9	57.4
Voit, Luke	29	9	1.5	14.9	38	4.5	56.2
Matz, Steven	29	0	-1.0	-4.1	25	6.9	52.4
Boyd, Matthew	29	0	-0.6	-2.4	27	6.3	52.1

Hall of Fame Values by Age Group

Player	Age	2020 Season			Career		
		Win Shares	WAR	HoF Value	Win Shares	WAR	HoF Value
Green, Chad	29	3	0.4	4.4	27	5.9	50.6
Freeman, Freddie	**30**	**17**	**2.9**	**28.6**	**243**	**39.4**	**400.7**
Altuve, Jose	30	2	-0.4	0.5	200	37.7	351.0
Stanton, Giancarlo	30	2	0.4	3.8	175	40.6	337.6
Heyward, Jason	30	9	1.3	14.3	178	38.5	331.9
Rizzo, Anthony	30	5	0.8	8.1	192	33.5	325.9
Rendon, Anthony	30	7	1.8	14.3	158	29.8	277.2
Bumgarner, Madison	30	0	-0.3	-1.2	124	36.8	271.3
Simmons, Andrelton	30	2	0.3	3.4	122	37.2	270.7
Perez, Salvador	30	7	1.9	14.7	129	24.0	269.8
Springer, George	30	10	1.9	17.6	124	26.7	230.9
Castro, Starlin	30	1	0.4	2.5	158	17.9	229.7
Hosmer, Eric	30	6	0.9	9.8	163	16.3	228.4
Segura, Jean	30	6	1.1	10.6	134	19.8	213.2
Kiermaier, Kevin	30	6	1.5	12.2	78	27.6	188.6
Gregorius, Didi	30	9	0.9	12.6	111	17.7	181.9
Hendricks, Kyle	30	7	1.9	14.5	75	21.7	161.6
Hernandez, Cesar	30	8	1.5	13.8	104	11.1	148.5
Corbin, Patrick	30	2	1.8	9.0	71	19.3	148.0
Bradley Jr., Jackie	30	5	1.9	12.7	80	17.0	148.0
Gray, Sonny	30	5	0.6	7.5	72	19.0	147.9
Iglesias, Jose	30	8	1.1	12.6	85	11.7	131.7
Galvis, Freddy	30	4	0.1	4.4	88	7.5	118.2
Hicks, Aaron	30	7	0.6	9.3	70	11.9	117.7
Shaw, Travis	30	3	0.0	3.1	68	10.4	109.8
Odorizzi, Jake	30	0	-0.2	-0.8	56	13.0	108.1
Miller, Brad	30	5	0.7	7.8	73	8.3	106.2
Ahmed, Nick	30	6	1.2	10.9	54	12.5	104.0
McCann, James	30	5	1.2	9.8	56	7.5	103.0
Herrera, Kelvin	30	0	-0.1	-0.5	61	9.7	99.6
Wheeler, Zack	30	5	2.9	16.7	42	13.4	95.7
Cron, C.J.	30	2	0.2	3.0	67	6.9	94.7
Grossman, Robbie	30	7	1.0	10.9	68	6.2	92.9
Dietrich, Derek	30	2	0.1	2.3	71	5.2	91.7
Chatwood, Tyler	30	1	-0.1	0.6	46	11.2	90.9
Iglesias, Raisel	30	6	0.2	6.7	51	8.7	85.8
Hand, Brad	30	6	0.7	8.6	57	6.8	84.3
Familia, Jeurys	30	2	0.5	4.0	54	7.3	83.2
Eovaldi, Nathan	30	3	1.2	7.8	38	10.2	78.9
Rosenthal, Trevor	30	5	1.2	9.8	47	5.8	70.2
Wendle, Joey	30	7	1.2	11.9	34	7.3	63.1
Smith, Will	30	1	0.2	1.8	44	4.7	62.8
Lugo, Seth	30	2	0.3	3.2	31	7.4	60.6
Givens, Mychal	30	1	0.4	2.7	32	6.9	59.5
Aguilar, Jesus	30	8	0.4	9.7	44	3.6	58.4
Montgomery, Mike	30	0	-0.1	-0.6	28	6.4	53.6
DeSclafani, Anthony	30	0	-0.6	-2.5	27	6.1	51.3
Anderson, Tyler	30	3	0.4	4.6	24	6.6	50.6
Andrus, Elvis	**31**	**1**	**-0.6**	**-1.4**	**203**	**31.5**	**329.2**
Marte, Starling	31	6	1.2	10.8	137	30.4	258.8
LeMahieu, DJ	31	12	2.9	23.5	143	25.7	245.8
Strasburg, Stephen	31	0	-0.2	-0.9	107	33.6	241.4
Grandal, Yasmani	31	7	0.6	9.4	121	17.0	223.5
Quintana, Jose	31	0	0.0	0.0	89	24.9	188.4
Porcello, Rick	31	1	0.1	1.2	106	20.0	185.9
Eaton, Adam	31	4	-0.9	0.5	112	18.0	184.0
Moustakas, Mike	31	5	0.1	5.5	112	16.7	179.0
Tanaka, Masahiro	31	3	0.7	5.8	69	18.1	141.3
Merrifield, Whit	31	9	0.5	11.0	81	14.9	140.5
Escobar, Eduardo	31	2	-0.8	-1.0	96	10.7	138.7
Pillar, Kevin	31	5	0.7	7.8	73	15.9	136.6
Dickerson, Corey	31	3	0.0	2.8	83	12.8	134.2
Gonzalez, Marwin	31	4	0.0	4.1	80	13.4	133.4
Duffy, Danny	31	2	0.3	3.2	65	16.4	130.7
Gyorko, Jedd	31	3	0.6	5.6	78	10.4	119.4
Paxton, James	31	0	-0.4	-1.5	47	12.6	97.5
Pomeranz, Drew	31	4	1.0	8.0	50	11.9	97.4
Lagares, Juan	31	0	0.1	0.4	44	12.4	93.5
Pineda, Michael	31	2	0.4	3.6	47	11.4	92.4
Colome, Alex	31	5	0.9	8.8	59	7.7	89.6
Perez, Roberto	31	3	0.1	3.3	45	7.1	88.3
Adams, Matt	31	0	-0.5	-2.0	65	5.6	87.2
Canha, Mark	31	11	1.4	16.5	55	7.5	85.2

Hall of Fame Values by Age Group

Player	Age	2020 Season			Career		
		Win Shares	WAR	HoF Value	Win Shares	WAR	HoF Value
Hechavarria, Adeiny	31	1	-0.4	-0.5	66	4.8	85.2
Rojas, Miguel	31	10	1.5	16.0	51	8.4	84.5
d'Arnaud, Travis	31	6	0.6	8.5	55	3.8	83.6
Harvey, Matt	31	0	-0.6	-2.4	40	9.7	78.8
Smyly, Drew	31	2	0.4	3.8	40	9.6	78.4
Duvall, Adam	31	4	0.6	6.4	43	7.1	71.6
Neris, Hector	31	2	-0.1	1.8	42	6.4	67.8
Pressly, Ryan	31	2	0.3	3.0	37	6.8	64.3
Souza Jr., Steven	31	0	-0.1	-0.2	41	5.6	63.3
Hendriks, Liam	31	6	1.4	11.5	37	4.7	56.0
La Stella, Tommy	31	7	0.5	9.0	38	3.8	53.1
Leon, Sandy	31	1	-0.3	0.0	35	2.0	51.3
Martinez, Jose	31	2	-0.6	-0.4	41	2.5	50.8
Kershaw, Clayton	**32**	**6**	**1.7**	**12.9**	**207**	**69.3**	**484.2**
Goldschmidt, Paul	32	9	1.7	15.8	223	45.2	403.7
Upton, Justin	32	2	-0.6	-0.4	206	33.6	340.5
Seager, Kyle	32	10	0.6	12.5	180	30.9	303.7
Martinez, J.D.	32	2	-0.9	-1.6	154	23.1	246.4
deGrom, Jacob	32	6	2.5	16.2	95	37.7	245.6
Belt, Brandon	32	7	2.0	14.8	143	25.3	244.1
Ramos, Wilson	32	1	0.2	1.6	113	15.4	209.6
Kimbrel, Craig	32	1	-0.1	0.4	126	19.5	204.0
Jansen, Kenley	32	4	0.3	5.2	126	16.2	190.6
Chapman, Aroldis	32	2	0.4	3.6	113	18.0	185.0
Calhoun, Kole	32	7	1.0	11.0	114	16.8	181.3
Pollock, A.J.	32	5	0.6	7.5	97	20.8	180.4
Keuchel, Dallas	32	7	2.0	15.2	85	22.3	174.4
Gomes, Yan	32	2	0.6	4.6	74	13.6	153.0
Strange-Gordon, Dee	32	0	-0.6	-2.4	105	11.9	152.5
Chacin, Jhoulys	32	0	-0.1	-0.4	72	19.9	151.4
Harrison, Josh	32	2	0.2	2.8	91	13.5	145.0
Peralta, David	32	6	0.4	7.5	87	14.4	144.6
Britton, Zack	32	4	0.5	6.1	85	14.7	143.9
Davis, Khris	32	0	-0.4	-1.6	95	11.5	141.1
Minor, Mike	32	0	0.0	0.2	66	17.9	137.6
Pham, Tommy	32	2	-0.2	1.0	68	14.6	126.4
Cahill, Trevor	32	2	0.5	4.1	68	11.6	114.4
Betances, Dellin	32	0	-0.2	-1.0	58	11.4	103.6
Cobb, Alex	32	2	1.0	6.0	52	12.6	102.4
Morrison, Logan	32	0	-0.3	-1.4	79	4.4	96.4
Anderson, Brett	32	3	0.6	5.4	53	10.8	96.2
Gibson, Kyle	32	2	0.0	2.0	53	9.7	91.9
Holt, Brock	32	1	-0.7	-1.9	58	7.1	86.6
Jeffress, Jeremy	32	6	1.2	10.6	51	8.7	85.7
Treinen, Blake	32	2	-0.3	1.0	47	8.0	79.2
Anderson, Chase	32	0	-0.5	-1.9	46	8.0	78.0
Richards, Garrett	32	3	0.9	6.8	45	8.0	77.0
Wilson, Justin	32	2	0.2	2.7	44	7.3	73.2
Rondon, Hector	32	0	-0.6	-2.4	52	5.1	72.2
Shaw, Bryan	32	0	-0.7	-2.8	48	5.0	68.0
Maeda, Kenta	32	7	1.6	13.2	40	6.8	67.3
Kelly, Joe	32	1	0.2	1.8	43	5.8	66.0
Solano, Donovan	32	7	1.3	12.1	46	3.5	60.2
Peacock, Brad	32	0	-0.1	-0.4	30	5.4	51.6
McCutchen, Andrew	**33**	**6**	**-0.5**	**4.1**	**283**	**43.4**	**456.7**
Brantley, Michael	33	9	1.5	15.0	167	29.1	283.3
Kipnis, Jason	33	5	0.6	7.4	152	23.1	244.4
Bruce, Jay	33	1	0.1	1.2	168	19.1	244.3
Abreu, Jose	33	10	2.8	21.0	147	23.4	240.7
Dozier, Brian	33	0	-0.4	-1.6	142	24.2	238.7
Crawford, Brandon	33	6	1.2	11.0	142	24.1	238.3
Blackmon, Charlie	33	7	0.5	9.0	153	18.4	226.8
Sandoval, Pablo	33	0	-0.6	-2.4	148	19.5	226.6
Reddick, Josh	33	5	-0.7	2.3	127	24.2	224.0
Avila, Alex	33	1	0.4	2.5	103	16.3	200.2
Lynn, Lance	33	7	2.3	16.1	90	24.4	187.5
Darvish, Yu	33	9	2.6	19.5	81	24.7	179.7
Carrasco, Carlos	33	6	1.6	12.3	88	22.1	176.4
Maybin, Cameron	33	2	-0.3	0.6	107	14.1	163.4
Castro, Jason	33	3	-0.3	1.8	79	11.7	150.6
Roark, Tanner	33	0	-0.4	-1.4	66	19.1	142.4
Smoak, Justin	33	0	-0.8	-3.4	110	6.2	134.9
Ryu, Hyun-Jin	33	5	3.0	17.0	59	17.5	129.0

Hall of Fame Values by Age Group

Player	Age	2020 Season			Career		
		Win Shares	WAR	HoF Value	Win Shares	WAR	HoF Value
Forsythe, Logan	33	0	-0.4	-1.4	76	12.4	125.6
Nova, Ivan	33	0	-0.5	-2.0	64	12.2	112.8
Hunter, Tommy	33	2	0.6	4.5	67	10.9	110.6
Miley, Wade	33	0	-0.1	-0.5	67	10.7	109.6
Maldonado, Martin	33	7	0.7	9.9	61	6.9	105.6
Mercer, Jordy	33	0	-0.1	-0.4	72	8.2	104.8
Doolittle, Sean	33	0	0.0	0.1	62	9.3	99.2
Holland, Derek	33	0	-1.0	-4.2	60	8.0	92.0
McGee, Jake	33	3	0.4	4.7	53	7.4	82.7
Nunez, Eduardo	33	0	0.0	0.1	70	1.3	75.4
Hudson, Daniel	33	1	0.0	0.8	51	6.0	74.8
Ramos, AJ	33	0	0.1	0.2	44	6.1	68.3
Shoemaker, Matt	33	1	0.6	3.5	35	7.7	65.9
Phelps, David	33	2	0.2	3.0	38	5.7	60.8
Pina, Manny	33	2	0.5	3.9	29	5.0	58.8
Thames, Eric	33	1	-0.6	-1.4	48	2.5	57.9
Milone, Tommy	33	1	-0.4	-0.6	37	4.5	54.9
Vincent, Nick	33	1	0.4	2.4	32	5.4	53.7
Yates, Kirby	33	0	-0.3	-1.4	33	4.5	50.9
Longoria, Evan	**34**	**1**	**0.4**	**2.8**	**233**	**54.5**	**451.0**
Donaldson, Josh	34	3	0.4	4.7	187	44.6	366.1
Santana, Carlos	34	6	0.6	8.5	196	31.2	337.2
Cabrera, Asdrubal	34	4	-0.1	3.7	206	27.4	315.7
Cain, Lorenzo	34	1	0.2	1.8	145	37.0	293.1
Carpenter, Matt	34	3	-0.1	2.6	184	26.9	291.7
Cueto, Johnny	34	2	0.1	2.3	128	32.4	257.6
Walker, Neil	34	0	-0.2	-1.0	171	21.0	254.9
Lucroy, Jonathan	34	0	0.0	0.0	137	18.1	249.4
Wieters, Matt	34	1	0.0	0.8	134	18.2	247.9
Fowler, Dexter	34	2	-0.1	1.6	170	19.4	247.6
Kluber, Corey	34	0	0.1	0.2	109	33.2	241.7
Gonzalez, Gio	34	1	-0.3	-0.1	115	29.1	231.2
Frazier, Todd	34	3	0.1	3.4	125	25.9	228.6
Cespedes, Yoenis	34	0	-0.1	-0.4	118	21.6	204.5
Arrieta, Jake	34	2	0.8	5.0	95	26.2	199.9
Davis, Chris	34	0	-1.0	-4.0	140	12.3	189.0
Zimmermann, Jordan	34	0	-0.2	-0.7	84	21.2	168.9
Cervelli, Francisco	34	3	0.6	5.6	81	13.6	161.7
Moreland, Mitch	34	5	1.0	9.0	99	9.9	138.8
Davis, Wade	34	0	-0.7	-2.9	94	10.9	137.5
Holland, Greg	34	5	0.9	8.6	86	12.4	135.4
Cishek, Steve	34	1	-0.2	0.0	80	12.3	129.3
Flowers, Tyler	34	0	0.2	0.7	61	7.8	110.4
Ottavino, Adam	34	1	-0.1	0.4	53	10.7	95.8
Bailey, Homer	34	1	0.2	1.6	60	6.2	84.8
Sogard, Eric	34	3	-0.4	1.4	54	7.0	82.2
Hughes, Jared	34	1	-0.3	0.0	48	8.3	81.2
Brach, Brad	34	0	-0.1	-0.2	47	6.5	73.0
Joseph, Caleb	34	0	0.0	0.1	34	4.5	61.8
Jones, Nate	34	0	-0.3	-1.2	30	6.1	54.3
Scherzer, Max	**35**	**4**	**2.2**	**12.9**	**189**	**62.5**	**439.1**
Kemp, Matt	35	4	-0.1	3.6	218	21.2	302.8
Turner, Justin	35	8	1.3	13.2	154	30.0	274.0
Murphy, Daniel	35	2	-1.3	-3.2	191	18.2	263.9
Joyce, Matt	35	3	-0.6	0.4	110	14.1	166.4
Jay, Jon	35	0	-0.4	-1.7	111	12.5	160.8
Clippard, Tyler	35	3	0.4	4.4	95	15.3	156.4
Kennedy, Ian	35	0	-0.9	-3.5	90	15.9	153.6
Melancon, Mark	35	3	1.0	7.0	93	12.0	140.9
Dyson, Jarrod	35	1	-0.8	-2.0	69	15.6	131.5
Samardzija, Jeff	35	0	-0.7	-2.6	72	14.5	130.0
Watson, Tony	35	3	0.1	3.5	70	12.0	118.0
Fiers, Mike	35	3	0.6	5.6	61	11.8	108.1
Miller, Andrew	35	2	0.2	2.6	73	8.1	105.4
Vogt, Stephen	35	1	-0.1	0.6	57	8.0	103.4
Rodriguez, Sean	35	0	-0.3	-1.1	62	8.6	96.4
Strop, Pedro	35	0	-0.2	-0.7	60	9.1	96.4
Petit, Yusmeiro	35	3	0.8	6.3	49	7.5	79.2
Harris, Will	35	1	0.4	2.6	47	8.0	79.1
Kintzler, Brandon	35	3	1.3	8.0	47	7.5	76.9
Bonifacio, Emilio	35	0	-0.1	-0.4	60	3.9	75.8
Tomlin, Josh	35	2	0.5	4.0	45	6.5	70.9
LeBlanc, Wade	35	0	-0.4	-1.5	37	5.2	57.7

Hall of Fame Values by Age Group

Player	Age	2020 Season			Career		
		Win Shares	WAR	HoF Value	Win Shares	WAR	HoF Value
Votto, Joey	**36**	**3**	**-0.2**	**2.2**	**312**	**60.9**	**555.6**
Greinke, Zack	36	3	1.2	7.8	227	72.6	517.5
Braun, Ryan	36	4	-0.2	3.3	280	47.5	470.0
Hamels, Cole	36	0	-0.1	-0.4	189	59.7	427.9
Markakis, Nick	36	1	-0.3	-0.3	244	33.0	376.1
Lester, Jon	36	2	-0.3	1.0	177	45.4	358.8
Gardner, Brett	36	5	0.5	7.1	178	42.6	348.5
Gordon, Alex	36	1	-0.1	0.6	179	36.3	324.4
Kendrick, Howie	36	1	-0.3	-0.2	192	33.0	323.9
Suzuki, Kurt	36	2	0.1	2.5	139	20.3	264.1
Sanchez, Anibal	36	0	0.2	0.6	100	27.0	208.0
Soria, Joakim	36	3	0.4	4.7	109	18.3	182.2
Chirinos, Robinson	36	0	-0.8	-3.4	56	12.4	126.3
Morton, Charlie	36	2	0.2	2.6	68	8.0	100.0
Gurriel, Yuli	36	2	-0.3	0.6	61	8.5	95.0
Stammen, Craig	36	1	-0.3	-0.1	56	8.4	89.4
Volquez, Edinson	36	0	-0.1	-0.4	61	5.3	82.3
Rivera, Rene	36	0	0.1	0.4	44	2.1	62.6
Chavez, Jesse	36	0	-0.4	-1.6	43	3.4	56.5
Cabrera, Miguel	**37**	**9**	**-0.2**	**8.1**	**411**	**69.1**	**687.4**
Cano, Robinson	37	5	0.9	8.7	349	70.6	631.4
Molina, Yadier	37	4	0.1	4.5	281	40.1	527.6
Verlander, Justin	37	1	0.2	1.7	238	70.7	520.8
Encarnacion, Edwin	37	0	-0.5	-2.2	238	34.6	376.6
Choo, Shin-Soo	37	3	0.0	2.8	227	34.6	365.4
Pence, Hunter	37	0	-0.7	-2.8	218	30.4	339.8
Happ, J.A.	37	3	1.2	8.0	100	23.1	192.5
O'Day, Darren	37	2	0.7	4.8	73	17.2	141.8
Romo, Sergio	37	3	0.0	3.0	87	10.7	129.9
Mathis, Jeff	37	1	0.4	2.5	45	0.5	56.1
Wainwright, Adam	**38**	**5**	**0.5**	**7.2**	**156**	**40.5**	**317.9**
Perez, Oliver	38	3	0.6	5.2	72	11.2	116.7
Cruz, Nelson	**39**	**8**	**1.6**	**14.3**	**243**	**39.5**	**400.9**
Pujols, Albert	**40**	**1**	**-0.3**	**0.0**	**488**	**100.4**	**889.5**
Hill, Rich	40	3	0.8	6.1	67	14.2	123.7

Potential Players on 2021 Hall of Fame Ballot

Player	Win Shares	WAR	HOF Value	HOF Monitor
Bonds, Barry	704	162.8	1355.2	267
Clemens, Roger	437	139.6	995.3	283
Ramirez, Manny	408	69.3	685.4	169
Sheffield, Gary	430	60.5	672.1	103
Abreu, Bobby	356	60.0	596.1	76
Rolen, Scott	304	70.2	584.7	82
Schilling, Curt	252	79.6	570.4	122
Helton, Todd	318	61.2	562.8	128
Kent, Jeff	339	55.4	560.6	94
Sosa, Sammy	321	58.6	555.3	134
Jones, Andruw	276	62.8	527.2	57
Hunter, Torii	277	50.1	477.3	42
Pettitte, Andy	224	60.3	465.0	104
Vizquel, Omar	282	45.6	464.3	72
Buehrle, Mark	220	59.3	457.3	76
Hudson, Tim	219	58.2	451.8	67
Ramirez, Aramis	272	32.6	402.2	63
Wagner, Billy	182	27.7	292.8	81
Haren, Dan	144	35.0	284.0	46
Victorino, Shane	153	31.6	279.5	33
Zito, Barry	146	32.0	273.9	60
Rios, Alex	159	27.4	268.7	27
Swisher, Nick	172	22.0	260.2	20
Burnett, A.J.	137	29.1	253.5	51
Sizemore, Grady	139	27.3	248.1	23
Uggla, Dan	162	17.5	232.1	38
Cuddyer, Michael	153	17.3	222.2	23
LaRoche, Adam	161	14.2	217.6	23
Hawkins, LaTroy	124	17.8	195.2	39
Harang, Aaron	102	20.1	182.2	37
Hart, Corey	110	14.4	167.7	23
Wilson, C.J.	95	17.4	164.4	36
Soriano, Rafael	91	13.9	146.5	37
Marquis, Jason	85	6.9	112.4	20
Affeldt, Jeremy	67	9.8	106.3	29
Balfour, Grant	64	9.2	100.6	20
Schumaker, Skip	88	1.3	93.3	11
Gregg, Kevin	65	4.5	83.1	25

In Memoriam – Tom Seaver

Mark Simon

This was a sad year for baseball in many ways, one of which was the death of six baseball legends through the second week of October, whom we honor here.

Tom Seaver's arrival turned the Mets from lovable laughingstocks into eventual World Series champions in 1969, earning him the nicknames "Tom Terrific" and "The Franchise."

Seaver was a 12-time All-Star who won 311 games and three Cy Young Awards. His nine straight seasons of 200 or more strikeouts and 10 consecutive strikeouts within one game are both MLB records. It's important to note that Seaver pitched in an era in which strikeouts were harder to come by then they are now. He led the NL in strikeouts per 9 innings six times in seven seasons, but only once struck out more than a batter per inning in that stretch.

Seaver received 98.8% of the vote from the BBWAA for election to the Hall of Fame in 1992. That was the highest mark of any player up to that point. It was well-deserved. Just about any sabermetric stats rate Seaver as one of the best pitchers of the Live-Ball Era, including Pitching Win Shares, in which he ranks fifth.

Seaver died on August 31 at age 75.

In Memoriam – Lou Brock

John Dewan

This is one of my favorite baseball memories of all time. It's not about 938 stolen bases or about one of the best or worst trades in baseball history (depending on your perspective). It's a small glimpse of the type of man that Lou Brock was.

This is a very short story about the 60-year-old Lou Brock and my 8-year-old son Jason. My wife, Sue, and I were invited to attend the Players Choice Awards in 1999. We traveled from Chicago to Las Vegas to attend the event and our kids came along.

It was a black-tie affair that was aired on ESPN. I rented a tuxedo and Sue looked terrific in a beautiful evening gown. The hotel had a very nice childcare center on the first floor that could take care of Jason and our 6-year-old daughter Erica during the event.

Our room was on an upper floor and the four of us were waiting for the elevator on our way to dropping off the kids and then going straight to the event. And here comes a very distinguished older man to the elevator. I immediately knew it was Lou Brock. I turned to Jason and said,

"Jason, this is Lou Brock. He is one of the greatest base-stealers of all time!"

Jason looks at Lou and asks, "How many home runs did you hit?"

Lou smiles widely and says, "Oh, I hit a few."

In a loud voice Jason says, "Not as many as Babe Ruth!"

We all broke out laughing, especially Lou. During the entire elevator ride Lou engaged our son, smiling and laughing. It was an absolutely joyful experience.

And then I noticed the tie that Lou was wearing. It was covered with the handprints of children. That tie and his interaction with my son showed just how much Lou loved children.

It brings tears to my eyes just thinking about this short three-minute interaction between Lou Brock and Jason Dewan.

Brock died on September 6 at age 81.

In Memoriam – Al Kaline

Mark Simon

Lifelong Tigers outfielder Al Kaline was known as "Mr. Tiger" for a 22-year career in which he recorded 3,007 hits, 399 home runs, 18 All-Star Game selections and 10 Gold Gloves.

Kaline won a batting title in his second full season, as he hit .340 with 27 home runs at age 20 in 1955. Thus began an impressive run.

Kaline's stats didn't necessarily dazzle. He never hit more than 30 home runs in a season, but he was consistent and he had a very good batting eye, as he walked 257 more times than he struck out for his career. In the decade of the 1960s, his slashline was .296/.381/.494. His OPS for that decade, adjusted for ballpark, was 41% better than league average. He ranks in the top-35 all-time in Runs Created. Kaline was also highly capable in the field, highly regarded for his glove and arm.

Kaline was a huge part of the 1968 World Series championship team. He hit .379 with 11 hits and eight RBIs in a seven-game win over the Cardinals. His go-ahead single in the seventh inning of Game 5 set in motion the Tigers comeback from a 3-games-to-1 deficit.

Kaline died on April 6 at age 85.

In Memoriam – Bob Gibson

Mark Simon

Bob Gibson produced a greater level of collective fear among major league hitters than just about any pitcher during a career that spanned from 1959 to 1975. This came from Gibson's willingness to pitch inside and knock down any hitter at any time. That was a big part of what made Gibson a great pitcher for the only team he played for, the Cardinals.

Gibson's signature season is one of the most memorable pitching seasons of all time. He went 22-9 with a 1.12 ERA in 304 2/3 innings pitched in 1968. That is the lowest ERA for any pitcher in the Live Ball Era (since 1920). It's one of five seasons in which he won 20 games and nine seasons in which he had at least 200 strikeouts. It concluded with him winning the NL MVP and the first of his two Cy Young Awards.

Gibson wasn't a World Series winner that year, as the Cardinals lost in seven games to the Tigers. But he won titles with St. Louis in both 1964 and 1967, winning Game 7 in both of those and was named the MVP of each series. Gibson completed eight of his nine World Series starts, went eight innings in the other, and posted a 1.89 World Series ERA. His 17 strikeouts in Game 1 of the 1968 World Series are an MLB record.

Gibson was a first-ballot Hall of Fame inductee in 1981. Four decades later he is still the standard setter for pitchers when it comes to intimidation factor and big-game performance.

Bob Gibson died on October 2 at age 84.

In Memoriam – Whitey Ford

Mark Simon

Whitey Ford's many pitching accomplishments have stood the test of time more than 50 years after he retired.

In a 16-year career with the Yankees spanning 1950 to 1967, Ford went 236–106. The .690 winning percentage ranks second among retired pitchers whose career began in the modern era (since 1900).

Ford's combination of longevity and effectiveness in the postseason hold up against the best big-game pitchers in MLB history. His 10 World Series wins and 33-inning World Series scoreless streak are both all-time marks. He won one Cy Young Award and was named AL Pitcher of the Year by *The Sporting News* in two other seasons. He was inducted into the Baseball of Fame in 1974.

On the more serious side, he took two years off near the beginning of his career to serve in the military during the Korean War. He played baseball and basketball in the army, allowing him to stay in good pitching form.

When he returned to the game, he established himself as one of baseball's top left-handed pitchers. *The New York Times* once wrote "Possessed of an instinctive sense of gamesmanship, evidenced from his first appearance in Yankees pinstripes, Whitey is a cool and calculating operation…He revels in such challenges [of being the ace or the losing-streak stopper] because to his way of thinking, they are what make pitching fun."

Ford's fun came in the form of six World Series titles and 11 AL pennants, and a lifelong friendship with baseball legend and teammate, Mickey Mantle.

In describing Ford, Mantle used the phrase "Nerves of steel." That's the kind of approach needed to become an all-time baseball great.

Whitey Ford died on October 8 at age 91.

In Memoriam – Joe Morgan

Mark Simon

Five-foot-seven, 160-pound Joe Morgan was the little guy who could do just about everything on a baseball field. He was one of the leaders of the Big Red Machine, the Reds team that won World Series titles in 1975 and 1976 and played the game in a dynamic, exciting way that would have been a good fit in any era. He did it at a position, second base, that was not known for the offensive production of other spots.

Morgan finished his career with 2,517 hits, 689 stolen bases, and 268 home runs. He had an incredible batting eye, drawing 1,865 walks, which ranks fifth all-time. That helped him record an on-base percentage over .400 in six straight seasons from 1972 to 1977 (he led the NL four times in that span). He was also a standout fielder, winning five Gold Glove Awards.

Morgan was the MVP of both of those Reds championship teams and was a 10-time All-Star. He was inducted into the Baseball Hall of Fame in 1990. After his playing career ended, Morgan joined Jon Miller as the inaugural voices of Sunday Night Baseball on ESPN. They worked together as a broadcast team from 1990 to 2010.

It's reasonable to argue that he is one of the greatest second basemen in MLB history. In fact, *The Bill James New Historical Baseball Abstract* ranked him No. 1 at the position when it was published in 2001.

Morgan died on October 11 at age 77.

In Memoriam

Other notable baseball people who passed away in 2020 include **Don Larsen**, who pitched the only perfect game in World Series history for the Yankees against the Dodgers in 1956; shortstop **Tony Fernandez**, who totaled 2,276 hits in a 17-year career that began in 1983; **Jimmy Wynn**, who was known as "The Toy Cannon" and overcame both small stature and a tough home ballpark in the Astrodome to slug 291 home runs; **Bob Watson**, who played 19 years in the major leagues, then became the first African-American general manager to win a World Series, which he did with the Yankees; **Jay Johnstone**, who played 20 seasons with eight teams and was known as one of the game's great pranksters; **Ron Perranoski**, a top closer with the Dodgers and Twins, who led the majors in saves in 1969, the first year the save rule was official; **Ed Farmer**, who pitched 11 seasons in the majors and then spent 29 years as a broadcaster with the White Sox; super-scout **Gary Hughes**, who won five World Series titles in his more than 50 years in pro baseball; and longtime MLB executive **Jimmie Lee Solomon**, who was most recently the league's executive vice president for baseball development.

Rookie Roundup

Mark Simon

Some rookies were hot, some were cold, and for some, making the majors was all that was needed to say that things were just right.

Because of the circumstances of the season—expanded rosters with no minor league season—there were several hundred rookies in the major leagues in this shortened year, including a number who had never previously played above Single-A. Given that there were so many and that so many of you seem to enjoy following new players, we thought we'd spotlight the most notable, the most hyped, and the most interesting.

Jake Cronenworth was an unexpected standout in his debut season at age 26, though maybe he shouldn't have been. Cronenworth hit .334 with 10 home runs with Triple-A Durham in 2019 before the Rays sent him to San Diego as part of the package that netted outfielder Hunter Renfroe.

Cronenworth made his mark as someone who could hit, batting .285 in 54 games but who could also play three infield positions—first base, second base, and shortstop—and play them well (he also got an inning in at third base). Cronenworth was one of the toughest hitters in the majors to strike out, whiffing just 30 times in 172 at-bats.

Kyle Lewis picked up where he left off from his 2019 season, hitting .262 with 11 home runs. He fixed his biggest issue, bringing his strikeout rate down and raising his walk rate from 4% to 14%. Lewis also had a flare for the spectacular play in the outfield, including a takeaway of a potential grand slam.

Jared Walsh, after debuting as a two-way player with the Angels in 2019 (and hitting .203), looked like a star in a brief stint. The 27-year-old, who was a 39th-round pick out of Georgia in 2015, hit like Albert Pujols in his prime while spelling Pujols in 22 starts at first base.

Ryan Mountcastle made a name for himself when the Orioles gave him a look primarily in left field. He hit .333 with 5 home runs in 126 at-bats. Mountcastle made multiple top-100 prospect lists and showed that he has a promising future in the Orioles' rebuild.

The Phillies got a look at their future with third baseman **Alec Bohm**, who put up similar numbers to Mountcastle, a .338 batting average with 4 home runs and 11 doubles.

Infielder **Willi Castro** was a surprise standout for the Tigers, hitting .349 after hitting .230 in 100 at-bats with the Tigers last season. Castro would do well to work on his defense, which would make him a more complete player. He finished with minus-8 Runs Saved between shortstop and third base.

There was a group of rookies who made a big and immediate impact with their power: **Bobby Dalbec** of the Red Sox (8 home runs in 80 at-bats) , **Edwin Ríos** of the Dodgers (8 home runs in 76 at-bats) and **Randy Arozarena** of the Rays (7 home runs in 64 at-bats).

Some players looked good both at-bat and in the field, most notably Pirates third baseman **Ke'Bryan Hayes**, who had two hits, including a home run, in his first game. Hayes kept that up for a month, hitting .376 in 85 at-bats. He also showed why evaluators considered him one of the top defensive prospects in the minor leagues. Hayes saved 4 runs with his defense.

He wasn't the only one to look sharp in the field. White Sox center fielder **Luis Robert** hit .233 but finished with 8 Runs Saved, most among American League rookies and one behind another slick-fielding rookie, Rockies first baseman **Josh Fuentes**, for the MLB lead. Mariners first baseman **Evan White** led all players in our Good Fielding Plays stat (think Web Gems, plus things like scooping throws or keeping the ball on the infield to prevent a runner from taking an extra base) with 20.

Mets infielder **Andrés Giménez** displaced former top prospect Amed Rosario at shortstop and wowed with his baseball acumen and 3 Runs

Saved (one apiece at second base, shortstop and third base). Athletics catcher **Sean Murphy** pushed the team to its first season with a positive Runs Saved total at catcher since 2010. Cardinals outfielder **Dylan Carlson** didn't hit but played a role in helping the Cardinals lead the majors in Runs Saved.

Two highly-regarded prospects may turn out to be the best of the group eventually, but they struggled in their initial MLB appearance. **Jo Adell** of the Angels hit .161 in 124 at-bats. **Joey Bart**, pressed into duty after Buster Posey decided to sit out the season due to COVID concerns, hit .233 and went homerless in 103 at-bats.

Among pitchers, the most impressive was a rookie reliever armed not only with a 99-MPH fastball, but with perhaps the best changeup in the game— **Devin Williams** of the Brewers. Opponents went 2-for-62 in at-bats ending against the pitch, which some said resembled a screwball. He finished with an 0.33 ERA in 27 innings pitched.

The other rookie reliever with a unique approach was **James Karinchak** of the Indians, whose lean-back over-the-top delivery netted 53 strikeouts in 27 innings. The only issue was a little wildness. He walked 5.3 batters per 9 innings.

Marlins pitcher **Sixto Sánchez** lived up to the billing of a top starting pitcher prospect. He pitched to a 3.46 ERA in seven starts with 33 strikeouts in 39 innings pitched. Another top starting pitching prospect, **Triston McKenzie** of the Indians, dazzled with two starts allowing one run or fewer in his first three appearances. He finished the season with a 3.24 ERA and 11.3 strikeouts per 9 innings in 33 1/3 innings.

Others who looked good with a little less pizazz included **Tony Gonsolin** of the Dodgers, **Kwang-Hyun Kim** of the Cardinals, **Cristian Javier** of the Astros, and **Ian Anderson** of the Braves. By season's end, Royals pitcher **Brady Singer** was right there with them. He took a no-hit bid into the ninth inning against the Indians, then pitched six scoreless innings against the Tigers in his next start. Top prospect **Jesús Luzardo** had moments of excellence and finished the season with a 4.12 ERA.

One rookie pitcher skipped the minor leagues entirely and was thrust into the late-season spotlight—**Garrett Crochet** of the White Sox. Crochet, who was selected No. 11 overall from the University of Tennessee in the 2020 MLB Draft, averaged 100 MPH with his fastball in six scoreless innings and was included on the White Sox postseason roster.

The coolest story among rookies wasn't one related to statistics. **Eddy Alvarez** made his MLB debut with the Marlins at age 30 and hit .189 in 37 at-bats.

That Alvarez made it to the majors was amazing. He had previously won a silver medal in short track speed skating in the 5,000 men's relay for the United States at the 2014 Winter Olympics. Alvarez, who had previously played high school and JUCO baseball, signed with the White Sox after the Olympics and worked his way through the minors, finally earning the call-up this season. He made the most of it even if he didn't light up the stat sheet.

Super Scooper

Rookie Evan White became a good friend of Mariners infielders because of his steady defense at first base. White led first basemen in our Scoop Runs Saved (SRS) stat, recording 14 scoops of difficult-to-handle throws and only 1 mishandle, good for 1.3 SRS.

Matt Olson leads all first basemen over the last three seasons with 3.6 SRS, just ahead of Freddie Freeman's 3.4. Olson's 76 successful scoops are the most in the majors.

MLB Rule Changes Impact

Mark Simon

A season like no other featured a version of baseball like no other.

MLB had introduced a few new rules for the 2020 season before the pandemic, but coronavirus-related complications required additional alterations to a game that is long marked by tradition and consistency.

Trying to make evaluations of how these new rules worked using one shortened season as our basis is a complicated process. Ideally, we want to see how much these changes impacted games. The results of this are presented here.

The Designated Hitter

The designated hitter was finally adopted by the National League, perhaps for this season, perhaps for longer. It was one of the rule changes agreed to because of the pandemic, but it is not yet a permanent change, at least not as of when this book went to press in October 2020.

Under the circumstances of the season, NL teams didn't have an offseason to prepare and acquire players who would be well-suited to the DH role. Instead, they largely used who they had on the roster entering late July.

NL DHs hit .235/.319/.409. Their batting average was lower than that of any of the eight other batting positions. The .728 OPS ranked sixth, ahead of center field, catcher, and second base.

NL teams scored runs at about the same rate as in 2019 (4.84 runs per 9-inning team game compared to 4.78), had a batting average five points lower and an OPS seven points lower.

NL Offenses - Last 2 Seasons

	Runs per 9-Inning Game	Batting Average	OPS
2019	4.78	.251	.753
2020	4.84	.246	.746

Though DHs faltered, they certainly bested pitcher hitting by a considerable amount, with that .728 OPS being 399 points better than the combined OPS by pitchers in 2019.

If at-bats by DHs were replaced with pitcher at-bats proportional to the number of 9-slot at-bats that pitchers took in 2019, the NL batting average would have dropped to .241 rather than .246.

Three other consequences of the DH's arrival:

1) With no pitchers hitting, pinch-hitter usage in NL games also took a huge drop, going from 1.8 per game to 0.7.

2) Sacrifices plummeted as expected, from one every 4.6 NL team games to one every 15.0 team games.

3) Intentional walks also dropped from one every 5.1 games to one every 7.1.

The Braves were easily the biggest beneficiary of the addition of the DH. Their designated hitters hit .316 with 17 home runs and 55 RBI in 60 games and a 1.000 OPS.

Most of that came from NL MVP candidate Marcell Ozuna, who had a 1.155 OPS in 39 games at DH. The Phillies ranked second among teams in DH OPS at .832. The Mets (.827) were the only other NL team over .800.

Three-Batter Minimum

In trying to speed up the game, MLB attempted to cut down on pitching changes. It implemented a rule that a reliever had to either finish an inning or pitch to at least three batters before he could be removed (unless a move was necessary due to injury).

This nearly halved reliever appearances of one and two batters, slicing the percentage of relief outings that fit that description from 15% of relief appearances to 8%.

Comparing Reliever Usage

	% of Appearances facing 1 or 2 batters	Batters Faced per Relief Appearance
2015 - 2019	15%	4.5
2020	8%	4.9

The LOOGY and ROOGY (left- and right-handed one-out guy) didn't quite become extinct as a result of this rule, but their impact was lessened. For example, Dodgers left-handed reliever Adam Kolarek, who had an MLB-high 42 one-or-two batter appearances in 2019, had only two of those in 2020.

The MLB leader in one-or-two batter appearances was a right-handed pitcher, Marlins reliever James Hoyt, with 13. No one else had more than seven. The left-handed pitching leaders were Sam Selman of the Giants and Hoby Milner of the Angels with six, which prorates to 16 in a 162-game season. That's a big drop-off from Kolarek's 42.

Roster Expansion

MLB teams would have expanded their regular season rosters to 26 had there not been a pandemic. The circumstances of this season resulted in a one-season agreement for rosters to be expanded to 28.

The biggest outcome here was more pinch-runner usage, something that had been expected with 26-man rosters as well (hello Billy Hamilton, Jarrod Dyson, and Terrance Gore). Pinch running increased by 64% from 2019, from one pinch-runner used every 7.0 games to one every 4.3.

With more pitchers on the roster, the need to use any pitcher for a considerable workload lessened. There were only 40 qualifiers for the ERA title in 2020. By comparison, every other season in the expansion era (since 1961, the first year of the 162-game schedule) had at least 57 pitchers qualify.

The number of qualifiers was already in a decline. The four seasons with the fewest ERA-title qualifiers since 1961 are the most recent four.

The Extra-Inning Rule

MLB implemented a rule that had been tried in the minor leagues, putting a runner on second base with nobody out to start each extra inning.

This was done to try to speed up extra innings and cut down on marathon games, with the expectation that teams would score more quickly in extra innings if their chance began with a runner in scoring position.

There were 78 games played that went longer than scheduled, meaning either a nine-inning game that went at least 10 innings, or a seven-inning game that went at least eight.

Of those 78, two went four innings longer than scheduled and four more went three innings longer than scheduled. The other 72 games (92% of those played) went either one or two extra innings.

From 2015 to 2019, there were 301 games that went at least 3 innings longer than intended, an average of 60 per season. That's out of 1,003 extra-inning games in total, meaning 70% went one or two extra innings.

Percentage of Extra-Inning Games Completed in 1-2 Extra Innings

	Completed in 1-2 extra innings	Extra Inning Games	%
2015-2019	301	1,003	30%
2020	72	78	92%

MLB got its wish of producing scoring quickly, as the percentage of extra-inning half innings with a run scored was more than twice that of the previous five seasons.

Percentage of Extra-Inning half-innings with at least 1 run

	Extra Innings	% with At Least 1 Run
2015-2019	4,464	27%
2020	222	57%

Shortened Doubleheaders

Coronavirus outbreaks on teams during the season necessitated a change on the fly to have regulation doubleheader length be seven innings per game.

In total, there were 55 shortened doubleheaders. The two teams that played the most of them did well in them.

The Cardinals went 13-9 in doubleheaders and 17-19 in other games (one rescheduled doubleheader against the Tigers was unplayed).

The Marlins played seven seven-inning doubleheaders and went 10-4 in those compared to 21-25 in their other games.

The average doubleheader game featured slightly more scoring per inning but cut down on total batters faced by nearly 15.

Comparing 7-Inning Games to 9-Inning Games

	7-Inning Games	9-Inning Games
Runs Per Game	8.3	9.4
Batters Faced Per Game	61.0	75.9
Batters Faced Per Inning	8.7	8.4

One consequence of the doubleheaders and the shortened games was the need for more pitchers. The Marlins overhauled their roster after the team's COVID outbreak in the first week of the season resulted in the need for 17 new players after an eight-day hiatus.

As such, the Marlins used 37 pitchers this season, seven more than the Red Sox, who ranked second with 30.

Determining whether these rules worked will be in the eye of the beholder. The Commissioner's Office and the Players Association will need to unify their differing interests in order to evaluate this and will need to figure out what is in the best interests of their respective groups.

Then there's the other party that will mull these over in due time—the fans. Their view on these changes may turn out to be what matters most.

Major League Weirdness

Mark Simon

We are a numbers company. I'm part of a Research and Development team that looks at stats every day. We see the good, the bad, and the weird.

A 60-game season produces a lot of good numbers and a lot of bad numbers. But it also produces a lot of weirdness. Here are some of the … um, weirdlights?

Weird Batting Averages

Remember how you were a kid and you were on the verge of getting in trouble at school and the teacher would threaten you by saying, "This will go on your permanent record."?

There was some baseball trouble this year in the form of beleaguered batting averages. With only 60 games in the season, there was no way for a hitter to hide a prolonged slump no matter how good he used to be.

The greats of the game were not exempt. The last four NL MVPs—Kris Bryant, Giancarlo Stanton, Christian Yelich, and Cody Bellinger—combined to hit .223, with Stanton missing much of the season due to injury.

Among other prominent players whose batting averages tumbled were Edwin Encarnación (.157), Kyle Schwarber (.188), Shohei Ohtani (.190), Max Muncy (.192), Matt Olson (.195), Carlos Santana (.199), Eugenio Suárez (.202), Javier Báez (.203), Austin Meadows (.205) and J.D. Martinez (.213).

Those will appear on their permanent records, and five or 10 years from now, they're going to look downright weird.

Weird Splits

With only 30 games at home and 30 games on the road (for most, though not all teams), things like home–road splits had the potential to get a little kooky.

Joey Votto had the biggest differential between his home OPS and road OPS in 2020 (among hitters with at least 80 at-bats in each area).

Votto hit like Ted Williams at home, with a slash line of .333/.461/.699 (1.160 OPS) in 93 at-bats, but hit like a meek-hitting pitcher on the road, at .118/.241/.194 (.434 OPS), also in 93 at-bats. His OPS differential was a totally ridiculous 726 points.

A 60-game season also produced split weirdness of this nature. Rockies outfielder Charlie Blackmon chased both .400 and the Mendoza Line. He hit .405 in his first 28 games and .200 in his last 31. It will be the weirdest .303 anyone's probably ever hit.

Weirdly Lopsided Records

The White Sox went undefeated against left-handed pitching, going 14–0. This was both weird and an incredible accomplishment. In those 14 games, the White Sox totaled 99 runs, an average of 7.1 per game. This was powered by a predominantly right-handed hitting lineup led by Tim Anderson, who went 22-for-49 (.449) with 7 doubles and 6 home runs in 49 at-bats against lefties in 2020.

Weird Career Highs

It was going to be almost impossible for any hitter to achieve career highs in a counting stat. But Luke Voit defied the odds. His 22 home runs surpassed his previous mark of 21 (and led the majors).

The next-most home runs by a player, with at least two previous seasons played, that matched or beat a career high was Alex Dickerson of the Giants, who tied it with 10.

Weird Winning

The pandemic tested the depth of every team, especially the pitching depth. Only 40 pitchers qualified for the ERA title, which means averaging one inning per team game played. ERA qualifiers have gradually declined over time as the game has changed, but in this aberration of a season, the 40 pitchers averaging one inning per team game is the lowest total since only 33 did it in 1900.

Some teams were well equipped in pitching depth. The Dodgers won 43 games but had only one pitcher who won more than three (Clayton Kershaw, 6). Nine Dodgers pitchers won exactly three games.

In other words, 10 Dodgers pitchers had more wins than any of the Pirates' starting pitchers. The Pirates leader in wins by a starter were Chad Kuhl and Trevor Williams with only two each.

Weird Arrangements

The 16-team postseason created the strong possibility that a team could make the playoffs with a losing record. Two teams delivered on that. The Brewers and Astros will each get an asterisk next to their "accomplishment" of becoming the first teams to make the MLB playoffs with a losing regular season record. The Brewers even went one better. They made the playoffs despite never having a winning record during the season.

Weird Endgames

COVID and climate-related issues resulted in some rescheduled games being played in the other team's ballpark. In fact, 12 teams hosted more games than the 30 originally scheduled.

As such Amed Rosario and Trent Grisham went full weirdness, walk-off style. Rosario hit a walk-off home run to give the Mets a win over the Yankees in Yankee Stadium. And Trent Grisham dealt the Giants a painful defeat in the final series of the season, hitting a walk-off home run for the Padres at Oracle Park in San Francisco.

May It Never Be This Weird Again

The weirdest stat of all is going to be when we look back at 2020 and see a 0 for regular season attendance.

Weird. And sad.

Where to Find More of Us

If you like our work, there are other outlets at which you can find more of it

The Sports Info Solutions Baseball Podcast features interviews with players (Trevor Story, Kevin Kiermaier) and notable people who cover baseball (Joe Sheehan, Tyler Kepner) and provides insight into different projects our R&D team is working on. It can be found wherever you subscribe to podcasts.

The Sports Info Solutions Blog (SportsInfoSolutionsBlog.com) features articles and research written by our R&D team and our Baseball Operations department. Topics include examinations of player and team performance, as well as statistical updates and leaderboards.

You can also follow us on Twitter at @SportsInfo_SIS and on Instagram at @sportsinfosolutions.

Going Broader and Deeper into Baseball in Asia

Alex Vigderman

Our company has been going through a growth spurt over the last several years. Sure, we expanded into football in 2015 and amateur basketball this year. But just within baseball, we've ventured into parts less known, tracking Japanese Nippon Professional Baseball (NPB) starting in 2018 and Korean Baseball Organization (KBO) games dating to last season. It's a wonder we haven't needed to buy a whole new wardrobe.

The expansion into the Asian market was rather fortuitous this season, as the only major professional baseball being played early this summer was coming from Taiwan, Japan, and Korea. A thirst for any kind of sports normalcy and KBO broadcasts available on ESPN allowed all of us to acquaint ourselves with teams and players we'd have to scour the far corners of the internet to watch previously.

When faced with a new league, the obvious question is, "Who do I know that plays there?" Take this opportunity to remember some guys.

Notable Former Major Leaguers Playing in Asia in 2020
Ordered by MLB Playing Time

KBO	NPB
Dan Straily	Adam Jones
Odrisamer Despaigne	Alcides Escobar
Tyler Saladino	Gerardo Parra
David Buchanan	Jose Lopez
Aaron Altherr	Matt Moore
Seung-hwan Oh	Norichika Aoki
Aaron Brooks	Leonys Martín
Adrian Sampson	Kosuke Fukudome
Preston Tucker	Nick Martínez
Nick Kingham	Rubby De La Rosa
Hyun-soo Kim	Dayán Viciedo

The KBO and NPB seasons are still going on, so all stats discussion below is as of October 1st. Former Orioles centerpiece Adam Jones is the best-known name on this list, although he hasn't been the most successful in

2020. His .255/.330/.417 triple-slash line for the Orix Buffaloes is in line with his last two seasons in the majors, which is solid but unspectacular.

Not mentioned on either list is one expat who was anything but unspectacular this season. Mel Rojas Jr., who was a career minor leaguer before moving to Korea in 2018, leads KBO in slugging percentage and hard-hit rate and is fifth in batting average in 2020. "I just made a few adjustments," Rojas said, explaining his success in a July 2 appearance on the Sports Info Solutions Baseball Podcast. "Being successful with the inside pitch, fastballs away, breaking balls. I'm doing a lot better covering the plate."

Foreign-born players generally flood the pitching leaderboards in KBO, partially owing to native players tending not to throw as hard as their foreign-born counterparts (by 2-3 mph). At least seven of the top ten pitchers by ERA the last two seasons (min. 100 IP) have come from somewhere other than Korea.

While you'd recognize some names that cracked those leaderboards, it's cooler to see names that you don't. Drew Rucinski and Eric Jokisch, who have 68 career MLB innings between them, have made the ERA leaderboard both seasons.

The KBO player with the most previous MLB success, journeyman starting pitcher Dan Straily, is having the most success of any pitcher in Korea this season, leading the league in Pitching Runs Created. His 2.69 ERA, 9.2 Strikeouts per 9 Innings, and 2.5 Walks per 9 Innings for the Lotte Giants would each best any mark he posted in his 8-year MLB career.

The key to Straily's dominance has been finding his slider again. In 2019, batters missed on 13 percent of swings at Straily's slider, and they hit .441 on at-bats ending with it. This year, he's induced whiffs more than twice as often (30 percent), and hitters are only hitting .164 against the pitch.

Drop your innings cutoff a bit, though, and you'll find a local product who has been truly lights-out: NC Dinos ace Chang-Mo Koo. Koo, just 23 years old, has pitched to a sub-2.00 ERA with a K:BB ratio of over 5:1 in just shy of 100 innings. None of his pitches have allowed even a .200 batting average this season, but his splitter has been the most dominant, missing bats on more than half of swings.

One of the things that makes it harder to get into leagues besides MLB, at least for fans of our disposition, is that there isn't nearly the wealth of stats available. Sites like DeltaGraphs and MyKBOStats do a good job of making NPB and KBO statistics available, but since MLB's Statcast tracking data came around a few years ago, the thirst for on-field metrics is extreme.

A couple years ago, we devised Synthetic Statcast to bridge that gap. Synthetic Statcast is a data set that uses advanced modeling techniques to take data we collect and convert it into equivalent Statcast-like metrics, particularly Exit Velocity (the speed off the bat) and Launch Angle (the vertical angle of the ball's trajectory). This gives us a way to analyze the minor leagues or international ball in a similar way that we're starting to get used to for MLB.

Let's see who the hardest-hitting players in KBO were this season.

KBO Synthetic Statcast Average Exit Velocity Leaders, 2020

Player	Avg Exit Velocity (mph)	Avg Launch Angle (degrees)
Byung-ho Park	92.0	19.9
Roberto Ramos	91.7	19.2
Mel Rojas Jr.	90.9	15.5
Jae-hwan Kim	89.6	9.4
Hyun-soo Kim	89.1	11.5

While Mel Rojas Jr. should obviously be familiar, two of the Korean names should be as well. Byung-ho Park and Hyun-soo Kim had previously come to the US from Korea and have since returned to resume their raking.

Jae-hwan Kim's presence on this list is interesting, since his typical batted ball trajectory is quite a bit lower than those of the names above him. His flyball rate is one of the lowest in KBO, but he hits the ball hard much more often than his peers. At 31 years old, he's past his prime, but his prime included three consecutive 35-plus homer seasons with an OPS over 1.000.

And now, for NPB!

NPB Synthetic Statcast Average Exit Velocity Leaders, 2020

Player	Avg Exit Velocity (mph)	Avg Launch Angle (degrees)
Jerry Sands	90.4	16.5
Yurisbel Gracial	89.4	15.1
Munetaka Murakami	89.3	14.1
Kazuma Okamoto	89.3	15.7
Hotaka Yamakawa	89.0	17.2

Jerry Sands (Hanshin Tigers) is likely the only name you've heard of on this list. One of his claims to fame (as with Rubby de la Rosa, also playing in NPB) is that he was one of the Dodgers prospects who went to Boston in the famed Beckett/Crawford/Gonzalez megadeal of 2012. He has played in both NPB and KBO as well as the independent Atlantic League since his last MLB appearance in 2016. For his part, he's posted at least an .850 OPS in every stop he's made since that season, so it's no shock to see him here.

If you see a leaderboard like this where all the players look pretty similar, you'd probably expect that they all had similar results. And you'd be wrong.

Thanks to funky bounces and differences in defensive play against them, Munetaka Murakami hit 100 points better than Hotaka Yamakawa in terms of batting average. And next year, we'd expect them to have similar results, because they hit the ball way more similarly than the gulf between their batting averages suggests.

That's what bringing Synthetic Statcast into the picture allows us to do. We can take ourselves beyond the limited data generally available for non-MLB leagues and really get to know what kind of hitter a player is. We look forward to giving you more peeks into this data in future Handbooks.

Starting Pitcher Rankings

Brian Reiff

In a world of ever-shortening attention spans, consistent performance at the highest level often gets overlooked. Everyone wants to know who the best player was today or this week or this month, or what the next new blockbuster is going to be, or, for the younger generation out there, what the latest TikTok craze is. No one wants to read 600 pointless words written by someone who's going to ramble on about movies and social media and how amazing his dog is—they just want to get the data they came here for (for the record, incredibly amazing).

Maintaining that elite level of performance is incredibly difficult, but that is exactly what Gerrit Cole has done. Cole took over the No. 1 spot in the Starting Pitcher Rankings during last year's playoffs, knocking off then-teammate Justin Verlander, meaning he started the 2020 season atop the leaderboard.

As you can see on the following pages, he also finished 2020 as the top pitcher by this metric. This made him the first pitcher to both start and end a regular season as the No. 1 starting pitcher since Clayton Kershaw in 2016. (Kershaw did it in 2014 and 2015 as well.) Before Kershaw, the last pitcher to experience such sustained dominance was Johan Santana in 2007.

What the charts won't tell you is that Cole actually wasn't the No. 1 pitcher for the entire season, despite holding that status at the start and end of the season. Mets pitcher Jacob deGrom temporarily took over the top spot after his seven-inning, 12-strikeout game against the Phillies on September 6, and he held onto it for 10 days before it was reclaimed by Cole. It may still change hands yet again before the World Series wraps up, although Cole looks to have built up a large enough cushion, especially with deGrom's Mets missing out on the playoffs.

A new name can be found one spot below those two. Shane Bieber of the Indians finished the regular season at No. 3 in the rankings, improving his score more than any other pitcher from 385 to 460 points and moving up from the No. 24 spot in which he began the season. The biggest rank jump, meanwhile, belonged to the Brewers' Corbin Burnes, who started from the literal bottom (T-201st) and ended up inside the top 50 at No. 49.

Unlike last season, when two different teams—the Astros and Nationals— each had three pitchers in the top 10, no team dominated the leaderboards in 2020. The Cubs led the way with two pitchers in the top 10—Yu Darvish, who climbed his way back there for the first time since 2014, and Kyle Hendricks—but had no one else higher than No. 75 (Jon Lester). The Yankees, Rays, and Padres, on the other hand, combined for just one pitcher in the top 10, but each had four pitchers in the top 60, which tied for the MLB lead.

Looking at the sum of the scores of each team's five highest-ranked pitchers, it was actually the Reds who narrowly came out on top. Featuring a top-five rotation of Trevor Bauer (No. 4), Luis Castillo (14), Sonny Gray (18), Tyler Mahle (76) and Anthony DeSclafani (126) that combined for a score of 2,023 points, the Reds edged out the Yankees, who finished second with a cumulative score of 2,021 points.

The following pages provide the scores and rankings for baseball's top starting pitchers by month in 2020. The full leaderboard as well as all the details behind the methodology of the rankings can be found at BillJamesOnline.com.

No Ordinary Joe

With the understanding that 2020 was a shortened season, the pitcher whose strikeout percentage increased the most from 2019 to 2020 was Joe Musgrove of the Pirates. His rate increased from 22% to 33% (this among pitchers who threw at least 100 innings in 2019 and 30 in 2020). Put another way, his rate increased from 8.3 strikeouts per 9 innings to 12.5.

Musgrove ranked 54th in the Starting Pitcher Rankings, one of the bright spots for a team that finished with the worst record in MLB.

Starting Pitcher Rankings

Player	July 23 Score	Rank	Aug 1 Score	Rank	Sept 1 Score	Rank	Sept 27 Score	Rank
Cole, Gerrit	449.5	1	452.4	1	456.0	1	479.4	1
deGrom, Jacob	428.5	3	437.7	2	455.3	2	469.2	2
Bieber, Shane	384.7	24	407.6	9	444.9	3	459.6	3
Bauer, Trevor	388.1	21	395.7	15	423.0	10	453.9	4
Scherzer, Max	427.2	4	436.5	3	441.3	4	445.9	5
Darvish, Yu	378.9	34	386.1	23	417.3	12	438.0	6
Kershaw, Clayton	402.7	9	393.7	18	423.0	9	437.0	7
Nola, Aaron	396.5	14	396.9	13	436.1	5	435.6	8
Giolito, Lucas	383.1	27	383.2	27	421.9	11	431.8	9
Hendricks, Kyle	386.4	22	393.6	19	400.2	23	431.0	10
Ryu, Hyun-Jin	385.1	23	380.7	32	412.2	16	430.6	11
Lynn, Lance	395.5	15	405.7	10	428.8	6	427.7	12
Maeda, Kenta	368.0	53	380.3	34	408.2	17	427.7	13
Castillo, Luis	388.5	19	392.7	20	399.3	24	425.2	14
Verlander, Justin	431.8	2	435.9	4	428.2	7	421.7	15
Greinke, Zack	402.6	10	402.3	11	424.6	8	419.6	16
Lamet, Dinelson	347.0	111	359.1	73	387.4	37	419.6	17
Gray, Sonny	395.0	16	411.4	6	417.0	14	417.6	18
Carrasco, Carlos	373.9	44	380.4	33	392.4	33	417.3	19
Marquez, German	378.4	36	386.4	22	391.6	35	417.3	20
Woodruff, Brandon	359.5	78	374.9	42	386.2	38	416.7	21
Clevinger, Mike	399.6	11	401.1	12	404.0	18	416.1	22
Gonzales, Marco	368.8	52	376.4	38	398.6	27	414.0	23
Flaherty, Jack	408.5	6	412.3	5	417.3	13	412.9	24
Gallen, Zac	354.3	93	362.3	65	398.6	26	412.9	25
Wheeler, Zack	377.6	37	383.0	28	398.7	25	412.7	26
Berrios, Jose	383.8	25	383.5	26	395.7	29	411.1	27
Bundy, Dylan	366.4	55	378.7	35	403.1	19	409.9	28
Snell, Blake	380.7	31	381.6	29	400.7	22	409.4	29
Buehler, Walker	396.5	13	394.0	17	402.7	20	409.1	30
Keuchel, Dallas	360.7	73	365.8	56	393.4	32	405.5	31
Davies, Zach	361.2	71	359.7	72	392.1	34	405.5	32
Corbin, Patrick	403.4	8	409.9	8	412.7	15	404.7	33
Fried, Max	357.7	83	370.2	49	401.9	21	402.3	34
Tanaka, Masahiro	388.4	20	381.2	31	395.5	30	402.1	35
Gausman, Kevin	346.6	113	351.1	100	383.3	40	401.1	36
Morton, Charlie	397.9	12	394.5	16	393.5	31	400.8	37
Happ, J.A.	374.4	41	364.9	59	375.9	51	400.1	38
Bassitt, Chris	354.9	91	356.4	85	371.7	58	397.9	39
Plesac, Zach	351.8	101	360.6	69	377.5	48	397.6	40
Wainwright, Adam	361.8	66	367.0	54	383.8	39	396.2	41
Means, John	364.0	59	356.6	83	363.8	74	394.6	42
Minor, Mike	379.2	33	376.8	36	381.8	44	392.9	43
Glasnow, Tyler	345.3	116	353.3	92	374.7	53	392.6	44
Hill, Rich	374.3	42	373.8	45	372.3	57	392.1	45
Strasburg, Stephen	419.6	5	410.6	7	396.7	28	390.2	46
Fiers, Mike	377.4	38	375.7	41	382.4	42	389.8	47
Keller, Brad	358.6	80	349.6	102	374.2	55	389.2	48
Burnes, Corbin	325.0	201	329.6	173	357.4	88	389.0	49
Paddack, Chris	364.0	60	374.8	43	383.2	41	387.1	50
Hudson, Dakota	361.7	68	357.6	80	377.9	47	386.7	51
Ray, Robbie	380.9	29	376.2	39	379.9	45	385.5	52
Brault, Steven	339.3	139	340.7	127	360.3	78	385.4	53
Musgrove, Joe	356.8	85	363.3	62	353.1	105	384.9	54
Freeland, Kyle	351.9	100	363.3	63	376.7	49	384.9	55
Yarbrough, Ryan	353.5	96	365.1	58	376.4	50	383.2	56
Paxton, James	390.0	18	385.1	24	389.4	36	382.9	57
Heaney, Andrew	347.4	109	358.2	77	368.0	66	382.8	58
Valdez, Framber	325.0	201	327.3	187	370.3	63	382.2	59
Alcantara, Sandy	363.7	61	371.0	48	358.3	82	381.9	60
Duffy, Danny	358.1	82	364.0	61	382.0	43	381.6	61
Turnbull, Spencer	346.8	112	358.1	78	369.8	65	379.7	62
Senzatela, Antonio	326.1	197	327.8	184	363.5	75	378.8	63
Boyd, Matthew	372.4	48	370.2	50	371.6	59	378.2	64
Walker, Taijuan	325.0	201	335.3	140	357.2	92	378.2	65
Eflin, Zach	350.2	104	341.2	124	359.9	80	378.2	66
Canning, Griffin	345.5	115	351.4	97	361.3	77	377.2	67
Porcello, Rick	369.4	51	358.5	76	369.9	64	376.9	68
Perez, Martin	344.1	120	348.4	104	363.8	73	376.7	69
Singer, Brady			334.6	142	345.5	128	376.3	70
Bumgarner, Madison	380.8	30	383.6	25	365.2	71	375.4	71

Starting Pitcher Rankings

Player	July 23 Score	Rank	Aug 1 Score	Rank	Sept 1 Score	Rank	Sept 27 Score	Rank
May, Dustin	328.0	187	332.3	150	354.0	103	374.8	72
Gonsolin, Tony	331.4	165	331.8	156	348.9	117	374.7	73
Sanchez, Anibal	379.5	32	375.9	40	371.5	60	374.5	74
Lester, Jon	362.7	64	365.9	55	366.9	69	374.2	75
Mahle, Tyler	341.9	128	339.8	129	355.7	97	373.9	76
Urias, Julio	325.0	201	335.3	139	354.7	102	373.7	77
Soroka, Mike	378.6	35	387.9	21	378.4	46	371.9	78
McCullers Jr., Lance	325.0	201	330.3	170	348.2	120	371.3	79
Lopez, Pablo	336.0	149	327.0	189	356.8	94	370.9	80
Javier, Cristian			334.5	143	355.7	98	370.8	81
Manaea, Sean	341.3	131	340.8	126	350.5	112	370.2	82
Gray, Jon	373.4	47	376.6	37	374.6	54	369.6	83
Kelly, Merrill	358.2	81	361.6	66	375.8	52	369.3	84
Gibson, Kyle	361.2	70	357.6	79	357.4	87	368.6	85
Peterson, David			329.0	175	344.5	134	368.6	86
Eovaldi, Nathan	331.3	166	340.7	128	349.9	114	367.7	87
Civale, Aaron	342.4	125	343.7	119	370.6	61	367.3	88
Sheffield, Justus	328.9	180	324.0	445	347.1	123	367.1	89
Roark, Tanner	364.6	58	367.2	53	370.4	62	366.8	90
Anderson, Brett	354.1	95	345.1	113	357.8	85	366.5	91
Odorizzi, Jake	383.6	26	374.6	44	367.0	68	361.4	92
Anderson, Chase	365.6	57	356.6	84	374.1	56	365.4	93
Mills, Alec	327.5	190	332.1	154	343.1	137	364.7	94
Anderson, Ian					342.1	138	364.6	95
Cease, Dylan	332.6	158	325.3	195	357.3	91	363.9	96
Montas, Frankie	348.4	107	355.1	87	357.1	93	363.3	97
Teheran, Julio	382.1	28	373.1	47	367.3	67	362.7	98
Kikuchi, Yusei	338.3	141	345.1	112	346.1	125	361.9	99
Cueto, Johnny	330.3	170	331.0	166	362.8	76	361.9	100
Arrieta, Jake	356.6	87	347.6	105	352.7	107	361.5	101
Anderson, Tyler	326.2	195	325.4	194	344.6	133	361.4	102
Smyly, Drew	340.6	133	347.0	108	340.8	142	361.2	103
Lopez, Reynaldo	360.3	74	354.5	88	353.9	104	361.0	104
Luzardo, Jesus					345.9	127	360.6	105
Dunn, Justin	329.3	177	327.9	180	348.5	119	360.4	106
Williams, Trevor	354.7	92	355.5	86	360.0	79	360.3	107
Cobb, Alex	325.0	201	335.9	136	349.5	116	359.6	108
Kluber, Corey	375.5	40	373.6	46	365.8	70	359.3	109
Richards, Garrett	325.0	201	336.6	134	351.1	110	358.6	110
Webb, Logan	329.7	176	335.8	137	357.4	89	358.4	111
Velasquez, Vince	344.8	119	342.9	121	347.6	121	357.6	112
Montgomery, Jordan	325.0	201	331.3	163	343.2	136	356.6	113
Sanchez, Sixto					338.7	148	356.4	114
Smith, Caleb	351.2	102	353.1	93	345.3	130	355.6	115
Fedde, Erick	328.1	186	331.7	157	338.0	151	355.5	116
Bubic, Kris			328.6	178	338.9	147	355.4	117
Dobnak, Randy	333.2	157	344.4	115	355.4	100	355.2	118
Houser, Adrian	347.3	110	351.2	98	359.0	81	354.4	119
Barria, Jaime	337.7	142	328.7	177	337.0	158	354.3	120
McKenzie, Triston					337.5	155	354.2	121
Kim, Kwang-hyun					340.3	143	354.2	122
Dunning, Dane					337.7	153	353.6	123
Houck, Tanner							353.4	124
Urquidy, Jose	339.0	140	330.0	172	325.0	220	353.4	125
DeSclafani, Anthony	367.9	54	358.9	74	354.7	101	352.8	126
Wojciechowski, Asher	345.3	118	343.1	120	357.5	86	352.5	127
Weaver, Luke	334.9	153	324.2	444	339.8	146	352.5	128
Bailey, Homer	360.1	76	360.2	70	352.9	106	352.1	129
Ponce de Leon, Daniel	325.0	201	329.2	174	328.3	204	351.8	130
Foltynewicz, Mike	373.9	43	365.7	57	358.2	83	351.7	131
Hernandez, Elieser	340.4	134	331.4	162	356.4	95	351.4	132
Margevicius, Nick	325.0	201	325.0	196	344.6	132	351.1	133
Miley, Wade	360.1	75	352.5	96	357.4	90	351.1	134
Milone, Tommy	347.4	108	346.8	109	358.1	84	350.1	135
Voth, Austin	335.4	151	335.7	138	332.3	182	349.9	136
Gonzalez, Gio	360.8	72	357.3	81	356.3	96	349.8	137
Brubaker, Jonathan					336.0	164	349.4	138
Lindblom, Josh			15.1	456	338.0	150	349.4	139
Akin, Keegan					332.1	184	349.2	140
Chirinos, Yonny	353.1	98	352.8	94	355.5	99	349.0	141
Pineda, Michael	361.7	67	352.7	95	330.5	196	348.7	142
Cahill, Trevor	325.0	201	325.0	196	348.7	118	348.3	143
Castellani, Ryan					345.4	129	347.7	144
Cody, Kyle							347.3	145

Starting Pitcher Rankings

Player	July 23 Score	Rank	Aug 1 Score	Rank	Sept 1 Score	Rank	Sept 27 Score	Rank
Gomber, Austin	325.0	201	325.0	196	325.0	220	347.2	146
Alzolay, Adbert	325.0	201	325.0	196	331.5	188	347.0	147
Wacha, Michael	341.8	130	342.5	122	340.0	145	346.3	148
Lucchesi, Joey	362.1	65	358.6	75	352.4	108	345.9	149
Shoemaker, Matt	325.0	201	332.3	152	346.0	126	345.1	150
Lyles, Jordan	356.6	86	349.1	103	334.8	170	344.9	151
Wright, Kyle	325.0	201	322.3	451	325.7	216	344.8	152
Stripling, Ross	339.4	138	351.2	99	344.7	131	344.3	153
Keller, Mitch	328.5	182	332.3	151	326.1	214	343.9	154
Sandoval, Patrick	337.1	144	337.2	132	336.2	162	343.9	155
Fleming, Josh					337.6	154	343.4	156
Suter, Brent					15.4	487	343.3	157
Junis, Jakob	356.0	89	347.0	107	350.0	113	343.2	158
Samardzija, Jeff	365.8	56	356.8	82	347.5	122	343.2	159
Wisler, Matt	334.0	154	325.0	196	341.5	140	343.1	160
Nova, Ivan	358.7	79	361.5	67	349.5	115	343.0	161
Mazza, Chris	325.0	201	325.0	196	324.9	481	342.3	162
Eshelman, Tom	325.0	201	325.0	196	340.0	144	342.3	163
Kremer, Dean							342.1	164
Clarke, Taylor	328.5	181	325.0	196	337.7	152	341.6	165
Lorenzen, Michael	325.0	201	325.0	196	331.6	186	341.3	166
Garcia, Deivi					20.7	486	341.1	167
Young, Alex	345.3	117	336.3	135	336.1	163	341.1	168
Rogers, Trevor					335.5	166	340.7	169
Lopez, Jorge	330.1	172	325.0	196	333.1	180	340.7	170
Matz, Steven	361.3	69	367.7	51	351.5	109	340.5	171
Thornton, Trent	355.3	90	353.5	91	346.8	124	340.3	172
Pivetta, Nick	330.5	169	325.0	196	325.0	220	339.4	173
Sale, Chris	405.0	7	396.0	14	365.0	72	339.0	174
Antone, Tejay			332.0	155	334.7	172	338.9	175
Skubal, Tarik					331.0	191	338.9	176
Gonzalez, Chi Chi	339.4	136	330.4	168	334.4	174	337.8	177
Urena, Jose	342.1	126	333.1	147	325.0	220	337.7	178
Richards, Trevor	342.9	123	333.9	146	340.9	141	337.3	179
Norris, Daniel	353.4	97	344.4	116	343.7	135	337.2	180
Wilson, Bryse	325.0	201	325.0	196	325.0	220	337.0	181
Ponce, Cody					330.9	193	337.0	182
Garcia, Luis							336.4	183
Howard, Spencer					334.3	175	336.1	184
Mize, Casey					330.6	195	336.0	185
Merryweather, Julian					338.6	149	335.8	186
Quantrill, Cal	335.6	150	331.7	158	331.2	190	335.6	187
LeBlanc, Wade	339.4	137	346.7	110	341.8	139	335.3	188
Fairbanks, Peter							334.5	189
Castano, Daniel					335.0	169	334.3	190
Morejon, Adrian	325.0	201	325.0	196	330.7	194	334.1	191
Ynoa, Huascar					325.0	220	333.5	192
Benjamin, Wes					328.1	207	333.5	193
Braymer, Ben							333.2	194
Newsome, Ljay					330.2	198	333.2	195
Weber, Ryan	325.0	201	321.1	454	332.5	181	333.0	196
Hale, David	325.0	201	325.0	196	325.0	220	332.3	197
Zeuch, T.J.	328.2	185	325.0	196	325.0	220	332.1	198
Fulmer, Michael	325.0	201	323.9	446	335.5	165	331.5	199
Chatwood, Tyler	325.0	201	345.0	114	336.8	160	331.3	200
Allard, Kolby	332.4	160	325.0	196	337.2	157	331.2	201
Graterol, Brusdar							330.9	202
Zimmermann, Jordan	330.8	168	325.0	196	325.0	220	330.5	203
Tomlin, Josh	325.0	201	325.0	196	327.4	210	330.4	204
Plutko, Adam	342.6	124	343.9	117	336.9	159	330.4	205
Curtiss, John					325.6	218	330.0	206
Baragar, Caleb							329.8	207
Smith, Riley							329.8	208
Bielak, Brandon					334.2	176	329.4	209
Quintana, Jose	362.7	63	353.7	90	325.0	220	329.1	210
Herget, Jimmy							329.1	211
Gonzalez, Victor							329.0	212
Erlin, Robbie	325.0	201	325.0	196	337.5	156	329.0	213
Pearson, Nate			334.0	145	335.2	168	328.7	214
Parker, Blake	325.0	201	325.0	196	325.0	220	328.7	215
Medina, Adonis							328.6	216
Oswalt, Corey	325.0	201	322.4	450	334.8	171	328.3	217
Ramirez, Erasmo	325.0	201	325.0	196	325.0	220	328.2	218
Foster, Matt					334.5	173	328.0	219

Starting Pitcher Rankings

Player	July 23 Score	July 23 Rank	Aug 1 Score	Aug 1 Rank	Sept 1 Score	Sept 1 Rank	Sept 27 Score	Sept 27 Rank
Hernandez, Carlos							328.0	220
Rodriguez, Nivaldo							327.4	221
Loaisiga, Jonathan	325.0	201	330.2	171	333.4	178	327.4	222
Goody, Nick							327.3	223
Schmidt, Clarke							327.3	224
Brewer, Colten					332.2	183	326.9	225
Patino, Luis							326.7	226
King, Michael					326.8	211	326.7	227
Wood, Alex	325.0	201	325.7	193	325.0	220	326.1	228
Hamels, Cole	373.6	46	360.1	71	325.0	220	326.0	229
Yamaguchi, Shun					332.1	185	325.6	230
Leyer, Robinson							325.6	231
Yacabonis, Jimmy	325.0	201	325.0	196	325.0	220	325.4	232
Dugger, Robert	326.8	192	323.3	449	325.0	220	325.4	233
Lail, Brady							325.1	234
Rosso, Ramon							325.1	235
Tropeano, Nick	325.0	201	325.0	196	331.5	187	325.0	236
Toussaint, Touki	325.0	201	331.6	161	335.4	167	325.0	237
All Others							325.0	238

Team Statistics

Mark Simon

When I was little, I was a mystery-loving Encyclopedia Brown wanna-be. Eventually my interest in baseball work won out over my interest in detective work, but I always enjoy combining the two. And the next bunch of pages are great for that. I can get out my magnifying glass, dust for fingerprints (or in this case scan the agate type) and solve some baseball statistical mysteries:

There's

"Why were the White Sox so good?"
(They were 14-0 versus left-handed starters)

Or

"How did the Brewers make the playoffs?"
(They went an NL-best 11-5 in one-run games)

Or something more broad like

"How important was pitching to AL teams?"
(Very. Seven of the top eight teams in ERA made the playoffs)

Or

"Who had the biggest home-road home run disparity?"
(The Yankees hit 67 at home, 27 on the road)

There are so many options here whether you wish to investigate overall success or something more specific related to batting, pitching, or fielding. May you solve all the mysteries you wish to unravel.

2020 American League Standings

Overall

EAST Team	W-L	Pct	GB	D1	LD1	LLd	CENTRAL Team	W-L	Pct	GB	D1	LD1	LLd	WEST Team	W-L	Pct	GB	D1	LD1	LLd
Tampa Bay Rays	40-20	.667	0.0	41	9/27	7.0	Minnesota Twins	36-24	.600	0.0	39	9/27	3.0	Oakland Athletics	36-24	.600	0.0	64	9/27	7.0
New York Yankees	33-27	.550	7.0	28	8/24	4.0	Cleveland Indians	35-25	.583	1.0	14	9/8	1.0	Houston Astros	29-31	.483	7.0	10	8/2	1.0
Toronto Blue Jays	32-28	.533	8.0	2	7/25	0.0	Chicago White Sox	35-25	.583	1.0	24	9/22	3.0	Seattle Mariners	27-33	.450	9.0	0	-	0.0
Baltimore Orioles	25-35	.417	15.0	2	7/26	0.0	Kansas City Royals	26-34	.433	10.0	1	7/25	0.0	Los Angeles Angels	26-34	.433	10.0	0	-	0.0
Boston Red Sox	24-36	.400	16.0	2	7/25	0.0	Detroit Tigers	23-35	.397	12.0	2	7/26	0.0	Texas Rangers	22-38	.367	14.0	1	7/24	0.0

Division Clinch Dates: Oakland 9/21, Tampa Bay 9/24, Minnesota 9/27. Postseason Clinch Dates: Chicago 9/17, New York 9/20, Cleveland 9/22, Toronto 9/24, Houston 9/25.
D1 = Number of days a team had at least a share of first place of their division; LD1 = Last date the team had at least a share of first place; LLd = The largest number of games that a team led their division by.

East Division

Tm	AT Home	Road	VERSUS East	Cent	West	NL	LHS	RHS	CONDITIONS Day	Night	Grass	Turf	GAME 1-Rn	5+Rn	XInn	MONTHLY April	May	June	July	Aug	Sept	ALL-STAR Pre	Post
TB	20-9	20-11	27-13	0-0	0-0	13-7	9-8	31-12	11-6	29-14	20-11	20-9	14-5	8-3	4-3	0-0	0-0	0-0	4-4	21-7	15-9	0-0	40-20
NYY	22-9	11-18	23-17	0-0	0-0	10-10	7-8	26-19	8-7	25-20	32-24	1-3	6-7	11-8	5-2	0-0	0-0	0-0	5-1	14-13	14-13	0-0	33-27
Tor	17-9	15-19	22-18	0-0	0-0	10-10	12-8	20-20	8-8	24-20	29-24	3-4	13-10	8-7	5-6	0-0	0-0	0-0	3-4	15-11	14-13	0-0	32-28
Bal	13-20	12-15	14-26	0-0	0-0	11-9	7-6	18-29	10-6	15-29	25-33	0-2	7-12	7-12	4-4	0-0	0-0	0-0	3-3	12-16	10-16	0-0	25-35
Bos	11-20	13-16	14-26	0-0	0-0	10-10	7-17	17-19	7-5	17-31	21-33	3-3	4-9	8-13	0-4	0-0	0-0	0-0	3-5	9-18	12-13	0-0	24-36

Central Division

Tm	AT Home	Road	VERSUS East	Cent	West	NL	LHS	RHS	CONDITIONS Day	Night	Grass	Turf	GAME 1-Rn	5+Rn	XInn	MONTHLY April	May	June	July	Aug	Sept	ALL-STAR Pre	Post
Min	24-7	12-17	0-0	23-17	0-0	13-7	9-7	27-17	11-11	25-13	36-24	0-0	9-5	7-5	3-1	0-0	0-0	0-0	5-2	15-14	16-8	0-0	36-24
CWS	18-12	17-13	0-0	25-15	0-0	10-10	14-0	21-25	10-10	25-15	35-25	0-0	5-8	14-7	1-2	0-0	0-0	0-0	3-4	19-9	13-12	0-0	35-25
Cle	18-12	17-13	0-0	23-17	0-0	12-8	8-5	27-20	9-4	26-21	35-25	0-0	8-6	10-7	4-2	0-0	0-0	0-0	5-3	16-11	14-11	0-0	35-25
KC	15-15	11-19	0-0	17-23	0-0	9-11	4-7	22-27	5-8	21-26	26-34	0-0	8-9	6-14	1-2	0-0	0-0	0-0	3-5	11-16	12-13	0-0	26-34
Det	12-15	11-20	0-0	12-28	0-0	11-7	7-4	16-31	9-13	14-22	23-35	0-0	7-9	8-12	1-2	0-0	0-0	0-0	5-3	11-13	7-19	0-0	23-35

West Division

Tm	AT Home	Road	VERSUS East	Cent	West	NL	LHS	RHS	CONDITIONS Day	Night	Grass	Turf	GAME 1-Rn	5+Rn	XInn	MONTHLY April	May	June	July	Aug	Sept	ALL-STAR Pre	Post
Oak	22-10	14-14	0-0	0-0	26-14	10-10	11-3	25-21	17-13	19-11	32-19	4-5	7-6	9-7	6-1	0-0	0-0	0-0	3-4	19-8	14-12	0-0	36-24
Hou	20-8	9-23	0-0	0-0	19-21	10-10	12-10	17-21	11-12	18-19	27-26	2-5	10-14	8-8	2-7	0-0	0-0	0-0	4-3	15-11	10-17	0-0	29-31
Sea	14-10	13-23	0-0	0-0	20-20	7-13	8-12	19-21	13-11	14-22	24-30	3-3	7-8	6-14	2-3	0-0	0-0	0-0	4-4	11-18	12-11	0-0	27-33
LAA	16-15	10-19	0-0	0-0	19-21	7-13	9-10	17-24	12-13	14-21	25-29	1-5	9-9	5-9	3-5	0-0	0-0	0-0	2-6	10-18	14-10	0-0	26-34
Tex	16-14	6-24	0-0	0-0	16-24	6-14	7-15	15-23	6-13	16-25	6-22	16-16	7-6	3-9	2-2	0-0	0-0	0-0	2-4	10-17	10-17	0-0	22-38

Team vs. Team Breakdown

	EAST TB	NYY	Tor	Bal	Bos	CENTRAL Min	CWS	Cle	KC	Det	WEST Oak	Hou	Sea	LAA	Tex
Tampa Bay Rays	-	8	6	6	7	0	0	0	0	0	0	0	0	0	0
New York Yankees	2	-	5	7	9	0	0	0	0	0	0	0	0	0	0
Toronto Blue Jays	4	5	-	8	5	0	0	0	0	0	0	0	0	0	0
Baltimore Orioles	4	3	2	-	5	0	0	0	0	0	0	0	0	0	0
Boston Red Sox	3	1	5	5	-	0	0	0	0	0	0	0	0	0	0
Minnesota Twins	0	0	0	0	0	-	5	7	5	6	0	0	0	0	0
Chicago White Sox	0	0	0	0	0	5	-	2	9	9	0	0	0	0	0
Cleveland Indians	0	0	0	0	0	3	8	-	5	7	0	0	0	0	0
Kansas City Royals	0	0	0	0	0	5	1	5	-	6	0	0	0	0	0
Detroit Tigers	0	0	0	0	0	4	1	3	4	-	0	0	0	0	0
Oakland Athletics	0	0	0	0	0	0	0	0	0	0	-	7	6	6	7
Houston Astros	0	0	0	0	0	0	0	0	0	0	3	-	7	4	5
Seattle Mariners	0	0	0	0	0	0	0	0	0	0	7	3	-	5	8
Los Angeles Angels	0	0	0	0	0	0	0	0	0	0	4	6	5	-	4
Texas Rangers	0	0	0	0	0	0	0	0	0	0	3	5	2	6	-

2020 National League Standings

Overall

EAST Team	W-L	Pct	GB	D1	LD1	LLd	CENTRAL Team	W-L	Pct	GB	D1	LD1	LLd	WEST Team	W-L	Pct	GB	D1	LD1	LLd
Atlanta Braves	35-25	.583	0.0	46	9/27	6.0	Chicago Cubs	34-26	.567	0.0	65	9/27	6.5	Los Angeles Dodgers	43-17	.717	0.0	47	9/27	6.0
Miami Marlins	31-29	.517	4.0	23	8/16	2.0	St Louis Cardinals	30-28	.517	3.0	3	7/26	1.0	San Diego Padres	37-23	.617	6.0	5	7/31	1.0
Philadelphia Phillies	28-32	.467	7.0	1	7/25	0.0	Cincinnati Reds	31-29	.517	3.0	1	7/24	0.0	San Francisco Giants	29-31	.483	14.0	0	-	0.0
Washington Nationals	26-34	.433	9.0	2	7/25	0.0	Milwaukee Brewers	29-31	.483	5.0	0	-	0.0	Colorado Rockies	26-34	.433	17.0	16	8/13	1.5
New York Mets	26-34	.433	9.0	2	7/25	0.0	Pittsburgh Pirates	19-41	.317	15.0	0	-	0.0	Arizona Diamondbacks	25-35	.417	18.0	0	-	0.0

Division Clinch Dates: Los Angeles 9/22, Atlanta 9/22, Chicago 9/26. Postseason Clinch Dates: San Diego 9/20, Cincinnati 9/25, Miami 9/25, St. Louis 9/27, Milwaukee 9/27.

D1 = Number of days a team had at least a share of first place of their division; LD1 = Last date the team had at least a share of first place; LLd = The largest number of games that a team led their division

East Division

Tm	AT Home	Road	VERSUS East	Cent	West	AL	LHS	RHS	CONDITIONS Day	Night	Grass	Turf	GAME 1-Rn	5+Rn	XInn	MONTHLY April	May	June	July	Aug	Sept	ALL-STAR Pre	Post
Atl	19-11	16-14	24-16	0-0	0-0	11-9	8-4	27-21	8-4	27-21	35-23	0-2	11-6	13-11	2-3	0-0	0-0	0-0	5-3	15-11	15-11	0-0	35-25
Mia	11-15	20-14	21-19	0-0	0-0	10-10	7-12	24-17	8-9	23-20	30-27	1-2	11-8	6-13	3-2	0-0	0-0	0-0	2-1	13-14	16-14	0-0	31-29
Phi	19-13	9-19	21-19	0-0	0-0	7-13	13-9	15-23	5-15	23-17	28-29	0-3	8-10	10-7	3-2	0-0	0-0	0-0	1-2	14-13	13-17	0-0	28-32
Was	15-18	11-16	17-23	0-0	0-0	9-11	11-6	15-28	10-8	16-26	25-33	1-1	7-9	10-10	4-1	0-0	0-0	0-0	3-4	9-16	14-14	0-0	26-34
NYM	12-17	14-17	17-23	0-0	0-0	9-11	8-14	18-20	6-13	20-21	26-34	0-0	6-11	10-7	1-4	0-0	0-0	0-0	3-5	12-15	11-14	0-0	26-34

Central Division

Tm	AT Home	Road	VERSUS East	Cent	West	AL	LHS	RHS	CONDITIONS Day	Night	Grass	Turf	GAME 1-Rn	5+Rn	XInn	MONTHLY April	May	June	July	Aug	Sept	ALL-STAR Pre	Post
ChC	19-14	15-12	0-0	22-18	0-0	12-8	7-4	27-22	8-6	26-20	34-26	0-0	10-9	10-8	3-1	0-0	0-0	0-0	5-2	15-12	14-12	0-0	34-26
Cin	16-13	15-16	0-0	21-19	0-0	10-10	7-6	24-23	5-5	26-24	31-29	0-0	7-8	12-7	2-0	0-0	0-0	0-0	2-5	13-15	16-9	0-0	31-29
StL	14-13	16-15	0-0	22-18	0-0	8-10	4-7	26-21	10-10	20-18	30-28	0-0	7-6	10-6	1-3	0-0	0-0	0-0	2-3	11-10	17-15	0-0	30-28
Mil	15-14	14-17	0-0	19-21	0-0	10-10	11-7	18-24	6-7	23-24	29-31	0-0	11-5	10-13	3-2	0-0	0-0	0-0	3-3	13-15	13-13	0-0	29-31
Pit	13-19	6-22	0-0	16-24	0-0	3-17	2-10	17-31	10-9	9-32	19-41	0-0	8-15	4-12	1-5	0-0	0-0	0-0	2-5	8-17	9-19	0-0	19-41

West Division

Tm	AT Home	Road	VERSUS East	Cent	West	AL	LHS	RHS	CONDITIONS Day	Night	Grass	Turf	GAME 1-Rn	5+Rn	XInn	MONTHLY April	May	June	July	Aug	Sept	ALL-STAR Pre	Post
LAD	21-9	22-8	0-0	0-0	27-13	16-4	13-5	30-12	11-2	32-15	36-14	7-3	7-5	17-1	5-1	0-0	0-0	0-0	5-3	21-7	17-7	0-0	43-17
SD	21-11	16-12	0-0	0-0	24-16	13-7	10-10	27-13	11-8	26-15	35-20	2-3	8-8	14-5	4-0	0-0	0-0	0-0	6-2	16-13	15-8	0-0	37-23
SF	19-14	10-17	0-0	0-0	18-22	11-9	14-10	15-21	7-13	22-18	27-30	2-1	8-8	10-11	2-3	0-0	0-0	0-0	4-4	13-15	12-12	0-0	29-31
Col	12-18	14-16	0-0	0-0	17-23	9-11	10-10	16-24	9-11	17-23	20-30	6-4	9-8	5-14	1-2	0-0	0-0	0-0	4-2	13-16	9-16	0-0	26-34
Ari	16-14	9-21	0-0	0-0	14-26	11-9	5-11	20-24	9-10	16-25	8-20	17-15	9-9	6-5	0-3	0-0	0-0	0-0	3-5	11-16	11-14	0-0	25-35

Team vs. Team Breakdown

	EAST Atl	Mia	Phi	Was	NYM	CENTRAL ChC	StL	Cin	Mil	Pit	WEST LAD	SD	SF	Col	Ari
Atlanta Braves	-	6	5	6	7	0	0	0	0	0	0	0	0	0	0
Miami Marlins	4	-	7	6	4	0	0	0	0	0	0	0	0	0	0
Philadelphia Phillies	5	3	-	7	6	0	0	0	0	0	0	0	0	0	0
Washington Nationals	4	4	3	-	6	0	0	0	0	0	0	0	0	0	0
New York Mets	3	6	4	4	-	0	0	0	0	0	0	0	0	0	0
Chicago Cubs	0	0	0	0	0	-	5	6	5	6	0	0	0	0	0
St Louis Cardinals	0	0	0	0	0	5	-	6	5	6	0	0	0	0	0
Cincinnati Reds	0	0	0	0	0	4	4	-	6	7	0	0	0	0	0
Milwaukee Brewers	0	0	0	0	0	5	5	4	-	5	0	0	0	0	0
Pittsburgh Pirates	0	0	0	0	0	4	4	3	5	-	0	0	0	0	0
Los Angeles Dodgers	0	0	0	0	0	0	0	0	0	0	-	6	6	7	8
San Diego Padres	0	0	0	0	0	0	0	0	0	0	4	-	8	7	5
San Francisco Giants	0	0	0	0	0	0	0	0	0	0	4	2	-	4	8
Colorado Rockies	0	0	0	0	0	0	0	0	0	0	3	3	6	-	5
Arizona Diamondbacks	0	0	0	0	0	0	0	0	0	0	2	5	2	5	-

American League Batting

Tm	G	AB	H	2B	3B	HR	(Hm	Rd)	TB	R	RBI	TBB	IBB	SO	HBP	SH	SF	ShO	SB	CS	SB%	GDP	LOB	Avg	OBP	Slg
NYY	60	1915	473	87	7	94	(67	27)	856	315	301	251	5	480	30	1	11	2	27	7	.79	51	604	.247	.342	.447
CWS	60	2047	534	94	6	96	(52	44)	928	306	294	179	1	571	24	1	13	2	20	8	.71	44	593	.261	.326	.453
Tor	60	2023	516	104	4	88	(43	45)	892	302	288	203	4	508	12	8	14	2	33	6	.85	39	597	.255	.325	.441
LAA	60	2020	501	97	8	85	(50	35)	869	294	285	239	8	490	25	6	18	3	21	8	.72	49	633	.248	.332	.430
Bos	60	2083	552	118	7	81	(38	43)	927	292	278	187	8	545	21	4	9	1	31	9	.78	51	630	.265	.330	.445
TB	60	1975	470	105	12	80	(33	47)	839	289	274	243	9	608	28	0	14	1	48	9	.84	38	613	.238	.328	.425
Hou	60	1992	478	103	12	69	(29	40)	812	279	268	192	5	440	23	6	13	2	22	11	.67	39	596	.240	.312	.408
Oak	60	1908	430	91	11	71	(36	35)	756	274	264	238	5	524	39	2	14	2	26	3	.90	44	584	.225	.322	.396
Bal	60	2026	523	102	7	77	(45	32)	870	274	264	164	5	514	27	15	10	4	19	14	.58	32	612	.258	.321	.429
Min	60	1937	468	81	3	91	(43	48)	828	269	258	186	9	528	29	2	14	2	14	7	.67	38	558	.242	.315	.427
Sea	60	1929	435	88	5	60	(23	37)	713	254	244	207	5	545	30	3	12	2	50	16	.76	35	562	.226	.309	.370
Det	58	1893	463	78	12	62	(27	35)	751	249	242	147	1	567	19	1	14	7	19	6	.76	42	489	.245	.303	.397
KC	60	1988	485	97	7	68	(33	35)	800	248	242	172	3	527	18	8	10	7	49	20	.71	28	597	.244	.309	.402
Cle	60	1959	446	96	5	59	(25	34)	729	248	234	239	4	517	24	7	16	5	25	10	.71	40	604	.228	.317	.372
Tex	60	1936	420	80	9	62	(27	35)	704	224	204	167	3	548	24	2	18	1	49	14	.78	33	533	.217	.285	.364
AL	449	29631	7194	1421	115	1143	(571	572)	12274	4117	3935	3014	75	7912	373	66	200	43	453	148	.75	603	8805	.243	.319	.414

American League Pitching

	HOW MUCH THEY PITCHED					WHAT THEY GAVE UP												THE RESULTS									
Tm	G	CG	Rel	IP	BFP	H	R	ER	HR	SH	SF	HB	TBB	IBB	SO	WP	Bk	W	L	Pct.	ShO	Sv-Op	Hld	OAvg	OOBP	OSlg	ERA
Cle	60	1	181	536.0	2176	440	209	196	68	4	13	27	157	8	621	20	1	35	25	.583	7	20-27	35	.223	.288	.378	3.29
Min	60	0	202	513.1	2130	448	215	204	62	1	8	21	170	0	535	20	1	36	24	.600	4	17-26	49	.232	.301	.372	3.58
TB	60	0	219	527.2	2212	475	229	209	70	9	10	29	168	4	552	30	1	40	20	.667	4	23-29	38	.238	.305	.391	3.56
Oak	60	1	181	515.1	2164	471	232	216	69	4	15	15	165	6	506	16	1	36	24	.600	5	17-21	32	.240	.302	.392	3.77
CWS	60	1	224	527.0	2235	448	246	223	71	5	7	23	217	6	523	24	0	35	25	.583	6	13-22	29	.226	.309	.379	3.81
NYY	60	2	174	500.2	2133	455	270	242	83	4	5	25	168	5	528	22	2	33	27	.550	2	14-23	15	.236	.305	.421	4.35
KC	60	1	232	517.0	2233	500	272	247	76	4	18	29	211	7	517	28	3	26	34	.433	4	19-20	29	.254	.332	.415	4.30
Hou	60	0	193	524.0	2239	472	275	251	70	8	13	29	217	7	526	25	4	29	31	.483	0	16-29	27	.239	.322	.407	4.31
Bal	60	0	207	518.2	2246	489	294	260	79	4	23	34	192	2	487	35	4	25	35	.417	1	11-18	31	.246	.319	.421	4.51
Sea	60	1	189	516.2	2249	482	303	289	79	0	15	37	230	7	469	23	1	27	33	.450	0	15-23	28	.245	.333	.425	5.03
Tex	60	2	204	516.2	2273	479	312	288	81	8	17	30	236	3	489	21	2	22	38	.367	3	10-19	15	.242	.329	.419	5.02
Tor	60	0	226	524.2	2309	517	312	268	81	6	12	14	250	7	519	15	2	32	28	.533	1	17-28	31	.255	.339	.436	4.60
Det	58	1	218	492.1	2174	511	318	308	91	5	15	34	192	4	444	18	0	23	35	.397	1	11-19	25	.265	.340	.464	5.63
LAA	60	1	228	525.1	2256	492	321	297	82	3	21	21	199	8	523	25	1	26	34	.433	2	12-26	20	.245	.316	.430	5.09
Bos	60	0	232	524.0	2389	587	351	325	98	5	10	31	252	4	537	28	3	24	36	.400	2	14-25	37	.281	.365	.484	5.58
AL	449	11	3110	7779.1	33418	7266	4159	3823	1160	70	202	399	3024	76	7776	350	26	449	449	.500	42	229-355	441	.245	.321	.416	4.42

American League Fielding

Team	G	Inn	PO	Ast	OFAst	E	(Throw	Field)	TC	DP	GDP	SB	CS	SB%	CPkof	PPkof	PB	UER	UERA	FPct
Houston	60	524.0	1572	546	5	20	11	9	2138	48	43	28	9	.76	0	1	4	24	0.41	.991
Minnesota	60	513.1	1540	459	10	20	8	12	2019	39	33	33	10	.77	0	5	7	11	0.19	.990
Seattle	60	516.2	1550	502	10	23	6	17	2075	48	41	44	5	.90	0	3	9	14	0.24	.989
Oakland	60	515.1	1546	489	6	26	10	16	2061	33	29	23	10	.70	0	2	4	16	0.28	.987
Cleveland	60	536.0	1608	500	10	30	14	16	2138	46	41	17	14	.55	2	2	0	13	0.22	.986
Detroit	58	492.1	1477	502	5	29	12	17	2008	46	38	40	9	.82	0	0	4	10	0.18	.986
Kansas City	60	517.0	1551	503	6	31	16	15	2085	62	55	17	3	.85	0	3	2	25	0.44	.985
Tampa Bay	60	527.2	1583	541	8	33	13	20	2157	52	43	27	13	.68	0	0	7	20	0.34	.985
Los Angeles	60	525.1	1576	485	2	36	16	20	2097	36	29	50	17	.75	0	3	3	24	0.41	.983
Toronto	60	524.2	1574	530	12	39	17	22	2143	47	42	32	10	.76	0	2	6	44	0.75	.982
Chicago	60	527.0	1581	517	6	39	14	25	2137	48	44	16	10	.62	0	1	6	23	0.39	.982
Texas	60	516.2	1550	467	6	40	16	24	2057	40	34	27	7	.79	1	0	6	24	0.42	.981
Baltimore	60	518.2	1556	511	9	43	23	20	2110	42	39	23	8	.74	1	2	5	34	0.59	.980
Boston	60	524.0	1572	522	18	45	19	26	2139	59	50	33	13	.72	1	1	5	26	0.45	.979
New York	60	500.2	1502	472	8	48	17	31	2022	37	29	22	10	.69	1	1	6	28	0.50	.976
American League	449	7779.1	23338	7546	121	502	212	290	31386	683	590	432	148	.74	6	26	74	336	0.39	.984

National League Batting

Tm	G	AB	H	2B	3B	HR	(Hm	Rd)	TB	R	RBI	TBB	IBB	SO	HBP	SH	SF	ShO	SB	CS	SB%	GDP	LOB	Avg	OBP	Slg
LAD	60	2042	523	97	6	118	(64	54)	986	349	327	228	7	471	30	3	12	0	29	8	.78	46	611	.256	.338	.483
Atl	60	2074	556	130	3	103	(52	51)	1001	348	338	239	13	573	23	1	7	3	23	4	.85	39	628	.268	.349	.483
SD	60	1972	506	103	12	95	(55	40)	918	325	312	204	6	479	28	12	14	2	55	13	.81	37	568	.257	.333	.466
Phi	60	1948	500	90	10	82	(48	34)	856	306	289	229	16	480	28	8	10	2	35	8	.81	40	612	.257	.342	.439
SF	60	2019	532	107	14	81	(51	30)	910	299	290	195	8	499	27	4	13	5	19	8	.70	51	633	.263	.335	.451
Was	60	1968	519	112	12	66	(30	36)	853	293	279	192	16	451	32	5	21	3	33	12	.73	42	608	.264	.336	.433
NYM	60	2023	551	106	7	86	(41	45)	929	286	278	197	8	498	45	1	13	4	20	10	.67	53	656	.272	.348	.459
Col	60	2057	528	84	16	63	(35	28)	833	275	264	161	12	543	10	7	19	4	42	9	.82	41	595	.257	.311	.405
Ari	60	1997	482	101	12	58	(29	29)	781	269	255	181	5	461	36	1	23	2	23	7	.77	37	617	.241	.312	.391
ChC	60	1918	422	82	8	74	(30	44)	742	265	248	229	9	568	52	1	13	4	24	10	.71	42	593	.220	.318	.387
Mia	60	1935	472	82	5	60	(22	38)	744	263	247	191	6	537	25	6	9	7	51	14	.78	37	590	.244	.319	.384
Mil	60	1920	429	83	5	75	(39	36)	747	247	238	221	8	582	35	0	10	3	15	11	.58	53	545	.223	.313	.389
Cin	60	1842	390	76	3	90	(55	35)	742	243	237	239	4	534	33	0	7	7	29	9	.76	44	538	.212	.312	.403
StL	58	1752	410	73	7	51	(25	26)	650	240	231	205	3	477	33	4	16	5	18	10	.64	38	535	.234	.323	.371
Pit	60	1932	425	76	6	59	(29	30)	690	219	210	167	6	521	11	7	15	6	16	11	.59	34	547	.220	.284	.357
NL	449	29399	7245	1402	126	1161	(605	556)	12382	4227	4043	3078	127	7674	448	60	202	57	432	144	.75	634	8876	.246	.325	.421

National League Pitching

Tm	G	CG	Rel	IP	BFP	H	R	ER	HR	SH	SF	HB	TBB	IBB	SO	WP	Bk	W	L	Pct.	ShO	Sv-Op	Hld	OAvg	OOBP	OSlg	ERA
LAD	60	0	249	538.2	2172	424	213	181	66	6	12	21	145	4	517	24	0	43	17	.717	5	15-24	45	.213	.272	.355	3.02
StL	58	2	176	473.0	1989	376	229	205	69	3	14	26	204	8	464	21	1	30	28	.517	2	13-18	17	.216	.306	.380	3.90
ChC	60	2	188	518.1	2153	451	240	230	74	3	11	17	182	7	523	22	4	34	26	.567	8	16-21	24	.233	.302	.400	3.99
SD	60	1	218	520.1	2160	456	241	223	70	4	12	22	170	2	565	19	3	37	23	.617	5	13-24	39	.234	.301	.389	3.86
Cin	60	3	168	504.0	2125	401	243	215	67	2	14	29	213	6	615	23	5	31	29	.517	5	9-16	25	.215	.303	.374	3.84
Mil	60	1	189	517.1	2186	446	264	239	67	2	10	35	189	1	614	21	2	29	31	.483	8	14-22	20	.229	.307	.385	4.16
Atl	60	0	228	524.1	2276	494	288	257	69	6	17	33	220	13	506	23	2	35	25	.583	4	13-19	30	.247	.329	.408	4.41
Ari	60	0	200	518.1	2279	506	295	279	93	4	13	23	235	20	524	23	1	25	35	.417	2	13-22	19	.253	.336	.462	4.84
SF	60	1	236	517.2	2240	474	297	267	69	5	19	34	210	2	488	20	5	29	31	.483	0	13-23	42	.241	.322	.410	4.64
Pit	60	1	209	513.0	2227	451	298	267	80	2	18	37	249	3	536	22	2	19	41	.317	3	6-18	22	.235	.332	.416	4.68
Was	60	2	202	503.2	2273	548	301	285	94	3	7	22	216	22	508	23	4	26	34	.433	3	12-21	39	.271	.346	.466	5.09
Mia	60	1	215	504.0	2214	506	304	272	82	4	17	26	226	14	451	11	4	31	29	.517	6	18-22	25	.261	.343	.455	4.86
NYM	60	0	197	513.1	2262	511	308	284	81	4	8	29	219	7	574	24	0	26	34	.433	1	11-18	28	.255	.336	.438	4.98
Phi	60	3	189	497.0	2197	550	311	284	80	4	8	30	185	12	532	14	3	28	32	.467	5	11-23	26	.279	.348	.468	5.14
Col	60	1	189	526.1	2335	579	353	327	83	4	19	40	205	5	393	29	1	26	34	.433	1	16-24	20	.280	.353	.477	5.59
NL	449	18	3053	7689.1	33088	7173	4185	3815	1144	56	200	422	3068	126	7810	325	37	449	449	.500	58	193-315	421	.245	.323	.419	4.47

National League Fielding

Team	G	Inn	PO	Ast	OFAst	E	(Throw	Field)	TC	DP	GDP	SB	CS	SB%	CPkof	PPkof	PB	UER	UERA	FPct
Cincinnati	60	504.0	1512	442	6	27	12	15	1981	36	33	23	11	.68	0	0	5	28	0.50	.986
Chicago	60	518.1	1555	559	11	30	14	16	2144	45	41	22	11	.67	0	4	1	10	0.17	.986
New York	60	513.1	1540	494	14	32	17	15	2066	39	33	41	8	.84	1	3	6	24	0.42	.985
San Diego	60	520.1	1561	502	9	33	18	15	2096	46	41	23	12	.66	1	1	9	18	0.31	.984
Atlanta	60	524.1	1573	533	2	34	19	15	2140	52	45	42	5	.89	0	4	6	31	0.53	.984
Milwaukee	60	517.1	1552	494	5	35	21	14	2081	44	37	26	14	.65	1	0	2	25	0.43	.983
Arizona	60	518.1	1555	474	5	35	18	17	2064	54	51	40	8	.83	0	2	4	16	0.28	.983
St Louis	58	473.0	1419	489	8	33	18	15	1941	46	41	8	7	.53	1	0	6	24	0.46	.983
Philadelphia	60	497.0	1491	536	7	36	18	18	2063	57	46	23	7	.77	1	5	5	27	0.49	.983
Los Angeles	60	538.2	1616	544	6	40	24	16	2200	46	41	36	10	.78	1	1	1	32	0.53	.982
Miami	60	504.0	1512	549	6	40	21	19	2101	60	55	31	10	.76	2	3	6	32	0.57	.981
Colorado	60	526.1	1579	633	11	43	22	21	2255	78	66	29	6	.83	0	1	5	26	0.44	.981
Washington	60	503.2	1511	462	2	39	15	24	2012	48	40	46	9	.84	0	0	3	16	0.29	.981
San Francisco	60	517.2	1553	491	7	42	15	27	2086	43	37	18	13	.73	0	6	5	30	0.52	.980
Pittsburgh	60	513.0	1539	511	12	47	23	24	2097	53	40	27	13	.68	2	2	3	31	0.54	.978
National League	449	7689.1	23068	7713	111	546	275	271	31327	747	647	453	144	.76	10	32	67	370	0.43	.983

Team Pitching Staff Summary

Team	Starters				Bullpen					
	IP	ERA	ERA Rank	W-L	IP	ERA	ERA Rank	W-L	Sv-Opp	Sv Pct
Arizona Diamondbacks	291.1	5.04	22	10-25	227.0	4.60	18	15-10	13-22	59%
Atlanta Braves	251.2	5.51	28	14-16	272.2	3.50	4	21-9	13-19	68%
Baltimore Orioles	267.0	5.09	23	12-22	251.2	3.90	9	13-13	11-18	61%
Boston Red Sox	246.0	5.34	25	13-22	278.0	5.79	27	11-14	14-25	56%
Chicago Cubs	325.0	3.77	6	25-20	193.1	4.38	13	9-6	16-21	76%
Chicago White Sox	287.2	3.85	8	18-15	239.1	3.76	7	17-10	13-22	59%
Cincinnati Reds	311.1	3.50	4	18-22	192.2	4.53	17	13-7	9-16	56%
Cleveland Indians	349.2	3.17	1	23-17	186.1	3.53	5	12-8	20-27	74%
Colorado Rockies	320.1	4.83	20	14-23	206.0	6.77	29	12-11	16-24	67%
Detroit Tigers	237.1	6.37	30	9-22	255.0	4.94	25	14-13	11-19	58%
Houston Astros	312.2	4.26	13	19-15	211.1	4.39	15	10-16	16-29	55%
Kansas City Royals	275.2	4.70	18	14-26	241.1	3.84	8	12-8	19-20	95%
Los Angeles Angels	270.2	5.52	29	13-22	254.2	4.63	21	13-12	12-26	46%
Los Angeles Dodgers	276.1	3.29	2	17-6	262.1	2.74	2	26-11	15-24	63%
Miami Marlins	273.1	4.31	14	15-19	230.2	5.50	26	16-10	18-22	82%
Milwaukee Brewers	288.2	4.18	11	14-23	228.2	4.17	11	15-8	14-22	64%
Minnesota Twins	282.1	3.54	5	22-12	231.0	3.62	6	14-12	17-26	65%
New York Mets	278.1	5.37	26	13-22	235.0	4.60	18	13-12	11-18	61%
New York Yankees	295.1	4.24	12	18-17	205.1	4.51	16	15-10	14-23	61%
Oakland Athletics	307.0	4.49	16	22-19	208.1	2.72	1	14-5	17-21	81%
Philadelphia Phillies	311.0	4.08	10	19-18	186.0	7.06	30	9-14	11-23	48%
Pittsburgh Pirates	283.0	4.74	19	10-25	230.0	4.62	20	9-16	6-18	33%
San Diego Padres	286.0	3.46	3	18-15	234.1	4.38	13	19-8	13-24	54%
San Francisco Giants	279.2	4.99	21	11-17	238.0	4.24	12	18-14	13-23	57%
Seattle Mariners	304.0	4.41	15	21-20	212.2	5.92	28	6-13	15-23	65%
St Louis Cardinals	279.2	3.86	9	17-17	193.1	4.00	10	13-11	13-18	72%
Tampa Bay Rays	258.0	3.77	6	15-9	269.2	3.37	3	25-11	23-29	79%
Texas Rangers	287.1	5.32	24	10-28	229.1	4.63	21	12-10	10-19	53%
Toronto Blue Jays	255.1	4.55	17	10-10	269.1	4.71	24	22-18	17-28	61%
Washington Nationals	298.0	5.38	27	15-27	205.2	4.68	23	11-7	12-21	57%

Team Defense

Defensive Runs Saved by Position and Team

Team	P	C	1B	2B	3B	SS	LF	CF	RF	Shifts	Total
St Louis Cardinals	0	0	1	7	1	3	9	3	-1	8	32
Los Angeles Dodgers	-1	3	-4	18	-3	-1	-3	4	12	4	29
Cleveland Indians	6	7	5	7	-6	3	2	4	0	-3	27
Minnesota Twins	3	2	-3	1	0	-1	5	11	3	6	25
Pittsburgh Pirates	2	8	-2	3	0	-5	7	-3	2	11	24
Tampa Bay Rays	1	-2	5	3	-1	0	6	10	2	0	22
Chicago Cubs	6	2	2	5	0	6	-2	-3	1	4	22
Chicago White Sox	2	10	4	2	-2	5	-5	8	1	-1	21
Seattle Mariners	1	-8	7	-2	-6	6	5	-1	3	6	15
Texas Rangers	-1	1	1	-11	7	3	-3	3	15	-1	14
Colorado Rockies	-5	-1	4	-1	18	4	3	-8	2	-1	13
Houston Astros	-1	-2	1	-5	1	7	8	6	-5	1	8
San Diego Padres	-6	-2	6	-1	9	-2	2	8	-5	0	6
Cincinnati Reds	1	8	-8	0	-3	1	5	-1	-4	7	6
San Francisco Giants	1	0	2	4	-2	-1	-9	2	1	5	5
Miami Marlins	5	-5	0	-1	4	2	-4	4	-9	5	1
Baltimore Orioles	-3	-6	-4	-3	0	-4	2	1	7	7	-2
Boston Red Sox	1	-1	0	-2	-7	-5	14	5	-3	-6	-2
New York Yankees	0	0	-4	3	1	-9	-1	-7	6	9	-3
Arizona Diamondbacks	-5	-2	-2	5	-4	3	1	-1	0	2	-4
Atlanta Braves	1	-5	1	-2	-7	9	2	1	-7	-3	-8
Milwaukee Brewers	0	6	-2	-8	3	-3	-5	-3	-2	3	-9
Kansas City Royals	-7	2	-2	6	-2	0	-2	-9	-2	7	-10
Detroit Tigers	-2	-5	2	-2	0	-4	-2	-2	0	1	-12
Oakland Athletics	-9	3	5	-9	2	-9	-4	4	5	1	-20
New York Mets	2	-2	-6	-7	-5	-2	3	-5	5	-3	-20
Los Angeles Angels	3	3	0	-3	1	-1	-10	-8	-6	-2	-23
Philadelphia Phillies	0	-5	-5	-3	-3	-3	-9	-3	-4	0	-33
Toronto Blue Jays	-5	-3	-3	-3	-10	-1	-7	-7	-5	5	-39
Washington Nationals	-6	-7	-3	-2	8	-9	-8	-4	-9	-5	-45

Batting By Position

Pos	AB	H	2B	3B	HR	(Hm	Rd)	TB	R	RBI	TBB	IBB	SO	HBP	SH	SF	SB	CS	SB%	GDP	LOB	Avg	OBP	Slg
P	12	1	0	0	0	(0	0)	1	2	1	2	0	4	0	0	0	0	0	-	0	2	.083	.214	.083
C	5896	1369	257	9	227	(99	128)	2325	732	802	597	4	1767	102	37	37	27	9	.75	138	1850	.232	.312	.394
1B	6593	1627	330	19	342	(164	178)	3021	998	1040	743	37	1745	76	1	44	35	8	.81	156	2018	.247	.328	.458
2B	6528	1608	300	23	175	(86	89)	2479	841	735	542	5	1510	98	19	42	87	36	.71	122	1854	.246	.312	.380
3B	6518	1630	322	31	248	(109	139)	2758	908	908	729	28	1575	93	4	57	59	25	.70	164	2084	.250	.331	.423
SS	6716	1764	342	35	222	(118	104)	2842	971	843	571	14	1594	66	15	43	163	55	.75	155	1888	.263	.325	.423
LF	6441	1604	315	29	265	(137	128)	2772	925	872	683	25	1623	85	11	45	121	33	.79	111	1881	.249	.327	.430
CF	6408	1557	270	47	240	(118	122)	2641	937	796	670	16	1755	97	24	40	177	61	.74	80	1775	.243	.322	.412
RF	6472	1577	346	29	288	(139	149)	2845	962	929	704	20	1813	88	8	39	127	34	.79	125	1897	.244	.324	.440
DH	6438	1493	296	15	276	(144	132)	2647	851	916	719	41	1851	100	4	50	51	17	.75	162	2011	.232	.316	.411
PH	1003	209	45	4	21	(10	11)	325	94	136	132	12	344	16	3	5	3	0	1.00	24	421	.208	.309	.324
PR	0	0	0	0	0	(0	0)	0	123	0	0	0	0	0	0	0	35	14	.71	0	0	-	-	-

Fielding By Position

Pos	Inn	PO	Ast	E	(Throw	Field)	TC	DP	GDP	FPct
P	15468.2	864	1453	137	106	31	2454	107	61	.944
C	15468.2	15744	707	112	65	41	16563	68		.993
1B	15468.2	13153	1025	112	23	81	14290	1331	96	.992
2B	15468.2	2693	4178	144	57	87	7015	1012	326	.979
3B	15468.2	1230	3322	214	105	107	4766	370	294	.955
SS	15468.2	2153	4342	192	94	97	6687	927	460	.971
LF	15468.2	3057	84	41	10	31	3182	13		.987
CF	15468.2	4116	67	38	10	28	4221	15		.991
RF	15468.2	3396	81	58	17	40	3535	19		.984

86

Team Efficiency Summary

Mark Simon

I've been a comprehensive watcher of the New York Mets since 1982, and I feel like I've seen everything I could possible see—from the ground ball going through Bill Buckner's legs to Carlos Beltrán taking strike three in Game 7 of the NLCS to Luis Castillo dropping a popup against the Yankees. And oh, so much more.

So when I read the tables on the upcoming pages and found out that the Mets were the least efficient team in 2020 when comparing their Runs Created to their Expected Runs Allowed, I wasn't fazed in the least.

The Mets ranked first, second, and fourth in the National League in batting average, on-base percentage and slugging percentage, respectively but ranked seventh in runs scored. They ranked 11th in the NL in stolen bases and 12th in batting average with runners in scoring position, failing to take advantage of what they could have had. By Runs Created, they should have scored 314 runs. Instead, they totaled 286.

In the field, the Mets ranked 13th in the NL and 25th overall in Defensive Runs Saved, what you'd expect from a lineup that played Wilson Ramos, Robinson Canó, and Amed Rosario.

These deficiencies proved to be their downfall, one also observed by FanGraphs, which uses a similar formula (Marc Carig of The Athletic wrote about it).

We should also mention two of the most improbable defeats by any team this season. The Mets blew an 8-2 lead to the Braves on July 31 and a 7-2 ninth-inning lead against the Yankees on August 30.

The top two overachieving teams came from the state of Florida. The Marlins and Rays made baseball in the Sunshine State a winning proposition. By Runs Created and Expected Runs Allowed, the Marlins should have won 24 games (8 fewer than the Mets!) but won 31. The Rays won 40, six above their expected total.

The Marlins excelled in the shortened-game format, winning 10 of 14 seven-inning games. The Rays used an outstanding bullpen to go 14-5 in one-run games. They each found ways to win that other teams (like the Mets) could not.

2020 American League Team Efficiency Summary

	RC	Runs	Hit Eff	Exp RA	RA	Pit Eff	Exp Wins	Wins	Runs Eff	Eff Wins	Wins	Overall Eff
Tampa Bay Rays	277	289	104	240	229	105	37	40	109	34	40	117
Seattle Mariners	223	254	114	277	303	91	25	27	109	24	27	115
Oakland Athletics	246	274	111	233	232	101	35	36	103	32	36	114
Toronto Blue Jays	287	302	105	303	312	97	29	32	110	28	32	113
Detroit Tigers	222	249	112	302	318	95	22	23	104	20	23	113
Texas Rangers	200	224	112	286	312	92	20	22	108	20	22	111
Cleveland Indians	234	248	106	210	209	100	35	35	100	33	35	105
Boston Red Sox	295	292	99	375	351	107	25	24	98	23	24	105
Minnesota Twins	256	269	105	217	215	101	37	36	98	35	36	103
Chicago White Sox	293	306	105	243	246	99	36	35	96	36	35	99
New York Yankees	290	315	109	257	270	95	35	33	95	34	33	98
Kansas City Royals	245	248	101	275	272	101	27	26	95	26	26	98
Houston Astros	249	279	112	251	275	91	30	29	95	30	29	97
Baltimore Orioles	273	274	101	279	294	95	28	25	90	29	25	85
Los Angeles Angels	286	294	103	274	321	85	27	26	95	31	26	83

2020 National League Team Efficiency Summary

	RC	Runs	Hit Eff	Exp RA	RA	Pit Eff	Exp Wins	Wins	Runs Eff	Eff Wins	Wins	Overall Eff
Miami Marlins	240	263	110	296	304	97	26	31	121	24	31	131
Colorado Rockies	257	275	107	332	353	94	23	26	115	23	26	115
Chicago Cubs	236	265	112	233	240	97	33	34	103	30	34	112
Arizona Diamondbacks	246	269	110	302	295	102	27	25	92	24	25	104
Washington Nationals	284	293	103	330	301	110	29	26	89	25	26	102
St Louis Cardinals	214	240	112	212	229	93	30	30	99	29	30	102
Milwaukee Brewers	226	247	109	235	264	89	28	29	104	29	29	101
Cincinnati Reds	228	243	106	219	243	90	30	31	103	31	31	99
Pittsburgh Pirates	192	219	114	280	298	94	21	19	90	19	19	99
Philadelphia Phillies	294	306	104	308	311	99	30	28	95	29	28	98
Los Angeles Dodgers	326	349	107	197	213	93	44	43	98	44	43	98
San Diego Padres	304	325	107	231	241	96	39	37	96	38	37	97
Atlanta Braves	343	348	101	270	288	94	36	35	98	37	35	94
San Francisco Giants	294	299	102	265	297	89	30	29	96	33	29	87
New York Mets	314	286	91	297	308	97	28	26	94	32	26	82

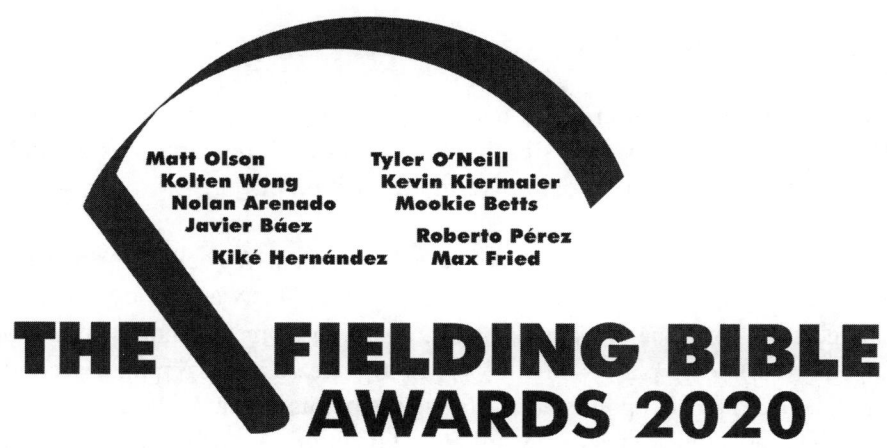

Matt Olson
Kolten Wong
Nolan Arenado
Javier Báez
Kiké Hernández

Tyler O'Neill
Kevin Kiermaier
Mookie Betts
Roberto Pérez
Max Fried

THE FIELDING BIBLE
AWARDS 2020

The Fielding Bible Awards 2020

Mark Simon

The 2020 Fielding Bible Award winners are a group whose reputation largely precedes them.

Seven of the 10 winners had previously won the Award, including Javier Báez who was a first-time winner at shortstop after taking the Multi-Position honor in three previous seasons.

The three newcomers are Cardinals left fielder Tyler O'Neill, Braves pitcher Max Fried, and Dodgers multi-position standout Kiké Hernández.

First baseman Matt Olson and second baseman Kolten Wong each won for the third straight year. Nolan Arenado, who had a dominant season at third base, won for the fourth time. Kevin Kiermaier won his second Award in center field. Mookie Betts won his fourth in right field.

Close votes were a big part of this year's voting, not surprising given how difficult it is to make determinations on players in a 60-game season. Kiermaier won on a tiebreaker, just beating another previous winner, Byron Buxton. Wong and Báez each won narrowly.

Congratulations to the winners!

The Fielding Bible Awards are determined by a 12-person expert voting panel. The panel awards 10 winners each year, one at each position plus an additional award that goes to the best defensive multi-position player.

Here's a refresher on how the awards are determined. We asked our panel to rank 5 players at each position on a scale from 1 to 5. This was a one-year temporary change from the usual 10-player ballot, resulting from the shortened season (we hope to return to 10 players in 2021). A first-place vote gets 5 points, second place 4 points, third place 3 points etc. Total up the points for each player and the player with the most points wins the award at that position. A perfect score is 60 points.

Here are the Fielding Bible Awards for the 2020 season.

First Base – Matt Olson, Oakland Athletics

Olson won his third straight Fielding Bible Award despite slipping to third place in Defensive Runs Saved with five in 2020.

But Olson is well-rounded, and that's what carried him to the honor. Over the last three seasons, he's well ahead of the rest of the field in the Range component of DRS. And he's the MLB leader in that time in Scoop Runs Saved (Runs Saved from handling difficult throws).

Olson joined Albert Pujols as the only first basemen to win a Fielding Bible Award in three straight seasons. Pujols, who has won five, did it in the first four years of the award, from 2006 to 2009.

Previous Winners:

2019	Matt Olson	2014	Adrián González	2009	Albert Pujols
2018	Matt Olson	2013	Paul Goldschmidt	2008	Albert Pujols
2017	Paul Goldschmidt	2012	Mark Teixeira	2007	Albert Pujols
2016	Anthony Rizzo	2011	Albert Pujols	2006	Albert Pujols
2015	Paul Goldschmidt	2010	Daric Barton		

Second Base – Kolten Wong, St. Louis Cardinals

Wong becomes the first second baseman to win a Fielding Bible Award in three straight seasons. He's now won two close votes (this year and 2018) sandwiched around a unanimous choice in 2019.

Wong was the only winner from a Cardinals infield that was the best in baseball in turning ground balls and bunts into outs. It's the second straight year that the team has done that. Wong wasn't flashy, but he finished with five Defensive Runs Saved. His 40 Runs Saved at the position over the last three seasons are easily the most in the majors.

Previous Winners:

2019	Kolten Wong	2014	Dustin Pedroia	2009	Aaron Hill
2018	Kolten Wong	2013	Dustin Pedroia	2008	Brandon Phillips
2017	DJ LeMahieu	2012	Darwin Barney	2007	Aaron Hill
2016	Dustin Pedroia	2011	Dustin Pedroia	2006	Orlando Hudson
2015	Ian Kinsler	2010	Chase Utley		

Third Base – Nolan Arenado, Colorado Rockies

After two years of losing out to Matt Chapman, Arenado takes his fourth Fielding Bible Award, tying Adrián Beltré for the most won at the hot corner since we began handing them out in 2006.

Arenado led all MLB players with 15 Runs Saved. No other third baseman was in double figures. Arenado stood out most on balls hit to his left, making 58-of-89 plays on which he had a greater-than zero chance of getting at least one out. That was 10 more than he was expected to record based on historical probabilities.

Previous Winners:

2019	Matt Chapman	2014	Josh Donaldson	2009	Ryan Zimmerman
2018	Matt Chapman	2013	Manny Machado	2008	Adrián Beltré
2017	Nolan Arenado	2012	Adrián Beltré	2007	Pedro Feliz
2016	Nolan Arenado	2011	Adrián Beltré	2006	Adrián Beltré
2015	Nolan Arenado	2010	Evan Longoria		

Shortstop – Javier Báez, Chicago Cubs

Báez lost out to Nick Ahmed of the Diamondbacks by two points last season but won a tight vote in 2020. This is his fourth Fielding Bible Award, his first at shortstop with the other three being the Multi-Position Award.

Báez finished tied for second among shortstops in the component of Defensive Runs Saved that measures range, throwing, and handling balls hit in the air. He finished tied for first in Double Play Runs Saved. His strength was in taking away base hits on balls hit up the middle. He made 67-of-111 such plays in which he had a greater-than-zero chance to record an out, six plays more than his expected total.

Previous Winners:

2019	Nick Ahmed	2014	Andrelton Simmons	2009	Jack Wilson
2018	Andrelton Simmons	2013	Andrelton Simmons	2008	Jimmy Rollins
2017	Andrelton Simmons	2012	Brendan Ryan	2007	Troy Tulowitzki
2016	Andrelton Simmons	2011	Troy Tulowitzki	2006	Adam Everett
2015	Andrelton Simmons	2010	Troy Tulowitzki		

Left Field – Tyler O'Neill, St. Louis Cardinals

O'Neill is the fifth different left fielder to win a Fielding Bible Award in the last five years. He earned it on the strength of an MLB-leading nine Runs Saved at the position. O'Neill won with his play on balls hit to the deepest part of the ballpark. He caught 46-of-54 chances on those balls, eight more than an average left fielder.

O'Neill can also thank the Cardinals coaching staff for positioning him well. His top three plays made in terms of plays saved value were all on balls sliced down the left field line that O'Neill was able to track down thanks to being in a good spot to get to the ball at the time of the pitch.

Previous Winners:

2019	David Peralta	2014	Alex Gordon	2009	Carl Crawford
2018	Alex Gordon	2013	Alex Gordon	2008	Carl Crawford
2017	Brett Garnder	2012	Alex Gordon	2007	Eric Byrnes
2016	Starling Marte	2011	Brett Gardner	2006	Carl Crawford
2015	Starling Marte	2010	Brett Gardner		

Center Field – Kevin Kiermaier, Tampa Bay Rays

This was the closest vote, with Kiermaier and Byron Buxton finishing even in Points. Kiermaier won on our first tiebreaker, recording six first-place votes to Buxton's five.

Kiermaier won this award in a little different fashion than his previous honor in 2015. He is normally known for catching up to balls with his great closing speed. But this year, he saved six runs for his Outfield Arm compared to only two for his Range & Positioning. The six Outfield Arm Runs Saved were double that of the next-closest player, with six also representing his MLB-leading center field assist total for 2020.

Previous Winners:

2019	Lorenzo Cain	2014	Juan Lagares	2009	Franklin Gutierrez
2018	Lorenzo Cain	2013	Carlos Gómez	2008	Carlos Beltrán
2017	Byron Buxton	2012	Mike Trout	2007	Andruw Jones
2016	Kevin Pillar	2011	Austin Jackson	2006	Carlos Beltrán
2015	Kevin Kiermaier	2010	Michael Bourn		

Right Field – Mookie Betts, Los Angeles Dodgers

Betts won for the fourth time in five seasons, making his first season with the Dodgers a highly successful one. Betts' four Fielding Bible Awards pass Ichiro Suzuki and Jason Heyward for most won by a right fielder since the Awards began in 2006.

Betts extended his streak of seasons with at least 10 Runs Saved at an outfield position to six (one season in center field and now five straight in right field). He led in the Range & Positioning component of Runs Saved in right field, rating above average at getting outs on balls hit to both the shallowest and deepest parts of the ballpark.

Previous Winners:

2019	Cody Bellinger	2014	Jason Heyward	2009	Ichiro Suzuki
2018	Mookie Betts	2013	Gerardo Parra	2008	Franklin Gutierrez
2017	Mookie Betts	2012	Jason Heyward	2007	Álex Ríos
2016	Mookie Betts	2011	Justin Upton	2006	Ichiro Suzuki
2015	Jason Heyward	2010	Ichiro Suzuki		

Catcher – Roberto Pérez, Cleveland Indians

In last year's Fielding Bible Awards, we said that Pérez might have some staying power at catcher. That turned out to be prescient. He became the first repeat winner at the position since Buster Posey in 2015 and 2016. Though Pérez finished third among catchers in Defensive Runs Saved, he had positive Runs Saved totals in pitch framing, pitch blocking, and stolen base deterrence. His MLB-best three Stolen Base Runs Saved came from catching 9-of-13 basestealers and picking off another.

If Pérez wins again next year, he would become the second catcher to do so in three straight seasons. Fellow Puerto Rico native Yadier Molina won four straight from 2007 to 2010.

Previous Winners:

2019	Roberto Pérez	2014	Jonathan Lucroy	2009	Yadier Molina
2018	Jeff Mathis	2013	Yadier Molina	2008	Yadier Molina
2017	Martin Maldonado	2012	Yadier Molina	2007	Yadier Molina
2016	Buster Posey	2011	Matt Wieters	2006	Iván Rodríguez
2015	Buster Posey	2010	Yadier Molina		

Pitcher – Max Fried, Atlanta Braves

Fried led pitchers with five Defensive Runs Saved, matching the total he recorded in 2019. Fried showed both quick reflexes to snag hard-hit ground balls and the ability to get off the mound to field a weak dribbler or bunt. His top plays are reminiscent of those made by past winners Dallas Keuchel (a former Fried teammate) and Zack Greinke.

Additionally, Fried is tough to run on. His four pickoffs tied Tyler Anderson of the Giants for the MLB lead. The completeness of his defensive game is what made him award worthy.

Previous Winners:

2019	Zack Greinke	2014	Dallas Keuchel	2009	Mark Buehrle
2018	Zack Greinke	2013	R.A. Dickey	2008	Kenny Rogers
2017	Dallas Keuchel	2012	Mark Buehrle	2007	Johan Santana
2016	Dallas Keuchel	2011	Mark Buehrle	2006	Greg Maddux
2015	Dallas Keuchel	2010	Mark Buehrle		

Multi-Position – Kiké Hernández, Los Angeles Dodgers

When we asked Hernández how many gloves he owned during his appearance on the SIS Baseball Podcast, he said "Too many," before rattling off a long list of practice mitts and gamers at the different positions he plays.

He needs them all.

In addition to making 22 starts at second base, where he saved an MLB-best nine runs, Hernández made three starts in right field, three starts in center field, two starts in left field, two starts at shortstop, as well as seven innings at first base. He was a major asset to the Dodgers defensively at each of those spots. And in winning his first Fielding Bible Award, he helped the team to the best record in the majors.

Previous Winners:

2019	Cody Bellinger	2017	Javier Báez	2015	Ender Inciarte
2018	Javier Báez	2016	Javier Báez	2014	Lorenzo Cain

Background of the Fielding Bible Awards

While the five volumes of *The Fielding Bible* put a lot of emphasis on the numbers, especially Defensive Runs Saved and the PART system (formerly the Range and Positioning System, and before that, the Plus-Minus System), we feel that visual observation and subjective judgment are still very important parts of determining the best defensive players. Also, we believe people have a right to know who is voting and all the players they are voting for. Therefore, in setting up the Fielding Bible Awards, we took the following steps:

1. ***We appointed a panel of experts to vote***. We have a panel of twelve experts plus three "tie-breaker" ballots. (See below.)

2. ***We rate everybody in one group.*** The Gold Glove vote is divided into National League and American League. We make ours different by putting everybody together. Besides, is playing shortstop in the American League one thing and playing shortstop in the National League a different thing, or are they really very much the same thing? A few years back we had a great example of this decision. Without the Fielding Bible Award, Jack Wilson wins *nada*, because he switched leagues in mid-year. According to our panelists (and unlike the Gold Glove

voters), Jack was the best fielding shortstop in baseball in 2009. Period. He deserved to be recognized for that.

3. *We use a ten-man ballot and a ten-point scale*. We use a ten-man ballot. We give ten points for first place, nine points for second place, etc, down to one point for tenth place. We feel strongly that a ten-man ballot with weighted positions leads to more accurate outcomes.
For 2020, we used a five-man ballot and a five-point scale because of the shortened season.

4. *We defined the list of candidates*. Only players who actually were regulars at the position are candidates. This eliminates the possibility of a vote going to somebody who wasn't really playing the position.

5. *We are publishing the balloting*. We summarize the voting at each position, clearly identifying whom everybody voted for. Publishing the actual vote totals encourages the voters to take their votes more seriously. Also, we feel the public will have more respect for the voting if they have more insight into the process.

A perfect score is 60 points. If all 12 voters place one player first on their ballot, he scores 60. Two players had perfect scores of 60 this year: Nolan Arenado and Mookie Betts.

Here are the tie-breaker rules, which came into play in our very first year (2006), 2010, 2016, 2019, and again this year. They are applied one at a time until we have a winner:

1. Most first-place votes wins.
2. Count the tie-breaker ballots, highest point tally wins.
3. Award goes to player with the higher defensive runs saved.

Ballots were due three days after the end of the regular season. Here is this year's panel:

Ben Lindbergh is a staff writer for *The Ringer*. He also hosts the *Effectively Wild* podcast for *FanGraphs*. He is a former staff writer for *FiveThirtyEight* and *Grantland*, a former editor-in-chief of *Baseball Prospectus*, and the *New York Times* bestselling co-author of *The MVP Machine: How Baseball's New Nonconformists Are Using Data to Build Better Players* and *The Only Rule Is It*

Has to Work: Our Wild Experiment Building a New Kind of Baseball Team. He lives in New York City.

Bill James has been writing about baseball since 1975, when he published his first articles in *The Baseball Digest*. He wrote annual books called *The Baseball Abstract* from 1977 to 1987, and followed that up with three editions of *The Historical Abstract*, the last one published almost 20 years ago. He worked for the Boston Red Sox for 17+ years, 2002 to 2019, and has written many other books on baseball and other subjects. He has collaborated with John Dewan and legions of others on annual editions of the *Bill James Handbook* for about 30 years. This book represents the work of many, many people.

The **BIS Video Scouts** at Baseball Info Solutions (BIS) study every game of the season, multiple times, charting a huge list of valuable game details.

Chris Singleton played six seasons in the major leagues primarily as a center fielder. As a rookie, he led American League center fielders in Total Zone Fielding Runs Above Average. Chris has been a Major League broadcaster for the past 13 seasons and has been a color commentator/analyst on over 1,000 live games for the Chicago White Sox, ESPN Radio, and ESPN *Baseball Tonight*.

Christina Kahrl is a senior editor for MLB coverage at ESPN.com, a member of the Baseball Writers Association of America, and a voter for the Hall of Fame in Cooperstown. Before joining ESPN, she was a co-founder of the sabermetric think-tank *Baseball Prospectus*, where she was the Executive Editor of the website as well as managing editor of the group's bestselling annual. Long based out of Chicago, she is now based at ESPN's Los Angeles campus.

The man who created Strat-O-Matic Baseball, **Hal Richman**, continues to lead his company's annual in-depth analysis of each player's season. Hal cautions SOM players that his voting on this ballot may or may not reflect the eventual fielding ratings for players in his game. Ballots were due prior to the completion of his annual research effort to evaluate player defense.

Joe Sheehan writes for *Sports Illustrated* and has published the Joe Sheehan Baseball Newsletter, one of the first subscription baseball newsletters, for a decade. He was a founding member of Baseball Prospectus and has contributed to ESPN, *Baseball America*, *The Wall Street Journal*, *The Washington Post*, and *The New York Times* in a 25-year career. He has never once participated in an infield shift.

For over twenty-five years, SIS CEO and owner **John Dewan** has collected, analyzed, and published in-depth baseball statistics and analysis. He has focused his analytics work in baseball on defense and has authored or co-authored five volumes of *The Fielding Bible*.

Mark Simon is a senior research analyst for Sports Info Solutions where he helps oversee the company's public-facing content. He formerly worked at ESPN for nearly 16 years, including eight years on *Baseball Tonight*, and has more than 20 years of sports broadcasting experience. He has written about baseball for many publications. His book, *The Yankees Index: Every Number Tells A Story,* was published by Triumph Books in 2016.

Peter Gammons is a senior writer for *The Athletic*, who regularly appears on MLB Network and NESN (New England Sports Network). He is the 56th recipient of the J. G. Taylor Spink Award for outstanding baseball writing given by the BBWAA (Baseball Writers Association of America).

Rob Neyer has been a working writer for more than 25 years, and most recently has contributed to *The New York Times*, Vice Sports, and Complex. When he's not writing, he's thinking about not writing. Rob will live in Portland, Oregon for as long as they let him.

Travis Sawchik is a sportswriter for *FiveThirtyEight*. He is the author of the *New York Times* best-selling book *Big Data Baseball: Math, Miracles, and the End of a 20-Year Losing Streak* and co-author of *The MVP Machine: How Baseball's New Nonconformists Are Using Data to Build Better Players*. He previously covered the Pittsburgh Pirates for the *Pittsburgh Tribune-Review*.

Our three tie-breakers are **Dan Casey**, veteran Video Scout and Senior Operations Analyst and MLB Coordinator at BIS, **Chris Dial**, who developed Runs Effectively Defended (RED), a component of the SABR Defensive Index, in 1997, and **Meg Rowley**, managing editor at *FanGraphs*.

Fielding Bible Awards Voting

Below we show the final point tally for The Fielding Bible Awards in the 2020 season. Given the shortened season, we had to adjust our voting criteria slightly. We asked a panel of experts to complete a 5-man ballot ranking players from 1 to 5 based on their defensive abilities. We show the ranks in the tables below. We then awarded 5 points for a first place vote, 4 for second, etc., down to 1 point for 5th place. We cover all nine positions, looking at only their fielding work for the 2020 season. Position players are eligible if they played at least 200 innings while catchers require a minimum of 150 innings. Either can qualify with 4 Runs Saved, as well. Pitchers require a minimum of 40 innings pitched or 2 Runs Saved.

In 2014, we introduced a Multi-Position Award for fielders who are excellent defensive players but do not call any one position their home. For a player to qualify for the Multi-Position Award, he must have played at least 200 innings (or saved at least 4 runs) across all positions and played no more than 70 percent of those innings at any one position.

First Basemen

First Basemen	Ben	Bill	BIS Video Scouts	Chris	Christina	Hal	Joe	John	Mark	Peter	Rob	Travis	Total Points
Matt Olson	1	1	2	1	1	1	1	1	3	3	1	3	53
Evan White	4	1	2	2	2	4	5	1	2	2	2		39
Josh Fuentes	3		3	3	5			2	5	1		1	25
Anthony Rizzo	2	2	5		4	4	5			5	3	4	20
José Abreu	5		4	4	3			3	2	4			17
Others receiving points: Yuli Gurriel 7, Carlos Santana 6, Paul Goldschmidt 5, Brandon Belt 3, Eric Hosmer 2, Freddie Freeman 2, Mitch Moreland 1														

Second Basemen

Second Basemen	Ben	Bill	BIS Video Scouts	Chris	Christina	Hal	Joe	John	Mark	Peter	Rob	Travis	Total Points
Kolten Wong	2	1	3	5	2	1	1	2	3	2	1	4	45
Kiké Hernández	3	3	4	1	3	4	2	1	1	1	3	2	44
Nicky Lopez	4	2	2	3	4	2	3	3	2	3	5	1	38
César Hernández	1	4	1	2	1			5	4	4	2	3	33
Adam Frazier	5		5	4						5		5	6
Others receiving points: Gavin Lux 3, Ketel Marte 3, DJ LeMahieu 3, Jonathan Schoop 2, Ozzie Albies 2, Jean Segura 1														

Third Basemen

Third Basemen	Ben	Bill	BIS Video Scouts	Chris	Christina	Hal	Joe	John	Mark	Peter	Rob	Travis	Total Points
Nolan Arenado	1	1	1	1	1	1	1	1	1	1	1	1	60
Manny Machado	3		3	3	2	4	3	3	4	2	4	4	31
Isiah Kiner-Falefa	4	4	2	2		5	2	2	2	4		5	28
Gio Urshela	2	3	4	5	5	3		4	3	5	3	2	27
Matt Chapman	5	2	5	4		2	5			3	2	3	23
Others receiving points: Ke'Bryan Hayes 5, Brian Anderson 4, Carter Kieboom 2														

Shortstops

Shortstops	Ben	Bill	BIS Video Scouts	Chris	Christina	Hal	Joe	John	Mark	Peter	Rob	Travis	Total Points
Javier Báez	1	2	2	1	3	3	4	1	1		5	1	42
Dansby Swanson	2	3	1	2	4		2	2	4	3		2	35
Trevor Story	3	4	4	4		2	1	5	3	2	2	4	32
Carlos Correa	5		3	3	5		5	3	2		1	3	24
Francisco Lindor		5			2	1				1			15
Others receiving points: Nick Ahmed 11, Fernando Tatis Jr. 9, J.P. Crawford 8, Paul DeJong 3, Andrelton Simmons 1														

Left Fielders

Left Fielders	Ben	Bill	BIS Video Scouts	Chris	Christina	Hal	Joe	John	Mark	Peter	Rob	Travis	Total Points
Tyler O'Neill	1	3	1	1	1	3	3	3	2	1	1	1	51
Bryan Reynolds	3	4	2	2	3		2	5	1	2		3	33
Michael Brantley	2	1	3	5			1	4	4	3		2	29
Shogo Akiyama		2	4	3	5	2				4		5	17
Alex Gordon	4		5				5	2	5		2		13

Others receiving points: Adam Duvall 8, Eddie Rosario 7, Brett Gardner 5, Jurickson Profar 4, David Peralta 5, Robbie Grossman 4, Kyle Tucker 2, Mike Tauchman 2

Center Fielders

Center Fielders	Ben	Bill	BIS Video Scouts	Chris	Christina	Hal	Joe	John	Mark	Peter	Rob	Travis	Total Points
Kevin Kiermaier	1	3	1	2	4	2	1	1	1	2	1	2	51
Byron Buxton	2	1	2	1	3	1	2	2	2	1	3	1	51
Luis Robert	3		3	4	1	5	4	3	4	5	4	3	27
Jackie Bradley Jr.	5	2	4	5	2	4	3	5	3	3			24
Ramón Laureano		4	5	3			5	4	5		2	5	15

Others receiving points: Trent Grisham 8, Harrison Bader 3, Víctor Robles 1

Right Fielders

Right Fielders	Ben	Bill	BIS Video Scouts	Chris	Christina	Hal	Joe	John	Mark	Peter	Rob	Travis	Total Points
Mookie Betts	1	1	1	1	1	1	1	1	1	1	1	1	60
Joey Gallo	2		2	2	2	4	3	2	2	2	2	2	41
Anthony Santander	5	2	3	3	3		5	3	4			3	23
Jason Heyward	4		4	4		2	4	5		4			15
Alex Verdugo		3					2			3			10

Others receiving points: Max Kepler 8, Clint Frazier 7, Whit Merrifield 5, Kole Calhoun 5, Stephen Piscotty 2, Adam Engel 2, Gregory Polanco 1, Bryce Harper 1

Catchers

Catchers	Ben	Bill	BIS Video Scouts	Chris	Christina	Hal	Joe	John	Mark	Peter	Rob	Travis	Total Points
Roberto Pérez	3	2	1	2	1	1	1	1	1	3	1	3	52
Tucker Barnhart		4	2	1	2			2	2	2	2		31
Jacob Stallings	4		3	3	4	5			4	1	3	4	23
Christian Vázquez	1	1			3						5	1	19
Yasmani Grandal	2	4					3	5	3			2	17
Others receiving points: Austin Barnes 8, Jeff Mathis 6, James McCann 4, Yadier Molina 4, Austin Hedges 4, J.T. Realmuto 4, Omar Narváez 3, Willson Contreras 2, Martín Maldonado 2, Tony Wolters 1														

Pitchers

Pitchers	Ben	Bill	BIS Video Scouts	Chris	Christina	Hal	Joe	John	Mark	Peter	Rob	Travis	Total Points
Max Fried	1	2	1	2	1	3	1	1	1	1	2	1	55
Zack Greinke	4	3	2	1	5	1	2	2	3	2	1		40
Kyle Hendricks	5	1	3	4	3		4	4	2	3		3	28
Nathan Eovaldi	2				4							2	10
Masahiro Tanaka				5		2		5			3		9
Others receiving points: Alec Mills 8, David Peterson 5, Dallas Keuchel 5, Luis Castillo 4, Griffin Canning 3, Steven Brault 3, Jack Flaherty 3, Vince Velasquez 2, Martín Pérez 2, Jacob deGrom 2, Jake Arrieta 1														

Multi-Position

Players	Ben	Bill	BIS Video Scouts	Chris	Christina	Hal	Joe	John	Mark	Peter	Rob	Travis	Total Points
Kiké Hernández	1	3	1	1	1	2	2	1		1	4	1	48
Tommy Edman	5	1	3	2	3		4	3	3	3			27
Alex Verdugo	2	2	5				1		4	2			20
David Fletcher	3	4		4				2	1				16
Chris Taylor						4	5	5			1	2	13
Others receiving points: Cody Bellinger 12, Nico Hoerner 11, Dylan Moore 4, Joey Wendle 4, Pat Valaika 4, Shogo Akiyama 3, Ronald Acuña Jr. 3, Jurickson Profar 3, Whit Merrifield 3, Mike Brosseau 2, Jean Segura 2, Tommy La Stella 2, Marwin González 1, Manuel Margot 1, Mike Yastrzemski 1														

Defensive Runs Saved Leaders

Brian Reiff

It was a surprising year on the Defensive Runs Saved Leaderboards, with seven players making their first appearance atop them despite never having previously earned even a top-five finish.

Those players were Tucker Barnhart (catcher), Josh Fuentes (first base), Nicky Lopez and Kiké Hernández (second base), Dansby Swanson (shortstop), Tyler O'Neill (left field) and Joey Gallo (right field).

Max Fried (pitcher), Nolan Arenado (third base) and Byron Buxton (center field), meanwhile, are all making at least a second appearance atop the leaderboards. Fried topped the pitcher leaderboard last year, while it's been three years for both Arenado and Buxton, with each last leading their position in 2017.

It's worth mentioning that these leaderboards use the updated DRS numbers first previewed in last year's *Bill James Handbook* and officially introduced in *The Fielding Bible—Volume V*. Totals are largely the same, but there are some differences from year to year. For example, despite appearing atop the pitcher leaderboard in last year's *Handbook*, Fried actually saved two fewer runs than the Astros' Zack Greinke last season according to what is now the official tally. So, in a way, this is also Fried's first time leading the position.

Given the short timeframe, even those that did lead their position did so narrowly, almost all by one or two runs. That wasn't the case for Arenado, who saved nearly twice as many runs as the next-highest-rated third baseman, Isiah Kiner-Falefa of the Rangers. Of course, he still trails the A's Matt Chapman on the three-year leaderboard with the two locked in a tight race for the title of MLB's best defensive third baseman.

Infield Runs Saved Leaders

First Basemen 3-Year Leaders		Second Basemen 3-Year Leaders		Third Basemen 3-Year Leaders		Shortstops 3-Year Leaders	
Olson, Matt	36	Wong, Kolten	40	Chapman, Matt	66	Ahmed, Nick	50
Belt, Brandon	18	Albies, Ozzie	26	Arenado, Nolan	40	DeJong, Paul	38
Votto, Joey	16	Hernandez, Kike	24	Kiner-Falefa, Isiah	19	Baez, Javier	33
Goldschmidt, Paul	12	Marte, Ketel	19	Machado, Manny	14	Simmons, Andrelton	33
Freeman, Freddie	10	Wendle, Joey	17	Fletcher, David	13	Lindor, Francisco	26
Walker, Christian	10	LeMahieu, DJ	17	Longoria, Evan	12	Correa, Carlos	22
Fuentes, Josh	9	Fletcher, David	15	Donaldson, Josh	10	Semien, Marcus	21
Rizzo, Anthony	8	Lopez, Nicky	11	5 tied with	9	Swanson, Dansby	21
Pujols, Albert	8	Schoop, Jonathan	11			Story, Trevor	20
3 tied with	7	Lux, Gavin	10			Riddle, JT	11

First Basemen 3-Year Trailers		Second Basemen 3-Year Trailers		Third Basemen 3-Year Trailers		Shortstops 3-Year Trailers	
Voit, Luke	-23	Profar, Jurickson	-17	Moran, Colin	-32	Bogaerts, Xander	-33
Bell, Josh	-22	Nunez, Eduardo	-17	Devers, Rafael	-30	Rosario, Amed	-29
Davis, Chris	-15	Cabrera, Asdrubal	-16	Andujar, Miguel	-29	Mercer, Jordy	-17
Healy, Ryon	-13	Murphy, Daniel	-14	Davis, J.D.	-19	Machado, Manny	-17
Smoak, Justin	-11	Dozier, Brian	-13	Franco, Maikel	-16	Polanco, Jorge	-15
O'Hearn, Ryan	-10	Hiura, Keston	-13	Sano, Miguel	-15	Newman, Kevin	-13

First Basemen 2020 Leaders		Second Basemen 2020 Leaders		Third Basemen 2020 Leaders		Shortstops 2020 Leaders	
Fuentes, Josh	8	Hernandez, Kike	8	Arenado, Nolan	15	Swanson, Dansby	9
White, Evan	7	Lopez, Nicky	8	Kiner-Falefa, Isiah	9	Correa, Carlos	7
Olson, Matt	5	Hernandez, Cesar	6	Machado, Manny	7	Crawford, J.P.	7
Santana, Carlos	5	Lux, Gavin	6	Urshela, Gio	5	Baez, Javier	6
Abreu, Jose	4	Hoerner, Nico	5	Kieboom, Carter	5	Story, Trevor	5
Hosmer, Eric	3	Wong, Kolten	5	Hayes, Ke'Bryan	4	7 tied with	3
Cronenworth, Jake	3	Frazier, Adam	4	Anderson, Brian	4		
Rizzo, Anthony	3	Marte, Ketel	4	McMahon, Ryan	3		
Pujols, Albert	3	VanMeter, Josh	4	Camargo, Johan	3		
7 tied with	2	Mendick, Danny	4	Gonzalez, Erik	3		

First Basemen 2020 Trailers		Second Basemen 2020 Trailers		Third Basemen 2020 Trailers		Shortstops 2020 Trailers	
Votto, Joey	-7	Hiura, Keston	-8	Davis, J.D.	-8	Torres, Gleyber	-9
Hoskins, Rhys	-5	Kemp, Tony	-6	Riley, Austin	-8	Turner, Trea	-8
Alonso, Pete	-4	La Stella, Tommy	-6	Devers, Rafael	-6	Castro, Willi	-7
Guerrero Jr., Vladimir	-4	Odor, Rougned	-5	Seager, Kyle	-6	Semien, Marcus	-5
Sano, Miguel	-4	Solak, Nick	-5	Ramirez, Jose	-6	Bogaerts, Xander	-5
3 tied with	-3	Kingery, Scott	-5	Bohm, Alec	-5	Arcia, Orlando	-4

Outfield Runs Saved Leaders

Left Fielders 3-Year Leaders	
Duvall, Adam	20
Gordon, Alex	20
Gardner, Brett	17
Pinder, Chad	16
Brantley, Michael	14
Verdugo, Alex	14
Jones, JaCoby	13
Tauchman, Mike	13
Gonzalez, Marwin	12
O'Neill, Tyler	11

Center Fielders 3-Year Leaders	
Cain, Lorenzo	41
Kiermaier, Kevin	36
Buxton, Byron	23
Bader, Harrison	23
Robles, Victor	20
Hamilton, Billy	20
DeShields, Delino	17
Margot, Manuel	16
3 tied with	15

Right Fielders 3-Year Leaders	
Betts, Mookie	44
Judge, Aaron	40
Bellinger, Cody	20
Kepler, Max	17
Gallo, Joey	17
Renfroe, Hunter	16
Reddick, Josh	12
Santander, Anthony	12
Naquin, Tyler	11
Heyward, Jason	11

Left Fielders 3-Year Trailers	
Hoskins, Rhys	-21
Dietrich, Derek	-19
Choo, Shin-Soo	-19
Smith Jr., Dwight	-17
Upton, Justin	-16
Jimenez, Eloy	-15

Center Fielders 3-Year Trailers	
Blackmon, Charlie	-29
Hicks, Aaron	-17
Pillar, Kevin	-14
Nimmo, Brandon	-11
Canha, Mark	-11
Conforto, Michael	-11

Right Fielders 3-Year Trailers	
Castellanos, Nick	-30
Soler, Jorge	-19
Martinez, Jose	-17
Reyes, Franmil	-13
Eaton, Adam	-12
4 tied with	-11

Left Fielders 2020 Leaders	
O'Neill, Tyler	9
Verdugo, Alex	8
Reynolds, Bryan	5
Brantley, Michael	5
Profar, Jurickson	4
Hays, Austin	4
Munoz, Yairo	4
Akiyama, Shogo	4
4 tied with	3

Center Fielders 2020 Leaders	
Buxton, Byron	11
Kiermaier, Kevin	10
Robert, Luis	8
Grisham, Trent	7
Taveras, Leody	6
Springer, George	6
Brinson, Lewis	5
Bellinger, Cody	5
Laureano, Ramon	5
Bradley Jr., Jackie	5

Right Fielders 2020 Leaders	
Gallo, Joey	13
Betts, Mookie	11
Santander, Anthony	8
Frazier, Clint	4
Merrifield, Whit	4
Canha, Mark	3
Judge, Aaron	3
Kepler, Max	3
15 tied with	2

Left Fielders 2020 Trailers	
Dickerson, Alex	-8
McCutchen, Andrew	-8
Soto, Juan	-8
Yelich, Christian	-6
Pollock, A.J.	-5
3 tied with	-4

Center Fielders 2020 Trailers	
Trout, Mike	-9
Grichuk, Randal	-8
Hicks, Aaron	-8
Solak, Nick	-6
Nimmo, Brandon	-5
5 tied with	-4

Right Fielders 2020 Trailers	
Eaton, Adam	-6
Joyce, Matt	-6
Markakis, Nick	-5
4 tied with	-4

Pitcher/Catcher Runs Saved Leaders

Pitchers 3-Year Leaders

Greinke, Zack	15
Fried, Max	11
Teheran, Julio	10
Tanaka, Masahiro	9
Brault, Steven	9
Velasquez, Vince	9
Eovaldi, Nathan	8
Arrieta, Jake	7
Castillo, Luis	7
Soroka, Mike	7

Catchers 3-Year Leaders

Perez, Roberto	40
Hedges, Austin	31
Mathis, Jeff	24
Barnes, Austin	21
Stallings, Jacob	21
Wolters, Tony	20
Grandal, Yasmani	17
Zunino, Mike	17
Pina, Manny	16
2 tied with	13

Pitchers 3-Year Trailers

Lynn, Lance	-10
Covey, Dylan	-9
Ottavino, Adam	-9
Scherzer, Max	-8
Manaea, Sean	-7
5 tied with	-6

Catchers 3-Year Trailers

Narvaez, Omar	-31
Suzuki, Kurt	-26
Lucroy, Jonathan	-25
Diaz, Elias	-22
Sisco, Chance	-19
Ramos, Wilson	-18

Pitchers 2020 Leaders

Fried, Max	5
Eovaldi, Nathan	3
Mills, Alec	3
Hendricks, Kyle	3
Canning, Griffin	3
17 tied with	2

Catchers 2020 Leaders

Barnhart, Tucker	9
Stallings, Jacob	7
Perez, Roberto	6
Mathis, Jeff	5
Grandal, Yasmani	5
Barnes, Austin	5
McCann, James	5
4 tied with	3

Pitchers 2020 Trailers

Valdez, Framber	-4
Stammen, Craig	-3
Manaea, Sean	-3
Turnbull, Spencer	-3
Webb, Logan	-3
16 tied with	-2

Catchers 2020 Trailers

Torrens, Luis	-7
Alfaro, Jorge	-7
d'Arnaud, Travis	-7
Sisco, Chance	-6
Chirinos, Robinson	-5
5 tied with	-4

Strike Zone Runs Saved

Mark Simon

In 2019, the White Sox had major issues with the defensive performance of their catchers, the primary one being their pitch framing. White Sox catchers cost their teams 11 runs in that area, as measured by our stat, Strike Zone Runs Saved (SZRS).

That's why the signing of free agent Yasmani Grandal was an important one. It wasn't just for his bat, but for his glove. Or to describe it more accurately, his still hand.

Grandal has separated himself from his fellow catchers in getting more strike calls than expected. Since becoming a regular in 2014, he's amassed 64 SZRS. Only Tyler Flowers (78) has more in that time. Grandal led all catchers with 5 SZRS in 2020.

Different catchers have different methods for catching pitches. Some tap the ground with the glove as their pitcher winds up, giving themselves a chance to catch a pitch on the way up, so that the momentum of their glove makes a borderline pitch look more like it's in the strike zone. Others just try to catch a pitch with as still a glove as they can to give the umpire the best possible look at it.

Grandal falls into the latter category. And it works well for him. Some of Grandal's success rubbed off on teammate James McCann, who moved from regular to oft-used backup. McCann finished tied for third with 3 SZRS a year after finishing with -2. The White Sox tallied 8 SZRS for the season. No other team totaled more than 3.

While we're talking White Sox, let's also give props to a former White Sox catcher, Omar Narváez. From 2017 to 2019, Narváez finished tied for last place in SZRS, costing his teams (the White Sox and Mariners) 20 runs. In 2020, he moved to the positive side of the ledger, finishing with 2 SZRS.

2020 Catcher Strike Zone Runs Saved Leaders

Catcher	Called Pitches	Called Strikes			Runs Saved	
		Actual	Expected	Extra	Per 1,000 Called Pitches	Total
Grandal, Yasmani	2691	816	776	40	1.86	5
Barnes, Austin	1935	717	686	31	2.07	4
McCann, James	2128	637	612	25	1.41	3
Kelly, Carson	2702	874	850	24	1.11	3
Nola, Austin	3257	1072	1048	24	0.61	2
Murphy, Sean	2959	988	970	18	0.68	2
Vazquez, Christian	3442	1053	1035	18	0.58	2
Perez, Roberto	2076	679	661	18	0.96	2
Stallings, Jacob	3345	978	961	17	0.60	2
Barnhart, Tucker	2662	821	805	16	0.75	2
Narvaez, Omar	2610	820	807	13	0.77	2
Castro, Jason	1813	593	584	9	1.10	2
Gallagher, Cam	1460	473	462	11	0.68	1
Bart, Joey	2224	707	698	9	0.45	1
Tromp, Chadwick	1520	478	470	8	0.66	1
Odom, Joseph	1163	370	362	8	0.86	1
Caratini, Victor	1525	546	539	7	0.66	1
Garver, Mitch	1471	463	456	7	0.68	1
Casali, Curt	1966	623	616	7	0.51	1
Perez, Salvador	2569	854	848	6	0.39	1
Bemboom, Anthony	1276	380	375	5	0.78	1
Jeffers, Ryan	1468	469	464	5	0.68	1
Contreras, Willson	2921	929	925	4	0.34	1
Trevino, Jose	1465	478	474	4	0.00	0
Wallach, Chad	1045	324	321	3	0.00	0
Flowers, Tyler	1621	497	494	3	0.00	0
Vogt, Stephen	1609	528	525	3	0.00	0
d'Arnaud, Travis	2819	878	877	1	0.00	0
Mathis, Jeff	1683	571	570	1	0.00	0
Molina, Yadier	3053	978	977	1	0.00	0
Nottingham, Jacob	1268	394	393	1	0.00	0
Realmuto, J.T.	2653	862	862	0	0.00	0
Leon, Sandy	1638	530	530	0	0.00	0
Hedges, Austin	1921	619	620	-1	0.00	0
Heineman, Tyler	1114	379	380	-1	0.00	0
Murphy, John Ryan	1523	487	489	-2	0.00	0
Wolters, Tony	2495	778	781	-3	0.00	0
Diaz, Elias	1066	310	313	-3	0.00	0
Cervelli, Francisco	1120	360	364	-4	0.00	0
Zunino, Mike	1828	584	589	-5	-0.55	-1
Sanchez, Gary	2880	895	901	-6	-0.35	-1
Maldonado, Martin	3587	1192	1199	-7	-0.28	-1
Suzuki, Kurt	2367	684	692	-8	-0.42	-1
Stassi, Max	2132	711	719	-8	-0.47	-1
Greiner, Grayson	1301	381	389	-8	-0.77	-1
Perez, Michael	1841	553	562	-9	-0.54	-1
Butera, Drew	1092	343	352	-9	-0.92	-1
Ramos, Wilson	2957	878	888	-10	-0.34	-1
Severino, Pedro	2517	753	763	-10	-0.40	-1
Smith, Will	2073	665	678	-13	-0.48	-1
Chirinos, Robinson	2030	617	629	-12	-0.99	-2
Romine, Austin	2958	844	859	-15	-0.68	-2
Avila, Alex	1270	385	401	-16	-1.57	-2
Sisco, Chance	1676	524	540	-16	-1.19	-2
Plawecki, Kevin	1579	463	482	-19	-1.27	-2
Torrens, Luis	1562	502	520	-18	-1.92	-3
Knapp, Andrew	1578	471	492	-21	-1.90	-3
Jansen, Danny	3377	900	922	-22	-0.89	-3
Alfaro, Jorge	1900	522	548	-26	-1.58	-3
Gomes, Yan	2281	643	670	-27	-1.32	-3

Shift Update

Mark Simon

If you're a new hard-core baseball fan, you're entering a baseball universe that is unusual to most of us, though to you, it will probably make a lot of sense once you learn about it.

Defensive shifts have reached a point in which they're basically normal. Teams are using a probabilistic approach to limiting base hits as best they can. Just as NBA and NFL teams adjust their defenses to the situation and moment, MLB teams do the same.

This requires alignments that look different to the longtime fan, with a second baseman or shortstop often behind second base or just to the side of it, and/or one infielder playing in a slot in shallow right field. These are defensive shifts.

There were 23,875 shifts on balls in play in 2020. If we prorate that number to a 162-game season, there would have been 64,606 shifts that season, a 31% increase from 2019. That is nearly two-and-a-half times as many as there were in 2017, more than three-and-a-half times as many as 2015, and more than 26 times as many as there were in 2010.

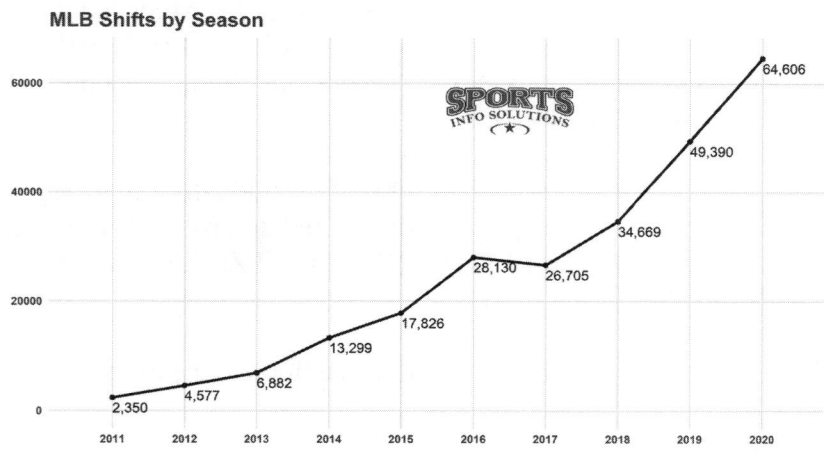

Only five teams were on pace to decrease their shift usage from 2019. Four teams more than doubled their usage: the Cubs, Angels, Nationals, and Braves. The Braves went from 22nd in shift usage in 2019 to 2nd in 2020.

Do shifts work? This chart indicates that in aggregate, they do what they're supposed to do.

Season	Shifts	Shift Runs Saved	Runs/100
2010	2,463	25	1.02
2011	2,350	28	1.19
2012	4,577	62	1.35
2013	6,882	117	1.70
2014	13,299	144	1.08
2015	17,826	238	1.34
2016	28,130	378	1.34
2017	26,705	346	1.30
2018	34,669	592	1.71
2019	49,390	679	1.37
2020	23,875*	192*	0.80

Prorates to 64,606 and 520, respectively, in a full season

The hitters shifted the most this season in terms of raw totals were Kyle Seager, Matt Olson, Max Muncy, Anthony Rizzo, Cody Bellinger and Francisco Lindor. All but Lindor hit below .200 when hitting a groundball or short line drive against a defensive shift.

Among the 14 super-shifted players (those with at least 200 plate appearances against a shift), Michael Conforto of the Mets had the highest batting average on groundballs and short line drives, .303. You'll get more data on who fared best versus shifts in the next essay in this book (Hits Lost and Gained To The Shift).

Two pitchers got outs on more than 90% of groundballs and bunts against shifts (minimum 30 balls in play versus shifted defenses): Dakota Hudson of the Cardinals (29 outs on 31 balls, 93.5%) and Zach Plesac of the Indians (30-of-33, 91%).

The Padres defense ranked last in shift usage but had the highest out rate on groundballs and bunts when shifting, turning 81% of them into outs. The top seven teams in converting groundballs and bunts into outs when shifted all made the postseason, as did 12 of the top 14 in that stat.

The Padres are an example of a team that benefited considerably from shifting. They converted outs on 71% of groundballs and bunts when using an unshifted defense, meaning their out rate when shifting was 10 percentage points higher than not.

The Padres also had the biggest improvement in groundball and bunt out rate when shifted, going from 72% in 2019 to 81% in 2020. The Cubs had the second-highest increase, going from 75% success to 80%.

BIS has software, called BIS-D, that it provides to teams that recommends which hitters should be shifted and which should not based on their batted ball spray charts. The Cubs ranked highest regarding their shift decision making according to BIS-D, following the tool's year-end recommendation 74% of the time.

There is still room for teams to make better shifting decisions. There have been nearly 19,000 balls put in play by non-shift candidates against unshifted defenses since the start of the 2019 season. And there have been more than 37,500 balls put in play by non-shift candidates against defensive shifts in that same time.

Weighted* Batting Average on Groundballs and Short Line Drives, 2019-20

BIS-D Recommendation	No Shift	Shift	Difference
Shift Candidates	.260	.221	Helps by 39 points
Non-Shift Candidate	.257	.252	Helps by 5 points

* The averages are weighted such that players with extreme shift tendencies (high or low) are not over-represented, thus separating the effect of the shift from batter quality.

The payoff is still very much there for teams that play the percentage and position their fielders in the best place to field ground balls for each hitter.

In the player stats table on the following pages, GSL stands for Grounders and Short Liners, i.e. the plays that the shift is designed to defend.

Shifts Employed
American League

Team	2019	2020	2020 Prorated	Change
Seattle	1601	953	2573	972
Texas	1460	935	2525	1065
Minnesota	2418	928	2506	88
Toronto	1878	859	2319	441
Baltimore	2568	854	2306	-262
Los Angeles	1033	851	2298	1265
Houston	1926	839	2265	339
Detroit	1536	838	2341	805
Kansas City	1340	813	2195	855
Tampa Bay	2065	787	2125	60
Chicago	1679	780	2106	427
Boston	1226	707	1909	683
Cleveland	1243	647	1747	504
New York	1844	633	1709	-135
Oakland	815	526	1420	605
Total	**24632**	**11950**	**32344**	**7712**
Average	**1642**	**797**	**2157**	**515**

Shifts Employed
National League

Team	2019	2020	2020 Prorated	Change
Los Angeles	2434	1113	3005	571
Atlanta	1344	1042	2813	1469
Pittsburgh	2170	949	2562	392
San Francisco	1603	884	2387	784
Philadelphia	1350	872	2354	1004
Washington	1114	868	2344	1230
Arizona	1950	827	2233	283
Milwaukee	1826	824	2225	399
Cincinnati	1845	788	2128	283
Miami	2151	761	2055	-96
Chicago	898	746	2014	1116
Colorado	1992	671	1812	-180
St Louis	1547	604	1687	140
New York	1114	513	1385	271
San Diego	1420	463	1250	-170
Total	**24758**	**11925**	**32254**	**7496**
Average	**1651**	**795**	**2151**	**500**

Top 30 Shifted Batters

Batter	Shifted PA	Shift Percent	Shift GSL BA	No Shift GSL BA
Seager, Kyle	218	92.4	.191	.800
Olson, Matt	215	93.5	.180	1.000
Muncy, Max	215	95.1	.152	.000
Rizzo, Anthony	213	94.2	.156	.200
Bellinger, Cody	212	91.0	.176	.750
Lindor, Francisco	212	82.5	.254	.167
Blackmon, Charlie	209	87.8	.266	.167
Seager, Corey	207	91.2	.209	.182
Biggio, Cavan	205	81.3	.222	.467
Yelich, Christian	203	91.9	.250	.143
Conforto, Michael	202	93.5	.303	.500
Rosario, Eddie	201	92.6	.145	.625
Grisham, Trent	200	86.2	.132	.417
Freeman, Freddie	200	84.0	.277	.263
Ramirez, Jose	199	85.4	.264	.222
Santana, Carlos	197	86.8	.176	.300
Harper, Bryce	196	89.1	.255	.333
Gallo, Joey	194	95.6	.156	.000
Votto, Joey	194	92.4	.211	.000
Calhoun, Kole	191	90.1	.164	.125
Schwarber, Kyle	190	94.1	.209	.000
Tucker, Kyle	186	87.3	.217	.400
Castellanos, Nicholas	181	82.6	.216	.091
Moran, Colin	179	95.2	.206	.333
Bell, Josh	179	89.1	.241	.714
Bradley Jr., Jackie	176	87.6	.265	.250
Gregorius, Didi	176	76.9	.241	.348
Devers, Rafael	175	76.4	.250	.227
Happ, Ian	174	83.7	.214	.308
Moncada, Yoan	169	81.3	.294	.333

Hits Lost and Gained to the Shift

Lindsay Zeck

Dominic Smith of the Mets saw a shift in over half of his plate appearances in 2020 (106 of 199). Those shifts caused him to lose 11 hits and gain 2 for a net loss of 9 hits. This was tied with Max Kepler for the biggest net loss of any player.

Even with that loss, Smith hit for the best batting average of his career—.316 (56 hits in 177 at bats). This was good enough to finish 8th in the National League among qualified hitters. If we imagine a world without shifts and add back his net loss of 9 hits, his batting average would be raised by 51 points to .367. That puts him just above DJ LeMahieu who finished with an average of .364 and the batting title.

The St. Louis Cardinals shifted only 604 times in 2020, the fourth fewest behind the San Diego Padres (463), New York Mets (513), and Oakland A's (526). Though the Cardinals did not shift that often, they shifted effectively. They gained 49 outs and lost 31 for a net gain of 18 outs, which was tied for the highest gain with the Chicago Cubs and Pittsburgh Pirates.

Conversely, the Philadelphia Phillies shifted 872 times, the eighth most in the league, but lost nine more outs than they gained when implementing the shift. This was the biggest net loss of any team. Along with the Phillies, four more teams—the Milwaukee Brewers, New York Mets, Boston Red Sox, and Washington Nationals—finished with more outs lost to the shift than gained.

The following pages detail this information. In addition to hits lost and gained to the shift for batters, there's also data for pitchers and teams. Only players who had at least 4 net hits gained or lost to the shift are listed.

Hits Lost and Gained to the Shift for Batters

Player	2020 Season				Career Since 2010			
	Shifts	Lost	Gained	Net	Shifts	Lost	Gained	Net
Kepler, Max	122	14	5	9	900	71	49	22
Smith, Dominic	106	11	2	9	357	35	18	17
Calhoun, Kole	112	12	4	8	1465	150	85	65
Suarez, Eugenio	103	10	2	8	643	56	38	18
Seager, Kyle	153	14	7	7	1999	161	102	59
Sogard, Eric	67	7	1	6	233	18	9	9
Muncy, Max	126	13	7	6	612	58	29	29
Sanchez, Gary	73	7	1	6	519	50	27	23
Gamel, Ben	54	9	3	6	241	28	15	13
Bellinger, Cody	144	13	7	6	1026	84	88	-4
Gallo, Joey	99	9	3	6	642	60	30	30
Bregman, Alex	72	7	1	6	435	35	22	13
Stewart, Christin	51	6	1	5	264	23	9	14
Cronenworth, Jake	89	7	2	5	89	7	2	5
Vogelbach, Daniel	73	7	2	5	382	37	16	21
Tatis Jr., Fernando	75	9	4	5	149	14	9	5
Pederson, Joc	72	9	4	5	1003	96	65	31
Shaw, Travis	77	8	3	5	921	73	44	29
Davis, Khris	40	5	0	5	643	64	43	21
Barnhart, Tucker	57	5	0	5	465	39	23	16
Rizzo, Anthony	147	13	8	5	2280	198	117	81
Cabrera, Asdrubal	115	13	8	5	952	78	53	25
Gordon, Alex	113	10	5	5	1444	131	96	35
Santana, Carlos	136	13	8	5	1970	176	111	65
Markakis, Nick	50	6	1	5	474	49	35	14
Escobar, Eduardo	128	9	5	4	704	45	36	9
Gonzalez, Marwin	93	9	5	4	590	39	41	-2
Pujols, Albert	78	8	4	4	1707	194	108	86
Bruce, Jay	66	6	2	4	1828	155	88	67
Smoak, Justin	64	6	2	4	1356	131	66	65
Winker, Jesse	83	9	5	4	400	34	24	10
Lamb, Jake	52	5	1	4	812	79	55	24
Polanco, Gregory	83	8	4	4	613	47	38	9
La Stella, Tommy	137	11	7	4	369	30	21	9
Harper, Bryce	124	10	6	4	1225	114	76	38
Grandal, Yasmani	75	7	3	4	933	84	53	31
Akiyama, Shogo	50	5	1	4	50	5	1	4
Tucker, Kyle	133	11	7	4	187	17	10	7
Riley, Austin	95	9	5	4	178	16	9	7
Grisham, Trent	117	9	5	4	189	14	9	5
Torres, Gleyber	68	6	2	4	317	26	21	5
Castro, Willi	56	2	6	-4	78	4	8	-4
Tapia, Raimel	50	5	9	-4	176	14	22	-8
Adames, Willy	52	2	6	-4	195	15	21	-6
Biggio, Cavan	118	7	11	-4	292	17	17	0
Hays, Austin	49	3	7	-4	86	8	10	-2
Alberto, Hanser	66	3	7	-4	171	11	14	-3
Ramirez, Jose	139	7	11	-4	714	50	39	11
Mondesi, Adalberto	74	5	10	-5	193	13	21	-8
Albies, Ozzie	61	4	9	-5	592	41	50	-9
Reyes, Franmil	74	5	10	-5	238	19	24	-5
Crawford, J.P.	109	6	11	-5	293	21	22	-1
Verdugo, Alex	108	7	12	-5	266	18	28	-10
Kipnis, Jason	62	2	8	-6	676	51	42	9
McNeil, Jeff	117	6	13	-7	381	27	35	-8
Anderson, Brian	62	2	10	-8	186	18	21	-3
Joyce, Matt	73	2	10	-8	1113	94	63	31
Betts, Mookie	94	5	13	-8	554	44	41	3

Outs Gained and Lost to the Shift for Pitchers

Player	2020 Season				Career Since 2010			
	Shifts	Gained	Lost	Net	Shifts	Gained	Lost	Net
McCullers Jr., Lance	83	11	4	7	602	58	38	20
Mills, Alec	119	14	7	7	153	18	10	8
Stripling, Ross	109	11	5	6	496	54	35	19
Cease, Dylan	102	9	3	6	171	14	8	6
Civale, Aaron	108	10	4	6	165	13	7	6
Fried, Max	99	10	4	6	269	27	20	7
Kershaw, Clayton	132	14	9	5	712	70	55	15
Lynn, Lance	147	11	6	5	660	59	40	19
Ponce, Cody	39	5	0	5	39	5	0	5
Fedde, Erick	95	10	5	5	230	25	18	7
Hudson, Dakota	61	7	2	5	290	31	12	19
May, Dustin	106	11	6	5	152	14	11	3
Kuhl, Chad	104	11	6	5	437	32	26	6
Teheran, Julio	68	7	2	5	739	65	44	21
Paddack, Chris	56	7	2	5	197	18	9	9
Berrios, Jose	125	13	8	5	775	69	49	20
Nola, Aaron	104	9	5	4	586	55	38	17
Lyles, Jordan	130	11	7	4	592	48	38	10
Shoemaker, Matt	50	7	3	4	471	45	34	11
Gonzales, Marco	116	9	5	4	542	46	37	9
Darvish, Yu	113	9	5	4	537	46	35	11
Duffey, Tyler	37	5	1	4	310	26	17	9
Sandoval, Patrick	54	6	2	4	83	9	6	3
Keller, Brad	112	12	8	4	412	45	36	9
Dunn, Justin	81	7	3	4	85	7	4	3
Eovaldi, Nathan	55	6	2	4	480	46	34	12
Gallen, Zac	114	10	6	4	226	19	12	7
Cueto, Johnny	147	11	7	4	575	44	25	19
Margevicius, Nick	79	7	3	4	137	12	9	3
Graterol, Brusdar	41	6	2	4	53	8	4	4
Lamet, Dinelson	56	6	2	4	168	11	11	0
LeBlanc, Wade	39	1	5	-4	485	37	29	8
Montgomery, Jordan	61	4	8	-4	175	12	19	-7
Waguespack, Jacob	44	1	5	-4	176	10	13	-3
Jackson, Luke	78	7	11	-4	189	16	20	-4
Suter, Brent	55	3	8	-5	283	27	23	4
Corbin, Patrick	123	13	18	-5	568	61	40	21
Yardley, Eric	37	2	7	-5	47	4	9	-5
Castro, Miguel	34	2	7	-5	266	19	24	-5
Woodruff, Brandon	106	6	11	-5	285	21	24	-3
Boyd, Matthew	102	5	10	-5	410	28	29	-1

Hits Lost and Gained to the Shift by Batting Team

Team	2020 Season				Totals Since 2010			
	Shifts	Lost	Gained	Net	Shifts	Lost	Gained	Net
Cincinnati Reds	895	74	44	30	6921	595	438	157
San Diego Padres	859	74	46	28	5350	477	369	108
Milwaukee Brewers	720	66	40	26	5374	455	352	103
Houston Astros	897	73	50	23	6922	578	433	145
New York Yankees	716	63	42	21	8961	805	545	260
Minnesota Twins	934	75	56	19	8169	669	561	108
Pittsburgh Pirates	735	69	53	16	5815	533	421	112
Washington Nationals	743	54	43	11	5924	477	379	98
New York Mets	909	76	66	10	7973	687	466	221
Oakland Athletics	872	56	46	10	8589	684	549	135
Toronto Blue Jays	851	70	61	9	8629	765	512	253
Los Angeles Dodgers	974	76	68	8	7811	683	511	172
Chicago Cubs	817	72	65	7	8509	734	585	149
Texas Rangers	658	51	44	7	8236	762	586	176
Kansas City Royals	771	58	52	6	7042	610	465	145
Seattle Mariners	685	51	45	6	8062	695	520	175
San Francisco Giants	686	53	47	6	5295	415	325	90
Detroit Tigers	638	47	42	5	5899	508	408	100
Arizona Diamondbacks	880	65	60	5	5304	472	377	95
Los Angeles Angels	765	62	58	4	7994	768	514	254
Philadelphia Phillies	837	58	55	3	7008	639	423	216
St Louis Cardinals	816	58	57	1	5758	454	378	76
Chicago White Sox	717	59	58	1	4973	428	361	67
Atlanta Braves	877	61	60	1	6896	574	455	119
Tampa Bay Rays	769	52	52	0	7603	644	522	122
Cleveland Indians	874	62	63	-1	7936	665	504	161
Baltimore Orioles	734	52	55	-3	7580	639	531	108
Colorado Rockies	786	53	61	-8	5826	460	488	-28
Boston Red Sox	808	58	70	-12	9683	831	651	180
Miami Marlins	652	40	66	-26	4124	365	314	51

Outs Gained and Lost to the Shift by Defensive Team

Team	2020 Season				Totals Since 2010			
	Shifts	Gained	Lost	Net	Shifts	Gained	Lost	Net
Chicago Cubs	746	65	47	18	4169	356	257	99
Pittsburgh Pirates	949	79	61	18	9722	819	700	119
St Louis Cardinals	604	49	31	18	4933	432	315	117
Minnesota Twins	928	74	57	17	8196	684	528	156
Seattle Mariners	953	76	59	17	8134	685	557	128
Chicago White Sox	780	71	57	14	7677	670	528	142
Kansas City Royals	813	71	58	13	6455	557	476	81
San Diego Padres	463	39	26	13	4959	451	328	123
San Francisco Giants	884	64	51	13	6154	512	377	135
Los Angeles Dodgers	1113	90	77	13	6988	631	457	174
Atlanta Braves	1042	74	62	12	5886	525	410	115
Houston Astros	839	68	58	10	11304	980	739	241
Cincinnati Reds	788	63	54	9	6688	574	418	156
Cleveland Indians	647	44	35	9	6478	556	355	201
Los Angeles Angels	851	62	53	9	6326	528	405	123
Baltimore Orioles	854	72	64	8	9099	760	594	166
Toronto Blue Jays	859	61	54	7	8029	670	500	170
Texas Rangers	935	68	62	6	6319	546	405	141
New York Yankees	633	50	45	5	8946	766	652	114
Oakland Athletics	526	40	36	4	5575	496	346	150
Arizona Diamondbacks	827	58	54	4	6848	648	426	222
Colorado Rockies	671	51	48	3	7112	632	493	139
Miami Marlins	761	57	55	2	6362	495	424	71
Tampa Bay Rays	787	58	56	2	11556	1036	778	258
Detroit Tigers	838	60	58	2	5630	493	366	127
Washington Nationals	868	66	70	-4	5025	407	357	50
Boston Red Sox	707	54	59	-5	6168	506	382	124
New York Mets	513	34	40	-6	4857	390	320	70
Milwaukee Brewers	824	64	71	-7	9110	819	652	167
Philadelphia Phillies	872	56	65	-9	5461	447	396	51

Four-Outfielder Alignments

Joe Rosales

I'm intrigued to see what's next.

I love baseball no matter what, so it's not that I necessarily need innovation in order to keep it interesting. But it's fun to see teams discovering new strategies to get an edge. And given that we've had so many innovations just in the last 10–15 years—infield shifts, four-outfielder alignments, and openers just to name a few that we keep track of in this book—it's kind of exciting to know that there must be more untapped possibilities.

In the tables on the following page are the total number of four-outfielder alignments that each team has used in each of the last three seasons (and overall) as well as the total number that any batter with two or more has seen in that same time frame. Not likely to be surprising for most people reading this book, the Rays are prominently involved in both.

After using more four-outfielder alignments than any other team in 2019, the Rays repeated that feat in 2020. The 26 four-outfielder alignments they used through the 60-game 2020 season ended up outpacing the 51 they used in the full 162-game 2019 season. So, there may be even more coming in 2021.

You'll also note that Justin Smoak tops the list of players that have had four outfielders used against them with 24. Of the 18 of those that occurred in 2018 and 2019 when he played for the Blue Jays, 10 of them were employed by the division-rival Rays.

Next on the leaderboard is Cavan Biggio. He's another member of the Blue Jays, and all 16 of the four-outfielder alignments used against him in 2019 and 2020 have been employed by the Rays. However, the strategy doesn't seem to have slowed Biggio down as much as it has Smoak. Biggio has a .563 batting average and .688 slugging percentage on those 16 balls in play.

Four-Outfielder Alignments Employed
On Balls In Play

Team	2018	2019	2020	Total
Tampa Bay Rays	2	51	26	79
Cincinnati Reds	0	36	0	36
Minnesota Twins	27	3	0	30
Pittsburgh Pirates	0	0	6	6
Toronto Blue Jays	0	4	1	5
Arizona Diamondbacks	0	5	0	5
San Francisco Giants	0	5	0	5
Houston Astros	5	0	0	5
Chicago Cubs	2	0	0	2
St Louis Cardinals	0	0	1	1
Los Angeles Dodgers	0	1	0	1
Seattle Mariners	0	1	0	1
Colorado Rockies	1	0	0	1
MLB	37	106	34	177

Four-Outfielder Alignments By Batter, Career
On Balls In Play (Minimum 2 BIP)

Batter	AB	H	2B	3B	BABIP	SlgBIP
Smoak, Justin	24	5	1	0	.208	.250
Biggio, Cavan	16	9	2	0	.563	.688
Gallo, Joey	14	6	1	0	.429	.500
Belt, Brandon	12	2	1	0	.167	.250
Olson, Matt	12	4	1	0	.333	.417
Duda, Lucas	11	3	0	0	.273	.273
Carpenter, Matt	9	5	0	1	.556	.778
Freeman, Freddie	6	4	0	0	.667	.667
Bellinger, Cody	5	3	2	0	.600	1.000
Grandal, Yasmani	5	3	0	0	.600	.600
Moreland, Mitch	5	0	0	0	.000	.000
Muncy, Max	5	1	0	0	.200	.200
Seager, Corey	5	5	1	0	1.000	1.200
Voit, Luke	4	2	0	0	.500	.500
Granderson, Curtis	3	0	0	0	.000	.000
Sisco, Chance	3	1	0	0	.333	.333
Alvarez, Yordan	2	1	0	0	.500	.500
Davis, Chris	2	0	0	0	.000	.000
Davis, Khris	2	1	0	0	.500	.500
Encarnacion, Edwin	2	1	0	0	.500	.500
Seager, Kyle	2	0	0	0	.000	.000
Shaw, Travis	2	0	0	0	.000	.000
Thaiss, Matt	2	0	0	0	.000	.000

Home Run Robberies

John Shirley

Even in a full season, home run robberies are relatively rare events, averaging only one every 52 games over the past 15 seasons. This is why it should be no surprise that in the pandemic-shortened 2020 season there were only 20 robberies after a record-breaking amount the year before.

While we were only treated to a few masterful robberies this year, 2020 actually had the fourth-highest rate—one every 45 games on average—of any season since we started tracking them in 2004.

All home run robberies impact the game, but none were more impactful than when Mariners outfielder Kyle Lewis robbed the Athletics Ramón Laureano on September 14. This robbery was only the 16th to come on a potential grand slam. It also helped Lewis tie Leody Taveras for the MLB lead in robberies with two.

Lewis and Taveras by themselves each had as many as any single team in 2020. Teams tied for the most robberies include Lewis' Mariners, Taveras' Rangers, Braves, Rockies and Twins.

On the other end of things, the Dodgers were the team that had the most potential home runs taken away, with three. Justin Turner was unlucky enough to be the batter on two of them, which tied for the MLB lead with Xander Bogaerts of the Red Sox.

If we stretch the timeline back to cover the last three seasons, Lorenzo Cain has the most home run takeaways with seven, one more than Josh Reddick. Cody Bellinger, Neil Walker, and Eric Hosmer have had the most potential home runs taken away, with three each.

Home Run Robberies

Date	Matchup	Fielder	Pos	Pitcher	Batter	Inn.	Outs	Men On	Score
08/23/2020	Marlins@Nationals	Lewis Brinson	8	Humberto Mejia	Juan Soto	1	1	1__	0-0
09/01/2020	White Sox@Twins	Byron Buxton	8	Michael Pineda	Edwin Encarnacion	6	0	___	2-1
08/29/2020	Twins@Tigers	Jake Cave	8	Tyler Clippard	Cameron Maybin	4	0	___	2-2
09/27/2020	Orioles@Blue Jays	Jonathan Davis	9	Tanner Roark	Cedric Mullins II	2	2	___	0-0
09/04/2020	Nationals@Braves	Adam Duvall	7	Tommy Milone	Yan Gomes	4	0	__3	0-3
09/15/2020	Pirates@Reds	Brian Goodwin	8	Amir Garrett	Colin Moran	9	0	___	1-4
07/25/2020	Rockies@Rangers	Garrett Hampson	7	Jon Gray	Shin-Soo Choo	1	0	___	0-0
08/19/2020	Phillies@Red Sox	Bryce Harper	9	Jake Arrieta	Xander Bogaerts	3	2	___	2-2
09/05/2020	Rockies@Dodgers	Sam Hilliard	9	German Marquez	Cody Bellinger	4	0	___	2-0
08/12/2020	Athletics@Angels	Ramon Laureano	8	Yusmeiro Petit	Brian Goodwin	7	2	___	5-4
08/04/2020	Angels@Mariners	Kyle Lewis	8	Erik Swanson	Jason Castro	7	1	___	3-1
09/14/2020	Athletics@Mariners	Kyle Lewis	8	Jimmy Yacabonis	Ramon Laureano	1	2	123	1-0
09/16/2020	Braves@Orioles	Marcell Ozuna	7	Cole Hamels	Renato Nunez	4	0	___	0-3
08/29/2020	Twins@Tigers	Victor Reyes	8	Tarik Skubal	Miguel Sano	4	2	___	2-2
08/18/2020	Nationals@Braves	Victor Robles	8	Wander Suero	Austin Riley	5	2	1__	6-5
07/26/2020	Orioles@Red Sox	Anthony Santander	9	Wade LeBlanc	Xander Bogaerts	4	2	___	6-1
08/28/2020	Dodgers@Rangers	Leody Taveras	8	Mike Minor	Justin Turner	3	1	12_	0-0
09/06/2020	Rangers@Mariners	Leody Taveras	8	Rafael Montero	Evan White	8	2	___	2-4
08/07/2020	Blue Jays@Red Sox	Alex Verdugo	9	Brandon Workman	Travis Shaw	9	0	___	3-5
08/27/2020	Dodgers@Giants	Mike Yastrzemski	8	Andrew Suarez	Justin Turner	7	0	___	5-0

2020 Career Register

Joe Rosales

We don't have Willie Mays' career achievements in this book. However, we do have the full career achievements of everyone that played in the majors in 2020, including the player that just edged past Mays on the all-time home run leaderboard, Albert Pujols. With his six home runs in 2020, Albert now has 662 for his career, only two more than Willie.

BIS has existed as a company since 2002. At this point it's starting to feel like we've been at this for a while. And yet, amazingly, Pujols' career—that of an *active* major league player—still spans further back.

If you look at Pujols' table in this section—which takes up nearly a third of a page—you'll note all the numbers in **boldface**. Those are all the times he led the league in things like home runs, total bases, runs scored, Runs Created, intentional walks, and OPS. Most are in the top half of the table during his time with St. Louis. However, there are also a couple in the lower half as the years started to wear on when he led the league in double plays.

This section of the book is a little shorter this year than it normally is. Because no minor league baseball was played, we don't have all the 2020 minor league stats that we normally would for players that split time between the majors and minors. However, you can still find some minor league stats in this section. For players that are generally considered among the top 25 prospects in baseball that have yet to make their major league debut or among the top 100 prospects in baseball that have made their debut, we have included the last five years of their minor league achievements.

Despite there not being any minor league baseball in 2020, there were still a number of players who were able to make their debuts anyway, leading to a few instances of the rare one-row table. In fact, two such players show up right next to each other in Nabil Crismatt and Garrett Crochet. The latter of those is particularly interesting because minor league stats aren't even an option for him. In 2020, he went from pitching at the University of Tennessee, to being drafted by the Chicago White Sox, to making his major league debut on September 18. And you can see from his one-row table that he made the most of his five relief appearances—six innings pitched, eight strikeouts, zero walks, zero runs allowed, all while averaging 100 mph on his fastball (which is shown in the Vel column in the table).

In addition to many of the traditional stats that most people are familiar with, this section also includes a couple of advanced metrics—Runs Created (RC) for hitters and Component ERA (ERC) for pitchers. You can find explanations of the details of both in the glossary at the back of the book.

A player's career postseason numbers appear in a row just above his career regular season numbers. However, because it is our goal to provide you with all of the great information contained within this book by November 1 every year, 2020 postseason data is not included here.

It may feel strange for some time to consistently have to remind ourselves that the 50-60 games' worth of 2020 stats that we see for most players aren't the result of an injury shortened season or anything like that. But that's part of what is nice about having a book like this. It captures a snapshot of what players have achieved at this point in their careers in the games that were able to be played.

CJ Abrams

Bats: L **Throws:** R **Pos:** CF **Ht:** 6'2" **Wt:** 185 **Born:** 10/3/2000 **Age:** 20

								BATTING												RUNNING			AVERAGES			
Year	Team	Lg	G	AB	H	2B	3B	HR	(Hm | Rd)	TB	R	RBI	RC	TBB	IBB	SO	HBP	SH	SF	SB	CS	GDP	Avg	OBP	Slg	OPS
2019	2 Tms	Low	34	150	59	13	8	3	(- | -)	97	41	22	41	11	0	14	2	0	2	15	6	3	.393	.436	.647	1.083

Albert Abreu

Pitches: R **Bats:** R **Pos:** RP-2 **Ht:** 6'2" **Wt:** 190 **Born:** 9/26/1995 **Age:** 25

			HOW MUCH PITCHED				WHAT HE GAVE UP										THE RESULTS							
Year	Team	Lg	G	GS	GF	IP	BFP	H	R	ER	HR	SH	SF	HB	TBB	IBB	SO	WP	W	L	Pct	Sv-Op	Hld	Vel	OPS	ERC	ERA
2020	NYY	AL	2	0	1	1.1	11	4	4	3	1	0	0	1	2	0	2	0	0	1	.000	0-0	0	96	1.511	36.34	20.25

Bryan Abreu

Pitches: R **Bats:** R **Pos:** RP-4 **Ht:** 6'1" **Wt:** 225 **Born:** 4/22/1997 **Age:** 24

Year	Team	Lg	G	GS	GF	IP	BFP	H	R	ER	HR	SH	SF	HB	TBB	IBB	SO	WP	W	L	Pct	Sv-Op	Hld	Vel	OPS	ERC	ERA
2019	Hou	AL	7	0	2	8.2	32	4	1	1	0	0	0	0	3	0	13	0	0	0	-	0-0	0	95	1.05	1.04	
2020	Hou	AL	4	0	1	3.1	20	1	2	1	0	0	0	2	7	0	3	0	0	0	-	0-0	0	93	.682	7.75	2.70
	Postseason		1	0	0	0.2	6	2	2	2	1	0	0	0	2	0	0	0	0	0	-	0-0	0	96	1.917	51.61	27.00
	2 ML YEARS		11	0	3	12.0	52	5	3	2	0	0	0	2	10	0	16	0	0	0	-	0-0	0	94	.502	2.46	1.50

Jose Abreu

Bats: R **Throws:** R **Pos:** 1B-54;DH-6 **Ht:** 6'3" **Wt:** 250 **Born:** 1/29/1987 **Age:** 34

								BATTING												RUNNING			AVERAGES			
Year	Team	Lg	G	AB	H	2B	3B	HR	(Hm	Rd)	TB	R	RBI	RC	TBB	IBB	SO	HBP	SH	SF	SB	CS	GDP	Avg	OBP	Slg	OPS
2014	CWS	AL	145	556	176	35	2	36	(15	21)	323	80	107	113	51	15	131	11	0	4	3	1	14	.317	.383	.581	.964
2015	CWS	AL	154	613	178	34	3	30	(16	14)	308	88	101	105	39	11	140	15	0	1	0	0	16	.290	.347	.502	.850
2016	CWS	AL	159	624	183	32	1	25	(15	10)	292	67	100	92	47	7	125	15	0	2	0	2	21	.293	.353	.468	.820
2017	CWS	AL	156	621	189	43	6	33	(16	17)	343	95	102	116	35	6	119	15	0	4	3	0	21	.304	.354	.552	.906
2018	CWS	AL	128	499	132	36	1	22	(11	11)	236	68	78	78	37	7	109	11	0	6	2	0	14	.265	.325	.473	.798
2019	CWS	AL	159	634	180	38	1	33	(15	18)	319	85	123	103	36	4	152	13	0	10	2	2	24	.284	.330	.503	.834
2020	CWS	AL	60	240	76	15	0	19	(8	11)	148	43	60	49	18	1	59	3	0	1	0	0	10	.317	.370	.617	.987
	7 ML YEARS		961	3787	1114	233	14	198	(96	102)	1969	526	671	656	263	51	835	83	0	35	10	5	120	.294	.350	.520	.870

Ronald Acuna Jr.

Bats: R **Throws:** R **Pos:** CF-34;RF-28 **Ht:** 6'0" **Wt:** 205 **Born:** 12/18/1997 **Age:** 23

								BATTING												RUNNING			AVERAGES			
Year	Team	Lg	G	AB	H	2B	3B	HR	(Hm	Rd)	TB	R	RBI	RC	TBB	IBB	SO	HBP	SH	SF	SB	CS	GDP	Avg	OBP	Slg	OPS
2018	Atl	NL	111	433	127	26	4	26	(14	12)	239	78	64	83	45	2	123	6	0	3	16	5	4	.293	.366	.552	.917
2019	Atl	NL	156	626	175	22	2	41	(18	23)	324	127	101	122	76	4	188	9	0	1	37	9	8	.280	.365	.518	.883
2020	Atl	NL	46	160	40	11	0	14	(8	6)	93	46	29	37	38	2	60	4	0	0	8	1	3	.250	.406	.581	.987
	Postseason		9	34	11	4	1	2	(2	0)	23	2	6	9	5	0	10	1	0	0	0	2	0	.324	.425	.676	1.101
	3 ML YEARS		313	1219	342	59	6	81	(40	41)	656	251	194	242	159	8	371	19	0	4	61	15	15	.281	.371	.538	.909

Jason Adam

Pitches: R **Bats:** R **Pos:** RP-13 **Ht:** 6'3" **Wt:** 229 **Born:** 8/4/1991 **Age:** 29

			HOW MUCH PITCHED				WHAT HE GAVE UP										THE RESULTS							
Year	Team	Lg	G	GS	GF	IP	BFP	H	R	ER	HR	SH	SF	HB	TBB	IBB	SO	WP	W	L	Pct	Sv-Op	Hld	Vel	OPS	ERC	ERA
2018	KC	AL	31	0	14	32.1	142	30	22	22	9	0	2	3	15	1	37	4	0	3	.000	0-2	2	94	.871	5.56	6.12
2019	Tor	AL	23	0	2	21.2	91	15	8	7	1	0	3	3	10	1	18	1	3	0	1.000	0-1	4	94	.601	2.75	2.91
2020	ChC	NL	13	0	5	13.2	58	9	7	5	2	0	0	0	8	0	21	0	2	1	.667	0-0	0	95	.673	3.19	3.29
	3 ML YEARS		67	0	21	67.2	291	54	37	34	12	0	5	6	33	2	76	5	5	4	.556	0-3	6	94	.749	4.13	4.52

Willy Adames

Bats: R **Throws:** R **Pos:** SS-53;PH-1;PR-1 **Ht:** 6'0" **Wt:** 210 **Born:** 9/2/1995 **Age:** 25

								BATTING												RUNNING			AVERAGES			
Year	Team	Lg	G	AB	H	2B	3B	HR	(Hm	Rd)	TB	R	RBI	RC	TBB	IBB	SO	HBP	SH	SF	SB	CS	GDP	Avg	OBP	Slg	OPS
2018	TB	AL	85	288	80	7	0	10	(7	3)	117	43	34	34	31	3	95	1	1	2	6	5	6	.278	.348	.406	.754
2019	TB	AL	152	531	135	25	1	20	(5	15)	222	69	52	60	46	1	153	3	3	1	4	2	9	.254	.317	.418	.735
2020	TB	AL	54	185	48	15	1	8	(1	7)	89	29	23	31	20	0	74	0	0	0	2	1	4	.259	.332	.481	.813
	Postseason		6	17	5	1	0	2	(2	0)	12	3	2	4	3	0	5	0	0	0	0	1	0	.294	.400	.706	1.106
	3 ML YEARS		291	1004	263	47	2	38	(13	25)	428	141	109	125	97	4	322	4	4	3	12	8	19	.262	.329	.426	.755

Austin L Adams

Pitches: R **Bats:** R **Pos:** RP-3 **Ht:** 6'3" **Wt:** 220 **Born:** 5/5/1991 **Age:** 30

			HOW MUCH PITCHED				WHAT HE GAVE UP										THE RESULTS							
Year	Team	Lg	G	GS	GF	IP	BFP	H	R	ER	HR	SH	SF	HB	TBB	IBB	SO	WP	W	L	Pct	Sv-Op	Hld	Vel	OPS	ERC	ERA
2017	Was	NL	6	0	3	5.0	29	4	4	2	0	0	1	1	8	0	10	1	0	0	-	0-0	0	95	.711	7.11	3.60
2018	Was	NL	2	0	0	1.0	7	1	0	0	0	0	0	0	3	0	0	0	0	0	-	0-0	0	95	.821	13.82	0.00
2019	2 Tms		30	2	3	32.0	130	20	14	14	4	0	1	1	16	0	53	4	2	2	.500	0-2	10	95	.615	2.77	3.94

Year	Team	Lg	G	GS	GF	IP	BFP	H	R	ER	HR	SH	SF	HB	TBB	IBB	SO	WP	W	L	Pct	Sv-Op	Hld	Vel	OPS	ERC	ERA
2020	SD	NL	3	0	1	4.0	17	3	2	2	1	0	0	0	2	0	7	1	0	0	-	0-0	1	93	.694	4.02	4.50
19	Was	NL	1	0	0	1.0	6	0	1	1	0	0	0	0	2	0	2	2	0	0	-	0-0	0	94	.500	7.00	9.00
19	Sea	AL	29	2	3	31.0	124	20	13	13	4	0	1	0	14	0	51	2	2	2	.500	0-2	10	95	.614	2.62	3.77
4 ML YEARS			41	2	7	42.0	183	28	20	18	5	0	2	2	29	0	70	6	2	2	.500	0-2	11	95	.649	3.64	3.86

Chance Adams

Pitches: R **Bats:** R **Pos:** RP-6   **Ht:** 6'1" **Wt:** 215 **Born:** 8/10/1994 **Age:** 26

Year	Team	Lg	G	GS	GF	IP	BFP	H	R	ER	HR	SH	SF	HB	TBB	IBB	SO	WP	W	L	Pct	Sv-Op	Hld	Vel	OPS	ERC	ERA
2018	NYY	AL	3	1	1	7.2	34	8	7	6	3	0	0	0	4	0	4	0	0	1	.000	0-0	0	93	.953	7.11	7.04
2019	NYY	AL	13	0	5	25.1	124	39	25	24	7	0	0	2	11	0	23	1	1	1	.500	1-1	0	92	1.068	9.56	8.53
2020	KC	AL	6	0	1	8.2	40	15	9	9	1	0	0	0	0	0	6	2	0	0	-	0-0	0	92	.950	6.92	9.35
3 ML YEARS			22	1	7	41.2	198	62	41	39	11	0	0	2	15	0	33	3	1	2	.333	1-1	0	92	1.023	8.54	8.42

Matt Adams

Bats: L **Throws:** R **Pos:** DH-11;PH-3;1B-2   **Ht:** 6'3" **Wt:** 245 **Born:** 8/31/1988 **Age:** 32

Year	Team	Lg	G	AB	H	2B	3B	HR	(Hm	Rd)	TB	R	RBI	RC	TBB	IBB	SO	HBP	SH	SF	SB	CS	GDP	Avg	OBP	Slg	OPS
2012	StL	NL	27	86	21	6	0	2	(1	1)	33	8	13	9	5	0	24	0	0	0	0	0	3	.244	.286	.384	.669
2013	StL	NL	108	296	84	14	0	17	(10	7)	149	46	51	49	23	0	80	0	0	0	0	1	9	.284	.335	.503	.839
2014	StL	NL	142	527	152	34	5	15	(8	7)	241	55	68	65	26	5	114	3	0	7	3	2	9	.288	.321	.457	.779
2015	StL	NL	60	175	42	9	0	5	(1	4)	66	14	24	16	10	1	41	0	0	1	1	0	1	.240	.280	.377	.657
2016	StL	NL	118	297	74	18	0	16	(11	5)	140	37	54	46	25	1	81	2	0	3	0	1	5	.249	.309	.471	.780
2017	2 Tms	NL	131	339	93	22	1	20	(12	8)	177	46	65	55	23	5	88	1	0	4	0	0	5	.274	.319	.522	.841
2018	2 Tms	NL	121	306	73	10	0	21	(12	9)	146	42	57	47	27	3	73	4	0	0	0	0	6	.239	.309	.477	.786
2019	Was	NL	111	310	70	14	0	20	(13	7)	144	42	56	42	20	1	115	0	0	1	0	0	7	.226	.276	.465	.741
2020	Atl	NL	16	49	9	2	0	2	(1	1)	17	4	9	5	2	0	18	0	0	0	0	0	3	.184	.216	.347	.563
17	StL	NL	31	48	14	2	0	1	(0	1)	19	4	7	6	4	0	17	0	0	1	0	0	0	.292	.340	.396	.735
17	Atl	NL	100	291	79	20	1	19	(12	7)	158	42	58	49	19	5	71	1	0	3	0	0	5	.271	.315	.543	.858
18	Was	NL	94	249	64	9	0	18	(11	7)	127	37	48	42	24	2	55	4	0	0	0	0	6	.257	.332	.510	.842
18	StL	NL	27	57	9	1	0	3	(1	2)	19	5	9	5	3	1	18	0	0	0	0	0	0	.158	.200	.333	.533
Postseason			30	96	22	3	0	4	(3	1)	37	11	11	13	9	2	25	1	0	0	0	0	2	.229	.302	.385	.687
9 ML YEARS			834	2385	618	129	6	118	(69	49)	1113	294	397	334	161	16	634	12	0	16	4	4	48	.259	.307	.467	.774

Jo Adell

Bats: R **Throws:** R **Pos:** RF-34;CF-4;PR-1   **Ht:** 6'3" **Wt:** 215 **Born:** 4/8/1999 **Age:** 22

Year	Team	Lg	G	AB	H	2B	3B	HR	(Hm	Rd)	TB	R	RBI	RC	TBB	IBB	SO	HBP	SH	SF	SB	CS	GDP	Avg	OBP	Slg	OPS
2017	2 Tms	Low	49	203	66	11	8	5	(-	-)	108	43	30	37	14	1	49	3	1	1	8	2	3	.325	.376	.532	.908
2018	2 Tms	Low	82	333	100	26	4	18	(-	-)	188	69	71	52	26	0	89	7	0	3	13	3	1	.300	.360	.565	.925
2018	Mobile	AA	17	63	15	6	0	2	(-	-)	27	14	6	9	6	0	22	2	0	0	2	0	0	.238	.324	.429	.753
2019	Mobile	AA	43	159	49	15	0	8	(-	-)	88	28	23	35	19	0	41	3	0	1	6	0	7	.308	.390	.553	.944
2019	Salt Lk	AAA	27	121	32	11	0	0	(-	-)	43	22	8	14	10	0	43	0	0	0	1	0	0	.264	.321	.355	.676
2020	LAA	AL	38	124	20	4	0	3	(3	0)	33	9	7	1	7	0	55	1	0	0	0	1	3	.161	.212	.266	.478

Ehire Adrianza

eh-EE-ray ah-dree-AHN-zah

Bats: B **Throws:** R **Pos:** 3B-23;SS-9;PH-6;2B-5;PR-5;DH-1   **Ht:** 6'1" **Wt:** 195 **Born:** 8/21/1989 **Age:** 31

Year	Team	Lg	G	AB	H	2B	3B	HR	(Hm	Rd)	TB	R	RBI	RC	TBB	IBB	SO	HBP	SH	SF	SB	CS	GDP	Avg	OBP	Slg	OPS
2013	SF	NL	9	18	4	1	0	1	(0	1)	8	3	3	1	1	0	5	0	1	0	0	0	1	.222	.263	.444	.708
2014	SF	NL	53	97	23	6	0	0	(0	0)	29	10	5	6	5	1	22	1	2	1	1	1	2	.237	.279	.299	.578
2015	SF	NL	52	113	21	7	1	0	(0	0)	30	11	11	12	15	0	20	4	2	0	3	2	2	.186	.303	.265	.569
2016	SF	NL	40	63	16	2	0	2	(1	1)	24	3	7	6	2	0	13	2	4	0	0	1	0	.254	.299	.381	.679
2017	Min	AL	70	162	43	9	2	2	(0	2)	62	30	24	24	16	1	25	1	1	6	8	1	0	.265	.324	.383	.707
2018	Min	AL	114	335	84	23	1	6	(2	4)	127	42	39	38	24	4	82	5	1	4	5	1	4	.251	.301	.379	.680
2019	Min	AL	84	202	55	8	3	5	(3	2)	84	34	22	31	20	1	40	6	2	4	0	2	3	.272	.349	.416	.765
2020	Min	AL	44	89	17	7	0	0	(0	0)	24	10	3	4	11	0	23	1	0	1	1	0	3	.191	.287	.270	.557
Postseason			1	1	0	0	0	0	(0	0)	0	0	0	0	0	0	1	0	0	0	0	0	0	.000	.000	.000	.000
8 ML YEARS			466	1079	263	63	7	16	(6	10)	388	143	114	122	94	5	230	16	16	13	18	8	14	.244	.310	.360	.670

Jesus Aguilar

Bats: R **Throws:** R **Pos:** 1B-31;DH-20;3B-1;PH-1   AGG-you-lahr   **Ht:** 6'3" **Wt:** 277 **Born:** 6/30/1990 **Age:** 31

Year	Team	Lg	G	AB	H	2B	3B	HR	(Hm	Rd)	TB	R	RBI	RC	TBB	IBB	SO	HBP	SH	SF	SB	CS	GDP	Avg	OBP	Slg	OPS
2014	Cle	AL	19	33	4	0	0	0	(0	0)	4	2	3	0	4	0	13	0	0	1	0	0	1	.121	.211	.121	.332
2015	Cle	AL	7	19	6	1	0	0	(0	0)	7	0	2	4	0	0	7	1	0	0	0	0	0	.316	.350	.368	.718
2016	Cle	AL	9	6	0	0	0	0	(0	0)	0	0	0	0	0	0	1	0	0	0	0	0	0	.000	.000	.000	.000
2017	Mil	NL	133	279	74	15	2	16	(4	12)	141	40	52	47	25	1	94	4	0	3	0	0	8	.265	.331	.505	.837
2018	Mil	NL	149	492	135	25	0	35	(18	17)	265	80	108	82	58	3	143	6	0	10	0	0	19	.274	.352	.539	.890
2019	2 Tms		131	314	74	12	0	12	(5	7)	122	39	50	43	43	0	81	2	0	7	0	0	12	.236	.325	.389	.714
2020	Mia	NL	51	188	52	10	0	8	(1	7)	86	31	34	31	23	0	40	1	0	4	0	1	5	.277	.352	.457	.809

Year Team	Lg	G	AB	H	2B	3B	HR	(Hm	Rd)	TB	R	RBI	RC	TBB	IBB	SO	HBP	SH	SF	SB	CS	GDP	Avg	OBP	Slg	OPS
19 Mil	NL	94	222	50	9	0	8	(3	5)	83	26	34	28	31	0	59	2	0	4	0	0	11	.225	.320	.374	.694
19 TB	AL	37	92	24	3	0	4	(2	2)	39	13	16	15	12	0	22	0	0	3	0	0	1	.261	.336	.424	.760
Postseason		10	37	8	3	0	2	(1	1)	17	5	5	3	3	1	15	0	0	0	0	0	1	.216	.275	.459	.734
7 ML YEARS		499	1331	345	63	2	71	(28	43)	625	192	249	207	153	4	379	14	0	25	0	1	45	.259	.336	.470	.806

Nick Ahmed

Bats: R **Throws:** R **Pos:** SS-57;PH-1   **Ht:** 6'2" **Wt:** 200 **Born:** 3/15/1990 **Age:** 31

Year Team	Lg	G	AB	H	2B	3B	HR	(Hm	Rd)	TB	R	RBI	RC	TBB	IBB	SO	HBP	SH	SF	SB	CS	GDP	Avg	OBP	Slg	OPS
2014 Ari	NL	25	70	14	2	0	1	(1	0)	19	9	4	3	3	0	10	0	2	0	1	0	2	.200	.233	.271	.504
2015 Ari	NL	134	421	95	17	6	9	(4	5)	151	49	34	38	29	1	81	1	5	3	4	5	4	.226	.275	.359	.634
2016 Ari	NL	90	284	62	9	1	4	(1	3)	85	26	20	18	15	3	58	4	2	3	5	2	9	.218	.265	.299	.564
2017 Ari	NL	53	167	42	8	1	6	(3	3)	70	24	21	18	10	3	39	1	0	0	3	4	6	.251	.298	.419	.717
2018 Ari	NL	153	516	121	33	5	16	(7	9)	212	61	70	62	40	2	109	2	1	5	5	4	15	.234	.290	.411	.700
2019 Ari	NL	158	556	141	33	6	19	(8	11)	243	79	82	73	52	2	113	4	1	12	8	2	15	.254	.316	.437	.753
2020 Ari	NL	57	199	53	10	1	5	(2	3)	80	29	29	32	18	0	46	0	0	0	2	0	3	.266	.327	.402	.729
7 ML YEARS		670	2213	528	112	20	60	(26	34)	860	277	260	244	167	11	456	12	11	23	29	18	54	.239	.293	.389	.681

Keegan Akin

Pitches: L **Bats:** L **Pos:** SP-6; RP-2   **Ht:** 6'0" **Wt:** 225 **Born:** 4/1/1995 **Age:** 26

	HOW MUCH PITCHED					WHAT HE GAVE UP										THE RESULTS						
Year Team	Lg	G	GS	GF	IP	BFP	H	R	ER	HR	SH	SF	HB	TBB	IBB	SO	WP	W	L	Pct	Sv-Op Hld	Vel	OPS	ERC	ERA
2020 Bal	AL	8	6	0	25.2	116	27	17	13	3	0	2	1	10	0	35	0	1	2	.333	0-0 0	92	.755	4.45	4.56

Shogo Akiyama

Bats: L **Throws:** R **Pos:** LF-36;CF-21;PH-5   ah-kee-ah-ma   **Ht:** 6'0" **Wt:** 190 **Born:** 4/16/1988 **Age:** 33

Year Team	Lg	G	AB	H	2B	3B	HR	(Hm	Rd)	TB	R	RBI	RC	TBB	IBB	SO	HBP	SH	SF	SB	CS	GDP	Avg	OBP	Slg	OPS
2020 Cin	NL	54	155	38	6	1	0	(0	0)	46	16	9	21	25	0	34	2	0	0	7	3	1	.245	.357	.297	.654

Hanser Alberto

Bats: R **Throws:** R **Pos:** 2B-52;3B-5;DH-1;PH-1   HAHN-zer al-BAIR-tow   **Ht:** 5'11" **Wt:** 215 **Born:** 10/17/1992 **Age:** 28

Year Team	Lg	G	AB	H	2B	3B	HR	(Hm	Rd)	TB	R	RBI	RC	TBB	IBB	SO	HBP	SH	SF	SB	CS	GDP	Avg	OBP	Slg	OPS
2015 Tex	AL	41	99	22	2	1	0	(0	0)	26	12	4	3	2	0	17	0	3	0	1	0	2	.222	.238	.263	.500
2016 Tex	AL	35	56	8	1	0	0	(0	0)	9	2	5	1	0	0	17	0	2	0	1	0	1	.143	.143	.161	.304
2018 Tex	AL	13	27	5	2	0	0	(0	0)	7	0	0	0	2	0	4	0	1	0	0	1	0	.185	.241	.259	.501
2019 Bal	AL	139	524	160	21	2	12	(9	3)	221	62	51	64	16	1	50	4	3	3	4	4	9	.305	.329	.422	.751
2020 Bal	AL	54	219	62	15	0	3	(3	0)	86	35	22	23	5	0	30	3	2	2	3	0	6	.283	.306	.393	.698
Postseason		3	10	2	1	0	0	(0	0)	3	0	2	1	0	0	2	0	0	1	0	0	0	.200	.182	.300	.482
5 ML YEARS		282	925	257	41	3	15	(12	3)	349	111	82	91	25	1	118	7	11	5	9	5	18	.278	.300	.377	.678

Ozzie Albies

Bats: B **Throws:** R **Pos:** 2B-29;PH-1   **Ht:** 5'8" **Wt:** 165 **Born:** 1/7/1997 **Age:** 24

Year Team	Lg	G	AB	H	2B	3B	HR	(Hm	Rd)	TB	R	RBI	RC	TBB	IBB	SO	HBP	SH	SF	SB	CS	GDP	Avg	OBP	Slg	OPS
2017 Atl	NL	57	217	62	9	5	6	(1	5)	99	34	28	36	21	0	36	3	1	2	8	1	3	.286	.354	.456	.810
2018 Atl	NL	158	639	167	40	5	24	(9	15)	289	105	72	82	36	0	116	5	1	3	14	3	9	.261	.305	.452	.757
2019 Atl	NL	160	640	189	43	8	24	(12	12)	320	102	86	113	54	6	112	4	0	4	15	4	2	.295	.352	.500	.852
2020 Atl	NL	29	118	32	5	0	6	(2	4)	55	21	19	20	5	0	30	1	0	0	3	1	0	.271	.306	.466	.773
Postseason		9	35	8	0	0	1	(0	1)	11	4	3	2	2	0	4	0	0	1	0	0	0	.229	.263	.314	.577
4 ML YEARS		404	1614	450	97	18	60	(24	36)	763	262	205	251	116	6	294	13	2	9	40	9	14	.279	.330	.473	.803

Jorge Alcala

Pitches: R **Bats:** R **Pos:** RP-16   **Ht:** 6'3" **Wt:** 205 **Born:** 7/28/1995 **Age:** 25

	HOW MUCH PITCHED					WHAT HE GAVE UP										THE RESULTS						
Year Team	Lg	G	GS	GF	IP	BFP	H	R	ER	HR	SH	SF	HB	TBB	IBB	SO	WP	W	L	Pct	Sv-Op Hld	Vel	OPS	ERC	ERA
2019 Min	AL	2	0	2	1.2	7	1	0	0	0	0	0	0	1	0	1	0	0	0	-	0-0 0	94	.452	2.03	0.00
2020 Min	AL	16	0	8	24.0	94	21	8	7	3	0	0	0	8	0	27	1	2	1	.667	0-1 0	97	.681	3.52	2.63
2 ML YEARS		18	0	10	25.2	101	22	8	7	3	0	0	0	9	0	28	1	2	1	.667	0-1 0	97	.666	3.42	2.45

Sandy Alcantara

Pitches: R **Bats:** R **Pos:** SP-7   **Ht:** 6'5" **Wt:** 200 **Born:** 9/7/1995 **Age:** 25

	HOW MUCH PITCHED					WHAT HE GAVE UP										THE RESULTS						
Year Team	Lg	G	GS	GF	IP	BFP	H	R	ER	HR	SH	SF	HB	TBB	IBB	SO	WP	W	L	Pct	Sv-Op Hld	Vel	OPS	ERC	ERA
2017 StL	NL	8	0	3	8.1	39	9	6	4	2	0	0	0	6	0	10	0	0	0	-	0-0 0	98	.869	7.04	4.32
2018 Mia	NL	6	6	0	34.0	146	25	13	13	3	2	2	2	23	0	30	0	2	3	.400	0-0 0	95	.706	3.90	3.44
2019 Mia	NL	32	32	0	197.1	838	179	94	85	23	5	1	8	81	5	151	4	6	14	.300	0-0 0	96	.719	3.86	3.88
2020 Mia	NL	7	7	0	42.0	172	35	22	14	4	1	0	1	15	0	39	1	3	2	.600	0-0 0	97	.653	3.11	3.00
4 ML YEARS		53	45	3	281.2	1195	248	135	116	32	8	3	11	125	5	230	5	11	19	.367	0-0 0	96	.713	3.84	3.71

Sergio Alcantara

Bats: B **Throws:** R **Pos:** 2B-6;3B-6;PR-1   **Ht:** 5'9" **Wt:** 151 **Born:** 7/10/1996 **Age:** 24

					BATTING																RUNNING			AVERAGES			
Year	Team	Lg	G	AB	H	2B	3B	HR	(Hm	Rd)	TB	R	RBI	RC	TBB	IBB	SO	HBP	SH	SF	SB	CS	GDP	Avg	OBP	Slg	OPS
2020	Det	AL	10	21	3	0	1	1	(0	1)	8	2	1	1	2	0	4	0	0	0	0	0	0	.143	.217	.381	.598

Scott Alexander

Pitches: L **Bats:** L **Pos:** RP-13   **Ht:** 6'2" **Wt:** 195 **Born:** 7/10/1989 **Age:** 31

			HOW MUCH PITCHED					WHAT HE GAVE UP										THE RESULTS								
Year	Team	Lg	G	GS	GF	IP	BFP	H	R	ER	HR	SH	SF	HB	TBB	IBB	SO	WP	W	L	Pct	Sv-Op	Hld	Vel	OPS	ERC	ERA
2015	KC	AL	4	0	3	6.0	25	5	3	3	0	0	0	0	3	0	3	1	0	0	-	0-0	0	93	.598	3.67	4.50
2016	KC	AL	17	0	4	19.0	84	24	7	7	1	0	1	0	7	0	16	0	0	0	-	0-1	0	91	.790	5.24	3.32
2017	KC	AL	58	0	9	69.0	283	62	23	19	3	1	2	0	28	0	59	3	5	4	.556	4-6	9	93	.645	3.27	2.48
2018	LAD	NL	73	1	8	66.0	268	57	28	27	4	1	0	2	27	2	56	2	2	1	.667	3-6	21	93	.667	3.32	3.68
2019	LAD	NL	28	0	4	17.1	76	17	7	7	2	0	0	1	7	2	9	0	3	2	.600	0-0	6	93	.741	4.09	3.63
2020	LAD	NL	13	0	1	12.1	52	9	6	4	2	1	0	1	9	1	9	0	2	0	1.000	0-2	3	93	.710	4.35	2.92
	Postseason		4	0	1	2.1	10	1	2	2	0	0	0	0	2	0	2	1	0	0	-	0-0	0	92	.425	2.03	7.71
	6 ML YEARS		193	1	29	189.2	788	174	74	67	12	3	3	4	81	5	152	6	12	7	.632	7-15	39	93	.680	3.63	3.18

Tyler Alexander

Pitches: L **Bats:** R **Pos:** RP-12; SP-2   **Ht:** 6'2" **Wt:** 200 **Born:** 7/14/1994 **Age:** 26

			HOW MUCH PITCHED					WHAT HE GAVE UP										THE RESULTS								
Year	Team	Lg	G	GS	GF	IP	BFP	H	R	ER	HR	SH	SF	HB	TBB	IBB	SO	WP	W	L	Pct	Sv-Op	Hld	Vel	OPS	ERC	ERA
2019	Det	AL	13	8	1	53.2	235	68	30	29	9	0	1	2	7	0	47	1	1	4	.200	0-0	0	91	.834	5.10	4.86
2020	Det	AL	14	2	0	36.1	152	39	16	16	8	0	1	4	9	0	34	0	2	3	.400	0-0	0	91	.849	5.40	3.96
	2 ML YEARS		27	10	1	90.0	387	107	46	45	17	0	2	6	16	0	81	1	3	7	.300	0-0	0	91	.840	5.22	4.50

Jorge Alfaro

Bats: R **Throws:** R **Pos:** C-29;RF-1;DH-1;PH-1   **Ht:** 6'3" **Wt:** 230 **Born:** 6/11/1993 **Age:** 28

					BATTING																RUNNING			AVERAGES			
Year	Team	Lg	G	AB	H	2B	3B	HR	(Hm	Rd)	TB	R	RBI	RC	TBB	IBB	SO	HBP	SH	SF	SB	CS	GDP	Avg	OBP	Slg	OPS
2016	Phi	NL	6	16	2	0	0	0	(0	0)	2	0	0	0	1	1	8	0	0	0	0	0	0	.125	.176	.125	.301
2017	Phi	NL	29	107	34	6	0	5	(3	2)	55	12	14	20	3	1	33	4	0	0	0	0	2	.318	.360	.514	.874
2018	Phi	NL	108	344	90	16	2	10	(8	2)	140	35	37	44	18	6	138	10	0	1	3	0	2	.262	.324	.407	.731
2019	Mia	NL	130	431	113	14	1	18	(7	11)	183	44	57	53	22	1	154	10	0	2	4	4	12	.262	.312	.425	.736
2020	Mia	NL	31	93	21	2	0	3	(2	1)	32	12	16	14	4	1	36	3	0	0	2	0	2	.226	.280	.344	.624
	5 ML YEARS		304	991	260	38	3	36	(20	16)	412	103	124	131	48	10	369	31	0	3	9	4	18	.262	.316	.416	.732

Anthony Alford

Bats: R **Throws:** R **Pos:** LF-6;CF-6;PR-6;RF-1;DH-1   **Ht:** 6'1" **Wt:** 210 **Born:** 7/20/1994 **Age:** 26

					BATTING																RUNNING			AVERAGES			
Year	Team	Lg	G	AB	H	2B	3B	HR	(Hm	Rd)	TB	R	RBI	RC	TBB	IBB	SO	HBP	SH	SF	SB	CS	GDP	Avg	OBP	Slg	OPS
2017	Tor	AL	4	8	1	1	0	0	(0	0)	2	0	0	0	0	0	3	0	0	0	0	0	0	.125	.125	.250	.375
2018	Tor	AL	13	19	2	0	0	0	(0	0)	2	3	1	1	2	0	9	0	0	0	1	0	0	.105	.190	.105	.296
2019	Tor	AL	16	28	5	0	0	1	(1	0)	8	3	1	2	1	0	11	1	0	0	2	0	0	.179	.233	.286	.519
2020	2 Tms		18	28	6	0	1	2	(2	0)	14	5	7	3	1	0	8	0	0	0	3	0	0	.214	.241	.500	.741
20	Tor	AL	13	16	3	0	0	1	(1	0)	6	3	3	2	0	0	7	0	0	0	3	0	0	.188	.188	.375	.563
20	Pit	NL	5	12	3	0	1	1	(1	0)	8	2	4	1	1	0	1	0	0	0	0	0	0	.250	.308	.667	.974
	4 ML YEARS		51	83	14	1	1	3	(3	0)	26	11	9	6	4	0	31	1	0	0	6	0	0	.169	.216	.313	.529

Kolby Allard

Pitches: L **Bats:** L **Pos:** SP-8; RP-3   **Ht:** 6'1" **Wt:** 195 **Born:** 8/13/1997 **Age:** 23

			HOW MUCH PITCHED					WHAT HE GAVE UP										THE RESULTS								
Year	Team	Lg	G	GS	GF	IP	BFP	H	R	ER	HR	SH	SF	HB	TBB	IBB	SO	WP	W	L	Pct	Sv-Op	Hld	Vel	OPS	ERC	ERA
2018	Atl	NL	3	1	0	8.0	47	19	12	11	3	1	0	1	4	0	3	0	1	1	.500	0-0	0	89	1.253	17.45	12.38
2019	Tex	AL	9	9	0	45.1	208	52	26	25	3	0	1	0	19	0	33	1	4	2	.667	0-0	0	92	.742	4.82	4.96
2020	Tex	AL	11	8	2	33.2	152	31	29	29	4	0	1	1	20	0	32	1	0	6	.000	0-0	0	92	.734	4.58	7.75
	3 ML YEARS		23	18	2	87.0	407	102	67	65	10	1	2	4	43	0	68	2	5	9	.357	0-0	0	92	.798	5.68	6.72

Austin Allen

Bats: L **Throws:** R **Pos:** C-14   **Ht:** 6'2" **Wt:** 219 **Born:** 1/16/1994 **Age:** 27

					BATTING																RUNNING			AVERAGES			
Year	Team	Lg	G	AB	H	2B	3B	HR	(Hm	Rd)	TB	R	RBI	RC	TBB	IBB	SO	HBP	SH	SF	SB	CS	GDP	Avg	OBP	Slg	OPS
2019	SD	NL	34	65	14	4	0	0	(0	0)	18	4	3	4	6	3	21	0	0	0	0	0	2	.215	.282	.277	.559
2020	Oak	AL	14	31	6	1	0	1	(1	0)	10	1	3	2	1	0	14	0	0	0	0	0	0	.194	.219	.323	.541
	2 ML YEARS		48	96	20	5	0	1	(1	0)	28	5	6	6	7	3	35	0	0	0	0	0	2	.208	.262	.292	.554

Greg Allen

Bats: B Throws: R Pos: LF-12;CF-4;PR-3;RF-1   Ht: 6'0" Wt: 185 Born: 3/15/1993 Age: 28

								BATTING													RUNNING			AVERAGES			
Year	Team	Lg	G	AB	H	2B	3B	HR	(Hm	Rd)	TB	R	RBI	RC	TBB	IBB	SO	HBP	SH	SF	SB	CS	GDP	Avg	OBP	Slg	OPS
2017	Cle	AL	25	35	8	1	0	1	(0	1)	12	7	6	4	2	0	8	1	0	1	1	0	0	.229	.282	.343	.625
2018	Cle	AL	91	265	68	11	3	2	(1	1)	91	36	20	26	14	1	58	7	4	1	21	4	5	.257	.310	.343	.654
2019	Cle	AL	89	231	53	9	3	4	(0	4)	80	30	27	24	11	1	53	9	4	1	8	2	3	.229	.290	.346	.636
2020	2 Tms		16	26	4	1	0	1	(1	0)	8	4	4	3	3	0	10	2	0	1	2	0	0	.154	.281	.308	.589
20	Cle	AL	15	25	4	1	0	1	(1	0)	8	3	4	2	1	0	9	1	0	1	1	0	0	.160	.214	.320	.534
20	SD	NL	1	1	0	0	0	0	(0	0)	0	1	0	1	2	0	1	1	0	0	1	0	0	.000	.750	.000	.750
	Postseason		3	1	0	0	0	0	(0	0)	0	0	0	0	0	0	0	0	0	0	0	0	1	.000	.000	.000	.000
	4 ML YEARS		221	557	133	22	6	8	(2	6)	191	77	57	57	30	2	129	19	8	4	32	6	8	.239	.298	.343	.641

Logan Allen

Pitches: L Bats: R Pos: RP-3   Ht: 6'3" Wt: 220 Born: 5/23/1997 Age: 24

			HOW MUCH PITCHED				WHAT HE GAVE UP										THE RESULTS						
Year	Team	Lg	G	GS	GF	IP	BFP	H	R	ER	HR	SH	SF	HB	TBB	IBB	SO	WP	W	L	Pct	Sv-Op	Hld	Vel	OPS	ERC	ERA
2019	2 Tms		9	4	3	27.2	127	36	20	19	4	2	1	2	13	0	17	0	2	3	.400	0-0	0	93	.958	7.07	6.18
2020	Cle	AL	3	0	2	10.2	49	12	4	4	1	0	0	1	7	0	7	1	0	0	-	0-0	0	94	.847	6.44	3.38
19	SD	NL	8	4	2	25.1	118	33	20	19	4	2	1	2	13	0	14	0	2	3	.400	0-0	0	93	.974	7.39	6.75
19	Cle	AL	1	0	1	2.1	9	3	0	0	0	0	0	0	0	0	3	0	0	0	-	0-0	0	94	.778	3.75	0.00
	2 ML YEARS		12	4	5	38.1	176	48	24	23	5	2	1	3	20	0	24	1	2	3	.400	0-0	0	93	.928	6.89	5.40

Abraham Almonte

Bats: B Throws: R Pos: DH-3;LF-2;CF-1;PH-1;PR-1   Ht: 5'10" Wt: 223 Born: 6/27/1989 Age: 32

								BATTING													RUNNING			AVERAGES			
Year	Team	Lg	G	AB	H	2B	3B	HR	(Hm	Rd)	TB	R	RBI	RC	TBB	IBB	SO	HBP	SH	SF	SB	CS	GDP	Avg	OBP	Slg	OPS
2013	Sea	AL	25	72	19	4	0	2	(1	1)	29	10	9	9	6	0	21	0	2	1	1	0	2	.264	.313	.403	.715
2014	2 Tms		59	204	47	10	1	3	(2	1)	68	19	15	18	12	0	60	1	2	1	4	3	5	.230	.275	.333	.609
2015	2 Tms		82	232	58	12	5	5	(4	1)	95	36	24	28	21	0	52	0	3	2	7	1	5	.250	.310	.409	.719
2016	Cle	AL	67	182	48	20	1	1	(1	0)	73	24	22	20	8	1	42	1	0	3	8	0	5	.264	.294	.401	.695
2017	Cle	AL	69	172	40	8	3	3	(2	1)	63	26	14	19	20	0	46	1	1	1	2	1	2	.233	.314	.366	.681
2018	KC	AL	50	134	24	1	2	3	(1	2)	38	15	9	5	15	0	36	0	1	1	2	2	6	.179	.260	.284	.544
2019	Ari	NL	17	31	9	3	1	1	(0	1)	17	11	4	6	7	0	8	0	0	0	0	0	1	.290	.421	.548	.969
2020	SD	NL	7	11	1	0	0	0	(0	0)	1	0	0	0	2	0	4	0	0	0	1	1	0	.091	.231	.091	.322
14	Sea	AL	27	106	21	5	1	1	(0	1)	31	10	8	10	6	0	40	1	0	0	3	1	1	.198	.248	.292	.540
14	SD	NL	32	98	26	5	0	2	(2	0)	37	9	7	8	6	0	20	0	2	1	1	2	4	.265	.305	.378	.682
15	SD	NL	31	54	11	3	0	0	(0	0)	14	6	4	3	5	0	19	0	3	0	1	1	1	.204	.271	.259	.530
15	Cle	AL	51	178	47	9	5	5	(4	1)	81	30	20	25	16	0	33	0	0	2	6	0	4	.264	.321	.455	.776
	8 ML YEARS		376	1038	246	58	13	18	(12	6)	384	141	97	105	91	1	269	3	9	10	25	8	26	.237	.298	.370	.668

Yency Almonte

Pitches: R Bats: B Pos: RP-24   Ht: 6'5" Wt: 223 Born: 6/4/1994 Age: 27

			HOW MUCH PITCHED				WHAT HE GAVE UP										THE RESULTS						
Year	Team	Lg	G	GS	GF	IP	BFP	H	R	ER	HR	SH	SF	HB	TBB	IBB	SO	WP	W	L	Pct	Sv-Op	Hld	Vel	OPS	ERC	ERA
2018	Col	NL	14	0	3	14.2	60	15	5	3	1	0	1	0	4	0	14	1	0	0	-	0-0	3	95	.735	3.61	1.84
2019	Col	NL	28	0	6	34.0	157	39	22	21	7	1	1	1	14	0	29	1	0	1	.000	0-1	1	96	.860	5.73	5.56
2020	Col	NL	24	0	4	27.2	113	25	13	9	2	0	1	3	6	0	23	0	3	0	1.000	1-3	4	95	.670	3.14	2.93
	3 ML YEARS		66	0	13	76.1	330	79	40	33	10	1	3	4	24	0	66	2	3	1	.750	1-4	8	95	.772	4.35	3.89

Albert Almora Jr.

Bats: R Throws: R Pos: CF-28;PR-5;PH-1   Ht: 6'2" Wt: 190 Born: 4/16/1994 Age: 27

								BATTING													RUNNING			AVERAGES			
Year	Team	Lg	G	AB	H	2B	3B	HR	(Hm	Rd)	TB	R	RBI	RC	TBB	IBB	SO	HBP	SH	SF	SB	CS	GDP	Avg	OBP	Slg	OPS
2016	ChC	NL	47	112	31	9	1	3	(1	2)	51	14	14	16	5	0	20	0	0	0	0	0	5	.277	.308	.455	.763
2017	ChC	NL	132	299	89	18	1	8	(4	4)	133	39	46	44	19	1	53	0	3	2	1	0	8	.298	.338	.445	.782
2018	ChC	NL	152	444	127	24	1	5	(3	2)	168	62	41	51	24	2	83	3	2	6	1	3	12	.286	.323	.378	.701
2019	ChC	NL	130	339	80	11	1	12	(6	6)	129	41	32	25	16	4	62	1	5	2	2	1	8	.236	.271	.381	.651
2020	ChC	NL	28	30	5	1	0	0	(0	0)	6	4	1	1	3	0	9	1	0	0	0	0	0	.167	.265	.200	.465
	Postseason		19	37	7	1	0	1	(0	1)	11	2	3	3	1	0	7	0	2	0	0	0	1	.189	.211	.297	.508
	5 ML YEARS		489	1224	332	63	4	28	(14	14)	487	160	134	137	67	6	227	5	10	10	4	4	33	.271	.309	.398	.707

Pete Alonso

Bats: R Throws: R Pos: 1B-39;DH-17;PH-2   Ht: 6'3" Wt: 245 Born: 12/7/1994 Age: 26

								BATTING													RUNNING			AVERAGES			
Year	Team	Lg	G	AB	H	2B	3B	HR	(Hm	Rd)	TB	R	RBI	RC	TBB	IBB	SO	HBP	SH	SF	SB	CS	GDP	Avg	OBP	Slg	OPS
2019	NYM	NL	161	597	155	30	2	53	(27	26)	348	103	120	112	72	6	183	21	0	3	1	0	13	.260	.358	.583	.941
2020	NYM	NL	57	208	48	6	0	16	(7	9)	102	31	35	31	24	4	61	6	0	1	1	0	4	.231	.326	.490	.817
	2 ML YEARS		218	805	203	36	2	69	(34	35)	450	134	155	143	96	10	244	27	0	4	2	0	17	.252	.350	.559	.909

Dan Altavilla

Pitches: R Bats: R Pos: RP-22 • all-ta-VILL-ah • Ht: 5'11" Wt: 226 Born: 9/8/1992 Age: 28

Year Team	Lg	G	GS	GF	IP	BFP	H	R	ER	HR	SH	SF	HB	TBB	IBB	SO	WP	W	L	Pct	Sv-Op	Hld	Vel	OPS	ERC	ERA
2016 Sea	AL	15	0	7	12.1	48	11	1	1	0	0	1	1	1	0	10	1	0	0	-	0-1	1	96	.560	2.09	0.73
2017 Sea	AL	41	0	13	46.2	203	43	27	22	9	0	4	1	20	1	52	9	1	1	.500	0-4	2	97	.765	4.38	4.24
2018 Sea	AL	22	0	3	20.2	85	11	7	6	2	0	0	2	15	0	23	4	3	2	.600	0-1	5	96	.609	3.27	2.61
2019 Sea	AL	17	0	3	14.2	64	9	9	9	1	1	1	0	12	1	18	2	2	1	.667	0-2	1	97	.613	3.20	5.52
2020 2 Tms		22	0	7	20.1	89	18	14	13	3	0	0	0	12	0	24	2	2	3	.400	1-1	3	97	.779	4.54	5.75
20 Sea	AL	13	0	5	11.2	54	12	11	10	3	0	0	0	7	0	14	0	1	2	.333	1-1	1	97	.884	6.13	7.71
20 SD	NL	9	0	2	8.2	35	6	3	3	0	0	0	0	5	0	10	2	1	1	.500	0-0	2	97	.614	2.54	3.12
5 ML YEARS		117	0	33	114.2	489	92	58	51	15	1	6	4	60	2	127	18	8	7	.533	1-9	12	97	.702	3.80	4.00

Jose Altuve

Bats: R Throws: R Pos: 2B-48 • al-TOO-vay • Ht: 5'6" Wt: 166 Born: 5/6/1990 Age: 31

Year Team	Lg	G	AB	H	2B	3B	HR	(Hm	Rd)	TB	R	RBI	RC	TBB	IBB	SO	HBP	SH	SF	SB	CS	GDP	Avg	OBP	Slg	OPS
2011 Hou	NL	57	221	61	10	1	2	(2	0)	79	26	12	18	5	0	29	2	5	1	7	3	5	.276	.297	.357	.654
2012 Hou	NL	147	576	167	34	4	7	(4	3)	230	80	37	76	40	0	74	6	4	4	33	11	8	.290	.340	.399	.740
2013 Hou	AL	152	626	177	31	2	5	(4	1)	227	64	52	67	32	5	85	2	4	8	35	13	24	.283	.316	.363	.678
2014 Hou	AL	158	660	225	47	3	7	(4	3)	299	85	59	106	36	7	53	5	1	5	56	9	20	.341	.377	.453	.830
2015 Hou	AL	154	638	200	40	4	15	(9	6)	293	86	66	98	33	8	67	9	3	6	38	13	17	.313	.353	.459	.812
2016 Hou	AL	161	640	216	42	5	24	(15	9)	340	108	96	132	60	11	70	7	3	7	30	10	15	.338	.396	.531	.928
2017 Hou	AL	153	590	204	39	4	24	(9	15)	323	112	81	118	58	3	84	9	1	4	32	6	19	.346	.410	.547	.957
2018 Hou	AL	137	534	169	29	2	13	(7	6)	241	84	61	91	55	4	79	6	3	1	17	4	17	.316	.386	.451	.837
2019 Hou	AL	124	500	149	27	3	31	(18	13)	275	89	74	81	41	0	82	3	1	3	6	5	19	.298	.353	.550	.903
2020 Hou	AL	48	192	42	9	0	5	(1	4)	66	32	18	14	17	0	39	1	0	0	2	3	5	.219	.286	.344	.629
Postseason		50	207	60	10	0	13	(10	3)	109	38	29	27	18	2	30	0	0	1	5	2	9	.290	.345	.527	.872
10 ML YEARS		1291	5177	1610	308	28	133	(73	60)	2373	766	556	801	377	38	662	50	25	39	256	77	149	.311	.361	.458	.819

Jose Alvarado

Pitches: L Bats: L Pos: RP-9 • Ht: 6'2" Wt: 245 Born: 5/21/1995 Age: 26

Year Team	Lg	G	GS	GF	IP	BFP	H	R	ER	HR	SH	SF	HB	TBB	IBB	SO	WP	W	L	Pct	Sv-Op	Hld	Vel	OPS	ERC	ERA
2017 TB	AL	35	0	6	29.2	123	24	12	12	1	2	1	0	9	1	29	2	0	3	.000	0-0	7	98	.570	2.19	3.64
2018 TB	AL	70	0	17	64.0	263	42	21	17	1	2	2	1	29	4	80	2	1	6	.143	8-12	32	98	.525	1.90	2.39
2019 TB	AL	35	1	16	30.0	146	29	18	16	2	3	2	0	27	3	39	8	1	6	.143	7-9	8	98	.751	5.28	4.80
2020 TB	AL	9	0	3	9.0	45	9	7	6	2	0	1	2	6	0	13	3	0	0	-	0-0	1	97	.850	6.78	6.00
4 ML YEARS		149	1	42	132.2	577	104	58	51	6	7	6	3	71	8	161	15	2	15	.118	15-21	48	98	.614	2.95	3.46

Eddy Alvarez

Bats: B Throws: R Pos: 2B-9;3B-3;PH-2;SS-1 • Ht: 5'9" Wt: 185 Born: 1/30/1990 Age: 31

Year Team	Lg	G	AB	H	2B	3B	HR	(Hm	Rd)	TB	R	RBI	RC	TBB	IBB	SO	HBP	SH	SF	SB	CS	GDP	Avg	OBP	Slg	OPS
2020 Mia	NL	12	37	7	1	0	0	(0	0)	8	6	2	3	3	0	16	1	0	0	2	0	0	.189	.268	.216	.485

Jose Alvarez

Pitches: L Bats: L Pos: RP-8 • Ht: 5'11" Wt: 195 Born: 5/6/1989 Age: 32

Year Team	Lg	G	GS	GF	IP	BFP	H	R	ER	HR	SH	SF	HB	TBB	IBB	SO	WP	W	L	Pct	Sv-Op	Hld	Vel	OPS	ERC	ERA
2013 Det	AL	14	6	0	38.2	172	42	26	25	7	2	2	2	16	1	31	0	1	5	.167	0-0	2	89	.866	5.41	5.82
2014 LAA	AL	2	0	1	0.2	3	1	0	0	0	0	0	0	0	0	1	0	0	0	-	0-0	0	89	.667	4.47	0.00
2015 LAA	AL	64	0	18	67.0	283	58	29	26	5	0	1	5	23	4	59	1	4	3	.571	0-1	7	91	.642	3.13	3.49
2016 LAA	AL	64	0	12	57.1	256	71	29	22	4	1	1	1	15	4	51	2	1	3	.250	0-1	11	91	.745	4.55	3.45
2017 LAA	AL	64	0	12	48.2	203	50	23	21	7	1	0	0	12	5	45	1	0	3	.000	1-3	13	91	.733	3.78	3.88
2018 LAA	AL	76	0	5	63.0	261	51	20	19	3	2	0	2	22	2	59	1	6	4	.600	1-4	14	92	.613	2.59	2.71
2019 Phi	NL	67	1	11	59.0	255	66	25	22	8	1	3	1	18	4	51	3	3	4	.429	1-3	16	91	.766	4.61	3.36
2020 Phi	NL	8	0	1	6.1	27	7	1	1	0	0	0	0	3	0	6	0	0	0	-	0-0	1	92	.745	4.44	1.42
Postseason		1	0	0	3.0	10	0	0	0	0	0	0	0	1	0	3	0	0	0	-	0-0	0	91	.100	0.13	0.00
8 ML YEARS		359	7	60	340.2	1460	346	153	136	34	7	7	11	109	20	303	8	15	22	.405	3-12	64	91	.717	3.87	3.59

Yordan Alvarez

Bats: L Throws: R Pos: DH-2 • Ht: 6'5" Wt: 225 Born: 6/27/1997 Age: 24

Year Team	Lg	G	AB	H	2B	3B	HR	(Hm	Rd)	TB	R	RBI	RC	TBB	IBB	SO	HBP	SH	SF	SB	CS	GDP	Avg	OBP	Slg	OPS
2019 Hou	AL	87	313	98	26	0	27	(14	13)	205	58	78	72	52	4	94	2	0	2	0	0	9	.313	.412	.655	1.067
2020 Hou	AL	2	8	2	0	0	1	(1	0)	5	2	4	2	0	0	1	1	0	0	0	0	1	.250	.333	.625	.958
Postseason		18	58	14	3	0	1	(0	1)	20	5	3	5	7	1	21	0	0	0	0	0	0	.241	.323	.345	.668
2 ML YEARS		89	321	100	26	0	28	(15	13)	210	60	82	74	52	4	95	3	0	2	0	0	10	.312	.410	.654	1.064

Adbert Alzolay

Pitches: R Bats: R Pos: SP-4; RP-2 Ht: 6'1" Wt: 208 Born: 3/1/1995 Age: 26

		HOW MUCH PITCHED				WHAT HE GAVE UP											THE RESULTS						
Year Team	Lg	G	GS	GF	IP	BFP	H	R	ER	HR	SH	SF	HB	TBB	IBB	SO	WP	W	L	Pct	Sv-Op	Hld	Vel	OPS	ERC	ERA
2019 ChC	NL	4	2	1	12.1	60	13	10	10	4	0	0	1	9	0	13	0	1	1	.500	0-0	0	94	.923	7.80	7.30
2020 ChC	NL	6	4	0	21.1	87	12	8	7	1	0	2	1	13	0	29	1	1	1	.500	0-0	0	95	.566	2.43	2.95
2 ML YEARS		10	6	1	33.2	147	25	18	17	5	0	2	2	22	0	42	1	2	2	.500	0-0	0	95	.713	4.21	4.54

Brett Anderson

Pitches: L Bats: L Pos: SP-10 Ht: 6'4" Wt: 230 Born: 2/1/1988 Age: 33

Year Team	Lg	G	GS	GF	IP	BFP	H	R	ER	HR	SH	SF	HB	TBB	IBB	SO	WP	W	L	Pct	Sv-Op	Hld	Vel	OPS	ERC	ERA
2009 Oak	AL	30	30	0	175.1	735	180	94	79	20	4	4	3	45	1	150	0	11	11	.500	0-0	0	93	.711	3.84	4.06
2010 Oak	AL	19	19	0	112.1	470	112	41	35	6	3	2	7	22	2	75	4	7	6	.538	0-0	0	92	.655	3.16	2.80
2011 Oak	AL	13	13	0	83.1	356	86	40	37	8	4	1	7	25	1	61	0	3	6	.333	0-0	0	91	.721	4.20	4.00
2012 Oak	AL	6	6	0	35.0	137	29	11	10	1	0	0	1	7	1	25	1	4	2	.667	0-0	0	92	.565	2.13	2.57
2013 Oak	AL	16	5	4	44.2	200	51	32	30	5	1	0	0	21	1	46	0	1	4	.200	3-3	0	92	.794	5.27	6.04
2014 Col	NL	8	8	0	43.1	180	44	18	14	1	1	1	0	13	3	29	0	1	3	.250	0-0	0	90	.688	3.20	2.91
2015 LAD	NL	31	31	0	180.1	750	194	82	74	18	3	2	2	46	2	116	4	10	9	.526	0-0	0	91	.726	4.05	3.69
2016 LAD	NL	4	3	0	11.1	62	25	15	15	4	1	1	0	4	0	5	2	1	2	.333	0-0	0	91	1.208	14.27	11.91
2017 2 Tms		13	13	0	55.1	251	73	41	39	5	0	3	0	21	0	38	2	4	4	.500	0-0	0	91	.872	5.87	6.34
2018 Oak	AL	17	17	0	80.1	333	90	42	40	10	2	0	2	13	0	47	3	4	5	.444	0-0	0	90	.770	4.15	4.48
2019 Oak	AL	31	31	0	176.0	743	181	80	76	20	4	4	4	49	2	90	4	13	9	.591	0-0	0	91	.724	3.94	3.89
2020 Mil	NL	10	10	0	47.0	202	50	24	22	6	0	3	4	10	0	32	0	4	4	.500	0-0	0	90	.771	4.19	4.21
17 ChC	NL	6	6	0	22.0	111	34	22	20	2	0	1	0	12	0	16	1	2	2	.500	0-0	0	90	.986	7.85	8.18
17 Tor	AL	7	7	0	33.1	140	39	19	19	3	0	2	0	9	0	22	1	2	2	.500	0-0	0	91	.785	4.62	5.13
Postseason		3	2	1	9.1	40	10	7	7	1	0	0	0	3	0	10	1	1	1	.500	0-0	0	92	.730	4.23	6.75
12 ML YEARS		198	186	4	1044.1	4419	1115	520	471	104	23	21	30	276	13	714	20	63	65	.492	3-3	1	91	.732	4.05	4.06

Brian Anderson

Bats: R Throws: R Pos: 3B-56;1B-1;2B-1;DH-1;PH-1 Ht: 6'3" Wt: 208 Born: 5/19/1993 Age: 28

		BATTING																		RUNNING			AVERAGES			
Year Team	Lg	G	AB	H	2B	3B	HR	(Hm	Rd)	TB	R	RBI	RC	TBB	IBB	SO	HBP	SH	SF	SB	CS	GDP	Avg	OBP	Slg	OPS
2017 Mia	NL	25	84	22	7	1	0	(0	0)	31	11	8	11	10	0	28	0	0	1	0	0	1	.262	.337	.369	.706
2018 Mia	NL	156	590	161	34	4	11	(7	4)	236	87	65	94	62	2	129	16	0	2	2	4	18	.273	.357	.400	.757
2019 Mia	NL	126	459	120	33	1	20	(10	10)	215	57	66	72	44	1	114	14	0	3	5	1	15	.261	.342	.468	.811
2020 Mia	NL	59	200	51	7	1	11	(4	7)	93	27	38	40	22	1	66	6	0	1	0	0	2	.255	.345	.465	.810
4 ML YEARS		366	1333	354	81	7	42	(21	21)	575	182	177	217	138	4	337	36	0	7	7	5	36	.266	.349	.431	.780

Chase Anderson

Pitches: R Bats: R Pos: SP-7; RP-3 Ht: 6'1" Wt: 210 Born: 11/30/1987 Age: 33

Year Team	Lg	G	GS	GF	IP	BFP	H	R	ER	HR	SH	SF	HB	TBB	IBB	SO	WP	W	L	Pct	Sv-Op	Hld	Vel	OPS	ERC	ERA
2014 Ari	NL	21	21	0	114.1	486	117	56	51	16	4	4	2	40	2	105	4	9	7	.563	0-0	0	91	.779	4.39	4.01
2015 Ari	NL	27	27	0	152.2	640	158	75	73	18	4	9	7	40	2	111	3	6	6	.500	0-0	0	92	.754	4.08	4.30
2016 Mil	NL	31	30	1	151.2	647	155	83	74	28	4	3	4	53	0	120	4	9	11	.450	0-0	0	91	.819	4.76	4.39
2017 Mil	NL	25	25	0	141.1	569	113	47	43	14	5	2	7	41	1	133	0	12	4	.750	0-0	0	93	.647	2.80	2.74
2018 Mil	NL	30	30	0	158.0	644	131	71	69	30	4	1	7	57	0	128	1	9	8	.529	0-0	0	92	.731	3.85	3.93
2019 Mil	NL	32	27	1	139.0	592	126	67	65	23	6	2	8	50	2	124	1	8	4	.667	0-0	0	93	.763	4.03	4.21
2020 Tor	AL	10	7	0	33.2	154	45	29	27	11	0	0	1	10	0	38	1	1	2	.333	0-0	0	92	.986	7.54	7.22
7 ML YEARS		176	167	2	890.2	3732	845	428	402	140	26	21	36	291	7	759	14	54	42	.563	0-0	0	92	.759	4.09	4.06

Drew Anderson

Pitches: R Bats: R Pos: RP-1 Ht: 6'3" Wt: 205 Born: 3/22/1994 Age: 27

Year Team	Lg	G	GS	GF	IP	BFP	H	R	ER	HR	SH	SF	HB	TBB	IBB	SO	WP	W	L	Pct	Sv-Op	Hld	Vel	OPS	ERC	ERA
2017 Phi	NL	2	0	1	2.1	14	6	7	6	0	0	1	0	1	0	2	0	0	0	-	0-0	0	94	1.167	13.44	23.14
2018 Phi	NL	5	1	1	12.2	59	17	7	7	0	0	0	2	2	0	11	0	0	1	.000	0-0	0	93	.792	4.81	4.97
2019 Phi	NL	2	0	1	6.0	30	6	5	5	1	0	0	0	6	2	6	0	0	0	-	0-0	0	93	.775	6.27	7.50
2020 CWS	AL	1	0	0	1.1	10	4	6	6	2	0	0	0	2	0	2	1	0	1	.000	0-0	0	92	1.975	41.86	40.50
4 ML YEARS		10	1	3	22.1	113	33	25	24	3	0	1	2	11	2	21	1	0	2	.000	0-0	0	93	.932	7.70	9.67

Ian Anderson

Pitches: R Bats: R Pos: SP-6 Ht: 6'3" Wt: 170 Born: 5/2/1998 Age: 23

Year Team	Lg	G	GS	GF	IP	BFP	H	R	ER	HR	SH	SF	HB	TBB	IBB	SO	WP	W	L	Pct	Sv-Op	Hld	Vel	OPS	ERC	ERA
2016 2 Tms	Low	10	10	0	39.2	157	33	12	9	1	3	1	0	12	0	36	6	1	2	.333	0- -	-	-	.583	2.43	2.04
2017 Rome	A	20	20	0	83.0	355	69	30	29	0	2	1	11	43	0	101	8	4	5	.444	0- -	-	-	.617	3.47	3.14
2018 Florida	A+	20	20	0	100.0	414	73	31	28	2	3	1	2	40	0	118	18	2	6	.250	0- -	-	-	.530	2.19	2.52
2019 Missi	AA	21	21	0	111.0	462	82	38	33	8	3	4	2	47	1	147	8	7	5	.583	0- -	-	-	.581	2.61	2.68
2019 Gwnntt	AAA	5	5	0	24.2	113	23	18	18	5	0	0		18	0	25	1	1	3	.333	0- -	-	-	.815	5.79	6.57
2020 Atl	NL	6	6	0	32.1	138	21	11	7	1	0	0	2	14	0	41	4	3	2	.600	0-0	0	94	.498	2.04	1.95

Justin Anderson

Pitches: R **Bats:** L **Pos:** P   **Ht:** 6'3" **Wt:** 230 **Born:** 9/28/1992 **Age:** 28

Year Team	Lg	G	GS	GF	IP	BFP	H	R	ER	HR	SH	SF	HB	TBB	IBB	SO	WP	W	L	Pct	Sv-Op	Hld	Vel	OPS	ERC	ERA
2018 LAA	AL	57	0	10	55.1	241	42	25	25	3	0	1	4	40	3	67	9	3	3	.500	4-6	22	97	.634	3.92	4.07
2019 LAA	AL	54	0	7	47.0	217	42	32	29	6	1	2	1	32	0	60	4	3	0	1.000	1-2	11	95	.778	4.74	5.55
2 ML YEARS		111	0	17	102.1	458	84	57	54	9	1	2	5	72	3	127	13	6	3	.667	5-8	33	96	.703	4.30	4.75

Nick Anderson

Pitches: R **Bats:** R **Pos:** RP-19   **Ht:** 6'4" **Wt:** 205 **Born:** 7/5/1990 **Age:** 30

Year Team	Lg	G	GS	GF	IP	BFP	H	R	ER	HR	SH	SF	HB	TBB	IBB	SO	WP	W	L	Pct	Sv-Op	Hld	Vel	OPS	ERC	ERA
2019 2 Tms		68	0	3	65.0	264	52	24	24	8	0	1	2	18	4	110	4	5	4	.556	1-5	16	96	.647	2.71	3.32
2020 TB	AL	19	0	9	16.1	58	5	2	1	1	0	0	0	3	0	26	0	2	1	.667	6-6	6	95	.320	0.55	0.55
19 Mia	NL	45	0	3	43.2	186	40	19	19	5	0	1	1	16	3	69	2	2	4	.333	1-2	7	96	.705	3.53	3.92
19 TB	NL	23	0	0	21.1	78	12	5	5	3	0	0	1	2	1	41	2	3	0	1.000	0-3	9	96	.512	1.33	2.11
Postseason		4	0	0	5.2	21	5	1	1	0	0	0	0	0	0	8	1	0	0	-	0-0	0	97	.476	1.58	1.59
2 ML YEARS		87	0	12	81.1	322	57	26	25	9	0	1	2	21	4	136	4	7	5	.583	7-11	22	96	.587	2.09	2.77

Shaun Anderson

Pitches: R **Bats:** R **Pos:** RP-18   **Ht:** 6'4" **Wt:** 228 **Born:** 10/29/1994 **Age:** 26

Year Team	Lg	G	GS	GF	IP	BFP	H	R	ER	HR	SH	SF	HB	TBB	IBB	SO	WP	W	L	Pct	Sv-Op	Hld	Vel	OPS	ERC	ERA
2019 SF	NL	28	16	4	96.0	427	111	61	58	13	4	1	2	38	3	70	6	3	5	.375	2-2	1	93	.818	5.29	5.44
2020 SF	NL	18	0	4	15.1	67	10	6	6	3	0	0	0	12	0	18	2	0	0	-	0-0	2	95	.710	4.30	3.52
2 ML YEARS		46	16	8	111.1	494	121	67	64	16	4	1	2	50	3	88	8	3	5	.375	2-2	3	93	.804	5.15	5.17

Tim Anderson

Bats: R **Throws:** R **Pos:** SS-49   **Ht:** 6'1" **Wt:** 185 **Born:** 6/23/1993 **Age:** 28

Year Team	Lg	G	AB	H	2B	3B	HR	(Hm	Rd)	TB	R	RBI	RC	TBB	IBB	SO	HBP	SH	SF	SB	CS	GDP	Avg	OBP	Slg	OPS
2016 CWS	AL	99	410	116	22	6	9	(5	4)	177	57	30	45	13	0	117	1	6	1	10	2	15	.283	.306	.432	.738
2017 CWS	AL	146	587	151	26	4	17	(7	10)	236	72	56	59	13	0	162	1	1	5	15	1	13	.257	.276	.402	.679
2018 CWS	AL	153	567	136	28	3	20	(10	10)	230	77	64	58	30	2	149	4	2	3	26	8	15	.240	.281	.406	.687
2019 CWS	AL	123	498	167	32	0	18	(9	9)	253	81	56	77	15	0	109	3	0	2	17	5	12	**.335**	.357	.508	.865
2020 CWS	AL	49	208	67	11	1	10	(5	5)	110	**45**	21	31	10	0	50	2	0	1	5	2	4	.322	.357	.529	.886
5 ML YEARS		570	2270	637	119	14	74	(36	38)	1006	332	227	270	81	2	587	13	10	8	73	18	59	.281	.308	.443	.751

Tyler Anderson

Pitches: L **Bats:** L **Pos:** SP-11; RP-2   **Ht:** 6'2" **Wt:** 213 **Born:** 12/30/1989 **Age:** 31

Year Team	Lg	G	GS	GF	IP	BFP	H	R	ER	HR	SH	SF	HB	TBB	IBB	SO	WP	W	L	Pct	Sv-Op	Hld	Vel	OPS	ERC	ERA
2016 Col	NL	19	19	0	114.1	478	119	50	45	12	6	3	3	28	2	99	4	5	6	.455	0-0	0	91	.742	3.85	3.54
2017 Col	NL	17	15	1	86.0	362	88	48	46	16	5	2	2	26	0	81	6	6	6	.500	0-0	0	92	.820	4.57	4.81
2018 Col	NL	32	32	0	176.0	737	165	94	89	30	3	7	3	59	1	164	9	7	9	.438	0-0	0	92	.757	4.04	4.55
2019 Col	NL	5	5	0	20.2	106	33	27	27	8	2	2	0	11	0	23	0	0	3	.000	0-0	0	91	1.159	10.75	11.76
2020 SF	NL	13	11	0	59.2	260	58	32	29	5	1	3	4	25	0	41	1	4	3	.571	0-0	0	90	.746	4.15	4.37
Postseason		2	1	0	7.0	28	6	3	3	1	0	0	0	2	0	6	0	0	1	.000	0-0	0	92	.709	3.21	3.86
5 ML YEARS		86	82	1	456.2	1943	463	251	236	71	17	17	12	149	3	408	20	22	27	.449	0-0	0	91	.785	4.37	4.65

Matt Andriese

ANN-dreese

Pitches: R **Bats:** R **Pos:** RP-15; SP-1   **Ht:** 6'2" **Wt:** 215 **Born:** 8/28/1989 **Age:** 31

Year Team	Lg	G	GS	GF	IP	BFP	H	R	ER	HR	SH	SF	HB	TBB	IBB	SO	WP	W	L	Pct	Sv-Op	Hld	Vel	OPS	ERC	ERA
2015 TB	AL	25	8	8	65.2	282	69	32	30	8	1	3	2	18	1	49	2	3	5	.375	2-2	0	91	.728	4.08	4.11
2016 TB	AL	29	19	3	127.2	527	131	64	62	17	0	6	1	25	1	109	3	8	8	.500	1-1	4	92	.720	3.68	4.37
2017 TB	AL	18	17	1	86.0	374	90	48	43	16	0	1	4	28	1	76	3	5	5	.500	1-1	0	92	.795	4.80	4.50
2018 2 Tms		41	5	13	78.2	340	84	54	46	15	1	1	2	25	5	78	3	3	7	.300	0-0	1	92	.819	4.77	5.26
2019 Ari	NL	54	0	13	70.2	310	72	37	37	8	1	3	3	27	4	79	9	5	5	.500	1-4	4	93	.757	4.24	4.71
2020 LAA	NL	16	1	3	32.0	126	21	17	16	5	0	0	1	11	0	33	0	2	4	.333	2-3	3	92	.622	2.56	4.50
18 TB	AL	27	4	6	59.2	251	55	32	27	7	1	1	2	18	3	59	3	3	4	.429	0-0	1	92	.702	3.41	4.07
18 Ari	NL	14	1	7	19.0	89	29	19	19	8	0	0	0	7	2	19	0	0	3	.000	0-0	0	92	1.148	9.93	9.00
6 ML YEARS		183	50	41	460.2	1959	467	249	234	69	3	14	13	134	12	424	20	26	34	.433	7-11	12	92	.752	4.13	4.57

Elvis Andrus

AHN-droos

Bats: R **Throws:** R **Pos:** SS-29; PR-1   **Ht:** 6'0" **Wt:** 210 **Born:** 8/26/1988 **Age:** 32

Year Team	Lg	G	AB	H	2B	3B	HR	(Hm	Rd)	TB	R	RBI	RC	TBB	IBB	SO	HBP	SH	SF	SB	CS	GDP	Avg	OBP	Slg	OPS
2009 Tex	AL	145	480	128	17	8	6	(3	3)	179	72	40	65	40	0	77	6	12	3	33	6	4	.267	.329	.373	.702
2010 Tex	AL	148	588	156	15	9	0	(0	0)	177	88	35	79	64	0	96	5	17	0	32	15	6	.265	.342	.301	.643
2011 Tex	AL	150	587	164	27	3	5	(2	3)	212	96	60	76	56	0	74	5	16	1	37	12	17	.279	.347	.361	.708
2012 Tex	AL	158	629	180	31	9	3	(1	2)	238	85	62	92	57	0	96	5	17	3	21	10	15	.286	.349	.378	.727
2013 Tex	AL	156	620	168	17	4	4	(0	4)	205	91	67	72	52	1	97	4	16	6	42	8	19	.271	.328	.331	.659
2014 Tex	AL	157	619	163	35	1	2	(1	1)	206	72	41	59	46	0	96	3	9	7	27	15	21	.263	.314	.333	.647
2015 Tex	AL	160	596	154	34	2	7	(4	3)	213	69	62	68	46	1	78	2	8	9	25	9	14	.258	.309	.357	.667

Year	Team	Lg	G	AB	H	2B	3B	HR	(Hm	Rd)	TB	R	RBI	RC	TBB	IBB	SO	HBP	SH	SF	SB	CS	GDP	Avg	OBP	Slg	OPS
2016	Tex	AL	147	506	153	31	7	8	(3	5)	222	75	69	87	47	2	70	4	4	7	24	8	18	.302	.362	.439	.800
2017	Tex	AL	158	643	191	44	4	20	(7	13)	303	100	88	104	38	0	101	3	1	4	25	10	18	.297	.337	.471	.808
2018	Tex	AL	97	395	101	20	3	6	(6	0)	145	53	33	44	28	0	66	3	0	2	5	3	8	.256	.308	.367	.675
2019	Tex	AL	147	600	165	27	4	12	(4	8)	236	81	72	76	34	1	96	4	0	10	31	8	16	.275	.313	.393	.707
2020	Tex	AL	29	103	20	5	0	3	(2	1)	34	11	7	6	8	0	15	0	0	0	3	1	5	.194	.252	.330	.582
	Postseason		42	173	46	4	1	1	(0	1)	55	21	7	15	12	0	24	1	4	1	9	5	6	.266	.316	.318	.633
	12 ML YEARS		1652	6366	1743	303	48	76	(33	43)	2370	893	636	828	516	5	962	44	100	52	305	105	161	.274	.330	.372	.702

Miguel Andujar

Bats: R **Throws:** R **Pos:** LF-7;DH-7;3B-6;PH-2;PR-1   **Ht:** 6'0" **Wt:** 211 **Born:** 3/2/1995 **Age:** 26

Year	Team	Lg	G	AB	H	2B	3B	HR	(Hm	Rd)	TB	R	RBI	RC	TBB	IBB	SO	HBP	SH	SF	SB	CS	GDP	Avg	OBP	Slg	OPS
2017	NYY	AL	5	7	4	2	0	0	(0	0)	6	0	4	4	1	0	0	0	0	0	0	0	0	.571	.625	.857	1.482
2018	NYY	AL	149	573	170	47	2	27	(16	11)	302	83	92	99	25	2	97	4	0	4	2	1	9	.297	.328	.527	.855
2019	NYY	AL	12	47	6	0	0	0	(0	0)	6	1	1	0	1	0	11	0	0	1	0	0	4	.128	.143	.128	.271
2020	NYY	AL	21	62	15	2	1	1	(0	1)	22	5	5	4	3	0	9	0	0	0	1	0	1	.242	.277	.355	.632
	Postseason		4	10	2	0	0	0	(0	0)	2	0	0	1	2	0	2	0	0	0	0	0	1	.200	.333	.200	.533
	4 ML YEARS		187	689	195	51	3	28	(16	12)	336	89	102	107	30	2	117	4	0	5	3	1	14	.283	.315	.488	.802

Tejay Antone

Pitches: R **Bats:** R **Pos:** RP-9; SP-4   **Ht:** 6'4" **Wt:** 230 **Born:** 12/5/1993 **Age:** 27

			HOW MUCH PITCHED					WHAT HE GAVE UP										THE RESULTS							
Year	Team	Lg	G	GS	GF	IP	BFP	H	R	ER	HR	SH	SF	HB	TBB	IBB	SO	WP	W	L	Pct	Sv-Op Hld	Vel	OPS	ERC	ERA
2020	Cin	NL	13	4	1	35.1	141	20	11	11	4	0	2	2	16	0	45	2	0	3	.000	0-1 1	96	.584	2.34	2.80

Sherten Apostel

Bats: R **Throws:** R **Pos:** 1B-5;3B-2   **Ht:** 6'4" **Wt:** 235 **Born:** 3/11/1999 **Age:** 22

Year	Team	Lg	G	AB	H	2B	3B	HR	(Hm	Rd)	TB	R	RBI	RC	TBB	IBB	SO	HBP	SH	SF	SB	CS	GDP	Avg	OBP	Slg	OPS
2020	Tex	AL	7	20	2	1	0	0	(0	0)	3	1	0	0	1	0	9	0	0	0	0	0	0	.100	.143	.150	.293

Aristides Aquino

Bats: R **Throws:** R **Pos:** LF-13;PH-5;RF-4;DH-4;PR-2;CF-1   **Ht:** 6'4" **Wt:** 220 **Born:** 4/22/1994 **Age:** 27

Year	Team	Lg	G	AB	H	2B	3B	HR	(Hm	Rd)	TB	R	RBI	RC	TBB	IBB	SO	HBP	SH	SF	SB	CS	GDP	Avg	OBP	Slg	OPS
2018	Cin	NL	1	1	0	0	0	0	(0	0)	0	0	0	0	0	0	1	0	0	0	0	0	0	.000	.000	.000	.000
2019	Cin	NL	56	205	53	8	0	19	(11	8)	118	31	47	39	16	2	60	2	0	2	7	0	5	.259	.316	.576	.891
2020	Cin	NL	23	47	8	1	0	2	(1	1)	15	7	8	9	6	0	18	3	0	0	1	0	1	.170	.304	.319	.623
	3 ML YEARS		80	253	61	9	0	21	(12	9)	133	38	55	48	22	2	79	5	0	2	8	0	6	.241	.312	.526	.838

Jonathan Arauz

Bats: B **Throws:** R **Pos:** 2B-16;3B-6;SS-4;PR-2;DH-1;PH-1   **Ht:** 6'0" **Wt:** 195 **Born:** 8/3/1998 **Age:** 22

Year	Team	Lg	G	AB	H	2B	3B	HR	(Hm	Rd)	TB	R	RBI	RC	TBB	IBB	SO	HBP	SH	SF	SB	CS	GDP	Avg	OBP	Slg	OPS
2020	Bos	AL	25	72	18	2	0	1	(0	1)	23	8	9	12	8	0	21	0	0	0	0	0	0	.250	.325	.319	.644

Chris Archer

Pitches: R **Bats:** R **Pos:** P   **Ht:** 6'2" **Wt:** 195 **Born:** 9/26/1988 **Age:** 32

			HOW MUCH PITCHED					WHAT HE GAVE UP										THE RESULTS							
Year	Team	Lg	G	GS	GF	IP	BFP	H	R	ER	HR	SH	SF	HB	TBB	IBB	SO	WP	W	L	Pct	Sv-Op Hld	Vel	OPS	ERC	ERA
2012	TB	AL	6	4	1	29.1	122	23	17	15	3	1	0	1	13	0	36	2	1	3	.250	0-0 0	94	.624	3.24	4.60
2013	TB	AL	23	23	0	128.2	525	107	49	46	15	1	5	8	38	2	101	7	9	7	.563	0-0 0	95	.660	3.13	3.22
2014	TB	AL	32	32	0	194.2	822	177	85	72	12	4	9	8	72	1	173	8	10	9	.526	0-0 0	95	.650	3.36	3.33
2015	TB	AL	34	34	0	212.0	868	175	85	76	19	2	2	3	66	0	252	13	12	13	.480	0-0 0	95	.613	2.79	3.23
2016	TB	AL	33	33	0	201.1	850	183	100	90	30	6	4	3	67	0	233	11	9	19	.321	0-0 0	94	.703	3.66	4.02
2017	TB	AL	34	34	0	201.0	852	193	101	91	27	1	2	5	60	0	249	15	10	12	.455	0-0 0	95	.710	3.75	4.07
2018	2 Tms		27	27	0	148.1	638	155	77	71	19	1	3	6	49	3	162	6	6	8	.429	0-0 0	95	.767	4.41	4.31
2019	Pit	NL	23	23	0	119.2	526	114	73	69	25	6	3	4	55	3	143	6	3	9	.250	0-0 0	94	.793	4.89	5.19
18	TB	AL	17	17	0	96.0	413	102	50	46	11	0	1	4	31	0	102	3	3	5	.375	0-0 0	95	.751	4.43	4.31
18	Pit	NL	10	10	0	52.1	225	53	27	25	8	1	2	2	18	3	60	3	3	3	.500	0-0 0	95	.796	4.36	4.30
	Postseason		2	0	0	1.2	6	1	0	0	0	0	1	0	0	0	2	0	0	0	-	0-0 0	96	.367	0.75	0.00
	8 ML YEARS		212	210	1	1235.0	5203	1127	587	530	150	22	28	38	420	8	1349	68	60	80	.429	0-0 0	95	.691	3.61	3.86

Orlando Arcia

Bats: R **Throws:** R **Pos:** SS-57;PH-2;PR-2;CF-1   ARR-see-ya   **Ht:** 6'0" **Wt:** 187 **Born:** 8/4/1994 **Age:** 26

Year	Team	Lg	G	AB	H	2B	3B	HR	(Hm	Rd)	TB	R	RBI	RC	TBB	IBB	SO	HBP	SH	SF	SB	CS	GDP	Avg	OBP	Slg	OPS
2016	Mil	NL	55	201	44	10	3	4	(2	2)	72	21	17	20	15	0	47	0	0	0	8	0	6	.219	.273	.358	.631
2017	Mil	NL	153	506	140	17	2	15	(8	7)	206	56	53	63	36	9	100	1	2	3	14	7	10	.277	.324	.407	.731
2018	Mil	NL	119	348	82	16	0	3	(2	1)	107	32	30	26	15	0	87	1	1	1	7	4	9	.236	.268	.307	.576

Year	Team	Lg	G	AB	H	2B	3B	HR	(Hm	Rd)	TB	R	RBI	RC	TBB	IBB	SO	HBP	SH	SF	SB	CS	GDP	Avg	OBP	Slg	OPS
2019	Mil	NL	152	494	110	16	1	15	(6	9)	197	51	59	48	43	5	109	1	2	6	8	5	15	.223	.301	.350	.633
2020	Mil	NL	59	173	45	10	1	5	(2	3)	72	22	20	19	14	0	32	1	0	1	2	0	10	.260	.317	.416	.734
	Postseason		11	37	12	0	0	3	(1	2)	21	7	4	4	1	1	5	0	0	0	0	0	1	.324	.342	.568	.910
	5 ML YEARS		538	1722	421	69	7	42	(20	22)	630	182	179	176	123	14	375	4	5	11	39	16	50	.244	.295	.366	.660

Nolan Arenado

Bats: R **Throws:** R **Pos:** 3B-48   ahr-eh-NOD-oh   **Ht:** 6'2" **Wt:** 215 **Born:** 4/16/1991 **Age:** 30

Year	Team	Lg	G	AB	H	2B	3B	HR	(Hm	Rd)	TB	R	RBI	RC	TBB	IBB	SO	HBP	SH	SF	SB	CS	GDP	Avg	OBP	Slg	OPS
2013	Col	NL	133	486	130	29	4	10	(5	5)	197	49	52	48	23	1	72	1	2	2	2	0	16	.267	.301	.405	.706
2014	Col	NL	111	432	124	34	2	18	(16	2)	216	58	61	60	25	1	58	4	1	5	2	1	13	.287	.328	.500	.828
2015	Col	NL	157	616	177	43	4	42	(20	22)	354	97	130	116	34	13	110	4	0	11	2	5	17	.287	.323	.575	.898
2016	Col	NL	160	618	182	35	6	41	(25	16)	352	116	133	128	68	10	103	2	0	8	2	3	17	.294	.362	.570	.932
2017	Col	NL	159	606	187	43	7	37	(19	18)	355	100	130	130	62	9	106	4	1	6	3	2	21	.309	.373	.586	.959
2018	Col	NL	156	590	175	38	2	38	(23	15)	331	104	110	117	73	10	122	3	1	6	2	2	16	.297	.374	.561	.935
2019	Col	NL	155	588	185	31	2	41	(21	20)	343	102	118	123	62	11	93	4	0	8	3	2	14	.315	.379	.583	.962
2020	Col	NL	48	182	46	9	0	8	(7	1)	79	23	26	18	15	3	20	0	0	4	0	0	7	.253	.303	.434	.738
	Postseason		5	21	4	0	0	1	(0	1)	7	2	3	0	0	0	7	0	0	2	0	0	0	.190	.174	.333	.507
	8 ML YEARS		1079	4118	1206	262	27	235	(136	99)	2227	649	760	740	362	58	684	22	5	50	16	15	121	.293	.349	.541	.890

Shawn Armstrong

Pitches: R **Bats:** R **Pos:** RP-14   **Ht:** 6'2" **Wt:** 225 **Born:** 9/11/1990 **Age:** 30

			HOW MUCH PITCHED				WHAT HE GAVE UP										THE RESULTS							
Year	Team	Lg	G	GS	GF	IP	BFP	H	R	ER	HR	SH	SF	HB	TBB	IBB	SO	WP	W	L	Pct	Sv-Op	Hld	Vel	OPS	ERC	ERA
2015	Cle	AL	8	0	5	8.0	30	5	2	2	1	1	0	0	2	0	11	0	0	0	-	0-0	0	94	.590	1.84	2.25
2016	Cle	AL	10	0	2	10.2	44	9	3	3	1	1	0	0	5	2	7	1	0	0	-	0-0	0	92	.668	3.25	2.53
2017	Cle	AL	21	0	14	24.2	108	23	12	12	5	0	0	1	10	0	20	1	1	0	1.000	0-0	0	93	.737	4.50	4.38
2018	Sea	AL	14	0	3	14.2	57	9	2	2	1	0	2	3	3	1	15	0	0	1	.000	1-1	0	94	.569	1.91	1.23
2019	2 Tms		55	0	10	58.0	271	66	38	37	8	1	3	4	29	1	63	4	1	1	.500	4-9	9	93	.815	5.74	5.74
2020	Bal	AL	14	0	2	15.0	57	9	6	3	1	0	0	1	9	0	14	2	2	0	1.000	0-0	0	94	.530	1.51	1.80
19	Sea		4	0	1	3.2	23	8	6	6	1	1	0	1	3	1	3	0	0	1	.000	0-0	0	93	1.268	16.16	14.73
19	Bal		51	0	9	54.1	248	58	32	31	7	0	3	3	26	0	60	4	1	0	1.000	4-9	9	93	.777	5.14	5.13
	6 ML YEARS		122	0	36	131.0	567	121	63	59	17	2	5	9	52	4	130	8	4	2	.667	5-10	14	93	.723	4.04	4.05

Randy Arozarena

Bats: R **Throws:** R **Pos:** LF-14;DH-5;RF-3;PH-3;CF-2;PR-1   ah-row-sah-RAY-nah   **Ht:** 5'11" **Wt:** 185 **Born:** 2/28/1995 **Age:** 26

Year	Team	Lg	G	AB	H	2B	3B	HR	(Hm	Rd)	TB	R	RBI	RC	TBB	IBB	SO	HBP	SH	SF	SB	CS	GDP	Avg	OBP	Slg	OPS
2019	StL	NL	19	20	6	1	0	1	(0	1)	10	4	2	3	2	0	4	1	0	0	2	1	0	.300	.391	.500	.891
2020	TB	AL	23	64	18	2	0	7	(2	5)	41	15	11	15	6	0	22	5	0	1	4	0	2	.281	.382	.641	1.022
	Postseason		5	4	0	0	0	0	(0	0)	0	0	0	0	0	0	3	1	0	0	1	0	0	.000	.200	.000	.200
	2 ML YEARS		42	84	24	3	0	8	(2	6)	51	19	13	18	8	0	26	6	0	1	6	1	2	.286	.384	.607	.991

Luis Arraez

Bats: L **Throws:** R **Pos:** 2B-31;PH-1   ah-RYE-ez   **Ht:** 5'10" **Wt:** 175 **Born:** 4/9/1997 **Age:** 24

Year	Team	Lg	G	AB	H	2B	3B	HR	(Hm	Rd)	TB	R	RBI	RC	TBB	IBB	SO	HBP	SH	SF	SB	CS	GDP	Avg	OBP	Slg	OPS
2019	Min	AL	92	326	109	20	1	4	(1	3)	143	54	28	59	36	1	29	1	0	3	2	2	2	.334	.399	.439	.838
2020	Min	AL	32	112	36	9	0	0	(0	0)	45	16	13	22	8	0	11	0	0	1	0	0	2	.321	.364	.402	.765
	Postseason		3	11	5	4	0	0	(0	0)	9	1	1	2	0	0	2	0	0	0	0	0	1	.455	.455	.818	1.273
	2 ML YEARS		124	438	145	29	1	4	(1	3)	188	70	41	81	44	1	40	1	0	4	2	2	4	.331	.390	.429	.819

Jake Arrieta

Pitches: R **Bats:** R **Pos:** SP-9   air-ee-ETT-uh   **Ht:** 6'4" **Wt:** 230 **Born:** 3/6/1986 **Age:** 35

			HOW MUCH PITCHED					WHAT HE GAVE UP										THE RESULTS							
Year	Team	Lg	G	GS	GF	IP	BFP	H	R	ER	HR	SH	SF	HB	TBB	IBB	SO	WP	W	L	Pct	Sv-Op	Hld	Vel	OPS	ERC	ERA
2010	Bal	AL	18	18	0	100.1	449	106	57	52	9	4	2	4	48	3	52	5	6	6	.500	0-0	0	93	.767	4.74	4.66
2011	Bal	AL	22	22	0	119.1	523	115	70	67	21	3	2	4	59	2	93	0	10	8	.556	0-0	0	92	.791	4.93	5.05
2012	Bal	AL	24	18	0	114.2	496	122	82	79	16	3	4	5	35	3	109	4	3	9	.250	0-0	1	93	.763	4.47	6.20
2013	2 Tms		14	14	0	75.1	324	59	41	40	9	2	3	5	41	1	60	1	5	4	.556	0-0	0	94	.718	3.82	4.78
2014	ChC	NL	25	25	0	156.2	614	114	46	44	5	3	3	3	41	2	167	8	10	5	.667	0-0	0	94	.535	1.85	2.53
2015	ChC	NL	33	33	0	229.0	870	150	52	45	10	4	1	6	48	2	236	6	22	6	.786	0-0	0	95	.507	1.53	1.77
2016	ChC	NL	31	31	0	197.1	795	138	72	68	16	2	1	6	76	1	190	16	18	8	.692	0-0	0	94	.583	2.45	3.10
2017	ChC	NL	30	30	0	168.1	707	150	82	66	23	1	4	10	55	3	163	14	14	10	.583	0-0	0	92	.716	3.64	3.53
2018	Phi	NL	31	31	0	172.2	724	165	93	76	21	1	8	7	57	0	138	11	10	11	.476	0-0	0	93	.724	3.92	3.96
2019	Phi	NL	24	24	0	135.2	594	149	76	70	21	5	4	7	51	3	110	7	8	8	.500	0-0	0	93	.799	5.19	4.64
2020	Phi	NL	9	9	0	44.1	190	51	25	25	6	0	2	1	16	0	32	4	4	4	.500	0-0	0	92	.814	5.34	5.08
13	Bal	AL	5	5	0	23.2	111	25	19	19	2	0	3	2	17	1	23	1	1	2	.333	0-0	0	94	.857	5.91	7.23
13	ChC	NL	9	9	0	51.2	213	34	22	21	7	2	0	3	24	0	37	0	4	2	.667	0-0	0	94	.648	2.94	3.66
	Postseason		9	9	0	52.2	218	36	19	18	6	1	1	5	21	1	66	3	5	3	.625	0-0	0	94	.623	2.79	3.08
	11 ML YEARS		261	255	1	1513.2	6286	1319	696	632	157	30	34	58	527	20	1350	76	110	79	.582	0-0	1	93	.677	3.35	3.76

Christian Arroyo

Bats: R **Throws:** R **Pos:** 2B-13;SS-2;3B-1   **Ht:** 6'1" **Wt:** 210 **Born:** 5/30/1995 **Age:** 26

Year	Team	Lg	G	AB	H	2B	3B	HR	(Hm	Rd)	TB	R	RBI	RC	TBB	IBB	SO	HBP	SH	SF	SB	CS	GDP	Avg	OBP	Slg	OPS
2017	SF	NL	34	125	24	5	0	3	(2	1)	38	9	14	7	8	1	32	1	0	1	1	2	4	.192	.244	.304	.548
2018	TB	AL	20	53	14	2	1	1	(1	0)	21	5	6	9	6	0	16	0	0	0	0	0	0	.264	.339	.396	.735
2019	TB	AL	16	50	11	2	0	2	(2	0)	19	8	7	6	5	0	18	1	1	0	0	0	0	.220	.304	.380	.684
2020	2 Tms	AL	15	50	12	1	0	3	(1	2)	22	7	8	10	4	0	11	0	0	0	0	0	2	.240	.296	.440	.736
20	Cle	AL	1	0	0	0	0	0	(0	0)	0	0	0	0	0	0	0	0	0	0	0	0	0	-	-	-	-
20	Bos	AL	14	50	12	1	0	3	(1	2)	22	7	8	10	4	0	11	0	0	0	0	0	2	.240	.296	.440	.736
	4 ML YEARS		85	278	61	10	1	9	(6	3)	100	29	35	32	23	1	77	2	1	1	1	2	6	.219	.283	.360	.643

Willians Astudillo

Bats: R **Throws:** R **Pos:** C-6;PH-3   **Ht:** 5'9" **Wt:** 225 **Born:** 10/14/1991 **Age:** 29

Year	Team	Lg	G	AB	H	2B	3B	HR	(Hm	Rd)	TB	R	RBI	RC	TBB	IBB	SO	HBP	SH	SF	SB	CS	GDP	Avg	OBP	Slg	OPS
2018	Min	AL	30	93	33	4	1	3	(1	2)	48	9	21	17	2	0	3	1	0	1	0	0	4	.355	.371	.516	.887
2019	Min	AL	58	190	51	9	0	4	(1	3)	72	28	21	19	5	0	8	5	0	4	0	0	6	.268	.299	.379	.678
2020	Min	AL	8	16	4	1	0	1	(1	0)	8	4	3	1	0	0	2	0	0	0	0	0	0	.250	.250	.500	.750
	3 ML YEARS		96	299	88	14	1	8	(3	5)	128	41	45	37	7	0	13	6	0	5	0	0	10	.294	.319	.428	.747

Alex Avila

Bats: L **Throws:** R **Pos:** C-22;DH-1;PH-1   ah-VEE-lah   **Ht:** 5'11" **Wt:** 210 **Born:** 1/29/1987 **Age:** 34

Year	Team	Lg	G	AB	H	2B	3B	HR	(Hm	Rd)	TB	R	RBI	RC	TBB	IBB	SO	HBP	SH	SF	SB	CS	GDP	Avg	OBP	Slg	OPS
2009	Det	AL	29	61	17	4	0	5	(4	1)	36	9	14	12	10	0	18	0	0	1	0	0	0	.279	.375	.590	.965
2010	Det	AL	104	294	67	12	0	7	(4	3)	100	28	31	26	36	0	71	2	1	0	2	2	12	.228	.316	.340	.656
2011	Det	AL	141	464	137	33	4	19	(10	9)	235	63	82	86	73	9	131	3	3	8	3	1	8	.295	.389	.506	.895
2012	Det	AL	116	367	89	21	2	9	(7	2)	141	42	48	53	61	2	104	2	2	2	2	0	12	.243	.352	.384	.736
2013	Det	AL	102	330	75	14	1	11	(7	4)	124	39	47	37	44	0	112	1	1	3	0	0	10	.227	.317	.376	.693
2014	Det	AL	124	390	85	22	0	11	(3	8)	140	44	47	48	61	1	151	3	1	2	0	3	6	.218	.327	.359	.686
2015	Det	AL	67	178	34	5	0	4	(2	2)	51	21	13	20	40	0	66	0	1	0	0	1	4	.191	.339	.287	.626
2016	CWS	AL	57	169	36	6	0	7	(5	2)	63	19	11	17	38	0	78	1	0	1	0	0	3	.213	.359	.373	.732
2017	2 Tms		112	311	82	13	1	14	(8	6)	139	41	49	55	62	2	120	1	1	1	0	1	10	.264	.387	.447	.834
2018	Ari	NL	80	194	32	6	0	7	(1	6)	59	13	20	17	37	2	90	1	0	2	0	0	4	.165	.299	.304	.603
2019	Ari	NL	63	164	34	8	0	9	(5	4)	69	22	24	23	36	7	68	1	0	0	1	0	8	.207	.353	.421	.774
2020	Min	AL	23	49	9	2	0	1	(1	0)	14	6	2	11	11	0	22	2	0	0	0	0	2	.184	.355	.286	.641
17	Det	AL	77	219	60	11	0	11	(6	5)	104	30	32	37	43	2	80	1	0	1	0	1	6	.274	.394	.475	.869
17	ChC	NL	35	92	22	2	1	3	(2	1)	35	11	17	18	19	0	40	0	1	0	0	0	4	.239	.369	.380	.750
	Postseason		35	111	17	2	0	3	(2	1)	28	6	7	5	11	0	43	1	1	0	0	0	1	.153	.236	.252	.488
	12 ML YEARS		1018	2971	697	146	8	104	(57	47)	1171	347	388	398	509	23	1031	17	10	20	8	8	79	.235	.348	.394	.742

Luis Avilan

Pitches: L **Bats:** L **Pos:** RP-10   ah-VEE-lan   **Ht:** 6'2" **Wt:** 220 **Born:** 7/19/1989 **Age:** 31

| | | | HOW MUCH PITCHED | | | | | WHAT HE GAVE UP | | | | | | | | | | | THE RESULTS | | | | | | | |
Year	Team	Lg	G	GS	GF	IP	BFP	H	R	ER	HR	SH	SF	HB	TBB	IBB	SO	WP	W	L	Pct	Sv-Op	Hld	Vel	OPS	ERC	ERA
2012	Atl	NL	31	0	2	36.0	142	27	9	8	1	3	0	1	10	1	33	3	1	0	1.000	0-0	5	92	.547	2.00	2.00
2013	Atl	NL	75	0	7	65.0	256	40	12	11	1	1	1	4	22	2	38	3	5	0	1.000	0-2	27	93	.478	1.62	1.52
2014	Atl	NL	62	0	14	43.1	193	47	22	22	2	3	2	3	21	7	25	5	4	1	.800	0-2	8	93	.764	4.55	4.57
2015	2 Tms	NL	73	0	9	53.1	220	48	24	24	6	1	2	1	15	2	49	2	2	5	.286	0-3	17	94	.665	3.18	4.05
2016	LAD	NL	27	0	3	19.2	82	12	8	7	2	2	0	1	10	4	28	1	3	0	1.000	0-1	3	92	.491	1.84	3.20
2017	LAD	NL	61	0	5	46.0	194	42	16	15	2	0	0	1	22	3	52	1	2	3	.400	0-2	13	93	.703	3.57	2.93
2018	2 Tms		70	0	8	45.1	197	44	22	19	3	1	1	2	18	3	51	2	2	1	.667	2-5	9	91	.692	3.70	3.77
2019	NYM	NL	45	0	8	32.0	141	33	18	18	5	0	0	3	14	0	30	2	4	0	1.000	0-0	9	90	.782	5.28	5.06
2020	NYY	AL	10	0	1	8.1	39	9	4	4	2	0	0	0	5	0	9	0	0	0	-	0-0	1	91	.830	6.32	4.32
15	Atl	AL	50	0	7	37.2	154	35	15	15	4	0	1	0	10	2	31	1	2	4	.333	0-3	11	94	.670	3.16	3.58
15	LAD	NL	23	0	2	15.2	66	13	9	9	2	1	1	1	5	0	18	1	0	1	.000	0-0	6	94	.654	3.21	5.17
18	CWS	AL	58	0	7	39.2	172	40	20	17	2	1	1	2	14	2	46	2	2	1	.667	2-4	9	91	.685	3.68	3.86
18	Phi	NL	12	0	1	5.2	25	4	2	2	1	0	0	0	4	1	5	0	0	0	-	0-1	0	91	.749	3.81	3.18
	Postseason		11	0	2	7.2	31	7	0	0	0	0	1	0	2	1	6	1	0	0	-	0-1	2	93	.576	2.30	0.00
	9 ML YEARS		454	0	57	349.0	1464	302	135	128	22	11	6	17	137	22	315	19	23	10	.697	2-15	85	93	.649	3.17	3.30

Dakota Bacus

Pitches: R **Bats:** R **Pos:** RP-11   **Ht:** 6'2" **Wt:** 220 **Born:** 4/2/1991 **Age:** 30

| | | | HOW MUCH PITCHED | | | | | WHAT HE GAVE UP | | | | | | | | | | | THE RESULTS | | | | | | | |
Year	Team	Lg	G	GS	GF	IP	BFP	H	R	ER	HR	SH	SF	HB	TBB	IBB	SO	WP	W	L	Pct	Sv-Op	Hld	Vel	OPS	ERC	ERA
2020	Was	NL	11	0	3	11.1	57	14	10	10	1	0	1	0	9	0	7	0	0	0	-	0-0	2	91	.808	6.85	7.94

Harrison Bader

Bats: R **Throws:** R **Pos:** CF-49;PR-5;PH-1   **Ht:** 6'0" **Wt:** 210 **Born:** 6/3/1994 **Age:** 27

Year	Team	Lg	G	AB	H	2B	3B	HR	(Hm	Rd)	TB	R	RBI	RC	TBB	IBB	SO	HBP	SH	SF	SB	CS	GDP	Avg	OBP	Slg	OPS
2017	StL	NL	32	85	20	3	0	3	(0	3)	32	10	10	10	5	1	24	1	0	1	2	1	1	.235	.283	.376	.659
2018	StL	NL	138	379	100	20	2	12	(2	10)	160	61	37	54	31	3	125	11	2	4	15	3	1	.264	.334	.422	.756

Year Team	Lg	G	AB	H	2B	3B	HR	(Hm	Rd)	TB	R	RBI	RC	TBB	IBB	SO	HBP	SH	SF	SB	CS	GDP	Avg	OBP	Slg	OPS
								BATTING												RUNNING			AVERAGES			
2019 StL	NL	128	347	71	14	3	12	(5	7)	127	54	39	41	46	4	117	10	1	2	11	3	3	.205	.314	.366	.680
2020 StL	NL	50	106	24	7	2	4	(4	0)	47	21	11	16	13	0	40	5	0	1	3	1	2	.226	.336	.443	.779
Postseason		6	12	2	0	0	0	(0	0)	2	2	1	0	1	0	6	0	0	0	1	1	0	.167	.231	.167	.397
4 ML YEARS		348	917	215	44	7	31	(11	20)	366	146	97	121	95	8	306	27	3	8	31	8	7	.234	.322	.399	.721

Javier Baez

Bats: R **Throws:** R **Pos:** SS-56;LF-1;DH-1;PH-1   BYE-ezz   **Ht:** 6'0" **Wt:** 190 **Born:** 12/1/1992 **Age:** 28

Year Team	Lg	G	AB	H	2B	3B	HR	(Hm	Rd)	TB	R	RBI	RC	TBB	IBB	SO	HBP	SH	SF	SB	CS	GDP	Avg	OBP	Slg	OPS
								BATTING												RUNNING			AVERAGES			
2014 ChC	NL	52	213	36	6	0	9	(3	6)	69	25	20	12	15	0	95	1	0	0	5	1	5	.169	.227	.324	.551
2015 ChC	NL	28	76	22	6	0	1	(1	0)	31	4	4	5	4	1	24	0	0	0	1	2	0	.289	.325	.408	.733
2016 ChC	NL	142	421	115	19	1	14	(8	6)	178	50	59	53	15	3	108	11	1	2	12	3	8	.273	.314	.423	.737
2017 ChC	NL	145	469	128	24	2	23	(13	10)	225	75	75	69	30	15	144	1	6	2	10	3	10	.273	.317	.480	.796
2018 ChC	NL	160	606	176	40	9	34	(13	21)	336	101	**111**	96	29	8	167	5	1	4	21	9	10	.290	.326	.554	.881
2019 ChC	NL	138	531	149	38	4	29	(15	14)	282	89	85	82	28	3	156	1	0	2	11	7	16	.281	.316	.531	.847
2020 ChC	NL	59	222	45	9	1	8	(2	6)	80	27	24	15	7	0	75	4	0	2	3	0	6	.203	.238	.360	.599
Postseason		34	114	26	5	0	5	(4	1)	46	12	14	13	5	0	38	0	0	1	7	0	3	.228	.258	.404	.662
7 ML YEARS		724	2538	671	142	17	118	(55	63)	1201	371	378	332	128	30	769	22	8	12	63	25	57	.264	.304	.473	.777

Michel Baez

Pitches: R **Bats:** R **Pos:** RP-2; SP-1   BYE-ezz   **Ht:** 6'8" **Wt:** 220 **Born:** 1/21/1996 **Age:** 25

Year Team	Lg	G	GS	GF	IP	BFP	H	R	ER	HR	SH	SF	HB	TBB	IBB	SO	WP	W	L	Pct	Sv-Op	Hld	Vel	OPS	ERC	ERA
			HOW MUCH PITCHED					WHAT HE GAVE UP												THE RESULTS						
2019 SD	NL	24	1	8	29.2	131	25	10	10	3	1	1	3	14	2	28	1	1	1	.500	0-0	0	95	.689	3.69	3.03
2020 SD	NL	3	1	1	4.2	23	7	4	4	0	0	0	0	2	0	7	0	0	0	-	0-1	0	95	.820	6.19	7.71
2 ML YEARS		27	2	9	34.1	154	32	14	14	3	1	1	3	16	2	35	1	1	1	.500	0-1	0	96	.709	4.01	3.67

Pedro Baez

Pitches: R **Bats:** R **Pos:** RP-18   BYE-ezz   **Ht:** 6'0" **Wt:** 232 **Born:** 3/11/1988 **Age:** 33

Year Team	Lg	G	GS	GF	IP	BFP	H	R	ER	HR	SH	SF	HB	TBB	IBB	SO	WP	W	L	Pct	Sv-Op	Hld	Vel	OPS	ERC	ERA
			HOW MUCH PITCHED					WHAT HE GAVE UP												THE RESULTS						
2014 LAD	NL	20	0	8	24.0	92	16	7	7	3	1	0	1	5	1	18	0	0	0	-	0-0	5	95	.537	1.79	2.63
2015 LAD	NL	52	0	8	51.0	208	47	22	19	4	3	3	1	11	1	60	1	4	2	.667	0-3	11	97	.693	2.87	3.35
2016 LAD	NL	73	0	10	74.0	295	52	27	25	11	1	2	2	22	0	83	3	3	2	.600	0-2	23	97	.615	2.52	3.04
2017 LAD	NL	66	0	6	64.0	280	56	24	21	9	0	0	2	29	2	64	1	3	6	.333	0-3	23	97	.728	3.84	2.95
2018 LAD	NL	55	0	6	56.1	237	46	19	18	4	2	2	1	23	2	62	0	4	3	.571	0-1	7	96	.652	2.91	2.88
2019 LAD	NL	71	0	9	69.2	276	43	30	24	6	2	0	4	23	1	69	0	7	2	.778	1-7	25	96	.543	1.97	3.10
2020 LAD	NL	18	0	2	17.0	70	10	8	6	2	0	0	0	7	0	13	0	0	0	-	2-2	6	94	.529	2.01	3.18
Postseason		23	0	1	21.2	95	17	14	10	4	1	0	2	13	1	23	0	1	0	1.000	0-0	2	97	.745	4.56	4.15
7 ML YEARS		355	0	51	356.0	1458	270	137	120	39	9	8	10	120	7	369	5	21	15	.583	3-18	100	96	.631	2.67	3.03

Brandon Bailey

Pitches: R **Bats:** R **Pos:** RP-5   **Ht:** 5'10" **Wt:** 195 **Born:** 10/19/1994 **Age:** 26

Year Team	Lg	G	GS	GF	IP	BFP	H	R	ER	HR	SH	SF	HB	TBB	IBB	SO	WP	W	L	Pct	Sv-Op	Hld	Vel	OPS	ERC	ERA
			HOW MUCH PITCHED					WHAT HE GAVE UP												THE RESULTS						
2020 Hou	AL	5	0	1	7.1	30	6	2	2	1	0	0	1	3	0	4	1	0	0	-	0-0	0	92	.756	4.10	2.45

Homer Bailey

Pitches: R **Bats:** R **Pos:** SP-2   **Ht:** 6'4" **Wt:** 223 **Born:** 5/3/1986 **Age:** 35

Year Team	Lg	G	GS	GF	IP	BFP	H	R	ER	HR	SH	SF	HB	TBB	IBB	SO	WP	W	L	Pct	Sv-Op	Hld	Vel	OPS	ERC	ERA
			HOW MUCH PITCHED					WHAT HE GAVE UP												THE RESULTS						
2007 Cin	NL	9	9	0	45.1	205	43	32	29	7	1	6	3	28	1	28	1	4	2	.667	0-0	0	92	.758	4.61	5.76
2008 Cin	NL	8	8	0	36.1	180	59	36	32	8	5	2	0	17	1	18	0	0	6	.000	0-0	0	91	1.024	9.31	7.93
2009 Cin	NL	20	20	0	113.1	496	115	61	57	12	4	4	3	52	1	86	6	8	5	.615	0-0	0	94	.740	4.56	4.53
2010 Cin	NL	19	19	0	109.0	465	109	55	54	11	2	1	3	40	6	100	3	4	3	.571	0-0	0	93	.744	4.01	4.46
2011 Cin	NL	22	22	0	132.0	561	136	68	65	18	4	4	5	33	2	106	4	9	7	.563	0-0	0	93	.728	4.01	4.43
2012 Cin	NL	33	**33**	0	208.0	874	206	97	85	26	5	5	8	52	3	168	3	13	10	.565	0-0	0	92	.718	3.73	3.68
2013 Cin	NL	32	32	0	209.0	849	181	85	81	20	8	4	10	54	2	199	5	11	12	.478	0-0	0	94	.660	2.99	3.49
2014 Cin	NL	23	23	0	145.2	604	134	60	60	16	5	4	7	45	1	124	1	9	5	.643	0-0	0	94	.703	3.57	3.71
2015 Cin	NL	2	2	0	11.1	51	16	7	7	3	0	0	0	4	2	3	0	0	1	.000	0-0	0	91	1.009	7.64	5.56
2016 Cin	NL	6	6	0	23.0	111	35	19	17	2	0	2	2	7	0	27	1	2	3	.400	0-0	0	93	.816	7.04	6.65
2017 Cin	NL	18	18	0	91.0	420	112	67	65	11	5	2	8	42	2	67	4	6	9	.400	0-0	0	93	.875	6.26	6.43
2018 Cin	NL	20	20	0	106.1	494	141	82	72	23	5	3	6	33	**9**	75	2	1	14	.067	0-0	0	93	.901	6.32	6.09
2019 2 Tms	AL	31	31	0	163.1	696	162	84	83	21	2	5	4	53	1	149	4	13	9	.591	0-0	0	93	.719	4.01	4.57
2020 Min	AL	2	2	0	8.0	33	6	3	3	1	0	0	1	3	0	7	0	1	0	1.000	0-0	0	91	.648	3.32	3.38
19 KC	AL	18	18	0	90.0	389	89	49	48	12	1	3	2	38	0	81	2	7	6	.538	0-0	0	93	.741	4.45	4.80
19 Oak	AL	13	13	0	73.1	307	73	35	35	9	1	2	2	15	1	68	2	6	3	.667	0-0	0	93	.691	3.49	4.30
Postseason		2	1	0	9.0	32	3	1	1	0	1	1	1	1	0	12	0	0	0	-	0-0	0	94	.268	0.52	1.00
14 ML YEARS		245	245	0	1401.2	6039	1455	756	710	175	46	42	56	463	31	1157	42	81	86	.485	0-0	0	93	.753	4.32	4.56

Anthony Banda

Pitches: L Bats: L Pos: RP-4   Ht: 6'2" Wt: 230 Born: 8/10/1993 Age: 27

Year	Team	Lg	G	GS	GF	IP	BFP	H	R	ER	HR	SH	SF	HB	TBB	IBB	SO	WP	W	L	Pct	Sv-Op	Hld	Vel	OPS	ERC	ERA
2017	Ari	NL	8	4	1	25.2	115	26	17	17	1	0	0	3	10	1	25	2	2	3	.400	0-0	0	94	.771	3.98	5.96
2018	TB	AL	3	1	1	14.2	56	12	6	6	1	1	1	0	3	0	10	0	1	0	1.000	0-0	0	95	.665	2.32	3.68
2019	TB	AL	3	0	1	4.0	18	6	3	3	0	0	0	0	0	0	2	0	0	0	-	0-0	0	93	.889	4.47	6.75
2020	TB	AL	4	0	3	7.0	36	10	9	8	1	0	0	2	5	0	4	0	1	0	1.000	1-1	0	92	1.127	10.08	10.29
4 ML YEARS			18	5	6	51.1	225	54	35	34	3	1	1	5	18	1	41	2	4	3	.571	1-1	0	94	.809	4.24	5.96

Caleb Baragar

Pitches: L Bats: R Pos: RP-23; SP-1   Ht: 6'3" Wt: 215 Born: 4/9/1994 Age: 27

Year	Team	Lg	G	GS	GF	IP	BFP	H	R	ER	HR	SH	SF	HB	TBB	IBB	SO	WP	W	L	Pct	Sv-Op	Hld	Vel	OPS	ERC	ERA
2020	SF	NL	24	1	2	22.1	88	17	10	10	3	0	1	1	5	0	19	1	5	1	.833	0-1	2	94	.656	2.57	4.03

Daniel Bard

Pitches: R Bats: R Pos: RP-23   Ht: 6'4" Wt: 197 Born: 6/25/1985 Age: 36

Year	Team	Lg	G	GS	GF	IP	BFP	H	R	ER	HR	SH	SF	HB	TBB	IBB	SO	WP	W	L	Pct	Sv-Op	Hld	Vel	OPS	ERC	ERA
2009	Bos	AL	49	0	12	49.1	212	41	24	20	5	4	3	3	22	3	63	1	2	2	.500	1-4	13	97	.690	3.43	3.65
2010	Bos	AL	73	0	12	74.2	295	45	18	16	6	2	5	2	30	3	76	2	1	2	.333	3-10	32	98	.540	1.99	1.93
2011	Bos	AL	70	0	10	73.0	288	46	29	27	5	5	0	2	24	3	74	2	2	9	.182	1-6	34	97	.546	1.80	3.33
2012	Bos	AL	17	10	2	59.1	277	60	42	41	9	3	8	3	43	1	38	1	5	6	.455	0-0	0	93	.852	6.55	6.22
2013	Bos	AL	2	0	1	1.0	6	1	1	1	0	0	0	0	2	0	1	0	0	0	-	0-0	0	99	.750	9.51	9.00
2020	Col	NL	23	0	10	24.2	106	22	10	10	2	0	0	3	10	2	27	1	4	2	.667	6-6	2	97	.674	3.73	3.65
Postseason			2	0	1	3.0	8	0	0	0	0	0	0	0	0	0	4	0	0	0	-	0-0	1	98	.000	0.00	0.00
6 ML YEARS			234	10	47	282.0	1184	215	124	115	27	14	11	18	131	12	279	7	14	21	.400	11-26	81	97	.652	3.20	3.67

Luke Bard

Pitches: R Bats: R Pos: RP-6   Ht: 6'3" Wt: 200 Born: 11/13/1990 Age: 30

Year	Team	Lg	G	GS	GF	IP	BFP	H	R	ER	HR	SH	SF	HB	TBB	IBB	SO	WP	W	L	Pct	Sv-Op	Hld	Vel	OPS	ERC	ERA
2018	LAA	AL	8	0	3	11.2	53	10	7	7	4	0	0	3	5	1	13	1	0	0	-	0-0	0	92	.829	5.95	5.40
2019	LAA	AL	32	3	5	49.0	199	41	27	26	8	0	1	5	13	1	40	5	3	3	.500	0-1	1	94	.691	3.52	4.78
2020	LAA	AL	6	0	3	5.1	23	7	4	4	2	0	0	0	0	0	7	0	0	0	-	0-0	1	94	1.000	5.96	6.75
3 ML YEARS			46	3	11	66.0	275	58	38	37	14	0	1	8	18	2	60	6	3	3	.500	0-1	2	94	.745	4.12	5.05

Scott Barlow

Pitches: R Bats: R Pos: RP-32   Ht: 6'3" Wt: 215 Born: 12/18/1992 Age: 28

Year	Team	Lg	G	GS	GF	IP	BFP	H	R	ER	HR	SH	SF	HB	TBB	IBB	SO	WP	W	L	Pct	Sv-Op	Hld	Vel	OPS	ERC	ERA
2018	KC	AL	6	0	3	15.0	65	16	7	6	2	0	0	0	3	0	15	0	1	1	.500	0-0	0	91	.679	3.73	3.60
2019	KC	AL	61	0	7	70.1	310	64	33	33	6	2	1	3	37	3	92	5	3	3	.500	1-3	14	94	.735	4.03	4.22
2020	KC	AL	32	0	7	30.0	125	27	14	14	4	0	1	2	9	2	39	2	2	1	.667	2-2	7	95	.693	3.54	4.20
3 ML YEARS			99	0	17	115.1	500	107	54	53	12	2	2	5	49	5	146	7	6	5	.545	3-5	21	94	.717	3.87	4.14

Austin Barnes

Bats: R Throws: R Pos: C-28;DH-1;PH-1   Ht: 5'10" Wt: 187 Born: 12/28/1989 Age: 31

Year	Team	Lg	G	AB	H	2B	3B	HR	(Hm	Rd)	TB	R	RBI	RC	TBB	IBB	SO	HBP	SH	SF	SB	CS	GDP	Avg	OBP	Slg	OPS
2015	LAD	NL	20	29	6	2	0	0	(0	0)	8	4	1	3	6	0	6	1	1	0	1	0	2	.207	.361	.276	.637
2016	LAD	NL	21	32	5	1	0	0	(0	0)	6	2	2	3	5	0	9	0	0	0	0	0	0	.156	.270	.188	.458
2017	LAD	NL	102	218	63	15	2	8	(6	2)	106	35	38	46	39	1	43	5	0	0	4	1	6	.289	.408	.486	.895
2018	LAD	NL	100	200	41	5	0	4	(2	2)	58	32	14	15	31	4	67	6	1	0	4	3	7	.205	.329	.290	.619
2019	LAD	NL	75	212	43	12	1	5	(4	1)	72	28	25	18	23	3	56	5	0	2	3	0	8	.203	.293	.340	.633
2020	LAD	NL	29	86	21	3	0	1	(1	0)	27	14	9	12	13	0	24	2	2	1	3	0	1	.244	.353	.314	.667
Postseason			27	76	12	2	0	1	(0	1)	17	9	7	4	7	0	25	1	0	1	1	0	2	.158	.235	.224	.459
6 ML YEARS			347	777	179	38	3	18	(13	5)	277	116	89	97	117	8	205	19	4	3	15	4	23	.230	.344	.356	.700

Jacob Barnes

Pitches: R Bats: R Pos: RP-18   Ht: 6'2" Wt: 231 Born: 4/14/1990 Age: 31

Year	Team	Lg	G	GS	GF	IP	BFP	H	R	ER	HR	SH	SF	HB	TBB	IBB	SO	WP	W	L	Pct	Sv-Op	Hld	Vel	OPS	ERC	ERA
2016	Mil	NL	27	0	7	26.2	106	24	9	8	1	1	1	0	6	1	26	2	0	1	.000	1-1	0	95	.612	2.50	2.70
2017	Mil	NL	73	0	8	72.0	304	57	35	32	8	0	3	3	33	4	80	6	3	4	.429	2-7	24	97	.664	3.31	4.00
2018	Mil	NL	49	0	19	48.2	217	51	24	18	4	1	1	0	23	2	47	4	0	1	.000	2-4	1	96	.723	4.39	3.33
2019	2 Tms		33	1	6	32.2	160	36	30	27	7	0	2	0	22	1	32	3	1	5	.167	0-0	1	94	.840	6.34	7.44
2020	LAA	AL	18	0	5	18.0	78	19	13	11	1	1	2	2	4	0	24	0	0	2	.000	0-0	1	95	.716	3.77	5.50
19	Mil	NL	18	1	3	19.2	95	22	17	15	3	0	1	0	11	1	22	1	1	1	.500	0-0	0	94	.769	5.40	6.86
19	KC	AL	15	0	3	13.0	65	14	13	12	4	0	1	0	11	0	10	2	0	4	.000	0-0	0	94	.951	7.85	8.31
5 ML YEARS			200	1	45	198.0	865	187	111	96	21	3	9	5	88	8	209	15	4	13	.235	5-12	30	95	.709	3.97	4.36

Matt Barnes

Pitches: R **Bats:** R **Pos:** RP-24 **Ht:** 6'4" **Wt:** 208 **Born:** 6/17/1990 **Age:** 31

Year	Team	Lg	HOW MUCH PITCHED					WHAT HE GAVE UP										THE RESULTS							
			G	GS	GF	IP	BFP	H	R	ER	HR	SH	SF	HB	TBB	IBB	SO	WP	W	L	Pct	Sv-Op	Hld	Vel	OPS	ERC	ERA
2014	Bos	AL	5	0	3	9.0	39	11	4	4	1	0	1	0	2	0	8	0	0	0	-	0-0	0	94	.861	4.72	4.00
2015	Bos	AL	32	2	7	43.0	199	56	28	26	9	2	0	2	15	0	39	4	3	4	.429	0-0	3	95	.887	6.66	5.44
2016	Bos	AL	62	0	13	66.2	287	62	32	30	6	2	1	3	31	1	71	4	4	3	.571	1-2	16	97	.709	4.06	4.05
2017	Bos	AL	70	0	15	69.2	287	57	31	30	7	1	3	1	28	0	83	3	7	3	.700	1-3	21	95	.655	3.20	3.88
2018	Bos	AL	62	0	8	61.2	265	47	25	25	5	0	2	2	31	1	96	8	6	4	.600	0-3	25	97	.624	3.08	3.65
2019	Bos	AL	70	0	14	64.1	285	51	29	27	8	0	1	2	38	2	110	13	5	4	.556	4-12	26	97	.666	3.81	3.78
2020	Bos	AL	24	0	14	23.0	102	18	13	11	4	1	1	2	14	1	31	4	1	3	.250	9-13	4	96	.706	4.43	4.30
	Postseason		11	0	0	10.1	42	6	2	1	1	0	0	0	6	0	10	2	2	0	1.000	0-0	3	96	.536	2.55	0.87
7 ML YEARS			325	2	74	337.1	1464	302	162	153	40	6	9	12	159	5	438	36	26	21	.553	15-33	95	96	.704	3.99	4.08

Tucker Barnhart

Bats: L **Throws:** R **Pos:** C-36;1B-2;PH-2 **Ht:** 5'11" **Wt:** 192 **Born:** 1/7/1991 **Age:** 30

Year	Team	Lg	BATTING																			RUNNING			AVERAGES			
			G	AB	H	2B	3B	HR	(Hm	Rd)	TB	R	RBI	RC	TBB	IBB	SO	HBP	SH	SF	SB	CS	GDP	Avg	OBP	Slg	OPS
2014	Cin	NL	21	54	10	0	0	1	(1	0)	13	3	1	2	4	1	10	0	2	0	0	0	0	.185	.241	.241	.482
2015	Cin	NL	81	242	61	9	0	3	(2	1)	79	23	18	22	25	5	45	2	2	3	0	1	10	.252	.324	.326	.650
2016	Cin	NL	115	377	97	23	1	7	(6	1)	143	34	51	51	36	8	72	2	2	3	1	0	12	.257	.323	.379	.702
2017	Cin	NL	121	370	100	24	2	7	(2	5)	149	26	44	50	42	11	68	3	5	3	4	0	12	.270	.347	.403	.750
2018	Cin	NL	138	460	114	21	3	10	(7	3)	171	50	46	48	54	2	96	2	3	3	0	4	13	.248	.328	.372	.699
2019	Cin	NL	114	316	73	14	0	11	(5	6)	120	32	40	40	44	7	83	2	1	1	1	0	5	.231	.328	.380	.708
2020	Cin	NL	38	98	20	3	0	5	(4	1)	38	10	13	11	12	0	28	0	0	0	0	0	2	.204	.291	.388	.679
7 ML YEARS			628	1917	475	94	6	44	(27	17)	713	178	213	224	217	34	402	11	15	13	6	5	54	.248	.326	.372	.698

Franklin Barreto

Bats: R **Throws:** R **Pos:** PR-8;2B-6;SS-4;PH-4;3B-2;LF-1;DH-1 **Ht:** 5'10" **Wt:** 208 **Born:** 2/27/1996 **Age:** 25

Year	Team	Lg	BATTING																			RUNNING			AVERAGES			
			G	AB	H	2B	3B	HR	(Hm	Rd)	TB	R	RBI	RC	TBB	IBB	SO	HBP	SH	SF	SB	CS	GDP	Avg	OBP	Slg	OPS
2017	Oak	AL	25	71	14	1	2	2	(1	1)	25	10	6	5	5	0	33	0	0	0	2	0	1	.197	.250	.352	.602
2018	Oak	AL	32	73	17	4	0	5	(1	4)	36	10	16	11	1	0	29	1	0	0	0	0	3	.233	.253	.493	.746
2019	Oak	AL	23	57	7	2	0	2	(1	1)	15	6	5	1	1	0	23	0	0	0	1	0	0	.123	.138	.263	.401
2020	2 Tms		21	27	2	0	0	0	(0	0)	2	5	2	0	0	0	15	1	0	0	1	0	0	.074	.107	.074	.181
20	Oak	AL	15	10	0	0	0	0	(0	0)	0	5	0	0	0	0	7	0	0	0	0	0	0	.000	.000	.000	.000
20	LAA	AL	6	17	2	0	0	0	(0	0)	2	0	2	0	0	0	8	1	0	0	1	0	0	.118	.167	.118	.284
4 ML YEARS			101	228	40	7	2	9	(3	6)	78	31	29	17	7	0	100	2	0	0	4	0	4	.175	.207	.342	.549

Aaron Barrett

Pitches: R **Bats:** R **Pos:** RP-2 **Ht:** 6'3" **Wt:** 230 **Born:** 1/2/1988 **Age:** 33

Year	Team	Lg	HOW MUCH PITCHED					WHAT HE GAVE UP											THE RESULTS							
			G	GS	GF	IP	BFP	H	R	ER	HR	SH	SF	HB	TBB	IBB	SO	WP	W	L	Pct	Sv-Op	Hld	Vel	OPS	ERC	ERA
2014	Was	NL	50	0	12	40.2	174	33	17	12	1	2	1	2	20	2	49	6	3	0	1.000	0-0	8	94	.605	2.87	2.66
2015	Was	NL	40	0	8	29.1	123	28	15	15	1	0	0	3	7	0	35	1	3	3	.500	0-3	10	94	.636	3.17	4.60
2019	Was	NL	3	0	0	2.1	16	5	4	4	1	0	0	0	4	0	1	1	0	0	-	0-0	0	92	1.229	21.72	15.43
2020	Was	NL	2	0	0	1.2	9	2	2	2	0	0	1	0	2	1	1	0	0	0	-	0-0	0	90	.889	9.50	10.80
	Postseason		2	0	0	0.1	3	1	0	0	0	0	0	0	2	1	0	1	0	0	-	0-0	0	94	3.000	44.72	0.00
4 ML YEARS			95	0	20	74.0	322	68	38	33	3	1	2	5	33	3	86	8	6	3	.667	0-3	18	94	.654	3.56	4.01

Jaime Barria

Pitches: R **Bats:** R **Pos:** SP-5; RP-2 HIGH-may **Ht:** 6'1" **Wt:** 210 **Born:** 7/18/1996 **Age:** 24

Year	Team	Lg	HOW MUCH PITCHED					WHAT HE GAVE UP											THE RESULTS							
			G	GS	GF	IP	BFP	H	R	ER	HR	SH	SF	HB	TBB	IBB	SO	WP	W	L	Pct	Sv-Op	Hld	Vel	OPS	ERC	ERA
2018	LAA	AL	26	26	0	129.1	537	117	50	49	17	0	0	6	47	0	98	3	10	9	.526	0-0	0	91	.719	3.89	3.41
2019	LAA	AL	19	13	1	82.2	365	92	61	59	24	0	2	2	27	0	75	1	4	10	.286	0-0	0	92	.903	5.85	6.42
2020	LAA	AL	7	5	2	32.1	132	27	13	13	3	0	1	1	9	1	27	0	1	0	1.000	0-0	0	92	.685	2.76	3.62
3 ML YEARS			52	44	3	244.1	1034	236	124	121	44	0	3	9	83	1	200	4	15	19	.441	0-0	0	91	.780	4.37	4.46

Joey Bart

Bats: R **Throws:** R **Pos:** C-32;DH-1;PH-1 **Ht:** 6'2" **Wt:** 238 **Born:** 12/15/1996 **Age:** 24

Year	Team	Lg	BATTING																			RUNNING			AVERAGES			
			G	AB	H	2B	3B	HR	(Hm	Rd)	TB	R	RBI	RC	TBB	IBB	SO	HBP	SH	SF	SB	CS	GDP	Avg	OBP	Slg	OPS
2018	2 Tms	Low	51	204	60	15	3	13	(-	-)	120	38	40	42	13	2	47	10	0	1	2	1	9	.294	.364	.588	.952
2019	SnJos	A+	57	234	62	10	2	12	(-	-)	112	37	37	36	14	0	50	3	0	0	5	2	10	.265	.315	.479	.793
2019	Rchmd	AA	22	79	25	4	1	4	(-	-)	43	9	11	14	7	1	21	0	0	0	0	2	2	.316	.368	.544	.912
2020	SF	NL	33	103	24	5	2	0	(0	0)	33	15	7	8	3	0	41	5	0	0	0	0	1	.233	.288	.320	.609

Luis Alexander Basabe

Bats: B **Throws:** R **Pos:** RF-5;LF-3;PR-2 **Ht:** 6'0" **Wt:** 180 **Born:** 8/26/1996 **Age:** 24

Year	Team	Lg	BATTING																			RUNNING			AVERAGES			
			G	AB	H	2B	3B	HR	(Hm	Rd)	TB	R	RBI	RC	TBB	IBB	SO	HBP	SH	SF	SB	CS	GDP	Avg	OBP	Slg	OPS
2020	SF	NL	9	14	2	0	0	0	(0	0)	2	5	1	2	4	0	5	0	0	0	2	0	0	.143	.333	.143	.476

Tyler Bashlor

Pitches: R Bats: R Pos: RP-8 **Ht: 6'0" Wt: 195 Born: 4/16/1993 Age: 28**

Year	Team	Lg	G	GS	GF	IP	BFP	H	R	ER	HR	SH	SF	HB	TBB	IBB	SO	WP	W	L	Pct	Sv-Op	Hld	Vel	OPS	ERC	ERA
2018	NYM	NL	24	0	6	32.0	135	26	16	15	6	1	0	3	12	0	25	1	0	3	.000	0-0	0	96	.726	3.89	4.22
2019	NYM	NL	24	0	7	22.0	103	21	17	17	6	1	1	0	17	2	20	0	0	3	.000	0-3	1	96	.861	6.46	6.95
2020	Pit	NL	8	0	3	8.1	38	9	8	8	2	0	0	2	4	0	6	1	0	0	-	0-0	0	95	1.020	7.24	8.64
3 ML YEARS			56	0	16	62.1	276	56	41	40	14	2	1	5	33	2	51	2	0	6	.000	0-3	1	96	.815	5.19	5.78

Anthony Bass

Pitches: R Bats: R Pos: RP-26 **Ht: 6'2" Wt: 200 Born: 11/1/1987 Age: 33**

Year	Team	Lg	G	GS	GF	IP	BFP	H	R	ER	HR	SH	SF	HB	TBB	IBB	SO	WP	W	L	Pct	Sv-Op	Hld	Vel	OPS	ERC	ERA
2011	SD	NL	27	3	6	48.1	198	41	9	9	3	2	0	1	21	1	24	1	2	0	1.000	0-0	4	93	.655	3.28	1.68
2012	SD	NL	24	15	3	97.0	411	89	59	51	10	2	2	1	39	3	80	5	2	8	.200	1-1	1	92	.719	3.65	4.73
2013	SD	NL	24	0	9	42.0	173	51	26	25	4	1	0	0	26	4	31	5	0	0	-	0-0	0	92	.829	5.41	5.36
2014	Hou	AL	21	0	8	27.0	119	32	20	19	6	0	1	2	7	1	7	2	1	1	.500	2-4	4	94	.840	5.74	6.33
2015	Tex	AL	33	0	9	64.0	272	66	33	32	5	3	3	1	20	1	45	1	0	0	-	0-1	0	93	.756	3.81	4.50
2017	Tex	AL	2	0	1	5.2	31	14	9	9	1	0	1	0	0	0	1	1	0	0	-	0-0	0	92	1.152	12.41	14.29
2018	ChC	NL	16	0	3	15.1	62	18	6	5	1	0	0	0	3	0	14	2	0	0	-	0-0	3	94	.729	4.26	2.93
2019	Sea	AL	44	0	14	48.0	189	30	20	19	5	2	1	1	17	2	43	6	2	4	.333	5-10	6	95	.560	2.04	3.56
2020	Tor	AL	26	0	14	25.2	100	17	13	10	2	1	0	0	9	2	21	0	2	3	.400	7-9	3	95	.563	1.97	3.51
9 ML YEARS			217	18	67	373.0	1575	358	195	179	37	11	8	6	136	14	266	23	9	16	.360	15-25	21	93	.721	3.74	4.32

Chris Bassitt

Pitches: R Bats: R Pos: SP-11 **Ht: 6'5" Wt: 217 Born: 2/22/1989 Age: 32**

Year	Team	Lg	G	GS	GF	IP	BFP	H	R	ER	HR	SH	SF	HB	TBB	IBB	SO	WP	W	L	Pct	Sv-Op	Hld	Vel	OPS	ERC	ERA
2014	CWS	AL	6	5	1	29.2	137	34	13	13	0	1	1	3	13	1	21	0	1	1	.500	0-0	0	92	.721	4.57	3.94
2015	Oak	AL	18	13	3	86.0	361	78	36	34	5	1	1	9	30	0	64	5	1	8	.111	0-0	0	93	.684	3.55	3.56
2016	Oak	AL	5	5	0	28.0	133	35	20	19	5	0	0	0	14	0	23	2	0	2	.000	0-0	0	93	.856	6.44	6.11
2018	Oak	AL	11	7	0	47.2	204	40	21	16	4	0	0	4	19	0	41	2	2	3	.400	0-0	0	92	.624	3.37	3.02
2019	Oak	AL	28	25	0	144.0	612	125	66	61	21	2	5	13	47	0	141	3	10	5	.667	0-0	0	94	.698	3.68	3.81
2020	Oak	AL	11	11	0	63.0	261	56	18	16	6	1	1	2	17	0	55	2	5	2	.714	0-0	0	93	.659	3.05	2.29
6 ML YEARS			79	66	6	398.1	1708	368	174	159	41	5	8	31	140	1	345	14	19	21	.475	0-0	0	93	.694	3.76	3.59

Trevor Bauer

Pitches: R Bats: R Pos: SP-11 **Ht: 6'1" Wt: 205 Born: 1/17/1991 Age: 30**

Year	Team	Lg	G	GS	GF	IP	BFP	H	R	ER	HR	SH	SF	HB	TBB	IBB	SO	WP	W	L	Pct	Sv-Op	Hld	Vel	OPS	ERC	ERA
2012	Ari	NL	4	4	0	16.1	77	14	13	11	2	1	1	1	13	0	17	2	1	2	.333	0-0	0	92	.795	5.12	6.06
2013	Cle	AL	4	4	0	17.0	81	15	11	10	3	0	1	1	16	0	11	1	1	2	.333	0-0	0	93	.840	6.47	5.29
2014	Cle	AL	26	26	0	153.0	663	151	76	71	16	1	8	11	60	4	143	6	5	8	.385	0-0	0	94	.737	4.27	4.18
2015	Cle	AL	31	30	1	176.0	744	152	90	89	23	4	1	5	79	1	170	7	11	12	.478	0-0	0	93	.713	3.86	4.55
2016	Cle	AL	35	28	3	190.0	811	179	96	90	20	4	7	9	70	1	168	3	12	8	.600	0-0	0	93	.712	3.85	4.26
2017	Cle	AL	32	31	1	176.1	749	181	84	82	25	1	3	5	60	0	196	3	17	9	.654	0-0	0	94	.774	4.46	4.19
2018	Cle	AL	28	27	1	175.1	717	134	51	43	9	3	3	9	57	2	221	12	12	6	.667	1-1	0	95	.582	2.41	2.21
2019	2 Tms		34	34	0	213.0	911	184	118	106	34	5	5	19	82	0	253	10	11	13	.458	0-0	0	95	.743	4.00	4.48
2020	Cin	NL	11	11	0	73.0	278	41	17	14	9	0	0	3	17	1	100	3	5	4	.556	0-0	0	94	.522	**1.59**	**1.73**
19	Cle	AL	24	24	0	156.2	664	127	76	66	22	2	3	14	63	0	185	8	9	8	.529	0-0	0	95	.707	3.65	3.79
19	Cin	NL	10	10	0	56.1	247	57	42	40	12	3	2	5	19	0	68	2	2	5	.286	0-0	0	94	.841	5.02	6.39
	Postseason		10	6	1	26.0	116	31	16	11	4	0	1	0	8	1	32	1	1	4	.200	0-1	0	94	.832	5.06	3.81
9 ML YEARS			205	195	6	1190.0	5031	1051	556	516	141	19	29	63	454	9	1279	47	75	64	.540	1-1	0	94	.704	3.69	3.90

Jeremy Beasley

Pitches: R Bats: R Pos: RP-1 **Ht: 6'3" Wt: 245 Born: 11/20/1995 Age: 25**

Year	Team	Lg	G	GS	GF	IP	BFP	H	R	ER	HR	SH	SF	HB	TBB	IBB	SO	WP	W	L	Pct	Sv-Op	Hld	Vel	OPS	ERC	ERA
2020	Ari	NL	1	0	1	0.1	3	2	0	0	0	0	0	0	0	0	1	0	0	0	-	0-0	0	92	1.667	39.65	0.00

Matt Beaty

Bats: L Throws: R Pos: 1B-13;DH-5;PH-3;LF-2;PR-1 **Ht: 6'0" Wt: 215 Born: 4/28/1993 Age: 28**

Year	Team	Lg	G	AB	H	2B	3B	HR	(Hm	Rd)	TB	R	RBI	RC	TBB	IBB	SO	HBP	SH	SF	SB	CS	GDP	Avg	OBP	Slg	OPS
2019	LAD	NL	99	249	66	19	1	9	(5	4)	114	36	46	42	17	2	33	2	0	6	5	0	6	.265	.317	.458	.775
2020	LAD	NL	21	50	11	1	0	2	(0	2)	18	8	5	5	2	0	14	2	0	0	0	0	3	.220	.278	.360	.638
	Postseason		4	8	3	0	0	0	(0	0)	3	1	0	0	0	0	1	0	0	0	0	0	0	.375	.375	.375	.750
2 ML YEARS			120	299	77	20	1	11	(5	6)	132	44	51	47	19	2	47	4	0	6	5	0	9	.258	.311	.441	.752

David Bednar

Pitches: R Bats: L Pos: RP-4   Ht: 6'1" Wt: 249 Born: 10/10/1994 Age: 26

Year Team	Lg	G	GS	GF	IP	BFP	H	R	ER	HR	SH	SF	HB	TBB	IBB	SO	WP	W	L	Pct	Sv-Op	Hld	Vel	OPS	ERC	ERA
2019 SD	NL	13	0	4	11.0	48	10	8	8	3	2	1	0	5	0	14	0	0	2	.000	0-0	2	95	.876	4.89	6.55
2020 SD	NL	4	0	3	6.1	32	11	6	5	1	0	0	0	2	0	5	0	0	0	-	0-0	0	96	.973	8.59	7.11
2 ML YEARS		17	0	7	17.1	80	21	14	13	4	2	1	0	7	0	19	0	0	2	.000	0-0	2	96	.916	6.19	6.75

Cam Bedrosian

Pitches: R Bats: R Pos: RP-11   beh-DROH-zhee-ann   Ht: 6'1" Wt: 225 Born: 10/2/1991 Age: 29

Year Team	Lg	G	GS	GF	IP	BFP	H	R	ER	HR	SH	SF	HB	TBB	IBB	SO	WP	W	L	Pct	Sv-Op	Hld	Vel	OPS	ERC	ERA
2014 LAA	AL	17	0	4	19.1	93	23	17	14	2	0	1	0	12	1	20	1	0	1	.000	0-1	1	94	.801	5.88	6.52
2015 LAA	AL	34	0	10	33.1	156	40	21	20	3	1	2	2	19	2	34	2	1	0	1.000	0-0	1	94	.833	6.05	5.40
2016 LAA	AL	45	0	9	40.1	162	30	7	5	1	0	1	2	14	1	51	3	2	0	1.000	1-2	7	95	.532	2.25	1.12
2017 LAA	AL	48	0	13	44.2	190	41	26	22	5	1	1	0	17	1	53	7	6	5	.545	6-11	10	94	.705	3.56	4.43
2018 LAA	AL	71	0	7	64.0	271	63	30	27	7	1	1	2	26	0	57	1	5	4	.556	1-8	10	93	.738	4.31	3.80
2019 LAA	AL	59	7	5	61.1	258	48	30	22	7	0	1	3	22	0	64	9	3	3	.500	1-3	15	93	.619	2.96	3.23
2020 LAA	AL	11	0	3	14.2	58	10	4	4	0	0	1	0	6	0	11	1	0	0	-	0-0	0	92	.531	1.90	2.45
7 ML YEARS		285	7	51	277.2	1188	255	135	114	25	3	8	9	116	5	290	24	17	13	.567	9-25	44	94	.685	3.72	3.70

Tyler Beede

Pitches: R Bats: R Pos: P   Ht: 6'2" Wt: 216 Born: 5/23/1993 Age: 28

Year Team	Lg	G	GS	GF	IP	BFP	H	R	ER	HR	SH	SF	HB	TBB	IBB	SO	WP	W	L	Pct	Sv-Op	Hld	Vel	OPS	ERC	ERA
2018 SF	NL	2	2	0	7.2	40	9	7	7	0	0	0	1	8	0	9	0	0	1	.000	0-0	0	92	.869	7.41	8.22
2019 SF	NL	24	22	0	117.0	523	127	70	66	22	1	3	5	46	1	113	9	5	10	.333	0-0	0	94	.803	5.29	5.08
2 ML YEARS		26	24	0	124.2	563	136	77	73	22	1	3	6	54	1	122	9	5	11	.313	0-0	0	94	.808	5.44	5.27

Jalen Beeks

Pitches: L Bats: L Pos: RP-12   Ht: 5'11" Wt: 215 Born: 7/10/1993 Age: 27

Year Team	Lg	G	GS	GF	IP	BFP	H	R	ER	HR	SH	SF	HB	TBB	IBB	SO	WP	W	L	Pct	Sv-Op	Hld	Vel	OPS	ERC	ERA
2018 2 Tms	AL	14	1	0	50.2	223	52	31	31	6	1	1	3	24	0	42	0	5	1	.833	0-0	0	92	.794	4.97	5.51
2019 TB	AL	33	3	5	104.1	464	115	56	50	12	1	5	9	40	1	89	3	6	3	.667	1-1	2	92	.789	5.07	4.31
2020 TB	AL	12	0	3	19.1	81	21	9	7	1	1	0	0	4	0	26	2	1	1	.500	1-1	2	93	.694	3.48	3.26
18 Bos	AL	2	1	0	6.1	34	11	9	9	1	0	0	1	4	0	5	0	0	1	.000	0-0	0	91	1.160	11.16	12.79
18 TB	AL	12	0	0	44.1	189	41	22	22	5	1	1	2	20	0	37	0	5	0	1.000	0-0	0	92	.729	4.20	4.47
3 ML YEARS		59	4	8	174.1	768	188	96	88	19	3	6	12	68	1	157	5	12	5	.706	2-2	4	92	.780	4.86	4.54

Josh Bell

Bats: B Throws: R Pos: 1B-35;DH-21;PH-2   Ht: 6'4" Wt: 250 Born: 8/14/1992 Age: 28

Year Team	Lg	G	AB	H	2B	3B	HR	(Hm	Rd)	TB	R	RBI	RC	TBB	IBB	SO	HBP	SH	SF	SB	CS	GDP	Avg	OBP	Slg	OPS
2016 Pit	NL	45	128	35	8	0	3	(2	1)	52	18	19	18	21	0	19	0	0	3	0	1	4	.273	.368	.406	.775
2017 Pit	NL	159	549	140	26	6	26	(11	15)	256	75	90	86	66	4	117	1	0	4	2	4	15	.255	.334	.466	.800
2018 Pit	NL	148	501	131	31	4	12	(5	7)	206	74	62	73	77	2	104	0	0	5	2	5	12	.261	.357	.411	.768
2019 Pit	NL	143	527	146	37	3	37	(17	20)	300	94	116	112	74	13	118	5	0	1	0	1	11	.277	.367	.569	.936
2020 Pit	NL	57	195	44	3	0	8	(2	6)	71	22	22	25	22	4	59	2	0	4	0	0	3	.226	.305	.364	.669
5 ML YEARS		552	1900	496	105	13	86	(37	49)	885	283	309	314	260	23	417	8	0	23	4	11	45	.261	.349	.466	.814

Cody Bellinger

Bats: L Throws: L Pos: CF-39;1B-19;DH-2;RF-1   Ht: 6'4" Wt: 203 Born: 7/13/1995 Age: 25

Year Team	Lg	G	AB	H	2B	3B	HR	(Hm	Rd)	TB	R	RBI	RC	TBB	IBB	SO	HBP	SH	SF	SB	CS	GDP	Avg	OBP	Slg	OPS
2017 LAD	NL	132	480	128	26	4	39	(19	20)	279	87	97	94	64	13	146	1	0	3	10	3	5	.267	.352	.581	.933
2018 LAD	NL	162	557	145	28	7	25	(11	14)	262	84	76	88	69	9	151	3	0	3	14	1	7	.260	.343	.470	.814
2019 LAD	NL	156	558	170	34	3	47	(27	20)	351	121	115	124	95	21	108	3	0	4	15	5	10	.305	.406	.629	1.035
2020 LAD	NL	56	213	51	10	0	12	(3	9)	97	33	30	34	30	2	42	0	0	0	6	1	4	.239	.333	.455	.789
Postseason		36	135	24	6	1	4	(0	4)	44	17	13	10	10	0	52	0	0	0	8	1	1	.178	.234	.326	.560
4 ML YEARS		506	1808	494	98	14	123	(60	63)	989	325	318	340	258	45	447	7	0	10	45	10	26	.273	.364	.547	.911

Brandon Belt

Bats: L Throws: L Pos: 1B-47;PH-6;DH-1   Ht: 6'3" Wt: 231 Born: 4/20/1988 Age: 33

Year Team	Lg	G	AB	H	2B	3B	HR	(Hm	Rd)	TB	R	RBI	RC	TBB	IBB	SO	HBP	SH	SF	SB	CS	GDP	Avg	OBP	Slg	OPS
2011 SF	NL	63	187	42	6	1	9	(2	7)	77	21	18	20	20	1	57	2	0	0	3	2	3	.225	.306	.412	.718
2012 SF	NL	145	411	113	27	6	7	(5	2)	173	47	56	63	54	5	106	3	4	1	12	2	2	.275	.360	.421	.781
2013 SF	NL	150	509	147	39	4	17	(6	11)	245	76	67	82	52	4	125	6	1	3	5	2	4	.289	.360	.481	.841
2014 SF	NL	61	214	52	8	0	12	(2	10)	96	30	27	24	18	2	64	2	0	1	3	1	4	.243	.306	.449	.755
2015 SF	NL	137	492	138	33	5	18	(5	13)	235	73	68	78	56	2	147	4	0	4	9	3	3	.280	.356	.478	.834
2016 SF	NL	156	542	149	41	8	17	(6	11)	257	77	82	105	104	4	148	5	0	4	0	4	7	.275	.394	.474	.868
2017 SF	NL	104	382	92	27	3	18	(8	10)	179	63	51	60	66	2	104	2	0	1	3	2	5	.241	.355	.469	.823
2018 SF	NL	112	399	101	18	2	14	(8	6)	165	50	46	63	49	6	107	6	0	2	4	0	2	.253	.342	.414	.756

Year Team	Lg	G	AB	H	2B	3B	HR	(Hm	Rd)	TB	R	RBI	RC	TBB	IBB	SO	HBP	SH	SF	SB	CS	GDP	Avg	OBP	Slg	OPS
2019 SF	NL	156	526	123	32	3	17	(5	12)	212	76	57	72	83	3	127	3	0	4	4	3	6	.234	.339	.403	.742
2020 SF	NL	51	149	46	13	1	9	(7	2)	88	25	30	32	30	1	36	0	0	0	0	0	5	.309	.425	.591	1.015
Postseason		37	127	29	2	2	2	(1	1)	41	14	13	16	21	1	40	0	0	3	1	2	6	.228	.331	.323	.654
10 ML YEARS		1135	3811	1003	244	33	138	(54	84)	1727	538	502	599	532	30	1021	33	1	23	43	19	41	.263	.356	.453	.810

Anthony Bemboom

Bats: L Throws: R Pos: C-20;PR-1 　　Ht: 6'2" Wt: 200 Born: 1/18/1990 Age: 31

Year Team	Lg	G	AB	H	2B	3B	HR	(Hm	Rd)	TB	R	RBI	RC	TBB	IBB	SO	HBP	SH	SF	SB	CS	GDP	Avg	OBP	Slg	OPS
2019 2 Tms	AL	25	54	7	1	0	1	(1	0)	11	2	4	1	1	0	21	0	1	0	0	0	0	.130	.145	.204	.349
2020 LAA	AL	21	48	10	1	0	3	(0	3)	20	9	5	5	7	0	13	2	2	1	0	1	0	.208	.328	.417	.744
19 TB	AL	3	5	2	1	0	0	(0	0)	3	0	1	1	0	0	2	0	0	0	0	0	0	.400	.400	.600	1.000
19 LAA	AL	22	49	5	0	0	1	(1	0)	8	2	3	0	1	0	19	0	1	0	0	0	0	.102	.120	.163	.283
2 ML YEARS		46	102	17	2	0	4	(1	3)	31	11	9	6	8	0	34	2	3	1	0	1	0	.167	.239	.304	.543

Andrew Benintendi

Bats: L Throws: L Pos: LF-13;PH-2 　　Ht: 5'9" Wt: 180 Born: 7/6/1994 Age: 26

Year Team	Lg	G	AB	H	2B	3B	HR	(Hm	Rd)	TB	R	RBI	RC	TBB	IBB	SO	HBP	SH	SF	SB	CS	GDP	Avg	OBP	Slg	OPS
2016 Bos	AL	34	105	31	11	1	2	(0	2)	50	16	14	20	10	0	25	1	1	1	1	0	0	.295	.359	.476	.835
2017 Bos	AL	151	573	155	26	1	20	(7	13)	243	84	90	96	70	7	112	6	1	8	20	5	16	.271	.352	.424	.776
2018 Bos	AL	148	579	168	41	6	16	(7	9)	269	103	87	105	71	1	106	2	2	7	21	3	9	.290	.366	.465	.830
2019 Bos	AL	138	541	144	40	5	13	(8	5)	233	72	68	88	59	1	140	7	3	5	10	3	6	.266	.343	.431	.774
2020 Bos	AL	14	39	4	1	0	0	(0	0)	5	4	1	1	11	0	17	1	1	0	1	2	1	.103	.314	.128	.442
Postseason		21	81	22	5	0	2	(1	1)	33	18	9	13	5	0	17	1	0	0	2	0	2	.272	.322	.407	.729
5 ML YEARS		485	1837	502	119	13	51	(22	29)	800	279	260	310	221	9	400	17	8	21	53	13	32	.273	.353	.435	.789

Wes Benjamin

Pitches: L Bats: R Pos: RP-7; SP-1 　　Ht: 6'2" Wt: 210 Born: 7/26/1993 Age: 27

Year Team	Lg	G	GS	GF	IP	BFP	H	R	ER	HR	SH	SF	HB	TBB	IBB	SO	WP	W	L	Pct	Sv-Op	Hld	Vel	OPS	ERC	ERA
2020 Tex	AL	8	1	0	22.1	98	24	12	12	4	0	0	0	7	0	21	0	2	1	.667	0-0	0	91	.745	4.60	4.84

Travis Bergen

Pitches: L Bats: L Pos: RP-8 　　Ht: 6'1" Wt: 215 Born: 10/8/1993 Age: 27

Year Team	Lg	G	GS	GF	IP	BFP	H	R	ER	HR	SH	SF	HB	TBB	IBB	SO	WP	W	L	Pct	Sv-Op	Hld	Vel	OPS	ERC	ERA
2019 SF	NL	21	0	8	19.2	85	18	12	12	4	0	0	1	9	2	18	1	2	0	1.000	0-0	0	91	.823	4.62	5.49
2020 2 Tms		8	0	2	8.1	36	5	3	3	1	0	0	0	9	0	11	0	1	0	1.000	1-1	0	92	.722	4.93	3.24
20 Tor	AL	1	0	0	1.2	6	1	0	0	0	0	0	0	1	0	3	0	0	0	-	0-0	0	94	.533	2.46	0.00
20 Ari	NL	7	0	2	6.2	30	4	3	3	1	0	0	0	8	0	8	0	1	0	1.000	1-1	0	92	.764	5.59	4.05
2 ML YEARS		29	0	10	28.0	121	23	15	15	5	0	0	1	18	2	29	1	3	0	1.000	1-1	0	91	.798	4.73	4.82

Jose Berrios

Pitches: R Bats: R Pos: SP-12 　　beh-REE-ohs 　　Ht: 6'0" Wt: 205 Born: 5/27/1994 Age: 27

Year Team	Lg	G	GS	GF	IP	BFP	H	R	ER	HR	SH	SF	HB	TBB	IBB	SO	WP	W	L	Pct	Sv-Op	Hld	Vel	OPS	ERC	ERA
2016 Min	AL	14	14	0	58.1	281	74	56	52	12	2	0	5	35	0	49	1	3	7	.300	0-0	0	93	.932	7.85	8.02
2017 Min	AL	26	25	0	145.2	616	131	71	63	15	3	4	13	48	0	139	7	14	8	.636	0-0	0	93	.693	3.62	3.89
2018 Min	AL	32	32	0	192.1	797	159	83	82	25	2	4	13	61	0	202	2	12	11	.522	0-0	0	93	.665	3.26	3.84
2019 Min	AL	32	32	0	200.1	842	194	94	82	26	2	6	9	51	0	195	8	14	8	.636	0-0	0	93	.707	3.69	3.68
2020 Min	AL	12	12	0	63.0	271	57	28	28	8	0	2	3	26	0	68	5	5	4	.556	0-0	0	94	.701	3.95	4.00
Postseason		2	1	0	7.0	33	9	6	4	1	0	0	0	3	0	10	0	0	1	.000	0-0	0	95	.864	6.07	5.14
5 ML YEARS		116	115	0	659.2	2807	615	332	307	86	9	16	43	221	1	653	23	48	38	.558	0-0	0	93	.713	3.90	4.19

Jon Berti

Bats: R Throws: R Pos: 2B-21;CF-9;RF-7;3B-5;SS-2;PH-2;PR-1 　　Ht: 5'10" Wt: 190 Born: 1/22/1990 Age: 31

Year Team	Lg	G	AB	H	2B	3B	HR	(Hm	Rd)	TB	R	RBI	RC	TBB	IBB	SO	HBP	SH	SF	SB	CS	GDP	Avg	OBP	Slg	OPS
2018 Tor	AL	4	15	4	1	1	0	(0	0)	7	2	2	2	0	0	4	0	0	0	1	0	0	.267	.267	.467	.733
2019 Mia	NL	73	256	70	14	1	6	(3	3)	104	52	24	37	24	0	73	6	0	1	17	3	2	.273	.348	.406	.755
2020 Mia	NL	39	120	31	5	0	2	(1	1)	42	21	14	22	23	0	37	3	2	1	9	2	1	.258	.388	.350	.738
3 ML YEARS		116	391	105	20	2	8	(4	4)	153	75	40	61	47	0	114	9	2	2	27	5	3	.269	.359	.391	.750

Dellin Betances

Pitches: R Bats: R Pos: RP-15 　　DELL-inn buh-TAN-siss 　　Ht: 6'8" Wt: 265 Born: 3/23/1988 Age: 33

Year Team	Lg	G	GS	GF	IP	BFP	H	R	ER	HR	SH	SF	HB	TBB	IBB	SO	WP	W	L	Pct	Sv-Op	Hld	Vel	OPS	ERC	ERA
2011 NYY	AL	2	1	0	2.2	16	1	2	2	0	0	1	1	6	0	2	0	0	0	-	0-0	0	93	.625	7.94	6.75
2013 NYY	AL	6	0	3	5.0	26	9	6	6	1	0	0	0	2	0	10	0	0	0	-	0-0	0	96	.965	9.81	10.80
2014 NYY	AL	70	0	8	90.0	341	46	15	14	4	2	3	4	24	1	135	2	5	0	1.000	1-5	22	97	.442	1.24	1.40
2015 NYY	AL	74	0	17	84.0	332	45	17	14	6	1	1	3	40	2	131	9	6	4	.600	9-13	28	97	.510	1.94	1.50

Year	Team	Lg	G	GS	GF	IP	BFP	H	R	ER	HR	SH	SF	HB	TBB	IBB	SO	WP	W	L	Pct	Sv-Op	Hld	Vel	OPS	ERC	ERA
2016	NYY	AL	73	0	20	73.0	299	54	31	25	5	1	1	1	28	0	126	6	3	6	.333	12-17	28	98	.577	2.48	3.08
2017	NYY	AL	66	0	21	59.2	261	29	20	19	3	1	0	11	44	0	100	5	3	6	.333	10-13	19	99	.538	2.86	2.87
2018	NYY	AL	66	0	15	66.2	272	44	22	20	7	3	1	5	26	2	115	4	4	6	.400	4-7	20	98	.578	2.51	2.70
2019	NYY	AL	1	0	0	0.2	2	0	0	0	0	0	0	0	0	0	2	0	0	0		0-0	0	94	.000	0.00	0.00
2020	NYM	NL	15	0	2	11.2	59	12	10	10	0	0	0	2	12	0	11	2	0	1	.000	0-0	4	94	.730	6.66	7.71
Postseason			9	0	3	11.0	47	6	4	4	0	0	1	0	7	1	17	1	1	1	.500	0-0	1	98	.482	1.72	3.27
9 ML YEARS			373	1	86	393.1	1608	240	123	110	26	8	7	27	182	5	632	28	21	23	.477	36-55	121	97	.541	2.29	2.52

Mookie Betts

Bats: R **Throws:** R **Pos:** RF-52;DH-2;2B-1;CF-1   **Ht:** 5'9" **Wt:** 180 **Born:** 10/7/1992 **Age:** 28

Year	Team	Lg	G	AB	H	2B	3B	HR	(Hm	Rd)	TB	R	RBI	RC	TBB	IBB	SO	HBP	SH	SF	SB	CS	GDP	Avg	OBP	Slg	OPS
2014	Bos	AL	52	189	55	12	1	5	(1	4)	84	34	18	30	21	0	31	2	1	0	7	3	2	.291	.368	.444	.812
2015	Bos	AL	145	597	174	42	8	18	(9	9)	286	92	77	100	46	1	82	2	3	6	21	6	2	.291	.341	.479	.820
2016	Bos	AL	158	672	214	42	5	31	(17	14)	359	122	113	130	49	1	80	2	0	7	26	4	12	.318	.363	.534	.897
2017	Bos	AL	153	628	166	46	2	24	(8	16)	288	101	102	115	77	9	79	2	0	5	26	3	9	.264	.344	.459	.803
2018	Bos	AL	136	520	180	47	5	32	(13	19)	333	129	80	134	81	8	91	8	0	5	30	6	5	.346	.438	.640	1.078
2019	Bos	AL	150	597	176	40	5	29	(17	12)	313	135	80	118	97	6	101	3	0	9	16	3	11	.295	.391	.524	.915
2020	LAD	NL	55	219	64	9	1	16	(11	5)	123	47	39	52	24	1	38	2	0	1	10	2	2	.292	.366	.562	.927
Postseason			21	88	20	7	0	1	(0	1)	30	16	4	8	10	4	17	1	0	0	2	0	1	.227	.313	.341	.654
7 ML YEARS			849	3422	1029	238	27	155	(76	79)	1786	660	509	679	395	26	502	21	4	33	136	27	43	.301	.373	.522	.895

Joe Biagini

Pitches: R **Bats:** R **Pos:** RP-4   bee-ah-gee-nee   **Ht:** 6'5" **Wt:** 235 **Born:** 5/29/1990 **Age:** 31

Year	Team	Lg	G	GS	GF	IP	BFP	H	R	ER	HR	SH	SF	HB	TBB	IBB	SO	WP	W	L	Pct	Sv-Op	Hld	Vel	OPS	ERC	ERA
2016	Tor	AL	60	0	12	67.2	295	69	28	23	3	2	3	5	19	1	62	3	4	3	.571	1-3	8	94	.678	3.52	3.06
2017	Tor	AL	44	18	3	119.2	517	125	78	71	15	0	2	2	42	0	97	6	3	13	.188	1-3	9	94	.752	4.38	5.34
2018	Tor	AL	50	4	7	72.0	328	96	50	48	14	0	1	6	24	0	53	8	4	7	.364	0-0	5	94	.913	7.04	6.00
2019	2 Tms	AL	63	0	15	64.2	281	71	35	33	14	1	0	1	26	3	60	3	3	2	.600	1-3	10	94	.864	5.60	4.59
2020	Hou		4	0	0	4.1	27	10	10	10	1	0	0	0	4	0	4	1	0	0		0-0	0	94	1.258	16.51	20.77
19	Tor	AL	50	0	11	50.0	212	50	22	21	8	1	0	1	17	3	50	2	3	1	.750	1-3	10	94	.783	4.28	3.78
19	Hou	AL	13	0	4	14.2	69	21	13	12	6	0	0	0	9	0	10	1	0	1	.000	0-0	0	94	1.118	10.95	7.36
Postseason			6	0	0	7.1	26	3	0	0	0	0	0	0	1	0	6	1	0	0		0-1	0	94	.354	0.55	0.00
5 ML YEARS			221	22	37	328.1	1448	371	201	185	47	3	6	14	115	4	276	21	14	25	.359	3-9	32	94	.804	5.11	5.07

Bo Bichette

Bats: R **Throws:** R **Pos:** SS-26;DH-3   **Ht:** 6'0" **Wt:** 185 **Born:** 3/5/1998 **Age:** 23

Year	Team	Lg	G	AB	H	2B	3B	HR	(Hm	Rd)	TB	R	RBI	RC	TBB	IBB	SO	HBP	SH	SF	SB	CS	GDP	Avg	OBP	Slg	OPS
2019	Tor	AL	46	196	61	18	0	11	(3	8)	112	32	21	32	14	0	50	1	0	1	4	4	2	.311	.358	.571	.930
2020	Tor	AL	29	123	37	9	1	5	(3	2)	63	18	23	23	5	1	27	0	0	0	4	1	2	.301	.328	.512	.840
2 ML YEARS			75	319	98	27	1	16	(6	10)	175	50	44	55	19	1	77	1	0	1	8	5	4	.307	.347	.549	.896

Phil Bickford

Pitches: R **Bats:** R **Pos:** RP-1   **Ht:** 6'4" **Wt:** 200 **Born:** 7/10/1995 **Age:** 25

Year	Team	Lg	G	GS	GF	IP	BFP	H	R	ER	HR	SH	SF	HB	TBB	IBB	SO	WP	W	L	Pct	Sv-Op	Hld	Vel	OPS	ERC	ERA
2020	Mil	NL	1	0	0	1.0	9	4	4	4	0	0	0	2	0	0	2	1	0	0		0-0	0	89	1.381	32.97	36.00

Jesse Biddle

Pitches: L **Bats:** L **Pos:** RP-1   **Ht:** 6'5" **Wt:** 220 **Born:** 10/22/1991 **Age:** 29

Year	Team	Lg	G	GS	GF	IP	BFP	H	R	ER	HR	SH	SF	HB	TBB	IBB	SO	WP	W	L	Pct	Sv-Op	Hld	Vel	OPS	ERC	ERA
2018	Atl	NL	60	0	14	63.2	266	50	26	22	6	2	1	3	31	5	67	2	6	1	.857	1-4	12	94	.654	3.31	3.11
2019	3 Tms		30	0	3	28.0	152	42	33	26	5	0	2	4	22	1	26	7	0	1	.000	0-1	1	94	.972	9.96	8.36
2020	Cin	NL	1	0	0	0.2	4	1	0	0	0	0	0	0	1	0	1	0	0	0		0-0	0	96	.833	10.76	0.00
19	Atl	NL	15	0	1	11.2	64	18	11	7	1	0	0	0	10	1	11	3	0	1	.000	0-0	0	94	.882	8.75	5.40
19	Sea	AL	11	0	1	11.0	60	20	14	12	2	0	2	1	7	0	8	4	0	0		0-1	1	94	1.067	11.55	9.82
19	Tex	AL	4	0	1	5.1	28	4	8	7	2	0	0	3	5	0	7	0	0	0		0-0	0	93	.979	9.44	11.81
3 ML YEARS			91	0	17	92.1	422	93	59	48	11	2	3	7	54	6	94	9	6	2	.750	1-5	13	94	.768	5.19	4.68

Shane Bieber

Pitches: R **Bats:** R **Pos:** SP-12   **Ht:** 6'3" **Wt:** 200 **Born:** 5/31/1995 **Age:** 26

Year	Team	Lg	G	GS	GF	IP	BFP	H	R	ER	HR	SH	SF	HB	TBB	IBB	SO	WP	W	L	Pct	Sv-Op	Hld	Vel	OPS	ERC	ERA
2018	Cle	AL	20	19	0	114.2	485	130	60	58	13	0	4	2	23	1	118	5	11	5	.688	0-0	0	93	.787	4.23	4.55
2019	Cle	AL	34	33	1	214.1	859	186	86	78	31	2	1	6	40	1	259	6	15	8	.652	0-0	0	93	.663	2.94	3.28
2020	Cle	AL	12	12	0	77.1	297	46	15	14	7	0	0	1	21	0	122	5	8	1	.889	0-0	0	94	.494	1.61	1.63
3 ML YEARS			66	64	1	406.1	1641	362	161	150	51	2	5	9	84	1	499	16	34	14	.708	0-0	0	93	.670	3.00	3.32

Brandon Bielak

Pitches: R **Bats:** L **Pos:** SP-6; RP-6

Ht: 6'2" **Wt:** 208 **Born:** 4/2/1996 **Age:** 25

			HOW MUCH PITCHED					WHAT HE GAVE UP									THE RESULTS								
Year	Team	Lg	G	GS	GF	IP	BFP	H	R	ER	HR	SH	SF	HB	TBB	IBB	SO	WP	W	L	Pct	Sv-Op	Hld	Vel	OPS	ERC	ERA
2020	Hou	AL	12	6	3	32.0	148	39	26	24	9	1	0	2	17	0	26	0	3	3	.500	0-0	0	93	.973	7.84	6.75

Cavan Biggio

Bats: L **Throws:** R **Pos:** 2B-37;RF-14;3B-10;CF-3;PH-2;LF-1;DH-1

Ht: 6'2" **Wt:** 200 **Born:** 4/11/1995 **Age:** 26

						BATTING											RUNNING			AVERAGES			
Year	Team	Lg	G	AB	H	2B	3B	HR	(Hm | Rd)	TB	R	RBI	RC	TBB	IBB	SO	HBP	SH	SF	SB	CS	GDP	Avg	OBP	Slg	OPS
2019	Tor	AL	100	354	83	17	2	16	(9 | 7)	152	66	48	65	71	0	123	2	0	2	14	0	0	.234	.364	.429	.793
2020	Tor	AL	59	220	55	16	0	8	(3 | 5)	95	41	28	42	41	0	61	3	0	0	6	0	2	.250	.375	.432	.807
	2 ML YEARS		159	574	138	33	2	24	(12 | 12)	247	107	76	107	112	0	184	5	0	2	20	0	2	.240	.368	.430	.798

Braden Bishop

Bats: R **Throws:** R **Pos:** RF-8;CF-3;LF-2

Ht: 6'1" **Wt:** 178 **Born:** 8/22/1993 **Age:** 27

						BATTING											RUNNING			AVERAGES			
Year	Team	Lg	G	AB	H	2B	3B	HR	(Hm | Rd)	TB	R	RBI	RC	TBB	IBB	SO	HBP	SH	SF	SB	CS	GDP	Avg	OBP	Slg	OPS
2019	Sea	AL	27	56	6	0	0	0	(0 | 0)	6	3	4	1	3	0	21	0	1	0	0	0	0	.107	.153	.107	.260
2020	Sea	AL	12	30	5	2	0	0	(0 | 0)	7	2	4	3	2	0	10	1	1	0	1	0	0	.167	.242	.233	.476
	2 ML YEARS		39	86	11	2	0	0	(0 | 0)	13	5	8	4	5	0	31	1	2	0	1	0	0	.128	.185	.151	.336

Ray Black

Pitches: R **Bats:** R **Pos:** RP-3

Ht: 6'3" **Wt:** 230 **Born:** 6/26/1990 **Age:** 31

					HOW MUCH PITCHED			WHAT HE GAVE UP										THE RESULTS								
Year	Team	Lg	G	GS	GF	IP	BFP	H	R	ER	HR	SH	SF	HB	TBB	IBB	SO	WP	W	L	Pct	Sv-Op	Hld	Vel	OPS	ERC	ERA
2018	SF	NL	26	0	4	23.1	95	17	16	16	4	2	0	1	10	0	33	1	2	2	.500	0-1	1	98	.728	3.41	6.17
2019	2 Tms	NL	17	0	3	16.0	70	14	9	9	5	0	0	1	9	0	18	0	1	0	.000	0-2	2	98	.860	5.89	5.06
2020	Mil	NL	3	0	2	3.0	14	2	1	1	0	0	0	0	3	0	3	0	0	0	-	0-0	0	96	.539	3.63	3.00
19	SF	NL	2	0	1	2.0	11	4	1	1	1	0	0	0	1	0	5	0	0	0	-	0-0	0	99	1.155	14.72	4.50
19	Mil	NL	15	0	2	14.0	59	10	8	8	4	0	0	1	8	0	13	0	1	0	.000	0-2	2	98	.802	4.82	5.14
	3 ML YEARS		46	0	9	42.1	179	33	26	26	9	2	0	2	22	0	54	1	2	3	.400	0-3	3	98	.766	4.33	5.53

Paul Blackburn

Pitches: R **Bats:** R **Pos:** SP-1

Ht: 6'1" **Wt:** 196 **Born:** 12/4/1993 **Age:** 27

					HOW MUCH PITCHED			WHAT HE GAVE UP										THE RESULTS								
Year	Team	Lg	G	GS	GF	IP	BFP	H	R	ER	HR	SH	SF	HB	TBB	IBB	SO	WP	W	L	Pct	Sv-Op	Hld	Vel	OPS	ERC	ERA
2017	Oak	AL	10	10	0	58.2	238	58	22	21	5	0	0	1	16	0	22	1	3	1	.750	0-0	0	90	.686	3.62	3.22
2018	Oak	AL	6	6	0	27.2	119	33	23	22	2	0	2	2	6	0	19	1	2	3	.400	0-0	0	90	.794	4.62	7.16
2019	Oak	AL	4	1	1	11.0	57	19	14	13	3	1	1	1	4	0	8	1	0	2	.000	0-0	0	91	1.089	10.24	10.64
2020	Oak	AL	1	1	0	2.1	14	5	7	7	0	0	0	0	2	0	2	1	0	1	.000	0-0	0	90	1.083	12.37	27.00
	4 ML YEARS		21	18	1	99.2	428	115	66	63	10	1	3	4	28	0	51	4	5	7	.417	0-0	0	90	.780	4.74	5.69

Charlie Blackmon

Bats: L **Throws:** L **Pos:** RF-50;DH-9

Ht: 6'3" **Wt:** 221 **Born:** 7/1/1986 **Age:** 34

						BATTING											RUNNING			AVERAGES			
Year	Team	Lg	G	AB	H	2B	3B	HR	(Hm | Rd)	TB	R	RBI	RC	TBB	IBB	SO	HBP	SH	SF	SB	CS	GDP	Avg	OBP	Slg	OPS
2011	Col	NL	27	98	25	1	0	1	(1 | 0)	29	9	8	10	3	1	8	0	1	0	5	1	2	.255	.277	.296	.573
2012	Col	NL	42	113	32	8	0	2	(1 | 1)	46	15	9	11	4	0	17	3	1	0	1	2	4	.283	.325	.407	.732
2013	Col	NL	82	246	76	17	2	6	(3 | 3)	115	35	22	35	7	0	49	3	2	0	7	0	1	.309	.336	.467	.803
2014	Col	NL	154	593	171	27	3	19	(13 | 6)	261	82	72	87	31	5	96	13	6	5	28	10	3	.288	.335	.440	.775
2015	Col	NL	157	614	176	31	9	17	(7 | 10)	276	93	58	95	46	2	112	13	5	4	43	13	4	.287	.347	.450	.797
2016	Col	NL	143	578	187	35	5	29	(12 | 17)	319	111	82	110	43	4	102	13	3	4	17	9	2	.324	.381	.552	.933
2017	Col	NL	159	644	213	35	14	37	(24 | 13)	387	137	104	151	65	9	135	10	3	3	14	10	4	.331	.399	.601	1.000
2018	Col	NL	156	626	182	31	7	29	(14 | 15)	314	119	70	110	59	2	134	8	1	2	12	4	10	.291	.358	.502	.860
2019	Col	NL	140	580	182	42	7	32	(22 | 10)	334	112	86	115	40	1	104	9	0	5	2	5	11	.314	.364	.576	.940
2020	Col	NL	59	221	67	12	1	6	(3 | 3)	99	31	42	36	19	4	44	2	0	5	2	1	4	.303	.356	.448	.804
	Postseason		5	19	2	0	0	0	(0 | 0)	2	1	2	0	1	0	2	0	1	0	0	0	0	.105	.150	.105	.255
	10 ML YEARS		1119	4313	1311	239	48	178	(100 | 78)	2180	744	553	760	317	28	801	74	22	28	131	55	45	.304	.360	.505	.865

Travis Blankenhorn

Bats: L **Throws:** R **Pos:** 2B-1

Ht: 6'2" **Wt:** 235 **Born:** 8/3/1996 **Age:** 24

						BATTING											RUNNING			AVERAGES			
Year	Team	Lg	G	AB	H	2B	3B	HR	(Hm | Rd)	TB	R	RBI	RC	TBB	IBB	SO	HBP	SH	SF	SB	CS	GDP	Avg	OBP	Slg	OPS
2020	Min	AL	1	3	1	1	0	0	(0 | 0)	2	0	0	1	0	0	0	1	0	0	0	0	0	.333	.500	.667	1.167

Richard Bleier

Pitches: L Bats: L Pos: RP-21

BLY-er

Ht: 6'3" Wt: 215 Born: 4/16/1987 Age: 34

			HOW MUCH PITCHED				WHAT HE GAVE UP									THE RESULTS							
Year Team	Lg	G	GS	GF	IP	BFP	H	R	ER	HR	SH	SF	HB	TBB	IBB	SO	WP	W	L	Pct	Sv-Op	Hld	Vel	OPS	ERC	ERA
2016 NYY	AL	23	0	8	23.0	92	20	6	5	0	0	1	1	4	0	13	0	0	0	-	0-0	2	89	.586	2.11	1.96
2017 Bal	AL	57	0	14	63.1	265	62	23	14	6	3	4	4	13	3	26	5	2	1	.667	0-0	3	89	.671	3.33	1.99
2018 Bal	AL	31	0	4	32.2	133	36	7	7	0	0	2	1	4	1	15	1	3	0	1.000	0-1	9	88	.673	3.05	1.93
2019 Bal	AL	53	1	13	55.1	235	62	34	33	6	1	2	4	8	2	30	1	3	0	1.000	4-5	6	89	.802	4.39	5.37
2020 2 Tms		21	0	1	16.2	67	14	6	4	0	0	2	1	4	1	11	2	1	1	.500	0-0	6	89	.590	2.18	2.16
20 Bal	AL	2	0	0	3.0	11	1	0	0	0	0	0	0	0	0	4	1	0	0	-	0-0	0	89	.282	0.69	0.00
20 Mia	NL	19	0	1	13.2	56	13	6	4	0	0	0	1	4	1	7	1	1	1	.500	0-0	6	89	.650	2.68	2.63
5 ML YEARS		185	1	40	191.0	792	197	76	63	12	4	9	11	33	7	95	9	9	2	.818	4-6	25	89	.694	3.31	2.97

Scott Blewett

Pitches: R Bats: R Pos: RP-2

Ht: 6'6" Wt: 245 Born: 4/10/1996 Age: 25

			HOW MUCH PITCHED				WHAT HE GAVE UP									THE RESULTS							
Year Team	Lg	G	GS	GF	IP	BFP	H	R	ER	HR	SH	SF	HB	TBB	IBB	SO	WP	W	L	Pct	Sv-Op	Hld	Vel	OPS	ERC	ERA
2020 KC	AL	2	0	1	3.0	16	6	2	2	0	0	0	0	1	0	4	0	0	0	-	0-0	0	93	1.038	8.97	6.00

Xander Bogaerts

Bats: R Throws: R Pos: SS-53;PH-3;DH-1

ZAN-derr BO-garts

Ht: 6'2" Wt: 218 Born: 10/1/1992 Age: 28

							BATTING													RUNNING			AVERAGES			
Year Team	Lg	G	AB	H	2B	3B	HR	(Hm	Rd)	TB	R	RBI	RC	TBB	IBB	SO	HBP	SH	SF	SB	CS	GDP	Avg	OBP	Slg	OPS
2013 Bos	AL	18	44	11	2	0	1	(0	1)	16	7	5	4	5	0	13	0	0	1	1	0	1	.250	.320	.364	.684
2014 Bos	AL	144	538	129	28	1	12	(7	5)	195	60	46	43	39	1	138	8	2	7	2	3	11	.240	.297	.362	.660
2015 Bos	AL	156	613	196	35	3	7	(5	2)	258	84	81	88	32	1	101	3	3	3	10	2	16	.320	.355	.421	.776
2016 Bos	AL	157	652	192	34	1	21	(11	10)	291	115	89	98	58	0	123	6	0	3	13	4	14	.294	.356	.446	.802
2017 Bos	AL	148	571	156	32	6	10	(4	6)	230	94	62	81	56	6	116	6	0	2	15	1	17	.273	.343	.403	.746
2018 Bos	AL	136	513	148	45	3	23	(15	8)	268	72	103	100	55	4	102	6	0	6	8	2	14	.288	.360	.522	.883
2019 Bos	AL	155	614	190	52	0	33	(17	16)	341	110	117	124	76	2	122	2	0	6	4	2	11	.309	.384	.555	.939
2020 Bos	AL	56	203	61	8	0	11	(5	6)	102	36	28	32	21	2	41	0	0	1	8	0	3	.300	.364	.502	.867
Postseason		33	114	25	5	1	2	(2	0)	38	17	10	11	14	1	25	0	0	2	0	0	4	.219	.300	.333	.633
8 ML YEARS		970	3748	1083	236	14	118	(64	54)	1701	578	531	570	342	16	756	31	5	29	61	14	87	.289	.351	.454	.805

Alec Bohm

Bats: R Throws: R Pos: 3B-38;1B-7;DH-1

Ht: 6'5" Wt: 218 Born: 8/3/1996 Age: 24

							BATTING													RUNNING			AVERAGES			
Year Team	Lg	G	AB	H	2B	3B	HR	(Hm	Rd)	TB	R	RBI	RC	TBB	IBB	SO	HBP	SH	SF	SB	CS	GDP	Avg	OBP	Slg	OPS
2018 3 Tms	Low	40	139	35	6	2	0	(-	-)	45	17	17	16	12	0	23	6	0	1	3	0	5	.252	.324	.324	.659
2019 Rdng	AA	63	238	64	11	1	14	(-	-)	119	38	42	42	28	0	38	1	0	3	2	2	11	.269	.344	.500	.844
2019 2 Tms	Low	62	237	81	19	3	7	(-	-)	127	38	38	51	29	2	35	1	0	3	4	2	4	.342	.411	.536	.947
2020 Phi	NL	44	160	54	11	0	4	(2	2)	77	24	23	33	16	0	36	2	0	2	1	1	4	.338	.400	.481	.881

Ronald Bolanos

Pitches: R Bats: R Pos: SP-2

boh-LAHN-yos

Ht: 6'2" Wt: 230 Born: 8/23/1996 Age: 24

			HOW MUCH PITCHED				WHAT HE GAVE UP									THE RESULTS							
Year Team	Lg	G	GS	GF	IP	BFP	H	R	ER	HR	SH	SF	HB	TBB	IBB	SO	WP	W	L	Pct	Sv-Op	Hld	Vel	OPS	ERC	ERA
2019 SD	NL	5	3	0	19.2	88	17	13	13	3	0	1	1	12	0	19	1	0	2	.000	0-0	0	94	.800	4.68	5.95
2020 KC	AL	2	2	0	3.2	21	8	7	5	2	0	0	1	3	0	2	2	0	2	.000	0-0	0	95	1.395	21.97	12.27
2 ML YEARS		7	5	0	23.1	109	25	20	18	5	0	1	2	15	0	21	3	0	4	.000	0-0	0	94	.913	6.82	6.94

Emilio Bonifacio

Bats: B Throws: R Pos: PR-2;LF-1

bone-ee-FAH-see-oh

Ht: 5'10" Wt: 200 Born: 4/23/1985 Age: 36

							BATTING													RUNNING			AVERAGES			
Year Team	Lg	G	AB	H	2B	3B	HR	(Hm	Rd)	TB	R	RBI	RC	TBB	IBB	SO	HBP	SH	SF	SB	CS	GDP	Avg	OBP	Slg	OPS
2007 Ari	NL	11	23	5	1	0	0	(0	0)	6	2	2	4	4	0	3	0	0	0	1	0	0	.217	.333	.261	.594
2008 2 Tms	NL	49	169	41	6	5	0	(0	0)	57	29	14	16	14	0	46	0	0	3	7	4	2	.243	.296	.337	.633
2009 Fla	NL	127	461	116	11	6	1	(1	0)	142	72	27	41	34	0	95	2	8	4	21	9	5	.252	.303	.308	.611
2010 Fla	NL	73	180	47	6	3	0	(0	0)	59	30	10	24	17	0	42	0	1	3	12	0	1	.261	.320	.328	.648
2011 Fla	NL	152	565	167	26	7	5	(1	4)	222	78	36	83	59	1	129	1	11	5	40	11	4	.296	.360	.393	.753
2012 Mia	NL	64	244	63	3	4	1	(1	0)	77	30	11	30	25	1	52	1	4	0	30	3	3	.258	.330	.316	.645
2013 2 Tms	NL	136	420	102	22	3	1	(1	2)	139	54	31	39	30	0	103	2	6	3	28	8	4	.243	.295	.331	.625
2014 2 Tms	NL	110	394	102	17	4	3	(2	1)	136	47	24	46	26	2	85	0	6	0	26	8	2	.259	.305	.345	.650
2015 CWS	AL	47	78	13	2	0	0	(0	0)	15	5	4	1	2	0	27	1	1	0	1	4	1	.167	.198	.192	.390
2016 Atl	NL	24	38	8	0	0	0	(0	0)	8	6	3	3	3	0	12	0	2	0	1	0	0	.211	.268	.211	.479
2017 Atl	NL	38	38	5	1	1	0	(0	0)	8	2	3	1	1	0	9	0	4	1	0	0	1	.132	.150	.211	.361
2020 Was	NL	3	3	0	0	0	0	(0	0)	0	1	0	0	0	0	2	0	0	0	1	0	0	.000	.000	.000	.000
08 Ari	NL	8	12	2	1	0	0	(0	0)	3	3	2	1	0	0	5	0	0	0	1	0	0	.167	.167	.250	.417
08 Was	NL	41	157	39	5	5	0	(0	0)	54	26	12	15	14	0	41	0	0	3	6	4	2	.248	.305	.344	.649
13 Tor	AL	94	262	57	16	1	3	(1	2)	84	33	20	19	13	0	66	2	3	2	12	6	3	.218	.258	.321	.579
13 KC	NL	42	158	45	6	2	0	(0	0)	55	21	11	20	17	0	37	0	3	1	16	2	1	.285	.352	.348	.700
14 ChC	NL	69	276	77	14	3	2	(2	0)	103	35	18	37	16	2	49	0	6	0	14	6	1	.279	.318	.373	.692
14 Atl	NL	41	118	25	3	1	1	(0	1)	33	12	6	9	10	0	36	0	0	0	12	2	1	.212	.273	.280	.553
12 ML YEARS		834	2613	669	95	33	13	(6	7)	869	356	165	287	215	4	605	7	43	19	166	49	23	.256	.312	.333	.645

Jorge Bonifacio

Bats: R **Throws:** R **Pos:** LF-19;RF-10;PH-4;PR-1   **Ht:** 6'1" **Wt:** 220 **Born:** 6/4/1993 **Age:** 28

Year Team	Lg	G	AB	H	2B	3B	HR	(Hm	Rd)	TB	R	RBI	RC	TBB	IBB	SO	HBP	SH	SF	SB	CS	GDP	Avg	OBP	Slg	OPS
2017 KC	AL	113	384	98	15	1	17	(8	9)	166	55	40	51	35	0	118	2	0	1	1	1	8	.255	.320	.432	.752
2018 KC	AL	69	236	53	16	2	4	(1	3)	85	31	23	29	29	1	71	2	1	2	0	1	3	.225	.312	.360	.672
2019 KC	AL	5	20	7	3	0	0	(0	0)	10	3	3	5	1	0	7	0	0	0	0	0	0	.350	.381	.500	.881
2020 Det	AL	30	86	19	3	0	2	(0	2)	28	8	17	15	5	0	26	2	0	1	0	0	1	.221	.277	.326	.602
4 ML YEARS		217	726	177	37	3	23	(9	14)	289	97	83	100	70	1	222	6	1	4	1	2	12	.244	.314	.398	.712

Ryan Borucki

Pitches: L **Bats:** L **Pos:** RP-21   **Ht:** 6'4" **Wt:** 215 **Born:** 3/31/1994 **Age:** 27

Year Team	Lg	G	GS	GF	IP	BFP	H	R	ER	HR	SH	SF	HB	TBB	IBB	SO	WP	W	L	Pct	Sv-Op	Hld	Vel	OPS	ERC	ERA
2018 Tor	AL	17	17	0	97.2	415	96	48	42	7	3	2	2	33	3	67	2	4	6	.400	0-0	0	92	.705	3.58	3.87
2019 Tor	AL	2	2	0	6.2	40	15	10	8	2	0	0	0	6	0	6	0	0	1	.000	0-0	0	92	1.319	17.16	10.80
2020 Tor	AL	21	0	1	16.2	73	12	5	5	1	0	1	0	12	1	21	0	1	1	.500	0-1	3	95	.629	3.35	2.70
3 ML YEARS		40	19	1	121.0	528	123	63	55	10	3	3	2	51	4	94	2	5	8	.385	0-1	3	92	.740	4.13	4.09

David Bote

Bats: R **Throws:** R **Pos:** 3B-33;2B-7;PH-4;DH-3;1B-1   BOH-tee   **Ht:** 6'1" **Wt:** 205 **Born:** 4/7/1993 **Age:** 28

Year Team	Lg	G	AB	H	2B	3B	HR	(Hm	Rd)	TB	R	RBI	RC	TBB	IBB	SO	HBP	SH	SF	SB	CS	GDP	Avg	OBP	Slg	OPS
2018 ChC	NL	74	184	44	9	2	6	(5	1)	75	23	33	26	19	1	60	4	0	3	3	4	3	.239	.319	.408	.727
2019 ChC	NL	127	303	78	17	0	11	(3	8)	128	47	41	44	44	4	93	7	0	2	5	1	11	.257	.362	.422	.785
2020 ChC	NL	45	125	25	3	1	7	(1	6)	51	15	29	23	17	0	40	2	0	1	2	0	6	.200	.303	.408	.711
Postseason		1	2	0	0	0	0	(0	0)	0	0	0	0	0	0	2	0	0	0	0	0	0	.000	.000	.000	.000
3 ML YEARS		246	612	147	29	3	24	(9	15)	254	85	103	93	80	5	193	13	0	6	10	5	20	.240	.338	.415	.753

James Bourque

Pitches: R **Bats:** R **Pos:** RP-6   **Ht:** 6'4" **Wt:** 215 **Born:** 7/9/1993 **Age:** 27

Year Team	Lg	G	GS	GF	IP	BFP	H	R	ER	HR	SH	SF	HB	TBB	IBB	SO	WP	W	L	Pct	Sv-Op	Hld	Vel	OPS	ERC	ERA
2019 Was	NL	1	0	0	0.2	6	3	4	4	0	0	0	0	2	0	0	0	0	0	-	0-0	0	96	2.083	49.74	54.00
2020 Was	NL	6	0	3	4.0	19	3	3	3	1	0	0	0	5	0	1	1	1	0	1.000	0-0	0	94	.992	7.58	6.75
2 ML YEARS		7	0	3	4.2	25	6	7	7	1	0	0	0	7	0	1	1	1	0	1.000	0-0	0	94	1.242	12.54	13.50

Matt Bowman

Pitches: R **Bats:** R **Pos:** P   **Ht:** 6'0" **Wt:** 185 **Born:** 5/31/1991 **Age:** 30

Year Team	Lg	G	GS	GF	IP	BFP	H	R	ER	HR	SH	SF	HB	TBB	IBB	SO	WP	W	L	Pct	Sv-Op	Hld	Vel	OPS	ERC	ERA
2016 StL	NL	59	0	12	67.2	281	59	31	26	4	1	1	1	20	2	52	0	2	5	.286	0-1	13	92	.623	2.71	3.46
2017 StL	NL	75	0	10	58.2	247	52	29	26	4	2	4	5	18	2	46	1	3	6	.333	2-5	23	91	.659	3.15	3.99
2018 StL	NL	22	0	5	23.0	109	29	16	16	4	2	1	1	11	3	26	1	0	2	.000	0-2	5	92	.894	6.39	6.26
2019 Cin	NL	27	0	10	32.0	137	27	15	13	2	0	2	0	13	3	25	0	2	0	1.000	0-0	0	93	.628	2.78	3.66
4 ML YEARS		183	0	37	181.1	774	167	91	81	14	5	8	7	62	10	149	2	7	13	.350	2-8	41	92	.672	3.28	4.02

Brad Boxberger

Pitches: R **Bats:** R **Pos:** RP-23   **Ht:** 5'10" **Wt:** 211 **Born:** 5/27/1988 **Age:** 33

Year Team	Lg	G	GS	GF	IP	BFP	H	R	ER	HR	SH	SF	HB	TBB	IBB	SO	WP	W	L	Pct	Sv-Op	Hld	Vel	OPS	ERC	ERA
2012 SD	NL	24	0	4	27.2	120	22	12	8	3	0	1	2	18	1	33	0	0	0	-	0-0	1	92	.734	4.28	2.60
2013 SD	NL	18	0	6	22.0	94	19	9	7	3	3	2	0	13	0	24	0	0	1	.000	1-1	0	92	.760	4.43	2.86
2014 TB	AL	63	0	10	64.2	247	34	17	17	9	2	2	4	20	0	104	3	5	2	.714	2-5	18	93	.538	1.84	2.37
2015 TB	AL	69	0	53	63.0	271	54	29	26	9	2	1	2	32	5	74	5	4	10	.286	**41-47**	2	93	.703	4.01	3.71
2016 TB	AL	27	0	3	24.1	114	23	13	13	3	0	1	2	19	1	22	0	4	3	.571	0-3	7	92	.734	5.75	4.81
2017 TB	AL	30	0	10	29.1	121	23	11	11	4	1	1	1	11	3	40	1	4	4	.500	0-2	5	92	.665	3.03	3.38
2018 Ari	NL	60	0	45	53.1	235	44	30	26	9	2	1	1	32	4	71	3	3	7	.300	32-40	1	91	.732	4.27	4.39
2019 KC	AL	29	0	9	26.2	122	25	16	16	3	0	1	1	17	0	27	1	1	3	.250	1-4	0	90	.751	4.83	5.40
2020 Mia	NL	23	0	0	18.0	79	17	7	7	3	0	1	1	8	0	18	0	1	0	1.000	0-1	5	93	.749	4.60	3.00
9 ML YEARS		343	0	140	329.0	1403	261	144	130	46	10	11	14	170	14	413	13	22	30	.423	77-103	39	92	.691	3.77	3.56

Matthew Boyd

Pitches: L **Bats:** L **Pos:** SP-12   **Ht:** 6'3" **Wt:** 234 **Born:** 2/2/1991 **Age:** 30

Year Team	Lg	G	GS	GF	IP	BFP	H	R	ER	HR	SH	SF	HB	TBB	IBB	SO	WP	W	L	Pct	Sv-Op	Hld	Vel	OPS	ERC	ERA
2015 2 Tms	AL	13	12	0	57.1	252	71	50	48	17	1	3	1	20	0	43	4	1	6	.143	0-0	0	91	.979	7.04	7.53
2016 Det	AL	20	18	1	97.1	412	97	51	49	17	0	3	4	29	0	82	1	6	5	.545	0-0	0	91	.765	4.35	4.53
2017 Det	AL	26	25	0	135.0	605	157	84	79	18	3	6	3	53	3	110	2	6	11	.353	0-0	0	92	.826	5.28	5.27
2018 Det	AL	31	31	0	170.1	709	146	87	83	27	2	6	11	51	0	159	6	9	13	.409	0-0	0	90	.704	3.53	4.39
2019 Det	AL	32	32	0	185.1	788	178	101	94	39	4	4	8	50	1	238	6	9	12	.429	0-0	0	92	.766	4.18	4.56
2020 Det	AL	12	12	0	60.1	271	67	46	45	15	1	2	5	22	0	60	5	3	7	.300	0-0	0	92	.900	5.99	6.71
15 Tor	AL	2	2	0	6.2	36	15	11	11	5	0	1	0	7	0	7	2	0	2	.000	0-0	0	91	1.327	17.16	14.85
15 Det	AL	11	10	0	50.2	216	56	39	37	12	1	2	1	19	0	36	2	1	4	.200	0-0	0	91	.918	5.88	6.57
6 ML YEARS		134	130	1	705.2	3037	716	419	398	133	11	24	32	225	4	692	24	34	54	.386	0-0	0	91	.793	4.61	5.08

Brad Brach

Pitches: R Bats: R Pos: RP-14   BROCK   Ht: 6'6" Wt: 215 Born: 4/12/1986 Age: 35

			HOW MUCH PITCHED				WHAT HE GAVE UP									THE RESULTS						
Year	Team	Lg	G	GS	GF	IP	BFP	H	R	ER	HR	SH	SF	HB	TBB	IBB	SO	WP	W	L	Pct	Sv-Op	Hld	Vel	OPS	ERC	ERA
2011	SD	NL	9	0	4	7.0	38	9	5	4	0	0	0	1	7	4	11	1	0	2	.000	0-0	0	93	.747	6.51	5.14
2012	SD	NL	67	0	13	66.2	280	50	28	28	11	1	3	2	33	7	75	4	2	4	.333	0-1	15	92	.674	3.47	3.78
2013	SD	NL	33	0	6	31.0	141	36	15	11	3	0	3	0	19	0	31	4	1	0	1.000	0-0	2	92	.819	6.03	3.19
2014	Bal	AL	46	0	8	62.1	254	48	24	22	6	2	4	1	25	1	54	2	7	1	.875	0-0	8	93	.640	2.90	3.18
2015	Bal	AL	62	0	12	79.1	324	57	25	24	7	3	2	0	38	3	89	1	5	3	.625	1-2	14	94	.627	2.78	2.72
2016	Bal	AL	71	0	16	79.0	311	57	23	18	7	0	3	0	25	1	92	4	10	4	.714	2-7	24	94	.578	2.27	2.05
2017	Bal	AL	67	0	36	68.0	275	51	27	24	7	1	3	0	26	1	70	4	4	5	.444	18-24	9	95	.620	2.70	3.18
2018	2 Tms		69	0	32	62.2	289	72	32	25	5	1	1	1	28	2	60	3	2	4	.333	12-16	11	94	.754	4.85	3.59
2019	2 Tms	NL	58	0	6	54.1	242	57	33	33	4	1	4	1	31	2	60	3	5	4	.556	0-3	6	94	.774	4.94	5.47
2020	NYM	NL	14	0	5	12.1	58	8	8	8	2	0	0	1	14	0	14	2	1	0	1.000	0-0	0	90	.745	5.87	5.84
18	Bal	AL	42	0	24	39.0	185	50	24	21	4	1	0	0	19	1	38	1	1	2	.333	11-13	3	93	.830	5.96	4.85
18	Atl		27	0	8	23.2	104	22	8	4	1	0	1	1	9	1	22	2	1	2	.333	1-3	8	95	.620	3.19	1.52
19	ChC	NL	42	0	6	39.2	181	42	27	27	3	0	4	1	28	1	45	3	4	3	.571	0-2	4	94	.811	5.66	6.13
19	NYM	NL	16	0	0	14.2	61	15	6	6	1	1	0	0	3	1	15	0	1	1	.500	0-1	2	94	.668	3.12	3.68
	Postseason		5	0	0	5.0	24	5	1	1	0	0	0	0	5	0	5	0	1	0	1.000	0-1	0	94	.890	7.14	1.80
	10 ML YEARS		496	0	138	522.2	2212	445	220	197	52	9	23	7	246	21	556	28	37	27	.578	33-53	89	94	.676	3.54	3.39

Silvino Bracho

Pitches: R Bats: R Pos: RP-1   BRAH-cho   Ht: 5'10" Wt: 190 Born: 7/17/1992 Age: 28

			HOW MUCH PITCHED				WHAT HE GAVE UP									THE RESULTS						
Year	Team	Lg	G	GS	GF	IP	BFP	H	R	ER	HR	SH	SF	HB	TBB	IBB	SO	WP	W	L	Pct	Sv-Op	Hld	Vel	OPS	ERC	ERA
2015	Ari	NL	13	0	3	12.1	50	9	2	2	2	0	0	1	4	1	17	1	0	0	-	1-1	0	93	.680	2.95	1.46
2016	Ari	NL	26	0	11	24.2	119	31	22	20	7	0	1	3	10	1	17	3	0	2	.000	0-0	0	93	.951	7.32	7.30
2017	Ari	NL	21	0	10	20.2	87	18	14	13	5	0	0	0	7	0	25	1	0	0	-	0-0	0	94	.725	3.98	5.66
2018	Ari	NL	31	0	7	31.0	129	25	12	11	2	1	1	3	12	2	34	2	2	0	1.000	0-4	2	93	.670	3.05	3.19
2020	Ari	NL	1	0	0	1.0	5	2	2	2	1	0	0	0	0	0	1	0	0	0	-	0-0	0	92	1.400	16.28	18.00
	5 ML YEARS		92	0	31	89.2	390	85	52	48	17	1	2	7	33	4	94	7	2	2	.500	1-5	2	93	.780	4.48	4.82

Archie Bradley

Pitches: R Bats: R Pos: RP-16   Ht: 6'4" Wt: 215 Born: 8/10/1992 Age: 28

			HOW MUCH PITCHED				WHAT HE GAVE UP									THE RESULTS						
Year	Team	Lg	G	GS	GF	IP	BFP	H	R	ER	HR	SH	SF	HB	TBB	IBB	SO	WP	W	L	Pct	Sv-Op	Hld	Vel	OPS	ERC	ERA
2015	Ari	NL	8	8	0	35.2	161	36	23	23	3	1	1	2	22	1	23	0	2	3	.400	0-0	0	92	.768	5.12	5.80
2016	Ari	NL	26	26	0	141.2	638	154	84	79	16	2	7	4	67	8	143	7	8	9	.471	0-0	0	92	.802	4.96	5.02
2017	Ari	NL	63	0	13	73.0	290	55	14	14	4	1	1	1	21	2	79	0	3	3	.500	1-7	25	96	.567	2.14	1.73
2018	Ari	NL	76	0	8	71.2	296	62	30	29	9	1	0	4	20	1	75	2	4	5	.444	3-11	34	96	.672	3.24	3.64
2019	Ari	NL	66	1	32	71.2	317	67	30	28	5	2	2	5	36	2	87	0	4	5	.444	18-21	7	96	.714	4.10	3.52
2020	2 Tms	NL	16	0	10	18.1	73	17	6	6	1	0	0	1	3	0	18	0	2	0	1.000	6-7	2	94	.635	2.78	2.95
20	Ari	NL	10	0	9	10.2	45	13	5	5	0	0	0	1	3	0	12	0	1	0	1.000	6-7	0	94	.792	4.78	4.22
20	Cin		6	0	1	7.2	28	4	1	1	1	0	0	0	0	0	6	0	1	0	1.000	0-0	2	94	.393	0.87	1.17
	Postseason		3	0	1	6.0	28	6	3	2	2	0	0	0	3	0	5	0	0	0	-	0-0	1	96	.841	5.84	3.00
	6 ML YEARS		255	35	63	412.0	1775	391	187	179	38	7	11	17	169	14	425	9	23	25	.479	28-46	68	94	.715	3.88	3.91

Jackie Bradley Jr.

Bats: L Throws: R Pos: CF-55   Ht: 5'10" Wt: 196 Born: 4/19/1990 Age: 31

			BATTING																		RUNNING			AVERAGES			
Year	Team	Lg	G	AB	H	2B	3B	HR	(Hm	Rd)	TB	R	RBI	RC	TBB	IBB	SO	HBP	SH	SF	SB	CS	GDP	Avg	OBP	Slg	OPS
2013	Bos	AL	37	95	18	5	0	3	(2	1)	32	18	10	8	10	0	31	2	0	0	2	0	1	.189	.280	.337	.617
2014	Bos	AL	127	384	76	19	2	1	(1	0)	102	45	30	27	31	1	121	5	1	2	8	0	10	.198	.265	.266	.531
2015	Bos	AL	74	221	55	17	4	10	(5	5)	110	43	43	41	27	0	69	3	1	3	3	0	5	.249	.335	.498	.832
2016	Bos	AL	156	558	149	30	7	26	(12	14)	271	94	87	86	63	5	143	10	0	5	9	2	10	.267	.349	.486	.835
2017	Bos	AL	133	482	118	19	3	17	(6	11)	194	58	63	70	48	4	124	9	0	2	8	3	8	.245	.323	.402	.726
2018	Bos	AL	144	474	111	33	4	13	(4	9)	191	76	59	67	46	3	137	11	0	4	17	1	6	.234	.314	.403	.717
2019	Bos	AL	147	494	111	28	3	21	(10	11)	208	69	62	61	56	3	155	12	3	2	8	6	6	.225	.317	.421	.738
2020	Bos	AL	55	191	54	11	0	7	(3	4)	86	32	22	28	23	1	48	2	0	1	5	2	2	.283	.364	.450	.814
	Postseason		21	65	12	2	0	4	(1	3)	26	7	15	12	9	0	22	2	0	0	1	2	2	.185	.303	.400	.703
	8 ML YEARS		873	2899	692	162	23	98	(43	55)	1194	435	376	388	304	17	828	54	5	19	60	14	48	.239	.321	.412	.732

Michael Brantley

Bats: L Throws: L Pos: DH-26;LF-19;PH-1   Ht: 6'2" Wt: 209 Born: 5/15/1987 Age: 34

			BATTING																		RUNNING			AVERAGES			
Year	Team	Lg	G	AB	H	2B	3B	HR	(Hm	Rd)	TB	R	RBI	RC	TBB	IBB	SO	HBP	SH	SF	SB	CS	GDP	Avg	OBP	Slg	OPS
2009	Cle	AL	28	112	35	4	0	0	(0	0)	39	10	11	16	8	0	19	0	1	0	4	4	3	.313	.358	.348	.707
2010	Cle	AL	72	297	73	9	3	3	(2	1)	97	38	22	32	22	0	38	0	4	2	10	2	6	.246	.296	.327	.623
2011	Cle	AL	114	451	120	24	4	7	(4	3)	173	63	46	56	34	2	76	3	3	5	13	5	11	.266	.318	.384	.702
2012	Cle	AL	149	552	159	37	4	6	(3	3)	222	63	60	76	53	12	56	0	0	4	12	9	7	.288	.348	.402	.750
2013	Cle	AL	151	556	158	26	3	10	(9	1)	220	66	73	86	40	1	67	4	3	8	17	4	11	.284	.332	.396	.728
2014	Cle	AL	156	611	200	45	2	20	(11	9)	309	94	97	114	52	4	56	0	0	5	23	1	16	.327	.385	.506	.890
2015	Cle	AL	137	529	164	45	0	15	(9	6)	254	68	84	94	60	8	51	2	0	5	15	1	14	.310	.379	.480	.859
2016	Cle	AL	11	39	9	2	0	0	(0	0)	11	5	7	5	3	1	6	0	0	1	1	0	1	.231	.279	.282	.561
2017	Cle	AL	90	338	101	20	1	9	(6	3)	150	47	52	51	31	3	50	2	0	4	11	1	8	.299	.357	.444	.801
2018	Cle	AL	143	570	176	36	2	17	(9	8)	267	89	76	86	48	0	60	5	1	6	12	3	15	.309	.364	.468	.832

Year Team	Lg	G	AB	H	2B	3B	HR	(Hm	Rd)	TB	R	RBI	RC	TBB	IBB	SO	HBP	SH	SF	SB	CS	GDP	Avg	OBP	Slg	OPS
								BATTING												RUNNING			AVERAGES			
2019 Hou	AL	148	575	179	40	2	22	(12	10)	289	88	90	103	51	3	66	7	0	4	3	2	21	.311	.372	.503	.875
2020 Hou	AL	46	170	51	15	0	5	(3	2)	81	24	22	35	17	0	28	0	0	0	0	0	3	.300	.364	.476	.840
Postseason		25	95	24	0	0	1	(1	0)	27	7	5	10	11	2	17	0	0	1	1	0	2	.253	.327	.284	.611
12 ML YEARS		1245	4800	1425	303	21	114	(68	46)	2112	655	640	754	419	34	573	31	12	44	123	32	116	.297	.354	.440	.794

Rob Brantly

Bats: L **Throws:** R **Pos:** C-1   **Ht:** 6'0" **Wt:** 191 **Born:** 7/14/1989 **Age:** 31

Year Team	Lg	G	AB	H	2B	3B	HR	(Hm	Rd)	TB	R	RBI	RC	TBB	IBB	SO	HBP	SH	SF	SB	CS	GDP	Avg	OBP	Slg	OPS
								BATTING												RUNNING			AVERAGES			
2012 Mia	NL	31	100	29	8	0	3	(1	2)	46	14	8	14	13	2	16	0	0	0	1	1	1	.290	.372	.460	.832
2013 Mia	NL	67	223	47	9	0	1	(1	0)	59	11	18	14	15	1	53	2	0	3	0	0	8	.211	.263	.265	.528
2015 CWS	AL	14	33	4	1	0	1	(1	0)	8	3	6	1	2	0	8	0	0	1	0	0	1	.121	.167	.242	.409
2017 CWS	AL	14	31	9	1	0	2	(1	1)	16	4	5	7	3	0	14	2	0	0	0	0	0	.290	.389	.516	.905
2019 Phi	NL	1	1	0	0	0	0	(0	0)	0	0	0	0	0	0	1	0	0	0	0	0	0	.000	.000	.000	.000
2020 SF	NL	1	3	0	0	0	0	(0	0)	0	0	0	0	0	0	0	0	0	0	0	0	0	.000	.000	.000	.000
6 ML YEARS		128	391	89	19	0	7	(4	3)	129	32	37	36	33	3	92	4	0	4	1	1	10	.228	.292	.330	.622

Ryan Brasier

Pitches: R **Bats:** R **Pos:** RP-24; SP-1   BRAY-zhur   **Ht:** 6'0" **Wt:** 227 **Born:** 8/26/1987 **Age:** 33

Year Team	Lg	G	GS	GF	IP	BFP	H	R	ER	HR	SH	SF	HB	TBB	IBB	SO	WP	W	L	Pct	Sv-Op	Hld	Vel	OPS	ERC	ERA
		HOW MUCH PITCHED					WHAT HE GAVE UP											THE RESULTS								
2013 LAA	AL	7	0	7	9.0	35	7	2	2	1	0	1	0	4	0	7	0	0	0	-	0-0	0	94	.648	3.37	2.00
2018 Bos	AL	34	0	5	33.2	124	19	6	6	2	1	5	0	7	0	29	1	2	0	1.000	0-2	10	97	.482	1.26	1.60
2019 Bos	AL	62	0	15	55.2	241	51	33	30	9	0	3	3	21	1	61	3	2	4	.333	7-11	9	96	.722	4.06	4.85
2020 Bos	AL	25	1	1	25.0	110	24	12	11	2	0	1	0	11	1	30	1	1	0	1.000	0-2	10	96	.696	3.71	3.96
Postseason		9	0	0	8.2	39	7	1	1	0	0	1	1	5	0	7	1	0	0	-	0-0	5	96	.583	3.31	1.04
4 ML YEARS		128	1	28	123.1	510	101	53	49	14	1	10	3	43	2	127	5	5	4	.556	7-15	29	96	.653	3.05	3.58

Steven Brault

Pitches: L **Bats:** L **Pos:** SP-10; RP-1   **Ht:** 6'0" **Wt:** 195 **Born:** 4/29/1992 **Age:** 29

Year Team	Lg	G	GS	GF	IP	BFP	H	R	ER	HR	SH	SF	HB	TBB	IBB	SO	WP	W	L	Pct	Sv-Op	Hld	Vel	OPS	ERC	ERA
		HOW MUCH PITCHED					WHAT HE GAVE UP											THE RESULTS								
2016 Pit	NL	8	7	0	33.1	166	45	26	18	5	3	0	2	17	1	29	1	0	3	.000	0-0	0	91	.893	6.99	4.86
2017 Pit	NL	11	4	2	34.2	162	41	21	18	3	2	1	2	14	1	23	0	1	0	1.000	1-1	0	92	.790	5.06	4.67
2018 Pit	NL	45	5	6	91.2	413	84	51	47	10	3	1	8	57	4	82	9	6	3	.667	0-0	3	93	.747	4.84	4.61
2019 Pit	NL	25	19	1	113.1	505	117	69	65	15	3	0	7	53	2	100	7	4	6	.400	0-0	0	92	.791	5.00	5.16
2020 Pit	NL	11	10	0	42.2	178	29	17	16	2	0	2	5	22	0	38	3	1	3	.250	0-0	0	92	.563	2.92	3.38
5 ML YEARS		100	45	9	315.2	1424	316	184	164	35	11	4	24	163	8	272	20	12	15	.444	1-1	3	92	.762	4.87	4.68

Ryan Braun

Bats: R **Throws:** R **Pos:** RF-20;DH-16;PH-5;1B-1   **Ht:** 6'2" **Wt:** 205 **Born:** 11/17/1983 **Age:** 37

Year Team	Lg	G	AB	H	2B	3B	HR	(Hm	Rd)	TB	R	RBI	RC	TBB	IBB	SO	HBP	SH	SF	SB	CS	GDP	Avg	OBP	Slg	OPS
								BATTING												RUNNING			AVERAGES			
2007 Mil	NL	113	451	146	26	6	34	(17	17)	286	91	97	94	29	1	112	7	0	5	15	5	13	.324	.370	.634	1.004
2008 Mil	NL	151	611	174	39	7	37	(23	14)	338	92	106	100	42	4	129	6	0	4	14	4	13	.285	.335	.553	.888
2009 Mil	NL	158	635	203	39	6	32	(15	17)	350	113	114	133	57	1	121	13	0	3	20	6	6	.320	.386	.551	.937
2010 Mil	NL	157	619	188	45	1	25	(13	12)	310	101	103	104	56	1	105	6	0	3	14	3	17	.304	.365	.501	.866
2011 Mil	NL	150	563	187	38	6	33	(16	17)	336	109	111	124	58	2	93	5	0	3	33	6	9	.332	.397	.597	.994
2012 Mil	NL	154	598	191	36	3	41	(24	17)	356	108	112	125	63	15	128	11	0	5	30	7	12	.319	.391	.595	.987
2013 Mil	NL	61	225	67	14	2	9	(5	4)	112	30	38	39	27	7	56	0	0	1	4	5	8	.298	.372	.498	.869
2014 Mil	NL	135	530	141	30	6	19	(8	11)	240	68	81	74	41	3	113	6	0	3	11	5	17	.266	.324	.453	.777
2015 Mil	NL	140	506	144	27	3	25	(8	17)	252	87	84	91	54	4	115	4	0	3	24	4	20	.285	.356	.498	.854
2016 Mil	NL	135	511	156	23	3	30	(15	15)	275	80	91	93	46	10	98	4	0	3	16	5	20	.305	.365	.538	.903
2017 Mil	NL	104	380	102	28	2	17	(7	10)	185	58	52	53	38	2	76	3	0	4	12	4	15	.268	.336	.487	.823
2018 Mil	NL	125	405	103	25	1	20	(8	12)	190	59	64	65	34	5	85	2	0	3	11	5	8	.254	.313	.469	.782
2019 Mil	NL	144	459	131	31	2	22	(9	13)	232	70	75	75	34	1	105	8	0	3	11	1	15	.285	.343	.505	.849
2020 Mil	NL	39	129	30	7	1	8	(5	3)	63	14	26	22	7	0	27	2	0	1	1	0	6	.233	.281	.488	.769
Postseason		26	104	35	11	0	2	(2	0)	52	9	16	18	6	0	26	1	0	1	3	0	0	.337	.375	.500	.875
14 ML YEARS		1766	6622	1963	408	49	352	(173	179)	3525	1080	1154	1192	586	56	1363	77	0	44	216	60	179	.296	.358	.532	.891

Ben Braymer

Pitches: L **Bats:** L **Pos:** RP-2; SP-1   **Ht:** 6'2" **Wt:** 220 **Born:** 4/28/1994 **Age:** 27

Year Team	Lg	G	GS	GF	IP	BFP	H	R	ER	HR	SH	SF	HB	TBB	IBB	SO	WP	W	L	Pct	Sv-Op	Hld	Vel	OPS	ERC	ERA
		HOW MUCH PITCHED					WHAT HE GAVE UP											THE RESULTS								
2020 Was	NL	3	1	0	7.1	34	7	1	1	0	0	0	0	5	0	8	0	1	0	1.000	0-0	0	89	.629	4.04	1.23

John Brebbia

Pitches: R Bats: L Pos: P

Ht: 6'1" Wt: 200 Born: 5/30/1990 Age: 31

Year	Team	Lg	G	GS	GF	IP	BFP	H	R	ER	HR	SH	SF	HB	TBB	IBB	SO	WP	W	L	Pct	Sv-Op	Hld	Vel	OPS	ERC	ERA
2017	StL	NL	50	0	13	51.2	209	37	15	14	8	1	0	5	11	3	51	2	0	0	-	0-1	5	94	.640	2.45	2.44
2018	StL	NL	45	0	17	50.2	209	43	18	18	5	1	2	0	16	2	60	1	3	3	.500	2-2	5	95	.647	2.85	3.20
2019	StL	NL	66	0	22	72.2	304	59	31	29	6	0	1	3	27	2	87	0	3	4	.429	0-1	12	93	.626	2.93	3.59
	Postseason		5	0		3.0	17	7	2	2	1	0	0	0	1	0	3	0	0	0	-	0-0	0	93	1.408	14.72	6.00
	3 ML YEARS		161	0	52	175.0	722	139	64	61	19	2	3	8	54	7	198	3	6	7	.462	2-4	22	94	.636	2.77	3.14

Alex Bregman

Bats: R Throws: R Pos: 3B-42;PH-1

Ht: 6'0" Wt: 192 Born: 3/30/1994 Age: 27

Year	Team	Lg	G	AB	H	2B	3B	HR	(Hm	Rd)	TB	R	RBI	RC	TBB	IBB	SO	HBP	SH	SF	SB	CS	GDP	Avg	OBP	Slg	OPS
2016	Hou	AL	49	201	53	13	3	8	(3	5)	96	31	34	37	15	0	52	0	0	1	2	0	1	.264	.313	.478	.791
2017	Hou	AL	155	556	158	39	5	19	(9	10)	264	88	71	87	55	2	97	7	1	7	17	5	15	.284	.352	.475	.827
2018	Hou	AL	157	594	170	51	1	31	(16	15)	316	105	103	135	96	2	85	12	0	3	10	4	15	.286	.394	.532	.926
2019	Hou	AL	156	554	164	37	2	41	(16	25)	328	122	112	126	119	2	83	9	0	8	5	1	9	.296	.423	.592	1.015
2020	Hou	AL	42	153	37	12	1	6	(2	4)	69	19	22	28	24	1	26	2	0	1	0	0	2	.242	.350	.451	.801
	Postseason		44	160	37	8	0	10	(7	3)	75	32	27	21	28	2	27	4	0	1	2	1	3	.231	.358	.469	.826
	5 ML YEARS		559	2058	582	152	12	105	(46	59)	1073	365	342	413	309	7	343	30	1	20	34	10	42	.283	.381	.521	.902

Brandon Brennan

Pitches: R Bats: R Pos: RP-5

Ht: 6'4" Wt: 207 Born: 7/26/1991 Age: 29

Year	Team	Lg	G	GS	GF	IP	BFP	H	R	ER	HR	SH	SF	HB	TBB	IBB	SO	WP	W	L	Pct	Sv-Op	Hld	Vel	OPS	ERC	ERA
2019	Sea	AL	44	0	7	47.1	196	34	25	24	6	0	3	0	24	4	47	6	3	6	.333	0-2	8	95	.651	3.03	4.56
2020	Sea	AL	5	0	0	7.1	33	7	3	3	2	0	0	0	5	1	7	0	0	0	-	0-0	0	93	.864	6.11	3.68
	2 ML YEARS		49	0	7	54.2	229	41	28	27	8	0	3	0	29	5	54	6	3	6	.333	0-2	8	95	.681	3.40	4.45

Colten Brewer

Pitches: R Bats: R Pos: RP-7; SP-4

Ht: 6'4" Wt: 222 Born: 10/29/1992 Age: 28

Year	Team	Lg	G	GS	GF	IP	BFP	H	R	ER	HR	SH	SF	HB	TBB	IBB	SO	WP	W	L	Pct	Sv-Op	Hld	Vel	OPS	ERC	ERA
2018	SD	NL	11	0	5	9.2	49	15	10	6	0	0	0	0	7	0	10	1	1	0	1.000	0-0	0	93	.878	8.08	5.59
2019	Bos	AL	58	0	10	54.2	253	59	26	25	6	1	3	2	34	1	52	9	1	2	.333	0-1	6	93	.804	5.63	4.12
2020	Bos	AL	11	4	1	25.2	122	31	17	16	6	0	0	1	14	0	25	1	0	3	.000	0-0	0	94	.900	7.07	5.61
	3 ML YEARS		80	4	14	90.0	424	105	53	47	12	1	3	3	55	1	87	11	2	5	.286	0-1	6	93	.841	6.30	4.70

Austin Brice

Pitches: R Bats: R Pos: RP-20; SP-1

Ht: 6'4" Wt: 238 Born: 6/19/1992 Age: 29

Year	Team	Lg	G	GS	GF	IP	BFP	H	R	ER	HR	SH	SF	HB	TBB	IBB	SO	WP	W	L	Pct	Sv-Op	Hld	Vel	OPS	ERC	ERA
2016	Mia	NL	15	0	2	14.0	59	9	12	11	2	0	0	2	5	1	14	0	0	1	.000	0-0	1	94	.598	2.63	7.07
2017	Cin	NL	22	0	4	32.2	137	33	18	18	6	1	1	3	7	0	26	0	0	0	-	0-0	1	94	.756	4.38	4.96
2018	Cin	NL	33	0	8	37.1	162	39	26	24	9	1	1	3	13	6	32	1	2	3	.400	0-0	3	94	.876	5.26	5.79
2019	Mia	NL	36	0	10	44.2	199	37	21	17	7	0	1	7	18	2	46	2	1	0	1.000	0-1	6	93	.676	3.92	3.43
2020	Bos	AL	21	1	2	19.2	87	17	13	13	3	0	0	2	13	0	25	1	1	0	1.000	0-0	4	94	.826	5.28	5.95
	5 ML YEARS		127	1	26	148.1	644	135	90	83	27	2	3	17	56	9	143	4	4	4	.500	0-1	15	94	.757	4.39	5.04

Jose Briceno

Bats: R Throws: R Pos: C-2

Ht: 6'1" Wt: 225 Born: 9/19/1992 Age: 28

Year	Team	Lg	G	AB	H	2B	3B	HR	(Hm	Rd)	TB	R	RBI	RC	TBB	IBB	SO	HBP	SH	SF	SB	CS	GDP	Avg	OBP	Slg	OPS
2018	LAA	AL	46	117	28	2	0	5	(1	4)	45	12	10	11	8	0	35	2	1	0	0	1	2	.239	.299	.385	.684
2020	LAA	AL	2	5	1	0	0	0	(0	0)	1	0	0	0	1	0	1	0	0	0	0	0	0	.200	.333	.200	.533
	2 ML YEARS		48	122	29	2	0	5	(1	4)	46	12	10	11	9	0	36	2	1	0	0	1	2	.238	.301	.377	.678

Jeff Brigham

Pitches: R Bats: R Pos: RP-1

Ht: 6'0" Wt: 195 Born: 2/16/1992 Age: 29

Year	Team	Lg	G	GS	GF	IP	BFP	H	R	ER	HR	SH	SF	HB	TBB	IBB	SO	WP	W	L	Pct	Sv-Op	Hld	Vel	OPS	ERC	ERA
2018	Mia	NL	4	4	0	16.1	77	16	11	11	2	0	3	2	13	0	12	0	0	4	.000	0-0	0	93	.860	6.35	6.06
2019	Mia	NL	32	0	10	38.1	161	36	20	19	8	0	1	1	14	2	39	6	3	2	.600	1-2	4	97	.765	4.43	4.46
2020	Mia	NL	1	0	0	1.0	5	2	1	1	0	0	0	0	0	0	0	0	0	0	-	0-0	0	94	1.000	7.48	9.00
	3 ML YEARS		37	4	10	55.2	243	54	32	31	10	0	4	3	27	2	51	6	3	6	.333	1-2	4	95	.800	5.05	5.01

Lewis Brinson

Bats: R **Throws:** R **Pos:** RF-31;LF-21;PH-10;CF-7;PR-2   **Ht:** 6'5" **Wt:** 212 **Born:** 5/8/1994 **Age:** 27

									BATTING													RUNNING			AVERAGES			
Year	Team	Lg	G	AB	H	2B	3B	HR	(Hm	Rd)	TB	R	RBI	RC	TBB	IBB	SO	HBP	SH	SF		SB	CS	GDP	Avg	OBP	Slg	OPS
2017	Mil	NL	21	47	5	0	1	2	(0	2)	13	2	3	4	7	1	17	1	0	0		1	0	0	.106	.236	.277	.513
2018	Mia	NL	109	382	76	10	5	11	(2	9)	129	31	42	29	17	2	120	4	0	2		2	1	6	.199	.240	.338	.577
2019	Mia	NL	75	226	39	9	1	0	(0	0)	50	15	15	10	13	1	74	6	2	1		1	1	8	.173	.236	.221	.457
2020	Mia	NL	47	106	24	6	0	3	(2	1)	39	14	12	12	6	0	30	0	0	0		4	0	2	.226	.268	.368	.636
	4 ML YEARS		252	761	144	25	7	16	(4	12)	231	62	72	55	43	4	241	11	2	3		8	2	16	.189	.242	.304	.546

Zack Britton

Pitches: L **Bats:** L **Pos:** RP-20   **Ht:** 6'1" **Wt:** 200 **Born:** 12/22/1987 **Age:** 33

			HOW MUCH PITCHED					WHAT HE GAVE UP											THE RESULTS							
Year	Team	Lg	G	GS	GF	IP	BFP	H	R	ER	HR	SH	SF	HB	TBB	IBB	SO	WP		W	L	Pct	Sv-Op	Hld	Vel	OPS	ERC	ERA
2011	Bal	AL	28	28	0	154.1	666	162	93	79	12	8	7	1	62	3	97	7		11	11	.500	0-0	0	92	.735	4.24	4.61
2012	Bal	AL	12	11	0	60.1	270	61	37	34	6	0	1	2	32	3	53	4		5	3	.625	0-0	0	92	.756	4.70	5.07
2013	Bal	AL	8	7	0	40.0	182	52	23	22	4	1	1	1	17	1	18	1		2	3	.400	0-0	0	92	.837	6.14	4.95
2014	Bal	AL	71	0	49	76.1	285	46	17	14	4	3	0	1	23	0	62	0		3	2	.600	37-41	7	95	.500	1.62	1.65
2015	Bal	AL	64	0	58	65.2	253	51	16	14	3	0	0	1	14	1	79	5		4	1	.800	36-40	0	96	.547	2.02	1.92
2016	Bal	AL	69	0	63	67.0	254	38	7	4	1	1	0	0	18	3	74	10		2	1	.667	47-47	0	96	.430	1.18	0.54
2017	Bal	AL	38	0	30	37.1	161	39	12	12	1	1	1	0	18	1	29	4		2	1	.667	15-17	0	96	.690	4.18	2.89
2018	2 Tms	AL	41	0	21	40.2	169	29	16	14	3	0	1	3	21	0	34	7		2	0	1.000	7-10	9	95	.605	3.13	3.10
2019	NYY	AL	66	0	15	61.1	245	38	13	13	3	1	2	1	32	1	53	3		3	1	.750	3-7	29	95	.545	2.32	1.91
2020	NYY	AL	20	0	10	19.0	76	12	6	4	0	0	0	0	7	0	16	4		1	2	.333	8-8	3	95	.482	1.54	1.89
	18	Bal	AL	16	0	11	15.2	63	11	6	6	1	0	0	1	10	0	13	2		1	0	1.000	4-5	1	94	.676	3.63	3.45
	18	NYY	AL	25	0	10	25.0	106	18	10	8	2	0	1	2	11	0	21	5		1	0	1.000	3-5	8	95	.564	2.84	2.88
	Postseason		17	0	4	17.2	78	12	6	6	3	1	1	0	13	3	15	2		0	0	-	2-2	4	95	.722	3.74	3.06
	10 ML YEARS		417	46	246	622.0	2561	528	240	210	37	15	13	10	244	13	515	45		35	25	.583	153-170	48	94	.631	3.04	3.04

Connor Brogdon

Pitches: R **Bats:** R **Pos:** RP-9   **Ht:** 6'6" **Wt:** 205 **Born:** 1/29/1995 **Age:** 26

			HOW MUCH PITCHED					WHAT HE GAVE UP										THE RESULTS							
Year	Team	Lg	G	GS	GF	IP	BFP	H	R	ER	HR	SH	SF	HB	TBB	IBB	SO	WP	W	L	Pct	Sv-Op	Hld	Vel	OPS	ERC	ERA
2020	Phi	NL	9	0	3	11.1	44	5	5	5	3	0	0	0	5	1	17	0	1	0	1.000	0-0	0	95	.612	2.17	3.97

Mike Brosseau

Bats: R **Throws:** R **Pos:** 1B-12;3B-11;2B-9;PH-4;PR-3;LF-2;RF-1   **Ht:** 5'10" **Wt:** 205 **Born:** 3/15/1994 **Age:** 27

									BATTING													RUNNING			AVERAGES			
Year	Team	Lg	G	AB	H	2B	3B	HR	(Hm	Rd)	TB	R	RBI	RC	TBB	IBB	SO	HBP	SH	SF		SB	CS	GDP	Avg	OBP	Slg	OPS
2019	TB	AL	51	132	36	7	0	6	(2	4)	61	17	16	18	7	0	39	2	1	0		1	0	3	.273	.319	.462	.781
2020	TB	AL	37	86	26	5	1	5	(1	4)	48	12	12	16	8	0	31	3	0	1		2	0	1	.302	.378	.558	.936
	Postseason		1	2	0	0	0	0	(0	0)	0	0	0	0	1	0	1	0	0	0		0	0	0	.000	.333	.000	.333
	2 ML YEARS		88	218	62	12	1	11	(3	8)	109	29	28	34	15	0	70	5	1	1		3	0	4	.284	.343	.500	.843

Rex Brothers

Pitches: L **Bats:** L **Pos:** RP-3   **Ht:** 6'0" **Wt:** 205 **Born:** 12/18/1987 **Age:** 33

			HOW MUCH PITCHED					WHAT HE GAVE UP											THE RESULTS							
Year	Team	Lg	G	GS	GF	IP	BFP	H	R	ER	HR	SH	SF	HB	TBB	IBB	SO	WP		W	L	Pct	Sv-Op	Hld	Vel	OPS	ERC	ERA
2011	Col	NL	48	0	6	40.2	172	33	14	13	4	0	0	0	20	2	59	2		1	2	.333	1-3	16	95	.644	3.31	2.88
2012	Col	NL	75	0	10	67.2	295	63	33	29	5	3	3	1	37	7	83	5		8	2	.800	0-5	18	95	.732	3.99	3.86
2013	Col	NL	72	0	40	67.1	281	51	16	13	5	1	0	0	36	2	76	3		2	1	.667	19-21	12	93	.618	3.09	1.74
2014	Col	NL	74	0	15	56.1	273	65	38	35	7	1	4	2	39	0	55	5		4	6	.400	0-6	15	93	.825	6.43	5.59
2015	Col	NL	17	0	1	10.1	46	9	2	2	0	0	1	0	8	0	5	1		1	0	1.000	0-0	0	93	.748	4.12	1.74
2017	Atl	NL	27	0	8	23.2	105	23	19	19	3	0	0	1	12	3	33	2		4	3	.571	0-0	2	95	.767	4.48	7.23
2018	Atl	NL	1	0	0	0.0	2	0	1	1	0	0	0	0	2	0	0	0		0	0	-	0-0	0	96	-	-	-
2020	ChC	NL	3	0	0	3.1	15	2	3	3	2	0	0	0	3	0	8	0		0	0	-	0-0	0	95	1.000	7.36	8.10
	8 ML YEARS		317	0	80	269.1	1189	246	126	115	26	5	8	4	157	14	319	18		20	14	.588	20-35	63	94	.721	4.25	3.84

Seth Brown

Bats: L **Throws:** L **Pos:** 1B-3;PH-3;DH-1;PR-1   **Ht:** 6'1" **Wt:** 223 **Born:** 7/13/1992 **Age:** 28

									BATTING													RUNNING			AVERAGES			
Year	Team	Lg	G	AB	H	2B	3B	HR	(Hm	Rd)	TB	R	RBI	RC	TBB	IBB	SO	HBP	SH	SF		SB	CS	GDP	Avg	OBP	Slg	OPS
2019	Oak	AL	26	75	22	8	2	0	(0	0)	34	11	13	13	7	0	23	1	0	0		1	0	2	.293	.361	.453	.815
2020	Oak	AL	7	5	0	0	0	0	(0	0)	0	0	0	0	0	0	2	0	0	0		0	0	0	.000	.000	.000	.000
	Postseason		1	1	0	0	0	0	(0	0)	0	0	0	0	0	0	0	0	0	0		0	0	0	.000	.000	.000	.000
	2 ML YEARS		33	80	22	8	2	0	(0	0)	34	11	13	13	7	0	25	1	0	0		1	0	2	.275	.341	.425	.766

JT Brubaker

Pitches: R **Bats:** R **Pos:** SP-9; RP-2   **Ht:** 6'3" **Wt:** 185 **Born:** 11/17/1993 **Age:** 27

			HOW MUCH PITCHED					WHAT HE GAVE UP										THE RESULTS							
Year	Team	Lg	G	GS	GF	IP	BFP	H	R	ER	HR	SH	SF	HB	TBB	IBB	SO	WP	W	L	Pct	Sv-Op	Hld	Vel	OPS	ERC	ERA
2020	Pit	NL	11	9	0	47.1	205	48	27	26	6	0	2	3	17	0	48	4	1	3	.250	0-0	1	94	.758	4.45	4.94

Jay Bruce

Bats: L **Throws:** L **Pos:** LF-11;DH-10;PH-8;RF-6;1B-2   **Ht:** 6'3" **Wt:** 230 **Born:** 4/3/1987 **Age:** 34

Year	Team	Lg	G	AB	H	2B	3B	HR	(Hm	Rd)	TB	R	RBI	RC	TBB	IBB	SO	HBP	SH	SF	SB	CS	GDP	Avg	OBP	Slg	OPS
2008	Cin	NL	108	413	105	17	1	21	(13	8)	187	63	52	49	33	1	110	4	0	2	4	6	8	.254	.314	.453	.767
2009	Cin	NL	101	345	77	15	2	22	(13	9)	162	47	58	47	38	2	75	2	1	1	3	3	5	.223	.303	.470	.773
2010	Cin	NL	148	509	143	23	5	25	(19	6)	251	80	70	71	58	5	136	1	0	5	5	4	12	.281	.353	.493	.846
2011	Cin	NL	157	585	150	27	2	32	(16	16)	277	84	97	96	71	14	158	5	1	2	8	7	8	.256	.341	.474	.814
2012	Cin	NL	155	560	141	35	5	34	(21	13)	288	89	99	85	62	11	155	4	0	7	9	3	5	.252	.327	.514	.841
2013	Cin	NL	160	626	164	43	1	30	(16	14)	299	89	109	88	63	13	185	2	0	5	7	3	9	.262	.329	.478	.807
2014	Cin	NL	137	493	107	21	1	18	(10	8)	184	71	66	54	44	5	149	2	1	5	12	3	8	.217	.281	.373	.654
2015	Cin	NL	157	580	131	35	4	26	(13	13)	252	72	87	61	58	8	145	2	0	9	9	5	10	.226	.294	.434	.729
2016	2 Tms	NL	147	539	135	27	6	33	(17	16)	273	74	99	87	44	7	126	3	0	3	4	2	14	.250	.309	.506	.815
2017	2 Tms		146	555	141	29	2	36	(15	21)	282	82	101	94	57	0	139	2	0	3	1	1	11	.254	.324	.508	.832
2018	NYM	NL	94	319	71	18	1	9	(3	6)	118	31	37	44	41	4	75	0	0	1	2	3	3	.223	.310	.370	.680
2019	2 Tms		98	310	67	17	0	26	(8	18)	162	43	59	36	19	0	82	1	0	3	1	0	5	.216	.261	.523	.784
2020	Phi	NL	32	96	19	4	2	6	(4	2)	45	11	14	10	7	1	24	0	0	0	0	0	1	.198	.252	.469	.721
16	Cin	NL	97	370	98	22	6	25	(14	11)	207	60	80	67	27	3	83	2	0	3	4	2	11	.265	.316	.559	.875
16	NYM	NL	50	169	37	5	0	8	(3	5)	66	14	19	20	17	4	43	1	0	0	0	0	3	.219	.294	.391	.685
17	NYM	NL	103	406	104	20	0	29	(11	18)	211	61	75	68	39	0	102	1	0	2	0	1	9	.256	.321	.520	.841
17	Cle	AL	43	149	37	9	2	7	(4	3)	71	21	26	26	18	0	37	1	0	1	1	0	2	.248	.331	.477	.808
19	Sea	AL	47	165	35	11	0	14	(5	9)	88	27	28	19	16	0	53	1	0	2	1	0	1	.212	.283	.533	.816
19	Phi	NL	51	145	32	6	0	12	(3	9)	74	16	31	17	3	0	29	0	0	1	0	0	4	.221	.235	.510	.745
	Postseason		15	52	13	3	0	4	(2	2)	28	8	10	7	6	0	13	1	0	1	0	1	0	.250	.333	.538	.872
	13 ML YEARS		1640	5930	1451	311	32	318	(168	150)	2780	836	948	822	595	71	1559	28	3	46	65	40	99	.245	.314	.469	.783

Kris Bryant

Bats: R **Throws:** R **Pos:** 3B-27;LF-4;DH-2;1B-1   **Ht:** 6'5" **Wt:** 230 **Born:** 1/4/1992 **Age:** 29

Year	Team	Lg	G	AB	H	2B	3B	HR	(Hm	Rd)	TB	R	RBI	RC	TBB	IBB	SO	HBP	SH	SF	SB	CS	GDP	Avg	OBP	Slg	OPS
2015	ChC	NL	151	559	154	31	5	26	(21	5)	273	87	99	104	77	0	199	9	0	5	13	4	7	.275	.369	.488	.858
2016	ChC	NL	155	603	176	35	3	39	(17	22)	334	121	102	120	75	5	154	18	0	3	8	5	3	.292	.385	.554	.939
2017	ChC	NL	151	549	162	38	4	29	(18	11)	295	111	73	113	95	5	128	15	0	6	7	5	8	.295	.409	.537	.946
2018	ChC	NL	102	389	106	28	3	13	(7	6)	179	59	52	65	48	6	107	17	0	3	2	4	5	.272	.374	.460	.834
2019	ChC	NL	147	543	153	35	1	31	(15	16)	283	108	77	107	74	1	145	15	0	2	4	0	10	.282	.382	.521	.903
2020	ChC	NL	34	131	27	5	1	4	(1	3)	46	20	11	15	12	0	40	4	0	0	0	0	1	.206	.293	.351	.644
	Postseason		37	145	35	8	1	6	(4	2)	63	17	16	18	13	0	50	1	0	0	1	0	3	.241	.308	.434	.743
	6 ML YEARS		740	2774	778	172	17	142	(79	63)	1410	506	414	524	381	17	773	78	0	19	34	18	34	.280	.380	.508	.889

Kris Bubic

Pitches: L **Bats:** L **Pos:** SP-10   **Ht:** 6'3" **Wt:** 220 **Born:** 8/19/1997 **Age:** 23

			HOW MUCH PITCHED				WHAT HE GAVE UP										THE RESULTS							
Year	Team	Lg	G	GS	GF	IP	BFP	H	R	ER	HR	SH	SF	HB	TBB	IBB	SO	WP	W	L	Pct	Sv-Op	Hld	Vel	OPS	ERC	ERA
2020	KC	AL	10	10	0	50.0	222	52	29	24	8	0	0	2	22	1	49	0	1	6	.143	0-0	0	91	.777	5.02	4.32

Ryan Buchter

Pitches: L **Bats:** L **Pos:** RP-10   BUCK-ter   **Ht:** 6'4" **Wt:** 232 **Born:** 2/13/1987 **Age:** 34

			HOW MUCH PITCHED				WHAT HE GAVE UP										THE RESULTS							
Year	Team	Lg	G	GS	GF	IP	BFP	H	R	ER	HR	SH	SF	HB	TBB	IBB	SO	WP	W	L	Pct	Sv-Op	Hld	Vel	OPS	ERC	ERA
2014	NL		1	0	0	1.0	0	0	0	0	0	0	0	0	1	0	1	0	1	0	1.000	0-0	0	92	.333	1.26	0.00
2016	SD	NL	67	0	10	63.0	247	34	20	20	4	0	2	2	31	3	78	3	3	0	1.000	1-2	20	92	.559	1.94	2.86
2017	2 Tms		71	0	12	65.1	268	44	25	21	10	0	3	4	26	1	65	0	4	3	.571	1-3	20	93	.642	2.86	2.89
2018	Oak	AL	54	0	4	39.1	163	32	17	12	4	1	1	0	15	1	41	1	6	0	1.000	0-0	16	92	.646	2.96	2.75
2019	Oak	AL	64	0	7	45.1	198	42	16	15	8	3	3	2	23	2	50	1	1	1	.500	0-4	12	93	.799	4.77	2.98
2020	LAA	AL	10	0	1	6.0	29	5	4	3	2	0	0	0	6	0	8	1	2	0	1.000	0-0	0	93	.901	7.31	4.50
17	SD	NL	42	0	5	38.1	161	28	15	13	7	0	1	1	18	0	47	0	3	3	.500	1-3	15	93	.696	3.48	3.05
17	KC	AL	29	0	7	27.0	107	16	10	8	3	0	2	3	8	1	18	0	1	0	1.000	0-0	5	93	.561	2.03	2.67
	6 ML YEARS		267	0	34	220.0	908	157	82	71	28	4	9	8	102	7	243	6	17	4	.810	2-9	68	93	.661	3.07	2.90

Walker Buehler

Pitches: R **Bats:** R **Pos:** SP-8   **Ht:** 6'2" **Wt:** 185 **Born:** 7/28/1994 **Age:** 26

			HOW MUCH PITCHED				WHAT HE GAVE UP										THE RESULTS							
Year	Team	Lg	G	GS	GF	IP	BFP	H	R	ER	HR	SH	SF	HB	TBB	IBB	SO	WP	W	L	Pct	Sv-Op	Hld	Vel	OPS	ERC	ERA
2017	LAD	NL	8	0	2	9.1	44	11	8	8	2	0	0	0	8	1	12	1	1	0	1.000	0-0	1	98	.932	8.22	7.71
2018	LAD	NL	24	23	0	137.1	541	95	43	40	12	2	3	6	37	1	151	4	8	5	.615	0-1	0	96	.556	2.10	2.62
2019	LAD	NL	30	30	0	182.1	737	153	77	66	20	2	6	7	37	0	215	4	14	4	.778	0-0	0	97	.636	2.66	3.26
2020	LAD	NL	8	8	0	36.2	147	24	18	14	7	0	0	1	11	0	42	4	1	0	1.000	0-0	0	97	.600	2.48	3.44
	Postseason		6	6	0	36.1	138	21	11	11	3	1	0	1	10	1	44	1	1	1	.500	0-0	0	97	.527	1.57	2.72
	4 ML YEARS		70	61	2	365.2	1469	283	146	128	41	4	9	14	93	2	420	13	24	9	.727	0-1	1	97	.612	2.54	3.15

Madison Bumgarner

Pitches: L Bats: R Pos: SP-9   Ht: 6'4" Wt: 255 Born: 8/1/1989 Age: 31

			HOW MUCH PITCHED				WHAT HE GAVE UP										THE RESULTS						
Year	Team	Lg	G	GS	GF	IP	BFP	H	R	ER	HR	SH	SF	HB	TBB	IBB	SO	WP	W	L	Pct	Sv-Op	Hld	Vel	OPS	ERC	ERA
2009	SF	NL	4	1	1	10.0	40	8	2	2	2	1	1	0	3	1	10	0	0	0	-	0-0	0	89	.739	3.14	1.80
2010	SF	NL	18	18	0	111.0	472	119	40	37	11	0	4	5	26	2	86	1	7	6	.538	0-0	0	91	.732	3.98	3.00
2011	SF	NL	33	33	0	204.2	844	202	82	73	12	12	4	4	46	5	191	0	13	13	.500	0-0	0	92	.670	3.14	3.21
2012	SF	NL	32	32	0	208.1	849	183	87	78	23	7	4	7	49	6	191	3	16	11	.593	0-0	0	91	.670	2.95	3.37
2013	SF	NL	31	31	0	201.1	803	146	68	62	15	10	4	6	62	6	199	6	13	9	.591	0-0	0	91	.577	2.23	2.77
2014	SF	NL	33	33	0	217.1	873	194	81	72	21	9	5	6	43	3	219	4	18	10	.643	0-0	0	92	.653	2.83	2.98
2015	SF	NL	32	32	0	218.1	869	181	73	71	21	5	4	7	39	2	234	1	18	9	.667	0-0	0	92	.612	2.43	2.93
2016	SF	NL	34	**34**	0	226.2	**912**	179	79	69	26	3	6	8	54	0	251	4	15	9	.625	0-0	0	91	.619	2.57	2.74
2017	SF	NL	17	17	0	111.0	460	101	41	41	17	2	1	3	20	3	101	0	4	9	.308	0-0	0	91	.704	3.14	3.32
2018	SF	NL	21	21	0	129.2	551	118	51	47	14	5	3	5	43	3	109	3	6	7	.462	0-0	0	91	.694	3.44	3.26
2019	SF	NL	34	**34**	0	207.2	844	191	99	90	30	5	5	10	43	3	203	3	9	9	.500	0-0	0	91	.717	3.38	3.90
2020	Ari		9	9	0	41.2	190	47	31	30	13	0	1	6	13	2	30	0	1	4	.200	0-0	0	88	.924	6.48	6.48
	Postseason		16	14	1	102.1	398	74	25	24	8	6	1	5	18	2	87	0	8	3	.727	1-1	0	92	.544	1.88	2.11
12 ML YEARS			298	295	1	1887.2	7697	1669	734	672	205	59	42	68	441	36	1824	25	120	96	.556	0-0	0	91	.665	2.99	3.20

Aaron Bummer

Pitches: L Bats: L Pos: RP-9   Ht: 6'3" Wt: 215 Born: 9/21/1993 Age: 27

			HOW MUCH PITCHED				WHAT HE GAVE UP										THE RESULTS						
Year	Team	Lg	G	GS	GF	IP	BFP	H	R	ER	HR	SH	SF	HB	TBB	IBB	SO	WP	W	L	Pct	Sv-Op	Hld	Vel	OPS	ERC	ERA
2017	CWS	AL	30	0	3	22.0	91	13	11	11	4	1	1	1	15	1	17	1	1	3	.250	0-1	7	93	.692	3.70	4.50
2018	CWS	AL	37	0	9	31.2	144	40	19	15	1	0	0	1	10	0	35	7	0	1	.000	0-1	2	93	.730	4.80	4.26
2019	CWS	AL	58	0	5	67.2	262	43	17	16	4	1	0	3	24	2	60	4	0	0	-	1-3	27	96	.520	1.99	2.13
2020	CWS	AL	9	0	1	9.1	38	5	1	1	0	0	0	0	5	0	14	0	1	0	1.000	0-0	3	96	.415	1.60	0.96
4 ML YEARS			134	0	18	130.2	535	101	48	43	9	2	1	5	54	3	126	12	2	4	.333	1-5	39	95	.598	2.86	2.96

Dylan Bundy

Pitches: R Bats: B Pos: SP-11   Ht: 6'1" Wt: 225 Born: 11/15/1992 Age: 28

			HOW MUCH PITCHED				WHAT HE GAVE UP										THE RESULTS						
Year	Team	Lg	G	GS	GF	IP	BFP	H	R	ER	HR	SH	SF	HB	TBB	IBB	SO	WP	W	L	Pct	Sv-Op	Hld	Vel	OPS	ERC	ERA
2012	Bal	AL	2	0	2	1.2	6	1	0	0	0	0	0	0	1	0	0	0	0	0	-	0-0	0	94	.533	2.46	0.00
2016	Bal	AL	36	14	6	109.2	474	109	52	49	18	1	1	6	42	4	104	0	10	6	.625	0-0	3	94	.766	4.61	4.02
2017	Bal	AL	28	28	0	169.2	698	152	82	80	26	0	7	7	51	0	152	0	13	9	.591	0-0	0	92	.721	3.68	4.24
2018	Bal	AL	31	31	0	171.2	750	188	116	104	**41**	3	2	6	54	1	184	6	8	**16**	.333	0-0	0	92	.855	5.39	5.45
2019	Bal	AL	30	30	0	161.2	700	161	95	86	29	1	7	6	58	0	162	7	7	14	.333	0-0	0	91	.784	4.57	4.79
2020	LAA	AL	11	11	0	65.2	267	51	27	24	5	0	4	4	17	1	72	2	6	3	.667	0-0	0	90	.614	2.41	3.29
6 ML YEARS			138	114	8	680.0	2895	662	372	343	119	5	17	29	223	6	674	15	44	48	.478	0-0	3	92	.768	4.32	4.54

Nick Burdi

Pitches: R Bats: R Pos: RP-3   Ht: 6'3" Wt: 225 Born: 1/19/1993 Age: 28

			HOW MUCH PITCHED				WHAT HE GAVE UP										THE RESULTS						
Year	Team	Lg	G	GS	GF	IP	BFP	H	R	ER	HR	SH	SF	HB	TBB	IBB	SO	WP	W	L	Pct	Sv-Op	Hld	Vel	OPS	ERC	ERA
2018	Pit	NL	2	0	1	1.1	10	3	4	3	1	0	0	0	2	0	2	0	0	0	-	0-0	0	96	1.250	22.77	20.25
2019	Pit	NL	11	0	3	8.2	40	11	9	9	1	0	0	0	3	0	17	1	2	1	.667	0-1	0	97	.836	5.40	9.35
2020	Pit	NL	3	0	3	2.1	10	2	1	1	0	0	0	0	2	0	4	0	0	1	.000	1-1	0	98	.650	4.61	3.86
3 ML YEARS			16	0	7	12.1	60	16	14	13	2	0	0	0	7	0	23	1	2	2	.500	1-2	0	97	.874	6.90	9.49

Zack Burdi

Pitches: R Bats: R Pos: RP-8   Ht: 6'3" Wt: 210 Born: 3/9/1995 Age: 26

			HOW MUCH PITCHED				WHAT HE GAVE UP										THE RESULTS						
Year	Team	Lg	G	GS	GF	IP	BFP	H	R	ER	HR	SH	SF	HB	TBB	IBB	SO	WP	W	L	Pct	Sv-Op	Hld	Vel	OPS	ERC	ERA
2020	CWS	AL	8	0	0	7.1	37	11	11	9	4	0	0	0	3	0	11	1	0	1	.000	0-1	1	98	1.084	10.46	11.05

Corbin Burnes

Pitches: R Bats: R Pos: SP-9; RP-3   Ht: 6'3" Wt: 225 Born: 10/22/1994 Age: 26

			HOW MUCH PITCHED				WHAT HE GAVE UP										THE RESULTS						
Year	Team	Lg	G	GS	GF	IP	BFP	H	R	ER	HR	SH	SF	HB	TBB	IBB	SO	WP	W	L	Pct	Sv-Op	Hld	Vel	OPS	ERC	ERA
2018	Mil	NL	30	0	6	38.0	152	27	11	11	4	1	1	3	11	2	35	2	7	0	1.000	1-2	3	95	.595	2.42	2.61
2019	Mil	NL	32	4	8	49.0	235	70	52	48	17	3	0	0	20	0	70	2	1	5	.167	1-1	4	95	1.011	8.65	8.82
2020	Mil	NL	12	9	2	59.2	240	37	15	14	2	0	0	3	24	0	88	5	4	1	.800	0-0	0	96	.515	1.91	2.11
	Postseason		6	0	1	9.0	31	4	2	2	0	0	0	1	1	0	11	0	1	0	1.000	0-0	1	96	.400	0.81	2.00
3 ML YEARS			74	13	16	146.2	627	134	78	73	23	4	1	6	55	2	193	9	12	6	.667	2-3	7	95	.721	4.00	4.48

Beau Burrows

Pitches: R Bats: R Pos: RP-5   Ht: 6'2" Wt: 210 Born: 9/18/1996 Age: 24

			HOW MUCH PITCHED				WHAT HE GAVE UP										THE RESULTS						
Year	Team	Lg	G	GS	GF	IP	BFP	H	R	ER	HR	SH	SF	HB	TBB	IBB	SO	WP	W	L	Pct	Sv-Op	Hld	Vel	OPS	ERC	ERA
2020	Det	AL	5	0	1	6.2	30	8	4	4	3	0	0	1	1	0	3	0	0	0	-	0-0	0	93	.976	7.26	5.40

Drew Butera

Bats: R **Throws:** R **Pos:** C-25;1B-5   bue-TARE-ah   **Ht:** 6'1" **Wt:** 212 **Born:** 8/9/1983 **Age:** 37

Year	Team	Lg	G	AB	H	2B	3B	HR	(Hm	Rd)	TB	R	RBI	RC	TBB	IBB	SO	HBP	SH	SF	SB	CS	GDP	Avg	OBP	Slg	OPS
2010	Min	AL	49	142	28	6	1	2	(0	2)	42	12	13	7	4	0	25	4	3	2	0	0	5	.197	.237	.296	.533
2011	Min	AL	93	234	39	9	1	2	(1	1)	56	19	23	11	11	0	42	2	6	1	0	0	7	.167	.210	.239	.449
2012	Min	AL	42	111	22	6	0	1	(1	0)	31	7	5	6	9	0	26	2	0	0	0	0	3	.198	.270	.279	.550
2013	2 Tms		6	10	1	0	0	0	(0	0)	1	0	0	0	0	0	5	0	0	0	0	0	0	.100	.100	.100	.200
2014	LAD	NL	61	170	32	6	1	3	(0	3)	49	16	14	10	17	1	41	2	1	2	0	0	1	.188	.267	.288	.555
2015	2 Tms	AL	55	107	21	3	0	1	(0	1)	27	9	5	6	6	0	26	2	5	0	0	1	0	.196	.252	.252	.505
2016	KC	AL	56	123	35	10	1	4	(0	4)	59	18	16	15	8	0	36	0	2	0	0	0	2	.285	.328	.480	.808
2017	KC	AL	75	163	37	4	1	3	(1	2)	52	18	14	18	12	0	41	1	1	0	0	0	0	.227	.284	.319	.603
2018	2 Tms		62	163	31	9	0	3	(2	1)	49	13	21	13	15	0	39	2	0	2	0	0	4	.190	.264	.301	.564
2019	Col	NL	16	43	7	3	0	0	(0	0)	10	6	3	1	4	0	14	0	1	1	0	0	0	.163	.229	.233	.462
2020	Col	NL	29	39	6	2	0	0	(0	0)	8	4	4	0	2	0	11	0	1	1	0	0	3	.154	.190	.205	.396
13	Min	AL	2	3	0	0	0	0	(0	0)	0	0	0	0	0	0	1	0	0	0	0	0	0	.000	.000	.000	.000
13	LAD	NL	4	7	1	0	0	0	(0	0)	1	0	0	0	0	0	4	0	0	0	0	0	0	.143	.143	.143	.286
15	LAA	AL	10	21	4	0	0	0	(0	0)	4	3	0	0	0	0	2	0	1	0	0	1	0	.190	.190	.190	.381
15	KC	AL	45	86	17	3	0	1	(0	1)	23	6	5	6	6	0	24	2	5	0	0	0	0	.198	.266	.267	.533
18	KC	AL	52	149	28	9	0	2	(1	1)	43	11	18	10	13	0	37	2	0	2	0	0	4	.188	.259	.289	.548
18	Col	NL	10	14	3	0	0	1	(1	0)	6	2	3	3	2	0	2	0	0	0	0	0	0	.214	.313	.429	.741
	Postseason		4	3	0	0	0	0	(0	0)	0	0	0	0	2	0	0	0	0	0	0	0	0	.000	.400	.000	.400
	11 ML YEARS		544	1305	259	58	5	19	(5	14)	384	122	118	87	88	1	306	15	20	9	0	1	27	.198	.255	.294	.550

Ty Buttrey

Pitches: R **Bats:** L **Pos:** RP-27   **Ht:** 6'6" **Wt:** 240 **Born:** 3/31/1993 **Age:** 28

Year	Team	Lg	G	GS	GF	IP	BFP	H	R	ER	HR	SH	SF	HB	TBB	IBB	SO	WP	W	L	Pct	Sv-Op	Hld	Vel	OPS	ERC	ERA
2018	LAA	AL	16	0	4	16.1	70	15	7	6	0	1	1	0	5	0	20	0	0	1	.000	4-6	6	96	.591	2.52	3.31
2019	LAA	AL	72	0	6	72.1	309	69	34	32	8	0	2	5	23	0	84	6	6	7	.462	2-6	26	97	.690	3.83	3.98
2020	LAA	AL	27	0	14	26.1	112	28	18	17	4	1	2	1	9	3	18	2	2	3	.400	5-9	2	96	.837	4.65	5.81
	3 ML YEARS		115	0	24	115.0	491	112	59	55	12	2	5	6	37	3	122	8	8	11	.421	11-21	34	97	.709	3.81	4.30

Byron Buxton

Bats: R **Throws:** R **Pos:** CF-39   **Ht:** 6'2" **Wt:** 190 **Born:** 12/18/1993 **Age:** 27

Year	Team	Lg	G	AB	H	2B	3B	HR	(Hm	Rd)	TB	R	RBI	RC	TBB	IBB	SO	HBP	SH	SF	SB	CS	GDP	Avg	OBP	Slg	OPS
2015	Min	AL	46	129	27	7	1	2	(0	2)	42	16	6	10	6	0	44	1	2	0	2	2	1	.209	.250	.326	.576
2016	Min	AL	92	298	67	19	6	10	(6	4)	128	44	38	33	23	0	118	3	4	3	10	2	2	.225	.284	.430	.714
2017	Min	AL	140	462	117	14	6	16	(8	8)	191	69	51	63	38	2	150	4	5	2	29	1	1	.253	.314	.413	.728
2018	Min	AL	28	90	14	4	0	0	(0	0)	18	8	4	4	3	0	28	0	1	0	5	0	1	.156	.183	.200	.383
2019	Min	AL	87	271	71	30	4	10	(4	6)	139	48	46	44	19	1	68	2	2	1	14	3	3	.262	.314	.513	.827
2020	Min	AL	39	130	33	3	0	13	(4	9)	75	19	27	17	2	0	36	1	0	2	2	1	2	.254	.267	.577	.844
	Postseason		1	2	0	0	0	0	(0	0)	0	0	0	1	0	0	1	0	0	0	1	0	0	.000	.000	.000	.000
	6 ML YEARS		432	1380	329	77	17	51	(22	29)	593	204	172	171	91	3	444	11	14	8	62	9	10	.238	.289	.430	.719

Asdrubal Cabrera

Bats: B **Throws:** R **Pos:** 1B-25;3B-17;DH-11;PH-1   azz-DRUE-bull   **Ht:** 6'0" **Wt:** 205 **Born:** 11/13/1985 **Age:** 35

Year	Team	Lg	G	AB	H	2B	3B	HR	(Hm	Rd)	TB	R	RBI	RC	TBB	IBB	SO	HBP	SH	SF	SB	CS	GDP	Avg	OBP	Slg	OPS
2007	Cle	AL	45	159	45	9	2	3	(1	2)	67	30	22	27	17	0	29	2	5	3	0	0	7	.283	.354	.421	.775
2008	Cle	AL	114	352	91	20	0	6	(5	1)	129	48	47	48	46	2	77	4	11	5	4	4	8	.259	.346	.366	.713
2009	Cle	AL	131	523	161	42	4	6	(4	2)	229	81	68	81	44	1	89	1	10	3	17	4	13	.308	.361	.438	.799
2010	Cle	AL	97	381	105	16	1	3	(2	1)	132	39	29	46	25	0	60	5	11	3	6	4	10	.276	.326	.346	.673
2011	Cle	AL	151	604	165	32	3	25	(13	12)	278	87	92	100	44	5	119	11	4	4	17	5	10	.273	.332	.460	.792
2012	Cle	AL	143	555	150	35	1	16	(10	6)	235	70	68	74	52	3	99	6	1	2	9	4	18	.270	.338	.423	.762
2013	Cle	AL	136	508	123	35	2	14	(8	6)	204	66	64	51	35	1	114	8	6	5	9	3	10	.242	.299	.402	.700
2014	2 Tms		146	553	133	31	4	14	(6	8)	214	74	61	57	49	2	108	7	1	6	10	2	15	.241	.307	.387	.694
2015	TB	AL	143	505	134	28	5	15	(7	8)	217	66	58	53	36	4	107	3	1	6	6	3	14	.265	.315	.430	.744
2016	NYM	NL	141	521	146	30	1	23	(18	5)	247	65	62	76	38	3	103	7	0	2	5	1	14	.280	.336	.474	.810
2017	NYM	NL	135	479	134	32	0	14	(5	9)	208	66	59	70	50	1	83	5	1	5	3	2	19	.280	.351	.434	.785
2018	2 Tms	NL	147	546	143	36	1	23	(10	13)	250	68	75	77	41	1	119	3	0	0	0	0	16	.262	.316	.458	.774
2019	2 Tms	NL	131	447	116	25	1	18	(13	5)	197	69	91	79	57	2	103	3	0	7	4	0	5	.260	.342	.441	.783
2020	Was	NL	52	190	46	9	3	8	(2	6)	85	23	31	26	19	0	40	0	0	4	0	0	6	.242	.305	.447	.753
14	Cle	AL	97	378	93	22	2	9	(5	4)	146	54	40	36	27	1	79	7	0	4	7	2	11	.246	.305	.386	.692
14	Was	NL	49	175	40	9	2	5	(1	4)	68	20	21	21	22	1	29	0	1	2	3	0	4	.229	.312	.389	.700
18	NYM	NL	98	375	104	23	1	18	(7	11)	183	48	58	57	29	1	81	1	0	2	0	0	12	.277	.329	.488	.817
18	Phi	NL	49	171	39	13	0	5	(3	2)	67	20	17	20	12	0	38	2	0	0	0	0	4	.228	.286	.392	.678
19	Tex	AL	93	323	76	15	0	12	(11	1)	127	45	51	47	38	1	85	3	0	4	4	0	6	.235	.318	.393	.711
19	Was	NL	38	124	40	10	1	6	(2	4)	70	24	40	32	19	1	18	0	0	3	0	0	3	.323	.404	.565	.969
	Postseason		29	98	21	2	0	2	(2	0)	29	8	13	10	4	0	28	0	4	2	0	0	3	.214	.240	.296	.536
	14 ML YEARS		1712	6323	1692	380	28	188	(104	84)	2692	852	827	865	553	25	1250	65	51	57	90	32	169	.268	.330	.426	.756

Genesis Cabrera

Pitches: L Bats: L Pos: RP-19

heh-NEH-sees

Ht: 6'2" Wt: 180 Born: 10/10/1996 Age: 24

Year	Team	Lg	G	GS	GF	IP	BFP	H	R	ER	HR	SH	SF	HB	TBB	IBB	SO	WP	W	L	Pct	Sv-Op	Hld	Vel	OPS	ERC	ERA
2019	StL	NL	13	2	5	20.1	99	23	16	11	2	1	1	2	11	0	19	1	0	2	.000	1-1	1	96	.760	5.53	4.87
2020	StL	NL	19	0	1	22.1	96	10	9	6	3	0	0	4	16	0	32	3	4	1	.800	1-1	2	96	.589	3.18	2.42
	Postseason		2	0	1	1.2	6	1	0	0	0	0	0	0	0	0	1	0	0	0	-	0-0	0	99	.333	0.75	0.00
	2 ML YEARS		32	2	6	42.2	195	33	25	17	5	1	1	6	27	0	51	4	4	3	.571	2-2	3	96	.678	4.26	3.59

Miguel Cabrera

Bats: R Throws: R Pos: DH-56;PH-1

Ht: 6'4" Wt: 249 Born: 4/18/1983 Age: 38

Year	Team	Lg	G	AB	H	2B	3B	HR	(Hm	Rd)	TB	R	RBI	RC	TBB	IBB	SO	HBP	SH	SF	SB	CS	GDP	Avg	OBP	Slg	OPS
2003	Fla	NL	87	314	84	21	3	12	(7	5)	147	39	62	51	25	3	84	2	4	1	0	2	12	.268	.325	.468	.793
2004	Fla	NL	160	603	177	31	1	33	(14	19)	309	101	112	92	68	5	148	6	0	8	5	2	20	.294	.366	.512	.879
2005	Fla	NL	158	613	198	43	2	33	(11	22)	344	106	116	108	64	12	125	2	0	6	1	0	20	.323	.385	.561	.947
2006	Fla	NL	158	576	195	50	2	26	(15	11)	327	112	114	132	86	27	108	10	0	4	9	6	18	.339	.430	.568	.998
2007	Fla	NL	157	588	188	38	2	34	(19	15)	332	91	119	122	79	23	127	5	1	7	2	1	17	.320	.401	.565	.965
2008	Det	AL	160	616	180	36	2	37	(19	18)	331	85	127	109	56	6	126	3	0	9	1	0	16	.292	.349	.537	.887
2009	Det	AL	160	611	198	34	0	34	(19	15)	334	96	103	114	68	14	107	5	0	1	6	2	22	.324	.396	.547	.942
2010	Det	AL	150	548	180	45	1	38	(17	21)	341	111	126	122	89	32	95	3	0	8	3	3	17	.328	.420	.622	1.042
2011	Det	AL	161	572	197	48	0	30	(15	15)	335	111	105	141	108	22	89	3	0	5	2	1	24	.344	.448	.586	1.033
2012	Det	AL	161	622	205	40	0	44	(28	16)	377	109	139	123	66	17	98	3	0	6	4	1	28	.330	.393	.606	.999
2013	Det	AL	148	555	193	26	1	44	(17	27)	353	103	137	146	90	19	94	5	0	2	3	0	19	.348	.442	.636	1.078
2014	Det	AL	159	611	191	52	1	25	(13	12)	320	101	109	110	60	10	117	3	0	11	1	1	21	.313	.371	.524	.895
2015	Det	AL	119	429	145	28	1	18	(7	11)	229	64	76	93	77	15	82	3	0	2	1	1	19	.338	.440	.534	.974
2016	Det	AL	158	595	188	31	1	38	(20	18)	335	92	108	106	75	15	116	4	0	5	0	0	26	.316	.393	.563	.956
2017	Det	AL	130	469	117	22	0	16	(11	5)	187	50	60	55	54	6	110	3	0	3	0	1	15	.249	.329	.399	.728
2018	Det	AL	38	134	40	11	0	3	(2	1)	60	17	22	23	22	4	27	0	0	1	0	0	6	.299	.395	.448	.843
2019	Det	AL	136	493	139	21	0	12	(5	7)	196	41	59	72	48	4	108	3	0	5	0	0	18	.282	.346	.398	.744
2020	Det	AL	57	204	51	4	0	10	(5	5)	85	28	35	39	24	1	51	1	0	2	1	0	3	.250	.329	.417	.746
	Postseason		55	205	57	10	0	13	(4	9)	106	29	38	34	27	7	48	2	1	0	3	0	7	.278	.368	.517	.885
	18 ML YEARS		2457	9153	2866	581	17	487	(244	243)	4942	1457	1729	1758	1159	235	1812	64	5	86	39	21	321	.313	.391	.540	.931

Trevor Cahill

Pitches: R Bats: R Pos: SP-6; RP-5

KAY-hill

Ht: 6'4" Wt: 223 Born: 3/1/1988 Age: 33

Year	Team	Lg	G	GS	GF	IP	BFP	H	R	ER	HR	SH	SF	HB	TBB	IBB	SO	WP	W	L	Pct	Sv-Op	Hld	Vel	OPS	ERC	ERA
2009	Oak	AL	32	32	0	178.2	783	185	99	92	27	4	7	4	72	1	90	5	10	13	.435	0-0	0	90	.810	4.79	4.63
2010	Oak	AL	30	30	0	196.2	783	155	73	65	19	3	6	6	63	1	118	2	18	8	.692	0-0	0	90	.619	2.81	2.97
2011	Oak	AL	34	34	0	207.2	901	214	102	96	19	8	6	8	82	1	147	15	12	14	.462	0-0	0	89	.738	4.34	4.16
2012	Ari	NL	32	32	0	200.0	839	184	93	84	16	12	6	11	74	0	156	10	13	12	.520	0-0	0	89	.706	3.66	3.78
2013	Ari	NL	26	25	1	146.2	636	143	70	65	13	9	9	6	65	2	102	17	8	10	.444	0-0	0	89	.745	4.19	3.99
2014	Ari	NL	32	17	8	110.2	499	123	76	69	9	6	3	4	55	2	105	5	3	12	.200	1-2	0	90	.791	5.11	5.61
2015	2 Tms	NL	26	3	6	43.1	187	44	27	26	4	3	1	2	16	1	36	2	1	3	.250	0-0	2	92	.725	4.15	5.40
2016	ChC	NL	50	1	16	65.2	284	49	22	20	7	0	0	5	35	3	66	3	4	4	.500	0-1	4	92	.621	3.42	2.74
2017	2 Tms	NL	21	14	1	84.0	381	91	50	46	16	2	0	3	45	1	87	16	4	3	.571	0-0	1	91	.850	5.97	4.93
2018	Oak	AL	21	20	0	110.0	450	90	52	46	8	3	3	5	41	0	100	8	7	4	.636	0-0	0	92	.653	3.05	3.76
2019	LAA	AL	37	11	12	102.1	455	111	71	68	25	0	4	6	39	0	81	14	4	9	.308	0-0	1	92	.880	5.78	5.98
2020	SF	NL	11	6	2	25.0	106	16	10	9	3	1	2	2	14	0	31	1	1	2	.333	0-0	1	91	.638	3.15	3.24
15	Atl	NL	15	3	6	26.1	124	36	23	22	2	2	1	1	11	1	14	1	0	3	.000	0-0	0	91	.843	6.22	7.52
15	ChC	NL	11	0	0	17.0	63	8	4	4	2	1	0	1	5	0	22	1	1	0	1.000	0-0	2	93	.494	1.52	2.12
17	SD	NL	11	11	0	61.0	263	58	29	25	6	1	0	3	24	1	72	14	4	3	.571	0-0	0	91	.712	3.92	3.69
17	KC	AL	10	3	1	23.0	118	33	21	21	10	1	0	0	21	0	15	2	0	0	-	0-0	1	91	1.180	12.52	8.22
	Postseason		6	0	1	5.1	24	7	2	2	0	1	0	0	0	0	8	1	1	1	.500	0-1	2	94	.783	3.29	3.38
	12 ML YEARS		352	225	46	1470.2	6294	1405	745	686	166	51	47	62	601	12	1119	98	85	94	.475	1-3	8	90	.736	4.14	4.20

Lorenzo Cain

Bats: R Throws: R Pos: CF-5

Ht: 6'2" Wt: 214 Born: 4/13/1986 Age: 35

Year	Team	Lg	G	AB	H	2B	3B	HR	(Hm	Rd)	TB	R	RBI	RC	TBB	IBB	SO	HBP	SH	SF	SB	CS	GDP	Avg	OBP	Slg	OPS
2010	Mil	NL	43	147	45	11	1	1	(1	0)	61	17	13	23	9	0	28	1	0	1	7	1	1	.306	.348	.415	.763
2011	KC	AL	6	22	6	1	0	0	(0	0)	7	4	1	2	1	0	4	0	0	0	0	0	0	.273	.304	.318	.623
2012	KC	AL	61	222	59	9	2	7	(3	4)	93	27	31	32	15	0	56	3	0	4	10	0	4	.266	.316	.419	.734
2013	KC	AL	115	399	100	21	3	4	(3	1)	139	54	46	46	33	2	90	4	0	6	14	6	10	.251	.310	.348	.658
2014	KC	AL	133	471	142	29	4	5	(3	2)	194	55	53	67	24	2	108	4	0	3	28	5	9	.301	.339	.412	.751
2015	KC	AL	140	551	169	34	6	16	(9	7)	263	101	72	90	37	4	98	12	0	4	28	6	16	.307	.361	.477	.838
2016	KC	AL	103	397	114	19	1	9	(3	6)	162	56	56	53	31	3	84	2	0	4	14	5	15	.287	.339	.408	.747
2017	KC	AL	155	584	175	27	5	15	(3	12)	257	86	49	90	54	1	100	5	0	2	26	2	20	.300	.363	.440	.803
2018	Mil	NL	141	539	166	25	2	10	(4	6)	225	90	38	94	71	1	94	8	0	2	30	7	10	.308	.395	.417	.813
2019	Mil	NL	148	562	146	30	4	11	(7	4)	209	75	48	61	50	0	106	4	0	4	18	8	14	.260	.325	.372	.697
2020	Mil	NL	5	18	6	1	0	0	(0	0)	7	4	2	5	3	1	2	0	0	1	0	0	1	.333	.429	.389	.817
	Postseason		42	171	48	11	0	1	(0	1)	62	28	20	29	19	3	36	1	1	2	8	2	1	.281	.352	.363	.715
	11 ML YEARS		1050	3912	1128	207	24	78	(36	42)	1617	569	409	563	328	14	770	45	0	30	175	40	100	.288	.348	.413	.761

Kole Calhoun

Bats: L Throws: L Pos: RF-48;DH-6;PH-1   Ht: 5'10" Wt: 210 Born: 10/14/1987 Age: 33

Year Team	Lg	G	AB	H	2B	3B	HR	(Hm	Rd)	TB	R	RBI	RC	TBB	IBB	SO	HBP	SH	SF	SB	CS	GDP	Avg	OBP	Slg	OPS
2012 LAA	AL	21	23	4	1	0	0	(0	0)	5	2	1	0	2	1	6	0	0	0	1	0	0	.174	.240	.217	.457
2013 LAA	AL	58	195	55	7	2	8	(5	3)	90	29	32	33	21	0	41	1	0	5	2	2	6	.282	.347	.462	.808
2014 LAA	AL	127	493	134	31	3	17	(7	10)	222	90	58	75	38	0	104	2	2	2	5	3	5	.272	.325	.450	.776
2015 LAA	AL	159	630	161	23	2	26	(16	10)	266	78	83	85	45	1	164	5	2	4	4	1	6	.256	.308	.422	.731
2016 LAA	AL	157	594	161	35	5	18	(7	11)	260	91	75	93	67	0	118	6	0	5	2	3	10	.271	.348	.438	.786
2017 LAA	AL	155	569	139	23	2	19	(8	11)	223	77	71	85	71	4	134	8	0	6	5	1	10	.244	.333	.392	.725
2018 LAA	AL	137	491	102	18	2	19	(9	10)	181	71	57	53	53	2	133	1	0	6	6	2	9	.208	.283	.369	.652
2019 LAA	AL	152	552	128	29	1	33	(16	17)	258	92	74	77	70	7	162	7	0	2	4	1	14	.232	.325	.467	.792
2020 Ari	NL	54	190	43	9	0	16	(7	9)	100	35	40	37	28	0	50	6	0	4	1	1	6	.226	.338	.526	.864
Postseason		3	15	5	0	0	0	(0	0)	5	1	0	1	0	0	1	0	0	0	0	0	0	.333	.333	.333	.667
9 ML YEARS		1020	3737	927	176	17	156	(75	81)	1605	565	491	538	395	15	912	36	4	34	30	14	66	.248	.323	.429	.753

Willie Calhoun

Bats: L Throws: R Pos: DH-21;LF-8;PH-3;PR-1   Ht: 5'8" Wt: 200 Born: 11/4/1994 Age: 26

Year Team	Lg	G	AB	H	2B	3B	HR	(Hm	Rd)	TB	R	RBI	RC	TBB	IBB	SO	HBP	SH	SF	SB	CS	GDP	Avg	OBP	Slg	OPS
2017 Tex	AL	13	34	9	0	0	1	(1	0)	12	3	4	6	2	0	7	1	0	0	0	0	0	.265	.324	.353	.677
2018 Tex	AL	35	99	22	5	0	2	(1	1)	33	8	11	11	6	0	24	1	0	2	0	0	2	.222	.269	.333	.602
2019 Tex	AL	83	309	83	14	1	21	(8	13)	162	51	48	49	23	0	53	3	0	2	0	0	5	.269	.323	.524	.848
2020 Tex	AL	29	100	19	2	1	1	(1	0)	26	3	13	9	5	0	17	1	0	2	0	0	1	.190	.231	.260	.491
4 ML YEARS		160	542	133	21	2	25	(11	14)	233	65	76	75	36	0	101	6	0	6	0	0	8	.245	.297	.430	.726

Johan Camargo

Bats: B Throws: R Pos: 2B-21;3B-10;PH-4;DH-3   Ht: 6'0" Wt: 195 Born: 12/13/1993 Age: 27

Year Team	Lg	G	AB	H	2B	3B	HR	(Hm	Rd)	TB	R	RBI	RC	TBB	IBB	SO	HBP	SH	SF	SB	CS	GDP	Avg	OBP	Slg	OPS
2017 Atl	NL	82	241	72	21	2	4	(2	2)	109	30	27	32	12	2	51	0	2	1	0	0	5	.299	.331	.452	.783
2018 Atl	NL	134	464	126	27	1	19	(7	12)	212	63	76	72	51	4	108	6	0	3	1	1	13	.272	.349	.457	.806
2019 Atl	NL	98	232	54	12	1	7	(2	5)	89	31	32	27	15	2	43	1	0	5	1	0	5	.233	.279	.384	.663
2020 Atl	NL	35	120	24	8	0	4	(1	3)	44	16	9	7	6	0	35	1	0	0	0	0	1	.200	.244	.367	.611
Postseason		4	15	0	0	0	0	(0	0)	0	1	0	0	1	0	5	0	0	0	0	0	1	.000	.063	.000	.063
4 ML YEARS		349	1057	276	68	4	34	(12	22)	454	140	144	138	84	8	237	7	3	4	2	1	24	.261	.319	.430	.748

Daz Cameron

Bats: R Throws: R Pos: RF-16;PH-1   Ht: 6'2" Wt: 185 Born: 1/15/1997 Age: 24

Year Team	Lg	G	AB	H	2B	3B	HR	(Hm	Rd)	TB	R	RBI	RC	TBB	IBB	SO	HBP	SH	SF	SB	CS	GDP	Avg	OBP	Slg	OPS
2020 Det	AL	17	57	11	2	1	0	(0	0)	15	4	3	3	2	0	19	0	0	0	1	0	1	.193	.220	.263	.483

Luis Campusano

Bats: R Throws: R Pos: DH-1   Ht: 5'11" Wt: 232 Born: 9/29/1998 Age: 22

Year Team	Lg	G	AB	H	2B	3B	HR	(Hm	Rd)	TB	R	RBI	RC	TBB	IBB	SO	HBP	SH	SF	SB	CS	GDP	Avg	OBP	Slg	OPS
2017 2 Tms	Low	37	134	36	4	0	4	(-	-)	52	8	25	19	15	0	25	1	0	1	0	2	5	.269	.344	.388	.732
2018 FtWyn	A	70	260	75	11	0	3	(-	-)	95	26	40	34	19	0	43	4	0	1	0	1	9	.288	.345	.365	.710
2019 Lk Els	A+	110	422	137	31	1	15	(-	-)	215	63	81	87	52	2	57	4	0	9	0	0	15	.325	.396	.509	.906
2020 SD	NL	1	3	1	0	0	1	(0	1)	4	2	1	1	0	0	2	1	0	0	0	0	0	.333	.500	1.333	1.833

Jeimer Candelario

Bats: B Throws: R Pos: 1B-43;3B-10;PH-1   Ht: 6'1" Wt: 221 Born: 11/24/1993 Age: 27

Year Team	Lg	G	AB	H	2B	3B	HR	(Hm	Rd)	TB	R	RBI	RC	TBB	IBB	SO	HBP	SH	SF	SB	CS	GDP	Avg	OBP	Slg	OPS
2016 ChC	NL	5	11	1	0	0	0	(0	0)	1	0	0	0	2	1	5	1	0	0	0	0	0	.091	.286	.091	.377
2017 2 Tms		38	127	36	9	0	3	(2	1)	54	18	16	19	13	0	30	2	0	0	0	0	3	.283	.359	.425	.784
2018 Det	AL	144	539	121	28	3	19	(10	9)	212	78	54	64	66	1	160	9	0	5	3	2	4	.224	.317	.393	.710
2019 Det	AL	94	335	68	17	2	8	(4	4)	113	33	32	35	43	1	99	7	0	1	3	1	3	.203	.306	.337	.643
2020 Det	AL	52	185	55	11	3	7	(3	4)	93	30	29	36	20	0	49	1	0	0	1	1	3	.297	.369	.503	.872
17 ChC	NL	11	33	5	2	0	1	(0	1)	10	2	3	1	1	0	12	2	0	0	0	0	1	.152	.222	.303	.525
17 Det		27	94	31	7	0	2	(2	0)	44	16	13	18	12	0	18	0	0	0	0	0	2	.330	.406	.468	.874
5 ML YEARS		333	1197	281	65	8	37	(19	18)	473	159	131	154	144	3	343	20	0	6	7	4	13	.235	.326	.395	.721

Mark Canha

Bats: R Throws: R Pos: DH-21;RF-17;LF-15;CF-9;1B-3   CAN-uh   Ht: 6'2" Wt: 209 Born: 2/15/1989 Age: 32

Year Team	Lg	G	AB	H	2B	3B	HR	(Hm	Rd)	TB	R	RBI	RC	TBB	IBB	SO	HBP	SH	SF	SB	CS	GDP	Avg	OBP	Slg	OPS
2015 Oak	AL	124	441	112	22	3	16	(8	8)	188	61	70	62	33	0	96	8	0	3	7	2	9	.254	.315	.426	.742
2016 Oak	AL	16	41	5	0	0	3	(1	2)	14	4	6	0	0	0	20	1	1	1	0	1	1	.122	.140	.341	.481
2017 Oak	AL	57	173	36	13	1	5	(3	2)	66	16	14	13	7	0	56	6	0	1	2	0	5	.208	.262	.382	.644
2018 Oak	AL	122	365	91	22	0	17	(8	9)	164	60	52	52	34	3	88	10	0	2	1	2	11	.249	.328	.449	.778

Year	Team	Lg	G	AB	H	2B	3B	HR	(Hm	Rd)	TB	R	RBI	RC	TBB	IBB	SO	HBP	SH	SF	SB	CS	GDP	Avg	OBP	Slg	OPS
2019	Oak	AL	126	410	112	16	3	26	(15	11)	212	80	58	80	67	1	107	18	0	2	3	2	10	.273	.396	.517	.913
2020	Oak	AL	59	191	47	12	2	5	(3	2)	78	32	33	43	37	1	54	10	0	5	4	0	2	.246	.387	.408	.795
	Postseason		2	4	0	0	0	0	(0	0)	0	0	0	0	1	0	3	0	0	0	0	0	0	.000	.200	.000	.200
	6 ML YEARS		504	1621	403	85	9	72	(38	34)	722	253	233	250	178	5	421	53	1	14	17	7	38	.249	.340	.445	.785

Griffin Canning

Pitches: R **Bats:** R **Pos:** SP-11

Ht: 6'2" **Wt:** 180 **Born:** 5/11/1996 **Age:** 25

			HOW MUCH PITCHED					WHAT HE GAVE UP									THE RESULTS							
Year	Team	Lg	G	GS	GF	IP	BFP	H	R	ER	HR	SH	SF	HB	TBB	IBB	SO	WP	W	L	Pct	Sv-Op	Hld	Vel	OPS	ERC	ERA
2019	LAA	AL	18	17	1	90.1	384	80	46	46	14	1	4	8	30	0	96	9	5	6	.455	0-0	0	94	.739	3.87	4.58
2020	LAA	AL	11	11	0	56.1	238	54	29	25	8	0	4	1	23	0	56	5	2	3	.400	0-0	0	93	.771	4.33	3.99
	2 ML YEARS		29	28	1	146.2	622	134	75	71	22	1	8	9	53	0	152	14	7	9	.438	0-0	0	94	.751	4.04	4.36

Robinson Cano

Bats: L **Throws:** R **Pos:** 2B-34;DH-13;PH-3   kuh-NOE

Ht: 6'0" **Wt:** 212 **Born:** 10/22/1982 **Age:** 38

									BATTING												RUNNING			AVERAGES			
Year	Team	Lg	G	AB	H	2B	3B	HR	(Hm	Rd)	TB	R	RBI	RC	TBB	IBB	SO	HBP	SH	SF	SB	CS	GDP	Avg	OBP	Slg	OPS
2005	NYY	AL	132	522	155	34	4	14	(5	9)	239	78	62	59	16	1	68	3	7	3	1	3	16	.297	.320	.458	.778
2006	NYY	AL	122	482	165	41	1	15	(9	6)	253	62	78	74	18	3	54	2	1	5	5	2	19	.342	.365	.525	.890
2007	NYY	AL	160	617	189	41	7	19	(10	9)	301	93	97	94	39	5	85	8	1	4	4	5	19	.306	.353	.488	.841
2008	NYY	AL	159	597	162	35	3	14	(7	7)	245	70	72	64	26	3	65	5	1	5	2	4	18	.271	.305	.410	.715
2009	NYY	AL	161	637	204	48	2	25	(14	11)	331	103	85	79	30	2	63	3	0	4	5	7	22	.320	.352	.520	.871
2010	NYY	AL	160	626	200	41	3	29	(16	13)	334	103	109	118	57	14	77	8	0	5	3	2	19	.319	.381	.534	.914
2011	NYY	AL	159	623	188	46	7	28	(16	12)	332	104	118	111	38	11	96	12	0	8	8	2	18	.302	.349	.533	.882
2012	NYY	AL	161	627	196	48	1	33	(22	11)	345	105	94	110	61	10	96	7	0	2	3	2	22	.313	.379	.550	.929
2013	NYY	AL	160	605	190	41	0	27	(11	16)	312	81	107	120	65	16	85	6	0	5	7	1	18	.314	.383	.516	.899
2014	Sea	AL	157	595	187	37	2	14	(9	5)	270	77	82	106	61	20	68	6	0	3	10	3	19	.314	.382	.454	.836
2015	Sea	AL	156	624	179	34	1	21	(11	10)	278	82	79	84	43	5	107	3	0	4	2	6	26	.287	.334	.446	.779
2016	Sea	AL	161	655	195	33	2	39	(17	22)	349	107	103	100	47	8	100	8	0	5	0	1	18	.298	.350	.533	.882
2017	Sea	AL	150	592	166	33	0	23	(11	12)	268	79	97	96	49	8	85	4	0	3	1	0	15	.280	.338	.453	.791
2018	Sea	AL	80	310	94	22	0	10	(5	5)	146	44	50	55	32	2	47	4	0	2	0	0	9	.303	.374	.471	.845
2019	NYM	NL	107	390	100	28	0	13	(6	7)	167	46	39	40	25	3	69	5	0	3	0	1	16	.256	.307	.428	.736
2020	NYM	NL	49	171	54	9	0	10	(3	7)	93	23	30	27	9	1	24	1	0	1	0	0	7	.316	.352	.544	.896
	Postseason		51	203	45	10	3	8	(5	3)	85	22	33	23	11	3	28	2	0	1	0	2	7	.222	.267	.419	.686
	16 ML YEARS		2234	8673	2624	571	33	334	(172	162)	4263	1257	1302	1337	616	112	1189	85	10	62	51	38	284	.303	.352	.492	.844

Victor Caratini

Bats: B **Throws:** R **Pos:** C-22;DH-18;PH-5;1B-3

Ht: 6'1" **Wt:** 215 **Born:** 8/17/1993 **Age:** 27

									BATTING												RUNNING			AVERAGES			
Year	Team	Lg	G	AB	H	2B	3B	HR	(Hm	Rd)	TB	R	RBI	RC	TBB	IBB	SO	HBP	SH	SF	SB	CS	GDP	Avg	OBP	Slg	OPS
2017	ChC	NL	31	59	15	3	0	1	(0	1)	21	6	2	3	4	1	13	3	0	0	0	0	3	.254	.333	.356	.689
2018	ChC	NL	76	181	42	7	0	2	(1	1)	55	21	21	15	12	0	42	4	2	1	0	0	5	.232	.293	.304	.597
2019	ChC	NL	95	244	65	11	0	11	(4	7)	109	31	34	35	29	0	59	3	0	3	1	0	6	.266	.348	.447	.794
2020	ChC	NL	44	116	28	7	0	1	(0	1)	38	10	16	15	12	1	31	4	0	0	0	1	4	.241	.333	.328	.661
	Postseason		1	1	0	0	0	0	(0	0)	0	0	0	0	0	0	0	0	0	0	0	0	0	.000	.000	.000	.000
	4 ML YEARS		246	600	150	28	0	15	(5	10)	223	68	73	68	57	2	145	14	2	4	1	1	18	.250	.327	.372	.699

Dylan Carlson

Bats: B **Throws:** L **Pos:** RF-18;CF-17;LF-10;PH-3

Ht: 6'2" **Wt:** 205 **Born:** 10/23/1998 **Age:** 22

									BATTING												RUNNING			AVERAGES			
Year	Team	Lg	G	AB	H	2B	3B	HR	(Hm	Rd)	TB	R	RBI	RC	TBB	IBB	SO	HBP	SH	SF	SB	CS	GDP	Avg	OBP	Slg	OPS
2016	Cards	R	50	183	46	13	3	3	(-	-)	74	30	22	22	16	0	52	1	0	1	4	2	5	.251	.313	.404	.718
2017	Peoria	A	115	383	92	18	1	7	(-	-)	133	63	42	53	52	1	116	9	4	3	6	6	5	.240	.342	.347	.690
2018	2 Tms	Low	112	423	104	22	3	11	(-	-)	165	68	62	59	62	4	88	7	1	5	8	3	15	.246	.348	.390	.738
2019	Sprgfld	AA	108	417	117	24	6	21	(-	-)	216	81	59	81	52	3	98	7	0	7	18	7	3	.281	.364	.518	.882
2019	Memp	AAA	18	72	26	4	2	5	(-	-)	49	14	9	18	6	0	18	1	0	0	2	1	0	.361	.418	.681	1.098
2020	StL	NL	35	110	22	7	1	3	(2	1)	40	11	16	11	8	0	35	0	0	1	1	1	3	.200	.252	.364	.616

Matt Carpenter

Bats: L **Throws:** R **Pos:** 3B-30;DH-14;1B-6;PH-3

Ht: 6'4" **Wt:** 210 **Born:** 11/26/1985 **Age:** 35

									BATTING												RUNNING			AVERAGES			
Year	Team	Lg	G	AB	H	2B	3B	HR	(Hm	Rd)	TB	R	RBI	RC	TBB	IBB	SO	HBP	SH	SF	SB	CS	GDP	Avg	OBP	Slg	OPS
2011	StL	NL	7	15	1	1	0	0	(0	0)	2	0	0	0	4	0	4	0	0	0	0	0	0	.067	.263	.133	.396
2012	StL	NL	114	296	87	22	5	6	(3	3)	137	44	46	46	34	2	63	3	0	7	1	1	10	.294	.365	.463	.828
2013	StL	NL	157	626	199	55	7	11	(5	6)	301	126	78	119	72	1	98	9	3	7	3	3	4	.318	.392	.481	.873
2014	StL	NL	158	595	162	33	2	8	(4	4)	223	99	59	93	95	2	111	8	2	9	5	3	5	.272	.375	.375	.750
2015	StL	NL	154	574	156	44	3	28	(13	15)	290	101	84	108	81	5	151	6	0	4	4	3	5	.272	.365	.505	.871
2016	StL	NL	129	473	128	36	6	21	(9	12)	239	81	68	87	81	6	108	5	3	4	0	4	4	.271	.380	.505	.885
2017	StL	NL	145	497	120	31	2	23	(9	14)	224	91	69	94	109	4	125	9	2	5	2	1	5	.241	.384	.451	.835
2018	StL	NL	156	564	145	42	0	36	(13	23)	295	111	81	107	102	17	158	6	0	4	4	1	4	.257	.374	.523	.897
2019	StL	NL	129	416	94	20	2	15	(8	7)	163	59	46	61	63	0	129	7	1	5	6	1	3	.226	.334	.392	.726
2020	StL	NL	50	140	26	6	0	4	(1	3)	44	22	24	24	23	1	48	6	0	0	0	0	1	.186	.325	.314	.640
	Postseason		47	149	34	8	1	6	(4	2)	62	21	19	21	14	0	45	1	0	3	1	0	1	.228	.293	.416	.710
	10 ML YEARS		1199	4196	1118	290	27	152	(66	86)	1918	734	555	733	664	38	995	59	11	45	25	17	35	.266	.371	.457	.828

Carlos Carrasco

Pitches: R **Bats:** R **Pos:** SP-12　　　　　　　　　　**Ht:** 6'4" **Wt:** 224 **Born:** 3/21/1987 **Age:** 34

			HOW MUCH PITCHED					WHAT HE GAVE UP										THE RESULTS								
Year	Team	Lg	G	GS	GF	IP	BFP	H	R	ER	HR	SH	SF	HB	TBB	IBB	SO	WP	W	L	Pct	Sv-Op	Hld	Vel	OPS	ERC	ERA
2009	Cle	AL	5	5	0	22.1	112	40	23	22	6	0	1	0	11	1	11	0	0	4	.000	0-0	0	92	1.125	11.36	8.87
2010	Cle	AL	7	7	0	44.2	188	47	20	19	6	2	1	1	14	1	38	1	2	2	.500	0-0	0	93	.816	4.42	3.83
2011	Cle	AL	21	21	0	124.2	536	130	68	64	15	3	7	4	40	3	85	3	8	9	.471	0-0	0	92	.754	4.24	4.62
2013	Cle	AL	15	7	5	46.2	218	64	36	35	4	2	3	1	18	2	30	2	1	4	.200	0-0	0	95	.864	6.11	6.75
2014	Cle	AL	40	14	12	134.0	529	103	40	38	7	2	3	3	29	1	140	4	8	7	.533	1-1	0	95	.543	2.00	2.55
2015	Cle	AL	30	30	0	183.2	730	154	75	74	18	1	6	5	43	2	216	5	14	12	.538	0-0	0	95	.646	2.72	3.63
2016	Cle	AL	25	25	0	146.1	599	134	64	54	21	1	3	3	34	2	150	4	11	8	.579	0-0	0	94	.711	3.31	3.32
2017	Cle	AL	32	32	0	200.0	798	173	73	73	21	1	6	10	46	2	226	10	**18**	6	.750	0-0	0	94	.674	2.99	3.29
2018	Cle	AL	32	30	1	192.0	784	173	78	72	21	4	5	6	43	4	231	9	17	10	.630	0-0	0	95	.669	3.02	3.38
2019	Cle	AL	23	12	3	80.0	341	92	48	47	18	2	2	2	16	1	96	2	6	7	.462	1-2	0	93	.867	5.11	5.29
2020	Cle	AL	12	12	0	68.0	280	55	22	22	8	1	1	2	27	0	82	6	3	4	.429	0-0	0	94	.663	3.30	2.91
	Postseason		2	2	0	11.0	44	9	2	2	0	1	0	1	4	0	10	0	0	1	.000	0-0	0	94	.562	2.79	1.64
11 ML YEARS			242	195	21	1242.1	5115	1165	547	520	145	19	38	37	321	19	1305	46	88	73	.547	2-3	0	94	.703	3.42	3.77

Cody Carroll

Pitches: R **Bats:** R **Pos:** RP-3　　　　　　　　　　**Ht:** 6'5" **Wt:** 215 **Born:** 10/15/1992 **Age:** 28

			HOW MUCH PITCHED					WHAT HE GAVE UP										THE RESULTS								
Year	Team	Lg	G	GS	GF	IP	BFP	H	R	ER	HR	SH	SF	HB	TBB	IBB	SO	WP	W	L	Pct	Sv-Op	Hld	Vel	OPS	ERC	ERA
2018	Bal	AL	15	0	3	17.0	84	21	17	17	6	0	0	0	13	0	16	3	0	2	.000	0-1	1	96	.982	9.17	9.00
2020	Bal	AL	3	0	0	2.0	21	9	12	12	0	0	1	1	5	0	3	2	0	0	-	0-0	0	95	1.571	42.55	54.00
2 ML YEARS			18	0	3	19.0	105	30	29	29	6	0	1	1	18	0	19	5	0	2	.000	0-1	1	96	1.090	12.44	13.74

Curt Casali

Bats: R **Throws:** R **Pos:** C-29;PH-5;DH-1　　cuh-SAL-ee　　　　**Ht:** 6'2" **Wt:** 220 **Born:** 11/9/1988 **Age:** 32

			BATTING																	RUNNING			AVERAGES			
Year	Team	Lg	G	AB	H	2B	3B	HR	(Hm	Rd)	TB	R	RBI	RC	TBB	IBB	SO	HBP	SH	SF	SB	CS	GDP	Avg	OBP	Slg	OPS
2014	TB	AL	30	72	12	3	0	0	(0	0)	15	10	3	3	8	0	23	2	2	0	0	0	2	.167	.268	.208	.477
2015	TB	AL	38	101	24	6	0	10	(7	3)	60	13	18	14	8	0	34	2	1	1	0	0	2	.238	.304	.594	.898
2016	TB	AL	84	226	42	10	0	8	(3	5)	76	23	25	18	25	1	82	2	3	0	0	0	2	.186	.273	.336	.609
2017	TB	AL	9	9	3	0	0	1	(1	0)	6	2	3	2	3	0	3	0	0	1	0	0	0	.333	.462	.667	1.128
2018	Cin	NL	52	140	41	10	0	4	(2	2)	63	15	16	17	12	1	32	2	1	1	0	2	5	.293	.355	.450	.805
2019	Cin	NL	84	207	52	9	0	8	(2	6)	85	24	32	24	25	1	59	1	0	3	0	0	1	.251	.331	.411	.741
2020	Cin	NL	31	76	17	3	0	6	(4	2)	38	10	8	12	14	0	29	3	0	0	2	0	2	.224	.366	.500	.866
7 ML YEARS			328	831	191	41	0	37	(19	18)	343	97	105	90	95	3	262	12	7	6	2	2	14	.230	.316	.413	.728

Daniel Castano

Pitches: L **Bats:** L **Pos:** SP-6; RP-1　　　　　　　　**Ht:** 6'3" **Wt:** 231 **Born:** 9/17/1994 **Age:** 26

			HOW MUCH PITCHED					WHAT HE GAVE UP										THE RESULTS								
Year	Team	Lg	G	GS	GF	IP	BFP	H	R	ER	HR	SH	SF	HB	TBB	IBB	SO	WP	W	L	Pct	Sv-Op	Hld	Vel	OPS	ERC	ERA
2020	Mia	NL	7	6	0	29.2	126	30	12	10	3	0	1	0	11	0	12	1	1	2	.333	0-0	0	89	.729	4.08	3.03

Ryan Castellani

Pitches: R **Bats:** R **Pos:** SP-9; RP-1　　　　　　　　**Ht:** 6'4" **Wt:** 218 **Born:** 4/1/1996 **Age:** 25

			HOW MUCH PITCHED					WHAT HE GAVE UP										THE RESULTS								
Year	Team	Lg	G	GS	GF	IP	BFP	H	R	ER	HR	SH	SF	HB	TBB	IBB	SO	WP	W	L	Pct	Sv-Op	Hld	Vel	OPS	ERC	ERA
2020	Col	NL	10	9	0	43.1	189	37	30	28	12	0	1	5	26	0	25	1	1	4	.200	0-0	0	92	.882	6.02	5.82

Humberto Castellanos

Pitches: R **Bats:** R **Pos:** RP-8　　　　　　　　　　**Ht:** 5'11" **Wt:** 218 **Born:** 4/3/1998 **Age:** 23

			HOW MUCH PITCHED					WHAT HE GAVE UP										THE RESULTS								
Year	Team	Lg	G	GS	GF	IP	BFP	H	R	ER	HR	SH	SF	HB	TBB	IBB	SO	WP	W	L	Pct	Sv-Op	Hld	Vel	OPS	ERC	ERA
2020	Hou	AL	8	0	4	10.2	51	12	8	8	2	0	0	2	5	0	12	0	0	1	.000	0-1	0	90	.850	6.42	6.75

Nick Castellanos

Bats: R **Throws:** R **Pos:** RF-57;DH-2;PH-1　　cahs-teh-YAHN-ohs　　**Ht:** 6'4" **Wt:** 203 **Born:** 3/4/1992 **Age:** 29

			BATTING																	RUNNING			AVERAGES			
Year	Team	Lg	G	AB	H	2B	3B	HR	(Hm	Rd)	TB	R	RBI	RC	TBB	IBB	SO	HBP	SH	SF	SB	CS	GDP	Avg	OBP	Slg	OPS
2013	Det	AL	11	18	5	0	0	0	(0	0)	5	1	0	1	0	0	1	0	0	0	0	0	0	.278	.278	.278	.556
2014	Det	AL	148	533	138	31	4	11	(6	5)	210	50	66	63	36	3	140	3	0	7	2	2	7	.259	.306	.394	.700
2015	Det	AL	154	549	140	33	6	15	(6	9)	230	42	73	66	39	1	152	1	0	6	0	3	21	.255	.303	.419	.721
2016	Det	AL	110	411	117	25	4	18	(5	13)	204	54	58	67	28	1	111	3	0	5	1	1	4	.285	.331	.496	.827
2017	Det	AL	157	614	167	36	**10**	26	(14	12)	301	73	101	97	41	0	142	5	0	5	4	5	12	.272	.320	.490	.811
2018	Det	AL	157	620	185	46	5	23	(10	13)	310	88	89	110	49	5	151	6	0	3	2	1	8	.298	.354	.500	.854
2019	2 Tms		151	615	178	58	3	27	(11	16)	323	100	73	94	41	1	143	5	0	3	2	2	12	.289	.337	.525	.863
2020	Cin	NL	60	218	49	11	2	14	(7	7)	106	37	34	29	19	1	69	4	0	1	0	2	5	.225	.298	.486	.784
19	Det	AL	100	403	110	37	3	11	(3	8)	186	57	37	54	31	1	96	3	0	2	2	1	7	.273	.328	.462	.790
19	ChC	NL	51	212	68	21	0	16	(8	8)	137	43	36	40	10	0	47	2	0	1	0	1	5	.321	.356	.646	1.002
	Postseason		3	10	1	0	0	1	(0	1)	4	1	1	0	2	1	1	0	0	0	0	0	0	.100	.250	.400	.650
8 ML YEARS			948	3578	979	240	34	134	(59	75)	1689	445	494	527	253	12	909	27	0	30	11	16	69	.274	.324	.472	.796

Diego Castillo

Pitches: R Bats: R Pos: RP-22 Ht: 6'3" Wt: 250 Born: 1/18/1994 Age: 27

		HOW MUCH PITCHED					WHAT HE GAVE UP										THE RESULTS						
Year	Team	Lg	G	GS	GF	IP	BFP	H	R	ER	HR	SH	SF	HB	TBB	IBB	SO	WP	W	L	Pct	Sv-Op	Hld	Vel	OPS	ERC	ERA
2018	TB	AL	43	11	5	56.2	222	36	21	20	6	0	0	2	18	0	65	5	4	2	.667	0-2	10	98	.554	2.09	3.18
2019	TB	AL	65	6	18	68.2	290	59	32	26	8	1	1	5	26	4	81	5	5	8	.385	8-10	17	98	.685	3.53	3.41
2020	TB	AL	22	0	5	21.2	89	12	4	4	3	0	0	1	11	0	23	0	3	0	1.000	4-5	5	96	.581	2.52	1.66
	Postseason		4	1	0	5.2	23	5	0	0	0	0	0	0	2	0	8	0	0	0	-	0-0	0	98	.542	2.68	0.00
	3 ML YEARS		130	17	28	147.0	601	107	57	50	17	1	1	8	55	4	169	10	12	10	.545	12-17	32	98	.621	2.80	3.06

Jose Castillo

Pitches: L Bats: L Pos: P Ht: 6'6" Wt: 252 Born: 1/10/1996 Age: 25

		HOW MUCH PITCHED					WHAT HE GAVE UP										THE RESULTS						
Year	Team	Lg	G	GS	GF	IP	BFP	H	R	ER	HR	SH	SF	HB	TBB	IBB	SO	WP	W	L	Pct	Sv-Op	Hld	Vel	OPS	ERC	ERA
2018	SD	NL	37	0	5	38.1	150	23	14	14	3	0	0	3	12	1	52	1	3	3	.500	0-1	12	95	.520	1.87	3.29
2019	SD	NL	1	0	0	0.2	4	0	0	0	0	0	0	1	1	0	2	1	0	0	-	0-0	0	95	.500	7.00	0.00
	2 ML YEARS		38	0	5	39.0	154	23	14	14	3	0	0	4	13	1	54	2	3	3	.500	0-1	12	95	.523	1.96	3.23

Luis Castillo

Pitches: R Bats: R Pos: SP-12 Ht: 6'2" Wt: 200 Born: 12/12/1992 Age: 28

		HOW MUCH PITCHED					WHAT HE GAVE UP										THE RESULTS						
Year	Team	Lg	G	GS	GF	IP	BFP	H	R	ER	HR	SH	SF	HB	TBB	IBB	SO	WP	W	L	Pct	Sv-Op	Hld	Vel	OPS	ERC	ERA
2017	Cin	NL	15	15	0	89.1	359	64	32	31	11	4	3	3	32	1	98	2	3	7	.300	0-0	0	97	.638	2.70	3.12
2018	Cin	NL	31	31	0	169.2	708	158	89	81	28	3	6	5	49	1	165	4	10	12	.455	0-0	0	96	.732	3.80	4.30
2019	Cin	NL	32	32	0	190.2	781	139	76	72	22	6	1	7	79	0	226	5	15	8	.652	0-0	0	96	.633	2.94	3.40
2020	Cin	NL	12	12	0	70.0	292	62	31	25	5	0	1	1	24	0	89	1	4	6	.400	0-0	0	97	.663	3.10	3.21
	4 ML YEARS		90	90	0	519.2	2140	423	228	209	66	13	11	16	184	2	578	12	32	33	.492	0-0	0	97	.671	3.19	3.62

Anthony Castro

Pitches: R Bats: R Pos: RP-1 Ht: 6'2" Wt: 182 Born: 4/13/1995 Age: 26

		HOW MUCH PITCHED					WHAT HE GAVE UP										THE RESULTS						
Year	Team	Lg	G	GS	GF	IP	BFP	H	R	ER	HR	SH	SF	HB	TBB	IBB	SO	WP	W	L	Pct	Sv-Op	Hld	Vel	OPS	ERC	ERA
2020	Det	AL	1	0	1	1.0	5	1	2	2	1	0	0	0	1	0	1	0	0	0	-	0-0	0	92	1.400	14.27	18.00

Harold Castro

Bats: L Throws: R Pos: LF-6;PH-5;3B-4;RF-4;1B-2;2B-2;SS-2;CF-2;DH-2;PR-2 Ht: 5'10" Wt: 151 Born: 11/30/1993 Age: 27

			BATTING																RUNNING			AVERAGES			
Year	Team	Lg	G	AB	H	2B	3B	HR	(Hm | Rd)	TB	R	RBI	RC	TBB	IBB	SO	HBP	SH	SF	SB	CS	GDP	Avg	OBP	Slg	OPS
2018	Det	AL	6	10	3	0	0	0	(0 | 0)	3	2	0	1	0	0	2	0	0	0	1	0	0	.300	.300	.300	.600
2019	Det	AL	97	354	103	10	4	5	(2 | 3)	136	30	38	44	9	0	86	0	2	4	4	2	6	.291	.305	.384	.689
2020	Det	AL	22	49	17	4	0	0	(0 | 0)	21	6	3	8	5	0	11	0	0	0	0	0	1	.347	.407	.429	.836
	3 ML YEARS		125	413	123	14	4	5	(2 | 3)	160	38	41	53	14	0	99	0	2	4	5	2	7	.298	.318	.387	.705

Jason Castro

Bats: L Throws: R Pos: C-26;PH-1 Ht: 6'3" Wt: 215 Born: 6/18/1987 Age: 34

			BATTING																RUNNING			AVERAGES			
Year	Team	Lg	G	AB	H	2B	3B	HR	(Hm | Rd)	TB	R	RBI	RC	TBB	IBB	SO	HBP	SH	SF	SB	CS	GDP	Avg	OBP	Slg	OPS
2010	Hou	NL	67	195	40	8	1	2	(1 | 1)	56	26	8	12	22	2	41	0	0	0	0	0	4	.205	.286	.287	.573
2012	Hou	NL	87	257	66	15	2	6	(3 | 3)	103	29	29	33	31	2	61	1	2	4	0	0	8	.257	.334	.401	.735
2013	Hou	AL	120	435	120	35	1	18	(13 | 5)	211	63	56	76	50	3	130	2	0	4	2	1	4	.276	.350	.485	.835
2014	Hou	AL	126	465	103	21	2	14	(10 | 4)	170	43	56	45	34	1	151	9	1	3	1	0	11	.222	.286	.366	.651
2015	Hou	AL	104	337	71	19	0	11	(8 | 3)	123	38	31	29	33	1	115	2	0	3	0	0	5	.211	.283	.365	.648
2016	Hou	AL	113	329	69	16	3	11	(5 | 6)	124	41	32	34	45	0	123	1	1	0	2	1	9	.210	.307	.377	.684
2017	Min	AL	110	356	86	22	0	10	(6 | 4)	138	49	47	45	45	1	108	4	1	1	0	0	10	.242	.333	.388	.720
2018	Min	AL	19	63	9	3	0	1	(0 | 1)	15	4	3	1	9	0	26	1	0	1	0	0	2	.143	.257	.238	.495
2019	Min	AL	79	237	55	9	0	13	(7 | 6)	103	39	30	31	33	0	88	3	1	1	0	0	4	.232	.332	.435	.767
2020	2 Tms		27	80	15	9	0	2	(1 | 1)	30	8	9	11	12	0	33	0	0	0	0	0	2	.188	.293	.375	.668
20	LAA	AL	18	52	10	4	0	2	(1 | 1)	20	5	6	8	10	0	23	0	0	0	0	0	1	.192	.323	.385	.707
20	SD	NL	9	28	5	5	0	0	(0 | 0)	10	3	3	3	2	0	10	0	0	0	0	0	1	.179	.233	.357	.590
	Postseason		7	19	1	0	0	0	(0 | 0)	1	1	2	0	2	0	11	0	0	0	0	0	2	.053	.143	.053	.195
	10 ML YEARS		852	2754	634	157	9	88	(54 | 34)	1073	340	301	317	314	10	876	23	6	17	5	2	55	.230	.312	.390	.702

Miguel Castro

Pitches: R Bats: R Pos: RP-26 Ht: 6'7" Wt: 205 Born: 12/24/1994 Age: 26

		HOW MUCH PITCHED					WHAT HE GAVE UP										THE RESULTS						
Year	Team	Lg	G	GS	GF	IP	BFP	H	R	ER	HR	SH	SF	HB	TBB	IBB	SO	WP	W	L	Pct	Sv-Op	Hld	Vel	OPS	ERC	ERA
2015	2 Tms		18	0	12	17.2	83	21	13	12	4	0	2	0	10	2	18	2	0	3	.000	4-6	1	96	.937	6.61	6.11
2016	Col	NL	19	0	4	14.2	67	18	10	10	3	1	0	1	5	0	12	0	0	0	-	0-1	1	96	.880	6.21	6.14
2017	Bal	AL	39	1	8	66.1	274	53	29	26	8	3	4	2	28	4	38	2	3	3	.500	0-0	1	96	.682	3.27	3.53
2018	Bal	AL	63	1	16	86.1	376	75	41	38	9	0	3	5	50	7	57	9	2	7	.222	0-2	5	96	.714	4.22	3.96
2019	Bal	AL	65	0	28	73.1	319	63	42	38	10	0	6	0	41	3	71	11	1	3	.250	2-5	9	97	.712	4.08	4.66
2020	2 Tms		26	0	5	24.2	115	28	12	11	4	0	0	1	13	0	38	1	2	2	.500	1-3	5	98	.821	5.95	4.01
15	Tor	AL	13	0	9	12.1	57	15	7	6	2	0	2	0	6	2	12	2	0	2	.000	4-6	1	96	.858	5.86	4.38

Year Team	Lg	G	GS	GF	IP	BFP	H	R	ER	HR	SH	SF	HB	TBB	IBB	SO	WP	W	L	Pct	Sv-Op	Hld	Vel	OPS	ERC	ERA
15 Col	NL	5	0	3	5.1	26	6	6	6	2	0	0	0	4	0	6	0	0	1	.000	0-0	0	96	1.112	8.41	10.13
20 Bal	AL	16	0	4	15.2	70	17	7	7	3	0	0	1	5	0	24	0	1	0	1.000	1-3	4	98	.782	5.04	4.02
20 NYM	NL	10	0	1	9.0	45	11	5	4	1	0	0	0	8	0	14	0	1	2	.333	0-0	1	99	.882	7.55	4.00
6 ML YEARS		230	2	73	283.0	1234	258	147	135	38	4	15	9	147	16	234	24	8	18	.308	7-17	28	96	.741	4.34	4.29

Starlin Castro

Bats: R **Throws:** R **Pos:** 2B-16   STARR-linn   **Ht:** 6'2" **Wt:** 220 **Born:** 3/24/1990 **Age:** 31

Year Team	Lg	G	AB	H	2B	3B	HR	(Hm	Rd)	TB	R	RBI	RC	TBB	IBB	SO	HBP	SH	SF	SB	CS	GDP	Avg	OBP	Slg	OPS
2010 ChC	NL	125	463	139	31	5	3	(1	2)	189	53	41	56	29	7	71	6	4	4	10	8	14	.300	.347	.408	.755
2011 ChC	NL	158	674	207	36	9	10	(4	6)	291	91	66	93	35	2	96	2	0	4	22	9	20	.307	.341	.432	.773
2012 ChC	NL	162	646	183	29	12	14	(7	7)	278	78	78	91	36	5	100	4	0	5	25	13	15	.283	.323	.430	.753
2013 ChC	NL	161	666	163	34	2	10	(9	1)	231	59	44	55	30	0	129	7	1	1	9	6	21	.245	.284	.347	.631
2014 ChC	NL	134	528	154	33	1	14	(3	11)	231	58	65	72	35	4	100	4	0	2	4	4	18	.292	.339	.438	.777
2015 ChC	NL	151	547	145	23	2	11	(3	8)	205	52	69	54	21	6	91	5	1	4	5	5	18	.265	.296	.375	.671
2016 NYY	AL	151	577	156	29	1	21	(15	6)	250	63	70	69	24	1	118	3	1	5	4	0	15	.270	.300	.433	.734
2017 NYY	AL	112	443	133	18	1	16	(10	6)	201	66	63	69	23	1	93	4	0	3	2	0	9	.300	.338	.454	.792
2018 Mia	NL	154	593	165	32	2	12	(7	5)	237	76	54	70	48	3	124	0	0	6	6	4	18	.278	.329	.400	.729
2019 Mia	NL	162	636	172	31	4	22	(11	11)	277	68	86	77	28	2	111	3	0	9	2	2	23	.270	.300	.436	.736
2020 Was	NL	16	60	16	3	1	2	(1	1)	27	9	4	7	3	0	13	0	0	0	0	0	0	.267	.302	.450	.752
Postseason		22	84	17	4	0	1	(1	0)	24	7	3	6	3	1	15	1	0	0	0	0	1	.202	.239	.286	.524
11 ML YEARS		1486	5833	1633	299	40	135	(71	64)	2417	673	640	713	312	31	1046	38	7	43	89	51	171	.280	.319	.414	.733

Willi Castro

Bats: B **Throws:** R **Pos:** SS-27;3B-8;2B-1;DH-1;PR-1   **Ht:** 6'1" **Wt:** 170 **Born:** 4/24/1997 **Age:** 24

Year Team	Lg	G	AB	H	2B	3B	HR	(Hm	Rd)	TB	R	RBI	RC	TBB	IBB	SO	HBP	SH	SF	SB	CS	GDP	Avg	OBP	Slg	OPS
2019 Det	AL	30	100	23	6	1	1	(1	0)	34	10	8	9	6	0	34	2	1	0	0	1	4	.230	.284	.340	.624
2020 Det	AL	36	129	45	4	2	6	(3	3)	71	21	24	30	7	0	38	1	1	2	0	1	0	.349	.381	.550	.932
2 ML YEARS		66	229	68	10	3	7	(4	3)	105	31	32	39	13	0	72	3	2	3	0	2	4	.297	.339	.459	.797

Jake Cave

Bats: L **Throws:** L **Pos:** CF-22;RF-12;PR-8;LF-7;DH-2;PH-2   **Ht:** 6'0" **Wt:** 200 **Born:** 12/4/1992 **Age:** 28

Year Team	Lg	G	AB	H	2B	3B	HR	(Hm	Rd)	TB	R	RBI	RC	TBB	IBB	SO	HBP	SH	SF	SB	CS	GDP	Avg	OBP	Slg	OPS
2018 Min	AL	91	283	75	16	2	13	(6	7)	134	54	45	46	18	2	102	3	2	3	2	1	2	.265	.313	.473	.786
2019 Min	AL	72	198	51	11	2	8	(3	5)	90	28	25	27	21	0	71	8	0	1	0	0	5	.258	.351	.455	.805
2020 Min	AL	42	113	25	3	2	4	(3	1)	44	17	15	15	5	0	44	5	0	0	0	2	0	.221	.285	.389	.674
Postseason		2	4	1	0	0	0	(0	0)	1	0	0	0	0	0	2	0	0	0	0	0	0	.250	.250	.250	.500
3 ML YEARS		205	594	151	30	6	25	(12	13)	268	99	85	88	44	2	217	16	2	4	2	3	7	.254	.321	.451	.772

Dylan Cease

Pitches: R **Bats:** R **Pos:** SP-12   **Ht:** 6'2" **Wt:** 200 **Born:** 12/28/1995 **Age:** 25

Year Team	Lg	G	GS	GF	IP	BFP	H	R	ER	HR	SH	SF	HB	TBB	IBB	SO	WP	W	L	Pct	Sv-Op	Hld	Vel	OPS	ERC	ERA
2019 CWS	AL	14	14	0	73.0	326	78	51	47	15	0	1	2	35	1	81	4	4	7	.364	0-0	0	97	.839	5.70	5.79
2020 CWS	AL	12	12	0	58.1	255	50	30	26	12	0	1	5	34	1	44	1	5	4	.556	0-0	0	98	.827	5.17	4.01
2 ML YEARS		26	26	0	131.1	581	128	81	73	27	0	2	7	69	2	125	5	9	11	.450	0-0	0	97	.834	5.46	5.00

Blake Cederlind

Pitches: R **Bats:** R **Pos:** RP-5   **Ht:** 6'4" **Wt:** 215 **Born:** 1/4/1996 **Age:** 25

Year Team	Lg	G	GS	GF	IP	BFP	H	R	ER	HR	SH	SF	HB	TBB	IBB	SO	WP	W	L	Pct	Sv-Op	Hld	Vel	OPS	ERC	ERA
2020 Pit	NL	5	0	2	4.0	16	3	2	2	0	0	0	0	1	0	4	1	0	0	-	0-0	0	98	.517	1.65	4.50

Francisco Cervelli

Bats: R **Throws:** R **Pos:** C-16   sir-VEL-lee   **Ht:** 6'0" **Wt:** 220 **Born:** 3/6/1986 **Age:** 35

Year Team	Lg	G	AB	H	2B	3B	HR	(Hm	Rd)	TB	R	RBI	RC	TBB	IBB	SO	HBP	SH	SF	SB	CS	GDP	Avg	OBP	Slg	OPS
2008 NYY	AL	3	5	0	0	0	0	(0	0)	0	0	0	0	0	0	3	0	0	0	0	0	1	.000	.000	.000	.000
2009 NYY	AL	42	94	28	4	0	1	(0	1)	35	13	11	11	2	0	11	0	4	1	0	3	1	.298	.309	.372	.682
2010 NYY	AL	93	266	72	11	3	0	(0	0)	89	27	38	40	33	1	42	6	8	4	1	1	7	.271	.359	.335	.694
2011 NYY	AL	43	124	33	4	0	4	(2	2)	49	17	22	17	9	0	29	2	1	1	4	1	4	.266	.324	.395	.719
2012 NYY	AL	3	1	0	0	0	0	(0	0)	0	1	0	0	1	0	0	0	0	0	0	0	0	.000	.500	.000	.500
2013 NYY	AL	17	52	14	3	0	3	(3	0)	26	12	8	9	8	0	9	1	0	0	0	0	0	.269	.377	.500	.877
2014 NYY	AL	49	146	44	11	1	2	(1	1)	63	18	13	19	11	0	41	5	0	0	0	1	5	.301	.370	.432	.802
2015 Pit	NL	130	451	133	17	5	7	(6	1)	181	56	43	62	46	1	94	8	4	1	1	1	12	.295	.370	.401	.771
2016 Pit	NL	101	326	86	14	1	1	(0	1)	105	42	33	40	56	1	72	6	0	5	6	2	14	.264	.377	.322	.699
2017 Pit	NL	81	265	66	13	2	5	(2	3)	98	31	31	30	32	0	65	6	0	1	0	2	7	.249	.342	.370	.712
2018 Pit	NL	104	332	86	15	3	12	(5	7)	143	39	57	60	51	1	84	15	2	4	2	3	7	.259	.378	.431	.809
2019 2 Tms	NL	48	141	30	8	1	3	(1	2)	49	15	12	11	13	0	41	5	1	0	1	0	7	.213	.302	.348	.649
2020 Mia	NL	16	53	13	2	0	3	(0	3)	24	10	7	9	8	0	14	1	0	0	1	0	3	.245	.355	.453	.808

Year	Team	Lg	G	AB	H	2B	3B	HR	(Hm	Rd)	TB	R	RBI	RC	TBB	IBB	SO	HBP	SH	SF	SB	CS	GDP	Avg	OBP	Slg	OPS
19	Pit	NL	34	109	21	3	0	1	(0	1)	27	11	5	4	9	0	31	4	1	0	1	0	4	.193	.279	.248	.526
19	Atl	NL	14	32	9	5	1	2	(1	1)	22	4	7	7	4	0	10	1	0	0	0	0	0	.281	.378	.688	1.066
	Postseason		6	8	1	0	0	0	(0	0)	1	0	0	0	1	0	3	1	0	0	0	0	0	.125	.300	.125	.425
13 ML YEARS			730	2256	605	102	16	41	(20	21)	862	281	275	308	270	4	505	55	20	17	17	13	69	.268	.358	.382	.740

Yoenis Cespedes

Bats: R **Throws:** R **Pos:** DH-8   yo-EHN-ess SESS-peh-des   **Ht:** 5'11" **Wt:** 225 **Born:** 10/18/1985 **Age:** 35

Year	Team	Lg	G	AB	H	2B	3B	HR	(Hm	Rd)	TB	R	RBI	RC	TBB	IBB	SO	HBP	SH	SF	SB	CS	GDP	Avg	OBP	Slg	OPS
2012	Oak	AL	129	487	142	25	5	23	(11	12)	246	70	82	90	43	5	102	7	0	3	16	4	9	.292	.356	.505	.861
2013	Oak	AL	135	529	127	21	4	26	(14	12)	234	74	80	65	37	5	137	5	0	3	7	7	8	.240	.294	.442	.737
2014	2 Tms	AL	152	600	156	36	6	22	(13	9)	270	89	100	85	35	3	128	3	0	7	7	2	13	.260	.301	.450	.751
2015	2 Tms	AL	159	633	184	42	6	35	(10	25)	343	101	105	103	33	5	141	5	0	5	7	5	14	.291	.328	.542	.870
2016	NYM	NL	132	479	134	25	1	31	(14	17)	254	72	86	83	51	8	108	7	0	6	3	1	14	.280	.354	.530	.884
2017	NYM	NL	81	291	85	17	2	17	(5	12)	157	46	42	44	26	5	61	2	0	2	0	1	7	.292	.352	.540	.892
2018	NYM	NL	38	141	37	6	0	9	(4	5)	70	20	29	24	13	2	50	1	0	2	3	0	1	.262	.325	.496	.821
2020	NYM	NL	8	31	5	1	0	2	(2	0)	12	3	4	1	2	0	15	1	0	0	0	0	1	.161	.235	.387	.622
14	Oak	AL	101	399	102	26	3	17	(11	6)	185	62	67	55	28	3	80	1	0	4	3	2	8	.256	.303	.464	.767
14	Bos	AL	51	201	54	10	3	5	(2	3)	85	27	33	30	7	0	48	2	0	3	4	0	5	.269	.296	.423	.719
15	Det	AL	102	403	118	28	2	18	(5	13)	204	62	61	58	19	2	87	1	0	4	3	4	9	.293	.323	.506	.829
15	NYM	NL	57	230	66	14	4	17	(5	12)	139	39	44	45	14	3	54	4	0	1	4	1	5	.287	.337	.604	.942
	Postseason		25	98	26	3	1	3	(2	1)	40	11	14	14	3	0	25	1	0	1	3	0	1	.265	.291	.408	.699
8 ML YEARS			834	3191	870	173	24	165	(73	92)	1586	475	528	495	240	33	742	31	0	28	43	20	67	.273	.327	.497	.824

Luis Cessa

Pitches: R **Bats:** R **Pos:** RP-16   SESS-uh   **Ht:** 6'0" **Wt:** 208 **Born:** 4/25/1992 **Age:** 29

			HOW MUCH PITCHED					WHAT HE GAVE UP									THE RESULTS						
Year	Team	Lg	G	GS	GF	IP	BFP	H	R	ER	HR	SH	SF	HB	TBB	IBB	SO	WP	W	L	Pct	Sv-Op	Hld	Vel	OPS	ERC	ERA
2016	NYY	AL	17	9	5	70.1	285	64	36	34	16	1	1	3	14	0	46	2	4	4	.500	0-0	0	95	.744	3.81	4.35
2017	NYY	AL	10	5	2	36.0	160	36	21	19	7	0	0	3	17	0	30	2	0	3	.000	0-0	0	96	.829	5.43	4.75
2018	NYY	AL	16	5	6	44.2	195	51	27	26	5	1	0	0	13	0	39	7	1	4	.200	2-2	0	95	.761	4.50	5.24
2019	NYY	AL	43	0	14	81.0	343	75	42	37	14	0	4	3	31	1	75	1	2	1	.667	1-1	4	94	.751	4.26	4.11
2020	NYY	AL	16	0	6	21.2	93	20	10	8	2	0	0	0	7	0	17	1	0	0	-	1-1	1	94	.693	3.20	3.32
	Postseason		2	0	1	4.0	14	2	0	0	0	0	0	1	0	0	4	0	0	0	-	0-0	0	95	.368	1.01	0.00
5 ML YEARS			102	19	33	253.2	1076	246	136	124	44	2	5	9	82	1	207	13	7	12	.368	4-4	5	95	.757	4.25	4.40

Jhoulys Chacin

Pitches: R **Bats:** R **Pos:** RP-2   yoo-LEES cha-SEEN   **Ht:** 6'3" **Wt:** 215 **Born:** 1/7/1988 **Age:** 33

			HOW MUCH PITCHED					WHAT HE GAVE UP									THE RESULTS						
Year	Team	Lg	G	GS	GF	IP	BFP	H	R	ER	HR	SH	SF	HB	TBB	IBB	SO	WP	W	L	Pct	Sv-Op	Hld	Vel	OPS	ERC	ERA
2009	Col	NL	9	1	3	11.0	48	6	6	6	1	1	0	0	11	0	13	2	0	1	.000	0-0	0	91	.667	3.87	4.91
2010	Col	NL	28	21	3	137.1	583	114	64	50	10	6	5	9	61	5	138	4	9	11	.450	0-0	0	91	.650	3.33	3.28
2011	Col	NL	31	31	0	194.0	827	168	87	78	20	5	3	4	87	1	150	7	11	14	.440	0-0	0	91	.707	3.61	3.62
2012	Col	NL	14	14	0	69.0	314	80	35	34	10	1	1	2	32	0	45	3	3	5	.375	0-0	0	90	.821	5.73	4.43
2013	Col	NL	31	31	0	197.1	816	188	82	76	11	3	7	3	61	3	126	5	14	10	.583	0-0	0	91	.685	3.26	3.47
2014	Col	NL	11	11	0	63.1	272	63	38	38	8	2	3	1	28	1	42	4	1	7	.125	0-0	0	88	.790	4.52	5.40
2015	Ari	NL	5	4	0	26.2	111	24	11	10	4	1	0	0	10	0	21	0	2	1	.667	0-0	0	89	.729	3.80	3.38
2016	2 Tms		34	22	5	144.0	632	153	81	77	14	4	6	5	55	4	119	8	6	8	.429	0-0	0	91	.745	4.42	4.81
2017	SD	NL	32	32	0	180.1	765	157	82	78	19	6	6	14	72	5	153	7	13	10	.565	0-0	0	91	.693	3.67	3.89
2018	Mil	NL	35	35	0	192.2	796	153	83	75	18	8	9	11	71	3	156	5	15	8	.652	0-0	0	90	.655	3.01	3.50
2019	2 Tms		25	24	0	103.1	470	115	73	69	25	4	4	5	46	1	101	3	3	12	.200	0-0	0	90	.877	6.13	6.01
2020	Atl	NL	2	0	0	5.0	24	6	4	4	1	0	0	0	3	0	3	0	1	0	1.000	0-0	0	91	.661	6.75	7.20
16	Atl	NL	5	5	0	26.2	117	29	17	16	4	2	1	0	8	0	27	0	1	2	.333	0-0	0	89	.756	4.42	5.40
16	LAA	AL	29	17	5	117.1	515	124	64	61	10	2	5	5	47	4	92	8	5	6	.455	0-0	0	91	.742	4.42	4.68
19	Mil	NL	19	19	0	88.2	403	99	61	57	19	4	4	5	39	1	80	3	3	10	.231	0-0	0	90	.857	5.96	5.79
19	Bos	AL	6	5	0	14.2	67	16	12	12	6	0	0	0	7	0	21	0	0	2	.000	0-0	0	90	.993	7.12	7.36
	Postseason		3	3	0	12.1	51	9	2	2	1	0	0	0	6	1	9	0	2	1	.667	0-0	0	91	.627	2.72	1.46
12 ML YEARS			257	226	10	1324.0	5658	1227	646	595	141	41	44	54	537	23	1067	48	78	87	.473	0-0	0	90	.718	3.88	4.04

Andrew Chafin

Pitches: L **Bats:** R **Pos:** RP-15   **Ht:** 6'2" **Wt:** 235 **Born:** 6/17/1990 **Age:** 31

			HOW MUCH PITCHED					WHAT HE GAVE UP									THE RESULTS						
Year	Team	Lg	G	GS	GF	IP	BFP	H	R	ER	HR	SH	SF	HB	TBB	IBB	SO	WP	W	L	Pct	Sv-Op	Hld	Vel	OPS	ERC	ERA
2014	Ari	NL	3	3	0	14.0	60	13	6	6	0	2	0	1	8	1	10	2	0	1	.000	0-0	0	91	.685	3.92	3.86
2015	Ari	NL	66	0	6	75.0	306	56	23	23	3	3	2	1	30	6	58	2	5	1	.833	2-2	16	92	.587	2.30	2.76
2016	Ari	NL	32	0	1	22.2	98	22	18	17	1	1	0	1	11	1	28	2	0	1	.000	0-1	6	93	.703	4.01	6.75
2017	Ari	NL	71	0	11	51.1	221	48	21	20	5	2	1	2	21	3	61	1	1	0	1.000	0-0	17	94	.699	3.78	3.51
2018	Ari	NL	77	0	13	49.1	211	41	18	17	0	0	3	2	25	1	53	3	1	6	.143	0-0	17	94	.621	2.99	3.10
2019	Ari	NL	77	0	6	52.2	225	52	23	22	6	3	0	2	18	0	68	1	2	2	.500	0-4	23	94	.691	4.03	3.76
2020	2 Tms		15	0	5	9.2	45	11	7	7	2	0	0	0	5	1	13	0	1	2	.333	1-3	5	94	.856	5.87	6.52
20	Ari	NL	11	0	1	6.2	33	9	6	6	1	0	0	0	4	0	10	0	1	1	.500	0-2	3	94	.877	7.28	8.10
20	ChC	NL	4	0	4	3.0	12	2	1	1	1	0	0	0	1	1	3	0	0	1	.000	1-1	0	94	.795	2.95	3.00
	Postseason		3	0	1	0.2	3	2	1	1	0	0	0	0	0	0	0	0	1	0	1.000	0-0	0	94	1.333	19.55	13.50
7 ML YEARS			341	3	43	274.2	1166	243	116	112	17	11	6	9	118	13	291	12	10	13	.435	3-10	82	93	.660	3.36	3.67

Yu Chang

Bats: R **Throws:** R **Pos:** SS-4;3B-3;2B-2;PH-2;PR-2   **Ht:** 6'1" **Wt:** 180 **Born:** 8/18/1995 **Age:** 25

Year	Team	Lg	G	AB	H	2B	3B	HR	(Hm	Rd)	TB	R	RBI	RC	TBB	IBB	SO	HBP	SH	SF	SB	CS	GDP	Avg	OBP	Slg	OPS
2019	Cle	AL	28	73	13	2	1	1	(0	1)	20	8	6	5	11	0	22	0	0	0	0	0	4	.178	.286	.274	.560
2020	Cle	AL	10	11	2	0	0	0	(0	0)	2	1	1	0	2	0	4	0	0	0	0	0	2	.182	.308	.182	.490
2 ML YEARS			38	84	15	2	1	1	(0	1)	22	9	7	5	13	0	26	0	0	0	0	0	6	.179	.289	.262	.551

Aroldis Chapman

Pitches: L **Bats:** L **Pos:** RP-13   ah-ROLL-diss   **Ht:** 6'4" **Wt:** 218 **Born:** 2/28/1988 **Age:** 33

Year	Team	Lg	G	GS	GF	IP	BFP	H	R	ER	HR	SH	SF	HB	TBB	IBB	SO	WP	W	L	Pct	Sv-Op	Hld	Vel	OPS	ERC	ERA
2010	Cin	NL	15	0	3	13.1	51	9	4	3	0	0	0	0	5	0	19	2	2	2	.500	0-1	4	100	.492	1.82	2.03
2011	Cin	NL	54	0	13	50.0	207	24	21	20	2	1	0	2	41	0	71	4	4	1	.800	1-3	13	98	.534	2.69	3.60
2012	Cin	NL	68	0	52	71.2	276	35	13	12	4	0	1	4	23	0	122	4	5	5	.500	38-43	6	98	.450	1.35	1.51
2013	Cin	NL	68	0	55	63.2	258	37	18	18	7	1	0	3	29	0	112	6	4	5	.444	38-43	0	98	.544	2.33	2.54
2014	Cin	NL	54	0	44	54.0	202	21	12	12	1	1	1	2	24	0	106	4	0	3	.000	36-38	0	100	.406	1.18	2.00
2015	Cin	NL	65	0	54	66.1	278	43	13	12	3	0	2	5	33	1	116	7	4	4	.500	33-36	0	99	.527	2.45	1.63
2016	2 Tms		59	0	52	58.0	222	32	12	10	2	0	1	0	18	0	90	8	4	1	.800	36-39	0	100	.452	1.33	1.55
2017	NYY	AL	52	0	42	50.1	210	37	20	18	3	0	1	3	20	2	69	5	4	3	.571	22-26	1	100	.584	2.53	3.22
2018	NYY	AL	55	0	43	51.1	212	24	15	14	2	0	0	5	30	0	93	9	3	0	1.000	32-34	1	99	.493	1.94	2.45
2019	NYY	AL	60	0	53	57.0	235	38	18	14	3	0	3	1	25	0	85	6	3	2	.600	37-42	0	98	.537	2.21	2.21
2020	NYY	AL	13	0	8	11.2	45	6	4	4	2	0	0	1	4	0	22	0	1	1	.500	3-5	0	98	.619	2.15	3.09
16	NYY	AL	31	0	29	31.1	120	20	8	7	2	0	0	0	8	0	44	2	3	0	1.000	20-21	0	100	.519	1.59	2.01
16	ChC	NL	28	0	23	26.2	102	12	4	3	0	0	1	0	10	0	46	6	1	1	.500	16-18	0	101	.370	1.04	1.01
Postseason			32	0	24	36.2	151	26	13	10	2	1	1	2	15	1	54	2	2	3	.400	9-13	0	100	.575	2.44	2.45
11 ML YEARS			563	0	419	547.1	2196	306	150	137	29	3	9	26	252	3	905	55	34	27	.557	276-310	25	99	.506	1.92	2.25

Matt Chapman

Bats: R **Throws:** R **Pos:** 3B-36;SS-1   **Ht:** 6'0" **Wt:** 215 **Born:** 4/28/1993 **Age:** 28

Year	Team	Lg	G	AB	H	2B	3B	HR	(Hm	Rd)	TB	R	RBI	RC	TBB	IBB	SO	HBP	SH	SF	SB	CS	GDP	Avg	OBP	Slg	OPS
2017	Oak	AL	84	290	68	23	2	14	(8	6)	137	39	40	42	32	0	92	6	0	2	0	3	2	.234	.313	.472	.785
2018	Oak	AL	145	547	152	42	6	24	(8	16)	278	100	68	94	58	0	146	9	0	2	1	2	18	.278	.356	.508	.864
2019	Oak	AL	156	583	145	36	3	36	(21	15)	295	102	91	109	73	0	147	11	0	3	1	1	12	.249	.342	.506	.848
2020	Oak	AL	37	142	33	9	2	10	(7	3)	76	22	25	20	8	0	54	1	0	1	0	0	2	.232	.276	.535	.812
Postseason			2	8	2	0	0	0	(0	0)	2	0	0	0	1	0	0	0	0	0	0	0	0	.250	.333	.250	.583
4 ML YEARS			422	1562	398	110	13	84	(44	40)	786	263	224	265	171	0	439	23	0	8	2	6	34	.255	.336	.503	.839

Tyler Chatwood

Pitches: R **Bats:** R **Pos:** SP-5   **Ht:** 5'11" **Wt:** 200 **Born:** 12/16/1989 **Age:** 31

Year	Team	Lg	G	GS	GF	IP	BFP	H	R	ER	HR	SH	SF	HB	TBB	IBB	SO	WP	W	L	Pct	Sv-Op	Hld	Vel	OPS	ERC	ERA
2011	LAA	AL	27	25	0	142.0	633	166	81	75	14	6	3	6	71	4	74	3	6	11	.353	0-0	0	93	.830	5.78	4.75
2012	Col	NL	19	12	3	64.2	294	74	43	39	9	4	2	0	33	2	41	4	5	6	.455	1-1	0	94	.836	5.62	5.43
2013	Col	NL	20	20	0	111.1	476	118	44	39	5	2	4	4	41	5	66	10	8	5	.615	0-0	0	93	.711	4.05	3.15
2014	Col	NL	4	4	0	24.0	101	21	13	12	4	0	2	2	8	0	20	2	1	0	1.000	0-0	0	93	.711	3.91	4.50
2016	Col	NL	27	27	0	158.0	669	147	75	68	15	2	3	5	70	2	117	7	12	9	.571	0-0	0	95	.723	4.01	3.87
2017	Col	NL	33	25	3	147.2	631	136	79	77	20	4	3	4	77	2	120	12	8	15	.348	1-1	0	95	.788	4.58	4.69
2018	ChC	NL	24	20	4	103.2	486	92	62	61	9	4	5	4	95	1	85	8	4	6	.400	0-0	0	95	.774	5.72	5.30
2019	ChC	NL	38	5	9	76.2	324	65	33	32	8	1	1	5	37	0	74	8	5	3	.625	2-4	3	96	.685	3.92	3.76
2020	ChC	NL	5	5	0	18.2	86	22	11	11	2	0	1	0	9	0	25	1	2	2	.500	0-0	0	94	.834	5.44	5.30
9 ML YEARS			197	143	19	846.2	3700	841	441	414	86	24	23	33	441	16	622	55	51	57	.472	4-6	3	93	.766	4.75	4.40

Jesse Chavez

Pitches: R **Bats:** R **Pos:** RP-18   CHAH-vezz   **Ht:** 6'1" **Wt:** 175 **Born:** 8/21/1983 **Age:** 37

Year	Team	Lg	G	GS	GF	IP	BFP	H	R	ER	HR	SH	SF	HB	TBB	IBB	SO	WP	W	L	Pct	Sv-Op	Hld	Vel	OPS	ERC	ERA
2008	Pit	NL	15	0	6	15.0	74	20	11	11	2	3	1	0	9	2	16	2	0	1	.000	0-2	0	94	.900	6.76	6.60
2009	Pit	NL	73	0	24	67.1	286	69	33	30	11	1	1	1	22	3	47	5	1	4	.200	0-4	15	94	.783	4.39	4.01
2010	2 Tms		51	0	26	62.2	280	69	44	41	11	5	3	1	23	7	45	2	5	5	.500	0-1	6	95	.834	4.85	5.89
2011	KC	AL	4	0	3	7.2	39	12	9	9	3	0	0	0	5	0	6	0	0	0	-	0-0	0	93	1.112	11.48	10.57
2012	2 Tms	AL	13	2	3	24.2	123	34	29	27	7	0	1	3	11	1	30	1	1	1	.500	0-0	0	93	.983	8.32	9.85
2013	Oak	AL	35	0	16	57.1	248	50	27	25	3	6	2	3	20	4	55	5	2	4	.333	1-2	1	92	.620	2.85	3.92
2014	Oak	AL	32	21	6	146.0	621	142	64	56	17	1	4	5	49	3	136	7	8	8	.500	0-0	0	91	.692	3.89	3.45
2015	Oak	AL	30	26	3	157.0	672	164	78	73	18	4	6	2	48	2	136	3	7	15	.318	1-1	0	91	.730	4.08	4.18
2016	2 Tms		62	0	19	67.0	282	71	36	33	12	0	1	8	18	3	63	1	2	2	.500	0-3	10	93	.779	4.56	4.43
2017	LAA	AL	38	21	6	138.0	586	148	83	82	28	0	2	4	45	2	119	1	7	11	.389	0-1	1	93	.826	5.06	5.35
2018	2 Tms		62	0	26	95.1	377	84	28	27	13	0	2	1	17	1	92	1	5	2	.714	5-6	7	93	.645	2.84	2.55
2019	Tex	AL	48	9	5	78.0	337	82	48	42	12	1	2	5	22	0	72	1	3	5	.375	1-2	8	91	.787	4.52	4.85
2020	Tex	AL	18	0	5	17.0	77	20	13	13	6	0	3	1	7	0	13	0	0	0	-	0-3	2	91	.985	7.42	6.88
10	Atl	NL	28	0	16	36.2	162	40	24	24	6	3	2	1	12	3	29	1	3	2	.600	0-0	0	95	.812	4.65	5.89
10	KC	AL	23	0	10	26.0	118	29	20	17	5	2	1	0	11	4	16	2	2	3	.400	0-1	6	94	.864	5.13	5.88
12	Tor	AL	9	2	2	21.1	102	25	22	20	6	0	1	2	10	1	27	0	1	1	.500	0-0	0	93	.925	6.90	8.44
12	Oak	AL	4	0	1	3.1	21	9	7	7	1	0	0	1	1	0	3	1	0	0	-	0-0	0	93	1.261	18.70	18.90
16	Tor	AL	39	0	6	41.1	173	43	22	21	9	0	1	2	10	0	42	1	1	2	.333	0-2	7	93	.799	4.75	4.57
16	LAD	NL	23	0	3	25.2	109	28	14	12	3	0	0	6	8	3	21	0	1	0	1.000	0-1	3	93	.746	4.24	4.21

158

Year	Team	Lg	G	GS	GF	IP	BFP	H	R	ER	HR	SH	SF	HB	TBB	IBB	SO	WP	W	L	Pct	Sv-Op	Hld	Vel	OPS	ERC	ERA
18	Tex	AL	30	0	15	56.1	234	58	23	22	10	0	1	0	12	1	50	1	3	1	.750	1-1	5	93	.747	4.00	3.51
18	ChC	NL	32	0	11	39.0	143	26	5	5	3	0	1	0	5	0	42	0	2	1	.667	4-5	4	93	.480	1.47	1.15
	Postseason		1	0	0	1.0	3	1	0	0	0	0	0	0	0	0	0	0	0	0	-	0-0	0	93	.667	2.79	0.00
13 ML YEARS			481	79	137	933.0	4002	965	503	469	143	21	28	25	296	28	832	29	41	58	.414	8-25	50	92	.762	4.37	4.52

Michael Chavis

Bats: R **Throws:** R **Pos:** 1B-24;LF-12;2B-8;DH-1;PH-1   **Ht:** 5'10" **Wt:** 210 **Born:** 8/11/1995 **Age:** 25

Year	Team	Lg	G	AB	H	2B	3B	HR	(Hm	Rd)	TB	R	RBI	RC	TBB	IBB	SO	HBP	SH	SF	SB	CS	GDP	Avg	OBP	Slg	OPS
2019	Bos	AL	95	347	88	10	1	18	(10	8)	154	46	58	47	31	2	127	4	0	0	2	1	11	.254	.322	.444	.766
2020	Bos	AL	42	146	31	5	2	5	(2	3)	55	16	19	13	8	0	50	2	0	2	3	0	6	.212	.259	.377	.636
2 ML YEARS			137	493	119	15	3	23	(12	11)	209	62	77	60	39	2	177	6	0	2	5	1	17	.241	.304	.424	.728

Robinson Chirinos

Bats: R **Throws:** R **Pos:** C-25;DH-1;PH-1   chee-REE-nos   **Ht:** 6'1" **Wt:** 220 **Born:** 6/5/1984 **Age:** 37

Year	Team	Lg	G	AB	H	2B	3B	HR	(Hm	Rd)	TB	R	RBI	RC	TBB	IBB	SO	HBP	SH	SF	SB	CS	GDP	Avg	OBP	Slg	OPS
2011	TB	AL	20	55	12	2	0	1	(1	0)	17	4	7	5	5	0	13	0	0	0	0	0	0	.218	.283	.309	.592
2013	Tex	AL	13	28	5	3	0	0	(0	0)	8	3	0	0	2	0	6	0	0	0	0	0	1	.179	.233	.286	.519
2014	Tex	AL	93	306	73	15	0	13	(6	7)	127	36	40	38	17	1	71	7	4	4	0	1	4	.239	.290	.415	.705
2015	Tex	AL	78	233	54	16	1	10	(4	6)	102	33	34	28	28	0	62	5	5	2	0	0	4	.232	.325	.438	.762
2016	Tex	AL	57	147	33	11	0	9	(1	8)	71	21	20	21	15	0	44	5	1	2	0	1	4	.224	.314	.483	.797
2017	Tex	AL	88	263	67	13	1	17	(10	7)	133	46	38	44	34	0	79	10	1	1	1	0	5	.255	.360	.506	.866
2018	Tex	AL	113	360	80	15	1	18	(10	8)	151	48	65	66	45	0	140	19	0	2	0	2	7	.222	.338	.419	.757
2019	Hou	AL	114	366	87	22	1	17	(10	7)	162	57	58	55	51	1	125	13	2	5	1	2	11	.238	.347	.443	.790
2020	2 Tms		26	74	12	3	0	1	(0	1)	18	4	7	2	6	0	21	1	0	1	0	0	5	.162	.232	.243	.475
20	Tex	AL	14	42	5	1	0	0	(0	0)	6	3	2	0	5	0	12	1	0	1	0	0	3	.119	.224	.143	.367
20	NYM	NL	12	32	7	2	0	1	(0	1)	12	1	5	2	1	0	9	0	0	0	0	0	2	.219	.242	.375	.617
	Postseason		18	52	9	1	0	4	(0	4)	22	5	7	5	4	0	19	1	0	0	0	0	2	.173	.246	.423	.669
9 ML YEARS			602	1832	423	100	4	86	(42	44)	789	252	269	259	203	2	561	60	13	17	4	4	41	.231	.325	.431	.755

Yonny Chirinos

Pitches: R **Bats:** R **Pos:** SP-3   chih-REE-nos   **Ht:** 6'2" **Wt:** 225 **Born:** 12/26/1993 **Age:** 27

Year	Team	Lg	G	GS	GF	IP	BFP	H	R	ER	HR	SH	SF	HB	TBB	IBB	SO	WP	W	L	Pct	Sv-Op	Hld	Vel	OPS	ERC	ERA
2018	TB	AL	18	7	2	89.2	370	84	40	35	7	2	7	5	25	2	75	5	5	5	.500	0-0	0	94	.687	3.36	3.51
2019	TB	AL	26	18	0	133.1	530	112	61	57	23	0	1	3	28	1	114	4	9	5	.643	0-0	0	94	.683	3.05	3.85
2020	TB	AL	3	3	0	11.1	52	14	4	3	2	0	0	2	4	0	10	0	0	0	-	0-0	0	93	.863	6.73	2.38
3 ML YEARS			47	28	2	234.1	952	210	105	95	32	2	8	10	57	3	199	9	14	10	.583	0-0	0	94	.695	3.34	3.65

Jazz Chisholm

Bats: L **Throws:** R **Pos:** 2B-13;SS-9;PH-1;PR-1   **Ht:** 5'11" **Wt:** 184 **Born:** 2/1/1998 **Age:** 23

Year	Team	Lg	G	AB	H	2B	3B	HR	(Hm	Rd)	TB	R	RBI	RC	TBB	IBB	SO	HBP	SH	SF	SB	CS	GDP	Avg	OBP	Slg	OPS
2016	Msoula	R+	62	249	70	12	1	9	(-	-)	111	42	37	41	19	0	73	1	0	1	13	4	1	.281	.333	.446	.779
2017	Kane	A	29	109	27	5	2	1	(-	-)	39	14	12	14	10	0	39	3	2	1	3	0	1	.248	.325	.358	.683
2018	2 Tms	Low	112	456	124	23	6	25	(-	-)	234	79	70	56	39	0	149	2	0	4	17	4	3	.272	.329	.513	.842
2019	Jacksn	AA	89	315	65	7	5	18	(-	-)	136	51	45	45	41	0	123	6	0	3	13	4	6	.206	.307	.432	.739
2019	Jaxnvl	AA	23	81	23	4	2	3	(-	-)	40	6	10	16	11	0	24	2	0	0	3	0	0	.284	.383	.494	.877
2020	Mia	NL	21	56	9	1	1	2	(0	2)	18	8	6	3	5	0	19	1	0	0	2	2	0	.161	.242	.321	.563

Ji-Man Choi

Bats: L **Throws:** R **Pos:** 1B-38;PH-10;DH-1   gee-man choy   **Ht:** 6'1" **Wt:** 260 **Born:** 5/19/1991 **Age:** 30

Year	Team	Lg	G	AB	H	2B	3B	HR	(Hm	Rd)	TB	R	RBI	RC	TBB	IBB	SO	HBP	SH	SF	SB	CS	GDP	Avg	OBP	Slg	OPS
2016	LAA	AL	54	112	19	4	0	5	(3	2)	38	9	12	8	16	1	27	0	0	1	2	4	2	.170	.271	.339	.611
2017	NYY	AL	6	15	4	1	0	2	(2	0)	11	2	5	3	2	0	5	0	0	1	0	0	0	.267	.333	.733	1.067
2018	2 Tms	Low	61	190	50	14	1	10	(5	5)	96	25	32	30	26	1	55	3	0	2	2	0	1	.263	.357	.505	.863
2019	TB	AL	127	410	107	20	2	19	(8	11)	188	54	63	68	64	2	108	6	0	7	2	3	7	.261	.363	.459	.822
2020	TB	AL	42	122	28	13	0	3	(1	2)	50	16	16	17	20	2	36	0	0	3	0	0	3	.230	.331	.410	.741
18	Mil	NL	12	30	7	2	0	2	(0	2)	15	4	5	5	2	1	14	0	0	0	0	0	0	.233	.281	.500	.781
18	TB	AL	49	160	43	12	1	8	(5	3)	81	21	27	25	24	0	41	3	0	2	2	0	0	.269	.370	.506	.877
	Postseason		6	16	3	0	0	1	(1	0)	6	2	1	3	7	0	10	0	0	0	0	0	0	.188	.435	.375	.810
5 ML YEARS			290	849	208	52	3	39	(19	20)	383	106	128	126	128	6	231	9	0	14	6	7	12	.245	.345	.451	.796

Shin-Soo Choo

Bats: L **Throws:** L **Pos:** LF-16;DH-14;RF-3;PH-3   SHIN-sue CHEW   **Ht:** 5'11" **Wt:** 205 **Born:** 7/13/1982 **Age:** 38

Year	Team	Lg	G	AB	H	2B	3B	HR	(Hm	Rd)	TB	R	RBI	RC	TBB	IBB	SO	HBP	SH	SF	SB	CS	GDP	Avg	OBP	Slg	OPS
2005	Sea	AL	10	18	1	0	0	0	(0	0)	1	1	1	0	3	0	4	0	0	0	0	0	0	.056	.190	.056	.246
2006	2 Tms	AL	49	157	44	12	3	3	(2	1)	71	23	22	24	18	2	50	2	1	1	5	3	1	.280	.360	.452	.812
2007	Cle	AL	6	17	5	0	0	0	(0	0)	5	5	5	3	2	1	5	0	0	1	0	1	0	.294	.350	.294	.644
2008	Cle	AL	94	317	98	28	3	14	(10	4)	174	68	66	72	44	4	78	5	0	4	4	3	5	.309	.397	.549	.946

Year Team	Lg	G	AB	H	2B	3B	HR	(Hm	Rd)	TB	R	RBI	RC	TBB	IBB	SO	HBP	SH	SF	SB	CS	GDP	Avg	OBP	Slg	OPS
2009 Cle	AL	156	583	175	38	6	20	(11	9)	285	87	86	111	78	5	151	17	0	7	21	2	9	.300	.394	.489	.883
2010 Cle	AL	144	550	165	31	2	22	(8	14)	266	81	90	106	83	11	118	11	0	2	22	7	11	.300	.401	.484	.885
2011 Cle	AL	85	313	81	11	3	8	(7	1)	122	37	36	38	36	3	78	6	0	3	12	5	7	.259	.344	.390	.733
2012 Cle	AL	155	598	169	43	2	16	(8	8)	264	88	67	96	73	0	150	14	0	1	21	7	10	.283	.373	.441	.815
2013 Cin	NL	154	569	162	34	2	21	(10	11)	263	107	54	111	112	5	133	26	3	2	20	11	3	.285	.423	.462	.885
2014 Tex	AL	123	455	110	19	1	13	(5	8)	170	58	40	54	58	3	131	12	0	4	3	4	9	.242	.340	.374	.714
2015 Tex	AL	149	555	153	32	3	22	(12	10)	257	94	82	99	76	1	147	15	2	5	4	2	7	.276	.375	.463	.838
2016 Tex	AL	48	178	43	7	0	7	(2	5)	71	27	17	25	25	1	46	7	0	0	6	3	1	.242	.357	.399	.756
2017 Tex	AL	149	544	142	20	1	22	(9	13)	230	96	78	97	77	1	134	7	3	5	12	3	18	.261	.357	.423	.780
2018 Tex	AL	146	560	148	30	1	21	(7	14)	243	83	62	94	92	2	156	10	1	2	6	1	11	.264	.377	.434	.810
2019 Tex	AL	151	563	149	31	2	24	(12	12)	256	93	61	103	78	3	165	18	0	1	15	1	6	.265	.371	.455	.826
2020 Tex	AL	33	110	26	3	0	5	(0	5)	44	13	15	17	13	1	33	2	0	2	6	2	1	.236	.323	.400	.723
06 Sea	AL	4	11	1	1	0	0	(0	0)	2	0	0	0	0	0	4	1	0	0	0	0	0	.091	.167	.182	.348
06 Cle	AL	45	146	43	11	3	3	(2	1)	69	23	22	24	18	2	46	1	1	1	5	3	2	.295	.373	.473	.846
Postseason		7	27	6	0	0	2	(0	2)	12	6	4	3	1	0	9	1	1	0	0	0	0	.222	.276	.444	.720
16 ML YEARS		1652	6087	1671	339	29	218	(103	115)	2722	961	782	1050	868	43	1579	152	10	40	157	55	101	.275	.377	.447	.824

Adam Cimber

Pitches: R **Bats:** R **Pos:** RP-14 **Ht:** 6'3" **Wt:** 195 **Born:** 8/15/1990 **Age:** 30

		HOW MUCH PITCHED					WHAT HE GAVE UP										THE RESULTS						
Year Team	Lg	G	GS	GF	IP	BFP	H	R	ER	HR	SH	SF	HB	TBB	IBB	SO	WP	W	L	Pct	Sv-Op	Hld	Vel	OPS	ERC	ERA
2018 2 Tms		70	0	16	68.1	284	68	28	26	5	2	2	6	17	9	58	1	3	8	.273	0-1	12	87	.743	3.49	3.42
2019 Cle	AL	68	0	12	56.2	244	56	29	28	6	1	2	4	19	2	41	0	6	3	.667	1-3	19	85	.720	4.01	4.45
2020 Cle	AL	14	0	5	11.1	49	13	5	5	1	0	2	0	2	0	5	0	0	1	.000	0-0	3	86	.751	3.84	3.97
18 SD	NL	42	0	10	48.1	192	42	19	17	2	1	2	2	10	3	51	0	3	5	.375	0-1	5	86	.644	2.42	3.17
18 Cle	AL	28	0	6	20.0	92	26	9	9	3	1	0	4	7	6	7	1	0	3	.000	0-0	7	87	.957	6.53	4.05
Postseason		2	0	1	2.0	8	2	1	1	0	0	0	0	1	0	0	0	0	0	-	0-0	0	87	.661	4.15	4.50
3 ML YEARS		152	0	33	136.1	577	137	62	59	12	3	6	10	38	11	104	1	9	12	.429	1-4	34	86	.734	3.74	3.89

Steve Cishek

Pitches: R **Bats:** R **Pos:** RP-22 SEE-sheck **Ht:** 6'6" **Wt:** 215 **Born:** 6/18/1986 **Age:** 35

		HOW MUCH PITCHED					WHAT HE GAVE UP										THE RESULTS						
Year Team	Lg	G	GS	GF	IP	BFP	H	R	ER	HR	SH	SF	HB	TBB	IBB	SO	WP	W	L	Pct	Sv-Op	Hld	Vel	OPS	ERC	ERA
2010 Fla	NL	3	0	2	4.1	15	1	0	0	0	0	0	0	1	0	3	0	0	0	-	0-0	0	93	.276	0.35	0.00
2011 Fla	NL	45	0	21	54.2	229	45	18	16	1	3	0	3	19	7	55	5	2	1	.667	3-2	3	93	.591	2.38	2.63
2012 Mia	NL	68	0	36	63.2	275	54	26	19	3	3	2	6	29	6	68	1	5	2	.714	15-19	13	92	.663	3.28	2.69
2013 Mia	NL	69	0	62	69.2	281	53	19	18	3	3	3	2	22	6	74	1	4	6	.400	34-36	1	92	.568	2.15	2.33
2014 Mia	NL	67	0	55	65.1	275	58	26	23	3	5	3	1	21	2	84	1	4	5	.444	39-43	0	92	.643	2.78	3.17
2015 2 Tms	NL	59	0	23	55.1	243	55	26	22	4	1	2	1	27	3	48	1	2	6	.250	4-9	6	91	.720	4.17	3.58
2016 Sea	AL	62	0	40	64.0	258	44	21	20	8	1	0	4	21	2	76	4	4	6	.400	25-32	9	91	.600	2.51	2.81
2017 2 Tms	AL	49	0	11	44.2	174	26	10	10	3	0	1	3	14	1	41	3	3	2	.600	1-4	15	90	.491	1.70	2.01
2018 ChC	NL	80	0	10	70.1	288	45	19	17	5	2	1	9	28	4	78	2	4	3	.571	4-7	25	90	.593	2.39	2.18
2019 ChC	NL	70	0	23	64.0	267	48	22	21	7	0	2	7	29	1	57	0	4	6	.400	7-11	11	91	.642	3.44	2.95
2020 CWS	AL	22	0	8	20.0	93	21	12	12	4	0	2	4	9	0	21	0	0	0	-	0-1	0	90	.853	6.10	5.40
15 Mia	NL	32	0	15	32.0	144	37	19	16	2	1	2	0	14	3	28	0	2	6	.250	3-7	3	91	.782	4.66	4.50
15 StL	NL	27	0	8	23.1	99	18	7	6	2	0	0	1	13	0	20	1	0	0	-	1-2	3	91	.629	3.53	2.31
17 Sea	AL	23	0	8	20.0	80	13	7	7	3	0	1	1	7	1	15	1	1	1	.500	1-4	6	90	.601	2.48	3.15
17 TB	AL	26	0	3	24.2	94	13	3	3	0	0	0	2	7	0	26	2	2	1	.667	0-0	9	91	.399	1.25	1.09
Postseason		1	0	0	0.2	1	0	0	0	0	0	0	0	0	0	0	0	0	0	-	0-0	0	92	.000	0.00	0.00
11 ML YEARS		594	0	291	576.0	2398	450	199	178	41	18	16	40	220	32	605	22	32	37	.464	132-165	82	91	.623	2.82	2.78

Jose Cisnero

Pitches: R **Bats:** R **Pos:** RP-29 siss-NEHR-oh **Ht:** 6'3" **Wt:** 245 **Born:** 4/11/1989 **Age:** 32

		HOW MUCH PITCHED					WHAT HE GAVE UP										THE RESULTS						
Year Team	Lg	G	GS	GF	IP	BFP	H	R	ER	HR	SH	SF	HB	TBB	IBB	SO	WP	W	L	Pct	Sv-Op	Hld	Vel	OPS	ERC	ERA
2013 Hou	AL	28	0	11	43.2	198	49	23	20	5	0	2	1	22	5	41	1	2	2	.500	0-2	5	93	.826	5.21	4.12
2014 Hou	AL	5	0	1	4.2	25	8	5	5	0	0	1	0	4	0	5	0	0	0	-	0-1	0	94	.930	9.79	9.64
2019 Det	AL	35	0	10	35.1	162	35	21	17	5	2	2	3	19	3	40	1	0	4	.000	0-2	4	96	.805	4.99	4.33
2020 Det	AL	29	0	2	29.2	123	23	10	10	1	0	0	3	10	0	34	0	3	3	.500	0-2	6	96	.584	2.58	3.03
4 ML YEARS		97	0	24	113.1	508	115	59	52	11	2	5	7	55	8	120	2	5	9	.357	0-7	15	95	.764	4.57	4.13

Aaron Civale

Pitches: R **Bats:** R **Pos:** SP-12 **Ht:** 6'2" **Wt:** 215 **Born:** 6/12/1995 **Age:** 26

		HOW MUCH PITCHED					WHAT HE GAVE UP										THE RESULTS						
Year Team	Lg	G	GS	GF	IP	BFP	H	R	ER	HR	SH	SF	HB	TBB	IBB	SO	WP	W	L	Pct	Sv-Op	Hld	Vel	OPS	ERC	ERA
2019 Cle	AL	10	10	0	57.2	227	44	18	15	4	1	5	1	16	0	46	2	3	4	.429	0-0	0	93	.638	2.31	2.34
2020 Cle	AL	12	12	0	74.0	312	82	39	39	11	0	2	3	16	0	69	0	4	6	.400	0-0	0	92	.798	4.52	4.74
2 ML YEARS		22	22	0	131.2	539	126	57	54	15	1	7	4	32	0	115	2	7	10	.412	0-0	0	92	.731	3.50	3.69

Taylor Clarke

Pitches: R **Bats:** R **Pos:** RP-7; SP-5   Ht: 6'4" **Wt:** 220 **Born:** 5/13/1993 **Age:** 28

Year Team	Lg	G	GS	GF	IP	BFP	H	R	ER	HR	SH	SF	HB	TBB	IBB	SO	WP	W	L	Pct	Sv-Op	Hld	Vel	OPS	ERC	ERA
2019 Ari	NL	23	15	3	84.2	369	86	55	50	23	1	5	6	30	0	68	3	5	5	.500	1-1	0	94	.882	5.50	5.31
2020 Ari	NL	12	5	2	43.1	183	35	23	21	8	0	1	0	21	2	40	0	3	0	1.000	0-0	0	94	.728	3.84	4.36
2 ML YEARS		35	20	5	128.0	552	121	78	71	31	1	6	6	51	2	108	3	8	5	.615	1-1	0	94	.831	4.92	4.99

Emmanuel Clase

Pitches: R **Bats:** R **Pos:** P   Ht: 6'2" **Wt:** 206 **Born:** 3/18/1998 **Age:** 23

Year Team	Lg	G	GS	GF	IP	BFP	H	R	ER	HR	SH	SF	HB	TBB	IBB	SO	WP	W	L	Pct	Sv-Op	Hld	Vel	OPS	ERC	ERA
2019 Tex	AL	21	1	7	23.1	94	20	8	6	2	0	0	1	6	0	21	1	2	3	.400	1-1	4	99	.678	2.89	2.31

Alex Claudio

Pitches: L **Bats:** L **Pos:** RP-20   Ht: 6'3" **Wt:** 188 **Born:** 1/31/1992 **Age:** 29

Year Team	Lg	G	GS	GF	IP	BFP	H	R	ER	HR	SH	SF	HB	TBB	IBB	SO	WP	W	L	Pct	Sv-Op	Hld	Vel	OPS	ERC	ERA
2014 Tex	AL	15	0	5	12.1	54	14	4	4	0	0	0	0	4	0	14	0	0	0	-	0-0	0	84	.693	3.79	2.92
2015 Tex	AL	18	0	6	15.2	66	12	6	5	4	0	2	1	6	2	13	1	1	1	.500	0-1	3	84	.762	3.74	2.87
2016 Tex	AL	39	0	15	51.2	217	55	19	16	2	0	2	1	10	0	34	0	4	1	.800	0-0	2	85	.662	3.28	2.79
2017 Tex	AL	70	1	38	82.2	323	71	26	23	5	1	3	2	15	4	56	0	4	2	.667	11-15	7	87	.591	2.37	2.50
2018 Tex	AL	66	1	20	68.1	299	91	35	34	4	3	3	3	13	3	41	0	4	2	.667	1-3	14	86	.827	5.03	4.48
2019 Mil	NL	83	0	9	62.0	267	57	29	28	8	1	3	6	24	2	44	1	2	2	.500	0-3	22	86	.751	4.12	4.06
2020 Mil	NL	20	0	7	19.0	81	18	10	9	2	0	0	1	6	0	15	2	0	0	-	1-1	1	86	.687	3.67	4.26
Postseason		2	0	0	5.0	18	3	0	0	0	0	0	0	3	0	0	0	0	0	-	0-0	0	86	.600	2.46	0.00
7 ML YEARS		311	2	100	311.2	1307	318	129	119	25	5	13	14	78	11	217	4	15	8	.652	13-23	49	86	.707	3.62	3.44

Garrett Cleavinger

Pitches: L **Bats:** R **Pos:** RP-1   Ht: 6'1" **Wt:** 220 **Born:** 4/23/1994 **Age:** 27

Year Team	Lg	G	GS	GF	IP	BFP	H	R	ER	HR	SH	SF	HB	TBB	IBB	SO	WP	W	L	Pct	Sv-Op	Hld	Vel	OPS	ERC	ERA
2020 Phi	NL	1	0	1	0.2	4	2	1	1	0	0	0	0	0	0	1	0	0	0	-	0-0	0	94	1.750	31.01	13.50

Mike Clevinger

Pitches: R **Bats:** R **Pos:** SP-8   Ht: 6'4" **Wt:** 215 **Born:** 12/21/1990 **Age:** 30

Year Team	Lg	G	GS	GF	IP	BFP	H	R	ER	HR	SH	SF	HB	TBB	IBB	SO	WP	W	L	Pct	Sv-Op	Hld	Vel	OPS	ERC	ERA
2016 Cle	AL	17	10	3	53.0	233	50	31	31	8	0	1	0	29	0	50	2	3	3	.500	0-0	0	93	.768	4.72	5.26
2017 Cle	AL	27	21	1	121.2	502	92	46	42	13	1	0	3	60	2	137	3	12	6	.667	0-0	0	92	.667	3.29	3.11
2018 Cle	AL	32	32	0	200.0	810	164	71	67	21	0	1	4	67	0	207	4	13	8	.619	0-0	0	94	.655	3.02	3.02
2019 Cle	AL	21	21	0	126.0	499	96	38	38	10	0	1	4	37	0	169	0	13	4	.765	0-0	0	95	.602	2.41	2.71
2020 2 Tms		8	8	0	41.2	162	34	14	14	6	0	0	0	14	0	40	2	3	2	.600	0-0	0	95	.713	3.31	3.02
20 Cle	AL	4	4	0	22.2	93	20	8	8	5	0	0	0	11	0	21	0	1	1	.500	0-0	0	95	.818	4.83	3.18
20 SD	NL	4	4	0	19.0	69	14	6	6	1	0	0	0	3	0	19	2	2	1	.667	0-0	0	96	.580	1.75	2.84
Postseason		7	1	3	12.0	57	8	7	6	3	0	1	1	12	0	15	1	0	0	-	0-0	0	95	.857	5.95	4.50
5 ML YEARS		105	92	4	542.1	2206	436	200	192	58	1	3	9	207	2	603	11	44	23	.657	0-0	0	94	.662	3.11	3.19

Tyler Clippard

Pitches: R **Bats:** R **Pos:** RP-24; SP-2   Ht: 6'3" **Wt:** 200 **Born:** 2/14/1985 **Age:** 36

Year Team	Lg	G	GS	GF	IP	BFP	H	R	ER	HR	SH	SF	HB	TBB	IBB	SO	WP	W	L	Pct	Sv-Op	Hld	Vel	OPS	ERC	ERA
2007 NYY	AL	6	6	0	27.0	124	29	19	19	6	0	0	0	17	1	18	2	3	1	.750	0-0	0	88	.876	6.37	6.33
2008 Was	NL	2	2	0	10.1	48	12	5	5	2	0	0	0	7	1	8	1	1	1	.500	0-0	0	89	.957	6.90	4.35
2009 Was	NL	41	0	8	60.1	246	36	20	18	9	3	1	1	32	1	67	1	4	2	.667	0-1	3	90	.633	2.79	2.69
2010 Was	NL	78	0	18	91.0	378	69	33	31	8	3	7	2	41	4	112	1	11	8	.579	1-11	23	92	.646	2.91	3.07
2011 Was	NL	72	0	8	88.1	329	48	18	18	11	4	3	0	26	2	104	1	3	0	1.000	0-7	38	93	.535	1.61	1.83
2012 Was	NL	74	0	42	72.2	307	55	32	30	7	3	4	2	29	2	84	5	2	6	.250	32-37	13	93	.621	2.73	3.72
2013 Was	NL	72	0	71	71.0	275	37	19	19	9	2	1	4	24	1	73	2	6	3	.667	0-3	33	92	.517	1.79	2.41
2014 Was	NL	75	0	6	70.1	278	47	22	17	5	2	2	1	23	1	82	0	7	4	.636	1-7	40	92	.541	1.98	2.18
2015 2 Tms		69	0	36	70.1	301	49	25	23	8	1	2	4	31	2	64	6	5	4	.556	19-25	8	92	.599	2.72	2.92
2016 2 Tms		69	0	17	63.0	262	54	27	25	10	1	0	1	26	2	72	5	4	6	.400	3-6	25	91	.716	3.80	3.57
2017 3 Tms	AL	67	0	23	60.1	264	47	33	32	10	3	3	2	31	1	72	11	2	8	.200	5-11	9	91	.711	3.73	4.77
2018 Tor	AL	73	0	22	68.2	285	57	29	28	13	2	2	2	23	0	85	1	3	5	.571	7-13	15	91	.719	3.57	3.67
2019 Cle	AL	53	3	7	62.0	241	38	20	20	8	2	1	7	15	0	64	3	1	0	1.000	0-0	8	90	.608	2.13	2.90
2020 Min	AL	26	2	1	26.0	98	19	9	8	2	0	0	0	4	0	26	2	2	1	.667	0-2	7	89	.543	1.74	2.77
15 Oak	AL	37	0	30	38.2	167	25	12	12	3	0	1	2	21	1	38	1	1	3	.250	17-21	0	91	.567	2.62	2.79
15 NYM	NL	32	0	6	32.1	134	24	13	11	5	1	1	2	10	1	26	5	4	1	.800	2-4	8	92	.637	2.82	3.06
16 Ari	NL	40	0	10	37.2	155	34	18	18	7	1	0	0	15	0	46	1	2	3	.400	1-3	13	91	.764	4.23	4.30
16 NYY	AL	29	0	7	25.1	107	20	9	7	3	0	0	1	11	2	26	4	2	3	.400	2-3	12	92	.646	3.19	2.49
17 NYY	AL	40	0	7	36.1	158	28	21	20	7	3	1	1	19	1	42	5	1	5	.167	1-6	8	91	.735	3.88	4.95
17 CWS	AL	11	0	7	10.0	44	8	2	2	0	0	1	0	5	0	12	3	1	0	1.000	2-2	0	91	.585	2.56	1.80
17 Hou	AL	16	0	9	14.0	62	11	10	10	3	0	1	1	7	0	18	3	0	2	.000	2-3	1	90	.740	4.19	6.43
Postseason		14	0	1	12.2	53	9	6	6	2	1	0	0	5	0	11	1	0	1	.000	0-0	8	92	.673	2.77	4.26
14 ML YEARS		777	14	194	842.0	3436	597	311	293	108	26	26	26	329	18	931	47	55	47	.539	68-123	222	91	.632	2.76	3.13

Alex Cobb

Pitches: R **Bats:** R **Pos:** SP-10   **Ht:** 6'3" **Wt:** 205 **Born:** 10/7/1987 **Age:** 33

Year	Team	Lg	G	GS	GF	IP	BFP	H	R	ER	HR	SH	SF	HB	TBB	IBB	SO	WP	W	L	Pct	Sv-Op	Hld	Vel	OPS	ERC	ERA
2011	TB	AL	9	9	0	52.2	224	49	21	20	3	0	1	1	21	1	37	2	3	2	.600	0-0	0	91	.655	3.44	3.42
2012	TB	AL	23	23	0	136.1	569	130	67	61	11	3	6	9	40	2	106	8	11	9	.550	0-0	0	90	.690	3.56	4.03
2013	TB	AL	22	22	0	143.1	578	120	46	44	13	1	2	3	45	4	134	5	11	3	.786	0-0	0	92	.644	2.92	2.76
2014	TB	AL	27	27	0	166.1	681	142	56	53	11	4	4	10	47	1	149	8	10	9	.526	0-0	0	92	.619	2.87	2.87
2016	TB	AL	5	5	0	22.0	104	32	22	21	5	1	1	0	7	0	16	0	1	2	.333	0-0	0	90	.968	7.40	8.59
2017	TB	AL	29	29	0	179.1	742	175	78	73	22	2	1	6	44	2	128	8	12	10	.545	0-0	0	92	.709	3.64	3.66
2018	Bal	AL	28	28	0	152.1	661	172	93	83	24	2	6	4	43	5	102	4	5	15	.250	0-0	0	92	.814	4.81	4.90
2019	Bal	AL	3	3	0	12.1	60	21	16	15	9	0	0	0	2	0	8	0	0	2	.000	0-0	0	92	1.297	12.47	10.95
2020	Bal	AL	10	10	0	52.1	226	52	27	25	8	0	0	2	18	0	38	1	2	5	.286	0-0	0	92	.736	4.31	4.30
	Postseason		2	2	0	11.2	51	13	3	2	0	0	0	1	3	0	10	1	1	0	1.000	0-0	0	92	.695	3.75	1.54
	9 ML YEARS		156	156	0	917.0	3845	893	426	395	106	13	21	35	267	15	718	36	55	57	.491	0-0	0	91	.714	3.76	3.88

Kyle Cody

Pitches: R **Bats:** R **Pos:** SP-5; RP-3   **Ht:** 6'7" **Wt:** 225 **Born:** 8/9/1994 **Age:** 26

Year	Team	Lg	G	GS	GF	IP	BFP	H	R	ER	HR	SH	SF	HB	TBB	IBB	SO	WP	W	L	Pct	Sv-Op	Hld	Vel	OPS	ERC	ERA
2020	Tex	AL	8	5	3	22.2	92	15	5	4	1	0	0	0	13	0	18	3	1	1	.500	0-0	0	94	.583	2.64	1.59

A.J. Cole

Pitches: R **Bats:** R **Pos:** RP-24   **Ht:** 6'5" **Wt:** 240 **Born:** 1/5/1992 **Age:** 29

Year	Team	Lg	G	GS	GF	IP	BFP	H	R	ER	HR	SH	SF	HB	TBB	IBB	SO	WP	W	L	Pct	Sv-Op	Hld	Vel	OPS	ERC	ERA
2015	Was	NL	3	1	1	9.1	44	14	11	6	1	1	1	0	1	1	9	1	0	0	--	1-1	0	90	.812	5.38	5.79
2016	Was	NL	8	8	0	38.1	168	37	24	22	7	0	3	2	14	1	39	1	1	2	.333	0-0	0	93	.779	4.39	5.17
2017	Was	NL	11	8	0	52.0	229	51	23	22	8	3	1	3	27	0	44	2	3	5	.375	0-0	0	93	.799	5.15	3.81
2018	2 Tms		32	2	14	48.1	221	55	38	33	15	2	1	0	22	1	59	2	4	2	.667	0-1	0	93	.928	6.57	6.14
2019	Cle	AL	25	0	9	26.0	118	31	16	11	4	1	2	0	8	0	30	0	3	1	.750	1-1	0	94	.819	5.03	3.81
2020	Tor	AL	24	0	7	23.1	95	19	9	8	3	1	1	0	9	2	20	3	3	0	1.000	1-4	2	93	.691	3.13	3.09
	18 Was	NL	4	2	1	10.1	53	16	15	15	6	2	0	0	6	0	10	0	1	1	.500	0-0	0	92	1.298	12.42	13.06
	18 NYY	AL	28	0	13	38.0	168	39	23	18	9	0	1	0	16	1	49	2	3	1	.750	0-1	0	94	.817	5.17	4.26
	6 ML YEARS		103	19	31	197.1	875	207	121	102	38	8	9	5	81	5	201	9	14	10	.583	3-7	2	93	.820	5.08	4.65

Gerrit Cole

Pitches: R **Bats:** R **Pos:** SP-12   **Ht:** 6'4" **Wt:** 220 **Born:** 9/8/1990 **Age:** 30

Year	Team	Lg	G	GS	GF	IP	BFP	H	R	ER	HR	SH	SF	HB	TBB	IBB	SO	WP	W	L	Pct	Sv-Op	Hld	Vel	OPS	ERC	ERA
2013	Pit	NL	19	19	0	117.1	469	109	43	42	7	5	2	3	28	0	100	4	10	7	.588	0-0	0	96	.638	3.02	3.22
2014	Pit	NL	22	22	0	138.0	571	127	58	56	11	10	0	9	40	1	138	9	11	5	.688	0-0	0	96	.693	3.37	3.65
2015	Pit	NL	32	32	0	208.0	832	183	71	60	11	7	6	10	44	1	202	7	19	8	.704	0-0	0	96	.623	2.66	2.60
2016	Pit	NL	21	21	0	116.0	506	131	57	50	7	4	6	6	36	3	98	5	7	10	.412	0-0	0	95	.754	4.35	3.88
2017	Pit	NL	33	**33**	0	203.0	849	199	98	96	31	5	1	4	55	1	196	7	12	12	.500	0-0	0	96	.739	3.89	4.26
2018	Hou	AL	32	32	0	200.1	799	143	68	64	19	2	3	7	64	0	276	9	15	5	.750	0-0	0	97	.600	2.40	2.88
2019	Hou	AL	33	33	0	212.1	817	142	66	59	29	1	3	3	48	0	**326**	4	20	5	.800	0-0	0	97	.579	2.02	**2.50**
2020	NYY	AL	12	12	0	73.0	288	53	27	23	14	0	0	2	17	0	94	2	7	3	.700	0-0	0	97	.655	2.65	2.84
	Postseason		10	10	0	65.2	250	41	20	19	9	0	0	0	16	0	78	0	6	4	.600	0-0	0	97	.549	1.84	2.60
	8 ML YEARS		204	204	0	1268.0	5131	1087	488	450	129	34	21	44	332	6	1430	47	101	55	.647	0-0	0	96	.656	2.95	3.19

Edwar Colina

Pitches: R **Bats:** R **Pos:** RP-1   **Ht:** 5'11" **Wt:** 240 **Born:** 5/3/1997 **Age:** 24

Year	Team	Lg	G	GS	GF	IP	BFP	H	R	ER	HR	SH	SF	HB	TBB	IBB	SO	WP	W	L	Pct	Sv-Op	Hld	Vel	OPS	ERC	ERA
2020	Min	AL	1	0	0	0.1	7	4	3	3	1	0	0	0	2	0	0	0	0	0	--	0-0	0	97	2.257	185.3	81.00

Zack Collins

Bats: L **Throws:** R **Pos:** DH-5;PH-3;C-2;1B-1;PR-1   **Ht:** 6'3" **Wt:** 230 **Born:** 2/6/1995 **Age:** 26

Year	Team	Lg	G	AB	H	2B	3B	HR	(Hm	Rd)	TB	R	RBI	RC	TBB	IBB	SO	HBP	SH	SF	SB	CS	GDP	Avg	OBP	Slg	OPS
2019	CWS	AL	27	86	16	3	1	3	(0	3)	30	10	12	11	14	1	39	1	0	0	0	0	0	.186	.307	.349	.656
2020	CWS	AL	9	16	1	1	0	0	(0	0)	2	1	0	0	2	0	5	0	0	0	0	0	0	.063	.167	.125	.292
	2 ML YEARS		36	102	17	4	1	3	(0	3)	32	11	12	11	16	1	44	1	0	0	0	0	1	.167	.286	.314	.599

Alex Colome

Pitches: R **Bats:** R **Pos:** RP-21   COH-loh-may   **Ht:** 6'1" **Wt:** 225 **Born:** 12/31/1988 **Age:** 32

Year	Team	Lg	G	GS	GF	IP	BFP	H	R	ER	HR	SH	SF	HB	TBB	IBB	SO	WP	W	L	Pct	Sv-Op	Hld	Vel	OPS	ERC	ERA
2013	TB	AL	3	3	0	16.0	71	14	8	4	2	0	0	1	9	0	12	1	1	1	.500	0-0	0	95	.715	4.41	2.25
2014	TB	AL	5	3	1	23.2	97	19	7	7	1	0	1	0	10	0	13	3	2	0	1.000	0-0	0	94	.590	2.77	2.66
2015	TB	AL	43	13	0	109.2	457	112	50	48	9	2	7	4	31	4	88	8	8	5	.615	0-5	8	94	.698	3.78	3.94
2016	TB	AL	57	0	48	56.2	226	43	12	12	6	0	0	2	15	1	71	0	2	4	.333	37-40	1	95	.572	2.46	1.91
2017	TB	AL	65	0	53	66.2	281	57	27	24	4	3	6	3	23	**7**	58	4	2	3	.400	**47-53**	1	95	.636	2.79	3.24
2018	2 Tms	AL	70	0	24	68.0	282	59	26	23	7	0	1	3	21	2	72	10	7	5	.583	12-17	30	95	.645	3.15	3.04

			HOW MUCH PITCHED					WHAT HE GAVE UP											THE RESULTS							
Year	Team	Lg	G	GS	GF	IP	BFP	H	R	ER	HR	SH	SF	HB	TBB	IBB	SO	WP	W	L	Pct	Sv-Op	Hld	Vel	OPS	ERC	ERA
2019	CWS	AL	62	0	54	61.0	249	42	28	19	7	2	3	1	23	2	55	4	4	5	.444	30-33	0	94	.617	2.43	2.87
2020	CWS	AL	21	0	18	22.1	90	13	3	2	0	0	0	1	8	0	16	0	2	0	1.000	12-13	0	94	.460	1.45	0.81
18	TB	AL	23	0	21	21.2	97	24	12	10	1	0	1	0	8	1	23	4	2	5	.286	11-13	0	95	.728	3.99	4.15
18	Sea	AL	47	0	3	46.1	185	35	14	13	6	0	0	3	13	1	49	6	5	0	1.000	1-4	30	95	.601	2.77	2.53
	8 ML YEARS		326	19	203	424.0	1753	359	161	139	36	7	18	15	140	16	385	31	28	23	.549	138-161	40	95	.634	2.97	2.95

Christian Colon

Bats: R **Throws:** R **Pos:** 2B-7;DH-3;PH-2;1B-1   co-LONE   **Ht:** 5'10" **Wt:** 215 **Born:** 5/14/1989 **Age:** 32

			BATTING																	RUNNING			AVERAGES			
Year	Team	Lg	G	AB	H	2B	3B	HR	(Hm	Rd)	TB	R	RBI	RC	TBB	IBB	SO	HBP	SH	SF	SB	CS	GDP	Avg	OBP	Slg	OPS
2014	KC	AL	21	45	15	5	1	0	(0	0)	22	8	6	9	3	0	4	0	1	0	2	0	1	.333	.375	.489	.864
2015	KC	AL	43	107	31	5	0	0	(0	0)	36	8	6	12	11	0	17	0	1	0	3	2	2	.290	.356	.336	.692
2016	KC	AL	54	147	34	6	0	1	(1	0)	43	13	13	13	11	0	31	2	1	0	0	1	4	.231	.294	.293	.586
2017	2 Tms		24	50	8	1	0	0	(0	0)	9	4	0	0	5	1	10	0	2	0	0	0	0	.160	.236	.180	.416
2019	Cin	NL	8	6	3	0	0	0	(0	0)	3	1	1	2	0	0	0	2	0	0	0	0	0	.500	.625	.500	1.125
2020	Cin	NL	11	23	3	1	0	0	(0	0)	4	3	2	1	1	0	3	0	0	0	1	0	1	.130	.167	.174	.341
17	KC	AL	7	17	3	0	0	0	(0	0)	3	1	0	0	1	0	3	0	1	0	0	0	2	.176	.222	.176	.399
17	Mia		17	33	5	1	0	0	(0	0)	6	3	0	0	4	1	7	0	1	0	0	0	2	.152	.243	.182	.425
	Postseason		3	2	2	0	0	0	(0	0)	2	2	2	2	0	0	0	0	1	0	1	0	0	1.000	1.000	1.000	2.000
	6 ML YEARS		161	378	94	18	1	1	(1	0)	117	37	28	37	31	1	65	4	5	0	6	3	12	.249	.312	.310	.622

Michael Conforto

Bats: L **Throws:** R **Pos:** RF-52;DH-1;PH-1   **Ht:** 6'1" **Wt:** 215 **Born:** 3/1/1993 **Age:** 28

			BATTING																	RUNNING			AVERAGES			
Year	Team	Lg	G	AB	H	2B	3B	HR	(Hm	Rd)	TB	R	RBI	RC	TBB	IBB	SO	HBP	SH	SF	SB	CS	GDP	Avg	OBP	Slg	OPS
2015	NYM	NL	56	174	47	14	0	9	(4	5)	88	30	26	29	17	0	39	1	0	2	0	1	4	.270	.335	.506	.841
2016	NYM	NL	109	304	67	21	1	12	(7	5)	126	38	42	35	36	2	89	5	0	3	2	1	6	.220	.310	.414	.725
2017	NYM	NL	109	373	104	20	1	27	(16	11)	207	72	68	77	57	5	113	8	0	2	2	0	3	.279	.384	.555	.939
2018	NYM	NL	153	543	132	25	1	28	(11	17)	243	78	82	87	84	8	159	7	0	4	3	4	10	.243	.350	.448	.797
2019	NYM	NL	151	549	141	29	1	33	(18	15)	271	90	92	97	84	5	149	10	0	5	7	2	11	.257	.363	.494	.856
2020	NYM	NL	54	202	65	12	0	9	(4	5)	104	40	31	39	24	0	57	7	0	0	3	3	6	.322	.412	.515	.927
	Postseason		12	30	6	0	0	3	(2	1)	15	3	6	5	1	0	8	1	0	2	0	0	0	.200	.235	.500	.735
	6 ML YEARS		632	2145	556	121	4	118	(60	58)	1039	348	341	364	302	20	606	38	0	16	17	11	40	.259	.358	.484	.843

William Contreras

Bats: R **Throws:** R **Pos:** C-4   **Ht:** 6'0" **Wt:** 180 **Born:** 12/24/1997 **Age:** 23

			BATTING																	RUNNING			AVERAGES			
Year	Team	Lg	G	AB	H	2B	3B	HR	(Hm	Rd)	TB	R	RBI	RC	TBB	IBB	SO	HBP	SH	SF	SB	CS	GDP	Avg	OBP	Slg	OPS
2020	Atl	NL	4	10	4	1	0	0	(0	0)	5	0	1	2	0	0	4	0	0	0	0	0	0	.400	.400	.500	.900

Willson Contreras

Bats: R **Throws:** R **Pos:** C-41;DH-18   **Ht:** 6'1" **Wt:** 225 **Born:** 5/13/1992 **Age:** 29

			BATTING																	RUNNING			AVERAGES			
Year	Team	Lg	G	AB	H	2B	3B	HR	(Hm	Rd)	TB	R	RBI	RC	TBB	IBB	SO	HBP	SH	SF	SB	CS	GDP	Avg	OBP	Slg	OPS
2016	ChC	NL	76	252	71	14	1	12	(8	4)	123	33	35	41	26	0	67	4	0	1	2	2	7	.282	.357	.488	.845
2017	ChC	NL	117	377	104	21	0	21	(10	11)	188	50	74	76	45	2	98	3	1	2	5	4	13	.276	.356	.499	.855
2018	ChC	NL	138	474	118	27	5	10	(6	4)	185	50	54	58	53	2	121	13	2	2	4	1	14	.249	.339	.390	.730
2019	ChC	NL	105	360	98	18	2	24	(15	9)	192	57	64	62	38	2	102	9	0	2	1	2	4	.272	.355	.533	.888
2020	ChC	NL	57	189	46	10	0	7	(3	4)	77	37	26	32	20	1	57	14	0	2	1	2	6	.243	.356	.407	.763
	Postseason		28	74	17	2	0	3	(2	1)	28	9	7	11	12	1	21	0	0	0	0	0	0	.230	.337	.378	.716
	5 ML YEARS		493	1652	437	90	8	74	(42	32)	765	227	253	269	182	7	445	43	3	9	13	11	44	.265	.351	.463	.814

Sam Coonrod

Pitches: R **Bats:** R **Pos:** RP-18   **Ht:** 6'1" **Wt:** 225 **Born:** 9/22/1992 **Age:** 28

			HOW MUCH PITCHED					WHAT HE GAVE UP											THE RESULTS							
Year	Team	Lg	G	GS	GF	IP	BFP	H	R	ER	HR	SH	SF	HB	TBB	IBB	SO	WP	W	L	Pct	Sv-Op	Hld	Vel	OPS	ERC	ERA
2019	SF	NL	33	0	9	27.2	114	19	11	11	3	1	0	4	15	1	20	2	5	1	.833	0-1	0	97	.655	3.63	3.58
2020	SF	NL	18	0	5	14.2	71	17	16	16	2	0	1	2	7	0	15	1	0	2	.000	3-5	2	98	.871	5.94	9.82
	2 ML YEARS		51	0	14	42.1	185	36	27	27	5	1	1	6	22	1	35	3	5	3	.625	3-6	2	97	.739	4.41	5.74

Garrett Cooper

Bats: R **Throws:** R **Pos:** DH-18;1B-15;PH-1   **Ht:** 6'5" **Wt:** 235 **Born:** 12/25/1990 **Age:** 30

			BATTING																	RUNNING			AVERAGES			
Year	Team	Lg	G	AB	H	2B	3B	HR	(Hm	Rd)	TB	R	RBI	RC	TBB	IBB	SO	HBP	SH	SF	SB	CS	GDP	Avg	OBP	Slg	OPS
2017	NYY	AL	13	43	14	5	1	0	(0	0)	21	3	6	6	1	0	12	0	0	1	0	0	0	.326	.333	.488	.822
2018	Mia	NL	14	33	7	1	0	0	(0	0)	8	2	2	3	4	0	12	1	0	0	0	0	1	.212	.316	.242	.558
2019	Mia	NL	107	381	107	16	1	15	(6	9)	170	52	50	57	33	0	110	5	0	2	0	0	10	.281	.344	.446	.791
2020	Mia	NL	34	120	34	8	0	6	(3	3)	60	20	20	22	11	0	31	2	0	0	0	0	5	.283	.353	.500	.853
	4 ML YEARS		168	577	162	30	2	21	(9	12)	259	77	78	88	49	0	165	8	0	3	0	0	16	.281	.344	.449	.793

Patrick Corbin

Pitches: L Bats: L Pos: SP-11   Ht: 6'3" Wt: 210 Born: 7/19/1989 Age: 31

			HOW MUCH PITCHED					WHAT HE GAVE UP									THE RESULTS						
Year	Team	Lg	G	GS	GF	IP	BFP	H	R	ER	HR	SH	SF	HB	TBB	IBB	SO	WP	W	L	Pct	Sv-Op	Hld	Vel	OPS	ERC	ERA
2012	Ari	NL	22	17	3	107.0	454	117	56	54	14	2	5	4	25	2	86	1	6	8	.429	1-1	0	91	.782	4.31	4.54
2013	Ari	NL	32	32	0	208.1	860	189	81	79	19	8	1	9	54	1	178	13	14	8	.636	0-0	0	92	.671	3.14	3.41
2015	Ari	NL	16	16	0	85.0	357	91	34	34	9	2	1	2	17	0	78	4	6	5	.545	0-0	0	92	.743	3.82	3.60
2016	Ari	NL	36	24	6	155.2	701	177	**109**	89	24	6	5	5	66	2	131	9	5	13	.278	1-1	2	92	.825	5.47	5.15
2017	Ari	NL	33	32	0	189.2	826	208	97	85	26	4	5	3	61	8	178	10	14	13	.519	0-0	0	92	.792	4.55	4.03
2018	Ari	NL	33	33	0	200.0	800	162	70	70	15	3	2	5	48	3	246	8	11	7	.611	0-0	0	91	.607	2.41	3.15
2019	Was	NL	33	33	0	202.0	835	169	81	73	24	8	8	3	70	4	238	4	14	7	.667	0-0	0	92	.668	3.15	3.25
2020	Was	NL	11	11	0	65.2	295	**85**	35	34	10	0	1	0	18	1	60	1	2	7	.222	0-0	0	90	.838	5.61	4.66
	Postseason		8	3	0	23.1	103	21	16	15	2	0	0	1	12	1	36	0	2	3	.400	0-1	2	93	.663	3.90	5.79
	8 ML YEARS		216	198	9	1213.1	5128	1198	563	518	141	33	28	31	359	19	1195	50	72	68	.514	2-2	2	92	.725	3.78	3.84

Ryan Cordell

Bats: R Throws: R Pos: CF-4;RF-1;PR-1   Ht: 6'4" Wt: 200 Born: 3/31/1992 Age: 29

						BATTING													RUNNING			AVERAGES			
Year	Team	Lg	G	AB	H	2B	3B	HR	(Hm | Rd)	TB	R	RBI	RC	TBB	IBB	SO	HBP	SH	SF	SB	CS	GDP	Avg	OBP	Slg	OPS
2018	CWS	AL	19	37	4	1	0	1	(0 | 1)	8	3	4	0	0	0	15	1	0	2	0	0	0	.108	.125	.216	.341
2019	CWS	AL	97	217	48	8	0	7	(3 | 4)	77	22	24	21	19	0	69	3	6	2	3	1	2	.221	.290	.355	.645
2020	NYM	NL	5	8	1	0	0	0	(0 | 0)	1	0	0	0	0	0	3	0	0	0	1	0	0	.125	.125	.125	.250
	3 ML YEARS		121	262	53	9	0	8	(3 | 5)	86	25	28	21	19	0	87	4	6	4	4	1	2	.202	.263	.328	.591

Franchy Cordero

Bats: L Throws: R Pos: RF-8;CF-5;PH-5;DH-2;LF-1   Ht: 6'3" Wt: 226 Born: 9/2/1994 Age: 26

						BATTING													RUNNING			AVERAGES			
Year	Team	Lg	G	AB	H	2B	3B	HR	(Hm | Rd)	TB	R	RBI	RC	TBB	IBB	SO	HBP	SH	SF	SB	CS	GDP	Avg	OBP	Slg	OPS
2017	SD	NL	30	92	21	3	3	3	(3 | 0)	39	15	9	9	6	0	44	0	1	0	1	1	0	.228	.276	.424	.699
2018	SD	NL	40	139	33	5	1	7	(3 | 4)	61	19	19	19	14	0	55	0	1	0	5	2	1	.237	.307	.439	.746
2019	SD	NL	9	15	5	1	0	0	(0 | 0)	6	2	1	3	4	0	7	0	0	1	1	0	0	.333	.450	.400	.850
2020	KC	AL	16	38	8	3	0	2	(2 | 0)	17	7	7	7	4	0	4	0	0	0	1	0	1	.211	.286	.447	.733
	4 ML YEARS		95	284	67	12	4	12	(8 | 4)	123	43	36	38	28	0	110	0	2	1	8	3	2	.236	.304	.433	.737

Jimmy Cordero

Pitches: R Bats: R Pos: RP-30   Ht: 6'4" Wt: 235 Born: 10/19/1991 Age: 29

				HOW MUCH PITCHED				WHAT HE GAVE UP									THE RESULTS						
Year	Team	Lg	G	GS	GF	IP	BFP	H	R	ER	HR	SH	SF	HB	TBB	IBB	SO	WP	W	L	Pct	Sv-Op	Hld	Vel	OPS	ERC	ERA
2018	Was	NL	22	0	3	19.0	94	23	13	12	2	0	0	2	12	2	12	0	1	2	.333	0-1	0	98	.794	6.39	5.68
2019	2 Tms	AL	31	0	7	37.1	146	26	12	12	4	0	0	3	11	0	31	1	1	1	.500	0-0	4	97	.615	2.52	2.89
2020	CWS	AL	30	0	4	26.2	124	33	21	18	2	1	1	3	9	2	22	3	1	2	.333	0-1	8	97	.784	5.24	6.08
19	Tor	AL	1	0	1	1.1	5	2	1	1	1	0	0	0	0	0	0	0	0	1	.000	0-0	0	97	1.400	12.07	6.75
19	CWS	AL	30	0	6	36.0	141	24	11	11	3	0	0	3	11	0	31	1	1	0	1.000	0-0	4	97	.584	2.27	2.75
	3 ML YEARS		83	0	14	83.0	364	82	46	42	8	1	1	8	32	4	65	4	3	5	.375	0-2	12	97	.718	4.21	4.55

Carlos Correa

Bats: R Throws: R Pos: SS-57;PH-2   coh-RAY-uh   Ht: 6'4" Wt: 220 Born: 9/22/1994 Age: 26

						BATTING													RUNNING			AVERAGES			
Year	Team	Lg	G	AB	H	2B	3B	HR	(Hm | Rd)	TB	R	RBI	RC	TBB	IBB	SO	HBP	SH	SF	SB	CS	GDP	Avg	OBP	Slg	OPS
2015	Hou	AL	99	387	108	22	1	22	(12 | 10)	198	52	68	68	40	2	78	1	0	4	14	4	10	.279	.345	.512	.857
2016	Hou	AL	153	577	158	36	3	20	(8 | 12)	260	76	96	93	75	5	139	5	0	3	13	3	12	.274	.361	.451	.811
2017	Hou	AL	109	422	133	25	1	24	(11 | 13)	232	82	84	86	53	5	92	2	0	4	2	1	12	.315	.391	.550	.941
2018	Hou	AL	110	402	96	20	1	15	(7 | 8)	163	60	65	49	53	3	111	2	0	**11**	3	0	17	.239	.323	.405	.728
2019	Hou	AL	75	280	78	16	1	21	(11 | 10)	159	42	59	52	35	0	75	2	0	4	1	0	8	.279	.358	.568	.926
2020	Hou	AL	58	201	53	9	0	5	(1 | 4)	77	22	25	23	16	2	49	3	0	0	0	0	4	.264	.326	.383	.709
	Postseason		50	194	48	11	0	11	(6 | 5)	92	20	33	30	16	0	55	1	0	0	1	0	3	.247	.308	.474	.782
	6 ML YEARS		604	2269	626	128	7	107	(50 | 57)	1089	334	397	371	272	17	544	15	0	27	33	8	63	.276	.353	.480	.833

Nestor Cortes

Pitches: L Bats: R Pos: RP-4; SP-1   Ht: 5'11" Wt: 210 Born: 12/10/1994 Age: 26

				HOW MUCH PITCHED				WHAT HE GAVE UP									THE RESULTS						
Year	Team	Lg	G	GS	GF	IP	BFP	H	R	ER	HR	SH	SF	HB	TBB	IBB	SO	WP	W	L	Pct	Sv-Op	Hld	Vel	OPS	ERC	ERA
2018	Bal	AL	4	0	3	4.2	26	10	4	4	2	0	0	0	4	0	3	0	0	0	-	0-0	0	88	1.357	18.44	7.71
2019	NYY	AL	33	1	7	66.2	298	75	44	42	16	0	2	1	28	1	69	1	5	1	.833	0-1	1	90	.843	5.97	5.67
2020	Sea	AL	5	1	2	7.2	44	12	14	13	6	0	0	2	6	0	8	0	0	1	.000	0-0	0	88	1.379	16.80	15.26
	3 ML YEARS		42	2	12	79.0	368	97	62	59	24	0	2	3	38	1	80	1	5	2	.714	0-1	1	89	.938	7.53	6.72

Danny Coulombe

Pitches: L Bats: L Pos: RP-2   KOO-lohm   Ht: 5'10" Wt: 190 Born: 10/26/1989 Age: 31

				HOW MUCH PITCHED				WHAT HE GAVE UP									THE RESULTS						
Year	Team	Lg	G	GS	GF	IP	BFP	H	R	ER	HR	SH	SF	HB	TBB	IBB	SO	WP	W	L	Pct	Sv-Op	Hld	Vel	OPS	ERC	ERA
2014	LAD	NL	5	0	4	4.1	22	5	3	2	1	0	0	0	2	0	4	2	0	0	-	0-0	0	91	.768	5.49	4.15
2015	2 Tms	AL	14	0	4	16.0	72	17	10	10	0	0	0	0	9	0	11	2	0	0	-	0-1	0	90	.742	4.32	5.63
2016	Oak	AL	35	0	11	47.2	193	37	24	24	6	2	3	0	17	2	54	3	3	1	.750	0-1	2	90	.634	2.84	4.53
2017	Oak	AL	72	0	10	51.2	219	46	22	20	4	0	1	4	22	1	39	5	2	2	.500	0-1	13	91	.714	3.74	3.48

Year	Team	Lg	HOW MUCH PITCHED					WHAT HE GAVE UP											THE RESULTS								
			G	GS	GF	IP	BFP	H	R	ER	HR	SH	SF	HB	TBB	IBB	SO	WP	W	L	Pct	Sv-Op	Hld	Vel	OPS	ERC	ERA
2018	Oak	AL	27	0	3	23.2	98	24	13	12	5	0	1	0	11	0	26	2	1	1	.500	0-0	0	90	.846	5.58	4.56
2020	Min	AL	2	0	2	2.2	13	2	0	0	0	0	0	0	3	0	3	0	0	0	-	0-0	0	90	.585	4.52	0.00
15	LAD	NL	5	0	3	8.1	40	9	7	7	0	0	0	0	6	0	7	1	0	0	-	0-0	0	90	.816	4.87	7.56
15	Oak	AL	9	0	1	7.2	32	8	3	3	0	0	0	0	3	0	4	1	0	0	-	0-1	0	89	.654	3.72	3.52
6 ML YEARS			155	0	30	146.0	617	131	72	68	16	2	5	4	64	3	137	14	6	4	.600	0-3	15	90	.713	3.85	4.19

Dylan Covey

Pitches: R **Bats:** R **Pos:** RP-8
COE-vee
Ht: 6'1" **Wt:** 215 **Born:** 8/14/1991 **Age:** 29

Year	Team	Lg	HOW MUCH PITCHED					WHAT HE GAVE UP											THE RESULTS								
			G	GS	GF	IP	BFP	H	R	ER	HR	SH	SF	HB	TBB	IBB	SO	WP	W	L	Pct	Sv-Op	Hld	Vel	OPS	ERC	ERA
2017	CWS	AL	18	12	4	70.0	309	83	60	60	20	1	1	1	34	1	41	6	0	7	.000	0-0	0	93	.979	7.33	7.71
2018	CWS	AL	27	21	2	121.2	542	129	81	70	13	5	3	2	52	4	91	5	5	14	.263	0-0	0	94	.735	4.53	5.18
2019	CWS	AL	18	12	2	58.2	280	75	54	52	12	3	1	3	28	2	41	3	1	8	.111	0-1	0	94	.889	6.95	7.98
2020	Bos	AL	8	0	2	14.0	60	18	11	11	2	0	0	0	2	0	11	1	0	0	-	0-0	1	92	.799	5.04	7.07
4 ML YEARS			71	45	10	264.1	1191	305	206	193	47	9	5	6	116	7	184	15	6	29	.171	0-1	1	94	.837	5.79	6.57

Will Craig

Bats: R **Throws:** R **Pos:** 1B-2
Ht: 6'3" **Wt:** 220 **Born:** 11/16/1994 **Age:** 26

Year	Team	Lg	BATTING																	RUNNING			AVERAGES			
			G	AB	H	2B	3B	HR	(Hm | Rd)	TB	R	RBI	RC	TBB	IBB	SO	HBP	SH	SF	SB	CS	GDP	Avg	OBP	Slg	OPS
2020	Pit	NL	2	4	0	0	0	0	(0 | 0)	0	0	0	0	0	0	1	0	0	0	0	0	0	.000	.000	.000	.000

Brandon Crawford

Bats: L **Throws:** R **Pos:** SS-53;PH-1
Ht: 6'1" **Wt:** 223 **Born:** 1/21/1987 **Age:** 34

Year	Team	Lg	BATTING																	RUNNING			AVERAGES			
			G	AB	H	2B	3B	HR	(Hm | Rd)	TB	R	RBI	RC	TBB	IBB	SO	HBP	SH	SF	SB	CS	GDP	Avg	OBP	Slg	OPS
2011	SF	NL	66	196	40	5	2	3	(0 | 3)	58	22	21	20	23	1	31	0	1	0	1	3	4	.204	.288	.296	.584
2012	SF	NL	143	435	108	26	3	4	(1 | 3)	152	44	45	40	33	6	95	3	2	3	1	4	4	.248	.304	.349	.653
2013	SF	NL	149	499	124	24	3	9	(2 | 7)	181	52	43	42	42	6	96	5	1	3	1	2	10	.248	.311	.363	.674
2014	SF	NL	153	491	121	20	10	10	(4 | 6)	191	54	69	72	59	10	129	2	2	10	5	3	4	.246	.324	.389	.713
2015	SF	NL	143	507	130	33	4	21	(8 | 13)	234	65	84	84	39	9	119	11	0	4	6	4	18	.256	.321	.462	.782
2016	SF	NL	155	553	152	28	11	12	(4 | 8)	238	67	84	82	57	10	115	4	0	9	7	0	13	.275	.342	.430	.772
2017	SF	NL	144	518	131	34	1	14	(6 | 8)	209	58	77	61	42	3	113	1	0	9	3	5	18	.253	.305	.403	.709
2018	SF	NL	151	531	135	28	2	14	(7 | 7)	209	63	54	60	50	13	122	8	0	5	4	5	12	.254	.325	.394	.719
2019	SF	NL	147	500	114	24	2	11	(2 | 9)	175	58	59	55	53	5	117	3	0	4	3	2	10	.228	.304	.350	.654
2020	SF	NL	54	172	44	12	0	8	(5 | 3)	80	26	28	27	15	2	47	4	0	2	1	2	3	.256	.326	.465	.792
Postseason			38	127	30	6	1	1	(0 | 1)	41	13	17	14	15	2	32	0	1	2	2	0	2	.236	.313	.323	.635
10 ML YEARS			1305	4402	1099	234	38	106	(39 | 67)	1727	509	564	528	413	65	984	41	6	49	32	30	96	.250	.317	.392	.709

J.P. Crawford

Bats: L **Throws:** R **Pos:** SS-53
Ht: 6'2" **Wt:** 199 **Born:** 1/11/1995 **Age:** 26

Year	Team	Lg	BATTING																	RUNNING			AVERAGES			
			G	AB	H	2B	3B	HR	(Hm | Rd)	TB	R	RBI	RC	TBB	IBB	SO	HBP	SH	SF	SB	CS	GDP	Avg	OBP	Slg	OPS
2017	Phi	NL	23	70	15	4	1	0	(0 | 0)	21	8	6	9	16	0	22	0	0	1	1	0	1	.214	.356	.300	.656
2018	Phi	NL	49	117	25	6	3	3	(2 | 1)	46	17	12	17	13	0	37	5	2	0	2	0	2	.214	.319	.393	.712
2019	Sea	AL	93	345	78	21	4	7	(4 | 3)	128	43	46	46	43	0	83	2	3	3	5	3	4	.226	.313	.371	.684
2020	Sea	AL	53	204	52	7	2	2	(1 | 1)	69	33	24	30	23	0	39	3	0	2	6	3	4	.255	.336	.338	.674
4 ML YEARS			218	736	170	38	10	12	(7 | 5)	264	101	88	102	95	0	181	10	5	6	14	6	11	.231	.325	.359	.683

Stefan Crichton

Pitches: R **Bats:** R **Pos:** RP-26
CRY-ton
Ht: 6'3" **Wt:** 205 **Born:** 2/29/1992 **Age:** 29

Year	Team	Lg	HOW MUCH PITCHED					WHAT HE GAVE UP											THE RESULTS								
			G	GS	GF	IP	BFP	H	R	ER	HR	SH	SF	HB	TBB	IBB	SO	WP	W	L	Pct	Sv-Op	Hld	Vel	OPS	ERC	ERA
2017	Bal	AL	8	0	1	12.1	62	26	11	11	2	0	1	0	4	0	8	2	0	0	-	0-0	1	94	1.151	12.21	8.03
2019	Ari	NL	28	0	9	30.1	123	23	12	12	3	0	0	2	8	1	33	1	1	0	1.000	0-0	3	93	.578	2.47	3.56
2020	Ari	NL	26	0	8	26.0	109	22	7	7	1	0	0	4	9	4	23	2	2	2	.500	5-7	2	92	.665	3.00	2.42
3 ML YEARS			62	0	18	68.2	294	71	30	30	6	0	1	6	21	5	64	5	3	2	.600	5-7	6	93	.732	4.08	3.93

Kyle Crick

Pitches: R **Bats:** L **Pos:** RP-7
Ht: 6'4" **Wt:** 225 **Born:** 11/30/1992 **Age:** 28

Year	Team	Lg	HOW MUCH PITCHED					WHAT HE GAVE UP											THE RESULTS								
			G	GS	GF	IP	BFP	H	R	ER	HR	SH	SF	HB	TBB	IBB	SO	WP	W	L	Pct	Sv-Op	Hld	Vel	OPS	ERC	ERA
2017	SF	NL	30	0	14	32.1	134	22	13	11	2	1	0	1	17	1	28	6	0	0	-	0-0	1	96	.596	2.68	3.06
2018	Pit	NL	64	0	13	60.1	255	45	18	16	3	1	1	7	23	3	65	9	3	2	.600	2-3	16	96	.569	2.63	2.39
2019	Pit	NL	52	0	9	49.0	226	41	30	27	10	0	1	7	35	1	61	1	3	7	.300	0-6	13	95	.799	5.73	4.96
2020	Pit	NL	7	0	2	5.2	29	7	6	1	0	0	0	0	4	0	7	0	0	1	.000	0-1	0	91	.699	5.50	1.59
4 ML YEARS			153	0	38	147.1	644	115	67	55	15	2	2	15	79	5	161	16	6	10	.375	2-10	30	95	.659	3.70	3.36

Nabil Crismatt

Pitches: R **Bats:** R **Pos:** RP-6   **Ht:** 6'1" **Wt:** 220 **Born:** 12/25/1994 **Age:** 26

			HOW MUCH PITCHED				WHAT HE GAVE UP										THE RESULTS						
Year	Team	Lg	G	GS	GF	IP	BFP	H	R	ER	HR	SH	SF	HB	TBB	IBB	SO	WP	W	L	Pct	Sv-Op	Hld	Vel	OPS	ERC	ERA
2020	StL	NL	6	0	6	8.1	31	6	3	3	2	0	0	1	1	1	8	0	0	0	-	0-0	0	90	.692	2.27	3.24

Garrett Crochet

Pitches: L **Bats:** L **Pos:** RP-5   CROH-shay   **Ht:** 6'6" **Wt:** 218 **Born:** 6/21/1999 **Age:** 22

Year	Team	Lg	G	GS	GF	IP	BFP	H	R	ER	HR	SH	SF	HB	TBB	IBB	SO	WP	W	L	Pct	Sv-Op	Hld	Vel	OPS	ERC	ERA
2020	CWS	AL	5	0	1	6.0	22	3	0	0	0	0	0	0	0	0	8	0	0	0	-	0-0	0	100	.325	0.80	0.00

C.J. Cron

Bats: R **Throws:** R **Pos:** 1B-13   CROHN   **Ht:** 6'4" **Wt:** 235 **Born:** 1/5/1990 **Age:** 31

Year	Team	Lg	G	AB	H	2B	3B	HR	(Hm	Rd)	TB	R	RBI	RC	TBB	IBB	SO	HBP	SH	SF	SB	CS	GDP	Avg	OBP	Slg	OPS
2014	LAA	AL	79	242	62	12	1	11	(5	6)	109	28	37	35	10	0	61	1	0	0	0	0	10	.256	.289	.450	.739
2015	LAA	AL	113	378	99	17	1	16	(11	5)	166	37	51	46	17	1	82	5	0	3	3	1	9	.262	.300	.439	.739
2016	LAA	AL	116	407	113	25	2	16	(7	9)	190	51	69	66	24	1	75	7	0	5	2	3	9	.278	.325	.467	.792
2017	LAA	AL	100	339	84	14	1	16	(8	8)	148	39	56	51	22	0	96	7	0	3	3	2	5	.248	.305	.437	.741
2018	LAA	AL	140	501	127	28	1	30	(11	19)	247	68	74	65	37	2	145	17	0	5	1	2	11	.253	.323	.493	.816
2019	Min	AL	125	458	116	24	0	25	(10	15)	215	51	78	66	29	3	107	10	0	2	0	0	13	.253	.311	.469	.780
2020	Det	AL	13	42	8	3	0	4	(0	4)	23	9	8	7	9	0	16	1	0	0	0	0	2	.190	.346	.548	.894
	Postseason		5	14	2	1	0	0	(0	0)	3	0	0	0	3	0	5	0	0	0	0	0	0	.143	.294	.214	.508
	7 ML YEARS		686	2367	609	123	6	118	(52	66)	1098	283	373	336	148	7	582	48	0	18	9	8	59	.257	.312	.464	.776

Kevin Cron

Bats: R **Throws:** R **Pos:** DH-6;PH-3;1B-1   CROHN   **Ht:** 6'5" **Wt:** 255 **Born:** 2/17/1993 **Age:** 28

Year	Team	Lg	G	AB	H	2B	3B	HR	(Hm	Rd)	TB	R	RBI	RC	TBB	IBB	SO	HBP	SH	SF	SB	CS	GDP	Avg	OBP	Slg	OPS
2019	Ari	NL	39	71	15	4	0	6	(2	4)	37	12	16	11	4	0	28	2	0	1	0	1	2	.211	.269	.521	.790
2020	Ari	NL	8	17	0	0	0	0	(0	0)	0	0	0	0	1	0	7	2	0	0	0	0	0	.000	.150	.000	.150
	2 ML YEARS		47	88	15	4	0	6	(2	4)	37	12	16	11	5	0	35	4	0	1	0	1	2	.170	.245	.420	.665

Jake Cronenworth

Bats: L **Throws:** R **Pos:** 2B-38;SS-11;1B-10;PR-2;3B-1;PH-1   **Ht:** 6'0" **Wt:** 187 **Born:** 1/21/1994 **Age:** 27

Year	Team	Lg	G	AB	H	2B	3B	HR	(Hm	Rd)	TB	R	RBI	RC	TBB	IBB	SO	HBP	SH	SF	SB	CS	GDP	Avg	OBP	Slg	OPS
2020	SD	NL	54	172	49	15	3	4	(3	1)	82	26	20	28	18	0	30	1	0	1	3	1	4	.285	.354	.477	.831

Wil Crowe

Pitches: R **Bats:** R **Pos:** SP-3   **Ht:** 6'2" **Wt:** 228 **Born:** 9/9/1994 **Age:** 26

Year	Team	Lg	G	GS	GF	IP	BFP	H	R	ER	HR	SH	SF	HB	TBB	IBB	SO	WP	W	L	Pct	Sv-Op	Hld	Vel	OPS	ERC	ERA
2020	Was	NL	3	3	0	8.1	46	14	13	11	5	0	0	1	8	0	8	0	0	2	.000	0-0	0	91	1.338	17.20	11.88

Jesus Cruz

Pitches: R **Bats:** R **Pos:** RP-1   **Ht:** 6'1" **Wt:** 230 **Born:** 4/15/1995 **Age:** 26

Year	Team	Lg	G	GS	GF	IP	BFP	H	R	ER	HR	SH	SF	HB	TBB	IBB	SO	WP	W	L	Pct	Sv-Op	Hld	Vel	OPS	ERC	ERA
2020	StL	NL	1	0	0	1.0	7	3	2	2	0	0	0	0	1	0	2	0	0	0	-	0-0	0	91	1.371	19.55	18.00

Nelson Cruz

Bats: R **Throws:** R **Pos:** DH-52;PH-1   **Ht:** 6'2" **Wt:** 230 **Born:** 7/1/1980 **Age:** 40

Year	Team	Lg	G	AB	H	2B	3B	HR	(Hm	Rd)	TB	R	RBI	RC	TBB	IBB	SO	HBP	SH	SF	SB	CS	GDP	Avg	OBP	Slg	OPS
2005	Mil	NL	8	5	1	1	0	0	(0	0)	2	1	0	1	2	0	0	0	0	0	0	0	0	.200	.429	.400	.829
2006	Tex	AL	41	130	29	3	0	6	(3	3)	50	15	22	18	7	0	32	0	0	1	1	0	1	.223	.261	.385	.645
2007	Tex	AL	96	307	72	15	2	9	(4	5)	118	35	34	32	21	1	87	2	1	1	2	4	5	.235	.287	.384	.671
2008	Tex	AL	31	115	38	9	1	7	(4	3)	70	19	26	30	17	2	28	1	0	0	3	1	1	.330	.421	.609	1.030
2009	Tex	AL	128	462	120	21	1	33	(18	15)	242	75	76	72	49	6	118	2	0	2	20	4	9	.260	.332	.524	.856
2010	Tex	AL	108	399	127	31	3	22	(13	9)	230	60	78	77	38	5	81	1	1	6	17	4	12	.318	.374	.576	.950
2011	Tex	AL	124	475	125	28	1	29	(19	10)	242	64	87	79	33	1	116	2	0	3	9	5	8	.263	.312	.509	.821
2012	Tex	AL	159	585	152	45	0	24	(18	6)	269	86	90	80	48	2	140	5	0	4	8	4	7	.260	.319	.460	.779
2013	Tex	AL	109	413	110	18	0	27	(13	14)	209	49	76	69	35	2	109	4	0	4	5	1	14	.266	.327	.506	.833
2014	Bal	AL	159	613	166	32	2	**40**	(15	**25**)	322	87	108	93	55	8	140	5	0	5	4	5	17	.271	.333	.525	.859
2015	Sea	AL	152	590	178	22	1	44	(17	**27**)	334	90	93	108	59	9	164	5	0	1	3	2	6	.302	.369	.566	.936
2016	Sea	AL	155	589	169	27	1	43	(17	**26**)	327	96	105	101	62	5	159	9	0	7	2	0	15	.287	.360	.555	.915
2017	Sea	AL	155	556	160	28	0	39	(19	20)	305	91	**119**	112	70	7	140	12	0	7	1	1	15	.288	.375	.549	.924
2018	Sea	AL	144	519	133	18	1	37	(21	16)	264	70	97	90	55	5	122	14	0	3	1	0	15	.256	.342	.509	.850

Year	Team	Lg	G	AB	H	2B	3B	HR	(Hm	Rd)	TB	R	RBI	RC	TBB	IBB	SO	HBP	SH	SF	SB	CS	GDP	Avg	OBP	Slg	OPS
									BATTING												RUNNING			AVERAGES			
2019	Min	AL	120	454	141	26	0	41	(21	20)	290	81	108	102	56	8	131	7	0	3	0	1	14	.311	.392	.639	1.031
2020	Min	AL	53	185	56	6	0	16	(6	10)	110	33	33	38	25	5	58	4	0	0	0	0	8	.303	.397	.595	.992
	Postseason		44	164	47	10	0	17	(10	7)	108	33	35	36	16	2	39	1	0	0	1	1	5	.287	.354	.659	1.012
	16 ML YEARS		1742	6397	1777	330	13	417	(208	209)	3384	952	1152	1102	632	66	1625	73	2	47	76	32	147	.278	.347	.529	.876

Johnny Cueto

Pitches: R **Bats:** R **Pos:** SP-12   KWAY-toe   **Ht:** 5'11" **Wt:** 229 **Born:** 2/15/1986 **Age:** 35

Year	Team	Lg	G	GS	GF	IP	BFP	H	R	ER	HR	SH	SF	HB	TBB	IBB	SO	WP	W	L	Pct	Sv-Op	Hld	Vel	OPS	ERC	ERA
					HOW MUCH PITCHED						WHAT HE GAVE UP											THE RESULTS					
2008	Cin	NL	31	31	0	174.0	769	178	101	94	29	9	5	14	68	1	158	6	9	14	.391	0-0	0	93	.803	4.95	4.81
2009	Cin	NL	30	30	0	171.1	740	172	90	84	24	5	3	14	61	0	132	4	11	11	.500	0-0	0	93	.780	4.57	4.41
2010	Cin	NL	31	31	0	185.2	780	181	79	75	19	9	3	9	56	5	138	5	12	7	.632	0-0	0	93	.727	3.75	3.64
2011	Cin	NL	24	24	0	156.0	631	123	51	40	8	10	4	10	47	0	104	5	9	5	.643	0-0	0	93	.593	2.55	2.31
2012	Cin	NL	33	33	0	217.0	888	205	73	67	15	6	6	12	49	5	170	1	19	9	.679	0-0	0	93	.667	3.13	2.78
2013	Cin	NL	11	11	0	60.2	242	46	20	19	7	2	1	4	18	1	51	1	5	2	.714	0-0	0	92	.607	2.57	2.82
2014	Cin	NL	34	34	0	243.2	961	169	69	61	22	7	1	15	65	2	242	1	20	9	.690	0-0	0	93	.574	2.18	2.25
2015	2 Tms	NL	32	32	0	212.0	866	194	87	81	21	5	4	8	46	1	176	0	11	13	.458	0-0	0	92	.675	3.06	3.44
2016	SF	NL	32	32	0	219.2	881	195	71	68	15	7	3	8	45	1	198	3	18	5	.783	0-0	0	91	.633	2.71	2.79
2017	SF	NL	25	25	0	147.1	648	160	77	74	22	7	3	8	53	2	136	4	8	8	.500	0-0	0	91	.814	4.97	4.52
2018	SF	NL	9	9	0	53.0	214	46	19	19	8	3	0	5	13	0	38	2	3	2	.600	0-0	0	89	.702	3.55	3.23
2019	SF	NL	4	4	0	16.0	67	11	9	9	3	2	0	0	9	0	13	1	1	2	.333	0-0	0	91	.754	3.58	5.06
2020	SF	NL	12	12	0	63.1	277	61	41	38	9	0	2	3	26	0	56	1	2	3	.400	0-0	0	91	.748	4.35	5.40
15	Cin	NL	19	19	0	130.2	516	93	42	38	11	4	3	6	29	1	120	0	7	6	.538	0-0	0	93	.577	2.00	2.62
15	KC	NL	13	13	0	81.1	350	101	45	43	10	1	1	2	17	0	56	0	4	7	.364	0-0	0	92	.818	5.05	4.76
	Postseason		8	8	0	41.2	170	33	22	21	7	1	1	1	12	0	32	0	2	4	.333	0-0	0	93	.646	3.02	4.54
	13 ML YEARS		308	308	0	1919.2	7964	1741	787	728	202	72	35	107	556	18	1612	34	128	90	.587	0-0	0	93	.691	3.40	3.41

Charlie Culberson

Bats: R **Throws:** R **Pos:** 1B-4;PR-4;PH-2;2B-1;DH-1   **Ht:** 6'1" **Wt:** 200 **Born:** 4/10/1989 **Age:** 32

Year	Team	Lg	G	AB	H	2B	3B	HR	(Hm	Rd)	TB	R	RBI	RC	TBB	IBB	SO	HBP	SH	SF	SB	CS	GDP	Avg	OBP	Slg	OPS
									BATTING												RUNNING			AVERAGES			
2012	SF	NL	6	22	3	0	0	0	(0	0)	3	0	1	0	0	0	7	0	1	0	0	0	0	.136	.136	.136	.273
2013	Col	NL	47	99	29	5	0	2	(0	2)	40	12	12	13	4	1	23	0	0	1	5	1	5	.293	.317	.404	.721
2014	Col	NL	95	210	41	7	2	3	(2	1)	61	17	24	14	12	2	62	5	4	2	2	2	6	.195	.253	.290	.544
2016	LAD	NL	34	67	20	3	0	1	(1	0)	26	6	7	9	1	0	13	0	0	0	1	0	2	.299	.309	.388	.697
2017	LAD	NL	15	13	2	1	0	0	(0	0)	3	0	1	0	2	0	4	0	0	0	0	0	2	.154	.267	.231	.497
2018	Atl	NL	113	296	80	18	2	12	(5	7)	138	47	45	50	21	5	85	4	0	1	4	2	5	.270	.326	.466	.792
2019	Atl	NL	108	135	35	5	2	5	(3	2)	59	14	20	11	6	0	44	1	1	1	0	1	5	.259	.294	.437	.731
2020	Atl	NL	10	7	1	1	0	0	(0	0)	2	2	1	1	0	0	4	0	0	0	0	0	0	.143	.143	.286	.429
	Postseason		18	35	10	2	1	1	(1	0)	17	5	2	5	1	1	9	0	1	1	0	0	0	.286	.297	.486	.783
	8 ML YEARS		428	849	211	40	6	23	(11	12)	332	98	111	98	46	8	242	10	6	5	12	6	25	.249	.293	.391	.684

John Curtiss

Pitches: R **Bats:** R **Pos:** RP-14; SP-3   **Ht:** 6'5" **Wt:** 220 **Born:** 4/5/1993 **Age:** 28

Year	Team	Lg	G	GS	GF	IP	BFP	H	R	ER	HR	SH	SF	HB	TBB	IBB	SO	WP	W	L	Pct	Sv-Op	Hld	Vel	OPS	ERC	ERA
					HOW MUCH PITCHED						WHAT HE GAVE UP											THE RESULTS					
2017	Min	AL	9	0	4	8.2	38	9	8	8	2	0	0	1	2	0	10	2	0	0	-	0-0	0	95	.802	4.89	8.31
2018	Min	AL	8	0	2	6.1	30	8	4	4	0	0	0	0	4	1	7	3	0	1	.000	0-0	0	94	.900	5.47	5.68
2019	LAA	AL	1	0	1	2.1	12	2	1	1	0	0	0	0	3	0	1	0	0	0	-	0-0	0	92	.750	5.73	3.86
2020	TB	AL	17	3	7	25.0	99	21	7	5	3	0	0	2	3	0	25	0	3	0	1.000	2-2	0	94	.614	2.62	1.80
	4 ML YEARS		35	3	14	42.1	179	40	20	18	5	0	0	3	12	1	43	5	3	1	.750	2-2	0	94	.710	3.67	3.83

Cheslor Cuthbert

Bats: R **Throws:** R **Pos:** 3B-1;PH-1   CHESS-lohr   **Ht:** 6'1" **Wt:** 205 **Born:** 11/16/1992 **Age:** 28

Year	Team	Lg	G	AB	H	2B	3B	HR	(Hm	Rd)	TB	R	RBI	RC	TBB	IBB	SO	HBP	SH	SF	SB	CS	GDP	Avg	OBP	Slg	OPS
									BATTING												RUNNING			AVERAGES			
2015	KC	AL	19	46	10	2	1	1	(1	0)	17	6	8	6	4	0	9	0	0	0	0	0	0	.217	.280	.370	.650
2016	KC	AL	128	475	130	28	1	12	(4	8)	196	49	46	57	32	0	96	0	1	2	2	0	14	.274	.318	.413	.731
2017	KC	AL	58	143	33	7	0	2	(1	1)	46	10	18	11	9	0	39	0	0	1	0	0	2	.231	.275	.322	.596
2018	KC	AL	30	103	20	2	0	3	(2	1)	31	11	7	4	11	0	23	2	0	1	0	1	5	.194	.282	.301	.583
2019	KC	AL	87	309	76	14	0	9	(5	4)	117	24	40	35	19	1	67	2	0	0	1	0	14	.246	.294	.379	.673
2020	CWS	AL	1	1	0	0	0	0	(0	0)	0	0	0	0	0	0	0	0	0	0	0	0	0	.000	.000	.000	.000
	6 ML YEARS		323	1077	269	53	2	27	(13	14)	407	100	119	113	75	1	234	4	1	4	3	1	35	.250	.300	.378	.678

David Dahl

Bats: L **Throws:** R **Pos:** CF-17;LF-4;RF-2;DH-2   **Ht:** 6'2" **Wt:** 197 **Born:** 4/1/1994 **Age:** 27

Year	Team	Lg	G	AB	H	2B	3B	HR	(Hm	Rd)	TB	R	RBI	RC	TBB	IBB	SO	HBP	SH	SF	SB	CS	GDP	Avg	OBP	Slg	OPS
									BATTING												RUNNING			AVERAGES			
2016	Col	NL	63	222	70	14	3	7	(3	4)	111	42	24	35	15	0	59	0	0	0	5	0	3	.315	.359	.500	.859
2018	Col	NL	77	249	68	11	3	16	(13	3)	133	31	48	43	19	4	68	1	0	2	5	3	4	.273	.325	.534	.859
2019	Col	NL	100	374	113	28	5	15	(9	6)	196	67	61	70	28	0	110	4	2	5	4	4	3	.302	.353	.524	.877
2020	Col	NL	24	93	17	2	0	0	(0	0)	23	9	9	8	4	0	28	1	0	1	1	0	0	.183	.222	.247	.470
	Postseason		3	11	0	0	0	0	(0	0)	0	0	0	0	0	0	3	0	0	0	0	0	0	.000	.000	.000	.000
	4 ML YEARS		264	938	268	53	14	38	(25	13)	463	149	142	156	66	4	265	6	2	8	15	7	10	.286	.334	.494	.828

Bobby Dalbec

Bats: R Throws: R Pos: 1B-21;3B-2;DH-1   Ht: 6'4" Wt: 227 Born: 6/29/1995 Age: 26

							BATTING												RUNNING			AVERAGES			
Year Team	Lg	G	AB	H	2B	3B	HR	(Hm Rd)	TB	R	RBI	RC	TBB	IBB	SO	HBP	SH	SF	SB	CS	GDP	Avg	OBP	Slg	OPS
2020 Bos	AL	23	80	21	3	0	8	(4 4)	48	13	16	15	10	0	39	2	0	0	0	0	0	.263	.359	.600	.959

Travis d'Arnaud

Bats: R Throws: R Pos: C-35;DH-7;PH-4   dar-NO   Ht: 6'2" Wt: 210 Born: 2/10/1989 Age: 32

							BATTING												RUNNING			AVERAGES			
Year Team	Lg	G	AB	H	2B	3B	HR	(Hm Rd)	TB	R	RBI	RC	TBB	IBB	SO	HBP	SH	SF	SB	CS	GDP	Avg	OBP	Slg	OPS
2013 NYM	NL	31	99	20	3	0	1	(1 0)	26	4	5	6	12	0	21	0	0	1	0	0	3	.202	.286	.263	.548
2014 NYM	NL	108	385	93	22	3	13	(5 8)	160	48	41	39	32	5	64	2	1	1	1	0	15	.242	.302	.416	.718
2015 NYM	NL	67	239	64	14	1	12	(6 6)	116	31	41	36	23	0	49	4	0	2	0	0	7	.268	.340	.485	.825
2016 NYM	NL	75	251	62	7	0	4	(4 0)	81	27	15	17	19	1	50	3	2	1	0	0	7	.247	.307	.323	.629
2017 NYM	NL	112	348	85	19	1	16	(5 11)	154	39	57	41	23	3	59	2	0	3	0	0	12	.244	.293	.443	.735
2018 NYM	NL	4	15	3	0	0	1	(1 0)	6	1	3	2	1	0	5	0	0	0	0	0	0	.200	.250	.400	.650
2019 3 Tms		103	351	88	16	0	16	(6 10)	152	52	69	59	32	0	85	2	0	6	0	1	4	.251	.312	.433	.745
2020 Atl		44	165	53	8	0	9	(5 4)	88	19	34	31	16	0	50	2	0	1	1	0	8	.321	.386	.533	.919
19 NYM	NL	10	23	2	0	0	0	(0 0)	2	2	2	2	2	0	5	0	0	0	0	0	1	.087	.160	.087	.247
19 LAD	NL	1	1	0	0	0	0	(0 0)	0	0	0	0	0	0	0	0	0	0	0	0	0	.000	.000	.000	.000
19 TB	AL	92	327	86	16	0	16	(6 10)	150	50	67	59	30	0	80	2	0	6	0	1	3	.263	.323	.459	.782
Postseason		20	74	12	1	0	3	(2 1)	22	6	9	4	1	0	23	3	0	2	0	0	2	.162	.200	.297	.497
8 ML YEARS		544	1853	468	89	5	72	(33 39)	783	221	265	231	158	9	383	15	3	15	2	1	56	.253	.314	.423	.737

Yu Darvish

Pitches: R Bats: R Pos: SP-12   YOO DARR-vish   Ht: 6'5" Wt: 220 Born: 8/16/1986 Age: 34

			HOW MUCH PITCHED					WHAT HE GAVE UP											THE RESULTS						
Year Team	Lg	G	GS	GF	IP	BFP	H	R	ER	HR	SH	SF	HB	TBB	IBB	SO	WP	W	L	Pct	Sv-Op	Hld	Vel	OPS	ERC	ERA
2012 Tex	AL	29	29	0	191.1	816	156	89	83	14	2	7	10	89	1	221	8	16	9	.640	0-0	0	93	.659	3.31	3.90
2013 Tex	AL	32	32	0	209.2	841	145	68	66	26	0	5	8	80	1	277	7	13	9	.591	0-0	0	93	.611	2.70	2.83
2014 Tex	AL	22	22	0	144.1	605	133	54	49	13	1	2	2	49	1	182	14	10	7	.588	0-0	0	92	.679	3.39	3.06
2016 Tex	AL	17	17	0	100.1	416	81	43	38	12	0	4	3	31	1	132	6	7	5	.583	0-0	0	93	.636	2.87	3.41
2017 2 Tms		31	31	0	186.2	766	159	83	80	27	2	3	6	58	1	209	12	10	12	.455	0-0	0	94	.689	3.35	3.86
2018 ChC	NL	8	8	0	40.0	180	36	24	22	7	1	1	4	21	0	49	2	1	3	.250	0-0	0	94	.766	4.88	4.95
2019 ChC	NL	31	31	0	178.2	731	140	82	79	33	3	4	11	56	1	229	11	6	8	.429	0-0	0	94	.695	3.35	3.98
2020 ChC	NL	12	12	0	76.0	297	59	18	17	5	0	0	2	14	1	93	3	8	3	.727	0-0	0	96	.575	2.03	2.01
17 Tex	AL	22	22	0	137.0	564	115	63	61	20	1	3	5	45	0	148	9	6	9	.400	0-0	0	94	.689	3.39	4.01
17 LAD	NL	9	9	0	49.2	202	44	20	19	7	1	0	1	13	1	61	3	4	3	.571	0-0	0	94	.690	3.27	3.86
Postseason		6	6	0	26.1	114	27	19	17	8	1	2	3	4	0	25	0	2	4	.333	0-0	0	94	.839	4.91	5.81
8 ML YEARS		182	182	0	1127.0	4652	909	461	434	137	9	26	46	398	7	1392	63	71	56	.559	0-0	0	93	.660	3.14	3.47

Matt Davidson

Bats: R Throws: R Pos: DH-10;PH-10;1B-2   Ht: 6'3" Wt: 230 Born: 3/26/1991 Age: 30

							BATTING												RUNNING			AVERAGES			
Year Team	Lg	G	AB	H	2B	3B	HR	(Hm Rd)	TB	R	RBI	RC	TBB	IBB	SO	HBP	SH	SF	SB	CS	GDP	Avg	OBP	Slg	OPS
2013 Ari	NL	31	76	18	6	0	3	(1 2)	33	8	12	12	10	1	24	1	0	0	0	1	1	.237	.333	.434	.768
2016 CWS	AL	1	2	1	0	0	0	(0 0)	1	1	1	0	0	0	1	0	0	0	0	0	0	.500	.500	.500	1.000
2017 CWS	AL	118	414	91	16	1	26	(15 11)	187	43	68	48	19	0	165	5	0	5	0	1	12	.220	.260	.452	.711
2018 CWS	AL	126	434	99	23	0	20	(5 15)	182	51	62	64	52	0	165	7	0	3	0	0	8	.228	.319	.419	.738
2020 Cin	NL	22	43	7	1	0	3	(1 2)	17	3	11	8	4	0	13	0	0	0	0	0	2	.163	.234	.395	.726
5 ML YEARS		298	969	216	46	1	52	(22 30)	420	106	154	132	85	1	368	13	0	8	0	2	23	.223	.292	.433	.726

Tucker Davidson

Pitches: L Bats: L Pos: SP-1   Ht: 6'2" Wt: 215 Born: 3/25/1996 Age: 25

			HOW MUCH PITCHED					WHAT HE GAVE UP											THE RESULTS						
Year Team	Lg	G	GS	GF	IP	BFP	H	R	ER	HR	SH	SF	HB	TBB	IBB	SO	WP	W	L	Pct	Sv-Op	Hld	Vel	OPS	ERC	ERA
2020 Atl	NL	1	1	0	1.2	13	3	7	2	1	0	0	0	4	0	2	0	0	1	.000	0-0	0	92	1.205	22.80	10.80

Zach Davies

Pitches: R Bats: R Pos: SP-12   Ht: 6'0" Wt: 180 Born: 2/7/1993 Age: 28

			HOW MUCH PITCHED					WHAT HE GAVE UP											THE RESULTS						
Year Team	Lg	G	GS	GF	IP	BFP	H	R	ER	HR	SH	SF	HB	TBB	IBB	SO	WP	W	L	Pct	Sv-Op	Hld	Vel	OPS	ERC	ERA
2015 Mil	NL	6	6	0	34.0	139	26	14	14	2	1	0	0	15	0	24	0	3	2	.600	0-0	0	89	.614	2.74	3.71
2016 Mil	NL	28	28	0	163.1	682	166	79	72	20	3	4	6	38	0	135	3	11	7	.611	0-0	0	89	.728	3.83	3.97
2017 Mil	NL	33	33	0	191.1	817	204	90	83	20	7	5	9	55	3	124	2	17	9	.654	0-0	0	90	.755	4.24	3.90
2018 Mil	NL	13	13	0	66.0	280	67	36	35	8	0	5	4	21	3	49	1	2	7	.222	0-0	0	90	.768	4.22	4.77
2019 Mil	NL	31	31	0	159.2	672	155	73	63	20	7	5	2	51	0	102	4	10	7	.588	0-0	0	88	.729	3.83	3.55
2020 SD	NL	12	12	0	69.1	276	55	26	21	9	1	1	0	19	0	63	2	7	4	.636	0-0	0	89	.630	2.71	2.73
Postseason		1	0	1	1.0	4	1	0	0	0	0	0	0	0	0	1	0	0	0	-	0-0	0	91	.750	1.95	0.00
6 ML YEARS		123	123	0	683.2	2866	673	318	288	79	19	20	21	199	6	497	12	50	36	.581	0-0	0	89	.725	3.81	3.79

Austin Davis

Pitches: L **Bats:** L **Pos:** RP-9   **Ht:** 6'4" **Wt:** 225 **Born:** 2/3/1993 **Age:** 28

			HOW MUCH PITCHED					WHAT HE GAVE UP											THE RESULTS						
Year	Team	Lg	G	GS	GF	IP	BFP	H	R	ER	HR	SH	SF	HB	TBB	IBB	SO	WP	W	L	Pct	Sv-Op	Hld	Vel	OPS	ERC	ERA
2018	Phi	NL	32	0	10	34.2	151	35	20	16	4	1	4	2	12	1	38	4	1	2	.333	0-0	2	93	.812	4.17	4.15
2019	Phi	NL	14	0	7	20.2	98	22	15	15	6	0	0	3	14	1	24	0	0	0	-	0-0	0	94	.929	7.79	6.53
2020	2 Tms	NL	9	0	3	6.2	32	11	8	8	1	0	0	0	2	0	5	0	0	0	-	0-0	1	93	.906	8.13	10.80
20	Phi	NL	4	0	1	3.0	20	10	7	7	1	0	0	0	1	0	2	0	0	0	-	0-0	0	94	1.287	22.82	21.00
20	Pit	NL	5	0	2	3.2	12	1	1	1	0	0	0	0	1	0	3	0	0	0	-	0-0	1	93	.258	0.51	2.45
3 ML YEARS			55	0	20	62.0	281	68	43	39	11	1	4	5	28	2	67	4	1	2	.333	0-0	3	93	.863	5.71	5.66

Chris Davis

Bats: L **Throws:** R **Pos:** 1B-15;PH-2   **Ht:** 6'3" **Wt:** 245 **Born:** 3/17/1986 **Age:** 35

			BATTING																RUNNING			AVERAGES			
Year	Team	Lg	G	AB	H	2B	3B	HR	(Hm | Rd)	TB	R	RBI	RC	TBB	IBB	SO	HBP	SH	SF	SB	CS	GDP	Avg	OBP	Slg	OPS
2008	Tex	AL	80	295	84	23	2	17	(8 | 9)	162	51	55	44	20	1	88	1	0	1	1	2	5	.285	.331	.549	.880
2009	Tex	AL	113	391	93	15	1	21	(11 | 10)	173	48	59	50	24	2	150	2	0	2	0	0	6	.238	.284	.442	.726
2010	Tex	AL	45	120	23	9	0	1	(0 | 1)	35	7	4	5	15	3	40	0	0	1	3	0	3	.192	.279	.292	.571
2011	2 Tms	AL	59	199	53	12	0	5	(2 | 3)	80	25	19	23	11	1	63	0	0	0	1	0	4	.266	.305	.402	.707
2012	Bal	AL	139	515	139	20	0	33	(22 | 11)	258	75	85	85	37	6	169	7	0	3	2	3	8	.270	.326	.501	.827
2013	Bal	AL	160	584	167	42	1	53	(28 | 25)	370	103	138	134	72	12	199	10	0	7	4	1	4	.286	.370	.634	1.004
2014	Bal	AL	127	450	88	16	0	26	(13 | 13)	182	65	72	58	60	9	173	9	1	5	2	1	2	.196	.300	.404	.704
2015	Bal	AL	160	573	150	31	0	47	(29 | 18)	322	100	117	117	84	6	208	8	0	5	2	3	6	.262	.361	.562	.923
2016	Bal	AL	157	566	125	21	0	38	(17 | 21)	260	99	84	82	88	3	219	8	0	3	1	0	6	.221	.332	.459	.792
2017	Bal	AL	128	456	98	15	1	26	(15 | 11)	193	65	61	55	61	4	195	3	0	4	1	1	7	.215	.309	.423	.732
2018	Bal	AL	128	470	79	12	0	16	(10 | 6)	139	40	49	36	41	2	192	7	0	4	2	0	5	.168	.243	.296	.539
2019	Bal	AL	105	307	55	9	0	12	(5 | 7)	100	26	36	29	39	1	139	3	0	3	0	0	6	.179	.276	.326	.601
2020	Bal	AL	16	52	6	3	0	0	(0 | 0)	9	3	1	0	3	0	17	0	0	0	0	0	0	.115	.164	.173	.337
11	Tex	AL	28	76	19	3	0	3	(1 | 2)	31	9	6	7	5	0	24	0	0	0	0	0	2	.250	.296	.408	.704
11	Bal	AL	31	123	34	9	0	2	(1 | 1)	49	16	13	16	6	1	39	0	0	0	1	0	2	.276	.310	.398	.708
	Postseason		7	27	5	0	0	0	(0 | 0)	5	1	2	1	2	0	11	1	0	0	0	0	0	.185	.267	.185	.452
13 ML YEARS			1417	4978	1160	228	5	295	(160 | 135)	2283	707	780	718	555	50	1852	58	1	38	19	11	62	.233	.315	.459	.774

J.D. Davis

Bats: R **Throws:** R **Pos:** 3B-34;DH-13;LF-8;PH-4   **Ht:** 6'3" **Wt:** 218 **Born:** 4/27/1993 **Age:** 28

			BATTING																RUNNING			AVERAGES			
Year	Team	Lg	G	AB	H	2B	3B	HR	(Hm | Rd)	TB	R	RBI	RC	TBB	IBB	SO	HBP	SH	SF	SB	CS	GDP	Avg	OBP	Slg	OPS
2017	Hou	AL	25	62	14	4	0	4	(2 | 2)	30	8	7	4	4	0	20	1	0	1	1	1	3	.226	.279	.484	.763
2018	Hou	AL	42	103	18	2	0	1	(0 | 1)	23	9	5	3	10	0	29	0	0	0	0	0	3	.175	.248	.223	.471
2019	NYM	NL	140	410	126	22	1	22	(16 | 6)	216	65	57	66	38	2	97	3	0	2	3	0	14	.307	.369	.527	.895
2020	NYM	NL	56	190	47	9	0	6	(2 | 4)	74	26	19	25	31	1	56	7	0	1	0	0	8	.247	.371	.389	.761
4 ML YEARS			263	765	205	37	1	33	(20 | 13)	343	108	88	98	83	3	202	11	0	4	4	1	28	.268	.346	.448	.795

Jaylin Davis

Bats: R **Throws:** R **Pos:** RF-4   **Ht:** 5'11" **Wt:** 205 **Born:** 7/1/1994 **Age:** 26

			BATTING																RUNNING			AVERAGES			
Year	Team	Lg	G	AB	H	2B	3B	HR	(Hm | Rd)	TB	R	RBI	RC	TBB	IBB	SO	HBP	SH	SF	SB	CS	GDP	Avg	OBP	Slg	OPS
2019	SF	NL	17	42	7	0	0	1	(1 | 0)	10	2	3	1	3	0	11	2	0	0	1	2	1	.167	.255	.238	.493
2020	SF	NL	4	12	2	0	0	1	(0 | 1)	5	2	1	0	0	0	6	0	0	0	0	0	0	.167	.167	.417	.583
2 ML YEARS			21	54	9	0	0	2	(1 | 1)	15	4	4	1	3	0	17	2	0	0	1	2	1	.167	.237	.278	.515

Jonathan Davis

Bats: R **Throws:** R **Pos:** RF-6;CF-5;LF-3;PR-1   **Ht:** 5'8" **Wt:** 190 **Born:** 5/12/1992 **Age:** 29

			BATTING																RUNNING			AVERAGES			
Year	Team	Lg	G	AB	H	2B	3B	HR	(Hm | Rd)	TB	R	RBI	RC	TBB	IBB	SO	HBP	SH	SF	SB	CS	GDP	Avg	OBP	Slg	OPS
2018	Tor	AL	20	25	5	1	0	0	(0 | 0)	6	3	0	0	1	0	6	1	0	0	3	0	2	.200	.259	.240	.499
2019	Tor	AL	37	83	15	1	0	2	(1 | 1)	22	8	6	5	5	0	24	5	1	1	3	1	1	.181	.266	.265	.531
2020	Tor	AL	13	27	7	2	0	1	(1 | 0)	12	4	6	7	3	0	11	2	0	1	1	0	1	.259	.364	.444	.808
3 ML YEARS			70	135	27	4	0	3	(2 | 1)	40	15	12	12	9	0	41	8	1	2	7	1	4	.200	.286	.296	.582

Khris Davis

Bats: R **Throws:** R **Pos:** DH-27;PH-5   **Ht:** 5'11" **Wt:** 205 **Born:** 12/21/1987 **Age:** 33

			BATTING																RUNNING			AVERAGES			
Year	Team	Lg	G	AB	H	2B	3B	HR	(Hm | Rd)	TB	R	RBI	RC	TBB	IBB	SO	HBP	SH	SF	SB	CS	GDP	Avg	OBP	Slg	OPS
2013	Mil	NL	56	136	38	10	0	11	(5 | 6)	81	27	27	25	11	0	34	5	0	1	3	0	4	.279	.353	.596	.949
2014	Mil	NL	144	501	122	37	2	22	(12 | 10)	229	70	69	58	32	0	122	10	0	6	4	1	13	.244	.299	.457	.756
2015	Mil	NL	121	392	97	16	2	27	(16 | 11)	198	54	66	57	44	1	122	1	0	3	6	2	9	.247	.323	.505	.828
2016	Oak	AL	150	555	137	24	2	42	(19 | 23)	291	85	102	77	42	0	166	8	0	5	1	2	19	.247	.307	.524	.831
2017	Oak	AL	153	566	140	28	1	43	(26 | 17)	299	91	110	98	73	1	195	6	0	7	4	0	20	.247	.336	.528	.864
2018	Oak	AL	151	576	142	28	1	48	(23 | 25)	316	98	123	104	59	5	175	12	0	7	0	0	16	.247	.326	.549	.874
2019	Oak	AL	133	481	106	11	0	23	(9 | 14)	186	61	73	60	47	3	146	3	0	2	0	0	11	.220	.293	.387	.679
2020	Oak	AL	30	85	17	5	0	2	(1 | 1)	28	9	10	4	10	0	26	3	0	1	0	0	5	.200	.303	.329	.632
	Postseason		2	8	1	0	0	1	(0 | 1)	4	1	2	1	0	0	5	0	0	0	0	0	0	.125	.125	.500	.625
8 ML YEARS			938	3292	799	159	8	218	(111 | 107)	1628	495	580	483	318	10	986	48	0	32	18	5	97	.243	.316	.495	.810

Wade Davis

Pitches: R **Bats:** R **Pos:** RP-5 **Ht:** 6'5" **Wt:** 225 **Born:** 9/7/1985 **Age:** 35

Year	Team	Lg	G	GS	GF	IP	BFP	H	R	ER	HR	SH	SF	HB	TBB	IBB	SO	WP	W	L	Pct	Sv-Op	Hld	Vel	OPS	ERC	ERA
			HOW MUCH PITCHED					**WHAT HE GAVE UP**											**THE RESULTS**								
2009	TB	AL	6	6	0	36.1	150	33	19	15	2	0	0	0	13	1	36	1	2	2	.500	0-0	0	92	.640	3.12	3.72
2010	TB	AL	29	29	0	168.0	722	165	77	76	24	3	6	5	62	2	113	4	12	10	.545	0-0	0	92	.756	4.25	4.07
2011	TB	AL	29	29	0	184.0	795	190	96	91	23	5	7	8	63	1	105	6	11	10	.524	0-0	0	91	.771	4.38	4.45
2012	TB	AL	54	0	15	70.1	284	48	20	19	5	0	1	0	29	2	87	2	3	0	1.000	0-1	6	94	.570	2.25	2.43
2013	KC	AL	31	24	2	135.1	618	169	89	80	15	1	5	4	58	2	114	7	8	11	.421	0-0	0	92	.822	5.88	5.32
2014	KC	AL	71	0	11	72.0	279	38	8	8	0	0	1	3	23	0	109	1	9	2	.818	3-6	33	96	.408	1.23	1.00
2015	KC	AL	69	0	24	67.1	251	33	8	7	3	0	2	0	20	1	78	1	8	1	.889	17-18	18	96	.451	1.16	0.94
2016	KC	AL	45	0	40	43.1	176	33	9	9	9	0	0	3	16	0	47	4	2	1	.667	27-30	0	95	.537	2.35	1.87
2017	ChC	NL	59	0	56	58.2	242	39	16	15	6	1	0	3	28	1	79	7	4	2	.667	32-33	0	94	.600	2.77	2.30
2018	Col	NL	69	0	63	65.1	261	43	31	30	8	0	0	2	26	0	78	6	3	6	.333	**43-49**	0	94	.615	2.56	4.13
2019	Col	NL	50	0	32	42.2	206	51	42	41	7	0	0	2	29	0	42	1	1	6	.143	15-18	0	93	.872	7.12	8.65
2020	Col	NL	5	0	2	4.1	25	9	10	10	3	0	0	0	3	1	3	2	0	1	.000	2-3	0	92	1.435	17.88	20.77
	Postseason		30	1	14	40.0	160	29	9	8	5	0	0	0	18	0	57	2	4	0	1.000	8-8	3	95	.639	3.05	1.80
12 ML YEARS			517	88	245	947.2	4009	851	425	401	96	10	22	30	370	11	891	42	63	52	.548	139-158	57	93	.690	3.60	3.81

Grant Dayton

Pitches: L **Bats:** L **Pos:** RP-18 **Ht:** 6'2" **Wt:** 210 **Born:** 11/25/1987 **Age:** 33

Year	Team	Lg	G	GS	GF	IP	BFP	H	R	ER	HR	SH	SF	HB	TBB	IBB	SO	WP	W	L	Pct	Sv-Op	Hld	Vel	OPS	ERC	ERA
			HOW MUCH PITCHED					**WHAT HE GAVE UP**											**THE RESULTS**								
2016	LAD	NL	25	0	0	26.1	101	14	7	6	4	0	0	1	6	0	39	0	0	1	.000	0-2	6	91	.495	1.56	2.05
2017	LAD	NL	29	0	6	23.2	102	19	13	13	5	1	3	0	12	1	20	0	1	1	.500	0-1	4	91	.749	4.02	4.94
2019	Atl	NL	14	0	4	12.0	51	12	5	4	4	0	0	0	4	0	14	0	0	1	.000	0-1	1	91	.824	5.42	3.00
2020	Atl	NL	18	0	5	27.1	117	22	9	7	4	1	1	1	11	1	32	0	2	1	.667	0-0	0	91	.662	3.32	2.30
	Postseason		7	0	1	3.1	18	6	3	3	1	0	0	0	2	0	6	0	0	0	-	0-0	1	93	1.132	11.76	8.10
4 ML YEARS			86	0	15	89.1	371	67	34	30	17	2	4	2	33	2	105	0	3	4	.429	0-4	11	91	.661	3.18	3.02

Chase De Jong

Pitches: R **Bats:** L **Pos:** SP-2; RP-1 **Ht:** 6'4" **Wt:** 230 **Born:** 12/29/1993 **Age:** 27

Year	Team	Lg	G	GS	GF	IP	BFP	H	R	ER	HR	SH	SF	HB	TBB	IBB	SO	WP	W	L	Pct	Sv-Op	Hld	Vel	OPS	ERC	ERA
			HOW MUCH PITCHED					**WHAT HE GAVE UP**											**THE RESULTS**								
2017	Sea	AL	7	4	2	28.1	125	31	20	20	5	1	1	0	13	0	13	0	0	3	.000	0-1	0	90	.837	5.49	6.35
2018	Min	AL	4	4	0	17.2	74	18	9	7	3	0	0	0	6	0	13	2	1	1	.500	0-0	0	89	.810	4.53	3.57
2019	Min	AL	1	0	1	1.0	9	3	4	4	1	0	0	0	3	0	0	0	0	0	-	0-0	0	91	1.667	44.28	36.00
2020	Hou	AL	3	2	0	7.1	38	12	12	12	2	0	1	1	4	0	9	0	0	1	.000	0-0	0	93	1.010	11.02	14.73
4 ML YEARS			15	10	3	54.1	246	64	45	43	11	1	2	1	26	0	35	2	1	5	.167	0-1	0	90	.881	6.39	7.12

Jose De Leon

Pitches: R **Bats:** R **Pos:** RP-5 **Ht:** 6'2" **Wt:** 215 **Born:** 8/7/1992 **Age:** 28

Year	Team	Lg	G	GS	GF	IP	BFP	H	R	ER	HR	SH	SF	HB	TBB	IBB	SO	WP	W	L	Pct	Sv-Op	Hld	Vel	OPS	ERC	ERA
			HOW MUCH PITCHED					**WHAT HE GAVE UP**											**THE RESULTS**								
2016	LAD	NL	4	4	0	17.0	80	19	17	12	5	3	1	3	7	1	15	0	2	0	1.000	0-0	0	92	.937	6.82	6.35
2017	TB	AL	1	0	0	2.2	15	4	3	3	1	0	0	0	3	0	2	2	1	0	1.000	0-0	0	92	1.133	12.97	10.13
2019	TB	AL	3	0	1	4.0	21	3	2	1	0	0	0	2	3	1	7	1	1	0	1.000	0-0	0	92	.568	4.23	2.25
2020	Cin	NL	5	0	2	6.0	35	6	12	12	1	0	0	0	11	2	10	0	0	0	-	0-0	0	95	.861	9.77	18.00
4 ML YEARS			13	4	3	29.2	151	32	34	28	7	3	1	5	24	4	34	3	4	0	1.000	0-0	0	93	.895	7.63	8.49

Austin Dean

Bats: R **Throws:** R **Pos:** LF-2;1B-1;RF-1;PH-1 **Ht:** 6'0" **Wt:** 215 **Born:** 10/14/1993 **Age:** 27

Year	Team	Lg	G	AB	H	2B	3B	HR	(Hm	Rd)	TB	R	RBI	RC	TBB	IBB	SO	HBP	SH	SF	SB	CS	GDP	Avg	OBP	Slg	OPS
			BATTING																		**RUNNING**			**AVERAGES**			
2018	Mia	NL	34	113	25	4	0	4	(2	2)	41	16	14	12	7	0	22	2	0	1	1	0	1	.221	.279	.363	.642
2019	Mia	NL	64	178	40	14	0	6	(4	2)	72	17	21	16	9	1	47	0	1	1	0	2	5	.225	.261	.404	.665
2020	StL	NL	3	4	1	1	0	0	(0	0)	2	1	0	1	3	0	2	0	0	0	0	0	0	.250	.571	.500	1.071
3 ML YEARS			101	295	66	19	0	10	(6	4)	115	34	35	29	19	1	71	2	1	1	1	2	6	.224	.274	.390	.664

Jacob deGrom

Pitches: R **Bats:** L **Pos:** SP-12 duh-GRAHM **Ht:** 6'4" **Wt:** 180 **Born:** 6/19/1988 **Age:** 33

Year	Team	Lg	G	GS	GF	IP	BFP	H	R	ER	HR	SH	SF	HB	TBB	IBB	SO	WP	W	L	Pct	Sv-Op	Hld	Vel	OPS	ERC	ERA
			HOW MUCH PITCHED					**WHAT HE GAVE UP**											**THE RESULTS**								
2014	NYM	NL	22	22	0	140.1	565	117	44	42	7	5	3	4	43	4	144	1	9	6	.600	0-0	0	93	.613	2.57	2.69
2015	NYM	NL	30	30	0	191.0	751	149	59	54	16	10	7	2	38	2	205	6	14	8	.636	0-0	0	95	.574	2.13	2.54
2016	NYM	NL	24	24	0	148.0	604	142	53	50	15	5	3	3	36	0	143	4	7	8	.467	0-0	0	93	.685	3.40	3.04
2017	NYM	NL	31	31	0	201.1	827	180	87	79	28	3	5	2	59	5	239	7	15	10	.600	0-0	0	95	.682	3.36	3.53
2018	NYM	NL	32	32	0	217.0	835	152	48	41	10	3	5	5	46	3	269	2	10	9	.526	0-0	0	96	.521	**1.67**	**1.70**
2019	NYM	NL	32	32	0	204.0	804	154	59	55	19	5	3	7	44	1	255	2	11	8	.579	0-0	0	97	.580	**2.21**	2.43
2020	NYM	NL	12	12	0	68.0	268	47	21	18	7	0	2	0	18	0	104	4	4	2	.667	0-0	0	99	.565	2.00	2.38
	Postseason		4	4	0	25.0	105	21	8	8	2	2	0	0	8	1	29	0	3	1	.750	0-0	0	96	.608	2.65	2.88
7 ML YEARS			183	183	0	1169.2	4654	941	371	339	102	31	28	20	284	13	1359	26	70	51	.579	0-0	0	95	.603	2.45	2.61

Paul DeJong

Bats: R **Throws:** R **Pos:** SS-45 **Ht:** 6'0" **Wt:** 205 **Born:** 8/2/1993 **Age:** 27

Year	Team	Lg	G	AB	H	2B	3B	HR	(Hm	Rd)	TB	R	RBI	RC	TBB	IBB	SO	HBP	SH	SF	SB	CS	GDP	Avg	OBP	Slg	OPS
2017	StL	NL	108	417	119	26	1	25	(11	14)	222	55	65	57	21	1	124	4	0	1	1	0	8	.285	.325	.532	.857
2018	StL	NL	115	436	105	25	1	19	(4	15)	189	68	68	67	36	2	123	12	0	5	1	1	6	.241	.313	.433	.746
2019	StL	NL	159	583	136	31	1	30	(10	20)	259	97	78	76	62	1	149	13	0	6	9	5	15	.233	.318	.444	.762
2020	StL	NL	45	152	38	6	0	3	(1	2)	53	17	25	23	17	0	50	1	0	4	1	0	4	.250	.322	.349	.671
	Postseason		9	30	7	1	0	0	(0	0)	8	3	2	4	3	2	14	0	0	0	0	0	0	.233	.303	.267	.570
	4 ML YEARS		427	1588	398	88	3	77	(26	51)	723	237	236	223	136	4	446	30	0	16	12	6	33	.251	.319	.455	.774

Miguel Del Pozo

Pitches: L **Bats:** L **Pos:** RP-5 **Ht:** 6'1" **Wt:** 205 **Born:** 10/14/1992 **Age:** 28

Year	Team	Lg	G	GS	GF	IP	BFP	H	R	ER	HR	SH	SF	HB	TBB	IBB	SO	WP	W	L	Pct	Sv-Op	Hld	Vel	OPS	ERC	ERA
2019	LAA	AL	17	0	1	9.1	45	10	11	11	3	1	1	0	8	0	11	0	1	1	.500	0-0	0	95	.981	8.30	10.61
2020	Pit	NL	5	0	1	3.2	25	7	7	7	0	0	0	0	8	1	2	1	0	0	-	0-2	0	93	1.129	16.73	17.18
	2 ML YEARS		22	0	2	13.0	70	17	18	18	3	1	1	0	16	1	13	1	1	1	.500	0-2	0	94	1.036	10.77	12.46

Nicky Delmonico

Bats: L **Throws:** R **Pos:** RF-4;LF-3 **Ht:** 6'3" **Wt:** 230 **Born:** 7/12/1992 **Age:** 28

Year	Team	Lg	G	AB	H	2B	3B	HR	(Hm	Rd)	TB	R	RBI	RC	TBB	IBB	SO	HBP	SH	SF	SB	CS	GDP	Avg	OBP	Slg	OPS
2017	CWS	AL	43	141	37	4	0	9	(3	6)	68	25	23	23	23	0	31	2	0	0	2	0	5	.262	.373	.482	.856
2018	CWS	AL	88	284	61	11	5	8	(7	1)	106	31	25	30	27	1	80	6	0	1	1	2	7	.215	.296	.373	.669
2019	CWS	AL	21	63	13	2	0	1	(1	0)	18	6	6	7	4	0	25	1	0	0	0	1	1	.206	.265	.286	.550
2020	CWS	AL	6	20	3	0	0	0	(0	0)	3	0	3	1	2	0	2	0	0	0	0	0	2	.150	.227	.150	.377
	4 ML YEARS		158	508	114	17	5	18	(11	7)	195	62	57	61	56	1	138	9	0	1	3	3	15	.224	.312	.384	.696

Travis Demeritte

Bats: R **Throws:** R **Pos:** RF-12;PR-5;PH-4;LF-2;DH-2 **Ht:** 6'0" **Wt:** 180 **Born:** 9/30/1994 **Age:** 26

Year	Team	Lg	G	AB	H	2B	3B	HR	(Hm	Rd)	TB	R	RBI	RC	TBB	IBB	SO	HBP	SH	SF	SB	CS	GDP	Avg	OBP	Slg	OPS
2019	Det	AL	48	169	38	7	2	3	(2	1)	58	24	10	13	14	0	63	1	1	1	3	0	3	.225	.286	.343	.630
2020	Det	AL	18	29	5	1	0	0	(0	0)	6	5	4	3	3	0	14	1	0	0	0	0	0	.172	.273	.207	.480
	2 ML YEARS		66	198	43	8	2	3	(2	1)	64	29	14	16	17	0	77	2	1	1	3	0	3	.217	.284	.323	.608

Matt Dermody

Pitches: L **Bats:** R **Pos:** RP-1 **Ht:** 6'5" **Wt:** 190 **Born:** 7/4/1990 **Age:** 30

Year	Team	Lg	G	GS	GF	IP	BFP	H	R	ER	HR	SH	SF	HB	TBB	IBB	SO	WP	W	L	Pct	Sv-Op	Hld	Vel	OPS	ERC	ERA
2016	Tor	AL	5	0	1	3.0	16	6	4	4	1	0	0	1	0	0	5	1	0	0	-	0-0	0	91	1.104	12.18	12.00
2017	Tor	AL	23	0	3	22.1	95	23	13	11	6	0	1	2	5	1	15	1	2	0	1.000	0-0	1	92	.822	5.00	4.43
2020	ChC	NL	1	0	1	1.0	3	0	0	0	0	0	0	0	0	0	1	0	0	0	-	0-0	0	95	.000	0.00	0.00
	3 ML YEARS		29	0	5	26.1	114	29	17	15	7	0	1	3	5	1	21	2	2	0	1.000	0-0	1	92	.839	5.36	5.13

Daniel Descalso

Bats: L **Throws:** R **Pos:** IF dess-CAL-so **Ht:** 5'10" **Wt:** 190 **Born:** 10/19/1986 **Age:** 34

Year	Team	Lg	G	AB	H	2B	3B	HR	(Hm	Rd)	TB	R	RBI	RC	TBB	IBB	SO	HBP	SH	SF	SB	CS	GDP	Avg	OBP	Slg	OPS
2010	StL	NL	11	34	9	2	0	0	(0	0)	11	6	4	5	2	0	6	1	0	0	1	0	0	.265	.324	.324	.648
2011	StL	NL	148	326	86	20	3	1	(1	0)	115	35	28	40	33	9	65	3	10	3	2	2	3	.264	.334	.353	.687
2012	StL	NL	143	374	85	10	7	4	(0	4)	121	41	26	29	37	3	83	5	7	3	6	3	5	.227	.303	.324	.627
2013	StL	NL	123	328	78	25	1	5	(1	4)	120	43	43	40	22	5	56	3	3	2	6	3	7	.238	.290	.366	.656
2014	StL	NL	104	161	39	11	0	0	(0	0)	50	20	10	15	20	0	33	2	1	0	1	3	2	.242	.333	.311	.644
2015	Col	NL	101	185	38	3	2	5	(1	4)	60	22	19	24	20	6	45	0	4	0	1	2	3	.205	.283	.324	.607
2016	Col	NL	99	250	66	12	2	8	(3	5)	106	38	38	45	34	3	56	1	0	4	3	0	2	.264	.349	.424	.773
2017	Ari	NL	131	344	80	16	5	10	(7	3)	136	47	51	49	48	0	89	4	0	6	2	0	6	.233	.332	.395	.727
2018	Ari	NL	138	349	83	22	4	13	(5	8)	152	54	57	57	64	2	110	2	0	7	0	1	2	.238	.353	.436	.789
2019	ChC	NL	82	168	29	5	1	2	(0	2)	42	20	15	16	23	0	57	0	1	1	2	1	3	.173	.271	.250	.521
	Postseason		48	93	21	3	0	4	(3	1)	36	19	9	8	8	3	23	0	5	1	2	0	2	.226	.284	.387	.671
	10 ML YEARS		1080	2519	593	126	25	48	(18	30)	913	326	294	310	303	28	600	21	26	22	26	15	33	.235	.320	.362	.683

Anthony DeSclafani

Pitches: R **Bats:** R **Pos:** SP-7; RP-2 DEE-skla-fa-nee **Ht:** 6'1" **Wt:** 200 **Born:** 4/18/1990 **Age:** 31

Year	Team	Lg	G	GS	GF	IP	BFP	H	R	ER	HR	SH	SF	HB	TBB	IBB	SO	WP	W	L	Pct	Sv-Op	Hld	Vel	OPS	ERC	ERA
2014	Mia	NL	13	5	4	33.0	146	40	23	23	4	4	3	2	5	0	26	2	2	2	.500	0-0	0	93	.801	4.56	6.27
2015	Cin	NL	31	31	0	184.2	785	194	93	83	17	10	5	5	55	5	151	6	9	13	.409	0-0	0	93	.742	4.00	4.05
2016	Cin	NL	20	20	0	123.1	507	120	51	45	16	7	3	4	30	2	105	6	9	5	.643	0-0	0	93	.723	3.67	3.28
2018	Cin	NL	21	21	0	115.0	484	118	68	63	24	5	4	2	30	2	108	4	7	8	.467	0-0	0	94	.792	4.47	4.93
2019	Cin	NL	31	31	0	166.2	696	151	77	72	29	5	3	4	49	5	167	2	9	9	.500	0-0	0	95	.717	3.66	3.89
2020	Cin	NL	9	7	1	33.2	158	41	27	27	7	0	3	3	16	0	25	1	1	2	.333	0-0	0	95	.909	6.91	7.22
	6 ML YEARS		125	115	5	656.1	2776	664	339	313	97	31	21	20	185	14	582	21	37	39	.487	0-0	0	93	.753	4.10	4.29

Delino DeShields

Bats: R **Throws:** R **Pos:** CF-35;PR-3;DH-1;PH-1   **Ht:** 5'9" **Wt:** 190 **Born:** 8/16/1992 **Age:** 28

Year	Team	Lg	G	AB	H	2B	3B	HR	(Hm	Rd)	TB	R	RBI	RC	TBB	IBB	SO	HBP	SH	SF	SB	CS	GDP	Avg	OBP	Slg	OPS
2015	Tex	AL	121	425	111	22	10	2	(2	0)	159	83	37	66	53	1	101	3	7	4	25	8	1	.261	.344	.374	.718
2016	Tex	AL	74	182	38	7	0	4	(0	4)	57	36	13	16	15	0	54	2	3	1	8	3	1	.209	.275	.313	.588
2017	Tex	AL	120	376	101	15	2	6	(5	1)	138	75	22	54	44	0	109	3	13	4	29	8	2	.269	.347	.367	.714
2018	Tex	AL	106	334	72	14	1	2	(1	1)	94	52	22	38	43	0	83	3	12	1	20	4	1	.216	.310	.281	.591
2019	Tex	AL	118	357	89	15	4	4	(3	1)	124	42	32	51	38	0	100	3	8	2	24	6	8	.249	.325	.347	.672
2020	Cle	AL	37	107	27	3	2	0	(0	0)	34	10	7	10	9	0	29	0	4	0	3	2	0	.252	.310	.318	.628
	Postseason		5	24	7	3	0	0	(0	0)	10	4	2	4	0	0	2	0	0	0	1	0	0	.292	.292	.417	.708
	6 ML YEARS		576	1781	438	76	19	18	(11	7)	606	298	133	235	202	1	476	14	47	12	109	31	13	.246	.326	.340	.666

Ian Desmond

Bats: R **Throws:** R **Pos:** OF   **Ht:** 6'3" **Wt:** 217 **Born:** 9/20/1985 **Age:** 35

Year	Team	Lg	G	AB	H	2B	3B	HR	(Hm	Rd)	TB	R	RBI	RC	TBB	IBB	SO	HBP	SH	SF	SB	CS	GDP	Avg	OBP	Slg	OPS
2009	Was	NL	21	82	23	7	2	4	(2	2)	46	9	12	10	5	0	14	0	1	1	1	0	2	.280	.318	.561	.879
2010	Was	NL	154	525	141	27	4	10	(8	2)	206	59	65	58	28	3	109	5	9	7	17	5	9	.269	.308	.392	.700
2011	Was	NL	154	584	148	27	5	8	(7	1)	209	65	49	65	35	2	139	4	11	5	25	10	9	.253	.298	.358	.656
2012	Was	NL	130	513	150	33	2	25	(16	9)	262	72	73	73	30	1	113	3	0	1	21	6	17	.292	.335	.511	.845
2013	Was	NL	158	600	168	38	3	20	(10	10)	272	77	80	81	43	3	145	5	2	5	21	6	16	.280	.331	.453	.784
2014	Was	NL	154	593	151	26	3	24	(12	12)	255	73	91	78	46	0	183	6	0	3	24	5	17	.255	.313	.430	.743
2015	Was	NL	156	583	136	27	2	19	(11	8)	224	69	62	59	45	0	187	3	6	4	13	5	9	.233	.290	.384	.674
2016	Tex	AL	156	625	178	29	3	22	(10	12)	279	107	86	92	44	2	160	5	0	3	21	6	11	.285	.335	.446	.782
2017	Col	NL	95	339	93	11	1	7	(2	5)	127	47	40	47	24	1	87	4	2	4	15	4	13	.274	.326	.375	.701
2018	Col	NL	160	555	131	21	8	22	(8	14)	234	82	88	75	53	0	146	6	1	4	20	6	17	.236	.307	.422	.729
2019	Col	NL	140	443	113	31	4	20	(11	9)	212	64	65	59	34	1	119	2	1	2	3	3	12	.255	.310	.479	.788
	Postseason		17	70	16	2	0	0	(0	0)	18	5	2	3	1	0	18	0	0	0	2	0	0	.229	.239	.257	.497
	11 ML YEARS		1478	5442	1432	277	37	181	(97	84)	2326	724	711	697	387	13	1402	43	33	39	181	56	132	.263	.315	.427	.742

Ross Detwiler

Pitches: L **Bats:** R **Pos:** RP-16   DETT-why-lerr   **Ht:** 6'5" **Wt:** 210 **Born:** 3/6/1986 **Age:** 35

Year	Team	Lg	G	GS	GF	IP	BFP	H	R	ER	HR	SH	SF	HB	TBB	IBB	SO	WP	W	L	Pct	Sv-Op	Hld	Vel	OPS	ERC	ERA
2007	Was	NL	1	0	1	1.0	4	0	0	0	0	0	0	0	0	0	1	0	0	0	-	0-0	0	93	.000	0.00	0.00
2009	Was	NL	15	14	0	75.2	341	87	43	42	3	4	1	2	33	3	43	4	1	6	.143	0-0	0	91	.767	4.65	5.00
2010	Was	NL	8	5	1	29.2	136	34	22	14	5	2	0	1	14	1	17	1	1	3	.250	0-0	0	90	.826	5.83	4.25
2011	Was	NL	15	10	0	66.0	277	63	26	22	7	7	3	3	20	2	41	2	4	5	.444	0-0	0	92	.704	3.64	3.00
2012	Was	NL	33	27	1	164.1	686	149	75	62	15	8	3	5	52	0	105	4	10	8	.556	0-0	1	93	.681	3.30	3.40
2013	Was	NL	13	13	0	71.1	316	92	37	32	5	4	1	5	14	2	39	0	2	7	.222	0-0	0	92	.811	4.96	4.04
2014	Was	NL	47	0	15	63.0	274	68	34	28	5	4	3	5	21	4	39	3	2	3	.400	1-2	3	93	.734	4.36	4.00
2015	2 Tms		41	7	7	58.1	288	82	51	47	10	1	4	6	36	1	41	3	1	5	.167	0-2	2	92	.984	8.67	7.25
2016	2 Tms		16	7	0	48.2	220	59	34	33	5	0	1	1	19	0	26	3	4	4	.333	0-1	0	92	.806	5.37	6.10
2018	Sea	AL	1	0	0	6.0	23	8	3	3	1	0	1	0	2	0	2	0	0	1	.000	0-0	0	90	.985	7.59	4.50
2019	CWS	AL	18	12	2	85.0	315	86	54	51	20	2	1	3	27	3	46	1	3	5	.375	0-0	0	91	.942	7.05	6.59
2020	CWS	AL	16	0	4	19.2	81	19	8	7	2	0	0	1	5	1	15	1	1	1	.500	0-0	0	92	.695	3.52	3.20
15	Tex	AL	17	7	4	43.0	208	62	37	34	9	1	3	3	20	0	28	3	0	5	.000	0-1	1	91	.991	8.35	7.12
15	Atl	NL	24	0	3	15.1	80	20	14	13	1	0	1	3	16	1	13	0	1	0	1.000	0-1	1	93	.954	9.42	7.63
16	Cle	AL	7	0	0	4.2	21	3	3	3	1	0	1	0	4	0	3	0	0	0	-	0-1	0	91	.833	4.60	5.79
16	Oak	AL	9	7	0	44.0	199	56	31	30	4	0	0	1	15	0	23	3	4	4	.333	0-0	0	92	.804	5.46	6.14
	Postseason		1	1	0	6.0	25	3	1	0	0	1	1	0	3	1	2	0	0	0	-	0-0	0	92	.400	1.21	0.00
	12 ML YEARS		224	95	31	673.1	2960	747	387	341	78	32	18	32	243	17	415	22	27	48	.360	1-5	8	92	.786	4.84	4.56

Chris Devenski

Pitches: R **Bats:** R **Pos:** RP-4   **Ht:** 6'3" **Wt:** 219 **Born:** 11/13/1990 **Age:** 30

Year	Team	Lg	G	GS	GF	IP	BFP	H	R	ER	HR	SH	SF	HB	TBB	IBB	SO	WP	W	L	Pct	Sv-Op	Hld	Vel	OPS	ERC	ERA
2016	Hou	AL	48	5	16	108.1	408	79	26	26	4	1	1	3	20	0	104	2	4	4	.500	1-1	5	92	.551	1.74	2.16
2017	Hou	AL	62	0	10	80.2	316	50	26	24	11	0	1	2	26	3	100	2	8	5	.615	4-10	24	94	.588	2.10	2.68
2018	Hou	AL	50	1	8	47.1	196	42	23	22	9	1	3	3	13	1	51	1	2	3	.400	2-5	18	94	.719	3.79	4.18
2019	Hou	AL	61	1	19	69.0	298	69	39	37	13	1	3	3	21	0	72	2	2	3	.400	0-1	7	95	.784	4.42	4.83
2020	Hou	AL	4	0	0	3.2	21	7	6	6	1	0	0	0	3	0	5	0	0	1	.000	0-1	0	93	1.143	13.40	14.73
	Postseason		13	0	5	11.0	50	12	11	11	3	0	1	1	4	0	11	0	1	0	1.000	0-1	3	95	.954	5.99	9.00
	5 ML YEARS		225	7	53	309.0	1239	247	120	115	38	3	6	11	83	4	332	7	16	16	.500	7-18	54	94	.652	2.80	3.35

Rafael Devers

Bats: L **Throws:** R **Pos:** 3B-57;PH-2   **Ht:** 6'0" **Wt:** 240 **Born:** 10/24/1996 **Age:** 24

Year	Team	Lg	G	AB	H	2B	3B	HR	(Hm	Rd)	TB	R	RBI	RC	TBB	IBB	SO	HBP	SH	SF	SB	CS	GDP	Avg	OBP	Slg	OPS
2017	Bos	AL	58	222	63	14	0	10	(6	4)	107	34	30	34	18	3	57	0	0	0	3	1	5	.284	.338	.482	.819
2018	Bos	AL	121	450	108	24	0	21	(9	12)	195	59	66	47	38	6	121	0	0	2	5	2	9	.240	.298	.433	.731
2019	Bos	AL	156	647	201	54	4	32	(13	19)	359	129	115	119	48	7	119	4	1	2	8	8	8	.311	.361	.555	.916
2020	Bos	AL	57	232	61	16	1	11	(5	6)	112	32	43	34	13	0	67	3	0	0	0	0	8	.263	.310	.483	.793
	Postseason		15	45	14	0	0	3	(2	1)	23	10	14	10	5	0	17	0	0	1	0	0	1	.311	.373	.511	.884
	4 ML YEARS		392	1551	433	108	5	74	(33	41)	773	254	254	234	117	16	364	7	1	4	16	11	30	.279	.332	.498	.830

Aledmys Diaz

Bats: R **Throws:** R **Pos:** 2B-10;3B-3;1B-2;DH-2;LF-1;PH-1   ah-LED-mees   **Ht:** 6'1" **Wt:** 195 **Born:** 8/1/1990 **Age:** 30

Year	Team	Lg	G	AB	H	2B	3B	HR	(Hm	Rd)	TB	R	RBI	RC	TBB	IBB	SO	HBP	SH	SF	SB	CS	GDP	Avg	OBP	Slg	OPS
2016	StL	NL	111	404	121	28	3	17	(7	10)	206	71	65	75	41	6	60	7	2	6	4	4	10	.300	.369	.510	.879
2017	StL	NL	79	286	74	17	0	7	(5	2)	112	31	20	27	13	1	42	0	1	1	4	1	9	.259	.290	.392	.682
2018	Tor	AL	130	422	111	26	0	18	(7	11)	191	55	55	50	23	2	62	3	0	4	3	4	9	.263	.303	.453	.756
2019	Hou	AL	69	210	57	12	1	9	(5	4)	98	36	40	36	26	1	28	5	0	6	2	0	10	.271	.356	.467	.823
2020	Hou	AL	17	58	14	5	0	3	(1	2)	28	8	6	5	1	0	12	0	0	0	0	0	1	.241	.254	.483	.737
	Postseason		8	9	0	0	0	0	(0	0)	0	0	0	0	1	0	2	0	0	0	0	0	0	.000	.100	.000	.100
	5 ML YEARS		406	1380	377	88	4	54	(25	29)	635	201	186	193	104	10	204	15	3	17	13	9	39	.273	.327	.460	.787

Edwin Diaz

Pitches: R **Bats:** R **Pos:** RP-26   **Ht:** 6'3" **Wt:** 165 **Born:** 3/22/1994 **Age:** 27

			HOW MUCH PITCHED					WHAT HE GAVE UP									THE RESULTS							
Year	Team	Lg	G	GS	GF	IP	BFP	H	R	ER	HR	SH	SF	HB	TBB	IBB	SO	WP	W	L	Pct	Sv-Op	Hld	Vel	OPS	ERC	ERA
2016	Sea	AL	49	0	23	51.2	217	45	16	16	5	0	0	3	15	2	88	6	0	4	.000	18-21	13	97	.627	3.05	2.79
2017	Sea	AL	66	0	52	66.0	278	44	28	24	10	1	2	3	32	2	89	3	4	6	.400	34-39	2	97	.619	3.01	3.27
2018	Sea	AL	73	0	65	73.1	280	41	17	16	5	0	0	6	17	0	124	3	0	4	.000	57-61	0	97	.470	1.49	1.96
2019	NYM	NL	66	0	48	58.0	254	58	36	36	15	1	2	4	22	3	99	3	2	7	.222	26-33	1	97	.834	5.31	5.59
2020	NYM	NL	26	0	19	25.2	110	18	6	5	2	0	0	2	14	0	50	1	2	1	.667	6-10	1	98	.596	3.12	1.75
	5 ML YEARS		280	0	207	274.2	1139	206	103	97	37	2	4	18	100	7	450	16	8	22	.267	141-164	17	97	.629	3.01	3.18

Elias Diaz

Bats: R **Throws:** R **Pos:** C-24;PH-7;DH-2   eh-LEE-ahs   **Ht:** 6'1" **Wt:** 223 **Born:** 11/17/1990 **Age:** 30

Year	Team	Lg	G	AB	H	2B	3B	HR	(Hm	Rd)	TB	R	RBI	RC	TBB	IBB	SO	HBP	SH	SF	SB	CS	GDP	Avg	OBP	Slg	OPS
2015	Pit	NL	2	2	0	0	0	0	(0	0)	0	0	0	0	0	0	1	0	0	0	0	0	0	.000	.000	.000	.000
2016	Pit	NL	1	4	0	0	0	0	(0	0)	0	0	1	0	0	0	1	0	0	0	0	0	0	.000	.000	.000	.000
2017	Pit	NL	64	188	42	14	0	1	(0	1)	59	18	19	15	11	0	38	0	0	1	1	0	8	.223	.265	.314	.579
2018	Pit	NL	82	252	72	12	0	10	(3	7)	114	33	34	36	21	1	40	1	0	3	0	1	4	.286	.339	.452	.792
2019	Pit	NL	101	303	73	14	0	2	(2	0)	93	31	28	30	23	0	56	2	1	3	0	0	11	.241	.296	.307	.603
2020	Col	NL	26	68	16	2	0	2	(1	1)	24	4	9	6	5	0	15	0	0	0	0	0	4	.235	.288	.353	.641
	6 ML YEARS		276	817	203	42	0	15	(6	9)	290	86	91	87	60	1	151	3	1	7	1	1	27	.248	.300	.355	.655

Isan Diaz

Bats: L **Throws:** R **Pos:** 2B-7   **Ht:** 5'11" **Wt:** 201 **Born:** 5/27/1996 **Age:** 25

Year	Team	Lg	G	AB	H	2B	3B	HR	(Hm	Rd)	TB	R	RBI	RC	TBB	IBB	SO	HBP	SH	SF	SB	CS	GDP	Avg	OBP	Slg	OPS
2019	Mia	NL	49	179	31	5	2	5	(2	3)	55	17	23	19	19	0	59	2	0	1	0	3	2	.173	.259	.307	.566
2020	Mia	NL	7	22	4	0	0	0	(0	0)	4	3	1	0	0	0	7	0	0	0	0	0	0	.182	.182	.182	.364
	2 ML YEARS		56	201	35	5	2	5	(2	3)	59	20	24	19	19	0	66	2	0	1	0	3	2	.174	.251	.294	.545

Jairo Diaz

Pitches: R **Bats:** R **Pos:** RP-24   HIGH-row   **Ht:** 6'0" **Wt:** 254 **Born:** 5/27/1991 **Age:** 30

			HOW MUCH PITCHED					WHAT HE GAVE UP									THE RESULTS							
Year	Team	Lg	G	GS	GF	IP	BFP	H	R	ER	HR	SH	SF	HB	TBB	IBB	SO	WP	W	L	Pct	Sv-Op	Hld	Vel	OPS	ERC	ERA
2014	LAA	AL	5	0	2	5.2	24	4	2	2	0	0	0	0	3	0	8	0	0	0	-	0-0	0	97	.592	2.29	3.18
2015	Col	NL	21	0	5	19.0	78	16	6	5	2	0	0	0	6	0	18	0	0	1	.000	0-1	7	97	.615	2.93	2.37
2017	Col	NL	4	0	3	5.0	30	12	6	5	0	0	0	1	5	0	2	0	0	0	-	0-0	0	97	1.267	17.54	9.00
2019	Col	NL	56	0	20	57.2	245	56	34	29	7	0	1	2	19	0	63	4	6	4	.600	5-8	7	97	.745	3.92	4.53
2020	Col	NL	24	0	12	20.0	106	31	21	17	4	2	2	3	14	1	17	2	1	2	.333	4-4	3	95	1.073	10.31	7.65
	5 ML YEARS		110	0	42	107.1	483	119	69	58	13	2	4	6	47	1	108	6	7	7	.500	9-13	17	97	.815	5.23	4.86

Lewin Diaz

Bats: L **Throws:** L **Pos:** 1B-11;PH-2;DH-1   **Ht:** 6'4" **Wt:** 217 **Born:** 11/19/1996 **Age:** 24

Year	Team	Lg	G	AB	H	2B	3B	HR	(Hm	Rd)	TB	R	RBI	RC	TBB	IBB	SO	HBP	SH	SF	SB	CS	GDP	Avg	OBP	Slg	OPS
2020	Mia	NL	14	39	6	2	0	0	(0	0)	8	2	3	2	2	0	12	0	0	0	0	0	2	.154	.195	.205	.400

Yandy Diaz

Bats: R **Throws:** R **Pos:** 3B-25;DH-7;PH-4;1B-2   **Ht:** 6'2" **Wt:** 215 **Born:** 8/8/1991 **Age:** 29

Year	Team	Lg	G	AB	H	2B	3B	HR	(Hm	Rd)	TB	R	RBI	RC	TBB	IBB	SO	HBP	SH	SF	SB	CS	GDP	Avg	OBP	Slg	OPS
2017	Cle	AL	49	156	41	8	1	0	(0	0)	51	25	13	18	21	0	35	1	0	1	2	0	5	.263	.352	.327	.679
2018	Cle	AL	39	109	34	5	2	1	(1	0)	46	15	15	16	11	1	19	0	0	0	0	0	6	.312	.375	.422	.797
2019	TB	AL	79	307	82	20	1	14	(7	7)	146	53	38	38	35	1	61	1	0	4	2	2	9	.267	.340	.476	.816
2020	TB	AL	34	114	35	3	0	2	(1	1)	44	16	11	21	23	1	17	1	0	0	0	0	6	.307	.428	.386	.814
	Postseason		5	16	4	1	0	2	(0	2)	11	2	2	3	0	0	5	0	0	0	0	0	0	.250	.250	.688	.938
	4 ML YEARS		201	686	192	36	4	17	(9	8)	287	109	77	93	90	3	132	3	0	5	4	2	26	.280	.364	.418	.782

Alex Dickerson

Bats: L **Throws:** L **Pos:** LF-41;PH-14;RF-5;DH-3   **Ht:** 6'2" **Wt:** 226 **Born:** 5/26/1990 **Age:** 31

Year Team	Lg	G	AB	H	2B	3B	HR	(Hm	Rd)	TB	R	RBI	RC	TBB	IBB	SO	HBP	SH	SF	SB	CS	GDP	Avg	OBP	Slg	OPS
2015 SD	NL	11	8	2	0	0	0	(0	0)	2	0	0	0	0	0	3	0	0	0	0	0	1	.250	.250	.250	.500
2016 SD	NL	84	253	65	16	2	10	(5	5)	115	39	37	40	26	2	44	4	0	2	5	1	5	.257	.333	.455	.788
2019 2 Tms	NL	68	174	48	13	3	6	(4	2)	85	29	28	27	13	1	42	2	0	1	1	1	5	.276	.332	.489	.820
2020 SF	NL	52	151	45	10	1	10	(5	5)	87	28	27	27	16	2	30	2	0	1	0	0	5	.298	.371	.576	.947
19 SD	NL	12	19	3	0	0	0	(0	0)	3	1	2	2	0	0	7	0	0	0	0	0	0	.158	.158	.158	.316
19 SF	NL	56	155	45	13	3	6	(4	2)	82	28	26	25	13	1	35	2	0	1	1	1	5	.290	.351	.529	.880
4 ML YEARS		215	586	160	39	6	26	(14	12)	289	96	92	94	55	5	119	8	0	4	6	2	16	.273	.342	.493	.835

Corey Dickerson

Bats: L **Throws:** R **Pos:** LF-46;DH-6;RF-1;PH-1   **Ht:** 6'1" **Wt:** 200 **Born:** 5/22/1989 **Age:** 32

Year Team	Lg	G	AB	H	2B	3B	HR	(Hm	Rd)	TB	R	RBI	RC	TBB	IBB	SO	HBP	SH	SF	SB	CS	GDP	Avg	OBP	Slg	OPS
2013 Col	NL	69	194	51	13	5	5	(4	1)	89	32	17	23	16	0	41	0	1	2	2	2	1	.263	.316	.459	.775
2014 Col	NL	131	436	136	27	6	24	(15	9)	247	74	76	79	37	6	101	1	0	4	8	7	6	.312	.364	.567	.931
2015 Col	NL	65	224	68	18	2	10	(5	5)	120	30	31	39	10	0	56	0	0	0	0	1	3	.304	.333	.536	.869
2016 TB	AL	148	510	125	36	3	24	(7	17)	239	57	70	59	33	6	134	2	0	2	0	2	12	.245	.293	.469	.761
2017 TB	AL	150	588	166	33	4	27	(14	13)	288	84	62	87	35	6	152	3	0	2	4	3	11	.282	.325	.490	.815
2018 Pit	NL	135	504	151	35	7	13	(4	9)	239	65	55	69	21	4	80	4	0	4	8	3	14	.300	.330	.474	.804
2019 2 Tms	NL	78	260	79	28	2	12	(6	6)	147	33	59	50	16	4	56	0	0	3	1	0	4	.304	.341	.565	.906
2020 Mia	NL	52	194	50	5	1	7	(2	5)	78	25	17	20	15	1	35	0	0	0	1	1	5	.258	.311	.402	.713
19 Pit	NL	44	127	40	18	0	4	(0	4)	70	20	25	24	13	4	23	0	0	2	1	0	3	.315	.373	.551	.924
19 Phi	NL	34	133	39	10	2	8	(6	2)	77	13	34	26	3	0	33	0	0	1	0	0	1	.293	.307	.579	.886
8 ML YEARS		828	2910	826	195	30	122	(57	65)	1447	400	387	426	183	27	655	10	1	17	24	19	56	.284	.327	.497	.824

Phillip Diehl

Pitches: L **Bats:** L **Pos:** RP-6   **Ht:** 6'2" **Wt:** 169 **Born:** 7/16/1994 **Age:** 26

Year Team	Lg	G	GS	GF	IP	BFP	H	R	ER	HR	SH	SF	HB	TBB	IBB	SO	WP	W	L	Pct	Sv-Op	Hld	Vel	OPS	ERC	ERA
2019 Col	NL	10	0	2	7.1	35	10	6	6	1	0	0	1	2	0	8	1	0	0	-	0-0	0	91	.934	6.41	7.36
2020 Col	NL	6	0	2	6.0	25	7	7	7	2	0	0	1	1	0	4	0	0	0	-	0-0	0	90	.945	5.81	10.50
2 ML YEARS		16	0	4	13.1	60	17	13	13	3	0	0	1	3	0	12	1	0	0	-	0-0	0	91	.939	6.19	8.78

Jake Diekman

Pitches: L **Bats:** L **Pos:** RP-21   DEEK-man   **Ht:** 6'4" **Wt:** 195 **Born:** 1/21/1987 **Age:** 34

Year Team	Lg	G	GS	GF	IP	BFP	H	R	ER	HR	SH	SF	HB	TBB	IBB	SO	WP	W	L	Pct	Sv-Op	Hld	Vel	OPS	ERC	ERA
2012 Phi	NL	32	0	7	27.1	131	25	17	12	1	1	0	3	20	3	35	1	1	1	.500	0-1	4	95	.696	4.45	3.95
2013 Phi	NL	45	0	11	38.1	164	34	15	11	1	2	1	0	16	2	41	2	1	4	.200	0-1	11	96	.598	2.89	2.58
2014 Phi	NL	73	0	19	71.0	313	66	36	30	4	2	7	3	35	5	100	7	5	5	.500	0-4	18	97	.692	3.73	3.80
2015 2 Tms		67	0	7	58.1	260	53	28	26	5	0	0	3	31	0	69	2	2	1	.667	0-3	16	96	.689	4.11	4.01
2016 Tex	AL	66	0	14	53.0	221	36	22	20	4	0	2	3	26	1	59	3	4	2	.667	4-5	26	95	.594	2.72	3.40
2017 Tex	AL	11	0	2	10.2	45	4	3	3	1	0	2	0	10	1	13	0	0	0	-	1-1	5	95	.523	2.58	2.53
2018 2 Tms		71	0	15	53.1	243	49	33	28	4	0	2	6	31	2	66	3	1	2	.333	2-3	17	95	.717	4.46	4.73
2019 2 Tms	AL	76	0	5	62.0	282	49	34	32	3	1	3	11	39	1	84	6	1	7	.125	0-2	31	96	.668	4.00	4.65
2020 Oak	AL	21	0	2	21.1	84	8	2	1	1	1	0	1	12	1	31	0	2	0	1.000	0-1	13	95	.410	1.43	0.42
15 Phi	NL	41	0	6	36.2	175	40	23	21	3	0	0	2	24	0	49	1	2	1	.667	0-2	6	96	.773	5.60	5.15
15 Tex	AL	26	0	1	21.2	85	13	5	5	2	0	0	1	7	0	20	1	0	0	-	0-1	10	97	.520	1.89	2.08
18 Tex	AL	47	0	10	39.0	172	31	18	16	2	0	2	3	23	1	48	0	1	1	.500	2-3	14	95	.651	3.53	3.69
18 Ari	NL	24	0	5	14.1	71	18	15	12	2	0	0	3	8	1	18	3	0	1	.000	0-0	3	96	.875	7.29	7.53
19 KC	AL	48	0	4	41.2	188	33	23	22	3	0	1	8	23	0	63	4	0	6	.000	0-2	18	96	.667	3.97	4.75
19 Oak	AL	28	0	1	20.1	94	16	11	10	0	1	2	3	16	1	21	2	1	1	.500	0-0	13	96	.668	4.05	4.43
Postseason		7	0	2	7.1	30	7	4	4	1	0	0	0	2	1	6	0	0	0	-	0-0	1	97	.729	3.42	4.91
9 ML YEARS		462	0	82	395.1	1743	324	190	163	24	7	17	30	220	16	498	24	17	22	.436	7-21	141	96	.653	3.58	3.71

Derek Dietrich

Bats: L **Throws:** R **Pos:** DH-9;1B-6;PH-6;2B-3;3B-3   DEE-trick   **Ht:** 6'2" **Wt:** 205 **Born:** 7/18/1989 **Age:** 31

Year Team	Lg	G	AB	H	2B	3B	HR	(Hm	Rd)	TB	R	RBI	RC	TBB	IBB	SO	HBP	SH	SF	SB	CS	GDP	Avg	OBP	Slg	OPS
2013 Mia	NL	57	215	46	10	2	9	(3	6)	87	32	23	22	11	1	56	7	0	0	1	0	1	.214	.275	.405	.679
2014 Mia	NL	49	158	36	6	2	5	(1	4)	61	31	17	22	13	0	38	10	2	0	1	0	1	.228	.326	.386	.712
2015 Mia	NL	90	250	64	14	3	10	(3	7)	114	38	24	32	23	2	65	13	0	3	0	2	4	.256	.346	.456	.802
2016 Mia	NL	128	351	98	20	5	7	(3	4)	149	39	42	57	32	2	84	24	0	5	1	0	6	.279	.374	.425	.798
2017 Mia	NL	135	406	101	22	5	13	(7	6)	172	56	53	59	36	5	98	18	0	4	0	1	4	.249	.334	.424	.758
2018 Mia	NL	149	499	132	26	2	16	(4	12)	210	72	45	63	29	2	140	21	0	2	2	0	5	.265	.330	.421	.751
2019 Cin	NL	113	251	47	8	2	19	(12	7)	116	41	43	45	28	2	74	25	0	1	1	1	2	.187	.328	.462	.790
2020 Tex	AL	25	61	12	1	0	5	(2	3)	28	9	8	10	9	0	21	5	0	0	1	1	4	.197	.347	.459	.806
8 ML YEARS		746	2191	536	107	21	84	(35	49)	937	318	255	312	181	14	576	123	2	15	7	5	27	.245	.335	.428	.762

Wilmer Difo

Bats: B **Throws:** R **Pos:** 2B-4;SS-4;PH-3;3B-2;PR-1   DEE-fo   **Ht:** 5'11" **Wt:** 200 **Born:** 4/2/1992 **Age:** 29

Year Team	Lg	G	AB	H	2B	3B	HR	(Hm	Rd)	TB	R	RBI	RC	TBB	IBB	SO	HBP	SH	SF	SB	CS	GDP	Avg	OBP	Slg	OPS
2015 Was	NL	15	11	2	0	0	0	(0	0)	2	1	0	0	0	0	2	0	0	0	0	0	0	.182	.182	.182	.364
2016 Was	NL	31	58	16	3	0	1	(1	0)	22	14	7	9	8	1	12	0	0	0	3	0	0	.276	.364	.379	.743
2017 Was	NL	124	332	90	10	4	5	(3	2)	123	47	21	34	24	6	74	1	5	3	10	1	7	.271	.319	.370	.690
2018 Was	NL	148	408	94	14	7	7	(5	2)	143	55	42	38	39	5	82	2	3	4	10	3	8	.230	.298	.350	.649
2019 Was	NL	43	131	33	2	0	2	(1	1)	41	15	8	15	12	3	29	0	1	0	0	1	2	.252	.315	.313	.628
2020 Was	NL	12	14	1	0	0	0	(0	0)	1	1	1	0	3	0	4	0	0	1	0	0	0	.071	.222	.071	.294
Postseason		3	3	0	0	0	0	(0	0)	0	0	0	0	0	0	1	0	0	0	0	0	0	.000	.000	.000	.000
6 ML YEARS		373	954	236	29	11	15	(10	5)	332	133	79	96	86	15	203	3	9	8	23	5	17	.247	.309	.348	.657

Brandon Dixon

Bats: R **Throws:** R **Pos:** 1B-4;LF-2;2B-1;PH-1;PR-1   **Ht:** 6'2" **Wt:** 215 **Born:** 1/29/1992 **Age:** 29

Year Team	Lg	G	AB	H	2B	3B	HR	(Hm	Rd)	TB	R	RBI	RC	TBB	IBB	SO	HBP	SH	SF	SB	CS	GDP	Avg	OBP	Slg	OPS
2018 Cin	NL	74	118	21	6	0	5	(2	3)	42	14	10	2	6	0	43	0	0	0	0	0	2	.178	.218	.356	.574
2019 Det	AL	118	391	97	20	4	15	(5	10)	170	41	52	50	21	0	136	4	0	4	5	1	5	.248	.290	.435	.725
2020 Det	AL	5	13	1	1	0	0	(0	0)	2	0	2	0	1	0	4	0	0	0	0	0	1	.077	.143	.154	.297
3 ML YEARS		197	522	119	27	4	20	(7	13)	214	55	64	52	28	0	183	4	0	4	5	1	8	.228	.271	.410	.681

Randy Dobnak

Pitches: R **Bats:** R **Pos:** SP-10   **Ht:** 6'1" **Wt:** 230 **Born:** 1/17/1995 **Age:** 26

Year Team	Lg	G	GS	GF	IP	BFP	H	R	ER	HR	SH	SF	HB	TBB	IBB	SO	WP	W	L	Pct	Sv-Op	Hld	Vel	OPS	ERC	ERA
2019 Min	AL	9	5	4	28.1	118	27	9	5	1	0	0	3	5	0	23	0	2	1	.667	1-1	0	93	.597	2.93	1.59
2020 Min	AL	10	10	0	46.2	200	50	21	21	3	0	1	4	13	0	27	0	6	4	.600	0-0	0	92	.705	4.14	4.05
Postseason		1	1	0	2.0	13	6	4	4	0	0	0	0	2	0	0	0	0	1	.000	0-0	0	92	1.252	21.10	18.00
2 ML YEARS		19	15	4	75.0	318	77	30	26	4	0	1	7	18	0	50	0	8	5	.615	1-1	0	92	.664	3.67	3.12

Rafael Dolis

Pitches: R **Bats:** R **Pos:** RP-24   DOE-leese   **Ht:** 6'4" **Wt:** 235 **Born:** 1/10/1988 **Age:** 33

Year Team	Lg	G	GS	GF	IP	BFP	H	R	ER	HR	SH	SF	HB	TBB	IBB	SO	WP	W	L	Pct	Sv-Op	Hld	Vel	OPS	ERC	ERA
2011 ChC	NL	1	0	0	1.1	4	0	0	0	0	0	0	0	1	0	1	0	0	0	-	0-0	0	95	.250	0.71	0.00
2012 ChC	NL	34	0	15	38.0	173	40	29	27	5	2	1	3	23	1	24	1	2	4	.333	4-6	3	95	.858	5.85	6.39
2013 ChC	NL	5	0	2	5.0	21	3	2	0	0	0	0	0	2	0	0	0	0	0	-	0-0	0	95	.554	1.44	0.00
2020 Tor	AL	24	0	9	24.0	100	16	9	4	1	2	0	1	14	0	31	3	2	2	.500	5-6	7	95	.593	2.78	1.50
4 ML YEARS		64	0	26	68.1	298	59	40	31	6	4	1	4	40	1	56	4	4	6	.400	9-12	10	95	.740	4.20	4.08

Seranthony Dominguez

Pitches: R **Bats:** R **Pos:** P   **Ht:** 6'1" **Wt:** 225 **Born:** 11/25/1994 **Age:** 26

Year Team	Lg	G	GS	GF	IP	BFP	H	R	ER	HR	SH	SF	HB	TBB	IBB	SO	WP	W	L	Pct	Sv-Op	Hld	Vel	OPS	ERC	ERA
2018 Phi	NL	53	0	24	58.0	231	32	19	19	4	0	1	4	22	2	74	10	2	5	.286	16-20	14	98	.501	1.74	2.95
2019 Phi	NL	27	0	2	24.2	110	24	13	11	3	1	0	1	12	0	29	1	3	0	1.000	0-2	9	97	.725	4.52	4.01
2 ML YEARS		80	0	26	82.2	341	56	32	30	7	1	1	5	34	2	103	11	5	5	.500	16-22	23	98	.573	2.48	3.27

Josh Donaldson

Bats: R **Throws:** R **Pos:** 3B-26;PH-3   **Ht:** 6'1" **Wt:** 210 **Born:** 12/8/1985 **Age:** 35

Year Team	Lg	G	AB	H	2B	3B	HR	(Hm	Rd)	TB	R	RBI	RC	TBB	IBB	SO	HBP	SH	SF	SB	CS	GDP	Avg	OBP	Slg	OPS
2010 Oak	AL	14	32	5	1	0	1	(0	1)	9	1	4	3	2	0	12	0	0	0	0	0	0	.156	.206	.281	.487
2012 Oak	AL	75	274	66	16	0	9	(3	6)	109	34	33	33	14	0	61	5	0	1	4	1	6	.241	.289	.398	.687
2013 Oak	AL	158	579	174	37	3	24	(13	11)	289	89	93	112	76	2	110	6	1	6	5	2	15	.301	.384	.499	.883
2014 Oak	AL	158	608	155	31	2	29	(11	18)	277	93	98	105	76	5	130	7	0	4	8	0	16	.255	.342	.456	.798
2015 Tor	AL	158	620	184	41	2	41	(24	17)	352	122	123	131	73	0	133	6	2	10	6	0	16	.297	.371	.568	.939
2016 Tor	AL	155	577	164	32	5	37	(21	16)	317	122	99	121	109	6	119	9	2	3	7	1	16	.284	.404	.549	.953
2017 Tor	AL	113	415	112	21	0	33	(14	19)	232	65	78	98	76	1	111	3	0	2	2	2	5	.270	.385	.559	.944
2018 2 Tms	AL	52	187	46	14	0	8	(4	4)	84	30	23	32	37	4	54	0	0	1	2	0	3	.246	.352	.449	.801
2019 Atl	NL	155	549	142	33	4	37	(22	15)	286	96	94	103	100	2	155	8	0	2	4	2	13	.259	.379	.521	.900
2020 Min	AL	28	81	18	2	0	6	(3	3)	38	14	11	14	18	1	24	2	0	1	0	0	4	.222	.373	.469	.842
18 Tor	AL	36	137	32	11	0	5	(2	3)	58	22	16	24	21	2	44	0	0	1	2	0	1	.234	.333	.423	.757
18 Cle	AL	16	50	14	3	0	3	(2	1)	26	8	7	8	10	0	10	0	0	0	0	0	2	.280	.400	.520	.920
Postseason		39	150	39	11	0	5	(4	1)	65	19	16	22	15	2	39	2	0	0	1	0	2	.260	.335	.433	.769
10 ML YEARS		1066	3922	1066	228	12	225	(115	110)	1993	666	656	752	575	19	909	46	5	30	38	8	94	.272	.369	.508	.877

Sean Doolittle

Pitches: L **Bats:** L **Pos:** RP-11   **Ht:** 6'2" **Wt:** 204 **Born:** 9/26/1986 **Age:** 34

Year	Team	Lg	G	GS	GF	IP	BFP	H	R	ER	HR	SH	SF	HB	TBB	IBB	SO	WP	W	L	Pct	Sv-Op	Hld	Vel	OPS	ERC	ERA
2012	Oak	AL	44	0	7	47.1	191	40	18	16	3	2	2	0	11	1	60	0	2	1	.667	1-2	18	94	.611	2.36	3.04
2013	Oak	AL	70	0	11	69.0	266	53	24	24	4	3	0	2	13	1	60	2	5	5	.500	2-7	26	94	.573	2.00	3.13
2014	Oak	AL	61	0	40	62.2	236	38	19	19	5	2	1	0	8	1	89	0	2	4	.333	22-26	5	94	.459	1.23	2.73
2015	Oak	AL	12	0	7	13.2	57	12	6	6	1	0	1	0	5	0	15	0	1	0	1.000	4-5	1	92	.651	3.10	3.95
2016	Oak	AL	44	0	13	39.0	155	33	14	14	6	4	0	0	8	2	45	1	2	3	.400	4-6	10	95	.705	2.79	3.23
2017	2 Tms		53	0	34	51.1	197	34	18	16	5	0	3	0	10	1	62	3	2	0	1.000	24-26	9	95	.517	1.62	2.81
2018	Was	NL	43	0	35	45.0	163	21	8	8	3	0	0	2	6	1	60	1	3	3	.500	25-26	1	94	.391	0.93	1.60
2019	Was	NL	63	0	55	60.0	260	63	27	27	11	1	2	0	15	2	66	0	6	5	.545	29-35	2	93	.772	4.32	4.05
2020	Was	NL	11	0	3	7.2	36	9	6	5	3	1	1	0	4	2	6	0	0	2	.000	0-0	3	91	1.005	7.28	5.87
17	Oak	AL	23	0	6	21.1	79	12	8	8	3	0	1	0	2	0	31	1	1	0	1.000	3-4	8	94	.467	1.23	3.38
17	Was		30	0	28	30.0	118	22	10	8	2	0	2	0	8	1	31	2	1	0	1.000	21-22	1	95	.551	1.99	2.40
	Postseason		20	0	8	22.1	87	17	8	6	2	3	1	0	3	0	23	0	0	1	.000	3-6	5	95	.563	1.81	2.42
	9 ML YEARS		401	0	205	395.2	1561	303	140	135	41	13	8	6	80	11	463	7	23	23	.500	111-133	75	94	.592	2.16	3.07

Tommy Doyle

Pitches: R **Bats:** R **Pos:** RP-3   **Ht:** 6'6" **Wt:** 244 **Born:** 5/1/1996 **Age:** 25

Year	Team	Lg	G	GS	GF	IP	BFP	H	R	ER	HR	SH	SF	HB	TBB	IBB	SO	WP	W	L	Pct	Sv-Op	Hld	Vel	OPS	ERC	ERA
2020	Col	NL	3	0	2	2.1	17	6	6	6	0	0	0	0	4	0	2	0	0	0	-	0-0	0	95	1.357	19.73	23.14

Brian Dozier

Bats: R **Throws:** R **Pos:** 2B-5;DH-1;PH-1   DOE-zhur   **Ht:** 5'11" **Wt:** 200 **Born:** 5/15/1987 **Age:** 34

Year	Team	Lg	G	AB	H	2B	3B	HR	(Hm	Rd)	TB	R	RBI	RC	TBB	IBB	SO	HBP	SH	SF	SB	CS	GDP	Avg	OBP	Slg	OPS
2012	Min	AL	84	316	74	11	1	6	(4	2)	105	33	33	24	16	0	58	1	4	3	9	2	10	.234	.271	.332	.603
2013	Min	AL	147	558	136	33	4	18	(8	10)	231	72	66	74	51	0	120	6	3	4	14	7	14	.244	.312	.414	.726
2014	Min	AL	156	598	145	33	1	23	(11	12)	249	112	71	87	89	1	129	9	3	8	21	7	8	.242	.345	.416	.762
2015	Min	AL	157	628	148	39	4	28	(13	15)	279	101	77	87	61	2	148	7	0	8	12	4	10	.236	.307	.444	.751
2016	Min	AL	155	615	165	35	5	42	(21	21)	336	104	99	102	61	6	138	8	2	5	18	2	12	.268	.340	.546	.886
2017	Min	AL	152	617	167	30	4	34	(18	16)	307	106	93	106	78	6	141	8	0	2	16	7	11	.271	.359	.498	.856
2018	2 Tms		151	553	119	30	2	21	(7	14)	216	81	72	69	70	1	129	4	0	5	12	3	12	.215	.305	.391	.696
2019	Was	NL	135	416	99	20	0	20	(10	10)	179	54	50	58	61	2	105	4	0	1	3	4	11	.238	.340	.430	.771
2020	NYM	NL	7	15	2	0	0	0	(0	0)	2	1	0	0	1	0	5	0	0	0	0	0	1	.133	.188	.133	.321
18	Min		104	410	93	21	2	16	(5	11)	166	65	52	47	46	1	96	3	0	3	8	3	7	.227	.307	.405	.712
18	LAD	NL	47	143	26	9	0	5	(2	3)	50	16	20	22	24	0	33	1	0	2	4	0	5	.182	.300	.350	.650
	Postseason		20	26	4	0	0	1	(0	1)	7	4	3	2	7	0	8	1	0	0	1	1	0	.154	.353	.269	.622
	9 ML YEARS		1144	4316	1055	231	21	192	(92	100)	1904	664	561	607	488	18	973	47	12	36	105	36	89	.244	.325	.441	.767

Hunter Dozier

Bats: R **Throws:** R **Pos:** 1B-28;RF-18;LF-2;3B-1   DOE-zhur   **Ht:** 6'4" **Wt:** 220 **Born:** 8/22/1991 **Age:** 29

Year	Team	Lg	G	AB	H	2B	3B	HR	(Hm	Rd)	TB	R	RBI	RC	TBB	IBB	SO	HBP	SH	SF	SB	CS	GDP	Avg	OBP	Slg	OPS
2016	KC	AL	8	19	4	1	0	0	(0	0)	5	4	1	1	2	0	8	0	0	0	0	0	0	.211	.286	.263	.549
2018	KC	AL	102	362	83	19	4	11	(5	6)	143	36	34	26	24	0	109	1	0	1	2	3	12	.229	.278	.395	.673
2019	KC	AL	139	523	146	29	10	26	(8	18)	273	75	84	91	55	2	148	3	0	5	2	2	9	.279	.348	.522	.870
2020	KC	AL	44	158	36	4	2	6	(4	2)	62	29	12	20	27	0	48	1	0	0	4	0	3	.228	.344	.392	.736
	4 ML YEARS		293	1062	269	53	16	43	(17	26)	483	144	131	138	108	2	313	5	0	6	8	5	24	.253	.323	.455	.778

Oliver Drake

Pitches: R **Bats:** R **Pos:** RP-11   **Ht:** 6'4" **Wt:** 220 **Born:** 1/13/1987 **Age:** 34

Year	Team	Lg	G	GS	GF	IP	BFP	H	R	ER	HR	SH	SF	HB	TBB	IBB	SO	WP	W	L	Pct	Sv-Op	Hld	Vel	OPS	ERC	ERA
2015	Bal	AL	13	0	5	15.2	72	16	7	5	1	0	2	0	9	0	17	3	0	0	-	0-0	2	91	.708	4.50	2.87
2016	Bal	AL	14	0	5	18.0	74	11	11	8	2	1	0	0	7	0	21	1	1	0	1.000	0-1	9	90	.595	2.01	4.00
2017	2 Tms		64	0	15	56.0	251	63	31	29	6	3	0	0	25	2	62	3	3	5	.375	1-4	5	92	.808	4.96	4.66
2018	5 Tms		44	0	19	47.2	209	52	29	28	4	1	0	1	17	1	51	5	1	1	.500	0-1	5	92	.758	4.33	5.29
2019	TB	AL	50	0	9	56.0	219	36	20	20	9	0	0	1	19	1	70	1	5	2	.714	2-3	10	94	.612	2.43	3.21
2020	TB	AL	11	0	4	11.0	45	7	8	7	2	1	1	0	6	1	7	1	0	2	.000	2-4	1	91	.701	3.10	5.73
17	Bal		3	0	1	3.1	18	6	3	3	0	0	0	0	3	0	3	1	0	0	-	0-0	0	92	1.033	10.76	8.10
17	Mil	NL	61	0	14	52.2	233	57	28	26	6	3	0	0	22	2	59	2	3	5	.375	1-4	5	92	.791	4.63	4.44
18	Mil	NL	11	0	3	12.2	58	14	9	9	0	1	0	0	8	1	15	2	1	0	1.000	0-1	2	92	.794	4.71	6.39
18	Cle		4	0	0	4.1	22	7	6	6	0	0	0	1	1	0	4	0	0	0	-	0-0	0	93	.859	7.03	12.46
18	LAA	AL	8	0	6	8.2	40	15	5	5	2	0	0	0	1	0	8	0	0	1	.000	0-0	0	93	.990	8.66	5.19
18	Tor	AL	2	0	2	1.2	9	4	3	3	0	0	0	0	0	0	2	1	0	0	-	0-0	1	92	1.333	10.16	16.20
18	Min	AL	19	0	8	20.1	80	12	6	5	2	0	0	0	7	0	22	2	0	0	-	0-0	1	92	.511	1.77	2.21
	Postseason		2	0	0	3.0	13	3	2	2	0	0	0	0	1	0	4	0	0	0	-	0-0	0	94	.724	3.05	6.00
	6 ML YEARS		196	0	57	204.1	870	185	106	97	24	6	3	2	83	5	228	14	10	10	.500	5-13	19	92	.715	3.68	4.27

Brandon Drury

Bats: R Throws: R Pos: 3B-16;2B-4;SS-2;PH-1   DROO-ree   Ht: 6'2" Wt: 230 Born: 8/21/1992 Age: 28

Year	Team	Lg	G	AB	H	2B	3B	HR	(Hm	Rd)	TB	R	RBI	RC	TBB	IBB	SO	HBP	SH	SF	SB	CS	GDP	Avg	OBP	Slg	OPS
2015	Ari	NL	20	56	12	3	0	2	(0	2)	21	3	8	4	2	0	8	1	0	0	0	0	5	.214	.254	.375	.629
2016	Ari	NL	134	461	130	31	1	16	(12	4)	211	59	53	59	31	2	100	3	0	4	1	1	14	.282	.329	.458	.786
2017	Ari	NL	135	445	119	37	2	13	(7	6)	199	41	63	62	28	1	103	5	0	2	1	1	9	.267	.317	.447	.764
2018	2 Tms	AL	26	77	13	4	0	1	(0	1)	20	5	10	7	7	0	20	2	0	0	0	0	5	.169	.256	.260	.516
2019	Tor	AL	120	418	91	21	1	15	(9	6)	159	43	41	37	25	0	113	1	0	3	0	1	6	.218	.262	.380	.642
2020	Tor	AL	21	46	7	1	0	0	(0	0)	8	3	1	0	2	0	9	0	0	1	0	0	0	.152	.184	.174	.358
18	NYY	AL	18	51	9	2	0	1	(0	1)	14	2	7	5	5	0	12	1	0	0	0	0	4	.176	.263	.275	.538
18	Tor	AL	8	26	4	2	0	0	(0	0)	6	3	3	2	2	0	8	1	0	0	0	0	1	.154	.241	.231	.472
	Postseason		3	6	1	0	0	1	(0	1)	4	1	3	1	0	0	2	0	0	0	0	0	2	.167	.167	.667	.833
	6 ML YEARS		456	1503	372	97	4	47	(28	19)	618	154	176	169	95	3	353	12	0	10	2	3	39	.248	.296	.411	.707

Mauricio Dubon

Bats: R Throws: R Pos: CF-44;2B-8;SS-8;PH-1   Ht: 6'0" Wt: 173 Born: 7/19/1994 Age: 26

Year	Team	Lg	G	AB	H	2B	3B	HR	(Hm	Rd)	TB	R	RBI	RC	TBB	IBB	SO	HBP	SH	SF	SB	CS	GDP	Avg	OBP	Slg	OPS
2019	2 Tms	NL	30	106	29	5	0	4	(2	2)	46	12	9	11	5	0	20	0	0	0	3	1	3	.274	.306	.434	.740
2020	SF	NL	54	157	43	4	1	4	(3	1)	61	21	19	22	15	0	36	1	1	2	2	3	4	.274	.337	.389	.726
19	Mil	NL	2	2	0	0	0	0	(0	0)	0	0	0	0	0	0	1	0	0	0	0	0	0	.000	.000	.000	.000
19	SF	NL	28	104	29	5	0	4	(2	2)	46	12	9	11	5	0	19	0	0	0	3	1	3	.279	.312	.442	.754
	2 ML YEARS		84	263	72	9	1	8	(5	3)	107	33	28	33	20	0	56	1	1	2	5	4	7	.274	.325	.407	.732

Tyler Duffey

Pitches: R Bats: R Pos: RP-22   Ht: 6'3" Wt: 220 Born: 12/27/1990 Age: 30

Year	Team	Lg	G	GS	GF	IP	BFP	H	R	ER	HR	SH	SF	HB	TBB	IBB	SO	WP	W	L	Pct	Sv-Op	Hld	Vel	OPS	ERC	ERA
2015	Min	AL	10	10	0	58.0	242	56	20	20	4	3	0	0	20	0	53	1	5	1	.833	0-0	0	90	.702	3.51	3.10
2016	Min	AL	26	26	0	133.0	596	167	103	95	25	2	2	6	32	3	114	9	9	12	.429	0-0	0	90	.876	5.66	6.43
2017	Min	AL	56	0	7	71.0	310	79	41	39	9	1	3	1	18	5	67	4	2	3	.400	1-3	12	92	.721	4.17	4.94
2018	Min	AL	19	1	4	25.0	107	26	22	20	6	0	2	1	4	0	19	2	2	2	.500	0-0	2	93	.830	4.29	7.20
2019	Min	AL	58	0	12	57.2	238	44	23	16	8	1	1	3	14	1	82	3	5	1	.833	0-2	15	94	.595	2.55	2.50
2020	Min	AL	22	0	1	24.0	92	13	6	5	2	0	0	1	6	0	31	0	1	1	.500	0-2	12	93	.488	1.43	1.88
	Postseason		2	0	0	1.2	11	3	4	4	1	0	1	1	2	0	4	0	0	0		0-0	0	94	1.545	21.45	21.60
	6 ML YEARS		191	37	24	368.2	1585	385	215	195	54	7	8	12	94	9	366	19	24	20	.545	1-7	41	92	.752	4.10	4.76

Danny Duffy

Pitches: L Bats: L Pos: SP-11; RP-1   Ht: 6'3" Wt: 185 Born: 12/21/1988 Age: 32

Year	Team	Lg	G	GS	GF	IP	BFP	H	R	ER	HR	SH	SF	HB	TBB	IBB	SO	WP	W	L	Pct	Sv-Op	Hld	Vel	OPS	ERC	ERA
2011	KC	AL	20	20	0	105.1	474	119	66	66	15	2	2	5	51	1	87	4	4	8	.333	0-0	0	93	.864	5.76	5.64
2012	KC	AL	6	6	0	27.2	121	26	13	12	2	0	0	0	18	1	28	0	2	2	.500	0-0	0	95	.771	4.58	3.90
2013	KC	AL	5	5	0	24.1	104	19	5	5	0	0	0	1	14	0	22	2	2	0	1.000	0-0	0	94	.608	3.02	1.85
2014	KC	AL	31	25	1	149.1	606	113	52	42	12	3	4	5	53	2	113	5	9	12	.429	0-0	1	93	.605	2.62	2.53
2015	KC	AL	30	24	1	136.2	588	137	64	62	15	3	5	9	53	0	102	11	7	8	.467	1-1	2	94	.746	4.44	4.08
2016	KC	AL	42	26	5	179.2	731	163	71	70	27	4	2	7	42	0	188	4	12	3	.800	0-0	1	95	.710	3.44	3.51
2017	KC	AL	24	24	0	146.1	609	143	67	62	13	6	2	4	41	0	130	2	9	10	.474	0-0	0	93	.709	3.55	3.81
2018	KC	AL	28	28	0	155.0	692	161	86	84	23	2	6	4	70	1	141	14	8	12	.400	0-0	0	93	.767	4.90	4.88
2019	KC	AL	23	23	0	130.2	555	125	69	63	21	0	3	8	46	0	115	4	7	6	.538	0-0	0	92	.760	4.35	4.34
2020	KC	AL	12	11	0	56.1	242	53	33	31	10	1	4	2	22	0	57	3	4	4	.500	0-0	1	92	.756	4.37	4.95
	Postseason		9	0	1	10.2	44	10	6	6	2	1	1	0	4	0	14	0	2	0	1.000	0-0	0	95	.878	4.35	5.06
	10 ML YEARS		221	192	7	1111.1	4722	1059	526	497	138	21	28	45	410	5	983	49	64	65	.496	1-1	5	93	.732	4.04	4.02

Steven Duggar

Bats: L Throws: R Pos: LF-11;RF-7;CF-4;PR-3;PH-1   Ht: 6'1" Wt: 187 Born: 11/4/1993 Age: 27

Year	Team	Lg	G	AB	H	2B	3B	HR	(Hm	Rd)	TB	R	RBI	RC	TBB	IBB	SO	HBP	SH	SF	SB	CS	GDP	Avg	OBP	Slg	OPS
2018	SF	NL	41	141	36	11	1	2	(1	1)	55	20	17	19	10	1	44	0	0	1	5	1	0	.255	.303	.390	.693
2019	SF	NL	73	261	61	12	2	4	(1	3)	89	26	28	29	16	0	78	1	0	3	1	4	1	.234	.278	.341	.619
2020	SF	NL	21	34	6	2	0	0	(0	0)	8	3	3	1	1	0	11	1	0	0	1	0	1	.176	.222	.235	.458
	3 ML YEARS		135	436	103	25	3	6	(2	4)	152	49	48	49	27	1	133	2	0	4	7	5	2	.236	.281	.349	.630

Robert Dugger

Pitches: R Bats: R Pos: RP-3; SP-1   Ht: 6'0" Wt: 198 Born: 7/3/1995 Age: 25

Year	Team	Lg	G	GS	GF	IP	BFP	H	R	ER	HR	SH	SF	HB	TBB	IBB	SO	WP	W	L	Pct	Sv-Op	Hld	Vel	OPS	ERC	ERA
2019	Mia	NL	7	7	0	34.1	156	33	26	22	6	1	3	5	17	1	25	2	0	4	.000	0-0	0	90	.824	5.29	5.77
2020	Mia	NL	4	1	2	10.2	56	21	16	15	5	0	0	0	3	0	4	1	0	0	-	0-0	0	92	1.315	12.95	12.66
	2 ML YEARS		11	8	2	45.0	212	54	42	37	11	1	3	5	20	1	29	3	0	4	.000	0-0	0	90	.965	6.94	7.40

Justin Dunn

Pitches: R **Bats:** R **Pos:** SP-10   **Ht:** 6'2" **Wt:** 185 **Born:** 9/22/1995 **Age:** 25

Year	Team	Lg	G	GS	GF	IP	BFP	H	R	ER	HR	SH	SF	HB	TBB	IBB	SO	WP	W	L	Pct	Sv-Op	Hld	Vel	OPS	ERC	ERA
2019	Sea	AL	4	4	0	6.2	30	2	2	2	0	2	0	0	9	0	5	0	0	0	-	0-0	0	92	.472	3.04	2.70
2020	Sea	AL	10	10	0	45.2	198	31	23	22	10	0	1	2	31	1	38	0	4	1	.800	0-0	0	91	.732	4.34	4.34
	2 ML YEARS		14	14	0	52.1	228	33	25	24	10	0	3	2	40	1	43	0	4	1	.800	0-0	0	91	.706	4.21	4.13

Dane Dunning

Pitches: R **Bats:** R **Pos:** SP-7   **Ht:** 6'4" **Wt:** 225 **Born:** 12/20/1994 **Age:** 26

Year	Team	Lg	G	GS	GF	IP	BFP	H	R	ER	HR	SH	SF	HB	TBB	IBB	SO	WP	W	L	Pct	Sv-Op	Hld	Vel	OPS	ERC	ERA
2020	CWS	AL	7	7	0	34.0	142	25	17	15	4	0	0	2	13	0	35	5	2	0	1.000	0-0	0	92	.597	2.88	3.97

Adam Duvall

Bats: R **Throws:** R **Pos:** LF-45;RF-17;PH-5;CF-1;DH-1   **Ht:** 6'1" **Wt:** 215 **Born:** 9/4/1988 **Age:** 32

Year	Team	Lg	G	AB	H	2B	3B	HR	(Hm	Rd)	TB	R	RBI	RC	TBB	IBB	SO	HBP	SH	SF	SB	CS	GDP	Avg	OBP	Slg	OPS
2014	SF	NL	28	73	14	2	0	3	(2	1)	25	8	5	4	3	0	20	1	0	0	0	0	0	.192	.234	.342	.576
2015	Cin	NL	27	64	14	2	0	5	(3	2)	31	6	9	9	6	1	26	2	0	0	0	0	0	.219	.306	.484	.790
2016	Cin	NL	150	552	133	31	6	33	(16	17)	275	85	103	80	41	1	164	6	0	8	6	5	7	.241	.297	.498	.795
2017	Cin	NL	157	587	146	37	3	31	(12	19)	282	78	99	75	39	1	170	10	0	11	5	3	11	.249	.301	.480	.782
2018	2 Tms	NL	138	384	75	20	0	15	(8	7)	140	48	61	37	37	3	117	5	0	1	2	2	9	.195	.274	.365	.639
2019	Atl	NL	41	120	32	4	1	10	(4	6)	68	17	19	19	7	0	39	2	0	1	0	0	0	.267	.315	.567	.882
2020	Atl	NL	57	190	45	8	0	16	(7	9)	101	34	33	24	15	0	54	3	0	1	0	0	2	.237	.301	.532	.833
18	Cin	NL	105	331	68	19	0	15	(8	7)	132	40	61	37	34	3	100	4	0	1	2	2	8	.205	.286	.399	.685
18	Atl	NL	33	53	7	1	0	0	(0	0)	8	8	0	0	3	0	17	1	0	0	0	0	1	.132	.193	.151	.344
	Postseason		5	11	3	0	0	1	(1	0)	6	2	5	2	1	1	5	0	0	0	0	0	0	.273	.333	.545	.879
	7 ML YEARS		598	1970	459	104	10	113	(52	61)	922	276	329	248	148	6	590	29	0	22	13	10	29	.233	.293	.468	.761

Jarrod Dyson

Bats: L **Throws:** R **Pos:** CF-23;PR-8;LF-6;DH-2;RF-1;PH-1   juh-ROD   **Ht:** 5'9" **Wt:** 165 **Born:** 8/15/1984 **Age:** 36

Year	Team	Lg	G	AB	H	2B	3B	HR	(Hm	Rd)	TB	R	RBI	RC	TBB	IBB	SO	HBP	SH	SF	SB	CS	GDP	Avg	OBP	Slg	OPS
2010	KC	AL	18	57	12	4	2	1	(1	0)	23	11	5	9	6	0	16	0	2	0	9	1	2	.211	.286	.404	.689
2011	KC	AL	26	44	9	1	0	0	(0	0)	10	8	3	7	7	0	14	0	1	1	11	1	0	.205	.308	.227	.535
2012	KC	AL	102	292	76	8	5	0	(0	0)	94	52	9	36	30	1	56	1	4	3	30	5	5	.260	.328	.322	.650
2013	KC	AL	87	213	55	9	4	2	(2	0)	78	30	17	28	21	1	45	1	3	1	34	6	4	.258	.326	.366	.692
2014	KC	AL	120	260	70	4	4	1	(1	0)	85	33	24	32	22	0	52	0	6	2	36	7	5	.269	.324	.327	.651
2015	KC	AL	90	200	50	8	6	2	(2	0)	76	31	18	25	14	0	37	4	6	1	26	3	3	.250	.311	.380	.691
2016	KC	AL	107	299	83	14	8	1	(1	0)	116	46	25	45	26	2	39	3	8	1	30	7	4	.278	.340	.388	.728
2017	Sea	AL	111	346	87	13	3	5	(2	3)	121	56	30	40	28	2	55	10	4	2	28	7	3	.251	.324	.350	.674
2018	Ari	NL	67	206	39	4	2	2	(0	2)	53	29	12	19	27	2	34	0	3	1	16	3	3	.189	.282	.257	.539
2019	Ari	NL	130	400	92	11	2	7	(1	6)	128	65	27	52	47	0	86	2	1	2	30	4	1	.230	.313	.320	.633
2020	2 Tms		32	61	11	0	0	0	(0	0)	11	9	5	5	4	0	11	0	1	0	6	0	0	.180	.231	.180	.411
20	Pit	NL	21	51	8	0	0	0	(0	0)	8	6	5	4	4	0	10	0	0	0	4	0	0	.157	.218	.157	.375
20	CWS		11	10	3	0	0	0	(0	0)	3	3	0	1	0	0	1	0	1	0	2	0	0	.300	.300	.300	.600
	Postseason		19	20	2	0	0	0	(0	0)	2	3	0	0	2	0	6	0	1	0	4	2	1	.100	.182	.100	.282
	11 ML YEARS		890	2378	584	76	36	21	(10	11)	795	370	175	298	232	8	445	21	39	14	256	44	30	.246	.316	.334	.651

Adam Eaton

Bats: L **Throws:** L **Pos:** RF-41;PH-1   **Ht:** 5'9" **Wt:** 176 **Born:** 12/6/1988 **Age:** 32

Year	Team	Lg	G	AB	H	2B	3B	HR	(Hm	Rd)	TB	R	RBI	RC	TBB	IBB	SO	HBP	SH	SF	SB	CS	GDP	Avg	OBP	Slg	OPS
2012	Ari	NL	22	85	22	3	2	2	(1	1)	35	19	5	14	14	0	15	3	1	0	2	3	0	.259	.382	.412	.794
2013	Ari	NL	66	250	63	10	4	3	(2	1)	90	40	22	27	17	0	44	6	3	1	5	2	4	.252	.314	.360	.674
2014	CWS	AL	123	486	146	26	10	1	(1	0)	195	76	35	77	43	0	83	5	2	2	15	9	4	.300	.362	.401	.763
2015	CWS	AL	153	610	175	28	9	14	(6	8)	263	98	56	96	58	2	131	14	5	2	18	8	5	.287	.361	.431	.792
2016	CWS	AL	157	619	176	29	9	14	(7	7)	265	91	59	92	63	2	115	14	7	3	14	5	6	.284	.362	.428	.790
2017	Was	NL	23	91	27	7	1	2	(1	1)	42	24	13	19	14	0	18	1	0	1	3	1	0	.297	.393	.462	.854
2018	Was	NL	95	319	96	18	1	5	(1	4)	131	55	33	58	38	0	64	11	2	0	9	1	2	.301	.394	.411	.805
2019	Was	NL	151	566	158	25	7	15	(8	7)	242	103	49	88	65	0	106	13	9	3	15	3	8	.279	.365	.428	.792
2020	Was	NL	41	159	36	11	1	4	(4	0)	61	22	17	22	12	1	32	1	4	0	3	0	4	.226	.285	.384	.669
	Postseason		17	61	15	2	1	2	(0	2)	25	11	10	12	10	0	9	1	3	0	1	0	1	.246	.361	.410	.771
	9 ML YEARS		831	3185	899	157	44	60	(31	29)	1324	528	289	492	324	5	608	68	33	12	84	32	33	.282	.360	.416	.775

Tommy Edman

Bats: B **Throws:** R **Pos:** 3B-31;SS-13;RF-13;2B-8;LF-8;PH-1   **Ht:** 5'10" **Wt:** 180 **Born:** 5/9/1995 **Age:** 26

Year	Team	Lg	G	AB	H	2B	3B	HR	(Hm	Rd)	TB	R	RBI	RC	TBB	IBB	SO	HBP	SH	SF	SB	CS	GDP	Avg	OBP	Slg	OPS
2019	StL	NL	92	326	99	17	7	11	(4	7)	163	59	36	52	16	0	61	7	0	0	15	1	3	.304	.350	.500	.850
2020	StL	NL	55	204	51	7	1	5	(3	2)	75	29	26	26	16	0	48	5	0	2	2	4	5	.250	.317	.368	.685
	Postseason		9	33	6	3	1	0	(0	0)	11	3	3	4	3	0	7	0	0	0	1	0	1	.182	.250	.333	.583
	2 ML YEARS		147	530	150	24	8	16	(7	9)	238	88	62	78	32	0	109	12	0	2	17	5	8	.283	.337	.449	.786

Carl Edwards Jr.

Pitches: R **Bats:** R **Pos:** RP-5   **Ht:** 6'3" **Wt:** 170 **Born:** 9/3/1991 **Age:** 29

			HOW MUCH PITCHED					WHAT HE GAVE UP									THE RESULTS							
Year	Team	Lg	G	GS	GF	IP	BFP	H	R	ER	HR	SH	SF	HB	TBB	IBB	SO	WP	W	L	Pct	Sv-Op	Hld	Vel	OPS	ERC	ERA
2015	ChC	NL	5	0	3	4.2	19	3	3	2	0	0	0	0	3	0	4	0	0	0	-	0-0	0	93	.566	2.50	3.86
2016	ChC	NL	36	0	10	36.0	138	15	15	15	4	0	2	0	14	1	52	5	0	1	.000	2-3	6	95	.456	1.33	3.75
2017	ChC	NL	73	0	8	66.1	262	29	22	22	6	1	1	4	38	2	94	4	5	4	.556	0-4	25	95	.503	1.99	2.98
2018	ChC	NL	58	0	2	52.0	222	36	17	15	2	1	0	0	32	1	67	4	3	2	.600	0-2	23	95	.583	2.75	2.60
2019	2 Tms	NL	22	0	4	17.0	78	12	17	16	3	0	1	1	13	0	19	4	1	1	.500	0-2	4	94	.683	4.48	8.47
2020	Sea	AL	5	0	1	4.2	17	2	1	1	0	0	0	0	6	0	6	0	0	0	-	1-1	1	93	.489	0.71	1.93
19	ChC	NL	20	0	3	15.1	64	8	11	10	3	0	1	1	9	0	17	2	1	1	.500	0-2	4	94	.621	3.05	5.87
19	SD	NL	2	0	1	1.2	14	4	6	6	0	0	0	0	4	0	2	2	0	0	-	0-0	0	94	.971	20.14	32.40
	Postseason		15	0	0	11.0	48	7	8	8	1	1	0	0	10	0	12	2	1	2	.333	0-1	5	95	.632	4.04	6.55
	6 ML YEARS		199	0	28	180.2	736	97	75	71	15	2	4	5	101	4	242	17	9	8	.529	3-12	59	95	.539	2.22	3.54

Zach Eflin

Pitches: R **Bats:** R **Pos:** SP-10; RP-1   **Ht:** 6'6" **Wt:** 220 **Born:** 4/8/1994 **Age:** 27

			HOW MUCH PITCHED					WHAT HE GAVE UP									THE RESULTS							
Year	Team	Lg	G	GS	GF	IP	BFP	H	R	ER	HR	SH	SF	HB	TBB	IBB	SO	WP	W	L	Pct	Sv-Op	Hld	Vel	OPS	ERC	ERA
2016	Phi	NL	11	11	0	63.1	272	67	42	39	12	1	4	1	17	1	31	1	3	5	.375	0-0	0	92	.828	4.49	5.54
2017	Phi	NL	11	11	0	64.1	280	79	45	44	16	2	5	5	12	0	35	2	1	5	.167	0-0	0	93	.896	6.00	6.16
2018	Phi	NL	24	24	0	128.0	548	130	69	62	16	5	4	3	37	4	123	4	11	8	.579	0-0	0	94	.746	3.90	4.36
2019	Phi	NL	32	28	3	163.1	705	172	88	75	28	6	3	6	48	5	129	1	10	13	.435	0-0	0	94	.775	4.53	4.13
2020	Phi	NL	11	10	0	59.0	245	60	28	26	8	1	0	1	15	0	70	1	4	2	.667	0-0	0	94	.759	3.96	3.97
	5 ML YEARS		89	84	3	478.0	2050	508	272	246	80	15	16	16	129	10	388	9	29	33	.468	0-0	0	93	.789	4.47	4.63

Brett Eibner

Pitches: R **Bats:** R **Pos:** RP-3   eye-b-nur   **Ht:** 6'4" **Wt:** 215 **Born:** 12/2/1988 **Age:** 32

			HOW MUCH PITCHED					WHAT HE GAVE UP									THE RESULTS							
Year	Team	Lg	G	GS	GF	IP	BFP	H	R	ER	HR	SH	SF	HB	TBB	IBB	SO	WP	W	L	Pct	Sv-Op	Hld	Vel	OPS	ERC	ERA
2020	Mia	NL	3	0	2	3.1	21	7	7	5	2	0	0	0	4	1	4	1	0	0	-	0-0	0	94	1.347	19.78	13.50

Roenis Elias

Pitches: L **Bats:** L **Pos:** P   roh-EN-ees ehl-LEE-us   **Ht:** 6'1" **Wt:** 205 **Born:** 8/1/1988 **Age:** 32

			HOW MUCH PITCHED					WHAT HE GAVE UP									THE RESULTS							
Year	Team	Lg	G	GS	GF	IP	BFP	H	R	ER	HR	SH	SF	HB	TBB	IBB	SO	WP	W	L	Pct	Sv-Op	Hld	Vel	OPS	ERC	ERA
2014	Sea	AL	29	29	0	163.2	693	151	77	70	16	4	4	11	64	3	143	6	10	12	.455	0-0	0	92	.713	3.89	3.85
2015	Sea	AL	22	20	0	115.1	490	106	57	53	15	1	4	9	44	1	97	1	5	8	.385	0-0	1	92	.730	4.10	4.14
2016	Bos	AL	3	1	2	7.2	41	15	11	11	2	0	0	0	5	1	3	0	0	1	.000	0-0	0	93	1.210	13.11	12.91
2017	Bos	AL	1	0	1	0.1	2	0	0	0	0	0	0	0	1	0	1	0	0	0	-	0-0	0	92	.500	7.00	0.00
2018	Sea	AL	23	4	13	51.0	210	46	17	15	1	0	3	1	16	1	34	3	3	1	.750	0-0	4	94	.642	2.76	2.65
2019	2 Tms	AL	48	0	28	50.0	216	46	32	22	10	1	1	1	18	1	47	1	4	2	.667	14-17	2	94	.728	4.09	3.96
19	Sea	AL	44	0	28	47.0	203	41	28	19	8	1	1	1	17	1	45	1	4	2	.667	14-16	1	94	.686	3.61	3.64
19	Was	NL	4	0	0	3.0	13	5	4	3	2	0	0	0	1	0	2	0	0	0	-	0-1	1	94	1.378	14.71	9.00
	6 ML YEARS		126	54	44	388.0	1652	364	194	171	44	6	12	22	148	7	325	11	22	24	.478	14-17	3	92	.723	3.98	3.97

Seth Elledge

Pitches: R **Bats:** R **Pos:** RP-12   **Ht:** 6'3" **Wt:** 240 **Born:** 5/20/1996 **Age:** 25

			HOW MUCH PITCHED					WHAT HE GAVE UP									THE RESULTS							
Year	Team	Lg	G	GS	GF	IP	BFP	H	R	ER	HR	SH	SF	HB	TBB	IBB	SO	WP	W	L	Pct	Sv-Op	Hld	Vel	OPS	ERC	ERA
2020	StL	NL	12	0	5	11.2	52	11	6	6	2	0	0	1	8	0	14	2	1	0	1.000	0-0	0	93	.964	6.03	4.63

Edwin Encarnacion

Bats: R **Throws:** R **Pos:** DH-43;PH-1   **Ht:** 6'1" **Wt:** 230 **Born:** 1/7/1983 **Age:** 38

			BATTING																			RUNNING			AVERAGES			
Year	Team	Lg	G	AB	H	2B	3B	HR	(Hm	Rd)	TB	R	RBI	RC	TBB	IBB	SO	HBP	SH	SF	SB	CS	GDP	Avg	OBP	Slg	OPS
2005	Cin	NL	69	211	49	16	0	9	(3	6)	92	25	31	24	20	2	60	3	0	0	8			.232	.308	.436	.744
2006	Cin	NL	117	406	112	33	1	15	(7	8)	192	60	72	66	41	3	78	13	0	3	6	3	9	.276	.359	.473	.831
2007	Cin	NL	139	502	145	25	1	16	(10	6)	220	66	76	86	39	4	86	14	0	1	8	1	5	.289	.356	.438	.794
2008	Cin	NL	146	506	127	29	1	26	(15	11)	236	75	68	72	61	1	102	10	0	5	1	0	13	.251	.340	.466	.807
2009	2 Tms		85	293	66	11	2	13	(5	8)	120	35	39	37	37	0	57	5	0	3	2	1	5	.225	.320	.410	.729
2010	Tor	AL	96	332	81	16	0	21	(7	14)	160	47	51	41	29	1	60	2	0	4	1	0	9	.244	.305	.482	.787
2011	Tor	AL	134	481	131	36	0	17	(14	3)	218	70	55	67	43	2	77	3	0	3	8	2	17	.272	.334	.453	.787
2012	Tor	AL	151	542	152	24	0	42	(23	19)	302	93	110	124	84	12	94	11	0	7	13	3	6	.280	.384	.557	.941
2013	Tor	AL	142	530	144	29	1	36	(12	24)	283	90	104	102	82	7	62	4	0	5	7	1	20	.272	.370	.534	.904
2014	Tor	AL	128	477	128	27	2	34	(19	15)	261	75	98	86	62	6	82	2	0	1	2	0	18	.268	.354	.547	.901
2015	Tor	AL	146	528	146	31	0	39	(18	21)	294	94	111	110	77	5	98	9	0	10	3	2	14	.277	.372	.557	.929
2016	Tor	AL	160	601	158	34	0	42	(20	22)	318	99	127	104	87	3	138	5	0	4	0	0	22	.263	.357	.529	.886
2017	Cle	AL	157	554	143	20	1	38	(15	23)	279	96	107	102	104	5	133	4	0	5	2	0	18	.258	.377	.504	.881
2018	Cle	AL	137	500	123	16	1	32	(16	16)	237	74	107	85	63	2	132	8	0	7	3	0	14	.246	.336	.474	.810
2019	2 Tms	AL	109	418	102	18	0	34	(17	17)	222	81	86	84	58	1	103	7	0	3	0	1	4	.244	.344	.531	.875
2020	CWS	AL	44	159	25	5	0	10	(6	4)	60	19	19	16	16	0	54	4	0	1	0	0	3	.157	.250	.377	.627
09	Cin	NL	43	139	29	6	1	5	(3	2)	52	10	16	19	24	0	38	2	0	1	1	1	3	.209	.333	.374	.707
09	Tor	AL	42	154	37	5	1	8	(2	6)	68	25	23	18	13	0	29	3	0	3	1	0	2	.240	.306	.442	.748

Year	Team	Lg	G	AB	H	2B	3B	HR	(Hm	Rd)	TB	R	RBI	RC	TBB	IBB	SO	HBP	SH	SF	SB	CS	GDP	Avg	OBP	Slg	OPS
19	Sea	AL	65	241	58	7	0	21	(9	12)	128	48	49	52	41	0	55	4	0	3	0	1	3	.241	.356	.531	.888
19	NYY	AL	44	177	44	11	0	13	(8	5)	94	33	37	32	17	1	48	3	0	0	0	0	1	.249	.325	.531	.856
	Postseason		34	123	27	6	0	4	(3	1)	45	14	16	18	19	5	33	1	0	0	0	0	2	.220	.329	.366	.695
	16 ML YEARS		1960	7040	1832	370	10	424	(207	217)	3494	1099	1261	1200	903	54	1426	105	0	66	61	14	185	.260	.350	.496	.846

Adam Engel

Bats: R Throws: R Pos: RF-25;LF-9;PR-6;PH-4;CF-3　　　　**Ht: 6'2" Wt: 220 Born: 12/9/1991 Age: 29**

Year	Team	Lg	G	AB	H	2B	3B	HR	(Hm	Rd)	TB	R	RBI	RC	TBB	IBB	SO	HBP	SH	SF	SB	CS	GDP	Avg	OBP	Slg	OPS
2017	CWS	AL	97	301	50	11	3	6	(4	2)	85	34	21	16	19	0	117	8	8	0	8	1	1	.166	.235	.282	.517
2018	CWS	AL	143	429	101	17	4	6	(4	2)	144	49	29	31	18	0	129	8	7	1	16	8	1	.235	.279	.336	.614
2019	CWS	AL	89	227	55	10	2	6	(3	3)	87	26	26	26	14	0	78	6	1	0	3	3	5	.242	.304	.383	.687
2020	CWS	AL	36	88	26	5	1	3	(2	1)	42	11	12	14	3	0	19	2	0	0	1	0	1	.295	.333	.477	.811
	4 ML YEARS		365	1045	232	43	10	21	(13	8)	358	120	88	87	54	0	343	24	16	1	28	12	8	.222	.276	.343	.618

Nathan Eovaldi

Pitches: R Bats: R Pos: SP-9　　ee-VAUL-dee　　**Ht: 6'2" Wt: 217 Born: 2/13/1990 Age: 31**

Year	Team	Lg	G	GS	GF	IP	BFP	H	R	ER	HR	SH	SF	HB	TBB	IBB	SO	WP	W	L	Pct	Sv-Op	Hld	Vel	OPS	ERC	ERA
2011	LAD	NL	10	6	1	34.2	146	28	14	14	2	2	0	2	20	0	23	0	1	2	.333	0-0	1	94	.667	3.75	3.63
2012	2 Tms	NL	22	22	0	119.1	526	133	59	57	10	1	6	3	47	3	78	1	4	13	.235	0-0	0	94	.771	4.67	4.30
2013	Mia	NL	18	18	0	106.1	451	100	44	40	7	6	1	4	40	3	78	3	4	6	.400	0-0	0	96	.681	3.41	4.37
2014	Mia	NL	33	33	0	199.2	854	223	107	97	14	9	5	7	43	5	142	6	6	14	.300	0-0	0	96	.732	3.89	4.37
2015	NYY	AL	27	27	0	154.1	673	175	72	72	10	3	3	3	49	0	121	8	14	3	.824	0-0	0	97	.716	4.34	4.20
2016	NYY	AL	24	21	0	124.2	525	123	66	66	23	1	1	1	40	2	97	5	9	8	.529	0-0	0	97	.778	4.30	4.76
2018	2 Tms	AL	22	21	0	111.0	455	105	55	47	14	1	4	3	20	1	101	4	6	7	.462	0-0	0	97	.685	3.18	3.81
2019	Bos	AL	23	12	2	67.2	302	72	46	45	16	1	2	3	35	0	70	6	2	1	.667	0-1	4	98	.875	6.26	5.99
2020	Bos	AL	9	9	0	48.1	199	51	20	20	8	1	0	4	7	0	52	2	4	2	.667	0-0	0	97	.789	4.24	3.72
12	LAD	NL	10	10	0	56.1	241	63	27	26	5	0	3	0	20	0	34	1	1	6	.143	0-0	0	94	.771	4.54	4.15
12	Mia	NL	12	12	0	63.0	285	70	32	31	5	1	3	3	27	1	44	0	3	7	.300	0-0	0	94	.770	4.79	4.43
18	TB	AL	10	10	0	57.0	224	48	27	27	11	0	2	1	8	1	53	1	3	4	.429	0-0	0	97	.682	2.85	4.26
18	Bos	AL	12	11	0	54.0	231	57	28	20	3	1	2	2	12	0	48	3	3	3	.500	0-0	0	97	.687	3.48	3.33
	Postseason		6	2	1	22.1	85	15	5	4	1	1	0	0	3	0	16	0	2	1	.667	0-0	2	99	.449	1.34	1.61
	9 ML YEARS		188	169	5	966.0	4131	1010	483	458	104	25	22	27	301	14	762	35	50	56	.472	0-1	5	96	.740	4.14	4.27

Robbie Erlin

Pitches: L Bats: R Pos: SP-5; RP-4　　　　**Ht: 5'11" Wt: 200 Born: 10/8/1990 Age: 30**

Year	Team	Lg	G	GS	GF	IP	BFP	H	R	ER	HR	SH	SF	HB	TBB	IBB	SO	WP	W	L	Pct	Sv-Op	Hld	Vel	OPS	ERC	ERA
2013	SD	NL	11	9	2	54.2	227	53	26	25	6	3	1	0	15	0	40	3	3	3	.500	0-0	0	90	.698	3.50	4.12
2014	SD	NL	13	11	1	61.1	264	71	34	34	6	2	4	1	15	1	46	4	4	5	.444	0-0	0	90	.787	4.39	4.99
2015	SD	NL	3	3	0	17.0	65	16	9	9	1	0	0	1	2	0	10	1	1	2	.333	0-0	0	90	.663	2.84	4.76
2016	SD	NL	3	2	0	15.2	58	12	7	7	3	0	0	0	3	0	13	2	1	2	.333	0-0	0	88	.750	2.77	4.02
2018	SD	NL	39	12	8	109.0	439	112	57	51	12	3	5	0	12	0	88	2	4	7	.364	0-0	0	90	.695	3.20	4.21
2019	SD	NL	37	1	10	55.1	251	72	36	33	6	1	3	1	15	0	52	3	0	1	.000	0-1	5	91	.789	5.37	5.37
2020	2 Tms	NL	9	5	1	26.2	122	33	24	24	8	0	1	2	7	1	25	1	0	0	-	0-0	0	89	.987	6.51	8.10
20	Pit	NL	2	0	1	3.1	17	5	2	2	0	0	0	1	1	1	4	0	0	0	-	0-0	0	90	1.012	6.27	5.40
20	Atl	NL	7	5	0	23.1	105	28	22	22	8	0	1	1	6	0	21	1	0	0	-	0-0	0	89	.983	6.48	8.49
	7 ML YEARS		115	43	22	339.2	1426	369	193	183	42	9	14	5	69	2	274	16	13	20	.394	0-1	6	90	.754	4.01	4.85

Phillip Ervin

Bats: R Throws: R Pos: RF-19;PH-14;LF-10;CF-7;DH-1;PR-1　　　　**Ht: 5'10" Wt: 207 Born: 7/15/1992 Age: 28**

Year	Team	Lg	G	AB	H	2B	3B	HR	(Hm	Rd)	TB	R	RBI	RC	TBB	IBB	SO	HBP	SH	SF	SB	CS	GDP	Avg	OBP	Slg	OPS
2017	Cin	NL	28	58	15	2	0	3	(1	2)	26	8	10	10	4	0	15	1	1	0	4	1	1	.259	.317	.448	.766
2018	Cin	NL	78	218	55	10	1	7	(3	4)	88	27	31	27	20	1	60	5	0	4	6	1	5	.252	.324	.404	.728
2019	Cin	NL	94	236	64	11	7	7	(3	4)	110	30	23	32	18	0	63	4	0	2	4	3	4	.271	.331	.466	.797
2020	2 Tms	NL	37	74	11	3	0	0	(0	0)	14	10	4	6	14	0	22	1	0	0	1	0	2	.149	.292	.189	.481
20	Cin	NL	19	35	3	0	0	0	(0	0)	3	5	0	0	6	0	8	1	0	1	1	0	1	.086	.238	.086	.324
20	Sea	AL	18	39	8	3	0	0	(0	0)	11	5	4	6	8	0	14	0	0	0	0	0	1	.205	.340	.282	.622
	4 ML YEARS		237	586	145	26	8	17	(7	10)	238	75	68	75	56	1	160	11	1	6	15	5	12	.247	.322	.406	.728

Eduardo Escobar

Bats: B Throws: R Pos: 3B-47;DH-4;2B-3　　　　**Ht: 5'10" Wt: 210 Born: 1/5/1989 Age: 32**

Year	Team	Lg	G	AB	H	2B	3B	HR	(Hm	Rd)	TB	R	RBI	RC	TBB	IBB	SO	HBP	SH	SF	SB	CS	GDP	Avg	OBP	Slg	OPS
2011	CWS	AL	9	7	2	0	0	0	(0	0)	2	0	0	0	0	0	1	0	0	0	0	0	0	.286	.286	.286	.571
2012	2 Tms	AL	50	131	28	4	1	0	(0	0)	34	18	9	12	11	0	31	0	2	1	3	0	0	.214	.278	.260	.537
2013	Min	AL	66	165	39	5	2	3	(2	1)	57	23	10	14	11	0	34	0	2	1	0	2	0	.236	.282	.345	.628
2014	Min	AL	133	433	119	35	6	6	(2	4)	176	52	37	53	24	1	93	2	4	2	1	1	6	.275	.315	.406	.721
2015	Min	AL	127	409	107	31	4	12	(2	10)	182	48	58	55	28	1	86	2	2	5	2	3	7	.262	.309	.445	.754
2016	Min	AL	105	352	83	14	6	6	(3	3)	119	32	37	38	21	1	72	1	2	1	1	3	7	.236	.280	.338	.618
2017	Min	AL	129	457	116	16	5	21	(12	9)	205	62	73	72	33	3	98	5	1	3	5	1	5	.254	.309	.449	.758
2018	2 Tms		151	566	154	48	3	23	(9	14)	277	75	84	93	52	8	126	5	0	8	2	4	12	.272	.334	.489	.824
2019	Ari	NL	158	636	171	29	10	35	(18	17)	325	94	118	108	50	3	130	3	0	10	5	1	8	.269	.320	.511	.831

Year Team	Lg	G	AB	H	2B	3B	HR	(Hm Rd)	TB	R	RBI	RC	TBB	IBB	SO	HBP	SH	SF	SB	CS	GDP	Avg	OBP	Slg	OPS
2020 Ari	NL	54	203	43	7	3	4	(3 1)	68	22	20	19	15	4	41	2	0	2	1	0	5	.212	.270	.335	.605
12 CWS	AL	36	87	18	4	1	0	(0 0)	24	14	3	7	9	0	23	0	1	0	2	0	0	.207	.281	.276	.557
12 Min	AL	14	44	10	0	0	0	(0 0)	10	4	6	5	2	0	8	1	1	1	1	0	0	.227	.271	.227	.498
18 Min	AL	97	368	101	37	3	15	(7 8)	189	45	63	70	34	6	91	3	0	3	1	3	7	.274	.338	.514	.852
18 Ari	NL	54	198	53	11	0	8	(2 6)	88	30	21	23	18	2	35	2	0	5	1	1	5	.268	.327	.444	.772
Postseason		1	4	2	0	0	0	(0 0)	2	0	0	0	0	0	0	0	0	0	0	0	0	.500	.500	.500	1.000
10 ML YEARS		982	3359	862	189	32	110	(51 59)	1445	426	446	465	245	21	712	21	13	33	20	15	50	.257	.308	.430	.739

Thomas Eshelman

Pitches: R **Bats:** R **Pos:** RP-8; SP-4   **Ht:** 6'3" **Wt:** 210 **Born:** 6/20/1994 **Age:** 27

Year Team	Lg	G	GS	GF	IP	BFP	H	R	ER	HR	SH	SF	HB	TBB	IBB	SO	WP	W	L	Pct	Sv-Op	Hld	Vel	OPS	ERC	ERA
2019 Bal	AL	10	4	2	36.0	164	47	31	26	12	0	2	1	11	1	22	0	1	2	.333	0-0	0	86	.953	7.35	6.50
2020 Bal	AL	12	4	3	34.2	143	34	17	15	7	0	2	1	9	0	16	1	3	1	.750	0-1	0	86	.812	4.29	3.89
2 ML YEARS		22	8	5	70.2	307	81	48	41	19	0	4	2	20	1	38	1	4	3	.571	0-1	0	86	.887	5.79	5.22

Santiago Espinal

Bats: R **Throws:** R **Pos:** SS-21;PR-4;3B-2   **Ht:** 5'10" **Wt:** 181 **Born:** 11/13/1994 **Age:** 26

Year Team	Lg	G	AB	H	2B	3B	HR	(Hm Rd)	TB	R	RBI	RC	TBB	IBB	SO	HBP	SH	SF	SB	CS	GDP	Avg	OBP	Slg	OPS
2020 Tor	AL	27	60	16	4	0	0	(0 0)	20	10	6	6	4	0	16	0	1	1	1	0	1	.267	.308	.333	.641

Paolo Espino

Pitches: R **Bats:** R **Pos:** SP-1; RP-1   **Ht:** 5'10" **Wt:** 215 **Born:** 1/10/1987 **Age:** 34

Year Team	Lg	G	GS	GF	IP	BFP	H	R	ER	HR	SH	SF	HB	TBB	IBB	SO	WP	W	L	Pct	Sv-Op	Hld	Vel	OPS	ERC	ERA
2017 2 Tms		12	2	7	24.0	109	23	17	16	7	1	0	3	10	0	20	0	0	0	-	0-0	1	89	.870	5.64	6.00
2020 Was	NL	2	1	1	6.0	27	8	3	3	1	0	0	0	2	0	7	0	0	0	-	0-0	0	90	.850	6.38	4.50
17 Mil	NL	6	2	3	17.2	82	17	13	12	5	1	0	3	8	0	13	0	0	0	-	0-0	0	88	.860	5.94	6.11
17 Tex	AL	6	0	4	6.1	27	6	4	4	2	0	0	0	2	0	7	0	0	0	-	0-0	1	90	.896	4.79	5.68
2 ML YEARS		14	3	8	30.0	136	31	20	19	8	1	0	3	12	0	27	0	0	0	-	0-0	1	89	.866	5.79	5.70

Carlos Estevez

Pitches: R **Bats:** R **Pos:** RP-26   **Ht:** 6'6" **Wt:** 277 **Born:** 12/28/1992 **Age:** 28

Year Team	Lg	G	GS	GF	IP	BFP	H	R	ER	HR	SH	SF	HB	TBB	IBB	SO	WP	W	L	Pct	Sv-Op	Hld	Vel	OPS	ERC	ERA
2016 Col	NL	63	0	26	55.0	246	50	32	32	6	1	4	5	28	4	59	3	3	7	.300	11-18	11	97	.728	4.23	5.24
2017 Col	NL	35	0	9	32.1	149	39	21	20	3	1	0	1	14	2	31	1	5	0	1.000	0-0	6	97	.778	5.31	5.57
2019 Col	NL	71	0	13	72.0	308	70	34	30	12	1	3	1	23	1	81	1	2	2	.500	0-2	11	98	.756	4.03	3.75
2020 Col	NL	26	0	6	24.0	116	33	21	20	6	0	0	3	9	0	27	2	1	3	.250	1-4	6	97	1.003	7.91	7.50
Postseason		1	0	0	0.1	2	1	1	1	0	0	0	0	0	0	1	0	0	0	-	0-0	0	99	1.000	14.52	27.00
4 ML YEARS		195	0	54	183.1	819	192	108	102	27	3	7	10	74	7	198	7	11	12	.478	12-24	34	97	.788	4.79	5.01

Thairo Estrada

Bats: R **Throws:** R **Pos:** 2B-20;3B-6;SS-3;PR-3;PH-1   **Ht:** 5'10" **Wt:** 185 **Born:** 2/22/1996 **Age:** 25

Year Team	Lg	G	AB	H	2B	3B	HR	(Hm Rd)	TB	R	RBI	RC	TBB	IBB	SO	HBP	SH	SF	SB	CS	GDP	Avg	OBP	Slg	OPS
2019 NYY	AL	35	64	16	3	0	3	(1 2)	28	12	12	12	3	0	15	1	1	0	4	0	1	.250	.294	.438	.732
2020 NYY	AL	26	48	8	0	0	1	(1 0)	11	8	3	1	1	0	19	3	0	0	1	0	0	.167	.231	.229	.460
2 ML YEARS		61	112	24	3	0	4	(2 2)	39	20	15	13	4	0	34	4	1	0	5	0	1	.214	.267	.348	.615

Demarcus Evans

Pitches: R **Bats:** R **Pos:** RP-4   **Ht:** 6'5" **Wt:** 265 **Born:** 10/22/1996 **Age:** 24

Year Team	Lg	G	GS	GF	IP	BFP	H	R	ER	HR	SH	SF	HB	TBB	IBB	SO	WP	W	L	Pct	Sv-Op	Hld	Vel	OPS	ERC	ERA
2020 Tex	AL	4	0	0	4.0	14	3	1	1	1	0	0	1	0	0	4	0	0	0	-	0-0	0	94	.747	3.52	2.25

Phillip Evans

Bats: R **Throws:** R **Pos:** 3B-8;1B-1;LF-1;RF-1   **Ht:** 5'10" **Wt:** 210 **Born:** 9/10/1992 **Age:** 28

Year Team	Lg	G	AB	H	2B	3B	HR	(Hm Rd)	TB	R	RBI	RC	TBB	IBB	SO	HBP	SH	SF	SB	CS	GDP	Avg	OBP	Slg	OPS
2017 NYM	NL	19	33	10	2	0	0	(0 0)	12	4	1	5	4	0	8	1	0	0	0	0	0	.303	.395	.364	.758
2018 NYM	NL	15	21	3	0	0	0	(0 0)	3	1	1	1	2	0	8	0	0	0	1	0	1	.143	.217	.143	.360
2020 Pit	NL	11	39	14	2	0	1	(1 0)	19	6	9	12	5	0	7	1	0	0	0	1	1	.359	.444	.487	.932
3 ML YEARS		45	93	27	4	0	1	(1 0)	34	11	11	18	11	0	23	2	0	0	1	1	2	.290	.377	.366	.743

Pete Fairbanks

Pitches: R Bats: R Pos: RP-25; SP-2   Ht: 6'6" Wt: 225 Born: 12/16/1993 Age: 27

		HOW MUCH PITCHED					WHAT HE GAVE UP										THE RESULTS						
Year Team	Lg	G	GS	GF	IP	BFP	H	R	ER	HR	SH	SF	HB	TBB	IBB	SO	WP	W	L	Pct	Sv-Op	Hld	Vel	OPS	ERC	ERA
2019 2 Tms	AL	21	0	3	21.0	99	25	20	16	5	0	0	0	10	0	28	2	2	3	.400	2-2	3	97	.882	6.37	6.86
2020 TB	AL	27	2	2	26.2	117	23	9	8	2	0	0	2	14	0	39	6	6	3	.667	0-2	7	97	.640	3.89	2.70
19 Tex	AL	8	0	0	8.2	41	8	10	9	4	0	0	0	7	0	15	1	0	2	.000	0-0	0	97	.954	8.04	9.35
19 TB	AL	13	0	3	12.1	58	17	10	7	1	0	0	0	3	0	13	1	2	1	.667	2-2	3	98	.836	5.26	5.11
2 ML YEARS		48	2	5	47.2	216	48	29	24	7	0	0	2	24	0	67	8	8	6	.571	2-4	10	97	.753	4.96	4.53

Jeurys Familia

jer-ISS fa-MEAL-ya

Pitches: R Bats: R Pos: RP-25   Ht: 6'3" Wt: 240 Born: 10/10/1989 Age: 31

		HOW MUCH PITCHED					WHAT HE GAVE UP										THE RESULTS						
Year Team	Lg	G	GS	GF	IP	BFP	H	R	ER	HR	SH	SF	HB	TBB	IBB	SO	WP	W	L	Pct	Sv-Op	Hld	Vel	OPS	ERC	ERA
2012 NYM	NL	8	1	4	12.1	52	10	8	8	0	0	0	0	9	0	10	0	0	0	-	0-0	0	96	.644	3.76	5.84
2013 NYM	NL	9	0	3	10.2	52	12	5	5	2	2	0	0	9	1	8	3	0	0	-	1-1	0	95	.908	7.20	4.22
2014 NYM	NL	76	0	16	77.1	322	59	26	19	3	4	2	2	32	5	73	9	2	5	.286	5-10	23	96	.587	2.45	2.21
2015 NYM	NL	76	0	65	78.0	308	59	16	16	6	1	1	2	19	1	86	4	2	2	.500	43-48	1	97	.569	2.19	1.85
2016 NYM	NL	78	0	67	77.2	321	63	25	22	1	1	1	1	31	6	84	3	3	4	.429	51-56	0	96	.574	2.44	2.55
2017 NYM	NL	26	0	15	24.2	111	21	14	12	1	2	2	1	15	3	25	1	2	2	.500	6-7	2	96	.636	3.48	4.38
2018 2 Tms		70	0	36	72.0	302	60	26	25	3	0	1	2	28	1	83	2	8	6	.571	18-24	7	96	.601	2.81	3.13
2019 NYM	NL	66	0	14	60.0	274	62	39	38	7	2	1	3	42	4	63	3	4	2	.667	0-4	14	96	.831	5.84	5.70
2020 NYM	NL	25	0	4	26.2	120	20	11	11	2	0	0	3	19	2	23	1	2	0	1.000	0-1	5	97	.687	3.98	3.71
18 NYM	NL	40	0	29	40.2	171	36	13	13	1	0	1	2	14	1	43	1	4	4	.500	17-21	1	96	.616	2.88	2.88
18 Oak	AL	30	0	7	31.1	131	24	13	12	2	0	0	0	14	0	40	1	4	2	.667	1-3	6	97	.581	2.73	3.45
Postseason		14	0	11	16.2	60	7	5	4	2	0	0	0	3	0	11	0	0	1	.000	5-8	0	96	.412	0.97	2.16
9 ML YEARS		434	1	224	439.1	1862	366	170	156	25	13	8	14	204	23	455	26	23	21	.523	124-151	52	96	.638	3.16	3.20

Buck Farmer

Pitches: R Bats: L Pos: RP-23   Ht: 6'4" Wt: 232 Born: 2/20/1991 Age: 30

		HOW MUCH PITCHED					WHAT HE GAVE UP										THE RESULTS						
Year Team	Lg	G	GS	GF	IP	BFP	H	R	ER	HR	SH	SF	HB	TBB	IBB	SO	WP	W	L	Pct	Sv-Op	Hld	Vel	OPS	ERC	ERA
2014 Det	AL	4	2	1	9.1	46	12	12	12	2	0	0	2	5	0	11	0	0	1	.000	0-0	0	93	1.054	8.29	11.57
2015 Det	AL	14	5	0	40.1	186	53	35	33	10	1	1	3	17	2	24	1	0	4	.000	0-0	0	93	.986	7.65	7.36
2016 Det	AL	14	1	7	29.1	131	25	15	15	4	1	1	1	20	1	27	2	0	1	.000	0-0	0	93	.771	4.71	4.60
2017 Det	AL	11	11	0	48.0	219	55	38	36	9	0	2	4	20	0	49	1	5	5	.500	0-0	0	92	.843	5.99	6.75
2018 Det	AL	66	1	12	69.1	308	67	34	32	6	1	2	1	41	1	57	2	3	4	.429	0-0	7	94	.754	4.61	4.15
2019 Det	AL	73	1	8	67.2	288	62	32	28	8	4	4	5	24	2	73	4	6	6	.500	0-3	15	95	.743	3.81	3.72
2020 Det	AL	23	0	9	21.1	89	20	9	9	3	1	1	0	5	0	14	1	1	0	1.000	0-1	7	93	.674	3.29	3.80
7 ML YEARS		205	21	37	285.1	1267	294	175	165	42	8	11	16	132	6	255	11	15	21	.417	0-4	29	93	.808	5.06	5.20

Kyle Farmer

Bats: R Throws: R Pos: SS-15;2B-13;3B-2;LF-2;1B-1;PR-1   Ht: 6'0" Wt: 205 Born: 8/17/1990 Age: 30

		BATTING																			RUNNING			AVERAGES			
Year Team	Lg	G	AB	H	2B	3B	HR	(Hm	Rd)	TB	R	RBI	RC	TBB	IBB	SO	HBP	SH	SF	SB	CS	GDP	Avg	OBP	Slg	OPS
2017 LAD	NL	20	20	6	1	0	0	(0	0)	7	1	2	1	0	0	3	0	0	0	0	0	2	.300	.300	.350	.650
2018 LAD	NL	39	68	16	4	1	0	(0	0)	22	1	9	7	5	1	15	3	0	1	0	0	1	.235	.312	.324	.635
2019 Cin	NL	97	183	42	6	0	9	(6	3)	75	22	27	22	10	1	59	3	0	0	4	1	1	.230	.279	.410	.689
2020 Cin	NL	32	64	17	3	0	0	(0	0)	20	4	4	7	5	0	13	1	0	0	1	0	0	.266	.329	.313	.641
Postseason		5	4	0	0	0	0	(0	0)	0	0	1	0	0	0	2	0	0	1	0	0	0	.000	.000	.000	.000
4 ML YEARS		188	335	81	14	1	9	(6	3)	124	28	42	37	20	2	90	7	0	2	5	1	4	.242	.297	.370	.667

Luke Farrell

Pitches: R Bats: L Pos: RP-4   Ht: 6'6" Wt: 200 Born: 6/7/1991 Age: 30

		HOW MUCH PITCHED					WHAT HE GAVE UP										THE RESULTS						
Year Team	Lg	G	GS	GF	IP	BFP	H	R	ER	HR	SH	SF	HB	TBB	IBB	SO	WP	W	L	Pct	Sv-Op	Hld	Vel	OPS	ERC	ERA
2017 2 Tms		10	1	3	13.0	61	12	8	8	2	0	0	0	10	0	9	0	0	0	-	0-0	1	91	.753	5.40	5.54
2018 ChC	NL	20	2	8	31.1	141	30	22	18	7	0	1	1	16	2	39	1	3	4	.429	0-1	1	92	.797	5.09	5.17
2019 Tex	AL	9	1	3	13.1	48	6	4	4	3	0	1	0	3	0	12	0	1	0	1.000	0-0	0	92	.574	1.49	2.70
2020 Tex	AL	4	0	1	5.1	27	5	5	5	1	1	0	1	5	0	8	2	0	0	-	0-0	0	91	.923	7.27	8.44
17 KC	AL	1	1	0	2.2	18	7	5	5	1	0	0	0	3	0	2	0	0	0	-	0-0	0	90	1.289	21.83	16.88
17 Cin	NL	9	0	3	10.1	43	5	3	3	1	0	0	0	7	0	7	0	0	0	-	0-0	1	91	.529	2.34	2.61
4 ML YEARS		43	4	15	63.0	277	53	39	35	13	1	2	2	34	2	68	3	4	4	.500	0-1	2	92	.759	4.49	5.00

Erick Fedde

Pitches: R Bats: R Pos: SP-8; RP-3   Ht: 6'4" Wt: 200 Born: 2/25/1993 Age: 28

		HOW MUCH PITCHED					WHAT HE GAVE UP										THE RESULTS						
Year Team	Lg	G	GS	GF	IP	BFP	H	R	ER	HR	SH	SF	HB	TBB	IBB	SO	WP	W	L	Pct	Sv-Op	Hld	Vel	OPS	ERC	ERA
2017 Was	NL	3	3	0	15.1	76	25	16	16	5	2	0	1	8	2	15	0	0	1	.000	0-0	0	93	1.106	11.01	9.39
2018 Was	NL	12	8	1	50.1	217	55	31	31	8	1	2	0	22	1	46	0	2	4	.333	0-0	0	94	.846	5.32	5.54
2019 Was	NL	21	12	3	78.0	334	81	39	39	11	4	2	2	33	2	41	1	4	2	.667	0-0	0	92	.802	4.88	4.50
2020 Was	NL	11	8	1	50.1	222	47	25	24	10	1	1	3	22	2	28	2	2	4	.333	0-0	0	93	.767	4.65	4.29
4 ML YEARS		46	34	4	194.0	849	208	111	110	34	8	5	6	85	7	130	3	8	11	.421	0-0	0	93	.831	5.36	5.10

Michael Feliz

Pitches: R **Bats:** R **Pos:** RP-3 **Ht:** 6'4" **Wt:** 240 **Born:** 6/28/1993 **Age:** 28

Year	Team	Lg	G	GS	GF	IP	BFP	H	R	ER	HR	SH	SF	HB	TBB	IBB	SO	WP	W	L	Pct	Sv-Op	Hld	Vel	OPS	ERC	ERA
2015	Hou	AL	5	0	5	8.0	38	9	7	7	2	0	0	1	4	0	7	0	0	0	-	0-0	0	94	.884	6.79	7.88
2016	Hou	AL	47	0	17	65.0	270	55	33	32	10	0	2	0	22	0	95	6	8	1	.889	0-3	5	95	.659	3.32	4.43
2017	Hou	AL	46	0	13	48.0	218	53	31	30	8	0	4	0	22	1	70	7	4	2	.667	0-2	5	96	.854	5.28	5.63
2018	Pit	NL	47	0	7	47.2	217	49	33	30	6	0	3	3	23	0	55	3	1	2	.333	0-2	12	95	.776	4.92	5.66
2019	Pit	NL	58	1	5	56.1	239	44	27	25	11	1	1	2	27	1	73	0	4	4	.500	0-1	3	95	.720	3.91	3.99
2020	Pit	NL	3	0	0	1.2	12	4	6	6	1	0	0	1	2	0	2	0	0	0	-	0-0	0	94	1.361	26.50	32.40
6 ML YEARS			206	1	47	226.2	994	214	137	130	38	1	10	7	100	2	302	16	17	9	.654	0-8	22	95	.758	4.45	5.16

Caleb Ferguson

Pitches: L **Bats:** R **Pos:** RP-20; SP-1 **Ht:** 6'3" **Wt:** 226 **Born:** 7/2/1996 **Age:** 24

Year	Team	Lg	G	GS	GF	IP	BFP	H	R	ER	HR	SH	SF	HB	TBB	IBB	SO	WP	W	L	Pct	Sv-Op	Hld	Vel	OPS	ERC	ERA
2018	LAD	NL	29	3	7	49.0	202	43	21	19	8	0	0	3	12	1	59	1	7	2	.778	2-3	5	94	.688	3.42	3.49
2019	LAD	NL	46	2	5	44.2	204	39	26	24	7	1	3	6	27	2	54	1	1	2	.333	0-0	4	94	.774	4.99	4.84
2020	LAD	NL	21	1	0	18.2	75	16	7	6	4	0	0	0	3	0	27	0	2	1	.667	0-2	5	95	.670	3.02	2.89
Postseason			6	0	0	3.0	10	0	0	0	0	0	0	0	1	0	3	0	0	0	-	0-0	1	95	.100	0.13	0.00
3 ML YEARS			96	6	12	112.1	481	98	54	49	19	1	3	9	42	3	140	2	10	5	.667	2-5	14	94	.721	3.98	3.93

Junior Fernandez

Pitches: R **Bats:** R **Pos:** RP-3 **Ht:** 6'3" **Wt:** 215 **Born:** 3/2/1997 **Age:** 24

Year	Team	Lg	G	GS	GF	IP	BFP	H	R	ER	HR	SH	SF	HB	TBB	IBB	SO	WP	W	L	Pct	Sv-Op	Hld	Vel	OPS	ERC	ERA
2019	StL	NL	13	0	5	11.2	54	9	7	7	2	0	0	4	6	0	16	2	0	1	.000	0-3	0	97	.693	5.01	5.40
2020	StL	NL	3	0	2	3.0	16	6	6	6	1	0	0	0	2	0	2	0	0	0	-	0-0	0	94	1.286	14.84	18.00
2 ML YEARS			16	0	7	14.2	70	15	13	13	3	0	0	4	8	0	18	2	0	1	.000	0-3	0	96	.834	6.73	7.98

J.P. Feyereisen

Pitches: R **Bats:** R **Pos:** RP-6 FIRE-eye-zehn **Ht:** 6'2" **Wt:** 215 **Born:** 2/7/1993 **Age:** 28

Year	Team	Lg	G	GS	GF	IP	BFP	H	R	ER	HR	SH	SF	HB	TBB	IBB	SO	WP	W	L	Pct	Sv-Op	Hld	Vel	OPS	ERC	ERA
2020	Mil	NL	6	0	4	9.1	37	4	6	6	3	0	2	1	5	0	7	0	0	0	-	0-0	0	93	.719	3.39	5.79

Mike Fiers

Pitches: R **Bats:** R **Pos:** SP-11 FIRES **Ht:** 6'2" **Wt:** 211 **Born:** 6/15/1985 **Age:** 36

Year	Team	Lg	G	GS	GF	IP	BFP	H	R	ER	HR	SH	SF	HB	TBB	IBB	SO	WP	W	L	Pct	Sv-Op	Hld	Vel	OPS	ERC	ERA
2011	Mil	NL	2	0	2	2.0	10	2	0	0	0	0	0	0	3	0	2	0	0	0	-	0-0	0	88	.786	8.25	0.00
2012	Mil	NL	23	22	1	127.2	539	125	56	53	12	4	4	2	36	0	135	4	9	10	.474	0-0	0	88	.694	3.50	3.74
2013	Mil	NL	11	3	4	22.1	103	28	20	18	8	1	2	0	6	0	15	1	1	4	.200	0-0	0	88	.972	6.65	7.25
2014	Mil	NL	14	10	1	71.2	274	46	19	17	7	2	1	0	17	1	76	1	6	5	.545	0-0	0	90	.531	1.68	2.13
2015	2 Tms		31	30	0	180.1	761	162	83	74	24	3	8	6	64	5	180	8	7	10	.412	0-0	0	89	.713	3.64	3.69
2016	Hou	AL	31	30	0	168.2	724	187	89	84	26	3	5	7	42	0	134	17	11	8	.579	0-0	0	90	.801	4.66	4.48
2017	Hou	AL	29	28	0	153.1	671	157	95	89	32	3	1	13	62	0	146	11	8	10	.444	0-0	0	90	.827	5.44	5.22
2018	2 Tms		31	30	0	172.0	714	166	71	68	32	1	2	8	37	1	139	4	12	8	.600	0-0	0	89	.746	3.90	3.56
2019	Oak	AL	33	33	0	184.2	754	166	82	80	30	4	5	9	53	0	126	13	15	4	.789	0-0	0	90	.712	3.76	3.90
2020	Oak	AL	11	11	0	59.0	257	65	31	30	9	0	1	4	16	0	37	1	6	3	.667	0-0	0	88	.767	4.78	4.58
15	Mil	NL	21	21	0	118.0	509	117	57	51	14	3	6	5	43	5	121	6	5	9	.357	0-0	0	89	.749	4.11	3.89
15	Hou	AL	10	9	0	62.1	252	45	26	23	10	0	2	1	21	0	59	2	2	1	.667	0-0	0	90	.643	2.78	3.32
18	Det	AL	21	21	0	119.0	502	121	49	46	20	1	1	5	26	1	87	2	7	6	.538	0-0	0	89	.749	4.04	3.48
18	Oak	AL	10	9	0	53.0	212	45	22	22	12	0	1	3	11	0	52	2	5	2	.714	0-0	0	90	.740	3.57	3.74
Postseason			1	0	0	1.0	4	1	1	1	0	1	1	0	0	0	0	0	0	0	-	0-0	0	90	1.333	1.95	9.00
10 ML YEARS			216	197	8	1141.2	4807	1104	546	513	180	21	29	49	336	7	990	60	75	62	.547	0-0	0	89	.743	4.04	4.04

Kyle Finnegan

Pitches: R **Bats:** R **Pos:** RP-25 **Ht:** 6'2" **Wt:** 200 **Born:** 9/4/1991 **Age:** 29

Year	Team	Lg	G	GS	GF	IP	BFP	H	R	ER	HR	SH	SF	HB	TBB	IBB	SO	WP	W	L	Pct	Sv-Op	Hld	Vel	OPS	ERC	ERA
2020	Was	NL	25	0	4	24.2	107	21	10	8	2	0	0	1	13	4	27	2	1	0	1.000	0-1	4	95	.639	3.49	2.92

Derek Fisher

Bats: L **Throws:** R **Pos:** RF-10;LF-5;PR-2;DH-1;PH-1 **Ht:** 6'3" **Wt:** 215 **Born:** 8/21/1993 **Age:** 27

Year	Team	Lg	G	AB	H	2B	3B	HR	(Hm	Rd)	TB	R	RBI	RC	TBB	IBB	SO	HBP	SH	SF	SB	CS	GDP	Avg	OBP	Slg	OPS
2017	Hou	AL	53	146	31	4	1	5	(3	2)	52	21	17	18	17	1	54	3	0	0	3	3	1	.212	.307	.356	.663
2018	Hou	AL	42	79	13	2	2	4	(2	2)	31	13	11	4	5	0	42	0	0	2	2	0	0	.165	.209	.392	.602
2019	2 Tms	AL	57	146	27	4	1	7	(4	3)	54	23	17	13	21	0	57	0	0	3	5	1	3	.185	.287	.370	.657
2020	Tor	AL	16	31	7	2	1	1	(1	0)	14	5	7	6	7	0	11	0	0	1	0	1	0	.226	.359	.452	.811
19	Hou	AL	17	53	12	2	1	1	(0	1)	19	9	5	7	7	0	14	0	0	0	4	1	0	.226	.317	.358	.675
19	Tor	AL	40	93	15	2	0	6	(4	2)	35	14	12	6	14	0	43	0	0	3	1	0	3	.161	.271	.376	.647
Postseason			5	0	0	0	0	0	(0	0)	0	1	0	0	1	0	0	0	0	1	0	1	0	-	1.000	-	-
4 ML YEARS			168	402	78	12	5	17	(10	7)	151	62	52	41	50	1	164	3	0	3	10	5	4	.194	.286	.376	.662

Jack Flaherty

Pitches: R **Bats:** R **Pos:** SP-9   **Ht:** 6'4" **Wt:** 225 **Born:** 10/15/1995 **Age:** 25

			HOW MUCH PITCHED				WHAT HE GAVE UP											THE RESULTS					
Year	Team	Lg	G	GS	GF	IP	BFP	H	R	ER	HR	SH	SF	HB	TBB	IBB	SO	WP	W	L	Pct	Sv-Op	Hld	Vel	OPS	ERC	ERA
2017	StL	NL	6	5	0	21.1	94	23	15	15	4	0	2	1	10	1	20	0	0	2	.000	0-0	0	93	.843	5.71	6.33
2018	StL	NL	28	28	0	151.0	615	108	59	56	20	2	1	11	59	3	182	6	8	9	.471	0-0	0	93	.635	3.01	3.34
2019	StL	NL	33	33	0	196.1	772	135	62	60	25	3	3	7	55	2	231	6	11	8	.579	0-0	0	94	.591	2.31	2.75
2020	StL	NL	9	9	0	40.1	170	33	22	22	6	1	1	3	16	0	49	1	4	3	.571	0-0	0	94	.677	3.68	4.91
	Postseason		3	3	0	17.0	72	17	8	8	2	2	0	1	4	0	22	3	1	2	.333	0-0	0	95	.714	3.75	4.24
	4 ML YEARS		76	75	0	409.0	1651	299	158	153	55	6	7	22	140	6	482	13	23	22	.511	0-0	0	93	.631	2.85	3.37

Josh Fleming

Pitches: L **Bats:** R **Pos:** SP-5; RP-2   **Ht:** 6'2" **Wt:** 220 **Born:** 5/18/1996 **Age:** 25

			HOW MUCH PITCHED				WHAT HE GAVE UP											THE RESULTS					
Year	Team	Lg	G	GS	GF	IP	BFP	H	R	ER	HR	SH	SF	HB	TBB	IBB	SO	WP	W	L	Pct	Sv-Op	Hld	Vel	OPS	ERC	ERA
2020	TB	AL	7	5	0	32.1	130	28	10	10	5	0	0	1	7	0	25	0	5	0	1.000	0-0	0	91	.670	3.14	2.78

Aaron Fletcher

Pitches: L **Bats:** L **Pos:** RP-6   **Ht:** 6'0" **Wt:** 220 **Born:** 2/25/1996 **Age:** 25

			HOW MUCH PITCHED				WHAT HE GAVE UP											THE RESULTS					
Year	Team	Lg	G	GS	GF	IP	BFP	H	R	ER	HR	SH	SF	HB	TBB	IBB	SO	WP	W	L	Pct	Sv-Op	Hld	Vel	OPS	ERC	ERA
2020	Sea	AL	6	0	0	4.1	29	7	6	6	1	0	0	2	7	0	7	0	0	0	-	0-0	1	93	1.102	16.97	12.46

David Fletcher

Bats: R **Throws:** R **Pos:** SS-27;2B-15;3B-8;RF-1   **Ht:** 5'9" **Wt:** 185 **Born:** 5/31/1994 **Age:** 27

								BATTING													RUNNING			AVERAGES			
Year	Team	Lg	G	AB	H	2B	3B	HR	(Hm	Rd)	TB	R	RBI	RC	TBB	IBB	SO	HBP	SH	SF	SB	CS	GDP	Avg	OBP	Slg	OPS
2018	LAA	AL	80	284	78	18	2	1	(1	0)	103	35	25	35	15	0	34	3	3	2	3	0	7	.275	.316	.363	.678
2019	LAA	AL	154	596	173	30	4	6	(3	3)	229	83	49	89	55	2	64	0	1	1	8	3	8	.290	.350	.384	.734
2020	LAA	AL	49	207	66	13	0	3	(1	2)	88	31	18	38	20	0	25	0	1	2	2	1	4	.319	.376	.425	.801
	3 ML YEARS		283	1087	317	61	6	10	(5	5)	420	149	92	162	90	2	123	3	5	5	13	4	19	.292	.346	.386	.732

Wilmer Flores

Bats: R **Throws:** R **Pos:** DH-22;1B-14;2B-14;PH-5;3B-3   **Ht:** 6'2" **Wt:** 213 **Born:** 8/6/1991 **Age:** 29

								BATTING													RUNNING			AVERAGES			
Year	Team	Lg	G	AB	H	2B	3B	HR	(Hm	Rd)	TB	R	RBI	RC	TBB	IBB	SO	HBP	SH	SF	SB	CS	GDP	Avg	OBP	Slg	OPS
2013	NYM	NL	27	95	20	5	0	1	(0	1)	28	8	13	7	5	0	23	0	0	1	0	0	1	.211	.248	.295	.542
2014	NYM	NL	78	259	65	13	1	6	(4	2)	98	28	29	25	12	2	31	1	1	1	1	0	6	.251	.286	.378	.664
2015	NYM	NL	137	483	127	22	0	16	(8	8)	197	55	59	58	19	2	63	4	2	2	0	1	12	.263	.295	.408	.703
2016	NYM	NL	103	307	82	14	0	16	(12	4)	144	38	49	39	23	0	48	2	0	3	1	1	9	.267	.319	.469	.788
2017	NYM	NL	110	336	91	17	1	18	(9	9)	164	42	52	39	17	1	54	3	0	6	1	1	14	.271	.307	.488	.796
2018	NYM	NL	126	386	103	25	0	11	(4	7)	161	43	51	51	29	1	42	5	0	9	0	0	8	.267	.319	.417	.736
2019	Ari	NL	89	265	84	18	0	9	(6	3)	129	31	37	38	15	0	31	4	0	1	0	0	9	.317	.361	.487	.848
2020	SF	NL	55	198	53	11	1	12	(7	5)	102	30	32	30	13	1	36	1	0	1	1	0	5	.268	.315	.515	.830
	Postseason		13	41	8	2	1	0	(0	0)	12	4	0	5	5	2	9	1	1	0	1	0	1	.195	.298	.293	.591
	8 ML YEARS		725	2329	625	125	3	89	(50	39)	1023	275	322	287	133	7	328	20	3	24	4	3	64	.268	.310	.439	.750

Bernardo Flores Jr.

Pitches: L **Bats:** L **Pos:** RP-2   **Ht:** 6'4" **Wt:** 190 **Born:** 8/23/1995 **Age:** 25

			HOW MUCH PITCHED				WHAT HE GAVE UP											THE RESULTS					
Year	Team	Lg	G	GS	GF	IP	BFP	H	R	ER	HR	SH	SF	HB	TBB	IBB	SO	WP	W	L	Pct	Sv-Op	Hld	Vel	OPS	ERC	ERA
2020	CWS	AL	2	0	1	2.0	10	4	2	2	0	0	0	0	0	0	2	0	0	0	-	0-0	0	92	.900	7.48	9.00

Estevan Florial

Bats: L **Throws:** R **Pos:** CF-1   **Ht:** 6'1" **Wt:** 195 **Born:** 11/25/1997 **Age:** 23

								BATTING													RUNNING			AVERAGES			
Year	Team	Lg	G	AB	H	2B	3B	HR	(Hm	Rd)	TB	R	RBI	RC	TBB	IBB	SO	HBP	SH	SF	SB	CS	GDP	Avg	OBP	Slg	OPS
2020	NYY	AL	1	3	1	0	0	0	(0	0)	1	0	0	0	0	0	2	0	0	0	0	0	0	.333	.333	.333	.667

Dylan Floro

Pitches: R **Bats:** L **Pos:** RP-25   **Ht:** 6'2" **Wt:** 203 **Born:** 12/27/1990 **Age:** 30

			HOW MUCH PITCHED				WHAT HE GAVE UP											THE RESULTS					
Year	Team	Lg	G	GS	GF	IP	BFP	H	R	ER	HR	SH	SF	HB	TBB	IBB	SO	WP	W	L	Pct	Sv-Op	Hld	Vel	OPS	ERC	ERA
2016	TB	AL	12	0	4	15.0	72	23	8	7	0	0	1	0	5	1	14	2	0	1	.000	0-0	0	93	.813	5.96	4.20
2017	ChC	NL	3	0	2	9.2	45	15	7	7	2	0	1	2	2	0	6	0	0	0	-	0-0	0	91	.971	8.12	6.52
2018	2 Tms	NL	54	0	20	64.0	271	57	17	16	3	3	3	1	23	6	58	1	6	3	.667	0-0	7	93	.634	2.85	2.25
2019	LAD	NL	50	0	4	46.2	201	46	25	22	4	2	1	2	14	5	42	1	5	3	.625	0-3	6	94	.685	3.44	4.24
2020	LAD	NL	25	0	4	24.1	98	23	7	7	1	0	2	0	4	1	19	1	3	0	1.000	0-0	4	93	.623	2.48	2.59
18	Cin	NL	25	0	13	36.1	159	39	12	11	2	2	3	0	12	3	27	0	3	2	.600	0-0	1	93	.726	3.69	2.72
18	LAD	NL	29	0	7	27.2	112	18	5	5	1	1	0	1	11	3	31	1	3	1	.750	0-0	6	94	.503	1.84	1.63
	Postseason		8	0	2	7.0	29	6	3	3	0	0	0	0	4	2	8	0	1	0	.000	0-0	0	93	.665	2.91	3.86
	5 ML YEARS		144	0	34	159.2	687	164	64	59	10	5	7	4	48	13	139	5	14	7	.667	0-3	17	93	.689	3.51	3.33

Tyler Flowers

Bats: R **Throws:** R **Pos:** C-22   **Ht:** 6'4" **Wt:** 260 **Born:** 1/24/1986 **Age:** 35

Year	Team	Lg	G	AB	H	2B	3B	HR	(Hm	Rd)	TB	R	RBI	RC	TBB	IBB	SO	HBP	SH	SF	SB	CS	GDP	Avg	OBP	Slg	OPS
2009	CWS	AL	10	16	3	1	0	0	(0	0)	4	3	0	2	3	0	8	1	0	0	0	0	1	.188	.350	.250	.600
2010	CWS	AL	8	11	1	0	0	0	(0	0)	1	2	0	1	4	0	5	0	0	0	0	0	0	.091	.333	.091	.424
2011	CWS	AL	38	110	23	5	1	5	(3	2)	45	13	16	13	14	0	38	3	0	2	0	1	2	.209	.310	.409	.719
2012	CWS	AL	52	136	29	6	0	7	(5	2)	56	19	13	13	12	0	56	4	1	0	2	1	2	.213	.296	.412	.708
2013	CWS	AL	84	256	50	11	0	10	(7	3)	91	24	24	14	14	1	94	4	0	1	0	1	9	.195	.247	.355	.603
2014	CWS	AL	127	407	98	16	1	15	(7	8)	161	42	50	43	25	0	159	8	1	1	0	1	10	.241	.297	.396	.693
2015	CWS	AL	112	331	79	12	4	9	(3	6)	118	21	39	36	21	0	104	6	2	1	0	1	8	.239	.295	.356	.652
2016	Atl	NL	83	281	76	18	0	8	(5	3)	118	27	41	46	29	1	91	11	0	4	0	0	3	.270	.357	.420	.777
2017	Atl	NL	99	317	89	16	0	12	(6	6)	141	41	49	50	31	1	82	20	0	2	0	1	6	.281	.378	.445	.823
2018	Atl	NL	82	251	57	9	0	8	(5	3)	90	34	30	33	35	0	76	9	0	1	0	0	6	.227	.341	.359	.700
2019	Atl	NL	85	271	62	11	3	11	(7	4)	112	36	34	31	31	3	105	6	0	2	0	0	8	.229	.319	.413	.733
2020	Atl	NL	22	69	15	6	0	1	(1	0)	24	5	5	5	8	0	34	3	0	0	0	0	1	.217	.325	.348	.673
	Postseason		5	8	2	0	0	0	(0	0)	2	1	0	1	1	0	3	0	0	0	0	0	0	.250	.333	.250	.583
	12 ML YEARS		802	2456	582	111	5	86	(49	37)	961	267	301	287	227	6	852	75	4	14	2	6	56	.237	.319	.391	.710

Mike Foltynewicz

Pitches: R **Bats:** R **Pos:** SP-1   fohl-tuh-neh-vich   **Ht:** 6'4" **Wt:** 195 **Born:** 10/7/1991 **Age:** 29

Year	Team	Lg	G	GS	GF	IP	BFP	H	R	ER	HR	SH	SF	HB	TBB	IBB	SO	WP	W	L	Pct	Sv-Op	Hld	Vel	OPS	ERC	ERA
2014	Hou	AL	16	0	9	18.2	84	23	11	11	3	0	0	0	7	0	14	3	0	1	.000	0-0	1	97	.864	5.80	5.30
2015	Atl	NL	18	15	1	86.2	399	112	63	55	17	2	6	4	29	0	77	3	4	6	.400	0-0	1	95	.896	6.43	5.71
2016	Atl	NL	22	22	0	123.1	525	125	61	59	18	5	4	6	35	2	111	13	9	5	.643	0-0	0	95	.761	4.18	4.31
2017	Atl	NL	29	28	0	154.0	692	169	86	82	20	11	2	10	59	2	143	4	10	13	.435	0-0	0	95	.795	4.97	4.79
2018	Atl	NL	31	31	0	183.0	744	130	65	58	17	2	1	6	68	3	202	7	13	10	.565	0-0	0	96	.600	2.49	2.85
2019	Atl	NL	21	21	0	117.0	491	109	65	59	23	5	1	2	37	2	105	5	8	6	.571	0-0	0	95	.764	4.05	4.54
2020	Atl	NL	1	1	0	3.1	16	4	6	6	3	0	0	0	4	0	3	0	0	1	.000	0-0	0	90	1.583	18.39	16.20
	Postseason		4	4	0	13.1	63	11	12	11	2	2	0	1	10	2	17	0	1	2	.333	0-0	0	95	.761	4.68	7.43
	7 ML YEARS		138	118	10	686.0	2951	672	357	330	101	25	14	28	239	9	655	35	44	42	.512	0-0	2	95	.754	4.21	4.33

Wilmer Font

Pitches: R **Bats:** R **Pos:** RP-21   FAHNT   **Ht:** 6'4" **Wt:** 255 **Born:** 5/24/1990 **Age:** 31

Year	Team	Lg	G	GS	GF	IP	BFP	H	R	ER	HR	SH	SF	HB	TBB	IBB	SO	WP	W	L	Pct	Sv-Op	Hld	Vel	OPS	ERC	ERA
2012	Tex	AL	3	0	0	2.0	10	0	2	2	0	0	0	0	4	0	1	1	0	0	-	0-0	0	95	.400	3.47	9.00
2013	Tex	AL	2	0	2	1.1	7	1	0	0	0	0	0	0	2	0	0	0	0	0	-	0-0	0	95	.629	5.91	0.00
2017	LAD	NL	3	0	2	3.2	22	7	7	7	2	0	0	0	4	0	3	0	0	0	-	0-0	0	94	1.389	17.78	17.18
2018	3 Tms		19	5	8	44.0	192	46	29	29	12	0	0	1	16	1	36	1	2	3	.400	0-1	0	94	.842	5.46	5.93
2019	3 Tms		48	17	6	84.1	356	78	42	42	17	0	2	3	29	2	95	2	4	5	.444	0-1	2	94	.797	4.24	4.48
2020	Tor	AL	21	0	5	16.1	85	28	19	18	2	0	1	1	9	0	15	1	1	3	.250	0-1	2	95	.974	9.73	9.92
18	LAD	NL	6	0	6	10.1	48	18	13	13	5	0	0	0	1	1	7	0	0	2	.000	0-1	0	93	1.119	10.58	11.32
18	Oak	AL	4	0	2	6.2	37	13	11	11	5	0	0	0	4	0	9	1	0	0	-	0-0	0	94	1.369	17.41	14.85
18	TB	AL	9	5	0	27.0	107	15	5	5	2	0	0	1	11	0	20	0	2	1	.667	0-0	0	95	.526	1.83	1.67
19	TB	AL	10	0	3	14.0	60	15	9	9	2	0	0	0	5	0	18	1	1	0	1.000	0-0	1	94	.806	4.68	5.79
19	NYM	NL	15	3	1	31.0	134	29	17	17	8	0	0	2	13	1	24	1	1	2	.333	0-1	0	94	.858	5.14	4.94
19	Tor	AL	23	14	2	39.1	162	34	16	16	7	0	2	1	11	1	53	0	2	3	.400	0-0	1	95	.743	3.42	3.66
	6 ML YEARS		96	22	23	151.2	672	160	99	98	33	0	3	5	64	3	150	5	7	11	.389	0-3	4	94	.846	5.43	5.82

Mike Ford

Bats: L **Throws:** R **Pos:** 1B-13;PH-10;DH-7   **Ht:** 6'0" **Wt:** 225 **Born:** 7/4/1992 **Age:** 28

Year	Team	Lg	G	AB	H	2B	3B	HR	(Hm	Rd)	TB	R	RBI	RC	TBB	IBB	SO	HBP	SH	SF	SB	CS	GDP	Avg	OBP	Slg	OPS
2019	NYY	AL	50	143	37	7	0	12	(2	10)	80	30	25	27	17	2	28	3	0	0	0	0	0	.259	.350	.559	.909
2020	NYY	AL	29	74	10	4	0	2	(1	1)	20	5	11	3	7	0	16	2	0	1	0	0	4	.135	.226	.270	.496
	2 ML YEARS		79	217	47	11	0	14	(3	11)	100	35	36	30	24	2	44	5	0	1	0	0	4	.217	.308	.461	.769

Logan Forsythe

Bats: R **Throws:** R **Pos:** 2B-6;1B-4;DH-2   **Ht:** 6'1" **Wt:** 205 **Born:** 1/14/1987 **Age:** 34

Year	Team	Lg	G	AB	H	2B	3B	HR	(Hm	Rd)	TB	R	RBI	RC	TBB	IBB	SO	HBP	SH	SF	SB	CS	GDP	Avg	OBP	Slg	OPS
2011	SD	NL	62	150	32	9	1	0	(0	0)	43	12	12	15	12	3	33	3	2	2	3	1	3	.213	.281	.287	.568
2012	SD	NL	91	315	86	13	3	6	(5	1)	123	45	26	37	28	0	57	6	0	1	8	2	6	.273	.343	.390	.733
2013	SD	NL	75	220	47	6	1	6	(2	4)	73	22	19	16	19	2	54	2	1	1	6	1	5	.214	.281	.332	.613
2014	TB	AL	110	301	67	12	1	6	(2	4)	99	32	26	26	21	0	71	4	2	4	2	0	9	.223	.287	.329	.616
2015	TB	AL	153	540	152	33	2	17	(8	9)	240	69	68	73	55	2	111	14	0	6	9	4	12	.281	.359	.444	.804
2016	TB	AL	127	511	135	24	4	20	(12	8)	227	76	52	74	46	0	127	8	0	2	6	6	8	.264	.333	.444	.778
2017	LAD	NL	119	361	81	19	0	6	(4	2)	118	56	36	45	69	1	109	4	0	5	3	2	12	.224	.351	.327	.678
2018	2 Tms		120	371	86	16	2	2	(1	1)	108	37	27	40	41	1	83	3	0	1	3	0	10	.232	.313	.291	.604
2019	Tex	AL	101	317	72	17	1	7	(2	5)	112	38	39	41	44	0	100	3	0	2	2	0	8	.227	.325	.353	.678
2020	Mia	NL	13	34	4	1	0	1	(0	1)	8	2	2	2	4	0	12	0	0	0	0	0	0	.118	.211	.235	.446
18	LAD	NL	70	193	40	10	0	2	(1	1)	56	18	13	15	17	1	43	0	0	0	1	0	5	.207	.270	.290	.560
18	Min	AL	50	178	46	6	2	0	(0	0)	52	19	14	25	24	0	40	3	0	1	2	0	5	.258	.356	.292	.648
	Postseason		14	37	11	2	0	0	(0	0)	13	9	6	8	9	3	7	0	0	0	2	1	1	.297	.435	.351	.786
	10 ML YEARS		971	3120	762	150	13	71	(36	35)	1151	389	307	367	343	9	757	47	5	24	42	16	73	.244	.326	.369	.695

Matt Foster

Pitches: R **Bats:** R **Pos:** RP-21; SP-2 **Ht:** 6'0" **Wt:** 210 **Born:** 1/27/1995 **Age:** 26

			HOW MUCH PITCHED					WHAT HE GAVE UP										THE RESULTS						
Year	Team	Lg	G	GS	GF	IP	BFP	H	R	ER	HR	SH	SF	HB	TBB	IBB	SO	WP	W	L	Pct	Sv-Op	Hld	Vel	OPS	ERC	ERA
2020	CWS	AL	23	2	4	28.2	109	16	8	7	2	1	0	0	9	0	31	0	6	1	.857	0-1	2	94	.504	1.50	2.20

Dexter Fowler

Bats: B **Throws:** R **Pos:** RF-27;DH-2;PH-2 **Ht:** 6'5" **Wt:** 205 **Born:** 3/22/1986 **Age:** 35

						BATTING															RUNNING			AVERAGES			
Year	Team	Lg	G	AB	H	2B	3B	HR	(Hm	Rd)	TB	R	RBI	RC	TBB	IBB	SO	HBP	SH	SF	SB	CS	GDP	Avg	OBP	Slg	OPS
2008	Col	NL	13	26	4	0	0	0	(0	0)	4	3	0	0	0	0	5	1	0	0	0	1	0	.154	.185	.154	.339
2009	Col	NL	135	433	115	29	10	4	(2	2)	176	73	34	68	67	1	116	1	14	3	27	10	4	.266	.363	.406	.770
2010	Col	NL	132	439	114	20	14	6	(5	1)	180	73	36	68	57	0	104	2	7	0	13	8	5	.260	.347	.410	.757
2011	Col	NL	125	481	128	35	15	5	(3	2)	208	84	45	79	68	3	130	6	7	1	12	9	6	.266	.363	.432	.796
2012	Col	NL	143	454	136	18	11	13	(10	3)	215	72	53	81	68	1	128	0	6	2	12	5	5	.300	.389	.474	.863
2013	Col	NL	119	415	109	18	3	12	(7	5)	169	71	42	62	65	1	105	6	4	2	19	9	5	.263	.369	.407	.776
2014	Hou	AL	116	434	120	21	4	8	(5	3)	173	61	35	65	66	2	108	3	1	1	11	4	6	.276	.375	.399	.774
2015	ChC	NL	156	596	149	29	8	17	(11	6)	245	102	46	77	84	1	154	5	2	3	20	7	4	.250	.346	.411	.757
2016	ChC	NL	125	456	126	25	7	13	(4	9)	204	84	48	83	79	0	124	11	1	4	13	4	3	.276	.393	.447	.840
2017	StL	NL	118	420	111	22	9	18	(11	7)	205	68	64	74	63	6	101	4	0	4	7	3	10	.264	.363	.488	.851
2018	StL	NL	90	289	52	10	0	8	(4	4)	86	40	31	27	38	0	75	3	0	4	5	2	2	.180	.278	.298	.576
2019	StL	NL	150	487	116	24	1	19	(9	10)	199	69	67	81	74	1	142	8	1	4	8	5	6	.238	.346	.409	.754
2020	StL	NL	31	90	21	2	0	4	(3	1)	35	14	15	11	10	0	28	1	0	1	1	1	2	.233	.317	.389	.706
	Postseason		39	155	33	8	0	5	(3	2)	56	22	14	14	9	0	36	1	2	2	2	1	1	.213	.257	.361	.619
	13 ML YEARS		1453	5020	1301	253	82	127	(74	53)	2099	814	516	776	739	16	1320	51	43	28	148	68	58	.259	.358	.418	.776

Jake Fraley

Bats: L **Throws:** L **Pos:** RF-6;LF-1 **Ht:** 6'0" **Wt:** 195 **Born:** 5/25/1995 **Age:** 26

						BATTING															RUNNING			AVERAGES			
Year	Team	Lg	G	AB	H	2B	3B	HR	(Hm	Rd)	TB	R	RBI	RC	TBB	IBB	SO	HBP	SH	SF	SB	CS	GDP	Avg	OBP	Slg	OPS
2019	Sea	AL	12	40	6	2	0	0	(0	0)	8	3	1	2	0	0	14	1	0	0	2	1	0	.150	.171	.200	.371
2020	Sea	AL	7	26	4	1	1	0	(0	0)	7	3	0	1	2	0	11	1	0	0	2	1	0	.154	.241	.269	.511
	2 ML YEARS		19	66	10	3	1	0	(0	0)	15	6	1	3	2	0	25	2	0	0	2	1	0	.152	.200	.227	.427

Ty France

Bats: R **Throws:** R **Pos:** DH-19;2B-10;PH-8;3B-6;1B-5 **Ht:** 5'11" **Wt:** 217 **Born:** 7/13/1994 **Age:** 26

						BATTING															RUNNING			AVERAGES			
Year	Team	Lg	G	AB	H	2B	3B	HR	(Hm	Rd)	TB	R	RBI	RC	TBB	IBB	SO	HBP	SH	SF	SB	CS	GDP	Avg	OBP	Slg	OPS
2019	SD	NL	69	184	43	8	1	7	(4	3)	74	20	24	25	9	0	49	7	0	1	0	2	8	.234	.294	.402	.696
2020	2 Tms		43	141	43	9	1	4	(2	2)	66	19	23	29	11	0	37	3	0	0	0	0	3	.305	.368	.468	.836
20	SD	NL	20	55	17	4	0	2	(2	0)	27	9	10	11	5	0	15	1	0	0	0	0	1	.309	.377	.491	.868
20	Sea	AL	23	86	26	5	1	2	(0	2)	39	10	13	18	6	0	22	2	0	0	0	0	2	.302	.362	.453	.815
	2 ML YEARS		112	325	86	17	2	11	(6	5)	140	39	47	54	20	0	86	10	0	1	0	2	11	.265	.326	.431	.757

Maikel Franco

Bats: R **Throws:** R **Pos:** 3B-51;DH-8;1B-2 MY-kell **Ht:** 6'1" **Wt:** 225 **Born:** 8/26/1992 **Age:** 28

						BATTING															RUNNING			AVERAGES			
Year	Team	Lg	G	AB	H	2B	3B	HR	(Hm	Rd)	TB	R	RBI	RC	TBB	IBB	SO	HBP	SH	SF	SB	CS	GDP	Avg	OBP	Slg	OPS
2014	Phi	NL	16	56	10	2	0	0	(0	0)	12	5	5	1	1	0	13	0	0	1	0	0	1	.179	.190	.214	.404
2015	Phi	NL	80	304	85	22	1	14	(7	7)	151	45	50	48	26	2	52	4	0	1	0	0	8	.280	.343	.497	.840
2016	Phi	NL	152	581	148	23	1	25	(10	15)	248	67	88	74	40	7	106	5	0	4	1	1	13	.255	.306	.427	.733
2017	Phi	NL	154	575	132	29	1	24	(14	10)	235	66	76	53	41	3	95	2	0	5	0	0	21	.230	.281	.409	.690
2018	Phi	NL	131	433	117	17	1	22	(10	12)	202	48	68	55	29	7	62	0	0	3	1	0	15	.270	.314	.467	.780
2019	Phi	NL	123	389	91	17	0	17	(13	4)	159	48	56	44	36	19	61	0	0	3	0	0	14	.234	.297	.409	.705
2020	KC	AL	60	223	62	16	0	8	(3	5)	102	23	38	36	16	1	38	0	0	4	1	0	4	.278	.321	.457	.778
	7 ML YEARS		716	2561	645	126	4	110	(57	53)	1109	302	381	311	189	39	427	11	0	21	4	1	76	.252	.304	.433	.737

Wander Franco

Bats: B **Throws:** R **Pos:** SS **Ht:** 5'10" **Wt:** 189 **Born:** 3/1/2001 **Age:** 20

						BATTING															RUNNING			AVERAGES			
Year	Team	Lg	G	AB	H	2B	3B	HR	(Hm	Rd)	TB	R	RBI	RC	TBB	IBB	SO	HBP	SH	SF	SB	CS	GDP	Avg	OBP	Slg	OPS
2018	Prnctn	R+	61	242	85	10	7	11	(-	-)	142	46	57	57	27	1	19	2	0	2	4	3	5	.351	.418	.587	1.004
2019	2 Tms	Low	114	425	139	27	7	9	(-	-)	207	82	53	89	56	3	35	2	0	12	18	14	6	.327	.398	.487	.885

Seth Frankoff

Pitches: R **Bats:** R **Pos:** RP-2 **Ht:** 6'5" **Wt:** 215 **Born:** 8/27/1988 **Age:** 32

			HOW MUCH PITCHED					WHAT HE GAVE UP											THE RESULTS						
Year	Team	Lg	G	GS	GF	IP	BFP	H	R	ER	HR	SH	SF	HB	TBB	IBB	SO	WP	W	L	Pct	Sv-Op	Hld	Vel	OPS	ERC	ERA
2017	ChC	NL	1	0	0	2.0	9	4	2	2	1	0	0	0	0	0	2	0	0	1	.000	0-0	0	92	1.222	13.26	9.00
2020	Sea	AL	2	0	1	2.2	16	6	5	5	0	0	0	0	2	0	0	0	0	0	-	0-0	0	93	1.071	12.64	16.88
	2 ML YEARS		3	0	1	4.2	25	10	7	7	1	0	0	0	2	0	2	0	0	1	.000	0-0	0	92	1.132	13.08	13.50

Adam Frazier

Bats: L **Throws:** R **Pos:** 2B-41;LF-14;PH-3;DH-2

Ht: 5'10" **Wt:** 185 **Born:** 12/14/1991 **Age:** 29

									BATTING											RUNNING			AVERAGES			
Year	Team	Lg	G	AB	H	2B	3B	HR	(Hm | Rd)	TB	R	RBI	RC	TBB	IBB	SO	HBP	SH	SF	SB	CS	GDP	Avg	OBP	Slg	OPS
2016	Pit	NL	66	146	44	8	1	2	(2 | 0)	60	21	11	23	12	0	26	1	0	1	4	1	0	.301	.356	.411	.767
2017	Pit	NL	121	406	112	20	6	6	(2 | 4)	162	55	53	61	36	2	57	8	1	3	9	5	9	.276	.344	.399	.743
2018	Pit	NL	113	318	88	23	2	10	(6 | 4)	145	52	35	49	29	2	53	3	1	1	1	3	3	.277	.342	.456	.798
2019	Pit	NL	152	554	154	33	7	10	(5 | 5)	231	80	50	72	40	4	75	9	4	1	5	5	6	.278	.336	.417	.753
2020	Pit	NL	58	209	48	7	0	7	(5 | 2)	76	22	23	23	17	0	35	3	1	0	1	3	3	.230	.297	.364	.661
	5 ML YEARS		510	1633	446	91	16	35	(20 | 15)	674	230	172	228	134	8	246	24	7	6	20	17	21	.273	.336	.413	.749

Clint Frazier

Bats: R **Throws:** R **Pos:** RF-28;LF-8;DH-5

Ht: 5'11" **Wt:** 212 **Born:** 9/6/1994 **Age:** 26

									BATTING											RUNNING			AVERAGES			
Year	Team	Lg	G	AB	H	2B	3B	HR	(Hm	Rd)	TB	R	RBI	RC	TBB	IBB	SO	HBP	SH	SF	SB	CS	GDP	Avg	OBP	Slg	OPS
2017	NYY	AL	39	134	31	9	4	4	(3	1)	60	16	17	17	7	0	43	0	0	1	1	0	2	.231	.268	.448	.715
2018	NYY	AL	15	34	9	3	0	0	(0	0)	12	9	1	3	5	0	13	2	0	0	0	0	3	.265	.390	.353	.743
2019	NYY	AL	69	225	60	14	0	12	(5	7)	110	31	38	40	16	1	70	2	0	3	1	2	2	.267	.317	.489	.806
2020	NYY	AL	39	131	35	6	1	8	(6	2)	67	24	26	29	25	0	44	3	0	1	3	0	5	.267	.394	.511	.905
	4 ML YEARS		162	524	135	32	5	24	(14	10)	249	80	82	89	53	1	170	7	0	5	5	2	12	.258	.331	.475	.806

Todd Frazier

Bats: R **Throws:** R **Pos:** 3B-29;1B-16;PH-1

Ht: 6'3" **Wt:** 220 **Born:** 2/12/1986 **Age:** 35

									BATTING											RUNNING			AVERAGES			
Year	Team	Lg	G	AB	H	2B	3B	HR	(Hm	Rd)	TB	R	RBI	RC	TBB	IBB	SO	HBP	SH	SF	SB	CS	GDP	Avg	OBP	Slg	OPS
2011	Cin	NL	41	112	26	5	0	6	(2	4)	49	17	15	13	7	0	27	2	0	0	1	0	2	.232	.289	.438	.727
2012	Cin	NL	128	422	115	26	6	19	(10	9)	210	55	67	59	36	1	103	3	0	4	3	2	9	.273	.331	.498	.829
2013	Cin	NL	150	531	124	29	3	19	(12	7)	216	63	73	67	50	1	125	14	2	3	6	5	14	.234	.314	.407	.721
2014	Cin	NL	157	597	163	22	1	29	(20	9)	274	88	80	84	52	2	139	7	0	4	20	8	9	.273	.336	.459	.795
2015	Cin	NL	157	619	158	43	1	35	(19	16)	308	82	89	73	44	3	137	7	1	7	13	8	19	.255	.309	.498	.806
2016	CWS	AL	158	590	133	21	0	40	(16	24)	274	89	98	71	64	1	163	4	1	7	15	5	11	.225	.302	.464	.767
2017	2 Tms	AL	147	474	101	19	1	27	(9	18)	203	74	76	69	83	2	125	14	0	5	4	3	10	.213	.344	.428	.772
2018	NYM	NL	115	408	87	18	0	18	(10	8)	159	54	59	48	48	1	112	8	0	8	9	4	10	.213	.303	.390	.693
2019	NYM	NL	133	447	112	19	2	21	(10	11)	198	63	67	70	40	1	106	12	0	0	1	2	9	.251	.329	.443	.772
2020	2 Tms		45	157	37	9	1	4	(3	1)	60	16	12	17	11	0	42	4	0	0	1	1	1	.236	.302	.382	.684
17	CWS	AL	81	280	58	15	0	16	(5	11)	121	41	44	39	48	1	71	4	0	3	4	3	4	.207	.328	.432	.761
17	NYY	AL	66	194	43	4	1	11	(4	7)	82	33	32	30	35	1	54	10	0	2	0	0	6	.222	.365	.423	.788
20	Tex	AL	31	108	26	7	1	2	(1	1)	41	11	7	12	10	0	26	3	0	0	1	1	0	.241	.322	.380	.702
20	NYM	NL	14	49	11	2	0	2	(2	0)	19	5	5	5	1	0	16	1	0	0	0	0	1	.224	.255	.388	.643
	Postseason		18	53	10	3	0	1	(1	0)	16	6	6	5	5	0	13	0	0	0	0	1	0	.189	.259	.302	.561
	10 ML YEARS		1231	4357	1056	211	15	218	(111	107)	1951	601	636	571	435	12	1079	75	4	38	73	38	94	.242	.319	.448	.767

Kyle Freeland

Pitches: L **Bats:** L **Pos:** SP-13

Ht: 6'4" **Wt:** 204 **Born:** 5/14/1993 **Age:** 28

			HOW MUCH PITCHED					WHAT HE GAVE UP										THE RESULTS							
Year	Team	Lg	G	GS	GF	IP	BFP	H	R	ER	HR	SH	SF	HB	TBB	IBB	SO	WP	W	L	Pct	Sv-Op	Hld	Vel	OPS	ERC	ERA
2017	Col	NL	33	28	0	156.0	688	169	78	71	17	14	7	8	63	4	107	1	11	11	.500	0-0	0	92	.792	4.83	4.10
2018	Col	NL	33	33	0	202.1	844	182	64	64	17	5	6	6	70	2	173	1	17	7	.708	0-0	0	92	.666	3.33	2.85
2019	Col	NL	22	22	0	104.1	473	126	85	78	25	2	4	2	39	3	79	4	3	11	.214	0-0	0	92	.909	6.23	6.73
2020	Col	NL	13	13	0	70.2	304	77	34	34	9	0	1	3	23	0	46	0	2	3	.400	0-0	0	92	.772	4.73	4.33
	Postseason		1	1	0	6.2	24	4	0	0	0	0	0	0	1	0	6	0	0	0	-	0-0	0	93	.382	1.06	0.00
	4 ML YEARS		101	96	0	533.1	2309	554	261	247	68	21	18	19	195	9	405	7	33	32	.508	0-0	0	92	.767	4.49	4.17

Freddie Freeman

Bats: L **Throws:** R **Pos:** 1B-58;DH-2;PH-2

Ht: 6'5" **Wt:** 220 **Born:** 9/12/1989 **Age:** 31

									BATTING											RUNNING			AVERAGES			
Year	Team	Lg	G	AB	H	2B	3B	HR	(Hm	Rd)	TB	R	RBI	RC	TBB	IBB	SO	HBP	SH	SF	SB	CS	GDP	Avg	OBP	Slg	OPS
2010	Atl	NL	20	24	4	1	0	1	(0	1)	8	3	1	0	0	0	8	0	0	0	0	0	1	.167	.167	.333	.500
2011	Atl	NL	157	571	161	32	0	21	(9	12)	256	67	76	79	53	3	142	6	0	5	4	4	15	.282	.346	.448	.795
2012	Atl	NL	147	540	140	33	2	23	(12	11)	246	91	94	82	64	4	129	7	0	9	2	0	10	.259	.340	.456	.796
2013	Atl	NL	147	551	176	27	2	23	(16	7)	276	89	109	124	66	10	121	7	0	5	1	0	11	.319	.396	.501	.897
2014	Atl	NL	162	607	175	43	4	18	(7	11)	280	93	78	101	90	4	145	8	0	3	3	4	18	.288	.386	.461	.847
2015	Atl	NL	118	416	115	27	0	18	(5	13)	196	62	66	77	56	4	98	7	0	2	3	1	6	.276	.370	.471	.841
2016	Atl	NL	158	589	178	43	6	34	(15	19)	335	102	91	119	89	18	171	10	0	5	6	1	12	.302	.400	.569	.968
2017	Atl	NL	117	440	135	35	2	28	(11	17)	258	84	71	93	65	14	95	7	0	3	8	5	9	.307	.403	.586	.989
2018	Atl	NL	162	618	191	44	4	23	(13	10)	312	94	98	115	76	12	132	7	0	6	10	3	11	.309	.388	.505	.892
2019	Atl	NL	158	597	176	34	2	38	(22	16)	328	113	121	126	87	11	127	6	0	2	6	3	17	.295	.389	.549	.938
2020	Atl	NL	60	214	73	23	1	13	(9	4)	137	51	53	68	45	7	37	3	0	0	2	0	6	.341	.462	.640	1.102
	Postseason		14	56	16	3	0	2	(2	0)	25	6	2	4	4	0	14	1	0	0	0	0	1	.286	.344	.446	.791
	11 ML YEARS		1406	5167	1524	342	23	240	(119	121)	2632	849	858	984	691	87	1205	68	0	39	45	21	116	.295	.383	.509	.892

Mike Freeman

Bats: L Throws: R Pos: PH-8;3B-6;2B-4;LF-4;SS-3;PR-2;1B-1;DH-1   Ht: 6'0" Wt: 195 Born: 8/4/1987 Age: 33

Year	Team	Lg	G	AB	H	2B	3B	HR	(Hm	Rd)	TB	R	RBI	RC	TBB	IBB	SO	HBP	SH	SF	SB	CS	GDP	Avg	OBP	Slg	OPS
2016	2 Tms		21	22	5	1	0	0	(0	0)	6	1	1	1	2	0	7	0	0	0	0	0	2	.227	.292	.273	.564
2017	3 Tms		35	60	6	2	0	1	(1	0)	11	6	1	2	6	1	19	0	0	0	0	0	0	.100	.182	.183	.365
2018	ChC	NL	1	0	0	0	0	0	(0	0)	0	0	0	0	0	0	0	0	1	0	0	0	0	-	-	-	-
2019	Cle	AL	75	177	49	8	0	4	(3	1)	69	27	24	28	22	0	61	4	6	4	1	2	2	.277	.362	.390	.752
2020	Cle	AL	24	38	9	3	0	0	(0	0)	12	5	3	4	3	0	11	1	0	1	0	0	0	.237	.302	.316	.618
16	Ari	NL	8	9	0	0	0	0	(0	0)	0	0	0	0	2	0	5	0	0	0	0	0	1	.000	.182	.000	.182
16	Sea	AL	13	13	5	1	0	0	(0	0)	6	1	1	1	0	0	2	0	0	0	0	0	1	.385	.385	.462	.846
17	Sea	AL	16	30	2	0	0	1	(1	0)	5	3	1	0	4	1	9	0	0	0	0	0	0	.067	.176	.167	.343
17	LAD	NL	4	5	0	0	0	0	(0	0)	0	0	0	0	0	0	2	0	0	0	0	0	0	.000	.000	.000	.000
17	ChC	NL	15	25	4	2	0	0	(0	0)	6	3	0	2	2	0	8	0	0	0	0	0	0	.160	.222	.240	.462
5 ML YEARS			156	297	69	14	0	5	(4	1)	98	39	29	35	33	1	98	5	7	5	1	2	5	.232	.315	.330	.645

Sam Freeman

Pitches: L Bats: R Pos: RP-7   Ht: 5'11" Wt: 180 Born: 6/24/1987 Age: 34

Year	Team	Lg	G	GS	GF	IP	BFP	H	R	ER	HR	SH	SF	HB	TBB	IBB	SO	WP	W	L	Pct	Sv-Op	Hld	Vel	OPS	ERC	ERA
2012	StL	NL	24	0	7	20.0	86	17	13	12	2	1	0	1	10	0	18	0	0	2	.000	0-0	2	93	.654	3.84	5.40
2013	StL	NL	13	0	2	12.1	50	8	3	3	0	1	0	0	5	0	8	2	1	0	1.000	0-0	1	95	.515	1.67	2.19
2014	StL	NL	44	0	9	38.0	169	34	13	11	2	1	1	4	19	0	35	3	2	0	1.000	0-0	11	94	.638	3.89	2.61
2015	Tex	AL	54	0	10	38.1	171	31	13	13	4	0	1	3	25	0	40	0	0	0	-	0-0	12	94	.683	4.31	3.05
2016	Mil	NL	7	0	4	7.2	44	13	11	11	2	0	2	0	9	0	8	1	0	0	-	0-0	0	94	1.136	13.79	12.91
2017	Atl	NL	58	0	5	60.0	254	48	19	17	3	1	1	3	27	2	59	2	2	0	1.000	0-3	12	95	.592	2.97	2.55
2018	Atl	NL	63	0	4	50.1	216	41	26	24	3	1	2	2	32	2	58	4	3	5	.375	0-3	9	95	.667	3.85	4.29
2019	LAA	AL	1	0	0	2.0	11	3	1	1	1	0	0	0	2	0	0	0	0	0	-	0-0	0	93	1.121	13.58	4.50
2020	Was	NL	7	0	1	5.0	25	2	1	1	0	0	0	0	7	1	6	0	0	0	-	0-0	1	94	.471	3.06	1.80
Postseason			1	0	0	0.0	2	0	0	0	0	0	0	0	2	0	0	0	0	0	-	0-0	0	94	-	-	-
9 ML YEARS			271	0	42	233.2	1026	197	100	93	17	5	7	13	136	5	232	12	8	7	.533	0-6	48	94	.657	3.88	3.58

Max Fried

Pitches: L Bats: L Pos: SP-11   Ht: 6'4" Wt: 190 Born: 1/18/1994 Age: 27

Year	Team	Lg	G	GS	GF	IP	BFP	H	R	ER	HR	SH	SF	HB	TBB	IBB	SO	WP	W	L	Pct	Sv-Op	Hld	Vel	OPS	ERC	ERA
2017	Atl	NL	9	4	4	26.0	121	30	15	11	3	0	0	4	12	1	22	0	1	1	.500	0-0	0	92	.818	5.92	3.81
2018	Atl	NL	14	5	5	33.2	142	26	12	11	3	2	2	2	20	0	44	2	1	4	.200	0-0	1	93	.688	3.84	2.94
2019	Atl	NL	33	30	1	165.2	702	174	80	74	21	3	2	5	47	3	173	11	17	6	.739	0-0	0	94	.743	4.22	4.02
2020	Atl	NL	11	11	0	56.0	224	42	14	14	2	0	2	4	19	0	50	1	7	0	1.000	0-0	0	93	.622	2.46	2.25
Postseason			8	0	0	6.1	29	6	5	5	1	0	0	0	4	0	7	1	0	0	-	0-0	2	95	.905	5.02	7.11
4 ML YEARS			67	50	10	281.1	1189	272	121	110	29	5	6	15	98	4	289	14	26	11	.703	0-0	1	93	.722	3.95	3.52

Jace Fry

Pitches: L Bats: L Pos: RP-18   Ht: 6'1" Wt: 220 Born: 7/9/1993 Age: 27

Year	Team	Lg	G	GS	GF	IP	BFP	H	R	ER	HR	SH	SF	HB	TBB	IBB	SO	WP	W	L	Pct	Sv-Op	Hld	Vel	OPS	ERC	ERA
2017	CWS	AL	11	0	3	6.2	36	12	8	8	1	0	0	0	5	1	3	3	0	0	-	0-0	0	94	1.085	10.97	10.80
2018	CWS	AL	59	1	12	51.1	214	37	28	25	4	2	0	1	20	0	70	5	2	3	.400	4-5	16	93	.567	2.43	4.38
2019	CWS	AL	68	0	6	55.0	251	44	33	29	7	2	1	3	43	3	68	4	3	4	.429	0-2	11	92	.733	4.74	4.75
2020	CWS	AL	18	0	4	19.2	83	16	9	8	3	0	0	0	12	2	24	1	0	1	.000	0-0	1	90	.732	4.19	3.66
4 ML YEARS			156	1	25	132.2	584	109	78	70	15	4	1	4	80	6	165	13	5	8	.385	4-7	28	92	.692	3.97	4.75

Paul Fry

Pitches: L Bats: L Pos: RP-22   Ht: 6'0" Wt: 205 Born: 7/26/1992 Age: 28

Year	Team	Lg	G	GS	GF	IP	BFP	H	R	ER	HR	SH	SF	HB	TBB	IBB	SO	WP	W	L	Pct	Sv-Op	Hld	Vel	OPS	ERC	ERA
2018	Bal	AL	35	0	11	37.2	159	33	20	14	1	0	0	4	15	0	36	3	1	2	.333	2-4	9	91	.613	3.34	3.35
2019	Bal	AL	66	0	8	57.1	255	54	39	34	7	1	0	6	29	1	55	2	1	9	.100	3-8	11	91	.752	4.72	5.34
2020	Bal	AL	22	0	4	22.0	98	22	7	6	3	0	0	1	9	0	29	3	1	0	1.000	0-0	4	93	.724	4.45	2.45
3 ML YEARS			123	0	23	117.0	512	109	66	54	11	1	0	11	53	1	120	8	3	11	.214	5-12	24	91	.703	4.22	4.15

Josh Fuentes

Bats: R Throws: R Pos: 1B-26;3B-6;PH-4;LF-2;RF-1   Ht: 6'2" Wt: 209 Born: 2/19/1993 Age: 28

Year	Team	Lg	G	AB	H	2B	3B	HR	(Hm	Rd)	TB	R	RBI	RC	TBB	IBB	SO	HBP	SH	SF	SB	CS	GDP	Avg	OBP	Slg	OPS
2019	Col	NL	24	55	12	1	0	3	(2	1)	22	8	7	4	1	0	20	0	0	0	1	0	0	.218	.232	.400	.632
2020	Col	NL	30	98	30	7	0	2	(1	1)	43	14	17	15	2	0	29	1	0	2	1	0	1	.306	.320	.439	.759
2 ML YEARS			54	153	42	8	0	5	(3	2)	65	22	24	19	3	0	49	1	0	2	2	0	1	.275	.289	.425	.714

Carson Fulmer

Pitches: R Bats: R Pos: RP-10
Ht: 6'0" Wt: 215 Born: 12/13/1993 Age: 27

Year	Team	Lg	G	GS	GF	IP	BFP	H	R	ER	HR	SH	SF	HB	TBB	IBB	SO	WP	W	L	Pct	Sv-Op	Hld	Vel	OPS	ERC	ERA
2016	CWS	AL	8	0	4	11.2	53	12	11	11	2	0	0	2	7	0	10	2	0	2	.000	0-1	0	93	.873	6.57	8.49
2017	CWS	AL	7	5	0	23.1	101	16	10	10	4	1	0	2	13	0	19	0	3	1	.750	0-0	0	93	.639	3.71	3.86
2018	CWS	AL	9	8	1	32.1	164	37	32	29	8	1	2	5	24	0	29	2	2	4	.333	0-0	0	93	.935	8.08	8.07
2019	CWS	AL	20	2	3	27.1	133	26	22	19	5	0	3	3	20	0	25	1	1	2	.333	0-0	1	94	.780	6.01	6.26
2020	2 Tms	AL	10	0	3	10.1	46	8	5	5	1	0	0	2	5	0	11	3	0	0	-	0-0	0	92	.685	3.78	4.35
20	Det	AL	7	0	1	6.2	32	8	5	5	1	0	0	1	3	0	7	1	0	0	-	0-0	0	92	.875	6.33	6.75
20	Bal	AL	3	0	2	3.2	14	0	0	0	0	0	0	1	2	0	4	2	0	0	-	0-0	0	93	.214	0.66	0.00
5 ML YEARS			54	15	11	105.0	497	99	80	74	20	2	5	14	69	0	94	8	6	9	.400	0-1	1	93	.803	5.90	6.34

Michael Fulmer

Pitches: R Bats: R Pos: SP-10
Ht: 6'3" Wt: 246 Born: 3/15/1993 Age: 28

Year	Team	Lg	G	GS	GF	IP	BFP	H	R	ER	HR	SH	SF	HB	TBB	IBB	SO	WP	W	L	Pct	Sv-Op	Hld	Vel	OPS	ERC	ERA
2016	Det	AL	26	26	0	159.0	647	136	57	54	16	4	2	9	42	1	132	1	11	7	.611	0-0	0	95	.652	3.02	3.06
2017	Det	AL	25	25	0	164.2	676	150	80	70	13	3	8	8	40	2	114	3	10	12	.455	0-0	0	96	.644	3.04	3.83
2018	Det	AL	24	24	0	132.1	558	128	75	69	19	1	2	5	46	1	110	1	3	12	.200	0-0	0	96	.758	4.18	4.69
2020	Det	AL	10	10	0	27.2	136	45	27	27	8	1	2	1	12	0	20	0	0	2	.000	0-0	0	93	1.046	10.13	8.78
4 ML YEARS			85	85	0	483.2	2017	459	239	220	56	9	14	23	140	4	376	5	24	33	.421	0-0	0	95	.705	3.68	4.09

Kyle Funkhouser

Pitches: R Bats: R Pos: RP-13
Ht: 6'3" Wt: 225 Born: 3/16/1994 Age: 27

Year	Team	Lg	G	GS	GF	IP	BFP	H	R	ER	HR	SH	SF	HB	TBB	IBB	SO	WP	W	L	Pct	Sv-Op	Hld	Vel	OPS	ERC	ERA
2020	Det	AL	13	0	4	17.1	81	22	14	14	3	0	1	0	11	0	12	1	1	1	.500	0-0	0	95	.929	7.49	7.27

Cam Gallagher

Bats: R Throws: R Pos: C-25
Ht: 6'3" Wt: 230 Born: 12/6/1992 Age: 28

Year	Team	Lg	G	AB	H	2B	3B	HR	(Hm	Rd)	TB	R	RBI	RC	TBB	IBB	SO	HBP	SH	SF	SB	CS	GDP	Avg	OBP	Slg	OPS
2017	KC	AL	13	24	6	1	0	1	(0	1)	10	2	5	4	3	0	4	0	0	0	0	0	1	.250	.333	.417	.750
2018	KC	AL	22	63	13	3	0	1	(1	0)	19	5	7	5	3	0	15	1	0	1	0	0	1	.206	.250	.302	.552
2019	KC	AL	45	126	30	7	0	3	(2	1)	46	14	12	14	11	0	28	3	1	1	0	1	3	.238	.312	.365	.677
2020	KC	AL	25	53	15	5	0	1	(0	1)	23	10	3	6	6	0	11	0	1	0	0	0	0	.283	.356	.434	.790
4 ML YEARS			105	266	64	16	0	6	(3	3)	98	31	27	29	23	0	58	4	3	2	0	1	5	.241	.308	.368	.677

Giovanny Gallegos

Pitches: R Bats: R Pos: RP-16
gah-YAY-gohss
Ht: 6'2" Wt: 215 Born: 8/14/1991 Age: 29

Year	Team	Lg	G	GS	GF	IP	BFP	H	R	ER	HR	SH	SF	HB	TBB	IBB	SO	WP	W	L	Pct	Sv-Op	Hld	Vel	OPS	ERC	ERA
2017	NYY	AL	16	0	7	20.1	88	21	12	11	3	1	1	0	5	1	22	1	0	1	.000	0-1	0	94	.740	3.76	4.87
2018	2 Tms		6	0	4	11.1	45	11	5	5	2	1	0	0	3	0	12	0	0	0	-	1-1	0	94	.782	4.10	3.97
2019	StL	NL	66	0	10	74.0	279	44	19	19	9	0	1	3	16	2	93	3	3	2	.600	1-4	19	94	.546	1.66	2.31
2020	StL	NL	16	0	7	15.0	57	9	6	6	1	0	0	0	4	0	21	1	2	2	.500	4-4	1	94	.473	1.51	3.60
18	NYY	AL	4	0	2	10.0	40	10	5	5	2	1	0	0	3	0	10	0	0	0	-	1-1	0	94	.833	4.63	4.50
18	StL	NL	2	0	2	1.1	5	1	0	0	0	0	0	0	0	0	2	0	0	0	-	0-0	0	95	.400	1.13	0.00
	Postseason		5	0	0	4.1	19	3	1	1	0	0	0	0	3	1	6	0	0	0	-	0-0	0		.628	2.37	2.08
4 ML YEARS			104	0	28	120.2	469	85	42	41	15	2	2	3	28	3	148	5	5	5	.500	6-10	20	94	.595	2.16	3.06

Zac Gallen

Pitches: R Bats: R Pos: SP-12
Ht: 6'2" Wt: 198 Born: 8/3/1995 Age: 25

Year	Team	Lg	G	GS	GF	IP	BFP	H	R	ER	HR	SH	SF	HB	TBB	IBB	SO	WP	W	L	Pct	Sv-Op	Hld	Vel	OPS	ERC	ERA
2019	2 Tms	NL	15	15	0	80.0	334	62	26	25	8	0	1	4	36	1	96	3	3	6	.333	0-0	0	93	.660	3.24	2.81
2020	Ari	NL	12	12	0	72.0	291	55	24	22	9	1	0	2	25	0	82	4	3	2	.600	0-0	0	93	.620	2.91	2.75
19	Mia	NL	7	7	0	36.1	151	25	12	11	3	0	0	2	18	1	43	1	1	3	.250	0-0	0	93	.603	2.83	2.72
19	Ari	NL	8	8	0	43.2	183	37	14	14	5	0	1	2	18	0	53	2	2	3	.400	0-0	0	93	.707	3.60	2.89
2 ML YEARS			27	27	0	152.0	625	117	50	47	17	1	1	6	61	1	178	7	6	8	.429	0-0	0	93	.641	3.09	2.78

Joey Gallo

Bats: L Throws: R Pos: RF-53;DH-2;PH-2;CF-1
Ht: 6'5" Wt: 250 Born: 11/19/1993 Age: 27

Year	Team	Lg	G	AB	H	2B	3B	HR	(Hm	Rd)	TB	R	RBI	RC	TBB	IBB	SO	HBP	SH	SF	SB	CS	GDP	Avg	OBP	Slg	OPS
2015	Tex	AL	36	108	22	3	1	6	(4	2)	45	16	14	13	15	3	57	0	0	0	3	0	0	.204	.301	.417	.717
2016	Tex	AL	17	25	1	0	0	1	(1	0)	4	2	1	0	5	0	19	0	0	0	1	0	0	.040	.200	.160	.360
2017	Tex	AL	145	449	94	18	3	41	(22	19)	241	85	80	84	75	1	196	8	0	0	7	2	3	.209	.333	.537	.869
2018	Tex	AL	148	500	103	24	1	40	(23	17)	249	82	92	80	74	4	207	3	0	3	3	4	3	.206	.312	.498	.810
2019	Tex	AL	70	241	61	15	1	22	(13	9)	144	54	49	50	52	4	114	2	1	1	4	2	0	.253	.389	.598	.986
2020	Tex	AL	57	193	35	8	0	10	(5	5)	73	23	26	29	29	2	79	4	0	0	2	0	0	.181	.301	.378	.679
6 ML YEARS			473	1516	316	68	6	120	(68	52)	756	262	262	256	250	14	672	17	1	1	20	8	6	.208	.327	.499	.825

Freddy Galvis

Bats: B **Throws:** R **Pos:** SS-33;2B-16;PH-3;PR-1 GAL-viss **Ht:** 5'10" **Wt:** 195 **Born:** 11/14/1989 **Age:** 31

Year	Team	Lg	G	AB	H	2B	3B	HR	(Hm	Rd)	TB	R	RBI	RC	TBB	IBB	SO	HBP	SH	SF	SB	CS	GDP	Avg	OBP	Slg	OPS
2012	Phi	NL	58	190	43	15	1	3	(3	0)	69	14	24	14	7	0	29	0	3	0			6	.226	.254	.363	.617
2013	Phi	NL	70	205	48	5	4	6	(4	2)	79	13	19	20	13	2	45	1	3	0	1	0	5	.234	.283	.385	.668
2014	Phi	NL	43	119	21	3	1	4	(2	2)	38	14	12	9	8	0	30	0	0	1	1	0	0	.176	.227	.319	.546
2015	Phi	NL	151	559	147	14	5	7	(6	1)	192	63	50	64	30	1	103	3	7	4	10	1	11	.263	.302	.343	.645
2016	Phi	NL	158	584	141	26	3	20	(11	9)	233	61	67	59	25	6	136	3	8	4	17	6	16	.241	.274	.399	.673
2017	Phi	NL	162	608	155	29	6	12	(10	2)	232	71	61	77	45	2	111	4	2	4	14	5	12	.255	.309	.382	.690
2018	SD	NL	162	602	149	31	5	13	(5	8)	229	62	67	65	45	2	147	2	1	6	8	6	8	.248	.299	.380	.680
2019	2 Tms	NL	147	557	145	28	1	23	(9	14)	244	67	70	69	28	1	145	1	1	2	4	2	14	.260	.296	.438	.734
2020	Cin	NL	47	141	31	5	0	7	(5	2)	57	18	16	17	13	0	30	5	0	0	1	1	5	.220	.308	.404	.712
19	Tor	AL	115	450	120	24	1	18	(7	11)	200	55	54	56	21	1	112	0	1	1	4	1	11	.267	.299	.444	.743
19	Cin	NL	32	107	25	4	0	5	(2	3)	44	12	16	13	7	0	33	1	0	1	0	1	3	.234	.284	.411	.696
	9 ML YEARS		998	3565	880	156	26	95	(55	40)	1373	383	386	394	214	14	776	19	25	21	56	21	77	.247	.291	.385	.677

Ben Gamel

Bats: L **Throws:** L **Pos:** RF-27;CF-11;PH-3;PR-2;LF-1 **Ht:** 5'11" **Wt:** 177 **Born:** 5/17/1992 **Age:** 29

Year	Team	Lg	G	AB	H	2B	3B	HR	(Hm	Rd)	TB	R	RBI	RC	TBB	IBB	SO	HBP	SH	SF	SB	CS	GDP	Avg	OBP	Slg	OPS
2016	2 Tms	AL	33	48	9	2	0	1	(0	1)	14	9	5	4	6	0	16	0	3	0	0	0	1	.188	.278	.292	.569
2017	Sea	AL	134	509	140	27	5	11	(5	6)	210	68	59	68	36	1	122	1	1	3	4	1	8	.275	.322	.413	.735
2018	Sea	AL	101	257	70	14	4	1	(1	0)	95	37	19	38	31	1	61	4	0	1	7	3	4	.272	.358	.370	.728
2019	Mil	NL	134	311	77	18	0	7	(4	3)	116	47	33	40	40	2	104	3	0	2	2	2	0	.248	.337	.373	.710
2020	Mil	NL	40	114	27	8	1	3	(1	2)	46	13	10	15	13	0	39	0	0	0	0	0	4	.237	.315	.404	.718
16	NYY	AL	6	8	1	0	0	0	(0	0)	1	1	0	0	1	0	1	0	1	0	0	0	1	.125	.222	.125	.347
16	Sea	AL	27	40	8	2	0	1	(0	1)	13	8	5	4	5	0	15	0	2	0	0	0	0	.200	.289	.325	.614
	Postseason		1	1	0	0	0	0	(0	0)	0	0	0	0	0	0	0	0	0	0	0	0	0	.000	.000	.000	.000
	5 ML YEARS		442	1239	323	69	10	23	(11	12)	481	174	126	165	126	4	342	8	4	6	13	8	17	.261	.331	.388	.720

John Gant

Pitches: R **Bats:** R **Pos:** RP-17 **Ht:** 6'4" **Wt:** 200 **Born:** 8/6/1992 **Age:** 28

			HOW MUCH PITCHED						WHAT HE GAVE UP									THE RESULTS							
Year	Team	Lg	G	GS	GF	IP	BFP	H	R	ER	HR	SH	SF	HB	TBB	IBB	SO	WP	W	L	Pct	Sv-Op	Hld	Vel	OPS	ERC	ERA
2016	Atl	NL	20	7	6	50.0	222	54	32	27	7	3	2	2	21	3	49	4	1	4	.200	0-0	0	92	.831	4.97	4.86
2017	StL	NL	7	2	1	17.1	76	17	9	9	4	0	1	1	10	1	11	0	0	1	.000	0-0	0	93	.884	6.01	4.67
2018	StL	NL	26	19	1	114.0	487	91	54	44	9	2	4	2	57	3	95	5	7	6	.538	0-0	0	93	.646	3.21	3.47
2019	StL	NL	64	0	13	66.1	269	51	29	27	4	0	0	0	34	1	60	1	11	1	.917	3-6	18	96	.639	3.09	3.66
2020	StL	NL	17	0	2	15.0	61	9	6	4	0	0	0	0	7	0	18	1	0	3	.000	0-0	5	94	.447	1.65	2.40
	5 ML YEARS		134	28	23	262.2	1115	222	130	111	24	5	7	5	129	8	233	11	19	15	.559	3-6	23	94	.686	3.57	3.80

Adolis Garcia

Bats: R **Throws:** R **Pos:** LF-3 **Ht:** 6'1" **Wt:** 205 **Born:** 3/2/1993 **Age:** 28

Year	Team	Lg	G	AB	H	2B	3B	HR	(Hm	Rd)	TB	R	RBI	RC	TBB	IBB	SO	HBP	SH	SF	SB	CS	GDP	Avg	OBP	Slg	OPS
2018	StL	NL	21	17	2	1	0	0	(0	0)	3	3	1	0	0	0	7	0	0	0	0	0	0	.118	.118	.176	.294
2020	Tex	AL	3	6	0	0	0	0	(0	0)	0	0	0	0	1	0	4	0	0	0	0	0	0	.000	.143	.000	.143
	2 ML YEARS		24	23	2	1	0	0	(0	0)	3	3	1	0	1	0	11	0	0	0	0	0	0	.087	.125	.130	.255

Avisail Garcia

Bats: R **Throws:** R **Pos:** CF-44;RF-5;DH-3;PH-3 ah-vee-SAH-eel **Ht:** 6'4" **Wt:** 250 **Born:** 6/12/1991 **Age:** 30

Year	Team	Lg	G	AB	H	2B	3B	HR	(Hm	Rd)	TB	R	RBI	RC	TBB	IBB	SO	HBP	SH	SF	SB	CS	GDP	Avg	OBP	Slg	OPS
2012	Det	AL	23	47	15	0	0	0	(0	0)	15	7	3	5	3	1	10	1	0	0	0	2	1	.319	.373	.319	.692
2013	2 Tms	AL	72	244	69	7	3	7	(3	4)	103	31	31	30	9	0	59	1	0	2	3	3	8	.283	.309	.422	.731
2014	CWS	AL	46	172	42	8	0	7	(2	5)	71	19	29	20	14	1	44	2	0	2	4	1	5	.244	.305	.413	.718
2015	CWS	AL	148	553	142	17	2	13	(8	5)	202	66	59	58	36	3	141	8	0	4	7	7	13	.257	.309	.365	.675
2016	CWS	AL	120	413	101	18	2	12	(5	7)	159	59	51	56	34	0	115	4	0	2	4	4	9	.245	.307	.385	.692
2017	CWS	AL	136	518	171	27	5	18	(9	9)	262	75	80	96	33	5	111	9	0	1	5	3	14	.330	.380	.506	.885
2018	CWS	AL	93	356	84	11	2	19	(6	13)	156	47	49	38	20	2	102	4	0	5	3	1	9	.236	.281	.438	.719
2019	TB	AL	125	489	138	25	2	20	(13	7)	227	61	72	70	31	2	125	7	0	3	10	4	15	.282	.332	.464	.796
2020	Mil	NL	53	181	43	10	0	2	(1	1)	59	20	15	21	20	2	49	6	0	0	1	3	2	.238	.333	.326	.659
13	Det	AL	30	83	20	3	1	2	(1	1)	31	12	10	7	4	0	21	0	0	1	0	1	3	.241	.273	.373	.646
13	CWS	AL	42	161	49	4	2	5	(2	3)	72	19	21	23	5	0	38	1	0	1	3	2	5	.304	.327	.447	.775
	Postseason		17	43	12	1	0	1	(0	1)	16	4	7	5	2	0	10	0	0	0	1	0	1	.279	.311	.372	.683
	9 ML YEARS		816	2973	805	123	16	98	(47	51)	1254	385	389	394	200	16	756	42	0	19	37	28	76	.271	.324	.422	.746

Bryan Garcia

Pitches: R **Bats:** R **Pos:** RP-26 **Ht:** 6'1" **Wt:** 215 **Born:** 4/19/1995 **Age:** 26

			HOW MUCH PITCHED						WHAT HE GAVE UP									THE RESULTS							
Year	Team	Lg	G	GS	GF	IP	BFP	H	R	ER	HR	SH	SF	HB	TBB	IBB	SO	WP	W	L	Pct	Sv-Op	Hld	Vel	OPS	ERC	ERA
2019	Det	AL	7	0	1	6.2	33	9	9	9	1	0	0	0	5	1	7	1	0	0	-	0-1	1	94	.924	7.88	12.15
2020	Det	AL	26	0	12	21.2	93	18	6	4	0	0	1	1	10	0	12	1	2	1	.667	4-6	3	94	.559	2.84	1.66
	2 ML YEARS		33	0	13	28.1	126	27	15	13	1	0	1	1	15	1	19	2	2	1	.667	4-7	4	94	.653	3.88	4.13

Deivi Garcia

Pitches: R **Bats:** R **Pos:** SP-6 **Ht:** 5'9" **Wt:** 163 **Born:** 5/19/1999 **Age:** 22

Year	Team	Lg	G	GS	GF	IP	BFP	H	R	ER	HR	SH	SF	HB	TBB	IBB	SO	WP	W	L	Pct	Sv-Op	Hld	Vel	OPS	ERC	ERA
2017	2 Tms	Low	10	7	1	44.2	178	32	20	20	6	1	0	3	17	1	67	5	5	1	.833	0- -	-	-	.643	3.03	4.03
2018	2 Tms	Low	13	13	0	69.0	279	50	25	21	5	3	1	7	18	0	98	5	4	4	.500	0- -	-	-	.617	2.32	2.74
2019	Trntn	AA	11	11	0	53.2	235	43	23	23	2	1	0	6	26	0	87	3	4	4	.500	0- -	-	-	.622	3.23	3.86
2019	S-WB	AAA	11	6	0	40.0	178	39	25	24	8	2	3	4	20	0	45	1	1	3	.250	0- -	-	-	.848	5.54	5.40
2020	NYY	AL	6	6	0	34.1	146	35	20	19	6	1	0	1	6	0	33	0	3	2	.600	0-0	0	92	.710	3.79	4.98

Edgar Garcia

Pitches: R **Bats:** R **Pos:** RP-4 **Ht:** 6'1" **Wt:** 205 **Born:** 10/4/1996 **Age:** 24

Year	Team	Lg	G	GS	GF	IP	BFP	H	R	ER	HR	SH	SF	HB	TBB	IBB	SO	WP	W	L	Pct	Sv-Op	Hld	Vel	OPS	ERC	ERA
2019	Phi	NL	37	0	9	39.0	172	38	25	25	11	1	2	0	26	2	45	4	2	0	1.000	0-0	2	94	.906	6.55	5.77
2020	TB	AL	4	0	1	3.1	16	3	4	4	2	0	0	0	4	0	1	0	0	0	-	1-1	2	93	1.188	11.82	10.80
	2 ML YEARS		41	0	10	42.1	188	41	29	29	13	1	2	0	30	2	46	4	2	0	1.000	1-1	4	94	.928	6.93	6.17

Greg Garcia

Bats: L **Throws:** R **Pos:** PH-12;2B-11;3B-10;DH-9 **Ht:** 6'0" **Wt:** 200 **Born:** 8/8/1989 **Age:** 31

Year	Team	Lg	G	AB	H	2B	3B	HR	(Hm	Rd)	TB	R	RBI	RC	TBB	IBB	SO	HBP	SH	SF	SB	CS	GDP	Avg	OBP	Slg	OPS
2014	StL	NL	14	14	2	1	0	0	(0	0)	3	2	1	1	1	0	6	3	0	0	0	0	0	.143	.333	.214	.548
2015	StL	NL	49	75	18	5	0	2	(1	1)	29	7	4	7	10	1	12	1	1	0	0	0	2	.240	.337	.387	.724
2016	StL	NL	99	214	59	11	0	3	(0	3)	79	33	17	31	38	4	50	4	0	1	1	1	3	.276	.393	.369	.762
2017	StL	NL	133	241	61	9	2	2	(1	1)	80	27	20	30	37	0	64	6	5	1	2	1	6	.253	.365	.332	.697
2018	StL	NL	114	181	40	6	0	3	(0	3)	55	15	15	18	20	1	37	4	1	2	3	1	3	.221	.309	.304	.613
2019	SD	NL	134	311	77	13	4	4	(0	4)	110	52	31	45	53	1	83	5	1	2	0	2	4	.248	.364	.354	.718
2020	SD	NL	35	60	12	3	0	0	(0	0)	15	6	11	7	7	0	18	0	3	1	1	0	0	.200	.279	.250	.529
	Postseason		3	3	0	0	0	0	(0	0)	0	0	0	0	0	0	1	0	0	0	0	0	0	.000	.000	.000	.000
	7 ML YEARS		578	1096	269	48	6	14	(2	12)	371	142	99	139	166	7	270	23	11	7	7	5	18	.245	.354	.339	.693

Jarlin Garcia

Pitches: L **Bats:** L **Pos:** RP-19 HAR-lin **Ht:** 6'3" **Wt:** 215 **Born:** 1/18/1993 **Age:** 28

Year	Team	Lg	G	GS	GF	IP	BFP	H	R	ER	HR	SH	SF	HB	TBB	IBB	SO	WP	W	L	Pct	Sv-Op	Hld	Vel	OPS	ERC	ERA
2017	Mia	NL	68	0	14	53.1	225	47	29	28	6	2	2	4	17	0	42	5	1	2	.333	0-1	15	94	.695	3.46	4.73
2018	Mia	NL	29	7	3	66.0	278	59	37	36	16	1	2	0	28	3	40	0	3	3	.500	0-0	2	92	.792	4.52	4.91
2019	Mia	NL	53	0	11	50.2	206	40	17	17	4	1	2	2	16	2	39	4	4	2	.667	0-1	6	93	.602	2.61	3.02
2020	SF	NL	19	0	5	18.1	73	11	6	1	0	0	3	2	7	1	14	0	2	1	.667	0-0	6	94	.487	1.70	0.49
	4 ML YEARS		169	7	33	188.1	782	157	89	82	26	4	9	8	68	6	135	9	10	8	.556	0-2	29	93	.686	3.40	3.92

Jose Garcia

Bats: R **Throws:** R **Pos:** SS-21;DH-2;PH-2;PR-2 **Ht:** 6'2" **Wt:** 175 **Born:** 4/5/1998 **Age:** 23

Year	Team	Lg	G	AB	H	2B	3B	HR	(Hm	Rd)	TB	R	RBI	RC	TBB	IBB	SO	HBP	SH	SF	SB	CS	GDP	Avg	OBP	Slg	OPS
2020	Cin	NL	24	67	13	0	0	0	(0	0)	13	4	2	0	1	0	26	0	0	0	1	1	1	.194	.206	.194	.400

Leury Garcia

Bats: B **Throws:** R **Pos:** SS-10;2B-5;RF-3;PH-1 lay-OOH-ree **Ht:** 5'8" **Wt:** 185 **Born:** 3/18/1991 **Age:** 30

Year	Team	Lg	G	AB	H	2B	3B	HR	(Hm	Rd)	TB	R	RBI	RC	TBB	IBB	SO	HBP	SH	SF	SB	CS	GDP	Avg	OBP	Slg	OPS
2013	2 Tms	AL	45	101	20	1	1	0	(0	0)	23	10	2	4	7	0	34	0	2	1	7	2	0	.198	.248	.228	.475
2014	CWS	AL	74	145	24	3	0	1	(0	1)	30	13	6	0	5	1	48	0	4	1	11	1	6	.166	.192	.207	.399
2015	CWS	AL	18	14	3	0	0	0	(0	0)	3	0	1	2	1	0	7	0	0	0	1	0	0	.214	.267	.214	.481
2016	CWS	AL	18	48	11	1	1	1	(0	1)	17	6	5	5	1	0	13	1	0	0	2	1	0	.229	.260	.354	.614
2017	CWS	AL	87	300	81	15	2	9	(5	4)	127	41	33	39	13	0	69	8	3	2	8	5	4	.270	.316	.423	.739
2018	CWS	AL	82	258	70	7	4	4	(2	2)	97	23	32	38	9	0	69	3	4	1	12	1	2	.271	.303	.376	.679
2019	CWS	AL	140	577	161	27	3	8	(6	2)	218	93	40	60	21	0	139	6	11	3	15	5	6	.279	.310	.378	.688
2020	CWS	AL	16	59	16	1	0	3	(3	0)	26	6	8	9	4	0	9	0	0	0	0	0	0	.271	.317	.441	.758
13	Tex	AL	25	52	10	0	1	0	(0	0)	12	8	1	2	3	0	16	0	2	0	1	0	0	.192	.236	.231	.467
13	CWS	AL	20	49	10	1	0	0	(0	0)	11	2	1	2	4	0	18	0	0	1	6	2	0	.204	.259	.224	.484
	8 ML YEARS		480	1502	386	55	11	26	(17	9)	541	192	127	157	61	1	388	18	24	8	56	15	18	.257	.293	.360	.653

Luis Garcia

Pitches: R **Bats:** R **Pos:** RP-9; SP-2 **Ht:** 6'2" **Wt:** 240 **Born:** 1/30/1987 **Age:** 34

Year	Team	Lg	G	GS	GF	IP	BFP	H	R	ER	HR	SH	SF	HB	TBB	IBB	SO	WP	W	L	Pct	Sv-Op	Hld	Vel	OPS	ERC	ERA
2013	Phi	NL	24	0	6	31.1	138	27	15	13	3	0	0	1	23	0	23	3	1	1	.500	0-0	1	94	.764	4.85	3.73
2014	Phi	NL	13	0	5	14.0	69	14	12	10	2	1	0	2	13	0	12	2	1	0	1.000	0-0	0	95	.815	6.43	6.43
2015	Phi	NL	72	0	14	66.2	304	72	28	26	4	3	2	0	37	8	63	6	4	6	.400	2-4	16	96	.748	4.59	3.51
2016	Phi	NL	17	0	7	15.1	76	21	11	11	2	0	1	1	8	1	14	2	1	1	.500	0-1	1	97	.895	7.04	6.46
2017	Phi	NL	66	0	16	71.1	295	61	22	21	3	1	2	0	26	5	60	9	2	5	.286	2-7	14	97	.593	2.69	2.65

Year Team	Lg	G	GS	GF	IP	BFP	H	R	ER	HR	SH	SF	HB	TBB	IBB	SO	WP	W	L	Pct	Sv-Op	Hld	Vel	OPS	ERC	ERA
											HOW MUCH PITCHED / **WHAT HE GAVE UP** / **THE RESULTS**															
2018 Phi	NL	59	0	7	46.0	204	49	31	31	4	0	1	4	18	1	51	7	3	1	.750	1-4	13	97	.773	4.63	6.07
2019 LAA	AL	64	2	18	62.0	278	61	35	30	13	1	2	5	33	1	57	7	2	1	.667	1-3	6	97	.800	5.68	4.35
2020 Tex	AL	11	2	3	8.1	45	10	9	7	1	0	0	0	9	1	11	2	0	2	.000	0-0	0	97	.839	7.69	7.56
8 ML YEARS		326	4	76	315.0	1409	315	163	149	32	6	8	11	167	17	291	40	14	17	.452	6-19	51	96	.744	4.64	4.26

Luis Garcia

Bats: L Throws: R Pos: 2B-37;SS-3;PH-1
Ht: 6'2" Wt: 211 Born: 5/16/2000 Age: 21

Year Team	Lg	G	AB	H	2B	3B	HR	(Hm	Rd)	TB	R	RBI	RC	TBB	IBB	SO	HBP	SH	SF	SB	CS	GDP	Avg	OBP	Slg	OPS
2017 Nats	R	49	199	60	8	3	1	(-	-)	77	25	22	26	9	0	32	1	1	2	11	2	4	.302	.330	.387	.717
2018 2 Tms	Low	127	500	149	21	6	7	(-	-)	203	82	54	46	31	0	82	1	6	6	12	6	11	.298	.336	.406	.742
2019 Hrsbrg	AA	129	525	135	22	4	4	(-	-)	177	66	30	50	17	0	86	1	7	3	11	5	11	.257	.280	.337	.617
2020 Was	NL	40	134	37	6	0	2	(0	2)	49	18	16	16	5	0	29	0	0	0	1	1	3	.276	.302	.366	.668

Luis Garcia

Pitches: R Bats: R Pos: RP-4; SP-1
Ht: 6'1" Wt: 244 Born: 12/13/1996 Age: 24

Year Team	Lg	G	GS	GF	IP	BFP	H	R	ER	HR	SH	SF	HB	TBB	IBB	SO	WP	W	L	Pct	Sv-Op	Hld	Vel	OPS	ERC	ERA
2020 Hou	AL	5	1	1	12.1	49	7	4	4	1	0	1	1	5	0	9	1	0	1	.000	0-0	0	94	.622	2.08	2.92

Rico Garcia

Pitches: R Bats: R Pos: RP-12
Ht: 5'9" Wt: 201 Born: 1/10/1994 Age: 27

Year Team	Lg	G	GS	GF	IP	BFP	H	R	ER	HR	SH	SF	HB	TBB	IBB	SO	WP	W	L	Pct	Sv-Op	Hld	Vel	OPS	ERC	ERA
2019 Col	NL	2	1	1	6.0	30	9	7	7	3	0	0	0	5	0	2	0	0	1	.000	0-0	0	90	1.307	13.57	10.50
2020 SF	NL	12	0	2	10.0	44	13	6	6	1	0	1	0	4	0	7	2	1	1	.500	0-1	2	96	.874	6.12	5.40
2 ML YEARS		14	1	3	16.0	74	22	13	13	4	0	1	0	9	0	9	2	1	2	.333	0-1	2	94	1.044	8.72	7.31

Rony Garcia

Pitches: R Bats: R Pos: RP-13; SP-2
Ht: 6'3" Wt: 200 Born: 12/19/1997 Age: 23

Year Team	Lg	G	GS	GF	IP	BFP	H	R	ER	HR	SH	SF	HB	TBB	IBB	SO	WP	W	L	Pct	Sv-Op	Hld	Vel	OPS	ERC	ERA
2020 Det	AL	15	2	7	21.0	96	25	20	19	7	0	0	0	9	0	14	1	1	0	1.000	0-0	0	93	.940	7.04	8.14

Yimi Garcia

Pitches: R Bats: R Pos: RP-14
yee-mee
Ht: 6'2" Wt: 228 Born: 8/18/1990 Age: 30

Year Team	Lg	G	GS	GF	IP	BFP	H	R	ER	HR	SH	SF	HB	TBB	IBB	SO	WP	W	L	Pct	Sv-Op	Hld	Vel	OPS	ERC	ERA
2014 LAD	NL	8	0	5	10.0	36	6	2	2	2	0	0	0	1	0	9	0	0	0	-	0-0	1	92	.537	1.59	1.80
2015 LAD	NL	59	1	15	56.2	225	44	23	21	8	0	2	2	10	1	68	1	3	5	.375	1-6	11	93	.595	2.40	3.34
2016 LAD	NL	9	0	1	8.1	35	9	3	3	0	2	2	1	1	0	4	0	0	0	-	0-2	1	93	.644	3.23	3.24
2018 LAD	NL	25	0	3	22.1	101	29	18	14	7	0	0	2	4	1	19	0	1	2	.333	0-1	2	94	.957	6.74	5.64
2019 LAD	NL	64	0	22	62.1	247	40	28	25	15	1	1	6	14	2	66	1	1	4	.200	0-3	4	94	.671	2.65	3.61
2020 Mia	NL	14	0	4	15.0	60	9	1	1	0	0	0	0	5	0	19	0	3	0	1.000	1-2	4	94	.452	1.35	0.60
Postseason		1	0	0	1.0	4	0	0	0	0	0	0	0	1	0	3	0	0	0	-	0-0	0	94	.250	0.95	0.00
6 ML YEARS		179	1	50	174.2	704	137	75	66	32	3	5	11	35	4	185	2	8	11	.421	2-14	23	94	.661	2.85	3.40

Brett Gardner

Bats: L Throws: L Pos: LF-39;CF-10;PR-2;DH-1
Ht: 5'11" Wt: 195 Born: 8/24/1983 Age: 37

Year Team	Lg	G	AB	H	2B	3B	HR	(Hm	Rd)	TB	R	RBI	RC	TBB	IBB	SO	HBP	SH	SF	SB	CS	GDP	Avg	OBP	Slg	OPS
2008 NYY	AL	42	127	29	5	2	0	(0	0)	38	18	16	17	8	0	30	2	3	1	13	1	0	.228	.283	.299	.582
2009 NYY	AL	108	248	67	6	6	3	(1	2)	94	48	23	38	26	0	40	3	6	1	26	5	3	.270	.345	.379	.724
2010 NYY	AL	150	477	132	20	7	5	(5	0)	181	97	47	77	79	1	101	5	5	3	47	9	6	.277	.383	.379	.762
2011 NYY	AL	159	510	132	19	8	7	(4	3)	188	87	36	77	60	1	93	8	8	2	49	13	5	.259	.345	.369	.713
2012 NYY	AL	16	31	10	2	0	0	(0	0)	12	7	3	7	5	0	7	0	1	0	2	2	0	.323	.417	.387	.804
2013 NYY	AL	145	539	147	33	**10**	8	(6	2)	224	81	52	88	52	1	127	8	7	3	24	8	8	.273	.344	.416	.759
2014 NYY	AL	148	555	142	25	8	17	(8	9)	234	87	58	81	56	0	134	6	**13**	6	21	5	3	.256	.327	.422	.749
2015 NYY	AL	151	571	148	26	3	16	(12	4)	228	94	66	90	68	1	135	8	4	5	20	5	8	.259	.343	.399	.742
2016 NYY	AL	148	547	143	22	6	7	(5	2)	198	80	41	77	70	0	106	8	4	5	16	4	6	.261	.351	.362	.713
2017 NYY	AL	151	594	157	26	4	21	(11	10)	254	96	63	95	72	2	122	8	5	3	23	5	4	.264	.350	.428	.778
2018 NYY	AL	140	530	125	20	7	12	(5	7)	195	95	45	70	65	0	107	8	4	5	16	2	6	.236	.322	.368	.690
2019 NYY	AL	141	491	123	26	7	28	(12	16)	247	86	74	77	52	0	108	4	0	3	10	2	6	.251	.325	.503	.829
2020 NYY	AL	49	130	29	5	1	5	(4	1)	51	20	15	24	26	0	35	1	0	1	3	3	0	.223	.354	.392	.747
Postseason		61	163	32	3	0	2	(2	0)	41	20	16	13	13	0	48	2	3	3	6	3	2	.196	.260	.252	.511
13 ML YEARS		1548	5350	1384	235	69	129	(73	56)	2144	896	539	818	639	6	1145	64	64	36	270	64	55	.259	.343	.401	.743

Kyle Garlick

Bats: R **Throws:** R **Pos:** LF-5;RF-5;PH-2;DH-1 **Ht:** 6'1" **Wt:** 210 **Born:** 1/26/1992 **Age:** 29

Year	Team	Lg	G	AB	H	2B	3B	HR	(Hm	Rd)	TB	R	RBI	RC	TBB	IBB	SO	HBP	SH	SF	SB	CS	GDP	Avg	OBP	Slg	OPS
2019	LAD	NL	30	48	12	4	0	3	(2	1)	25	8	6	7	5	1	19	0	0	0	0	0	0	.250	.321	.521	.842
2020	Phi	NL	12	22	3	1	0	0	(0	0)	4	0	3	0	0	0	7	1	0	0	0	0	0	.136	.174	.182	.356
	2 ML YEARS		42	70	15	5	0	3	(2	1)	29	8	9	7	5	1	26	1	0	0	0	0	0	.214	.276	.414	.691

Dustin Garneau

Bats: R **Throws:** R **Pos:** C-17;PH-1 GARR-noh **Ht:** 6'2" **Wt:** 205 **Born:** 8/13/1987 **Age:** 33

Year	Team	Lg	G	AB	H	2B	3B	HR	(Hm	Rd)	TB	R	RBI	RC	TBB	IBB	SO	HBP	SH	SF	SB	CS	GDP	Avg	OBP	Slg	OPS
2015	Col	NL	22	70	11	3	0	2	(0	2)	20	6	8	5	6	2	14	0	0	0	0	0	2	.157	.224	.286	.509
2016	Col	NL	24	68	16	6	0	1	(0	1)	25	7	6	6	6	0	22	0	0	1	0	0	1	.235	.293	.368	.661
2017	2 Tms		41	112	21	8	0	2	(1	1)	35	10	9	6	12	0	36	1	1	0	0	0	3	.188	.272	.313	.585
2018	CWS	AL	1	2	1	0	0	0	(0	0)	1	0	1	1	1	0	0	0	0	0	0	0	0	.500	.667	.500	1.167
2019	2 Tms	AL	35	86	21	5	0	3	(1	2)	35	14	14	15	10	0	22	4	0	0	0	0	1	.244	.350	.407	.757
2020	Hou	AL	17	38	6	0	1	1	(1	0)	11	4	4	2	6	0	15	0	2	0	0	0	1	.158	.273	.289	.562
17	Col	NL	22	68	14	7	0	1	(1	0)	24	5	6	4	4	0	24	1	1	0	0	0	1	.206	.260	.353	.613
17	Oak	AL	19	44	7	1	0	1	(0	1)	11	5	3	2	8	0	12	0	0	0	0	0	2	.159	.288	.250	.538
19	LAA	AL	28	69	16	3	0	2	(1	1)	25	11	7	9	8	0	18	4	0	0	0	0	1	.232	.346	.362	.708
19	Oak	AL	7	17	5	2	0	1	(0	1)	10	3	7	6	2	0	4	0	0	0	0	0	0	.294	.368	.588	.957
	6 ML YEARS		140	376	76	22	1	9	(3	6)	127	41	42	35	41	2	109	5	3	1	0	0	8	.202	.288	.338	.626

Amir Garrett

Pitches: L **Bats:** R **Pos:** RP-21 **Ht:** 6'5" **Wt:** 239 **Born:** 5/3/1992 **Age:** 29

Year	Team	Lg	G	GS	GF	IP	BFP	H	R	ER	HR	SH	SF	HB	TBB	IBB	SO	WP	W	L	Pct	Sv-Op	Hld	Vel	OPS	ERC	ERA
2017	Cin	NL	16	14	0	70.2	321	74	60	58	23	1	3	2	40	2	63	1	3	8	.273	0-0	1	92	.937	6.86	7.39
2018	Cin	NL	66	0	7	63.0	264	56	30	30	8	1	1	3	25	3	71	3	1	2	.333	0-2	15	95	.734	3.81	4.29
2019	Cin	NL	69	0	4	56.0	246	44	22	20	7	0	0	4	35	1	78	5	5	3	.625	0-3	22	95	.695	4.19	3.21
2020	Cin	NL	21	0	1	18.1	69	10	5	5	4	0	0	0	7	0	26	0	1	0	1.000	1-2	6	95	.601	2.45	2.45
	4 ML YEARS		172	14	12	208.0	900	184	117	113	42	2	4	9	107	6	238	9	10	13	.435	1-7	50	94	.785	4.77	4.89

Braxton Garrett

Pitches: L **Bats:** L **Pos:** SP-2 **Ht:** 6'2" **Wt:** 202 **Born:** 8/5/1997 **Age:** 23

Year	Team	Lg	G	GS	GF	IP	BFP	H	R	ER	HR	SH	SF	HB	TBB	IBB	SO	WP	W	L	Pct	Sv-Op	Hld	Vel	OPS	ERC	ERA
2020	Mia	NL	2	2	0	7.2	34	8	6	5	3	0	0	0	5	0	8	1	1	1	.500	0-0	0	90	1.003	8.00	5.87

Mitch Garver

Bats: R **Throws:** R **Pos:** C-22;PH-2;1B-1 **Ht:** 6'1" **Wt:** 220 **Born:** 1/15/1991 **Age:** 30

Year	Team	Lg	G	AB	H	2B	3B	HR	(Hm	Rd)	TB	R	RBI	RC	TBB	IBB	SO	HBP	SH	SF	SB	CS	GDP	Avg	OBP	Slg	OPS
2017	Min	AL	23	46	9	1	3	0	(0	0)	16	5	3	5	6	0	15	0	0	0	0	0	1	.196	.288	.348	.636
2018	Min	AL	103	302	81	19	2	7	(4	3)	125	38	45	45	29	2	72	2	1	1	0	0	8	.268	.335	.414	.749
2019	Min	AL	93	311	85	16	1	31	(16	15)	196	70	67	71	41	0	87	5	0	2	0	0	5	.273	.365	.630	.995
2020	Min	AL	23	72	12	1	0	2	(2	0)	19	8	5	3	7	0	37	1	0	1	0	0	1	.167	.247	.264	.511
	Postseason		3	12	2	0	0	0	(0	0)	2	1	1	1	1	0	5	0	0	0	0	0	0	.167	.231	.167	.397
	4 ML YEARS		242	731	187	37	6	40	(22	18)	356	121	120	124	83	2	211	8	1	4	0	0	15	.256	.337	.487	.824

Kevin Gausman

Pitches: R **Bats:** L **Pos:** SP-10; RP-2 gauze-min **Ht:** 6'2" **Wt:** 190 **Born:** 1/6/1991 **Age:** 30

Year	Team	Lg	G	GS	GF	IP	BFP	H	R	ER	HR	SH	SF	HB	TBB	IBB	SO	WP	W	L	Pct	Sv-Op	Hld	Vel	OPS	ERC	ERA
2013	Bal	AL	20	5	3	47.2	201	51	30	30	8	2	1	0	13	2	49	4	3	5	.375	0-2	2	96	.792	4.41	5.66
2014	Bal	AL	20	20	0	113.1	476	111	48	45	7	3	7	1	38	0	88	9	7	7	.500	0-0	0	95	.685	3.52	3.57
2015	Bal	AL	25	17	1	112.1	470	109	56	53	17	2	3	2	29	1	103	7	4	7	.364	0-0	1	95	.739	3.74	4.25
2016	Bal	AL	30	30	0	179.2	757	183	76	72	28	4	3	5	47	1	174	8	9	12	.429	0-0	0	95	.742	4.13	3.61
2017	Bal	AL	34	34	0	186.2	816	208	99	97	29	1	3	5	71	0	179	8	11	12	.478	0-0	0	95	.808	5.24	4.68
2018	2 Tms		31	31	0	183.2	776	189	85	80	26	4	4	7	50	1	148	6	10	11	.476	0-0	0	94	.741	3.81	3.92
2019	2 Tms	NL	31	17	6	102.1	451	113	71	65	15	7	6	5	32	3	114	2	3	9	.250	0-0	2	94	.792	4.76	5.72
2020	SF	NL	12	10	1	59.2	245	50	26	24	8	0	2	0	16	0	79	4	3	3	.500	0-0	0	95	.660	2.87	3.62
18	Bal	AL	21	21	0	124.0	534	139	62	61	21	0	2	5	32	0	104	6	5	8	.385	0-0	0	94	.806	4.88	4.43
18	Atl	NL	10	10	0	59.2	242	50	23	19	5	0	2	2	18	1	44	0	5	3	.625	0-0	0	95	.635	2.87	2.87
19	Atl	NL	16	16	0	80.0	360	92	60	55	12	6	6	4	27	2	85	2	3	7	.300	0-0	0	94	.814	5.14	6.19
19	Cin	NL	15	1	6	22.1	91	21	11	10	3	1	0	1	5	1	29	0	0	2	.000	0-0	2	95	.705	3.46	4.03
	Postseason		4	0	1	10.0	37	6	3	3	1	0	1	0	4	0	11	0	0	0	-	0-0	0	97	.583	2.21	2.70
	8 ML YEARS		203	164	11	985.1	4192	1014	491	466	138	19	29	25	296	8	934	48	50	66	.431	0-2	5	95	.753	4.23	4.26

Sam Gaviglio

Pitches: R **Bats:** R **Pos:** RP-4   guh-VEE-lee-oh   **Ht:** 6'1" **Wt:** 215 **Born:** 5/22/1990 **Age:** 31

			HOW MUCH PITCHED					WHAT HE GAVE UP											THE RESULTS							
Year	Team	Lg	G	GS	GF	IP	BFP	H	R	ER	HR	SH	SF	HB	TBB	IBB	SO	WP	W	L	Pct	Sv-Op	Hld	Vel	OPS	ERC	ERA
2017	2 Tms	AL	16	13	1	74.1	313	76	41	36	16	1	2	3	26	1	49	1	4	5	.444	0-0	0	89	.849	5.11	4.36
2018	Tor	AL	26	24	1	123.2	548	140	77	73	21	4	4	4	38	1	105	6	3	10	.231	0-0	0	88	.804	5.01	5.31
2019	Tor	AL	52	0	9	95.2	392	85	51	49	18	1	3	4	22	0	88	0	4	2	.667	0-0	3	89	.718	3.53	4.61
2020	Tor	AL	4	0	1	3.0	17	3	3	3	0	0	1	0	5	0	1	0	0	1	.000	0-0	0	88	.925	8.12	9.00
17	Sea	AL	12	11	1	62.1	259	63	37	32	15	1	2	2	21	1	40	1	3	5	.375	0-0	0	89	.866	5.16	4.62
17	KC	AL	4	2	0	12.0	54	13	4	4	1	0	0	1	5	0	9	0	1	0	1.000	0-0	0	89	.769	4.80	3.00
	4 ML YEARS		98	37	12	296.2	1270	304	172	161	55	6	10	11	91	2	243	7	11	18	.379	0-0	3	88	.790	4.58	4.88

Cory Gearrin

Pitches: R **Bats:** R **Pos:** RP-1   GARE-inn   **Ht:** 6'1" **Wt:** 205 **Born:** 4/14/1986 **Age:** 35

			HOW MUCH PITCHED					WHAT HE GAVE UP											THE RESULTS							
Year	Team	Lg	G	GS	GF	IP	BFP	H	R	ER	HR	SH	SF	HB	TBB	IBB	SO	WP	W	L	Pct	Sv-Op	Hld	Vel	OPS	ERC	ERA
2011	Atl	NL	18	0	4	18.1	85	17	16	16	0	0	1	2	12	4	25	1	1	1	.500	0-1	3	90	.722	3.84	7.85
2012	Atl	NL	22	0	7	20.0	80	17	4	4	1	0	0	2	5	0	20	2	0	1	.000	0-1	4	91	.642	2.86	1.80
2013	Atl	NL	37	0	12	31.0	133	30	13	13	2	1	0	4	16	2	23	3	2	1	.667	1-3	1	88	.754	4.73	3.77
2015	SF	NL	7	0	0	3.2	13	1	2	2	0	0	0	0	1	0	5	0	0	0	-	0-0	3	93	.237	0.47	4.91
2016	SF	NL	56	0	10	48.1	197	42	24	23	4	0	2	1	14	2	45	1	3	2	.600	3-7	15	92	.650	2.89	4.28
2017	SF	NL	68	0	21	68.0	285	50	16	15	4	1	2	7	35	4	64	3	4	3	.571	0-0	8	92	.645	3.15	1.99
2018	3 Tms		62	0	12	57.1	248	56	24	24	7	1	0	6	21	1	53	4	2	1	.667	1-3	9	92	.741	4.39	3.77
2019	2 Tms	AL	66	2	8	55.1	241	55	25	25	5	0	1	4	25	1	47	4	1	3	.250	0-0	13	91	.732	4.50	4.07
2020	Min	AL	1	0	1	2.0	7	0	0	0	0	0	0	0	2	0	1	0	0	0	-	0-0	0	91	.286	1.08	0.00
18	SF	NL	35	0	8	30.0	137	33	14	14	5	1	0	3	13	1	31	0	1	1	.500	1-3	2	92	.810	5.61	4.20
18	Tex	AL	21	0	3	21.1	82	13	6	6	2	0	0	2	6	0	20	1	1	0	1.000	0-0	7	92	.540	2.02	2.53
18	Oak	AL	6	0	1	6.0	29	10	4	4	0	0	0	1	2	0	2	3	0	0	-	0-0	0	92	.987	8.08	6.00
19	Sea	AL	48	2	3	41.1	180	38	18	18	3	0	1	4	21	1	39	4	0	2	.000	0-0	11	91	.701	4.26	3.92
19	NYY	AL	18	0	5	14.0	61	17	7	7	2	0	0	0	4	0	8	0	1	1	.500	0-2	2	91	.818	5.22	4.50
	9 ML YEARS		337	2	75	304.0	1289	268	124	122	23	3	6	26	131	14	283	18	13	12	.520	5-15	56	91	.691	3.69	3.61

Joey Gerber

Pitches: R **Bats:** R **Pos:** RP-17   **Ht:** 6'4" **Wt:** 215 **Born:** 5/3/1997 **Age:** 24

			HOW MUCH PITCHED					WHAT HE GAVE UP											THE RESULTS							
Year	Team	Lg	G	GS	GF	IP	BFP	H	R	ER	HR	SH	SF	HB	TBB	IBB	SO	WP	W	L	Pct	Sv-Op	Hld	Vel	OPS	ERC	ERA
2020	Sea	AL	17	0	3	15.2	62	13	8	7	1	0	2	1	5	0	6	1	1	1	.500	0-1	4	93	.714	3.02	4.02

Domingo German

Pitches: R **Bats:** R **Pos:** P   hair-MAHN   **Ht:** 6'2" **Wt:** 181 **Born:** 8/4/1992 **Age:** 28

			HOW MUCH PITCHED					WHAT HE GAVE UP											THE RESULTS							
Year	Team	Lg	G	GS	GF	IP	BFP	H	R	ER	HR	SH	SF	HB	TBB	IBB	SO	WP	W	L	Pct	Sv-Op	Hld	Vel	OPS	ERC	ERA
2017	NYY	AL	7	0	5	14.1	62	11	6	5	1	1	1	0	9	0	18	3	1	0	1.000	0-0	0	96	.661	3.44	3.14
2018	NYY	AL	21	14	2	85.2	375	81	55	53	15	0	2	5	33	0	102	7	2	6	.250	0-0	0	95	.774	4.39	5.57
2019	NYY	AL	27	24	0	143.0	594	125	69	64	30	1	1	5	39	0	153	5	18	4	.818	0-0	0	94	.727	3.69	4.03
	3 ML YEARS		55	38	7	243.0	1031	217	130	122	46	2	4	10	81	0	273	15	20	11	.645	0-0	0	94	.740	3.93	4.52

Ian Gibaut

Pitches: R **Bats:** R **Pos:** RP-14   jih-BOH   **Ht:** 6'3" **Wt:** 250 **Born:** 11/19/1993 **Age:** 27

			HOW MUCH PITCHED					WHAT HE GAVE UP											THE RESULTS							
Year	Team	Lg	G	GS	GF	IP	BFP	H	R	ER	HR	SH	SF	HB	TBB	IBB	SO	WP	W	L	Pct	Sv-Op	Hld	Vel	OPS	ERC	ERA
2019	2 Tms	AL	10	0	1	14.1	64	12	9	9	1	0	2	1	10	1	16	1	1	1	.500	0-0	0	95	.732	4.28	5.65
2020	Tex	AL	14	0	0	12.1	59	11	10	9	2	1	0	1	9	0	14	2	0	1	.000	0-1	2	95	.779	5.35	6.57
19	TB	AL	1	0	1	2.0	9	1	2	2	0	0	1	0	2	0	2	0	0	0	-	0-0	0	95	.667	2.80	9.00
19	Tex	AL	9	0	0	12.1	55	11	7	7	1	0	1	1	8	1	14	1	1	1	.500	0-0	0	95	.741	4.54	5.11
	2 ML YEARS		24	0	1	26.2	123	23	19	18	3	1	2	2	19	1	30	3	1	2	.333	0-1	2	95	.755	4.78	6.08

Kyle Gibson

Pitches: R **Bats:** R **Pos:** SP-12   **Ht:** 6'6" **Wt:** 215 **Born:** 10/23/1987 **Age:** 33

			HOW MUCH PITCHED					WHAT HE GAVE UP											THE RESULTS							
Year	Team	Lg	G	GS	GF	IP	BFP	H	R	ER	HR	SH	SF	HB	TBB	IBB	SO	WP	W	L	Pct	Sv-Op	Hld	Vel	OPS	ERC	ERA
2013	Min	AL	10	10	0	51.0	238	69	38	37	7	0	2	5	20	0	29	4	2	4	.333	0-0	0	92	.874	6.98	6.53
2014	Min	AL	31	31	0	179.1	757	178	91	89	12	4	3	2	57	0	107	11	13	12	.520	0-0	0	91	.679	3.54	4.47
2015	Min	AL	32	32	0	194.2	821	186	88	83	18	6	6	7	65	0	145	7	11	11	.500	0-0	0	92	.698	3.63	3.84
2016	Min	AL	25	25	0	147.1	653	175	89	83	20	3	4	4	55	3	104	9	6	11	.353	0-0	0	91	.820	5.47	5.07
2017	Min	AL	29	29	0	158.0	693	182	93	89	24	1	2	6	60	0	121	4	12	10	.545	0-0	0	92	.826	5.53	5.07
2018	Min	AL	32	32	0	196.2	826	177	88	79	23	3	7	4	79	2	179	8	10	13	.435	0-0	0	93	.701	3.75	3.62
2019	Min	AL	34	29	0	160.0	706	175	99	86	23	3	2	7	56	0	160	8	13	7	.650	0-1	2	93	.782	4.88	4.84
2020	Tex	AL	12	12	0	67.1	301	73	44	40	12	0	0	6	30	1	58	1	2	6	.250	0-0	0	92	.823	5.75	5.35
	Postseason		1	0	0	1.0	7	1	3	3	0	0	0	0	3	0	1	0	0	0	-	0-0	0	94	1.071	13.82	27.00
	8 ML YEARS		205	200	0	1154.1	4995	1215	630	586	139	20	26	41	422	12	903	52	69	74	.483	0-1	2	92	.757	4.55	4.57

Ken Giles

Pitches: R **Bats:** R **Pos:** RP-4 **Ht:** 6'3" **Wt:** 210 **Born:** 9/20/1990 **Age:** 30

Year	Team	Lg	G	GS	GF	IP	BFP	H	R	ER	HR	SH	SF	HB	TBB	IBB	SO	WP	W	L	Pct	Sv-Op	Hld	Vel	OPS	ERC	ERA
2014	Phi	NL	44	0	11	45.2	166	25	7	6	1	2	1	0	11	1	64	1	3	1	.750	1-1	13	97	.450	1.15	1.18
2015	Phi	NL	69	0	28	70.0	298	59	23	14	2	1	2	1	25	2	87	1	6	3	.667	15-20	12	97	.569	2.53	1.80
2016	Hou	AL	69	0	24	65.2	286	60	32	30	8	2	1	2	25	1	102	14	2	5	.286	15-20	18	97	.709	3.66	4.11
2017	Hou	AL	63	0	55	62.2	247	44	16	16	4	1	2	1	21	0	83	3	1	3	.250	34-38	2	98	.566	2.17	2.30
2018	2 Tms	AL	55	0	42	50.1	212	54	28	26	6	1	0	1	7	0	53	2	0	3	.000	26-26	1	97	.722	3.59	4.65
2019	Tor	AL	53	0	44	53.0	208	36	11	11	5	0	0	0	17	1	83	2	2	3	.400	23-24	0	97	.516	2.10	1.87
2020	Tor	AL	4	0	1	3.2	19	4	4	4	2	0	0	0	4	0	6	0	0	0	-	1-1	1	94	1.154	11.42	9.82
18	Hou	AL	34	0	24	30.2	129	36	17	17	2	0	0	0	3	0	31	1	0	2	.000	12-12	1	97	.723	3.59	4.99
18	Tor	AL	21	0	18	19.2	83	18	11	9	4	1	0	1	4	0	22	1	0	1	.000	14-14	0	97	.722	3.58	4.12
Postseason			7	0	4	7.2	40	12	10	10	3	0	0	0	5	1	10	3	0	2	.000	2-3	0	98	1.111	10.90	11.74
7 ML YEARS			357	0	205	351.0	1436	282	121	107	28	7	6	5	110	5	478	23	14	18	.438	115-130	47	97	.613	2.59	2.74

Sean Gilmartin

Pitches: L **Bats:** L **Pos:** RP-2 **Ht:** 6'2" **Wt:** 205 **Born:** 5/8/1990 **Age:** 31

Year	Team	Lg	G	GS	GF	IP	BFP	H	R	ER	HR	SH	SF	HB	TBB	IBB	SO	WP	W	L	Pct	Sv-Op	Hld	Vel	OPS	ERC	ERA
2015	NYM	NL	50	1	13	57.1	235	50	17	17	2	2	1	2	18	5	54	1	3	2	.600	0-1	2	89	.626	2.67	2.67
2016	NYM	NL	14	1	3	17.2	79	21	14	14	4	1	0	1	7	1	11	0	0	1	.000	0-0	0	88	.872	6.39	7.13
2017	NYM	NL	2	0	1	3.1	19	8	5	5	2	1	1	0	1	0	4	1	0	0	-	0-0	0	90	1.375	17.83	13.50
2018	Bal	AL	12	0	2	27.0	113	23	9	9	4	0	0	2	11	0	15	0	1	1	.500	0-0	0	88	.729	3.98	3.00
2019	Bal	AL	1	1	0	2.1	16	7	5	5	2	0	0	0	2	0	1	0	0	1	.000	0-0	0	90	1.563	29.43	19.29
2020	TB	AL	2	0	0	4.1	24	7	4	4	2	0	0	0	4	0	5	0	0	0	-	0-0	0	87	1.108	13.67	8.31
Postseason			1	0	1	0.2	2	0	0	0	0	0	0	0	0	0	0	0	0	0	-	0-0	0	89	.000	0.00	0.00
6 ML YEARS			81	3	19	112.0	486	116	54	54	16	4	2	5	43	6	90	2	4	5	.444	0-1	3	89	.771	4.65	4.34

Andres Gimenez

Bats: L **Throws:** R **Pos:** SS-23;2B-19;3B-10;PR-5;PH-4 **Ht:** 5'11" **Wt:** 161 **Born:** 9/4/1998 **Age:** 22

Year	Team	Lg	G	AB	H	2B	3B	HR	(Hm	Rd)	TB	R	RBI	RC	TBB	IBB	SO	HBP	SH	SF	SB	CS	GDP	Avg	OBP	Slg	OPS
2018	Bnghtn	AA	37	137	38	9	1	0	(-	-)	49	19	16	18	9	0	22	5	2	0	10	3	1	.277	.344	.358	.702
2018	Stluci	A+	85	308	87	20	4	6	(-	-)	133	43	30	49	22	1	70	11	6	4	28	11	3	.282	.348	.432	.780
2019	Bnghtn	AA	117	432	108	22	5	9	(-	-)	167	54	37	53	24	6	102	14	6	3	28	15	8	.250	.309	.387	.695
2020	NYM	NL	49	118	31	3	2	3	(2	1)	47	22	12	15	7	0	28	6	0	1	8	1	0	.263	.333	.398	.732

Kevin Ginkel

Pitches: R **Bats:** L **Pos:** RP-19 **Ht:** 6'4" **Wt:** 235 **Born:** 3/24/1994 **Age:** 27

Year	Team	Lg	G	GS	GF	IP	BFP	H	R	ER	HR	SH	SF	HB	TBB	IBB	SO	WP	W	L	Pct	Sv-Op	Hld	Vel	OPS	ERC	ERA
2019	Ari	NL	25	0	4	24.1	96	15	7	4	2	0	0	0	9	0	28	2	3	0	1.000	2-2	8	94	.532	1.91	1.48
2020	Ari	NL	19	0	2	16.0	79	21	13	12	3	0	0	0	13	2	18	4	0	2	.000	1-2	0	96	.961	8.38	6.75
2 ML YEARS			44	0	6	40.1	175	36	20	16	5	0	0	0	22	2	46	6	3	2	.600	3-4	8	95	.721	4.15	3.57

Lucas Giolito

Pitches: R **Bats:** R **Pos:** SP-12 jee-oh-LEE-toh **Ht:** 6'6" **Wt:** 245 **Born:** 7/14/1994 **Age:** 26

Year	Team	Lg	G	GS	GF	IP	BFP	H	R	ER	HR	SH	SF	HB	TBB	IBB	SO	WP	W	L	Pct	Sv-Op	Hld	Vel	OPS	ERC	ERA
2016	Was	NL	6	4	1	21.1	101	26	18	16	7	0	0	1	12	0	11	1	0	1	.000	0-0	0	93	.988	8.14	6.75
2017	CWS	AL	7	7	0	45.1	179	31	14	12	8	1	0	3	12	0	34	2	3	3	.500	0-0	0	92	.645	2.63	2.38
2018	CWS	AL	32	32	0	173.1	775	166	123	118	27	1	5	15	90	2	125	13	10	13	.435	0-0	0	92	.794	5.05	6.13
2019	CWS	AL	29	29	0	176.2	705	131	69	67	24	1	3	4	57	1	228	6	14	9	.609	0-0	0	94	.646	2.75	3.41
2020	CWS	AL	12	12	0	72.1	288	47	31	28	8	0	3	2	28	0	97	3	4	3	.571	0-0	0	94	.577	2.40	3.48
5 ML YEARS			86	84	1	489.0	2048	401	255	241	74	3	11	25	199	3	495	25	31	29	.517	0-0	0	93	.708	3.67	4.44

Mychal Givens

Pitches: R **Bats:** R **Pos:** RP-22 michael **Ht:** 6'0" **Wt:** 230 **Born:** 5/13/1990 **Age:** 31

Year	Team	Lg	G	GS	GF	IP	BFP	H	R	ER	HR	SH	SF	HB	TBB	IBB	SO	WP	W	L	Pct	Sv-Op	Hld	Vel	OPS	ERC	ERA
2015	Bal	AL	22	0	5	30.0	117	20	7	6	1	1	1	1	6	0	38	0	2	0	1.000	0-0	4	94	.538	1.49	1.80
2016	Bal	AL	66	0	8	74.2	313	59	28	26	6	2	1	6	36	2	96	3	8	2	.800	0-1	13	94	.664	3.44	3.13
2017	Bal	AL	69	0	8	78.2	315	57	24	24	10	0	0	5	25	1	88	2	8	1	.889	0-5	21	96	.617	2.74	2.75
2018	Bal	AL	69	0	32	76.2	317	61	37	34	4	1	3	3	30	4	79	4	0	7	.000	9-13	15	95	.622	2.72	3.99
2019	Bal	AL	58	0	33	63.0	260	49	35	32	13	0	2	2	26	1	86	5	2	6	.250	11-19	7	95	.722	3.74	4.57
2020	2 Tms	AL	22	0	5	22.1	93	16	10	9	5	0	1	2	10	0	25	2	1	1	.500	1-3	6	95	.751	3.91	3.63
20	Bal	AL	12	0	3	13.0	51	7	2	2	1	0	1	0	6	0	19	0	0	1	.000	0-0	5	95	.573	1.84	1.38
20	Col	NL	10	0	2	9.1	42	9	8	7	4	0	0	2	4	0	6	2	1	0	1.000	1-3	1	95	.968	7.42	6.75
Postseason			1	0	0	2.1	6	0	0	0	0	0	0	0	0	0	3	0	0	0	-	0-0	0	96	.000	0.00	0.00
6 ML YEARS			306	0	91	345.1	1415	262	141	131	39	4	8	19	133	8	412	16	21	17	.553	21-41	66	95	.650	3.01	3.41

Tyler Glasnow

Pitches: R Bats: L Pos: SP-11   Ht: 6'8" Wt: 225 Born: 8/23/1993 Age: 27

			HOW MUCH PITCHED					WHAT HE GAVE UP										THE RESULTS						
Year	Team	Lg	G	GS	GF	IP	BFP	H	R	ER	HR	SH	SF	HB	TBB	IBB	SO	WP	W	L	Pct	Sv-Op	Hld	Vel	OPS	ERC	ERA
2016	Pit	NL	7	4	0	23.1	105	22	13	11	2	1	0	3	13	0	24	2	0	2	.000	0-0	0	94	.774	4.80	4.24
2017	Pit	NL	15	13	0	62.0	305	81	61	53	13	4	1	2	44	0	56	3	2	7	.222	0-0	1	95	.997	8.32	7.69
2018	2 Tms		45	11	9	111.2	468	89	55	53	15	0	1	4	53	3	136	12	2	7	.222	0-0	4	97	.688	3.62	4.27
2019	TB	AL	12	12	0	60.2	230	40	13	12	4	0	1	0	14	0	76	2	6	1	.857	0-0	0	97	.509	1.63	1.78
2020	TB	AL	11	11	0	57.1	238	43	26	26	11	0	1	0	22	0	91	7	5	1	.833	0-0	0	97	.673	3.18	4.08
18	Pit	AL	34	0	9	56.0	243	47	28	27	5	0	0	1	34	2	72	7	1	2	.333	0-0	4	97	.698	3.95	4.34
18	TB	AL	11	11	0	55.2	225	42	27	26	10	0	1	3	19	1	64	5	1	5	.167	0-0	0	97	.676	3.26	4.20
	Postseason		2	2	0	7.0	33	9	6	6	1	0	0	0	3	0	8	0	0	2	.000	0-0	0	98	.797	6.07	7.71
	5 ML YEARS		90	51	9	315.0	1346	275	168	155	45	5	4	9	146	5	383	26	15	18	.455	0-0	5	96	.728	4.01	4.43

Zack Godley

Pitches: R Bats: R Pos: SP-7; RP-1   Ht: 6'3" Wt: 250 Born: 4/21/1990 Age: 31

			HOW MUCH PITCHED					WHAT HE GAVE UP										THE RESULTS						
Year	Team	Lg	G	GS	GF	IP	BFP	H	R	ER	HR	SH	SF	HB	TBB	IBB	SO	WP	W	L	Pct	Sv-Op	Hld	Vel	OPS	ERC	ERA
2015	Ari	NL	9	6	1	36.2	150	29	13	13	4	1	1	3	17	1	34	2	5	1	.833	0-0	0	91	.688	3.67	3.19
2016	Ari	NL	27	9	1	74.2	335	86	54	53	13	7	1	4	25	4	60	5	5	4	.556	0-1	0	91	.844	5.31	6.39
2017	Ari	NL	26	25	1	155.0	627	124	61	58	15	6	2	5	53	2	165	13	8	9	.471	0-0	0	92	.657	2.92	3.37
2018	Ari	NL	33	32	0	178.1	791	177	103	94	16	8	8	12	81	2	185	17	15	11	.577	0-0	0	90	.733	4.40	4.74
2019	2 Tms		33	9	10	92.0	407	96	62	61	14	3	2	5	42	2	70	3	4	5	.444	2-2	0	90	.824	5.17	5.97
2020	Bos	AL	8	7	0	28.2	143	42	26	26	9	0	1	3	14	0	28	3	0	4	.000	0-0	0	90	1.037	9.60	8.16
19	Ari	NL	27	9	9	76.0	338	81	55	54	12	3	2	4	35	2	58	3	3	5	.375	2-2	0	90	.834	5.35	6.39
19	Tor	AL	6	0	1	16.0	69	15	7	7	2	0	0	1	7	0	12	0	1	0	1.000	0-0	0	90	.776	4.34	3.94
	Postseason		1	0	0	5.0	22	4	3	2	0	1	0	0	2	0	5	1	0	0	-	0-0	0	90	.496	2.18	3.60
	6 ML YEARS		136	88	13	565.1	2453	554	319	305	71	25	15	32	232	11	542	43	37	34	.521	2-3	0	91	.759	4.40	4.86

Ryan Goins

Bats: L Throws: R Pos: PR-8;DH-5;3B-2;SS-2;2B-1;PH-1   GO-inns   Ht: 5'10" Wt: 180 Born: 2/13/1988 Age: 33

			BATTING																	RUNNING			AVERAGES			
Year	Team	Lg	G	AB	H	2B	3B	HR	(Hm	Rd)	TB	R	RBI	RC	TBB	IBB	SO	HBP	SH	SF	SB	CS	GDP	Avg	OBP	Slg	OPS
2013	Tor	AL	34	119	30	5	0	2	(2	0)	41	11	8	11	2	0	28	0	0	0	0	0	1	.252	.264	.345	.609
2014	Tor	AL	67	181	34	6	3	1	(1	0)	49	14	15	7	5	0	42	0	1	4	1	1	4	.188	.209	.271	.479
2015	Tor	AL	128	376	94	16	4	5	(4	1)	133	52	45	48	39	0	83	1	7	5	2	1	12	.250	.318	.354	.672
2016	Tor	AL	77	183	34	9	2	3	(1	2)	56	13	12	9	9	0	48	1	3	0	1	1	6	.186	.228	.306	.534
2017	Tor	AL	143	418	99	21	1	9	(3	6)	149	37	62	53	31	0	96	0	5	5	3	2	14	.237	.286	.356	.643
2018	KC	AL	41	115	26	8	1	0	(0	0)	36	10	6	7	4	0	29	0	1	0	0	0	2	.226	.252	.313	.565
2019	CWS	AL	52	144	36	6	1	2	(1	1)	50	13	10	16	17	1	44	1	1	0	0	1	7	.250	.333	.347	.681
2020	CWS	AL	14	9	0	0	0	0	(0	0)	0	4	0	0	1	0	1	0	0	0	0	0	0	.000	.100	.000	.100
	Postseason		14	41	6	1	0	1	(1	0)	10	5	5	3	2	0	14	0	3	0	0	0	2	.146	.186	.244	.430
	8 ML YEARS		556	1545	353	71	12	22	(12	10)	514	154	158	151	108	1	371	3	23	11	6	6	46	.228	.278	.333	.611

Paul Goldschmidt

Bats: R Throws: R Pos: 1B-52;DH-6   Ht: 6'3" Wt: 220 Born: 9/10/1987 Age: 33

			BATTING																	RUNNING			AVERAGES			
Year	Team	Lg	G	AB	H	2B	3B	HR	(Hm	Rd)	TB	R	RBI	RC	TBB	IBB	SO	HBP	SH	SF	SB	CS	GDP	Avg	OBP	Slg	OPS
2011	Ari	NL	48	156	39	9	1	8	(2	6)	74	28	26	26	20	0	53	0	0	1	4	0	4	.250	.333	.474	.808
2012	Ari	NL	145	514	147	43	1	20	(10	10)	252	82	82	86	60	4	130	4	0	9	18	3	9	.286	.359	.490	.850
2013	Ari	NL	160	602	182	36	3	36	(17	19)	332	103	125	131	99	19	145	3	0	5	15	7	25	.302	.401	.551	.952
2014	Ari	NL	109	406	122	39	1	19	(10	9)	220	75	69	83	64	10	110	2	0	3	9	3	10	.300	.396	.542	.938
2015	Ari	NL	159	567	182	38	2	33	(13	20)	323	103	110	135	118	29	151	2	0	7	21	5	16	.321	.435	.570	1.005
2016	Ari	NL	158	579	172	33	3	24	(15	9)	283	106	95	113	110	15	150	7	0	8	32	5	14	.297	.411	.489	.899
2017	Ari	NL	155	558	166	34	3	36	(20	16)	314	117	120	131	94	15	147	8	0	4	18	5	14	.297	.404	.563	.966
2018	Ari	NL	158	593	172	35	5	33	(12	21)	316	95	83	118	90	11	173	6	0	7	7	4	7	.290	.389	.533	.922
2019	StL	NL	161	597	155	25	1	34	(17	17)	284	97	97	103	78	2	166	2	0	3	3	1	11	.260	.346	.476	.821
2020	StL	NL	58	191	58	13	0	6	(4	2)	89	31	21	38	37	0	43	1	0	1	1	0	4	.304	.417	.466	.883
	Postseason		17	69	20	4	0	6	(3	3)	42	11	13	14	5	1	20	1	0	0	1	0	1	.290	.347	.609	.955
	10 ML YEARS		1311	4763	1395	305	20	249	(120	129)	2487	837	828	964	770	105	1268	35	0	41	128	33	114	.293	.392	.522	.914

Austin Gomber

Pitches: L Bats: L Pos: RP-10; SP-4   Ht: 6'5" Wt: 220 Born: 11/23/1993 Age: 27

			HOW MUCH PITCHED					WHAT HE GAVE UP										THE RESULTS						
Year	Team	Lg	G	GS	GF	IP	BFP	H	R	ER	HR	SH	SF	HB	TBB	IBB	SO	WP	W	L	Pct	Sv-Op	Hld	Vel	OPS	ERC	ERA
2018	StL	NL	29	11	1	75.0	334	81	40	37	7	4	2	4	32	4	67	3	6	2	.750	0-0	7	92	.786	4.72	4.44
2020	StL	NL	14	4	2	29.0	119	19	6	6	1	0	2	2	15	0	27	1	1	1	.500	0-0	1	93	.563	2.56	1.86
	2 ML YEARS		43	15	3	104.0	453	100	46	43	8	4	4	6	47	4	94	4	7	3	.700	0-0	8	92	.729	4.08	3.72

Yan Gomes

Bats: R Throws: R Pos: C-30   YAHN GOHMS   Ht: 6'2" Wt: 215 Born: 7/19/1987 Age: 33

Year	Team	Lg	G	AB	H	2B	3B	HR	(Hm	Rd)	TB	R	RBI	RC	TBB	IBB	SO	HBP	SH	SF	SB	CS	GDP	Avg	OBP	Slg	OPS
2012	Tor	AL	43	98	20	4	0	4	(3	1)	36	9	13	11	6	0	32	3	1	3	0	0	3	.204	.264	.367	.631
2013	Cle	AL	88	293	86	18	2	11	(6	5)	141	45	38	42	18	0	67	7	0	4	2	0	12	.294	.345	.481	.826
2014	Cle	AL	135	485	135	25	3	21	(9	12)	229	61	74	65	24	3	120	3	0	6	0	0	13	.278	.313	.472	.785
2015	Cle	AL	95	363	84	22	0	12	(5	7)	142	38	45	25	13	1	104	7	0	6	0	0	11	.231	.267	.391	.659
2016	Cle	AL	74	251	42	11	1	9	(4	5)	82	22	34	18	9	0	69	2	0	2	0	0	7	.167	.201	.327	.527
2017	Cle	AL	105	341	79	15	0	14	(5	9)	136	43	56	41	31	0	99	8	1	2	0	0	9	.232	.309	.399	.708
2018	Cle	AL	112	403	107	26	4	16	(5	11)	181	52	48	47	21	2	119	8	0	3	0	0	4	.266	.313	.449	.762
2019	Was	NL	97	314	70	16	0	12	(8	4)	122	36	43	39	38	6	84	5	0	1	2	0	7	.223	.316	.389	.704
2020	Was	NL	30	109	31	6	1	4	(4	0)	51	14	13	12	6	0	22	1	0	3	1	0	1	.284	.319	.468	.787
	Postseason		22	51	13	4	0	0	(0	0)	17	6	4	6	5	2	17	0	0	1	0	0	1	.255	.321	.333	.655
	9 ML YEARS		779	2657	654	143	7	103	(49	54)	1120	320	364	300	166	12	716	44	2	30	5	0	67	.246	.298	.422	.720

Tony Gonsolin

Pitches: R Bats: R Pos: SP-8; RP-1   Ht: 6'3" Wt: 205 Born: 5/14/1994 Age: 27

Year	Team	Lg	G	GS	GF	IP	BFP	H	R	ER	HR	SH	SF	HB	TBB	IBB	SO	WP	W	L	Pct	Sv-Op	Hld	Vel	OPS	ERC	ERA
2016	2 Tms	Low	19	0	10	31.0	127	29	14	13	1	2	1	1	8	0	25	1	1	2	.333	4- -	-		.643	2.90	3.77
2017	2 Tms	Low	42	0	20	70.0	292	69	32	30	7	0	1	0	18	0	85	5	7	6	.538	6- -	-		.708	3.53	4.05
2018	Rcuca	A+	17	17	0	83.2	347	72	31	25	5	1	3	0	26	0	106	10	4	2	.667	0- -	-		.633	2.70	2.69
2018	Tulsa	AA	9	9	0	44.1	180	32	14	12	3	3	2	1	16	1	49	4	6	0	1.000	0- -	-		.606	2.32	2.44
2019	OkCity	AAA	13	13	0	41.1	191	41	25	20	4	0	2	3	21	0	50	3	2	4	.333	0- -	-		.734	4.55	4.35
2019	LAD	NL	11	6	1	40.0	163	26	15	13	4	0	1	1	15	0	37	2	4	2	.667	1-1	0	94	.580	2.21	2.93
2020	LAD	NL	9	8	1	46.2	176	32	13	12	2	1	1	1	7	0	46	3	2	2	.500	0-0	0	95	.518	1.48	2.31
	2 ML YEARS		20	14	2	86.2	339	58	28	25	6	1	2	2	22	0	83	5	6	4	.600	1-1	0	94	.547	1.77	2.60

Marco Gonzales

Pitches: L Bats: L Pos: SP-11   Ht: 6'1" Wt: 197 Born: 2/16/1992 Age: 29

Year	Team	Lg	G	GS	GF	IP	BFP	H	R	ER	HR	SH	SF	HB	TBB	IBB	SO	WP	W	L	Pct	Sv-Op	Hld	Vel	OPS	ERC	ERA
2014	StL	NL	10	5	0	34.2	156	32	16	16	4	0	1	1	21	1	31	0	4	2	.667	0-0	1	90	.737	4.59	4.15
2015	StL	NL	1	1	0	2.2	16	7	4	4	1	0	1	0	1	0	1	0				0-0	0	89	1.286	17.70	13.50
2017	2 Tms		11	8	1	40.0	185	59	27	27	8	0	1	1	11	0	32	2	1	1	.500	0-0	0	92	.924	7.40	6.08
2018	Sea	AL	29	29	0	166.2	686	172	76	74	17	1	4	6	32	0	145	2	13	9	.591	0-0	0	90	.720	3.65	4.00
2019	Sea	AL	34	34	0	203.0	866	210	106	90	23	1	9	6	56	1	147	2	16	13	.552	0-0	0	89	.736	3.96	3.99
2020	Sea	AL	11	11	0	69.2	277	59	27	24	8	0	4	2	7	0	64	0	7	2	.778	0-0	0	88	.614	2.43	3.10
17	StL	NL	1	1	0	3.1	16	6	5	5	3	0	0	0	0	0	2	0	0	0		0-0	0	91	1.500	13.65	13.50
17	Sea	AL	10	7	1	36.2	169	53	22	22	5	0	1	1	11	0	30	2	1	1	.500	0-0	0	92	.865	6.82	5.40
	Postseason		6	0	0	6.0	24	4	3	3	0	1	0	0	2	0	4	0	2	1	.667	0-1	0	91	.451	1.57	4.50
	6 ML YEARS		96	88	1	516.2	2186	539	256	235	61	2	16	18	128	2	420	6	41	27	.603	0-0	1	89	.736	3.98	4.09

Chi Chi Gonzalez

Pitches: R Bats: R Pos: SP-4; RP-2   Ht: 6'3" Wt: 210 Born: 1/15/1992 Age: 29

Year	Team	Lg	G	GS	GF	IP	BFP	H	R	ER	HR	SH	SF	HB	TBB	IBB	SO	WP	W	L	Pct	Sv-Op	Hld	Vel	OPS	ERC	ERA
2015	Tex	AL	14	10	1	67.0	280	49	33	29	6	1	2	3	32	1	30	2	4	6	.400	0-0	0	91	.632	3.00	3.90
2016	Tex	AL	3	3	0	10.1	62	21	13	10	1	0	1	0	9	0	7	0	0	2	.000	0-0	0	91	.984	12.48	8.71
2019	Col	NL	14	12	0	63.0	278	59	39	37	11	3	1	1	33	0	46	1	2	6	.250	0-0	0	92	.784	4.78	5.29
2020	Col	NL	6	4	0	19.2	91	22	16	15	3	1	1	3	10	0	16	2	0	2	.000	0-0	0	92	.889	6.34	6.86
	Postseason		1	0	0	1.2	8	2	1	1	1	0	0	0	2	0	0	0	0	0	-	0-0	0	93	1.333	15.09	5.40
	4 ML YEARS		37	29	1	160.0	711	151	101	91	21	5	5	7	84	1	99	5	6	16	.273	0-0	0	92	.754	4.62	5.12

Erik Gonzalez

Bats: R Throws: R Pos: SS-38;3B-13;PH-2   Ht: 6'3" Wt: 210 Born: 8/31/1991 Age: 29

Year	Team	Lg	G	AB	H	2B	3B	HR	(Hm	Rd)	TB	R	RBI	RC	TBB	IBB	SO	HBP	SH	SF	SB	CS	GDP	Avg	OBP	Slg	OPS
2016	Cle	AL	21	16	5	0	0	0	(0	0)	5	2	0	1	1	0	8	0	0	0	0	1	0	.313	.353	.313	.665
2017	Cle	AL	60	110	28	6	0	4	(1	3)	46	18	11	9	3	0	37	0	1	1	1	2	1	.255	.272	.418	.690
2018	Cle	AL	81	136	36	10	1	1	(1	0)	51	17	16	14	5	0	34	2	0	0	3	0	0	.265	.301	.375	.676
2019	Pit	NL	53	142	36	4	1	1	(1	0)	45	15	6	7	9	3	37	1	3	1	4	1	5	.254	.301	.317	.618
2020	Pit	NL	50	181	41	13	1	3	(1	2)	65	14	20	21	8	0	51	0	1	3	2	3	5	.227	.255	.359	.614
	Postseason		2	2	0	0	0	0	(0	0)	0	0	0	0	0	0	0	0	0	0	0	0	0	.000	.000	.000	.000
	5 ML YEARS		265	585	146	33	3	9	(3	6)	212	66	53	52	26	3	167	3	5	5	10	7	11	.250	.283	.362	.645

Gio Gonzalez

Pitches: L Bats: R Pos: RP-8; SP-4   JEE-oh   Ht: 6'0" Wt: 205 Born: 9/19/1985 Age: 35

Year	Team	Lg	G	GS	GF	IP	BFP	H	R	ER	HR	SH	SF	HB	TBB	IBB	SO	WP	W	L	Pct	Sv-Op	Hld	Vel	OPS	ERC	ERA
2008	Oak	AL	10	7	3	34.0	163	32	34	29	9	2	1	3	25	1	34	1	1	4	.200	0-0	0	90	.911	6.74	7.68
2009	Oak	AL	20	17	0	98.2	455	113	68	63	14	2	3	1	56	2	109	2	6	7	.462	0-0	0	92	.846	5.96	5.75
2010	Oak	AL	33	33	0	200.2	851	171	75	72	15	5	2	4	92	1	171	4	15	9	.625	0-0	0	92	.644	3.39	3.23
2011	Oak	AL	32	32	0	202.0	864	175	81	70	17	3	2	8	91	1	197	6	16	12	.571	0-0	0	92	.654	3.56	3.12
2012	Was	NL	32	32	0	199.1	822	149	69	64	9	9	7	5	76	3	207	10	21	8	.724	0-0	0	93	.582	2.37	2.89

Year	Team	Lg	G	GS	GF	IP	BFP	H	R	ER	HR	SH	SF	HB	TBB	IBB	SO	WP	W	L	Pct	Sv-Op	Hld	Vel	OPS	ERC	ERA
2013	Was	NL	32	32	0	195.2	819	169	79	73	17	7	1	2	76	1	192	4	11	8	.579	0-0	0	93	.668	3.23	3.36
2014	Was	NL	27	27	0	158.2	653	134	66	63	10	7	4	3	56	0	162	2	10	10	.500	0-0	0	92	.647	2.91	3.57
2015	Was	NL	31	31	0	175.2	758	181	79	74	8	3	9	4	69	3	169	4	11	8	.579	0-0	0	92	.711	3.92	3.79
2016	Was	NL	32	32	0	177.1	765	179	98	90	19	8	5	9	59	2	171	7	11	11	.500	0-0	0	91	.730	4.08	4.57
2017	Was	NL	32	32	0	201.0	827	158	69	66	21	7	3	7	**79**	5	188	7	15	9	.625	0-0	0	90	.642	3.05	2.96
2018	2 Tms	NL	32	32	0	171.0	746	167	84	80	17	3	**9**	2	80	2	148	5	10	11	.476	0-0	0	90	.734	4.23	4.21
2019	Mil	NL	19	17	0	87.1	366	76	36	34	9	4	0	0	37	0	78	5	3	2	.600	0-0	0	89	.709	3.50	3.50
2020	CWS	AL	12	4	1	31.2	153	40	19	17	6	0	0	2	19	0	34	2	1	2	.333	0-0	0	90	.875	7.50	4.83
18	Was	NL	27	27	0	145.2	646	153	77	74	15	3	8	2	70	2	126	4	7	11	.389	0-0	0	90	.769	4.75	4.57
18	Mil	NL	5	5	0	25.1	100	14	7	6	2	0	1	0	10	0	22	1	3	0	1.000	0-0	0	90	.510	1.67	2.13
Postseason			8	8	0	29.1	131	23	18	16	4	1	1	1	21	0	27	4	0	0	-	0-0	0	92	.739	4.48	4.91
13 ML YEARS			344	328	4	1933.0	8242	1744	857	795	171	60	46	50	815	21	1860	59	131	101	.565	0-0	0	92	.687	3.62	3.70

Luis Gonzalez

Bats: L **Throws:** L **Pos:** LF-1;CF-1;DH-1;PH-1;PR-1   **Ht:** 6'1" **Wt:** 180 **Born:** 9/10/1995 **Age:** 25

Year	Team	Lg	G	AB	H	2B	3B	HR	(Hm	Rd)	TB	R	RBI	RC	TBB	IBB	SO	HBP	SH	SF	SB	CS	GDP	Avg	OBP	Slg	OPS
2020	CWS	AL	3	1	0	0	0	0	(0	0)	0	1	0	0	0	0	1	1	0	0	0	0	0	.000	.500	.000	.500

Marwin Gonzalez

Bats: B **Throws:** R **Pos:** 3B-23;2B-21;1B-14;RF-8;PR-1   MARR-win   **Ht:** 6'1" **Wt:** 205 **Born:** 3/14/1989 **Age:** 32

Year	Team	Lg	G	AB	H	2B	3B	HR	(Hm	Rd)	TB	R	RBI	RC	TBB	IBB	SO	HBP	SH	SF	SB	CS	GDP	Avg	OBP	Slg	OPS
2012	Hou	NL	80	205	48	13	0	2	(1	1)	67	21	12	12	13	0	29	0	1	0	3	3	9	.234	.280	.327	.607
2013	Hou	AL	72	204	45	8	0	4	(2	2)	65	22	14	10	9	0	37	0	8	1	6	2	5	.221	.252	.319	.571
2014	Hou	AL	103	285	79	15	1	6	(3	3)	114	33	23	26	17	0	58	4	4	0	2	4	6	.277	.327	.400	.727
2015	Hou	AL	120	344	96	18	1	12	(6	6)	152	44	34	39	16	0	74	3	7	0	4	5	9	.279	.317	.442	.759
2016	Hou	AL	141	484	123	26	3	13	(8	5)	194	55	51	47	22	1	118	5	6	1	12	6	16	.254	.293	.401	.694
2017	Hou	AL	134	455	138	34	0	23	(15	8)	241	67	90	93	49	4	99	6	3	2	8	3	8	.303	.377	.530	.907
2018	Hou	AL	145	489	121	25	3	16	(5	11)	200	61	68	61	53	3	126	3	5	2	2	3	14	.247	.324	.409	.733
2019	Min	AL	114	425	112	19	0	15	(10	5)	176	52	55	58	31	2	98	6	0	1	1	0	7	.264	.322	.414	.736
2020	Min	AL	53	175	37	4	0	5	(3	2)	56	15	22	21	17	0	41	3	0	4	0	0	1	.211	.286	.320	.606
Postseason			33	108	25	7	0	3	(1	2)	41	10	13	8	7	2	30	4	0	0	0	2	1	.231	.303	.380	.682
9 ML YEARS			962	3066	799	162	8	96	(53	43)	1265	370	369	367	227	10	680	30	34	11	38	26	75	.261	.317	.413	.729

Victor Gonzalez

Pitches: L **Bats:** L **Pos:** RP-14;SP-1   **Ht:** 6'0" **Wt:** 180 **Born:** 11/16/1995 **Age:** 25

Year	Team	Lg	G	GS	GF	IP	BFP	H	R	ER	HR	SH	SF	HB	TBB	IBB	SO	WP	W	L	Pct	Sv-Op	Hld	Vel	OPS	ERC	ERA
2020	LAD	NL	15	1	1	20.1	80	13	3	3	0	0	1	3	2	0	23	2	3	0	1.000	0-0	2	95	.428	1.29	1.33

Niko Goodrum

Bats: B **Throws:** R **Pos:** SS-31;2B-11;PH-2   **Ht:** 6'3" **Wt:** 198 **Born:** 2/28/1992 **Age:** 29

Year	Team	Lg	G	AB	H	2B	3B	HR	(Hm	Rd)	TB	R	RBI	RC	TBB	IBB	SO	HBP	SH	SF	SB	CS	GDP	Avg	OBP	Slg	OPS
2017	Min	AL	11	17	1	0	0	0	(0	0)	1	1	0	0	1	0	10	0	0	0	0	0	0	.059	.111	.059	.170
2018	Det	AL	131	444	109	29	3	16	(8	8)	192	55	53	63	42	1	132	4	0	2	12	4	9	.245	.315	.432	.747
2019	Det	AL	112	423	105	27	5	12	(4	8)	178	61	45	50	46	1	138	1	0	2	12	3	7	.248	.322	.421	.743
2020	Det	AL	43	158	29	7	1	5	(2	3)	53	15	20	13	18	0	69	0	0	3	7	1	4	.184	.263	.335	.598
4 ML YEARS			297	1042	244	63	9	33	(14	19)	424	132	118	126	107	2	349	5	0	7	31	8	20	.234	.307	.407	.714

Brian Goodwin

Bats: L **Throws:** R **Pos:** CF-20;LF-16;RF-12;PH-6;DH-1   **Ht:** 6'0" **Wt:** 200 **Born:** 11/2/1990 **Age:** 30

Year	Team	Lg	G	AB	H	2B	3B	HR	(Hm	Rd)	TB	R	RBI	RC	TBB	IBB	SO	HBP	SH	SF	SB	CS	GDP	Avg	OBP	Slg	OPS
2016	Was	NL	22	42	12	4	1	0	(0	0)	18	1	5	6	2	0	14	0	0	0	0	0	1	.286	.318	.429	.747
2017	Was	NL	74	251	63	21	1	13	(9	4)	125	41	30	31	23	2	69	1	0	3	6	0	3	.251	.313	.498	.811
2018	2 Tms		75	159	38	6	0	6	(2	4)	62	20	25	27	16	0	57	3	1	1	4	2	0	.239	.318	.390	.708
2019	LAA	AL	136	413	108	29	3	17	(10	7)	194	65	47	57	38	2	129	3	1	3	7	3	3	.262	.326	.470	.796
2020	2 Tms		50	144	31	9	1	6	(5	1)	60	17	22	18	17	1	54	1	0	2	5	0	1	.215	.299	.417	.715
18	Was	NL	48	65	13	1	0	3	(1	2)	23	9	12	10	10	0	26	2	1	1	3	1	0	.200	.321	.354	.674
18	KC	AL	27	94	25	5	0	3	(1	2)	39	11	13	17	6	0	31	1	0	0	1	1	0	.266	.317	.415	.732
20	LAA	AL	30	95	23	7	1	4	(4	0)	44	12	17	15	12	1	35	1	0	1	1	0	0	.242	.330	.463	.793
20	Cin	NL	20	49	8	2	0	2	(1	1)	16	5	5	3	5	0	19	0	0	1	4	0	1	.163	.236	.327	.563
Postseason			1	0	0	0	0	0	(0	0)	0	0	0	0	0	0	0	0	0	0	0	0	0	-	-	-	-
5 ML YEARS			357	1009	252	69	6	42	(26	16)	459	144	129	139	96	5	323	8	2	9	22	5	8	.250	.317	.455	.772

Nick Goody

Pitches: R Bats: R Pos: RP-16; SP-1   Ht: 5'11" Wt: 200 Born: 7/6/1991 Age: 29

			HOW MUCH PITCHED					WHAT HE GAVE UP											THE RESULTS						
Year	Team	Lg	G	GS	GF	IP	BFP	H	R	ER	HR	SH	SF	HB	TBB	IBB	SO	WP	W	L	Pct	Sv-Op Hld	Vel	OPS	ERC	ERA
2015	NYY	AL	7	0	5	5.2	26	6	3	3	0	0	0	0	3	0	3	0	0	0	-	0-0 0	91	.794	4.90	4.76
2016	NYY	AL	27	0	10	29.0	128	30	15	15	7	1	1	1	12	1	34	0	0	0	-	0-0 0	91	.878	5.42	4.66
2017	Cle	AL	56	0	14	54.2	221	39	20	17	7	1	0	3	20	2	72	4	1	2	.333	0-0 6	92	.632	2.78	2.80
2018	Cle	AL	12	0	1	11.2	58	15	9	9	4	0	0	1	5	1	12	1	0	2	.000	0-1 2	91	1.016	7.63	6.94
2019	Cle	AL	39	0	6	40.2	173	30	18	16	7	0	2	0	22	1	50	0	3	2	.600	0-0 10	93	.690	3.59	3.54
2020	Tex	AL	17	1	3	11.0	55	14	12	11	3	0	1	0	8	0	13	1	0	2	.000	1-3 0	92	1.052	8.42	9.00
	6 ML YEARS		158	1	39	152.2	661	134	77	71	28	2	4	6	70	5	184	6	4	8	.333	1-4 18	92	.769	4.27	4.19

Alex Gordon

Bats: L Throws: R Pos: LF-49;PH-2   Ht: 6'1" Wt: 220 Born: 2/10/1984 Age: 37

									BATTING													RUNNING			AVERAGES			
Year	Team	Lg	G	AB	H	2B	3B	HR	(Hm	Rd)	TB	R	RBI	RC	TBB	IBB	SO	HBP	SH	SF	SB	CS	GDP	Avg	OBP	Slg	OPS
2007	KC	AL	151	543	134	36	4	15	(8	7)	223	60	60	69	41	4	137	13	1	2	14	4	12	.247	.314	.411	.725
2008	KC	AL	134	493	128	35	1	16	(9	7)	213	72	59	71	66	5	120	6	1	5	9	2	8	.260	.351	.432	.783
2009	KC	AL	49	164	38	6	0	6	(2	4)	62	28	22	16	21	0	43	2	1	1	5	0	5	.232	.324	.378	.703
2010	KC	AL	74	242	52	10	0	8	(5	3)	86	34	20	23	34	1	62	2	2	1	1	5	9	.215	.315	.355	.671
2011	KC	AL	151	611	185	45	4	23	(12	11)	307	101	87	103	67	2	139	7	0	3	17	8	9	.303	.376	.502	.879
2012	KC	AL	161	642	189	51	5	14	(6	8)	292	93	72	94	73	7	140	3	0	3	10	5	14	.294	.368	.455	.822
2013	KC	AL	156	633	168	27	6	20	(10	10)	267	90	81	90	52	7	141	9	0	6	11	3	4	.265	.327	.422	.749
2014	KC	AL	156	563	150	34	1	19	(11	8)	243	87	74	95	65	5	126	11	0	4	12	3	11	.266	.351	.432	.783
2015	KC	AL	104	354	96	18	0	13	(4	9)	153	40	48	60	49	7	92	14	0	5	2	5	2	.271	.377	.432	.809
2016	KC	AL	128	445	98	16	2	17	(8	9)	169	62	40	48	52	3	148	8	0	1	8	1	9	.220	.312	.380	.692
2017	KC	AL	148	476	99	20	2	9	(3	6)	150	52	45	45	45	3	126	14	2	4	7	4	7	.208	.293	.315	.608
2018	KC	AL	141	506	124	24	0	13	(2	11)	187	56	54	66	50	4	124	10	0	2	12	2	7	.245	.324	.370	.694
2019	KC	AL	150	556	148	31	1	13	(5	8)	220	77	76	81	51	4	100	19	1	6	5	3	13	.266	.345	.396	.741
2020	KC	AL	50	163	34	4	0	4	(2	2)	50	15	11	13	18	0	37	3	0	0	0	0	0	.209	.299	.307	.606
	Postseason		31	108	24	10	0	3	(1	2)	43	17	17	13	14	2	30	4	0	0	4	0	3	.222	.333	.398	.731
	14 ML YEARS		1753	6391	1643	357	26	190	(87	103)	2622	867	749	874	684	48	1535	121	8	43	113	45	110	.257	.338	.410	.748

MacKenzie Gore

Pitches: L Bats: L Pos: P   Ht: 6'2" Wt: 197 Born: 2/24/1999 Age: 22

			HOW MUCH PITCHED					WHAT HE GAVE UP											THE RESULTS						
Year	Team	Lg	G	GS	GF	IP	BFP	H	R	ER	HR	SH	SF	HB	TBB	IBB	SO	WP	W	L	Pct	Sv-Op Hld	Vel	OPS	ERC	ERA
2017	Padres	R	7	7	0	21.1	84	14	5	3	0	0	0	1	7	0	34	1	1	0	.000	0- -	-	.424	1.67	1.27
2018	FtWyn	A	16	16	0	60.2	261	61	35	30	5	0	2	5	18	0	74	9	2	5	.286	0- -	-	.899	3.89	4.45
2019	Lk Els	A+	15	15	0	79.1	288	36	9	9	4	1	3	2	20	0	110	4	7	1	.875	0- -	-	.420	1.07	1.02
2019	Amrillo	AA	5	5	0	21.2	90	20	10	10	3	0	1	1	8	0	25	2	2	1	.667	0- -	-	.735	4.09	4.15

Terrance Gore

Bats: R Throws: R Pos: CF-1;DH-1;PR-1   Ht: 5'7" Wt: 160 Born: 6/8/1991 Age: 30

									BATTING													RUNNING			AVERAGES			
Year	Team	Lg	G	AB	H	2B	3B	HR	(Hm	Rd)	TB	R	RBI	RC	TBB	IBB	SO	HBP	SH	SF	SB	CS	GDP	Avg	OBP	Slg	OPS
2014	KC	AL	11	1	0	0	0	0	(0	0)	0	5	0	1	0	0	0	1	0	0	5	0	0	.000	.500	.000	.500
2015	KC	AL	9	3	0	0	0	0	(0	0)	0	1	0	0	0	0	1	1	0	0	3	0	0	.000	.250	.000	.250
2016	KC	AL	17	3	0	0	0	0	(0	0)	0	6	0	0	0	0	1	0	0	0	11	2	0	.000	.000	.000	.000
2017	KC	AL	12	4	0	0	0	0	(0	0)	0	2	0	0	1	0	2	0	0	0	2	2	0	.000	.200	.000	.200
2018	ChC	NL	14	5	1	0	0	0	(0	0)	1	5	0	1	0	0	1	0	0	0	6	0	0	.200	.200	.200	.400
2019	KC	AL	37	51	14	2	1	0	(0	0)	18	13	1	8	6	0	18	1	0	0	13	5	0	.275	.362	.353	.715
2020	LAD	NL	2	0	0	0	0	0	(0	0)	0	0	0	0	0	0	0	0	0	0	0	0	0	-	-	-	-
	Postseason		9	2	0	0	0	0	(0	0)	0	3	0	0	0	0	2	0	0	0	5	1	0	.000	.000	.000	.000
	7 ML YEARS		102	67	15	2	1	0	(0	0)	19	32	1	10	7	0	23	3	0	0	40	9	0	.224	.325	.284	.608

Phil Gosselin

GOSS-lin

Bats: R Throws: R Pos: DH-11;1B-8;PH-8;LF-7;RF-7;2B-4;3B-2;PR-1   Ht: 6'1" Wt: 188 Born: 10/3/1988 Age: 32

									BATTING													RUNNING			AVERAGES			
Year	Team	Lg	G	AB	H	2B	3B	HR	(Hm	Rd)	TB	R	RBI	RC	TBB	IBB	SO	HBP	SH	SF	SB	CS	GDP	Avg	OBP	Slg	OPS
2013	Atl	NL	4	6	2	0	0	0	(0	0)	2	2	0	1	1	1	2	0	0	0	0	0	0	.333	.429	.333	.762
2014	Atl	NL	46	128	34	4	0	1	(1	0)	41	17	3	10	5	0	27	2	1	0	2	2	1	.266	.304	.320	.624
2015	2 Tms	NL	44	106	33	9	1	3	(2	1)	53	19	15	22	9	0	16	2	0	1	2	1	2	.311	.373	.500	.873
2016	Ari	NL	122	220	61	12	1	2	(1	1)	81	26	13	24	15	0	46	1	2	2	3	0	0	.277	.324	.368	.692
2017	2 Tms	NL	40	48	7	2	0	0	(0	0)	9	3	2	0	2	0	12	0	0	0	0	1	0	.146	.180	.188	.368
2018	Cin	NL	20	24	3	0	0	1	(1	0)	6	5	2	2	4	1	8	0	0	0	0	0	1	.125	.250	.250	.500
2019	Phi	NL	44	65	17	3	0	0	(0	0)	20	5	7	8	3	0	16	0	0	0	0	0	1	.262	.294	.308	.602
2020	Phi	NL	39	92	23	5	0	3	(2	1)	37	14	12	11	10	1	27	0	0	0	0	0	3	.250	.324	.402	.726
15	Atl	NL	20	40	13	4	0	0	(0	0)	17	2	2	6	2	0	5	0	0	1	2	0	0	.325	.357	.425	.782
15	Ari	NL	24	66	20	5	1	3	(2	1)	36	17	13	16	7	0	11	2	0	0	0	1	2	.303	.382	.545	.927
17	Pit	NL	28	40	6	1	0	0	(0	0)	7	3	2	0	2	0	9	0	0	0	0	0	0	.150	.190	.175	.365
17	Tex	AL	12	8	1	1	0	0	(0	0)	2	0	0	0	0	0	3	0	0	0	0	1	0	.125	.125	.250	.375
	8 ML YEARS		359	689	180	35	2	10	(7	3)	249	91	54	78	49	3	154	5	3	3	7	4	9	.261	.314	.361	.675

Trevor Gott

Pitches: R **Bats:** R **Pos:** RP-15   **Ht:** 5'10" **Wt:** 182 **Born:** 8/26/1992 **Age:** 28

			HOW MUCH PITCHED					WHAT HE GAVE UP											THE RESULTS							
Year	Team	Lg	G	GS	GF	IP	BFP	H	R	ER	HR	SH	SF	HB	TBB	IBB	SO	WP	W	L	Pct	Sv-Op	Hld	Vel	OPS	ERC	ERA
2015	LAA	AL	48	0	7	47.2	202	43	18	16	2	2	3	3	16	3	27	1	4	2	.667	0-4	14	96	.625	3.03	3.02
2016	Was	NL	9	0	1	6.0	28	6	1	1	0	0	0	1	3	1	6	0	0	0	-	0-0	1	94	.690	3.93	1.50
2017	Was	NL	4	0	1	3.0	23	11	10	10	1	0	0	0	3	1	3	1	1	0	1.000	0-0	0	95	1.359	28.38	30.00
2018	Was	NL	20	0	5	19.0	84	19	13	12	4	0	2	2	10	1	15	2	0	2	.000	0-0	2	95	.869	5.94	5.68
2019	SF	NL	50	0	6	52.2	214	41	26	26	4	1	4	2	17	0	57	1	7	0	1.000	1-2	1	95	.597	2.61	4.44
2020	SF	NL	15	0	5	11.2	57	13	13	13	7	0	0	1	8	0	8	0	1	2	.333	4-6	3	96	1.198	10.36	10.03
	6 ML YEARS		146	0	25	140.0	608	133	81	78	18	3	9	9	57	6	116	5	13	6	.684	5-12	21	95	.731	4.20	5.01

Ashton Goudeau

Pitches: R **Bats:** R **Pos:** RP-4   **Ht:** 6'6" **Wt:** 210 **Born:** 7/23/1992 **Age:** 28

			HOW MUCH PITCHED					WHAT HE GAVE UP											THE RESULTS							
Year	Team	Lg	G	GS	GF	IP	BFP	H	R	ER	HR	SH	SF	HB	TBB	IBB	SO	WP	W	L	Pct	Sv-Op	Hld	Vel	OPS	ERC	ERA
2020	Col	NL	4	0	2	8.1	39	15	7	7	3	0	2	1	2	0	2	1	0	0	-	0-0	0	93	1.226	12.28	7.56

Matt Grace

Pitches: L **Bats:** L **Pos:** RP-3   **Ht:** 6'4" **Wt:** 215 **Born:** 12/14/1988 **Age:** 32

			HOW MUCH PITCHED					WHAT HE GAVE UP											THE RESULTS							
Year	Team	Lg	G	GS	GF	IP	BFP	H	R	ER	HR	SH	SF	HB	TBB	IBB	SO	WP	W	L	Pct	Sv-Op	Hld	Vel	OPS	ERC	ERA
2015	Was	NL	26	0	5	17.0	84	26	11	8	0	0	2	1	8	2	14	1	2	1	.667	0-2	4	91	.855	6.71	4.24
2016	Was	NL	5	0	1	3.0	10	1	0	0	0	0	0	0	0	0	4	0	0	0	-	0-0	0	89	.200	0.25	0.00
2017	Was	NL	40	1	11	50.0	215	50	25	24	3	3	3	3	18	4	31	2	1	0	1.000	2-2	4	91	.702	3.76	4.32
2018	Was	NL	56	0	12	59.2	247	55	22	19	5	1	2	2	13	2	48	1	1	1	.500	0-0	8	91	.638	2.90	2.87
2019	Was	NL	51	1	12	46.2	206	61	34	33	11	1	2	2	10	0	35	1	1	2	.333	0-0	4	91	.916	6.39	6.36
2020	Ari	NL	3	0	1	1.0	10	5	6	6	1	0	0	0	2	0	2	0	0	1	.000	0-0	0	89	1.825	57.07	54.00
	6 ML YEARS		181	2	42	177.1	772	198	98	90	20	5	9	8	51	8	134	5	5	5	.500	2-4	20	91	.763	4.48	4.57

Yasmani Grandal

Bats: B **Throws:** R **Pos:** C-32;DH-7;1B-6;PH-1   yahz-MAH-nee gran-DAHL   **Ht:** 6'2" **Wt:** 230 **Born:** 11/8/1988 **Age:** 32

							BATTING															RUNNING			AVERAGES			
Year	Team	Lg	G	AB	H	2B	3B	HR	(Hm	Rd)	TB	R	RBI	RC	TBB	IBB	SO	HBP	SH	SF	SB	CS	GDP	Avg	OBP	Slg	OPS
2012	SD	NL	60	192	57	7	1	8	(3	5)	90	28	36	37	31	1	39	1	0	2	0	0	8	.297	.394	.469	.863
2013	SD	NL	28	88	19	8	0	1	(1	0)	30	13	9	12	18	2	18	1	0	1	0	0	1	.216	.352	.341	.693
2014	SD	NL	128	377	85	19	1	15	(7	8)	151	47	49	45	58	1	115	2	0	6	3	0	7	.225	.327	.401	.728
2015	LAD	NL	115	355	83	12	0	16	(8	8)	143	43	47	47	65	1	92	2	1	3	0	1	16	.234	.353	.403	.756
2016	LAD	NL	126	390	89	14	1	27	(20	7)	186	49	72	63	64	1	116	2	0	1	1	3	11	.228	.339	.477	.816
2017	LAD	NL	129	438	108	27	0	22	(13	9)	201	50	58	48	40	0	130	0	1	3	0	1	10	.247	.308	.459	.767
2018	LAD	NL	140	440	106	23	2	24	(11	13)	205	65	68	65	72	1	124	3	0	3	2	1	12	.241	.349	.466	.815
2019	Mil	NL	153	513	126	26	2	28	(13	15)	240	79	77	94	109	2	139	5	0	5	5	1	16	.246	.380	.468	.848
2020	CWS	NL	46	161	37	7	0	8	(5	3)	68	27	27	29	30	0	58	1	0	2	0	0	4	.230	.351	.422	.773
	Postseason		33	78	9	1	0	3	(2	1)	19	4	8	5	17	0	36	0	1	0	0	0	2	.115	.274	.244	.517
	9 ML YEARS		925	2954	710	143	7	149	(79	70)	1314	401	443	440	487	9	831	17	2	26	11	7	85	.240	.348	.445	.793

Brusdar Graterol

Pitches: R **Bats:** R **Pos:** RP-21; SP-2   BROOS-dar   **Ht:** 6'1" **Wt:** 265 **Born:** 8/26/1998 **Age:** 22

			HOW MUCH PITCHED					WHAT HE GAVE UP											THE RESULTS							
Year	Team	Lg	G	GS	GF	IP	BFP	H	R	ER	HR	SH	SF	HB	TBB	IBB	SO	WP	W	L	Pct	Sv-Op	Hld	Vel	OPS	ERC	ERA
2017	2 Tms	Low	10	7	0	40.0	157	26	12	12	2	0	0	3	13	0	45	3	4	1	.800	0--	-	-	.523	2.02	2.70
2018	2 Tms	Low	19	19	0	102.0	419	89	34	31	3	0	2	9	28	0	107	8	8	4	.667	0--	-	-	.606	2.82	2.74
2019	Pnscla	AA	12	9	1	52.2	205	32	10	10	2	1	1	3	21	0	50	2	6	0	1.000	1--	-	-	.537	1.96	1.71
2019	Min	AL	10	0	4	9.2	40	10	5	5	1	0	1	1	2	1	10	2	1	1	.500	0-0	1	99	.714	3.90	4.66
2020	LAD	NL	23	2	1	23.1	88	18	9	8	1	0	2	3	3	0	13	0	1	2	.333	0-1	5	99	.560	2.17	3.09
	Postseason		1	0	1	1.0	3	0	0	0	0	0	0	0	0	0	2	0	0	0	-	0-0	0	100	.000	0.00	0.00
	2 ML YEARS		33	2	5	33.0	128	28	14	13	2	0	3	4	5	1	23	2	2	3	.400	0-1	6	99	.608	2.64	3.55

Kendall Graveman

Pitches: R **Bats:** R **Pos:** RP-9; SP-2   **Ht:** 6'2" **Wt:** 200 **Born:** 12/21/1990 **Age:** 30

			HOW MUCH PITCHED					WHAT HE GAVE UP											THE RESULTS							
Year	Team	Lg	G	GS	GF	IP	BFP	H	R	ER	HR	SH	SF	HB	TBB	IBB	SO	WP	W	L	Pct	Sv-Op	Hld	Vel	OPS	ERC	ERA
2014	Tor	AL	5	0	1	4.2	18	4	2	2	0	0	0	0	0	0	4	1	0	0	-	0-0	0	93	.556	1.44	3.86
2015	Oak	AL	21	21	0	115.2	502	126	57	52	15	1	2	5	38	0	77	4	6	9	.400	0-0	0	91	.761	4.72	4.05
2016	Oak	AL	31	31	0	186.0	786	196	87	85	22	2	6	7	47	2	108	2	10	11	.476	0-0	0	93	.734	4.08	4.11
2017	Oak	AL	19	19	0	105.1	444	114	50	49	12	0	1	4	32	1	70	5	6	4	.600	0-0	0	93	.780	4.53	4.19
2018	Oak	AL	7	7	0	34.1	158	44	32	29	9	0	0	1	13	0	27	2	1	5	.167	0-0	0	94	.909	7.04	7.60
2020	Sea	AL	11	2	1	18.2	77	15	13	12	2	0	1	0	8	0	15	0	1	3	.250	0-1	5	95	.710	3.20	5.79
	6 ML YEARS		94	80	2	464.2	1985	499	241	229	60	3	10	17	138	3	301	14	24	32	.429	0-1	5	93	.762	4.48	4.44

Jon Gray

Pitches: R Bats: R Pos: SP-8   Ht: 6'4" Wt: 225 Born: 11/5/1991 Age: 29

Year	Team	Lg	G	GS	GF	IP	BFP	H	R	ER	HR	SH	SF	HB	TBB	IBB	SO	WP	W	L	Pct	Sv-Op	Hld	Vel	OPS	ERC	ERA
2015	Col	NL	9	9	0	40.2	185	52	26	25	4	2	4	2	14	2	40	3	0	2	.000	0-0	0	94	.856	5.60	5.53
2016	Col	NL	29	29	0	168.0	712	153	92	86	18	5	5	12	59	2	185	7	10	10	.500	0-0	0	95	.703	3.71	4.61
2017	Col	NL	20	20	0	110.1	461	113	47	45	10	2	2	2	30	0	112	3	10	4	.714	0-0	0	96	.716	3.76	3.67
2018	Col	NL	31	31	0	172.1	743	180	102	98	27	4	3	6	52	1	183	6	12	9	.571	0-0	0	95	.773	4.44	5.12
2019	Col	NL	26	25	1	150.0	637	147	70	64	19	7	3	4	56	4	150	7	11	8	.579	0-0	0	96	.766	4.16	3.84
2020	Col	NL	8	8	0	39.0	174	45	31	29	6	0	1	2	11	0	22	2	2	4	.333	0-0	0	94	.815	4.99	6.69
Postseason			1	1	0	1.1	11	7	4	4	1	0	0	0	0	0	2	0	0	1	.000	0-0	0	97	1.818	43.52	27.00
6 ML YEARS			123	122	1	680.1	2912	690	368	347	84	20	18	28	222	9	692	28	45	37	.549	0-0	0	95	.753	4.18	4.59

Sonny Gray

Pitches: R Bats: R Pos: SP-11   Ht: 5'10" Wt: 195 Born: 11/7/1989 Age: 31

Year	Team	Lg	G	GS	GF	IP	BFP	H	R	ER	HR	SH	SF	HB	TBB	IBB	SO	WP	W	L	Pct	Sv-Op	Hld	Vel	OPS	ERC	ERA
2013	Oak	AL	12	10	0	64.0	198	51	22	19	4	0	3	0	20	0	67	1	5	3	.625	0-0	0	93	.570	2.42	2.67
2014	Oak	AL	33	33	0	219.0	899	187	84	75	15	8	5	7	74	2	183	15	14	10	.583	0-0	0	93	.627	2.99	3.08
2015	Oak	AL	31	31	0	208.0	831	166	71	63	17	1	4	2	59	0	169	13	14	7	.667	0-0	0	93	.590	2.53	2.73
2016	Oak	AL	22	22	0	117.0	517	133	80	74	18	0	7	2	42	0	94	15	5	11	.313	0-0	0	93	.818	5.16	5.69
2017	2 Tms	AL	27	27	0	162.1	678	139	79	64	19	1	2	3	57	1	153	11	10	12	.455	0-0	0	93	.668	3.26	3.55
2018	NYY	AL	30	23	2	130.1	582	138	73	71	14	1	5	8	57	0	123	9	11	9	.550	0-0	0	93	.768	4.85	4.90
2019	Cin	NL	31	31	0	175.1	708	122	59	56	17	6	5	7	68	1	205	7	11	8	.579	0-0	0	93	.605	2.57	2.87
2020	Cin	NL	11	11	0	56.0	235	42	26	23	4	0	0	2	26	0	72	7	5	3	.625	0-0	0	93	.607	2.90	3.70
17	Oak	AL	16	16	0	97.0	400	84	48	37	8	0	2	1	30	0	94	7	6	5	.545	0-0	0	93	.644	2.93	3.43
17	NYY	AL	11	11	0	65.1	278	55	31	27	11	1	0	2	27	1	59	4	4	7	.364	0-0	0	93	.702	3.77	3.72
Postseason			4	4	0	21.1	90	14	8	7	2	1	0	2	12	1	18	2	0	2	.000	0-0	0	93	.615	3.09	2.95
8 ML YEARS			197	188	2	1132.0	4711	978	494	445	108	17	31	31	403	4	1066	79	75	63	.543	0-0	0	93	.657	3.25	3.54

Chad Green

Pitches: R Bats: L Pos: RP-22   Ht: 6'3" Wt: 215 Born: 5/24/1991 Age: 30

Year	Team	Lg	G	GS	GF	IP	BFP	H	R	ER	HR	SH	SF	HB	TBB	IBB	SO	WP	W	L	Pct	Sv-Op	Hld	Vel	OPS	ERC	ERA
2016	NYY	AL	12	8	4	45.2	198	49	26	24	12	1	1	1	15	0	52	1	2	4	.333	1-1	0	94	.852	5.46	4.73
2017	NYY	AL	40	1	4	69.0	253	34	14	14	4	2	1	2	17	0	103	3	5	0	1.000	0-1	9	96	.454	1.20	1.83
2018	NYY	AL	63	0	3	75.2	298	64	22	21	9	0	3	1	15	2	94	3	8	3	.727	0-4	12	96	.641	2.67	2.50
2019	NYY	AL	54	15	10	69.0	295	66	35	32	10	0	3	6	19	0	98	2	4	4	.500	2-2	4	96	.735	3.95	4.17
2020	NYY	AL	22	0	5	25.2	100	13	13	10	5	1	0	2	8	2	32	3	3	3	.500	1-3	6	95	.534	1.66	3.51
Postseason			13	1	1	19.0	81	16	11	10	3	1	1	1	7	1	17	0	2	0	1.000	0-0	1	96	.737	3.53	4.74
5 ML YEARS			191	24	26	285.0	1144	226	110	101	40	4	9	10	74	4	379	12	22	14	.611	4-11	31	96	.651	2.82	3.19

Shane Greene

Pitches: R Bats: R Pos: RP-28   Ht: 6'4" Wt: 200 Born: 11/17/1988 Age: 32

Year	Team	Lg	G	GS	GF	IP	BFP	H	R	ER	HR	SH	SF	HB	TBB	IBB	SO	WP	W	L	Pct	Sv-Op	Hld	Vel	OPS	ERC	ERA
2014	NYY	AL	15	14	0	78.2	345	81	38	33	8	4	6	6	29	0	81	1	5	4	.556	0-0	0	93	.715	4.43	3.78
2015	Det	AL	18	16	1	83.2	373	103	67	64	13	2	4	6	27	4	50	1	4	8	.333	0-0	0	92	.897	5.83	6.88
2016	Det	AL	50	3	4	60.1	256	58	39	39	3	2	2	4	22	1	59	0	5	4	.556	2-3	16	94	.680	3.65	5.82
2017	Det	AL	71	0	26	67.2	283	50	21	20	6	0	1	4	34	4	73	1	4	3	.571	9-13	14	95	.631	3.14	2.66
2018	Det	AL	66	0	58	63.1	279	68	39	36	12	0	3	3	19	1	65	3	4	6	.400	32-38	0	94	.787	4.80	5.12
2019	2 Tms	AL	65	0	37	62.2	252	46	22	16	8	1	1	3	17	1	64	0	0	3	.000	23-28	10	93	.598	2.51	2.30
2020	Atl	NL	28	0	6	27.2	109	22	9	8	2	1	1	2	9	1	21	0	1	0	1.000	0-0	9	92	.639	2.89	2.60
19	Det	AL	38	0	32	38.0	151	21	11	5	5	1	0	1	12	1	43	0	0	2	.000	22-25	0	93	.504	1.70	1.18
19	Atl	AL	27	0	5	24.2	101	25	11	11	3	0	1	2	5	0	21	0	0	1	.000	1-3	10	92	.736	3.97	4.01
Postseason			2	0	0	2.2	13	4	1	1	0	0	0	0	1	1	3	0	0	0	-	0-1	2	92	.885	5.24	3.38
7 ML YEARS			313	33	132	444.0	1897	428	235	216	52	6	13	28	157	12	413	6	23	28	.451	66-82	49	93	.725	4.04	4.38

Didi Gregorius

Bats: L Throws: R Pos: SS-59;PH-3   dee-dee greh-GORE-ee-us   Ht: 6'3" Wt: 205 Born: 2/18/1990 Age: 31

Year	Team	Lg	G	AB	H	2B	3B	HR	(Hm	Rd)	TB	R	RBI	RC	TBB	IBB	SO	HBP	SH	SF	SB	CS	GDP	Avg	OBP	Slg	OPS
2012	Cin	NL	8	20	6	0	0	0	(0	0)	6	1	2	2	0	0	5	0	1	0	0	0	0	.300	.300	.300	.600
2013	Ari	NL	103	357	90	16	3	7	(3	4)	133	47	28	42	37	5	65	6	2	1	0	2	4	.252	.332	.373	.704
2014	Ari	NL	80	270	61	9	5	6	(3	3)	98	35	27	37	22	3	52	3	2	2	3	0	1	.226	.290	.363	.653
2015	NYY	AL	155	525	139	24	2	9	(6	3)	194	57	56	64	33	0	85	11	3	6	5	3	4	.265	.318	.370	.688
2016	NYY	AL	153	562	155	32	2	20	(11	9)	251	68	70	71	19	2	82	6	5	5	7	1	9	.276	.304	.447	.751
2017	NYY	AL	136	534	153	27	0	25	(12	13)	255	73	87	84	25	1	70	3	0	7	3	1	7	.287	.318	.478	.796
2018	NYY	AL	134	504	135	23	5	27	(19	8)	249	89	86	79	48	3	69	7	1	9	10	6	8	.268	.335	.494	.829
2019	NYY	AL	82	324	77	14	2	16	(6	10)	143	47	61	45	17	1	53	1	0	2	2	1	5	.238	.276	.441	.718
2020	Phi	NL	60	215	61	10	2	10	(7	3)	105	34	40	40	15	3	28	4	1	2	3	2	4	.284	.339	.488	.827
Postseason			28	101	26	3	1	4	(2	2)	43	11	16	16	9	3	22	0	1	0	0	0	0	.257	.315	.426	.741
9 ML YEARS			911	3311	877	155	21	120	(67	53)	1434	451	457	462	216	18	509	41	15	34	33	16	42	.265	.315	.433	.748

Grayson Greiner

Bats: R **Throws:** R **Pos:** C-18   **Ht:** 6'6" **Wt:** 239 **Born:** 10/11/1992 **Age:** 28

								BATTING												RUNNING			AVERAGES			
Year	Team	Lg	G	AB	H	2B	3B	HR	(Hm | Rd)	TB	R	RBI	RC	TBB	IBB	SO	HBP	SH	SF	SB	CS	GDP	Avg	OBP	Slg	OPS
2018	Det	AL	30	96	21	6	0	0	(0 | 0)	27	9	12	13	17	0	32	0	0	3	0	1	0	.219	.328	.281	.609
2019	Det	AL	58	208	42	5	1	5	(1 | 4)	64	18	19	15	13	0	70	1	1	1	0	0	5	.202	.251	.308	.559
2020	Det	AL	18	51	6	2	0	3	(0 | 3)	17	8	8	3	3	0	20	1	0	0	0	0	2	.118	.182	.333	.515
	3 ML YEARS		106	355	69	13	1	8	(1 | 7)	108	35	39	31	33	0	122	2	1	4	0	1	7	.194	.264	.304	.568

Zack Greinke

Pitches: R **Bats:** R **Pos:** SP-12   GRAIN-key   **Ht:** 6'2" **Wt:** 200 **Born:** 10/21/1983 **Age:** 37

			HOW MUCH PITCHED					WHAT HE GAVE UP										THE RESULTS							
Year	Team	Lg	G	GS	GF	IP	BFP	H	R	ER	HR	SH	SF	HB	TBB	IBB	SO	WP	W	L	Pct	Sv-Op	Hld	Vel	OPS	ERC	ERA
2004	KC	AL	24	24	0	145.0	599	143	64	64	26	3	2	8	26	3	100	1	8	11	.421	0-0	0	89	.752	3.85	3.97
2005	KC	AL	33	33	0	183.0	829	233	125	118	23	4	4	13	53	0	114	4	5	17	.227	0-0	0	90	.846	5.71	5.80
2006	KC	AL	3	0	1	6.1	28	7	3	3	1	0	0	0	3	2	5	0	1	0	1.000	0-0	0	93	.757	4.93	4.26
2007	KC	AL	52	14	7	122.0	507	122	52	50	12	3	4	3	36	5	106	3	7	7	.500	1-1	12	94	.747	3.77	3.69
2008	KC	AL	32	32	0	202.1	851	202	87	78	21	2	4	4	56	1	183	3	13	10	.565	0-0	0	93	.715	3.68	3.47
2009	KC	AL	33	33	0	229.1	915	195	64	55	11	8	3	4	51	0	242	5	16	8	.667	0-0	0	94	.611	**2.39**	**2.16**
2010	KC	AL	33	33	0	220.0	919	219	114	102	18	6	7	7	55	1	181	4	10	14	.417	0-0	0	93	.696	3.48	4.17
2011	Mil	NL	28	28	0	171.2	715	161	82	73	19	6	1	4	45	0	201	10	16	6	.727	0-0	0	93	.708	3.35	3.83
2012	2 Tms		34	34	0	212.1	868	200	84	82	18	7	2	2	54	0	200	8	15	5	.750	0-0	0	92	.663	3.17	3.48
2013	LAD	NL	28	28	0	177.2	717	152	54	52	13	**13**	1	7	46	1	148	5	15	4	**.789**	0-0	0	92	.647	2.78	2.63
2014	LAD	NL	32	32	0	202.1	821	190	69	61	19	6	2	4	43	3	207	12	17	8	.680	0-0	0	92	.660	3.03	2.71
2015	LAD	NL	32	32	0	222.2	843	148	43	41	14	6	2	5	40	1	200	7	19	3	**.864**	0-0	0	92	.507	1.56	**1.66**
2016	Ari	NL	26	26	0	158.2	667	161	80	77	23	7	4	0	41	3	134	1	13	7	.650	0-0	0	91	.750	3.86	4.37
2017	Ari	NL	32	32	0	202.1	801	172	80	72	25	4	3	0	45	0	215	12	17	7	.708	0-0	0	91	.659	2.79	3.20
2018	Ari	NL	33	33	0	207.2	839	181	77	74	28	3	3	6	43	3	199	4	15	11	.577	0-0	0	90	.665	2.96	3.21
2019	2 Tms		33	33	0	208.2	810	175	73	68	21	5	4	4	30	2	187	2	18	5	.783	0-0	0	90	.623	2.39	2.93
2020	Hou	AL	12	12	0	67.0	273	67	30	30	6	0	1	1	9	0	67	3	3	3	.500	0-0	0	87	.687	3.04	4.03
12	Mil	NL	21	21	0	123.0	504	120	49	47	7	3	0	0	28	0	122	4	9	3	.750	0-0	0	92	.653	3.02	3.44
12	LAA		13	13	0	89.1	364	80	35	35	11	4	2	2	26	0	78	4	6	2	.750	0-0	0	92	.679	3.38	3.53
19	Ari	NL	23	23	0	146.0	562	117	48	47	15	4	3	3	21	2	135	1	10	4	.714	0-0	0	90	.614	2.22	2.90
19	Hou	AL	10	10	0	62.2	248	58	25	21	6	1	1	1	9	0	52	1	8	1	.889	0-0	0	90	.644	2.79	3.02
	Postseason		16	16	0	92.0	381	84	46	43	15	3	1	3	25	0	84	2	3	6	.333	0-0	0	92	.726	3.64	4.21
	17 ML YEARS		500	459	8	2939.0	12002	2728	1181	1100	298	79	49	70	676	25	2689	89	208	126	.623	1-1	12	92	.679	3.14	3.37

Randal Grichuk

Bats: R **Throws:** R **Pos:** CF-48;DH-7   GRICH-ick   **Ht:** 6'2" **Wt:** 216 **Born:** 8/13/1991 **Age:** 29

								BATTING												RUNNING			AVERAGES			
Year	Team	Lg	G	AB	H	2B	3B	HR	(Hm	Rd)	TB	R	RBI	RC	TBB	IBB	SO	HBP	SH	SF	SB	CS	GDP	Avg	OBP	Slg	OPS
2014	StL	NL	47	110	27	6	1	3	(2	1)	44	11	8	7	5	0	31	0	1	0	0	2	4	.245	.278	.400	.678
2015	StL	NL	103	323	89	23	7	17	(10	7)	177	49	47	47	22	2	110	4	0	1	4	2	6	.276	.329	.548	.877
2016	StL	NL	132	446	107	29	3	24	(12	12)	214	66	68	62	28	0	141	3	0	1	5	4	9	.240	.289	.480	.769
2017	StL	NL	122	412	98	25	3	22	(13	9)	195	53	59	47	26	3	133	2	0	2	6	1	9	.238	.285	.473	.758
2018	Tor	AL	124	424	104	32	1	25	(17	8)	213	60	61	61	27	0	122	8	0	3	3	2	5	.245	.301	.502	.803
2019	Tor	AL	151	586	136	29	5	31	(19	12)	268	75	80	68	35	0	163	5	0	2	2	1	20	.232	.280	.457	.738
2020	Tor	AL	55	216	59	9	0	12	(7	5)	104	38	35	35	13	1	49	0	0	2	1	1	5	.273	.312	.481	.793
	Postseason		13	43	8	0	0	3	(1	2)	17	5	4	2	1	0	17	0	0	0	0	0	0	.186	.205	.395	.600
	7 ML YEARS		734	2517	620	153	20	134	(80	54)	1215	352	358	327	156	6	749	22	1	11	21	13	58	.246	.295	.483	.778

Foster Griffin

Pitches: L **Bats:** R **Pos:** RP-1   **Ht:** 6'3" **Wt:** 225 **Born:** 7/27/1995 **Age:** 25

			HOW MUCH PITCHED					WHAT HE GAVE UP										THE RESULTS							
Year	Team	Lg	G	GS	GF	IP	BFP	H	R	ER	HR	SH	SF	HB	TBB	IBB	SO	WP	W	L	Pct	Sv-Op	Hld	Vel	OPS	ERC	ERA
2020	KC	AL	1	0	0	1.2	6	0	0	0	0	0	0	0	0	0	1	0	1	0	1.000	0-0	0	92	.000	0.00	0.00

Justin Grimm

Pitches: R **Bats:** R **Pos:** RP-4   **Ht:** 6'3" **Wt:** 210 **Born:** 8/16/1988 **Age:** 32

			HOW MUCH PITCHED					WHAT HE GAVE UP										THE RESULTS							
Year	Team	Lg	G	GS	GF	IP	BFP	H	R	ER	HR	SH	SF	HB	TBB	IBB	SO	WP	W	L	Pct	Sv-Op	Hld	Vel	OPS	ERC	ERA
2012	Tex	AL	5	2	3	14.0	65	22	14	14	1	0	2	0	3	0	13	3	1	1	.500	0-0	0	92	.935	6.54	9.00
2013	2 Tms		27	17	3	98.0	442	120	70	65	15	4	2	2	34	1	76	4	7	9	.438	0-0	3	92	.846	5.61	5.97
2014	ChC	NL	73	0	19	69.0	292	59	32	29	4	1	3	4	27	2	70	6	5	2	.714	0-1	11	94	.632	3.14	3.78
2015	ChC	NL	62	0	11	49.2	204	31	18	11	4	0	3	1	26	1	67	8	3	5	.375	3-6	15	95	.572	2.48	1.99
2016	ChC	NL	68	0	11	52.2	225	47	24	24	5	0	0	1	23	2	65	7	2	1	.667	0-0	10	94	.679	3.59	4.10
2017	ChC	NL	50	0	13	55.1	232	47	34	34	12	1	1	1	27	0	59	4	1	2	.333	1-3	4	95	.760	4.57	5.53
2018	2 Tms	AL	21	0	5	17.1	83	19	20	20	3	2	3	0	14	1	11	1	1	3	.250	0-2	3	93	.907	6.84	10.38
2020	Mil	NL	4	0	2	4.2	27	9	9	9	4	0	0	0	4	0	6	0	0	0	-	0-0	0	93	1.395	19.93	17.36
13	Tex	AL	17	17	0	89.0	406	116	67	63	15	2	2	1	31	1	68	4	7	7	.500	0-0	0	91	.883	6.21	6.37
13	ChC	NL	10	0	3	9.0	36	4	3	2	0	2	0	1	3	0	8	0	0	2	.000	0-0	3	94	.402	1.12	2.00
18	KC	AL	16	0	3	12.2	67	17	19	19	2	2	2	0	14	1	8	1	1	3	.250	0-2	3	94	1.008	9.68	13.50
18	Sea	AL	5	0	2	4.2	16	2	1	1	1	0	1	0	0	0	3	0	0	0	-	0-0	0	93	.525	0.85	1.93
	Postseason		9	0	0	6.1	28	7	6	6	0	0	0	0	1	0	7	1	0	0	-	0-0	0	95	.706	3.52	8.53
	8 ML YEARS		310	19	67	360.2	1570	354	221	206	48	8	14	9	158	7	367	35	20	23	.465	4-12	46	94	.751	4.43	5.14

Trent Grisham

Bats: L Throws: L Pos: CF-59;PH-1   Ht: 5'11" Wt: 224 Born: 11/1/1996 Age: 24

Year	Team	Lg	G	AB	H	2B	3B	HR	(Hm	Rd)	TB	R	RBI	RC	TBB	IBB	SO	HBP	SH	SF	SB	CS	GDP	Avg	OBP	Slg	OPS
2019	Mil	NL	51	156	36	6	2	6	(3	3)	64	24	24	20	20	0	48	4	0	3	1	0	3	.231	.328	.410	.738
2020	SD	NL	59	215	54	8	3	10	(6	4)	98	42	26	35	31	0	64	3	1	1	10	1	1	.251	.352	.456	.808
	Postseason		1	3	0	0	0	0	(0	0)	0	1	0	0	1	0	2	0	0	0	0	0	0	.000	.250	.000	.250
	2 ML YEARS		110	371	90	14	5	16	(9	7)	162	66	50	55	51	0	112	7	1	4	11	1	4	.243	.342	.437	.778

Robbie Grossman

Bats: B Throws: L Pos: LF-46;PH-5;CF-2;DH-2;RF-1   Ht: 6'0" Wt: 216 Born: 9/16/1989 Age: 31

Year	Team	Lg	G	AB	H	2B	3B	HR	(Hm	Rd)	TB	R	RBI	RC	TBB	IBB	SO	HBP	SH	SF	SB	CS	GDP	Avg	OBP	Slg	OPS
2013	Hou	AL	63	257	69	14	0	4	(3	1)	95	29	21	37	23	0	70	2	5	1	6	7	2	.268	.332	.370	.702
2014	Hou	AL	103	360	84	14	2	6	(2	4)	120	42	37	48	55	1	105	2	3	2	9	3	7	.233	.337	.333	.670
2015	Hou	AL	24	49	7	2	0	1	(1	0)	12	7	5	4	5	0	17	0	0	0	0	0	0	.143	.222	.245	.467
2016	Min	AL	99	332	93	19	1	11	(8	3)	147	49	37	52	55	0	96	2	0	0	2	3	3	.280	.386	.443	.828
2017	Min	AL	119	382	94	22	1	9	(5	4)	145	62	45	58	67	0	79	3	2	2	3	1	6	.246	.361	.380	.741
2018	Min	AL	129	396	108	27	1	5	(2	3)	152	50	48	62	60	0	83	2	2	5	0	1	2	.273	.367	.384	.751
2019	Oak	AL	138	420	101	21	3	6	(2	4)	146	57	38	58	59	2	86	1	0	2	9	4	7	.240	.334	.348	.682
2020	Oak	AL	51	166	40	12	2	8	(4	4)	80	23	23	27	21	2	38	5	0	0	8	1	1	.241	.344	.482	.826
	Postseason		2	8	2	0	0	0	(0	0)	2	0	0	0	0	0	4	0	0	0	0	0	0	.250	.250	.250	.500
	8 ML YEARS		726	2362	596	131	10	50	(27	23)	897	319	254	346	345	5	574	17	12	12	37	20	28	.252	.350	.380	.730

Zac Grotz

Pitches: R Bats: R Pos: RP-5   Ht: 6'2" Wt: 195 Born: 2/17/1993 Age: 28

			HOW MUCH PITCHED				WHAT HE GAVE UP										THE RESULTS							
Year	Team	Lg	G	GS	GF	IP	BFP	H	R	ER	HR	SH	SF	HB	TBB	IBB	SO	WP	W	L	Pct	Sv-Op	Hld	Vel	OPS	ERC	ERA
2019	Sea	AL	14	0	4	17.1	73	14	9	8	0	0	1	1	8	1	18	6	1	0	1.000	0-0	1	92	.585	2.73	4.15
2020	Sea	AL	5	0	1	7.1	46	11	12	12	4	0	1	4	11	0	4	1	0	0	-	0-0	0	92	1.399	20.57	14.73
	2 ML YEARS		19	0	5	24.2	119	25	21	20	4	0	2	5	19	1	22	7	1	0	1.000	0-0	1	92	.863	7.04	7.30

Deivy Grullon

Bats: R Throws: R Pos: C-1   DAY-vee groo-YOHN   Ht: 5'11" Wt: 240 Born: 2/17/1996 Age: 25

Year	Team	Lg	G	AB	H	2B	3B	HR	(Hm	Rd)	TB	R	RBI	RC	TBB	IBB	SO	HBP	SH	SF	SB	CS	GDP	Avg	OBP	Slg	OPS
2019	Phi	NL	4	9	1	1	0	0	(0	0)	2	0	1	0	0	0	2	0	0	0	0	0	1	.111	.111	.222	.333
2020	Bos	AL	1	3	1	0	0	0	(0	0)	1	0	1	1	1	0	1	0	0	0	0	0	0	.333	.500	.333	.833
	2 ML YEARS		5	12	2	1	0	0	(0	0)	3	0	2	1	1	0	3	0	0	0	0	0	1	.167	.231	.250	.481

Robert Gsellman

Pitches: R Bats: R Pos: SP-4; RP-2   guh-ZELL-man   Ht: 6'4" Wt: 200 Born: 7/18/1993 Age: 27

			HOW MUCH PITCHED				WHAT HE GAVE UP										THE RESULTS							
Year	Team	Lg	G	GS	GF	IP	BFP	H	R	ER	HR	SH	SF	HB	TBB	IBB	SO	WP	W	L	Pct	Sv-Op	Hld	Vel	OPS	ERC	ERA
2016	NYM	NL	8	7	0	44.2	185	42	12	12	1	4	2	1	15	2	42	1	4	2	.667	0-0	0	94	.639	3.05	2.42
2017	NYM	NL	25	22	1	119.2	549	138	85	69	17	4	2	8	42	3	82	4	8	7	.533	0-1	1	93	.807	5.16	5.19
2018	NYM	NL	68	0	24	80.0	345	76	44	38	8	3	5	5	28	6	70	1	6	3	.667	13-19	15	94	.700	3.69	4.28
2019	NYM	NL	52	0	9	63.2	277	64	36	33	7	1	2	6	23	2	60	4	2	3	.400	1-5	7	95	.766	4.36	4.66
2020	NYM	NL	6	4	0	14.0	71	22	15	15	4	0	1	1	8	0	9	2	0	0	-	0-0	1	94	1.109	10.49	9.64
	5 ML YEARS		159	33	34	322.0	1427	342	192	167	37	12	12	21	116	13	263	12	20	15	.571	14-25	24	94	.767	4.52	4.67

Deolis Guerra

Pitches: R Bats: R Pos: RP-9   day-OH-lis   Ht: 6'5" Wt: 245 Born: 4/17/1989 Age: 32

			HOW MUCH PITCHED				WHAT HE GAVE UP										THE RESULTS							
Year	Team	Lg	G	GS	GF	IP	BFP	H	R	ER	HR	SH	SF	HB	TBB	IBB	SO	WP	W	L	Pct	Sv-Op	Hld	Vel	OPS	ERC	ERA
2015	Pit	NL	10	0	4	16.2	74	26	12	12	5	0	0	1	3	0	17	2	2	0	1.000	0-0	0	91	1.077	8.96	6.48
2016	LAA	AL	44	0	11	53.1	220	52	23	19	6	1	1	2	7	0	36	2	3	0	1.000	0-4	5	90	.671	3.08	3.21
2017	LAA	AL	19	0	5	25.0	105	20	13	13	4	0	1	0	12	0	22	2	2	2	.500	0-1	0	92	.729	3.70	4.68
2019	Mil	NL	1	0	0	0.2	6	4	4	4	1	0	1	0	0	0	0	0	0	0	-	0-0	0	92	2.067	61.64	54.00
2020	Phi	NL	9	0	5	7.1	36	10	9	7	3	0	0	2	2	0	8	0	1	3	.250	0-0	0	92	1.014	9.34	8.59
	5 ML YEARS		83	0	25	103.0	441	112	61	55	19	1	3	5	24	0	83	6	8	5	.615	0-5	5	91	.798	4.69	4.81

Javy Guerra

Pitches: R Bats: R Pos: RP-14   Ht: 6'1" Wt: 216 Born: 10/31/1985 Age: 35

			HOW MUCH PITCHED				WHAT HE GAVE UP										THE RESULTS							
Year	Team	Lg	G	GS	GF	IP	BFP	H	R	ER	HR	SH	SF	HB	TBB	IBB	SO	WP	W	L	Pct	Sv-Op	Hld	Vel	OPS	ERC	ERA
2011	LAD	NL	47	0	38	46.2	195	37	12	12	2	3	1	3	18	1	38	2	2	2	.500	21-23	0	94	.608	2.73	2.31
2012	LAD	NL	45	0	17	45.0	196	44	13	13	1	4	2	1	23	5	37	1	2	3	.400	8-13	4	93	.685	3.76	2.60
2013	LAD	NL	9	0	5	10.2	55	15	9	8	1	0	1	1	6	0	12	0	0	0	-	0-0	0	93	.826	7.24	6.75
2014	CWS	AL	42	0	10	46.1	198	41	15	15	3	2	4	5	20	5	38	2	2	4	.333	1-6	7	94	.696	3.60	2.91
2015	CWS	AL	3	0	1	1.2	7	2	0	0	0	0	0	0	1	0	0	0	0	0	-	0-0	0	92	.762	5.91	0.00
2016	LAA	AL	7	0	1	6.1	30	5	4	4	1	0	0	0	7	1	4	1	0	0	-	0-0	0	92	.842	6.80	5.68
2017	Mia	NL	16	0	5	21.0	88	23	8	7	2	1	0	1	7	1	12	0	1	1	.500	0-1	0	94	.757	4.40	3.00
2018	Mia	NL	32	0	12	35.2	162	42	27	22	4	2	1	3	12	2	30	3	1	1	.500	1-1	0	93	.835	5.12	5.55
2019	2 Tms		51	0	21	67.2	287	67	36	35	10	1	1	1	17	3	57	3	3	1	.750	2-2	5	93	.724	3.68	4.66

Year Team	Lg	G	GS	GF	IP	BFP	H	R	ER	HR	SH	SF	HB	TBB	IBB	SO	WP	W	L	Pct	Sv-Op	Hld	Vel	OPS	ERC	ERA
2020 Was	NL	14	0	2	15.2	70	19	7	7	2	0	0	0	7	0	13	0	0	0		0-0	5	92	.816	5.85	4.02
19 Tor	AL	11	0	6	14.0	59	12	6	6	1	1	0	1	5	1	15	0	0	0	-	1-1	1	93	.714	3.10	3.86
19 Was	NL	40	0	15	53.2	228	55	30	29	9	0	1	0	12	2	42	3	3	1	.750	1-1	4	93	.726	3.83	4.86
Postseason		2	0	2	3.0	15	6	1	1	1	0	0	0	0	0	1	0	0	0		0-0	0	93	1.067	10.41	3.00
10 ML YEARS		266	0	111	296.2	1288	295	131	123	26	13	10	15	118	18	241	12	11	12	.478	33-46	23	93	.726	4.05	3.73

Javy Guerra

Pitches: R **Bats:** L **Pos:** RP-14   **Ht:** 6'0" **Wt:** 185 **Born:** 9/25/1995 **Age:** 25

Year Team	Lg	G	GS	GF	IP	BFP	H	R	ER	HR	SH	SF	HB	TBB	IBB	SO	WP	W	L	Pct	Sv-Op	Hld	Vel	OPS	ERC	ERA
2019 SD	NL	8	0	1	8.2	36	7	5	5	3	0	1	0	3	0	6	0	0	0	-	0-0	0	98	.840	4.29	5.19
2020 SD	NL	14	0	5	13.1	67	25	16	15	1	0	1	1	5	0	12	2	1	0	1.000	0-0	2	98	.979	9.97	10.13
2 ML YEARS		22	0	6	22.0	103	32	21	20	4	0	2	1	8	0	18	2	1	0	1.000	0-0	2	98	.931	7.67	8.18

Junior Guerra

Pitches: R **Bats:** R **Pos:** RP-25   **Ht:** 6'0" **Wt:** 235 **Born:** 1/16/1985 **Age:** 36

Year Team	Lg	G	GS	GF	IP	BFP	H	R	ER	HR	SH	SF	HB	TBB	IBB	SO	WP	W	L	Pct	Sv-Op	Hld	Vel	OPS	ERC	ERA
2015 CWS	AL	3	0	3	4.0	18	7	3	3	1	0	0	0	1	1	3	1	0	0	-	0-0	0	94	1.033	9.70	6.75
2016 Mil	NL	20	20	0	121.2	492	94	40	38	10	3	2	3	43	2	100	7	9	3	.750	0-0	0	93	.633	2.68	2.81
2017 Mil	NL	21	14	2	70.1	314	61	44	40	18	1	1	4	43	0	67	5	1	4	.200	0-0	0	92	.817	5.53	5.12
2018 Mil	NL	31	26	1	141.0	611	143	74	64	19	5	4	4	55	0	136	11	6	9	.400	0-0	1	93	.767	4.49	4.09
2019 Mil	NL	72	0	11	83.2	344	58	35	33	11	3	2	4	36	2	77	5	9	5	.643	3-11	20	95	.639	2.90	3.55
2020 Ari	NL	25	0	5	23.2	103	17	10	8	1	2	1	2	15	2	21	2	1	2	.333	0-2	4	94	.638	3.18	3.04
Postseason		2	0	2	4.2	15	2	1	1	0	0	0	0	0	0	5	1	0	1	.000	0-0	0	94	.267	0.43	1.93
6 ML YEARS		172	60	22	444.1	1882	380	206	186	60	14	10	17	193	7	404	31	26	23	.531	3-13	25	93	.712	3.79	3.77

Vladimir Guerrero Jr.

Bats: R **Throws:** R **Pos:** 1B-34;DH-23;PH-3   **Ht:** 6'2" **Wt:** 250 **Born:** 3/16/1999 **Age:** 22

								BATTING												RUNNING			AVERAGES			
Year Team	Lg	G	AB	H	2B	3B	HR	(Hm	Rd)	TB	R	RBI	RC	TBB	IBB	SO	HBP	SH	SF	SB	CS	GDP	Avg	OBP	Slg	OPS
2019 Tor	AL	123	464	126	26	2	15	(5	10)	201	52	69	67	46	0	91	2	0	2	0	1	17	.272	.339	.433	.772
2020 Tor	AL	60	221	58	13	2	9	(5	4)	102	34	33	30	20	1	38	2	0	0	1	0	6	.262	.329	.462	.791
2 ML YEARS		183	685	184	39	4	24	(10	14)	303	86	102	97	66	1	129	4	0	2	1	1	23	.269	.336	.442	.778

Taylor Guilbeau

Pitches: L **Bats:** L **Pos:** RP-8   **Ht:** 6'4" **Wt:** 190 **Born:** 5/12/1993 **Age:** 28

Year Team	Lg	G	GS	GF	IP	BFP	H	R	ER	HR	SH	SF	HB	TBB	IBB	SO	WP	W	L	Pct	Sv-Op	Hld	Vel	OPS	ERC	ERA
2019 Sea	AL	17	0	1	12.1	51	10	6	5	2	0	0	1	3	1	7	0	0	0	-	0-2	3	94	.657	2.99	3.65
2020 Sea	AL	8	0	3	7.2	36	8	1	1	0	0	0	0	6	0	3	1	0	0	-	0-0	1	91	.756	5.05	1.17
2 ML YEARS		25	0	4	20.0	87	18	7	6	2	0	0	1	9	1	10	1	0	0	-	0-2	4	93	.698	3.79	2.70

Luis Guillorme

Bats: L **Throws:** R **Pos:** 2B-17;PH-7;3B-4;SS-3;PR-1   ghee-YOR-may   **Ht:** 5'10" **Wt:** 190 **Born:** 9/27/1994 **Age:** 26

								BATTING												RUNNING			AVERAGES			
Year Team	Lg	G	AB	H	2B	3B	HR	(Hm	Rd)	TB	R	RBI	RC	TBB	IBB	SO	HBP	SH	SF	SB	CS	GDP	Avg	OBP	Slg	OPS
2018 NYM	NL	35	67	14	2	0	0	(0	0)	16	4	5	6	7	0	3	0	0	0	1	0	1	.209	.284	.239	.523
2019 NYM	NL	45	61	15	4	0	1	(1	0)	22	8	3	5	7	0	14	0	2	0	0	0	2	.246	.324	.361	.684
2020 NYM	NL	30	57	19	6	0	0	(0	0)	25	6	9	11	10	0	17	0	0	1	2	0	3	.333	.426	.439	.865
3 ML YEARS		110	185	48	12	0	1	(1	0)	63	18	17	22	24	0	34	0	2	1	3	0	6	.259	.343	.341	.683

Yuli Gurriel

Bats: R **Throws:** R **Pos:** 1B-55;DH-2;PH-1   yoo-lee goo-REE-el   **Ht:** 6'0" **Wt:** 215 **Born:** 6/9/1984 **Age:** 37

								BATTING												RUNNING			AVERAGES			
Year Team	Lg	G	AB	H	2B	3B	HR	(Hm	Rd)	TB	R	RBI	RC	TBB	IBB	SO	HBP	SH	SF	SB	CS	GDP	Avg	OBP	Slg	OPS
2016 Hou	AL	36	130	34	7	0	3	(1	2)	50	13	15	13	5	0	12	1	0	1	1	1	7	.262	.292	.385	.677
2017 Hou	AL	139	529	158	43	1	18	(8	10)	257	69	75	83	22	1	62	7	0	6	3	2	12	.299	.332	.486	.817
2018 Hou	AL	136	537	156	33	1	13	(10	3)	230	70	85	88	23	0	63	6	0	7	5	1	22	.291	.323	.428	.751
2019 Hou	AL	144	564	168	40	2	31	(19	12)	305	85	104	98	37	2	65	5	0	6	5	3	12	.298	.343	.541	.884
2020 Hou	AL	57	211	49	12	1	6	(3	3)	81	27	22	18	12	0	27	2	0	5	0	1	6	.232	.274	.384	.658
Postseason		44	172	46	12	1	5	(4	1)	75	15	24	25	13	1	20	0	0	1	1	0	1	.267	.317	.436	.753
5 ML YEARS		512	1971	565	135	5	71	(41	30)	923	264	301	300	99	3	229	21	0	25	14	8	59	.287	.324	.468	.792

Lourdes Gurriel Jr.

Bats: R **Throws:** R **Pos:** LF-53;PH-4;DH-3;1B-1   goo-REE-el   **Ht:** 6'4" **Wt:** 215 **Born:** 10/10/1993 **Age:** 27

								BATTING												RUNNING			AVERAGES			
Year Team	Lg	G	AB	H	2B	3B	HR	(Hm	Rd)	TB	R	RBI	RC	TBB	IBB	SO	HBP	SH	SF	SB	CS	GDP	Avg	OBP	Slg	OPS
2018 Tor	AL	65	249	70	8	0	11	(6	5)	111	30	35	30	9	1	59	2	1	2	1	2	5	.281	.309	.446	.755
2019 Tor	AL	84	314	87	19	2	20	(10	10)	170	52	50	51	20	0	86	5	1	3	6	4	4	.277	.327	.541	.869
2020 Tor	AL	57	208	64	14	0	11	(3	8)	111	28	33	37	14	0	48	0	0	2	3	1	4	.308	.348	.534	.882
3 ML YEARS		206	771	221	41	2	42	(19	23)	392	110	118	118	43	1	193	7	2	7	10	7	13	.287	.327	.508	.836

Kelvin Gutierrez

Bats: R **Throws:** R **Pos:** 3B-3;PR-1 **Ht:** 6'2" **Wt:** 220 **Born:** 8/28/1994 **Age:** 26

Year	Team	Lg	G	AB	H	2B	3B	HR	(Hm	Rd)	TB	R	RBI	RC	TBB	IBB	SO	HBP	SH	SF	SB	CS	GDP	Avg	OBP	Slg	OPS
2019	KC	AL	20	73	19	2	1	1	(1	0)	26	4	11	9	5	0	24	0	0	1	1	0	2	.260	.304	.356	.660
2020	KC	AL	4	9	1	0	0	0	(0	0)	1	0	0	0	3	0	6	0	0	0	0	0	0	.111	.333	.111	.444
	2 ML YEARS		24	82	20	2	1	1	(1	0)	27	4	11	9	8	0	30	0	0	1	1	0	2	.244	.308	.329	.637

Jorge Guzman

Pitches: R **Bats:** R **Pos:** RP-1 **Ht:** 6'1" **Wt:** 246 **Born:** 1/28/1996 **Age:** 25

			HOW MUCH PITCHED					WHAT HE GAVE UP										THE RESULTS							
Year	Team	Lg	G	GS	GF	IP	BFP	H	R	ER	HR	SH	SF	HB	TBB	IBB	SO	WP	W	L	Pct	Sv-Op	Hld	Vel	OPS	ERC	ERA
2020	Mia	NL	1	0	0	1.0	7	2	2	2	2	0	0	1	1	0	0	0	0	0	-	0-0	0	97	2.171	41.82	18.00

Ronald Guzman

Bats: L **Throws:** L **Pos:** 1B-24;PH-2 **Ht:** 6'5" **Wt:** 235 **Born:** 10/20/1994 **Age:** 26

Year	Team	Lg	G	AB	H	2B	3B	HR	(Hm	Rd)	TB	R	RBI	RC	TBB	IBB	SO	HBP	SH	SF	SB	CS	GDP	Avg	OBP	Slg	OPS
2018	Tex	AL	123	387	91	18	2	16	(7	9)	161	46	58	55	33	2	121	7	0	1	1	0	8	.235	.306	.416	.722
2019	Tex	AL	87	256	56	20	0	10	(2	8)	106	34	36	36	32	1	87	3	0	4	1	2	7	.219	.308	.414	.723
2020	Tex	AL	26	78	19	1	1	4	(3	1)	34	10	9	12	7	0	24	1	0	0	1	0	0	.244	.314	.436	.750
	3 ML YEARS		236	721	166	39	3	30	(12	18)	301	90	103	103	72	3	232	11	0	5	3	2	15	.230	.308	.417	.725

Jedd Gyorko

Bats: R **Throws:** R **Pos:** 1B-30;3B-11;PH-7;DH-1   JERK-oh   **Ht:** 5'10" **Wt:** 205 **Born:** 9/23/1988 **Age:** 32

Year	Team	Lg	G	AB	H	2B	3B	HR	(Hm	Rd)	TB	R	RBI	RC	TBB	IBB	SO	HBP	SH	SF	SB	CS	GDP	Avg	OBP	Slg	OPS
2013	SD	NL	125	486	121	26	0	23	(13	10)	216	62	63	48	33	1	123	4	0	2	1	1	14	.249	.301	.444	.745
2014	SD	NL	111	400	84	17	1	10	(7	3)	133	37	51	42	36	1	100	4	0	3	3	2	8	.210	.280	.333	.612
2015	SD	NL	128	421	104	15	0	16	(9	7)	167	34	57	46	27	1	107	5	0	5	0	1	13	.247	.297	.397	.694
2016	StL	NL	128	400	97	9	1	30	(12	18)	198	58	59	54	37	1	96	0	0	1	0	0	11	.243	.306	.495	.801
2017	StL	NL	125	426	116	21	2	20	(9	11)	201	52	67	65	47	1	105	1	0	7	6	2	12	.272	.341	.472	.813
2018	StL	NL	125	351	92	19	1	11	(6	5)	146	49	47	53	44	0	77	3	0	4	2	0	12	.262	.346	.416	.762
2019	2 Tms	NL	62	92	16	1	0	2	(1	1)	23	6	9	7	9	0	24	0	0	0	2	0	3	.174	.248	.250	.498
2020	Mil	NL	43	117	29	3	0	9	(4	5)	59	19	17	16	15	1	38	1	0	2	0	0	4	.248	.333	.504	.838
19	StL	NL	38	56	11	0	0	2	(1	1)	17	5	7	7	6	0	14	0	0	0	2	0	1	.196	.274	.304	.578
19	LAD	NL	24	36	5	1	0	0	(0	0)	6	1	2	0	3	0	10	0	0	0	0	0	2	.139	.205	.167	.372
	8 ML YEARS		847	2693	659	111	5	121	(61	60)	1143	317	370	331	248	6	670	18	0	24	14	6	77	.245	.310	.424	.735

Eric Haase

Bats: R **Throws:** R **Pos:** C-7 **Ht:** 5'10" **Wt:** 210 **Born:** 12/18/1992 **Age:** 28

Year	Team	Lg	G	AB	H	2B	3B	HR	(Hm	Rd)	TB	R	RBI	RC	TBB	IBB	SO	HBP	SH	SF	SB	CS	GDP	Avg	OBP	Slg	OPS
2018	Cle	AL	9	16	2	0	0	0	(0	0)	2	0	1	1	0	0	6	1	0	0	0	0	1	.125	.176	.125	.301
2019	Cle	AL	10	16	1	0	0	1	(0	1)	4	1	3	1	1	0	8	0	0	0	0	0	0	.063	.118	.250	.368
2020	Det	AL	7	17	3	0	0	0	(0	0)	3	1	2	1	1	0	6	0	0	1	0	0	0	.176	.211	.176	.387
	3 ML YEARS		26	49	6	0	0	1	(0	1)	9	2	6	3	2	0	20	1	0	1	0	0	1	.122	.170	.184	.353

Josh Hader

Pitches: L **Bats:** L **Pos:** RP-21 **Ht:** 6'3" **Wt:** 180 **Born:** 4/7/1994 **Age:** 27

			HOW MUCH PITCHED					WHAT HE GAVE UP										THE RESULTS							
Year	Team	Lg	G	GS	GF	IP	BFP	H	R	ER	HR	SH	SF	HB	TBB	IBB	SO	WP	W	L	Pct	Sv-Op	Hld	Vel	OPS	ERC	ERA
2017	Mil	NL	35	0	2	47.2	188	25	11	11	4	1	4	4	22	1	68	0	2	3	.400	0-1	12	94	.554	2.09	2.08
2018	Mil	NL	55	0	14	81.1	306	36	23	22	9	1	2	1	30	0	143	0	6	1	.857	12-17	21	95	.484	1.45	2.43
2019	Mil	NL	61	0	46	75.2	289	41	24	22	15	0	0	4	20	2	138	0	3	5	.375	37-44	6	96	.591	1.98	2.62
2020	Mil	NL	21	0	17	19.0	78	8	8	8	3	0	0	3	10	0	31	2	1	2	.333	13-15	0	95	.562	2.44	3.79
	Postseason		8	0	2	11.0	41	7	3	2	0	1	0	1	2	0	18	0	0	1	.000	0-1	2	96	.439	1.42	1.64
	4 ML YEARS		172	0	79	223.2	861	110	66	63	31	2	3	12	82	3	380	2	12	11	.522	62-77	39	95	.543	1.82	2.54

Sam Haggerty

Bats: B **Throws:** R **Pos:** LF-10;3B-1;RF-1;DH-1 **Ht:** 5'11" **Wt:** 175 **Born:** 5/26/1994 **Age:** 27

Year	Team	Lg	G	AB	H	2B	3B	HR	(Hm	Rd)	TB	R	RBI	RC	TBB	IBB	SO	HBP	SH	SF	SB	CS	GDP	Avg	OBP	Slg	OPS
2019	NYM	NL	11	4	0	0	0	0	(0	0)	0	2	0	0	0	0	3	0	0	0	0	0	0	.000	.000	.000	.000
2020	Sea	AL	13	50	13	4	0	1	(1	0)	20	7	6	10	4	0	16	0	0	0	4	0	0	.260	.315	.400	.715
	2 ML YEARS		24	54	13	4	0	1	(1	0)	20	9	6	10	4	0	19	0	0	0	4	0	0	.241	.293	.370	.663

Jesse Hahn

Pitches: R Bats: R Pos: RP-18 **Ht: 6'5" Wt: 210 Born: 7/30/1989 Age: 31**

			HOW MUCH PITCHED					WHAT HE GAVE UP										THE RESULTS						
Year	Team	Lg	G	GS	GF	IP	BFP	H	R	ER	HR	SH	SF	HB	TBB	IBB	SO	WP	W	L	Pct	Sv-Op	Hld	Vel	OPS	ERC	ERA
2014	SD	NL	14	12	2	73.1	306	57	26	25	4	3	1	4	32	1	70	4	7	4	.636	0-0	0	91	.623	2.91	3.07
2015	Oak	AL	16	16	0	96.2	406	88	46	36	5	1	2	8	25	1	64	7	6	6	.500	0-0	0	92	.623	3.00	3.35
2016	Oak	AL	9	9	0	46.1	203	57	32	31	8	1	1	0	19	1	23	2	2	4	.333	0-0	0	94	.860	6.22	6.02
2017	Oak	AL	14	13	1	69.2	316	78	46	41	4	3	6	3	27	0	55	2	3	6	.333	0-0	0	94	.748	4.46	5.30
2019	KC	AL	6	0	2	4.2	27	7	7	7	1	0	0	0	6	1	7	0	0	1	.000	0-0	0	95	1.053	11.57	13.50
2020	KC	AL	18	0	3	17.1	65	4	1	1	0	0	0	1	8	0	19	2	1	0	1.000	3-3	5	95	.289	0.74	0.52
	6 ML YEARS		77	50	8	308.0	1323	291	158	141	22	8	10	16	117	4	238	17	19	21	.475	3-3	5	93	.681	3.66	4.12

David Hale

Pitches: R Bats: R Pos: RP-9; SP-2 **Ht: 6'2" Wt: 210 Born: 9/27/1987 Age: 33**

			HOW MUCH PITCHED					WHAT HE GAVE UP										THE RESULTS						
Year	Team	Lg	G	GS	GF	IP	BFP	H	R	ER	HR	SH	SF	HB	TBB	IBB	SO	WP	W	L	Pct	Sv-Op	Hld	Vel	OPS	ERC	ERA
2013	Atl	NL	2	2	0	11.0	46	11	1	1	0	0	0	0	1	0	14	0	1	0	1.000	0-0	0	91	.572	2.18	0.82
2014	Atl	NL	45	6	13	87.1	383	89	38	32	5	1	3	3	39	8	44	5	4	5	.444	0-0	4	91	.714	4.05	3.30
2015	Col	NL	17	12	0	78.1	346	95	56	53	14	3	2	2	20	2	61	11	5	5	.500	0-0	0	90	.861	5.33	6.09
2016	Col	NL	2	0	0	2.0	12	4	3	3	1	0	0	0	2	0	1	0	0	0	-	0-0	0	90	1.200	17.51	13.50
2018	2 Tms	AL	4	0	1	13.2	62	16	7	7	3	0	0	1	5	0	8	0	0	0	-	0-0	0	91	.891	6.11	4.61
2019	NYY	AL	20	0	10	37.2	157	39	13	13	2	0	1	1	7	1	23	2	3	0	1.000	2-2	0	93	.712	3.19	3.11
2020	2 Tms	NL	11	2	3	17.0	75	23	7	7	2	0	0	0	4	0	14	0	1	1	.500	0-0	0	93	.867	5.69	3.71
18	NYY	AL	3	0	1	10.2	46	12	3	3	2	0	0	1	1	0	6	0	0	0	-	0-0	0	91	.804	4.42	2.53
18	Min	AL	1	0	0	3.0	16	4	4	4	1	0	0	0	4	0	2	0	0	0	-	0-0	0	92	1.167	13.17	12.00
20	NYY	AL	5	0	1	6.0	26	7	2	2	0	0	0	0	3	0	7	0	1	1	.500	0-0	0	93	.776	4.92	3.00
20	Phi	NL	6	2	2	11.0	49	16	5	5	2	0	0	0	1	0	7	0	0	0	-	0-0	0	93	.909	6.06	4.09
	Postseason		1	0	1	0.1	1	0	0	0	0	0	0	0	0	0	0	0	0	0	-	0-0	0	92	.000	0.00	0.00
	7 ML YEARS		101	22	27	247.0	1081	277	125	116	27	4	6	7	78	11	165	18	13	10	.565	3-3	4	91	.781	4.53	4.23

Matt Hall

Pitches: L Bats: L Pos: RP-3; SP-1 **Ht: 6'0" Wt: 200 Born: 7/23/1993 Age: 27**

			HOW MUCH PITCHED					WHAT HE GAVE UP										THE RESULTS						
Year	Team	Lg	G	GS	GF	IP	BFP	H	R	ER	HR	SH	SF	HB	TBB	IBB	SO	WP	W	L	Pct	Sv-Op	Hld	Vel	OPS	ERC	ERA
2018	Det	AL	5	0	2	8.0	48	19	16	13	1	0	2	1	3	0	5	2	0	0	-	0-0	0	89	1.146	13.40	14.63
2019	Det	AL	16	0	7	23.1	113	28	20	20	4	0	0	1	15	1	27	1	0	1	.000	0-1	0	90	.853	6.87	7.71
2020	Bos	AL	4	1	0	8.2	54	17	18	18	2	0	0	1	10	0	9	0	0	3	.000	0-0	0	88	1.146	15.61	18.69
	3 ML YEARS		25	1	9	40.0	215	64	54	51	7	0	2	3	28	1	41	3	0	4	.000	0-1	0	90	.991	9.92	11.48

Cole Hamels

Pitches: L Bats: L Pos: SP-1 **Ht: 6'4" Wt: 205 Born: 12/27/1983 Age: 37**

			HOW MUCH PITCHED					WHAT HE GAVE UP										THE RESULTS						
Year	Team	Lg	G	GS	GF	IP	BFP	H	R	ER	HR	SH	SF	HB	TBB	IBB	SO	WP	W	L	Pct	Sv-Op	Hld	Vel	OPS	ERC	ERA
2006	Phi	NL	23	23	0	132.1	558	117	66	60	19	6	8	3	48	4	145	5	9	8	.529	0-0	0	91	.730	3.61	4.08
2007	Phi	NL	28	28	0	183.1	743	163	72	69	25	6	5	3	43	4	177	5	15	5	.750	0-0	0	90	.686	3.12	3.39
2008	Phi	NL	33	33	0	227.1	914	193	89	78	28	6	2	1	53	7	196	0	14	10	.583	0-0	0	90	.657	2.76	3.09
2009	Phi	NL	32	32	0	193.2	814	206	95	93	24	7	5	6	43	4	168	1	10	11	.476	0-0	0	90	.755	3.98	4.32
2010	Phi	NL	33	33	0	208.2	856	185	74	71	26	7	0	8	61	5	211	3	12	11	.522	0-0	0	92	.693	3.36	3.06
2011	Phi	NL	32	31	0	216.0	850	169	68	67	19	9	3	5	44	2	194	3	14	9	.609	0-0	0	92	.596	2.23	2.79
2012	Phi	NL	31	31	0	215.1	867	190	80	73	24	6	4	3	52	3	216	3	17	6	.739	0-0	0	91	.661	2.98	3.05
2013	Phi	NL	33	33	0	220.0	905	205	94	88	21	11	3	9	50	5	202	4	8	14	.364	0-0	0	92	.699	3.15	3.60
2014	Phi	NL	30	30	0	204.2	829	176	60	56	14	7	7	8	59	3	198	6	9	9	.500	0-0	0	92	.641	2.82	2.46
2015	2 Tms		32	32	0	212.1	880	190	88	86	22	6	2	10	62	3	215	9	13	8	.619	0-0	0	93	.669	3.28	3.65
2016	Tex	AL	32	32	0	200.2	848	185	83	74	24	1	2	8	77	1	200	4	15	5	.750	0-0	0	93	.699	3.90	3.32
2017	Tex	AL	24	24	0	148.0	614	125	74	69	18	0	2	1	53	1	105	6	11	6	.647	0-0	0	92	.693	3.54	4.20
2018	2 Tms		32	32	0	190.2	806	176	93	80	29	1	4	19	65	0	188	7	9	12	.429	0-0	0	92	.746	4.23	3.78
2019	ChC	NL	27	27	0	141.2	617	141	64	60	17	4	6	7	56	1	143	1	7	7	.500	0-0	0	91	.740	4.35	3.81
2020	Atl	NL	1	1	0	3.1	14	3	3	3	0	0	1	0	1	0	2	0	0	1	.000	0-0	0	88	.702	2.46	8.10
15	Phi	NL	20	20	0	128.2	537	113	53	52	12	5	1	6	39	3	137	7	6	7	.462	0-0	0	92	.645	3.13	3.64
15	Tex	AL	12	12	0	83.2	343	77	35	34	10	1	1	4	23	0	78	2	7	1	.875	0-0	0	93	.705	3.54	3.66
18	Tex	AL	20	20	0	114.1	502	115	70	60	23	0	3	12	42	0	114	6	5	9	.357	0-0	0	91	.811	5.13	4.72
18	ChC	NL	12	12	0	76.1	304	61	23	20	6	1	1	7	23	0	74	1	4	3	.571	0-0	0	93	.639	2.95	2.36
	Postseason		17	16	0	100.1	411	83	45	38	12	4	2	2	27	2	93	1	7	6	.538	0-0	0	92	.653	2.79	3.41
	15 ML YEARS		423	422	0	2698.0	11115	2424	1103	1027	310	76	54	100	767	43	2560	57	163	122	.572	0-0	0	92	.688	3.32	3.43

Billy Hamilton

Bats: B Throws: R Pos: CF-25;PR-12;DH-2;PH-2 **Ht: 6'0" Wt: 155 Born: 9/9/1990 Age: 30**

			BATTING																	RUNNING			AVERAGES			
Year	Team	Lg	G	AB	H	2B	3B	HR	(Hm	Rd)	TB	R	RBI	RC	TBB	IBB	SO	HBP	SH	SF	SB	CS	GDP	Avg	OBP	Slg	OPS
2013	Cin	NL	13	19	7	2	0	0	(0	0)	9	9	1	5	2	0	4	0	1	0	13	1	0	.368	.429	.474	.902
2014	Cin	NL	152	563	141	25	8	6	(3	3)	200	72	48	64	34	0	117	1	9	4	56	23	1	.250	.292	.355	.648
2015	Cin	NL	114	412	93	8	3	4	(2	2)	119	56	28	32	28	0	75	1	9	4	57	8	5	.226	.274	.289	.563
2016	Cin	NL	119	411	107	19	3	3	(2	1)	141	69	17	46	36	0	93	1	11	1	58	8	5	.260	.321	.343	.664
2017	Cin	NL	139	582	144	17	11	4	(3	1)	195	85	38	62	44	0	133	0	5	2	59	13	5	.247	.299	.335	.634
2018	Cin	NL	153	504	119	16	9	4	(4	0)	165	74	29	51	46	0	132	1	1	4	34	10	1	.236	.299	.327	.626
2019	2 Tms	NL	119	316	69	14	2	0	(0	0)	87	41	15	29	32	1	87	0	3	2	22	6	1	.218	.289	.275	.564
2020	2 Tms	NL	31	32	4	0	0	1	(0	1)	7	10	2	2	2	0	7	0	1	1	6	2	0	.125	.171	.219	.390
19	KC	AL	93	275	58	12	2	0	(0	0)	74	32	12	22	25	0	74	0	3	2	18	5	1	.211	.275	.269	.544

Year Team	Lg	G	AB	H	2B	3B	HR	(Hm Rd)	TB	R	RBI	RC	TBB	IBB	SO	HBP	SH	SF	SB	CS	GDP	Avg	OBP	Slg	OPS
19 Atl	NL	26	41	11	2	0	0	(0 0)	13	9	3	7	7	1	13	0	0	0	4	1	0	.268	.375	.317	.692
20 NYM	NL	17	22	1	0	0	0	(0 0)	1	4	1	0	1	0	3	0	1	1	3	1	0	.045	.083	.045	.129
20 ChC	NL	14	10	3	0	0	1	(0 1)	6	6	1	2	1	0	4	0	0	0	3	1	0	.300	.364	.600	.964
Postseason		2	0	0	0	0	0	(0 0)	0	2	0		1	0	0	0	0	0	1	0	0	-	1.000	-	-
8 ML YEARS		840	2839	684	101	36	22	(14 8)	923	416	178	291	224	1	648	4	40	18	305	71	18	.241	.296	.325	.621

Ian Hamilton

Pitches: R Bats: R Pos: RP-4   **Ht: 6'1" Wt: 200 Born: 6/16/1995 Age: 26**

Year Team	Lg	G	GS	GF	IP	BFP	H	R	ER	HR	SH	SF	HB	TBB	IBB	SO	WP	W	L	Pct	Sv-Op	Hld	Vel	OPS	ERC	ERA
2018 CWS	AL	10	0	3	8.0	33	6	5	4	2	0	1	1	2	0	5	0	1	2	.333	0-1	1	97	.687	3.51	4.50
2020 CWS	AL	4	0	0	4.0	20	4	2	2	0	0	0	0	5	0	4	2	0	0	-	0-0	0	94	.717	6.80	4.50
2 ML YEARS		14	0	3	12.0	53	10	7	6	2	0	1	1	7	0	9	2	1	2	.333	0-1	1	96	.703	4.67	4.50

Garrett Hampson

Bats: R Throws: R Pos: 2B-26;CF-20;LF-7;SS-6;PH-5;PR-3;DH-1   **Ht: 5'11" Wt: 196 Born: 10/10/1994 Age: 26**

Year Team	Lg	G	AB	H	2B	3B	HR	(Hm Rd)	TB	R	RBI	RC	TBB	IBB	SO	HBP	SH	SF	SB	CS	GDP	Avg	OBP	Slg	OPS
2018 Col	NL	24	40	11	3	1	0	(0 0)	16	3	4	9	7	0	12	1	0	0	2	0	0	.275	.396	.400	.796
2019 Col	NL	105	299	74	9	4	8	(1 7)	115	40	27	29	24	1	88	0	2	2	15	3	2	.247	.302	.385	.686
2020 Col	NL	53	167	39	4	3	5	(3 2)	64	25	11	16	13	0	60	0	3	1	6	1	1	.234	.287	.383	.671
Postseason		2	1	0	0	0	0	(0 0)	0	1	0		0	0	0	0	0	0	0	0	0	.000	.000	.000	.000
3 ML YEARS		182	506	124	16	8	13	(4 9)	195	68	42	54	44	1	160	1	5	3	23	4	3	.245	.305	.385	.690

Brad Hand

Pitches: L Bats: L Pos: RP-23   **Ht: 6'3" Wt: 215 Born: 3/20/1990 Age: 31**

Year Team	Lg	G	GS	GF	IP	BFP	H	R	ER	HR	SH	SF	HB	TBB	IBB	SO	WP	W	L	Pct	Sv-Op	Hld	Vel	OPS	ERC	ERA
2011 Fla	NL	12	12	0	60.0	263	53	32	28	10	4	3	1	35	1	38	0	1	8	.111	0-0	0	90	.789	4.68	4.20
2012 Mia	NL	1	1	0	3.2	23	6	7	7	1	0	0	0	6	1	3	0	0	1	1.000	0-0	0	90	1.169	14.74	17.18
2013 Mia	NL	7	2	2	20.2	82	13	7	7	2	0	0	0	8	0	15	1	1	1	.500	0-0	0	93	.553	2.10	3.05
2014 Mia	NL	32	16	5	111.0	474	112	56	54	10	6	2	2	39	3	67	5	3	8	.273	1-1	0	92	.732	3.91	4.38
2015 Mia	NL	38	12	7	93.1	408	107	55	55	9	5	2	3	32	1	67	2	4	7	.364	0-0	2	92	.784	4.83	5.30
2016 SD	NL	82	0	16	89.1	364	63	32	29	8	2	2	1	36	4	111	7	4	4	.500	1-7	21	93	.589	2.44	2.92
2017 SD	NL	72	0	32	79.1	311	54	20	19	9	1	1	7	20	1	104	4	3	4	.429	21-26	16	94	.580	2.30	2.16
2018 2 Tms		69	0	42	72.0	301	52	28	22	8	2	2	9	28	2	106	2	2	5	.286	32-39	10	94	.656	3.03	2.75
2019 Cle	AL	60	0	54	57.1	242	53	21	21	6	1	0	4	18	5	84	0	6	4	.600	34-39	0	93	.695	3.50	3.30
2020 Cle	AL	23	0	21	22.0	86	13	8	5	0	0	1	2	4	0	29	1	2	1	.667	16-16	1	94	.486	1.21	2.05
18 SD	NL	41	0	31	44.1	186	33	21	15	5	1	0	7	15	1	65	1	2	4	.333	24-29	3	94	.672	3.09	3.05
18 Cle	AL	28	0	11	27.2	115	19	7	7	3	1	0	2	13	1	41	1	0	1	.000	8-10	7	93	.632	2.94	2.28
Postseason		2	0	1	1.2	9	3	2	2	1	0	0	0	1	1	4	1	0	0	-	0-0	0	93	1.194	13.35	10.80
10 ML YEARS		396	43	179	608.2	2554	526	266	247	63	21	11	29	226	18	624	22	26	43	.377	105-128	50	92	.684	3.39	3.65

Mitch Haniger

Bats: R Throws: R Pos: RF   **Ht: 6'2" Wt: 199 Born: 12/23/1990 Age: 30**

Year Team	Lg	G	AB	H	2B	3B	HR	(Hm Rd)	TB	R	RBI	RC	TBB	IBB	SO	HBP	SH	SF	SB	CS	GDP	Avg	OBP	Slg	OPS
2016 Ari	NL	34	109	25	2	1	5	(4 1)	44	9	17	16	12	2	27	1	0	1	0	0	3	.229	.309	.404	.713
2017 Sea	AL	96	369	104	25	2	16	(6 10)	181	58	47	55	31	0	93	9	1	0	5	4	9	.282	.352	.491	.843
2018 Sea	AL	157	596	170	38	4	26	(12 14)	294	90	93	102	70	4	148	10	0	7	8	2	8	.285	.366	.493	.859
2019 Sea	AL	63	246	54	13	1	15	(7 8)	114	46	32	35	30	1	81	5	0	2	4	0	3	.220	.314	.463	.778
4 ML YEARS		350	1320	353	78	8	62	(29 33)	633	203	189	208	143	7	349	25	1	10	17	6	23	.267	.348	.480	.827

Ian Happ

Bats: B Throws: R Pos: CF-51;LF-28;RF-7;PH-3;1B-2;DH-1   **Ht: 6'0" Wt: 205 Born: 8/12/1994 Age: 26**

Year Team	Lg	G	AB	H	2B	3B	HR	(Hm Rd)	TB	R	RBI	RC	TBB	IBB	SO	HBP	SH	SF	SB	CS	GDP	Avg	OBP	Slg	OPS
2017 ChC	NL	115	364	92	17	3	24	(15 9)	187	62	68	57	39	5	129	4	2	4	8	4	12	.253	.328	.514	.842
2018 ChC	NL	142	387	90	19	2	15	(7 8)	158	56	44	56	70	9	167	3	0	2	8	4	6	.233	.353	.408	.761
2019 ChC	NL	58	140	37	7	1	11	(4 7)	79	25	30	30	15	0	39	0	0	0	2	0	1	.264	.333	.564	.898
2020 ChC	NL	57	198	51	11	1	12	(8 4)	100	27	28	35	30	1	63	2	1	0	1	3	1	.258	.361	.505	.866
Postseason		6	7	1	0	0	0	(0 0)	1	0	0		0	0	2	0	5	0	0	0	0	1	.143	.333	.143	.476
4 ML YEARS		372	1089	270	54	7	62	(34 28)	524	170	170	178	154	15	398	9	3	7	19	11	20	.248	.344	.481	.825

J.A. Happ

JAY

Pitches: L Bats: L Pos: SP-9   **Ht: 6'5" Wt: 205 Born: 10/19/1982 Age: 38**

Year Team	Lg	G	GS	GF	IP	BFP	H	R	ER	HR	SH	SF	HB	TBB	IBB	SO	WP	W	L	Pct	Sv-Op	Hld	Vel	OPS	ERC	ERA
2007 Phi	NL	1	1	0	4.0	21	7	5	5	3	0	0	0	2	0	5	0	0	1	.000	0-0	0	88	1.323	15.13	11.25
2008 Phi	NL	8	4	1	31.2	138	28	13	13	3	2	1	1	14	1	26	1	1	0	1.000	0-0	0	89	.658	3.55	3.69
2009 Phi	NL	35	23	4	166.0	685	149	55	54	20	7	6	5	56	2	119	2	12	4	.750	0-0	0	90	.710	3.57	2.93
2010 2 Tms	NL	16	16	0	87.1	374	73	37	33	8	5	4	1	47	1	70	4	6	4	.600	0-0	0	90	.688	3.69	3.40
2011 Hou	NL	28	28	0	156.1	698	157	103	93	21	12	8	2	83	5	134	3	6	15	.286	0-0	0	90	.806	4.86	5.35

Year Team	Lg	HOW MUCH PITCHED					WHAT HE GAVE UP											THE RESULTS								
		G	GS	GF	IP	BFP	H	R	ER	HR	SH	SF	HB	TBB	IBB	SO	WP	W	L	Pct	Sv-Op	Hld	Vel	OPS	ERC	ERA
2012 2 Tms		28	24	3	144.2	627	147	79	77	19	9	4	2	56	1	144	7	10	11	.476	0-0	1	90	.787	4.37	4.79
2013 Tor	AL	18	18	0	92.2	415	91	53	47	10	1	3	2	45	0	77	5	5	7	.417	0-0	0	91	.734	4.36	4.56
2014 Tor	AL	30	26	2	158.0	673	160	79	74	22	1	5	2	51	0	133	1	11	11	.500	0-0	0	93	.770	4.17	4.22
2015 2 Tms		32	31	0	172.0	717	173	71	69	16	2	0	2	45	4	151	6	11	8	.579	0-0	0	92	.698	3.56	3.61
2016 Tor	AL	32	32	0	195.0	796	168	72	69	22	2	2	6	60	0	163	3	20	4	.833	0-0	0	92	.665	3.22	3.18
2017 Tor	AL	25	25	0	145.1	626	145	64	57	18	1	4	0	46	1	142	4	10	11	.476	0-0	0	92	.700	3.81	3.53
2018 2 Tms		31	31	0	177.2	733	150	81	72	27	2	2	9	51	0	193	4	17	6	.739	0-0	0	92	.677	3.32	3.65
2019 NYY	AL	31	30	0	161.1	678	160	88	88	34	0	2	5	49	1	140	3	12	8	.600	0-0	0	91	.785	4.57	4.91
2020 NYY	AL	9	9	0	49.1	196	37	19	19	8	1	0	1	15	0	42	0	2	2	.500	0-0	0	91	.655	2.88	3.47
10 Phi	NL	3	3	0	15.1	70	13	4	3	1	1	1	0	12	0	9	1	1	0	1.000	0-0	0	89	.702	4.40	1.76
10 Hou	NL	13	13	0	72.0	304	60	33	30	7	4	3	1	35	1	61	3	5	4	.556	0-0	0	90	.684	3.53	3.75
12 Hou	NL	18	18	0	104.1	457	112	58	56	17	7	2	1	39	0	98	5	7	9	.438	0-0	0	90	.818	4.86	4.83
12 Tor	AL	10	6	3	40.1	170	35	21	21	2	2	2	1	17	1	46	2	3	2	.600	0-0	1	91	.701	3.16	4.69
15 Sea	AL	21	20	0	108.2	468	121	58	56	13	1	0	2	32	3	82	4	4	6	.400	0-0	0	92	.764	4.49	4.64
15 Pit	NL	11	11	0	63.1	249	52	13	13	3	1	0	0	13	1	69	2	7	2	.778	0-0	0	92	.577	2.12	1.85
18 Tor	AL	20	20	0	114.0	475	99	61	53	17	1	1	4	35	0	130	1	10	6	.625	0-0	0	92	.677	3.43	4.18
18 NYY	AL	11	11	0	63.2	258	51	20	19	10	1	1	5	16	0	63	3	7	0	1.000	0-0	0	92	.676	3.11	2.69
Postseason		14	4	1	25.0	117	31	14	14	4	0	0	0	13	0	24	1	1	3	.250	0-0	1	91	.818	6.44	5.04
14 ML YEARS		324	298	10	1741.1	7377	1645	819	770	231	45	41	38	620	16	1539	43	123	92	.572	0-0	2	91	.727	3.90	3.98

Bryce Harper

Bats: L **Throws:** R **Pos:** RF-48;DH-10;CF-3   **Ht:** 6'3" **Wt:** 210 **Born:** 10/16/1992 **Age:** 28

Year Team	Lg	BATTING																			RUNNING			AVERAGES			
		G	AB	H	2B	3B	HR	(Hm	Rd)	TB	R	RBI	RC	TBB	IBB	SO	HBP	SH	SF	SB	CS	GDP	Avg	OBP	Slg	OPS
2012 Was	NL	139	533	144	26	9	22	(10	12)	254	98	59	82	56	0	120	2	3	3	18	6	8	.270	.340	.477	.817
2013 Was	NL	118	424	116	24	3	20	(13	7)	206	71	58	73	61	4	94	5	3	4	11	4	4	.274	.368	.486	.854
2014 Was	NL	100	352	96	10	2	13	(5	8)	149	41	32	43	38	4	104	1	3	1	2	2	6	.273	.344	.423	.768
2015 Was	NL	153	521	172	38	1	42	(23	19)	338	118	99	138	124	15	131	5	0	4	6	4	15	.330	.460	.649	1.109
2016 Was	NL	147	506	123	24	2	24	(12	12)	223	84	86	90	108	20	117	3	0	10	21	10	11	.243	.373	.441	.814
2017 Was	NL	111	420	134	27	1	29	(12	17)	250	95	87	93	68	11	99	1	0	3	4	2	15	.319	.413	.595	1.008
2018 Was	NL	159	550	137	34	0	34	(17	17)	273	103	100	111	130	16	169	6	0	9	13	3	7	.249	.393	.496	.889
2019 Phi	NL	157	573	149	36	1	35	(20	15)	292	98	114	125	99	11	178	6	0	4	15	3	10	.260	.372	.510	.882
2020 Phi	NL	58	190	51	9	2	13	(7	6)	103	41	33	44	49	8	43	2	1	2	8	2	5	.268	.420	.542	.962
Postseason		19	76	16	4	1	5	(3	2)	37	12	10	12	11	1	23	1	0	1	4	0	0	.211	.315	.487	.801
9 ML YEARS		1142	4069	1122	228	21	232	(119	113)	2088	749	668	799	733	89	1055	31	10	40	98	36	81	.276	.387	.513	.900

Ryne Harper

Pitches: R **Bats:** R **Pos:** RP-23   **Ht:** 6'3" **Wt:** 215 **Born:** 3/27/1989 **Age:** 32

Year Team	Lg	HOW MUCH PITCHED					WHAT HE GAVE UP											THE RESULTS								
		G	GS	GF	IP	BFP	H	R	ER	HR	SH	SF	HB	TBB	IBB	SO	WP	W	L	Pct	Sv-Op	Hld	Vel	OPS	ERC	ERA
2019 Min	AL	61	0	7	54.1	225	54	25	23	7	0	3	1	10	0	50	5	4	2	.667	1-4	12	89	.709	3.44	3.81
2020 Was		23	0	12	23.2	110	29	21	20	5	0	0	1	9	2	25	2	1	0	1.000	0-0	1	88	.865	6.06	7.61
2 ML YEARS		84	0	19	78.0	335	83	46	43	12	0	3	2	19	2	75	7	5	2	.714	1-4	13	89	.760	4.19	4.96

Will Harris

Pitches: R **Bats:** R **Pos:** RP-20   **Ht:** 6'4" **Wt:** 240 **Born:** 8/28/1984 **Age:** 36

Year Team	Lg	HOW MUCH PITCHED					WHAT HE GAVE UP											THE RESULTS								
		G	GS	GF	IP	BFP	H	R	ER	HR	SH	SF	HB	TBB	IBB	SO	WP	W	L	Pct	Sv-Op	Hld	Vel	OPS	ERC	ERA
2012 Col	NL	20	0	10	17.2	89	27	18	16	3	2	1	1	6	1	19	4	1	1	.500	0-0	3	91	.922	7.39	8.15
2013 Ari	NL	61	0	11	52.2	217	50	17	17	3	0	4	2	15	1	53	4	4	1	.800	0-1	3	92	.661	3.25	2.91
2014 Ari	NL	29	0	8	29.0	120	27	14	14	3	1	1	2	9	2	35	1	0	3	.000	0-1	3	92	.740	3.62	4.34
2015 Hou	AL	68	0	18	71.0	276	42	18	15	8	2	1	1	22	1	68	2	5	5	.500	2-6	13	92	.525	1.79	1.90
2016 Hou	AL	66	0	19	64.0	255	52	17	16	3	1	2	1	15	1	69	4	1	2	.333	12-15	28	92	.560	2.21	2.25
2017 Hou	AL	46	0	5	45.1	177	37	15	15	7	0	0	0	7	0	52	1	3	2	.600	2-4	20	92	.613	2.52	2.98
2018 Hou	AL	61	0	11	56.2	230	48	22	22	3	1	1	2	14	1	64	6	5	3	.625	0-3	16	92	.591	2.50	3.49
2019 Hou	AL	68	0	10	60.0	229	42	14	10	6	1	0	0	14	0	62	3	4	1	.800	4-5	26	88	.540	1.99	1.50
2020 Was	NL	20	0	5	17.2	84	21	9	6	3	0	0	0	9	0	21	1	0	1	.000	1-4	6	91	.797	5.96	3.06
Postseason		23	0	3	17.2	77	23	9	8	3	0	0	0	3	0	16	3	0	2	.000	1-3	10	92	.824	5.41	4.08
9 ML YEARS		439	0	97	414.0	1677	346	144	131	39	8	10	9	111	7	443	26	23	19	.548	21-39	119	92	.618	2.73	2.85

Josh Harrison

Bats: R **Throws:** R **Pos:** 2B-12;3B-10;DH-6;LF-5;PH-5;PR-4;RF-2;1B-1   **Ht:** 5'8" **Wt:** 190 **Born:** 7/8/1987 **Age:** 33

Year Team	Lg	BATTING																			RUNNING			AVERAGES			
		G	AB	H	2B	3B	HR	(Hm	Rd)	TB	R	RBI	RC	TBB	IBB	SO	HBP	SH	SF	SB	CS	GDP	Avg	OBP	Slg	OPS
2011 Pit	NL	65	195	53	13	2	1	(1	0)	73	21	16	19	3	0	24	0	5	1	4	1	6	.272	.281	.374	.656
2012 Pit	NL	104	249	58	9	5	3	(1	2)	86	34	16	22	10	0	37	7	7	3	7	3	3	.233	.279	.345	.624
2013 Pit	NL	60	88	22	1	2	3	(1	2)	36	10	14	11	2	0	10	3	2	0	2	0	4	.250	.290	.409	.699
2014 Pit	NL	143	520	164	38	7	13	(4	9)	255	77	52	84	22	1	81	4	2	2	18	7	6	.315	.347	.490	.837
2015 Pit	NL	114	418	120	29	1	4	(2	2)	163	57	28	48	19	1	71	7	3	2	10	8	4	.287	.327	.390	.717
2016 Pit	NL	131	487	138	25	7	4	(2	2)	189	57	59	61	18	0	76	5	4	8	19	4	10	.283	.311	.388	.699
2017 Pit	NL	128	486	132	26	2	16	(9	7)	210	66	47	65	28	2	90	23	2	3	12	4	5	.272	.339	.432	.771
2018 Pit	NL	97	344	86	13	1	8	(3	5)	125	41	37	42	18	1	68	5	2	5	3	0	8	.250	.293	.363	.656
2019 Det	AL	36	137	24	7	1	1	(1	0)	36	10	8	3	6	0	27	2	0	2	4	2	0	.175	.218	.263	.480
2020 Was	NL	33	79	22	2	0	3	(1	2)	33	11	14	12	6	0	12	4	0	2	1	2	1	.278	.352	.418	.769
Postseason		4	7	2	0	0	0	(0	0)	2	1	0	0	0	0	2	0	0	0	0	0	0	.286	.375	.286	.661
10 ML YEARS		911	3003	819	163	28	56	(25	31)	1206	384	291	367	132	5	496	60	27	28	80	31	48	.273	.314	.402	.715

Monte Harrison

Bats: R **Throws:** R **Pos:** CF-16;RF-13;PR-9;PH-2   **Ht:** 6'3" **Wt:** 225 **Born:** 8/10/1995 **Age:** 25

Year	Team	Lg	G	AB	H	2B	3B	HR	(Hm	Rd)	TB	R	RBI	RC	TBB	IBB	SO	HBP	SH	SF	SB	CS	GDP	Avg	OBP	Slg	OPS
2020	Mia	NL	32	47	8	1	0	1	(1	0)	12	8	3	1	4	0	26	0	0	0	6	0	0	.170	.235	.255	.491

Kyle Hart

Pitches: L **Bats:** L **Pos:** SP-3; RP-1   **Ht:** 6'5" **Wt:** 200 **Born:** 11/23/1992 **Age:** 28

Year	Team	Lg	G	GS	GF	IP	BFP	H	R	ER	HR	SH	SF	HB	TBB	IBB	SO	WP	W	L	Pct	Sv-Op	Hld	Vel	OPS	ERC	ERA
2020	Bos	AL	4	3	0	11.0	67	24	21	19	4	0	1	0	10	0	13	0	0	1	.000	0-0	0	89	1.222	16.95	15.55

Geoff Hartlieb

Pitches: R **Bats:** R **Pos:** RP-21   **Ht:** 6'5" **Wt:** 235 **Born:** 12/9/1993 **Age:** 27

Year	Team	Lg	G	GS	GF	IP	BFP	H	R	ER	HR	SH	SF	HB	TBB	IBB	SO	WP	W	L	Pct	Sv-Op	Hld	Vel	OPS	ERC	ERA
2019	Pit	NL	29	0	10	35.0	171	52	35	35	8	1	4	0	18	0	38	5	0	1	.000	0-0	2	96	1.020	8.67	9.00
2020	Pit	NL	21	0	1	22.1	101	16	11	9	1	0	1	3	19	0	19	2	1	0	1.000	0-0	5	94	.658	4.39	3.63
2 ML YEARS			50	0	11	57.1	272	68	46	44	9	1	5	3	37	0	57	7	1	1	.500	0-0	7	95	.894	6.94	6.91

Hunter Harvey

Pitches: R **Bats:** R **Pos:** RP-10   **Ht:** 6'3" **Wt:** 210 **Born:** 12/9/1994 **Age:** 26

Year	Team	Lg	G	GS	GF	IP	BFP	H	R	ER	HR	SH	SF	HB	TBB	IBB	SO	WP	W	L	Pct	Sv-Op	Hld	Vel	OPS	ERC	ERA
2019	Bal	AL	7	0	1	6.1	26	3	1	1	1	0	0	0	4	0	11	0	1	0	1.000	0-1	1	98	.678	2.51	1.42
2020	Bal	AL	10	0	2	8.2	37	8	6	4	2	0	1	1	2	0	6	2	0	2	.000	0-0	4	97	.722	4.23	4.15
2 ML YEARS			17	0	3	15.0	63	11	7	5	3	0	1	1	6	0	17	2	1	2	.333	0-1	5	98	.704	3.47	3.00

Joe Harvey

Pitches: R **Bats:** R **Pos:** RP-4   **Ht:** 6'2" **Wt:** 236 **Born:** 1/9/1992 **Age:** 29

Year	Team	Lg	G	GS	GF	IP	BFP	H	R	ER	HR	SH	SF	HB	TBB	IBB	SO	WP	W	L	Pct	Sv-Op	Hld	Vel	OPS	ERC	ERA
2019	2 Tms		18	0	7	18.0	84	18	11	10	3	0	1	2	13	0	17	0	1	0	1.000	0-0	0	95	.834	6.48	5.00
2020	Col	NL	4	0	1	3.1	14	3	0	0	0	0	0	0	0	0	2	0	0	0		0-0	0	95	.593	2.46	0.00
19	NYY	AL	9	0	4	10.0	48	11	6	5	1	0	1	1	7	0	11	0	1	0	1.000	0-0	0	95	.832	6.28	4.50
19	Col	NL	9	0	3	8.0	36	7	5	5	2	0	0	1	6	0	6	0	0	0		0-0	0	95	.837	6.71	5.63
2 ML YEARS			22	0	8	21.1	98	21	11	10	3	0	1	3	13	0	19	0	1	0	1.000	0-0	0	95	.797	5.77	4.22

Matt Harvey

Pitches: R **Bats:** R **Pos:** SP-4; RP-3   **Ht:** 6'4" **Wt:** 220 **Born:** 3/27/1989 **Age:** 32

Year	Team	Lg	G	GS	GF	IP	BFP	H	R	ER	HR	SH	SF	HB	TBB	IBB	SO	WP	W	L	Pct	Sv-Op	Hld	Vel	OPS	ERC	ERA
2012	NYM	NL	10	10	0	59.1	245	42	19	18	5	3	3	3	26	0	70	3	3	5	.375	0-0	0	95	.631	2.75	2.73
2013	NYM	NL	26	26	0	178.1	690	135	46	45	7	5	4	4	31	1	191	2	9	5	.643	0-0	0	96	.530	1.76	2.27
2015	NYM	NL	29	29	0	189.1	755	156	62	57	18	7	2	5	37	2	188	4	13	8	.619	0-0	0	96	.609	2.44	2.71
2016	NYM	NL	17	17	0	92.2	402	111	55	50	8	5	4	1	25	1	76	4	4	10	.286	0-0	0	94	.797	4.65	4.86
2017	NYM	NL	19	18	0	92.2	431	110	70	69	21	3	2	4	47	3	67	6	5	7	.417	0-0	0	94	.890	6.87	6.70
2018	2 Tms	NL	32	28	2	155.0	663	165	87	85	27	6	5	6	37	2	131	2	7	9	.438	0-0	0	94	.783	4.42	4.94
2019	LAA	AL	12	12	0	59.2	266	63	48	47	13	1	4	3	29	0	39	3	3	5	.375	0-0	0	93	.887	5.91	7.09
2020	KC	AL	7	4	1	11.2	65	27	15	15	6	0	0	0	5	0	10	0	0	3	.000	0-0	0	94	1.309	17.52	11.57
18	NYM	NL	8	4	2	27.0	123	33	21	21	6	2	2	1	9	0	20	1	0	2	.000	0-0	0	93	.906	6.10	7.00
18	Cin	NL	24	24	0	128.0	540	132	66	64	21	4	3	5	28	2	111	1	7	7	.500	0-0	0	94	.756	4.08	4.50
Postseason			4	4	0	26.2	109	21	10	9	2	0	1	1	8	1	27	0	2	0	1.000	0-0	0	95	.578	2.49	3.04
8 ML YEARS			152	144	3	838.2	3517	809	402	386	105	30	24	28	237	9	772	24	44	52	.458	0-0	0	95	.716	3.71	4.14

Adam Haseley

Bats: L **Throws:** L **Pos:** CF-24;LF-11;RF-9;PH-5;PR-1   **Ht:** 6'1" **Wt:** 190 **Born:** 4/12/1996 **Age:** 25

Year	Team	Lg	G	AB	H	2B	3B	HR	(Hm	Rd)	TB	R	RBI	RC	TBB	IBB	SO	HBP	SH	SF	SB	CS	GDP	Avg	OBP	Slg	OPS
2019	Phi	NL	67	222	59	14	0	5	(3	2)	88	30	26	28	14	1	60	5	1	0	4	0	7	.266	.324	.396	.720
2020	Phi	NL	40	79	22	5	0	0	(0	0)	27	7	13	12	7	1	17	2	3	1	0	0	3	.278	.348	.342	.690
2 ML YEARS			107	301	81	19	0	5	(3	2)	115	37	39	40	21	2	77	7	4	1	4	0	10	.269	.330	.382	.712

Thomas Hatch

Pitches: R **Bats:** R **Pos:** RP-16; SP-1   **Ht:** 6'1" **Wt:** 205 **Born:** 9/29/1994 **Age:** 26

Year	Team	Lg	G	GS	GF	IP	BFP	H	R	ER	HR	SH	SF	HB	TBB	IBB	SO	WP	W	L	Pct	Sv-Op	Hld	Vel	OPS	ERC	ERA
2020	Tor	AL	17	1	1	26.1	109	18	11	8	2	0	0	2	13	0	23	0	3	1	.750	0-0	3	95	.601	2.90	2.73

Ke'Bryan Hayes

Bats: R **Throws:** R **Pos:** 3B-24   **Ht:** 5'10" **Wt:** 205 **Born:** 1/28/1997 **Age:** 24

Year	Team	Lg	G	AB	H	2B	3B	HR	(Hm	Rd)	TB	R	RBI	RC	TBB	IBB	SO	HBP	SH	SF	SB	CS	GDP	Avg	OBP	Slg	OPS
									BATTING												RUNNING			AVERAGES			
2016	2 Tms	Low	67	252	67	13	1	6	(-	-)	100	27	37	32	17	1	52	6	3	4	6	5	5	.266	.323	.397	.719
2017	Bradtn	A+	108	421	117	16	7	2	(-	-)	153	66	43	60	41	0	76	4	12	4	27	5	12	.278	.345	.363	.708
2018	Altna	AA	117	437	128	31	7	7	(-	-)	194	64	47	77	57	0	84	4	4	6	12	5	10	.293	.375	.444	.819
2019	Indy	AAA	110	427	113	30	2	10	(-	-)	177	64	53	64	43	0	90	5	1	4	12	1	8	.265	.336	.415	.751
2020	Pit	NL	24	85	32	7	2	5	(3	2)	58	17	11	24	9	2	20	1	0	0	1	0	2	.376	.442	.682	1.124

Austin Hays

Bats: R **Throws:** R **Pos:** CF-23;LF-10;RF-3;PH-2   **Ht:** 6'0" **Wt:** 205 **Born:** 7/5/1995 **Age:** 25

Year	Team	Lg	G	AB	H	2B	3B	HR	(Hm	Rd)	TB	R	RBI	RC	TBB	IBB	SO	HBP	SH	SF	SB	CS	GDP	Avg	OBP	Slg	OPS
									BATTING												RUNNING			AVERAGES			
2017	Bal	AL	20	60	13	3	0	1	(0	1)	19	4	8	5	2	0	16	0	0	1	0	0	2	.217	.238	.317	.555
2019	Bal	AL	21	68	21	6	0	4	(2	2)	39	12	13	16	7	0	13	0	0	0	2	0	0	.309	.373	.574	.947
2020	Bal	AL	33	122	34	2	0	4	(1	3)	48	20	9	14	8	0	25	2	0	2	2	3	1	.279	.328	.393	.722
	3 ML YEARS		74	250	68	11	0	9	(3	6)	106	36	30	35	17	0	54	2	0	3	4	3	3	.272	.320	.424	.744

Ryon Healy

Bats: R **Throws:** R **Pos:** 1B-2;DH-2;PH-1   **Ht:** 6'4" **Wt:** 230 **Born:** 1/10/1992 **Age:** 29

Year	Team	Lg	G	AB	H	2B	3B	HR	(Hm	Rd)	TB	R	RBI	RC	TBB	IBB	SO	HBP	SH	SF	SB	CS	GDP	Avg	OBP	Slg	OPS
									BATTING												RUNNING			AVERAGES			
2016	Oak	AL	72	269	82	20	0	13	(8	5)	141	36	37	43	12	1	60	1	1	0	0	0	7	.305	.337	.524	.861
2017	Oak	AL	149	576	156	29	0	25	(14	11)	260	66	78	75	23	0	142	4	0	2	0	1	16	.271	.302	.451	.754
2018	Sea	AL	133	493	116	15	0	24	(15	9)	203	51	73	52	27	0	113	2	0	2	0	0	21	.235	.277	.412	.688
2019	Sea	AL	47	169	40	16	0	7	(2	5)	77	24	26	23	13	0	40	1	0	4	0	0	1	.237	.289	.456	.744
2020	Mil	NL	4	7	1	0	0	0	(0	0)	1	0	0	0	0	0	2	0	0	0	0	0	0	.143	.143	.143	.286
	5 ML YEARS		405	1514	395	80	0	69	(39	30)	682	177	214	193	75	1	357	8	1	8	0	1	45	.261	.298	.450	.748

Andrew Heaney

Pitches: L **Bats:** L **Pos:** SP-12   HEE-nee   **Ht:** 6'2" **Wt:** 200 **Born:** 6/5/1991 **Age:** 30

Year	Team	Lg	G	GS	GF	IP	BFP	H	R	ER	HR	SH	SF	HB	TBB	IBB	SO	WP	W	L	Pct	Sv-Op	Hld	Vel	OPS	ERC	ERA
				HOW MUCH PITCHED						WHAT HE GAVE UP										THE RESULTS						
2014	Mia	NL	7	5	2	29.1	126	32	19	19	6	2	0	3	7	0	20	2	0	3	.000	0-0		90	.847	5.17	5.83
2015	LAA	AL	18	18	0	105.2	438	99	41	41	9	1	3	6	28	1	78	4	6	4	.600	0-0		91	.679	3.35	3.49
2016	LAA	AL	1	1	0	6.0	25	7	4	4	2	0	0	0	0	0	7	0	1	0	.000	0-0		91	.840	4.78	6.00
2017	LAA	AL	5	5	0	21.2	101	27	17	17	12	2	0	0	9	0	27	2	1	2	.333	0-0		92	1.108	8.99	7.06
2018	LAA	AL	30	30	0	180.0	749	171	91	83	27	2	5	8	45	0	180	9	9	10	.474	0-0		92	.719	3.73	4.15
2019	LAA	AL	18	18	0	95.1	409	93	53	52	20	0	2	7	30	1	118	4	4	6	.400	0-0		93	.772	4.63	4.91
2020	LAA	AL	12	12	0	66.2	279	63	35	33	9	0	2	2	19	1	70	2	4	3	.571	0-0		92	.715	3.65	4.46
	7 ML YEARS		91	89	2	504.2	2127	492	260	249	85	7	12	26	138	3	500	23	24	29	.453	0-0		92	.748	4.10	4.44

Taylor Hearn

Pitches: L **Bats:** L **Pos:** RP-14   **Ht:** 6'6" **Wt:** 230 **Born:** 8/30/1994 **Age:** 26

Year	Team	Lg	G	GS	GF	IP	BFP	H	R	ER	HR	SH	SF	HB	TBB	IBB	SO	WP	W	L	Pct	Sv-Op	Hld	Vel	OPS	ERC	ERA
				HOW MUCH PITCHED						WHAT HE GAVE UP										THE RESULTS						
2019	Tex	AL	1	1	0	0.1	8	3	5	4	0	0	0	0	4	0	0	0	0	1	.000	0-0		92	1.875	131.5	108.0
2020	Tex	AL	14	0	3	17.1	76	13	8	7	2	0	1	1	11	0	23	2	0	0	-	0-0		95	.646	3.90	3.63
	2 ML YEARS		15	1	3	17.2	84	16	13	11	2	0	1	1	15	0	23	2	0	1	.000	0-0		95	.739	5.60	5.60

Nick Heath

Bats: L **Throws:** L **Pos:** CF-6;PR-6;DH-3;PH-3;LF-1   **Ht:** 6'1" **Wt:** 190 **Born:** 11/27/1993 **Age:** 27

Year	Team	Lg	G	AB	H	2B	3B	HR	(Hm	Rd)	TB	R	RBI	RC	TBB	IBB	SO	HBP	SH	SF	SB	CS	GDP	Avg	OBP	Slg	OPS
									BATTING												RUNNING			AVERAGES			
2020	KC	AL	15	13	2	1	0	0	(0	0)	3	2	3	1	2	0	6	1	1	0	2	2	0	.154	.313	.231	.543

Adeiny Hechavarria

Bats: R **Throws:** R **Pos:** 2B-12;3B-8;SS-4;PH-3;DH-1;PR-1   a-DAY-nee etch-eh-vah-REE-ah   **Ht:** 6'0" **Wt:** 195 **Born:** 4/15/1989 **Age:** 32

Year	Team	Lg	G	AB	H	2B	3B	HR	(Hm	Rd)	TB	R	RBI	RC	TBB	IBB	SO	HBP	SH	SF	SB	CS	GDP	Avg	OBP	Slg	OPS
									BATTING												RUNNING			AVERAGES			
2012	Tor	AL	41	126	32	8	0	2	(1	1)	46	10	15	15	4	0	32	1	5	1	0	0	2	.254	.280	.365	.645
2013	Mia	NL	148	543	123	14	8	3	(1	2)	162	30	42	37	30	1	96	0	4	1	11	10	19	.227	.267	.298	.565
2014	Mia	NL	146	536	148	20	10	1	(0	1)	191	53	34	49	26	5	86	1	4	6	7	5	21	.276	.308	.356	.664
2015	Mia	NL	130	470	132	17	6	5	(3	2)	176	54	48	49	23	4	78	2	0	4	7	2	18	.281	.315	.374	.689
2016	Mia	NL	155	508	120	17	6	3	(1	2)	158	52	38	40	33	7	73	1	2	3	1	0	10	.236	.283	.311	.594
2017	2 Tms		97	330	86	14	5	8	(4	4)	134	37	30	36	13	1	67	1	2	2	4	1	7	.261	.289	.406	.695
2018	3 Tms		94	296	73	11	0	6	(2	4)	102	34	31	24	16	2	58	0	2	7	2	0	7	.247	.279	.345	.624
2019	2 Tms	NL	84	203	49	12	1	9	(6	3)	90	34	33	29	14	0	48	3	0	1	3	1	3	.241	.294	.443	.742
2020	Atl	NL	27	59	15	3	0	0	(0	0)	18	7	2	2	4	0	12	0	0	0	0	0	1	.254	.302	.305	.607
17	Mia	NL	20	65	18	2	1	1	(0	1)	25	8	6	8	1	0	9	1	0	1	0	0	1	.277	.288	.385	.672
17	TB		77	265	68	12	4	7	(4	3)	109	29	24	28	12	1	58	1	1	2	4	1	6	.257	.289	.411	.701
18	TB	AL	61	217	56	7	0	3	(2	1)	72	29	26	22	12	1	37	0	2	6	1	0	4	.258	.289	.332	.621
18	Pit	NL	15	43	10	4	0	1	(0	1)	17	2	3	0	3	1	11	0	0	1	0	0	3	.233	.277	.395	.672

Year	Team	Lg	G	AB	H	2B	3B	HR	(Hm	Rd)	TB	R	RBI	RC	TBB	IBB	SO	HBP	SH	SF	SB	CS	GDP	Avg	OBP	Slg	OPS
18	NYY	AL	18	36	7	0	0	2	(0	2)	13	3	2	2	1	0	10	0	0	0	1	0	0	.194	.216	.361	.577
19	NYM	NL	60	142	29	7	0	5	(4	1)	51	20	18	13	8	0	33	1	0	0	3	1	2	.204	.252	.359	.611
19	Atl	NL	24	61	20	5	1	4	(2	2)	39	14	15	16	6	0	15	2	0	1	0	0	1	.328	.400	.639	1.039
	Postseason		7	6	0	0	0	0	(0	0)	0	0	0	0	1	0	2	0	0	0	0	0	0	.000	.143	.000	.143
	9 ML YEARS		922	3071	778	116	36	37	(18	19)	1077	311	273	281	163	20	550	9	19	25	35	19	88	.253	.291	.351	.641

Austin Hedges

Bats: R **Throws:** R **Pos:** C-34;DH-1;PH-1   **Ht:** 6'1" **Wt:** 223 **Born:** 8/18/1992 **Age:** 28

Year	Team	Lg	G	AB	H	2B	3B	HR	(Hm	Rd)	TB	R	RBI	RC	TBB	IBB	SO	HBP	SH	SF	SB	CS	GDP	Avg	OBP	Slg	OPS
2015	SD	NL	56	137	23	2	0	3	(2	1)	34	13	11	7	8	1	38	1	3	3	0	0	1	.168	.215	.248	.463
2016	SD	NL	8	24	3	1	0	0	(0	0)	4	2	1	0	0	0	7	1	0	1	0	1	0	.125	.154	.167	.321
2017	SD	NL	120	387	83	17	0	18	(9	9)	154	36	55	39	23	3	122	3	1	3	4	1	10	.214	.262	.398	.660
2018	SD	NL	91	303	70	14	2	14	(5	9)	130	29	37	28	21	3	90	1	0	1	3	0	9	.231	.282	.429	.711
2019	SD	NL	102	312	55	9	0	11	(3	8)	97	28	36	28	27	3	109	5	2	1	1	0	3	.176	.252	.311	.563
2020	2 Tms		35	69	10	1	0	3	(1	2)	20	7	6	3	6	0	23	2	5	1	1	1	3	.145	.231	.290	.521
20	SD	NL	29	57	9	1	0	3	(1	2)	19	7	6	3	6	0	18	2	5	1	1	1	3	.158	.258	.333	.591
20	Cle	AL	6	12	1	0	0	0	(0	0)	1	0	0	0	0	0	5	0	0	0	0	0	0	.083	.083	.083	.167
	6 ML YEARS		412	1232	244	44	2	49	(20	29)	439	115	146	105	85	10	389	13	11	10	9	3	26	.198	.255	.356	.612

Jonah Heim

Bats: B **Throws:** R **Pos:** C-12;DH-1;PH-1   **Ht:** 6'4" **Wt:** 220 **Born:** 6/27/1995 **Age:** 26

Year	Team	Lg	G	AB	H	2B	3B	HR	(Hm	Rd)	TB	R	RBI	RC	TBB	IBB	SO	HBP	SH	SF	SB	CS	GDP	Avg	OBP	Slg	OPS
2020	Oak	AL	13	38	8	0	0	0	(0	0)	8	5	5	5	3	0	3	0	0	0	0	0	1	.211	.268	.211	.479

Scott Heineman

Bats: R **Throws:** R **Pos:** CF-17;PR-4;LF-3;DH-2;PH-2;1B-1;RF-1   **Ht:** 6'1" **Wt:** 205 **Born:** 12/4/1992 **Age:** 28

Year	Team	Lg	G	AB	H	2B	3B	HR	(Hm	Rd)	TB	R	RBI	RC	TBB	IBB	SO	HBP	SH	SF	SB	CS	GDP	Avg	OBP	Slg	OPS
2019	Tex	AL	25	75	16	6	0	2	(1	1)	28	8	7	7	9	0	20	1	0	0	1	2	3	.213	.306	.373	.679
2020	Tex	AL	24	52	8	3	0	1	(0	1)	14	6	7	4	2	0	11	0	0	0	3	0	1	.154	.185	.269	.454
	2 ML YEARS		49	127	24	9	0	3	(1	2)	42	14	14	11	11	0	31	1	0	0	4	2	4	.189	.259	.331	.590

Tyler Heineman

Bats: B **Throws:** R **Pos:** C-15   **Ht:** 5'10" **Wt:** 199 **Born:** 6/19/1991 **Age:** 30

Year	Team	Lg	G	AB	H	2B	3B	HR	(Hm	Rd)	TB	R	RBI	RC	TBB	IBB	SO	HBP	SH	SF	SB	CS	GDP	Avg	OBP	Slg	OPS
2019	Mia	NL	5	11	3	1	0	1	(0	1)	7	1	2	3	0	0	4	0	1	0	0	0	0	.273	.273	.636	.909
2020	SF	NL	15	42	8	1	0	0	(0	0)	9	3	1	3	4	0	6	2	2	0	1	0	0	.190	.292	.214	.506
	2 ML YEARS		20	53	11	2	0	1	(0	1)	16	4	3	6	4	0	10	2	3	0	1	0	0	.208	.288	.302	.590

Ben Heller

Pitches: R **Bats:** R **Pos:** RP-6   **Ht:** 6'3" **Wt:** 210 **Born:** 8/5/1991 **Age:** 29

			HOW MUCH PITCHED				WHAT HE GAVE UP									THE RESULTS							
Year	Team	Lg	G	GS	GF	IP	BFP	H	R	ER	HR	SH	SF	HB	TBB	IBB	SO	WP	W	L	Pct	Sv-Op	Hld	Vel	OPS	ERC	ERA
2016	NYY	AL	10	0	4	7.0	40	11	5	5	3	0	0	2	4	1	6	0	1	0	1.000	0-1	1	96	1.101	11.69	6.43
2017	NYY	AL	9	0	4	11.0	43	5	1	1	0	0	1	0	6	1	9	1	1	0	1.000	0-0	0	95	.450	1.40	0.82
2019	NYY	AL	6	0	1	7.1	28	6	1	1	1	1	0	0	3	1	9	0	0	0	-	0-0	0	93	.750	3.49	1.23
2020	NYY	AL	6	0	2	6.0	27	5	2	2	2	0	0	2	2	0	6	0	0	0	-	0-0	0	93	.855	5.80	3.00
	4 ML YEARS		31	0	11	31.1	138	27	9	9	6	1	1	4	15	2	30	1	2	0	1.000	0-1	1	94	.780	4.64	2.59

Ryan Helsley

Pitches: R **Bats:** R **Pos:** RP-12   **Ht:** 6'2" **Wt:** 230 **Born:** 7/18/1994 **Age:** 26

			HOW MUCH PITCHED				WHAT HE GAVE UP									THE RESULTS							
Year	Team	Lg	G	GS	GF	IP	BFP	H	R	ER	HR	SH	SF	HB	TBB	IBB	SO	WP	W	L	Pct	Sv-Op	Hld	Vel	OPS	ERC	ERA
2019	StL	NL	24	0	4	36.2	153	34	13	12	5	1	1	0	12	2	32	2	2	0	1.000	0-1	1	98	.734	3.56	2.95
2020	StL	NL	12	0	4	12.0	52	8	8	7	3	0	0	1	8	1	10	0	1	1	.500	1-3	2	97	.769	4.53	5.25
	Postseason		5	0	1	5.1	18	1	0	0	0	0	0	0	1	0	8	0	0	0	-	0-0	0	98	.170	0.24	0.00
	2 ML YEARS		36	0	8	48.2	205	42	21	19	8	1	1	1	20	3	42	2	3	1	.750	1-4	3	98	.743	3.79	3.51

Heath Hembree

Pitches: R **Bats:** R **Pos:** RP-22   HEHM-bree   **Ht:** 6'4" **Wt:** 220 **Born:** 1/13/1989 **Age:** 32

			HOW MUCH PITCHED				WHAT HE GAVE UP									THE RESULTS							
Year	Team	Lg	G	GS	GF	IP	BFP	H	R	ER	HR	SH	SF	HB	TBB	IBB	SO	WP	W	L	Pct	Sv-Op	Hld	Vel	OPS	ERC	ERA
2013	SF	NL	9	0	2	7.2	29	4	0	0	0	0	0	0	2	0	12	0	0	0	-	0-0	0	92	.392	1.02	0.00
2014	Bos	AL	6	0	3	10.0	43	11	5	5	1	0	0	0	5	2	6	1	0	0	-	0-0	0	92	.846	4.94	4.50
2015	Bos	AL	22	0	9	25.1	106	25	10	10	5	0	0	0	9	2	15	1	0	0	-	0-0	0	94	.795	4.46	3.55
2016	Bos	AL	38	0	8	51.0	223	51	23	15	6	0	1	0	17	1	47	0	4	1	.800	0-2	5	94	.695	3.78	2.65
2017	Bos	AL	62	0	8	62.0	260	72	29	25	10	1	2	1	18	0	70	2	2	3	.400	0-3	14	95	.803	5.07	3.63
2018	Bos	AL	67	0	10	60.0	260	53	30	28	10	0	5	1	27	3	76	4	4	1	.800	0-3	20	95	.734	4.05	4.20
2019	Bos	AL	45	0	14	39.2	173	34	20	17	7	0	0	3	18	2	46	2	1	0	1.000	2-3	4	94	.772	4.18	3.86

Year Team	Lg	G	GS	GF	IP	BFP	H	R	ER	HR	SH	SF	HB	TBB	IBB	SO	WP	W	L	Pct	Sv-Op	Hld	Vel	OPS	ERC	ERA
2020 2 Tms		22	0	2	19.0	90	26	19	19	9	0	1	2	8	0	20	0	3	0	1.000	0-1	3	94	1.159	10.17	9.00
20 Bos	AL	11	0	1	9.2	40	9	6	6	2	0	0	0	3	0	10	0	2	0	1.000	0-1	1	94	.786	4.08	5.59
20 Phi	NL	11	0	1	9.1	50	17	13	13	7	0	1	2	5	0	10	0	1	0	1.000	0-0	2	94	1.480	17.96	12.54
Postseason		4	0	2	4.2	16	0	0	0	0	0	0	0	5	0	3	0	0	0	-	0-0	0	94	.313	1.27	0.00
8 ML YEARS		271	0	56	274.2	1195	276	136	119	48	1	9	7	104	8	292	10	16	5	.762	2-12	47	94	.780	4.57	3.90

Kyle Hendricks

Pitches: R **Bats:** R **Pos:** SP-12   **Ht:** 6'3" **Wt:** 190 **Born:** 12/7/1989 **Age:** 31

Year Team	Lg	G	GS	GF	IP	BFP	H	R	ER	HR	SH	SF	HB	TBB	IBB	SO	WP	W	L	Pct	Sv-Op	Hld	Vel	OPS	ERC	ERA
2014 ChC	NL	13	13	0	80.1	321	72	24	22	4	4	1	4	15	2	47	0	7	2	.778	0-0	0	88	.610	2.61	2.46
2015 ChC	NL	32	32	0	180.0	739	166	82	79	17	6	0	8	43	1	167	3	8	7	.533	0-0	0	88	.677	3.18	3.95
2016 ChC	NL	31	30	0	190.0	742	142	53	45	15	4	3	8	44	3	170	5	16	8	.667	0-0	0	88	.581	2.19	2.13
2017 ChC	NL	24	24	0	139.2	570	126	49	47	17	6	1	2	40	1	123	0	7	5	.583	0-0	0	86	.670	3.34	3.03
2018 ChC	NL	33	33	0	199.0	812	184	82	76	22	7	7	9	44	4	161	0	14	11	.560	0-0	0	87	.685	3.22	3.44
2019 ChC	NL	30	30	0	177.0	730	168	78	68	19	8	5	9	32	1	150	1	11	10	.524	0-0	0	87	.687	3.17	3.46
2020 ChC	NL	12	12	0	81.1	315	73	26	26	10	0	2	1	8	1	64	1	6	5	.545	0-0	0	87	.632	2.62	2.88
Postseason		11	10	0	51.1	214	48	19	17	9	2	1	2	13	1	48	0	2	3	.400	0-0	0	88	.724	3.75	2.98
7 ML YEARS		175	174	0	1047.1	4232	931	394	363	104	35	19	41	226	13	882	10	69	48	.590	0-0	0	87	.654	2.93	3.12

Liam Hendriks

Pitches: R **Bats:** R **Pos:** RP-24   **Ht:** 6'0" **Wt:** 230 **Born:** 2/10/1989 **Age:** 32

Year Team	Lg	G	GS	GF	IP	BFP	H	R	ER	HR	SH	SF	HB	TBB	IBB	SO	WP	W	L	Pct	Sv-Op	Hld	Vel	OPS	ERC	ERA
2011 Min	AL	4	4	0	23.1	100	29	16	16	3	0	1	0	6	0	16	1	0	2	.000	0-0	0	90	.866	5.26	6.17
2012 Min	AL	16	16	0	85.1	381	106	61	53	17	3	1	4	26	3	50	4	1	8	.111	0-0	0	90	.890	6.03	5.59
2013 Min	AL	10	8	1	47.1	224	67	39	36	10	0	2	3	14	1	34	1	1	3	.250	0-0	0	91	.907	7.16	6.85
2014 2 Tms	AL	9	6	0	32.2	143	38	21	19	3	0	2	3	7	0	23	1	1	2	.333	0-0	1	91	.786	4.56	5.23
2015 Tor	AL	58	0	14	64.2	261	59	23	21	3	0	2	2	11	1	71	4	5	0	1.000	0-2	5	95	.605	2.51	2.92
2016 Oak	AL	53	0	10	64.2	275	69	31	27	6	0	4	1	14	3	71	3	0	4	.000	0-1	10	94	.704	3.63	3.76
2017 Oak	AL	70	0	13	64.0	273	57	34	30	7	0	1	0	23	0	78	6	4	2	.667	1-4	16	95	.663	3.30	4.22
2018 Oak	AL	25	8	1	24.0	104	25	11	11	3	0	1	1	10	0	22	1	0	1	.000	0-0	4	94	.759	4.82	4.13
2019 Oak	AL	75	2	41	85.0	332	61	18	17	5	2	3	2	21	5	124	7	4	4	.500	25-32	8	96	.564	1.86	1.80
2020 Oak	AL	24	0	20	25.1	92	14	6	5	1	1	1	0	3	1	37	0	3	1	.750	14-15	0	96	.405	0.95	1.78
14 Tor	AL	3	3	0	13.1	57	12	9	9	3	0	0	2	4	0	8	0	1	0	1.000	0-0	0	91	.767	4.58	6.08
14 KC	AL	6	3	0	19.1	86	26	12	10	0	0	2	1	3	0	15	1	0	2	.000	0-0	1	92	.799	4.52	4.66
Postseason		5	1	2	7.0	26	6	5	5	1	0	1	0	1	0	4	0	0	1	.000	0-0	0	96	.686	2.80	6.43
10 ML YEARS		344	44	100	516.1	2185	525	260	235	58	6	18	16	135	14	526	28	19	27	.413	40-54	40	93	.721	3.78	4.10

Guillermo Heredia

Bats: R **Throws:** L **Pos:** CF-9;RF-5;PR-3;PH-1   ghee-YAIR-moh   **Ht:** 5'10" **Wt:** 195 **Born:** 1/31/1991 **Age:** 30

Year Team	Lg	G	AB	H	2B	3B	HR	(Hm	Rd)	TB	R	RBI	RC	TBB	IBB	SO	HBP	SH	SF	SB	CS	GDP	Avg	OBP	Slg	OPS
2016 Sea	AL	45	92	23	3	0	1	(1	0)	29	12	9	12	12	0	15	2	1	0	1	1	1	.250	.349	.315	.664
2017 Sea	AL	123	386	96	16	0	6	(4	2)	130	43	24	37	27	2	64	11	1	1	1	5	9	.249	.315	.337	.652
2018 Sea	AL	125	292	69	14	1	5	(1	4)	100	29	19	33	32	0	52	4	7	2	2	4	4	.236	.318	.342	.661
2019 TB	AL	89	204	46	13	0	5	(1	4)	74	31	20	20	18	0	60	6	2	1	2	2	4	.225	.306	.363	.668
2020 2 Tms	NL	15	33	7	0	0	2	(1	1)	13	6	5	4	3	0	9	0	0	0	1	0	0	.212	.278	.394	.672
20 Pit	NL	8	16	3	0	0	0	(0	0)	3	2	2	2	2	0	4	0	0	0	1	0	0	.188	.278	.188	.465
20 NYM	NL	7	17	4	0	0	2	(1	1)	10	4	3	2	1	0	5	0	0	0	0	0	0	.235	.278	.588	.866
5 ML YEARS		397	1007	241	46	1	19	(8	11)	346	121	80	106	92	2	200	23	11	4	7	12	18	.239	.316	.344	.660

Jimmy Herget

Pitches: R **Bats:** R **Pos:** RP-19; SP-1   **Ht:** 6'3" **Wt:** 170 **Born:** 9/9/1993 **Age:** 27

Year Team	Lg	G	GS	GF	IP	BFP	H	R	ER	HR	SH	SF	HB	TBB	IBB	SO	WP	W	L	Pct	Sv-Op	Hld	Vel	OPS	ERC	ERA
2019 Cin	NL	5	0	4	6.1	26	8	3	3	2	0	0	0	3	0	0	0	0	0	-	0-0	0	93	1.119	8.76	4.26
2020 Tex	AL	20	1	6	19.2	87	13	7	7	2	1	1	2	14	1	17	0	1	0	1.000	0-1	1	93	.671	3.68	3.20
2 ML YEARS		25	1	10	26.0	113	21	10	10	4	1	1	2	17	1	17	0	1	0	1.000	0-1	1	93	.781	4.75	3.46

Michael Hermosillo

Bats: R **Throws:** R **Pos:** LF-5;CF-1;PH-1   air-moh-SEE-yo   **Ht:** 6'0" **Wt:** 205 **Born:** 1/17/1995 **Age:** 26

Year Team	Lg	G	AB	H	2B	3B	HR	(Hm	Rd)	TB	R	RBI	RC	TBB	IBB	SO	HBP	SH	SF	SB	CS	GDP	Avg	OBP	Slg	OPS
2018 LAA	AL	31	57	12	4	0	1	(1	0)	19	7	1	3	3	0	17	2	0	0	0	1	0	.211	.274	.333	.608
2019 LAA	AL	18	36	5	1	1	0	(0	0)	8	7	3	3	5	0	19	4	0	1	2	0	1	.139	.304	.222	.527
2020 LAA	AL	7	8	2	0	0	0	(0	0)	2	0	2	1	1	0	1	0	0	1	1	0	0	.250	.300	.250	.550
3 ML YEARS		56	101	19	5	1	1	(1	0)	29	14	6	7	9	0	37	6	0	2	3	1	1	.188	.288	.287	.575

Carlos Hernandez

Pitches: R Bats: R Pos: SP-3; RP-2

Ht: 6'4" Wt: 250 Born: 3/11/1997 Age: 24

Year Team	Lg	G	GS	GF	IP	BFP	H	R	ER	HR	SH	SF	HB	TBB	IBB	SO	WP	W	L	Pct	Sv-Op	Hld	Vel	OPS	ERC	ERA
2020 KC	AL	5	3	0	14.2	67	19	9	8	4	0	0	1	6	0	13	0	0	1	.000	0-0	0	96	.955	7.75	4.91

Cesar Hernandez

Bats: B Throws: R Pos: 2B-58; PH-1

Ht: 5'10" Wt: 195 Born: 5/23/1990 Age: 31

Year Team	Lg	G	AB	H	2B	3B	HR	(Hm	Rd)	TB	R	RBI	RC	TBB	IBB	SO	HBP	SH	SF	SB	CS	GDP	Avg	OBP	Slg	OPS
2013 Phi	NL	34	121	35	5	0	0	(0	0)	40	17	10	13	9	0	26	1	0	0	3	2	.289	.344	.331	.674
2014 Phi	NL	66	114	27	2	0	1	(1	0)	32	13	4	7	9	1	33	0	1	1	1	1	1	.237	.290	.281	.571
2015 Phi	NL	127	405	110	20	4	1	(1	0)	141	57	35	52	40	1	86	2	4	1	19	5	6	.272	.339	.348	.687
2016 Phi	NL	155	547	161	14	11	6	(4	2)	215	67	39	82	66	4	116	2	5	2	17	13	6	.294	.371	.393	.764
2017 Phi	NL	128	511	150	26	6	9	(6	3)	215	85	34	80	61	1	104	4	0	1	15	5	8	.294	.373	.421	.793
2018 Phi	NL	161	605	153	15	3	15	(7	8)	219	91	60	85	95	4	155	4	1	3	19	6	12	.253	.356	.362	.718
2019 Phi	NL	161	612	171	31	3	14	(7	7)	250	77	71	82	45	4	100	6	0	4	9	2	9	.279	.333	.408	.741
2020 Cle	AL	58	233	66	20	0	3	(3	0)	95	35	20	36	24	0	57	2	1	0	0	0	3	.283	.355	.408	.763
8 ML YEARS		890	3148	873	133	27	49	(29	20)	1207	442	273	437	349	15	677	21	12	12	80	35	47	.277	.352	.383	.736

Darwinzon Hernandez

Pitches: L Bats: L Pos: RP-7

Ht: 6'2" Wt: 255 Born: 12/17/1996 Age: 24

Year Team	Lg	G	GS	GF	IP	BFP	H	R	ER	HR	SH	SF	HB	TBB	IBB	SO	WP	W	L	Pct	Sv-Op	Hld	Vel	OPS	ERC	ERA
2019 Bos	AL	29	1	2	30.1	147	27	18	15	1	1	0	3	26	1	57	4	0	1	.000	0-0	2	96	.725	4.90	4.45
2020 Bos	AL	7	0	0	8.1	40	5	2	2	0	0	0	1	8	0	13	1	1	0	1.000	0-0	2	94	.511	3.46	2.16
2 ML YEARS		36	1	2	38.2	187	32	20	17	1	1	0	4	34	1	70	5	1	1	.500	0-0	4	95	.680	4.57	3.96

Elieser Hernandez

Pitches: R Bats: R Pos: SP-6

eh-LEE-eh-ser

Ht: 6'0" Wt: 214 Born: 5/3/1995 Age: 26

Year Team	Lg	G	GS	GF	IP	BFP	H	R	ER	HR	SH	SF	HB	TBB	IBB	SO	WP	W	L	Pct	Sv-Op	Hld	Vel	OPS	ERC	ERA
2018 Mia	NL	32	6	6	65.2	284	68	38	38	11	3	2	2	27	3	45	1	2	7	.222	0-0	2	91	.809	4.94	5.21
2019 Mia	NL	21	15	1	82.1	353	76	49	46	20	3	1	9	26	1	85	2	3	5	.375	0-0	0	91	.820	4.69	5.03
2020 Mia	NL	6	6	0	25.2	106	21	10	9	5	0	0	2	5	0	34	0	1	0	1.000	0-0	0	91	.678	3.11	3.16
3 ML YEARS		59	27	7	173.2	743	165	97	93	36	6	3	13	58	4	164	3	6	12	.333	0-0	2	91	.795	4.54	4.82

Felix Hernandez

Pitches: R Bats: R Pos: P

Ht: 6'3" Wt: 208 Born: 4/8/1986 Age: 35

Year Team	Lg	G	GS	GF	IP	BFP	H	R	ER	HR	SH	SF	HB	TBB	IBB	SO	WP	W	L	Pct	Sv-Op	Hld	Vel	OPS	ERC	ERA
2005 Sea	AL	12	12	0	84.1	328	61	26	25	5	1	2	2	23	0	77	3	4	4	.500	0-0	0	96	.546	2.08	2.67
2006 Sea	AL	31	31	0	191.0	816	195	105	96	23	2	3	6	60	2	176	11	12	14	.462	0-0	0	95	.729	4.11	4.52
2007 Sea	AL	30	30	0	190.1	808	209	88	83	20	6	1	3	53	4	165	7	14	7	.667	0-0	0	96	.751	4.27	3.92
2008 Sea	AL	31	31	0	200.2	857	198	85	77	17	4	6	8	80	7	175	8	9	11	.450	0-0	0	95	.727	4.05	3.45
2009 Sea	AL	34	34	0	238.2	977	200	81	66	15	6	11	8	71	0	217	17	19	5	.792	0-0	0	94	.605	2.72	2.49
2010 Sea	AL	34	34	0	249.2	1001	194	80	63	17	6	3	8	70	1	232	14	13	12	.520	0-0	0	94	.585	2.39	2.27
2011 Sea	AL	33	33	0	233.2	964	218	99	90	19	3	7	7	67	0	222	12	14	14	.500	0-0	0	93	.660	3.31	3.47
2012 Sea	AL	33	33	0	232.0	939	209	84	79	14	2	2	12	56	0	223	13	13	9	.591	0-0	0	92	.629	2.94	3.06
2013 Sea	AL	31	31	0	204.1	823	185	74	69	15	4	6	3	46	1	216	13	12	10	.545	0-0	0	92	.644	2.82	3.04
2014 Sea	AL	34	34	0	236.0	912	170	68	56	16	4	5	5	46	1	248	18	15	6	.714	0-0	0	92	.546	1.81	2.14
2015 Sea	AL	31	31	0	201.2	826	180	80	79	23	4	4	9	58	0	191	10	18	9	.667	0-0	0	92	.682	3.37	3.53
2016 Sea	AL	25	25	0	153.1	655	138	76	65	19	3	0	10	65	0	122	6	11	8	.579	0-0	0	90	.718	4.07	3.82
2017 Sea	AL	16	16	0	86.2	368	86	46	42	17	1	1	6	26	0	78	8	6	5	.545	0-0	0	90	.791	4.62	4.36
2018 Sea	AL	29	28	0	155.2	685	159	107	96	27	3	4	12	59	0	125	11	8	14	.364	0-0	0	89	.798	4.94	5.55
2019 Sea	AL	15	15	0	71.2	325	85	58	51	17	1	1	6	25	0	57	5	1	8	.111	0-0	0	90	.909	6.34	6.40
15 ML YEARS		419	418	0	2729.2	11284	2487	1157	1037	264	50	56	105	805	16	2524	156	169	136	.554	0-0	0	93	.673	3.33	3.42

Jonathan Hernandez

Pitches: R Bats: R Pos: RP-27

Ht: 6'3" Wt: 190 Born: 7/6/1996 Age: 24

Year Team	Lg	G	GS	GF	IP	BFP	H	R	ER	HR	SH	SF	HB	TBB	IBB	SO	WP	W	L	Pct	Sv-Op	Hld	Vel	OPS	ERC	ERA
2019 Tex	AL	9	2	1	16.2	78	14	10	8	3	0	1	0	13	0	19	1	2	1	.667	0-0	1	97	.721	5.09	4.32
2020 Tex	AL	27	0	5	31.0	125	24	10	10	2	1	2	4	8	0	31	0	5	1	.833	0-0	5	98	.618	2.65	2.90
2 ML YEARS		36	2	6	47.2	203	38	20	18	5	1	3	4	21	0	50	1	7	2	.778	0-0	6	97	.657	3.46	3.40

Kike Hernandez

kee-KAY

Bats: R **Throws:** R **Pos:** 2B-30;PH-10;RF-9;LF-5;CF-3;1B-2;SS-2;DH-2   **Ht:** 5'11" **Wt:** 190 **Born:** 8/24/1991 **Age:** 29

								BATTING												RUNNING			AVERAGES			
Year Team	Lg	G	AB	H	2B	3B	HR	(Hm Rd)	TB	R	RBI	RC	TBB	IBB	SO	HBP	SH	SF	SB	CS	GDP	Avg	OBP	Slg	OPS
2014 2 Tms		42	121	30	6	3	3	(1 2)	51	13	14	18	12	0	21	1	0	0	0	0	1	.248	.321	.421	.742
2015 LAD	NL	76	202	62	12	2	7	(2 5)	99	24	22	32	11	0	46	2	1	2	0	2	3	.307	.346	.490	.836
2016 LAD	NL	109	216	41	8	0	7	(5 2)	70	25	18	16	28	1	64	0	0	0	2	0	3	.190	.283	.324	.607
2017 LAD	NL	140	297	64	24	2	11	(7 4)	125	46	37	39	41	2	80	0	1	3	3	0	4	.215	.308	.421	.729
2018 LAD	NL	145	402	103	17	3	21	(14 7)	189	67	52	58	50	5	78	1	4	5	3	0	3	.256	.336	.470	.806
2019 LAD	NL	130	414	98	19	1	17	(8 9)	170	57	64	57	36	3	97	6	0	4	4	0	9	.237	.304	.411	.715
2020 LAD	NL	48	139	32	8	1	5	(4 1)	57	20	20	18	6	0	31	2	0	1	0	1	5	.230	.270	.410	.680
14 Hou	AL	24	81	23	4	2	1	(1 0)	34	10	8	14	8	0	11	0	0	0	0	0	0	.284	.348	.420	.768
14 Mia		18	40	7	2	1	2	(0 2)	17	3	6	4	4	0	10	1	0	0	0	0	1	.175	.267	.425	.692
Postseason		41	94	20	2	0	6	(3 3)	40	14	14	12	16	2	26	1	0	0	3	2	2	.213	.333	.426	.759
7 ML YEARS		690	1791	430	94	12	71	(41 30)	761	252	227	238	184	11	417	12	6	15	12	3	28	.240	.313	.425	.738

Oscar Hernandez

Bats: R **Throws:** R **Pos:** C-3;PH-1   **Ht:** 6'1" **Wt:** 230 **Born:** 7/9/1993 **Age:** 27

								BATTING												RUNNING			AVERAGES			
Year Team	Lg	G	AB	H	2B	3B	HR	(Hm Rd)	TB	R	RBI	RC	TBB	IBB	SO	HBP	SH	SF	SB	CS	GDP	Avg	OBP	Slg	OPS
2015 Ari	NL	18	31	5	1	0	0	(0 0)	6	4	1	2	3	0	15	1	1	0	0	0	0	.161	.257	.194	.451
2016 Ari	NL	4	11	2	0	0	1	(0 1)	5	1	1	0	0	0	0	0	0	0	0	0	1	.182	.182	.455	.636
2020 KC	AL	4	4	2	0	0	0	(0 0)	2	1	0	0	0	0	1	0	0	0	0	0	1	.500	.500	.500	1.000
3 ML YEARS		26	46	9	1	0	1	(0 1)	13	6	2	2	3	0	16	1	1	0	0	0	2	.196	.260	.283	.543

Teoscar Hernandez

tay-OH-skar

Bats: R **Throws:** R **Pos:** RF-40;CF-9;DH-4;PH-3   **Ht:** 6'2" **Wt:** 205 **Born:** 10/15/1992 **Age:** 28

								BATTING												RUNNING			AVERAGES			
Year Team	Lg	G	AB	H	2B	3B	HR	(Hm Rd)	TB	R	RBI	RC	TBB	IBB	SO	HBP	SH	SF	SB	CS	GDP	Avg	OBP	Slg	OPS
2016 Hou	AL	41	100	23	7	0	4	(1 3)	42	15	11	11	11	1	28	0	0	1	0	2	5	.230	.304	.420	.724
2017 2 Tms	AL	27	88	23	6	0	8	(5 3)	53	16	20	15	6	0	36	0	0	1	0	1	0	.261	.305	.602	.908
2018 Tor	AL	134	476	114	29	7	22	(9 13)	223	67	57	60	41	0	163	3	0	3	5	5	14	.239	.302	.468	.771
2019 Tor	AL	125	417	96	19	2	26	(15 11)	197	58	65	67	45	1	153	1	0	1	6	3	8	.230	.306	.472	.778
2020 Tor	AL	50	190	55	7	0	16	(6 10)	110	33	34	31	14	0	63	1	0	1	6	1	4	.289	.340	.579	.919
17 Hou	AL	1	0	0	0	0	0	(0 0)	0	0	0	0	0	0	0	0	0	0	0	0	0				
17 Tor	AL	26	88	23	6	0	8	(5 3)	53	16	20	15	6	0	36	0	0	1	0	1	0	.261	.305	.602	.908
5 ML YEARS		377	1271	311	68	9	76	(36 40)	625	189	187	184	117	2	443	5	0	7	17	12	31	.245	.309	.492	.801

Yadiel Hernandez

Bats: L **Throws:** R **Pos:** DH-7;PH-3;PR-2;RF-1   **Ht:** 5'9" **Wt:** 185 **Born:** 10/9/1987 **Age:** 33

								BATTING												RUNNING			AVERAGES			
Year Team	Lg	G	AB	H	2B	3B	HR	(Hm Rd)	TB	R	RBI	RC	TBB	IBB	SO	HBP	SH	SF	SB	CS	GDP	Avg	OBP	Slg	OPS
2020 Was	NL	12	26	5	3	0	1	(1 0)	11	3	6	4	1	0	12	0	0	1	0	0	0	.192	.214	.423	.637

Dilson Herrera

DILL-sun

Bats: R **Throws:** R **Pos:** 1B-2;CF-1;PH-1   **Ht:** 5'10" **Wt:** 210 **Born:** 3/3/1994 **Age:** 27

								BATTING												RUNNING			AVERAGES			
Year Team	Lg	G	AB	H	2B	3B	HR	(Hm Rd)	TB	R	RBI	RC	TBB	IBB	SO	HBP	SH	SF	SB	CS	GDP	Avg	OBP	Slg	OPS
2014 NYM	NL	18	59	13	0	1	3	(0 3)	24	6	11	7	7	0	17	0	0	0	0	0	3	.220	.303	.407	.710
2015 NYM	NL	31	90	19	3	1	3	(2 1)	33	7	6	11	11	1	23	2	0	0	2	0	2	.211	.311	.367	.677
2018 Cin	NL	53	87	16	5	0	5	(3 2)	36	11	11	8	8	0	39	2	0	0	0	0	0	.184	.268	.414	.682
2020 Bal	AL	3	5	0	0	0	0	(0 0)	0	0	0	0	0	0	4	1	0	0	0	0	0	.000	.167	.000	.167
4 ML YEARS		105	241	48	8	2	11	(5 6)	93	24	28	26	26	1	83	5	0	0	2	0	5	.199	.290	.386	.676

Kelvin Herrera

Pitches: R **Bats:** R **Pos:** RP-2   **Ht:** 5'10" **Wt:** 220 **Born:** 12/31/1989 **Age:** 31

		HOW MUCH PITCHED					WHAT HE GAVE UP											THE RESULTS							
Year Team	Lg	G	GS	GF	IP	BFP	H	R	ER	HR	SH	SF	HB	TBB	IBB	SO	WP	W	L	Pct	Sv-Op	Hld	Vel	OPS	ERC	ERA
2011 KC	AL	2	0	0	2.0	9	2	3	3	1	1	0	1	0	0	0	0	0	1	.000	0-0	1	96	1.232	7.30	13.50
2012 KC	AL	76	0	10	84.1	344	79	24	22	4	5	0	2	21	6	77	3	4	3	.571	3-4	19	99	.643	2.84	2.35
2013 KC	AL	59	0	16	58.1	245	48	27	25	9	0	3	2	21	2	74	5	5	7	.417	2-4	20	98	.701	3.35	3.86
2014 KC	AL	70	0	12	70.0	285	54	12	11	0	4	0	3	26	0	59	1	4	3	.571	0-1	20	98	.561	2.31	1.41
2015 KC	AL	72	0	8	69.2	286	52	23	21	5	1	5	2	26	1	64	4	4	3	.571	0-7	21	98	.578	2.53	2.71
2016 KC	AL	72	0	23	72.0	283	57	23	22	6	1	1	3	12	0	86	3	2	6	.250	12-15	26	97	.590	2.20	2.75
2017 KC	AL	64	0	48	59.1	259	60	33	28	9	1	2	1	20	2	56	2	3	3	.500	26-31	4	97	.786	4.17	4.25
2018 2 Tms		48	0	32	44.1	184	43	12	12	6	1	0	1	10	0	38	0	2	3	.400	17-19	2	97	.689	3.54	2.44
2019 CWS	AL	57	0	16	51.1	235	60	36	35	8	1	2	1	23	6	53	8	3	3	.500	1-3	6	96	.821	5.50	6.14
2020 CWS	AL	2	0	1	2.1	11	3	4	4	2	0	0	1	0	3	0	0	0	-	0-0	0	94	1.264	11.78	15.43
18 KC	AL	27	0	21	25.2	95	19	3	3	2	1	0	0	2	0	22	0	1	1	.500	14-16	0	96	.506	1.58	1.05
18 Wsh	NL	21	0	11	18.2	89	24	9	9	4	0	0	1	8	0	16	0	1	2	.333	3-3	2	97	.894	6.88	4.34
Postseason		22	0	0	28.2	115	21	5	4	0	0	1	0	10	0	38	0	2	0	1.000	0-0	6	98	.491	1.90	1.26
10 ML YEARS		522	0	166	513.2	2141	458	197	183	50	15	13	16	160	17	510	26	27	32	.458	61-84	119	98	.669	3.19	3.21

David Hess

Pitches: R Bats: R Pos: RP-3

Ht: 6'1" Wt: 215 Born: 7/10/1993 Age: 27

Year	Team	Lg	G	GS	GF	IP	BFP	H	R	ER	HR	SH	SF	HB	TBB	IBB	SO	WP	W	L	Pct	Sv-Op	Hld	Vel	OPS	ERC	ERA
2018	Bal	AL	21	19	1	103.1	454	106	64	56	22	1	4	8	37	2	74	3	3	10	.231	0-0	0	92	.821	5.12	4.88
2019	Bal	AL	23	14	5	80.0	365	94	73	63	28	3	3	2	30	0	68	1	1	10	.091	0-0	0	93	.957	6.87	7.09
2020	Bal	AL	3	0	3	7.0	32	10	5	5	1	0	0	0	2	0	1	0	0	0	-	0-0	0	93	.975	6.54	6.43
	3 ML YEARS		47	33	9	190.1	851	210	142	124	51	4	7	10	69	2	143	4	4	20	.167	0-0	0	92	.885	5.90	5.86

Codi Heuer

Pitches: R Bats: R Pos: RP-21

Ht: 6'5" Wt: 190 Born: 7/3/1996 Age: 24

Year	Team	Lg	G	GS	GF	IP	BFP	H	R	ER	HR	SH	SF	HB	TBB	IBB	SO	WP	W	L	Pct	Sv-Op	Hld	Vel	OPS	ERC	ERA
2020	CWS	AL	21	0	4	23.2	92	12	4	4	1	0	0	0	9	0	25	0	3	0	1.000	1-1	5	98	.433	1.36	1.52

Jason Heyward

Bats: L Throws: L Pos: RF-50;PH-1

Ht: 6'5" Wt: 240 Born: 8/9/1989 Age: 31

Year	Team	Lg	G	AB	H	2B	3B	HR	(Hm	Rd)	TB	R	RBI	RC	TBB	IBB	SO	HBP	SH	SF	SB	CS	GDP	Avg	OBP	Slg	OPS
2010	Atl	NL	142	520	144	29	5	18	(9	9)	237	83	72	96	91	2	128	10	0	2	11	6	13	.277	.393	.456	.849
2011	Atl	NL	128	396	90	18	2	14	(5	9)	154	50	42	49	51	4	93	4	0	3	9	2	7	.227	.319	.389	.708
2012	Atl	NL	158	587	158	30	6	27	(9	18)	281	93	82	87	58	1	152	2	0	3	21	8	4	.269	.335	.479	.814
2013	Atl	NL	104	382	97	22	1	14	(10	4)	163	67	38	55	48	1	73	8	1	0	2	4	7	.254	.349	.427	.776
2014	Atl	NL	149	573	155	26	3	11	(5	6)	220	74	58	84	67	3	98	6	0	3	20	4	2	.271	.351	.384	.735
2015	StL	NL	154	547	160	33	4	13	(5	8)	240	79	60	78	56	4	90	2	0	3	23	3	13	.293	.359	.439	.797
2016	ChC	NL	142	530	122	27	1	7	(3	4)	172	61	49	53	54	0	93	5	1	2	11	4	12	.230	.306	.325	.631
2017	ChC	NL	126	432	112	15	4	11	(4	7)	168	59	59	60	41	1	67	3	2	2	4	4	8	.259	.326	.389	.715
2018	ChC	NL	127	440	119	23	4	8	(5	3)	174	67	57	67	42	1	60	2	2	2	1	1	7	.270	.335	.395	.731
2019	ChC	NL	147	513	129	20	4	21	(8	13)	220	78	62	74	68	5	110	5	0	3	8	3	12	.251	.343	.429	.772
2020	ChC	NL	50	147	39	6	2	6	(1	5)	67	20	22	30	30	1	37	2	0	2	2	0	1	.265	.392	.456	.848
	Postseason		38	121	18	3	1	2	(0	2)	29	8	7	5	7	2	35	2	0	0	4	0	2	.149	.208	.240	.447
	11 ML YEARS		1427	5067	1325	249	36	150	(64	86)	2096	731	601	733	606	23	1001	49	6	25	112	39	86	.261	.345	.414	.758

Aaron Hicks

Bats: B Throws: R Pos: CF-50;PH-5;DH-1

Ht: 6'1" Wt: 205 Born: 10/2/1989 Age: 31

Year	Team	Lg	G	AB	H	2B	3B	HR	(Hm	Rd)	TB	R	RBI	RC	TBB	IBB	SO	HBP	SH	SF	SB	CS	GDP	Avg	OBP	Slg	OPS
2013	Min	AL	81	281	54	11	3	8	(3	5)	95	37	27	25	24	0	84	2	4	2	9	3	0	.192	.259	.338	.597
2014	Min	AL	69	186	40	8	0	1	(0	1)	51	22	18	22	36	0	56	0	2	1	4	3	2	.215	.341	.274	.615
2015	Min	AL	97	352	90	11	3	11	(6	5)	140	48	33	45	34	2	66	2	0	2	13	3	6	.256	.323	.398	.721
2016	NYY	AL	123	327	71	13	1	8	(7	1)	110	32	31	28	30	1	68	0	1	3	3	4	7	.217	.281	.336	.617
2017	NYY	AL	88	301	80	18	0	15	(12	3)	143	54	52	52	51	0	67	3	1	5	10	5	8	.266	.372	.475	.847
2018	NYY	AL	137	480	119	18	3	27	(15	12)	224	90	79	94	90	1	111	3	2	6	11	2	1	.248	.366	.467	.833
2019	NYY	AL	59	221	52	10	0	12	(4	8)	98	41	36	34	31	0	72	0	0	3	1	2	2	.235	.325	.443	.769
2020	NYY	AL	54	169	38	10	2	6	(4	2)	70	28	21	32	41	1	38	1	0	4	4	1	4	.225	.379	.414	.793
	Postseason		21	68	13	3	0	2	(1	1)	22	7	9	10	9	0	20	0	0	0	1	0	1	.191	.286	.324	.609
	8 ML YEARS		708	2317	544	99	12	88	(51	37)	931	352	297	332	337	5	562	11	10	22	55	23	30	.235	.332	.402	.734

Jordan Hicks

Pitches: R Bats: R Pos: P

Ht: 6'2" Wt: 220 Born: 9/6/1996 Age: 24

Year	Team	Lg	G	GS	GF	IP	BFP	H	R	ER	HR	SH	SF	HB	TBB	IBB	SO	WP	W	L	Pct	Sv-Op	Hld	Vel	OPS	ERC	ERA
2018	StL	NL	73	0	20	77.2	339	59	33	31	2	0	8	8	45	2	70	9	3	4	.429	6-13	24	101	.587	3.24	3.59
2019	StL	NL	29	0	21	28.2	110	16	10	10	2	0	1	1	11	0	31	2	2	2	.500	14-15	3	101	.510	1.80	3.14
	2 ML YEARS		102	0	41	106.1	449	75	43	41	4	0	9	9	56	2	101	11	5	6	.455	20-28	27	101	.568	2.84	3.47

Kyle Higashioka

Bats: R Throws: R Pos: C-14;PH-2;DH-1

he-gah-shi-oh-kah

Ht: 6'1" Wt: 202 Born: 4/20/1990 Age: 31

Year	Team	Lg	G	AB	H	2B	3B	HR	(Hm	Rd)	TB	R	RBI	RC	TBB	IBB	SO	HBP	SH	SF	SB	CS	GDP	Avg	OBP	Slg	OPS
2017	NYY	AL	9	18	0	0	0	0	(0	0)	0	2	0	0	2	0	6	0	0	0	0	0	0	.000	.100	.000	.100
2018	NYY	AL	29	72	12	2	0	3	(3	0)	23	6	6	2	6	0	16	1	0	0	0	0	2	.167	.241	.319	.560
2019	NYY	AL	18	56	12	5	0	3	(0	3)	26	8	11	7	0	0	26	0	0	1	0	0	1	.214	.211	.464	.675
2020	NYY	AL	16	48	12	1	0	4	(4	0)	25	7	10	8	0	0	11	0	0	0	0	0	0	.250	.250	.521	.771
	4 ML YEARS		72	194	36	8	0	10	(7	3)	74	23	27	17	8	0	59	1	0	1	0	0	3	.186	.221	.381	.602

Cam Hill

Pitches: R Bats: R Pos: RP-18

Ht: 6'1" Wt: 200 Born: 5/24/1994 Age: 27

Year	Team	Lg	G	GS	GF	IP	BFP	H	R	ER	HR	SH	SF	HB	TBB	IBB	SO	WP	W	L	Pct	Sv-Op	Hld	Vel	OPS	ERC	ERA
2020	Cle	AL	18	0	5	18.1	72	11	11	10	4	0	2	2	5	1	16	0	2	0	1.000	1-1	2	92	.647	2.56	4.91

Derek Hill

Bats: R **Throws:** R **Pos:** CF-10;PR-6;DH-4;PH-3

Ht: 6'2" **Wt:** 190 **Born:** 12/30/1995 **Age:** 25

								BATTING												RUNNING			AVERAGES			
Year	Team	Lg	G	AB	H	2B	3B	HR	(Hm | Rd)	TB	R	RBI	RC	TBB	IBB	SO	HBP	SH	SF	SB	CS	GDP	Avg	OBP	Slg	OPS
2020	Det	AL	15	11	1	0	0	0	(0 | 0)	1	3	0	1	1	0	6	0	0	0	0	0	0	.091	.167	.091	.258

Rich Hill

Pitches: L **Bats:** L **Pos:** SP-8

Ht: 6'5" **Wt:** 221 **Born:** 3/11/1980 **Age:** 41

			HOW MUCH PITCHED				WHAT HE GAVE UP										THE RESULTS							
Year	Team	Lg	G	GS	GF	IP	BFP	H	R	ER	HR	SH	SF	HB	TBB	IBB	SO	WP	W	L	Pct	Sv-Op	Hld	Vel	OPS	ERC	ERA
2005	ChC	NL	10	4	1	23.2	115	25	24	24	3	1	0	1	17	1	21	0	0	2	.000	0-0	0	90	.794	5.81	9.13
2006	ChC	NL	17	16	1	99.1	417	83	51	46	16	8	3	2	39	1	90	3	6	7	.462	0-0	0	90	.725	3.59	4.17
2007	ChC	NL	32	32	0	195.0	812	170	89	85	27	9	4	12	63	3	183	1	11	8	.579	0-0	0	89	.699	3.56	3.92
2008	ChC	NL	5	5	0	19.2	89	13	9	9	2	0	2	1	18	0	15	1	1	0	1.000	0-0	0	88	.683	4.38	4.12
2009	Bal	AL	14	13	0	57.2	275	68	53	50	7	2	2	1	40	2	46	1	3	3	.500	0-0	0	88	.886	6.55	7.80
2010	Bos	AL	6	0	0	4.0	18	5	0	0	0	0	0	0	1	0	3	0	1	0	1.000	0-0	1	89	.627	4.05	0.00
2011	Bos	AL	9	0	3	8.0	30	3	0	0	0	0	0	0	3	0	12	1	0	0	-	0-0	3	91	.349	1.10	0.00
2012	Bos	AL	25	0	3	19.2	83	17	4	4	0	0	0	0	11	1	21	0	1	0	1.000	0-0	6	92	.685	3.24	1.83
2013	Cle	AL	63	0	3	38.2	182	38	30	27	3	1	2	2	29	6	51	6	1	2	.333	0-2	13	91	.719	5.07	6.28
2014	2 Tms		16	0	2	5.1	29	7	2	2	0	0	0	1	6	1	9	1	0	0	-	0-0	1	90	.801	8.55	3.38
2015	Bos	AL	4	4	0	29.0	106	14	5	5	2	0	0	0	5	0	36	0	2	1	.667	0-0	0	90	.410	1.13	1.55
2016	2 Tms		20	20	0	110.1	439	77	29	26	4	1	2	8	33	0	129	0	12	5	.706	0-0	0	90	.530	2.04	2.12
2017	LAD	NL	25	25	0	135.2	552	99	51	50	18	4	2	9	49	1	166	2	12	8	.600	0-0	0	89	.639	2.96	3.32
2018	LAD	NL	25	24	0	132.2	547	108	57	54	20	4	1	8	41	3	150	2	11	5	.688	0-0	0	89	.689	3.24	3.66
2019	LAD	NL	13	13	0	58.2	242	48	20	16	10	4	1	4	18	2	72	0	4	1	.800	0-0	0	90	.689	3.40	2.45
2020	Min	AL	8	8	0	38.2	156	28	13	13	3	0	1	1	17	0	31	1	2	2	.500	0-0	0	88	.601	2.78	3.03
14	LAA	AL	2	0	0	0.0	4	1	1	1	0	0	0	0	3	0	0	1	0	0	-	0-0	0	92	2.000		
14	NYY	AL	14	0	2	5.1	25	6	1	1	0	0	0	1	3	1	9	0	0	0	-	0-0	1	90	.686	5.10	1.69
16	Oak	AL	14	14	0	76.0	311	55	22	19	2	0	1	8	28	0	90	0	9	3	.750	0-0	0	90	.559	2.44	2.25
16	Oak	NL	6	6	0	34.1	128	22	7	7	2	1	1	0	5	0	39	0	3	2	.600	0-0	0	90	.461	1.34	1.83
	Postseason		13	12	1	53.0	234	41	18	18	5	3	1	4	32	3	65	1	1	2	.333	0-0	0	90	.643	3.71	3.06
	16 ML YEARS		292	164	13	976.0	4092	803	437	411	115	34	20	53	390	21	1035	19	67	44	.604	0-2	24	89	.675	3.41	3.79

Tim Hill

Pitches: L **Bats:** R **Pos:** RP-23

Ht: 6'4" **Wt:** 200 **Born:** 2/10/1990 **Age:** 31

			HOW MUCH PITCHED				WHAT HE GAVE UP										THE RESULTS							
Year	Team	Lg	G	GS	GF	IP	BFP	H	R	ER	HR	SH	SF	HB	TBB	IBB	SO	WP	W	L	Pct	Sv-Op	Hld	Vel	OPS	ERC	ERA
2018	KC	AL	70	0	9	45.2	198	46	28	23	4	2	1	2	14	0	42	0	1	4	.200	2-4	13	91	.691	3.77	4.53
2019	KC	AL	46	0	4	39.2	161	31	17	16	4	1	0	4	13	2	39	0	2	0	1.000	1-2	9	90	.636	3.01	3.63
2020	SD	NL	23	0	3	18.0	79	17	9	9	3	0	0	2	6	1	20	1	3	0	1.000	0-0	5	91	.739	4.22	4.50
	3 ML YEARS		139	0	16	103.1	438	94	54	48	11	3	1	8	33	3	101	1	6	4	.600	3-6	27	91	.679	3.55	4.18

Sam Hilliard

Bats: L **Throws:** L **Pos:** LF-14;RF-13;CF-10;PH-3;PR-2

Ht: 6'5" **Wt:** 236 **Born:** 2/21/1994 **Age:** 27

								BATTING												RUNNING			AVERAGES			
Year	Team	Lg	G	AB	H	2B	3B	HR	(Hm	Rd)	TB	R	RBI	RC	TBB	IBB	SO	HBP	SH	SF	SB	CS	GDP	Avg	OBP	Slg	OPS
2019	Col	NL	27	77	21	4	2	7	(5	2)	50	13	13	17	9	0	23	1	0	0	2	0	1	.273	.356	.649	1.006
2020	Col	NL	36	105	22	2	2	6	(1	5)	46	13	10	12	9	0	42	0	0	0	3	0	0	.210	.272	.438	.710
	2 ML YEARS		63	182	43	6	4	13	(6	7)	96	26	23	29	18	0	65	1	0	0	5	0	1	.236	.308	.527	.836

Yoshihisa Hirano

Pitches: R **Bats:** R **Pos:** RP-13

Ht: 6'1" **Wt:** 185 **Born:** 3/8/1984 **Age:** 37

			HOW MUCH PITCHED				WHAT HE GAVE UP										THE RESULTS							
Year	Team	Lg	G	GS	GF	IP	BFP	H	R	ER	HR	SH	SF	HB	TBB	IBB	SO	WP	W	L	Pct	Sv-Op	Hld	Vel	OPS	ERC	ERA
2018	Ari	NL	75	0	10	66.1	262	49	22	18	6	1	1	2	23	4	59	6	4	3	.571	3-7	32	91	.615	2.55	2.44
2019	Ari	NL	62	0	11	53.0	233	51	31	28	7	1	2	3	22	2	61	2	5	5	.500	1-6	15	91	.723	4.26	4.75
2020	Sea	AL	13	0	9	12.1	63	18	9	8	2	0	1	1	8	0	11	0	0	1	.000	4-4	1	90	.938	8.83	5.84
	3 ML YEARS		150	0	30	131.2	558	118	62	54	15	2	4	6	53	6	131	8	9	9	.500	8-17	48	91	.696	3.74	3.69

Keston Hiura

Bats: R **Throws:** R **Pos:** 2B-49;DH-10

Ht: 6'0" **Wt:** 202 **Born:** 8/2/1996 **Age:** 24

								BATTING												RUNNING			AVERAGES			
Year	Team	Lg	G	AB	H	2B	3B	HR	(Hm	Rd)	TB	R	RBI	RC	TBB	IBB	SO	HBP	SH	SF	SB	CS	GDP	Avg	OBP	Slg	OPS
2019	Mil	NL	84	314	95	23	2	19	(10	9)	179	51	49	53	25	1	107	8	0	1	9	3	6	.303	.368	.570	.938
2020	Mil	NL	59	217	46	4	0	13	(6	7)	89	30	32	28	16	2	85	11	0	2	3	2	7	.212	.297	.410	.707
	Postseason		1	4	1	1	0	0	(0	0)	2	0	0	0	0	0	3	0	0	0	0	0	0	.250	.250	.500	.750
	2 ML YEARS		143	531	141	27	2	32	(16	16)	268	81	81	81	41	3	192	19	0	3	12	5	13	.266	.338	.505	.843

Nico Hoerner

Bats: R **Throws:** R **Pos:** 2B-37;SS-10;3B-6;PH-3;PR-3;LF-1;CF-1   **Ht:** 6'1" **Wt:** 200 **Born:** 5/13/1997 **Age:** 24

Year	Team	Lg	G	AB	H	2B	3B	HR	(Hm	Rd)	TB	R	RBI	RC	TBB	IBB	SO	HBP	SH	SF	SB	CS	GDP	Avg	OBP	Slg	OPS
2018	3 Tms	Low	14	49	16	2	2	2	(-	-)	28	10	6	12	9	0	4	2	0	0	6	1	2	.327	.450	.571	1.021
2019	Tenn	AA	70	268	76	16	3	3	(-	-)	107	37	22	38	21	0	31	4	0	5	8	4	5	.284	.344	.399	.743
2019	ChC	NL	20	78	22	1	1	3	(3	0)	34	13	17	14	3	1	11	0	0	1	0	0	3	.282	.305	.436	.741
2020	ChC	NL	48	108	24	4	0	0	(0	0)	28	19	13	14	12	0	24	3	0	2	3	2	3	.222	.312	.259	.571
	2 ML YEARS		68	186	46	5	1	3	(3	0)	62	32	30	28	15	1	35	3	0	3	3	2	6	.247	.309	.333	.643

Jeff Hoffman

Pitches: R **Bats:** R **Pos:** RP-16   **Ht:** 6'5" **Wt:** 215 **Born:** 1/8/1993 **Age:** 28

			HOW MUCH PITCHED					WHAT HE GAVE UP										THE RESULTS						
Year	Team	Lg	G	GS	GF	IP	BFP	H	R	ER	HR	SH	SF	HB	TBB	IBB	SO	WP	W	L	Pct	Sv-Op	Hld	Vel	OPS	ERC	ERA
2016	Col	NL	8	6	0	31.1	147	37	29	17	7	1	0	0	17	1	22	4	0	4	.000	0-0	0	94	.881	6.55	4.88
2017	Col	NL	23	16	3	99.1	440	106	66	65	15	3	5	4	40	1	82	2	6	5	.545	0-0	0	94	.833	4.97	5.89
2018	Col	NL	6	1	1	8.2	44	15	9	9	0	0	0	0	7	1	5	1	0	0	-	0-0	1	93	.986	9.88	9.35
2019	Col	NL	15	15	0	70.0	315	77	51	51	21	3	2	4	34	3	68	2	2	6	.250	0-0	0	94	.957	6.81	6.56
2020	Col	NL	16	0	5	21.1	104	32	23	22	3	0	2	2	9	1	20	4	2	1	.667	1-1	0	94	.985	7.93	9.28
	5 ML YEARS		68	38	9	230.2	1050	267	178	164	46	7	9	10	107	7	197	13	10	16	.385	1-1	1	94	.898	6.18	6.40

Bryan Holaday

Bats: R **Throws:** R **Pos:** C-10;1B-6;PH-5;DH-3;PR-3   HAHL-ih-daye   **Ht:** 6'0" **Wt:** 215 **Born:** 11/19/1987 **Age:** 33

Year	Team	Lg	G	AB	H	2B	3B	HR	(Hm	Rd)	TB	R	RBI	RC	TBB	IBB	SO	HBP	SH	SF	SB	CS	GDP	Avg	OBP	Slg	OPS
2012	Det	AL	6	12	3	1	0	0	(0	0)	4	3	0	1	0	0	2	0	1	0	0	0	0	.250	.250	.333	.583
2013	Det	AL	16	27	8	1	0	1	(1	0)	12	8	2	3	2	0	3	1	3	0	0	0	0	.296	.367	.444	.811
2014	Det	AL	62	156	36	5	1	0	(0	0)	43	14	15	11	8	0	37	1	2	4	1	1	4	.231	.266	.276	.542
2015	Det	AL	24	64	18	5	0	2	(1	1)	29	3	13	9	1	0	13	0	0	0	0	0	0	.281	.292	.453	.745
2016	2 Tms		44	117	27	7	1	2	(1	1)	42	17	14	14	7	0	28	2	1	2	0	1	1	.231	.281	.359	.640
2017	Det	AL	13	29	7	2	0	0	(0	0)	9	1	2	2	0	0	1	0	0	0	0	0	2	.241	.241	.310	.552
2018	Mia	NL	61	151	31	5	0	1	(0	1)	39	7	16	10	10	2	29	2	1	2	0	0	4	.205	.261	.258	.519
2019	Mia	NL	43	115	32	6	0	4	(0	4)	50	12	12	14	11	2	21	1	1	1	0	1	5	.278	.344	.435	.779
2020	Bal	AL	21	31	5	1	0	0	(0	0)	6	5	4	2	2	0	9	0	0	0	0	0	1	.161	.212	.194	.406
16	Tex	AL	30	84	20	6	1	2	(1	1)	34	14	13	12	5	0	16	2	1	2	0	1	0	.238	.290	.405	.695
16	Bos	AL	14	33	7	1	0	0	(0	0)	8	3	1	2	2	0	12	0	0	0	0	0	1	.212	.257	.242	.500
	Postseason		1	2	0	0	0	0	(0	0)	0	0	0	0	0	0	1	0	0	0	0	0	0	.000	.000	.000	.000
	9 ML YEARS		290	702	167	33	2	10	(3	7)	234	70	78	66	41	4	143	7	9	9	1	3	17	.238	.283	.333	.617

Jonathan Holder

Pitches: R **Bats:** R **Pos:** RP-18   **Ht:** 6'2" **Wt:** 232 **Born:** 6/9/1993 **Age:** 28

			HOW MUCH PITCHED					WHAT HE GAVE UP										THE RESULTS						
Year	Team	Lg	G	GS	GF	IP	BFP	H	R	ER	HR	SH	SF	HB	TBB	IBB	SO	WP	W	L	Pct	Sv-Op	Hld	Vel	OPS	ERC	ERA
2016	NYY	AL	8	0	1	8.1	36	8	5	5	1	0	1	0	4	0	5	0	0	0	-	0-0	0	93	.753	4.34	5.40
2017	NYY	AL	37	0	12	39.1	171	45	17	17	5	1	0	3	8	1	40	2	1	1	.500	0-2	3	93	.770	4.54	3.89
2018	NYY	AL	60	1	14	66.0	272	53	27	23	4	2	2	1	19	3	60	1	1	3	.250	0-0	7	93	.589	2.31	3.14
2019	NYY	AL	34	1	8	41.1	181	43	32	29	8	0	0	2	11	1	46	0	5	2	.714	0-2	4	92	.762	4.44	6.31
2020	NYY	AL	18	0	4	21.2	101	25	13	12	3	0	1	0	11	1	14	1	3	0	1.000	0-0	0	92	.806	5.49	4.98
	Postseason		1	0	0	2.0	9	2	1	1	0	0	0	0	1	0	1	0	0	0	-	0-0	0	92	.708	3.63	4.50
	5 ML YEARS		157	2	39	176.2	761	174	94	86	21	3	4	6	53	6	165	4	10	6	.625	0-4	14	93	.707	3.73	4.38

Derek Holland

Pitches: L **Bats:** B **Pos:** RP-7; SP-5   **Ht:** 6'2" **Wt:** 213 **Born:** 10/9/1986 **Age:** 34

			HOW MUCH PITCHED					WHAT HE GAVE UP										THE RESULTS						
Year	Team	Lg	G	GS	GF	IP	BFP	H	R	ER	HR	SH	SF	HB	TBB	IBB	SO	WP	W	L	Pct	Sv-Op	Hld	Vel	OPS	ERC	ERA
2009	Tex	AL	33	21	0	138.1	611	160	98	94	26	2	3	4	47	0	107	3	8	13	.381	0-1	2	93	.856	5.52	6.12
2010	Tex	AL	14	10	2	57.1	253	55	30	26	6	0	2	4	24	0	54	0	3	4	.429	0-0	1	92	.727	4.17	4.08
2011	Tex	AL	32	32	0	198.0	843	201	97	87	22	1	3	6	67	1	162	2	16	5	.762	0-0	0	94	.724	4.15	3.95
2012	Tex	AL	29	27	1	175.1	730	162	100	91	32	5	4	3	52	0	145	1	12	7	.632	0-0	0	93	.745	3.86	4.67
2013	Tex	AL	33	33	0	213.0	894	210	90	81	20	8	9	3	64	0	189	9	10	9	.526	0-0	0	94	.711	3.64	3.42
2014	Tex	AL	6	5	0	37.0	145	34	8	6	0	2	1	0	5	1	25	1	2	0	1.000	0-0	0	92	.601	2.07	1.46
2015	Tex	AL	10	10	0	58.2	245	59	32	32	11	3	1	5	17	2	41	1	4	3	.571	0-0	0	93	.828	4.51	4.91
2016	Tex	AL	22	20	0	107.1	461	116	62	59	15	1	2	2	35	2	67	2	7	9	.438	0-0	0	92	.770	4.61	4.95
2017	CWS	AL	29	26	0	135.0	626	156	106	93	31	1	3	8	75	2	104	7	7	14	.333	0-0	0	91	.918	6.96	6.20
2018	SF	NL	36	30	1	171.1	727	154	74	68	19	9	7	4	67	6	169	2	7	9	.438	0-0	5	92	.718	3.58	3.57
2019	2 Tms		51	8	19	84.1	376	82	61	57	20	7	2	4	45	2	82	1	2	5	.286	0-1	2	92	.852	5.64	6.08
2020	Pit	NL	12	5	3	40.2	179	42	33	31	12	0	0	3	15	0	45	0	1	3	.250	0-1	0	92	.876	5.84	6.86
19	SF	NL	31	7	10	68.2	308	68	49	45	17	6	2	4	35	2	71	0	2	4	.333	0-0	0	92	.860	5.73	5.90
19	ChC	NL	20	1	9	15.2	68	14	12	12	3	1	0	0	10	0	11	1	0	1	.000	0-1	2	94	.814	5.23	6.89
	Postseason		14	5	2	37.2	161	37	23	21	10	0	0	1	16	0	24	2	3	1	.750	0-0	2	94	.870	5.47	5.02
	12 ML YEARS		307	227	26	1416.1	6090	1431	791	725	214	39	37	46	513	16	1190	31	79	81	.494	0-3	5	93	.774	4.48	4.61

Greg Holland

Pitches: R Bats: R Pos: RP-28

Ht: 5'10" Wt: 205 Born: 11/20/1985 Age: 35

			HOW MUCH PITCHED				WHAT HE GAVE UP											THE RESULTS							
Year	Team	Lg	G	GS	GF	IP	BFP	H	R	ER	HR	SH	SF	HB	TBB	IBB	SO	WP	W	L	Pct	Sv-Op	Hld	Vel	OPS	ERC	ERA
2010	KC	AL	15	0	10	18.2	87	23	15	14	3	1	0	0	8	0	23	2	0	1	.000	0-0	0	96	.835	5.88	6.75
2011	KC	AL	46	0	15	60.0	233	37	13	12	3	1	1	1	19	3	74	7	5	1	.833	4-6	18	95	.521	1.60	1.80
2012	KC	AL	67	0	36	67.0	289	58	22	22	2	4	3	0	34	7	91	3	7	4	.636	16-20	9	96	.653	3.07	2.96
2013	KC	AL	68	0	61	67.0	255	40	11	9	3	1	1	0	18	1	103	2	2	1	.667	47-50	1	96	.479	1.41	1.21
2014	KC	AL	65	0	60	62.1	240	37	13	10	3	1	1	0	20	0	90	9	1	3	.250	46-48	0	96	.472	1.54	1.44
2015	KC	AL	48	0	40	44.2	193	39	20	19	2	3	1	0	26	1	49	7	3	2	.600	32-37	0	94	.692	3.68	3.83
2017	Col	NL	61	0	58	57.1	235	40	24	23	7	0	1	1	26	1	70	7	3	6	.333	41-45	1	93	.623	2.86	3.61
2018	2 Tms	NL	56	0	13	46.1	212	43	30	24	2	1	0	1	32	2	47	0	2	2	.500	3-6	6	93	.697	4.33	4.66
2019	Ari	NL	40	0	27	35.2	152	25	18	18	5	0	2	0	24	2	41	6	1	2	.333	17-22	0	92	.687	3.71	4.54
2020	KC	AL	28	0	9	28.1	112	20	8	6	1	1	1	3	7	1	31	1	3	0	1.000	6-6	2	93	.580	1.98	1.91
18	StL	NL	32	0	7	25.0	132	34	28	22	1	1	0	0	22	2	22	0	0	2	.000	0-3	2	93	.859	7.32	7.92
18	Was	NL	24	0	6	21.1	80	9	2	2	1	0	0	1	10	0	25	0	2	0	1.000	3-3	4	93	.438	1.48	0.84
	Postseason		12	0	11	11.2	49	7	3	3	0	0	0	0	6	2	15	1	0	0	-	7-7	0	95	.475	1.54	2.31
10 ML YEARS			494	0	329	487.1	2008	362	174	157	31	13	11	6	214	18	619	44	27	22	.551	212-240	37	95	.604	2.62	2.90

Jordan Holloway

Pitches: R Bats: R Pos: RP-1

Ht: 6'6" Wt: 230 Born: 6/13/1996 Age: 25

			HOW MUCH PITCHED				WHAT HE GAVE UP											THE RESULTS							
Year	Team	Lg	G	GS	GF	IP	BFP	H	R	ER	HR	SH	SF	HB	TBB	IBB	SO	WP	W	L	Pct	Sv-Op	Hld	Vel	OPS	ERC	ERA
2020	Mia	NL	1	0	0	0.1	4	2	0	0	0	0	0	0	1	0	0	0	0	0	-	0-0	0	97	1.417	56.02	0.00

Clay Holmes

Pitches: R Bats: R Pos: RP-1

Ht: 6'5" Wt: 230 Born: 3/27/1993 Age: 28

			HOW MUCH PITCHED				WHAT HE GAVE UP											THE RESULTS							
Year	Team	Lg	G	GS	GF	IP	BFP	H	R	ER	HR	SH	SF	HB	TBB	IBB	SO	WP	W	L	Pct	Sv-Op	Hld	Vel	OPS	ERC	ERA
2018	Pit	NL	11	4	6	26.1	129	30	21	20	2	0	1	2	23	1	21	4	1	3	.250	0-1	0	94	.824	6.99	6.84
2019	Pit	NL	35	0	10	50.0	240	45	36	31	5	0	0	9	36	1	56	4	1	2	.333	0-1	1	94	.743	5.32	5.58
2020	Pit	NL	1	0	0	1.1	6	2	0	0	0	0	0	0	0	0	1	0	0	0	-	0-0	0	92	.667	4.47	0.00
3 ML YEARS			47	4	16	77.2	375	77	57	51	7	0	1	11	59	2	78	8	2	5	.286	0-2	1	94	.769	5.85	5.91

Brock Holt

Bats: L Throws: R Pos: 3B-18;LF-9;PH-7;1B-4;RF-3;DH-2;PR-1

Ht: 5'10" Wt: 180 Born: 6/11/1988 Age: 33

			BATTING																		RUNNING			AVERAGES			
Year	Team	Lg	G	AB	H	2B	3B	HR	(Hm	Rd)	TB	R	RBI	RC	TBB	IBB	SO	HBP	SH	SF	SB	CS	GDP	Avg	OBP	Slg	OPS
2012	Pit	NL	24	65	19	2	1	0	(0	0)	23	6	3	10	4	0	14	0	2	1	0	0	1	.292	.329	.354	.682
2013	Bos	AL	26	59	12	2	0	0	(0	0)	14	9	11	7	7	0	4	0	3	3	1	0	0	.203	.275	.237	.513
2014	Bos	AL	106	449	126	23	5	4	(1	3)	171	68	29	56	33	0	98	2	5	3	12	2	7	.281	.331	.381	.711
2015	Bos	AL	129	454	127	27	6	2	(1	1)	172	56	45	65	46	0	97	3	4	2	8	1	7	.280	.349	.379	.727
2016	Bos	AL	94	290	74	16	0	7	(4	3)	111	45	34	36	27	0	58	3	1	3	4	3	5	.255	.322	.383	.705
2017	Bos	AL	64	140	28	6	0	0	(0	0)	34	20	7	12	19	0	34	3	0	2	2	1	3	.200	.305	.243	.548
2018	Bos	AL	109	321	89	18	2	7	(3	4)	132	41	46	48	37	2	73	7	0	2	7	7	7	.277	.362	.411	.774
2019	Bos	AL	87	259	77	14	2	3	(1	2)	104	38	31	40	28	1	57	4	0	4	1	0	4	.297	.369	.402	.771
2020	2 Tms	NL	37	95	20	6	0	0	(0	0)	26	12	5	8	9	0	24	1	0	1	1	0	3	.211	.283	.274	.557
20	Mil	NL	16	30	3	0	0	0	(0	0)	3	1	1	0	4	0	9	1	0	1	0	0	2	.100	.222	.100	.322
20	Was	NL	21	65	17	6	0	0	(0	0)	23	11	4	8	5	0	15	0	0	0	1	0	1	.262	.314	.354	.668
	Postseason		12	37	11	3	1	2	(0	2)	22	8	7	7	4	0	6	1	0	0	1	0	1	.297	.381	.595	.976
9 ML YEARS			676	2132	572	114	16	23	(10	13)	787	295	211	282	210	3	459	23	15	21	36	14	37	.268	.337	.369	.707

Rhys Hoskins

Bats: R Throws: R Pos: 1B-40;DH-1

Ht: 6'4" Wt: 245 Born: 3/17/1993 Age: 28

			BATTING																		RUNNING			AVERAGES			
Year	Team	Lg	G	AB	H	2B	3B	HR	(Hm	Rd)	TB	R	RBI	RC	TBB	IBB	SO	HBP	SH	SF	SB	CS	GDP	Avg	OBP	Slg	OPS
2017	Phi	NL	50	170	44	7	0	18	(10	8)	105	37	48	45	37	1	46	3	0	2	2	0	2	.259	.396	.618	1.014
2018	Phi	NL	153	558	137	38	0	34	(20	14)	277	89	96	97	87	2	150	9	0	5	5	3	7	.246	.354	.496	.850
2019	Phi	NL	160	570	129	33	5	29	(16	13)	259	86	85	97	116	6	173	11	0	6	2	2	10	.226	.364	.454	.819
2020	Phi	NL	41	151	37	9	0	10	(4	6)	76	35	26	29	29	0	43	5	0	0	1	0	4	.245	.384	.503	.887
4 ML YEARS			404	1449	347	87	5	91	(50	41)	717	247	255	268	269	9	412	28	0	13	10	5	23	.239	.366	.495	.861

Eric Hosmer

Bats: L Throws: L Pos: 1B-32;DH-5;PH-1

HOZ-mur

Ht: 6'4" Wt: 226 Born: 10/24/1989 Age: 31

			BATTING																		RUNNING			AVERAGES			
Year	Team	Lg	G	AB	H	2B	3B	HR	(Hm	Rd)	TB	R	RBI	RC	TBB	IBB	SO	HBP	SH	SF	SB	CS	GDP	Avg	OBP	Slg	OPS
2011	KC	AL	128	523	153	27	3	19	(3	16)	243	66	78	71	34	7	82	1	0	5	11	5	13	.293	.334	.465	.799
2012	KC	AL	152	535	124	22	2	14	(8	6)	192	65	60	61	56	4	95	2	0	5	16	1	10	.232	.304	.359	.663
2013	KC	AL	159	623	188	34	3	17	(10	7)	279	86	79	88	51	4	100	1	1	4	11	4	15	.302	.353	.448	.801
2014	KC	AL	131	503	136	35	1	9	(4	5)	200	54	58	62	35	4	93	3	0	6	4	2	12	.270	.318	.398	.716
2015	KC	AL	158	599	178	33	5	18	(10	8)	275	98	93	94	61	6	108	3	1	3	7	3	16	.297	.363	.459	.822
2016	KC	AL	158	605	161	24	1	25	(8	17)	262	80	104	87	57	5	132	1	0	4	5	3	18	.266	.328	.433	.761
2017	KC	AL	162	603	192	31	1	25	(16	9)	300	98	94	116	66	3	104	0	0	2	6	1	20	.318	.385	.498	.882
2018	SD	NL	157	613	155	31	2	18	(10	8)	244	72	69	77	62	10	142	1	0	1	7	4	18	.253	.322	.398	.720

Year	Team	Lg	G	AB	H	2B	3B	HR	(Hm	Rd)	TB	R	RBI	RC	TBB	IBB	SO	HBP	SH	SF	SB	CS	GDP	Avg	OBP	Slg	OPS
2019	SD	NL	160	619	164	29	2	22	(11	11)	263	72	99	87	40	3	163	3	0	5	0	3	12	.265	.310	.425	.735
2020	SD	NL	38	143	41	6	0	9	(4	5)	74	23	36	27	9	0	28	2	0	2	4	0	3	.287	.333	.517	.851
	Postseason		31	123	34	5	1	3	(1	2)	50	18	29	21	12	2	33	0	0	3	1	1	1	.276	.333	.407	.740
	10 ML YEARS		1403	5366	1492	272	20	176	(85	91)	2332	714	770	770	471	46	1047	17	2	37	71	26	137	.278	.336	.435	.771

Tanner Houck

Pitches: R Bats: R Pos: SP-3

Ht: 6'5" Wt: 230 Born: 6/29/1996 Age: 25

| | | | HOW MUCH PITCHED | | | | WHAT HE GAVE UP | | | | | | | | | | THE RESULTS | | | | | | |
Year	Team	Lg	G	GS	GF	IP	BFP	H	R	ER	HR	SH	SF	HB	TBB	IBB	SO	WP	W	L	Pct	Sv-Op	Hld	Vel	OPS	ERC	ERA
2020	Bos	AL	3	3	0	17.0	63	6	2	1	1	0	0	1	9	0	21	1	3	0	1.000	0-0	0	92	.443	1.49	0.53

Adrian Houser

Pitches: R Bats: R Pos: SP-11; RP-1

HOW-zer

Ht: 6'3" Wt: 222 Born: 2/2/1993 Age: 28

| | | | HOW MUCH PITCHED | | | | WHAT HE GAVE UP | | | | | | | | | | THE RESULTS | | | | | | |
Year	Team	Lg	G	GS	GF	IP	BFP	H	R	ER	HR	SH	SF	HB	TBB	IBB	SO	WP	W	L	Pct	Sv-Op	Hld	Vel	OPS	ERC	ERA
2015	Mil	NL	2	0	2	2.0	8	1	0	0	0	0	0	0	2	0	0	0	0	0	-	0-0	0	94	.542	3.21	0.00
2018	Mil	NL	7	0	5	13.2	59	13	5	5	0	0	0	1	7	0	8	1	0	0	-	0-0	0	94	.728	3.89	3.29
2019	Mil	NL	35	18	7	111.1	462	101	49	46	14	3	3	5	37	2	117	2	6	7	.462	0-0	1	94	.710	3.68	3.72
2020	Mil	NL	12	11	1	56.0	246	63	41	33	8	0	0	4	21	0	44	1	1	6	.143	0-0	0	93	.815	5.41	5.30
	4 ML YEARS		56	29	15	183.0	775	178	95	84	22	3	3	10	67	2	169	4	7	13	.350	0-0	1	94	.744	4.21	4.13

Sam Howard

Pitches: L Bats: R Pos: RP-22

Ht: 6'4" Wt: 200 Born: 3/5/1993 Age: 28

| | | | HOW MUCH PITCHED | | | | WHAT HE GAVE UP | | | | | | | | | | THE RESULTS | | | | | | |
Year	Team	Lg	G	GS	GF	IP	BFP	H	R	ER	HR	SH	SF	HB	TBB	IBB	SO	WP	W	L	Pct	Sv-Op	Hld	Vel	OPS	ERC	ERA
2018	Col	NL	4	0	4	4.0	20	5	1	1	0	0	0	1	3	0	1	0	0	0	-	0-0	0	92	.888	7.36	2.25
2019	Col	NL	20	0	3	19.0	91	21	16	14	5	2	0	3	10	0	23	2	2	1	1.000	0-0	0	93	.895	7.04	6.63
2020	Pit	NL	22	0	4	21.0	90	17	10	9	4	0	1	3	9	0	27	0	2	3	.400	0-2	4	92	.764	4.34	3.86
	3 ML YEARS		46	0	11	44.0	201	43	27	24	9	2	1	7	22	0	51	2	4	3	.571	0-2	4	92	.835	5.76	4.91

Spencer Howard

Pitches: R Bats: R Pos: SP-6

Ht: 6'3" Wt: 210 Born: 7/28/1996 Age: 24

| | | | HOW MUCH PITCHED | | | | WHAT HE GAVE UP | | | | | | | | | | THE RESULTS | | | | | | |
Year	Team	Lg	G	GS	GF	IP	BFP	H	R	ER	HR	SH	SF	HB	TBB	IBB	SO	WP	W	L	Pct	Sv-Op	Hld	Vel	OPS	ERC	ERA
2017	Wmspt	A-	9	9	0	28.1	123	22	15	14	0	0	0	2	18	0	40	5	1	1	.500	0--	-	-	.623	3.32	4.45
2018	Lakwd	A	23	23	0	112.0	465	101	52	47	6	1	4	0	40	0	147	15	9	8	.529	0--	-	-	.745	3.09	3.78
2019	Rdng	AA	6	6	0	30.2	122	20	9	8	2	0	0	2	9	0	38	3	1	0	1.000	0--	-	-	.542	1.93	2.35
2019	3 Tms	Low	9	9	0	40.1	148	23	8	8	2	0	1	4	7	0	56	0	2	1	.667	0--	-	-	.437	1.41	1.79
2020	Phi	NL	6	6	0	24.1	113	30	17	16	6	0	2	1	10	0	23	0	1	2	.333	0-0	0	94	.893	6.73	5.92

James Hoyt

Pitches: R Bats: R Pos: RP-24

Ht: 6'6" Wt: 230 Born: 9/30/1986 Age: 34

| | | | HOW MUCH PITCHED | | | | WHAT HE GAVE UP | | | | | | | | | | THE RESULTS | | | | | | |
Year	Team	Lg	G	GS	GF	IP	BFP	H	R	ER	HR	SH	SF	HB	TBB	IBB	SO	WP	W	L	Pct	Sv-Op	Hld	Vel	OPS	ERC	ERA
2016	Hou	AL	22	0	7	22.0	91	16	12	11	5	1	1	1	9	1	28	3	1	1	.500	0-1	1	93	.707	3.55	4.50
2017	Hou	AL	43	0	7	49.1	211	51	24	24	7	0	0	2	14	0	66	4	1	0	1.000	0-0	7	93	.748	4.25	4.38
2018	Hou	AL	1	0	0	0.1	3	1	0	0	0	0	0	0	1	0	0	0	0	0	-	0-0	0	93	1.167	29.63	0.00
2019	Cle	AL	8	0	2	8.1	32	6	2	2	2	0	0	0	2	0	10	0	0	0	-	0-0	1	94	.717	2.87	2.16
2020	Mia	NL	24	0	3	14.2	62	9	2	2	1	0	1	1	8	1	20	2	2	0	1.000	0-0	5	88	.598	2.46	1.23
	5 ML YEARS		98	0	19	94.2	399	83	40	39	15	1	2	4	34	2	124	9	4	1	.800	0-1	14	93	.717	3.75	3.71

Dakota Hudson

Pitches: R Bats: R Pos: SP-8

Ht: 6'5" Wt: 215 Born: 9/15/1994 Age: 26

| | | | HOW MUCH PITCHED | | | | WHAT HE GAVE UP | | | | | | | | | | THE RESULTS | | | | | | |
Year	Team	Lg	G	GS	GF	IP	BFP	H	R	ER	HR	SH	SF	HB	TBB	IBB	SO	WP	W	L	Pct	Sv-Op	Hld	Vel	OPS	ERC	ERA
2018	StL	NL	26	0	2	27.1	118	19	9	8	0	0	2	1	18	0	19	2	4	1	.800	0-0	11	96	.559	2.82	2.63
2019	StL	NL	33	32	1	174.2	757	160	80	65	22	3	7	9	86	8	136	5	16	7	.696	1-1	0	94	.742	4.32	3.35
2020	StL	NL	8	8	0	39.0	151	24	13	12	5	0	0	1	15	1	31	0	3	2	.600	0-0	0	93	.583	2.34	2.77
	Postseason		2	2	0	5.0	28	10	11	5	1	0	2	0	3	1	2	0	0	1	.000	0-0	0	93	1.160	11.75	9.00
	3 ML YEARS		67	40	3	241.0	1026	203	102	85	27	3	9	11	119	9	186	7	23	10	.697	1-1	11	94	.698	3.81	3.17

Daniel Hudson

Pitches: R Bats: R Pos: RP-21

Ht: 6'3" Wt: 215 Born: 3/9/1987 Age: 34

| | | | HOW MUCH PITCHED | | | | WHAT HE GAVE UP | | | | | | | | | | THE RESULTS | | | | | | |
Year	Team	Lg	G	GS	GF	IP	BFP	H	R	ER	HR	SH	SF	HB	TBB	IBB	SO	WP	W	L	Pct	Sv-Op	Hld	Vel	OPS	ERC	ERA
2009	CWS	AL	6	2	1	18.2	82	16	9	7	3	0	1	1	9	0	14	1	1	1	.500	0-0	0	93	.711	4.15	3.38
2010	2 Tms		14	14	0	95.1	372	68	26	26	8	2	2	4	27	1	84	5	8	2	.800	0-0	0	93	.579	2.26	2.45
2011	Ari	NL	33	33	0	222.0	921	217	98	86	17	6	6	8	50	1	169	4	16	12	.571	0-0	0	93	.694	3.26	3.49
2012	Ari	NL	9	9	0	45.1	202	62	37	37	9	2	1	0	12	0	37	2	3	2	.600	0-0	0	93	.910	6.56	7.35
2014	Ari	NL	3	0	0	2.2	13	4	4	4	0	0	0	0	2	0	2	0	1	0	1.000	0-0	0	95	.769	4.08	13.50
2015	Ari	NL	64	1	13	67.2	290	64	34	29	7	1	3	0	25	2	71	5	4	3	.571	4-6	20	96	.691	3.58	3.86
2016	Ari	NL	70	0	17	60.1	268	65	40	35	6	0	0	4	22	3	58	5	3	2	.600	5-7	17	96	.753	4.51	5.22

Year	Team	Lg	G	GS	GF	IP	BFP	H	R	ER	HR	SH	SF	HB	TBB	IBB	SO	WP	W	L	Pct	Sv-Op	Hld	Vel	OPS	ERC	ERA
2017	Pit	NL	71	0	18	61.2	271	57	34	30	7	1	2	5	33	1	66	4	2	7	.222	0-2	21	96	.761	4.63	4.38
2018	LAD	NL	40	1	11	46.0	197	38	25	21	6	0	0	4	18	1	44	3	3	2	.600	0-1	3	95	.653	3.54	4.11
2019	2 Tms	NL	69	1	25	73.0	304	56	25	20	8	1	5	4	27	2	71	2	9	3	.750	8-12	11	96	.650	2.91	2.47
2020	Was	NL	21	0	15	20.2	92	15	15	14	6	1	0	3	11	0	28	0	3	2	.600	10-15	1	96	.786	4.83	6.10
10	CWS	AL	3	3	0	15.2	71	17	11	11	1	1	1	0	11	0	14	2	1	1	.500	0-0	0	93	.797	5.69	6.32
10	Ari	NL	11	11	0	79.2	301	51	15	15	7	1	1	4	16	1	70	3	7	1	.875	0-0	0	92	.531	1.70	1.69
19	Tor	AL	45	1	11	48.0	207	38	18	16	5	1	3	3	23	0	48	1	6	3	.667	2-4	8	96	.678	3.45	3.00
19	Was	NL	24	0	14	25.0	97	18	7	4	3	0	2	1	4	2	23	1	3	0	1.000	6-8	3	96	.593	1.93	1.44
	Postseason		10	1	6	15.0	69	20	9	9	2	0	0	1	4	2	16	0	1	1	.500	4-4	1	96	.878	5.72	5.40
11 ML YEARS			400	61	100	713.1	3012	662	347	309	77	14	20	33	234	11	644	31	52	37	.584	27-43	72	94	.702	3.61	3.90

Joe Hudson

Bats: R **Throws:** R **Pos:** C-9 **Ht:** 6'0" **Wt:** 210 **Born:** 5/21/1991 **Age:** 30

								BATTING															RUNNING			AVERAGES			
Year	Team	Lg	G	AB	H	2B	3B	HR	(Hm	Rd)	TB	R	RBI	RC	TBB	IBB	SO	HBP	SH	SF		SB	CS	GDP	Avg	OBP	Slg	OPS
2018	LAA	AL	8	12	2	1	0	0	(0	0)	3	0	1	0	0	0	0	0	0	0		0	0	0	.167	.167	.250	.417
2019	StL	NL	1	1	0	0	0	0	(0	0)	0	0	0	0	0	0	1	0	0	0		0	0	0	.000	.000	.000	.000
2020	Sea	AL	9	17	3	0	0	0	(0	0)	3	0	0	1	2	0	5	0	1	0		0	0	0	.176	.263	.176	.440
3 ML YEARS			18	30	5	1	0	0	(0	0)	6	0	1	1	2	0	6	0	1	0		0	0	0	.167	.219	.200	.419

Sam Huff

Bats: R **Throws:** R **Pos:** C-10 **Ht:** 6'5" **Wt:** 240 **Born:** 1/14/1998 **Age:** 23

								BATTING															RUNNING			AVERAGES			
Year	Team	Lg	G	AB	H	2B	3B	HR	(Hm	Rd)	TB	R	RBI	RC	TBB	IBB	SO	HBP	SH	SF		SB	CS	GDP	Avg	OBP	Slg	OPS
2020	Tex	AL	10	31	11	3	0	3	(2	1)	23	5	4	7	2	0	11	0	0	0		0	0	0	.355	.394	.742	1.136

Jared Hughes

Pitches: R **Bats:** R **Pos:** RP-18 **Ht:** 6'7" **Wt:** 240 **Born:** 7/4/1985 **Age:** 35

Year	Team	Lg	G	GS	GF	IP	BFP	H	R	ER	HR	SH	SF	HB	TBB	IBB	SO	WP	W	L	Pct	Sv-Op	Hld	Vel	OPS	ERC	ERA
2011	Pit	NL	12	0	1	11.0	46	9	5	5	1	1	0	0	4	0	10	0	0	1	.000	0-0	2	93	.630	2.85	4.09
2012	Pit	NL	66	0	20	75.2	316	65	30	24	7	1	0	5	22	4	50	5	2	2	.500	2-4	11	92	.677	2.99	2.85
2013	Pit	NL	29	0	8	32.0	148	37	17	17	2	2	1	2	16	1	23	2	2	3	.400	0-0	3	92	.786	5.27	4.78
2014	Pit	NL	63	0	16	64.1	256	51	21	14	4	6	2	6	19	5	36	2	7	5	.583	0-2	13	92	.609	2.68	1.96
2015	Pit	NL	76	0	11	67.0	284	70	21	17	3	6	4	7	19	2	36	3	3	1	.750	0-3	21	93	.720	3.93	2.28
2016	Pit	NL	67	0	18	59.1	257	62	24	20	6	4	2	5	22	3	34	5	1	1	.500	1-3	4	93	.794	4.55	3.03
2017	Mil	NL	67	0	15	59.2	244	49	21	20	4	2	0	6	24	5	48	6	5	3	.625	1-4	12	93	.723	3.27	3.02
2018	Cin	NL	72	0	23	78.2	298	57	17	17	4	1	3	2	23	2	59	5	4	3	.571	7-11	15	92	.566	2.16	1.94
2019	2 Tms	NL	72	0	13	71.1	289	57	37	32	13	4	1	2	27	1	54	1	5	5	.500	1-4	7	91	.725	3.61	4.04
2020	NYM	NL	18	0	4	22.1	109	23	17	12	3	0	0	5	14	2	21	0	1	2	.333	0-0	2	91	.808	6.05	4.84
19	Cin	NL	47	0	12	48.1	199	41	27	22	6	3	1	2	19	0	34	0	3	4	.429	1-3	3	91	.707	3.63	4.10
19	Phi	NL	25	0	1	23.0	90	16	10	10	7	1	0	0	8	1	20	1	2	1	.667	0-1	4	92	.763	3.50	3.91
	Postseason		1	0	0	1.0	7	3	2	2	0	0	0	0	1	0	1	0	0	0	-	0-0	0	93	1.071	19.55	18.00
10 ML YEARS			542	0	129	541.1	2247	480	210	178	47	27	13	40	190	25	371	29	30	26	.536	12-31	90	92	.697	3.46	2.96

Tommy Hunter

Pitches: R **Bats:** R **Pos:** RP-24 **Ht:** 6'3" **Wt:** 250 **Born:** 7/3/1986 **Age:** 34

Year	Team	Lg	G	GS	GF	IP	BFP	H	R	ER	HR	SH	SF	HB	TBB	IBB	SO	WP	W	L	Pct	Sv-Op	Hld	Vel	OPS	ERC	ERA
2008	Tex	AL	3	3	0	11.0	63	23	20	20	4	0	0	1	3	0	9	0	0	2	.000	0-0	0	91	1.144	12.66	16.36
2009	Tex	AL	19	19	0	112.0	475	113	55	51	13	2	1	2	33	2	64	6	9	6	.600	0-0	0	89	.736	3.86	4.10
2010	Tex	AL	23	22	0	128.0	536	126	55	53	21	3	2	3	33	0	68	1	13	4	.765	0-0	0	90	.740	3.95	3.73
2011	2 Tms	AL	20	11	2	84.2	367	100	50	44	12	2	2	4	15	1	45	0	4	4	.500	0-1	1	92	.782	4.65	4.68
2012	Bal	AL	33	20	5	133.2	573	161	85	81	32	3	6	4	27	0	77	0	7	8	.467	0-1	0	92	.864	5.63	5.45
2013	Bal	AL	68	0	28	86.1	336	71	28	27	11	1	0	2	14	1	68	0	6	5	.545	0-1	4	96	.617	2.53	2.81
2014	Bal	AL	60	0	24	60.2	241	55	22	20	4	1	2	1	12	3	45	2	3	2	.600	11-17	12	96	.643	2.65	2.97
2015	2 Tms	AL	58	0	17	60.1	249	61	29	28	7	1	3	1	14	2	47	2	4	2	.667	1-2	7	96	.711	3.65	4.18
2016	2 Tms	AL	33	0	8	34.0	139	35	13	12	1	1	0	2	8	1	23	0	2	2	.500	0-1	1	94	.678	3.43	3.18
2017	TB	AL	61	0	11	58.2	228	43	18	17	6	0	1	0	14	0	64	2	3	5	.375	1-1	25	96	.588	2.21	2.61
2018	Phi	NL	65	0	10	64.0	270	65	28	27	6	1	1	3	15	1	51	1	5	4	.556	4-6	25	96	.745	3.62	3.80
2019	Phi	NL	5	0	1	5.1	22	2	0	0	0	0	0	0	0	0	5	0	0	0	-	0-0	1	94	.222	0.31	0.00
2020	Phi	NL	24	0	1	24.2	102	22	11	11	2	1	0	3	6	0	25	0	0	1	.000	1-3	8	93	.698	3.27	4.01
11	Tex	AL	8	0	2	15.1	62	12	6	5	1	1	1	0	5	0	10	0	1	1	.500	0-1	0	93	.570	2.44	2.93
11	Bal	AL	12	11	0	69.1	305	88	44	39	11	1	1	4	10	1	35	0	3	3	.500	0-0	1	92	.823	5.19	5.06
15	Bal	AL	39	0	12	44.2	180	41	19	18	3	1	3	1	11	2	32	2	2	2	.500	0-1	6	96	.650	2.92	3.63
15	ChC	NL	19	0	5	15.2	69	20	10	10	4	0	0	0	3	0	15	0	2	0	1.000	1-1	1	97	.864	5.91	5.74
16	Cle	AL	21	0	5	21.2	90	21	10	9	1	1	0	2	5	1	17	0	2	2	.500	0-1	0	94	.668	3.22	3.74
16	Bal	AL	12	0	3	12.1	49	14	3	3	0	0	0	0	3	0	6	0	0	0	-	0-0	1	95	.695	3.82	2.19
	Postseason		7	3	2	14.1	65	19	8	7	2	0	2	1	2	0	15	0	0	2	.000	0-0	0	93	.888	5.35	4.40
13 ML YEARS			472	75	99	863.1	3597	877	414	391	119	16	17	27	194	13	591	14	56	45	.554	22-38	101	93	.735	3.85	4.08

Jose Iglesias

Bats: R **Throws:** R **Pos:** SS-24;DH-14;PH-3 ee-GLAY-see-us **Ht:** 5'11" **Wt:** 195 **Born:** 1/5/1990 **Age:** 31

								BATTING													RUNNING			AVERAGES			
Year	Team	Lg	G	AB	H	2B	3B	HR	(Hm	Rd)	TB	R	RBI	RC	TBB	IBB	SO	HBP	SH	SF	SB	CS	GDP	Avg	OBP	Slg	OPS
2011	Bos	AL	10	6	2	0	0	0	(0	0)	2	3	0	0	0	0	2	0	0	0	0	0	0	.333	.333	.333	.667
2012	Bos	AL	25	68	8	2	0	1	(0	1)	13	5	2	0	4	0	16	3	2	0	1	0	2	.118	.200	.191	.391
2013	2 Tms	AL	109	350	106	16	2	3	(1	2)	135	39	29	45	15	0	60	11	4	2	5	2	7	.303	.349	.386	.735
2015	Det	AL	120	416	125	17	3	2	(1	1)	154	44	23	47	25	2	44	6	4	3	11	8	10	.300	.347	.370	.717
2016	Det	AL	137	467	119	26	0	4	(1	3)	157	57	32	47	28	1	50	8	7	3	7	4	12	.255	.306	.336	.643
2017	Det	AL	130	463	118	33	1	6	(4	2)	171	56	54	54	21	0	65	1	3	1	7	4	6	.255	.288	.369	.657
2018	Det	AL	125	432	116	31	3	5	(3	2)	168	43	48	60	19	0	47	8	3	2	15	6	11	.269	.310	.389	.699
2019	Cin	NL	146	504	145	21	3	11	(9	2)	205	62	59	61	20	3	70	3	1	2	6	6	17	.288	.318	.407	.724
2020	Bal	AL	39	142	53	17	0	3	(1	2)	79	16	24	32	3	0	17	4	0	1	0	0	1	.373	.400	.556	.956
13	Bos	AL	63	215	71	10	2	1	(0	1)	88	27	19	34	11	0	30	6	0	2	3	1	4	.330	.376	.409	.785
13	Det	AL	46	135	35	6	0	2	(1	1)	47	12	10	11	4	0	30	5	4	0	2	1	3	.259	.306	.348	.654
	Postseason		11	26	6	0	0	0	(0	0)	6	2	1	0	1	0	5	1	3	0	0	1	1	.231	.286	.231	.516
	9 ML YEARS		841	2848	792	163	12	35	(20	15)	1084	325	271	346	135	6	371	44	24	14	52	30	66	.278	.319	.381	.700

Raisel Iglesias

Pitches: R **Bats:** R **Pos:** RP-22 rye-SELL **Ht:** 6'2" **Wt:** 190 **Born:** 1/4/1990 **Age:** 31

			HOW MUCH PITCHED					WHAT HE GAVE UP										THE RESULTS							
Year	Team	Lg	G	GS	GF	IP	BFP	H	R	ER	HR	SH	SF	HB	TBB	IBB	SO	WP	W	L	Pct	Sv-Op	Hld	Vel	OPS	ERC	ERA
2015	Cin	NL	18	16	1	95.1	395	81	45	44	11	4	0	7	28	0	104	2	3	7	.300	0-0	0	92	.682	3.24	4.15
2016	Cin	NL	37	5	15	78.1	325	63	22	22	7	1	2	5	26	1	83	3	3	2	.600	6-8	7	93	.623	2.90	2.53
2017	Cin	NL	63	0	57	76.0	306	57	22	21	5	1	1	1	27	1	92	1	3	3	.500	28-30	0	96	.576	2.43	2.49
2018	Cin	NL	66	0	57	72.0	291	52	22	19	12	1	2	2	25	2	80	2	2	5	.286	30-34	0	95	.644	2.88	2.38
2019	Cin	NL	68	0	55	67.0	279	61	31	31	12	1	1	2	21	4	89	3	3	12	.200	34-40	3	95	.743	3.81	4.16
2020	Cin	NL	22	0	17	23.0	91	16	11	7	1	1	1	1	5	1	31	0	4	3	.571	8-10	2	96	.510	1.64	2.74
	6 ML YEARS		274	21	202	411.2	1687	330	153	144	48	9	7	18	132	9	479	11	18	32	.360	106-122	12	94	.646	2.95	3.15

Ender Inciarte

Bats: L **Throws:** L **Pos:** CF-46;PR-3;PH-1 END-er in-see-ARR-tay **Ht:** 5'11" **Wt:** 190 **Born:** 10/29/1990 **Age:** 30

								BATTING													RUNNING			AVERAGES			
Year	Team	Lg	G	AB	H	2B	3B	HR	(Hm	Rd)	TB	R	RBI	RC	TBB	IBB	SO	HBP	SH	SF	SB	CS	GDP	Avg	OBP	Slg	OPS
2014	Ari	NL	118	418	116	18	2	4	(1	3)	150	54	27	49	25	0	53	1	0	4	19	3	3	.278	.318	.359	.677
2015	Ari	NL	132	524	159	27	5	6	(1	5)	214	73	45	69	26	0	58	4	2	5	21	10	8	.303	.338	.408	.747
2016	Atl	NL	131	522	152	24	7	3	(1	2)	199	85	29	58	45	5	68	4	5	2	16	7	8	.291	.351	.381	.732
2017	Atl	NL	158	662	201	27	5	11	(6	5)	271	93	57	95	49	3	94	0	3	4	22	9	8	.304	.350	.409	.759
2018	Atl	NL	156	597	158	27	6	10	(3	7)	227	83	61	70	49	1	86	6	4	4	28	14	6	.265	.325	.380	.705
2019	Atl	NL	65	199	49	11	2	5	(2	3)	79	30	24	32	26	2	41	4	0	1	7	1	1	.246	.343	.397	.740
2020	Atl	NL	46	116	22	2	1	1	(0	1)	29	17	10	9	12	0	25	0	1	2	4	1	0	.190	.262	.250	.512
	Postseason		4	13	3	0	0	0	(0	0)	3	0	0	1	0	0	4	1	0	0	0	0	0	.231	.231	.231	.462
	7 ML YEARS		806	3038	857	136	28	40	(14	26)	1169	435	253	382	232	11	425	18	19	18	117	45	34	.282	.335	.385	.720

Cole Irvin

Pitches: L **Bats:** L **Pos:** RP-3 **Ht:** 6'4" **Wt:** 217 **Born:** 1/31/1994 **Age:** 27

			HOW MUCH PITCHED					WHAT HE GAVE UP										THE RESULTS							
Year	Team	Lg	G	GS	GF	IP	BFP	H	R	ER	HR	SH	SF	HB	TBB	IBB	SO	WP	W	L	Pct	Sv-Op	Hld	Vel	OPS	ERC	ERA
2019	Phi	NL	16	3	1	41.2	181	45	28	27	7	1	2	3	13	1	31	1	2	1	.667	1-1	0	90	.796	4.96	5.83
2020	Phi	NL	3	0	1	3.2	22	11	7	7	1	0	0	0	1	0	4	0	0	1	.000	0-0	0	92	1.355	19.91	17.18
	2 ML YEARS		19	3	2	45.1	203	56	35	34	8	1	2	3	14	1	35	1	2	2	.500	1-1	0	90	.859	5.94	6.75

Alex Jackson

Bats: R **Throws:** R **Pos:** C-4;PR-1 **Ht:** 6'2" **Wt:** 215 **Born:** 12/25/1995 **Age:** 25

								BATTING													RUNNING			AVERAGES			
Year	Team	Lg	G	AB	H	2B	3B	HR	(Hm	Rd)	TB	R	RBI	RC	TBB	IBB	SO	HBP	SH	SF	SB	CS	GDP	Avg	OBP	Slg	OPS
2019	Atl	NL	4	13	0	0	0	0	(0	0)	0	0	0	0	1	1	5	1	0	0	0	0	1	.000	.133	.000	.133
2020	Atl	NL	5	7	2	1	0	0	(0	0)	3	0	0	0	0	0	4	0	0	0	0	0	1	.286	.286	.429	.714
	2 ML YEARS		9	20	2	1	0	0	(0	0)	3	0	0	0	1	1	9	1	0	0	0	0	2	.100	.182	.150	.332

Luke Jackson

Pitches: R **Bats:** R **Pos:** RP-19 **Ht:** 6'2" **Wt:** 210 **Born:** 8/24/1991 **Age:** 29

			HOW MUCH PITCHED					WHAT HE GAVE UP										THE RESULTS							
Year	Team	Lg	G	GS	GF	IP	BFP	H	R	ER	HR	SH	SF	HB	TBB	IBB	SO	WP	W	L	Pct	Sv-Op	Hld	Vel	OPS	ERC	ERA
2015	Tex	AL	7	0	4	6.1	27	5	3	3	1	0	0	0	2	0	6	1	0	0	-	0-0	0	96	.619	2.81	4.26
2016	Tex	AL	8	0	2	11.2	62	22	14	14	4	0	1	0	8	0	3	0	0	0	-	0-0	0	94	1.201	13.93	10.80
2017	Atl	NL	43	0	17	50.2	224	55	26	26	4	1	2	4	19	4	53	4	1	0	1.000	0-0	1	95	.759	4.50	4.62
2018	Atl	NL	35	0	11	40.2	184	41	22	20	3	1	2	2	21	3	46	6	1	2	.333	1-2	3	94	.742	4.39	4.43
2019	Atl	NL	70	0	35	72.2	315	76	34	31	10	1	0	2	26	4	106	3	9	2	.818	18-25	9	96	.733	4.46	3.84
2020	Atl	NL	19	0	3	26.1	132	39	23	20	2	0	4	2	13	0	20	3	1	0	1.000	0-0	1	94	.852	7.39	6.84
	Postseason		3	0	0	2.2	18	6	4	3	1	0	0	1	2	0	6	0	0	0	-	0-0	1	96	1.167	17.71	10.13
	6 ML YEARS		182	0	72	208.1	944	238	122	114	24	3	9	10	89	11	214	17	14	4	.778	19-27	14	95	.784	5.20	4.92

Josh James

Pitches: R **Bats:** R **Pos:** RP-11; SP-2   **Ht:** 6'3" **Wt:** 234 **Born:** 3/8/1993 **Age:** 28

			HOW MUCH PITCHED					WHAT HE GAVE UP											THE RESULTS								
Year	Team	Lg	G	GS	GF	IP	BFP	H	R	ER	HR	SH	SF	HB	TBB	IBB	SO	WP	W	L	Pct	Sv-Op	Hld	Vel	OPS	ERC	ERA
2018	Hou	AL	6	3	0	23.0	91	15	6	6	3	0	0	2	7	0	29	0	2	0	1.000	0-0	2	97	.605	2.45	2.35
2019	Hou	AL	49	1	18	61.1	266	46	34	32	10	0	0	4	35	0	100	6	5	1	.833	1-3	6	97	.694	4.02	4.70
2020	Hou	AL	13	2	1	17.1	83	15	14	14	4	0	0	2	17	0	21	2	1	0	1.000	0-2	4	96	.894	7.35	7.27
Postseason			11	0	2	11.1	56	14	10	8	3	0	0		9	0	21	0	2	1	.667	0-0	0	98	.964	8.57	6.35
3 ML YEARS			68	6	19	101.2	440	76	54	52	17	0	0	8	59	0	150	8	8	1	.889	1-5	12	97	.711	4.16	4.60

Travis Jankowski

Bats: L **Throws:** R **Pos:** CF-9;PR-7;RF-3;LF-1;DH-1;PH-1   **Ht:** 6'2" **Wt:** 190 **Born:** 6/15/1991 **Age:** 30

			BATTING																				RUNNING			AVERAGES			
Year	Team	Lg	G	AB	H	2B	3B	HR	(Hm	Rd)	TB	R	RBI	RC	TBB	IBB	SO	HBP	SH	SF	SB	CS	GDP	Avg	OBP	Slg	OPS
2015	SD	NL	34	90	19	2	2	2	(0	2)	31	9	12	10	4	0	24	0	2	0	2	1	1	.211	.245	.344	.589
2016	SD	NL	131	335	82	13	2	2	(1	1)	105	53	12	34	42	0	100	2	3	0	30	12	5	.245	.332	.313	.646
2017	SD	NL	27	75	14	2	0	0	(0	0)	16	10	1	5	9	0	28	1	2	0	4	0	2	.187	.282	.213	.496
2018	SD	NL	117	347	90	12	3	4	(3	1)	120	45	17	42	37	0	73	1	2	0	24	7	7	.259	.332	.346	.678
2019	SD	NL	25	22	4	0	0	0	(0	0)	4	4	0	0	2	0	4	0	0	0	2	2	0	.182	.250	.182	.432
2020	Cin	NL	16	15	1	0	0	0	(0	0)	1	3	0	0	2	0	7	0	0	0	2	1	1	.067	.176	.067	.243
6 ML YEARS			350	884	210	29	7	8	(4	4)	277	124	42	91	96	0	236	4	9	0	64	23	16	.238	.315	.313	.628

Danny Jansen

Bats: R **Throws:** R **Pos:** C-43;PH-1   **Ht:** 6'2" **Wt:** 225 **Born:** 4/15/1995 **Age:** 26

			BATTING																				RUNNING			AVERAGES			
Year	Team	Lg	G	AB	H	2B	3B	HR	(Hm	Rd)	TB	R	RBI	RC	TBB	IBB	SO	HBP	SH	SF	SB	CS	GDP	Avg	OBP	Slg	OPS
2018	Tor	AL	31	81	20	6	0	3	(1	2)	35	12	8	14	9	0	17	4	0	1	0	0	1	.247	.347	.432	.779
2019	Tor	AL	107	347	72	12	1	13	(8	5)	125	41	43	40	31	1	79	4	1	1	0	1	8	.207	.279	.360	.640
2020	Tor	AL	43	120	22	3	0	6	(4	2)	43	18	20	17	21	0	31	2	3	1	0	0	1	.183	.313	.358	.671
3 ML YEARS			181	548	114	21	1	22	(13	9)	203	71	71	71	61	1	127	10	4	3	0	1	10	.208	.297	.370	.668

Kenley Jansen

Pitches: R **Bats:** B **Pos:** RP-27   KEN-lee JANN-sen   **Ht:** 6'5" **Wt:** 265 **Born:** 9/30/1987 **Age:** 33

			HOW MUCH PITCHED					WHAT HE GAVE UP											THE RESULTS								
Year	Team	Lg	G	GS	GF	IP	BFP	H	R	ER	HR	SH	SF	HB	TBB	IBB	SO	WP	W	L	Pct	Sv-Op	Hld	Vel	OPS	ERC	ERA
2010	LAD	NL	25	0	8	27.0	109	12	2	2	0	1	0	1	15	1	41	1	1	0	1.000	4-4	4	94	.422	1.40	0.67
2011	LAD	NL	51	0	13	53.2	218	30	17	17	3	0	1	2	26	0	96	0	2	1	.667	5-6	9	93	.494	1.96	2.85
2012	LAD	NL	65	0	40	65.0	252	33	18	17	6	0	1	3	22	1	99	3	5	3	.625	25-32	8	92	.504	1.55	2.35
2013	LAD	NL	75	0	45	76.2	292	48	16	16	6	0	0	3	18	1	111	2	4	3	.571	28-32	16	92	.605	1.65	1.88
2014	LAD	NL	68	0	57	65.1	268	55	20	20	5	1	2	0	19	2	101	2	2	3	.400	44-49	0	94	.610	2.60	2.76
2015	LAD	NL	54	0	50	52.1	200	33	14	14	6	0	2	2	8	0	80	0	2	1	.667	36-38	1	93	.513	1.58	2.41
2016	LAD	NL	71	0	63	68.2	251	35	14	14	4	3	1	2	11	2	104	1	3	2	.600	47-53	0	94	.446	1.03	1.83
2017	LAD	NL	65	0	57	68.1	258	44	11	10	5	0	0	2	7	0	109	2	5	0	1.000	**41**-42	1	95	.476	1.35	1.32
2018	LAD	NL	69	0	59	71.2	289	54	28	24	13	0	1	2	17	1	82	0	1	5	.167	38-42	0	94	.635	2.68	3.01
2019	LAD	NL	62	0	51	63.0	263	51	28	26	9	0	3	4	16	0	80	2	5	3	.625	33-41	0	93	.653	2.92	3.71
2020	LAD	NL	27	0	24	24.1	102	19	11	9	2	0	0	3	9	0	33	0	3	1	.750	11-13	0	92	.615	3.13	3.33
Postseason			41	0	33	49.1	189	24	12	11	5	0	0	3	15	2	70	0	1	1	.500	16-19	1	94	.485	1.46	2.01
11 ML YEARS			632	0	467	636.0	2502	414	179	169	59	5	11	24	168	8	936	13	33	22	.600	312-352	39	93	.540	1.87	2.39

Cristian Javier

Pitches: R **Bats:** R **Pos:** SP-10; RP-2   **Ht:** 6'1" **Wt:** 213 **Born:** 3/26/1997 **Age:** 24

			HOW MUCH PITCHED					WHAT HE GAVE UP											THE RESULTS								
Year	Team	Lg	G	GS	GF	IP	BFP	H	R	ER	HR	SH	SF	HB	TBB	IBB	SO	WP	W	L	Pct	Sv-Op	Hld	Vel	OPS	ERC	ERA
2020	Hou	AL	12	10	0	54.1	214	36	21	21	11	0	2	2	18	0	54	4	5	2	.714	0-0	0	92	.652	2.83	3.48

Jon Jay

Bats: L **Throws:** L **Pos:** RF-9;CF-5;LF-4;DH-1;PH-1   **Ht:** 5'11" **Wt:** 200 **Born:** 3/15/1985 **Age:** 36

			BATTING																				RUNNING			AVERAGES			
Year	Team	Lg	G	AB	H	2B	3B	HR	(Hm	Rd)	TB	R	RBI	RC	TBB	IBB	SO	HBP	SH	SF	SB	CS	GDP	Avg	OBP	Slg	OPS
2010	StL	NL	105	287	86	19	2	4	(2	2)	121	47	27	40	24	0	50	3	8	1	2	4	5	.300	.359	.422	.780
2011	StL	NL	159	455	135	24	2	10	(5	5)	193	56	37	56	28	1	81	7	9	4	6	7	11	.297	.344	.424	.768
2012	StL	NL	117	443	135	22	4	4	(3	1)	177	70	40	65	34	3	71	15	9	1	19	7	9	.305	.373	.400	.773
2013	StL	NL	157	548	151	27	2	7	(2	5)	203	75	67	74	52	7	103	14	9	5	10	5	13	.276	.351	.370	.721
2014	StL	NL	140	413	125	16	3	0	(0	3)	156	52	46	57	28	3	78	**20**	3	4	6	3	17	.303	.372	.378	.750
2015	StL	NL	79	210	44	5	1	1	(0	1)	54	25	10	11	19	5	36	11	3	2	0	2	7	.210	.306	.257	.563
2016	SD	NL	90	347	101	26	1	2	(1	1)	135	49	26	55	19	0	78	6	1	0	2	0	5	.291	.339	.389	.728
2017	ChC	NL	141	379	112	18	3	2	(1	1)	142	65	34	58	37	3	80	12	3	2	6	2	11	.296	.374	.355	.749
2018	2 Tms		143	527	141	19	7	3	(2	1)	183	74	40	64	33	0	95	18	5	3	4	3	11	.268	.330	.347	.678
2019	CWS	AL	47	165	44	8	0	0	(0	0)	52	12	9	23	8	0	30	3	5	1	0	0	1	.267	.311	.315	.626
2020	Ari	NL	18	50	8	1	0	1	(0	0)	12	5	4	0	3	0	12	1	0	3	0	0	0	.160	.211	.240	.451
18	KC	AL	59	238	73	9	2	1	(1	0)	89	28	18	31	19	0	39	3	4	2	3	2	4	.307	.363	.374	.737
18	Ari	NL	84	289	68	10	5	2	(1	1)	94	46	22	33	14	0	56	15	1	1	1	1	7	.235	.304	.325	.629
Postseason			67	213	48	6	1	0	(1	0)	56	26	16	23	19	1	36	8	6	2	5	2	5	.225	.310	.263	.573
11 ML YEARS			1196	3824	1082	185	25	37	(17	20)	1428	530	340	503	285	22	714	110	55	26	55	33	90	.283	.348	.373	.721

Daulton Jefferies

Pitches: R Bats: L Pos: SP-1   Ht: 6'0" Wt: 182 Born: 8/2/1995 Age: 25

		HOW MUCH PITCHED					WHAT HE GAVE UP										THE RESULTS							
Year	Team	Lg	G	GS	GF	IP	BFP	H	R	ER	HR	SH	SF	HB	TBB	IBB	SO	WP	W	L	Pct	Sv-Op	Hld	Vel	OPS	ERC	ERA
2020	Oak	AL	1	1	0	2.0	13	5	5	5	2	0	0	0	2	0	1	0	0	1	.000	0-0	0	94	1.538	27.53	22.50

Ryan Jeffers

Bats: R Throws: R Pos: C-25;DH-1;PH-1   Ht: 6'4" Wt: 235 Born: 6/3/1997 Age: 24

							BATTING												RUNNING			AVERAGES			
Year	Team	Lg	G	AB	H	2B	3B	HR	(Hm | Rd)	TB	R	RBI	RC	TBB	IBB	SO	HBP	SH	SF	SB	CS	GDP	Avg	OBP	Slg	OPS
2020	Min	AL	26	55	15	0	0	3	(3 | 0)	24	5	7	8	5	0	19	2	0	0	0	0	0	.273	.355	.436	.791

Jeremy Jeffress

Pitches: R Bats: R Pos: RP-22   JEFF-ress   Ht: 6'0" Wt: 205 Born: 9/21/1987 Age: 33

			HOW MUCH PITCHED					WHAT HE GAVE UP										THE RESULTS							
Year	Team	Lg	G	GS	GF	IP	BFP	H	R	ER	HR	SH	SF	HB	TBB	IBB	SO	WP	W	L	Pct	Sv-Op	Hld	Vel	OPS	ERC	ERA
2010	Mil	NL	10	0	5	10.0	42	8	4	3	0	0	1	0	6	1	8	1	1	0	1.000	0-0	0	95	.676	2.96	2.70
2011	KC	AL	14	0	6	15.1	67	12	8	8	1	2	0	0	11	0	13	1	1	1	.500	1-2	0	97	.706	3.87	4.70
2012	KC	AL	13	0	6	13.1	73	19	14	10	0	0	0	0	13	0	13	1	0	0	—	0-0	0	95	.838	7.87	6.75
2013	Tor	AL	10	0	3	10.1	43	8	1	1	1	0	0	0	5	0	12	0	1	0	1.000	0-0	0	97	.592	3.17	0.87
2014	2 Tms		32	0	12	32.0	135	35	10	10	1	3	1	2	10	2	29	1	1	1	.500	0-1	6	96	.709	4.06	2.81
2015	Mil	NL	72	0	8	68.0	285	64	22	20	5	3	0	3	22	5	67	4	5	0	1.000	0-5	23	95	.666	3.36	2.65
2016	2 Tms		59	0	41	58.0	241	55	17	15	2	2	1	4	18	3	42	3	3	2	.600	27-28	6	95	.656	3.26	2.33
2017	2 Tms		61	1	12	65.1	295	73	35	34	10	1	1	2	34	4	51	6	5	2	.714	0-1	8	95	.830	5.75	4.68
2018	Mil	NL	73	0	24	76.2	299	49	12	11	5	1	1	1	27	4	89	1	8	1	.889	15-20	18	95	.530	1.87	1.29
2019	Mil	NL	48	0	12	52.0	225	54	32	29	5	2	0	5	17	0	46	1	3	4	.429	1-4	12	94	.734	4.40	5.02
2020	ChC	NL	22	0	15	23.1	88	10	5	4	1	0	1	2	12	1	17	0	4	1	.800	8-10	3	93	.465	1.65	1.54
14	Tor	AL	3	0	3	3.1	21	8	4	4	0	0	1	2	3	0	4	0	0	0	—	0-0	0	96	1.219	19.06	10.80
14	Mil	NL	29	0	9	28.2	114	27	6	6	1	3	0	0	7	2	25	1	1	1	.500	0-1	6	97	.624	2.75	1.88
16	Mil	NL	47	0	40	44.2	190	45	13	11	2	2	1	4	11	3	35	0	2	2	.500	27-28	6	96	.662	3.38	2.22
16	Tex	AL	12	0	1	13.1	51	10	4	4	0	0	0	0	7	0	7	3	1	0	1.000	0-0	0	94	.629	2.84	2.70
17	Tex	AL	39	0	10	40.2	183	49	25	24	8	0	1	2	19	2	29	3	1	2	.333	0-0	4	95	.898	6.63	5.31
17	Mil	NL	22	1	2	24.2	112	24	10	10	2	1	0	0	15	2	22	3	4	0	1.000	0-1	4	95	.716	4.39	3.65
	Postseason		9	0	2	9.0	48	17	7	6	2	0	1	0	5	0	12	0	0	1	.000	1-3	2	95	1.054	11.67	6.00
11 ML YEARS			414	1	144	424.1	1793	387	160	145	31	14	6	19	175	20	387	22	32	12	.727	52-71	76	95	.677	3.60	3.08

Dany Jimenez

Pitches: R Bats: R Pos: RP-2   Ht: 6'1" Wt: 182 Born: 12/23/1993 Age: 27

			HOW MUCH PITCHED					WHAT HE GAVE UP										THE RESULTS							
Year	Team	Lg	G	GS	GF	IP	BFP	H	R	ER	HR	SH	SF	HB	TBB	IBB	SO	WP	W	L	Pct	Sv-Op	Hld	Vel	OPS	ERC	ERA
2020	SF	NL	2	0	1	1.1	8	1	1	1	0	0	0	0	3	0	1	0	0	0	—	0-0	0	93	.700	8.88	6.75

Eloy Jimenez

Bats: R Throws: R Pos: LF-54;DH-1   Ht: 6'4" Wt: 235 Born: 11/27/1996 Age: 24

							BATTING												RUNNING			AVERAGES			
Year	Team	Lg	G	AB	H	2B	3B	HR	(Hm | Rd)	TB	R	RBI	RC	TBB	IBB	SO	HBP	SH	SF	SB	CS	GDP	Avg	OBP	Slg	OPS
2019	CWS	AL	122	468	125	18	2	31	(12 | 19)	240	69	79	68	30	0	134	4	0	2	0	0	11	.267	.315	.513	.828
2020	CWS	AL	55	213	63	14	0	14	(8 | 6)	119	26	41	44	12	0	56	0	0	1	0	0	4	.296	.332	.559	.891
2 ML YEARS			177	681	188	32	2	45	(20 | 25)	359	95	120	112	42	0	190	4	0	3	0	0	15	.276	.321	.527	.848

Joe Jimenez

Pitches: R Bats: R Pos: RP-25   Ht: 6'3" Wt: 272 Born: 1/17/1995 Age: 26

			HOW MUCH PITCHED					WHAT HE GAVE UP										THE RESULTS							
Year	Team	Lg	G	GS	GF	IP	BFP	H	R	ER	HR	SH	SF	HB	TBB	IBB	SO	WP	W	L	Pct	Sv-Op	Hld	Vel	OPS	ERC	ERA
2017	Det	AL	24	0	6	19.0	99	31	28	26	4	0	1	2	9	0	17	0	0	2	.000	0-1	0	95	.999	9.60	12.32
2018	Det	AL	68	0	17	62.2	267	53	34	30	5	0	2	3	22	3	78	3	4	5	.556	3-7	23	96	.645	2.99	4.31
2019	Det	AL	66	0	29	59.2	257	56	33	29	13	0	0	4	23	1	82	1	4	7	.364	9-14	15	95	.797	4.74	4.37
2020	Det	AL	25	0	9	22.2	101	25	19	18	7	0	2	5	6	0	22	1	1	3	.250	5-6	4	94	.936	6.68	7.15
4 ML YEARS			183	0	61	164.0	724	165	114	103	29	0	5	14	60	4	199	5	10	16	.385	17-28	42	95	.787	4.77	5.65

Pierce Johnson

Pitches: R Bats: R Pos: RP-24   Ht: 6'2" Wt: 202 Born: 5/10/1991 Age: 30

			HOW MUCH PITCHED					WHAT HE GAVE UP										THE RESULTS							
Year	Team	Lg	G	GS	GF	IP	BFP	H	R	ER	HR	SH	SF	HB	TBB	IBB	SO	WP	W	L	Pct	Sv-Op	Hld	Vel	OPS	ERC	ERA
2017	ChC	NL	1	0	0	1.0	7	2	2	0	0	0	0	0	1	0	2	0	0	0	—	0-0	0	92	.762	10.22	0.00
2018	SF	NL	37	0	7	43.2	186	38	27	27	5	1	2	0	22	1	36	1	3	2	.600	0-0	1	94	.740	3.86	5.56
2020	SD	NL	24	0	7	20.0	80	15	7	6	2	0	1	0	9	0	27	1	3	1	.750	0-0	1	96	.643	3.04	2.70
3 ML YEARS			62	0	14	64.2	273	55	36	33	7	1	3	0	32	1	65	2	6	3	.667	0-0	2	94	.712	3.69	4.59

Daniel Johnson

Bats: L **Throws:** L **Pos:** RF-4;LF-1;PR-1   **Ht:** 5'10" **Wt:** 200 **Born:** 7/11/1995 **Age:** 25

Year	Team	Lg	G	AB	H	2B	3B	HR	(Hm	Rd)	TB	R	RBI	RC	TBB	IBB	SO	HBP	SH	SF	SB	CS	GDP	Avg	OBP	Slg	OPS
2020	Cle	AL	5	12	1	0	0	0	(0	0)	1	0	0	1	1	1	5	0	0	0	0	0	0	.083	.154	.083	.237

JaCoby Jones

Bats: R **Throws:** R **Pos:** CF-28;PH-2   **Ht:** 6'2" **Wt:** 201 **Born:** 5/10/1992 **Age:** 29

Year	Team	Lg	G	AB	H	2B	3B	HR	(Hm	Rd)	TB	R	RBI	RC	TBB	IBB	SO	HBP	SH	SF	SB	CS	GDP	Avg	OBP	Slg	OPS
2016	Det	AL	13	28	6	3	0	0	(0	0)	9	3	2	2	0	0	12	0	0	0	0	0	1	.214	.214	.321	.536
2017	Det	AL	56	141	24	3	1	3	(2	1)	38	14	13	7	9	0	65	4	0	0	6	2	5	.170	.240	.270	.510
2018	Det	AL	129	429	89	22	6	11	(8	3)	156	54	34	36	24	0	142	11	1	2	13	5	9	.207	.266	.364	.630
2019	Det	AL	88	298	70	19	3	11	(7	4)	128	39	26	35	27	2	94	6	1	1	7	2	6	.235	.310	.430	.740
2020	Det	AL	30	97	26	9	0	5	(3	2)	50	19	14	14	7	0	34	3	0	1	1	1	1	.268	.333	.515	.849
	5 ML YEARS		316	993	215	56	10	30	(20	10)	381	129	89	94	67	2	347	24	2	4	27	10	22	.217	.281	.384	.665

Jahmai Jones

Bats: R **Throws:** R **Pos:** 2B-2;PR-1   **Ht:** 6'0" **Wt:** 204 **Born:** 8/4/1997 **Age:** 23

Year	Team	Lg	G	AB	H	2B	3B	HR	(Hm	Rd)	TB	R	RBI	RC	TBB	IBB	SO	HBP	SH	SF	SB	CS	GDP	Avg	OBP	Slg	OPS
2020	LAA	AL	3	7	3	0	0	0	(0	0)	3	2	1	2	0	0	2	0	0	0	0	0	0	.429	.429	.429	.857

Nate Jones

Pitches: R **Bats:** R **Pos:** RP-21   **Ht:** 6'5" **Wt:** 230 **Born:** 1/28/1986 **Age:** 35

Year	Team	Lg	G	GS	GF	IP	BFP	H	R	ER	HR	SH	SF	HB	TBB	IBB	SO	WP	W	L	Pct	Sv-Op	Hld	Vel	OPS	ERC	ERA
2012	CWS	AL	65	0	11	71.2	301	67	19	19	4	2	4	1	32	3	65	5	8	0	1.000	0-3	7	98	.686	3.67	2.39
2013	CWS	AL	70	0	17	78.0	315	69	40	36	5	3	6	1	26	1	89	8	4	5	.444	0-4	16	98	.659	3.09	4.15
2014	CWS	AL	2	0	0	0.0	5	2	4	4	0	0	0	0	3	0	0	0	0	0	—	0-1	0	96	2.500		
2015	CWS	AL	19	0	3	19.0	72	12	7	7	5	2	0	0	6	0	27	0	2	2	.500	0-1	6	98	.695	2.87	3.32
2016	CWS	AL	71	0	11	70.2	274	48	20	18	7	2	2	3	15	3	80	7	5	3	.625	3-12	28	97	.552	1.87	2.29
2017	CWS	AL	11	0	1	11.2	49	9	3	3	1	0	1	0	6	1	15	1	1	0	1.000	0-0	4	97	.675	3.43	2.31
2018	CWS	AL	33	0	15	30.0	137	28	14	10	4	1	1	3	15	0	32	2	2	2	.500	5-8	6	97	.723	4.59	3.00
2019	CWS	AL	13	0	5	10.1	47	10	4	4	2	0	0	1	7	1	10	2	0	1	.000	1-1	2	95	.793	6.10	3.48
2020	Cin	NL	21	0	8	18.2	86	25	13	13	5	0	1	2	6	1	23	2	0	1	.000	0-0	4	96	.955	7.59	6.27
	9 ML YEARS		305	0	71	310.0	1286	270	124	114	33	11	14	12	116	10	341	27	22	14	.611	9-30	73	97	.681	3.47	3.31

Taylor Jones

Bats: R **Throws:** R **Pos:** DH-4;1B-3;PH-1   **Ht:** 6'7" **Wt:** 230 **Born:** 12/6/1993 **Age:** 27

Year	Team	Lg	G	AB	H	2B	3B	HR	(Hm	Rd)	TB	R	RBI	RC	TBB	IBB	SO	HBP	SH	SF	SB	CS	GDP	Avg	OBP	Slg	OPS
2020	Hou	AL	7	21	4	1	0	1	(0	1)	8	3	3	1	1	0	7	0	0	0	0	0	2	.190	.227	.381	.608

Caleb Joseph

Bats: R **Throws:** R **Pos:** C-3   **Ht:** 6'3" **Wt:** 205 **Born:** 6/18/1986 **Age:** 35

Year	Team	Lg	G	AB	H	2B	3B	HR	(Hm	Rd)	TB	R	RBI	RC	TBB	IBB	SO	HBP	SH	SF	SB	CS	GDP	Avg	OBP	Slg	OPS
2014	Bal	AL	82	246	51	9	0	9	(4	5)	87	22	28	22	17	0	69	3	6	3	0	1	6	.207	.264	.354	.618
2015	Bal	AL	100	320	75	16	1	11	(5	6)	126	38	49	44	27	2	72	3	3	1	0	0	7	.234	.299	.394	.693
2016	Bal	AL	49	132	23	3	0	0	(0	0)	26	7	0	0	7	0	28	0	2	0	0	0	6	.174	.216	.197	.413
2017	Bal	AL	89	254	65	14	1	8	(3	5)	105	31	28	28	10	0	72	1	1	0	0	0	7	.256	.287	.413	.700
2018	Bal	AL	82	265	58	14	2	3	(1	2)	85	28	17	19	10	0	68	3	1	1	2	1	3	.219	.254	.321	.575
2019	Ari	NL	20	38	8	2	0	0	(0	0)	10	5	3	3	1	0	10	1	1	0	0	0	0	.211	.250	.263	.513
2020	Tor	AL	3	8	1	0	0	1	(0	1)	4	2	2	0	1	0	1	0	0	0	0	0	0	.125	.222	.500	.722
	Postseason		3	9	2	0	0	0	(0	0)	2	0	1	1	0	0	4	0	0	1	0	0	0	.222	.200	.222	.422
	7 ML YEARS		425	1263	281	58	4	32	(13	19)	443	133	127	116	73	2	320	11	14	5	2	2	29	.222	.270	.351	.621

Matt Joyce

Bats: L **Throws:** R **Pos:** RF-27;LF-15;DH-10;PH-8   **Ht:** 6'2" **Wt:** 194 **Born:** 8/3/1984 **Age:** 36

Year	Team	Lg	G	AB	H	2B	3B	HR	(Hm	Rd)	TB	R	RBI	RC	TBB	IBB	SO	HBP	SH	SF	SB	CS	GDP	Avg	OBP	Slg	OPS
2008	Det	AL	92	242	61	16	3	12	(6	6)	119	40	33	36	31	0	65	2	0	2	0	2	3	.252	.339	.492	.831
2009	TB	AL	11	32	6	1	0	3	(2	1)	16	3	7	5	3	0	7	1	0	1	1	0	0	.188	.270	.500	.770
2010	TB	AL	77	216	52	15	3	10	(4	6)	103	30	40	41	40	2	55	2	0	3	2	2	2	.241	.360	.477	.837
2011	TB	AL	141	462	128	32	2	19	(11	8)	221	69	75	77	49	9	106	4	0	7	13	1	7	.277	.347	.478	.825
2012	TB	AL	124	399	96	18	3	17	(4	13)	171	55	59	59	55	4	102	6	1	1	4	3	10	.241	.341	.429	.769
2013	TB	AL	140	413	97	22	0	18	(8	10)	173	61	47	51	59	0	87	2	0	7	7	3	8	.235	.328	.419	.747
2014	TB	AL	140	418	106	23	2	9	(2	7)	160	51	52	52	62	4	111	4	0	9	2	5	11	.254	.349	.383	.732
2015	LAA	AL	93	247	43	12	1	5	(4	1)	72	17	21	15	30	1	67	4	1	2	0	3	5	.174	.272	.291	.564
2016	Pit	NL	140	231	56	10	2	13	(10	3)	107	45	42	47	59	4	67	3	0	0	1	1	9	.242	.403	.463	.866
2017	Oak	AL	141	469	114	33	0	25	(11	14)	222	78	68	70	66	0	113	2	0	7	4	1	10	.243	.335	.473	.808
2018	Oak	AL	83	207	43	9	0	7	(2	5)	73	34	15	20	35	2	53	1	1	2	0	2	3	.208	.322	.353	.675

Year Team	Lg	G	AB	H	2B	3B	HR	(Hm	Rd)	TB	R	RBI	RC	TBB	IBB	SO	HBP	SH	SF	SB	CS	GDP	Avg	OBP	Slg	OPS
2019 Atl	NL	129	200	59	10	0	7	(4	3)	90	32	23	39	38	0	45	0	0	0	0	1	3	.295	.408	.450	.858
2020 Mia	NL	46	127	32	4	0	2	(0	2)	42	16	14	17	20	0	41	0	0	1	1	0	3	.252	.351	.331	.682
Postseason		17	42	6	1	0	1	(0	1)	10	1	4	3	2	0	15	0	0	0	1	0	0	.143	.182	.238	.420
13 ML YEARS		1357	3663	893	205	15	147	(68	79)	1569	531	496	529	547	26	919	31	3	42	35	23	74	.244	.343	.428	.772

Aaron Judge

Bats: R **Throws:** R **Pos:** RF-25;DH-3;PH-2   **Ht:** 6'7" **Wt:** 282 **Born:** 4/26/1992 **Age:** 29

Year Team	Lg	G	AB	H	2B	3B	HR	(Hm	Rd)	TB	R	RBI	RC	TBB	IBB	SO	HBP	SH	SF	SB	CS	GDP	Avg	OBP	Slg	OPS
2016 NYY	AL	27	84	15	2	0	4	(3	1)	29	10	10	6	9	0	42	1	0	1	0	1	2	.179	.263	.345	.608
2017 NYY	AL	155	542	154	24	3	52	(33	19)	340	128	114	131	127	11	208	5	0	4	9	4	15	.284	.422	.627	1.049
2018 NYY	AL	112	413	115	22	0	27	(18	9)	218	77	67	82	76	3	152	4	0	5	6	3	10	.278	.392	.528	.919
2019 NYY	AL	102	378	103	18	1	27	(11	16)	204	75	55	70	64	4	141	3	0	1	3	2	11	.272	.381	.540	.921
2020 NYY	AL	28	101	26	3	0	9	(5	4)	56	23	22	19	10	0	32	2	0	0	0	1	5	.257	.336	.554	.891
Postseason		27	101	26	4	0	8	(4	4)	54	21	17	20	19	0	41	0	0	0	2	1	1	.257	.375	.535	.910
5 ML YEARS		424	1518	413	69	4	119	(70	49)	847	313	268	308	286	18	575	15	0	11	18	11	43	.272	.390	.558	.948

Jakob Junis

Pitches: R **Bats:** R **Pos:** SP-6; RP-2   JOO-nis   **Ht:** 6'3" **Wt:** 220 **Born:** 9/16/1992 **Age:** 28

Year Team	Lg	G	GS	GF	IP	BFP	H	R	ER	HR	SH	SF	HB	TBB	IBB	SO	WP	W	L	Pct	Sv-Op	Hld	Vel	OPS	ERC	ERA
2017 KC	AL	20	16	1	98.1	422	101	52	47	15	3	3	9	25	1	80	3	9	3	.750	0-0	0	91	.762	4.36	4.30
2018 KC	AL	30	30	0	177.0	758	182	94	86	32	4	8	15	43	1	164	9	9	12	.429	0-0	0	91	.773	4.49	4.37
2019 KC	AL	31	31	0	175.1	771	192	108	102	31	0	5	11	58	1	164	4	9	14	.391	0-0	0	92	.807	5.14	5.24
2020 KC	AL	8	6	0	25.1	114	35	18	18	7	0	1	2	6	1	19	2	0	2	.000	0-0	0	91	.958	7.50	6.39
4 ML YEARS		89	83	1	476.0	2065	510	272	253	85	7	17	37	132	4	427	18	27	31	.466	0-0	1	91	.794	4.85	4.78

Ariel Jurado

Pitches: R **Bats:** R **Pos:** SP-1   hurr-RAH-doe   **Ht:** 6'2" **Wt:** 240 **Born:** 1/30/1996 **Age:** 25

Year Team	Lg	G	GS	GF	IP	BFP	H	R	ER	HR	SH	SF	HB	TBB	IBB	SO	WP	W	L	Pct	Sv-Op	Hld	Vel	OPS	ERC	ERA
2018 Tex	AL	12	8	0	54.2	241	66	36	36	7	1	0	0	18	1	22	0	5	5	.500	0-0	0	92	.809	5.20	5.93
2019 Tex	AL	32	18	3	122.1	541	148	94	79	21	5	9	4	36	1	81	3	7	11	.389	0-0	1	92	.876	5.54	5.81
2020 NYM	NL	1	1	0	4.0	21	9	5	5	1	1	0	0	0	0	2	0	0	0	-	0-0	0	91	1.150	11.49	11.25
3 ML YEARS		45	27	3	181.0	803	223	135	120	29	7	9	4	54	2	105	3	12	16	.429	0-0	1	92	.863	5.55	5.97

Tommy Kahnle

Pitches: R **Bats:** R **Pos:** RP-1   KAIN-lee   **Ht:** 6'1" **Wt:** 230 **Born:** 8/7/1989 **Age:** 31

Year Team	Lg	G	GS	GF	IP	BFP	H	R	ER	HR	SH	SF	HB	TBB	IBB	SO	WP	W	L	Pct	Sv-Op	Hld	Vel	OPS	ERC	ERA
2014 Col	NL	54	0	7	68.2	285	51	39	32	7	2	3	1	31	2	63	7	2	1	.667	0-2	8	95	.628	2.91	4.19
2015 Col	NL	36	0	8	33.1	155	31	22	18	3	1	2	0	28	1	39	3	0	1	.000	2-3	10	96	.778	5.31	4.86
2016 CWS	AL	29	0	12	27.1	119	21	8	8	2	0	0	0	20	3	25	3	0	1	.000	1-2	4	97	.678	3.74	2.63
2017 2 Tms	AL	69	0	17	62.2	256	53	20	18	4	1	4	2	17	1	96	5	2	4	.333	0-6	15	98	.606	2.63	2.59
2018 NYY	AL	24	0	6	23.1	107	23	22	17	3	0	2	0	15	0	30	2	2	0	1.000	1-2	2	95	.811	5.11	6.56
2019 NYY	AL	72	0	5	61.1	248	45	27	25	9	0	1	2	20	0	88	8	3	2	.600	0-5	27	96	.635	2.79	3.67
2020 NYY	AL	1	0	0	1.0	6	1	0	0	0	0	0	0	1	1	3	0	0	0	-	0-0	1	98	.733	2.79	0.00
17 CWS	AL	37	0	10	36.0	141	28	12	10	3	1	2	0	7	1	60	2	1	3	.250	0-4	7	98	.571	2.04	2.50
17 NYY	AL	32	0	7	26.2	115	25	8	8	1	0	2	2	10	0	36	3	1	1	.500	0-2	8	98	.648	3.47	2.70
Postseason		15	0	3	19.1	71	10	5	5	2	0	0	0	5	0	18	0	1	0	1.000	1-1	2	98	.484	1.39	2.33
7 ML YEARS		285	0	56	277.2	1176	225	138	118	28	4	12	5	132	8	344	28	9	9	.500	4-20	67	96	.666	3.35	3.82

Rob Kaminsky

Pitches: L **Bats:** R **Pos:** RP-5   **Ht:** 6'0" **Wt:** 195 **Born:** 9/2/1994 **Age:** 26

Year Team	Lg	G	GS	GF	IP	BFP	H	R	ER	HR	SH	SF	HB	TBB	IBB	SO	WP	W	L	Pct	Sv-Op	Hld	Vel	OPS	ERC	ERA
2020 StL	NL	5	0	3	4.2	21	3	3	1	0	0	2	0	2	0	3	0	0	0	-	0-0	0	92	.438	1.54	1.93

James Kaprielian

Pitches: R **Bats:** R **Pos:** RP-2   ka-PRELL-ee-an   **Ht:** 6'3" **Wt:** 225 **Born:** 3/2/1994 **Age:** 27

Year Team	Lg	G	GS	GF	IP	BFP	H	R	ER	HR	SH	SF	HB	TBB	IBB	SO	WP	W	L	Pct	Sv-Op	Hld	Vel	OPS	ERC	ERA
2020 Oak	AL	2	0	0	3.2	17	4	3	3	2	0	0	0	2	0	4	0	0	0	-	0-0	0	95	1.020	8.51	7.36

James Karinchak

Pitches: R **Bats:** R **Pos:** RP-27   **Ht:** 6'3" **Wt:** 215 **Born:** 9/22/1995 **Age:** 25

Year Team	Lg	G	GS	GF	IP	BFP	H	R	ER	HR	SH	SF	HB	TBB	IBB	SO	WP	W	L	Pct	Sv-Op	Hld	Vel	OPS	ERC	ERA
2019 Cle	AL	5	0	4	5.1	22	3	1	1	0	0	1	0	1	0	8	2	0	0	-	0-0	0	97	.382	0.90	1.69
2020 Cle	AL	27	0	4	27.0	109	14	9	8	1	1	4	0	16	1	53	5	1	2	.333	1-4	8	96	.505	1.87	2.67
2 ML YEARS		32	0	8	32.1	131	17	10	9	1	1	5	0	17	1	61	7	1	2	.333	1-4	8	96	.484	1.65	2.51

Anthony Kay

Pitches: L Bats: L Pos: RP-13 **Ht: 6'0" Wt: 225 Born: 3/21/1995 Age: 26**

Year	Team	Lg	G	GS	GF	IP	BFP	H	R	ER	HR	SH	SF	HB	TBB	IBB	SO	WP	W	L	Pct	Sv-Op	Hld	Vel	OPS	ERC	ERA
2019	Tor	AL	3	2	0	14.0	63	15	9	9	0	0	0	1	5	0	13	1	1	0	1.000	0-0	0	93	.649	3.75	5.79
2020	Tor	AL	13	0	0	21.0	98	22	13	12	3	0	2	0	14	1	22	0	2	0	1.000	0-0	2	94	.867	5.61	5.14
	2 ML YEARS		16	2	0	35.0	161	37	22	21	3	0	2	1	19	1	35	1	3	0	1.000	0-0	2	94	.778	4.84	5.40

Keone Kela

Pitches: R Bats: R Pos: RP-3 KEY-oh-nee KELL-uh **Ht: 6'1" Wt: 220 Born: 4/16/1993 Age: 28**

Year	Team	Lg	G	GS	GF	IP	BFP	H	R	ER	HR	SH	SF	HB	TBB	IBB	SO	WP	W	L	Pct	Sv-Op	Hld	Vel	OPS	ERC	ERA
2015	Tex	AL	68	0	11	60.1	243	52	18	16	4	1	0	0	18	0	68	6	7	5	.583	1-4	22	96	.615	2.79	2.39
2016	Tex	AL	35	0	2	34.0	150	30	23	23	6	2	1	3	17	0	45	2	5	1	.833	0-1	15	96	.779	4.68	6.09
2017	Tex	AL	39	0	13	38.2	151	18	12	12	4	0	0	1	17	1	51	1	4	1	.800	2-3	11	96	.479	1.64	2.79
2018	2 Tms		54	0	36	52.0	212	38	19	19	5	1	1	0	19	2	66	6	3	4	.429	24-26	4	97	.605	2.43	3.29
2019	Pit	NL	32	0	8	29.2	119	19	7	7	3	0	0	1	11	0	33	1	2	0	1.000	1-5	6	96	.606	2.23	2.12
2020	Pit	NL	3	0	1	2.0	10	3	1	1	1	0	0	0	1	0	3	0	0	0	—	0-0	0	96	1.067	10.88	4.50
18	Tex	AL	38	0	31	36.2	152	28	14	14	3	1	1	0	14	1	44	4	3	3	.500	24-25	0	97	.602	2.55	3.44
18	Pit	NL	16	0	5	15.1	60	10	5	5	2	0	0	0	5	1	22	2	0	1	.000	0-1	4	97	.614	2.12	2.93
	Postseason		4	0	1	4.2	16	1	1	1	1	0	0	0	2	0	3	0	1	0	1.000	0-1	1	97	.473	1.27	1.93
	6 ML YEARS		231	0	71	216.2	885	160	80	78	23	4	2	5	83	3	266	16	21	11	.656	28-39	58	96	.620	2.73	3.24

Jarred Kelenic

Bats: L Throws: L Pos: CF KELL-nick **Ht: 6'1" Wt: 190 Born: 7/16/1999 Age: 21**

Year	Team	Lg	G	AB	H	2B	3B	HR	(Hm	Rd)	TB	R	RBI	RC	TBB	IBB	SO	HBP	SH	SF	SB	CS	GDP	Avg	OBP	Slg	OPS
2018	2 Tms	Low	56	220	63	10	6	6	(-	-)	103	42	42	40	26	0	50	4	0	1	15	1	1	.286	.371	.468	.839
2019	2 Tms	Low	96	360	108	27	4	17	(-	-)	194	69	51	75	42	0	94	3	0	3	17	7	4	.300	.375	.539	.914
2019	Ark	AA	21	83	21	4	1	6	(-	-)	45	11	17	15	8	0	17	0	0	1	3	0	2	.253	.315	.542	.857

Brad Keller

Pitches: R Bats: R Pos: SP-9 **Ht: 6'5" Wt: 250 Born: 7/27/1995 Age: 25**

Year	Team	Lg	G	GS	GF	IP	BFP	H	R	ER	HR	SH	SF	HB	TBB	IBB	SO	WP	W	L	Pct	Sv-Op	Hld	Vel	OPS	ERC	ERA
2018	KC	AL	41	20	2	140.1	583	133	50	48	7	0	3	2	50	1	96	8	9	6	.600	0-2	5	94	.653	3.39	3.08
2019	KC	AL	28	28	0	165.1	709	154	80	77	15	1	5	9	70	2	122	9	7	14	.333	0-0	0	93	.711	3.94	4.19
2020	KC	AL	9	9	0	54.2	215	39	16	15	2	0	3	2	17	0	35	1	5	3	.625	0-0	0	93	.513	2.06	2.47
	3 ML YEARS		78	57	2	360.1	1507	326	146	140	24	1	11	13	137	3	253	18	21	23	.477	0-2	5	94	.660	3.42	3.50

Kyle Keller

Pitches: R Bats: R Pos: RP-2 **Ht: 6'4" Wt: 205 Born: 4/28/1993 Age: 28**

Year	Team	Lg	G	GS	GF	IP	BFP	H	R	ER	HR	SH	SF	HB	TBB	IBB	SO	WP	W	L	Pct	Sv-Op	Hld	Vel	OPS	ERC	ERA
2019	Mia	NL	10	0	4	10.2	46	5	4	4	3	0	0	2	8	0	11	0	0	0	—	0-0	0	95	.715	4.53	3.38
2020	LAA	AL	2	0	1	2.1	13	3	2	2	0	0	0	0	2	0	1	1	0	0	—	0-0	0	94	.657	6.07	7.71
	2 ML YEARS		12	0	5	13.0	59	8	6	6	3	0	0	2	10	0	12	1	0	0	—	0-0	0	95	.701	4.83	4.15

Mitch Keller

Pitches: R Bats: R Pos: SP-5 **Ht: 6'2" Wt: 205 Born: 4/4/1996 Age: 25**

Year	Team	Lg	G	GS	GF	IP	BFP	H	R	ER	HR	SH	SF	HB	TBB	IBB	SO	WP	W	L	Pct	Sv-Op	Hld	Vel	OPS	ERC	ERA
2016	2 Tms	Low	24	24	0	130.1	511	101	36	34	4	3	2	11	19	0	138	10	9	5	.643	0--	-		.539	1.91	2.35
2017	2 Tms	Low	17	17	0	81.1	322	59	29	27	5	2	2	8	21	0	71	7	6	3	.667	0--	-		.552	2.29	2.99
2017	Altna	AA	6	6	0	34.2	142	25	14	12	2	1	1	2	11	0	45	0	2	2	.500	0--	-		.569	2.23	3.12
2018	Altna	AA	14	14	0	86.0	342	64	29	26	7	1	1	0	32	0	76	6	9	2	.818	0--	-		.632	2.57	2.72
2018	Indy	AAA	10	10	0	52.1	236	59	34	28	3	1	1	1	22	0	57	1	3	2	.600	0--	-		.771	4.59	4.82
2019	Indy	AAA	19	19	0	103.2	436	94	44	41	9	5	2	7	35	0	123	5	7	5	.583	0--	-		.695	3.52	3.56
2019	Pit	NL	11	11	0	48.0	227	72	41	38	6	1	2	1	16	0	65	2	1	5	.167	0-0	0	95	.940	7.13	7.13
2020	Pit	NL	5	5	0	21.2	87	9	7	7	4	0	0	1	18	0	16	2	1	1	.500	0-0	0	94	.660	3.51	2.91
	2 ML YEARS		16	16	0	69.2	314	81	48	45	10	1	2	2	34	0	81	4	2	6	.250	0-0	0	95	.868	5.94	5.81

Trevor Kelley

Pitches: R Bats: R Pos: RP-4 **Ht: 6'2" Wt: 210 Born: 10/20/1993 Age: 27**

Year	Team	Lg	G	GS	GF	IP	BFP	H	R	ER	HR	SH	SF	HB	TBB	IBB	SO	WP	W	L	Pct	Sv-Op	Hld	Vel	OPS	ERC	ERA
2019	Bos	AL	10	0	3	8.1	40	9	8	8	2	0	4	0	5	0	6	2	0	3	.000	0-0	0	89	.963	6.15	8.64
2020	Phi	NL	4	0	2	3.1	19	8	4	4	2	0	0	0	1	0	5	1	0	0	—	0-0	0	90	1.307	17.83	10.80
	2 ML YEARS		14	0	5	11.2	59	17	12	12	4	0	4	0	6	0	11	3	0	3	.000	0-0	0	89	1.084	9.10	9.26

Carson Kelly

Bats: R **Throws:** R **Pos:** C-38;PH-2;DH-1   **Ht:** 6'2" **Wt:** 210 **Born:** 7/14/1994 **Age:** 26

Year	Team	Lg	G	AB	H	2B	3B	HR	(Hm	Rd)	TB	R	RBI	RC	TBB	IBB	SO	HBP	SH	SF	SB	CS	GDP	Avg	OBP	Slg	OPS
2016	StL	NL	10	13	2	1	0	0	(0	0)	3	1	1	0	1	0	2	1	0	0	0	0	0	.154	.214	.231	.445
2017	StL	NL	34	69	12	3	0	0	(0	0)	15	5	6	4	5	0	11	1	0	0	0	0	3	.174	.240	.217	.457
2018	StL	NL	19	35	4	0	0	0	(0	0)	4	1	3	1	3	0	7	1	3	0	0	0	0	.114	.205	.114	.319
2019	Ari	NL	111	314	77	19	0	18	(4	14)	150	46	47	46	48	10	79	2	0	1	0	0	11	.245	.348	.478	.826
2020	Ari	NL	39	122	27	5	0	5	(2	3)	47	11	19	16	6	0	29	1	0	0	0	0	4	.221	.264	.385	.649
5 ML YEARS			213	553	122	28	0	23	(6	17)	219	64	76	67	62	10	128	6	3	1	0	0	18	.221	.305	.396	.701

Joe Kelly

Pitches: R **Bats:** R **Pos:** RP-11; SP-1   **Ht:** 6'1" **Wt:** 174 **Born:** 6/9/1988 **Age:** 33

Year	Team	Lg	G	GS	GF	IP	BFP	H	R	ER	HR	SH	SF	HB	TBB	IBB	SO	WP	W	L	Pct	Sv-Op	Hld	Vel	OPS	ERC	ERA
2012	StL	NL	24	16	4	107.0	457	112	50	42	10	4	1	3	36	2	75	4	5	7	.417	0-0	0	94	.740	4.17	3.53
2013	StL	NL	37	15	8	124.0	532	124	42	37	10	2	2	5	44	4	79	3	10	5	.667	0-1	0	95	.694	3.88	2.69
2014	2 Tms		17	17	0	96.1	415	88	48	45	8	2	4	7	42	0	66	3	6	4	.600	0-0	0	95	.693	3.92	4.20
2015	Bos	AL	25	25	0	134.1	587	145	76	72	15	0	5	6	49	0	110	9	10	6	.625	0-0	0	95	.769	4.68	4.82
2016	Bos	AL	20	6	6	40.0	188	44	23	23	5	0	4	2	24	0	48	0	4	0	1.000	0-1	2	96	.828	5.80	5.18
2017	Bos	AL	54	0	14	58.0	238	42	19	18	3	0	2	1	27	1	52	4	4	1	.800	0-4	13	99	.573	2.61	2.79
2018	Bos	AL	73	0	9	65.2	285	57	34	32	4	0	4	5	32	0	68	4	4	2	.667	2-7	21	98	.662	3.70	4.39
2019	LAD	NL	55	0	13	51.1	226	49	31	26	6	0	0	3	22	2	62	10	5	4	.556	1-6	8	98	.711	4.16	4.56
2020	LAD	NL	12	1	2	10.0	42	8	3	2	0	1	0	0	7	0	9	3	0	0	-	0-0	3	97	.681	3.57	1.80
14	StL	NL	7	7	0	35.0	156	41	19	17	3	1	1	3	10	0	25	3	2	2	.500	0-0	0	95	.774	4.82	4.37
14	Bos	AL	10	10	0	61.1	259	47	29	28	5	1	3	4	32	0	41	0	4	2	.667	0-0	0	95	.641	3.43	4.11
Postseason			28	4	2	49.1	210	43	21	19	3	1	0	2	18	2	45	5	3	3	.500	0-0	2	97	.614	3.02	3.47
9 ML YEARS			317	80	56	686.2	2970	669	326	297	61	8	23	32	283	9	569	40	48	29	.623	3-19	49	96	.713	4.08	3.89

Merrill Kelly

Pitches: R **Bats:** R **Pos:** SP-5   **Ht:** 6'2" **Wt:** 210 **Born:** 10/14/1988 **Age:** 32

Year	Team	Lg	G	GS	GF	IP	BFP	H	R	ER	HR	SH	SF	HB	TBB	IBB	SO	WP	W	L	Pct	Sv-Op	Hld	Vel	OPS	ERC	ERA
2019	Ari	NL	32	32	0	183.1	777	184	95	90	29	2	5	2	57	4	158	4	13	14	.481	0-0	0	92	.761	4.16	4.42
2020	Ari	NL	5	5	0	31.1	125	26	9	9	5	0	0	1	5	1	29	0	3	2	.600	0-0	0	92	.651	2.68	2.59
2 ML YEARS			37	37	0	214.2	902	210	104	99	34	2	5	3	62	5	187	4	16	16	.500	0-0	0	92	.746	3.93	4.15

Matt Kemp

Bats: R **Throws:** R **Pos:** DH-32;PH-13;LF-1   **Ht:** 6'4" **Wt:** 225 **Born:** 9/23/1984 **Age:** 36

Year	Team	Lg	G	AB	H	2B	3B	HR	(Hm	Rd)	TB	R	RBI	RC	TBB	IBB	SO	HBP	SH	SF	SB	CS	GDP	Avg	OBP	Slg	OPS
2006	LAD	NL	52	154	39	7	1	7	(4	3)	69	30	23	20	9	1	53	0	0	3	6	0	1	.253	.289	.448	.737
2007	LAD	NL	98	292	100	12	5	10	(9	1)	152	47	42	49	16	0	66	0	0	3	10	5	6	.342	.373	.521	.894
2008	LAD	NL	155	606	176	38	5	18	(14	4)	278	93	76	86	46	6	153	1	1	3	35	11	11	.290	.340	.459	.799
2009	LAD	NL	159	606	180	25	7	26	(13	13)	297	97	101	100	52	6	139	3	0	6	34	8	14	.297	.352	.490	.842
2010	LAD	NL	162	602	150	25	6	28	(15	13)	271	82	89	74	53	4	170	4	0	9	19	15	14	.249	.310	.450	.760
2011	LAD	NL	161	602	195	33	4	39	(19	20)	353	115	126	129	74	24	159	6	0	7	40	11	16	.324	.399	.586	.986
2012	LAD	NL	106	403	122	22	2	23	(13	10)	217	74	69	75	40	8	103	3	0	3	9	4	10	.303	.367	.538	.906
2013	LAD	NL	73	263	71	15	0	6	(0	6)	104	35	33	27	22	3	76	2	0	3	9	0	11	.270	.328	.395	.723
2014	LAD	NL	150	541	155	38	3	25	(17	8)	274	77	89	79	52	3	145	0	0	6	8	5	21	.287	.346	.506	.852
2015	SD	NL	154	596	158	31	3	23	(13	10)	264	80	100	81	39	0	147	5	0	8	12	2	17	.265	.312	.443	.755
2016	2 Tms		156	623	167	39	0	35	(14	21)	311	89	108	85	36	6	156	1	0	12	1	0	17	.268	.304	.499	.803
2017	Atl	NL	115	438	121	23	1	19	(7	12)	203	47	64	46	27	5	99	0	0	2	0	0	25	.276	.318	.463	.781
2018	LAD	NL	146	462	134	25	0	21	(11	10)	222	62	85	80	36	2	115	1	0	7	0	0	14	.290	.338	.481	.818
2019	Cin	NL	20	60	12	2	0	1	(1	0)	17	4	5	3	1	0	19	0	0	1	0	0	2	.200	.210	.283	.493
2020	Col	NL	43	117	28	3	0	6	(4	2)	49	18	21	22	15	1	41	0	0	0	1	0	5	.239	.326	.419	.745
16	SD	NL	100	409	107	24	0	23	(8	15)	200	54	69	58	16	3	100	0	0	6	0	0	8	.262	.285	.489	.774
16	Atl	NL	56	214	60	15	0	12	(6	6)	111	35	39	27	20	3	56	1	0	6	1	0	9	.280	.336	.519	.855
Postseason			33	102	24	4	0	4	(2	2)	40	7	10	3	6	1	34	0	0	1	0	2	4	.235	.275	.392	.667
15 ML YEARS			1750	6365	1808	338	37	287	(154	133)	3081	950	1031	956	518	69	1641	26	1	72	184	63	184	.284	.337	.484	.821

Tony Kemp

Bats: L **Throws:** R **Pos:** 2B-43;PR-5;PH-4;LF-3;DH-2   **Ht:** 5'6" **Wt:** 160 **Born:** 10/31/1991 **Age:** 29

Year	Team	Lg	G	AB	H	2B	3B	HR	(Hm	Rd)	TB	R	RBI	RC	TBB	IBB	SO	HBP	SH	SF	SB	CS	GDP	Avg	OBP	Slg	OPS
2016	Hou	AL	59	120	26	4	3	1	(1	0)	39	15	7	11	14	0	27	0	1	1	2	1	5	.217	.296	.325	.621
2017	Hou	AL	17	37	8	1	0	0	(0	0)	9	6	4	4	1	0	5	1	0	0	1	0	0	.216	.256	.243	.500
2018	Hou	AL	97	255	67	15	0	6	(1	5)	100	37	30	41	32	1	44	3	3	1	9	3	1	.263	.351	.392	.743
2019	2 Tms		110	245	52	9	4	8	(7	1)	93	31	29	28	23	1	47	6	1	4	4	4	4	.212	.291	.380	.671
2020	Oak	AL	49	93	23	5	0	0	(0	0)	28	15	4	11	15	0	14	3	1	2	3	1	0	.247	.363	.301	.664
19	Hou	AL	66	163	37	6	2	7	(6	1)	68	23	17	18	16	1	29	4	1	2	4	3	2	.227	.308	.417	.725
19	ChC	NL	44	82	15	3	2	1	(1	0)	25	8	12	10	7	0	18	2	0	2	0	1	2	.183	.258	.305	.563
Postseason			6	14	4	1	0	1	(1	0)	8	3	1	3	5	0	3	0	0	0	0	0	0	.286	.474	.571	1.045
5 ML YEARS			332	750	176	34	7	15	(9	6)	269	104	74	95	85	2	137	13	6	8	19	9	16	.235	.320	.359	.679

Howie Kendrick

Bats: R **Throws:** R **Pos:** DH-19;1B-6   **Ht:** 5'11" **Wt:** 225 **Born:** 7/12/1983 **Age:** 37

Year	Team	Lg	G	AB	H	2B	3B	HR	(Hm	Rd)	TB	R	RBI	RC	TBB	IBB	SO	HBP	SH	SF	SB	CS	GDP	Avg	OBP	Slg	OPS
2006	LAA	AL	72	267	76	21	1	4	(2	2)	111	25	30	32	9	2	44	4	0	3	6	0	5	.285	.314	.416	.730
2007	LAA	AL	88	338	109	24	2	5	(3	2)	152	55	39	41	9	2	61	4	1	1	5	4	15	.322	.347	.450	.796
2008	LAA	AL	92	340	104	26	2	3	(1	2)	143	43	37	50	12	3	58	4	1	4	11	4	8	.306	.333	.421	.754
2009	LAA	AL	105	374	109	21	3	10	(5	5)	166	61	61	58	20	1	71	4	2	0	11	4	8	.291	.334	.444	.778
2010	LAA	AL	158	616	172	41	4	10	(4	6)	251	67	75	81	28	2	94	5	4	5	14	4	16	.279	.313	.407	.721
2011	LAA	AL	140	537	153	30	6	18	(5	13)	249	86	63	69	33	3	119	10	3	0	14	6	18	.285	.338	.464	.802
2012	LAA	AL	147	550	158	32	3	8	(4	4)	220	57	57	65	29	1	115	4	6	5	14	6	26	.287	.325	.400	.725
2013	LAA	AL	122	478	142	21	4	13	(9	4)	210	55	54	57	23	5	89	6	3	3	6	3	16	.297	.335	.439	.775
2014	LAA	AL	157	617	181	33	5	7	(0	7)	245	85	75	94	48	8	110	4	3	2	14	5	15	.293	.347	.397	.744
2015	LAD	NL	117	464	137	22	2	9	(6	3)	190	64	54	62	27	1	82	2	1	1	6	2	17	.295	.336	.409	.746
2016	LAD	NL	146	487	124	26	2	8	(3	5)	178	65	40	55	50	2	96	3	0	3	10	2	20	.255	.326	.366	.691
2017	2 Tms	NL	91	305	96	16	3	9	(4	5)	145	40	41	47	22	0	68	5	0	2	12	5	8	.315	.368	.475	.844
2018	Was	NL	40	152	46	14	0	4	(3	1)	72	17	12	15	5	1	29	2	0	1	1	1	6	.303	.331	.474	.805
2019	Was	NL	121	334	115	23	1	17	(10	7)	191	61	62	58	27	1	49	4	0	5	2	1	11	.344	.395	.572	.966
2020	Was	NL	25	91	25	4	0	2	(1	1)	35	11	14	8	7	2	17	0	0	2	0	0	4	.275	.320	.385	.705
17	Phi	NL	39	141	48	8	1	2	(0	2)	64	16	16	23	11	0	30	3	0	1	8	3	4	.340	.397	.454	.851
17	Was	NL	52	164	48	8	2	7	(4	3)	81	24	25	24	11	0	38	2	0	1	4	2	4	.293	.343	.494	.837
	Postseason		50	168	40	8	1	4	(1	3)	62	19	18	16	7	3	34	0	2	1	4	0	6	.238	.267	.369	.636
	15 ML YEARS		1621	5950	1747	354	38	127	(60	67)	2558	792	724	792	349	34	1102	61	24	37	126	47	193	.294	.337	.430	.767

Ian Kennedy

Pitches: R **Bats:** R **Pos:** RP-14; SP-1   **Ht:** 6'0" **Wt:** 210 **Born:** 12/19/1984 **Age:** 36

Year	Team	Lg	G	GS	GF	IP	BFP	H	R	ER	HR	SH	SF	HB	TBB	IBB	SO	WP	W	L	Pct	Sv-Op	Hld	Vel	OPS	ERC	ERA
2007	NYY	AL	3	3	0	19.0	77	13	6	4	1	0	0	0	9	0	15	0	1	0	1.000	0-0	0	89	.565	2.42	1.89
2008	NYY	AL	10	9	1	39.2	194	50	37	36	5	1	4	1	26	0	27	3	0	4	.000	0-0	0	89	.917	6.93	8.17
2009	NYY	AL	1	0	0	1.0	6	0	0	0	0	0	0	1	2	0	1	0	0	0	-	0-0	1	92	.500	7.00	0.00
2010	Ari	NL	32	32	0	194.0	810	163	87	82	26	11	5	10	70	2	168	16	9	10	.474	0-0	0	89	.696	3.47	3.80
2011	Ari	NL	33	33	0	222.0	900	186	73	71	19	9	9	9	55	0	198	11	21	4	.840	0-0	0	90	.641	2.71	2.88
2012	Ari	NL	33	33	0	208.1	899	216	101	93	28	13	5	14	55	4	187	5	15	12	.556	0-0	0	90	.775	4.18	4.02
2013	2 Tms	NL	31	31	0	181.1	794	180	108	99	27	8	5	12	73	1	163	10	7	10	.412	0-0	0	90	.781	4.64	4.91
2014	SD	NL	33	33	0	201.0	846	189	85	81	16	9	8	4	70	4	207	11	13	13	.500	0-0	0	92	.698	3.47	3.63
2015	SD	NL	30	30	0	168.1	713	166	95	80	31	8	2	7	52	4	174	5	9	15	.375	0-0	0	91	.816	4.37	4.28
2016	KC	AL	33	33	0	195.2	818	173	81	80	33	1	5	13	66	1	184	4	11	11	.500	0-0	0	92	.722	3.94	3.68
2017	KC	AL	30	30	0	154.0	655	143	99	92	34	1	6	5	61	2	131	4	5	13	.278	0-0	0	92	.804	4.64	5.38
2018	KC	AL	22	22	0	119.2	518	125	66	62	20	4	2	1	40	2	105	4	3	9	.250	0-0	0	92	.779	4.51	4.66
2019	KC	AL	63	0	51	63.1	266	64	24	24	6	3	0	1	17	1	73	3	3	2	.600	30-34	1	94	.675	3.63	3.41
2020	KC	AL	15	1	1	14.0	69	20	17	14	7	1	0	1	5	1	15	0	0	2	.000	0-0	2	94	1.076	9.67	9.00
13	Ari	NL	21	21	0	124.0	549	128	79	72	18	8	5	10	48	1	108	9	3	8	.273	0-0	0	90	.798	4.82	5.23
13	SD	NL	10	10	0	57.1	245	52	29	27	9	0	0	2	25	0	55	1	4	2	.667	0-0	0	90	.744	4.26	4.24
	Postseason		2	2	0	12.2	57	13	6	6	1	0	2	3	3	0	8	1	0	1	.000	0-0	0	92	.782	4.25	4.26
	14 ML YEARS		369	290	53	1781.1	7565	1688	879	818	253	69	51	79	601	22	1648	76	97	105	.480	30-34	4	91	.744	3.98	4.13

Max Kepler

Bats: L **Throws:** L **Pos:** RF-44;CF-2;PH-1;PR-1   **Ht:** 6'4" **Wt:** 225 **Born:** 2/10/1993 **Age:** 28

Year	Team	Lg	G	AB	H	2B	3B	HR	(Hm	Rd)	TB	R	RBI	RC	TBB	IBB	SO	HBP	SH	SF	SB	CS	GDP	Avg	OBP	Slg	OPS
2015	Min	AL	3	7	1	0	0	0	(0	0)	1	0	0	0	0	0	3	0	0	0	0	0	0	.143	.143	.143	.286
2016	Min	AL	113	396	93	20	2	17	(8	9)	168	52	63	52	42	3	93	3	1	5	6	2	2	.235	.309	.424	.734
2017	Min	AL	147	511	124	32	2	19	(9	10)	217	67	69	68	47	2	114	6	1	3	6	1	5	.243	.312	.425	.737
2018	Min	AL	156	532	119	30	4	20	(12	8)	217	80	58	65	71	2	96	5	0	3	4	5	8	.224	.319	.408	.727
2019	Min	AL	134	524	132	32	0	36	(17	19)	272	98	90	90	60	0	99	8	0	4	1	5	5	.252	.336	.519	.855
2020	Min	AL	48	171	39	9	0	9	(3	6)	75	27	23	27	22	0	36	2	0	1	3	0	1	.228	.321	.439	.760
	Postseason		4	13	1	1	0	0	(0	0)	2	0	0	1	4	0	3	0	0	0	0	0	0	.077	.294	.154	.448
	6 ML YEARS		601	2141	508	123	8	101	(49	52)	950	324	303	302	242	7	441	24	2	16	20	13	21	.237	.319	.444	.763

Clayton Kershaw

Pitches: L **Bats:** L **Pos:** SP-10   **Ht:** 6'4" **Wt:** 225 **Born:** 3/19/1988 **Age:** 33

Year	Team	Lg	G	GS	GF	IP	BFP	H	R	ER	HR	SH	SF	HB	TBB	IBB	SO	WP	W	L	Pct	Sv-Op	Hld	Vel	OPS	ERC	ERA
2008	LAD	NL	22	21	0	107.2	470	109	51	51	11	3	3	1	52	3	100	7	5	5	.500	0-0	1	94	.756	4.53	4.26
2009	LAD	NL	31	30	1	171.0	701	119	55	53	7	11	2	1	91	4	185	11	8	8	.500	0-0	0	94	.588	2.60	2.79
2010	LAD	NL	32	32	0	204.1	848	160	73	66	13	8	4	7	81	9	212	15	13	10	.565	0-0	0	93	.615	2.72	2.91
2011	LAD	NL	33	33	0	233.1	912	174	66	59	15	11	2	3	54	2	248	5	21	5	.808	0-0	0	93	.554	2.00	2.28
2012	LAD	NL	33	33	0	227.2	901	170	70	64	16	18	4	5	63	5	229	6	14	9	.609	0-0	0	93	.593	2.20	2.53
2013	LAD	NL	33	33	0	236.0	908	164	55	48	11	8	3	3	52	2	232	12	16	9	.640	0-0	0	93	.521	1.65	1.83
2014	LAD	NL	27	27	0	198.1	749	139	42	39	9	6	1	2	31	0	239	7	21	3	.875	0-0	0	93	.521	1.53	1.77
2015	LAD	NL	33	33	0	232.2	890	163	62	55	15	4	0	5	42	1	301	9	16	7	.696	0-0	0	93	.521	1.67	2.13
2016	LAD	NL	21	21	0	149.0	544	97	31	28	8	4	1	2	11	1	172	6	12	4	.750	0-0	0	93	.472	1.23	1.69
2017	LAD	NL	27	27	0	175.0	679	136	49	45	23	4	3	0	30	0	202	4	18	4	.818	0-0	0	93	.604	2.27	2.31
2018	LAD	NL	26	26	0	161.1	650	139	55	49	17	3	2	2	29	0	155	10	9	5	.643	0-0	0	90	.630	2.56	2.73
2019	LAD	NL	29	28	0	178.1	706	145	63	60	28	6	1	2	41	0	189	1	16	5	.762	0-0	0	90	.664	2.86	3.03
2020	LAD	NL	10	10	0	58.1	221	41	18	14	8	0	1	1	8	0	62	0	6	2	.750	0-0	0	91	.591	1.90	2.16
	Postseason		32	25	2	158.1	645	130	83	78	24	6	5	4	45	5	170	10	9	11	.450	1-2	0	93	.664	3.04	4.43
	13 ML YEARS		357	354	1	2333.0	9179	1756	690	631	181	86	27	34	585	27	2526	88	175	76	.697	0-0	1	93	.581	2.17	2.43

228

Dallas Keuchel

Pitches: L **Bats:** L **Pos:** SP-11   KY-kull   **Ht:** 6'2" **Wt:** 220 **Born:** 1/1/1988 **Age:** 33

Year Team	Lg	G	GS	GF	IP	BFP	H	R	ER	HR	SH	SF	HB	TBB	IBB	SO	WP	W	L	Pct	Sv-Op	Hld	Vel	OPS	ERC	ERA
2012 Hou	NL	16	16	0	85.1	377	93	56	50	14	9	3	1	39	1	38	2	3	8	.273	0-0	0	88	.823	5.39	5.27
2013 Hou	AL	31	22	2	153.2	682	184	96	88	20	2	3	5	52	3	123	7	6	10	.375	0-0	2	89	.812	5.33	5.15
2014 Hou	AL	29	29	0	200.0	808	187	71	65	11	4	5	7	48	2	146	7	12	9	.571	0-0	0	90	.655	3.02	2.93
2015 Hou	AL	33	33	0	232.0	911	185	68	64	17	1	3	2	51	0	216	9	20	8	.714	0-0	0	90	.575	2.26	2.48
2016 Hou	AL	26	26	0	168.0	701	168	88	85	20	2	1	2	48	1	144	9	9	12	.429	0-0	0	89	.736	3.84	4.55
2017 Hou	AL	23	23	0	145.2	584	116	50	47	15	1	0	2	47	0	125	1	14	5	.737	0-0	0	89	.619	2.82	2.90
2018 Hou	AL	34	34	0	204.2	874	211	92	85	18	3	9	2	58	0	153	9	12	11	.522	0-0	0	89	.704	3.71	3.74
2019 Atl	NL	19	19	0	112.2	487	115	50	47	16	5	0	9	39	1	91	6	8	8	.500	0-0	0	88	.764	4.62	3.75
2020 CWS	AL	11	11	0	63.1	257	52	15	14	2	2	0	0	17	0	42	0	6	2	.750	0-0	0	87	.556	2.21	1.99
Postseason		12	11	1	59.2	247	52	24	23	8	4	1	0	20	3	52	1	4	2	.667	0-0	0	90	.702	3.27	3.47
9 ML YEARS		222	213	2	1365.1	5681	1311	586	545	133	29	24	30	399	8	1078	50	90	73	.552	0-0	2	89	.690	3.53	3.59

Mike Kickham

Pitches: L **Bats:** L **Pos:** RP-4; SP-2   KICK-em   **Ht:** 6'4" **Wt:** 220 **Born:** 12/12/1988 **Age:** 32

Year Team	Lg	G	GS	GF	IP	BFP	H	R	ER	HR	SH	SF	HB	TBB	IBB	SO	WP	W	L	Pct	Sv-Op	Hld	Vel	OPS	ERC	ERA
2013 SF	NL	12	3	5	28.1	144	46	34	32	8	2	1	0	10	2	29	2	0	3	.000	0-0	0	90	1.036	8.75	10.16
2014 SF	NL	2	0	0	2.0	16	8	5	5	1	0	0	0	1	0	1	0	0	0	-	0-0	0	91	1.296	29.66	22.50
2020 Bos	AL	6	2	2	14.0	70	21	12	12	6	0	0	2	5	1	17	0	1	1	.500	0-0	0	89	1.083	10.10	7.71
3 ML YEARS		20	5	7	44.1	230	75	51	49	15	2	1	2	16	3	47	2	1	4	.200	0-0	0	90	1.068	10.01	9.95

Carter Kieboom

Bats: R **Throws:** R **Pos:** 3B-31;DH-1;PH-1;PR-1   **Ht:** 6'2" **Wt:** 210 **Born:** 9/3/1997 **Age:** 23

Year Team	Lg	G	AB	H	2B	3B	HR	(Hm	Rd)	TB	R	RBI	RC	TBB	IBB	SO	HBP	SH	SF	SB	CS	GDP	Avg	OBP	Slg	OPS
2016 Nats	R	36	135	33	8	4	4	(-	-)	61	22	25	20	12	0	43	5	0	3	1	2	4	.244	.323	.452	.774
2017 3 Tms	Low	61	219	65	16	0	9	(-	-)	108	41	35	43	32	3	42	4	0	0	3	2	5	.297	.396	.493	.889
2018 Ptomc	A+	61	245	73	15	0	11	(-	-)	121	48	46	49	36	0	50	1	0	3	1	0	5	.298	.386	.494	.880
2018 Hrsbrg	AA	62	248	66	16	1	5	(-	-)	99	36	23	34	22	0	59	2	0	1	3	1	5	.266	.330	.399	.729
2019 Fresno	AAA	109	412	125	24	3	16	(-	-)	203	79	79	87	68	1	100	9	0	5	5	2	11	.303	.409	.493	.902
2019 Was	NL	11	39	5	0	0	2	(2	0)	11	4	2	0	4	1	16	0	0	0	0	0	0	.128	.209	.282	.491
2020 Was	NL	33	99	20	1	0	0	(0	0)	21	15	9	10	17	0	33	5	0	1	0	1	6	.202	.344	.212	.556
2 ML YEARS		44	138	25	1	0	2	(2	0)	32	19	11	10	21	1	49	5	0	1	0	1	6	.181	.309	.232	.541

Kevin Kiermaier

Bats: L **Throws:** R **Pos:** CF-46;PH-6;PR-1   KEER-my-urr   **Ht:** 6'1" **Wt:** 210 **Born:** 4/22/1990 **Age:** 31

Year Team	Lg	G	AB	H	2B	3B	HR	(Hm	Rd)	TB	R	RBI	RC	TBB	IBB	SO	HBP	SH	SF	SB	CS	GDP	Avg	OBP	Slg	OPS
2013 TB	AL	1	0	0	0	0	0	(0	0)	0	0	0	0	0	0	0	0	0	0	0	0	0	-	-	-	-
2014 TB	AL	108	331	87	16	8	10	(4	6)	149	35	35	37	23	2	71	3	5	2	5	4	3	.263	.315	.450	.765
2015 TB	AL	151	505	133	25	12	10	(5	5)	212	62	40	66	24	0	95	2	2	2	18	5	7	.263	.298	.420	.718
2016 TB	AL	105	366	90	20	2	12	(5	7)	150	55	37	54	40	1	74	7	0	1	21	3	5	.246	.331	.410	.741
2017 TB	AL	98	380	105	15	3	15	(8	7)	171	56	39	53	31	2	99	5	4	1	16	7	3	.276	.338	.450	.788
2018 TB	AL	88	332	72	12	9	7	(4	3)	123	44	29	30	25	2	91	6	2	2	10	5	4	.217	.282	.370	.653
2019 TB	AL	129	447	102	20	7	14	(7	7)	178	60	55	56	26	2	104	5	1	1	19	5	8	.228	.278	.398	.676
2020 TB	AL	49	138	30	5	3	3	(0	3)	50	16	22	20	20	1	42	1	0	0	8	1	2	.217	.321	.362	.683
Postseason		7	22	3	1	0	1	(1	0)	7	1	3	2	0	0	7	0	0	0	0	0	0	.136	.136	.318	.455
8 ML YEARS		729	2499	619	113	44	71	(33	38)	1033	328	257	316	189	10	576	29	14	9	97	30	32	.248	.307	.413	.720

Yusei Kikuchi

Pitches: L **Bats:** L **Pos:** SP-9   **Ht:** 6'0" **Wt:** 200 **Born:** 6/17/1991 **Age:** 30

Year Team	Lg	G	GS	GF	IP	BFP	H	R	ER	HR	SH	SF	HB	TBB	IBB	SO	WP	W	L	Pct	Sv-Op	Hld	Vel	OPS	ERC	ERA
2019 Sea	AL	32	32	0	161.2	721	195	109	98	36	0	5	6	50	0	116	5	6	11	.353	0-0	0	92	.888	5.97	5.46
2020 Sea	AL	9	9	0	47.0	194	41	27	27	3	0	2	0	20	0	47	3	2	4	.333	0-0	0	95	.681	3.31	5.17
2 ML YEARS		41	41	0	208.2	915	236	136	125	39	0	7	6	70	0	163	8	8	15	.348	0-0	0	93	.845	5.34	5.39

Franklyn Kilome

Pitches: R **Bats:** R **Pos:** RP-4   **Ht:** 6'6" **Wt:** 175 **Born:** 6/25/1995 **Age:** 26

Year Team	Lg	G	GS	GF	IP	BFP	H	R	ER	HR	SH	SF	HB	TBB	IBB	SO	WP	W	L	Pct	Sv-Op	Hld	Vel	OPS	ERC	ERA
2020 NYM	NL	4	0	2	11.1	58	14	14	14	5	1	0	1	9	0	13	1	0	1	.000	1-1	0	94	1.102	10.43	11.12

Kwang-hyun Kim

Pitches: L **Bats:** L **Pos:** SP-7; RP-1   **Ht:** 6'2" **Wt:** 195 **Born:** 7/22/1988 **Age:** 32

Year Team	Lg	G	GS	GF	IP	BFP	H	R	ER	HR	SH	SF	HB	TBB	IBB	SO	WP	W	L	Pct	Sv-Op	Hld	Vel	OPS	ERC	ERA
2020 StL	NL	8	7	1	39.0	154	28	9	7	3	0	0	0	12	2	24	1	3	0	1.000	1-1	0	90	.584	2.09	1.62

Craig Kimbrel

Pitches: R **Bats:** R **Pos:** RP-18 KIM-brull **Ht:** 6'0" **Wt:** 215 **Born:** 5/28/1988 **Age:** 33

Year	Team	Lg	G	GS	GF	IP	BFP	H	R	ER	HR	SH	SF	HB	TBB	IBB	SO	WP	W	L	Pct	Sv-Op	Hld	Vel	OPS	ERC	ERA
2010	Atl	NL	21	0	7	20.2	88	9	2	1	0	0	0	0	16	1	40	4	4	0	1.000	1-1	2	95	.437	1.72	0.44
2011	Atl	NL	79	0	64	77.0	306	48	19	18	3	1	2	1	32	1	127	4	4	3	.571	**46-54**	0	96	.499	1.88	2.10
2012	Atl	NL	63	0	56	62.2	231	27	7	7	3	0	0	2	14	0	116	5	3	1	.750	42-45	0	97	.358	0.93	1.01
2013	Atl	NL	68	0	60	67.0	258	39	10	9	4	0	0	3	20	2	98	3	4	3	.571	50-54	0	97	.487	1.58	1.21
2014	Atl	NL	63	0	54	61.2	244	30	13	11	2	3	0	2	26	0	95	6	0	3	.000	**47-51**	0	97	.430	1.41	1.61
2015	SD	NL	61	0	53	59.1	239	40	19	17	6	0	0	1	22	1	87	4	4	2	.667	39-43	0	97	.569	2.31	2.58
2016	Bos	AL	57	0	47	53.0	220	28	22	20	4	1	1	4	30	0	83	6	2	6	.250	31-33	1	97	.539	2.32	3.40
2017	Bos	AL	67	0	51	69.0	254	33	11	11	6	1	0	4	14	0	126	5	5	0	1.000	35-39	1	98	.444	1.21	1.43
2018	Bos	AL	63	0	57	62.1	247	31	19	19	7	1	0	2	31	0	96	7	5	1	.833	42-47	0	97	.565	2.07	2.74
2019	ChC	NL	23	0	17	20.2	96	21	15	15	9	0	1	2	12	0	30	0	0	4	.000	13-16	0	96	1.019	7.90	6.53
2020	ChC	NL	18	0	11	15.1	69	10	9	9	2	0	0	2	12	1	28	4	0	1	.000	2-3	0	97	.693	4.20	5.28
	Postseason		19	0	15	20.2	87	14	10	9	2	0	1	3	12	0	25	2	0	1	.000	7-7	1	98	.671	3.64	3.92
	11 ML YEARS		583	0	477	568.2	2252	316	146	137	46	7	4	23	229	6	926	48	31	24	.564	348-386	7	97	.513	1.85	2.17

Isiah Kiner-Falefa

Bats: R **Throws:** R **Pos:** 3B-46;SS-15;PH-1 **Ht:** 5'11" **Wt:** 190 **Born:** 3/23/1995 **Age:** 26

Year	Team	Lg	G	AB	H	2B	3B	HR	(Hm	Rd)	TB	R	RBI	RC	TBB	IBB	SO	HBP	SH	SF	SB	CS	GDP	Avg	OBP	Slg	OPS
2018	Tex	AL	111	356	93	18	2	4	(0	4)	127	43	34	34	28	1	62	6	5	1	7	5	14	.261	.325	.357	.682
2019	Tex	AL	65	202	48	12	1	1	(0	1)	65	23	21	18	14	0	49	4	1	1	3	0	9	.238	.299	.322	.620
2020	Tex	AL	58	211	59	4	3	3	(1	2)	78	28	10	26	14	0	32	2	0	1	8	5	6	.280	.329	.370	.699
	3 ML YEARS		234	769	200	34	6	8	(1	7)	270	94	65	78	56	1	143	12	6	3	18	10	29	.260	.319	.351	.670

John King

Pitches: L **Bats:** L **Pos:** RP-6 **Ht:** 6'2" **Wt:** 215 **Born:** 9/14/1994 **Age:** 26

Year	Team	Lg	G	GS	GF	IP	BFP	H	R	ER	HR	SH	SF	HB	TBB	IBB	SO	WP	W	L	Pct	Sv-Op	Hld	Vel	OPS	ERC	ERA
2020	Tex	AL	6	0	0	10.1	51	13	8	7	2	0	0	2	4	0	9	0	1	0	1.000	0-1	0	93	.839	6.83	6.10

Michael King

Pitches: R **Bats:** R **Pos:** RP-5; SP-4 **Ht:** 6'3" **Wt:** 210 **Born:** 5/25/1995 **Age:** 26

Year	Team	Lg	G	GS	GF	IP	BFP	H	R	ER	HR	SH	SF	HB	TBB	IBB	SO	WP	W	L	Pct	Sv-Op	Hld	Vel	OPS	ERC	ERA
2019	NYY	AL	1	0	0	2.0	9	2	1	0	0	0	0	0	0	0	1	0	0	0	-	0-0	0	92	.444	1.68	0.00
2020	NYY	AL	9	4	1	26.2	121	30	23	23	5	0	0	2	11	0	26	0	1	2	.333	0-0	0	93	.846	5.80	7.76
	2 ML YEARS		10	4	1	28.2	130	32	24	23	5	0	0	2	11	0	27	0	1	2	.333	0-0	0	93	.816	5.44	7.22

Scott Kingery

Bats: R **Throws:** R **Pos:** 2B-29;CF-9;PR-2;SS-1 **Ht:** 5'10" **Wt:** 180 **Born:** 4/29/1994 **Age:** 27

Year	Team	Lg	G	AB	H	2B	3B	HR	(Hm	Rd)	TB	R	RBI	RC	TBB	IBB	SO	HBP	SH	SF	SB	CS	GDP	Avg	OBP	Slg	OPS
2018	Phi	NL	147	452	102	23	2	8	(6	2)	153	55	35	39	24	1	126	3	0	5	10	3	2	.226	.267	.338	.605
2019	Phi	NL	126	458	118	34	4	19	(10	9)	217	64	55	63	34	1	147	5	1	2	15	4	3	.258	.315	.474	.788
2020	Phi	NL	36	113	18	5	0	3	(1	2)	32	12	6	6	9	0	35	1	1	0	0	0	1	.159	.228	.283	.511
	3 ML YEARS		309	1023	238	62	6	30	(17	13)	402	131	96	108	67	2	308	9	2	7	25	7	6	.233	.284	.393	.677

Tyler Kinley

Pitches: R **Bats:** R **Pos:** RP-24 **Ht:** 6'4" **Wt:** 220 **Born:** 1/31/1991 **Age:** 30

Year	Team	Lg	G	GS	GF	IP	BFP	H	R	ER	HR	SH	SF	HB	TBB	IBB	SO	WP	W	L	Pct	Sv-Op	Hld	Vel	OPS	ERC	ERA
2018	2 Tms		13	0	4	11.0	57	15	15	15	2	0	0	1	8	2	13	3	0	0		0-0	0	97	.942	8.25	12.27
2019	Mia	NL	52	0	13	49.1	221	43	20	20	5	1	2	1	36	2	46	3	3	1	.750	1-3	1	95	.723	4.71	3.65
2020	Col	NL	24	0	4	23.2	96	13	15	14	2	1	2	3	12	0	26	4	0	2	.000	0-0	4	96	.564	2.52	5.32
18	Min	AL	4	0	3	3.1	23	9	9	9	2	0	0	0	4	0	4	2	0	0	-	0-0	0	96	1.407	25.66	24.30
18	Mia	NL	9	0	1	7.2	34	6	6	6	0	0	0	1	4	2	9	1	0	0		0-0	0	97	.634	2.62	7.04
	3 ML YEARS		89	0	21	84.0	374	71	50	49	9	2	4	5	56	4	85	10	3	3	.500	1-3	5	96	.716	4.48	5.25

Brandon Kintzler

Pitches: R **Bats:** R **Pos:** RP-24 **Ht:** 5'10" **Wt:** 200 **Born:** 8/1/1984 **Age:** 36

Year	Team	Lg	G	GS	GF	IP	BFP	H	R	ER	HR	SH	SF	HB	TBB	IBB	SO	WP	W	L	Pct	Sv-Op	Hld	Vel	OPS	ERC	ERA
2010	Mil	NL	7	0	2	7.1	33	10	6	6	2	1	0	0	4	1	9	1	0	1	.000	0-0	0	93	1.045	8.67	7.36
2011	Mil	NL	9	0	3	14.2	61	14	9	6	3	0	2	0	3	0	15	0	1	1	.500	0-0	0	93	.725	3.65	3.68
2012	Mil	NL	14	0	1	16.2	72	18	7	7	1	0	0	0	7	1	14	1	3	0	1.000	0-0	2	93	.732	4.30	3.78
2013	Mil	NL	71	0	11	77.0	305	66	26	23	2	4	2	1	16	2	58	1	3	3	.500	0-4	26	92	.567	2.21	2.69
2014	Mil	NL	64	0	13	58.1	239	62	22	21	8	4	1	0	16	3	31	1	3	3	.500	0-3	8	92	.781	4.28	3.24
2015	Mil	NL	7	0	4	7.0	36	12	6	5	1	0	0	0	5	0	7	1	0	1	.000	0-0	0	91	1.021	10.76	6.43
2016	Min	AL	54	0	36	54.1	224	59	22	19	5	0	0	2	8	1	35	0	2	3	.400	17-20	1	93	.705	3.68	3.15
2017	2 Tms		72	0	45	71.1	288	66	25	24	5	1	2	3	16	2	39	1	4	3	.571	29-35	10	93	.638	2.99	3.03
2018	2 Tms	NL	70	0	15	60.2	263	67	31	31	5	1	2	4	22	5	43	1	3	3	.500	2-5	19	93	.787	4.62	4.60
2019	ChC	NL	62	0	10	57.0	227	45	18	17	5	4	4	4	13	4	48	0	3	3	.500	1-3	17	93	.632	2.47	2.68

Year	Team	Lg	G	GS	GF	IP	BFP	H	R	ER	HR	SH	SF	HB	TBB	IBB	SO	WP	W	L	Pct	Sv-Op	Hld	Vel	OPS	ERC	ERA
2020	Mia	NL	24	0	21	24.1	101	21	7	6	3	0	1	0	11	3	14	0	2	3	.400	12-14	1	91	.710	3.57	2.22
17	Min	AL	45	0	41	45.1	182	41	15	14	3	0	2	2	11	1	27	1	2	2	.500	28-32	0	93	.626	2.97	2.78
17	Was	NL	27	0	4	26.0	106	25	10	10	2	1	0	1	5	1	12	0	2	1	.667	1-3	10	93	.659	3.04	3.46
18	Was	NL	45	0	8	42.2	175	40	17	17	2	1	0	3	13	3	31	1	1	2	.333	2-5	15	93	.689	3.28	3.59
18	ChC	NL	25	0	7	18.0	88	27	14	14	3	0	2	1	9	2	12	0	2	1	.667	0-0	4	93	.986	8.26	7.00
Postseason			3	0	1	3.1	12	1	2	2	0	1	0	1	2	0	2	0	0	1	.000	0-0	0	93	.614	1.96	5.40
11 ML YEARS			454	0	161	448.2	1849	440	179	165	40	11	11	14	121	21	313	7	22	23	.489	61-84	84	93	.698	3.51	3.31

Jason Kipnis

Bats: L **Throws:** R **Pos:** 2B-36;DH-6;PH-3;1B-1 KIP-niss **Ht:** 5'11" **Wt:** 200 **Born:** 4/3/1987 **Age:** 34

Year	Team	Lg	G	AB	H	2B	3B	HR	(Hm	Rd)	TB	R	RBI	RC	TBB	IBB	SO	HBP	SH	SF	SB	CS	GDP	Avg	OBP	Slg	OPS
2011	Cle	AL	36	136	37	9	1	7	(3	4)	69	24	19	22	11	0	34	2	0	1	5	0	0	.272	.333	.507	.841
2012	Cle	AL	152	591	152	22	4	14	(5	9)	224	86	76	88	67	2	109	5	3	6	31	7	12	.257	.335	.379	.714
2013	Cle	AL	149	564	160	36	4	17	(7	10)	255	86	84	99	76	3	143	3	5	10	30	7	10	.284	.366	.452	.818
2014	Cle	AL	129	500	120	25	1	6	(3	3)	165	61	41	44	50	2	100	2	1	2	22	3	15	.240	.310	.330	.640
2015	Cle	AL	141	565	171	43	7	9	(6	3)	255	86	52	92	57	6	107	9	4	6	12	8	5	.303	.372	.451	.823
2016	Cle	AL	156	610	168	41	4	23	(13	10)	286	91	82	90	60	0	146	6	5	7	15	3	21	.275	.343	.469	.811
2017	Cle	AL	90	336	78	25	0	12	(5	7)	139	43	35	42	28	0	71	2	2	5	6	2	0	.232	.291	.414	.705
2018	Cle	AL	147	530	122	28	1	18	(13	5)	206	65	75	80	60	1	112	7	1	3	7	1	5	.230	.315	.389	.704
2019	Cle	AL	121	458	112	23	1	17	(6	11)	188	52	65	63	40	2	88	2	5	6	7	2	7	.245	.304	.410	.715
2020	ChC	NL	44	114	27	8	1	3	(3	0)	46	13	16	20	18	0	41	1	0	2	1	0	1	.237	.341	.404	.744
Postseason			24	96	19	3	1	4	(2	2)	36	9	9	9	2	0	30	1	0	0	0	0	1	.198	.222	.375	.597
10 ML YEARS			1165	4404	1147	260	24	126	(64	62)	1833	607	545	640	467	16	951	39	26	48	136	33	76	.260	.333	.416	.750

Alejandro Kirk

Bats: R **Throws:** R **Pos:** C-7;DH-1;PH-1 **Ht:** 5'8" **Wt:** 265 **Born:** 11/6/1998 **Age:** 22

Year	Team	Lg	G	AB	H	2B	3B	HR	(Hm	Rd)	TB	R	RBI	RC	TBB	IBB	SO	HBP	SH	SF	SB	CS	GDP	Avg	OBP	Slg	OPS
2020	Tor	AL	9	24	9	2	0	1	(1	0)	14	4	3	5	1	0	4	0	0	0	0	0	0	.375	.400	.583	.983

Andrew Kittredge

Pitches: R **Bats:** R **Pos:** RP-7; SP-1 **Ht:** 6'1" **Wt:** 230 **Born:** 3/17/1990 **Age:** 31

Year	Team	Lg	G	GS	GF	IP	BFP	H	R	ER	HR	SH	SF	HB	TBB	IBB	SO	WP	W	L	Pct	Sv-Op	Hld	Vel	OPS	ERC	ERA
2017	TB	AL	15	0	2	15.1	66	13	4	3	2	1	0	0	6	1	14	1	0	1	.000	0-0	0	94	.665	3.19	1.76
2018	TB	AL	33	3	4	38.1	181	54	34	33	7	1	2	1	17	5	30	1	3	2	.600	0-0	0	93	.956	7.35	7.75
2019	TB	AL	37	7	10	49.2	210	51	25	23	7	0	2	2	12	0	58	2	1	0	1.000	0-0	2	95	.717	4.03	4.17
2020	TB	AL	8	1	1	8.0	31	8	2	2	0	0	0	0	2	0	3	0	0	0	-	1-1	1	94	.667	3.09	2.25
4 ML YEARS			93	11	17	111.1	488	126	65	61	16	2	4	3	37	6	105	4	4	3	.571	1-1	4	94	.794	4.91	4.93

Branden Kline

Pitches: R **Bats:** R **Pos:** RP-3 **Ht:** 6'3" **Wt:** 210 **Born:** 9/29/1991 **Age:** 29

Year	Team	Lg	G	GS	GF	IP	BFP	H	R	ER	HR	SH	SF	HB	TBB	IBB	SO	WP	W	L	Pct	Sv-Op	Hld	Vel	OPS	ERC	ERA
2019	Bal	AL	34	0	8	41.0	183	44	28	27	9	1	1	1	19	0	34	3	1	4	.200	0-1	5	96	.860	5.76	5.93
2020	Bal	AL	3	0	1	5.0	20	2	1	1	0	0	0	0	3	0	7	0	0	0	-	0-0	0	95	.426	1.32	1.80
2 ML YEARS			37	0	9	46.0	203	46	29	28	9	1	1	1	22	0	41	3	1	4	.200	0-1	5	96	.818	5.18	5.48

Corey Kluber

Pitches: R **Bats:** R **Pos:** SP-1 CLUE-burr **Ht:** 6'4" **Wt:** 215 **Born:** 4/10/1986 **Age:** 35

Year	Team	Lg	G	GS	GF	IP	BFP	H	R	ER	HR	SH	SF	HB	TBB	IBB	SO	WP	W	L	Pct	Sv-Op	Hld	Vel	OPS	ERC	ERA
2011	Cle	AL	3	0	2	4.1	25	6	4	4	0	0	0	2	3	0	5	1	0	0	-	0-0	0	92	.740	8.12	8.31
2012	Cle	AL	12	12	0	63.0	281	76	44	36	9	1	0	4	18	0	54	2	2	5	.286	0-0	0	93	.834	5.38	5.14
2013	Cle	AL	26	24	1	147.1	608	153	67	63	15	4	2	5	33	0	136	1	11	5	.688	0-0	0	93	.729	3.83	3.85
2014	Cle	AL	34	34	0	235.2	951	207	72	64	14	5	2	6	51	3	269	3	18	9	.667	0-0	0	93	.624	2.57	2.44
2015	Cle	AL	32	32	0	222.0	886	189	92	86	22	7	4	11	45	3	245	6	9	16	.360	0-0	0	95	.650	2.74	3.49
2016	Cle	AL	32	32	0	215.0	860	170	82	75	22	6	2	7	57	1	227	5	18	9	.667	0-0	0	92	.631	2.62	3.14
2017	Cle	AL	29	29	0	203.2	777	141	56	51	21	3	1	5	36	2	265	4	18	4	.818	0-0	0	93	.556	1.83	2.25
2018	Cle	AL	33	33	0	215.0	842	179	75	69	25	2	2	3	34	0	222	2	20	7	.741	0-0	0	92	.624	2.47	2.89
2019	Cle	AL	7	7	0	35.2	168	44	26	23	4	1	1	3	15	0	38	1	2	3	.400	0-0	0	92	.824	5.87	5.80
2020	Tex	AL	1	1	0	1.0	3	0	0	0	0	0	0	0	1	0	1	0	0	0	-	0-0	0	92	.333	1.26	0.00
Postseason			9	9	0	45.1	194	44	20	20	10	0	1	5	13	0	47	1	4	3	.571	0-0	0	92	.787	4.75	3.97
10 ML YEARS			209	204	3	1342.2	5401	1165	518	471	132	29	14	46	293	9	1462	25	98	58	.628	0-0	0	93	.649	2.82	3.16

Andrew Knapp

Bats: B Throws: R Pos: C-29;PH-5;DH-2;1B-1   Ht: 6'1" Wt: 189 Born: 11/9/1991 Age: 29

Year	Team	Lg	G	AB	H	2B	3B	HR	(Hm	Rd)	TB	R	RBI	RC	TBB	IBB	SO	HBP	SH	SF	SB	CS	GDP	Avg	OBP	Slg	OPS
2017	Phi	NL	56	171	44	8	1	3	(2	1)	63	26	13	20	31	4	56	0	0	2	1	0	5	.257	.368	.368	.736
2018	Phi	NL	84	187	37	6	2	4	(1	3)	59	19	15	15	24	1	75	2	1	1	1	0	2	.198	.294	.316	.610
2019	Phi	NL	74	136	29	9	0	2	(0	2)	44	12	8	11	18	2	51	3	3	0	0	0	2	.213	.318	.324	.642
2020	Phi	NL	33	72	20	4	1	2	(0	2)	32	9	15	17	15	0	19	1	0	1	0	0	1	.278	.404	.444	.849
	4 ML YEARS		247	566	130	27	4	11	(3	8)	198	66	51	63	88	7	201	6	4	4	2	0	10	.230	.337	.350	.687

Corey Knebel

Pitches: R Bats: R Pos: RP-15   kuh-NAY-bull   Ht: 6'3" Wt: 224 Born: 11/26/1991 Age: 29

Year	Team	Lg	G	GS	GF	IP	BFP	H	R	ER	HR	SH	SF	HB	TBB	IBB	SO	WP	W	L	Pct	Sv-Op	Hld	Vel	OPS	ERC	ERA
2014	Det	AL	8	0	4	8.2	39	11	7	6	0	0	0	0	3	0	11	1	0	0	-	0-0	0	94	.776	4.65	6.23
2015	Mil	NL	48	0	15	50.1	209	44	18	18	8	0	0	2	17	1	58	1	0	0	-	0-1	3	95	.744	3.69	3.22
2016	Mil	NL	35	0	7	32.2	145	32	20	17	3	0	1	1	16	3	38	1	1	4	.200	2-4	13	95	.708	4.18	4.68
2017	Mil	NL	76	0	48	76.0	309	48	15	15	6	0	0	2	40	5	126	2	1	4	.200	39-45	11	97	.568	2.51	1.78
2018	Mil	NL	57	0	29	55.1	223	38	23	22	7	0	1	4	22	0	88	0	4	3	.571	16-19	6	97	.659	2.90	3.58
2020	Mil	NL	15	0	2	13.1	62	15	9	9	4	0	0	0	8	0	15	0	0	0	-	0-2	0	94	.927	7.20	6.08
	Postseason		9	0	1	10.0	33	2	1	1	0	0	0	1	3	0	14	0	1	0	1.000	1-1	3	97	.320	0.55	0.90
	6 ML YEARS		239	0	105	236.1	987	188	92	87	28	0	2	9	106	9	336	5	6	11	.353	57-71	33	96	.678	3.39	3.31

Andrew Knizner

Bats: R Throws: R Pos: C-7;PH-2;DH-1;PR-1   KIZZ-ner   Ht: 6'1" Wt: 225 Born: 2/3/1995 Age: 26

Year	Team	Lg	G	AB	H	2B	3B	HR	(Hm	Rd)	TB	R	RBI	RC	TBB	IBB	SO	HBP	SH	SF	SB	CS	GDP	Avg	OBP	Slg	OPS
2019	StL	NL	18	53	12	2	0	2	(1	1)	20	7	7	7	4	0	14	1	0	0	0	0	3	.226	.293	.377	.670
2020	StL	NL	8	16	4	1	0	0	(0	0)	5	1	4	2	0	0	5	0	0	1	0	0	2	.250	.235	.313	.548
	2 ML YEARS		26	69	16	3	0	2	(1	1)	25	8	11	9	4	0	19	1	0	1	0	0	5	.232	.280	.362	.642

Adam Kolarek

Pitches: L Bats: L Pos: RP-20   Ht: 6'3" Wt: 215 Born: 1/14/1989 Age: 32

Year	Team	Lg	G	GS	GF	IP	BFP	H	R	ER	HR	SH	SF	HB	TBB	IBB	SO	WP	W	L	Pct	Sv-Op	Hld	Vel	OPS	ERC	ERA
2017	TB	AL	12	0	5	8.1	40	9	6	6	2	1	0	4	4	2	4	1	1	0	1.000	0-0	2	88	.984	7.84	6.48
2018	TB	AL	31	0	5	34.1	141	38	15	15	0	0	1	1	5	1	19	0	1	0	1.000	2-4	10	90	.685	3.14	3.93
2019	2 Tms		80	0	18	55.0	229	48	22	20	7	0	0	3	16	4	45	1	6	3	.667	1-1	17	89	.669	3.23	3.27
2020	LAD	NL	20	0	3	19.0	72	11	2	2	1	0	1	0	4	0	13	2	3	0	1.000	1-1	3	89	.432	1.26	0.95
19	TB	AL	54	0	15	43.1	184	39	19	19	6	0	0	3	14	4	36	1	4	3	.571	1-1	14	89	.700	3.58	3.95
19	LAD	NL	26	0	3	11.2	45	9	3	1	1	0	0	0	2	0	9	0	2	0	1.000	0-0	3	89	.547	2.01	0.77
	Postseason		3	0	0	1.0	3	0	0	0	0	0	0	0	0	0	2	0	0	0	-	0-0	1	90	.000	0.00	0.00
	4 ML YEARS		143	0	31	116.2	482	106	45	43	10	1	2	8	29	7	81	4	11	3	.786	4-6	32	89	.662	3.09	3.32

Michael Kopech

Pitches: R Bats: R Pos: P   Ht: 6'3" Wt: 225 Born: 4/30/1996 Age: 25

Year	Team	Lg	G	GS	GF	IP	BFP	H	R	ER	HR	SH	SF	HB	TBB	IBB	SO	WP	W	L	Pct	Sv-Op	Hld	Vel	OPS	ERC	ERA
2016	2 Tms	Low	12	12	0	56.1	225	29	15	13	1	0	1	5	33	0	86	11	4	1	.800	0- -	-	-	.497	2.11	2.08
2017	Brham	AA	22	22	0	119.1	488	77	45	38	6	0	3	6	60	0	155	8	8	7	.533	0- -	-	-	.570	2.48	2.87
2018	Charllt	AAA	24	24	0	126.1	543	101	58	52	9	3	6	13	60	0	170	12	7	7	.500	0- -	-	-	.658	3.45	3.70
2018	CWS	AL	4	4	0	14.1	68	20	8	8	4	0	0	5	2	0	15	1	1	1	.500	0-0	0	95	1.004	8.42	5.02

Erik Kratz

Bats: R Throws: R Pos: C-12;1B-4   Ht: 6'4" Wt: 250 Born: 6/15/1980 Age: 41

Year	Team	Lg	G	AB	H	2B	3B	HR	(Hm	Rd)	TB	R	RBI	RC	TBB	IBB	SO	HBP	SH	SF	SB	CS	GDP	Avg	OBP	Slg	OPS
2010	Pit	NL	9	34	4	0	0	0	(0	0)	4	2	1	0	2	0	9	0	0	0	0	0	0	.118	.167	.118	.284
2011	Phi	NL	2	6	2	1	0	0	(0	0)	3	0	0	1	0	0	1	0	0	0	0	0	0	.333	.333	.500	.833
2012	Phi	NL	50	141	35	9	0	9	(6	3)	71	14	26	20	11	2	34	2	0	3	0	0	2	.248	.306	.504	.809
2013	Phi	NL	68	197	42	7	0	9	(5	4)	76	21	26	15	18	4	45	1	0	2	0	0	11	.213	.280	.386	.666
2014	2 Tms	AL	47	110	24	4	0	5	(1	4)	43	12	13	7	4	1	22	0	0	1	0	0	4	.218	.243	.391	.634
2015	2 Tms		16	26	5	2	0	0	(0	0)	7	3	3	3	1	0	5	0	0	0	0	0	1	.192	.214	.269	.484
2016	2 Tms		33	85	8	2	0	1	(1	0)	13	3	4	4	1	0	32	0	1	0	0	0	3	.094	.105	.153	.258
2017	NYY	AL	4	2	2	1	0	0	(0	0)	3	0	2	2	0	0	0	0	0	0	0	0	0	1.000	1.000	1.500	2.500
2018	Mil	NL	67	203	48	6	0	6	(2	4)	72	18	23	16	6	0	40	7	1	2	1	0	8	.236	.280	.355	.634
2019	2 Tms		21	49	5	2	0	1	(1	0)	10	1	3	2	0	0	14	2	0	0	0	0	0	.102	.170	.204	.374
2020	NYY	AL	18	28	9	2	0	0	(0	0)	11	2	4	4	2	0	6	0	0	0	0	0	0	.321	.367	.393	.760
14	Tor	AL	34	81	16	3	0	3	(1	2)	28	8	10	5	3	0	12	0	0	0	0	0	3	.198	.226	.346	.572
14	KC	AL	13	29	8	1	0	2	(0	2)	15	4	3	2	1	1	10	0	0	1	0	0	1	.276	.290	.517	.808
15	KC	AL	4	4	0	0	0	0	(0	0)	0	0	0	1	0	0	2	0	0	0	0	0	0	.000	.000	.000	.000
15	Phi	NL	12	22	5	2	0	0	(0	0)	7	3	2	1	1	0	3	0	0	0	0	0	0	.227	.261	.318	.579
16	Hou	AL	15	29	2	1	0	0	(0	0)	3	0	0	1	0	0	14	0	0	0	0	0	1	.069	.100	.103	.203
16	Pit	NL	18	56	6	1	0	1	(1	0)	10	3	4	0	0	0	18	0	1	0	0	0	2	.107	.107	.179	.286

Year	Team	Lg	G	AB	H	2B	3B	HR	(Hm	Rd)	TB	R	RBI	RC	TBB	IBB	SO	HBP	SH	SF	SB	CS	GDP	Avg	OBP	Slg	OPS
19 SF		NL	15	32	4	2	0	1	(1	0)	9	1	3	2	2	0	6	2	0	0	0	0	0	.125	.222	.281	.503
19 TB		AL	6	17	1	0	0	0	(0	0)	1	0	0	0	0	0	8	0	0	0	0	0	0	.059	.059	.059	.118
Postseason			9	24	7	2	0	0	(0	0)	9	2	3	2	1	0	6	1	0	0	0	0	1	.292	.346	.375	.721
11 ML YEARS			335	881	184	36	0	31	(16	15)	313	76	105	68	47	7	208	12	2	9	1	0	28	.209	.256	.355	.611

Dean Kremer

Pitches: R Bats: R Pos: SP-4   Ht: 6'3" Wt: 185 Born: 1/7/1996 Age: 25

Year	Team	Lg	G	GS	GF	IP	BFP	H	R	ER	HR	SH	SF	HB	TBB	IBB	SO	WP	W	L	Pct	Sv-Op	Hld	Vel	OPS	ERC	ERA
2020 Bal		AL	4	4	0	18.2	83	15	10	10	0	0	1	0	12	0	22	0	1	1	.500	0-0	0	93	.711	3.12	4.82

Brooks Kriske

Pitches: R Bats: R Pos: RP-4   Ht: 6'3" Wt: 190 Born: 2/3/1994 Age: 27

Year	Team	Lg	G	GS	GF	IP	BFP	H	R	ER	HR	SH	SF	HB	TBB	IBB	SO	WP	W	L	Pct	Sv-Op	Hld	Vel	OPS	ERC	ERA
2020 NYY		AL	4	0	2	3.2	22	3	6	6	1	0	0	0	7	0	8	2	0	0	-	0-0	0	95	.855	10.28	14.73

Chad Kuhl

Pitches: R Bats: R Pos: SP-9; RP-2   cool   Ht: 6'3" Wt: 215 Born: 9/10/1992 Age: 28

Year	Team	Lg	G	GS	GF	IP	BFP	H	R	ER	HR	SH	SF	HB	TBB	IBB	SO	WP	W	L	Pct	Sv-Op	Hld	Vel	OPS	ERC	ERA
2016 Pit		NL	14	14	0	70.2	301	73	34	33	7	2	2	4	20	0	53	2	5	4	.556	0-0	0	93	.757	4.04	4.20
2017 Pit		NL	31	31	0	157.1	680	159	81	76	17	6	4	6	72	7	142	8	8	11	.421	0-0	0	96	.793	4.60	4.35
2018 Pit		NL	16	16	0	85.0	373	89	47	43	14	6	6	4	33	1	81	7	5	5	.500	0-0	0	95	.806	4.94	4.55
2020 Pit		NL	11	9	0	46.1	197	35	26	22	8	1	0	2	28	0	44	1	2	3	.400	0-0	0	94	.727	4.27	4.27
4 ML YEARS			72	70	0	359.1	1551	356	188	174	46	15	12	16	153	8	320	18	20	23	.465	0-0	0	95	.781	4.53	4.36

Joel Kuhnel

Pitches: R Bats: R Pos: RP-3   Ht: 6'4" Wt: 280 Born: 2/19/1995 Age: 26

Year	Team	Lg	G	GS	GF	IP	BFP	H	R	ER	HR	SH	SF	HB	TBB	IBB	SO	WP	W	L	Pct	Sv-Op	Hld	Vel	OPS	ERC	ERA
2019 Cin		NL	11	0	2	9.2	42	8	5	5	1	0	0	0	5	0	9	0	1	0	1.000	0-0	0	96	.634	3.53	4.66
2020 Cin		NL	3	0	1	3.0	13	4	2	2	2	0	0	0	0	0	3	0	1	0	1.000	0-0	0	95	1.077	8.07	6.00
2 ML YEARS			14	0	3	12.2	55	12	7	7	3	0	0	0	5	0	12	0	2	0	1.000	0-0	1	96	.749	4.61	4.97

Tommy La Stella

Bats: L Throws: R Pos: 2B-33;1B-10;DH-9;3B-6;PH-2   Ht: 5'11" Wt: 180 Born: 1/31/1989 Age: 32

Year	Team	Lg	G	AB	H	2B	3B	HR	(Hm	Rd)	TB	R	RBI	RC	TBB	IBB	SO	HBP	SH	SF	SB	CS	GDP	Avg	OBP	Slg	OPS
2014 Atl		NL	93	319	80	16	1	1	(1	0)	101	22	31	36	36	2	40	1	3	1	2	1	8	.251	.328	.317	.644
2015 ChC		NL	33	67	18	6	0	1	(1	0)	27	4	11	10	5	0	7	1	0	1	2	0	1	.269	.324	.403	.727
2016 ChC		NL	74	148	40	12	1	2	(1	1)	60	17	11	20	18	1	27	2	0	0	0	1	2	.270	.357	.405	.763
2017 ChC		NL	73	125	36	8	0	5	(0	5)	59	18	22	24	20	1	18	2	0	2	0	0	3	.288	.389	.472	.861
2018 ChC		NL	123	169	45	8	0	1	(0	1)	56	23	19	17	17	1	27	2	0	0	0	1	5	.266	.331	.331	.662
2019 LAA		AL	80	292	86	8	0	16	(11	5)	142	49	44	43	20	0	28	3	0	0	1	0	8	.295	.346	.486	.832
2020 2 Tms		AL	55	196	55	14	2	5	(2	3)	88	31	25	36	27	0	12	2	1	2	1	0	6	.281	.370	.449	.819
20 LAA		AL	28	99	27	8	0	4	(2	2)	47	15	14	19	15	0	7	1	1	1	1	0	3	.273	.375	.475	.845
20 Oak		AL	27	97	28	6	2	1	(0	1)	41	16	11	17	12	0	5	1	0	1	0	0	3	.289	.369	.423	.792
Postseason			12	13	0	0	0	0	(0	0)	0	0	0	0	1	0	4	0	0	0	0	0	0	.000	.071	.000	.071
7 ML YEARS			531	1316	360	72	4	31	(16	15)	533	164	163	186	143	5	159	13	4	6	5	3	33	.274	.349	.405	.754

Juan Lagares

Bats: R Throws: R Pos: CF-2;PR-1   luh-GAR-ess   Ht: 6'2" Wt: 219 Born: 3/17/1989 Age: 32

Year	Team	Lg	G	AB	H	2B	3B	HR	(Hm	Rd)	TB	R	RBI	RC	TBB	IBB	SO	HBP	SH	SF	SB	CS	GDP	Avg	OBP	Slg	OPS
2013 NYM		NL	121	392	95	21	5	4	(1	3)	138	35	34	36	20	4	96	2	5	2	6	3	6	.242	.281	.352	.633
2014 NYM		NL	116	416	117	24	3	4	(2	2)	159	46	47	53	20	1	87	7	3	6	13	4	6	.281	.321	.382	.703
2015 NYM		NL	143	441	114	16	5	6	(2	4)	158	47	41	51	16	2	87	4	1	3	7	3	6	.259	.289	.358	.647
2016 NYM		NL	79	142	34	7	2	3	(2	1)	54	15	9	12	11	1	27	2	4	1	4	2	4	.239	.301	.380	.682
2017 NYM		NL	94	252	63	16	2	3	(1	2)	92	37	15	20	14	0	56	3	2	1	7	3	6	.250	.296	.365	.661
2018 NYM		NL	30	59	20	1	1	0	(0	0)	23	9	6	10	3	1	9	1	0	1	3	1	2	.339	.375	.390	.765
2019 NYM		NL	133	258	55	12	1	5	(2	3)	84	38	27	23	22	4	75	2	2	1	4	1	8	.213	.279	.326	.605
2020 NYM		NL	2	0	0	0	0	0	(0	0)	0	0	0	0	0	0	0	0	0	0	0	0	0	-	-	-	-
Postseason			13	23	8	2	0	0	(0	0)	10	7	0	3	1	0	3	0	1	0	2	0	0	.348	.375	.435	.810
8 ML YEARS			718	1960	498	97	19	25	(10	15)	708	227	179	205	106	13	437	21	17	15	44	17	38	.254	.297	.361	.659

Brady Lail

Pitches: R **Bats:** R **Pos:** RP-8   **Ht:** 6'2" **Wt:** 200 **Born:** 8/9/1993 **Age:** 27

Year Team	Lg	G	GS	GF	IP	BFP	H	R	ER	HR	SH	SF	HB	TBB	IBB	SO	WP	W	L	Pct	Sv-Op	Hld	Vel	OPS	ERC	ERA
2019 NYY	AL	1	0	0	2.2	10	2	3	3	1	0	0	0	1	0	2	0	0	0	-	0-0	0	92	.856	4.74	10.13
2020 2 Tms	AL	8	0	7	16.1	71	14	8	8	5	0	0	2	7	0	12	0	0	0	-	0-0	0	90	.808	5.31	4.41
20 CWS	AL	1	0	1	1.1	6	2	0	0	0	0	0	0	0	0	1	0	0	0	-	0-0	0	90	.667	4.47	0.00
20 Sea	AL	7	0	6	15.0	65	12	8	8	5	0	0	2	7	0	11	0	0	0	-	0-0	0	90	.823	5.38	4.80
2 ML YEARS		9	0	7	19.0	81	16	11	11	6	0	0	2	8	0	14	0	0	0	-	0-0	0	90	.814	5.24	5.21

Travis Lakins

Pitches: R **Bats:** R **Pos:** RP-22   **Ht:** 6'1" **Wt:** 215 **Born:** 6/29/1994 **Age:** 27

Year Team	Lg	G	GS	GF	IP	BFP	H	R	ER	HR	SH	SF	HB	TBB	IBB	SO	WP	W	L	Pct	Sv-Op	Hld	Vel	OPS	ERC	ERA
2019 Bos	AL	16	3	4	23.1	102	23	11	10	1	0	2	1	10	1	18	1	0	1	.000	0-0	1	94	.738	3.78	3.86
2020 Bal	AL	22	0	5	25.2	116	25	11	8	2	0	1	2	13	0	25	3	3	2	.600	1-1	1	93	.725	4.42	2.81
2 ML YEARS		38	3	9	49.0	218	48	22	18	3	0	3	3	23	1	43	4	3	3	.500	1-1	2	94	.731	4.11	3.31

Jake Lamb

Bats: L **Throws:** R **Pos:** 3B-14;1B-12;DH-5   **Ht:** 6'3" **Wt:** 215 **Born:** 10/9/1990 **Age:** 30

Year Team	Lg	G	AB	H	2B	3B	HR	(Hm	Rd)	TB	R	RBI	RC	TBB	IBB	SO	HBP	SH	SF	SB	CS	GDP	Avg	OBP	Slg	OPS
2014 Ari	NL	37	126	29	4	1	4	(2	2)	47	15	11	7	6	0	37	0	0	1	1	1	4	.230	.263	.373	.636
2015 Ari	NL	107	350	92	15	5	6	(1	5)	135	38	34	39	36	3	97	1	0	3	3	2	5	.263	.331	.386	.716
2016 Ari	NL	151	523	130	31	9	29	(19	10)	266	81	91	84	64	5	154	3	0	4	6	1	13	.249	.332	.509	.840
2017 Ari	NL	149	536	133	30	4	30	(16	14)	261	89	105	90	87	13	152	7	0	5	6	4	15	.248	.357	.487	.844
2018 Ari	NL	56	207	46	8	0	6	(3	3)	72	34	31	26	26	0	65	1	0	4	1	2	4	.222	.307	.348	.655
2019 Ari	NL	78	187	36	8	2	6	(3	3)	66	26	30	27	32	1	55	5	0	2	1	0	4	.193	.323	.353	.676
2020 2 Tms		31	88	17	5	0	3	(2	1)	31	7	10	11	8	0	25	3	0	0	0	1	1	.193	.283	.352	.635
20 Ari	NL	18	43	5	1	0	0	(0	0)	6	2	1	1	6	0	17	1	0	0	0	1	0	.116	.240	.140	.380
20 Oak	AL	13	45	12	4	0	3	(2	1)	25	5	9	10	2	0	8	2	0	0	0	0	1	.267	.327	.556	.882
Postseason		4	13	6	0	0	0	(0	0)	6	4	0	1	0	0	2	0	0	0	0	0	0	.462	.462	.462	.923
7 ML YEARS		609	2017	483	101	21	84	(46	38)	878	290	312	284	259	22	585	20	0	19	18	11	46	.239	.329	.435	.764

Jimmy Lambert

Pitches: R **Bats:** R **Pos:** RP-2   **Ht:** 6'2" **Wt:** 190 **Born:** 11/18/1994 **Age:** 26

Year Team	Lg	G	GS	GF	IP	BFP	H	R	ER	HR	SH	SF	HB	TBB	IBB	SO	WP	W	L	Pct	Sv-Op	Hld	Vel	OPS	ERC	ERA
2020 CWS	AL	2	0	1	2.0	8	2	0	0	0	0	0	0	0	0	2	0	0	0	-	0-0	0	93	.500	1.95	0.00

Peter Lambert

Pitches: R **Bats:** R **Pos:** P   **Ht:** 6'2" **Wt:** 208 **Born:** 4/18/1997 **Age:** 24

Year Team	Lg	G	GS	GF	IP	BFP	H	R	ER	HR	SH	SF	HB	TBB	IBB	SO	WP	W	L	Pct	Sv-Op	Hld	Vel	OPS	ERC	ERA
2019 Col	NL	19	19	0	89.1	420	119	74	72	18	4	3	6	36	3	57	5	3	7	.300	0-0	0	93	.958	7.11	7.25

Dinelson Lamet

Pitches: R **Bats:** R **Pos:** SP-12   dee-NEL-sun luh-MET   **Ht:** 6'3" **Wt:** 228 **Born:** 7/18/1992 **Age:** 28

Year Team	Lg	G	GS	GF	IP	BFP	H	R	ER	HR	SH	SF	HB	TBB	IBB	SO	WP	W	L	Pct	Sv-Op	Hld	Vel	OPS	ERC	ERA
2017 SD	NL	21	21	0	114.1	485	88	63	58	18	1	5	6	54	2	139	9	7	8	.467	0-0	0	95	.707	3.64	4.57
2019 SD	NL	14	14	0	73.0	313	62	38	33	12	2	2	5	30	0	105	6	3	5	.375	0-0	0	96	.721	3.95	4.07
2020 SD	NL	12	12	0	69.0	267	39	18	16	5	0	1	4	20	0	93	1	3	1	.750	0-0	0	97	.496	1.60	2.09
3 ML YEARS		47	47	0	256.1	1065	189	119	107	35	3	8	15	104	2	337	16	13	14	.481	0-0	0	96	.657	3.12	3.76

Eric Lauer

Pitches: L **Bats:** R **Pos:** SP-2; RP-2   **Ht:** 6'3" **Wt:** 228 **Born:** 6/3/1995 **Age:** 26

Year Team	Lg	G	GS	GF	IP	BFP	H	R	ER	HR	SH	SF	HB	TBB	IBB	SO	WP	W	L	Pct	Sv-Op	Hld	Vel	OPS	ERC	ERA
2018 SD	NL	23	23	0	112.0	504	127	61	54	15	4	2	6	46	2	100	2	6	7	.462	0-0	0	91	.800	5.33	4.34
2019 SD	NL	30	29	0	149.2	651	158	82	74	20	3	3	5	51	4	138	4	8	10	.444	0-0	0	92	.760	4.47	4.45
2020 Mil	NL	4	2	0	11.0	61	17	16	16	2	0	1	2	9	0	12	1	0	2	.000	0-0	0	92	1.030	10.72	13.09
3 ML YEARS		57	54	0	272.2	1216	302	159	144	37	7	6	13	106	6	250	7	14	19	.424	0-0	0	92	.789	5.05	4.75

Ramon Laureano

Bats: R **Throws:** R **Pos:** CF-53;DH-1   **Ht:** 5'11" **Wt:** 203 **Born:** 7/15/1994 **Age:** 26

Year Team	Lg	G	AB	H	2B	3B	HR	(Hm	Rd)	TB	R	RBI	RC	TBB	IBB	SO	HBP	SH	SF	SB	CS	GDP	Avg	OBP	Slg	OPS
2018 Oak	AL	48	156	45	12	1	5	(4	1)	74	27	19	29	16	0	50	2	0	2	7	1	0	.288	.358	.474	.832
2019 Oak	AL	123	434	125	29	0	24	(13	11)	226	79	67	69	27	0	123	11	1	8	13	2	7	.288	.340	.521	.860
2020 Oak	AL	54	183	39	8	1	6	(3	3)	67	27	25	28	24	0	58	12	0	3	2	1	7	.213	.338	.366	.704
Postseason		2	6	1	0	0	0	(0	0)	1	0	1	0	1	0	3	0	0	1	0	0	0	.167	.250	.167	.417
3 ML YEARS		225	773	209	49	2	35	(20	15)	367	133	111	126	67	0	231	25	1	13	22	4	14	.270	.343	.475	.818

Ryan Lavarnway

Bats: R Throws: R Pos: C-5   luh-VARN-way   **Ht: 6'3" Wt: 239 Born: 8/7/1987 Age: 33**

Year	Team	Lg	G	AB	H	2B	3B	HR	(Hm	Rd)	TB	R	RBI	RC	TBB	IBB	SO	HBP	SH	SF	SB	CS	GDP	Avg	OBP	Slg	OPS
2011	Bos	AL	17	39	9	2	0	2	(0	2)	17	5	8	4	4	0	10	0	0	0	0	0	1	.231	.302	.436	.738
2012	Bos	AL	46	153	24	8	0	2	(0	2)	38	11	12	4	11	0	41	0	0	2	0	0	4	.157	.211	.248	.459
2013	Bos	AL	25	77	23	7	0	1	(1	0)	33	8	14	11	2	0	17	2	0	1	0	0	3	.299	.329	.429	.758
2014	Bos	AL	9	10	0	0	0	0	(0	0)	0	0	0	0	0	0	3	0	0	0	0	0	0	.000	.000	.000	.000
2015	2 Tms		37	94	18	6	0	2	(0	2)	30	6	6	4	12	1	28	0	0	0	0	0	5	.191	.283	.319	.602
2017	Oak	AL	6	11	3	1	0	0	(0	0)	4	0	2	2	1	0	3	1	0	0	0	0	1	.273	.385	.364	.748
2018	Pit	NL	6	6	4	1	0	0	(0	0)	5	1	1	2	0	0	1	0	0	0	0	0	0	.667	.667	.833	1.500
2019	Cin	NL	5	18	5	2	0	2	(2	0)	13	4	7	5	1	0	5	0	0	0	0	0	0	.278	.316	.722	1.038
2020	Mia	NL	5	11	4	0	0	0	(0	0)	4	0	0	1	0	0	2	0	0	0	0	0	0	.364	.364	.364	.727
15	Bal	AL	10	28	3	1	0	0	(0	0)	4	1	0	4	4	0	7	0	0	0	0	0	1	.107	.219	.143	.362
15	Atl	NL	27	66	15	5	0	2	(0	2)	26	5	6	4	8	1	21	0	0	0	0	0	4	.227	.311	.394	.705
	9 ML YEARS		156	419	90	27	0	9	(3	6)	144	35	50	33	31	1	110	3	0	3	0	0	15	.215	.272	.344	.616

Mike Leake

Pitches: R Bats: R Pos: P   LEEK   **Ht: 5'10" Wt: 165 Born: 11/12/1987 Age: 33**

Year	Team	Lg	G	GS	GF	IP	BFP	H	R	ER	HR	SH	SF	HB	TBB	IBB	SO	WP	W	L	Pct	Sv-Op	Hld	Vel	OPS	ERC	ERA
2010	Cin	NL	24	22	0	138.1	604	158	77	65	19	7	3	3	49	2	91	2	8	4	.667	0-0	0	89	.804	5.12	4.23
2011	Cin	NL	29	26	2	167.2	693	159	74	72	23	3	6	8	38	3	118	2	12	9	.571	0-0	0	89	.714	3.53	3.86
2012	Cin	NL	30	30	0	179.0	757	201	97	91	26	6	7	3	41	3	116	3	8	9	.471	0-0	0	90	.805	4.50	4.58
2013	Cin	NL	31	31	0	192.1	801	193	78	72	21	8	5	6	48	4	122	2	14	7	.667	0-0	0	90	.719	3.69	3.37
2014	Cin	NL	33	33	0	214.1	902	217	93	88	23	7	7	13	50	3	164	4	11	13	.458	0-0	0	91	.730	3.77	3.70
2015	2 Tms	NL	30	30	0	192.0	778	174	80	79	22	6	3	3	49	5	119	6	11	10	.524	0-0	0	91	.686	3.18	3.70
2016	StL	NL	30	30	0	176.2	757	203	101	92	20	5	**10**	7	30	1	125	7	9	12	.429	0-0	0	91	.756	4.22	4.69
2017	2 Tms		31	31	0	186.0	782	201	93	81	20	6	6	9	37	3	130	3	10	13	.435	0-0	0	90	.742	3.99	3.92
2018	Sea	AL	31	31	0	185.2	784	207	98	90	23	1	3	6	34	3	119	2	10	10	.500	0-0	0	89	.762	4.15	4.36
2019	2 Tms		32	32	0	197.0	835	227	114	94	41	2	3	10	27	2	127	2	12	11	.522	0-0	0	88	.823	4.83	4.29
15	Cin	NL	21	21	0	136.2	556	123	55	54	14	6	2	2	34	4	90	3	9	5	.643	0-0	0	91	.666	3.01	3.56
15	SF	NL	9	9	0	55.1	222	51	25	25	8	0	1	1	15	1	29	3	2	5	.286	0-0	0	91	.736	3.61	4.07
17	StL	NL	26	26	0	154.0	654	169	83	72	19	6	6	7	35	3	103	2	7	12	.368	0-0	0	90	.761	4.29	4.21
17	Sea	AL	5	5	0	32.0	128	32	10	9	1	0	0	2	2	0	27	1	3	1	.750	0-0	0	90	.652	2.64	2.53
19	Sea	AL	22	22	0	137.0	576	153	78	65	26	1	1	4	19	1	100	2	9	8	.529	0-0	0	88	.796	4.39	4.27
19	Ari	NL	10	10	0	60.0	259	74	36	29	15	1	2	6	8	1	27	0	3	3	.500	0-0	0	89	.882	5.89	4.35
	Postseason		1	1	0	4.1	20	6	5	5	2	1	0	0	2	0	1	0	0	1	.000	0-0	0	90	1.303	10.00	10.38
	10 ML YEARS		301	296	2	1829.0	7693	1940	905	824	238	51	53	68	403	29	1231	33	105	98	.517	0-0	0	90	.754	4.06	4.05

Wade LeBlanc

Pitches: L Bats: L Pos: SP-6   lah-BLAHNK   **Ht: 6'3" Wt: 215 Born: 8/7/1984 Age: 36**

Year	Team	Lg	G	GS	GF	IP	BFP	H	R	ER	HR	SH	SF	HB	TBB	IBB	SO	WP	W	L	Pct	Sv-Op	Hld	Vel	OPS	ERC	ERA
2008	SD	NL	5	4	0	21.1	104	29	19	19	7	1	0	0	15	2	14	0	1	3	.250	0-0	0	86	1.086	9.57	8.02
2009	SD	NL	9	9	0	46.1	194	35	19	19	6	3	1	4	19	1	30	0	3	1	.750	0-0	0	85	.669	3.28	3.69
2010	SD	NL	26	25	0	146.0	625	157	69	69	24	7	2	2	51	5	110	2	8	12	.400	0-0	0	87	.818	4.84	4.25
2011	SD	NL	14	14	0	79.2	339	84	42	41	7	3	3	1	28	1	51	1	5	6	.455	0-0	0	87	.757	4.21	4.63
2012	Mia	NL	25	9	1	68.2	284	71	30	28	7	5	1	1	19	1	43	1	2	5	.286	0-0	1	87	.729	3.94	3.67
2013	2 Tms		17	7	1	55.0	259	72	40	33	7	2	1	3	20	3	33	0	1	5	.167	0-0	0	86	.855	5.97	5.40
2014	2 Tms	AL	11	3	3	29.2	121	27	13	13	2	0	2	2	7	2	21	1	1	1	.500	0-0	0	88	.625	2.96	3.94
2016	2 Tms		19	8	7	62.0	252	59	30	26	14	0	2	0	11	0	51	0	4	0	1.000	2-2	1	87	.776	3.72	3.77
2017	Pit	NL	50	0	18	68.0	283	64	35	34	10	1	1	1	17	1	54	2	5	2	.714	1-3	4	87	.717	3.48	4.50
2018	Sea	AL	32	27	5	162.0	662	151	74	67	24	1	4	3	40	1	130	1	9	5	.643	0-0	0	86	.712	3.52	3.72
2019	Sea	AL	26	8	4	121.1	532	145	80	77	28	1	1	1	31	1	92	0	6	7	.462	0-0	0	86	.867	5.55	5.71
2020	Bal	AL	6	6	0	22.1	103	27	20	20	6	0	2	1	8	0	13	0	1	0	1.000	0-0	0	87	.882	6.46	8.06
13	Mia	NL	13	7	0	48.2	222	63	30	28	6	2	1	2	15	2	31	0	1	5	.167	0-0	0	86	.834	5.67	5.18
13	Hou	AL	4	0	1	6.1	37	9	10	5	1	0	0	1	5	1	2	0	0	0	-	0-0	0	87	.986	8.25	7.11
14	LAA	AL	10	3	2	28.2	114	25	11	11	2	0	1	1	6	1	21	1	1	1	.500	0-0	0	88	.601	2.63	3.45
14	NYY	AL	1	0	1	1.0	7	2	2	2	0	0	1	1	1	1	0	0	0	0	-	0-0	0	89	1.071	13.81	18.00
16	Sea	AL	11	8	3	50.0	208	52	27	25	14	0	0	0	9	0	41	0	3	0	1.000	1-1	0	87	.841	4.58	4.50
16	Pit	NL	8	0	4	12.0	44	7	3	1	0	0	2	0	2	0	10	0	1	0	1.000	1-1	1	87	.455	1.03	0.75
	12 ML YEARS		240	120	39	882.1	3758	921	471	446	142	24	20	19	266	18	642	8	46	47	.495	3-5	6	87	.781	4.43	4.55

Jose Leclerc

Pitches: R Bats: R Pos: RP-2   leh-KLURK   **Ht: 6'0" Wt: 195 Born: 12/19/1993 Age: 27**

Year	Team	Lg	G	GS	GF	IP	BFP	H	R	ER	HR	SH	SF	HB	TBB	IBB	SO	WP	W	L	Pct	Sv-Op	Hld	Vel	OPS	ERC	ERA
2016	Tex	AL	12	0	5	15.0	66	11	4	3	0	0	1	0	13	2	15	1	0	0	-	0-0	0	94	.710	3.46	1.80
2017	Tex	AL	47	0	15	45.2	200	23	21	20	4	0	0	8	40	1	60	5	2	3	.400	2-3	10	94	.585	3.28	3.94
2018	Tex	AL	59	0	21	57.2	223	24	16	10	1	4	0	3	25	1	85	2	2	3	.400	12-16	15	95	.431	1.21	1.56
2019	Tex	AL	70	3	40	68.2	299	52	34	33	7	3	2	6	39	1	100	7	2	4	.333	14-18	7	97	.701	3.68	4.33
2020	Tex	AL	2	0	2	2.0	10	2	1	1	0	0	0	0	2	0	3	0	0	0	-	1-1	0	95	.775	5.48	4.50
	5 ML YEARS		190	3	83	189.0	798	112	76	67	12	7	3	12	119	5	263	15	6	10	.375	29-38	32	96	.598	2.70	3.19

Brandon Leibrandt

Pitches: L Bats: L Pos: RP-5 Ht: 6'4" Wt: 190 Born: 12/13/1992 Age: 28

		HOW MUCH PITCHED					WHAT HE GAVE UP										THE RESULTS							
Year	Team	Lg	G	GS	GF	IP	BFP	H	R	ER	HR	SH	SF	HB	TBB	IBB	SO	WP	W	L	Pct	Sv-Op	Hld	Vel	OPS	ERC	ERA
2020	Mia	NL	5	0	2	9.0	36	3	2	2	0	0	0	0	7	1	3	0	0	0	-	0-0	0	89	.381	1.40	2.00

DJ LeMahieu

Bats: R Throws: R Pos: 2B-37;1B-11;3B-11;PH-3;DH-1   la-MAY-hugh   Ht: 6'4" Wt: 220 Born: 7/13/1988 Age: 32

			BATTING																			RUNNING			AVERAGES			
Year	Team	Lg	G	AB	H	2B	3B	HR	(Hm	Rd)	TB	R	RBI	RC	TBB	IBB	SO	HBP	SH	SF	SB	CS	GDP	Avg	OBP	Slg	OPS
2011	ChC	NL	37	60	15	2	0	0	(0	0)	17	3	4	3	1	0	12	0	1	0	0	0	2	.250	.262	.283	.546
2012	Col	NL	81	229	68	12	4	2	(1	1)	94	26	22	28	13	4	42	0	3	2	1	2	8	.297	.332	.410	.742
2013	Col	NL	109	404	113	21	3	2	(1	1)	146	39	28	42	19	2	67	1	7	3	18	7	13	.280	.311	.361	.673
2014	Col	NL	149	494	132	15	5	5	(2	3)	172	59	42	47	33	7	97	2	7	2	10	10	13	.267	.315	.348	.663
2015	Col	NL	150	564	170	21	5	6	(3	3)	219	85	61	75	50	4	107	1	3	2	23	3	20	.301	.358	.388	.746
2016	Col	NL	146	552	192	32	8	11	(7	4)	273	104	66	104	66	2	80	3	8	6	11	7	19	.348	.416	.495	.911
2017	Col	NL	155	609	189	28	4	8	(3	5)	249	95	64	87	59	1	90	6	3	5	6	5	24	.310	.374	.409	.783
2018	Col	NL	128	533	147	32	2	15	(4	11)	228	90	62	72	37	0	82	2	2	7	6	5	14	.276	.321	.428	.749
2019	NYY	AL	145	602	197	33	2	26	(19	7)	312	109	102	122	46	0	90	2	1	4	5	2	14	.327	.375	.518	.893
2020	NYY	AL	50	195	71	10	2	10	(8	2)	115	41	27	46	18	0	21	2	0	1	3	0	3	.364	.421	.590	1.011
	Postseason		14	60	16	5	0	3	(2	1)	30	10	7	8	7	0	11	0	0	0	0	1	1	.267	.343	.500	.843
	10 ML YEARS		1150	4242	1294	206	35	85	(48	37)	1825	651	478	626	342	20	688	19	35	32	83	41	130	.305	.357	.430	.787

Sandy Leon

Bats: B Throws: R Pos: C-24;PH-2;DH-1   lay-OHN   Ht: 5'10" Wt: 235 Born: 3/13/1989 Age: 32

			BATTING																			RUNNING			AVERAGES			
Year	Team	Lg	G	AB	H	2B	3B	HR	(Hm	Rd)	TB	R	RBI	RC	TBB	IBB	SO	HBP	SH	SF	SB	CS	GDP	Avg	OBP	Slg	OPS
2012	Was	NL	12	30	8	2	0	0	(0	0)	10	2	2	2	4	0	11	2	0	0	0	0	1	.267	.389	.333	.722
2013	Was	NL	2	1	0	0	0	0	(0	0)	0	0	0	0	0	0	1	0	0	0	0	0	0	.000	.000	.000	.000
2014	Was	NL	20	64	10	1	0	1	(0	1)	14	7	3	2	6	0	20	0	0	0	0	0	1	.156	.229	.219	.447
2015	Bos	AL	41	114	21	2	0	0	(0	0)	23	8	3	1	7	1	28	1	6	0	0	1	4	.184	.238	.202	.439
2016	Bos	AL	78	252	78	17	2	7	(2	5)	120	36	35	44	23	1	66	2	4	2	0	0	3	.310	.369	.476	.845
2017	Bos	AL	85	271	61	14	0	7	(3	4)	96	32	39	32	25	1	74	1	1	3	0	0	5	.225	.290	.354	.644
2018	Bos	AL	89	265	47	12	0	5	(2	3)	74	30	22	17	15	0	75	4	3	1	1	0	6	.177	.232	.279	.511
2019	Bos	AL	65	172	33	3	0	5	(4	1)	51	14	19	15	13	0	47	1	4	1	0	0	0	.192	.251	.297	.548
2020	Cle	AL	25	66	9	1	0	2	(1	1)	16	4	4	3	14	0	21	1	0	0	0	0	2	.136	.296	.242	.539
	Postseason		15	31	8	1	0	1	(0	1)	12	2	3	4	2	0	11	0	1	0	0	0	0	.258	.303	.387	.690
	9 ML YEARS		417	1235	267	52	2	27	(12	15)	404	133	127	116	107	3	343	12	18	7	1	1	23	.216	.284	.327	.611

Dominic Leone

Pitches: R Bats: R Pos: RP-12   LEE-own   Ht: 5'10" Wt: 215 Born: 10/26/1991 Age: 29

			HOW MUCH PITCHED					WHAT HE GAVE UP										THE RESULTS							
Year	Team	Lg	G	GS	GF	IP	BFP	H	R	ER	HR	SH	SF	HB	TBB	IBB	SO	WP	W	L	Pct	Sv-Op	Hld	Vel	OPS	ERC	ERA
2014	Sea	AL	57	0	3	66.1	272	52	18	16	4	1	3	3	25	3	70	4	8	2	.800	0-2	7	95	.624	2.71	2.17
2015	2 Tms		13	0	6	15.0	74	19	15	14	2	0	1	1	9	2	9	2	0	5	.000	0-1	1	93	.884	6.63	8.40
2016	Ari	NL	25	0	8	27.0	131	45	21	19	7	0	3	1	12	1	23	4	0	1	.000	0-1	0	93	1.095	10.37	6.33
2017	Tor	AL	65	0	6	70.1	279	51	22	20	6	3	0	0	23	3	81	8	3	0	1.000	1-5	11	94	.625	2.25	2.56
2018	StL	NL	29	0	8	24.0	106	27	12	12	3	1	3	0	8	3	26	0	1	2	.333	0-2	5	94	.727	4.43	4.50
2019	StL	NL	40	0	11	40.2	180	39	28	25	9	1	1	0	22	2	46	1	1	0	1.000	1-2	0	94	.822	5.20	5.53
2020	Cle	AL	12	0	4	9.2	47	14	9	9	3	0	0	0	5	0	16	1	0	0	-	0-0	3	95	1.023	9.14	8.38
15	Sea	AL	10	0	5	11.1	54	11	9	8	1	0	0	0	9	2	7	2	0	4	.000	0-0	1	93	.770	4.93	6.35
15	Ari	NL	3	0	1	3.2	20	8	6	6	1	0	1	1	0	0	2	0	0	1	.000	0-1	0	93	1.172	12.63	14.73
	7 ML YEARS		241	0	46	253.0	1089	247	125	115	34	3	14	5	104	14	271	20	13	10	.565	2-13	27	94	.758	4.23	4.09

Jon Lester

Pitches: L Bats: L Pos: SP-12 Ht: 6'4" Wt: 240 Born: 1/7/1984 Age: 37

			HOW MUCH PITCHED					WHAT HE GAVE UP										THE RESULTS							
Year	Team	Lg	G	GS	GF	IP	BFP	H	R	ER	HR	SH	SF	HB	TBB	IBB	SO	WP	W	L	Pct	Sv-Op	Hld	Vel	OPS	ERC	ERA
2006	Bos	AL	15	15	0	81.1	367	91	43	43	7	2	8	5	43	1	60	5	7	2	.778	0-0	0	90	.814	5.52	4.76
2007	Bos	AL	12	11	0	63.0	275	61	33	32	10	1	5	1	31	0	50	1	4	0	1.000	0-0	0	90	.753	4.78	4.57
2008	Bos	AL	33	33	0	210.1	874	202	78	75	14	6	3	10	66	1	152	3	16	6	.727	0-0	0	92	.688	3.55	3.21
2009	Bos	AL	32	32	0	203.1	843	186	80	77	20	2	6	3	64	0	225	6	15	8	.652	0-0	0	94	.667	3.35	3.41
2010	Bos	AL	32	32	0	208.0	861	167	81	75	14	6	4	10	83	0	225	6	19	9	.679	0-0	0	93	.628	3.00	3.25
2011	Bos	AL	31	31	0	191.2	799	166	77	74	20	2	2	11	75	0	182	4	15	9	.625	0-0	0	93	.690	3.62	3.47
2012	Bos	AL	33	33	0	205.1	876	216	117	110	25	5	7	4	68	2	166	6	9	14	.391	0-0	0	93	.773	4.36	4.82
2013	Bos	AL	33	33	0	213.1	903	209	94	89	19	1	1	7	67	0	177	5	15	8	.652	0-0	0	93	.703	3.69	3.75
2014	2 Tms	AL	32	32	0	219.2	885	194	76	60	16	6	5	4	48	0	220	3	16	11	.593	0-0	0	92	.635	2.70	2.46
2015	ChC	NL	32	32	0	205.0	828	183	83	76	16	5	4	7	47	0	207	8	11	12	.478	0-0	0	92	.661	2.88	3.34
2016	ChC	NL	32	32	0	202.2	795	154	57	55	21	4	4	6	52	0	197	4	19	5	.792	0-0	0	92	.602	2.47	2.44
2017	ChC	NL	32	32	0	180.2	763	179	101	87	26	4	4	4	60	3	180	3	13	8	.619	0-0	0	91	.750	4.16	4.33
2018	ChC	NL	32	32	0	181.2	761	174	75	67	24	7	3	6	64	1	149	4	18	6	.750	0-0	0	91	.733	4.07	3.32
2019	ChC	NL	31	31	0	171.2	746	205	101	95	26	5	5	2	52	0	165	3	13	10	.565	0-0	0	90	.815	5.27	4.46
2020	ChC	NL	12	12	0	61.0	265	64	35	35	11	1	0	3	17	0	42	2	3	3	.500	0-0	0	89	.777	4.56	5.16
14	Bos	AL	21	21	0	143.0	580	128	52	40	9	5	2	4	32	0	149	2	10	7	.588	0-0	0	92	.637	2.73	2.52
14	Oak	AL	11	11	0	76.2	305	66	24	20	7	1	3	0	16	0	71	1	6	4	.600	0-0	0	91	.632	2.65	2.35
	Postseason		26	22	2	154.0	610	117	46	43	15	6	2	3	40	0	133	4	9	7	.563	0-0	0	93	.594	2.37	2.51
	15 ML YEARS		424	423	0	2598.2	10860	2451	1131	1040	269	55	62	87	837	8	2397	63	193	111	.635	0-0	0	92	.702	3.65	3.60

Artie Lewicki

Pitches: R **Bats:** R **Pos:** RP-2   **Ht:** 6'3" **Wt:** 195 **Born:** 4/8/1992 **Age:** 29

Year	Team	Lg	G	GS	GF	IP	BFP	H	R	ER	HR	SH	SF	HB	TBB	IBB	SO	WP	W	L	Pct	Sv-Op	Hld	Vel	OPS	ERC	ERA
2017	Det	AL	4	1	1	10.1	52	19	8	7	1	0	0	0	4	0	6	0	0	1	.000	0-0	0	92	.921	9.42	6.10
2018	Det	AL	13	3	6	38.2	170	48	24	21	4	0	5	1	14	1	30	0	0	2	.000	0-0	1	92	.844	5.58	4.89
2020	Ari	NL	2	0	2	3.1	18	7	2	2	0	0	0	0	1	0	5	0	0	0	-	0-0	0	93	1.150	9.49	5.40
	3 ML YEARS		19	4	9	52.1	240	74	34	30	5	0	5	1	19	1	41	0	0	3	.000	0-0	1	92	.885	6.55	5.16

Kyle Lewis

Bats: R **Throws:** R **Pos:** CF-57;DH-1;PR-1   **Ht:** 6'4" **Wt:** 205 **Born:** 7/13/1995 **Age:** 25

Year	Team	Lg	G	AB	H	2B	3B	HR	(Hm	Rd)	TB	R	RBI	RC	TBB	IBB	SO	HBP	SH	SF	SB	CS	GDP	Avg	OBP	Slg	OPS
2019	Sea	AL	18	71	19	5	0	6	(4	2)	42	10	13	13	3	0	29	0	0	0	0	0	0	.268	.293	.592	.885
2020	Sea	AL	58	206	54	3	0	11	(5	6)	90	37	28	31	34	0	71	0	0	2	5	1	5	.262	.364	.437	.801
	2 ML YEARS		76	277	73	8	0	17	(9	8)	132	47	41	44	37	0	100	0	0	3	5	1	5	.264	.347	.477	.824

Royce Lewis

Bats: R **Throws:** R **Pos:** SS   **Ht:** 6'2" **Wt:** 200 **Born:** 6/5/1999 **Age:** 22

Year	Team	Lg	G	AB	H	2B	3B	HR	(Hm	Rd)	TB	R	RBI	RC	TBB	IBB	SO	HBP	SH	SF	SB	CS	GDP	Avg	OBP	Slg	OPS
2017	2 Tms	Low	54	204	57	8	3	4	(-	-)	83	34	27	38	25	0	33	9	0	1	18	3	3	.279	.381	.407	.788
2018	2 Tms	Low	121	483	141	29	3	14	(-	-)	218	83	74	65	43	1	84	4	1	4	28	8	8	.292	.352	.451	.803
2019	FtMyrs	A+	94	383	91	17	3	10	(-	-)	144	55	35	46	27	1	90	3	0	5	16	8	5	.238	.289	.376	.665
2019	Pnscla	AA	33	134	31	9	1	2	(-	-)	48	18	14	15	11	0	33	1	0	2	6	2	0	.231	.291	.358	.649

Robinson Leyer

Pitches: R **Bats:** R **Pos:** RP-5; SP-1   **Ht:** 6'2" **Wt:** 185 **Born:** 3/13/1993 **Age:** 28

Year	Team	Lg	G	GS	GF	IP	BFP	H	R	ER	HR	SH	SF	HB	TBB	IBB	SO	WP	W	L	Pct	Sv-Op	Hld	Vel	OPS	ERC	ERA
2020	Bos	AL	6	1	0	4.2	34	12	11	11	3	0	0	0	8	0	9	0	0	0	-	0-0	1	95	1.473	28.04	21.21

Tzu-Wei Lin

zoo-way

Bats: L **Throws:** R **Pos:** SS-12;2B-6;LF-4;PR-4;RF-3;CF-2;C-1;DH-1;PH-1   **Ht:** 5'9" **Wt:** 180 **Born:** 2/15/1994 **Age:** 27

Year	Team	Lg	G	AB	H	2B	3B	HR	(Hm	Rd)	TB	R	RBI	RC	TBB	IBB	SO	HBP	SH	SF	SB	CS	GDP	Avg	OBP	Slg	OPS
2017	Bos	AL	25	56	15	0	2	0	(0	0)	19	7	2	7	9	0	17	0	1	0	1	1	0	.268	.369	.339	.709
2018	Bos	AL	37	65	16	6	1	1	(0	1)	27	15	6	8	8	0	17	0	0	0	0	1	0	.246	.329	.415	.744
2019	Bos	AL	13	20	4	2	0	0	(0	0)	6	3	1	2	2	0	6	0	0	0	1	1	0	.200	.273	.300	.573
2020	Bos	AL	26	52	8	1	0	0	(0	0)	9	2	3	2	2	0	17	0	2	1	0	0	1	.154	.182	.173	.355
	4 ML YEARS		101	193	43	9	3	1	(0	1)	61	27	12	18	21	0	57	0	3	1	2	3	1	.223	.298	.316	.614

Josh Lindblom

Pitches: R **Bats:** R **Pos:** SP-10; RP-2   LIN-bloom   **Ht:** 6'4" **Wt:** 240 **Born:** 6/15/1987 **Age:** 34

Year	Team	Lg	G	GS	GF	IP	BFP	H	R	ER	HR	SH	SF	HB	TBB	IBB	SO	WP	W	L	Pct	Sv-Op	Hld	Vel	OPS	ERC	ERA
2011	LAD	NL	27	0	8	29.2	116	21	9	9	0	2	3	2	10	3	28	3	1	0	1.000	0-1	3	92	.572	1.90	2.73
2012	2 Tms	NL	74	0	18	71.0	304	61	31	28	13	2	0	4	35	2	70	2	3	5	.375	1-4	22	92	.753	4.47	3.55
2013	Tex	AL	8	5	2	31.1	137	35	19	19	4	0	0	0	11	2	21	2	1	3	.250	0-0	0	90	.788	4.64	5.46
2014	Oak	AL	1	1	0	4.2	22	5	2	2	1	0	0	1	2	0	2	0	0	0	-	0-0	0	90	.837	6.25	3.86
2017	Pit	NL	4	0	1	10.1	51	18	9	9	0	0	0	0	3	0	10	0	0	0	-	0-0	0	91	.849	7.25	7.84
2020	Mil	NL	12	10	1	45.1	191	42	26	26	6	0	0	3	16	0	52	2	2	4	.333	0-0	0	90	.732	4.02	5.16
	12 LAD	NL	48	0	12	47.2	197	42	16	16	9	2	0	3	18	0	43	1	2	2	.500	0-2	15	92	.754	4.31	3.02
	12 Phi	NL	26	0	6	23.1	107	19	15	12	4	0	0	1	17	2	27	1	1	3	.250	1-2	7	92	.750	4.77	4.63
	6 ML YEARS		126	16	30	192.1	821	182	96	93	24	4	3	10	77	7	183	9	7	12	.368	1-5	25	91	.738	4.14	4.35

Francisco Lindor

Bats: B **Throws:** R **Pos:** SS-58;DH-2   lin-DOHR   **Ht:** 5'11" **Wt:** 190 **Born:** 11/14/1993 **Age:** 27

Year	Team	Lg	G	AB	H	2B	3B	HR	(Hm	Rd)	TB	R	RBI	RC	TBB	IBB	SO	HBP	SH	SF	SB	CS	GDP	Avg	OBP	Slg	OPS
2015	Cle	AL	99	390	122	22	4	12	(8	4)	188	50	51	64	27	0	69	1	**13**	7	12	2	12	.313	.353	.482	.835
2016	Cle	AL	158	604	182	30	3	15	(6	9)	263	99	78	87	57	3	88	5	3	**15**	19	5	18	.301	.358	.435	.794
2017	Cle	AL	159	**651**	178	44	4	33	(16	17)	329	99	89	107	60	6	93	4	5	3	15	3	11	.273	.337	.505	.842
2018	Cle	AL	158	**661**	183	42	2	38	(20	18)	343	**129**	92	117	70	7	107	8	3	3	25	10	5	.277	.352	.519	.871
2019	Cle	AL	143	598	170	40	2	32	(14	18)	310	101	74	89	46	9	98	3	1	6	22	5	13	.284	.335	.518	.854
2020	Cle	AL	60	236	61	13	0	8	(3	5)	98	30	27	29	24	2	41	4	0	2	6	2	8	.258	.335	.415	.750
	Postseason		23	87	24	3	0	5	(4	1)	42	10	12	14	8	2	24	0	1	0	1	3	2	.276	.337	.483	.820
	6 ML YEARS		777	3140	896	191	15	138	(67	71)	1531	508	411	493	284	27	496	25	25	36	99	27	67	.285	.346	.488	.833

Francisco Liriano

Pitches: L **Bats:** L **Pos:** P   **Ht:** 6'3" **Wt:** 220 **Born:** 10/26/1983 **Age:** 37

			HOW MUCH PITCHED				WHAT HE GAVE UP									THE RESULTS							
Year	Team	Lg	G	GS	GF	IP	BFP	H	R	ER	HR	SH	SF	HB	TBB	IBB	SO	WP	W	L	Pct	Sv-Op	Hld	Vel	OPS	ERC	ERA
2005	Min	AL	6	4	2	23.2	93	19	15	15	4	0	0	0	7	0	33	0	1	2	.333	0-0	0	95	.687	3.15	5.70
2006	Min	AL	28	16	2	121.0	473	89	31	29	9	4	2	1	32	0	144	9	12	3	.800	1-1	1	95	.567	2.12	2.16
2008	Min	AL	14	14	0	76.0	329	74	40	33	7	2	3	1	32	1	67	3	6	4	.600	0-0	0	91	.719	3.97	3.91
2009	Min	AL	29	24	3	136.2	609	147	93	88	21	5	6	6	65	0	122	5	5	13	.278	0-0	0	92	.830	5.46	5.80
2010	Min	AL	31	31	0	191.2	806	184	77	77	9	6	2	10	58	0	201	10	14	10	.583	0-0	0	94	.670	3.34	3.62
2011	Min	AL	26	24	0	134.1	591	125	81	76	14	0	6	7	75	1	112	9	9	10	.474	0-0	0	93	.726	4.58	5.09
2012	2 Tms		34	28	0	156.2	693	143	97	93	19	4	3	7	87	5	167	11	6	12	.333	0-0	1	93	.741	4.47	5.34
2013	Pit	NL	26	26	0	161.0	666	134	54	54	9	3	1	0	63	0	163	7	16	8	.667	0-0	0	93	.611	2.86	3.02
2014	Pit	NL	29	29	0	162.1	691	130	68	61	13	6	5	4	81	3	175	12	7	10	.412	0-0	0	93	.645	3.28	3.38
2015	Pit	NL	31	31	0	186.2	773	155	75	70	15	2	1	5	70	1	205	10	12	7	.632	0-0	0	92	.631	3.04	3.38
2016	2 Tms		31	29	0	163.0	731	157	98	85	26	7	6	9	85	1	168	9	8	13	.381	0-0	0	93	.773	4.96	4.69
2017	2 Tms		38	18	3	97.0	439	105	66	61	11	2	3	4	53	2	85	5	6	7	.462	0-0	6	93	.824	5.43	5.66
2018	Det	AL	27	26	0	133.2	586	127	84	68	19	0	5	5	73	0	110	9	5	12	.294	0-0	0	92	.771	4.90	4.58
2019	Pit	NL	69	0	8	70.0	301	60	32	27	8	2	2	3	35	1	63	1	5	3	.625	0-4	12	93	.710	3.93	3.47
12	Min	AL	22	17	2	100.0	440	89	63	59	12	2	7	4	55	4	109	6	3	10	.231	0-0	1	93	.730	4.27	5.31
12	CWS	AL	12	11	0	56.2	253	54	34	34	7	2	1	3	32	1	58	5	3	2	.600	0-0	0	93	.759	4.83	5.40
16	Pit	NL	21	21	0	113.2	523	115	76	69	19	7	5	7	69	1	116	8	6	11	.353	0-0	0	92	.814	5.71	5.46
16	Tor	AL	10	8	0	49.1	208	42	22	16	7	0	1	2	16	0	52	1	2	2	.500	0-0	0	93	.675	3.34	2.92
17	Tor	AL	18	18	0	82.2	375	91	57	54	11	2	3	2	43	1	74	4	6	5	.545	0-0	0	93	.832	5.49	5.88
17	Hou	AL	20	0	3	14.1	64	14	9	7	0	0	0	2	10	1	11	1	0	2	.000	0-0	6	94	.772	5.00	4.40
	Postseason		11	3	3	25.0	103	18	12	11	2	0	0	2	9	0	21	3	2	1	.667	0-0	0	94	.619	2.60	3.96
	14 ML YEARS		419	300	19	1813.2	7781	1649	911	837	184	43	50	62	816	15	1815	100	112	114	.496	1-5	20	93	.705	3.91	4.15

Zack Littell

Pitches: R **Bats:** R **Pos:** RP-6   lah-TELL   **Ht:** 6'4" **Wt:** 220 **Born:** 10/5/1995 **Age:** 25

			HOW MUCH PITCHED				WHAT HE GAVE UP									THE RESULTS							
Year	Team	Lg	G	GS	GF	IP	BFP	H	R	ER	HR	SH	SF	HB	TBB	IBB	SO	WP	W	L	Pct	Sv-Op	Hld	Vel	OPS	ERC	ERA
2018	Min	AL	8	2	1	20.1	101	25	17	14	3	1	1	4	11	0	14	0	0	2	.000	0-0	0	92	.924	7.09	6.20
2019	Min	AL	29	0	7	37.0	146	34	12	11	4	1	0	0	9	1	32	0	6	0	1.000	0-1	9	94	.708	3.18	2.68
2020	Min	AL	6	0	3	6.1	31	12	7	7	5	0	0	1	3	0	3	1	0	0	-	0-0	1	94	1.516	19.87	9.95
	Postseason		2	0	1	0.1	3	0	2	2	0	0	0	1	1	0	0	1	0	1	.000	0-0	0	95	.667	19.60	54.00
	3 ML YEARS		43	2	11	63.2	278	71	36	32	12	2	1	5	23	1	49	1	6	2	.750	0-1	1	93	.873	5.67	4.52

Mauricio Llovera

Pitches: R **Bats:** R **Pos:** RP-1   yo-VAIR-uh   **Ht:** 5'11" **Wt:** 224 **Born:** 4/17/1996 **Age:** 25

			HOW MUCH PITCHED				WHAT HE GAVE UP									THE RESULTS							
Year	Team	Lg	G	GS	GF	IP	BFP	H	R	ER	HR	SH	SF	HB	TBB	IBB	SO	WP	W	L	Pct	Sv-Op	Hld	Vel	OPS	ERC	ERA
2020	Phi	NL	1	0	0	1.0	10	5	4	4	0	0	0	1	1	0	1	0	0	0	-	0-0	0	93	1.575	41.68	36.00

Jonathan Loaisiga

Pitches: R **Bats:** R **Pos:** RP-9; SP-3   loh-AYE-sig-ah   **Ht:** 5'11" **Wt:** 165 **Born:** 11/2/1994 **Age:** 26

			HOW MUCH PITCHED				WHAT HE GAVE UP									THE RESULTS							
Year	Team	Lg	G	GS	GF	IP	BFP	H	R	ER	HR	SH	SF	HB	TBB	IBB	SO	WP	W	L	Pct	Sv-Op	Hld	Vel	OPS	ERC	ERA
2018	NYY	AL	9	4	2	24.2	108	26	17	14	3	0	0	0	12	0	33	0	2	0	1.000	0-0	0	96	.789	4.97	5.11
2019	NYY	AL	15	4	3	31.2	139	31	16	16	6	0	4	1	16	0	37	1	2	2	.500	0-1	0	97	.820	5.21	4.55
2020	NYY	AL	12	3	2	23.0	100	21	11	9	3	1	0	4	7	1	22	1	3	0	1.000	0-2	2	97	.740	4.00	3.52
	Postseason		4	0	2	2.2	15	3	2	1	0	0	0	0	3	0	3	2	0	0	-	0-0	0	98	.733	6.23	3.38
	3 ML YEARS		36	11	7	79.1	347	78	44	39	12	1	4	5	35	1	92	2	7	2	.778	0-3	2	97	.787	4.77	4.42

Tim Locastro

Bats: R **Throws:** R **Pos:** CF-13;PR-8;LF-7;RF-6;PH-5;DH-2   **Ht:** 6'1" **Wt:** 195 **Born:** 7/14/1992 **Age:** 28

			BATTING																			RUNNING			AVERAGES			
Year	Team	Lg	G	AB	H	2B	3B	HR	(Hm	Rd)	TB	R	RBI	RC	TBB	IBB	SO	HBP	SH	SF	SB	CS	GDP	Avg	OBP	Slg	OPS
2017	LAD	NL	3	1	0	0	0	0	(0	0)	0	0	0	0	0	0	0	0	0	0	1	0	0	.000	.000	.000	.000
2018	LAD	NL	18	11	2	1	0	0	(0	0)	3	6	0	2	2	0	5	1	0	0	4	0	0	.182	.357	.273	.630
2019	Ari	NL	91	212	53	12	2	1	(0	1)	72	38	17	35	14	0	44	22	1	1	17	0	1	.250	.357	.340	.697
2020	Ari	NL	33	69	20	4	1	2	(1	1)	32	15	7	15	8	0	14	4	1	0	4	0	0	.290	.395	.464	.859
	4 ML YEARS		145	293	75	17	3	3	(1	2)	107	59	24	52	24	0	63	27	2	1	26	0	1	.256	.365	.365	.730

Walker Lockett

Pitches: R **Bats:** R **Pos:** RP-6; SP-1   **Ht:** 6'5" **Wt:** 225 **Born:** 5/3/1994 **Age:** 27

			HOW MUCH PITCHED				WHAT HE GAVE UP									THE RESULTS							
Year	Team	Lg	G	GS	GF	IP	BFP	H	R	ER	HR	SH	SF	HB	TBB	IBB	SO	WP	W	L	Pct	Sv-Op	Hld	Vel	OPS	ERC	ERA
2018	SD	NL	4	3	1	15.0	76	22	16	16	4	0	0	0	10	1	12	0	0	3	.000	0-0	0	93	1.042	9.39	9.60
2019	NYM	NL	9	4	1	22.2	103	33	21	21	6	1	0	1	6	0	16	1	1	1	.500	0-0	0	93	1.003	7.99	8.34
2020	2 Tms		7	1	3	16.1	73	21	9	9	2	0	0	2	4	0	11	0	1	0	1.000	0-0	0	93	.833	5.90	4.96
20	NYM	NL	2	1	0	8.0	37	9	5	5	1	0	0	2	3	0	8	0	1	0	1.000	0-0	0	93	.847	5.95	5.63
20	Sea	AL	5	0	3	8.1	36	12	4	4	1	0	0	0	1	0	3	0	0	0	-	0-0	0	94	.818	5.84	4.32
	3 ML YEARS		20	8	5	54.0	252	76	46	46	12	1	0	3	20	1	39	1	2	4	.333	0-0	0	93	.965	7.72	7.67

Shed Long Jr.

Bats: L **Throws:** R **Pos:** 2B-32;PH-3;LF-1;DH-1   **Ht:** 5'8" **Wt:** 184 **Born:** 8/22/1995 **Age:** 25

Year	Team	Lg	G	AB	H	2B	3B	HR	(Hm	Rd)	TB	R	RBI	RC	TBB	IBB	SO	HBP	SH	SF	SB	CS	GDP	Avg	OBP	Slg	OPS
2019	Sea	AL	42	152	40	12	1	5	(1	4)	69	21	15	19	16	0	40	0	0	0	3	3	1	.263	.333	.454	.787
2020	Sea	AL	34	117	20	5	0	3	(0	3)	34	10	9	9	11	0	37	0	0	0	4	0	1	.171	.242	.291	.533
	2 ML YEARS		76	269	60	17	1	8	(1	7)	103	31	24	28	27	0	77	0	0	0	7	3	2	.223	.294	.383	.677

Evan Longoria

Bats: R **Throws:** R **Pos:** 3B-52;PH-1   **Ht:** 6'1" **Wt:** 213 **Born:** 10/7/1985 **Age:** 35

Year	Team	Lg	G	AB	H	2B	3B	HR	(Hm	Rd)	TB	R	RBI	RC	TBB	IBB	SO	HBP	SH	SF	SB	CS	GDP	Avg	OBP	Slg	OPS
2008	TB	AL	122	448	122	31	2	27	(18	9)	238	67	85	72	46	4	122	6	0	8	7	0	8	.272	.343	.531	.874
2009	TB	AL	157	584	164	44	0	33	(16	17)	307	100	113	102	72	11	140	8	0	7	9	0	27	.281	.364	.526	.889
2010	TB	AL	151	574	169	46	5	22	(10	12)	291	96	104	99	72	12	124	5	0	10	15	5	15	.294	.372	.507	.879
2011	TB	AL	133	483	118	26	1	31	(14	17)	239	78	99	91	80	6	93	6	0	5	3	2	11	.244	.355	.495	.850
2012	TB	AL	74	273	79	14	0	17	(8	9)	144	39	55	55	33	6	61	3	0	3	2	3	14	.289	.369	.527	.896
2013	TB	AL	160	614	165	39	3	32	(15	17)	306	91	88	90	70	10	162	3	0	6	1	0	16	.269	.343	.498	.842
2014	TB	AL	**162**	624	158	26	1	22	(12	10)	252	83	91	83	57	11	133	9	1	9	5	0	15	.253	.320	.404	.724
2015	TB	AL	160	604	163	35	1	21	(10	11)	263	74	73	77	51	8	132	6	0	9	3	1	11	.270	.328	.435	.764
2016	TB	AL	160	633	173	41	4	36	(17	19)	330	81	98	95	42	6	144	3	0	7	0	3	13	.273	.318	.521	.840
2017	TB	AL	156	613	160	36	2	20	(10	10)	260	71	86	81	46	3	109	6	0	12	6	1	18	.261	.313	.424	.737
2018	SF	NL	125	480	117	25	4	16	(4	12)	198	51	54	46	22	3	101	5	0	5	3	1	11	.244	.281	.413	.694
2019	SF	NL	129	453	115	19	2	20	(6	14)	198	59	69	63	43	1	112	7	0	5	3	1	14	.254	.325	.437	.762
2020	SF	NL	53	193	49	10	1	7	(6	1)	82	26	28	16	11	0	39	2	0	3	0	1	10	.254	.297	.425	.722
	Postseason		30	115	22	5	0	9	(4	5)	54	16	21	13	11	0	38	0	0	0	1	0	4	.191	.262	.470	.731
	13 ML YEARS		1742	6576	1752	392	26	304	(146	158)	3108	916	1043	970	645	81	1472	69	1	89	57	18	183	.266	.334	.473	.807

Tim Lopes

Bats: R **Throws:** R **Pos:** LF-17;DH-17;RF-12;PH-7;3B-1   **Ht:** 5'11" **Wt:** 180 **Born:** 6/24/1994 **Age:** 27

Year	Team	Lg	G	AB	H	2B	3B	HR	(Hm	Rd)	TB	R	RBI	RC	TBB	IBB	SO	HBP	SH	SF	SB	CS	GDP	Avg	OBP	Slg	OPS
2019	Sea	AL	41	111	30	7	0	1	(1	0)	40	11	12	16	15	0	29	1	0	1	6	3	1	.270	.359	.360	.720
2020	Sea	AL	46	143	34	12	0	2	(0	2)	52	16	15	16	6	0	34	2	0	0	5	0	2	.238	.278	.364	.642
	2 ML YEARS		87	254	64	19	0	3	(1	2)	92	27	27	32	21	0	63	3	0	1	11	3	3	.252	.315	.362	.678

Jorge Lopez

Pitches: R **Bats:** R **Pos:** SP-6; RP-4   **Ht:** 6'2" **Wt:** 205 **Born:** 2/10/1993 **Age:** 28

Year	Team	Lg	G	GS	GF	IP	BFP	H	R	ER	HR	SH	SF	HB	TBB	IBB	SO	WP	W	L	Pct	Sv-Op	Hld	Vel	OPS	ERC	ERA
2015	Mil	NL	2	2	0	10.0	46	14	6	6	0	0	0	1	5	0	10	1	1	1	.500	0-0	0	94	.860	6.87	5.40
2017	Mil	NL	1	0	1	2.0	10	4	1	1	0	0	0	0	1	0	0	0	0	0	-	0-0	0	95	1.056	10.75	4.50
2018	2 Tms		17	7	8	53.2	234	57	30	30	6	0	2	1	22	1	38	3	2	5	.286	0-0	0	94	.763	4.64	5.03
2019	KC	AL	39	18	8	123.2	548	140	94	87	27	0	7	10	42	0	109	6	4	9	.308	1-2	0	94	.864	5.85	6.33
2020	2 Tms	AL	10	6	1	39.0	174	46	32	29	7	1	3	3	12	1	28	4	2	2	.500	0-0	0	94	.817	5.61	6.69
18	Mil	NL	10	0	8	19.2	85	16	6	6	1	0	1	0	13	1	15	1	0	1	.000	0-0	0	94	.665	3.66	2.75
18	KC	AL	7	7	0	34.0	149	41	24	24	5	0	1	1	9	0	23	2	2	4	.333	0-0	0	93	.813	5.20	6.35
20	KC	AL	1	0	0	0.2	5	3	2	2	0	0	0	0	0	0	0	0	0	0	-	0-0	0	94	1.400	26.58	27.00
20	Bal	AL	9	6	1	38.1	169	43	30	27	7	1	3	3	12	1	28	4	2	2	.500	0-0	0	94	.799	5.32	6.34
	5 ML YEARS		69	33	18	228.1	1012	261	163	153	40	1	12	15	82	2	185	14	9	17	.346	1-2	0	94	.834	5.61	6.03

Nicky Lopez

Bats: L **Throws:** R **Pos:** 2B-53;SS-4;3B-2;PH-2   **Ht:** 5'11" **Wt:** 175 **Born:** 3/13/1995 **Age:** 26

Year	Team	Lg	G	AB	H	2B	3B	HR	(Hm	Rd)	TB	R	RBI	RC	TBB	IBB	SO	HBP	SH	SF	SB	CS	GDP	Avg	OBP	Slg	OPS
2019	KC	AL	103	379	91	22	2	2	(1	1)	123	44	30	38	18	0	51	1	4	0	1	1	5	.240	.276	.325	.601
2020	KC	AL	56	169	34	8	0	1	(1	0)	45	15	13	12	18	0	41	2	3	0	0	5	1	.201	.286	.266	.552
	2 ML YEARS		159	548	125	30	2	3	(2	1)	168	59	43	50	36	0	92	3	7	0	1	6	6	.228	.279	.307	.586

Pablo Lopez

Pitches: R **Bats:** L **Pos:** SP-11   **Ht:** 6'4" **Wt:** 225 **Born:** 3/7/1996 **Age:** 25

Year	Team	Lg	G	GS	GF	IP	BFP	H	R	ER	HR	SH	SF	HB	TBB	IBB	SO	WP	W	L	Pct	Sv-Op	Hld	Vel	OPS	ERC	ERA
2018	Mia	NL	10	10	0	58.2	247	56	28	27	8	1	2	4	18	5	46	2	2	4	.333	0-0	0	5	.745	3.88	4.14
2019	Mia	NL	21	21	0	111.1	469	111	64	63	15	4	2	11	27	3	95	6	5	8	.385	0-0	0	94	.756	4.07	5.09
2020	Mia	NL	11	11	0	57.1	240	50	27	23	4	0	3	2	18	1	59	0	6	4	.600	0-0	0	94	.637	2.93	3.61
	3 ML YEARS		42	42	0	227.1	956	217	119	113	27	5	7	17	63	9	200	8	13	16	.448	0-0	0	93	.723	3.72	4.47

Reynaldo Lopez

Pitches: R **Bats:** R **Pos:** SP-8 — ray-NAHL-doh — **Ht:** 6'1" **Wt:** 220 **Born:** 1/4/1994 **Age:** 27

Year	Team	Lg	G	GS	GF	IP	BFP	H	R	ER	HR	SH	SF	HB	TBB	IBB	SO	WP	W	L	Pct	Sv-Op	Hld	Vel	OPS	ERC	ERA
2016	Was	NL	11	6	1	44.0	201	47	27	24	4	3	2	0	22	2	42	5	5	3	.625	0-0	1	96	.772	4.60	4.91
2017	CWS	AL	8	8	0	47.2	207	49	29	25	7	0	2	1	14	0	30	3	3	3	.500	0-0	0	94	.741	4.12	4.72
2018	CWS	AL	32	32	0	188.2	799	165	88	82	25	0	9	10	75	1	151	7	7	10	.412	0-0	0	96	.713	3.80	3.91
2019	CWS	AL	33	33	0	184.0	809	203	**119**	110	35	2	5	8	65	0	169	5	10	15	.400	0-0	0	95	.833	5.33	5.38
2020	CWS	AL	8	8	0	26.1	121	28	21	19	9	1	0	1	15	0	24	1	1	3	.250			94	.944	7.17	6.49
	Postseason		1	0	0	2.0	9	2	1	1	0	0	0	0	1	0	3	0	0	0		0-0	0	96	.708	3.63	4.50
	5 ML YEARS		92	87	1	490.2	2137	492	284	260	80	6	18	20	191	3	416	21	26	34	.433	0-0	1	95	.780	4.64	4.77

Yoan Lopez

Pitches: R **Bats:** R **Pos:** RP-20 — **Ht:** 6'3" **Wt:** 205 **Born:** 1/2/1993 **Age:** 28

Year	Team	Lg	G	GS	GF	IP	BFP	H	R	ER	HR	SH	SF	HB	TBB	IBB	SO	WP	W	L	Pct	Sv-Op	Hld	Vel	OPS	ERC	ERA
2018	Ari	NL	10	0	5	9.0	35	7	3	3	2	1	0	0	1	0	11	0	0	0	-	0-0	1	97	.720	2.47	3.00
2019	Ari	NL	70	0	13	60.2	246	52	27	23	11	1	4	0	17	2	42	1	2	7	.222	1-4	21	96	.728	3.32	3.41
2020	Ari	NL	20	0	7	19.2	87	21	15	13	4	0	0	0	9	2	16	0	0	1	.000	0-0	1	95	.870	5.30	5.95
	3 ML YEARS		100	0	25	89.1	368	80	45	39	17	2	4	0	27	4	69	1	2	8	.200	1-4	23	96	.761	3.65	3.93

Michael Lorenzen

Pitches: R **Bats:** R **Pos:** RP-16; SP-2 — **Ht:** 6'3" **Wt:** 220 **Born:** 1/4/1992 **Age:** 29

Year	Team	Lg	G	GS	GF	IP	BFP	H	R	ER	HR	SH	SF	HB	TBB	IBB	SO	WP	W	L	Pct	Sv-Op	Hld	Vel	OPS	ERC	ERA
2015	Cin	NL	27	21	1	113.1	515	131	70	68	18	2	1	6	57	6	83	4	4	9	.308	0-0	1	94	.882	6.09	5.40
2016	Cin	NL	35	0	4	50.0	202	41	16	16	5	0	0	6	13	0	48	2	2	1	.667	0-2	10	96	.630	3.11	2.88
2017	Cin	NL	70	0	14	83.0	361	78	43	41	9	2	1	4	34	5	80	12	8	4	.667	2-7	18	96	.695	3.89	4.45
2018	Cin	NL	45	3	10	81.0	344	78	32	28	6	2	3	3	34	2	54	2	4	2	.667	1-2	8	95	.707	3.95	3.11
2019	Cin	NL	73	0	16	83.1	343	68	29	27	9	4	2	2	28	1	85	2	1	4	.200	7-11	21	97	.644	2.96	2.92
2020	Cin	NL	18	2	2	33.2	147	30	17	16	3	1	1	1	17	1	35	2	3	1	.750	0-1	2	97	.691	3.84	4.28
	6 ML YEARS		268	26	47	444.1	1912	426	207	196	50	11	8	22	183	15	385	24	22	21	.512	10-23	60	95	.731	4.15	3.97

Aaron Loup

Pitches: L **Bats:** L **Pos:** RP-24 — LOOP — **Ht:** 5'11" **Wt:** 210 **Born:** 12/19/1987 **Age:** 33

Year	Team	Lg	G	GS	GF	IP	BFP	H	R	ER	HR	SH	SF	HB	TBB	IBB	SO	WP	W	L	Pct	Sv-Op	Hld	Vel	OPS	ERC	ERA
2012	Tor	AL	33	0	3	30.2	117	26	10	9	2	1	0	2	2	0	21	1	0	2	.000	0-1	6	92	.547	1.59	2.64
2013	Tor	AL	64	0	12	69.1	282	66	23	19	5	2	4	7	13	4	53	2	4	6	.400	2-3	8	92	.670	3.20	2.47
2014	Tor	AL	71	0	15	68.2	283	50	25	24	4	3	3	6	30	5	56	5	4	4	.500	4-8	13	92	.647	2.75	3.15
2015	Tor	AL	60	0	6	42.1	186	47	24	21	6	2	0	6	7	0	46	0	2	5	.286	0-4	9	93	.776	4.54	4.46
2016	Tor	AL	21	0	8	14.1	62	15	8	8	2	0	3	3	4	0	15	3	0	1		0-1	1	91	.855	5.13	5.02
2017	Tor	AL	70	0	8	57.2	265	59	27	24	4	5	0	6	29	5	64	3	2	3	.400	0-0	6	92	.722	4.56	3.75
2018	2 Tms		59	0	8	39.2	183	48	23	20	4	0	3	4	14	0	44	0	0	0	-	0-0	11	92	.805	5.45	4.54
2019	SD	NL	4	0	1	3.1	14	2	0	0	0	0	1	1	1	0	5	0	0	0	-	0-0	1	92	.558	2.03	0.00
2020	TB	AL	24	0	6	25.0	96	17	9	7	3	**2**	1	3	4	0	22	0	3	2	.600	0-1	4	92	.635	2.16	2.52
18	Tor	AL	50	0	7	35.2	166	44	21	18	4	0	3	3	13	0	42	0	0	0	-	0-0	9	92	.824	5.63	4.54
18	Phi	NL	9	0	1	4.0	17	4	2	2	0	0	0	1	1	0	2	0	0	0	-	0-0	2	91	.620	3.88	4.50
	Postseason		4	0	1	2.0	7	1	1	1	0	0	0	0	2	0	1	0	0	0		0-0	1	91	.629	3.75	4.50
	9 ML YEARS		406	0	61	351.0	1488	330	149	132	28	16	16	36	104	14	326	14	15	22	.405	6-18	59	92	.700	3.55	3.38

Richard Lovelady

Pitches: L **Bats:** L **Pos:** RP-1 — **Ht:** 6'0" **Wt:** 185 **Born:** 7/7/1995 **Age:** 25

Year	Team	Lg	G	GS	GF	IP	BFP	H	R	ER	HR	SH	SF	HB	TBB	IBB	SO	WP	W	L	Pct	Sv-Op	Hld	Vel	OPS	ERC	ERA
2019	KC	AL	25	0	5	20.0	96	30	17	17	2	1	1	1	8	2	17	1	0	3	.000	0-1	2	94	.952	7.18	7.65
2020	KC	AL	1	0	0	1.0	4	1	1	1	1	0	0	0	1	0	0	0	0	0	-	0-0	0	92	1.833	17.98	9.00
	2 ML YEARS		26	0	5	21.0	100	31	18	18	3	1	1	1	9	2	17	1	0	3	.000	0-1	2	94	.982	7.60	7.71

Brandon Lowe

Bats: L **Throws:** R **Pos:** 2B-44;RF-7;PH-7;LF-5;DH-4;1B-1 — LAOW — **Ht:** 5'10" **Wt:** 185 **Born:** 7/6/1994 **Age:** 26

Year	Team	Lg	G	AB	H	2B	3B	HR	(Hm	Rd)	TB	R	RBI	RC	TBB	IBB	SO	HBP	SH	SF	SB	CS	GDP	Avg	OBP	Slg	OPS
2018	TB	AL	43	129	30	6	2	6	(2	4)	58	16	25	21	16	0	38	2	0	1	2	1	3	.233	.324	.450	.774
2019	TB	AL	82	296	80	17	2	17	(8	9)	152	42	51	50	25	0	113	5	0	1	5	0	1	.270	.336	.514	.850
2020	TB	AL	56	193	52	9	2	14	(6	8)	107	36	37	39	25	0	58	4	0	2	3	0	2	.269	.362	.554	.916
	Postseason		5	19	4	1	0	1	(1	0)	8	1	1	1	1	0	10	0	0	0	0	0	0	.211	.250	.421	.671
	3 ML YEARS		181	618	162	32	6	37	(16	21)	317	94	113	110	66	0	209	11	0	4	10	1	6	.262	.342	.513	.855

Nate Lowe

Bats: L **Throws:** R **Pos:** 1B-15;DH-3;3B-2;PH-2 **Ht:** 6'4" **Wt:** 220 **Born:** 7/7/1995 **Age:** 25

Year	Team	Lg	G	AB	H	2B	3B	HR	(Hm	Rd)	TB	R	RBI	RC	TBB	IBB	SO	HBP	SH	SF	SB	CS	GDP	Avg	OBP	Slg	OPS
2019	TB	AL	50	152	40	8	0	7	(4	3)	69	24	19	19	13	0	50	2	0	2	0	0	4	.263	.325	.454	.779
2020	TB	AL	21	67	15	2	0	4	(3	1)	29	10	11	8	9	2	28	0	0	0	1	0	2	.224	.316	.433	.749
	2 ML YEARS		71	219	55	10	0	11	(7	4)	98	34	30	27	22	2	78	2	0	2	1	0	6	.251	.322	.447	.770

Jed Lowrie

Bats: B **Throws:** R **Pos:** IF LAU-ree **Ht:** 6'0" **Wt:** 180 **Born:** 4/17/1984 **Age:** 37

Year	Team	Lg	G	AB	H	2B	3B	HR	(Hm	Rd)	TB	R	RBI	RC	TBB	IBB	SO	HBP	SH	SF	SB	CS	GDP	Avg	OBP	Slg	OPS
2008	Bos	AL	81	260	67	25	3	2	(0	2)	104	34	46	35	35	0	68	1	2	8	1	0	8	.258	.339	.400	.739
2009	Bos	AL	32	68	10	2	0	2	(1	1)	18	5	11	5	6	0	20	0	0	0	0	0	0	.147	.211	.265	.475
2010	Bos	AL	55	171	49	14	0	9	(3	6)	90	31	24	32	25	0	25	1	0	0	1	1	2	.287	.381	.526	.907
2011	Bos	AL	88	309	78	14	4	6	(3	3)	118	40	36	33	23	2	60	2	1	6	1	1	6	.252	.303	.382	.685
2012	Hou	NL	97	340	83	18	0	16	(9	7)	149	43	42	45	43	0	65	2	0	2	2	0	3	.244	.331	.438	.769
2013	Oak	AL	154	603	175	45	2	15	(7	8)	269	80	75	88	50	3	91	2	3	4	1	0	17	.290	.344	.446	.791
2014	Oak	AL	136	502	125	29	3	6	(4	2)	178	59	50	52	51	5	79	5	2	6	0	0	14	.249	.321	.355	.676
2015	Hou	AL	69	230	51	14	0	9	(5	4)	92	35	30	29	28	5	43	3	0	2	1	0	3	.222	.312	.400	.712
2016	Oak	AL	87	338	89	12	1	2	(1	1)	109	30	27	36	26	0	65	1	0	4	0	0	10	.263	.314	.322	.637
2017	Oak	AL	153	567	157	49	3	14	(8	6)	254	86	69	94	73	2	100	2	0	3	0	1	10	.277	.360	.448	.808
2018	Oak	AL	157	596	159	37	1	23	(4	19)	267	78	99	106	78	1	128	3	0	3	0	0	8	.267	.353	.448	.801
2019	NYM	NL	9	7	0	0	0	0	(0	0)	0	0	0	0	1	0	4	0	0	0	0	0	0	.000	.125	.000	.125
	Postseason		23	64	9	2	0	1	(0	1)	14	7	5	4	7	0	17	1	1	1	0	0	1	.141	.233	.219	.452
	12 ML YEARS		1118	3991	1043	259	17	104	(45	59)	1648	521	509	555	439	18	748	22	8	40	7	3	81	.261	.335	.413	.748

Joey Lucchesi

Pitches: L **Bats:** L **Pos:** SP-2; RP-1 loo-KAY-zee **Ht:** 6'5" **Wt:** 225 **Born:** 6/6/1993 **Age:** 28

			HOW MUCH PITCHED					WHAT HE GAVE UP											THE RESULTS								
Year	Team	Lg	G	GS	GF	IP	BFP	H	R	ER	HR	SH	SF	HB	TBB	IBB	SO	WP	W	L	Pct	Sv-Op	Hld	Vel	OPS	ERC	ERA
2018	SD	NL	26	26	0	130.0	548	125	63	59	23	3	4	4	43	2	145	4	8	9	.471	0-0	0	90	.766	4.24	4.08
2019	SD	NL	30	30	0	163.2	686	144	78	76	23	5	4	2	56	0	158	8	10	10	.500	0-0	0	90	.702	3.48	4.18
2020	SD	NL	3	2	0	5.2	32	13	5	5	0	0	1	1	2	0	5	0	0	1	.000	0-0	0	90	1.036	12.30	7.94
	3 ML YEARS		59	58	0	299.1	1266	282	146	140	46	8	9	7	101	2	308	12	18	20	.474	0-0	0	90	.738	3.95	4.21

Marco Luciano

Bats: R **Throws:** R **Pos:** SS **Ht:** 6'2" **Wt:** 178 **Born:** 9/10/2001 **Age:** 19

Year	Team	Lg	G	AB	H	2B	3B	HR	(Hm	Rd)	TB	R	RBI	RC	TBB	IBB	SO	HBP	SH	SF	SB	CS	GDP	Avg	OBP	Slg	OPS
2019	2 Tms	Low	47	179	54	13	2	10	(-	-)	101	52	42	44	32	0	45	4	0	1	9	6	4	.302	.417	.564	.981

Jonathan Lucroy

Bats: R **Throws:** R **Pos:** C-1 LOO-croy **Ht:** 6'0" **Wt:** 200 **Born:** 6/13/1986 **Age:** 35

Year	Team	Lg	G	AB	H	2B	3B	HR	(Hm	Rd)	TB	R	RBI	RC	TBB	IBB	SO	HBP	SH	SF	SB	CS	GDP	Avg	OBP	Slg	OPS
2010	Mil	NL	75	277	70	9	0	4	(4	0)	91	24	26	23	18	1	44	1	0	1	4	2	9	.253	.300	.329	.628
2011	Mil	NL	136	430	114	16	1	12	(8	4)	168	45	59	50	29	0	99	2	4	3	2	1	7	.265	.313	.391	.703
2012	Mil	NL	96	316	101	17	4	12	(7	5)	162	46	58	61	22	1	44	4	1	3	4	1	12	.320	.368	.513	.881
2013	Mil	NL	147	521	146	25	6	18	(9	9)	237	59	82	78	46	2	69	5	0	8	9	1	16	.280	.340	.455	.795
2014	Mil	NL	153	585	176	53	2	13	(6	7)	272	73	69	90	66	3	71	2	0	2	4	4	13	.301	.373	.465	.837
2015	Mil	NL	103	371	98	20	3	7	(3	4)	145	51	43	46	36	0	64	1	1	6	1	0	18	.264	.326	.391	.717
2016	2 Tms		142	490	143	24	3	24	(15	9)	245	67	81	74	47	5	100	3	0	4	5	0	16	.292	.355	.500	.855
2017	2 Tms		123	423	112	21	3	6	(2	4)	157	45	40	53	46	6	51	8	0	4	1	0	16	.265	.345	.371	.716
2018	Oak	AL	126	415	100	21	1	4	(1	3)	135	41	51	44	29	1	65	3	1	6	0	0	12	.241	.291	.325	.617
2019	2 Tms		101	293	68	10	1	8	(6	2)	104	30	36	32	27	1	51	5	0	3	0	0	17	.232	.305	.355	.660
2020	Bos	AL	1	0	0	0	0	0	(0	0)	0	0	0	0	0	0	0	0	0	0	0	0	0	-	-	-	-
16	Mil	NL	95	338	101	17	3	13	(9	4)	163	48	50	46	33	3	70	1	0	4	5	0	12	.299	.359	.482	.841
16	Tex	AL	47	152	42	7	0	11	(6	5)	82	19	31	28	14	2	30	2	0	0	0	0	4	.276	.345	.539	.885
17	Tex	AL	77	281	68	15	0	4	(0	4)	95	27	27	28	19	0	32	4	0	2	1	0	10	.242	.297	.338	.635
17	Col	NL	46	142	44	6	3	2	(2	0)	62	18	13	25	27	6	19	4	0	2	0	0	6	.310	.429	.437	.865
19	LAA	AL	74	240	58	8	1	7	(5	2)	89	28	30	28	21	0	39	4	0	3	0	0	15	.242	.310	.371	.681
19	ChC	NL	27	53	10	2	0	1	(1	0)	15	2	6	4	6	1	12	1	0	0	0	0	2	.189	.283	.283	.566
	Postseason		15	51	12	3	0	1	(1	0)	18	6	6	5	1	0	12	0	0	0	0	0	0	.235	.250	.353	.603
	11 ML YEARS		1203	4121	1128	216	24	108	(61	47)	1716	481	545	551	366	20	658	34	7	40	30	9	136	.274	.335	.416	.751

Dawel Lugo

Bats: R **Throws:** R **Pos:** 3B-5;PR-3;DH-2;2B-1;PH-1 **Ht:** 6'0" **Wt:** 190 **Born:** 12/31/1994 **Age:** 26

Year	Team	Lg	G	AB	H	2B	3B	HR	(Hm	Rd)	TB	R	RBI	RC	TBB	IBB	SO	HBP	SH	SF	SB	CS	GDP	Avg	OBP	Slg	OPS
2018	Det	AL	27	94	20	4	1	1	(0	1)	29	10	8	10	7	0	20	0	0	0	0	0	2	.213	.267	.309	.576
2019	Det	AL	77	273	67	11	4	6	(3	3)	104	28	26	22	8	1	59	3	0	4	0	0	8	.245	.271	.381	.652
2020	Det	AL	9	10	2	0	0	0	(0	0)	2	3	1	1	1	0	1	0	0	0	0	0	1	.200	.273	.200	.473
	3 ML YEARS		113	377	89	15	5	7	(3	4)	135	41	35	33	16	1	80	3	0	4	0	0	11	.236	.270	.358	.628

Seth Lugo

Pitches: R Bats: R Pos: RP-9; SP-7   **Ht: 6'4" Wt: 225 Born: 11/17/1989 Age: 31**

Year	Team	Lg	G	GS	GF	IP	BFP	H	R	ER	HR	SH	SF	HB	TBB	IBB	SO	WP	W	L	Pct	Sv-Op	Hld	Vel	OPS	ERC	ERA
2016	NYM	NL	17	8	2	64.0	260	49	19	19	7	8	4	4	21	3	45	1	5	2	.714	0-0	0	92	.666	2.81	2.67
2017	NYM	NL	19	18	1	101.1	436	114	57	53	13	2	5	2	25	1	85	2	7	5	.583	0-0	0	91	.770	4.43	4.71
2018	NYM	NL	54	5	13	101.1	410	81	36	30	9	1	5	2	28	4	103	2	3	4	.429	3-4	11	94	.595	2.49	2.66
2019	NYM	NL	61	0	14	80.0	314	56	28	24	8	1	1	5	16	4	104	2	7	4	.636	6-11	21	94	.562	1.97	2.70
2020	NYM	NL	16	7	6	36.2	160	40	22	21	8	0	2	2	10	1	47	1	3	4	.429	3-5	0	93	.825	5.05	5.15
	5 ML YEARS		167	38	36	383.1	1580	340	162	147	45	12	17	15	100	13	384	8	25	19	.568	12-20	32	93	.672	3.14	3.45

Jordan Luplow

Bats: R Throws: R Pos: LF-21;RF-9;PH-5   **Ht: 6'1" Wt: 195 Born: 9/26/1993 Age: 27**

Year	Team	Lg	G	AB	H	2B	3B	HR	(Hm	Rd)	TB	R	RBI	RC	TBB	IBB	SO	HBP	SH	SF	SB	CS	GDP	Avg	OBP	Slg	OPS
2017	Pit	NL	27	78	16	3	1	3	(3	0)	30	6	11	8	6	0	22	2	0	1	0	1	4	.205	.276	.385	.660
2018	Pit	NL	37	92	17	1	3	3	(3	0)	33	16	7	4	10	0	18	1	0	0	2	2	7	.185	.272	.359	.631
2019	Cle	AL	85	225	62	15	1	15	(8	7)	124	42	38	42	33	0	61	2	0	1	3	2	7	.276	.372	.551	.923
2020	Cle	AL	29	78	15	5	1	2	(1	1)	28	8	8	8	12	0	19	1	0	1	0	1	3	.192	.304	.359	.663
	4 ML YEARS		178	473	110	24	6	23	(15	8)	215	72	64	62	61	0	120	6	0	3	5	6	21	.233	.326	.455	.781

Gavin Lux

Bats: L Throws: R Pos: 2B-18;DH-1   **Ht: 6'2" Wt: 190 Born: 11/23/1997 Age: 23**

Year	Team	Lg	G	AB	H	2B	3B	HR	(Hm	Rd)	TB	R	RBI	RC	TBB	IBB	SO	HBP	SH	SF	SB	CS	GDP	Avg	OBP	Slg	OPS
2016	2 Tms	Low	56	223	66	13	5	0	(-	-)	89	41	21	37	28	0	51	1	0	1	2	0	4	.296	.375	.399	.775
2017	Gt Lks	A	111	434	106	14	8	7	(-	-)	157	68	39	57	56	0	88	3	3	5	27	10	6	.244	.331	.362	.693
2018	Rcuca	A+	88	358	116	23	7	11	(-	-)	186	64	48	79	43	0	68	1	0	2	11	7	3	.324	.396	.520	.916
2018	Tulsa	AA	28	105	34	4	1	4	(-	-)	52	21	9	21	14	2	20	1	0	0	2	2	0	.324	.408	.495	.904
2019	Tulsa	AA	64	259	81	7	4	13	(-	-)	135	45	37	51	28	1	60	0	0	4	7	3	1	.313	.375	.521	.896
2019	OkCity	AAA	49	199	78	18	4	13	(-	-)	143	54	39	61	33	0	42	0	0	0	3	2	0	.392	.478	.719	1.197
2019	LAD	NL	23	75	18	4	1	2	(0	2)	30	12	9	10	7	0	24	0	0	0	2	0	0	.240	.305	.400	.705
2020	LAD	NL	19	63	11	2	0	3	(0	3)	22	8	8	8	6	0	19	0	0	0	1	0	0	.175	.246	.349	.596
	Postseason		4	9	2	0	0	1	(1	0)	5	1	1	1	1	0	6	0	0	0	0	0	0	.222	.300	.556	.856
	2 ML YEARS		42	138	29	6	1	5	(0	5)	52	20	17	18	13	0	43	0	0	0	3	0	0	.210	.278	.377	.655

Jesus Luzardo

Pitches: L Bats: L Pos: SP-9; RP-3   **Ht: 6'0" Wt: 218 Born: 9/30/1997 Age: 23**

Year	Team	Lg	G	GS	GF	IP	BFP	H	R	ER	HR	SH	SF	HB	TBB	IBB	SO	WP	W	L	Pct	Sv-Op	Hld	Vel	OPS	ERC	ERA
2017	3 Tms	Low	12	11	0	43.1	171	35	9	8	2	1	0	3	5	0	48	3	2	1	.667	0--	-	-	.216	1.97	1.66
2018	Mdlnd	AA	16	16	0	78.2	310	58	22	20	5	2	2	3	18	0	86	2	7	3	.700	0--	-	-	.579	2.03	2.29
2019	LsVgs	AAA	7	7	0	31.0	131	29	12	11	3	1	1	0	8	0	34	3	1	1	.500	0--	-	-	.673	3.06	3.19
2019	Oak	AL	6	0	2	12.0	46	5	2	2	1	0	0	1	3	0	16	2	0	0	-	2-2	0	96	.434	1.13	1.50
2020	Oak	AL	12	9	1	59.0	248	58	27	27	9	1	1	3	17	1	59	3	3	2	.600	0-0	0	96	.745	4.11	4.12
	Postseason		1	0	0	3.0	12	1	0	0	0	0	0	0	2	0	4	0	0	0	-	0-0	0	97	.350	1.26	0.00
	2 ML YEARS		18	9	3	71.0	294	63	29	29	10	1	1	4	20	1	75	5	3	2	.600	2-2	2	96	.696	3.48	3.68

Jordan Lyles

Pitches: R Bats: R Pos: SP-9; RP-3   **Ht: 6'5" Wt: 230 Born: 10/19/1990 Age: 30**

Year	Team	Lg	G	GS	GF	IP	BFP	H	R	ER	HR	SH	SF	HB	TBB	IBB	SO	WP	W	L	Pct	Sv-Op	Hld	Vel	OPS	ERC	ERA
2011	Hou	NL	20	15	2	94.0	415	107	61	56	14	7	1	5	26	1	67	0	2	8	.200	0-0	0	90	.817	4.87	5.36
2012	Hou	NL	25	25	0	141.1	628	159	97	80	20	6	4	5	42	4	99	2	5	12	.294	0-0	0	92	.772	4.67	5.09
2013	Hou	AL	27	22	1	141.2	642	165	98	88	17	0	3	11	49	1	93	5	7	9	.438	1-1	1	92	.801	5.20	5.59
2014	Col	NL	22	22	0	126.2	546	127	64	61	12	4	3	8	46	1	90	6	7	4	.636	0-0	0	91	.750	4.17	4.33
2015	Col	NL	10	10	0	49.0	212	54	32	28	2	3	1	4	19	1	30	2	2	5	.286	0-0	0	92	.751	4.51	5.14
2016	Col	NL	40	5	7	58.2	273	69	46	38	4	1	2	4	22	2	32	5	4	5	.444	1-4	3	93	.790	5.32	5.83
2017	2 Tms	NL	38	5	12	69.2	324	96	61	60	16	2	1	4	22	1	55	4	1	5	.167	0-0	2	94	.948	7.24	7.75
2018	2 Tms	NL	35	8	10	87.2	371	83	42	40	12	3	4	3	28	3	84	5	3	4	.429	0-0	2	94	.718	3.78	4.11
2019	2 Tms	NL	28	28	0	141.0	591	131	72	65	25	2	3	1	55	2	146	6	12	8	.600	0-0	0	93	.767	4.18	4.15
2020	Tex	AL	12	9	0	57.2	266	67	49	45	12	1	5	2	23	0	36	3	1	6	.143	0-0	0	92	.841	5.82	7.02
17	Col	NL	33	0	12	46.2	211	61	37	36	11	1	1	4	12	1	33	2	0	2	.000	0-0	2	94	.921	6.72	6.94
17	SD	NL	5	5	0	23.0	113	35	24	24	5	1	0	0	10	0	22	2	1	3	.250	0-0	0	93	1.000	8.31	9.39
18	SD	NL	24	8	5	71.1	300	71	35	34	12	3	3	1	19	0	62	4	2	4	.333	0-0	1	93	.741	4.03	4.29
18	Mil	NL	11	0	5	16.1	71	12	7	6	0	0	1	2	9	3	22	1	1	0	1.000	0-0	1	94	.612	2.63	3.31
19	Pit	NL	17	17	0	82.1	361	88	53	49	16	1	1	1	33	1	90	4	5	7	.417	0-0	0	93	.853	5.20	5.36
19	Mil	NL	11	11	0	58.2	238	43	19	16	9	1	2	0	22	1	56	0	7	1	.875	0-0	0	94	.636	2.87	2.45
	10 ML YEARS		257	152	32	967.1	4276	1058	622	561	134	29	27	46	338	16	732	36	44	66	.400	2-5	8	92	.791	4.82	5.22

Lance Lynn

Pitches: R Bats: B Pos: SP-13   Ht: 6'5" Wt: 250 Born: 5/12/1987 Age: 34

Year	Team	Lg	G	GS	GF	IP	BFP	H	R	ER	HR	SH	SF	HB	TBB	IBB	SO	WP	W	L	Pct	Sv-Op	Hld	Vel	OPS	ERC	ERA
2011	StL	NL	18	2	2	34.2	136	25	12	12	3	1	0	1	11	1	40	1	1	1	.500	1-2	3	93	.591	2.37	3.12
2012	StL	NL	35	29	2	176.0	744	168	76	74	16	4	3	10	64	3	180	3	18	7	.720	0-0	1	93	.728	3.87	3.78
2013	StL	NL	33	33	0	201.2	856	189	92	89	14	11	8	11	76	0	198	6	15	10	.600	0-0	0	92	.701	3.67	3.97
2014	StL	NL	33	33	0	203.2	866	185	72	62	13	6	4	7	72	1	181	7	15	10	.600	0-0	0	92	.662	3.24	2.74
2015	StL	NL	31	31	0	175.1	751	172	66	59	13	9	2	5	68	5	167	2	12	11	.522	0-0	0	92	.708	3.83	3.03
2017	StL	NL	33	33	0	186.1	776	151	80	71	27	9	3	10	78	5	153	2	11	8	.579	0-0	0	92	.707	3.62	3.43
2018 2 Tms		AL	31	29	0	156.2	700	163	87	83	14	0	2	6	76	3	161	5	10	10	.500	0-0	0	93	.744	4.68	4.77
2019	Tex	AL	33	33	0	208.1	875	195	89	85	21	1	6	8	59	0	246	18	16	11	.593	0-0	0	94	.689	3.41	3.67
2020	Tex	AL	13	13	0	84.0	344	64	34	31	13	1	1	6	25	0	89	2	6	3	.667	0-0	0	93	.663	3.01	3.32
18	Min	AL	20	20	0	102.1	469	105	61	58	12	0	2	6	62	3	100	3	7	8	.467	0-0	0	93	.780	5.38	5.10
18	NYY	AL	11	9	0	54.1	231	58	26	25	2	0	0	0	14	0	61	2	3	2	.600	0-0	0	93	.676	3.44	4.14
Postseason			26	7	3	54.1	244	59	33	29	6	2	3	1	28	5	52	0	5	4	.556	0-0	3	94	.792	5.06	4.80
9 ML YEARS			260	236	4	1426.2	6048	1312	608	566	134	42	29	64	529	18	1415	46	104	71	.594	1-2	4	93	.699	3.64	3.57

Tyler Lyons

Pitches: L Bats: L Pos: RP-1   Ht: 6'2" Wt: 210 Born: 2/21/1988 Age: 33

Year	Team	Lg	G	GS	GF	IP	BFP	H	R	ER	HR	SH	SF	HB	TBB	IBB	SO	WP	W	L	Pct	Sv-Op	Hld	Vel	OPS	ERC	ERA
2013	StL	NL	12	8	1	53.0	223	49	29	28	5	1	0	3	16	0	43	0	2	4	.333	0-0	0	90	.725	3.46	4.75
2014	StL	NL	11	4	1	36.2	155	33	23	18	4	1	1	2	11	2	36	0	0	4	.000	0-0	0	90	.677	3.29	4.42
2015	StL	NL	17	8	1	60.0	255	59	29	25	12	3	2	1	15	0	60	4	3	1	.750	0-0	0	90	.751	4.04	3.75
2016	StL	NL	30	0	10	48.0	187	35	18	18	9	1	1	0	14	0	46	2	2	0	1.000	0-0	4	91	.667	2.83	3.38
2017	StL	NL	50	0	12	54.0	220	39	17	17	3	1	3	7	20	2	68	1	4	1	.800	3-4	15	90	.608	2.68	2.83
2018	StL	NL	27	0	2	16.2	83	24	16	16	3	1	2	2	8	2	19	2	1	0	1.000	0-2	9	89	.986	7.98	8.64
2019 2 Tms			14	0	7	12.2	54	13	9	9	4	0	0	1	5	2	17	0	1	2	.333	0-0	1	90	.956	6.07	6.39
2020	NYY	AL	1	0	0	1.2	10	3	4	4	0	0	0	1	1	0	0	0	0	0	-	0-0	0	88	1.125	11.51	21.60
19	Pit	NL	3	0	2	4.0	20	6	5	5	1	0	0	0	3	1	5	0	1	1	.500	0-0	1	90	1.156	9.83	11.25
19	NYY	AL	11	0	5	8.2	34	7	4	4	3	0	0	1	2	1	12	0	0	1	.000	0-0	0	90	.843	4.41	4.15
Postseason			2	0	1	1.2	5	0	0	0	0	0	0	0	0	4	0	0	0		-	0-0	0	90	.000	0.00	0.00
8 ML YEARS			162	20	34	282.2	1187	255	145	135	40	8	9	17	90	8	289	9	13	12	.520	3-6	29	90	.726	3.69	4.30

Manny Machado

muh-CHAH-doe

Bats: R Throws: R Pos: 3B-56;DH-4   Ht: 6'3" Wt: 218 Born: 7/6/1992 Age: 28

Year	Team	Lg	G	AB	H	2B	3B	HR	(Hm	Rd)	TB	R	RBI	RC	TBB	IBB	SO	HBP	SH	SF	SB	CS	GDP	Avg	OBP	Slg	OPS
2012	Bal	AL	51	191	50	8	3	7	(7	0)	85	24	26	29	9	0	38	0	1	1	2	0	6	.262	.294	.445	.739
2013	Bal	AL	156	667	189	51	3	14	(5	9)	288	88	71	87	29	0	113	2	9	3	6	7	15	.283	.314	.432	.746
2014	Bal	AL	82	327	91	14	0	12	(9	3)	141	38	32	44	20	2	68	3	2	2	2	0	13	.278	.324	.431	.755
2015	Bal	AL	162	633	181	30	1	35	(21	14)	318	102	86	107	70	2	111	4	2	4	20	8	17	.286	.359	.502	.861
2016	Bal	AL	157	640	188	40	1	37	(18	19)	341	105	96	103	48	9	120	3	0	5	0	3	14	.294	.343	.533	.876
2017	Bal	AL	156	630	163	33	1	33	(22	11)	297	81	95	94	50	3	115	1	0	9	9	4	17	.259	.310	.471	.782
2018 2 Tms			162	632	188	35	3	37	(24	13)	340	84	107	115	70	18	104	2	0	5	14	2	26	.297	.367	.538	.905
2019	SD	NL	156	587	150	21	2	32	(15	17)	271	81	85	86	65	3	128	6	0	3	5	3	24	.256	.334	.462	.796
2020	SD	NL	60	224	68	12	1	16	(13	3)	130	44	47	46	26	4	37	0	0	4	6	3	9	.304	.370	.580	.950
18	Bal	AL	96	365	115	21	1	24	(17	7)	210	48	65	74	45	12	51	0	0	3	8	1	14	.315	.387	.575	.963
18	LAD	NL	66	267	73	14	2	13	(7	6)	130	36	42	41	25	6	53	2	0	2	6	1	12	.273	.338	.487	.825
Postseason			23	89	19	3	0	4	(1	3)	34	11	14	8	6	2	24	1	2	1	1	0	5	.213	.268	.382	.650
9 ML YEARS			1142	4531	1268	244	15	223	(134	89)	2211	647	645	711	387	41	834	21	14	36	64	30	141	.280	.337	.488	.825

Vimael Machin

Bats: L Throws: R Pos: 3B-10;SS-6;DH-4;2B-3;1B-2;PH-1   Ht: 5'11" Wt: 185 Born: 9/25/1993 Age: 27

Year	Team	Lg	G	AB	H	2B	3B	HR	(Hm	Rd)	TB	R	RBI	RC	TBB	IBB	SO	HBP	SH	SF	SB	CS	GDP	Avg	OBP	Slg	OPS
2020	Oak	AL	24	63	13	2	0	0	(0	0)	15	11	0	0	8	0	10	0	0	0	0	0	4	.206	.296	.238	.534

Nick Madrigal

Bats: R Throws: R Pos: 2B-29   Ht: 5'8" Wt: 175 Born: 3/5/1997 Age: 24

Year	Team	Lg	G	AB	H	2B	3B	HR	(Hm	Rd)	TB	R	RBI	RC	TBB	IBB	SO	HBP	SH	SF	SB	CS	GDP	Avg	OBP	Slg	OPS
2018 3 Tms		Low	43	155	47	7	0	0	(-	-)	54	25	16	20	7	0	5	7	0	4	8	6	4	.303	.353	.348	.701
2019	WinSa	A+	49	191	52	10	2	2	(-	-)	72	20	27	30	17	2	6	6	1	3	17	4	6	.272	.346	.377	.723
2019	Brham	AA	42	164	56	11	2	1	(-	-)	74	30	16	30	14	0	5	2	0	0	14	6	1	.341	.400	.451	.851
2019	Charllt	AAA	29	118	39	6	1	1	(-	-)	50	26	12	20	13	0	5	1	1	1	4	3	3	.331	.398	.424	.822
2020	CWS	AL	29	103	35	3	0	0	(0	0)	38	8	11	16	4	0	7	2	0	0	2	1	5	.340	.376	.369	.745

Kenta Maeda

Pitches: R Bats: R Pos: SP-11
mah-AY-duh
Ht: 6'1" Wt: 185 Born: 4/11/1988 Age: 33

Year	Team	Lg	HOW MUCH PITCHED					WHAT HE GAVE UP										THE RESULTS								
			G	GS	GF	IP	BFP	H	R	ER	HR	SH	SF	HB	TBB	IBB	SO	WP	W	L	Pct	Sv-Op	Hld	Vel	OPS	ERC	ERA
2016	LAD	NL	32	32	0	175.2	716	150	72	68	20	2	3	8	50	6	179	6	16	11	.593	0-0	0	90	.649	3.09	3.48
2017	LAD	NL	29	25	1	134.1	557	121	68	63	22	6	4	5	34	1	140	4	13	6	.684	1-1	0	92	.714	3.48	4.22
2018	LAD	NL	39	20	4	125.1	532	115	58	53	13	2	3	5	43	4	153	2	8	10	.444	2-2	5	92	.706	3.51	3.81
2019	LAD	NL	37	26	3	153.2	624	114	70	69	22	2	3	4	51	3	169	3	10	8	.556	3-3	4	92	.642	2.79	4.04
2020	Min	AL	11	11	0	66.2	248	40	20	20	9	0	0	0	10	0	80	0	6	1	.857	0-0	0	91	.508	**1.48**	2.70
	Postseason		24	3	2	32.2	139	27	12	12	2	0	0	2	12	2	39	2	2	1	.667	0-0	4	93	.647	2.83	3.31
	5 ML YEARS		148	114	8	655.2	2677	540	288	273	86	10	13	22	188	12	721	15	53	36	.596	6-6	9	91	.659	2.99	3.75

Matt Magill

Pitches: R Bats: R Pos: RP-11
Ht: 6'3" Wt: 210 Born: 11/10/1989 Age: 31

Year	Team	Lg	HOW MUCH PITCHED					WHAT HE GAVE UP										THE RESULTS								
			G	GS	GF	IP	BFP	H	R	ER	HR	SH	SF	HB	TBB	IBB	SO	WP	W	L	Pct	Sv-Op	Hld	Vel	OPS	ERC	ERA
2013	LAD	NL	6	6	0	27.2	137	27	25	20	6	1	2	1	28	1	26	1	0	2	.000	0-0	0	91	.869	7.48	6.51
2016	Cin	NL	5	0	2	4.1	20	5	3	3	1	1	0	0	5	0	1	0	0	0		0-0	0	93	1.098	10.68	6.23
2018	Min	AL	40	0	9	56.2	249	58	24	24	11	1	1	3	23	0	56	0	3	3	.500	0-1	6	95	.809	5.13	3.81
2019	2 Tms		50	0	20	50.2	229	51	31	23	7	2	2	2	20	3	64	5	5	2	.714	5-7	1	95	.760	4.24	4.09
2020	Sea	AL	11	0	0	10.1	45	9	9	7	3	0	0	0	6	0	11	1	0	1	.000	0-2	2	92	.795	5.46	6.10
19	Min	AL	28	0	8	28.1	133	30	21	14	4	1	2	1	15	1	36	2	2	0	1.000	0-0	0	95	.830	5.30	4.45
19	Sea	AL	22	0	12	22.1	96	21	10	9	3	1	1	0	5	2	28	3	3	2	.600	5-7	1	95	.667	2.98	3.63
	5 ML YEARS		112	6	31	149.2	680	150	90	77	28	5	5	6	82	4	158	7	8	8	.500	5-10	9	94	.811	5.40	4.63

Tyler Mahle

Pitches: R Bats: R Pos: SP-9; RP-1
Ht: 6'3" Wt: 210 Born: 9/29/1994 Age: 26

Year	Team	Lg	HOW MUCH PITCHED					WHAT HE GAVE UP										THE RESULTS								
			G	GS	GF	IP	BFP	H	R	ER	HR	SH	SF	HB	TBB	IBB	SO	WP	W	L	Pct	Sv-Op	Hld	Vel	OPS	ERC	ERA
2017	Cin	NL	4	4	0	20.0	92	19	6	6	2	0	4	1	14	1	14	1	1	2	.333	0-0	0	93	.684	4.27	2.70
2018	Cin	NL	23	23	0	112.0	507	125	68	62	22	5	3	4	53	7	110	1	7	9	.438	0-0	0	92	.848	5.77	4.98
2019	Cin	NL	25	25	0	129.2	556	136	82	74	25	2	2	6	34	0	129	2	3	12	.200	0-0	0	93	.775	4.61	5.14
2020	Cin	NL	10	9	0	47.2	201	34	21	19	6	0	4	4	21	0	60	2	2	2	.500	0-0	0	94	.666	3.13	3.59
	4 ML YEARS		62	61	0	309.1	1356	314	177	161	53	9	9	17	119	8	313	6	13	25	.342	0-0	0	93	.781	4.77	4.68

Luke Maile

Bats: R Throws: R Pos: C
MAY-lee
Ht: 6'3" Wt: 225 Born: 2/6/1991 Age: 30

Year	Team	Lg	BATTING																			RUNNING			AVERAGES			
			G	AB	H	2B	3B	HR	(Hm	Rd)	TB	R	RBI	RC	TBB	IBB	SO	HBP	SH	SF	SB	CS	GDP	Avg	OBP	Slg	OPS
2015	TB	AL	15	35	6	3	0	0	(0	0)	9	2	2	0	0	0	8	0	0	0	0	0	3	.171	.171	.257	.429
2016	TB	AL	42	119	27	7	0	3	(2	1)	43	10	15	11	4	1	36	0	3	0	0	0	2	.227	.252	.361	.613
2017	Tor	AL	46	130	19	5	0	2	(1	1)	30	10	7	2	3	0	35	2	0	1	1	0	2	.146	.176	.231	.407
2018	Tor	AL	68	202	50	13	1	3	(2	1)	74	22	27	28	25	0	67	2	0	2	2	0	4	.248	.333	.366	.700
2019	Tor	AL	45	119	18	2	1	2	(2	0)	28	9	9	4	8	0	33	0	2	0	1	0	1	.151	.205	.235	.440
	5 ML YEARS		216	605	120	30	2	10	(7	3)	184	53	60	45	40	1	179	4	5	3	4	0	12	.198	.252	.304	.556

Martin Maldonado

Bats: R Throws: R Pos: C-47
mar-TEEN
Ht: 6'0" Wt: 230 Born: 8/16/1986 Age: 34

Year	Team	Lg	BATTING																			RUNNING			AVERAGES			
			G	AB	H	2B	3B	HR	(Hm	Rd)	TB	R	RBI	RC	TBB	IBB	SO	HBP	SH	SF	SB	CS	GDP	Avg	OBP	Slg	OPS
2011	Mil	NL	3	1	0	0	0	0	(0	0)	0	0	0	0	0	0	1	0	0	0	0	0	0	.000	.000	.000	.000
2012	Mil	NL	78	233	62	9	0	8	(6	2)	95	22	30	28	17	0	56	2	4	0	1	1	5	.266	.321	.408	.729
2013	Mil	NL	67	183	31	7	1	4	(1	3)	52	13	22	14	13	1	53	3	3	0	0	0	2	.169	.236	.284	.520
2014	Mil	NL	52	111	26	5	0	4	(2	2)	43	14	16	14	11	1	32	3	1	0	0	0	4	.234	.320	.387	.707
2015	Mil	NL	79	229	48	7	0	4	(4	0)	67	19	22	20	23	4	65	1	1	2	0	1	6	.210	.282	.293	.575
2016	Mil	NL	76	208	42	7	0	8	(6	2)	73	21	24	23	35	9	56	6	3	1	1	0	6	.202	.332	.351	.683
2017	LAA	AL	138	429	95	19	1	14	(5	9)	158	43	38	37	15	1	119	18	8	1	0	2	12	.221	.276	.368	.645
2018	2 Tms	AL	119	373	84	18	1	9	(2	7)	131	39	44	38	16	0	98	11	2	2	0	1	8	.225	.276	.351	.627
2019	3 Tms	AL	105	333	71	19	0	12	(8	4)	126	46	27	29	32	1	86	6	2	1	0	0	11	.213	.293	.378	.671
2020	Hou	AL	47	135	29	4	0	6	(4	2)	51	19	24	27	27	0	51	1	2	0	1	0	2	.215	.350	.378	.727
18	LAA	AL	78	265	59	14	0	5	(2	3)	88	24	32	30	13	0	73	10	1	1	0	1	3	.223	.284	.332	.616
18	Hou	AL	41	108	25	4	1	4	(0	4)	43	15	12	8	3	0	25	1	1	1	0	0	5	.231	.257	.398	.655
19	KC	AL	74	238	54	15	0	6	(2	4)	87	26	17	21	17	0	55	5	2	1	0	0	9	.227	.291	.366	.657
19	ChC	NL	4	11	0	0	0	0	(0	0)	0	0	0	0	2	1	5	0	0	0	0	0	0	.000	.154	.000	.154
19	Hou	AL	27	84	17	4	0	6	(6	0)	39	20	10	8	13	0	26	1	0	0	0	0	2	.202	.316	.464	.781
	Postseason		14	39	8	2	0	2	(2	0)	16	5	3	3	1	0	13	1	1	0	0	0	2	.205	.244	.410	.654
	10 ML YEARS		764	2235	488	95	3	69	(38	31)	796	236	244	230	189	16	617	51	26	7	3	5	56	.218	.293	.356	.649

Sean Manaea

Pitches: L Bats: R Pos: SP-11
muh-NIE-uh
Ht: 6'5" Wt: 245 Born: 2/1/1992 Age: 29

Year	Team	Lg	HOW MUCH PITCHED					WHAT HE GAVE UP										THE RESULTS								
			G	GS	GF	IP	BFP	H	R	ER	HR	SH	SF	HB	TBB	IBB	SO	WP	W	L	Pct	Sv-Op	Hld	Vel	OPS	ERC	ERA
2016	Oak	AL	25	24	0	144.2	594	135	65	62	20	4	4	4	37	1	124	3	7	9	.438	0-0	0	92	.713	3.53	3.86
2017	Oak	AL	29	29	0	158.2	692	167	88	77	18	1	2	10	55	1	140	8	12	10	.545	0-0	0	92	.763	4.51	4.37
2018	Oak	AL	27	27	0	160.2	654	141	67	64	21	4	2	8	32	1	108	9	12	9	.571	0-0	0	90	.663	3.02	3.59

Year Team	Lg	G	GS	GF	IP	BFP	H	R	ER	HR	SH	SF	HB	TBB	IBB	SO	WP	W	L	Pct	Sv-Op	Hld	Vel	OPS	ERC	ERA
2019 Oak	AL	5	5	0	29.2	109	16	4	4	3	0	0	2	7	0	30	1	4	0	1.000	0-0	0	90	.509	1.58	1.21
2020 Oak	AL	11	11	0	54.0	222	57	32	27	7	0	2	1	8	0	45	1	4	3	.571	0-0	0	90	.724	3.69	4.50
Postseason		1	1	0	2.0	10	4	4	4	3	0	0	0	0	0	5	0	0	1	.000	0-0	0	91	1.700	20.67	18.00
5 ML YEARS		97	96	0	547.2	2271	516	256	234	69	9	10	25	139	3	447	22	39	31	.557	0-0	0	91	.705	3.55	3.85

Trey Mancini

Bats: R **Throws:** R **Pos:** OF   **Ht:** 6'4" **Wt:** 230 **Born:** 3/18/1992 **Age:** 29

Year Team	Lg	G	AB	H	2B	3B	HR	(Hm	Rd)	TB	R	RBI	RC	TBB	IBB	SO	HBP	SH	SF	SB	CS	GDP	Avg	OBP	Slg	OPS
2016 Bal	AL	5	14	5	1	0	3	(3	0)	15	3	5	5	0	0	4	1	0	0	0	0	0	.357	.400	1.071	1.471
2017 Bal	AL	147	543	159	26	4	24	(11	13)	265	65	78	90	33	1	139	6	0	4	1	0	12	.293	.338	.488	.826
2018 Bal	AL	156	582	141	23	3	24	(13	11)	242	69	58	55	44	1	153	5	0	5	0	1	17	.242	.299	.416	.715
2019 Bal	AL	154	602	175	38	2	35	(18	17)	322	106	97	101	63	3	143	9	0	5	1	0	22	.291	.364	.535	.899
4 ML YEARS		462	1741	480	88	9	86	(45	41)	844	243	238	251	140	5	439	21	0	14	2	1	51	.276	.335	.485	.819

Matt Manning

Pitches: R **Bats:** R **Pos:** P   **Ht:** 6'6" **Wt:** 195 **Born:** 1/28/1998 **Age:** 23

Year Team	Lg	G	GS	GF	IP	BFP	H	R	ER	HR	SH	SF	HB	TBB	IBB	SO	WP	W	L	Pct	Sv-Op	Hld	Vel	OPS	ERC	ERA
2016 TigersW	R	10	10	0	29.1	122	27	18	13	2	0	0	1	7	0	46	0	0	2	.000	0- -	-	-	.682	2.92	3.99
2017 2 Tms	Low	14	14	0	51.0	218	41	21	18	0	1	1	3	25	0	62	3	4	2	.667	0- -	-	-	.605	2.87	3.18
2018 2 Tms	Low	20	20	0	107.0	442	79	39	38	7	3	3	2	47	0	141	6	7	7	.500	0- -	-	-	.583	2.71	3.20
2019 Erie	AA	24	24	0	133.2	527	93	42	38	7	0	3	2	38	1	148	5	11	5	.688	0- -	-	-	.540	1.87	2.56

Joe Mantiply

Pitches: L **Bats:** R **Pos:** RP-4   **Ht:** 6'4" **Wt:** 215 **Born:** 3/1/1991 **Age:** 30

Year Team	Lg	G	GS	GF	IP	BFP	H	R	ER	HR	SH	SF	HB	TBB	IBB	SO	WP	W	L	Pct	Sv-Op	Hld	Vel	OPS	ERC	ERA
2016 Det	AL	5	0	3	2.2	16	7	5	5	1	1	0	0	2	1	2	0	0	0	-	0-0	0	88	1.446	19.98	16.88
2019 NYY	AL	1	0	0	3.0	14	3	3	3	1	0	0	0	2	0	2	0	1	0	1.000	0-0	0	89	1.024	6.85	9.00
2020 Ari	NL	4	0	1	2.1	15	3	4	4	0	0	0	0	4	0	2	0	0	0	-	0-0	0	91	.830	9.50	15.43
3 ML YEARS		10	0	4	8.0	45	13	12	12	2	1	0	0	8	1	6	0	1	0	1.000	0-0	0	89	1.116	11.69	13.50

Dillon Maples

Pitches: R **Bats:** R **Pos:** RP-2   **Ht:** 6'2" **Wt:** 230 **Born:** 5/9/1992 **Age:** 29

Year Team	Lg	G	GS	GF	IP	BFP	H	R	ER	HR	SH	SF	HB	TBB	IBB	SO	WP	W	L	Pct	Sv-Op	Hld	Vel	OPS	ERC	ERA
2017 ChC	NL	6	0	1	5.1	27	6	6	6	0	0	0	0	6	0	11	1	0	0	-	0-0	0	97	.825	6.99	10.13
2018 ChC	NL	9	0	1	5.1	29	7	7	7	2	0	0	2	5	0	9	2	1	0	1.000	0-0	0	97	1.210	12.98	11.81
2019 ChC	NL	14	0	3	11.2	54	6	7	7	2	0	0	4	10	0	18	0	1	0	1.000	0-0	0	97	.670	4.99	5.40
2020 ChC	NL	2	0	1	1.0	9	1	3	2	0	0	0	0	4	0	1	0	0	0	-	0-0	0	96	.956	16.22	18.00
4 ML YEARS		31	0	6	23.1	119	20	23	22	4	0	0	6	25	0	39	3	2	0	1.000	0-0	0	97	.860	7.62	8.49

Rafael Marchan

Bats: B **Throws:** R **Pos:** C-3   **Ht:** 5'9" **Wt:** 170 **Born:** 2/25/1999 **Age:** 22

Year Team	Lg	G	AB	H	2B	3B	HR	(Hm	Rd)	TB	R	RBI	RC	TBB	IBB	SO	HBP	SH	SF	SB	CS	GDP	Avg	OBP	Slg	OPS
2020 Phi	NL	3	8	4	0	0	1	(1	0)	7	3	3	4	1	0	2	0	0	0	0	0	0	.500	.556	.875	1.431

Nick Margevicius

Pitches: L **Bats:** L **Pos:** SP-7; RP-3   mahr-GAH-vih-chus   **Ht:** 6'5" **Wt:** 220 **Born:** 6/18/1996 **Age:** 25

Year Team	Lg	G	GS	GF	IP	BFP	H	R	ER	HR	SH	SF	HB	TBB	IBB	SO	WP	W	L	Pct	Sv-Op	Hld	Vel	OPS	ERC	ERA
2019 SD	NL	17	12	1	57.0	263	73	46	43	12	3	0	3	19	1	42	1	2	6	.250	0-0	0	88	.912	6.43	6.79
2020 Sea	AL	10	7	1	41.1	170	38	21	21	6	0	0	0	14	2	36	2	2	3	.400	0-1	0	90	.742	3.69	4.57
2 ML YEARS		27	19	2	98.1	433	111	67	64	18	3	0	3	33	3	78	3	4	9	.308	0-1	0	89	.844	5.23	5.86

Manuel Margot

Bats: R **Throws:** R **Pos:** CF-21;LF-18;RF-15;PH-2;PR-2;DH-1 mar-GOH   **Ht:** 5'11" **Wt:** 180 **Born:** 9/28/1994 **Age:** 26

Year Team	Lg	G	AB	H	2B	3B	HR	(Hm	Rd)	TB	R	RBI	RC	TBB	IBB	SO	HBP	SH	SF	SB	CS	GDP	Avg	OBP	Slg	OPS
2016 SD	NL	10	37	9	4	1	0	(0	0)	15	4	3	5	0	0	7	0	0	0	2	0	0	.243	.243	.405	.649
2017 SD	NL	126	487	128	18	7	13	(7	6)	199	53	39	55	35	0	106	2	1	4	17	7	6	.263	.313	.409	.721
2018 SD	NL	141	477	117	26	8	8	(5	3)	183	50	51	56	32	4	88	2	1	7	11	10	9	.245	.292	.384	.675
2019 SD	NL	151	398	93	19	3	12	(3	9)	154	59	37	47	38	1	88	2	3	0	20	4	6	.234	.304	.387	.691
2020 TB	AL	47	145	39	9	0	1	(1	0)	51	19	11	17	13	0	25	0	0	1	12	4	0	.269	.327	.352	.679
5 ML YEARS		475	1544	386	76	19	34	(16	18)	602	185	141	180	118	5	314	6	5	12	62	25	21	.250	.304	.390	.693

Jake Marisnick

Bats: R **Throws:** R **Pos:** CF-16;PR-1 muh-RIZ-nick **Ht:** 6'4" **Wt:** 220 **Born:** 3/30/1991 **Age:** 30

Year Team	Lg	G	AB	H	2B	3B	HR	(Hm	Rd)	TB	R	RBI	RC	TBB	IBB	SO	HBP	SH	SF	SB	CS	GDP	Avg	OBP	Slg	OPS
2013 Mia	NL	40	109	20	2	1	1	(1	0)	27	6	5	7	6	0	27	1	1	1	3	1	1	.183	.231	.248	.478
2014 2 Tms		65	221	55	8	0	3	(3	0)	72	21	19	19	8	3	67	3	2	3	11	3	2	.249	.281	.326	.607
2015 Hou	AL	133	339	80	15	4	9	(4	5)	130	46	36	40	18	0	105	5	6	4	24	9	2	.236	.281	.383	.665
2016 Hou	AL	118	287	60	18	1	5	(1	4)	95	40	21	23	16	0	83	3	4	1	10	5	4	.209	.257	.331	.588
2017 Hou	AL	106	230	56	10	0	16	(10	6)	114	50	35	31	20	1	90	6	2	1	9	4	5	.243	.319	.496	.815
2018 Hou	AL	103	213	45	8	1	10	(2	8)	85	34	28	24	15	1	84	4	1	1	6	2	6	.211	.275	.399	.674
2019 Hou	AL	120	292	68	16	3	10	(5	5)	120	46	34	31	17	0	95	6	3	0	10	3	6	.233	.289	.411	.700
2020 NYM	NL	16	33	11	3	0	2	(1	1)	20	4	5	6	1	0	10	0	0	0	0	0	0	.333	.353	.606	.959
14 Mia	NL	14	48	8	0	0	0	(0	0)	8	3	0	1	3	1	19	0	0	0	5	0	0	.167	.216	.167	.382
14 Hou	AL	51	173	47	8	0	3	(3	0)	64	18	19	18	5	2	48	3	2	3	6	3	2	.272	.299	.370	.669
Postseason		23	21	7	1	0	0	(0	0)	8	1	0	3	1	0	8	0	0	0	2	0	0	.333	.364	.381	.745
8 ML YEARS		701	1724	395	80	10	56	(27	29)	663	247	183	181	101	5	561	28	19	11	73	27	26	.229	.281	.385	.666

Nick Markakis

Bats: L **Throws:** L **Pos:** RF-29;LF-7;PH-3;DH-2 mar-KAY-kiss **Ht:** 6'1" **Wt:** 210 **Born:** 11/17/1983 **Age:** 37

Year Team	Lg	G	AB	H	2B	3B	HR	(Hm	Rd)	TB	R	RBI	RC	TBB	IBB	SO	HBP	SH	SF	SB	CS	GDP	Avg	OBP	Slg	OPS
2006 Bal	AL	147	491	143	25	2	16	(9	7)	220	72	62	67	43	3	72	3	3	2	2	0	15	.291	.351	.448	.799
2007 Bal	AL	161	637	191	43	3	23	(15	8)	309	97	112	103	61	5	112	5	1	6	18	6	22	.300	.362	.485	.848
2008 Bal	AL	157	595	182	48	1	20	(11	9)	292	106	87	113	99	7	113	2	0	1	10	7	10	.306	.406	.491	.897
2009 Bal	AL	161	642	188	45	2	18	(8	10)	291	94	101	97	56	0	98	3	0	10	6	2	12	.293	.347	.453	.801
2010 Bal	AL	160	629	187	45	3	12	(8	4)	274	79	60	99	73	9	93	2	0	5	7	2	18	.297	.370	.436	.805
2011 Bal	AL	160	641	182	31	1	15	(8	7)	260	72	73	90	62	6	75	7	0	6	12	3	16	.284	.351	.406	.756
2012 Bal	AL	104	420	125	28	3	13	(8	4)	198	59	54	69	42	3	51	4	0	5	1	1	11	.298	.363	.471	.834
2013 Bal	AL	160	634	172	24	0	10	(6	4)	226	89	59	66	55	3	76	3	0	8	1	2	17	.271	.329	.356	.685
2014 Bal	AL	155	642	177	27	1	14	(8	6)	248	81	50	82	62	4	84	4	0	2	4	2	10	.276	.342	.386	.729
2015 Atl	NL	156	612	181	38	1	3	(1	2)	230	73	53	81	70	11	83	3	0	1	2	1	17	.296	.370	.376	.746
2016 Atl	NL	158	599	161	38	0	13	(7	6)	238	67	89	82	71	9	101	5	0	9	0	2	16	.269	.346	.397	.744
2017 Atl	NL	160	593	163	39	1	8	(4	4)	228	76	76	77	68	8	110	6	0	3	0	2	16	.275	.354	.384	.738
2018 Atl	NL	162	623	185	43	2	14	(4	10)	274	78	93	96	72	10	80	1	0	9	1	1	18	.297	.366	.440	.806
2019 Atl	NL	116	414	118	25	2	9	(5	4)	174	61	62	60	47	1	59	2	0	6	2	0	11	.285	.356	.420	.776
2020 Atl	NL	37	130	33	15	0	1	(1	0)	51	15	15	12	10	0	23	1	0	0	1	0	5	.254	.312	.392	.704
Postseason		16	64	12	2	0	1	(1	0)	17	6	3	4	5	0	9	0	0	0	1	1	1	.188	.246	.266	.512
15 ML YEARS		2154	8302	2388	514	22	189	(104	85)	3513	1119	1046	1194	891	79	1230	51	4	73	66	32	214	.288	.357	.423	.781

Jose Marmolejos

Bats: L **Throws:** L **Pos:** LF-18;DH-10;1B-5;PH-3;RF-2 marr-mo-LEH-hose **Ht:** 6'2" **Wt:** 239 **Born:** 1/2/1993 **Age:** 28

Year Team	Lg	G	AB	H	2B	3B	HR	(Hm	Rd)	TB	R	RBI	RC	TBB	IBB	SO	HBP	SH	SF	SB	CS	GDP	Avg	OBP	Slg	OPS
2020 Sea	AL	35	107	22	4	0	6	(1	5)	44	12	18	15	7	0	32	1	0	0	0	1	2	.206	.261	.411	.672

Brailyn Marquez

Pitches: L **Bats:** L **Pos:** RP-1 **Ht:** 6'4" **Wt:** 185 **Born:** 1/30/1999 **Age:** 22

		HOW MUCH PITCHED					WHAT HE GAVE UP											THE RESULTS								
Year Team	Lg	G	GS	GF	IP	BFP	H	R	ER	HR	SH	SF	HB	TBB	IBB	SO	WP	W	L	Pct	Sv-Op	Hld	Vel	OPS	ERC	ERA
2017 Cubs	R	11	9	0	44.0	199	50	34	27	3	1	0	4	12	0	52	9	2	1	.667	0--	-	-	.672	4.33	5.52
2018 2 Tms	Low	12	7	0	54.2	228	53	25	19	5	0	1	2	16	0	59	6	1	4	.200	0--	-	-	1.185	3.62	3.13
2019 2 Tms	Low	22	17	0	103.2	438	85	46	36	5	0	2	6	50	0	128	23	9	5	.643	0--	-	-	.493	3.31	3.13
2020 ChC	NL	1	0	0	0.2	7	2	5	5	0	0	0	0	3	0	1	2	0	0	-	0-0	0	98	1.464	37.18	67.50

German Marquez

Pitches: R **Bats:** R **Pos:** SP-13 hair-MAHN **Ht:** 6'1" **Wt:** 230 **Born:** 2/22/1995 **Age:** 26

		HOW MUCH PITCHED					WHAT HE GAVE UP											THE RESULTS								
Year Team	Lg	G	GS	GF	IP	BFP	H	R	ER	HR	SH	SF	HB	TBB	IBB	SO	WP	W	L	Pct	Sv-Op	Hld	Vel	OPS	ERC	ERA
2016 Col	NL	6	3	0	20.2	98	28	12	12	3	2	1	3	6	0	15	0	1	1	.500	0-0	0	93	.932	6.21	5.23
2017 Col	NL	29	29	0	162.0	701	174	82	79	25	5	4	8	49	3	147	6	11	7	.611	0-0	0	95	.806	4.67	4.39
2018 Col	NL	33	33	0	196.0	817	179	90	82	24	2	6	8	57	5	230	8	14	11	.560	0-0	0	95	.698	3.45	3.77
2019 Col	NL	28	28	0	174.0	721	174	96	92	29	6	4	5	35	0	175	14	12	5	.706	0-0	0	95	.740	3.86	4.76
2020 Col	NL	13	13	0	81.2	344	78	41	34	6	0	3	0	25	0	73	4	4	6	.400	0-0	0	96	.673	3.26	3.75
Postseason		1	1	0	5.0	22	7	2	2	1	0	0	0	1	0	5	0	0	1	.000	0-0	0	96	.840	6.52	3.60
5 ML YEARS		109	106	0	634.1	2681	633	321	299	86	15	18	24	172	8	640	32	42	30	.583	0-0	0	95	.742	3.93	4.24

Evan Marshall

Pitches: R **Bats:** R **Pos:** RP-23 **Ht:** 6'2" **Wt:** 235 **Born:** 4/18/1990 **Age:** 31

		HOW MUCH PITCHED					WHAT HE GAVE UP											THE RESULTS								
Year Team	Lg	G	GS	GF	IP	BFP	H	R	ER	HR	SH	SF	HB	TBB	IBB	SO	WP	W	L	Pct	Sv-Op	Hld	Vel	OPS	ERC	ERA
2014 Ari	NL	57	0	11	49.1	210	50	17	15	3	2	1	2	17	3	54	3	4	4	.500	0-1	19	94	.709	3.76	2.74
2015 Ari	NL	13	0	4	13.1	61	20	9	9	3	0	0	0	5	1	7	1	0	2	.000	0-2	2	94	.827	8.27	6.08
2016 Ari	NL	15	0	8	15.1	79	28	18	15	2	0	1	0	8	2	9	1	0	0	.000	0-0	1	93	1.083	10.46	8.80
2017 Sea	AL	6	0	2	7.2	38	12	8	8	1	0	0	0	5	1	4	0	0	0	-	0-0	0	94	.993	8.94	9.39

Year Team	Lg	G	GS	GF	IP	BFP	H	R	ER	HR	SH	SF	HB	TBB	IBB	SO	WP	W	L	Pct	Sv-Op	Hld	Vel	OPS	ERC	ERA
2018 Cle	AL	10	0	1	7.0	37	12	6	6	0	0	0	1	4	0	9	1	0	0	-	0-1	3	93	.866	9.01	7.71
2019 CWS	AL	55	0	2	50.2	209	42	16	14	5	0	1	0	24	2	41	1	4	2	.667	0-4	19	94	.669	3.45	2.49
2020 CWS	AL	23	0	0	22.2	93	17	6	6	1	0	0	0	7	0	30	2	2	1	.667	0-2	8	93	.537	2.04	2.38
7 ML YEARS		179	0	28	166.0	727	181	80	73	15	2	2	4	70	9	154	9	10	10	.500	0-10	52	94	.763	4.67	3.96

Ketel Marte

Bats: B Throws: R Pos: 2B-41;CF-3;SS-2;DH-1 kuh-TELL marr-TAY **Ht: 6'1" Wt: 210 Born: 10/12/1993 Age: 27**

Year Team	Lg	G	AB	H	2B	3B	HR	(Hm	Rd)	TB	R	RBI	RC	TBB	IBB	SO	HBP	SH	SF	SB	CS	GDP	Avg	OBP	Slg	OPS
2015 Sea	AL	57	219	62	14	3	2	(1	1)	88	25	17	33	24	0	43	0	2	2	8	4	1	.283	.351	.402	.753
2016 Sea	AL	119	437	113	21	2	1	(1	0)	141	55	33	41	18	0	84	2	3	6	11	5	10	.259	.287	.323	.610
2017 Ari	NL	73	223	58	11	2	5	(1	4)	88	30	18	27	29	3	37	1	0	2	3	1	3	.260	.345	.395	.740
2018 Ari	NL	153	520	135	26	4	14	(8	6)	227	68	59	67	54	3	79	3	1	2	6	1	12	.260	.332	.437	.768
2019 Ari	NL	144	569	187	36	9	32	(13	19)	337	97	92	121	53	2	86	4	0	2	10	2	7	.329	.389	.592	.981
2020 Ari	NL	45	181	52	14	1	2	(1	1)	74	19	17	27	7	0	21	4	0	3	1	0	2	.287	.323	.409	.732
Postseason		4	17	7	0	2	1	(0	1)	14	4	2	4	0	0	5	0	0	0	0	0	0	.412	.412	.824	1.235
6 ML YEARS		591	2149	607	122	29	56	(25	31)	955	294	236	316	185	8	350	14	6	17	39	13	35	.282	.341	.444	.785

Starling Marte

Bats: R Throws: R Pos: CF-61;LF-1;PH-1 marr-TAY **Ht: 6'1" Wt: 195 Born: 10/9/1988 Age: 32**

Year Team	Lg	G	AB	H	2B	3B	HR	(Hm	Rd)	TB	R	RBI	RC	TBB	IBB	SO	HBP	SH	SF	SB	CS	GDP	Avg	OBP	Slg	OPS
2012 Pit	NL	47	167	43	3	6	5	(3	2)	73	18	17	21	8	0	50	3	2	2	12	5	5	.257	.300	.437	.737
2013 Pit	NL	135	510	143	26	10	12	(5	7)	225	83	35	74	25	2	138	24	6	1	41	15	6	.280	.343	.441	.784
2014 Pit	NL	135	495	144	29	6	13	(5	8)	224	73	56	70	33	0	131	17	0	0	30	11	5	.291	.356	.453	.808
2015 Pit	NL	153	579	166	30	2	19	(10	9)	257	84	81	81	27	3	123	19	3	5	30	10	14	.287	.337	.444	.780
2016 Pit	NL	129	489	152	34	5	9	(2	7)	223	71	46	77	23	5	104	16	1	0	47	12	8	.311	.362	.456	.818
2017 Pit	NL	77	309	85	7	2	7	(5	2)	117	48	31	46	20	0	63	8	0	2	21	4	5	.275	.333	.379	.712
2018 Pit	NL	145	559	155	32	5	20	(8	12)	257	81	72	83	35	2	109	8	1	3	33	14	11	.277	.327	.460	.787
2019 Pit	NL	132	539	159	31	6	23	(9	14)	271	97	82	95	25	1	94	16	2	4	25	6	15	.295	.342	.503	.845
2020 2 Tms	NL	61	228	64	14	1	6	(2	4)	98	36	27	32	12	1	41	9	0	1	10	2	5	.281	.340	.430	.770
20 Ari	NL	33	122	38	8	1	2	(0	2)	54	23	14	21	10	1	19	5	0	1	5	2	3	.311	.384	.443	.827
20 Mia	NL	28	106	26	6	0	4	(2	2)	44	13	13	11	2	0	22	4	0	0	5	0	2	.245	.286	.415	.701
Postseason		8	32	4	1	0	1	(0	1)	8	2	1	1	1	0	7	1	0	0	1	0	2	.125	.176	.250	.426
9 ML YEARS		1014	3875	1111	206	43	114	(49	65)	1745	591	447	579	208	14	853	120	15	18	249	79	74	.287	.341	.450	.791

Brett Martin

Pitches: L Bats: L Pos: RP-15 **Ht: 6'4" Wt: 200 Born: 4/28/1995 Age: 26**

Year Team	Lg	G	GS	GF	IP	BFP	H	R	ER	HR	SH	SF	HB	TBB	IBB	SO	WP	W	L	Pct	Sv-Op	Hld	Vel	OPS	ERC	ERA
2019 Tex	AL	51	2	7	62.1	280	72	38	33	7	0	3	2	18	2	62	3	2	3	.400	0-1	4	94	.745	4.54	4.76
2020 Tex	AL	15	0	4	14.2	61	8	5	3	2	0	1	0	9	0	8	1	1	1	.500	0-0	2	94	.612	2.67	1.84
2 ML YEARS		66	2	11	77.0	341	80	43	36	9	0	4	2	27	2	70	4	3	4	.429	0-1	6	94	.722	4.16	4.21

Chris Martin

Pitches: R Bats: R Pos: RP-19 **Ht: 6'8" Wt: 225 Born: 6/2/1986 Age: 35**

Year Team	Lg	G	GS	GF	IP	BFP	H	R	ER	HR	SH	SF	HB	TBB	IBB	SO	WP	W	L	Pct	Sv-Op	Hld	Vel	OPS	ERC	ERA
2014 Col	NL	16	0	1	15.2	69	22	12	12	2	0	0	0	4	0	14	1	0	0	-	0-0	3	94	.915	6.30	6.89
2015 NYY	AL	24	0	8	20.2	99	28	13	13	2	0	0	1	6	1	18	3	0	2	.000	1-1	5	94	.777	5.52	5.66
2018 Tex	AL	46	0	8	41.2	177	46	21	21	5	0	1	3	5	2	37	4	1	5	.167	0-3	14	95	.722	3.85	4.54
2019 2 Tms	NL	58	0	20	55.2	216	52	23	21	9	0	2	0	5	0	65	0	1	3	.250	4-6	18	96	.675	2.98	3.40
2020 Atl	NL	19	0	3	18.0	66	8	3	2	1	0	0	1	3	1	20	0	1	1	.500	1-1	6	94	.375	0.89	1.00
19 Tex	AL	38	0	15	38.0	147	35	13	13	8	0	1	0	4	0	43	0	0	2	.000	4-5	12	96	.716	3.27	3.08
19 Atl	NL	20	0	5	17.2	69	17	10	8	1	0	1	0	1	0	22	0	1	1	.500	0-1	6	95	.589	2.36	4.08
5 ML YEARS		163	0	40	151.2	627	156	72	69	19	0	3	5	23	4	154	8	3	11	.214	6-11	46	95	.700	3.52	4.09

Jason Martin

Bats: L Throws: R Pos: CF-4;PR-2;LF-1 **Ht: 5'9" Wt: 185 Born: 9/5/1995 Age: 25**

Year Team	Lg	G	AB	H	2B	3B	HR	(Hm	Rd)	TB	R	RBI	RC	TBB	IBB	SO	HBP	SH	SF	SB	CS	GDP	Avg	OBP	Slg	OPS
2019 Pit	NL	20	36	9	2	0	0	(0	0)	11	5	2	5	4	0	10	0	0	0	2	0	0	.250	.325	.306	.631
2020 Pit	NL	7	9	0	0	0	0	(0	0)	0	2	0	0	2	0	4	0	0	0	0	0	0	.000	.182	.000	.182
2 ML YEARS		27	45	9	2	0	0	(0	0)	11	7	2	5	6	0	14	0	0	0	2	0	0	.200	.294	.244	.539

Richie Martin Jr.

Bats: R Throws: R Pos: SS **Ht: 5'11" Wt: 190 Born: 12/22/1994 Age: 26**

Year Team	Lg	G	AB	H	2B	3B	HR	(Hm	Rd)	TB	R	RBI	RC	TBB	IBB	SO	HBP	SH	SF	SB	CS	GDP	Avg	OBP	Slg	OPS
2019 Bal	AL	120	283	59	8	3	6	(3	3)	91	29	23	17	14	0	83	6	5	1	10	1	6	.208	.260	.322	.581

Carlos Martinez

Pitches: R Bats: R Pos: SP-5   Ht: 6'0" Wt: 200 Born: 9/21/1991 Age: 29

			HOW MUCH PITCHED				WHAT HE GAVE UP										THE RESULTS						
Year	Team	Lg	G	GS	GF	IP	BFP	H	R	ER	HR	SH	SF	HB	TBB	IBB	SO	WP	W	L	Pct	Sv-Op	Hld	Vel	OPS	ERC	ERA
2013	StL	NL	21	1	5	28.1	124	31	16	16	1	1	1	3	9	1	24	0	2	1	.667	1-1	3	97	.704	4.20	5.08
2014	StL	NL	57	7	13	89.1	386	90	41	40	4	7	1	4	36	8	84	8	2	4	.333	1-6	17	97	.713	3.79	4.03
2015	StL	NL	31	29	1	179.2	755	168	65	60	13	9	4	8	63	5	184	8	14	7	.667	0-0	1	95	.687	3.51	3.01
2016	StL	NL	31	31	0	195.1	809	169	68	66	15	2	2	11	70	1	174	6	16	9	.640	0-0	0	96	.643	3.29	3.04
2017	StL	NL	32	32	0	205.0	858	179	93	83	27	4	2	8	71	3	217	9	12	11	.522	0-0	0	96	.694	3.51	3.64
2018	StL	NL	33	18	9	118.2	521	100	48	41	5	7	4	11	60	4	117	5	8	6	.571	5-5	3	94	.647	3.46	3.11
2019	StL	NL	48	0	38	48.1	200	39	18	17	2	1	1	3	18	1	53	2	4	2	.667	24-27	3	96	.590	2.77	3.17
2020	StL	NL	5	5	0	20.0	104	32	26	22	6	0	2	0	10	2	17	0	0	3	.000	0-0	0	93	1.045	9.41	9.90
	Postseason		20	0	4	20.1	86	16	12	12	2	1	1	1	11	3	18	2	1	2	.333	0-1	5	97	.718	3.45	5.31
	8 ML YEARS		258	123	66	884.2	3757	808	375	345	73	31	17	48	337	25	870	40	58	43	.574	31-39	27	95	.682	3.58	3.51

J.D. Martinez

Bats: R Throws: R Pos: DH-48;RF-4;LF-3   Ht: 6'3" Wt: 230 Born: 8/21/1987 Age: 33

			BATTING																		RUNNING			AVERAGES			
Year	Team	Lg	G	AB	H	2B	3B	HR	(Hm	Rd)	TB	R	RBI	RC	TBB	IBB	SO	HBP	SH	SF	SB	CS	GDP	Avg	OBP	Slg	OPS
2011	Hou	NL	53	208	57	13	0	6	(3	3)	88	29	35	30	13	1	48	2	0	3	0	1	4	.274	.319	.423	.742
2012	Hou	NL	113	395	95	14	3	11	(5	6)	148	34	55	45	40	0	96	1	0	2	0	2	18	.241	.311	.375	.685
2013	Hou	AL	86	296	74	17	0	7	(4	3)	112	24	36	29	10	0	82	0	0	3	0	0	8	.250	.272	.378	.650
2014	Det	AL	123	441	139	30	3	23	(13	10)	244	57	76	75	30	5	126	3	0	6	6	3	8	.315	.358	.553	.912
2015	Det	AL	158	596	168	33	2	38	(20	18)	319	93	102	100	53	7	178	5	0	3	3	2	11	.282	.344	.535	.879
2016	Det	AL	120	460	141	35	2	22	(13	9)	246	69	68	77	49	2	128	3	0	5	1	2	13	.307	.373	.535	.908
2017	2 Tms		119	432	131	26	3	45	(27	18)	298	85	104	92	53	8	128	0	0	4	4	0	23	.303	.376	.690	1.066
2018	Bos	AL	150	569	188	37	2	43	(26	17)	358	111	130	138	69	11	146	4	0	7	6	1	19	.330	.402	.629	1.031
2019	Bos	AL	146	575	175	33	2	36	(18	18)	320	98	105	117	72	9	138	4	0	5	2	0	19	.304	.383	.557	.939
2020	Bos	AL	54	211	45	16	0	7	(4	3)	82	22	27	23	22	3	59	2	0	2	1	0	6	.213	.291	.389	.680
17	Det	AL	57	200	61	13	2	16	(11	5)	126	38	39	39	29	5	54	0	0	3	2	0	10	.305	.388	.630	1.018
17	Ari	NL	62	232	70	13	1	29	(16	13)	172	47	65	53	24	3	74	0	0	1	2	0	13	.302	.366	.741	1.107
	Postseason		21	77	22	3	0	6	(1	5)	43	10	20	18	11	3	21	0	0	2	0	1	1	.286	.367	.558	.925
	10 ML YEARS		1122	4183	1213	254	17	238	(133	105)	2215	622	738	726	411	46	1129	24	0	40	25	11	129	.290	.354	.530	.883

Jose Martinez

Bats: R Throws: R Pos: DH-20;PH-13;1B-6   Ht: 6'6" Wt: 215 Born: 7/25/1988 Age: 32

			BATTING																		RUNNING			AVERAGES			
Year	Team	Lg	G	AB	H	2B	3B	HR	(Hm	Rd)	TB	R	RBI	RC	TBB	IBB	SO	HBP	SH	SF	SB	CS	GDP	Avg	OBP	Slg	OPS
2016	StL	NL	12	16	7	1	0	0	(0	0)	8	4	1	4	2	0	1	0	0	0	0	0	0	.438	.500	.500	1.000
2017	StL	NL	106	272	84	13	1	14	(8	6)	141	47	46	47	32	2	60	0	1	2	4	0	9	.309	.379	.518	.897
2018	StL	NL	152	534	163	30	0	17	(9	8)	244	64	83	89	49	0	104	2	2	3	0	3	15	.305	.364	.457	.821
2019	StL	NL	128	334	90	13	2	10	(3	7)	137	45	42	46	35	0	82	2	0	2	3	0	14	.269	.340	.410	.751
2020	2 Tms		34	88	16	4	0	2	(2	0)	26	10	10	9	10	1	27	0	0	0	0	0	6	.182	.265	.295	.561
20	TB	AL	24	67	16	4	0	2	(2	0)	26	10	10	9	9	1	20	0	0	0	0	0	5	.239	.329	.388	.717
20	ChC	NL	10	21	0	0	0	0	(0	0)	0	0	0	0	1	0	7	0	0	0	0	0	1	.000	.045	.000	.045
	Postseason		7	13	7	2	0	0	(0	0)	9	1	3	3	0	0	3	0	0	0	0	0	0	.538	.538	.692	1.231
	5 ML YEARS		432	1244	360	61	3	43	(22	21)	556	170	182	195	128	3	274	4	3	7	7	3	44	.289	.356	.447	.803

Jorge Mateo

Bats: R Throws: R Pos: PR-7;2B-5;PH-4;LF-3;RF-3;DH-3;CF-1   Ht: 6'0" Wt: 182 Born: 6/23/1995 Age: 26

			BATTING																		RUNNING			AVERAGES			
Year	Team	Lg	G	AB	H	2B	3B	HR	(Hm	Rd)	TB	R	RBI	RC	TBB	IBB	SO	HBP	SH	SF	SB	CS	GDP	Avg	OBP	Slg	OPS
2020	SD	NL	22	26	4	3	0	0	(0	0)	7	4	2	2	1	0	11	0	1	0	1	0	1	.154	.185	.269	.454

Mark Mathias

Bats: R Throws: R Pos: RF-8;PH-5;LF-4;1B-1;2B-1;CF-1;DH-1;PR-1   Ht: 6'0" Wt: 200 Born: 8/2/1994 Age: 26

			BATTING																		RUNNING			AVERAGES			
Year	Team	Lg	G	AB	H	2B	3B	HR	(Hm	Rd)	TB	R	RBI	RC	TBB	IBB	SO	HBP	SH	SF	SB	CS	GDP	Avg	OBP	Slg	OPS
2020	Mil	NL	16	36	10	3	0	0	(0	0)	13	2	4	3	0	0	7	0	0	0	1	0	1	.278	.278	.361	.639

Jeff Mathis

Bats: R Throws: R Pos: C-24;PH-1   Ht: 6'0" Wt: 205 Born: 3/31/1983 Age: 38

			BATTING																		RUNNING			AVERAGES			
Year	Team	Lg	G	AB	H	2B	3B	HR	(Hm	Rd)	TB	R	RBI	RC	TBB	IBB	SO	HBP	SH	SF	SB	CS	GDP	Avg	OBP	Slg	OPS
2005	LAA	AL	5	3	1	0	0	0	(0	0)	1	1	0	0	0	0	1	0	0	0	0	0	0	.333	.333	.333	.667
2006	LAA	AL	23	55	8	2	0	2	(1	1)	16	9	6	4	7	1	14	0	0	1	0	0	0	.145	.238	.291	.529
2007	LAA	AL	59	171	36	12	0	4	(3	1)	60	24	23	13	15	0	49	2	3	1	3	1	3	.211	.276	.351	.627
2008	LAA	AL	94	283	55	8	0	9	(4	5)	90	35	42	33	30	4	90	3	8	4	2	2	1	.194	.275	.318	.593
2009	LAA	AL	84	237	50	8	0	5	(3	2)	73	26	28	24	22	0	73	4	8	1	2	3	2	.211	.288	.308	.596
2010	LAA	AL	68	205	40	6	1	3	(2	1)	57	19	18	10	6	0	59	1	3	3	3	0	3	.195	.225	.278	.497
2011	LAA	AL	93	247	43	12	0	3	(1	2)	64	18	22	12	15	2	75	2	14	3	1	2	3	.174	.225	.259	.484
2012	Tor	AL	71	211	46	13	0	8	(5	3)	83	25	27	18	9	0	68	0	6	1	1	0	2	.218	.249	.393	.642
2013	Mia	NL	73	232	42	7	1	5	(3	2)	66	14	29	15	21	4	76	1	1	1	0	0	5	.181	.251	.284	.535
2014	Mia	NL	64	175	35	7	0	2	(1	1)	48	12	12	11	15	2	64	0	5	0	0	0	2	.200	.263	.274	.537
2015	Mia	NL	32	93	15	4	1	2	(1	1)	27	9	12	3	7	1	24	0	0	3	0	0	2	.161	.214	.290	.504
2016	Mia	NL	41	126	30	4	1	2	(0	2)	42	12	15	10	4	0	36	1	1	0	0	0	1	.238	.267	.333	.601

Year Team	Lg	G	AB	H	2B	3B	HR	(Hm	Rd)	TB	R	RBI	RC	TBB	IBB	SO	HBP	SH	SF	SB	CS	GDP	Avg	OBP	Slg	OPS
								BATTING												RUNNING			AVERAGES			
2017 Ari	NL	60	186	40	10	2	2	(2	0)	60	13	11	14	14	1	61	2	1	0	1	0	6	.215	.277	.323	.600
2018 Ari	NL	69	195	39	9	1	1	(1	0)	53	15	20	15	20	1	66	0	1	2	0	0	7	.200	.272	.272	.544
2019 Tex	AL	88	228	36	9	0	2	(1	1)	51	17	12	9	15	1	87	0	0	0	1	0	2	.158	.209	.224	.433
2020 Tex	AL	24	62	10	1	1	3	(2	1)	22	6	9	7	5	0	24	0	0	1	1	0	0	.161	.221	.355	.575
Postseason		13	29	11	5	0	1	(0	1)	19	3	4	5	1	0	8	0	1	0	0	0	0	.379	.400	.655	1.055
16 ML YEARS		948	2709	526	112	8	53	(30	23)	813	255	286	198	205	17	867	16	51	25	12	8	39	.194	.253	.300	.553

Wyatt Mathisen

Bats: R Throws: R Pos: 3B-7;DH-2;PH-1　　　　**Ht: 6'0" Wt: 210 Born: 12/30/1993 Age: 27**

Year Team	Lg	G	AB	H	2B	3B	HR	(Hm	Rd)	TB	R	RBI	RC	TBB	IBB	SO	HBP	SH	SF	SB	CS	GDP	Avg	OBP	Slg	OPS
								BATTING												RUNNING			AVERAGES			
2020 Ari	NL	9	27	6	0	0	2	(2	0)	12	5	5	5	5	0	12	1	0	0	0	0	0	.222	.364	.444	.808

Phil Maton

Pitches: R Bats: R Pos: RP-23　　　　**Ht: 6'2" Wt: 206 Born: 3/25/1993 Age: 28**

Year Team	Lg	G	GS	GF	IP	BFP	H	R	ER	HR	SH	SF	HB	TBB	IBB	SO	WP	W	L	Pct	Sv-Op	Hld	Vel	OPS	ERC	ERA
			HOW MUCH PITCHED						WHAT HE GAVE UP											THE RESULTS						
2017 SD	NL	46	0	12	43.0	180	41	23	20	10	0	0	1	14	0	46	0	3	2	.600	1-1	8	93	.778	4.56	4.19
2018 SD	NL	45	0	12	47.1	214	50	25	23	3	2	1	2	23	1	55	4	0	2	.000	0-1	3	91	.757	4.55	4.37
2019 2 Tms		30	0	13	36.2	163	38	27	25	7	2	0	2	12	0	33	3	0	0	-	0-0	2	91	.806	4.72	6.14
2020 Cle	AL	23	0	4	21.2	96	23	14	11	1	0	0	4	6	1	32	1	3	3	.500	0-1	4	94	.716	4.18	4.57
19 SD	NL	21	0	5	24.1	115	34	22	21	6	2	0	1	6	0	20	1	0	0	-	0-0	2	91	.948	6.90	7.77
19 Cle	AL	9	0	8	12.1	48	4	5	4	1	0	0	1	6	0	13	2	0	0	-	0-0	0	90	.449	1.36	2.92
4 ML YEARS		144	0	41	148.2	653	152	89	79	21	4	1	9	55	2	166	8	6	7	.462	1-3	17	92	.769	4.56	4.78

Steven Matz

Pitches: L Bats: R Pos: SP-6; RP-3　　　　**Ht: 6'2" Wt: 201 Born: 5/29/1991 Age: 30**

Year Team	Lg	G	GS	GF	IP	BFP	H	R	ER	HR	SH	SF	HB	TBB	IBB	SO	WP	W	L	Pct	Sv-Op	Hld	Vel	OPS	ERC	ERA
			HOW MUCH PITCHED						WHAT HE GAVE UP											THE RESULTS						
2015 NYM	NL	6	6	0	35.2	149	34	9	9	4	1	1	1	10	0	34	0	4	0	1.000	0-0	0	94	.650	3.55	2.27
2016 NYM	NL	22	22	0	132.1	547	129	53	50	14	8	1	5	31	2	129	3	9	8	.529	0-0	0	94	.689	3.49	3.40
2017 NYM	NL	13	13	0	66.2	298	83	46	45	12	3	1	3	19	2	48	1	2	7	.222	0-0	0	93	.860	5.78	6.08
2018 NYM	NL	30	30	0	154.0	654	134	77	68	25	6	2	10	58	2	152	0	5	11	.313	0-0	0	93	.730	3.91	3.97
2019 NYM	NL	32	30	0	160.1	691	163	83	75	27	5	1	7	52	7	153	3	11	10	.524	0-0	1	93	.777	4.44	4.21
2020 NYM	NL	9	6	1	30.2	142	42	33	33	14	1	1	0	10	0	36	2	0	5	.000	0-0	0	95	1.069	8.76	9.68
Postseason		3	3	0	14.2	64	17	6	6	0	0	0	0	4	1	13	0	1	1	.500	0-0	0	94	.678	3.60	3.68
6 ML YEARS		112	107	1	579.2	2481	585	301	280	96	24	7	26	180	13	552	9	31	41	.431	0-0	1	94	.764	4.37	4.35

Tyler Matzek

Pitches: L Bats: L Pos: RP-21　　　MATT-zick　　　**Ht: 6'3" Wt: 230 Born: 10/19/1990 Age: 30**

Year Team	Lg	G	GS	GF	IP	BFP	H	R	ER	HR	SH	SF	HB	TBB	IBB	SO	WP	W	L	Pct	Sv-Op	Hld	Vel	OPS	ERC	ERA
			HOW MUCH PITCHED						WHAT HE GAVE UP											THE RESULTS						
2014 Col	NL	20	19	1	117.2	503	120	53	53	9	4	3	3	44	1	91	3	6	11	.353	0-0	0	93	.749	4.06	4.05
2015 Col	NL	5	5	0	22.0	102	21	10	10	2	1	1	3	19	0	15	2	2	1	.667	0-0	0	92	.823	6.45	4.09
2020 Atl	NL	21	0	3	29.0	121	23	9	9	1	0	0	2	10	0	43	1	4	3	.571	0-2	1	94	.574	2.57	2.79
3 ML YEARS		46	24	4	168.2	726	164	72	72	12	5	4	8	73	1	149	6	12	15	.444	0-2	1	93	.730	4.07	3.84

Dustin May

Pitches: R Bats: R Pos: SP-10; RP-2　　　　**Ht: 6'6" Wt: 180 Born: 9/6/1997 Age: 23**

Year Team	Lg	G	GS	GF	IP	BFP	H	R	ER	HR	SH	SF	HB	TBB	IBB	SO	WP	W	L	Pct	Sv-Op	Hld	Vel	OPS	ERC	ERA
			HOW MUCH PITCHED						WHAT HE GAVE UP											THE RESULTS						
2016 Ddgrs	R	10	6	1	30.1	135	37	16	13	0	0	1	3	4	0	34	3	0	1	.000	1--	-	-	.696	3.82	3.86
2017 2 Tms	Low	25	24	0	134.0	566	127	63	54	8	3	2	9	27	0	128	10	9	6	.600	0--	-	-	.638	2.95	3.63
2018 Rcuca	A+	17	17	0	98.1	407	91	42	36	9	2	2	8	17	0	94	6	7	3	.700	0--	-	-	.641	3.03	3.29
2018 Tulsa	AA	6	6	0	34.1	145	27	14	14	0	0	0	4	12	0	28	4	2	2	.500	0--	-	-	.560	2.48	3.67
2019 Tulsa	AA	15	15	0	79.1	333	71	41	33	5	3	3	7	20	0	86	8	3	5	.375	0--	-	-	.627	3.00	3.74
2019 OkCity	AAA	5	5	0	27.1	114	21	8	7	0	1	0	5	9	0	24	1	3	0	1.000	0--	-	-	.562	2.60	2.30
2019 LAD	NL	14	4	0	34.2	141	33	17	14	2	0	0	4	5	0	32	0	2	3	.400	0-1	4	96	.639	3.06	3.63
2020 LAD	NL	12	10	0	56.0	224	45	18	16	9	1	1	1	16	0	44	2	3	1	.750	0-0	0	98	.649	3.08	2.57
Postseason		2	0	1	3.1	12	3	1	1	0	1	0	0	1	0	1	0	0	0	-	0-0	0	98	.764	2.96	2.70
2 ML YEARS		26	14	0	90.2	365	78	35	30	11	1	1	5	21	0	76	2	5	4	.556	0-1	4	97	.645	3.08	2.98

Trevor May

Pitches: R Bats: R Pos: RP-24　　　　**Ht: 6'5" Wt: 240 Born: 9/23/1989 Age: 31**

Year Team	Lg	G	GS	GF	IP	BFP	H	R	ER	HR	SH	SF	HB	TBB	IBB	SO	WP	W	L	Pct	Sv-Op	Hld	Vel	OPS	ERC	ERA
			HOW MUCH PITCHED						WHAT HE GAVE UP											THE RESULTS						
2014 Min	AL	10	9	0	45.2	213	59	41	40	7	0	1	2	22	1	44	3	3	6	.333	0-0	0	92	.900	6.80	7.88
2015 Min	AL	48	16	9	114.2	492	127	53	51	11	3	4	4	26	2	110	4	8	9	.471	0-2	7	93	.752	4.06	4.00
2016 Min	AL	44	0	10	42.2	187	39	26	25	7	0	0	2	17	1	60	10	2	2	.500	0-2	6	94	.757	4.07	5.27
2018 Min	AL	24	1	6	25.1	103	21	9	9	4	2	0	1	5	0	36	1	4	1	.800	3-3	5	94	.646	2.85	3.20

(continued)

Year	Team	Lg	G	GS	GF	IP	BFP	H	R	ER	HR	SH	SF	HB	TBB	IBB	SO	WP	W	L	Pct	Sv-Op	Hld	Vel	OPS	ERC	ERA
2019	Min	AL	65	0	13	64.1	266	43	24	21	8	0	3	3	26	1	79	3	5	3	.625	2-4	17	96	.587	2.59	2.94
2020	Min	AL	24	0	4	23.1	96	20	11	10	5	0	1	0	7	0	38	2	1	0	1.000	2-2	8	96	.679	3.61	3.86
	Postseason		2	0	1	1.0	4	1	0	0	0	0	0	0	0	0	2	0	0	0	-	0-0	0	97	.500	1.95	0.00
	6 ML YEARS		215	26	42	316.0	1357	309	164	156	42	5	9	12	103	5	367	23	23	21	.523	7-13	43	94	.731	3.97	4.44

Cameron Maybin

Bats: R **Throws:** R **Pos:** RF-19;LF-5;PH-5;CF-4;DH-3;PR-2   **Ht:** 6'3" **Wt:** 215 **Born:** 4/4/1987 **Age:** 34

Year	Team	Lg	G	AB	H	2B	3B	HR	(Hm	Rd)	TB	R	RBI	RC	TBB	IBB	SO	HBP	SH	SF	SB	CS	GDP	Avg	OBP	Slg	OPS
2007	Det	AL	24	49	7	3	0	1	(0	1)	13	8	2	2	3	0	21	1	0	0	5	0	0	.143	.208	.265	.473
2008	Fla	NL	8	32	16	2	0	0	(0	0)	18	9	2	8	3	0	8	0	1	0	4	0	0	.500	.543	.563	1.105
2009	Fla	NL	54	176	44	12	2	4	(1	3)	72	30	13	15	17	1	51	1	4	1	1	3	2	.250	.318	.409	.727
2010	Fla	NL	82	291	68	7	3	8	(5	3)	105	46	28	37	24	1	92	5	1	2	9	2	4	.234	.302	.361	.663
2011	SD	NL	137	516	136	24	8	9	(2	7)	203	82	40	69	44	2	125	2	4	2	40	8	6	.264	.323	.393	.716
2012	SD	NL	147	507	123	20	5	8	(3	5)	177	67	45	52	44	1	110	4	3	3	26	7	12	.243	.306	.349	.656
2013	SD	NL	14	51	8	1	0	1	(0	1)	12	7	5	0	4	1	9	1	1	0	4	1	3	.157	.232	.235	.467
2014	SD	NL	95	251	59	13	4	1	(0	1)	83	24	15	22	19	2	56	1	0	1	4	3	8	.235	.290	.331	.621
2015	Atl	NL	141	505	135	18	2	10	(5	5)	187	65	59	64	45	1	102	1	1	3	23	6	16	.267	.327	.370	.697
2016	Det	AL	94	349	110	14	5	4	(3	1)	146	65	43	60	36	0	69	3	2	1	15	6	8	.315	.383	.418	.801
2017	2 Tms	AL	114	395	90	20	4	10	(3	7)	144	63	35	51	51	1	94	2	1	1	33	8	12	.228	.318	.365	.683
2018	2 Tms		129	342	85	14	2	4	(2	2)	115	32	28	38	38	1	75	2	0	2	10	5	7	.249	.326	.336	.662
2019	NYY	AL	82	239	68	17	0	11	(5	6)	118	48	32	36	30	0	72	0	0	0	9	6	5	.285	.364	.494	.858
2020	2 Tms		32	93	23	8	1	1	(1	0)	36	8	7	9	7	0	25	1	0	0	3	0	4	.247	.307	.387	.694
17	LAA	AL	93	336	79	19	1	6	(2	4)	118	57	22	42	48	1	78	2	0	1	29	5	11	.235	.333	.351	.685
17	Hou	AL	21	59	11	1	1	4	(1	3)	26	6	13	9	3	0	16	0	1	0	4	3	1	.186	.226	.441	.666
18	Mia	NL	99	251	63	12	1	3	(2	1)	86	20	20	29	32	1	55	2	0	2	8	5	3	.251	.338	.343	.681
18	Sea	AL	30	91	22	2	1	1	(0	1)	29	12	8	9	6	0	20	0	0	0	2	0	4	.242	.289	.319	.607
20	Det	AL	14	41	10	4	0	1	(1	0)	17	5	2	2	4	0	13	0	0	0	0	0	3	.244	.311	.415	.726
20	ChC	NL	18	52	13	4	1	0	(0	0)	19	3	5	7	3	0	12	1	0	0	3	0	1	.250	.304	.365	.669
	Postseason		11	13	4	0	0	1	(0	1)	7	4	1	3	2	0	5	0	0	0	3	0	0	.308	.400	.538	.938
	14 ML YEARS		1153	3796	972	173	34	72	(30	42)	1429	554	354	463	365	11	909	24	18	15	186	55	87	.256	.324	.376	.700

Mike Mayers

Pitches: R **Bats:** R **Pos:** RP-29   MY-erz   **Ht:** 6'2" **Wt:** 220 **Born:** 12/6/1991 **Age:** 29

Year	Team	Lg	G	GS	GF	IP	BFP	H	R	ER	HR	SH	SF	HB	TBB	IBB	SO	WP	W	L	Pct	Sv-Op	Hld	Vel	OPS	ERC	ERA
2016	StL	NL	4	1	0	5.1	35	16	16	16	3	0	1	1	3	0	2	0	1	1	.500	0-0	0	93	1.438	25.90	27.00
2017	StL	NL	3	0	1	4.2	25	8	8	8	2	0	2	0	4	1	3	0	0	0	-	0-0	0	94	1.427	13.79	11.57
2018	StL	NL	50	0	15	51.2	226	59	28	27	7	3	3	1	15	1	49	4	2	1	.667	1-1	6	96	.822	4.72	4.70
2019	StL	NL	16	0	4	19.0	88	21	14	14	3	0	0	1	11	2	16	1	0	1	.000	0-0	1	95	.888	5.90	6.63
2020	LAA	AL	29	0	4	30.0	121	18	10	7	2	0	0	1	9	0	43	0	2	0	1.000	2-4	5	94	.484	1.59	2.10
	5 ML YEARS		102	1	24	110.2	495	122	76	70	17	3	6	4	42	4	113	5	5	3	.625	3-5	12	95	.819	5.00	5.69

Jack Mayfield

Bats: R **Throws:** R **Pos:** 3B-8;SS-8;2B-5;PH-2;PR-2;DH-1   **Ht:** 5'11" **Wt:** 190 **Born:** 9/30/1990 **Age:** 30

Year	Team	Lg	G	AB	H	2B	3B	HR	(Hm	Rd)	TB	R	RBI	RC	TBB	IBB	SO	HBP	SH	SF	SB	CS	GDP	Avg	OBP	Slg	OPS
2019	Hou	AL	26	64	10	5	0	2	(0	2)	21	8	5	3	1	0	16	0	0	0	0	0	0	.156	.169	.328	.497
2020	Hou	AL	21	42	8	1	0	0	(0	0)	9	5	3	1	2	0	14	1	1	1	0	0	1	.190	.239	.214	.453
	2 ML YEARS		47	106	18	6	0	2	(0	2)	30	13	8	4	3	0	30	1	1	1	0	0	1	.170	.198	.283	.481

Nomar Mazara

Bats: L **Throws:** L **Pos:** RF-42;PH-4   **Ht:** 6'4" **Wt:** 215 **Born:** 4/26/1995 **Age:** 26

Year	Team	Lg	G	AB	H	2B	3B	HR	(Hm	Rd)	TB	R	RBI	RC	TBB	IBB	SO	HBP	SH	SF	SB	CS	GDP	Avg	OBP	Slg	OPS
2016	Tex	AL	145	516	137	13	3	20	(7	13)	216	59	64	67	39	1	112	6	0	7	0	2	12	.266	.320	.419	.739
2017	Tex	AL	148	554	140	30	2	20	(11	9)	234	64	101	87	55	6	127	4	0	3	2	2	12	.253	.323	.422	.745
2018	Tex	AL	128	489	126	25	1	20	(15	5)	213	61	77	80	40	2	116	4	0	3	1	0	13	.258	.317	.436	.753
2019	Tex	AL	116	429	115	27	1	19	(8	11)	201	69	66	60	28	2	108	6	0	6	4	1	5	.268	.318	.469	.786
2020	CWS	AL	42	136	31	6	0	1	(0	1)	40	13	15	16	10	0	44	3	0	0	0	1	0	.228	.295	.294	.589
	Postseason		2	6	1	0	0	0	(0	0)	1	1	0	0	0	0	3	0	0	0	0	0	0	.167	.167	.167	.333
	5 ML YEARS		579	2124	549	101	7	80	(41	39)	904	266	323	297	172	11	507	23	0	19	7	6	42	.258	.318	.426	.744

Chris Mazza

Pitches: R **Bats:** R **Pos:** SP-6; RP-3   **Ht:** 6'4" **Wt:** 190 **Born:** 10/17/1989 **Age:** 31

Year	Team	Lg	G	GS	GF	IP	BFP	H	R	ER	HR	SH	SF	HB	TBB	IBB	SO	WP	W	L	Pct	Sv-Op	Hld	Vel	OPS	ERC	ERA
2019	NYM	NL	9	0	6	16.1	74	21	10	10	0	1	0	4	5	0	11	0	1	1	.500	0-0	0	92	.905	5.81	5.51
2020	Bos	AL	9	6	0	30.0	136	34	18	16	3	0	1	2	15	0	29	4	1	2	.333	0-0	0	92	.790	5.61	4.80
	2 ML YEARS		18	6	6	46.1	210	55	28	26	3	0	2	6	20	0	40	4	2	3	.400	0-0	0	92	.831	5.68	5.05

Ryan McBroom

Bats: R **Throws:** L **Pos:** PH-17;1B-10;DH-9;LF-3;RF-1   **Ht:** 6'3" **Wt:** 225 **Born:** 4/9/1992 **Age:** 29

Year Team	Lg	G	AB	H	2B	3B	HR	(Hm	Rd)	TB	R	RBI	RC	TBB	IBB	SO	HBP	SH	SF	SB	CS	GDP	Avg	OBP	Slg	OPS
2019 KC	AL	23	75	22	5	0	0	(0	0)	27	8	6	7	7	0	25	1	0	0	0	0	3	.293	.361	.360	.721
2020 KC	AL	36	81	20	3	0	6	(3	3)	41	8	10	8	4	0	30	0	0	0	0	0	2	.247	.282	.506	.789
2 ML YEARS		59	156	42	8	0	6	(3	3)	68	16	16	15	11	0	55	1	0	0	0	0	5	.269	.321	.436	.757

James McCann

Bats: R **Throws:** R **Pos:** C-30;PH-1   **Ht:** 6'3" **Wt:** 220 **Born:** 6/13/1990 **Age:** 31

Year Team	Lg	G	AB	H	2B	3B	HR	(Hm	Rd)	TB	R	RBI	RC	TBB	IBB	SO	HBP	SH	SF	SB	CS	GDP	Avg	OBP	Slg	OPS
2014 Det	AL	9	12	3	1	0	0	(0	0)	4	2	0	1	0	0	2	0	0	0	1	0	0	.250	.250	.333	.583
2015 Det	AL	114	401	106	18	5	7	(5	2)	155	32	41	34	16	0	90	3	4	1	0	1	17	.264	.297	.387	.683
2016 Det	AL	105	344	76	9	1	12	(7	5)	123	31	48	30	23	0	109	2	1	3	0	1	12	.221	.272	.358	.629
2017 Det	AL	106	352	89	14	2	13	(8	5)	146	39	49	46	26	0	89	9	1	3	1	0	8	.253	.318	.415	.733
2018 Det	AL	118	427	94	16	0	8	(5	3)	134	31	39	31	26	0	116	2	0	2	0	3	9	.220	.267	.314	.581
2019 CWS	AL	118	439	120	26	1	18	(8	10)	202	62	60	67	30	1	137	6	1	0	4	1	10	.273	.328	.460	.789
2020 CWS	AL	31	97	28	3	0	7	(4	3)	52	20	15	16	8	0	30	4	0	2	1	1	2	.289	.360	.536	.896
7 ML YEARS		601	2072	516	87	9	65	(37	28)	816	217	252	225	129	1	573	26	7	11	7	7	58	.249	.300	.394	.694

Joe McCarthy

Bats: L **Throws:** L **Pos:** LF-3;RF-1   **Ht:** 6'3" **Wt:** 220 **Born:** 2/23/1994 **Age:** 27

Year Team	Lg	G	AB	H	2B	3B	HR	(Hm	Rd)	TB	R	RBI	RC	TBB	IBB	SO	HBP	SH	SF	SB	CS	GDP	Avg	OBP	Slg	OPS
2020 SF	NL	4	10	0	0	0	0	(0	0)	0	0	0	0	0	0	5	0	0	0	0	0	0	.000	.000	.000	.000

Kevin McCarthy

Pitches: R **Bats:** R **Pos:** RP-5   **Ht:** 6'3" **Wt:** 210 **Born:** 2/22/1992 **Age:** 29

		HOW MUCH PITCHED					WHAT HE GAVE UP										THE RESULTS							
Year Team	Lg	G	GS	GF	IP	BFP	H	R	ER	HR	SH	SF	HB	TBB	IBB	SO	WP	W	L	Pct	Sv-Op	Hld	Vel	OPS	ERC	ERA
2016 KC	AL	10	0	1	8.1	41	11	8	6	1	1	0	0	5	0	7	0	1	0	1.000	0-1	0	94	.857	6.83	6.48
2017 KC	AL	33	0	14	45.0	196	50	23	16	4	1	1	0	13	0	27	1	1	0	1.000	0-0	1	93	.704	4.13	3.20
2018 KC	AL	65	0	10	72.0	293	70	28	26	7	0	1	2	20	2	46	2	5	4	.556	0-4	15	92	.703	3.62	3.25
2019 KC	AL	56	0	14	60.1	268	68	31	30	4	2	4	2	21	6	38	2	4	2	.667	1-5	6	91	.756	4.26	4.48
2020 KC	AL	5	0	2	6.0	29	10	3	3	1	0	0	1	2	0	2	0	0	0	-	0-0	0	90	.948	9.72	4.50
5 ML YEARS		169	0	41	191.2	827	209	93	81	17	4	6	5	61	8	120	5	11	6	.647	1-10	22	92	.736	4.24	3.80

Reggie McClain

Pitches: R **Bats:** R **Pos:** RP-5   **Ht:** 6'2" **Wt:** 180 **Born:** 11/16/1992 **Age:** 28

		HOW MUCH PITCHED					WHAT HE GAVE UP										THE RESULTS							
Year Team	Lg	G	GS	GF	IP	BFP	H	R	ER	HR	SH	SF	HB	TBB	IBB	SO	WP	W	L	Pct	Sv-Op	Hld	Vel	OPS	ERC	ERA
2019 Sea	AL	14	2	6	21.0	95	22	14	14	2	0	1	0	13	0	11	1	1	1	.500	0-1	0	94	.795	5.24	6.00
2020 Phi	NL	5	0	1	5.1	29	9	6	3	1	0	1	0	3	0	2	0	0	0	-	0-0	0	93	.974	9.34	5.06
2 ML YEARS		19	2	7	26.1	124	31	20	17	3	0	1	0	16	0	13	1	1	1	.500	0-1	0	94	.837	6.04	5.81

Lance McCullers Jr.

Pitches: R **Bats:** L **Pos:** SP-11   **Ht:** 6'1" **Wt:** 202 **Born:** 10/2/1993 **Age:** 27

		HOW MUCH PITCHED					WHAT HE GAVE UP										THE RESULTS							
Year Team	Lg	G	GS	GF	IP	BFP	H	R	ER	HR	SH	SF	HB	TBB	IBB	SO	WP	W	L	Pct	Sv-Op	Hld	Vel	OPS	ERC	ERA
2015 Hou	AL	22	22	0	125.2	520	106	49	45	10	4	0	5	43	2	129	8	6	7	.462	0-0	0	94	.659	3.02	3.22
2016 Hou	AL	14	14	0	81.0	352	80	29	29	5	0	0	4	45	1	106	9	6	5	.545	0-0	0	94	.736	4.42	3.22
2017 Hou	AL	22	22	0	118.2	512	114	61	56	8	2	2	11	40	1	132	8	7	4	.636	0-0	0	94	.696	3.71	4.25
2018 Hou	AL	25	22	0	128.1	527	100	60	55	12	1	4	7	50	0	142	14	10	6	.625	0-0	1	94	.653	3.05	3.86
2020 Hou	AL	11	11	0	55.0	227	44	29	24	5	1	1	5	20	0	56	0	3	3	.500	0-0	0	94	.710	3.19	3.93
Postseason		11	4	1	32.0	127	19	10	9	2	0	0	6	13	0	30	2	1	0	1.000	1-1	1	94	.558	2.53	2.53
5 ML YEARS		94	91	0	508.2	2138	444	228	209	40	4	10	28	198	4	565	39	32	25	.561	0-0	1	94	.684	3.42	3.70

Andrew McCutchen

Bats: R **Throws:** R **Pos:** LF-39;DH-16;PH-4   **Ht:** 5'11" **Wt:** 195 **Born:** 10/10/1986 **Age:** 34

Year Team	Lg	G	AB	H	2B	3B	HR	(Hm	Rd)	TB	R	RBI	RC	TBB	IBB	SO	HBP	SH	SF	SB	CS	GDP	Avg	OBP	Slg	OPS
2009 Pit	NL	108	433	124	26	9	12	(8	4)	204	74	54	78	54	2	83	2	0	4	22	5	3	.286	.365	.471	.836
2010 Pit	NL	154	570	163	35	5	16	(8	8)	256	94	56	86	70	1	89	5	1	7	33	10	6	.286	.365	.449	.814
2011 Pit	NL	158	572	148	34	5	23	(10	13)	261	87	89	102	89	3	126	9	2	6	23	10	7	.259	.364	.456	.820
2012 Pit	NL	157	593	**194**	29	6	31	(15	16)	328	107	96	**125**	70	13	132	5	0	9	20	12	9	.327	.400	.553	.953
2013 Pit	NL	157	583	185	38	5	21	(9	12)	296	97	84	105	78	12	101	9	0	4	27	10	13	.317	.404	.508	.911
2014 Pit	NL	146	548	172	38	6	25	(10	15)	297	89	83	**109**	84	8	115	10	0	9	18	3	9	.314	**.410**	.542	**.952**
2015 Pit	NL	157	566	165	36	3	23	(13	10)	276	91	96	120	98	12	133	12	0	11	11	5	9	.292	.401	.488	.889
2016 Pit	NL	153	598	153	26	3	24	(14	10)	257	81	79	83	69	7	143	5	0	3	6	7	15	.256	.336	.430	.766
2017 Pit	NL	156	570	159	30	2	28	(9	19)	277	94	88	98	73	5	116	4	0	3	11	5	10	.279	.363	.486	.849
2018 2 Tms		155	569	145	30	3	20	(7	13)	241	83	65	88	95	1	145	11	0	7	14	9	12	.255	.368	.424	.792
2019 Phi	NL	59	219	56	12	1	10	(5	5)	100	45	29	41	43	0	55	0	0	0	2	1	1	.256	.378	.457	.834
2020 Phi	NL	57	217	55	9	0	10	(5	5)	94	32	34	34	22	0	48	1	0	4	4	0	4	.253	.324	.433	.757

Year	Team	Lg	G	AB	H	2B	3B	HR	(Hm	Rd)	TB	R	RBI	RC	TBB	IBB	SO	HBP	SH	SF	SB	CS	GDP	Avg	OBP	Slg	OPS
18	SF	NL	130	482	123	28	2	15	(5	10)	200	65	55	70	73	1	123	7	0	6	13	6	11	.255	.357	.415	.772
18	NYY	AL	25	87	22	2	1	5	(2	3)	41	18	10	18	22	0	22	4	0	1	1	3	1	.253	.421	.471	.892
	Postseason		13	46	11	1	0	0	(0	0)	12	5	1	3	7	1	7	0	0	0	0	0	1	.239	.340	.261	.600
	12 ML YEARS		1617	6038	1719	343	48	243	(109	134)	2887	974	853	1069	845	64	1286	73	3	55	191	77	98	.285	.376	.478	.854

T.J. McFarland

Pitches: L Bats: L Pos: RP-23 **Ht: 6'3" Wt: 200 Born: 6/8/1989 Age: 32**

			HOW MUCH PITCHED					WHAT HE GAVE UP										THE RESULTS							
Year	Team	Lg	G	GS	GF	IP	BFP	H	R	ER	HR	SH	SF	HB	TBB	IBB	SO	WP	W	L	Pct	Sv-Op	Hld	Vel	OPS	ERC	ERA
2013	Bal	AL	38	1	8	74.2	331	83	37	35	7	2	1	0	28	5	58	2	4	1	.800	0-0	0	88	.737	4.40	4.22
2014	Bal	AL	37	1	14	58.2	255	70	22	18	2	5	0	4	13	2	34	0	4	2	.667	0-0	5	91	.739	4.23	2.76
2015	Bal	AL	30	0	7	40.1	188	52	26	22	4	0	0	0	18	5	26	3	2	2	.500	0-0	3	92	.814	5.68	4.91
2016	Bal	AL	16	0	3	24.2	112	33	19	19	3	0	3	2	10	2	7	1	2	2	.500	0-3	0	92	.928	6.74	6.93
2017	Ari	NL	43	1	22	54.0	241	65	42	32	4	2	3	2	17	6	29	2	4	5	.444	0-0	2	92	.757	4.65	5.33
2018	Ari	NL	47	0	21	72.0	292	64	18	16	4	1	1	0	22	3	42	2	2	2	.500	1-1	1	91	.631	2.82	2.00
2019	Ari	NL	51	0	13	56.0	250	71	35	30	6	2	2	1	20	5	35	1	0	0		0-0	4	89	.842	5.53	4.82
2020	Oak	AL	23	0	2	20.2	92	26	10	10	5	0	0	1	5	0	9	1	2	0	1.000	0-0	6	88	.894	6.20	4.35
	8 ML YEARS		285	3	89	401.0	1761	464	209	182	35	12	10	10	133	28	240	12	20	14	.588	1-4	26	90	.766	4.61	4.08

Jake McGee

Pitches: L Bats: L Pos: RP-24 **Ht: 6'4" Wt: 229 Born: 8/6/1986 Age: 34**

			HOW MUCH PITCHED					WHAT HE GAVE UP										THE RESULTS							
Year	Team	Lg	G	GS	GF	IP	BFP	H	R	ER	HR	SH	SF	HB	TBB	IBB	SO	WP	W	L	Pct	Sv-Op	Hld	Vel	OPS	ERC	ERA
2010	TB	AL	8	0	3	5.0	20	2	1	1	0	0	0	0	3	0	6	0	0	0		0-0	0	94	.426	1.32	1.80
2011	TB	AL	37	0	9	28.0	124	30	14	14	5	1	0	0	12	1	27	0	5	2	.714	0-0	4	95	.801	5.09	4.50
2012	TB	AL	69	0	13	55.1	212	33	13	12	3	0	2	1	11	4	73	3	5	2	.714	0-2	19	96	.452	1.26	1.95
2013	TB	AL	71	0	6	62.2	260	52	28	28	8	1	3	1	22	5	75	4	5	3	.625	1-5	27	96	.659	3.07	4.02
2014	TB	AL	73	0	31	71.1	274	48	15	15	2	1	1	2	16	1	90	1	5	2	.714	19-23	14	96	.486	1.55	1.89
2015	TB	AL	39	0	6	37.1	147	27	11	10	3	0	1	1	8	1	48	1	1	2	.333	6-10	19	95	.544	1.92	2.41
2016	Col	NL	57	0	25	45.2	205	56	25	24	9	0	0	3	16	1	38	4	2	3	.400	15-19	4	93	.887	6.26	4.73
2017	Col	NL	62	0	13	57.1	229	47	23	23	4	1	1	1	16	0	58	5	0	0	.000	3-6	20	95	.624	2.59	3.61
2018	Col	NL	61	0	9	51.1	227	59	39	37	10	2	0	2	16	1	47	5	2	4	.333	1-3	14	94	.883	5.38	6.49
2019	Col	NL	45	0	10	41.1	180	47	25	20	11	0	3	3	11	1	35	0	0	0	.000	0-2	4	94	.903	5.83	4.35
2020	LAD	NL	24	0	4	20.1	79	14	6	6	2	1	0	0	3	0	33	0	3	1	.750	0-0	4	95	.565	1.59	2.66
	Postseason		6	0	1	3.2	18	3	2	2	0	1	0	1	3	1	3	0	0	1	.000	0-0	2	96	.643	4.24	4.91
	11 ML YEARS		546	0	129	475.2	1957	415	200	190	57	7	11	14	134	15	530	23	28	23	.549	45-70	129	95	.674	3.13	3.59

Kyle McGowin

Pitches: R Bats: R Pos: RP-9 **Ht: 6'3" Wt: 195 Born: 11/27/1991 Age: 29**

			HOW MUCH PITCHED					WHAT HE GAVE UP										THE RESULTS							
Year	Team	Lg	G	GS	GF	IP	BFP	H	R	ER	HR	SH	SF	HB	TBB	IBB	SO	WP	W	L	Pct	Sv-Op	Hld	Vel	OPS	ERC	ERA
2018	Was	NL	5	1	2	7.2	34	6	5	5	2	0	1	0	5	0	8	2	0	0	-	0-0	0	91	.824	4.90	5.87
2019	Was	NL	7	1	4	16.0	76	22	19	18	7	1	1	1	4	0	18	4	0	0	-	1-1	0	91	1.012	8.33	10.13
2020	Was	NL	9	0	3	11.0	47	9	6	6	2	0	0	0	5	1	16	1	1	0	1.000	1-1	1	91	.655	3.63	4.91
	3 ML YEARS		21	2	9	34.2	157	37	30	29	11	1	2	1	14	1	42	7	1	0	1.000	2-2	1	91	.866	5.98	7.53

Reese McGuire

Bats: L Throws: R Pos: C-18;PH-1 **Ht: 6'0" Wt: 215 Born: 3/2/1995 Age: 26**

			BATTING																RUNNING			AVERAGES			
Year	Team	Lg	G	AB	H	2B	3B	HR	(Hm | Rd)	TB	R	RBI	RC	TBB	IBB	SO	HBP	SH	SF	SB	CS	GDP	Avg	OBP	Slg	OPS
2018	Tor	AL	14	31	9	3	0	2	(1 | 1)	18	5	4	5	2	0	9	0	0	0	1	0	0	.290	.333	.581	.914
2019	Tor	AL	30	97	29	7	0	5	(4 | 1)	51	14	11	14	7	0	18	0	0	0	0	0	1	.299	.346	.526	.872
2020	Tor	AL	19	41	3	0	0	1	(0 | 1)	6	2	1	0	0	0	11	0	4	0	0	0	1	.073	.073	.146	.220
	3 ML YEARS		63	169	41	10	0	8	(5 | 3)	75	21	16	19	9	0	38	0	4	0	1	0	2	.243	.281	.444	.725

Collin McHugh

Pitches: R Bats: R Pos: P mick-HYOO **Ht: 6'2" Wt: 191 Born: 6/19/1987 Age: 34**

			HOW MUCH PITCHED					WHAT HE GAVE UP										THE RESULTS							
Year	Team	Lg	G	GS	GF	IP	BFP	H	R	ER	HR	SH	SF	HB	TBB	IBB	SO	WP	W	L	Pct	Sv-Op	Hld	Vel	OPS	ERC	ERA
2012	NYM	NL	8	4	1	21.1	99	27	21	18	5	2	1	2	8	2	17	0	0	4	.000	0-0	0	90	1.044	6.83	7.59
2013	2 Tms	NL	7	5	2	26.0	125	45	29	29	6	2	2	0	5	0	11	0	0	4	.000	0-0	0	90	1.053	8.82	10.04
2014	Hou	AL	25	25	0	154.2	619	117	53	47	13	6	4	6	41	1	157	6	11	9	.550	0-0	0	90	.588	2.34	2.73
2015	Hou	AL	32	32	0	203.2	859	207	89	88	19	5	4	9	53	2	171	5	19	7	.731	0-0	0	90	.705	3.75	3.89
2016	Hou	AL	33	33	0	184.2	796	206	90	89	25	1	5	5	54	1	177	9	13	10	.565	0-0	0	90	.790	4.69	4.34
2017	Hou	AL	12	12	0	63.1	271	62	27	25	7	0	0	5	20	0	62	0	5	2	.714	0-0	0	90	.747	4.02	3.55
2018	Hou	AL	58	0	18	72.1	283	45	18	16	6	1	1	5	21	0	94	0	6	2	.750	0-1	12	92	.542	1.92	1.99
2019	Hou	AL	35	8	6	74.2	317	62	41	39	12	0	3	3	30	0	82	0	4	5	.444	0-0	0	91	.733	3.67	4.70
13	NYM	NL	3	1	2	7.0	34	12	8	8	2	0	1	0	3	0	3	0	0	1	.000	0-0	0	91	1.141	10.77	10.29
13	Col	NL	4	4	0	19.0	91	33	21	21	4	2	1	0	2	0	8	0	0	3	.000	0-0	0	90	1.021	8.14	9.95
	Postseason		8	2	3	20.0	77	11	8	8	3	0	2	0	6	0	14	0	2	1	.667	0-0	0	91	.551	2.12	3.60
	8 ML YEARS		210	119	29	800.2	3369	771	370	351	93	17	20	35	232	6	771	24	58	43	.574	0-1	16	91	.718	3.72	3.95

Brendan McKay

Pitches: L Bats: L Pos: P   Ht: 6'2" Wt: 220 Born: 12/18/1995 Age: 25

Year	Team	Lg	G	GS	GF	IP	BFP	H	R	ER	HR	SH	SF	HB	TBB	IBB	SO	WP	W	L	Pct	Sv-Op	Hld	Vel	OPS	ERC	ERA
			HOW MUCH PITCHED					**WHAT HE GAVE UP**											**THE RESULTS**								
2017	HudVal	A-	6	6	0	20.0	73	10	4	4	3	1	0	0	5	0	21	1	1	0	1.000	0- -	-	-	.507	1.48	1.80
2018	3 Tms	Low	19	17	0	78.1	299	55	22	21	3	2	1	1	14	0	103	0	5	2	.714	0- -	-	-	.511	1.56	2.41
2019	Mont	AA	8	7	0	41.2	156	25	6	6	2	0	1	1	9	0	62	3	3	0	1.000	0- -	-	-	.466	1.41	1.30
2019	Drham	AAA	7	6	0	32.0	122	17	4	3	1	1	1	2	9	0	40	0	3	0	1.000	0- -	-	-	.452	1.34	0.84
2019	TB	AL	13	11	0	49.0	216	53	32	28	8	1	1	0	16	0	56	0	2	4	.333	0-0	0	94	.796	4.59	5.14
	Postseason		3	0	1	1.1	6	2	2	0	0	0	0	0	0	0	2	0	0	0	-	0-0	0	96	.833	4.47	0.00

David McKay

Pitches: R Bats: R Pos: RP-1   Ht: 6'3" Wt: 205 Born: 3/31/1995 Age: 26

Year	Team	Lg	G	GS	GF	IP	BFP	H	R	ER	HR	SH	SF	HB	TBB	IBB	SO	WP	W	L	Pct	Sv-Op	Hld	Vel	OPS	ERC	ERA
			HOW MUCH PITCHED					**WHAT HE GAVE UP**											**THE RESULTS**								
2019	2 Tms	AL	25	0	11	26.1	115	20	17	16	3	0	0	1	17	1	34	2	0	0	-	0-1	1	94	.647	5.47	5.47
2020	Det	AL	1	0	0	0.1	3	1	2	2	1	0	0	0	1	0	0	0	0	0	-	0-0	0	92	2.667	73.60	54.00
19	Det	AL	18	0	6	19.1	81	15	12	12	2	0	0	1	9	1	29	2	0	0	-	0-1	1	94	.647	3.27	5.59
19	Sea	AL	7	0	5	7.0	34	5	5	4	1	0	0	0	8	0	5	0	0	0	-	0-0	0	93	.767	5.59	5.14
	2 ML YEARS		26	0	11	26.2	118	21	19	18	4	0	0	1	18	1	34	2	0	0	-	0-1	1	94	.723	4.39	6.08

Triston McKenzie

Pitches: R Bats: R Pos: SP-6; RP-2   Ht: 6'5" Wt: 165 Born: 8/2/1997 Age: 23

Year	Team	Lg	G	GS	GF	IP	BFP	H	R	ER	HR	SH	SF	HB	TBB	IBB	SO	WP	W	L	Pct	Sv-Op	Hld	Vel	OPS	ERC	ERA
			HOW MUCH PITCHED					**WHAT HE GAVE UP**											**THE RESULTS**								
2020	Cle	AL	8	6	0	33.1	127	21	12	12	6	0	0	1	9	0	42	0	2	1	.667	0-0	0	93	.612	2.32	3.24

Billy McKinney

Bats: L Throws: L Pos: LF-1;RF-1;PR-1   Ht: 6'1" Wt: 205 Born: 8/23/1994 Age: 26

Year	Team	Lg	G	AB	H	2B	3B	HR	(Hm	Rd)	TB	R	RBI	RC	TBB	IBB	SO	HBP	SH	SF	SB	CS	GDP	Avg	OBP	Slg	OPS
								BATTING													**RUNNING**			**AVERAGES**			
2018	2 Tms	AL	38	119	30	7	0	6	(5	1)	55	14	13	14	11	0	33	1	0	1	1	0	0	.252	.318	.462	.780
2019	Tor	AL	84	251	54	14	1	12	(7	5)	106	37	28	35	19	0	73	2	2	2	0	0	0	.215	.274	.422	.696
2020	Tor	AL	2	3	2	0	0	0	(0	0)	2	1	0	0	0	0	0	0	0	0	0	0	0	.667	.667	.667	1.333
18	NYY	AL	2	4	1	0	0	0	(0	0)	1	0	0	0	0	0	1	0	0	0	0	0	0	.250	.250	.250	.500
18	Tor	AL	36	115	29	7	0	6	(5	1)	54	14	13	14	11	0	32	1	0	1	1	0	0	.252	.320	.470	.790
	3 ML YEARS		124	373	86	21	1	18	(12	6)	163	52	41	49	30	0	106	3	2	3	1	2	0	.231	.291	.437	.728

Zach McKinstry

Bats: L Throws: R Pos: PH-3;DH-2;2B-1;RF-1   Ht: 6'0" Wt: 180 Born: 4/29/1995 Age: 26

Year	Team	Lg	G	AB	H	2B	3B	HR	(Hm	Rd)	TB	R	RBI	RC	TBB	IBB	SO	HBP	SH	SF	SB	CS	GDP	Avg	OBP	Slg	OPS
								BATTING													**RUNNING**			**AVERAGES**			
2020	LAD	NL	4	7	2	1	0	0	(0	0)	3	1	0	1	0	0	3	0	0	0	0	0	1	.286	.286	.429	.714

Ryan McMahon

Bats: L Throws: R Pos: 2B-33;3B-14;1B-12;PH-3;SS-2   Ht: 6'2" Wt: 219 Born: 12/14/1994 Age: 26

Year	Team	Lg	G	AB	H	2B	3B	HR	(Hm	Rd)	TB	R	RBI	RC	TBB	IBB	SO	HBP	SH	SF	SB	CS	GDP	Avg	OBP	Slg	OPS
								BATTING													**RUNNING**			**AVERAGES**			
2017	Col	NL	17	19	3	1	0	0	(0	0)	4	2	1	1	5	0	5	0	0	0	0	0	1	.158	.333	.211	.544
2018	Col	NL	91	181	42	9	1	5	(4	1)	68	17	19	23	18	2	64	2	0	1	1	0	0	.232	.307	.376	.683
2019	Col	NL	141	480	120	22	1	24	(18	6)	216	70	83	69	56	1	160	1	1	1	5	1	14	.250	.329	.450	.779
2020	Col	NL	52	172	37	6	1	9	(6	3)	72	23	26	24	18	0	66	2	0	1	0	1	4	.215	.295	.419	.714
	Postseason		4	3	0	0	0	0	(0	0)	0	0	0	0	0	0	1	0	1	0	0	0	0	.000	.250	.000	.250
	4 ML YEARS		301	852	202	38	3	38	(28	10)	360	112	129	117	97	3	295	5	1	3	6	2	19	.237	.318	.423	.740

Jeff McNeil

Bats: L Throws: R Pos: LF-28;2B-12;3B-9;RF-4;DH-2;PH-2   Ht: 6'1" Wt: 195 Born: 4/8/1992 Age: 29

Year	Team	Lg	G	AB	H	2B	3B	HR	(Hm	Rd)	TB	R	RBI	RC	TBB	IBB	SO	HBP	SH	SF	SB	CS	GDP	Avg	OBP	Slg	OPS
								BATTING													**RUNNING**			**AVERAGES**			
2018	NYM	NL	63	225	74	11	6	3	(1	2)	106	35	19	39	14	1	24	5	4	0	7	1	2	.329	.381	.471	.852
2019	NYM	NL	133	510	162	38	1	23	(9	14)	271	83	75	103	35	2	75	21	0	1	5	6	5	.318	.384	.531	.916
2020	NYM	NL	52	183	57	14	0	4	(4	0)	83	19	23	30	20	2	24	3	0	3	0	2	3	.311	.383	.454	.836
	3 ML YEARS		248	918	293	63	7	30	(14	16)	460	137	117	172	69	5	123	29	4	4	12	9	10	.319	.383	.501	.884

Alex McRae

Pitches: R Bats: R Pos: RP-2   Ht: 6'2" Wt: 220 Born: 4/6/1993 Age: 28

Year	Team	Lg	G	GS	GF	IP	BFP	H	R	ER	HR	SH	SF	HB	TBB	IBB	SO	WP	W	L	Pct	Sv-Op	Hld	Vel	OPS	ERC	ERA
			HOW MUCH PITCHED					**WHAT HE GAVE UP**											**THE RESULTS**								
2018	Pit	NL	2	0	0	6.1	32	8	4	4	0	0	0	1	5	0	5	2	0	1	.000	0-0	0	92	.899	7.08	5.68
2019	Pit	NL	11	2	3	26.2	132	36	30	26	9	0	0	3	16	1	19	2	0	4	.000	0-0	0	93	1.027	9.60	8.78
2020	CWS	AL	2	0	1	3.0	10	1	0	0	0	0	0	0	0	0	2	0	0	0	-	0-0	0	92	.200	0.25	0.00
	3 ML YEARS		15	2	4	36.0	174	45	34	30	9	0	0	4	21	1	26	4	0	5	.000	0-0	0	93	.953	8.06	7.50

Austin Meadows

Bats: L **Throws:** L **Pos:** LF-23;DH-9;RF-4;PH-3   **Ht:** 6'3" **Wt:** 225 **Born:** 5/3/1995 **Age:** 26

Year	Team	Lg	G	AB	H	2B	3B	HR	(Hm	Rd)	TB	R	RBI	RC	TBB	IBB	SO	HBP	SH	SF	SB	CS	GDP	Avg	OBP	Slg	OPS
2018	2 Tms		59	178	51	9	2	6	(3	3)	82	19	17	23	10	2	40	1	0	2	5	1	1	.287	.325	.461	.785
2019	TB	AL	138	530	154	29	7	33	(13	20)	296	83	89	103	54	6	131	7	0	0	12	7	3	.291	.364	.558	.922
2020	TB	AL	36	132	27	8	1	4	(1	3)	49	19	13	13	17	0	50	1	0	2	2	1	0	.205	.296	.371	.667
18	Pit	NL	49	154	45	8	2	5	(2	3)	72	16	13	20	8	2	35	1	0	2	4	1	1	.292	.327	.468	.795
18	TB	AL	10	24	6	1	0	1	(1	0)	10	3	4	3	2	0	5	0	0	0	1	0	0	.250	.308	.417	.724
	Postseason		6	23	3	2	0	0	(0	0)	5	2	3	1	3	0	10	0	0	0	0	0	1	.130	.231	.217	.448
	3 ML YEARS		233	840	232	46	10	43	(17	26)	427	121	119	139	81	8	221	9	0	4	19	9	4	.276	.345	.508	.853

John Means

Pitches: L **Bats:** L **Pos:** SP-10   **Ht:** 6'3" **Wt:** 230 **Born:** 4/24/1993 **Age:** 28

Year	Team	Lg	G	GS	GF	IP	BFP	H	R	ER	HR	SH	SF	HB	TBB	IBB	SO	WP	W	L	Pct	Sv-Op	Hld	Vel	OPS	ERC	ERA
2018	Bal	AL	1	0	0	3.1	16	6	5	5	1	0	0	0	0	0	4	0	0	0	-	0-0	0	90	1.125	8.70	13.50
2019	Bal	AL	31	27	1	155.0	637	138	68	62	23	0	3	5	38	0	121	5	12	11	.522	0-0	0	92	.702	3.31	3.60
2020	Bal	AL	10	10	0	43.2	176	36	22	22	12	0	1	4	7	0	42	2	2	4	.333	0-0	0	94	.718	3.61	4.53
	3 ML YEARS		42	37	1	202.0	829	180	95	89	36	0	4	9	45	0	167	7	14	15	.483	0-0	0	92	.714	3.45	3.97

Nick Mears

Pitches: R **Bats:** R **Pos:** RP-4   **Ht:** 6'2" **Wt:** 215 **Born:** 10/7/1996 **Age:** 24

Year	Team	Lg	G	GS	GF	IP	BFP	H	R	ER	HR	SH	SF	HB	TBB	IBB	SO	WP	W	L	Pct	Sv-Op	Hld	Vel	OPS	ERC	ERA
2020	Pit	NL	4	0	2	5.0	26	4	3	3	1	0	1	0	7	0	7	1	0	0	-	0-0	0	96	.868	7.69	5.40

Adonis Medina

Pitches: R **Bats:** R **Pos:** SP-1   **Ht:** 6'1" **Wt:** 187 **Born:** 12/18/1996 **Age:** 24

Year	Team	Lg	G	GS	GF	IP	BFP	H	R	ER	HR	SH	SF	HB	TBB	IBB	SO	WP	W	L	Pct	Sv-Op	Hld	Vel	OPS	ERC	ERA
2020	Phi	NL	1	1	0	4.0	18	3	2	2	0	0	0	0	3	0	4	0	0	1	.000	0-0	0	92	.600	3.21	4.50

Ryan Meisinger

Pitches: R **Bats:** R **Pos:** RP-2   **Ht:** 6'4" **Wt:** 235 **Born:** 5/4/1994 **Age:** 27

Year	Team	Lg	G	GS	GF	IP	BFP	H	R	ER	HR	SH	SF	HB	TBB	IBB	SO	WP	W	L	Pct	Sv-Op	Hld	Vel	OPS	ERC	ERA
2018	Bal	AL	18	1	2	21.0	87	18	15	15	6	1	1	0	10	0	21	4	2	1	.667	0-0	0	91	.886	5.01	6.43
2020	StL	NL	2	0	0	2.2	13	1	0	0	0	0	0	1	4	0	3	0	0	0	-	0-0	0	91	.587	5.54	0.00
	2 ML YEARS		20	1	2	23.2	100	19	15	15	6	1	1	1	14	0	24	4	2	1	.667	0-0	0	91	.862	5.17	5.70

Erick Mejia

Bats: B **Throws:** R **Pos:** 3B-4;LF-2;PH-2;2B-1;PR-1   **Ht:** 5'11" **Wt:** 155 **Born:** 11/9/1994 **Age:** 26

Year	Team	Lg	G	AB	H	2B	3B	HR	(Hm	Rd)	TB	R	RBI	RC	TBB	IBB	SO	HBP	SH	SF	SB	CS	GDP	Avg	OBP	Slg	OPS
2019	KC	AL	9	22	5	1	0	0	(0	0)	6	3	4	3	4	0	7	0	0	1	0	0	1	.227	.333	.273	.606
2020	KC	AL	8	14	1	1	0	0	(0	0)	2	1	0	0	0	0	7	0	1	0	1	0	0	.071	.071	.143	.214
	2 ML YEARS		17	36	6	2	0	0	(0	0)	8	4	4	3	4	0	14	0	1	1	1	0	1	.167	.244	.222	.466

Francisco Mejia

Bats: B **Throws:** R **Pos:** C-16;PH-3   **Ht:** 5'8" **Wt:** 188 **Born:** 10/27/1995 **Age:** 25

Year	Team	Lg	G	AB	H	2B	3B	HR	(Hm	Rd)	TB	R	RBI	RC	TBB	IBB	SO	HBP	SH	SF	SB	CS	GDP	Avg	OBP	Slg	OPS
2017	Cle	AL	11	13	2	0	0	0	(0	0)	2	1	1	0	1	1	3	0	0	0	0	0	0	.154	.214	.154	.368
2018	2 Tms		21	56	10	2	0	3	(1	2)	21	6	8	5	5	0	19	1	0	0	0	0	2	.179	.258	.375	.633
2019	SD	NL	79	226	60	11	2	8	(3	5)	99	27	22	27	13	1	56	4	0	1	1	1	6	.265	.316	.438	.754
2020	SD	NL	17	39	3	1	0	1	(1	0)	7	5	2	0	1	0	9	2	0	0	0	0	1	.077	.143	.179	.322
18	Cle	AL	1	2	0	0	0	0	(0	0)	0	0	0	0	2	0	0	0	0	0	0	0	0	.000	.500	.000	.500
18	SD	NL	20	54	10	2	0	3	(1	2)	21	6	8	5	3	0	19	1	0	0	0	0	2	.185	.241	.389	.630
	4 ML YEARS		128	334	75	14	2	12	(5	7)	129	39	33	32	20	2	87	7	0	1	1	1	9	.225	.282	.386	.668

Humberto Mejia

Pitches: R **Bats:** R **Pos:** SP-3   **Ht:** 6'4" **Wt:** 235 **Born:** 3/3/1997 **Age:** 24

Year	Team	Lg	G	GS	GF	IP	BFP	H	R	ER	HR	SH	SF	HB	TBB	IBB	SO	WP	W	L	Pct	Sv-Op	Hld	Vel	OPS	ERC	ERA
2020	Mia	NL	3	3	0	10.0	49	13	8	6	3	0	0	1	6	0	11	0	0	2	.000	0-0	0	93	1.027	8.91	5.40

Mark Melancon

Pitches: R Bats: R Pos: RP-23 | muh-LANN-sun | Ht: 6'1" Wt: 215 Born: 3/28/1985 Age: 36

Year	Team	Lg	G	GS	GF	IP	BFP	H	R	ER	HR	SH	SF	HB	TBB	IBB	SO	WP	W	L	Pct	Sv-Op	Hld	Vel	OPS	ERC	ERA
2009	NYY	AL	13	0	4	16.1	74	13	8	7	0	0	0	4	10	0	10	3	0	1	.000	0-1	0	93	.665	3.94	3.86
2010	2 Tms		22	0	4	21.1	90	19	13	10	2	0	1	1	8	0	22	2	2	0	1.000	0-1	8	93	.674	3.53	4.22
2011	Hou	NL	71	0	47	74.1	309	65	28	23	5	2	0	2	26	6	66	1	8	4	.667	20-25	3	93	.631	2.98	2.78
2012	Bos	AL	41	0	17	45.0	194	45	31	31	8	1	2	3	12	1	41	2	0	2	.000	1-2	2	93	.754	4.24	6.20
2013	Pit	NL	72	0	24	71.0	279	60	15	11	1	0	1	1	8	0	70	6	3	2	.600	16-21	26	93	.511	1.78	1.39
2014	Pit	NL	72	0	48	71.0	277	51	15	15	2	1	1	3	11	1	71	3	3	5	.375	33-37	14	93	.473	1.54	1.90
2015	Pit	NL	78	0	63	76.2	293	57	22	19	4	1	1	2	14	2	62	3	3	2	.600	**51-53**	1	92	.541	1.82	2.23
2016	2 Tms	NL	75	0	67	71.1	270	52	16	13	3	0	2	1	12	0	65	4	2	2	.500	47-51	0	92	.511	1.66	1.64
2017	SF	NL	32	0	18	30.0	130	37	16	15	3	0	0	1	6	0	29	2	1	2	.333	11-16	5	92	.794	4.78	4.50
2018	SF	NL	41	0	18	39.0	174	48	18	14	2	0	0	1	14	2	31	4	1	4	.200	3-7	8	92	.771	4.94	3.23
2019	2 Tms	NL	66	0	34	67.1	284	71	28	27	4	0	1	2	18	2	68	3	5	2	.714	12-12	5	92	.678	3.69	3.61
2020	Atl	NL	23	0	19	22.2	95	22	8	7	1	1	1	2	7	3	14	1	2	1	.667	11-13	0	92	.639	3.38	2.78
10	NYY	AL	2	0	2	4.0	19	7	5	4	1	0	1	0	0	0	3	0	0	0	-	0-0	0	93	.980	7.95	9.00
10	Hou	NL	20	0	2	17.1	71	12	8	6	1	0	0	1	8	0	19	2	2	0	1.000	0-1	8	93	.586	2.65	3.12
16	Pit	NL	45	0	39	41.2	163	31	10	7	2	0	2	1	9	0	38	1	1	1	.500	30-33	0	92	.516	1.89	1.51
16	Was	NL	30	0	28	29.2	107	21	6	6	1	0	0	0	3	0	27	3	1	1	.500	17-18	0	93	.503	1.41	1.82
19	SF	NL	43	0	16	46.1	195	49	19	18	3	0	1	2	16	2	44	3	4	2	.667	1-1	5	92	.724	4.18	3.50
19	Atl	NL	23	0	18	21.0	89	22	9	9	1	0	0	0	2	0	24	1	1	0	1.000	11-11	0	93	.580	2.69	3.86
	Postseason		13	0	9	13.0	58	17	8	8	2	0	0	0	5	3	12	0	1	1	.500	3-5	0	93	.870	6.00	5.54
	12 ML YEARS		606	0	353	606.0	2469	540	218	192	35	6	10	23	146	17	549	35	30	27	.526	205-239	72	93	.612	2.74	2.85

Keury Mella

Pitches: R Bats: R Pos: RP-11 | Ht: 6'2" Wt: 230 Born: 8/2/1993 Age: 27

Year	Team	Lg	G	GS	GF	IP	BFP	H	R	ER	HR	SH	SF	HB	TBB	IBB	SO	WP	W	L	Pct	Sv-Op	Hld	Vel	OPS	ERC	ERA
2017	Cin	NL	2	0	1	4.0	19	5	3	3	1	0	0	0	2	1	1	0	0	0	-	0-0	0	96	.957	6.56	6.75
2018	Cin	NL	4	0	1	9.1	48	13	9	9	4	2	0	1	8	0	8	1	0	0	-	0-0	0	94	1.262	12.40	8.68
2019	Cin	NL	2	0	1	3.2	18	5	3	3	0	0	0	0	2	1	4	0	0	0	-	0-0	0	95	.826	5.31	7.36
2020	Ari	NL	11	0	3	10.0	42	10	3	2	1	0	1	0	3	1	10	1	2	0	1.000	0-0	0	95	.704	3.54	1.80
	4 ML YEARS		19	0	6	27.0	127	33	18	17	6	2	1	1	15	3	23	2	2	0	1.000	0-0	0	95	.957	7.00	5.67

Danny Mendick

Bats: R Throws: R Pos: 2B-28;SS-4;3B-3 | Ht: 5'10" Wt: 195 Born: 9/28/1993 Age: 27

Year	Team	Lg	G	AB	H	2B	3B	HR	(Hm	Rd)	TB	R	RBI	RC	TBB	IBB	SO	HBP	SH	SF	SB	CS	GDP	Avg	OBP	Slg	OPS
2019	CWS	AL	16	39	12	0	0	2	(2	0)	18	6	4	6	1	0	11	0	0	0	0	0	1	.308	.325	.462	.787
2020	CWS	AL	33	107	26	4	1	3	(2	1)	41	11	6	6	6	0	25	0	0	1	0	1	3	.243	.281	.383	.664
	2 ML YEARS		49	146	38	4	1	5	(4	1)	59	17	10	12	7	0	36	0	0	1	0	1	4	.260	.292	.404	.696

Conner Menez

Pitches: L Bats: L Pos: RP-7 | Ht: 6'2" Wt: 206 Born: 5/29/1995 Age: 26

Year	Team	Lg	G	GS	GF	IP	BFP	H	R	ER	HR	SH	SF	HB	TBB	IBB	SO	WP	W	L	Pct	Sv-Op	Hld	Vel	OPS	ERC	ERA
2019	SF	NL	8	3	2	17.0	73	13	10	10	4	1	1	0	12	0	22	2	0	1	.000	0-0	0	91	.805	5.06	5.29
2020	SF	NL	7	0	3	11.1	45	6	4	3	2	1	0	1	5	0	8	0	1	0	1.000	0-0	0	92	.641	2.61	2.38
	2 ML YEARS		15	3	5	28.1	118	19	14	13	6	2	1	1	17	0	30	2	1	1	.500	0-0	0	91	.742	4.02	4.13

Daniel Mengden

Pitches: R Bats: R Pos: RP-3; SP-1 | MENG-den | Ht: 6'1" Wt: 215 Born: 2/19/1993 Age: 28

Year	Team	Lg	G	GS	GF	IP	BFP	H	R	ER	HR	SH	SF	HB	TBB	IBB	SO	WP	W	L	Pct	Sv-Op	Hld	Vel	OPS	ERC	ERA
2016	Oak	AL	14	14	0	72.0	332	83	54	52	9	2	1	4	33	0	71	5	2	9	.182	0-0	0	92	.819	6.56	6.50
2017	Oak	AL	7	7	0	43.0	169	36	16	15	6	1	2	0	9	0	29	2	3	2	.600	0-0	0	92	.650	2.78	3.14
2018	Oak	AL	22	17	0	115.2	476	103	58	52	18	4	2	3	26	0	72	6	7	6	.538	0-0	0	92	.699	3.22	4.05
2019	Oak	AL	13	9	2	59.2	260	59	32	32	7	0	1	0	27	0	42	1	5	2	.714	1-1	0	91	.753	4.34	4.83
2020	Oak	AL	4	1	2	12.1	58	14	5	5	2	0	1	1	7	0	10	0	0	1	.000	0-0	0	90	.869	6.36	3.65
	5 ML YEARS		60	48	4	302.2	1295	295	165	156	42	7	7	8	102	0	224	14	17	20	.459	1-1	0	92	.741	4.03	4.64

Oscar Mercado

Bats: R Throws: R Pos: CF-21;LF-12;PR-4;PH-3;DH-1 | Ht: 6'2" Wt: 197 Born: 12/16/1994 Age: 26

Year	Team	Lg	G	AB	H	2B	3B	HR	(Hm	Rd)	TB	R	RBI	RC	TBB	IBB	SO	HBP	SH	SF	SB	CS	GDP	Avg	OBP	Slg	OPS
2019	Cle	AL	115	438	118	25	3	15	(11	4)	194	70	54	69	28	0	84	5	7	4	15	4	9	.269	.318	.443	.761
2020	Cle	AL	36	86	11	1	0	1	(0	1)	15	6	6	1	5	0	27	0	1	1	3	0	0	.128	.174	.174	.348
	2 ML YEARS		151	524	129	26	3	16	(11	5)	209	76	60	70	33	0	111	5	8	5	18	4	9	.246	.295	.399	.693

Yermin Mercedes

Bats: R Throws: R Pos: DH-1;PH-1 | Ht: 5'11" Wt: 235 Born: 2/14/1993 Age: 28

Year	Team	Lg	G	AB	H	2B	3B	HR	(Hm	Rd)	TB	R	RBI	RC	TBB	IBB	SO	HBP	SH	SF	SB	CS	GDP	Avg	OBP	Slg	OPS
2020	CWS	AL	1	1	0	0	0	0	(0	0)	0	0	0	0	0	0	0	0	0	0	0	0	0	.000	.000	.000	.000

Jordy Mercer

Bats: R **Throws:** R **Pos:** SS-6;1B-2;3B-2;PH-1   **Ht:** 6'3" **Wt:** 210 **Born:** 8/27/1986 **Age:** 34

Year	Team	Lg	G	AB	H	2B	3B	HR	(Hm	Rd)	TB	R	RBI	RC	TBB	IBB	SO	HBP	SH	SF	SB	CS	GDP	Avg	OBP	Slg	OPS
2012	Pit	NL	42	62	13	5	1	1	(1	0)	23	7	5	6	4	0	14	1	0	1	0	1	0	.210	.265	.371	.636
2013	Pit	NL	103	333	95	22	2	8	(1	7)	145	33	27	46	22	6	62	4	5	1	3	2	7	.285	.336	.435	.772
2014	Pit	NL	149	506	129	27	2	12	(3	9)	196	56	55	45	35	12	89	4	5	5	4	1	14	.255	.305	.387	.693
2015	Pit	NL	116	394	96	21	0	3	(0	3)	126	34	34	34	27	7	73	2	4	3	3	2	7	.244	.293	.320	.613
2016	Pit	NL	149	519	133	22	3	11	(4	7)	194	66	59	58	51	8	83	5	7	2	1	1	11	.256	.328	.374	.701
2017	Pit	NL	145	502	128	24	5	14	(5	9)	204	52	58	60	51	13	88	3	0	2	0	4	16	.255	.326	.406	.733
2018	Pit	NL	117	394	99	29	2	6	(1	5)	150	43	39	41	32	9	87	6	1	3	2	0	12	.251	.315	.381	.696
2019	Det	AL	74	256	69	16	0	9	(4	5)	112	24	22	28	13	1	57	2	0	0	0	0	4	.270	.310	.438	.747
2020	2 Tms	AL	9	20	4	0	0	0	(0	0)	4	2	0	1	2	0	2	0	0	0	0	0	1	.200	.273	.200	.473
20	Det	AL	3	9	2	0	0	0	(0	0)	2	1	0	0	0	0	1	0	0	0	0	0	0	.222	.222	.222	.444
20	NYY	AL	6	11	2	0	0	0	(0	0)	2	1	0	1	2	0	1	0	0	0	0	0	0	.182	.308	.182	.490
	Postseason		7	14	2	0	0	0	(0	0)	2	0	0	0	1	1	5	0	0	0	0	0	0	.143	.200	.143	.343
	9 ML YEARS		904	2986	766	166	15	64	(19	45)	1154	317	299	319	237	56	555	27	22	17	13	11	72	.257	.315	.386	.702

Whit Merrifield

Bats: R **Throws:** R **Pos:** RF-34;CF-23;2B-15;LF-6;1B-1   **Ht:** 6'1" **Wt:** 195 **Born:** 1/24/1989 **Age:** 32

Year	Team	Lg	G	AB	H	2B	3B	HR	(Hm	Rd)	TB	R	RBI	RC	TBB	IBB	SO	HBP	SH	SF	SB	CS	GDP	Avg	OBP	Slg	OPS
2016	KC	AL	81	311	88	22	3	2	(2	0)	122	44	29	38	19	1	72	0	1	1	8	3	1	.283	.323	.392	.716
2017	KC	AL	145	587	169	32	6	19	(13	6)	270	80	78	88	29	0	88	6	1	7	34	8	13	.288	.324	.460	.784
2018	KC	AL	158	632	192	43	3	12	(5	7)	277	88	60	103	61	2	114	6	2	6	45	10	12	.304	.367	.438	.806
2019	KC	AL	162	681	206	41	10	16	(4	12)	315	105	74	114	45	5	126	5	0	4	20	10	8	.302	.348	.463	.811
2020	KC	AL	60	248	70	12	0	9	(3	6)	109	38	30	41	12	0	33	4	0	1	12	3	3	.282	.325	.440	.764
	5 ML YEARS		606	2459	725	150	22	58	(27	31)	1093	355	271	384	166	8	433	21	4	19	119	34	37	.295	.342	.444	.787

Julian Merryweather

Pitches: R **Bats:** R **Pos:** RP-5; SP-3   **Ht:** 6'4" **Wt:** 215 **Born:** 10/14/1991 **Age:** 29

Year	Team	Lg	G	GS	GF	IP	BFP	H	R	ER	HR	SH	SF	HB	TBB	IBB	SO	WP	W	L	Pct	Sv-Op	Hld	Vel	OPS	ERC	ERA
2020	Tor	AL	8	3	0	13.0	55	11	6	6	0	0	0	0	6	0	15	0	0	0	-	0-0	1	97	.595	2.79	4.15

Keynan Middleton

Pitches: R **Bats:** R **Pos:** RP-13   **Ht:** 6'3" **Wt:** 215 **Born:** 9/12/1993 **Age:** 27

Year	Team	Lg	G	GS	GF	IP	BFP	H	R	ER	HR	SH	SF	HB	TBB	IBB	SO	WP	W	L	Pct	Sv-Op	Hld	Vel	OPS	ERC	ERA
2017	LAA	AL	64	0	17	58.1	246	60	25	25	11	0	2	0	18	2	63	2	6	1	.857	3-5	10	97	.791	4.47	3.86
2018	LAA	AL	16	0	9	17.2	71	14	4	4	1	0	1	1	9	1	16	1	0	0	-	6-7	2	96	.688	3.42	2.04
2019	LAA	AL	11	0	0	7.2	33	4	1	1	0	0	0	0	7	0	6	1	0	0	-	0-0	0	94	.564	2.72	1.17
2020	LAA	AL	13	0	4	12.0	53	12	8	7	2	0	3	0	6	0	11	1	0	1	.000	0-0	2	97	.817	4.95	5.25
	4 ML YEARS		104	0	30	95.2	403	90	38	37	14	0	6	1	40	3	96	5	6	2	.750	9-12	14	97	.760	4.21	3.48

Miles Mikolas

Pitches: R **Bats:** R **Pos:** P   MIKE-uh-liss   **Ht:** 6'4" **Wt:** 230 **Born:** 8/23/1988 **Age:** 32

Year	Team	Lg	G	GS	GF	IP	BFP	H	R	ER	HR	SH	SF	HB	TBB	IBB	SO	WP	W	L	Pct	Sv-Op	Hld	Vel	OPS	ERC	ERA
2012	SD	NL	25	0	9	32.1	144	32	15	13	4	2	0	2	15	0	23	2	2	1	.667	0-1	1	93	.761	4.65	3.62
2013	SD	NL	2	0	1	1.2	7	0	0	0	0	0	0	1	1	0	1	0	0	0	-	0-0	0	93	.286	1.30	0.00
2014	Tex	AL	10	10	0	57.1	255	64	43	41	8	1	2	4	18	2	38	0	2	5	.286	0-0	0	93	.769	4.85	6.44
2018	StL	NL	32	32	0	200.2	808	186	70	63	16	8	4	7	29	4	146	2	18	4	.818	0-0	0	94	.628	2.70	2.83
2019	StL	NL	32	32	0	184.0	764	193	90	85	27	3	7	12	32	1	144	5	9	14	.391	0-0	0	94	.761	4.08	4.16
	Postseason		3	2	1	12.0	50	10	2	2	0	0	0	0	4	1	9	0	1	1	.500	0-0	0	94	.606	2.14	1.50
	5 ML YEARS		101	74	10	476.0	1978	475	218	202	55	14	13	26	95	7	352	9	31	24	.564	0-1	1	94	.706	3.59	3.82

Wade Miley

Pitches: L **Bats:** L **Pos:** SP-4; RP-2   MY-lee   **Ht:** 6'2" **Wt:** 220 **Born:** 11/13/1986 **Age:** 34

Year	Team	Lg	G	GS	GF	IP	BFP	H	R	ER	HR	SH	SF	HB	TBB	IBB	SO	WP	W	L	Pct	Sv-Op	Hld	Vel	OPS	ERC	ERA
2011	Ari	NL	8	7	0	40.0	180	48	20	20	6	3	1	0	18	0	25	1	4	2	.667	0-0	0	90	.873	5.90	4.50
2012	Ari	NL	32	29	0	194.2	807	193	79	72	14	8	3	2	37	0	144	6	16	11	.593	0-0	0	91	.685	3.05	3.33
2013	Ari	NL	33	33	0	202.2	847	201	88	80	21	6	2	4	66	4	147	13	10	10	.500	0-0	0	91	.727	3.88	3.55
2014	Ari	NL	33	33	0	201.1	866	207	103	97	23	8	9	4	75	3	183	9	8	12	.400	0-0	0	91	.746	4.31	4.34
2015	Bos	AL	32	32	0	193.2	831	201	98	96	17	3	2	4	64	0	147	10	11	11	.500	0-0	0	91	.740	4.01	4.46
2016	2 Tms	AL	30	30	0	166.0	711	187	100	99	25	2	5	6	49	1	137	8	9	13	.409	0-0	0	90	.808	4.98	5.37
2017	Bal	AL	32	32	0	157.1	728	179	104	98	25	1	6	4	93	1	142	1	8	15	.348	0-0	0	91	.841	6.27	5.61
2018	Mil	NL	16	16	0	80.2	338	71	28	23	3	5	1	5	27	1	50	1	5	2	.714	0-0	0	91	.636	2.98	2.57
2019	Hou	AL	33	33	0	167.1	720	164	83	74	23	2	5	5	61	0	140	4	14	6	.700	0-0	0	90	.726	4.19	3.98
2020	Cin	NL	6	4	2	14.1	67	15	10	9	1	0	0	2	9	0	12	0	0	3	.000	0-0	0	90	.799	5.62	5.65
16	Sea	AL	19	19	0	112.0	469	117	62	62	18	2	3	3	34	1	82	5	7	8	.467	0-0	0	90	.786	4.58	4.98
16	Bal	AL	11	11	0	54.0	242	70	38	37	7	0	2	3	15	0	55	3	2	5	.286	0-0	0	90	.850	5.83	6.17
	Postseason		5	4	0	17.1	72	14	5	4	2	0	0	0	5	0	10	0	0	0	-	0-0	0	91	.607	2.64	2.08
	10 ML YEARS		255	249	2	1418.0	6095	1466	713	668	158	38	34	36	499	10	1127	53	85	85	.500	0-0	0	91	.749	4.27	4.24

Andrew Miller

Pitches: L **Bats:** L **Pos:** RP-16   **Ht:** 6'7" **Wt:** 200 **Born:** 5/21/1985 **Age:** 36

Year Team	Lg	G	GS	GF	IP	BFP	H	R	ER	HR	SH	SF	HB	TBB	IBB	SO	WP	W	L	Pct	Sv-Op	Hld	Vel	OPS	ERC	ERA
2006 Det	AL	8	0	3	10.1	51	8	9	7	0	0	0	2	10	0	6	1	0	1	.000	0-0	1	94	.700	4.79	6.10
2007 Det	AL	13	13	0	64.0	309	73	43	40	8	3	1	7	39	0	56	4	5	5	.500	0-0	0	92	.821	6.31	5.63
2008 Fla	NL	29	20	1	107.1	492	120	78	70	7	10	7	4	56	4	89	4	6	10	.375	0-0	2	91	.798	5.04	5.87
2009 Fla	NL	20	14	1	80.0	366	85	52	43	7	6	4	2	43	1	59	10	3	5	.375	0-0	1	91	.792	4.90	4.84
2010 Fla	NL	9	7	1	32.2	171	51	34	31	6	5	2	1	26	2	28	5	1	5	.167	0-0	0	91	1.054	10.20	8.54
2011 Bos	AL	17	12	2	65.0	310	77	43	40	8	6	5	3	41	0	50	2	6	3	.667	0-0	0	93	.857	6.48	5.54
2012 Bos	AL	53	0	4	40.1	169	28	15	15	3	0	3	2	20	1	51	1	3	2	.600	0-0	13	95	.588	2.76	3.35
2013 Bos	AL	37	0	11	30.2	135	25	12	9	3	1	0	2	17	0	48	2	1	2	.333	0-1	6	95	.624	3.83	2.64
2014 2 Tms	AL	73	0	15	62.1	242	33	16	14	3	2	2	5	17	2	103	3	5	5	.500	1-2	22	94	.456	1.36	2.02
2015 NYY	AL	60	0	53	61.2	246	33	16	14	5	1	2	5	20	1	100	2	3	2	.600	36-38	0	94	.475	1.61	2.04
2016 2 Tms	AL	70	0	23	74.1	275	42	13	12	8	1	1	2	9	0	123	1	10	1	.909	12-14	25	95	.487	1.27	1.45
2017 Cle	AL	57	0	6	62.2	244	31	11	10	3	2	1	5	21	0	95	1	4	3	.571	2-4	27	94	.440	1.42	1.44
2018 Cle	AL	37	0	5	34.0	154	31	16	16	3	0	0	5	16	1	45	1	2	4	.333	2-5	10	93	.729	4.19	4.24
2019 StL	NL	73	0	11	54.2	236	45	32	27	11	0	1	8	27	1	70	4	5	6	.455	6-11	28	92	.739	4.81	4.45
2020 StL	NL	16	0	5	13.0	55	9	4	4	0	0	0	3	5	0	16	2	1	1	.500	4-5	2	90	.522	2.55	2.77
14 Bos	AL	50	0	12	42.1	170	25	13	11	2	2	2	4	13	2	69	2	3	5	.375	0-0	13	94	.492	1.62	2.34
14 Bal	AL	23	0	3	20.0	72	8	3	3	1	0	0	1	4	0	34	1	2	0	1.000	1-2	9	94	.375	0.86	1.35
16 NYY	AL	44	0	16	45.1	172	28	8	7	5	1	1	2	7	0	77	0	6	1	.857	9-11	16	95	.521	1.55	1.39
16 Cle	AL	26	0	7	29.0	103	14	5	5	3	0	0	0	2	0	46	1	4	0	1.000	3-3	9	95	.433	0.87	1.55
Postseason		28	0	3	38.0	144	19	4	4	3	1	1	2	13	2	54	1	2	1	.667	1-2	8	94	.482	1.50	0.95
15 ML YEARS		572	66	141	793.0	3455	691	394	352	75	37	29	56	367	13	939	43	55	55	.500	63-80	137	93	.687	3.78	3.99

Brad Miller

Bats: L **Throws:** R **Pos:** DH-32;3B-15;PH-3;SS-2;2B-1   **Ht:** 6'2" **Wt:** 195 **Born:** 10/18/1989 **Age:** 31

Year Team	Lg	G	AB	H	2B	3B	HR	(Hm	Rd)	TB	R	RBI	RC	TBB	IBB	SO	HBP	SH	SF	SB	CS	GDP	Avg	OBP	Slg	OPS
2013 Sea	AL	76	306	81	11	6	8	(3	5)	128	41	36	41	24	0	52	1	2	2	5	3	2	.265	.318	.418	.737
2014 Sea	AL	123	367	81	15	4	10	(4	6)	134	47	36	41	34	2	95	2	3	3	4	2	2	.221	.288	.365	.653
2015 Sea	AL	144	438	113	22	4	11	(6	5)	176	44	46	58	47	0	101	2	4	6	13	4	7	.258	.329	.402	.730
2016 TB	AL	152	548	133	29	6	30	(22	8)	264	73	81	74	47	0	149	3	0	3	6	4	5	.243	.304	.482	.786
2017 TB	AL	110	338	68	13	3	9	(6	3)	114	43	40	37	63	4	110	2	0	4	5	3	5	.201	.327	.337	.664
2018 2 Tms		75	230	57	13	2	7	(5	2)	95	21	29	27	22	1	82	0	0	2	0	0	4	.248	.311	.413	.724
2019 2 Tms		79	154	40	6	1	13	(6	7)	87	24	25	26	15	0	45	1	0	0	2	0	2	.260	.329	.565	.894
2020 StL	NL	48	142	33	8	1	7	(1	6)	64	21	25	25	25	1	46	3	0	1	1	0	2	.232	.357	.451	.807
18 TB	AL	48	156	40	10	1	5	(3	2)	67	16	21	18	16	0	51	0	0	2	0	0	2	.256	.322	.429	.751
18 Mil	NL	27	74	17	3	1	2	(2	0)	28	5	8	9	6	1	31	0	0	0	0	0	2	.230	.288	.378	.666
19 Cle	AL	13	36	9	3	0	1	(0	1)	15	4	4	7	4	0	10	0	0	0	0	0	0	.250	.325	.417	.742
19 Phi	NL	66	118	31	3	1	12	(6	6)	72	22	21	19	11	0	35	1	0	0	2	0	2	.263	.331	.610	.941
8 ML YEARS		807	2523	606	117	27	95	(53	42)	1062	316	318	329	277	8	680	14	9	21	36	16	29	.240	.316	.421	.737

Ian Miller

Bats: L **Throws:** R **Pos:** PR-1   **Ht:** 6'0" **Wt:** 170 **Born:** 2/21/1992 **Age:** 29

Year Team	Lg	G	AB	H	2B	3B	HR	(Hm	Rd)	TB	R	RBI	RC	TBB	IBB	SO	HBP	SH	SF	SB	CS	GDP	Avg	OBP	Slg	OPS
2019 Min	AL	12	17	3	1	0	0	(0	0)	4	2	1	1	0	0	3	0	0	0	0	0	0	.176	.176	.235	.412
2020 ChC	NL	1	0	0	0	0	0	(0	0)	0	0	0	0	0	0	0	0	0	0	0	0	0	-	-	-	-
2 ML YEARS		13	17	3	1	0	0	(0	0)	4	2	1	1	0	0	3	0	0	0	0	0	0	.176	.176	.235	.412

Shelby Miller

Pitches: R **Bats:** R **Pos:** P   **Ht:** 6'3" **Wt:** 225 **Born:** 10/10/1990 **Age:** 30

Year Team	Lg	G	GS	GF	IP	BFP	H	R	ER	HR	SH	SF	HB	TBB	IBB	SO	WP	W	L	Pct	Sv-Op	Hld	Vel	OPS	ERC	ERA
2012 StL	NL	6	1	1	13.2	54	9	2	2	0	0	0	1	4	0	16	0	1	0	1.000	0-0	1	93	.463	1.65	1.32
2013 StL	NL	31	31	0	173.1	722	152	65	59	20	7	3	5	57	0	169	2	15	9	.625	0-0	0	94	.670	3.34	3.06
2014 StL	NL	32	31	0	183.0	764	160	78	76	22	7	4	2	73	4	127	4	10	9	.526	0-0	0	93	.698	3.56	3.74
2015 Atl	NL	33	33	0	205.1	860	183	82	69	13	8	4	6	73	8	171	5	6	17	.261	0-0	0	94	.663	3.12	3.02
2016 Ari	NL	20	20	0	101.0	460	127	72	69	14	3	3	2	42	3	70	3	3	12	.200	0-0	0	93	.867	6.03	6.15
2017 Ari	NL	4	4	0	22.0	99	20	10	10	1	0	0	0	12	1	20	1	2	2	.500	0-0	0	95	.668	3.53	4.09
2018 Ari	NL	5	4	0	16.0	79	24	21	19	5	0	1	0	8	0	19	1	0	4	.000	0-0	1	94	1.048	9.35	10.69
2019 Tex	AL	19	8	4	44.0	220	58	46	42	8	4	0	3	29	1	30	1	1	3	.250	0-1	1	94	.908	7.95	8.59
Postseason		5	2	0	13.2	61	16	8	8	1	1	1	1	6	0	12	0	0	0	-	0-0	0	94	.768	5.46	5.27
8 ML YEARS		150	132	5	758.1	3258	733	376	346	83	25	19	19	298	17	622	17	38	56	.404	0-1	3	94	.724	3.99	4.11

Tyson Miller

Pitches: R **Bats:** R **Pos:** SP-1; RP-1   **Ht:** 6'4" **Wt:** 225 **Born:** 7/29/1995 **Age:** 25

Year Team	Lg	G	GS	GF	IP	BFP	H	R	ER	HR	SH	SF	HB	TBB	IBB	SO	WP	W	L	Pct	Sv-Op	Hld	Vel	OPS	ERC	ERA
2020 ChC	NL	2	1	1	5.0	20	2	3	3	1	0	1	0	3	0	0	0	0	0	-	0-0	0	93	.625	2.30	5.40

Alec Mills

Pitches: R Bats: R Pos: SP-11 Ht: 6'4" Wt: 205 Born: 11/30/1991 Age: 29

Year Team	Lg	G	GS	GF	IP	BFP	H	R	ER	HR	SH	SF	HB	TBB	IBB	SO	WP	W	L	Pct	Sv-Op	Hld	Vel	OPS	ERC	ERA
2016 KC	AL	3	0	2	3.1	19	3	5	5	0	0	1	1	5	0	4	0	0	0	-	0-0	0	92	.858	8.02	13.50
2018 ChC	NL	7	2	1	18.0	71	11	8	8	1	0	0	0	7	0	23	1	0	1	.000	0-0	0	91	.550	1.80	4.00
2019 ChC	NL	9	4	3	36.0	152	31	11	11	5	0	0	7	11	0	42	0	1	0	1.000	1-1	0	90	.718	4.03	2.75
2020 ChC	NL	11	11	0	62.1	252	53	31	31	13	0	1	2	19	0	46	0	5	5	.500	0-0	0	90	.741	3.80	4.48
4 ML YEARS		30	17	6	119.2	494	98	55	55	19	0	1	10	42	0	115	1	6	6	.500	1-1	0	90	.712	3.66	4.14

Hoby Milner

Pitches: L Bats: L Pos: RP-19 Ht: 6'3" Wt: 175 Born: 1/13/1991 Age: 30

Year Team	Lg	G	GS	GF	IP	BFP	H	R	ER	HR	SH	SF	HB	TBB	IBB	SO	WP	W	L	Pct	Sv-Op	Hld	Vel	OPS	ERC	ERA
2017 Phi	NL	37	0	5	31.1	139	30	7	7	2	2	1	4	16	3	22	0	0	0	-	0-1	7	89	.736	4.39	2.01
2018 2 Tms		14	0	3	7.1	38	9	8	6	3	0	0	1	5	1	8	0	0	0	-	0-0	1	89	.988	9.22	7.36
2019 TB	AL	4	0	1	3.2	17	4	3	3	0	0	0	1	1	0	3	0	0	0	-	0-0	1	88	.820	4.28	7.36
2020 LAA	AL	19	0	4	13.1	59	13	12	12	5	0	0	1	6	0	13	0	0	0	-	0-0	1	88	.897	6.45	8.10
18 Phi	NL	10	0	2	4.2	25	6	4	4	1	0	0	1	3	1	4	0	0	0	-	0-0	0	89	.829	7.79	7.71
18 TB	AL	4	0	1	2.2	13	3	4	2	2	0	0	0	2	0	4	0	0	0	-	0-0	1	89	1.294	11.59	6.75
4 ML YEARS		74	0	13	55.2	253	56	30	28	10	2	1	7	28	4	46	0	0	0	-	0-1	10	89	.818	5.51	4.53

Tommy Milone

Pitches: L Bats: L Pos: SP-9 mah-LONE Ht: 6'0" Wt: 215 Born: 2/16/1987 Age: 34

Year Team	Lg	G	GS	GF	IP	BFP	H	R	ER	HR	SH	SF	HB	TBB	IBB	SO	WP	W	L	Pct	Sv-Op	Hld	Vel	OPS	ERC	ERA
2011 Was	NL	5	5	0	26.0	110	28	11	11	2	3	2	2	4	2	15	0	1	0	1.000	0-0	0	88	.742	3.55	3.81
2012 Oak	AL	31	31	0	190.0	791	207	90	79	24	3	3	4	36	2	137	2	13	10	.565	0-0	0	88	.738	4.04	3.74
2013 Oak	AL	28	26	0	156.1	667	160	83	72	25	0	6	2	39	2	126	1	12	9	.571	0-0	0	87	.738	3.98	4.14
2014 2 Tms	AL	22	21	1	118.0	519	128	63	55	16	1	2	5	37	2	75	0	6	4	.600	0-0	0	87	.763	4.55	4.19
2015 Min	AL	24	23	1	128.2	543	128	64	56	17	6	7	1	36	1	91	3	9	5	.643	1-1	0	88	.731	3.79	3.92
2016 Min	AL	19	12	3	69.1	311	84	53	44	15	4	3	1	22	3	49	3	3	5	.375	0-0	1	88	.857	5.77	5.71
2017 2 Tms	NL	17	8	2	48.1	221	65	43	41	15	2	0	0	14	3	38	0	1	3	.250	1-1	0	88	.970	7.12	7.63
2018 Was	NL	5	4	1	26.1	118	37	17	17	7	2	2	1	1	0	23	0	1	1	.500	0-0	0	88	.917	6.17	5.81
2019 Sea	AL	23	6	0	111.2	453	102	61	59	24	0	5	2	23	2	94	1	4	10	.286	0-0	0	87	.765	3.63	4.76
2020 2 Tms		9	9	0	39.0	181	55	34	29	9	1	2	2	6	0	40	1	1	4	.200	0-0	0	86	.950	6.50	6.69
14 Oak	AL	16	16	0	96.1	405	91	42	38	12	1	2	4	26	2	61	0	6	3	.667	0-0	0	87	.705	3.53	3.55
14 Min	AL	6	5	1	21.2	114	37	21	17	4	0	0	1	11	0	14	0	0	1	.000	0-0	0	88	.969	9.76	7.06
17 Mil	NL	6	3	1	21.0	93	29	15	15	6	0	0	0	2	0	16	0	1	0	1.000	1-1	0	88	.905	6.32	6.43
17 NYM	NL	11	5	1	27.1	128	36	28	26	9	2	0	0	12	3	22	0	0	3	.000	0-0	0	88	1.021	7.74	8.56
20 Bal	AL	6	6	0	29.1	129	33	18	13	5	1	1	2	4	0	31	1	1	4	.200	0-0	0	86	.776	4.30	3.99
20 Atl	NL	3	3	0	9.2	52	22	16	16	4	0	1	0	2	0	9	0	0	0	-	0-0	0	86	1.380	14.68	14.90
Postseason		1	1	0	6.0	25	5	1	1	0	0	0	1	1	0	6	1	0	0	-	0-0	0	88	.584	2.26	1.50
10 ML YEARS		183	145	8	913.2	3914	994	519	463	154	22	32	20	218	17	688	11	51	51	.500	2-2	1	87	.781	4.43	4.56

Mike Minor

Pitches: L Bats: R Pos: SP-11; RP-1 Ht: 6'4" Wt: 210 Born: 12/26/1987 Age: 33

Year Team	Lg	G	GS	GF	IP	BFP	H	R	ER	HR	SH	SF	HB	TBB	IBB	SO	WP	W	L	Pct	Sv-Op	Hld	Vel	OPS	ERC	ERA
2010 Atl	NL	9	8	1	40.2	185	53	28	27	6	1	3	1	11	0	43	0	3	2	.600	0-0	0	91	.880	5.71	5.98
2011 Atl	NL	15	15	0	82.2	361	93	39	38	7	3	1	1	30	5	77	2	5	3	.625	0-0	0	91	.785	4.51	4.14
2012 Atl	NL	30	30	0	179.1	728	151	88	82	26	8	8	5	56	7	145	3	11	10	.524	0-0	0	90	.702	3.28	4.12
2013 Atl	NL	32	32	0	204.2	820	177	79	73	22	5	6	1	46	2	181	5	13	9	.591	0-0	0	90	.657	2.76	3.21
2014 Atl	NL	25	25	0	145.1	637	165	77	77	21	6	2	6	44	2	120	5	6	12	.333	0-0	0	90	.798	4.93	4.77
2017 KC	AL	65	0	13	77.2	307	57	23	22	5	3	1	1	22	3	88	5	6	6	.500	6-9	17	94	.585	2.07	2.55
2018 Tex	AL	28	28	0	157.0	640	138	76	73	25	1	6	8	38	1	132	3	12	8	.600	0-0	0	93	.733	3.40	4.18
2019 Tex	AL	32	32	0	208.1	863	190	86	83	30	3	6	7	68	1	200	2	14	10	.583	0-0	0	93	.704	3.78	3.59
2020 2 Tms	AL	12	11	0	56.2	239	50	36	35	11	0	1	1	20	0	62	0	1	6	.143	0-0	0	91	.712	3.90	5.56
20 Tex	AL	7	7	0	35.1	155	35	23	22	7	0	1	0	13	0	35	0	0	5	.000	0-0	0	91	.742	4.45	5.60
20 Oak	AL	5	4	0	21.1	84	15	13	13	4	0	0	1	7	0	27	0	1	1	.500	0-0	0	91	.655	3.02	5.48
Postseason		1	1	0	6.1	26	8	1	1	0	1	0	0	1	0	5	0	1	0	1.000	0-0	0	92	.777	4.11	1.42
9 ML YEARS		248	181	14	1152.1	4780	1074	532	510	153	30	34	31	335	21	1048	25	71	66	.518	6-9	17	91	.717	3.60	3.98

A.J. Minter

Pitches: L Bats: L Pos: RP-22 Ht: 6'0" Wt: 215 Born: 9/2/1993 Age: 27

Year Team	Lg	G	GS	GF	IP	BFP	H	R	ER	HR	SH	SF	HB	TBB	IBB	SO	WP	W	L	Pct	Sv-Op	Hld	Vel	OPS	ERC	ERA
2017 Atl	NL	16	0	3	15.0	60	13	5	5	1	0	0	0	2	0	26	0	0	1	.000	0-0	5	96	.595	2.15	3.00
2018 Atl	NL	65	0	31	61.1	260	57	23	22	3	1	1	2	22	1	69	5	4	3	.571	15-17	12	97	.642	3.27	3.23
2019 Atl	NL	36	0	12	29.1	147	36	23	23	3	1	1	1	23	5	35	5	3	4	.429	5-7	5	96	.857	6.73	7.06
2020 Atl	NL	22	0	6	21.2	85	15	3	2	1	1	0	0	9	2	24	1	1	1	.500	0-0	5	96	.606	2.15	0.83
Postseason		2	0	1	2.0	8	1	0	0	0	0	0	0	1	0	3	1	0	0	-	0-0	1	97	.393	1.41	0.00
4 ML YEARS		139	0	52	127.1	552	121	54	52	8	3	2	3	56	8	154	11	8	9	.471	20-24	27	96	.686	3.66	3.68

Anthony Misiewicz

Pitches: L **Bats:** R **Pos:** RP-21   mih-SEV-itch   **Ht:** 6'1" **Wt:** 200 **Born:** 11/1/1994 **Age:** 26

		HOW MUCH PITCHED				WHAT HE GAVE UP										THE RESULTS							
Year Team	Lg	G	GS	GF	IP	BFP	H	R	ER	HR	SH	SF	HB	TBB	IBB	SO	WP	W	L	Pct	Sv-Op	Hld	Vel	OPS	ERC	ERA
2020 Sea	AL	21	0	1	20.0	83	20	9	9	2	0	0	1	6	1	25	2	0	2	.000	0-1	8	94	.746	3.92	4.05

Casey Mize

Pitches: R **Bats:** R **Pos:** SP-7   **Ht:** 6'3" **Wt:** 220 **Born:** 5/1/1997 **Age:** 24

Year Team	Lg	G	GS	GF	IP	BFP	H	R	ER	HR	SH	SF	HB	TBB	IBB	SO	WP	W	L	Pct	Sv-Op	Hld	Vel	OPS	ERC	ERA
2018 2 Tms	Low	5	5	0	13.2	55	13	6	6	2	0	0	2	3	0	14	0	0	1	.000	0- -	-	-	.747	4.23	3.95
2019 Lkland	A+	6	6	0	30.2	107	11	3	3	0	1	0	1	5	0	30	0	2	0	1.000	0- -	-	-	.300	0.55	0.88
2019 Erie	AA	15	15	0	78.2	323	69	30	28	5	1	3	6	18	0	76	0	6	3	.667	0- -	-	-	.635	2.82	3.20
2020 Det	AL	7	7	0	28.1	133	29	25	22	7	0	0	5	13	0	26	2	0	3	.000	0-0	0	94	.832	6.13	6.99

Yadier Molina

Bats: R **Throws:** R **Pos:** C-42;1B-2   YAH-dee-air   **Ht:** 5'11" **Wt:** 225 **Born:** 7/13/1982 **Age:** 38

								BATTING												RUNNING			AVERAGES			
Year Team	Lg	G	AB	H	2B	3B	HR	(Hm	Rd)	TB	R	RBI	RC	TBB	IBB	SO	HBP	SH	SF	SB	CS	GDP	Avg	OBP	Slg	OPS
2004 StL	NL	51	135	36	6	0	2	(1	1)	48	12	15	15	13	3	20	0	2	1	0	1	4	.267	.329	.356	.684
2005 StL	NL	114	385	97	15	1	8	(6	2)	138	36	49	46	23	3	30	2	8	3	2	3	10	.252	.295	.358	.654
2006 StL	NL	129	417	90	26	0	6	(2	4)	134	29	49	35	26	2	41	8	8	2	1	2	15	.216	.274	.321	.595
2007 StL	NL	111	353	97	15	0	6	(4	2)	130	30	40	38	34	5	43	3	2	4	1	1	18	.275	.340	.368	.708
2008 StL	NL	124	444	135	18	0	7	(2	5)	174	37	56	57	32	4	29	1	3	5	0	2	21	.304	.349	.392	.740
2009 StL	NL	140	481	141	23	1	6	(5	1)	184	45	54	64	50	2	39	6	6	1	9	3	27	.293	.366	.383	.749
2010 StL	NL	136	465	122	19	0	6	(1	5)	159	34	62	55	42	6	51	7	2	5	8	4	19	.262	.329	.342	.671
2011 StL	NL	139	475	145	32	1	14	(5	9)	221	55	65	64	33	4	44	1	5	4	4	5	21	.305	.349	.465	.814
2012 StL	NL	138	505	159	28	0	22	(9	13)	253	65	76	91	45	4	55	5	3	5	12	3	10	.315	.373	.501	.874
2013 StL	NL	136	505	161	44	0	12	(5	7)	241	68	80	84	30	4	55	3	0	3	3	2	14	.319	.359	.477	.836
2014 StL	NL	110	404	114	21	0	7	(3	4)	156	40	38	47	28	4	55	6	1	6	1	1	14	.282	.333	.386	.719
2015 StL	NL	136	488	132	23	2	4	(3	1)	171	34	61	48	32	3	59	0	1	9	3	1	16	.270	.310	.350	.660
2016 StL	NL	147	534	164	38	1	8	(4	4)	228	56	58	74	39	1	63	6	0	2	3	2	22	.307	.360	.427	.787
2017 StL	NL	136	501	137	27	1	18	(7	11)	220	60	82	67	28	4	74	4	1	9	9	4	14	.273	.312	.439	.751
2018 StL	NL	123	459	120	20	0	20	(3	17)	200	55	74	65	29	0	66	9	0	6	4	3	15	.261	.314	.436	.750
2019 StL	NL	113	419	113	24	0	10	(4	6)	167	45	57	56	23	0	58	5	0	5	6	0	14	.270	.312	.399	.711
2020 StL	NL	42	145	38	2	0	4	(2	2)	52	12	16	16	6	0	21	3	1	1	0	0	7	.262	.303	.359	.662
Postseason		98	348	95	17	0	4	(2	2)	124	27	34	33	26	6	41	3	1	2	1	1	13	.273	.327	.356	.683
17 ML YEARS		2025	7115	2001	381	7	160	(66	94)	2876	713	932	922	513	49	803	69	43	71	66	37	261	.281	.333	.404	.737

Yoan Moncada

Bats: B **Throws:** R **Pos:** 3B-52;PH-1   yo-AHN   **Ht:** 6'2" **Wt:** 225 **Born:** 5/27/1995 **Age:** 26

								BATTING												RUNNING			AVERAGES			
Year Team	Lg	G	AB	H	2B	3B	HR	(Hm	Rd)	TB	R	RBI	RC	TBB	IBB	SO	HBP	SH	SF	SB	CS	GDP	Avg	OBP	Slg	OPS
2016 Bos	AL	8	19	4	1	0	0	(0	0)	5	3	1	0	1	0	12	0	0	0	0	0	0	.211	.250	.263	.513
2017 CWS	AL	54	199	46	8	2	8	(4	4)	82	31	22	27	29	0	74	3	0	0	3	2	0	.231	.338	.412	.750
2018 CWS	AL	149	578	136	32	6	17	(10	7)	231	73	61	73	67	1	**217**	1	2	2	12	6	4	.235	.315	.400	.714
2019 CWS	AL	132	511	161	34	5	25	(16	9)	280	83	79	94	40	2	154	4	1	3	10	3	1	.315	.367	.548	.915
2020 CWS	AL	52	200	45	8	3	6	(5	1)	77	28	24	30	28	0	72	1	0	2	0	0	1	.225	.320	.385	.705
5 ML YEARS		395	1507	392	83	16	56	(35	21)	675	218	187	224	165	3	529	9	3	7	25	11	6	.260	.335	.448	.783

Adalberto Mondesi

Bats: B **Throws:** R **Pos:** SS-59   **Ht:** 6'1" **Wt:** 200 **Born:** 7/27/1995 **Age:** 25

								BATTING												RUNNING			AVERAGES			
Year Team	Lg	G	AB	H	2B	3B	HR	(Hm	Rd)	TB	R	RBI	RC	TBB	IBB	SO	HBP	SH	SF	SB	CS	GDP	Avg	OBP	Slg	OPS
2016 KC	AL	47	135	25	1	3	2	(0	2)	38	16	13	9	6	0	48	2	6	0	9	1	1	.185	.231	.281	.512
2017 KC	AL	25	53	9	1	0	1	(1	0)	13	4	3	0	3	0	22	0	4	0	5	2	2	.170	.214	.245	.460
2018 KC	AL	75	275	76	13	3	14	(7	7)	137	47	37	39	11	0	77	1	3	1	32	7	2	.276	.306	.498	.804
2019 KC	AL	102	415	109	20	10	9	(4	5)	176	58	62	60	19	0	132	0	3	6	43	7	6	.263	.291	.424	.715
2020 KC	AL	59	219	56	11	3	6	(4	2)	91	33	22	24	11	0	70	1	2	0	24	8	4	.256	.294	.416	.710
Postseason		1	1	0	0	0	0	(0	0)	0	0	0	0	0	0	1	0	0	0	0	0	0	.000	.000	.000	.000
5 ML YEARS		308	1097	275	46	19	32	(16	16)	455	158	137	132	50	0	349	4	18	7	113	25	15	.251	.284	.415	.699

Mickey Moniak

Bats: L **Throws:** R **Pos:** LF-5;PR-2;RF-1;DH-1;PH-1   **Ht:** 6'2" **Wt:** 195 **Born:** 5/13/1998 **Age:** 23

								BATTING												RUNNING			AVERAGES			
Year Team	Lg	G	AB	H	2B	3B	HR	(Hm	Rd)	TB	R	RBI	RC	TBB	IBB	SO	HBP	SH	SF	SB	CS	GDP	Avg	OBP·	Slg	OPS
2020 Phi	NL	8	14	3	0	0	0	(0	0)	3	3	0	1	4	0	6	0	0	0	0	0	0	.214	.389	.214	.603

Frankie Montas

Pitches: R Bats: R Pos: SP-11 MOHN-tahs Ht: 6'2" Wt: 255 Born: 3/21/1993 Age: 28

		HOW MUCH PITCHED					WHAT HE GAVE UP											THE RESULTS						
Year	Team	Lg	G	GS	GF	IP	BFP	H	R	ER	HR	SH	SF	HB	TBB	IBB	SO	WP	W	L	Pct	Sv-Op	Hld	Vel	OPS	ERC	ERA
2015	CWS	AL	7	2	2	15.0	66	14	8	8	1	0	0	0	9	1	20	0	0	2	.000	0-0	0	97	.699	4.16	4.80
2017	Oak	AL	23	0	5	32.0	152	39	25	25	10	0	0	3	20	0	36	1	1	1	.500	0-0	1	98	.974	8.72	7.03
2018	Oak	AL	13	11	1	65.0	283	74	34	28	5	2	3	2	21	0	43	5	5	4	.556	0-0	0	96	.796	4.55	3.88
2019	Oak	AL	16	16	0	96.0	394	84	35	28	8	0	2	4	23	1	103	5	9	2	.818	0-0	0	97	.646	2.82	2.63
2020	Oak	AL	11	11	0	53.0	237	57	35	33	10	0	2	1	23	0	60	2	3	5	.375	0-0	0	96	.806	5.33	5.60
	5 ML YEARS		70	40	8	261.0	1132	268	137	122	34	2	7	10	96	2	262	13	18	14	.563	0-0	1	96	.763	4.46	4.21

Rafael Montero

Pitches: R Bats: R Pos: RP-17 Ht: 6'0" Wt: 190 Born: 10/17/1990 Age: 30

		HOW MUCH PITCHED					WHAT HE GAVE UP											THE RESULTS						
Year	Team	Lg	G	GS	GF	IP	BFP	H	R	ER	HR	SH	SF	HB	TBB	IBB	SO	WP	W	L	Pct	Sv-Op	Hld	Vel	OPS	ERC	ERA
2014	NYM	NL	10	8	1	44.1	194	44	21	20	8	0	0	0	23	0	42	0	1	3	.250	0-0	0	92	.825	5.16	4.06
2015	NYM	NL	5	1	1	10.0	46	9	6	5	0	1	0	0	5	3	13	0	0	1	.000	0-0	1	92	.661	2.50	4.50
2016	NYM	NL	9	3	1	19.0	93	23	17	17	4	0	0	0	16	1	20	2	0	1	.000	0-0	0	93	.965	8.15	8.05
2017	NYM	NL	34	18	4	119.0	550	141	75	73	12	9	8	5	67	5	114	6	5	11	.313	0-0	0	94	.832	6.01	5.52
2019	Tex	AL	22	0	6	29.0	113	23	8	8	5	0	0	2	5	0	34	0	2	0	1.000	0-1	7	96	.671	2.89	2.48
2020	Tex	AL	17	0	16	17.2	72	12	11	8	2	1	0	1	6	0	19	0	0	1	.000	8-8	0	96	.652	2.43	4.08
	6 ML YEARS		97	30	29	239.0	1068	252	138	131	31	11	8	8	122	9	242	8	8	17	.320	8-9	8	93	.805	5.16	4.93

Jordan Montgomery

Pitches: L Bats: L Pos: SP-10 Ht: 6'6" Wt: 228 Born: 12/27/1992 Age: 28

		HOW MUCH PITCHED					WHAT HE GAVE UP											THE RESULTS						
Year	Team	Lg	G	GS	GF	IP	BFP	H	R	ER	HR	SH	SF	HB	TBB	IBB	SO	WP	W	L	Pct	Sv-Op	Hld	Vel	OPS	ERC	ERA
2017	NYY	AL	29	29	0	155.1	649	140	72	67	21	2	3	1	51	0	144	7	9	7	.563	0-0	0	92	.684	3.50	3.88
2018	NYY	AL	6	6	0	27.1	116	25	11	11	3	0	0	0	12	0	23	0	2	0	1.000	0-0	0	90	.675	3.85	3.62
2019	NYY	AL	2	1	0	4.0	19	7	3	3	1	0	0	0	0	0	5	0	0	0	—	0-0	0	92	1.053	7.95	6.75
2020	NYY	AL	10	10	0	44.0	193	48	27	25	7	0	0	2	9	0	47	3	2	3	.400	0-0	0	93	.749	4.25	5.11
	4 ML YEARS		47	46	0	230.2	977	220	113	106	32	2	3	3	72	0	219	10	13	10	.565	0-0	0	92	.704	3.75	4.14

Mike Montgomery

Pitches: L Bats: L Pos: RP-2; SP-1 Ht: 6'5" Wt: 220 Born: 7/1/1989 Age: 31

		HOW MUCH PITCHED					WHAT HE GAVE UP											THE RESULTS						
Year	Team	Lg	G	GS	GF	IP	BFP	H	R	ER	HR	SH	SF	HB	TBB	IBB	SO	WP	W	L	Pct	Sv-Op	Hld	Vel	OPS	ERC	ERA
2015	Sea	AL	16	16	0	90.0	395	92	49	46	11	0	0	4	37	1	64	10	4	6	.400	0-0	0	91	.754	4.56	4.60
2016	2 Tms		49	7	18	100.0	414	79	33	28	8	3	2	10	38	2	92	10	4	5	.444	0-0	5	94	.652	3.13	2.52
2017	ChC	NL	44	14	11	130.2	540	103	52	49	10	5	2	8	55	4	100	7	7	8	.467	3-3	1	92	.632	3.09	3.38
2018	ChC	NL	38	19	6	124.0	534	131	58	55	10	3	4	7	39	4	86	4	5	6	.455	0-0	0	92	.724	4.11	3.99
2019	2 Tms		33	13	6	91.0	402	113	55	50	18	3	1	4	34	1	69	3	3	9	.250	0-1	3	92	.914	6.53	4.95
2020	KC	AL	3	1	0	5.1	23	6	5	3	1	0	1	0	1	0	4	0	0	0	—	0-0	0	90	.828	4.42	5.06
	16	Sea	AL	32	2	13	61.2	250	49	18	16	3	2	1	6	18	2	54	5	3	4	.429	0-0	3	94	.617	2.61	2.34
	16	ChC	NL	17	5	5	38.1	164	30	15	12	5	1	1	4	20	0	38	5	1	1	.500	0-0	2	93	.708	4.01	2.82
	19	ChC	NL	20	0	6	27.0	123	35	18	17	6	1	1	0	13	1	18	0	1	2	.333	0-1	3	93	1.004	7.31	5.67
	19	KC	AL	13	13	0	64.0	279	78	37	33	12	2	0	4	21	0	51	3	2	7	.222	0-0	0	92	.876	6.21	4.64
	Postseason		16	0	5	18.2	95	28	14	13	3	1	2	0	11	1	15	3	1	1	.500	1-1	2	93	.970	8.19	6.27
	6 ML YEARS		183	70	41	541.0	2308	524	252	231	58	14	10	33	204	12	415	34	23	34	.404	3-4	9	92	.730	4.12	3.84

Dylan Moore

Bats: R Throws: R Pos: LF-13;RF-13;2B-10;1B-3;SS-3;3B-2;CF-1;PR-1 Ht: 6'0" Wt: 185 Born: 8/2/1992 Age: 28

			BATTING																	RUNNING			AVERAGES			
Year	Team	Lg	G	AB	H	2B	3B	HR	(Hm	Rd)	TB	R	RBI	RC	TBB	IBB	SO	HBP	SH	SF	SB	CS	GDP	Avg	OBP	Slg	OPS
2019	Sea	AL	113	247	51	14	2	9	(6	3)	96	31	28	29	25	0	93	9	1	0	11	9	6	.206	.302	.389	.691
2020	Sea	AL	38	137	35	9	0	8	(4	4)	68	26	17	22	14	0	43	8	0	0	12	5	4	.255	.358	.496	.855
	2 ML YEARS		151	384	86	23	2	17	(10	7)	164	57	45	51	39	0	136	17	1	0	23	14	10	.224	.323	.427	.750

Brian Moran

Pitches: L Bats: L Pos: RP-7 Ht: 6'4" Wt: 225 Born: 9/30/1988 Age: 32

		HOW MUCH PITCHED					WHAT HE GAVE UP											THE RESULTS						
Year	Team	Lg	G	GS	GF	IP	BFP	H	R	ER	HR	SH	SF	HB	TBB	IBB	SO	WP	W	L	Pct	Sv-Op	Hld	Vel	OPS	ERC	ERA
2019	Mia	NL	10	0	0	6.1	29	6	3	3	1	1	0	2	2	1	10	0	1	0	1.000	0-1	2	84	.857	4.74	4.26
2020	2 Tms		7	0	2	4.2	26	6	5	5	1	0	0	0	6	0	7	0	1	0	1.000	0-1	0	82	1.012	10.57	9.64
	20	Tor	AL	2	0	1	1.0	4	1	0	0	0	0	0	0	0	0	1	0	0	0	—	0-1	0	81	.500	1.95	0.00
	20	Mia	NL	5	0	1	3.2	22	5	5	5	1	0	0	0	6	0	6	0	1	0	1.000	0-0	0	82	1.125	13.42	12.27
	2 ML YEARS		17	0	2	11.0	55	12	8	8	2	1	0	2	8	1	17	0	2	0	1.000	0-2	2	83	.930	7.08	6.55

Colin Moran

Bats: L **Throws:** R **Pos:** DH-26;1B-22;3B-4;PH-1   **Ht:** 6'4" **Wt:** 200 **Born:** 10/1/1992 **Age:** 28

Year	Team	Lg	G	AB	H	2B	3B	HR	(Hm	Rd)	TB	R	RBI	RC	TBB	IBB	SO	HBP	SH	SF	SB	CS	GDP	Avg	OBP	Slg	OPS
2016	Hou	AL	9	23	3	1	0	0	(0	0)	4	1	2	0	1	0	8	1	0	0	0	0	4	.130	.200	.174	.374
2017	Hou	AL	7	11	4	0	1	1	(0	1)	9	3	3	4	1	0	1	0	0	0	0	0	0	.364	.417	.818	1.235
2018	Pit	NL	144	415	115	19	1	11	(5	6)	169	49	58	55	39	4	82	4	0	7	0	2	6	.277	.340	.407	.747
2019	Pit	NL	149	466	129	30	1	13	(6	7)	200	46	80	69	30	4	117	3	0	4	0	1	13	.277	.322	.429	.751
2020	Pit	NL	52	178	44	10	0	10	(4	6)	84	28	23	22	19	0	52	2	0	1	0	0	9	.247	.325	.472	.797
	5 ML YEARS		361	1093	295	60	3	35	(15	20)	466	127	166	150	90	8	260	10	0	12	0	3	32	.270	.328	.426	.754

Adrian Morejon

Pitches: L **Bats:** L **Pos:** RP-5; SP-4   moh-ray-HOHN   **Ht:** 5'11" **Wt:** 224 **Born:** 2/27/1999 **Age:** 22

Year	Team	Lg	G	GS	GF	IP	BFP	H	R	ER	HR	SH	SF	HB	TBB	IBB	SO	WP	W	L	Pct	Sv-Op	Hld	Vel	OPS	ERC	ERA
2019	SD	NL	5	2	1	8.0	42	15	9	9	1	0	0	0	3	0	9	0	0	0	-	0-0	0	96	1.044	9.51	10.13
2020	SD	NL	9	4	0	19.1	79	20	11	10	7	0	0	0	4	0	25	0	2	2	.500	0-0	0	97	.877	5.33	4.66
	2 ML YEARS		14	6	1	27.1	121	35	20	19	8	0	0	0	7	0	34	0	2	2	.500	0-0	0	97	.935	6.59	6.26

Mitch Moreland

Bats: L **Throws:** L **Pos:** 1B-38;PH-4;DH-3   **Ht:** 6'3" **Wt:** 245 **Born:** 9/6/1985 **Age:** 35

Year	Team	Lg	G	AB	H	2B	3B	HR	(Hm	Rd)	TB	R	RBI	RC	TBB	IBB	SO	HBP	SH	SF	SB	CS	GDP	Avg	OBP	Slg	OPS
2010	Tex	AL	47	145	37	4	0	9	(3	6)	68	20	25	27	25	5	36	1	0	2	3	1	3	.255	.364	.469	.833
2011	Tex	AL	134	464	120	22	1	16	(7	9)	192	60	51	56	39	6	92	4	2	3	2	2	9	.259	.320	.414	.733
2012	Tex	AL	114	327	90	18	0	15	(10	5)	153	41	50	46	23	5	71	1	2	4	1	1	8	.275	.321	.468	.789
2013	Tex	AL	147	462	107	24	1	23	(10	13)	202	60	60	55	45	1	117	3	0	8	0	0	11	.232	.299	.437	.736
2014	Tex	AL	52	167	41	9	1	2	(1	1)	58	18	23	20	12	0	43	1	2	2	0	0	7	.246	.297	.347	.644
2015	Tex	AL	132	471	131	27	0	23	(9	14)	227	51	85	74	32	2	112	7	0	5	1	0	9	.278	.330	.482	.812
2016	Tex	AL	147	460	107	21	0	22	(13	9)	194	49	60	56	35	5	118	8	0	1	0	0	8	.233	.298	.422	.720
2017	Bos	AL	149	508	125	34	2	22	(10	12)	225	73	79	69	57	6	120	6	0	5	0	1	14	.246	.326	.443	.769
2018	Bos	AL	124	404	99	23	4	15	(6	9)	175	57	68	60	50	2	102	0	0	5	2	0	12	.245	.325	.433	.758
2019	Bos	AL	91	298	75	17	1	19	(8	11)	151	48	58	49	34	0	74	1	0	2	1	0	12	.252	.328	.507	.835
2020	2 Tms		42	136	36	9	0	10	(6	4)	75	22	29	27	15	2	32	1	0	0	0	0	0	.265	.342	.551	.894
20	Bos	AL	22	67	22	4	0	8	(5	3)	50	14	21	19	11	1	18	1	0	0	0	0	0	.328	.430	.746	1.177
20	SD	NL	20	69	14	5	0	2	(1	1)	25	8	8	8	4	1	14	0	0	0	0	0	0	.203	.247	.362	.609
	Postseason		48	127	31	9	0	4	(3	1)	52	15	18	20	12	1	30	2	1	0	0	0	3	.244	.319	.409	.729
	11 ML YEARS		1179	3842	968	208	8	176	(83	93)	1720	499	588	539	367	34	917	33	6	36	11	5	93	.252	.320	.448	.767

Adam Morgan

Pitches: L **Bats:** L **Pos:** RP-17   **Ht:** 6'1" **Wt:** 200 **Born:** 2/27/1990 **Age:** 31

Year	Team	Lg	G	GS	GF	IP	BFP	H	R	ER	HR	SH	SF	HB	TBB	IBB	SO	WP	W	L	Pct	Sv-Op	Hld	Vel	OPS	ERC	ERA
2015	Phi	NL	15	15	0	84.1	352	88	45	42	14	1	3	4	17	0	49	2	5	7	.417	0-0	0	89	.775	4.21	4.48
2016	Phi	NL	23	21	1	113.1	507	141	81	76	23	3	4	4	29	3	95	2	2	11	.154	0-0	0	91	.880	5.72	6.04
2017	Phi	NL	37	0	6	54.2	229	51	25	25	10	0	0	0	18	2	63	1	3	3	.500	0-1	6	94	.737	3.92	4.12
2018	Phi	NL	67	0	9	49.1	214	49	25	21	5	0	2	0	22	3	50	3	0	2	.000	0-0	2	94	.698	4.14	3.83
2019	Phi	NL	40	0	4	29.2	120	20	14	13	4	0	0	3	10	1	29	0	3	3	.500	0-2	19	93	.621	2.68	3.94
2020	Phi	NL	17	0	4	13.0	58	14	8	8	3	0	0	0	6	0	16	0	0	1	.000	0-2	2	92	.845	5.72	5.54
	6 ML YEARS		199	36	20	344.1	1480	363	198	185	59	4	9	11	102	9	302	8	13	27	.325	1-9	41	91	.785	4.55	4.84

Mike Morin

Pitches: R **Bats:** R **Pos:** RP-3   MORE-in   **Ht:** 6'4" **Wt:** 220 **Born:** 5/3/1991 **Age:** 30

Year	Team	Lg	G	GS	GF	IP	BFP	H	R	ER	HR	SH	SF	HB	TBB	IBB	SO	WP	W	L	Pct	Sv-Op	Hld	Vel	OPS	ERC	ERA
2014	LAA	AL	60	0	10	59.0	246	51	22	19	7	3	4	3	19	6	54	3	4	4	.500	0-2	9	92	.629	2.76	2.90
2015	LAA	AL	47	0	10	35.1	151	36	28	25	3	2	2	2	9	2	41	0	4	2	.667	1-1	5	92	.720	3.61	6.37
2016	LAA	AL	60	0	8	55.2	227	52	31	27	6	2	1	1	15	1	49	1	2	2	.500	0-1	12	91	.677	3.37	4.37
2017	2 Tms	AL	16	0	6	20.0	93	29	16	16	3	1	2	1	5	1	16	0	0	0	-	0-0	0	91	.916	6.64	7.20
2018	Sea	AL	3	0	1	4.0	18	6	3	3	0	0	1	0	1	1	6	0	0	0	-	0-1	0	91	1.014	5.30	6.75
2019	2 Tms	AL	52	0	13	50.2	210	46	29	26	6	2	1	4	10	0	26	2	1	3	.250	1-2	8	91	.672	3.19	4.62
2020	Mia	NL	3	0	0	4.0	12	1	0	0	0	0	0	0	1	0	2	0	1	0	1.000	0-0	0	92	.348	0.47	0.00
17	LAA	AL	10	0	3	14.1	65	21	11	11	3	1	1	1	2	1	10	0	0	0	-	0-0	0	91	.958	6.84	6.91
17	KC	AL	6	0	3	5.2	28	8	5	5	0	0	1	0	3	0	6	0	0	0	-	0-0	0	90	.810	6.06	7.94
19	Min	AL	23	0	10	22.2	92	20	11	8	3	0	0	2	2	0	11	0	0	0	-	1-1	1	91	.647	2.75	3.18
19	Phi	NL	29	0	3	28.0	118	26	18	18	3	2	1	2	8	0	15	2	1	3	.250	0-1	7	91	.691	3.56	5.79
	Postseason		1	0	0	1.0	6	3	2	2	1	0	1	0	0	0	1	1	0	0	-	0-0	0	93	1.700	25.51	18.00
	7 ML YEARS		241	0	50	228.2	957	221	129	116	21	9	11	11	60	11	194	6	12	11	.522	2-7	34	91	.696	3.42	4.57

Reyes Moronta

Pitches: R **Bats:** R **Pos:** P   **Ht:** 5'10" **Wt:** 265 **Born:** 1/6/1993 **Age:** 28

Year	Team	Lg	HOW MUCH PITCHED						WHAT HE GAVE UP											THE RESULTS						
			G	GS	GF	IP	BFP	H	R	ER	HR	SH	SF	HB	TBB	IBB	SO	WP	W	L	Pct	Sv-Op	Hld	Vel	OPS	ERC	ERA
2017	SF	NL	7	0	1	6.2	29	6	2	2	1	0	0	0	3	1	11	0	0	0	-	0-1	0	96	.656	3.74	2.70
2018	SF	NL	69	0	9	65.0	262	34	20	18	4	1	3	0	37	4	79	5	5	2	.714	1-6	12	97	.507	1.93	2.49
2019	SF	NL	56	0	5	56.2	246	41	19	18	4	1	1	3	33	1	70	3	3	7	.300	0-5	15	97	.612	3.18	2.86
	3 ML YEARS		132	0	15	128.1	537	81	41	38	9	2	4	3	73	6	160	8	8	9	.471	1-12	27	97	.564	2.55	2.66

Logan Morrison

Bats: L **Throws:** L **Pos:** DH-6;PH-3;1B-2   **Ht:** 6'3" **Wt:** 245 **Born:** 8/25/1987 **Age:** 33

Year	Team	Lg	BATTING																		RUNNING			AVERAGES			
			G	AB	H	2B	3B	HR	(Hm	Rd)	TB	R	RBI	RC	TBB	IBB	SO	HBP	SH	SF	SB	CS	GDP	Avg	OBP	Slg	OPS
2010	Fla	NL	62	244	69	20	7	2	(1	1)	109	43	18	41	41	0	51	2	0	0	0	1	4	.283	.390	.447	.837
2011	Fla	NL	123	462	114	25	4	23	(12	11)	216	54	72	55	54	3	99	5	0	4	2	1	9	.247	.330	.468	.797
2012	Mia	NL	93	296	68	15	1	11	(4	7)	118	30	36	27	31	2	58	4	0	3	1	0	9	.230	.308	.399	.707
2013	Mia	NL	85	293	71	13	4	6	(1	5)	110	32	36	37	38	5	56	2	0	0	0	0	10	.242	.333	.375	.709
2014	Sea	AL	99	336	88	20	0	11	(7	4)	141	41	38	46	24	1	59	3	0	2	5	2	9	.262	.315	.420	.735
2015	Sea	AL	146	457	103	15	3	17	(7	10)	175	47	54	53	47	5	81	4	1	2	8	4	7	.225	.302	.383	.685
2016	TB	AL	107	353	84	18	1	14	(6	8)	146	45	43	50	37	1	89	6	0	2	4	2	4	.238	.319	.414	.733
2017	TB	AL	149	512	126	22	1	38	(11	27)	264	75	85	77	81	8	149	5	0	3	2	0	12	.246	.353	.516	.868
2018	Min	AL	95	318	59	13	0	15	(9	6)	117	41	39	31	34	0	80	6	0	1	1	0	3	.186	.276	.368	.644
2019	Phi	NL	29	35	7	1	0	2	(1	1)	14	5	3	4	3	0	10	0	0	0	0	0	1	.200	.263	.400	.663
2020	Mil	NL	9	25	3	1	0	1	(1	0)	7	3	2	0	3	0	8	0	0	0	0	0	0	.120	.214	.280	.494
	11 ML YEARS		997	3331	792	163	21	140	(60	80)	1417	416	426	421	393	25	740	37	1	17	23	10	68	.238	.323	.425	.749

Charlie Morton

Pitches: R **Bats:** R **Pos:** SP-9   **Ht:** 6'5" **Wt:** 215 **Born:** 11/12/1983 **Age:** 37

Year	Team	Lg	HOW MUCH PITCHED						WHAT HE GAVE UP											THE RESULTS						
			G	GS	GF	IP	BFP	H	R	ER	HR	SH	SF	HB	TBB	IBB	SO	WP	W	L	Pct	Sv-Op	Hld	Vel	OPS	ERC	ERA
2008	Atl	NL	16	15	0	74.2	345	80	56	51	9	5	4	2	41	2	48	2	4	8	.333	0-0	0	91	.816	5.21	6.15
2009	Pit	NL	18	18	0	97.0	416	102	49	49	7	1	1	5	40	1	62	4	5	9	.357	0-0	0	91	.761	4.56	4.55
2010	Pit	NL	17	17	0	79.2	382	112	79	67	15	6	6	7	26	3	59	5	2	12	.143	0-0	0	93	.908	7.10	7.57
2011	Pit	NL	29	29	0	171.2	769	186	82	73	6	12	6	13	77	5	110	9	10	10	.500	0-0	0	91	.737	4.52	3.83
2012	Pit	NL	9	9	0	50.1	223	62	30	26	5	5	2	2	11	1	25	4	2	6	.250	0-0	0	90	.812	4.74	4.65
2013	Pit	NL	20	20	0	116.0	493	113	51	42	6	2	16	8	36	1	85	5	7	4	.636	0-0	0	93	.683	3.84	3.26
2014	Pit	NL	26	26	0	157.1	666	143	76	65	9	7	5	19	57	2	126	8	6	12	.333	0-0	0	91	.682	3.64	3.72
2015	Pit	NL	23	23	0	129.0	563	137	77	69	13	4	0	12	41	6	96	2	9	9	.500	0-0	0	93	.769	4.41	4.81
2016	Phi	NL	4	4	0	17.1	71	15	8	8	1	1	0	0	8	0	19	1	1	1	.500	0-0	0	94	.651	3.42	4.15
2017	Hou	AL	25	25	0	146.2	617	125	65	59	14	2	2	13	50	1	163	4	14	7	.667	0-0	0	95	.692	3.34	3.62
2018	Hou	AL	30	30	0	167.0	695	130	63	58	18	1	4	16	64	0	201	4	15	3	.833	0-0	0	96	.659	3.25	3.13
2019	TB	AL	33	33	0	194.2	790	154	71	66	15	1	3	12	57	0	240	5	16	6	.727	0-0	0	94	.623	2.67	3.05
2020	TB	AL	9	9	0	38.0	170	43	21	20	4	0	2	4	10	0	42	1	2	2	.500	0-0	0	93	.764	4.65	4.74
	Postseason		9	8	1	41.1	174	34	18	17	4	1	1	3	17	0	44	3	4	2	.667	0-0	0	95	.661	3.42	3.70
	13 ML YEARS		259	258	0	1439.1	6200	1402	728	653	122	51	37	121	518	21	1276	54	93	89	.511	0-0	0	93	.721	3.99	4.08

Ryan Mountcastle

Bats: R **Throws:** R **Pos:** LF-25;1B-10;DH-2;PH-1   **Ht:** 6'3" **Wt:** 210 **Born:** 2/18/1997 **Age:** 24

Year	Team	Lg	BATTING																		RUNNING			AVERAGES			
			G	AB	H	2B	3B	HR	(Hm	Rd)	TB	R	RBI	RC	TBB	IBB	SO	HBP	SH	SF	SB	CS	GDP	Avg	OBP	Slg	OPS
2016	Dlmrva	A	115	455	128	28	4	10	(-	-)	194	53	51	58	25	0	95	3	0	6	5	4	10	.281	.319	.426	.745
2017	Frdrck	A+	88	360	113	35	1	15	(-	-)	195	63	47	66	14	2	61	3	0	2	8	2	9	.314	.343	.542	.885
2017	Bowie	AA	39	153	34	13	0	3	(-	-)	56	18	15	13	3	0	35	1	0	2	0	0	2	.222	.239	.366	.605
2018	Bowie	AA	102	394	117	19	4	13	(-	-)	183	63	59	64	26	2	79	3	0	5	2	0	10	.297	.341	.464	.806
2019	Norfolk	AAA	127	520	162	35	1	25	(-	-)	274	81	83	93	24	1	130	4	0	5	2	1	10	.312	.344	.527	.871
2020	Bal	AL	35	126	42	5	0	5	(2	3)	62	16	23	25	11	0	30	1	0	2	0	1	2	.333	.386	.492	.878

Mike Moustakas

Bats: L **Throws:** R **Pos:** 2B-32;1B-10;DH-3;3B-2;PH-1   moo-STOCK-us   **Ht:** 6'0" **Wt:** 225 **Born:** 9/11/1988 **Age:** 32

Year	Team	Lg	BATTING																		RUNNING			AVERAGES			
			G	AB	H	2B	3B	HR	(Hm	Rd)	TB	R	RBI	RC	TBB	IBB	SO	HBP	SH	SF	SB	CS	GDP	Avg	OBP	Slg	OPS
2011	KC	AL	89	338	89	18	1	5	(3	2)	124	26	30	31	22	0	51	1	2	2	2	0	5	.263	.309	.367	.675
2012	KC	AL	149	563	136	34	1	20	(10	10)	232	69	73	64	39	4	124	7	0	5	5	2	4	.242	.296	.412	.708
2013	KC	AL	136	472	110	26	0	12	(5	7)	172	42	42	35	32	1	83	5	1	4	2	4	13	.233	.287	.364	.651
2014	KC	AL	140	457	97	21	0	15	(5	10)	165	45	54	44	35	1	74	3	1	4	1	0	12	.212	.271	.361	.632
2015	KC	AL	147	549	156	34	1	22	(9	13)	258	73	82	85	43	1	76	13	4	5	1	2	14	.284	.348	.470	.817
2016	KC	AL	27	104	25	6	0	7	(4	3)	52	12	13	10	9	0	13	0	0	0	0	1	5	.240	.301	.500	.801
2017	KC	AL	148	555	151	24	0	38	(14	24)	289	75	85	77	34	7	94	3	0	6	0	0	18	.272	.314	.521	.835
2018	2 Tms		152	573	144	33	1	28	(14	14)	263	66	95	89	49	5	103	7	0	6	4	1	13	.251	.315	.459	.774
2019	Mil	NL	143	523	133	30	1	35	(14	21)	270	80	87	82	53	5	98	6	0	2	3	0	12	.254	.329	.516	.845
2020	Cin	NL	44	139	32	9	0	8	(4	4)	65	13	27	26	18	1	36	4	0	2	1	0	5	.230	.331	.468	.799
	18 KC	AL	98	378	94	21	1	20	(9	11)	177	46	62	54	30	3	63	6	0	4	3	0	10	.249	.309	.468	.778
	18 Mil	NL	54	195	50	12	0	8	(5	3)	86	20	33	35	19	2	40	1	0	2	1	1	3	.256	.326	.441	.767
	Postseason		42	161	34	5	0	6	(3	3)	57	17	18	15	9	3	31	1	1	1	0	0	2	.211	.256	.354	.610
	10 ML YEARS		1175	4273	1073	235	6	190	(82	108)	1890	501	588	543	334	25	752	49	8	36	19	10	101	.251	.310	.442	.753

Jose Mujica

Pitches: R **Bats:** R **Pos:** RP-2 **Ht:** 6'2" **Wt:** 249 **Born:** 6/29/1996 **Age:** 25

			HOW MUCH PITCHED				WHAT HE GAVE UP										THE RESULTS							
Year	Team	Lg	G	GS	GF	IP	BFP	H	R	ER	HR	SH	SF	HB	TBB	IBB	SO	WP	W	L	Pct	Sv-Op	Hld	Vel	OPS	ERC	ERA
2020	Col	NL	2	0	1	4.1	23	10	7	6	2	0	0	0	2	0	1	0	0	0	-	0-0	0	93	1.379	18.05	12.46

Cedric Mullins II

Bats: B **Throws:** L **Pos:** CF-41;LF-4;RF-4;PR-3;DH-1 **Ht:** 5'8" **Wt:** 175 **Born:** 10/1/1994 **Age:** 26

			BATTING																		RUNNING			AVERAGES			
Year	Team	Lg	G	AB	H	2B	3B	HR	(Hm	Rd)	TB	R	RBI	RC	TBB	IBB	SO	HBP	SH	SF	SB	CS	GDP	Avg	OBP	Slg	OPS
2018	Bal	AL	45	170	40	9	0	4	(1	3)	61	23	11	17	17	0	37	2	2	0	2	3	1	.235	.312	.359	.671
2019	Bal	AL	22	64	6	0	2	0	(0	0)	10	7	4	1	4	0	14	3	2	1	1	0	2	.094	.181	.156	.337
2020	Bal	AL	48	140	38	4	3	3	(2	1)	57	16	12	17	8	0	37	1	4	0	7	2	0	.271	.315	.407	.723
	3 ML YEARS		115	374	84	13	5	7	(3	4)	128	46	27	35	29	0	88	6	8	1	10	5	3	.225	.290	.342	.632

Max Muncy

Bats: L **Throws:** R **Pos:** 1B-35;3B-16;2B-12;DH-2 **Ht:** 6'0" **Wt:** 215 **Born:** 8/25/1990 **Age:** 30

			BATTING																		RUNNING			AVERAGES			
Year	Team	Lg	G	AB	H	2B	3B	HR	(Hm	Rd)	TB	R	RBI	RC	TBB	IBB	SO	HBP	SH	SF	SB	CS	GDP	Avg	OBP	Slg	OPS
2015	Oak	AL	45	102	21	8	1	3	(1	2)	40	14	9	9	9	0	31	0	0	1	0	0	0	.206	.268	.392	.660
2016	Oak	AL	51	113	21	2	0	2	(1	1)	29	13	8	10	20	1	24	0	0	0	0	0	2	.186	.308	.257	.565
2018	LAD	NL	137	395	104	17	2	35	(20	15)	230	75	79	87	79	6	131	5	0	2	3	0	4	.263	.391	.582	.973
2019	LAD	NL	141	487	122	22	1	35	(13	22)	251	101	98	93	90	1	149	8	0	4	4	1	5	.251	.374	.515	.889
2020	LAD	NL	58	203	39	4	0	12	(7	5)	79	36	27	28	39	2	60	4	0	2	1	0	3	.192	.331	.389	.720
	Postseason		21	69	15	1	0	6	(4	2)	34	14	13	14	16	2	25	0	0	0	2	0	0	.217	.365	.493	.857
	5 ML YEARS		432	1300	307	53	4	87	(42	45)	629	239	221	227	237	10	395	17	0	9	8	1	14	.236	.359	.484	.843

Andres Munoz

Pitches: R **Bats:** R **Pos:** P **Ht:** 6'2" **Wt:** 243 **Born:** 1/16/1999 **Age:** 22

			HOW MUCH PITCHED				WHAT HE GAVE UP										THE RESULTS							
Year	Team	Lg	G	GS	GF	IP	BFP	H	R	ER	HR	SH	SF	HB	TBB	IBB	SO	WP	W	L	Pct	Sv-Op	Hld	Vel	OPS	ERC	ERA
2019	SD	NL	22	0	3	23.0	97	16	10	10	2	1	0	0	11	0	30	1	1	1	.500	1-2	8	100	.611	2.59	3.91

Yairo Munoz

Bats: R **Throws:** R **Pos:** LF-7;RF-4;DH-1 | JYE-roh MOON-yohs | **Ht:** 5'11" **Wt:** 200 **Born:** 1/23/1995 **Age:** 26

			BATTING																		RUNNING			AVERAGES			
Year	Team	Lg	G	AB	H	2B	3B	HR	(Hm	Rd)	TB	R	RBI	RC	TBB	IBB	SO	HBP	SH	SF	SB	CS	GDP	Avg	OBP	Slg	OPS
2018	StL	NL	108	293	81	16	0	8	(1	7)	121	39	42	46	30	7	71	4	0	2	5	6	3	.276	.330	.413	.763
2019	StL	NL	88	172	46	7	1	2	(0	2)	61	20	13	19	7	0	37	1	0	1	8	3	5	.267	.298	.355	.653
2020	Bos	AL	12	45	15	5	0	1	(1	0)	23	6	4	7	0	0	11	0	0	0	2	0	1	.333	.333	.511	.844
	Postseason		1	1	0	0	0	0	(0	0)	0	0	0	0	0	0	1	0	0	0	0	0	0	.000	.000	.000	.000
	3 ML YEARS		208	510	142	28	1	11	(2	9)	205	65	59	72	37	7	119	5	0	3	15	9	9	.278	.332	.402	.733

Daniel Murphy

Bats: L **Throws:** R **Pos:** 1B-29;PH-8;DH-4 **Ht:** 6'1" **Wt:** 223 **Born:** 4/1/1985 **Age:** 36

			BATTING																		RUNNING			AVERAGES			
Year	Team	Lg	G	AB	H	2B	3B	HR	(Hm	Rd)	TB	R	RBI	RC	TBB	IBB	SO	HBP	SH	SF	SB	CS	GDP	Avg	OBP	Slg	OPS
2008	NYM	NL	49	131	41	9	3	2	(1	1)	62	24	17	26	18	1	28	1	0	1	0	2	4	.313	.397	.473	.871
2009	NYM	NL	155	508	135	38	4	12	(7	5)	217	60	63	60	38	4	69	0	4	6	4	2	13	.266	.313	.427	.741
2011	NYM	NL	109	391	125	28	2	6	(2	4)	175	49	49	57	24	2	42	3	3	2	5	5	14	.320	.362	.448	.809
2012	NYM	NL	156	571	166	40	3	6	(1	5)	230	62	65	78	36	5	82	1	0	4	10	2	12	.291	.332	.403	.735
2013	NYM	NL	161	658	188	38	4	13	(6	7)	273	92	78	86	32	2	95	2	0	5	23	3	13	.286	.319	.415	.733
2014	NYM	NL	143	596	172	37	2	9	(4	5)	240	79	57	78	39	3	86	2	0	5	13	5	15	.289	.332	.403	.734
2015	NYM	NL	130	499	140	38	2	14	(7	7)	224	56	73	71	31	10	38	2	0	6	2	2	15	.281	.322	.449	.770
2016	Was	NL	142	531	184	**47**	5	25	(10	15)	316	88	104	115	35	10	57	8	0	8	5	3	4	.347	.390	**.595**	**.985**
2017	Was	NL	144	534	172	**43**	3	23	(6	17)	290	94	93	103	52	14	77	4	0	3	2	0	16	.322	.384	.543	.928
2018	2 Tms	NL	91	328	98	15	0	12	(5	7)	149	40	42	49	20	2	40	0	0	3	3	0	5	.299	.336	.454	.790
2019	Col	NL	132	438	122	35	1	13	(3	10)	198	56	78	64	32	1	74	2	0	4	1	1	10	.279	.328	.452	.780
2020	Col	NL	40	123	29	3	0	3	(2	1)	41	10	16	17	7	2	21	0	0	1	0	0	1	.236	.275	.333	.608
	18 Was	NL	56	190	57	9	0	6	(3	3)	84	17	29	27	13	2	17	0	0	2	1	0	4	.300	.341	.442	.784
	18 ChC	NL	35	138	41	6	0	6	(2	4)	65	23	13	22	7	0	23	0	0	1	2	0	1	.297	.329	.471	.800
	Postseason		25	97	30	3	0	8	(4	4)	57	21	19	22	15	4	21	0	0	1	3	2	1	.309	.398	.588	.986
	12 ML YEARS		1452	5308	1572	371	29	138	(54	84)	2415	710	735	804	364	56	709	25	7	48	68	25	124	.296	.341	.455	.796

John Ryan Murphy

Bats: R **Throws:** R **Pos:** C-23;PH-1 **Ht:** 5'11" **Wt:** 200 **Born:** 5/13/1991 **Age:** 30

			BATTING																		RUNNING			AVERAGES			
Year	Team	Lg	G	AB	H	2B	3B	HR	(Hm	Rd)	TB	R	RBI	RC	TBB	IBB	SO	HBP	SH	SF	SB	CS	GDP	Avg	OBP	Slg	OPS
2013	NYY	AL	16	26	4	1	0	0	(0	0)	5	3	1	0	1	0	9	0	0	0	0	0	0	.154	.185	.192	.377
2014	NYY	AL	32	81	23	4	0	1	(1	0)	30	7	9	10	4	0	22	0	0	0	0	0	0	.284	.318	.370	.688
2015	NYY	AL	67	155	43	9	1	3	(1	2)	63	21	14	17	12	0	43	1	1	3	0	0	4	.277	.327	.406	.734
2016	Min	AL	26	82	12	3	0	1	(1	0)	18	4	3	0	5	0	19	0	2	1	0	0	3	.146	.193	.220	.413
2017	Ari	AL	5	7	1	1	0	0	(0	0)	2	0	1	0	0	0	1	0	0	0	0	0	1	.143	.143	.286	.429
2018	Ari	NL	87	208	42	9	0	9	(4	5)	78	19	24	17	11	1	71	1	2	1	0	0	1	.202	.244	.375	.619
2019	2 Tms	NL	26	63	11	3	0	4	(1	3)	26	9	7	5	6	0	28	0	1	0	0	0	0	.175	.246	.413	.659

Year	Team	Lg	G	AB	H	2B	3B	HR	(Hm	Rd)	TB	R	RBI	RC	TBB	IBB	SO	HBP	SH	SF	SB	CS	GDP	Avg	OBP	Slg	OPS
2020	Pit	NL	25	58	10	2	0	0	(0	0)	12	6	2	1	4	0	28	0	1	0	0	0	1	.172	.226	.207	.433
19	Ari	NL	25	62	11	3	0	4	(1	3)	26	9	7	5	6	0	28	0	1	0	0	0	0	.177	.250	.419	.669
19	Atl	NL	1	1	0	0	0	0	(0	0)	0	0	0	0	0	0	0	0	0	0	0	0	0	.000	.000	.000	.000
	8 ML YEARS		284	680	146	32	1	18	(8	10)	234	69	61	50	43	1	221	2	7	5	0	0	10	.215	.262	.344	.606

Patrick Murphy

Pitches: R **Bats:** R **Pos:** RP-4   **Ht:** 6'5" **Wt:** 235 **Born:** 6/10/1995 **Age:** 26

			HOW MUCH PITCHED				WHAT HE GAVE UP								THE RESULTS							
Year	Team	Lg	G	GS	GF	IP	BFP	H	R	ER	HR	SH	SF	HB	TBB	IBB	SO	WP	W	L	Pct	Sv-Op	Hld	Vel	OPS	ERC	ERA
2020	Tor	AL	4	0	2	6.0	25	6	1	1	0	0	0	0	2	0	5	0	0	0	-	0-0	0	97	.711	3.19	1.50

Sean Murphy

Bats: R **Throws:** R **Pos:** C-43;PH-1   **Ht:** 6'3" **Wt:** 228 **Born:** 10/4/1994 **Age:** 26

Year	Team	Lg	G	AB	H	2B	3B	HR	(Hm	Rd)	TB	R	RBI	RC	TBB	IBB	SO	HBP	SH	SF	SB	CS	GDP	Avg	OBP	Slg	OPS
2016	2 Tms	Low	23	79	18	1	0	2	(-	-)	25	11	7	8	9	0	12	0	0	0	1	0	6	.228	.307	.316	.623
2017	Stcktn	A+	45	165	49	11	0	9	(-	-)	87	22	26	29	11	0	33	1	0	1	0	0	9	.297	.343	.527	.870
2017	Mdlnd	AA	53	191	40	7	0	4	(-	-)	59	25	22	18	21	0	34	1	2	2	0	0	9	.209	.288	.309	.597
2018	Mdlnd	AA	68	257	74	26	2	8	(-	-)	128	51	43	47	23	2	47	6	1	2	3	0	9	.288	.358	.498	.856
2019	LsVgs	AAA	31	120	37	6	1	10	(-	-)	75	25	30	28	15	0	31	2	0	3	0	1	2	.308	.386	.625	1.011
2019	2 Tms	Low	10	30	7	2	0	1	(-	-)	12	9	1	4	7	1	5	0	0	0	0	0	3	.233	.378	.400	.778
2019	Oak	AL	20	53	13	5	0	4	(1	3)	30	14	8	7	6	0	16	1	0	0	0	0	3	.245	.333	.566	.899
2020	Oak	AL	43	116	27	5	0	7	(3	4)	53	21	14	15	24	0	37	0	0	0	0	0	6	.233	.364	.457	.821
	Postseason		1	1	0	0	0	0	(0	0)	0	0	0	0	0	0	0	0	0	0	0	0	1	.000	.000	.000	.000
	2 ML YEARS		63	169	40	10	0	11	(4	7)	83	35	22	22	30	0	53	1	0	0	0	0	9	.237	.355	.491	.846

Tom Murphy

Bats: R **Throws:** R **Pos:** C   **Ht:** 6'1" **Wt:** 218 **Born:** 4/3/1991 **Age:** 30

Year	Team	Lg	G	AB	H	2B	3B	HR	(Hm	Rd)	TB	R	RBI	RC	TBB	IBB	SO	HBP	SH	SF	SB	CS	GDP	Avg	OBP	Slg	OPS
2015	Col	NL	11	35	9	1	0	3	(3	0)	19	5	9	9	4	1	10	0	0	0	0	0	0	.257	.333	.543	.876
2016	Col	NL	21	44	12	2	0	5	(5	0)	29	8	13	10	4	0	19	1	0	0	1	0	2	.273	.347	.659	1.006
2017	Col	NL	12	24	1	1	0	0	(0	0)	2	1	1	0	2	1	9	0	0	0	0	0	0	.042	.115	.083	.199
2018	Col	NL	37	93	21	7	1	2	(1	1)	36	5	11	8	3	1	44	0	0	0	0	1	2	.226	.250	.387	.637
2019	Sea	AL	76	260	71	12	1	18	(6	12)	139	32	40	43	19	0	87	1	0	1	2	0	0	.273	.324	.535	.858
	5 ML YEARS		157	456	114	23	2	28	(15	13)	225	51	74	70	32	3	169	2	0	1	3	1	4	.250	.301	.493	.795

Joe Musgrove

Pitches: R **Bats:** R **Pos:** SP-8   **Ht:** 6'5" **Wt:** 235 **Born:** 12/4/1992 **Age:** 28

			HOW MUCH PITCHED				WHAT HE GAVE UP								THE RESULTS							
Year	Team	Lg	G	GS	GF	IP	BFP	H	R	ER	HR	SH	SF	HB	TBB	IBB	SO	WP	W	L	Pct	Sv-Op	Hld	Vel	OPS	ERC	ERA
2016	Hou	AL	11	10	1	62.0	256	59	28	28	9	0	1	3	16	0	55	0	4	4	.500	0-0	0	92	.758	3.80	4.06
2017	Hou	AL	38	15	5	109.1	462	117	59	58	18	5	2	4	28	1	98	4	7	8	.467	2-4	5	93	.798	4.54	4.77
2018	Pit	NL	19	19	0	115.1	486	113	56	52	12	3	5	8	23	3	100	5	6	9	.400	0-0	0	93	.687	3.40	4.06
2019	Pit	NL	32	31	0	170.1	718	168	98	84	21	1	6	9	39	1	157	2	11	12	.478	0-0	1	92	.738	3.66	4.44
2020	Pit	NL	8	8	0	39.2	166	33	17	17	5	0	2	2	16	0	55	1	1	5	.167	0-0	0	92	.711	3.56	3.86
	Postseason		7	0	3	6.2	27	6	6	6	3	0	1	0	1	1	3	0	1	0	1.000	0-0	1	95	.859	4.35	8.10
	5 ML YEARS		108	83	6	496.2	2088	490	258	239	65	9	16	26	122	5	465	12	29	38	.433	2-4	6	93	.740	3.79	4.33

Wil Myers

Bats: R **Throws:** R **Pos:** RF-52;1B-2;DH-2   **Ht:** 6'3" **Wt:** 207 **Born:** 12/10/1990 **Age:** 30

Year	Team	Lg	G	AB	H	2B	3B	HR	(Hm	Rd)	TB	R	RBI	RC	TBB	IBB	SO	HBP	SH	SF	SB	CS	GDP	Avg	OBP	Slg	OPS
2013	TB	AL	88	335	98	23	0	13	(5	8)	160	50	53	52	33	6	91	1	0	4	5	2	10	.293	.354	.478	.831
2014	TB	AL	87	325	72	14	0	6	(2	4)	104	37	35	32	34	3	90	0	0	2	6	1	10	.222	.294	.320	.614
2015	SD	NL	60	225	57	13	1	8	(3	5)	96	40	29	35	27	0	55	1	0	0	5	2	2	.253	.336	.427	.763
2016	SD	NL	157	599	155	29	4	28	(18	10)	276	99	94	97	68	1	160	4	0	5	28	6	12	.259	.336	.461	.797
2017	SD	NL	155	567	138	29	3	30	(8	22)	263	80	74	80	70	3	180	5	0	7	20	6	15	.243	.328	.464	.792
2018	SD	NL	83	312	79	25	4	11	(6	5)	139	39	39	45	30	1	94	0	0	1	13	1	10	.253	.318	.446	.763
2019	SD	NL	155	435	104	22	1	18	(9	9)	182	58	53	54	51	0	168	2	1	1	16	7	12	.239	.321	.418	.739
2020	SD	NL	55	198	57	14	2	15	(11	4)	120	34	40	44	18	0	56	2	0	0	2	1	0	.288	.353	.606	.959
	Postseason		5	20	2	0	0	0	(0	0)	2	0	0	0	1	0	7	0	0	0	0	0	0	.100	.143	.100	.243
	8 ML YEARS		840	2996	760	169	12	129	(62	67)	1340	437	417	439	331	14	894	15	1	20	95	26	71	.254	.329	.447	.776

Tyler Naquin

Bats: L **Throws:** R **Pos:** RF-39;PH-7   NAY-kwin   **Ht:** 6'2" **Wt:** 195 **Born:** 4/24/1991 **Age:** 30

Year	Team	Lg	G	AB	H	2B	3B	HR	(Hm	Rd)	TB	R	RBI	RC	TBB	IBB	SO	HBP	SH	SF	SB	CS	GDP	Avg	OBP	Slg	OPS
2016	Cle	AL	116	321	95	18	5	14	(9	5)	165	52	43	53	36	4	112	4	2	2	6	3	4	.296	.372	.514	.886
2017	Cle	AL	19	37	8	2	0	0	(0	0)	10	4	1	2	2	0	9	0	0	1	0	1	1	.216	.250	.270	.520
2018	Cle	AL	61	174	46	7	0	3	(0	3)	62	22	23	21	6	1	42	2	0	1	1	1	1	.264	.295	.356	.651

Year	Team	Lg	G	AB	H	2B	3B	HR	(Hm	Rd)	TB	R	RBI	RC	TBB	IBB	SO	HBP	SH	SF	SB	CS	GDP	Avg	OBP	Slg	OPS
2019	Cle	AL	89	274	79	19	0	10	(6	4)	128	34	34	36	14	2	66	2	2	2	4	2	8	.288	.325	.467	.792
2020	Cle	AL	40	133	29	8	1	4	(0	4)	51	15	20	14	5	0	40	1	0	2			3	.218	.248	.383	.632
	Postseason		11	23	4	2	0	0	(0	0)	6	0	2	1	1	1	14	0	1	0	0	0	0	.174	.208	.261	.469
	5 ML YEARS		325	939	257	54	6	31	(15	16)	416	127	121	126	63	7	269	9	4	8	11	8	17	.274	.323	.443	.766

Omar Narvaez

Bats: L **Throws:** R **Pos:** C-39;PH-5;PR-1   nar-VAH-es   **Ht:** 5'11" **Wt:** 220 **Born:** 2/10/1992 **Age:** 29

Year	Team	Lg	G	AB	H	2B	3B	HR	(Hm	Rd)	TB	R	RBI	RC	TBB	IBB	SO	HBP	SH	SF	SB	CS	GDP	Avg	OBP	Slg	OPS
2016	CWS	AL	34	101	27	4	0	1	(1	0)	34	13	10	15	14	1	14	0	0	2	0	0	0	.267	.350	.337	.687
2017	CWS	AL	90	253	70	10	0	2	(2	0)	86	23	14	33	38	1	45	1	3	0	0	0	8	.277	.373	.340	.713
2018	CWS	AL	97	280	77	14	1	9	(4	5)	120	30	30	48	38	1	65	2	2	0	0	2	5	.275	.366	.429	.794
2019	Sea	AL	132	428	119	12	0	22	(13	9)	197	63	55	66	47	1	92	4	0	3	0	0	5	.278	.353	.460	.813
2020	Mil	NL	40	108	19	4	0	2	(2	0)	29	8	10	13	16	0	39	2	0	0	0	0	1	.176	.294	.269	.562
	5 ML YEARS		393	1170	312	44	1	36	(22	14)	466	137	119	170	153	4	255	9	5	5	0	2	19	.267	.355	.398	.753

Brian Navarreto

Bats: R **Throws:** R **Pos:** C-2   **Ht:** 6'0" **Wt:** 237 **Born:** 12/29/1994 **Age:** 26

Year	Team	Lg	G	AB	H	2B	3B	HR	(Hm	Rd)	TB	R	RBI	RC	TBB	IBB	SO	HBP	SH	SF	SB	CS	GDP	Avg	OBP	Slg	OPS
2020	Mia	NL	2	5	2	0	0	0	(0	0)	2	0	0	1	0	0	1	0	0	0	0	0	0	.400	.400	.400	.800

Josh Naylor

Bats: L **Throws:** L **Pos:** LF-22;PH-11;DH-8;1B-5;RF-4   **Ht:** 5'11" **Wt:** 250 **Born:** 6/22/1997 **Age:** 24

Year	Team	Lg	G	AB	H	2B	3B	HR	(Hm	Rd)	TB	R	RBI	RC	TBB	IBB	SO	HBP	SH	SF	SB	CS	GDP	Avg	OBP	Slg	OPS
2019	SD	NL	94	253	63	15	0	8	(4	4)	102	29	32	36	25	1	64	0	0	1	1	1	4	.249	.315	.403	.719
2020	2 Tms		40	97	24	3	1	1	(0	1)	32	13	6	9	5	0	12	1	0	0	1	0	2	.247	.291	.330	.621
20	SD	NL	18	36	10	0	1	1	(0	1)	15	4	4	4	1	0	4	1	0	0	1	0	2	.278	.316	.417	.732
20	Cle	AL	22	61	14	3	0	0	(0	0)	17	9	2	5	4	0	8	0	0	0	0	0	0	.230	.277	.279	.556
	2 ML YEARS		134	350	87	18	1	9	(4	5)	134	42	38	45	30	1	76	1	0	1	2	1	6	.249	.309	.383	.692

Nick Neidert

Pitches: R **Bats:** R **Pos:** RP-4   NY-dert   **Ht:** 6'1" **Wt:** 202 **Born:** 11/20/1996 **Age:** 24

Year	Team	Lg	G	GS	GF	IP	BFP	H	R	ER	HR	SH	SF	HB	TBB	IBB	SO	WP	W	L	Pct	Sv-Op	Hld	Vel	OPS	ERC	ERA
2020	Mia	NL	4	0	1	8.1	34	10	5	5	1	0	0	0	2	0	4	0	0	0	-	0-0	0	92	.853	5.06	5.40

Jimmy Nelson

Pitches: R **Bats:** R **Pos:** P   **Ht:** 6'6" **Wt:** 250 **Born:** 6/5/1989 **Age:** 32

Year	Team	Lg	G	GS	GF	IP	BFP	H	R	ER	HR	SH	SF	HB	TBB	IBB	SO	WP	W	L	Pct	Sv-Op	Hld	Vel	OPS	ERC	ERA
2013	Mil	NL	4	1	0	10.0	37	2	1	1	0	0	1	0	5	0	8	1	0	0	-	0-0	0	94	.286	0.64	0.90
2014	Mil	NL	14	12	1	69.1	311	82	42	38	6	1	2	8	19	0	57	4	2	9	.182	0-0	0	94	.793	4.96	4.93
2015	Mil	NL	30	30	0	177.1	752	163	89	81	18	4	7	13	65	4	148	11	11	13	.458	0-0	0	93	.704	3.79	4.11
2016	Mil	NL	32	32	0	179.1	807	186	108	92	25	7	4	17	86	2	140	8	8	16	.333	0-0	0	93	.791	5.29	4.62
2017	Mil	NL	29	29	0	175.1	728	171	75	68	16	4	2	9	48	1	199	6	12	6	.667	0-0	0	94	.689	3.64	3.49
2019	Mil	NL	10	3	2	22.0	105	25	18	17	4	0	0	2	17	1	26	1	0	2	.000	0-0	0	93	.966	7.63	6.95
	6 ML YEARS		119	107	3	633.1	2740	629	333	297	69	16	16	49	240	8	578	31	33	46	.418	0-0	0	93	.740	4.34	4.22

Kyle Nelson

Pitches: L **Bats:** L **Pos:** RP-1   **Ht:** 6'1" **Wt:** 175 **Born:** 7/8/1996 **Age:** 24

Year	Team	Lg	G	GS	GF	IP	BFP	H	R	ER	HR	SH	SF	HB	TBB	IBB	SO	WP	W	L	Pct	Sv-Op	Hld	Vel	OPS	ERC	ERA
2020	Cle	AL	1	0	0	0.2	6	3	4	4	1	0	0	0	1	0	0	0	0	0	-	0-0	0	90	1.867	56.63	54.00

Nick Nelson

Pitches: R **Bats:** R **Pos:** RP-11   **Ht:** 6'1" **Wt:** 205 **Born:** 12/5/1995 **Age:** 25

Year	Team	Lg	G	GS	GF	IP	BFP	H	R	ER	HR	SH	SF	HB	TBB	IBB	SO	WP	W	L	Pct	Sv-Op	Hld	Vel	OPS	ERC	ERA
2020	NYY	AL	11	0	4	20.2	90	20	13	11	4	0	1	0	11	0	18	0	1	0	1.000	0-0	0	96	.780	5.18	4.79

Hector Neris

Pitches: R **Bats:** R **Pos:** RP-24   NAIR-ess   **Ht:** 6'2" **Wt:** 227 **Born:** 6/14/1989 **Age:** 32

Year	Team	Lg	G	GS	GF	IP	BFP	H	R	ER	HR	SH	SF	HB	TBB	IBB	SO	WP	W	L	Pct	Sv-Op	Hld	Vel	OPS	ERC	ERA
2014	Phi	NL	1	0	0	1.0	3	0	0	0	0	0	0	0	0	0	1	0	1	0	1.000	0-0	0	93	.000	0.00	0.00
2015	Phi	NL	32	0	8	40.1	170	38	19	17	8	1	0	4	10	0	41	3	2	2	.500	0-0	2	93	.772	4.21	3.79
2016	Phi	NL	79	0	13	80.1	328	59	26	23	9	1	2	3	30	3	102	4	4	4	.500	2-6	28	94	.620	2.73	2.58
2017	Phi	NL	74	0	56	74.2	320	68	26	25	9	1	2	6	26	3	86	2	4	5	.444	26-29	4	95	.689	3.74	3.01

Year	Team	Lg	G	GS	GF	IP	BFP	H	R	ER	HR	SH	SF	HB	TBB	IBB	SO	WP	W	L	Pct	Sv-Op	Hld	Vel	OPS	ERC	ERA
2018	Phi	NL	53	0	28	47.2	203	46	27	27	11	2	0	1	16	1	76	5	1	3	.250	11-14	4	95	.803	4.55	5.10
2019	Phi	NL	68	0	49	67.2	275	45	24	22	10	1	2	6	24	1	89	2	3	6	.333	28-34	2	95	.613	2.74	2.93
2020	Phi	NL	24	0	13	21.2	103	24	15	11	0	0	0	0	13	2	27	3	2	2	.500	5-8	4	94	.670	4.36	4.57
7 ML YEARS			331	0	168	333.1	1402	280	137	125	47	6	6	20	119	10	422	19	17	22	.436	72-91	44	94	.682	3.47	3.38

Dovydas Neverauskas

Pitches: R **Bats:** R **Pos:** RP-17 · DOE-vee-duss nev-er-OWS-kiss · **Ht:** 6'3" **Wt:** 225 **Born:** 1/14/1993 **Age:** 28

Year	Team	Lg	G	GS	GF	IP	BFP	H	R	ER	HR	SH	SF	HB	TBB	IBB	SO	WP	W	L	Pct	Sv-Op	Hld	Vel	OPS	ERC	ERA
2017	Pit	NL	24	0	11	25.1	105	24	11	11	4	1	0	1	8	0	17	2	1	1	.500	0-1	2	97	.749	4.09	3.91
2018	Pit	NL	25	0	8	27.0	119	30	25	24	9	0	1	1	10	0	27	2	0	0	-	0-1	2	97	.943	6.52	8.00
2019	Pit	NL	10	0	3	9.1	53	15	11	11	2	0	1	2	7	1	10	1	0	0	-	0-0	1	96	1.081	10.85	10.61
2020	Pit	NL	17	0	7	19.0	89	24	17	15	5	0	0	0	10	0	23	2	0	3	.000	0-0	0	95	.939	7.51	7.11
4 ML YEARS			76	0	29	80.2	366	93	64	61	20	1	2	4	35	1	77	7	1	4	.200	0-2	5	96	.905	6.44	6.81

Jake Newberry

Pitches: R **Bats:** R **Pos:** RP-20 · **Ht:** 6'2" **Wt:** 205 **Born:** 11/20/1994 **Age:** 26

Year	Team	Lg	G	GS	GF	IP	BFP	H	R	ER	HR	SH	SF	HB	TBB	IBB	SO	WP	W	L	Pct	Sv-Op	Hld	Vel	OPS	ERC	ERA
2018	KC	AL	14	0	3	13.1	60	13	8	7	3	0	0	0	9	0	11	1	2	0	1.000	0-0	1	94	.857	6.10	4.73
2019	KC	AL	27	0	6	31.0	137	29	13	13	7	0	3	1	16	2	29	0	1	0	1.000	0-1	4	94	.849	5.08	3.77
2020	KC	AL	20	0	6	22.0	94	20	12	10	3	0	2	2	12	0	24	3	1	0	1.000	1-1	1	93	.772	4.99	4.09
3 ML YEARS			61	0	15	66.1	291	62	33	30	13	0	5	3	37	2	64	4	4	0	1.000	1-2	6	94	.826	5.26	4.07

Sean Newcomb

Pitches: L **Bats:** L **Pos:** SP-4 · **Ht:** 6'5" **Wt:** 255 **Born:** 6/12/1993 **Age:** 28

Year	Team	Lg	G	GS	GF	IP	BFP	H	R	ER	HR	SH	SF	HB	TBB	IBB	SO	WP	W	L	Pct	Sv-Op	Hld	Vel	OPS	ERC	ERA
2017	Atl	NL	19	19	0	100.0	456	100	51	48	10	5	3	6	57	6	108	3	4	9	.308	0-0	0	94	.780	4.85	4.32
2018	Atl	NL	31	30	0	164.0	696	137	74	71	18	4	3	1	81	1	160	4	12	9	.571	0-0	0	93	.679	3.62	3.90
2019	Atl	NL	55	4	4	68.1	293	61	28	24	8	0	2	3	29	1	65	4	6	3	.667	1-3	16	94	.692	3.83	3.16
2020	Atl	NL	4	4	0	13.2	70	20	17	17	4	0	1	3	6	0	10	1	0	2	.000	0-0	0	93	.998	9.58	11.20
Postseason			6	1	1	8.1	28	2	2	1	0	1	0	0	3	0	6	0	1	0	1.000	0-0	1	96	.269	0.57	1.08
4 ML YEARS			109	57	4	346.0	1515	318	170	160	40	9	9	13	173	8	343	12	22	23	.489	1-3	16	94	.726	4.22	4.16

Kevin Newman

Bats: R **Throws:** R **Pos:** SS-23;2B-20;PH-3 · **Ht:** 6'0" **Wt:** 200 **Born:** 8/4/1993 **Age:** 27

Year	Team	Lg					BATTING																RUNNING			AVERAGES			
			G	AB	H	2B	3B	HR	(Hm	Rd)	TB	R	RBI	RC	TBB	IBB	SO	HBP	SH	SF	SB	CS	GDP	Avg	OBP	Slg	OPS
2018	Pit	NL	31	91	19	2	0	0	(0	0)	21	7	6	5	4	1	23	1	0	1	0	1	2	.209	.247	.231	.478
2019	Pit	NL	130	493	152	20	6	12	(3	9)	220	61	64	73	28	2	62	7	2	1	16	8	5	.308	.353	.446	.800
2020	Pit	NL	44	156	35	5	0	1	(0	1)	43	12	10	15	12	0	21	1	1	2	0	1	1	.224	.281	.276	.556
3 ML YEARS			205	740	206	27	6	13	(3	10)	284	80	80	93	44	3	106	9	3	4	16	10	8	.278	.325	.384	.709

Ljay Newsome

Pitches: R **Bats:** R **Pos:** SP-4; RP-1 · **Ht:** 5'11" **Wt:** 210 **Born:** 11/8/1996 **Age:** 24

Year	Team	Lg	G	GS	GF	IP	BFP	H	R	ER	HR	SH	SF	HB	TBB	IBB	SO	WP	W	L	Pct	Sv-Op	Hld	Vel	OPS	ERC	ERA
2020	Sea	AL	5	4	0	15.2	68	20	9	9	4	0	0	1	1	0	9	0	0	1	.000	0-0	0	91	.914	5.62	5.17

Juan Nicasio

Pitches: R **Bats:** R **Pos:** RP-2 · nih-KAH-see-oh · **Ht:** 6'4" **Wt:** 250 **Born:** 8/31/1986 **Age:** 34

Year	Team	Lg	G	GS	GF	IP	BFP	H	R	ER	HR	SH	SF	HB	TBB	IBB	SO	WP	W	L	Pct	Sv-Op	Hld	Vel	OPS	ERC	ERA
2011	Col	NL	13	13	0	71.2	299	73	35	33	8	1	0	1	18	3	58	1	4	4	.500	0-0	0	94	.735	3.69	4.14
2012	Col	NL	11	11	0	58.0	257	72	37	34	7	3	1	1	22	1	54	4	2	3	.400	0-0	0	93	.861	5.74	5.28
2013	Col	NL	31	31	0	157.2	703	168	97	90	17	6	1	5	64	7	119	6	9	9	.500	0-0	0	92	.785	4.52	5.14
2014	Col	NL	33	14	7	93.2	409	107	59	56	19	5	2	1	31	1	63	3	6	6	.500	0-0	1	93	.860	5.43	5.38
2015	LAD	NL	53	1	12	58.1	260	59	25	25	1	3	0	1	32	6	65	2	1	3	.250	1-3	14	95	.742	4.00	3.86
2016	Pit	NL	52	12	9	118.0	513	117	64	59	15	5	7	7	45	3	138	3	10	7	.588	0-2	6	94	.774	4.33	4.50
2017	3 Tms		76	0	15	72.1	291	58	22	21	5	1	0	2	20	2	72	1	5	5	.500	6-10	21	95	.610	2.46	2.61
2018	Sea	AL	46	0	6	42.0	183	53	30	28	6	0	4	2	5	0	53	0	1	6	.143	1-7	19	94	.828	4.90	6.00
2019	Phi	NL	47	0	10	47.1	217	57	27	25	4	1	2	2	21	5	45	0	2	3	.400	1-2	10	94	.810	5.29	4.75
2020	Tex	AL	2	0	1	1.1	11	5	6	6	1	0	0	0	2	0	1	0	0	0	-	0-0	0	94	1.747	38.73	40.50
17	Pit	NL	65	0	8	60.0	243	49	20	19	4	1	0	2	18	2	60	1	2	5	.286	2-6	21	95	.617	2.62	2.85
17	Phi	NL	2	0	0	1.1	4	0	0	0	0	0	0	0	0	0	1	0	1	0	1.000	0-0	0	96	.000	0.00	0.00
17	StL	NL	9	0	7	11.0	44	9	2	2	1	0	0	0	2	0	11	0	2	0	1.000	4-4	0	95	.631	2.23	1.64
10 ML YEARS			364	82	59	720.1	3143	769	402	377	83	25	17	22	260	28	668	20	40	46	.465	9-24	71	93	.782	4.47	4.71

266

Tomas Nido

Bats: R **Throws:** R **Pos:** C-7 **Ht:** 6'0" **Wt:** 211 **Born:** 4/12/1994 **Age:** 27

Year	Team	Lg	G	AB	H	2B	3B	HR	(Hm	Rd)	TB	R	RBI	RC	TBB	IBB	SO	HBP	SH	SF	SB	CS	GDP	Avg	OBP	Slg	OPS
2017	NYM	NL	5	10	3	1	0	0	(0	0)	4	0	3	2	0	0	2	0	0	0	0	0	0	.300	.300	.400	.700
2018	NYM	NL	34	84	14	3	0	1	(1	0)	20	10	9	2	4	0	27	0	0	2	0	0	4	.167	.200	.238	.438
2019	NYM	NL	50	136	26	5	0	4	(2	2)	43	9	14	5	7	2	37	0	1	0	0	0	4	.191	.231	.316	.547
2020	NYM	NL	7	24	7	1	0	2	(2	0)	14	4	6	4	2	0	6	0	0	0	0	0	2	.292	.346	.583	.929
	4 ML YEARS		96	254	50	10	0	7	(5	2)	81	23	32	13	13	2	72	0	1	2	0	0	10	.197	.234	.319	.553

Brandon Nimmo

Bats: L **Throws:** R **Pos:** CF-44;LF-22;RF-10;PH-1;PR-1 NIH-moe **Ht:** 6'3" **Wt:** 206 **Born:** 3/27/1993 **Age:** 28

Year	Team	Lg	G	AB	H	2B	3B	HR	(Hm	Rd)	TB	R	RBI	RC	TBB	IBB	SO	HBP	SH	SF	SB	CS	GDP	Avg	OBP	Slg	OPS
2016	NYM	NL	32	73	20	1	0	1	(1	0)	24	12	6	9	6	0	20	1	0	0	0	0	0	.274	.338	.329	.666
2017	NYM	NL	69	177	46	11	1	5	(3	2)	74	26	21	26	33	1	60	2	1	2	2	0	3	.260	.379	.418	.797
2018	NYM	NL	140	433	114	28	8	17	(8	9)	209	77	47	84	80	2	140	22	0	4	9	6	8	.263	.404	.483	.886
2019	NYM	NL	69	199	44	11	1	8	(2	6)	81	34	29	38	46	2	71	5	1	3	3	0	1	.221	.375	.407	.783
2020	NYM	NL	55	186	52	8	3	8	(5	3)	90	33	18	33	33	0	43	6	0	0	1	2	1	.280	.404	.484	.888
	5 ML YEARS		365	1068	276	59	13	39	(19	20)	478	182	121	190	198	5	334	36	2	5	15	8	13	.258	.390	.448	.838

John Nogowski

Bats: R **Throws:** L **Pos:** 1B-1 **Ht:** 6'0" **Wt:** 245 **Born:** 1/5/1993 **Age:** 28

Year	Team	Lg	G	AB	H	2B	3B	HR	(Hm	Rd)	TB	R	RBI	RC	TBB	IBB	SO	HBP	SH	SF	SB	CS	GDP	Avg	OBP	Slg	OPS
2020	StL	NL	1	4	1	0	0	0	(0	0)	1	0	0	0	0	0	1	0	0	0	0	0	0	.250	.250	.250	.500

Aaron Nola

Pitches: R **Bats:** R **Pos:** SP-12 **Ht:** 6'2" **Wt:** 200 **Born:** 6/4/1993 **Age:** 28

Year	Team	Lg	G	GS	GF	IP	BFP	H	R	ER	HR	SH	SF	HB	TBB	IBB	SO	WP	W	L	Pct	Sv-Op	Hld	Vel	OPS	ERC	ERA
2015	Phi	NL	13	13	0	77.2	318	74	31	31	11	1	1	2	19	1	68	0	6	2	.750	0-0	0	91	.703	3.62	3.59
2016	Phi	NL	20	20	0	111.0	483	116	68	59	10	5	4	6	29	3	121	2	6	9	.400	0-0	0	90	.712	3.80	4.78
2017	Phi	NL	27	27	0	168.0	693	154	67	66	18	2	0	2	49	2	184	1	12	11	.522	0-0	0	92	.679	3.30	3.54
2018	Phi	NL	33	33	0	212.1	831	149	57	56	17	6	4	7	58	3	224	4	17	6	.739	0-0	0	92	.570	2.09	2.37
2019	Phi	NL	34	34	0	202.1	852	176	91	87	27	4	2	11	80	3	229	3	12	7	.632	0-0	0	93	.708	3.79	3.87
2020	Phi	NL	12	12	0	71.1	289	54	31	26	9	0	1	2	23	2	96	1	5	5	.500	0-0	0	92	.627	2.72	3.28
	6 ML YEARS		139	139	0	842.2	3466	723	345	325	92	18	12	30	258	14	922	11	58	40	.592	0-0	0	92	.663	3.13	3.47

Austin Nola

Bats: R **Throws:** R **Pos:** C-44;DH-4;PH-3;1B-2;3B-1 **Ht:** 6'0" **Wt:** 197 **Born:** 12/28/1989 **Age:** 31

Year	Team	Lg	G	AB	H	2B	3B	HR	(Hm	Rd)	TB	R	RBI	RC	TBB	IBB	SO	HBP	SH	SF	SB	CS	GDP	Avg	OBP	Slg	OPS
2019	Sea	AL	79	238	64	12	1	10	(1	9)	108	37	31	34	23	1	63	4	1	1	1	0	8	.269	.342	.454	.796
2020	2 Tms		48	161	44	9	1	7	(4	3)	76	24	28	27	18	1	34	3	0	2	0	0	3	.273	.353	.472	.825
20	Sea	AL	29	98	30	5	1	5	(3	2)	52	15	19	19	9	1	17	2	0	1	0	0	1	.306	.373	.531	.903
20	SD	NL	19	63	14	4	0	2	(1	1)	24	9	9	8	9	0	17	1	0	1	0	0	2	.222	.324	.381	.705
	2 ML YEARS		127	399	108	21	2	17	(5	12)	184	61	59	61	41	2	97	7	1	3	1	0	11	.271	.347	.461	.808

Jake Noll

Bats: R **Throws:** R **Pos:** 1B-4;PH-3;3B-1;DH-1 **Ht:** 6'2" **Wt:** 215 **Born:** 3/8/1994 **Age:** 27

Year	Team	Lg	G	AB	H	2B	3B	HR	(Hm	Rd)	TB	R	RBI	RC	TBB	IBB	SO	HBP	SH	SF	SB	CS	GDP	Avg	OBP	Slg	OPS
2019	Was	NL	8	12	2	1	0	0	(0	0)	3	1	2	1	1	0	4	0	0	0	0	0	0	.167	.231	.250	.481
2020	Was	NL	7	17	6	1	0	0	(0	0)	7	2	0	1	0	0	4	0	0	0	0	0	1	.353	.353	.412	.765
	2 ML YEARS		15	29	8	2	0	0	(0	0)	10	3	2	2	1	0	8	0	0	0	0	0	1	.276	.300	.345	.645

Daniel Norris

Pitches: L **Bats:** L **Pos:** RP-13; SP-1 **Ht:** 6'2" **Wt:** 185 **Born:** 4/25/1993 **Age:** 28

Year	Team	Lg	G	GS	GF	IP	BFP	H	R	ER	HR	SH	SF	HB	TBB	IBB	SO	WP	W	L	Pct	Sv-Op	Hld	Vel	OPS	ERC	ERA
2014	Tor	AL	5	1	2	6.2	30	5	4	4	1	0	1	0	5	0	4	0	0	0	-	0-0	1	91	.667	4.31	5.40
2015	2 Tms	AL	13	13	0	60.0	251	53	31	25	9	1	4	2	19	0	45	3	3	2	.600	0-0	0	92	.732	3.55	3.75
2016	Det	AL	14	13	1	69.1	302	75	30	26	10	0	3	0	22	0	71	1	4	2	.667	0-0	0	93	.762	4.46	3.38
2017	Det	AL	22	18	0	101.2	460	120	64	60	12	2	3	3	44	3	86	1	5	8	.385	0-0	0	93	.840	5.48	5.31
2018	Det	AL	11	8	0	44.1	200	46	28	28	8	1	2	2	19	0	51	2	0	5	.000	0-0	0	90	.791	5.06	5.68
2019	Det	AL	32	29	0	144.1	610	154	75	72	25	5	3	4	38	0	125	5	3	13	.188	0-0	0	91	.797	4.58	4.49
2020	Det	AL	14	1	0	27.2	116	25	10	10	8	2	2	0	7	0	28	0	3	1	.750	0-0	0	93	.639	2.74	3.25
15	Tor	AL	5	5	0	23.1	103	23	11	10	3	1	2	2	12	0	18	2	1	1	.500	0-0	0	91	.816	5.10	3.86
15	Det	AL	8	8	0	36.2	148	30	20	15	6	0	2	0	7	0	27	1	2	1	.667	0-0	0	92	.674	2.64	3.68
	7 ML YEARS		111	83	5	454.0	1969	478	242	225	67	9	16	11	154	3	410	12	18	31	.367	0-0	1	92	.781	4.54	4.46

James Norwood

Pitches: R Bats: R Pos: RP-3 Ht: 6'2" Wt: 215 Born: 12/24/1993 Age: 27

Year	Team	Lg	G	GS	GF	IP	BFP	H	R	ER	HR	SH	SF	HB	TBB	IBB	SO	WP	W	L	Pct	Sv-Op	Hld	Vel	OPS	ERC	ERA
2018	ChC	NL	11	0	5	11.0	54	14	7	5	0	0	2	0	5	0	10	1	0	1	.000	0-0	2	98	.714	4.75	4.09
2019	ChC	NL	9	0	3	9.1	44	9	4	3	1	0	0	0	8	0	11	1	0	1	.000	0-0	0	96	.803	5.76	2.89
2020	ChC	NL	3	0	0	1.2	9	4	3	3	0	0	0	0	1	0	0	1	0	0	-	0-0	0	97	1.181	14.52	16.20
3 ML YEARS			23	0	8	22.0	107	27	14	11	1	0	2	0	14	0	21	3	0	2	.000	0-0	2	97	.790	5.78	4.50

Jacob Nottingham

Bats: R Throws: R Pos: C-19;PH-1;PR-1 Ht: 6'2" Wt: 220 Born: 4/3/1995 Age: 26

Year	Team	Lg	G	AB	H	2B	3B	HR	(Hm	Rd)	TB	R	RBI	RC	TBB	IBB	SO	HBP	SH	SF	SB	CS	GDP	Avg	OBP	Slg	OPS
2018	Mil	NL	9	20	4	1	0	0	(0	0)	5	2	0	1	4	0	8	0	0	0	0	0	0	.200	.333	.250	.583
2019	Mil	NL	9	6	2	0	0	1	(0	1)	5	1	4	3	0	0	2	1	0	0	0	0	0	.333	.429	.833	1.262
2020	Mil	NL	20	48	9	1	0	4	(3	1)	22	8	13	9	5	0	20	1	0	0	0	0	1	.188	.278	.458	.736
3 ML YEARS			38	74	15	2	0	5	(3	2)	32	11	17	13	9	0	30	2	0	0	0	0	1	.203	.306	.432	.738

Ivan Nova

ee-VAHN

Pitches: R Bats: R Pos: SP-4 Ht: 6'5" Wt: 250 Born: 1/12/1987 Age: 34

Year	Team	Lg	G	GS	GF	IP	BFP	H	R	ER	HR	SH	SF	HB	TBB	IBB	SO	WP	W	L	Pct	Sv-Op	Hld	Vel	OPS	ERC	ERA
2010	NYY	AL	10	7	3	42.0	185	44	22	21	4	1	1	1	17	2	26	2	1	2	.333	0-1	0	93	.729	4.31	4.50
2011	NYY	AL	28	27	1	165.1	704	163	74	68	13	2	6	6	57	3	98	11	16	4	.800	0-0	0	93	.706	3.76	3.70
2012	NYY	AL	28	28	0	170.1	748	194	100	95	28	3	6	10	56	3	153	6	12	8	.600	0-0	0	93	.860	5.32	5.02
2013	NYY	AL	23	20	2	139.1	586	135	49	48	9	2	3	14	44	3	116	3	9	6	.600	0-0	0	93	.678	3.77	3.10
2014	NYY	AL	4	4	0	20.2	96	32	19	19	6	0	2	2	6	0	12	1	2	2	.500	0-0	0	92	1.033	9.40	8.27
2015	NYY	AL	17	17	0	94.0	413	99	54	53	13	3	2	7	33	0	63	5	6	11	.353	0-0	0	93	.793	4.75	5.07
2016	2 Tms		32	26	3	162.0	684	175	81	75	23	5	6	9	28	1	127	10	12	8	.600	1-1	0	93	.778	4.12	4.17
2017	Pit	NL	31	31	0	187.0	785	203	96	86	29	7	3	7	36	2	131	8	11	14	.440	0-0	0	93	.781	4.27	4.14
2018	Pit	NL	29	29	0	161.0	683	171	82	75	26	4	2	4	35	4	114	9	9	9	.500	0-0	0	93	.769	4.15	4.19
2019	CWS	AL	34	34	0	187.0	806	225	107	98	30	2	4	9	47	1	114	7	11	12	.478	0-0	0	92	.833	5.40	4.72
2020	Det	AL	4	4	0	19.0	88	22	18	18	4	0	0	0	9	0	9	2	1	1	.500	0-0	0	92	.833	6.01	8.53
16	NYY	AL	21	15	3	97.1	421	107	54	53	19	1	2	6	25	1	75	7	7	6	.538	1-1	0	92	.827	4.98	4.90
16	Pit	NL	11	11	0	64.2	263	68	27	22	4	4	4	3	3	0	52	3	5	2	.714	0-0	0	93	.699	2.93	3.06
Postseason			2	1	0	8.1	34	7	4	4	2	0	0	0	4	0	8	0	1	1	.500	0-0	0	92	.790	4.66	4.32
11 ML YEARS			240	227	9	1347.2	5778	1463	702	656	185	29	35	69	368	19	963	64	90	77	.539	1-2	0	93	.782	4.54	4.38

Eduardo Nunez

Bats: R Throws: R Pos: RF-1;DH-1;PR-1 Ht: 6'0" Wt: 195 Born: 6/15/1987 Age: 34

Year	Team	Lg	G	AB	H	2B	3B	HR	(Hm	Rd)	TB	R	RBI	RC	TBB	IBB	SO	HBP	SH	SF	SB	CS	GDP	Avg	OBP	Slg	OPS
2010	NYY	AL	30	50	14	1	0	1	(0	1)	18	12	7	8	3	0	2	0	0	0	5	0	4	.280	.321	.360	.681
2011	NYY	AL	112	309	82	18	2	5	(2	3)	119	38	30	42	22	2	37	0	6	1	22	6	6	.265	.313	.385	.698
2012	NYY	AL	38	89	26	4	1	1	(1	0)	35	14	11	15	6	0	12	1	0	4	11	2	1	.292	.330	.393	.723
2013	NYY	AL	90	304	79	17	4	3	(2	1)	113	38	28	31	20	1	51	3	4	5	10	3	3	.260	.307	.372	.679
2014	Min	AL	72	204	51	7	4	4	(4	0)	78	26	24	21	5	0	31	1	3	0	9	3	7	.250	.271	.382	.654
2015	Min	AL	72	188	53	14	1	4	(3	1)	81	23	20	25	12	0	29	1	2	1	8	4	1	.282	.327	.431	.758
2016	2 Tms		141	553	159	24	4	16	(8	8)	239	73	67	74	29	3	88	5	2	6	40	10	8	.288	.325	.432	.758
2017	2 Tms		114	467	146	33	0	12	(5	7)	215	60	58	76	18	0	54	3	1	2	24	7	11	.313	.341	.460	.801
2018	Bos	AL	127	480	127	23	3	10	(6	4)	186	56	44	47	16	0	69	2	1	3	7	2	17	.265	.289	.388	.677
2019	Bos	AL	60	167	38	7	0	2	(0	2)	51	13	20	13	4	0	27	0	1	2	5	1	6	.228	.243	.305	.548
2020	NYM	NL	2	2	1	0	0	0	(0	0)	1	0	0	0	0	0	0	0	0	0	1	0	0	.500	.500	.500	1.000
16	Min	AL	91	371	110	15	1	12	(6	6)	163	49	47	54	15	0	58	3	2	5	27	6	6	.296	.325	.439	.764
16	SF		50	182	49	9	3	4	(2	2)	76	24	20	20	14	3	30	2	0	1	13	4	2	.269	.327	.418	.744
17	SF	NL	76	302	93	21	0	4	(1	3)	126	37	31	45	12	0	29	1	1	2	18	5	8	.308	.334	.417	.752
17	Bos	AL	38	165	53	12	0	8	(4	4)	89	23	27	31	6	0	25	2	0	0	6	2	3	.321	.353	.539	.892
Postseason			18	41	9	2	1	2	(1	1)	19	5	5	5	2	0	5	0	0	0	2	0	0	.220	.256	.463	.719
11 ML YEARS			858	2813	776	148	19	58	(31	27)	1136	353	309	352	135	6	400	16	20	24	142	38	64	.276	.310	.404	.714

Renato Nunez

Bats: R Throws: R Pos: 1B-28;DH-21;3B-4;PH-1 Ht: 6'1" Wt: 220 Born: 4/4/1994 Age: 27

Year	Team	Lg	G	AB	H	2B	3B	HR	(Hm	Rd)	TB	R	RBI	RC	TBB	IBB	SO	HBP	SH	SF	SB	CS	GDP	Avg	OBP	Slg	OPS
2016	Oak	AL	9	15	2	0	0	0	(0	0)	2	0	1	0	0	0	3	0	0	0	0	0	0	.133	.133	.133	.267
2017	Oak	AL	8	15	3	0	0	1	(0	1)	6	1	3	3	1	0	8	0	0	0	0	0	0	.200	.250	.400	.650
2018	2 Tms		73	236	61	14	0	8	(0	8)	99	28	22	26	19	0	62	4	0	2	0	0	4	.258	.322	.419	.741
2019	Bal	AL	151	541	132	24	0	31	(16	15)	249	72	90	81	44	1	143	10	0	4	1	1	9	.244	.311	.460	.771
2020	Bal	AL	52	195	50	10	0	12	(7	5)	96	29	31	26	17	0	64	3	0	1	0	0	4	.256	.324	.492	.816
18	Tex	AL	13	36	6	1	0	1	(0	1)	10	2	2	1	3	0	12	1	0	1	0	0	0	.167	.244	.278	.522
18	Bal	AL	60	200	55	13	0	7	(0	7)	89	26	20	25	16	0	50	3	0	1	0	0	4	.275	.336	.445	.781
5 ML YEARS			293	1002	248	48	0	52	(23	29)	452	130	147	136	81	1	280	17	0	7	1	1	17	.248	.313	.451	.764

Scott Oberg

Pitches: R **Bats:** R **Pos:** P

Ht: 6'2" **Wt:** 207 **Born:** 3/13/1990 **Age:** 31

Year	Team	Lg	HOW MUCH PITCHED					WHAT HE GAVE UP										THE RESULTS						
			G	GS	GF	IP	BFP	H	R	ER	HR	SH	SF	HB	TBB	IBB	SO	WP	W	L	Pct	Sv-Op	Hld	Vel	OPS	ERC	ERA
2015	Col	NL	64	0	11	58.1	259	58	35	33	10	3	1	6	31	2	44	6	3	4	.429	1-3	15	95	.839	5.60	5.09
2016	Col	NL	24	0	9	26.0	113	26	15	15	3	0	0	1	11	2	20	3	1	1	.500	1-2	1	95	.713	4.33	5.19
2017	Col	NL	66	0	12	58.1	265	70	35	32	4	1	2	2	24	2	55	3	0	1	.000	0-1	14	96	.800	5.11	4.94
2018	Col	NL	56	0	7	58.2	228	45	17	16	4	0	2	3	12	0	57	3	8	1	.889	0-4	14	95	.571	2.20	2.45
2019	Col	NL	49	0	18	56.0	223	39	18	14	5	0	1	0	23	2	58	3	6	1	.857	5-8	8	94	.569	2.46	2.25
	Postseason		5	0	1	4.1	17	4	2	0	0	0	0	0	0	0	12	1	1	0	1.000	0-0	0	97	.588	1.64	4.15
	5 ML YEARS		259	0	57	257.1	1088	238	120	110	26	4	6	12	101	8	234	18	18	8	.692	7-18	52	95	.703	3.82	3.85

Darren O'Day

Pitches: R **Bats:** R **Pos:** RP-19

Ht: 6'4" **Wt:** 220 **Born:** 10/22/1982 **Age:** 38

Year	Team	Lg	HOW MUCH PITCHED					WHAT HE GAVE UP										THE RESULTS						
			G	GS	GF	IP	BFP	H	R	ER	HR	SH	SF	HB	TBB	IBB	SO	WP	W	L	Pct	Sv-Op	Hld	Vel	OPS	ERC	ERA
2008	LAA	AL	30	0	17	43.1	194	49	24	22	2	2	1	4	14	6	29	1	0	1	.000	0-0	1	87	.719	4.20	4.57
2009	2 Tms		68	0	15	58.2	233	41	14	12	3	1	3	5	18	1	56	1	2	1	.667	2-2	20	85	.543	2.20	1.84
2010	Tex	AL	72	0	14	62.0	240	43	15	14	5	1	3	5	12	2	45	0	6	2	.750	0-2	22	86	.548	1.93	2.03
2011	Tex	AL	16	0	7	16.2	74	17	10	10	7	1	1	2	5	0	18	0	0	1	.000	0-0	3	84	.929	6.45	5.40
2012	Bal	AL	69	0	10	67.0	263	49	17	17	6	3	1	3	14	2	69	0	7	1	.875	0-2	15	85	.613	2.06	2.28
2013	Bal	AL	68	0	18	62.0	247	47	16	15	7	1	1	5	15	1	59	1	5	3	.625	2-6	20	86	.617	2.60	2.18
2014	Bal	AL	68	0	18	68.2	271	42	14	13	6	1	2	8	19	4	73	0	5	2	.714	4-8	25	87	.550	1.92	1.70
2015	Bal	AL	68	0	19	65.1	257	47	13	11	5	0	1	5	14	1	82	0	6	2	.750	6-11	18	87	.540	2.09	1.52
2016	Bal	AL	34	0	6	31.0	131	25	13	13	6	0	0	1	13	2	38	0	3	1	.750	3-5	10	86	.717	3.70	3.77
2017	Bal	AL	64	0	16	60.1	240	41	24	23	8	0	1	3	24	2	76	0	2	3	.400	2-4	17	88	.609	2.79	3.43
2018	Bal	AL	20	0	10	20.0	83	18	9	8	3	0	0	3	4	1	27	0	0	2	.000	2-4	4	87	.722	3.61	3.60
2019	Atl	NL	8	0	0	5.1	21	3	1	1	0	0	0	1	1	0	6	0	0	0	-	0-0	0	87	.554	1.35	1.69
2020	Atl	NL	19	0	1	16.1	67	8	3	2	1	0	0	3	5	0	22	0	4	0	1.000	0-1	2	86	.442	1.57	1.10
09	NYM	NL	4	0	1	3.0	17	5	2	0	0	0	1	1	1	0	2	0	0	0	-	0-0	0	84	.769	7.72	0.00
09	Tex	AL	64	0	14	55.2	216	36	12	12	3	1	2	4	17	1	54	1	2	1	.667	2-2	20	85	.526	1.95	1.94
	Postseason		25	0	1	18.0	67	12	8	8	4	1	0	1	3	0	18	0	0	3	.000	0-0	5	86	.630	2.47	4.00
	13 ML YEARS		604	0	151	576.2	2321	430	173	161	59	10	14	48	158	22	600	3	40	19	.678	21-45	157	86	.607	2.55	2.51

Joseph Odom

Bats: R **Throws:** R **Pos:** C-18;PH-1

Ht: 6'2" **Wt:** 215 **Born:** 1/9/1992 **Age:** 29

Year	Team	Lg	BATTING																RUNNING			AVERAGES			
			G	AB	H	2B	3B	HR	(Hm | Rd)	TB	R	RBI	RC	TBB	IBB	SO	HBP	SH	SF	SB	CS	GDP	Avg	OBP	Slg	OPS
2020	Sea	AL	18	39	5	0	0	0	(0 | 0)	5	2	2	1	4	0	20	0	1	0	0	0	1	.128	.209	.128	.338

Rougned Odor

Bats: L **Throws:** R **Pos:** 2B-37;DH-1

ROOG-ned oh-DORE

Ht: 5'11" **Wt:** 200 **Born:** 2/3/1994 **Age:** 27

Year	Team	Lg	BATTING																RUNNING			AVERAGES			
			G	AB	H	2B	3B	HR	(Hm | Rd)	TB	R	RBI	RC	TBB	IBB	SO	HBP	SH	SF	SB	CS	GDP	Avg	OBP	Slg	OPS
2014	Tex	AL	114	386	100	14	7	9	(4 | 5)	155	39	48	46	17	1	71	5	6	3	4	7	7	.259	.297	.402	.698
2015	Tex	AL	120	426	111	21	9	16	(7 | 9)	198	54	61	62	23	2	79	14	2	5	6	7	3	.261	.316	.465	.781
2016	Tex	AL	150	605	164	33	4	33	(17 | 16)	304	89	88	77	19	0	135	4	0	4	14	7	6	.271	.296	.502	.798
2017	Tex	AL	162	607	124	21	3	30	(18 | 12)	241	79	75	61	32	5	162	8	0	4	15	6	13	.204	.252	.397	.649
2018	Tex	AL	129	474	120	23	2	18	(10 | 8)	201	76	63	67	43	2	127	11	2	5	12	12	5	.253	.326	.424	.751
2019	Tex	AL	145	522	107	30	1	30	(15 | 15)	229	77	93	77	52	2	178	5	1	1	11	9	4	.205	.283	.439	.721
2020	Tex	AL	38	138	23	4	0	10	(6 | 4)	57	15	30	16	7	0	47	1	0	2	0	1	2	.167	.209	.413	.623
	Postseason		8	28	7	1	0	2	(0 | 2)	14	9	4	5	3	0	5	2	0	0	0	0	0	.250	.364	.500	.864
	7 ML YEARS		858	3158	749	146	26	146	(77 | 69)	1385	429	458	406	193	12	799	48	11	24	62	49	40	.237	.289	.439	.728

Jake Odorizzi

Pitches: R **Bats:** R **Pos:** SP-4

oh-duh-RIZZ-ee

Ht: 6'2" **Wt:** 190 **Born:** 3/27/1990 **Age:** 31

Year	Team	Lg	HOW MUCH PITCHED					WHAT HE GAVE UP										THE RESULTS						
			G	GS	GF	IP	BFP	H	R	ER	HR	SH	SF	HB	TBB	IBB	SO	WP	W	L	Pct	Sv-Op	Hld	Vel	OPS	ERC	ERA
2012	KC	AL	2	2	0	7.1	34	8	4	4	1	0	0	4	4	0	4	0	0	1	.000	0-0	0	90	.820	5.34	4.91
2013	TB	AL	7	4	2	29.2	122	28	13	13	3	0	1	2	8	0	22	1	0	1	.000	1-1	0	91	.744	3.62	3.94
2014	TB	AL	31	31	0	168.0	719	156	79	77	20	3	8	5	59	0	174	3	11	13	.458	0-0	0	90	.692	3.68	4.13
2015	TB	AL	28	28	0	169.1	700	149	65	63	18	4	3	3	46	0	150	5	9	9	.500	0-0	0	91	.680	3.02	3.35
2016	TB	AL	33	33	0	187.2	773	170	80	77	29	3	6	4	54	3	166	3	10	6	.625	0-0	0	92	.715	3.56	3.69
2017	TB	AL	28	28	0	143.1	604	117	80	66	30	2	7	2	61	1	127	1	10	8	.556	0-0	0	92	.736	3.91	4.14
2018	Min	AL	32	32	0	164.1	711	151	89	82	20	4	4	8	70	3	162	1	7	10	.412	0-0	0	91	.743	4.02	4.49
2019	Min	AL	30	30	0	159.0	658	139	65	62	16	4	4	4	53	0	178	4	15	7	.682	0-0	0	93	.671	3.25	3.51
2020	Min	AL	4	4	0	13.2	60	16	10	10	4	0	0	1	3	0	12	0	0	1	.000	0-0	0	93	.903	6.00	6.59
	Postseason		1	1	0	5.0	20	5	2	2	1	0	0	0	0	0	5	1	0	1	.000	0-0	0	93	.737	3.05	3.60
	9 ML YEARS		195	192	2	1042.1	4381	934	485	454	141	20	33	29	358	7	995	18	62	56	.525	1-1	0	91	.711	3.61	3.92

Brian O'Grady

Bats: L **Throws:** R **Pos:** 1B-1;LF-1;CF-1   **Ht:** 6'2" **Wt:** 215 **Born:** 5/17/1992 **Age:** 29

| | | | | BATTING | | | | | | | | | | | | | | | | | RUNNING | | | AVERAGES | | | |
Year	Team	Lg	G	AB	H	2B	3B	HR	(Hm	Rd)	TB	R	RBI	RC	TBB	IBB	SO	HBP	SH	SF	SB	CS	GDP	Avg	OBP	Slg	OPS
2019	Cin	NL	28	42	8	2	1	2	(0	2)	18	4	3	4	4	0	17	2	0	0	0	0	0	.190	.292	.429	.720
2020	TB	AL	2	5	2	1	0	0	(0	0)	3	2	0	0	0	0	1	0	0	0	1	0	0	.400	.400	.600	1.000
	2 ML YEARS		30	47	10	3	1	2	(0	2)	21	6	3	4	4	0	18	2	0	0	1	0	0	.213	.302	.447	.749

Ryan O'Hearn

Bats: L **Throws:** L **Pos:** 1B-27;PH-11;DH-8   **Ht:** 6'3" **Wt:** 220 **Born:** 7/26/1993 **Age:** 27

| | | | | BATTING | | | | | | | | | | | | | | | | | RUNNING | | | AVERAGES | | | |
Year	Team	Lg	G	AB	H	2B	3B	HR	(Hm	Rd)	TB	R	RBI	RC	TBB	IBB	SO	HBP	SH	SF	SB	CS	GDP	Avg	OBP	Slg	OPS
2018	KC	AL	44	149	39	11	2	12	(5	7)	89	23	30	20	20	0	45	1	0	0	0	0	0	.262	.353	.597	.950
2019	KC	AL	105	328	64	13	1	14	(6	8)	121	32	38	25	39	1	99	1	0	2	0	1	7	.195	.281	.369	.650
2020	KC	AL	42	113	22	6	0	2	(0	2)	34	7	18	14	18	2	37	0	0	1	0	0	5	.195	.303	.301	.604
	3 ML YEARS		191	590	125	29	3	28	(11	17)	244	62	86	72	77	3	181	2	0	3	0	1	12	.212	.304	.414	.717

Shohei Ohtani

Bats: L **Throws:** R **Pos:** DH-40;PH-3;PR-1   **Ht:** 6'4" **Wt:** 210 **Born:** 7/5/1994 **Age:** 26

| | | | | BATTING | | | | | | | | | | | | | | | | | RUNNING | | | AVERAGES | | | |
Year	Team	Lg	G	AB	H	2B	3B	HR	(Hm	Rd)	TB	R	RBI	RC	TBB	IBB	SO	HBP	SH	SF	SB	CS	GDP	Avg	OBP	Slg	OPS
2018	LAA	AL	114	326	93	21	2	22	(15	7)	184	59	61	70	37	2	102	2	0	1	10	4	2	.285	.361	.564	.925
2019	LAA	AL	106	384	110	20	5	18	(11	7)	194	51	62	68	33	1	110	2	0	4	12	3	6	.286	.343	.505	.848
2020	LAA	AL	46	153	29	6	0	7	(4	3)	56	23	24	16	22	0	50	0	0	0	7	1	3	.190	.291	.366	.657
	3 ML YEARS		266	863	232	47	7	47	(30	17)	434	133	147	154	92	3	262	4	0	5	29	8	11	.269	.340	.503	.843

Shohei Ohtani

Pitches: R **Bats:** L **Pos:** SP-2   **Ht:** 6'4" **Wt:** 210 **Born:** 7/5/1994 **Age:** 26

| | | | HOW MUCH PITCHED | | | | | WHAT HE GAVE UP | | | | | | | | | | THE RESULTS | | | | | | | |
Year	Team	Lg	G	GS	GF	IP	BFP	H	R	ER	HR	SH	SF	HB	TBB	IBB	SO	WP	W	L	Pct	Sv-Op	Hld	Vel	OPS	ERC	ERA
2018	LAA	AL	10	10	0	51.2	211	38	19	19	6	0	1	1	22	0	63	5	4	2	.667	0-0	0	97	.621	2.96	3.31
2020	LAA	AL	2	2	0	1.2	16	3	7	7	0	0	0	0	8	0	3	1	0	1	.000	0-0	0	94	1.063	28.51	37.80
	2 ML YEARS		12	12	0	53.1	227	41	26	26	6	0	1	1	30	0	66	6	4	3	.571	0-0	0	96	.651	3.60	4.39

Jared Oliva

Bats: R **Throws:** R **Pos:** LF-4;CF-1;PH-1   **Ht:** 6'2" **Wt:** 195 **Born:** 11/27/1995 **Age:** 25

| | | | | BATTING | | | | | | | | | | | | | | | | | RUNNING | | | AVERAGES | | | |
Year	Team	Lg	G	AB	H	2B	3B	HR	(Hm	Rd)	TB	R	RBI	RC	TBB	IBB	SO	HBP	SH	SF	SB	CS	GDP	Avg	OBP	Slg	OPS
2020	Pit	NL	6	16	3	0	0	0	(0	0)	3	0	0	0	0	0	6	0	0	0	1	0	0	.188	.188	.188	.375

Edward Olivares

Bats: R **Throws:** R **Pos:** LF-14;CF-11;RF-11;PH-2   **Ht:** 6'2" **Wt:** 188 **Born:** 3/6/1996 **Age:** 25

| | | | | BATTING | | | | | | | | | | | | | | | | | RUNNING | | | AVERAGES | | | |
Year	Team	Lg	G	AB	H	2B	3B	HR	(Hm	Rd)	TB	R	RBI	RC	TBB	IBB	SO	HBP	SH	SF	SB	CS	GDP	Avg	OBP	Slg	OPS
2020	2 Tms		31	96	23	2	1	3	(2	1)	36	9	10	8	4	0	25	0	0	1	0	2	1	.240	.267	.375	.642
20	SD	NL	13	34	6	1	0	1	(1	0)	10	4	3	2	2	0	14	0	0	0	0	1	0	.176	.222	.294	.516
20	KC	AL	18	62	17	1	1	2	(1	1)	26	5	7	6	2	0	11	0	0	1	0	1	1	.274	.292	.419	.712

Matt Olson

Bats: L **Throws:** R **Pos:** 1B-60   **Ht:** 6'5" **Wt:** 225 **Born:** 3/29/1994 **Age:** 27

| | | | | BATTING | | | | | | | | | | | | | | | | | RUNNING | | | AVERAGES | | | |
Year	Team	Lg	G	AB	H	2B	3B	HR	(Hm	Rd)	TB	R	RBI	RC	TBB	IBB	SO	HBP	SH	SF	SB	CS	GDP	Avg	OBP	Slg	OPS
2016	Oak	AL	11	21	2	1	0	0	(0	0)	3	3	0	1	7	0	4	0	0	0	0	0	1	.095	.321	.143	.464
2017	Oak	AL	59	189	49	2	0	24	(12	12)	123	33	45	40	22	1	60	5	0	0	0	0	6	.259	.352	.651	1.003
2018	Oak	AL	**162**	580	143	33	0	29	(14	15)	263	85	84	86	70	3	163	8	0	2	2	1	13	.247	.335	.453	.788
2019	Oak	AL	127	483	129	26	0	36	(13	23)	263	73	91	92	51	7	138	12	0	1	0	0	11	.267	.351	.545	.896
2020	Oak	AL	60	210	41	4	1	14	(9	5)	89	28	42	34	34	2	77	1	0	0	1	0	2	.195	.310	.424	.734
	Postseason		2	5	1	0	0	0	(0	0)	1	0	0	0	3	0	1	0	0	0	0	0	1	.200	.500	.200	.700
	5 ML YEARS		419	1483	364	66	1	103	(48	55)	741	222	262	253	184	13	442	26	0	3	3	1	33	.245	.338	.500	.838

Jorge Ona

Bats: R **Throws:** R **Pos:** DH-4;RF-1   **Ht:** 6'0" **Wt:** 235 **Born:** 12/31/1996 **Age:** 24

| | | | | BATTING | | | | | | | | | | | | | | | | | RUNNING | | | AVERAGES | | | |
Year	Team	Lg	G	AB	H	2B	3B	HR	(Hm	Rd)	TB	R	RBI	RC	TBB	IBB	SO	HBP	SH	SF	SB	CS	GDP	Avg	OBP	Slg	OPS
2020	SD	NL	5	12	3	1	0	1	(1	0)	7	3	2	2	2	0	7	1	0	0	0	0	0	.250	.400	.583	.983

Tyler O'Neill

Bats: R Throws: R Pos: LF-48;DH-2;PH-2;PR-1   Ht: 5'11" Wt: 200 Born: 6/22/1995 Age: 26

							BATTING												RUNNING			AVERAGES			
Year	Team	Lg	G	AB	H	2B	3B	HR	(Hm | Rd)	TB	R	RBI	RC	TBB	IBB	SO	HBP	SH	SF	SB	CS	GDP	Avg	OBP	Slg	OPS
2018	StL	NL	61	130	33	5	0	9	(6 | 3)	65	29	23	24	7	0	57	3	0	2	2	0	0	.254	.303	.500	.803
2019	StL	NL	60	141	37	6	0	5	(4 | 1)	58	18	16	19	10	0	53	0	0	0	1	0	3	.262	.311	.411	.723
2020	StL	NL	50	139	24	5	0	7	(2 | 5)	50	20	19	15	15	0	43	2	0	1	3	1	3	.173	.261	.360	.621
	3 ML YEARS		171	410	94	16	0	21	(12 | 9)	173	67	58	58	32	0	153	5	0	3	6	1	6	.229	.291	.422	.713

Nate Orf

Bats: R Throws: R Pos: SS-3;2B-2;PH-2;PR-1   Ht: 5'8" Wt: 181 Born: 2/1/1990 Age: 31

							BATTING												RUNNING			AVERAGES			
Year	Team	Lg	G	AB	H	2B	3B	HR	(Hm	Rd)	TB	R	RBI	RC	TBB	IBB	SO	HBP	SH	SF	SB	CS	GDP	Avg	OBP	Slg	OPS
2018	Mil	NL	15	21	2	0	0	1	(1	0)	5	4	1	0	3	0	8	1	0	0	1	0	1	.095	.240	.238	.478
2020	Oak	AL	6	7	0	0	0	0	(0	0)	0	1	0	0	0	0	1	0	0	0	0	0	0	.000	.000	.000	.000
	2 ML YEARS		21	28	2	0	0	1	(1	0)	5	5	1	0	3	0	9	1	0	0	1	0	1	.071	.188	.179	.366

Josh Osich

Pitches: L Bats: L Pos: RP-16; SP-1   OH-sitch   Ht: 6'2" Wt: 235 Born: 9/3/1988 Age: 32

			HOW MUCH PITCHED				WHAT HE GAVE UP									THE RESULTS							
Year	Team	Lg	G	GS	GF	IP	BFP	H	R	ER	HR	SH	SF	HB	TBB	IBB	SO	WP	W	L	Pct	Sv-Op	Hld	Vel	OPS	ERC	ERA
2015	SF	NL	35	0	6	28.2	120	24	12	7	4	1	1	0	8	0	27	2	2	0	1.000	0-2	11	96	.633	2.88	2.20
2016	SF	NL	59	0	9	36.1	160	31	20	19	7	1	0	3	19	1	25	2	1	3	.250	0-3	18	95	.769	4.65	4.71
2017	SF	NL	54	0	12	43.1	201	48	32	30	7	1	0	1	27	1	43	5	3	2	.600	0-1	6	95	.839	6.18	6.23
2018	SF	NL	12	0	2	12.0	61	20	11	11	2	0	0	2	7	0	10	3	0	0	-	0-1	2	95	1.052	10.94	8.25
2019	CWS	AL	57	0	14	67.2	272	62	38	35	15	0	1	0	15	1	61	3	4	0	1.000	0-1	2	94	.752	3.72	4.66
2020	2 Tms		17	1	3	18.1	86	21	16	13	6	0	0	2	5	0	24	0	1	1	.500	0-0	1	92	.832	6.16	6.38
20	Bos	AL	13	1	3	15.2	70	16	10	10	6	0	0	1	5	0	20	0	1	1	.500	0-0	1	92	.846	5.92	5.74
20	ChC	NL	4	0	0	2.2	16	5	6	3	0	0	0	1	0	0	4	0	0	0	-	0-0	0	93	.775	7.22	10.13
	6 ML YEARS		234	1	46	206.1	900	206	129	115	41	3	2	8	81	3	190	15	11	6	.647	0-8	40	95	.786	4.85	5.02

Jose Osuna

Bats: R Throws: R Pos: 1B-9;RF-7;3B-5;LF-4;DH-4;PH-2   Ht: 6'2" Wt: 235 Born: 12/12/1992 Age: 28

							BATTING												RUNNING			AVERAGES			
Year	Team	Lg	G	AB	H	2B	3B	HR	(Hm	Rd)	TB	R	RBI	RC	TBB	IBB	SO	HBP	SH	SF	SB	CS	GDP	Avg	OBP	Slg	OPS
2017	Pit	NL	104	215	50	13	4	7	(3	4)	92	31	30	19	9	0	40	2	0	1	0	0	10	.233	.269	.428	.697
2018	Pit	NL	51	106	24	9	0	3	(2	1)	42	14	11	8	3	0	22	1	0	1	0	0	2	.226	.252	.396	.648
2019	Pit	NL	95	261	69	20	0	10	(4	6)	119	41	36	33	18	0	48	1	0	4	0	0	6	.264	.310	.456	.766
2020	Pit	NL	26	78	16	3	0	4	(1	3)	31	6	11	10	4	0	16	0	0	0	0	1	1	.205	.244	.397	.641
	4 ML YEARS		276	660	159	45	4	24	(10	14)	284	92	88	70	34	0	126	4	0	6	0	1	19	.241	.280	.430	.710

Roberto Osuna

Pitches: R Bats: R Pos: RP-4   Ht: 6'2" Wt: 217 Born: 2/7/1995 Age: 26

			HOW MUCH PITCHED				WHAT HE GAVE UP									THE RESULTS							
Year	Team	Lg	G	GS	GF	IP	BFP	H	R	ER	HR	SH	SF	HB	TBB	IBB	SO	WP	W	L	Pct	Sv-Op	Hld	Vel	OPS	ERC	ERA
2015	Tor	AL	68	0	39	69.2	271	48	21	20	7	1	2	1	16	2	75	5	1	6	.143	20-23	7	96	.591	1.89	2.58
2016	Tor	AL	72	0	61	74.0	288	55	23	22	9	1	3	3	14	4	82	4	4	3	.571	36-42	0	96	.603	2.20	2.68
2017	Tor	AL	66	0	58	64.0	249	46	26	24	3	1	2	3	9	0	83	4	3	4	.429	39-49	0	95	.507	1.61	3.38
2018	2 Tms	AL	38	0	31	38.0	150	33	10	10	1	0	1	4	4	0	32	3	2	2	.500	21-22	2	95	.578	2.27	2.37
2019	Hou	AL	66	0	56	65.0	253	45	20	19	8	1	1	2	12	0	73	1	4	3	.571	38-44	1	97	.555	1.95	2.63
2020	Hou	AL	4	0	2	4.1	16	3	1	1	0	0	0	0	0	0	3	0	0	0	-	1-1	1	94	.500	0.98	2.08
18	Tor	AL	15	0	13	15.1	63	16	5	5	0	0	0	2	1	0	13	1	0	0	-	9-10	0	95	.618	2.90	2.93
18	Hou	AL	23	0	18	22.2	87	17	5	5	1	0	1	2	3	0	19	2	2	2	.500	12-12	2	95	.549	1.87	1.99
	Postseason		27	0	21	33.1	127	19	11	11	3	0	0	2	7	0	30	2	2	1	.667	5-6	1	96	.492	1.50	2.97
	6 ML YEARS		314	0	247	315.0	1227	230	101	96	28	4	9	13	55	6	348	17	14	18	.438	155-181	10	96	.567	1.94	2.74

Corey Oswalt

Pitches: R Bats: R Pos: RP-3; SP-1   Ht: 6'5" Wt: 250 Born: 9/3/1993 Age: 27

			HOW MUCH PITCHED				WHAT HE GAVE UP									THE RESULTS							
Year	Team	Lg	G	GS	GF	IP	BFP	H	R	ER	HR	SH	SF	HB	TBB	IBB	SO	WP	W	L	Pct	Sv-Op	Hld	Vel	OPS	ERC	ERA
2018	NYM	NL	17	12	2	64.2	282	69	43	42	14	1	0	4	20	1	45	4	3	3	.500	0-0	1	90	.806	5.14	5.85
2019	NYM	NL	2	0	0	6.2	34	9	9	9	1	0	0	0	6	1	5	0	0	1	.000	0-0	0	92	1.013	8.55	12.15
2020	NYM	NL	4	1	2	13.0	55	14	7	7	3	0	0	1	2	0	11	0	0	0	-	0-0	1	92	.886	4.71	4.85
	3 ML YEARS		23	13	4	84.1	371	92	59	58	18	1	0	5	28	2	61	4	3	4	.429	0-0	1	91	.836	5.34	6.19

Adam Ottavino

Pitches: R Bats: B Pos: RP-24   ott-tah-VEE-no   Ht: 6'5" Wt: 246 Born: 11/22/1985 Age: 35

			HOW MUCH PITCHED				WHAT HE GAVE UP									THE RESULTS							
Year	Team	Lg	G	GS	GF	IP	BFP	H	R	ER	HR	SH	SF	HB	TBB	IBB	SO	WP	W	L	Pct	Sv-Op	Hld	Vel	OPS	ERC	ERA
2010	StL	NL	5	3	0	22.1	110	37	21	21	5	1	0	0	9	1	12	1	0	2	.000	0-0	0	93	1.072	9.22	8.46
2012	Col	NL	53	0	6	79.0	339	76	42	40	9	3	1	1	34	4	81	8	5	1	.833	0-2	5	94	.717	4.01	4.56
2013	Col	NL	51	0	5	78.1	335	73	27	23	5	6	4	2	31	5	78	9	1	3	.250	0-0	8	91	.672	3.42	2.64
2014	Col	NL	75	0	16	65.0	272	67	26	26	6	2	3	4	16	1	70	4	1	4	.200	1-6	21	94	.735	3.87	3.60
2015	Col	NL	10	0	5	10.1	35	3	0	0	0	0	0	0	2	0	13	0	1	0	1.000	3-3	3	96	.265	0.56	0.00
2016	Col	NL	34	0	19	27.0	107	18	9	8	3	0	0	2	7	0	35	4	1	3	.250	7-12	4	94	.528	2.17	2.67

Year	Team	Lg	G	GS	GF	IP	BFP	H	R	ER	HR	SH	SF	HB	TBB	IBB	SO	WP	W	L	Pct	Sv-Op	Hld	Vel	OPS	ERC	ERA
2017	Col	NL	63	0	11	53.1	243	48	30	30	8	0	3	4	39	2	63	8	2	3	.400	0-2	21	94	.786	5.51	5.06
2018	Col	NL	75	0	16	77.2	309	41	25	21	5	1	5	6	36	5	112	7	6	4	.600	6-11	34	94	.509	1.89	2.43
2019	NYY	AL	73	0	7	66.1	283	47	17	14	5	0	3	2	40	3	88	3	6	5	.545	2-9	28	94	.624	3.13	1.90
2020	NYY	AL	24	0	4	18.1	85	20	12	12	2	0	1	1	9	0	25	1	2	3	.400	0-3	2	93	.772	5.13	5.89
	Postseason		11	0	1	7.0	39	10	6	5	1	0	0	0	6	1	7	3	0	1	.000	0-1	0	94	.921	8.10	6.43
	10 ML YEARS		463	3	89	497.2	2118	430	209	195	48	13	20	23	223	24	577	45	25	28	.472	19-48	127	94	.682	3.61	3.53

Johan Oviedo

Pitches: R **Bats:** R **Pos:** SP-5

Ht: 6'5" **Wt:** 245 **Born:** 3/2/1998 **Age:** 23

Year	Team	Lg	G	GS	GF	IP	BFP	H	R	ER	HR	SH	SF	HB	TBB	IBB	SO	WP	W	L	Pct	Sv-Op	Hld	Vel	OPS	ERC	ERA
2020	StL	NL	5	5	0	24.2	112	24	18	15	3	0	2	5	10	0	16	4	0	3	.000	0-0	0	95	.780	4.84	5.47

Chris Owings

Bats: R **Throws:** R **Pos:** 2B-8;PH-3;3B-2;LF-2;CF-2;RF-2;PR-2;SS-1

Ht: 5'10" **Wt:** 185 **Born:** 8/12/1991 **Age:** 29

Year	Team	Lg	G	AB	H	2B	3B	HR	(Hm	Rd)	TB	R	RBI	RC	TBB	IBB	SO	HBP	SH	SF	SB	CS	GDP	Avg	OBP	Slg	OPS
2013	Ari	NL	20	55	16	5	0	0	(0	0)	21	5	5	7	6	1	10	0	0	0	2	0	0	.291	.361	.382	.742
2014	Ari	NL	91	310	81	15	6	6	(1	5)	126	34	26	38	16	0	67	2	2	2	8	1	4	.261	.300	.406	.706
2015	Ari	NL	147	515	117	27	5	4	(3	1)	166	59	43	41	26	3	144	1	7	3	16	4	9	.227	.264	.322	.587
2016	Ari	NL	119	437	121	24	11	5	(5	0)	182	52	49	60	20	4	87	5	2	2	21	2	8	.277	.315	.416	.731
2017	Ari	NL	97	362	97	25	1	12	(8	4)	160	41	51	48	17	0	87	1	2	4	12	2	3	.268	.299	.442	.741
2018	Ari	NL	106	281	58	15	0	4	(3	1)	85	34	22	25	24	4	75	2	0	2	11	4	4	.206	.272	.302	.574
2019	2 Tms	NL	67	180	25	6	1	3	(0	3)	42	13	14	7	14	0	78	2	0	0	5	2	2	.139	.209	.233	.443
2020	Col	NL	17	41	11	1	0	2	(2	0)	18	9	5	6	3	0	11	0	0	0	1	0	0	.268	.318	.439	.757
19	KC	AL	41	135	18	4	1	2	(0	2)	30	9	9	4	8	0	55	2	0	0	4	1	1	.133	.193	.222	.415
19	Bos	AL	26	45	7	2	0	1	(0	1)	12	4	5	3	6	0	23	0	0	0	1	1	1	.156	.255	.267	.522
	8 ML YEARS		664	2181	526	118	24	36	(22	14)	800	247	215	232	126	12	559	13	13	13	76	15	30	.241	.285	.367	.652

Marcell Ozuna

Bats: R **Throws:** R **Pos:** DH-39;LF-19;RF-2

oh-ZUNE-uh

Ht: 6'1" **Wt:** 225 **Born:** 11/12/1990 **Age:** 30

Year	Team	Lg	G	AB	H	2B	3B	HR	(Hm	Rd)	TB	R	RBI	RC	TBB	IBB	SO	HBP	SH	SF	SB	CS	GDP	Avg	OBP	Slg	OPS
2013	Mia	NL	70	275	73	17	4	3	(0	3)	107	31	32	35	13	0	57	2	1	0	5	1	6	.265	.303	.389	.693
2014	Mia	NL	153	565	152	26	5	23	(12	11)	257	72	85	74	41	1	164	1	0	5	3	1	12	.269	.317	.455	.772
2015	Mia	NL	123	459	119	27	0	10	(2	8)	176	47	44	48	30	1	110	3	0	2	2	3	10	.259	.308	.383	.691
2016	Mia	NL	148	557	148	23	6	23	(12	11)	252	75	76	69	43	2	115	4	0	4	0	3	11	.266	.321	.452	.773
2017	Mia	NL	159	613	191	30	2	37	(22	15)	336	93	124	117	64	4	144	0	0	2	1	3	18	.312	.376	.548	.924
2018	StL	NL	148	582	163	16	2	23	(13	10)	252	69	88	86	38	2	110	3	0	4	3	0	10	.280	.325	.433	.758
2019	StL	NL	130	485	117	23	1	29	(13	16)	229	80	89	73	62	2	114	1	0	1	12	2	21	.241	.328	.472	.800
2020	Atl	NL	60	228	77	14	0	18	(8	10)	145	38	56	56	38	3	60	0	0	1	0	0	3	.338	.431	.636	1.067
	Postseason		9	37	12	4	0	2	(2	0)	22	6	5	5	1	0	13	1	0	0	0	0	1	.324	.359	.595	.954
	8 ML YEARS		991	3764	1040	176	20	166	(82	84)	1754	505	594	560	329	15	874	14	1	19	26	13	91	.276	.335	.466	.801

Cristian Pache

Bats: R **Throws:** R **Pos:** LF-2

PAH-chay

Ht: 6'2" **Wt:** 215 **Born:** 11/19/1998 **Age:** 22

Year	Team	Lg	G	AB	H	2B	3B	HR	(Hm	Rd)	TB	R	RBI	RC	TBB	IBB	SO	HBP	SH	SF	SB	CS	GDP	Avg	OBP	Slg	OPS
2016	2 Tms	Low	57	220	68	4	7	0	(-	-)	86	28	21	30	13	0	24	1	1	1	11	5	5	.309	.349	.391	.740
2017	Rome	A	119	469	132	13	8	0	(-	-)	161	60	42	57	39	1	104	0	4	2	32	14	6	.281	.335	.343	.679
2018	Florida	A+	93	369	105	20	5	8	(-	-)	159	46	40	49	15	2	69	0	0	2	7	6	5	.285	.311	.431	.742
2018	Missi	AA	29	104	27	3	1	1	(-	-)	35	10	7	9	5	0	28	0	0	0	0	2	1	.260	.294	.337	.630
2019	Missi	AA	104	392	109	28	8	11	(-	-)	186	50	53	61	34	1	104	4	1	2	8	11	7	.278	.340	.474	.815
2019	Gwnntt	AAA	26	95	26	8	1	1	(-	-)	39	13	8	13	9	0	18	0	1	0	0	0	3	.274	.337	.411	.747
2020	Atl	NL	2	4	1	0	0	0	(0	0)	1	0	0	0	0	0	2	0	0	0	0	0	0	.250	.250	.250	.500

Chris Paddack

Pitches: R **Bats:** R **Pos:** SP-12

Ht: 6'5" **Wt:** 217 **Born:** 1/8/1996 **Age:** 25

Year	Team	Lg	G	GS	GF	IP	BFP	H	R	ER	HR	SH	SF	HB	TBB	IBB	SO	WP	W	L	Pct	Sv-Op	Hld	Vel	OPS	ERC	ERA
2019	SD	NL	26	26	0	140.2	568	107	58	52	23	4	3	6	31	1	153	1	9	7	.563	0-0	0	94	.635	2.62	3.33
2020	SD	NL	12	12	0	59.0	245	60	33	31	14	0	2	2	12	0	58	0	4	5	.444	0-0	0	94	.817	4.46	4.73
	2 ML YEARS		38	38	0	199.2	813	167	91	83	37	4	5	8	43	1	211	1	13	12	.520	0-0	0	94	.690	3.13	3.74

Emilio Pagan

Pitches: R **Bats:** L **Pos:** RP-22

Ht: 6'2" **Wt:** 208 **Born:** 5/7/1991 **Age:** 30

Year	Team	Lg	G	GS	GF	IP	BFP	H	R	ER	HR	SH	SF	HB	TBB	IBB	SO	WP	W	L	Pct	Sv-Op	Hld	Vel	OPS	ERC	ERA
2017	Sea	AL	34	0	9	50.1	196	39	20	18	7	1	2	1	8	0	56	1	2	3	.400	0-1	8	94	.610	2.32	3.22
2018	Oak	AL	55	0	17	62.0	262	55	30	30	13	0	1	3	19	1	63	3	3	1	.750	0-0	6	94	.767	3.92	4.35

Year	Team	Lg	G	GS	GF	IP	BFP	H	R	ER	HR	SH	SF	HB	TBB	IBB	SO	WP	W	L	Pct	Sv-Op	Hld	Vel	OPS	ERC	ERA
												WHAT HE GAVE UP							**THE RESULTS**								
2019	TB	AL	66	0	29	70.0	267	45	19	18	12	0	1	1	13	1	96	3	4	2	.667	20-28	7	96	.590	1.91	2.31
2020	SD	NL	22	0	5	22.0	87	14	11	11	4	0	1	0	9	0	23	0	0	1	.000	2-7	7	95	.641	2.73	4.50
	Postseason		4	0	1	3.0	17	5	3	2	2	0	0	0	2	0	2	0	0	0	-	0-0	1	97	1.212	13.76	6.00
	4 ML YEARS		177	0	60	204.1	812	153	80	77	36	1	5	5	49	2	238	7	9	7	.563	22-36	28	94	.657	2.67	3.39

Joe Palumbo

Pitches: L Bats: L Pos: RP-2 **Ht: 6'0" Wt: 195 Born: 10/26/1994 Age: 26**

Year	Team	Lg	G	GS	GF	IP	BFP	H	R	ER	HR	SH	SF	HB	TBB	IBB	SO	WP	W	L	Pct	Sv-Op	Hld	Vel	OPS	ERC	ERA
2019	Tex	AL	7	4	0	16.2	81	21	17	17	7	1	0	2	8	0	21	0	0	3	.000	0-0	0	94	1.073	8.98	9.18
2020	Tex	AL	2	0	0	2.1	14	3	3	3	1	0	0	0	3	0	5	0	0	1	.000	0-0	0	92	.974	11.79	11.57
	2 ML YEARS		9	4	0	19.0	95	24	20	20	8	1	0	2	11	0	26	0	0	4	.000	0-0	0	94	1.060	9.33	9.47

Joe Panik

Bats: L Throws: R Pos: 2B-18;SS-14;3B-12;PH-6;DH-2 PAN-ick **Ht: 6'1" Wt: 205 Born: 10/30/1990 Age: 30**

Year	Team	Lg	G	AB	H	2B	3B	HR	(Hm	Rd)	TB	R	RBI	RC	TBB	IBB	SO	HBP	SH	SF	SB	CS	GDP	Avg	OBP	Slg	OPS
2014	SF	NL	73	269	82	10	2	1	(0	1)	99	31	18	33	16	0	33	0	1	1	0	0	4	.305	.343	.368	.711
2015	SF	NL	100	382	119	27	2	8	(4	4)	174	59	37	60	38	0	42	5	3	4	3	2	7	.312	.378	.455	.833
2016	SF	NL	127	464	111	21	7	10	(3	7)	176	67	62	56	50	5	47	4	3	5	5	0	14	.239	.315	.379	.695
2017	SF	NL	138	511	147	28	5	10	(0	10)	215	60	53	73	46	4	54	5	3	8	4	1	10	.288	.347	.421	.768
2018	SF	NL	102	358	91	14	1	4	(1	3)	119	38	24	31	26	3	30	3	1	4	4	2	10	.254	.307	.332	.639
2019	2 Tms	NL	142	438	107	21	2	5	(1	4)	147	50	39	51	43	2	47	4	2	4	2	2	6	.244	.315	.336	.651
2020	Tor	AL	41	120	27	6	0	1	(0	1)	36	18	7	14	20	0	27	1	0	0	0	0	4	.225	.340	.300	.640
19	SF	NL	103	344	81	17	1	3	(0	3)	109	33	27	37	36	2	38	3	1	4	4	2	5	.235	.307	.317	.627
19	NYM	NL	39	94	26	4	1	2	(1	1)	38	17	12	14	7	0	9	1	1	0	0	0	1	.277	.333	.404	.738
	Postseason		21	86	23	4	2	1	(1	0)	34	10	10	11	7	0	10	0	1	1	0	0	1	.267	.319	.395	.714
	7 ML YEARS		723	2542	684	127	19	39	(9	30)	966	323	240	318	239	14	280	22	13	26	20	7	55	.269	.334	.380	.714

Enoli Paredes

Pitches: R Bats: R Pos: RP-22 **Ht: 5'11" Wt: 171 Born: 9/28/1995 Age: 25**

Year	Team	Lg	G	GS	GF	IP	BFP	H	R	ER	HR	SH	SF	HB	TBB	IBB	SO	WP	W	L	Pct	Sv-Op	Hld	Vel	OPS	ERC	ERA
2020	Hou	AL	22	0	4	20.2	90	18	9	7	1	1	1	1	11	0	20	0	3	3	.500	0-2	4	96	.666	3.69	3.05

Isaac Paredes

Bats: R Throws: R Pos: 3B-33;PR-2;DH-1 **Ht: 5'11" Wt: 213 Born: 2/18/1999 Age: 22**

Year	Team	Lg	G	AB	H	2B	3B	HR	(Hm	Rd)	TB	R	RBI	RC	TBB	IBB	SO	HBP	SH	SF	SB	CS	GDP	Avg	OBP	Slg	OPS
2020	Det	AL	34	100	22	4	0	1	(0	1)	29	7	6	8	8	0	24	0	0	0	0	0	1	.220	.278	.290	.568

Blake Parker

Pitches: R Bats: R Pos: RP-13; SP-1 **Ht: 6'3" Wt: 225 Born: 6/19/1985 Age: 36**

Year	Team	Lg	G	GS	GF	IP	BFP	H	R	ER	HR	SH	SF	HB	TBB	IBB	SO	WP	W	L	Pct	Sv-Op	Hld	Vel	OPS	ERC	ERA
2012	ChC	NL	7	0	0	6.0	32	10	7	4	3	0	0	0	5	1	6	0	0	0	-	0-0	0	92	1.172	14.02	6.00
2013	ChC	NL	49	0	18	46.1	195	39	17	14	4	0	1	2	15	1	55	2	1	2	.333	1-1	7	92	.626	2.91	2.72
2014	ChC	NL	18	0	10	21.0	91	24	13	12	3	0	1	0	4	0	24	1	1	1	.500	0-1	1	91	.784	4.24	5.14
2016	2 Tms	AL	17	0	5	17.1	79	17	9	9	1	0	0	2	9	1	15	0	1	0	1.000	1-1	0	92	.707	4.41	4.67
2017	LAA	AL	71	0	17	67.1	254	40	20	19	7	1	4	1	16	0	86	4	3	3	.500	8-11	15	94	.527	1.60	2.54
2018	LAA	AL	67	0	41	66.1	276	63	24	24	12	0	1	3	19	1	70	8	2	1	.667	14-17	6	92	.751	4.10	3.26
2019	2 Tms	NL	60	2	21	61.1	255	53	32	31	13	2	2	3	22	0	65	4	3	3	.500	10-11	13	91	.746	4.15	4.55
2020	Phi	NL	14	1	4	16.0	69	12	7	5	2	0	1	0	9	2	25	0	3	0	1.000	0-1	1	91	.677	3.24	2.81
16	Sea	AL	1	0	0	1.0	5	1	0	0	0	0	0	0	1	0	0	0	0	0	-	0-0	0	93	.650	5.48	0.00
16	NYY	AL	16	0	5	16.1	74	16	9	9	1	0	0	2	8	1	15	0	1	0	1.000	1-1	0	92	.711	4.35	4.96
19	Min	AL	37	0	19	36.1	157	34	18	17	7	0	1	2	16	0	34	4	2	3	.333	10-11	9	92	.773	4.79	4.21
19	Phi	NL	23	2	2	25.0	98	19	14	14	6	2	1	1	6	0	31	0	1	0	.667	0-0	4	91	.703	3.24	5.04
	8 ML YEARS		303	3	116	301.2	1251	258	129	118	45	3	10	11	99	6	346	19	14	10	.583	34-42	43	92	.691	3.45	3.52

Luis Patino

Pitches: R Bats: R Pos: RP-10; SP-1 **Ht: 6'0" Wt: 192 Born: 10/26/1999 Age: 21**

Year	Team	Lg	G	GS	GF	IP	BFP	H	R	ER	HR	SH	SF	HB	TBB	IBB	SO	WP	W	L	Pct	Sv-Op	Hld	Vel	OPS	ERC	ERA
2017	Padres	R	9	8	0	40.0	168	32	14	11	2	0	0	2	16	0	43	4	2	1	.667	0--	-	-	.598	2.84	2.48
2018	FtWyn	A	17	17	0	83.1	330	65	25	20	1	2	2	5	24	0	98	13	6	3	.667	0--	-	-	.686	2.25	2.16
2019	Lk Els	A+	18	17	0	87.0	357	61	30	26	4	0	4	1	34	0	113	8	6	8	.429	0--	-	-	.592	2.34	2.69
2020	SD	NL	11	1	1	17.1	85	18	10	10	3	0	0	1	14	0	21	1	1	0	1.000	0-0	1	97	.788	6.66	5.19

James Paxton

Pitches: L **Bats:** L **Pos:** SP-5 **Ht:** 6'4" **Wt:** 227 **Born:** 11/6/1988 **Age:** 32

			HOW MUCH PITCHED				WHAT HE GAVE UP										THE RESULTS							
Year	Team	Lg	G	GS	GF	IP	BFP	H	R	ER	HR	SH	SF	HB	TBB	IBB	SO	WP	W	L	Pct	Sv-Op	Hld	Vel	OPS	ERC	ERA
2013	Sea	AL	4	4	0	24.0	94	15	5	4	2	0	0	0	7	2	21	0	3	0	1.000	0-0	0	95	.533	1.61	1.50
2014	Sea	AL	13	13	0	74.0	303	60	29	25	3	3	1	1	29	2	59	7	6	4	.600	0-0	0	95	.612	2.69	3.04
2015	Sea	AL	13	13	0	67.0	297	67	34	29	8	0	3	0	29	1	56	5	3	4	.429	0-0	0	94	.704	4.22	3.90
2016	Sea	AL	20	20	0	121.0	511	134	62	51	9	0	6	1	24	3	117	5	6	7	.462	0-0	0	97	.717	3.70	3.79
2017	Sea	AL	24	24	0	136.0	552	113	47	45	9	1	5	3	37	1	156	15	12	5	.706	0-0	0	95	.602	2.56	2.98
2018	Sea	AL	28	28	0	160.1	645	134	67	67	23	2	2	1	42	0	208	8	11	6	.647	0-0	0	95	.662	2.98	3.76
2019	NYY	AL	29	29	0	150.2	633	138	71	64	23	2	4	2	55	0	186	7	15	6	.714	0-0	0	95	.732	3.90	3.82
2020	NYY	AL	5	5	0	20.1	90	23	17	15	4	0	1	1	7	0	26	2	1	1	.500	0-0	0	92	.875	5.53	6.64
	Postseason		3	3	0	13.0	58	13	5	5	2	0	0	0	7	0	20	1	1	0	1.000	0-0	0	96	.776	5.01	3.46
8 ML YEARS			136	136	0	753.1	3125	684	332	300	81	8	22	9	230	9	829	49	57	33	.633	0-0	0	95	.676	3.29	3.58

Joel Payamps

Pitches: R **Bats:** R **Pos:** RP-2 **Ht:** 6'2" **Wt:** 225 **Born:** 4/7/1994 **Age:** 27

			HOW MUCH PITCHED				WHAT HE GAVE UP										THE RESULTS							
Year	Team	Lg	G	GS	GF	IP	BFP	H	R	ER	HR	SH	SF	HB	TBB	IBB	SO	WP	W	L	Pct	Sv-Op	Hld	Vel	OPS	ERC	ERA
2019	Ari	NL	2	0	1	4.0	17	4	2	2	0	1	0	0	3	0	3	0	0	0	–	0-0	0	93	.745	5.14	4.50
2020	Ari	NL	2	0	1	3.0	13	2	2	1	0	0	0	0	3	0	2	0	0	0	–	0-0	0	94	.685	3.96	3.00
2 ML YEARS			4	0	2	7.0	30	6	4	3	0	1	0	0	6	0	5	0	0	0	–	0-0	0	93	.718	4.61	3.86

Mark Payton

Bats: L **Throws:** L **Pos:** LF-6;PH-2;DH-1 **Ht:** 5'8" **Wt:** 180 **Born:** 12/7/1991 **Age:** 29

			BATTING																	RUNNING			AVERAGES			
Year	Team	Lg	G	AB	H	2B	3B	HR	(Hm	Rd)	TB	R	RBI	RC	TBB	IBB	SO	HBP	SH	SF	SB	CS	GDP	Avg	OBP	Slg	OPS
2020	Cin	NL	8	18	3	1	0	0	(0	0)	4	0	0	0	2	0	5	0	0	0	1	0	1	.167	.250	.222	.472

James Pazos

Pitches: L **Bats:** R **Pos:** RP-6 pah-ZOHSS **Ht:** 6'2" **Wt:** 252 **Born:** 5/5/1991 **Age:** 30

			HOW MUCH PITCHED				WHAT HE GAVE UP										THE RESULTS							
Year	Team	Lg	G	GS	GF	IP	BFP	H	R	ER	HR	SH	SF	HB	TBB	IBB	SO	WP	W	L	Pct	Sv-Op	Hld	Vel	OPS	ERC	ERA
2015	NYY	AL	11	0	4	5.0	21	3	0	0	0	1	0	0	3	0	3	1	0	0	–	0-0	0	94	.476	2.03	0.00
2016	NYY	AL	7	0	1	3.1	17	7	5	5	2	0	0	0	1	0	3	0	1	0	1.000	0-0	0	95	1.408	16.29	13.50
2017	Sea	AL	59	0	7	53.2	240	51	30	23	7	1	4	5	24	0	65	4	4	5	.444	0-3	10	96	.723	4.49	3.86
2018	Sea	AL	60	0	4	50.0	211	47	19	16	4	0	2	5	15	1	45	2	4	1	.800	0-2	19	94	.683	3.61	2.88
2019	Col	NL	12	0	0	10.1	39	7	2	2	1	0	0	0	4	1	10	0	0	0	–	0-0	3	94	.596	2.37	1.74
2020	Col	NL	6	0	3	5.1	29	10	10	10	3	0	1	0	5	0	1	0	0	0	–	0-0	0	92	1.474	18.03	16.88
6 ML YEARS			155	0	16	127.2	557	125	66	56	17	2	7	10	52	2	127	7	9	6	.600	0-5	32	94	.748	4.52	3.95

Brad Peacock

Pitches: R **Bats:** R **Pos:** RP-3 **Ht:** 6'1" **Wt:** 207 **Born:** 2/2/1988 **Age:** 33

			HOW MUCH PITCHED				WHAT HE GAVE UP										THE RESULTS							
Year	Team	Lg	G	GS	GF	IP	BFP	H	R	ER	HR	SH	SF	HB	TBB	IBB	SO	WP	W	L	Pct	Sv-Op	Hld	Vel	OPS	ERC	ERA
2011	Was	NL	3	2	0	12.0	48	7	1	1	0	0	0	0	6	0	4	1	2	0	1.000	0-1	0	93	.437	1.71	0.75
2013	Hou	AL	18	14	1	83.1	365	78	51	48	15	1	1	3	37	0	77	4	5	6	.455	0-0	2	93	.779	4.54	5.18
2014	Hou	AL	28	24	3	131.2	589	136	80	69	20	0	6	4	70	4	119	6	4	9	.308	0-0	0	92	.801	5.29	4.72
2015	Hou	AL	1	1	0	5.0	22	5	3	3	0	0	1	1	2	0	3	0	0	1	.000	0-0	0	90	.808	4.20	5.40
2016	Hou	AL	10	5	3	31.2	127	21	15	13	6	0	0	0	14	0	28	2	0	1	.000	0-0	0	92	.700	3.04	3.69
2017	Hou	AL	34	21	7	132.0	546	100	46	44	10	1	0	3	57	0	161	6	13	2	.867	0-0	0	92	.615	2.83	3.00
2018	Hou	AL	61	1	20	65.0	272	56	26	25	11	0	1	3	20	0	96	5	3	5	.375	3-6	10	93	.722	3.55	3.46
2019	Hou	AL	23	15	1	91.2	383	78	43	42	15	0	3	5	31	0	96	1	7	6	.538	0-0	0	92	.725	3.65	4.12
2020	Hou	AL	3	0	0	2.1	12	3	2	2	0	0	0	1	1	0	3	0	0	0	–	0-0	0	90	.817	6.63	7.71
	Postseason		12	2	2	18.0	80	16	9	9	2	0	0	1	8	0	23	1	0	0	–	1-1	2	93	.721	3.78	4.50
9 ML YEARS			181	83	35	554.2	2364	484	267	247	77	2	12	20	238	4	587	25	34	30	.531	3-7	13	92	.720	3.88	4.01

Nate Pearson

Pitches: R **Bats:** R **Pos:** SP-4; RP-1 **Ht:** 6'6" **Wt:** 250 **Born:** 8/20/1996 **Age:** 24

			HOW MUCH PITCHED				WHAT HE GAVE UP										THE RESULTS							
Year	Team	Lg	G	GS	GF	IP	BFP	H	R	ER	HR	SH	SF	HB	TBB	IBB	SO	WP	W	L	Pct	Sv-Op	Hld	Vel	OPS	ERC	ERA
2017	2 Tms	Low	8	8	0	20.0	71	7	2	2	0	0	0	0	5	0	26	2	0	0	–	0--	–	–	.287	0.61	0.90
2019	Dnedin	A+	6	6	0	21.0	75	10	2	2	2	0	0	0	3	0	35	0	3	0	1.000	0--	–	–	.409	0.99	0.86
2019	Nham	AA	16	16	0	62.2	244	41	18	18	4	0	0	2	21	0	69	6	1	4	.200	0--	–	–	.538	2.02	2.59
2020	Tor	AL	5	4	0	18.0	81	14	15	12	5	0	0	0	13	0	16	1	1	0	1.000	0-0	0	96	.781	5.30	6.00

Joc Pederson

Bats: L **Throws:** L **Pos:** LF-23;DH-12;RF-8;PH-5 JOCK **Ht:** 6'1" **Wt:** 220 **Born:** 4/21/1992 **Age:** 29

			BATTING																	RUNNING			AVERAGES			
Year	Team	Lg	G	AB	H	2B	3B	HR	(Hm	Rd)	TB	R	RBI	RC	TBB	IBB	SO	HBP	SH	SF	SB	CS	GDP	Avg	OBP	Slg	OPS
2014	LAD	NL	18	28	4	0	0	0	(0	0)	4	1	0	1	9	0	11	0	1	0	0	0	1	.143	.351	.143	.494
2015	LAD	NL	151	480	101	19	1	26	(13	13)	200	67	54	62	92	6	170	9	2	2	4	7	5	.210	.346	.417	.763
2016	LAD	NL	137	406	100	26	0	25	(13	12)	201	64	68	71	63	4	130	4	1	2	6	2	5	.246	.352	.495	.847
2017	LAD	NL	102	273	58	20	0	11	(8	3)	111	44	35	35	39	1	68	10	0	1	4	3	7	.212	.331	.407	.738
2018	LAD	NL	148	395	98	27	3	25	(13	12)	206	65	56	55	40	3	85	4	1	3	1	5	6	.248	.321	.522	.843

Year	Team	Lg	G	AB	H	2B	3B	HR	(Hm	Rd)	TB	R	RBI	RC	TBB	IBB	SO	HBP	SH	SF	SB	CS	GDP	Avg	OBP	Slg	OPS
2019	LAD	NL	149	450	112	16	3	36	(24	12)	242	83	74	82	50	2	111	12	0	2	1	1	4	.249	.339	.538	.876
2020	LAD	NL	43	121	23	4	0	7	(2	5)	48	21	16	15	11	0	34	5	0	0	1	0	5	.190	.285	.397	.681
Postseason			48	117	28	8	0	7	(5	2)	57	21	12	16	12	2	43	3	1	0	2	0	1	.239	.326	.487	.813
7 ML YEARS			748	2153	496	112	7	130	(73	57)	1012	345	303	321	304	16	609	44	5	10	17	18	33	.230	.336	.470	.806

Dustin Pedroia

Bats: R **Throws:** R **Pos:** 2B   peh-DROY-uh   **Ht:** 5'9" **Wt:** 170 **Born:** 8/17/1983 **Age:** 37

Year	Team	Lg	G	AB	H	2B	3B	HR	(Hm	Rd)	TB	R	RBI	RC	TBB	IBB	SO	HBP	SH	SF	SB	CS	GDP	Avg	OBP	Slg	OPS
2006	Bos	AL	31	89	17	4	0	2	(1	1)	27	5	7	3	7	0	7	1	1	0	0	1	1	.191	.258	.303	.561
2007	Bos	AL	139	520	165	39	1	8	(5	3)	230	86	50	79	47	1	42	7	5	2	7	1	8	.317	.380	.442	.823
2008	Bos	AL	157	653	**213**	**54**	2	17	(7	10)	322	**118**	83	107	50	1	52	7	7	9	20	1	17	.326	.376	.493	.869
2009	Bos	AL	154	626	185	48	1	15	(10	5)	280	**115**	72	104	74	3	45	5	3	6	20	8	19	.296	.371	.447	.819
2010	Bos	AL	75	302	87	24	1	12	(4	8)	149	53	41	52	37	1	38	4	2	6	9	1	7	.288	.367	.493	.860
2011	Bos	AL	159	635	195	37	3	21	(13	8)	301	102	91	114	86	6	85	1	2	7	26	8	12	.307	.387	.474	.861
2012	Bos	AL	141	563	163	39	3	15	(9	6)	253	81	65	84	48	3	60	5	1	6	20	6	9	.290	.347	.449	.797
2013	Bos	AL	160	641	193	42	2	9	(7	2)	266	91	84	99	73	4	75	3	0	7	17	5	24	.301	.372	.415	.787
2014	Bos	AL	135	551	153	33	0	7	(2	5)	207	72	53	65	51	1	75	1	0	6	6	6	14	.278	.337	.376	.712
2015	Bos	AL	93	381	111	19	1	12	(4	8)	168	46	42	55	38	1	51	2	1	3	2	2	6	.291	.356	.441	.797
2016	Bos	AL	154	633	201	36	1	15	(7	8)	284	105	74	100	61	0	73	0	1	3	7	4	24	.318	.376	.449	.825
2017	Bos	AL	105	406	119	19	0	7	(4	3)	159	46	62	65	49	4	48	2	2	4	4	3	11	.293	.369	.392	.760
2018	Bos	AL	3	11	1	0	0	0	(0	0)	1	1	0	0	2	0	1	0	0	0	0	0	0	.091	.231	.091	.322
2019	Bos	AL	6	20	2	0	0	0	(0	0)	2	1	1	0	1	0	2	0	0	0	0	0	2	.100	.143	.100	.243
Postseason			51	206	48	14	0	5	(2	3)	77	32	25	23	23	0	32	2	1	2	3	1	4	.233	.313	.374	.687
14 ML YEARS			1512	6031	1805	394	15	140	(73	67)	2649	922	725	927	624	25	654	38	25	59	138	46	154	.299	.365	.439	.805

Felix Pena

Pitches: R **Bats:** R **Pos:** RP-25   **Ht:** 6'2" **Wt:** 220 **Born:** 2/25/1990 **Age:** 31

			HOW MUCH PITCHED					WHAT HE GAVE UP										THE RESULTS						
Year	Team	Lg	G	GS	GF	IP	BFP	H	R	ER	HR	SH	SF	HB	TBB	IBB	SO	WP	W	L	Pct	Sv-Op Hld	Vel	OPS	ERC	ERA
2016	ChC	NL	11	0	2	9.0	35	5	4	4	1	0	0	0	3	1	13	1	0	0		1-1	93	.479	1.57	4.00
2017	ChC	NL	25	0	15	34.1	155	35	21	20	8	0	0	2	18	1	37	3	1	0	1.000	0-0 1	94	.866	5.88	5.24
2018	LAA	AL	19	17	1	92.2	389	87	45	43	12	1	4	4	28	0	85	7	3	5	.375	0-0 0	92	.699	3.73	4.18
2019	LAA	AL	22	7	1	96.1	407	80	56	49	16	0	1	6	34	0	101	8	8	3	.727	0-0 1	92	.696	3.60	4.58
2020	LAA	AL	25	0	5	26.2	115	27	12	12	2	0	0	1	8	0	29	3	3	0	1.000	2-5 4	94	.672	3.67	4.05
5 ML YEARS			102	24	24	259.0	1101	234	138	128	39	1	5	13	91	2	265	22	15	8	.652	3-6 8	93	.711	3.85	4.45

Hunter Pence

Bats: R **Throws:** R **Pos:** DH-7;LF-5;RF-5;PH-3;PR-1   **Ht:** 6'4" **Wt:** 216 **Born:** 4/13/1983 **Age:** 38

Year	Team	Lg	G	AB	H	2B	3B	HR	(Hm	Rd)	TB	R	RBI	RC	TBB	IBB	SO	HBP	SH	SF	SB	CS	GDP	Avg	OBP	Slg	OPS
2007	Hou	NL	108	456	147	30	9	17	(7	10)	246	57	69	77	26	0	95	1	0	1	11	5	10	.322	.360	.539	.899
2008	Hou	NL	157	595	160	34	4	25	(14	11)	277	78	83	82	40	2	124	4	0	3	11	10	14	.269	.318	.466	.783
2009	Hou	NL	159	585	165	26	5	25	(14	11)	276	76	72	80	58	1	109	1	0	3	14	11	25	.282	.346	.472	.818
2010	Hou	NL	156	614	173	29	5	25	(14	11)	283	93	91	89	41	2	105	0	0	3	18	9	11	.282	.325	.461	.786
2011	2 Tms	NL	154	606	190	38	5	22	(5	17)	304	84	97	102	56	3	124	1	0	5	8	2	15	.314	.370	.502	.871
2012	2 Tms	NL	160	617	156	26	4	24	(9	15)	262	87	104	81	56	2	145	7	1	7	5	2	14	.253	.319	.425	.743
2013	SF	NL	162	629	178	35	6	27	(10	17)	304	91	99	91	52	3	115	3	0	3	22	3	17	.283	.339	.483	.822
2014	SF	NL	162	**650**	180	29	10	20	(5	15)	289	106	74	96	52	3	130	3	0	3	13	6	13	.277	.332	.445	.777
2015	SF	NL	52	207	57	13	1	9	(3	6)	99	30	40	28	16	0	48	0	0	0	4	1	8	.275	.327	.478	.806
2016	SF	NL	106	395	114	23	1	13	(6	7)	178	58	57	65	43	1	95	1	0	3	1	1	10	.289	.357	.451	.808
2017	SF	NL	134	493	128	13	5	13	(4	9)	190	55	67	68	40	1	102	2	0	4	2	3	8	.260	.315	.385	.701
2018	SF	NL	97	235	53	11	1	4	(2	2)	78	19	24	20	11	1	59	0	0	2	5	1	1	.226	.258	.332	.590
2019	Tex	AL	83	286	85	17	1	18	(7	11)	158	53	59	61	26	0	69	2	0	2	6	1	2	.297	.358	.552	.910
2020	SF	NL	17	52	5	0	1	2	(1	1)	13	4	6	1	3	0	15	1	0	0	0	0	3	.096	.161	.250	.411
11	Hou	NL	100	399	123	26	3	11	(4	7)	188	49	62	63	30	1	86	1	0	2	7	1	7	.308	.356	.471	.828
11	Phi	NL	54	207	67	12	2	11	(1	10)	116	35	35	39	26	2	38	0	0	3	1	1	8	.324	.394	.560	.954
12	Phi	NL	101	398	108	15	2	17	(7	10)	178	59	59	50	37	1	85	3	0	2	4	2	13	.271	.336	.447	.784
12	SF	NL	59	219	48	11	2	7	(2	5)	84	28	45	31	19	1	60	4	1	5	1	0	1	.219	.287	.384	.671
Postseason			43	169	43	8	0	2	(0	2)	57	23	16	14	12	1	33	0	0	1	4	3	3	.254	.302	.337	.639
14 ML YEARS			1707	6420	1791	324	55	244	(101	143)	2957	891	942	941	520	19	1335	26	1	39	120	55	151	.279	.334	.461	.794

David Peralta

Bats: L **Throws:** L **Pos:** LF-45;DH-8;PH-1   **Ht:** 6'1" **Wt:** 220 **Born:** 8/14/1987 **Age:** 33

Year	Team	Lg	G	AB	H	2B	3B	HR	(Hm	Rd)	TB	R	RBI	RC	TBB	IBB	SO	HBP	SH	SF	SB	CS	GDP	Avg	OBP	Slg	OPS
2014	Ari	NL	88	329	94	12	9	8	(5	3)	148	40	36	38	16	0	60	1	1	1	6	3	9	.286	.320	.450	.770
2015	Ari	NL	149	462	144	26	**10**	17	(8	9)	241	61	78	83	44	2	107	4	0	7	9	4	7	.312	.371	.522	.893
2016	Ari	NL	48	171	43	9	5	4	(3	1)	74	23	15	15	8	1	42	3	0	1	2	0	3	.251	.295	.433	.728
2017	Ari	NL	140	525	154	31	3	14	(8	6)	233	82	57	77	43	1	94	6	0	3	8	4	7	.293	.352	.444	.796
2018	Ari	NL	146	560	164	25	5	30	(16	14)	289	75	87	104	48	4	124	4	0	2	4	0	14	.293	.352	.516	.868
2019	Ari	NL	99	382	105	29	3	12	(6	6)	176	48	57	62	35	3	87	5	0	1	0	0	9	.275	.343	.461	.804
2020	Ari	NL	54	203	61	10	1	5	(2	3)	88	19	34	33	13	0	45	0	0	2	1	0	4	.300	.339	.433	.773
Postseason			4	18	4	0	0	0	(0	0)	4	2	0	1	1	0	1	0	0	0	0	0	1	.222	.263	.222	.485
7 ML YEARS			724	2632	765	142	36	90	(48	42)	1249	348	364	412	207	11	559	23	1	17	30	11	53	.291	.346	.475	.820

Freddy Peralta

Pitches: R **Bats:** R **Pos:** RP-14; SP-1   **Ht:** 5'11" **Wt:** 199 **Born:** 6/4/1996 **Age:** 25

			HOW MUCH PITCHED					WHAT HE GAVE UP											THE RESULTS						
Year Team	Lg	G	GS	GF	IP	BFP	H	R	ER	HR	SH	SF	HB	TBB	IBB	SO	WP	W	L	Pct	Sv-Op	Hld	Vel	OPS	ERC	ERA
2018 Mil	NL	16	14	1	78.1	321	49	37	37	8	1	1	4	40	1	96	3	6	4	.600	0-0	0	91	.622	2.71	4.25
2019 Mil	NL	39	8	3	85.0	382	87	58	50	15	3	1	2	37	1	115	3	7	3	.700	1-2	5	94	.790	4.86	5.29
2020 Mil	NL	15	1	2	29.1	125	22	14	13	2	1	1	3	12	0	47	2	3	1	.750	0-1	3	93	.622	2.88	3.99
Postseason		1	0	0	3.0	12	0	0	0	0	0	0	0	3	0	6	0	0	0	-	0-0	0	92	.250	0.95	0.00
3 ML YEARS		70	23	6	192.2	828	158	109	100	25	5	3	9	89	2	258	8	16	8	.667	1-3	8	92	.700	3.65	4.67

Wandy Peralta

Pitches: L **Bats:** L **Pos:** RP-25   **Ht:** 6'0" **Wt:** 217 **Born:** 7/27/1991 **Age:** 29

			HOW MUCH PITCHED					WHAT HE GAVE UP											THE RESULTS						
Year Team	Lg	G	GS	GF	IP	BFP	H	R	ER	HR	SH	SF	HB	TBB	IBB	SO	WP	W	L	Pct	Sv-Op	Hld	Vel	OPS	ERC	ERA
2016 Cin	NL	10	0	3	7.1	39	11	7	7	1	0	0	1	7	0	5	0	0	0	-	0-0	2	95	1.036	10.93	8.59
2017 Cin	NL	69	0	10	64.2	263	53	28	27	8	2	3	1	24	1	57	4	3	4	.429	0-2	16	96	.681	3.24	3.76
2018 Cin	NL	59	0	6	45.1	227	58	32	27	2	1	1	2	31	2	31	0	2	2	.500	0-0	7	96	.783	6.37	5.36
2019 2 Tms	NL	47	0	11	39.2	172	40	25	25	11	0	3	2	16	3	32	0	1	1	.500	0-1	3	95	.860	5.56	5.67
2020 SF	NL	25	0	9	27.1	114	22	13	10	3	0	1	2	11	0	25	0	1	1	.500	0-1	1	95	.657	3.40	3.29
19 Cin	NL	39	0	11	34.0	151	36	23	23	10	0	3	2	15	3	27	0	1	1	.500	0-1	2	95	.893	6.17	6.09
19 SF	NL	8	0	0	5.2	21	4	2	2	1	0	0	0	1	0	5	0	0	0	-	0-0	1	95	.638	2.27	3.18
5 ML YEARS		210	0	39	184.1	815	184	105	96	25	3	8	8	89	6	150	4	7	8	.467	0-4	29	96	.760	4.79	4.69

Jose Peraza

Bats: R **Throws:** R **Pos:** 2B-27;LF-5;SS-3;PH-2;3B-1;PR-1   per-AH-zuh   **Ht:** 6'0" **Wt:** 210 **Born:** 4/30/1994 **Age:** 27

					BATTING																RUNNING			AVERAGES			
Year Team	Lg	G	AB	H	2B	3B	HR	(Hm	Rd)	TB	R	RBI	RC	TBB	IBB	SO	HBP	SH	SF	SB	CS	GDP	Avg	OBP	Slg	OPS
2015 LAD	NL	7	22	4	1	0	0	(0	0)	7	3	1	2	2	1	2	0	1	0	0	1	0	.182	.250	.318	.568
2016 Cin	NL	72	241	78	8	2	3	(1	2)	99	25	25	32	7	0	33	5	0	3	21	10	3	.324	.352	.411	.762
2017 Cin	NL	143	487	126	9	4	5	(3	2)	158	50	37	43	20	1	70	7	3	1	23	8	7	.259	.297	.324	.622
2018 Cin	NL	157	632	182	31	4	14	(7	7)	263	85	58	79	29	4	75	9	8	5	23	6	12	.288	.326	.416	.742
2019 Cin	NL	141	376	90	18	2	6	(4	2)	130	37	33	34	17	0	58	8	0	2	7	6	9	.239	.285	.346	.631
2020 Bos	AL	34	111	25	8	1	1	(1	0)	38	13	8	8	5	0	18	3	0	1	1	1	3	.225	.275	.342	.617
6 ML YEARS		554	1869	505	75	14	29	(16	13)	695	213	162	198	80	6	256	32	12	12	78	31	34	.270	.310	.372	.681

Angel Perdomo

Pitches: L **Bats:** L **Pos:** RP-3   **Ht:** 6'8" **Wt:** 201 **Born:** 5/7/1994 **Age:** 27

			HOW MUCH PITCHED					WHAT HE GAVE UP											THE RESULTS						
Year Team	Lg	G	GS	GF	IP	BFP	H	R	ER	HR	SH	SF	HB	TBB	IBB	SO	WP	W	L	Pct	Sv-Op	Hld	Vel	OPS	ERC	ERA
2020 Mil	NL	3	0	1	2.2	19	3	7	6	0	0	0	1	7	1	5	0	0	0	-	0-0	0	95	1.033	13.65	20.25

Luis Perdomo

Pitches: R **Bats:** R **Pos:** RP-9; SP-1   **Ht:** 6'2" **Wt:** 185 **Born:** 5/9/1993 **Age:** 28

			HOW MUCH PITCHED					WHAT HE GAVE UP											THE RESULTS						
Year Team	Lg	G	GS	GF	IP	BFP	H	R	ER	HR	SH	SF	HB	TBB	IBB	SO	WP	W	L	Pct	Sv-Op	Hld	Vel	OPS	ERC	ERA
2016 SD	NL	35	20	8	146.2	662	187	99	93	23	0	4	7	46	7	105	10	9	10	.474	0-0	0	94	.847	5.91	5.71
2017 SD	NL	29	29	0	163.2	716	182	97	85	17	3	2	8	65	3	118	11	8	11	.421	0-0	0	94	.784	5.00	4.67
2018 SD	NL	12	10	2	44.2	217	62	37	35	4	1	2	3	22	2	39	4	1	6	.143	0-0	0	93	.895	6.86	7.05
2019 SD	NL	47	1	13	72.0	296	69	34	32	6	2	0	2	18	1	55	3	2	4	.333	0-1	7	94	.675	3.29	4.00
2020 SD	NL	10	1	3	17.1	74	13	12	11	3	0	0	0	10	0	16	0	0	0	-	0-0	0	94	.717	3.87	5.71
5 ML YEARS		133	61	26	444.1	1965	513	279	256	53	6	8	20	161	13	333	28	20	31	.392	0-1	7	94	.798	5.14	5.19

Cionel Perez

Pitches: L **Bats:** L **Pos:** RP-7   see-oh-NEHL   **Ht:** 5'11" **Wt:** 162 **Born:** 4/21/1996 **Age:** 25

			HOW MUCH PITCHED					WHAT HE GAVE UP											THE RESULTS						
Year Team	Lg	G	GS	GF	IP	BFP	H	R	ER	HR	SH	SF	HB	TBB	IBB	SO	WP	W	L	Pct	Sv-Op	Hld	Vel	OPS	ERC	ERA
2018 Hou	AL	8	0	3	11.1	45	6	5	5	3	0	0	0	7	0	12	0	0	0	-	0-0	0	95	.684	3.56	3.97
2019 Hou	AL	5	0	3	9.0	40	11	10	10	3	0	0	0	2	0	7	0	1	1	.500	0-0	0	95	.904	6.18	10.00
2020 Hou	AL	7	0	1	6.1	32	7	2	2	0	0	0	0	6	1	8	0	0	0	-	0-0	2	95	.675	5.57	2.84
3 ML YEARS		20	0	7	26.2	117	24	17	17	6	0	0	0	15	1	27	0	1	1	.500	0-0	2	95	.765	4.99	5.74

Hector Perez

Pitches: R **Bats:** R **Pos:** RP-1   **Ht:** 6'3" **Wt:** 223 **Born:** 6/6/1996 **Age:** 25

			HOW MUCH PITCHED					WHAT HE GAVE UP											THE RESULTS						
Year Team	Lg	G	GS	GF	IP	BFP	H	R	ER	HR	SH	SF	HB	TBB	IBB	SO	WP	W	L	Pct	Sv-Op	Hld	Vel	OPS	ERC	ERA
2020 Tor	AL	1	0	0	1.2	10	3	2	2	1	0	0	0	3	0	1	0	0	0	-	0-0	0	96	1.457	23.66	10.80

Hernan Perez

Bats: R **Throws:** R **Pos:** 1B-2;2B-1;LF-1;DH-1;PH-1   air-NAHN   **Ht:** 6'1" **Wt:** 213 **Born:** 3/26/1991 **Age:** 30

Year	Team	Lg	G	AB	H	2B	3B	HR	(Hm	Rd)	TB	R	RBI	RC	TBB	IBB	SO	HBP	SH	SF	SB	CS	GDP	Avg	OBP	Slg	OPS
2012	Det	AL	2	2	1	0	0	0	(0	0)	1	1	0	0	0	0	0	0	0	0	0	0	0	.500	.500	.500	1.000
2013	Det	AL	34	66	13	0	1	0	(0	0)	15	13	5	4	2	0	15	0	2	1	1	0	2	.197	.217	.227	.445
2014	Det	AL	8	5	1	0	0	0	(0	0)	1	1	0	0	1	0	1	0	0	0	0	0	0	.200	.333	.200	.533
2015	2 Tms		112	263	64	15	2	1	(0	1)	86	14	21	23	5	1	59	0	3	1	5	1	6	.243	.257	.327	.584
2016	Mil	NL	123	404	110	18	3	13	(7	6)	173	50	56	56	18	0	94	1	3	4	34	7	6	.272	.302	.428	.730
2017	Mil	NL	136	432	112	19	3	14	(7	7)	179	47	51	49	20	1	79	0	2	4	13	4	8	.259	.289	.414	.704
2018	Mil	NL	132	316	80	11	2	9	(5	4)	122	36	29	33	17	1	71	0	0	1	11	3	6	.253	.290	.386	.676
2019	Mil	NL	91	232	53	11	0	8	(3	5)	88	29	18	12	11	0	66	0	2	1	5	1	9	.228	.262	.379	.642
2020	ChC	NL	3	6	1	0	0	0	(0	0)	1	0	0	0	0	0	2	0	0	0	0	0	0	.167	.167	.167	.333
15	Det	AL	22	33	2	0	0	0	(0	0)	2	1	0	0	1	0	11	0	0	0	1	0	2	.061	.088	.061	.149
15	Mil	NL	90	230	62	15	2	1	(0	1)	84	13	21	23	4	1	48	0	3	1	4	1	4	.270	.281	.365	.646
	Postseason		13	16	3	2	0	0	(0	0)	5	1	2	1	1	0	3	0	0	1	2	2	1	.188	.222	.313	.535
	9 ML YEARS		641	1726	435	74	11	45	(22	23)	666	191	180	177	74	3	387	1	12	12	69	16	37	.252	.281	.386	.667

Martin Perez

Pitches: L **Bats:** L **Pos:** SP-12   mar-TEEN   **Ht:** 6'0" **Wt:** 200 **Born:** 4/4/1991 **Age:** 30

Year	Team	Lg	G	GS	GF	IP	BFP	H	R	ER	HR	SH	SF	HB	TBB	IBB	SO	WP	W	L	Pct	Sv-Op	Hld	Vel	OPS	ERC	ERA
2012	Tex	AL	12	6	2	38.0	177	47	26	23	3	1	1	2	15	1	25	5	1	4	.200	0-0	0	92	.819	5.33	5.45
2013	Tex	AL	20	20	0	124.1	529	129	55	50	15	2	3	3	37	0	84	9	10	6	.625	0-0	0	93	.728	4.14	3.62
2014	Tex	AL	8	8	0	51.1	207	50	25	25	3	1	0	1	19	1	35	1	4	3	.571	0-0	0	90	.743	3.82	4.38
2015	Tex	AL	14	14	0	78.2	339	88	45	39	3	0	3	2	24	1	48	1	3	6	.333	0-0	0	92	.729	4.04	4.46
2016	Tex	AL	33	33	0	198.2	855	205	110	97	18	9	8	4	76	0	103	3	10	11	.476	0-0	0	93	.741	4.24	4.39
2017	Tex	AL	32	32	0	185.0	811	221	108	99	23	4	3	6	63	3	115	4	13	12	.520	0-0	0	93	.812	5.35	4.82
2018	Tex	AL	22	15	3	85.1	397	116	68	59	16	1	5	2	36	1	52	3	2	7	.222	0-1	2	93	.916	7.19	6.22
2019	Min	AL	32	29	0	165.1	737	184	104	94	23	3	5	3	67	1	135	3	10	7	.588	0-0	0	94	.785	5.07	5.12
2020	Bos	AL	12	12	0	62.0	262	55	33	31	8	1	1	3	28	0	46	2	3	5	.375	0-0	0	92	.744	4.13	4.50
	Postseason		1	1	0	5.0	21	6	4	4	0	1	0	0	3	1	2	0	0	1	.000	0-0	0	92	.921	5.47	7.20
	9 ML YEARS		185	169	5	988.2	4314	1095	574	517	112	22	29	26	365	8	643	31	56	61	.479	0-1	2	93	.779	4.81	4.71

Michael Perez

Bats: L **Throws:** R **Pos:** C-38;1B-1;PH-1   **Ht:** 5'10" **Wt:** 195 **Born:** 8/7/1992 **Age:** 28

Year	Team	Lg	G	AB	H	2B	3B	HR	(Hm	Rd)	TB	R	RBI	RC	TBB	IBB	SO	HBP	SH	SF	SB	CS	GDP	Avg	OBP	Slg	OPS
2018	TB	AL	24	74	21	5	0	1	(0	1)	29	9	11	9	3	0	19	0	1	2	0	0	0	.284	.304	.392	.696
2019	TB	AL	22	46	10	5	0	0	(0	0)	15	6	2	6	8	0	19	1	0	0	0	0	0	.217	.345	.326	.672
2020	TB	AL	38	84	14	3	0	1	(1	0)	20	7	13	5	7	0	27	1	0	1	0	0	3	.167	.237	.238	.475
	3 ML YEARS		84	204	45	13	0	2	(1	1)	64	22	26	20	18	0	65	2	1	3	0	0	3	.221	.286	.314	.600

Oliver Perez

Pitches: L **Bats:** L **Pos:** RP-21   **Ht:** 6'3" **Wt:** 225 **Born:** 8/15/1981 **Age:** 39

Year	Team	Lg	G	GS	GF	IP	BFP	H	R	ER	HR	SH	SF	HB	TBB	IBB	SO	WP	W	L	Pct	Sv-Op	Hld	Vel	OPS	ERC	ERA
2002	SD	NL	16	15	0	90.0	387	71	37	35	13	5	3	5	48	1	94	3	4	5	.444	0-0	0	91	.702	3.93	3.50
2003	2 Tms	NL	24	24	0	126.2	579	129	80	77	22	5	2	4	77	3	141	7	4	10	.286	0-0	0	93	.830	5.66	5.47
2004	Pit	NL	30	30	0	196.0	805	145	71	65	22	9	5	9	81	2	239	2	12	10	.545	0-0	0	93	.655	2.99	2.98
2005	Pit	NL	20	20	0	103.0	471	102	68	67	23	5	4	6	70	1	97	3	7	5	.583	0-0	0	91	.874	6.44	5.85
2006	2 Tms	NL	22	22	0	112.2	529	129	90	82	20	5	10	6	68	0	102	5	3	13	.188	0-0	0	90	.865	6.62	6.55
2007	NYM	NL	29	29	0	177.0	765	153	90	70	22	4	7	7	79	1	174	6	15	10	.600	0-0	0	91	.696	3.76	3.56
2008	NYM	NL	34	34	0	194.0	847	167	100	91	24	9	7	11	105	4	180	9	10	7	.588	0-0	0	91	.725	4.21	4.22
2009	NYM	NL	14	14	0	66.0	324	69	51	50	12	5	4	4	58	2	62	2	3	4	.429	0-0	0	90	.897	7.16	6.82
2010	NYM	NL	17	7	4	46.1	234	54	37	35	9	1	3	4	42	3	37	4	0	5	.000	0-0	0	88	.935	8.27	6.80
2012	Sea	AL	33	0	6	29.2	123	27	7	7	1	1	1	0	10	2	24	2	1	3	.250	0-2	5	94	.628	2.82	2.12
2013	Sea	AL	61	0	22	53.0	229	50	23	22	6	1	0	3	26	3	74	1	3	3	.500	2-3	8	92	.731	4.23	3.74
2014	Ari	NL	68	0	11	58.2	256	50	25	19	5	4	0	7	24	2	76	3	3	4	.429	0-1	15	91	.679	3.53	2.91
2015	2 Tms	NL	70	0	15	41.0	183	39	24	19	4	1	0	4	15	2	51	3	2	4	.333	0-3	10	92	.681	3.81	4.17
2016	Was	NL	64	0	7	40.0	182	38	22	22	4	1	1	7	20	3	46	5	2	3	.400	0-1	15	92	.751	4.72	4.95
2017	Was	NL	50	0	8	33.0	143	32	17	17	4	0	1	4	12	2	39	1	0	0	-	1-1	12	93	.772	4.32	4.64
2018	Cle	AL	51	0	1	32.1	120	17	6	5	1	0	1	2	7	3	43	1	1	1	.500	0-0	15	92	.417	1.12	1.39
2019	Cle	AL	67	0	4	40.2	173	38	20	18	5	0	1	3	12	2	48	1	2	4	.333	1-5	22	92	.733	3.64	3.98
2020	Cle	AL	21	0	2	18.0	72	13	5	4	0	0	1	3	6	3	14	0	1	1	.500	1-2	3	90	.564	2.17	2.00
03	SD	NL	19	19	0	103.2	473	103	65	62	20	4	2	3	65	2	117	6	4	7	.364	0-0	0	92	.836	5.74	5.38
03	Pit	NL	5	5	0	23.0	106	26	15	15	2	1	0	1	12	1	24	1	0	3	.000	0-0	0	93	.806	5.29	5.87
06	Pit	NL	15	15	0	76.0	364	88	64	56	13	5	8	3	51	0	61	4	2	10	.167	0-0	0	90	.877	6.85	6.63
06	NYM	NL	7	7	0	36.2	165	41	26	26	7	0	2	3	17	0	41	1	1	3	.250	0-0	0	91	.838	6.16	6.38
15	Ari	NL	48	0	11	29.0	128	25	12	10	2	1	0	4	11	1	37	2	2	1	.667	0-3	7	92	.627	3.38	3.10
15	Hou	AL	22	0	4	12.0	55	14	12	9	2	0	0	0	4	1	14	1	0	3	.000	0-0	3	92	.798	4.89	6.75
	Postseason		10	2	1	16.1	69	17	7	7	3	3	0	2	5	1	10	0	2	0	1.000	0-0	3	93	.855	5.13	3.86
	18 ML YEARS		691	195	80	1458.0	6422	1323	773	705	197	66	51	87	760	39	1541	58	73	92	.442	5-18	105	91	.748	4.47	4.35

Roberto Perez

Bats: R Throws: R Pos: C-32   Ht: 5'11" Wt: 220 Born: 12/23/1988 Age: 32

Year	Team	Lg	G	AB	H	2B	3B	HR	(Hm	Rd)	TB	R	RBI	RC	TBB	IBB	SO	HBP	SH	SF	SB	CS	GDP	Avg	OBP	Slg	OPS
2014	Cle	AL	29	85	23	5	0	1	(1	0)	31	10	4	8	5	0	26	0	5	0	0	0	2	.271	.311	.365	.676
2015	Cle	AL	70	184	42	9	1	7	(4	3)	74	30	21	24	33	1	64	2	5	2	0	0	9	.228	.348	.402	.751
2016	Cle	AL	61	153	28	6	1	3	(1	2)	45	14	17	17	23	0	44	0	5	3	0	0	4	.183	.285	.294	.579
2017	Cle	AL	73	217	45	12	0	8	(6	2)	81	22	38	26	26	0	71	0	4	1	0	1	4	.207	.291	.373	.664
2018	Cle	AL	62	179	30	9	1	2	(1	1)	47	16	19	12	21	0	70	1	7	2	1	0	6	.168	.256	.263	.519
2019	Cle	AL	119	389	93	9	1	24	(12	12)	176	46	63	56	45	1	127	4	7	4	0	0	12	.239	.321	.452	.774
2020	Cle	AL	32	97	16	2	0	1	(0	1)	21	6	5	5	11	0	38	2	0	0	0	0	2	.165	.264	.216	.480
	Postseason		19	53	11	1	0	4	(3	1)	24	6	9	7	9	0	18	0	2	0	0	0	2	.208	.323	.453	.775
	7 ML YEARS		446	1304	277	52	4	46	(25	21)	475	144	167	148	164	2	440	9	33	12	1	1	39	.212	.302	.364	.666

Salvador Perez

Bats: R Throws: R Pos: C-34;1B-3;DH-3   Ht: 6'3" Wt: 250 Born: 5/10/1990 Age: 31

Year	Team	Lg	G	AB	H	2B	3B	HR	(Hm	Rd)	TB	R	RBI	RC	TBB	IBB	SO	HBP	SH	SF	SB	CS	GDP	Avg	OBP	Slg	OPS
2011	KC	AL	39	148	49	8	2	3	(1	2)	70	20	21	26	7	0	20	1	0	2	0	0	5	.331	.361	.473	.834
2012	KC	AL	76	289	87	16	0	11	(3	8)	136	38	39	36	12	3	27	1	0	3	0	0	14	.301	.328	.471	.798
2013	KC	AL	138	496	145	25	3	13	(6	7)	215	48	79	77	21	2	63	4	0	5	0	0	13	.292	.323	.433	.757
2014	KC	AL	150	578	150	28	2	17	(8	9)	233	57	70	55	22	2	85	3	0	3	1	0	22	.260	.289	.403	.692
2015	KC	AL	142	531	138	25	0	21	(9	12)	226	52	70	60	13	4	82	4	0	5	1	0	23	.260	.280	.426	.706
2016	KC	AL	139	514	127	28	2	22	(11	11)	225	57	64	61	22	3	119	8	0	2	0	0	12	.247	.288	.438	.725
2017	KC	AL	129	471	126	24	1	27	(6	21)	233	57	80	65	17	3	95	5	0	5	1	0	23	.268	.297	.495	.792
2018	KC	AL	129	510	120	23	0	27	(11	16)	224	52	80	58	17	0	108	12	0	5	1	1	19	.235	.274	.439	.713
2020	KC	AL	37	150	50	12	0	11	(5	6)	95	22	32	29	3	0	36	2	0	1	1	0	0	.333	.353	.633	.986
	Postseason		31	116	27	4	0	5	(3	2)	46	14	14	10	5	0	19	3	0	0	0	0	3	.233	.282	.397	.679
	9 ML YEARS		979	3687	992	189	10	152	(60	92)	1657	403	535	467	134	17	635	40	0	31	5	1	131	.269	.300	.449	.749

Dillon Peters

Pitches: L Bats: L Pos: SP-1   Ht: 5'11" Wt: 190 Born: 8/31/1992 Age: 28

Year	Team	Lg	G	GS	GF	IP	BFP	H	R	ER	HR	SH	SF	HB	TBB	IBB	SO	WP	W	L	Pct	Sv-Op	Hld	Vel	OPS	ERC	ERA
2017	Mia	NL	6	6	0	31.1	139	32	18	18	3	0	0	2	19	1	27	3	1	2	.333	0-0	0	91	.771	5.38	5.17
2018	Mia	NL	7	5	2	27.2	129	34	22	22	4	1	1	1	15	0	17	3	2	2	.500	0-0	0	91	.868	6.59	7.16
2019	LAA	AL	17	12	1	72.0	327	85	50	43	18	1	2	5	26	1	55	1	4	4	.500	0-0	0	91	.926	6.34	5.38
2020	LAA	AL	1	1	0	1.2	9	3	4	3	2	0	0	0	0	0	2	0	0	0	-	0-0	0	91	1.333	14.27	16.20
	4 ML YEARS		31	24	3	132.2	604	154	94	86	27	2	3	8	60	2	101	7	7	8	.467	0-0	0	91	.887	6.30	5.83

David Peterson

Pitches: L Bats: L Pos: SP-9; RP-1   Ht: 6'6" Wt: 240 Born: 9/3/1995 Age: 25

Year	Team	Lg	G	GS	GF	IP	BFP	H	R	ER	HR	SH	SF	HB	TBB	IBB	SO	WP	W	L	Pct	Sv-Op	Hld	Vel	OPS	ERC	ERA
2020	NYM	NL	10	9	0	49.2	205	36	20	19	5	0	0	3	24	0	40	1	6	2	.750	0-0	0	92	.644	3.20	3.44

Jace Peterson

Bats: L Throws: R Pos: RF-13;1B-4;3B-4;LF-4;2B-3;PH-3;PR-3   JAYCE   Ht: 6'0" Wt: 215 Born: 5/9/1990 Age: 31

Year	Team	Lg	G	AB	H	2B	3B	HR	(Hm	Rd)	TB	R	RBI	RC	TBB	IBB	SO	HBP	SH	SF	SB	CS	GDP	Avg	OBP	Slg	OPS
2014	SD	NL	27	53	6	0	0	0	(0	0)	6	3	0	0	2	1	18	1	2	0	2	0	1	.113	.161	.113	.274
2015	Atl	NL	152	528	126	23	5	6	(1	5)	177	55	52	56	56	4	120	3	7	3	12	10	5	.239	.314	.335	.649
2016	Atl	NL	115	350	89	16	1	7	(3	4)	128	45	29	42	52	2	69	1	2	3	5	5	9	.254	.350	.366	.715
2017	Atl	NL	89	186	40	9	2	2	(2	0)	59	15	17	20	27	3	48	1	1	0	3	0	4	.215	.318	.317	.635
2018	2 Tms	AL	96	210	42	13	2	3	(2	1)	68	21	28	26	31	0	58	3	1	1	13	3	8	.200	.310	.324	.634
2019	Bal	NL	29	100	22	3	1	2	(2	0)	33	14	11	13	6	0	24	1	0	1	4	1	1	.220	.269	.330	.599
2020	Mil	NL	26	45	9	1	0	2	(1	1)	16	6	5	10	15	0	20	0	1	0	1	0	0	.200	.393	.356	.749
18	NYY	AL	3	10	3	0	0	0	(0	0)	3	0	0	1	1	0	3	0	0	0	0	1	0	.300	.364	.300	.664
18	Bal	AL	93	200	39	13	2	3	(2	1)	65	21	28	25	30	0	55	3	1	1	13	2	8	.195	.308	.325	.633
	7 ML YEARS		534	1472	334	65	11	22	(11	11)	487	159	142	167	189	10	357	10	13	9	40	19	28	.227	.317	.331	.648

Yusmeiro Petit

Pitches: R Bats: R Pos: RP-26   yooz-MAY-roh peh-TEET   Ht: 6'1" Wt: 252 Born: 11/22/1984 Age: 36

Year	Team	Lg	G	GS	GF	IP	BFP	H	R	ER	HR	SH	SF	HB	TBB	IBB	SO	WP	W	L	Pct	Sv-Op	Hld	Vel	OPS	ERC	ERA
2006	Fla	NL	15	1	5	26.1	129	46	28	28	7	1	1	0	9	1	20	0	1	1	.500	0-0	0	89	1.125	10.07	9.57
2007	Ari	NL	14	10	2	57.0	243	58	30	29	12	1	1	0	18	1	40	0	3	4	.429	0-0	0	87	.830	4.56	4.58
2008	Ari	NL	19	8	6	56.1	229	45	29	27	12	4	2	1	14	2	42	3	3	5	.375	0-0	0	87	.704	3.08	4.31
2009	Ari	NL	23	17	2	89.2	407	102	62	58	19	3	0	0	34	1	74	3	3	10	.231	0-0	0	87	.837	5.44	5.82
2012	SF	NL	1	1	0	4.2	22	7	2	2	1	0	0	0	4	0	1	1	0	0	-	0-0	0	88	.936	9.14	3.86
2013	SF	NL	8	7	0	48.0	196	46	19	19	4	2	0	0	11	1	47	0	4	1	.800	0-0	0	88	.660	3.08	3.56
2014	SF	NL	39	12	14	117.0	461	97	51	48	12	0	3	1	22	5	133	0	5	5	.500	0-0	0	89	.635	2.40	3.69
2015	SF	NL	42	1	15	76.0	316	75	32	31	11	1	6	1	15	2	59	3	1	1	.500	1-1	0	89	.743	3.48	3.67
2016	Was	NL	36	1	16	62.0	265	67	33	31	12	3	1	0	15	3	49	0	3	5	.375	1-2	1	89	.793	4.42	4.50
2017	LAA	AL	60	1	10	91.1	354	69	32	28	9	1	1	1	18	4	101	0	5	2	.714	4-5	14	90	.571	2.07	2.76
2018	Oak	AL	74	0	12	93.0	368	76	32	31	13	1	5	0	18	4	76	1	7	3	.700	0-2	16	89	.649	2.52	3.00

Year Team	Lg	G	GS	GF	IP	BFP	H	R	ER	HR	SH	SF	HB	TBB	IBB	SO	WP	W	L	Pct	Sv-Op	Hld	Vel	OPS	ERC	ERA
2019 Oak	AL	**80**	0	6	83.0	308	57	25	25	11	1	3	0	10	0	71	2	5	3	.625	0-1	29	89	.579	1.71	2.71
2020 Oak	AL	26	0	6	21.2	88	19	4	4	3	0	1	0	5	0	17	0	2	1	.667	0-0	7	88	.639	2.99	1.66
Postseason		5	0	0	15.1	57	9	3	3	1	0	0	0	4	1	15	1	3	0	1.000	0-0		88	.511	1.42	1.76
13 ML YEARS		437	59	94	826.0	3386	764	379	361	125	19	24	4	193	24	730	16	42	41	.506	6-11	67	88	.711	3.32	3.93

Tommy Pham

Bats: R **Throws:** R **Pos:** LF-18;DH-13   FAM   **Ht:** 6'1" **Wt:** 223 **Born:** 3/8/1988 **Age:** 33

Year Team	Lg	G	AB	H	2B	3B	HR	(Hm	Rd)	TB	R	RBI	RC	TBB	IBB	SO	HBP	SH	SF	SB	CS	GDP	Avg	OBP	Slg	OPS
2014 StL	NL	6	2	0	0	0	0	(0	0)	0	0	0	0	0	0	2	0	0	0	0	0	0	.000	.000	.000	.000
2015 StL	NL	52	153	41	7	5	5	(1	4)	73	28	18	26	19	1	41	0	0	1	2	0	1	.268	.347	.477	.824
2016 StL	NL	78	159	36	7	0	9	(3	6)	70	26	17	21	20	1	71	3	1	0	2	2	3	.226	.324	.440	.764
2017 StL	NL	128	444	136	22	2	23	(6	17)	231	95	73	93	71	0	117	10	2	3	25	7	18	.306	.411	.520	.931
2018 2 Tms		137	494	136	18	6	21	(9	12)	229	102	63	76	67	2	140	6	0	3	15	7	18	.275	.367	.464	.830
2019 TB	AL	145	567	155	33	2	21	(11	10)	255	77	68	86	81	4	123	5	0	1	25	4	22	.273	.369	.450	.818
2020 SD	NL	31	109	23	2	0	3	(0	3)	34	13	12	14	15	0	27	1	0	0	6	0	2	.211	.312	.312	.624
18 StL	NL	98	351	87	11	0	14	(6	8)	140	67	41	45	42	1	97	2	0	1	10	6	12	.248	.331	.399	.730
18 TB	AL	39	143	49	7	6	7	(3	4)	89	35	22	31	25	1	43	4	0	2	5	1	6	.343	.448	.622	1.071
Postseason		9	30	10	0	0	3	(2	1)	19	3	5	5	1	0	6	0	0	0	1	0	2	.333	.355	.633	.988
7 ML YEARS		577	1928	527	89	15	82	(30	52)	892	341	251	316	273	8	521	25	3	8	75	20	64	.273	.369	.463	.832

Josh Phegley

Bats: R **Throws:** R **Pos:** DH-6;PH-6;C-4   FEG-lee   **Ht:** 5'10" **Wt:** 225 **Born:** 2/12/1988 **Age:** 33

Year Team	Lg	G	AB	H	2B	3B	HR	(Hm	Rd)	TB	R	RBI	RC	TBB	IBB	SO	HBP	SH	SF	SB	CS	GDP	Avg	OBP	Slg	OPS
2013 CWS	AL	65	204	42	7	0	4	(2	2)	61	14	22	12	5	0	41	0	2	2	2	0	6	.206	.223	.299	.522
2014 CWS	AL	11	37	8	2	0	3	(3	0)	19	4	7	2	0	0	11	0	0	1	0	0	0	.216	.211	.514	.724
2015 Oak	AL	73	225	56	16	1	9	(6	3)	101	27	34	32	14	0	51	3	0	1	0	0	5	.249	.300	.449	.749
2016 Oak	AL	26	78	20	6	0	1	(1	0)	29	11	10	8	5	0	13	2	0	1	0	0	4	.256	.314	.372	.686
2017 Oak	AL	57	149	30	11	0	3	(0	3)	50	14	10	11	9	0	26	2	0	1	0	1	4	.201	.255	.336	.590
2018 Oak	AL	39	93	19	7	0	2	(1	1)	32	13	15	8	6	0	27	1	0	2	0	0	3	.204	.255	.344	.599
2019 Oak	AL	106	314	75	18	0	12	(4	8)	129	44	62	40	15	0	63	6	2	5	0	1	11	.239	.282	.411	.693
2020 ChC	NL	11	16	1	0	0	1	(1	0)	4	4	2	1	1	0	3	1	0	0	0	0	0	.063	.167	.250	.417
Postseason		1	2	0	0	0	0	(0	0)	0	0	0	0	0	0	1	0	0	0	0	0	0	.000	.000	.000	.000
8 ML YEARS		388	1116	251	67	1	35	(18	17)	425	131	162	114	55	0	235	15	4	13	2	2	33	.225	.268	.381	.649

David Phelps

Pitches: R **Bats:** R **Pos:** RP-22   **Ht:** 6'2" **Wt:** 198 **Born:** 10/9/1986 **Age:** 34

Year Team	Lg	G	GS	GF	IP	BFP	H	R	ER	HR	SH	SF	HB	TBB	IBB	SO	WP	W	L	Pct	Sv-Op	Hld	Vel	OPS	ERC	ERA
2012 NYY	AL	33	11	5	99.2	414	81	38	37	14	4	3	6	33	2	96	2	4	4	.500	0-0	2	91	.682	3.48	3.34
2013 NYY	AL	22	12	3	86.2	376	88	50	48	8	1	2	5	35	1	79	2	6	5	.545	0-1	1	90	.749	4.38	4.98
2014 NYY	AL	32	17	5	113.0	497	115	62	55	13	4	3	7	46	2	92	2	5	5	.500	1-1	5	90	.753	4.52	4.38
2015 Mia	NL	23	19	1	112.0	482	119	59	56	11	2	5	4	33	0	77	2	4	8	.333	0-0	0	94	.729	4.13	4.50
2016 Mia	NL	64	5	6	86.2	352	61	23	22	6	1	2	2	38	6	114	0	7	6	.538	4-10	25	94	.582	2.47	2.28
2017 2 Tms		54	0	5	55.2	238	51	23	21	5	2	2	1	26	3	62	0	4	5	.444	0-8	21	94	.693	3.82	3.40
2019 2 Tms		41	1	4	34.1	147	31	14	13	5	0	1	1	17	1	36	3	2	1	.667	1-5	5	93	.755	4.36	3.41
2020 2 Tms		22	0	4	20.2	85	19	16	15	7	0	0	1	5	0	31	1	2	4	.333	0-2	6	94	.813	4.78	6.53
17 Mia	NL	44	0	4	47.0	197	42	20	18	5	2	1	0	21	3	51	0	2	4	.333	0-6	18	94	.699	3.68	3.45
17 Sea	AL	10	0	1	8.2	41	9	3	3	0	0	1	1	5	0	11	0	2	1	.667	0-2	3	94	.660	4.54	3.12
19 Tor	AL	17	1	1	17.1	71	14	7	7	3	0	0	1	7	1	18	1	0	0	-	0-2	4	92	.754	3.77	3.63
19 ChC	NL	24	0	3	17.0	76	17	7	6	2	0	1	0	10	0	18	2	2	1	.667	1-3	1	93	.755	4.98	3.18
20 Mil	NL	12	0	3	13.0	48	7	5	4	2	0	0	1	2	0	20	1	2	3	.400	0-1	4	94	.497	1.56	2.77
20 Phi	NL	10	0	1	7.2	37	12	11	11	5	0	0	0	3	0	11	0	0	1	.000	0-1	2	94	1.229	12.43	12.91
Postseason		3	0	1	3.1	19	7	4	3	0	0	0	0	1	0	2	0	0	2	.000	0-0	0	90	1.032	8.97	8.10
8 ML YEARS		291	65	33	608.2	2591	565	285	267	69	14	18	27	238	15	587	12	34	38	.472	6-27	65	91	.710	3.89	3.95

Brett Phillips

Bats: L **Throws:** R **Pos:** CF-15;RF-13;LF-7;PR-4;PH-3;DH-2   **Ht:** 6'0" **Wt:** 195 **Born:** 5/30/1994 **Age:** 27

Year Team	Lg	G	AB	H	2B	3B	HR	(Hm	Rd)	TB	R	RBI	RC	TBB	IBB	SO	HBP	SH	SF	SB	CS	GDP	Avg	OBP	Slg	OPS
2017 Mil	NL	37	87	24	3	0	4	(2	2)	39	9	12	14	9	2	34	1	1	0	5	0	0	.276	.351	.448	.799
2018 2 Tms		51	134	25	4	3	2	(1	1)	41	15	11	10	11	0	61	1	0	1	1	1	2	.187	.252	.306	.558
2019 KC	AL	30	65	9	2	0	2	(1	1)	17	7	6	2	10	0	23	0	2	2	3	0	1	.138	.247	.262	.508
2020 2 Tms		35	51	10	0	2	2	(1	1)	20	10	5	6	8	0	15	0	0	0	6	1	0	.196	.305	.392	.697
18 Mil	NL	15	22	4	0	1	0	(0	0)	6	2	4	2	2	0	11	0	0	0	0	0	1	.182	.250	.273	.523
18 KC	AL	36	112	21	4	2	2	(1	1)	35	13	7	8	9	0	50	1	0	1	1	1	1	.188	.252	.313	.565
20 KC	AL	18	31	7	0	1	1	(0	1)	12	8	2	3	3	0	8	0	0	0	3	1	0	.226	.294	.387	.681
20 TB	AL	17	20	3	0	1	1	(1	0)	8	2	3	3	5	0	7	0	0	0	3	0	0	.150	.320	.400	.720
4 ML YEARS		153	337	68	9	5	10	(5	5)	117	41	34	32	38	2	133	2	3	3	15	2	3	.202	.284	.347	.631

Evan Phillips

Pitches: R Bats: R Pos: RP-14   Ht: 6'2" Wt: 215 Born: 9/11/1994 Age: 26

			HOW MUCH PITCHED						WHAT HE GAVE UP										THE RESULTS							
Year	Team	Lg	G	GS	GF	IP	BFP	H	R	ER	HR	SH	SF	HB	TBB	IBB	SO	WP	W	L	Pct	Sv-Op	Hld	Vel	OPS	ERC	ERA
2018	2 Tms		9	1	4	11.2	59	13	19	17	5	0	0	1	10	0	8	1	0	1	.000	0-0	0	94	1.073	9.76	13.11
2019	Bal	AL	25	0	2	28.0	140	32	20	20	2	1	2	5	20	0	40	2	0	1	.000	0-0	3	94	.821	6.59	6.43
2020	Bal	AL	14	0	3	14.1	69	14	8	8	1	0	0	3	10	0	20	1	1	1	.500	0-0	2	95	.695	5.67	5.02
18	Atl	NL	4	0	4	6.1	29	6	6	6	3	0	0	0	4	0	3	0	0	0	-	0-0	0	94	.985	7.41	8.53
18	Bal	AL	5	1	0	5.1	30	7	13	11	2	0	0	1	6	0	5	1	0	1	.000	0-0	0	94	1.162	12.53	18.56
	3 ML YEARS		48	1	9	54.0	268	59	47	45	8	1	2	9	40	0	68	4	1	3	.250	0-0	5	94	.844	7.02	7.50

Kevin Pillar

Bats: R Throws: R Pos: CF-27;RF-25;PH-5;DH-3;LF-2   pih-LAHR   Ht: 6'0" Wt: 200 Born: 1/4/1989 Age: 32

						BATTING															RUNNING			AVERAGES			
Year	Team	Lg	G	AB	H	2B	3B	HR	(Hm	Rd)	TB	R	RBI	RC	TBB	IBB	SO	HBP	SH	SF	SB	CS	GDP	Avg	OBP	Slg	OPS
2013	Tor	AL	36	102	21	4	0	3	(1	2)	34	11	13	9	4	0	29	2	2	0	1	0	0	.206	.250	.333	.121
2014	Tor	AL	53	116	31	9	0	2	(2	0)	46	19	7	8	4	0	28	1	0	1	1	2	3	.267	.295	.397	.692
2015	Tor	AL	159	586	163	31	2	12	(6	6)	234	76	56	73	28	1	85	5	4	5	25	4	9	.278	.314	.399	.713
2016	Tor	AL	146	548	146	35	2	7	(3	4)	206	59	53	66	24	0	90	6	3	3	14	6	12	.266	.303	.376	.679
2017	Tor	AL	154	587	150	37	1	16	(6	10)	237	72	42	58	33	0	95	3	6	3	15	6	13	.256	.300	.404	.704
2018	Tor	AL	142	512	129	40	2	15	(11	4)	218	65	59	59	18	0	98	6	0	6	14	3	8	.252	.282	.426	.708
2019	2 Tms		161	611	158	37	3	21	(11	10)	264	83	88	76	18	4	89	9	0	7	14	5	15	.259	.287	.432	.719
2020	2 Tms		54	208	60	12	3	6	(2	4)	96	34	26	29	13	1	41	2	0	0	5	2	4	.288	.336	.462	.798
19	Tor	AL	5	16	1	0	0	0	(0	0)	1	1	1	0	0	0	3	0	0	1	0	0	0	.063	.059	.063	.121
19	SF		156	595	157	37	3	21	(11	10)	263	82	87	76	18	4	86	9	0	6	14	5	15	.264	.293	.442	.735
20	Bos	AL	30	117	32	7	2	4	(2	2)	55	20	13	14	8	0	23	1	0	0	1	1	4	.274	.325	.470	.795
20	Col	NL	24	91	28	5	1	2	(0	2)	41	14	13	15	5	1	18	1	0	0	4	1	0	.308	.351	.451	.801
	Postseason		20	74	15	6	0	2	(0	2)	27	7	8	8	5	1	14	0	0	1	3	1	1	.203	.250	.365	.615
	8 ML YEARS		905	3270	858	205	13	82	(42	40)	1335	419	344	378	142	6	555	37	12	25	88	29	64	.262	.299	.408	.707

Manny Pina

Bats: R Throws: R Pos: C-13;PH-3   PEEN-yah   Ht: 6'0" Wt: 222 Born: 6/5/1987 Age: 34

						BATTING															RUNNING			AVERAGES			
Year	Team	Lg	G	AB	H	2B	3B	HR	(Hm	Rd)	TB	R	RBI	RC	TBB	IBB	SO	HBP	SH	SF	SB	CS	GDP	Avg	OBP	Slg	OPS
2011	KC	AL	4	14	3	2	0	0	(0	0)	5	2	0	1	1	0	2	0	0	0	0	0	1	.214	.267	.357	.624
2012	KC	AL	1	2	0	0	0	0	(0	0)	0	0	0	0	0	0	0	0	0	0	0	0	0	.000	.000	.000	.000
2016	Mil	NL	33	71	18	4	0	2	(1	1)	28	4	12	8	10	0	15	0	0	0	0	1	2	.254	.346	.394	.740
2017	Mil	NL	107	330	92	21	0	9	(6	3)	140	45	43	46	20	0	79	5	1	3	2	0	8	.279	.327	.424	.751
2018	Mil	NL	98	306	77	13	2	9	(6	3)	121	39	28	27	21	3	62	5	1	4	2	0	13	.252	.307	.395	.702
2019	Mil	NL	76	158	36	8	0	7	(5	2)	65	10	25	20	16	1	50	4	0	1	0	0	1	.228	.313	.411	.724
2020	Mil	NL	15	39	9	1	0	2	(2	0)	16	4	5	6	3	0	11	3	0	0	0	0	0	.231	.333	.410	.744
	Postseason		5	7	3	1	0	0	(0	0)	4	1	0	3	5	0	1	0	0	0	0	0	0	.429	.667	.571	1.238
	7 ML YEARS		334	920	235	49	2	29	(20	9)	375	104	113	108	71	4	219	17	2	8	4	1	25	.255	.318	.408	.726

Chad Pinder

Bats: R Throws: R Pos: 2B-13;3B-7;PH-7;LF-2;RF-1;DH-1;PR-1   Ht: 6'2" Wt: 210 Born: 3/29/1992 Age: 29

						BATTING															RUNNING			AVERAGES			
Year	Team	Lg	G	AB	H	2B	3B	HR	(Hm	Rd)	TB	R	RBI	RC	TBB	IBB	SO	HBP	SH	SF	SB	CS	GDP	Avg	OBP	Slg	OPS
2016	Oak	AL	22	51	12	4	0	1	(0	1)	19	4	4	5	3	0	14	0	0	1	0	0	1	.235	.273	.373	.645
2017	Oak	AL	87	282	67	15	1	15	(10	5)	129	36	42	37	18	0	92	5	0	3	2	1	7	.238	.292	.457	.750
2018	Oak	AL	110	298	77	12	1	13	(6	7)	130	43	27	35	27	1	88	6	2	0	0	2	4	.258	.332	.436	.769
2019	Oak	AL	124	341	82	21	0	13	(6	7)	142	45	47	43	20	0	88	5	1	3	0	1	11	.240	.290	.416	.706
2020	Oak	AL	24	56	13	3	0	2	(0	2)	22	8	8	8	5	0	13	0	0	0	0	0	3	.232	.295	.393	.688
	5 ML YEARS		367	1028	251	55	2	44	(22	22)	442	136	128	128	73	1	295	16	3	7	2	4	26	.244	.302	.430	.732

Michael Pineda

Pitches: R Bats: R Pos: SP-5   pah-NAY-dah   Ht: 6'7" Wt: 280 Born: 1/18/1989 Age: 32

			HOW MUCH PITCHED						WHAT HE GAVE UP										THE RESULTS							
Year	Team	Lg	G	GS	GF	IP	BFP	H	R	ER	HR	SH	SF	HB	TBB	IBB	SO	WP	W	L	Pct	Sv-Op	Hld	Vel	OPS	ERC	ERA
2011	Sea	AL	28	28	0	171.0	696	133	76	71	18	4	3	5	55	1	173	9	9	10	.474	0-0	0	95	.621	2.73	3.74
2014	NYY	AL	13	13	0	76.1	290	56	18	16	5	2	1	0	7	0	59	3	5	5	.500	0-0	0	92	.526	1.51	1.89
2015	NYY	AL	27	27	0	160.2	668	176	83	78	21	4	6	3	21	0	156	4	12	10	.545	0-0	0	94	.752	3.82	4.37
2016	NYY	AL	32	32	0	175.2	756	184	98	94	27	0	3	6	53	1	207	7	6	12	.333	0-0	0	94	.784	4.45	4.82
2017	NYY	AL	17	17	0	96.1	410	103	55	47	20	0	4	2	21	0	92	5	8	4	.667	0-0	0	94	.769	4.52	4.39
2019	Min	AL	26	26	0	146.0	600	141	68	65	23	2	7	5	28	1	140	8	11	5	.688	0-0	0	93	.721	3.58	4.01
2020	Min	AL	5	5	0	26.2	111	25	10	10	0	0	2	1	7	0	25	0	2	0	1.000	0-0	0	92	.604	2.69	3.38
	7 ML YEARS		148	148	0	852.2	3531	818	408	381	114	12	26	22	192	3	852	36	53	46	.535	0-0	0	93	.707	3.48	4.02

Stephen Piscotty

Bats: R Throws: R Pos: RF-44;PR-1   Ht: 6'4" Wt: 211 Born: 1/14/1991 Age: 30

						BATTING															RUNNING			AVERAGES			
Year	Team	Lg	G	AB	H	2B	3B	HR	(Hm	Rd)	TB	R	RBI	RC	TBB	IBB	SO	HBP	SH	SF	SB	CS	GDP	Avg	OBP	Slg	OPS
2015	StL	NL	63	233	71	15	4	7	(4	3)	115	29	39	41	20	2	56	1	0	7	2	1	7	.305	.359	.494	.853
2016	StL	NL	153	582	159	35	3	22	(13	9)	266	86	85	97	51	0	133	12	1	2	7	5	14	.273	.343	.457	.800
2017	StL	NL	107	341	80	16	1	9	(1	8)	125	40	39	43	52	2	87	5	0	3	3	6	11	.235	.342	.367	.708
2018	Oak	AL	151	546	146	41	0	27	(10	17)	268	78	88	87	42	0	114	12	0	5	2	0	21	.267	.331	.491	.821

Year Team	Lg	G	AB	H	2B	3B	HR	(Hm	Rd)	TB	R	RBI	RC	TBB	IBB	SO	HBP	SH	SF	SB	CS	GDP	Avg	OBP	Slg	OPS
													BATTING						**RUNNING**			**AVERAGES**			
2019 Oak	AL	93	357	89	17	1	13	(8	5)	147	46	44	42	29	0	84	3	1	3	2	0	13	.249	.309	.412	.720
2020 Oak	AL	45	159	36	6	0	5	(1	4)	57	17	29	21	9	0	53	1	1	1	4	0	4	.226	.271	.358	.629
Postseason		5	19	6	1	0	3	(1	2)	16	5	6	8	3	0	10	0	0	0	0	0	0	.316	.409	.842	1.251
6 ML YEARS		612	2218	581	130	9	83	(37	46)	978	296	324	331	203	4	527	34	3	16	20	12	70	.262	.331	.441	.772

Nick Pivetta

Pitches: R **Bats:** R **Pos:** RP-3; SP-2

Ht: 6'5" **Wt:** 214 **Born:** 2/14/1993 **Age:** 28

Year Team	Lg	G	GS	GF	IP	BFP	H	R	ER	HR	SH	SF	HB	TBB	IBB	SO	WP	W	L	Pct	Sv-Op	Hld	Vel	OPS	ERC	ERA
			HOW MUCH PITCHED					**WHAT HE GAVE UP**												**THE RESULTS**						
2017 Phi	NL	26	26	0	133.0	584	144	91	89	25	4	7	4	57	0	140	11	8	10	.444	0-0	0	94	.846	5.52	6.02
2018 Phi	NL	33	32	1	164.0	694	163	91	87	24	8	5	5	51	0	188	8	7	14	.333	0-0	0	95	.743	4.15	4.77
2019 Phi	NL	30	13	8	93.2	421	103	64	56	20	4	4	4	39	2	89	4	4	6	.400	1-1	0	95	.866	5.67	5.38
2020 2 Tms		5	2	0	15.2	71	18	12	12	4	0	1	1	6	0	17	1	2	0	1.000	0-0	1	93	.924	6.28	6.89
20 Phi	NL	3	0	0	5.2	29	10	10	10	3	0	1	1	1	0	4	1	0	0	-	0-0	1	94	1.375	12.33	15.88
20 Bos	AL	2	2	0	10.0	42	8	2	2	1	0	0	0	5	0	13	0	2	0	1.000	0-0	0	92	.607	3.39	1.80
4 ML YEARS		94	73	9	406.1	1770	428	258	244	73	16	17	14	153	2	434	24	21	30	.412	1-1	2	95	.813	5.02	5.40

Kevin Plawecki

Bats: R **Throws:** R **Pos:** C-20;1B-2;DH-2

plah-WEH-kee

Ht: 6'2" **Wt:** 208 **Born:** 2/26/1991 **Age:** 30

Year Team	Lg	G	AB	H	2B	3B	HR	(Hm	Rd)	TB	R	RBI	RC	TBB	IBB	SO	HBP	SH	SF	SB	CS	GDP	Avg	OBP	Slg	OPS
						BATTING														**RUNNING**			**AVERAGES**			
2015 NYM	NL	73	233	51	9	0	3	(1	2)	69	18	21	22	17	4	60	4	1	3	0	0	4	.219	.280	.296	.576
2016 NYM	NL	48	132	26	6	0	1	(0	1)	35	6	11	11	17	2	33	2	0	0	0	0	1	.197	.298	.265	.563
2017 NYM	NL	37	100	26	5	0	3	(3	0)	40	11	13	15	14	2	17	3	0	1	1	0	2	.260	.364	.400	.764
2018 NYM	NL	79	238	50	13	2	7	(5	2)	88	33	30	25	28	2	65	9	1	1	0	1	12	.210	.315	.370	.685
2019 Cle	AL	60	158	35	10	0	3	(3	0)	54	13	17	14	12	0	31	3	0	1	0	1	4	.222	.287	.342	.629
2020 Bos	AL	24	82	28	5	1	1	(1	0)	38	8	17	17	5	0	14	2	0	0	1	0	4	.341	.393	.463	.857
6 ML YEARS		321	943	216	48	3	18	(13	5)	324	89	109	104	93	10	220	23	2	6	2	2	27	.229	.312	.344	.655

Zach Plesac

Pitches: R **Bats:** R **Pos:** SP-8

Ht: 6'3" **Wt:** 220 **Born:** 1/21/1995 **Age:** 26

Year Team	Lg	G	GS	GF	IP	BFP	H	R	ER	HR	SH	SF	HB	TBB	IBB	SO	WP	W	L	Pct	Sv-Op	Hld	Vel	OPS	ERC	ERA
			HOW MUCH PITCHED					**WHAT HE GAVE UP**												**THE RESULTS**						
2019 Cle	AL	21	21	0	115.2	475	102	52	49	19	2	0	3	40	0	88	1	8	6	.571	0-0	0	94	.744	3.82	3.81
2020 Cle	AL	8	8	0	55.1	206	38	14	14	8	0	0	1	6	0	57	0	4	2	.667	0-0	0	93	.565	1.78	2.28
2 ML YEARS		29	29	0	171.0	681	140	66	63	27	2	0	4	46	0	145	1	12	8	.600	0-0	0	94	.688	3.12	3.32

Adam Plutko

Pitches: R **Bats:** R **Pos:** RP-6; SP-4

PLET-ko

Ht: 6'3" **Wt:** 215 **Born:** 10/3/1991 **Age:** 29

Year Team	Lg	G	GS	GF	IP	BFP	H	R	ER	HR	SH	SF	HB	TBB	IBB	SO	WP	W	L	Pct	Sv-Op	Hld	Vel	OPS	ERC	ERA
			HOW MUCH PITCHED					**WHAT HE GAVE UP**												**THE RESULTS**						
2016 Cle	AL	2	0	1	3.2	18	5	3	3	1	0	0	0	2	0	3	1	0	0	-	0-0	0	91	.951	8.17	7.36
2018 Cle	AL	17	12	4	76.2	326	78	45	45	21	1	2	1	23	1	60	3	4	5	.444	1-1	0	91	.869	5.00	5.28
2019 Cle	AL	21	20	0	109.1	462	115	61	59	22	0	2	4	26	2	78	0	7	5	.583	0-0	0	91	.802	4.55	4.86
2020 Cle	AL	10	4	5	27.2	116	30	15	15	5	1	0	1	7	0	15	0	2	2	.500	1-1	0	91	.826	4.79	4.88
4 ML YEARS		50	36	10	217.1	922	228	124	122	49	2	4	6	58	3	156	4	13	12	.520	2-2	0	91	.831	4.80	5.05

Colin Poche

Pitches: L **Bats:** L **Pos:** P

poh-SHAY

Ht: 6'3" **Wt:** 225 **Born:** 1/17/1994 **Age:** 27

Year Team	Lg	G	GS	GF	IP	BFP	H	R	ER	HR	SH	SF	HB	TBB	IBB	SO	WP	W	L	Pct	Sv-Op	Hld	Vel	OPS	ERC	ERA
			HOW MUCH PITCHED					**WHAT HE GAVE UP**												**THE RESULTS**						
2019 TB	AL	51	0	8	51.2	207	33	27	27	9	1	0	5	19	1	72	2	5	5	.500	2-6	16	93	.650	2.88	4.70
Postseason		5	0	3	4.1	15	2	1	1	1	0	0	0	0	0	6	0	0	0	-	0-0	0	93	.467	0.97	2.08

Gregory Polanco

Bats: L **Throws:** L **Pos:** RF-39;DH-8;PH-5

poh-LAHN-koh

Ht: 6'5" **Wt:** 235 **Born:** 9/14/1991 **Age:** 29

Year Team	Lg	G	AB	H	2B	3B	HR	(Hm	Rd)	TB	R	RBI	RC	TBB	IBB	SO	HBP	SH	SF	SB	CS	GDP	Avg	OBP	Slg	OPS
						BATTING														**RUNNING**			**AVERAGES**			
2014 Pit	NL	89	277	65	9	4	7	(5	2)	95	50	33	32	30	1	59	0	2	2	14	5	1	.235	.307	.343	.650
2015 Pit	NL	153	593	152	35	6	9	(6	3)	226	83	52	73	55	6	121	1	1	2	27	10	5	.256	.320	.381	.701
2016 Pit	NL	144	527	136	34	4	22	(9	13)	244	79	86	73	53	6	119	0	1	6	17	6	13	.258	.323	.463	.786
2017 Pit	NL	108	379	95	20	0	11	(7	4)	148	39	35	39	27	4	60	3	0	1	8	1	5	.251	.305	.391	.695
2018 Pit	NL	130	461	117	32	6	23	(12	11)	230	75	81	76	61	5	117	3	0	7	12	2	11	.254	.340	.499	.839
2019 Pit	NL	42	153	37	8	1	6	(3	3)	65	23	17	17	12	1	49	1	0	1	3	1	4	.242	.301	.425	.726
2020 Pit	NL	50	157	24	6	0	7	(4	3)	51	12	22	12	13	0	65	0	0	3	3	1	1	.153	.214	.325	.539
Postseason		1	4	0	0	0	0	(0	0)	0	0	0	0	0	0	2	0	0	0	0	0	0	.000	.000	.000	.000
7 ML YEARS		716	2547	626	144	17	85	(46	39)	1059	361	326	322	251	23	590	8	4	21	84	26	40	.246	.313	.416	.729

Jorge Polanco

Bats: B Throws: R Pos: SS-53;PH-2
poh-LAHN-koh
Ht: 5'11" Wt: 208 Born: 7/5/1993 Age: 27

Year	Team	Lg	G	AB	H	2B	3B	HR	(Hm	Rd)	TB	R	RBI	RC	TBB	IBB	SO	HBP	SH	SF	SB	CS	GDP	Avg	OBP	Slg	OPS
2014	Min	AL	5	6	2	1	1	0	(0	0)	5	2	3	4	2	0	2	0	0	0	0	0	0	.333	.500	.833	1.333
2015	Min	AL	4	10	3	0	0	0	(0	0)	3	1	1	3	2	0	1	0	0	0	1	0	0	.300	.417	.300	.717
2016	Min	AL	69	245	69	15	4	4	(1	3)	104	24	27	36	17	0	46	3	2	3	4	3	3	.282	.332	.424	.757
2017	Min	AL	133	488	125	30	3	13	(4	9)	200	60	74	68	41	1	78	2	7	6	13	5	7	.256	.313	.410	.723
2018	Min	AL	77	302	87	18	3	6	(1	5)	129	38	42	50	25	0	62	2	3	1	7	7	5	.288	.345	.427	.773
2019	Min	AL	153	631	186	40	7	22	(9	13)	306	107	79	112	60	2	116	4	2	7	4	3	11	.295	.356	.485	.841
2020	Min	AL	55	209	54	8	0	4	(2	2)	74	22	19	23	13	0	35	1	2	1	4	2	7	.258	.304	.354	.658
	Postseason		4	15	4	0	0	1	(0	1)	7	3	2	3	3	0	3	1	0	0	1	0	0	.267	.421	.467	.888
	7 ML YEARS		496	1891	526	112	18	49	(17	32)	821	254	245	296	160	3	340	12	16	18	33	20	33	.278	.335	.434	.770

A.J. Pollock

Bats: R Throws: R Pos: LF-27;CF-16;DH-11;PH-8
Ht: 6'1" Wt: 210 Born: 12/5/1987 Age: 33

Year	Team	Lg	G	AB	H	2B	3B	HR	(Hm	Rd)	TB	R	RBI	RC	TBB	IBB	SO	HBP	SH	SF	SB	CS	GDP	Avg	OBP	Slg	OPS
2012	Ari	NL	31	81	20	4	1	2	(2	0)	32	8	8	9	9	1	11	0	1	2	1	2	2	.247	.315	.395	.710
2013	Ari	NL	137	443	119	28	5	8	(3	5)	181	64	38	58	33	1	82	2	3	1	12	3	5	.269	.322	.409	.730
2014	Ari	NL	75	265	80	19	6	7	(7	0)	132	41	24	43	19	0	46	2	1	0	14	3	4	.302	.353	.498	.851
2015	Ari	NL	157	609	192	39	6	20	(9	11)	303	111	76	106	53	0	89	2	0	9	39	7	19	.315	.367	.498	.865
2016	Ari	NL	12	41	10	0	0	0	(0	0)	10	6	4	5	5	0	8	0	0	0	4	0	1	.244	.326	.390	.716
2017	Ari	NL	112	425	113	33	6	14	(9	5)	200	73	49	66	35	1	71	6	0	0	20	6	8	.266	.330	.471	.801
2018	Ari	NL	113	413	106	21	5	21	(11	10)	200	61	65	57	31	2	100	8	1	7	13	2	6	.257	.316	.484	.800
2019	LAD	NL	86	308	82	15	1	15	(9	6)	144	49	47	50	23	1	74	7	0	4	5	1	7	.266	.327	.468	.795
2020	LAD	NL	55	196	54	9	0	16	(9	7)	111	30	34	29	12	1	45	0	0	2	2	2	6	.276	.314	.566	.881
	Postseason		9	27	3	1	1	1	(0	1)	9	4	3	3	3	0	15	0	0	0	0	0	0	.111	.200	.333	.533
	9 ML YEARS		778	2781	776	168	30	105	(59	46)	1319	446	345	423	220	7	526	27	6	25	110	26	58	.279	.335	.474	.809

Drew Pomeranz

Pitches: L Bats: R Pos: RP-20
POMM-er-anze
Ht: 6'5" Wt: 246 Born: 11/22/1988 Age: 32

			HOW MUCH PITCHED				WHAT HE GAVE UP										THE RESULTS						
Year	Team	Lg	G	GS	GF	IP	BFP	H	R	ER	HR	SH	SF	HB	TBB	IBB	SO	WP	W	L	Pct	Sv-Op	Hld	Vel	OPS	ERC	ERA
2011	Col	NL	4	4	0	18.1	77	19	11	11	0	1	0	1	5	0	13	1	2	1	.667	0-0	0	90	.700	3.36	5.40
2012	Col	NL	22	22	0	96.2	434	97	57	53	14	8	4	4	46	2	83	8	2	9	.182	0-0	0	91	.775	4.78	4.93
2013	Col	NL	8	4	0	21.2	105	25	15	15	4	1	1	1	19	1	19	0	0	4	.000	0-0	0	91	.951	8.04	6.23
2014	Oak	AL	20	10	4	69.0	278	51	22	18	7	1	0	1	26	0	64	0	5	4	.556	0-0	0	91	.586	2.70	2.35
2015	Oak	AL	53	9	9	86.0	357	71	44	35	8	4	5	3	31	1	82	2	5	6	.455	3-6	12	91	.651	3.05	3.66
2016	2 Tms		31	30	1	170.2	703	137	65	63	22	3	3	1	65	3	186	10	11	12	.478	0-0	0	90	.658	3.13	3.32
2017	Bos	AL	32	32	0	173.2	740	166	69	64	19	2	6	4	69	0	174	6	17	6	.739	0-0	0	91	.712	4.00	3.32
2018	Bos	AL	26	11	5	74.0	344	87	53	50	12	0	3	4	44	1	66	4	2	6	.250	0-0	1	89	.894	6.73	6.08
2019	2 Tms	NL	46	18	4	104.0	455	105	58	56	21	2	2	4	44	0	137	1	2	10	.167	2-2	12	93	.804	5.13	4.85
2020	SD	NL	20	0	5	18.2	73	9	3	3	1	0	0	0	10	0	29	0	1	0	1.000	4-5	9	95	.454	1.71	1.45
	16	SD	NL	17	17	0	102.0	411	67	30	28	8	2	3	1	41	2	115	7	8	7	.533	0-0	0	90	.555	2.17	2.47
	16	Bos	AL	14	13	1	68.2	292	70	35	35	14	1	0	0	24	1	71	3	3	5	.375	0-0	0	91	.799	4.73	4.59
	19	SF	NL	21	17	0	77.2	355	89	51	49	17	2	1	4	36	0	92	1	2	9	.182	0-0	0	92	.872	6.32	5.68
	19	Mil	NL	25	1	4	26.1	100	16	7	7	4	0	1	0	8	0	45	0	0	1	.000	2-2	12	94	.570	2.07	2.39
	Postseason		4	1	0	7.2	35	9	6	6	3	1	0	0	3	1	10	0	0	1	.000	0-0	1	93	.998	6.89	7.04
	10 ML YEARS		262	140	28	832.2	3566	767	397	368	108	22	25	23	359	8	853	32	47	58	.448	9-13	34	91	.723	4.07	3.98

Cody Ponce

Pitches: R Bats: R Pos: SP-3; RP-2
Ht: 6'5" Wt: 255 Born: 4/25/1994 Age: 27

			HOW MUCH PITCHED				WHAT HE GAVE UP										THE RESULTS						
Year	Team	Lg	G	GS	GF	IP	BFP	H	R	ER	HR	SH	SF	HB	TBB	IBB	SO	WP	W	L	Pct	Sv-Op	Hld	Vel	OPS	ERC	ERA
2020	Pit	NL	5	3	1	17.0	66	12	7	6	5	0	0	0	6	0	12	0	1	1	.500	0-0	0	93	.806	3.62	3.18

Daniel Ponce de Leon

Pitches: R Bats: R Pos: SP-8; RP-1
Ht: 6'3" Wt: 200 Born: 1/16/1992 Age: 29

			HOW MUCH PITCHED				WHAT HE GAVE UP										THE RESULTS						
Year	Team	Lg	G	GS	GF	IP	BFP	H	R	ER	HR	SH	SF	HB	TBB	IBB	SO	WP	W	L	Pct	Sv-Op	Hld	Vel	OPS	ERC	ERA
2018	StL	NL	11	4	2	33.0	132	24	10	10	2	0	1	1	13	0	31	0	2	0	.000	1-1	0	93	.596	2.54	2.73
2019	StL	NL	13	8	1	48.2	203	36	21	20	6	0	1	2	26	3	52	0	1	2	.333	0-0	0	93	.666	3.46	3.70
2020	StL	NL	9	8	1	32.2	143	23	18	18	8	0	0	2	20	0	45	0	1	3	.250	0-0	0	93	.744	4.43	4.96
	Postseason		1	0	1	2.0	9	2	1	1	0	0	0	0	1	0	4	0	0	0	-	0-0	0	95	.708	3.63	4.50
	3 ML YEARS		33	20	4	114.1	478	83	49	48	16	0	2	5	59	3	128	2	2	7	.222	1-1	0	93	.669	3.46	3.78

Sean Poppen

Pitches: R Bats: R Pos: RP-6
Ht: 6'3" Wt: 205 Born: 3/15/1994 Age: 27

			HOW MUCH PITCHED				WHAT HE GAVE UP										THE RESULTS						
Year	Team	Lg	G	GS	GF	IP	BFP	H	R	ER	HR	SH	SF	HB	TBB	IBB	SO	WP	W	L	Pct	Sv-Op	Hld	Vel	OPS	ERC	ERA
2019	Min	AL	4	0	3	8.1	36	10	7	7	1	0	0	0	5	0	9	0	0	0	-	0-0	0	95	.997	6.83	7.56
2020	Min	AL	6	0	4	7.2	35	9	4	4	0	0	0	0	4	0	10	3	0	0	-	0-0	1	94	.759	4.80	4.70
	2 ML YEARS		10	0	7	16.0	71	19	11	11	1	0	0	0	9	0	19	3	0	0	-	0-0	1	94	.878	5.81	6.19

Rick Porcello

Pitches: R Bats: R Pos: SP-12   pore-SELL-oh   Ht: 6'5" Wt: 205 Born: 12/27/1988 Age: 32

			HOW MUCH PITCHED					WHAT HE GAVE UP												THE RESULTS							
Year	Team	Lg	G	GS	GF	IP	BFP	H	R	ER	HR	SH	SF	HB	TBB	IBB	SO	WP	W	L	Pct	Sv-Op	Hld	Vel	OPS	ERC	ERA
2009	Det	AL	31	31	0	170.2	720	176	81	75	23	4	2	3	52	0	89	6	14	9	.609	0-0	0	91	.738	4.24	3.96
2010	Det	AL	27	27	0	162.2	700	188	96	89	18	1	2	7	38	2	84	11	10	12	.455	0-0	0	91	.752	4.56	4.92
2011	Det	AL	31	31	0	182.0	784	210	103	96	18	5	5	8	46	1	104	12	14	9	.609	0-0	0	90	.774	4.57	4.75
2012	Det	AL	31	31	0	176.1	783	226	101	90	16	2	3	6	44	3	107	6	10	12	.455	0-0	0	92	.808	5.16	4.59
2013	Det	AL	32	29	1	177.0	736	185	87	85	18	4	3	3	42	4	142	6	13	8	.619	0-0	0	91	.709	3.79	4.32
2014	Det	AL	32	31	1	204.2	840	211	89	78	18	3	4	4	41	4	129	0	15	13	.536	0-0	0	90	.712	3.50	3.43
2015	Bos	AL	28	28	0	172.0	737	196	103	94	25	2	5	10	38	0	149	12	9	15	.375	0-0	0	91	.787	4.76	4.92
2016	Bos	AL	33	33	0	223.0	890	193	85	78	23	2	3	13	32	0	189	3	22	4	.846	0-0	0	90	.635	2.64	3.15
2017	Bos	AL	33	33	0	203.1	885	236	125	105	38	1	6	6	48	1	181	5	11	17	.393	0-0	0	90	.826	5.04	4.65
2018	Bos	AL	33	33	0	191.1	808	177	97	91	27	3	6	16	48	0	190	1	17	7	.708	0-0	0	90	.698	3.64	4.28
2019	Bos	AL	32	32	0	174.1	768	198	114	107	31	3	1	6	45	2	143	5	14	12	.538	0-0	0	90	.809	4.87	5.52
2020	NYM	NL	12	12	0	59.0	261	74	41	37	5	0	0	2	15	0	54	1	1	7	.125	0-0	0	92	.783	4.99	5.64
Postseason			16	7	5	40.0	174	44	23	21	6	0	2	5	7	2	34	2	1	3	.250	0-0	2	92	.803	4.47	4.73
12 ML YEARS			355	351	2	2096.1	8912	2270	1122	1025	260	30	40	84	489	17	1561	70	150	125	.545	0-0	0	91	.750	4.21	4.40

Buster Posey

Bats: R Throws: R Pos: C   Ht: 6'1" Wt: 213 Born: 3/27/1987 Age: 34

			BATTING																		RUNNING			AVERAGES			
Year	Team	Lg	G	AB	H	2B	3B	HR	(Hm	Rd)	TB	R	RBI	RC	TBB	IBB	SO	HBP	SH	SF	SB	CS	GDP	Avg	OBP	Slg	OPS
2009	SF	NL	7	17	2	0	0	0	(0	0)	2	1	0	0	0	0	4	0	0	0	0	0	0	.118	.118	.118	.235
2010	SF	NL	108	406	124	23	2	18	(6	12)	205	58	67	70	30	5	55	4	0	3	0	2	12	.305	.357	.505	.862
2011	SF	NL	45	162	46	5	0	4	(1	3)	63	17	21	26	18	3	30	4	0	4	3	0	4	.284	.368	.389	.756
2012	SF	NL	148	530	178	39	1	24	(7	17)	291	78	103	111	69	7	96	2	0	9	1	1	19	.336	.408	.549	.957
2013	SF	NL	148	520	153	34	1	15	(8	7)	234	61	72	77	60	8	70	8	0	7	2	1	16	.294	.371	.450	.821
2014	SF	NL	147	547	170	28	2	22	(11	11)	268	72	89	94	47	5	69	3	0	8	0	1	16	.311	.364	.490	.854
2015	SF	NL	150	557	177	28	0	19	(6	13)	262	74	95	96	56	10	52	3	0	7	2	0	17	.318	.379	.470	.849
2016	SF	NL	146	539	155	33	2	14	(7	7)	234	82	80	82	64	7	68	3	0	8	6	1	18	.288	.362	.434	.796
2017	SF	NL	140	494	158	34	0	12	(3	9)	228	62	67	84	61	13	66	8	0	5	6	1	17	.320	.400	.462	.861
2018	SF	NL	105	398	102	22	1	5	(4	1)	152	47	41	58	45	3	53	3	0	2	3	2	12	.284	.359	.382	.741
2019	SF	NL	114	405	104	24	0	7	(1	6)	149	43	38	49	34	1	71	4	1	1	0	0	18	.257	.320	.368	.688
Postseason			53	206	51	4	0	4	(1	3)	67	17	23	21	23	5	41	1	0	2	1	1	4	.248	.323	.325	.649
11 ML YEARS			1258	4575	1380	270	9	140	(54	86)	2088	595	673	747	484	62	634	42	1	51	23	9	148	.302	.370	.456	.826

Ryan Pressly

Pitches: R Bats: R Pos: RP-23   Ht: 6'2" Wt: 206 Born: 12/15/1988 Age: 32

			HOW MUCH PITCHED					WHAT HE GAVE UP												THE RESULTS							
Year	Team	Lg	G	GS	GF	IP	BFP	H	R	ER	HR	SH	SF	HB	TBB	IBB	SO	WP	W	L	Pct	Sv-Op	Hld	Vel	OPS	ERC	ERA
2013	Min	AL	49	0	18	76.2	315	71	37	33	5	2	3	0	27	1	49	7	3	3	.500	0-0	0	93	.677	3.31	3.87
2014	Min	AL	25	0	5	28.1	122	30	10	9	3	2	3	1	8	2	14	1	2	0	1.000	0-1	2	93	.779	3.98	2.86
2015	Min	AL	27	0	6	27.2	119	27	9	9	0	1	1	0	12	1	22	2	2	2	.600	0-0	4	94	.645	3.31	2.93
2016	Min	AL	72	0	10	75.1	328	79	34	31	8	4	2	0	23	2	67	7	6	7	.462	1-6	13	95	.725	4.01	3.70
2017	Min	AL	57	0	10	61.1	252	52	34	32	10	2	1	3	19	5	61	5	2	3	.400	0-1	6	96	.697	3.41	4.70
2018	2 Tms	AL	77	0	11	71.0	292	57	21	20	6	1	2	3	22	1	101	8	2	1	.667	2-8	21	96	.604	2.71	2.54
2019	Hou	AL	55	0	2	54.1	211	37	15	14	6	0	1	0	12	0	72	4	2	3	.400	3-8	31	96	.543	1.85	2.32
2020	Hou	AL	23	0	15	21.0	91	21	10	8	2	0	0	1	7	1	29	1	1	3	.250	12-16	0	95	.728	3.85	3.43
18	Min	AL	51	0	7	47.2	208	46	19	18	5	1	2	2	19	1	69	6	1	1	.500	0-4	8	96	.699	3.99	3.40
18	Hou	AL	26	0	4	23.1	84	11	2	2	1	0	0	1	3	0	32	2	1	0	1.000	2-4	13	96	.379	0.88	0.77
Postseason			15	0	1	10.2	52	13	9	8	0	1	0	0	6	1	13	2	1	0	1.000	0-0	3	95	.684	4.78	6.75
8 ML YEARS			385	0	83	415.2	1730	374	170	156	40	12	13	10	130	13	415	35	21	22	.488	18-40	78	95	.668	3.21	3.38

David Price

Pitches: L Bats: L Pos: P   Ht: 6'5" Wt: 215 Born: 8/26/1985 Age: 35

			HOW MUCH PITCHED					WHAT HE GAVE UP												THE RESULTS							
Year	Team	Lg	G	GS	GF	IP	BFP	H	R	ER	HR	SH	SF	HB	TBB	IBB	SO	WP	W	L	Pct	Sv-Op	Hld	Vel	OPS	ERC	ERA
2008	TB	AL	5	1	0	14.0	57	9	4	3	1	0	1	1	4	0	12	0	0	0	-	0-0	0	94	.501	1.86	1.93
2009	TB	AL	23	23	0	128.1	557	119	72	63	17	3	2	4	54	0	102	2	10	7	.588	0-0	0	93	.716	4.05	4.42
2010	TB	AL	32	31	0	208.2	861	170	71	63	15	4	3	5	79	1	188	5	19	6	.760	0-0	0	95	.637	2.91	2.72
2011	TB	AL	34	34	0	224.1	918	192	93	87	22	4	7	9	63	5	218	1	12	13	.480	0-0	0	95	.659	2.97	3.49
2012	TB	AL	31	31	0	211.0	836	173	63	60	16	2	3	5	59	2	205	8	20	5	.800	0-0	0	96	.602	2.67	2.56
2013	TB	AL	27	27	0	186.2	740	178	78	69	16	1	2	3	27	0	151	6	10	8	.556	0-0	0	94	.661	2.89	3.33
2014	2 Tms	AL	34	34	0	248.1	1009	230	100	90	25	4	3	5	38	1	271	6	15	12	.556	0-0	0	93	.647	2.79	3.26
2015	2 Tms	AL	32	32	0	220.1	888	190	70	60	17	4	8	3	47	2	225	4	18	5	.783	0-0	0	94	.621	2.54	2.45
2016	Bos	AL	35	35	0	230.0	951	227	106	102	30	8	7	7	50	1	228	4	17	9	.654	0-0	0	93	.721	3.63	3.99
2017	Bos	AL	16	11	1	74.2	317	65	30	28	8	0	2	4	24	0	76	2	6	3	.667	0-0	1	94	.652	3.25	3.38
2018	Bos	AL	30	30	0	176.0	722	151	75	70	25	1	4	10	50	0	177	1	16	7	.696	0-0	0	93	.691	3.58	3.58
2019	Bos	AL	22	22	0	107.1	458	109	57	51	15	0	3	1	32	0	128	3	7	5	.583	0-0	0	92	.755	4.13	4.28
14	TB	AL	23	23	0	170.2	689	156	68	59	20	3	3	5	23	1	189	2	11	8	.579	0-0	0	93	.647	2.79	3.11
14	Det	AL	11	11	0	77.2	320	74	32	31	5	1	0	0	15	0	82	0	4	4	.500	0-0	0	93	.647	2.77	3.59
15	TB	AL	21	21	0	146.0	592	133	50	41	13	4	5	3	29	2	138	3	9	4	.692	0-0	0	94	.654	2.83	2.53
15	Tor	AL	11	11	0	74.1	296	57	20	19	4	0	3	0	18	0	87	1	9	1	.900	0-0	0	95	.555	2.00	2.30
Postseason			23	14	5	99.1	414	91	53	51	16	0	2	3	28	1	91	1	5	9	.357	1-1	0	94	.707	3.65	4.62
12 ML YEARS			321	311	1	2029.2	8314	1813	819	746	207	31	43	59	527	12	1981	39	150	80	.652	0-0	2	94	.663	3.09	3.31

Jurickson Profar

JURR-ick-sun PRO-farr

Bats: B **Throws:** R **Pos:** LF-36;2B-17;PH-3;RF-2;1B-1;CF-1;DH-1   **Ht:** 6'0" **Wt:** 184 **Born:** 2/20/1993 **Age:** 28

								BATTING														RUNNING			AVERAGES			
Year	Team	Lg	G	AB	H	2B	3B	HR	(Hm	Rd)	TB	R	RBI	RC	TBB	IBB	SO	HBP	SH	SF	SB	CS	GDP	Avg	OBP	Slg	OPS
2012	Tex	AL	9	17	3	2	0	1	(0	1)	8	2	2	1	0	0	4	0	0	0	0	0	1	.176	.176	.471	.647
2013	Tex	AL	85	286	67	11	0	6	(3	3)	96	30	26	30	26	0	63	5	6	1	2	4	1	.234	.308	.336	.644
2016	Tex	AL	90	272	65	6	3	5	(4	1)	92	35	20	30	30	0	61	3	2	0	2	1	7	.239	.321	.338	.660
2017	Tex	AL	22	58	10	2	0	0	(0	0)	12	8	5	5	9	0	14	1	2	0	1	1	0	.172	.294	.207	.501
2018	Tex	AL	146	524	133	35	6	20	(11	9)	240	82	77	88	54	1	88	12	0	4	10	0	9	.254	.335	.458	.793
2019	Oak	AL	139	459	100	24	2	20	(11	9)	188	65	67	58	48	2	75	8	0	3	9	1	12	.218	.301	.410	.711
2020	SD	NL	56	180	50	6	0	7	(2	5)	77	28	25	30	15	0	28	4	1	2	7	1	1	.278	.343	.428	.771
	Postseason		2	5	3	0	0	0	(0	0)	3	0	0	0	0	0	1	0	0	0	0	0	0	.600	.600	.600	1.200
	7 ML YEARS		547	1796	428	86	11	59	(31	28)	713	250	222	242	182	3	333	33	11	10	31	8	31	.238	.318	.397	.715

Austin Pruitt

Pitches: R **Bats:** R **Pos:** P   **Ht:** 5'10" **Wt:** 185 **Born:** 8/31/1989 **Age:** 31

			HOW MUCH PITCHED					WHAT HE GAVE UP											THE RESULTS						
Year	Team	Lg	G	GS	GF	IP	BFP	H	R	ER	HR	SH	SF	HB	TBB	IBB	SO	WP	W	L	Pct	Sv-Op	Hld	Vel	OPS	ERC	ERA
2017	TB	AL	30	8	7	83.0	371	103	55	49	11	1	0	5	22	2	66	4	7	5	.583	1-2	1	92	.827	5.36	5.31
2018	TB	AL	23	0	11	69.2	291	72	40	36	7	1	4	1	16	0	42	1	2	3	.400	4-5	0	92	.712	3.67	4.65
2019	TB	AL	14	2	4	47.0	193	47	23	23	7	2	2	0	12	2	39	1	3	0	1.000	0-0	0	92	.761	3.84	4.40
	3 ML YEARS		67	10	22	199.2	855	222	118	108	25	4	6	6	50	4	147	6	12	8	.600	5-7	1	92	.773	4.40	4.87

Cesar Puello

PWAY-oh

Bats: R **Throws:** R **Pos:** RF-3;LF-2   **Ht:** 6'2" **Wt:** 220 **Born:** 4/1/1991 **Age:** 30

								BATTING														RUNNING			AVERAGES			
Year	Team	Lg	G	AB	H	2B	3B	HR	(Hm	Rd)	TB	R	RBI	RC	TBB	IBB	SO	HBP	SH	SF	SB	CS	GDP	Avg	OBP	Slg	OPS
2017	2 Tms	AL	17	34	7	0	0	0	(0	0)	7	6	3	3	4	0	12	1	0	0	2	0	2	.206	.308	.206	.514
2019	2 Tms		44	125	31	5	0	4	(1	3)	48	14	18	19	10	1	38	11	1	0	0	0	0	.248	.356	.384	.740
2020	Bos	AL	5	8	3	0	0	0	(0	0)	3	1	0	1	2	0	2	0	1	0	0	0	0	.375	.500	.375	.875
17	LAA	AL	1	4	1	0	0	0	(0	0)	1	0	1	1	0	0	1	0	0	0	2	0	0	.250	.250	.250	.500
17	TB	AL	16	30	6	0	0	0	(0	0)	6	6	2	2	4	0	11	1	0	0	0	0	2	.200	.314	.200	.514
19	LAA	AL	12	41	16	3	0	3	(1	2)	28	6	12	15	3	0	8	6	0	0	0	0	0	.390	.500	.683	1.183
19	Mia	NL	32	84	15	2	0	1	(0	1)	20	8	6	4	7	1	30	5	1	0	0	0	0	.179	.281	.238	.519
	3 ML YEARS		66	167	41	5	0	4	(1	3)	58	21	21	23	16	1	52	12	2	0	2	0	4	.246	.354	.347	.701

Albert Pujols

POO-holes

Bats: R **Throws:** R **Pos:** 1B-26;DH-12;PH-1   **Ht:** 6'3" **Wt:** 235 **Born:** 1/16/1980 **Age:** 41

								BATTING														RUNNING			AVERAGES			
Year	Team	Lg	G	AB	H	2B	3B	HR	(Hm	Rd)	TB	R	RBI	RC	TBB	IBB	SO	HBP	SH	SF	SB	CS	GDP	Avg	OBP	Slg	OPS
2001	StL	NL	161	590	194	47	4	37	(18	19)	360	112	130	132	69	6	93	9	1	7	1	3	21	.329	.403	.610	1.013
2002	StL	NL	157	590	185	40	2	34	(14	20)	331	118	127	121	72	13	69	9	0	4	2	4	20	.314	.394	.561	.955
2003	StL	NL	157	591	212	51	1	43	(21	22)	394	137	124	160	79	12	65	10	0	5	5	1	13	.359	.439	.667	1.106
2004	StL	NL	154	592	196	51	2	46	(18	28)	389	133	123	143	84	12	52	7	0	9	5	5	21	.331	.415	.657	1.072
2005	StL	NL	161	591	195	38	2	41	(23	18)	360	129	117	139	97	27	65	9	0	3	16	2	19	.330	.430	.609	1.039
2006	StL	NL	143	535	177	33	1	49	(24	25)	359	119	137	146	92	28	50	4	0	3	7	2	27	.331	.431	.671	1.102
2007	StL	NL	158	565	185	38	1	32	(12	20)	321	99	103	118	99	22	58	7	0	8	2	6	27	.327	.429	.568	.997
2008	StL	NL	148	524	187	44	0	37	(19	18)	342	100	116	130	104	34	54	5	0	3	7	3	16	.357	.462	.653	1.114
2009	StL	NL	160	568	186	45	1	47	(22	25)	374	124	135	145	115	44	64	9	0	8	16	4	23	.327	.443	.658	1.101
2010	StL	NL	159	587	183	39	1	42	(17	25)	350	115	118	131	103	38	76	4	0	6	14	4	23	.312	.414	.596	1.011
2011	StL	NL	147	579	173	29	0	37	(16	21)	313	105	99	100	61	15	58	4	0	9	9	1	29	.299	.366	.541	.906
2012	LAA	AL	154	607	173	50	0	30	(14	16)	313	85	105	100	52	16	76	5	0	6	8	1	19	.285	.343	.516	.859
2013	LAA	AL	99	391	101	19	0	17	(8	9)	171	49	64	54	40	8	55	5	0	7	1	1	18	.258	.330	.437	.767
2014	LAA	AL	159	633	172	37	1	28	(13	15)	295	89	105	86	48	11	71	5	0	9	5	1	28	.272	.324	.466	.790
2015	LAA	AL	157	602	147	22	0	40	(20	20)	329	85	95	82	50	10	72	6	0	3	5	3	15	.244	.307	.480	.787
2016	LAA	AL	152	593	159	19	0	31	(18	13)	271	71	119	91	46	9	75	2	0	6	4	0	24	.268	.323	.457	.780
2017	LAA	AL	149	593	143	17	0	23	(13	10)	229	53	101	66	37	5	93	2	0	4	3	0	26	.241	.286	.386	.672
2018	LAA	AL	117	465	114	20	0	19	(10	9)	191	50	64	55	28	3	65	2	0	3	1	0	12	.245	.289	.411	.700
2019	LAA	AL	131	491	120	22	0	23	(9	14)	211	55	93	69	43	1	68	3	0	8	3	0	21	.244	.305	.430	.734
2020	LAA	AL	39	152	34	8	0	6	(4	2)	60	15	25	15	9	1	25	1	0	1	0	0	4	.224	.270	.395	.665
	Postseason		77	279	90	18	1	19	(7	12)	167	55	54	68	49	20	40	5	0	1	1	2	6	.323	.431	.599	1.030
	20 ML YEARS		2862	10839	3236	669	16	662	(313	349)	5923	1843	2100	2083	1331	312	1304	108	1	115	114	41	399	.299	.377	.546	.924

A.J. Puk

Pitches: L **Bats:** L **Pos:** P   **Ht:** 6'7" **Wt:** 248 **Born:** 4/25/1995 **Age:** 26

			HOW MUCH PITCHED					WHAT HE GAVE UP											THE RESULTS						
Year	Team	Lg	G	GS	GF	IP	BFP	H	R	ER	HR	SH	SF	HB	TBB	IBB	SO	WP	W	L	Pct	Sv-Op	Hld	Vel	OPS	ERC	ERA
2016	Vrmnt	A-	10	10	0	32.2	137	23	18	11	0	0	1	4	12	0	40	3	0	4	.000	0- -	-	-	.489	1.72	3.03
2017	Stcktn	A+	14	11	1	61.0	254	44	28	25	1	0	2	4	23	0	98	6	4	5	.444	0- -	-	-	.564	2.19	3.69
2017	Mdlnd	AA	13	13	0	64.0	279	64	34	31	2	0	1	3	25	0	86	7	2	5	.286	0- -	-	-	.674	3.71	4.36
2019	Mdlnd	AA	6	1	0	8.1	35	9	4	4	2	0	0	0	3	0	13	3	0	0		0- -	-	-	.843	5.59	4.32
2019	LsVgs	AAA	9	0	2	11.0	44	7	7	6	3	0	0	1	3	0	16	1	4	1	.800	0- -	-	-	.675	3.00	4.91
2019	Oak	AL	10	0	0	11.1	47	10	4	4	1	0	0	0	5	0	13	2	2	0	1.000	0-1	2	97	.652	3.60	3.18

Cal Quantrill

Pitches: R **Bats:** L **Pos:** RP-15; SP-3   **Ht:** 6'3" **Wt:** 195 **Born:** 2/10/1995 **Age:** 26

			HOW MUCH PITCHED					WHAT HE GAVE UP										THE RESULTS						
Year	Team	Lg	G	GS	GF	IP	BFP	H	R	ER	HR	SH	SF	HB	TBB	IBB	SO	WP	W	L	Pct	Sv-Op	Hld	Vel	OPS	ERC	ERA
2019	SD	NL	23	18	0	103.0	443	106	61	59	15	2	3	3	28	2	89	3	6	8	.429	0-0	1	94	.741	4.07	5.16
2020	2 Tms		18	3	2	32.0	135	31	12	8	4	1	0	3	8	1	31	0	2	0	1.000	1-2	2	95	.701	3.81	2.25
20	SD	NL	10	1	1	17.1	74	17	6	5	2	1	0	2	6	1	18	0	2	0	1.000	1-1	1	95	.727	4.32	2.60
20	Cle	AL	8	2	1	14.2	61	14	6	3	2	0	0	1	2	0	13	0	0	0	-	0-1	1	95	.669	3.24	1.84
	2 ML YEARS		41	21	2	135.0	578	137	73	67	19	3	3	6	36	3	120	3	8	8	.500	1-2	3	95	.732	4.01	4.47

Johan Quezada

Pitches: R **Bats:** R **Pos:** RP-3   **Ht:** 6'9" **Wt:** 255 **Born:** 8/25/1994 **Age:** 26

			HOW MUCH PITCHED					WHAT HE GAVE UP										THE RESULTS						
Year	Team	Lg	G	GS	GF	IP	BFP	H	R	ER	HR	SH	SF	HB	TBB	IBB	SO	WP	W	L	Pct	Sv-Op	Hld	Vel	OPS	ERC	ERA
2020	Mia	NL	3	0	2	3.0	12	4	3	3	1	0	0	0	1	0	2	0	0	0	-	0-0	0	97	1.053	8.78	9.00

Jose Quijada

Pitches: L **Bats:** L **Pos:** RP-6   kee-HAH-dah   **Ht:** 5'11" **Wt:** 215 **Born:** 11/9/1995 **Age:** 25

			HOW MUCH PITCHED					WHAT HE GAVE UP										THE RESULTS						
Year	Team	Lg	G	GS	GF	IP	BFP	H	R	ER	HR	SH	SF	HB	TBB	IBB	SO	WP	W	L	Pct	Sv-Op	Hld	Vel	OPS	ERC	ERA
2019	Mia	NL	34	0	9	29.2	144	27	20	19	10	1	0	4	26	3	44	2	2	3	.400	1-2	4	93	.974	7.81	5.76
2020	LAA	AL	6	0	1	3.2	20	6	4	3	1	0	1	1	2	0	6	0	0	1	.000	0-1	1	93	1.013	11.40	7.36
	2 ML YEARS		40	0	10	33.1	164	33	24	22	11	1	1	5	28	3	50	2	2	4	.333	1-3	5	93	.979	8.19	5.94

Roman Quinn

Bats: B **Throws:** R **Pos:** CF-37;PH-4;RF-2   **Ht:** 5'10" **Wt:** 175 **Born:** 5/14/1993 **Age:** 28

			BATTING																	RUNNING			AVERAGES			
Year	Team	Lg	G	AB	H	2B	3B	HR	(Hm	Rd)	TB	R	RBI	RC	TBB	IBB	SO	HBP	SH	SF	SB	CS	GDP	Avg	OBP	Slg	OPS
2016	Phi	NL	15	57	15	4	0	0	(0	0)	19	10	6	9	8	0	19	2	2	0	5	1	0	.263	.373	.333	.706
2018	Phi	NL	50	131	34	6	4	2	(1	1)	54	13	12	15	10	0	35	1	1	0	10	4	1	.260	.317	.412	.729
2019	Phi	NL	44	108	23	3	1	4	(3	1)	40	18	11	15	12	1	34	1	1	0	8	0	2	.213	.298	.370	.668
2020	Phi	NL	41	108	23	3	1	2	(2	0)	34	14	7	9	5	0	39	2	1	0	12	0	0	.213	.261	.315	.576
	4 ML YEARS		150	404	95	16	6	8	(6	2)	147	55	36	48	35	0	127	6	5	0	35	5	3	.235	.306	.364	.669

Jose Quintana

Pitches: L **Bats:** R **Pos:** RP-3; SP-1   KIN-tahn-ah   **Ht:** 6'1" **Wt:** 220 **Born:** 1/24/1989 **Age:** 32

			HOW MUCH PITCHED					WHAT HE GAVE UP										THE RESULTS						
Year	Team	Lg	G	GS	GF	IP	BFP	H	R	ER	HR	SH	SF	HB	TBB	IBB	SO	WP	W	L	Pct	Sv-Op	Hld	Vel	OPS	ERC	ERA
2012	CWS	AL	25	22	2	136.1	568	142	62	57	14	5	1	3	42	4	81	10	6	6	.500	0-0	0	90	.754	4.13	3.76
2013	CWS	AL	33	33	0	200.0	832	188	83	78	23	3	6	5	56	2	164	2	9	7	.563	0-0	0	91	.695	3.47	3.51
2014	CWS	AL	32	32	0	200.1	830	197	87	74	10	4	6	2	52	3	178	7	9	11	.450	0-0	0	92	.662	3.15	3.32
2015	CWS	AL	32	32	0	206.1	862	218	81	77	16	4	4	8	44	4	177	5	9	10	.474	0-0	0	92	.722	3.67	3.36
2016	CWS	AL	32	32	0	208.0	837	192	76	74	22	2	2	4	50	1	181	10	13	12	.520	0-0	0	92	.687	3.23	3.20
2017	2 Tms		32	32	0	188.2	790	170	92	87	23	1	3	10	61	4	207	8	11	11	.500	0-0	0	92	.701	3.57	4.15
2018	ChC	NL	32	32	0	174.1	739	162	81	78	25	8	3	3	68	3	158	3	13	11	.542	0-0	0	91	.737	4.00	4.03
2019	ChC	NL	32	31	0	171.0	745	191	100	89	20	5	13	2	46	0	152	11	13	9	.591	0-0	0	91	.763	4.32	4.68
2020	ChC	NL	4	1	0	10.0	41	10	5	5	1	0	0	1	3	0	12	1	0	0	-	0-0	0	91	.738	3.80	4.50
17	CWS	AL	18	18	0	104.1	444	98	55	52	14	1	2	2	40	1	109	7	4	8	.333	0-0	0	92	.735	3.97	4.49
17	ChC	NL	14	14	0	84.1	346	72	37	35	9	0	1	8	21	3	98	1	7	3	.700	0-0	0	92	.659	3.08	3.74
	Postseason		4	3	0	13.1	57	11	9	8	1	0	2	0	5	0	12	0	1	1	.500	0-0	1	92	.621	2.76	5.40
	9 ML YEARS		254	247	2	1495.0	6244	1470	667	619	154	32	37	37	422	21	1310	57	83	77	.519	0-0	0	92	.713	3.65	3.73

Tanner Rainey

Pitches: R **Bats:** R **Pos:** RP-20   **Ht:** 6'2" **Wt:** 235 **Born:** 12/25/1992 **Age:** 28

			HOW MUCH PITCHED					WHAT HE GAVE UP										THE RESULTS						
Year	Team	Lg	G	GS	GF	IP	BFP	H	R	ER	HR	SH	SF	HB	TBB	IBB	SO	WP	W	L	Pct	Sv-Op	Hld	Vel	OPS	ERC	ERA
2018	Cin	NL	8	0	2	7.0	45	13	19	19	4	0	1	0	12	1	7	0	0	0	-	0-0	0	98	1.462	21.19	24.43
2019	Was	NL	52	0	7	48.1	214	32	22	21	6	2	0	4	38	2	74	7	2	3	.400	0-3	9	98	.696	4.13	3.91
2020	Was	NL	20	0	1	20.1	75	8	6	6	4	0	0	1	7	1	32	3	1	1	.500	0-0	9	97	.542	1.60	2.66
	Postseason		9	0	1	6.2	28	3	5	5	1	0	0	0	5	0	6	1	0	0	-	0-0	2	99	.547	2.75	6.75
	3 ML YEARS		80	0	10	75.2	334	53	47	46	14	2	1	5	57	4	113	10	3	4	.429	0-3	18	98	.755	4.60	5.47

Brooks Raley

Pitches: L **Bats:** L **Pos:** RP-21   RAIL-ee   **Ht:** 6'3" **Wt:** 200 **Born:** 6/29/1988 **Age:** 33

			HOW MUCH PITCHED					WHAT HE GAVE UP										THE RESULTS						
Year	Team	Lg	G	GS	GF	IP	BFP	H	R	ER	HR	SH	SF	HB	TBB	IBB	SO	WP	W	L	Pct	Sv-Op	Hld	Vel	OPS	ERC	ERA
2012	ChC	NL	5	5	0	24.1	116	33	23	22	7	1	0	0	11	0	16	0	1	2	.333	0-0	0	88	.931	7.87	8.14
2013	ChC	NL	9	0	1	14.0	61	11	9	8	2	1	1	2	8	0	14	0	0	0	-	0-0	0	89	.758	4.48	5.14
2020	2 Tms		21	0	7	20.0	84	13	12	11	3	1	0	4	6	0	27	0	0	1	.000	1-1	6	90	.633	2.82	4.95
20	Cin	NL	4	0	2	4.0	22	5	4	4	0	0	0	3	2	0	6	0	0	0	-	0-0	0	90	.866	8.02	9.00
20	Hou	AL	17	0	5	16.0	62	8	8	7	3	1	0	1	4	0	21	0	0	1	.000	1-1	6	90	.552	1.69	3.94
	3 ML YEARS		35	5	8	58.1	261	57	44	41	12	3	1	6	25	0	57	0	1	3	.250	1-1	6	89	.797	5.18	6.33

Erasmo Ramirez

Pitches: R Bats: R Pos: RP-6
eh-RASS-moh
Ht: 6'0" Wt: 220 Born: 5/2/1990 Age: 31

Year Team	Lg	G	GS	GF	IP	BFP	H	R	ER	HR	SH	SF	HB	TBB	IBB	SO	WP	W	L	Pct	Sv-Op	Hld	Vel	OPS	ERC	ERA
2012 Sea	AL	16	8	2	59.0	238	47	26	22	6	1	3	4	12	1	48	0	1	3	.250	0-0	0	93	.616	2.42	3.36
2013 Sea	AL	14	13	0	72.1	321	79	44	40	12	0	3	3	26	0	57	0	5	3	.625	0-0	0	92	.772	5.04	4.98
2014 Sea	AL	17	14	0	75.1	338	82	44	44	13	1	1	6	34	2	60	3	1	6	.143	0-0	0	91	.815	5.68	5.26
2015 TB	AL	34	27	5	163.1	666	145	73	68	16	1	1	9	40	0	126	3	11	6	.647	0-0	0	91	.655	3.11	3.75
2016 TB	AL	64	1	13	90.2	378	90	39	38	14	7	2	4	26	5	63	7	7	11	.389	2-6	15	91	.766	4.13	3.77
2017 2 Tms		37	19	4	131.1	539	123	70	64	22	2	7	2	31	2	109	1	5	6	.455	1-2	6	92	.733	3.58	4.39
2018 Sea	AL	10	10	0	45.2	202	52	35	33	14	0	4	3	12	0	33	0	2	4	.333	0-0	0	90	.916	6.02	6.50
2019 Bos	AL	1	0	1	3.0	15	4	4	4	2	1	0	1	1	0	1	0	0	0	-	0-0	0	90	1.345	12.01	12.00
2020 NYM	NL	6	0	3	14.1	53	8	1	1	1	0	0	0	4	0	9	0	0	0	-	1-1	0	90	.471	1.45	0.63
17 TB	AL	26	8	4	69.1	282	66	39	37	10	1	2	1	16	1	55	1	4	3	.571	1-2	6	92	.719	3.53	4.80
17 Sea	AL	11	11	0	62.0	257	57	31	27	12	1	5	1	15	1	54	0	1	3	.250	0-0	0	92	.749	3.62	3.92
9 ML YEARS		199	92	28	655.0	2750	630	336	314	100	13	23	31	186	10	506	14	32	39	.451	4-9	21	91	.734	3.94	4.31

Harold Ramirez

Bats: R Throws: R Pos: RF-2;LF-1
Ht: 5'10" Wt: 232 Born: 9/6/1994 Age: 26

Year Team	Lg	G	AB	H	2B	3B	HR	(Hm	Rd)	TB	R	RBI	RC	TBB	IBB	SO	HBP	SH	SF	SB	CS	GDP	Avg	OBP	Slg	OPS
2019 Mia	NL	119	421	116	20	3	11	(5	6)	175	54	50	52	18	1	91	5	0	1	2	1	8	.276	.312	.416	.728
2020 Mia	NL	3	10	2	0	0	0	(0	0)	2	2	1	1	1	0	2	0	0	0	0	1	0	.200	.273	.200	.473
2 ML YEARS		122	431	118	20	3	11	(5	6)	177	56	51	53	19	1	93	5	0	1	2	2	8	.274	.311	.411	.722

Jose Ramirez

Bats: B Throws: R Pos: 3B-57;DH-1
Ht: 5'9" Wt: 190 Born: 9/17/1992 Age: 28

Year Team	Lg	G	AB	H	2B	3B	HR	(Hm	Rd)	TB	R	RBI	RC	TBB	IBB	SO	HBP	SH	SF	SB	CS	GDP	Avg	OBP	Slg	OPS
2013 Cle	AL	15	12	4	0	1	0	(0	0)	6	5	0	2	2	0	2	0	0	0	0	1	0	.333	.429	.500	.929
2014 Cle	AL	68	237	62	10	2	2	(1	1)	82	27	17	25	13	0	35	1	13	2	10	1	3	.262	.300	.346	.646
2015 Cle	AL	97	315	69	14	3	6	(1	5)	107	50	27	28	32	0	39	1	5	2	10	4	5	.219	.291	.340	.631
2016 Cle	AL	152	565	176	46	3	11	(8	3)	261	84	76	101	44	1	62	4	1	4	22	7	10	.312	.363	.462	.825
2017 Cle	AL	152	585	186	56	6	29	(10	19)	341	107	83	113	52	5	69	3	0	5	17	5	13	.318	.374	.583	.957
2018 Cle	AL	157	578	156	38	4	39	(19	20)	319	110	105	130	106	15	80	8	0	6	34	6	2	.270	.387	.552	.939
2019 Cle	AL	129	482	123	33	3	23	(8	15)	231	68	83	80	52	3	74	2	0	6	24	4	8	.255	.327	.479	.806
2020 Cle	AL	58	219	64	16	1	17	(8	9)	133	45	46	52	31	0	43	3	0	1	10	3	2	.292	.386	.607	.993
Postseason		23	87	17	2	0	1	(0	1)	22	8	4	4	6	1	18	0	0	0	0	1	2	.195	.247	.253	.500
8 ML YEARS		828	2993	840	213	23	127	(55	72)	1480	496	437	531	332	24	404	22	19	26	127	31	43	.281	.354	.494	.848

Nick Ramirez

Pitches: L Bats: L Pos: RP-5
Ht: 6'4" Wt: 232 Born: 8/1/1989 Age: 31

Year Team	Lg	G	GS	GF	IP	BFP	H	R	ER	HR	SH	SF	HB	TBB	IBB	SO	WP	W	L	Pct	Sv-Op	Hld	Vel	OPS	ERC	ERA
2019 Det	AL	46	0	7	79.2	348	76	45	36	11	1	3	1	35	4	74	6	5	4	.556	0-1	1	90	.748	4.16	4.07
2020 Det	AL	5	0	1	10.2	46	8	7	7	3	0	1	1	4	0	11	0	0	0	-	0-0	0	90	.708	3.99	5.91
2 ML YEARS		51	0	8	90.1	394	84	52	43	14	1	4	2	39	4	85	6	5	4	.556	0-1	1	90	.743	4.14	4.28

Noe Ramirez

Pitches: R Bats: R Pos: RP-21
no-EH
Ht: 6'3" Wt: 205 Born: 12/22/1989 Age: 31

Year Team	Lg	G	GS	GF	IP	BFP	H	R	ER	HR	SH	SF	HB	TBB	IBB	SO	WP	W	L	Pct	Sv-Op	Hld	Vel	OPS	ERC	ERA
2015 Bos	AL	17	0	7	13.0	61	13	12	6	3	0	0	2	7	0	13	1	0	1	.000	0-0	4	90	.803	6.15	4.15
2016 Bos	AL	14	0	7	13.0	61	16	9	9	4	0	2	2	8	1	15	0	0	0	-	0-0	0	90	1.059	9.08	6.23
2017 2 Tms		12	0	1	13.0	49	6	5	4	2	0	0	0	5	0	14	0	0	0	-	0-0	0	90	.520	1.68	2.77
2018 LAA	AL	69	1	12	83.1	353	75	43	42	15	0	0	6	30	3	95	4	7	5	.583	1-4	5	90	.750	4.16	4.54
2019 LAA	AL	51	7	10	67.2	280	59	30	30	9	0	1	5	20	1	79	2	5	4	.556	0-0	3	89	.698	3.48	3.99
2020 LAA	AL	21	0	3	21.0	85	15	7	7	2	0	1	1	9	2	14	1	1	0	1.000	0-1	0	89	.618	2.73	3.00
17 Bos	AL	2	0	1	4.2	18	3	2	2	2	0	0	0	1	0	4	0	0	0	-	0-0	0	89	.752	3.21	3.86
17 LAA	AL	10	0	0	8.1	31	3	3	2	0	0	0	0	4	0	10	0	0	0	-	0-0	0	89	.374	1.02	2.16
6 ML YEARS		184	8	36	211.0	889	184	106	98	35	0	4	16	79	7	230	8	13	10	.565	1-5	12	90	.732	4.00	4.18

Roel Ramirez

Pitches: R Bats: R Pos: RP-1
Ht: 6'0" Wt: 235 Born: 5/26/1995 Age: 26

Year Team	Lg	G	GS	GF	IP	BFP	H	R	ER	HR	SH	SF	HB	TBB	IBB	SO	WP	W	L	Pct	Sv-Op	Hld	Vel	OPS	ERC	ERA
2020 StL	NL	1	0	0	0.2	8	6	6	6	4	0	0	0	1	0	1	1	0	0	-	0-0	0	92	3.446	200.7	81.00

Yohan Ramirez

Pitches: R Bats: R Pos: RP-16
Ht: 6'4" Wt: 190 Born: 5/6/1995 Age: 26

Year Team	Lg	G	GS	GF	IP	BFP	H	R	ER	HR	SH	SF	HB	TBB	IBB	SO	WP	W	L	Pct	Sv-Op	Hld	Vel	OPS	ERC	ERA
2020 Sea	AL	16	0	7	20.2	94	9	6	6	3	0	1	4	20	1	26	2	0	0	-	3-3	1	96	.626	4.07	2.61

AJ Ramos

Pitches: R **Bats:** R **Pos:** RP-3   **Ht:** 5'10" **Wt:** 200 **Born:** 9/20/1986 **Age:** 34

			HOW MUCH PITCHED					WHAT HE GAVE UP											THE RESULTS						
Year Team	Lg	G	GS	GF	IP	BFP	H	R	ER	HR	SH	SF	HB	TBB	IBB	SO	WP	W	L	Pct	Sv-Op Hld	Vel	OPS	ERC	ERA
2012 Mia	NL	11	0	4	9.1	40	8	4	4	2	0	1	4	4	0	13	0	0	0	-	0-1 1	94	.754	4.65	3.86
2013 Mia	NL	68	0	18	80.0	338	58	32	28	4	1	3	2	43	3	86	1	3	4	.429	0-4 11	93	.603	2.80	3.15
2014 Mia	NL	68	0	12	64.0	270	36	16	15	1	3	1	3	43	7	73	7	7	0	1.000	0-3 20	91	.543	2.19	2.11
2015 Mia	NL	71	0	51	70.1	277	45	18	18	6	1	2	3	26	0	87	2	2	4	.333	32-38 4	93	.562	2.21	2.30
2016 Mia	NL	67	0	52	64.0	278	52	21	20	1	2	4	4	35	3	73	6	1	4	.200	40-43 2	92	.600	3.15	2.81
2017 2 Tms	NL	61	0	55	58.2	258	49	27	26	7	1	1	2	34	1	72	7	2	4	.333	27-30 1	92	.694	4.36	3.99
2018 NYM	NL	28	0	5	19.2	88	17	14	14	3	0	1	0	15	0	22	1	2	2	.500	0-0 7	91	.766	5.22	6.41
2020 Col	NL	3	0	0	2.2	15	4	1	1	1	0	0	0	3	0	1	0	0	0	-	0-0 0	92	1.133	12.97	3.38
17 Mia	NL	40	0	38	39.2	171	30	17	16	4	1	0	2	22	1	47	4	2	4	.333	20-22 0	92	.646	3.46	3.63
17 NYM	NL	21	0	17	19.0	87	19	10	10	3	0	1	0	12	0	25	3	0	0	-	7-8 1	92	.789	5.39	4.74
8 ML YEARS		377	0	197	368.2	1564	269	133	126	25	8	12	15	203	14	427	24	17	18	.486	99-119 46	92	.618	3.06	3.08

Wilson Ramos

Bats: R **Throws:** R **Pos:** C-41;PH-4;DH-1   **Ht:** 6'1" **Wt:** 245 **Born:** 8/10/1987 **Age:** 33

				BATTING													RUNNING			AVERAGES			
Year Team	Lg	G	AB	H	2B	3B	HR	(Hm Rd)	TB	R	RBI	RC	TBB	IBB	SO	HBP	SH	SF	SB	CS	GDP	Avg	OBP	Slg	OPS
2010 2 Tms		22	79	22	7	0	1	(1 0)	32	5	5	10	2	0	12	1	0	0	0	0	2	.278	.305	.405	.710
2011 Was	NL	113	389	104	22	1	15	(8 7)	173	48	52	43	38	8	76	2	4	2	0	2	19	.267	.334	.445	.779
2012 Was	NL	25	83	22	2	0	3	(1 2)	33	11	10	12	12	2	19	0	0	1	0	0	1	.265	.354	.398	.752
2013 Was	NL	78	287	78	9	0	16	(6 10)	135	29	59	40	15	1	42	0	0	1	0	1	12	.272	.307	.470	.777
2014 Was	NL	88	341	91	12	0	11	(3 8)	136	32	47	35	17	2	57	0	0	3	0	0	17	.267	.299	.399	.698
2015 Was	NL	128	475	109	16	0	15	(10 5)	170	41	68	39	21	2	101	0	0	6	0	0	16	.229	.258	.358	.616
2016 Was	NL	131	482	148	25	0	22	(12 10)	239	58	80	78	35	2	79	2	0	4	0	0	17	.307	.354	.496	.850
2017 TB	AL	64	208	54	6	0	11	(3 8)	93	19	35	27	10	2	36	0	0	3	0	0	11	.260	.290	.447	.737
2018 2 Tms		111	382	117	22	1	15	(6 9)	186	39	70	70	32	2	80	0	0	2	0	0	20	.306	.358	.487	.845
2019 NYM	NL	141	473	136	19	0	14	(8 6)	197	52	73	70	44	5	69	4	0	3	1	0	16	.288	.351	.416	.768
2020 NYM	NL	45	142	34	6	0	5	(1 4)	55	13	15	11	10	0	31	2	0	1	0	0	5	.239	.297	.387	.684
10 Min	AL	7	27	8	3	0	0	(0 0)	11	2	1	3	0	0	3	1	0	0	0	0	1	.296	.321	.407	.729
10 Was	NL	15	52	14	4	0	1	(1 0)	21	3	4	7	2	0	9	0	0	0	0	0	1	.269	.296	.404	.700
18 TB	AL	78	293	87	14	0	14	(6 8)	143	30	53	50	22	1	61	0	0	0	0	0	17	.297	.346	.488	.834
18 Phi	NL	33	89	30	8	1	1	(0 1)	43	9	17	20	10	1	19	0	0	2	0	0	3	.337	.396	.483	.879
Postseason		4	17	2	0	0	0	(0 0)	2	1	0	0	1	0	6	0	1	0	0	0	1	.118	.167	.118	.284
11 ML YEARS		946	3341	915	146	2	128	(59 69)	1449	347	514	435	236	26	602	11	4	28	1	3	136	.274	.321	.434	.755

Drew Rasmussen

Pitches: R **Bats:** R **Pos:** RP-12   **Ht:** 6'1" **Wt:** 211 **Born:** 7/27/1995 **Age:** 25

			HOW MUCH PITCHED					WHAT HE GAVE UP										THE RESULTS						
Year Team	Lg	G	GS	GF	IP	BFP	H	R	ER	HR	SH	SF	HB	TBB	IBB	SO	WP	W	L	Pct	Sv-Op Hld	Vel	OPS	ERC	ERA
2020 Mil	NL	12	0	3	15.1	71	17	10	10	3	0	0	0	9	0	21	0	1	0	1.000	0-0 0	98	.834	6.18	5.87

Rangel Ravelo

Bats: R **Throws:** R **Pos:** DH-6;RF-4;1B-3;PH-3;LF-1   RAHN-hel   **Ht:** 6'1" **Wt:** 235 **Born:** 4/24/1992 **Age:** 29

				BATTING													RUNNING			AVERAGES			
Year Team	Lg	G	AB	H	2B	3B	HR	(Hm Rd)	TB	R	RBI	RC	TBB	IBB	SO	HBP	SH	SF	SB	CS	GDP	Avg	OBP	Slg	OPS
2019 StL	NL	29	39	8	2	0	2	(1 1)	16	4	7	4	3	0	12	0	0	1	0	0	1	.205	.256	.410	.666
2020 StL	NL	13	35	6	1	0	1	(1 0)	10	5	6	3	4	0	6	0	0	2	0	0	0	.171	.244	.286	.530
2 ML YEARS		42	74	14	3	0	3	(2 1)	26	9	13	7	7	0	18	0	0	3	0	0	1	.189	.250	.351	.601

Robbie Ray

Pitches: L **Bats:** L **Pos:** SP-11; RP-1   **Ht:** 6'2" **Wt:** 215 **Born:** 10/1/1991 **Age:** 29

			HOW MUCH PITCHED					WHAT HE GAVE UP										THE RESULTS						
Year Team	Lg	G	GS	GF	IP	BFP	H	R	ER	HR	SH	SF	HB	TBB	IBB	SO	WP	W	L	Pct	Sv-Op Hld	Vel	OPS	ERC	ERA
2014 Det	AL	9	6	1	28.2	136	43	26	26	5	1	1	0	11	0	19	2	1	4	.200	0-0 1	91	.993	7.72	8.16
2015 Ari	NL	23	23	0	127.2	545	121	56	50	9	7	6	8	49	3	119	2	5	12	.294	0-0 0	93	.731	3.75	3.52
2016 Ari	NL	32	32	0	174.1	776	185	105	95	24	3	2	6	71	4	218	8	8	15	.348	0-0 0	94	.770	4.78	4.90
2017 Ari	NL	28	28	0	162.0	665	116	57	52	23	4	3	5	71	3	218	8	15	5	.750	0-0 0	94	.646	3.08	2.89
2018 Ari	NL	24	24	0	123.2	526	97	55	54	19	1	1	5	70	3	165	5	6	2	.750	0-0 0	94	.706	4.08	3.93
2019 Ari	NL	33	33	0	174.1	747	150	91	84	30	11	4	5	84	5	235	7	12	8	.600	0-0 0	92	.766	4.19	4.34
2020 2 Tms		12	11	0	51.2	251	53	40	38	13	0	2	1	45	1	68	6	2	5	.286	0-0 0	94	.917	7.42	6.62
20 Ari	NL	7	7	0	31.0	154	31	27	27	9	0	2	1	31	1	43	6	1	4	.200	0-0 0	94	.967	8.23	7.84
20 Tor	AL	5	4	0	20.2	97	22	13	11	4	0	0	0	14	0	25	0	1	1	.500	0-0 0	94	.841	6.26	4.79
Postseason		2	1	0	6.2	30	6	5	5	0	0	0	1	4	0	9	4	0	1	.000	0-0 0	94	.647	4.14	6.75
7 ML YEARS		161	157	1	842.1	3646	765	430	399	123	27	19	30	401	19	1042	38	49	51	.490	0-0 1	94	.750	4.30	4.26

Colin Rea

Pitches: R **Bats:** R **Pos:** RP-7; SP-2   ray   **Ht:** 6'5" **Wt:** 235 **Born:** 7/1/1990 **Age:** 30

			HOW MUCH PITCHED					WHAT HE GAVE UP										THE RESULTS						
Year Team	Lg	G	GS	GF	IP	BFP	H	R	ER	HR	SH	SF	HB	TBB	IBB	SO	WP	W	L	Pct	Sv-Op Hld	Vel	OPS	ERC	ERA
2015 SD	NL	6	6	0	31.2	133	29	16	15	2	1	2	1	11	0	26	0	2	2	.500	0-0 0	91	.700	3.29	4.26
2016 2 Tms	NL	20	19	0	102.2	454	102	63	55	12	4	2	8	44	4	80	0	5	5	.500	0-0 0	92	.768	4.50	4.82

Year	Team	Lg	G	GS	GF	IP	BFP	H	R	ER	HR	SH	SF	HB	TBB	IBB	SO	WP	W	L	Pct	Sv-Op	Hld	Vel	OPS	ERC	ERA
2020	ChC	NL	9	2	3	14.0	62	15	9	9	3	0	1	0	2	0	10	0	1	1	.500	0-0	1	93	.715	3.88	5.79
16	SD	NL	19	18	0	99.1	443	101	63	55	12	3	2	8	44	4	76	0	5	5	.500	0-0	0	92	.782	4.73	4.98
16	Mia	NL	1	1	0	3.1	11	1	0	0	0	1	0	0	0	0	4	0	0	0	-	0-0	0	90	.200	0.21	0.00
	3 ML YEARS		35	27	3	148.1	649	146	88	79	17	5	5	9	57	4	116	0	8	8	.500	0-0	1	92	.749	4.18	4.79

J.T. Realmuto

Bats: R **Throws:** R **Pos:** C-36;DH-8;1B-6;PH-2 ray-al-MOO-toh **Ht:** 6'1" **Wt:** 212 **Born:** 3/18/1991 **Age:** 30

Year	Team	Lg	G	AB	H	2B	3B	HR	(Hm	Rd)	TB	R	RBI	RC	TBB	IBB	SO	HBP	SH	SF	SB	CS	GDP	Avg	OBP	Slg	OPS
2014	Mia	NL	11	29	7	1	1	0	(0	0)	10	4	9	4	1	0	8	0	0	0	0	0	2	.241	.267	.345	.611
2015	Mia	NL	126	441	114	21	7	10	(6	4)	179	49	47	44	19	2	70	2	1	4	8	4	11	.259	.290	.406	.696
2016	Mia	NL	137	509	154	31	0	11	(3	8)	218	60	48	63	28	1	100	5	0	3	12	4	12	.303	.343	.428	.771
2017	Mia	NL	141	532	148	31	5	17	(5	12)	240	68	65	74	36	4	106	8	0	3	8	2	13	.278	.332	.451	.783
2018	Mia	NL	125	477	132	30	3	21	(8	13)	231	74	74	74	38	0	104	10	0	4	3	2	9	.277	.340	.484	.825
2019	Phi	NL	145	538	148	36	3	25	(16	9)	265	92	83	78	41	2	123	5	0	8	9	1	12	.275	.328	.493	.820
2020	Phi	NL	47	173	46	6	0	11	(8	3)	85	33	32	28	16	0	48	6	0	0	4	1	3	.266	.349	.491	.840
	7 ML YEARS		732	2699	749	156	19	95	(46	49)	1228	380	358	365	179	9	559	36	1	22	44	14	62	.278	.328	.455	.783

Josh Reddick

Bats: L **Throws:** R **Pos:** RF-50;DH-5;PH-2 **Ht:** 6'2" **Wt:** 197 **Born:** 2/19/1987 **Age:** 34

Year	Team	Lg	G	AB	H	2B	3B	HR	(Hm	Rd)	TB	R	RBI	RC	TBB	IBB	SO	HBP	SH	SF	SB	CS	GDP	Avg	OBP	Slg	OPS
2009	Bos	AL	27	59	10	4	0	2	(0	2)	20	5	4	4	2	0	17	1	0	0	0	0	0	.169	.210	.339	.549
2010	Bos	AL	29	62	12	3	1	1	(1	0)	20	5	5	1	1	0	15	1	0	0	1	0	1	.194	.206	.323	.529
2011	Bos	AL	87	254	71	18	3	7	(2	5)	116	41	28	33	19	1	50	1	0	4	1	2	1	.280	.327	.457	.784
2012	Oak	AL	156	611	148	29	5	32	(18	14)	283	85	85	73	55	8	151	2	1	4	11	1	15	.242	.305	.463	.768
2013	Oak	AL	114	385	87	19	2	12	(2	10)	146	54	56	53	46	1	86	2	1	7	9	2	4	.226	.307	.379	.686
2014	Oak	AL	109	363	96	16	7	12	(5	7)	162	53	54	54	28	0	63	1	0	3	3	1	3	.264	.316	.446	.763
2015	Oak	AL	149	526	143	25	4	20	(7	13)	236	67	77	83	49	1	65	0	1	2	10	2	7	.272	.333	.449	.781
2016	2 Tms		115	398	112	17	1	10	(5	5)	161	53	37	54	39	5	56	0	0	1	8	3	8	.281	.345	.405	.749
2017	Hou	AL	134	477	150	34	4	13	(6	7)	231	77	82	88	43	1	72	0	1	**12**	7	3	9	.314	.363	.484	.847
2018	Hou	AL	134	433	105	13	2	17	(6	11)	173	63	47	50	49	3	77	0	1	2	7	2	9	.242	.318	.400	.718
2019	Hou	AL	141	501	138	19	3	14	(6	8)	205	57	56	65	36	1	66	0	1	9	5	2	9	.275	.319	.409	.728
2020	Hou	AL	56	188	46	11	1	4	(1	3)	71	22	23	25	20	0	42	0	0	1	1	0	5	.245	.316	.378	.693
16	Oak	AL	68	243	72	11	1	8	(3	5)	109	33	28	42	28	5	34	0	0	1	5	0	7	.296	.368	.449	.816
16	LAD	NL	47	155	40	6	0	2	(2	0)	52	20	9	12	11	0	22	0	0	0	3	3	1	.258	.307	.335	.643
	Postseason		61	191	40	3	0	4	(0	4)	55	19	12	14	15	2	44	0	0	0	3	0	7	.209	.267	.288	.555
	12 ML YEARS		1251	4257	1118	208	33	144	(59	85)	1824	582	554	583	387	21	760	7	6	45	61	18	71	.263	.322	.428	.750

Cody Reed

Pitches: L **Bats:** L **Pos:** RP-11 **Ht:** 6'5" **Wt:** 230 **Born:** 4/15/1993 **Age:** 28

Year	Team	Lg	G	GS	GF	IP	BFP	H	R	ER	HR	SH	SF	HB	TBB	IBB	SO	WP	W	L	Pct	Sv-Op	Hld	Vel	OPS	ERC	ERA
2016	Cin	NL	10	10	0	47.2	230	67	47	39	12	1	4	4	19	2	43	2	0	7	.000	0-0	0	93	.968	8.00	7.36
2017	Cin	NL	12	1	3	17.2	79	11	11	10	3	0	0	0	19	3	17	2	1	1	.500	1-1	0	94	.780	4.97	5.09
2018	Cin	NL	17	7	2	43.0	188	45	21	19	5	2	2	2	15	0	42	2	1	3	.250	0-0	1	92	.729	4.41	3.98
2019	Cin	NL	3	0	1	6.1	25	6	1	1	0	0	0	0	1	1	7	1	0	0	-	0-0	0	94	.530	2.11	1.42
2020	2 Tms		11	0	5	12.0	55	11	6	6	2	0	0	1	8	0	12	1	0	1	.000	0-0	0	94	.798	5.50	4.50
20	Cin	NL	9	0	4	9.1	46	10	6	6	2	0	0	1	8	0	10	1	0	1	.000	0-0	0	95	.927	7.84	5.79
20	TB	AL	2	0	1	2.2	9	1	0	0	0	0	0	0	0	0	2	0	0	0	-	0-0	0	94	.222	0.31	0.00
	5 ML YEARS		53	18	11	126.2	577	140	86	75	22	3	3	7	62	6	121	8	2	12	.143	1-1	1	93	.830	5.76	5.33

Rob Refsnyder

Bats: R **Throws:** R **Pos:** DH-7;1B-4;PH-4;RF-2;LF-1 REF-snide-er **Ht:** 6'0" **Wt:** 205 **Born:** 3/26/1991 **Age:** 30

Year	Team	Lg	G	AB	H	2B	3B	HR	(Hm	Rd)	TB	R	RBI	RC	TBB	IBB	SO	HBP	SH	SF	SB	CS	GDP	Avg	OBP	Slg	OPS
2015	NYY	AL	16	43	13	3	0	2	(1	1)	22	3	5	6	3	1	7	0	0	0	2	0	3	.302	.348	.512	.859
2016	NYY	AL	58	152	38	9	0	0	(0	0)	47	25	12	14	18	2	30	1	0	3	2	1	5	.250	.328	.309	.637
2017	2 Tms		52	88	15	2	1	0	(0	0)	19	8	0	0	8	1	17	1	0	0	4	1	2	.170	.247	.216	.463
2018	TB	AL	40	84	14	3	0	2	(0	2)	23	10	5	6	18	0	26	0	0	0	0	2	5	.167	.314	.274	.588
2020	Tex	AL	15	30	6	1	0	0	(0	0)	7	4	1	2	2	0	11	1	0	1	0	0	0	.200	.265	.233	.498
17	NYY	AL	20	37	5	1	1	0	(0	0)	8	3	0	0	3	0	8	0	0	0	2	0	0	.135	.200	.216	.416
17	Tor	AL	32	51	10	1	0	0	(0	0)	11	5	0	0	5	1	9	1	0	0	2	1	2	.196	.281	.216	.496
	Postseason		1	3	0	0	0	0	(0	0)	0	0	0	0	0	0	0	0	0	0	0	0	0	.000	.000	.000	.000
	5 ML YEARS		181	397	86	18	1	4	(1	3)	118	50	23	28	49	4	91	3	0	4	8	4	15	.217	.305	.297	.602

Sean Reid-Foley

Pitches: R **Bats:** R **Pos:** RP-5 **Ht:** 6'3" **Wt:** 230 **Born:** 8/30/1995 **Age:** 25

Year	Team	Lg	G	GS	GF	IP	BFP	H	R	ER	HR	SH	SF	HB	TBB	IBB	SO	WP	W	L	Pct	Sv-Op	Hld	Vel	OPS	ERC	ERA
2018	Tor	AL	7	7	0	33.1	150	31	23	19	6	0	1	1	21	0	42	3	2	4	.333	0-0	0	94	.794	5.32	5.13
2019	Tor	AL	9	6	0	31.2	150	33	20	15	5	0	1	2	21	0	28	3	2	4	.333	0-0	0	93	.818	6.01	4.26
2020	Tor	AL	5	0	2	6.2	30	3	3	1	0	0	0	0	6	1	6	0	1	0	1.000	0-0	0	95	.425	1.93	1.35
	3 ML YEARS		21	13	2	71.2	330	67	46	35	11	0	2	3	48	1	76	6	5	8	.385	0-0	0	93	.773	5.26	4.40

Anthony Rendon

Bats: R **Throws:** R **Pos:** 3B-52   ren-DOAN   **Ht:** 6'1" **Wt:** 200 **Born:** 6/6/1990 **Age:** 31

							BATTING													RUNNING			AVERAGES			
Year Team	Lg	G	AB	H	2B	3B	HR	(Hm	Rd)	TB	R	RBI	RC	TBB	IBB	SO	HBP	SH	SF	SB	CS	GDP	Avg	OBP	Slg	OPS
2013 Was	NL	98	351	93	23	1	7	(3	4)	139	40	35	43	31	3	69	5	2	5	1	1	7	.265	.329	.396	.725
2014 Was	NL	153	613	176	39	6	21	(10	11)	290	111	83	97	58	2	104	5	2	5	17	3	11	.287	.351	.473	.824
2015 Was	NL	80	311	82	16	0	5	(3	2)	113	43	25	39	36	0	70	4	0	4	1	2	8	.264	.344	.363	.707
2016 Was	NL	156	567	153	38	2	20	(11	9)	255	91	85	95	65	2	117	7	0	8	12	6	5	.270	.348	.450	.797
2017 Was	NL	147	508	153	41	1	25	(14	11)	271	81	100	115	84	6	82	7	0	6	7	2	7	.301	.403	.533	.937
2018 Was	NL	136	529	163	44	2	24	(10	14)	283	88	92	99	55	5	82	5	0	8	2	1	5	.308	.374	.535	.909
2019 Was	NL	146	545	174	44	3	34	(20	14)	326	117	126	130	80	8	86	12	0	5	5	1	13	.319	.412	.598	1.010
2020 LAA	AL	52	189	54	11	1	9	(9	0)	94	29	31	38	38	2	31	5	0	0	0	0	10	.286	.418	.497	.915
Postseason		31	117	33	8	0	5	(1	4)	56	16	21	22	18	3	19	0	0	3	1	0	0	.282	.370	.479	.848
8 ML YEARS		968	3613	1048	256	16	145	(80	65)	1771	600	577	656	447	28	641	50	4	45	45	16	66	.290	.372	.490	.862

Hunter Renfroe

Bats: R **Throws:** R **Pos:** RF-39;PH-3;PR-3;1B-2;DH-1   **Ht:** 6'1" **Wt:** 230 **Born:** 1/28/1992 **Age:** 29

							BATTING													RUNNING			AVERAGES			
Year Team	Lg	G	AB	H	2B	3B	HR	(Hm	Rd)	TB	R	RBI	RC	TBB	IBB	SO	HBP	SH	SF	SB	CS	GDP	Avg	OBP	Slg	OPS
2016 SD	NL	11	35	13	3	0	4	(4	0)	28	8	14	10	1	1	5	0	0	0	0	0	1	.371	.389	.800	1.189
2017 SD	NL	122	445	103	25	1	26	(14	12)	208	51	58	48	27	1	140	6	0	1	3	0	4	.231	.284	.467	.751
2018 SD	NL	117	403	100	23	1	26	(13	13)	203	53	68	58	30	2	109	3	0	5	2	1	9	.248	.302	.504	.805
2019 SD	NL	140	440	95	19	1	33	(14	19)	215	64	64	57	46	1	154	2	0	6	5	0	6	.216	.289	.489	.778
2020 TB	AL	42	122	19	5	0	8	(5	3)	48	18	22	13	14	0	37	2	0	1	2	0	3	.156	.252	.393	.645
5 ML YEARS		432	1445	330	75	3	97	(50	47)	702	194	226	186	118	5	445	13	0	13	12	1	23	.228	.290	.486	.776

Luis Rengifo

Bats: B **Throws:** R **Pos:** 2B-32;3B-1;SS-1;PR-1   ren-HEE-foh   **Ht:** 5'10" **Wt:** 195 **Born:** 2/26/1997 **Age:** 24

							BATTING													RUNNING			AVERAGES			
Year Team	Lg	G	AB	H	2B	3B	HR	(Hm	Rd)	TB	R	RBI	RC	TBB	IBB	SO	HBP	SH	SF	SB	CS	GDP	Avg	OBP	Slg	OPS
2019 LAA	AL	108	357	85	18	3	7	(1	6)	130	44	33	45	40	0	93	5	1	3	2	5	6	.238	.321	.364	.685
2020 LAA	AL	33	90	14	1	0	1	(0	1)	18	12	3	2	14	0	26	0	2	0	3	1	2	.156	.269	.200	.469
2 ML YEARS		141	447	99	19	3	8	(1	7)	148	56	36	47	54	0	119	5	3	3	5	6	8	.221	.310	.331	.642

Alex Reyes

Pitches: R **Bats:** R **Pos:** RP-14; SP-1   **Ht:** 6'4" **Wt:** 220 **Born:** 8/29/1994 **Age:** 26

			HOW MUCH PITCHED				WHAT HE GAVE UP										THE RESULTS							
Year Team	Lg	G	GS	GF	IP	BFP	H	R	ER	HR	SH	SF	HB	TBB	IBB	SO	WP	W	L	Pct	Sv-Op	Hld	Vel	OPS	ERC	ERA
2016 StL	NL	12	5	3	46.0	189	33	8	8	1	1	0	1	23	1	52	3	4	1	.800	1-1	1	97	.578	2.43	1.57
2018 StL	NL	1	1	0	4.0	15	3	0	0	0	0	0	1	2	0	2	0	0	0	-	0-0	0	95	.650	3.97	0.00
2019 StL	NL	4	0	0	3.0	17	2	5	5	1	0	1	0	6	0	1	1	0	0	1.000	0-0	2	97	.971	10.79	15.00
2020 StL	NL	15	1	5	19.2	86	14	10	7	1	1	0	0	14	1	27	2	2	1	.667	1-1	2	98	.611	3.22	3.20
4 ML YEARS		32	7	8	72.2	307	52	23	20	3	2	2	1	45	2	82	6	6	3	.667	2-2	5	97	.609	3.00	2.48

Franmil Reyes

Bats: R **Throws:** R **Pos:** DH-57;LF-1;PH-1   **Ht:** 6'5" **Wt:** 265 **Born:** 7/7/1995 **Age:** 25

							BATTING													RUNNING			AVERAGES			
Year Team	Lg	G	AB	H	2B	3B	HR	(Hm	Rd)	TB	R	RBI	RC	TBB	IBB	SO	HBP	SH	SF	SB	CS	GDP	Avg	OBP	Slg	OPS
2018 SD	NL	87	261	73	9	0	16	(8	8)	130	36	31	37	24	0	80	0	0	0	0	0	5	.280	.340	.498	.838
2019 2 Tms		150	494	123	19	0	37	(25	12)	253	69	81	71	47	1	156	0	0	7	0	0	15	.249	.310	.512	.822
2020 Cle	AL	59	211	58	10	0	9	(2	7)	95	27	34	32	24	0	69	1	0	5	0	0	6	.275	.344	.450	.795
19 SD	NL	99	321	82	9	0	27	(17	10)	172	43	46	41	29	1	93	0	0	4	0	0	12	.255	.314	.536	.849
19 Cle	AL	51	173	41	10	0	10	(8	2)	81	26	35	30	18	0	63	0	0	3	0	0	3	.237	.304	.468	.772
3 ML YEARS		296	966	254	38	0	62	(35	27)	478	132	146	140	95	1	305	1	0	12	0	0	26	.263	.326	.495	.821

Victor Reyes

Bats: B **Throws:** R **Pos:** CF-30;LF-22;RF-18;PH-1;PR-1   **Ht:** 6'5" **Wt:** 194 **Born:** 10/5/1994 **Age:** 26

							BATTING													RUNNING			AVERAGES			
Year Team	Lg	G	AB	H	2B	3B	HR	(Hm	Rd)	TB	R	RBI	RC	TBB	IBB	SO	HBP	SH	SF	SB	CS	GDP	Avg	OBP	Slg	OPS
2018 Det	AL	100	212	47	5	3	1	(0	1)	61	35	12	12	5	0	46	0	1	1	9	1	4	.222	.239	.288	.526
2019 Det	AL	69	276	84	16	5	3	(2	1)	119	29	25	35	14	0	64	0	0	2	9	3	5	.304	.336	.431	.767
2020 Det	AL	57	202	56	7	2	4	(1	3)	79	30	14	23	9	0	45	2	0	0	8	2	4	.277	.315	.391	.706
3 ML YEARS		226	690	187	28	10	8	(3	5)	259	94	51	70	28	0	155	2	1	3	26	6	13	.271	.300	.375	.676

Bryan Reynolds

Bats: B **Throws:** R **Pos:** LF-37;CF-17;PH-3;DH-1   **Ht:** 6'3" **Wt:** 205 **Born:** 1/27/1995 **Age:** 26

							BATTING													RUNNING			AVERAGES			
Year Team	Lg	G	AB	H	2B	3B	HR	(Hm	Rd)	TB	R	RBI	RC	TBB	IBB	SO	HBP	SH	SF	SB	CS	GDP	Avg	OBP	Slg	OPS
2019 Pit	NL	134	491	154	37	4	16	(8	8)	247	83	68	89	46	0	121	6	0	3	3	2	9	.314	.377	.503	.880
2020 Pit	NL	55	185	35	6	2	7	(4	3)	66	24	19	22	21	0	57	1	0	0	1	1	2	.189	.275	.357	.632
2 ML YEARS		189	676	189	43	6	23	(12	11)	313	107	87	111	67	0	178	7	0	3	4	3	11	.280	.349	.463	.812

Matt Reynolds

Bats: R Throws: R Pos: 3B-3   Ht: 6'1" Wt: 200 Born: 12/3/1990 Age: 30

Year	Team	Lg	G	AB	H	2B	3B	HR	(Hm	Rd)	TB	R	RBI	RC	TBB	IBB	SO	HBP	SH	SF	SB	CS	GDP	Avg	OBP	Slg	OPS
2016	NYM	NL	47	89	20	8	0	3	(2	1)	37	11	13	10	4	0	34	1	2	0	0	1	2	.225	.266	.416	.682
2017	NYM	NL	68	113	26	1	2	1	(1	0)	34	12	5	11	14	1	37	2	1	0	0	1	2	.230	.326	.301	.626
2018	Was	NL	12	13	2	0	0	0	(0	0)	2	1	1	0	1	0	4	0	0	0	0	0	0	.154	.214	.154	.368
2020	KC	AL	3	11	0	0	0	0	(0	0)	0	1	0	0	0	0	7	0	0	0	0	0	0	.000	.000	.000	.000
	4 ML YEARS		130	226	48	9	2	4	(3	1)	73	25	19	21	19	1	82	3	3	0	0	2	4	.212	.282	.323	.605

Garrett Richards

Pitches: R Bats: R Pos: SP-10; RP-4   Ht: 6'2" Wt: 210 Born: 5/27/1988 Age: 33

Year	Team	Lg	G	GS	GF	IP	BFP	H	R	ER	HR	SH	SF	HB	TBB	IBB	SO	WP	W	L	Pct	Sv-Op	Hld	Vel	OPS	ERC	ERA
2011	LAA	AL	7	3	2	14.0	62	16	11	9	4	0	0	0	7	0	9	2	0	2	.000	0-0	0	95	.989	6.97	5.79
2012	LAA	AL	30	9	4	71.0	318	77	46	37	7	2	4	3	34	1	47	2	4	3	.571	1-3	5	95	.793	5.04	4.69
2013	LAA	AL	47	17	6	145.0	620	151	73	67	12	9	3	1	44	4	101	11	7	8	.467	1-2	5	95	.699	3.78	4.16
2014	LAA	AL	26	26	0	168.2	678	124	51	49	5	0	3	7	51	1	164	22	13	4	.765	0-0	0	96	.529	2.06	2.61
2015	LAA	AL	32	32	0	207.1	865	181	94	84	20	6	10	5	76	2	176	17	15	12	.556	0-0	0	95	.664	3.32	3.65
2016	LAA	AL	6	6	0	34.2	148	31	16	9	2	2	0	1	15	1	34	3	1	3	.250	0-0	0	96	.683	3.39	2.34
2017	LAA	AL	6	6	0	27.2	108	18	8	7	1	1	0	0	7	0	27	2	0	2	.000	0-0	0	96	.494	1.49	2.28
2018	LAA	AL	16	16	0	76.1	324	64	43	31	11	1	0	1	34	0	87	15	5	4	.556	0-0	0	96	.688	3.69	3.66
2019	SD	NL	3	3	0	8.2	41	10	8	8	2	1	0	0	6	0	11	1	0	1	.000	0-0	0	95	1.076	7.31	8.31
2020	SD	NL	14	10	2	51.1	213	47	23	23	7	0	1	2	17	0	46	3	2	2	.500	0-0	1	95	.724	3.80	4.03
	10 ML YEARS		187	128	14	804.2	3377	719	373	324	71	22	21	20	291	9	702	78	47	41	.534	2-5	11	95	.667	3.35	3.62

Trevor Richards

Pitches: R Bats: R Pos: RP-5; SP-4   Ht: 6'2" Wt: 195 Born: 5/15/1993 Age: 28

Year	Team	Lg	G	GS	GF	IP	BFP	H	R	ER	HR	SH	SF	HB	TBB	IBB	SO	WP	W	L	Pct	Sv-Op	Hld	Vel	OPS	ERC	ERA
2018	Mia	NL	25	25	0	126.1	547	121	65	62	15	4	4	5	54	5	130	8	4	9	.308	0-0	0	91	.754	4.18	4.42
2019	2 Tms		30	23	1	135.1	580	127	63	61	19	5	4	5	56	6	127	4	6	12	.333	0-0	1	91	.749	4.16	4.06
2020	TB	AL	9	4	1	32.0	150	44	24	21	6	1	1	0	11	0	27	1	0	0	-	0-0	0	91	.880	6.66	5.91
19	TB	NL	23	20	1	112.0	483	104	56	56	16	4	4	5	51	6	103	3	3	12	.200	0-0	1	91	.759	4.32	4.50
19	TB	AL	7	3	0	23.1	97	23	7	5	3	1	0	0	5	0	24	0	3	0	1.000	0-0	0	90	.698	3.43	1.93
	3 ML YEARS		64	52	2	293.2	1277	292	152	144	40	11	9	10	121	11	284	13	10	21	.323	0-0	1	91	.767	4.43	4.41

Joey Rickard

Bats: R Throws: L Pos: RF-3; PR-1   Ht: 6'0" Wt: 192 Born: 5/21/1991 Age: 30

Year	Team	Lg	G	AB	H	2B	3B	HR	(Hm	Rd)	TB	R	RBI	RC	TBB	IBB	SO	HBP	SH	SF	SB	CS	GDP	Avg	OBP	Slg	OPS
2016	Bal	AL	85	257	69	13	0	5	(2	3)	97	32	19	32	18	0	54	2	3	2	4	1	3	.268	.319	.377	.696
2017	Bal	AL	111	261	63	15	0	4	(3	1)	90	29	19	20	9	0	63	4	2	1	8	1	6	.241	.276	.345	.621
2018	Bal	AL	79	213	52	10	1	8	(6	2)	88	27	23	22	15	0	55	2	0	0	4	2	3	.244	.300	.413	.713
2019	2 Tms		68	168	38	9	2	3	(2	1)	60	14	10	20	18	1	50	3	0	0	4	2	1	.226	.312	.357	.669
2020	SF	NL	4	5	0	0	0	0	(0	0)	0	1	0	0	1	0	1	0	0	0	0	0	0	.000	.167	.000	.167
19	Bal	AL	42	118	24	7	2	2	(1	1)	41	10	6	15	14	1	33	3	0	0	3	2	0	.203	.304	.347	.651
19	SF	NL	26	50	14	2	0	1	(1	0)	19	4	4	5	4	0	17	0	0	0	1	0	1	.280	.333	.380	.713
	5 ML YEARS		347	904	222	47	3	20	(13	7)	335	103	71	94	61	1	223	11	5	3	20	6	13	.246	.300	.371	.671

JT Riddle

Bats: L Throws: R Pos: 3B-11;SS-3;LF-2;CF-2;RF-2;1B-1;2B-1;PH-1;PR-1   Ht: 6'1" Wt: 190 Born: 10/12/1991 Age: 29

Year	Team	Lg	G	AB	H	2B	3B	HR	(Hm	Rd)	TB	R	RBI	RC	TBB	IBB	SO	HBP	SH	SF	SB	CS	GDP	Avg	OBP	Slg	OPS
2017	Mia	NL	70	228	57	13	1	3	(2	1)	81	20	31	24	12	2	50	0	2	5	0	2	6	.250	.282	.355	.637
2018	Mia	NL	102	308	71	10	4	9	(4	5)	116	28	36	31	20	1	67	0	3	1	0	3	4	.231	.277	.377	.653
2019	Mia	NL	51	132	25	6	0	6	(3	3)	49	15	12	7	5	1	42	2	0	0	0	0	3	.189	.230	.371	.601
2020	Pit	NL	23	67	10	2	0	1	(0	1)	15	8	1	0	2	0	13	0	0	0	1	0	0	.149	.174	.224	.398
	4 ML YEARS		246	735	163	31	5	19	(9	10)	261	71	80	62	39	4	172	2	5	6	1	5	13	.222	.261	.355	.616

Austin Riley

Bats: R Throws: R Pos: 3B-46;1B-4;LF-4   Ht: 6'3" Wt: 240 Born: 4/2/1997 Age: 24

Year	Team	Lg	G	AB	H	2B	3B	HR	(Hm	Rd)	TB	R	RBI	RC	TBB	IBB	SO	HBP	SH	SF	SB	CS	GDP	Avg	OBP	Slg	OPS
2019	Atl	NL	80	274	62	11	1	18	(11	7)	129	41	49	38	16	3	108	5	0	2	0	2	2	.226	.279	.471	.750
2020	Atl	NL	51	188	45	7	1	8	(3	5)	78	24	27	24	16	1	49	1	0	1	0	0	5	.239	.301	.415	.716
	2 ML YEARS		131	462	107	18	2	26	(14	12)	207	65	76	62	32	4	157	6	0	3	0	2	9	.232	.288	.448	.736

Edwin Rios

Bats: L Throws: R Pos: 3B-21;1B-6;PH-6;PR-2;DH-1   Ht: 6'3" Wt: 220 Born: 4/21/1994 Age: 27

Year	Team	Lg	G	AB	H	2B	3B	HR	(Hm	Rd)	TB	R	RBI	RC	TBB	IBB	SO	HBP	SH	SF	SB	CS	GDP	Avg	OBP	Slg	OPS
2019	LAD	NL	28	47	13	2	1	4	(0	4)	29	10	8	10	9	0	21	0	0	0	0	0	0	.277	.393	.617	1.010
2020	LAD	NL	32	76	19	6	0	8	(4	4)	49	13	17	15	4	0	18	2	0	1	0	0	2	.250	.301	.645	.946
	2 ML YEARS		60	123	32	8	1	12	(4	8)	78	23	25	25	13	0	39	2	0	1	0	0	3	.260	.338	.634	.972

Yacksel Rios

Pitches: R Bats: R Pos: RP-3   Ht: 6'3" Wt: 215 Born: 6/27/1993 Age: 28

Year Team	Lg	G	GS	GF	IP	BFP	H	R	ER	HR	SH	SF	HB	TBB	IBB	SO	WP	W	L	Pct	Sv-Op	Hld	Vel	OPS	ERC	ERA
2017 Phi	NL	13	0	7	16.1	73	15	8	8	4	1	0	0	9	1	17	0	1	0	1.000	0-0		94	.825	5.06	4.41
2018 Phi	NL	36	0	10	36.0	165	43	28	27	6	0	1	2	15	2	36	2	3	2	.600	0-0	2	96	.853	5.90	6.75
2019 2 Tms	NL	14	0	5	13.0	65	16	13	10	4	1	2	3	8	0	12	1	1	0	1.000	0-0	1	96	1.049	9.16	6.92
2020 Pit	NL	3	0	1	4.0	17	3	4	4	0	0	0	1	2	0	3	0			-	0-0		95	.639	3.44	9.00
19 Phi	NL	4	0	3	2.2	19	6	7	4	2	1	1	1	3	0	2	1	0	0	-	0-0		96	1.632	24.00	13.50
19 Pit	NL	10	0	2	10.1	46	10	6	6	2	0	1	2	5	0	10	0	1	0	1.000	0-0	1	96	.843	5.87	5.23
4 ML YEARS		66	0	23	69.1	320	77	53	49	14	2	3	6	34	3	68	3	5	2	.714	0-0	4	96	.873	6.13	6.36

Rene Rivera

Bats: R Throws: R Pos: C-1;PH-1   ruh-NAY   Ht: 5'10" Wt: 215 Born: 7/31/1983 Age: 37

Year Team	Lg	G	AB	H	2B	3B	HR	(Hm	Rd)	TB	R	RBI	RC	TBB	IBB	SO	HBP	SH	SF	SB	CS	GDP	Avg	OBP	Slg	OPS
2004 Sea	AL	2	3	0	0	0	0	(0	0)	0	0	0	0	0	0	1	0	0	0	0	0	0	.000	.000	.000	.000
2005 Sea	AL	16	48	19	3	0	1	(0	1)	25	3	6	8	1	0	11	0	1	0	0	0	0	.396	.408	.521	.929
2006 Sea	AL	35	99	15	4	0	2	(1	1)	25	8	4	4	3	0	29	1	3	0	1	0	2	.152	.184	.253	.437
2011 Min	AL	45	104	15	3	0	1	(0	1)	21	9	5	3	8	0	32	1	0	1	0	0	2	.144	.211	.202	.412
2013 SD	NL	23	67	17	3	1	0	(0	0)	22	4	7	6	2	1	16	0	0	2	0	0	1	.254	.268	.328	.596
2014 SD	NL	103	294	74	18	1	11	(1	10)	127	27	44	41	27	3	76	3	3	2	0	0	6	.252	.319	.432	.751
2015 TB	AL	110	298	53	14	0	5	(4	1)	82	26	26	16	11	0	86	3	5	2	0	0	4	.178	.213	.275	.489
2016 NYM	NL	65	185	41	4	0	6	(4	2)	63	12	26	19	16	3	54	3	1	2	0	0	4	.222	.291	.341	.632
2017 2 Tms	NL	74	218	55	9	0	10	(5	5)	94	23	35	29	14	3	70	3	1	1	0	1	4	.252	.305	.431	.736
2018 2 Tms		33	86	20	4	0	4	(2	2)	36	8	11	8	4	0	35	1	0	0	0	0	3	.233	.275	.419	.693
2019 NYM	NL	9	17	4	0	0	1	(1	0)	7	2	3	4	3	0	4	0	0	0	0	0	0	.235	.350	.412	.762
2020 NYM	NL	2	4	1	0	0	0	(0	0)	1	0	0	0	0	0	3	0	0	0	0	0	0	.250	.250	.250	.500
17 NYM	NL	54	174	40	4	0	8	(3	5)	68	15	23	18	9	3	54	3	0	1	0	1	3	.230	.278	.391	.669
17 ChC	NL	20	44	15	5	0	2	(2	0)	26	8	12	11	5	0	16	0	1	0	0	0	1	.341	.408	.591	.999
18 LAA	AL	30	82	20	4	0	4	(2	2)	36	8	11	8	4	0	32	1	0	0	0	0	3	.244	.287	.439	.726
18 Atl	NL	3	4	0	0	0	0	(0	0)	0	0	0	0	0	0	3	0	0	0	0	0	0	.000	.000	.000	.000
Postseason		1	3	1	0	0	0	(0	0)	1	0	0	0	0	0	0	0	0	0	0	0	0	.333	.333	.333	.667
12 ML YEARS		517	1423	314	62	2	41	(18	23)	503	112	167	138	89	10	417	15	14	10	1	1	26	.221	.272	.353	.625

Yadiel Rivera

Bats: R Throws: R Pos: SS-2;PR-2;1B-1;2B-1   YA-dee-el   Ht: 6'3" Wt: 190 Born: 5/2/1992 Age: 29

Year Team	Lg	G	AB	H	2B	3B	HR	(Hm	Rd)	TB	R	RBI	RC	TBB	IBB	SO	HBP	SH	SF	SB	CS	GDP	Avg	OBP	Slg	OPS
2015 Mil	NL	7	14	1	0	0	0	(0	0)	1	0	0	0	0	0	4	0	1	0	0	0	0	.071	.071	.071	.143
2016 Mil	NL	35	66	14	4	0	0	(0	0)	18	12	3	3	2	0	20	0	3	0	0	0	4	.212	.235	.273	.508
2017 Mil	NL	1	2	0	0	0	0	(0	0)	0	0	0	0	0	0	1	0	0	0	0	0	0	.000	.000	.000	.000
2018 Mia	NL	111	139	24	3	0	1	(0	1)	30	13	9	7	19	3	51	0	0	2	2	1	3	.173	.269	.216	.485
2019 Mia	NL	34	60	11	2	0	0	(0	0)	13	8	3	5	6	0	20	0	0	0	0	0	1	.183	.258	.217	.474
2020 Tex	AL	4	5	0	0	0	0	(0	0)	0	0	0	0	0	0	1	0	0	0	1	0	0	.000	.000	.000	.000
6 ML YEARS		192	286	50	9	0	1	(0	1)	62	33	15	15	27	3	97	0	4	2	5	1	8	.175	.244	.217	.461

Anthony Rizzo

Bats: L Throws: L Pos: 1B-57;PH-1   Ht: 6'3" Wt: 240 Born: 8/8/1989 Age: 31

Year Team	Lg	G	AB	H	2B	3B	HR	(Hm	Rd)	TB	R	RBI	RC	TBB	IBB	SO	HBP	SH	SF	SB	CS	GDP	Avg	OBP	Slg	OPS
2011 SD	NL	49	128	18	8	1	1	(1	0)	31	9	9	7	21	1	46	4	0	0	2	1	2	.141	.281	.242	.523
2012 ChC	NL	87	337	96	15	0	15	(7	8)	156	44	48	57	27	1	62	3	0	1	3	2	7	.285	.342	.463	.805
2013 ChC	NL	160	606	141	40	2	23	(13	10)	254	71	80	74	76	7	127	6	0	2	6	5	12	.233	.323	.419	.742
2014 ChC	NL	140	524	150	28	1	32	(14	18)	276	89	78	99	73	7	116	15	0	4	5	4	8	.286	.386	.527	.913
2015 ChC	NL	160	586	163	38	3	31	(11	20)	300	94	101	115	78	9	105	30	0	7	17	6	9	.278	.387	.512	.899
2016 ChC	NL	155	583	170	43	4	32	(12	20)	317	94	109	119	74	8	108	16	0	3	3	5	13	.292	.385	.544	.928
2017 ChC	NL	157	572	156	32	3	32	(15	17)	290	99	109	116	91	11	90	24	0	4	10	4	21	.273	.392	.507	.899
2018 ChC	NL	153	566	160	29	1	25	(13	12)	266	74	101	97	70	15	80	20	0	9	6	4	11	.283	.376	.470	.846
2019 ChC	NL	146	512	150	29	3	27	(13	14)	266	89	94	111	71	3	86	27	0	3	5	2	15	.293	.405	.520	.924
2020 ChC	NL	58	203	45	6	0	11	(4	7)	84	26	24	25	28	4	84	10	0	2	3	1	6	.222	.342	.414	.755
Postseason		37	138	30	6	0	6	(3	3)	54	16	18	16	12	2	35	4	0	0	2	0	4	.217	.299	.391	.690
10 ML YEARS		1265	4617	1249	268	18	229	(103	126)	2240	689	753	820	609	66	858	155	0	35	60	34	104	.271	.372	.485	.857

Tanner Roark

Pitches: R Bats: R Pos: SP-11   ROW-ark   Ht: 6'2" Wt: 238 Born: 10/5/1986 Age: 34

Year Team	Lg	G	GS	GF	IP	BFP	H	R	ER	HR	SH	SF	HB	TBB	IBB	SO	WP	W	L	Pct	Sv-Op	Hld	Vel	OPS	ERC	ERA
2013 Was	NL	14	5	1	53.2	204	38	11	9	1	3	2	0	11	0	40	0	7	1	.875	0-0		93	.473	1.54	1.51
2014 Was	NL	31	31	0	198.2	798	178	64	63	16	5	2	6	39	1	138	0	15	10	.600	0-0		91	.632	2.76	2.85
2015 Was	NL	40	12	8	111.0	467	119	55	54	17	4	4	5	26	3	70	0	4	7	.364	1-2	4	93	.784	4.39	4.38
2016 Was	NL	34	33	0	210.0	855	173	72	66	17	10	1	13	73	4	172	6	16	10	.615	0-0		92	.634	3.08	2.83
2017 Was	NL	32	30	0	181.1	776	178	105	94	27	3	2	6	64	5	166	3	13	11	.542	0-0		92	.729	4.06	4.67
2018 Was	NL	31	30	1	180.1	760	181	90	87	24	4	6	10	50	3	146	5	9	15	.375	0-0		91	.741	4.07	4.34
2019 2 Tms	NL	31	31	0	165.1	722	180	84	80	28	0	2	13	51	1	158	3	10	10	.500	0-0		92	.806	5.05	4.35
2020 Tor	AL	11	11	0	47.2	220	60	39	36	14	1	2	1	23	0	41	2	2	3	.400	0-0		91	1.000	7.85	6.80

Year	Team	Lg	G	GS	GF	IP	BFP	H	R	ER	HR	SH	SF	HB	TBB	IBB	SO	WP	W	L	Pct	Sv-Op	Hld	Vel	OPS	ERC	ERA
19	Cin	NL	21	21	0	110.1	484	119	55	52	14	0	1	9	38	1	108	0	6	7	.462	0-0	0	92	.774	4.84	4.24
19	Oak	AL	10	10	0	55.0	238	61	29	28	14	0	1	4	13	0	50	3	4	3	.571	0-0	0	92	.868	5.44	4.58
	Postseason		3	1	1	7.0	35	10	3	3	2	0	0	1	3	1	4	0	0	1	.000	0-0	0	94	.916	8.56	3.86
	8 ML YEARS		224	183	10	1148.0	4802	1107	520	489	140	29	20	55	337	17	931	19	76	67	.531	1-2	6	92	.716	3.82	3.83

Luis Robert

Bats: R **Throws:** R **Pos:** CF-56;PH-1 **Ht:** 6'2" **Wt:** 210 **Born:** 8/3/1997 **Age:** 23

										BATTING											RUNNING			AVERAGES			
Year	Team	Lg	G	AB	H	2B	3B	HR	(Hm	Rd)	TB	R	RBI	RC	TBB	IBB	SO	HBP	SH	SF	SB	CS	GDP	Avg	OBP	Slg	OPS
2018	3 Tms	Low	50	186	50	11	3	0	(-	-)	67	31	17	18	12	0	52	1	1	2	15	4	1	.269	.333	.360	.694
2019	WinSa	A+	19	75	34	5	3	8	(-	-)	69	21	24	30	4	0	20	5	0	0	8	2	1	.453	.512	.920	1.432
2019	Brham	AA	56	226	71	16	3	8	(-	-)	117	43	29	43	13	0	54	4	1	0	21	5	3	.314	.362	.518	.880
2019	Charllt	AAA	47	202	60	10	5	16	(-	-)	128	44	39	43	11	0	55	5	0	5	7	3	6	.297	.341	.634	.974
2020	CWS	AL	56	202	47	8	0	11	(6	5)	88	33	31	30	20	0	73	1	0	2	9	2	4	.233	.302	.436	.738

Daniel Robertson

Bats: R **Throws:** R **Pos:** SS-5;2B-3;3B-2;LF-2;PR-2;RF-1 **Ht:** 5'11" **Wt:** 210 **Born:** 3/22/1994 **Age:** 27

										BATTING											RUNNING			AVERAGES			
Year	Team	Lg	G	AB	H	2B	3B	HR	(Hm	Rd)	TB	R	RBI	RC	TBB	IBB	SO	HBP	SH	SF	SB	CS	GDP	Avg	OBP	Slg	OPS
2017	TB	AL	75	218	45	7	2	5	(4	1)	71	22	19	23	29	0	73	4	1	2	1	1	5	.206	.308	.326	.634
2018	TB	AL	88	282	74	16	0	9	(5	4)	117	46	34	40	43	0	77	13	0	2	2	2	7	.262	.382	.415	.797
2019	TB	AL	74	207	44	9	1	2	(0	2)	61	23	19	16	24	0	59	6	0	0	2	2	10	.213	.312	.295	.607
2020	SF	NL	13	21	7	0	0	0	(0	0)	7	4	2	4	3	0	6	0	0	0	0	0	0	.333	.417	.333	.750
	4 ML YEARS		250	728	170	32	3	16	(9	7)	256	95	74	83	99	0	215	23	1	4	5	5	22	.234	.342	.352	.694

David Robertson

Pitches: R **Bats:** R **Pos:** P **Ht:** 5'11" **Wt:** 195 **Born:** 4/9/1985 **Age:** 36

Year	Team	Lg	G	GS	GF	IP	BFP	H	R	ER	HR	SH	SF	HB	TBB	IBB	SO	WP	W	L	Pct	Sv-Op	Hld	Vel	OPS	ERC	ERA
2008	NYY	AL	25	0	8	30.1	131	29	18	18	3	0	3	0	15	2	36	6	4	0	1.000	0-0	0	91	.690	4.12	5.34
2009	NYY	AL	45	0	20	43.2	191	36	19	16	4	0	0	1	23	1	63	6	2	1	.667	1-1	5	92	.685	3.51	3.30
2010	NYY	AL	64	0	10	61.1	273	59	26	26	5	5	3	3	33	6	71	7	4	5	.444	1-3	14	92	.721	4.29	3.82
2011	NYY	AL	70	0	8	66.2	272	40	9	8	1	1	0	1	35	6	100	6	4	0	1.000	1-4	34	93	.506	1.85	1.08
2012	NYY	AL	65	0	17	60.2	248	52	19	18	5	0	1	1	19	0	81	1	2	7	.222	2-5	30	92	.638	2.95	2.67
2013	NYY	AL	70	0	9	66.1	262	51	15	15	5	3	0	2	18	1	77	1	5	1	.833	3-5	33	92	.584	2.37	2.04
2014	NYY	AL	63	0	55	64.1	259	45	23	22	7	1	0	1	23	2	96	0	4	5	.444	39-44	0	92	.588	2.41	3.08
2015	CWS	AL	60	0	53	63.1	250	46	27	24	7	0	0	1	13	2	86	4	6	5	.545	34-41	0	92	.573	2.00	3.41
2016	CWS	AL	62	0	48	62.1	267	53	24	24	6	3	2	1	32	4	75	1	5	3	.625	37-44	0	91	.684	3.63	3.47
2017	2 Tms	AL	61	0	34	68.1	264	35	14	14	6	0	1	3	23	5	98	7	9	2	.818	14-16	8	91	.488	1.50	1.84
2018	NYY	AL	69	0	11	69.2	283	46	30	25	7	4	1	0	26	1	91	1	8	3	.727	5-9	21	92	.595	2.15	3.23
2019	Phi	NL	7	0	3	6.2	33	8	4	4	1	0	0	0	6	0	6	0	0	1	.000	0-0	2	92	.869	7.88	5.40
	17 CWS	AL	31	0	28	33.1	132	21	10	10	4	0	0	2	11	3	47	3	4	2	.667	13-14	0	91	.577	2.14	2.70
	17 NYY	AL	30	0	6	35.0	132	14	4	4	2	0	1	1	12	2	51	4	5	0	1.000	1-2	8	92	.399	1.05	1.03
	Postseason		30	0	9	33.2	136	26	13	13	4	1	0	1	10	3	40	2	5	0	1.000	0-1	3	92	.637	2.59	3.48
	12 ML YEARS		661	0	276	663.2	2733	500	228	214	57	17	11	14	266	30	880	40	53	33	.616	137-172	147	92	.611	2.68	2.90

Hansel Robles

Pitches: R **Bats:** R **Pos:** RP-18 **Ht:** 6'0" **Wt:** 220 **Born:** 8/13/1990 **Age:** 30

Year	Team	Lg	G	GS	GF	IP	BFP	H	R	ER	HR	SH	SF	HB	TBB	IBB	SO	WP	W	L	Pct	Sv-Op	Hld	Vel	OPS	ERC	ERA
2015	NYM	NL	57	0	7	54.0	217	37	27	22	8	1	1	2	18	1	61	2	4	3	.571	0-4	12	96	.659	2.57	3.67
2016	NYM	NL	68	0	15	77.2	331	69	32	30	7	1	5	1	36	4	85	3	6	4	.600	1-3	13	95	.703	3.62	3.48
2017	NYM	NL	46	0	9	56.2	247	47	31	31	10	3	2	5	29	2	60	2	7	5	.583	0-2	5	95	.750	4.38	4.92
2018	2 Tms		53	0	14	56.0	242	53	26	23	9	2	3	2	25	1	59	2	2	3	.400	2-3	8	96	.771	4.53	3.70
2019	LAA	AL	71	0	51	72.2	283	58	20	20	6	3	3	0	16	1	75	4	5	1	.833	23-27	2	97	.595	2.28	2.48
2020	LAA	AL	18	0	5	16.2	80	19	20	19	4	1	1	1	10	0	20	1	0	2	.000	1-3	0	96	.917	6.96	10.26
	18 NYM	NL	16	0	3	19.2	88	21	11	11	7	1	1	1	10	1	23	1	2	2	.500	0-0	2	95	.981	7.12	5.03
	18 LAA	AL	37	0	11	36.1	154	32	15	12	2	1	2	1	15	0	36	1	0	1	.000	2-3	6	97	.654	3.27	2.97
	Postseason		3	0	2	3.0	9	0	0	0	0	0	0	0	0	0	4	0	0	0	-	0-0	0	97	.000	0.00	0.00
	6 ML YEARS		313	1	101	333.2	1400	283	156	145	44	10	15	11	134	9	360	14	24	18	.571	27-42	40	96	.705	3.56	3.91

Victor Robles

Bats: R **Throws:** R **Pos:** CF-52 **Ht:** 6'0" **Wt:** 205 **Born:** 5/19/1997 **Age:** 24

										BATTING											RUNNING			AVERAGES			
Year	Team	Lg	G	AB	H	2B	3B	HR	(Hm	Rd)	TB	R	RBI	RC	TBB	IBB	SO	HBP	SH	SF	SB	CS	GDP	Avg	OBP	Slg	OPS
2017	Was	NL	13	24	6	1	2	0	(0	0)	11	2	4	3	0	0	6	2	1	0	0	1	2	.250	.308	.458	.766
2018	Was	NL	21	59	17	3	1	3	(2	1)	31	8	10	10	4	0	12	2	0	1	3	2	2	.288	.348	.525	.874
2019	Was	NL	155	546	139	33	3	17	(10	7)	229	86	65	79	35	3	140	25	6	5	28	9	6	.255	.326	.419	.745
2020	Was	NL	52	168	37	5	1	3	(2	1)	53	20	15	18	9	0	53	9	1	2	4	1	0	.220	.293	.315	.608
	Postseason		14	42	9	1	1	1	(1	0)	15	9	3	3	2	0	16	1	1	0	1	0	2	.214	.267	.357	.624
	4 ML YEARS		241	797	199	42	7	23	(14	9)	324	116	94	110	48	3	211	38	8	8	35	13	10	.250	.320	.407	.726

Brendan Rodgers

Bats: R Throws: R Pos: 2B-5;SS-1;DH-1;PH-1;PR-1   Ht: 6'0" Wt: 204 Born: 8/9/1996 Age: 24

Year	Team	Lg	G	AB	H	2B	3B	HR	(Hm	Rd)	TB	R	RBI	RC	TBB	IBB	SO	HBP	SH	SF	SB	CS	GDP	Avg	OBP	Slg	OPS
2016	Ashvll	A	110	442	124	31	0	19	(-	-)	212	73	73	78	35	0	98	8	2	4	6	3	3	.281	.342	.480	.821
2017	Lancst	A+	51	222	86	21	3	12	(-	-)	149	44	47	55	6	0	35	4	0	4	2	1	3	.387	.407	.671	1.078
2017	Hrtfrd	AA	38	150	39	5	0	6	(-	-)	62	20	17	19	8	0	36	6	0	0	2	2	6	.260	.323	.413	.737
2018	Hrtfrd	AA	95	357	98	23	2	17	(-	-)	176	49	62	63	30	1	76	9	1	5	12	3	9	.275	.342	.493	.835
2018	Albq	AAA	19	69	16	4	0	0	(-	-)	20	5	5	5	1	0	16	2	0	0	0	0	3	.232	.264	.290	.554
2019	Albq	AAA	37	143	50	10	1	9	(-	-)	89	34	21	34	14	1	27	2	0	1	0	0	1	.350	.413	.622	1.035
2019	Col	NL	25	76	17	2	0	0	(0	0)	19	8	7	5	4	0	27	1	0	0	0	0	2	.224	.272	.250	.522
2020	Col	NL	7	21	2	1	0	0	(0	0)	3	1	2	0	0	0	6	0	0	0	0	0	0	.095	.095	.143	.238
	2 ML YEARS		32	97	19	3	0	0	(0	0)	22	9	9	5	4	0	33	1	0	0	0	0	2	.196	.235	.227	.462

Carlos Rodon

Pitches: L Bats: L Pos: SP-2; RP-2   roh-DON   Ht: 6'3" Wt: 250 Born: 12/10/1992 Age: 28

Year	Team	Lg	G	GS	GF	IP	BFP	H	R	ER	HR	SH	SF	HB	TBB	IBB	SO	WP	W	L	Pct	Sv-Op	Hld	Vel	OPS	ERC	ERA
2015	CWS	AL	26	23	1	139.1	607	130	63	58	11	6	5	8	71	0	139	7	9	6	.600	0-0	0	93	.725	4.25	3.75
2016	CWS	AL	28	28	0	165.0	715	176	82	74	23	4	6	6	54	3	168	11	9	10	.474	0-0	0	93	.763	4.57	4.04
2017	CWS	AL	12	12	0	69.1	297	64	35	32	12	1	2	3	31	0	76	4	2	5	.286	0-0	0	93	.770	4.57	4.15
2018	CWS	AL	20	20	0	120.2	511	97	61	56	15	0	2	12	55	1	90	4	6	8	.429	0-0	0	93	.698	3.80	4.18
2019	CWS	AL	7	7	0	34.2	158	33	22	20	4	0	2	1	17	0	46	5	3	2	.600	0-0	0	92	.714	4.19	5.19
2020	CWS	AL	4	2	0	7.2	35	9	7	7	1	0	1	0	3	0	6	1	0	2	.000	0-1	0	93	.920	5.87	8.22
	6 ML YEARS		97	92	1	536.2	2323	509	270	247	66	11	17	31	231	4	525	32	29	33	.468	0-1	0	93	.739	4.31	4.14

Dereck Rodriguez

Pitches: R Bats: R Pos: RP-2   Ht: 6'0" Wt: 208 Born: 6/5/1992 Age: 29

Year	Team	Lg	G	GS	GF	IP	BFP	H	R	ER	HR	SH	SF	HB	TBB	IBB	SO	WP	W	L	Pct	Sv-Op	Hld	Vel	OPS	ERC	ERA
2018	SF	NL	21	19	1	118.1	487	98	43	37	9	2	3	7	36	2	89	1	6	4	.600	0-0	0	91	.667	2.84	2.81
2019	SF	NL	28	16	4	99.0	439	108	74	62	21	3	0	2	36	0	71	1	6	11	.353	0-0	0	91	.827	5.28	5.64
2020	SF	NL	2	0	0	4.0	24	10	6	6	2	0	0	0	3	0	2	0	0	0	-	0-0	0	93	1.399	21.06	13.50
	3 ML YEARS		51	35	5	221.1	950	216	123	105	32	5	3	9	75	2	162	2	12	15	.444	0-0	0	91	.759	4.13	4.27

Eduardo Rodriguez

Pitches: L Bats: L Pos: P   Ht: 6'2" Wt: 231 Born: 4/7/1993 Age: 28

Year	Team	Lg	G	GS	GF	IP	BFP	H	R	ER	HR	SH	SF	HB	TBB	IBB	SO	WP	W	L	Pct	Sv-Op	Hld	Vel	OPS	ERC	ERA
2015	Bos	AL	21	21	0	121.2	522	120	55	52	13	5	4	4	37	1	98	4	10	6	.625	0-0	0	94	.701	3.73	3.85
2016	Bos	AL	20	20	0	107.0	458	99	58	56	16	1	4	3	40	1	100	0	3	7	.300	0-0	0	93	.728	3.96	4.71
2017	Bos	AL	25	24	0	137.1	582	126	66	64	19	1	3	5	50	1	150	1	6	7	.462	0-0	0	93	.736	3.87	4.19
2018	Bos	AL	27	23	0	129.2	553	119	56	55	16	0	3	4	45	1	146	1	13	5	.722	0-0	0	93	.681	3.63	3.82
2019	Bos	AL	34	34	0	203.1	859	195	88	86	24	2	5	7	75	2	213	3	19	6	.760	0-0	0	93	.714	4.03	3.81
	Postseason		8	1	2	10.0	44	7	9	9	2	0	0	2	5	1	11	0	0	0	-	0-0	1	94	.697	4.04	8.10
	5 ML YEARS		127	122	1	699.0	2974	659	323	313	88	9	19	23	247	6	707	9	51	31	.622	0-0	0	93	.712	3.86	4.03

Joely Rodriguez

Pitches: L Bats: L Pos: RP-12   joe-EL-ee   Ht: 6'1" Wt: 200 Born: 11/14/1991 Age: 29

Year	Team	Lg	G	GS	GF	IP	BFP	H	R	ER	HR	SH	SF	HB	TBB	IBB	SO	WP	W	L	Pct	Sv-Op	Hld	Vel	OPS	ERC	ERA
2016	Phi	NL	12	0	1	9.2	39	8	3	3	0	0	0	1	4	1	7	0	0	0	-	0-0	3	95	.598	2.91	2.79
2017	Phi	NL	26	0	4	27.0	134	37	26	19	4	1	0	4	15	3	18	0	1	2	.333	0-2	3	93	.930	7.81	6.33
2020	Tex	AL	12	0	2	12.2	52	8	3	3	0	1	0	0	5	0	17	1	0	0	-	0-1	3	95	.494	1.56	2.13
	3 ML YEARS		50	0	7	49.1	225	53	32	25	4	2	0	5	24	4	42	1	1	2	.333	0-3	9	94	.770	4.96	4.56

Jose Rodriguez

Pitches: R Bats: R Pos: RP-1   Ht: 6'2" Wt: 175 Born: 8/29/1995 Age: 25

Year	Team	Lg	G	GS	GF	IP	BFP	H	R	ER	HR	SH	SF	HB	TBB	IBB	SO	WP	W	L	Pct	Sv-Op	Hld	Vel	OPS	ERC	ERA
2019	LAA	AL	9	1	2	19.2	84	17	6	6	5	0	0	0	11	0	13	1	0	1	.000	0-0	3	93	.785	5.14	2.75
2020	LAA	AL	1	0	0	1.2	8	2	0	0	0	0	0	0	1	0	0	0	0	0	-	0-0	0	91	.661	5.10	0.00
	2 ML YEARS		10	1	2	21.1	92	19	6	6	5	0	0	0	12	0	13	1	0	1	.000	0-0	3	93	.774	5.15	2.53

Julio Rodriguez

Bats: R Throws: R Pos: RF   Ht: 6'3" Wt: 180 Born: 12/29/2000 Age: 20

Year	Team	Lg	G	AB	H	2B	3B	HR	(Hm	Rd)	TB	R	RBI	RC	TBB	IBB	SO	HBP	SH	SF	SB	CS	GDP	Avg	OBP	Slg	OPS
2019	2 Tms	Low	84	328	107	26	4	12	(-	-)	177	63	69	68	25	1	76	11	0	3	1	3	10	.326	.390	.540	.929

Nivaldo Rodriguez

Pitches: R Bats: R Pos: RP-5 Ht: 6'1" Wt: 214 Born: 4/16/1997 Age: 24

			HOW MUCH PITCHED					WHAT HE GAVE UP										THE RESULTS						
Year	Team	Lg	G	GS	GF	IP	BFP	H	R	ER	HR	SH	SF	HB	TBB	IBB	SO	WP	W	L	Pct	Sv-Op Hld	Vel	OPS	ERC	ERA
2020	Hou	AL	5	0	3	8.2	46	15	7	6	3	0	1	0	6	1	8	1	0	1	.000	0-0 0	93	1.123	12.18	6.23

Richard Rodriguez

Pitches: R Bats: R Pos: RP-24 Ht: 6'4" Wt: 218 Born: 3/4/1990 Age: 31

			HOW MUCH PITCHED					WHAT HE GAVE UP										THE RESULTS						
Year	Team	Lg	G	GS	GF	IP	BFP	H	R	ER	HR	SH	SF	HB	TBB	IBB	SO	WP	W	L	Pct	Sv-Op Hld	Vel	OPS	ERC	ERA
2017	Bal	AL	5	0	1	5.2	31	12	9	9	4	0	0	1	3	1	3	0	0	0	-	0-0 0	94	1.516	19.81	14.29
2018	Pit	NL	63	0	20	69.1	279	55	19	19	5	1	1	5	19	3	88	11	4	3	.571	0-0 15	93	.596	2.58	2.47
2019	Pit	NL	72	0	12	65.1	285	65	30	27	14	0	1	2	23	3	103	3	4	5	.444	1-5 16	93	.751	4.62	3.72
2020	Pit	NL	24	0	15	23.1	93	15	8	7	3	0	1	2	5	0	34	1	3	2	.600	4-5 2	93	.537	2.00	2.70
	4 ML YEARS		164	0	48	163.2	688	147	66	62	26	1	3	10	50	7	188	15	11	10	.524	5-10 33	93	.693	3.70	3.41

Sean Rodriguez

Bats: R Throws: R Pos: 2B-3;LF-1 Ht: 6'0" Wt: 199 Born: 4/26/1985 Age: 36

			BATTING																		RUNNING			AVERAGES			
Year	Team	Lg	G	AB	H	2B	3B	HR	(Hm	Rd)	TB	R	RBI	RC	TBB	IBB	SO	HBP	SH	SF	SB	CS	GDP	Avg	OBP	Slg	OPS
2008	LAA	AL	59	167	34	8	1	3	(2	1)	53	18	10	12	14	0	55	3	2	1	3	1	3	.204	.276	.317	.593
2009	LAA	AL	12	25	5	0	0	2	(0	2)	11	4	4	2	3	0	7	0	0	1	0	0	2	.200	.276	.440	.716
2010	TB	AL	118	343	86	19	2	9	(5	4)	136	53	40	38	21	1	97	8	5	1	13	3	10	.251	.308	.397	.705
2011	TB	AL	131	373	83	20	3	8	(4	4)	133	45	36	41	38	2	87	18	5	2	11	7	8	.223	.323	.357	.679
2012	TB	AL	112	301	64	14	1	6	(3	3)	98	36	32	32	27	1	75	3	8	3	5	0	7	.213	.281	.326	.607
2013	TB	AL	96	195	48	10	1	5	(3	2)	75	21	23	21	17	0	59	5	3	2	1	3	5	.246	.320	.385	.704
2014	TB	AL	96	237	50	13	3	12	(7	5)	105	30	41	29	10	0	66	6	3	3	2	1	3	.211	.258	.443	.701
2015	Pit	NL	139	224	55	12	1	4	(2	2)	81	25	17	17	5	0	63	6	5	0	2	2	9	.246	.281	.362	.642
2016	Pit	NL	140	300	81	16	1	18	(7	11)	153	49	56	53	33	2	102	5	1	3	2	1	6	.270	.349	.510	.859
2017	2 Tms	NL	54	132	22	2	0	5	(2	3)	39	18	8	8	16	1	57	4	1	0	1	0	3	.167	.276	.295	.572
2018	Pit	NL	66	150	25	5	1	5	(1	4)	47	21	19	14	22	1	60	1	0	0	1	0	1	.167	.277	.313	.591
2019	Phi	NL	76	112	25	5	0	4	(3	1)	42	24	14	14	19	0	41	3	4	1	1	1	2	.223	.348	.375	.723
2020	Mia	NL	4	13	2	0	0	0	(0	0)	2	0	0	0	0	0	6	0	0	0	0	0	0	.154	.154	.154	.308
	17 Atl	NL	15	37	6	1	0	2	(0	2)	13	6	3	4	8	1	19	1	1	0	1	0	1	.162	.326	.351	.677
	17 Pit	NL	39	95	16	1	0	3	(2	1)	26	12	5	4	8	0	38	3	0	0	0	0	2	.168	.255	.274	.528
	Postseason		13	28	5	1	0	1	(0	1)	9	6	2	1	2	0	5	0	0	0	0	0	0	.179	.233	.321	.555
	13 ML YEARS		1103	2572	580	124	14	81	(39	42)	975	344	298	281	225	8	775	62	37	17	42	19	57	.226	.301	.379	.681

Chaz Roe
ROW

Pitches: R Bats: R Pos: RP-10 Ht: 6'5" Wt: 190 Born: 10/9/1986 Age: 34

			HOW MUCH PITCHED					WHAT HE GAVE UP										THE RESULTS						
Year	Team	Lg	G	GS	GF	IP	BFP	H	R	ER	HR	SH	SF	HB	TBB	IBB	SO	WP	W	L	Pct	Sv-Op Hld	Vel	OPS	ERC	ERA
2013	Ari	NL	21	0	4	22.1	95	18	10	10	3	2	1	0	13	3	24	1	1	0	1.000	0-2 1	91	.726	3.78	4.03
2014	NYY	AL	3	0	2	2.0	13	3	3	2	0	1	0	0	3	0	4	1	0	0	-	0-0 0	93	1.239	9.89	9.00
2015	Bal	AL	36	0	6	41.1	177	44	19	19	4	1	1	1	17	2	38	0	4	2	.667	0-1 4	93	.798	4.62	4.14
2016	2 Tms	AL	30	0	11	29.2	124	22	12	12	2	0	2	1	14	1	37	1	2	0	1.000	0-1 3	93	.672	2.82	3.64
2017	2 Tms	AL	12	0	3	10.2	44	7	5	3	1	0	0	1	5	0	13	1	0	0	-	0-0 1	93	.585	2.84	2.53
2018	TB	AL	61	0	6	50.1	203	35	21	20	6	1	0	8	16	1	53	1	1	3	.250	1-2 31	92	.629	2.90	3.58
2019	TB	AL	71	0	11	51.0	229	49	27	23	3	0	1	1	31	2	65	3	1	3	.250	1-5 23	92	.704	4.36	4.06
2020	TB	AL	10	0	4	9.1	39	10	4	3	0	0	1	1	3	0	9	0	2	0	1.000	1-1 2	91	.771	4.08	2.89
	16 Bal	AL	9	0	6	9.2	44	8	4	4	2	0	0	0	7	0	11	1	1	0	1.000	0-0 0	92	.800	5.07	3.72
	16 Atl	AL	21	0	5	20.0	80	14	8	8	0	0	2	1	7	1	26	0	1	0	1.000	0-1 3	93	.604	1.86	3.60
	17 Atl	NL	3	0	0	2.0	13	3	4	2	0	0	0	1	2	0	1	0	0	0	-	0-0 0	93	.762	9.89	9.00
	17 TB	AL	9	0	3	8.2	31	4	1	1	1	0	0	0	3	0	12	1	0	0	-	0-0 1	93	.512	1.51	1.04
	Postseason		3	0	0	2.2	12	3	2	2	0	0	0	0	1	0	2	0	0	0	-	0-0 0	94	.697	3.84	6.75
	8 ML YEARS		244	0	47	216.2	924	188	101	92	19	4	7	13	102	9	243	8	11	8	.579	3-12 65	92	.707	3.74	3.82

Taylor Rogers

Pitches: L Bats: L Pos: RP-21 Ht: 6'3" Wt: 190 Born: 12/17/1990 Age: 30

			HOW MUCH PITCHED					WHAT HE GAVE UP										THE RESULTS						
Year	Team	Lg	G	GS	GF	IP	BFP	H	R	ER	HR	SH	SF	HB	TBB	IBB	SO	WP	W	L	Pct	Sv-Op Hld	Vel	OPS	ERC	ERA
2016	Min	AL	57	0	8	61.1	264	63	29	27	7	0	5	16	3	64	1	3	1	.750	0-0 9	93	.719	3.99	3.96
2017	Min	AL	69	0	7	55.2	237	52	20	19	6	2	0	3	21	5	49	1	7	3	.700	0-4 30	93	.693	3.76	3.07
2018	Min	AL	72	0	6	68.1	260	49	20	20	3	1	3	2	16	3	75	0	1	2	.333	2-4 18	93	.553	1.83	2.63
2019	Min	AL	60	0	36	69.0	278	58	20	20	8	3	0	6	11	2	90	2	2	4	.333	30-36 10	95	.625	2.70	2.61
2020	Min	AL	21	0	16	20.0	91	26	14	9	2	0	0	1	4	0	24	1	2	4	.333	9-11 2	95	.806	5.07	4.05
	Postseason		2	0	1	2.1	8	2	1	1	0	0	0	0	0	0	3	0	0	0	-	0-0 0	95	.625	1.62	3.86
	5 ML YEARS		279	0	73	274.1	1130	248	103	95	26	6	4	17	68	13	302	5	15	14	.517	41-55 69	94	.660	3.12	3.12

Trevor Rogers

Pitches: L Bats: L Pos: SP-7 Ht: 6'5" Wt: 217 Born: 11/13/1997 Age: 23

			HOW MUCH PITCHED					WHAT HE GAVE UP										THE RESULTS						
Year	Team	Lg	G	GS	GF	IP	BFP	H	R	ER	HR	SH	SF	HB	TBB	IBB	SO	WP	W	L	Pct	Sv-Op Hld	Vel	OPS	ERC	ERA
2020	Mia	NL	7	7	0	28.0	130	32	20	19	5	0	2	2	13	0	39	0	1	2	.333	0-0 0	94	.866	5.99	6.11

Tyler Rogers

Pitches: R **Bats:** R **Pos:** RP-29   **Ht:** 6'3" **Wt:** 181 **Born:** 12/17/1990 **Age:** 30

		HOW MUCH PITCHED					WHAT HE GAVE UP										THE RESULTS						
Year	Team	Lg	G	GS	GF	IP	BFP	H	R	ER	HR	SH	SF	HB	TBB	IBB	SO	WP	W	L	Pct	Sv-Op	Hld	Vel	OPS	ERC	ERA
2019	SF	NL	17	0	4	17.2	70	12	3	2	0	1	0	1	3	0	16	1	2	0	1.000	0-2	5	82	.463	1.37	1.02
2020	SF	NL	**29**	0	6	28.0	123	31	16	14	2	1	0	4	6	0	27	0	3	3	.500	3-6	**10**	83	.711	4.27	4.50
	2 ML YEARS		46	0	10	45.2	193	43	19	16	2	2	0	5	9	0	43	1	5	3	.625	3-8	15	82	.620	2.98	3.15

Josh Rojas

Bats: L **Throws:** R **Pos:** 2B-8;DH-5;SS-2;LF-1;PH-1   **Ht:** 6'1" **Wt:** 200 **Born:** 6/30/1994 **Age:** 27

									BATTING											RUNNING			AVERAGES			
Year	Team	Lg	G	AB	H	2B	3B	HR	(Hm	Rd)	TB	R	RBI	RC	TBB	IBB	SO	HBP	SH	SF	SB	CS	GDP	Avg	OBP	Slg	OPS
2019	Ari	NL	41	138	30	7	0	2	(2	0)	43	17	16	15	18	0	41	1	0	0	4	2	3	.217	.312	.312	.624
2020	Ari	NL	17	61	11	0	0	0	(0	0)	11	9	2	2	7	0	16	0	0	2	1	1	1	.180	.257	.180	.437
	2 ML YEARS		58	199	41	7	0	2	(2	0)	54	26	18	17	25	0	57	1	0	2	5	3	4	.206	.295	.271	.567

Miguel Rojas

Bats: R **Throws:** R **Pos:** SS-39;1B-1;3B-1;PH-1   **Ht:** 6'0" **Wt:** 188 **Born:** 2/24/1989 **Age:** 32

									BATTING											RUNNING			AVERAGES			
Year	Team	Lg	G	AB	H	2B	3B	HR	(Hm	Rd)	TB	R	RBI	RC	TBB	IBB	SO	HBP	SH	SF	SB	CS	GDP	Avg	OBP	Slg	OPS
2014	LAD	NL	85	149	27	3	0	1	(0	1)	33	16	9	6	10	1	28	2	1	0	0	0	5	.181	.242	.221	.464
2015	Mia	NL	60	142	40	7	1	1	(1	0)	52	13	17	15	11	1	16	0	2	2	0	1	4	.282	.329	.366	.695
2016	Mia	NL	123	194	48	12	0	1	(0	1)	63	27	14	14	11	2	27	1	6	2	2	1	10	.247	.288	.325	.613
2017	Mia	NL	90	272	79	16	2	1	(1	0)	102	37	26	32	27	5	32	4	1	2	2	1	6	.290	.361	.375	.736
2018	Mia	NL	153	488	123	13	0	11	(4	7)	169	44	53	51	24	2	69	9	2	4	6	3	**23**	.252	.297	.346	.643
2019	Mia	NL	132	483	137	29	1	5	(3	2)	183	52	46	63	32	2	62	5	1	5	9	5	15	.284	.331	.379	.710
2020	Mia	NL	40	125	38	10	1	4	(2	2)	62	20	20	28	16	2	18	2	0	0	5	1	1	.304	.392	.496	.888
	Postseason		1	1	0	0	0	0	(0	0)	0	0	0	0	0	0	0	0	0	0	0	0	0	.000	.000	.000	.000
	7 ML YEARS		683	1853	492	90	5	24	(11	13)	664	209	185	209	131	15	252	23	13	15	24	12	64	.266	.319	.358	.678

Jordan Romano

Pitches: R **Bats:** R **Pos:** RP-15   **Ht:** 6'5" **Wt:** 225 **Born:** 4/21/1993 **Age:** 28

				HOW MUCH PITCHED					WHAT HE GAVE UP										THE RESULTS						
Year	Team	Lg	G	GS	GF	IP	BFP	H	R	ER	HR	SH	SF	HB	TBB	IBB	SO	WP	W	L	Pct	Sv-Op	Hld	Vel	OPS	ERC	ERA
2019	Tor	AL	17	0	2	15.1	75	17	14	13	4	0	0	4	9	0	21	0	0	2	.000	0-0	5	95	.884	7.90	7.63
2020	Tor	AL	15	0	3	14.2	57	8	3	2	2	0	0	0	5	0	21	0	2	1	.667	2-3	5	97	.517	1.77	1.23
	2 ML YEARS		32	0	5	30.0	132	25	17	15	6	0	0	4	14	0	42	0	2	3	.400	2-3	10	95	.720	4.59	4.50

Sal Romano

Pitches: R **Bats:** L **Pos:** RP-2   **Ht:** 6'5" **Wt:** 255 **Born:** 10/12/1993 **Age:** 27

				HOW MUCH PITCHED					WHAT HE GAVE UP										THE RESULTS						
Year	Team	Lg	G	GS	GF	IP	BFP	H	R	ER	HR	SH	SF	HB	TBB	IBB	SO	WP	W	L	Pct	Sv-Op	Hld	Vel	OPS	ERC	ERA
2017	Cin	NL	16	16	0	87.0	384	91	49	43	9	6	6	4	37	2	73	5	5	8	.385	0-0	0	95	.799	4.61	4.45
2018	Cin	NL	39	25	1	145.2	644	155	92	86	23	3	4	4	53	6	105	7	8	11	.421	0-0	2	94	.784	4.69	5.31
2019	Cin	NL	12	0	4	16.1	77	22	14	14	4	0	1	1	8	1	16	1	1	0	1.000	2-2	1	96	1.029	8.05	7.71
2020	Cin	NL	2	0	1	1.1	4	0	0	0	0	0	0	0	0	0	0	0	1	0	1.000	0-0	0	95	.000	0.00	0.00
	4 ML YEARS		69	41	6	250.1	1109	268	155	143	36	9	11	9	98	9	194	13	15	19	.441	2-2	3	95	.803	4.82	5.14

JoJo Romero

Pitches: L **Bats:** L **Pos:** RP-12   **Ht:** 5'11" **Wt:** 200 **Born:** 9/9/1996 **Age:** 24

				HOW MUCH PITCHED					WHAT HE GAVE UP										THE RESULTS						
Year	Team	Lg	G	GS	GF	IP	BFP	H	R	ER	HR	SH	SF	HB	TBB	IBB	SO	WP	W	L	Pct	Sv-Op	Hld	Vel	OPS	ERC	ERA
2020	Phi	NL	12	0	2	10.2	47	13	10	9	1	1	0	2	5	0	10	0	0	0	-	0-0	4	95	.822	5.30	7.59

Seth Romero

Pitches: L **Bats:** L **Pos:** RP-3   **Ht:** 6'3" **Wt:** 240 **Born:** 4/19/1996 **Age:** 25

				HOW MUCH PITCHED					WHAT HE GAVE UP										THE RESULTS						
Year	Team	Lg	G	GS	GF	IP	BFP	H	R	ER	HR	SH	SF	HB	TBB	IBB	SO	WP	W	L	Pct	Sv-Op	Hld	Vel	OPS	ERC	ERA
2020	Was	NL	3	0	0	2.2	18	5	4	4	1	0	0	0	3	0	5	1	0	0	-	0-0	1	92	.978	14.00	13.50

Andrew Romine

Bats: B **Throws:** R **Pos:** SS-1;PR-1   ROW-mine   **Ht:** 6'1" **Wt:** 190 **Born:** 12/24/1985 **Age:** 35

									BATTING											RUNNING			AVERAGES			
Year	Team	Lg	G	AB	H	2B	3B	HR	(Hm	Rd)	TB	R	RBI	RC	TBB	IBB	SO	HBP	SH	SF	SB	CS	GDP	Avg	OBP	Slg	OPS
2010	LAA	AL	5	11	1	0	0	0	(0	0)	1	0	0	0	0	0	4	0	1	0	0	0	0	.091	.091	.091	.182
2011	LAA	AL	10	16	2	0	0	0	(0	0)	2	2	0	0	1	0	6	0	1	0	1	0	0	.125	.176	.125	.301
2012	LAA	AL	12	17	7	0	0	0	(0	0)	7	2	1	5	3	0	3	0	1	0	1	0	0	.412	.500	.412	.912
2013	LAA	AL	47	108	28	3	0	0	(0	0)	31	9	10	12	7	0	24	1	6	1	1	0	2	.259	.308	.287	.595
2014	Det	AL	94	251	57	6	0	2	(1	1)	69	30	12	17	18	0	60	0	4	0	12	2	5	.227	.279	.275	.554
2015	Det	AL	109	184	47	5	0	2	(0	2)	58	25	15	13	11	1	46	3	4	1	10	5	4	.255	.307	.315	.622
2016	Det	AL	109	174	41	5	2	2	(1	1)	56	21	16	15	13	0	38	4	3	0	8	0	5	.236	.304	.322	.626
2017	Det	AL	124	318	74	17	2	4	(3	1)	107	45	25	27	22	0	67	4	2	2	6	4	7	.233	.289	.336	.625

295

Year Team	Lg	BATTING G	AB	H	2B	3B	HR	(Hm	Rd)	TB	R	RBI	RC	TBB	IBB	SO	HBP	SH	SF	RUNNING SB	CS	GDP	AVERAGES Avg	OBP	Slg	OPS
2018 Sea	AL	75	119	25	2	1	0	(0	0)	29	15	2	4	7	0	39	1	4	0	1	0	2	.210	.260	.244	.504
2020 Tex	AL	2	4	1	1	0	0	(0	0)	2	1	0	0	0	0	0	0	0	0	0	0	0	.250	.250	.500	.750
Postseason		3	11	2	0	0	0	(0	0)	2	0	0	0	0	0	4	0	0	0	0	0	0	.182	.182	.182	.364
10 ML YEARS		587	1202	283	39	5	10	(5	5)	362	150	81	93	82	1	288	13	26	4	40	11	25	.235	.291	.301	.592

Austin Romine

Bats: R **Throws:** R **Pos:** C-37;1B-1   ROW-mine   **Ht:** 6'1" **Wt:** 216 **Born:** 11/22/1988 **Age:** 32

Year Team	Lg	BATTING G	AB	H	2B	3B	HR	(Hm	Rd)	TB	R	RBI	RC	TBB	IBB	SO	HBP	SH	SF	RUNNING SB	CS	GDP	AVERAGES Avg	OBP	Slg	OPS
2011 NYY	AL	9	19	3	0	0	0	(0	0)	3	2	0	0	1	0	5	0	0	0	0	0	0	.158	.200	.158	.358
2013 NYY	AL	60	135	28	9	0	1	(0	1)	40	15	10	8	8	0	37	1	3	1	1	0	7	.207	.255	.296	.551
2014 NYY	AL	7	13	3	1	0	0	(0	0)	4	2	1	2	0	0	4	0	0	0	0	0	0	.231	.231	.308	.538
2015 NYY	AL	1	2	0	0	0	0	(0	0)	0	0	0	0	0	0	0	0	0	0	0	0	0	.000	.000	.000	.000
2016 NYY	AL	62	165	40	11	0	4	(1	3)	63	17	26	19	7	1	31	0	1	3	1	0	7	.242	.269	.382	.650
2017 NYY	AL	80	229	50	9	1	2	(2	0)	67	19	21	18	16	0	57	2	2	3	0	0	7	.218	.272	.293	.565
2018 NYY	AL	77	242	59	12	0	10	(3	7)	101	30	42	32	17	0	67	2	1	3	1	0	10	.244	.295	.417	.713
2019 NYY	AL	73	228	64	12	0	8	(2	6)	100	29	35	30	10	0	50	0	1	1	1	1	7	.281	.310	.439	.748
2020 Det	AL	37	130	31	5	0	2	(1	1)	42	12	17	13	4	0	47	0	0	0	0	0	3	.238	.259	.323	.582
Postseason		3	2	0	0	0	0	(0	0)	0	0	0	0	0	0	0	0	0	0	0	0	0	.000	.000	.000	.000
9 ML YEARS		406	1163	278	59	1	27	(9	18)	420	126	152	122	63	1	298	5	8	12	4	1	41	.239	.278	.361	.639

Sergio Romo

Pitches: R **Bats:** R **Pos:** RP-24   **Ht:** 5'11" **Wt:** 185 **Born:** 3/4/1983 **Age:** 38

Year Team	Lg	HOW MUCH PITCHED G	GS	GF	IP	BFP	WHAT HE GAVE UP H	R	ER	HR	SH	SF	HB	TBB	IBB	SO	WP	THE RESULTS W	L	Pct	Sv-Op	Hld	Vel	OPS	ERC	ERA
2008 SF	NL	29	0	8	34.0	130	16	13	8	3	2	1	3	8	1	33	0	3	1	.750	0-0	5	89	.470	1.27	2.12
2009 SF	NL	45	0	9	34.0	143	34	15	15	1	2	0	1	11	0	41	2	5	2	.714	2-2	10	90	.631	2.76	3.97
2010 SF	NL	68	0	13	62.0	247	46	16	15	6	2	2	4	14	2	70	0	5	3	.625	0-4	21	89	.599	2.26	2.18
2011 SF	NL	65	0	16	48.0	175	29	8	8	2	2	0	0	5	1	70	0	3	1	.750	1-2	23	89	.458	1.08	1.50
2012 SF	NL	69	0	27	55.1	215	37	11	11	5	2	0	3	10	1	63	2	4	2	.667	14-15	23	88	.525	1.72	1.79
2013 SF	NL	65	0	52	60.1	250	53	20	17	5	1	1	1	12	3	58	1	5	8	.385	38-43	0	88	.614	2.47	2.54
2014 SF	NL	64	0	35	58.0	230	43	24	24	9	2	0	4	12	2	59	2	6	4	.600	23-28	11	88	.622	2.54	3.72
2015 SF	NL	70	0	14	57.1	230	51	20	19	3	2	0	1	10	2	71	4	0	5	.000	2-4	34	87	.622	2.37	2.98
2016 SF	NL	40	0	13	30.2	117	26	9	9	5	0	0	0	7	1	33	1	1	0	1.000	4-4	14	86	.709	3.13	2.64
2017 2 Tms		55	0	12	55.2	224	42	23	22	9	0	1	1	19	2	59	2	3	1	.750	0-1	11	86	.661	2.97	3.56
2018 TB	AL	73	5	39	67.1	284	65	31	31	11	2	2	2	20	0	75	2	3	4	.429	25-33	9	86	.718	4.02	4.14
2019 2 Tms		65	0	33	60.1	249	50	27	23	7	0	4	2	17	3	60	3	2	1	.667	20-23	17	86	.649	2.83	3.43
2020 Min	AL	24	0	7	20.0	87	16	9	8	3	0	1	3	7	0	23	0	1	2	.333	5-6	10	86	.667	3.58	4.05
17 LAD	NL	30	0	8	25.0	108	23	17	17	7	0	0	0	12	1	31	0	1	1	.500	0-0	7	87	.845	5.15	6.12
17 TB	AL	25	0	4	30.2	116	19	6	5	2	0	1	1	7	1	28	2	2	0	1.000	0-1	4	86	.494	1.54	1.47
19 Mia	NL	38	0	28	37.2	156	33	18	15	4	0	3	0	13	3	33	2	2	0	1.000	17-18	1	86	.673	3.12	3.58
19 Min	AL	27	0	5	22.2	93	17	9	8	3	0	1	2	4	0	27	1	0	1	.000	3-5	16	86	.608	2.35	3.18
Postseason		29	0	13	25.1	100	20	10	10	4	0	0	0	5	0	23	1	3	1	.750	4-7	4	88	.618	2.54	3.55
13 ML YEARS		732	5	278	643.0	2581	504	226	211	69	17	12	25	152	18	715	19	41	34	.547	134-165	188	88	.614	2.47	2.95

Hector Rondon

Pitches: R **Bats:** R **Pos:** RP-23   rohn-DOHN   **Ht:** 6'3" **Wt:** 225 **Born:** 2/26/1988 **Age:** 33

Year Team	Lg	HOW MUCH PITCHED G	GS	GF	IP	BFP	WHAT HE GAVE UP H	R	ER	HR	SH	SF	HB	TBB	IBB	SO	WP	THE RESULTS W	L	Pct	Sv-Op	Hld	Vel	OPS	ERC	ERA
2013 ChC	NL	45	0	14	54.2	242	52	29	29	6	4	3	3	25	5	44	4	2	1	.667	0-1	5	94	.737	4.10	4.77
2014 ChC	NL	64	0	44	63.1	255	52	21	17	2	0	1	0	15	0	63	0	4	4	.500	29-33	1	96	.526	2.10	2.42
2015 ChC	NL	72	0	47	70.0	281	55	19	13	4	3	1	3	15	2	69	5	6	4	.600	30-34	8	96	.568	2.12	1.67
2016 ChC	NL	54	0	35	51.0	209	42	20	20	8	1	2	2	8	0	58	3	2	3	.400	18-23	7	96	.641	2.75	3.53
2017 ChC	NL	61	0	14	57.1	237	50	30	27	10	1	0	1	20	0	69	3	4	1	.800	0-3	10	96	.724	3.77	4.24
2018 Hou	AL	63	0	26	59.0	250	58	22	21	4	0	0	0	20	2	67	1	2	5	.286	15-22	9	97	.695	3.47	3.20
2019 Hou	AL	62	1	5	60.2	257	56	25	25	10	1	1	4	20	0	48	0	3	2	.600	0-3	19	97	.754	4.08	3.71
2020 Ari	NL	23	0	5	20.0	97	25	18	17	6	0	1	1	11	2	23	3	1	0	1.000	0-1	7	96	1.012	7.71	7.65
Postseason		21	0	12	16.1	70	23	8	8	4	0	0	0	3	0	14	0	1	1	.500	2-2	1	97	.954	7.04	4.41
8 ML YEARS		444	1	190	436.0	1819	390	184	169	50	10	9	14	134	11	441	19	24	20	.545	92-120	63	96	.679	3.31	3.49

Brent Rooker

Bats: R **Throws:** R **Pos:** RF-4;DH-2;LF-1   **Ht:** 6'3" **Wt:** 225 **Born:** 11/1/1994 **Age:** 26

Year Team	Lg	BATTING G	AB	H	2B	3B	HR	(Hm	Rd)	TB	R	RBI	RC	TBB	IBB	SO	HBP	SH	SF	RUNNING SB	CS	GDP	AVERAGES Avg	OBP	Slg	OPS
2020 Min	AL	7	19	6	2	0	1	(0	1)	11	4	5	5	0	0	5	2	0	0	0	0	0	.316	.381	.579	.960

Amed Rosario

Bats: R **Throws:** R **Pos:** SS-44;PH-3;PR-1   **Ht:** 6'2" **Wt:** 190 **Born:** 11/20/1995 **Age:** 25

Year Team	Lg	BATTING G	AB	H	2B	3B	HR	(Hm	Rd)	TB	R	RBI	RC	TBB	IBB	SO	HBP	SH	SF	RUNNING SB	CS	GDP	AVERAGES Avg	OBP	Slg	OPS
2017 NYM	NL	46	165	41	4	4	4	(1	3)	65	16	10	14	3	0	49	2	0	0	7	3	3	.248	.271	.394	.665
2018 NYM	NL	154	554	142	26	8	9	(4	5)	211	76	51	60	29	4	119	3	3	3	24	11	9	.256	.295	.381	.676
2019 NYM	NL	157	616	177	30	7	15	(8	7)	266	75	72	79	31	2	124	3	2	3	19	**10**	13	.287	.323	.432	.755
2020 NYM	NL	46	143	36	3	1	4	(0	4)	53	20	15	10	4	0	34	0	0	0	0	1	5	.252	.272	.371	.643
4 ML YEARS		403	1478	396	63	20	32	(13	19)	595	187	148	163	67	6	326	8	5	6	50	25	30	.268	.302	.403	.705

Eddie Rosario

Bats: L Throws: R Pos: LF-51;DH-4;PH-2   Ht: 6'1" Wt: 180 Born: 9/28/1991 Age: 29

Year Team	Lg	G	AB	H	2B	3B	HR	(Hm	Rd)	TB	R	RBI	RC	TBB	IBB	SO	HBP	SH	SF	SB	CS	GDP	Avg	OBP	Slg	OPS
2015 Min	AL	122	453	121	18	15	13	(10	3)	208	60	50	58	15	3	118	0	3	3	11	6	5	.267	.289	.459	.748
2016 Min	AL	92	335	90	17	2	10	(4	6)	141	52	32	35	12	2	91	2	2	3	5	2	4	.269	.295	.421	.716
2017 Min	AL	151	542	157	33	2	27	(20	7)	275	79	78	77	35	1	106	0	4	8	9	8	10	.290	.328	.507	.836
2018 Min	AL	138	559	161	31	2	24	(15	9)	268	87	77	79	30	5	104	0	1	2	8	2	4	.288	.323	.479	.803
2019 Min	AL	137	562	155	28	1	32	(12	20)	281	91	109	88	22	2	86	0	0	6	3	1	10	.276	.300	.500	.800
2020 Min	AL	57	210	54	7	0	13	(6	7)	100	31	42	37	19	2	34	0	0	2	3	1	3	.257	.316	.476	.792
Postseason		4	16	5	1	0	2	(1	1)	12	2	3	1	1	0	5	0	0	0	0	0	1	.313	.353	.750	1.103
6 ML YEARS		697	2661	738	134	22	119	(67	52)	1273	400	388	374	133	15	539	2	10	24	39	20	36	.277	.310	.478	.788

Randy Rosario

Pitches: L Bats: L Pos: RP-4   Ht: 6'1" Wt: 210 Born: 5/18/1994 Age: 27

Year Team	Lg	G	GS	GF	IP	BFP	H	R	ER	HR	SH	SF	HB	TBB	IBB	SO	WP	W	L	Pct	Sv-Op	Hld	Vel	OPS	ERC	ERA
2017 Min	AL	2	0	1	2.1	15	7	8	8	1	0	0	1	0	0	2	0	0	0	-	0-0	0	94	1.390	21.70	30.86
2018 ChC	NL	44	0	8	46.2	200	47	22	19	5	0	0	0	22	2	30	1	4	0	1.000	1-2	8	93	.721	4.49	3.66
2019 2 Tms		19	0	4	14.1	63	15	9	7	2	0	0	0	5	0	13	3	2	0	1.000	0-1	0	94	.748	4.31	4.40
2020 KC	AL	4	0	1	3.1	21	7	3	3	1	0	1	1	3	0	4	1	0	1	.000	0-1	0	92	1.211	17.12	8.10
19 ChC	NL	13	0	2	10.2	49	12	8	7	2	0	0	0	5	0	10	2	1	0	1.000	0-1	0	94	.824	5.61	5.91
19 KC	AL	6	0	2	3.2	14	3	1	0	0	0	0	0	0	0	3	1	1	0	1.000	0-0	0	94	.500	1.32	0.00
Postseason		1	0	0	0.1	2	0	0	0	0	0	0	0	1	0	0	0	0	0	-	0-0	0	94	.500	7.00	0.00
4 ML YEARS		69	0	14	66.2	299	76	42	37	9	0	1	2	30	2	49	5	6	1	.857	1-4	8	93	.794	5.47	5.00

Trevor Rosenthal

Pitches: R Bats: R Pos: RP-23   Ht: 6'2" Wt: 230 Born: 5/29/1990 Age: 31

Year Team	Lg	G	GS	GF	IP	BFP	H	R	ER	HR	SH	SF	HB	TBB	IBB	SO	WP	W	L	Pct	Sv-Op	Hld	Vel	OPS	ERC	ERA
2012 StL	NL	19	0	7	22.2	89	14	7	7	2	1	0	1	7	0	25	1	0	2	.000	0-0	3	98	.513	1.89	2.78
2013 StL	NL	74	0	15	75.1	311	63	25	22	4	3	0	6	20	0	108	3	2	4	.333	3-8	29	97	.608	2.68	2.63
2014 StL	NL	72	0	59	70.1	308	57	25	25	2	2	4	4	42	5	87	1	2	6	.250	45-51	0	97	.641	3.36	3.20
2015 StL	NL	68	0	57	68.2	287	62	16	16	3	1	0	1	25	3	83	7	2	4	.333	48-51	0	98	.619	3.04	2.10
2016 StL	NL	45	0	27	40.1	197	48	22	20	3	1	0	3	29	0	56	0	2	4	.333	14-18	0	97	.792	6.59	4.46
2017 StL	NL	50	0	16	47.2	202	37	20	18	3	1	3	2	20	0	76	2	3	4	.429	11-13	12	98	.572	2.80	3.40
2019 2 Tms		22	0	8	15.1	85	11	24	23	0	1	1	4	26	0	17	9	0	1	.000	0-0	2	98	.715	7.67	13.50
2020 2 Tms		23	0	18	23.2	91	12	6	5	2	0	1	1	8	0	38	0	1	0	1.000	11-12	1	98	.527	1.54	1.90
19 Was	NL	12	0	5	6.1	43	8	16	16	0	0	1	3	15	0	5	5	0	1	.000	0-0	1	98	.938	15.78	22.74
19 Det	AL	10	0	3	9.0	42	3	8	7	0	1	0	1	11	0	12	4	0	0	-	0-0	1	98	.504	3.04	7.00
20 KC	AL	14	0	9	13.2	56	9	5	5	2	0	0	1	7	0	21	0	0	0	-	7-7	1	98	.699	3.32	3.29
20 SD	NL	9	0	9	10.0	35	3	1	0	0	0	1	0	1	0	17	0	1	0	1.000	4-5	0	98	.266	0.30	0.00
Postseason		23	0	15	26.0	102	15	2	2	0	0	0	0	11	3	42	1	1	0	1.000	7-9	2	98	.475	1.41	0.69
8 ML YEARS		373	0	207	364.0	1570	304	145	136	19	10	9	22	177	8	490	23	12	25	.324	132-153	49	97	.632	3.34	3.36

Joe Ross

Pitches: R Bats: R Pos: P   Ht: 6'4" Wt: 220 Born: 5/21/1993 Age: 28

Year Team	Lg	G	GS	GF	IP	BFP	H	R	ER	HR	SH	SF	HB	TBB	IBB	SO	WP	W	L	Pct	Sv-Op	Hld	Vel	OPS	ERC	ERA
2015 Was	NL	16	13	0	76.2	314	64	33	31	7	3	1	2	21	0	69	1	5	5	.500	0-0	0	93	.628	2.74	3.64
2016 Was	NL	19	19	0	105.0	447	108	43	40	9	7	3	6	29	3	93	2	7	5	.583	0-0	0	93	.713	3.84	3.43
2017 Was	NL	13	13	0	73.2	323	84	44	41	16	5	0	1	20	2	68	2	5	3	.625	0-0	0	91	.867	5.54	5.01
2018 Was	NL	3	3	0	16.0	68	17	10	9	3	0	0	2	4	0	7	0	0	2	.000	0-0	0	93	.870	5.09	5.06
2019 Was	NL	27	9	3	64.0	295	74	41	39	7	3	1	4	33	1	57	2	4	4	.500	0-2	2	94	.829	5.79	5.48
Postseason		3	2	0	9.2	42	9	8	8	3	0	0	2	4	0	4	1	0	1	.000	0-0	0	95	.885	6.34	7.45
5 ML YEARS		78	57	4	335.1	1447	351	171	160	42	18	5	15	107	6	294	7	21	19	.525	0-2	2	93	.760	4.35	4.29

Tyson Ross

Pitches: R Bats: R Pos: P   Ht: 6'5" Wt: 254 Born: 4/22/1987 Age: 34

Year Team	Lg	G	GS	GF	IP	BFP	H	R	ER	HR	SH	SF	HB	TBB	IBB	SO	WP	W	L	Pct	Sv-Op	Hld	Vel	OPS	ERC	ERA
2010 Oak	AL	26	2	9	39.1	169	39	24	24	4	1	4	0	20	0	32	5	1	4	.200	1-2	0	93	.754	4.60	5.49
2011 Oak	AL	9	6	1	36.0	145	33	12	11	1	1	0	0	13	1	24	2	3	3	.500	0-0	0	92	.617	3.09	2.75
2012 Oak	AL	18	13	3	73.1	342	96	56	53	7	3	3	5	37	3	46	2	2	11	.154	0-0	0	92	.870	6.68	6.50
2013 SD	NL	35	16	8	125.0	504	100	51	44	8	3	5	7	44	4	119	7	3	8	.273	0-0	0	94	.627	2.84	3.17
2014 SD	NL	31	31	0	195.2	811	165	75	61	13	10	4	9	72	2	195	12	13	14	.481	0-0	0	93	.634	3.07	2.81
2015 SD	NL	33	33	0	196.0	823	172	78	71	9	3	3	8	84	3	212	14	10	12	.455	0-0	0	93	.652	3.33	3.26
2016 SD	NL	1	1	0	5.1	27	9	8	7	0	0	0	2	1	0	5	1	0	1	.000	0-0	0	92	.986	8.24	11.81
2017 Tex	AL	12	10	0	49.0	238	53	46	42	7	0	1	6	37	0	36	4	3	3	.500	0-0	0	92	.856	6.88	7.71
2018 2 Tms	NL	31	23	0	149.2	634	132	73	69	17	3	6	7	62	4	122	4	8	9	.471	0-0	0	91	.712	3.74	4.15
2019 Det	AL	7	7	0	35.1	162	41	28	24	7	0	1	1	18	0	25	1	1	5	.167	0-0	0	90	.863	6.38	6.11
18 SD	NL	22	22	0	123.1	530	112	64	61	16	1	4	7	52	3	107	4	6	9	.400	0-0	0	91	.729	4.04	4.45
18 StL	NL	9	1	0	26.1	104	20	9	8	1	2	2	0	10	1	15	0	2	0	1.000	0-0	0	92	.627	2.38	2.73
10 ML YEARS		203	142	21	904.2	3855	840	451	406	73	24	27	45	388	17	816	52	44	70	.386	1-2	2	93	.700	3.87	4.04

Ramon Rosso

Pitches: R **Bats:** R **Pos:** RP-6; SP-1 **Ht:** 6'4" **Wt:** 240 **Born:** 6/9/1996 **Age:** 25

Year Team	Lg	HOW MUCH PITCHED					WHAT HE GAVE UP										THE RESULTS							
		G	GS	GF	IP	BFP	H	R	ER	HR	SH	SF	HB	TBB	IBB	SO	WP	W	L	Pct	Sv-Op	Hld	Vel	OPS	ERC	ERA
2020 Phi	NL	7	1	3	9.2	46	9	7	7	1	0	0	1	8	0	11	3	0	1	.000	0-0	0	94	.824	5.83	6.52

Darin Ruf

Bats: R **Throws:** R **Pos:** LF-22;PH-15;DH-8;1B-4;RF-3;PR-1 ROUGH **Ht:** 6'2" **Wt:** 232 **Born:** 7/28/1986 **Age:** 34

Year Team	Lg	BATTING																	RUNNING			AVERAGES			
		G	AB	H	2B	3B	HR	(Hm | Rd)	TB	R	RBI	RC	TBB	IBB	SO	HBP	SH	SF	SB	CS	GDP	Avg	OBP	Slg	OPS
2012 Phi	NL	12	33	11	2	1	3	(1 | 2)	24	4	10	5	2	1	12	0	0	2	0	0	1	.333	.351	.727	1.079
2013 Phi	NL	73	251	62	11	0	14	(11 | 3)	115	36	30	33	33	1	91	7	0	2	0	0	4	.247	.348	.458	.806
2014 Phi	NL	52	102	24	8	0	3	(3 | 0)	41	13	8	9	8	0	32	4	1	2	0	0	2	.235	.310	.402	.712
2015 Phi	NL	106	268	63	12	0	12	(6 | 6)	111	30	39	34	21	0	69	5	0	3	1	0	7	.235	.300	.414	.714
2016 Phi	NL	43	83	17	2	0	3	(1 | 2)	28	8	9	4	4	0	25	0	0	2	0	1	5	.205	.236	.337	.573
2020 SF	NL	40	87	24	6	0	5	(4 | 1)	45	11	18	18	13	0	23	0	0	0	1	0	1	.276	.370	.517	.887
6 ML YEARS		326	824	201	41	1	40	(26 | 14)	364	102	114	103	81	2	252	16	1	11	2	1	20	.244	.320	.442	.761

Jose Ruiz

Pitches: R **Bats:** R **Pos:** RP-5 **Ht:** 6'1" **Wt:** 250 **Born:** 10/21/1994 **Age:** 26

Year Team	Lg	HOW MUCH PITCHED					WHAT HE GAVE UP										THE RESULTS							
		G	GS	GF	IP	BFP	H	R	ER	HR	SH	SF	HB	TBB	IBB	SO	WP	W	L	Pct	Sv-Op	Hld	Vel	OPS	ERC	ERA
2017 SD	NL	1	0	1	1.0	4	0	0	0	0	0	0	0	1	0	1	0	0	0	-	0-0	0	95	.250	0.95	0.00
2018 CWS	AL	6	0	2	4.1	21	5	2	2	1	0	0	0	3	0	6	2	0	0	-	0-0	0	96	.825	7.12	4.15
2019 CWS	AL	40	1	16	40.0	198	56	27	25	6	2	2	2	24	2	35	4	1	4	.200	0-1	1	96	.924	7.89	5.63
2020 CWS	AL	5	0	4	4.0	14	2	1	1	1	0	0	0	0	0	5	0	0	0	-	0-1	0	97	.500	1.13	2.25
4 ML YEARS		52	1	23	49.1	237	63	30	28	8	2	2	2	28	2	47	6	1	4	.200	0-2	1	96	.878	7.00	5.11

Keibert Ruiz

Bats: B **Throws:** R **Pos:** C-2 **Ht:** 6'0" **Wt:** 225 **Born:** 7/20/1998 **Age:** 22

Year Team	Lg	BATTING																	RUNNING			AVERAGES			
		G	AB	H	2B	3B	HR	(Hm | Rd)	TB	R	RBI	RC	TBB	IBB	SO	HBP	SH	SF	SB	CS	GDP	Avg	OBP	Slg	OPS
2016 2 Tms	Low	56	222	83	22	3	2	(- | -)	117	33	48	47	15	0	27	3	0	5	0	0	5	.374	.412	.527	.939
2017 2 Tms	Low	101	376	119	23	2	8	(- | -)	170	58	51	70	25	2	53	4	1	5	0	0	12	.316	.361	.452	.813
2018 Tulsa	AA	101	377	100	14	0	12	(- | -)	150	44	47	51	26	1	33	9	0	3	0	1	14	.265	.325	.398	.723
2019 Tulsa	AA	76	276	70	9	0	4	(- | -)	91	33	25	33	28	2	21	4	0	2	0	0	10	.254	.329	.330	.659
2020 LAD	NL	2	8	2	0	0	1	(0 | 1)	5	1	1	1	0	0	3	0	0	0	0	0	0	.250	.250	.625	.875

Rio Ruiz

Bats: L **Throws:** R **Pos:** 3B-53;PH-3;2B-1;LF-1;PR-1 **Ht:** 6'1" **Wt:** 215 **Born:** 5/22/1994 **Age:** 27

Year Team	Lg	BATTING																	RUNNING			AVERAGES			
		G	AB	H	2B	3B	HR	(Hm | Rd)	TB	R	RBI	RC	TBB	IBB	SO	HBP	SH	SF	SB	CS	GDP	Avg	OBP	Slg	OPS
2016 Atl	NL	5	7	2	0	1	0	(0 | 0)	4	1	2	2	0	0	2	0	0	0	1	0	0	.286	.286	.571	.857
2017 Atl	NL	53	150	29	5	0	4	(2 | 2)	46	22	19	15	19	1	41	1	0	3	1	0	4	.193	.283	.307	.590
2018 Atl	NL	14	12	1	0	0	0	(0 | 0)	1	1	0	0	2	0	5	1	0	0	0	0	0	.083	.267	.083	.350
2019 Bal	AL	127	370	86	13	2	12	(6 | 6)	139	35	46	50	40	0	88	0	1	2	0	1	12	.232	.306	.376	.682
2020 Bal	AL	54	185	41	11	0	9	(4 | 5)	79	25	32	23	17	1	46	0	1	1	1	2	4	.222	.286	.427	.713
5 ML YEARS		253	724	159	29	3	25	(12 | 13)	269	84	99	90	78	2	182	2	2	6	3	3	20	.220	.295	.372	.667

Chris Rusin

Pitches: L **Bats:** L **Pos:** RP-1 RUH-sin **Ht:** 6'2" **Wt:** 200 **Born:** 10/22/1986 **Age:** 34

Year Team	Lg	HOW MUCH PITCHED					WHAT HE GAVE UP										THE RESULTS							
		G	GS	GF	IP	BFP	H	R	ER	HR	SH	SF	HB	TBB	IBB	SO	WP	W	L	Pct	Sv-Op	Hld	Vel	OPS	ERC	ERA
2012 ChC	NL	7	7	0	29.2	135	38	22	21	4	0	0	3	11	0	21	0	2	3	.400	0-0	0	88	.881	6.46	6.37
2013 ChC	NL	13	13	0	66.1	282	66	30	29	8	1	1	3	24	3	36	1	2	6	.250	0-0	0	88	.750	4.21	3.93
2014 ChC	NL	4	0	2	12.2	58	16	10	10	1	1	0	0	5	1	8	1	0	0	-	0-0	0	88	.830	5.24	7.11
2015 Col	NL	24	22	0	131.2	594	170	88	78	19	2	0	3	41	5	86	2	6	10	.375	0-0	0	90	.867	5.80	5.33
2016 Col	NL	29	7	1	84.1	350	82	36	35	5	7	0	3	23	2	69	4	3	5	.375	0-1	3	90	.706	3.30	3.74
2017 Col	NL	60	0	7	85.0	340	75	31	25	9	2	3	3	19	1	71	4	5	1	.833	2-3	12	91	.645	2.99	2.65
2018 Col	NL	49	0	11	54.2	241	56	42	37	7	1	3	2	26	1	47	4	2	3	.400	0-1	7	90	.785	4.88	6.09
2019 Col	NL	2	0	0	1.0	9	5	4	4	1	0	1	0	3	0	0	0	0	0	-	0-0	0	89	2.095	50.97	36.00
2020 Atl	NL	1	0	0	3.1	17	6	3	3	1	0	0	0	3	0	3	0	0	0	-	0-0	0	87	1.244	14.91	8.10
Postseason		5	0	2	6.1	26	4	0	0	0	0	0	0	4	1	5	0	0	0	-	0-0	0	90	.580	2.13	0.00
9 ML YEARS		189	49	21	468.2	2026	514	266	242	55	14	8	17	153	13	341	16	20	28	.417	2-5	22	89	.784	4.60	4.65

Adley Rutschman

Bats: B **Throws:** R **Pos:** C **Ht:** 6'2" **Wt:** 220 **Born:** 2/6/1998 **Age:** 23

Year Team	Lg	BATTING																	RUNNING			AVERAGES			
		G	AB	H	2B	3B	HR	(Hm | Rd)	TB	R	RBI	RC	TBB	IBB	SO	HBP	SH	SF	SB	CS	GDP	Avg	OBP	Slg	OPS
2019 3 Tms	Low	37	130	33	8	1	4	(- | -)	55	19	26	20	20	1	27	1	0	3	1	0	2	.254	.351	.423	.774

Kyle Ryan

Pitches: L Bats: L Pos: RP-18
Ht: 6'5" Wt: 215 Born: 9/25/1991 Age: 29

		HOW MUCH PITCHED					WHAT HE GAVE UP											THE RESULTS								
Year Team	Lg	G	GS	GF	IP	BFP	H	R	ER	HR	SH	SF	HB	TBB	IBB	SO	WP	W	L	Pct	Sv-Op	Hld	Vel	OPS	ERC	ERA
2014 Det	AL	6	1	1	10.1	41	10	3	3	0	0	0	0	2	0	4	0	2	0	1.000	0-0	0	89	.626	2.57	2.61
2015 Det	AL	16	6	3	56.1	237	60	29	28	9	2	1	1	20	0	30	1	2	4	.333	0-0	0	88	.795	4.94	4.47
2016 Det	AL	56	0	14	55.2	226	48	21	19	2	2	1	3	15	5	35	1	4	2	.667	0-1	4	89	.636	2.55	3.07
2017 Det	AL	8	0	0	5.2	29	9	5	5	0	0	1	0	7	1	1	0	0	0	-	0-1	4	90	1.028	11.19	7.94
2019 ChC	NL	73	0	12	61.0	260	55	26	24	5	0	3	1	29	2	58	1	4	2	.667	0-2	14	90	.669	3.75	3.54
2020 ChC	NL	18	0	2	15.2	66	16	9	9	5	0	0	0	6	0	11	0	1	0	1.000	1-1	4	88	.900	5.84	5.17
6 ML YEARS		177	7	32	204.2	859	198	93	88	21	4	6	5	79	8	139	3	13	8	.619	1-5	26	89	.723	3.99	3.87

Hyun-Jin Ryu

Pitches: L Bats: R Pos: SP-12
he-YUN-jin ree-YOO
Ht: 6'3" Wt: 255 Born: 3/25/1987 Age: 34

		HOW MUCH PITCHED					WHAT HE GAVE UP											THE RESULTS								
Year Team	Lg	G	GS	GF	IP	BFP	H	R	ER	HR	SH	SF	HB	TBB	IBB	SO	WP	W	L	Pct	Sv-Op	Hld	Vel	OPS	ERC	ERA
2013 LAD	NL	30	30	0	192.0	783	182	67	64	15	7	3	1	49	4	154	5	14	8	.636	0-0	0	90	.660	3.13	3.00
2014 LAD	NL	26	26	0	152.0	631	152	60	57	8	6	2	3	29	2	139	2	14	7	.667	0-0	0	91	.658	3.00	3.38
2016 LAD	NL	1	1	0	4.2	24	8	6	6	1	0	0	0	2	1	4	0	0	1	.000	0-0	0	90	1.144	9.03	11.57
2017 LAD	NL	25	24	1	126.2	541	128	58	53	22	4	1	4	45	3	116	4	5	9	.357	1-1	0	90	.792	4.61	3.77
2018 LAD	NL	15	15	0	82.1	324	68	23	18	9	1	0	1	15	1	89	0	7	3	.700	0-0	0	90	.622	2.45	1.97
2019 LAD	NL	29	29	0	182.2	723	160	53	47	17	8	2	4	24	2	163	0	14	5	.737	0-0	0	91	.622	2.45	**2.32**
2020 Tor	AL	12	12	0	67.0	275	60	22	20	6	1	0	1	17	0	72	1	5	2	.714	0-0	0	90	.636	2.94	2.69
Postseason		8	8	0	40.0	165	41	18	18	3	0	0	0	8	2	32	0	3	2	.600	0-0	0	92	.666	3.21	4.05
7 ML YEARS		138	137	1	807.1	3301	758	289	265	78	27	8	14	181	13	737	12	59	35	.628	1-1	0	90	.670	3.11	2.95

Casey Sadler

Pitches: R Bats: R Pos: RP-17
Ht: 6'3" Wt: 205 Born: 7/13/1990 Age: 30

		HOW MUCH PITCHED					WHAT HE GAVE UP											THE RESULTS								
Year Team	Lg	G	GS	GF	IP	BFP	H	R	ER	HR	SH	SF	HB	TBB	IBB	SO	WP	W	L	Pct	Sv-Op	Hld	Vel	OPS	ERC	ERA
2014 Pit	NL	6	0	2	10.1	49	12	9	9	0	0	0	1	5	0	7	1	0	1	.000	0-0	0	92	.782	4.80	7.84
2015 Pit	NL	1	1	0	5.0	19	4	2	2	1	0	0	0	1	0	5	0	1	0	1.000	0-0	0	91	.763	2.98	3.60
2018 Pit	NL	2	0	1	4.1	25	9	7	4	0	0	0	0	3	0	3	1	0	0	-	0-0	0	92	1.116	11.14	8.31
2019 2 Tms		33	1	16	46.1	194	41	14	11	5	2	1	4	13	2	31	0	4	0	1.000	1-2	2	93	.664	3.30	2.14
2020 2 Tms		17	0	2	19.1	86	15	13	11	3	1	0	0	12	0	21	5	1	2	.333	0-0	5	93	.715	3.94	5.12
19 TB	AL	9	0	8	19.1	79	16	5	4	2	0	0	1	5	0	11	0	0	0	-	0-0	0	93	.621	2.83	1.86
19 LAD	NL	24	1	8	27.0	115	25	9	7	3	2	1	3	8	2	20	0	4	0	1.000	1-2	2	94	.695	3.64	2.33
20 ChC	NL	10	0	1	9.1	44	8	6	6	2	1	0	0	8	0	9	3	0	0	-	0-0	4	93	.801	5.86	5.79
20 Sea	AL	7	0	1	10.0	42	7	7	5	1	0	0	0	4	0	12	2	1	2	.333	0-0	1	93	.630	2.39	4.50
5 ML YEARS		59	2	21	85.1	373	81	45	37	9	3	3	5	34	2	67	7	6	3	.667	1-2	7	93	.727	3.96	3.90

Chris Sale

Pitches: L Bats: L Pos: P
SAIL
Ht: 6'6" Wt: 183 Born: 3/30/1989 Age: 32

		HOW MUCH PITCHED					WHAT HE GAVE UP											THE RESULTS								
Year Team	Lg	G	GS	GF	IP	BFP	H	R	ER	HR	SH	SF	HB	TBB	IBB	SO	WP	W	L	Pct	Sv-Op	Hld	Vel	OPS	ERC	ERA
2010 CWS	AL	21	0	8	23.1	92	15	5	5	2	1	0	0	10	0	32	1	2	1	.667	4-4	2	96	.546	2.30	1.93
2011 CWS	AL	58	0	17	71.0	288	52	22	22	6	3	2	2	27	3	79	2	2	2	.500	8-10	16	95	.612	2.55	2.79
2012 CWS	AL	30	29	0	192.0	772	167	66	65	19	1	3	6	51	5	192	6	17	8	.680	0-1	0	92	.660	3.00	3.05
2013 CWS	AL	30	30	0	214.1	866	184	81	73	23	2	4	14	46	2	226	8	11	14	.440	0-0	0	93	.636	2.92	3.07
2014 CWS	AL	26	26	0	174.0	685	129	48	42	13	2	3	11	39	2	208	3	12	4	.750	0-0	0	94	.567	2.18	2.17
2015 CWS	AL	31	31	0	208.2	854	185	88	79	23	2	4	**13**	42	0	274	7	13	11	.542	0-0	0	94	.649	3.00	3.41
2016 CWS	AL	32	32	0	226.2	907	190	88	84	27	5	3	**17**	45	2	233	2	17	10	.630	0-0	0	93	.651	2.88	3.34
2017 Bos	AL	32	32	0	214.1	851	165	73	69	24	2	4	8	43	0	308	3	17	8	.680	0-0	0	94	.603	2.33	2.90
2018 Bos	AL	27	27	0	158.0	617	102	39	37	11	0	4	14	34	0	237	4	12	4	.750	0-0	0	95	.532	1.76	2.11
2019 Bos	AL	25	25	0	147.1	612	123	80	72	24		4	13	37	0	218	2	6	11	.353	0-0	0	93	.695	3.31	4.40
Postseason		7	4	1	25.0	107	24	16	16	5	0	0	1	9	0	36	0	1	2	.333	0-0	1	94	.751	4.54	5.76
10 ML YEARS		312	232	25	1629.2	6544	1312	590	548	172	20	28	98	374	14	2007	38	109	73	.599	12-15	18	94	.625	2.67	3.03

Jeff Samardzija

Pitches: R Bats: R Pos: SP-4
suh-MAHR-jah
Ht: 6'4" Wt: 233 Born: 1/23/1985 Age: 36

		HOW MUCH PITCHED					WHAT HE GAVE UP											THE RESULTS								
Year Team	Lg	G	GS	GF	IP	BFP	H	R	ER	HR	SH	SF	HB	TBB	IBB	SO	WP	W	L	Pct	Sv-Op	Hld	Vel	OPS	ERC	ERA
2008 ChC	NL	26	0	6	27.2	124	24	12	7	0	1	1	1	15	2	25	2	1	0	1.000	1-4	3	95	.599	3.08	2.28
2009 ChC	NL	20	2	7	34.2	161	46	29	29	7	4	1	1	15	1	21	2	1	3	.250	0-0	0	94	.981	7.13	7.53
2010 ChC	NL	7	3	0	19.1	100	21	22	18	4	0	0	2	20	1	9	1	2	2	.500	0-0	0	93	.930	8.45	8.38
2011 ChC	NL	75	0	18	88.0	380	64	35	29	5	3	2	5	50	3	87	8	8	4	.667	0-2	13	95	.613	3.05	2.97
2012 ChC	NL	28	28	0	174.2	723	157	79	74	20	5	4	4	56	2	180	10	9	13	.409	0-0	0	95	.698	3.41	3.81
2013 ChC	NL	33	33	0	213.2	914	210	109	103	25	4	2	8	78	3	214	11	8	13	.381	0-0	0	95	.736	4.11	4.34
2014 2 Tms		33	33	0	219.2	879	191	86	73	20	3	7	10	43	3	202	10	7	13	.350	0-0	0	94	.646	2.74	2.99
2015 CWS	AL	32	32	0	214.0	910	**228**	**122**	**118**	**29**	4	9	12	49	0	163	5	11	13	.458	0-0	0	94	.765	4.24	4.96
2016 SF	NL	32	32	0	203.1	829	190	88	86	24	6	4	1	54	4	167	2	12	11	.522	0-0	0	94	.710	3.36	3.81
2017 SF	NL	32	32	0	**207.2**	847	204	107	102	30	4	4	6	32	1	205	2	9	**15**	.375	0-0	0	94	.734	3.43	4.42
2018 SF	NL	10	10	0	44.2	207	47	32	31	6	1	4	2	26	1	30	2	1	5	.167	0-0	0	92	.789	5.45	6.25
2019 SF	NL	32	32	0	181.1	740	152	78	71	28	4	4	6	49	4	140	5	11	12	.478	0-0	0	92	.692	3.14	3.52
2020 SF	NL	4	4	0	16.2	77	21	19	18	7	0	0	2	4	0	6	0	0	2	.000	0-0	0	91	.984	7.76	9.72

Year Team	Lg	G	GS	GF	IP	BFP	H	R	ER	HR	SH	SF	HB	TBB	IBB	SO	WP	W	L	Pct	Sv-Op	Hld	Vel	OPS	ERC	ERA
14 ChC	NL	17	17	0	108.0	449	99	44	34	7	3	4	6	31	3	103	6	2	7	.222	0-0	0	94	.672	3.14	2.83
14 Oak	AL	16	16	0	111.2	430	92	42	39	13	0	3	4	12	0	99	4	5	6	.455	0-0	0	95	.619	2.34	3.14
Postseason		2	1	0	3.0	17	8	5	5	0	0	0	0	1	0	1	0	0	1	.000	0-0	0	96	1.217	14.52	15.00
13 ML YEARS		364	241	31	1645.1	6891	1555	818	759	205	39	42	60	491	25	1449	60	80	106	.430	1-6	16	94	.720	3.67	4.15

Carlos Sanabria

Pitches: R Bats: R Pos: RP-2   Ht: 6'3" Wt: 165 Born: 1/24/1997 Age: 24

Year Team	Lg	G	GS	GF	IP	BFP	H	R	ER	HR	SH	SF	HB	TBB	IBB	SO	WP	W	L	Pct	Sv-Op	Hld	Vel	OPS	ERC	ERA
2020 Hou	AL	2	0	2	2.0	12	3	2	2	1	0	0	0	3	0	2	2	0	0	-	0-0	0	93	1.278	16.26	9.00

Aaron Sanchez

Pitches: R Bats: R Pos: P   Ht: 6'4" Wt: 210 Born: 7/1/1992 Age: 28

Year Team	Lg	G	GS	GF	IP	BFP	H	R	ER	HR	SH	SF	HB	TBB	IBB	SO	WP	W	L	Pct	Sv-Op	Hld	Vel	OPS	ERC	ERA
2014 Tor	AL	24	0	6	33.0	121	14	5	4	1	2	0	1	9	0	27	1	2	2	.500	3-3	7	97	.367	0.96	1.09
2015 Tor	AL	41	11	4	92.1	380	74	35	33	9	2	1	3	44	2	61	8	7	6	.538	0-1	10	95	.666	3.47	3.22
2016 Tor	AL	30	30	0	192.0	790	161	69	64	15	1	2	5	63	0	161	5	15	2	**.882**	0-0	0	95	.625	2.90	**3.00**
2017 Tor	AL	8	8	0	36.0	167	42	24	17	6	0	0	1	20	0	24	1	1	3	.250	0-0	0	95	.836	6.36	4.25
2018 Tor	AL	20	20	0	105.0	474	106	62	57	11	0	4	7	58	2	86	4	4	6	.400	0-0	0	94	.768	5.02	4.89
2019 2 Tms	AL	27	27	0	131.1	605	145	92	86	20	0	4	11	68	2	115	7	5	14	.263	0-0	0	94	.828	5.88	5.89
19 Tor	AL	23	23	0	112.2	524	131	82	76	15	0	3	10	59	2	99	7	3	14	.176	0-0	0	94	.835	6.16	6.07
19 Hou	AL	4	4	0	18.2	81	14	10	10	5	0	1	1	9	0	16	0	2	0	1.000	0-0	0	92	.782	4.22	4.82
Postseason		11	2	1	19.0	77	12	8	7	2	2	0	0	8	0	16	1	2	0	1.000	0-0	0	96	.565	2.24	3.32
6 ML YEARS		150	96	10	589.2	2537	542	287	261	62	5	11	28	262	6	474	26	34	33	.507	3-4	17	95	.707	4.02	3.98

Ali Sanchez

Bats: R Throws: R Pos: C-5   Ht: 6'1" Wt: 200 Born: 1/20/1997 Age: 24

Year Team	Lg	G	AB	H	2B	3B	HR	(Hm Rd)	TB	R	RBI	RC	TBB	IBB	SO	HBP	SH	SF	SB	CS	GDP	Avg	OBP	Slg	OPS
2020 NYM	NL	5	9	1	0	0	0	(0 0)	1	0	0	0	1	0	3	0	0	0	0	0	2	.111	.200	.111	.311

Anibal Sanchez

Pitches: R Bats: R Pos: SP-11   ah-NEE-bahl   Ht: 6'0" Wt: 205 Born: 2/27/1984 Age: 37

Year Team	Lg	G	GS	GF	IP	BFP	H	R	ER	HR	SH	SF	HB	TBB	IBB	SO	WP	W	L	Pct	Sv-Op	Hld	Vel	OPS	ERC	ERA
2006 Fla	NL	18	17	0	114.1	469	90	39	36	9	3	1	4	46	1	72	4	10	3	.769	0-0	0	91	.635	2.96	2.83
2007 Fla	NL	6	6	0	30.0	151	43	17	16	3	2	2	2	19	1	14	3	2	1	.667	0-0	0	90	.930	7.90	4.80
2008 Fla	NL	10	10	0	51.2	241	54	35	32	7	4	2	6	27	2	50	1	2	5	.286	0-0	0	90	.788	5.40	5.57
2009 Fla	NL	16	16	0	86.0	383	84	39	37	10	2	2	1	46	5	71	0	4	8	.333	0-0	0	91	.756	4.51	3.87
2010 Fla	NL	32	32	0	195.0	841	192	89	77	10	13	3	7	70	5	157	1	13	12	.520	0-0	0	91	.680	3.56	3.55
2011 Fla	NL	32	32	0	196.1	830	187	85	80	20	12	1	5	64	8	202	4	8	9	.471	0-0	0	92	.711	3.57	3.67
2012 2 Tms		31	31	0	195.2	820	200	95	84	20	5	7	5	48	3	167	7	9	13	.409	0-0	0	92	.716	3.70	3.86
2013 Det	AL	29	29	0	182.0	746	156	56	52	9	4	4	2	54	1	202	7	14	8	.636	0-0	0	93	.616	2.63	2.57
2014 Det	AL	22	21	0	126.0	514	108	55	48	4	3	4	3	30	1	102	5	8	5	.615	0-0	0	92	.599	2.35	3.43
2015 Det	AL	25	25	0	157.0	660	152	89	87	29	5	2	1	49	1	138	5	10	10	.500	0-0	0	92	.768	4.14	4.99
2016 Det	AL	35	26	3	153.1	668	171	108	100	30	4	6	5	53	1	135	7	7	13	.350	0-0	0	91	.828	5.40	5.87
2017 Det	AL	28	17	6	105.1	482	139	81	75	26	2	3	4	29	1	104	5	3	7	.300	0-0	0	91	.906	6.66	6.41
2018 Atl	NL	25	24	0	136.2	553	106	48	43	15	7	3	4	42	0	135	4	7	6	.538	0-0	0	91	.633	2.71	2.83
2019 Was	NL	30	30	0	166.0	712	153	77	71	22	1	2	4	58	10	134	1	11	8	.579	0-0	0	90	.709	3.59	3.85
2020 Was	NL	11	11	0	53.0	245	70	40	39	11	0	0	3	18	2	43	0	4	5	.444	0-0	0	90	.907	6.74	6.62
12 Mia	NL	19	19	0	121.0	504	119	59	53	12	4	5	2	33	2	110	4	5	7	.417	0-0	0	91	.717	3.55	3.94
12 Det	AL	12	12	0	74.2	316	81	36	31	8	1	2	3	15	1	57	3	4	6	.400	0-0	0	93	.714	3.95	3.74
Postseason		11	10	0	61.1	256	51	22	20	9	1	1	2	19	1	64	4	3	6	.333	0-0	1	92	.677	3.16	2.93
15 ML YEARS		350	327	9	1948.1	8315	1905	953	877	225	67	42	56	653	42	1726	60	112	113	.498	0-0	0	91	.723	3.87	4.05

Gary Sanchez

Bats: R Throws: R Pos: C-41;DH-7;PH-4   Ht: 6'2" Wt: 230 Born: 12/2/1992 Age: 28

Year Team	Lg	G	AB	H	2B	3B	HR	(Hm Rd)	TB	R	RBI	RC	TBB	IBB	SO	HBP	SH	SF	SB	CS	GDP	Avg	OBP	Slg	OPS
2015 NYY	AL	2	2	0	0	0	0	(0 0)	0	0	0	0	0	0	1	0	0	0	0	0	0	.000	.000	.000	.000
2016 NYY	AL	53	201	60	12	0	20	(10 10)	132	34	42	40	24	2	57	2	0	2	1	0	5	.299	.376	.657	1.032
2017 NYY	AL	122	471	131	20	0	33	(15 18)	250	79	90	81	40	1	120	10	0	4	2	1	9	.278	.345	.531	.876
2018 NYY	AL	89	323	60	17	0	18	(8 10)	131	51	53	41	46	0	94	3	0	2	1	0	10	.186	.291	.406	.697
2019 NYY	AL	106	396	92	12	1	34	(19 15)	208	62	77	64	40	3	125	9	0	1	0	1	3	.232	.316	.525	.841
2020 NYY	AL	49	156	23	4	0	10	(7 3)	57	19	24	12	18	0	64	4	0	0	0	0	6	.147	.253	.365	.618
Postseason		27	102	18	3	0	6	(3 3)	39	10	16	9	6	0	40	1	0	2	0	0	3	.176	.225	.382	.608
6 ML YEARS		421	1549	366	65	1	115	(59 56)	778	245	286	238	168	6	461	28	0	9	4	2	33	.236	.320	.502	.823

Jesus Sanchez

Bats: L **Throws:** R **Pos:** RF-10;PH-1   **Ht:** 6'3" **Wt:** 222 **Born:** 10/7/1997 **Age:** 23

Year	Team	Lg	G	AB	H	2B	3B	HR	(Hm	Rd)	TB	R	RBI	RC	TBB	IBB	SO	HBP	SH	SF	SB	CS	GDP	Avg	OBP	Slg	OPS
2016	2 Tms	Low	56	213	70	10	8	7	(-	-)	117	33	39	39	9	0	43	0	1	3	2	5	4	.329	.351	.549	.900
2017	BG	A	117	475	145	29	4	15	(-	-)	227	81	82	80	32	2	91	1	0	4	7	2	12	.305	.348	.478	.826
2018	Charltt	A+	90	359	108	24	2	10	(-	-)	166	56	64	55	15	1	71	2	0	2	6	3	6	.301	.331	.462	.793
2018	Mont	AA	27	98	21	8	0	1	(-	-)	32	14	11	10	11	1	21	1	0	0	1	1	3	.214	.300	.327	.627
2019	Mont	AA	78	287	79	11	1	8	(-	-)	116	32	49	39	24	0	65	2	0	3	5	4	9	.275	.332	.404	.736
2019	Drham	AAA	18	63	13	2	1	1	(-	-)	20	6	5	5	6	0	20	1	0	1	0	0	5	.206	.282	.317	.599
2019	NewOr	AAA	17	65	16	1	0	4	(-	-)	29	11	9	10	9	0	15	1	1	2	0	0	1	.246	.338	.446	.784
2020	Mia	NL	10	25	1	1	0	0	(0	0)	2	1	2	0	4	0	11	0	0	0	0	0	1	.040	.172	.080	.252

Ricardo Sanchez

Pitches: L **Bats:** L **Pos:** RP-3   **Ht:** 5'10" **Wt:** 220 **Born:** 4/11/1997 **Age:** 24

Year	Team	Lg	G	GS	GF	IP	BFP	H	R	ER	HR	SH	SF	HB	TBB	IBB	SO	WP	W	L	Pct	Sv-Op	Hld	Vel	OPS	ERC	ERA
2020	StL	NL	3	0	1	5.1	27	5	4	4	1	0	1	1	5	0	4	0	0	0	-	0-0	0	92	.907	7.27	6.75

Sixto Sanchez

Pitches: R **Bats:** R **Pos:** SP-7   **Ht:** 6'0" **Wt:** 234 **Born:** 7/29/1998 **Age:** 22

Year	Team	Lg	G	GS	GF	IP	BFP	H	R	ER	HR	SH	SF	HB	TBB	IBB	SO	WP	W	L	Pct	Sv-Op	Hld	Vel	OPS	ERC	ERA
2016	Phillies	R	11	11	0	54.0	194	33	4	3	0	1	1	2	8	0	44	1	5	0	1.000	0--	-	-	.377	1.18	0.50
2017	2 Tms	Low	18	18	0	95.0	375	73	35	32	2	2	3	4	18	0	84	5	5	7	.417	0--	-	-	.436	1.81	3.03
2018	Clrwtr	A+	8	8	0	46.2	188	39	14	13	1	0	1	2	11	0	45	0	4	3	.571	0--	-	-	.604	2.28	2.51
2019	Jaxnvl	AA	18	18	0	103.0	411	87	33	29	5	2	0	3	19	0	97	0	8	4	.667	0--	-	-	.600	2.26	2.53
2020	Mia	NL	7	7	0	39.0	158	36	15	15	3	0	1	2	11	1	33	1	3	2	.600	0-0	0	98	.643	3.32	3.46

Yolmer Sanchez

Bats: B **Throws:** R **Pos:** 3B-5;PR-4;SS-3;DH-3;2B-1   **Ht:** 5'8" **Wt:** 205 **Born:** 6/29/1992 **Age:** 29

Year	Team	Lg	G	AB	H	2B	3B	HR	(Hm	Rd)	TB	R	RBI	RC	TBB	IBB	SO	HBP	SH	SF	SB	CS	GDP	Avg	OBP	Slg	OPS
2014	CWS	AL	28	100	25	5	0	0	(0	0)	30	6	5	5	3	0	25	0	0	1	1	1	1	.250	.269	.300	.569
2015	CWS	AL	120	389	87	23	1	5	(2	3)	127	40	31	30	19	0	81	5	6	1	2	2	9	.224	.268	.326	.595
2016	CWS	AL	53	154	32	9	1	4	(2	2)	55	15	21	14	5	0	42	1	2	1	0	1	1	.208	.236	.357	.593
2017	CWS	AL	141	484	129	19	8	12	(8	4)	200	63	59	68	35	2	111	4	7	4	8	9	10	.267	.319	.413	.732
2018	CWS	AL	155	600	145	34	**10**	8	(4	4)	223	62	55	72	49	0	138	8	2	3	14	6	9	.242	.306	.372	.678
2019	CWS	AL	149	496	125	20	4	2	(0	2)	159	59	43	55	44	1	117	5	7	3	5	4	7	.252	.318	.321	.638
2020	CWS	AL	12	16	5	3	0	1	(0	1)	11	7	1	4	5	0	5	0	0	0	0	0	1	.313	.476	.688	1.164
	7 ML YEARS		658	2239	548	113	24	32	(16	16)	805	252	215	248	160	3	519	23	24	13	30	23	38	.245	.300	.360	.660

Pablo Sandoval

Bats: B **Throws:** R **Pos:** DH-14;PH-13;1B-8;3B-5   **Ht:** 5'10" **Wt:** 268 **Born:** 8/11/1986 **Age:** 34

Year	Team	Lg	G	AB	H	2B	3B	HR	(Hm	Rd)	TB	R	RBI	RC	TBB	IBB	SO	HBP	SH	SF	SB	CS	GDP	Avg	OBP	Slg	OPS
2008	SF	NL	41	145	50	10	1	3	(1	2)	71	24	24	24	4	1	14	1	0	4	0	0	6	.345	.357	.490	.847
2009	SF	NL	153	572	189	44	5	25	(13	12)	318	79	90	113	52	13	83	4	0	5	5	5	10	.330	.387	.556	.943
2010	SF	NL	152	563	151	34	3	13	(9	4)	230	61	63	55	47	12	81	1	0	5	3	2	**26**	.268	.323	.409	.732
2011	SF	NL	117	426	134	26	3	23	(7	16)	235	55	70	72	32	9	63	0	1	7	2	4	12	.315	.357	.552	.909
2012	SF	NL	108	396	112	25	2	12	(7	5)	177	59	63	60	38	4	59	1	0	7	1	1	13	.283	.342	.447	.789
2013	SF	NL	141	525	146	27	2	14	(6	8)	219	52	79	78	47	5	79	6	0	6	0	0	19	.278	.341	.417	.758
2014	SF	NL	157	588	164	26	3	16	(9	7)	244	68	73	78	39	6	85	4	0	7	0	0	16	.279	.324	.415	.739
2015	Bos	AL	126	470	115	25	1	10	(4	6)	172	43	47	46	25	1	73	7	1	2	0	0	14	.245	.292	.366	.658
2016	Bos	AL	3	6	0	0	0	0	(0	0)	0	0	0	0	1	0	4	0	0	0	0	0	0	.000	.143	.000	.143
2017	2 Tms		79	259	57	11	0	9	(4	5)	95	27	32	20	16	0	53	1	0	3	0	1	11	.220	.265	.367	.632
2018	SF	NL	92	230	57	10	1	9	(6	3)	96	22	40	31	19	2	52	2	0	1	0	0	9	.248	.310	.417	.727
2019	SF	NL	108	272	73	23	0	14	(6	8)	138	42	41	38	18	2	67	1	2	3	1	0	8	.268	.313	.507	.820
2020	2 Tms	NL	34	84	18	1	0	1	(0	1)	22	5	6	5	8	0	19	1	0	1	0	0	3	.214	.287	.262	.549
17	Bos	AL	32	99	21	2	0	4	(2	2)	35	10	12	9	8	0	24	0	0	1	0	1	4	.212	.269	.354	.622
17	SF	NL	47	160	36	9	0	5	(2	3)	60	17	20	11	8	0	29	1	0	2	0	0	7	.225	.263	.375	.638
20	SF	NL	33	82	18	1	0	1	(0	1)	22	5	6	5	6	0	18	1	0	1	0	0	3	.220	.278	.268	.546
20	Atl	NL	1	2	0	0	0	0	(0	0)	0	0	0	0	2	0	1	0	0	0	0	0	0	.000	.500	.000	.500
	Postseason		39	154	53	13	0	6	(3	3)	84	21	20	27	10	3	22	2	0	1	0	0	7	.344	.389	.545	.935
	13 ML YEARS		1311	4536	1266	262	21	149	(72	77)	2017	537	628	620	346	55	732	29	4	51	12	13	147	.279	.331	.445	.775

Patrick Sandoval

Pitches: L **Bats:** L **Pos:** SP-6; RP-3   **Ht:** 6'3" **Wt:** 190 **Born:** 10/18/1996 **Age:** 24

Year	Team	Lg	G	GS	GF	IP	BFP	H	R	ER	HR	SH	SF	HB	TBB	IBB	SO	WP	W	L	Pct	Sv-Op	Hld	Vel	OPS	ERC	ERA
2019	LAA	AL	10	9	0	39.1	169	35	22	22	6	2	1	1	19	0	42	4	0	4	.000	0-0	0	93	.754	4.28	5.03
2020	LAA	AL	9	6	0	36.2	159	37	26	23	10	0	0	0	12	0	33	2	1	5	.167	0-0	0	93	.818	4.92	5.65
	2 ML YEARS		19	15	0	76.0	328	72	48	45	16	2	1	1	31	0	75	6	1	9	.100	0-0	0	93	.787	4.60	5.33

Miguel Sano

Bats: R **Throws:** R **Pos:** 1B-52;DH-1
sah-NO
Ht: 6'4" **Wt:** 272 **Born:** 5/11/1993 **Age:** 28

Year Team	Lg	G	AB	H	2B	3B	HR	(Hm	Rd)	TB	R	RBI	RC	TBB	IBB	SO	HBP	SH	SF	SB	CS	GDP	Avg	OBP	Slg	OPS
2015 Min	AL	80	279	75	17	1	18	(10	8)	148	46	52	62	53	1	119	1	0	2	1	1	4	.269	.385	.530	.916
2016 Min	AL	116	437	103	22	1	25	(11	14)	202	57	66	62	54	1	178	1	0	3	1	0	8	.236	.319	.462	.781
2017 Min	AL	114	424	112	15	2	28	(12	16)	215	75	77	71	54	5	173	4	0	1	0	0	12	.264	.352	.507	.859
2018 Min	AL	71	266	53	14	0	13	(7	6)	106	32	41	28	31	0	115	0	0	2	0	0	7	.199	.281	.398	.679
2019 Min	AL	105	380	94	19	2	34	(14	20)	219	76	79	74	55	0	159	3	0	1	0	1	5	.247	.346	.576	.923
2020 Min	AL	53	186	38	12	0	13	(6	7)	89	31	25	22	18	1	90	1	0	0	0	0	3	.204	.278	.478	.757
Postseason		3	12	1	0	0	1	(0	1)	4	1	1	0	0	0	0	0	0	0	0	0	0	.083	.083	.333	.417
6 ML YEARS		539	1972	475	99	6	131	(60	71)	979	317	340	319	265	8	834	10	0	9	2	2	39	.241	.332	.496	.829

Carlos Santana

Bats: B **Throws:** R **Pos:** 1B-60
Ht: 5'11" **Wt:** 210 **Born:** 4/8/1986 **Age:** 35

Year Team	Lg	G	AB	H	2B	3B	HR	(Hm	Rd)	TB	R	RBI	RC	TBB	IBB	SO	HBP	SH	SF	SB	CS	GDP	Avg	OBP	Slg	OPS
2010 Cle	AL	46	150	39	13	0	6	(2	4)	70	23	22	25	37	2	29	1	0	4	3	0	3	.260	.401	.467	.868
2011 Cle	AL	155	552	132	35	2	27	(14	13)	252	84	79	81	97	7	133	2	0	7	5	3	15	.239	.351	.457	.808
2012 Cle	AL	143	507	128	27	2	18	(7	11)	213	72	76	77	91	4	101	3	0	8	3	5	21	.252	.365	.420	.785
2013 Cle	AL	154	541	145	39	1	20	(8	12)	246	75	74	93	93	6	110	4	0	4	3	1	7	.268	.377	.455	.832
2014 Cle	AL	152	541	125	25	0	27	(13	14)	231	68	85	88	113	5	124	3	0	3	5	2	13	.231	.365	.427	.792
2015 Cle	AL	154	550	127	29	2	19	(6	13)	217	72	85	80	108	8	122	3	0	5	11	3	20	.231	.357	.395	.752
2016 Cle	AL	158	582	151	31	3	34	(20	14)	290	89	87	104	99	0	99	2	0	5	5	2	18	.259	.366	.498	.865
2017 Cle	AL	154	571	148	37	3	23	(11	12)	260	90	79	89	88	6	94	6	0	2	5	1	11	.259	.363	.455	.818
2018 Phi	NL	161	560	128	28	2	24	(13	11)	232	82	86	87	110	6	93	1	0	8	2	1	12	.229	.352	.414	.766
2019 Cle	AL	158	573	161	30	1	34	(19	15)	295	110	93	114	108	12	108	3	0	2	4	0	13	.281	.397	.515	.911
2020 Cle	AL	60	206	41	7	0	8	(5	3)	72	34	30	35	47	1	43	1	0	1	0	0	0	.199	.349	.350	.699
Postseason		21	75	16	2	0	4	(1	3)	30	8	8	10	11	0	16	1	0	0	0	0	0	.213	.322	.400	.722
11 ML YEARS		1495	5333	1325	301	16	240	(122	118)	2378	799	796	873	991	57	1056	29	0	49	46	18	138	.248	.366	.446	.812

Danny Santana

Bats: B **Throws:** R **Pos:** 1B-9;CF-4;DH-2;LF-1;PH-1
Ht: 5'11" **Wt:** 195 **Born:** 11/7/1990 **Age:** 30

Year Team	Lg	G	AB	H	2B	3B	HR	(Hm	Rd)	TB	R	RBI	RC	TBB	IBB	SO	HBP	SH	SF	SB	CS	GDP	Avg	OBP	Slg	OPS
2014 Min	AL	101	405	129	27	7	7	(3	4)	191	70	40	72	19	0	98	3	2	1	20	4	3	.319	.353	.472	.824
2015 Min	AL	91	261	56	10	5	0	(0	0)	76	30	21	16	6	1	68	3	7	0	8	4	7	.215	.241	.291	.532
2016 Min	AL	75	233	56	10	2	2	(0	2)	76	29	14	18	12	0	55	1	1	1	12	9	1	.240	.279	.326	.606
2017 2 Tms		82	168	34	10	2	4	(3	1)	60	19	23	17	8	1	41	1	1	0	7	0	3	.202	.243	.357	.600
2018 Atl	NL	15	28	5	3	0	0	(0	0)	8	4	2	2	3	0	11	1	0	0	1	1	0	.179	.281	.286	.567
2019 Tex	AL	130	474	134	23	6	28	(19	9)	253	81	81	83	25	2	151	6	0	5	21	6	8	.283	.324	.534	.857
2020 Tex	AL	15	55	8	4	0	1	(0	1)	15	6	7	4	7	0	24	1	1	2	2	0	1	.145	.238	.273	.511
17 Min	AL	13	25	5	1	0	1	(1	0)	9	3	1	0	1	0	8	0	0	0	1	0	1	.200	.231	.360	.591
17 Min	NL	69	143	29	9	2	3	(2	1)	51	16	22	17	7	1	33	1	1	0	6	0	2	.203	.245	.357	.602
7 ML YEARS		509	1624	422	87	22	42	(25	17)	679	239	188	212	80	4	448	15	11	8	71	24	23	.260	.299	.418	.717

Dennis Santana

Pitches: R **Bats:** R **Pos:** RP-12
Ht: 6'2" **Wt:** 190 **Born:** 4/12/1996 **Age:** 25

Year Team	Lg	G	GS	GF	IP	BFP	H	R	ER	HR	SH	SF	HB	TBB	IBB	SO	WP	W	L	Pct	Sv-Op	Hld	Vel	OPS	ERC	ERA
2018 LAD	NL	1	0	0	3.2	19	6	5	5	0	1	0	1	1	0	4	1	1	0	1.000	0-0	0	93	1.007	7.52	12.27
2019 LAD	NL	3	0	1	5.0	27	6	4	4	1	0	1	2	4	0	6	1	0	0	-	0-0	0	93	.994	9.44	7.20
2020 LAD	NL	12	0	7	17.0	73	15	11	10	4	0	0	2	7	0	18	1	1	2	.333	0-1	0	94	.782	4.93	5.29
3 ML YEARS		16	0	8	25.2	119	27	20	19	5	1	1	5	12	0	28	3	2	2	.500	0-1	0	94	.863	6.17	6.66

Domingo Santana

Bats: R **Throws:** R **Pos:** RF-16;LF-9;PH-1
Ht: 6'5" **Wt:** 232 **Born:** 8/5/1992 **Age:** 28

Year Team	Lg	G	AB	H	2B	3B	HR	(Hm	Rd)	TB	R	RBI	RC	TBB	IBB	SO	HBP	SH	SF	SB	CS	GDP	Avg	OBP	Slg	OPS
2014 Hou	AL	6	17	0	0	0	0	(0	0)	0	1	0	0	1	0	14	0	0	0	0	0	0	.000	.056	.000	.056
2015 2 Tms		52	160	38	7	0	8	(3	5)	69	20	26	28	20	0	63	5	0	2	4	1	2	.238	.337	.431	.768
2016 Mil	NL	77	246	63	14	0	11	(3	8)	110	34	32	36	32	0	91	2	0	1	2	3	7	.256	.345	.447	.792
2017 Mil	NL	151	525	146	29	0	30	(19	11)	265	88	85	98	73	2	178	6	0	3	15	4	12	.278	.371	.505	.875
2018 Mil	NL	85	211	56	14	1	5	(4	1)	87	21	20	24	20	1	77	1	0	3	1	1	3	.265	.328	.412	.740
2019 Sea	AL	121	451	114	20	1	21	(9	12)	199	63	69	64	50	1	164	2	0	2	8	3	11	.253	.329	.441	.770
2020 Cle	AL	24	70	11	3	0	2	(0	2)	20	6	12	8	13	0	25	1	0	0	0	0	2	.157	.298	.286	.583
15 Hou	AL	14	39	10	2	0	2	(0	2)	18	6	8	8	2	0	17	1	0	0	2	1	1	.256	.310	.462	.771
15 Mil	NL	38	121	28	5	0	6	(3	3)	51	14	18	20	18	0	46	4	0	2	2	0	1	.231	.345	.421	.766
Postseason		10	8	2	1	0	0	(0	0)	3	1	3	2	2	1	5	0	0	0	1	0	0	.250	.400	.375	.775
7 ML YEARS		516	1680	428	87	2	77	(38	39)	750	233	244	258	209	4	612	17	0	11	30	12	37	.255	.341	.446	.788

Anthony Santander

Bats: B **Throws:** R **Pos:** RF-35;LF-2;DH-1   **Ht:** 6'2" **Wt:** 225 **Born:** 10/19/1994 **Age:** 26

Year	Team	Lg	G	AB	H	2B	3B	HR	(Hm	Rd)	TB	R	RBI	RC	TBB	IBB	SO	HBP	SH	SF	SB	CS	GDP	Avg	OBP	Slg	OPS
2017	Bal	AL	13	30	8	3	0	0	(0	0)	11	1	2	2	0	0	8	0	0	1	0	0	0	.267	.258	.367	.625
2018	Bal	AL	33	101	20	5	1	1	(0	1)	30	8	6	10	6	0	21	1	0	0	1	0	1	.198	.250	.297	.547
2019	Bal	AL	93	380	99	20	1	20	(10	10)	181	46	59	55	19	0	86	2	1	3	1	2	1	.261	.297	.476	.773
2020	Bal	AL	37	153	40	13	1	11	(8	3)	88	24	32	28	10	3	25	2	0	0	0	1	2	.261	.315	.575	.890
	4 ML YEARS		176	664	167	41	3	32	(18	14)	310	79	99	95	35	3	140	5	1	4	2	3	4	.252	.292	.467	.759

Antonio Santos

Pitches: R **Bats:** R **Pos:** RP-2; SP-1   **Ht:** 6'3" **Wt:** 223 **Born:** 10/6/1996 **Age:** 24

Year	Team	Lg	G	GS	GF	IP	BFP	H	R	ER	HR	SH	SF	HB	TBB	IBB	SO	WP	W	L	Pct	Sv-Op	Hld	Vel	OPS	ERC	ERA
2020	Col	NL	3	1	0	6.0	35	14	11	11	1	0	0	2	4	0	4	0	0	1	.000	0-0	0	93	1.330	17.82	16.50

Josh Sborz

Pitches: R **Bats:** R **Pos:** RP-4   **Ht:** 6'3" **Wt:** 215 **Born:** 12/17/1993 **Age:** 27

Year	Team	Lg	G	GS	GF	IP	BFP	H	R	ER	HR	SH	SF	HB	TBB	IBB	SO	WP	W	L	Pct	Sv-Op	Hld	Vel	OPS	ERC	ERA
2019	LAD	NL	7	0	6	9.0	40	10	8	8	2	0	1	0	4	0	7	0	0	1	.000	0-0	0	95	.921	5.84	8.00
2020	LAD	NL	4	0	3	4.1	16	2	1	1	1	0	0	0	1	0	2	0	0	0	-	0-0	0	96	.588	1.53	2.08
	2 ML YEARS		11	0	9	13.1	56	12	9	9	3	0	1	0	5	0	9	0	0	1	.000	0-0	0	95	.824	4.26	6.08

Scott Schebler

Bats: L **Throws:** R **Pos:** RF-1;PH-1   SHEB-ler   **Ht:** 6'1" **Wt:** 228 **Born:** 10/6/1990 **Age:** 30

Year	Team	Lg	G	AB	H	2B	3B	HR	(Hm	Rd)	TB	R	RBI	RC	TBB	IBB	SO	HBP	SH	SF	SB	CS	GDP	Avg	OBP	Slg	OPS
2015	LAD	NL	19	36	9	0	0	3	(1	2)	18	6	4	4	3	1	13	1	0	0	2	1	0	.250	.325	.500	.825
2016	Cin	NL	82	257	68	12	2	9	(5	4)	111	36	40	36	19	2	59	6	0	0	2	4	5	.265	.330	.432	.762
2017	Cin	NL	141	473	110	25	2	30	(13	17)	229	63	67	58	39	5	125	14	0	5	5	3	7	.233	.307	.484	.791
2018	Cin	NL	107	380	97	19	0	17	(7	10)	167	55	49	47	39	1	99	9	0	2	4	2	5	.255	.337	.439	.777
2019	Cin	NL	30	81	10	2	0	2	(1	1)	18	11	7	3	14	0	27	0	0	0	0	1	3	.123	.250	.222	.475
2020	Atl	NL	1	1	0	0	0	0	(0	0)	0	0	0	0	0	0	0	0	0	0	0	0	0	.000	.000	.000	.000
	6 ML YEARS		380	1228	294	58	4	61	(27	34)	543	171	167	148	114	9	323	30	0	7	13	11	20	.239	.318	.442	.760

Max Scherzer

Pitches: R **Bats:** R **Pos:** SP-12   SHERR-zer   **Ht:** 6'3" **Wt:** 215 **Born:** 7/27/1984 **Age:** 36

Year	Team	Lg	G	GS	GF	IP	BFP	H	R	ER	HR	SH	SF	HB	TBB	IBB	SO	WP	W	L	Pct	Sv-Op	Hld	Vel	OPS	ERC	ERA
2008	Ari	NL	16	7	2	56.0	237	48	24	19	5	4	2	5	21	1	66	2	0	4	.000	0-0	0	94	.649	3.45	3.05
2009	Ari	NL	30	30	0	170.1	741	166	94	78	20	5	6	10	63	1	174	5	9	11	.450	0-0	0	94	.751	4.12	4.12
2010	Det	AL	31	31	0	195.2	800	174	84	76	20	5	5	7	70	1	184	8	12	11	.522	0-0	0	93	.700	3.56	3.50
2011	Det	AL	33	33	0	195.0	833	207	101	96	29	3	7	7	56	1	174	12	15	9	.625	0-0	0	93	.781	4.48	4.43
2012	Det	AL	32	32	0	187.2	787	179	82	78	23	5	1	5	60	2	231	2	16	7	.696	0-0	0	94	.721	3.77	3.74
2013	Det	AL	32	32	0	214.1	836	152	73	69	18	2	8	4	56	0	240	6	21	3	.875	0-0	0	93	.583	2.07	2.90
2014	Det	AL	33	33	0	220.1	904	196	80	77	18	4	8	6	63	1	252	10	18	5	.783	0-0	0	94	.663	3.04	3.15
2015	Was	NL	33	33	0	228.2	899	176	74	71	27	11	2	5	34	2	276	10	14	12	.538	0-0	0	94	.600	2.11	2.79
2016	Was	NL	34	34	0	228.1	902	165	77	75	31	7	3	6	56	2	284	2	20	7	.741	0-0	0	94	.619	2.35	2.96
2017	Was	NL	31	31	0	200.2	780	126	62	56	22	4	1	11	55	2	268	4	16	6	.727	0-0	0	94	.566	1.98	2.51
2018	Was	NL	33	33	0	220.2	866	150	66	62	23	4	2	12	51	4	300	4	18	7	.720	0-0	0	94	.580	2.02	2.53
2019	Was	NL	27	27	0	172.1	693	144	59	56	18	0	7	3	33	0	243	0	11	7	.611	0-0	0	95	.637	2.58	2.92
2020	Was	NL	12	12	0	67.1	295	70	30	28	10	0	2	1	23	1	92	6	5	4	.556	0-0	0	94	.742	4.36	3.74
	Postseason		22	18	0	112.0	463	81	45	42	12	3	0	7	46	3	137	5	7	5	.583	0-0	2	94	.639	2.88	3.38
	13 ML YEARS		377	368	2	2357.1	9573	1953	906	841	264	54	49	86	641	20	2784	71	175	93	.653	0-0	0	94	.655	2.88	3.21

Clarke Schmidt

Pitches: R **Bats:** R **Pos:** RP-2; SP-1   **Ht:** 6'1" **Wt:** 200 **Born:** 2/20/1996 **Age:** 25

Year	Team	Lg	G	GS	GF	IP	BFP	H	R	ER	HR	SH	SF	HB	TBB	IBB	SO	WP	W	L	Pct	Sv-Op	Hld	Vel	OPS	ERC	ERA
2020	NYY	AL	3	1	2	6.1	33	7	5	5	0	0	0	2	5	0	7	1	0	1	.000	0-0	0	95	.770	6.52	7.11

Jonathan Schoop

Bats: R **Throws:** R **Pos:** 2B-44   SCOPE   **Ht:** 6'1" **Wt:** 225 **Born:** 10/16/1991 **Age:** 29

Year	Team	Lg	G	AB	H	2B	3B	HR	(Hm	Rd)	TB	R	RBI	RC	TBB	IBB	SO	HBP	SH	SF	SB	CS	GDP	Avg	OBP	Slg	OPS
2013	Bal	AL	5	14	4	0	0	1	(1	0)	7	5	1	1	1	0	2	0	0	0	0	0	2	.286	.333	.500	.833
2014	Bal	AL	137	455	95	18	0	16	(5	11)	161	48	45	32	13	0	122	8	5	0	2	0	12	.209	.244	.354	.598
2015	Bal	AL	86	305	85	17	0	15	(9	6)	147	34	39	40	9	0	79	4	1	2	2	0	9	.279	.306	.482	.788
2016	Bal	AL	162	615	164	38	1	25	(13	12)	279	82	82	72	21	0	137	8	0	3	1	2	16	.267	.298	.454	.752
2017	Bal	AL	160	622	182	35	0	32	(18	14)	313	92	105	100	35	0	142	11	0	7	1	0	20	.293	.338	.503	.841
2018	2 Tms		131	473	110	22	1	21	(12	9)	197	61	61	45	19	2	115	4	1	4	1	1	11	.233	.266	.416	.682
2019	Min	AL	121	433	111	23	1	23	(7	16)	205	61	59	52	20	1	116	10	0	1	1	1	13	.256	.304	.473	.777
2020	Det	AL	44	162	45	4	2	8	(6	2)	77	26	23	23	8	0	39	4	0	2	0	0	8	.278	.324	.475	.799

Year Team	Lg	G	AB	H	2B	3B	HR	(Hm	Rd)	TB	R	RBI	RC	TBB	IBB	SO	HBP	SH	SF	SB	CS	GDP	Avg	OBP	Slg	OPS
18 Bal	AL	85	349	85	18	1	17	(9	8)	156	45	40	34	12	1	74	3	1	2	0	1	8	.244	.273	.447	.720
18 Mil	NL	46	124	25	4	0	4	(3	1)	41	16	21	11	7	1	41	1	0	2	1	0	3	.202	.246	.331	.577
Postseason		14	35	4	1	0	0	(0	0)	5	3	2	2	3	0	10	0	0	0	2	0	1	.114	.184	.143	.327
8 ML YEARS		846	3079	796	157	5	141	(71	70)	1386	409	415	365	126	3	752	49	7	19	8	4	91	.259	.297	.450	.747

John Schreiber

Pitches: R **Bats:** R **Pos:** RP-15   **Ht:** 6'2" **Wt:** 210 **Born:** 3/5/1994 **Age:** 27

		HOW MUCH PITCHED					WHAT HE GAVE UP									THE RESULTS							
Year Team	Lg	G	GS	GF	IP	BFP	H	R	ER	HR	SH	SF	HB	TBB	IBB	SO	WP	W	L	Pct	Sv-Op	Hld	Vel	OPS	ERC	ERA
2019 Det	AL	13	0	3	13.0	59	16	9	9	3	0	0	1	4	0	19	1	2	0	1.000	0-1	1	92	.837	6.34	6.23
2020 Det	AL	15	0	2	15.2	70	19	11	11	2	0	1	1	4	1	14	0	0	1	.000	0-1	1	90	.827	5.02	6.32
2 ML YEARS		28	0	5	28.2	129	35	20	20	5	0	1	2	8	1	33	1	2	1	.667	0-2	2	91	.832	5.61	6.28

Max Schrock

Bats: L **Throws:** R **Pos:** 2B-5;PH-5;3B-2;DH-1   **Ht:** 5'9" **Wt:** 185 **Born:** 10/12/1994 **Age:** 26

		BATTING																		RUNNING			AVERAGES			
Year Team	Lg	G	AB	H	2B	3B	HR	(Hm	Rd)	TB	R	RBI	RC	TBB	IBB	SO	HBP	SH	SF	SB	CS	GDP	Avg	OBP	Slg	OPS
2020 StL	NL	11	17	3	0	0	1	(0	1)	6	1	1	0	0	0	6	0	0	0	0	0	0	.176	.176	.353	.529

Kyle Schwarber

Bats: L **Throws:** R **Pos:** LF-48;DH-9;PH-3   SHWAR-burr   **Ht:** 6'0" **Wt:** 225 **Born:** 3/5/1993 **Age:** 28

Year Team	Lg	G	AB	H	2B	3B	HR	(Hm	Rd)	TB	R	RBI	RC	TBB	IBB	SO	HBP	SH	SF	SB	CS	GDP	Avg	OBP	Slg	OPS
2015 ChC	NL	69	232	57	6	1	16	(7	9)	113	52	43	39	36	1	77	4	0	1	3	3	4	.246	.355	.487	.842
2016 ChC	NL	2	4	0	0	0	0	(0	0)	0	0	0	0	1	0	2	0	0	0	0	0	0	.000	.200	.000	.200
2017 ChC	NL	129	422	89	16	1	30	(18	12)	197	67	59	55	59	1	150	5	0	0	1	1	6	.211	.315	.467	.782
2018 ChC	NL	137	428	102	14	3	26	(11	15)	200	64	61	65	78	20	140	1	1	2	4	3	6	.238	.356	.467	.823
2019 ChC	NL	155	529	132	29	3	38	(18	20)	281	82	92	92	70	5	156	5	0	6	2	3	6	.250	.339	.531	.871
2020 ChC	NL	59	191	36	6	0	11	(5	6)	75	30	24	27	30	1	66	3	0	0	1	0	3	.188	.308	.393	.701
Postseason		22	62	19	1	0	6	(4	2)	38	10	11	12	10	0	18	0	0	0	1	0	1	.306	.403	.613	1.016
6 ML YEARS		551	1806	416	71	8	121	(59	62)	866	295	279	278	274	28	591	18	1	9	11	10	25	.230	.336	.480	.816

Tanner Scott

Pitches: L **Bats:** R **Pos:** RP-25   **Ht:** 6'2" **Wt:** 220 **Born:** 7/22/1994 **Age:** 26

		HOW MUCH PITCHED					WHAT HE GAVE UP									THE RESULTS							
Year Team	Lg	G	GS	GF	IP	BFP	H	R	ER	HR	SH	SF	HB	TBB	IBB	SO	WP	W	L	Pct	Sv-Op	Hld	Vel	OPS	ERC	ERA
2017 Bal	AL	2	0	1	1.2	9	2	2	2	0	0	0	0	2	0	2	0	0	0	-	0-0	0	98	.873	7.49	10.80
2018 Bal	AL	53	0	8	53.1	240	55	33	32	6	1	1	1	28	1	76	7	3	3	.500	0-3	5	97	.777	4.86	5.40
2019 Bal	AL	28	0	5	26.1	122	28	17	14	4	0	0	2	19	2	37	2	1	1	.500	0-1	2	96	.847	6.54	4.78
2020 Bal	AL	25	0	6	20.2	86	12	5	3	1	0	0	3	10	0	23	4	0	0		1-2	5	96	.524	2.37	1.31
4 ML YEARS		108	0	20	102.0	457	97	57	51	11	1	1	6	59	3	138	13	4	4	.500	1-6	12	97	.750	4.76	4.50

Andre Scrubb

Pitches: R **Bats:** R **Pos:** RP-20   **Ht:** 6'4" **Wt:** 270 **Born:** 1/13/1995 **Age:** 26

		HOW MUCH PITCHED					WHAT HE GAVE UP									THE RESULTS							
Year Team	Lg	G	GS	GF	IP	BFP	H	R	ER	HR	SH	SF	HB	TBB	IBB	SO	WP	W	L	Pct	Sv-Op	Hld	Vel	OPS	ERC	ERA
2020 Hou	AL	20	0	4	23.2	102	15	5	5	1	1	2	0	20	1	24	1	1	0	1.000	1-1	2	93	.587	3.33	1.90

Corey Seager

Bats: L **Throws:** R **Pos:** SS-43;DH-9   SEE-gurr   **Ht:** 6'4" **Wt:** 215 **Born:** 4/27/1994 **Age:** 27

Year Team	Lg	G	AB	H	2B	3B	HR	(Hm	Rd)	TB	R	RBI	RC	TBB	IBB	SO	HBP	SH	SF	SB	CS	GDP	Avg	OBP	Slg	OPS
2015 LAD	NL	27	98	33	8	1	4	(3	1)	55	17	17	19	14	1	19	1	0	0	2	0	2	.337	.425	.561	.986
2016 LAD	NL	157	627	193	40	5	26	(18	8)	321	105	72	110	54	5	133	4	0	2	3	3	12	.308	.365	.512	.877
2017 LAD	NL	145	539	159	33	0	22	(12	10)	258	85	77	104	67	5	131	4	0	3	4	2	14	.295	.375	.479	.854
2018 LAD	NL	26	101	27	5	1	2	(1	1)	40	13	13	17	11	1	17	2	0	1	0	0	2	.267	.348	.396	.744
2019 LAD	NL	134	489	133	44	1	19	(9	10)	236	82	87	81	44	3	98	4	0	4	1	0	8	.272	.335	.483	.817
2020 LAD	NL	52	212	65	12	1	15	(7	8)	124	38	41	36	17	0	37	1	0	1	1	0	8	.307	.358	.585	.943
Postseason		31	118	24	4	1	3	(1	2)	39	12	10	8	11	0	41	1	0	1	1	0	5	.203	.275	.331	.605
6 ML YEARS		541	2066	610	142	9	88	(50	38)	1034	340	307	367	207	15	435	16	0	12	11	5	46	.295	.362	.500	.863

Kyle Seager

Bats: L **Throws:** R **Pos:** 3B-53;DH-6;PH-1   SEE-gurr   **Ht:** 6'0" **Wt:** 216 **Born:** 11/3/1987 **Age:** 33

Year Team	Lg	G	AB	H	2B	3B	HR	(Hm	Rd)	TB	R	RBI	RC	TBB	IBB	SO	HBP	SH	SF	SB	CS	GDP	Avg	OBP	Slg	OPS
2011 Sea	AL	53	182	47	13	0	3	(0	3)	69	22	13	16	13	0	36	2	2	2	3	1	4	.258	.312	.379	.691
2012 Sea	AL	155	594	154	35	1	20	(5	15)	251	62	86	88	46	1	110	5	2	4	13	5	9	.259	.316	.423	.738
2013 Sea	AL	160	615	160	32	2	22	(8	14)	262	79	69	90	68	1	122	7	0	5	9	3	8	.260	.338	.426	.764
2014 Sea	AL	159	590	158	27	4	25	(16	9)	268	71	96	96	52	3	118	8	1	3	7	5	12	.268	.334	.454	.788
2015 Sea	AL	161	623	166	37	0	26	(7	19)	281	85	74	75	54	6	98	5	0	4	6	6	17	.266	.328	.451	.779
2016 Sea	AL	158	597	166	36	3	30	(11	19)	298	89	99	110	69	10	108	8	0	2	3	1	18	.278	.359	.499	.859
2017 Sea	AL	154	578	144	33	1	27	(12	15)	260	72	88	84	58	6	110	8	0	6	2	1	6	.249	.323	.450	.773

304

Year	Team	Lg	G	AB	H	2B	3B	HR	(Hm	Rd)	TB	R	RBI	RC	TBB	IBB	SO	HBP	SH	SF	SB	CS	GDP	Avg	OBP	Slg	OPS
2018	Sea	AL	155	583	129	36	1	22	(8	14)	233	62	78	59	38	3	138	5	0	4	2	2	10	.221	.273	.400	.673
2019	Sea	AL	106	393	94	19	1	23	(10	13)	184	55	57	57	44	0	86	4	0	2	2	2	12	.239	.321	.468	.789
2020	Sea	AL	60	203	49	12	0	9	(4	5)	88	35	40	37	32	3	33	7	0	6	5	0	4	.241	.355	.433	.788
10 ML YEARS			1321	4958	1267	280	13	207	(81	126)	2194	632	706	712	474	33	959	59	5	38	52	26	100	.256	.326	.443	.768

Jean Segura

Bats: R **Throws:** R **Pos:** 2B-32;3B-24;SS-4;DH-1   JEEN seh-GOO-ruh   **Ht:** 5'10" **Wt:** 220 **Born:** 3/17/1990 **Age:** 31

Year	Team	Lg	G	AB	H	2B	3B	HR	(Hm	Rd)	TB	R	RBI	RC	TBB	IBB	SO	HBP	SH	SF	SB	CS	GDP	Avg	OBP	Slg	OPS
2012	2 Tms		45	151	39	4	3	0	(0	0)	49	19	14	16	13	3	23	0	1	1	7	1	1	.258	.315	.325	.640
2013	Mil	NL	146	588	173	20	10	12	(7	5)	249	74	49	72	25	1	84	6	2	2	44	13	17	.294	.329	.423	.752
2014	Mil	NL	146	513	126	14	6	5	(3	2)	167	61	31	45	28	5	70	4	10	2	20	9	13	.246	.289	.326	.614
2015	Mil	NL	142	560	144	16	5	6	(4	2)	188	57	50	57	13	2	93	6	3	2	25	6	14	.257	.281	.336	.616
2016	Ari	NL	153	637	203	41	7	20	(12	8)	318	102	64	107	39	1	101	12	4	2	33	10	6	.319	.368	.499	.867
2017	Sea	AL	125	524	157	30	2	11	(7	4)	224	80	45	71	34	3	83	6	0	1	22	8	14	.300	.349	.427	.776
2018	Sea	AL	144	586	178	29	3	10	(7	3)	243	91	63	77	32	2	69	4	4	6	20	11	17	.304	.341	.415	.755
2019	Phi	NL	144	576	161	37	4	12	(9	3)	242	79	60	79	30	1	73	8	1	3	10	2	11	.280	.323	.420	.743
2020	Phi	NL	54	192	51	5	2	7	(5	2)	81	28	25	28	23	2	45	1	1	0	2	2	6	.266	.347	.422	.769
12	LAA	AL	1	3	0	0	0	0	(0	0)	0	0	0	0	0	0	2	0	0	0	0	0	0	.000	.000	.000	.000
12	Mil	NL	44	148	39	4	3	0	(0	0)	49	19	14	16	13	3	21	0	1	1	7	1	1	.264	.321	.331	.652
9 ML YEARS			1099	4327	1232	196	42	83	(54	29)	1761	591	401	552	237	20	641	47	26	19	183	62	99	.285	.327	.407	.734

Sam Selman

Pitches: L **Bats:** R **Pos:** RP-24   **Ht:** 6'2" **Wt:** 198 **Born:** 11/14/1990 **Age:** 30

Year	Team	Lg		HOW MUCH PITCHED					WHAT HE GAVE UP										THE RESULTS							
			G	GS	GF	IP	BFP	H	R	ER	HR	SH	SF	HB	TBB	IBB	SO	WP	W	L	Pct	Sv-Op	Hld	Vel	OPS	ERC	ERA
2019	SF	NL	10	0	3	10.1	44	6	5	5	2	1	0	2	6	0	10	0	0	0	-	0-1	1	90	.697	3.89	4.35
2020	SF	NL	24	0	8	19.1	82	13	8	8	2	1	0	2	9	0	23	2	1	1	.500	1-1	3	91	.611	2.92	3.72
2 ML YEARS			34	0	11	29.2	126	19	13	13	4	2	0	4	15	0	33	2	1	1	.500	1-2	4	91	.640	3.25	3.94

Marcus Semien

Bats: R **Throws:** R **Pos:** SS-53   SIM-ee-inn   **Ht:** 6'0" **Wt:** 195 **Born:** 9/17/1990 **Age:** 30

Year	Team	Lg	G	AB	H	2B	3B	HR	(Hm	Rd)	TB	R	RBI	RC	TBB	IBB	SO	HBP	SH	SF	SB	CS	GDP	Avg	OBP	Slg	OPS
2013	CWS	AL	21	69	18	4	0	2	(2	0)	28	7	7	7	7	0	22	0	0	1	2	2	1	.261	.268	.406	.673
2014	CWS	AL	64	231	54	10	2	6	(4	2)	86	30	28	31	21	0	70	1	2	0	3	0	6	.234	.300	.372	.673
2015	Oak	AL	155	556	143	23	7	15	(5	10)	225	65	45	57	42	1	132	1	1	1	11	5	16	.257	.310	.405	.715
2016	Oak	AL	159	568	135	27	2	27	(10	17)	247	72	75	77	51	1	139	0	1	1	10	2	12	.238	.300	.435	.735
2017	Oak	AL	85	342	85	19	1	10	(5	5)	136	53	40	48	38	0	85	2	1	3	12	1	3	.249	.325	.398	.722
2018	Oak	AL	159	632	161	35	2	15	(6	9)	245	89	70	85	61	1	131	1	2	7	14	6	12	.255	.318	.388	.706
2019	Oak	AL	162	657	187	43	7	33	(15	18)	343	123	92	136	87	2	102	2	0	1	10	8	11	.285	.369	.522	.892
2020	Oak	AL	53	211	47	9	1	7	(2	5)	79	28	23	30	25	0	50	0	0	4	4	0	3	.223	.305	.374	.679
Postseason			2	8	2	0	0	0	(0	0)	2	1	0	0	1	0	3	0	0	0	0	0	0	.250	.333	.250	.583
8 ML YEARS			858	3266	830	170	22	115	(49	66)	1389	467	380	471	326	5	731	7	7	14	66	24	64	.254	.322	.425	.747

Antonio Senzatela

Pitches: R **Bats:** R **Pos:** SP-12   **Ht:** 6'1" **Wt:** 236 **Born:** 1/21/1995 **Age:** 26

Year	Team	Lg		HOW MUCH PITCHED					WHAT HE GAVE UP										THE RESULTS							
			G	GS	GF	IP	BFP	H	R	ER	HR	SH	SF	HB	TBB	IBB	SO	WP	W	L	Pct	Sv-Op	Hld	Vel	OPS	ERC	ERA
2017	Col	NL	36	20	3	134.2	564	128	72	70	18	4	5	4	47	1	102	1	10	5	.667	0-0	0	94	.756	4.00	4.68
2018	Col	NL	23	13	2	90.1	390	94	45	44	10	1	3	3	30	1	69	1	6	6	.500	0-0	0	94	.763	4.22	4.38
2019	Col	NL	25	25	0	124.2	582	161	99	93	19	4	3	4	57	5	76	1	11	11	.500	0-0	0	94	.890	6.53	6.71
2020	Col	NL	12	12	0	73.1	303	71	29	28	9	0	2	4	18	0	41	0	5	3	.625	0-0	0	94	.716	3.72	3.44
Postseason			1	1	0	5.0	19	3	2	2	1	0	0	0	2	0	1	2	0	0	-	0-0	0	94	.616	2.72	3.60
4 ML YEARS			96	70	5	423.0	1839	454	245	235	56	9	13	15	152	7	288	3	32	25	.561	0-0	1	94	.793	4.71	5.00

Nick Senzel

Bats: R **Throws:** R **Pos:** CF-23;PH-1   **Ht:** 6'1" **Wt:** 205 **Born:** 6/29/1995 **Age:** 26

Year	Team	Lg	G	AB	H	2B	3B	HR	(Hm	Rd)	TB	R	RBI	RC	TBB	IBB	SO	HBP	SH	SF	SB	CS	GDP	Avg	OBP	Slg	OPS
2019	Cin	NL	104	375	96	20	4	12	(7	5)	160	55	42	49	30	0	101	3	0	1	14	5	6	.256	.315	.427	.742
2020	Cin	NL	23	70	13	6	0	2	(2	0)	25	8	8	7	6	0	15	0	0	1	2	1	2	.186	.247	.357	.604
2 ML YEARS			127	445	109	26	4	14	(9	5)	185	63	50	56	36	0	116	3	0	2	16	6	8	.245	.305	.416	.720

Luis Severino

Pitches: R **Bats:** R **Pos:** P   **Ht:** 6'2" **Wt:** 218 **Born:** 2/20/1994 **Age:** 27

Year	Team	Lg		HOW MUCH PITCHED					WHAT HE GAVE UP										THE RESULTS							
			G	GS	GF	IP	BFP	H	R	ER	HR	SH	SF	HB	TBB	IBB	SO	WP	W	L	Pct	Sv-Op	Hld	Vel	OPS	ERC	ERA
2015	NYY	AL	11	11	0	62.1	255	53	21	20	9	0	0	2	22	0	56	2	5	3	.625	0-0	0	95	.705	3.57	2.89
2016	NYY	AL	22	11	3	71.0	312	78	48	46	11	0	0	3	25	1	66	3	3	8	.273	0-0	1	96	.812	5.00	5.83
2017	NYY	AL	31	31	0	193.1	783	150	73	64	21	3	2	6	51	0	230	6	14	6	.700	0-0	0	98	.603	2.53	2.98

Year Team	Lg	G	GS	GF	IP	BFP	H	R	ER	HR	SH	SF	HB	TBB	IBB	SO	WP	W	L	Pct	Sv-Op	Hld	Vel	OPS	ERC	ERA
2018 NYY	AL	32	32	0	191.1	780	173	76	72	19	1	2	5	46	0	220	8	19	8	.704	0-0	0	98	.666	3.06	3.39
2019 NYY	AL	3	3	0	12.0	48	6	2	2	0	0	1	0	6	0	17	0	1	1	.500	0-0	0	96	.442	1.62	1.50
Postseason		8	8	0	31.1	144	31	18	18	7	0	1	0	19	0	31	0	1	3	.250	0-0	0	97	.799	5.66	5.17
5 ML YEARS		99	88	3	530.0	2178	460	220	204	60	4	4	17	150	1	589	19	42	26	.618	0-0	1	97	.664	3.12	3.46

Pedro Severino

Bats: R **Throws:** R **Pos:** C-35;DH-10;PH-6   **Ht:** 6'1" **Wt:** 220 **Born:** 7/20/1993 **Age:** 27

| | | | | | | | | | | BATTING | | | | | | | | | | | | | RUNNING | | | AVERAGES | | | |
Year Team	Lg	G	AB	H	2B	3B	HR	(Hm	Rd)	TB	R	RBI	RC	TBB	IBB	SO	HBP	SH	SF	SB	CS	GDP	Avg	OBP	Slg	OPS
2015 Was	NL	2	4	1	1	0	0	(0	0)	2	1	0	0	0	0	1	0	0	0	0	0	0	.250	.250	.500	.750
2016 Was	NL	16	28	9	2	0	2	(1	1)	17	6	4	5	5	0	3	1	0	0	0	0	0	.321	.441	.607	1.048
2017 Was	NL	17	29	5	1	0	0	(0	0)	6	0	3	2	2	1	10	0	0	0	0	0	0	.172	.226	.207	.433
2018 Was	NL	70	190	32	9	0	2	(2	0)	47	14	15	12	18	4	47	4	0	1	1	0	3	.168	.254	.247	.501
2019 Bal	AL	96	305	76	13	0	13	(7	6)	128	37	44	39	29	0	73	4	1	2	3	1	5	.249	.321	.420	.740
2020 Bal	AL	48	160	40	5	1	5	(3	2)	62	17	21	20	16	0	40	1	1	0	1	0	3	.250	.322	.388	.710
Postseason		4	10	1	1	0	0	(0	0)	2	1	0	0	0	0	3	0	0	0	0	0	0	.100	.100	.200	.300
6 ML YEARS		249	716	163	31	1	22	(13	9)	262	75	87	78	70	5	174	10	2	3	5	1	11	.228	.304	.366	.670

Paul Sewald

Pitches: R **Bats:** R **Pos:** RP-5   **Ht:** 6'3" **Wt:** 207 **Born:** 5/26/1990 **Age:** 31

Year Team	Lg	G	GS	GF	IP	BFP	H	R	ER	HR	SH	SF	HB	TBB	IBB	SO	WP	W	L	Pct	Sv-Op	Hld	Vel	OPS	ERC	ERA
2017 NYM	NL	57	0	12	65.1	275	58	36	33	8	3	3	3	21	2	69	3	0	6	.000	0-3	13	91	.706	3.41	4.55
2018 NYM	NL	46	0	9	56.1	253	62	39	38	8	2	3	1	23	2	58	1	0	7	.000	2-4	2	90	.820	4.93	6.07
2019 NYM	NL	17	0	6	19.2	80	18	10	10	3	1	1	1	3	0	22	0	1	1	.500	1-1	0	91	.724	3.17	4.58
2020 NYM	NL	5	0	1	6.0	35	12	9	9	1	0	1	1	4	0	2	0	0	0	-	0-0	0	92	1.072	13.03	13.50
4 ML YEARS		125	0	28	147.1	643	150	94	90	20	6	8	6	51	4	151	4	1	14	.067	3-8	15	91	.773	4.28	5.50

Justin Shafer

Pitches: R **Bats:** R **Pos:** RP-5   **Ht:** 6'2" **Wt:** 205 **Born:** 9/18/1992 **Age:** 28

Year Team	Lg	G	GS	GF	IP	BFP	H	R	ER	HR	SH	SF	HB	TBB	IBB	SO	WP	W	L	Pct	Sv-Op	Hld	Vel	OPS	ERC	ERA
2018 Tor	AL	6	0	1	8.1	39	6	4	3	1	0	0	1	7	0	2	0	0	0	-	0-0	0	93	.714	4.72	3.24
2019 Tor	AL	34	0	11	39.2	182	41	19	17	6	1	0	1	25	4	39	1	2	1	.667	1-1	3	94	.854	5.52	3.86
2020 Mia	NL	5	0	0	5.2	30	8	8	8	2	0	1	1	4	0	5	0	0	0	-	0-0	0	91	1.142	10.88	12.71
3 ML YEARS		45	0	12	53.2	251	55	31	28	9	1	1	3	36	4	46	1	2	1	.667	1-1	3	94	.866	5.91	4.70

Sterling Sharp

Pitches: R **Bats:** R **Pos:** RP-4   **Ht:** 6'3" **Wt:** 182 **Born:** 5/30/1995 **Age:** 26

Year Team	Lg	G	GS	GF	IP	BFP	H	R	ER	HR	SH	SF	HB	TBB	IBB	SO	WP	W	L	Pct	Sv-Op	Hld	Vel	OPS	ERC	ERA
2020 Mia	NL	4	0	0	5.1	29	7	7	6	1	0	0	1	5	0	3	0	0	0	-	0-0	0	88	1.057	9.74	10.13

Bryan Shaw

Pitches: R **Bats:** B **Pos:** RP-6   **Ht:** 6'1" **Wt:** 226 **Born:** 11/8/1987 **Age:** 33

Year Team	Lg	G	GS	GF	IP	BFP	H	R	ER	HR	SH	SF	HB	TBB	IBB	SO	WP	W	L	Pct	Sv-Op	Hld	Vel	OPS	ERC	ERA
2011 Ari	NL	33	0	8	28.1	122	30	9	8	2	0	0	4	8	1	24	1	1	0	1.000	0-0	9	91	.699	4.31	2.54
2012 Ari	NL	64	0	19	59.1	252	60	29	23	4	4	2	2	24	3	41	4	1	6	.143	2-4	10	92	.747	4.08	3.49
2013 Cle	AL	70	0	11	75.0	316	60	31	27	4	4	2	4	28	2	73	5	7	3	.700	1-5	12	91	.586	2.71	3.24
2014 Cle	AL	80	0	16	76.1	313	61	26	22	6	5	2	2	22	4	64	4	5	5	.500	2-9	24	93	.602	2.45	2.59
2015 Cle	AL	74	0	19	64.0	265	59	24	21	8	1	0	1	19	1	54	3	3	3	.500	2-6	23	92	.693	3.47	2.95
2016 Cle	AL	75	0	9	66.2	275	56	26	24	8	2	1	1	28	3	69	2	2	5	.286	1-4	25	93	.686	3.47	3.24
2017 Cle	AL	79	0	16	76.2	312	71	36	30	5	1	1	0	22	3	73	1	4	6	.400	3-6	26	94	.653	3.01	3.52
2018 Col	NL	61	0	14	54.2	257	70	43	36	9	1	3	1	28	1	54	8	4	6	.400	0-5	13	93	.896	6.79	5.93
2019 Col	NL	70	0	18	72.0	311	69	44	43	12	1	1	5	29	1	58	1	3	2	.600	1-6	12	93	.798	4.61	5.38
2020 Sea	AL	6	0	1	6.0	38	13	12	12	1	0	1	1	6	0	4	0	1	0	1.000	0-1	0	93	1.293	15.93	18.00
Postseason		19	0	2	22.0	89	19	8	6	2	0	1	0	6	3	22	1	2	1	.667	0-0	5	95	.622	2.63	2.45
10 ML YEARS		612	0	131	579.0	2461	549	280	246	59	19	13	21	214	19	514	31	31	36	.463	12-46	154	93	.710	3.79	3.82

Travis Shaw

Bats: L **Throws:** R **Pos:** 3B-37;1B-14;PH-6;DH-2   **Ht:** 6'4" **Wt:** 230 **Born:** 4/16/1990 **Age:** 31

| | | | | | | | | | | BATTING | | | | | | | | | | | | | RUNNING | | | AVERAGES | | | |
Year Team	Lg	G	AB	H	2B	3B	HR	(Hm	Rd)	TB	R	RBI	RC	TBB	IBB	SO	HBP	SH	SF	SB	CS	GDP	Avg	OBP	Slg	OPS
2015 Bos	AL	65	226	61	10	0	13	(8	5)	111	31	36	35	18	1	57	2	0	1	0	1	1	.270	.327	.487	.813
2016 Bos	AL	145	480	116	34	2	16	(7	9)	202	63	71	64	43	4	133	3	0	4	5	1	10	.242	.306	.421	.726
2017 Mil	NL	144	538	147	34	1	31	(13	18)	276	84	101	93	60	6	138	4	1	3	10	0	20	.273	.349	.513	.862
2018 Mil	NL	152	498	120	23	0	32	(16	16)	239	73	86	84	78	6	108	4	1	6	5	2	7	.241	.345	.480	.825
2019 Mil	NL	86	230	36	5	0	7	(3	4)	62	22	16	11	36	3	89	4	0	0	0	0	5	.157	.281	.270	.551
2020 Tor	AL	50	163	39	10	0	6	(3	3)	67	17	17	19	16	0	50	0	0	0	1	0	4	.239	.306	.411	.717
Postseason		12	32	9	2	1	1	(1	0)	16	2	2	3	5	1	10	0	0	0	1	0	0	.281	.378	.500	.878
6 ML YEARS		642	2135	519	116	3	105	(50	55)	957	290	327	306	251	20	575	17	2	16	20	4	47	.243	.325	.448	.773

Justus Sheffield

Pitches: L **Bats:** L **Pos:** SP-10 **Ht:** 5'10" **Wt:** 195 **Born:** 5/13/1996 **Age:** 25

Year	Team	Lg	G	GS	GF	IP	BFP	H	R	ER	HR	SH	SF	HB	TBB	IBB	SO	WP	W	L	Pct	Sv-Op	Hld	Vel	OPS	ERC	ERA
2018	NYY	AL	3	0	2	2.2	14	4	3	3	1	0	0	0	3	0	0	1	0	0	-	0-0	0	94	1.227	13.94	10.13
2019	Sea	AL	8	7	0	36.0	168	44	22	22	5	1	0	3	18	0	37	3	0	1	.000	0-0	0	93	.881	6.51	5.50
2020	Sea	AL	10	10	0	55.1	232	52	23	22	2	0	2	3	20	0	48	1	4	3	.571	0-0	0	92	.628	3.43	3.58
	3 ML YEARS		21	17	2	94.0	414	100	48	47	8	1	2	6	41	0	85	5	4	4	.500	0-0	0	92	.748	4.80	4.50

Ryan Sherriff

Pitches: L **Bats:** L **Pos:** RP-10 **Ht:** 6'1" **Wt:** 190 **Born:** 5/25/1990 **Age:** 31

Year	Team	Lg	G	GS	GF	IP	BFP	H	R	ER	HR	SH	SF	HB	TBB	IBB	SO	WP	W	L	Pct	Sv-Op	Hld	Vel	OPS	ERC	ERA
2017	StL	NL	13	0	2	14.1	60	13	5	5	2	0	0	1	4	0	15	0	2	1	.667	0-0	1	92	.682	3.62	3.14
2018	StL	NL	5	0	0	5.2	27	8	4	4	1	0	0	1	2	0	3	0	0	0	-	0-0	1	91	.949	7.89	6.35
2020	TB	AL	10	0	3	9.2	34	6	0	0	0	0	0	0	2	0	2	0	1	0	1.000	1-1	1	91	.423	1.29	0.00
	3 ML YEARS		28	0	5	29.2	121	27	9	9	3	0	0	2	8	0	20	0	3	1	.750	1-1	3	91	.666	3.44	2.73

Matt Shoemaker

Pitches: R **Bats:** R **Pos:** SP-6 SHOO-may-kerr **Ht:** 6'2" **Wt:** 225 **Born:** 9/27/1986 **Age:** 34

Year	Team	Lg	G	GS	GF	IP	BFP	H	R	ER	HR	SH	SF	HB	TBB	IBB	SO	WP	W	L	Pct	Sv-Op	Hld	Vel	OPS	ERC	ERA
2013	LAA	AL	1	1	0	5.0	19	2	0	0	0	0	0	0	2	0	5	1	0	0	-	0-0	0	91	.328	0.95	0.00
2014	LAA	AL	27	20	5	136.0	543	122	49	46	14	3	5	4	24	0	124	5	16	4	.800	0-0	0	91	.658	2.84	3.04
2015	LAA	AL	25	24	1	135.1	569	135	70	67	24	4	4	4	35	2	116	3	7	10	.412	0-0	0	90	.758	4.12	4.46
2016	LAA	AL	27	27	0	160.0	668	166	71	69	18	2	5	7	30	1	143	2	9	13	.409	0-0	0	91	.723	3.71	3.88
2017	LAA	AL	14	14	0	77.2	326	73	41	39	15	1	1	4	28	0	69	2	6	3	.667	0-0	0	92	.788	4.52	4.52
2018	LAA	AL	7	7	0	31.0	130	29	17	17	3	0	0	1	10	0	33	3	2	2	.500	0-0	0	91	.694	3.54	4.94
2019	Tor	AL	5	5	0	28.2	108	16	7	5	3	0	0	1	9	0	24	1	3	0	1.000	0-0	0	91	.547	1.77	1.57
2020	Tor	AL	6	6	0	28.2	115	22	16	15	8	1	0	0	9	0	26	0	0	1	.000	0-0	0	92	.739	3.60	4.71
	Postseason		1	1	0	6.0	23	5	1	1	0	1	0	0	0	0	6	0	0	0	-	0-0	0	91	.500	1.37	1.50
	8 ML YEARS		112	104	6	602.1	2478	565	271	258	85	11	15	21	147	3	540	17	43	33	.566	0-0	0	91	.714	3.56	3.86

Chasen Shreve

Pitches: L **Bats:** L **Pos:** RP-17 CHAY-sen shreev **Ht:** 6'4" **Wt:** 195 **Born:** 7/12/1990 **Age:** 30

Year	Team	Lg	G	GS	GF	IP	BFP	H	R	ER	HR	SH	SF	HB	TBB	IBB	SO	WP	W	L	Pct	Sv-Op	Hld	Vel	OPS	ERC	ERA
2014	Atl	NL	15	0	4	12.1	50	10	1	1	0	1	0	0	3	0	15	1	0	0	-	0-0	2	91	.526	1.88	0.73
2015	NYY	AL	59	0	13	58.1	251	49	21	20	10	2	0	1	33	2	64	4	6	2	.750	0-1	10	91	.738	4.39	3.09
2016	NYY	AL	37	0	11	33.0	142	29	19	19	8	1	0	3	13	0	33	0	2	1	.667	1-1	1	92	.823	4.70	5.18
2017	NYY	AL	44	0	15	45.1	198	35	20	19	8	0	2	0	25	3	58	4	4	1	.800	0-1	1	93	.712	3.71	3.77
2018	2 Tms		60	0	20	52.2	235	53	28	23	11	0	4	1	27	0	62	2	3	4	.429	1-1	6	92	.832	5.43	3.93
2019	StL	NL	3	0	0	2.0	10	2	2	2	0	0	0	1	1	0	2	0	1	0	1.000	0-0	1	91	.900	5.48	9.00
2020	NYM	NL	17	0	1	25.0	102	19	12	11	4	0	1	0	12	0	34	0	1	0	1.000	0-0	1	92	.655	3.07	3.96
18	NYY	AL	40	0	17	38.0	170	39	23	18	8	0	2	1	18	0	46	2	2	2	.500	1-1	3	92	.831	5.40	4.26
18	StL	NL	20	0	3	14.2	65	14	5	5	3	0	2	0	9	0	16	0	1	2	.333	0-0	3	92	.835	5.52	3.07
	7 ML YEARS		235	0	64	228.2	988	195	103	95	41	4	7	6	114	5	268	11	17	8	.680	2-4	22	92	.750	4.24	3.74

Magneuris Sierra

Bats: L **Throws:** L **Pos:** CF-11;LF-5;RF-4;PR-2;DH-1 **Ht:** 5'11" **Wt:** 178 **Born:** 4/7/1996 **Age:** 25

Year	Team	Lg	G	AB	H	2B	3B	HR	(Hm	Rd)	TB	R	RBI	RC	TBB	IBB	SO	HBP	SH	SF	SB	CS	GDP	Avg	OBP	Slg	OPS
2017	StL	NL	22	60	19	0	0	0	(0	0)	19	10	5	10	4	0	14	0	0	0	2	2	0	.317	.359	.317	.676
2018	Mia	NL	54	147	28	3	0	0	(0	0)	31	10	7	6	6	1	39	0	3	0	3	2	0	.190	.222	.211	.433
2019	Mia	NL	15	40	14	1	1	0	(0	0)	17	5	1	5	2	0	7	0	0	0	3	3	0	.350	.381	.425	.806
2020	Mia	NL	19	44	11	3	1	0	(0	0)	16	8	7	8	5	0	9	1	2	1	4	1	0	.250	.333	.364	.697
	4 ML YEARS		110	291	72	7	2	0	(0	0)	83	33	20	29	17	1	69	1	5	1	12	8	0	.247	.290	.285	.576

Andrelton Simmons

Bats: R **Throws:** R **Pos:** SS-30 ANN-drel-ton **Ht:** 6'2" **Wt:** 195 **Born:** 9/4/1989 **Age:** 31

Year	Team	Lg	G	AB	H	2B	3B	HR	(Hm	Rd)	TB	R	RBI	RC	TBB	IBB	SO	HBP	SH	SF	SB	CS	GDP	Avg	OBP	Slg	OPS
2012	Atl	NL	49	166	48	8	2	3	(3	0)	69	17	19	23	12	1	21	1	0	3	1	0	5	.289	.335	.416	.751
2013	Atl	NL	157	606	150	27	6	17	(5	12)	240	76	59	60	40	1	55	3	5	4	6	5	16	.248	.296	.396	.692
2014	Atl	NL	146	540	132	18	4	7	(3	4)	179	44	46	41	32	4	60	0	2	4	4	5	25	.244	.286	.331	.617
2015	Atl	NL	147	535	142	23	2	4	(2	2)	181	60	44	48	39	6	48	6	1	2	5	3	19	.265	.321	.338	.660
2016	LAA	AL	124	448	126	22	2	4	(4	0)	164	48	44	52	28	0	38	2	1	4	10	1	16	.281	.324	.366	.690
2017	LAA	AL	158	589	164	38	2	14	(10	4)	248	77	69	91	47	0	67	3	0	8	19	6	20	.278	.331	.421	.752
2018	LAA	AL	146	554	162	26	5	11	(1	10)	231	68	75	80	35	2	44	5	1	5	10	2	17	.292	.337	.417	.754
2019	LAA	AL	103	398	105	19	0	7	(5	2)	145	47	40	36	24	1	37	2	0	0	10	2	21	.264	.309	.364	.673
2020	LAA	AL	30	118	35	7	0	0	(0	0)	42	19	10	15	8	0	16	1	0	2	2	0	5	.297	.346	.356	.702
	Postseason		5	16	4	1	0	0	(0	0)	5	0	2	1	2	0	3	0	1	0	0	0	1	.250	.333	.313	.646
	9 ML YEARS		1060	3954	1064	188	23	67	(33	34)	1499	456	406	446	265	15	386	23	10	28	67	24	144	.269	.317	.379	.696

Lucas Sims

Pitches: R Bats: R Pos: RP-20   Ht: 6'2" Wt: 225 Born: 5/10/1994 Age: 27

Year	Team	Lg	G	GS	GF	IP	BFP	H	R	ER	HR	SH	SF	HB	TBB	IBB	SO	WP	W	L	Pct	Sv-Op	Hld	Vel	OPS	ERC	ERA
2017	Atl	NL	14	10	1	57.2	255	64	37	36	9	5	1	4	23	2	44	0	3	6	.333	0-0	1	92	.869	5.43	5.62
2018	2 Tms	NL	9	0	2	15.2	77	15	13	13	3	0	0	2	13	1	16	0	0	0	-	0-1	0	92	.825	6.59	7.47
2019	Cin	NL	24	4	2	43.0	177	31	22	22	8	1	1	2	19	0	57	1	2	1	.667	0-0	3	94	.711	3.49	4.60
2020	Cin	NL	20	0	5	25.2	103	13	10	7	3	0	0	3	11	0	34	0	3	0	1.000	0-2	5	94	.554	2.17	2.45
18	Atl	NL	6	0	2	10.1	52	12	9	9	2	0	0	1	8	1	10	0	0	0	-	0-1	0	93	.869	7.45	7.84
18	Cin	NL	3	0	0	5.1	25	3	4	4	1	0	0	1	5	0	6	0	0	0	-	0-0	0	92	.728	5.00	6.75
4 ML YEARS			67	14	10	142.0	612	123	82	78	23	6	2	11	66	3	151	1	8	7	.533	0-3	9	93	.765	4.31	4.94

Brady Singer

Pitches: R Bats: R Pos: SP-12   Ht: 6'5" Wt: 210 Born: 8/4/1996 Age: 24

Year	Team	Lg	G	GS	GF	IP	BFP	H	R	ER	HR	SH	SF	HB	TBB	IBB	SO	WP	W	L	Pct	Sv-Op	Hld	Vel	OPS	ERC	ERA
2020	KC	AL	12	12	0	64.1	263	52	29	29	8	0	2	2	23	0	61	5	4	5	.444	0-0	0	93	.649	3.19	4.06

Chance Sisco

Bats: L Throws: R Pos: C-26;DH-9;PH-5   Ht: 6'2" Wt: 195 Born: 2/24/1995 Age: 26

Year	Team	Lg	G	AB	H	2B	3B	HR	(Hm	Rd)	TB	R	RBI	RC	TBB	IBB	SO	HBP	SH	SF	SB	CS	GDP	Avg	OBP	Slg	OPS
2017	Bal	AL	10	18	6	2	0	2	(1	1)	14	3	4	6	3	0	7	1	0	0	0	0	0	.333	.455	.778	1.232
2018	Bal	AL	63	160	29	8	0	2	(2	0)	43	13	16	13	13	0	66	11	0	0	1	0	5	.181	.288	.269	.557
2019	Bal	AL	59	167	35	7	0	8	(3	5)	66	29	20	21	22	0	61	9	0	0	0	1	1	.210	.333	.395	.729
2020	Bal	AL	36	98	21	4	0	4	(3	1)	37	11	10	12	17	0	41	6	0	0	0	0	1	.214	.364	.378	.741
4 ML YEARS			168	443	91	21	0	16	(9	7)	160	56	50	52	55	0	175	27	0	0	1	1	8	.205	.330	.361	.691

Tarik Skubal

Pitches: L Bats: L Pos: SP-7; RP-1   Ht: 6'3" Wt: 215 Born: 11/20/1996 Age: 24

Year	Team	Lg	G	GS	GF	IP	BFP	H	R	ER	HR	SH	SF	HB	TBB	IBB	SO	WP	W	L	Pct	Sv-Op	Hld	Vel	OPS	ERC	ERA
2018	3 Tms	Low	9	1	3	22.1	82	15	3	1	0	0	0	4	1	1	33	1	3	0	1.000	2--	-	-	.536	1.29	0.40
2019	Lkland	A+	15	15	0	80.1	320	62	29	23	5	1	0	4	19	0	97	4	4	5	.444	0--	-	-	.591	2.25	2.58
2019	Erie	AA	9	9	0	42.1	170	25	13	10	2	0	2	1	18	0	82	1	2	3	.400	0--	-	-	.527	1.83	2.13
2020	Det	AL	8	7	0	32.0	134	28	21	20	9	0	2	2	11	0	37	0	1	4	.200	0-0	0	94	.802	4.65	5.63

Austin Slater

Bats: R Throws: R Pos: DH-13;RF-9;PH-4;LF-3;PR-3   Ht: 6'1" Wt: 204 Born: 12/13/1992 Age: 28

Year	Team	Lg	G	AB	H	2B	3B	HR	(Hm	Rd)	TB	R	RBI	RC	TBB	IBB	SO	HBP	SH	SF	SB	CS	GDP	Avg	OBP	Slg	OPS
2017	SF	NL	34	117	33	3	1	3	(0	3)	47	15	16	17	8	0	29	2	0	0	0	0	3	.282	.339	.402	.740
2018	SF	NL	74	199	50	6	1	1	(0	1)	61	21	23	23	20	2	69	5	0	1	7	0	5	.251	.333	.307	.640
2019	SF	NL	68	168	40	9	3	5	(2	3)	70	20	21	28	22	1	59	2	0	0	1	0	1	.238	.333	.417	.750
2020	SF	NL	31	85	24	2	1	5	(2	3)	43	18	7	18	16	0	22	2	1	0	8	1	2	.282	.408	.506	.914
4 ML YEARS			207	569	147	20	6	14	(4	10)	221	74	67	86	66	3	179	11	1	1	16	1	11	.258	.346	.388	.735

Aaron Slegers

Pitches: R Bats: R Pos: RP-10; SP-1   Ht: 6'10" Wt: 260 Born: 9/4/1992 Age: 28

Year	Team	Lg	G	GS	GF	IP	BFP	H	R	ER	HR	SH	SF	HB	TBB	IBB	SO	WP	W	L	Pct	Sv-Op	Hld	Vel	OPS	ERC	ERA
2017	Min	AL	4	3	0	15.1	63	12	12	11	3	0	0	0	6	0	9	0	0	1	.000	0-0	0	91	.689	3.48	6.46
2018	Min	AL	4	2	1	13.2	60	17	8	8	3	0	0	1	2	0	6	0	1	1	.500	0-0	0	90	.877	5.59	5.27
2019	TB	AL	1	0	1	3.0	12	3	1	1	1	0	0	1	0	0	0	0	0	0	-	1-1	0	90	.879	5.79	3.00
2020	TB	AL	11	1	3	26.0	101	18	10	10	1	1	0	2	5	2	19	0	0	0	-	2-2	2	91	.487	1.63	3.46
4 ML YEARS			20	6	5	58.0	236	50	31	30	8	1	0	4	13	2	34	0	1	2	.333	3-3	2	91	.661	3.13	4.66

Devin Smeltzer

Pitches: L Bats: R Pos: RP-6; SP-1   Ht: 6'3" Wt: 195 Born: 9/7/1995 Age: 25

Year	Team	Lg	G	GS	GF	IP	BFP	H	R	ER	HR	SH	SF	HB	TBB	IBB	SO	WP	W	L	Pct	Sv-Op	Hld	Vel	OPS	ERC	ERA
2019	Min	AL	11	6	2	49.0	202	50	23	21	8	0	0	1	12	0	38	1	2	2	.500	1-1	1	89	.777	4.18	3.86
2020	Min	AL	7	1	2	16.0	72	19	12	12	2	1	0	1	5	0	15	0	2	0	1.000	0-0	0	88	.829	5.20	6.75
Postseason			1	0	0	3.1	14	2	0	0	0	0	0	0	3	0	4	0	0	0	-	0-0	0	89	.539	3.21	0.00
2 ML YEARS			18	7	4	65.0	274	69	35	33	10	1	0	2	17	0	53	1	4	2	.667	1-1	1	89	.791	4.43	4.57

Burch Smith

Pitches: R Bats: R Pos: RP-6

Ht: 6'4" Wt: 225 Born: 4/12/1990 Age: 31

Year	Team	Lg		HOW MUCH PITCHED					WHAT HE GAVE UP										THE RESULTS						
			G	GS	GF	IP	BFP	H	R	ER	HR	SH	SF	HB	TBB	IBB	SO	WP	W	L	Pct	Sv-Op	Hld	Vel	OPS	ERC	ERA
2013	SD	NL	10	7	3	36.1	167	39	26	26	9	1	0	0	21	1	46	0	1	3	.250	0-0	0	92	.899	6.27	6.44
2018	KC	AL	38	6	16	78.0	358	90	60	60	15	2	4	4	40	2	77	0	1	6	.143	0-0	1	93	.873	6.38	6.92
2019	2 Tms	NL	17	0	6	21.1	106	26	14	13	3	1	0	1	14	2	20	1	0	1	.000	0-1	0	93	.857	6.56	5.48
2020	Oak	AL	6	0	3	12.0	44	7	3	3	1	0	0	0	1	0	13	0	2	0	1.000	1-1	0	94	.461	1.11	2.25
19	Mil	NL	7	0	4	12.2	65	16	11	11	3	0	0	1	10	2	14	1	0	1	.000	0-0	0	93	.952	8.37	7.82
19	SF	NL	10	0	2	8.2	41	10	3	2	0	1	0	0	4	0	6	0	0	0	-	0-1	0	93	.711	4.19	2.08
4 ML YEARS			71	13	28	147.2	675	162	103	102	28	4	4	5	76	5	156	1	4	10	.286	1-2	1	93	.848	5.84	6.22

Caleb Smith

Pitches: L Bats: R Pos: SP-4; RP-1

Ht: 6'0" Wt: 206 Born: 7/28/1991 Age: 29

Year	Team	Lg		HOW MUCH PITCHED					WHAT HE GAVE UP										THE RESULTS						
			G	GS	GF	IP	BFP	H	R	ER	HR	SH	SF	HB	TBB	IBB	SO	WP	W	L	Pct	Sv-Op	Hld	Vel	OPS	ERC	ERA
2017	NYY	AL	9	2	6	18.2	86	21	16	16	4	0	1	0	10	1	18	1	0	1	.000	0-0	0	94	.854	6.09	7.71
2018	Mia	NL	16	16	0	77.1	326	63	36	36	10	2	2	3	33	2	88	0	5	6	.455	0-0	0	93	.694	3.46	4.19
2019	Mia	NL	28	28	0	153.1	646	128	82	77	33	2	5	6	60	2	168	6	10	11	.476	0-0	0	92	.755	4.01	4.52
2020	2 Tms	NL	5	4	0	14.0	60	6	4	4	3	0	0	0	12	0	15	0	0	0	-	0-0	0	92	.613	3.44	2.57
20	Mia	NL	1	1	0	3.0	15	1	1	1	1	0	0	0	6	0	3	0	0	0	-	0-0	0	92	.911	9.13	3.00
20	Ari	NL	4	3	0	11.0	45	5	3	3	2	0	0	0	6	0	12	0	0	0	-	0-0	0	92	.526	2.21	2.45
4 ML YEARS			58	50	6	263.1	1118	218	138	133	50	4	8	9	115	5	289	7	15	18	.455	0-0	0	92	.738	3.96	4.55

Dominic Smith

Bats: L Throws: L Pos: 1B-25;LF-23;DH-5;PH-2

Ht: 6'0" Wt: 239 Born: 6/15/1995 Age: 26

Year	Team	Lg		BATTING																	RUNNING			AVERAGES			
			G	AB	H	2B	3B	HR	(Hm	Rd)	TB	R	RBI	RC	TBB	IBB	SO	HBP	SH	SF	SB	CS	GDP	Avg	OBP	Slg	OPS
2017	NYM	NL	49	167	33	6	0	9	(4	5)	66	17	26	19	14	0	49	1	0	1	0	0	5	.198	.262	.395	.658
2018	NYM	NL	56	143	32	11	1	5	(4	1)	60	14	11	9	4	0	47	2	0	0	0	0	2	.224	.255	.420	.675
2019	NYM	NL	89	177	50	10	0	11	(3	8)	93	35	25	26	19	0	44	1	0	0	1	2	5	.282	.355	.525	.881
2020	NYM	NL	50	177	56	21	1	10	(5	5)	109	27	42	35	14	0	45	5	0	3	0	0	2	.316	.377	.616	.993
4 ML YEARS			244	664	171	48	2	35	(16	19)	328	93	104	89	51	0	185	9	0	4	1	2	14	.258	.317	.494	.811

Drew Smith

Pitches: R Bats: R Pos: RP-8

Ht: 6'2" Wt: 190 Born: 9/24/1993 Age: 27

Year	Team	Lg		HOW MUCH PITCHED					WHAT HE GAVE UP										THE RESULTS						
			G	GS	GF	IP	BFP	H	R	ER	HR	SH	SF	HB	TBB	IBB	SO	WP	W	L	Pct	Sv-Op	Hld	Vel	OPS	ERC	ERA
2018	NYM	NL	27	0	8	28.0	120	34	11	11	2	0	2	2	6	0	18	1	1	1	.500	0-2	4	96	.795	4.77	3.54
2020	NYM	NL	8	0	3	7.0	29	6	6	5	2	0	0	0	2	1	7	1	0	1	.000	0-0	2	95	.757	3.75	6.43
2 ML YEARS			35	0	11	35.0	149	40	17	16	4	0	2	2	8	1	25	2	1	2	.333	0-2	6	96	.788	4.57	4.11

Joe Smith

Pitches: R Bats: R Pos: P

Ht: 6'2" Wt: 211 Born: 3/22/1984 Age: 37

Year	Team	Lg		HOW MUCH PITCHED					WHAT HE GAVE UP										THE RESULTS						
			G	GS	GF	IP	BFP	H	R	ER	HR	SH	SF	HB	TBB	IBB	SO	WP	W	L	Pct	Sv-Op	Hld	Vel	OPS	ERC	ERA
2007	NYM	NL	54	0	14	44.1	205	48	18	17	3	2	0	7	21	4	45	2	3	2	.600	0-0	10	86	.757	5.04	3.45
2008	NYM	NL	82	0	12	63.1	271	51	28	25	4	4	0	4	31	4	52	1	6	3	.667	0-3	18	89	.658	3.23	3.55
2009	Cle	AL	37	0	5	34.0	142	30	16	13	4	1	1	0	13	0	30	2	0	1	.000	0-1	10	90	.707	3.49	3.44
2010	Cle	AL	53	0	7	40.0	170	30	18	17	4	1	0	1	24	2	32	0	2	2	.500	0-1	17	91	.659	3.53	3.83
2011	Cle	AL	71	0	13	67.0	267	52	16	15	1	2	2	2	21	1	45	2	3	3	.500	0-3	16	90	.541	2.19	2.01
2012	Cle	AL	72	0	12	67.0	278	53	27	22	4	1	1	2	25	4	53	1	7	4	.636	0-3	21	89	.594	2.60	2.96
2013	Cle	AL	70	0	20	63.0	259	54	17	16	5	3	0	3	23	2	54	3	6	2	.750	3-8	25	90	.643	3.23	2.29
2014	LAA	AL	76	0	26	74.2	285	45	16	15	4	3	0	6	15	3	68	4	7	2	.778	15-19	18	89	.491	1.47	1.81
2015	LAA	AL	70	0	13	65.1	271	64	26	26	4	2	1	2	19	4	57	1	5	5	.500	5-9	32	88	.684	3.36	3.58
2016	2 Tms		54	0	19	52.0	217	47	20	20	8	1	1	6	18	3	40	0	2	5	.286	6-9	7	88	.716	4.19	3.46
2017	2 Tms		59	0	3	54.0	214	46	20	20	4	1	1	1	10	1	71	0	3	0	1.000	1-2	21	89	.601	2.40	3.33
2018	Hou	AL	56	0	13	45.2	180	34	20	19	7	0	2	2	12	0	46	1	5	1	.833	0-2	11	88	.645	2.75	3.74
2019	Hou	AL	28	0	4	25.0	96	19	6	5	2	0	0	0	5	0	22	0	1	0	1.000	0-1	4	88	.569	2.04	1.80
16	LAA	AL	38	0	16	37.2	160	36	16	16	4	1	1	5	13	3	25	0	1	4	.200	6-9	6	88	.697	4.15	3.82
16	ChC	NL	16	0	3	14.1	57	11	4	4	4	0	0	1	5	0	15	0	1	1	.500	0-0	1	89	.769	4.20	2.51
17	Tor	AL	38	0	1	35.2	144	30	13	13	3	1	1	1	10	1	51	0	3	0	1.000	0-1	13	89	.623	2.78	3.28
17	Cle	AL	21	0	2	18.1	70	16	7	7	1	0	0	0	0	0	20	0	0	0	-	1-1	8	89	.557	1.72	3.44
Postseason			18	0	4	14.0	54	8	4	4	2	0	1	0	3	1	13	0	0	1	.000	0-0	2	89	.484	1.47	2.57
13 ML YEARS			782	0	161	695.1	2855	573	248	230	54	21	9	36	237	28	615	17	50	29	.633	30-61	210	89	.631	2.93	2.98

Josh A. Smith

Pitches: R Bats: R Pos: RP-15; SP-1

Ht: 6'2" Wt: 210 Born: 8/7/1987 Age: 33

Year	Team	Lg		HOW MUCH PITCHED					WHAT HE GAVE UP										THE RESULTS						
			G	GS	GF	IP	BFP	H	R	ER	HR	SH	SF	HB	TBB	IBB	SO	WP	W	L	Pct	Sv-Op	Hld	Vel	OPS	ERC	ERA
2015	Cin	NL	9	7	0	32.2	161	42	27	25	5	0	2	5	21	3	30	0	0	4	.000	0-0	0	90	.926	7.82	6.89
2016	Cin	NL	32	2	8	59.2	260	57	32	31	11	1	1	1	26	1	48	1	3	3	.500	0-0	1	91	.757	4.56	4.68
2017	Oak	AL	26	0	15	35.0	151	35	20	19	3	0	1	0	15	1	25	1	2	1	.667	0-0	1	91	.805	4.06	4.89
2019	Bos	AL	18	0	13	31.0	139	36	22	20	10	0	0	3	8	1	29	0	0	3	.000	1-2	0	91	.885	6.34	5.81
2020	Mia	NL	16	1	2	26.1	121	33	21	20	3	1	3	1	11	2	18	0	1	1	.500	1-1	1	90	.870	5.77	6.84
5 ML YEARS			101	12	38	184.2	832	203	122	115	32	2	7	10	81	8	150	2	6	12	.333	2-3	3	91	.836	5.49	5.60

Josh D. Smith

Pitches: L Bats: L Pos: RP-2　　　　**Ht:** 6'3" **Wt:** 200 **Born:** 10/11/1989 **Age:** 31

Year	Team	Lg	G	GS	GF	IP	BFP	H	R	ER	HR	SH	SF	HB	TBB	IBB	SO	WP	W	L	Pct	Sv-Op	Hld	Vel	OPS	ERC	ERA
2019	2 Tms		14	0	6	12.2	64	11	9	9	0	0	1	3	11	2	14	0	0	0	-	0-0	0	91	.738	4.72	6.39
2020	Mia	NL	2	0	0	1.2	10	2	2	2	1	0	0	2	1	0	4	0	0	0	-	0-0	0	89	1.357	16.60	10.80
19	Cle	AL	8	0	3	8.1	43	8	5	5	0	0	0	2	8	1	12	0	0	0	-	0-0	0	91	.782	5.76	5.40
19	Mia	NL	6	0	3	4.1	21	3	4	4	0	0	1	1	3	1	2	0	0	0	-	0-0	0	90	.646	2.92	8.31
	2 ML YEARS		16	0	6	14.1	74	13	11	11	1	0	1	5	12	2	18	0	0	0	-	0-0	0	90	.816	5.90	6.91

Kevan Smith

Bats: R Throws: R Pos: C-16;PH-2;DH-1　　　　**Ht:** 6'4" **Wt:** 230 **Born:** 6/28/1988 **Age:** 33

Year	Team	Lg	G	AB	H	2B	3B	HR	(Hm	Rd)	TB	R	RBI	RC	TBB	IBB	SO	HBP	SH	SF	SB	CS	GDP	Avg	OBP	Slg	OPS
2016	CWS	AL	7	16	2	0	0	0	(0	0)	2	2	0	0	0	0	6	0	0	0	0	0	1	.125	.125	.125	.250
2017	CWS	AL	87	276	78	17	0	4	(4	0)	107	23	30	29	9	0	46	3	2	3	0	0	9	.283	.309	.388	.697
2018	CWS	AL	52	171	50	6	0	3	(1	2)	65	21	21	25	10	0	18	5	0	5	1	0	5	.292	.348	.380	.728
2019	LAA	AL	67	191	48	12	0	5	(1	4)	75	21	20	19	16	0	37	3	0	1	2	0	8	.251	.318	.393	.710
2020	TB	AL	17	31	8	3	0	1	(1	0)	14	3	8	7	5	0	11	1	0	0	0	0	1	.258	.378	.452	.830
	5 ML YEARS		230	685	186	38	0	13	(7	6)	263	70	79	80	40	0	118	12	2	5	3	0	24	.272	.321	.384	.705

Mallex Smith

Bats: L Throws: R Pos: RF-12;CF-3　　　　**Ht:** 5'10" **Wt:** 180 **Born:** 5/6/1993 **Age:** 28

Year	Team	Lg	G	AB	H	2B	3B	HR	(Hm	Rd)	TB	R	RBI	RC	TBB	IBB	SO	HBP	SH	SF	SB	CS	GDP	Avg	OBP	Slg	OPS
2016	Atl	NL	72	189	45	7	4	3	(0	3)	69	28	22	26	20	0	48	2	3	1	16	8	3	.238	.316	.365	.681
2017	TB	AL	81	256	69	8	4	2	(2	0)	91	33	12	30	23	0	62	0	2	1	16	5	2	.270	.329	.355	.684
2018	TB	AL	141	480	142	27	10	2	(1	1)	195	65	40	74	47	0	98	8	7	2	40	12	11	.296	.367	.406	.773
2019	Sea	AL	134	510	116	19	9	6	(4	2)	171	70	37	56	42	0	141	11	2	4	46	9	7	.227	.300	.335	.635
2020	Sea	AL	14	45	6	2	0	0	(0	0)	8	2	3	1	2	0	13	0	0	0	2	0	1	.133	.170	.178	.348
	5 ML YEARS		442	1480	378	63	27	13	(7	6)	534	198	114	187	134	0	362	21	14	5	120	34	24	.255	.325	.361	.686

Pavin Smith

Bats: L Throws: L Pos: 1B-5;LF-3;RF-2;DH-2　　　　**Ht:** 6'2" **Wt:** 210 **Born:** 2/6/1996 **Age:** 25

Year	Team	Lg	G	AB	H	2B	3B	HR	(Hm	Rd)	TB	R	RBI	RC	TBB	IBB	SO	HBP	SH	SF	SB	CS	GDP	Avg	OBP	Slg	OPS
2020	Ari	NL	12	37	10	0	1	1	(1	0)	15	7	4	5	5	0	8	0	0	2	1	0	0	.270	.341	.405	.746

Riley Smith

Pitches: R Bats: R Pos: RP-6　　　　**Ht:** 6'1" **Wt:** 175 **Born:** 1/15/1995 **Age:** 26

Year	Team	Lg	G	GS	GF	IP	BFP	H	R	ER	HR	SH	SF	HB	TBB	IBB	SO	WP	W	L	Pct	Sv-Op	Hld	Vel	OPS	ERC	ERA
2020	Ari	NL	6	0	5	18.1	70	15	3	3	1	1	0	0	5	0	18	0	2	0	1.000	0-0	0	93	.602	2.53	1.47

Will Smith

Pitches: L Bats: R Pos: RP-18　　　　**Ht:** 6'5" **Wt:** 255 **Born:** 7/10/1989 **Age:** 31

Year	Team	Lg	G	GS	GF	IP	BFP	H	R	ER	HR	SH	SF	HB	TBB	IBB	SO	WP	W	L	Pct	Sv-Op	Hld	Vel	OPS	ERC	ERA
2012	KC	AL	16	16	0	89.2	396	111	54	53	12	2	5	1	33	1	59	4	6	9	.400	0-0	0	90	.853	5.75	5.32
2013	KC	AL	19	1	4	33.1	131	24	16	12	6	0	4	1	7	0	43	0	2	1	.667	0-3	6	91	.631	2.47	3.24
2014	Mil	NL	78	0	6	65.2	286	62	31	27	6	1	1	3	31	6	86	7	1	3	.250	1-6	30	93	.737	4.02	3.70
2015	Mil	NL	76	0	11	63.1	264	52	23	19	5	1	2	1	24	1	91	5	7	2	.778	0-4	20	93	.649	2.91	2.70
2016	2 Tms	NL	53	0	40	40.1	167	31	19	15	3	1	1	1	18	1	48	3	2	4	.333	0-5	23	92	.637	2.92	3.35
2018	SF	NL	54	0	27	53.0	210	37	18	15	3	2	2	0	15	4	71	2	2	3	.400	14-18	6	93	.533	1.74	2.55
2019	SF	NL	63	0	52	65.1	257	46	20	20	10	0	1	0	21	2	96	3	6	0	1.000	34-38	0	93	.618	2.54	2.76
2020	Atl	NL	18	0	11	16.0	62	11	8	8	7	0	0	0	4	0	18	0	2	2	.500	0-1	5	93	.794	3.74	4.50
16	Mil	NL	27	0	3	22.0	92	18	13	9	3	1	1	1	9	1	22	3	1	3	.250	0-4	12	92	.708	3.48	3.68
16	SF	NL	26	0	1	18.1	75	13	6	6	0	0	0	0	9	0	26	0	1	1	.500	0-1	11	92	.551	2.26	2.95
	Postseason		2	0	0	1.1	5	1	1	0	0	0	0	0	0	0	1	0	0	1	.000	0-1	0	93	.400	1.13	0.00
	8 ML YEARS		377	17	105	426.2	1773	374	189	169	52	7	16	7	153	15	512	24	28	24	.538	49-75	90	92	.693	3.42	3.56

Will Smith

Bats: R Throws: R Pos: C-34;DH-3;PH-1　　　　**Ht:** 5'10" **Wt:** 195 **Born:** 3/28/1995 **Age:** 26

Year	Team	Lg	G	AB	H	2B	3B	HR	(Hm	Rd)	TB	R	RBI	RC	TBB	IBB	SO	HBP	SH	SF	SB	CS	GDP	Avg	OBP	Slg	OPS
2019	LAD	NL	54	170	43	9	0	15	(7	8)	97	30	42	38	18	1	52	5	0	3	2	0	3	.253	.337	.571	.907
2020	LAD	NL	37	114	33	9	0	8	(7	1)	66	23	25	27	20	1	22	2	0	1	0	0	2	.289	.401	.579	.980
	Postseason		4	13	1	0	0	0	(0	0)	1	0	0	0	3	1	5	0	0	0	0	0	0	.077	.250	.077	.327
	2 ML YEARS		91	284	76	18	0	23	(14	9)	163	53	67	65	38	2	74	7	0	4	2	0	5	.268	.363	.574	.937

Dwight Smith Jr.

Bats: L Throws: R Pos: LF-16;DH-5;PH-2;PR-1   Ht: 6'0" Wt: 210 Born: 10/26/1992 Age: 28

Year	Team	Lg	G	AB	H	2B	3B	HR	(Hm	Rd)	TB	R	RBI	RC	TBB	IBB	SO	HBP	SH	SF	SB	CS	GDP	Avg	OBP	Slg	OPS
2017	Tor	AL	12	27	10	2	0	0	(0	0)	12	2	1	4	1	0	10	1	0	0	1	0	0	.370	.414	.444	.858
2018	Tor	AL	35	65	17	8	0	2	(1	1)	31	9	8	10	7	0	13	2	0	1	0	0	1	.262	.347	.477	.824
2019	Bal	AL	101	357	86	16	3	13	(7	6)	147	46	53	55	26	0	82	4	1	4	5	1	8	.241	.297	.412	.708
2020	Bal	AL	21	63	14	3	0	2	(2	0)	23	9	6	9	7	1	19	1	0	1	1	0	1	.222	.306	.365	.671
4 ML YEARS			169	512	127	29	3	17	(10	7)	213	66	68	78	41	1	124	8	1	6	7	1	10	.248	.310	.416	.726

Justin Smoak

Bats: B Throws: L Pos: 1B-31;PH-5;DH-4   SMOKE   Ht: 6'4" Wt: 220 Born: 12/5/1986 Age: 34

Year	Team	Lg	G	AB	H	2B	3B	HR	(Hm	Rd)	TB	R	RBI	RC	TBB	IBB	SO	HBP	SH	SF	SB	CS	GDP	Avg	OBP	Slg	OPS
2010	2 Tms	AL	100	348	76	14	0	13	(4	9)	129	40	48	42	46	4	91	0	0	3	1	0	9	.218	.307	.371	.678
2011	Sea	AL	123	427	100	24	0	15	(10	5)	169	38	55	55	55	4	105	3	0	4	0	0	10	.234	.323	.396	.719
2012	Sea	AL	132	483	105	14	0	19	(4	15)	176	49	51	50	49	2	111	1	0	2	1	0	12	.217	.290	.364	.654
2013	Sea	AL	131	454	108	19	0	20	(9	11)	187	53	50	60	64	1	119	2	0	1	0	0	11	.238	.334	.412	.746
2014	Sea	AL	80	248	50	13	0	7	(4	3)	84	28	30	23	24	0	66	2	0	2	0	1	8	.202	.275	.339	.614
2015	Tor	AL	132	296	67	16	1	18	(8	10)	139	44	59	49	29	0	86	2	0	1	0	0	10	.226	.299	.470	.768
2016	Tor	AL	126	299	65	10	0	14	(10	4)	117	33	34	33	40	1	112	2	0	0	1	0	7	.217	.314	.391	.705
2017	Tor	AL	158	560	151	24	1	38	(19	19)	296	85	90	100	73	3	128	2	0	2	0	1	17	.270	.355	.529	.883
2018	Tor	AL	147	505	122	34	0	25	(11	14)	231	67	77	86	83	2	156	3	0	3	0	1	11	.242	.350	.457	.808
2019	Tor	AL	121	414	86	16	0	22	(13	9)	168	54	61	64	79	3	106	6	0	1	0	0	11	.208	.342	.406	.748
2020	2 Tms	AL	36	119	21	7	0	5	(1	4)	43	14	15	9	10	0	42	2	0	1	0	0	4	.176	.250	.361	.611
10	Tex	AL	70	235	49	10	0	8	(4	4)	83	29	34	30	38	4	57	0	0	2	1	0	6	.209	.316	.353	.670
10	Sea	AL	30	113	27	4	0	5	(0	5)	46	11	14	12	8	0	34	0	0	1	0	0	3	.239	.287	.407	.694
20	Mil	NL	33	113	21	7	0	5	(1	4)	43	14	15	9	10	0	40	2	0	1	0	0	3	.186	.262	.381	.642
20	SF	NL	3	6	0	0	0	0	(0	0)	0	0	0	0	0	0	2	0	0	0	0	0	1	.000	.000	.000	.000
Postseason			11	10	0	0	0	0	(0	0)	0	0	0	0	0	0	5	0	0	0	0	0	0	.000	.000	.000	.000
11 ML YEARS			1286	4153	951	196	2	196	(93	103)	1739	505	570	571	552	20	1122	25	0	20	3	3	110	.229	.322	.419	.740

Drew Smyly

Pitches: L Bats: L Pos: SP-5; RP-2   SMY-lee   Ht: 6'2" Wt: 188 Born: 6/13/1989 Age: 32

Year	Team	Lg	G	GS	GF	IP	BFP	H	R	ER	HR	SH	SF	HB	TBB	IBB	SO	WP	W	L	Pct	Sv-Op	Hld	Vel	OPS	ERC	ERA
2012	Det	AL	23	18	0	99.1	416	93	49	44	12	2	3	2	33	1	94	3	4	3	.571	0-0	0	92	.732	3.68	3.99
2013	Det	AL	63	0	9	76.0	303	62	20	20	4	0	1	1	17	1	81	5	6	0	1.000	2-6	21	91	.601	2.21	2.37
2014	2 Tms	AL	28	25	0	153.0	618	136	57	55	18	1	3	1	42	2	133	8	9	10	.474	0-0	1	90	.688	3.17	3.24
2015	TB	AL	12	12	0	66.2	275	58	24	23	11	1	1	1	20	0	77	2	5	2	.714	0-0	0	90	.701	3.45	3.11
2016	TB	AL	30	30	0	175.1	738	174	103	95	32	5	11	2	49	2	167	10	7	12	.368	0-0	0	90	.763	4.13	4.88
2019	2 Tms		25	21	1	114.0	514	126	83	79	32	2	2	2	55	0	120	7	4	7	.364	1-1	0	91	.916	6.49	6.24
2020	SF	NL	7	5	0	26.1	111	20	11	10	2	0	1	0	9	0	42	1	1	0	1.000	0-0	0	94	.558	2.32	3.42
14	Det	AL	21	18	0	105.1	445	111	48	46	14	0	3	1	31	1	89	4	6	9	.400	0-0	1	90	.770	4.26	3.93
14	TB	AL	7	7	0	47.2	173	25	9	9	4	1	0	0	11	1	44	4	3	1	.750	0-0	0	90	.476	1.28	1.70
19	Tex	AL	13	9	1	51.1	251	64	49	48	19	0	2	1	34	0	52	5	1	5	.167	1-1	0	91	1.021	8.95	8.42
19	Phi	NL	12	12	0	62.2	263	62	34	31	13	2	0	1	21	0	68	2	3	2	.600	0-0	0	92	.820	4.64	4.45
Postseason			10	0	1	7.0	30	3	3	2	0	0	0	0	6	1	7	0	1	0	1.000	0-0	2	91	.467	1.81	2.57
7 ML YEARS			188	111	10	710.2	2975	669	347	326	111	11	22	9	225	6	714	36	35	35	.500	3-7	23	91	.738	3.85	4.13

Cy Sneed

Pitches: R Bats: R Pos: RP-18   Ht: 6'4" Wt: 213 Born: 10/1/1992 Age: 28

Year	Team	Lg	G	GS	GF	IP	BFP	H	R	ER	HR	SH	SF	HB	TBB	IBB	SO	WP	W	L	Pct	Sv-Op	Hld	Vel	OPS	ERC	ERA
2019	Hou	AL	8	0	4	21.1	93	26	13	13	5	1	0	0	5	0	23	0	0	1	.000	0-0	0	93	.866	5.64	5.48
2020	Hou	AL	18	0	8	17.1	83	22	15	11	3	2	0	0	10	2	21	1	0	3	.000	0-2	3	94	.930	6.72	5.71
2 ML YEARS			26	0	12	38.2	176	48	28	24	8	3	0	0	15	2	44	1	0	4	.000	0-2	3	93	.896	6.14	5.59

Blake Snell

Pitches: L Bats: L Pos: SP-11   Ht: 6'4" Wt: 225 Born: 12/4/1992 Age: 28

Year	Team	Lg	G	GS	GF	IP	BFP	H	R	ER	HR	SH	SF	HB	TBB	IBB	SO	WP	W	L	Pct	Sv-Op	Hld	Vel	OPS	ERC	ERA
2016	TB	AL	19	19	0	89.0	401	93	44	35	5	2	2	0	51	0	98	6	6	8	.429	0-0	0	94	.728	4.69	3.54
2017	TB	AL	24	24	0	129.1	547	113	65	58	15	4	1	0	59	1	119	8	5	7	.417	0-0	0	94	.707	3.71	4.04
2018	TB	AL	31	31	0	180.2	700	112	41	38	16	2	3	1	64	2	221	13	21	5	.808	0-0	0	96	.554	1.95	1.89
2019	TB	AL	23	23	0	107.0	441	96	53	51	14	0	1	1	40	1	147	11	6	8	.429	0-0	0	96	.702	3.72	4.29
2020	TB	AL	11	11	0	50.0	203	42	19	18	10	1	0	0	18	0	63	7	4	2	.667	0-0	0	95	.726	3.77	3.24
Postseason			3	1	1	5.1	20	4	1	1	0	0	0	0	7	0	7	0	0	1	.000	1-1	0	96	.600	1.77	1.69
5 ML YEARS			108	108	0	556.0	2292	456	222	200	60	9	7	2	232	4	648	45	42	30	.583	0-0	0	95	.664	3.26	3.24

Chad Sobotka

Pitches: R Bats: R Pos: RP-4

Ht: 6'7" Wt: 225 Born: 7/10/1993 Age: 27

			HOW MUCH PITCHED					WHAT HE GAVE UP										THE RESULTS							
Year	Team	Lg	G	GS	GF	IP	BFP	H	R	ER	HR	SH	SF	HB	TBB	IBB	SO	WP	W	L	Pct	Sv-Op	Hld	Vel	OPS	ERC	ERA
2018	Atl	NL	14	0	5	14.1	58	5	3	3	2	1	0	0	9	2	21	3	1	0	1.000	0-0	1	97	.496	1.64	1.88
2019	Atl	NL	32	0	5	29.0	134	28	22	20	6	0	0	3	19	0	38	3	0	0	-	0-0	6	96	.820	6.19	6.21
2020	Atl	NL	4	0	3	3.2	20	6	5	5	0	0	0	0	2	0	2	2	0	0	-	0-0	0	94	.900	7.12	12.27
	Postseason		3	0	1	2.1	13	2	4	3	1	0	1	0	4	0	0	0	0	0	-	0-0	1	97	1.087	11.75	11.57
	3 ML YEARS		50	0	13	47.0	212	39	30	28	8	1	0	3	30	2	61	8	1	0	1.000	0-0	7	96	.740	4.67	5.36

Eric Sogard

Bats: L Throws: R Pos: 3B-30;PH-10;2B-9;SS-7;LF-2;DH-2;PR-1   SO-guard

Ht: 5'10" Wt: 180 Born: 5/22/1986 Age: 35

						BATTING															RUNNING			AVERAGES			
Year	Team	Lg	G	AB	H	2B	3B	HR	(Hm	Rd)	TB	R	RBI	RC	TBB	IBB	SO	HBP	SH	SF	SB	CS	GDP	Avg	OBP	Slg	OPS
2010	Oak	AL	4	7	3	0	0	0	(0	0)	3	0	0	1	2	0	1	0	0	0	0	1	0	.429	.556	.429	.984
2011	Oak	AL	27	70	14	3	0	2	(0	2)	23	7	4	3	4	0	13	0	0	0	0	0	2	.200	.243	.329	.572
2012	Oak	AL	37	102	17	3	1	2	(0	2)	28	8	7	7	5	0	17	0	1	0	2	0	1	.167	.206	.275	.480
2013	Oak	AL	130	368	98	24	3	2	(0	2)	134	45	35	43	27	2	51	5	6	4	10	5	4	.266	.322	.364	.686
2014	Oak	AL	117	291	65	10	0	1	(1	0)	78	38	22	27	31	0	37	1	4	2	11	4	6	.223	.298	.268	.567
2015	Oak	AL	120	372	92	12	3	1	(1	0)	113	40	37	36	23	1	50	2	3	1	6	1	9	.247	.294	.304	.598
2017	Mil	NL	94	249	68	15	1	3	(2	1)	94	37	18	37	45	2	37	4	1	0	3	3	7	.273	.393	.378	.770
2018	Mil	NL	55	97	13	3	0	0	(0	0)	16	7	2	2	12	1	23	2	1	1	3	0	3	.134	.241	.165	.406
2019	2 Tms	AL	110	396	115	23	2	13	(8	5)	181	59	40	67	38	2	63	2	3	3	8	0	4	.290	.353	.457	.810
2020	Mil	NL	43	115	24	5	0	1	(1	0)	32	14	10	13	11	0	20	1	0	1	0	0	1	.209	.281	.278	.560
19	Tor	AL	73	287	86	17	2	10	(6	4)	137	45	30	52	29	0	47	1	3	3	6	0	2	.300	.363	.477	.840
19	TB	AL	37	109	29	6	0	3	(2	1)	44	14	10	15	9	2	16	1	0	0	2	0	2	.266	.328	.404	.731
	Postseason		7	17	3	0	0	1	(0	1)	6	2	2	1	1	0	4	0	1	0	0	0	0	.176	.222	.353	.575
	10 ML YEARS		737	2067	509	98	10	25	(13	12)	702	251	175	236	198	8	312	17	19	12	43	14	37	.246	.316	.340	.655

Nick Solak

Bats: R Throws: R Pos: LF-29;2B-17;CF-13;DH-5;1B-1;PH-1

Ht: 5'11" Wt: 185 Born: 1/11/1995 Age: 26

						BATTING															RUNNING			AVERAGES			
Year	Team	Lg	G	AB	H	2B	3B	HR	(Hm	Rd)	TB	R	RBI	RC	TBB	IBB	SO	HBP	SH	SF	SB	CS	GDP	Avg	OBP	Slg	OPS
2019	Tex	AL	33	116	34	6	1	5	(3	2)	57	19	17	25	15	1	29	4	0	0	2	0	2	.293	.393	.491	.884
2020	Tex	AL	58	209	56	10	0	2	(0	2)	72	27	23	30	18	0	42	2	0	4	7	1	6	.268	.326	.344	.671
	2 ML YEARS		91	325	90	16	1	7	(3	4)	129	46	40	55	33	1	71	6	0	4	9	1	8	.277	.351	.397	.747

Donovan Solano

Bats: R Throws: R Pos: 2B-45;3B-5;PH-5;SS-2   sol-ON-oh

Ht: 5'8" Wt: 210 Born: 12/17/1987 Age: 33

						BATTING															RUNNING			AVERAGES			
Year	Team	Lg	G	AB	H	2B	3B	HR	(Hm	Rd)	TB	R	RBI	RC	TBB	IBB	SO	HBP	SH	SF	SB	CS	GDP	Avg	OBP	Slg	OPS
2012	Mia	NL	93	285	84	11	3	2	(0	2)	107	29	28	35	21	1	58	2	3	5	7	0	5	.295	.342	.375	.717
2013	Mia	NL	102	361	90	13	1	3	(0	3)	114	33	34	38	23	3	57	7	2	2	3	1	11	.249	.305	.316	.621
2014	Mia	NL	111	310	78	11	1	3	(1	2)	100	26	28	35	19	0	61	3	7	1	1	2	5	.252	.300	.323	.623
2015	Mia	NL	55	90	17	3	1	0	(0	0)	22	6	7	3	1	0	18	2	1	0	0	0	4	.189	.215	.244	.459
2016	NYY	AL	9	22	5	2	0	1	(0	1)	10	5	2	3	1	0	3	0	0	0	0	0	0	.227	.261	.455	.715
2019	SF	NL	81	215	71	13	1	4	(0	4)	98	27	23	36	10	0	49	1	0	2	0	1	4	.330	.360	.456	.815
2020	SF	NL	54	190	62	15	1	3	(3	0)	88	22	29	36	10	0	39	2	0	1	0	0	2	.326	.365	.463	.828
	7 ML YEARS		505	1473	407	68	8	16	(4	12)	539	148	151	186	85	4	285	17	13	11	11	4	31	.276	.321	.366	.687

Jorge Soler

Bats: R Throws: R Pos: DH-35;RF-8;PH-1   HOR-hay so-LAIR

Ht: 6'4" Wt: 235 Born: 2/25/1992 Age: 29

						BATTING															RUNNING			AVERAGES			
Year	Team	Lg	G	AB	H	2B	3B	HR	(Hm	Rd)	TB	R	RBI	RC	TBB	IBB	SO	HBP	SH	SF	SB	CS	GDP	Avg	OBP	Slg	OPS
2014	ChC	NL	24	89	26	8	1	5	(1	4)	51	11	20	15	6	0	24	0	0	2	1	0	3	.292	.330	.573	.903
2015	ChC	NL	101	366	96	18	1	10	(7	3)	146	39	47	43	32	5	121	3	0	3	3	1	9	.262	.324	.399	.723
2016	ChC	NL	86	227	54	9	0	12	(6	6)	99	37	31	31	31	0	66	3	0	3	0	0	5	.238	.333	.436	.769
2017	KC	AL	35	97	14	5	0	2	(1	1)	25	7	6	5	12	1	36	1	0	0	0	0	5	.144	.245	.258	.503
2018	KC	AL	61	223	59	18	0	9	(5	4)	104	27	28	32	28	0	69	4	0	2	3	1	6	.265	.354	.466	.820
2019	KC	AL	162	589	156	33	1	48	(21	27)	335	95	117	109	73	3	178	10	0	4	3	1	16	.265	.354	.569	.922
2020	KC	AL	43	149	34	8	0	8	(4	4)	66	17	24	24	19	0	60	3	0	1	0	0	3	.228	.326	.443	.769
	Postseason		15	32	11	3	1	3	(2	1)	25	6	5	9	9	0	9	0	0	0	0	0	1	.344	.488	.781	1.269
	7 ML YEARS		512	1740	439	99	3	94	(46	48)	826	233	273	259	201	9	554	24	0	15	10	3	47	.252	.335	.475	.810

Joakim Soria

Pitches: R Bats: R Pos: RP-22   wah-KEEM SORE-ee-uh

Ht: 6'3" Wt: 208 Born: 5/18/1984 Age: 37

						HOW MUCH PITCHED				WHAT HE GAVE UP									THE RESULTS							
Year	Team	Lg	G	GS	GF	IP	BFP	H	R	ER	HR	SH	SF	HB	TBB	IBB	SO	WP	W	L	Pct	Sv-Op	Hld	Vel	OPS	ERC	ERA
2007	KC	AL	62	0	38	69.0	270	46	20	19	3	1	3		19	3	75	2	2	3	.400	17-21	9	91	.510	1.63	2.48
2008	KC	AL	63	0	57	67.1	260	39	13	12	5	2	2	6	19	1	66	1	2	3	.400	42-45	0	91	.503	1.72	1.60
2009	KC	AL	47	0	41	53.0	222	44	14	13	5	1	2	2	16	1	69	3	3	2	.600	30-33	0	92	.614	2.80	2.21
2010	KC	AL	66	0	56	65.2	270	53	13	13	4	3	4	2	16	1	71	3	1	2	.333	43-46	0	92	.568	2.27	1.78
2011	KC	AL	60	0	47	60.1	256	60	29	27	7	3	2	2	17	0	60	1	5	5	.500	28-35	0	91	.709	3.80	4.03
2013	Tex	AL	26	0	9	23.2	101	18	10	10	2	1	0	1	14	2	28	2	1	0	1.000	0-0	6	91	.624	3.45	3.80
2014	2 Tms	AL	48	0	37	44.1	182	38	19	16	2	1	2	2	6	2	48	1	2	4	.333	18-20	1	90	.605	2.04	3.25
2015	2 Tms	AL	72	0	40	67.2	272	55	20	19	8	1	2	1	19	1	64	5	3	1	.750	24-30	11	92	.628	2.87	2.53

			HOW MUCH PITCHED					WHAT HE GAVE UP											THE RESULTS						
Year	Team	Lg	G	GS	GF	IP	BFP	H	R	ER	HR	SH	SF	HB	TBB	IBB	SO	WP	W	L	Pct	Sv-Op	Hld	Vel	OPS	ERC	ERA
2016	KC	AL	70	0	18	66.2	293	70	31	30	10	4	2	2	27	0	68	2	5	8	.385	1-8	20	93	.800	4.86	4.05
2017	KC	AL	59	0	10	56.0	232	49	24	23	1	0	1	1	20	2	64	4	4	3	.571	1-8	20	93	.592	2.73	3.70
2018	2 Tms		66	0	29	60.2	255	53	24	21	4	1	0	2	16	1	75	2	3	4	.429	16-21	13	92	.619	2.68	3.12
2019	Oak	AL	71	1	21	69.0	278	51	33	33	9	1	2	3	20	1	79	5	2	4	.333	1-6	21	93	.608	2.61	4.30
2020	Oak	AL	22	0	4	22.1	96	18	8	7	1	0	3	0	10	3	24	0	2	2	.500	2-3	4	92	.581	2.55	2.82
14	Tex	AL	35	0	32	33.1	133	25	12	10	0	1	1	1	4	1	42	0	1	3	.250	17-19	2	90	.521	1.38	2.70
14	Det	AL	13	0	5	11.0	49	13	7	6	2	0	1	1	2	1	6	1	1	1	.500	1-1	1	91	.838	4.92	4.91
15	Det	AL	43	0	35	41.0	165	32	13	13	8	1	0	2	11	1	36	0	3	1	.750	23-26	0	92	.665	3.15	2.85
15	Pit	NL	29	0	5	26.2	107	23	7	6	0	0	1	0	8	0	28	5	0	0	-	1-4	11	92	.571	2.39	2.03
18	CWS	AL	40	0	29	38.2	164	35	13	11	2	1	0	1	10	1	49	1	0	3	.000	16-19	2	92	.591	2.68	2.56
18	Mil	NL	26	0	0	22.0	91	18	11	10	2	0	0	1	6	0	26	1	1	1	.750	0-2	11	93	.668	2.69	4.09
	Postseason		10	0	2	6.2	35	9	9	9	0	0	0	0	6	1	11	0	1	1	.500	0-1	1	93	.842	6.88	12.15
13 ML YEARS			732	1	407	725.2	2987	594	258	243	61	19	24	26	219	18	791	31	35	41	.461	223-276	105	92	.615	2.71	3.01

Mike Soroka

Pitches: R **Bats:** R **Pos:** SP-3

suh-ROH-kah

Ht: 6'5" **Wt:** 225 **Born:** 8/4/1997 **Age:** 23

			HOW MUCH PITCHED					WHAT HE GAVE UP											THE RESULTS						
Year	Team	Lg	G	GS	GF	IP	BFP	H	R	ER	HR	SH	SF	HB	TBB	IBB	SO	WP	W	L	Pct	Sv-Op	Hld	Vel	OPS	ERC	ERA
2018	Atl	NL	5	5	0	25.2	113	30	14	10	1	1	1	0	7	0	21	2	2	1	.667	0-0	0	93	.744	4.02	3.51
2019	Atl	NL	29	29	0	174.2	701	153	56	52	14	3	2	7	41	1	142	3	13	4	.765	0-0	0	92	.628	2.86	2.68
2020	Atl	NL	3	3	0	13.2	57	11	7	6	0	0	0	1	7	0	8	1	0	1	.000	0-0	0	92	.578	3.12	3.95
	Postseason		1	1	0	7.0	23	2	1	1	0	0	1	0	0	0	7	0	0	0	-	0-0	0	93	.223	0.19	1.29
3 ML YEARS			37	37	0	214.0	871	194	77	68	15	4	3	8	55	1	171	6	15	6	.714	0-0	0	92	.641	3.01	2.86

Elliot Soto

Bats: R **Throws:** R **Pos:** SS-2;2B-1;PR-1

Ht: 5'9" **Wt:** 160 **Born:** 8/21/1989 **Age:** 31

						BATTING															RUNNING			AVERAGES			
Year	Team	Lg	G	AB	H	2B	3B	HR	(Hm	Rd)	TB	R	RBI	RC	TBB	IBB	SO	HBP	SH	SF	SB	CS	GDP	Avg	OBP	Slg	OPS
2020	LAA	AL	3	6	2	1	0	0	(0	0)	3	2	0	1	1	0	1	0	0	0	0	0	0	.333	.429	.500	.929

Gregory Soto

Pitches: L **Bats:** L **Pos:** RP-27

Ht: 6'1" **Wt:** 236 **Born:** 2/11/1995 **Age:** 26

			HOW MUCH PITCHED					WHAT HE GAVE UP											THE RESULTS						
Year	Team	Lg	G	GS	GF	IP	BFP	H	R	ER	HR	SH	SF	HB	TBB	IBB	SO	WP	W	L	Pct	Sv-Op	Hld	Vel	OPS	ERC	ERA
2019	Det	AL	33	7	9	57.2	276	74	39	37	9	0	3	0	33	1	45	5	0	5	.000	0-1	2	95	.884	6.86	5.77
2020	Det	AL	27	0	6	23.0	98	16	11	11	2	0	0	2	13	0	29	3	0	1	.000	2-3	4	97	.605	3.30	4.30
2 ML YEARS			60	7	15	80.2	374	90	50	48	11	0	3	2	46	1	74	8	0	6	.000	2-4	6	96	.812	5.77	5.36

Juan Soto

Bats: L **Throws:** L **Pos:** LF-36;RF-6;DH-5

Ht: 6'1" **Wt:** 220 **Born:** 10/25/1998 **Age:** 22

						BATTING															RUNNING			AVERAGES			
Year	Team	Lg	G	AB	H	2B	3B	HR	(Hm	Rd)	TB	R	RBI	RC	TBB	IBB	SO	HBP	SH	SF	SB	CS	GDP	Avg	OBP	Slg	OPS
2018	Was	NL	116	414	121	25	1	22	(6	16)	214	77	70	73	79	10	99	0	1	4	5	2	9	.292	.406	.517	.923
2019	Was	NL	150	542	153	32	5	34	(18	16)	297	110	110	117	108	3	132	3	0	6	12	1	11	.282	.401	.548	.949
2020	Was	NL	47	154	54	14	0	13	(4	9)	107	39	37	53	41	12	28	1	0	0	6	2	1	.351	.490	.695	1.185
	Postseason		17	65	18	3	0	5	(2	3)	36	12	14	12	9	2	21	1	0	0	1	0	0	.277	.373	.554	.927
3 ML YEARS			313	1110	328	71	6	69	(28	41)	618	226	217	243	228	25	259	4	1	6	23	5	21	.295	.415	.557	.972

Steven Souza Jr.

Bats: R **Throws:** R **Pos:** RF-6;LF-3;PH-3;DH-1

SOO-zuh

Ht: 6'4" **Wt:** 225 **Born:** 4/24/1989 **Age:** 32

						BATTING															RUNNING			AVERAGES			
Year	Team	Lg	G	AB	H	2B	3B	HR	(Hm	Rd)	TB	R	RBI	RC	TBB	IBB	SO	HBP	SH	SF	SB	CS	GDP	Avg	OBP	Slg	OPS
2014	Was	NL	21	23	3	0	0	2	(1	1)	9	2	2	1	3	0	7	0	0	0	0	0	1	.130	.231	.391	.622
2015	TB	AL	110	373	84	15	1	16	(6	10)	149	59	40	40	46	0	144	5	1	1	12	6	7	.225	.318	.399	.717
2016	TB	AL	120	430	106	17	1	17	(7	10)	176	58	49	53	31	0	159	5	0	2	7	6	5	.247	.303	.409	.713
2017	TB	AL	148	523	125	21	2	30	(14	16)	240	78	78	85	84	2	179	7	2	1	16	4	9	.239	.351	.459	.810
2018	Ari	NL	72	241	53	15	3	5	(3	2)	89	21	29	29	24	0	75	3	0	4	6	1	4	.220	.309	.369	.678
2020	ChC	NL	11	27	4	2	0	1	(1	0)	9	3	5	3	4	0	15	0	0	0	1	0	0	.148	.258	.333	.591
6 ML YEARS			482	1617	375	70	7	71	(32	39)	672	221	203	211	196	2	579	20	3	4	42	17	26	.232	.322	.416	.737

Glenn Sparkman

Pitches: R **Bats:** R **Pos:** RP-4

Ht: 6'2" **Wt:** 215 **Born:** 5/11/1992 **Age:** 29

			HOW MUCH PITCHED					WHAT HE GAVE UP											THE RESULTS						
Year	Team	Lg	G	GS	GF	IP	BFP	H	R	ER	HR	SH	SF	HB	TBB	IBB	SO	WP	W	L	Pct	Sv-Op	Hld	Vel	OPS	ERC	ERA
2017	Tor	AL	2	0	1	1.0	12	9	7	7	0	0	0	0	1	0	1	0	0	0		0-0	0	94	1.924	79.03	63.00
2018	KC	AL	15	3	3	38.1	176	47	20	19	3	0	5	1	15	3	27	3	0	3	.000	0-0	0	94	.816	5.08	4.46
2019	KC	AL	31	23	2	136.0	606	164	96	91	30	1	4	6	41	1	81	6	4	11	.267	0-0	0	93	.876	5.94	6.02
2020	KC	AL	4	0	0	5.0	27	9	6	3	0	0	1	0	1	0	2	0	0	0		0-0	0	93	.810	6.52	5.40
4 ML YEARS			52	26	6	180.1	821	229	129	120	33	1	10	7	58	4	111	9	4	14	.222	0-0	0	94	.877	6.06	5.99

Gabe Speier

Pitches: L Bats: L Pos: RP-8   Ht: 5'11" Wt: 175 Born: 4/12/1995 Age: 26

		HOW MUCH PITCHED					WHAT HE GAVE UP										THE RESULTS							
Year Team	Lg	G	GS	GF	IP	BFP	H	R	ER	HR	SH	SF	HB	TBB	IBB	SO	WP	W	L	Pct	Sv-Op	Hld	Vel	OPS	ERC	ERA
2019 KC	AL	9	0	1	7.1	33	5	6	6	2	0	0	0	6	0	10	1	0	0	-	0-0	1	95	.778	5.10	7.36
2020 KC	AL	8	0	3	5.2	30	9	5	5	1	0	0	0	4	0	6	0	0	1	.000	0-0	1	92	.972	9.58	7.94
2 ML YEARS		17	0	4	13.0	63	14	11	11	3	0	0	0	10	0	16	1	0	1	.000	0-0	2	94	.872	6.97	7.62

George Springer

Bats: R Throws: R Pos: CF-42;RF-9;DH-3;PH-1;PR-1   Ht: 6'3" Wt: 221 Born: 9/19/1989 Age: 31

								BATTING													RUNNING			AVERAGES			
Year Team	Lg	G	AB	H	2B	3B	HR	(Hm	Rd)	TB	R	RBI	RC	TBB	IBB	SO	HBP	SH	SF	SB	CS	GDP	Avg	OBP	Slg	OPS
2014 Hou	AL	78	295	68	8	1	20	(5	15)	138	45	51	45	39	4	114	9	0	2	5	2	4	.231	.336	.468	.804
2015 Hou	AL	102	388	107	19	2	16	(9	7)	178	59	41	60	50	0	109	8	2	3	16	4	4	.276	.367	.459	.826
2016 Hou	AL	162	644	168	29	5	29	(13	16)	294	116	82	100	88	2	178	11	0	1	9	10	12	.261	.359	.457	.815
2017 Hou	AL	140	548	155	29	0	34	(16	18)	286	112	85	99	64	1	111	11	0	4	5	7	11	.283	.367	.522	.889
2018 Hou	AL	140	544	144	26	0	22	(12	10)	236	102	71	84	64	0	122	6	0	4	6	4	12	.265	.346	.434	.780
2019 Hou	AL	122	479	140	20	3	39	(18	21)	283	96	96	103	67	1	113	6	0	4	6	2	12	.292	.383	.591	.974
2020 Hou	AL	51	189	50	6	2	14	(6	8)	102	37	32	42	24	0	38	5	0	2	1	2	3	.265	.359	.540	.899
Postseason		50	203	55	14	0	15	(7	8)	114	35	28	40	29	1	57	0	0	0	4	0	3	.271	.362	.562	.924
7 ML YEARS		795	3087	832	137	13	174	(79	95)	1517	567	458	533	396	8	785	55	2	19	48	31	58	.270	.361	.491	.852

Jeffrey Springs

Pitches: L Bats: L Pos: RP-16   Ht: 6'3" Wt: 218 Born: 9/20/1992 Age: 28

		HOW MUCH PITCHED					WHAT HE GAVE UP										THE RESULTS							
Year Team	Lg	G	GS	GF	IP	BFP	H	R	ER	HR	SH	SF	HB	TBB	IBB	SO	WP	W	L	Pct	Sv-Op	Hld	Vel	OPS	ERC	ERA
2018 Tex	AL	18	2	4	32.0	141	32	14	12	4	1	0	1	14	1	31	3	1	1	.500	0-1	2	91	.744	4.44	3.38
2019 Tex	AL	25	0	7	32.1	155	38	23	23	4	0	2	0	23	0	32	0	4	1	.800	0-0	1	92	.884	6.57	6.40
2020 Bos	AL	16	0	8	20.1	99	30	18	16	5	0	1	1	7	1	28	2	0	2	.000	0-1	1	92	.973	7.87	7.08
3 ML YEARS		59	2	19	84.2	395	100	55	51	13	1	3	2	44	2	91	5	5	4	.556	0-2	4	92	.857	6.04	5.42

Jacob Stallings

Bats: R Throws: R Pos: C-42   Ht: 6'5" Wt: 220 Born: 12/22/1989 Age: 31

								BATTING													RUNNING			AVERAGES			
Year Team	Lg	G	AB	H	2B	3B	HR	(Hm	Rd)	TB	R	RBI	RC	TBB	IBB	SO	HBP	SH	SF	SB	CS	GDP	Avg	OBP	Slg	OPS
2016 Pit	NL	5	15	6	1	0	0	(0	0)	7	0	2	3	0	0	4	0	0	0	1	0	0	.400	.400	.467	.867
2017 Pit	NL	5	14	5	2	0	0	(0	0)	7	3	3	3	2	1	2	0	0	0	0	0	0	.357	.438	.500	.938
2018 Pit	NL	14	37	8	0	0	0	(0	0)	8	2	5	3	3	0	9	0	0	1	0	0	2	.216	.268	.216	.485
2019 Pit	NL	71	191	50	5	0	6	(1	5)	73	26	13	18	16	5	40	2	1	0	0	0	3	.262	.325	.382	.708
2020 Pit	NL	42	125	31	7	0	3	(3	0)	47	13	18	18	15	0	40	0	2	1	0	0	2	.248	.326	.376	.702
5 ML YEARS		137	382	100	15	0	9	(4	5)	142	44	41	45	36	6	95	2	3	2	1	0	7	.262	.327	.372	.699

Craig Stammen

Pitches: R Bats: R Pos: RP-24   Ht: 6'2" Wt: 228 Born: 3/9/1984 Age: 37

STAMM-enn

		HOW MUCH PITCHED					WHAT HE GAVE UP										THE RESULTS							
Year Team	Lg	G	GS	GF	IP	BFP	H	R	ER	HR	SH	SF	HB	TBB	IBB	SO	WP	W	L	Pct	Sv-Op	Hld	Vel	OPS	ERC	ERA
2009 Was	NL	19	19	0	105.2	448	112	67	60	14	4	3	3	24	1	48	7	4	7	.364	0-0	0	89	.774	4.03	5.11
2010 Was	NL	35	19	3	128.0	562	151	78	73	13	5	6	1	41	4	85	3	4	4	.500	0-0	1	91	.814	4.79	5.13
2011 Was	NL	7	0	2	10.1	38	3	1	1	0	0	0	0	4	0	12	1	1	1	.500	0-0	1	91	.272	0.67	0.87
2012 Was	NL	59	0	15	88.1	370	70	27	23	7	5	1	2	36	4	87	3	6	1	.857	1-2	10	92	.636	2.84	2.34
2013 Was	NL	55	0	14	81.2	339	78	30	25	4	8	4	2	27	3	79	2	7	6	.538	0-1	7	92	.682	3.32	2.76
2014 Was	NL	49	0	15	72.2	304	78	34	31	5	3	1	3	14	2	56	1	4	5	.444	0-0	7	92	.708	3.61	3.84
2015 Was	NL	5	0	0	4.0	17	2	0	0	0	1	0	1	3	1	3	0	0	0	-	0-0	2	92	.525	1.66	0.00
2017 SD	NL	60	0	9	80.1	329	68	29	28	12	2	0	2	28	3	74	2	2	3	.400	0-2	11	92	.684	3.46	3.14
2018 SD	NL	73	0	7	79.0	317	65	25	24	3	2	1	3	17	3	88	3	8	3	.727	0-5	23	92	.583	2.17	2.73
2019 SD	NL	76	0	12	82.0	339	80	36	30	13	0	3	2	15	2	73	0	8	7	.533	4-13	31	92	.719	3.51	3.29
2020 SD	NL	24	0	6	24.0	105	27	16	15	2	2	0	2	4	0	20	0	4	2	.667	0-1	5	92	.702	3.97	5.63
Postseason		6	0	0	7.0	34	8	4	4	1	1	1	3	2	0	5	0	0	0	-	0-0	1	91	.912	6.41	5.14
11 ML YEARS		462	38	83	756.0	3168	734	343	310	73	31	20	20	213	23	625	22	48	39	.552	5-24	98	91	.705	3.49	3.69

Ryne Stanek

Pitches: R Bats: R Pos: RP-9   Ht: 6'4" Wt: 226 Born: 7/26/1991 Age: 29

		HOW MUCH PITCHED					WHAT HE GAVE UP										THE RESULTS							
Year Team	Lg	G	GS	GF	IP	BFP	H	R	ER	HR	SH	SF	HB	TBB	IBB	SO	WP	W	L	Pct	Sv-Op	Hld	Vel	OPS	ERC	ERA
2017 TB	AL	21	0	4	20.0	95	26	13	13	6	0	1	0	12	2	29	4	0	0	-	0-1	4	98	.985	8.31	5.85
2018 TB	AL	59	29	10	66.1	263	45	23	22	8	0	0	1	27	1	81	5	2	3	.400	0-0	8	98	.618	2.64	2.98
2019 2 Tms		63	27	12	77.0	327	61	39	34	11	0	3	0	39	3	89	5	0	4	.000	1-5	7	98	.686	3.56	3.97
2020 Mia	NL	9	0	3	10.0	48	11	8	8	3	0	0	0	8	1	11	0	0	0	-	0-0	0	96	.921	7.82	7.20
19 TB	AL	41	27	3	55.2	228	44	24	21	7	0	2	0	20	1	61	2	0	2	.000	0-0	2	98	.654	2.93	3.40
19 Mia	NL	22	0	9	21.1	99	17	15	13	4	0	1	0	19	2	28	3	0	2	.000	1-5	5	98	.769	5.31	5.48
4 ML YEARS		152	56	29	173.1	733	143	83	77	28	0	4	1	86	7	210	14	2	7	.222	1-6	19	98	.716	3.89	4.00

Giancarlo Stanton

Bats: R **Throws:** R **Pos:** DH-23   john-CAHR-loh   **Ht:** 6'6" **Wt:** 245 **Born:** 11/8/1989 **Age:** 31

Year	Team	Lg	G	AB	H	2B	3B	HR	(Hm	Rd)	TB	R	RBI	RC	TBB	IBB	SO	HBP	SH	SF	SB	CS	GDP	Avg	OBP	Slg	OPS
2010	Fla	NL	100	359	93	21	1	22	(7	15)	182	45	59	56	34	6	123	2	0	1	5	2	7	.259	.326	.507	.833
2011	Fla	NL	150	516	135	30	5	34	(16	18)	277	79	87	81	70	6	166	9	0	6	5	5	11	.262	.356	.537	.893
2012	Mia	NL	123	449	130	30	1	37	(16	21)	273	75	86	79	46	9	143	5	0	1	6	2	5	.290	.361	.608	.969
2013	Mia	NL	116	425	106	26	0	24	(15	9)	204	62	62	66	74	5	140	4	0	1	1	0	10	.249	.365	.480	.845
2014	Mia	NL	145	539	155	31	1	37	(24	13)	299	89	105	109	94	24	170	3	0	2	13	1	16	.288	.395	.555	.950
2015	Mia	NL	74	279	74	12	1	27	(13	14)	169	47	67	54	34	6	95	2	0	3	4	2	5	.265	.346	.606	.952
2016	Mia	NL	119	413	99	20	1	27	(13	14)	202	56	74	56	50	5	140	4	0	2	0	0	6	.240	.326	.489	.815
2017	Mia	NL	159	597	168	32	0	59	(31	28)	377	123	132	117	85	13	163	7	0	3	2	2	13	.281	.376	.631	1.007
2018	NYY	AL	158	617	164	34	1	38	(20	18)	314	102	100	98	70	5	211	8	0	10	5	0	17	.266	.343	.509	.852
2019	NYY	AL	18	59	17	3	0	3	(1	2)	29	8	13	14	12	0	24	0	0	1	0	0	1	.288	.403	.492	.894
2020	NYY	AL	23	76	19	7	0	4	(1	3)	38	12	11	14	15	1	27	2	0	0	1	1	4	.250	.387	.500	.887
	Postseason		10	34	8	0	0	2	(1	1)	14	5	3	2	5	0	12	0	0	1	0	0	2	.235	.325	.412	.737
	11 ML YEARS		1185	4329	1160	246	11	312	(158	154)	2364	698	796	744	584	80	1402	46	0	30	42	15	95	.268	.359	.546	.905

Bubba Starling

Bats: R **Throws:** R **Pos:** CF-29;PR-5;PH-3;DH-2;LF-1;RF-1   **Ht:** 6'4" **Wt:** 215 **Born:** 8/3/1992 **Age:** 28

Year	Team	Lg	G	AB	H	2B	3B	HR	(Hm	Rd)	TB	R	RBI	RC	TBB	IBB	SO	HBP	SH	SF	SB	CS	GDP	Avg	OBP	Slg	OPS
2019	KC	AL	56	186	40	7	4	4	(1	3)	59	26	12	10	9	0	56	1	1	0	2	0	4	.215	.255	.317	.572
2020	KC	AL	35	59	10	1	0	1	(1	0)	14	5	5	2	4	0	27	0	0	1	0	0	0	.169	.219	.237	.456
	2 ML YEARS		91	245	50	8	0	5	(2	3)	73	31	17	12	13	0	83	1	1	1	2	0	4	.204	.246	.298	.544

Cody Stashak

Pitches: R **Bats:** R **Pos:** RP-11   **Ht:** 6'2" **Wt:** 180 **Born:** 6/4/1994 **Age:** 27

			HOW MUCH PITCHED				WHAT HE GAVE UP											THE RESULTS							
Year	Team	Lg	G	GS	GF	IP	BFP	H	R	ER	HR	SH	SF	HB	TBB	IBB	SO	WP	W	L	Pct	Sv-Op	Hld	Vel	OPS	ERC	ERA
2019	Min	AL	18	1	4	25.0	104	29	9	9	3	0	1	1	1	0	25	0	0	0	.000	0-0	1	92	.773	3.82	3.24
2020	Min	AL	11	0	1	15.0	57	11	5	5	2	0	0	0	3	0	17	1	1	0	1.000	0-0	5	92	.635	2.22	3.00
	Postseason		2	0	0	1.2	9	3	2	2	2	0	0	0	1	0	0	0	0	0	-	0-0	0	92	1.569	20.55	10.80
	2 ML YEARS		29	1	5	40.0	161	40	14	14	5	0	1	1	4	0	42	1	1	1	.500	0-0	6	92	.725	3.19	3.15

Max Stassi

Bats: R **Throws:** R **Pos:** C-31;PH-3   STASS-ee   **Ht:** 5'10" **Wt:** 200 **Born:** 3/15/1991 **Age:** 30

Year	Team	Lg	G	AB	H	2B	3B	HR	(Hm	Rd)	TB	R	RBI	RC	TBB	IBB	SO	HBP	SH	SF	SB	CS	GDP	Avg	OBP	Slg	OPS
2013	Hou	AL	3	7	2	0	0	0	(0	0)	2	0	1	0	0	0	2	1	0	0	0	0	1	.286	.375	.286	.661
2014	Hou	AL	7	20	7	2	0	0	(0	0)	9	2	4	4	0	0	6	0	0	0	0	0	0	.350	.350	.450	.800
2015	Hou	AL	11	15	6	0	0	1	(1	0)	9	4	2	3	1	0	5	0	1	0	0	0	1	.400	.438	.600	1.038
2016	Hou	AL	9	13	1	0	0	0	(0	0)	1	1	0	0	0	0	5	0	0	0	0	0	0	.077	.077	.077	.154
2017	Hou	AL	14	24	4	1	0	2	(1	1)	11	5	4	3	6	0	4	0	0	1	0	0	2	.167	.323	.458	.781
2018	Hou	AL	88	221	50	13	0	8	(1	7)	87	28	27	33	23	0	74	6	0	0	0	0	3	.226	.316	.394	.710
2019	2 Tms	AL	51	132	18	1	0	1	(0	1)	22	7	5	2	12	0	49	1	0	2	0	0	3	.136	.211	.167	.378
2020	LAA	AL	31	90	25	2	0	7	(3	4)	48	12	20	18	11	0	21	1	0	3	0	0	5	.278	.352	.533	.886
19	Hou	AL	31	90	15	1	0	1	(0	1)	19	4	3	2	7	0	34	1	0	0	0	0	1	.167	.235	.211	.446
19	LAA	AL	20	42	3	0	0	0	(0	0)	3	3	2	0	5	0	15	0	0	2	0	0	2	.071	.163	.071	.235
	8 ML YEARS		214	522	113	19	0	19	(6	13)	189	59	63	63	53	0	166	9	1	6	0	0	18	.216	.297	.362	.659

Josh Staumont

Pitches: R **Bats:** R **Pos:** RP-26   **Ht:** 6'3" **Wt:** 205 **Born:** 12/21/1993 **Age:** 27

			HOW MUCH PITCHED				WHAT HE GAVE UP											THE RESULTS							
Year	Team	Lg	G	GS	GF	IP	BFP	H	R	ER	HR	SH	SF	HB	TBB	IBB	SO	WP	W	L	Pct	Sv-Op	Hld	Vel	OPS	ERC	ERA
2019	KC	AL	16	0	7	19.1	88	21	13	8	4	0	0	1	10	1	15	0	0	0	-	0-1	0	96	.870	6.01	3.72
2020	KC	AL	26	0	3	25.2	112	20	8	7	2	0	0	3	16	0	37	1	2	1	.667	0-0	8	98	.639	4.06	2.45
	2 ML YEARS		42	0	10	45.0	200	41	21	15	6	0	0	4	26	1	52	1	2	1	.667	0-1	8	97	.743	4.89	3.00

Drew Steckenrider

Pitches: R **Bats:** R **Pos:** P   **Ht:** 6'4" **Wt:** 217 **Born:** 1/10/1991 **Age:** 30

			HOW MUCH PITCHED				WHAT HE GAVE UP											THE RESULTS							
Year	Team	Lg	G	GS	GF	IP	BFP	H	R	ER	HR	SH	SF	HB	TBB	IBB	SO	WP	W	L	Pct	Sv-Op	Hld	Vel	OPS	ERC	ERA
2017	Mia	NL	37	0	7	34.2	151	30	13	9	4	0	1	0	18	1	54	1	1	1	.500	1-1	10	95	.674	3.80	2.34
2018	Mia	NL	71	0	17	64.2	272	55	29	28	7	0	1	2	27	5	74	0	4	4	.500	5-10	19	95	.664	3.39	3.90
2019	Mia	NL	15	0	4	14.1	58	9	10	10	6	0	0	1	5	0	14	0	0	2	.000	0-1	3	95	.778	4.00	6.28
	3 ML YEARS		123	0	28	113.2	481	94	52	47	17	0	2	3	50	6	142	1	5	7	.417	6-12	32	95	.681	3.62	3.72

Robert Stephenson

Pitches: R **Bats:** R **Pos:** RP-10   **Ht:** 6'3" **Wt:** 205 **Born:** 2/24/1993 **Age:** 28

Year	Team	Lg	G	GS	GF	IP	BFP	H	R	ER	HR	SH	SF	HB	TBB	IBB	SO	WP	W	L	Pct	Sv-Op	Hld	Vel	OPS	ERC	ERA
2016	Cin	NL	8	8	0	37.0	170	41	26	25	9	0	0	4	19	1	31	2	2	3	.400	0-0	0	93	.893	6.78	6.08
2017	Cin	NL	25	11	6	84.2	383	81	52	44	12	5	6	2	53	3	86	5	5	6	.455	1-1	0	94	.805	5.06	4.68
2018	Cin	NL	4	3	0	11.2	63	17	12	12	2	0	1	0	12	3	11	2	0	2	.000	0-0	0	93	1.040	9.71	9.26
2019	Cin	NL	57	0	16	64.2	262	43	30	27	9	0	1	0	24	4	81	3	2	4	.600	0-4	11	95	.634	2.33	3.76
2020	Cin	NL	10	0	4	10.0	43	11	11	11	8	0	0	1	3	0	13	0	0	0	-	0-0	1	95	1.246	10.14	9.90
	5 ML YEARS		104	22	26	208.0	921	193	131	119	40	5	8	7	111	11	222	12	10	13	.435	1-5	12	94	.809	4.89	5.15

Tyler Stephenson

Bats: R **Throws:** R **Pos:** C-4;DH-3;PH-3   **Ht:** 6'4" **Wt:** 225 **Born:** 8/16/1996 **Age:** 24

Year	Team	Lg	G	AB	H	2B	3B	HR	(Hm	Rd)	TB	R	RBI	RC	TBB	IBB	SO	HBP	SH	SF	SB	CS	GDP	Avg	OBP	Slg	OPS
2020	Cin	NL	8	17	5	0	0	2	(2	0)	11	4	6	3	2	0	9	1	0	0	0	0	0	.294	.400	.647	1.047

Andrew Stevenson

Bats: L **Throws:** L **Pos:** LF-9;RF-4;PH-2;CF-1;PR-1   **Ht:** 6'0" **Wt:** 192 **Born:** 6/1/1994 **Age:** 27

Year	Team	Lg	G	AB	H	2B	3B	HR	(Hm	Rd)	TB	R	RBI	RC	TBB	IBB	SO	HBP	SH	SF	SB	CS	GDP	Avg	OBP	Slg	OPS
2017	Was	NL	37	57	9	2	0	0	(0	0)	11	5	1	1	7	0	20	0	2	0	1	0	0	.158	.250	.193	.443
2018	Was	NL	57	75	19	2	0	1	(1	0)	24	9	13	11	6	0	23	1	1	3	1	1	0	.253	.306	.320	.626
2019	Was	NL	30	30	11	1	1	0	(0	0)	14	4	0	6	6	0	11	1	0	0	0	1	1	.367	.486	.467	.953
2020	Was	NL	15	41	15	7	1	2	(0	0)	30	11	12	13	5	0	11	1	0	0	2	0	0	.366	.447	.732	1.179
	Postseason		1	0	0	0	0	0	(0	0)	0	1	0	0	0	0	0	0	0	0	0	0	0	-	-	-	-
	4 ML YEARS		139	203	54	12	2	3	(3	0)	79	29	26	31	24	0	65	3	3	3	4	2	1	.266	.348	.389	.737

Christin Stewart

Bats: L **Throws:** R **Pos:** LF-32;PH-3;DH-1;PR-1   **Ht:** 6'0" **Wt:** 220 **Born:** 12/10/1993 **Age:** 27

Year	Team	Lg	G	AB	H	2B	3B	HR	(Hm	Rd)	TB	R	RBI	RC	TBB	IBB	SO	HBP	SH	SF	SB	CS	GDP	Avg	OBP	Slg	OPS
2018	Det	AL	17	60	16	1	1	2	(0	2)	25	7	10	13	10	0	13	1	0	1	0	0	1	.267	.375	.417	.792
2019	Det	AL	104	369	86	25	1	10	(3	7)	143	32	40	42	34	3	103	7	0	6	0	1	4	.233	.305	.388	.693
2020	Det	AL	36	90	15	3	0	3	(2	1)	27	6	9	5	5	0	30	2	0	1	0	0	2	.167	.224	.300	.524
	3 ML YEARS		157	519	117	29	2	15	(7	8)	195	45	59	60	49	3	146	10	0	8	0	1	7	.225	.300	.376	.676

D.J. Stewart

Bats: L **Throws:** R **Pos:** RF-21;LF-10;PH-1   **Ht:** 6'0" **Wt:** 230 **Born:** 11/30/1993 **Age:** 27

Year	Team	Lg	G	AB	H	2B	3B	HR	(Hm	Rd)	TB	R	RBI	RC	TBB	IBB	SO	HBP	SH	SF	SB	CS	GDP	Avg	OBP	Slg	OPS
2018	Bal	AL	17	40	10	3	0	3	(2	1)	22	8	10	8	4	0	12	2	0	1	2	1	0	.250	.340	.550	.890
2019	Bal	AL	44	126	30	6	0	4	(1	3)	48	15	15	17	14	1	26	1	0	1	1	2	3	.238	.317	.381	.698
2020	Bal	AL	31	88	17	2	0	7	(4	3)	40	13	15	18	20	0	38	2	2	0	0	0	0	.193	.355	.455	.809
	3 ML YEARS		92	254	57	11	0	14	(7	7)	110	36	40	43	38	1	76	5	2	2	3	3	3	.224	.334	.433	.768

Kohl Stewart

Pitches: R **Bats:** R **Pos:** P   **Ht:** 6'3" **Wt:** 200 **Born:** 10/7/1994 **Age:** 26

Year	Team	Lg	G	GS	GF	IP	BFP	H	R	ER	HR	SH	SF	HB	TBB	IBB	SO	WP	W	L	Pct	Sv-Op	Hld	Vel	OPS	ERC	ERA
2018	Min	AL	8	4	0	36.2	159	34	16	15	1	0	0	3	18	0	24	4	2	1	.667	0-0	0	93	.672	3.87	3.68
2019	Min	AL	9	2	5	25.1	109	29	18	18	5	0	0	1	8	0	10	6	2	2	.500	0-0	1	92	.869	5.59	6.39
	2 ML YEARS		17	6	5	62.0	268	63	34	33	6	0	0	4	26	0	34	10	4	3	.571	0-0	1	92	.755	4.57	4.79

Jonathan Stiever

Pitches: R **Bats:** R **Pos:** SP-2   **Ht:** 6'2" **Wt:** 215 **Born:** 5/12/1997 **Age:** 24

Year	Team	Lg	G	GS	GF	IP	BFP	H	R	ER	HR	SH	SF	HB	TBB	IBB	SO	WP	W	L	Pct	Sv-Op	Hld	Vel	OPS	ERC	ERA
2020	CWS	AL	2	2	0	6.1	29	7	7	7	4	0	0	0	4	0	3	0	0	1	.000	0-0	0	92	1.139	10.13	9.95

Robert Stock

Pitches: R **Bats:** L **Pos:** RP-10   **Ht:** 6'1" **Wt:** 214 **Born:** 11/21/1989 **Age:** 31

Year	Team	Lg	G	GS	GF	IP	BFP	H	R	ER	HR	SH	SF	HB	TBB	IBB	SO	WP	W	L	Pct	Sv-Op	Hld	Vel	OPS	ERC	ERA
2018	SD	NL	32	0	6	39.2	166	37	13	11	1	1	0	2	13	1	38	3	1	1	.500	0-1	4	98	.615	3.11	2.50
2019	SD	NL	10	0	4	10.2	56	14	14	12	2	0	0	1	8	0	15	4	1	0	1.000	0-1	0	98	.900	8.30	10.13
2020	Bos	AL	10	0	4	13.1	62	16	9	7	0	1	1	0	10	0	14	3	0	1	.000	0-0	0	97	.826	6.08	4.73
	3 ML YEARS		52	0	14	63.2	284	67	36	30	3	2	1	3	31	1	67	10	2	2	.500	0-2	4	97	.714	4.50	4.24

Trevor Story

Bats: R **Throws:** R **Pos:** SS-57;DH-2   **Ht:** 6'2" **Wt:** 213 **Born:** 11/15/1992 **Age:** 28

Year	Team	Lg	G	AB	H	2B	3B	HR	(Hm	Rd)	TB	R	RBI	RC	TBB	IBB	SO	HBP	SH	SF	SB	CS	GDP	Avg	OBP	Slg	OPS
2016	Col	NL	97	372	101	21	4	27	(16	11)	211	67	72	67	35	2	130	5	2	1	8	5	5	.272	.341	.567	.909
2017	Col	NL	145	503	120	32	3	24	(13	11)	230	68	82	66	49	4	**191**	2	0	1	7	2	12	.239	.308	.457	.765
2018	Col	NL	157	598	174	42	6	37	(26	11)	339	88	108	107	47	3	168	7	0	4	27	6	12	.291	.348	.567	.914
2019	Col	NL	145	588	173	38	5	35	(24	11)	326	111	85	113	58	0	174	7	0	3	23	8	3	.294	.363	.554	.917
2020	Col	NL	59	235	68	13	**4**	11	(5	6)	122	41	28	35	24	1	63	0	0	0	**15**	3	5	.289	.355	.519	.874
	Postseason		5	22	7	2	0	1	(0	1)	12	3	1	2	0	0	7	0	0	0	0	0	0	.318	.318	.545	.864
	5 ML YEARS		603	2296	636	146	22	134	(84	50)	1228	375	375	388	213	10	726	21	2	9	80	24	37	.277	.343	.535	.877

Matt Strahm

Pitches: L **Bats:** R **Pos:** RP-19   **Ht:** 6'2" **Wt:** 190 **Born:** 11/12/1991 **Age:** 29

Year	Team	Lg	G	GS	GF	IP	BFP	H	R	ER	HR	SH	SF	HB	TBB	IBB	SO	WP	W	L	Pct	Sv-Op	Hld	Vel	OPS	ERC	ERA
2016	KC	AL	21	0	1	22.0	88	13	4	3	0	0	1	1	11	1	30	1	2	2	.500	0-0	5	94	.484	1.84	1.23
2017	KC	AL	24	3	3	34.2	154	30	22	21	6	2	0	3	22	2	37	3	2	5	.286	0-0	5	94	.779	5.10	5.45
2018	SD	NL	41	5	5	61.1	245	39	16	14	6	1	1	3	21	1	69	2	3	4	.429	0-0	7	93	.564	2.12	2.05
2019	SD	NL	46	16	4	114.2	487	121	61	60	22	4	1	7	22	4	118	3	6	11	.353	0-1	6	92	.787	4.35	4.71
2020	SD	NL	19	0	2	20.2	83	14	6	6	3	0	0	5	4	0	15	1	0	1	.000	0-2	3	93	.615	2.82	2.61
	5 ML YEARS		151	24	15	253.1	1057	217	109	104	37	7	3	19	80	8	269	10	13	23	.361	0-3	27	93	.698	3.52	3.69

Dee Strange-Gordon

Bats: L **Throws:** R **Pos:** 2B-13;LF-13;PR-7;SS-3;DH-2;PH-1   **Ht:** 5'11" **Wt:** 166 **Born:** 4/22/1988 **Age:** 33

Year	Team	Lg	G	AB	H	2B	3B	HR	(Hm	Rd)	TB	R	RBI	RC	TBB	IBB	SO	HBP	SH	SF	SB	CS	GDP	Avg	OBP	Slg	OPS
2011	LAD	NL	56	224	68	9	2	0	(0	0)	81	34	11	25	7	0	27	0	2	0	24	7	1	.304	.325	.362	.686
2012	LAD	NL	87	303	69	9	2	1	(0	1)	85	38	17	22	20	0	62	3	2	2	32	10	5	.228	.280	.281	.561
2013	LAD	NL	38	94	22	1	1	0	(1	0)	28	9	6	9	10	2	21	1	1	0	10	2	0	.234	.314	.298	.612
2014	LAD	NL	148	609	176	24	**12**	2	(2	0)	230	92	34	76	31	0	107	4	3	3	**64**	19	6	.289	.326	.378	.704
2015	Mia	NL	145	615	**205**	24	8	4	(2	2)	257	88	46	94	25	2	91	2	6	5	58	**20**	6	**.333**	.359	.418	.776
2016	Mia	NL	79	325	87	7	6	1	(1	0)	109	47	14	33	18	1	55	0	1	1	30	7	4	.268	.305	.335	.641
2017	Mia	NL	158	653	201	20	9	2	(0	2)	245	114	33	81	25	0	93	10	2	4	60	16	7	.308	.341	.375	.716
2018	Sea	AL	141	556	149	17	8	4	(2	2)	194	62	36	50	9	0	80	9	9	5	30	**12**	10	.268	.288	.349	.637
2019	Sea	AL	117	393	108	12	6	3	(0	3)	141	36	34	51	18	1	61	1	3	6	22	5	8	.275	.304	.359	.663
2020	Sea	AL	33	75	15	1	0	0	(0	0)	16	12	3	5	5	0	13	2	0	0	3	2	1	.200	.268	.213	.482
	Postseason		6	17	3	0	0	0	(0	0)	3	0	2	0	2	0	6	0	0	0	1	1	0	.176	.263	.176	.440
	10 ML YEARS		1002	3847	1100	124	54	18	(8	10)	1386	532	234	446	168	6	610	32	29	26	333	100	45	.286	.319	.360	.679

Stephen Strasburg

Pitches: R **Bats:** R **Pos:** SP-2   **Ht:** 6'5" **Wt:** 235 **Born:** 7/20/1988 **Age:** 32

Year	Team	Lg	G	GS	GF	IP	BFP	H	R	ER	HR	SH	SF	HB	TBB	IBB	SO	WP	W	L	Pct	Sv-Op	Hld	Vel	OPS	ERC	ERA
2010	Was	NL	12	12	0	68.0	274	56	25	22	5	2	0	2	17	0	92	2	5	3	.625	0-0	0	97	.596	2.41	2.91
2011	Was	NL	5	5	0	24.0	88	15	5	4	0	1	1	0	2	0	24	0	1	1	.500	0-0	0	96	.398	0.97	1.50
2012	Was	NL	28	28	0	159.1	653	136	62	56	15	6	4	4	48	1	197	5	15	6	.714	0-0	0	96	.649	2.97	3.16
2013	Was	NL	30	30	0	183.0	731	136	71	61	16	5	1	12	56	1	191	7	8	9	.471	0-0	0	95	.588	2.58	3.00
2014	Was	NL	34	**34**	0	215.0	868	198	86	75	23	9	4	5	43	4	**242**	7	14	11	.560	0-0	0	95	.672	3.02	3.14
2015	Was	NL	23	23	0	127.1	523	115	56	49	14	5	1	3	26	0	155	4	11	7	.611	0-0	0	95	.653	2.92	3.46
2016	Was	NL	24	24	0	147.2	598	119	59	59	15	5	1	2	44	1	183	2	15	4	.789	0-0	0	96	.637	2.72	3.60
2017	Was	NL	28	28	0	175.1	701	131	55	49	13	2	4	7	47	5	204	3	15	4	.789	0-0	0	96	.581	2.22	2.52
2018	Was	NL	22	22	0	130.0	544	118	59	54	18	1	5	8	38	2	156	5	10	7	.588	0-0	0	95	.620	3.62	3.74
2019	Was	NL	33	33	0	209.0	841	161	79	77	24	3	4	10	56	4	251	8	**18**	6	.750	0-0	0	94	.620	2.62	3.32
2020	Was	NL	2	2	0	5.0	23	8	6	6	1	0	0	0	1	0	2	0	0	1	.000	0-0	0	92	.937	7.85	10.80
	Postseason		9	8	0	55.1	218	44	13	9	4	2	2	1	8	1	71	1	6	2	.750	0-0	0	95	.562	1.95	1.46
	11 ML YEARS		241	241	0	1443.2	5844	1193	563	512	144	39	27	51	378	18	1697	43	112	59	.655	0-0	0	95	.632	2.75	3.19

Chris Stratton

Pitches: R **Bats:** R **Pos:** RP-27   **Ht:** 6'2" **Wt:** 210 **Born:** 8/22/1990 **Age:** 30

Year	Team	Lg	G	GS	GF	IP	BFP	H	R	ER	HR	SH	SF	HB	TBB	IBB	SO	WP	W	L	Pct	Sv-Op	Hld	Vel	OPS	ERC	ERA
2016	SF	NL	7	0	7	10.0	43	11	4	4	1	0	0	0	5	0	6	0	1	0	1.000	0-0	0	91	.767	5.31	3.60
2017	SF	NL	13	10	1	58.2	256	59	25	24	5	2	3	1	28	0	51	2	4	4	.500	1-2	0	92	.738	4.42	3.68
2018	SF	NL	28	26	1	145.0	625	153	87	82	19	3	6	2	54	1	112	6	10	10	.500	0-0	0	91	.791	4.59	5.09
2019	2 Tms		35	5	7	76.0	344	93	50	47	13	0	1	0	33	1	69	2	1	3	.250	0-0	0	92	.873	6.10	5.57
2020	Pit	NL	27	0	3	30.0	131	26	19	13	2	0	2	0	13	0	39	1	2	1	.667	0-2	5	93	.651	3.34	3.90
	19	LAA	AL	7	5	0	29.1	144	43	28	28	6	0	1	0	18	0	22	1	0	2	.000	0-0	0	91	1.000	8.90	8.59
	19	Pit	NL	28	0	7	46.2	200	50	22	19	7	0	0	0	15	1	47	1	1	1	.500	0-0	0	93	.784	4.50	3.66
	5 ML YEARS		110	41	19	319.2	1399	342	185	170	41	5	12	3	133	2	277	11	18	18	.500	1-4	5	92	.788	4.80	4.79

Myles Straw

Bats: R Throws: R Pos: CF-27;PR-6;DH-2;PH-2;SS-1 Ht: 5'10" Wt: 178 Born: 10/17/1994 Age: 26

Year	Team	Lg	G	AB	H	2B	3B	HR	(Hm	Rd)	TB	R	RBI	RC	TBB	IBB	SO	HBP	SH	SF	SB	CS	GDP	Avg	OBP	Slg	OPS
2018	Hou	AL	9	9	3	0	0	1	(0	1)	6	4	1	2	1	0	0	0	0	0	2	0	0	.333	.400	.667	1.067
2019	Hou	AL	56	108	29	4	2	0	(0	0)	37	27	7	17	19	1	24	0	1	0	8	1	2	.269	.378	.343	.721
2020	Hou	AL	33	82	17	4	0	0	(0	0)	21	8	8	8	4	0	22	0	0	0	6	2	0	.207	.244	.256	.500
	Postseason		2	0	0	0	0	0	(0	0)	0	1	0	0	0	0	0	0	0	0	1	0	0	-	-	-	-
	3 ML YEARS		98	199	49	8	2	1	(0	1)	64	39	16	27	24	1	46	0	1	0	16	3	2	.246	.327	.322	.649

Hunter Strickland

Pitches: R Bats: R Pos: RP-4 Ht: 6'3" Wt: 225 Born: 9/24/1988 Age: 32

Year	Team	Lg	G	GS	GF	IP	BFP	H	R	ER	HR	SH	SF	HB	TBB	IBB	SO	WP	W	L	Pct	Sv-Op	Hld	Vel	OPS	ERC	ERA
2014	SF	NL	9	0	5	7.0	25	5	0	0	0	0	0	0	0	0	9	0	1	0	1.000	1-1	1	98	.440	1.08	0.00
2015	SF	NL	55	0	11	51.1	191	34	14	14	4	0	0	2	10	1	50	1	3	3	.500	0-2	20	97	.543	1.72	2.45
2016	SF	NL	72	0	14	61.0	250	50	21	21	4	0	3	2	19	3	57	3	3	3	.500	3-8	18	97	.589	2.61	3.10
2017	SF	NL	68	0	17	61.1	268	59	20	18	4	1	3	2	29	4	58	3	4	3	.571	1-3	21	96	.702	3.91	2.64
2018	SF	NL	49	0	35	45.1	201	43	25	20	5	2	3	1	21	2	37	4	3	5	.375	14-18	0	95	.758	4.03	3.97
2019	2 Tms		28	0	3	24.1	105	22	15	15	6	0	1	3	8	0	18	1	2	1	.667	2-3	10	96	.809	4.72	5.55
2020	NYM	NL	4	0	2	3.1	16	5	4	3	0	0	0	0	1	0	4	0	0	1	.000	0-0	0	95	.842	5.66	8.10
19	Sea	AL	4	0	2	3.1	13	2	3	3	1	0	0	1	0	0	3	0	1	0	1.000	2-3	0	96	.731	8.10	8.10
19	Was	NL	24	0	1	21.0	92	20	12	12	5	0	1	2	8	0	15	1	2	1	.000	0-0	10	96	.820	5.05	5.14
	Postseason		13	0	7	13.0	54	14	11	11	9	0	0	0	4	0	14	1	1	0	1.000	1-2	1	97	1.193	8.64	7.62
	7 ML YEARS		285	0	87	253.2	1056	218	99	91	23	3	10	10	88	10	233	12	16	16	.500	21-35	70	96	.662	3.14	3.23

Ross Stripling

Pitches: R Bats: R Pos: SP-9; RP-3 Ht: 6'3" Wt: 220 Born: 11/23/1989 Age: 31

Year	Team	Lg	G	GS	GF	IP	BFP	H	R	ER	HR	SH	SF	HB	TBB	IBB	SO	WP	W	L	Pct	Sv-Op	Hld	Vel	OPS	ERC	ERA
2016	LAD	NL	22	14	4	100.0	419	96	46	44	10	3	1	4	30	3	74	6	5	9	.357	0-0	0	90	.709	3.46	3.96
2017	LAD	NL	49	2	12	74.1	304	69	31	31	10	2	3	0	19	4	74	2	3	5	.375	2-5	4	93	.691	3.29	3.75
2018	LAD	NL	33	21	2	122.0	503	123	42	41	18	2	0	1	22	2	136	3	8	6	.571	0-0	3	92	.722	3.58	3.02
2019	LAD	NL	32	15	3	90.2	370	84	40	35	11	0	4	2	20	0	93	4	4	4	.500	0-0	3	91	.699	3.22	3.47
2020	2 Tms		12	9	1	49.1	220	56	37	32	13	2	0	1	18	0	40	1	3	3	.500	1-1	0	92	.882	5.97	5.84
20	LAD	NL	7	7	0	33.2	150	38	26	21	12	2	0	1	11	0	27	1	3	1	.750	0-0	0	92	.933	6.43	5.61
20	Tor	AL	5	2	1	15.2	70	18	11	11	1	0	0	0	7	0	13	0	0	2	.000	1-1	0	92	.770	4.87	6.32
	Postseason		11	0	4	8.1	36	11	6	5	0	0	2	0	2	0	4	1	0	0	-	0-0	0	92	.799	4.67	5.40
	5 ML YEARS		148	61	23	436.1	1816	428	196	183	62	9	8	5	109	9	417	16	23	27	.460	3-6	10	91	.728	3.68	3.77

Marcus Stroman

Pitches: R Bats: R Pos: P Ht: 5'7" Wt: 180 Born: 5/1/1991 Age: 30

Year	Team	Lg	G	GS	GF	IP	BFP	H	R	ER	HR	SH	SF	HB	TBB	IBB	SO	WP	W	L	Pct	Sv-Op	Hld	Vel	OPS	ERC	ERA
2014	Tor	AL	26	20	1	130.2	534	125	56	53	7	0	2	3	28	1	111	9	11	6	.647	1-1	0	94	.633	2.93	3.65
2015	Tor	AL	4	4	0	27.0	103	20	5	5	2	0	0	1	6	0	18	2	4	0	1.000	0-0	0	92	.554	2.16	1.67
2016	Tor	AL	32	32	0	204.0	855	209	104	99	21	2	2	4	54	0	166	9	9	10	.474	0-0	0	92	.720	3.58	4.37
2017	Tor	AL	33	33	0	201.0	834	201	82	69	21	0	4	6	62	1	164	3	13	9	.591	0-0	0	93	.715	3.97	3.09
2018	Tor	AL	19	19	0	102.1	449	115	68	63	9	2	3	2	36	0	77	3	4	9	.308	0-0	0	93	.759	4.59	5.54
2019	2 Tms		32	32	0	184.1	774	183	77	66	18	1	2	1	58	1	159	7	10	13	.435	0-0	0	93	.697	3.73	3.22
19	Tor	AL	21	21	0	124.2	513	118	50	41	10	0	1	0	35	0	99	4	6	11	.353	0-0	0	93	.656	3.23	2.96
19	NYM	NL	11	11	0	59.2	261	65	27	25	8	1	1	1	23	1	60	3	4	2	.667	0-0	0	92	.781	4.84	3.77
	Postseason		5	5	0	30.2	128	29	16	15	4	0	1	0	7	0	21	2	1	1	.500	0-0	0	93	.690	3.24	4.40
	6 ML YEARS		146	140	1	849.1	3549	853	392	355	78	5	13	17	244	3	695	33	51	47	.520	1-1	0	93	.701	3.72	3.76

Pedro Strop

Pitches: R Bats: R Pos: RP-4 STROPE Ht: 6'1" Wt: 220 Born: 6/13/1985 Age: 36

Year	Team	Lg	G	GS	GF	IP	BFP	H	R	ER	HR	SH	SF	HB	TBB	IBB	SO	WP	W	L	Pct	Sv-Op	Hld	Vel	OPS	ERC	ERA
2009	Tex	AL	7	0	3	7.0	30	6	6	6	0	0	0	0	4	0	9	0	0	0	-	0-0	0	95	.679	3.27	7.71
2010	Tex	AL	15	0	5	10.2	60	17	12	12	2	1	0	1	11	0	11	5	0	0	-	0-0	1	95	1.109	11.92	10.13
2011	2 Tms		23	0	5	22.0	90	15	5	5	0	2	1	1	10	0	21	2	2	1	.667	0-2	4	94	.519	2.15	2.05
2012	Bal	AL	70	0	17	66.1	283	52	18	18	2	1	1	4	37	2	58	5	5	2	.714	3-10	24	97	.613	3.22	2.44
2013	2 Tms		66	0	22	57.1	254	45	30	29	5	7	0	6	26	2	66	8	2	5	.286	1-4	17	96	.663	3.21	4.55
2014	ChC	NL	65	0	13	61.0	244	40	19	15	4	0	1	4	25	3	71	6	2	4	.333	2-6	21	95	.535	2.12	2.21
2015	ChC	NL	76	0	12	68.0	270	39	24	22	5	1	3	4	29	6	81	6	2	6	.250	3-5	28	95	.538	1.94	2.91
2016	ChC	NL	54	0	8	47.1	187	27	16	15	4	0	2	4	15	1	60	7	2	2	.500	0-4	21	95	.517	1.78	2.85
2017	ChC	NL	69	0	8	60.1	250	45	22	19	4	2	1	3	26	1	65	7	5	4	.556	0-4	21	96	.619	2.78	2.83
2018	ChC	NL	60	0	20	59.2	240	38	15	15	4	1	1	5	21	3	57	3	6	1	.857	13-17	9	95	.541	2.06	2.26
2019	ChC	NL	50	0	27	41.2	178	33	24	23	6	0	1	5	20	1	49	4	2	5	.286	10-16	6	94	.734	4.01	4.97
2020	Cin	NL	4	0	0	2.1	15	1	3	1	0	0	1	0	6	0	3	1	0	0	-	0-0	1	92	.592	7.50	3.86
11	Tex	AL	11	0	4	9.2	44	7	4	4	0	1	0	1	9	0	9	2	0	1	.000	0-1	0	94	.555	3.34	3.72
11	Bal	AL	12	0	2	12.1	46	8	1	1	0	1	0	0	3	0	12	0	2	0	1.000	0-1	4	95	.481	1.39	0.73
13	Bal	AL	29	0	15	22.1	111	23	19	18	4	4	0	2	15	2	24	5	0	3	.000	0-3	3	96	.861	5.81	7.25
13	ChC	NL	37	0	7	35.0	143	22	11	11	1	3	0	4	11	0	42	3	2	2	.500	1-1	14	96	.520	1.80	2.83
	Postseason		22	0	7	19.1	75	9	4	4	1	1	0	4	7	0	14	1	1	0	1.000	0-0	4	95	.524	1.76	1.86
	12 ML YEARS		559	0	141	503.2	2101	358	194	180	34	15	12	37	230	19	551	54	28	30	.483	32-68	153	95	.605	2.75	3.22

Garrett Stubbs

Bats: L **Throws:** R **Pos:** C-8;LF-3;PR-3;PH-2 **Ht:** 5'10" **Wt:** 170 **Born:** 5/26/1993 **Age:** 28

| | | | | | | | | | BATTING | | | | | | | | | | | | RUNNING | | | AVERAGES | | | |
Year	Team	Lg	G	AB	H	2B	3B	HR	(Hm	Rd)	TB	R	RBI	RC	TBB	IBB	SO	HBP	SH	SF	SB	CS	GDP	Avg	OBP	Slg	OPS
2019	Hou	AL	19	35	7	3	0	0	(0	0)	10	8	2	1	4	0	7	0	0	0	1	0	1	.200	.282	.286	.568
2020	Hou	AL	14	8	1	0	0	0	(0	0)	1	1	1	0	0	0	0	0	1	1	0	1	0	.125	.111	.125	.236
	2 ML YEARS		33	43	8	3	0	0	(0	0)	11	9	3	1	4	0	7	0	1	1	1	1	1	.186	.250	.256	.506

Andrew Suarez

Pitches: L **Bats:** L **Pos:** RP-6 **Ht:** 6'0" **Wt:** 202 **Born:** 9/11/1992 **Age:** 28

| | | | HOW MUCH PITCHED | | | | | WHAT HE GAVE UP | | | | | | | | | | THE RESULTS | | | | | | | | |
Year	Team	Lg	G	GS	GF	IP	BFP	H	R	ER	HR	SH	SF	HB	TBB	IBB	SO	WP	W	L	Pct	Sv-Op	Hld	Vel	OPS	ERC	ERA
2018	SF	NL	29	29	0	160.1	665	163	85	80	23	5	6	3	45	1	130	4	7	13	.350	0-0	0	92	.767	4.15	4.49
2019	SF	NL	21	2	4	32.2	148	39	23	21	7	0	4	1	14	2	25	2	1	3	.250	0-1	1	93	.923	6.27	5.79
2020	SF	NL	6	0	1	9.2	42	9	4	4	1	0	0	0	6	0	5	1	0	0	-	0-0	0	92	.774	4.71	3.72
	3 ML YEARS		56	31	5	202.2	855	211	112	105	31	5	10	4	65	3	160	7	7	15	.318	0-1	1	92	.794	4.51	4.66

Eugenio Suarez

Bats: R **Throws:** R **Pos:** 3B-57 ay-yoo-HAY-nee-oh SWAH-rez **Ht:** 5'11" **Wt:** 213 **Born:** 7/18/1991 **Age:** 29

| | | | | | | | | | BATTING | | | | | | | | | | | | RUNNING | | | AVERAGES | | | |
Year	Team	Lg	G	AB	H	2B	3B	HR	(Hm	Rd)	TB	R	RBI	RC	TBB	IBB	SO	HBP	SH	SF	SB	CS	GDP	Avg	OBP	Slg	OPS
2014	Det	AL	85	244	59	9	1	4	(2	2)	82	33	23	30	22	1	67	5	5	1	3	2	3	.242	.316	.336	.652
2015	Cin	NL	97	372	104	19	2	13	(4	9)	166	42	48	49	17	0	94	3	4	2	4	1	7	.280	.315	.446	.761
2016	Cin	NL	159	565	140	25	2	21	(10	11)	232	78	70	77	51	0	155	8	0	3	11	5	10	.248	.317	.411	.728
2017	Cin	NL	156	534	139	25	2	26	(21	5)	246	87	82	81	84	1	147	9	0	5	4	5	16	.260	.367	.461	.828
2018	Cin	NL	143	527	149	22	2	34	(19	15)	277	79	104	95	64	7	142	9	0	6	1	1	20	.283	.366	.526	.892
2019	Cin	NL	159	575	156	22	2	49	(24	25)	329	87	103	103	70	4	189	11	0	6	3	2	12	.271	.358	.572	.930
2020	Cin	NL	57	198	40	8	0	15	(5	10)	93	29	38	32	30	1	67	2	0	1	2	0	5	.202	.312	.470	.781
	Postseason		1	1	0	0	0	0	(0	0)	0	0	0	0	0	0	0	0	0	0	0	0	0	.000	.000	.000	.000
	7 ML YEARS		856	3015	787	130	11	162	(85	77)	1425	435	468	467	338	14	861	47	9	24	28	16	73	.261	.342	.473	.815

Jose Suarez

Pitches: L **Bats:** L **Pos:** SP-2 **Ht:** 5'10" **Wt:** 225 **Born:** 1/3/1998 **Age:** 23

| | | | HOW MUCH PITCHED | | | | | WHAT HE GAVE UP | | | | | | | | | | THE RESULTS | | | | | | | | |
Year	Team	Lg	G	GS	GF	IP	BFP	H	R	ER	HR	SH	SF	HB	TBB	IBB	SO	WP	W	L	Pct	Sv-Op	Hld	Vel	OPS	ERC	ERA
2019	LAA	AL	19	15	0	81.0	375	100	67	64	23	1	2	10	33	1	72	5	2	6	.250	0-0	0	92	.948	7.33	7.11
2020	LAA	AL	2	2	0	2.1	23	10	10	10	1	0	0	1	5	0	2	1	0	2	.000	0-0	0	93	1.578	44.98	38.57
	2 ML YEARS		21	17	0	83.1	398	110	77	74	24	1	2	11	38	1	74	6	2	8	.200	0-0	0	92	.981	8.43	7.99

Ranger Suarez

Pitches: L **Bats:** L **Pos:** RP-3 **Ht:** 6'1" **Wt:** 217 **Born:** 8/26/1995 **Age:** 25

| | | | HOW MUCH PITCHED | | | | | WHAT HE GAVE UP | | | | | | | | | | THE RESULTS | | | | | | | | |
Year	Team	Lg	G	GS	GF	IP	BFP	H	R	ER	HR	SH	SF	HB	TBB	IBB	SO	WP	W	L	Pct	Sv-Op	Hld	Vel	OPS	ERC	ERA
2018	Phi	NL	4	3	0	15.0	69	21	14	9	3	1	0	0	6	1	11	0	1	1	.500	0-0	0	92	.945	7.33	5.40
2019	Phi	NL	37	0	8	48.2	205	52	18	17	6	3	2	1	12	2	42	1	6	1	.857	0-1	6	92	.739	4.07	3.14
2020	Phi	NL	3	0	1	4.0	26	10	9	9	1	0	0	1	4	0	1	0	0	1	.000	0-0	0	91	1.291	20.74	20.25
	3 ML YEARS		44	3	9	67.2	300	83	41	35	10	4	2	2	22	3	54	1	7	3	.700	0-1	6	92	.832	5.55	4.66

Wander Suero

Pitches: R **Bats:** R **Pos:** RP-22 **Ht:** 6'4" **Wt:** 211 **Born:** 9/15/1991 **Age:** 29

| | | | HOW MUCH PITCHED | | | | | WHAT HE GAVE UP | | | | | | | | | | THE RESULTS | | | | | | | | |
Year	Team	Lg	G	GS	GF	IP	BFP	H	R	ER	HR	SH	SF	HB	TBB	IBB	SO	WP	W	L	Pct	Sv-Op	Hld	Vel	OPS	ERC	ERA
2018	Was	NL	40	0	11	47.2	200	43	20	19	4	1	1	4	15	2	47	3	4	1	.800	0-0	2	92	.719	3.38	3.59
2019	Was	NL	78	0	10	71.1	296	64	36	36	5	0	3	3	26	3	81	2	6	9	.400	1-7	19	93	.666	3.34	4.54
2020	Was	NL	22	0	2	23.2	102	20	10	10	1	0	1	3	10	2	28	2	2	0	1.000	0-0	6	91	.642	3.25	3.80
	Postseason		4	0	2	2.0	8	2	1	1	1	0	0	0	0	0	2	0	0	0	-	0-0	0	93	1.000	4.70	4.50
	3 ML YEARS		140	0	23	142.2	598	127	66	65	10	1	5	10	51	7	156	7	12	10	.545	1-7	27	92	.680	3.34	4.10

Cole Sulser

Pitches: R **Bats:** R **Pos:** RP-19 **Ht:** 6'1" **Wt:** 190 **Born:** 3/12/1990 **Age:** 31

| | | | HOW MUCH PITCHED | | | | | WHAT HE GAVE UP | | | | | | | | | | THE RESULTS | | | | | | | | |
Year	Team	Lg	G	GS	GF	IP	BFP	H	R	ER	HR	SH	SF	HB	TBB	IBB	SO	WP	W	L	Pct	Sv-Op	Hld	Vel	OPS	ERC	ERA
2019	TB	AL	7	0	4	7.1	29	5	0	0	0	0	0	0	3	0	9	0	0	0	-	0-0	0	93	.507	1.90	0.00
2020	Bal	AL	19	0	9	22.2	100	17	18	14	2	2	0	0	17	1	19	1	1	5	.167	5-8	1	94	.705	3.87	5.56
	2 ML YEARS		26	0	13	30.0	129	22	18	14	2	2	0	0	20	1	28	1	1	5	.167	5-8	1	94	.658	3.36	4.20

Andrew Susac

Bats: R Throws: R Pos: C-1 SOO-sack Ht: 6'1" Wt: 220 Born: 3/22/1990 Age: 31

Year Team	Lg	G	AB	H	2B	3B	HR	(Hm	Rd)	TB	R	RBI	RC	TBB	IBB	SO	HBP	SH	SF	SB	CS	GDP	Avg	OBP	Slg	OPS
2014 SF	NL	35	88	24	8	0	3	(1	2)	41	13	19	16	7	0	28	0	0	0	0	0	0	.273	.326	.466	.792
2015 SF	NL	52	133	29	7	2	3	(2	1)	49	14	14	13	14	0	43	1	0	0	0	0	2	.218	.297	.368	.666
2016 Mil	NL	9	17	4	1	0	1	(0	1)	8	3	2	2	2	0	5	0	0	0	0	0	0	.235	.316	.471	.786
2017 Mil	NL	8	12	1	0	0	0	(0	0)	1	0	0	0	0	0	6	0	0	0	0	0	0	.083	.083	.083	.167
2018 Bal	AL	9	26	3	1	0	0	(0	0)	4	1	0	0	0	0	12	0	0	0	0	0	0	.115	.115	.154	.269
2020 Pit	NL	1	2	0	0	0	0	(0	0)	0	0	0	1	2	0	0	0	0	0	0	0	0	.000	.500	.000	.500
Postseason		4	4	1	0	0	0	(0	0)	1	0	0	1	0	0	1	0	0	0	0	0	0	.250	.250	.250	.500
6 ML YEARS		114	278	61	17	2	7	(3	4)	103	31	35	32	25	0	94	1	0	0	0	0	2	.219	.286	.371	.657

Brent Suter

Pitches: L Bats: L Pos: RP-12; SP-4 SOO-ter Ht: 6'4" Wt: 213 Born: 8/29/1989 Age: 31

Year Team	Lg	G	GS	GF	IP	BFP	H	R	ER	HR	SH	SF	HB	TBB	IBB	SO	WP	W	L	Pct	Sv-Op	Hld	Vel	OPS	ERC	ERA
2016 Mil	NL	14	2	4	21.2	91	25	8	8	3	1	0	1	5	0	15	1	2	2	.500	0-0	2	84	.773	4.90	3.32
2017 Mil	NL	22	14	1	81.2	341	83	33	31	8	1	1	2	22	2	64	1	3	2	.600	0-0	0	86	.702	3.75	3.42
2018 Mil	NL	20	18	0	101.1	424	102	55	50	18	5	1	4	19	2	84	1	8	7	.533	0-0	0	87	.754	3.88	4.44
2019 Mil	NL	9	0	0	18.1	65	10	1	1	1	0	0	0	1	0	15	0	4	0	1.000	0-0	2	88	.435	0.88	0.49
2020 Mil	NL	16	4	1	31.2	129	30	13	11	4	0	0	1	5	0	38	0	2	0	1.000	0-0	2	86	.645	3.14	3.13
Postseason		1	0	0	1.0	5	1	0	0	0	0	0	0	0	0	0	0	0	0	-	0-0	0	87	.400	1.51	0.00
5 ML YEARS		81	38	6	254.2	1050	250	110	101	34	7	2	8	52	4	216	3	19	11	.633	0-0	6	86	.705	3.55	3.57

Kurt Suzuki

Bats: R Throws: R Pos: C-30;DH-2;PH-1 Ht: 5'11" Wt: 210 Born: 10/4/1983 Age: 37

Year Team	Lg	G	AB	H	2B	3B	HR	(Hm	Rd)	TB	R	RBI	RC	TBB	IBB	SO	HBP	SH	SF	SB	CS	GDP	Avg	OBP	Slg	OPS
2007 Oak	AL	68	213	53	13	0	7	(4	3)	87	27	39	33	24	0	39	3	3	5	0	0	4	.249	.327	.408	.735
2008 Oak	AL	148	530	148	25	1	7	(5	2)	196	54	42	66	44	2	69	11	2	1	2	3	20	.279	.346	.370	.716
2009 Oak	AL	147	570	156	37	1	15	(8	7)	240	74	88	77	28	0	59	8	1	7	8	2	14	.274	.313	.421	.734
2010 Oak	AL	131	495	120	18	2	13	(8	5)	181	55	71	54	33	3	49	12	0	4	3	2	22	.242	.303	.366	.669
2011 Oak	AL	134	460	109	26	0	14	(8	6)	177	54	44	42	38	1	64	7	3	7	2	2	14	.237	.301	.385	.686
2012 2 Tms		118	408	96	20	0	6	(3	3)	134	36	43	39	20	3	73	5	4	5	2	0	5	.235	.276	.328	.605
2013 2 Tms		94	285	66	13	1	5	(2	3)	96	25	32	34	22	6	35	3	2	4	2	0	7	.232	.290	.337	.627
2014 Min	AL	131	452	130	34	0	3	(1	2)	173	37	61	65	34	0	46	9	1	7	0	1	9	.288	.345	.383	.727
2015 Min	AL	131	433	104	17	0	5	(3	2)	136	36	50	46	29	4	59	7	6	4	0	0	14	.240	.296	.314	.610
2016 Min	AL	106	345	89	24	1	8	(4	4)	139	34	49	45	18	0	48	5	1	4	0	0	4	.258	.301	.403	.704
2017 Atl	NL	81	276	78	13	0	19	(8	11)	148	38	50	49	17	2	39	13	1	2	0	0	5	.283	.351	.536	.887
2018 Atl	NL	105	347	94	24	0	12	(5	7)	154	45	50	45	22	0	43	13	0	6	0	0	6	.271	.332	.444	.776
2019 Was	NL	85	280	74	11	0	17	(10	7)	136	37	63	53	20	1	36	6	0	3	0	1	10	.264	.324	.486	.809
2020 Was	NL	33	111	30	8	0	2	(0	2)	44	15	17	11	11	0	19	4	0	3	1	0	4	.270	.349	.396	.745
12 Oak	AL	75	262	57	15	0	1	(1	0)	75	19	18	16	9	0	53	3	2	2	1	0	3	.218	.250	.286	.536
12 Was		43	146	39	5	0	5	(2	3)	59	17	25	23	11	3	20	2	2	3	1	0	2	.267	.321	.404	.725
13 Was	NL	79	252	56	11	1	3	(0	3)	78	19	25	26	20	6	32	3	2	4	2	0	2	.222	.283	.310	.593
13 Oak	AL	15	33	10	2	0	2	(2	0)	18	6	7	8	2	0	3	0	0	0	0	0	0	.303	.343	.545	.888
Postseason		19	55	9	0	0	1	(0	1)	12	2	5	4	6	0	16	1	0	0	0	0	3	.164	.258	.218	.476
14 ML YEARS		1512	5205	1347	283	6	133	(69	64)	2041	567	699	659	360	22	678	106	24	62	20	11	138	.259	.316	.392	.708

Dansby Swanson

Bats: R Throws: R Pos: SS-60 Ht: 6'1" Wt: 190 Born: 2/11/1994 Age: 27

Year Team	Lg	G	AB	H	2B	3B	HR	(Hm	Rd)	TB	R	RBI	RC	TBB	IBB	SO	HBP	SH	SF	SB	CS	GDP	Avg	OBP	Slg	OPS
2016 Atl	NL	38	129	39	7	1	3	(1	2)	57	20	17	17	13	5	34	0	1	2	3	0	2	.302	.361	.442	.803
2017 Atl	NL	144	488	113	23	2	6	(2	4)	158	59	51	55	59	10	120	0	0	4	3	3	5	.232	.312	.324	.636
2018 Atl	NL	136	478	114	25	4	14	(7	7)	189	51	59	59	44	15	122	2	6	3	10	4	5	.238	.304	.395	.699
2019 Atl	NL	127	483	121	26	3	17	(8	9)	204	77	65	61	51	2	124	5	1	5	10	5	7	.251	.325	.422	.748
2020 Atl	NL	60	237	65	15	0	10	(6	4)	110	49	35	40	22	0	71	4	0	1	5	0	0	.274	.345	.464	.809
Postseason		5	18	7	3	0	0	(0	0)	10	3	2	3	1	0	6	0	0	0	0	0	0	.389	.421	.556	.977
5 ML YEARS		505	1815	452	96	10	50	(24	26)	718	256	227	232	189	32	471	11	8	15	31	12	21	.249	.321	.396	.717

Erik Swanson

Pitches: R Bats: R Pos: RP-9 Ht: 6'3" Wt: 220 Born: 9/4/1993 Age: 27

Year Team	Lg	G	GS	GF	IP	BFP	H	R	ER	HR	SH	SF	HB	TBB	IBB	SO	WP	W	L	Pct	Sv-Op	Hld	Vel	OPS	ERC	ERA
2019 Sea	AL	27	8	7	58.0	245	56	41	37	17	0	1	2	12	1	52	2	1	5	.167	2-2	1	93	.803	4.38	5.74
2020 Sea	AL	9	0	2	7.2	37	11	12	11	3	0	1	2	2	0	9	1	0	2	.000	0-1	1	96	1.093	9.84	12.91
2 ML YEARS		36	8	9	65.2	282	67	53	48	20	0	2	4	14	1	61	3	1	7	.125	2-3	2	93	.840	4.94	6.58

Noah Syndergaard

Pitches: R **Bats:** L **Pos:** P sin-DER-gard **Ht:** 6'6" **Wt:** 242 **Born:** 8/29/1992 **Age:** 28

Year Team	Lg	G	GS	GF	IP	BFP	H	R	ER	HR	SH	SF	HB	TBB	IBB	SO	WP	W	L	Pct	Sv-Op	Hld	Vel	OPS	ERC	ERA
2015 NYM	NL	24	24	0	150.0	603	126	60	54	19	5	3	3	31	2	166	6	9	7	.563	0-0	0	97	.645	2.70	3.24
2016 NYM	NL	31	30	0	183.2	744	168	61	53	11	3	4	2	43	2	218	10	14	9	.609	0-0	1	98	.639	2.79	2.60
2017 NYM	NL	7	7	0	30.1	124	29	14	10	0	1	1	1	3	1	34	3	1	2	.333	0-0	0	98	.573	2.13	2.97
2018 NYM	NL	25	25	0	154.1	644	148	55	52	9	3	3	7	39	2	155	2	13	4	.765	0-0	0	97	.651	3.16	3.03
2019 NYM	NL	32	32	0	197.2	825	194	101	94	24	3	8	6	50	2	202	4	10	8	.556	0-0	0	98	.714	3.66	4.28
Postseason		5	4	0	26.0	103	17	7	7	0	1	0	0	11	1	36	1	2	1	.667	0-0	1	98	.505	1.75	2.42
5 ML YEARS		119	118	0	716.0	2940	665	291	263	63	15	19	19	166	9	775	25	47	30	.610	0-0	1	98	.661	3.06	3.31

Jameson Taillon

Pitches: R **Bats:** R **Pos:** P TIE-yohn **Ht:** 6'5" **Wt:** 230 **Born:** 11/18/1991 **Age:** 29

Year Team	Lg	G	GS	GF	IP	BFP	H	R	ER	HR	SH	SF	HB	TBB	IBB	SO	WP	W	L	Pct	Sv-Op	Hld	Vel	OPS	ERC	ERA
2016 Pit	NL	18	18	0	104.0	418	99	40	39	13	4	1	3	17	1	85	1	5	4	.556	0-0	0	94	.702	3.21	3.38
2017 Pit	NL	25	25	0	133.2	587	152	69	66	11	8	4	4	46	3	125	7	8	7	.533	0-0	0	95	.789	4.61	4.44
2018 Pit	NL	32	32	0	191.0	785	179	69	68	20	4	2	6	46	4	179	2	14	10	.583	0-0	0	95	.681	3.26	3.20
2019 Pit	NL	7	7	0	37.1	158	34	24	17	4	0	1	2	8	1	30	1	2	3	.400	0-0	0	95	.680	2.98	4.10
4 ML YEARS		82	82	0	466.0	1948	464	202	190	48	16	8	15	117	9	419	11	29	24	.547	0-0	0	95	.718	3.60	3.67

Masahiro Tanaka

Pitches: R **Bats:** R **Pos:** SP-10 mah-sah-HEE-roh tuh-NAH-kah **Ht:** 6'3" **Wt:** 218 **Born:** 11/1/1988 **Age:** 32

Year Team	Lg	G	GS	GF	IP	BFP	H	R	ER	HR	SH	SF	HB	TBB	IBB	SO	WP	W	L	Pct	Sv-Op	Hld	Vel	OPS	ERC	ERA
2014 NYY	AL	20	20	0	136.1	542	123	47	42	15	2	3	4	21	0	141	4	13	5	.722	0-0	0	91	.657	2.83	2.77
2015 NYY	AL	24	24	0	154.0	609	126	66	60	25	1	8	1	27	0	139	4	12	7	.632	0-0	0	92	.674	2.65	3.51
2016 NYY	AL	31	31	0	199.2	805	179	75	68	22	4	3	3	36	0	165	7	14	4	.778	0-0	0	91	.645	2.80	3.07
2017 NYY	AL	30	30	0	178.1	752	180	100	94	35	1	2	7	41	1	194	7	13	12	.520	0-0	0	92	.771	4.23	4.74
2018 NYY	AL	27	27	0	156.0	635	141	68	65	25	3	2	7	35	0	159	3	12	6	.667	0-0	0	91	.711	3.46	3.75
2019 NYY	AL	32	31	0	182.0	759	186	95	90	28	0	4	4	40	0	149	7	11	9	.550	0-0	0	91	.751	3.89	4.45
2020 NYY	AL	10	10	0	48.0	197	48	25	19	9	0	0	2	8	0	44	0	3	3	.500	0-0	0	92	.749	3.92	3.56
Postseason		8	8	0	46.0	171	25	10	9	4	0	0	1	11	0	37	2	5	3	.625	0-0	0	92	.474	1.41	1.76
7 ML YEARS		174	173	0	1054.1	4299	983	476	438	159	11	22	26	208	1	991	32	78	46	.629	0-0	0	91	.706	3.35	3.74

Domingo Tapia

Pitches: R **Bats:** R **Pos:** RP-5 **Ht:** 6'3" **Wt:** 263 **Born:** 8/4/1991 **Age:** 29

Year Team	Lg	G	GS	GF	IP	BFP	H	R	ER	HR	SH	SF	HB	TBB	IBB	SO	WP	W	L	Pct	Sv-Op	Hld	Vel	OPS	ERC	ERA
2020 Bos	AL	5	0	0	4.1	19	4	1	1	1	0	0	0	2	0	4	0	0	0	-	0-0	0	99	.786	4.71	2.08

Raimel Tapia

Bats: L **Throws:** L **Pos:** LF-36;DH-12;RF-3;PR-2;PH-1 rye-MELL **Ht:** 6'3" **Wt:** 175 **Born:** 2/4/1994 **Age:** 27

Year Team	Lg	G	AB	H	2B	3B	HR	(Hm	Rd)	TB	R	RBI	RC	TBB	IBB	SO	HBP	SH	SF	SB	CS	GDP	Avg	OBP	Slg	OPS
2016 Col	NL	22	38	10	0	0	0	(0	0)	10	4	3	5	2	0	11	0	0	1	3	0	0	.263	.293	.263	.556
2017 Col	NL	70	160	46	12	2	2	(1	1)	68	27	16	20	8	1	36	2	1	0	5	2	3	.288	.329	.425	.754
2018 Col	NL	25	25	5	2	1	1	(0	1)	12	6	6	5	2	0	7	0	0	0	0	0	0	.200	.259	.480	.739
2019 Col	NL	138	426	117	23	5	9	(6	3)	177	54	44	54	21	0	100	0	0	2	9	3	2	.275	.309	.415	.724
2020 Col	NL	51	184	59	8	2	1	(0	1)	74	26	17	33	14	0	38	2	1	3	8	2	3	.321	.369	.402	.772
Postseason		1	1	1	0	0	0	(0	0)	1	0	0	1	0	0	0	0	0	0	0	0	0	1.000	1.000	1.000	2.000
5 ML YEARS		306	833	237	45	10	13	(7	6)	341	117	86	117	47	1	192	4	2	4	25	7	8	.285	.324	.409	.734

Stephen Tarpley

Pitches: L **Bats:** R **Pos:** RP-12 **Ht:** 6'0" **Wt:** 202 **Born:** 2/17/1993 **Age:** 28

Year Team	Lg	G	GS	GF	IP	BFP	H	R	ER	HR	SH	SF	HB	TBB	IBB	SO	WP	W	L	Pct	Sv-Op	Hld	Vel	OPS	ERC	ERA
2018 NYY	AL	10	0	3	9.0	40	6	3	3	0	0	0	0	6	0	13	0	0	0	-	0-0	0	93	.506	2.46	3.00
2019 NYY	AL	21	1	3	24.2	120	34	20	19	6	0	0	2	15	1	34	5	1	0	1.000	2-2	2	92	.988	8.99	6.93
2020 Mia	NL	12	0	3	11.0	53	11	12	11	2	2	1	3	8	2	11	0	2	2	.500	1-1	2	91	.944	6.98	9.00
Postseason		1	0	1	1.0	8	4	3	3	0	0	0	0	1	0	1	1	0	0	-	0-0	0	93	1.339	27.72	27.00
3 ML YEARS		43	1	9	44.2	213	51	35	33	8	2	1	5	29	3	58	5	3	2	.600	3-3	4	92	.886	6.99	6.65

Dillon Tate

Pitches: R **Bats:** R **Pos:** RP-12 **Ht:** 6'2" **Wt:** 195 **Born:** 5/1/1994 **Age:** 27

Year Team	Lg	G	GS	GF	IP	BFP	H	R	ER	HR	SH	SF	HB	TBB	IBB	SO	WP	W	L	Pct	Sv-Op	Hld	Vel	OPS	ERC	ERA
2019 Bal	AL	16	0	5	21.0	93	18	15	15	3	0	1	5	9	0	20	2	0	2	.000	0-0	0	94	.729	4.64	6.43
2020 Bal	AL	12	0	1	16.2	64	9	7	6	1	0	2	2	5	0	14	1	1	1	.500	0-0	2	94	.486	1.66	3.24
2 ML YEARS		28	0	6	37.2	157	27	22	21	4	0	3	7	14	0	34	3	1	3	.250	0-0	3	94	.629	3.22	5.02

Fernando Tatis Jr.

Bats: R **Throws:** R **Pos:** SS-57;DH-2   **Ht:** 6'3" **Wt:** 217 **Born:** 1/2/1999 **Age:** 22

Year	Team	Lg	G	AB	H	2B	3B	HR	(Hm	Rd)	TB	R	RBI	RC	TBB	IBB	SO	HBP	SH	SF	SB	CS	GDP	Avg	OBP	Slg	OPS
2019	SD	NL	84	334	106	13	6	22	(10	12)	197	61	53	73	30	1	110	5	0	3	16	6	4	.317	.379	.590	.969
2020	SD	NL	59	224	62	11	2	17	(8	9)	128	50	45	48	27	1	61	5	0	1	11	3	6	.277	.366	.571	.937
	2 ML YEARS		143	558	168	24	8	39	(18	21)	325	111	98	121	57	2	171	10	0	4	27	9	10	.301	.374	.582	.956

Mike Tauchman

Bats: L **Throws:** L **Pos:** LF-20;RF-19;CF-5;PH-2;PR-2;DH-1   **Ht:** 6'2" **Wt:** 220 **Born:** 12/3/1990 **Age:** 30

Year	Team	Lg	G	AB	H	2B	3B	HR	(Hm	Rd)	TB	R	RBI	RC	TBB	IBB	SO	HBP	SH	SF	SB	CS	GDP	Avg	OBP	Slg	OPS
2017	Col	NL	31	27	6	0	1	0	(0	0)	8	2	2	2	5	0	10	0	0	0	1	2	1	.222	.344	.296	.640
2018	Col	NL	21	32	3	1	0	0	(0	0)	4	5	0	0	4	0	15	0	1	0	1	0	0	.094	.194	.125	.319
2019	NYY	AL	87	260	72	18	1	13	(7	6)	131	46	47	50	34	0	71	1	0	1	6	0	9	.277	.361	.504	.865
2020	NYY	AL	43	95	23	6	0	0	(0	0)	29	18	14	13	14	3	26	1	0	1	6	0	3	.242	.342	.305	.648
	4 ML YEARS		182	414	104	25	2	13	(7	6)	172	71	63	65	57	3	122	2	1	2	14	2	13	.251	.343	.415	.759

Leody Taveras

Bats: B **Throws:** R **Pos:** CF-33   **Ht:** 6'2" **Wt:** 195 **Born:** 9/8/1998 **Age:** 22

Year	Team	Lg	G	AB	H	2B	3B	HR	(Hm	Rd)	TB	R	RBI	RC	TBB	IBB	SO	HBP	SH	SF	SB	CS	GDP	Avg	OBP	Slg	OPS
2016	2 Tms	Low	62	267	68	12	4	1	(-	-)	91	36	24	31	19	0	50	0	0	2	14	5	4	.255	.302	.341	.643
2017	Hkry	A	134	522	130	20	7	8	(-	-)	188	73	50	73	47	0	92	2	3	3	20	6	10	.249	.312	.360	.672
2018	DwnEast	A+	132	521	128	16	7	5	(-	-)	173	65	48	62	51	1	96	0	7	1	19	11	6	.246	.312	.332	.644
2019	Frisco	AA	65	264	70	12	4	3	(-	-)	99	32	31	32	23	0	60	0	2	4	11	8	8	.265	.320	.375	.695
2019	DwnEast	A+	66	255	75	7	4	2	(-	-)	96	44	25	42	31	3	62	0	2	2	21	5	3	.294	.368	.376	.745
2020	Tex	AL	33	119	27	6	1	4	(2	2)	47	20	6	15	14	0	43	0	1	0	8	0	0	.227	.308	.395	.703

Beau Taylor

Bats: L **Throws:** R **Pos:** C-7   **Ht:** 5'11" **Wt:** 205 **Born:** 2/13/1990 **Age:** 31

Year	Team	Lg	G	AB	H	2B	3B	HR	(Hm	Rd)	TB	R	RBI	RC	TBB	IBB	SO	HBP	SH	SF	SB	CS	GDP	Avg	OBP	Slg	OPS
2018	Oak	AL	7	5	1	1	0	0	(0	0)	2	0	0	0	1	0	2	0	0	0	0	0	0	.200	.333	.400	.733
2019	2 Tms	AL	11	25	4	0	0	2	(1	1)	10	3	2	2	4	0	7	1	0	0	0	0	0	.160	.300	.400	.700
2020	Cle	AL	7	21	1	0	0	0	(0	0)	1	1	2	0	2	0	9	0	1	0	0	0	0	.048	.130	.048	.178
19	Oak	AL	10	23	4	0	0	2	(1	1)	10	3	2	2	4	0	6	1	0	0	0	0	0	.174	.321	.435	.756
19	Tor	AL	1	2	0	0	0	0	(0	0)	0	0	0	0	0	0	1	0	0	0	0	0	0	.000	.000	.000	.000
	3 ML YEARS		25	51	6	1	0	2	(1	1)	13	4	4	2	7	0	18	1	1	0	0	0	0	.118	.237	.255	.492

Blake Taylor

Pitches: L **Bats:** L **Pos:** RP-22   **Ht:** 6'3" **Wt:** 220 **Born:** 8/17/1995 **Age:** 25

	HOW MUCH PITCHED						WHAT HE GAVE UP											THE RESULTS							
Year	Team	Lg	G	GS	GF	IP	BFP	H	R	ER	HR	SH	SF	HB	TBB	IBB	SO	WP	W	L	Pct	Sv-Op	Hld	Vel	OPS	ERC	ERA
2020	Hou	AL	22	0	5	20.2	87	13	7	5	2	0	0	0	12	1	17	1	2	1	.667	1-2	5	94	.567	2.64	2.18

Chris Taylor

Bats: R **Throws:** R **Pos:** SS-20;LF-19;2B-13;CF-6;DH-6;PH-4;PR-1   **Ht:** 6'1" **Wt:** 196 **Born:** 8/29/1990 **Age:** 30

Year	Team	Lg	G	AB	H	2B	3B	HR	(Hm	Rd)	TB	R	RBI	RC	TBB	IBB	SO	HBP	SH	SF	SB	CS	GDP	Avg	OBP	Slg	OPS
2014	Sea	AL	47	136	39	8	0	0	(0	0)	47	16	9	18	11	0	39	2	1	1	5	2	3	.287	.347	.346	.692
2015	Sea	AL	37	94	16	3	1	0	(0	0)	21	9	1	1	6	0	31	0	2	0	3	2	0	.170	.220	.223	.443
2016	2 Tms		36	61	13	2	2	1	(0	1)	22	8	7	5	4	1	15	0	0	0	0	0	3	.213	.262	.361	.622
2017	LAD	NL	140	514	148	34	5	21	(7	14)	255	85	72	88	50	0	142	3	0	1	17	4	2	.288	.354	.496	.850
2018	LAD	NL	155	536	136	35	8	17	(10	7)	238	85	63	75	55	0	178	9	0	4	9	6	5	.254	.331	.444	.775
2019	LAD	NL	124	366	96	29	4	12	(8	4)	169	52	52	60	37	3	115	4	2	5	8	0	6	.262	.333	.462	.794
2020	LAD	NL	56	185	50	10	2	8	(5	3)	88	30	32	36	26	0	55	2	1	0	3	2	3	.270	.366	.476	.842
16	Sea	AL	2	3	1	0	0	0	(0	0)	1	0	0	0	0	0	2	0	0	0	0	0	0	.333	.333	.333	.667
16	LAD	NL	34	58	12	2	2	1	(0	1)	21	8	7	5	4	1	13	0	0	0	0	0	3	.207	.258	.362	.620
	Postseason		35	106	27	5	2	4	(2	2)	48	19	10	19	23	0	27	1	0	0	1	1	0	.255	.392	.453	.845
	7 ML YEARS		595	1892	498	121	22	59	(30	29)	840	285	236	283	189	4	575	20	6	11	45	16	22	.263	.335	.444	.779

Josh Taylor

Pitches: L **Bats:** L **Pos:** RP-8   **Ht:** 6'5" **Wt:** 245 **Born:** 3/2/1993 **Age:** 28

	HOW MUCH PITCHED						WHAT HE GAVE UP											THE RESULTS							
Year	Team	Lg	G	GS	GF	IP	BFP	H	R	ER	HR	SH	SF	HB	TBB	IBB	SO	WP	W	L	Pct	Sv-Op	Hld	Vel	OPS	ERC	ERA
2019	Bos	AL	52	1	8	47.1	194	40	17	16	5	0	1	2	16	1	62	3	2	2	.500	0-1	4	95	.642	3.22	3.04
2020	Bos	AL	8	0	1	7.1	36	7	8	8	2	0	0	1	5	0	7	0	1	1	.500	0-2	1	94	.861	6.56	9.82
	2 ML YEARS		60	1	9	54.2	230	47	25	24	7	0	1	3	21	1	69	3	3	3	.500	0-3	5	95	.675	3.63	3.95

Michael A. Taylor

Bats: R **Throws:** R **Pos:** LF-14;CF-11;RF-11;PH-4;DH-2;PR-2 **Ht:** 6'4" **Wt:** 215 **Born:** 3/26/1991 **Age:** 30

							BATTING														RUNNING			AVERAGES			
Year Team	Lg	G	AB	H	2B	3B	HR	(Hm	Rd)	TB	R	RBI	RC	TBB	IBB	SO	HBP	SH	SF	SB	CS	GDP	Avg	OBP	Slg	OPS
2014 Was	NL	17	39	8	3	0	1	(0	1)	14	5	5	3	3	0	17	1	0	0	0	2	1	.205	.279	.359	.638
2015 Was	NL	138	472	108	15	2	14	(6	8)	169	49	63	60	35	9	158	1	1	2	16	3	5	.229	.282	.358	.640
2016 Was	NL	76	221	51	11	0	7	(1	6)	83	28	16	20	14	0	77	1	0	1	14	3	2	.231	.278	.376	.654
2017 Was	NL	118	399	108	23	3	19	(11	8)	194	55	53	57	29	3	137	1	1	2	17	7	3	.271	.320	.486	.806
2018 Was	NL	134	353	80	22	3	6	(2	4)	126	46	28	33	29	2	116	1	2	0	24	6	9	.227	.287	.357	.644
2019 Was	NL	53	88	22	7	0	1	(1	0)	32	10	3	7	7	0	34	0	2	0	6	0	0	.250	.305	.364	.669
2020 Was	NL	38	92	18	6	0	5	(2	3)	39	11	16	9	6	0	27	1	0	0	0	0	2	.196	.253	.424	.676
Postseason		16	38	12	0	0	4	(1	3)	24	7	10	11	4	0	13	1	0	0	0	0	0	.316	.395	.632	1.027
7 ML YEARS		574	1664	395	87	8	53	(23	30)	657	204	184	189	123	14	566	6	6	5	77	21	22	.237	.291	.395	.686

Tyrone Taylor

Bats: R **Throws:** R **Pos:** RF-10;CF-9;PH-5;LF-2;PR-1 **Ht:** 6'0" **Wt:** 194 **Born:** 1/22/1994 **Age:** 27

							BATTING														RUNNING			AVERAGES			
Year Team	Lg	G	AB	H	2B	3B	HR	(Hm	Rd)	TB	R	RBI	RC	TBB	IBB	SO	HBP	SH	SF	SB	CS	GDP	Avg	OBP	Slg	OPS
2019 Mil	NL	15	10	4	2	0	0	(0	0)	6	1	1	3	1	0	1	1	0	0	0	0	0	.400	.500	.600	1.100
2020 Mil	NL	22	38	9	4	0	2	(0	2)	19	6	6	5	2	0	8	1	0	0	0	0	0	.237	.293	.500	.793
2 ML YEARS		37	48	13	6	0	2	(0	2)	25	7	7	8	3	0	9	2	0	0	0	0	1	.271	.340	.521	.860

Julio Teheran

Pitches: R **Bats:** R **Pos:** SP-9; RP-1   tay-RAHN   **Ht:** 6'2" **Wt:** 205 **Born:** 1/27/1991 **Age:** 30

		HOW MUCH PITCHED					WHAT HE GAVE UP										THE RESULTS								
Year Team	Lg	G	GS	GF	IP	BFP	H	R	ER	HR	SH	SF	HB	TBB	IBB	SO	WP	W	L	Pct	Sv-Op	Hld	Vel	OPS	ERC	ERA
2011 Atl	NL	5	3	0	19.2	87	21	11	11	4	2	1	0	8	0	10	1	1	1	.500	0-0	0	93	.828	5.19	5.03
2012 Atl	NL	2	1	0	6.1	24	5	4	4	0	0	0	0	1	0	5	0	0	0	-	0-0	0	92	.467	1.64	5.68
2013 Atl	NL	30	30	0	185.2	774	173	69	66	22	8	5	13	45	4	170	2	14	8	.636	0-0	0	92	.700	3.45	3.20
2014 Atl	NL	33	33	0	221.0	884	188	82	71	22	13	4	4	51	4	186	1	14	13	.519	0-0	0	90	.639	2.71	2.89
2015 Atl	NL	33	33	0	200.2	843	189	99	90	27	10	3	9	73	3	171	2	11	8	.579	0-0	0	91	.737	4.07	4.04
2016 Atl	NL	30	30	0	188.0	758	157	70	67	22	4	1	9	41	2	167	7	7	10	.412	0-0	0	91	.650	2.79	3.21
2017 Atl	NL	32	32	0	188.1	812	186	103	94	31	7	3	7	72	3	151	6	11	13	.458	0-0	0	91	.772	4.52	4.49
2018 Atl	NL	31	31	0	175.2	724	122	80	77	26	3	5	9	84	3	162	2	9	9	.500	0-0	0	90	.672	3.25	3.94
2019 Atl	NL	33	33	0	174.2	754	148	81	74	22	6	5	14	83	3	162	5	10	11	.476	0-0	0	90	.717	3.99	3.81
2020 LAA	AL	10	9	0	31.1	149	39	35	35	12	0	3	2	16	0	20	1	0	4	.000	0-0	0	89	1.023	8.56	10.05
Postseason		4	1	2	6.0	29	10	7	7	1	0	2	0	2	1	9	1	0	2	.000	0-0	0	93	1.014	8.24	10.50
10 ML YEARS		239	235	0	1391.1	5809	1228	634	589	188	53	30	67	474	22	1204	27	77	77	.500	0-0	0	91	.707	3.62	3.81

Anderson Tejeda

Bats: B **Throws:** R **Pos:** SS-18;2B-4;DH-1 **Ht:** 6'0" **Wt:** 200 **Born:** 5/1/1998 **Age:** 23

							BATTING														RUNNING			AVERAGES			
Year Team	Lg	G	AB	H	2B	3B	HR	(Hm	Rd)	TB	R	RBI	RC	TBB	IBB	SO	HBP	SH	SF	SB	CS	GDP	Avg	OBP	Slg	OPS
2020 Tex	AL	23	75	19	4	1	3	(0	3)	34	7	8	7	2	0	30	0	0	0	4	1	2	.253	.273	.453	.726

Rowdy Tellez

Bats: L **Throws:** L **Pos:** 1B-19;DH-11;PH-6 **Ht:** 6'4" **Wt:** 255 **Born:** 3/16/1995 **Age:** 26

							BATTING														RUNNING			AVERAGES			
Year Team	Lg	G	AB	H	2B	3B	HR	(Hm	Rd)	TB	R	RBI	RC	TBB	IBB	SO	HBP	SH	SF	SB	CS	GDP	Avg	OBP	Slg	OPS
2018 Tor	AL	23	70	22	9	0	4	(3	1)	43	10	14	17	2	0	21	0	0	1	0	0	0	.314	.329	.614	.943
2019 Tor	AL	111	370	84	19	0	21	(12	9)	166	49	54	47	29	3	116	7	0	3	1	1	9	.227	.293	.449	.742
2020 Tor	AL	35	113	32	5	0	8	(5	3)	61	20	23	22	11	1	20	1	0	2	0	1	1	.283	.346	.540	.886
3 ML YEARS		169	553	138	33	0	33	(20	13)	270	79	91	86	42	4	157	8	0	6	1	2	10	.250	.309	.488	.797

Ryan Tepera

Pitches: R **Bats:** R **Pos:** RP-21   tuh-PAIR-uh   **Ht:** 6'1" **Wt:** 195 **Born:** 11/3/1987 **Age:** 33

		HOW MUCH PITCHED					WHAT HE GAVE UP										THE RESULTS								
Year Team	Lg	G	GS	GF	IP	BFP	H	R	ER	HR	SH	SF	HB	TBB	IBB	SO	WP	W	L	Pct	Sv-Op	Hld	Vel	OPS	ERC	ERA
2015 Tor	AL	32	0	12	33.0	128	23	14	12	8	0	0	3	6	0	22	2	0	2	.000	1-1	0	95	.670	2.87	3.27
2016 Tor	AL	20	0	13	18.1	85	17	8	6	1	1	0	3	8	1	18	3	0	1	.000	0-0	0	95	.635	3.81	2.95
2017 Tor	AL	73	0	12	77.2	319	57	35	31	7	1	1	8	31	4	81	5	7	1	.875	2-4	17	95	.633	2.94	3.59
2018 Tor	AL	68	0	19	64.2	263	55	27	26	9	0	3	4	24	1	68	5	5	5	.500	7-15	19	95	.738	3.77	3.62
2019 Tor	AL	23	1	7	21.2	91	20	12	12	5	1	2	0	8	2	14	2	0	2	.000	0-0	2	94	.824	4.29	4.98
2020 ChC	NL	21	0	1	20.2	89	17	9	9	2	0	1	1	12	0	31	1	0	1	.000	0-1	2	94	.684	4.01	3.92
Postseason		2	0	1	2.1	14	5	4	4	0	0	3	0	2	0	1	0	0	0	-	0-0	0	93	1.167	12.37	15.43
6 ML YEARS		237	1	64	236.0	975	189	105	96	32	3	7	19	89	8	234	18	12	12	.500	10-21	40	95	.689	3.45	3.66

Matt Thaiss

Bats: L **Throws:** R **Pos:** 1B-2;DH-2;2B-1;3B-1;LF-1;PR-1   THICE   **Ht:** 6'0" **Wt:** 215 **Born:** 5/6/1995 **Age:** 26

							BATTING														RUNNING			AVERAGES			
Year Team	Lg	G	AB	H	2B	3B	HR	(Hm	Rd)	TB	R	RBI	RC	TBB	IBB	SO	HBP	SH	SF	SB	CS	GDP	Avg	OBP	Slg	OPS
2019 LAA	AL	53	147	31	7	0	8	(8	0)	62	17	23	20	17	0	52	0	0	0	0	0	4	.211	.293	.422	.714
2020 LAA	AL	8	21	3	0	0	1	(0	1)	6	3	1	0	4	0	8	0	0	0	0	0	1	.143	.280	.286	.566
2 ML YEARS		61	168	34	7	0	9	(8	1)	68	20	24	20	21	0	60	0	0	0	0	0	5	.202	.291	.405	.696

Eric Thames

Bats: L **Throws:** R **Pos:** 1B-27;DH-12;PH-3   **Ht:** 5'11" **Wt:** 235 **Born:** 11/10/1986 **Age:** 34

Year	Team	Lg	G	AB	H	2B	3B	HR	(Hm	Rd)	TB	R	RBI	RC	TBB	IBB	SO	HBP	SH	SF	SB	CS	GDP	Avg	OBP	Slg	OPS
2011	Tor	AL	95	362	95	24	5	12	(10	2)	165	58	37	42	23	0	88	5	1	3	2	1	7	.262	.313	.456	.769
2012	2 Tms	AL	86	271	63	12	3	9	(6	3)	108	27	25	25	15	0	87	1	1	2	1	1	7	.232	.273	.399	.672
2017	Mil	NL	138	469	116	26	4	31	(20	11)	243	83	63	70	75	5	163	7	0	0	4	2	6	.247	.359	.518	.877
2018	Mil	NL	96	247	54	10	3	16	(11	5)	118	41	37	40	29	4	97	2	0	0	7	0	3	.219	.306	.478	.783
2019	Mil	NL	149	396	98	23	2	25	(14	11)	200	67	61	64	51	4	140	10	0	2	3	2	0	.247	.346	.505	.851
2020	Was	NL	41	123	25	5	0	3	(1	2)	39	10	12	11	14	1	42	3	0	0	1	0	2	.203	.300	.317	.617
12	Tor	AL	46	148	36	7	1	3	(1	2)	54	17	11	13	9	0	40	1	0	2	0	1	7	.243	.288	.365	.652
12	Sea	AL	40	123	27	5	2	6	(5	1)	54	10	14	12	6	0	47	0	1	0	1	0	0	.220	.256	.439	.695
	Postseason		1	4	2	1	0	1	(0	1)	6	1	1	1	0	0	1	0	0	0	0	0	1	.500	.500	1.500	2.000
	6 ML YEARS		605	1868	451	100	17	96	(62	34)	873	286	235	259	207	14	617	28	2	7	18	6	25	.241	.325	.467	.792

Caleb Thielbar

Pitches: L **Bats:** R **Pos:** RP-17   THEEL-bar   **Ht:** 6'0" **Wt:** 205 **Born:** 1/31/1987 **Age:** 34

Year	Team	Lg	G	GS	GF	IP	BFP	H	R	ER	HR	SH	SF	HB	TBB	IBB	SO	WP	W	L	Pct	Sv-Op	Hld	Vel	OPS	ERC	ERA
2013	Min	AL	49	0	16	46.0	171	24	11	9	4	0	1	0	14	4	39	1	3	2	.600	0-0	1	90	.530	1.38	1.76
2014	Min	AL	54	0	7	47.2	206	51	19	18	3	1	6	1	16	1	35	0	2	1	.667	0-1	7	89	.738	4.01	3.40
2015	Min	AL	6	0	1	5.0	20	5	3	3	0	1	0	0	0	0	5	1	0	0	-	0-0	1	90	.579	1.95	5.40
2020	Min	AL	17	0	3	20.0	82	14	6	5	0	0	0	0	9	0	22	2	2	1	.667	0-0	1	90	.500	2.05	2.25
	4 ML YEARS		126	0	27	118.2	479	94	39	35	7	2	7	1	39	5	101	4	7	4	.636	0-1	10	89	.616	2.45	2.65

Lane Thomas

Bats: R **Throws:** R **Pos:** RF-14;CF-7;PH-2;PR-1   **Ht:** 6'0" **Wt:** 185 **Born:** 8/23/1995 **Age:** 25

Year	Team	Lg	G	AB	H	2B	3B	HR	(Hm	Rd)	TB	R	RBI	RC	TBB	IBB	SO	HBP	SH	SF	SB	CS	GDP	Avg	OBP	Slg	OPS
2019	StL	NL	34	38	12	0	1	4	(3	1)	26	6	12	12	4	0	8	2	0	0	1	1	1	.316	.409	.684	1.093
2020	StL	NL	18	36	4	2	0	1	(1	0)	9	5	2	1	4	0	13	0	0	0	0	0	1	.111	.200	.250	.450
	2 ML YEARS		52	74	16	2	1	5	(4	1)	35	11	14	13	8	0	21	2	0	0	1	1	2	.216	.310	.473	.782

Ryan Thompson

Pitches: R **Bats:** R **Pos:** RP-24; SP-1   **Ht:** 6'5" **Wt:** 210 **Born:** 6/26/1992 **Age:** 29

Year	Team	Lg	G	GS	GF	IP	BFP	H	R	ER	HR	SH	SF	HB	TBB	IBB	SO	WP	W	L	Pct	Sv-Op	Hld	Vel	OPS	ERC	ERA
2020	TB	AL	25	1	3	26.1	114	29	15	13	4	0	0	0	8	0	23	0	1	2	.333	1-1	4	91	.749	4.61	4.44

Tyler Thornburg

Pitches: R **Bats:** R **Pos:** RP-7   **Ht:** 5'11" **Wt:** 190 **Born:** 9/29/1988 **Age:** 32

Year	Team	Lg	G	GS	GF	IP	BFP	H	R	ER	HR	SH	SF	HB	TBB	IBB	SO	WP	W	L	Pct	Sv-Op	Hld	Vel	OPS	ERC	ERA
2012	Mil	NL	8	3	3	22.0	95	24	11	11	8	1	0	0	7	0	20	1	0	0	-	0-0	0	93	.922	6.44	4.50
2013	Mil	NL	18	7	4	66.2	270	53	17	15	1	4	1	3	26	2	48	1	3	1	.750	0-0	0	94	.575	2.59	2.03
2014	Mil	NL	27	0	4	29.2	131	24	14	14	1	1	1	0	21	0	28	4	3	1	.750	0-0	5	94	.670	3.71	4.25
2015	Mil	NL	24	0	9	34.1	151	31	22	14	7	0	2	3	12	1	34	3	0	2	.000	0-0	1	92	.723	4.20	3.67
2016	Mil	NL	67	0	23	67.0	263	38	19	16	6	6	1	2	25	1	90	4	8	5	.615	13-21	20	94	.541	1.82	2.15
2018	Bos	AL	25	0	9	24.0	107	28	15	15	6	0	1	1	10	0	21	2	2	0	1.000	0-0	3	93	.901	6.56	5.63
2019	Bos	AL	16	0	4	18.2	86	21	16	16	4	0	0	1	10	0	22	1	0	0	-	0-0	0	94	.972	6.51	7.71
2020	Cin	NL	7	0	2	7.0	32	6	3	3	0	0	0	1	5	0	10	1	0	0	-	0-0	1	93	.603	3.64	3.86
	8 ML YEARS		192	10	58	269.1	1135	225	117	104	33	6	6	11	116	4	273	18	16	9	.640	13-21	30	93	.689	3.59	3.48

Trent Thornton

Pitches: R **Bats:** R **Pos:** SP-3   **Ht:** 6'0" **Wt:** 195 **Born:** 9/30/1993 **Age:** 27

Year	Team	Lg	G	GS	GF	IP	BFP	H	R	ER	HR	SH	SF	HB	TBB	IBB	SO	WP	W	L	Pct	Sv-Op	Hld	Vel	OPS	ERC	ERA
2019	Tor	AL	32	29	0	154.1	677	156	87	83	24	1	7	5	61	0	149	5	6	9	.400	0-0	0	93	.768	4.60	4.84
2020	Tor	AL	3	3	0	5.2	33	15	7	7	0	0	1	0	3	0	6	0	0	0	-	0-0	0	92	1.166	15.41	11.12
	2 ML YEARS		35	32	0	160.0	710	171	94	90	24	1	8	5	64	0	155	5	6	9	.400	0-0	0	93	.786	4.92	5.06

Lewis Thorpe

Pitches: L **Bats:** R **Pos:** RP-6; SP-1   **Ht:** 6'1" **Wt:** 218 **Born:** 11/23/1995 **Age:** 25

Year	Team	Lg	G	GS	GF	IP	BFP	H	R	ER	HR	SH	SF	HB	TBB	IBB	SO	WP	W	L	Pct	Sv-Op	Hld	Vel	OPS	ERC	ERA
2019	Min	AL	12	2	3	27.2	124	38	19	19	3	0	1	0	10	0	31	3	3	2	.600	0-2	0	91	.918	6.41	6.18
2020	Min	AL	7	1	3	16.1	77	24	12	11	4	0	0	0	10	0	10	0	0	1	.000	0-0	0	90	1.039	9.70	6.06
	2 ML YEARS		19	3	6	44.0	201	62	31	30	7	0	1	0	20	0	41	3	3	3	.500	0-2	0	91	.964	7.58	6.14

Jesus Tinoco

Pitches: R Bats: R Pos: RP-6   hay-SOOS tih-NO-ko   Ht: 6'4" Wt: 258 Born: 4/30/1995 Age: 26

Year Team	Lg	G	GS	GF	IP	BFP	H	R	ER	HR	SH	SF	HB	TBB	IBB	SO	WP	W	L	Pct	Sv-Op	Hld	Vel	OPS	ERC	ERA
2019 Col	NL	24	0	3	36.0	161	36	23	19	12	0	1	1	22	1	28	1	0	3	.000	1-1	2	94	.965	6.94	4.75
2020 2 Tms	NL	6	0	3	8.2	32	3	1	1	0	0	0	0	7	0	6	2	0	0	-	0-0	0	94	.433	1.80	1.04
20 Mia		3	0	1	5.0	15	0	0	0	0	0	0	0	3	0	3	0	0	0	-	0-0	0	94	.200	0.45	0.00
20 Col		3	0	2	3.2	17	3	1	1	0	0	0	0	4	0	3	2	0	0	-	0-0	0	94	.643	5.09	2.45
2 ML YEARS		30	0	6	44.2	193	39	24	20	12	0	1	1	29	1	34	3	0	3	.000	1-1	2	94	.882	5.86	4.03

Josh Tomlin

Pitches: R Bats: R Pos: RP-12; SP-5   Ht: 6'1" Wt: 190 Born: 10/19/1984 Age: 36

Year Team	Lg	G	GS	GF	IP	BFP	H	R	ER	HR	SH	SF	HB	TBB	IBB	SO	WP	W	L	Pct	Sv-Op	Hld	Vel	OPS	ERC	ERA
2010 Cle	AL	12	12	0	73.0	301	72	38	37	10	3	3	3	19	3	43	1	6	4	.600	0-0	0	89	.773	3.89	4.56
2011 Cle	AL	26	26	0	165.1	662	157	80	78	24	1	3	3	21	2	89	3	12	7	.632	0-0	0	88	.712	3.11	4.25
2012 Cle	AL	21	16	0	103.1	452	126	74	73	18	2	3	3	25	3	56	4	5	8	.385	0-0	0	89	.860	5.34	6.36
2013 Cle	AL	1	0	0	2.0	9	2	0	0	0	0	0	0	0	0	0	0	0	0	-	0-0	0	90	.500	1.68	0.00
2014 Cle	AL	25	16	6	104.0	446	120	66	55	18	1	3	1	14	3	94	6	6	9	.400	0-0	0	89	.781	4.28	4.76
2015 Cle	AL	10	10	0	65.2	251	47	22	22	13	0	0	2	8	0	57	1	7	2	.778	0-0	0	88	.642	2.24	3.02
2016 Cle	AL	30	29	1	174.0	725	187	97	85	36	4	4	3	20	2	118	4	13	9	.591	0-0	0	88	.778	4.06	4.40
2017 Cle	AL	26	26	0	141.0	585	166	80	78	23	0	3	4	14	0	109	1	10	9	.526	0-0	0	88	.807	4.49	4.98
2018 Cle	AL	32	9	19	70.1	321	92	52	48	25	0	2	4	12	1	46	5	2	5	.286	0-0	0	88	.947	6.86	6.14
2019 Atl	NL	51	1	21	79.1	320	82	35	33	14	4	2	0	7	0	51	2	2	1	.667	2-4	7	89	.744	3.53	3.74
2020 Atl	NL	17	5	2	39.2	163	40	22	21	6	1	1	1	8	2	36	1	2	2	.500	0-0	1	88	.737	3.75	4.76
Postseason		8	4	2	24.1	93	17	9	9	1	0	0	0	5	0	17	0	3	1	.750	0-0	1	88	.498	1.59	3.33
11 ML YEARS		251	150	49	1017.2	4235	1091	566	530	187	16	24	24	148	16	699	28	65	56	.537	2-4	8	88	.781	4.09	4.69

Justin Topa

Pitches: R Bats: R Pos: RP-6   Ht: 6'4" Wt: 200 Born: 3/7/1991 Age: 30

Year Team	Lg	G	GS	GF	IP	BFP	H	R	ER	HR	SH	SF	HB	TBB	IBB	SO	WP	W	L	Pct	Sv-Op	Hld	Vel	OPS	ERC	ERA
2020 Mil	NL	6	0	2	7.2	30	7	3	2	1	0	0	0	0	0	12	0	0	1	.000	0-0	0	98	.633	2.25	2.35

Abraham Toro

Bats: B Throws: R Pos: 3B-14;DH-11;PH-10;1B-4;2B-1;PR-1   Ht: 6'0" Wt: 206 Born: 12/20/1996 Age: 24

Year Team	Lg	G	AB	H	2B	3B	HR	(Hm	Rd)	TB	R	RBI	RC	TBB	IBB	SO	HBP	SH	SF	SB	CS	GDP	Avg	OBP	Slg	OPS
2019 Hou	AL	25	78	17	3	2	2	(1	1)	30	13	9	8	9	0	19	1	0	1	1	1	2	.218	.303	.385	.688
2020 Hou	AL	33	87	13	2	0	3	(1	2)	24	13	9	5	3	0	23	7	0	0	1	1	1	.149	.237	.276	.513
2 ML YEARS		58	165	30	5	2	5	(2	3)	54	26	18	13	12	0	42	8	0	1	2	2	3	.182	.269	.327	.596

Luis Torrens

Bats: R Throws: R Pos: C-24;PH-2;DH-1   Ht: 6'0" Wt: 208 Born: 5/2/1996 Age: 25

Year Team	Lg	G	AB	H	2B	3B	HR	(Hm	Rd)	TB	R	RBI	RC	TBB	IBB	SO	HBP	SH	SF	SB	CS	GDP	Avg	OBP	Slg	OPS
2017 SD	NL	56	123	20	3	1	0	(0	0)	25	7	7	4	12	3	30	1	3	0	0	0	4	.163	.243	.203	.446
2019 SD	NL	7	14	3	1	0	0	(0	0)	4	2	0	1	2	0	6	0	0	0	0	0	1	.214	.313	.286	.598
2020 2 Tms		25	70	18	5	0	1	(1	0)	26	5	6	7	7	0	15	0	1	0	0	0	1	.257	.325	.371	.696
20 SD	NL	7	11	3	1	0	0	(0	0)	4	0	0	1	1	0	2	0	1	0	0	0	0	.273	.333	.364	.697
20 Sea	AL	18	59	15	4	0	1	(1	0)	22	5	6	6	6	0	13	0	0	0	0	0	1	.254	.323	.373	.696
3 ML YEARS		88	207	41	9	1	1	(1	0)	55	14	13	12	21	3	51	1	4	0	0	0	6	.198	.275	.266	.541

Gleyber Torres

Bats: R Throws: R Pos: SS-40;PH-2   Ht: 6'1" Wt: 205 Born: 12/13/1996 Age: 24

Year Team	Lg	G	AB	H	2B	3B	HR	(Hm	Rd)	TB	R	RBI	RC	TBB	IBB	SO	HBP	SH	SF	SB	CS	GDP	Avg	OBP	Slg	OPS
2018 NYY	AL	123	431	117	16	1	24	(13	11)	207	54	77	78	42	3	122	5	1	5	6	2	8	.271	.340	.480	.820
2019 NYY	AL	144	546	152	26	0	38	(20	18)	292	96	90	101	48	3	129	3	1	6	5	2	10	.278	.337	.535	.871
2020 NYY	AL	42	136	33	8	0	3	(1	2)	50	17	16	18	22	0	28	2	0	1	1	0	5	.243	.356	.368	.724
Postseason		14	53	16	5	0	3	(1	2)	30	9	10	10	5	0	9	0	0	0	2	0	2	.302	.362	.566	.928
3 ML YEARS		309	1113	302	50	1	65	(34	31)	549	167	183	197	112	6	279	10	2	11	12	4	23	.271	.340	.493	.834

Ronald Torreyes

Bats: R Throws: R Pos: SS-2;2B-1;CF-1   toh-RAY-ess   Ht: 5'8" Wt: 155 Born: 9/2/1992 Age: 28

Year Team	Lg	G	AB	H	2B	3B	HR	(Hm	Rd)	TB	R	RBI	RC	TBB	IBB	SO	HBP	SH	SF	SB	CS	GDP	Avg	OBP	Slg	OPS
2015 LAD	NL	8	6	2	1	0	0	(0	0)	3	1	1	2	1	0	1	0	1	0	0	0	0	.333	.429	.500	.929
2016 NYY	AL	72	155	40	7	4	1	(0	1)	58	20	12	19	10	0	20	1	1	1	2	1	4	.258	.305	.374	.680
2017 NYY	AL	108	315	92	15	1	3	(2	1)	118	35	36	37	11	0	43	1	5	4	2	0	9	.292	.314	.375	.688
2018 NYY	AL	41	100	28	7	1	0	(0	0)	37	9	7	12	2	0	16	0	0	0	0	0	2	.280	.294	.370	.664
2019 Min	AL	7	16	3	0	0	0	(0	0)	3	3	1	0	0	0	3	1	0	0	1	0	0	.188	.235	.188	.423
2020 Phi	NL	4	7	1	1	0	0	(0	0)	2	1	0	0	0	0	0	0	0	0	0	0	1	.143	.143	.286	.429
Postseason		2	1	0	0	0	0	(0	0)	0	0	0	0	0	0	1	0	0	0	0	0	0	.000	.000	.000	.000
6 ML YEARS		240	599	166	31	6	4	(2	2)	221	69	57	70	24	0	83	3	7	5	5	1	17	.277	.306	.369	.675

Touki Toussaint

Pitches: R **Bats:** R **Pos:** SP-5; RP-2   TOO-key TOO-sahnt   **Ht:** 6'3" **Wt:** 215 **Born:** 6/20/1996 **Age:** 25

			HOW MUCH PITCHED						WHAT HE GAVE UP									THE RESULTS							
Year Team	Lg	G	GS	GF	IP	BFP	H	R	ER	HR	SH	SF	HB	TBB	IBB	SO	WP	W	L	Pct	Sv-Op	Hld	Vel	OPS	ERC	ERA
2018 Atl	NL	7	5	1	29.0	123	18	13	13	1	1	0	2	21	1	32	1	2	1	.667	0-0	0	93	.619	3.05	4.03
2019 Atl	NL	24	1	3	41.2	198	44	28	26	5	2	0	7	26	2	45	6	4	0	1.000	0-0	2	93	.810	6.05	5.62
2020 Atl	NL	7	5	0	24.1	120	27	28	24	7	1	0	5	16	0	30	2	0	2	.000	0-0	0	94	.954	8.17	8.88
Postseason		2	0	0	3.0	13	1	0	0	0	0	0	0	4	0	2	0	1	0	1.000	0-0	0	95	.607	3.31	0.00
3 ML YEARS		38	11	4	95.0	441	89	69	63	13	4	0	14	63	3	107	9	6	3	.667	0-0	2	94	.797	5.60	5.97

Blake Treinen

Pitches: R **Bats:** R **Pos:** RP-27   TRY-nen   **Ht:** 6'5" **Wt:** 225 **Born:** 6/30/1988 **Age:** 33

			HOW MUCH PITCHED						WHAT HE GAVE UP									THE RESULTS							
Year Team	Lg	G	GS	GF	IP	BFP	H	R	ER	HR	SH	SF	HB	TBB	IBB	SO	WP	W	L	Pct	Sv-Op	Hld	Vel	OPS	ERC	ERA
2014 Was	NL	15	7	6	50.2	214	57	17	14	1	0	0	2	13	1	30	1	2	3	.400	0-0	0	95	.678	3.86	2.49
2015 Was	NL	60	0	17	67.2	280	62	32	29	4	1	1	2	32	6	65	4	2	5	.286	0-3	16	96	.692	3.76	3.86
2016 Was	NL	73	0	17	67.0	263	51	19	17	5	2	2	0	31	6	63	1	4	1	.800	1-3	22	95	.648	2.92	2.28
2017 2 Tms		72	0	35	75.2	325	80	35	33	6	0	3	5	25	3	74	4	3	6	.333	16-21	10	97	.736	4.24	3.93
2018 Oak	AL	68	0	58	80.1	315	46	12	7	2	1	0	1	21	3	100	1	9	2	.818	38-43	0	97	.417	1.21	0.78
2019 Oak	AL	57	0	35	58.2	266	58	33	32	9	1	1	1	37	1	59	1	6	5	.545	16-21	9	97	.778	5.39	4.91
2020 LAD	NL	27	0	3	25.2	107	23	15	11	1	0	1	2	8	1	22	2	3	3	.500	1-2	9	97	.621	3.03	3.86
17 Was	NL	37	0	11	37.2	169	48	24	24	3	0	3	3	13	1	32	1	1	2	.333	3-5	5	97	.832	5.71	5.73
17 Oak	AL	35	0	24	38.0	156	32	11	9	3	0	0	2	12	2	42	3	3	4	.429	13-16	5	97	.633	2.92	2.13
Postseason		4	0	0	4.2	22	5	5	5	1	0	1	1	2	0	5	0	1	1	.500	0-0	0	97	.919	6.25	9.64
7 ML YEARS		372	7	171	425.2	1770	377	163	143	28	5	8	13	167	21	413	19	29	25	.537	72-93	54	96	.650	3.29	3.02

Jose Trevino

Bats: R **Throws:** R **Pos:** C-21;DH-3;1B-1;PH-1   treh-VEEN-yo   **Ht:** 5'11" **Wt:** 210 **Born:** 11/28/1992 **Age:** 28

					BATTING													RUNNING			AVERAGES			
Year Team	Lg	G	AB	H	2B	3B	HR	(Hm | Rd)	TB	R	RBI	RC	TBB	IBB	SO	HBP	SH	SF	SB	CS	GDP	Avg	OBP	Slg	OPS
2018 Tex	AL	3	8	2	0	0	0	(0 | 0)	2	0	3	2	0	0	1	0	0	0	0	0	1	.250	.250	.250	.500
2019 Tex	AL	40	120	31	9	0	2	(1 | 1)	46	18	13	11	3	0	27	0	1	2	0	0	6	.258	.272	.383	.655
2020 Tex	AL	24	76	19	8	0	2	(0 | 2)	33	10	9	9	3	0	15	1	1	2	0	0	1	.250	.280	.434	.715
3 ML YEARS		67	204	52	17	0	4	(1 | 3)	81	28	25	22	6	0	43	1	2	4	0	0	8	.255	.274	.397	.671

Andrew Triggs

Pitches: R **Bats:** R **Pos:** RP-3; SP-2   **Ht:** 6'4" **Wt:** 233 **Born:** 3/16/1989 **Age:** 32

			HOW MUCH PITCHED						WHAT HE GAVE UP									THE RESULTS							
Year Team	Lg	G	GS	GF	IP	BFP	H	R	ER	HR	SH	SF	HB	TBB	IBB	SO	WP	W	L	Pct	Sv-Op	Hld	Vel	OPS	ERC	ERA
2016 Oak	AL	24	6	7	56.1	238	56	30	27	5	1	1	3	13	1	55	2	1	1	.500	0-0	0	91	.699	3.46	4.31
2017 Oak	AL	12	12	0	65.1	283	68	42	31	9	1	3	4	19	0	50	5	5	6	.455	0-0	0	89	.733	4.35	4.27
2018 Oak	AL	9	9	0	41.1	182	37	24	24	7	0	1	3	18	0	43	3	3	1	.750	0-0	0	89	.731	4.31	5.23
2020 2 Tms		5	2	1	8.1	39	8	7	7	3	0	0	0	6	0	7	0	0	2	.000	0-0	0	88	.874	7.05	7.56
20 SF	NL	1	0	0	0.1	4	0	3	3	0	0	0	0	3	0	0	0	0	1	.000	0-0	0	88	.750	33.46	81.00
20 Bos	AL	4	2	1	8.0	35	8	4	4	3	0	0	0	3	0	7	0	0	1	.000	0-0	0	88	.846	5.78	4.50
4 ML YEARS		50	29	8	171.1	742	169	103	89	24	2	5	10	56	1	155	10	9	10	.474	0-0	0	90	.729	4.16	4.68

Lou Trivino

Pitches: R **Bats:** R **Pos:** RP-20   **Ht:** 6'5" **Wt:** 235 **Born:** 10/1/1991 **Age:** 29

			HOW MUCH PITCHED						WHAT HE GAVE UP									THE RESULTS							
Year Team	Lg	G	GS	GF	IP	BFP	H	R	ER	HR	SH	SF	HB	TBB	IBB	SO	WP	W	L	Pct	Sv-Op	Hld	Vel	OPS	ERC	ERA
2018 Oak	AL	69	1	10	74.0	299	53	24	24	8	1	1	2	31	4	82	4	8	3	.727	4-9	23	98	.603	2.76	2.92
2019 Oak	AL	61	0	10	60.0	269	64	40	35	7	2	3	3	31	2	57	7	4	6	.400	0-5	17	97	.782	4.90	5.25
2020 Oak	AL	20	0	9	23.1	93	16	10	10	3	0	0	0	10	0	26	1	0	0	-	0-1	0	96	.605	2.76	3.86
Postseason		1	0	0	3.0	10	1	0	0	0	0	0	0	1	0	4	0	0	0	-	0-0	0	98	.311	0.75	0.00
3 ML YEARS		150	1	29	157.1	661	130	74	69	18	3	4	5	72	6	165	12	12	9	.571	4-15	40	97	.675	3.54	3.95

Chadwick Tromp

Bats: R **Throws:** R **Pos:** C-23;DH-1;PH-1   **Ht:** 5'8" **Wt:** 221 **Born:** 3/21/1995 **Age:** 26

					BATTING													RUNNING			AVERAGES			
Year Team	Lg	G	AB	H	2B	3B	HR	(Hm | Rd)	TB	R	RBI	RC	TBB	IBB	SO	HBP	SH	SF	SB	CS	GDP	Avg	OBP	Slg	OPS
2020 SF	NL	24	61	13	1	0	4	(2 | 2)	26	11	10	4	1	0	20	0	0	2	0	0	3	.213	.219	.426	.645

Nick Tropeano

Pitches: R **Bats:** R **Pos:** RP-7   TROH-pee-ah-no   **Ht:** 6'4" **Wt:** 205 **Born:** 8/27/1990 **Age:** 30

			HOW MUCH PITCHED						WHAT HE GAVE UP									THE RESULTS							
Year Team	Lg	G	GS	GF	IP	BFP	H	R	ER	HR	SH	SF	HB	TBB	IBB	SO	WP	W	L	Pct	Sv-Op	Hld	Vel	OPS	ERC	ERA
2014 Hou	AL	4	4	0	21.2	91	19	12	11	0	1	1	1	9	1	13	1	1	3	.250	0-0	0	90	.626	2.92	4.57
2015 LAA	AL	8	7	0	37.2	161	40	18	16	2	2	1	0	10	0	38	0	3	2	.600	0-0	0	91	.700	3.53	3.82
2016 LAA	AL	13	13	0	68.1	296	70	27	27	14	1	3	2	31	1	60	8	3	2	.600	0-0	0	90	.843	5.41	3.56
2018 LAA	AL	14	14	0	76.0	316	68	41	40	16	0	2	2	31	2	64	0	5	6	.455	0-0	0	90	.807	4.45	4.74
2019 LAA	AL	3	1	0	13.2	66	18	15	15	6	0	1	2	6	0	10	0	0	1	.000	0-0	0	91	1.061	9.62	9.88
2020 Pit	NL	7	0	2	15.2	66	14	2	2	1	0	0	1	4	0	19	1	1	0	1.000	0-0	0	91	.676	2.89	1.15
6 ML YEARS		49	39	2	233.0	996	229	115	111	39	4	8	8	91	4	212	8	13	14	.481	0-0	0	91	.791	4.58	4.29

Mike Trout

Bats: R Throws: R Pos: CF-52;DH-1   Ht: 6'2" Wt: 235 Born: 8/7/1991 Age: 29

									BATTING													RUNNING			AVERAGES			
Year	Team	Lg	G	AB	H	2B	3B	HR	(Hm	Rd)	TB	R	RBI	RC	TBB	IBB	SO	HBP	SH	SF	SB	CS	GDP	Avg	OBP	Slg	OPS
2011	LAA	AL	40	123	27	6	0	5	(1	4)	48	20	16	14	9	0	30	2	0	1	4	0	2	.220	.281	.390	.672
2012	LAA	AL	139	559	182	27	8	30	(16	14)	315	129	83	127	67	4	139	6	0	7	49	5	7	.326	.399	.564	.963
2013	LAA	AL	157	589	190	39	9	27	(13	14)	328	109	97	141	110	10	136	9	0	8	33	7	8	.323	.432	.557	.988
2014	LAA	AL	157	602	173	39	9	36	(19	17)	338	115	111	131	83	6	184	10	0	10	16	2	6	.287	.377	.561	.939
2015	LAA	AL	159	575	172	32	6	41	(20	21)	339	104	90	131	92	14	158	10	0	5	11	7	11	.299	.402	.590	.991
2016	LAA	AL	159	549	173	32	5	29	(14	15)	302	123	100	137	116	12	137	11	0	5	30	7	5	.315	.441	.550	.991
2017	LAA	AL	114	402	123	25	3	33	(20	13)	253	92	72	110	94	15	90	7	0	4	22	4	8	.306	.442	.629	1.071
2018	LAA	AL	140	471	147	24	4	39	(17	22)	296	101	79	140	122	25	124	10	0	4	24	2	5	.312	.460	.628	1.088
2019	LAA	AL	134	470	137	27	2	45	(21	24)	303	110	104	132	110	14	120	16	0	4	11	2	5	.291	.438	.645	1.083
2020	LAA	AL	53	199	56	9	2	17	(10	7)	120	41	46	49	35	4	56	3	0	4	1	1	1	.281	.390	.603	.993
	Postseason		3	12	1	0	0	1	(0	1)	4	1	1	0	3	0	2	0	0	0	0	1	0	.083	.267	.333	.600
	10 ML YEARS		1252	4539	1380	260	48	302	(151	151)	2642	944	798	1112	838	104	1174	84	0	52	201	37	58	.304	.418	.582	1.000

Yoshi Tsutsugo

Bats: L Throws: R Pos: DH-22;LF-16;3B-14;PH-9   yo-shee-toh-mo tsoo-tsoo-go   Ht: 6'1" Wt: 225 Born: 11/26/1991 Age: 29

									BATTING													RUNNING			AVERAGES			
Year	Team	Lg	G	AB	H	2B	3B	HR	(Hm	Rd)	TB	R	RBI	RC	TBB	IBB	SO	HBP	SH	SF	SB	CS	GDP	Avg	OBP	Slg	OPS
2020	TB	AL	51	157	31	5	1	8	(4	4)	62	27	24	22	26	1	50	1	0	1	0	0	5	.197	.314	.395	.708

Cole Tucker

Bats: B Throws: R Pos: CF-20;RF-16;PR-5;PH-2;2B-1;DH-1   Ht: 6'3" Wt: 205 Born: 7/3/1996 Age: 24

									BATTING													RUNNING			AVERAGES			
Year	Team	Lg	G	AB	H	2B	3B	HR	(Hm	Rd)	TB	R	RBI	RC	TBB	IBB	SO	HBP	SH	SF	SB	CS	GDP	Avg	OBP	Slg	OPS
2019	Pit	NL	56	147	31	10	3	2	(1	1)	53	16	13	14	10	1	40	1	1	0	0	0	2	.211	.266	.361	.626
2020	Pit	NL	37	109	24	3	0	1	(0	1)	30	17	8	6	5	0	31	0	1	1	1	0	3	.220	.252	.275	.527
	2 ML YEARS		93	256	55	13	3	3	(1	2)	83	33	21	20	15	1	71	1	2	1	1	0	5	.215	.260	.324	.584

Kyle Tucker

Bats: L Throws: R Pos: LF-41;DH-10;RF-7;PH-1   Ht: 6'4" Wt: 199 Born: 1/17/1997 Age: 24

									BATTING													RUNNING			AVERAGES			
Year	Team	Lg	G	AB	H	2B	3B	HR	(Hm	Rd)	TB	R	RBI	RC	TBB	IBB	SO	HBP	SH	SF	SB	CS	GDP	Avg	OBP	Slg	OPS
2018	Hou	AL	28	64	9	2	1	0	(0	0)	13	10	4	0	6	0	13	2	0	0	1	1	1	.141	.236	.203	.439
2019	Hou	AL	22	67	18	6	0	4	(1	3)	36	15	11	10	4	1	20	1	0	0	5	0	1	.269	.319	.537	.857
2020	Hou	AL	58	209	56	12	6	9	(4	5)	107	33	42	44	18	2	46	0	0	1	8	1	2	.268	.325	.512	.837
	Postseason		9	12	2	0	0	0	(0	0)	2	2	0	0	3	0	7	0	0	0	1	0	0	.167	.333	.167	.500
	3 ML YEARS		108	340	83	20	7	13	(5	8)	156	58	57	54	28	3	79	3	0	1	14	2	4	.244	.306	.459	.765

Nik Turley

Pitches: L Bats: L Pos: RP-25   Ht: 6'4" Wt: 235 Born: 9/11/1989 Age: 31

			HOW MUCH PITCHED					WHAT HE GAVE UP										THE RESULTS							
Year	Team	Lg	G	GS	GF	IP	BFP	H	R	ER	HR	SH	SF	HB	TBB	IBB	SO	WP	W	L	Pct	Sv-Op	Hld	Vel	OPS	ERC	ERA
2017	Min	AL	10	3	3	17.2	89	30	22	22	5	1	2	2	8	1	13	2	0	2	.000	0-0	0	93	1.178	11.06	11.21
2020	Pit	NL	25	0	3	21.2	92	13	13	12	1	0	3	3	11	1	20	1	0	3	.000	1-4	3	94	.587	2.40	4.98
	2 ML YEARS		35	3	6	39.1	181	43	35	34	6	1	5	5	19	2	33	3	0	5	.000	1-4	3	94	.882	5.79	7.78

Spencer Turnbull

Pitches: R Bats: R Pos: SP-11   Ht: 6'3" Wt: 211 Born: 9/18/1992 Age: 28

			HOW MUCH PITCHED					WHAT HE GAVE UP										THE RESULTS							
Year	Team	Lg	G	GS	GF	IP	BFP	H	R	ER	HR	SH	SF	HB	TBB	IBB	SO	WP	W	L	Pct	Sv-Op	Hld	Vel	OPS	ERC	ERA
2018	Det	AL	4	3	0	16.1	69	17	11	11	1	0	0	4	4	0	15	1	0	2	.000	0-0	0	94	.658	3.41	6.06
2019	Det	AL	30	30	0	148.1	656	154	86	76	14	1	4	16	59	1	146	9	3	17	.150	0-0	0	94	.763	4.69	4.61
2020	Det	AL	11	11	0	56.2	242	47	25	25	2	2	1	2	29	1	51	0	4	4	.500	0-0	0	94	.662	3.24	3.97
	3 ML YEARS		45	44	0	221.1	967	218	122	112	17	3	5	18	92	2	212	10	7	23	.233	0-0	1	94	.730	4.21	4.55

Justin Turner

Bats: R Throws: R Pos: 3B-32;DH-10   Ht: 5'11" Wt: 202 Born: 11/23/1984 Age: 36

									BATTING													RUNNING			AVERAGES			
Year	Team	Lg	G	AB	H	2B	3B	HR	(Hm	Rd)	TB	R	RBI	RC	TBB	IBB	SO	HBP	SH	SF	SB	CS	GDP	Avg	OBP	Slg	OPS
2009	Bal	AL	12	18	3	0	0	0	(0	0)	3	2	3	1	4	0	3	0	0	0	0	0	1	.167	.318	.167	.485
2010	2 Tms		9	17	1	1	0	0	(0	0)	2	1	0	0	1	0	3	0	0	0	0	0	0	.059	.111	.118	.229
2011	NYM	NL	117	435	113	30	0	4	(3	1)	155	49	51	59	39	2	59	10	2	1	7	2	9	.260	.334	.356	.690
2012	NYM	NL	94	171	46	13	1	2	(2	0)	67	20	19	19	9	0	24	4	0	1	1	1	9	.269	.319	.392	.711
2013	NYM	NL	86	200	56	13	1	2	(0	2)	77	12	16	17	11	1	34	1	1	1	0	1	6	.280	.319	.385	.704
2014	LAD	NL	109	288	98	21	1	7	(5	2)	142	46	43	55	28	1	58	4	0	2	6	1	6	.340	.404	.493	.897
2015	LAD	NL	126	385	113	26	1	16	(8	8)	189	55	60	65	36	1	71	13	1	4	5	2	10	.294	.370	.491	.861
2016	LAD	NL	151	556	153	34	3	27	(11	16)	274	79	90	96	48	1	107	10	0	8	4	1	16	.275	.339	.493	.832
2017	LAD	NL	130	457	147	32	0	21	(10	11)	242	72	71	95	59	5	56	19	1	7	7	1	12	.322	.415	.530	.945
2018	LAD	NL	103	365	114	31	1	14	(9	5)	189	62	52	71	47	3	54	12	0	2	2	1	10	.312	.406	.518	.924
2019	LAD	NL	135	479	139	24	0	27	(14	13)	244	80	67	84	51	1	88	14	0	5	2	0	11	.290	.372	.509	.881
2020	LAD	NL	42	150	46	9	1	4	(4	0)	69	26	23	32	18	0	26	6	0	1	1	0	2	.307	.400	.460	.860

Year Team	Lg		BATTING																	RUNNING			AVERAGES			
		G	AB	H	2B	3B	HR	(Hm Rd)	TB	R	RBI	RC	TBB	IBB	SO	HBP	SH	SF	SB	CS	GDP	Avg	OBP	Slg	OPS
10 Bal	AL	5	9	0	0	0	0	(0 0)	0	0	0	0	0	0	3	0	0	0	0	0	0	.000	.000	.000	.000
10 NYM	NL	4	8	1	1	0	0	(0 0)	2	1	0	0	1	0	0	0	0	0	0	0	0	.125	.222	.250	.472
Postseason		54	200	62	13	1	9	(4 5)	104	25	35	48	26	1	33	9	0	1	5	0	2	.310	.411	.520	.931
12 ML YEARS		1114	3521	1029	234	9	124	(66 58)	1653	504	495	594	351	15	583	93	5	32	35	10	92	.292	.369	.469	.838

Trea Turner

Bats: R Throws: R Pos: SS-59 TRAY **Ht:** 6'2" **Wt:** 185 **Born:** 6/30/1993 **Age:** 28

Year Team	Lg		BATTING																	RUNNING			AVERAGES			
		G	AB	H	2B	3B	HR	(Hm Rd)	TB	R	RBI	RC	TBB	IBB	SO	HBP	SH	SF	SB	CS	GDP	Avg	OBP	Slg	OPS
2015 Was	NL	27	40	9	1	0	1	(0 1)	13	5	1	2	4	0	12	0	0	0	2	2	0	.225	.295	.325	.620
2016 Was	NL	73	307	105	14	8	13	(7 6)	174	53	40	62	14	0	59	1	0	2	33	6	1	.342	.370	.567	.937
2017 Was	NL	98	412	117	24	6	11	(6 5)	186	75	45	67	30	0	80	4	0	1	46	8	4	.284	.338	.451	.789
2018 Was	NL	162	664	180	27	6	19	(10 9)	276	103	73	105	69	3	132	5	2	0	43	9	7	.271	.344	.416	.760
2019 Was	NL	122	521	155	37	5	19	(11 8)	259	96	57	87	43	2	113	3	0	5	35	5	10	.298	.353	.497	.850
2020 Was	NL	59	233	78	15	4	12	(5 7)	137	46	41	52	22	0	36	3	0	2	12	4	5	.335	.394	.588	.982
Postseason		27	116	27	5	0	1	(1 0)	35	16	4	8	9	1	33	0	0	1	4	0	0	.233	.286	.302	.587
6 ML YEARS		541	2177	644	118	29	75	(39 36)	1045	378	257	375	182	5	432	15	2	7	171	34	27	.296	.353	.480	.833

Duane Underwood Jr.

Pitches: R Bats: R Pos: RP-17 **Ht:** 6'2" **Wt:** 210 **Born:** 7/20/1994 **Age:** 26

Year Team	Lg	HOW MUCH PITCHED					WHAT HE GAVE UP										THE RESULTS						
		G	GS	GF	IP	BFP	H	R	ER	HR	SH	SF	HB	TBB	IBB	SO	WP	W	L	Pct	Sv-Op	Hld	Vel	OPS	ERC	ERA
2018 ChC	NL	1	1	0	4.0	16	2	1	1	1	0	0	0	3	0	3	0	0	1	.000	0-0	0	92	.697	3.91	2.25
2019 ChC	NL	12	0	1	11.2	51	13	7	7	2	0	0	1	3	0	13	1	0	0	-	0-0	0	95	.865	5.01	5.40
2020 ChC	NL	17	0	3	20.2	88	25	13	13	5	0	1	1	6	1	27	2	1	0	1.000	0-0	1	95	.939	6.33	5.66
3 ML YEARS		30	1	4	36.1	155	40	21	21	8	0	1	2	12	1	43	3	1	1	.500	0-0	1	94	.891	5.61	5.20

Justin Upton

Bats: R Throws: R Pos: LF-39;DH-3 **Ht:** 6'1" **Wt:** 215 **Born:** 8/25/1987 **Age:** 33

Year Team	Lg		BATTING																	RUNNING			AVERAGES			
		G	AB	H	2B	3B	HR	(Hm Rd)	TB	R	RBI	RC	TBB	IBB	SO	HBP	SH	SF	SB	CS	GDP	Avg	OBP	Slg	OPS
2007 Ari	NL	43	140	31	8	3	2	(2 0)	51	17	11	13	11	4	37	1	0	0	2	0	3	.221	.283	.364	.647
2008 Ari	NL	108	356	89	19	6	15	(12 3)	165	52	42	47	54	6	121	4	0	3	1	4	3	.250	.353	.463	.816
2009 Ari	NL	138	526	158	30	7	26	(14 12)	280	84	86	94	55	3	137	2	1	4	20	5	10	.300	.366	.532	.899
2010 Ari	NL	133	495	135	27	3	17	(8 9)	219	73	69	73	64	5	152	4	1	7	18	8	20	.273	.356	.442	.799
2011 Ari	NL	159	592	171	39	5	31	(20 11)	313	105	88	103	59	9	126	19	0	4	21	9	8	.289	.369	.529	.898
2012 Ari	NL	150	554	155	24	4	17	(11 6)	238	107	67	82	63	5	121	5	0	6	18	8	7	.280	.355	.430	.785
2013 Atl	NL	149	558	147	27	2	27	(13 14)	259	94	70	84	75	4	161	5	1	4	8	1	12	.263	.354	.464	.818
2014 Atl	NL	154	566	153	34	2	29	(18 11)	278	77	102	84	60	1	171	6	0	8	8	4	11	.270	.342	.491	.833
2015 SD	NL	150	542	136	26	3	26	(15 11)	246	85	81	85	68	5	159	4	0	5	19	5	10	.251	.336	.454	.790
2016 Det	AL	153	570	140	28	2	31	(14 17)	265	81	87	77	50	3	179	4	0	2	9	4	15	.246	.310	.465	.775
2017 2 Tms	AL	152	557	152	44	2	35	(17 18)	301	100	109	109	74	3	180	3	0	1	14	5	9	.273	.361	.540	.901
2018 LAA	AL	145	533	137	18	1	30	(22 8)	247	80	85	79	64	1	176	10	0	6	8	2	12	.257	.344	.463	.808
2019 LAA	AL	63	219	47	8	0	12	(5 7)	91	34	40	30	32	0	78	0	0	5	1	1	5	.215	.309	.416	.724
2020 LAA	AL	42	147	30	5	0	9	(5 4)	62	20	22	17	11	0	43	7	0	1	0	2	6	.204	.289	.422	.711
17 Det	AL	125	459	128	37	0	28	(13 15)	249	81	94	98	57	2	147	3	0	1	10	5	6	.279	.362	.542	.904
17 LAA	AL	27	98	24	7	2	7	(4 3)	52	19	15	11	17	1	33	0	0	0	4	0	3	.245	.357	.531	.887
Postseason		15	48	11	2	1	2	(0 2)	21	7	4	7	10	0	13	2	0	0	1	0	0	.229	.383	.438	.821
14 ML YEARS		1739	6355	1681	337	38	307	(176 131)	3015	1009	959	977	740	49	1841	74	3	56	147	58	130	.265	.345	.474	.820

Jose Urena

Pitches: R Bats: R Pos: SP-5 oo-RAY-nuh **Ht:** 6'2" **Wt:** 208 **Born:** 9/12/1991 **Age:** 29

Year Team	Lg	HOW MUCH PITCHED					WHAT HE GAVE UP										THE RESULTS						
		G	GS	GF	IP	BFP	H	R	ER	HR	SH	SF	HB	TBB	IBB	SO	WP	W	L	Pct	Sv-Op	Hld	Vel	OPS	ERC	ERA
2015 Mia	NL	20	9	4	61.2	274	73	37	36	5	3	5	3	25	2	28	2	1	5	.167	0-1	0	94	.818	5.27	5.25
2016 Mia	NL	28	12	4	83.2	373	91	59	57	11	3	4	6	29	6	58	0	4	9	.308	1-3	1	95	.800	4.70	6.13
2017 Mia	NL	34	28	2	169.2	724	152	77	72	26	5	3	14	64	4	113	5	14	7	.667	0-0	0	95	.735	4.07	3.82
2018 Mia	NL	31	31	0	174.0	712	155	78	77	19	5	4	12	51	8	130	2	9	12	.429	0-0	0	96	.690	3.40	3.98
2019 Mia	NL	24	13	8	84.2	369	99	53	49	13	1	2	2	26	3	62	2	4	10	.286	3-5	0	96	.818	5.16	5.21
2020 Mia	NL	5	5	0	23.1	104	22	15	14	4	0	0	2	13	0	15	1	0	3	.000	0-0	0	95	.783	5.31	5.40
6 ML YEARS		142	98	18	597.0	2556	592	319	305	78	17	18	39	208	23	406	12	32	46	.410	4-9	1	95	.755	4.28	4.60

Julio Urias

Pitches: L Bats: L Pos: SP-10; RP-1 oo-ree-AHS **Ht:** 6'0" **Wt:** 225 **Born:** 8/12/1996 **Age:** 24

Year Team	Lg	HOW MUCH PITCHED					WHAT HE GAVE UP										THE RESULTS						
		G	GS	GF	IP	BFP	H	R	ER	HR	SH	SF	HB	TBB	IBB	SO	WP	W	L	Pct	Sv-Op	Hld	Vel	OPS	ERC	ERA
2016 LAD	NL	18	15	1	77.0	336	81	32	29	5	4	1	4	31	0	84	3	5	2	.714	0-0	0	93	.728	3.39	3.39
2017 LAD	NL	5	5	0	23.1	102	23	15	14	1	2	0	1	14	1	11	1	0	2	.000	0-0	0	93	.768	4.61	5.40
2018 LAD	NL	3	0	3	4.0	13	1	0	0	0	0	0	0	0	0	7	0	0	0	-	0-0	0	95	.154	0.14	0.00
2019 LAD	NL	37	8	7	79.2	326	59	28	22	7	0	1	5	27	1	85	2	4	3	.571	4-5	5	95	.603	2.60	2.49
2020 LAD	NL	11	10	0	55.0	224	45	20	20	5	0	1	0	18	0	45	2	3	0	1.000	0-0	0	94	.608	2.78	3.27
Postseason		12	1	2	15.2	64	13	9	9	2	1	1	0	5	0	10	0	2	2	.500	0-0	1	94	.654	3.03	5.17
5 ML YEARS		74	38	11	239.0	1001	209	95	85	18	6	3	10	90	2	232	8	12	7	.632	4-5	5	94	.656	3.30	3.20

Luis Urias

Bats: R **Throws:** R **Pos:** 3B-30;2B-10;SS-8;PR-1   oo-REE-ahs   **Ht:** 5'9" **Wt:** 186 **Born:** 6/3/1997 **Age:** 24

							BATTING													RUNNING			AVERAGES			
Year	Team	Lg	G	AB	H	2B	3B	HR	(Hm | Rd)	TB	R	RBI	RC	TBB	IBB	SO	HBP	SH	SF	SB	CS	GDP	Avg	OBP	Slg	OPS
2018	SD	NL	12	48	10	1	0	2	(1 | 1)	17	5	5	6	3	0	10	1	0	1	1	0	0	.208	.264	.354	.618
2019	SD	NL	71	215	48	8	1	4	(1 | 3)	70	27	24	22	25	0	56	9	0	0	0	1	8	.223	.329	.326	.655
2020	Mil	NL	41	109	26	4	1	0	(0 | 0)	32	11	11	11	10	0	32	1	0	0	2	2	4	.239	.308	.294	.602
	3 ML YEARS		124	372	84	13	2	6	(2 | 4)	119	43	40	39	38	0	98	11	0	1	3	3	12	.226	.315	.320	.635

Ramon Urias

Bats: R **Throws:** R **Pos:** SS-5;2B-4;PH-2   **Ht:** 5'11" **Wt:** 180 **Born:** 6/3/1994 **Age:** 27

							BATTING													RUNNING			AVERAGES			
Year	Team	Lg	G	AB	H	2B	3B	HR	(Hm | Rd)	TB	R	RBI	RC	TBB	IBB	SO	HBP	SH	SF	SB	CS	GDP	Avg	OBP	Slg	OPS
2020	Bal	AL	10	25	9	2	0	1	(0 | 1)	14	3	3	6	2	0	6	0	0	0	0	0	1	.360	.407	.560	.967

Jose Urquidy

Pitches: R **Bats:** R **Pos:** SP-5   **Ht:** 6'0" **Wt:** 217 **Born:** 5/1/1995 **Age:** 26

			HOW MUCH PITCHED					WHAT HE GAVE UP									THE RESULTS						
Year	Team	Lg	G	GS	GF	IP	BFP	H	R	ER	HR	SH	SF	HB	TBB	IBB	SO	WP	W	L	Pct	Sv-Op	Hld	Vel	OPS	ERC	ERA
2019	Hou	AL	9	7	0	41.0	167	38	18	18	6	2	0	0	7	0	40	4	2	1	.667	0-0	0	93	.678	3.05	3.95
2020	Hou	AL	5	5	0	29.2	116	22	9	9	4	0	0	1	8	0	17	0	1	1	.500	0-0	0	93	.594	2.63	2.73
	Postseason		4	1	1	10.0	41	9	1	1	1	0	0	1	2	0	12	0	1	0	1.000	0-0	0	94	.635	3.17	0.90
	2 ML YEARS		14	12	0	70.2	283	60	27	27	10	2	0	1	15	0	57	4	3	2	.600	0-0	0	93	.644	2.87	3.44

Gio Urshela

Bats: R **Throws:** R **Pos:** 3B-43;PH-1   urr-SHELL-ah   **Ht:** 6'0" **Wt:** 215 **Born:** 10/11/1991 **Age:** 29

							BATTING													RUNNING			AVERAGES			
Year	Team	Lg	G	AB	H	2B	3B	HR	(Hm | Rd)	TB	R	RBI	RC	TBB	IBB	SO	HBP	SH	SF	SB	CS	GDP	Avg	OBP	Slg	OPS
2015	Cle	AL	81	267	60	8	1	6	(3 | 3)	88	25	21	19	18	0	58	2	1	0	0	1	9	.225	.279	.330	.608
2017	Cle	AL	67	156	35	7	0	1	(0 | 1)	45	14	15	10	8	0	22	0	1	0	0	0	6	.224	.262	.288	.551
2018	Tor	AL	19	43	10	1	0	1	(1 | 0)	14	7	3	2	2	0	10	1	0	0	0	0	1	.233	.283	.326	.608
2019	NYY	AL	132	442	139	34	0	21	(8 | 13)	236	73	74	80	25	1	87	5	0	4	1	1	13	.314	.355	.534	.889
2020	NYY	AL	43	151	45	11	0	6	(6 | 0)	74	24	30	31	18	0	25	1	0	4	1	0	6	.298	.368	.490	.858
	Postseason		14	45	10	1	0	2	(0 | 2)	17	4	3	5	2	0	10	0	1	0	0	0	1	.222	.255	.378	.633
	5 ML YEARS		342	1059	289	61	1	35	(18 | 17)	457	143	143	142	71	1	202	9	2	8	2	2	35	.273	.322	.432	.753

Pat Valaika

Bats: R **Throws:** R **Pos:** SS-24;1B-13;2B-13;PH-6;3B-4;LF-3;PR-2;RF-1   **Ht:** 5'11" **Wt:** 210 **Born:** 9/9/1992 **Age:** 28

							BATTING													RUNNING			AVERAGES			
Year	Team	Lg	G	AB	H	2B	3B	HR	(Hm | Rd)	TB	R	RBI	RC	TBB	IBB	SO	HBP	SH	SF	SB	CS	GDP	Avg	OBP	Slg	OPS
2016	Col	NL	13	19	5	1	0	1	(0 | 1)	9	3	2	2	0	0	8	0	0	0	0	0	0	.263	.263	.474	.737
2017	Col	NL	110	182	47	11	0	13	(9 | 4)	97	28	40	31	7	0	53	0	5	1	0	0	1	.258	.284	.533	.817
2018	Col	NL	68	122	19	5	0	2	(1 | 1)	30	8	5	2	9	0	30	0	2	0	0	0	4	.156	.214	.246	.460
2019	Col	NL	40	79	15	5	1	1	(1 | 0)	25	11	4	8	7	0	34	0	0	0	0	0	1	.190	.256	.316	.572
2020	Bal	AL	52	141	39	4	0	8	(5 | 3)	67	24	16	16	8	0	34	0	1	0	0	2	3	.277	.315	.475	.791
	Postseason		2	2	1	1	0	0	(0 | 0)	2	0	0	1	0	0	1	0	0	0	0	0	0	.500	.500	1.000	1.500
	5 ML YEARS		283	543	125	26	1	25	(16 | 9)	228	74	67	58	31	0	159	0	8	1	0	2	9	.230	.271	.420	.691

Cesar Valdez

Pitches: R **Bats:** R **Pos:** RP-9   **Ht:** 6'2" **Wt:** 200 **Born:** 3/17/1985 **Age:** 36

			HOW MUCH PITCHED					WHAT HE GAVE UP									THE RESULTS						
Year	Team	Lg	G	GS	GF	IP	BFP	H	R	ER	HR	SH	SF	HB	TBB	IBB	SO	WP	W	L	Pct	Sv-Op	Hld	Vel	OPS	ERC	ERA
2010	Ari	NL	9	2	3	20.0	97	29	19	17	2	0	0	1	10	2	13	3	1	2	.333	0-0	0	89	.889	7.29	7.65
2017	2 Tms	AL	11	4	5	30.2	140	41	29	26	7	0	0	1	11	1	21	1	1	1	.500	0-0	0	88	.988	7.11	7.63
2020	Bal	AL	9	0	7	14.1	53	7	3	2	0	0	1	0	3	0	12	1	1	1	.500	3-3	0	86	.413	0.84	1.26
17	Oak	AL	4	1	2	9.1	44	14	10	10	4	0	0	0	4	0	5	0	0	0	-	0-0	0	88	1.134	10.35	9.64
17	Tor	AL	7	3	3	21.1	96	27	19	16	3	0	0	1	7	1	16	1	1	1	.500	0-0	0	88	.921	5.81	6.75
	3 ML YEARS		29	6	15	65.0	290	77	51	45	9	0	1	2	24	3	46	5	3	4	.429	3-3	0	88	.849	5.38	6.23

Framber Valdez

Pitches: L **Bats:** L **Pos:** SP-10; RP-1   **Ht:** 5'11" **Wt:** 239 **Born:** 11/19/1993 **Age:** 27

			HOW MUCH PITCHED					WHAT HE GAVE UP									THE RESULTS						
Year	Team	Lg	G	GS	GF	IP	BFP	H	R	ER	HR	SH	SF	HB	TBB	IBB	SO	WP	W	L	Pct	Sv-Op	Hld	Vel	OPS	ERC	ERA
2018	Hou	AL	8	5	0	37.0	154	22	10	9	3	0	4	4	24	0	34	5	4	1	.800	0-0	0	92	.595	3.20	2.19
2019	Hou	AL	26	8	7	70.2	329	74	51	46	9	0	4	4	44	0	68	4	4	7	.364	0-0	0	93	.790	5.65	5.86
2020	Hou	AL	11	10	0	70.2	288	63	32	28	5	1	3	5	16	0	76	6	5	3	.625	0-0	0	93	.635	2.94	3.57
	3 ML YEARS		45	23	7	178.1	771	159	93	83	17	1	7	13	84	0	178	15	13	11	.542	0-0	0	93	.693	4.02	4.19

Phillips Valdez

Pitches: R **Bats:** R **Pos:** RP-24   **Ht:** 6'2" **Wt:** 160 **Born:** 11/16/1991 **Age:** 29

Year	Team	Lg	G	GS	GF	IP	BFP	H	R	ER	HR	SH	SF	HB	TBB	IBB	SO	WP	W	L	Pct	Sv-Op	Hld	Vel	OPS	ERC	ERA
2019	Tex	AL	11	0	2	16.0	75	17	7	7	3	0	1	2	9	0	18	1	0	0	-	0-0	0	92	.818	6.26	3.94
2020	Bos	AL	24	0	5	30.1	137	33	16	11	3	0	1	3	16	0	30	0	1	1	.500	0-1	4	92	.790	5.61	3.26
	2 ML YEARS		35	0	7	46.1	212	50	23	18	6	0	2	5	25	0	48	1	1	1	.500	0-1	4	92	.800	5.84	3.50

Josh VanMeter

Bats: L **Throws:** R **Pos:** 2B-17;DH-4;PH-4;1B-3;3B-2;PR-1   **Ht:** 5'11" **Wt:** 190 **Born:** 3/10/1995 **Age:** 26

Year	Team	Lg	G	AB	H	2B	3B	HR	(Hm	Rd)	TB	R	RBI	RC	TBB	IBB	SO	HBP	SH	SF	SB	CS	GDP	Avg	OBP	Slg	OPS
2019	Cin	NL	95	228	54	13	1	8	(3	5)	93	33	23	28	29	0	56	2	0	1	9	3	5	.237	.327	.408	.735
2020	2 Tms	NL	26	70	9	3	0	2	(2	0)	18	9	6	5	7	0	24	2	0	0	1	0	0	.129	.228	.257	.485
20	Cin	NL	14	34	2	1	0	1	(1	0)	6	3	1	0	3	0	16	1	0	0	1	0	0	.059	.158	.176	.334
20	Ari	NL	12	36	7	2	0	1	(1	0)	12	6	5	5	4	0	8	1	0	0	0	0	0	.194	.293	.333	.626
	2 ML YEARS		121	298	63	16	1	10	(5	5)	111	42	29	33	36	0	80	4	0	1	10	3	5	.211	.304	.372	.676

Ildemaro Vargas

Bats: B **Throws:** R **Pos:** 2B-16;PH-6;1B-5;3B-3;PR-1   **Ht:** 6'0" **Wt:** 180 **Born:** 7/16/1991 **Age:** 29

Year	Team	Lg	G	AB	H	2B	3B	HR	(Hm	Rd)	TB	R	RBI	RC	TBB	IBB	SO	HBP	SH	SF	SB	CS	GDP	Avg	OBP	Slg	OPS
2017	Ari	NL	12	13	4	1	0	0	(0	0)	5	4	4	2	0	0	3	0	0	0	0	0	1	.308	.308	.385	.692
2018	Ari	NL	14	19	4	0	0	1	(0	1)	7	2	4	4	1	0	4	0	0	0	1	0	1	.211	.250	.368	.618
2019	Ari	NL	92	201	54	9	1	6	(2	4)	83	25	24	26	9	0	24	0	0	1	1	0	6	.269	.299	.413	.712
2020	3 Tms		24	51	10	1	1	1	(0	1)	16	6	3	2	2	0	10	0	0	1	0	0	2	.196	.222	.314	.536
20	Ari	NL	8	20	3	0	0	0	(0	0)	3	2	0	0	1	0	5	0	0	0	0	0	1	.150	.190	.150	.340
20	Min	AL	10	22	5	1	1	0	(0	0)	8	3	2	1	1	0	2	0	0	1	0	0	1	.227	.250	.364	.614
20	ChC	NL	6	9	2	0	0	1	(0	1)	5	1	1	1	0	0	3	0	0	0	0	0	0	.222	.222	.556	.778
	4 ML YEARS		142	284	72	11	2	8	(2	6)	111	37	35	34	12	0	41	0	0	2	2	0	10	.254	.282	.391	.673

Daulton Varsho

Bats: L **Throws:** R **Pos:** CF-14;C-10;LF-5;DH-5;PR-3;PH-2   **Ht:** 5'10" **Wt:** 205 **Born:** 7/2/1996 **Age:** 24

Year	Team	Lg	G	AB	H	2B	3B	HR	(Hm	Rd)	TB	R	RBI	RC	TBB	IBB	SO	HBP	SH	SF	SB	CS	GDP	Avg	OBP	Slg	OPS
2017	Hlsbro	A-	50	193	60	16	3	7	(-	-)	103	36	39	38	17	0	30	1	0	1	7	2	1	.311	.368	.534	.902
2018	2 Tms	Low	83	316	93	13	4	12	(-	-)	150	48	45	56	30	1	72	7	0	1	19	3	3	.294	.367	.475	.842
2019	Jacksn	AA	108	396	119	25	4	18	(-	-)	206	85	58	81	42	1	63	10	0	4	21	5	3	.301	.378	.520	.899
2020	Ari	NL	37	101	19	5	2	3	(1	2)	37	16	9	8	12	0	33	2	0	0	3	1	1	.188	.287	.366	.653

Andrew Vaughn

Bats: R **Throws:** R **Pos:** 1B   **Ht:** 6'0" **Wt:** 215 **Born:** 4/3/1998 **Age:** 23

Year	Team	Lg	G	AB	H	2B	3B	HR	(Hm	Rd)	TB	R	RBI	RC	TBB	IBB	SO	HBP	SH	SF	SB	CS	GDP	Avg	OBP	Slg	OPS
2019	3 Tms	Low	55	205	57	17	0	6	(-	-)	92	33	36	36	30	0	38	7	0	3	0	1	9	.278	.384	.449	.832

Christian Vazquez

Bats: R **Throws:** R **Pos:** C-42;DH-4;2B-1;PH-1   VAZ-kehz   **Ht:** 5'9" **Wt:** 205 **Born:** 8/21/1990 **Age:** 30

Year	Team	Lg	G	AB	H	2B	3B	HR	(Hm	Rd)	TB	R	RBI	RC	TBB	IBB	SO	HBP	SH	SF	SB	CS	GDP	Avg	OBP	Slg	OPS
2014	Bos	AL	55	175	42	9	0	1	(1	0)	54	15	20	19	19	1	33	0	3	4	0	0	4	.240	.308	.309	.617
2016	Bos	AL	57	172	39	9	1	1	(1	0)	53	21	12	11	10	1	39	2	0	0	0	0	3	.227	.277	.308	.585
2017	Bos	AL	99	324	94	18	2	5	(4	1)	131	43	32	41	17	0	64	3	0	1	7	2	14	.290	.330	.404	.735
2018	Bos	AL	80	251	52	10	0	3	(2	1)	71	24	16	13	13	1	41	4	1	0	4	1	5	.207	.257	.283	.540
2019	Bos	AL	138	482	133	26	1	23	(8	15)	230	66	72	69	33	3	101	4	0	3	4	2	17	.276	.320	.477	.798
2020	Bos	AL	47	173	49	9	0	7	(2	5)	79	22	23	25	16	0	43	0	0	0	4	3	6	.283	.344	.457	.801
	Postseason		14	43	10	1	0	1	(0	1)	14	5	2	2	3	0	10	0	0	0	0	0	0	.233	.283	.326	.608
	6 ML YEARS		476	1577	409	81	4	40	(18	22)	618	191	175	178	108	6	321	9	7	8	19	8	49	.259	.309	.392	.701

Vince Velasquez

Pitches: R **Bats:** R **Pos:** SP-7; RP-2   **Ht:** 6'3" **Wt:** 212 **Born:** 6/7/1992 **Age:** 29

Year	Team	Lg	G	GS	GF	IP	BFP	H	R	ER	HR	SH	SF	HB	TBB	IBB	SO	WP	W	L	Pct	Sv-Op	Hld	Vel	OPS	ERC	ERA
2015	Hou	AL	19	7	5	55.2	231	50	28	27	5	0	0	2	21	0	58	3	1	1	.500	0-0	0	95	.720	3.58	4.37
2016	Phi	NL	24	24	0	131.0	551	129	64	60	21	9	5	1	45	1	152	3	8	6	.571	0-0	0	94	.765	4.25	4.12
2017	Phi	NL	15	15	0	72.0	315	74	44	41	15	2	2	3	34	1	68	2	2	7	.222	0-0	0	94	.851	5.58	5.13
2018	Phi	NL	31	30	1	146.2	630	138	83	79	16	7	3	8	59	1	161	9	9	12	.429	0-0	0	94	.747	4.04	4.85
2019	Phi	NL	33	23	2	117.1	516	120	69	64	26	3	3	9	43	2	130	5	7	8	.467	0-0	2	94	.833	5.21	4.91
2020	Phi	NL	9	7	0	34.0	154	36	21	21	5	0	0	3	17	1	46	0	1	1	.500	0-0	0	94	.804	5.51	5.56
	6 ML YEARS		131	106	8	556.2	2397	547	309	292	88	21	13	26	219	6	615	22	28	35	.444	0-0	2	94	.784	4.57	4.72

Andrew Velazquez

Bats: B **Throws:** R **Pos:** SS-30;PR-9;LF-7;CF-3;2B-2;PH-1 **Ht:** 5'9" **Wt:** 170 **Born:** 7/14/1994 **Age:** 26

							BATTING														RUNNING			AVERAGES			
Year Team	Lg	G	AB	H	2B	3B	HR	(Hm	Rd)	TB	R	RBI	RC	TBB	IBB	SO	HBP	SH	SF	SB	CS	GDP	Avg	OBP	Slg	OPS
2018 TB	AL	13	10	3	1	0	0	(0	0)	4	3	0	3	1	0	3	1	0	0	1	0	0	.300	.417	.400	.817
2019 2 Tms	AL	15	23	2	2	0	0	(0	0)	4	3	0	0	1	0	13	0	0	0	1	0	0	.087	.125	.174	.299
2020 Bal	AL	40	63	10	1	1	0	(0	0)	13	11	3	3	10	0	23	0	4	0	4	2	2	.159	.274	.206	.480
19 TB	AL	10	12	1	1	0	0	(0	0)	2	2	0	0	0	0	6	0	0	0	0	0	0	.083	.083	.167	.250
19 Cle	AL	5	11	1	1	0	0	(0	0)	2	1	0	0	1	0	7	0	0	0	1	0	0	.091	.167	.182	.348
3 ML YEARS		68	96	15	4	1	0	(0	0)	21	17	3	6	12	0	39	1	4	0	6	2	2	.156	.257	.219	.476

Pat Venditte

Pitches: B **Bats:** L **Pos:** RP-3 ven-DET-ee **Ht:** 6'0" **Wt:** 186 **Born:** 6/30/1985 **Age:** 36

		HOW MUCH PITCHED					WHAT HE GAVE UP										THE RESULTS							
Year Team	Lg	G	GS	GF	IP	BFP	H	R	ER	HR	SH	SF	HB	TBB	IBB	SO	WP	W	L	Pct	Sv-Op	Hld	Vel	OPS	ERC	ERA
2015 Oak	AL	26	0	7	28.2	119	22	14	14	1	1	0	1	12	0	23	0	2	2	.500	0-0	0	85	.679	2.90	4.40
2016 2 Tms	AL	15	0	7	22.0	102	24	18	14	5	0	3	2	11	1	19	0	0	0	-	0-0	1	84	.898	6.23	5.73
2018 LAD	NL	15	0	6	14.0	57	11	4	4	1	0	0	2	3	1	9	0	0	0	-	0-0	0	86	.608	2.50	2.57
2019 SF	NL	2	0	0	3.1	19	4	6	6	1	0	0	3	2	0	2	0	0	0	-	0-0	0	85	.974	11.86	16.20
2020 Mia	NL	3	0	2	4.1	15	1	0	0	0	0	0	2	0	0	5	0	0	0	-	0-0	0	84	.431	0.70	0.00
16 Tor	AL	8	0	3	8.2	44	11	8	5	1	0	2	1	4	0	7	0	0	0	-	0-0	1	84	.796	6.06	5.19
16 Sea	AL	7	0	4	13.1	58	13	10	9	4	0	1	1	7	1	12	0	0	0	-	0-0	0	84	.974	6.34	6.08
5 ML YEARS		61	0	22	72.1	312	62	42	38	10	1	4	9	28	2	58	0	2	2	.500	0-0	3	85	.741	3.91	4.73

Alex Verdugo

Bats: L **Throws:** L **Pos:** RF-31;LF-22;PH-2;CF-1;DH-1 **Ht:** 6'0" **Wt:** 192 **Born:** 5/15/1996 **Age:** 25

							BATTING														RUNNING			AVERAGES			
Year Team	Lg	G	AB	H	2B	3B	HR	(Hm	Rd)	TB	R	RBI	RC	TBB	IBB	SO	HBP	SH	SF	SB	CS	GDP	Avg	OBP	Slg	OPS
2017 LAD	NL	15	23	4	0	0	1	(1	0)	7	1	1	0	2	0	4	0	0	0	0	1	1	.174	.240	.304	.544
2018 LAD	NL	37	77	20	6	0	1	(0	1)	29	11	4	6	8	0	14	0	1	0	0	0	4	.260	.329	.377	.706
2019 LAD	NL	106	343	101	22	2	12	(5	7)	163	43	44	51	26	1	49	2	0	6	4	1	8	.294	.342	.475	.817
2020 Bos	AL	53	201	62	16	0	6	(2	4)	96	36	15	31	17	1	45	2	0	1	4	0	4	.308	.367	.478	.844
4 ML YEARS		211	644	187	44	2	20	(8	12)	295	91	64	88	53	2	112	4	1	7	8	2	17	.290	.345	.458	.803

Justin Verlander

Pitches: R **Bats:** R **Pos:** SP-1 **Ht:** 6'5" **Wt:** 235 **Born:** 2/20/1983 **Age:** 38

		HOW MUCH PITCHED					WHAT HE GAVE UP										THE RESULTS							
Year Team	Lg	G	GS	GF	IP	BFP	H	R	ER	HR	SH	SF	HB	TBB	IBB	SO	WP	W	L	Pct	Sv-Op	Hld	Vel	OPS	ERC	ERA
2005 Det	AL	2	2	0	11.1	54	15	9	9	1	0	0	1	5	0	7	1	0	2	.000	0-0	0	95	.868	6.41	7.15
2006 Det	AL	30	30	0	186.0	776	187	78	75	21	2	4	6	60	1	124	5	17	9	.654	0-0	0	95	.741	4.12	3.63
2007 Det	AL	32	32	0	201.2	866	181	88	82	20	3	1	19	67	3	183	17	18	6	.750	0-0	0	95	.668	3.53	3.66
2008 Det	AL	33	33	0	201.0	880	195	119	108	18	4	6	14	87	8	163	6	11	17	.393	0-0	0	94	.715	4.17	4.84
2009 Det	AL	35	35	0	240.0	982	219	99	92	20	6	4	6	63	5	269	8	19	9	.679	0-0	0	96	.665	3.06	3.45
2010 Det	AL	33	33	0	224.1	925	190	89	84	14	6	8	6	71	0	219	11	18	9	.667	0-0	0	95	.630	2.79	3.37
2011 Det	AL	34	34	0	251.0	969	174	73	67	24	2	3	3	57	0	250	7	24	5	.828	0-0	0	95	.555	1.92	2.40
2012 Det	AL	33	33	0	238.1	956	192	81	70	19	4	3	5	60	2	239	2	17	8	.680	0-0	0	94	.601	2.45	2.64
2013 Det	AL	34	34	0	218.1	925	212	94	84	19	6	2	4	75	1	217	3	13	12	.520	0-0	0	93	.691	3.68	3.46
2014 Det	AL	32	32	0	206.0	893	223	114	104	18	6	5	5	65	1	159	1	15	12	.556	0-0	0	92	.756	4.19	4.54
2015 Det	AL	20	20	0	133.1	535	113	56	50	13	1	6	3	32	1	113	2	5	8	.385	0-0	0	93	.634	2.75	3.38
2016 Det	AL	34	34	0	227.2	903	171	81	77	30	4	7	8	57	1	254	6	16	9	.640	0-0	0	93	.630	2.54	3.04
2017 2 Tms	AL	33	33	0	206.0	849	170	80	77	27	1	4	4	72	4	219	5	15	8	.652	0-0	0	95	.660	3.19	3.36
2018 Hou	AL	34	34	0	214.0	833	156	63	60	28	2	5	8	37	0	290	5	16	9	.640	0-0	0	95	.602	2.16	2.52
2019 Hou	AL	34	34	0	223.0	847	137	66	64	36	0	2	6	42	0	300	4	21	6	.778	0-0	0	95	.579	1.80	2.58
2020 Hou	AL	1	1	0	6.0	21	3	2	2	2	0	0	0	1	0	7	0	1	0	1.000	0-0	0	95	.640	1.95	3.00
17 Det	AL	28	28	0	172.0	729	153	76	73	23	1	4	3	67	4	176	5	10	8	.556	0-0	0	95	.693	3.67	3.82
17 Hou	AL	5	5	0	34.0	120	17	4	4	4	0	0	1	5	0	43	0	5	0	1.000	0-0	0	95	.464	1.22	1.06
Postseason		31	30	0	187.2	754	140	74	71	26	2	3	3	60	0	205	8	14	11	.560	0-0	0	95	.629	2.73	3.40
16 ML YEARS		454	454	0	2988.0	12214	2538	1192	1105	310	43	64	98	851	27	3013	87	226	129	.637	0-0	0	94	.652	2.97	3.33

Alex Vesia

Pitches: L **Bats:** L **Pos:** RP-5 **Ht:** 6'1" **Wt:** 209 **Born:** 4/11/1996 **Age:** 25

		HOW MUCH PITCHED					WHAT HE GAVE UP										THE RESULTS							
Year Team	Lg	G	GS	GF	IP	BFP	H	R	ER	HR	SH	SF	HB	TBB	IBB	SO	WP	W	L	Pct	Sv-Op	Hld	Vel	OPS	ERC	ERA
2020 Mia	NL	5	0	0	4.1	27	7	10	9	3	0	0	0	7	0	5	0	0	1	.000	0-0	1	92	1.319	19.97	18.69

Jonathan Villar

Bats: B **Throws:** R **Pos:** 2B-25;SS-21;DH-6;CF-2;PH-2;PR-1 vee-YARR **Ht:** 6'0" **Wt:** 233 **Born:** 5/2/1991 **Age:** 30

							BATTING														RUNNING			AVERAGES			
Year Team	Lg	G	AB	H	2B	3B	HR	(Hm	Rd)	TB	R	RBI	RC	TBB	IBB	SO	HBP	SH	SF	SB	CS	GDP	Avg	OBP	Slg	OPS
2013 Hou	AL	58	210	51	9	2	1	(0	1)	67	26	8	22	24	1	71	0	7	0	18	8	5	.243	.321	.319	.640
2014 Hou	AL	87	263	55	13	2	7	(3	4)	93	31	27	24	19	1	80	2	4	1	17	4	4	.209	.267	.354	.620
2015 Hou	AL	53	116	33	7	1	2	(0	2)	48	18	11	15	10	0	29	0	1	1	7	2	3	.284	.339	.414	.752
2016 Mil	NL	156	589	168	38	3	19	(6	13)	269	92	63	102	79	4	174	2	5	4	62	18	7	.285	.369	.457	.826
2017 Mil	NL	122	403	97	18	4	11	(7	4)	156	49	40	45	30	1	132	0	2	1	23	8	6	.241	.293	.372	.665
2018 2 Tms		141	466	121	14	1	14	(6	8)	179	54	46	67	41	0	138	5	1	2	35	5	13	.260	.325	.384	.709
2019 Bal	AL	162	642	176	33	5	24	(16	8)	291	111	73	100	61	0	176	4	2	4	40	9	8	.274	.339	.453	.792

Year	Team	Lg	G	AB	H	2B	3B	HR	(Hm	Rd)	TB	R	RBI	RC	TBB	IBB	SO	HBP	SH	SF	SB	CS	GDP	Avg	OBP	Slg	OPS
2020	2 Tms		52	185	43	5	0	2	(1	1)	54	13	15	15	19	1	54	0	1	2	16	5	2	.232	.301	.292	.593
18	Mil	NL	87	257	67	10	1	6	(2	4)	97	26	22	29	19	0	80	2	0	1	14	2	9	.261	.315	.377	.693
18	Bal	AL	54	209	54	4	0	8	(4	4)	82	28	24	38	22	0	58	3	1	1	21	3	4	.258	.336	.392	.729
20	Mia	NL	30	116	30	4	0	2	(1	1)	40	10	9	9	10	1	32	0	1	1	9	5	2	.259	.315	.345	.660
20	Tor	AL	22	69	13	1	0	0	(0	0)	14	3	6	6	9	0	22	0	0	1	7	0	0	.188	.278	.203	.481
	Postseason		1	0	0	0	0	0	(0	0)	0	1	0	0	0	0	0	0	0	0	1	0	0	-	-	-	-
	8 ML YEARS		831	2874	744	137	15	80	(39	41)	1151	394	283	390	283	8	854	13	23	15	218	59	46	.259	.327	.400	.727

Meibrys Viloria

Bats: L Throws: R Pos: C-15

MAY-breez

Ht: 5'11" Wt: 225 Born: 2/15/1997 Age: 24

								BATTING												RUNNING			AVERAGES			
Year	Team	Lg	G	AB	H	2B	3B	HR	(Hm	Rd)	TB	R	RBI	RC	TBB	IBB	SO	HBP	SH	SF	SB	CS	GDP	Avg	OBP	Slg	OPS
2018	KC	AL	10	27	7	2	0	0	(0	0)	9	4	4	3	1	0	9	0	1	0	0	0	1	.259	.286	.333	.619
2019	KC	AL	42	133	28	7	0	1	(0	1)	38	7	15	9	10	0	44	0	1	4	0	1	4	.211	.259	.286	.544
2020	KC	AL	15	21	4	1	0	0	(0	0)	5	1	0	2	2	0	9	1	0	0	0	0	0	.190	.292	.238	.530
	3 ML YEARS		67	181	39	10	0	1	(0	1)	52	12	19	14	13	0	62	1	2	4	0	1	5	.215	.266	.287	.554

Nick Vincent

Pitches: R Bats: R Pos: RP-21

Ht: 5'10" Wt: 185 Born: 7/12/1986 Age: 34

			HOW MUCH PITCHED					WHAT HE GAVE UP											THE RESULTS									
Year	Team	Lg	G	GS	GF	IP	BFP	H	R	ER	HR	SH	SF	HB	TBB	IBB	SO	WP	W	L	Pct	Sv-Op	Hld	Vel	OPS	ERC	ERA
2012	SD	NL	27	0	3	26.1	105	19	5	5	2	1	0	1	7	0	28	1	2	0	1.000	0-1	5	90	.551	2.13	1.71
2013	SD	NL	45	0	7	46.1	180	33	11	11	1	4	0	2	11	3	49	0	6	3	.667	1-1	10	90	.525	1.67	2.14
2014	SD	NL	63	0	7	55.0	215	44	22	22	5	3	0	2	11	1	62	1	1	2	.333	0-2	20	90	.626	2.39	3.60
2015	SD	NL	26	0	8	23.0	100	25	8	6	0	0	1	0	10	1	22	0	1	0	1.000	0-2	5	90	.698	3.95	2.35
2016	Sea	AL	60	0	15	60.1	247	53	26	25	11	1	1	1	15	1	65	0	4	4	.500	3-9	17	90	.700	3.28	3.73
2017	Sea	AL	69	0	7	64.2	262	62	23	23	3	4	4	0	13	5	50	0	3	3	.500	0-2	29	90	.643	2.67	3.20
2018	Sea	AL	62	0	8	56.1	239	50	28	25	7	1	2	3	15	4	56	0	4	4	.500	0-2	15	90	.662	3.11	3.99
2019	2 Tms	NL	32	1	8	44.2	194	47	23	22	8	0	2	4	12	3	47	0	1	4	.200	0-0	1	89	.785	4.63	4.43
2020	Mia	NL	21	0	8	22.1	92	23	11	11	5	0	0	1	6	0	17	0	1	2	.333	3-3		89	.844	4.94	4.43
19	SF	NL	18	1	4	30.2	138	36	20	19	7	0	1	3	8	2	30	0	0	2	.000	0-0	1	89	.856	5.67	5.58
19	Phi	NL	14	0	4	14.0	56	11	3	3	1	0	1	1	4	1	17	0	1	2	.333	0-0	1	89	.606	2.56	1.93
	9 ML YEARS		405	2	71	399.0	1634	356	157	150	42	14	10	14	100	22	396	2	22	23	.489	7-22	97	90	.665	3.02	3.38

Daniel Vogelbach

Bats: L Throws: R Pos: DH-34;PH-3;1B-2

VOH-guhl-back

Ht: 6'0" Wt: 270 Born: 12/17/1992 Age: 28

								BATTING												RUNNING			AVERAGES			
Year	Team	Lg	G	AB	H	2B	3B	HR	(Hm	Rd)	TB	R	RBI	RC	TBB	IBB	SO	HBP	SH	SF	SB	CS	GDP	Avg	OBP	Slg	OPS
2016	Sea	AL	8	12	1	0	0	0	(0	0)	1	0	0	0	1	0	6	0	0	0	0	0	0	.083	.154	.083	.237
2017	Sea	AL	16	28	6	1	0	0	(0	0)	7	0	2	2	3	0	9	0	0	0	0	0	2	.214	.290	.250	.540
2018	Sea	AL	37	87	18	2	0	4	(0	4)	32	9	13	11	13	0	25	2	0	0	0	0	4	.207	.324	.368	.691
2019	Sea	AL	144	462	96	17	0	30	(12	18)	203	73	76	72	92	2	149	2	0	2	0	0	4	.208	.341	.439	.780
2020	3 Tms		39	115	24	3	0	6	(4	2)	45	16	16	15	20	1	33	1	0	0	0	0	3	.209	.331	.391	.722
20	Sea	AL	18	53	5	1	0	2	(1	1)	12	3	4	3	11	1	13	0	0	0	0	0	1	.094	.250	.226	.476
20	Tor	AL	2	4	0	0	0	0	(0	0)	0	0	0	0	1	0	2	0	0	0	0	0	0	.000	.200	.000	.200
20	Mil	NL	19	58	19	2	0	4	(3	1)	33	13	12	12	8	0	18	1	0	0	0	0	2	.328	.418	.569	.987
	5 ML YEARS		244	704	145	23	0	40	(18	22)	288	98	107	100	129	3	223	5	0	2	0	0	13	.206	.332	.409	.741

Stephen Vogt

Bats: L Throws: R Pos: C-23;PH-3;1B-1;DH-1

VOTE

Ht: 6'0" Wt: 211 Born: 11/1/1984 Age: 36

								BATTING												RUNNING			AVERAGES			
Year	Team	Lg	G	AB	H	2B	3B	HR	(Hm	Rd)	TB	R	RBI	RC	TBB	IBB	SO	HBP	SH	SF	SB	CS	GDP	Avg	OBP	Slg	OPS
2012	TB	AL	18	25	0	0	0	0	(0	0)	0	0	0	0	2	0	2	0	0	0	0	0	0	.000	.074	.000	.074
2013	Oak	AL	47	135	34	6	1	4	(3	1)	54	18	16	15	9	1	28	0	2	2	0	1	2	.252	.295	.400	.695
2014	Oak	AL	84	269	75	10	2	9	(4	5)	116	26	35	38	16	2	39	1	0	1	1	0	2	.279	.321	.431	.752
2015	Oak	AL	136	445	116	21	3	18	(5	13)	197	58	71	75	56	6	97	2	0	8	0	2	9	.261	.341	.443	.783
2016	Oak	AL	137	490	123	30	2	14	(4	10)	199	54	56	51	35	3	83	4	0	3	0	0	6	.251	.305	.406	.711
2017	2 Tms		99	279	65	15	1	12	(6	6)	118	25	40	33	21	1	56	0	1	2	0	1	2	.233	.285	.423	.708
2019	SF	NL	99	255	67	24	2	10	(3	7)	125	30	40	42	20	1	66	1	0	4	3	1	1	.263	.314	.490	.804
2020	Ari	NL	26	72	12	5	0	1	(0	1)	20	6	7	5	8	0	18	0	0	1	0	0	1	.167	.247	.278	.525
17	Oak	AL	54	157	34	8	1	4	(1	3)	56	12	20	19	16	1	31	0	1	1	0	1	1	.217	.287	.357	.644
17	Mil	NL	45	122	31	7	0	8	(5	3)	62	13	20	14	5	0	25	0	0	1	0	0	1	.254	.281	.508	.789
	Postseason		6	19	3	0	1	0	(0	0)	5	2	1	1	2	0	8	0	0	0	0	0	0	.158	.238	.263	.501
	8 ML YEARS		646	1970	492	111	11	68	(25	43)	829	217	265	259	167	14	389	8	3	21	4	5	23	.250	.308	.421	.729

Luke Voit

Bats: R Throws: R Pos: 1B-48;DH-8;PH-1

Ht: 6'3" Wt: 255 Born: 2/13/1991 Age: 30

								BATTING												RUNNING			AVERAGES			
Year	Team	Lg	G	AB	H	2B	3B	HR	(Hm	Rd)	TB	R	RBI	RC	TBB	IBB	SO	HBP	SH	SF	SB	CS	GDP	Avg	OBP	Slg	OPS
2017	StL	NL	62	114	28	9	0	4	(4	0)	49	18	18	12	7	0	31	3	0	0	0	0	4	.246	.306	.430	.736
2018	2 Tms		47	143	46	5	0	15	(7	8)	96	30	36	40	17	0	43	1	0	0	0	0	3	.322	.398	.671	1.069
2019	NYY	AL	118	429	113	21	1	21	(7	14)	199	72	62	79	71	2	142	9	0	1	0	0	12	.263	.378	.464	.842
2020	NYY	AL	56	213	59	5	0	22	(16	6)	130	41	52	46	17	0	54	3	0	1	0	0	4	.277	.338	.610	.948

Year	Team	Lg	G	AB	H	2B	3B	HR	(Hm	Rd)	TB	R	RBI	RC	TBB	IBB	SO	HBP	SH	SF	SB	CS	GDP	Avg	OBP	Slg	OPS
18	StL	NL	8	11	2	0	0	1	(1	0)	5	2	3	2	2	0	4	0	0	0	0	0	0	.182	.308	.455	.762
18	NYY	AL	39	132	44	5	0	14	(6	8)	91	28	33	38	15	0	39	1	0	0	0	0	3	.333	.405	.689	1.095
	Postseason		5	17	4	0	1	0	(0	0)	6	2	4	4	4	0	6	0	0	0	0	0	0	.235	.381	.353	.734
	4 ML YEARS		283	899	246	40	1	62	(34	28)	474	161	168	177	112	2	270	16	0	2	0	0	23	.274	.363	.527	.891

Edinson Volquez

Pitches: R **Bats:** R **Pos:** RP-7

VOHL-kezz

Ht: 6'0" **Wt:** 220 **Born:** 7/3/1983 **Age:** 37

			HOW MUCH PITCHED					WHAT HE GAVE UP										THE RESULTS						
Year	Team	Lg	G	GS	GF	IP	BFP	H	R	ER	HR	SH	SF	HB	TBB	IBB	SO	WP	W	L	Pct	Sv-Op	Hld	Vel	OPS	ERC	ERA
2005	Tex	AL	6	3	0	12.2	75	25	22	20	3	0	1	2	10	0	11	0	0	4	.000	0-0	0	94	1.155	14.15	14.21
2006	Tex	AL	8	8	0	33.1	164	52	28	27	7	0	1	1	17	0	15	0	1	6	.143	0-0	0	94	.965	9.27	7.29
2007	Tex	AL	6	6	0	34.0	149	34	18	17	4	0	2	2	15	0	29	0	2	1	.667	0-0	0	94	.750	4.63	4.50
2008	Cin	NL	33	32	1	196.0	838	167	82	70	14	6	5	14	93	5	206	10	17	6	.739	0-0	0	94	.681	3.61	3.21
2009	Cin	NL	9	9	0	49.2	218	34	25	24	6	2	1	5	32	0	47	2	4	2	.667	0-0	0	94	.683	3.77	4.35
2010	Cin	NL	12	12	0	62.2	275	59	30	30	6	3	1	3	35	0	67	5	4	3	.571	0-0	0	94	.739	4.60	4.31
2011	Cin	NL	20	20	0	108.2	489	106	72	69	19	5	6	4	65	3	104	5	5	7	.417	0-0	0	94	.833	5.42	5.71
2012	SD	NL	32	32	0	182.2	802	160	88	84	14	5	4	9	105	6	174	9	11	11	.500	0-0	0	94	.706	4.04	4.14
2013	2 Tms	NL	33	32	0	170.1	777	193	114	108	19	9	4	3	77	2	142	16	9	12	.429	0-0	0	92	.804	5.11	5.71
2014	Pit	NL	32	31	0	192.2	809	166	75	65	17	13	6	14	71	6	140	15	13	7	.650	0-0	0	93	.674	3.37	3.04
2015	KC	AL	34	33	0	200.1	850	190	89	79	16	5	7	8	72	1	155	3	13	9	.591	0-0	0	93	.692	3.66	3.55
2016	KC	AL	34	34	0	189.1	853	217	124	113	23	6	6	7	76	1	139	5	10	11	.476	0-0	0	93	.794	5.20	5.37
2017	Mia	NL	17	17	0	92.1	397	78	46	43	8	5	5	3	53	3	81	4	4	8	.333	0-0	0	93	.719	3.93	4.19
2019	Tex	AL	11	4	1	16.0	75	20	12	12	3	0	0	1	12	0	10	3	0	1	.000	0-0	1	93	.935	8.17	6.75
2020	Tex	AL	7	0	3	5.2	26	6	4	4	0	0	0	1	2	0	3	0	2	1	.667	0-0	0	94	.651	4.05	6.35
13	SD	NL	27	27	0	142.1	659	168	100	95	14	7	3	3	69	2	116	11	9	10	.474	0-0	0	92	.820	5.45	6.01
13	LAD	NL	6	5	0	28.0	118	25	14	13	5	2	1	0	8	0	26	5	0	2	.000	0-0	0	93	.714	3.45	4.18
	Postseason		7	7	0	35.1	154	27	22	21	4	1	3	2	23	2	26	0	1	4	.200	0-0	0	95	.676	3.98	5.35
	15 ML YEARS		294	273	5	1546.1	6797	1507	829	765	159	59	49	76	735	27	1323	77	95	89	.516	0-0	1	93	.745	4.42	4.45

Austin Voth

Pitches: R **Bats:** R **Pos:** SP-11

Ht: 6'2" **Wt:** 210 **Born:** 6/26/1992 **Age:** 29

			HOW MUCH PITCHED					WHAT HE GAVE UP										THE RESULTS						
Year	Team	Lg	G	GS	GF	IP	BFP	H	R	ER	HR	SH	SF	HB	TBB	IBB	SO	WP	W	L	Pct	Sv-Op	Hld	Vel	OPS	ERC	ERA
2018	Was	NL	4	2	0	12.1	55	12	9	9	3	1	1	0	6	0	11	1	1	1	.500	0-0	0	91	.780	5.19	6.57
2019	Was	NL	9	8	0	43.2	174	33	16	16	5	1	2	3	13	2	44	0	2	1	.667	0-0	0	93	.677	2.74	3.30
2020	Was	NL	11	11	0	49.2	225	57	36	35	14	0	0	4	18	2	44	1	2	5	.286	0-0	0	92	.923	6.38	6.34
	3 ML YEARS		24	21	0	105.2	454	102	61	60	22	2	3	7	37	4	99	2	5	7	.417	0-0	0	92	.812	4.65	5.11

Joey Votto

Bats: L **Throws:** R **Pos:** 1B-50;DH-5

VAH-toe

Ht: 6'2" **Wt:** 220 **Born:** 9/10/1983 **Age:** 37

			BATTING																	RUNNING			AVERAGES			
Year	Team	Lg	G	AB	H	2B	3B	HR	(Hm	Rd)	TB	R	RBI	RC	TBB	IBB	SO	HBP	SH	SF	SB	CS	GDP	Avg	OBP	Slg	OPS
2007	Cin	NL	24	84	27	7	0	4	(4	0)	46	11	17	17	5	1	15	0	0	0	1	0	0	.321	.360	.548	.907
2008	Cin	NL	151	526	156	32	3	24	(14	10)	266	69	84	91	59	9	102	2	0	2	7	5	7	.297	.368	.506	.874
2009	Cin	NL	131	469	151	38	1	25	(14	11)	266	82	84	99	70	10	106	4	0	1	4	1	8	.322	.414	.567	.981
2010	Cin	NL	150	547	177	36	2	37	(18	19)	328	106	113	132	91	8	125	7	0	3	16	5	11	.324	.424	.600	1.024
2011	Cin	NL	161	599	185	40	3	29	(13	16)	318	101	103	131	110	15	129	4	0	6	8	6	20	.309	.416	.531	.947
2012	Cin	NL	111	374	126	44	0	14	(10	4)	212	59	56	97	94	18	85	5	0	2	5	3	8	.337	.474	.567	1.041
2013	Cin	NL	162	581	177	30	3	24	(11	13)	285	101	73	121	135	19	138	4	0	6	6	3	15	.305	.435	.491	.926
2014	Cin	NL	62	220	56	16	0	6	(6	0)	90	32	23	36	47	2	49	3	0	2	1	1	5	.255	.390	.409	.799
2015	Cin	NL	158	545	171	33	2	29	(14	15)	295	95	80	135	143	15	135	5	0	2	11	3	11	.314	.459	.541	1.000
2016	Cin	NL	158	556	181	34	2	29	(16	13)	306	101	97	130	108	15	120	5	0	8	8	1	16	.326	.434	.550	.985
2017	Cin	NL	162	559	179	34	1	36	(20	16)	323	106	100	139	134	20	83	8	0	6	5	1	16	.320	.454	.578	1.032
2018	Cin	NL	145	503	143	28	2	12	(8	4)	211	67	67	98	108	6	101	9	0	3	2	0	15	.284	.417	.419	.837
2019	Cin	NL	142	525	137	32	1	15	(4	11)	216	79	47	72	76	2	123	4	0	3	5	0	14	.261	.357	.411	.768
2020	Cin	NL	54	186	42	8	0	11	(10	1)	83	32	22	26	37	1	43	0	0	0	0	0	5	.226	.354	.446	.800
	Postseason		9	32	8	0	0	0	(0	0)	8	3	1	3	4	0	9	0	0	1	0	0	1	.250	.324	.250	.574
	14 ML YEARS		1771	6274	1908	412	20	295	(162	133)	3245	1041	966	1324	1217	141	1354	60	0	44	79	29	151	.304	.419	.517	.937

Michael Wacha

Pitches: R **Bats:** R **Pos:** SP-7; RP-1

WAHK-ah

Ht: 6'6" **Wt:** 215 **Born:** 7/1/1991 **Age:** 29

			HOW MUCH PITCHED					WHAT HE GAVE UP										THE RESULTS						
Year	Team	Lg	G	GS	GF	IP	BFP	H	R	ER	HR	SH	SF	HB	TBB	IBB	SO	WP	W	L	Pct	Sv-Op	Hld	Vel	OPS	ERC	ERA
2013	StL	NL	15	9	2	64.2	260	52	20	20	5	1	0	0	19	0	65	3	4	1	.800	0-1	0	93	.603	2.52	2.78
2014	StL	NL	19	19	0	107.0	447	95	41	38	6	1	2	5	33	0	94	2	5	6	.455	0-0	0	93	.636	3.00	3.20
2015	StL	NL	30	30	0	181.1	762	162	74	68	19	8	3	6	58	4	153	4	17	7	.708	0-0	0	94	.672	3.28	3.38
2016	StL	NL	27	24	1	138.0	606	159	86	78	15	4	5	1	45	6	114	6	7	7	.500	0-0	0	93	.800	4.66	5.09
2017	StL	NL	30	30	0	165.2	701	170	82	76	17	3	4	3	55	3	158	5	12	9	.571	0-0	0	95	.735	4.07	4.13
2018	StL	NL	15	15	0	84.1	355	68	36	30	9	4	5	2	36	0	71	2	8	2	.800	0-0	0	94	.646	3.24	3.20
2019	StL	NL	29	24	0	126.2	562	143	71	67	26	6	5	3	55	4	104	2	6	7	.462	0-0	0	93	.865	5.88	4.76
2020	NYM	NL	8	7	0	34.0	156	46	26	25	9	0	0	2	7	0	37	2	1	4	.200	0-0	0	94	.951	6.76	6.62
	Postseason		7	6	1	35.1	144	24	16	16	7	0	0	1	16	4	38	0	4	3	.571	0-0	0	94	.694	3.15	4.08
	8 ML YEARS		173	158	3	901.2	3849	895	436	402	106	27	27	22	308	17	796	26	60	43	.583	0-1	0	94	.732	4.00	4.01

Brandon Waddell

Pitches: L **Bats:** L **Pos:** RP-2 **Ht:** 6'3" **Wt:** 180 **Born:** 6/3/1994 **Age:** 27

			HOW MUCH PITCHED				WHAT HE GAVE UP											THE RESULTS						
Year	Team	Lg	G	GS	GF	IP	BFP	H	R	ER	HR	SH	SF	HB	TBB	IBB	SO	WP	W	L	Pct	Sv-Op Hld	Vel	OPS	ERC	ERA
2020	Pit	NL	2	0	1	3.1	14	2	1	1	0	0	0	0	2	0	2	0	0	0	-	0-0	93	.619	2.03	2.70

Tyler Wade

Bats: L **Throws:** R **Pos:** 2B-31;SS-22;PR-7;PH-1 **Ht:** 6'1" **Wt:** 188 **Born:** 11/23/1994 **Age:** 26

							BATTING													RUNNING			AVERAGES			
Year	Team	Lg	G	AB	H	2B	3B	HR	(Hm	Rd)	TB	R	RBI	RC	TBB	IBB	SO	HBP	SH	SF	SB	CS	GDP	Avg	OBP	Slg	OPS
2017	NYY	AL	30	58	9	4	0	0	(0	0)	13	7	2	1	5	0	19	0	0	0	1	1	2	.155	.222	.224	.446
2018	NYY	AL	36	66	11	4	0	1	(0	1)	18	8	5	4	4	0	23	0	0	0	1	0	1	.167	.214	.273	.487
2019	NYY	AL	43	94	23	3	1	2	(2	0)	34	16	11	12	11	0	28	1	2	0	7	0	0	.245	.330	.362	.692
2020	NYY	AL	52	88	15	3	0	3	(3	0)	27	19	10	10	12	0	22	3	1	1	4	1	1	.170	.288	.307	.595
	4 ML YEARS		161	306	58	14	1	6	(5	1)	92	50	28	27	32	0	92	4	3	1	13	2	4	.190	.274	.301	.575

LaMonte Wade Jr.

Bats: L **Throws:** L **Pos:** 1B-4;CF-4;LF-3;PH-3;RF-2;PR-1 lah-MONT **Ht:** 6'1" **Wt:** 205 **Born:** 1/1/1994 **Age:** 27

							BATTING													RUNNING			AVERAGES			
Year	Team	Lg	G	AB	H	2B	3B	HR	(Hm	Rd)	TB	R	RBI	RC	TBB	IBB	SO	HBP	SH	SF	SB	CS	GDP	Avg	OBP	Slg	OPS
2019	Min	AL	26	56	11	2	1	2	(1	1)	21	10	5	9	11	0	9	2	0	0	0	1	0	.196	.348	.375	.723
2020	Min	AL	16	39	9	3	0	0	(0	0)	12	3	1	5	4	0	9	1	0	0	1	1	0	.231	.318	.308	.626
	2 ML YEARS		42	95	20	5	1	2	(1	1)	33	13	6	14	15	0	18	3	0	0	1	2	0	.211	.336	.347	.684

Jacob Waguespack

Pitches: R **Bats:** R **Pos:** RP-11 **Ht:** 6'6" **Wt:** 235 **Born:** 11/5/1993 **Age:** 27

				HOW MUCH PITCHED				WHAT HE GAVE UP											THE RESULTS					
Year	Team	Lg	G	GS	GF	IP	BFP	H	R	ER	HR	SH	SF	HB	TBB	IBB	SO	WP	W	L	Pct	Sv-Op Hld	Vel	OPS	ERC	ERA
2019	Tor	AL	16	13	0	78.0	335	75	43	38	12	0	0	5	29	0	63	2	5	5	.500	0-0	92	.764	4.40	4.38
2020	Tor	AL	11	0	2	17.2	90	27	20	16	2	0	1	2	9	0	16	0	0	0	-	0-0 1	92	.897	8.30	8.15
	2 ML YEARS		27	13	2	95.2	425	102	63	54	14	0	1	7	38	0	79	2	5	5	.500	0-0 1	92	.792	5.08	5.08

Bobby Wahl

Pitches: R **Bats:** R **Pos:** RP-3 **Ht:** 6'3" **Wt:** 216 **Born:** 3/21/1992 **Age:** 29

				HOW MUCH PITCHED				WHAT HE GAVE UP											THE RESULTS					
Year	Team	Lg	G	GS	GF	IP	BFP	H	R	ER	HR	SH	SF	HB	TBB	IBB	SO	WP	W	L	Pct	Sv-Op Hld	Vel	OPS	ERC	ERA
2017	Oak	AL	7	0	1	7.2	36	8	4	4	0	0	0	1	4	0	8	2	0	0	-	0-0	95	.716	4.41	4.70
2018	NYM	NL	7	0	0	5.1	29	9	6	6	2	0	0	0	4	0	7	0	0	1	.000	0-0 2	95	1.088	12.44	10.13
2020	Mil	NL	3	0	1	2.1	11	4	3	3	2	1	0	0	0	0	1	0	0	1	.000	0-0 1	94	1.500	12.56	11.57
	3 ML YEARS		17	0	2	15.1	76	21	13	13	4	1	0	1	8	0	16	2	0	2	.000	0-0 2	95	.976	8.31	7.63

Adam Wainwright

Pitches: R **Bats:** R **Pos:** SP-10 **Ht:** 6'7" **Wt:** 230 **Born:** 8/30/1981 **Age:** 39

				HOW MUCH PITCHED				WHAT HE GAVE UP											THE RESULTS					
Year	Team	Lg	G	GS	GF	IP	BFP	H	R	ER	HR	SH	SF	HB	TBB	IBB	SO	WP	W	L	Pct	Sv-Op Hld	Vel	OPS	ERC	ERA
2005	StL	NL	2	0	1	2.0	9	2	3	3	1	0	0	0	1	0	0	0	0	0	-	0-0	91	.958	7.30	13.50
2006	StL	NL	61	0	10	75.0	309	64	26	26	6	4	1	4	22	2	72	3	2	1	.667	3-5 17	91	.644	2.92	3.12
2007	StL	NL	32	32	0	202.0	882	212	93	83	13	9	5	9	70	4	136	6	14	12	.538	0-0	89	.721	4.01	3.70
2008	StL	NL	20	20	0	132.0	544	122	51	47	12	6	4	3	34	1	91	3	11	3	.786	0-0	90	.688	3.14	3.20
2009	StL	NL	34	34	0	233.0	970	216	75	64	17	10	5	3	66	1	212	7	19	8	.704	0-0	91	.646	3.08	2.63
2010	StL	NL	33	33	0	230.1	910	186	68	62	15	13	6	4	56	2	213	2	20	11	.645	0-0	91	.604	2.36	2.42
2012	StL	NL	32	32	0	198.2	831	196	96	87	15	9	6	6	52	3	184	5	14	13	.519	0-0	90	.701	3.41	3.94
2013	StL	NL	34	34	0	241.2	956	223	83	79	15	13	2	6	35	2	219	5	19	9	.679	0-0	91	.636	2.60	2.94
2014	StL	NL	32	32	0	227.0	898	184	64	60	10	8	3	7	50	5	179	4	20	9	.690	0-0	90	.580	2.20	2.38
2015	StL	NL	7	4	2	28.0	111	25	7	5	0	2	0	0	4	0	20	0	2	1	.667	0-0	90	.590	1.97	1.61
2016	StL	NL	33	33	0	198.2	847	220	108	102	22	8	9	5	59	4	161	1	13	9	.591	0-0	90	.785	4.50	4.62
2017	StL	NL	24	23	0	123.1	546	140	73	70	14	5	1	5	45	4	96	2	12	5	.706	0-0	90	.794	4.93	5.11
2018	StL	NL	8	8	0	40.1	181	41	21	20	5	3	2	2	18	1	40	1	2	4	.333	0-0	89	.753	4.60	4.46
2019	StL	NL	31	31	0	171.2	745	181	83	80	22	6	5	8	64	7	153	2	14	10	.583	0-0	90	.782	4.64	4.19
2020	StL	NL	10	10	0	65.2	262	54	25	23	9	0	1	2	15	0	54	0	5	3	.625	0-0	89	.640	2.85	3.15
	Postseason		27	14	9	105.2	426	95	36	33	10	3	2	2	18	1	115	3	4	5	.444	4-5 0	92	.646	2.69	2.81
	15 ML YEARS		393	326	13	2169.1	9001	2066	876	815	176	96	50	64	591	36	1830	41	167	98	.630	3-5 17	90	.683	3.31	3.38

Marcus Walden

Pitches: R **Bats:** R **Pos:** RP-15 **Ht:** 5'10" **Wt:** 198 **Born:** 9/13/1988 **Age:** 32

				HOW MUCH PITCHED				WHAT HE GAVE UP											THE RESULTS					
Year	Team	Lg	G	GS	GF	IP	BFP	H	R	ER	HR	SH	SF	HB	TBB	IBB	SO	WP	W	L	Pct	Sv-Op Hld	Vel	OPS	ERC	ERA
2018	Bos	AL	8	0	5	14.2	59	14	7	6	0	0	0	1	9	0	14	2	0	0	-	1-1 1	94	.669	2.79	3.68
2019	Bos	AL	70	0	8	78.0	327	61	38	33	6	1	2	5	32	1	76	6	9	2	.818	2-6 6	94	.642	3.00	3.81
2020	Bos	AL	15	0	4	13.1	71	23	18	14	5	0	0	0	9	0	10	1	0	2	.000	1-1 2	93	1.209	12.50	9.45
	3 ML YEARS		93	0	17	106.0	457	98	63	53	11	1	2	6	44	1	100	9	9	4	.692	4-8 9	94	.733	3.94	4.50

Christian Walker

Bats: R **Throws:** R **Pos:** 1B-43;DH-14;PH-1   **Ht:** 6'0" **Wt:** 210 **Born:** 3/28/1991 **Age:** 30

Year	Team	Lg	G	AB	H	2B	3B	HR	(Hm	Rd)	TB	R	RBI	RC	TBB	IBB	SO	HBP	SH	SF	SB	CS	GDP	Avg	OBP	Slg	OPS
2014	Bal	AL	6	18	3	1	0	1	(1	0)	7	1	1	1	1	0	9	0	0	0	0	0	0	.167	.211	.389	.599
2015	Bal	AL	7	9	1	0	0	0	(0	0)	1	0	0	1	3	0	4	0	0	0	0	0	0	.111	.333	.111	.444
2017	Ari	NL	11	12	3	1	0	2	(2	0)	10	2	2	2	1	0	5	2	0	0	0	0	0	.250	.400	.833	1.233
2018	Ari	NL	37	49	8	2	0	3	(2	1)	19	6	6	3	3	0	22	1	0	0	1	0	1	.163	.226	.388	.614
2019	Ari	NL	152	529	137	26	1	29	(16	13)	252	86	73	83	67	6	155	6	0	1	8	1	11	.259	.348	.476	.825
2020	Ari	NL	57	218	59	18	1	7	(5	2)	100	35	34	34	19	0	50	3	0	3	1	1	6	.271	.333	.459	.792
	Postseason		2	1	1	0	0	0	(0	0)	1	0	0	1	0	0	0	1	0	0	0	0	0	1.000	1.000	1.000	2.000
	6 ML YEARS		270	835	211	48	2	42	(26	16)	389	130	116	123	94	6	245	12	0	4	10	2	18	.253	.335	.466	.801

Neil Walker

Bats: B **Throws:** R **Pos:** 2B-9;DH-4;PH-4;1B-3;3B-2;LF-1;PR-1   **Ht:** 6'2" **Wt:** 214 **Born:** 9/10/1985 **Age:** 35

Year	Team	Lg	G	AB	H	2B	3B	HR	(Hm	Rd)	TB	R	RBI	RC	TBB	IBB	SO	HBP	SH	SF	SB	CS	GDP	Avg	OBP	Slg	OPS
2009	Pit	NL	17	36	7	1	0	0	(0	0)	8	5	0	2	4	0	11	0	0	0	1	0	1	.194	.275	.222	.497
2010	Pit	NL	110	426	126	29	3	12	(5	7)	197	57	66	66	34	1	83	3	2	4	2	3	4	.296	.349	.462	.811
2011	Pit	NL	159	596	163	36	4	12	(4	8)	243	76	83	77	54	5	112	4	0	8	9	6	15	.273	.334	.408	.742
2012	Pit	NL	129	472	132	27	0	14	(7	7)	201	62	69	72	47	1	104	2	1	8	7	5	11	.280	.342	.426	.768
2013	Pit	NL	133	478	120	24	4	16	(8	8)	200	62	53	62	50	4	85	15	5	3	1	2	14	.251	.339	.418	.757
2014	Pit	NL	137	512	139	25	3	23	(10	13)	239	74	76	72	45	2	88	11	1	2	2	2	12	.271	.342	.467	.809
2015	Pit	NL	151	543	146	32	3	16	(8	8)	232	69	71	73	44	5	110	8	0	8	4	1	9	.269	.328	.427	.756
2016	NYM	NL	113	412	116	9	1	23	(10	13)	196	57	55	66	42	3	84	1	0	3	3	1	11	.282	.347	.476	.823
2017	2 Tms	NL	111	385	102	21	2	14	(7	7)	169	59	49	66	55	2	77	5	1	2	0	2	9	.265	.362	.439	.801
2018	NYY	AL	113	347	76	12	1	11	(5	6)	123	48	46	46	42	3	87	5	0	4	0	0	3	.219	.309	.354	.664
2019	Mia	NL	115	337	88	19	1	8	(4	4)	133	37	38	50	42	1	77	1	0	1	3	0	8	.261	.344	.395	.738
2020	Phi	NL	18	39	9	3	0	0	(0	0)	12	5	3	2	1	0	13	0	0	1	0	0	0	.231	.244	.308	.552
17	NYM	NL	73	265	70	13	2	10	(4	6)	117	40	36	46	27	1	47	4	1	2	0	1	4	.264	.339	.442	.780
17	Mil	NL	38	120	32	8	0	4	(3	1)	52	19	13	20	28	1	30	1	0	0	0	1	5	.267	.409	.433	.843
	Postseason		12	35	3	1	0	0	(0	0)	4	1	2	2	2	0	11	1	0	0	0	0	0	.086	.158	.114	.272
	12 ML YEARS		1306	4583	1224	238	22	149	(68	81)	1953	611	609	654	460	27	931	55	10	44	32	22	97	.267	.338	.426	.764

Taijuan Walker

Pitches: R **Bats:** R **Pos:** SP-11   TIE-wahn   **Ht:** 6'4" **Wt:** 235 **Born:** 8/13/1992 **Age:** 28

Year	Team	Lg	G	GS	GF	IP	BFP	H	R	ER	HR	SH	SF	HB	TBB	IBB	SO	WP	W	L	Pct	Sv-Op	Hld	Vel	OPS	ERC	ERA
2013	Sea	AL	3	3	0	15.0	60	11	7	6	0	0	2	0	4	0	12	0	1	0	1.000	0-0	0	95	.546	1.63	3.60
2014	Sea	AL	8	5	2	38.0	160	31	12	11	2	0	0	3	18	1	34	2	2	3	.400	0-0	0	95	.642	3.34	2.61
2015	Sea	AL	29	29	0	169.2	706	163	92	86	25	4	5	9	40	1	157	4	11	8	.579	0-0	0	94	.717	3.74	4.56
2016	Sea	AL	25	25	0	134.1	573	129	75	63	27	3	3	8	37	2	119	4	8	11	.421	0-0	0	94	.767	4.20	4.22
2017	Ari	NL	28	28	0	157.1	684	148	76	61	17	5	8	9	61	7	146	7	9	9	.500	0-0	0	94	.732	3.85	3.49
2018	Ari	NL	3	3	0	13.0	56	15	5	5	1	0	0	0	5	0	9	0	0	0	-	0-0	0	94	.749	4.88	3.46
2019	Ari	NL	1	1	0	1.0	4	1	0	0	0	0	0	0	0	0	1	0	0	0	-	0-0	0	93	.750	1.95	0.00
2020	2 Tms	AL	11	11	0	53.1	225	43	23	16	8	0	1	4	19	0	50	1	4	3	.571	0-0	0	93	.661	3.42	2.70
20	Sea	AL	5	5	0	27.0	112	21	13	12	5	0	1	3	8	0	25	0	2	2	.500	0-0	0	93	.676	3.42	4.00
20	Tor	AL	6	6	0	26.1	113	22	10	4	3	0	0	1	11	0	25	1	2	1	.667	0-0	0	93	.647	3.41	1.37
	Postseason		1	1	0	1.0	9	4	4	4	1	0	0	0	2	1	3	0	0	1	.000	0-0	0	93	1.810	44.27	36.00
	8 ML YEARS		108	105	2	581.2	2468	541	290	248	80	12	19	33	184	11	528	18	35	34	.507	0-0	0	94	.720	3.79	3.84

Chad Wallach

Bats: R **Throws:** R **Pos:** C-15;PH-1   **Ht:** 6'2" **Wt:** 246 **Born:** 11/4/1991 **Age:** 29

Year	Team	Lg	G	AB	H	2B	3B	HR	(Hm	Rd)	TB	R	RBI	RC	TBB	IBB	SO	HBP	SH	SF	SB	CS	GDP	Avg	OBP	Slg	OPS
2017	Cin	NL	6	11	1	0	0	0	(0	0)	1	0	0	0	0	0	5	0	0	0	0	0	0	.091	.091	.091	.182
2018	Mia	NL	15	45	8	1	0	1	(1	0)	12	4	5	4	4	0	23	2	1	0	0	0	0	.178	.275	.267	.541
2019	Mia	NL	19	48	12	3	0	1	(1	0)	18	4	3	5	6	0	12	0	0	0	0	0	0	.250	.333	.375	.708
2020	Mia	NL	15	44	10	3	0	1	(1	0)	16	4	6	7	3	0	12	0	1	0	0	0	1	.227	.277	.364	.640
	4 ML YEARS		55	148	31	7	0	3	(3	0)	47	12	14	16	13	0	52	2	2	0	0	0	1	.209	.282	.318	.600

Jared Walsh

Bats: L **Throws:** L **Pos:** 1B-29;PR-5;RF-2;PH-2;DH-1   **Ht:** 6'0" **Wt:** 210 **Born:** 7/30/1993 **Age:** 27

Year	Team	Lg	G	AB	H	2B	3B	HR	(Hm	Rd)	TB	R	RBI	RC	TBB	IBB	SO	HBP	SH	SF	SB	CS	GDP	Avg	OBP	Slg	OPS
2019	LAA	AL	34	79	16	5	1	1	(1	0)	26	6	5	8	6	1	35	2	0	0	0	0	0	.203	.276	.329	.605
2020	LAA	AL	32	99	29	4	2	9	(4	5)	64	19	26	21	5	0	15	1	0	3	0	0	0	.293	.324	.646	.971
	2 ML YEARS		66	178	45	9	3	10	(5	5)	90	25	31	29	11	1	50	3	0	3	0	0	0	.253	.303	.506	.808

Donovan Walton

Bats: L **Throws:** R **Pos:** SS-4;2B-1   **Ht:** 5'10" **Wt:** 175 **Born:** 5/25/1994 **Age:** 27

Year	Team	Lg	G	AB	H	2B	3B	HR	(Hm	Rd)	TB	R	RBI	RC	TBB	IBB	SO	HBP	SH	SF	SB	CS	GDP	Avg	OBP	Slg	OPS
2019	Sea	AL	7	16	3	0	0	0	(0	0)	3	2	2	1	3	0	5	0	0	0	0	1	0	.188	.316	.188	.503
2020	Sea	AL	5	13	2	1	0	0	(0	0)	3	0	3	0	1	0	5	0	0	0	0	1	1	.154	.214	.231	.445
	2 ML YEARS		12	29	5	1	0	0	(0	0)	6	2	5	1	4	0	10	0	0	0	0	2	1	.172	.273	.207	.480

Taylor Ward

Bats: R **Throws:** R **Pos:** RF-19;LF-17;PH-4;1B-2;DH-1;PR-1
Ht: 6'1" **Wt:** 200 **Born:** 12/14/1993 **Age:** 27

							BATTING																RUNNING			AVERAGES			
Year	Team	Lg	G	AB	H	2B	3B	HR	(Hm	Rd)	TB	R	RBI	RC	TBB	IBB	SO	HBP	SH	SF		SB	CS	GDP		Avg	OBP	Slg	OPS
2018	LAA	AL	40	135	24	3	0	6	(4	2)	45	14	15	14	9	0	45	3	0	0		2	0	0		.178	.245	.333	.578
2019	LAA	AL	20	42	8	3	0	1	(1	0)	14	4	2	2	6	0	23	0	0	0		0	0	1		.190	.292	.333	.625
2020	LAA	AL	34	94	26	6	2	0	(0	0)	36	16	5	14	8	0	28	0	0	0		2	0	1		.277	.333	.383	.716
3 ML YEARS			94	271	58	12	2	7	(5	2)	95	34	22	30	23	0	96	3	0	0		4	0	2		.214	.283	.351	.633

Drew Waters

Bats: B **Throws:** R **Pos:** CF
Ht: 6'2" **Wt:** 185 **Born:** 12/30/1998 **Age:** 22

							BATTING														RUNNING			AVERAGES			
Year	Team	Lg	G	AB	H	2B	3B	HR	(-	-)	TB	R	RBI	RC	TBB	IBB	SO	HBP	SH	SF	SB	CS	GDP	Avg	OBP	Slg	OPS
2017	2 Tms	Low	50	198	55	14	2	4	(-	-)	85	33	24	33	23	0	70	3	0	0	6	3	3	.278	.362	.429	.791
2018	2 Tms	Low	114	460	135	39	9	9	(-	-)	219	72	39	48	29	0	105	7	0	2	23	5	8	.293	.343	.476	.819
2019	Missi	AA	108	420	134	35	9	5	(-	-)	202	63	41	73	28	1	121	4	0	2	13	6	3	.319	.366	.481	.847
2019	Gwnntt	AAA	26	107	29	5	0	2	(-	-)	40	17	11	14	11	0	43	0	0	1	3	0	3	.271	.336	.374	.710

Tony Watson

Pitches: L **Bats:** L **Pos:** RP-21
Ht: 6'3" **Wt:** 224 **Born:** 5/30/1985 **Age:** 36

			HOW MUCH PITCHED					WHAT HE GAVE UP									THE RESULTS						
Year	Team	Lg	G	GS	GF	IP	BFP	H	R	ER	HR	SH	SF	HB	TBB	IBB	SO	WP	W	L	Pct	Sv-Op	Hld	Vel	OPS	ERC	ERA
2011	Pit	NL	43	0	6	41.0	174	34	18	18	6	2	1	1	20	4	37	0	2	2	.500	0-1	10	91	.711	3.75	3.95
2012	Pit	NL	68	0	10	53.1	215	37	21	20	5	2	2	1	23	1	53	1	5	2	.714	0-2	16	94	.623	2.62	3.38
2013	Pit	NL	67	0	14	71.2	280	51	19	19	5	3	1	6	12	1	54	2	3	1	.750	2-4	22	94	.544	1.88	2.39
2014	Pit	NL	78	0	3	77.1	305	64	16	14	5	5	3	6	15	0	81	0	10	2	.833	2-9	34	94	.613	2.54	1.63
2015	Pit	NL	77	0	4	75.1	293	55	17	16	3	1	3	4	17	1	62	1	4	1	.800	1-3	41	94	.525	1.92	1.91
2016	Pit	NL	70	0	27	67.2	272	52	26	23	10	4	3	3	20	1	58	0	2	5	.286	15-20	23	93	.672	2.92	3.06
2017	2 Tms	NL	71	0	23	66.2	291	72	26	25	9	5	2	5	20	7	53	0	7	4	.636	10-18	14	94	.764	4.50	3.38
2018	SF	NL	72	0	10	66.0	261	54	19	19	4	3	2	1	14	3	72	0	4	6	.400	0-4	32	92	.599	2.21	2.59
2019	SF	NL	60	0	4	54.0	231	56	26	25	9	2	0	5	12	1	41	1	2	2	.500	0-3	25	93	.757	4.36	4.17
2020	SF	NL	21	0	4	18.0	73	13	8	5	3	0	1	1	3	0	15	0	1	0	1.000	2-2	10	90	.571	2.24	2.50
17	Pit	NL	47	0	22	46.2	209	57	20	19	7	3	2	3	14	4	35	0	5	3	.625	10-17	6	93	.824	5.45	3.66
17	LAD	NL	24	0	1	20.0	82	15	6	6	2	2	0	2	6	3	18	0	2	1	.667	0-1	8	94	.607	2.52	2.70
	Postseason		16	0	0	12.0	48	9	4	3	1	0	0	2	2	0	5	0	2	0	1.000	0-0	4	94	.566	2.43	2.25
10 ML YEARS			627	0	105	591.0	2395	488	196	184	59	27	18	33	156	19	526	5	40	25	.615	32-66	227	93	.638	2.82	2.80

Luke Weaver

Pitches: R **Bats:** R **Pos:** SP-12
Ht: 6'2" **Wt:** 185 **Born:** 8/21/1993 **Age:** 27

			HOW MUCH PITCHED					WHAT HE GAVE UP									THE RESULTS						
Year	Team	Lg	G	GS	GF	IP	BFP	H	R	ER	HR	SH	SF	HB	TBB	IBB	SO	WP	W	L	Pct	Sv-Op	Hld	Vel	OPS	ERC	ERA
2016	StL	NL	9	8	0	36.1	167	46	29	23	7	2	3	2	12	0	45	1	1	4	.200	0-0	0	92	.870	6.23	5.70
2017	StL	NL	13	10	0	60.1	252	59	27	26	7	1	1	1	17	1	72	0	7	2	.778	0-0	0	93	.699	3.66	3.88
2018	StL	NL	30	25	0	136.1	609	150	83	75	19	9	1	3	54	2	121	3	7	11	.389	0-0	0	94	.786	4.93	4.95
2019	Ari	NL	12	12	0	64.1	260	55	22	21	6	0	1	1	14	1	69	0	4	3	.571	0-0	0	94	.645	2.73	2.94
2020	Ari	NL	12	12	0	52.0	236	63	39	38	10	0	1	1	18	0	55	0	1	9	.100	0-0	0	94	.871	5.78	6.58
5 ML YEARS			76	67	3	349.1	1524	373	200	183	49	12	7	10	115	4	362	4	20	29	.408	0-0	0	93	.769	4.53	4.71

Jacob Webb

Pitches: R **Bats:** R **Pos:** RP-8
Ht: 6'2" **Wt:** 210 **Born:** 8/15/1993 **Age:** 27

			HOW MUCH PITCHED					WHAT HE GAVE UP									THE RESULTS						
Year	Team	Lg	G	GS	GF	IP	BFP	H	R	ER	HR	SH	SF	HB	TBB	IBB	SO	WP	W	L	Pct	Sv-Op	Hld	Vel	OPS	ERC	ERA
2019	Atl	NL	36	0	12	32.1	131	24	10	5	4	1	0	1	12	0	28	3	4	0	1.000	2-4	9	95	.661	2.89	1.39
2020	Atl	NL	8	0	4	10.0	40	7	2	0	0	0	0	0	5	1	10	0	0	0	-	0-0	0	94	.529	2.16	0.00
2 ML YEARS			44	0	16	42.1	171	31	12	5	4	1	0	1	17	1	38	3	4	0	1.000	2-4	9	95	.630	2.72	1.06

Logan Webb

Pitches: R **Bats:** R **Pos:** SP-11; RP-2
Ht: 6'1" **Wt:** 220 **Born:** 11/18/1996 **Age:** 24

			HOW MUCH PITCHED					WHAT HE GAVE UP									THE RESULTS						
Year	Team	Lg	G	GS	GF	IP	BFP	H	R	ER	HR	SH	SF	HB	TBB	IBB	SO	WP	W	L	Pct	Sv-Op	Hld	Vel	OPS	ERC	ERA
2019	SF	NL	8	8	0	39.2	174	44	25	23	5	0	1	4	14	0	37	4	2	3	.400	0-0	0	93	.795	4.81	5.22
2020	SF	NL	13	11	0	54.1	246	61	38	33	4	0	1	7	24	1	46	3	3	4	.429	0-0	0	93	.806	5.31	5.47
2 ML YEARS			21	19	0	94.0	420	105	63	56	9	0	2	8	38	1	83	7	5	7	.417	0-0	0	93	.802	5.10	5.36

Tyler Webb

Pitches: L **Bats:** L **Pos:** RP-21
Ht: 6'5" **Wt:** 240 **Born:** 7/20/1990 **Age:** 30

			HOW MUCH PITCHED					WHAT HE GAVE UP									THE RESULTS						
Year	Team	Lg	G	GS	GF	IP	BFP	H	R	ER	HR	SH	SF	HB	TBB	IBB	SO	WP	W	L	Pct	Sv-Op	Hld	Vel	OPS	ERC	ERA
2017	2 Tms		9	0	3	8.0	36	9	5	5	2	0	0	0	5	1	8	0	0	0	-	0-1	0	91	.905	6.96	5.63
2018	2 Tms	NL	22	0	5	20.1	90	22	15	10	3	1	0	1	9	2	15	0	1	0	1.000	0-0	0	90	.828	5.17	4.43
2019	StL	NL	65	0	11	55.0	221	33	23	23	7	2	2	2	23	3	48	2	2	1	.667	1-1	8	90	.593	2.29	3.76
2020	StL	NL	21	0	5	21.2	87	17	5	5	2	1	1	0	7	0	19	1	1	1	.500	1-3	2	90	.600	2.62	2.08
17	NYY	AL	7	0	2	6.0	23	3	3	3	1	0	0	0	4	0	5	0	0	0	-	0-0	0	91	.673	3.11	4.50
17	Mil	NL	2	0	1	2.0	13	6	2	2	1	0	0	0	1	1	3	0	0	0	-	0-1	0	92	1.288	21.60	9.00

Year	Team	Lg	G	GS	GF	IP	BFP	H	R	ER	HR	SH	SF	HB	TBB	IBB	SO	WP	W	L	Pct	Sv-Op	Hld	Vel	OPS	ERC	ERA
18	SD	NL	4	0	1	5.0	24	6	7	7	2	0	0	0	3	0	4	0	0	1	.000	0-0	0	89	1.042	8.40	12.60
18	StL	NL	18	0	4	15.1	66	16	8	3	1	1	0	1	6	2	11	0	0	0	-	0-0	0	90	.750	4.17	1.76
Postseason			5	0	1	3.1	16	4	3	2	0	0	0	1	1	1	5	0	0	0	-	0-0	0	91	.732	4.53	5.40
4 ML YEARS			117	0	24	105.0	434	81	48	43	14	4	3	3	44	6	90	3	3	3	.500	2-5	10	90	.669	3.17	3.69

Ryan Weber

Pitches: R **Bats:** R **Pos:** RP-12; SP-5   **Ht:** 6'1" **Wt:** 175 **Born:** 8/12/1990 **Age:** 30

Year	Team	Lg	G	GS	GF	IP	BFP	H	R	ER	HR	SH	SF	HB	TBB	IBB	SO	WP	W	L	Pct	Sv-Op	Hld	Vel	OPS	ERC	ERA
2015	Atl	NL	5	5	0	28.1	109	25	15	15	3	0	0	2	6	0	19	0	0	3	.000	0-0	0	90	.699	3.26	4.76
2016	Atl	NL	16	2	6	36.1	157	46	22	22	7	1	0	2	5	2	23	1	1	1	.500	0-1	0	91	.877	5.40	5.45
2017	Sea	AL	1	1	0	3.2	14	3	1	1	0	0	0	0	0	0	0	0	0	0	-	0-0	0	90	.500	1.32	2.45
2018	TB	AL	2	0	0	5.1	25	5	5	3	0	0	1	1	2	0	1	0	0	1	.000	0-0	0	89	.701	3.36	5.06
2019	Bos	AL	18	3	8	40.2	181	48	25	23	5	1	0	3	8	0	29	2	2	4	.333	0-0	0	89	.789	4.63	5.09
2020	Bos	AL	17	5	3	43.0	185	44	23	21	8	1	1	3	14	0	27	1	1	3	.250	0-0	5	89	.807	4.84	4.40
6 ML YEARS			59	16	17	157.1	671	171	91	85	23	3	2	11	35	2	99	4	4	12	.250	0-1	5	89	.791	4.47	4.86

Jordan Weems

Pitches: R **Bats:** L **Pos:** RP-9   **Ht:** 6'3" **Wt:** 175 **Born:** 11/7/1992 **Age:** 28

Year	Team	Lg	G	GS	GF	IP	BFP	H	R	ER	HR	SH	SF	HB	TBB	IBB	SO	WP	W	L	Pct	Sv-Op	Hld	Vel	OPS	ERC	ERA
2020	Oak	AL	9	0	4	14.0	58	10	5	5	1	0	1	0	7	0	18	2	0	0	-	0-0	0	95	.593	2.74	3.21

Patrick Weigel

Pitches: R **Bats:** R **Pos:** RP-1   **Ht:** 6'6" **Wt:** 240 **Born:** 7/8/1994 **Age:** 26

Year	Team	Lg	G	GS	GF	IP	BFP	H	R	ER	HR	SH	SF	HB	TBB	IBB	SO	WP	W	L	Pct	Sv-Op	Hld	Vel	OPS	ERC	ERA
2020	Atl	NL	1	0	0	0.2	7	2	2	2	0	0	1	0	3	0	0	1	0	0	-	0-0	0	94	1.714	37.18	27.00

J.B. Wendelken

Pitches: R **Bats:** R **Pos:** RP-21   **Ht:** 6'1" **Wt:** 242 **Born:** 3/24/1993 **Age:** 28

Year	Team	Lg	G	GS	GF	IP	BFP	H	R	ER	HR	SH	SF	HB	TBB	IBB	SO	WP	W	L	Pct	Sv-Op	Hld	Vel	OPS	ERC	ERA
2016	Oak	AL	8	0	3	12.2	64	18	15	14	3	0	0	0	9	0	12	2	0	0	-	0-0	0	93	.931	9.17	9.95
2018	Oak	AL	13	0	3	16.2	62	8	1	1	1	0	0	0	5	0	14	1	0	0	-	0-0	1	95	.438	1.20	0.54
2019	Oak	AL	27	0	4	32.2	131	21	14	13	2	1	1	2	9	2	34	2	3	1	.750	0-1	1	95	.543	1.69	3.58
2020	Oak	AL	21	0	6	25.0	106	17	8	5	2	0	1	0	11	0	31	2	1	1	.500	0-0	2	95	.546	2.30	1.80
4 ML YEARS			69	0	16	87.0	363	64	38	33	8	1	2	2	34	2	91	7	4	2	.667	0-1	4	94	.593	2.58	3.41

Joey Wendle

Bats: L **Throws:** R **Pos:** 3B-28;2B-20;SS-10;PH-2;PR-1   **Ht:** 6'1" **Wt:** 195 **Born:** 4/26/1990 **Age:** 31

Year	Team	Lg	G	AB	H	2B	3B	HR	(Hm	Rd)	TB	R	RBI	RC	TBB	IBB	SO	HBP	SH	SF	SB	CS	GDP	Avg	OBP	Slg	OPS
2016	Oak	AL	28	96	25	1	0	1	(0	1)	29	11	11	10	6	0	16	0	0	2	2	0	3	.260	.298	.302	.600
2017	Oak	AL	8	13	4	1	0	1	(0	1)	8	3	5	4	1	1	3	0	0	0	0	0	0	.308	.357	.615	.973
2018	TB	AL	139	487	146	33	6	7	(2	5)	212	62	61	70	37	4	96	9	2	10	16	4	11	.300	.354	.435	.789
2019	TB	AL	75	238	55	13	2	3	(2	1)	81	32	19	23	14	0	47	8	0	3	8	3	4	.231	.293	.340	.633
2020	TB	AL	50	168	48	9	2	4	(1	3)	73	24	17	24	10	1	35	5	0	1	8	2	1	.286	.342	.435	.777
Postseason			5	10	2	1	0	0	(0	0)	3	1	1	1	0	0	5	0	0	0	0	0	1	.200	.200	.300	.500
5 ML YEARS			300	1002	278	57	10	16	(5	11)	403	132	113	131	68	6	197	22	2	16	34	9	19	.277	.332	.402	.734

Zack Wheeler

Pitches: R **Bats:** L **Pos:** SP-11   **Ht:** 6'4" **Wt:** 195 **Born:** 5/30/1990 **Age:** 31

Year	Team	Lg	G	GS	GF	IP	BFP	H	R	ER	HR	SH	SF	HB	TBB	IBB	SO	WP	W	L	Pct	Sv-Op	Hld	Vel	OPS	ERC	ERA
2013	NYM	NL	17	17	0	100.0	431	90	42	38	10	3	7	4	46	2	84	6	7	5	.583	0-0	0	94	.696	3.88	3.42
2014	NYM	NL	32	32	0	185.1	794	167	84	73	14	5	3	11	79	3	187	9	11	11	.500	0-0	0	95	.678	3.68	3.54
2017	NYM	NL	17	17	0	86.1	386	97	53	50	15	0	1	3	40	1	81	1	3	7	.300	0-0	0	95	.828	5.81	5.21
2018	NYM	NL	29	29	0	182.1	744	150	69	67	14	8	4	9	55	0	179	2	12	7	.632	0-0	0	96	.611	2.81	3.31
2019	NYM	NL	31	31	0	195.1	828	196	93	86	22	8	7	2	50	4	195	5	11	8	.579	0-0	0	97	.694	3.57	3.96
2020	Phi	NL	11	11	0	71.0	288	67	26	23	3	1	0	7	16	2	53	0	4	2	.667	0-0	0	97	.662	3.16	2.92
6 ML YEARS			137	137	0	820.1	3471	767	367	337	78	25	22	36	286	12	779	23	48	40	.545	0-0	0	96	.685	3.64	3.70

Eli White

Bats: R **Throws:** R **Pos:** LF-13;RF-3;CF-1;DH-1;PH-1;PR-1   **Ht:** 6'3" **Wt:** 195 **Born:** 6/26/1994 **Age:** 27

Year	Team	Lg	G	AB	H	2B	3B	HR	(Hm	Rd)	TB	R	RBI	RC	TBB	IBB	SO	HBP	SH	SF	SB	CS	GDP	Avg	OBP	Slg	OPS
2020	Tex	AL	19	48	9	2	0	0	(0	0)	11	5	3	2	3	0	16	0	0	1	1	1	0	.188	.231	.229	.460

Evan White

Bats: R **Throws:** L **Pos:** 1B-54;PH-1   **Ht:** 6'3" **Wt:** 220 **Born:** 4/26/1996 **Age:** 25

								BATTING														RUNNING			AVERAGES			
Year	Team	Lg	G	AB	H	2B	3B	HR	(Hm	Rd)	TB	R	RBI	RC	TBB	IBB	SO	HBP	SH	SF		SB	CS	GDP	Avg	OBP	Slg	OPS
2017	Everett	A-	14	47	13	1	1	3	(-	-)	25	6	12	7	6	0	6	0	0	2		1	1	0	.277	.345	.532	.877
2018	Mdest	A+	120	476	144	27	7	11	(-	-)	218	72	66	85	52	0	103	6	0	4		4	3	9	.303	.375	.458	.833
2019	Ark	AA	92	365	107	13	2	18	(-	-)	178	61	55	63	29	2	92	4	0	2		2	0	7	.293	.350	.488	.838
2020	Sea	AL	54	182	32	7	0	8	(2	6)	63	19	26	22	18	0	84	1	0	1		1	2	3	.176	.252	.346	.599

Mitch White

Pitches: R **Bats:** R **Pos:** RP-2   **Ht:** 6'3" **Wt:** 210 **Born:** 12/28/1994 **Age:** 26

				HOW MUCH PITCHED					WHAT HE GAVE UP									THE RESULTS							
Year	Team	Lg	G GS GF	IP	BFP	H	R	ER	HR	SH	SF	HB	TBB	IBB	SO	WP	W	L	Pct	Sv-Op	Hld	Vel	OPS	ERC	ERA
2020	LAD	NL	2 0 2	3.0	11	1	0	0	0	0	0	0	1	0	2	0	1	0	1.000	0-0	0	94	.282	0.69	0.00

Aaron Whitefield

Bats: R **Throws:** R **Pos:** CF-2;PR-2   **Ht:** 6'4" **Wt:** 210 **Born:** 9/2/1996 **Age:** 24

								BATTING														RUNNING			AVERAGES			
Year	Team	Lg	G	AB	H	2B	3B	HR	(Hm	Rd)	TB	R	RBI	RC	TBB	IBB	SO	HBP	SH	SF		SB	CS	GDP	Avg	OBP	Slg	OPS
2020	Min	AL	3	1	0	0	0	0	(0	0)	0	1	0	0	0	0	0	0	0	0		0	0	0	.000	.000	.000	.000

Forrest Whitley

Pitches: R **Bats:** R **Pos:** P   **Ht:** 6'7" **Wt:** 238 **Born:** 9/15/1997 **Age:** 23

				HOW MUCH PITCHED					WHAT HE GAVE UP									THE RESULTS							
Year	Team	Lg	G GS GF	IP	BFP	H	R	ER	HR	SH	SF	HB	TBB	IBB	SO	WP	W	L	Pct	Sv-Op	Hld	Vel	OPS	ERC	ERA
2016	2 Tms	Low	8 6 0	18.2	81	19	12	10	0	0	0	6	6	0	26	2	1	2	.333	0- -	-	-	.629	3.10	4.82
2017	2 Tms	Low	19 16 1	77.2	324	70	27	26	4	1	1	4	30	0	117	7	5	4	.556	0- -	-	-	.662	3.42	3.01
2018	CpChr	AA	8 8 0	26.1	108	15	11	11	2	0	1	2	11	0	34	0	0	2	.000	0- -	-	-	.504	2.00	3.76
2019	RdRck	AAA	8 5 0	24.1	119	35	33	33	9	1	1	0	15	0	29	1	0	3	.000	0- -	-	-	1.149	10.24	12.21
2019	CpChr	AA	6 6 0	22.2	103	18	14	14	2	0	0	3	19	0	36	7	2	2	.500	0- -	-	-	.722	5.19	5.56

Kodi Whitley

Pitches: R **Bats:** R **Pos:** RP-4   **Ht:** 6'3" **Wt:** 220 **Born:** 2/21/1995 **Age:** 26

				HOW MUCH PITCHED					WHAT HE GAVE UP									THE RESULTS							
Year	Team	Lg	G GS GF	IP	BFP	H	R	ER	HR	SH	SF	HB	TBB	IBB	SO	WP	W	L	Pct	Sv-Op	Hld	Vel	OPS	ERC	ERA
2020	StL	NL	4 0 1	4.2	17	2	1	1	1	0	0	0	1	0	5	0	0	0	-	0-0	0	94	.489	1.34	1.93

Rowan Wick

Pitches: R **Bats:** L **Pos:** RP-19   **Ht:** 6'3" **Wt:** 234 **Born:** 11/9/1992 **Age:** 28

				HOW MUCH PITCHED					WHAT HE GAVE UP									THE RESULTS							
Year	Team	Lg	G GS GF	IP	BFP	H	R	ER	HR	SH	SF	HB	TBB	IBB	SO	WP	W	L	Pct	Sv-Op	Hld	Vel	OPS	ERC	ERA
2018	SD	NL	10 0 3	8.1	38	13	6	6	1	0	0	0	7	0	7	0	0	1	.000	0-0	0	92	.936	6.41	6.48
2019	ChC	NL	31 0 7	33.1	140	22	13	9	1	0	1	3	16	1	35	0	2	0	1.000	2-2	5	96	.528	2.18	2.43
2020	ChC	NL	19 0 6	17.1	74	18	6	6	1	0	0	0	6	1	20	0	0	1	.000	4-4	5	95	.721	3.71	3.12
	3 ML YEARS		60 0 16	59.0	252	53	25	21	2	1	0	3	23	2	62	0	2	2	.500	6-6	10	95	.653	3.15	3.20

Taylor Widener

Pitches: R **Bats:** L **Pos:** RP-12   **Ht:** 6'0" **Wt:** 230 **Born:** 10/24/1994 **Age:** 26

				HOW MUCH PITCHED					WHAT HE GAVE UP									THE RESULTS							
Year	Team	Lg	G GS GF	IP	BFP	H	R	ER	HR	SH	SF	HB	TBB	IBB	SO	WP	W	L	Pct	Sv-Op	Hld	Vel	OPS	ERC	ERA
2020	Ari	NL	12 0 4	20.0	88	14	10	10	5	0	0	3	12	1	22	0	0	1	.000	0-0	1	95	.782	4.73	4.50

Brad Wieck

Pitches: L **Bats:** L **Pos:** RP-1   **Ht:** 6'8" **Wt:** 257 **Born:** 10/14/1991 **Age:** 29

				HOW MUCH PITCHED					WHAT HE GAVE UP									THE RESULTS							
Year	Team	Lg	G GS GF	IP	BFP	H	R	ER	HR	SH	SF	HB	TBB	IBB	SO	WP	W	L	Pct	Sv-Op	Hld	Vel	OPS	ERC	ERA
2018	SD	NL	5 0 0	7.0	24	3	1	1	1	0	0	0	1	0	10	0	0	0		0-0	0	92	.417	0.70	1.29
2019	2 Tms	NL	44 0 5	34.2	148	28	23	22	8	0	1	3	13	0	49	1	2	2	.500	0-2	9	94	.748	4.05	5.71
2020	ChC	NL	1 0 0	1.0	5	1	2	2	1	0	0	0	1	0	2	0	0	0		0-0	0	91	1.400	14.27	18.00
19	SD	NL	30 0 3	24.2	110	26	19	18	7	0	1	1	9	0	31	0	0	1	.000	0-2	8	94	.863	5.62	6.57
19	ChC	NL	14 0 2	10.0	38	2	4	4	1	0	0	2	4	0	18	1	2	1	.667	0-0	1	94	.398	1.14	3.60
	3 ML YEARS		50 0 5	42.2	177	32	26	25	10	0	1	3	14	0	61	1	2	2	.500	0-2	9	94	.717	3.51	5.27

Matt Wieters

Bats: B **Throws:** R **Pos:** C-18;PH-2   WEE-ters   **Ht:** 6'5" **Wt:** 235 **Born:** 5/21/1986 **Age:** 35

								BATTING														RUNNING			AVERAGES			
Year	Team	Lg	G	AB	H	2B	3B	HR	(Hm	Rd)	TB	R	RBI	RC	TBB	IBB	SO	HBP	SH	SF		SB	CS	GDP	Avg	OBP	Slg	OPS
2009	Bal	AL	96	354	102	15	1	9	(5	4)	146	35	43	43	28	2	86	1	0	2		0	0	11	.288	.340	.412	.753
2010	Bal	AL	130	446	111	22	1	11	(3	8)	168	37	55	47	47	7	94	2	0	7		0	1	13	.249	.319	.377	.695
2011	Bal	AL	139	500	131	28	0	22	(13	9)	225	72	68	76	48	3	84	2	0	1		1	0	16	.262	.328	.450	.778
2012	Bal	AL	144	526	131	27	1	23	(11	12)	229	67	83	73	60	4	112	4	0	3		3	0	17	.249	.329	.435	.764

Year	Team	Lg	G	AB	H	2B	3B	HR	(Hm	Rd)	TB	R	RBI	RC	TBB	IBB	SO	HBP	SH	SF	SB	CS	GDP	Avg	OBP	Slg	OPS
2013	Bal	AL	148	523	123	29	0	22	(13	9)	218	59	79	65	43	5	104	0	1	12	2	0	7	.235	.287	.417	.704
2014	Bal	AL	26	104	32	5	0	5	(2	3)	52	13	18	17	6	0	19	0	0	2	0	1	1	.308	.339	.500	.839
2015	Bal	AL	75	258	69	14	1	8	(3	5)	109	24	25	33	21	0	67	0	0	0	0	0	4	.267	.319	.422	.742
2016	Bal	AL	124	423	103	17	1	17	(10	7)	173	48	66	56	32	1	85	5	1	3	1	0	10	.243	.302	.409	.711
2017	Was	NL	123	422	95	20	0	10	(5	5)	145	43	52	41	38	4	94	1	0	4	1	0	14	.225	.288	.344	.632
2018	Was	NL	76	235	56	8	0	8	(7	1)	88	24	30	26	30	3	45	3	1	2	0	1	5	.238	.330	.374	.704
2019	StL	NL	67	168	36	4	0	11	(5	6)	73	15	27	16	12	0	47	1	0	2	1	1	3	.214	.268	.435	.702
2020	StL	NL	19	35	7	1	0	0	(0	0)	8	3	4	3	3	0	10	2	1	0	0	0	1	.200	.300	.229	.529
	Postseason		15	45	5	1	0	0	(0	0)	6	4	0	1	4	0	11	2	0	0	0	0	0	.111	.216	.133	.349
	12 ML YEARS		1167	3994	996	190	5	146	(77	69)	1634	440	550	496	368	29	847	21	4	41	9	4	102	.249	.313	.409	.722

Devin Williams

Pitches: R **Bats:** R **Pos:** RP-22

Ht: 6'2" **Wt:** 200 **Born:** 9/21/1994 **Age:** 26

			HOW MUCH PITCHED					WHAT HE GAVE UP									THE RESULTS						
Year	Team	Lg	G	GS	GF	IP	BFP	H	R	ER	HR	SH	SF	HB	TBB	IBB	SO	WP	W	L	Pct	Sv-Op	Hld	Vel	OPS	ERC	ERA
2019	Mil	NL	13	0	1	13.2	67	18	9	6	2	1	0	2	6	0	14	1	0	0		0-0	2	96	.894	6.97	3.95
2020	Mil	NL	22	0	1	27.0	100	8	4	1	1	0	0	1	9	0	53	3	4	1	.800	0-0	9	97	.339	0.76	0.33
	2 ML YEARS		35	0	2	40.2	167	26	13	7	3	1	0	3	15	0	67	4	4	1	.800	0-0	11	96	.559	2.15	1.55

Justin Williams

Bats: L **Throws:** R **Pos:** RF-2;PH-1

Ht: 6'1" **Wt:** 235 **Born:** 8/20/1995 **Age:** 25

									BATTING											RUNNING			AVERAGES			
Year	Team	Lg	G	AB	H	2B	3B	HR	(Hm	Rd)	TB	R	RBI	RC	TBB	IBB	SO	HBP	SH	SF	SB	CS	GDP	Avg	OBP	Slg	OPS
2018	TB	AL	1	1	0	0	0	0	(0	0)	0	0	0	0	0	0	0	0	0	0	0	0	1	.000	.000	.000	.000
2020	StL	NL	3	5	1	0	0	0	(0	0)	1	0	0	0	1	0	2	0	0	0	0	0	0	.200	.333	.200	.533
	2 ML YEARS		4	6	1	0	0	0	(0	0)	1	0	0	0	1	0	2	0	0	0	0	0	1	.167	.286	.167	.452

Mason Williams

Bats: L **Throws:** R **Pos:** LF-5;CF-4;RF-2;PH-2;PR-2

Ht: 6'1" **Wt:** 195 **Born:** 8/21/1991 **Age:** 29

									BATTING											RUNNING			AVERAGES			
Year	Team	Lg	G	AB	H	2B	3B	HR	(Hm	Rd)	TB	R	RBI	RC	TBB	IBB	SO	HBP	SH	SF	SB	CS	GDP	Avg	OBP	Slg	OPS
2015	NYY	AL	8	21	6	3	0	1	(0	1)	12	3	3	4	1	0	3	0	0	0	0	0	0	.286	.318	.571	.890
2016	NYY	AL	12	27	8	1	0	0	(0	0)	9	4	2	3	1	0	12	0	1	0	0	0	0	.296	.321	.333	.655
2017	NYY	AL	5	16	4	0	0	0	(0	0)	4	3	1	1	1	0	2	0	0	0	2	0	0	.250	.294	.250	.544
2018	Cin	NL	51	123	36	5	1	2	(2	0)	49	10	6	11	7	1	29	0	2	0	1	2	5	.293	.331	.398	.729
2019	Bal	AL	11	30	8	1	0	0	(0	0)	9	4	2	2	3	0	6	0	0	1	1	0	0	.267	.324	.300	.624
2020	Bal	AL	10	18	2	0	1	0	(0	0)	4	0	0	0	0	0	9	0	0	0	0	1	0	.111	.111	.222	.333
	6 ML YEARS		97	235	64	10	2	3	(2	1)	87	24	14	21	13	1	61	0	3	1	4	3	5	.272	.309	.370	.679

Taylor Williams

Pitches: R **Bats:** B **Pos:** RP-15

Ht: 5'11" **Wt:** 185 **Born:** 7/21/1991 **Age:** 29

			HOW MUCH PITCHED					WHAT HE GAVE UP									THE RESULTS						
Year	Team	Lg	G	GS	GF	IP	BFP	H	R	ER	HR	SH	SF	HB	TBB	IBB	SO	WP	W	L	Pct	Sv-Op	Hld	Vel	OPS	ERC	ERA
2017	Mil	NL	5	0	5	4.2	20	4	1	1	0	0	0	0	2	0	4	0	0	0		0-0	0	96	.633	2.67	1.93
2018	Mil	NL	56	0	10	53.0	236	53	28	25	6	4	2	1	25	4	57	4	1	3	.250	0-1	4	96	.747	4.34	4.25
2019	Mil	NL	10	0	4	14.2	73	22	17	16	1	0	0	2	7	2	15	1	1	1	.500	0-1	5	95	.878	7.50	9.82
2020	2 Tms		15	0	9	14.2	67	14	10	10	1	0	0	3	7	1	20	6	1	1	.500	6-6	1	95	.709	4.52	6.14
20	Sea	AL	14	0	9	13.2	62	12	9	9	1	0	0	3	7	1	19	6	1	1	.500	6-6	1	95	.682	4.32	5.93
20	SD	NL	1	0	0	1.0	5	2	1	1	0	0	0	0	0	0	1	0	0	0	-	0-0	0	96	1.000	7.48	9.00
	4 ML YEARS		86	0	28	87.0	396	93	56	52	8	4	2	6	41	7	96	11	3	5	.375	6-8	5	96	.759	4.77	5.38

Trevor Williams

Pitches: R **Bats:** R **Pos:** SP-11

Ht: 6'3" **Wt:** 235 **Born:** 4/25/1992 **Age:** 29

			HOW MUCH PITCHED					WHAT HE GAVE UP									THE RESULTS						
Year	Team	Lg	G	GS	GF	IP	BFP	H	R	ER	HR	SH	SF	HB	TBB	IBB	SO	WP	W	L	Pct	Sv-Op	Hld	Vel	OPS	ERC	ERA
2016	Pit	NL	7	1	1	12.2	61	19	13	11	4	0	0	0	5	0	11	0	1	1	.500	0-1	0	93	1.054	8.89	7.82
2017	Pit	NL	31	25	1	150.1	642	145	73	68	14	8	4	9	52	4	117	2	7	9	.438	0-0	0	92	.715	3.82	4.07
2018	Pit	NL	31	31	0	170.2	701	146	64	59	15	6	4	4	55	3	126	4	14	10	.583	0-0	0	90	.659	3.00	3.11
2019	Pit	NL	26	26	0	145.2	636	162	93	87	27	6	8	7	44	3	113	2	7	9	.438	0-0	0	91	.851	5.11	5.38
2020	Pit	NL	11	11	0	55.1	252	66	42	38	15	1	3	4	21	0	49	1	2	8	.200	0-0	0	91	.905	6.74	6.18
	5 ML YEARS		106	94	2	534.2	2292	538	285	263	75	21	19	24	177	10	416	9	31	37	.456	0-1	0	91	.766	4.28	4.43

Bryse Wilson

Pitches: R **Bats:** R **Pos:** RP-4; SP-2

Ht: 6'2" **Wt:** 225 **Born:** 12/20/1997 **Age:** 23

			HOW MUCH PITCHED					WHAT HE GAVE UP									THE RESULTS						
Year	Team	Lg	G	GS	GF	IP	BFP	H	R	ER	HR	SH	SF	HB	TBB	IBB	SO	WP	W	L	Pct	Sv-Op	Hld	Vel	OPS	ERC	ERA
2018	Atl	NL	3	1	2	7.0	33	8	5	5	0	0	1	0	6	2	6	0	1	0	1.000	0-0	0	95	.886	5.54	6.43
2019	Atl	NL	6	4	1	20.0	93	26	18	16	5	2	0	0	10	1	16	1	1	1	.500	0-0	0	95	1.050	7.50	7.20
2020	Atl	NL	6	2	2	15.2	73	18	7	7	2	0	0	1	9	0	15	0	1	0	1.000	1-1	0	94	.828	6.18	4.02
	3 ML YEARS		15	7	5	42.2	199	52	30	28	7	2	1	1	25	3	37	1	3	1	.750	1-1	0	94	.943	6.72	5.91

Justin Wilson

Pitches: L **Bats:** L **Pos:** RP-23   **Ht:** 6'2" **Wt:** 205 **Born:** 8/18/1987 **Age:** 33

			HOW MUCH PITCHED				WHAT HE GAVE UP											THE RESULTS						
Year Team	Lg	G	GS	GF	IP	BFP	H	R	ER	HR	SH	SF	HB	TBB	IBB	SO	WP	W	L	Pct	Sv-Op	Hld	Vel	OPS	ERC	ERA
2012 Pit	NL	8	0	3	4.2	26	10	1	1	0	1	0	0	3	0	7	1	0	0	-	0-0	0	94	1.111	11.83	1.93
2013 Pit	NL	58	0	8	73.2	295	50	17	17	4	3	1	3	28	1	59	5	6	1	.857	0-3	14	95	.543	2.20	2.08
2014 Pit	NL	70	0	15	60.0	256	49	30	28	4	0	0	3	30	5	61	4	3	4	.429	0-3	16	95	.643	3.29	3.10
2015 NYY	AL	74	0	3	61.0	244	49	21	21	3	2	0	2	20	0	66	4	5	0	1.000	0-2	29	95	.602	2.63	3.10
2016 Det	AL	66	0	10	58.2	251	61	29	27	6	1	0	1	17	2	65	4	4	5	.444	1-6	25	95	.708	3.87	4.14
2017 2 Tms		65	0	30	58.0	248	40	23	22	5	0	1	1	35	1	80	4	4	4	.500	13-16	9	96	.633	3.08	3.41
2018 ChC	NL	71	0	12	54.2	236	45	22	21	5	0	1	0	33	1	69	4	4	5	.444	0-3	16	95	.682	3.81	3.46
2019 NYM	NL	45	0	9	39.0	166	33	12	11	4	0	0	2	19	1	44	4	4	2	.667	4-5	9	95	.670	3.78	2.54
2020 NYM	NL	23	0	2	19.2	86	18	10	8	1	1	0	1	9	1	23	3	2	1	.667	0-0	10	95	.623	3.55	3.66
17 Det	AL	42	0	26	40.1	157	22	12	12	5	0	1	0	16	0	55	3	3	4	.429	13-15	8	96	.563	1.91	2.68
17 ChC	NL	23	0	4	17.2	91	18	11	10	0	0	0	1	19	1	25	1	1	0	1.000	0-1	1	96	.756	5.98	5.09
Postseason		6	0	1	5.1	23	3	1	1	0	0	0	0	3	0	4	1	0	0	-	0-0	0	96	.452	1.87	1.69
9 ML YEARS		480	0	92	429.1	1808	355	165	156	32	8	3	13	194	12	474	33	32	22	.593	18-38	128	95	.642	3.24	3.27

Trey Wingenter

Pitches: R **Bats:** R **Pos:** P   **Ht:** 6'7" **Wt:** 237 **Born:** 4/15/1994 **Age:** 27

			HOW MUCH PITCHED				WHAT HE GAVE UP											THE RESULTS						
Year Team	Lg	G	GS	GF	IP	BFP	H	R	ER	HR	SH	SF	HB	TBB	IBB	SO	WP	W	L	Pct	Sv-Op	Hld	Vel	OPS	ERC	ERA
2018 SD	NL	22	0	5	19.0	81	13	8	8	3	0	1	1	11	0	27	1	0	0	-	0-2	5	97	.647	3.62	3.79
2019 SD	NL	51	1	8	51.0	218	34	32	32	5	1	2	5	28	0	72	4	1	3	.250	1-4	16	96	.633	3.16	5.65
2 ML YEARS		73	1	13	70.0	299	47	40	40	8	1	3	6	39	0	99	5	1	3	.250	1-6	21	96	.637	3.29	5.14

Jesse Winker

Bats: L **Throws:** L **Pos:** DH-37;LF-15;PH-6;RF-1   **Ht:** 6'3" **Wt:** 215 **Born:** 8/17/1993 **Age:** 27

			BATTING																	RUNNING			AVERAGES			
Year Team	Lg	G	AB	H	2B	3B	HR	(Hm	Rd)	TB	R	RBI	RC	TBB	IBB	SO	HBP	SH	SF	SB	CS	GDP	Avg	OBP	Slg	OPS
2017 Cin	NL	47	121	36	7	0	7	(2	5)	64	21	15	18	15	0	24	0	1	0	1	1	2	.298	.375	.529	.904
2018 Cin	NL	89	281	84	16	0	7	(6	1)	121	38	43	54	49	4	46	2	1	1	0	0	6	.299	.405	.431	.836
2019 Cin	NL	113	338	91	17	2	16	(10	6)	160	51	38	48	38	2	60	8	0	0	0	2	10	.269	.357	.473	.830
2020 Cin	NL	54	149	38	7	0	12	(8	4)	81	27	23	31	28	0	46	5	0	1	1	0	3	.255	.388	.544	.932
4 ML YEARS		303	889	249	47	2	42	(26	16)	426	137	119	151	130	6	176	15	2	2	2	3	21	.280	.380	.479	.859

Dan Winkler

Pitches: R **Bats:** R **Pos:** RP-18   **Ht:** 6'3" **Wt:** 205 **Born:** 2/2/1990 **Age:** 31

			HOW MUCH PITCHED				WHAT HE GAVE UP											THE RESULTS						
Year Team	Lg	G	GS	GF	IP	BFP	H	R	ER	HR	SH	SF	HB	TBB	IBB	SO	WP	W	L	Pct	Sv-Op	Hld	Vel	OPS	ERC	ERA
2015 Atl	NL	2	0	0	1.2	8	2	2	2	2	0	0	0	1	0	2	0	0	0	-	0-0	0	89	1.518	14.99	10.80
2016 Atl	NL	3	0	0	2.1	8	0	0	0	0	0	0	0	1	0	4	0	0	0	-	0-0	0	92	.125	0.20	0.00
2017 Atl	NL	16	0	1	14.1	53	7	4	4	1	1	0	0	6	0	18	0	1	1	.500	0-0	4	94	.511	1.57	2.51
2018 Atl	NL	69	0	11	60.1	255	52	27	23	3	1	1	5	20	1	69	2	4	0	1.000	2-5	23	93	.645	2.99	3.43
2019 Atl	NL	27	0	4	21.2	93	18	14	12	5	0	0	1	11	0	22	1	3	1	.750	0-1	6	93	.804	4.67	4.98
2020 ChC	NL	18	0	4	18.1	76	11	7	6	3	1	0	1	11	0	18	0	0	0	-	0-1	1	93	.624	3.35	2.95
6 ML YEARS		135	0	20	118.2	493	90	54	47	14	3	1	7	50	1	133	3	8	2	.800	2-7	34	93	.663	3.20	3.56

Patrick Wisdom

Bats: R **Throws:** R **Pos:** 1B-2;PH-2   **Ht:** 6'2" **Wt:** 220 **Born:** 8/27/1991 **Age:** 29

			BATTING																	RUNNING			AVERAGES			
Year Team	Lg	G	AB	H	2B	3B	HR	(Hm	Rd)	TB	R	RBI	RC	TBB	IBB	SO	HBP	SH	SF	SB	CS	GDP	Avg	OBP	Slg	OPS
2018 StL	NL	32	50	13	1	0	4	(3	1)	26	11	10	8	6	0	19	2	0	0	2	1	1	.260	.362	.520	.882
2019 Tex	AL	9	26	4	1	0	0	(0	0)	5	1	1	1	1	0	15	0	1	0	0	0	0	.154	.185	.192	.377
2020 ChC	NL	2	2	0	0	0	0	(0	0)	0	0	0	0	0	0	0	0	0	0	0	0	0	.000	.000	.000	.000
3 ML YEARS		43	78	17	2	0	4	(3	1)	31	12	11	9	7	0	34	2	1	0	2	1	1	.218	.299	.397	.696

Matt Wisler

Pitches: R **Bats:** R **Pos:** RP-14; SP-4   WISS-lurr   **Ht:** 6'3" **Wt:** 215 **Born:** 9/12/1992 **Age:** 28

			HOW MUCH PITCHED				WHAT HE GAVE UP											THE RESULTS						
Year Team	Lg	G	GS	GF	IP	BFP	H	R	ER	HR	SH	SF	HB	TBB	IBB	SO	WP	W	L	Pct	Sv-Op	Hld	Vel	OPS	ERC	ERA
2015 Atl	NL	20	19	0	109.0	478	119	59	57	16	4	5	4	40	4	72	2	8	8	.500	0-0	0	93	.819	4.91	4.71
2016 Atl	NL	27	26	1	156.2	671	159	90	87	26	2	3	4	49	3	115	5	7	13	.350	1-1	0	93	.756	4.32	5.00
2017 Atl	NL	20	1	8	32.1	153	43	31	30	5	2	3	2	13	0	22	0	0	1	.000	0-0	0	93	.971	6.68	8.35
2018 2 Tms	NL	18	3	3	40.0	166	41	20	19	8	1	3	0	7	0	32	1	1	1	.500	0-1	0	92	.781	3.95	4.28
2019 2 Tms		44	8	7	51.1	224	56	34	32	10	1	1	0	16	0	63	3	3	4	.429	0-3	8	93	.813	4.85	5.61
2020 Min	AL	18	4	3	25.1	107	15	3	3	2	0	0	2	14	0	35	1	0	1	.000	1-2	3	92	.564	2.59	1.07
18 Atl	NL	7	3	1	26.2	112	30	16	16	6	0	1	0	5	0	21	1	1	1	.500	0-0	0	93	.850	4.82	5.40
18 Cin	NL	11	0	2	13.1	54	11	4	3	2	1	2	0	2	0	11	0	0	0	-	0-1	0	92	.633	2.41	2.03
19 SD	NL	21	0	5	29.0	129	34	17	17	5	1	0	0	10	0	34	3	2	2	.500	0-0	0	93	.822	5.35	5.28
19 Sea	AL	23	8	2	22.1	95	22	17	15	5	0	0	0	6	0	29	0	1	2	.333	0-1	4	93	.800	4.21	6.04
6 ML YEARS		147	61	22	414.2	1799	433	237	228	67	10	15	12	139	7	339	12	19	28	.404	2-7	11	93	.789	4.57	4.95

Bobby Witt Jr.

Bats: R Throws: R Pos: SS   Ht: 6'1" Wt: 190 Born: 6/14/2000 Age: 21

						BATTING																		RUNNING			AVERAGES			
Year	Team	Lg	G	AB	H	2B	3B	HR	(Hm	Rd)	TB	R	RBI	RC	TBB	IBB	SO	HBP	SH	SF	SB	CS	GDP	Avg	OBP	Slg	OPS
2019	Royals	R	37	164	43	2	5	1	(-	-)	58	30	27	21	13	0	35	1	0	2	9	1	4	.262	.317	.354	.670

Nick Wittgren

Pitches: R Bats: R Pos: RP-25   Ht: 6'2" Wt: 216 Born: 5/29/1991 Age: 30

			HOW MUCH PITCHED				WHAT HE GAVE UP									THE RESULTS						
Year	Team	Lg	G	GS	GF	IP	BFP	H	R	ER	HR	SH	SF	HB	TBB	IBB	SO	WP	W	L	Pct	Sv-Op	Hld	Vel	OPS	ERC	ERA
2016	Mia	NL	48	0	9	51.2	213	50	18	18	6	3	2	1	10	2	42	1	4	3	.571	0-2	6	92	.671	3.21	3.14
2017	Mia	NL	38	0	3	42.1	182	46	22	22	5	0	3	0	13	1	43	2	3	1	.750	0-0	5	92	.800	4.29	4.68
2018	Mia	NL	32	0	6	33.2	148	29	13	11	1	1	1	1	15	3	31	2	2	1	.667	0-0	4	92	.629	2.86	2.94
2019	Cle	AL	55	0	13	57.2	231	47	22	18	10	0	0	0	15	1	60	0	5	1	.833	4-6	12	92	.676	2.99	2.81
2020	Cle	AL	25	0	6	23.2	98	18	9	9	4	1	0	5	6	2	28	0	2	0	1.000	0-1	10	93	.706	3.37	3.42
	5 ML YEARS		198	0	37	209.0	872	190	84	78	26	5	6	7	59	9	204	5	16	6	.727	4-9	37	92	.697	3.33	3.36

Asher Wojciechowski

Pitches: R Bats: R Pos: SP-7; RP-3   wo-juh-HOW-ski   Ht: 6'4" Wt: 235 Born: 12/21/1988 Age: 32

			HOW MUCH PITCHED				WHAT HE GAVE UP									THE RESULTS						
Year	Team	Lg	G	GS	GF	IP	BFP	H	R	ER	HR	SH	SF	HB	TBB	IBB	SO	WP	W	L	Pct	Sv-Op	Hld	Vel	OPS	ERC	ERA
2015	Hou	AL	5	3	2	16.1	79	23	13	13	2	0	2	0	7	0	16	1	0	1	.000	0-0	0	91	.965	6.66	7.16
2017	Cin	NL	25	8	3	62.1	279	71	48	45	14	5	2	5	19	1	64	1	4	3	.571	0-0	2	93	.899	5.65	6.50
2019	Bal	AL	17	16	0	82.1	361	80	46	45	17	1	0	9	28	0	80	3	4	8	.333	0-0	0	92	.808	4.81	4.92
2020	Bal	AL	10	7	2	37.0	168	45	29	28	11	0	4	1	15	0	31	0	1	3	.250	0-0	0	91	.963	7.04	6.81
	4 ML YEARS		57	34	6	198.0	887	219	136	131	44	6	8	15	69	1	191	5	9	15	.375	0-0	2	92	.879	5.63	5.95

Tony Wolters

Bats: L Throws: R Pos: C-39;2B-4;PH-2   WAHL-ters   Ht: 5'10" Wt: 207 Born: 6/9/1992 Age: 29

						BATTING																		RUNNING			AVERAGES			
Year	Team	Lg	G	AB	H	2B	3B	HR	(Hm	Rd)	TB	R	RBI	RC	TBB	IBB	SO	HBP	SH	SF	SB	CS	GDP	Avg	OBP	Slg	OPS
2016	Col	NL	71	205	53	15	2	3	(2	1)	81	27	30	30	21	2	53	0	4	0	4	1	1	.259	.327	.395	.723
2017	Col	NL	83	229	55	8	1	0	(0	0)	65	30	16	25	33	9	55	2	2	0	0	1	9	.240	.341	.284	.625
2018	Col	NL	74	182	31	4	4	3	(1	2)	52	19	27	18	26	2	33	6	0	2	2	0	6	.170	.292	.286	.577
2019	Col	NL	121	359	94	17	2	1	(0	1)	118	42	42	42	36	5	68	8	2	6	0	1	9	.262	.337	.329	.666
2020	Col	NL	42	100	23	4	0	0	(0	0)	27	10	8	11	6	0	30	1	2	0	0	0	1	.230	.280	.270	.550
	Postseason		3	3	2	0	0	0	(0	0)	2	0	1	0	0	0	0	0	0	0	0	0	0	.667	.667	.667	1.333
	5 ML YEARS		391	1075	256	48	9	7	(3	4)	343	128	123	126	122	18	239	17	10	8	6	3	26	.238	.323	.319	.642

Kolten Wong

Bats: L Throws: R Pos: 2B-53;PH-1;PR-1   COLT-enn   Ht: 5'7" Wt: 185 Born: 10/10/1990 Age: 30

						BATTING																		RUNNING			AVERAGES			
Year	Team	Lg	G	AB	H	2B	3B	HR	(Hm	Rd)	TB	R	RBI	RC	TBB	IBB	SO	HBP	SH	SF	SB	CS	GDP	Avg	OBP	Slg	OPS
2013	StL	NL	32	59	9	1	0	0	(0	0)	10	6	0	0	3	0	12	0	0	0	3	0	2	.153	.194	.169	.363
2014	StL	NL	113	402	100	14	3	12	(10	2)	156	52	42	41	21	3	71	4	5	1	20	4	12	.249	.292	.388	.680
2015	StL	NL	150	557	146	28	4	11	(5	6)	215	71	61	67	36	2	95	15	0	5	15	8	10	.262	.321	.386	.707
2016	StL	NL	121	313	75	7	7	5	(3	2)	111	39	23	36	34	2	52	9	0	5	7	0	3	.240	.327	.355	.682
2017	StL	NL	108	354	101	27	3	4	(3	1)	146	55	42	56	41	11	60	12	1	3	8	2	4	.285	.376	.412	.788
2018	StL	NL	127	353	88	18	2	9	(6	3)	137	41	38	46	31	3	60	14	6	3	6	5	6	.249	.332	.388	.720
2019	StL	NL	148	478	136	25	4	11	(1	10)	202	61	59	81	47	5	83	13	6	5	24	4	2	.285	.361	.423	.784
2020	StL	NL	53	181	48	4	2	1	(0	1)	59	26	16	30	20	1	30	4	2	1	5	2	1	.265	.350	.326	.675
	Postseason		28	83	17	7	1	4	(3	1)	38	9	11	9	5	2	17	0	1	0	4	0	3	.205	.250	.458	.708
	8 ML YEARS		852	2697	703	124	25	53	(28	25)	1036	351	281	357	233	27	463	71	20	23	88	25	40	.261	.333	.384	.717

Alex Wood

Pitches: L Bats: R Pos: RP-7; SP-2   Ht: 6'4" Wt: 215 Born: 1/12/1991 Age: 30

			HOW MUCH PITCHED				WHAT HE GAVE UP									THE RESULTS						
Year	Team	Lg	G	GS	GF	IP	BFP	H	R	ER	HR	SH	SF	HB	TBB	IBB	SO	WP	W	L	Pct	Sv-Op	Hld	Vel	OPS	ERC	ERA
2013	Atl	NL	31	11	9	77.2	327	76	29	27	3	6	4	1	27	1	77	4	3	3	.500	0-0	1	92	.670	3.40	3.13
2014	Atl	NL	35	24	2	171.2	694	151	58	53	16	7	3	6	45	1	170	1	11	11	.500	0-0	2	90	.651	3.04	2.78
2015	2 Tms	NL	32	32	0	189.2	801	198	86	81	15	15	3	4	59	4	139	6	12	12	.500	0-0	0	89	.724	3.94	3.84
2016	LAD	NL	14	10	1	60.1	255	56	30	25	5	0	2	3	20	0	66	4	1	4	.200	0-0	0	91	.660	3.49	3.73
2017	LAD	NL	27	25	0	152.1	614	123	50	46	15	4	0	6	38	6	151	2	16	3	.842	0-0	1	92	.620	2.58	2.72
2018	LAD	NL	33	27	0	151.2	637	143	70	62	14	3	7	8	40	5	135	2	9	7	.563	0-0	1	90	.664	3.32	3.68
2019	Cin	NL	7	7	0	35.2	153	41	25	23	11	2	0	1	9	0	30	0	1	3	.250	0-0	0	91	.926	6.02	5.80
2020	LAD	NL	9	2	2	12.2	65	17	11	9	2	0	0	3	6	1	15	1	0	1	.000	0-0	1	91	.918	7.50	6.39
	15 Atl	NL	20	20	0	119.1	509	132	50	47	8	11	1	2	36	2	90	5	7	6	.538	0-0	0	89	.729	4.15	3.54
	15 LAD	NL	12	12	0	70.1	292	66	36	34	7	4	2	2	23	2	49	1	5	6	.455	0-0	0	88	.714	3.58	4.35
	Postseason		16	2	4	26.1	110	22	16	12	9	0	0	2	8	3	28	1	1	2	.333	0-0	0	91	.821	4.46	4.10
	8 ML YEARS		188	138	13	851.2	3546	805	359	326	81	37	19	32	244	18	783	24	53	44	.546	0-0	6	90	.684	3.44	3.45

Jake Woodford

Pitches: R **Bats:** R **Pos:** RP-11; SP-1   **Ht:** 6'4" **Wt:** 215 **Born:** 10/28/1996 **Age:** 24

			HOW MUCH PITCHED					WHAT HE GAVE UP											THE RESULTS							
Year	Team	Lg	G	GS	GF	IP	BFP	H	R	ER	HR	SH	SF	HB	TBB	IBB	SO	WP	W	L	Pct	Sv-Op	Hld	Vel	OPS	ERC	ERA
2020	StL	NL	12	1	4	21.0	85	20	13	13	7	0	1	0	5	0	16	1	1	0	1.000	0-0	0	93	.826	4.76	5.57

Brandon Woodruff

Pitches: R **Bats:** L **Pos:** SP-13   **Ht:** 6'4" **Wt:** 243 **Born:** 2/10/1993 **Age:** 28

			HOW MUCH PITCHED					WHAT HE GAVE UP											THE RESULTS							
Year	Team	Lg	G	GS	GF	IP	BFP	H	R	ER	HR	SH	SF	HB	TBB	IBB	SO	WP	W	L	Pct	Sv-Op	Hld	Vel	OPS	ERC	ERA
2017	Mil	NL	8	8	0	43.0	184	43	23	23	5	1	0	3	14	1	32	0	2	3	.400	0-0	0	94	.719	4.16	4.81
2018	Mil	NL	19	4	4	42.1	176	36	18	17	4	0	1	2	14	0	47	1	3	0	1.000	1-1	2	95	.641	3.14	3.61
2019	Mil	NL	22	22	0	121.2	493	109	49	49	12	2	2	5	30	0	143	1	11	3	.786	0-0	0	96	.650	3.13	3.62
2020	Mil	NL	13	13	0	73.2	293	55	26	25	9	0	1	4	18	0	91	1	3	5	.375	0-0	0	97	.604	2.51	3.05
	Postseason		5	2	1	16.1	60	9	4	3	1	1	0	2	3	1	23	0	1	1	.500	0-0	0	97	.478	1.42	1.65
	4 ML YEARS		62	47	4	280.2	1146	243	116	114	30	3	4	14	76	1	313	3	19	11	.633	1-1	2	96	.648	3.12	3.66

Brandon Workman

Pitches: R **Bats:** R **Pos:** RP-21   **Ht:** 6'5" **Wt:** 235 **Born:** 8/13/1988 **Age:** 32

			HOW MUCH PITCHED					WHAT HE GAVE UP											THE RESULTS							
Year	Team	Lg	G	GS	GF	IP	BFP	H	R	ER	HR	SH	SF	HB	TBB	IBB	SO	WP	W	L	Pct	Sv-Op	Hld	Vel	OPS	ERC	ERA
2013	Bos	AL	20	3	5	41.2	180	44	23	23	5	2	1	0	15	1	47	1	6	3	.667	0-1	5	92	.751	4.34	4.97
2014	Bos	AL	19	15	2	87.0	378	88	57	50	11	3	3	1	36	0	70	2	1	10	.091	0-0	1	90	.748	4.43	5.17
2017	Bos	AL	33	0	8	39.2	162	37	17	14	7	2	1	1	11	2	37	1	1	1	.500	0-1	4	92	.782	3.83	3.18
2018	Bos	AL	43	0	4	41.1	167	34	15	15	6	0	3	0	16	0	37	0	6	1	.857	0-0	7	91	.705	3.46	3.27
2019	Bos	AL	73	0	30	71.2	286	29	18	15	1	1	3	2	45	4	104	4	10	1	.909	16-22	15	93	.433	1.47	1.88
2020	2 Tms		21	0	15	19.2	101	31	14	13	4	0	0	0	13	2	23	0	1	4	.200	9-12	1	93	1.004	9.52	5.95
20	Bos	AL	7	0	6	6.2	31	8	3	3	0	0	0	0	4	0	8	0	0	0	-	4-4	0	93	.683	5.28	4.05
20	Phi	NL	14	0	9	13.0	70	23	11	10	4	0	0	0	9	2	15	0	1	4	.200	5-8	1	93	1.146	11.90	6.92
	Postseason		10	0	0	9.2	48	14	6	5	2	1	0	0	6	1	7	0	0	1	.000	0-0	0	92	.938	8.49	4.66
	6 ML YEARS		209	18	64	301.0	1274	263	144	130	34	8	11	4	136	9	318	8	25	20	.556	25-36	29	92	.700	3.70	3.89

Kyle Wright

Pitches: R **Bats:** R **Pos:** SP-8   **Ht:** 6'4" **Wt:** 215 **Born:** 10/2/1995 **Age:** 25

			HOW MUCH PITCHED					WHAT HE GAVE UP											THE RESULTS							
Year	Team	Lg	G	GS	GF	IP	BFP	H	R	ER	HR	SH	SF	HB	TBB	IBB	SO	WP	W	L	Pct	Sv-Op	Hld	Vel	OPS	ERC	ERA
2018	Atl	NL	4	0	1	6.0	28	4	3	3	2	0	0	0	6	0	5	0	0	0	-	0-0	0	94	.812	6.25	4.50
2019	Atl	NL	7	4	2	19.2	93	24	19	19	4	0	0	1	13	1	18	2	0	3	.000	0-0	0	95	.966	7.64	8.69
2020	Atl	NL	8	8	0	38.0	168	35	23	22	7	0	0	0	24	1	30	1	2	4	.333	0-0	0	94	.782	5.19	5.21
	3 ML YEARS		19	12	3	63.2	289	63	45	44	13	0	0	1	43	2	53	3	2	7	.222	0-0	0	94	.844	6.02	6.22

Jimmy Yacabonis

Pitches: R **Bats:** R **Pos:** SP-1; RP-1   **Ht:** 6'3" **Wt:** 225 **Born:** 3/21/1992 **Age:** 29

			HOW MUCH PITCHED					WHAT HE GAVE UP											THE RESULTS							
Year	Team	Lg	G	GS	GF	IP	BFP	H	R	ER	HR	SH	SF	HB	TBB	IBB	SO	WP	W	L	Pct	Sv-Op	Hld	Vel	OPS	ERC	ERA
2017	Bal	AL	14	0	7	20.2	90	18	10	10	2	0	3	0	14	1	8	1	2	0	1.000	0-0	0	95	.725	4.44	4.35
2018	Bal	AL	12	7	0	40.0	177	40	25	24	8	1	0	5	18	1	33	4	0	2	.000	0-0	0	93	.829	5.57	5.40
2019	Bal	AL	29	4	6	41.0	193	51	32	31	9	0	1	2	24	0	33	4	1	2	.333	0-0	3	94	.953	7.63	6.80
2020	Sea	AL	2	1	1	2.1	13	2	1	1	0	0	0	1	3	0	1	0	0	1	.000	0-0	0	93	.684	7.40	3.86
	4 ML YEARS		57	12	14	104.0	473	111	68	66	19	1	4	8	59	2	75	9	3	5	.375	0-0	3	94	.858	6.17	5.71

Miguel Yajure

Pitches: R **Bats:** R **Pos:** RP-3   **Ht:** 6'1" **Wt:** 175 **Born:** 5/1/1998 **Age:** 23

			HOW MUCH PITCHED					WHAT HE GAVE UP											THE RESULTS							
Year	Team	Lg	G	GS	GF	IP	BFP	H	R	ER	HR	SH	SF	HB	TBB	IBB	SO	WP	W	L	Pct	Sv-Op	Hld	Vel	OPS	ERC	ERA
2020	NYY	AL	3	0	3	7.0	29	3	1	1	1	0	0	1	5	0	8	1	0	0	-	0-0	0	92	.571	3.09	1.29

Shun Yamaguchi

Pitches: R **Bats:** R **Pos:** RP-17   **Ht:** 6'2" **Wt:** 225 **Born:** 7/11/1987 **Age:** 33

			HOW MUCH PITCHED					WHAT HE GAVE UP											THE RESULTS							
Year	Team	Lg	G	GS	GF	IP	BFP	H	R	ER	HR	SH	SF	HB	TBB	IBB	SO	WP	W	L	Pct	Sv-Op	Hld	Vel	OPS	ERC	ERA
2020	Tor	AL	17	0	7	25.2	120	28	25	23	6	0	2	2	17	0	26	2	2	4	.333	0-1	1	91	.947	7.21	8.06

Jordan Yamamoto

Pitches: R **Bats:** R **Pos:** SP-3; RP-1   **Ht:** 6'0" **Wt:** 185 **Born:** 5/11/1996 **Age:** 25

			HOW MUCH PITCHED					WHAT HE GAVE UP											THE RESULTS							
Year	Team	Lg	G	GS	GF	IP	BFP	H	R	ER	HR	SH	SF	HB	TBB	IBB	SO	WP	W	L	Pct	Sv-Op	Hld	Vel	OPS	ERC	ERA
2019	Mia	NL	15	15	0	78.2	325	54	42	39	11	0	2	5	36	1	82	5	4	5	.444	0-0	0	92	.647	3.10	4.46
2020	Mia	NL	4	3	0	11.1	67	27	24	23	8	0	1	0	7	0	13	0	0	1	.000	0-0	0	90	1.491	21.05	18.26
	2 ML YEARS		19	18	0	90.0	392	81	66	62	19	0	3	5	43	1	95	5	4	6	.400	0-0	0	91	.792	4.81	6.20

Ryan Yarbrough

Pitches: L **Bats:** R **Pos:** SP-9; RP-2   **Ht:** 6'5" **Wt:** 205 **Born:** 12/31/1991 **Age:** 29

Year	Team	Lg	G	GS	GF	IP	BFP	H	R	ER	HR	SH	SF	HB	TBB	IBB	SO	WP	W	L	Pct	Sv-Op	Hld	Vel	OPS	ERC	ERA
2018	TB	AL	38	6	3	147.1	628	140	70	64	18	1	1	8	50	6	128	1	16	6	.727	0-0	0	89	.730	3.86	3.91
2019	TB	AL	28	14	1	141.2	563	121	69	65	15	0	3	9	20	2	117	0	11	6	.647	0-0	0	88	.650	2.60	4.13
2020	TB	AL	11	9	0	55.2	234	54	22	22	5	2	2	7	12	1	44	2	1	4	.200	0-0	0	87	.689	3.61	3.56
	Postseason		3	0	0	3.0	11	2	0	0	0	0	0	0	1	0	1	0	1	0	1.000	0-0	0	89	.573	1.73	0.00
3 ML YEARS			77	29	4	344.2	1425	315	161	151	38	3	6	24	82	9	289	3	28	16	.636	0-0	0	89	.691	3.29	3.94

Eric Yardley

Pitches: R **Bats:** R **Pos:** RP-24   **Ht:** 6'0" **Wt:** 170 **Born:** 8/18/1990 **Age:** 30

Year	Team	Lg	G	GS	GF	IP	BFP	H	R	ER	HR	SH	SF	HB	TBB	IBB	SO	WP	W	L	Pct	Sv-Op	Hld	Vel	OPS	ERC	ERA
2019	SD	NL	10	0	2	11.2	52	12	5	3	1	2	0	1	3	0	7	0	0	1	.000	0-0	0	86	.668	3.73	2.31
2020	Mil	NL	24	0	4	23.1	97	19	6	4	2	0	1	1	10	0	19	0	2	0	1.000	0-2	1	88	.662	3.29	1.54
2 ML YEARS			34	0	6	35.0	149	31	11	7	3	2	1	2	13	0	26	0	2	1	.667	0-2	1	87	.664	3.44	1.80

Mike Yastrzemski

Bats: L **Throws:** L **Pos:** RF-31;CF-24;LF-8;PH-1   yuh-STREM-skee   **Ht:** 5'10" **Wt:** 178 **Born:** 8/23/1990 **Age:** 30

Year	Team	Lg	G	AB	H	2B	3B	HR	(Hm	Rd)	TB	R	RBI	RC	TBB	IBB	SO	HBP	SH	SF	SB	CS	GDP	Avg	OBP	Slg	OPS
2019	SF	NL	107	371	101	22	3	21	(8	13)	192	64	55	61	32	1	107	4	1	3	2	4	4	.272	.334	.518	.852
2020	SF	NL	54	192	57	14	4	10	(6	4)	109	39	35	43	30	2	55	3	0	0	2	1	2	.297	.400	.568	.968
2 ML YEARS			161	563	158	36	7	31	(14	17)	301	103	90	104	62	3	162	7	1	3	4	5	6	.281	.357	.535	.892

Kirby Yates

Pitches: R **Bats:** L **Pos:** RP-6   **Ht:** 5'10" **Wt:** 205 **Born:** 3/25/1987 **Age:** 34

Year	Team	Lg	G	GS	GF	IP	BFP	H	R	ER	HR	SH	SF	HB	TBB	IBB	SO	WP	W	L	Pct	Sv-Op	Hld	Vel	OPS	ERC	ERA
2014	TB	AL	37	0	12	36.0	156	33	16	15	4	0	1	3	15	3	42	2	0	2	.000	1-2	0	92	.699	3.94	3.75
2015	TB	AL	20	0	10	20.1	92	23	18	18	10	0	1	4	7	0	21	0	1	0	1.000	0-0	0	92	1.004	7.58	7.97
2016	NYY	AL	41	0	11	41.1	184	41	24	24	5	1	1	4	19	1	50	1	2	1	.667	0-2	2	93	.746	4.77	5.23
2017	2 Tms		62	0	12	56.2	231	44	28	25	12	0	1	2	19	2	88	0	4	5	.444	1-4	20	94	.698	3.42	3.97
2018	SD	NL	65	0	28	63.0	250	41	15	15	6	0	3	4	17	0	90	2	5	3	.625	12-13	16	94	.527	2.00	2.14
2019	SD	NL	60	0	51	60.2	243	41	14	8	2	1	1	7	13	1	101	2	0	5	.000	**41-44**	0	94	.515	1.72	1.19
2020	SD	NL	6	0	3	4.1	25	7	6	6	1	0	1	0	4	0	8	2	0	1	.000	2-2	1	94	.940	10.86	12.46
	17 LAA	AL	1	0	0	1.0	5	2	2	2	2	0	0	0	0	0	1	0	0	0	-	0-0	0	94	2.000	25.07	18.00
	17 SD	NL	61	0	12	55.2	226	42	26	23	10	0	1	2	19	2	87	0	4	5	.444	1-4	20	94	.666	3.13	3.72
7 ML YEARS			291	0	127	282.1	1181	230	121	111	40	2	8	21	94	7	400	9	12	17	.414	57-67	39	93	.660	3.31	3.54

Christian Yelich

Bats: L **Throws:** R **Pos:** LF-51;DH-7   YELL-itch   **Ht:** 6'3" **Wt:** 195 **Born:** 12/5/1991 **Age:** 29

Year	Team	Lg	G	AB	H	2B	3B	HR	(Hm	Rd)	TB	R	RBI	RC	TBB	IBB	SO	HBP	SH	SF	SB	CS	GDP	Avg	OBP	Slg	OPS
2013	Mia	NL	62	240	69	12	1	4	(0	4)	95	34	16	35	31	1	66	1	0	1	10	4	4	.288	.370	.396	.766
2014	Mia	NL	144	582	165	30	6	9	(2	7)	234	94	54	87	70	3	137	3	3	2	21	7	9	.284	.362	.402	.764
2015	Mia	NL	126	476	143	30	2	7	(1	6)	198	63	44	64	47	2	101	2	0	6	16	5	13	.300	.366	.416	.782
2016	Mia	NL	155	578	172	38	3	21	(8	13)	279	78	98	89	72	4	138	4	0	5	9	4	20	.298	.376	.483	.859
2017	Mia	NL	156	602	170	36	2	18	(7	11)	264	100	81	99	80	4	137	6	0	6	16	2	13	.282	.369	.439	.807
2018	Mil	NL	147	574	187	34	7	36	(22	14)	343	118	110	**128**	68	2	135	7	0	2	22	4	14	**.326**	.402	**.598**	**1.000**
2019	Mil	NL	130	489	161	29	3	44	**(27**	17)	328	100	97	126	80	16	118	8	0	3	30	2	8	**.329**	**.429**	**.671**	**1.100**
2020	Mil	NL	58	200	41	7	1	12	(6	6)	86	39	22	28	46	2	76	1	0	0	4	2	4	.205	.356	.430	.786
	Postseason		10	36	7	1	0	2	(2	0)	14	7	3	4	11	1	7	0	0	0	2	0	2	.194	.383	.389	.772
8 ML YEARS			978	3741	1108	216	25	151	(73	78)	1827	626	522	656	494	34	908	32	3	19	128	26	85	.296	.381	.488	.870

Huascar Ynoa

Pitches: R **Bats:** R **Pos:** SP-5; RP-4   WAH-scar ee-NOH-ah   **Ht:** 6'2" **Wt:** 220 **Born:** 5/28/1998 **Age:** 23

Year	Team	Lg	G	GS	GF	IP	BFP	H	R	ER	HR	SH	SF	HB	TBB	IBB	SO	WP	W	L	Pct	Sv-Op	Hld	Vel	OPS	ERC	ERA
2019	Atl	NL	2	0	1	3.0	16	6	6	6	1	0	0	0	1	0	3	0	0	0	-	0-0	0	98	1.171	12.18	18.00
2020	Atl	NL	9	5	1	21.2	100	23	14	14	2	0	2	2	13	1	17	2	0	0	-	0-0	0	95	.802	5.50	5.82
2 ML YEARS			11	5	2	24.2	116	29	20	20	3	0	2	2	14	1	20	2	0	0	-	0-0	0	95	.857	6.25	7.30

Alex Young

Pitches: L **Bats:** L **Pos:** RP-8; SP-7   **Ht:** 6'3" **Wt:** 220 **Born:** 9/9/1993 **Age:** 27

Year	Team	Lg	G	GS	GF	IP	BFP	H	R	ER	HR	SH	SF	HB	TBB	IBB	SO	WP	W	L	Pct	Sv-Op	Hld	Vel	OPS	ERC	ERA
2019	Ari	NL	17	15	0	83.1	349	72	40	33	14	3	0	4	27	4	71	2	7	5	.583	0-0	0	89	.710	3.58	3.56
2020	Ari	NL	15	7	0	46.1	204	51	30	28	11	0	5	1	14	0	39	1	2	4	.333	0-0	1	91	.872	5.24	5.44
2 ML YEARS			32	22	0	129.2	553	123	70	61	25	3	5	5	41	4	110	3	9	9	.500	0-0	1	90	.770	4.15	4.23

Andy Young

Bats: R **Throws:** R **Pos:** 2B-4;DH-4;3B-3;PH-2;LF-1   **Ht:** 6'0" **Wt:** 200 **Born:** 5/10/1994 **Age:** 27

							BATTING													RUNNING			AVERAGES			
Year	Team	Lg	G	AB	H	2B	3B	HR	(Hm | Rd)	TB	R	RBI	RC	TBB	IBB	SO	HBP	SH	SF	SB	CS	GDP	Avg	OBP	Slg	OPS
2020	Ari	NL	12	26	5	2	0	1	(0 | 1)	10	3	4	4	5	0	10	3	0	0	0	0	0	.192	.382	.385	.767

T.J. Zeuch

Pitches: R **Bats:** R **Pos:** RP-2; SP-1

ZOYK   **Ht:** 6'7" **Wt:** 245 **Born:** 8/1/1995 **Age:** 25

			HOW MUCH PITCHED					WHAT HE GAVE UP										THE RESULTS							
Year	Team	Lg	G	GS	GF	IP	BFP	H	R	ER	HR	SH	SF	HB	TBB	IBB	SO	WP	W	L	Pct	Sv-Op	Hld	Vel	OPS	ERC	ERA
2019	Tor	AL	5	3	0	22.2	99	22	13	12	2	0	0	0	11	0	20	2	1	2	.333	0-0	0	92	.731	4.15	4.76
2020	Tor	AL	3	1	1	11.1	47	9	2	2	1	0	0	0	4	0	3	0	1	0	1.000	0-0	0	92	.625	2.68	1.59
	2 ML YEARS		8	4	1	34.0	146	31	15	14	3	0	0	0	15	0	23	2	2	2	.500	0-0	0	92	.697	3.64	3.71

Bradley Zimmer

Bats: L **Throws:** R **Pos:** LF-8;CF-7;RF-7;PR-3;PH-1   **Ht:** 6'5" **Wt:** 220 **Born:** 11/27/1992 **Age:** 28

							BATTING													RUNNING			AVERAGES			
Year	Team	Lg	G	AB	H	2B	3B	HR	(Hm	Rd)	TB	R	RBI	RC	TBB	IBB	SO	HBP	SH	SF	SB	CS	GDP	Avg	OBP	Slg	OPS
2017	Cle	AL	101	299	72	15	2	8	(5	3)	115	41	39	37	26	1	99	4	0	3	18	5	5	.241	.307	.385	.692
2018	Cle	AL	34	106	24	5	0	2	(1	1)	35	14	9	9	7	0	44	1	0	0	4	1	1	.226	.281	.330	.611
2019	Cle	AL	9	13	0	0	0	0	(0	0)	0	1	0	1	1	0	7	0	0	0	0	0	0	.000	.071	.000	.071
2020	Cle	AL	20	37	6	0	0	1	(1	0)	9	3	3	3	7	0	14	5	0	1	2	1	2	.162	.360	.243	.603
	4 ML YEARS		164	455	102	20	2	11	(7	4)	159	59	51	49	41	1	164	10	0	4	24	3	8	.224	.300	.349	.649

Kyle Zimmer

Pitches: R **Bats:** R **Pos:** RP-15; SP-1   **Ht:** 6'3" **Wt:** 225 **Born:** 9/13/1991 **Age:** 29

			HOW MUCH PITCHED					WHAT HE GAVE UP										THE RESULTS							
Year	Team	Lg	G	GS	GF	IP	BFP	H	R	ER	HR	SH	SF	HB	TBB	IBB	SO	WP	W	L	Pct	Sv-Op	Hld	Vel	OPS	ERC	ERA
2019	KC	AL	15	0	3	18.1	102	28	22	22	2	0	0	0	19	0	18	2	0	1	.000	0-0	0	97	.991	10.03	10.80
2020	KC	AL	16	1	4	23.0	91	14	4	4	0	0	0	1	10	0	26	2	1	0	1.000	0-0	0	94	.537	1.78	1.57
	2 ML YEARS		31	1	7	41.1	193	42	26	26	2	0	0	1	29	0	44	4	1	1	.500	0-0	0	96	.772	5.01	5.66

Ryan Zimmerman

Bats: R **Throws:** R **Pos:** 1B   **Ht:** 6'3" **Wt:** 215 **Born:** 9/28/1984 **Age:** 36

							BATTING													RUNNING			AVERAGES			
Year	Team	Lg	G	AB	H	2B	3B	HR	(Hm	Rd)	TB	R	RBI	RC	TBB	IBB	SO	HBP	SH	SF	SB	CS	GDP	Avg	OBP	Slg	OPS
2005	Was	NL	20	58	23	10	0	0	(0	0)	33	6	6	9	3	0	12	0	0	1	0	0	1	.397	.419	.569	.988
2006	Was	NL	157	614	176	47	3	20	(10	10)	289	84	110	101	61	7	120	2	1	4	11	8	15	.287	.351	.471	.822
2007	Was	NL	162	653	174	43	5	24	(11	13)	299	99	91	83	61	3	125	3	0	5	4	1	26	.266	.330	.458	.788
2008	Was	NL	106	428	121	24	1	14	(7	7)	189	51	51	48	31	1	71	3	0	4	1	1	12	.283	.333	.442	.774
2009	Was	NL	157	610	178	37	3	33	(17	16)	320	110	106	96	72	9	119	2	0	9	2	0	22	.292	.364	.525	.888
2010	Was	NL	142	525	161	32	0	25	(9	16)	268	85	85	97	69	6	98	4	0	5	4	1	16	.307	.388	.510	.899
2011	Was	NL	101	395	114	21	2	12	(7	5)	175	52	49	58	41	4	73	1	0	3	3	1	14	.289	.355	.443	.798
2012	Was	NL	145	578	163	36	1	25	(16	9)	276	93	95	84	57	8	116	2	0	4	5	2	**20**	.282	.346	.478	.824
2013	Was	NL	147	568	156	26	2	26	(7	19)	264	84	79	83	60	2	133	2	0	3	6	0	16	.275	.344	.465	.809
2014	Was	NL	61	214	60	19	1	5	(1	4)	96	26	38	32	22	0	37	0	0	4	0	0	6	.280	.342	.449	.790
2015	Was	NL	95	346	86	25	1	16	(9	7)	161	43	73	49	33	0	79	1	0	10	1	0	13	.249	.308	.465	.773
2016	Was	NL	115	427	93	18	1	15	(9	6)	158	60	46	36	29	1	104	5	0	6	4	1	12	.218	.272	.370	.642
2017	Was	NL	144	524	159	33	0	36	(19	17)	300	90	108	94	44	1	126	3	0	5	1	0	16	.303	.358	.573	.930
2018	Was	NL	85	288	76	21	2	13	(7	6)	140	33	51	41	30	1	55	3	0	2	1	1	10	.264	.337	.486	.824
2019	Was	NL	52	171	44	9	0	6	(2	4)	71	20	27	22	17	0	39	0	0	2	0	0	4	.257	.321	.415	.736
	Postseason		35	117	32	7	0	5	(3	2)	54	10	17	19	10	0	30	0	0	1	1	0	2	.274	.328	.462	.790
	15 ML YEARS		1689	6399	1784	401	22	270	(131	139)	3039	936	1015	933	630	43	1307	31	1	67	43	16	203	.279	.343	.475	.818

Bruce Zimmermann

Pitches: L **Bats:** L **Pos:** SP-1; RP-1   **Ht:** 6'2" **Wt:** 215 **Born:** 2/9/1995 **Age:** 26

			HOW MUCH PITCHED					WHAT HE GAVE UP										THE RESULTS							
Year	Team	Lg	G	GS	GF	IP	BFP	H	R	ER	HR	SH	SF	HB	TBB	IBB	SO	WP	W	L	Pct	Sv-Op	Hld	Vel	OPS	ERC	ERA
2020	Bal	AL	2	1	1	7.0	31	6	6	6	2	0	0	2	2	0	7	2	0	0	-	0-0	0	91	.767	5.18	7.71

Jordan Zimmermann

Pitches: R **Bats:** R **Pos:** SP-2; RP-1   **Ht:** 6'2" **Wt:** 225 **Born:** 5/23/1986 **Age:** 35

			HOW MUCH PITCHED					WHAT HE GAVE UP										THE RESULTS							
Year	Team	Lg	G	GS	GF	IP	BFP	H	R	ER	HR	SH	SF	HB	TBB	IBB	SO	WP	W	L	Pct	Sv-Op	Hld	Vel	OPS	ERC	ERA
2009	Was	NL	16	16	0	91.1	391	95	51	47	10	5	3	4	29	0	92	0	3	5	.375	0-0	0	93	.760	4.25	4.63
2010	Was	NL	7	7	0	31.0	135	31	20	17	8	1	1	2	10	1	27	0	1	2	.333	0-0	0	92	.817	5.02	4.94
2011	Was	NL	26	26	0	161.1	662	154	62	57	12	8	2	7	31	2	124	3	8	11	.421	0-0	0	93	.671	3.02	3.18
2012	Was	NL	32	32	0	195.2	805	186	69	64	18	8	4	8	43	2	153	3	12	8	.600	0-0	0	94	.686	3.22	2.94
2013	Was	NL	32	32	0	213.1	865	192	81	77	19	9	4	7	40	0	161	3	**19**	9	.679	0-0	0	94	.654	2.79	3.25
2014	Was	NL	32	32	0	199.2	800	185	67	59	13	5	3	6	29	0	182	4	14	5	.737	0-0	0	93	.631	2.64	2.66
2015	Was	NL	33	**33**	0	201.2	831	204	89	82	24	8	2	8	39	3	164	2	13	10	.565	0-0	0	93	.699	3.63	3.66
2016	Det	AL	19	18	0	105.1	450	118	63	57	14	1	5	2	26	0	66	3	9	7	.563	0-0	0	92	.804	4.48	4.87
2017	Det	AL	29	29	0	160.0	713	204	111	**108**	29	3	8	7	44	2	103	3	8	13	.381	0-0	0	92	.888	6.00	6.08
2018	Det	AL	25	25	0	131.1	556	140	76	66	28	6	2	2	26	0	111	1	7	8	.467	0-0	0	91	.800	4.42	4.52

Year	Team	Lg	HOW MUCH PITCHED					WHAT HE GAVE UP												THE RESULTS						
			G	GS	GF	IP	BFP	H	R	ER	HR	SH	SF	HB	TBB	IBB	SO	WP	W	L	Pct	Sv-Op	Hld	Vel	OPS	ERC	ERA
2019	Det	AL	23	23	0	112.0	504	145	89	86	19	3	4	6	25	2	82	3	1	13	.071	0-0	0	90	.877	5.74	6.91
2020	Det	AL	3	2	0	5.2	28	11	6	5	0	0	0	0	2	0	6	0	0	0	-	0-0	0	89	.964	9.33	7.94
	Postseason		3	2	0	12.2	47	10	6	6	1	1	0	0	1	0	11	0	0	1	.000	0-0	0	94	.550	1.80	4.26
	12 ML YEARS		277	275	1	1608.1	6740	1665	784	725	194	53	41	59	344	12	1271	25	95	91	.511	0-0	0	93	.736	3.82	4.06

Tyler Zuber

Pitches: R **Bats:** R **Pos:** RP-23

Ht: 5'11" **Wt:** 175 **Born:** 6/16/1995 **Age:** 26

Year	Team	Lg	HOW MUCH PITCHED					WHAT HE GAVE UP												THE RESULTS						
			G	GS	GF	IP	BFP	H	R	ER	HR	SH	SF	HB	TBB	IBB	SO	WP	W	L	Pct	Sv-Op	Hld	Vel	OPS	ERC	ERA
2020	KC	AL	23	0	8	22.0	99	15	11	10	4	1	1	1	20	1	30	1	1	2	.333	0-0	0	94	.736	5.05	4.09

Mike Zunino

zoo-NEE-no

Bats: R **Throws:** R **Pos:** C-28

Ht: 6'2" **Wt:** 235 **Born:** 3/25/1991 **Age:** 30

Year	Team	Lg	BATTING																				RUNNING			AVERAGES			
			G	AB	H	2B	3B	HR	(Hm	Rd)	TB	R	RBI	RC	TBB	IBB	SO	HBP	SH	SF	SB	CS	GDP	Avg	OBP	Slg	OPS
2013	Sea	AL	52	173	37	5	0	5	(3	2)	57	22	14	13	16	0	49	3	0	1	1	0	5	.214	.290	.329	.620
2014	Sea	AL	131	438	87	20	2	22	(10	12)	177	51	60	39	17	1	158	17	0	4	0	3	12	.199	.254	.404	.658
2015	Sea	AL	112	350	61	11	0	11	(6	5)	105	28	28	14	21	0	132	5	8	2	0	1	6	.174	.230	.300	.530
2016	Sea	AL	55	164	34	7	0	12	(9	3)	77	16	31	28	21	0	65	6	0	1	0	0	0	.207	.318	.470	.787
2017	Sea	AL	124	387	97	25	0	25	(14	11)	197	52	64	55	39	0	160	8	0	1	1	0	8	.251	.331	.509	.840
2018	Sea	AL	113	373	75	18	0	20	(5	15)	153	37	44	29	24	0	150	6	0	2	0	0	7	.201	.259	.410	.669
2019	TB	AL	90	266	44	10	1	9	(5	4)	83	30	32	18	20	0	98	3	0	0	0	0	4	.165	.232	.312	.544
2020	TB	AL	28	75	11	4	0	4	(1	3)	27	8	10	7	6	0	37	3	0	0	0	0	0	.147	.238	.360	.598
	8 ML YEARS		705	2226	446	100	3	108	(53	55)	876	244	283	203	164	1	849	51	8	11	2	4	42	.200	.270	.394	.663

Fielding Statistics

Lindsay Zeck

Colorado Rockies third baseman Nolan Arenado saved 15 runs this season—the most of any player. He was outstanding on balls hit to his left, saving 11 plays. He also had 16 Good Fielding Plays, tied for fourth in the league. He was only behind Evan White with 20 at first base, teammate Trevor Story with 19 at shortstop, and Carlos Santana with 17 at first base.

Arenado led the Rockies infield to saving an MLB-leading 25 runs. Rockies first baseman Josh Fuentes saved eight runs at first base, which led all players at his position despite him playing just over 196 innings—less than half the innings played by second place White, who saved seven runs. Story also contributed to the outstanding defensive infield saving five runs.

The Rockies center fielders, however, left a lot to be desired. Three of their four fielders who played more than 50 innings at the position cost the Rockies runs. Kevin Pillar cost the team four runs, David Dahl cost three, and Sam Hilliard cost the team one run. Garrett Hampson, their fourth center fielder, did not save or cost any. They combined for the second-worst defensive center field in baseball after the Kansas City Royals.

The outfielder who saved the most runs this season was Joey Gallo of the Rangers with 13. Right behind him was Byron Buxton of the Twins finishing with two fewer runs saved in 144 fewer innings. He saved 11 runs—more than he did in 2019 when he played twice as many innings. Like Arenado led his team's infield, Buxton led the Twins outfield to the highest number of Runs Saved in the league with 19.

Matt Chapman has been outstanding defensively since he entered the league in 2017. He finished with the most Runs Saved in 2019, tied for most in 2018 with Nick Ahmed, and tied for the most of any third basemen in 2017 with Arenado and Evan Longoria. This season, however, he was limited to 37 games by injuries and finished with two Runs Saved.

The numbers on the accompanying pages include the use of the PART System, which was introduced in last year's *Handbook* and *The Fielding Bible — Volume V*.

The PART System (Positioning, Airballs, Range, and Throwing) takes the place of its predecessor, the Range and Positioning System, for non-outfielders in seasons since 2013. At its core, the system's goal is to split a fielder's contributions into its individual components.

The primary benefit of this is that players can be credited for what they can actually control. In the PART System, positioning has been effectively removed from a player's DRS total on the premise that teams now control where a player is standing more than the player does. Consequently, whatever credit the fielder may receive or lose on a play is based on where they were standing when the ball was hit, rather than simply assuming they were standing in a traditional starting location.

Baseball Info Solutions has tracked the starting position of infielders on groundballs and short line drives for eight years now, which is what allows the system to work. The Range and Positioning System continues to be used for outfielders.

In the following tables, you will see columns labeled ART to denote Runs Saved totals for non-outfielders (which exclude Positioning) and R/P to denote Range and Positioning Runs Saved for outfielders.

First Basemen - Regulars

Player	Tm	G	GS	Inn	PO	A	E	DP	Pct.	ART	Runs Saved GFP/ DME	Bunts/ GDP	Total
White, Evan	Sea	54	52	443	370	32	1	36	.998	5	2	0	7
Santana, Carlos	Cle	60	60	531	413	36	4	44	.991	4	1	0	5
Olson, Matt	Oak	60	59	499	393	48	1	30	.998	3	1	1	5
Abreu, Jose	CWS	54	54	470	430	27	5	39	.989	4	-1	1	4
Rizzo, Anthony	ChC	57	57	474	418	44	1	39	.998	3	0	0	3
Gurriel, Yuli	Hou	55	54	472	412	50	1	40	.998	2	0	0	2
Candelario, Jeimer	Det	43	41	345	297	19	4	35	.988	1	1	0	2
Goldschmidt, Paul	StL	52	52	411	383	27	1	41	.998	1	0	0	1
Belt, Brandon	SF	47	41	351	278	28	2	27	.994	0	1	0	1
Freeman, Freddie	Atl	58	56	477	427	32	1	44	.998	0	1	-1	0
Walker, Christian	Ari	43	42	366	268	28	3	40	.990	0	-1	0	-1
Voit, Luke	NYY	48	47	378	308	20	3	23	.991	-3	0	0	-3
Sano, Miguel	Min	52	52	423	355	13	4	30	.989	-2	-2	0	-4
Alonso, Pete	NYM	39	38	320	264	14	5	21	.982	-4	0	0	-4
Hoskins, Rhys	Phi	40	40	334	315	21	4	34	.988	-5	0	0	-5
Votto, Joey	Cin	50	49	406	299	40	5	25	.985	-5	-2	0	-7

Second Basemen - Regulars

Player	Tm	G	GS	Inn	PO	A	E	DP	Pct.	Range	ART	Runs Saved GFP/ DME	GDP	Total
Lopez, Nicky	KC	53	50	424	74	135	2	34	.991	4.44	5	2	1	8
Hernandez, Cesar	Cle	58	57	504	67	139	4	33	.981	3.68	5	0	1	6
Wong, Kolten	StL	53	48	397	59	129	2	29	.989	4.26	3	1	1	5
Marte, Ketel	Ari	41	40	332	65	90	1	22	.994	4.20	4	0	0	4
Frazier, Adam	Pit	41	40	343	63	90	1	24	.994	4.01	3	0	1	4
Cronenworth, Jake	SD	38	37	303	47	76	2	19	.984	3.65	2	-1	0	1
Solano, Donovan	SF	45	39	344	56	79	7	19	.951	3.54	1	1	-1	1
Schoop, Jonathan	Det	44	44	356	60	113	1	25	.994	4.38	0	0	1	1
Lowe, Brandon	TB	44	35	324	54	68	2	21	.984	3.39	-2	1	1	0
Alberto, Hanser	Bal	52	48	413	84	107	2	24	.990	4.17	-1	-1	0	-2
Altuve, Jose	Hou	48	48	416	64	126	4	36	.979	4.11	-3	-1	1	-3
Odor, Rougned	Tex	37	37	315	54	86	4	18	.972	4.00	-4	-1	0	-5
Hiura, Keston	Mil	49	49	406	66	83	6	15	.961	3.30	-8	0	0	-8

Third Basemen - Regulars

Player	Tm	G	GS	Inn	PO	A	E	DP	Pct.	Range	ART	Runs Saved GFP/ DME	Bunts/ GDP	Total
Arenado, Nolan	Col	48	48	417	43	117	3	19	.982	3.45	13	1	1	15
Kiner-Falefa, Isiah	Tex	46	42	366	32	79	5	4	.957	2.73	9	0	0	9
Machado, Manny	SD	56	56	464	44	105	2	10	.987	2.89	7	1	-1	7
Urshela, Gio	NYY	43	42	358	35	86	1	10	.992	3.04	4	1	0	5
Anderson, Brian	Mia	56	55	460	32	119	9	11	.944	2.95	5	-1	0	4
Longoria, Evan	SF	52	50	427	41	84	2	9	.984	2.64	4	0	-2	2
Ruiz, Rio	Bal	53	50	434	37	100	6	13	.958	2.84	1	0	1	2
Chapman, Matt	Oak	36	35	304	28	57	5	9	.944	2.51	1	0	1	2
Bregman, Alex	Hou	42	41	363	23	72	2	2	.979	2.35	0	0	0	0
Escobar, Eduardo	Ari	47	46	395	26	87	8	13	.934	2.57	0	0	0	0
Franco, Maikel	KC	51	51	435	29	89	6	17	.952	2.44	-3	1	2	0
Rendon, Anthony	LAA	52	52	455	48	73	3	7	.976	2.39	-2	1	0	-1
Moncada, Yoan	CWS	52	51	448	33	101	6	17	.957	2.69	-1	-1	0	-2
Suarez, Eugenio	Cin	57	57	473	47	75	5	10	.961	2.32	-2	-1	-1	-4
Bohm, Alec	Phi	38	37	300	26	64	4	6	.957	2.70	-4	-1	0	-5
Seager, Kyle	Sea	53	53	451	39	115	4	11	.975	3.08	-5	0	-1	-6
Ramirez, Jose	Cle	57	57	497	39	65	6	13	.945	1.88	-6	0	0	-6
Devers, Rafael	Bos	57	55	475	30	84	14	12	.891	2.16	-6	0	0	-6
Riley, Austin	Atl	46	45	383	31	95	6	6	.955	2.96	-7	0	-1	-8

Shortstops - Regulars

Player	Tm	G	GS	Inn	PO	A	E	DP	Pct.	Range	ART	Runs Saved GFP/ DME	GDP	Total
Swanson, Dansby	Atl	60	60	513	74	152	2	39	.991	3.96	7	1	1	9
Crawford, J.P.	Sea	53	53	455	73	145	3	31	.986	4.32	5	0	2	7
Correa, Carlos	Hou	57	56	475	69	142	1	35	.995	4.00	4	2	1	7
Baez, Javier	ChC	56	56	469	86	159	8	34	.968	4.70	5	-1	2	6

Player	Tm	G	GS	Inn	PO	A	E	DP	Pct.	Range	Runs Saved ART	GFP/ DME	GDP	Total
Story, Trevor	Col	57	57	491	88	161	10	49	.961	4.56	4	0	1	5
Anderson, Tim	CWS	49	49	417	65	109	6	23	.967	3.75	3	0	0	3
Ahmed, Nick	Ari	57	56	484	61	121	7	33	.963	3.38	2	0	1	3
Crawford, Brandon	SF	53	47	418	69	124	8	24	.960	4.16	4	-1	-1	2
Adames, Willy	TB	53	51	450	53	132	9	27	.954	3.70	3	0	-1	2
Lindor, Francisco	Cle	58	58	508	79	128	1	30	.995	3.67	2	-1	1	2
Rojas, Miguel	Mia	39	37	309	49	113	3	30	.982	4.72	2	-1	1	2
Mondesi, Adalberto	KC	59	59	497	85	144	4	37	.983	4.15	1	1	0	2
Tatis Jr., Fernando	SD	57	57	473	72	116	3	32	.984	3.57	2	0	-1	1
DeJong, Paul	StL	45	45	369	52	100	4	24	.974	3.71	0	0	0	0
Seager, Corey	LAD	43	43	376	46	113	8	16	.952	3.81	0	-2	0	-2
Gonzalez, Erik	Pit	38	36	309	32	79	5	22	.957	3.24	-3	0	1	-2
Gregorius, Didi	Phi	59	56	470	79	132	7	34	.968	4.04	-3	1	0	-2
Rosario, Amed	NYM	44	37	322	33	72	2	11	.981	2.93	-3	0	0	-3
Polanco, Jorge	Min	53	53	448	49	117	2	17	.988	3.33	-4	1	0	-3
Arcia, Orlando	Mil	57	52	439	58	120	3	26	.983	3.65	-4	1	-1	-4
Semien, Marcus	Oak	53	53	451	59	147	7	17	.967	4.11	-3	0	-2	-5
Bogaerts, Xander	Bos	53	52	438	59	130	5	26	.974	3.88	-5	1	-1	-5
Turner, Trea	Was	59	59	480	77	120	9	33	.956	3.70	-7	-1	0	-8
Torres, Gleyber	NYY	40	40	321	40	86	9	13	.933	3.54	-6	-1	-2	-9

Left Fielders - Regulars

Player	Tm	G	GS	Inn	PO	A	E	DP	Pct.	Range	Bases Saved	Runs Saved R/P	GFP/ DME	Throws	Total
O'Neill, Tyler	StL	48	41	344	89	0	0	0	1.000	2.33	+17	9	-1	1	9
Reynolds, Bryan	Pit	37	36	306	62	4	2	1	.971	1.94	+4	2	1	2	5
Tucker, Kyle	Hou	41	40	352	76	1	1	1	.987	1.97	+7	5	-1	-1	3
Rosario, Eddie	Min	51	51	438	84	5	2	1	.978	1.83	-1	-1	1	3	3
Tapia, Raimel	Col	36	36	311	63	3	2	0	.971	1.91	+5	2	-1	0	1
Gordon, Alex	KC	49	48	391	81	4	0	1	1.000	1.96	-4	-3	1	3	1
Peralta, David	Ari	45	45	380	86	1	0	1	1.000	2.06	+2	0	-1	0	-1
Grossman, Robbie	Oak	46	44	379	84	1	0	0	1.000	2.02	+2	0	-1	-1	-2
Gurriel Jr., Lourdes	Tor	53	49	438	100	3	1	0	.990	2.12	-5	-2	0	-1	-3
Dickerson, Corey	Mia	46	45	344	62	3	2	0	.970	1.70	-9	-4	0	1	-3
Schwarber, Kyle	ChC	48	48	363	70	3	0	0	1.000	1.81	-9	-5	1	1	-3
Jimenez, Eloy	CWS	54	54	454	68	0	1	0	.986	1.35	-5	-2	-1	-1	-4
Upton, Justin	LAA	39	39	312	65	0	2	0	.970	1.87	-4	-3	0	-1	-4
Yelich, Christian	Mil	51	51	431	60	1	0	0	1.000	1.27	-6	-4	-1	-1	-6
McCutchen, Andrew	Phi	39	36	302	47	0	0	0	1.000	1.40	-4	-3	-2	-3	-8

Center Fielders - Regulars

Player	Tm	G	GS	Inn	PO	A	E	DP	Pct.	Range	Bases Saved	Runs Saved R/P	GFP/ DME	Throws	Total
Buxton, Byron	Min	39	35	313	104	1	0	0	1.000	3.02	+15	8	2	1	11
Kiermaier, Kevin	TB	46	41	351	86	6	0	0	1.000	2.36	+5	2	2	6	10
Robert, Luis	CWS	56	55	483	151	2	1	0	.994	2.85	+22	10	-1	-1	8
Grisham, Trent	SD	59	57	496	134	3	2	1	.986	2.48	+11	6	0	1	7
Springer, George	Hou	42	41	338	82	0	0	0	1.000	2.18	+10	6	1	-1	6
Bellinger, Cody	LAD	39	38	336	103	1	1	0	.990	2.79	+14	7	-1	-1	5
Bradley Jr., Jackie	Bos	55	54	471	120	3	0	0	1.000	2.35	+8	5	0	0	5
Laureano, Ramon	Oak	53	53	447	144	2	0	0	1.000	2.94	-1	1	1	3	5
Dubon, Mauricio	SF	44	33	308	87	1	1	1	.989	2.57	0	2	-1	0	1
Bader, Harrison	StL	49	36	318	75	2	2	0	.975	2.18	+5	1	0	0	1
Inciarte, Ender	Atl	46	30	308	70	1	1	0	.986	2.07	-1	-1	-1	1	-1
Lewis, Kyle	Sea	57	56	479	133	1	2	0	.985	2.52	-3	-2	2	-1	-1
Happ, Ian	ChC	51	49	361	73	3	0	1	1.000	1.90	-9	-4	1	1	-2
Marte, Starling	TOT	61	60	487	122	3	1	0	.992	2.31	-1	-2	0	-1	-3
Garcia, Avisail	Mil	44	42	348	61	2	0	1	1.000	1.63	-9	-5	0	1	-4
Robles, Victor	Was	52	51	423	121	1	0	0	1.000	2.60	-9	-5	1	0	-4
Nimmo, Brandon	NYM	44	41	308	81	1	2	0	.976	2.39	-5	-3	0	-2	-5
Hicks, Aaron	NYY	50	48	394	97	3	2	2	.980	2.29	-9	-6	-2	0	-8
Grichuk, Randal	Tor	48	47	400	96	2	1	0	.990	2.21	-16	-8	0	0	-8
Trout, Mike	LAA	52	52	454	120	0	0	0	1.000	2.38	-16	-8	-1	0	-9

Right Fielders - Regulars

Player	Tm	G	GS	Inn	PO	A	E	DP	Pct.	Range	Bases Saved	Runs Saved R/P	GFP/ DME	Throws	Total
Gallo, Joey	Tex	53	53	457	120	3	0	1	1.000	2.42	+16	9	1	3	13
Betts, Mookie	LAD	52	50	439	113	1	4	0	.966	2.34	+18	11	0	0	11
Santander, Anthony	Bal	35	35	303	73	4	2	0	.975	2.28	+7	4	2	2	8
Kepler, Max	Min	44	44	366	72	2	1	0	.987	1.82	+3	2	0	1	3
Mazara, Nomar	CWS	42	38	336	72	1	0	0	1.000	1.96	+3	2	-1	1	2
Piscotty, Stephen	Oak	44	44	376	73	2	0	0	1.000	1.79	+3	1	0	1	2
Conforto, Michael	NYM	52	52	438	92	6	0	1	1.000	2.01	-8	-3	1	4	2
Polanco, Gregory	Pit	39	38	316	67	1	2	1	.971	1.93	+4	3	-1	-1	1
Heyward, Jason	ChC	50	49	404	98	2	0	1	1.000	2.23	+2	0	1	0	1
Calhoun, Kole	Ari	48	48	403	102	1	1	1	.990	2.30	+1	-1	0	1	0
Blackmon, Charlie	Col	50	50	428	101	4	0	2	1.000	2.21	+6	2	0	-3	-1
Harper, Bryce	Phi	48	45	370	64	2	1	0	.985	1.61	-2	0	0	-1	-1
Myers, Wil	SD	52	52	432	89	2	3	0	.968	1.89	+4	1	0	-3	-2
Hernandez, Teoscar	Tor	40	38	326	62	6	3	2	.958	1.88	-6	-5	0	2	-3
Reddick, Josh	Hou	50	49	421	89	1	2	0	.978	1.93	-1	-1	-1	-2	-4
Castellanos, Nick	Cin	57	57	467	77	1	3	0	.963	1.50	-5	-2	0	-2	-4
Eaton, Adam	Was	41	40	335	81	0	1	0	.988	2.18	-9	-5	0	-1	-6

Catchers - Regulars

Player	Tm	G	GS	Inn	PO	A	E	DP	PB	Pct.	SB Att	CS	Pit CS	CS Pct	Cat ERA	Stk Sav	Runs Saved GFP/ DME	SB	SZ	Other	Total
Barnhart, Tucker	Cin	36	33	272	341	15	0	0	2	1.000	22	8	0	.36	3.87	16	3	2	2	2	9
Stallings, Jacob	Pit	42	40	345	379	22	4	2	3	.990	24	6	3	.25	5.03	17	2	1	2	2	7
Perez, Roberto	Cle	32	30	256	291	21	0	2	0	1.000	13	9	1	.69	3.23	18	1	3	2	0	6
Grandal, Yasmani	CWS	32	32	271	271	13	2	2	4	.993	12	5	1	.42	4.74	40	-1	2	5	-1	5
Murphy, Sean	Oak	43	39	339	334	14	2	1	4	.994	21	6	0	.29	3.79	18	0	1	2	-1	2
Perez, Salvador	KC	34	33	274	295	6	0	1	0	1.000	11	3	0	.27	3.81	6	1	-1	1	1	2
Molina, Yadier	StL	42	42	337	307	16	5	1	3	.985	11	5	0	.45	3.84	1	1	1	0	-1	1
Severino, Pedro	Bal	35	32	276	272	11	4	1	5	.986	12	3	1	.25	3.89	-10	-2	1	-1	3	1
Vazquez, Christian	Bos	42	41	356	370	19	1	3	4	.997	28	7	2	.25	5.23	18	-1	1	2	-1	1
Contreras, Willson	ChC	41	39	324	311	13	2	0	0	.994	25	8	1	.32	4.16	4	1	2	1	-3	1
Narvaez, Omar	Mil	39	32	285	333	9	3	1	0	.991	21	5	2	.24	4.39	13	1	0	2	-2	1
Ramos, Wilson	NYM	41	38	327	396	9	1	3	4	.998	33	5	1	.15	4.95	-10	-2	0	-1	2	-1
Maldonado, Martin	Hou	47	46	392	375	22	2	0	3	.995	19	6	0	.32	3.95	-7	1	0	-1	-1	-1
Realmuto, J.T.	Phi	36	35	291	296	8	2	3	1	.993	19	4	1	.21	5.01	0	1	0	0	-2	-1
Kelly, Carson	Ari	38	34	289	291	13	2	1	3	.993	20	1	2	.05	5.01	24	1	-2	3	-4	-2
Nola, Austin	TOT	44	38	330	352	13	2	3	4	.995	25	6	1	.24	4.58	24	0	1	2	-5	-2
Smith, Will	LAD	34	31	277	270	10	0	3	1	1.000	21	4	1	.19	3.29	-13	-1	1	-1	-1	-2
Wolters, Tony	Col	39	35	284	230	13	1	2	4	.996	20	3	0	.15	5.62	-3	-1	-1	0	0	-2
Gomes, Yan	Was	30	30	252	229	15	2	0	2	.992	20	2	2	.10	5.25	-27	2	-2	-3	0	-3
Romine, Austin	Det	37	37	307	269	7	0	1	2	1.000	26	3	3	.12	5.89	-15	1	-2	-2	-1	-4
Suzuki, Kurt	Was	30	30	252	271	10	0	2	1	1.000	33	5	0	.15	4.94	-8	0	-2	-1	-1	-4
Jansen, Danny	Tor	43	40	342	332	20	2	2	3	.994	24	4	2	.17	4.81	-22	1	0	-3	-2	-4
Sanchez, Gary	NYY	41	38	322	347	14	6	2	5	.984	19	5	0	.26	4.53	-6	-1	1	-1	-3	-4
d'Arnaud, Travis	Atl	35	33	295	289	4	3	1	5	.990	26	2	1	.08	4.88	1	0	-2	0	-5	-7

Player	Pos	G	GS	Inn	Pct.	DRS
Acuna Jr., R	CF	34	30	215	1.000	2
	RF	28	16	162	1.000	1
Adams, M	1B	2	2	17	1.000	0
Adell, J	CF	4	4	32	.917	1
	RF	34	29	263	.969	-4
Adrianza, E	2B	5	3	28	1.000	1
	3B	23	14	145	.978	0
	SS	9	7	65	1.000	2
Aguilar, J	1B	31	31	261	.989	0
	3B	1	0	1	-	0
Akiyama, S	LF	36	30	246	1.000	4
	CF	21	17	135	1.000	1
Alberto, H	3B	5	4	35	1.000	0
Albies, O	2B	29	28	253	.982	-1
Alcantara, S	2B	6	2	28	1.000	-2
	3B	6	5	34	.818	-1
Alfaro, J	RF	1	0	3	.000	0
Alford, A	LF	6	5	33	1.000	-2
	CF	6	5	39	1.000	-1
	RF	1	0	1	-	0
Allen, G	LF	12	3	49	1.000	1
	CF	4	3	28	1.000	0
	RF	1	1	8	1.000	0
Almonte, A	LF	2	2	14	1.000	0
	CF	1	0	2	-	0
Almora Jr., A	CF	28	6	93	1.000	0
Alvarez, E	2B	9	7	62	1.000	-2
	3B	3	2	18	1.000	0
	SS	1	1	9	1.000	1
Anderson, B	1B	1	1	7	1.000	0
	2B	1	0	8	1.000	0
Andrus, E	SS	29	28	242	.969	-3
Andujar, M	3B	6	5	33	.750	-4
	LF	7	7	41	.800	0
Apostel, S	1B	5	4	38	.973	-1
	3B	2	2	8	.500	-1
Aquino, A	LF	13	9	84	1.000	0
	CF	1	1	4	-	0
	RF	4	2	20	1.000	-1
Arauz, J	2B	16	13	119	.965	-3
	3B	6	2	26	1.000	0
	SS	4	2	21	1.000	1
Arcia, O	CF	1	0	4	-	0
Arozarena, R	LF	14	12	93	1.000	1
	CF	2	0	9	1.000	0
	RF	3	1	11	-	0
Arraez, L	2B	31	31	259	.992	2
Arroyo, C	2B	13	13	109	1.000	2
	3B	1	0	1	-	0
	SS	2	1	11	1.000	-1
Baez, J	LF	1	0	0	-	0
Barnhart, T	1B	2	0	6	1.000	0
Barreto, F	2B	6	3	27	1.000	0
	3B	2	1	8	1.000	0
	SS	4	1	13	.833	-1
	LF	1	1	7	1.000	0
Basabe, L	LF	3	0	7	1.000	0
	RF	5	4	37	1.000	1
Beaty, M	1B	13	8	76	1.000	-2
	LF	2	1	6	1.000	0
Bell, J	1B	35	34	286	.984	-1
Bellinger, C	1B	19	16	143	1.000	0
	RF	1	0	1	-	0
Benintendi, A	LF	13	12	100	1.000	1
Berti, J	2B	21	17	147	.988	0
	3B	5	2	22	1.000	0
	SS	2	2	17	1.000	0
	CF	9	7	60	1.000	-1
	RF	7	7	57	1.000	0
Betts, M	2B	1	1	8	1.000	0
	CF	1	0	2	-	-1
Bichette, B	SS	26	26	217	.971	-1
Biggio, C	2B	37	32	281	.977	2
	3B	10	10	81	.964	-2
	LF	1	0	3	1.000	0
	CF	3	3	23	1.000	0
	RF	14	11	103	.957	-1
Bishop, B	LF	2	1	8	-	1
	CF	3	2	18	1.000	0
	RF	8	6	56	1.000	1
Blankenhorn, T	2B	1	1	8	1.000	-2
Bohm, A	1B	7	6	51	1.000	0

Player	Pos	G	GS	Inn	Pct.	DRS
Bonifacio, E	LF	1	1	9	1.000	0
Bonifacio, J	LF	19	13	126	1.000	-2
	RF	10	9	80	.952	-1
Bote, D	1B	1	1	6	1.000	0
	2B	7	4	40	.950	0
	3B	33	27	251	.941	-2
Brantley, M	LF	19	19	158	1.000	5
Braun, R	1B	1	1	0	-	0
	RF	20	19	127	.963	-1
Brinson, L	LF	21	4	59	1.000	-2
	CF	7	5	44	1.000	5
	RF	31	19	160	.971	0
Brosseau, M	1B	12	7	61	1.000	2
	2B	9	7	55	1.000	1
	3B	11	8	77	.933	2
	LF	2	1	10	1.000	0
	RF	1	0	4	1.000	0
Brown, S	1B	3	0	4	1.000	0
Bruce, J	1B	2	2	13	1.000	0
	LF	11	9	71	1.000	0
	RF	6	5	41	1.000	0
Bryant, K	1B	1	1	9	1.000	-1
	3B	27	27	225	.937	1
	LF	4	4	29	1.000	1
Butera, D	1B	5	0	7	1.000	0
Cabrera, A	1B	25	23	199	.995	-1
	3B	17	17	141	1.000	1
Cain, L	CF	5	5	44	1.000	1
Calhoun, W	LF	8	6	51	1.000	-2
Camargo, J	2B	21	21	175	.988	0
	3B	10	10	88	1.000	3
Cameron, D	RF	16	16	133	.972	-1
Candelario, J	3B	10	10	83	1.000	2
Canha, M	1B	3	1	9	1.000	0
	LF	15	15	120	.966	-1
	CF	9	7	65	1.000	-1
	RF	17	15	132	1.000	3
Cano, R	2B	34	33	249	.989	-4
Caratini, V	1B	3	2	7	1.000	0
Carlson, D	LF	10	8	69	1.000	0
	CF	17	16	113	1.000	2
	RF	18	8	81	1.000	2
Carpenter, M	1B	6	4	31	1.000	0
	3B	30	29	214	.960	0
Castro, H	1B	2	2	7	1.000	0
	2B	2	0	4	1.000	0
	3B	4	2	17	1.000	0
	SS	2	2	16	1.000	0
	LF	6	1	18	1.000	0
	CF	2	1	16	1.000	0
	RF	4	3	21	1.000	-1
Castro, S	2B	16	16	134	.955	1
Castro, W	2B	1	1	9	1.000	0
	3B	8	8	64	.938	-1
	SS	27	26	212	.941	-7
Cave, J	LF	7	5	45	1.000	2
	CF	22	19	161	1.000	0
	RF	12	5	62	1.000	0
Chang, Y	2B	2	2	16	.917	1
	3B	3	1	12	1.000	0
	SS	4	4	8	1.000	1
Chapman, M	SS	1	1	6	1.000	0
Chavis, M	1B	24	21	181	1.000	-1
	2B	8	7	61	.931	0
	LF	12	11	96	.895	-2
Chisholm, J	2B	13	11	93	1.000	1
	SS	9	6	52	.962	0
Choi, J	1B	38	31	278	.989	1
Choo, S	LF	16	15	131	.969	-1
	RF	3	2	18	1.000	0
Collins, Z	1B	1	0	1	1.000	0
Colon, C	1B	1	0	1	-	0
	2B	7	4	39	1.000	1
Cooper, G	1B	15	15	122	1.000	-2
Cordell, R	CF	4	1	11	1.000	0
	RF	1	1	8	1.000	0
Cordero, F	LF	1	1	8	1.000	0
	CF	5	3	34	.857	0
	RF	8	4	36	.857	0
Craig, W	1B	2	1	8	1.000	0
Cron, C	1B	13	13	108	.984	0
Cron, K	1B	1	0	1	1.000	0

Player	Pos	G	GS	Inn	Pct.	DRS
Cronenworth, J	1B	10	9	78	1.000	3
	3B	1	0	1	1.000	1
	SS	11	3	47	.917	-3
Culberson, C	1B	4	0	9	1.000	0
	2B	1	1	8	1.000	0
Cuthbert, C	3B	1	0	1	1.000	0
Dahl, D	LF	4	3	30	1.000	-1
	CF	17	17	152	.969	-3
	RF	2	1	11	1.000	0
Dalbec, B	1B	21	20	176	.981	0
	3B	2	2	15	1.000	-1
Davidson, M	1B	2	2	16	1.000	0
Davis, C	1B	15	13	114	.974	-2
Davis, J	3B	34	33	269	.958	-8
	LF	8	7	52	.900	-1
Davis, J	RF	4	4	31	.900	0
Davis, J	LF	3	2	22	1.000	0
	CF	5	3	29	1.000	0
	RF	6	4	36	1.000	2
Dean, A	1B	1	0	2	1.000	0
	LF	2	2	11	1.000	-1
	RF	1	0	2	-	0
Delmonico, N	LF	3	2	23	1.000	0
	RF	4	4	23	1.000	0
Demeritte, T	LF	2	2	15	1.000	0
	RF	12	6	56	.947	2
DeShields, D	CF	35	32	285	1.000	0
Diaz, A	1B	2	2	17	1.000	1
	2B	10	8	76	1.000	-2
	3B	3	3	17	1.000	0
	LF	1	1	4	1.000	0
Diaz, I	2B	7	6	47	1.000	-1
Diaz, L	1B	11	10	85	1.000	2
Diaz, Y	1B	2	2	14	1.000	0
	3B	25	22	185	.981	-2
Dickerson, A	LF	41	33	270	1.000	-8
	RF	5	3	28	.909	1
Dickerson, C	RF	1	0	0	-	0
Dietrich, D	1B	6	6	47	.977	0
	2B	3	2	20	1.000	0
	3B	3	1	12	1.000	0
Difo, W	2B	4	1	14	1.000	0
	3B	2	1	12	1.000	0
	SS	4	0	11	1.000	0
Dixon, B	1B	4	1	17	1.000	0
	2B	1	0	6	1.000	0
	LF	2	2	8	1.000	0
Donaldson, J	3B	26	25	197	1.000	-1
Dozier, B	2B	5	3	28	.941	-2
Dozier, H	1B	28	24	212	1.000	0
	3B	1	0	3	-	0
	LF	2	2	16	1.000	0
	RF	18	14	147	1.000	-4
Drury, B	2B	4	4	28	1.000	-3
	3B	16	9	88	1.000	-3
	SS	2	1	9	1.000	0
Dubon, M	2B	8	7	56	.963	2
	SS	8	6	48	.947	0
Duggar, S	LF	11	3	40	1.000	1
	CF	4	3	24	1.000	0
	RF	4	4	39	1.000	-1
Duvall, A	LF	45	31	290	.983	2
	CF	1	0	1	-	0
	RF	17	16	129	.955	-2
Dyson, J	LF	6	0	7	-	-1
	CF	23	17	160	.976	-2
	RF	1	1	8	1.000	0
Edman, T	2B	8	6	52	.964	1
	3B	31	17	162	.946	2
	SS	13	12	96	.946	3
	LF	8	6	42	1.000	0
	RF	13	13	86	.929	2
Engel, A	LF	9	4	43	1.000	1
	CF	3	3	25	1.000	0
	RF	25	16	150	.967	-2
Ervin, P	LF	10	3	38	1.000	0
	CF	7	4	34	1.000	0
	RF	19	13	123	1.000	2
Escobar, E	2B	3	3	27	1.000	0
Espinal, S	3B	2	1	7	1.000	0
	SS	21	18	156	.975	-1
Estrada, T	2B	20	13	103	1.000	0

All Other Fielders

Player	Pos	G	GS	Inn	Pct.	DRS
	3B	6	2	23	.800	0
	SS	3	0	5	-	0
Evans, P	1B	1	1	5	.750	-1
	3B	8	8	68	.882	-3
	LF	1	1	8	1.000	0
	RF	1	1	9	1.000	0
Farmer, K	1B	1	0	1	-	0
	2B	13	8	73	.935	1
	3B	2	1	13	1.000	0
	SS	15	10	86	1.000	2
	LF	2	0	2	-	0
Fisher, D	LF	5	4	33	1.000	-3
	RF	10	7	57	.917	-3
Fletcher, D	2B	15	15	128	.983	1
	3B	8	7	59	.944	2
	SS	27	27	233	.971	2
	RF	1	0	4	.500	-1
Flores, W	1B	14	12	98	.989	1
	2B	14	14	112	1.000	1
	3B	3	3	25	.778	0
Florial, E	CF	1	1	7	1.000	0
Ford, M	1B	13	12	92	.969	-1
Forsythe, L	1B	4	3	27	1.000	0
	2B	6	6	48	1.000	0
Fowler, D	RF	27	27	208	1.000	-2
Fraley, J	LF	1	1	9	1.000	1
	RF	6	6	52	1.000	0
France, T	1B	5	4	36	1.000	0
	2B	10	10	83	.971	0
	3B	6	6	52	.962	1
Franco, M	1B	2	1	9	1.000	0
Frazier, A	LF	14	13	109	1.000	2
Frazier, C	LF	8	7	64	1.000	-2
	RF	28	27	216	.981	4
Frazier, T	1B	16	15	130	1.000	0
	3B	29	27	235	.957	1
Freeman, M	1B	1	0	1	1.000	0
	2B	4	1	16	1.000	0
	3B	6	2	26	.900	0
	SS	3	2	20	1.000	0
	LF	4	3	25	.875	-1
Fuentes, J	1B	26	23	196	.996	8
	3B	6	1	16	1.000	0
	LF	2	0	3	-	0
	RF	1	0	1	-	0
Gallo, J	CF	1	0	1	-	0
Galvis, F	2B	16	11	100	1.000	1
	SS	33	31	261	.967	-1
Gamel, B	LF	1	1	9	1.000	0
	CF	11	10	85	1.000	-1
	RF	27	20	187	1.000	-1
Garcia, A	LF	3	2	21	1.000	0
Garcia, A	RF	5	5	45	1.000	1
Garcia, G	2B	11	6	59	.963	0
	3B	10	2	37	1.000	0
Garcia, J	SS	21	19	157	.969	0
Garcia, L	2B	5	5	42	1.000	-1
	SS	10	9	82	1.000	2
	RF	3	1	10	1.000	1
Garcia, L	2B	37	35	285	.954	-4
	SS	3	1	13	.889	-1
Gardner, B	LF	39	39	311	.956	0
	CF	10	9	78	1.000	1
Garlick, K	LF	5	5	32	1.000	-1
	RF	5	2	15	1.000	-1
Garver, M	1B	1	0	2	1.000	0
Gimenez, A	2B	19	4	65	1.000	1
	3B	10	3	34	.923	1
	SS	23	22	182	.987	1
Goins, R	2B	1	0	2	1.000	-1
	3B	2	1	18	1.000	0
	SS	2	0	2	1.000	0
Gonzalez, E	3B	13	11	96	.967	3
Gonzalez, L	LF	1	0	1	-	0
	CF	1	0	2	.500	0
Gonzalez, M	1B	14	5	60	1.000	0
	2B	21	19	166	.984	1
	3B	23	21	169	1.000	1
	RF	8	6	50	.900	1
Goodrum, N	2B	11	11	89	.976	-1
	SS	31	30	264	.991	3
Goodwin, B	LF	16	12	108	1.000	-4

Player	Pos	G	GS	Inn	Pct.	DRS
	CF	20	18	149	.969	-2
	RF	12	11	91	1.000	0
Gore, T	CF	1	0	1	-	0
Gosselin, P	1B	8	7	50	1.000	0
	2B	4	2	18	1.000	1
	3B	2	1	5	1.000	0
	LF	7	4	32	.800	-1
	RF	7	4	26	1.000	-1
Grandal, Y	1B	6	6	56	.983	0
Grossman, R	CF	2	0	3	1.000	0
Guerrero Jr., V	1B	34	34	299	.990	-4
Guillorme, L	2B	17	11	102	1.000	0
	3B	4	3	30	1.000	0
	SS	3	1	9	1.000	0
Gurriel Jr., L	1B	1	0	1	1.000	0
Gutierrez, K	3B	3	3	26	1.000	-1
Guzman, R	1B	24	23	192	.995	0
Gyorko, J	1B	30	26	209	.994	0
	3B	11	8	60	1.000	2
Haggerty, S	3B	1	1	10	1.000	0
	LF	10	10	85	1.000	1
	RF	1	1	9	1.000	0
Hamilton, B	CF	25	6	94	1.000	2
Hampson, G	2B	26	22	189	.981	-1
	SS	6	2	22	1.000	-1
	LF	7	5	50	1.000	2
	CF	20	14	120	1.000	0
Happ, I	1B	2	0	6	1.000	0
	LF	28	2	61	1.000	1
	RF	7	2	25	.800	-1
Harper, B	CF	3	3	14	1.000	0
Harrison, J	1B	1	0	1	1.000	0
	2B	12	8	70	1.000	1
	3B	10	7	59	.944	1
	LF	5	3	20	1.000	1
	RF	2	1	10	1.000	-1
Harrison, M	CF	16	11	101	1.000	1
	RF	13	1	24	1.000	-2
Haseley, A	LF	11	3	29	1.000	-1
	CF	24	19	160	1.000	-1
	RF	9	1	26	1.000	-1
Hayes, K	3B	24	24	198	.985	4
Hays, A	LF	10	8	69	1.000	4
	CF	23	20	180	1.000	1
	RF	3	3	25	1.000	-2
Healy, R	1B	2	1	9	1.000	0
Heath, N	LF	1	0	2	1.000	0
	CF	6	4	33	1.000	1
Hechavarria, A	2B	12	10	89	1.000	-1
	3B	8	4	44	.714	-2
	SS	4	0	11	1.000	0
Heineman, S	1B	1	1	8	1.000	0
	LF	3	2	19	1.000	-1
	CF	17	10	90	.970	2
	RF	1	1	9	1.000	0
Heredia, G	CF	9	7	58	1.000	2
	RF	5	3	30	1.000	1
Hermosillo, M	LF	5	1	18	1.000	0
	CF	1	1	5	1.000	0
Hernandez, K	1B	2	0	7	1.000	0
	2B	30	22	220	.960	8
	SS	2	2	15	1.000	0
	LF	5	3	32	1.000	1
	CF	3	3	20	1.000	0
	RF	9	3	43	1.000	0
Hernandez, T	CF	9	5	55	1.000	1
Hernandez, Y	RF	1	1	8	1.000	0
Herrera, D	1B	2	1	10	1.000	1
	CF	1	0	1	-	0
Hill, D	CF	10	1	33	.900	0
Hilliard, S	LF	14	13	109	1.000	0
	CF	10	8	77	1.000	-1
	RF	13	6	61	1.000	2
Hoerner, N	2B	37	22	208	.977	5
	3B	6	4	40	1.000	0
	SS	10	4	49	1.000	0
	LF	1	0	2	-	0
	CF	1	1	6	1.000	0
Holaday, B	1B	6	1	14	1.000	0
Holt, B	1B	4	4	24	.950	0
	3B	18	12	98	.960	0

Player	Pos	G	GS	Inn	Pct.	DRS
	LF	9	7	68	1.000	-1
	RF	3	2	20	1.000	-1
Hosmer, E	1B	32	32	257	.992	3
Iglesias, J	SS	24	22	168	.986	-2
Jankowski, T	LF	1	0	4	-	0
	CF	9	3	40	1.000	0
	RF	3	0	5	1.000	1
Jay, J	LF	4	2	21	1.000	0
	CF	5	5	37	1.000	-1
	RF	9	6	60	1.000	2
Johnson Jr., D	LF	1	1	8	1.000	0
	RF	4	3	25	1.000	0
Jones, J	CF	28	28	233	1.000	-1
Jones, J	2B	2	2	16	1.000	0
Jones, T	1B	3	2	18	1.000	-1
Joyce, M	LF	15	6	59	1.000	0
	RF	27	22	164	.939	-6
Judge, A	RF	25	23	188	1.000	3
Kemp, M	LF	1	1	6	1.000	1
Kemp, T	2B	43	31	258	.990	-6
	LF	3	1	13	1.000	-1
Kendrick, H	1B	6	6	50	.970	0
Kepler, M	CF	2	2	14	1.000	-1
Kieboom, C	3B	31	30	256	.966	5
Kiner-Falefa, I	SS	15	15	121	1.000	3
Kingery, S	2B	29	25	209	.952	-5
	SS	1	0	1	-	0
	CF	9	9	66	1.000	0
Kipnis, J	1B	1	1	9	1.000	0
	2B	36	31	246	.972	0
Knapp, A	1B	1	0	4	1.000	-1
Kolarek, A	RF	1	0	2	-	0
Kratz, E	1B	4	0	7	1.000	0
La Stella, T	1B	10	10	83	1.000	1
	2B	33	30	243	.964	-6
	3B	6	5	34	1.000	0
Lagares, J	CF	2	0	3	1.000	1
Lamb, J	1B	12	11	83	1.000	-1
	3B	14	12	110	.963	-4
LeMahieu, D	1B	11	1	24	1.000	0
	2B	37	34	271	.971	0
	3B	11	11	87	.929	0
Lin, T	2B	6	3	31	1.000	0
	SS	12	4	43	.929	0
	LF	4	3	27	1.000	1
	CF	2	1	10	1.000	0
	RF	3	2	21	1.000	0
Locastro, T	LF	7	5	44	.889	0
	CF	13	7	76	1.000	1
	RF	6	4	37	1.000	2
Long Jr., S	2B	32	29	260	.991	-1
	LF	1	1	7	1.000	1
Lopes, T	3B	1	1	8	.833	0
	LF	17	14	124	1.000	0
	RF	12	9	68	1.000	-1
Lopez, N	3B	2	0	3	-	0
	SS	4	1	20	1.000	-2
Lorenzen, M	CF	3	0	4	1.000	0
Lowe, B	1B	1	0	1	-	0
	LF	5	4	34	1.000	0
	RF	7	7	51	1.000	1
Lowe, N	1B	15	15	123	1.000	2
	3B	2	1	16	1.000	0
Lugo, D	2B	1	0	1	-	0
	3B	5	2	27	1.000	0
Luplow, J	LF	21	18	155	1.000	2
	RF	9	6	53	1.000	-1
Lux, G	2B	18	15	143	.958	6
Machin, V	1B	2	0	3	1.000	0
	2B	3	2	17	1.000	0
	3B	10	7	53	1.000	1
	SS	6	5	44	.931	-3
Madrigal, N	2B	29	29	249	.964	0
Margot, M	LF	18	9	93	.958	1
	CF	21	18	156	.979	1
	RF	15	10	96	1.000	0
Marisnick, J	CF	16	8	86	.968	-3
Markakis, N	LF	7	5	53	1.000	2
	RF	29	26	216	1.000	-5
Marmolejos, J	1B	5	4	35	1.000	0
	LF	18	15	120	.962	-1
	RF	2	1	8	1.000	0

Player	Pos	G	GS	Inn	Pct.	DRS
Marte, K	SS	2	2	16	.875	0
	CF	3	2	20	1.000	0
Marte, S	LF	1	0	3	1.000	0
Martin, J	LF	1	0	2	-	0
	CF	4	3	26	1.000	-1
Martinez, J	LF	3	3	22	1.000	1
	RF	4	3	30	1.000	-3
Martinez, J	1B	6	4	34	1.000	0
Mateo, J	2B	5	1	20	1.000	0
	LF	3	3	24	1.000	-1
	CF	1	1	7	1.000	0
	RF	3	0	4	-	0
Mathias, M	1B	1	0	3	1.000	0
	2B	1	0	1		0
	LF	4	3	25	1.000	0
	CF	1	0	1	-	0
	RF	8	5	45	1.000	0
Mathisen, W	3B	7	7	61	.905	0
Maybin, C	LF	5	3	36	1.000	-1
	CF	4	3	27	1.000	-1
	RF	19	17	146	.973	0
Mayfield, J	2B	5	3	23	1.000	0
	3B	8	6	47	1.000	1
	SS	8	4	46	1.000	1
McBroom, R	1B	10	9	74	.985	-2
	LF	3	2	15	1.000	0
	RF	1	0	2	1.000	0
McCarthy, J	LF	3	2	16	1.000	0
	RF	1	1	8	-	-1
McKinney, B	LF	1	1	5	-	0
	RF	1	0	2	1.000	0
McKinstry, Z	2B	1	0	1	-	0
	RF	1	1	8	1.000	0
McMahon, R	1B	12	10	89	.989	-1
	2B	33	28	248	.947	1
	3B	14	10	84	.946	3
	SS	2	0	3		0
McNeil, J	2B	12	9	69	1.000	-2
	3B	9	9	75	.865	0
	LF	28	26	215	1.000	2
	RF	4	4	30	1.000	2
Meadows, A	LF	23	21	184	1.000	2
	RF	4	3	23	1.000	0
Mejia, E	2B	1	0	1	-	0
	3B	4	3	26	.875	-1
	LF	2	0	6	1.000	-1
Mendick, D	2B	28	25	226	.991	4
	3B	3	3	27	1.000	0
	SS	4	1	15	1.000	0
Mercado, O	LF	12	7	64	1.000	0
	CF	21	19	171	1.000	4
Mercer, J	1B	2	1	9	1.000	0
	3B	2	1	10	1.000	0
	SS	6	4	33	1.000	0
Merrifield, W	1B	1	0	4	1.000	0
	2B	15	10	92	.966	-2
	LF	6	2	21	1.000	-3
	CF	23	20	159	.977	-1
	RF	34	28	235	1.000	4
Miller, B	2B	1	1	5	1.000	0
	3B	15	11	87	.783	-1
	SS	2	1	8	1.000	0
Molina, Y	1B	2	0	5	1.000	0
Moniak, M	LF	5	3	29	.818	0
	RF	1	1	7	1.000	0
Moore, D	1B	3	2	21	1.000	0
	2B	10	10	81	.957	1
	3B	2	1	10	1.000	0
	SS	3	2	17	.800	0
	LF	13	8	74	1.000	2
	CF	1	1	7	1.000	0
	RF	13	12	104	1.000	2
Moran, C	1B	22	20	166	.988	0
	3B	4	4	35	.923	0
Moreland, M	1B	38	33	296	.992	1
Morrison, L	1B	2	2	16	1.000	-1
Mountcastle, R	1B	10	9	75	.982	-3
	LF	25	23	192	1.000	-1
Moustakas, M	1B	10	8	64	.980	-1
	2B	32	31	243	1.000	-3
	3B	2	2	18	1.000	1
Mullins II, C	LF	4	0	11	1.000	1
	CF	41	36	299	1.000	-1
	RF	4	2	23	1.000	0
Muncy, M	1B	35	31	274	.988	-2
	2B	12	11	82	1.000	2
	3B	16	14	135	.975	-1
Munoz, Y	LF	7	7	56	1.000	4
	RF	4	4	25	1.000	0
Murphy, D	1B	29	27	234	.985	-3
Myers, W	1B	2	1	11	1.000	0
Naquin, T	RF	39	32	299	1.000	-1
Naylor, J	1B	5	0	9	1.000	0
	LF	22	18	151	1.000	2
	RF	4	2	22	1.000	-1
Newman, K	2B	20	19	159	.960	-1
	SS	23	22	184	.930	-3
Nimmo, B	LF	22	6	85	1.000	2
	RF	10	3	36	1.000	1
Nogowski, J	1B	1	1	8	1.000	0
Nola, A	1B	2	2	18	1.000	0
	3B	1	0	3	1.000	0
Noll, J	1B	4	3	28	1.000	-1
	3B	1	0	0	1.000	0
Nunez, E	RF	1	0	1	1.000	0
Nunez, R	1B	28	28	236	.995	-1
	3B	4	2	18	.750	-1
O'Grady, B	1B	1	0	1	1.000	0
	LF	1	1	4	-	0
	CF	1	0	5	-	0
O'Hearn, R	1B	27	25	203	.990	-1
Oliva, J	LF	4	3	29	1.000	0
	CF	1	1	9	1.000	0
Olivares, E	LF	14	7	81	1.000	1
	CF	11	11	82	.917	-4
	RF	11	6	61	1.000	-2
Ona, J	RF	1	0	2	-	0
Orf, N	2B	2	0	8	1.000	0
	SS	3	1	8	1.000	-1
Osuna, J	1B	9	4	46	1.000	0
	3B	5	3	27	1.000	0
	LF	4	4	34	1.000	0
	RF	7	7	48	1.000	2
Owings, C	2B	8	6	50	1.000	0
	3B	2	1	9	.500	-1
	SS	1	1	9	1.000	0
	LF	2	2	18	1.000	0
	CF	2	1	9	1.000	0
	RF	2	0	2	1.000	1
Ozuna, M	LF	19	19	145	.975	-2
	RF	2	2	17	.750	-1
Pache, C	LF	2	1	10	1.000	-1
Panik, J	2B	18	12	116	.980	-1
	3B	12	8	73	1.000	-3
	SS	14	10	94	1.000	-1
Paredes, I	3B	33	30	257	.975	-1
Payton, M	LF	6	6	38	1.000	0
Pederson, J	LF	23	20	165	1.000	-2
	RF	8	6	46	1.000	1
Pence, H	LF	5	4	34	1.000	-1
	RF	5	5	42	1.000	1
Peraza, J	2B	27	24	203	.972	-1
	3B	1	1	8	.333	0
	SS	3	1	11	1.000	0
	LF	5	4	39	1.000	1
Perez, H	1B	2	0	3	1.000	0
	2B	1	1	7	1.000	0
	LF	1	0	4	1.000	0
Perez, M	1B	1	0	7	1.000	0
Perez, S	1B	3	1	15	1.000	1
Peterson, J	1B	4	2	22	1.000	0
	2B	3	1	15	.833	0
	3B	4	3	20	.818	-1
	LF	4	2	20	1.000	1
	RF	13	6	58	1.000	0
Pham, T	LF	18	18	149	.967	-1
Phillips, B	LF	7	1	15	1.000	0
	CF	15	8	67	1.000	-1
	RF	13	7	69	1.000	2
Pillar, K	LF	2	2	14	1.000	1
	CF	27	24	203	.982	-4
	RF	25	20	186	1.000	0
Pinder, C	2B	13	10	95	.972	-1
	3B	7	2	30	1.000	2
	LF	2	0	3	-	0
	RF	1	0	1	1.000	0
Plawecki, K	1B	2	0	2	1.000	0
Pollock, A	LF	27	22	198	.966	-5
	CF	16	15	134	1.000	1
Profar, J	1B	1	0	2	1.000	0
	2B	17	16	138	.979	-2
	LF	36	32	282	1.000	4
	CF	1	1	9	1.000	0
	RF	2	1	13	1.000	0
Puello, C	LF	2	0	3	1.000	-1
	RF	3	2	22	1.000	1
Pujols, A	1B	26	26	216	.989	3
Quinn, R	CF	37	28	251	.984	-2
	RF	2	2	12	1.000	0
Ramirez, H	LF	1	1	4	1.000	0
	RF	2	2	17	1.000	0
Ravelo, R	1B	3	1	16	1.000	0
	LF	1	1	7	1.000	0
	RF	4	4	27	1.000	0
Realmuto, J	1B	6	2	21	1.000	0
Refsnyder, R	1B	4	2	20	1.000	0
	LF	1	1	8	1.000	0
	RF	2	1	9	1.000	2
Renfroe, H	1B	2	1	9	1.000	0
	RF	39	32	285	.953	-1
Rengifo, L	2B	32	26	238	.981	0
	3B	1	0	2	1.000	0
	SS	1	0	4	.500	0
Reyes, F	LF	1	1	5	-	-1
Reyes, V	LF	22	10	116	1.000	0
	CF	30	28	211	.985	-1
	RF	18	12	107	1.000	1
Reynolds, B	CF	17	15	129	1.000	2
Reynolds, M	3B	3	3	24	1.000	0
Rickard, J	RF	3	3	20	1.000	0
Riddle, J	1B	1	0	2	1.000	0
	2B	1	1	8	1.000	0
	3B	11	10	88	.885	-4
	SS	3	2	20	.917	0
	LF	2	2	17	1.000	1
	CF	2	2	14	1.000	0
	RF	2	2	17	1.000	0
Riley, A	1B	4	2	21	.944	1
	LF	4	4	27	1.000	-1
Rios, E	1B	6	5	39	1.000	0
	3B	21	14	140	.939	-1
Rivera, Y	1B	1	0	2	-	0
	2B	1	1	7	1.000	0
	SS	2	1	9	1.000	0
Robertson, D	2B	3	0	6	-	0
	3B	2	0	6	1.000	0
	SS	5	5	37	1.000	-2
	LF	2	0	5	1.000	0
	RF	1	0	2	-	0
Rodgers, B	2B	5	4	33	1.000	-1
	SS	1	0	1	1.000	0
Rodriguez, S	2B	3	2	18	1.000	0
	LF	1	1	9	-	-1
Rojas, J	2B	8	8	66	1.000	0
	SS	2	2	18	1.000	0
	LF	1	1	9	1.000	0
Rojas, M	1B	1	0	2	-	0
	3B	1	1	3	1.000	0
Romine, A	SS	1	0	8	1.000	0
Romine, A	1B	1	0	6	1.000	0
Rooker, B	LF	1	1	4	-	0
	RF	4	4	21	1.000	-2
Ruf, D	1B	4	2	18	1.000	0
	LF	22	15	106	.960	-1
	RF	3	1	16	1.000	0
Ruiz, R	2B	1	0	1	1.000	0
	LF	1	1	0	-	0
Sanchez, J	RF	10	8	66	.944	-1
Sanchez, Y	2B	1	1	8	1.000	0
	3B	5	4	33	.889	0
	SS	3	1	11	1.000	0
Sandoval, P	1B	8	5	50	1.000	0
	3B	5	3	27	1.000	-1
Santana, D	1B	9	9	78	1.000	2
	LF	1	0	1	-	0
	CF	4	4	35	1.000	1

Player	Pos	G	GS	Inn	Pct.	DRS
Santana, D	LF	9	7	49	1.000	-1
	RF	16	16	124	1.000	1
Santander, A	LF	2	1	8	.667	0
Schebler, S	RF	1	0	1	-	0
Schrock, M	2B	5	3	19	1.000	1
	3B	2	1	10	1.000	0
Segura, J	2B	32	30	239	1.000	3
	3B	24	21	180	.964	2
	SS	4	2	15	.909	-1
Senzel, N	CF	23	20	172	.976	1
Shaw, T	1B	14	8	72	.986	2
	3B	37	32	275	.977	-2
Sierra, M	LF	5	3	28	1.000	2
	CF	11	9	75	1.000	0
	RF	4	1	13	1.000	0
Simmons, A	SS	30	30	265	.960	-2
Slater, A	LF	3	2	19	1.000	0
	RF	9	8	67	1.000	0
Smith, D	1B	25	22	193	.988	-2
	LF	23	21	161	1.000	0
Smith, M	CF	3	1	13	.667	0
	RF	12	12	99	1.000	0
Smith, P	1B	5	5	41	1.000	1
	LF	3	2	16	1.000	1
	RF	2	2	18	1.000	0
Smith Jr., D	LF	16	14	117	.963	-3
Smoak, J	1B	31	27	243	.986	-1
Sogard, E	2B	9	2	30	1.000	0
	3B	30	22	199	.962	1
	SS	7	4	40	.941	0
	LF	2	0	2	-	0
Solak, N	1B	1	0	1	-	0
	2B	17	16	140	.981	-5
	LF	29	23	191	.974	-2
	CF	13	13	108	1.000	-6
Solano, D	3B	5	5	42	.692	-3
	SS	2	2	15	1.000	-1
Soler, J	RF	8	8	61	1.000	-1
Soto, E	2B	1	0	2	1.000	0
	SS	2	2	16	1.000	0
Soto, J	LF	36	36	289	1.000	-8
	RF	6	6	43	1.000	-1
Souza Jr., S	LF	3	3	23	1.000	0
	RF	6	4	39	1.000	1
Springer, G	RF	9	5	53	1.000	-3
Starling, B	LF	1	0	2	-	0
	CF	29	16	155	1.000	-4
	RF	1	0	3	-	0
Stevenson, A	LF	9	7	58	1.000	0
	CF	1	1	6	1.000	0
	RF	4	4	31	1.000	1
Stewart, C	LF	32	30	210	1.000	0
Stewart, D	LF	10	10	68	.933	-1
	RF	21	20	163	.962	1
Strange-Gordon, D	2B	13	10	84	.923	-2
	SS	3	2	19	1.000	-1
	LF	13	10	90	1.000	0
Straw, M	SS	1	0	3	-	-1
	CF	27	19	186	1.000	0
Stubbs, G	LF	3	0	10	1.000	0
Tapia, R	RF	3	2	17	1.000	-1
Tauchman, M	LF	20	15	129	1.000	1
	CF	5	2	22	1.000	0
	RF	19	10	97	1.000	-1
Taveras, L	CF	33	32	273	.976	6
Taylor, C	2B	13	11	84	.973	2
	SS	20	15	148	1.000	0
	LF	19	14	138	.971	3
	CF	6	5	46	1.000	-1
Taylor, M	LF	14	8	80	1.000	0
	CF	11	8	75	1.000	0
	RF	11	7	65	.938	-2
Taylor, T	LF	2	1	9	1.000	0
	CF	9	3	35	1.000	1
	RF	10	4	47	1.000	1
Tejeda, A	2B	4	4	34	1.000	-1
	SS	18	16	137	.944	3
Tellez, R	1B	19	18	153	1.000	-1
Thaiss, M	1B	2	2	21	1.000	-1
	2B	1	1	8	.750	0
	3B	1	0	1	-	0
	LF	1	1	8	1.000	-1

Player	Pos	G	GS	Inn	Pct.	DRS
Thames, E	1B	27	24	202	.989	-1
Thomas, L	CF	7	6	42	1.000	0
	RF	14	4	55	.929	0
Toro, A	1B	4	2	17	1.000	-1
	2B	1	1	9	1.000	0
	3B	14	10	97	1.000	0
Torreyes, R	2B	1	0	3	1.000	0
	SS	2	2	11	1.000	0
	CF	1	1	6	1.000	0
Trevino, J	1B	1	0	0	1.000	0
Tsutsugo, Y	3B	14	11	89	.846	-3
	LF	16	12	106	1.000	2
Tucker, C	2B	1	0	3	-	0
	CF	20	19	155	1.000	-3
	RF	16	9	92	1.000	-2
Tucker, K	RF	7	6	50	1.000	2
Turner, J	3B	32	32	264	.952	-1
Urias, L	2B	10	7	65	.980	0
	3B	30	20	176	.981	2
	SS	8	4	38	.929	1
Urias, R	2B	4	2	19	.900	0
	SS	5	4	35	.850	-2
Valaika, P	1B	13	8	70	1.000	1
	2B	13	8	73	1.000	-1
	3B	4	4	32	1.000	-1
	SS	24	15	145	.911	-3
	LF	3	3	24	1.000	2
	RF	1	0	1	-	0
VanMeter, J	1B	3	1	10	1.000	0
	2B	17	13	115	.982	4
	3B	2	2	18	.833	-1
Vargas, I	1B	5	2	23	.952	-1
	2B	16	9	84	.980	-1
	3B	3	1	13	1.000	0
Varsho, D	LF	5	5	43	1.000	1
	CF	14	13	112	1.000	2
Vazquez, C	2B	1	0	1	-	0
Velazquez, A	2B	2	2	13	1.000	0
	SS	30	19	171	1.000	3
	LF	7	0	15	1.000	0
	CF	3	1	11	1.000	1
Verdugo, A	LF	22	18	167	.956	8
	CF	1	1	8	1.000	0
	RF	31	30	247	.961	-1
Villar, J	2B	25	23	187	.950	0
	SS	21	19	166	.946	-1
	CF	2	1	10	.500	-1
Vogelbach, D	1B	2	2	15	1.000	0
Vogt, S	1B	1	0	4	1.000	0
Wade, T	2B	31	13	127	.983	3
	SS	22	16	142	1.000	0
Wade Jr., L	1B	4	3	28	1.000	1
	LF	3	3	26	1.000	0
	CF	4	4	20	1.000	0
	RF	2	1	14	.800	1
Walker, N	1B	3	3	24	1.000	1
	2B	9	3	28	1.000	-2
	3B	2	1	12	1.000	0
	LF	1	0	2	-	0
Walsh, J	1B	29	22	203	.994	-2
	RF	2	2	16	1.000	0
Walton, D	2B	1	1	9	1.000	0
	SS	4	3	26	1.000	0
Ward, T	1B	2	0	2	1.000	-1
	LF	17	6	75	1.000	-1
	RF	19	18	155	1.000	-2
Wendle, J	2B	20	18	149	1.000	2
	3B	28	18	161	.934	2
	SS	10	9	78	.974	-2
White, E	LF	13	11	94	1.000	3
	CF	1	1	10	1.000	0
	RF	3	3	24	1.000	0
Whitefield, A	CF	2	0	5	1.000	1
Williams, J	RF	2	2	13	1.000	0
Williams, M	LF	5	1	13	1.000	0
	CF	4	3	28	1.000	0
	RF	2	0	3	1.000	0
Winker, J	LF	15	12	89	1.000	1
	RF	1	1	6	1.000	0
Wisdom, P	1B	2	0	4	1.000	0
Wolters, T	2B	4	0	6	1.000	0
Yastrzemski, M	LF	8	1	20	1.000	0

Player	Pos	G	GS	Inn	Pct.	DRS
	CF	24	24	186	1.000	1
	RF	31	27	227	1.000	1
Young, A	2B	4	1	15	1.000	-1
	3B	3	3	19	.000	-2
	LF	1	0	2	-	0
Zimmer, B	LF	8	4	45	.875	0
	CF	7	6	52	.917	0
	RF	7	3	35	1.000	1

All Other Catchers

Player	Tm	G	GS	Inn	PO	A	E	DP	PB	Pct.	SB Att	CS	Pit CS	CS Pct	Cat ERA	Stk Sav	Runs Saved GFP/DME	SB	SZ	Other	Total
Alfaro, Jorge	Mia	29	26	217	182	9	2	0	4	.990	20	4	0	.20	5.18	-26	0	0	-3	-4	-7
Allen, Austin	Oak	14	9	81	76	1	0	0	0	1.000	6	0	1	.00	3.89	2	0	-1	0	0	-1
Astudillo, Willians	Min	6	4	32	40	1	0	0	2	1.000	1	0	0	.00	4.22	-1	-1	0	0	0	-1
Avila, Alex	Min	22	19	150	153	6	3	1	1	.981	11	3	0	.27	2.87	-16	0	1	-2	1	0
Barnes, Austin	LAD	28	27	245	245	6	2	0	0	.992	18	2	3	.11	2.61	31	0	-1	4	2	5
Bart, Joey	SF	32	27	231	234	12	2	0	2	.992	27	4	1	.15	4.36	9	0	-1	1	0	0
Bemboom, Anthony	LAA	20	16	144	143	8	0	2	0	1.000	17	7	0	.41	5.44	5	0	2	1	0	3
Brantly, Rob	SF	1	1	8	4	1	0	0	0	1.000	2	1	0	.50	6.75	-1	0	0	0	0	0
Briceno, Jose	LAA	2	2	15	16	0	1	0	1	.941	1	0	0	.00	6.00	0	0	0	0	0	0
Butera, Drew	Col	25	12	117	91	3	0	1	1	1.000	7	2	0	.29	4.86	-9	1	0	-1	1	1
Caratini, Victor	ChC	22	21	180	198	5	1	1	0	.995	5	1	1	.20	3.45	7	-1	0	1	1	1
Casali, Curt	Cin	29	25	213	258	9	1	1	3	.996	10	2	0	.20	3.68	7	-1	-1	1	0	-1
Castro, Jason	TOT	26	25	201	216	14	1	0	1	.996	14	3	1	.21	4.66	9	-2	0	2	-1	-1
Cervelli, Francisco	Mia	16	16	130	124	3	1	0	2	.992	5	0	0	.00	4.56	-4	0	0	0	1	1
Chirinos, Robinson	TOT	25	22	191	210	6	0	0	2	1.000	13	1	1	.08	5.03	-12	1	-2	-2	-2	-5
Collins, Zack	CWS	2	1	10	11	0	0	0	0	1.000	1	0	0	.00	2.70	-1	0	0	0	0	0
Contreras, William	Atl	4	2	21	21	1	0	0	0	1.000	2	0	0	.00	6.43	1	0	0	0	0	0
Diaz, Elias	Col	24	13	126	79	9	0	1	0	1.000	8	1	0	.13	6.21	-3	0	0	0	0	0
Flowers, Tyler	Atl	22	18	184	181	5	1	0	1	.995	17	2	0	.12	3.77	3	0	0	0	2	2
Gallagher, Cam	KC	25	19	162	156	4	1	0	0	.994	4	0	0	.00	3.72	11	0	0	1	2	3
Garneau, Dustin	Hou	17	13	111	120	6	4	1	1	.969	16	2	1	.13	5.69	5	-1	-1	1	0	-1
Garver, Mitch	Min	19	19	169	173	11	0	2	3	1.000	13	3	2	.23	3.78	7	-1	1	1	2	3
Greiner, Grayson	Det	18	16	137	134	4	0	0	2	1.000	10	2	0	.20	5.85	-8	0	0	-1	0	-1
Grullon, Deivy	Bos	1	1	7	4	1	0	0	0	1.000	0	0	0	-	2.57	-1	-1	0	0	0	-1
Haase, Eric	Det	7	5	48	52	2	1	0	0	.982	10	1	0	.10	3.35	-1	0	0	0	0	0
Hedges, Austin	TOT	34	22	210	220	15	2	0	4	.992	14	5	1	.36	4.58	-1	0	1	0	-1	0
Heim, Jonah	Oak	12	12	95	105	6	0	0	0	1.000	3	1	2	.33	3.60	-4	0	0	0	2	2
Heineman, Tyler	SF	15	13	118	110	9	3	0	0	.975	13	5	0	.38	5.03	-1	1	1	0	-1	1
Hernandez, Oscar	KC	3	1	10	7	2	0	0	0	1.000	0	0	0	.00	4.50	-1	0	0	0	0	0
Higashioka, Kyle	NYY	14	13	107	108	7	2	1	1	.983	8	3	0	.38	3.79	7	0	1	1	0	2
Holaday, Bryan	Bal	10	6	59	51	2	0	0	0	1.000	2	1	0	.50	3.20	-5	0	0	-1	0	-1
Hudson, Joe	Sea	9	6	57	57	3	0	0	1	1.000	4	0	0	.00	3.95	-6	-1	0	-1	0	-2
Huff, Sam	Tex	10	9	78	62	2	2	1	2	.970	2	0	0	.00	5.65	-5	0	0	-1	0	-1
Jackson, Alex	Atl	4	3	24	24	0	0	0	0	1.000	1	0	0	.00	3.00	-1	0	0	0	0	0
Jeffers, Ryan	Min	25	18	162	183	4	0	1	1	1.000	15	1	1	.07	3.89	5	1	-1	1	-1	0
Joseph, Caleb	Tor	3	2	19	18	0	2	0	1	.900	4	0	0	.00	6.98	-2	0	0	0	0	0
Kirk, Alejandro	Tor	7	6	52	48	1	0	0	0	1.000	4	0	0	.00	7.44	-4	0	0	0	0	0
Knapp, Andrew	Phi	29	22	183	218	13	2	1	4	.991	9	2	0	.22	5.21	-21	0	0	-3	-1	-4
Knizner, Andrew	StL	7	4	38	40	6	1	0	1	.979	3	2	0	.67	5.68	-1	0	0	0	0	0
Kratz, Erik	NYY	12	9	72	74	3	0	1	0	1.000	5	2	0	.40	4.38	1	1	1	0	0	2
Lavarnway, Ryan	Mia	5	3	29	35	1	0	0	0	1.000	2	1	0	.50	2.79	-2	0	0	0	0	0
Leon, Sandy	Cle	24	20	186	213	14	5	0	0	.978	10	1	1	.10	3.24	0	0	-1	0	1	0
Lin, Tzu-Wei	Bos	1	0	1	0	0	0	0	0	-	0	0	0	-	0.00	0	0	0	0	0	0
Lucroy, Jonathan	Bos	1	0	2	2	0	0	0	0	1.000	0	0	0	-	0.00	0	0	0	0	0	0
Marchan, Rafael	Phi	3	3	23	25	1	1	0	0	.963	1	0	0	.00	7.43	-3	0	0	0	0	0
Mathis, Jeff	Tex	24	22	182	169	15	2	1	2	.989	12	4	0	.33	4.69	1	2	1	0	2	5
McCann, James	CWS	30	27	246	250	7	4	0	2	.985	10	2	2	.20	2.82	25	-1	0	3	3	5
McGuire, Reese	Tor	18	12	111	131	5	3	1	2	.978	6	2	2	.33	2.35	-6	0	0	-1	2	1
Mejia, Francisco	SD	16	12	101	93	7	1	0	1	.990	2	0	0	.00	4.54	-7	0	0	-1	1	0
Murphy, John Ryan	Pit	23	19	160	159	11	2	3	0	.988	13	4	0	.31	3.55	-2	0	0	0	1	1
Navarreto, Brian	Mia	2	2	15	13	1	0	0	0	1.000	2	1	0	.50	3.60	0	0	0	0	0	0
Nido, Tomas	NYM	7	7	60	57	1	1	0	1	.983	6	1	0	.17	5.10	5	0	0	1	-1	0
Nottingham, Jacob	Mil	19	16	134	178	7	2	0	2	.989	8	2	0	.25	3.49	1	0	0	0	2	2
Odom, Joseph	Sea	18	15	123	110	3	0	0	2	1.000	17	1	0	.06	4.62	8	0	0	1	0	1
Perez, Michael	TB	38	27	232	222	25	1	2	1	.996	19	6	0	.32	2.83	-9	-1	1	-1	2	1
Phegley, Josh	ChC	4	0	14	21	0	0	0	1	1.000	1	0	0	.00	5.14	-2	0	0	0	0	0
Pina, Manny	Mil	13	12	98	117	7	0	2	0	1.000	9	5	0	.56	4.48	0	1	2	0	0	3
Plawecki, Kevin	Bos	20	18	158	168	7	1	0	1	.994	16	4	0	.25	6.59	-19	0	1	-2	0	-1
Rivera, Rene	NYM	1	1	8	7	1	0	0	0	1.000	4	4	0	1.00	6.75	-1	0	1	0	0	1
Ruiz, Keibert	LAD	2	2	17	12	1	0	0	0	1.000	3	0	0	.00	4.76	-2	0	0	0	0	0
Sanchez, Ali	NYM	5	4	32	29	0	0	0	1	1.000	3	0	0	.00	5.91	1	0	0	0	0	0
Sisco, Chance	Bal	26	22	184	172	6	2	0	3	.989	16	3	0	.19	5.87	-16	-2	-1	-2	-1	-6
Smith, Kevan	TB	16	8	80	73	3	0	0	1	1.000	4	0	3	.00	4.16	-5	1	-1	-1	0	-1
Stassi, Max	LAA	31	26	239	242	14	1	1	1	.996	37	5	1	.14	4.83	-8	2	-3	-1	3	1
Stephenson, Tyler	Cin	4	2	19	23	1	0	0	0	1.000	2	1	0	.50	6.63	-1	0	0	0	0	0
Stubbs, Garrett	Hou	8	1	21	24	0	0	0	0	1.000	1	0	0	.00	3.80	1	0	0	0	0	0
Susac, Andrew	Pit	1	1	8	5	0	0	0	0	1.000	0	0	0	-	9.00	-1	0	0	0	0	0
Taylor, Beau	Cle	7	7	60	73	6	1	0	0	.988	4	2	0	.50	2.70	3	0	1	0	0	1
Torrens, Luis	TOT	24	21	177	156	6	0	1	6	1.000	16	1	2	.06	4.37	-18	-2	-2	-3	0	-7
Trevino, Jose	Tex	21	17	151	153	3	1	0	0	1.000	11	1	0	.09	4.89	4	0	0	0	0	0
Tromp, Chadwick	SF	23	19	160	144	3	1	1	3	.993	4	0	0	.00	4.66	8	-1	-1	1	0	-1
Varsho, Daulton	Ari	10	6	59	52	3	0	0	1	1.000	7	1	0	.14	5.03	1	-1	-1	0	0	-2
Viloria, Meibrys	KC	5	1	71	62	3	1	0	1	.985	5	0	0	.00	7.48	-1	-1	-1	0	-1	-3
Vogt, Stephen	Ari	23	20	170	184	7	0	1	0	1.000	18	3	1	.17	4.50	3	1	0	0	1	2
Wallach, Chad	Mia	15	13	112	110	4	0	1	0	1.000	12	4	0	.33	5.29	3	0	0	0	1	1
Wieters, Matt	StL	18	12	98	119	2	0	0	2	1.000	1	0	0	.00	3.50	-7	0	0	-1	0	-1
Zunino, Mike	TB	28	25	216	244	15	1	2	5	.996	15	4	0	.27	4.13	-5	-2	1	-1	0	-2

Runs Saved Multi-Year Summary

Alex Vigderman

In baseball, so many aspects of a player's performance are heavily affected by the performance of other players, or just by the fickle fancies of fate.

While the stats might make you think otherwise, defense is one aspect of the game where your performance is heavily dictated by your own effort. It's one of the reasons that we find it so fascinating despite it not getting the air time of pitching and hitting.

In his walk year in Washington, Bryce Harper's defense dropped off a cliff (costing 24 runs after saving 25 runs over his career prior). Data we collect suggested that he was making fewer hustle plays, not diving or sliding when he might have done so previously. Now in Philadelphia, Harper is making much more of those kinds of plays, and he's saved nine runs since 2019.

Understanding that this season's numbers should all be taken with a grain of salt, some players' surprising defensive seasons merit a closer look. For example, Omar Narváez came down on the plus side of the ledger in both avoiding misplays and pitch framing—he'd done neither previously in his four MLB seasons.

Of course, with a short season amid a health crisis, we see proven elites missing on leaderboards. One Fielding Bible Award back-to-back winner, Matt Chapman, saved only two runs and was limited due to injury. Another, Lorenzo Cain, opted out of the season early on.

Use this section to see where we've come from and where we're going, but use it responsibly. Players won't appear if they haven't played enough over recent seasons, and their runs saved totals are collapsed together even if they played positions of varying difficulty (e.g. Manny Machado in 2018).

Defensive Runs Saved By Season

Player	YOB	Position 1	2	DRS <16	16	17	18	19	20
Abreu, Jose	1987	1B		-13	-1	2	-5	-8	4
Adams, Matt	1988	1B		7	-1	-6	3	4	0
Ahmed, Nick	1990	SS		9	15	5	30	17	3
Albies, Ozzie	1997	2B			1	16	11	-1
Almora Jr., Albert	1994	CF			3	0	10	-5	0
Altuve, Jose	1990	2B		-35	0	-1	-1	-1	-3
Anderson, Tim	1993	SS			3	-22	6	-12	3
Andrus, Elvis	1988	SS		6	-11	10	8	-4	-3
Arcia, Orlando	1994	SS			4	3	7	2	-4
Arenado, Nolan	1991	3B		52	13	15	7	18	15
Avila, Alex	1987	C		-9	-1	-5	6	7	0
Baez, Javier	1992	SS	2B	0	12	2	4	27	6
Barnhart, Tucker	1991	C		-1	-1	14	-8	4	9
Bell, Josh	1992	1B			-11	-4	-13	-8	-1
Belt, Brandon	1988	1B		21	5	9	11	2	1
Benintendi, Andrew	1994	LF			1	10	3	-2	1
Betts, Mookie	1992	RF	CF	16	30	30	18	16	10
Blackmon, Charlie	1986	CF	RF	-15	-1	-9	-29	-9	-1
Bogaerts, Xander	1992	SS		-14	-10	-12	-14	-14	-5
Bradley Jr., Jackie	1990	CF		20	14	15	1	-2	5
Brantley, Michael	1987	LF		-1	1	7	-2	10	5
Braun, Ryan	1983	LF	RF	-24	5	-8	-1	-3	-1
Bregman, Alex	1994	3B			6	-3	0	12	0
Bruce, Jay	1987	RF		37	-7	3	-9	1	2
Bryant, Kris	1992	3B		-4	9	-3	-5	-8	1
Buxton, Byron	1993	CF		5	2	23	2	10	11
Cabrera, Asdrubal	1985	SS	2B	-25	-2	-15	-19	-10	0
Cain, Lorenzo	1986	CF		70	11	4	18	22	1
Calhoun, Kole	1987	RF		0	1	2	7	0	0
Cano, Robinson	1982	2B		7	11	-7	2	-6	-4
Carpenter, Matt	1985	3B	1B	-13	1	0	3	5	0
Castellanos, Nick	1992	3B	RF	-22	-4	-21	-17	-9	-4
Castro, Jason	1987	C		1	3	11	1	-7	-1
Castro, Starlin	1990	2B		-29	-9	-6	-7	4	1
Cervelli, Francisco	1986	C		22	5	-6	-3	3	1
Chapman, Matt	1993	3B			15	30	34	2
Chirinos, Robinson	1984	C		0	-2	1	-9	3	-5
Choo, Shin-Soo	1982	RF		-32	-5	-7	-6	-17	-1
Contreras, Willson	1992	C		-1	0	3	-2	1
Correa, Carlos	1994	SS		4	6	9	8	7	7
Crawford, Brandon	1987	SS		47	25	9	1	-4	2
Cron, C.J.	1990	1B		-6	2	5	1	5	0
d'Arnaud, Travis	1989	C		-7	-3	-2	-1	-6	-7
Davis, Chris	1986	1B		-24	4	-12	-11	-2	-2
DeJong, Paul	1993	SS			-1	12	26	0
DeShields, Delino	1992	CF		-11	1	4	9	8	0
Devers, Rafael	1996	3B			-5	-14	-10	-6
Dickerson, Corey	1989	LF		-12	3	2	13	-6	-3
Donaldson, Josh	1985	3B		20	-1	-1	-5	15	-1
Dozier, Brian	1987	2B		-3	-2	-1	-6	-5	-2
Duvall, Adam	1988	LF		-2	17	11	17	1	0
Dyson, Jarrod	1984	CF		36	16	15	7	14	-3
Eaton, Adam	1988	RF	CF	-5	25	-6	-6	-2	-6
Engel, Adam	1991	CF			0	4	1	-1
Escobar, Eduardo	1989	3B	SS	-13	-6	-7	-1	1	0
Flowers, Tyler	1986	C		42	3	11	8	2	2
Forsythe, Logan	1987	2B		2	2	8	0	-4	0
Fowler, Dexter	1986	CF	RF	-65	0	-16	-4	-1	-2
Franco, Maikel	1992	3B		-8	-10	-2	-14	-2	0
Frazier, Todd	1986	3B		10	0	4	5	-3	1
Freeman, Freddie	1989	1B		-7	7	4	9	1	0
Galvis, Freddy	1989	SS		-13	4	3	3	6	0
Garcia, Avisail	1991	RF	CF	-17	3	0	-3	2	-3
Gardner, Brett	1983	LF	CF	90	10	21	12	5	1
Goldschmidt, Paul	1987	1B		19	6	14	11	0	1
Gomes, Yan	1987	C		33	-1	-1	4	5	-3
Gordon, Alex	1984	LF		79	2	9	12	2	1
Grandal, Yasmani	1988	C		21	17	18	12	-3	5
Gregorius, Didi	1990	SS		5	-8	8	1	-10	-2
Gurriel, Yuli	1984	1B			4	-1	0	3	2
Hamilton, Billy	1990	CF		24	18	13	10	8	2

Player	YOB	Position 1	2	DRS <16	16	17	18	19	20
Harper, Bryce	1992	RF		23	-3	5	-24	10	-1
Harrison, Josh	1987	2B		19	9	8	0	0	2
Hechavarria, Adeiny	1989	SS		13	7	-3	0	0	-3
Hedges, Austin	1992	C		5	-1	21	10	21	0
Hernandez, Cesar	1990	2B		-16	2	-4	-8	-3	6
Heyward, Jason	1989	RF	CF	101	15	17	8	2	1
Hicks, Aaron	1989	CF		1	5	15	-8	-1	-8
Hosmer, Eric	1989	1B		-6	-2	-4	6	-3	3
Iglesias, Jose	1990	SS		5	10	0	3	7	-2
Inciarte, Ender	1990	CF		46	15	4	17	-1	-1
Joseph, Caleb	1986	C		25	3	9	-1	1	0
Judge, Aaron	1992	RF		0	8	17	20	3
Kepler, Max	1993	RF		0	8	5	13	8	2
Kiermaier, Kevin	1990	CF		52	25	22	13	13	10
Kipnis, Jason	1987	2B		-23	-5	-6	-5	0
Lagares, Juan	1989	CF		53	8	17	6	-3	1
Lamb, Jake	1990	3B		15	-5	-9	5	1	-5
LeMahieu, DJ	1988	2B		25	3	12	14	6	0
Leon, Sandy	1989	C		8	0	15	11	-1	0
Lindor, Francisco	1993	SS		4	9	7	13	11	2
Longoria, Evan	1985	3B		81	-4	15	3	7	2
Lucroy, Jonathan	1986	C		90	2	-15	-10	-14	0
Machado, Manny	1992	3B	SS	55	20	9	-8	-2	1
Maldonado, Martin	1986	C		38	7	22	2	7	-1
Margot, Manuel	1994	CF			4	9	6	2
Marisnick, Jake	1991	CF		35	18	4	11	6	-3
Markakis, Nick	1983	RF		4	9	-2	3	-2	-3
Marte, Starling	1988	CF	LF	47	16	6	2	-9	-3
Martinez, J.D.	1987	RF		-1	-22	-8	-4	-7	-2
Maybin, Cameron	1987	CF	LF	3	-13	1	3	1	2
Mazara, Nomar	1995	RF			-7	-8	-5	-4	2
McCann, James	1990	C		-9	8	-7	-2	4	5
McCutchen, Andrew	1986	CF		-25	-26	-10	1	4	-8
Mercer, Jordy	1986	SS		0	-6	-12	-9	-7	0
Merrifield, Whit	1989	2B	RF		4	-3	6	2	-2
Molina, Yadier	1982	C		164	1	5	-3	2	1
Moreland, Mitch	1985	1B		-2	10	9	2	-1	1
Morrison, Logan	1987	1B		-36	-5	-1	4	0	-1
Moustakas, Mike	1988	3B	2B	3	1	-10	2	-2	-3
Murphy, Daniel	1985	2B	1B	-20	-11	-11	-15	3	-3
Myers, Wil	1990	1B	RF	-13	7	1	4	-9	-2
Narvaez, Omar	1992	C		-2	-7	-14	-18	1
Odor, Rougned	1994	2B		-12	-7	2	13	-5	-5
Olson, Matt	1994	1B		0	7	13	18	5
Ozuna, Marcell	1990	LF	CF	12	-10	6	5	1	-4
Panik, Joe	1990	2B		9	2	-8	0	-7	-5
Pederson, Joc	1992	CF	LF	-1	2	-13	-1	7	-1
Pence, Hunter	1983	RF		19	-2	-3	-5	-5	0
Peralta, David	1987	LF	RF	-4	2	3	2	10	-1
Perez, Roberto	1988	C		13	9	15	4	30	6
Perez, Salvador	1990	C		23	3	0	1		3
Pillar, Kevin	1989	CF		30	22	14	-4	-4	-2
Piscotty, Stephen	1991	RF		-5	1	6	-6	1	2
Polanco, Gregory	1991	RF		11	0	2	-3	-5	1
Polanco, Jorge	1993	SS		-2	-9	-8	-5	-7	-3
Pollock, A.J.	1987	CF		27	2	6	4	-10	-4
Pujols, Albert	1980	1B		138	-2	-1	5	0	3
Ramirez, Jose	1992	3B	2B	8	6	7	0	4	-6
Ramos, Wilson	1987	C		35	-3	-4	-6	-11	-1
Realmuto, J.T.	1991	C		0	-13	2	-2	11	-1
Reddick, Josh	1987	RF		50	5	8	6	10	-4
Rendon, Anthony	1990	3B		6	13	8	-1	2	-1
Rizzo, Anthony	1989	1B		37	13	12	3	2	3
Rojas, Miguel	1989	SS		16	0	4	7	2	2
Rosario, Amed	1995	SS			-6	-16	-10	-3
Rosario, Eddie	1991	LF		9	3	-11	9	-8	3
Sanchez, Gary	1992	C		3	0	4	-2	-4
Sanchez, Yolmer	1992	2B	3B	-3	-1	12	2	4	0
Santana, Carlos	1986	1B		-71	4	8	0	0	5
Santana, Domingo	1992	RF		-7	-10	-9	5	-16	0
Schoop, Jonathan	1991	2B		10	9	13	9	0	1

Player	YOB	Position 1	Position 2	DRS By Season <16	DRS By Season 16	DRS By Season 17	DRS By Season 18	DRS By Season 19	DRS By Season 20
Schwarber, Kyle	1993	LF		-6	0	-7	3	-3	-3
Seager, Corey	1994	SS		0	-7	6	-3	2	-2
Seager, Kyle	1987	3B		13	13	6	-10	3	-6
Segura, Jean	1990	SS	2B	6	9	-1	-6	-4	4
Semien, Marcus	1990	SS		-6	1	-3	14	12	-5
Shaw, Travis	1990	3B		-1	8	-2	9	1	0
Simmons, Andrelton	1989	SS		98	20	40	23	12	-2
Smoak, Justin	1986	1B		-10	-6	-4	-3	-7	-1
Soto, Juan	1998	LF					-6	0	-9
Souza Jr., Steven	1989	RF		-2	1	8	-2		1
Springer, George	1989	RF	CF	6	6	1	-3	12	3
Story, Trevor	1992	SS			14	11	1	14	5
Strange-Gordon, Dee	1988	2B		-12	-3	5	-7	-5	-3
Suarez, Eugenio	1991	3B		-13	1	3	1	-4	-4
Suzuki, Kurt	1983	C		-41	-12	3	-7	-15	-4
Swanson, Dansby	1994	SS			2	-6	10	2	9
Taylor, Michael A.	1991	CF		7	-1	12	13	0	-2
Trout, Mike	1991	CF		2	6	-5	9	-2	-9
Turner, Justin	1984	3B		-14	9	3	5	-3	-1
Turner, Trea	1993	SS		2	0	1	2	-1	-8
Upton, Justin	1987	LF		-5	-2	10	1	-13	-4
Vazquez, Christian	1990	C		14	6	10	-1	5	1
Villar, Jonathan	1991	2B	SS	-8	-7	-1	5	-11	-2
Vogt, Stephen	1984	C		-5	-10	-8		-3	2
Votto, Joey	1983	1B		37	-12	17	13	10	-7
Walker, Neil	1985	2B		-23	-4	-4	-4	-1	-1
Wieters, Matt	1986	C		33	-3	-5	-3	-2	-1
Wolters, Tony	1992	C			4	0	14	9	-2
Wong, Kolten	1990	2B		15	2	-4	16	19	5
Yelich, Christian	1991	LF	CF	16	1	-12	1	-2	-6
Zunino, Mike	1991	C		17	8	4	11	8	-2

Baserunning

Mark Simon

In 1983, when I was eight years old, I was given my first *Bill James Baseball Abstract* (I pronounced it "Abscart"). I had moved to the point of advanced understanding of the game, enough to learn a few important things from my father: Willie Mays is the greatest player of all-time. Keith Hernandez is an incredible first baseman. And the most fun thing to watch in baseball is when Mookie Wilson tries to score from second on a single (or sometimes on a ground out).

The numbers back up that Wilson was a very good baserunner. Thirty seven years later they'll tell you that Mookie Betts is just as good, if not better.

Betts was the leader in Baserunning Net Gain in 2020. He tallied +22 bases for the Dodgers from his baserunning. This was the first time in his career that Betts led the majors in this stat. He previously finished tied-sixth in 2015, third in 2016 and 2018, and second in 2017.

Betts stole 10 bases in 12 attempts, but it wasn't stolen bases where Betts made his mark. Betts rated an MLB-best +16 in Baserunning Gain, which measures how often a player takes extra bases on hits (such as going second to home on a single), how often he advances on wild pitches and passed balls, and how he fares at avoiding being thrown out or doubled off, or hitting into a double play.

This marked the second time he had the best Baserunning Gain numbers (as opposed to Net Gain), the other instance being in 2017.

In 2020, Betts went first to third on seven singles in 13 opportunities (the average runner advances to third 28% of the time), scored from second on a single seven times in eight opportunities (the average success rate is 59%), recorded 12 bases taken, made no baserunning outs, and hit into two double plays in 39 opportunities (his rate was about half the MLB double play rate of 10%).

That's a level of success that Mookie Wilson could appreciate.

Largest Baserunning Net Gain - 2020 Season

Player	Net Gain
Mookie Betts	+22
Trevor Story	+20
Kyle Tucker	+17
Brandon Lowe	+17
4 Players Tied*	+16

Xander Bogaerts, Adalberto Mondesi, Robbie Grossman, Starling Marte

The runner up to Betts for the Net Baserunning crown was Rockies shortstop Trevor Story.

Story, primarily known outside of Colorado for his hitting and his defense, led the National League with 15 stolen bases after previous seasons of 27 and 23. He finished with a Net Gain of +20 bases.

Story's Rockies led the majors in Net Gain, finishing with a +67. The Diamondbacks (+59), Rays (+43), Athletics (+43), and Rangers (+36) rounded out the top five.

Colorado separated itself from other teams in how well it did at taking extra bases on hits. For example, the Rockies scored 42 times in the 55 instances a runner was on second base when a single was hit. Their 76% success rate led the majors.

The Rockies ranked second in Baserunning Gain (+43) and third in Stolen Base Gain (+24) en route to being first overall. The rest of the Dodgers didn't take after Betts. His team ranked 17th overall (+6).

Net Gain is a statistic that measures baserunning production that includes all baserunning advancements on both hits and outs (BR Gain) and stolen bases (SB Gain). It estimates the number of bases a player gained or lost for a team due to his baserunning. BR Gain is the sum of extra baserunning advances a player made over the league average, minus a penalty for the number of baserunning outs he made above the league average. SB Gain estimates how many bases each runner gained or lost his team based on his successful and unsuccessful stolen base attempts.

The following pages show baserunning performance for players listed in alphabetical order for both 2020 and for the careers of those who qualify. It also includes baserunning numbers for 2020 for each team, ordered by Net Gain.

Redbirds Defense Soars Again

The MLB team leader in turning groundballs and bunts into outs was the Cardinals (78.3%). The Cardinals led in 2019 as well with an almost identical percentage (78.0%).

Chad Kuhl of the Pirates benefited most from his infield defense in that regard, as Pittsburgh recorded an 87.0% out conversion rate. Jack Flaherty of the Cardinals ranked second (86.4%).

2020 Baserunning

Player	1st to 3rd		2nd to Home		1st to Home		Bases Taken	Out Adv	Doubled Off	BR Outs	GDP	GDP Opps	BR Gain	SB Gain	Net Gain
	Moved	Chances	Moved	Chances	Moved	Chances									
Abreu, Jose	4	11	3	4	3	9	5	0	0	0	10	53	-3	0	-3
Acuna Jr., Ronald	3	9	6	9	5	6	3	1	0	1	3	31	+1	+6	+7
Adames, Willy	4	7	2	5	1	2	7	0	1	1	4	42	+3	0	+3
Adell, Jo	1	5	2	3	0	0	4	1	0	1	2	20	0	-2	-2
Adrianza, Ehire	3	6	4	4	0	0	2	0	0	0	3	17	+2	+1	+3
Aguilar, Jesus	0	8	9	10	0	2	2	1	0	1	5	29	-6	-2	-8
Ahmed, Nick	7	12	4	8	1	1	7	0	1	1	3	35	+5	+4	+9
Akiyama, Shogo	2	4	3	3	2	2	3	2	0	2	1	27	-1	+1	0
Alberto, Hanser	7	9	7	9	4	4	11	0	3	3	6	39	+5	+3	+8
Albies, Ozzie	4	8	1	1	1	1	4	1	0	1	0	26	+5	+1	+6
Alfaro, Jorge	1	7	1	3	0	1	2	0	0	0	2	17	-2	+2	0
Alonso, Pete	2	14	2	5	1	4	3	2	0	2	4	62	-7	+1	-6
Altuve, Jose	3	12	6	9	3	3	3	0	0	0	5	43	+1	-4	-3
Anderson, Brian	3	13	5	7	1	2	3	0	0	0	2	41	+2	0	+2
Anderson, Tim	3	9	5	7	1	3	11	0	0	0	4	33	+8	+1	+9
Andrus, Elvis	2	6	2	3	0	0	5	0	0	0	5	17	+1	+1	+2
Andujar, Miguel	1	3	2	2	0	1	3	0	0	0	1	8	+2	0	+2
Arauz, Jonathan	2	4	3	4	0	0	1	0	0	0	0	10	+2	0	+2
Arcia, Orlando	3	5	3	4	1	2	2	0	0	1	10	33	-8	+2	-6
Arenado, Nolan	3	8	0	2	0	1	4	0	0	0	7	49	-1	0	-1
Arozarena, Randy	2	4	3	4	1	2	0	0	0	0	2	15	0	+4	+4
Arraez, Luis	2	6	3	3	1	3	4	1	1	3	2	22	-6	0	-6
Avila, Alex	1	2	0	2	0	2	4	0	0	0	2	9	0	0	0
Bader, Harrison	1	6	2	7	0	1	6	0	0	0	2	19	+1	+1	+2
Baez, Javier	5	7	2	2	1	2	6	2	1	3	8	62	-4	+3	-1
Barnes, Austin	1	5	2	3	0	2	6	0	1	1	0	13	+2	+3	+5
Barnhart, Tucker	0	6	0	0	0	0	0	0	0	0	2	20	-3	0	-3
Bart, Joey	0	4	0	4	1	2	5	0	0	0	1	20	+1	0	+1
Bell, Josh	1	13	2	4	1	3	3	1	0	1	3	39	-5	0	-5
Bellinger, Cody	4	13	3	5	1	3	8	1	0	1	4	50	+3	+4	+7
Belt, Brandon	4	9	2	4	2	3	5	0	0	0	5	40	+3	0	+3
Berti, Jon	2	10	5	7	1	3	6	0	0	0	1	20	+4	+5	+9
Betts, Mookie	7	13	7	8	1	3	12	0	0	0	2	39	+16	+6	+22
Bichette, Bo	0	3	3	4	0	0	5	1	0	1	2	25	+1	+2	+3
Biggio, Cavan	2	17	4	9	2	6	14	0	0	1	2	36	+4	+6	+10
Blackmon, Charlie	5	18	7	8	0	3	12	1	0	1	4	46	+6	0	+6
Bogaerts, Xander	8	11	5	5	2	3	2	0	0	0	3	43	+8	+8	+16
Bohm, Alec	2	14	3	6	2	3	3	1	0	0	4	35	-6	-1	-7
Bonifacio, Jorge	0	2	2	2	1	2	4	0	0	0	1	25	+5	0	+5
Bote, David	3	6	1	2	0	2	4	1	0	1	6	33	-3	+2	-1
Bradley Jr., Jackie	5	17	3	6	0	3	6	0	0	0	2	38	+3	+1	+4
Brantley, Michael	3	10	1	4	0	4	8	0	0	0	3	46	+4	+2	+6
Braun, Ryan	0	5	0	1	1	1	3	1	0	1	6	32	-6	+1	-5
Bregman, Alex	5	14	0	3	1	2	6	1	0	1	2	32	+1	0	+1
Brinson, Lewis	1	4	3	4	1	2	3	0	0	0	2	16	+2	+4	+6
Brosseau, Mike	1	4	2	5	1	2	3	0	0	0	1	20	+1	+2	+3
Bruce, Jay	0	3	0	1	0	2	2	0	0	0	1	22	0	0	0
Bryant, Kris	5	7	2	3	2	2	5	0	0	0	1	22	+9	0	+9
Buxton, Byron	2	3	1	1	0	0	4	2	0	2	2	24	-1	0	-1
Cabrera, Asdrubal	2	11	2	9	1	2	6	1	0	0	6	49	-5	0	-5
Cabrera, Miguel	2	11	1	8	0	2	3	1	0	1	3	47	-7	+1	-6
Calhoun, Kole	3	7	6	9	0	1	8	0	0	0	6	45	+5	-1	+4
Calhoun, Willie	1	4	1	2	0	1	2	1	0	0	1	17	-2	0	-2
Camargo, Johan	1	3	3	3	0	1	4	0	1	1	1	26	+2	0	+2
Candelario, Jeimer	3	18	5	10	1	2	10	0	1	1	3	52	+3	-1	+2
Canha, Mark	4	12	6	7	3	5	6	2	0	2	2	44	+2	+4	+6
Cano, Robinson	1	6	3	7	0	3	2	1	0	1	7	44	-9	0	-9
Caratini, Victor	2	7	1	3	1	2	1	0	1	1	4	21	-6	-2	-8
Carlson, Dylan	2	3	5	5	0	1	1	1	0	1	3	25	-1	-1	-2
Carpenter, Matt	4	9	1	1	0	3	4	1	1	2	1	44	0	0	0
Casali, Curt	1	5	0	2	0	1	2	1	1	2	2	13	-8	+2	-6
Castellanos, Nick	1	4	2	3	0	2	8	0	0	0	5	48	+4	-4	0
Castro, Harold	0	3	4	5	0	1	2	0	0	0	1	9	+1	0	+1

2020 Baserunning

Player	1st to 3rd Moved	Chances	2nd to Home Moved	Chances	1st to Home Moved	Chances	Bases Taken	Out Adv	Doubled Off	BR Outs	GDP	GDP Opps	BR Gain	SB Gain	Net Gain
Castro, Jason	1	3	1	2	2	2	0	1	0	1	2	15	-3	0	-3
Castro, Starlin	0	1	1	1	1	1	3	0	0	0	0	11	+4	0	+4
Castro, Willi	7	14	1	3	0	1	2	1	0	1	0	22	+1	-2	-1
Cave, Jake	4	7	5	6	0	2	3	0	0	0	0	16	+5	-4	+1
Cervelli, Francisco	1	6	0	4	0	0	3	0	0	0	3	10	-3	+1	-2
Chapman, Matt	0	3	3	3	0	0	3	0	1	1	2	33	0	0	0
Chavis, Michael	0	4	2	4	1	1	6	1	1	2	6	33	-5	+3	-2
Choi, Ji-Man	0	4	2	2	0	2	2	1	0	1	1	32	-2	0	-2
Choo, Shin-Soo	2	5	1	1	1	2	4	1	1	2	1	16	-2	+2	0
Conforto, Michael	4	15	4	6	3	5	1	0	0	0	6	61	-2	-3	-5
Contreras, Willson	4	11	6	8	3	5	6	1	0	1	6	41	+1	-3	-2
Cooper, Garrett	1	9	4	7	0	1	1	0	0	0	5	40	-4	0	-4
Correa, Carlos	6	13	3	7	0	1	3	0	0	0	4	37	0	0	0
Crawford, Brandon	2	7	3	5	0	4	9	0	0	0	3	35	+5	-3	+2
Crawford, J.P.	5	11	5	8	3	3	5	1	1	2	4	28	-2	0	-2
Cronenworth, Jake	4	8	4	5	1	2	2	0	0	0	4	29	+1	+1	+2
Cruz, Nelson	0	10	1	2	1	3	9	0	0	0	8	47	-1	0	-1
d'Arnaud, Travis	1	4	1	3	1	4	3	1	0	1	8	43	-8	+1	-7
Dahl, David	0	1	3	3	0	0	3	0	0	0	0	15	+4	+1	+5
Dalbec, Bobby	0	3	0	1	1	3	2	0	0	0	0	22	+1	0	+1
Davis, J.D.	7	18	2	5	0	4	2	1	1	2	8	57	-11	0	-11
Davis, Khris	2	5	0	1	1	2	1	0	0	0	5	24	-3	0	-3
DeJong, Paul	2	7	2	5	2	4	5	1	0	1	4	34	-2	+1	-1
DeShields, Delino	4	6	2	2	1	2	4	1	0	1	0	19	+4	-1	+3
Devers, Rafael	7	14	6	7	0	0	7	0	0	0	8	65	+7	0	+7
Diaz, Elias	1	4	0	0	0	1	3	0	0	0	4	13	-1	0	-1
Diaz, Yandy	3	7	1	2	2	6	2	1	1	2	6	24	-10	0	-10
Dickerson, Alex	3	10	3	6	2	4	6	0	0	0	5	41	+3	0	+3
Dickerson, Corey	2	14	2	4	4	4	4	1	1	2	5	29	-7	-1	-8
Dietrich, Derek	1	2	0	1	0	2	2	1	1	2	4	11	-9	-1	-10
Donaldson, Josh	0	10	0	1	0	0	1	0	0	0	4	25	-6	0	-6
Dozier, Hunter	2	6	7	7	1	3	5	0	1	1	3	35	+3	+4	+7
Dubon, Mauricio	2	5	3	3	3	5	4	2	1	3	4	34	-5	-4	-9
Duvall, Adam	4	7	1	2	3	6	4	0	1	1	2	40	+3	0	+3
Dyson, Jarrod	2	3	1	2	1	1	3	0	0	0	0	6	+4	+6	+10
Eaton, Adam	1	3	2	3	0	0	2	0	0	0	4	27	-1	+3	+2
Edman, Tommy	6	11	4	4	2	2	4	0	0	0	5	49	+6	-6	0
Encarnacion, Edwin	3	5	1	4	1	1	3	1	1	2	3	39	-3	0	-3
Engel, Adam	4	8	0	0	1	2	3	0	0	0	1	17	+4	+1	+5
Ervin, Phillip	2	6	2	2	2	2	2	0	0	0	2	19	+3	+1	+4
Escobar, Eduardo	5	15	1	1	2	2	7	1	0	1	5	41	+3	+1	+4
Espinal, Santiago	2	3	1	3	0	0	2	0	0	0	1	14	+2	+1	+3
Evans, Phillip	1	4	2	2	0	0	1	1	0	1	1	7	-2	-2	-4
Farmer, Kyle	0	2	0	1	0	1	2	0	0	0	0	14	+1	+1	+2
Fletcher, David	6	14	4	10	1	3	10	1	1	2	4	40	0	0	0
Flores, Wilmer	2	6	2	5	0	3	8	0	1	1	5	48	0	+1	+1
Flowers, Tyler	0	1	0	1	0	1	2	0	0	0	1	12	0	0	0
Ford, Mike	1	2	1	1	0	0	2	0	0	0	4	22	0	0	0
Fowler, Dexter	1	5	2	4	2	2	3	2	1	3	2	21	-7	-1	-8
France, Ty	3	8	1	4	0	2	2	1	1	2	3	34	-7	0	-7
Franco, Maikel	2	8	2	6	0	1	4	1	1	2	4	34	-8	+1	-7
Frazier, Adam	1	8	3	3	2	3	10	3	0	3	3	36	0	-5	-5
Frazier, Clint	3	9	2	3	3	6	7	1	0	1	5	32	+1	+3	+4
Frazier, Todd	1	4	1	3	0	2	4	2	0	2	1	24	-4	-1	-5
Freeman, Freddie	9	19	5	9	3	8	9	2	1	3	6	56	-2	+2	0
Fuentes, Josh	3	6	3	6	1	1	2	0	0	0	1	20	+3	+1	+4
Gallagher, Cam	1	6	2	2	0	0	0	0	0	0	0	7	0	0	0
Gallo, Joey	5	16	3	4	1	1	3	0	0	0	0	27	+5	+2	+7
Galvis, Freddy	2	5	3	5	0	2	3	0	0	0	5	23	-2	-1	-3
Gamel, Ben	1	7	2	7	0	1	3	2	0	2	4	22	-10	-4	-14
Garcia, Avisail	4	8	1	5	3	4	7	0	0	0	2	31	+6	-5	+1
Garcia, Greg	2	4	0	3	0	0	1	0	0	0	0	12	0	+1	+1
Garcia, Leury	2	4	0	0	0	0	2	0	0	0	0	9	+3	0	+3
Garcia, Luis	3	11	4	5	0	1	5	1	1	2	3	35	-2	-1	-3

2020 Baserunning

Player	1st to 3rd Moved	1st to 3rd Chances	2nd to Home Moved	2nd to Home Chances	1st to Home Moved	1st to Home Chances	Bases Taken	Out Adv	Doubled Off	BR Outs	GDP	GDP Opps	BR Gain	SB Gain	Net Gain
Gardner, Brett	1	8	2	4	1	1	8	1	0	1	0	32	+5	-3	+2
Gimenez, Andres	2	5	2	2	3	3	4	1	0	1	0	23	+4	+6	+10
Goldschmidt, Paul	7	12	5	6	0	3	14	1	0	1	4	55	+12	+1	+13
Gomes, Yan	1	4	0	2	0	1	4	0	0	0	1	23	+2	+1	+3
Gonzalez, Erik	3	8	4	4	1	2	8	0	0	0	5	31	+6	-4	+2
Gonzalez, Marwin	3	9	3	4	0	1	8	1	0	1	1	35	+6	0	+6
Goodrum, Niko	1	3	2	4	1	3	6	0	0	0	4	27	+3	+5	+8
Goodwin, Brian	1	7	2	3	0	0	4	1	1	2	1	26	-3	+5	+2
Gordon, Alex	4	10	3	4	0	1	3	0	0	0	0	20	+4	0	+4
Gosselin, Phil	2	3	3	4	1	1	3	0	1	1	3	19	0	0	0
Grandal, Yasmani	2	10	2	4	0	2	5	1	0	1	4	34	-3	0	-3
Gregorius, Didi	4	12	5	7	4	5	5	1	0	1	4	48	+3	-1	+2
Grichuk, Randal	1	5	9	10	3	5	7	1	0	1	5	41	+4	-1	+3
Grisham, Trent	5	14	5	11	0	1	5	2	0	2	1	41	-3	+8	+5
Grossman, Robbie	6	10	1	3	1	1	8	0	0	0	1	28	+10	+6	+16
Guerrero Jr., Vladimir	6	12	4	11	1	2	8	2	1	3	6	41	-6	+1	-5
Guillorme, Luis	0	3	0	0	0	0	1	0	0	0	3	12	-3	+2	-1
Gurriel Jr., Lourdes	3	12	2	7	1	4	4	2	0	2	7	47	-11	+1	-10
Gurriel, Yuli	1	14	5	6	2	2	7	0	1	1	6	53	0	-2	-2
Guzman, Ronald	1	2	1	1	0	1	3	0	0	0	0	6	+3	+1	+4
Gyorko, Jedd	3	6	2	4	0	1	4	0	0	0	4	27	+1	0	+1
Hamilton, Billy	3	3	2	2	0	0	2	0	0	0	0	11	+5	+2	+7
Hampson, Garrett	6	15	5	5	2	2	8	2	0	2	1	20	+6	+4	+10
Happ, Ian	2	9	5	8	1	2	4	0	1	1	1	33	0	-5	-5
Harper, Bryce	4	16	6	9	0	1	5	2	0	2	5	62	-4	+4	0
Harrison, Josh	2	8	0	0	0	1	4	1	0	1	2	17	-2	-3	-5
Harrison, Monte	0	0	2	3	1	1	1	1	0	1	0	10	-1	+6	+5
Haseley, Adam	2	5	0	1	1	2	4	0	0	0	3	23	+2	0	+2
Hayes, Ke'Bryan	1	2	2	5	0	1	4	0	0	0	2	20	+1	+1	+2
Hays, Austin	1	5	4	5	4	7	0	0	0	0	1	21	+1	-4	-3
Hechavarria, Adeiny	0	1	3	3	0	1	1	0	1	1	1	14	-2	0	-2
Hernandez, Cesar	8	11	4	6	1	7	10	1	2	3	3	45	+2	0	+2
Hernandez, Kike	3	6	3	5	0	2	2	0	0	0	5	28	-1	-2	-3
Hernandez, Teoscar	3	9	3	4	1	2	1	0	0	0	4	38	0	+4	+4
Heyward, Jason	8	12	2	2	2	3	5	0	0	0	1	40	+11	+2	+13
Hicks, Aaron	2	10	6	8	2	2	6	0	0	0	4	52	+5	+2	+7
Hilliard, Sam	2	2	1	1	1	1	4	0	2	2	0	16	+1	+3	+4
Hiura, Keston	2	7	2	3	2	2	4	0	0	0	7	50	+1	-1	0
Hoerner, Nico	3	8	2	5	2	3	4	1	1	2	3	19	-5	-1	-6
Holt, Brock	4	8	1	2	1	1	1	0	0	0	3	23	+1	+1	+2
Hoskins, Rhys	2	8	3	7	0	0	7	0	0	0	4	44	+3	+1	+4
Hosmer, Eric	3	9	2	4	0	0	4	0	1	1	3	35	0	+4	+4
Iglesias, Jose	0	5	3	5	1	1	2	1	0	1	1	20	-3	0	-3
Inciarte, Ender	2	13	4	7	2	4	1	0	0	0	0	29	0	+2	+2
Jansen, Danny	1	5	2	4	0	6	4	1	2	3	1	31	-8	0	-8
Jeffers, Ryan	0	2	0	1	0	0	0	0	0	0	0	10	-1	0	-1
Jimenez, Eloy	2	8	3	4	1	2	5	0	0	0	4	44	+3	0	+3
Jones, JaCoby	0	1	1	3	2	2	3	2	0	2	1	20	-3	-1	-4
Joyce, Matt	1	6	3	4	1	1	1	0	0	0	3	30	-1	+1	0
Judge, Aaron	0	1	4	5	2	2	4	1	0	1	5	33	0	-2	-2
Kelly, Carson	1	3	1	2	0	3	6	0	0	0	4	24	+2	0	+2
Kemp, Matt	1	8	4	4	0	0	8	0	0	0	5	25	+4	+1	+5
Kemp, Tony	6	8	0	0	1	1	3	0	0	0	0	21	+7	+1	+8
Kendrick, Howie	1	6	4	6	1	2	2	0	2	2	4	23	-7	0	-7
Kepler, Max	3	6	3	8	3	4	8	0	1	1	1	29	+5	+3	+8
Kieboom, Carter	6	11	0	3	0	3	4	0	0	0	6	25	-2	-2	-4
Kiermaier, Kevin	3	3	6	6	1	1	5	1	1	2	2	25	+3	+6	+9
Kiner-Falefa, Isiah	2	11	7	7	0	0	9	1	1	2	6	39	-1	-2	-3
Kingery, Scott	2	7	2	4	1	2	4	0	0	0	1	20	+3	0	+3
Kipnis, Jason	2	5	0	0	2	3	4	0	1	1	1	22	+2	+1	+3
Knapp, Andrew	5	6	1	4	0	1	3	1	1	2	1	18	-2	0	-2
La Stella, Tommy	2	10	5	9	1	3	4	1	0	1	6	47	-5	-1	-4
Lamb, Jake	1	2	0	1	1	1	1	0	0	0	1	16	+1	-2	-1
Laureano, Ramon	4	7	4	5	1	1	7	0	1	1	7	51	+3	0	+3

2020 Baserunning

Player	1st to 3rd		2nd to Home		1st to Home		Bases Taken	Out Adv	Doubled Off	BR Outs	GDP	GDP Opps	BR Gain	SB Gain	Net Gain
	Moved	Chances	Moved	Chances	Moved	Chances									
LeMahieu, DJ	2	6	3	6	1	6	12	0	0	0	3	28	+7	+3	+10
Leon, Sandy	0	4	0	3	0	2	1	1	0	1	2	12	-8	0	-8
Lewis, Kyle	8	17	4	6	3	4	7	1	1	2	5	48	+2	+3	+5
Lindor, Francisco	4	11	5	10	1	1	8	5	0	5	8	52	-13	+2	-11
Locastro, Tim	2	7	4	8	1	2	3	0	0	0	0	11	+2	+4	+6
Long Jr., Shed	2	4	2	2	1	1	4	1	0	1	1	15	+3	+4	+7
Longoria, Evan	1	11	2	4	2	2	5	0	0	0	10	43	-5	-2	-7
Lopes, Tim	1	7	4	7	0	1	2	0	0	0	2	25	-1	+5	+4
Lopez, Nicky	5	11	4	4	4	5	2	2	0	2	1	27	+1	-10	-9
Lowe, Brandon	7	12	6	9	0	1	11	0	0	0	2	38	+14	+3	+17
Lowe, Nate	0	3	1	2	1	2	3	0	0	0	2	14	+1	+1	+2
Luplow, Jordan	2	2	3	3	1	1	0	0	2	2	3	24	-4	-2	-6
Machado, Manny	0	10	4	7	3	3	6	2	0	2	9	50	-9	0	-9
Machin, Vimael	2	2	2	3	0	2	3	0	0	0	4	14	0	0	0
Madrigal, Nick	4	8	0	2	0	2	5	3	0	3	5	26	-9	0	-9
Maldonado, Martin	2	8	0	4	1	4	4	1	0	1	2	21	-4	+1	-3
Margot, Manuel	4	6	4	6	3	4	5	0	0	0	0	23	+9	+4	+13
Markakis, Nick	1	4	1	3	0	1	4	0	0	0	5	32	-1	-2	-3
Marmolejos, Jose	0	2	1	2	1	2	2	2	0	2	2	23	-5	-2	-7
Marte, Ketel	5	11	8	11	1	2	3	1	0	1	2	41	+2	+1	+3
Marte, Starling	5	14	10	11	3	4	15	1	1	2	5	44	+10	+6	+16
Martinez, J.D.	1	13	2	3	1	4	4	1	1	2	6	56	-9	+1	-8
Martinez, Jose	2	4	2	2	0	0	3	0	0	0	6	21	0	0	0
Maybin, Cameron	1	3	0	1	0	1	2	0	0	0	4	20	-2	+3	+1
Mazara, Nomar	4	10	0	1	0	1	5	0	0	0	0	20	+5	-2	+3
McCann, James	2	5	2	3	1	1	1	0	0	0	2	24	+1	-1	0
McCutchen, Andrew	2	14	2	4	1	3	6	1	0	1	4	33	-4	+4	0
McMahon, Ryan	3	7	2	6	2	2	6	0	0	0	4	36	+4	-2	+2
McNeil, Jeff	3	16	5	10	0	2	6	0	0	1	3	51	-2	-4	-6
Meadows, Austin	2	4	1	2	0	1	2	0	0	0	0	19	+3	0	+3
Mendick, Danny	1	3	2	4	0	1	4	0	1	1	3	21	-2	-2	-4
Mercado, Oscar	0	3	0	0	1	2	4	0	0	0	2	23	+5	+3	+8
Merrifield, Whit	3	10	4	6	1	4	7	2	2	4	3	33	-8	+6	-2
Miller, Brad	2	8	4	5	0	2	6	1	0	1	2	40	+2	+1	+3
Molina, Yadier	0	9	1	3	0	4	5	2	1	3	7	38	-14	0	-14
Moncada, Yoan	2	8	4	5	5	6	11	0	1	1	1	44	+12	0	+12
Mondesi, Adalberto	2	6	4	6	2	2	11	1	0	1	4	51	+8	+8	+16
Moore, Dylan	4	5	6	8	0	0	4	1	0	1	4	24	+1	+2	+3
Moran, Colin	5	10	2	5	0	5	2	0	0	0	9	43	-6	0	-6
Moreland, Mitch	3	7	0	1	0	2	7	0	1	1	0	25	+4	0	+4
Mountcastle, Ryan	2	8	0	0	1	1	2	1	0	1	2	29	-2	-2	-4
Moustakas, Mike	1	4	1	1	0	0	1	0	0	0	5	27	-3	+1	-2
Mullins II, Cedric	4	8	2	4	1	2	5	0	0	0	0	20	+6	+3	+9
Muncy, Max	3	14	4	7	2	4	5	0	0	0	3	45	+3	+1	+4
Murphy, Daniel	2	5	0	0	1	2	2	1	0	1	3	24	-2	0	-2
Murphy, Sean	3	5	1	2	1	4	5	0	0	0	6	33	+1	0	+1
Myers, Wil	1	6	5	9	2	2	2	0	0	0	0	25	+2	0	+2
Naquin, Tyler	2	5	1	2	2	2	1	0	0	0	3	33	+1	-2	-1
Narvaez, Omar	1	9	2	5	0	1	2	0	1	1	1	22	-4	0	-4
Naylor, Josh	1	3	3	4	2	2	1	0	0	0	2	22	+2	+1	+3
Newman, Kevin	2	6	1	1	1	1	3	1	0	1	1	35	+2	-2	0
Nimmo, Brandon	9	14	1	3	1	4	7	0	1	1	1	31	+6	-3	+3
Nola, Austin	2	6	2	3	1	3	6	0	0	0	3	28	+4	0	+4
Nunez, Renato	2	10	1	5	1	3	9	3	1	4	4	41	-9	0	-9
O'Hearn, Ryan	0	2	0	1	1	2	1	0	0	0	5	32	-3	0	-3
O'Neill, Tyler	1	5	4	7	1	1	9	1	0	1	3	37	+5	+1	+6
Odor, Rougned	1	2	1	1	1	1	2	0	0	0	2	26	+3	-2	+1
Ohtani, Shohei	2	8	2	2	2	3	5	0	1	1	3	46	+3	+4	+7
Olivares, Edward	3	4	0	0	1	2	1	0	0	0	1	18	+3	-4	-1
Olson, Matt	1	9	4	5	0	4	5	1	1	2	2	51	-3	+1	-2
Osuna, Jose	1	3	0	0	0	0	0	0	0	0	1	18	0	-2	-2
Ozuna, Marcell	6	17	3	4	4	7	7	0	0	0	3	55	+8	0	+8
Panik, Joe	1	10	3	8	2	2	5	0	0	0	4	33	0	0	0
Paredes, Isaac	1	5	1	1	0	1	1	0	1	1	1	17	-3	0	-3

2020 Baserunning

Player	1st to 3rd Moved	Chances	2nd to Home Moved	Chances	1st to Home Moved	Chances	Bases Taken	Out Adv	Doubled Off	BR Outs	GDP	GDP Opps	BR Gain	SB Gain	Net Gain
Pederson, Joc	1	3	3	6	1	2	2	1	1	2	5	23	-8	+1	-7
Peralta, David	4	11	3	4	0	2	9	1	1	2	4	42	+1	+1	+2
Peraza, Jose	0	3	0	2	1	2	4	1	0	1	3	26	-3	-1	-4
Perez, Michael	0	2	1	1	1	3	2	2	0	2	3	10	-7	0	-7
Perez, Roberto	1	9	0	1	0	2	1	1	0	1	2	15	-7	0	-7
Perez, Salvador	2	6	1	8	0	2	6	0	0	0	0	24	+2	+1	+3
Peterson, Jace	1	8	2	3	0	0	0	0	0	0	0	9	-1	+1	0
Pham, Tommy	3	4	1	4	0	1	4	0	1	1	2	23	0	+6	+6
Phillips, Brett	2	3	0	1	0	1	2	0	0	0	0	8	+2	+4	+6
Pillar, Kevin	4	11	7	10	2	3	5	1	1	2	4	47	-1	+1	0
Pinder, Chad	1	2	1	1	0	2	3	0	1	1	3	16	-2	0	-2
Piscotty, Stephen	0	4	5	6	1	2	3	0	0	0	4	37	+1	+4	+5
Plawecki, Kevin	1	4	1	4	0	0	1	1	0	1	4	17	-7	+1	-6
Polanco, Gregory	0	5	1	1	1	1	1	0	0	0	1	27	+1	+1	+2
Polanco, Jorge	3	11	2	5	1	3	12	1	0	1	7	44	+2	0	+2
Pollock, A.J.	1	8	4	6	0	0	5	1	0	1	6	39	-3	-2	-5
Profar, Jurickson	1	3	2	3	2	4	5	2	0	2	1	42	0	+5	+5
Pujols, Albert	0	3	3	5	0	1	2	0	0	0	4	25	-2	0	-2
Quinn, Roman	2	3	4	4	1	1	2	0	1	1	0	25	+3	+12	+15
Ramirez, Jose	3	8	2	4	0	4	12	1	0	1	2	53	+8	+4	+12
Ramos, Wilson	0	8	0	3	0	2	1	1	0	1	5	28	-11	0	-11
Realmuto, J.T.	6	11	4	5	4	4	4	0	0	1	3	48	+6	+2	+8
Reddick, Josh	1	4	1	5	0	4	0	1	0	1	5	40	-10	+1	-9
Rendon, Anthony	4	8	2	4	2	4	9	0	1	1	10	51	-1	0	-1
Renfroe, Hunter	1	5	2	5	0	0	3	0	0	0	3	24	0	+2	+2
Rengifo, Luis	3	5	1	1	0	1	3	1	1	2	2	17	-3	0	-3
Reyes, Franmil	3	12	2	3	0	3	4	1	2	3	6	51	-11	0	-11
Reyes, Victor	5	12	7	9	0	1	6	1	0	1	4	32	+2	+4	+6
Reynolds, Bryan	2	7	5	8	0	1	5	1	2	3	2	40	-5	-1	-6
Riley, Austin	2	8	1	2	2	4	4	1	0	1	5	40	-3	0	-3
Rios, Edwin	2	2	1	3	0	0	0	0	0	0	2	11	-1	0	-1
Rizzo, Anthony	4	10	5	6	0	4	7	1	0	1	6	54	+1	+1	+2
Robert, Luis	3	10	4	6	1	2	6	0	0	0	4	48	+5	+5	+10
Robles, Victor	4	9	2	3	0	2	7	2	1	3	0	35	0	+2	+2
Rojas, Josh	0	2	1	1	1	2	3	0	0	0	1	16	+3	-1	+2
Rojas, Miguel	3	4	3	4	1	3	4	1	0	1	1	34	+3	+3	+6
Romine, Austin	1	4	2	3	0	1	4	1	0	1	3	24	-1	0	-1
Rosario, Amed	2	4	3	6	2	3	6	1	0	1	5	34	+1	-2	-1
Rosario, Eddie	3	7	4	6	1	5	10	5	0	5	3	43	-6	+1	-5
Ruf, Darin	0	9	2	2	1	2	1	0	0	0	1	27	-1	+1	0
Ruiz, Rio	0	9	3	5	2	4	8	1	0	1	4	40	0	-3	-3
Sanchez, Gary	1	4	0	1	0	0	5	0	0	0	6	32	0	0	0
Sandoval, Pablo	1	10	1	2	0	0	3	0	0	0	3	27	-1	0	-1
Sano, Miguel	1	7	8	10	2	2	4	0	0	0	3	50	+6	0	+6
Santana, Carlos	4	14	2	6	2	4	12	0	0	0	5	43	+6	0	+6
Santana, Domingo	0	1	2	2	0	0	0	2	0	2	2	19	-7	0	-7
Santander, Anthony	2	8	5	6	1	3	1	1	0	1	2	34	-2	-2	-4
Schoop, Jonathan	6	14	7	7	1	2	6	0	0	0	8	37	+4	0	+4
Schwarber, Kyle	4	8	5	7	2	4	5	0	0	1	3	32	+2	+1	+3
Seager, Corey	4	15	4	8	1	3	7	1	2	3	8	48	-10	+1	-9
Seager, Kyle	3	14	7	9	2	6	4	1	0	1	4	51	-1	+5	+4
Segura, Jean	6	11	3	4	0	2	2	1	2	3	6	35	-10	-2	-12
Semien, Marcus	2	11	2	2	1	1	10	0	0	0	3	48	+9	+4	+13
Senzel, Nick	1	2	1	2	0	0	1	1	0	1	2	11	-4	0	-4
Severino, Pedro	1	7	1	3	1	1	3	0	0	0	3	29	-1	+1	0
Shaw, Travis	2	14	3	7	0	0	3	4	0	4	4	39	-15	0	-15
Sierra, Magneuris	1	3	4	4	1	1	3	0	0	0	0	15	+6	+2	+8
Simmons, Andrelton	3	9	3	3	0	1	3	0	0	0	5	25	0	+2	+2
Sisco, Chance	0	5	1	4	0	1	7	1	0	1	1	27	+1	0	+1
Slater, Austin	2	10	3	4	1	2	4	0	0	0	2	20	+2	+6	+8
Smith Jr., Dwight	1	5	1	2	0	0	1	1	0	1	1	12	-3	+1	-2
Smith, Dominic	1	12	4	7	0	2	3	1	0	1	2	52	-3	0	-3
Smith, Will	2	5	3	6	1	2	6	2	0	2	2	29	-1	0	-1
Smoak, Justin	0	4	3	8	0	2	3	0	0	0	3	14	-4	0	-4

2020 Baserunning

Player	1st to 3rd Moved	Chances	2nd to Home Moved	Chances	1st to Home Moved	Chances	Bases Taken	Out Adv	Doubled Off	BR Outs	GDP	GDP Opps	BR Gain	SB Gain	Net Gain
Sogard, Eric	0	5	1	3	0	2	3	1	0	1	1	19	-4	0	-4
Solak, Nick	3	7	4	5	3	5	7	0	0	0	6	50	+6	+5	+11
Solano, Donovan	3	11	4	6	1	2	4	2	0	2	2	50	-2	0	-2
Soler, Jorge	7	12	3	3	0	1	2	0	0	0	3	34	+5	0	+5
Soto, Juan	0	9	6	12	0	3	11	1	1	2	1	39	-1	+2	+1
Springer, George	8	12	3	7	2	3	3	0	0	0	3	38	+5	-3	+2
Stallings, Jacob	1	7	1	3	0	3	3	1	0	1	2	23	-5	0	-5
Stanton, Giancarlo	0	2	0	1	1	2	3	0	0	0	4	19	-1	-1	-2
Stassi, Max	2	6	0	2	0	1	2	0	0	0	5	28	-3	0	-3
Stevenson, Andrew	0	3	3	4	0	0	1	1	0	1	0	10	-2	+2	0
Stewart, Christin	3	4	0	1	0	0	0	0	1	1	2	25	-2	0	-2
Stewart, D.J.	0	9	1	1	1	1	3	0	0	0	0	17	+2	0	+2
Story, Trevor	6	13	7	8	5	5	8	0	1	1	5	70	+11	+9	+20
Strange-Gordon, Dee	2	2	3	4	0	0	3	0	0	0	1	16	+5	+1	+6
Straw, Myles	1	3	3	4	1	1	1	0	0	0	0	12	+2	+2	+4
Suarez, Eugenio	5	8	4	6	1	2	3	0	0	0	5	40	+3	+2	+5
Suzuki, Kurt	3	12	3	6	0	1	2	1	0	1	4	28	-6	+1	-5
Swanson, Dansby	5	13	7	9	5	7	5	1	1	2	0	54	+5	+5	+10
Tapia, Raimel	3	13	2	2	6	9	8	0	1	1	3	40	+5	+4	+9
Tatis Jr., Fernando	6	11	4	7	3	3	10	2	1	3	6	57	+2	+5	+7
Tauchman, Mike	4	7	3	6	1	2	4	1	1	2	3	30	-2	+6	+4
Taveras, Leody	0	7	2	3	0	0	7	1	0	1	0	17	+2	+8	+10
Taylor, Chris	2	6	3	4	1	3	9	3	1	4	3	42	-4	-1	-5
Taylor, Michael A.	0	3	1	3	0	1	1	0	0	0	2	21	-2	0	-2
Tejeda, Anderson	0	1	2	2	0	0	0	0	0	0	2	13	-1	+2	+1
Tellez, Rowdy	2	5	1	3	2	4	1	1	0	1	1	18	-3	-2	-5
Thames, Eric	0	5	0	3	2	2	3	1	0	1	2	27	-3	+1	-2
Toro, Abraham	3	5	1	3	0	1	2	0	1	1	1	21	-1	-1	-2
Torrens, Luis	1	3	0	0	0	0	2	1	2	3	1	15	-7	0	-7
Torres, Gleyber	0	10	2	2	2	4	9	1	0	1	5	33	0	+1	+1
Trevino, Jose	1	5	3	5	0	0	2	0	0	0	1	21	+2	0	+2
Trout, Mike	4	10	2	5	1	1	6	0	0	0	1	59	+8	-1	+7
Tsutsugo, Yoshi	1	8	2	3	1	1	3	0	0	0	5	38	-1	0	-1
Tucker, Cole	3	5	3	4	0	1	4	0	0	0	3	24	+4	+1	+5
Tucker, Kyle	2	6	3	4	1	2	10	0	0	0	2	47	+11	+6	+17
Turner, Justin	2	11	3	5	1	5	4	0	1	1	2	31	-3	+1	-2
Turner, Trea	2	11	4	6	4	5	14	0	0	0	5	40	+10	+4	+14
Upton, Justin	0	1	4	4	1	2	1	1	0	1	6	34	-5	-4	-9
Urias, Luis	2	4	1	1	1	2	2	1	0	1	4	16	-4	-2	-6
Urshela, Gio	2	8	3	4	0	3	7	0	0	0	6	42	+2	+1	+3
Valaika, Pat	2	8	2	4	1	2	0	2	0	2	3	27	-9	-4	-13
VanMeter, Josh	1	4	2	3	0	0	4	0	0	0	0	16	+5	+1	+6
Varsho, Daulton	2	6	0	0	0	0	4	0	0	0	1	20	+4	+1	+5
Vazquez, Christian	0	7	3	6	0	5	6	0	0	0	6	42	-3	-2	-5
Velazquez, Andrew	3	3	0	1	0	1	4	0	0	0	2	24	+4	0	+4
Verdugo, Alex	5	14	4	5	4	5	8	0	0	0	4	32	+8	+4	+12
Villar, Jonathan	4	10	2	5	2	3	7	3	0	3	2	27	-3	+6	+3
Vogelbach, Daniel	0	4	1	3	0	2	3	0	0	0	3	20	-2	0	-2
Vogt, Stephen	0	2	1	1	0	0	1	0	0	0	1	10	0	0	0
Voit, Luke	2	12	2	5	2	5	5	0	0	1	4	43	-3	0	-3
Votto, Joey	1	7	4	4	1	3	6	1	0	1	5	41	0	0	0
Wade, Tyler	2	3	3	4	5	6	4	0	2	2	1	15	+1	+2	+3
Walker, Christian	3	7	7	11	0	4	10	0	0	0	6	53	+6	-1	+5
Walsh, Jared	1	6	3	3	0	2	2	0	0	0	0	24	+3	0	+3
Ward, Taylor	3	7	3	5	1	1	4	0	0	0	1	16	+4	+2	+6
Wendle, Joey	3	7	5	6	3	5	6	2	1	3	1	36	0	+4	+4
White, Evan	2	4	3	3	2	6	6	0	1	1	3	39	+3	-3	0
Winker, Jesse	1	6	3	3	0	4	3	0	1	1	3	27	-4	+1	-3
Wolters, Tony	4	7	1	1	2	5	3	1	0	1	1	18	+2	0	+2
Wong, Kolten	5	13	9	9	2	2	9	1	2	3	1	19	+4	+1	+5
Yastrzemski, Mike	2	14	5	8	0	1	7	2	0	2	2	43	-2	0	-2
Yelich, Christian	4	14	3	5	0	0	6	0	0	0	4	44	+3	0	+3
Zimmer, Bradley	0	1	1	3	0	0	0	0	0	0	2	13	-3	0	-3

Career Baserunning

Players with 1000 Career Games
(Data goes back to 2002)

Player	1st to 3rd Moved	1st to 3rd Chances	2nd to Home Moved	2nd to Home Chances	1st to Home Moved	1st to Home Chances	Bases Taken	Out Adv	Doubled Off	BR Outs	GDP	GDP Opps	BR Gain	SB Gain	Net Gain
Altuve, Jose	93	270	121	205	46	78	186	44	10	57	149	1031	-46	+102	+56
Andrus, Elvis	182	360	162	217	66	100	272	31	23	55	161	1269	+165	+95	+260
Arenado, Nolan	73	227	77	117	23	49	98	13	7	20	121	939	-1	-14	-15
Avila, Alex	29	180	40	97	9	46	73	17	16	33	79	668	-109	-8	-117
Belt, Brandon	63	255	77	130	21	63	126	31	6	37	42	887	+17	+5	+22
Blackmon, Charlie	83	282	104	159	34	60	161	23	9	33	45	591	+59	+21	+80
Brantley, Michael	81	286	79	142	37	89	166	15	5	21	116	1019	+45	+59	+104
Braun, Ryan	115	343	136	200	57	102	211	33	14	47	180	1512	+49	+96	+145
Bruce, Jay	69	266	86	165	34	74	141	27	8	35	99	1289	+23	-15	+8
Cabrera, Asdrubal	103	339	126	211	39	97	223	58	9	71	169	1420	-49	+26	-23
Cabrera, Miguel	142	658	186	350	49	166	268	51	14	67	321	2152	-183	-3	-186
Cain, Lorenzo	91	212	98	142	39	56	143	16	10	26	100	764	+69	+95	+164
Calhoun, Kole	66	191	70	117	31	68	149	24	7	31	66	713	+49	+2	+51
Cano, Robinson	125	457	198	321	48	118	258	43	23	67	284	2014	-72	-25	-97
Carpenter, Matt	88	310	95	173	28	69	147	33	13	46	35	718	-1	-9	-10
Castro, Starlin	79	291	103	159	40	83	140	24	12	36	171	1125	-58	-13	-71
Choo, Shin-Soo	110	411	148	234	47	109	250	30	22	52	102	1142	+62	+47	+109
Crawford, Brandon	52	223	88	137	21	49	144	18	4	22	96	992	+45	-28	+17
Cruz, Nelson	65	341	91	161	17	89	169	29	12	41	147	1350	-65	+12	-53
Davis, Chris	54	266	78	149	27	71	116	20	9	31	62	1005	+2	-3	-1
Descalso, Daniel	48	138	62	86	15	39	93	8	1	9	33	473	+81	-4	+77
Desmond, Ian	98	250	108	165	40	63	180	23	11	35	132	1096	+70	+69	+139
Donaldson, Josh	66	228	72	116	27	70	145	25	14	39	94	897	-7	+22	+15
Dozier, Brian	97	237	84	131	33	58	128	20	10	31	89	806	+42	+33	+75
Encarnacion, Edwin	98	374	114	196	40	119	169	32	11	43	185	1594	-47	+33	-14
Fowler, Dexter	164	302	120	181	40	70	210	51	29	81	59	839	+55	+12	+67
Frazier, Todd	70	211	61	111	32	64	133	32	10	43	94	919	-16	-3	-19
Freeman, Freddie	89	317	124	196	36	103	170	25	8	33	116	1234	+33	+3	+36
Gardner, Brett	118	297	120	191	47	79	240	22	19	41	55	975	+173	+142	+315
Goldschmidt, Paul	97	299	114	181	47	90	182	11	6	17	114	1159	+117	+62	+179
Gordon, Alex	112	391	151	231	57	105	195	23	9	32	110	1202	+93	+23	+116
Harper, Bryce	90	234	82	147	59	105	136	41	19	60	81	1047	-24	+26	+2
Heyward, Jason	119	316	123	186	52	81	174	21	7	28	87	1100	+134	+34	+168
Hosmer, Eric	77	307	114	182	45	79	143	27	15	44	137	1112	-44	+19	-25
Jay, Jon	87	276	107	138	36	61	135	21	7	29	90	718	+44	-11	+33
Joyce, Matt	69	217	85	126	33	59	109	14	9	23	74	839	+49	-11	+38
Kemp, Matt	121	338	139	202	42	84	182	48	25	74	184	1467	-61	+58	-3
Kendrick, Howie	129	323	134	217	51	95	183	31	21	54	193	1213	-33	+32	-1
Kipnis, Jason	71	240	96	150	33	70	147	12	16	28	76	895	+58	+70	+128
LeMahieu, DJ	62	220	98	161	41	85	151	12	12	24	130	795	-1	+1	0
Longoria, Evan	83	332	129	201	36	92	177	18	13	32	183	1489	+2	+21	+23
Lowrie, Jed	50	222	79	127	25	72	133	19	3	22	81	866	+31	+1	+32
Lucroy, Jonathan	44	198	64	123	22	64	100	25	11	38	136	870	-119	+12	-107
Machado, Manny	70	221	85	145	29	55	152	27	9	36	141	1008	-17	+4	-13
Markakis, Nick	132	567	184	307	54	151	231	29	9	39	214	1679	-26	+2	-24
Marte, Starling	78	188	101	139	31	56	128	29	10	39	74	730	+26	+91	+117
Martinez, J.D.	54	227	65	132	20	73	118	16	10	26	129	948	-63	+3	-60
Maybin, Cameron	66	174	102	140	41	61	124	15	17	33	87	772	+39	+76	+115
McCutchen, Andrew	106	414	145	222	51	107	167	20	12	33	98	1183	+46	+37	+83
Molina, Yadier	71	389	96	211	19	97	165	32	14	48	261	1521	-218	-8	-226
Moreland, Mitch	36	196	59	108	14	54	90	12	10	23	93	842	-46	+1	-45
Moustakas, Mike	35	221	66	122	13	57	110	23	8	31	101	940	-62	-1	-63
Murphy, Daniel	93	285	101	149	52	94	141	30	9	40	124	1105	+9	+18	+27
Pedroia, Dustin	92	368	137	217	52	147	191	45	15	62	154	1250	-76	+46	-30
Pence, Hunter	112	357	128	193	75	108	208	20	13	35	152	1345	+101	+10	+111
Posey, Buster	62	267	78	161	30	96	160	15	6	21	148	1018	-28	+5	-23
Pujols, Albert	185	599	218	328	60	163	297	75	23	101	378	2608	-156	+37	-119
Reddick, Josh	78	226	63	110	31	64	137	11	12	25	71	917	+67	+25	+92
Rizzo, Anthony	71	261	78	141	21	87	143	38	16	54	104	1158	-69	-8	-77
Rodriguez, Sean	48	136	56	85	17	29	95	14	6	20	57	547	+35	+4	+39
Sandoval, Pablo	45	268	74	139	15	59	140	24	7	31	147	1013	-75	-14	-89

Career Baserunning
Players with 1000 Career Games
(Data goes back to 2002)

Player	1st to 3rd		2nd to Home		1st to Home		Bases Taken	Out Adv	Doubled Off	BR Outs	GDP	GDP Opps	BR Gain	SB Gain	Net Gain
	Moved	Chances	Moved	Chances	Moved	Chances									
Santana, Carlos	87	333	105	178	38	107	175	33	8	43	138	1201	-32	+10	-22
Seager, Kyle	81	233	81	143	23	57	142	28	10	39	100	1049	+7	0	+7
Segura, Jean	82	207	109	148	31	56	160	23	22	46	99	737	+12	+59	+71
Simmons, Andrelton	64	181	81	114	20	55	110	15	7	23	144	825	-28	+19	-9
Smoak, Justin	36	213	56	123	11	66	78	17	6	23	109	860	-101	-3	-104
Stanton, Giancarlo	43	208	73	131	22	62	140	23	4	28	95	1026	+9	+12	+21
Strange-Gordon, Dee	67	169	85	117	29	51	134	11	8	20	45	575	+97	+135	+232
Suzuki, Kurt	72	283	89	173	31	74	121	18	2	21	138	1134	-17	-2	-19
Trout, Mike	162	331	130	187	44	73	189	18	18	37	58	1062	+181	+127	+308
Turner, Justin	75	231	75	126	20	63	115	21	6	30	92	852	-11	+15	+4
Upton, Justin	130	363	147	209	62	105	172	25	17	42	130	1464	+89	+31	+120
Votto, Joey	115	484	128	243	41	135	191	47	23	71	151	1496	-131	+21	-110
Walker, Neil	64	245	84	141	37	85	133	13	11	24	97	952	+24	-12	+12
Wieters, Matt	25	199	48	117	11	55	72	15	2	17	102	803	-88	+1	-87
Zimmerman, Ryan	107	350	140	210	54	109	183	26	7	33	203	1506	+29	+11	+40

2002-2020 MLB Averages

1st to 3rd	2nd to Home	1st to Home
28%	59%	44%

2020 Team Baserunning

Team	1st to 3rd Moved	Chances	2nd to Home Moved	Chances	1st to Home Moved	Chances	Bases Taken	Out Adv	Doubled Off	BR Outs	GDP	GDP Opps	BR Gain	SB Gain	Net Gain
Colorado Rockies	45	118	42	55	20	34	72	5	4	9	41	425	+43	+24	+67
Arizona D-Backs	41	107	47	71	10	24	84	5	3	8	37	421	+50	+9	+59
Oakland Athletics	34	86	33	46	11	28	61	3	5	8	44	448	+23	+20	+43
Tampa Bay Rays	34	83	41	61	15	32	61	8	4	12	38	397	+13	+30	+43
Texas Rangers	23	82	32	46	8	18	62	6	3	9	33	334	+15	+21	+36
New York Yankees	23	93	35	55	20	40	84	5	4	10	51	454	+20	+13	+33
Chicago White Sox	38	106	29	48	15	34	68	5	3	8	44	431	+21	+4	+25
Seattle Mariners	36	89	43	60	14	32	49	8	5	13	34	371	+4	+20	+24
Philadelphia Phillies	40	117	40	65	15	29	57	7	5	13	40	451	+2	+19	+21
Miami Marlins	25	112	49	76	16	30	49	6	2	8	37	391	-3	+23	+20
Atlanta Braves	39	113	36	58	26	51	53	8	5	13	39	475	+2	+15	+17
Kansas City Royals	34	86	33	52	12	30	50	7	4	11	28	361	+8	+9	+17
Chicago Cubs	45	96	34	51	16	34	56	6	5	12	42	411	+12	+4	+16
Boston Red Sox	38	117	35	58	13	32	58	6	4	10	51	474	-3	+13	+10
San Diego Padres	28	87	32	62	14	24	48	10	5	15	37	422	-19	+29	+10
Minnesota Twins	28	94	37	59	10	26	74	11	2	14	38	397	+8	0	+8
Los Angeles Dodgers	35	112	41	67	11	32	74	10	6	16	46	423	-7	+13	+6
St Louis Cardinals	33	95	41	61	9	27	71	11	5	16	38	417	+7	-2	+5
Houston Astros	35	106	30	61	13	31	50	3	3	6	39	428	+4	0	+4
Detroit Tigers	34	107	39	64	7	21	52	7	3	10	42	399	-5	+7	+2
San Francisco Giants	25	120	33	61	15	36	70	7	2	9	50	490	-2	+3	+1
Los Angeles Angels	32	103	32	57	10	22	62	7	5	12	48	460	-5	+3	-2
Washington Nationals	29	116	34	69	10	26	73	10	5	15	42	437	-14	+9	-5
Cincinnati Reds	20	69	25	39	6	19	45	7	3	10	44	356	-19	+11	-8
Toronto Blue Jays	27	114	38	77	15	35	62	14	3	18	39	422	-33	+21	-12
Cleveland Indians	32	97	29	52	11	32	60	13	6	19	40	448	-22	+5	-17
Pittsburgh Pirates	22	88	33	51	6	23	53	10	3	13	34	372	-13	-6	-19
Baltimore Orioles	26	105	32	56	18	34	59	13	5	18	32	411	-17	-9	-26
Milwaukee Brewers	25	95	26	58	9	22	46	5	1	7	53	378	-29	-7	-36
New York Mets	38	129	28	59	10	35	42	9	3	13	53	513	-43	0	-43
MLB Totals	964	3042	1059	1755	385	893	1805	232	116	355	1234	12617			

Stolen Base Attempt Times

Mark Simon

Jarrod Dyson's still got it.

Even at ages 35/36, Dyson still runs like someone 10 years younger. He went 6-for-6 in stolen base attempts during the 2020 season, and on the three instances we timed him trying to steal second base, he clocked in at 3.50 seconds. The combination of speed and base-stealing instincts (he's the active leader among those with at least 100 steal attempts with an 85% success rate) make Dyson a useful player even as his batting average dipped below .200 in 2018 and 2020.

The only player faster among those whom we timed at least three times was Dyson's teammate, Tim Anderson, at 3.48. Anderson's speed shows up more in his hitting than in his basestealing (he went 5-for-7 in steal attempts in 2020). Anderson's 30 infield hits since the start of 2019 rank tied for fourth most.

We saluted Blue Jays standout Cavan Biggio in this space last season and we'll do it again here. Biggio is now 20-for-20 on stolen base attempts in his two-year career. He's done this without breakout speed. He timed at 3.76 seconds on the three attempts we measured in 2020, which is within 11-hundredths of a second of the worst time on the list.

Those of you who watch the Phillies regularly might have thought that Roman Quinn would top our list given that Quinn went 12-for-12 in steal attempts (11-for-11 stealing second). That was the most steals of anyone without a caught stealing in 2020. He's tied for ninth timewise at 3.60 seconds.

Lastly, props to the last name on the list on the next page, Cubs first baseman Anthony Rizzo. Despite tying for the slowest average time (3.87 seconds), Rizzo was safe 3-of-4 times trying to steal second base.

Stolen Base Times - 2B Only

Runner	Timed Attempts	Average
Anderson, Tim	4	3.48
Dyson, Jarrod	3	3.50
Hamilton, Billy	4	3.54
Harrison, Monte	3	3.54
Locastro, Tim	4	3.55
Tucker, Kyle	8	3.56
Lewis, Kyle	4	3.57
Berti, Jon	4	3.58
Ohtani, Shohei	6	3.60
Wong, Kolten	3	3.60
Story, Trevor	10	3.60
Taveras, Leody	5	3.60
O'Neill, Tyler	3	3.60
Acuna Jr., Ronald	6	3.60
Quinn, Roman	8	3.60
Solak, Nick	3	3.60
Dubon, Mauricio	3	3.60
Fraley, Jake	3	3.61
Straw, Myles	4	3.61
Mullins II, Cedric	7	3.62
Bogaerts, Xander	4	3.62
Villar, Jonathan	9	3.62
Mondesi, Adalberto	16	3.62
Polanco, Gregory	4	3.62
Marte, Starling	4	3.63
Mercado, Oscar	3	3.63
Zimmer, Bradley	3	3.64
Edman, Tommy	4	3.64
Wade, Tyler	3	3.64
Kiermaier, Kevin	5	3.64
Tatis Jr., Fernando	7	3.64
Hilliard, Sam	3	3.64
Betts, Mookie	8	3.64
Robert, Luis	8	3.64
Kemp, Tony	3	3.65
Velazquez, Andrew	4	3.65
Grisham, Trent	7	3.65
Albies, Ozzie	3	3.65
Fletcher, David	3	3.66
Moore, Dylan	8	3.66
Swanson, Dansby	3	3.66
Profar, Jurickson	3	3.66
Turner, Trea	6	3.67
Margot, Manuel	10	3.67
DeShields, Delino	3	3.68
Tapia, Raimel	7	3.68
Nimmo, Brandon	3	3.68
Reyes, Victor	6	3.68
Hoerner, Nico	3	3.68
Lopes, Tim	4	3.68
Bellinger, Cody	3	3.68
Piscotty, Stephen	3	3.69
Tauchman, Mike	4	3.69
Goodrum, Niko	7	3.69
Merrifield, Whit	7	3.69
Heath, Nick	3	3.69
Kiner-Falefa, Isiah	6	3.70
Ramirez, Jose	8	3.70
Gimenez, Andres	5	3.70
Pollock, A.J.	3	3.70
Crawford, J.P.	6	3.70
Gardner, Brett	4	3.71
Realmuto, J.T.	4	3.71
Lindor, Francisco	7	3.72
Sierra, Magneuris	4	3.72
Goodwin, Brian	4	3.73
Wendle, Joey	5	3.73
Slater, Austin	7	3.73
Segura, Jean	4	3.73
Polanco, Jorge	4	3.73
Garcia, Avisail	4	3.73

Runner	Timed Attempts	Average
Bichette, Bo	3	3.73
Grossman, Robbie	7	3.73
Yelich, Christian	6	3.74
Semien, Marcus	4	3.74
Phillips, Brett	4	3.74
Akiyama, Shogo	8	3.74
Hosmer, Eric	3	3.74
Chisholm, Jazz	3	3.74
Arozarena, Randy	4	3.74
Choo, Shin-Soo	3	3.76
Benintendi, Andrew	3	3.76
Biggio, Cavan	3	3.76
Rojas, Miguel	3	3.77
Inciarte, Ender	3	3.77
Machado, Manny	3	3.81
Soto, Juan	4	3.81
Conforto, Michael	5	3.82
Harper, Bryce	7	3.82
Hays, Austin	3	3.82
Dozier, Hunter	3	3.83
Meadows, Austin	3	3.86
Lopez, Nicky	3	3.87
Rizzo, Anthony	4	3.87

Pitchers' Repertoires

Alex Vigderman

Playoff baseball looks different in part because frequent days off allow teams to deploy their pitchers differently, leading to more pitchers appearing for short high-effort stints. That leads to more pitching changes, yes, but also to faster fastballs and more filthy breaking balls.

While days off were but a myth in 2020, the short season did offer a bit of that all-out feel that the playoffs bring out. Jacob deGrom, coming off consecutive Cy Young Awards and in no need of tweaking his approach, threw four percent fewer fastballs and threw them as fast as any starter.

And speaking of going all out, the leader in fastball velocity this year was Garrett Crochet, who was drafted this year and therefore never played above the SEC. He averaged 100 MPH after the White Sox brought him up in the midst of a playoff push.

Joe Kelly has his own postseason pitching stories, but let's focus on his pitch mix. His curveball usage has jumped in two seasons from 19% to 63% after he ditched the changeup and cut back on his fastball. That said, his fastball velocity has declined each of the last three seasons, so he's not going full-postseason.

His team didn't make the postseason, but it would be irresponsible not to mention the transformation of Daniel Bard in 2020. A first-round pick in 2006 who was throwing 97 early in his career, Bard's last two MLB seasons featured an ignominious 39:45 strikeout-to-walk ratio and four ticks lost off his fastball. He returned this season after a six-year hiatus, back up to 97 and featuring his slider and changeup more. It was an inspiring comeback, and it's interesting to compare his current and former selves.

This section is teeming with trends, quirks, and insights about any pitcher you can think of from the 2020 season. Come and stay a while, but make sure to leave bread crumbs lest you get lost in the numbers.

Player	Tommy John SX	Fastball Velocity	Fastball	Slider	Change	Cutter	Curve	Splitter	Other
Abreu, Bryan	-	92.9	36%	43%	-	-	21%	-	
Adam, Jason	-	94.8	53%	19%	15%	-	12%	-	
Adams, Austin	-	93.3	16%	84%	-	-	-	-	
Adams, Chance	-	91.8	48%	5%	4%	-	44%	-	
Akin, Keegan	-	91.9	62%	10%	17%	-	11%	-	
Alcala, Jorge	-	97.0	46%	45%	9%	-	-	-	
Alcantara, Sandy	-	96.5	60%	24%	10%	-	6%	-	
Alexander, Scott	-	93.1	83%	17%	-	-	-	-	
Alexander, Tyler	-	90.6	44%	21%	18%	17%	-	-	
Allard, Kolby	-	91.6	47%	-	13%	31%	10%	-	
Allen, Logan	-	94.1	46%	27%	15%	-	13%	-	
Almonte, Yency	-	94.8	43%	45%	12%	-	-	-	
Altavilla, Dan	-	97.3	47%	53%	-	-	-	-	
Alvarado, Jose	-	96.9	77%	12%	-	-	11%	-	
Alvarez, Jose	-	91.7	53%	12%	22%	12%	-	-	
Alzolay, Adbert	-	94.7	52%	6%	8%	-	34%	-	
Anderson, Brett	July `11	89.8	43%	11%	24%	11%	10%	-	
Anderson, Chase	-	92.5	40%	-	23%	20%	16%	-	
Anderson, Drew	Apr `15	92.5	70%	4%	16%	-	10%	-	
Anderson, Ian	-	94.1	49%	-	30%	-	21%	-	
Anderson, Nick	-	95.2	65%	-	-	-	35%	-	
Anderson, Shaun	-	94.6	40%	53%	7%	-	-	-	
Anderson, Tyler	-	90.2	47%	-	33%	18%	2%	-	
Andriese, Matt	-	91.8	43%	6%	39%	-	12%	-	
Antone, Tejay	Apr `17	95.7	41%	40%	3%	-	17%	-	
Armstrong, Shawn	-	93.7	43%	-	-	46%	11%	-	
Arrieta, Jake	-	92.1	52%	-	17%	23%	7%	-	
Avilan, Luis	-	90.7	36%	-	58%	-	6%	-	
Bacus, Dakota	-	90.7	34%	60%	-	-	5%	-	
Baez, Michel	-	95.4	56%	3%	41%	-	-	-	
Baez, Pedro	-	94.4	42%	22%	36%	-	-	-	
Bailey, Brandon	July `12	92.1	53%	13%	18%	9%	7%	-	
Bailey, Homer	May `15	91.0	47%	18%	-	4%	11%	20%	
Banda, Anthony	June `18	92.4	42%	5%	52%	-	<1%	-	
Baragar, Caleb	-	93.9	75%	15%	<1%	-	10%	-	
Bard, Daniel	-	97.1	56%	31%	13%	-	-	-	
Bard, Luke	-	94.0	46%	49%	5%	-	-	-	
Barlow, Scott	June `12	94.9	37%	41%	-	-	21%	-	
Barnes, Jacob	-	95.3	47%	<1%	-	51%	-	<1%	
Barnes, Matt	-	95.6	54%	-	3%	-	43%	-	
Barria, Jaime	-	92.1	43%	46%	11%	-	-	-	
Bashlor, Tyler	May `14	95.1	48%	-	14%	-	37%	-	
Bass, Anthony	-	94.7	54%	39%	-	-	-	7%	
Bassitt, Chris	May `16	92.9	54%	3%	10%	23%	9%	-	
Bauer, Trevor	-	93.5	48%	16%	<1%	20%	16%	-	
Bednar, David	-	95.8	59%	-	-	-	14%	26%	
Bedrosian, Cam	May `11	92.3	53%	46%	-	-	-	1%	
Beeks, Jalen	Sept `20	93.1	42%	-	44%	14%	-	-	
Benjamin, Wes	Apr `14	91.0	50%	23%	12%	-	14%	-	
Bergen, Travis	Jan `16	92.4	64%	-	<1%	-	35%	-	
Berrios, Jose	-	94.3	51%	-	19%	-	30%	-	
Betances, Dellin	-	93.6	49%	40%	-	-	11%	-	
Biagini, Joe	-	93.6	64%	15%	3%	-	18%	-	
Bieber, Shane	-	94.2	37%	12%	8%	16%	26%	-	
Bielak, Brandon	-	93.3	49%	10%	17%	14%	8%	-	
Black, Ray	Apr `08	95.8	60%	40%	-	-	-	-	
Bleier, Richard	-	88.9	53%	24%	6%	17%	-	-	

Player	Tommy John SX	Fastball Velocity	Pitch Repertoire						
			Fastball	Slider	Change	Cutter	Curve	Splitter	Other
Blewett, Scott	-	93.0	58%	34%	8%	-	-	-	
Bolanos, Ronald	-	95.3	59%	27%	3%	-	11%	-	
Borucki, Ryan	Mar '13	94.9	48%	-	14%	38%	-	-	
Bourque, James	May '15	93.6	68%	-	-	-	32%	-	
Boxberger, Brad	-	92.5	55%	18%	27%	-	<1%	-	
Boyd, Matthew	-	91.7	53%	23%	17%	-	7%	-	
Brach, Brad	-	90.4	37%	8%	24%	31%	-	-	
Bradley, Archie	-	94.2	66%	-	12%	-	22%	-	
Brasier, Ryan	June '14	96.2	62%	33%	5%	-	-	-	
Brault, Steven	-	92.1	51%	23%	24%	-	3%	-	
Braymer, Ben	-	88.7	54%	-	22%	-	24%	-	
Brennan, Brandon	Aug '13	92.9	51%	11%	38%	-	-	-	
Brewer, Colten	-	93.7	2%	20%	<1%	45%	33%	-	
Brice, Austin	-	93.7	62%	38%	<1%	-	-	-	
Britton, Zack	-	94.8	80%	20%	-	-	-	-	
Brogdon, Connor	-	95.3	51%	-	35%	14%	-	-	
Brothers, Rex	-	95.3	53%	47%	-	-	-	-	
Brubaker, JT	-	93.7	49%	33%	4%	-	14%	-	
Bubic, Kris	-	91.5	54%	-	30%	-	16%	-	
Buchter, Ryan	-	92.6	61%	-	-	8%	31%	-	
Buehler, Walker	Aug '15	96.9	62%	9%	-	15%	14%	-	
Bumgarner, Madison	-	88.4	40%	36%	1%	-	23%	-	
Bummer, Aaron	Aug '15	95.7	86%	6%	-	8%	-	-	
Bundy, Dylan	June '13	90.2	42%	25%	21%	-	12%	-	
Burdi, Zack	July '17	97.8	50%	36%	14%	-	-	-	
Burnes, Corbin	-	96.0	37%	13%	11%	31%	9%	-	
Burrows, Beau	-	93.3	55%	25%	15%	-	5%	-	
Buttrey, Ty	-	96.1	58%	-	20%	-	22%	-	
Cabrera, Genesis	-	96.2	56%	-	13%	-	30%	-	
Cahill, Trevor	-	90.9	35%	12%	29%	-	23%	-	
Canning, Griffin	-	92.8	41%	21%	15%	-	23%	-	
Carrasco, Carlos	Sept '11	93.6	39%	23%	27%	<1%	11%	-	
Carroll, Cody	Jan '11	95.5	80%	19%	-	-	-		1%
Castano, Daniel	-	89.2	49%	26%	25%	-	-	-	
Castellani, Ryan	-	92.4	50%	17%	15%	-	17%	-	
Castellanos, Humberto	-	90.0	50%	17%	14%	10%	9%	-	
Castillo, Diego	-	96.2	35%	65%	-	-	-	-	
Castillo, Luis	-	97.5	52%	18%	30%	-	-	-	
Castro, Miguel	-	98.1	51%	31%	18%	-	-	-	
Cease, Dylan	July '14	97.5	48%	30%	13%	-	9%	-	
Cederlind, Blake	-	98.3	61%	39%	-	-	-	-	
Cessa, Luis	-	93.7	31%	54%	13%	-	2%	-	
Chacin, Jhoulys	-	91.2	42%	49%	9%	-	-	-	
Chafin, Andrew	June '09	93.6	73%	27%	-	-	-	-	
Chapman, Aroldis	-	98.1	77%	21%	-	-	-	2%	
Chatwood, Tyler	July '14 Jan '06	94.3	51%	-	5%	30%	14%	-	
Chavez, Jesse	-	91.0	49%	14%	5%	32%	-	-	
Chirinos, Yonny	Aug '20	93.4	61%	16%	-	-	-	24%	
Cimber, Adam	-	85.9	51%	49%	-	-	-	-	
Cishek, Steve	-	90.4	48%	51%	1%	-	-	-	
Cisnero, Jose	May '14	96.3	63%	28%	9%	-	-	-	
Civale, Aaron	-	91.8	31%	9%	9%	29%	21%	-	
Clarke, Taylor	Jan '13	94.4	46%	27%	17%	-	11%	-	
Claudio, Alex	-	85.9	39%	23%	38%	-	-	-	
Clevinger, Mike	Aug '12	95.2	40%	32%	8%	7%	12%	-	
Clippard, Tyler	-	89.2	38%	-	35%	<1%	7%	20%	
Cobb, Alex	May '15	92.5	48%	-	35%	-	17%	-	

Player	Tommy John SX	Fastball Velocity	Fastball	Slider	Change	Cutter	Curve	Splitter	Other
Cody, Kyle	July `18	94.3	50%	37%	12%	-	-	-	
Cole, A.J.	-	93.4	35%	48%	8%	7%	2%	-	
Cole, Gerrit	-	96.7	53%	24%	6%	-	17%	-	
Colome, Alex	-	94.4	28%	-	-	72%	-	-	
Coonrod, Sam	Sept `17	98.0	59%	13%	19%	6%	2%	-	
Corbin, Patrick	Mar `14	90.2	52%	40%	6%	-	2%	-	
Cordero, Jimmy	-	96.7	68%	16%	11%	3%	3%	-	
Cortes, Nestor	-	88.1	41%	40%	5%	-	14%	-	
Coulombe, Danny	Mar `11	89.6	38%	16%	-	-	46%	-	
Covey, Dylan	-	92.2	39%	10%	-	34%	-	16%	
Crichton, Stefan	-	92.3	62%	37%	<1%	-	-	-	
Crick, Kyle	-	90.9	45%	55%	-	-	-	-	
Crismatt, Nabil	-	89.5	41%	-	36%	-	23%	-	
Crochet, Garrett	-	100.2	85%	11%	5%	-	-	-	
Crowe, Wil	Apr `15	91.4	57%	27%	12%	-	4%	-	
Cueto, Johnny	Aug `18	91.3	44%	14%	27%	8%	8%	-	
Curtiss, John	Aug `12	94.0	57%	43%	-	-	-	-	
Darvish, Yu	Mar `15	95.5	25%	14%	4%	40%	13%	4%	
Davidson, Tucker	-	92.0	75%	13%	-	-	11%	-	
Davies, Zach	-	88.6	38%	-	41%	17%	3%	-	
Davis, Austin	-	93.5	53%	31%	16%	-	<1%	-	
Davis, Wade	-	91.7	40%	-	13%	29%	18%	-	
Dayton, Grant	Aug `17	90.6	63%	-	<1%	-	37%	-	
De Jong, Chase	-	93.1	47%	22%	7%	-	24%	-	
De Leon, Jose	Mar `18	95.1	69%	9%	22%	-	-	-	
deGrom, Jacob	Oct `10	98.6	45%	36%	17%	-	3%	-	
Del Pozo, Miguel	Apr `16	93.3	55%	-	2%	-	44%	-	
DeSclafani, Anthony	-	94.9	51%	31%	7%	-	11%	-	
Detwiler, Ross	-	91.5	57%	31%	9%	-	3%	-	
Devenski, Chris	-	92.9	38%	16%	43%	-	2%	-	
Diaz, Edwin	-	97.8	61%	38%	<1%	-	-	-	
Diaz, Jairo	Mar `16	95.1	58%	42%	-	-	-	-	
Diehl, Phillip	-	90.3	55%	44%	<1%	-	-	-	
Diekman, Jake	-	95.1	59%	40%	<1%	-	-	-	
Dobnak, Randy	-	91.6	49%	35%	16%	-	-	-	
Dolis, Rafael	July `07	94.7	61%	20%	-	-	-	19%	
Doolittle, Sean	-	90.7	82%	13%	6%	-	-	-	
Doyle, Tommy	-	94.8	59%	39%	1%	-	-	-	
Drake, Oliver	-	91.3	48%	1%	-	-	-	51%	
Duffey, Tyler	-	92.6	44%	-	-	-	56%	-	
Duffy, Danny	June `12	92.2	53%	17%	15%	-	14%	-	
Dugger, Robert	-	92.0	54%	27%	3%	-	17%	-	
Dunn, Justin	-	91.2	55%	15%	6%	-	24%	-	
Dunning, Dane	Mar `19	91.9	60%	22%	11%	-	7%	-	
Edwards Jr., Carl	-	93.3	66%	-	-	-	34%	-	
Eflin, Zach	-	93.9	61%	14%	5%	6%	13%	-	
Eibner, Brett	Aug `17	94.2	50%	21%	-	26%	3%	-	
Elledge, Seth	-	93.3	65%	-	-	-	35%	-	
Eovaldi, Nathan	Aug `16 May `07	97.4	38%	6%	-	26%	17%	14%	
Erlin, Robbie	May `16	89.4	57%	-	16%	-	27%	-	
Eshelman, Thomas	-	86.3	44%	24%	13%	-	19%	-	
Espino, Paolo	-	90.3	55%	9%	5%	-	31%	-	
Estevez, Carlos	-	96.9	61%	26%	12%	-	-	-	
Evans, Demarcus	-	93.9	67%	33%	-	-	-	-	
Fairbanks, Pete	Aug `17 Jan `11	97.5	57%	41%	2%	-	-	-	
Familia, Jeurys	-	96.6	60%	29%	-	-	-	11%	

Player	Tommy John SX	Fastball Velocity	Fastball	Slider	Change	Cutter	Curve	Splitter	Other
Farmer, Buck	-	93.3	53%	-	33%	-	15%	-	
Farrell, Luke	-	91.5	36%	42%	-	-	21%	<1%	
Fedde, Erick	June `14	93.5	56%	18%	10%	17%	-	-	
Feliz, Michael	-	93.9	54%	38%	8%	-	-	-	
Ferguson, Caleb	Sept `20 May `14	95.5	80%	20%	-	-	-	-	
Fernandez, Junior	-	94.1	56%	13%	31%	-	-	-	
Feyereisen, J.P.	-	93.4	54%	28%	18%	-	-	-	
Fiers, Mike	-	88.0	45%	-	-	27%	12%	16%	
Finnegan, Kyle	-	95.1	70%	21%	-	-	-	9%	
Flaherty, Jack	-	93.6	56%	29%	2%	-	14%	-	
Fleming, Josh	-	90.6	54%	-	16%	29%	<1%	-	
Fletcher, Aaron	Mar `16	93.3	65%	21%	13%	-	-	-	
Floro, Dylan	-	93.4	47%	-	21%	32%	-	-	
Foltynewicz, Mike	-	90.5	44%	29%	13%	-	14%	-	
Font, Wilmer	Oct `10	94.9	70%	15%	-	-	9%	6%	
Foster, Matt	-	93.8	57%	9%	33%	-	-	-	
Frankoff, Seth	-	92.8	32%	-	37%	26%	4%	-	
Freeland, Kyle	-	91.9	33%	24%	24%	-	19%	-	
Freeman, Sam	Aug `20 Mar `10	93.9	71%	21%	-	-	-	8%	
Fried, Max	Aug `14	93.0	52%	21%	5%	-	22%	-	
Fry, Jace	June `15 June `12	89.8	40%	39%	4%	-	17%	-	
Fry, Paul	-	92.8	53%	46%	1%	-	-	-	
Fulmer, Carson	-	92.5	54%	-	23%	12%	11%	-	
Fulmer, Michael	Mar `19	93.1	62%	23%	10%	-	5%	-	
Funkhouser, Kyle	-	95.3	62%	31%	7%	-	-	-	
Gallegos, Giovanny	Jan `11	93.7	49%	51%	<1%	-	-	-	
Gallen, Zac	-	93.3	39%	5%	19%	20%	17%	-	
Gant, John	-	93.9	52%	12%	23%	-	13%	-	
Garcia, Bryan	Feb `18	94.5	64%	22%	14%	-	-	-	
Garcia, Deivi	-	92.0	60%	9%	17%	-	14%	-	
Garcia, Edgar	-	92.6	54%	43%	3%	-	-	-	
Garcia, Jarlin	-	93.8	49%	33%	18%	-	-	-	
Garcia, Luis (Hou)	-	94.0	54%	15%	18%	5%	7%	-	
Garcia, Luis (Tex)	-	96.6	57%	26%	-	-	-	18%	
Garcia, Rico	-	95.9	56%	-	32%	<1%	12%	-	
Garcia, Rony	-	93.3	63%	22%	13%	-	2%	-	
Garcia, Yimi	Oct `16	94.5	49%	12%	10%	29%	-	-	
Garrett, Amir	-	94.7	44%	56%	-	-	-	-	
Garrett, Braxton	June `17	89.7	49%	6%	15%	-	31%	-	
Gausman, Kevin	-	95.1	51%	7%	13%	-	-	29%	
Gaviglio, Sam	-	88.0	51%	45%	4%	-	-	-	
Gerber, Joey	-	93.4	65%	35%	-	-	-	-	
Gibaut, Ian	-	95.3	54%	29%	16%	<1%	-	-	
Gibson, Kyle	Sept `11	92.3	49%	24%	18%	<1%	8%	-	
Giles, Ken	-	94.4	38%	62%	-	-	-	-	
Gilmartin, Sean	-	86.8	36%	27%	28%	-	8%	-	
Ginkel, Kevin	-	95.6	60%	39%	<1%	-	-	-	
Giolito, Lucas	Aug `12	94.0	51%	15%	34%	-	<1%	-	
Givens, Mychal	-	94.7	65%	16%	19%	-	-	-	
Glasnow, Tyler	-	97.0	61%	-	5%	-	35%	-	
Godley, Zack	-	89.7	12%	-	10%	40%	38%	-	
Gomber, Austin	-	92.5	52%	16%	7%	-	24%	-	
Gonsolin, Tony	-	95.1	48%	17%	-	-	6%	30%	
Gonzales, Marco	Apr `16	88.2	45%	-	14%	24%	16%	-	
Gonzalez, Chi Chi	July `17	92.2	59%	20%	14%	-	7%	-	

379

Player	Tommy John SX	Fastball Velocity	Pitch Repertoire						
			Fastball	Slider	Change	Cutter	Curve	Splitter	Other
Gonzalez, Gio	-	89.9	47%	-	33%	1%	19%	-	
Gonzalez, Victor	Jan `17	95.0	63%	36%	1%	-	-	-	
Goody, Nick	Apr `13	91.6	43%	57%	-	-	-	-	
Gott, Trevor	-	95.5	64%	8%	3%	-	25%	-	
Goudeau, Ashton	-	93.3	47%	-	28%	-	25%	-	
Graterol, Brusdar	Aug `15	99.3	71%	29%	-	-	-	-	
Graveman, Kendall	July `18	94.8	68%	3%	17%	7%	5%	-	
Gray, Jon	-	94.0	49%	29%	13%	-	8%	-	
Gray, Sonny	-	93.0	54%	15%	3%	-	29%	-	
Green, Chad	-	95.5	75%	-	-	-	25%	-	
Greene, Shane	May `08	92.1	39%	21%	13%	26%	-	-	
Greinke, Zack	-	87.1	46%	16%	23%	-	16%	-	
Grimm, Justin	-	93.4	38%	50%	-	-	12%	-	
Grotz, Zac	-	91.7	53%	20%	-	6%	-	20%	
Gsellman, Robert	-	93.6	64%	22%	7%	-	7%	-	
Guerra, Deolis	-	91.8	42%	-	40%	7%	11%	-	
Guerra, Javy (SD)	-	98.5	68%	27%	5%	-	-	-	
Guerra, Javy (Was)	Jan `05	91.8	67%	17%	-	-	8%	8%	
Guerra, Junior	-	94.0	61%	-	-	-	22%	18%	
Guilbeau, Taylor	-	91.4	58%	16%	25%	-	-	-	
Hader, Josh	-	94.6	68%	32%	-	-	-	-	
Hahn, Jesse	Jan `10	95.0	57%	13%	-	-	31%	-	
Hale, David	-	92.8	53%	16%	31%	-	-	-	
Hall, Matt	-	88.1	47%	-	3%	19%	31%	-	
Hamels, Cole	-	88.2	25%	-	29%	31%	15%	-	
Hamilton, Ian	-	94.3	75%	22%	4%	-	-	-	
Hand, Brad	-	91.4	48%	52%	-	-	<1%	-	
Happ, J.A.	-	90.9	66%	20%	-	-	<1%	14%	
Harper, Ryne	-	88.5	38%	-	<1%	-	62%	<1%	
Harris, Will	July `09	90.5	-	-	-	78%	22%	-	
Hart, Kyle	Apr `14	89.2	42%	4%	18%	31%	5%	-	
Hartlieb, Geoff	-	93.6	54%	45%	<1%	-	-	-	
Harvey, Hunter	July `16	97.4	77%	-	-	-	14%	8%	
Harvey, Joe	June `15	95.1	56%	43%	2%	-	-	-	
Harvey, Matt	Oct `13	94.1	53%	23%	10%	-	15%	-	
Hatch, Thomas	-	95.5	54%	21%	25%	-	-	-	
Heaney, Andrew	July `16	91.5	58%	25%	17%	-	-	-	
Hearn, Taylor	-	95.0	61%	28%	12%	-	-	-	
Heller, Ben	Apr `18	93.4	51%	36%	13%	-	-	-	
Helsley, Ryan	-	96.9	43%	-	4%	36%	17%	-	
Hembree, Heath	-	94.0	58%	33%	-	-	10%	-	
Hendricks, Kyle	-	87.4	54%	-	29%	-	17%	-	
Hendriks, Liam	-	96.1	70%	22%	<1%	-	7%	-	
Herget, Jimmy	-	93.1	54%	41%	3%	-	1%	-	
Hernandez, Carlos	-	96.2	51%	6%	15%	-	27%	-	
Hernandez, Darwinzon	-	94.3	73%	24%	-	-	3%	-	
Hernandez, Elieser	-	91.4	59%	35%	6%	-	-	-	
Hernandez, Jonathan	-	97.8	47%	40%	13%	-	-	-	
Hess, David	-	92.8	68%	21%	8%	-	3%	-	
Heuer, Codi	-	97.6	66%	25%	9%	-	-	-	
Hill, Cam	July `18	92.2	48%	36%	-	-	16%	-	
Hill, Rich	June `11	87.7	47%	3%	-	4%	47%	<1%	
Hill, Tim	-	90.7	90%	10%	-	-	-	-	
Hirano, Yoshihisa	-	89.9	45%	-	-	-	-	55%	
Hoffman, Jeff	May `14	94.5	55%	-	27%	-	18%	-	
Holder, Jonathan	-	92.1	52%	10%	24%	10%	3%	-	
Holland, Derek	-	92.3	47%	22%	16%	-	15%	-	
Holland, Greg	Oct `15	93.0	37%	51%	<1%	-	12%	-	

Player	Tommy John SX	Fastball Velocity	Pitch Repertoire						
			Fastball	Slider	Change	Cutter	Curve	Splitter	Other
Houck, Tanner	-	92.1	62%	35%	-	-	-	2%	
Houser, Adrian	July `16	93.4	64%	12%	12%	-	12%	-	
Howard, Sam	-	92.1	37%	62%	<1%	-	-	-	
Howard, Spencer	-	94.1	56%	22%	16%	-	6%	-	
Hoyt, James	-	88.4	31%	67%	-	-	-	2%	
Hudson, Dakota	Sept `20	92.9	59%	21%	2%	-	19%	-	
Hudson, Daniel	June `13 July `12	96.5	76%	17%	6%	-	2%	-	
Hughes, Jared	-	91.4	59%	27%	14%	-	-	-	
Hunter, Tommy	-	92.7	43%	-	-	34%	23%	-	
Iglesias, Raisel	-	96.2	46%	33%	20%	-	-	-	
Irvin, Cole	Feb `14	92.4	52%	18%	27%	-	2%	-	
Jackson, Luke	-	94.4	36%	43%	-	1%	20%	-	
James, Josh	-	96.3	58%	24%	14%	-	5%	-	
Jansen, Kenley	-	92.4	28%	10%	-	62%	-	-	
Javier, Cristian	-	92.3	63%	26%	7%	-	3%	-	
Jefferies, Daulton	Apr `17	94.3	60%	8%	11%	21%	-	-	
Jeffress, Jeremy	-	93.3	41%	-	-	-	25%	34%	
Jimenez, Joe	-	94.3	62%	31%	7%	-	-	-	
Johnson, Pierce	-	96.4	46%	-	-	-	54%	-	
Jones, Nate	July `14	95.9	53%	46%	<1%	-	-	-	
Junis, Jakob	-	91.0	49%	46%	5%	-	-	-	
Jurado, Ariel	-	91.3	50%	31%	15%	-	4%	-	
Kaminsky, Rob	-	91.7	44%	39%	18%	-	-	-	
Kaprielian, James	Apr `17	95.0	69%	18%	10%	-	3%	-	
Karinchak, James	-	95.5	50%	-	-	-	50%	-	
Kay, Anthony	Oct `16	93.7	56%	-	18%	2%	23%	-	
Kela, Keone	-	96.4	49%	-	-	-	51%	-	
Keller, Brad	-	92.8	59%	38%	3%	-	-	-	
Keller, Mitch	-	94.0	56%	22%	3%	-	19%	-	
Kelley, Trevor	-	90.3	55%	16%	1%	29%	-	-	
Kelly, Joe	-	97.0	37%	-	-	-	63%	-	
Kelly, Merrill	-	92.1	42%	-	15%	21%	22%	-	
Kennedy, Ian	-	93.6	50%	-	7%	32%	11%		
Kershaw, Clayton	-	91.6	41%	40%	<1%	-	19%		
Keuchel, Dallas	-	87.3	35%	7%	28%	31%	-	-	
Kickham, Mike	-	89.5	19%	49%	<1%	-	32%	-	
Kikuchi, Yusei	-	95.0	38%	16%	-	40%	-	6%	
Kilome, Franklyn	Oct `18	94.4	54%	4%	-	-	28%	14%	
Kim, Kwang-hyun	Jan `17	89.9	48%	32%	-	-	11%	8%	
Kimbrel, Craig	-	96.9	62%	-	-	-	38%	-	
King, John	Jan `17	93.1	63%	18%	17%	-	1%	-	
King, Michael	-	93.1	66%	19%	15%	-	-	-	
Kinley, Tyler	-	95.9	34%	60%	6%	-	-	-	
Kintzler, Brandon	-	91.3	76%	10%	14%	-	-	-	
Kittredge, Andrew	-	94.0	48%	46%	-	-	-	6%	
Kline, Branden	Oct `15	95.2	60%	16%	24%	-	-	-	
Knebel, Corey	Apr `19	94.4	63%	-	3%	-	34%	-	
Kolarek, Adam	-	89.3	84%	9%	7%	-	-	-	
Kremer, Dean	-	93.0	51%	-	3%	19%	27%	-	
Kriske, Brooks	Sept `16	94.9	69%	7%	-	-	-	24%	
Kuhl, Chad	Sept `18	93.9	44%	35%	4%	-	17%	-	
Kuhnel, Joel	-	95.4	58%	35%	7%	-	-	-	
Lail, Brady	-	90.1	49%	15%	16%	-	19%	-	
Lakins, Travis	-	93.4	32%	<1%	3%	42%	22%	-	
Lamet, Dinelson	Apr `18	97.1	46%	53%	<1%	-	-	-	
Lauer, Eric	-	91.6	52%	16%	5%	18%	8%	-	
LeBlanc, Wade	-	86.8	25%	<1%	34%	28%	13%	-	

Player	Tommy John SX	Fastball Velocity	Fastball	Slider	Change	Cutter	Curve	Splitter	Other
Leibrandt, Brandon	July `18	89.0	47%	29%	12%	-	12%	-	
Leone, Dominic	-	94.8	34%	36%	-	30%	-	-	
Lester, Jon	-	89.2	42%	-	13%	32%	13%	-	
Lewicki, Artie	Aug `18	93.4	33%	49%	7%	-	11%	-	
	Aug `12								
Leyer, Robinson	-	95.0	50%	50%	-	-	-	-	
Lindblom, Josh	-	90.1	35%	17%	9%	19%	9%	10%	
Littell, Zack	-	94.0	54%	-	3%	44%	-	-	
Loaisiga, Jonathan	May `16	96.7	67%	<1%	15%	-	17%	-	
Lockett, Walker	-	93.4	35%	-	22%	20%	22%	-	
Lopez, Jorge	-	93.8	60%	-	9%	-	31%	-	
Lopez, Pablo	Nov `13	93.7	55%	-	30%	8%	7%	-	
Lopez, Reynaldo	-	94.2	51%	28%	20%	-	-	-	
Lopez, Yoan	-	95.5	55%	45%	-	-	-	-	
Lorenzen, Michael	-	96.7	40%	17%	18%	18%	7%	-	
Loup, Aaron	-	92.1	50%	10%	9%	31%	-	-	
Lucchesi, Joey	-	90.0	57%	-	34%	8%	-	<1%	
Lugo, Seth	-	93.4	55%	15%	10%	-	19%	-	
Luzardo, Jesus	Mar `16	95.5	53%	22%	24%	-	<1%	-	
Lyles, Jordan	-	92.2	48%	12%	10%	<1%	30%	-	
Lynn, Lance	Nov `15	93.5	68%	23%	<1%	-	8%	-	
Maeda, Kenta	-	91.4	26%	40%	29%	2%	3%	-	
Magill, Matt	May `15	91.9	33%	39%	-	-	28%	-	
Mahle, Tyler	-	93.9	56%	33%	-	-	<1%	11%	
Manaea, Sean	-	90.4	54%	7%	28%	3%	7%	-	
Mantiply, Joe	Mar `18	91.1	47%	46%	7%	-	-	-	
Margevicius, Nick	-	90.0	64%	16%	-	-	11%	9%	
Marquez, German	-	95.7	52%	17%	6%	-	25%	-	
Marshall, Evan	-	92.9	29%	-	39%	-	32%	-	
Martin, Brett	-	94.0	53%	33%	-	-	14%	-	
Martin, Chris	-	94.1	45%	26%	-	19%	-	10%	
Martinez, Carlos	-	92.9	50%	27%	20%	<1%	1%	-	
Maton, Phil	-	93.6	48%	32%	-	-	20%	-	
Matz, Steven	May `10	94.5	54%	5%	26%	-	15%	-	
Matzek, Tyler	-	94.4	62%	19%	-	9%	11%	-	
May, Dustin	-	98.1	57%	-	5%	25%	13%	-	
May, Trevor	Mar `17	96.4	52%	33%	16%	-	-	-	
Mayers, Mike	-	94.2	34%	40%	-	24%	3%	-	
Mazza, Chris	-	92.1	39%	28%	3%	30%	-	-	
McCarthy, Kevin	-	90.0	54%	6%	25%	3%	-	12%	
McClain, Reggie	-	93.4	79%	12%	9%	-	-	-	
McCullers Jr., Lance	Nov `18	93.8	43%	-	18%	1%	38%	-	
McFarland, T.J.	-	88.5	60%	24%	17%	-	-	-	
McGee, Jake	July `08	95.0	97%	3%	-	-	-	-	
McGowin, Kyle	-	91.3	28%	71%	<1%	-	-	-	
McKenzie, Triston	-	92.8	53%	20%	10%	-	17%	-	
Means, John	-	93.8	52%	10%	25%	-	13%	-	
Mears, Nick	-	95.7	68%	-	-	-	32%	-	
Medina, Adonis	-	92.2	54%	26%	20%	-	-	-	
Meisinger, Ryan	-	91.2	63%	34%	3%	-	-	-	
Mejia, Humberto	-	92.8	52%	17%	10%	-	21%	-	
Melancon, Mark	Oct `06	91.7	3%	-	3%	54%	39%	-	
Mella, Keury	-	95.2	68%	32%	-	-	-	-	
Menez, Conner	-	91.8	54%	25%	4%	-	17%	-	
Mengden, Daniel	-	90.1	52%	15%	13%	12%	9%	-	
Merryweather, Julian	Mar `18	96.7	58%	15%	18%	-	9%	-	
Middleton, Keynan	May `18	97.1	59%	22%	19%	-	-	-	
Miley, Wade	-	90.2	14%	2%	24%	50%	11%	-	

Player	Tommy John SX	Fastball Velocity	Pitch Repertoire						
			Fastball	Slider	Change	Cutter	Curve	Splitter	Other
Miller, Andrew	-	90.3	40%	60%	-	-	-	-	
Miller, Tyson	-	93.4	57%	13%	24%	-	7%	-	
Mills, Alec	July `13	90.0	59%	10%	16%	-	15%	-	
Milner, Hoby	-	87.9	54%	44%	2%	-	-	-	
Milone, Tommy	-	86.1	45%	11%	39%	-	5%	-	
Minor, Mike	-	90.6	51%	21%	22%	-	6%	-	
Minter, A.J.	Mar `15	95.6	39%	43%	19%	-	-	-	
Misiewicz, Anthony	-	94.1	24%	-	-	53%	23%	-	
Mize, Casey	-	93.7	49%	-	-	23%	10%	18%	
Montas, Frankie	-	95.8	62%	25%	-	-	-	13%	
Montero, Rafael	Mar `18	95.5	72%	7%	21%	-	-	-	
Montgomery, Jordan	June `18	92.5	47%	-	26%	5%	22%	-	
Montgomery, Mike	-	89.7	37%	-	22%	31%	10%	-	
Moran, Brian	Apr `14	81.8	61%	39%	-	-	-	-	
Morejon, Adrian	-	96.6	56%	12%	-	-	15%	17%	
Morgan, Adam	-	91.6	34%	45%	16%	-	5%	-	
Morton, Charlie	June `12	93.3	56%	-	2%	9%	33%	-	
Mujica, Jose	Sept `18	93.3	59%	9%	28%	-	4%	-	
Murphy, Patrick	July `12	96.8	60%	-	-	-	40%	-	
Musgrove, Joe	-	92.5	39%	24%	11%	6%	20%	-	
Neidert, Nick	-	91.6	60%	14%	18%	-	8%	-	
Nelson, Nick	-	96.4	57%	12%	25%	-	6%	-	
Neris, Hector	-	94.0	52%	-	-	-	-	48%	
Neverauskas, Dovydas	-	94.8	46%	-	<1%	20%	34%	-	
Newberry, Jake	-	93.5	45%	51%	4%	-	-	-	
Newcomb, Sean	-	93.4	54%	10%	20%	-	16%	-	
Newsome, Ljay	-	91.5	49%	-	24%	-	27%	-	
Nola, Aaron	-	92.4	46%	-	27%	-	27%	-	
Norris, Daniel	-	92.7	48%	22%	31%	-	<1%	-	
Nova, Ivan	Apr `14	92.2	59%	-	15%	-	25%	-	
O'Day, Darren	-	86.0	57%	43%	-	-	-	-	
Odorizzi, Jake	-	93.0	42%	19%	23%	10%	5%	-	
Ohtani, Shohei	Oct `18	93.8	49%	29%	-	-	6%	16%	
Osich, Josh	Jan `10	92.4	37%	-	-	48%	15%	-	
Osuna, Roberto	July `13	94.4	44%	16%	18%	22%	-	-	
Oswalt, Corey	-	92.2	53%	-	17%	28%	2%	-	
Ottavino, Adam	May `15	93.5	45%	46%	4%	5%	-	-	
Oviedo, Johan	-	94.9	56%	30%	4%	-	10%	-	
Paddack, Chris	Aug `16	94.2	58%	-	31%	4%	7%	-	
Pagan, Emilio	-	94.5	63%	35%	-	-	2%	-	
Palumbo, Joseph	Apr `17	92.2	58%	24%	-	-	19%	-	
Paredes, Enoli	-	95.7	68%	25%	2%	-	4%	-	
Parker, Blake	-	90.7	41%	-	-	-	17%	42%	
Patino, Luis	-	96.8	65%	17%	18%	-	<1%	-	
Paxton, James	-	92.1	57%	-	13%	15%	16%	-	
Payamps, Joel	-	94.2	63%	32%	5%	-	-	-	
Pazos, James	-	92.1	69%	27%	4%	-	-	-	
Peacock, Brad	-	89.8	51%	34%	12%	-	3%	-	
Pearson, Nate	-	96.4	51%	35%	7%	-	7%	-	
Pena, Felix	-	94.5	48%	-	21%	-	30%	-	
Peralta, Freddy	-	93.0	66%	24%	-	-	10%	-	
Peralta, Wandy	-	94.8	35%	33%	31%	-	-	-	
Perdomo, Angel	-	94.6	68%	26%	6%	-	-	-	
Perdomo, Luis	-	94.0	43%	35%	22%	-	-	-	
Perez, Cionel	-	95.1	63%	34%	2%	-	<1%	-	
Perez, Martin	May `14	92.1	33%	-	26%	32%	9%	-	
Perez, Oliver	-	89.9	57%	43%	-	-	-	-	
Peterson, David	-	92.1	53%	26%	19%	-	2%	-	

Player	Tommy John SX	Fastball Velocity	Pitch Repertoire						
			Fastball	Slider	Change	Cutter	Curve	Splitter	Other
Petit, Yusmeiro	-	88.2	43%	<1%	18%	28%	11%	-	
Phelps, David	Mar '18	94.1	46%	-	-	27%	27%	-	
Phillips, Evan	-	94.6	66%	26%	7%	-	-	-	
Pineda, Michael	July '17	92.1	50%	38%	11%	-	-	-	
Pivetta, Nick	-	92.8	49%	20%	6%	-	24%	-	
Plesac, Zach	Apr '16	92.8	38%	28%	25%	-	9%	-	
Plutko, Adam	-	91.1	50%	3%	4%	30%	12%	-	
Pomeranz, Drew	-	94.7	80%	-	-	-	20%	-	
Ponce de Leon, Daniel	-	93.2	61%	-	4%	13%	22%	-	
Ponce, Cody	-	93.3	44%	-	8%	24%	24%	-	
Poppen, Sean	-	93.7	48%	45%	7%	-	-	-	
Porcello, Rick	-	90.4	53%	29%	13%	-	5%	-	
Pressly, Ryan	-	94.7	37%	42%	-	-	21%	-	
Quantrill, Cal	Mar '15	94.9	54%	35%	11%	-	-	-	
Quezada, Johan	-	97.0	62%	38%	-	-	-	-	
Quijada, Jose	-	93.3	69%	20%	11%	-	-	-	
Quintana, Jose	-	91.4	60%	13%	9%	-	18%	-	
Rainey, Tanner	-	96.6	61%	39%	-	-	-	-	
Raley, Brooks	-	90.2	23%	19%	4%	44%	10%	-	
Ramirez, Erasmo	-	90.4	45%	6%	11%	38%	-	-	
Ramirez, Nick	-	89.6	41%	6%	33%	16%	3%	-	
Ramirez, Noe	-	88.8	36%	31%	33%	-	-	-	
Ramirez, Yohan	-	95.7	60%	40%	-	-	-	-	
Ramos, AJ	Apr '08	91.7	33%	15%	20%	32%	-	-	
Rasmussen, Drew	Aug '17 Mar '16	97.7	68%	18%	4%	-	10%	-	
Ray, Robbie	-	93.7	53%	30%	<1%	-	16%	-	
Rea, Colin	Nov '16	93.0	52%	-	11%	18%	19%	-	
Reed, Cody	-	94.5	49%	47%	3%	1%	-	-	
Reid-Foley, Sean	-	94.6	62%	31%	6%	2%	-	-	
Reyes, Alex	Feb '17	97.6	60%	19%	4%	-	17%	-	
Richards, Garrett	July '18	95.2	55%	38%	-	-	7%	-	
Richards, Trevor	-	90.5	51%	18%	31%	-	-	-	
Rios, Yacksel	-	94.5	66%	8%	10%	-	16%	-	
Roark, Tanner	-	90.7	53%	15%	13%	3%	15%	-	
Robles, Hansel	-	95.5	52%	12%	-	-	-	-	36%
Rodon, Carlos	May '19	92.9	51%	30%	19%	-	-	-	
Rodriguez, Dereck	-	92.6	54%	15%	-	-	30%	-	
Rodriguez, Joely	-	94.6	68%	3%	30%	-	-	-	
Rodriguez, Nivaldo	-	93.0	49%	-	4%	23%	24%	-	
Rodriguez, Richard	-	93.0	72%	28%	-	-	-	-	
Roe, Chaz	-	91.2	26%	58%	-	16%	-	-	
Rogers, Taylor	-	94.6	54%	46%	-	-	-	-	
Rogers, Trevor	-	93.6	60%	21%	19%	-	-	-	
Rogers, Tyler	-	82.5	64%	36%	-	-	-	-	
Romano, Jordan	Mar '15	96.6	40%	60%	-	-	-	-	
Romero, JoJo	-	95.0	56%	27%	16%	-	-	-	
Romero, Seth	Aug '18	91.7	42%	38%	20%	-	-	-	
Romo, Sergio	-	85.6	24%	65%	11%	-	-	-	
Rondon, Hector	Aug '10	95.6	59%	37%	4%	-	-	-	
Rosario, Randy	May '14	91.8	54%	42%	4%	-	-	-	
Rosenthal, Trevor	Aug '17	98.0	71%	20%	8%	-	-	-	
Rosso, Ramon	-	93.8	68%	26%	3%	-	3%	-	
Ruiz, Jose	-	96.8	58%	25%	3%	-	13%	-	
Rusin, Chris	-	86.8	39%	12%	5%	44%	-	-	
Ryan, Kyle	-	87.9	53%	-	-	39%	9%	-	
Ryu, Hyun-Jin	Jan '04	89.6	35%	-	28%	24%	13%	-	
Sadler, Casey	Nov '15	92.9	36%	23%	4%	-	37%	-	

Player	Tommy John SX	Fastball Velocity	Pitch Repertoire						
			Fastball	Slider	Change	Cutter	Curve	Splitter	Other
Samardzija, Jeff	-	90.7	37%	22%	14%	20%	-	6%	
Sanchez, Anibal	Jan `03	89.6	32%	<1%	36%	26%	6%	-	
Sanchez, Ricardo	-	91.8	50%	15%	18%	-	17%	-	
Sanchez, Sixto	-	97.6	48%	21%	27%	-	5%	-	
Sandoval, Patrick	-	92.8	45%	25%	23%	-	7%	-	
Santana, Dennis	-	94.4	39%	46%	15%	-	-	-	
Santos, Antonio	-	93.2	59%	23%	16%	-	2%	-	
Scherzer, Max	-	94.7	46%	19%	16%	10%	9%	-	
Schmidt, Clarke	May `17	95.0	54%	-	9%	-	37%	-	
Schreiber, John	-	89.8	52%	35%	13%	-	-	-	
Scott, Tanner	-	96.5	61%	39%	-	-	-	-	
Scrubb, Andre	-	92.9	-	<1%	-	53%	47%	-	
Selman, Sam	-	91.2	41%	59%	-	-	-	-	
Senzatela, Antonio	-	94.4	56%	24%	10%	-	9%	-	
Sewald, Paul	-	91.8	60%	33%	7%	-	-	-	
Shafer, Justin	-	90.8	54%	38%	-	-	8%	-	
Sharp, Sterling	-	88.1	83%	5%	13%	-	-	-	
Shaw, Bryan	-	92.7	-	17%	5%	62%	16%	-	
Sheffield, Justus	-	92.0	48%	34%	19%	-	-	-	
Sherriff, Ryan	June `18	90.9	80%	17%	2%	-	-	-	
Shoemaker, Matt	-	92.1	44%	18%	-	-	6%	33%	
Shreve, Chasen	-	91.7	51%	8%	-	-	-	41%	
Sims, Lucas	-	94.0	48%	34%	2%	-	16%	-	
Singer, Brady	-	93.4	58%	37%	5%	-	-	-	
Skubal, Tarik	Apr `16	94.5	60%	16%	16%	-	8%	-	
Slegers, Aaron	-	91.2	62%	30%	8%	-	-	-	
Smeltzer, Devin	-	87.6	33%	18%	37%	-	12%	-	
Smith, Burch	Apr `15	94.4	72%	<1%	13%	-	14%	-	
Smith, Caleb	-	92.1	51%	27%	15%	-	7%	-	
Smith, Drew	Mar `19	95.2	47%	-	10%	30%	13%	-	
Smith, Josh A.	Jan `07	90.3	35%	<1%	3%	34%	28%	-	
Smith, Riley	-	93.4	62%	19%	2%	-	16%	<1%	
Smith, Will	Mar `17	92.6	45%	47%	-	-	8%	-	
Smyly, Drew	July `17	93.8	45%	-	-	18%	37%	-	
Sneed, Cy	-	93.9	36%	14%	1%	33%	15%	-	
Snell, Blake	-	95.1	51%	15%	20%	-	15%	-	
Sobotka, Chad	-	94.4	55%	38%	-	8%	-	-	
Soria, Joakim	Apr `12 Jan `03	92.4	66%	20%	9%	-	5%	-	
Soroka, Mike	-	92.1	59%	29%	12%	-	-	-	
Soto, Gregory	-	97.3	80%	20%	-	-	-	-	
Sparkman, Glenn	July `15	93.3	44%	47%	3%	-	6%	-	
Speier, Gabe	Sept `13	92.1	54%	25%	-	-	21%	-	
Springs, Jeffrey	-	92.1	47%	27%	26%	-	-	-	
Stammen, Craig	-	92.2	65%	7%	2%	14%	12%	-	
Stanek, Ryne	-	96.0	44%	39%	-	-	-	17%	
Stashak, Cody	-	91.9	55%	41%	4%	-	-	-	
Staumont, Josh	-	98.1	72%	-	-	-	28%	-	
Stephenson, Robert	-	94.8	30%	66%	4%	-	-	-	
Stiever, Jonathan	-	92.4	53%	20%	17%	-	9%	-	
Stock, Robert	-	96.8	64%	23%	13%	-	-	-	
Strahm, Matt	July `13	92.9	56%	15%	10%	-	19%	-	
Strasburg, Stephen	Sept `10	91.7	46%	-	21%	-	33%	-	
Stratton, Chris	-	93.3	46%	27%	10%	-	17%	-	
Strickland, Hunter	May `13	95.3	57%	41%	-	-	-	2%	
Stripling, Ross	Apr `14	91.7	44%	15%	17%	-	24%	-	
Strop, Pedro	-	91.8	48%	25%	-	18%	-	9%	
Suarez, Andrew	-	91.7	47%	29%	24%	-	-	-	

Player	Tommy John SX	Fastball Velocity	Pitch Repertoire						
			Fastball	Slider	Change	Cutter	Curve	Splitter	Other
Suarez, Jose	-	93.3	45%	3%	38%	-	14%	-	
Suarez, Ranger	-	91.2	61%	20%	19%	-	-	-	
Suero, Wander	-	91.1	<1%	-	13%	81%	5%	-	
Sulser, Cole	Jan `15 Apr `11	93.8	57%	17%	26%	-	-	-	
Suter, Brent	July `18	85.6	79%	-	14%	-	7%	-	
Swanson, Erik	-	95.6	74%	17%	8%	-	-	-	
Tanaka, Masahiro	-	92.2	32%	37%	5%	<1%	6%	19%	
Tapia, Domingo	May `15	98.9	79%	19%	3%	-	-	-	
Tarpley, Stephen	-	91.0	69%	31%	-	-	-	-	
Tate, Dillon	-	94.4	58%	26%	16%	-	-	-	
Taylor, Blake	July `15	93.8	77%	23%	<1%	-	-	-	
Taylor, Josh	-	93.6	52%	48%	-	-	-	-	
Teheran, Julio	-	89.0	60%	19%	11%	-	9%	-	
Tepera, Ryan	-	94.0	46%	5%	-	44%	-	5%	
Thielbar, Caleb	-	89.8	54%	20%	-	-	25%	-	
Thompson, Ryan	Jan `18	91.3	61%	38%	<1%	-	-	-	
Thornburg, Tyler	Sept `20	93.1	58%	-	20%	-	22%	-	
Thornton, Trent	-	92.2	44%	12%	11%	20%	14%	-	
Thorpe, Lewis	Apr `15	89.7	47%	30%	14%	-	8%	-	
Tinoco, Jesus	-	93.7	68%	10%	-	-	22%	-	
Tomlin, Josh	Aug `12	88.2	19%	-	4%	51%	26%	-	
Topa, Justin	Apr `15 Jan `11	97.5	70%	30%	-	-	-	-	
Toussaint, Touki	-	94.0	41%	10%	-	-	29%	20%	
Treinen, Blake	-	96.9	65%	26%	-	9%	-	-	
Triggs, Andrew	Jan `07	88.3	44%	24%	-	32%	-	-	
Trivino, Lou	-	95.5	59%	-	7%	23%	11%	-	
Tropeano, Nick	Aug `16	91.0	30%	-	13%	-	31%	26%	
Turley, Nik	Jan `18	94.2	55%	-	-	-	45%	-	
Turnbull, Spencer	-	94.1	66%	21%	9%	-	4%	-	
Underwood Jr., Duane	-	94.6	46%	-	29%	-	25%	-	
Urena, Jose	-	95.5	61%	32%	7%	-	-	-	
Urias, Julio	-	94.2	56%	5%	13%	-	25%	-	
Urquidy, Jose	Jan `17	93.1	55%	13%	21%	-	12%	-	
Valdez, Cesar	-	85.5	16%	1%	83%	-	-	-	
Valdez, Framber	-	93.1	58%	-	8%	-	33%	-	
Valdez, Phillips	-	92.2	45%	6%	49%	-	-	-	
Velasquez, Vince	Sept `10	93.7	58%	12%	14%	<1%	16%	-	
Venditte, Pat	-	83.9	44%	56%	-	-	-	-	
Verlander, Justin	-	94.9	55%	38%	5%	-	1%	-	
Vesia, Alex	-	91.8	73%	9%	18%	-	-	-	
Vincent, Nick	-	89.3	47%	-	8%	41%	4%	-	
Volquez, Edinson	Aug `17 Aug `09	94.3	51%	-	31%	-	19%	-	
Voth, Austin	-	92.1	61%	12%	3%	-	23%	1%	
Wacha, Michael	-	93.6	43%	-	29%	27%	1%	-	
Waguespack, Jacob	-	92.4	52%	-	19%	19%	11%	-	
Wainwright, Adam	Feb `11	89.3	37%	-	2%	22%	38%	-	
Walden, Marcus	Mar `10	92.7	39%	22%	-	40%	-	-	
Walker, Taijuan	Apr `18	93.2	50%	22%	-	-	10%	18%	
Watson, Tony	-	89.9	38%	14%	48%	-	-	-	
Weaver, Luke	-	94.1	54%	-	27%	12%	7%	-	
Webb, Jacob	Apr `15	93.6	52%	15%	33%	-	-	-	
Webb, Logan	June `16	92.7	49%	15%	31%	5%	-	-	
Webb, Tyler	Jan `08	90.1	60%	16%	24%	-	-	-	
Weber, Ryan	-	88.6	52%	16%	18%	8%	6%	-	
Weems, Jordan	-	95.3	62%	18%	-	-	<1%	19%	

Player	Tommy John SX	Fastball Velocity	Pitch Repertoire						
			Fastball	Slider	Change	Cutter	Curve	Splitter	Other
Wendelken, J.B.	Oct `16	94.5	58%	26%	7%	-	8%	-	
Wheeler, Zack	Mar `15	96.9	66%	16%	5%	-	10%	3%	
Whitley, Kodi	Mar `16	93.8	53%	18%	29%	-	-	-	
Wick, Rowan	-	95.0	52%	-	-	13%	34%	-	
Widener, Taylor	-	94.5	65%	21%	14%	-	-	-	
Williams, Devin	Mar `17	96.5	44%	3%	53%	-	-	-	
Williams, Taylor	Aug `15	95.1	45%	55%	-	-	-	-	
Williams, Trevor	-	91.3	51%	27%	15%	-	7%	-	
Wilson, Bryse	-	94.0	63%	19%	12%	-	7%	-	
Wilson, Justin	-	95.0	59%	3%	-	37%	-	-	
Winkler, Dan	July `14	92.8	33%	11%	1%	55%	-	-	
Wisler, Matt	-	91.9	17%	83%	-	-	-	-	
Wittgren, Nick	-	92.9	61%	15%	24%	-	-	-	
Wojciechowski, Asher	-	91.0	46%	27%	5%	22%	-	-	
Wood, Alex	Jan `09	91.2	48%	-	23%	-	29%	-	
Woodford, Jake	-	92.9	51%	27%	1%	-	21%	-	
Woodruff, Brandon	-	96.5	65%	11%	18%	-	7%	-	
Workman, Brandon	June `15	92.6	26%	-	-	34%	39%	-	
Wright, Kyle	-	94.3	48%	24%	14%	-	13%	-	
Yacabonis, Jimmy	-	92.9	65%	10%	25%	-	-	-	
Yajure, Miguel	Nov `16	92.4	35%	2%	27%	15%	21%	-	
Yamaguchi, Shun	-	90.8	41%	17%	-	-	2%	40%	
Yamamoto, Jordan	-	89.8	41%	22%	1%	21%	15%	-	
Yarbrough, Ryan	-	87.4	23%	11%	30%	36%	-	-	
Yardley, Eric	-	87.8	65%	34%	<1%	-	-	-	
Yates, Kirby	Jan `06	93.7	64%	-	-	-	-	36%	
Ynoa, Huascar	-	94.9	44%	47%	9%	-	-	-	
Young, Alex	-	90.9	33%	-	21%	22%	25%	-	
Zeuch, T.J.	-	92.2	56%	16%	7%	21%	-	-	
Zimmer, Kyle	-	94.1	48%	34%	4%	-	14%	-	
Zimmermann, Bruce	-	91.5	51%	15%	24%	-	9%	-	
Zimmermann, Jordan	Aug `09	89.5	54%	31%	-	-	10%	6%	
Zuber, Tyler	-	94.1	44%	36%	10%	-	10%	-	

Relief Pitching

Brian Reiff

For all the hubbub in response to the new three-batter-minimum rule for relief pitchers, it doesn't seem as though all that much has changed. In 2019, relief pitchers averaged 1.10 innings per appearance. In 2020, that number rose to…1.12.

Breaking it down by pitcher handedness does show a marginal increase in innings per appearance by lefty relievers, who averaged 1.11 innings a year after their 1.05 mark. But that jump isn't all that impressive relative to that of previous years—the average was 1.00 innings and 0.95 innings in 2018 and 2017, respectively.

One notable threshold was reached this season, though. For the first time in MLB history, the average start length failed to meet the minimum criteria for a win, coming in at 4.78 innings. This, too, is part of a larger trend, one in which the average start length plummeted from a recent high of 6.03 innings in 2011 and decreased every year since 2014.

On a more granular level, you may have already known that Brad Hand led all pitchers with 16 saves. However, only one of those was considered a tough save. (You can read more about how we classify saves in the Glossary.) In fact, 12 of Hand's saves were classified as easy saves, the most in MLB. Only three pitchers finished the season with multiple tough saves—Liam Hendriks, Jeremy Jeffress and Nick Vincent.

 As far as unsung heroes go, the Tigers' Bryan Garcia certainly stands out. Despite accumulating only seven total holds and saves, his 22 clean relief appearances tied for second behind only his teammate, José Cisnero. Most impressively, he stranded all 13 baserunners he inherited, the highest total among pitchers who didn't allow an inherited runner to score.

Arizona Diamondbacks

Pitcher	Pos	T	Usage					Inherited Runners			Saves			Relief Results						
			Rel G	Early Entry	Cons Days	Long	Lev Ind	#	Scrd	Pct	Easy	Reg	Tough	Clean	BS Win	BS	Holds	Sv/Hld Pct	Opp OPS	Rel ERA
Rondon, Hector	SU	R	23	3	3	2	1.1	6	2	.33	0 - 0	0 - 1	0 - 0	12	0	1	7	.88	1.012	7.65
Chafin, Andrew	LT	L	11	2	2	0	1.4	7	1	.14	0 - 1	0 - 0	0 - 1	6	0	2	3	.60	.877	8.10
Young, Alex	LT	L	8	5	3	4	0.9	2	2	1.00	0 - 0	0 - 0	0 - 0	3	0	0	1	1.00	.679	4.20
Bergen, Travis	LT	L	7	5	1	2	1.0	4	1	.25	1 - 1	0 - 0	0 - 0	4	0	0	0	1.00	.764	4.05
Ginkel, Kevin	LM	R	19	8	4	3	1.3	8	2	.25	0 - 0	0 - 1	0 - 0	12	0	1	0	.50	.961	6.75
Crichton, Stefan	UR	R	26	8	6	4	1.3	14	5	.36	3 - 3	2 - 4	0 - 0	21	0	2	2	.78	.665	2.42
Guerra, Junior	UR	R	25	7	5	5	1.2	17	7	.41	0 - 0	0 - 1	0 - 1	16	0	2	4	.67	.638	3.04
Lopez, Yoan	UR	R	20	8	2	1	0.6	11	1	.09	0 - 0	0 - 0	0 - 0	12	0	0	1	1.00	.870	5.95
Widener, Taylor	UR	R	12	5	1	6	0.4	4	1	.25	0 - 0	0 - 0	0 - 0	6	0	0	1	1.00	.782	4.50
Mella, Keury	UR	R	11	3	2	0	0.6	3	0	.00	0 - 0	0 - 0	0 - 0	9	0	0	0		.704	1.80
Bradley, Archie	UR	R	10	0	1	1	2.1	9	4	.44	3 - 3	3 - 3	0 - 1	6	1	1	0	.86	.792	4.22
Clarke, Taylor	UR	R	7	5	0	7	0.8	1	0	.00	0 - 0	0 - 0	0 - 0	3	0	0	0		.638	3.54
Smith, Riley	UR	R	6	3	0	4	0.5	4	2	.50	0 - 0	0 - 0	0 - 0	4	0	0	0		.602	1.47

Atlanta Braves

Pitcher	Pos	T	Usage					Inherited Runners			Saves			Relief Results						
			Rel G	Early Entry	Cons Days	Long	Lev Ind	#	Scrd	Pct	Easy	Reg	Tough	Clean	BS Win	BS	Holds	Sv/Hld Pct	Opp OPS	Rel ERA
Melancon, Mark	CL	R	23	0	6	0	2.3	0	0	.00	5 - 6	6 - 7	0 - 0	18	1	2	0	.85	.639	2.78
Greene, Shane	SU	R	28	2	5	2	1.1	4	0	.00	0 - 0	0 - 0	0 - 0	22	0	0	9	1.00	.639	2.60
Martin, Chris	SU	R	19	1	3	0	1.3	0	0	.00	0 - 0	1 - 1	0 - 0	17	0	0	6	1.00	.375	1.00
Smith, Will	SU	L	18	5	4	1	1.1	6	0	.00	0 - 0	0 - 1	0 - 0	11	1	1	5	.83	.794	4.50
Minter, A.J.	LT	L	22	8	1	3	0.9	15	2	.13	0 - 0	0 - 0	0 - 0	17	0	0	5	1.00	.606	0.83
Matzek, Tyler	LM	L	21	13	0	9	1.0	12	2	.17	0 - 0	0 - 1	0 - 1	15	0	2	1	.33	.574	2.79
ODay, Darren	LM	R	19	13	0	0	0.9	10	3	.30	0 - 0	0 - 0	0 - 1	15	1	1	2	.67	.442	1.10
Jackson, Luke	LM	R	19	11	1	10	0.7	11	7	.64	0 - 0	0 - 0	0 - 0	7	0	0	1	1.00	.852	6.84
Dayton, Grant	LM	L	18	10	2	8	0.6	10	6	.60	0 - 0	0 - 0	0 - 0	8	0	0	0		.662	2.30
Tomlin, Josh	UR	R	12	8	2	3	0.7	6	2	.33	0 - 0	0 - 0	0 - 0	7	0	0	1	1.00	.561	2.95
Webb, Jacob	UR	R	8	1	1	3	0.1	4	0	.00	0 - 0	0 - 0	0 - 0	7	0	0	0		.529	0.00

Baltimore Orioles

Pitcher	Pos	T	Usage					Inherited Runners			Saves			Relief Results						
			Rel G	Early Entry	Cons Days	Long	Lev Ind	#	Scrd	Pct	Easy	Reg	Tough	Clean	BS Win	BS	Holds	Sv/Hld Pct	Opp OPS	Rel ERA
Givens, Mychal	SU	R	12	0	3	1	1.0	5	2	.40	0 - 0	0 - 0	0 - 0	9	0	0	5	1.00	.573	1.38
Scott, Tanner	LT	L	25	8	6	0	1.5	22	6	.27	1 - 1	0 - 0	0 - 1	17	0	1	5	.86	.524	1.31
Fry, Paul	LM	L	22	10	2	2	1.2	11	3	.27	0 - 0	0 - 0	0 - 0	13	0	0	4	1.00	.724	2.45
Lakins, Travis	LM	R	22	13	1	7	1.0	15	10	.67	0 - 0	0 - 0	1 - 1	13	0	0	1	1.00	.725	2.81
Phillips, Evan	LM	R	14	9	1	2	0.8	6	4	.67	0 - 0	0 - 0	0 - 0	8	0	0	2	1.00	.695	5.02
Tate, Dillon	LM	R	12	9	3	6	1.1	9	2	.22	0 - 0	0 - 0	0 - 0	7	0	0	2	1.00	.486	3.24
Sulser, Cole	UR	R	19	3	3	5	1.9	7	1	.14	1 - 2	4 - 6	0 - 0	11	1	3	1	.67	.705	5.56
Castro, Miguel	UR	R	16	8	5	1	1.7	15	6	.40	1 - 2	0 - 0	0 - 1	10	0	2	4	.71	.782	4.02
Armstrong, Shawn	UR	R	14	8	4	1	0.9	13	2	.15	0 - 0	0 - 0	0 - 0	9	0	0	3	1.00	.530	1.80
Harvey, Hunter	UR	R	10	0	1	0	1.5	5	0	.00	0 - 0	0 - 0	0 - 0	6	0	0	4	1.00	.722	4.15
Valdez, Cesar	UR	R	9	2	2	3	1.2	4	0	.00	1 - 1	2 - 2	0 - 0	7	0	0	0	1.00	.413	1.26
Eshelman, Thomas	UR	R	8	6	0	6	0.6	6	1	.17	0 - 1	0 - 0	0 - 0	3	1	1	0	.00	.705	3.15

Boston Red Sox

Pitcher	Pos	T	Rel G	Early Entry	Cons Days	Long	Lev Ind	#	Scrd	Pct	Easy	Reg	Tough	Clean	BS Win	BS	Holds	Sv/Hld Pct	Opp OPS	Rel ERA
					Usage				**Inherited Runners**			**Saves**					**Relief Results**			
Barnes, Matt	CL	R	24	0	5	5	2.3	5	0	.00	7 - 7	2 - 5	0 - 1	17	0	4	4	.76	.706	4.30
Brasier, Ryan	SU	R	24	3	4	3	1.4	9	2	.22	0 - 0	0 - 1	0 - 1	16	0	2	10	.83	.687	4.13
Weber, Ryan	SU	R	12	6	1	7	1.0	7	2	.29	0 - 0	0 - 0	0 - 0	6	0	0	5	1.00	.583	2.25
Springs, Jeffrey	LT	L	16	5	1	7	1.0	12	7	.58	0 - 1	0 - 0	0 - 0	7	0	1	1	.50	.973	7.08
Osich, Josh	LT	L	12	5	2	3	0.6	3	0	.00	0 - 0	0 - 0	0 - 0	9	0	0	1	1.00	.815	5.27
Taylor, Josh	LT	L	8	5	2	1	1.1	0	0	.00	0 - 2	0 - 0	0 - 0	5	0	2	1	.33	.861	9.82
Hernandez, Darwinzon	LT	L	7	5	0	4	1.3	2	0	.00	0 - 0	0 - 0	0 - 0	6	0	0	2	1.00	.511	2.16
Valdez, Phillips	LM	R	24	14	1	7	0.9	12	6	.50	0 - 0	0 - 1	0 - 0	14	0	1	4	.80	.790	3.26
Hembree, Heath	LM	R	11	7	3	2	1.2	6	2	.33	0 - 0	0 - 1	0 - 0	7	0	1	1	.50	.786	5.59
Brice, Austin	UR	R	20	6	1	2	0.9	14	2	.14	0 - 0	0 - 0	0 - 0	13	0	0	4	1.00	.856	6.27
Walden, Marcus	UR	R	15	7	1	5	1.1	7	2	.29	0 - 0	1 - 1	0 - 0	6	0	0	2	1.00	1.209	9.45
Stock, Robert	UR	R	10	3	2	5	0.6	7	3	.43	0 - 0	0 - 0	0 - 0	3	0	0	0		.826	4.73
Covey, Dylan	UR	R	8	4	1	3	0.3	3	0	.00	0 - 0	0 - 0	0 - 0	4	0	0	1	1.00	.799	7.07
Brewer, Colten	UR	R	7	6	0	4	0.9	1	0	.00	0 - 0	0 - 0	0 - 0	4	0	0	0		.756	3.97
Workman, Brandon	UR	R	7	0	2	2	1.9	0	0	.00	4 - 4	0 - 0	0 - 0	5	0	0	0	1.00	.683	4.05
Tapia, Domingo	UR	R	5	2	0	0	0.1	0	0	.00	0 - 0	0 - 0	0 - 0	4	0	0	0		.786	2.08
Leyer, Robinson	UR	R	5	4	0	4	1.2	2	2	1.00	0 - 0	0 - 0	0 - 0	0	0	0	1	1.00	1.621	27.00

Chicago Cubs

Pitcher	Pos	T	Rel G	Early Entry	Cons Days	Long	Lev Ind	#	Scrd	Pct	Easy	Reg	Tough	Clean	BS Win	BS	Holds	Sv/Hld Pct	Opp OPS	Rel ERA
					Usage				**Inherited Runners**			**Saves**					**Relief Results**			
Jeffress, Jeremy	CL	R	22	1	5	3	2.1	11	1	.09	4 - 5	2 - 3	2 - 2	18	2	2	3	.85	.465	1.54
Wick, Rowan	SU	R	19	4	6	1	1.3	15	7	.47	1 - 1	3 - 3	0 - 0	9	0	0	5	1.00	.721	3.12
Ryan, Kyle	LT	L	18	5	3	0	0.7	9	3	.33	0 - 0	1 - 1	0 - 0	12	0	0	4	1.00	.900	5.17
Tepera, Ryan	LM	R	21	10	3	2	1.0	12	6	.50	0 - 0	0 - 0	0 - 1	14	0	1	2	.67	.684	3.92
Winkler, Dan	UR	R	18	5	3	1	1.0	5	2	.40	0 - 0	0 - 1	0 - 0	11	0	1	1	.50	.624	2.95
Kimbrel, Craig	UR	R	18	0	1	1	1.6	1	0	.00	2 - 2	0 - 1	0 - 0	13	0	1	3	.83	.693	5.28
Underwood Jr., Duane	UR	R	17	7	2	4	0.3	16	6	.38	0 - 0	0 - 0	0 - 0	9	0	0	1	1.00	.939	5.66
Adam, Jason	UR	R	13	5	2	5	0.7	3	2	.67	0 - 0	0 - 0	0 - 0	8	0	0	0		.673	3.29
Sadler, Casey	UR	R	10	2	2	2	1.0	3	2	.67	0 - 0	0 - 0	0 - 0	6	0	0	4	1.00	.801	5.79
Rea, Colin	UR	R	7	3	0	2	0.5	3	1	.33	0 - 0	0 - 0	0 - 0	4	0	0	1	1.00	.436	2.08

Chicago White Sox

Pitcher	Pos	T	Rel G	Early Entry	Cons Days	Long	Lev Ind	#	Scrd	Pct	Easy	Reg	Tough	Clean	BS Win	BS	Holds	Sv/Hld Pct	Opp OPS	Rel ERA
					Usage				**Inherited Runners**			**Saves**					**Relief Results**			
Colome, Alex	CL	R	21	0	5	3	1.9	7	0	.00	7 - 7	4 - 4	1 - 2	18	1	1	0	.92	.460	0.81
Cordero, Jimmy	SU	R	30	18	10	2	1.2	16	1	.06	0 - 0	0 - 1	0 - 0	17	0	1	8	.89	.784	6.08
Marshall, Evan	SU	R	23	5	3	0	1.5	16	4	.25	0 - 1	0 - 1	0 - 0	17	0	2	8	.80	.537	2.38
Fry, Jace	LT	L	18	8	2	3	0.6	6	2	.33	0 - 0	0 - 0	0 - 0	12	0	0	1	1.00	.732	3.66
Detwiler, Ross	LT	L	16	6	3	4	0.6	11	4	.36	0 - 0	0 - 0	0 - 0	11	0	0	1	1.00	.695	3.20
Bummer, Aaron	LT	L	9	1	2	2	1.0	3	3	1.00	0 - 0	0 - 0	0 - 0	7	0	0	3	1.00	.415	0.96
Gonzalez, Gio	LT	L	8	4	0	5	0.9	5	0	.00	0 - 0	0 - 0	0 - 0	4	0	0	0		.861	5.65
Crochet, Garrett	LT	L	5	2	1	0	0.8	0	0	.00	0 - 0	0 - 0	0 - 0	5	0	0	0		.325	0.00
Foster, Matt	LM	R	21	10	5	6	0.9	5	2	.40	0 - 0	0 - 1	0 - 0	16	0	1	2	.67	.557	2.55
Cishek, Steve	UR	R	22	6	3	2	0.6	12	8	.67	0 - 0	0 - 1	0 - 0	10	0	1	0	.00	.853	5.40
Heuer, Codi	UR	R	21	8	3	4	1.2	10	0	.00	0 - 0	1 - 1	0 - 0	18	0	0	5	1.00	.433	1.52
Burdi, Zack	UR	R	8	3	1	2	0.6	0	0	.00	0 - 0	0 - 1	0 - 0	3	0	1	1	.50	1.084	11.05
Ruiz, Jose	UR	R	5	0	0	0	0.6	2	2	1.00	0 - 0	0 - 0	0 - 1	4	0	1	0	.00	.500	2.25

Cincinnati Reds

Pitcher	Pos	T	Rel G	Early Entry	Cons Days	Long	Lev Ind	#	Scrd	Pct	Easy	Reg	Tough	Clean	BS Win	BS	Holds	Sv/Hld Pct	Opp OPS	Rel ERA
Iglesias, Raisel	CL	R	22	1	6	1	2.0	9	0	.00	4 - 5	4 - 4	0 - 1	16	0	2	2	.83	.510	2.74
Garrett, Amir	SU	L	21	5	6	1	1.1	10	3	.30	1 - 2	0 - 0	0 - 0	17	0	1	6	.88	.601	2.45
Sims, Lucas	SU	R	20	6	2	6	1.0	17	5	.29	0 - 1	0 - 0	0 - 1	14	0	2	5	.71	.554	2.45
Reed, Cody	LT	L	9	3	3	2	0.3	7	5	.71	0 - 0	0 - 0	0 - 0	5	0	0	0		.927	5.79
Lorenzen, Michael	LM	R	16	10	3	7	1.1	11	6	.55	0 - 0	0 - 0	0 - 1	6	0	1	2	.67	.765	4.88
Jones, Nate	UR	R	21	4	4	2	1.0	9	4	.44	0 - 0	0 - 0	0 - 0	10	0	0	4	1.00	.955	6.27
Stephenson, Robert	UR	R	10	3	1	2	0.4	6	0	.00	0 - 0	0 - 0	0 - 0	5	0	0	1	1.00	1.246	9.90
Antone, Tejay	UR	R	9	8	0	6	0.8	8	2	.25	0 - 0	0 - 1	0 - 0	4	0	1	1	.50	.377	1.89
Thornburg, Tyler	UR	R	7	4	0	3	0.6	1	0	.00	0 - 0	0 - 0	0 - 0	5	0	0	1	1.00	.603	3.86
Bradley, Archie	UR	R	6	3	1	0	0.8	1	0	.00	0 - 0	0 - 0	0 - 0	5	0	0	2	1.00	.393	1.17
De Leon, Jose	UR	R	5	3	1	3	0.2	2	0	.00	0 - 0	0 - 0	0 - 0	3	0	0	0		.861	18.00

Cleveland Indians

Pitcher	Pos	T	Rel G	Early Entry	Cons Days	Long	Lev Ind	#	Scrd	Pct	Easy	Reg	Tough	Clean	BS Win	BS	Holds	Sv/Hld Pct	Opp OPS	Rel ERA
Hand, Brad	CL	L	23	0	7	2	1.9	2	0	.00	12 - 12	3 - 3	1 - 1	18	0	0	1	1.00	.486	2.05
Karinchak, James	SU	R	27	2	3	4	1.4	9	1	.11	1 - 1	0 - 3	0 - 0	19	0	3	8	.75	.505	2.67
Wittgren, Nick	SU	R	25	1	4	3	1.7	9	1	.11	0 - 0	0 - 0	0 - 0	18	0	1	10	.91	.706	3.42
Perez, Oliver	LT	L	21	6	4	0	1.5	13	6	.46	0 - 0	0 - 1	1 - 1	14	0	1	3	.80	.564	2.00
Maton, Phil	UR	R	23	6	3	2	1.4	6	2	.33	0 - 0	0 - 1	0 - 0	16	0	1	4	.80	.716	4.57
Hill, Cam	UR	R	18	5	2	1	0.5	5	2	.40	1 - 1	0 - 0	0 - 0	12	0	0	2	1.00	.647	4.91
Cimber, Adam	UR	R	14	1	4	0	0.6	5	4	.80	0 - 0	0 - 0	0 - 0	8	0	0	3	1.00	.751	3.97
Leone, Dominic	UR	R	12	3	0	1	0.5	3	0	.00	0 - 0	0 - 0	0 - 0	7	0	0	3	1.00	1.023	8.38
Plutko, Adam	UR	R	6	2	0	2	0.8	3	0	.00	0 - 0	1 - 1	0 - 0	4	0	0	0	1.00	.726	1.54
Quantrill, Cal	UR	R	6	2	0	2	1.0	0	0	.00	0 - 1	0 - 0	0 - 0	4	0	1	1	.50	.761	2.35

Colorado Rockies

Pitcher	Pos	T	Rel G	Early Entry	Cons Days	Long	Lev Ind	#	Scrd	Pct	Easy	Reg	Tough	Clean	BS Win	BS	Holds	Sv/Hld Pct	Opp OPS	Rel ERA
Estevez, Carlos	SU	R	26	3	7	1	1.4	16	5	.31	0 - 1	1 - 2	0 - 1	17	0	3	6	.70	1.003	7.50
Pazos, James	LT	L	6	0	0	1	0.1	1	1	1.00	0 - 0	0 - 0	0 - 0	1	0	0	0		1.474	16.88
Diehl, Phillip	LT	L	6	3	0	2	0.4	3	2	.67	0 - 0	0 - 0	0 - 0	2	0	0	0		.945	10.50
Hoffman, Jeff	LM	R	16	9	1	9	0.8	15	5	.33	0 - 0	0 - 0	1 - 1	6	0	0	0	1.00	.985	9.28
Kinley, Tyler	UR	R	24	7	3	3	0.9	9	2	.22	0 - 0	0 - 0	0 - 0	17	0	0	4	1.00	.564	5.32
Almonte, Yency	UR	R	24	3	4	4	1.1	15	5	.33	0 - 0	1 - 1	0 - 2	14	0	2	4	.71	.670	2.93
Diaz, Jairo	UR	R	24	2	5	3	1.4	9	6	.67	2 - 2	1 - 1	1 - 1	14	0	0	3	1.00	1.073	7.65
Bard, Daniel	UR	R	23	3	5	4	1.7	7	0	.00	3 - 3	2 - 2	1 - 1	14	0	0	2	1.00	.674	3.65
Givens, Mychal	UR	R	10	1	3	2	1.3	4	0	.00	0 - 0	1 - 3	0 - 0	5	0	2	1	.50	.968	6.75
Davis, Wade	UR	R	5	0	2	3	1.3	0	0	.00	2 - 2	0 - 1	0 - 0	1	0	1	0	.67	1.435	20.77

Detroit Tigers

Pitcher	Pos	T	Usage Rel G	Early Entry	Cons Days	Long	Lev Ind	Inherited Runners #	Scrd	Pct	Saves Easy	Reg	Tough	Clean	BS Win	BS	Holds	Sv/Hld Pct	Opp OPS	Rel ERA
Farmer, Buck	SU	R	23	1	5	1	1.2	2	0	.00	0 - 0	0 - 1	0 - 0	18	0	1	7	.88	.674	3.80
Soto, Gregory	LT	L	27	4	5	0	1.0	5	1	.20	1 - 1	1 - 2	0 - 0	21	0	1	4	.86	.605	4.30
Ramirez, Nick	LT	L	5	5	0	5	0.1	3	0	.00	0 - 0	0 - 0	0 - 0	1	0	0	0		.708	5.91
Schreiber, John	LM	R	15	11	1	2	0.8	14	8	.57	0 - 0	0 - 0	0 - 1	8	0	1	1	.50	.827	6.32
Norris, Daniel	LM	L	13	10	0	8	0.7	10	4	.40	0 - 0	0 - 0	0 - 0	7	0	0	0		.583	2.77
Alexander, Tyler	LM	L	12	12	0	9	0.8	5	1	.20	0 - 0	0 - 0	0 - 0	5	0	0	0		.815	3.14
Cisnero, Jose	UR	R	29	11	7	6	1.2	17	1	.06	0 - 0	0 - 2	0 - 0	23	0	2	6	.75	.584	3.03
Garcia, Bryan	UR	R	26	4	4	0	1.3	13	0	.00	0 - 0	0 - 0	0 - 2	22	1	2	3	.78	.559	1.66
Jimenez, Joe	UR	R	25	4	5	2	1.2	6	4	.67	2 - 3	3 - 3	0 - 0	14	0	1	4	.90	.936	7.15
Funkhouser, Kyle	UR	R	13	4	1	7	0.5	3	1	.33	0 - 0	0 - 0	0 - 0	7	0	0	0		.929	7.27
Garcia, Rony	UR	R	13	6	1	6	0.5	7	4	.57	0 - 0	0 - 0	0 - 0	6	0	0	0		.902	7.88
Fulmer, Carson	UR	R	7	1	0	1	0.4	2	0	.00	0 - 0	0 - 0	0 - 0	4	0	0	0		.875	6.75
Burrows, Beau	UR	R	5	2	0	2	0.1	2	2	1.00	0 - 0	0 - 0	0 - 0	3	0	0	0		.976	5.40

Houston Astros

Pitcher	Pos	T	Usage Rel G	Early Entry	Cons Days	Long	Lev Ind	Inherited Runners #	Scrd	Pct	Saves Easy	Reg	Tough	Clean	BS Win	BS	Holds	Sv/Hld Pct	Opp OPS	Rel ERA
Pressly, Ryan	CL	R	23	0	8	1	2.3	2	2	1.00	7 - 7	5 - 9	0 - 0	13	0	4	0	.75	.728	3.43
Taylor, Blake	SU	L	22	8	4	2	1.7	15	5	.33	0 - 0	1 - 1	0 - 1	16	0	1	5	.86	.567	2.18
Raley, Brooks	SU	L	17	3	2	1	1.3	13	1	.08	0 - 0	1 - 1	0 - 0	11	0	0	6	1.00	.552	3.94
Perez, Cionel	LT	L	7	4	1	2	0.7	4	0	.00	0 - 0	0 - 0	0 - 0	5	0	0	2	1.00	.675	2.84
Paredes, Enoli	UR	R	22	4	5	3	1.9	16	7	.44	0 - 0	0 - 0	0 - 2	15	0	2	4	.67	.666	3.05
Scrubb, Andre	UR	R	20	8	2	3	1.1	15	2	.13	1 - 1	0 - 0	0 - 0	14	0	0	2	1.00	.587	1.90
Sneed, Cy	UR	R	18	4	2	4	1.4	9	5	.56	0 - 0	0 - 0	0 - 2	8	0	2	3	.60	.930	5.71
James, Josh	UR	R	11	1	1	1	1.3	4	3	.75	0 - 0	0 - 2	0 - 0	6	0	2	4	.67	.848	5.56
Castellanos, Humberto	UR	R	8	3	0	2	0.8	2	1	.50	0 - 0	0 - 1	0 - 0	5	0	1	0	.00	.850	6.75
Bielak, Brandon	UR	R	6	3	0	3	1.0	0	0	.00	0 - 0	0 - 0	0 - 0	3	0	0	0		.940	6.10
Bailey, Brandon	UR	R	5	2	0	3	0.2	3	0	.00	0 - 0	0 - 0	0 - 0	3	0	0	0		.756	2.45
Rodriguez, Nivaldo	UR	R	5	2	0	3	0.6	4	3	.75	0 - 0	0 - 0	0 - 0	1	0	0	0		1.123	6.23

Kansas City Royals

Pitcher	Pos	T	Usage Rel G	Early Entry	Cons Days	Long	Lev Ind	Inherited Runners #	Scrd	Pct	Saves Easy	Reg	Tough	Clean	BS Win	BS	Holds	Sv/Hld Pct	Opp OPS	Rel ERA
Rosenthal, Trevor	CL	R	14	0	4	2	2.3	6	0	.00	3 - 3	4 - 4	0 - 0	11	0	0	1	1.00	.699	3.29
Staumont, Josh	SU	R	26	6	6	3	1.2	1	0	.00	0 - 0	0 - 0	0 - 0	22	0	0	8	1.00	.639	2.45
Hahn, Jesse	SU	R	18	10	3	2	1.2	10	2	.20	2 - 2	1 - 1	0 - 0	16	0	0	5	1.00	.289	0.52
Speier, Gabe	LT	L	8	3	2	0	0.4	6	1	.17	0 - 0	0 - 0	0 - 0	3	0	0	1	1.00	.972	7.94
Zuber, Tyler	LM	R	23	12	4	5	0.8	7	3	.43	0 - 0	0 - 0	0 - 0	16	0	0	0		.736	4.09
Newberry, Jake	LM	R	20	11	4	3	0.7	18	3	.17	0 - 0	0 - 0	1 - 1	13	0	0	1	1.00	.772	4.09
Barlow, Scott	UR	R	32	10	9	0	1.3	10	4	.40	2 - 2	0 - 0	0 - 0	22	0	0	7	1.00	.693	4.20
Holland, Greg	UR	R	28	13	12	0	1.2	17	7	.41	3 - 3	2 - 2	1 - 1	22	0	0	2	1.00	.580	1.91
Zimmer, Kyle	UR	T	15	7	1	5	0.4	1	0	.00	0 - 0	0 - 0	0 - 0	12	0	0	0		.529	1.29
Kennedy, Ian	UR	R	14	4	4	1	0.9	1	0	.00	0 - 0	0 - 0	0 - 0	4	0	0	2	1.00	1.164	10.50
Adams, Chance	UR	R	6	3	0	4	0.1	3	0	.00	0 - 0	0 - 0	0 - 0	3	0	0	0		.950	9.35
McCarthy, Kevin	UR	R	5	3	1	1	0.3	4	2	.50	0 - 0	0 - 0	0 - 0	3	0	0	0		.948	4.50

Los Angeles Angels

Pitcher	Pos	T	Usage					Inherited Runners			Saves			Relief Results						
			Rel G	Early Entry	Cons Days	Long	Lev Ind	#	Scrd	Pct	Easy	Reg	Tough	Clean	BS Win	BS	Holds	Sv/Hld Pct	Opp OPS	Rel ERA
Mayers, Mike	SU	R	29	13	9	6	1.2	19	8	.42	0 - 1	2 - 2	0 - 1	20	0	2	5	.78	.484	2.10
Milner, Hoby	LT	L	19	9	6	2	0.9	18	9	.50	0 - 0	0 - 0	0 - 0	10	0	0	1	1.00	.897	8.10
Buchter, Ryan	LT	L	10	5	2	0	1.0	8	3	.38	0 - 0	0 - 0	0 - 0	7	0	0	0		.901	4.50
Quijada, Jose	LT	L	6	4	2	0	2.3	4	3	.75	0 - 0	0 - 1	0 - 0	2	0	1	1	.50	1.013	7.36
Ramirez, Noe	LM	R	21	11	4	2	1.0	13	6	.46	0 - 0	0 - 0	0 - 1	16	0	1	0	.00	.618	3.00
Andriese, Matt	LM	R	15	10	1	8	1.1	11	5	.45	1 - 1	1 - 1	0 - 1	6	1	1	3	.83	.559	3.56
Buttrey, Ty	UR	R	27	1	8	3	1.9	16	6	.38	0 - 0	5 - 7	0 - 2	15	0	4	2	.64	.837	5.81
Pena, Felix	UR	R	25	3	6	5	1.3	6	1	.17	2 - 3	0 - 2	0 - 0	15	1	3	4	.67	.672	4.05
Robles, Hansel	UR	R	18	3	5	1	0.8	1	1	1.00	1 - 2	0 - 1	0 - 0	10	0	2	0	.33	.917	10.26
Barnes, Jacob	UR	R	18	7	3	2	0.9	4	2	.50	0 - 0	0 - 0	0 - 0	8	0	0	1	1.00	.716	5.50
Middleton, Keynan	UR	R	13	5	1	0	0.9	5	2	.40	0 - 0	0 - 0	0 - 0	5	0	0	2	1.00	.817	5.25
Bedrosian, Cam	UR	R	11	8	1	3	0.5	8	0	.00	0 - 0	0 - 0	0 - 0	7	0	0	0		.531	2.45
Bard, Luke	UR	R	6	2	2	0	0.5	4	0	.00	0 - 0	0 - 0	0 - 0	3	0	0	1	1.00	1.000	6.75

Los Angeles Dodgers

Pitcher	Pos	T	Usage					Inherited Runners			Saves			Relief Results						
			Rel G	Early Entry	Cons Days	Long	Lev Ind	#	Scrd	Pct	Easy	Reg	Tough	Clean	BS Win	BS	Holds	Sv/Hld Pct	Opp OPS	Rel ERA
Jansen, Kenley	CL	R	27	0	7	4	1.7	8	0	.00	10 - 11	0 - 1	1 - 1	22	0	2	0	.85	.615	3.33
Treinen, Blake	SU	R	27	6	7	1	1.6	14	4	.29	1 - 2	0 - 0	0 - 0	17	0	1	9	.91	.621	3.86
Ferguson, Caleb	SU	L	20	6	3	0	1.3	9	3	.33	0 - 0	0 - 2	0 - 0	14	1	2	5	.71	.699	3.06
McGee, Jake	LT	L	24	8	4	0	0.8	6	2	.33	0 - 0	0 - 0	0 - 0	19	0	0	4	1.00	.565	2.66
Alexander, Scott	LT	L	13	3	0	0	1.6	7	1	.14	0 - 0	0 - 0	0 - 2	7	0	2	3	.60	.710	2.92
Wood, Alex	LT	L	7	1	0	4	1.1	2	2	1.00	0 - 0	0 - 0	0 - 0	3	0	0	1	1.00	.787	3.52
Floro, Dylan	LM	R	25	14	5	1	0.8	18	6	.33	0 - 0	0 - 0	0 - 0	17	0	0	4	1.00	.623	2.59
Graterol, Brusdar	LM	R	21	11	1	0	1.1	6	0	.00	0 - 0	0 - 1	0 - 0	15	0	1	5	.83	.544	3.00
Kolarek, Adam	LM	L	20	11	5	0	1.1	14	4	.29	0 - 0	0 - 0	1 - 1	14	0	3	3	1.00	.432	0.95
Gonzalez, Victor	LM	L	14	9	0	2	1.0	2	2	1.00	0 - 0	0 - 0	0 - 0	10	0	0	2	1.00	.424	1.40
Baez, Pedro	UR	R	18	6	1	1	0.8	3	3	1.00	2 - 2	0 - 0	0 - 0	12	0	0	6	1.00	.529	3.18
Santana, Dennis	UR	R	12	3	0	5	1.0	6	0	.00	0 - 0	0 - 0	0 - 1	7	0	1	0	.00	.782	5.29
Kelly, Joe	UR	R	11	2	3	0	0.9	3	1	.33	0 - 0	0 - 0	0 - 0	10	0	0	3	1.00	.567	0.00

Miami Marlins

Pitcher	Pos	T	Usage					Inherited Runners			Saves			Relief Results						
			Rel G	Early Entry	Cons Days	Long	Lev Ind	#	Scrd	Pct	Easy	Reg	Tough	Clean	BS Win	BS	Holds	Sv/Hld Pct	Opp OPS	Rel ERA
Kintzler, Brandon	CL	R	24	1	9	1	2.2	7	2	.29	6 - 6	5 - 6	1 - 2	18	1	2	1	.87	.710	2.22
Bleier, Richard	SU	R	19	4	4	0	1.1	12	1	.08	0 - 0	0 - 0	0 - 0	14	0	0	6	1.00	.650	2.63
Tarpley, Stephen	LT	L	12	7	2	0	1.4	4	1	.25	0 - 0	0 - 0	1 - 1	6	0	0	2	1.00	.944	9.00
Moran, Brian	LT	L	5	3	1	0	1.2	3	2	.67	0 - 0	0 - 0	0 - 0	2	0	0	0		1.125	12.27
Vesia, Alex	LT	L	5	4	0	1	0.6	1	1	1.00	0 - 0	0 - 0	0 - 0	1	0	0	1	1.00	1.319	18.69
Leibrandt, Brandon	LT	L	5	3	0	3	0.1	5	1	.20	0 - 0	0 - 0	0 - 0	3	0	0	0		.381	2.00
Smith, Josh A.	LM	R	15	8	0	8	0.9	11	6	.55	1 - 1	0 - 0	0 - 0	7	0	0	1	1.00	.904	7.40
Hoyt, James	UR	R	24	9	7	0	1.0	24	7	.29	0 - 0	0 - 0	0 - 0	16	0	0	5	1.00	.598	1.23
Boxberger, Brad	UR	R	23	4	6	1	1.2	7	5	.71	0 - 1	0 - 0	0 - 0	15	0	1	5	.83	.749	4.43
Vincent, Nick	UR	R	21	8	4	2	1.1	11	2	.18	1 - 1	0 - 0	2 - 2	14	0	0	0	1.00	.844	4.43
Garcia, Yimi	UR	R	14	4	4	2	1.1	3	2	.67	1 - 1	0 - 0	0 - 1	11	0	1	4	.83	.452	0.60
Stanek, Ryne	UR	R	9	3	2	4	0.5	2	0	.00	0 - 0	0 - 0	0 - 0	6	0	0	0		.921	7.20
Shafer, Justin	UR	R	5	3	1	1	0.7	2	0	.00	0 - 0	0 - 0	0 - 0	1	0	0	0		1.142	12.71

Milwaukee Brewers

Pitcher	Pos	T	Usage					Inherited Runners			Saves			Relief Results						
			Rel G	Early Entry	Cons Days	Long	Lev Ind	#	Scrd	Pct	Easy	Reg	Tough	Clean	BS Win	BS	Holds	Sv/Hld Pct	Opp OPS	Rel ERA
Hader, Josh	CL	L	21	0	3	3	2.2	2	0	.00	6-7	6-7	1-1	17	0	2	0	.87	.562	3.79
Williams, Devin	SU	R	22	4	2	5	1.5	4	0	.00	0-0	0-0	0-0	20	0	0	9	1.00	.339	0.33
Suter, Brent	LT	L	12	6	0	5	1.0	7	4	.57	0-0	0-0	0-0	6	0	0	2	1.00	.777	4.34
Yardley, Eric	LM	R	24	13	5	2	0.7	12	5	.42	0-0	0-1	0-1	16	1	2	1	.33	.662	1.54
Claudio, Alex	LM	L	20	10	2	2	0.7	11	5	.45	1-1	0-0	0-0	12	0	0	1	1.00	.687	4.26
Peralta, Freddy	LM	R	14	13	0	10	1.0	11	5	.45	0-0	0-1	0-0	7	0	1	3	.75	.586	3.08
Knebel, Corey	UR	R	15	3	1	3	0.4	6	3	.50	0-0	0-1	0-1	7	0	2	0	.00	.927	6.08
Phelps, David	UR	R	12	0	2	1	2.2	1	0	.00	0-0	0-1	0-0	8	0	1	4	.80	.497	2.77
Rasmussen, Drew	UR	R	12	3	2	6	0.7	6	3	.50	0-0	0-0	0-0	8	0	0	0		.834	5.87
Feyereisen, J.P.	UR	R	6	3	0	3	0.1	2	2	1.00	0-0	0-0	0-0	2	0	0	0		.719	5.79
Topa, Justin	UR	R	6	3	0	3	0.6	1	0	.00	0-0	0-0	0-0	4	0	0	0		.633	2.35

Minnesota Twins

Pitcher	Pos	T	Usage					Inherited Runners			Saves			Relief Results						
			Rel G	Early Entry	Cons Days	Long	Lev Ind	#	Scrd	Pct	Easy	Reg	Tough	Clean	BS Win	BS	Holds	Sv/Hld Pct	Opp OPS	Rel ERA
Rogers, Taylor	CL	L	21	0	5	1	1.9	3	2	.67	8-9	1-2	0-0	12	0	2	2	.85	.806	4.05
Romo, Sergio	SU	R	24	1	5	1	1.7	6	6	1.00	5-5	0-0	0-1	16	0	1	10	.94	.667	4.05
May, Trevor	SU	R	24	11	5	1	1.4	12	1	.08	1-1	0-0	1-1	16	0	0	8	1.00	.679	3.86
Clippard, Tyler	SU	R	24	13	6	1	1.2	13	2	.15	0-1	0-1	0-0	17	0	2	7	.78	.548	2.74
Duffey, Tyler	SU	R	22	9	1	3	1.4	9	2	.22	0-0	0-0	0-2	17	0	2	12	.86	.488	1.88
Thielbar, Caleb	LT	L	17	6	2	4	1.0	11	1	.09	0-0	0-0	0-0	12	0	0	1	1.00	.500	2.25
Thorpe, Lewis	LT	L	6	4	0	4	0.4	3	2	.67	0-0	0-0	0-0	3	0	0	0		1.009	5.84
Smeltzer, Devin	LT	L	6	4	0	5	0.8	0	0	.00	0-0	0-0	0-0	2	0	0	0		.884	7.71
Alcala, Jorge	LM	R	16	7	1	7	0.8	11	2	.18	0-0	0-1	0-0	9	0	1	0	.00	.681	2.63
Wisler, Matt	LM	R	14	8	2	4	1.1	4	2	.50	0-0	1-1	0-1	9	0	1	3	.80	.642	1.53
Stashak, Cody	UR	R	11	5	0	3	0.9	4	1	.25	0-0	0-0	0-0	8	0	0	5	1.00	.635	3.00
Poppen, Sean	UR	R	6	3	1	2	0.7	2	1	.50	0-0	0-0	0-0	2	0	0	1	1.00	.759	4.70
Littell, Zack	UR	R	6	2	1	1	0.5	0	0	.00	0-0	0-0	0-0	3	0	0	0		1.516	9.95

New York Mets

Pitcher	Pos	T	Usage					Inherited Runners			Saves			Relief Results						
			Rel G	Early Entry	Cons Days	Long	Lev Ind	#	Scrd	Pct	Easy	Reg	Tough	Clean	BS Win	BS	Holds	Sv/Hld Pct	Opp OPS	Rel ERA
Diaz, Edwin	CL	R	26	1	6	5	1.5	10	6	.60	3-3	3-5	0-1	18	1	4	1	.73	.596	1.75
Wilson, Justin	SU	L	23	4	7	3	1.5	16	2	.13	0-0	0-0	0-0	16	0	0	10	1.00	.623	3.66
Hughes, Jared	LM	R	18	10	3	4	0.6	7	4	.57	0-0	0-0	0-0	10	0	0	2	1.00	.808	4.84
Shreve, Chasen	LM	L	17	13	1	9	0.6	15	4	.27	0-0	0-0	0-0	9	0	0	1	1.00	.655	3.96
Familia, Jeurys	UR	R	25	9	5	4	1.0	8	1	.13	0-0	0-1	0-0	16	0	1	5	.83	.687	3.71
Betances, Dellin	UR	R	15	3	5	1	1.3	3	0	.00	0-0	0-0	0-0	11	0	0	4	1.00	.730	7.71
Brach, Brad	UR	R	14	4	2	1	0.6	8	2	.25	0-0	0-0	0-0	8	0	0	0		.745	5.84
Castro, Miguel	UR	R	10	2	1	2	1.5	3	0	.00	0-0	0-0	0-0	7	0	0	1	1.00	.882	4.00
Lugo, Seth	UR	R	9	1	1	1	1.2	3	2	.67	1-1	2-3	0-1	6	0	2	0	.60	.592	2.61
Smith, Drew	UR	R	8	3	0	0	1.0	6	2	.33	0-0	0-0	0-0	4	0	0	2	1.00	.757	6.43
Ramirez, Erasmo	UR	R	6	3	0	4	0.2	2	0	.00	0-0	1-1	0-0	5	0	0	0	1.00	.471	0.63
Sewald, Paul	UR	R	5	3	1	3	0.4	7	4	.57	0-0	0-0	0-0	2	0	0	0		1.072	13.50

New York Yankees

Pitcher	Pos	T	Usage					Inherited Runners			Saves			Relief Results						
			Rel G	Early Entry	Cons Days	Long	Lev Ind	#	Scrd	Pct	Easy	Reg	Tough	Clean	BS Win	BS	Holds	Sv/Hld Pct	Opp OPS	Rel ERA
Britton, Zack	CL	L	20	1	5	2	1.8	2	0	.00	7 - 7	1 - 1	0 - 0	16	0	0	3	1.00	.482	1.89
Green, Chad	SU	R	22	9	5	5	1.3	11	2	.18	1 - 1	0 - 2	0 - 0	15	0	2	6	.78	.534	3.51
Chapman, Aroldis	LT	L	13	0	5	1	2.0	3	2	.67	3 - 3	0 - 2	0 - 0	9	0	2	0	.60	.619	3.09
Avilan, Luis	LT	L	10	5	0	0	1.1	9	4	.44	0 - 0	0 - 0	0 - 0	6	0	0	0		.830	4.32
Holder, Jonathan	LM	R	19	7	2	9	0.9	6	1	.17	0 - 0	0 - 0	0 - 0	10	0	0	0		.806	4.98
Cessa, Luis	LM	R	16	11	1	6	0.5	11	4	.36	0 - 0	0 - 0	1 - 1	9	0	0	1	1.00	.693	3.32
Ottavino, Adam	UR	R	24	10	7	1	1.1	11	6	.55	0 - 0	0 - 2	0 - 1	17	0	3	2	.40	.772	5.89
Nelson, Nick	UR	R	11	7	0	8	0.5	5	0	.00	0 - 0	0 - 0	0 - 0	4	0	0	0		.780	4.79
Loaisiga, Jonathan	UR	R	9	5	0	5	1.3	5	2	.40	0 - 0	0 - 1	0 - 1	5	2	2	2	.50	.739	3.68
Heller, Ben	UR	R	6	4	0	1	0.4	5	3	.60	0 - 0	0 - 0	0 - 0	3	0	0	0		.855	3.00
Hale, David	UR	R	5	3	1	2	0.7	2	0	.00	0 - 0	1 - 1	0 - 0	3	0	0	0	1.00	.776	3.00
King, Michael	UR	R	5	3	0	4	1.0	3	1	.33	0 - 0	0 - 0	0 - 0	1	0	0	0		.861	7.11

Oakland Athletics

Pitcher	Pos	T	Usage					Inherited Runners			Saves			Relief Results						
			Rel G	Early Entry	Cons Days	Long	Lev Ind	#	Scrd	Pct	Easy	Reg	Tough	Clean	BS Win	BS	Holds	Sv/Hld Pct	Opp OPS	Rel ERA
Hendriks, Liam	CL	R	24	0	9	2	2.0	2	0	.00	8 - 8	4 - 5	2 - 2	20	0	1	0	.93	.405	1.78
Diekman, Jake	SU	L	21	2	4	2	1.6	2	1	.50	0 - 0	0 - 1	0 - 0	18	1	1	13	.93	.410	0.42
McFarland, T.J.	LT	L	23	11	5	1	0.8	5	1	.20	0 - 0	0 - 0	0 - 0	15	0	0	6	1.00	.894	4.35
Wendelken, J.B.	LM	R	21	13	2	8	1.0	24	8	.33	0 - 0	0 - 0	0 - 0	13	0	0	2	1.00	.546	1.80
Trivino, Lou	LM	R	20	6	6	6	0.3	8	4	.50	0 - 0	0 - 1	0 - 0	14	0	1	0	.00	.605	3.86
Petit, Yusmeiro	UR	R	26	10	6	1	1.3	18	5	.28	0 - 0	0 - 0	0 - 0	20	0	0	7	1.00	.639	1.66
Soria, Joakim	UR	R	22	3	2	2	1.7	2	0	.00	1 - 1	0 - 1	1 - 1	16	0	1	4	.86	.581	2.82
Weems, Jordan	UR	R	9	4	0	5	0.2	0	0	.00	0 - 0	0 - 0	0 - 0	6	0	0	0		.593	3.21
Smith, Burch	UR	R	6	3	0	3	1.1	1	0	.00	0 - 0	1 - 1	0 - 0	5	0	0	0	1.00	.461	2.25

Philadelphia Phillies

Pitcher	Pos	T	Usage					Inherited Runners			Saves			Relief Results						
			Rel G	Early Entry	Cons Days	Long	Lev Ind	#	Scrd	Pct	Easy	Reg	Tough	Clean	BS Win	BS	Holds	Sv/Hld Pct	Opp OPS	Rel ERA
Neris, Hector	CL	R	24	4	6	4	2.2	9	2	.22	3 - 3	1 - 4	1 - 1	15	1	3	4	.75	.670	4.57
Workman, Brandon	CL	R	14	1	2	3	2.4	7	6	.86	4 - 4	1 - 1	0 - 3	7	0	3	1	.67	1.146	6.92
Hunter, Tommy	SU	R	24	6	3	3	1.4	14	2	.14	1 - 1	0 - 2	0 - 0	17	0	2	8	.82	.698	4.01
Morgan, Adam	LT	L	17	7	1	1	1.0	13	1	.08	0 - 0	0 - 1	0 - 1	12	0	2	2	.50	.845	5.54
Romero, JoJo	LT	L	12	8	2	0	1.2	9	3	.33	0 - 0	0 - 0	0 - 0	8	0	0	4	1.00	.822	7.59
Alvarez, Jose	LT	L	8	3	1	0	0.8	4	0	.00	0 - 0	0 - 0	0 - 0	7	0	0	1	1.00	.745	1.42
Hembree, Heath	LM	R	11	7	2	1	1.2	2	0	.00	0 - 0	0 - 0	0 - 0	3	0	0	2	1.00	1.480	12.54
Parker, Blake	UR	R	13	7	0	4	1.3	14	5	.36	0 - 0	0 - 1	0 - 0	7	0	1	1	.50	.748	3.21
Phelps, David	UR	R	10	5	4	0	0.9	5	1	.20	0 - 0	0 - 1	0 - 0	4	0	1	2	.67	1.229	12.91
Guerra, Deolis	UR	R	9	3	2	0	0.8	1	1	1.00	0 - 0	0 - 0	0 - 0	4	0	0	0		1.014	8.59
Brogdon, Connor	UR	R	9	3	2	3	0.8	11	4	.36	0 - 0	0 - 0	0 - 0	6	0	0	0		.612	3.97
Rosso, Ramon	UR	R	6	2	0	3	0.8	3	1	.33	0 - 0	0 - 0	0 - 0	3	0	0	0		.864	6.14
McClain, Reggie	UR	R	5	5	1	2	0.6	6	2	.33	0 - 0	0 - 0	0 - 0	2	0	0	0		.974	5.06

Pittsburgh Pirates

Pitcher	Pos	T	Usage					Inherited Runners			Saves			Relief Results						
			Rel G	Early Entry	Cons Days	Long	Lev Ind	#	Scrd	Pct	Easy	Reg	Tough	Clean	BS Win	BS	Holds	Sv/Hld Pct	Opp OPS	Rel ERA
Turley, Nik	LT	L	25	8	1	1	1.5	5	2	.40	1 - 1	0 - 3	0 - 0	17	0	3	3	.57	.587	4.98
Holland, Derek	LT	L	7	3	1	3	0.8	0	0	.00	0 - 0	0 - 1	0 - 0	3	0	1	0	.00	.612	4.40
Del Pozo, Miguel	LT	L	5	1	1	2	1.2	8	6	.75	0 - 0	0 - 0	0 - 2	1	0	2	0	.00	1.129	17.18
Davis, Austin	LT	L	5	3	2	0	1.0	8	0	.00	0 - 0	0 - 0	0 - 0	4	0	0	1	1.00	.258	2.45
Stratton, Chris	LM	R	27	11	5	6	1.3	14	4	.29	0 - 0	0 - 1	0 - 1	15	0	2	5	.71	.651	3.90
Howard, Sam	LM	L	22	12	4	4	1.4	15	5	.33	0 - 0	0 - 2	0 - 0	15	0	2	4	.67	.764	3.86
Hartlieb, Geoff	LM	R	21	12	1	5	1.1	18	2	.11	0 - 0	0 - 0	0 - 0	14	0	0	5	1.00	.658	3.63
Rodriguez, Richard	UR	R	24	0	5	2	1.5	2	0	.00	1 - 1	3 - 4	0 - 0	19	0	1	2	.86	.537	2.70
Neverauskas, Dovydas	UR	R	17	9	1	4	0.8	6	4	.67	0 - 0	0 - 0	0 - 0	9	0	0	0		.939	7.11
Bashlor, Tyler	UR	R	8	3	2	1	0.4	2	1	.50	0 - 0	0 - 0	0 - 0	4	0	0	0		1.020	8.64
Tropeano, Nick	UR	R	7	4	0	5	0.3	7	5	.71	0 - 0	0 - 0	0 - 0	5	0	0	0		.676	1.15
Crick, Kyle	UR	R	7	2	0	1	0.9	2	2	1.00	0 - 0	0 - 0	0 - 1	3	0	1	0	.00	.699	1.59
Cederlind, Blake	UR	R	5	1	0	0	0.4	1	1	1.00	0 - 0	0 - 0	0 - 0	4	0	0	0		.517	4.50

San Diego Padres

Pitcher	Pos	T	Usage					Inherited Runners			Saves			Relief Results						
			Rel G	Early Entry	Cons Days	Long	Lev Ind	#	Scrd	Pct	Easy	Reg	Tough	Clean	BS Win	BS	Holds	Sv/Hld Pct	Opp OPS	Rel ERA
Rosenthal, Trevor	CL	R	9	0	2	1	1.2	1	0	.00	3 - 3	1 - 1	0 - 1	8	1	1	0	.80	.266	0.00
Pagan, Emilio	SU	R	22	1	2	3	1.3	1	0	.00	1 - 4	1 - 3	0 - 0	16	0	5	7	.64	.641	4.50
Pomeranz, Drew	SU	L	20	2	4	1	1.9	8	2	.25	2 - 2	1 - 2	1 - 1	18	0	1	9	.93	.454	1.45
Hill, Tim	LT	L	23	10	5	1	1.2	17	5	.29	0 - 0	0 - 0	0 - 0	15	0	0	5	1.00	.739	4.50
Morejon, Adrian	LT	L	5	4	0	4	0.7	0	0	.00	0 - 0	0 - 0	0 - 0	3	0	0	0		1.008	4.50
Strahm, Matt	LM	L	19	13	3	0	1.1	13	5	.38	0 - 0	0 - 1	0 - 1	13	0	2	3	.60	.615	2.61
Stammen, Craig	UR	R	24	8	3	1	1.0	6	3	.50	0 - 1	0 - 0	0 - 0	14	0	1	5	.83	.702	5.63
Johnson, Pierce	UR	R	24	2	2	0	1.0	18	4	.22	0 - 0	0 - 0	0 - 0	17	0	0	1	1.00	.643	2.70
Guerra, Javy	UR	R	14	5	0	1	0.5	4	1	.25	0 - 0	0 - 0	0 - 0	7	0	0	2	1.00	.979	10.13
Patino, Luis	UR	R	10	7	0	7	0.7	3	1	.33	0 - 0	0 - 0	0 - 0	5	0	0	1	1.00	.777	5.17
Altavilla, Dan	UR	R	9	5	3	1	1.3	7	1	.14	0 - 0	0 - 0	0 - 0	6	0	0	2	1.00	.614	3.12
Quantrill, Cal	UR	R	9	4	1	3	1.1	6	0	.00	0 - 0	0 - 0	1 - 1	6	0	0	1	1.00	.693	2.63
Perdomo, Luis	UR	R	9	5	0	5	0.4	2	0	.00	0 - 0	0 - 0	0 - 0	5	0	0	0		.701	5.51
Yates, Kirby	UR	R	6	0	1	2	1.8	0	0	.00	2 - 2	0 - 0	0 - 0	2	0	0	1	1.00	.940	12.46

San Francisco Giants

Pitcher	Pos	T	Usage					Inherited Runners			Saves			Relief Results						
			Rel G	Early Entry	Cons Days	Long	Lev Ind	#	Scrd	Pct	Easy	Reg	Tough	Clean	BS Win	BS	Holds	Sv/Hld Pct	Opp OPS	Rel ERA
Rogers, Tyler	SU	R	29	2	8	2	1.8	11	5	.45	2 - 2	0 - 1	1 - 3	21	1	3	10	.81	.711	4.50
Watson, Tony	SU	L	21	2	6	0	1.3	3	1	.33	0 - 0	2 - 2	0 - 0	17	0	0	10	1.00	.571	2.50
Garcia, Jarlin	SU	L	19	5	3	0	1.1	2	2	1.00	0 - 0	0 - 0	0 - 0	14	0	0	6	1.00	.487	0.49
Selman, Sam	LT	L	24	8	7	1	0.7	11	1	.09	1 - 1	0 - 0	0 - 0	19	0	0	3	1.00	.611	3.72
Menez, Conner	LT	L	7	3	0	2	0.3	4	0	.00	0 - 0	0 - 0	0 - 0	4	0	0	0		.641	2.38
Suarez, Andrew	LT	L	6	6	0	3	0.3	5	1	.20	0 - 0	0 - 0	0 - 0	3	0	0	0		.774	3.72
Peralta, Wandy	LM	L	25	10	6	6	0.5	18	5	.28	0 - 0	0 - 1	0 - 0	15	0	1	1	.50	.657	3.29
Baragar, Caleb	LM	L	23	14	4	1	1.0	22	3	.14	0 - 0	0 - 0	0 - 1	17	1	1	2	.67	.652	4.22
Anderson, Shaun	LM	R	18	8	5	2	0.6	10	3	.30	0 - 0	0 - 0	0 - 0	13	0	0	2	1.00	.710	3.52
Coonrod, Sam	UR	R	18	3	4	1	0.9	3	1	.33	2 - 3	1 - 2	0 - 0	10	0	2	2	.71	.871	9.82
Gott, Trevor	UR	R	15	3	3	1	1.6	3	0	.00	2 - 3	2 - 3	0 - 0	10	0	2	3	.78	1.198	10.03
Garcia, Rico	UR	R	12	7	3	1	0.7	5	2	.40	0 - 1	0 - 0	0 - 0	7	0	1	2	.67	.874	5.40
Cahill, Trevor	UR	R	5	2	1	1	1.1	5	0	.00	0 - 0	0 - 0	0 - 0	4	0	0	1	1.00	.433	0.00

Seattle Mariners

Pitcher	Pos	T	Usage					Inherited Runners			Saves			Relief Results						
			Rel G	Early Entry	Cons Days	Long	Lev Ind	#	Scrd	Pct	Easy	Reg	Tough	Clean	BS Win	BS	Holds	Sv/Hld Pct	Opp OPS	Rel ERA
Misiewicz, Anthony	SU	L	21	7	0	2	1.2	8	4	.50	0-0	0-1	0-0	12	0	1	8	.89	.746	4.05
Graveman, Kendall	SU	R	9	0	2	1	1.2	3	2	.67	0-0	0-1	0-0	6	0	1	5	.83	.516	3.60
Guilbeau, Taylor	LT	L	8	5	0	0	0.6	6	3	.50	0-0	0-0	0-0	5	0	0	1	1.00	.756	1.17
Fletcher, Aaron	LT	L	6	2	0	2	0.4	0	0	.00	0-0	0-0	0-0	4	0	0	1	1.00	1.102	12.46
Gerber, Joey	LM		17	10	1	1	1.3	16	7	.44	0-0	0-0	0-1	10	0	1	4	.80	.714	4.02
Ramirez, Yohan	UR	R	16	2	0	6	0.7	4	1	.25	2-2	0-0	1-1	11	0	0	1	1.00	.626	2.61
Williams, Taylor	UR	R	14	1	2	3	1.7	6	4	.67	4-4	2-2	0-0	9	0	0	1	1.00	.682	5.93
Hirano, Yoshihisa	UR	R	13	1	3	3	1.4	0	0	.00	3-3	1-1	0-0	8	0	0	1	1.00	.938	5.84
Altavilla, Dan	UR	R	13	0	1	3	0.9	1	1	1.00	1-1	0-0	0-0	7	0	0	1	1.00	.884	7.71
Magill, Matt	UR	R	11	3	1	1	1.3	0	0	.00	0-2	0-0	0-0	9	0	2	2	.50	.795	6.10
Swanson, Erik	UR	R	9	2	0	1	1.2	1	0	.00	0-1	0-0	0-0	4	0	1	1	.50	1.093	12.91
Lail, Brady	UR	R	7	3	0	6	0.3	0	0	.00	0-0	0-0	0-0	4	0	0	0		.823	4.80
Sadler, Casey	UR	R	7	5	1	4	1.2	3	1	.33	0-0	0-0	0-0	4	0	0	1	1.00	.630	4.50
Shaw, Bryan	UR	R	6	3	0	2	0.6	3	3	1.00	0-1	0-0	0-0	2	1	1	0	.00	1.293	18.00
Grotz, Zac	UR		5	5	0	3	0.2	6	3	.50	0-0	0-0	0-0	1	0	0	0		1.399	14.73
Edwards Jr., Carl	UR	R	5	2	1	0	1.2	1	0	.00	0-0	0-1	0-0	4	0	0	1	1.00	.489	1.93
Lockett, Walker	UR	R	5	2	0	2	0.1	3	3	1.00	0-0	0-0	0-0	3	0	0	0		.818	4.32
Brennan, Brandon	UR	R	5	3	0	2	0.2	6	4	.67	0-0	0-0	0-0	2	0	0	0		.864	3.68

St Louis Cardinals

Pitcher	Pos	T	Usage					Inherited Runners			Saves			Relief Results						
			Rel G	Early Entry	Cons Days	Long	Lev Ind	#	Scrd	Pct	Easy	Reg	Tough	Clean	BS Win	BS	Holds	Sv/Hld Pct	Opp OPS	Rel ERA
Webb, Tyler	LT	L	21	9	5	4	0.7	16	5	.31	0-1	0-0	1-2	17	0	2	2	.60	.600	2.08
Miller, Andrew	LT	L	16	3	3	0	1.2	8	3	.38	2-2	2-2	0-1	12	0	1	2	.86	.522	2.77
Gomber, Austin	LT	L	10	6	0	4	1.0	7	2	.29	0-0	0-0	0-0	6	0	0	1	1.00	.582	3.38
Kaminsky, Rob	LT	L	5	2	1	1	0.2	2	2	1.00	0-0	0-0	0-0	4	0	0	0		.438	1.93
Cabrera, Genesis	LM	L	20	12	3	4	1.4	6	1	.17	0-0	0-1	0-0	12	0	0	2	1.00	.589	2.42
Reyes, Alex	LM	R	14	6	2	7	1.5	10	1	.10	0-0	0-1	0-0	8	0	0	2	1.00	.602	3.38
Gant, John	UR	R	17	6	1	2	1.3	5	0	.00	0-0	0-0	0-0	13	0	0	5	1.00	.447	2.40
Gallegos, Giovanny	UR	R	16	6	1	0	1.3	8	2	.25	1-1	3-3	0-0	11	0	0	1	1.00	.473	3.60
Elledge, Seth	UR	R	12	6	3	4	0.3	6	2	.33	0-0	0-0	0-0	9	0	0	0		.964	4.63
Helsley, Ryan	UR	R	12	3	2	1	1.5	8	2	.25	0-0	0-1	0-2	7	0	2	2	.60	.769	5.25
Woodford, Jake	UR	R	11	5	1	8	0.3	10	4	.40	0-0	0-0	0-0	4	0	0	0		.871	6.00
Crismatt, Nabil	UR	R	6	1	2	1	0.2	2	0	.00	0-0	0-0	0-0	4	0	0	0		.692	3.24

Tampa Bay Rays

Pitcher	Pos	T	Usage					Inherited Runners			Saves			Relief Results						
			Rel G	Early Entry	Cons Days	Long	Lev Ind	#	Scrd	Pct	Easy	Reg	Tough	Clean	BS Win	BS	Holds	Sv/Hld Pct	Opp OPS	Rel ERA
Fairbanks, Pete	SU	R	25	11	4	3	1.4	8	2	.25	0-0	0-2	0-0	16	0	2	7	.78	.665	3.00
Castillo, Diego	SU	R	22	8	3	1	1.8	8	2	.25	2-2	2-2	0-1	18	1	1	5	.90	.581	1.66
Anderson, Nick	SU	R	19	0	4	0	1.9	14	1	.07	1-1	5-5	0-0	17	0	0	6	1.00	.320	0.55
Loup, Aaron	LT	L	24	7	9	0	0.8	8	2	.25	0-0	0-0	0-1	19	0	1	4	.80	.635	2.52
Beeks, Jalen	LT	L	12	6	1	7	0.9	6	0	.00	0-0	0-0	1-1	8	0	0	2	1.00	.694	3.26
Sherriff, Ryan	LT	L	10	1	2	0	0.8	0	0	.00	0-0	0-1	0-0	10	0	0	1	1.00	.423	0.00
Alvarado, Jose	LT	L	9	1	2	3	0.7	2	2	1.00	0-0	0-0	0-0	5	0	0	1	1.00	.850	6.00
Thompson, Ryan	LM	R	24	18	2	4	1.1	10	0	.00	1-1	0-0	0-0	16	0	0	4	1.00	.781	4.81
Curtiss, John	UR	R	14	5	2	5	0.9	4	2	.50	1-1	1-1	0-0	10	0	0	0	1.00	.530	1.66
Drake, Oliver	UR	R	11	4	1	0	1.1	2	1	.50	2-2	0-1	0-1	6	0	2	1	.60	.701	5.73
Roe, Chaz	UR	R	10	3	3	1	1.9	6	2	.33	1-1	0-0	0-0	6	0	0	2	1.00	.771	2.89
Slegers, Aaron	UR	R	10	4	0	6	0.9	5	0	.00	1-1	1-1	0-0	5	0	0	2	1.00	.562	4.09
Kittredge, Andrew	UR	R	7	6	1	1	1.2	6	3	.50	0-0	1-1	0-0	4	0	0	1	1.00	.644	2.35
Richards, Trevor	UR	R	5	5	0	5	0.9	3	0	.00	0-0	0-0	0-0	0	0	0	0		.825	6.46

Texas Rangers

Pitcher	Pos	T	Usage					Inherited Runners			Saves			Relief Results						
			Rel G	Early Entry	Cons Days	Long	Lev Ind	#	Scrd	Pct	Easy	Reg	Tough	Clean	BS Win	BS	Holds	Sv/Hld Pct	Opp OPS	Rel ERA
Montero, Rafael	CL	R	17	0	4	2	1.6	2	0	.00	5 - 5	2 - 2	1 - 1	11	0	0	0	1.00	.652	4.08
Martin, Brett	LT	L	15	6	2	1	0.9	9	1	.11	0 - 0	0 - 0	0 - 0	9	0	0	2	1.00	.612	1.84
Hearn, Taylor	LT	L	14	7	0	6	0.3	7	4	.57	0 - 0	0 - 0	0 - 0	9	0	0	0		.646	3.63
Rodriguez, Joely	LT	L	12	3	2	3	1.0	3	0	.00	0 - 1	0 - 0	0 - 0	10	0	1	3	.75	.494	2.13
Benjamin, Wes	LT	L	7	7	0	6	0.7	3	0	.00	0 - 0	0 - 0	0 - 0	2	0	0	0		.727	4.67
King, John	LT	L	6	6	0	5	0.9	0	0	.00	0 - 0	0 - 1	0 - 0	1	0	1	0	.00	.839	6.10
Hernandez, Jonathan	UR	R	27	1	5	3	1.2	10	3	.30	0 - 0	0 - 0	0 - 0	18	0	0	5	1.00	.618	2.90
Herget, Jimmy	UR	R	19	8	6	1	0.6	15	8	.53	0 - 0	0 - 1	0 - 0	12	1	1	1	.50	.682	3.38
Chavez, Jesse	UR	R	18	4	2	2	0.8	10	5	.50	0 - 1	0 - 2	0 - 0	8	0	3	2	.40	.985	6.88
Goody, Nick	UR	R	16	6	2	0	1.0	17	4	.24	1 - 1	0 - 0	0 - 2	9	0	2	0	.33	1.121	9.90
Gibaut, Ian	UR	R	14	6	3	2	0.9	8	2	.25	0 - 0	0 - 1	0 - 0	9	0	1	2	.67	.779	6.57
Garcia, Luis	UR	R	9	3	1	0	0.9	5	3	.60	0 - 0	0 - 0	0 - 0	3	0	0	0		.684	3.68
Volquez, Edinson	UR	R	7	3	1	0	1.0	1	0	.00	0 - 0	0 - 0	0 - 0	5	0	0	0		.651	6.35

Toronto Blue Jays

Pitcher	Pos	T	Usage					Inherited Runners			Saves			Relief Results						
			Rel G	Early Entry	Cons Days	Long	Lev Ind	#	Scrd	Pct	Easy	Reg	Tough	Clean	BS Win	BS	Holds	Sv/Hld Pct	Opp OPS	Rel ERA
Bass, Anthony	CL	R	26	2	5	2	1.8	7	0	.00	1 - 2	6 - 7	0 - 0	18	0	2	3	.83	.563	3.51
Dolis, Rafael	SU	R	24	4	5	2	1.9	12	2	.17	2 - 2	2 - 2	1 - 2	17	0	1	7	.92	.593	1.50
Romano, Jordan	SU	R	15	2	4	1	2.1	8	0	.00	1 - 1	1 - 2	0 - 0	12	0	1	5	.88	.517	1.23
Borucki, Ryan	LT	L	21	7	2	1	1.0	11	5	.45	0 - 1	0 - 0	0 - 0	16	0	1	3	.75	.629	2.70
Font, Wilmer	LM	R	21	10	3	3	0.9	7	1	.14	0 - 0	0 - 1	0 - 0	12	0	1	2	.67	.974	9.92
Yamaguchi, Shun	LM	R	17	11	1	11	1.0	8	0	.00	0 - 0	0 - 0	0 - 1	7	0	1	1	.50	.947	8.06
Hatch, Thomas	LM	R	16	7	0	8	1.1	13	4	.31	0 - 0	0 - 0	0 - 0	9	0	0	3	1.00	.632	3.00
Kay, Anthony	LM	L	13	11	0	7	1.2	15	5	.33	0 - 0	0 - 0	0 - 0	5	0	0	2	1.00	.867	5.14
Waguespack, Jacob	LM	R	11	9	1	8	0.5	10	7	.70	0 - 0	0 - 0	0 - 0	3	0	0	1	1.00	.897	8.15
Cole, A.J.	UR	R	24	7	4	2	1.8	16	7	.44	0 - 0	0 - 1	1 - 3	15	0	3	2	.50	.691	3.09
Reid-Foley, Sean	UR	R	5	2	0	4	0.7	2	1	.50	0 - 0	0 - 0	0 - 0	2	0	0	0		.425	1.35
Merryweather, Julian	UR	R	5	3	0	3	1.4	5	0	.00	0 - 0	0 - 0	0 - 0	3	0	0	1	1.00	.596	4.50

Washington Nationals

Pitcher	Pos	T	Usage					Inherited Runners			Saves			Relief Results						
			Rel G	Early Entry	Cons Days	Long	Lev Ind	#	Scrd	Pct	Easy	Reg	Tough	Clean	BS Win	BS	Holds	Sv/Hld Pct	Opp OPS	Rel ERA
Hudson, Daniel	CL	R	21	0	6	3	1.8	8	1	.13	7 - 9	3 - 5	0 - 1	13	1	5	0	.67	.786	6.10
Harris, Will	SU	R	20	2	5	1	1.4	4	1	.25	0 - 1	1 - 2	0 - 1	13	0	3	6	.70	.797	3.06
Rainey, Tanner	SU	R	20	4	9	2	1.5	12	2	.17	0 - 0	0 - 0	0 - 0	15	0	0	9	1.00	.542	2.66
Doolittle, Sean	LT	L	11	0	1	0	1.6	0	0	.00	0 - 0	0 - 0	0 - 0	6	0	0	3	1.00	1.005	5.87
Freeman, Sam	LT	L	7	5	1	0	0.7	2	0	.00	0 - 0	0 - 0	0 - 0	6	0	0	1	1.00	.471	1.80
Suero, Wander	LM	R	22	15	5	2	1.1	17	6	.35	0 - 0	0 - 0	0 - 0	13	0	0	6	1.00	.642	3.80
Finnegan, Kyle	UR	R	25	10	6	1	1.2	18	5	.28	0 - 0	0 - 0	0 - 1	18	0	1	4	.80	.639	2.92
Harper, Ryne	UR	R	23	8	6	5	0.3	19	2	.11	0 - 0	0 - 0	0 - 0	14	0	0	1	1.00	.865	7.61
Guerra, Javy	UR	R	14	8	3	3	0.6	5	2	.40	0 - 0	0 - 0	0 - 0	9	0	0	5	1.00	.816	4.02
Bacus, Dakota	UR	R	11	7	2	3	0.4	8	0	.00	0 - 0	0 - 0	0 - 0	7	0	0	2	1.00	.808	7.94
McGowin, Kyle	UR	R	9	5	3	3	0.9	9	4	.44	0 - 0	1 - 1	0 - 0	4	0	0	1	1.00	.655	4.91
Bourque, James	UR	R	6	2	0	1	1.0	3	1	.33	0 - 0	0 - 0	0 - 0	4	0	0	0		.992	6.75

Openers

Brian Reiff

The Opener is dead. Long live the traditional start.

Okay, maybe that proclamation is a bit premature. After all, there were countless statistical oddities that reared their heads during this shortened season—it's probably more likely that this was just one of them.

For those unfamiliar with the term, an Opener is…well, it doesn't really have a formal definition. Basically, when a nominal "starter" doesn't start the game, but rather comes in after one or two innings from a nominal "reliever" to then pitch a normal starter's innings…that's an Opener. It's different from a bullpen game, in which several pitchers each pitch an inning or two. The Opener, at least in its current form, was first seen in 2018, utilized primarily by the Tampa Bay Rays.

Because Openers don't have a formal definition, different sources may come up with different numbers. By our reckoning, teams used 11 Openers this year. This follows a two-year span in which 204 were collectively used by more than half the teams in the league.

So why were Openers down? Well, perhaps because starting pitchers weren't going as deep into games. One of the primary motivations for the Opener was alleviating the third-time-through-the-order penalty, making it so that the would-be starter avoids the top of the lineup to begin the game (and doesn't have to face it immediately when the lineup turns over). With only 70% of starters facing more than 18 batters this season—compared to 84% in 2019—there was less of a reason to utilize the tactic.

The charts on the following page show the number of Openers used by each team over the last three years and the number of times each pitcher has appeared as an Opener, as well as their ERA in that role. Pitchers are included if they made at least one Opener appearance this season or two in the last three years.

Opener Usage

By Team				
Team	**2018**	**2019**	**2020**	**Total**
Tampa Bay Rays	39	35	3	77
Los Angeles Angels	0	27	0	27
Seattle Mariners	1	26	0	27
Toronto Blue Jays	1	15	3	19
Texas Rangers	3	9	3	15
New York Yankees	0	10	0	10
Oakland Athletics	7	3	0	10
Minnesota Twins	7	0	0	7
Baltimore Orioles	2	3	0	5
Los Angeles Dodgers	1	1	1	3
Pittsburgh Pirates	0	3	0	3
Houston Astros	1	2	0	3
San Francisco Giants	0	1	1	2
San Diego Padres	0	2	0	2
Philadelphia Phillies	0	1	0	1
Washington Nationals	0	1	0	1
Chicago White Sox	0	1	0	1
Arizona Diamondbacks	0	1	0	1
Milwaukee Brewers	1	0	0	1
New York Mets	0	0	0	0
St Louis Cardinals	0	0	0	0
Atlanta Braves	0	0	0	0
Chicago Cubs	0	0	0	0
Cincinnati Reds	0	0	0	0
Colorado Rockies	0	0	0	0
Miami Marlins	0	0	0	0
Cleveland Indians	0	0	0	0
Detroit Tigers	0	0	0	0
Kansas City Royals	0	0	0	0
Boston Red Sox	0	0	0	0
Total	63	141	11	215

Appearances By Pitcher					
Pitcher	**2018**	**2019**	**2020**	**Total**	**ERA**
Ryne Stanek	20	22	0	42	3.36
Diego Castillo	6	6	0	12	4.41
Wilmer Font	0	10	0	10	5.51
Hunter Wood	8	2	0	10	3.18
Chad Green	0	8	0	8	2.53
Matt Wisler	0	8	0	8	0.00
Liam Hendriks	6	2	0	8	2.25
Noe Ramirez	0	7	0	7	6.48
Cam Bedrosian	0	7	0	7	2.57
Taylor Cole	0	6	0	6	11.05
Matt Carasiti	0	5	0	5	10.38
Andrew Kittredge	1	4	0	5	11.37
Gabriel Moya	5	0	0	5	3.00
Julian Merryweather	0	0	3	3	3.60
John Curtiss	0	0	3	3	2.70
Luis Garcia	0	2	1	3	3.00
Jesse Chavez	0	3	0	3	0.00
Luke Bard	0	3	0	3	3.00
Jose Leclerc	0	3	0	3	2.45
Sergio Romo	3	0	0	3	3.00
Cory Gearrin	0	2	0	2	18.00
Derek Law	0	2	0	2	5.40
Sam Tuivailala	0	2	0	2	0.00
Tayler Scott	0	2	0	2	27.00
Jimmy Yacabonis	0	2	0	2	3.00
Austin Adams	0	2	0	2	16.20
Montana DuRapau	0	2	0	2	10.13
Gerson Bautista	0	2	0	2	13.50
Justin Dunn	0	2	0	2	0.00
Nick Vincent	1	1	0	2	9.00
Connor Sadzeck	2	0	0	2	0.00
Nick Goody	0	0	1	1	0.00
Jimmy Herget	0	0	1	1	0.00
Caleb Baragar	0	0	1	1	0.00
Victor Gonzalez	0	0	1	1	0.00

Pitchers Fielding & Holding Runners, and Hitters Pitching

John Shirley

In sports it's always fun and exciting to see athletes excel doing something outside of their traditional role. Nothing beats an offensive lineman scoring a touchdown on a trick play in football or a diminutive point guard throwing down a massive dunk in basketball.

While baseball doesn't generally have the trick plays featured in football or the assignment fluidity of basketball, it still features players who have expanded their role past traditional norms. There are pitchers who excel in their fielding and holding runners. Hitters have seen increased usage on the mound over the past few seasons.

Fielding is technically within the job description for pitchers, but is not one of the main aspects of their role most think of. Within this part of the game, Braves pitcher Max Fried excelled, as he led all pitchers in Runs Saved this past year with five. This was the second season in a row Fried topped the leaderboard, after also saving five runs in 2019. His 2020 season might be more impressive considering he pitched 109 2/3 fewer innings and had fewer opportunities to make plays in the field.

The number of pitches thrown by hitters had been increasing for three straight years before this season. Obviously that number declined in 2020 due to the shortened season, but the percentage of all pitches that were thrown by hitters also declined from last season. However, this was only a slight decline, as 2020 had the second-highest percentage since 2004.

Matt Davidson led all hitters with 3 1/3 innings pitched. He was one of only six hitters to pitch more than an inning. His ERA of 5.40 ranked tied-first among those six hitters. He was also one of only four hitters to record a strikeout, tying Mike Brosseau, Drew Butera, and Todd Frazier with one.

Pitchers Fielding and Holding Runners

	2020 Fielding and Holding Runners											
Pitcher	Inn	PO	A	E	DP	Pct	SBA	CS	PCS	PPO	CS%	RS
Abreu, Albert	1.1	0	0	0	0	-	0	0	0	0	-	0
Abreu, Bryan	3.1	2	0	0	0	1.000	0	0	0	0	-	0
Adam, Jason	13.2	0	2	1	0	.667	3	1	0	0	.33	0
Adams, Austin L	4.0	0	1	0	0	1.000	0	0	0	0	-	0
Adams, Chance	8.2	0	1	0	0	1.000	1	0	0	0	.00	0
Akin, Keegan	25.2	1	2	0	0	1.000	0	0	0	1	-	1
Alcala, Jorge	24.0	2	1	0	0	1.000	3	2	1	0	.67	-1
Alcantara, Sandy	42.0	1	4	0	0	1.000	5	2	0	0	.40	-1
Alexander, Scott	12.1	0	3	0	0	1.000	0	0	0	0	-	0
Alexander, Tyler	36.1	1	7	0	1	1.000	6	4	3	0	.67	2
Allard, Kolby	33.2	0	2	0	0	1.000	1	1	0	0	1.00	0
Allen, Logan	10.2	0	1	0	0	1.000	1	0	0	0	.00	0
Almonte, Yency	27.2	3	1	0	0	1.000	4	1	0	0	.25	0
Altavilla, Dan	20.1	0	3	0	0	1.000	3	0	0	0	.00	0
Alvarado, Jose	9.0	0	1	0	0	1.000	1	0	0	0	.00	0
Alvarez, Jose	6.1	0	2	0	0	1.000	2	1	1	0	.50	0
Alzolay, Adbert	21.1	0	3	0	0	1.000	3	1	0	0	.33	0
Anderson, Brett	47.0	2	6	0	0	1.000	2	2	0	0	1.00	1
Anderson, Chase	33.2	1	1	0	0	1.000	1	0	0	0	.00	0
Anderson, Drew	1.1	0	0	0	0	-	0	0	0	0	-	0
Anderson, Ian	32.1	2	1	1	0	.750	1	0	0	0	.00	-1
Anderson, Nick	16.1	1	0	0	0	1.000	0	0	0	0	-	0
Anderson, Shaun	15.1	1	2	0	0	1.000	1	1	0	0	1.00	0
Anderson, Tyler	59.2	2	8	1	1	.909	3	1	1	3	.33	2
Andriese, Matt	32.0	4	3	0	0	1.000	2	0	0	0	.00	0
Antone, Tejay	35.1	6	2	0	1	1.000	3	1	0	0	.33	0
Armstrong, Shawn	15.0	0	0	1	0	.000	2	0	0	0	.00	-1
Arrieta, Jake	44.1	2	8	0	0	1.000	0	0	0	1	-	2
Avilan, Luis	8.1	0	0	0	0	-	1	0	0	0	.00	0
Bacus, Dakota	11.1	1	5	0	0	1.000	0	0	0	0	-	1
Baez, Michel	4.2	0	1	0	0	1.000	0	0	0	0	-	0
Baez, Pedro	17.0	0	0	0	0	-	1	0	0	0	.00	0
Bailey, Brandon	7.1	0	0	0	0	-	1	1	0	0	1.00	0
Bailey, Homer	8.0	0	1	0	0	1.000	0	0	0	0	-	0
Banda, Anthony	7.0	0	0	0	0	-	0	0	0	0	-	-1
Baragar, Caleb	22.1	0	0	0	0	-	2	0	0	0	.00	0
Bard, Daniel	24.2	1	0	1	0	.500	2	0	0	0	.00	-1
Bard, Luke	5.1	0	0	0	0	-	1	0	0	0	.00	0
Barlow, Scott	30.0	0	2	1	0	.667	3	0	0	0	.00	-1
Barnes, Jacob	18.0	2	1	0	0	1.000	0	0	0	0	.00	0
Barnes, Matt	23.0	2	1	0	0	1.000	6	0	0	0	.00	-1
Barrett, Aaron	1.2	0	0	0	0	-	1	0	0	0	.00	0
Barria, Jaime	32.1	2	2	0	0	1.000	3	2	0	0	.67	0
Bashlor, Tyler	8.1	0	0	0	0	-	2	0	0	0	.00	0
Bass, Anthony	25.2	3	3	0	1	1.000	3	2	0	0	.67	0
Bassitt, Chris	63.0	3	4	1	1	.875	3	1	0	0	.33	-1
Bauer, Trevor	73.0	5	6	0	0	1.000	8	2	0	0	.25	0
Beasley, Jeremy	0.1	0	0	0	0	-	0	0	0	0	-	0
Bednar, David	1.0	1	0	0	0	1.000	0	0	0	0	-	0
Bedrosian, Cam	14.2	0	0	0	0	-	5	2	0	0	.40	0
Beeks, Jalen	19.1	1	1	0	0	1.000	0	0	0	0	-	0
Benjamin, Wes	22.1	2	0	0	0	1.000	1	0	0	0	.00	0
Bergen, Travis	8.1	0	0	1	0	.000	1	1	0	0	1.00	0
Berrios, Jose	63.0	1	6	0	0	1.000	3	0	0	2	.00	1
Betances, Dellin	11.2	0	0	0	0	-	2	0	0	0	.00	0
Biagini, Joe	4.1	1	0	0	0	1.000	0	0	0	0	-	0
Bickford, Phil	1.0	0	0	0	0	-	0	0	0	0	-	0
Biddle, Jesse	0.2	0	0	0	0	-	0	0	0	0	-	0
Bieber, Shane	77.1	2	8	1	0	.909	5	3	1	0	.60	0
Bielak, Brandon	32.0	3	4	0	1	1.000	6	0	0	1	.00	-1
Black, Ray	3.0	0	1	0	0	1.000	0	0	0	0	-	0
Blackburn, Paul	2.1	1	0	0	0	1.000	1	0	0	0	.00	0
Bleier, Richard	16.2	0	4	0	0	1.000	0	0	0	0	-	0
Blewett, Scott	3.0	0	0	0	0	-	0	0	0	0	-	0
Bolanos, Ronald	3.2	0	0	0	0	-	1	1	0	0	1.00	0
Borucki, Ryan	16.2	0	1	0	0	1.000	0	0	0	0	-	0
Bourque, James	4.0	0	1	0	0	1.000	0	0	0	0	-	0
Boxberger, Brad	18.0	3	2	0	1	1.000	0	0	0	0	-	1
Boyd, Matthew	60.1	1	3	0	0	1.000	2	1	0	0	.50	0
Brach, Brad	12.1	1	4	0	0	1.000	1	1	0	0	1.00	1
Bracho, Silvino	1.0	0	0	0	0	-	0	0	0	0	-	0

	2020 Fielding and Holding Runners											
Pitcher	Inn	PO	A	E	DP	Pct	SBA	CS	PCS	PPO	CS%	RS
Bradley, Archie	18.1	1	2	0	0	1.000	0	0	0	0	-	0
Brasier, Ryan	25.0	0	1	0	0	1.000	1	1	0	0	1.00	0
Brault, Steven	42.2	1	6	0	1	1.000	1	1	0	0	1.00	1
Braymer, Ben	7.1	0	1	0	0	1.000	0	0	0	0	-	0
Brennan, Brandon	7.1	0	1	0	0	1.000	1	0	0	0	.00	0
Brewer, Colten	25.2	1	3	0	0	1.000	3	0	0	0	.00	1
Brice, Austin	19.2	0	2	0	0	1.000	3	1	0	0	.33	0
Brigham, Jeff	1.0	0	0	0	0	-	0	0	0	0	-	0
Britton, Zack	19.0	1	3	2	0	.667	1	1	0	0	1.00	0
Brogdon, Connor	11.1	0	1	0	0	1.000	0	0	0	0	-	0
Brothers, Rex	3.1	0	0	0	0	-	0	0	0	0	-	0
Brubaker, JT	47.1	3	2	0	1	1.000	4	2	0	0	.50	0
Bubic, Kris	50.0	1	3	0	0	1.000	1	0	0	0	.00	0
Buchter, Ryan	6.0	0	0	0	0	-	1	0	0	0	.00	0
Buehler, Walker	36.2	3	3	0	0	1.000	6	1	0	0	.17	0
Bumgarner, M.	41.2	2	3	2	0	.714	4	0	0	0	.00	0
Bummer, Aaron	9.1	0	0	1	0	.000	0	0	0	0	-	0
Bundy, Dylan	65.2	7	6	0	0	1.000	11	1	0	0	.09	1
Burdi, Nick	2.1	0	0	0	0	-	0	0	0	0	-	0
Burdi, Zack	7.1	0	1	0	0	1.000	0	0	0	0	-	0
Burnes, Corbin	59.2	2	7	2	0	.818	10	1	0	0	.10	-1
Burrows, Beau	6.2	1	0	0	0	1.000	0	0	0	0	-	0
Buttrey, Ty	26.1	2	1	0	0	1.000	3	1	0	0	.33	0
Cabrera, Genesis	22.1	0	0	0	0	-	1	0	0	0	.00	-1
Cahill, Trevor	25.0	1	3	0	0	1.000	8	2	0	0	.25	-1
Canning, Griffin	56.1	7	8	1	0	.938	9	5	0	2	.56	3
Carrasco, Carlos	68.0	2	6	1	0	.889	4	2	0	0	.50	0
Carroll, Cody	2.0	0	0	0	0	-	0	0	0	0	-	0
Castano, Daniel	29.2	0	3	0	0	1.000	1	1	0	1	1.00	1
Castellani, Ryan	43.1	4	3	0	1	1.000	3	1	0	0	.33	0
Castellanos, H.	10.2	0	1	0	0	1.000	0	0	0	0	-	0
Castillo, Diego	21.2	2	1	0	0	1.000	0	0	0	0	-	0
Castillo, Luis	70.0	7	10	0	0	1.000	4	2	0	0	.50	2
Castro, Anthony	1.0	0	0	0	0	-	0	0	0	0	-	0
Castro, Miguel	24.2	1	1	0	0	1.000	5	0	0	0	.00	-1
Cease, Dylan	58.1	6	3	0	0	1.000	4	1	0	0	.25	0
Cederlind, Blake	4.0	0	0	0	0	-	0	0	0	0	-	0
Cessa, Luis	21.2	4	2	0	0	1.000	1	1	0	0	1.00	0
Chacin, Jhoulys	5.0	0	0	0	0	-	1	0	0	0	.00	0
Chafin, Andrew	9.2	1	2	0	0	1.000	1	1	1	0	1.00	0
Chapman, Aroldis	11.2	0	0	0	0	-	5	1	0	0	.20	-1
Chatwood, Tyler	18.2	0	1	0	0	1.000	2	0	0	0	.00	0
Chavez, Jesse	17.0	0	1	0	0	1.000	0	0	0	0	-	-1
Chirinos, Yonny	11.1	0	1	0	0	1.000	1	1	0	0	1.00	0
Cimber, Adam	11.1	0	3	0	0	1.000	2	0	0	0	.00	0
Cishek, Steve	20.0	1	0	0	0	1.000	0	0	0	0	-	0
Cisnero, Jose	29.2	2	1	0	0	1.000	1	0	0	0	.00	-1
Civale, Aaron	74.0	5	8	1	2	.929	8	3	0	0	.38	0
Clarke, Taylor	43.1	5	3	0	1	1.000	1	0	0	2	.00	0
Claudio, Alex	19.0	3	4	0	0	1.000	0	0	0	0	-	1
Cleavinger, Garrett	0.2	0	0	0	0	-	0	0	0	0	-	0
Clevinger, Mike	41.2	2	4	1	0	.857	5	4	1	0	.80	-1
Clippard, Tyler	26.0	1	1	0	0	1.000	5	0	0	0	.00	-2
Cobb, Alex	52.1	1	8	2	0	.818	3	2	0	0	.67	0
Cody, Kyle	22.2	3	3	1	1	.857	2	0	0	0	.00	0
Cole, A.J.	23.1	1	2	0	0	1.000	0	0	0	0	-	-1
Cole, Gerrit	73.0	5	2	0	0	1.000	2	1	0	0	.50	1
Colina, Edwar	0.1	0	0	0	0	-	0	0	0	0	-	0
Colome, Alex	22.1	1	3	0	0	1.000	2	0	0	0	.00	-1
Coonrod, Sam	14.2	2	2	0	0	1.000	3	0	0	0	.00	0
Corbin, Patrick	65.2	1	8	1	1	.900	6	2	2	0	.33	-2
Cordero, Jimmy	26.2	1	3	1	0	.800	4	2	0	0	.50	0
Cortes, Nestor	7.2	0	0	0	0	-	0	0	0	0	-	0
Coulombe, Daniel	2.2	0	0	0	0	-	0	0	0	0	-	0
Covey, Dylan	14.0	0	1	0	0	1.000	1	1	0	0	1.00	-1
Crichton, Stefan	26.0	1	0	0	0	1.000	5	1	0	0	.20	0
Crick, Kyle	5.2	1	0	1	0	.500	1	0	0	0	.00	-1
Crismatt, Nabil	8.1	1	4	0	1	1.000	0	0	0	0	-	-1
Crochet, Garrett	6.0	0	0	0	0	-	0	0	0	0	-	-1
Crowe, Wil	8.1	1	0	0	0	1.000	1	1	0	0	1.00	0
Cruz, Jesus	1.0	0	0	0	0	-	0	0	0	0	-	0

Pitcher	Inn	PO	A	E	DP	Pct	SBA	CS	PCS	PPO	CS%	RS
Cueto, Johnny	63.1	3	5	0	0	1.000	2	0	0	0	.00	2
Curtiss, John	25.0	0	1	0	0	1.000	2	1	0	0	.50	-1
Darvish, Yu	76.0	4	10	1	2	.933	4	0	0	1	.00	1
Davidson, Tucker	1.2	0	0	0	0	-	1	0	0	0	.00	0
Davies, Zach	69.1	5	7	0	0	1.000	2	0	0	0	.00	-1
Davis, Austin	6.2	0	0	0	0	-	2	0	0	0	.00	0
Davis, Wade	4.1	0	0	0	0	-	1	0	0	0	.00	0
Dayton, Grant	27.1	1	3	0	0	1.000	2	0	0	0	.00	0
De Jong, Chase	7.1	0	0	0	0	-	1	0	0	0	.00	0
De Leon, Jose	6.0	1	0	0	0	1.000	1	0	0	0	.00	0
deGrom, Jacob	68.0	7	8	0	0	1.000	15	2	0	0	.13	-2
Del Pozo, Miguel	3.2	1	0	0	0	1.000	1	1	0	0	1.00	0
Dermody, Matt	1.0	0	0	0	0	-	0	0	0	0	-	0
DeSclafani, A.	33.2	4	3	0	0	1.000	3	0	0	0	.00	0
Detwiler, Ross	19.2	1	5	0	0	1.000	3	2	2	0	.67	1
Devenski, Chris	3.2	0	1	0	0	1.000	2	0	0	0	.00	0
Diaz, Edwin	25.2	0	0	1	0	.000	2	0	0	0	.00	-1
Diaz, Jairo	20.0	1	3	0	0	1.000	0	0	0	0	-	0
Diehl, Phillip	6.0	0	2	0	0	1.000	0	0	0	0	-	0
Diekman, Jake	21.1	2	0	0	0	1.000	0	0	0	0	-	0
Dobnak, Randy	46.2	5	6	0	0	1.000	3	1	0	0	.33	0
Dolis, Rafael	24.0	0	2	2	0	.500	2	0	0	1	.00	-1
Doolittle, Sean	7.2	0	1	0	0	1.000	0	0	0	0	-	0
Doyle, Tommy	2.1	0	1	0	0	1.000	0	0	0	0	-	0
Drake, Oliver	11.0	2	1	0	0	1.000	1	0	0	0	.00	0
Duffey, Tyler	24.0	0	3	0	0	1.000	0	0	0	0	-	1
Duffy, Danny	56.1	0	5	0	1	1.000	0	0	0	0	-	-1
Dugger, Robert	10.2	1	0	0	0	1.000	0	0	0	0	-	0
Dunn, Justin	45.2	3	1	0	0	1.000	14	1	0	0	.07	-2
Dunning, Dane	34.0	3	3	1	0	.857	3	0	0	0	.00	1
Edwards Jr., Carl	4.2	0	0	0	0	-	1	0	0	0	.00	0
Eflin, Zach	59.0	1	9	0	0	1.000	2	1	0	0	.50	1
Eibner, Brett	3.1	0	0	0	0	-	0	0	0	0	-	0
Elledge, Seth	11.2	0	0	0	0	-	2	2	0	0	1.00	0
Eovaldi, Nathan	48.1	2	7	0	1	1.000	2	1	0	1	.50	3
Erlin, Robbie	26.2	0	5	0	0	1.000	2	0	0	0	.00	1
Eshelman, T.	34.2	1	2	0	0	1.000	3	2	0	0	.67	0
Espino, Paolo	6.0	0	0	0	0	-	0	0	0	0	-	0
Estevez, Carlos	24.0	1	1	0	0	1.000	1	0	0	0	.00	0
Evans, Demarcus	4.0	0	0	0	0	-	0	0	0	0	-	0
Fairbanks, Pete	26.2	5	1	0	0	1.000	8	1	0	0	.13	-1
Familia, Jeurys	26.2	1	4	0	0	1.000	7	1	0	0	.14	-1
Farmer, Buck	21.1	2	0	0	0	1.000	2	0	0	0	.00	-1
Farrell, Luke	5.1	0	0	0	0	-	0	0	0	0	-	0
Fedde, Erick	50.1	4	12	0	2	1.000	7	2	0	0	.29	2
Feliz, Michael	1.2	0	0	0	0	-	0	0	0	0	-	0
Ferguson, Caleb	18.2	0	3	1	1	.750	3	0	0	0	.00	0
Fernandez, Junior	3.0	0	1	0	0	1.000	0	0	0	0	-	0
Feyereisen, J.P.	9.1	0	1	0	0	1.000	0	0	0	0	-	0
Fiers, Mike	59.0	3	5	0	0	1.000	9	2	0	2	.22	-1
Finnegan, Kyle	24.2	3	5	1	1	.889	3	0	0	0	.00	-1
Flaherty, Jack	40.1	1	4	0	0	1.000	1	1	0	0	1.00	1
Fleming, Josh	32.1	0	8	0	1	1.000	1	1	0	0	1.00	1
Fletcher, Aaron	4.1	0	0	0	0	-	0	0	0	0	-	0
Flores Jr., B.	2.0	0	0	0	0	-	0	0	0	0	-	0
Floro, Dylan	24.1	1	7	0	2	1.000	0	0	0	0	-	1
Foltynewicz, Mike	3.1	0	0	0	0	-	0	0	0	0	-	0
Font, Wilmer	16.1	0	1	0	0	1.000	1	0	0	0	.00	-1
Foster, Matt	28.2	0	5	0	0	1.000	0	0	0	0	-	1
Frankoff, Seth	2.2	0	0	0	0	-	1	0	0	0	.00	0
Freeland, Kyle	70.2	3	11	1	1	.933	3	0	0	0	.00	0
Freeman, Sam	5.0	0	0	0	0	-	0	0	0	0	-	0
Fried, Max	56.0	1	15	1	1	.941	4	1	0	4	.25	5
Fry, Jace	19.2	1	0	1	0	.500	1	1	0	0	1.00	-1
Fry, Paul	22.0	2	1	0	0	1.000	1	0	0	0	.00	-1
Fulmer, Carson	10.1	1	1	0	0	1.000	0	0	0	0	-	0
Fulmer, Michael	27.2	2	3	0	2	1.000	3	0	0	0	.00	-1
Funkhouser, Kyle	17.1	2	1	0	0	1.000	2	0	0	0	.00	0
Gallegos, G.	15.0	0	0	0	0	-	1	0	0	0	.00	0
Gallen, Zac	72.0	3	4	0	1	1.000	8	1	1	0	.13	-2
Gant, John	15.0	1	2	0	0	1.000	0	0	0	0	-	0
Garcia, Bryan	21.2	0	1	1	0	.500	2	1	0	0	.50	-1
Garcia, Deivi	34.1	2	2	2	0	.667	3	1	0	0	.33	-1

Pitcher	Inn	PO	A	E	DP	Pct	SBA	CS	PCS	PPO	CS%	RS
Garcia, Edgar	3.1	1	0	0	1	1.000	0	0	0	0	-	0
Garcia, Jarlin	18.1	1	1	0	0	1.000	0	0	0	0	-	0
Garcia, Luis (Tex)	8.1	0	0	0	0	-	0	0	0	0	-	0
Garcia, Luis (Hou)	12.1	0	0	0	0	-	0	0	0	0	-	0
Garcia, Rico	10.0	1	0	0	0	1.000	0	0	0	0	-	0
Garcia, Rony	21.0	4	2	1	0	.857	0	0	0	0	-	1
Garcia, Yimi	15.0	1	1	1	0	.667	0	0	0	0	-	1
Garrett, Amir	18.1	0	0	1	0	.000	1	0	0	0	.00	0
Garrett, Braxton	7.2	0	1	0	0	1.000	0	0	0	0	-	0
Gausman, Kevin	59.2	3	2	0	1	1.000	6	1	0	1	.17	-1
Gaviglio, Sam	3.0	0	0	0	0	-	0	0	0	0	-	0
Gearrin, Cory	2.0	0	0	0	0	-	1	1	0	0	1.00	0
Gerber, Joey	15.2	2	0	0	1	1.000	1	0	0	0	.00	0
Gibaut, Ian	12.1	0	2	1	0	.667	1	0	0	0	.00	1
Gibson, Kyle	67.1	6	6	0	0	1.000	8	3	0	0	.38	0
Giles, Ken	3.2	0	0	0	0	-	0	0	0	0	-	0
Gilmartin, Sean	4.1	0	0	0	0	-	0	0	0	0	-	0
Ginkel, Kevin	16.0	1	0	0	0	1.000	6	1	0	0	.17	-1
Giolito, Lucas	72.1	2	5	1	0	.875	2	1	1	0	.50	1
Givens, Mychal	22.1	0	0	1	0	.000	4	1	0	0	.25	-1
Glasnow, Tyler	57.1	4	5	0	0	1.000	11	2	1	0	.18	-2
Godley, Zack	28.2	2	2	0	0	1.000	3	1	1	0	.33	-1
Gomber, Austin	29.0	0	2	0	0	1.000	1	1	0	0	1.00	0
Gonsolin, Tony	46.2	4	4	0	0	1.000	3	1	0	0	.33	1
Gonzales, Marco	69.2	1	6	0	1	1.000	0	0	0	0	-	0
Gonzalez, Chi Chi	19.2	1	3	0	0	1.000	0	0	0	0	-	0
Gonzalez, Gio	31.2	1	2	0	0	1.000	1	1	0	1	1.00	1
Gonzalez, Victor	20.1	1	2	0	0	1.000	1	0	0	0	.00	0
Goody, Nick	11.0	0	1	0	0	1.000	0	0	0	0	-	0
Gott, Trevor	11.2	1	0	0	0	1.000	0	0	0	0	-	0
Goudeau, Ashton	8.1	2	1	0	1	1.000	1	1	0	0	1.00	0
Grace, Matt	1.0	0	0	0	0	-	0	0	0	0	-	-1
Graterol, Brusdar	23.1	3	5	0	2	1.000	1	0	0	0	.00	0
Graveman, K.	18.2	2	1	0	0	1.000	1	0	0	0	.00	0
Gray, Jon	39.0	5	2	0	0	1.000	2	1	0	0	.50	0
Gray, Sonny	56.0	5	6	1	0	.917	2	1	0	0	.50	0
Green, Chad	25.2	0	3	0	0	1.000	3	0	0	0	.00	0
Greene, Shane	27.2	1	2	0	0	1.000	3	1	0	0	.33	0
Greinke, Zack	67.0	9	7	0	3	1.000	1	0	0	0	.00	1
Griffin, Foster	1.2	0	0	0	0	-	0	0	0	0	-	0
Grimm, Justin	4.2	0	0	0	0	-	0	0	0	0	-	0
Grotz, Zac	7.1	1	0	0	0	1.000	0	0	0	0	-	0
Gsellman, Robert	14.0	1	1	1	0	.667	1	0	0	0	.00	0
Guerra, Deolis	7.1	3	0	0	0	1.000	0	0	0	0	-	-1
Guerra, Javy (SD)	13.1	0	3	0	0	1.000	1	0	0	0	.00	0
Guerra, Javy (Was)	15.2	0	0	0	0	-	0	0	0	0	-	0
Guerra, Junior	23.2	2	3	1	0	.833	0	0	0	0	-	-2
Guilbeau, Taylor	7.2	1	0	0	0	1.000	1	0	0	0	.00	0
Guzman, Jorge	1.0	0	0	0	0	-	0	0	0	0	-	0
Hader, Josh	19.0	2	1	0	0	1.000	0	0	0	0	-	0
Hahn, Jesse	17.1	1	1	0	0	1.000	2	0	0	0	.00	0
Hale, David	17.0	0	4	0	0	1.000	1	0	0	1	.00	0
Hall, Matt	8.2	0	0	0	0	-	2	0	0	0	.00	0
Hamels, Cole	3.1	0	0	0	0	-	0	0	0	0	-	0
Hamilton, Ian	4.0	0	0	0	0	-	0	0	0	0	-	0
Hand, Brad	22.0	0	1	0	0	1.000	0	0	0	0	-	0
Happ, J.A.	49.1	2	5	0	0	1.000	3	2	0	0	.67	1
Harper, Ryne	23.2	1	2	0	0	1.000	1	0	0	0	.00	0
Harris, Will	17.2	0	1	1	0	.500	3	0	0	0	.00	-1
Hart, Kyle	11.0	0	1	0	0	1.000	0	0	0	0	-	0
Hartlieb, Geoff	22.1	2	3	1	0	.833	0	0	0	0	-	0
Harvey, Hunter	8.2	1	0	0	0	1.000	1	1	0	0	1.00	0
Harvey, Joe	3.1	0	0	0	0	-	0	0	0	0	-	0
Harvey, Matt	11.2	1	1	0	0	1.000	1	0	0	0	.00	0
Hatch, Thomas	26.1	1	3	0	0	1.000	3	1	0	0	.33	0
Heaney, Andrew	66.2	3	6	0	1	1.000	8	2	1	0	.25	0
Hearn, Taylor	17.1	0	0	0	0	-	3	1	0	0	.33	0
Heller, Ben	6.0	0	0	0	0	-	0	0	0	0	-	0
Helsley, Ryan	12.0	0	0	0	0	-	0	0	0	0	-	0
Hembree, Heath	19.0	1	1	0	0	1.000	5	0	0	0	.00	-1
Hendricks, Kyle	81.1	7	13	0	0	1.000	4	4	2	0	1.00	3
Hendriks, Liam	25.1	4	1	0	0	1.000	2	0	0	0	.00	0
Herget, Jimmy	19.2	0	1	0	0	1.000	1	0	0	0	.00	-1

Pitcher	Inn	PO	A	E	DP	Pct	SBA	CS	PCS	PPO	CS%	RS
2020 Fielding and Holding Runners												
Hernandez, Carlos	14.2	0	0	1	0	.000	1	0	0	0	.00	-1
Hernandez, D.	8.1	0	0	0	0		0	0	0	0	-	0
Hernandez, E.	25.2	1	2	2	0	.600	1	0	0	0	.00	0
Hernandez, J.	31.0	2	4	1	1	.857	1	0	0	0	.00	1
Herrera, Kelvin	2.1	0	0	0	0	-	0	0	0	0	-	0
Hess, David	7.0	1	0	0	0	1.000	0	0	0	0	-	0
Heuer, Codi	23.2	3	1	0	0	1.000	0	0	0	0	-	0
Hill, Cam	18.1	5	1	0	0	1.000	0	0	0	0	-	0
Hill, Rich	38.2	0	4	1	0	.800	5	1	1	0	.20	0
Hill, Tim	18.0	1	5	0	0	1.000	0	0	0	0	-	0
Hirano, Yoshihisa	12.1	0	3	0	1	1.000	0	0	0	0	-	0
Hoffman, Jeff	21.1	1	1	0	1	1.000	3	1	0	0	.33	0
Holder, Jonathan	21.2	1	1	0	0	1.000	0	0	0	0	-	-1
Holland, Derek	40.2	2	3	2	0	.714	1	1	1	1	1.00	1
Holland, Greg	28.1	0	1	0	0	1.000	2	0	0	0	.00	0
Holloway, Jordan	0.1	0	0	0	0	-	0	0	0	0	-	0
Holmes, Clay	1.1	1	0	0	0	1.000	0	0	0	0	-	0
Houck, Tanner	17.0	0	2	0	0	1.000	0	0	0	0	-	0
Houser, Adrian	56.0	2	7	0	0	1.000	9	5	0	0	.56	-1
Howard, Sam	21.0	1	2	0	0	1.000	3	1	1	0	.33	0
Howard, Spencer	24.1	3	1	0	0	1.000	1	0	0	0	.00	0
Hoyt, James	14.2	1	1	2	0	.500	2	0	0	0	.00	0
Hudson, Dakota	39.0	5	4	0	0	1.000	2	1	0	0	.50	0
Hudson, Daniel	20.2	0	3	0	0	1.000	0	0	0	0	-	1
Hughes, Jared	22.1	1	8	0	0	1.000	2	0	0	0	.00	1
Hunter, Tommy	24.2	1	5	0	1	1.000	3	1	0	0	.33	0
Iglesias, Raisel	23.0	2	6	0	0	1.000	1	0	0	0	.00	1
Irvin, Cole	3.2	0	0	0	0	-	0	0	0	0	-	0
Jackson, Luke	26.1	0	2	0	0	1.000	1	0	0	0	.00	0
James, Josh	17.1	1	1	0	0	1.000	3	1	0	0	.33	0
Jansen, Kenley	24.1	1	0	0	0	1.000	2	0	0	0	.00	-1
Javier, Cristian	54.1	3	2	0	1	1.000	3	2	0	0	.67	0
Jefferies, Daulton	2.0	1	0	0	0	1.000	0	0	0	0	-	0
Jeffress, Jeremy	23.1	1	1	0	0	1.000	0	0	0	0	-	0
Jimenez, Dany	1.1	0	0	0	0	-	0	0	0	0	-	0
Jimenez, Joe	22.2	0	1	0	0	1.000	4	0	0	0	.00	-1
Johnson, Pierce	20.0	0	2	0	0	1.000	1	1	0	1	1.00	1
Jones, Nate	18.2	0	0	0	0	-	1	0	0	0	.00	-2
Junis, Jakob	25.1	1	3	0	2	1.000	1	0	0	0	.00	0
Jurado, Ariel	4.0	0	1	0	0	1.000	0	0	0	0	-	0
Kahnle, Tommy	1.0	0	0	0	0	-	0	0	0	0	-	0
Kaminsky, Rob	4.2	0	0	0	0	-	0	0	0	0	-	-1
Kaprielian, James	3.2	0	0	0	0	-	0	0	0	0	-	0
Karinchak, James	27.0	0	0	0	0	-	3	2	0	0	.67	0
Kay, Anthony	21.0	0	2	0	0	1.000	1	1	0	1	1.00	0
Kela, Keone	2.0	0	0	0	0	-	1	0	0	0	.00	0
Keller, Brad	54.2	4	7	0	0	1.000	0	0	0	0	-	0
Keller, Kyle	2.1	0	0	0	0	-	2	0	0	0	.00	0
Keller, Mitch	21.2	3	4	0	0	1.000	2	1	0	0	.50	1
Kelley, Trevor	3.1	0	0	0	0	-	0	0	0	0	-	0
Kelly, Joe	10.0	0	2	0	1	1.000	1	1	0	0	1.00	0
Kelly, Merrill	31.1	7	3	0	0	1.000	3	0	0	0	.00	0
Kennedy, Ian	14.0	0	1	1	0	.500	1	0	0	0	.00	-1
Kershaw, Clayton	58.1	1	4	0	0	1.000	2	1	1	0	.50	0
Keuchel, Dallas	63.1	2	6	0	0	1.000	2	1	0	0	.50	0
Kickham, Mike	14.0	1	2	0	0	1.000	1	1	0	0	1.00	0
Kikuchi, Yusei	47.0	3	5	0	0	1.000	5	0	0	0	.00	1
Kilome, Franklyn	11.1	0	3	0	0	1.000	1	0	0	0	.00	0
Kim, Kwang-hyun	39.0	1	3	0	0	1.000	0	0	0	0	-	0
Kimbrel, Craig	15.1	0	1	0	0	1.000	2	0	0	1	.00	0
King, John	10.1	1	1	0	0	1.000	1	0	0	0	.00	0
King, Michael	26.2	2	4	1	0	.857	0	0	0	0	-	1
Kinley, Tyler	23.2	3	4	1	1	1.000	0	0	0	1	-	1
Kintzler, Brandon	24.1	2	3	1	0	.833	3	0	0	0	.00	1
Kittredge, Andrew	8.0	0	2	0	0	1.000	1	0	0	0	.00	0
Kline, Branden	5.0	1	0	0	0	1.000	0	0	0	0	-	0
Kluber, Corey	1.0	0	0	0	0	-	1	1	0	0	1.00	0
Knebel, Corey	13.1	2	1	0	0	1.000	2	1	0	0	.50	0
Kolarek, Adam	19.0	2	4	0	0	1.000	0	0	0	0	-	1
Kremer, Dean	18.2	2	1	0	0	1.000	0	0	0	0	-	0
Kriske, Brooks	3.2	0	0	0	0	-	0	0	0	0	-	0
Kuhl, Chad	46.1	6	5	0	1	1.000	4	2	0	0	.50	-1
Kuhnel, Joel	3.0	0	0	0	0	-	0	0	0	0	-	0

Pitcher	Inn	PO	A	E	DP	Pct	SBA	CS	PCS	PPO	CS%	RS
2020 Fielding and Holding Runners												
Lail, Brady	16.1	1	1	0	0	1.000	2	0	0	0	.00	0
Lakins, Travis	25.2	1	0	0	0	1.000	2	0	0	0	.00	0
Lambert, Jimmy	2.0	0	1	0	0	1.000	0	0	0	0	-	0
Lamet, Dinelson	69.0	3	2	0	0	1.000	5	1	0	0	.20	0
Lauer, Eric	11.0	0	0	0	0	-	0	0	0	0	-	0
LeBlanc, Wade	22.1	1	4	0	0	1.000	1	0	0	0	.00	1
Leclerc, Jose	2.0	0	0	0	0	-	0	0	0	0	-	0
Leibrandt, B.	9.0	1	0	0	0	1.000	0	0	0	0	-	0
Leone, Dominic	9.2	1	3	0	0	1.000	0	0	0	0	-	1
Lester, Jon	61.0	2	4	1	0	.857	5	2	0	0	.40	0
Lewicki, Artie	3.1	0	0	0	0	-	0	0	0	0	-	0
Leyer, Robinson	4.2	0	0	0	0	-	0	0	0	0	-	0
Lindblom, Josh	45.1	2	1	0	0	1.000	7	3	1	0	.43	0
Littell, Zack	6.1	0	2	0	1	1.000	0	0	0	1	-	0
Llovera, Mauricio	1.0	0	1	0	0	1.000	0	0	0	0	-	0
Loaisiga, Jonathan	23.0	1	5	0	0	1.000	1	1	0	0	1.00	1
Lockett, Walker	16.1	2	1	0	1	1.000	1	1	0	0	1.00	1
Lopez, Jorge	39.0	4	5	0	1	1.000	2	1	0	0	.50	0
Lopez, Pablo	57.1	11	4	0	0	1.000	6	1	0	0	.17	1
Lopez, Reynaldo	26.1	0	1	0	0	1.000	2	1	0	0	.50	0
Lopez, Yoan	19.2	2	1	0	1	1.000	1	0	0	0	.00	-1
Lorenzen, Michael	33.2	3	4	0	0	1.000	4	2	0	0	.50	0
Loup, Aaron	25.0	2	4	0	0	1.000	1	1	1	0	1.00	0
Lovelady, Richard	1.0	0	0	0	0	-	0	0	0	0	-	0
Lucchesi, Joey	5.2	0	1	1	0	.500	0	0	0	0	-	-1
Lugo, Seth	36.2	4	3	0	0	1.000	0	0	0	0	-	0
Luzardo, Jesus	59.0	6	6	1	1	.923	2	1	0	0	.50	0
Lyles, Jordan	57.2	1	8	2	0	.818	3	1	1	0	.33	1
Lynn, Lance	84.0	2	4	0	1	1.000	6	0	0	0	.00	-2
Lyons, Tyler	1.2	0	0	0	0	-	0	0	0	0	-	0
Maeda, Kenta	66.2	1	11	1	0	.923	4	1	0	1	.25	1
Magill, Matt	10.1	0	0	0	0	-	0	0	0	0	-	0
Mahle, Tyler	47.2	0	6	0	1	1.000	2	1	0	0	.50	1
Manaea, Sean	54.0	0	5	0	0	1.000	3	1	0	0	.33	-3
Mantiply, Joe	2.1	0	0	0	0	-	0	0	0	0	-	0
Maples, Dillon	1.0	0	0	0	0	-	0	0	0	0	-	0
Margevicius, Nick	41.1	2	4	0	1	1.000	3	1	0	0	.33	0
Marquez, Brailyn	0.2	0	0	0	0	-	0	0	0	0	-	0
Marquez, German	81.2	6	3	3	1	.750	4	0	0	0	.00	-2
Marshall, Evan	22.2	0	2	0	0	1.000	0	0	0	0	-	0
Martin, Brett	14.2	1	0	0	0	1.000	0	0	0	0	-	0
Martin, Chris	18.0	2	4	1	0	.857	0	0	0	0	-	0
Martinez, Carlos	20.0	3	3	1	1	.857	0	0	0	0	-	0
Maton, Phil	21.2	1	2	0	0	1.000	1	0	0	0	.00	0
Matz, Steven	30.2	0	2	0	0	1.000	1	1	0	0	1.00	0
Matzek, Tyler	29.0	0	4	1	0	.800	2	0	0	0	.00	-1
May, Dustin	56.0	1	6	1	0	.875	7	2	1	0	.29	0
May, Trevor	23.1	0	2	0	0	1.000	1	0	0	1	.00	0
Mayers, Mike	30.0	1	2	1	0	.750	1	1	0	0	1.00	-1
Mazza, Chris	30.0	0	4	1	0	.800	5	1	0	0	.20	0
McCarthy, Kevin	6.0	0	0	0	0	-	0	0	0	0	-	-1
McClain, Reggie	5.1	0	1	0	0	1.000	0	0	0	0	-	0
McCullers Jr., L.	55.0	11	6	1	0	.944	3	1	0	0	.33	2
McFarland, T.J.	20.2	3	5	0	0	1.000	2	1	1	0	.50	1
McGee, Jake	20.1	0	1	0	0	1.000	0	0	0	0	-	0
McGowin, Kyle	11.0	0	0	0	0	-	1	0	0	0	.00	0
McKay, David	0.1	0	0	0	0	-	1	0	0	0	.00	0
McKenzie, Triston	33.1	0	4	0	0	1.000	3	2	0	0	.67	1
McRae, Alex	3.0	0	0	0	0	-	0	0	0	0	-	0
Means, John	43.2	0	6	0	0	1.000	3	1	1	0	.33	0
Mears, Nick	5.0	0	0	0	0	-	0	0	0	0	-	0
Medina, Adonis	4.0	1	2	0	0	1.000	0	0	0	0	-	0
Meisinger, Ryan	2.2	0	0	0	0	-	0	0	0	0	-	0
Mejia, Humberto	10.0	0	0	0	0	-	2	1	0	0	.50	0
Melancon, Mark	22.2	3	6	0	2	1.000	2	1	0	0	.50	0
Mella, Keury	10.0	0	1	0	0	1.000	3	1	1	0	.33	0
Menez, Conner	11.1	1	1	1	0	.667	2	0	0	0	.00	0
Mengden, Daniel	12.1	1	0	0	0	1.000	1	0	0	0	.00	0
Merryweather, J.	13.0	0	3	0	0	1.000	0	0	0	0	-	0
Middleton, Keynan	12.0	1	1	0	0	1.000	3	0	0	0	.00	-1
Miley, Wade	14.1	3	1	0	0	1.000	1	0	0	0	.00	0
Miller, Andrew	13.0	0	1	0	0	1.000	0	0	0	0	-	0
Miller, Tyson	5.0	0	2	0	0	1.000	0	0	0	0	-	0

Pitcher	Inn	PO	A	E	DP	Pct	SBA	CS	PCS	PPO	CS%	RS
Mills, Alec	62.1	4	12	0	1	1.000	3	2	0	1	.67	3
Milner, Hoby	13.1	1	1	0	1	1.000	0	0	0	0	-	0
Milone, Tommy	39.0	0	2	0	0	1.000	2	0	0	1	.00	-1
Minor, Mike	56.2	4	6	1	0	.909	5	1	1	0	.20	0
Minter, A.J.	21.2	0	4	0	0	1.000	1	0	0	0	.00	0
Misiewicz, A.	20.0	2	1	0	0	1.000	1	0	0	1	.00	0
Mize, Casey	28.1	0	5	0	0	1.000	4	0	0	0	.00	-1
Montas, Frankie	53.0	3	1	0	0	1.000	2	1	0	0	.50	-1
Montero, Rafael	17.2	2	0	0	0	1.000	0	0	0	0	-	0
Montgomery, J.	44.0	1	4	3	0	.625	4	0	0	0	.00	-2
Montgomery, Mike	5.1	0	0	0	0	-	1	0	0	0	.00	0
Moran, Brian	4.2	0	0	0	0	-	2	0	0	0	.00	0
Morejon, Adrian	19.1	0	3	0	0	1.000	2	1	1	0	.50	1
Morgan, Adam	13.0	0	0	1	0	.000	0	0	0	0	-	-2
Morin, Mike	4.0	0	0	0	0	-	1	1	0	0	1.00	0
Morton, Charlie	38.0	2	1	0	0	1.000	2	2	0	0	1.00	1
Mujica, Jose	4.1	0	1	0	0	1.000	0	0	0	0	-	0
Murphy, Patrick	6.0	0	1	0	0	1.000	0	0	0	0	-	0
Musgrove, Joe	39.2	7	8	0	0	1.000	3	2	1	0	.67	2
Neidert, Nick	8.1	1	0	0	0	1.000	1	1	0	0	1.00	0
Nelson, Kyle	0.2	0	0	0	0	-	0	0	0	0	-	0
Nelson, Nick	20.2	1	1	0	0	1.000	1	0	0	0	.00	0
Neris, Hector	21.2	1	2	0	0	1.000	2	0	0	0	.00	0
Neverauskas, D.	19.0	1	5	0	0	1.000	2	0	0	0	.00	1
Newberry, Jake	22.0	0	0	1	0	.000	0	0	0	0	-	-1
Newcomb, Sean	13.2	0	2	0	0	1.000	1	0	0	0	.00	0
Newsome, Ljay	15.2	0	1	0	0	1.000	0	0	0	0	-	0
Nicasio, Juan	1.1	0	0	0	0	-	0	0	0	0	-	0
Nola, Aaron	71.1	5	4	0	0	1.000	9	2	0	0	.22	-2
Norris, Daniel	27.2	2	4	0	0	1.000	3	0	0	0	.00	0
Norwood, James	1.2	1	0	0	1	1.000	0	0	0	0	-	0
Nova, Ivan	19.0	2	5	0	0	1.000	0	0	0	0	-	2
O'Day, Darren	16.1	1	2	1	0	.750	3	0	0	0	.00	-1
Odorizzi, Jake	13.2	0	0	0	0	-	2	2	0	0	1.00	0
Ohtani, Shohei	1.2	0	0	0	0	-	0	0	0	0	-	0
Osich, Josh	18.1	1	1	0	0	1.000	2	1	1	0	.50	-1
Osuna, Roberto	4.1	2	0	0	0	1.000	0	0	0	0	-	0
Oswalt, Corey	13.0	2	1	0	0	1.000	2	0	0	1	.00	0
Ottavino, Adam	18.1	0	2	0	0	1.000	4	0	0	0	.00	-1
Oviedo, Johan	24.2	3	0	0	0	1.000	1	0	0	0	.00	0
Paddack, Chris	59.0	3	7	2	1	.833	5	3	0	0	.60	0
Pagan, Emilio	22.0	1	0	0	0	1.000	0	0	0	0	-	-1
Palumbo, Joseph	2.1	0	1	1	0	.500	0	0	0	0	-	0
Paredes, Enoli	20.2	1	2	0	0	1.000	1	1	0	0	1.00	0
Parker, Blake	16.0	0	2	0	0	1.000	2	1	0	0	.50	0
Patino, Luis	17.1	1	1	0	0	1.000	1	0	0	0	.00	0
Paxton, James	20.1	0	2	0	0	1.000	0	0	0	0	-	0
Payamps, Joel	3.0	0	0	0	0	-	0	0	0	0	-	0
Pazos, James	5.1	2	0	0	1	1.000	4	0	0	0	.00	-1
Peacock, Brad	2.1	0	1	0	0	1.000	0	0	0	0	-	0
Pearson, Nate	18.0	1	1	0	0	1.000	3	0	0	0	.00	0
Pena, Felix	26.2	2	3	0	0	1.000	3	1	0	1	.33	0
Peralta, Freddy	29.1	0	2	2	0	.500	3	0	0	0	.00	0
Peralta, Wandy	27.1	3	8	1	0	.917	1	1	1	2	1.00	2
Perdomo, Angel	2.2	0	0	0	0	-	1	0	0	0	.00	0
Perdomo, Luis	17.1	2	0	1	0	.667	1	0	0	0	.00	0
Perez, Cionel	6.1	0	3	0	0	1.000	0	0	0	0	-	1
Perez, Hector	1.2	0	0	0	0	-	0	0	0	0	-	0
Perez, Martin	62.0	0	3	0	0	1.000	3	2	0	0	.67	0
Perez, Oliver	18.0	0	2	0	0	1.000	0	0	0	0	-	0
Peters, Dillon	1.2	1	0	0	0	1.000	0	0	0	0	-	0
Peterson, David	49.2	3	6	0	0	1.000	0	0	0	1	-	2
Petit, Yusmeiro	21.2	3	1	0	0	1.000	1	0	0	0	.00	-1
Phelps, David	20.2	4	0	0	0	1.000	1	0	0	0	.00	-1
Phillips, Evan	14.1	1	0	0	0	1.000	2	0	0	0	.00	0
Pineda, Michael	26.2	1	2	0	0	1.000	1	0	0	0	.00	-1
Pivetta, Nick	15.2	0	1	0	0	1.000	1	0	0	0	.00	0
Plesac, Zach	55.1	5	8	0	0	1.000	2	1	0	2	.50	2
Plutko, Adam	27.2	1	4	0	1	1.000	1	0	0	0	.00	1
Pomeranz, Drew	18.2	0	1	0	0	1.000	1	0	0	0	.00	-1
Ponce, Cody	17.0	1	0	0	0	1.000	1	1	0	0	1.00	0
Ponce de Leon, D.	32.2	4	1	0	0	1.000	2	0	0	0	.00	0
Poppen, Sean	7.2	0	0	0	0	-	2	0	0	0	.00	0

Pitcher	Inn	PO	A	E	DP	Pct	SBA	CS	PCS	PPO	CS%	RS
Porcello, Rick	59.0	3	4	0	0	1.000	4	0	0	1	.00	0
Pressly, Ryan	21.0	2	2	0	1	1.000	0	0	0	0	-	0
Quantrill, Cal	32.0	0	4	2	0	.667	2	0	0	0	.00	0
Quezada, Johan	3.0	0	0	0	0	-	0	0	0	0	-	0
Quijada, Jose	3.2	0	0	0	0	-	0	0	0	0	-	0
Quintana, Jose	10.0	1	1	0	0	1.000	1	1	0	0	1.00	0
Rainey, Tanner	20.1	1	0	0	0	1.000	2	1	0	0	.50	0
Raley, Brooks	20.0	2	1	0	0	1.000	1	0	0	0	.00	-1
Ramirez, Erasmo	14.1	1	1	0	0	1.000	0	0	0	0	-	0
Ramirez, Nick	10.2	1	2	0	0	1.000	0	0	0	0	-	1
Ramirez, Noe	21.0	2	5	0	0	1.000	7	1	0	0	.14	0
Ramirez, Roel	0.2	0	0	0	0	-	1	1	0	0	1.00	-1
Ramirez, Yohan	20.2	0	1	0	0	1.000	2	0	0	1	.00	0
Ramos, AJ	2.2	0	0	0	0	-	0	0	0	0	-	0
Rasmussen, Drew	15.1	1	2	0	0	1.000	0	0	0	0	-	0
Ray, Robbie	51.2	1	6	0	0	1.000	7	1	1	0	.14	0
Rea, Colin	14.0	4	0	0	0	1.000	1	0	0	0	.00	0
Reed, Cody	12.0	0	0	0	0	-	0	0	0	0	-	0
Reid-Foley, Sean	6.2	0	1	0	0	1.000	3	0	0	0	.00	-1
Reyes, Alex	19.2	3	1	0	0	1.000	1	0	0	0	.00	0
Richards, Garrett	51.1	7	3	0	1	1.000	3	1	1	0	.33	0
Richards, Trevor	32.0	0	3	0	1	1.000	1	0	0	0	.00	0
Rios, Yacksel	4.0	1	1	0	0	1.000	0	0	0	0	-	0
Roark, Tanner	47.2	3	2	0	0	1.000	2	0	0	0	.00	-1
Robles, Hansel	16.2	1	1	0	0	1.000	2	0	0	0	.00	0
Rodon, Carlos	7.2	0	1	0	0	1.000	2	0	0	0	.00	0
Rodriguez, Dereck	4.0	1	0	0	0	1.000	1	1	0	0	1.00	0
Rodriguez, Joely	12.2	0	2	1	0	.667	1	0	0	0	.00	0
Rodriguez, Jose	1.2	0	0	0	0	-	0	0	0	0	-	0
Rodriguez, N.	8.2	2	0	0	0	1.000	2	0	0	0	.00	0
Rodriguez, R.	23.1	2	1	0	0	1.000	3	0	0	0	.00	-1
Roe, Chaz	9.1	0	0	0	0	-	2	0	0	0	.00	0
Rogers, Taylor	20.0	1	1	0	0	1.000	0	0	0	0	-	0
Rogers, Trevor	28.0	0	2	0	0	1.000	3	0	0	0	.00	0
Rogers, Tyler	28.0	3	6	0	0	1.000	1	1	0	0	1.00	1
Romano, Jordan	14.2	3	2	0	0	1.000	2	0	0	0	.00	0
Romano, Sal	1.1	0	0	0	0	-	0	0	0	0	-	0
Romero, JoJo	10.2	1	0	0	0	1.000	0	0	0	0	-	-1
Romero, Seth	2.2	0	1	1	0	.500	0	0	0	0	-	-1
Romo, Sergio	20.0	0	2	0	0	1.000	4	0	0	0	.00	0
Rondon, Hector	20.0	0	2	0	0	1.000	2	0	0	0	.00	0
Rosario, Randy	3.1	0	0	0	0	-	0	0	0	0	-	0
Rosenthal, Trevor	23.2	1	1	0	0	1.000	0	0	0	0	-	0
Rosso, Ramon	9.2	0	0	0	0	-	1	0	0	0	.00	0
Ruiz, Jose	4.0	0	0	0	0	-	0	0	0	0	-	0
Rusin, Chris	3.1	0	0	0	0	-	1	0	0	0	.00	0
Ryan, Kyle	15.2	3	5	0	0	1.000	1	0	0	0	.00	0
Ryu, Hyun-Jin	67.0	1	5	0	0	1.000	2	1	1	0	.50	1
Sadler, Casey	19.1	1	4	0	0	1.000	1	0	0	0	.00	0
Samardzija, Jeff	16.2	3	1	0	0	1.000	0	0	0	0	-	0
Sanabria, Carlos	2.0	0	0	0	0	-	0	0	0	0	-	0
Sanchez, Anibal	53.0	5	5	1	1	.909	13	2	0	0	.15	0
Sanchez, Ricardo	5.1	0	1	0	0	1.000	0	0	0	0	-	0
Sanchez, Sixto	39.0	3	5	0	1	1.000	3	1	0	0	.33	1
Sandoval, Patrick	36.2	1	5	1	0	.857	1	0	0	0	.00	1
Santana, Dennis	17.0	1	2	1	0	.750	1	0	0	0	.00	-1
Santos, Antonio	6.0	0	0	0	0	-	0	0	0	0	-	0
Sborz, Josh	4.1	0	0	0	0	-	0	0	0	0	-	0
Scherzer, Max	67.1	3	5	2	1	.800	7	0	0	0	.00	-2
Schmidt, Clarke	6.1	1	0	0	0	1.000	1	0	0	0	.00	0
Schreiber, John	15.2	3	0	0	0	1.000	0	0	0	0	-	0
Scott, Tanner	20.2	0	3	2	0	.600	0	0	0	0	-	0
Scrubb, Andre	23.2	1	4	0	0	1.000	2	1	0	0	.50	0
Selman, Sam	19.1	1	2	0	0	1.000	1	0	0	0	.00	1
Senzatela, Antonio	73.1	7	4	0	4	1.000	4	0	0	0	.00	-1
Sewald, Paul	6.0	0	0	0	0	-	1	0	0	0	.00	0
Shafer, Justin	5.2	0	0	0	0	-	1	0	0	0	.00	0
Sharp, Sterling	5.1	0	2	0	0	1.000	0	0	0	0	-	0
Shaw, Bryan	6.0	0	1	0	0	1.000	0	0	0	0	-	0
Sheffield, Justus	55.1	4	7	0	1	1.000	8	2	2	0	.25	1
Sherriff, Ryan	9.2	1	0	0	0	1.000	0	0	0	0	-	0
Shoemaker, Matt	28.2	2	1	2	0	.600	2	0	0	1	.00	-2
Shreve, Chasen	25.0	1	5	1	0	.857	2	1	1	0	.50	1

2020 Fielding and Holding Runners

Pitcher	Inn	PO	A	E	DP	Pct	SBA	CS	PCS	PPO	CS%	RS
Sims, Lucas	25.2	7	0	0	0	1.000	0	0	0	0	-	0
Singer, Brady	64.1	3	7	2	0	.833	1	1	0	2	1.00	0
Skubal, Tarik	32.0	0	3	0	1	1.000	3	0	0	0	.00	1
Slegers, Aaron	26.0	2	3	0	0	1.000	0	0	0	0	-	1
Smeltzer, Devin	16.0	1	4	0	0	1.000	1	1	1	0	1.00	2
Smith, Burch	12.0	0	1	0	0	1.000	1	0	0	0	.00	0
Smith, Caleb	14.0	0	0	0	0	-	3	1	0	0	.33	0
Smith, Drew	7.0	2	2	0	0	1.000	0	0	0	0	-	1
Smith, Josh A.	26.1	0	1	1	0	.500	1	0	0	1	.00	-1
Smith, Josh D.	1.2	0	1	0	0	1.000	0	0	0	0	-	0
Smith, Riley	18.1	1	2	0	0	1.000	1	1	0	0	1.00	0
Smith, Will	16.0	1	2	0	0	1.000	0	0	0	0	-	0
Smyly, Drew	26.1	2	1	0	0	1.000	7	0	0	0	.00	-1
Sneed, Cy	17.1	1	3	0	0	1.000	0	0	0	0	-	0
Snell, Blake	50.0	1	7	0	0	1.000	4	3	1	0	.75	1
Sobotka, Chad	3.2	0	0	0	0	-	0	0	0	0	-	0
Soria, Joakim	22.1	0	1	0	0	1.000	2	1	0	0	.50	-1
Soroka, Mike	13.2	3	0	0	0	1.000	0	0	0	0	-	0
Soto, Gregory	23.0	1	1	0	0	1.000	2	0	0	0	.00	0
Sparkman, Glenn	5.0	0	0	1	0	.000	0	0	0	0	-	-1
Speier, Gabe	5.2	0	1	0	0	1.000	2	0	0	0	.00	0
Springs, Jeffrey	20.1	0	2	0	0	1.000	1	0	0	0	.00	0
Stammen, Craig	24.0	1	2	2	1	.600	3	1	0	0	.33	-3
Stanek, Ryne	10.0	1	0	0	0	1.000	0	0	0	0	-	0
Stashak, Cody	15.0	0	0	0	0	-	2	0	0	0	.00	0
Staumont, Josh	25.2	1	1	0	0	1.000	2	1	0	0	.50	0
Stephenson, R.	10.0	2	0	0	0	1.000	2	2	0	0	1.00	0
Stiever, Jonathan	6.1	0	0	0	0	-	0	0	0	0	-	0
Stock, Robert	13.1	1	1	0	1	1.000	0	0	0	0	-	0
Strahm, Matt	20.2	1	0	0	0	1.000	2	1	0	0	.50	0
Strasburg, S.	5.0	0	0	0	0	-	0	0	0	0	-	0
Stratton, Chris	30.0	2	3	0	0	1.000	5	1	0	0	.20	0
Strickland, Hunter	3.1	0	1	0	0	1.000	1	1	0	0	1.00	0
Stripling, Ross	49.1	4	5	1	0	.900	2	0	0	1	.00	-1
Strop, Pedro	2.1	1	0	0	0	1.000	0	0	0	0	-	0
Suarez, Andrew	9.2	0	0	0	0	-	0	0	0	0	-	-1
Suarez, Jose	2.1	0	1	1	0	.500	0	0	0	0	-	0
Suarez, Ranger	4.0	0	1	0	1	1.000	0	0	0	0	-	0
Suero, Wander	23.2	2	2	0	1	1.000	5	0	0	0	.00	-1
Sulser, Cole	22.2	2	3	0	0	1.000	2	0	0	0	.00	0
Suter, Brent	31.2	0	5	1	0	.833	0	0	0	0	-	-1
Swanson, Erik	7.2	0	0	0	0	-	0	0	0	0	-	0
Tanaka, Masahiro	48.0	3	7	0	0	1.000	2	2	0	0	1.00	2
Tapia, Domingo	4.1	0	1	0	0	1.000	0	0	0	0	-	0
Tarpley, Stephen	11.0	0	1	0	0	1.000	1	0	0	0	.00	0
Tate, Dillon	16.2	2	1	0	0	1.000	1	1	0	0	1.00	0
Taylor, Blake	20.2	3	2	0	0	1.000	1	0	0	0	.00	0
Taylor, Josh	7.1	0	0	1	0	.000	0	0	0	0	-	0
Teheran, Julio	31.1	2	5	1	0	.875	4	1	1	0	.25	0
Tepera, Ryan	20.2	3	2	0	0	1.000	0	0	0	1	-	0
Thielbar, Caleb	20.0	0	3	0	0	1.000	1	0	0	0	.00	1
Thompson, Ryan	26.1	1	5	0	1	1.000	1	0	0	0	.00	1
Thornburg, Tyler	7.0	0	0	0	0	-	1	0	0	0	.00	0
Thornton, Trent	5.2	0	0	0	0	-	0	0	0	0	-	0
Thorpe, Lewis	16.1	0	3	0	3	1.000	1	1	0	0	1.00	1
Tinoco, Jesus	8.2	0	2	0	0	1.000	1	1	0	0	1.00	1
Tomlin, Josh	39.2	2	3	0	1	1.000	6	1	0	0	.17	-1
Topa, Justin	7.2	0	1	0	0	1.000	1	0	0	0	.00	0
Toussaint, Touki	24.1	1	2	2	0	.600	4	1	1	0	.25	-1
Treinen, Blake	25.2	2	3	0	0	1.000	8	2	1	0	.25	0
Triggs, Andrew	8.1	0	0	0	0	-	1	0	0	0	.00	0
Trivino, Lou	23.1	1	1	0	0	1.000	2	1	0	0	.50	0
Tropeano, Nick	15.2	0	1	0	0	1.000	0	0	0	0	-	0
Turley, Nik	21.2	0	0	0	0	-	0	0	0	0	-	0
Turnbull, Spencer	56.2	7	5	1	3	.923	13	2	0	0	.15	-3
Underwood Jr., D.	20.2	3	1	0	1	1.000	3	0	0	0	.00	0
Urena, Jose	23.1	3	2	0	0	1.000	3	0	0	1	.00	0
Urias, Julio	55.0	2	3	0	0	1.000	7	1	0	0	.14	-1
Urquidy, Jose	29.2	4	2	0	0	1.000	3	1	0	0	.33	0
Valdez, Cesar	14.1	1	2	0	0	1.000	1	0	0	0	.00	0
Valdez, Framber	70.2	5	5	2	1	.833	7	1	1	0	.14	-4
Valdez, Phillips	30.1	0	6	1	1	.857	3	1	0	0	.33	1
Velasquez, Vince	34.0	1	8	1	0	.900	2	1	0	3	.50	2

2020 Fielding and Holding Runners

Pitcher	Inn	PO	A	E	DP	Pct	SBA	CS	PCS	PPO	CS%	RS
Venditte, Pat	4.1	0	0	0	0	-	0	0	0	0	-	0
Verlander, Justin	6.0	2	1	0	0	1.000	0	0	0	0	-	0
Vesia, Alex	4.1	0	0	0	0	-	0	0	0	0	-	0
Vincent, Nick	22.1	3	3	0	0	1.000	0	0	0	0	-	0
Volquez, Edinson	5.2	0	0	0	0	-	1	0	0	0	.00	0
Voth, Austin	49.2	4	2	0	1	1.000	5	1	0	0	.20	-1
Wacha, Michael	34.0	2	3	0	0	1.000	3	1	0	0	.33	0
Waddell, Brandon	3.1	0	0	0	0	-	0	0	0	0	-	0
Waguespack, J.	17.2	2	1	0	0	1.000	6	1	1	0	.17	0
Wahl, Bobby	2.1	0	1	0	0	1.000	0	0	0	0	-	0
Wainwright, Adam	65.2	2	8	0	0	1.000	1	1	0	0	1.00	1
Walden, Marcus	13.1	0	1	0	0	1.000	2	1	0	0	.50	0
Walker, Taijuan	53.1	1	5	1	0	.857	8	1	0	1	.13	0
Watson, Tony	18.0	2	2	1	0	.800	2	1	1	0	.50	0
Weaver, Luke	52.0	2	4	0	0	1.000	3	2	0	0	.67	2
Webb, Jacob	10.0	0	1	1	0	.500	1	0	0	0	.00	0
Webb, Logan	54.1	4	1	0	0	1.000	11	4	0	0	.36	-3
Webb, Tyler	21.2	2	4	1	1	.857	1	0	0	0	.00	0
Weber, Ryan	43.0	5	6	0	0	1.000	2	1	0	0	.50	0
Weems, Jordan	14.0	0	0	0	0	-	0	0	0	0	-	0
Weigel, Patrick	0.2	0	0	0	0	-	0	0	0	0	-	0
Wendelken, J.B.	25.0	0	1	2	1	.333	0	0	0	0	-	-2
Wheeler, Zack	71.0	4	12	1	3	.941	1	0	0	1	.00	1
White, Mitch	3.0	0	0	0	0	-	1	0	0	0	.00	0
Whitley, Kodi	4.2	0	1	0	0	1.000	0	0	0	0	-	0
Wick, Rowan	17.1	1	0	0	0	1.000	1	0	0	0	.00	0
Widener, Taylor	20.0	3	0	0	0	1.000	1	0	0	0	.00	0
Wieck, Brad	1.0	0	0	0	0	-	0	0	0	0	-	0
Williams, Devin	27.0	2	1	1	0	.750	1	1	0	0	1.00	-1
Williams, Taylor	14.2	0	1	0	0	1.000	0	0	0	0	-	0
Williams, Trevor	55.1	3	6	2	0	.818	4	0	0	1	.00	-1
Wilson, Bryse	15.2	1	2	0	0	1.000	0	0	0	0	-	0
Wilson, Justin	19.2	2	2	1	0	.800	2	0	0	0	.00	-1
Winkler, Dan	18.1	0	2	0	0	1.000	0	0	0	0	-	-1
Wisler, Matt	25.1	0	0	0	0	-	3	0	0	0	.00	0
Wittgren, Nick	23.2	0	1	0	0	1.000	0	0	0	0	-	-1
Wojciechowski, A.	37.0	3	2	0	0	1.000	2	0	0	0	.00	0
Wood, Alex	12.2	0	1	0	0	1.000	1	1	1	0	1.00	1
Woodford, Jake	21.0	2	1	0	0	1.000	0	0	0	0	-	0
Woodruff, Brandon	73.2	0	10	0	0	1.000	4	1	1	0	.25	2
Workman, B.	19.2	0	3	0	0	1.000	2	0	0	0	.00	0
Wright, Kyle	38.0	4	3	0	0	1.000	6	0	0	0	.00	-1
Yacabonis, Jimmy	2.1	0	0	0	0	-	1	0	0	0	.00	0
Yajure, Miguel	7.0	0	0	0	0	-	0	0	0	0	-	0
Yamaguchi, Shun	25.2	1	3	0	1	1.000	1	1	1	0	1.00	0
Yamamoto, J.	11.1	0	1	0	0	1.000	3	0	0	0	.00	0
Yarbrough, Ryan	55.2	2	8	0	0	1.000	3	1	0	0	.33	0
Yardley, Eric	23.1	0	3	0	0	1.000	0	0	0	0	-	1
Yates, Kirby	4.1	1	1	1	0	.667	0	0	0	0	-	0
Ynoa, Huascar	21.2	4	4	0	0	1.000	4	0	0	0	.00	0
Young, Alex	46.1	2	4	0	0	1.000	3	0	0	0	.00	1
Zeuch, T.J.	11.1	0	0	0	0	-	0	0	0	0	-	0
Zimmer, Kyle	23.0	2	4	0	1	1.000	0	0	0	1	-	1
Zimmermann, B.	7.0	0	0	0	0	-	0	0	0	0	-	-1
Zimmermann, J.	5.2	0	1	0	0	1.000	1	1	0	0	1.00	0
Zuber, Tyler	22.0	0	2	0	0	1.000	0	0	0	0	-	-1

Hitters Pitching

Player	2020 Pitching											Career Pitching										
	G	W	L	Sv	IP	H	R	ER	BB	SO	ERA	G	W	L	Sv	IP	H	R	ER	BB	SO	ERA
Adrianza, Ehire	1	-	-	-	1.0	1	1	1	-	-	9.00	2	0	0	0	2.0	6	4	4	0	1	18.00
Alberto, Hanser	-	-	-	-	-	-	-	-	-	-	-	1	0	0	0	1.0	1	2	2	2	0	18.00
Arcia, Orlando	2	-	-	-	2.0	4	4	4	1	-	18.00	2	0	0	0	2.0	4	4	4	1	0	18.00
Astudillo, Willians	-	-	-	-	-	-	-	-	-	-	-	1	0	0	0	1.0	5	5	5	0	0	45.00
Avila, Alex	-	-	-	-	-	-	-	-	-	-	-	3	0	0	0	4.0	3	1	1	1	1	2.25
Bemboom, Anthony	1	-	-	-	1.0	-	-	-	1	-	0.00	1	0	0	0	1.0	0	0	0	1	0	0.00
Brantly, Rob	-	-	-	-	-	-	-	-	-	-	-	1	0	0	0	1.0	1	1	1	0	0	9.00
Brosseau, Mike	1	-	-	-	0.1	-	-	-	-	1	0.00	4	0	0	0	4.1	5	2	2	0	1	4.15
Butera, Drew	1	-	-	-	1.2	3	1	1	-	1	5.40	7	0	0	0	6.0	8	5	5	4	5	7.50
Caratini, Victor	-	-	-	-	-	-	-	-	-	-	-	4	0	0	0	4.0	5	4	4	1	0	9.00
Culberson, Charlie	1	-	-	-	0.1	-	-	-	-	-	0.00	4	0	0	0	3.1	4	1	1	2	1	2.70
Davidson, Matt	3	-	-	-	3.1	4	2	2	2	1	5.40	6	0	0	0	6.1	5	2	2	3	3	2.84
Davis, Chris	-	-	-	-	-	-	-	-	-	-	-	2	1	0	0	3.0	4	1	1	1	3	3.00
Davis, J.D.	-	-	-	-	-	-	-	-	-	-	-	3	0	0	0	2.2	2	1	1	1	4	3.38
Demeritte, Travis	1	-	-	-	1.0	4	4	4	-	-	36.00	1	0	0	0	1.0	4	4	4	0	0	36.00
Descalso, Daniel	-	-	-	-	-	-	-	-	-	-	-	6	0	0	0	6.2	6	5	5	1	2	6.75
Desmond, Ian	-	-	-	-	-	-	-	-	-	-	-	1	0	0	0	1.0	1	0	0	0	0	0.00
Dixon, Brandon	-	-	-	-	-	-	-	-	-	-	-	4	0	0	0	3.1	1	2	2	0	2	5.40
Dozier, Brian	-	-	-	-	-	-	-	-	-	-	-	1	0	0	0	1.0	2	2	2	0	0	18.00
Ervin, Phillip	-	-	-	-	-	-	-	-	-	-	-	1	0	0	0	0.1	0	0	0	0	0	0.00
Escobar, Eduardo	-	-	-	-	-	-	-	-	-	-	-	1	0	0	0	1.0	1	0	0	0	0	0.00
Espinal, Santiago	2	-	-	-	2.0	3	2	2	1	-	9.00	2	0	0	0	2.0	3	2	2	1	0	9.00
Farmer, Kyle	-	-	-	-	-	-	-	-	-	-	-	1	0	0	0	1.1	1	0	0	0	0	0.00
Ford, Mike	-	-	-	-	-	-	-	-	-	-	-	1	0	0	0	2.0	6	5	5	0	1	22.50
Forsythe, Logan	1	-	-	-	1.0	2	1	1	1	-	9.00	1	0	0	0	1.0	2	1	1	1	0	9.00
France, Ty	-	-	-	-	-	-	-	-	-	-	-	2	0	0	0	2.0	2	1	1	0	0	4.50
Frazier, Todd	1	-	-	-	1.0	-	-	-	-	1	0.00	1	0	0	0	1.0	0	0	0	0	1	0.00
Freeman, Mike	-	-	-	-	-	-	-	-	-	-	-	2	0	0	0	3.0	5	3	3	0	0	9.00
Garcia, Greg	-	-	-	-	-	-	-	-	-	-	-	1	0	0	0	1.0	1	0	0	0	0	0.00
Garcia, Leury	-	-	-	-	-	-	-	-	-	-	-	2	0	1	0	2.0	2	2	2	2	1	9.00
Garver, Mitch	-	-	-	-	-	-	-	-	-	-	-	1	0	0	0	1.0	1	0	0	0	0	0.00
Goins, Ryan	-	-	-	-	-	-	-	-	-	-	-	1	0	0	0	1.0	2	0	0	1	0	0.00
Gordon, Alex	-	-	-	-	-	-	-	-	-	-	-	2	0	0	0	2.1	8	5	5	2	0	19.29
Guillorme, Luis	1	-	-	-	1.0	-	-	-	-	-	0.00	1	0	0	0	1.0	0	0	0	0	0	0.00
Gyorko, Jedd	1	-	-	-	1.0	1	-	-	-	-	0.00	3	0	0	0	2.1	3	1	1	0	1	3.86
Happ, Ian	-	-	-	-	-	-	-	-	-	-	-	1	0	0	0	1.0	1	0	0	0	0	0.00
Harrison, Josh	-	-	-	-	-	-	-	-	-	-	-	1	0	0	0	0.1	0	0	0	2	0	0.00
Heineman, Tyler	1	-	-	-	1.0	1	-	-	-	-	0.00	1	0	0	0	1.0	1	0	0	0	0	0.00
Hernandez, Kike	-	-	-	-	-	-	-	-	-	-	-	1	0	1	0	0.1	1	3	3	2	0	81.00
Holaday, Bryan	1	-	-	-	0.1	2	-	-	-	-	0.00	5	0	0	0	4.0	6	3	3	0	1	6.75
Holt, Brock	2	-	-	-	1.1	5	2	2	-	-	13.50	2	0	0	0	1.1	5	2	2	0	0	13.50
Jay, Jon	-	-	-	-	-	-	-	-	-	-	-	1	0	0	0	1.0	1	0	0	0	0	0.00
Joseph, Caleb	-	-	-	-	-	-	-	-	-	-	-	2	0	0	0	1.1	0	0	0	0	0	0.00
Kelly, Carson	1	-	-	-	1.0	1	-	-	-	-	0.00	1	0	0	0	1.0	1	0	0	0	0	0.00
Kingery, Scott	-	-	-	-	-	-	-	-	-	-	-	1	0	0	0	1.1	4	2	2	0	0	13.50
Kratz, Erik	2	-	-	-	2.0	2	2	2	-	-	9.00	7	0	0	0	7.0	10	6	4	1	3	5.14
La Stella, Tommy	-	-	-	-	-	-	-	-	-	-	-	1	0	0	0	1.1	3	1	1	0	0	6.75
Lin, Tzu-Wei	1	-	-	-	1.0	4	3	3	-	-	27.00	1	0	0	0	1.0	4	3	3	0	0	27.00
Lopes, Tim	1	-	-	-	1.0	2	2	2	1	-	18.00	1	0	0	0	1.0	2	2	2	1	0	18.00
Maile, Luke	-	-	-	-	-	-	-	-	-	-	-	2	0	0	0	2.0	1	0	0	0	3	0.00
Maldonado, Martin	-	-	-	-	-	-	-	-	-	-	-	1	0	0	0	1.0	1	0	0	0	0	0.00
Mathis, Jeff	-	-	-	-	-	-	-	-	-	-	-	5	0	1	0	5.0	8	5	5	1	2	9.00
Moore, Dylan	-	-	-	-	-	-	-	-	-	-	-	1	0	0	0	1.0	5	4	4	2	0	36.00
Moreland, Mitch	-	-	-	-	-	-	-	-	-	-	-	2	0	0	0	2.0	2	0	0	0	1	0.00
Murphy, John Ryan	1	-	-	-	1.0	-	-	-	-	-	0.00	3	0	0	0	4.0	10	9	9	3	0	20.25
Murphy, Tom	-	-	-	-	-	-	-	-	-	-	-	3	0	0	0	3.0	1	2	2	1	2	6.00
Nunez, Eduardo	-	-	-	-	-	-	-	-	-	-	-	1	0	0	0	1.0	1	1	1	0	0	9.00
Osuna, Jose	-	-	-	-	-	-	-	-	-	-	-	2	0	0	0	2.1	3	1	1	0	0	3.86
Owings, Chris	-	-	-	-	-	-	-	-	-	-	-	1	0	0	0	1.2	6	4	4	1	0	21.60
Peraza, Jose	1	-	-	-	0.1	2	1	1	-	-	27.00	3	0	0	0	1.2	3	1	1	0	0	5.40
Perez, Hernan	-	-	-	-	-	-	-	-	-	-	-	7	0	0	0	7.1	10	6	6	4	3	7.36
Peterson, Jace	-	-	-	-	-	-	-	-	-	-	-	1	0	0	0	1.0	6	4	4	0	1	36.00
Phegley, Josh	-	-	-	-	-	-	-	-	-	-	-	1	0	0	0	0.2	0	0	0	0	1	0.00
Plawecki, Kevin	1	-	-	-	0.2	-	-	-	1	-	0.00	5	0	0	0	5.2	5	4	4	1	0	6.35
Quinn, Roman	-	-	-	-	-	-	-	-	-	-	-	3	0	1	0	5.0	13	10	10	5	1	18.00
Rizzo, Anthony	-	-	-	-	-	-	-	-	-	-	-	1	0	0	0	0.1	0	0	0	0	0	0.00
Robertson, Daniel	-	-	-	-	-	-	-	-	-	-	-	2	0	0	0	2.0	1	0	0	0	0	0.00
Rodriguez, Sean	-	-	-	-	-	-	-	-	-	-	-	2	0	0	0	1.1	0	0	0	0	1	0.00

Hitters Pitching

Player	2020 Pitching											Career Pitching										
	G	W	L	Sv	IP	H	R	ER	BB	SO	ERA	G	W	L	Sv	IP	H	R	ER	BB	SO	ERA
Romine, Andrew	-	-	-	-	-	-	-	-	-	-		7	0	0	0	5.2	10	8	8	5	1	12.71
Romine, Austin	-	-	-	-	-	-	-	-	-	-		1	0	0	0	1.0	4	3	3	0	0	27.00
Sanchez, Yolmer	1	-	-	-	1.0	2	1	1	-	-	9.00	1	0	0	0	1.0	2	1	1	0	0	9.00
Sandoval, Pablo	-	-	-	-	-	-	-	-	-	-		2	0	0	0	2.0	0	0	0	0	0	0.00
Schrock, Max	1	-	-	-	1.0	-	-	-	-	-	0.00	1	0	0	0	1.0	0	0	0	0	0	0.00
Stallings, Jacob	-	-	-	-	-	-	-	-	-	-		1	0	0	0	1.0	0	0	0	0	0	0.00
Stassi, Max	-	-	-	-	-	-	-	-	-	-		1	0	0	0	0.1	0	0	0	0	0	0.00
Walker, Neil	1	-	-	-	0.2	-	-	-	1	-	0.00	1	0	0	0	0.2	0	0	0	1	0	0.00
Walsh, Jared	-	-	-	-	-	-	-	-	-	-		5	0	0	0	5.0	3	1	1	6	5	1.80

Lords of the Flies

Lindsay Zeck

Prior to the 2020 season, if someone had picked a Yankee to be the player to hit the most home runs of the season, I doubt anyone would think it was a crazy pick. Maybe they picked Aaron Judge—the 2017 AL home run leader—or perhaps Giancarlo Stanton, the 2014 NL and 2017 MLB home run leader. Both have been plagued with injuries, but if they are able to stay healthy…

Well, a Yankee did hit the most home runs in 2020. The home run champion was… drumroll please… Luke Voit. He hit 22 home runs in just 56 games. That was one more than his home run total that took him 118 games to reach in 2019. Nineteen of his 22 home runs had a calculated distance of more than 380 feet.

In his first season as a Dodger, Mookie Betts hit more long flies (at least 300 feet) than any other player, but finished tied for seventh in home runs with 16. Along with his 16 home runs, he hit 41 long fly ball outs, two of which were hit over 400 feet. The only player with more outs hit that distance was Kole Calhoun with three.

Marcell Ozuna hit 15 balls over 400 feet—the most in baseball—and they were all hit for home runs. The longest home run of the season was hit by Ronald Acuña Jr. of the Braves. He hit the ball 495 feet against rookie Chris Mazza of the Red Sox on September 25 at Truist Park. This was one of his nine balls hit over 400 feet in 2020.

In the tables that follow, batted balls are grouped by distance. Each group includes balls +/- 10 feet of the listed distance. The Long column includes the total long fly ball outs, and the HR column excludes inside-the-park home runs.

Long Outs and Home Runs

Player	Long Out Distances						Home Run Distances					
	330	350	370	390	400+	Long	330	350	370	390	400+	HR
Voit, Luke	6	3	5	1	0	20	0	0	3	12	7	22
Abreu, Jose	10	2	3	1	1	24	0	1	2	6	10	19
Ozuna, Marcell	5	3	7	2	0	19	0	0	0	3	15	18
Trout, Mike	6	7	3	4	0	25	0	0	1	2	14	17
Tatis Jr., Fernando	3	5	7	3	1	22	0	1	0	5	11	17
Ramirez, Jose	7	11	2	1	0	26	0	2	2	5	8	17
Hernandez, Teoscar	7	4	6	1	0	22	0	0	1	3	12	16
Machado, Manny	5	6	5	0	0	23	0	0	1	3	12	16
Cruz, Nelson	3	2	0	0	0	10	0	1	0	3	12	16
Alonso, Pete	5	4	2	1	0	15	0	0	3	2	11	16
Pollock, A.J.	7	9	2	2	0	25	0	0	1	6	9	16
Duvall, Adam	9	4	1	2	0	23	0	3	1	3	9	16
Betts, Mookie	10	11	10	2	2	41	0	0	1	10	5	16
Myers, Wil	6	7	7	3	0	25	0	1	0	3	11	15
Seager, Corey	11	6	7	4	0	30	0	0	3	1	11	15
Suarez, Eugenio	5	7	2	0	0	19	0	2	1	2	10	15
Calhoun, Kole	5	5	6	0	3	26	0	0	4	4	7	15
Castellanos, Nick	1	10	6	5	1	28	0	0	1	2	11	14
Olson, Matt	8	8	3	1	0	24	0	0	1	3	10	14
Lowe, Brandon	4	4	5	0	1	19	0	1	1	2	10	14
Acuna Jr., Ronald	3	6	1	1	0	18	0	1	3	1	9	14
Jimenez, Eloy	6	3	1	2	0	18	0	3	3	2	6	14
Springer, George	5	4	2	2	1	23	0	1	0	1	11	13
Sano, Miguel	4	1	3	1	1	11	0	0	3	0	10	13
Freeman, Freddie	9	6	2	1	0	26	0	0	1	3	9	13
Soto, Juan	5	2	2	2	0	11	0	0	1	3	9	13
Hiura, Keston	5	2	3	3	0	17	0	0	2	2	9	13
Rosario, Eddie	8	9	4	3	0	28	0	2	1	3	7	13
Harper, Bryce	8	6	7	1	1	27	0	1	3	3	6	13
Buxton, Byron	6	2	2	1	0	16	0	0	1	3	8	12
Nunez, Renato	1	2	4	1	0	10	2	0	0	2	8	12
Muncy, Max	2	9	10	3	0	24	0	0	1	4	7	12
Grichuk, Randal	8	3	1	1	0	19	0	2	1	3	6	12
Bellinger, Cody	6	7	5	4	0	26	0	0	4	3	5	12
Winker, Jesse	4	3	2	0	0	14	0	1	2	5	4	12
Happ, Ian	7	3	3	2	0	18	1	0	4	3	4	12
Flores, Wilmer	6	10	4	1	0	26	1	0	1	8	2	12
Lewis, Kyle	9	3	3	1	0	21	0	1	1	0	9	11
Bogaerts, Xander	6	4	2	2	0	24	0	0	1	2	8	11
Devers, Rafael	4	1	4	0	0	18	0	0	2	1	8	11
Yelich, Christian	2	7	2	1	0	16	0	0	0	4	7	11
Robert, Luis	3	6	2	2	0	19	0	0	1	3	7	11
Perez, Salvador	1	5	5	3	0	16	0	1	0	3	7	11
Story, Trevor	9	10	6	3	0	33	0	0	2	2	7	11
Gurriel Jr., Lourdes	5	3	3	0	0	18	0	0	1	4	6	11
Turner, Trea	5	8	8	2	0	30	0	1	1	3	6	11
Schwarber, Kyle	4	6	4	0	0	19	0	0	3	2	6	11
Realmuto, J.T.	3	5	3	1	1	18	0	2	1	2	6	11
Santander, Anthony	6	5	2	0	0	16	1	2	0	2	6	11
Votto, Joey	6	8	5	2	0	27	0	0	4	2	5	11
Anderson, Brian	3	4	3	2	0	15	0	2	1	4	4	11
Rizzo, Anthony	8	3	4	1	1	24	0	2	3	2	4	11
Gallo, Joey	3	3	9	1	0	20	0	0	0	2	8	10
Smith, Dominic	1	1	2	2	0	8	0	1	0	2	7	10
Moran, Colin	1	2	1	4	0	10	0	0	2	1	7	10
Dickerson, Alex	2	2	3	0	1	13	0	1	2	0	7	10
Chapman, Matt	4	4	2	0	0	13	0	0	0	4	6	10
Grisham, Trent	4	5	3	2	0	17	0	0	1	3	6	10
Encarnacion, Edwin	6	3	2	3	0	17	0	0	2	2	6	10
Swanson, Dansby	5	5	4	5	0	21	0	2	0	2	6	10
Cano, Robinson	3	2	2	2	0	13	0	1	2	1	6	10
Moreland, Mitch	0	5	1	0	0	11	0	1	1	3	5	10
Anderson, Tim	5	1	4	3	1	20	0	2	0	3	5	10
Odor, Rougned	4	2	2	0	1	15	0	2	1	2	5	10
Sanchez, Gary	1	6	3	0	0	14	0	1	1	4	4	10
McCutchen, Andrew	7	10	6	4	0	31	0	1	2	3	4	10
Cabrera, Miguel	3	3	2	0	2	14	0	1	3	2	4	10
Hoskins, Rhys	4	3	6	1	1	17	0	1	1	5	3	10
Yastrzemski, Mike	3	3	6	2	0	16	0	1	2	5	2	10
Gregorius, Didi	7	5	4	0	0	21	0	1	4	3	2	10
LeMahieu, DJ	1	4	3	0	0	12	1	5	2	2	0	10
Reyes, Franmil	6	6	2	3	0	24	0	0	0	1	8	9
d'Arnaud, Travis	1	2	3	4	0	14	0	0	0	1	8	9

Long Outs and Home Runs

Player	Long Out Distances						Home Run Distances					
	330	350	370	390	400+	Long	330	350	370	390	400+	HR
McMahon, Ryan	3	4	2	3	1	17	0	0	1	0	8	9
Hosmer, Eric	6	7	1	1	1	17	0	0	3	0	6	9
Belt, Brandon	7	2	4	3	0	18	0	1	2	0	6	9
Kepler, Max	5	4	3	2	0	18	0	0	2	2	5	9
Conforto, Michael	5	7	2	1	0	17	0	0	2	2	5	9
Rendon, Anthony	6	7	4	2	0	25	0	0	3	1	5	9
Guerrero Jr., Vladimir	6	4	1	0	0	20	0	0	1	4	4	9
Upton, Justin	4	4	2	2	0	13	0	0	2	3	4	9
Seager, Kyle	7	7	10	4	2	35	0	1	1	4	3	9
Tucker, Kyle	4	7	2	1	1	20	0	0	3	3	3	9
Merrifield, Whit	7	10	6	1	0	35	0	0	2	6	1	9
Ruiz, Rio	3	2	4	1	1	18	0	2	2	4	1	9
Baez, Javier	2	4	2	2	0	14	0	0	1	0	7	8
Santana, Carlos	8	2	6	5	0	22	0	0	0	2	6	8
Riley, Austin	2	2	1	2	1	13	0	0	1	1	6	8
Arenado, Nolan	11	3	9	3	1	33	0	0	1	1	6	8
Tellez, Rowdy	3	5	3	1	0	13	1	1	0	0	6	8
Bell, Josh	6	3	1	1	0	12	0	0	1	2	5	8
Crawford, Brandon	4	5	5	0	0	17	0	0	1	2	5	8
White, Evan	3	3	1	5	0	13	0	0	1	2	5	8
Soler, Jorge	4	0	3	3	0	13	0	0	1	2	5	8
Schoop, Jonathan	4	4	1	0	0	11	0	1	0	2	5	8
Renfroe, Hunter	0	5	1	0	0	9	1	0	0	2	5	8
Tsutsugo, Yoshi	3	1	3	3	0	14	0	1	2	0	5	8
Grandal, Yasmani	3	5	5	0	0	18	0	0	0	4	4	8
Aguilar, Jesus	4	7	4	1	0	23	0	0	1	3	4	8
Franco, Maikel	7	5	2	3	1	24	0	0	1	3	4	8
Moustakas, Mike	5	4	4	2	0	22	0	1	1	2	4	8
Adames, Willy	3	5	2	2	0	13	0	1	2	1	4	8
Nimmo, Brandon	5	2	1	2	0	14	0	0	0	5	3	8
Braun, Ryan	2	3	2	1	0	10	0	0	1	4	3	8
Cabrera, Asdrubal	6	5	7	1	1	26	0	0	1	4	3	8
Lindor, Francisco	7	4	5	2	0	27	0	0	2	3	3	8
Taylor, Chris	4	6	2	3	2	21	0	0	3	2	3	8
Moore, Dylan	3	6	2	0	0	13	0	1	2	2	3	8
Grossman, Robbie	1	4	6	0	0	17	0	3	2	0	3	8
Smith, Will	2	3	5	2	0	12	0	0	2	4	2	8
Valaika, Pat	5	5	1	1	0	17	0	1	1	4	2	8
Biggio, Cavan	3	9	6	2	0	24	0	2	1	4	1	8
Frazier, Clint	1	3	3	1	0	10	0	1	4	2	1	8
Reynolds, Bryan	5	5	4	0	0	21	0	0	0	2	5	7
Bradley Jr., Jackie	1	3	1	0	0	9	0	0	0	2	5	7
Polanco, Gregory	8	5	5	3	0	25	0	0	1	1	5	7
Candelario, Jeimer	2	5	2	3	0	15	0	0	1	1	5	7
Contreras, Willson	1	9	2	4	0	20	0	0	1	1	5	7
Ohtani, Shohei	1	6	3	0	0	12	0	1	0	1	5	7
Miller, Brad	2	2	3	1	0	13	0	0	2	0	5	7
O'Neill, Tyler	5	5	5	1	0	21	0	0	1	2	4	7
Longoria, Evan	8	6	2	2	2	29	0	0	1	2	4	7
Walker, Christian	11	6	7	3	0	33	0	0	1	2	4	7
Martinez, J.D.	9	6	4	7	0	35	0	1	1	1	4	7
Dickerson, Corey	4	5	4	1	1	20	1	0	1	1	4	7
Frazier, Adam	2	7	1	2	0	22	0	0	0	4	3	7
Semien, Marcus	2	12	3	1	0	25	0	0	1	3	3	7
Vazquez, Christian	9	4	0	0	0	18	0	0	2	2	3	7
Nola, Austin	6	3	2	4	0	20	0	0	1	4	2	7
Segura, Jean	7	2	2	2	0	20	0	2	1	2	2	7
Profar, Jurickson	9	4	4	0	0	20	0	0	2	4	1	7
Galvis, Freddy	1	6	1	2	0	14	0	2	2	2	1	7
Mondesi, Adalberto	1	5	3	1	0	14	0	0	0	2	4	6
Albies, Ozzie	3	1	2	1	0	8	0	0	0	2	4	6
Pillar, Kevin	3	7	4	1	2	29	0	0	0	2	4	6
Jansen, Danny	3	2	3	1	0	13	0	0	0	2	4	6
Blackmon, Charlie	4	6	2	2	1	27	0	0	1	1	4	6
Goldschmidt, Paul	6	6	5	4	0	25	0	0	1	1	4	6
Marte, Starling	10	2	1	3	1	22	0	1	0	1	4	6
Goodwin, Brian	6	2	0	1	0	14	0	1	1	0	4	6
Castro, Willi	2	2	1	2	0	10	0	1	1	0	4	6
Dozier, Hunter	7	1	1	1	0	11	0	1	1	0	4	6
Moncada, Yoan	5	3	1	1	0	13	0	2	0	0	4	6
Bregman, Alex	4	5	3	1	1	19	0	0	1	2	3	6
Pujols, Albert	5	4	2	2	0	19	0	0	2	1	3	6
Shaw, Travis	8	2	2	2	1	18	0	1	1	1	3	6
Gurriel, Yuli	7	12	6	5	0	40	0	1	1	1	3	6
Davis, J.D.	6	0	3	2	2	19	1	0	1	1	3	6
Hicks, Aaron	7	2	3	2	0	17	0	1	2	0	3	6

Long Outs and Home Runs

Player	Long Out Distances						Home Run Distances					
	330	350	370	390	400+	Long	330	350	370	390	400+	HR
Laureano, Ramon	2	5	1	4	1	19	0	0	1	3	2	6
Urshela, Gio	4	6	0	2	0	22	0	1	2	1	2	6
Heyward, Jason	3	5	1	5	0	16	0	2	1	1	2	6
Verdugo, Alex	5	2	2	3	0	17	1	1	2	0	2	6
Maldonado, Martin	3	1	0	0	2	9	0	0	3	2	1	6
Peralta, David	3	2	4	0	0	12	0	0	0	0	5	5
Ahmed, Nick	7	2	4	1	0	18	0	0	0	0	5	5
Hampson, Garrett	4	2	7	0	2	17	0	0	0	1	4	5
Mountcastle, Ryan	4	6	1	0	0	15	0	0	0	1	4	5
Correa, Carlos	2	6	7	2	0	17	0	0	1	0	4	5
Chavis, Michael	3	2	2	0	0	10	0	0	1	0	4	5
Severino, Pedro	5	5	4	1	0	19	0	0	1	0	4	5
Piscotty, Stephen	4	4	0	2	0	17	0	0	1	0	4	5
Gonzalez, Marwin	10	5	3	5	0	28	0	0	0	2	3	5
Goodrum, Niko	9	5	4	3	0	24	0	0	1	1	3	5
Edman, Tommy	4	6	3	1	0	16	0	0	1	1	3	5
Bichette, Bo	3	3	5	0	0	18	0	0	1	1	3	5
Ramos, Wilson	4	2	5	0	0	13	0	0	1	1	3	5
Altuve, Jose	7	4	2	1	0	17	1	0	0	1	3	5
Canha, Mark	11	6	5	2	0	34	0	0	1	2	2	5
Kelly, Carson	1	4	4	2	0	13	0	0	2	1	2	5
La Stella, Tommy	9	6	4	2	0	27	0	1	1	1	2	5
Gardner, Brett	4	7	3	2	0	20	0	1	1	1	2	5
Arcia, Orlando	2	5	4	2	1	19	0	0	0	4	1	5
Hernandez, Kike	6	1	6	1	0	17	1	0	2	1	1	5
Brantley, Michael	7	7	4	1	0	26	0	0	4	1	0	5
Reddick, Josh	6	4	4	1	0	23	0	0	0	1	3	4
Turner, Justin	3	6	9	6	0	27	0	0	0	2	2	4
Carpenter, Matt	10	6	5	1	0	25	0	0	0	2	2	4
Frazier, Todd	5	7	3	0	0	20	0	1	0	1	2	4
Escobar, Eduardo	11	3	5	1	2	26	0	0	0	3	1	4
Reyes, Victor	9	4	3	1	0	21	0	0	1	2	1	4
McNeil, Jeff	6	4	5	1	0	26	0	0	1	2	1	4
Molina, Yadier	3	7	5	0	0	22	0	0	2	1	1	4
Dubon, Mauricio	9	5	2	2	0	23	1	0	1	1	1	4
Wendle, Joey	2	5	2	2	0	20	0	0	2	2	0	4
Polanco, Jorge	7	3	6	6	0	32	0	0	3	1	0	4
Hernandez, Cesar	4	3	5	1	1	21	0	0	0	1	2	3
Solano, Donovan	9	6	2	1	0	25	0	0	0	1	2	3
DeJong, Paul	6	7	7	2	0	23	0	0	1	0	2	3
Gonzalez, Erik	7	4	2	2	0	23	0	0	1	1	1	3
Crawford, J.P.	4	10	5	2	0	23	0	0	1	0	1	2
Marte, Ketel	6	5	3	3	0	22	0	0	0	2	0	2
Solak, Nick	6	8	7	2	0	28	0	0	1	1	0	2
Margot, Manuel	6	5	1	3	0	20	0	0	0	0	1	1
Tapia, Raimel	6	6	3	1	0	21	0	0	0	0	1	1
Newman, Kevin	7	2	6	3	0	22	0	0	0	1	0	1
Arraez, Luis	7	4	5	1	0	20	0	0	0	0	0	0

Hard Hit Balls

Brian Reiff

This is not a leaderboard of the best hitters in baseball. But it comes pretty close.

Hitting the ball hard is almost certainly the best outcome that can come out of an at-bat, at least for the hitter. Hitting the ball hard in the air might be the only thing better. The ability to do so on a consistent basis generally indicates an elite hitter, which is a good way to describe this year's leader in hard-hit percentage, Fernando Tatis Jr.

Given how impressive his rookie season was, it was difficult to imagine Tatis improving on it, but that's exactly what he did in many ways. His hard-hit percentage increased from 41.9% in 2019 to the MLB-leading 54.9% mark in 2020, the largest increase among all players with at least 100 PA in both seasons. Moreover, he both increased his walk rate and lowered his strikeout rate, keeping his on-base and slugging percentages nearly steady despite his batting average on balls in play dropping over 100 points. Taking all that together, his OPS+ actually increased a point from last season from 154 to 155, and for a player only 21 years of age, the ceiling is likely even higher.

Joining Tatis in the top five were Corey Seager, Ronald Acuña Jr., Jesse Winker and Teoscar Hernández, all of whom increased their hard-hit percentage from last season by at least five points. Acuña's .930 slugging percentage on balls in play (including home runs) led MLB, although that may not have been the most impressive stat of his campaign. Acuña scored 46 runs in 46 games, averaging a run per game. That would be an amazing feat over a 162-game season—the last player to do that and be batting-title eligible was Rickey Henderson in 1985.

This section includes a full leaderboard of hard, medium, and soft hit rates, reported per batted ball, and also includes count and slugging percentage for each. Players with at least 100 plate appearances in 2020 are included.

Hard Hit Balls
Highest Percentage of Hard Hit Balls - Players with 100+ PA in 2020

Player	In Play	Hard Count	Hard SLG	Medium Count	Medium SLG	Soft Count	Soft SLG	Hard Pct	Medium Pct	Soft Pct	SLG
Tatis Jr., Fernando	164	90	1.258	61	.246	13	.077	54.9%	37.2%	7.9%	.785
Seager, Corey	177	92	1.165	70	.217	15	.200	52.0%	39.5%	8.5%	.709
Acuna Jr., Ronald	100	51	1.569	32	.281	17	.235	51.0%	32.0%	17.0%	.930
Hernandez, Teoscar	128	63	1.403	50	.340	15	.400	49.2%	39.1%	11.7%	.866
Winker, Jesse	104	51	1.380	42	.262	11	.091	49.0%	40.4%	10.6%	.786
Turner, Justin	125	61	.787	50	.286	14	.500	48.8%	40.0%	11.2%	.556
Sano, Miguel	96	46	1.674	40	.275	10	.100	47.9%	41.7%	10.4%	.927
Myers, Wil	142	68	1.324	58	.431	16	.313	47.9%	40.8%	11.3%	.845
Pham, Tommy	82	39	.615	32	.188	11	.364	47.6%	39.0%	13.4%	.415
Polanco, Gregory	95	45	.977	41	.225	9	.000	47.4%	43.2%	9.5%	.554
Ozuna, Marcell	169	78	1.468	66	.424	25	.160	46.2%	39.1%	14.8%	.863
d'Arnaud, Travis	116	53	1.170	51	.460	12	.250	45.7%	44.0%	10.3%	.765
Alfaro, Jorge	57	26	.923	21	.286	10	.200	45.6%	36.8%	17.5%	.561
Walker, Christian	171	77	.961	70	.294	24	.292	45.0%	40.9%	14.0%	.595
Smoak, Justin	78	35	.886	32	.387	11	.000	44.9%	41.0%	14.1%	.558
Betts, Mookie	182	81	1.113	77	.351	24	.292	44.5%	42.3%	13.2%	.680
Jimenez, Eloy	158	70	1.362	69	.290	19	.263	44.3%	43.7%	12.0%	.758
Freeman, Freddie	177	77	1.234	83	.422	17	.412	43.5%	46.9%	9.6%	.774
Lowe, Brandon	137	59	1.500	59	.310	19	.105	43.1%	43.1%	13.9%	.793
Olson, Matt	133	57	1.333	59	.169	17	.176	42.9%	44.4%	12.8%	.669
Perez, Salvador	115	49	1.396	52	.462	14	.286	42.6%	45.2%	12.2%	.833
Walsh, Jared	87	37	1.361	38	.417	12	.000	42.5%	43.7%	13.8%	.762
Rendon, Anthony	158	67	1.030	75	.280	16	.250	42.4%	47.5%	10.1%	.595
Soler, Jorge	90	38	1.432	36	.306	16	.125	42.2%	40.0%	17.8%	.742
Judge, Aaron	69	29	1.552	31	.290	9	.222	42.0%	44.9%	13.0%	.812
Grandal, Yasmani	105	44	1.279	47	.261	14	.071	41.9%	44.8%	13.3%	.660
Upton, Justin	105	44	1.227	48	.128	13	.154	41.9%	45.7%	12.4%	.596
Hosmer, Eric	117	49	1.167	49	.292	19	.211	41.9%	41.9%	16.2%	.643
Pollock, A.J.	153	64	1.419	72	.278	17	.176	41.8%	47.1%	11.1%	.735
Devers, Rafael	165	69	1.217	78	.295	18	.278	41.8%	47.3%	10.9%	.679
O'Hearn, Ryan	77	32	.613	37	.378	8	.125	41.6%	48.1%	10.4%	.447
Chapman, Matt	89	37	1.806	34	.294	18	.056	41.6%	38.2%	20.2%	.864
Trout, Mike	147	61	1.508	69	.418	17	.176	41.5%	46.9%	11.6%	.839
Muncy, Max	145	60	1.052	70	.214	15	.200	41.4%	48.3%	10.3%	.552
Bell, Josh	140	58	.947	68	.185	14	.357	41.4%	48.6%	10.0%	.522
Soto, Juan	126	52	1.635	55	.345	19	.158	41.3%	43.7%	15.1%	.849
Gallo, Joey	114	47	1.149	52	.308	15	.200	41.2%	45.6%	13.2%	.640
Yelich, Christian	124	51	1.294	63	.302	10	.100	41.1%	50.8%	8.1%	.694
Smith, Will	93	38	1.342	47	.261	8	.375	40.9%	50.5%	8.6%	.717
Schwarber, Kyle	125	51	1.196	61	.197	13	.154	40.8%	48.8%	10.4%	.600
Belt, Brandon	113	46	1.326	54	.426	13	.308	40.7%	47.8%	11.5%	.779
Voit, Luke	160	65	1.692	68	.224	27	.185	40.6%	42.5%	16.9%	.818
Sisco, Chance	57	23	1.130	24	.375	10	.200	40.4%	42.1%	17.5%	.649
Calhoun, Kole	144	58	1.400	68	.299	18	.167	40.3%	47.2%	12.5%	.714
Bruce, Jay	72	29	1.276	32	.219	11	.091	40.3%	44.4%	15.3%	.625
Carpenter, Matt	92	37	.811	49	.245	6	.333	40.2%	53.3%	6.5%	.478
Goodrum, Niko	92	37	1.139	39	.216	16	.250	40.2%	42.4%	17.4%	.596
Sanchez, Gary	92	37	1.351	41	.171	14	.000	40.2%	44.6%	15.2%	.620
McMahon, Ryan	107	43	1.286	52	.288	12	.250	40.2%	48.6%	11.2%	.679
Abreu, Jose	182	73	1.556	85	.329	24	.333	40.1%	46.7%	13.2%	.818
Story, Trevor	172	69	1.246	78	.385	25	.240	40.1%	45.3%	14.5%	.709
McCutchen, Andrew	170	68	.956	75	.324	27	.185	40.0%	44.1%	15.9%	.556
Harper, Bryce	150	60	1.350	76	.247	14	.286	40.0%	50.7%	9.3%	.701
Piscotty, Stephen	108	43	.907	48	.326	17	.176	39.8%	44.4%	15.7%	.538
Thames, Eric	81	32	.844	33	.303	16	.125	39.5%	40.7%	19.8%	.481
Moran, Colin	127	50	1.280	65	.297	12	.083	39.4%	51.2%	9.4%	.667
Heyward, Jason	112	44	1.047	52	.373	16	.188	39.3%	46.4%	14.3%	.609
Dickerson, Alex	122	48	1.396	57	.321	17	.118	39.3%	46.7%	13.9%	.719
Seager, Kyle	176	69	.969	81	.266	26	.154	39.2%	46.0%	14.8%	.518
Swanson, Dansby	167	65	1.156	83	.373	19	.263	38.9%	49.7%	11.4%	.663
Guerrero Jr., Vladimir	183	71	1.099	86	.256	26	.077	38.8%	47.0%	14.2%	.557
Bart, Joey	62	24	1.042	26	.269	12	.083	38.7%	41.9%	19.4%	.532
Machado, Manny	191	74	1.389	91	.281	26	.192	38.7%	47.6%	13.6%	.695
DeJong, Paul	106	41	.744	49	.447	16	.188	38.7%	46.2%	15.1%	.520
Cruz, Nelson	127	49	1.776	60	.350	18	.111	38.6%	47.2%	14.2%	.866
Stewart, D.J.	52	20	1.650	20	.278	12	.167	38.5%	38.5%	23.1%	.800
Kendrick, Howie	76	29	.778	35	.343	12	.167	38.2%	46.1%	15.8%	.473
Longoria, Evan	157	60	.983	80	.269	17	.176	38.2%	51.0%	10.8%	.532
Moustakas, Mike	105	40	1.100	46	.422	19	.111	38.1%	43.8%	18.1%	.631
Bellinger, Cody	171	65	1.031	78	.321	28	.179	38.0%	45.6%	16.4%	.567
Naquin, Tyler	95	36	1.056	50	.250	9	.111	37.9%	52.6%	9.5%	.548
Tucker, Kyle	164	62	1.323	85	.274	17	.118	37.8%	51.8%	10.4%	.656

416

Hard Hit Balls
Highest Percentage of Hard Hit Balls - Players with 100+ PA in 2020

Player	In Play	Hard Count	Hard SLG	Medium Count	Medium SLG	Soft Count	Soft SLG	Hard Pct	Medium Pct	Soft Pct	SLG
Smith, Dominic	135	51	1.412	70	.478	14	.357	37.8%	51.9%	10.4%	.826
Realmuto, J.T.	125	47	1.468	57	.158	21	.333	37.6%	45.6%	16.8%	.680
Calhoun, Willie	85	32	.467	36	.222	17	.235	37.6%	42.4%	20.0%	.313
Reynolds, Bryan	128	48	1.021	65	.200	15	.267	37.5%	50.8%	11.7%	.516
Canha, Mark	142	53	1.115	69	.246	20	.200	37.3%	48.6%	14.1%	.569
Brantley, Michael	142	53	.962	75	.347	14	.286	37.3%	52.8%	9.9%	.570
Marmolejos, Jose	75	28	1.250	36	.222	11	.091	37.3%	48.0%	14.7%	.587
Nola, Austin	129	48	1.196	61	.246	20	.300	37.2%	47.3%	15.5%	.598
Yastrzemski, Mike	137	51	1.431	59	.508	27	.222	37.2%	43.1%	19.7%	.796
Cabrera, Asdrubal	154	57	1.109	68	.318	29	.103	37.0%	44.2%	18.8%	.567
Meadows, Austin	84	31	1.323	40	.158	13	.154	36.9%	47.6%	15.5%	.598
Tellez, Rowdy	95	35	1.118	41	.500	19	.158	36.8%	43.2%	20.0%	.656
Pederson, Joc	87	32	1.156	44	.182	11	.273	36.8%	50.6%	12.6%	.552
Castellanos, Nick	150	55	1.315	80	.363	15	.400	36.7%	53.3%	10.0%	.711
Bregman, Alex	128	47	.935	63	.349	18	.222	36.7%	49.2%	14.1%	.543
Santander, Anthony	128	47	1.383	54	.333	27	.185	36.7%	42.2%	21.1%	.688
Turner, Trea	199	73	1.139	94	.516	32	.219	36.7%	47.2%	16.1%	.695
Reyes, Franmil	147	54	1.240	72	.352	21	.381	36.7%	49.0%	14.3%	.669
Taylor, Chris	131	48	1.083	64	.444	19	.421	36.6%	48.9%	14.5%	.677
Springer, George	153	56	1.345	66	.338	31	.194	36.6%	43.1%	20.3%	.675
Arcia, Orlando	142	52	1.020	67	.254	23	.130	36.6%	47.2%	16.2%	.511
Conforto, Michael	145	53	1.208	71	.465	21	.333	36.6%	49.0%	14.5%	.717
Cano, Robinson	148	54	1.245	64	.313	30	.233	36.5%	43.2%	20.3%	.633
Hilliard, Sam	63	23	1.609	25	.200	15	.267	36.5%	39.7%	23.8%	.730
Votto, Joey	143	52	1.269	76	.197	15	.133	36.4%	53.1%	10.5%	.580
Mondesi, Adalberto	151	55	1.109	77	.333	19	.263	36.4%	51.0%	12.6%	.611
Cronenworth, Jake	143	52	1.059	65	.323	26	.269	36.4%	45.5%	18.2%	.577
Bogaerts, Xander	163	59	1.288	77	.263	27	.222	36.2%	47.2%	16.6%	.630
McCann, James	69	25	1.522	34	.441	10	.200	36.2%	49.3%	14.5%	.776
Bote, David	86	31	1.300	42	.214	13	.231	36.0%	48.8%	15.1%	.600
Gurriel, Yuli	189	68	.857	93	.247	28	.143	36.0%	49.2%	14.8%	.440
Adames, Willy	111	40	1.425	50	.560	21	.190	36.0%	45.0%	18.9%	.802
Candelario, Jeimer	136	49	1.204	64	.438	23	.261	36.0%	47.1%	16.9%	.684
Correa, Carlos	153	55	.852	72	.389	26	.115	35.9%	47.1%	17.0%	.507
Pillar, Kevin	167	60	1.050	80	.350	27	.185	35.9%	47.9%	16.2%	.575
Bader, Harrison	67	24	1.522	27	.333	16	.188	35.8%	40.3%	23.9%	.712
Contreras, Willson	134	48	1.152	65	.308	21	.190	35.8%	48.5%	15.7%	.583
Solak, Nick	171	61	.627	85	.337	25	.280	35.7%	49.7%	14.6%	.431
Martinez, J.D.	154	55	1.148	82	.210	17	.176	35.7%	53.2%	11.0%	.539
Flores, Wilmer	163	58	1.241	77	.355	28	.107	35.6%	47.2%	17.2%	.630
Anderson, Brian	135	48	1.542	67	.258	20	.100	35.6%	49.6%	14.8%	.694
Davis, J.D.	135	48	.875	65	.406	22	.273	35.6%	48.1%	16.3%	.552
Baez, Javier	149	53	1.212	70	.203	26	.115	35.6%	47.0%	17.4%	.544
Aguilar, Jesus	152	54	1.094	76	.315	22	.227	35.5%	50.0%	14.5%	.581
Kelly, Carson	93	33	.939	49	.327	11	.000	35.5%	52.7%	11.8%	.505
Choo, Shin-Soo	79	28	1.107	42	.325	9	.000	35.4%	53.2%	11.4%	.571
Buxton, Byron	96	34	1.824	42	.200	20	.250	35.4%	43.8%	20.8%	.798
White, Evan	99	35	1.382	50	.240	14	.286	35.4%	50.5%	14.1%	.643
LeMahieu, DJ	175	62	1.213	90	.378	23	.304	35.4%	51.4%	13.1%	.661
Happ, Ian	136	48	1.417	71	.414	17	.176	35.3%	52.2%	12.5%	.741
Taveras, Leody	77	27	1.000	34	.424	16	.375	35.1%	44.2%	20.8%	.618
Miller, Brad	97	34	1.455	44	.205	19	.368	35.1%	45.4%	19.6%	.667
Moore, Dylan	94	33	1.606	52	.231	9	.333	35.1%	55.3%	9.6%	.723
Arenado, Nolan	166	58	.982	72	.319	36	.028	34.9%	43.4%	21.7%	.488
Grichuk, Randal	169	59	1.305	78	.237	32	.281	34.9%	46.2%	18.9%	.623
Renfroe, Hunter	86	30	1.400	38	.162	18	.000	34.9%	44.2%	20.9%	.565
Choi, Ji-Man	89	31	1.200	40	.316	18	.111	34.8%	44.9%	20.2%	.581
Cave, Jake	69	24	1.375	36	.250	9	.222	34.8%	52.2%	13.0%	.638
Suarez, Eugenio	132	46	1.652	64	.206	22	.182	34.8%	48.5%	16.7%	.710
Rizzo, Anthony	167	58	1.035	81	.288	28	.071	34.7%	48.5%	16.8%	.509
Mountcastle, Ryan	98	34	1.030	45	.477	19	.368	34.7%	45.9%	19.4%	.646
Donaldson, Josh	58	20	1.526	29	.207	9	.333	34.5%	50.0%	15.5%	.667
Kemp, Matt	76	26	1.192	37	.378	13	.308	34.2%	48.7%	17.1%	.645
Murphy, Sean	79	27	1.519	43	.256	9	.111	34.2%	54.4%	11.4%	.671
Solano, Donovan	152	52	.865	75	.486	25	.280	34.2%	49.3%	16.4%	.583
Carlson, Dylan	76	26	1.077	38	.324	12	.000	34.2%	50.0%	15.8%	.533
Andrus, Elvis	88	30	.833	41	.171	17	.118	34.1%	46.6%	19.3%	.386
Santana, Carlos	164	56	.839	75	.257	33	.182	34.1%	45.7%	20.1%	.442
Ohtani, Shohei	103	35	1.114	48	.292	20	.150	34.0%	46.6%	19.4%	.544
Hernandez, Kike	109	37	1.056	48	.313	24	.167	33.9%	44.0%	22.0%	.528
Crawford, Brandon	127	43	1.381	65	.281	19	.211	33.9%	51.2%	15.0%	.640
Barnes, Austin	65	22	.857	31	.276	12	.083	33.8%	47.7%	18.5%	.435
Riley, Austin	139	47	1.149	71	.243	22	.318	33.8%	51.1%	15.8%	.565

417

Hard Hit Balls
Highest Percentage of Hard Hit Balls - Players with 100+ PA in 2020

Player	In Play	Hard Count	Hard SLG	Medium Count	Medium SLG	Soft Count	Soft SLG	Hard Pct	Medium Pct	Soft Pct	SLG
Peralta, David	160	54	1.019	79	.354	27	.259	33.8%	49.4%	16.9%	.557
Chavis, Michael	98	33	1.063	51	.400	14	.071	33.7%	52.0%	14.3%	.573
Moreland, Mitch	104	35	1.686	53	.283	16	.063	33.7%	51.0%	15.4%	.721
Goodwin, Brian	92	31	1.233	53	.385	8	.375	33.7%	57.6%	8.7%	.667
Grisham, Trent	153	51	1.320	75	.419	27	.037	33.3%	49.0%	17.6%	.649
Ramirez, Jose	177	59	1.407	83	.512	35	.229	33.3%	46.9%	19.8%	.756
Stassi, Max	72	24	1.522	43	.317	5	.000	33.3%	59.7%	6.9%	.696
Gardner, Brett	96	32	1.094	47	.261	17	.235	33.3%	49.0%	17.7%	.537
Moncada, Yoan	130	43	1.190	65	.313	22	.318	33.1%	50.0%	16.9%	.602
O'Neill, Tyler	97	32	1.156	52	.216	13	.154	33.0%	53.6%	13.4%	.521
Kingery, Scott	79	26	.769	38	.297	15	.067	32.9%	48.1%	19.0%	.410
Franco, Maikel	189	62	1.233	81	.304	46	.087	32.8%	42.9%	24.3%	.551
Laureano, Ramon	128	42	1.143	64	.262	22	.136	32.8%	50.0%	17.2%	.536
Lewis, Kyle	137	45	1.273	67	.379	25	.360	32.8%	48.9%	18.2%	.667
Anderson, Tim	159	52	1.423	83	.366	24	.250	32.7%	52.2%	15.1%	.696
Mazara, Nomar	92	30	.733	51	.294	11	.273	32.6%	55.4%	12.0%	.435
Verdugo, Alex	157	51	1.080	83	.446	23	.217	32.5%	52.9%	14.6%	.615
Hoskins, Rhys	108	35	1.571	52	.269	21	.333	32.4%	48.1%	19.4%	.704
Valaika, Pat	108	35	1.114	57	.357	16	.500	32.4%	52.8%	14.8%	.626
Kepler, Max	136	44	1.182	60	.339	32	.094	32.4%	44.1%	23.5%	.556
Panik, Joe	93	30	.633	50	.340	13	.000	32.3%	53.8%	14.0%	.387
Bichette, Bo	96	31	1.258	51	.471	14	.000	32.3%	53.1%	14.6%	.656
Ramos, Wilson	112	36	.943	54	.370	22	.091	32.1%	48.2%	19.6%	.495
Gyorko, Jedd	81	26	1.792	39	.333	16	.188	32.1%	48.1%	19.8%	.747
Gonzalez, Erik	134	43	.929	67	.281	24	.333	32.1%	50.0%	17.9%	.500
Kipnis, Jason	75	24	1.043	41	.450	10	.400	32.0%	54.7%	13.3%	.630
Braun, Ryan	103	33	1.500	51	.235	19	.158	32.0%	49.5%	18.4%	.618
Tapia, Raimel	150	48	.667	75	.437	27	.407	32.0%	50.0%	18.0%	.507
Peraza, Jose	94	30	.900	45	.205	19	.105	31.9%	47.9%	20.2%	.409
Marte, Ketel	163	52	.880	82	.284	29	.241	31.9%	50.3%	17.8%	.463
Adell, Jo	69	22	.864	35	.371	12	.083	31.9%	50.7%	17.4%	.478
Ward, Taylor	66	21	.667	39	.487	6	.500	31.8%	59.1%	9.1%	.545
Alonso, Pete	148	47	1.766	76	.200	25	.160	31.8%	51.4%	16.9%	.694
Frazier, Clint	88	28	1.429	48	.532	12	.167	31.8%	54.5%	13.6%	.770
Vogelbach, Daniel	82	26	1.269	45	.222	11	.182	31.7%	54.9%	13.4%	.549
Cooper, Garrett	89	28	1.250	49	.408	12	.417	31.5%	55.1%	13.5%	.674
Tsutsugo, Yoshi	108	34	1.441	54	.226	20	.050	31.5%	50.0%	18.5%	.579
Urshela, Gio	130	41	1.026	71	.406	18	.333	31.5%	54.6%	13.8%	.587
Eaton, Adam	131	41	1.024	67	.254	23	.130	31.3%	51.1%	17.6%	.480
Slater, Austin	64	20	1.300	35	.382	9	.444	31.3%	54.7%	14.1%	.683
Kiermaier, Kevin	96	30	1.100	48	.271	18	.222	31.3%	50.0%	18.8%	.521
Odor, Rougned	93	29	1.786	43	.167	21	.000	31.2%	46.2%	22.6%	.626
Ruiz, Rio	141	44	1.302	70	.319	27	.037	31.2%	49.6%	19.1%	.568
Hernandez, Cesar	177	55	.927	99	.367	23	.348	31.1%	55.9%	13.0%	.540
Gomes, Yan	90	28	1.111	49	.362	13	.308	31.1%	54.4%	14.4%	.586
Segura, Jean	148	46	1.065	70	.348	32	.250	31.1%	47.3%	21.6%	.551
McNeil, Jeff	162	50	.917	88	.379	24	.250	30.9%	54.3%	14.8%	.522
Dozier, Hunter	110	34	1.294	52	.212	24	.292	30.9%	47.3%	21.8%	.564
Vazquez, Christian	130	40	1.250	57	.368	33	.242	30.8%	43.8%	25.4%	.608
Dickerson, Corey	159	49	.959	83	.277	27	.296	30.8%	52.2%	17.0%	.491
Rojas, Miguel	107	33	.970	60	.483	14	.071	30.8%	56.1%	13.1%	.579
France, Ty	104	32	1.188	55	.436	17	.235	30.8%	52.9%	16.3%	.635
Gosselin, Phil	65	20	1.300	31	.258	14	.214	30.8%	47.7%	21.5%	.569
Duvall, Adam	137	42	1.952	67	.182	28	.250	30.7%	48.9%	20.4%	.743
Altuve, Jose	153	47	.766	82	.329	24	.125	30.7%	53.6%	15.7%	.431
Stallings, Jacob	88	27	1.000	51	.347	10	.333	30.7%	58.0%	11.4%	.553
Torres, Gleyber	108	33	.879	60	.300	15	.200	30.6%	55.6%	13.9%	.463
Dubon, Mauricio	124	38	.737	65	.403	21	.381	30.6%	52.4%	16.9%	.504
Wolters, Tony	72	22	.409	41	.436	9	.111	30.6%	56.9%	12.5%	.386
Wendle, Joey	134	41	1.075	68	.382	25	.160	30.6%	50.7%	18.7%	.549
Lindor, Francisco	197	60	.983	118	.325	19	.105	30.5%	59.9%	9.6%	.503
Pujols, Albert	128	39	1.051	65	.281	24	.042	30.5%	50.8%	18.8%	.472
Cabrera, Miguel	155	47	1.217	89	.295	19	.158	30.3%	57.4%	12.3%	.556
Rengifo, Luis	66	20	.450	34	.188	12	.250	30.3%	51.5%	18.2%	.281
Rosario, Eddie	178	54	1.340	86	.294	38	.105	30.3%	48.3%	21.3%	.568
Biggio, Cavan	159	48	1.083	90	.389	21	.381	30.2%	56.6%	13.2%	.597
Blackmon, Charlie	182	55	1.096	100	.337	27	.333	30.2%	54.9%	14.8%	.559
Encarnacion, Edwin	106	32	1.452	50	.260	24	.083	30.2%	47.2%	22.6%	.571
Gurriel Jr., Lourdes	162	49	1.490	95	.376	18	.167	30.2%	58.6%	11.1%	.694
La Stella, Tommy	187	56	.982	104	.272	27	.231	29.9%	55.6%	14.4%	.478
Escobar, Eduardo	164	49	.771	95	.309	20	.100	29.9%	57.9%	12.2%	.420
Robert, Luis	131	39	1.513	58	.411	34	.176	29.8%	44.3%	26.0%	.682
Romine, Austin	84	25	1.040	36	.371	23	.130	29.8%	42.9%	27.4%	.506

418

Hard Hit Balls
Highest Percentage of Hard Hit Balls - Players with 100+ PA in 2020

Player	In Play	Hard Count	Hard SLG	Medium Count	Medium SLG	Soft Count	Soft SLG	Hard Pct	Medium Pct	Soft Pct	SLG
Hicks, Aaron	131	39	1.026	70	.371	22	.182	29.8%	53.4%	16.8%	.534
Ruf, Darin	64	19	1.789	33	.303	12	.083	29.7%	51.6%	18.8%	.703
Edman, Tommy	158	47	.956	78	.295	33	.273	29.7%	49.4%	20.9%	.481
Jones, JaCoby	64	19	1.526	33	.563	12	.250	29.7%	51.6%	18.8%	.794
Fuentes, Josh	71	21	1.100	38	.459	12	.333	29.6%	53.5%	16.9%	.623
Frazier, Todd	115	34	1.147	58	.310	23	.130	29.6%	50.4%	20.0%	.522
Caratini, Victor	85	25	.880	42	.310	18	.167	29.4%	49.4%	21.2%	.447
Ahmed, Nick	153	45	1.044	83	.337	25	.200	29.4%	54.2%	16.3%	.523
Maybin, Cameron	68	20	1.000	41	.341	7	.286	29.4%	60.3%	10.3%	.529
Lopes, Tim	109	32	.906	54	.352	23	.174	29.4%	49.5%	21.1%	.477
Gamel, Ben	75	22	1.455	41	.341	12	.000	29.3%	54.7%	16.0%	.613
Marte, Starling	188	55	.891	111	.391	22	.273	29.3%	59.0%	11.7%	.524
Hiura, Keston	134	39	1.658	69	.279	26	.269	29.1%	51.5%	19.4%	.674
Hoerner, Nico	86	25	.520	41	.308	20	.150	29.1%	47.7%	23.3%	.333
Markakis, Nick	107	31	.935	52	.385	24	.083	29.0%	48.6%	22.4%	.477
Profar, Jurickson	155	45	1.000	79	.286	31	.355	29.0%	51.0%	20.0%	.507
Kiner-Falefa, Isiah	180	52	.647	97	.392	31	.226	28.9%	53.9%	17.2%	.436
Margot, Manuel	121	35	.588	68	.412	18	.167	28.9%	56.2%	14.9%	.425
Brinson, Lewis	76	22	1.182	41	.268	13	.154	28.9%	53.9%	17.1%	.513
Shaw, Travis	114	33	1.333	66	.323	15	.133	28.9%	57.9%	13.2%	.593
Gregorius, Didi	190	55	1.302	90	.292	45	.222	28.9%	47.4%	23.7%	.561
Crawford, J.P.	167	48	.625	81	.342	38	.316	28.7%	48.5%	22.8%	.418
Castro, Willi	94	27	1.615	46	.432	21	.476	28.7%	48.9%	22.3%	.780
Iglesias, Jose	126	36	1.139	61	.517	29	.241	28.6%	48.4%	23.0%	.632
Bryant, Kris	91	26	1.077	49	.286	16	.250	28.6%	53.8%	17.6%	.505
Arraez, Luis	102	29	.571	62	.403	11	.364	28.4%	60.8%	10.8%	.446
Newman, Kevin	138	39	.486	69	.235	30	.300	28.3%	50.0%	21.7%	.319
Naylor, Josh	85	24	.792	43	.233	18	.167	28.2%	50.6%	21.2%	.376
Severino, Pedro	121	34	1.029	60	.322	27	.296	28.1%	49.6%	22.3%	.517
Grossman, Robbie	128	36	1.278	75	.413	17	.176	28.1%	58.6%	13.3%	.625
Semien, Marcus	161	45	1.000	79	.342	37	.189	28.0%	49.1%	23.0%	.491
Reddick, Josh	147	41	.829	73	.417	33	.212	27.9%	49.7%	22.4%	.486
Varsho, Daulton	68	19	1.211	38	.368	11	.000	27.9%	55.9%	16.2%	.544
Diaz, Yandy	97	27	.926	47	.298	23	.217	27.8%	48.5%	23.7%	.454
Bohm, Alec	126	35	1.171	71	.391	20	.450	27.8%	56.3%	15.9%	.621
Joyce, Matt	87	24	.739	48	.438	15	.267	27.6%	55.2%	17.2%	.488
Goldschmidt, Paul	149	41	1.125	86	.430	22	.318	27.5%	57.7%	14.8%	.601
Long Jr., Shed	80	22	1.091	41	.195	17	.118	27.5%	51.3%	21.3%	.425
Fowler, Dexter	62	17	1.176	32	.375	13	.231	27.4%	51.6%	21.0%	.565
Suzuki, Kurt	95	26	.960	48	.283	21	.333	27.4%	50.5%	22.1%	.478
Garcia, Avisail	132	36	.722	74	.392	22	.182	27.3%	56.1%	16.7%	.447
Albies, Ozzie	88	24	1.625	49	.265	15	.200	27.3%	55.7%	17.0%	.625
Adrianza, Ehire	66	18	.667	41	.293	7	.000	27.3%	62.1%	10.6%	.364
Bradley Jr., Jackie	144	39	1.359	78	.351	27	.222	27.1%	54.2%	18.8%	.601
Barnhart, Tucker	70	19	1.263	37	.270	14	.286	27.1%	52.9%	20.0%	.543
Tauchman, Mike	70	19	.737	34	.242	17	.412	27.1%	48.6%	24.3%	.420
Galvis, Freddy	111	30	1.333	58	.259	23	.087	27.0%	52.3%	20.7%	.514
Reyes, Victor	157	42	1.024	102	.314	13	.308	26.8%	65.0%	8.3%	.503
Kemp, Tony	82	22	.350	49	.333	11	.455	26.8%	59.8%	13.4%	.354
Holt, Brock	72	19	.778	39	.256	14	.143	26.4%	54.2%	19.4%	.366
Olivares, Edward	72	19	1.053	38	.378	15	.133	26.4%	52.8%	20.8%	.507
Hampson, Garrett	111	29	1.321	68	.308	14	.500	26.1%	61.3%	12.6%	.598
Gonzalez, Marwin	138	36	.829	81	.295	21	.190	26.1%	58.7%	15.2%	.418
Villar, Jonathan	134	35	.771	67	.344	32	.156	26.1%	50.0%	23.9%	.412
Nunez, Renato	132	34	1.824	67	.439	31	.161	25.8%	50.8%	23.5%	.733
Garcia, Luis	105	27	.963	50	.400	28	.107	25.7%	47.6%	26.7%	.467
Maldonado, Martin	86	22	1.500	51	.286	13	.308	25.6%	59.3%	15.1%	.607
Simmons, Andrelton	102	26	.692	54	.370	22	.182	25.5%	52.9%	21.6%	.412
Perez, Roberto	59	15	.800	28	.286	16	.063	25.4%	47.5%	27.1%	.356
Molina, Yadier	126	32	.935	71	.243	23	.261	25.4%	56.3%	18.3%	.419
Frazier, Adam	175	44	1.023	100	.293	31	.065	25.1%	57.1%	17.7%	.437
Akiyama, Shogo	121	30	.767	70	.300	21	.095	24.8%	57.9%	17.4%	.380
Camargo, Johan	85	21	1.571	49	.184	15	.133	24.7%	57.6%	17.6%	.518
Urias, Luis	77	19	.684	45	.289	13	.462	24.7%	58.4%	16.9%	.416
Polanco, Jorge	177	43	.698	93	.344	41	.317	24.3%	52.5%	23.2%	.425
Schoop, Jonathan	125	30	1.433	68	.379	27	.333	24.0%	54.4%	21.6%	.626
Wong, Kolten	154	37	.649	94	.308	23	.304	24.0%	61.0%	14.9%	.391
Lopez, Nicky	131	31	.581	69	.364	31	.097	23.7%	52.7%	23.7%	.352
Merrifield, Whit	216	51	1.059	135	.351	30	.267	23.6%	62.5%	13.9%	.507
Wade, Tyler	68	16	.938	39	.297	13	.077	23.5%	57.4%	19.1%	.409
DeShields, Delino	82	19	.579	52	.438	11	.182	23.2%	63.4%	13.4%	.436
Robles, Victor	118	27	1.000	65	.266	26	.423	22.9%	55.1%	22.0%	.461
Quinn, Roman	70	16	1.000	41	.350	13	.308	22.9%	58.6%	18.6%	.493

419

Hard Hit Balls

Highest Percentage of Hard Hit Balls - Players with 100+ PA in 2020

Player	In Play	Hard Count	Hard SLG	Medium Count	Medium SLG	Soft Count	Soft SLG	Overall Hard Pct	Overall Medium Pct	Overall Soft Pct	Overall SLG
Murphy, Daniel	103	23	.909	65	.277	15	.200	22.3%	63.1%	14.6%	.402
Gordon, Alex	126	28	.964	67	.224	31	.258	22.2%	53.2%	24.6%	.397
Berti, Jon	86	19	1.158	51	.271	16	.438	22.1%	59.3%	18.6%	.506
Rosario, Amed	109	24	1.167	65	.308	20	.250	22.0%	59.6%	18.3%	.486
Madrigal, Nick	96	21	.524	55	.345	20	.400	21.9%	57.3%	20.8%	.396
Nimmo, Brandon	143	31	1.839	82	.317	30	.233	21.7%	57.3%	21.0%	.629
Mendick, Danny	83	18	1.471	48	.292	17	.118	21.7%	57.8%	20.5%	.500
Fletcher, David	185	40	.975	112	.376	33	.242	21.6%	60.5%	17.8%	.484
Jansen, Danny	93	20	1.600	58	.111	15	.333	21.5%	62.4%	16.1%	.483
Mullins II, Cedric	107	23	1.130	67	.460	17	.118	21.5%	62.6%	15.9%	.553
Alberto, Hanser	193	41	1.075	109	.321	43	.209	21.2%	56.5%	22.3%	.455
Gimenez, Andres	91	19	1.421	56	.327	16	.125	20.9%	61.5%	17.6%	.522
Narvaez, Omar	69	14	1.214	39	.256	16	.125	20.3%	56.5%	23.2%	.420
Sogard, Eric	96	19	.526	64	.302	13	.231	19.8%	66.7%	13.5%	.337
Kieboom, Carter	67	13	.462	44	.279	10	.300	19.4%	65.7%	14.9%	.318
Hays, Austin	99	19	1.111	68	.358	12	.333	19.2%	68.7%	12.1%	.495
Tucker, Cole	80	15	.714	41	.325	24	.292	18.8%	51.3%	30.0%	.385
Paredes, Isaac	76	14	.643	45	.356	17	.235	18.4%	59.2%	22.4%	.382
Inciarte, Ender	94	13	.667	56	.296	25	.200	13.8%	59.6%	26.6%	.319
All MLB	43970	14584	1.129	22121	.318	7266	.205	33.2%	50.3%	16.5%	.568

RBI Percentages

Alex Vigderman

Fans of every team in baseball history have complained about a batter coming up who they're sure won't knock the runner in from second base because he's terrible in those spots. Batting average with runners in scoring position operationalizes this feeling in a way, but it misses out on other ways a hitter could succeed or fail with a runner on.

Bill James devised a method for measuring a player's RBI Opportunities over a decade ago, but it didn't make it onto these pages until last year. The guts of it are available in last season's edition or in the glossary at the end of this book, but in essence it's taking actual RBI and adding in "missed opportunities" based on the situation and what happened in that at-bat. RBI Percentage is just RBI divided by the total of RBI and RBI Opportunities.

As you might expect, good hitters knock in runs more often than bad hitters. Names like Soto, Freeman, Tatis, Voit, and Trout adorn the top of the leaderboard that follows. Tatis and Trout are also joined by teammates in Wil Myers and Jared Walsh, so fans of the Padres and Angels might have experienced a little less agita than average in big spots.

Well, that is, unless you saw the bottom of the list. Then you'll find more of Trout's teammates (Jo Adell and Luis Rengifo), who were responsible for only 10 RBI in 86.4 opportunities.

While you're down there, extend your pity to A's rookie infielder Vimael Machin, whose name is ripe for a pun that I cannot conceive of and who failed to knock in a run in 63 at-bats (24 opportunities). His unfortunate first foray into the major leagues wasn't on the level of former Orioles catcher Caleb Joseph (who came to the plate 141 times in 2016 without recording an RBI), but it's deserving of some sympathy.

The "RBI Man" isn't as celebrated as he once was, but we all know the feeling of dread when the player you're sure will choke comes up to the plate. Use this section to confirm or discredit your beliefs.

RBI Percentages by Batter

Player	AB	RBI	RBI Opps	Pct
Soto, Juan	154	37	70.2	.527
Freeman, Freddie	214	53	105.5	.502
Myers, Wil	198	40	79.8	.501
Perez, Salvador	150	32	64.2	.498
Tatis Jr., Fernando	224	45	92.6	.486
Walsh, Jared	99	26	54.0	.481
Voit, Luke	213	52	109.1	.477
Iglesias, Jose	142	24	50.4	.476
Trout, Mike	199	46	99.0	.465
Tellez, Rowdy	113	23	49.6	.464
Abreu, Jose	240	60	130.0	.462
Turner, Trea	233	41	88.8	.462
Betts, Mookie	219	39	85.0	.459
Moreland, Mitch	136	29	63.2	.459
Maldonado, Martin	135	24	52.6	.456
Lowe, Brandon	193	37	81.7	.453
Yastrzemski, Mike	192	35	77.4	.452
Hosmer, Eric	143	36	79.8	.451
Ozuna, Marcell	228	56	124.3	.451
Bichette, Bo	123	23	51.1	.450
Rojas, Miguel	125	20	44.6	.448
Jimenez, Eloy	213	41	91.8	.447
Smith, Dominic	177	42	94.1	.446
Ramirez, Jose	219	46	103.4	.445
Bote, David	125	29	65.5	.443
Judge, Aaron	101	22	49.7	.443
Taylor, Chris	185	32	72.2	.443
Knapp, Andrew	72	15	34.0	.441
Smith, Will	114	25	57.0	.439
Arraez, Luis	112	13	29.7	.438
Machado, Manny	224	47	107.2	.438
Garcia, Greg	60	11	25.2	.437
Moustakas, Mike	139	27	62.5	.432
Cabrera, Miguel	204	35	81.2	.431
Acuna Jr., Ronald	160	29	67.5	.430
Anderson, Brian	200	38	88.4	.430
Buxton, Byron	130	27	62.8	.430
Calhoun, Kole	190	40	93.5	.428
Rios, Edwin	76	17	39.9	.426
Bonifacio, Jorge	86	17	40.5	.420
Harrison, Josh	79	14	33.3	.420
Castro, Willi	129	24	57.3	.419
Ruf, Darin	87	18	43.0	.419
Braun, Ryan	129	26	62.3	.417
Hayes, Ke'Bryan	85	11	26.4	.417
Tucker, Kyle	209	42	100.8	.417
Winker, Jesse	149	23	55.1	.417
Osuna, Jose	78	11	26.5	.415
Rosario, Eddie	210	42	101.7	.413
Dickerson, Alex	151	27	65.7	.411
Frazier, Clint	131	26	63.2	.411
Mountcastle, Ryan	126	23	56.1	.410
Plawecki, Kevin	82	17	41.5	.410
Soler, Jorge	149	24	58.5	.410
LeMahieu, DJ	195	27	66.0	.409
Stewart, D.J.	88	15	36.8	.408
Urshela, Gio	151	30	73.8	.407
McCutchen, Andrew	217	34	83.7	.406
Springer, George	189	32	79.1	.405
Garcia, Leury	59	8	19.8	.404
Santander, Anthony	153	32	79.3	.404
Canha, Mark	191	33	81.8	.403
Stassi, Max	90	20	49.8	.402
Gregorius, Didi	215	40	99.8	.401
Kemp, Matt	117	21	52.4	.401
Arroyo, Christian	50	8	20.1	.398
Belt, Brandon	149	30	75.4	.398
Blackmon, Charlie	221	42	105.4	.398

Player	AB	RBI	RBI Opps	Pct
Bohm, Alec	160	23	57.8	.398
Alfaro, Jorge	93	16	40.4	.396
Cano, Robinson	171	30	75.7	.396
Hernandez, Teoscar	190	34	85.8	.396
Piscotty, Stephen	159	29	73.3	.396
Aguilar, Jesus	188	34	86.1	.395
Devers, Rafael	232	43	108.9	.395
Seager, Kyle	203	40	101.3	.395
Suarez, Eugenio	198	38	96.1	.395
Fuentes, Josh	98	17	43.1	.394
Turner, Justin	150	23	58.4	.394
Mathis, Jeff	62	9	23.0	.391
Pollock, A.J.	196	34	87.1	.390
Nola, Austin	161	28	72.2	.388
Candelario, Jeimer	185	29	75.0	.387
Donaldson, Josh	81	11	28.4	.387
Gurriel Jr., Lourdes	208	33	85.3	.387
Grandal, Yasmani	161	27	70.1	.385
Seager, Corey	212	41	106.5	.385
Choo, Shin-Soo	110	15	39.1	.384
Swanson, Dansby	237	35	91.3	.383
Peralta, David	203	34	88.9	.382
Cooper, Garrett	120	20	52.5	.381
Dalbec, Bobby	80	16	42.0	.381
Lux, Gavin	63	8	21.0	.381
Arozarena, Randy	64	11	29.0	.379
Franco, Maikel	223	38	100.2	.379
Cruz, Nelson	185	33	87.3	.378
Grichuk, Randal	216	35	92.6	.378
Solano, Donovan	190	29	76.9	.377
France, Ty	141	23	61.1	.376
Guerrero Jr., Vladimir	221	33	88.1	.375
Hoskins, Rhys	151	26	69.6	.374
Miller, Brad	142	25	66.8	.374
Conforto, Michael	202	31	83.0	.373
Kepler, Max	171	23	61.7	.373
Reyes, Franmil	211	34	91.4	.372
d'Arnaud, Travis	165	34	91.6	.371
Happ, Ian	198	28	75.5	.371
Heyward, Jason	147	22	59.5	.370
Renfroe, Hunter	122	22	59.5	.370
Nunez, Renato	195	31	84.1	.369
Albies, Ozzie	118	19	51.8	.367
Castellanos, Nick	218	34	92.7	.367
Jansen, Danny	120	20	54.5	.367
Ahmed, Nick	199	29	79.3	.366
Jeffers, Ryan	55	7	19.1	.366
Santana, Domingo	70	12	32.8	.366
Biggio, Cavan	220	28	76.8	.365
Odor, Rougned	138	30	82.3	.365
Brantley, Michael	170	22	60.5	.364
Grossman, Robbie	166	23	63.3	.363
Merrifield, Whit	248	30	82.6	.363
Brosseau, Mike	86	12	33.3	.360
Crawford, Brandon	172	28	78.1	.359
Harper, Bryce	190	33	91.8	.359
Schoop, Jonathan	162	23	64.1	.359
Stallings, Jacob	125	18	50.2	.359
Bregman, Alex	153	22	61.5	.358
DeJong, Paul	152	25	69.8	.358
Gonzalez, Marwin	175	22	61.4	.358
Naquin, Tyler	133	20	56.1	.357
Contreras, Willson	189	26	73.2	.355
Hicks, Aaron	169	21	59.1	.355
Locastro, Tim	69	7	19.7	.355
McCann, James	97	15	42.3	.355
McMahon, Ryan	172	26	73.9	.352
Carpenter, Matt	140	24	68.4	.351

Player	AB	RBI	RBI Opps	Pct
Olson, Matt	210	42	119.5	.351
Haseley, Adam	79	13	37.1	.350
Kelly, Carson	122	19	54.3	.350
Tromp, Chadwick	61	10	28.6	.350
Barnhart, Tucker	98	13	37.2	.349
Guzman, Ronald	78	9	25.8	.349
Fowler, Dexter	90	15	43.1	.348
McNeil, Jeff	183	23	66.1	.348
Stanton, Giancarlo	76	11	31.6	.348
Walker, Christian	218	34	97.8	.348
Engel, Adam	88	12	34.7	.346
Ruiz, Rio	185	32	92.6	.346
Edman, Tommy	204	26	75.3	.345
Pujols, Albert	152	25	72.4	.345
La Stella, Tommy	196	25	72.6	.344
Chapman, Matt	142	25	72.9	.343
Greiner, Grayson	51	8	23.3	.343
Gallo, Joey	193	26	76.3	.341
Laureano, Ramon	183	25	73.3	.341
Cabrera, Asdrubal	190	31	91.1	.340
Lowe, Nate	67	11	32.4	.340
Hiura, Keston	217	32	94.3	.339
Profar, Jurickson	180	25	73.8	.339
Kiermaier, Kevin	138	22	65.0	.338
Duvall, Adam	190	33	97.9	.337
Marte, Ketel	181	17	50.4	.337
Bogaerts, Xander	203	28	83.7	.335
Rendon, Anthony	189	31	92.8	.334
Cave, Jake	113	15	45.0	.333
Hernandez, Kike	139	20	60.0	.333
Guillorme, Luis	57	9	27.1	.332
Robert, Luis	202	31	93.4	.332
Moore, Dylan	137	17	51.4	.331
Bellinger, Cody	213	30	90.8	.330
Crawford, J.P.	204	24	72.8	.330
Mazara, Nomar	136	15	45.4	.330
White, Evan	182	26	78.7	.330
Flores, Wilmer	198	32	97.4	.329
Murphy, Daniel	123	16	48.6	.329
Pederson, Joc	121	16	48.6	.329
Caratini, Victor	116	16	48.8	.328
Solak, Nick	209	23	70.1	.328
Taylor, Michael A.	92	16	48.8	.328
Gyorko, Jedd	117	17	52.1	.326
Marte, Starling	228	27	82.9	.326
Sano, Miguel	186	25	76.8	.326
Frazier, Adam	209	23	70.8	.325
Marmolejos, Jose	107	18	55.5	.324
Arauz, Jonathan	72	9	27.9	.323
Jones, JaCoby	97	14	43.5	.322
Tapia, Raimel	184	17	52.8	.322
Segura, Jean	192	25	77.9	.321
Gosselin, Phil	92	12	37.5	.320
Grisham, Trent	215	26	81.3	.320
Heineman, Scott	52	7	21.9	.320
Pillar, Kevin	208	26	81.2	.320
Realmuto, J.T.	173	32	100.0	.320
Santana, Danny	55	7	21.9	.320
Alonso, Pete	208	35	110.1	.318
Lewis, Kyle	206	28	88.1	.318
Vazquez, Christian	173	23	72.4	.318
Kipnis, Jason	114	16	50.5	.317
Muncy, Max	203	27	85.1	.317
Tsutsugo, Yoshi	157	24	75.7	.317
Anderson, Tim	208	21	66.5	.316
Cronenworth, Jake	172	20	63.2	.316
Bradley Jr., Jackie	191	22	69.9	.315
Moncada, Yoan	200	24	76.2	.315
Upton, Justin	147	22	69.8	.315

Player	AB	RBI	RBI Opps	Pct
Casali, Curt	76	8	25.5	.314
Galvis, Freddy	141	16	51.0	.314
Gonzalez, Erik	181	20	63.9	.313
O'Hearn, Ryan	113	18	57.5	.313
Riley, Austin	188	27	86.2	.313
Votto, Joey	186	22	70.5	.312
Santana, Carlos	206	30	96.6	.311
Vogelbach, Daniel	115	16	51.5	.311
Zunino, Mike	75	10	32.2	.311
Perez, Michael	84	13	41.9	.310
Adames, Willy	185	23	74.5	.309
Wong, Kolten	181	16	51.8	.309
Correa, Carlos	201	25	81.2	.308
Meadows, Austin	132	13	42.3	.307
O'Neill, Tyler	139	19	61.8	.307
Eaton, Adam	159	17	55.5	.306
Fletcher, David	207	18	58.9	.306
Brinson, Lewis	106	12	39.3	.305
Moran, Colin	178	23	75.3	.305
Ohtani, Shohei	153	24	78.8	.305
Suzuki, Kurt	111	17	55.7	.305
Pham, Tommy	109	12	39.5	.304
Dietrich, Derek	61	8	26.4	.303
Haggerty, Sam	50	6	19.8	.303
Bruce, Jay	96	14	46.4	.302
Castro, Jason	80	9	29.8	.302
Kendrick, Howie	91	14	46.3	.302
Lopes, Tim	143	15	49.6	.302
Joyce, Matt	127	14	46.5	.301
Tauchman, Mike	95	14	46.7	.300
Calhoun, Willie	100	13	43.5	.299
Madrigal, Nick	103	11	36.8	.299
McBroom, Ryan	81	10	33.4	.299
Semien, Marcus	211	23	77.0	.299
Senzel, Nick	70	8	26.8	.299
Romine, Austin	130	17	57.1	.298
Wade, Tyler	88	10	33.6	.298
Cervelli, Francisco	53	7	23.6	.297
Goldschmidt, Paul	191	21	70.7	.297
Story, Trevor	235	28	94.2	.297
Alberto, Hanser	219	22	74.4	.296
Reynolds, Bryan	185	19	64.1	.296
Wendle, Joey	168	17	57.4	.296
Trevino, Jose	76	9	30.6	.294
Rizzo, Anthony	203	24	81.9	.293
Arenado, Nolan	182	26	88.9	.292
Longoria, Evan	193	28	95.8	.292
Martinez, Jose	88	10	34.3	.292
Diaz, Yandy	114	11	37.8	.291
Gardner, Brett	130	15	51.5	.291
Goodwin, Brian	144	22	75.7	.291
Schwarber, Kyle	191	24	82.5	.291
Urias, Luis	109	11	37.8	.291
Pinder, Chad	56	8	27.6	.290
Carlson, Dylan	110	16	55.4	.289
Gomes, Yan	109	13	45.0	.289
Hernandez, Cesar	233	20	69.2	.289
Nimmo, Brandon	186	18	62.3	.289
Phillips, Brett	51	5	17.3	.289
Polanco, Gregory	157	22	76.0	.289
Valaika, Pat	141	16	55.4	.289
Reddick, Josh	188	23	80.0	.288
Polanco, Jorge	209	19	66.2	.287
Smoak, Justin	119	15	52.3	.287
Martinez, J.D.	211	27	94.4	.286
Choi, Ji-Man	122	16	56.2	.285
Garcia, Luis	134	16	56.6	.283
Bader, Harrison	106	11	39.2	.281
Garcia, Avisail	181	15	53.4	.281

Player	AB	RBI	RBI Opps	Pct
Molina, Yadier	145	16	56.9	.281
Dahl, David	93	9	32.1	.280
Diaz, Elias	68	9	32.2	.280
Goodrum, Niko	158	20	71.7	.279
Mullins II, Cedric	140	12	43.2	.278
Berti, Jon	120	14	50.6	.277
Hoerner, Nico	108	13	47.0	.277
Severino, Pedro	160	21	75.7	.277
Straw, Myles	82	8	28.9	.277
Narvaez, Omar	108	10	36.5	.274
Dubon, Mauricio	157	19	69.5	.273
Ford, Mike	74	11	40.3	.273
Bell, Josh	195	22	80.9	.272
Lamb, Jake	88	10	36.8	.272
Yelich, Christian	200	22	80.8	.272
Verdugo, Alex	201	15	56.1	.267
Baez, Javier	222	24	90.6	.265
Wolters, Tony	100	8	30.3	.264
Encarnacion, Edwin	159	19	72.2	.263
Hilliard, Sam	105	10	38.1	.262
Espinal, Santiago	60	6	23.0	.261
Bryant, Kris	131	11	42.3	.260
Sanchez, Gary	156	24	92.2	.260
Arcia, Orlando	173	20	77.3	.259
Lindor, Francisco	236	27	104.3	.259
Markakis, Nick	130	15	57.9	.259
Torres, Gleyber	136	16	62.0	.258
Murphy, Sean	116	14	54.7	.256
Smith Jr., Dwight	63	6	23.4	.256
Altuve, Jose	192	18	70.5	.255
Chavis, Michael	146	19	74.8	.254
Davis, J.D.	190	19	75.5	.252
Luplow, Jordan	78	8	31.7	.252
Robles, Victor	168	15	59.5	.252
Mondesi, Adalberto	219	22	87.7	.251
Olivares, Edward	96	10	39.8	.251
Shaw, Travis	163	17	68.0	.250
Ward, Taylor	94	5	20.0	.250
Gimenez, Andres	118	12	48.2	.249
Sisco, Chance	98	10	40.5	.247
Gurriel, Yuli	211	22	89.3	.246
Tejeda, Anderson	75	8	32.6	.245
Gamel, Ben	114	10	41.0	.244
Dyson, Jarrod	61	5	20.7	.242
Beaty, Matt	50	5	20.9	.239
Dickerson, Corey	194	17	71.1	.239
Vogt, Stephen	72	7	29.4	.238
Starling, Bubba	59	5	21.1	.237
Thames, Eric	123	12	50.6	.237
Chisholm, Jazz	56	6	25.4	.236
Reyes, Victor	202	14	59.3	.236
Akiyama, Shogo	155	9	38.4	.234
Rosario, Amed	143	15	64.0	.234
Diaz, Aledmys	58	6	25.7	.233
Barnes, Austin	86	9	38.8	.232
Hays, Austin	122	9	39.0	.231
Stewart, Christin	90	9	39.2	.230
Escobar, Eduardo	203	20	87.3	.229
Ramos, Wilson	142	15	65.5	.229
Frazier, Todd	157	12	53.1	.226
Toro, Abraham	87	9	40.0	.225
DeShields, Delino	107	7	31.3	.224
Simmons, Andrelton	118	10	44.8	.223
Inciarte, Ender	116	10	45.4	.220
Sogard, Eric	115	10	45.4	.220
Kieboom, Carter	99	9	41.2	.218
Long Jr., Shed	117	9	41.2	.218
Andujar, Miguel	62	5	23.0	.217
Davis, Khris	85	10	46.0	.217

Player	AB	RBI	RBI Opps	Pct
Pence, Hunter	52	6	27.9	.215
Slater, Austin	85	7	32.6	.215
Newman, Kevin	156	10	46.7	.214
Lopez, Nicky	169	13	61.1	.213
Taveras, Leody	119	6	28.2	.213
Margot, Manuel	145	11	52.2	.211
Torrens, Luis	70	6	28.6	.210
Varsho, Daulton	101	9	42.8	.210
Villar, Jonathan	185	15	71.4	.210
Maybin, Cameron	93	7	33.5	.209
Hedges, Austin	69	6	29.0	.207
Kiner-Falefa, Isiah	211	10	49.4	.202
Dozier, Hunter	158	12	60.7	.198
Castro, Starlin	60	4	20.3	.197
Garver, Mitch	72	5	25.4	.197
Gordon, Alex	163	11	56.1	.196
Farmer, Kyle	64	4	20.5	.195
Hampson, Garrett	167	11	56.7	.194
Camargo, Johan	120	9	46.9	.192
VanMeter, Josh	70	6	31.4	.191
Paredes, Isaac	100	6	31.5	.190
Peraza, Jose	111	8	42.4	.189
Panik, Joe	120	7	37.5	.187
Chirinos, Robinson	74	7	37.6	.186
Tucker, Cole	109	8	43.2	.185
Bart, Joey	103	7	38.9	.180
Naylor, Josh	97	6	33.8	.178
Mendick, Danny	107	6	33.9	.177
Andrus, Elvis	103	7	40.1	.175
Mercado, Oscar	86	6	34.6	.173
Ervin, Phillip	74	4	23.3	.172
Holt, Brock	95	5	29.1	.172
Flowers, Tyler	69	5	29.2	.171
Quinn, Roman	108	7	42.2	.166
Gallagher, Cam	53	3	18.2	.165
Kingery, Scott	113	6	36.4	.165
Sandoval, Pablo	84	6	36.7	.163
Kemp, Tony	93	4	25.0	.160
Perez, Roberto	97	5	31.9	.157
Lin, Tzu-Wei	52	3	19.7	.152
Cameron, Daz	57	3	20.6	.146
Jay, Jon	50	4	27.9	.143
Leon, Sandy	66	4	28.3	.141
Adell, Jo	124	7	51.1	.137
Vargas, Ildemaro	51	3	23.6	.127
Strange-Gordon, Dee	75	3	24.3	.123
Rojas, Josh	61	2	18.0	.111
Velazquez, Andrew	63	3	29.3	.102
Adrianza, Ehire	89	3	31.3	.096
Garcia, Jose	67	2	21.8	.092
Hechavarria, Adeiny	59	2	22.0	.091
Murphy, John Ryan	58	2	22.1	.090
Rengifo, Luis	90	3	35.3	.085
Riddle, JT	67	1	17.0	.059
Davis, Chris	52	1	21.8	.046
Machin, Vimael	63	0	24.0	.000

Pinch Hitting

Mark Simon

As is noted elsewhere in the book, the unified usage of the designated hitter greatly reduced the reliance on pinch-hitters. NL teams went from using a combined 1.79 pinch-hitters per game to 0.73, a drop of 59%.

You can see it in the pages of this book. This year's pinch-hitter data section is a page shorter than the 2020 edition.

There was a time in which the pinch-hitter was a highly-specialized role on a team. Manny Mota, Greg Gross and Rusty Staub are among the players who had their careers prolonged by their team's need for a guy who could come off the bench and be highly effective in a one at-bat role.

As we've noted previously, pinch-hitting is hard. Pinch-hitters these days typically hit just over .200 as a group. Coming into a game and facing a hard-throwing pitcher while barely being warmed up is a less-than-ideal situation.

The spirit of Mota, Gross, and Staub lives on in Ryan McBroom of the Kansas City Royals. McBroom was 5-for-15 with three home runs in a pinch-hitting role this season. He led the majors in pinch hits and was the only player with multiple pinch-hit home runs. His pinch-hitting teammates were a combined 4-for-30.

McBroom was clutch. Those three home runs came in a three-week span in August. Two of them were game-tying home runs. The other was a go-ahead homer. All three came in the seventh inning or later.

Josh Naylor of the Indians ranked second with four pinch hits, though his lacked the impact of McBroom's.

From pinch-hitting greatness, we pivot to pinch-hitting futility, and that shows up for one of McBroom's teammates and name-mates. Ryan O'Hearn went 0-for-9 as a pinch-hitter, though he did walk twice. He had the most at-bats without a hit among pinch-hitters in 2020.

Teamwise, a shortened season makes for some weird stats, and there were a few on the pinch-hitting side. Diamondbacks pinch-hitters went a combined 0-for-22 this season. Cardinals pinch-hitters went 1-for-29.

The Giants had the most pinch-hit at-bats in 2020, 60, which seems appropriate given how intentional that team was at mixing and matching with its roster to gain advantages in games. They had fair success, batting .267 with an MLB-leading four pinch-hit homers. Nationals hitters had the highest pinch-hit batting average, .321 (9-for-28).

The following pages in this section feature pinch-hitting records for every batter with at least 5 pinch-hit plate appearances or pinch total bases in 2020 as well as career totals for every active player with at least 100 pinch-hit plate appearances.

The Flat Bat Award

Bunting, like pinch-hitting, is on the decline. But some players are still good at it. The most successful bunter in 2020 was Orioles outfielder Cedric Mullins, who went 9-for-10 when trying to bunt for a hit and had four successful sacrifices with no failed sacrifice attempts. The nine bunt hits led MLB.

Pinch Hitting

Pinch Hitters with 5+ PAs or 5+ Total Bases in 2020

Batter	B	AB	H	2B	3B	HR	RBI	TBB	IBB	SO	GDP	Avg	OBP	Slg	OPS
Adrianza, Ehire	B	6	1	1	0	0	0	0	0	3	0	.167	.167	.333	.500
Akiyama, Shogo	L	4	2	0	1	0	2	1	0	0	0	.500	.600	1.000	1.600
Aquino, Aristides	R	3	0	0	0	0	1	0	0	2	0	.000	.400	.000	.400
Belt, Brandon	L	6	2	1	0	1	3	0	0	3	0	.333	.333	1.000	1.333
Braun, Ryan	R	5	3	0	0	0	1	0	0	1	0	.600	.600	.600	1.200
Brinson, Lewis	R	8	2	1	0	0	2	1	0	4	0	.250	.333	.375	.708
Bruce, Jay	L	8	2	0	0	0	0	0	0	2	0	.250	.250	.250	.500
Caratini, Victor	B	5	2	1	0	0	0	0	0	1	1	.400	.400	.600	1.000
Casali, Curt	R	4	0	0	0	0	0	1	0	4	0	.000	.200	.000	.200
Castro, Harold	L	5	3	0	0	0	2	0	0	0	0	.600	.600	.600	1.200
Choi, Ji-Man	L	7	3	1	0	0	3	2	1	2	0	.429	.500	.571	1.071
Cordero, Franchy	L	5	1	1	0	0	1	0	0	1	0	.200	.200	.400	.600
Davidson, Matt	R	9	1	0	0	1	4	1	0	4	0	.111	.200	.444	.644
Davis, Khris	R	4	0	0	0	0	0	1	0	2	1	.000	.200	.000	.200
Diaz, Elias	R	6	1	0	0	0	0	1	0	3	0	.167	.286	.167	.452
Dickerson, Alex	L	8	3	1	0	1	3	6	2	3	0	.375	.643	.875	1.518
Dietrich, Derek	L	4	1	0	0	0	0	0	0	0	0	.250	.500	.250	.750
Duvall, Adam	R	5	2	1	0	1	4	0	0	1	0	.400	.400	1.200	1.600
Ervin, Phillip	R	9	1	0	0	0	0	4	0	3	1	.111	.429	.111	.540
Flores, Wilmer	R	4	1	1	0	0	1	0	0	2	0	.250	.200	.500	.700
Ford, Mike	L	6	1	0	0	0	0	3	0	2	0	.167	.500	.167	.667
France, Ty	R	6	0	0	0	0	0	2	0	2	1	.000	.250	.000	.250
Freeman, Mike	L	7	1	0	0	0	0	1	0	2	0	.143	.250	.143	.393
Garcia, Greg	L	9	3	0	0	0	4	1	0	1	0	.333	.400	.333	.733
Goodwin, Brian	L	6	2	1	0	0	1	0	0	2	0	.333	.333	.500	.833
Gosselin, Phil	R	7	2	1	0	0	1	1	1	3	0	.286	.375	.429	.804
Grossman, Robbie	B	4	2	1	0	0	1	1	1	1	0	.500	.600	.750	1.350
Guillorme, Luis	L	6	0	0	0	0	0	1	0	3	0	.000	.143	.000	.143
Gyorko, Jedd	R	5	1	1	0	0	1	2	0	1	0	.200	.429	.400	.829
Hampson, Garrett	R	5	0	0	0	0	0	0	0	3	0	.000	.000	.000	.000
Harrison, Josh	R	5	0	0	0	0	0	1	0	1	0	.000	.000	.000	.000
Haseley, Adam	L	5	2	0	0	0	2	0	0	1	0	.400	.400	.400	.800
Hernandez, Kike	R	10	1	0	0	0	1	0	0	4	0	.100	.100	.100	.200
Hicks, Aaron	B	4	2	0	0	0	0	1	0	1	1	.500	.600	.500	1.100
Holaday, Bryan	R	4	0	0	0	0	0	1	0	2	0	.000	.200	.000	.200
Holt, Brock	L	7	0	0	0	0	0	0	0	3	0	.000	.000	.000	.000
Joyce, Matt	L	6	2	1	0	0	1	2	0	1	1	.333	.500	.500	1.000
Kemp, Matt	R	9	2	1	0	0	3	4	0	3	0	.222	.462	.333	.795
Kiermaier, Kevin	L	5	2	0	0	0	2	1	0	3	0	.400	.500	.400	.900
Knapp, Andrew	B	3	1	0	0	0	0	2	0	0	0	.333	.600	.333	.933
Locastro, Tim	R	4	0	0	0	0	0	1	0	2	0	.000	.200	.000	.200
Lopes, Tim	R	7	1	0	0	0	2	0	0	2	1	.143	.143	.143	.286
Lowe, Brandon	L	6	1	1	0	0	2	1	0	1	0	.167	.286	.333	.619
Luplow, Jordan	R	5	1	0	0	0	0	0	0	2	2	.200	.200	.200	.400
Martinez, Jose	R	11	2	1	0	0	3	2	0	6	1	.182	.308	.273	.580
Mathias, Mark	R	5	0	0	0	0	0	0	0	2	0	.000	.000	.000	.000
Maybin, Cameron	R	3	0	0	0	0	1	1	0	0	1	.000	.400	.000	.400
McBroom, Ryan	R	15	5	0	0	3	4	2	0	6	0	.333	.412	.933	1.345
Murphy, Daniel	L	7	2	0	0	1	3	1	1	2	0	.286	.375	.714	1.089
Naquin, Tyler	L	5	2	1	0	1	2	2	0	1	0	.400	.571	.600	1.171
Narvaez, Omar	L	4	0	0	0	0	0	1	0	2	0	.000	.200	.000	.200
Naylor, Josh	L	10	4	0	1	0	1	1	0	0	0	.400	.455	.600	1.055
O'Hearn, Ryan	L	9	0	0	0	0	0	2	0	5	0	.000	.182	.000	.182
Panik, Joe	L	5	0	0	0	0	0	1	0	1	0	.000	.167	.000	.167
Pederson, Joc	L	4	2	1	0	0	1	1	0	0	0	.500	.600	.750	1.350
Peterson, Jace	L	3	2	0	0	1	2	0	0	1	0	.667	.667	1.667	2.333
Phegley, Josh	R	6	0	0	0	0	0	0	0	2	0	.000	.000	.000	.000
Pillar, Kevin	R	5	1	0	0	0	0	0	0	2	0	.200	.200	.200	.400
Pinder, Chad	R	7	1	0	0	1	2	0	0	2	1	.143	.143	.571	.714
Polanco, Gregory	L	5	0	0	0	0	0	0	0	3	0	.000	.000	.000	.000
Pollock, A.J.	R	7	3	2	0	1	3	0	0	2	1	.429	.375	1.143	1.518
Rios, Edwin	L	4	0	0	0	0	0	1	0	3	0	.000	.333	.000	.333
Ruf, Darin	R	11	1	0	0	1	1	3	0	6	0	.091	.286	.364	.649
Sanchez, Gary	R	4	2	0	0	1	4	0	0	1	0	.500	.500	1.250	1.750
Sandoval, Pablo	B	13	3	0	0	0	0	0	0	5	0	.231	.231	.231	.462
Schrock, Max	L	5	0	0	0	0	0	0	0	3	0	.000	.000	.000	.000
Severino, Pedro	R	5	3	0	0	1	2	1	0	1	0	.600	.667	1.200	1.867
Shaw, Travis	L	4	0	0	0	0	0	1	0	4	0	.000	.200	.000	.200

427

Pinch Hitting
Pinch Hitters with 5+ PAs or 5+ Total Bases in 2020

		Pinch Hitting													
Batter	B	AB	H	2B	3B	HR	RBI	TBB	IBB	SO	GDP	Avg	OBP	Slg	OPS
Sisco, Chance	L	4	0	0	0	0	0	1	0	3	0	.000	.200	.000	.200
Smoak, Justin	B	5	0	0	0	0	0	0	0	2	1	.000	.000	.000	.000
Sogard, Eric	L	9	3	0	0	0	1	1	0	1	1	.333	.400	.333	.733
Solano, Donovan	R	5	2	0	0	0	0	0	0	1	0	.400	.400	.400	.800
Taylor, Tyrone	R	5	2	2	0	0	1	0	0	0	0	.400	.400	.800	1.200
Tellez, Rowdy	L	5	1	1	0	0	0	0	0	2	0	.200	.333	.400	.733
Toro, Abraham	B	10	1	1	0	0	0	0	0	4	0	.100	.100	.200	.300
Tsutsugo, Yoshi	L	9	1	0	0	0	1	0	0	3	0	.111	.111	.111	.222
Valaika, Pat	R	5	1	0	0	1	1	0	0	2	0	.200	.200	.800	1.000
Vargas, Ildemaro	B	6	0	0	0	0	0	0	0	4	0	.000	.000	.000	.000
Winker, Jesse	L	5	2	1	0	0	1	1	0	1	0	.400	.500	.600	1.100

Career Pinch Hitting
Active Pinch Hitters with 100+ PAs in their careers

		Pinch Hitting													
Batter	B	AB	H	2B	3B	HR	RBI	TBB	IBB	SO	GDP	Avg	OBP	Slg	OPS
Adams, Matt	L	220	56	10	0	11	49	11	3	76	4	.255	.291	.450	.741
Aguilar, Jesus	R	123	27	6	0	5	18	14	0	44	6	.220	.300	.390	.690
Almora Jr., Albert	R	102	19	3	0	1	14	3	1	17	5	.186	.213	.245	.458
Bonifacio, Emilio	B	121	24	2	2	0	7	8	1	40	1	.198	.252	.248	.500
Culberson, Charlie	R	140	32	3	3	6	27	6	0	40	6	.229	.262	.421	.683
Dickerson, Corey	L	97	21	7	1	0	9	6	4	29	1	.216	.262	.309	.571
Dietrich, Derek	L	116	23	9	1	5	18	8	1	39	2	.198	.326	.422	.749
Flores, Wilmer	R	90	21	5	0	5	18	10	1	24	0	.233	.314	.456	.769
Forsythe, Logan	R	92	19	5	0	2	12	11	0	29	3	.207	.302	.326	.628
Fowler, Dexter	B	90	22	5	1	3	11	15	0	30	0	.244	.358	.422	.781
Garcia, Greg	L	192	50	7	0	2	19	34	0	55	3	.260	.387	.328	.715
Gosselin, Phil	R	171	43	8	0	1	12	13	2	54	2	.251	.301	.316	.617
Grandal, Yasmani	B	86	18	3	0	3	16	19	0	37	3	.209	.352	.349	.701
Gyorko, Jedd	R	103	22	6	0	2	13	14	1	28	0	.214	.303	.330	.633
Harrison, Josh	R	118	19	2	1	3	14	4	0	22	2	.161	.194	.271	.465
Hernandez, Kike	R	159	33	8	0	6	20	17	3	50	1	.208	.281	.371	.652
Jay, Jon	L	152	42	3	1	3	19	14	1	37	7	.276	.356	.368	.725
Joyce, Matt	L	280	59	16	1	8	40	57	3	84	10	.211	.344	.361	.705
Kemp, Matt	R	98	19	3	0	3	17	9	1	39	6	.194	.262	.316	.578
Kendrick, Howie	R	91	27	6	0	2	13	8	0	20	4	.297	.353	.429	.782
La Stella, Tommy	L	164	45	14	0	1	23	26	1	27	5	.274	.387	.378	.765
Martinez, Jose	R	98	30	5	1	3	18	12	2	26	4	.306	.382	.469	.851
Moreland, Mitch	L	98	28	5	0	4	23	15	2	26	3	.286	.386	.459	.845
Murphy, Daniel	L	144	35	6	2	5	31	11	3	35	3	.243	.293	.417	.710
Osuna, Jose	R	106	21	5	0	7	14	1	0	21	8	.198	.213	.443	.656
Pederson, Joc	L	99	19	5	0	4	11	20	0	31	0	.192	.325	.364	.689
Perez, Hernan	R	101	20	5	1	1	8	7	0	26	4	.198	.250	.297	.547
Rodriguez, Sean	R	153	23	2	0	5	19	23	0	70	2	.150	.280	.261	.542
Sandoval, Pablo	B	127	39	13	0	3	22	8	3	37	4	.307	.350	.480	.831
Solano, Donovan	R	117	28	0	3	0	9	5	0	29	2	.239	.288	.291	.579
Thames, Eric	L	97	16	2	1	3	10	16	0	45	1	.165	.283	.299	.582
Turner, Justin	R	172	45	10	0	6	38	16	1	34	8	.262	.325	.424	.749
Valaika, Pat	R	106	29	11	0	6	21	5	0	40	3	.274	.304	.547	.851
Vogt, Stephen	L	98	17	6	1	2	11	17	3	29	0	.173	.291	.316	.607

Manufactured Runs, Productive Outs & Unproductive Outs

Alex Vigderman

With the analytics-ization (that's an industry term) of baseball over the last two decades, "doing the little things right" has lost some of its cachet in baseball culture. After all, if you hit the ball over the fence, you don't need to worry about moving the runner over anymore.

Sure, we see less of the typical small-ball tactics and execution these days. Let's leave that part be. What I find interesting is how different teams get to the runs they do score.

The Dodgers led the league in runs per game, which shocked no one considering the lineups they put out every day. But even their star players did the little things well. Mookie Betts led the league in manufactured runs, and Corey Seager was near the lead in productive outs. As a team, the Dodgers had the fourth-fewest unproductive outs.

Now, consider the Braves. They trailed only the Dodgers in runs per game (5.8), but they trailed all of the other six teams with at least five runs per game in manufactured runs. They also made 17 more unproductive outs than any other team. They mashed, and they didn't seem too hampered by their lack of traditional fundamental hitting.

The Nationals had a disappointing season defending their World Series title, but it wasn't for a lack of effort and situational hitting. They tied for the lead in manufactured runs and made more productive outs than anyone. Shortstop Trea Turner led the way, finishing in the top five in both categories.

If you need a run-down of what we consider manufactured runs, productive outs, and unproductive outs, check out the glossary at the end of the book, then come back and enjoy some good old blue-collar baseball.

Players with the most Manufactured Runs, Productive Outs, & Unproductive Outs

Manufactured Runs		Productive Outs		Unproductive Outs	
Betts, Mookie	14	Seager, Kyle	20	Baez, Javier	45
Alberto, Hanser	13	Blackmon, Charlie	19	Mondesi, Adalberto	45
Turner, Trea	13	Seager, Corey	18	Story, Trevor	44
Soto, Juan	13	Turner, Trea	18	Ozuna, Marcell	43
Marte, Starling	12	Heyward, Jason	16	Alonso, Pete	43
Kiner-Falefa, Isiah	11	Gurriel, Yuli	15	Devers, Rafael	42
Mondesi, Adalberto	11	Cano, Robinson	14	Trout, Mike	40
Ahmed, Nick	10	Smith, Dominic	14	Harper, Bryce	37
Biggio, Cavan	10	Walker, Christian	14	Lewis, Kyle	37
Fletcher, David	9	Ohtani, Shohei	14	Hiura, Keston	36
Segura, Jean	9	Arenado, Nolan	14	Swanson, Dansby	35
Wong, Kolten	9	Rizzo, Anthony	13	Sano, Miguel	35
Goldschmidt, Paul	8	Cabrera, Asdrubal	13	Castellanos, Nick	35
Quinn, Roman	8	Bell, Josh	13	Nunez, Renato	35
Crawford, J.P.	8	Abreu, Jose	13	Davis, J.D.	35
Robert, Luis	8	Solak, Nick	12	Lindor, Francisco	35
Robles, Victor	8	Peralta, David	12	Olson, Matt	34
Grisham, Trent	8	Martinez, J.D.	12	Gurriel, Yuli	34
Solak, Nick	8	Miller, Brad	12	Ramirez, Jose	34
Hampson, Garrett	8	Marte, Ketel	12	Robert, Luis	34
Adames, Willy	8	Grossman, Robbie	12	Arenado, Nolan	34
Blackmon, Charlie	7	Gonzalez, Marwin	11	Blackmon, Charlie	34
Lewis, Kyle	7	Altuve, Jose	11	Conforto, Michael	34
Berti, Jon	7	Laureano, Ramon	11	Moncada, Yoan	33
Swanson, Dansby	7	Cronenworth, Jake	11	Voit, Luke	33
Moore, Dylan	7	Reyes, Franmil	11	Tatis Jr., Fernando	33
Harper, Bryce	7	Brantley, Michael	11	Arcia, Orlando	33
Candelario, Jeimer	7	Flores, Wilmer	11	Solano, Donovan	33
Ramirez, Jose	7	Olson, Matt	11	Semien, Marcus	32
Story, Trevor	7	Suzuki, Kurt	11	Martinez, J.D.	32
Polanco, Jorge	7	Escobar, Eduardo	11	Flores, Wilmer	32
Yelich, Christian	7	Profar, Jurickson	11	Santander, Anthony	32
Calhoun, Kole	7	Kiner-Falefa, Isiah	11	Smith, Dominic	32
Machado, Manny	7	Bellinger, Cody	11	Reynolds, Bryan	32
Gurriel Jr., Lourdes	7	Lindor, Francisco	11	Ruiz, Rio	31
Anderson, Tim	7			Grisham, Trent	31
				Marte, Starling	31
				Longoria, Evan	31

Manufactured Runs, Productive Outs, & Unproductive Outs Produced by Team

Team	Manufactured Runs	Productive Outs	Unproductive Outs
Arizona Diamondbacks	66	98	261
Atlanta Braves	42	69	330
Baltimore Orioles	47	73	300
Boston Red Sox	38	66	299
Chicago White Sox	47	73	269
Chicago Cubs	49	76	256
Cincinnati Reds	27	51	229
Cleveland Indians	41	76	277
Colorado Rockies	58	99	286
Detroit Tigers	31	50	266
Houston Astros	40	86	275
Kansas City Royals	40	78	275
Los Angeles Dodgers	54	74	242
Los Angeles Angels	49	80	309
Miami Marlins	51	63	269
Milwaukee Brewers	23	47	261
Minnesota Twins	47	69	250
New York Yankees	48	67	264
New York Mets	30	80	308
Oakland Athletics	39	90	279
Philadelphia Phillies	67	67	272
Pittsburgh Pirates	45	77	260
San Diego Padres	46	83	264
San Francisco Giants	31	77	313
Seattle Mariners	54	80	255
St Louis Cardinals	43	73	234
Tampa Bay Rays	56	73	268
Texas Rangers	49	75	231
Toronto Blue Jays	45	81	248
Washington Nationals	67	109	255

Manufactured Runs, Productive Outs, & Unproductive Outs Allowed by Team

Team	Manufactured Runs	Productive Outs	Unproductive Outs
Arizona Diamondbacks	39	76	272
Atlanta Braves	57	79	271
Baltimore Orioles	54	82	283
Boston Red Sox	53	78	313
Chicago White Sox	40	62	261
Chicago Cubs	39	72	224
Cincinnati Reds	37	68	253
Cleveland Indians	23	52	271
Colorado Rockies	67	98	271
Detroit Tigers	46	85	267
Houston Astros	46	87	272
Kansas City Royals	45	60	277
Los Angeles Dodgers	44	93	276
Los Angeles Angels	56	93	272
Miami Marlins	53	81	281
Milwaukee Brewers	42	82	271
Minnesota Twins	28	52	264
New York Yankees	39	66	250
New York Mets	50	76	285
Oakland Athletics	40	68	269
Philadelphia Phillies	50	73	288
Pittsburgh Pirates	53	78	253
San Diego Padres	44	66	269
San Francisco Giants	60	94	276
Seattle Mariners	43	80	253
St Louis Cardinals	40	59	236
Tampa Bay Rays	35	66	261
Texas Rangers	47	87	285
Toronto Blue Jays	52	78	287
Washington Nationals	48	69	294

Managers Record

Alex Vigderman

In 2020, three teams (Astros, Cubs, Giants) moved forward from managers who had unprecedented success for the franchise. Two other teams (Royals, Pirates) started anew after a decade with a familiar face. Let's see how some of the replacements shook things up.

After World-Series-winner A.J. Hinch was canned, the Astros turned to Dusty Baker. Baker's ledger over the last several years looks odd, as his teams won 90-plus games the two seasons prior to his firing in his last two stops, and he took multiple years off after each. Those who know his reputation for handling pitchers might be surprised that this was almost the first season he did not have more slow hooks than quick hooks since 2006.

The Cubs parted ways with Joe Maddon, bringing in a familiar face in 2016 team leader David Ross. Maddon's tactics in Chicago were marked by minimal infield shifting and heavy use of pinch hitters. Cubs fans saw a different team in these regards in 2020. In a short season, his Cubs shifted more than in all but one Maddon season. Sticking on the basepaths, Ross also put runners in motion as much as any manager this season, something that Maddon had cut back on dramatically in his last season in Chicago.

New Pirates manager Derek Shelton really pinched when it came to pinch hitters. Acknowledging that he didn't need to sub for pitchers, it's stark that he brought in pinch hitters at a rate one-quarter of that of the Pirates' former captain. In a season in which Pittsburgh failed to win a third of its games, it wasn't as crucial to squeeze the most out of the roster as Clint Hurdle did during his tenure.

The Royals parted ways with Ned Yost after consecutive sub-60-win seasons, bringing in ex-Cardinals manager Mike Matheny. He had caught some ire in St. Louis for his old school tactics and bullpen usage, and he didn't exactly keep a low profile in this regard in 2020. He used relievers on consecutive days more than anyone, and only five teams attempted more sacrifices this season.

Brad Ausmus

Year	Team	Lg	G	LUp	PL%	PH	PR	DS	Quick	Slow	LO	RCD	LS	Rel	SBA	SacA	RM	PO	#	Good	NG	Bomb	W	L	Pct
2014	Tigers	AL	162	103	.51	79	43	44	28	55	43	99	1	473	147	32	144	13	34	17	17	5	90	72	.556
2015	Tigers	AL	161	122	.47	83	38	50	33	59	30	131	4	505	134	37	161	7	32	18	14	7	74	87	.460
2016	Tigers	AL	161	111	.48	89	31	50	41	37	18	93	4	476	87	21	95	3	25	12	13	4	86	75	.534
2017	Tigers	AL	162	131	.50	103	30	24	28	52	17	97	6	510	99	16	104	3	42	26	16	8	64	98	.395
2019	Angels	AL	162	153	.57	98	27	44	34	29	0	105	5	589	85	4	78	1	11	5	6	4	72	90	.444
	162-Game Average			124	.50	91	34	43	33	47	22	105	4	512	111	22	117	5	29	16	13	6	77	85	.475

Dusty Baker

Year	Team	Lg	G	LUp	PL%	PH	PR	DS	Quick	Slow	LO	RCD	LS	Rel	SBA	SacA	RM	PO	#	Good	NG	Bomb	W	L	Pct
1994	Giants	NL	115	76	.53	177	16	9	29	25	2	86	12	288	154	88		78	40	24	16	8	55	60	.478
1995	Giants	NL	144	97	.41	230	36	13	32	50	8	90	8	381	184	101		77	51	32	19	14	67	77	.465
1996	Giants	NL	162	129	.51	250	17	15	24	58	15	94	8	425	166	103		96	60	37	23	15	68	94	.420
1997	Giants	NL	162	114	.71	212	17	22	46	25	17	132	4	481	170	85		93	57	36	21	12	90	72	.556
1998	Giants	NL	163	130	.62	224	20	12	43	38	8	113	5	433	153	111		41	68	42	26	9	89	74	.546
1999	Giants	NL	162	119	.62	233	16	16	30	51	27	111		450	165	113		40	41	25	16	10	86	76	.531
2000	Giants	NL	162	82	.56	233	26	22	38	50	25	91	3	384	118	86		37	26	17	9	2	97	65	.599
2001	Giants	NL	162	122	.48	261	22	19	40	48	10	114	4	439	99	95		45	49	33	16	6	90	72	.556
2002	Giants	NL	162	118	.43	223	32	38	29	56	53	106	8	417	95	89	42	41	44	28	16	10	95	66	.590
2003	Cubs	NL	162	114	.49	272	25	43	24	58	65	111	3	420	104	93	31	24	36	23	13	4	88	74	.543
2004	Cubs	NL	162	113	.44	254	16	19	37	41	42	129	8	460	94	108	71	62	33	22	11	7	89	73	.549
2005	Cubs	NL	162	121	.59	240	21	29	40	46	36	103	2	457	104	88	107	70	48	27	21	7	79	83	.488
2006	Cubs	NL	162	133	.56	271	9	26	45	39	22	165	2	542	170	108	139	46	44	28	16	11	66	96	.407
2008	Reds	NL	162	119	.58	285	28	27	26	63	39	124	2	507	132	100	101	37	40	28	12	4	74	88	.457
2009	Reds	NL	162	130	.45	252	15	35	30	62	35	115	1	478	136	120	118	23	36	29	7	4	78	84	.481
2010	Reds	NL	162	120	.46	258	19	49	36	41	22	140	0	502	136	91	157	13	32	22	10	9	91	71	.562
2011	Reds	NL	162	142	.42	240	29	42	34	51	20	115	0	501	147	102	226	33	47	26	21	5	79	83	.488
2012	Reds	NL	162	121	.43	201	19	39	33	39	30	78	4	425	114	108	148	19	33	22	11	3	97	65	.599
2013	Reds	NL	162	95	.54	236	20	27	39	40	14	93	4	461	102	110	157	21	28	23	5	3	90	72	.556
2016	Nationals	NL	162	112	.57	220	20	27	35	45	21	119	4	508	160	59	161	3	43	28	15	9	95	67	.586
2017	Nationals	NL	162	124	.59	241	33	26	22	53	27	90	2	487	138	57	113	3	39	29	10	6	97	65	.599
2020	Astros	AL	60	49	.48	28	13	7	14	15	1	24	0	193	33	7	36	3	7	4	3	1	29	31	.483
	162-Game Average			118	.52	240	22	27	35	47	26	112	4	460	137	96	120	43	43	28	15	8	85	77	.525

Rocco Baldelli

Year	Team	Lg	G	LUp	PL%	PH	PR	DS	Quick	Slow	LO	RCD	LS	Rel	SBA	SacA	RM	PO	#	Good	NG	Bomb	W	L	Pct
2019	Twins	AL	162	145	.62	84	24	35	42	43	1	94	16	524	49	16	56	4	10	9	1	1	101	61	.623
2020	Twins	AL	60	56	.65	29	19	20	14	11	1	29	0	202	21	3	18	0	0	0	0	0	36	24	.600
	162-Game Average			147	.63	82	31	40	41	39	1	90	12	530	51	14	54	3	7	7	1	1	100	62	.617

Jeff Banister

Year	Team	Lg	G	LUp	PL%	PH	PR	DS	Quick	Slow	LO	RCD	LS	Rel	SBA	SacA	RM	PO	#	Good	NG	Bomb	W	L	Pct
2015	Rangers	AL	162	127	.57	94	51	46	40	47	11	122	0	498	140	66	158	5	29	19	10	5	88	74	.543
2016	Rangers	AL	162	124	.55	84	58	38	47	44	7	85	1	479	135	26	136	3	16	5	11	8	95	67	.586
2017	Rangers	AL	162	134	.54	66	40	20	39	40	6	71	7	464	157	35	153	0	22	9	13	10	78	84	.481
2018	Rangers	AL	152	122	.61	74	40	21	29	44	1	61	3	465	108	42	135	1	22	13	9	5	64	88	.421
	162-Game Average			129	.57	81	48	32	39	44	6	86	3	484	137	43	148	2	23	12	11	7	83	79	.512

Rod Barajas

Year	Team	Lg	G	LUp	PL%	PH	PR	DS	Quick	Slow	LO	RCD	LS	Rel	SBA	SacA	RM	PO	#	Good	NG	Bomb	W	L	Pct
2019	Padres	NL	8	8	.69	28	2	1	5	0	0	4	0	34	4	2	8	0	0	0	0	0	1	7	.125
	162-Game Average			162	.69	567	41	20	101	0	0	81	0	689	81	41	162	0	0	0	0	0	20	142	.123

David Bell

Year	Team	Lg	G	LUp	PL%	PH	PR	DS	Quick	Slow	LO	RCD	LS	Rel	SBA	SacA	RM	PO	#	Good	NG	Bomb	W	L	Pct
2019	Reds	NL	162	140	.55	319	28	46	36	43	9	104	10	535	118	44	111	1	31	25	6	5	75	87	.463
2020	Reds	NL	60	54	.68	68	17	16	13	18	5	28	1	168	38	1	32	1	6	4	2	2	31	29	.517
	162-Game Average			142	.58	282	33	45	36	45	10	96	8	513	114	33	104	1	27	21	6	5	77	85	.475

Bud Black

Year	Team	Lg	G	LUp	PL%	PH	PR	DS	Quick	Slow	LO	RCD	LS	Rel	SBA	SacA	RM	PO	#	Good	NG	Bomb	W	L	Pct
				LINEUPS		SUBSTITUTION			PITCHER USAGE						TACTICS				INTENTIONAL BB				RESULTS		
2007	Padres	NL	163	115	.62	279	18	13	63	28	13	122	0	485	79	85	73	56	48	28	20	11	89	74	.546
2008	Padres	NL	162	113	.63	286	25	20	55	36	17	109	0	491	53	75	78	31	61	30	31	17	63	99	.389
2009	Padres	NL	162	137	.64	264	8	34	50	37	8	118	5	527	111	99	84	55	58	42	16	6	75	87	.463
2010	Padres	NL	162	135	.61	285	16	45	55	33	10	132	7	499	174	99	135	31	51	35	16	8	90	72	.556
2011	Padres	NL	162	140	.58	288	20	43	40	36	10	110	2	490	214	69	184	41	56	31	25	13	71	91	.438
2012	Padres	NL	162	132	.74	280	26	35	45	49	11	126	5	529	201	89	162	21	48	34	14	7	76	86	.469
2013	Padres	NL	162	145	.66	271	24	37	35	46	4	102	1	488	152	78	122	12	31	20	11	8	76	86	.469
2014	Padres	NL	162	157	.74	313	23	29	49	33	13	104	1	481	125	74	116	15	32	24	8	4	77	85	.475
2015	Padres	NL	65	50	.54	113	6	6	8	25	3	40	0	199	54	24	46	2	15	11	4	0	32	33	.492
2017	Rockies	NL	162	111	.51	261	19	14	44	36	4	100	2	549	93	76	149	4	20	14	6	3	87	75	.537
2018	Rockies	NL	163	126	.56	276	20	19	29	49	5	103	1	518	128	65	137	2	24	16	8	5	91	72	.558
2019	Rockies	NL	162	141	.60	305	8	13	27	58	1	114	3	590	102	71	96	5	33	21	12	3	71	91	.438
2020	Rockies	NL	60	52	.60	51	10	9	5	20	0	31	2	189	51	11	37	2	5	3	2	1	26	34	.433
	162-Game Average			132	.62	278	19	27	43	41	8	111	2	512	130	78	120	24	41	26	15	7	78	84	.481

Bruce Bochy

Year	Team	Lg	G	LUp	PL%	PH	PR	DS	Quick	Slow	LO	RCD	LS	Rel	SBA	SacA	RM	PO	#	Good	NG	Bomb	W	L	Pct
				LINEUPS		SUBSTITUTION			PITCHER USAGE						TACTICS				INTENTIONAL BB				RESULTS		
1995	Padres	NL	144	96	.59	262	30	23	44	41	17	38	3	337	170	68		13	37	19	18	11	70	74	.486
1996	Padres	NL	162	114	.52	289	29	15	51	33	10	67	12	411	164	73		65	47	29	18	12	91	71	.562
1997	Padres	NL	162	111	.60	291	26	9	45	45	3	81	11	426	200	84		58	37	20	17	11	76	86	.469
1998	Padres	NL	162	108	.65	280	62	44	44	45	9	81	12	369	116	84		27	45	31	14	10	98	64	.605
1999	Padres	NL	162	137	.60	298	51	21	44	36	4	68	5	403	241	60		29	48	29	19	13	74	88	.457
2000	Padres	NL	162	134	.52	285	44	14	41	47	14	105	5	443	184	52		27	50	21	29	11	76	86	.469
2001	Padres	NL	162	116	.60	255	54	27	32	47	6	85	10	422	173	43		23	54	31	23	13	79	83	.488
2002	Padres	NL	162	123	.66	259	44	56	39	40	17	106	4	459	115	63	74	14	61	38	23	14	66	96	.407
2003	Padres	NL	162	134	.58	339	20	29	34	43	16	100	3	473	115	63	41	6	52	33	19	12	64	98	.395
2004	Padres	NL	162	96	.54	261	28	47	47	32	15	76	3	437	77	75	96	14	39	24	15	10	87	75	.537
2005	Padres	NL	162	128	.58	285	31	49	46	36	23	87	1	456	128	89	111	16	45	33	12	8	82	80	.506
2006	Padres	NL	162	111	.60	264	64	48	43	42	24	111	2	475	154	77	110	21	63	43	20	10	88	74	.543
2007	Giants	NL	162	128	.72	264	50	45	26	50	36	132	2	496	152	86	119	10	41	29	12	3	71	91	.438
2008	Giants	NL	162	134	.68	276	32	39	24	59	42	97	6	478	154	77	155	5	59	40	19	8	72	90	.444
2009	Giants	NL	162	134	.65	231	21	52	42	40	32	84	8	457	106	93	118	5	49	32	17	10	88	74	.543
2010	Giants	NL	162	126	.55	224	45	70	29	37	40	118	12	477	87	102	144	12	58	41	17	8	92	70	.568
2011	Giants	NL	162	138	.62	245	49	42	38	38	44	108	3	480	136	79	175	11	46	36	10	6	86	76	.531
2012	Giants	NL	162	112	.75	220	32	55	22	50	31	136	9	526	157	87	176	15	42	30	12	5	94	68	.580
2013	Giants	NL	162	109	.70	263	19	45	33	52	23	143	4	524	93	78	164	7	64	46	18	6	76	86	.469
2014	Giants	NL	162	131	.66	236	29	64	45	41	19	102	1	475	83	53	147	12	35	25	10	9	88	74	.543
2015	Giants	NL	162	124	.63	230	12	21	45	32	11	137	2	557	129	54	173	8	28	20	8	3	84	78	.519
2016	Giants	NL	162	121	.66	268	7	29	31	42	28	148	4	575	115	54	178	6	30	25	5	4	87	75	.537
2017	Giants	NL	162	136	.61	298	22	12	22	59	20	93	2	502	110	51	135	3	42	29	13	11	64	98	.395
2018	Giants	NL	162	140	.59	305	16	30	36	38	6	100	1	549	111	43	139	2	37	25	12	5	73	89	.451
2019	Giants	NL	162	141	.67	362	11	25	34	43	4	94	2	587	75	37	101	4	26	16	10	4	77	85	.475
	162-Game Average			124	.62	273	33	37	38	43	20	100	5	474	135	69	131	18	46	30	16	9	80	82	.494

Aaron Boone

Year	Team	Lg	G	LUp	PL%	PH	PR	DS	Quick	Slow	LO	RCD	LS	Rel	SBA	SacA	RM	PO	#	Good	NG	Bomb	W	L	Pct
				LINEUPS		SUBSTITUTION			PITCHER USAGE						TACTICS				INTENTIONAL BB				RESULTS		
2018	Yankees	AL	162	137	.54	71	14	24	45	32	3	75	5	508	84	17	113	3	9	4	5	3	100	62	.617
2019	Yankees	AL	162	155	.48	57	24	32	43	27	1	80	5	545	77	19	81	2	12	9	3	1	103	59	.636
2020	Yankees	AL	60	57	.48	36	15	20	18	17	3	26	1	174	34	4	39	0	5	5	0	0	33	27	.550
	162-Game Average			147	.50	69	22	32	45	32	3	76	5	518	82	17	98	2	11	8	3	2	100	62	.617

Mickey Callaway

Year	Team	Lg	G	LUp	PL%	PH	PR	DS	Quick	Slow	LO	RCD	LS	Rel	SBA	SacA	RM	PO	#	Good	NG	Bomb	W	L	Pct
				LINEUPS		SUBSTITUTION			PITCHER USAGE						TACTICS				INTENTIONAL BB				RESULTS		
2018	Mets	NL	162	151	.58	258	17	30	41	43	11	72	10	501	110	39	119	6	32	17	15	9	77	85	.475
2019	Mets	NL	162	132	.50	273	42	65	35	57	16	87	6	502	83	42	102	10	40	27	13	6	86	76	.531
	162-Game Average			142	.54	266	30	48	38	50	14	80	8	502	97	41	111	8	36	22	14	8	82	81	.503

Kevin Cash

Year	Team	Lg	G	LUp	PL%	PH	PR	DS	Quick	Slow	LO	RCD	LS	Rel	SBA	SacA	RM	PO	#	Good	NG	Bomb	W	L	Pct
				LINEUPS		SUBSTITUTION			PITCHER USAGE						TACTICS				INTENTIONAL BB				RESULTS		
2015	Rays	AL	162	137	.62	219	23	38	72	33	10	134	3	530	132	27	173	2	23	17	6	3	80	82	.494
2016	Rays	AL	162	142	.55	103	11	28	42	52	18	100	8	485	97	24	146	12	25	16	9	4	68	94	.420
2017	Rays	AL	162	126	.57	123	21	24	39	47	16	89	9	511	122	24	143	12	37	25	12	8	80	82	.494

(continued)

Year	Team	Lg	G	LUp	PL%	PH	PR	DS	Quick	Slow	LO	RCD	LS	Rel	SBA	SacA	RM	PO	#	Good	NG	Bomb	W	L	Pct
				LINEUPS		SUBSTITUTION			PITCHER USAGE						TACTICS				INTENTIONAL BB				RESULTS		
2018	Rays	AL	162	151	.58	109	25	33	50	18	5	115	**10**	553	**179**	37	**190**	2	**34**	20	14	9	90	72	.556
2019	Rays	AL	162	152	.59	**131**	31	14	**50**	18	0	**136**	6	603	131	11	**166**	3	27	14	13	**8**	96	66	.593
2020	Rays	AL	60	**59**	.68	66	14	**24**	**22**	9	0	35	3	219	57	1	38	1	4	3	1	0	**40**	20	.667
	162-Game Average			143	.59	140	23	35	51	33	9	113	7	540	134	23	159	6	28	18	10	6	85	77	.525

Terry Collins

Year	Team	Lg	G	LUp	PL%	PH	PR	DS	Quick	Slow	LO	RCD	LS	Rel	SBA	SacA	RM	PO	#	Good	NG	Bomb	W	L	Pct
				LINEUPS		SUBSTITUTION			PITCHER USAGE						TACTICS				INTENTIONAL BB				RESULTS		
1994	Astros	NL	115	74	.54	185	20	13	6	6	0	37	4	268	168	90		37	28	17	11	5	66	49	.574
1995	Astros	NL	144	106	.49	302	38	11	15	7	8	100	8	394	236	97		44	39	27	12	8	76	68	.528
1996	Astros	NL	162	111	.41	257	30	38	13	12	9	70	10	371	243	94		35	42	30	12	6	82	80	.506
1997	Angels	AL	162	117	.70	86	34	22	10	16	15	67	8	400	198	55		60	25	13	12	4	84	78	.519
1998	Angels	AL	162	119	.57	100	64	33	15	11	28	86	11	415	138	69		38	16	6	10	4	85	77	.525
1999	Angels	AL	133	113	.56	93	26	16	10	16	10	68	2	315	93	39		7	10	1	8	3	51	82	.383
2011	Mets	NL	162	121	.68	**312**	18	28	32	44	23	126	5	514	165	88	151	9	48	35	13	9	77	85	.475
2012	Mets	NL	162	**141**	.69	**329**	16	38	39	36	19	113	0	505	117	75	149	8	29	18	11	3	74	88	.457
2013	Mets	NL	162	132	.61	266	12	33	33	42	15	131	**4**	**535**	135	67	128	3	38	30	8	3	74	88	.457
2014	Mets	NL	162	135	.55	247	17	26	28	46	23	111	**6**	489	135	73	119	2	38	23	15	4	79	83	.488
2015	Mets	NL	162	138	.52	255	21	40	47	36	6	119	**8**	485	76	49	117	1	43	33	10	6	90	72	.556
2016	Mets	NL	162	129	.68	292	17	50	53	33	6	141	4	538	60	55	80	6	39	26	13	9	87	75	.537
2017	Mets	NL	162	**149**	.66	247	20	32	25	54	8	**127**	6	568	81	52	97	3	51	27	**24**	**14**	70	92	.432
	162-Game Average			128	.59	239	27	31	26	29	14	104	6	467	150	73	120	20	36	23	13	6	80	82	.494

Alex Cora

Year	Team	Lg	G	LUp	PL%	PH	PR	DS	Quick	Slow	LO	RCD	LS	Rel	SBA	SacA	RM	PO	#	Good	NG	Bomb	W	L	Pct
				LINEUPS		SUBSTITUTION			PITCHER USAGE						TACTICS				INTENTIONAL BB				RESULTS		
2018	Red Sox	AL	162	134	.55	96	22	31	**58**	44	5	101	4	535	156	8	183	1	8	4	4	1	**108**	54	.667
2019	Red Sox	AL	162	135	.57	123	29	18	45	**52**	16	134	3	**632**	98	26	140	2	22	14	8	6	84	78	.519
	162-Game Average			135	.56	110	26	25	52	48	11	118	4	584	127	17	162	2	15	9	6	4	96	66	.593

Craig Counsell

Year	Team	Lg	G	LUp	PL%	PH	PR	DS	Quick	Slow	LO	RCD	LS	Rel	SBA	SacA	RM	PO	#	Good	NG	Bomb	W	L	Pct
				LINEUPS		SUBSTITUTION			PITCHER USAGE						TACTICS				INTENTIONAL BB				RESULTS		
2015	Brewers	NL	137	106	.54	247	14	30	30	47	3	85	1	424	99	56	106	2	30	26	4	3	61	76	.445
2016	Brewers	NL	162	123	.55	284	4	22	40	41	1	115	3	513	237	71	160	0	33	16	17	8	73	89	.451
2017	Brewers	NL	162	123	.58	285	18	44	58	33	5	124	5	550	**169**	56	**159**	0	45	30	15	9	86	76	.531
2018	Brewers	NL	163	137	.54	288	17	**77**	**64**	29	0	105	**18**	559	156	38	**148**	1	34	22	12	7	**96**	67	.589
2019	Brewers	NL	162	134	.64	317	14	56	**60**	26	1	97	**17**	588	126	29	78	3	28	22	6	2	89	73	.549
2020	Brewers	NL	60	53	.62	65	14	16	15	11	0	18	1	189	26	0	22	0	1	1	0	0	29	31	.483
	162-Game Average			129	.56	285	16	47	51	36	2	104	9	541	156	48	129	1	33	22	10	6	83	79	.512

John Farrell

Year	Team	Lg	G	LUp	PL%	PH	PR	DS	Quick	Slow	LO	RCD	LS	Rel	SBA	SacA	RM	PO	#	Good	NG	Bomb	W	L	Pct
				LINEUPS		SUBSTITUTION			PITCHER USAGE						TACTICS				INTENTIONAL BB				RESULTS		
2011	Blue Jays	AL	162	131	.43	64	**48**	22	40	41	26	62	3	474	183	40	181	22	28	17	11	5	81	81	.500
2012	Blue Jays	AL	162	131	.50	94	30	16	49	44	7	84	3	495	164	46	211	15	20	11	9	7	73	89	.451
2013	Red Sox	AL	162	126	.68	93	41	20	28	46	34	71	4	450	142	32	147	5	10	5	5	3	**97**	65	.599
2014	Red Sox	AL	162	**145**	.55	101	24	17	29	53	28	107	1	493	88	26	124	4	19	11	8	2	71	91	.438
2015	Red Sox	AL	114	96	.56	55	18	20	26	28	6	62	1	326	63	27	105	2	12	6	6	1	50	64	.439
2016	Red Sox	AL	162	118	.53	110	28	11	34	51	26	79	2	463	107	15	169	0	16	8	8	3	93	69	.574
2017	Red Sox	AL	162	137	.54	95	39	17	30	**63**	33	97	4	515	137	20	131	2	18	13	5	1	93	69	.574
	162-Game Average			132	.54	91	34	18	35	49	24	84	3	480	132	31	159	7	18	11	8	3	83	79	.512

Terry Francona

Year	Team	Lg	G	LUp	PL%	PH	PR	DS	Quick	Slow	LO	RCD	LS	Rel	SBA	SacA	RM	PO	#	Good	NG	Bomb	W	L	Pct
				LINEUPS		SUBSTITUTION			PITCHER USAGE						TACTICS				INTENTIONAL BB				RESULTS		
1997	Phillies	NL	162	98	.66	288	19	28	28	54	22	102	9	409	148	91		30	42	23	19	9	68	94	.420
1998	Phillies	NL	162	84	.53	256	20	19	34	57	20	88	7	385	142	85		16	27	10	17	8	75	87	.463
1999	Phillies	NL	162	85	.51	239	13	31	29	41	16	111	7	441	160	81		27	24	14	10	6	77	85	.475
2000	Phillies	NL	162	108	.53	278	17	14	38	43	25	102	5	414	132	89		16	32	22	10	7	65	97	.401
2004	Red Sox	AL	162	141	.65	116	65	**58**	41	48	32	105	8	437	98	18	91	28	28	22	6	4	98	64	.605
2005	Red Sox	AL	162	104	.67	110	46	37	35	55	30	99	3	442	57	21	79	11	28	18	10	5	95	67	.586
2006	Red Sox	AL	162	116	.59	93	**54**	49	36	44	13	94	9	454	74	33	98	16	25	11	14	7	86	76	.531
2007	Red Sox	AL	162	109	.60	84	34	23	41	35	32	89	4	451	120	45	90	14	20	14	6	4	**96**	66	.593
2008	Red Sox	AL	162	131	.59	62	40	40	50	30	20	90	**11**	466	155	40	87	8	17	10	7	4	95	67	.586
2009	Red Sox	AL	162	113	.58	85	47	28	36	50	30	68	6	463	165	29	68	9	24	15	9	6	95	67	.586

Year	Team	Lg	G	LUp	PL%	PH	PR	DS	Quick	Slow	LO	RCD	LS	Rel	SBA	SacA	RM	PO	#	Good	NG	Bomb	W	L	Pct
				LINEUPS		**SUBSTITUTION**			**PITCHER USAGE**						**TACTICS**				**INTENTIONAL BB**				**RESULTS**		
2010	Red Sox	AL	162	**143**	.62	125	48	34	32	**63**	49	84	3	443	85	36	125	26	30	17	13	4	89	73	.549
2011	Red Sox	AL	162	123	.67	89	44	11	**52**	46	27	89	4	444	144	29	163	34	11	6	5	2	90	72	.556
2013	Indians	AL	162	121	.75	78	45	24	47	34	18	122	2	**540**	153	41	158	5	26	15	11	6	92	70	.568
2014	Indians	AL	162	133	.78	123	16	24	37	37	18	**150**	7	**573**	131	**58**	128	3	**51**	29	**22**	**13**	85	77	.525
2015	Indians	AL	161	127	.75	138	21	13	40	36	23	85	8	476	114	63	87	4	27	20	7	5	81	80	.503
2016	Indians	AL	161	114	.73	114	27	29	47	39	18	103	3	504	**165**	44	126	2	**34**	**22**	12	7	94	67	.584
2017	Indians	AL	162	131	.73	93	**43**	**50**	48	31	20	106	4	497	111	35	95	2	15	11	4	3	**102**	60	.630
2018	Indians	AL	162	105	.75	97	**74**	42	29	48	**23**	121	**10**	508	171	**44**	152	6	29	19	10	6	91	71	.562
2019	Indians	AL	162	132	.73	101	25	15	30	44	**29**	89	9	522	138	**57**	100	2	19	11	8	7	93	69	.574
2020	Indians	AL	60	48	.74	37	18	10	8	18	2	27	2	181	35	14	33	0	**8**	4	4	1	35	25	.583
	162-Game Average			116	.66	135	37	30	38	44	24	99	6	468	129	49	109	13	27	16	11	6	88	74	.543

Ron Gardenhire

Year	Team	Lg	G	LUp	PL%	PH	PR	DS	Quick	Slow	LO	RCD	LS	Rel	SBA	SacA	RM	PO	#	Good	NG	Bomb	W	L	Pct
				LINEUPS		**SUBSTITUTION**			**PITCHER USAGE**						**TACTICS**				**INTENTIONAL BB**				**RESULTS**		
2002	Twins	AL	161	111	.69	141	36	42	54	25	10	84	1	435	141	48	44	11	24	16	8	4	94	67	.584
2003	Twins	AL	162	126	.63	144	50	26	49	33	13	85	2	399	138	59	37	14	35	16	19	6	90	72	.556
2004	Twins	AL	162	131	.59	129	45	29	**56**	21	20	106	4	435	162	66	121	18	27	15	12	7	92	70	.568
2005	Twins	AL	162	**135**	.58	104	45	26	50	21	5	87	1	396	146	59	138	16	38	**28**	10	3	83	79	.512
2006	Twins	AL	162	97	.62	93	36	21	**60**	31	9	82	5	421	143	48	130	11	25	14	11	4	96	66	.593
2007	Twins	AL	162	139	.63	104	42	25	45	30	8	99	4	438	142	45	118	11	33	14	19	9	79	83	.488
2008	Twins	AL	163	103	.64	109	26	12	47	29	5	**115**	3	485	144	**73**	143	17	38	25	13	8	88	75	.540
2009	Twins	AL	163	129	.63	83	54	34	43	25	12	115	3	480	117	**62**	100	21	20	9	11	6	87	76	.534
2010	Twins	AL	162	112	.62	86	**55**	30	**57**	28	5	106	1	465	96	47	140	14	19	12	7	4	94	68	.580
2011	Twins	AL	162	150	.58	93	**48**	21	34	44	17	82	1	457	131	44	170	5	37	21	16	9	63	**99**	.389
2012	Twins	AL	162	121	.62	64	45	24	42	31	4	82	1	499	172	49	207	10	43	27	16	6	66	**96**	.407
2013	Twins	AL	162	139	.66	103	42	28	41	43	6	78	1	511	85	37	137	14	31	13	18	7	66	96	.407
2014	Twins	AL	162	132	.64	97	44	23	40	40	2	82	2	491	135	31	149	5	24	11	13	6	70	**92**	.432
2018	Tigers	AL	162	144	.56	75	60	8	40	39	1	99	3	542	100	25	121	6	20	11	9	7	64	98	.395
2019	Tigers	AL	161	155	.48	68	**42**	7	45	46	2	87	0	577	77	19	93	**7**	24	13	11	6	47	**114**	.292
2020	Tigers	AL	50	44	.55	26	21	7	16	12	0	24	0	191	18	1	18	0	1	0	1	1	21	29	.420
	162-Game Average			129	.61	99	45	24	47	33	7	92	2	472	127	47	124	12	29	16	13	6	78	84	.481

John Gibbons

Year	Team	Lg	G	LUp	PL%	PH	PR	DS	Quick	Slow	LO	RCD	LS	Rel	SBA	SacA	RM	PO	#	Good	NG	Bomb	W	L	Pct
				LINEUPS		**SUBSTITUTION**			**PITCHER USAGE**						**TACTICS**				**INTENTIONAL BB**				**RESULTS**		
2004	Blue Jays	AL	50	36	.68	42	3	2	16	8	7	22	1	130	34	2	47	21	11	5	6	3	20	30	.400
2005	Blue Jays	AL	162	124	.66	**148**	11	37	**55**	18	9	77	12	432	107	28	128	45	29	13	16	9	80	82	.494
2006	Blue Jays	AL	162	120	.53	112	32	40	59	33	17	94	**16**	482	98	20	127	40	56	32	**24**	12	87	75	.537
2007	Blue Jays	AL	162	131	.46	**139**	**48**	33	45	37	31	75	9	420	79	35	99	37	34	17	17	6	83	79	.512
2008	Blue Jays	AL	74	60	.48	53	15	18	12	20	12	43	0	205	70	23	39	10	26	16	10	6	35	39	.473
2013	Blue Jays	AL	162	136	.63	124	31	24	**55**	44	14	69	2	487	153	41	160	4	33	17	16	6	74	88	.457
2014	Blue Jays	AL	162	128	.72	**202**	41	49	45	37	20	73	**8**	449	99	49	161	6	23	17	6	2	83	79	.512
2015	Blue Jays	AL	162	129	.48	97	41	47	46	37	13	85	6	469	111	45	152	2	20	10	10	3	93	69	.574
2016	Blue Jays	AL	162	141	.44	90	37	54	39	30	6	98	6	487	78	33	109	1	10	6	4	3	89	73	.549
2017	Blue Jays	AL	162	136	.56	**126**	39	33	41	33	8	100	4	**578**	77	35	132	4	25	14	11	5	76	86	.469
2018	Blue Jays	AL	162	**154**	.59	128	38	28	27	49	2	111	3	590	77	8	120	6	19	13	6	2	73	89	.451
	162-Game Average			133	.56	129	34	37	45	35	14	87	7	484	101	33	130	18	29	16	13	6	81	81	.500

Joe Girardi

Year	Team	Lg	G	LUp	PL%	PH	PR	DS	Quick	Slow	LO	RCD	LS	Rel	SBA	SacA	RM	PO	#	Good	NG	Bomb	W	L	Pct
				LINEUPS		**SUBSTITUTION**			**PITCHER USAGE**						**TACTICS**				**INTENTIONAL BB**				**RESULTS**		
2006	Marlins	NL	162	117	.50	250	44	66	46	40	28	76	3	438	168	97	108	42	58	37	21	7	78	84	.481
2008	Yankees	AL	162	114	.63	97	37	42	**60**	37	12	88	10	475	157	38	**173**	**36**	37	22	15	8	89	73	.549
2009	Yankees	AL	162	106	.73	97	**61**	42	36	45	27	88	**13**	461	139	44	83	33	28	14	14	9	**103**	59	.636
2010	Yankees	AL	162	114	.72	117	44	31	43	39	33	76	3	430	133	47	152	20	37	26	11	6	95	67	.586
2011	Yankees	AL	162	94	.69	72	41	53	51	36	21	88	2	465	193	50	151	26	43	30	13	4	**97**	65	.599
2012	Yankees	AL	162	107	.70	149	33	48	37	53	21	115	7	485	120	47	145	10	32	17	15	6	**95**	67	.586
2013	Yankees	AL	162	141	.59	119	15	29	42	50	23	82	4	428	146	49	131	4	34	20	14	6	85	77	.525
2014	Yankees	AL	162	142	.74	100	27	33	51	28	10	95	7	475	138	44	132	6	23	10	13	9	84	78	.519
2015	Yankees	AL	162	126	.79	118	50	57	48	34	9	80	**10**	497	88	32	92	6	16	8	8	4	87	75	.537
2016	Yankees	AL	162	143	.72	85	32	48	53	44	8	99	7	483	94	35	89	3	15	9	6	4	84	78	.519
2017	Yankees	AL	162	140	.56	112	22	10	49	29	9	79	7	477	112	28	117	3	18	11	7	4	91	71	.562
2020	Phillies	NL	60	51	.59	46	7	7	9	13	4	27	1	189	43	13	28	0	12	6	6	3	28	32	.467
	162-Game Average			123	.67	120	36	41	46	39	18	87	7	466	135	46	123	17	31	18	13	6	89	73	.549

Andy Green

Year	Team	Lg	G	LUp	PL%	PH	PR	DS	Quick	Slow	LO	RCD	LS	Rel	SBA	SacA	RM	PO	#	Good	NG	Bomb	W	L	Pct
2016	Padres	NL	162	130	.56	249	29	25	46	53	6	119	4	510	170	48	138	3	44	26	18	9	68	94	.420
2017	Padres	NL	162	138	.55	238	10	38	45	43	5	101	2	517	122	63	119	2	28	18	10	4	71	91	.438
2018	Padres	NL	162	146	.62	264	21	38	45	49	5	84	6	535	131	49	109	0	28	17	11	6	66	96	.407
2019	Padres	NL	154	139	.45	263	11	51	52	31	0	99	5	509	103	42	93	0	19	14	5	3	69	85	.448
	162-Game Average			140	.54	257	18	38	48	45	4	102	4	524	133	51	116	1	30	19	11	6	69	93	.426

A.J. Hinch

Year	Team	Lg	G	LUp	PL%	PH	PR	DS	Quick	Slow	LO	RCD	LS	Rel	SBA	SacA	RM	PO	#	Good	NG	Bomb	W	L	Pct
2009	Diamondbacks	NL	133	115	.63	222	10	13	24	50	24	61	5	392	113	64	41	5	24	12	12	6	58	75	.436
2010	Diamondbacks	NL	79	56	.53	120	7	4	12	40	21	39	1	207	58	19	51	7	19	9	10	9	31	48	.392
2015	Astros	AL	162	151	.63	122	40	37	33	41	19	97	0	482	169	31	128	6	17	11	6	2	86	76	.531
2016	Astros	AL	162	143	.55	118	35	27	42	35	9	87	1	500	146	38	137	5	19	11	8	6	84	78	.519
2017	Astros	AL	162	144	.56	73	29	39	57	35	3	83	8	519	140	21	148	6	17	12	5	3	101	61	.623
2018	Astros	AL	162	144	.54	92	34	39	31	35	10	80	4	510	97	9	154	2	4	3	1	0	103	59	.636
2019	Astros	AL	162	134	.46	81	41	26	38	30	7	92	2	492	94	15	96	0	0	0	0	0	107	55	.660
	162-Game Average			141	.56	131	31	29	38	42	15	85	3	492	130	31	120	5	16	9	7	4	90	72	.556

Clint Hurdle

Year	Team	Lg	G	LUp	PL%	PH	PR	DS	Quick	Slow	LO	RCD	LS	Rel	SBA	SacA	RM	PO	#	Good	NG	Bomb	W	L	Pct
2002	Rockies	NL	140	100	.52	274	28	41	33	45	17	104	3	437	139	46	50	13	38	22	16	11	67	73	.479
2003	Rockies	NL	162	108	.47	317	17	32	35	40	5	87	4	500	100	82	26	16	51	31	20	13	74	88	.457
2004	Rockies	NL	162	131	.57	289	18	35	36	63	20	74	1	473	77	128	67	12	84	54	30	12	68	94	.420
2005	Rockies	NL	162	135	.60	273	21	40	42	60	17	89	2	459	97	114	119	22	54	28	26	15	67	95	.414
2006	Rockies	NL	162	111	.49	259	17	22	34	52	17	107	2	499	135	156	114	28	81	45	36	23	76	86	.469
2007	Rockies	NL	163	96	.51	283	32	29	45	37	13	112	1	529	131	112	109	26	61	30	31	14	90	73	.552
2008	Rockies	NL	162	131	.49	253	20	31	40	43	16	85	2	485	178	111	116	43	49	31	18	6	74	88	.457
2009	Rockies	NL	46	42	.60	73	8	10	11	14	3	31	0	135	45	26	34	3	11	8	3	1	18	28	.391
2011	Pirates	NL	162	134	.60	278	26	63	58	27	1	134	3	549	160	101	173	20	65	39	26	13	72	90	.444
2012	Pirates	NL	162	133	.55	270	26	60	50	33	3	74	2	483	125	82	120	17	30	18	12	3	79	83	.488
2013	Pirates	NL	162	127	.51	289	24	61	61	25	7	76	3	465	136	83	172	20	26	22	4	2	94	68	.580
2014	Pirates	NL	162	123	.50	322	28	38	47	40	7	91	0	452	151	85	187	24	43	26	17	7	88	74	.543
2015	Pirates	NL	162	108	.50	269	48	76	39	40	9	124	1	500	143	81	173	9	38	31	7	3	98	64	.605
2016	Pirates	NL	162	125	.41	293	39	73	57	36	1	119	4	525	155	55	154	6	28	15	13	6	78	83	.484
2017	Pirates	NL	162	138	.51	277	23	37	42	39	6	110	8	502	103	59	124	7	32	17	15	7	75	87	.463
2018	Pirates	NL	161	128	.62	267	14	27	44	36	1	88	6	480	108	45	119	2	43	32	11	5	82	79	.509
2019	Pirates	NL	161	131	.67	281	30	38	40	49	0	85	7	548	93	60	117	16	22	15	7	5	69	92	.429
	162-Game Average			124	.53	283	26	44	44	42	9	99	3	497	129	88	122	18	47	29	18	9	79	83	.488

Brandon Hyde

Year	Team	Lg	G	LUp	PL%	PH	PR	DS	Quick	Slow	LO	RCD	LS	Rel	SBA	SacA	RM	PO	#	Good	NG	Bomb	W	L	Pct
2011	Marlins	NL	1		.44	0	0	0	0	0	1	0	1	3	0	1	0	0	1	1	0	0	0	1	.000
2019	Orioles	AL	162	150	.70	126	26	42	30	35	1	73	11	533	114	34	82	0	11	5	6	4	54	108	.333
2020	Orioles	AL	60	58	.56	44	21	14	15	10	0	31	4	207	33	15	32	0	2	1	1	1	25	35	.417
	162-Game Average			152	.66	123	34	41	33	33	1	76	11	540	107	36	84	0	10	5	5	4	57	105	.352

Gabe Kapler

Year	Team	Lg	G	LUp	PL%	PH	PR	DS	Quick	Slow	LO	RCD	LS	Rel	SBA	SacA	RM	PO	#	Good	NG	Bomb	W	L	Pct
2018	Phillies	NL	162	120	.66	295	22	38	38	38	3	117	11	596	95	46	65	0	35	25	10	5	80	82	.494
2019	Phillies	NL	162	106	.55	312	11	21	28	48	3	121	9	564	96	50	69	0	38	31	7	4	81	81	.500
2020	Giants	NL	60	53	.66	73	13	31	17	20	1	50	1	236	27	3	25	0	2	2	0	0	29	31	.483
	162-Game Average			125	.61	287	19	38	35	45	3	122	9	589	92	42	67	0	32	24	7	4	80	82	.494

Torey Lovullo

Year	Team	Lg	G	LUp	PL%	PH	PR	DS	Quick	Slow	LO	RCD	LS	Rel	SBA	SacA	RM	PO	#	Good	NG	Bomb	W	L	Pct
2015	Red Sox	AL	48	40	.58	17	17	4	9	16	10	28	0	149	35	10	32	0	5	3	2	1	28	20	.583
2017	Diamondbacks	NL	162	129	.55	254	28	36	34	45	6	116	2	513	133	50	85	3	45	32	13	6	93	69	.574
2018	Diamondbacks	NL	162	144	.66	258	13	32	31	45	2	143	2	573	104	60	92	4	43	29	14	4	82	80	.506
2019	Diamondbacks	NL	162	126	.66	256	21	46	32	38	0	105	9	557	102	49	105	5	38	19	19	8	85	77	.525
2020	Diamondbacks	NL	60	56	.69	27	12	3	11	16	0	31	1	200	30	2	14	0	20	13	7	5	25	35	.417
	162-Game Average			135	.63	221	25	33	32	44	5	115	4	543	110	47	89	3	41	26	15	7	85	77	.525

Pete Mackanin

Year	Team	Lg	G	LINEUPS		SUBSTITUTION			PITCHER USAGE						TACTICS				INTENTIONAL BB				RESULTS		
				LUp	PL%	PH	PR	DS	Quick	Slow	LO	RCD	LS	Rel	SBA	SacA	RM	PO	#	Good	NG	Bomb	W	L	Pct
2005	Pirates	NL	26	24	.52	54	1	5	11	4	1	22	0	94	19	19	20	2	5	2	3	1	12	14	.462
2007	Reds	NL	80	57	.59	130	10	26	20	22	9	58	3	266	62	44	36	12	18	10	8	3	41	39	.513
2015	Phillies	NL	88	82	.76	143	2	16	25	26	5	58	4	278	70	48	93	9	12	7	5	2	37	51	.420
2016	Phillies	NL	162	144	.64	260	14	46	44	44	4	128	2	505	141	61	138	17	30	19	11	10	71	91	.438
2017	Phillies	NL	162	135	.66	236	11	21	37	44	3	114	2	506	84	40	91	0	39	24	15	4	66	96	.407
	162-Game Average			138	.65	257	12	36	43	44	7	119	3	516	118	66	118	13	33	19	13	6	71	91	.438

Joe Maddon

Year	Team	Lg	G	LINEUPS		SUBSTITUTION			PITCHER USAGE						TACTICS				INTENTIONAL BB				RESULTS		
				LUp	PL%	PH	PR	DS	Quick	Slow	LO	RCD	LS	Rel	SBA	SacA	RM	PO	#	Good	NG	Bomb	W	L	Pct
1996	Angels	AL	22	19	.64	21	5	0	7	6	6	10	3	48	11	20		6	4	3	1	1	8	14	.364
1998	Angels	AL	8	4	.57	2	4	0	1	5	3	5	3	12	2	7		0	1	0	1	0	6	2	.750
1999	Angels	AL	29	19	.58	29	4	1	6	0	4	20	0	85	23	12		7	3	1	2	1	19	10	.655
2006	Devil Rays	AL	162	145	.54	81	26	51	41	39	16	79	10	444	186	51	132	48	39	19	20	13	61	101	.377
2007	Devil Rays	AL	162	122	.53	80	19	16	31	56	19	113	1	483	179	40	118	50	31	18	13	4	66	96	.407
2008	Rays	AL	162	115	.69	133	16	39	48	37	14	112	7	448	192	31	113	26	29	15	14	8	97	65	.599
2009	Rays	AL	162	123	.66	140	21	18	28	51	23	139	3	510	255	29	99	15	22	10	12	7	84	78	.519
2010	Rays	AL	162	129	.67	174	31	18	41	34	26	135	2	491	219	45	166	12	34	28	6	3	96	66	.593
2011	Rays	AL	162	130	.67	137	16	31	34	36	47	112	6	438	217	42	187	4	38	23	15	6	91	71	.562
2012	Rays	AL	162	151	.62	156	37	52	43	38	33	123	3	472	178	40	181	7	35	25	10	6	90	72	.556
2013	Rays	AL	163	147	.64	193	27	56	52	38	16	111	6	485	111	26	117	6	38	21	17	11	92	71	.564
2014	Rays	AL	162	130	.58	171	23	15	44	35	26	110	3	494	90	54	143	2	27	20	7	3	77	85	.475
2015	Cubs	NL	162	119	.60	288	22	32	41	31	14	129	2	552	132	48	180	3	38	22	16	10	97	65	.599
2016	Cubs	NL	162	130	.62	236	19	35	56	29	13	100	3	503	100	54	111	6	24	19	5	3	103	58	.640
2017	Cubs	NL	162	143	.65	296	7	51	47	30	10	85	3	531	93	54	122	1	29	18	11	7	92	70	.568
2018	Cubs	NL	163	152	.61	280	18	48	41	44	5	120	2	600	104	56	130	1	33	25	8	6	95	68	.583
2019	Cubs	NL	162	140	.56	244	15	43	40	41	7	103	4	576	69	46	87	3	16	11	5	3	84	78	.519
2020	Angels	AL	60	52	.53	20	13	15	16	17	1	51	6	228	29	6	37	2	8	6	2	1	26	34	.433
	162-Game Average			134	.62	182	22	35	42	38	19	112	5	502	149	45	134	14	30	19	11	6	87	75	.537

Dave Martinez

Year	Team	Lg	G	LINEUPS		SUBSTITUTION			PITCHER USAGE						TACTICS				INTENTIONAL BB				RESULTS		
				LUp	PL%	PH	PR	DS	Quick	Slow	LO	RCD	LS	Rel	SBA	SacA	RM	PO	#	Good	NG	Bomb	W	L	Pct
2018	Nationals	NL	162	125	.61	295	23	26	31	62	22	123	4	562	152	55	91	3	37	24	13	6	82	80	.506
2019	Nationals	NL	162	106	.49	253	15	19	32	41	13	136	8	530	145	77	81	0	41	31	10	6	93	69	.574
2020	Nationals	NL	60	54	.61	31	13	7	8	27	5	47	0	202	45	9	35	0	22	13	9	5	26	34	.433
	162-Game Average			120	.56	244	22	22	30	55	17	129	5	546	144	59	87	1	42	29	14	7	85	77	.525

Mike Matheny

Year	Team	Lg	G	LINEUPS		SUBSTITUTION			PITCHER USAGE						TACTICS				INTENTIONAL BB				RESULTS		
				LUp	PL%	PH	PR	DS	Quick	Slow	LO	RCD	LS	Rel	SBA	SacA	RM	PO	#	Good	NG	Bomb	W	L	Pct
2012	Cardinals	NL	162	122	.62	286	37	33	53	37	8	118	5	506	128	95	144	16	28	13	15	7	88	74	.543
2013	Cardinals	NL	162	89	.56	237	30	41	42	49	25	114	4	483	67	73	125	6	26	20	6	6	97	65	.599
2014	Cardinals	NL	162	119	.56	258	21	35	53	32	17	119	5	489	85	81	155	10	35	20	15	7	90	72	.556
2015	Cardinals	NL	162	135	.52	274	46	41	51	29	11	142	8	515	107	60	168	6	37	29	8	3	100	62	.617
2016	Cardinals	NL	162	146	.50	284	39	42	42	39	8	95	2	481	61	56	107	21	35	19	16	9	86	76	.531
2017	Cardinals	NL	162	144	.45	295	21	30	45	34	5	106	8	546	112	68	125	8	50	33	17	11	83	79	.512
2018	Cardinals	NL	93	69	.47	140	13	34	20	22	3	61	5	321	54	38	57	1	24	13	11	6	47	46	.505
2020	Royals	AL	60	52	.50	50	15	10	19	15	2	52	2	232	69	16	40	3	7	4	3	3	26	34	.433
	162-Game Average			126	.53	263	32	38	47	37	11	116	6	514	99	70	133	11	35	22	13	7	89	73	.549

Don Mattingly

Year	Team	Lg	G	LINEUPS		SUBSTITUTION			PITCHER USAGE						TACTICS				INTENTIONAL BB				RESULTS		
				LUp	PL%	PH	PR	DS	Quick	Slow	LO	RCD	LS	Rel	SBA	SacA	RM	PO	#	Good	NG	Bomb	W	L	Pct
2011	Dodgers	NL	161	140	.57	233	29	44	45	40	30	86	1	461	166	93	181	13	48	27	21	12	82	79	.509
2012	Dodgers	NL	162	127	.59	247	22	43	51	39	20	118	2	506	148	105	153	8	62	38	24	15	86	76	.531
2013	Dodgers	NL	162	145	.55	210	18	47	40	30	18	118	3	504	106	99	131	10	44	28	16	7	92	70	.568
2014	Dodgers	NL	162	124	.51	237	17	62	49	31	15	107	5	496	188	67	168	2	35	20	15	8	94	68	.580
2015	Dodgers	NL	162	136	.70	220	20	45	50	30	13	119	1	508	93	67	136	2	32	18	14	5	91	70	.565
2016	Marlins	NL	161	111	.48	281	28	69	48	35	10	145	1	559	99	63	101	2	62	42	20	14	79	82	.491
2017	Marlins	NL	162	98	.52	271	9	20	43	32	4	120	5	580	121	66	125	2	59	39	20	12	77	85	.475
2018	Marlins	NL	161	137	.46	283	19	53	47	43	2	114	0	546	76	45	121	1	73	40	33	19	63	98	.391
2019	Marlins	NL	162	143	.43	293	24	25	34	48	3	112	1	539	85	49	124	0	52	33	19	9	57	105	.352
2020	Marlins	NL	60	55	.54	37	15	14	20	12	0	40	3	215	65	8	36	0	14	8	6	3	31	29	.517
	162-Game Average			130	.53	253	22	45	46	36	12	115	2	526	123	71	137	4	51	31	20	11	80	82	.494

Lloyd McClendon

Year	Team	Lg	G	LUp	PL%	PH	PR	DS	Quick	Slow	LO	RCD	LS	Rel	SBA	SacA	RM	PO	#	Good	NG	Bomb	W	L	Pct
2001	Pirates	NL	162	131	.51	255	17	32	45	38	2	85	5	410	166	83		52	74	44	30	19	62	100	.383
2002	Pirates	NL	161	121	.45	261	38	65	62	30	3	98	2	458	135	93	73	67	93	61	32	22	72	89	.447
2003	Pirates	NL	162	114	.57	315	27	59	46	35	27	114	10	457	123	99	55	73	58	34	24	13	75	87	.463
2004	Pirates	NL	161	114	.50	278	13	58	50	40	26	133	1	464	103	100	91	61	64	37	27	16	72	89	.447
2005	Pirates	NL	136	123	.53	218	8	19	37	34	15	86	5	357	84	62	83	37	60	32	28	16	55	81	.404
2014	Mariners	AL	162	141	.69	93	48	33	61	21	11	87	3	497	138	48	187	30	36	21	15	9	87	75	.537
2015	Mariners	AL	162	140	.63	133	52	50	53	31	10	114	5	509	114	49	148	30	41	23	18	10	76	86	.469
2020	Tigers	AL	8	8	.56	5	4	3	2	3	0	5	0	27	7	0	7	0	1	0	1	0	2	6	.250
	162-Game Average			130	.56	227	30	46	52	34	14	105	5	462	127	78	110	51	62	37	25	15	73	89	.451

Bob Melvin

Year	Team	Lg	G	LUp	PL%	PH	PR	DS	Quick	Slow	LO	RCD	LS	Rel	SBA	SacA	RM	PO	#	Good	NG	Bomb	W	L	Pct
2003	Mariners	AL	162	111	.62	81	62	33	27	46	43	96	6	366	145	44	37	5	24	14	10	4	93	69	.574
2004	Mariners	AL	162	151	.59	109	66	26	26	63	43	82	5	414	152	56	123	24	32	18	14	8	63	99	.389
2005	Diamondbacks	NL	162	120	.68	310	26	38	26	56	36	123	11	458	93	93	101	30	43	27	16	9	77	85	.475
2006	Diamondbacks	NL	162	114	.72	278	11	35	37	42	15	86	0	461	106	83	61	30	44	28	16	8	76	86	.469
2007	Diamondbacks	NL	162	146	.57	243	11	61	35	42	31	96	2	469	133	74	70	25	38	30	8	4	90	72	.556
2008	Diamondbacks	NL	162	134	.57	263	27	30	41	39	16	102	0	444	81	87	79	28	41	27	14	9	82	80	.506
2009	Diamondbacks	NL	29	29	.62	47	6	8	7	4	3	17	0	91	29	17	13	3	3	1	2	2	12	17	.414
2011	Athletics	AL	99	87	.71	33	13	17	24	23	18	59	2	283	103	34	87	23	9	5	4	3	47	52	.475
2012	Athletics	AL	162	132	.71	111	17	18	63	29	5	93	2	462	154	41	116	30	34	21	13	6	94	68	.580
2013	Athletics	AL	162	133	.77	166	14	35	48	28	7	84	7	447	102	32	74	8	23	18	5	3	96	66	.593
2014	Athletics	AL	162	137	.77	187	38	44	45	30	11	101	2	441	103	28	91	16	28	20	8	5	88	74	.543
2015	Athletics	AL	162	137	.65	161	24	35	53	36	10	100	10	487	107	17	130	20	19	8	11	8	68	94	.420
2016	Athletics	AL	162	141	.64	135	28	39	55	36	7	96	3	492	73	19	79	5	28	14	14	8	69	93	.426
2017	Athletics	AL	162	137	.60	126	19	32	39	46	5	117	4	525	79	16	85	9	17	12	5	4	75	87	.463
2018	Athletics	AL	162	121	.55	138	16	23	49	22	1	115	9	578	56	10	74	8	19	14	5	3	97	65	.599
2019	Athletics	AL	162	138	.53	117	11	34	36	30	4	123	10	547	70	10	72	4	19	12	7	4	97	65	.599
2020	Athletics	AL	60	50	.53	32	17	10	12	9	1	34	4	181	29	2	33	1	6	4	2	1	36	24	.600
	162-Game Average			133	.64	167	27	34	41	38	17	98	5	471	107	44	87	18	28	18	10	6	83	79	.512

Paul Molitor

Year	Team	Lg	G	LUp	PL%	PH	PR	DS	Quick	Slow	LO	RCD	LS	Rel	SBA	SacA	RM	PO	#	Good	NG	Bomb	W	L	Pct
2015	Twins	AL	162	124	.59	75	34	27	51	27	7	123	4	520	108	44	132	5	34	20	14	8	83	79	.512
2016	Twins	AL	162	148	.61	72	25	18	33	57	4	117	4	533	123	47	157	5	26	13	13	8	59	103	.364
2017	Twins	AL	162	137	.71	104	22	31	54	32	4	95	8	520	123	46	164	4	37	19	18	11	85	77	.525
2018	Twins	AL	162	145	.70	102	21	23	35	43	14	104	3	566	74	21	134	5	34	18	16	11	78	84	.481
	162-Game Average			139	.65	88	26	25	43	40	7	110	5	535	107	40	147	5	33	18	15	10	76	86	.469

Charlie Montoyo

Year	Team	Lg	G	LUp	PL%	PH	PR	DS	Quick	Slow	LO	RCD	LS	Rel	SBA	SacA	RM	PO	#	Good	NG	Bomb	W	L	Pct
2019	Blue Jays	AL	162	158	.59	79	25	15	47	26	1	87	10	591	71	18	86	6	25	20	5	0	67	95	.414
2020	Blue Jays	AL	60	56	.53	37	14	15	14	15	0	26	4	226	39	9	28	3	7	4	3	0	32	28	.533
	162-Game Average			156	.57	85	28	22	45	30	1	82	10	596	80	20	83	7	23	18	6	0	72	90	.444

Bryan Price

Year	Team	Lg	G	LUp	PL%	PH	PR	DS	Quick	Slow	LO	RCD	LS	Rel	SBA	SacA	RM	PO	#	Good	NG	Bomb	W	L	Pct
2014	Reds	NL	162	130	.54	220	21	33	35	37	26	82	3	428	174	87	135	9	33	21	12	5	76	86	.469
2015	Reds	NL	162	118	.57	263	16	26	42	48	15	102	2	521	172	63	144	28	42	29	13	7	64	98	.395
2016	Reds	NL	162	109	.52	230	17	23	37	39	10	67	3	484	190	81	163	26	31	23	8	5	68	94	.420
2017	Reds	NL	162	94	.59	241	13	25	37	42	7	64	13	504	159	68	128	17	37	23	14	7	68	94	.420
2018	Reds	NL	18	18	.60	29	2	1	2	7	0	10	1	61	10	8	13	3	8	6	2	1	3	15	.167
	162-Game Average			114	.55	239	17	26	37	42	14	79	5	486	171	75	142	20	37	25	12	6	68	94	.420

Tom Prince

Year	Team	Lg	G	LUp	PL%	PH	PR	DS	Quick	Slow	LO	RCD	LS	Rel	SBA	SacA	RM	PO	#	Good	NG	Bomb	W	L	Pct
2019	Pirates	NL	1	1	.25	1	0	0	0	0	0	0	0	2	0	0	0	0	0	0	0	0	0	1	.000
	162-Game Average			162	.25	162	0	0	0	0	0	0	0	324	0	0	0	0	0	0	0	0	0	162	.000

Rick Renteria

Year	Team	Lg	G	LUp	PL%	PH	PR	DS	Quick	Slow	LO	RCD	LS	Rel	SBA	SacA	RM	PO	#	Good	NG	Bomb	W	L	Pct
2014	Cubs	NL	162	137	.63	275	9	20	50	42	12	103	1	537	105	77	106	5	37	23	14	8	73	89	.451
2017	White Sox	AL	162	**150**	.57	86	26	9	31	58	6	108	2	520	102	**47**	133	1	36	19	17	9	67	95	.414
2018	White Sox	AL	162	142	.60	90	30	25	18	**66**	9	99	5	553	139	28	126	**10**	25	15	10	6	62	100	.383
2019	White Sox	AL	161	143	.66	87	27	27	32	48	7	91	4	536	91	35	103	5	**30**	15	**14**	5	72	89	.447
2020	White Sox	AL	60	51	.49	22	**24**	8	15	17	3	37	3	224	28	2	31	0	6	1	**5**	2	35	25	.583
	162-Game Average			143	.60	128	27	20	33	53	8	100	3	543	107	43	114	5	31	17	14	7	71	91	.438

Jim Riggleman

Year	Team	Lg	G	LUp	PL%	PH	PR	DS	Quick	Slow	LO	RCD	LS	Rel	SBA	SacA	RM	PO	#	Good	NG	Bomb	W	L	Pct
1994	Padres	NL	117	93	.63	184	28	19	11	5	3	53	10	273	116	80	52		62	34	28	11	47	70	.402
1995	Cubs	NL	144	92	.56	196	9	30	15	8	13	119	12	414	142	90	53		68	45	23	12	73	71	.507
1996	Cubs	NL	162	87	.54	326	34	21	17	11	7	114	11	439	158	79	65		55	33	22	10	76	86	.469
1997	Cubs	NL	162	127	.50	280	40	44	13	5	2	113	9	441	176	103	74		51	38	13	6	68	94	.420
1998	Cubs	NL	163	104	.60	273	26	35	16	14	20	133	6	449	109	89	26		48	22	26	15	90	73	.552
1999	Cubs	NL	162	122	.61	312	25	30	16	19	8	105	4	441	104	94	20		48	21	27	15	67	95	.414
2008	Mariners	AL	90	70	.60	75	30	22	21	25	19	50	4	272	57	27	88	10	25	17	8	3	36	54	.400
2009	Nationals	NL	75	60	.51	115	15	33	24	16	4	63	6	250	59	44	36	8	33	17	16	8	33	42	.440
2010	Nationals	NL	162	131	.58	271	33	67	50	32	9	101	5	494	151	101	158	13	57	37	20	10	69	93	.426
2011	Nationals	NL	75	59	.58	105	22	23	24	15	2	54	5	220	80	47	89	3	22	16	6	3	38	37	.507
2018	Reds	NL	144	113	.65	215	16	34	31	40	4	93	15	483	100	68	138	10	52	30	22	9	64	80	.444
	162-Game Average			118	.58	262	31	40	26	21	10	111	10	465	139	91	151	37	58	34	23	11	74	88	.457

Dave Roberts

Year	Team	Lg	G	LUp	PL%	PH	PR	DS	Quick	Slow	LO	RCD	LS	Rel	SBA	SacA	RM	PO	#	Good	NG	Bomb	W	L	Pct
2015	Padres	NL	1	1	.63	3	0	0	0	1	0	2	0	3	1	1	0	0	1	1	0	0	0	1	.000
2016	Dodgers	NL	162	120	.69	**325**	11	26	**60**	26	6	143	**5**	**606**	71	45	120	2	51	36	15	10	91	71	.562
2017	Dodgers	NL	162	147	.64	**345**	10	30	**82**	22	3	104	**18**	536	105	45	97	3	33	23	10	6	**104**	58	.642
2018	Dodgers	NL	163	**155**	.67	**362**	16	51	**64**	29	3	112	9	593	99	51	87	0	39	26	13	5	92	71	.564
2019	Dodgers	NL	162	139	.62	309	13	16	57	28	2	108	9	545	67	61	44	3	24	12	12	8	**106**	56	.654
2020	Dodgers	NL	60	**57**	.56	41	5	11	**24**	7	0	37	0	**249**	37	3	32	0	4	2	2	2	**43**	17	.717
	162-Game Average			141	.65	316	13	31	65	26	3	115	9	578	87	47	87	2	35	23	12	7	99	63	.611

Ron Roenicke

Year	Team	Lg	G	LUp	PL%	PH	PR	DS	Quick	Slow	LO	RCD	LS	Rel	SBA	SacA	RM	PO	#	Good	NG	Bomb	W	L	Pct
2011	Brewers	NL	162	105	.45	260	31	36	36	43	31	92	1	434	125	**104**	141	14	16	9	7	4	96	66	.593
2012	Brewers	NL	162	110	.45	322	20	25	36	50	23	**149**	1	512	197	91	152	8	20	12	8	2	83	79	.512
2013	Brewers	NL	162	125	.47	275	15	34	39	47	7	96	2	501	**192**	86	157	6	29	22	7	6	74	88	.457
2014	Brewers	NL	162	115	.44	253	19	37	33	48	12	114	1	478	145	**92**	127	11	20	16	4	4	82	80	.506
2015	Brewers	NL	25	24	.39	48	4	5	3	9	2	15	0	72	14	18	17	2	6	5	1	1	7	18	.280
2020	Red Sox	AL	60	52	.57	22	7	2	**22**	12	0	26	0	**232**	40	3	25	1	4	2	2	1	24	36	.400
	162-Game Average			117	.46	261	21	31	37	46	17	109	1	493	158	87	137	9	21	15	6	4	81	81	.500

Luis Rojas

Year	Team	Lg	G	LUp	PL%	PH	PR	DS	Quick	Slow	LO	RCD	LS	Rel	SBA	SacA	RM	PO	#	Good	NG	Bomb	W	L	Pct
2020	Mets	NL	60	53	.60	37	**19**	19	14	15	2	33	**4**	197	30	3	35	**5**	7	2	5	3	26	34	.433
	162-Game Average			143	.60	100	51	51	38	41	5	89	11	532	81	8	95	14	19	5	14	8	70	92	.432

David Ross

Year	Team	Lg	G	LUp	PL%	PH	PR	DS	Quick	Slow	LO	RCD	LS	Rel	SBA	SacA	RM	PO	#	Good	NG	Bomb	W	L	Pct
2020	Cubs	NL	60	54	.61	51	16	23	12	14	1	27	3	188	34	0	**46**	0	7	4	3	1	34	26	.567
	162-Game Average			146	.61	138	43	62	32	38	3	73	8	508	92	0	124	0	19	11	8	3	92	70	.568

Mike Scioscia

Year	Team	Lg	G	LUp	PL%	PH	PR	DS	Quick	Slow	LO	RCD	LS	Rel	SBA	SacA	RM	PO	#	Good	NG	Bomb	W	L	Pct
2000	Angels	AL	162	75	.62	110	41	4	56	42	6	95	9	441	145	63		40	44	28	16	7	82	80	.506
2001	Angels	AL	162	130	.62	118	30	8	29	41	5	81	9	384	168	66		50	47	22	25	12	75	87	.463
2002	Angels	AL	162	102	.64	**162**	57	26	36	33	34	88	8	400	168	62	52	30	24	15	9	5	99	63	.611

				LINEUPS		SUBSTITUTION			PITCHER USAGE						TACTICS				INTENTIONAL BB				RESULTS		
Year	Team	Lg	G	LUp	PL%	PH	PR	DS	Quick	Slow	LO	RCD	LS	Rel	SBA	SacA	RM	PO	#	Good	NG	Bomb	W	L	Pct
2003	Angels	AL	162	130	.64	134	54	40	50	48	11	60	4	375	190	64	79	25	38	26	12	3	77	85	.475
2004	Angels	AL	162	126	.57	94	32	44	37	40	22	61	11	343	189	70	229	33	27	18	9	3	92	70	.568
2005	Angels	AL	162	124	.65	92	37	37	47	37	24	88	9	379	218	58	160	43	24	15	9	4	95	67	.586
2006	Angels	AL	162	114	.63	103	45	38	38	49	21	99	9	380	205	37	166	22	27	18	9	6	89	73	.549
2007	Angels	AL	162	127	.66	103	26	19	39	40	14	94	4	396	194	41	166	44	22	12	10	5	94	68	.580
2008	Angels	AL	162	125	.63	74	30	36	37	48	21	87	1	383	177	39	151	31	32	22	10	6	100	62	.617
2009	Angels	AL	162	123	.69	80	26	37	47	47	33	91	1	434	211	55	137	40	35	22	13	6	97	65	.599
2010	Angels	AL	162	133	.59	96	31	23	41	52	48	76	0	410	156	58	223	28	33	17	16	8	80	82	.494
2011	Angels	AL	162	129	.64	88	14	24	31	37	55	57	1	386	187	69	212	46	34	25	9	5	86	76	.531
2012	Angels	AL	162	121	.55	73	33	47	37	47	31	96	8	444	167	61	236	33	20	11	9	7	89	73	.549
2013	Angels	AL	162	118	.56	88	26	39	31	44	29	130	8	496	116	48	205	41	36	19	17	11	78	84	.481
2014	Angels	AL	162	125	.58	123	46	59	49	39	22	141	0	543	120	35	189	14	41	31	10	5	98	64	.605
2015	Angels	AL	162	125	.53	117	62	73	38	38	12	145	4	518	86	41	168	15	45	34	11	9	85	77	.525
2016	Angels	AL	162	133	.45	98	54	57	47	32	12	99	2	527	107	38	211	14	27	19	8	5	74	88	.457
2017	Angels	AL	162	116	.52	109	38	24	57	26	4	92	8	543	180	23	208	11	25	14	11	7	80	82	.494
2018	Angels	AL	162	132	.50	114	33	34	58	19	3	102	7	601	111	16	134	3	17	9	8	1	80	82	.494
	162-Game Average			121	.59	104	38	35	42	40	21	94	5	441	163	50	172	30	31	20	12	6	87	75	.537

Scott Servais

				LINEUPS		SUBSTITUTION			PITCHER USAGE						TACTICS				INTENTIONAL BB				RESULTS		
Year	Team	Lg	G	LUp	PL%	PH	PR	DS	Quick	Slow	LO	RCD	LS	Rel	SBA	SacA	RM	PO	#	Good	NG	Bomb	W	L	Pct
2016	Mariners	AL	162	114	.72	166	33	43	42	38	8	93	7	476	84	36	79	1	30	16	14	6	86	76	.531
2017	Mariners	AL	162	120	.52	93	29	18	55	32	3	98	7	527	124	26	99	4	28	15	13	7	78	84	.481
2018	Mariners	AL	162	124	.54	103	42	28	44	42	3	122	3	537	116	43	91	7	21	15	6	4	89	73	.549
2019	Mariners	AL	162	153	.58	82	33	35	33	37	4	58	3	538	162	17	100	7	25	11	14	7	68	94	.420
2020	Mariners	AL	60	59	.56	26	9	7	7	14	0	12	2	189	66	5	37	0	7	6	1	1	27	33	.450
	162-Game Average			130	.59	108	33	30	41	37	4	88	5	519	126	29	93	4	25	14	11	6	80	82	.494

Derek Shelton

				LINEUPS		SUBSTITUTION			PITCHER USAGE						TACTICS				INTENTIONAL BB				RESULTS		
Year	Team	Lg	G	LUp	PL%	PH	PR	DS	Quick	Slow	LO	RCD	LS	Rel	SBA	SacA	RM	PO	#	Good	NG	Bomb	W	L	Pct
2020	Pirates	NL	60	57	.65	26	15	5	16	18	2	26	0	209	27	7	31	2	3	1	2	0	19	41	.317
	162-Game Average			154	.65	70	41	14	43	49	5	70	0	564	73	19	84	5	8	3	5	0	51	111	.315

Mike Shildt

				LINEUPS		SUBSTITUTION			PITCHER USAGE						TACTICS				INTENTIONAL BB				RESULTS		
Year	Team	Lg	G	LUp	PL%	PH	PR	DS	Quick	Slow	LO	RCD	LS	Rel	SBA	SacA	RM	PO	#	Good	NG	Bomb	W	L	Pct
2018	Cardinals	NL	69	58	.49	117	22	30	21	11	1	44	3	244	40	29	82	0	25	16	9	2	41	28	.594
2019	Cardinals	NL	162	97	.48	268	30	44	47	33	9	111	10	542	145	57	154	2	41	29	12	4	91	71	.562
2020	Cardinals	NL	58	54	.60	32	9	11	19	13	1	25	4	176	28	5	36	0	8	6	2	1	30	28	.517
	162-Game Average			117	.51	234	34	48	49	32	6	101	10	539	119	51	152	1	41	29	13	4	91	71	.562

Buck Showalter

				LINEUPS		SUBSTITUTION			PITCHER USAGE						TACTICS				INTENTIONAL BB				RESULTS		
Year	Team	Lg	G	LUp	PL%	PH	PR	DS	Quick	Slow	LO	RCD	LS	Rel	SBA	SacA	RM	PO	#	Good	NG	Bomb	W	L	Pct
1994	Yankees	AL	113	79	.59	95	31	3	24	30	0	38	7	241	95	34		22	24	13	11	4	70	43	.619
1995	Yankees	AL	145	107	.68	124	30	20	29	42	37	57	6	302	80	27		29	21	14	7	1	79	65	.549
1998	Diamondbacks	NL	162	124	.62	252	17	15	34	40	7	43	6	368	111	68		13	32	16	16	9	65	97	.401
1999	Diamondbacks	NL	162	97	.63	220	20	17	37	48	25	74	3	382	176	75		15	48	29	19	8	100	62	.617
2000	Diamondbacks	NL	162	99	.60	250	32	11	46	26	18	74	12	390	141	89		10	53	28	25	16	85	77	.525
2003	Rangers	AL	162	133	.61	88	51	41	35	33	12	93	7	494	90	35	80	12	45	24	21	14	71	91	.438
2004	Rangers	AL	162	120	.62	86	15	24	53	30	12	82	10	468	105	30	88	5	29	19	10	3	89	73	.549
2005	Rangers	AL	162	98	.59	57	22	11	42	39	17	79	8	454	82	11	103	5	31	10	21	16	79	83	.488
2006	Rangers	AL	162	95	.57	39	34	22	41	27	10	85	4	489	77	30	72	8	18	11	7	5	80	82	.494
2010	Orioles	AL	57	42	.74	20	11	13	23	9	10	24	1	144	38	13	31	1	10	9	1	1	34	23	.596
2011	Orioles	AL	162	117	.53	60	39	27	43	40	14	61	2	478	106	32	133	6	42	31	11	5	69	93	.426
2012	Orioles	AL	162	120	.62	78	28	31	37	42	10	88	0	492	87	46	145	6	36	25	11	5	93	69	.574
2013	Orioles	AL	162	100	.65	90	23	21	31	39	19	84	4	473	108	37	104	4	32	11	21	13	85	77	.525
2014	Orioles	AL	162	120	.49	77	29	51	37	34	17	89	2	479	64	26	101	10	25	16	9	4	96	66	.593
2015	Orioles	AL	162	145	.60	89	21	35	35	41	6	76	8	453	69	26	95	10	27	12	15	8	81	81	.500
2016	Orioles	AL	162	125	.53	74	31	33	36	50	16	68	9	443	32	21	55	10	23	13	10	5	89	73	.549
2017	Orioles	AL	162	115	.44	95	31	40	27	57	21	93	3	492	45	19	40	8	21	15	6	5	75	87	.463
2018	Orioles	AL	162	152	.55	98	30	31	27	47	7	58	8	490	103	23	75	2	29	21	8	6	47	115	.290
	162-Game Average			117	.59	112	29	26	38	40	15	75	6	445	95	39	91	10	32	19	14	8	82	80	.506

Brian Snitker

Year	Team	Lg	G	LUp	PL%	PH	PR	DS	Quick	Slow	LO	RCD	LS	Rel	SBA	SacA	RM	PO	#	Good	NG	Bomb	W	L	Pct
2016	Braves	NL	124	85	.62	214	8	14	31	36	7	96	1	456	83	64	118	7	40	23	17	10	59	65	.476
2017	Braves	NL	162	108	.58	268	38	16	31	52	8	101	1	530	108	76	139	3	39	27	12	9	72	90	.444
2018	Braves	NL	162	103	.65	254	24	21	50	39	8	92	2	553	126	59	137	7	43	32	11	5	90	72	.556
2019	Braves	NL	162	95	.60	265	20	33	44	35	1	96	6	575	117	34	91	3	33	27	6	3	97	65	.599
2020	Braves	NL	60	51	.48	29	9	10	23	12	0	26	1	228	27	3	46	1	13	8	5	2	35	25	.583
	162-Game Average			107	.60	249	24	23	43	42	6	99	3	566	111	57	128	5	41	28	12	7	85	77	.525

Jayce Tingler

Year	Team	Lg	G	LUp	PL%	PH	PR	DS	Quick	Slow	LO	RCD	LS	Rel	SBA	SacA	RM	PO	#	Good	NG	Bomb	W	L	Pct
2020	Padres	NL	60	56	.59	44	10	13	23	9	1	27	0	218	68	14	46	0	2	1	1	0	37	23	.617
	162-Game Average			151	.59	119	27	35	62	24	3	73	0	589	184	38	124	0	5	3	3	0	100	62	.617

Don Wakamatsu

Year	Team	Lg	G	LUp	PL%	PH	PR	DS	Quick	Slow	LO	RCD	LS	Rel	SBA	SacA	RM	PO	#	Good	NG	Bomb	W	L	Pct
2009	Mariners	AL	162	138	.51	58	31	19	50	27	18	76	1	410	122	61	91	4	13	3	10	6	85	77	.525
2010	Mariners	AL	112	93	.61	49	21	12	37	21	20	39	2	254	129	40	124	17	25	11	14	7	42	70	.375
2018	Rangers	AL	10	10	.59	7	2	1	5	0	0	8	0	41	1	0	3	0	1	0	1	1	3	7	.300
	162-Game Average			137	.55	65	31	18	52	27	22	70	2	402	144	58	124	12	22	8	14	8	74	88	.457

Chris Woodward

Year	Team	Lg	G	LUp	PL%	PH	PR	DS	Quick	Slow	LO	RCD	LS	Rel	SBA	SacA	RM	PO	#	Good	NG	Bomb	W	L	Pct
2019	Rangers	AL	162	150	.62	82	14	19	32	48	24	70	2	499	169	19	115	0	11	4	7	5	78	84	.481
2020	Rangers	AL	60	58	.62	30	10	9	13	29	4	29	1	204	63	5	35	0	3	2	1	1	22	38	.367
	162-Game Average			152	.62	82	18	20	33	56	20	72	2	513	169	18	109	0	10	4	6	4	73	89	.451

Ned Yost

Year	Team	Lg	G	LUp	PL%	PH	PR	DS	Quick	Slow	LO	RCD	LS	Rel	SBA	SacA	RM	PO	#	Good	NG	Bomb	W	L	Pct
2003	Brewers	NL	162	97	.44	288	22	39	23	59	18	90	6	460	138	85	40	23	43	28	15	9	68	94	.420
2004	Brewers	NL	161	131	.60	283	25	20	39	41	27	63	2	423	178	79	108	8	27	16	11	8	67	94	.416
2005	Brewers	NL	162	99	.46	259	18	35	26	41	42	71	2	395	113	89	97	50	52	23	29	10	81	81	.500
2006	Brewers	NL	162	106	.48	238	12	14	33	44	18	77	4	427	108	80	82	16	34	14	20	12	75	87	.463
2007	Brewers	NL	162	109	.60	259	11	41	37	42	18	117	7	492	128	74	94	19	37	28	9	9	83	79	.512
2008	Brewers	NL	150	74	.48	217	5	16	37	39	23	69	5	399	141	61	105	31	30	17	13	7	83	67	.553
2010	Royals	AL	127	80	.57	56	25	6	22	39	20	65	0	332	127	40	128	18	25	16	9	5	55	72	.433
2011	Royals	AL	162	87	.58	36	28	16	42	42	21	56	7	420	211	65	203	19	42	27	15	5	71	91	.438
2012	Royals	AL	162	118	.57	60	34	15	48	37	10	108	1	500	170	37	149	25	44	29	15	11	72	90	.444
2013	Royals	AL	162	127	.60	79	48	39	43	44	21	72	2	427	185	48	168	25	21	12	9	5	86	76	.531
2014	Royals	AL	162	101	.52	51	63	46	37	51	26	93	1	451	189	45	159	3	14	7	7	3	89	73	.549
2015	Royals	AL	162	83	.57	40	40	26	51	42	13	90	3	493	138	45	126	5	10	7	3	1	95	67	.586
2016	Royals	AL	162	108	.54	50	38	12	49	44	10	85	2	472	156	55	130	0	8	6	2	2	81	81	.500
2017	Royals	AL	162	86	.53	48	29	25	53	31	2	120	0	538	122	20	110	6	24	14	10	6	80	82	.494
2018	Royals	AL	162	150	.58	48	7	12	32	52	6	75	0	483	155	42	136	1	28	15	13	7	58	104	.358
2019	Royals	AL	162	132	.56	58	25	16	30	52	5	85	3	520	156	32	92	0	25	15	10	5	59	103	.364
	162-Game Average			107	.54	133	27	24	38	45	18	85	3	461	154	57	123	15	30	17	12	7	77	85	.475

Categories of this record are Games Managed (G), Number of Different Lineups Used (LUp), the percentage of players who had the platoon advantage at the start of the game (PL%), Pinch Hitters Used (PH), Pinch Runners Used (PR), Defensive Substitutes Used (DS), Quick Hooks (Quick), Slow Hooks (Slow), Long Outings by Starting Pitchers (LO), Relievers Used on Consecutive Days (RCD), Long Saves (LS), Relievers Used (Rel), Stolen Base Attempts (SBA), Sacrifice Bunt Attempts (SacA), Runners Moving with the Pitch (RM), Pitchouts ordered (PO), Intentional Walks issued (#), Intentional Walks resulting in a Good Outcome (Good), Intentional Walks resulting Not in a Good Outcome (NG), Intentional Walks Blowing Up on the Manager (Bomb), Wins (W), Losses (L), and Winning Percentage (Pct).

2020 American League Managers

Manager	G	LINEUPS		SUBSTITUTION			PITCHER USAGE						TACTICS				INTENTIONAL BB				RESULTS		
		LUp	PL%	PH	PR	DS	Quick	Slow	LO	RCD	LS	Rel	SBA	SacA	RM	PO	#	Good	NG	Bomb	W	L	Pct
Brandon Hyde, Bal	60	58	.56	44	21	14	15	10	0	31	4	207	33	15	32	0	2	1	1	1	25	35	.417
Ron Roenicke, Bos	60	52	.57	22	7	2	22	12	0	26	0	232	40	3	25	1	4	2	2	1	24	36	.400
Terry Francona, Cle	60	48	.74	37	18	10	8	18	2	27	2	181	35	14	33	0	8	4	4	1	35	25	.583
Rick Renteria, CWS	60	51	.49	22	24	8	15	17	3	37	3	224	28	2	31	0	6	1	5	2	35	25	.583
Ron Gardenhire, Det	50	44	.55	26	21	7	16	12	0	24	0	191	18	1	18	0	1	0	1	1	21	29	.420
Dusty Baker, Hou	60	49	.48	28	13	7	14	15	1	24	0	193	33	7	36	3	7	4	3	1	29	31	.483
Mike Matheny, KC	60	52	.50	50	15	10	19	15	2	52	2	232	69	16	40	0	7	4	3	3	26	34	.433
Joe Maddon, LAA	60	52	.53	20	13	15	16	17	1	51	6	228	29	6	37	2	8	6	2	1	26	34	.433
Rocco Baldelli, Min	60	56	.65	29	19	20	14	11	1	29	0	202	21	3	18	0	0	0	0	0	36	24	.600
Aaron Boone, NYY	60	57	.48	36	15	20	18	17	3	26	1	174	34	4	39	0	5	5	0	0	33	27	.550
Bob Melvin, Oak	60	50	.53	32	17	10	12	9	1	34	4	181	29	2	33	1	6	4	2	1	36	24	.600
Scott Servais, Sea	60	59	.56	26	9	7	7	14	0	12	2	189	66	5	37	0	7	6	1	1	27	33	.450
Kevin Cash, TB	60	59	.68	66	14	24	22	9	0	35	3	219	57	1	38	1	4	3	1	0	40	20	.667
Chris Woodward, Tex	60	58	.62	30	10	9	13	29	4	29	1	204	63	5	35	0	3	2	1	1	22	38	.367
Charlie Montoyo, Tor	60	56	.53	37	14	15	14	15	0	26	4	226	39	9	28	3	7	4	3	0	32	28	.533
162-Game Average		146	.57	92	40	33	40	40	3	85	6	558	111	18	89	2	14	9	6	3	82	80	.506

Manager	G	LINEUPS		SUBSTITUTION			PITCHER USAGE						TACTICS				INTENTIONAL BB				RESULTS		
		LUp	PL%	PH	PR	DS	Quick	Slow	LO	RCD	LS	Rel	SBA	SacA	RM	PO	#	Good	NG	Bomb	W	L	Pct
Lloyd McClendon, Det	8	8	.56	5	4	3	2	3	0	5	0	27	7	0	7	0	1	0	1	0	2	6	.250

2020 National League Managers

Manager	G	LINEUPS		SUBSTITUTION			PITCHER USAGE						TACTICS				INTENTIONAL BB				RESULTS		
		LUp	PL%	PH	PR	DS	Quick	Slow	LO	RCD	LS	Rel	SBA	SacA	RM	PO	#	Good	NG	Bomb	W	L	Pct
Torey Lovullo, Ari	60	56	.69	27	12	3	11	16	0	31	1	200	30	2	14	0	20	13	7	5	25	35	.417
Brian Snitker, Atl	60	51	.48	29	9	10	23	12	0	26	1	228	27	3	46	1	13	8	5	2	35	25	.583
David Ross, ChC	60	54	.61	51	16	23	12	14	1	27	3	188	34	0	46	0	7	4	3	1	34	26	.567
David Bell, Cin	60	54	.68	68	17	16	13	18	5	28	1	168	38	1	32	1	6	4	2	2	31	29	.517
Bud Black, Col	60	52	.60	51	10	9	5	20	0	31	2	189	51	11	37	2	5	3	2	1	26	34	.433
Dave Roberts, LAD	60	57	.56	41	5	11	24	7	0	37	0	249	37	3	32	0	4	2	2	2	43	17	.717
Don Mattingly, Mia	60	55	.54	37	15	14	20	12	0	40	3	215	65	8	36	0	14	8	6	3	31	29	.517
Craig Counsell, Mil	60	53	.62	65	14	16	15	11	0	18	1	189	26	0	22	0	1	1	0	0	29	31	.483
Luis Rojas, NYM	60	53	.60	37	19	19	14	15	2	33	4	197	30	3	35	5	7	2	5	3	26	34	.433
Joe Girardi, Phi	60	51	.59	46	7	7	9	13	4	27	1	189	43	13	28	0	12	6	6	3	28	32	.467
Derek Shelton, Pit	60	57	.65	26	15	5	16	18	2	26	0	209	27	7	31	2	3	1	2	0	19	41	.317
Jayce Tingler, SD	60	56	.59	44	10	13	23	9	1	27	0	218	68	14	46	0	2	1	1	0	37	23	.617
Gabe Kapler, SF	60	53	.66	73	13	31	17	20	1	50	1	236	27	3	25	0	2	2	0	0	29	31	.483
Mike Shildt, StL	58	54	.60	32	9	11	19	13	1	25	4	176	28	5	36	0	8	6	2	1	30	28	.517
Dave Martinez, Was	60	54	.61	31	13	7	8	27	5	47	1	202	45	9	35	0	22	13	9	5	26	34	.433
162-Game Average		146	.60	119	33	35	41	41	4	85	4	551	104	15	90	2	23	13	9	5	81	81	.500

Ballparks and Park Indices

Lindsay Zeck

At the end of 2019, the Giants moved the Oracle Park bullpens from foul territory to beyond center field. In order to do this, they modified the dimensions of the field. Left-center went from 404 to 399 feet, right-center (Triples Alley) was reduced from 421 to 415 feet, and center field was lowered from 399 to 391 feet.

A one-season sample is already small, but with the reduced number of games in 2020, it is even more necessary to take the single season park factors with a grain of salt. However, we are seeing what we would expect to see when moving in the fences when it comes to the home run park factor. It has increased from 68 between 2017-2019 to 104 in 2020. From 2017-2019, the Giants and their opponents hit 403 total home runs at the now Oracle Park. In the Giants' road games, 590 total home runs were hit. This past season, the Giants and their opponents combined to hit 85 home runs in Oracle Park and 65 elsewhere. So far, it appears the new dimensions have made Oracle Park a more home run-friendly ballpark.

Due to COVID-19 travel restrictions to and from Canada, the Toronto Blue Jays played the 2020 season at Sahlen Field in Buffalo, New York. Again, it is an extremely small sample size, but home runs were hard to come by for both the Blue Jays and their opponents when playing in Buffalo compared to their away games, despite the Blue Jays, Rays, and Marlins combining for 25 homers in the first five home games of the season. The Blue Jays and their opponents combined for 67 total home runs at Sahlen Field and 102 when playing at the opponents' stadiums.

The Texas Rangers opened a brand-new stadium, Globe Life Field in Arlington, Texas. So far, home runs have been a bit harder to come by than at their old stadium, Globe Life Park. The Rangers and their opponents hit 66 home runs at home and 77 on the road for a park factor of 86. The home run park factor for the previous three years at Globe Life Park was 111. We will have to see how the home run factor is affected after more games have been played.

Arizona Diamondbacks - Chase Field Surface: FieldTurf
LF: 330   CF: 407   RF:334

| | 2020 Season | | | | | | | 2018-2020 | | | | | | |
| | Home Games | | | Away Games | | | | Home Games | | | Away Games | | | |
	D'Backs	Opp	Total	D'Backs	Opp	Total	Index	D'Backs	Opp	Total	D'Backs	Opp	Total	Index
G	30	30	60	30	30	60		192	192	384	192	192	384	
Avg	.261	.239	.250	.222	.267	.244	103	.248	.243	.245	.239	.250	.244	101
AB	987	1024	2011	1010	979	1989	101	6438	6721	13159	6652	6345	12997	101
R	156	142	298	113	153	266	112	914	840	1754	861	842	1703	103
H	258	245	503	224	261	485	104	1596	1634	3230	1588	1585	3173	102
2B	54	55	109	47	63	110	98	309	343	652	339	323	662	97
3B	10	6	16	2	5	7	226	68	38	106	34	21	55	190
HR	29	44	73	29	49	78	93	206	245	451	248	242	490	91
BB	104	121	225	77	114	191	117	676	625	1301	605	648	1253	103
SO	194	281	475	267	243	510	92	1559	1777	3336	1722	1622	3344	99
Foul Outs	18	21	39	16	20	36	107	126	128	254	105	130	235	107
E	20	22	42	15	16	31	135	100	135	235	96	97	193	122
E-Infield	9	6	15	7	7	14	107	42	53	95	39	39	78	122
LHB-Avg	.241	.226	.234	.204	.262	.226	104	.250	.238	.244	.220	.247	.232	105
LHB-HR	17	20	37	15	14	29	120	87	99	186	102	87	189	97
RHB-Avg	.284	.249	.264	.243	.269	.258	102	.246	.247	.247	.255	.252	.253	97
RHB-HR	12	24	36	14	35	49	76	119	146	265	146	155	301	87

Atlanta Braves - Truist Park
LF: 335   CF: 400   RF:325

| | 2020 Season | | | | | | | 2018-2020 | | | | | | |
| | Home Games | | | Away Games | | | | Home Games | | | Away Games | | | |
	Braves	Opp	Total	Braves	Opp	Total	Index	Braves	Opp	Total	Braves	Opp	Total	Index
G	30	30	60	30	30	60		192	192	384	192	192	384	
Avg	.277	.255	.266	.260	.238	.250	106	.261	.247	.254	.257	.239	.248	102
AB	1001	1023	2024	1073	977	2050	99	6388	6622	13010	6828	6328	13156	99
R	189	140	329	159	148	307	107	1013	864	1877	949	824	1773	106
H	277	261	538	279	233	512	105	1669	1636	3305	1752	1515	3267	101
2B	65	43	108	65	51	116	94	351	317	668	370	278	648	104
3B	1	4	5	2	6	8	63	28	26	54	33	33	66	83
HR	52	32	84	51	37	88	97	261	197	458	266	228	494	94
BB	132	109	241	107	111	218	112	711	689	1400	658	714	1372	103
SO	273	257	530	300	249	549	98	1611	1657	3268	1719	1665	3384	98
Foul Outs	22	15	37	19	18	37	101	118	112	230	132	126	258	90
E	23	22	45	11	15	26	173	112	143	255	80	110	190	134
E-Infield	7	5	12	2	10	12	100	49	51	100	24	40	64	156
LHB-Avg	.245	.273	.259	.273	.242	.257	101	.261	.238	.251	.269	.237	.255	99
LHB-HR	13	11	24	13	12	25	108	96	80	176	103	90	193	93
RHB-Avg	.293	.246	.269	.253	.236	.246	110	.261	.252	.256	.246	.241	.243	105
RHB-HR	39	21	60	38	25	63	91	165	117	282	163	138	301	94

Baltimore Orioles - Oriole Park at Camden Yards
LF: 333   CF: 410   RF:318

| | 2020 Season | | | | | | | 2018-2020 | | | | | | |
| | Home Games | | | Away Games | | | | Home Games | | | Away Games | | | |
	Orioles	Opp	Total	Orioles	Opp	Total	Index	Orioles	Opp	Total	Orioles	Opp	Total	Index
G	33	33	66	27	27	54		195	195	390	189	189	378	
Avg	.244	.239	.242	.273	.254	.264	91	.247	.268	.258	.243	.270	.257	101
AB	1064	1093	2157	962	898	1860	95	6507	6899	13406	6622	6414	13036	100
R	141	158	299	133	136	269	91	839	1101	1940	786	1066	1852	102
H	260	261	521	263	228	491	87	1607	1852	3459	1612	1733	3345	100
2B	44	40	84	58	53	111	65	300	346	646	296	383	679	93
3B	3	5	8	4	5	9	77	24	31	55	23	44	67	80
HR	45	43	88	32	36	68	112	259	341	600	219	277	496	118
BB	97	105	202	67	87	154	113	550	645	1195	498	697	1195	97
SO	277	267	544	237	220	457	103	1572	1514	3086	1789	1424	3213	93
Foul Outs	26	17	43	24	19	43	86	152	160	312	141	146	287	106
E	21	17	38	22	20	42	74	120	113	233	135	113	248	91
E-Infield	7	7	14	9	7	16	72	43	43	86	53	38	91	92
LHB-Avg	.214	.236	.225	.233	.246	.240	94	.225	.264	.246	.218	.265	.244	101
LHB-HR	20	16	36	13	14	27	116	88	131	219	77	116	193	112
RHB-Avg	.263	.241	.252	.297	.259	.279	90	.259	.271	.265	.257	.274	.265	100
RHB-HR	25	27	52	19	22	41	109	171	210	381	142	161	303	121

Boston Red Sox - Fenway Park
LF: 310   CF: 420   RF:302

	2020 Season							2018-2020						
	Home Games			Away Games				Home Games			Away Games			
	Red Sox	Opp	Total	Red Sox	Opp	Total	Index	Red Sox	Opp	Total	Red Sox	Opp	Total	Index
G	31	31	62	29	29	58		191	191	382	193	193	386	
Avg	.278	.301	.290	.251	.257	.254	114	.278	.251	.264	.259	.249	.254	104
AB	1076	1136	2212	1007	955	1962	105	6610	6709	13319	6866	6557	13423	100
R	160	205	365	132	146	278	123	1059	937	1996	1010	889	1899	106
H	299	342	641	253	245	498	120	1837	1681	3518	1778	1634	3412	104
2B	75	75	150	43	43	86	155	485	381	866	333	302	635	137
3B	4	4	8	3	3	6	118	40	33	73	25	35	60	123
HR	38	53	91	43	45	88	92	252	233	485	282	256	538	91
BB	98	131	229	89	121	210	97	656	694	1350	690	675	1365	100
SO	285	270	555	260	267	527	93	1544	1865	3409	1636	1863	3499	98
Foul Outs	10	13	23	14	15	29	70	81	106	187	156	121	277	68
E	31	24	55	14	12	26	198	118	133	251	92	113	205	124
E-Infield	15	10	25	6	6	12	195	56	59	115	43	44	87	134
LHB-Avg	.265	.272	.268	.270	.239	.255	105	.269	.246	.259	.252	.237	.245	105
LHB-HR	15	18	33	18	15	33	84	86	87	173	120	86	206	83
RHB-Avg	.287	.320	.304	.240	.267	.253	120	.285	.253	.268	.265	.256	.260	103
RHB-HR	23	35	58	25	30	55	97	166	146	312	162	170	332	96

Chicago Cubs - Wrigley Field
LF: 355   CF: 400   RF:353

	2020 Season							2018-2020						
	Home Games			Away Games				Home Games			Away Games			
	Cubs	Opp	Total	Cubs	Opp	Total	Index	Cubs	Opp	Total	Cubs	Opp	Total	Index
G	33	33	66	27	27	54		196	196	392	189	189	378	100
Avg	.210	.223	.217	.231	.243	.237	92	.254	.240	.247	.247	.247	.247	100
AB	1003	1056	2059	915	883	1798	94	6335	6624	12959	6668	6307	12975	96
R	114	122	236	151	118	269	72	921	787	1708	919	815	1734	95
H	211	236	447	211	215	426	86	1606	1589	3195	1647	1557	3204	96
2B	44	47	91	38	43	81	98	316	290	606	322	286	608	100
3B	5	5	10	3	1	4	218	42	32	74	26	27	53	140
HR	30	39	69	44	35	79	76	232	212	444	265	214	479	93
BB	128	89	217	101	93	194	98	723	662	1385	663	676	1339	104
SO	304	303	607	264	220	484	110	1618	1728	3346	1798	1572	3370	99
Foul Outs	11	7	18	15	13	28	56	81	72	153	109	117	226	68
E	14	16	30	16	25	41	60	120	107	227	132	135	267	82
E-Infield	5	10	15	9	11	20	61	42	51	93	55	47	102	88
LHB-Avg	.222	.210	.216	.243	.234	.239	90	.255	.239	.248	.250	.251	.250	99
LHB-HR	20	18	38	22	15	37	82	112	73	185	137	83	220	84
RHB-Avg	.200	.237	.219	.219	.250	.235	93	.252	.240	.246	.245	.244	.244	100
RHB-HR	10	21	31	22	20	42	70	120	139	259	128	131	259	100

Chicago White Sox - Guaranteed Rate Field
LF: 330   CF: 400   RF:334

	2020 Season							2018-2020						
	Home Games			Away Games				Home Games			Away Games			
	White Sox	Opp	Total	White Sox	Opp	Total	Index	White Sox	Opp	Total	White Sox	Opp	Total	Index
G	30	30	60	30	30	60		191	191	382	192	192	384	
Avg	.264	.218	.241	.258	.235	.247	98	.254	.245	.249	.252	.262	.257	97
AB	977	992	1969	1070	988	2058	96	6342	6587	12929	6757	6390	13147	99
R	154	130	284	152	116	268	106	810	956	1766	860	970	1830	97
H	258	216	474	276	232	508	93	1609	1614	3223	1700	1676	3376	96
2B	46	31	77	48	52	100	80	293	274	567	320	379	699	82
3B	0	0	0	6	3	9	0	25	13	38	41	33	74	52
HR	52	40	92	44	31	75	128	224	285	509	236	220	456	114
BB	91	117	208	88	100	188	116	485	730	1215	497	722	1219	101
SO	276	265	541	295	258	553	102	1822	1625	3447	1892	1469	3361	104
Foul Outs	22	22	44	16	18	34	135	119	151	270	126	149	275	100
E	18	16	34	21	26	47	72	126	119	245	144	128	272	91
E-Infield	9	5	14	12	8	20	70	61	56	117	60	51	111	106
LHB-Avg	.201	.185	.191	.233	.243	.239	80	.238	.232	.235	.245	.260	.253	93
LHB-HR	9	10	19	6	15	21	94	70	103	173	60	95	155	116
RHB-Avg	.287	.244	.269	.267	.228	.251	107	.263	.255	.259	.256	.264	.259	100
RHB-HR	43	30	73	38	16	54	142	154	182	336	176	125	301	112

Cincinnati Reds - Great American Ballpark
LF: 328   CF: 404   RF:325

	2020 Season							2018-2020						
	Home Games			Away Games				Home Games			Away Games			
	Reds	Opp	Total	Reds	Opp	Total	Index	Reds	Opp	Total	Reds	Opp	Total	Index
G	29	29	58	31	31	62		189	189	378	195	195	390	
Avg	.220	.215	.218	.204	.215	.209	104	.249	.243	.246	.238	.249	.243	101
AB	894	945	1839	948	922	1870	105	6237	6541	12778	6587	6326	12913	102
R	135	130	265	108	113	221	128	861	905	1766	779	868	1647	111
H	197	203	400	193	198	391	109	1556	1588	3144	1566	1574	3140	103
2B	37	36	73	39	41	80	93	280	311	591	282	317	599	100
3B	1	2	3	2	8	10	31	21	23	44	34	33	67	66
HR	55	50	105	35	17	52	205	267	296	563	222	213	435	131
BB	122	98	220	117	115	232	96	676	642	1318	614	639	1253	106
SO	266	329	595	268	286	554	109	1711	1835	3546	1635	1590	3225	111
Foul Outs	8	16	24	7	17	24	102	111	141	252	107	116	223	114
E	12	13	25	15	12	27	99	99	86	185	114	103	217	88
E-Infield	5	9	14	7	5	12	125	37	35	72	46	43	89	83
LHB-Avg	.238	.212	.225	.198	.208	.203	111	.261	.247	.254	.236	.263	.250	102
LHB-HR	31	27	58	13	10	23	265	106	163	269	89	114	203	132
RHB-Avg	.200	.217	.210	.209	.222	.215	97	.240	.239	.240	.239	.237	.238	101
RHB-HR	24	23	47	22	7	29	159	161	133	294	133	99	232	130

Cleveland Indians - Progressive Field
LF: 325   CF: 405   RF:325

	2020 Season							2018-2020						
	Home Games			Away Games				Home Games			Away Games			
	Indians	Opp	Total	Indians	Opp	Total	Index	Indians	Opp	Total	Indians	Opp	Total	Index
G	30	30	60	30	30	60		192	192	384	192	192	384	
Avg	.233	.235	.234	.222	.210	.216	108	.253	.239	.246	.247	.237	.242	102
AB	951	1020	1971	1008	951	1959	101	6297	6614	12911	6682	6372	13054	99
R	120	120	240	128	89	217	111	945	775	1720	890	739	1629	106
H	222	240	462	224	200	424	109	1595	1584	3179	1652	1513	3165	100
2B	49	47	96	47	36	83	115	332	380	712	347	329	676	106
3B	2	6	8	3	3	6	133	16	27	43	26	25	51	85
HR	25	35	60	34	33	67	89	239	251	490	259	224	483	103
BB	111	81	192	128	76	204	94	675	505	1180	681	509	1190	100
SO	259	321	580	258	300	558	103	1477	1903	3380	1561	1770	3331	103
Foul Outs	21	17	38	23	25	48	79	126	119	245	154	156	310	80
E	20	11	31	10	19	29	107	97	133	230	99	95	194	119
E-Infield	11	7	18	3	6	9	200	41	53	94	39	44	83	113
LHB-Avg	.248	.230	.239	.210	.192	.202	119	.254	.247	.251	.251	.234	.244	103
LHB-HR	17	11	28	15	12	27	118	142	123	265	148	107	255	108
RHB-Avg	.219	.239	.230	.237	.229	.233	99	.252	.233	.241	.242	.241	.241	100
RHB-HR	8	24	32	19	21	40	70	97	128	225	111	117	228	97

Colorado Rockies - Coors Field
LF: 347   CF: 415   RF:350

	2020 Season							2018-2020						
	Home Games			Away Games				Home Games			Away Games			
	Rockies	Opp	Total	Rockies	Opp	Total	Index	Rockies	Opp	Total	Rockies	Opp	Total	Index
G	30	30	60	30	30	60		192	192	384	193	193	386	
Avg	.280	.302	.291	.233	.255	.244	119	.292	.284	.288	.229	.247	.238	121
AB	1037	1103	2140	1020	964	1984	108	6624	6920	13544	6634	6340	12974	105
R	153	213	366	122	140	262	140	1098	1161	2259	792	895	1687	135
H	290	333	623	238	246	484	129	1931	1967	3898	1517	1565	3082	127
2B	37	69	106	47	50	97	101	381	418	799	306	294	600	128
3B	12	13	25	4	6	10	232	75	68	143	24	43	67	204
HR	35	43	78	28	40	68	106	286	288	574	211	249	460	120
BB	67	88	155	94	117	211	68	583	649	1232	574	670	1244	95
SO	244	205	449	299	188	487	85	1558	1579	3137	1885	1487	3372	89
Foul Outs	16	26	42	25	19	44	88	99	98	197	151	131	282	67
E	22	22	44	21	21	42	105	110	137	247	104	111	215	115
E-Infield	10	9	19	6	10	16	119	46	55	101	36	50	86	118
LHB-Avg	.272	.299	.285	.237	.244	.240	119	.297	.274	.286	.235	.257	.245	117
LHB-HR	12	26	38	13	18	31	119	122	117	239	85	104	189	121
RHB-Avg	.287	.305	.296	.230	.267	.248	120	.287	.292	.290	.223	.240	.232	125
RHB-HR	23	17	40	15	22	37	96	164	171	335	126	145	271	118

Detroit Tigers - Comerica Park
LF: 345   CF: 420   RF:330

| | 2020 Season | | | | | | | 2018-2020 | | | | | | |
| | Home Games | | | Away Games | | | | Home Games | | | Away Games | | | |
	Tigers	Opp	Total	Tigers	Opp	Total	Index	Tigers	Opp	Total	Tigers	Opp	Total	Index
G	27	27	54	31	31	62		189	189	378	192	192	384	
Avg	.245	.249	.247	.245	.279	.262	94	.247	.264	.256	.236	.269	.252	101
AB	846	910	1756	1047	1017	2064	98	6312	6721	13033	6624	6375	12999	102
R	111	141	252	138	177	315	92	726	1010	1736	735	1019	1754	101
H	207	227	434	256	284	540	92	1558	1776	3334	1564	1713	3277	103
2B	36	54	90	42	43	85	124	324	345	669	330	345	675	99
3B	9	6	15	3	1	4	441	59	52	111	29	33	62	179
HR	27	38	65	35	53	88	87	155	282	437	191	275	466	94
BB	71	87	158	76	105	181	103	466	595	1061	500	624	1124	94
SO	243	196	439	324	248	572	90	1633	1493	3126	1870	1534	3404	92
Foul Outs	15	26	41	23	17	40	120	149	179	328	136	117	253	129
E	15	12	27	14	18	32	97	126	99	225	108	109	217	105
E-Infield	8	6	14	4	7	11	146	57	41	98	45	37	82	121
LHB-Avg	.241	.193	.216	.247	.284	.266	81	.237	.251	.245	.241	.276	.259	94
LHB-HR	10	7	17	10	13	23	77	48	95	143	55	98	153	88
RHB-Avg	.247	.288	.268	.243	.277	.259	103	.252	.273	.262	.234	.265	.248	106
RHB-HR	17	31	48	25	40	65	93	107	187	294	136	177	313	97

Houston Astros - Minute Maid Park
LF: 315   CF: 409   RF:326

| | 2020 Season | | | | | | | 2018-2020 | | | | | | |
| | Home Games | | | Away Games | | | | Home Games | | | Away Games | | | |
	Astros	Opp	Total	Astros	Opp	Total	Index	Astros	Opp	Total	Astros	Opp	Total	Index
G	28	28	56	32	32	64		190	190	380	194	194	388	
Avg	.239	.200	.219	.241	.273	.256	86	.262	.215	.238	.259	.229	.245	97
AB	886	906	1792	1106	1066	2172	94	6241	6440	12681	6817	6358	13175	98
R	132	91	223	147	184	331	77	994	701	1695	1002	748	1750	99
H	212	181	393	266	291	557	81	1637	1387	3024	1769	1454	3223	96
2B	44	35	79	59	61	120	80	326	258	584	378	328	706	86
3B	6	5	11	6	7	13	103	23	28	51	35	26	61	87
HR	29	23	52	40	47	87	72	271	245	516	291	207	498	108
BB	99	84	183	93	133	226	98	711	508	1219	691	592	1283	99
SO	191	270	461	249	256	505	111	1343	2039	3382	1460	1845	3305	106
Foul Outs	20	17	37	24	21	45	100	127	124	251	158	138	296	88
E	12	19	31	8	18	26	136	76	117	193	78	103	181	109
E-Infield	3	9	12	3	4	7	196	22	47	69	28	45	73	97
LHB-Avg	.264	.173	.208	.248	.267	.259	80	.268	.197	.225	.253	.218	.232	97
LHB-HR	10	8	18	11	21	32	64	67	107	174	76	95	171	102
RHB-Avg	.228	.228	.228	.237	.278	.255	89	.260	.230	.246	.262	.237	.251	98
RHB-HR	19	15	34	29	26	55	79	204	138	342	215	112	327	111

Kansas City Royals - Kauffman Stadium
LF: 330   CF: 410   RF:330

| | 2020 Season | | | | | | | 2018-2020 | | | | | | |
| | Home Games | | | Away Games | | | | Home Games | | | Away Games | | | |
	Royals	Opp	Total	Royals	Opp	Total	Index	Royals	Opp	Total	Royals	Opp	Total	Index
G	30	30	60	30	30	60		191	191	382	193	193	386	
Avg	.257	.264	.261	.231	.242	.237	110	.256	.273	.265	.235	.269	.252	105
AB	980	1030	2010	1008	941	1949	103	6367	6761	13128	6622	6389	13011	102
R	129	137	266	119	135	254	105	799	1022	1821	778	952	1730	106
H	252	272	524	233	228	461	114	1632	1847	3479	1559	1720	3279	107
2B	49	42	91	48	38	86	103	356	341	697	305	309	614	113
3B	4	1	5	3	4	7	69	43	37	80	33	32	65	122
HR	33	34	67	35	42	77	84	161	238	399	224	264	488	81
BB	93	91	184	79	120	199	90	538	644	1182	517	698	1215	96
SO	258	244	502	269	273	542	90	1472	1413	2885	1770	1491	3261	88
Foul Outs	21	15	36	16	21	37	94	141	118	259	127	131	258	99
E	15	18	33	16	22	38	87	82	109	191	99	113	212	91
E-Infield	4	11	15	7	9	16	94	40	42	82	44	50	94	88
LHB-Avg	.231	.252	.243	.189	.246	.218	111	.256	.278	.268	.221	.262	.242	111
LHB-HR	6	12	18	6	18	24	71	52	91	143	78	109	187	75
RHB-Avg	.272	.274	.273	.255	.240	.248	110	.257	.270	.263	.245	.274	.259	101
RHB-HR	27	22	49	29	24	53	91	109	147	256	146	155	301	85

Los Angeles Angels - Angel Stadium of Anaheim
LF: 330 CF: 400 RF:330

| | 2020 Season | | | | | | | 2018-2020 | | | | | | |
| | Home Games | | | Away Games | | | | Home Games | | | Away Games | | | |
	Angels	Opp	Total	Angels	Opp	Total	Index	Angels	Opp	Total	Angels	Opp	Total	Index
G	31	31	62	29	29	58		191	191	382	193	193	386	
Avg	.268	.250	.259	.227	.238	.233	111	.247	.243	.245	.243	.258	.250	98
AB	1030	1088	2118	990	923	1913	104	6348	6668	13016	6686	6363	13049	101
R	179	174	353	115	147	262	126	919	940	1859	865	971	1836	102
H	276	272	548	225	220	445	115	1566	1621	3187	1626	1641	3267	99
2B	57	53	110	40	53	93	107	316	302	618	298	344	642	97
3B	5	4	9	3	6	9	90	24	22	46	28	35	63	73
HR	50	50	100	35	32	67	135	276	288	564	243	266	509	111
BB	134	103	237	105	96	201	106	687	661	1348	652	660	1312	103
SO	230	275	505	260	248	508	90	1482	1734	3216	1584	1579	3163	102
Foul Outs	18	23	41	30	23	53	70	146	128	274	163	141	304	90
E	20	11	31	16	18	34	85	110	96	206	94	116	210	99
E-Infield	8	7	15	6	10	16	88	54	39	93	38	55	93	101
LHB-Avg	.248	.252	.250	.208	.215	.211	118	.239	.237	.238	.228	.258	.244	97
LHB-HR	15	33	48	15	13	28	139	117	121	238	81	96	177	128
RHB-Avg	.276	.248	.264	.237	.254	.244	108	.251	.248	.249	.251	.258	.254	98
RHB-HR	35	17	52	20	19	39	128	159	167	326	162	170	332	101

Los Angeles Dodgers - Dodger Stadium
LF: 330 CF: 395 RF:330

| | 2020 Season | | | | | | | 2018-2020 | | | | | | |
| | Home Games | | | Away Games | | | | Home Games | | | Away Games | | | |
	Dodgers	Opp	Total	Dodgers	Opp	Total	Index	Dodgers	Opp	Total	Dodgers	Opp	Total	Index
G	30	30	60	30	30	60		193	193	386	192	192	384	
Avg	.271	.206	.238	.242	.220	.232	103	.256	.221	.238	.253	.228	.241	99
AB	978	993	1971	1064	995	2059	96	6328	6565	12893	6779	6372	13151	98
R	174	98	272	175	115	290	94	981	666	1647	1058	770	1828	90
H	265	205	470	258	219	477	99	1618	1454	3072	1713	1450	3163	97
2B	49	29	78	48	40	88	93	331	274	605	364	276	640	96
3B	2	3	5	4	4	8	65	17	12	29	42	44	86	34
HR	64	35	99	54	31	85	122	326	233	559	306	197	503	113
BB	104	74	178	124	71	195	95	679	434	1113	803	525	1328	85
SO	202	274	476	269	243	512	97	1556	1862	3418	1707	1739	3446	101
Foul Outs	20	18	38	15	12	27	147	132	130	262	122	115	237	113
E	18	24	42	22	24	46	91	113	109	222	133	105	238	93
E-Infield	5	10	15	8	9	17	88	45	47	92	58	49	107	86
LHB-Avg	.233	.172	.204	.235	.211	.224	91	.252	.218	.236	.258	.224	.243	97
LHB-HR	23	12	35	37	14	51	74	161	86	247	172	79	251	105
RHB-Avg	.302	.230	.264	.250	.227	.238	111	.259	.224	.240	.248	.230	.239	101
RHB-HR	41	23	64	17	17	34	192	165	147	312	134	118	252	123

Miami Marlins - Marlins Park Surface: FieldTurf
LF: 344 CF: 400 RF:335

| | 2020 Season | | | | | | | 2018-2020 | | | | | | |
| | Home Games | | | Away Games | | | | Home Games | | | Away Games | | | |
	Marlins	Opp	Total	Marlins	Opp	Total	Index	Marlins	Opp	Total	Marlins	Opp	Total	Index
G	26	26	52	34	34	68		188	188	376	195	195	390	
Avg	.240	.273	.257	.246	.251	.249	103	.241	.242	.242	.239	.260	.249	97
AB	799	849	1648	1136	1092	2228	97	6274	6482	12756	6661	6404	13065	101
R	98	128	226	165	176	341	87	703	866	1569	764	1055	1819	89
H	192	232	424	280	274	554	100	1512	1570	3082	1589	1664	3253	98
2B	40	59	99	42	58	100	134	264	362	626	305	345	650	99
3B	0	3	3	5	4	9	45	22	31	53	25	26	51	106
HR	22	31	53	38	51	89	81	143	210	353	191	300	491	74
BB	76	82	158	115	144	259	82	512	695	1207	529	751	1280	97
SO	225	188	413	312	263	575	97	1606	1580	3186	1784	1498	3282	99
Foul Outs	8	12	20	17	21	38	71	109	169	278	115	146	261	109
E	14	15	29	26	30	56	68	90	116	206	127	147	274	78
E-Infield	5	6	11	8	15	23	63	27	49	76	49	68	117	67
LHB-Avg	.197	.309	.266	.244	.271	.259	103	.213	.246	.234	.234	.278	.261	89
LHB-HR	3	11	14	9	20	29	65	40	90	130	49	124	173	77
RHB-Avg	.258	.245	.252	.248	.237	.243	104	.251	.240	.246	.240	.246	.242	101
RHB-HR	19	20	39	29	31	60	88	103	120	223	142	176	318	72

Milwaukee Brewers - Miller Park
LF: 344   CF: 400   RF:345

	2020 Season							2018-2020						
	Home Games			Away Games				Home Games			Away Games			
	Brewers	Opp	Total	Brewers	Opp	Total	Index	Brewers	Opp	Total	Brewers	Opp	Total	Index
G	29	29	58	31	31	62		191	191	382	194	194	388	
Avg	.221	.237	.229	.225	.221	.223	103	.245	.230	.238	.246	.246	.246	97
AB	885	959	1844	1035	990	2025	97	6212	6477	12689	6792	6429	13221	97
R	121	129	250	126	135	261	102	893	821	1714	877	868	1745	100
H	196	227	423	233	219	452	100	1525	1489	3014	1668	1580	3248	94
2B	38	34	72	45	49	94	84	292	264	556	322	305	627	92
3B	1	4	5	4	6	10	55	22	37	59	24	49	73	84
HR	39	35	74	36	32	68	120	280	240	520	263	225	488	111
BB	105	90	195	116	99	215	100	705	632	1337	682	680	1362	102
SO	287	295	582	295	319	614	104	1796	1870	3666	1807	1669	3476	110
Foul Outs	14	21	35	14	11	25	154	106	149	255	119	132	251	106
E	15	15	30	20	15	35	92	121	131	252	119	99	218	117
E-Infield	6	5	11	7	5	12	98	55	60	115	45	38	83	141
LHB-Avg	.212	.228	.221	.201	.249	.228	97	.253	.230	.241	.243	.258	.251	96
LHB-HR	16	15	31	14	23	37	92	146	97	243	130	104	234	108
RHB-Avg	.228	.244	.236	.240	.193	.220	108	.240	.230	.235	.247	.236	.242	97
RHB-HR	23	20	43	22	9	31	152	134	143	277	133	121	254	114

Minnesota Twins - Target Field
LF: 339   CF: 411   RF:328

	2020 Season							2018-2020						
	Home Games			Away Games				Home Games			Away Games			
	Twins	Opp	Total	Twins	Opp	Total	Index	Twins	Opp	Total	Twins	Opp	Total	Index
G	31	31	62	29	29	58		191	191	382	193	193	386	
Avg	.242	.216	.228	.241	.251	.246	93	.260	.251	.255	.255	.255	.255	100
AB	972	1011	1983	965	916	1881	99	6364	6684	13048	6831	6474	13305	99
R	140	99	239	129	116	245	91	976	847	1823	970	897	1867	99
H	235	218	453	233	230	463	92	1655	1677	3332	1739	1652	3391	99
2B	46	34	80	35	39	74	103	376	334	710	340	301	641	113
3B	2	4	6	1	1	2	285	28	25	53	20	29	49	110
HR	43	26	69	48	36	84	78	265	207	472	299	251	550	88
BB	95	88	183	91	82	173	100	651	591	1242	594	604	1198	106
SO	279	291	570	249	244	493	110	1539	1741	3280	1651	1634	3285	102
Foul Outs	32	18	50	22	25	47	101	156	123	279	159	146	305	93
E	12	16	28	8	11	19	138	97	96	193	131	107	238	82
E-Infield	4	5	9	6	6	12	70	37	35	72	53	57	110	66
LHB-Avg	.258	.221	.241	.225	.226	.226	107	.268	.251	.260	.253	.252	.253	103
LHB-HR	17	10	27	18	12	30	94	127	73	200	136	96	232	90
RHB-Avg	.226	.212	.218	.263	.269	.266	82	.251	.251	.251	.256	.258	.257	98
RHB-HR	26	16	42	30	24	54	68	138	134	272	163	155	318	85

New York Mets - Citi Field
LF: 335   CF: 408   RF:330

	2020 Season							2018-2020						
	Home Games			Away Games				Home Games			Away Games			
	Mets	Opp	Total	Mets	Opp	Total	Index	Mets	Opp	Total	Mets	Opp	Total	Index
G	29	29	58	31	31	62		191	191	382	193	193	386	
Avg	.259	.247	.253	.284	.263	.274	92	.237	.237	.237	.262	.262	.262	90
AB	956	996	1952	1067	1006	2073	101	6276	6572	12848	6839	6572	13411	97
R	127	157	284	159	151	310	98	781	807	1588	972	945	1917	84
H	248	246	494	303	265	568	93	1485	1558	3043	1793	1722	3515	87
2B	51	55	106	55	58	113	100	280	283	563	371	358	729	81
3B	3	1	4	4	4	8	53	25	16	41	33	32	65	66
HR	41	49	90	45	32	77	124	242	238	480	256	232	488	103
BB	88	111	199	109	108	217	97	602	578	1180	677	625	1302	95
SO	239	306	545	259	268	527	110	1600	1917	3517	1686	1623	3309	111
Foul Outs	18	14	32	22	17	39	87	158	133	291	134	116	250	122
E	14	14	28	18	19	37	81	99	95	194	120	113	233	84
E-Infield	7	4	11	5	7	12	98	37	40	77	59	43	102	76
LHB-Avg	.290	.229	.264	.314	.254	.289	91	.246	.244	.245	.270	.260	.265	92
LHB-HR	23	14	37	21	11	32	128	98	96	194	126	88	214	97
RHB-Avg	.223	.258	.243	.247	.270	.260	94	.229	.233	.231	.256	.264	.260	89
RHB-HR	18	35	53	24	21	45	120	144	142	286	130	144	274	107

New York Yankees - Yankee Stadium
LF: 318 CF: 408 RF:314

	2020 Season							2018-2020						
	Home Games			Away Games				Home Games			Away Games			
	Yankees	Opp	Total	Yankees	Opp	Total	Index	Yankees	Opp	Total	Yankees	Opp	Total	Index
G	31	31	62	29	29	58		193	193	386	191	191	382	
Avg	.266	.224	.245	.226	.250	.238	103	.263	.239	.250	.251	.244	.248	101
AB	991	1027	2018	924	900	1824	103	6333	6626	12959	6680	6379	13059	98
R	191	119	310	124	151	275	105	1084	787	1871	1025	891	1916	97
H	264	230	494	209	225	434	106	1663	1581	3244	1677	1559	3236	99
2B	50	43	93	37	52	89	94	288	312	600	358	353	711	85
3B	5	3	8	2	3	5	145	22	14	36	25	23	48	76
HR	67	40	107	27	43	70	138	354	249	603	313	259	572	106
BB	136	76	212	115	92	207	93	736	582	1318	709	587	1296	102
SO	238	280	518	242	248	490	96	1590	1914	3504	1748	1782	3530	100
Foul Outs	15	15	30	20	18	38	71	123	119	242	135	126	261	93
E	25	16	41	23	25	48	80	124	108	232	120	114	234	98
E-Infield	13	4	17	12	11	23	69	51	35	86	44	43	87	98
LHB-Avg	.234	.215	.223	.168	.225	.201	111	.245	.240	.243	.229	.243	.237	103
LHB-HR	11	16	27	3	14	17	126	90	96	186	86	88	174	108
RHB-Avg	.279	.230	.257	.246	.264	.254	101	.270	.237	.255	.261	.245	.254	100
RHB-HR	56	24	80	24	29	53	145	264	153	417	227	171	398	106

Oakland Athletics - RingCentral Coliseum
LF: 330 CF: 400 RF:330

	2020 Season							2018-2020						
	Home Games			Away Games				Home Games			Away Games			
	Athletics	Opp	Total	Athletics	Opp	Total	Index	Athletics	Opp	Total	Athletics	Opp	Total	Index
G	32	32	64	28	28	56		192	192	384	192	192	384	
Avg	.229	.227	.228	.222	.256	.239	95	.242	.231	.236	.251	.248	.250	95
AB	1002	1080	2082	906	884	1790	102	6323	6654	12977	6725	6368	13093	99
R	131	111	242	143	121	264	80	891	722	1613	1041	864	1905	85
H	229	245	474	201	226	427	97	1530	1538	3068	1691	1578	3269	94
2B	50	46	96	41	39	80	103	373	305	678	332	297	629	109
3B	5	1	6	6	2	8	64	24	19	43	30	26	56	77
HR	36	25	61	35	44	79	66	246	196	442	309	258	567	79
BB	124	81	205	114	84	198	89	699	522	1221	667	594	1261	98
SO	259	276	535	265	230	495	93	1517	1587	3104	1726	1455	3181	98
Foul Outs	39	30	69	23	21	44	135	194	196	390	143	137	280	141
E	14	10	24	12	16	28	75	95	109	204	100	109	209	98
E-Infield	10	4	14	5	8	13	94	41	40	81	42	51	93	87
LHB-Avg	.255	.241	.248	.205	.262	.234	106	.223	.234	.230	.255	.245	.249	92
LHB-HR	16	9	25	11	23	34	68	66	87	153	88	113	201	76
RHB-Avg	.213	.219	.216	.233	.251	.242	89	.250	.229	.240	.250	.250	.250	96
RHB-HR	20	16	36	24	21	45	66	180	109	289	221	145	366	80

Philadelphia Phillies - Citizens Bank Park
LF: 329 CF: 401 RF:329

	2020 Season							2018-2020						
	Home Games			Away Games				Home Games			Away Games			
	Phillies	Opp	Total	Phillies	Opp	Total	Index	Phillies	Opp	Total	Phillies	Opp	Total	Index
G	32	32	64	28	28	56		193	193	386	191	191	382	
Avg	.260	.273	.267	.252	.286	.269	99	.247	.253	.250	.238	.265	.251	100
AB	1029	1075	2104	919	896	1815	101	6378	6724	13102	6565	6308	12873	101
R	174	155	329	132	156	288	100	952	886	1838	805	947	1752	104
H	268	294	562	232	256	488	101	1577	1698	3275	1562	1670	3232	100
2B	49	54	103	41	63	104	85	318	307	625	324	351	675	91
3B	8	6	14	2	2	4	302	36	31	67	30	32	62	106
HR	48	49	97	34	31	65	129	274	271	545	209	238	447	120
BB	135	95	230	94	90	184	108	707	607	1314	666	624	1290	100
SO	244	280	524	236	252	488	93	1692	1810	3502	1761	1579	3340	103
Foul Outs	24	24	48	14	11	25	166	181	149	330	142	109	251	129
E	13	21	34	23	22	45	66	126	123	249	130	107	237	104
E-Infield	5	12	17	9	10	19	78	39	51	90	45	39	84	106
LHB-Avg	.275	.289	.283	.245	.278	.264	107	.248	.266	.258	.240	.268	.254	102
LHB-HR	19	22	41	13	13	26	133	110	136	246	101	106	207	119
RHB-Avg	.250	.261	.255	.257	.293	.273	94	.247	.242	.244	.236	.262	.249	98
RHB-HR	29	27	56	21	18	39	126	164	135	299	108	132	240	121

Pittsburgh Pirates - PNC Park
LF: 325   CF: 399   RF:320

	2020 Season							2018-2020						
	Home Games			Away Games				Home Games			Away Games			
	Pirates	Opp	Total	Pirates	Opp	Total	Index	Pirates	Opp	Total	Pirates	Opp	Total	Index
G	32	32	64	28	28	56		192	192	384	191	191	382	
Avg	.234	.219	.226	.204	.256	.229	99	.256	.250	.253	.251	.261	.256	99
AB	1030	1057	2087	902	861	1763	104	6408	6734	13142	6628	6338	12966	101
R	129	154	283	90	144	234	106	832	923	1755	837	979	1816	96
H	241	231	472	184	220	404	102	1638	1686	3324	1665	1656	3321	100
2B	47	56	103	29	44	73	119	355	415	770	326	323	649	117
3B	4	0	4	2	3	5	68	44	22	66	38	41	79	82
HR	29	40	69	30	40	70	83	163	245	408	216	250	466	86
BB	94	130	224	73	119	192	99	564	694	1258	502	636	1138	109
SO	262	311	573	259	225	484	100	1399	1712	3111	1564	1603	3167	97
Foul Outs	14	14	28	25	18	43	55	106	104	210	141	121	262	79
E	32	25	57	15	8	23	217	145	117	262	128	125	253	103
E-Infield	12	5	17	6	6	12	124	63	46	109	53	50	103	105
LHB-Avg	.226	.215	.221	.178	.240	.206	108	.273	.257	.265	.256	.264	.260	102
LHB-HR	18	16	34	20	16	36	79	89	114	203	100	115	215	94
RHB-Avg	.243	.221	.231	.233	.268	.251	92	.241	.245	.243	.247	.259	.253	96
RHB-HR	11	24	35	10	24	34	88	74	131	205	116	135	251	80

San Diego Padres - PETCO Park
LF: 336   CF: 396   RF:322

	2020 Season							2018-2020						
	Home Games			Away Games				Home Games			Away Games			
	Padres	Opp	Total	Padres	Opp	Total	Index	Padres	Opp	Total	Padres	Opp	Total	Index
G	32	32	64	28	28	56		191	191	382	193	193	386	
Avg	.253	.208	.230	.260	.262	.261	88	.233	.244	.239	.246	.257	.251	95
AB	1008	1036	2044	964	916	1880	95	6233	6653	12886	6616	6441	13057	100
R	166	114	280	159	127	286	86	781	864	1645	843	933	1776	94
H	255	216	471	251	240	491	84	1451	1623	3074	1625	1657	3282	95
2B	55	45	100	48	36	84	109	269	350	619	308	316	624	101
3B	3	1	4	9	5	14	26	29	22	51	37	38	75	69
HR	55	37	92	40	33	73	116	234	226	460	242	244	486	96
BB	117	88	205	87	82	169	112	636	590	1226	543	562	1105	112
SO	257	328	585	222	237	459	117	1745	1723	3468	1838	1716	3554	99
Foul Outs	17	15	32	27	12	39	75	119	115	234	148	113	261	91
E	18	13	31	15	15	30	90	118	103	221	131	100	231	97
E-Infield	6	5	11	3	6	9	107	39	33	72	41	41	82	89
LHB-Avg	.238	.183	.210	.260	.263	.261	80	.235	.244	.240	.238	.265	.251	96
LHB-HR	17	17	34	14	14	28	114	59	88	147	66	97	163	90
RHB-Avg	.265	.231	.248	.261	.261	.261	95	.231	.244	.238	.250	.252	.251	95
RHB-HR	38	20	58	26	19	45	116	175	138	313	176	147	323	99

San Francisco Giants - Oracle Park
LF: 339   CF: 391   RF:309

	2020 Season							2017-2019						
	Home Games			Away Games				Home Games			Away Games			
	Giants	Opp	Total	Giants	Opp	Total	Index	Giants	Opp	Total	Giants	Opp	Total	Index
G	33	33	66	27	27	54		243	243	486	243	243	486	
Avg	.273	.239	.256	.253	.243	.248	103	.241	.248	.245	.244	.265	.254	96
AB	1097	1121	2218	922	847	1769	103	8167	8627	16794	8504	8145	16649	101
R	180	158	338	119	139	258	107	908	1041	1949	1012	1207	2219	88
H	299	268	567	233	206	439	106	1967	2141	4108	2071	2156	4227	97
2B	65	61	126	42	36	78	129	419	402	821	426	430	856	95
3B	9	7	16	5	7	12	106	53	71	124	31	66	97	127
HR	51	34	85	30	35	65	104	171	232	403	257	333	590	68
BB	128	116	244	67	94	161	121	680	745	1425	710	794	1504	94
SO	257	313	570	242	175	417	109	1984	2016	4000	2122	1855	3977	100
Foul Outs	16	24	40	16	21	37	86	149	146	295	159	164	323	91
E	17	13	30	25	11	36	68	136	116	252	138	135	273	92
E-Infield	10	6	16	14	8	22	60	62	51	113	65	60	125	90
LHB-Avg	.281	.218	.248	.247	.230	.239	104	.240	.246	.243	.251	.266	.258	94
LHB-HR	23	14	37	15	12	27	122	80	68	148	128	116	244	59
RHB-Avg	.268	.254	.261	.257	.253	.255	102	.241	.249	.246	.237	.264	.251	98
RHB-HR	28	20	48	15	23	38	93	91	164	255	129	217	346	74

Seattle Mariners - T-Mobile Park
LF: 331   CF: 405   RF:326

| | 2020 Season | | | | | | | 2018-2020 | | | | | | |
| | Home Games | | | Away Games | | | | Home Games | | | Away Games | | | |
	Mariners	Opp	Total	Mariners	Opp	Total	Index	Mariners	Opp	Total	Mariners	Opp	Total	Index
G	24	24	48	36	36	72		186	186	372	198	198	396	
Avg	.217	.216	.217	.231	.264	.248	87	.236	.245	.241	.249	.265	.257	94
AB	748	790	1538	1181	1176	2357	98	6072	6488	12560	6870	6675	13545	99
R	97	105	202	157	198	355	85	763	880	1643	926	1027	1953	90
H	162	171	333	273	311	584	86	1433	1590	3023	1709	1772	3481	92
2B	36	33	69	52	64	116	91	271	307	578	327	415	742	84
3B	1	1	2	4	9	13	24	24	20	44	41	37	78	61
HR	23	33	56	37	46	83	103	214	267	481	261	267	528	98
BB	72	82	154	135	148	283	83	568	536	1104	657	599	1256	95
SO	202	202	404	343	267	610	101	1655	1570	3225	1692	1466	3158	110
Foul Outs	15	25	40	23	28	51	120	119	141	260	143	145	288	97
E	7	18	25	16	14	30	125	126	107	233	117	109	226	110
E-Infield	5	6	11	9	6	15	110	53	40	93	51	38	89	111
LHB-Avg	.191	.245	.216	.218	.253	.234	92	.230	.247	.238	.249	.259	.253	94
LHB-HR	7	13	20	15	15	30	112	78	86	164	104	99	203	88
RHB-Avg	.236	.202	.217	.243	.271	.258	84	.241	.244	.243	.248	.269	.259	94
RHB-HR	16	20	36	22	31	53	98	136	181	317	157	168	325	104

St Louis Cardinals - Busch Stadium
LF: 336   CF: 400   RF:335

| | 2020 Season | | | | | | | 2018-2020 | | | | | | |
| | Home Games | | | Away Games | | | | Home Games | | | Away Games | | | |
	Cardinals	Opp	Total	Cardinals	Opp	Total	Index	Cardinals	Opp	Total	Cardinals	Opp	Total	Index
G	27	27	54	31	31	62		189	189	378	193	193	386	
Avg	.241	.218	.229	.228	.214	.221	104	.247	.233	.240	.244	.244	.244	98
AB	813	857	1670	939	882	1821	105	6117	6396	12513	6582	6238	12820	100
R	118	101	219	122	128	250	101	857	741	1598	906	841	1747	93
H	196	187	383	214	189	403	109	1509	1492	3001	1606	1522	3128	98
2B	33	30	63	40	40	80	86	255	270	525	312	288	600	90
3B	6	0	6	1	4	5	131	24	18	42	16	31	47	92
HR	25	30	55	26	39	65	92	197	201	398	269	203	472	86
BB	114	89	203	91	115	206	107	643	610	1253	648	732	1380	93
SO	209	194	403	268	270	538	82	1491	1551	3042	1786	1649	3435	91
Foul Outs	16	20	36	15	9	24	164	132	132	264	125	105	230	118
E	16	10	26	17	13	30	100	117	113	230	115	118	233	101
E-Infield	5	4	9	6	6	12	86	40	46	86	45	50	95	92
LHB-Avg	.224	.196	.211	.232	.204	.220	96	.245	.234	.238	.240	.248	.245	97
LHB-HR	9	12	21	14	19	33	69	54	98	152	81	90	171	89
RHB-Avg	.257	.235	.245	.224	.222	.223	110	.248	.232	.241	.246	.240	.243	99
RHB-HR	16	18	34	12	20	32	117	143	103	246	188	113	301	85

Tampa Bay Rays - Tropicana Field Surface: FieldTurf
LF: 315   CF: 404   RF:322

| | 2020 Season | | | | | | | 2018-2020 | | | | | | |
| | Home Games | | | Away Games | | | | Home Games | | | Away Games | | | |
	Rays	Opp	Total	Rays	Opp	Total	Index	Rays	Opp	Total	Rays	Opp	Total	Index
G	29	29	58	31	31	62		191	191	382	193	193	386	
Avg	.228	.232	.230	.247	.244	.245	94	.251	.222	.236	.256	.241	.248	95
AB	917	986	1903	1058	1009	2067	98	6297	6476	12773	6781	6432	13213	98
R	134	103	237	155	126	281	90	871	694	1565	903	837	1740	91
H	209	229	438	261	246	507	92	1579	1435	3014	1733	1550	3283	93
2B	51	39	90	54	44	98	100	318	287	605	352	322	674	93
3B	7	3	10	5	3	8	136	46	28	74	38	24	62	123
HR	33	30	63	47	40	87	79	201	198	399	246	217	463	89
BB	130	83	213	113	85	198	117	687	531	1218	638	591	1229	103
SO	298	275	573	310	277	587	106	1722	1869	3591	1767	1725	3492	106
Foul Outs	18	19	37	20	15	35	115	143	163	306	138	117	255	124
E	20	13	33	13	24	37	95	86	107	193	119	116	235	83
E-Infield	12	6	18	4	9	13	148	37	51	88	49	32	81	110
LHB-Avg	.221	.220	.220	.239	.210	.228	97	.250	.205	.229	.255	.227	.243	95
LHB-HR	17	11	28	24	8	32	94	89	69	158	102	67	169	95
RHB-Avg	.237	.239	.238	.255	.263	.259	92	.251	.231	.240	.256	.249	.252	95
RHB-HR	16	19	35	23	32	55	70	112	129	241	144	150	294	86

Texas Rangers - Globe Life Field Surface: FieldTurf
LF: 329   CF: 407   RF:326

| | 2020 Season | | | | | | | 2017-2019 | | | | | | |
| | Home Games | | | Away Games | | | | Home Games | | | Away Games | | | |
	Rangers	Opp	Total	Rangers	Opp	Total	Index	Rangers	Opp	Total	Rangers	Opp	Total	Index
G	30	30	60	30	30	60		243	243	486	243	243	486	
Avg	.230	.233	.231	.205	.251	.228	102	.261	.276	.269	.227	.258	.242	111
AB	944	1014	1958	992	967	1959	100	8146	8739	16885	8277	8013	16290	104
R	123	145	268	101	167	268	100	1335	1398	2733	1011	1144	2155	127
H	217	236	453	203	243	446	102	2125	2410	4535	1883	2064	3947	115
2B	38	40	78	42	43	85	92	432	496	928	385	426	811	110
3B	6	5	11	3	8	11	100	42	54	96	27	35	62	149
HR	27	39	66	35	42	77	86	345	366	711	309	311	620	111
BB	94	132	226	73	104	177	128	884	844	1728	749	789	1538	108
SO	262	278	540	286	211	497	109	2128	1822	3950	2427	1785	4212	90
Foul Outs	20	26	46	26	22	48	96	151	186	337	168	169	337	96
E	18	20	38	22	13	35	109	180	178	358	153	147	300	119
E-Infield	9	8	17	9	7	16	106	68	74	142	61	66	127	112
LHB-Avg	.216	.233	.225	.185	.229	.206	109	.257	.271	.263	.224	.252	.236	112
LHB-HR	19	15	34	21	15	36	82	223	122	345	193	98	291	115
RHB-Avg	.242	.232	.237	.218	.264	.242	98	.265	.279	.273	.231	.261	.248	110
RHB-HR	8	24	32	14	27	41	87	122	244	366	116	213	329	107

Toronto Blue Jays - Sahlen Field
LF: 325   CF: 404   RF:325

| | 2020 Season | | | | | | | 2017-2019 | | | | | | |
| | Home Games | | | Away Games | | | | Home Games | | | Away Games | | | |
	Blue Jays	Opp	Total	Blue Jays	Opp	Total	Index	Blue Jays	Opp	Total	Blue Jays	Opp	Total	Index
G	26	26	52	34	34	68		243	243	486	243	243	486	
Avg	.276	.256	.266	.239	.254	.247	108	.241	.256	.249	.240	.265	.252	99
AB	880	903	1783	1143	1124	2267	103	8024	8616	16640	8445	8218	16663	100
R	159	136	295	143	176	319	121	1052	1209	2261	1076	1235	2311	98
H	243	231	474	273	286	559	111	1931	2206	4137	2024	2180	4204	98
2B	47	45	92	57	60	117	100	436	492	928	423	483	906	103
3B	1	5	6	3	4	7	109	24	35	59	18	46	64	92
HR	43	24	67	45	57	102	84	356	343	699	330	296	626	112
BB	88	98	186	115	152	267	89	739	851	1590	811	853	1664	96
SO	228	223	451	280	296	576	100	2011	2102	4113	2217	1900	4117	100
Foul Outs	10	23	33	17	20	37	113	207	198	405	185	211	396	102
E	19	24	43	20	21	41	137	144	121	265	145	130	275	96
E-Infield	8	11	19	8	11	19	131	52	52	104	68	50	118	88
LHB-Avg	.248	.246	.247	.225	.217	.221	112	.242	.243	.242	.238	.255	.247	98
LHB-HR	12	9	21	13	22	35	83	137	129	266	120	123	243	109
RHB-Avg	.292	.261	.277	.247	.282	.264	105	.240	.265	.252	.240	.273	.255	99
RHB-HR	31	15	46	32	35	67	83	219	214	433	210	173	383	113

Washington Nationals - Nationals Park
LF: 336   CF: 403   RF:335

| | 2020 Season | | | | | | | 2018-2020 | | | | | | |
| | Home Games | | | Away Games | | | | Home Games | | | Away Games | | | |
	Nationals	Opp	Total	Nationals	Opp	Total	Index	Nationals	Opp	Total	Nationals	Opp	Total	Index
G	33	33	66	27	27	54		195	195	390	189	189	378	
Avg	.243	.260	.252	.287	.284	.286	88	.265	.252	.258	.255	.243	.249	104
AB	1039	1130	2169	929	895	1824	97	6485	6786	13271	6512	6183	12695	101
R	144	150	294	149	151	300	80	1006	897	1903	931	810	1741	106
H	252	294	546	267	254	521	86	1720	1707	3427	1661	1501	3162	105
2B	63	48	111	49	53	102	92	385	344	729	309	311	620	112
3B	6	2	8	6	4	10	67	30	23	53	34	27	61	83
HR	30	47	77	36	47	83	78	256	273	529	232	221	453	112
BB	110	116	226	82	100	182	104	735	619	1354	672	601	1273	102
SO	251	290	541	200	218	418	109	1498	1805	3303	1550	1631	3181	99
Foul Outs	19	22	41	7	16	23	150	156	140	296	134	158	292	97
E	22	21	43	17	14	31	113	95	115	210	95	91	186	109
E-Infield	12	7	19	9	5	14	111	45	43	88	47	31	78	109
LHB-Avg	.243	.249	.247	.275	.276	.276	89	.272	.261	.266	.253	.237	.245	109
LHB-HR	14	14	28	15	18	33	69	108	112	220	104	83	187	114
RHB-Avg	.242	.268	.256	.297	.289	.293	87	.261	.245	.253	.257	.247	.252	100
RHB-HR	16	33	49	21	29	50	84	148	161	309	128	138	266	110

2020 American League Ballpark Index Rankings

Home Park	Avg	AB	R	H	2B	3B	HR	BB	SO	FO	E	E-Inf	LHB Avg	LHB HR	RHB Avg	RHB HR
Angels (Angel Stadium of Anaheim)	111	104	126	115	107	90	135	106	90	70	85	88	118	139	108	128
Red Sox (Fenway Park)	114	105	123	120	155	118	92	97	93	70	198	195	105	84	120	97
Blue Jays (Sahlen Field)	108	103	121	111	100	109	84	89	100	113	137	131	112	83	105	83
Indians (Progressive Field)	108	101	111	109	115	133	89	94	103	79	107	200	119	118	99	70
White Sox (Guaranteed Rate Field)	98	96	106	93	80	0	128	116	102	135	72	70	80	94	107	142
Yankees (Yankee Stadium)	103	103	105	106	94	145	138	93	96	71	80	69	111	126	101	145
Royals (Kauffman Stadium)	110	103	105	114	103	69	84	90	90	94	87	94	111	71	110	91
Rangers (Globe Life Field)	102	100	100	102	92	100	86	128	109	96	109	106	109	82	98	87
Tigers (Comerica Park)	94	98	92	92	124	441	87	103	90	120	97	146	81	77	103	93
Twins (Target Field)	93	99	91	92	103	285	78	100	110	101	138	70	107	94	82	68
Orioles (Oriole Park at Camden Yards)	91	95	91	87	65	77	112	113	103	86	74	72	94	116	90	109
Rays (Tropicana Field)	94	98	90	92	100	136	79	117	106	115	95	148	97	94	92	70
Mariners (T-Mobile Park)	87	98	85	86	91	24	103	83	101	120	125	110	92	112	84	98
Athletics (RingCentral Coliseum)	95	102	80	97	103	64	66	89	93	135	75	94	106	68	89	66
Astros (Minute Maid Park)	86	94	77	81	80	103	72	98	111	100	136	196	80	64	89	79

2020 National League Ballpark Index Rankings

Home Park	Avg	AB	R	H	2B	3B	HR	BB	SO	FO	E	E-Inf	LHB Avg	LHB HR	RHB Avg	RHB HR
Rockies (Coors Field)	119	108	140	129	101	232	106	68	85	88	105	119	119	119	120	96
Reds (Great American Ballpark)	104	105	128	109	93	31	205	96	109	102	99	125	111	265	97	159
Diamondbacks (Chase Field)	103	101	112	104	98	226	93	117	92	107	135	107	104	120	102	76
Giants (Oracle Park)	103	103	107	106	129	106	104	121	109	86	68	60	104	122	102	93
Braves (Truist Park)	106	99	107	105	94	63	97	112	98	101	173	100	101	108	110	91
Pirates (PNC Park)	99	104	106	102	119	68	83	99	100	55	217	124	108	79	92	88
Brewers (Miller Park)	103	97	102	100	84	55	120	100	104	154	92	98	97	92	108	152
Cardinals (Busch Stadium)	104	105	101	109	86	131	92	107	82	164	100	86	96	69	110	117
Phillies (Citizens Bank Park)	99	101	100	101	85	302	129	108	93	166	66	78	107	133	94	126
Mets (Citi Field)	92	101	98	93	100	53	124	97	110	87	81	98	91	128	94	120
Dodgers (Dodger Stadium)	103	96	94	99	93	65	122	95	97	147	91	88	91	74	111	192
Marlins (Marlins Park)	103	97	87	100	134	45	81	82	97	71	68	63	103	65	104	88
Padres (PETCO Park)	88	95	86	84	109	26	116	112	117	75	90	107	80	114	95	116
Nationals (Nationals Park)	88	97	80	86	92	67	78	104	109	150	113	111	89	69	87	84
Cubs (Wrigley Field)	92	94	72	86	98	218	76	98	110	56	60	61	90	82	93	70

2020 AL Home Runs

Home Park	Index
Yankees	138
Angels	135
White Sox	128
Orioles	112
Mariners	103
Red Sox	92
Indians	89
Tigers	87
Rangers	86
Royals	84
Blue Jays	84
Rays	79
Twins	78
Astros	72
Athletics	66

2020 AL LHB Home Runs

Home Park	Index
Angels	139
Yankees	126
Indians	118
Orioles	116
Mariners	112
Twins	94
Rays	94
White Sox	94
Red Sox	84
Blue Jays	83
Rangers	82
Tigers	77
Royals	71
Athletics	68
Astros	64

2020 AL RHB Home Runs

Home Park	Index
Yankees	145
White Sox	142
Angels	128
Orioles	109
Mariners	98
Red Sox	97
Tigers	93
Royals	91
Rangers	87
Blue Jays	83
Astros	79
Rays	70
Indians	70
Twins	68
Athletics	66

2020 NL Home Runs

Home Park	Index
Reds	205
Phillies	129
Mets	124
Dodgers	122
Brewers	120
Padres	116
Rockies	106
Giants	104
Braves	97
Diamondbacks	93
Cardinals	92
Pirates	83
Marlins	81
Nationals	78
Cubs	76

2020 NL LHB Home Runs

Home Park	Index
Reds	265
Phillies	133
Mets	128
Giants	122
Diamondbacks	120
Rockies	119
Padres	114
Braves	108
Brewers	92
Cubs	82
Pirates	79
Dodgers	74
Nationals	69
Cardinals	69
Marlins	65

2020 NL RHB Home Runs

Home Park	Index
Dodgers	192
Reds	159
Brewers	152
Phillies	126
Mets	120
Cardinals	117
Padres	116
Rockies	96
Giants	93
Braves	91
Marlins	88
Pirates	88
Nationals	84
Diamondbacks	76
Cubs	70

2020 AL Avg	
Home Park	Index
Red Sox	114
Angels	111
Royals	110
Indians	108
Blue Jays	108
Yankees	103
Rangers	102
White Sox	98
Athletics	95
Tigers	94
Rays	94
Twins	93
Orioles	91
Mariners	87
Astros	86

2020 AL LHB Avg	
Home Park	Index
Indians	119
Angels	118
Blue Jays	112
Royals	111
Yankees	111
Rangers	109
Twins	107
Athletics	106
Red Sox	105
Rays	97
Orioles	94
Mariners	92
Tigers	81
Astros	80
White Sox	80

2020 AL RHB Avg	
Home Park	Index
Red Sox	120
Royals	110
Angels	108
White Sox	107
Blue Jays	105
Tigers	103
Yankees	101
Indians	99
Rangers	98
Rays	92
Orioles	90
Athletics	89
Astros	89
Mariners	84
Twins	82

2020 NL Avg	
Home Park	Index
Rockies	119
Braves	106
Reds	104
Cardinals	104
Marlins	103
Giants	103
Dodgers	103
Brewers	103
Diamondbacks	103
Phillies	99
Pirates	99
Mets	92
Cubs	92
Padres	88
Nationals	88

2020 NL LHB Avg	
Home Park	Index
Rockies	119
Reds	111
Pirates	108
Phillies	107
Diamondbacks	104
Giants	104
Marlins	103
Braves	101
Brewers	97
Cardinals	96
Mets	91
Dodgers	91
Cubs	90
Nationals	89
Padres	80

2020 NL RHB Avg	
Home Park	Index
Rockies	120
Dodgers	111
Cardinals	110
Braves	110
Brewers	108
Marlins	104
Diamondbacks	102
Giants	102
Reds	97
Padres	95
Mets	94
Phillies	94
Cubs	93
Pirates	92
Nationals	87

2020 AL Doubles	
Home Park	Index
Red Sox	155
Tigers	124
Indians	115
Angels	107
Athletics	103
Royals	103
Twins	103
Blue Jays	100
Rays	100
Yankees	94
Rangers	92
Mariners	91
White Sox	80
Astros	80
Orioles	65

2020 AL Triples	
Home Park	Index
Tigers	441
Twins	285
Yankees	145
Rays	136
Indians	133
Red Sox	118
Blue Jays	109
Astros	103
Rangers	100
Angels	90
Orioles	77
Royals	69
Athletics	64
Mariners	24
White Sox	0

2020 AL Errors	
Home Park	Index
Red Sox	198
Twins	138
Blue Jays	137
Astros	136
Mariners	125
Rangers	109
Indians	107
Tigers	97
Rays	95
Royals	87
Angels	85
Yankees	80
Athletics	75
Orioles	74
White Sox	72

2020 NL Doubles	
Home Park	Index
Marlins	134
Giants	129
Pirates	119
Padres	109
Rockies	101
Mets	100
Cubs	98
Diamondbacks	98
Braves	94
Reds	93
Dodgers	93
Nationals	92
Cardinals	86
Phillies	85
Brewers	84

2020 NL Triples	
Home Park	Index
Phillies	302
Rockies	232
Diamondbacks	226
Cubs	218
Cardinals	131
Giants	106
Pirates	68
Nationals	67
Dodgers	65
Braves	63
Brewers	55
Mets	53
Marlins	45
Reds	31
Padres	26

2020 NL Errors	
Home Park	Index
Pirates	217
Braves	173
Diamondbacks	135
Nationals	113
Rockies	105
Cardinals	100
Reds	99
Brewers	92
Dodgers	91
Padres	90
Mets	81
Giants	68
Marlins	68
Phillies	66
Cubs	60

2018-2020 American League Ballpark Index Rankings

Home Park	TOTALS												LHB		RHB	
	Avg	AB	R	H	2B	3B	HR	BB	SO	FO	E	E-Inf	Avg	HR	Avg	HR
Blue Jays (Sahlen Field)[1]	108	103	121	111	100	109	84	89	100	113	137	131	112	83	105	83
Royals (Kauffman Stadium)	105	102	106	107	113	122	81	96	88	99	91	88	111	75	101	85
Red Sox (Fenway Park)	104	100	106	104	137	123	91	100	98	68	124	134	105	83	103	96
Rangers (Globe Life Field)[1]	102	100	100	102	92	100	86	128	109	96	109	106	109	82	98	87
Indians (Progressive Field)	102	99	106	100	106	85	103	100	103	80	119	113	103	108	100	97
Tigers (Comerica Park)	101	102	101	103	99	179	94	94	92	129	105	121	94	88	106	97
Yankees (Yankee Stadium)	101	98	97	99	85	76	106	102	100	93	98	98	103	108	100	106
Orioles (Oriole Park at Camden Yards)	101	100	102	100	93	80	118	97	93	106	91	92	101	112	100	121
Twins (Target Field)	100	99	99	99	113	110	88	106	102	93	82	66	103	90	98	85
Angels (Angel Stadium of Anaheim)	98	101	102	99	97	73	111	103	102	90	99	101	97	128	98	101
Astros (Minute Maid Park)	97	98	99	96	86	87	108	99	106	88	109	97	97	102	98	111
White Sox (Guaranteed Rate Field)	97	99	97	96	82	52	114	101	104	100	91	106	93	116	100	112
Rays (Tropicana Field)	95	98	91	93	93	123	89	103	106	124	83	110	95	95	95	86
Athletics (RingCentral Coliseum)	95	99	85	94	109	77	79	98	98	141	98	87	92	76	96	80
Mariners (T-Mobile Park)	94	99	90	92	84	61	98	95	110	97	110	111	94	88	94	104

2018-2020 National League Ballpark Index Rankings

Home Park	TOTALS												LHB		RHB	
	Avg	AB	R	H	2B	3B	HR	BB	SO	FO	E	E-Inf	Avg	HR	Avg	HR
Rockies (Coors Field)	121	105	135	127	128	204	120	95	89	67	115	118	117	121	125	118
Nationals (Nationals Park)	104	101	106	105	112	83	112	102	99	97	109	109	109	114	100	110
Giants (Oracle Park)[1]	103	103	107	106	129	106	104	121	109	86	68	60	104	122	102	93
Braves (Truist Park)	102	99	106	101	104	83	94	103	98	90	134	156	99	93	105	94
Reds (Great American Ballpark)	101	102	111	103	100	66	131	106	111	114	88	83	102	132	101	130
Diamondbacks (Chase Field)	101	101	103	102	97	190	91	103	99	107	122	122	105	97	97	87
Cubs (Wrigley Field)	100	96	95	96	100	140	93	104	99	68	82	88	99	84	100	100
Phillies (Citizens Bank Park)	100	101	104	100	91	106	120	100	103	129	104	106	102	119	98	121
Dodgers (Dodger Stadium)	99	98	90	97	96	34	113	85	101	113	93	86	97	105	101	123
Pirates (PNC Park)	99	101	96	100	117	82	86	109	97	79	103	105	102	94	96	80
Cardinals (Busch Stadium)	98	100	93	98	90	92	86	93	91	118	101	92	97	89	99	85
Marlins (Marlins Park)	97	101	89	98	99	106	74	97	99	109	78	67	89	77	101	72
Brewers (Miller Park)	97	97	100	94	92	84	111	102	110	106	117	141	96	108	97	114
Padres (PETCO Park)	95	100	94	95	101	69	96	112	99	91	97	89	96	90	95	99
Mets (Citi Field)	90	97	84	87	81	66	103	95	111	122	84	76	92	97	89	107

2018-2020 AL Home Runs

Home Park	Index
Orioles	118
White Sox	114
Angels	111
Astros	108
Yankees	106
Indians	103
Mariners	98
Tigers	94
Red Sox	91
Rays	89
Twins	88
Rangers[1]	86
Blue Jays[1]	84
Royals	81
Athletics	79

2018-2020 AL LHB Home Runs

Home Park	Index
Angels	128
White Sox	116
Orioles	112
Indians	108
Yankees	108
Astros	102
Rays	95
Twins	90
Mariners	88
Tigers	88
Red Sox	83
Blue Jays[1]	83
Rangers[1]	82
Athletics	76
Royals	75

2018-2020 AL RHB Home Runs

Home Park	Index
Orioles	121
White Sox	112
Astros	111
Yankees	106
Mariners	104
Angels	101
Indians	97
Tigers	97
Red Sox	96
Rangers[1]	87
Rays	86
Twins	85
Royals	85
Blue Jays[1]	83
Athletics	80

2018-2020 NL Home Runs

Home Park	Index
Reds	131
Phillies	120
Rockies	120
Dodgers	113
Nationals	112
Brewers	111
Giants[1]	104
Mets	103
Padres	96
Braves	94
Cubs	93
Diamondbacks	91
Cardinals	86
Pirates	86
Marlins	74

2018-2020 NL LHB Home Runs

Home Park	Index
Reds	132
Giants[1]	122
Rockies	121
Phillies	119
Nationals	114
Brewers	108
Dodgers	105
Mets	97
Diamondbacks	97
Pirates	94
Braves	93
Padres	90
Cardinals	89
Cubs	84
Marlins	77

2018-2020 NL RHB Home Runs

Home Park	Index
Reds	130
Dodgers	123
Phillies	121
Rockies	118
Brewers	114
Nationals	110
Mets	107
Cubs	100
Padres	99
Braves	94
Giants[1]	93
Diamondbacks	87
Cardinals	85
Pirates	80
Marlins	72

1. 2020 only

2018-2020 AL Avg	
Home Park	Index
Blue Jays[1]	108
Royals	105
Red Sox	104
Rangers[1]	102
Indians	102
Tigers	101
Yankees	101
Orioles	101
Twins	100
Angels	98
Astros	97
White Sox	97
Rays	95
Athletics	95
Mariners	94

2018-2020 AL LHB Avg	
Home Park	Index
Blue Jays[1]	112
Royals	111
Rangers[1]	109
Red Sox	105
Indians	103
Twins	103
Yankees	103
Orioles	101
Angels	97
Astros	97
Rays	95
Tigers	94
Mariners	94
White Sox	93
Athletics	92

2018-2020 AL RHB Avg	
Home Park	Index
Tigers	106
Blue Jays[1]	105
Red Sox	103
Royals	101
Yankees	100
Orioles	100
Indians	100
White Sox	100
Angels	98
Astros	98
Rangers[1]	98
Twins	98
Athletics	96
Rays	95
Mariners	94

2018-2020 NL Avg	
Home Park	Index
Rockies	121
Nationals	104
Giants[1]	103
Braves	102
Reds	101
Diamondbacks	101
Cubs	100
Phillies	100
Dodgers	99
Pirates	99
Cardinals	98
Marlins	97
Brewers	97
Padres	95
Mets	90

2018-2020 NL LHB Avg	
Home Park	Index
Rockies	117
Nationals	109
Diamondbacks	105
Giants[1]	104
Pirates	102
Reds	102
Phillies	102
Cubs	99
Braves	99
Cardinals	97
Dodgers	97
Brewers	96
Padres	96
Mets	92
Marlins	89

2018-2020 NL RHB Avg	
Home Park	Index
Rockies	125
Braves	105
Giants[1]	102
Marlins	101
Reds	101
Dodgers	101
Cubs	100
Nationals	100
Cardinals	99
Phillies	98
Diamondbacks	97
Brewers	97
Pirates	96
Padres	95
Mets	89

2018-2020 AL Doubles	
Home Park	Index
Red Sox	137
Twins	113
Royals	113
Athletics	109
Indians	106
Blue Jays[1]	100
Tigers	99
Angels	97
Rays	93
Orioles	93
Rangers[1]	92
Astros	86
Yankees	85
Mariners	84
White Sox	82

2018-2020 AL Triples	
Home Park	Index
Tigers	179
Rays	123
Red Sox	123
Royals	122
Twins	110
Blue Jays[1]	109
Rangers[1]	100
Astros	87
Indians	85
Orioles	80
Athletics	77
Yankees	76
Angels	73
Mariners	61
White Sox	52

2018-2020 AL Errors	
Home Park	Index
Blue Jays[1]	137
Red Sox	124
Indians	119
Mariners	110
Astros	109
Rangers[1]	109
Tigers	105
Angels	99
Yankees	98
Athletics	98
Orioles	91
Royals	91
White Sox	91
Rays	83
Twins	82

2018-2020 NL Doubles	
Home Park	Index
Giants[1]	129
Rockies	128
Pirates	117
Nationals	112
Braves	104
Padres	101
Cubs	100
Reds	100
Marlins	99
Diamondbacks	97
Dodgers	96
Brewers	92
Phillies	91
Cardinals	90
Mets	81

2018-2020 NL Triples	
Home Park	Index
Rockies	204
Diamondbacks	190
Cubs	140
Marlins	106
Giants[1]	106
Phillies	106
Cardinals	92
Brewers	84
Nationals	83
Braves	83
Pirates	82
Padres	69
Reds	66
Mets	66
Dodgers	34

2018-2020 NL Errors	
Home Park	Index
Braves	134
Diamondbacks	122
Brewers	117
Rockies	115
Nationals	109
Phillies	104
Pirates	103
Cardinals	101
Padres	97
Dodgers	93
Reds	88
Mets	84
Cubs	82
Marlins	78
Giants[1]	68

Lefty/Righty Statistics

Mark Simon

Right now, the most unstoppable hitter in baseball is the 22-year-old wonder playing left field in Washington D.C., Juan Soto.

Soto's numbers in 60 games were out of this world and make you wonder what kind of amazing numbers he'll put up in the next 162-game campaign.

What made Soto stand out from everyone else in 2020 was that he was a left-handed hitter who mashed against both right- and left-handed pitching.

Soto hit .346/.514/.654 vs. right-handed pitching and .360/.429/.780 with five home runs in 50 at-bats vs. left-handed pitching. His OPS vs. righties was 1.168. His OPS vs. lefties was 1.209.

Soto and Braves outfielder Marcell Ozuna were the only two players to have an OPS over 1.000 versus both right-handed pitchers and left-handed pitchers in 2020 (minimum 50 PA against each).

Two unusual sets of splits in this abbreviated season belonged to two of the best hitters in the game. Mike Trout finished the season with a reverse-split, sporting a 1.069 OPS vs. right-handed pitching and a .245 average with a .783 OPS in 53 at-bats against lefties.

Mookie Betts had an OPS nearly identical to Trout against righties, 1.061. But in 55 at-bats against lefties, he hit .200 with no home runs and just a .531 OPS.

For pitchers, the players whose splits I marvel at are those of former Dodger Kenta Maeda and current Dodger Tony Gonsolin. They were the two starting pitchers to hold both left- and right-handed hitting opponents to an OPS below .550 (White Sox reliever Matt Foster did it too).

Make sure to scroll across the entirety of Maeda's stat line to see his eye-popping strikeout-to-walk ratio against right-handed hitters (39-to-1 if you're not inclined to look!).

Shane Bieber and Dinelson Lamet came close to matching Maeda. Both had reverse splits, and though each had an opponents' OPS well below .550 versus left-handed hitters, each was a smidge above that line against right-handers (.565 and .574, respectively).

In terms of odd platoon splits, Zack Greinke's will get your attention. Left-handed and right-handed batters had the same number of at-bats against Greinke. But right-handed hitters hit .305 with an .845 OPS, and left-handed batters hit .206 with a .529 OPS. Greinke used his changeup with great effectiveness against lefties. They hit .102 against it. The 54 outs he got versus lefties with his changeup were the most outs he got with any pitch against left-handed batters.

Another pitcher to watch is Marlins rookie righty Sixto Sánchez, against whom left-handed batters had a .531 OPS and no home runs in 69 at-bats (righties had a .745 OPS). Sánchez was similarly excellent as Greinke with his changeup, a pitch against which left-handed hitters hit .152.

The following pages include platoon splits for all hitters with at least 20 plate appearances and pitchers with at least 20 batters faced in 2020. It contains batting average, on-base percentage and slugging percentage along with a count of at-bats, hits, doubles, triples, home runs, RBI, walks and strikeouts for hitters against both right- and left-handed pitchers.

The lists are alphabetical by last name. At the end of each set are MLB season numbers for context. If you're looking for split leaderboards, they can be found in the next section in this book.

Batters vs. Left-Handed and Right-Handed Pitchers

Batter	vs	Avg	AB	H	2B	3B	HR	RBI	BB	SO	OBP	Slg
Abreu, Jose	L	.250	52	13	4	0	4	17	4	12	.316	.558
Bats Right	R	.335	188	63	11	0	15	43	14	47	.385	.633
Acuna Jr., Ronald	L	.226	31	7	3	0	1	8	11	13	.429	.419
Bats Right	R	.256	129	33	8	0	13	21	27	47	.400	.620
Adames, Willy	L	.319	47	15	7	0	2	7	6	17	.396	.596
Bats Right	R	.239	138	33	8	1	6	16	14	57	.309	.442
Adams, Matt	L	.667	3	2	0	0	1	3	0	1	.667	1.667
Bats Left	R	.152	46	7	2	0	1	6	2	17	.188	.261
Adell, Jo	L	.171	41	7	1	0	2	3	2	21	.227	.341
Bats Right	R	.157	83	13	3	0	1	4	5	34	.205	.229
Adrianza, Ehire	L	.162	37	6	3	0	0	2	6	8	.295	.243
Bats Both	R	.212	52	11	4	0	0	1	5	15	.281	.288
Aguilar, Jesus	L	.321	53	17	4	0	3	5	6	12	.390	.566
Bats Right	R	.259	135	35	6	0	5	29	17	28	.338	.415
Ahmed, Nick	L	.274	62	17	4	0	2	9	5	13	.328	.435
Bats Right	R	.263	137	36	6	1	3	20	13	33	.327	.387
Akiyama, Shogo	L	.190	21	4	1	0	0	0	1	7	.261	.238
Bats Left	R	.254	134	34	5	1	0	9	24	27	.371	.306
Alberto, Hanser	L	.375	48	18	4	0	1	7	2	9	.396	.521
Bats Right	R	.257	171	44	11	0	2	15	3	21	.278	.357
Albies, Ozzie	L	.214	28	6	1	0	0	3	1	7	.241	.250
Bats Both	R	.289	90	26	4	0	6	16	4	23	.326	.533
Alcantara, Sergio	L	.333	3	1	0	0	1	1	0	1	.333	1.333
Bats Both	R	.111	18	2	0	1	0	0	2	3	.200	.222
Alfaro, Jorge	L	.258	31	8	0	0	1	4	1	10	.281	.355
Bats Right	R	.210	62	13	2	0	2	12	3	26	.279	.339
Allen, Austin	L	-	0	0	0	0	0	0	0	0	-	-
Bats Left	R	.194	31	6	1	0	1	3	1	14	.219	.323
Allen, Greg	L	.000	7	0	0	0	0	0	0	0	.000	.000
Bats Both	R	.211	19	4	1	0	1	4	3	6	.360	.421
Almora Jr., Albert	L	.200	10	2	0	0	0	0	1	2	.333	.200
Bats Right	R	.150	20	3	1	0	0	1	2	7	.227	.200
Alonso, Pete	L	.194	67	13	0	0	5	8	9	22	.299	.418
Bats Right	R	.248	141	35	6	0	11	27	15	39	.340	.525
Altuve, Jose	L	.167	48	8	1	0	1	3	6	13	.259	.250
Bats Right	R	.236	144	34	8	0	4	15	11	26	.295	.375
Alvarez, Eddy	L	.000	6	0	0	0	0	0	0	4	.000	.000
Bats Both	R	.226	31	7	1	0	0	2	3	12	.314	.258
Anderson, Brian	L	.286	56	16	2	0	2	8	6	15	.359	.429
Bats Right	R	.243	144	35	5	1	9	30	16	51	.339	.479
Anderson, Tim	L	.449	49	22	7	1	6	12	6	8	.509	1.000
Bats Right	R	.283	159	45	4	0	4	9	4	42	.307	.384
Andrus, Elvis	L	.206	34	7	2	0	1	2	1	6	.229	.353
Bats Right	R	.188	69	13	3	0	2	5	7	9	.263	.319
Andujar, Miguel	L	.308	26	8	1	0	1	3	1	3	.333	.462
Bats Right	R	.194	36	7	1	1	0	2	2	6	.237	.278
Apostel, Sherten	L	.091	11	1	1	0	0	0	1	5	.167	.182
Bats Right	R	.111	9	1	0	0	0	0	0	4	.111	.111
Aquino, Aristides	L	.190	21	4	0	0	1	4	1	9	.320	.333
Bats Right	R	.154	26	4	1	0	1	4	5	9	.290	.308
Arauz, Jonathan	L	.290	31	9	1	0	0	3	3	9	.353	.323
Bats Both	R	.220	41	9	1	0	1	6	5	12	.304	.317
Arcia, Orlando	L	.191	47	9	4	0	1	5	7	10	.296	.340
Bats Right	R	.286	126	36	6	1	4	15	7	22	.326	.444
Arenado, Nolan	L	.264	53	14	4	0	1	6	2	7	.286	.396
Bats Right	R	.248	129	32	5	0	7	20	13	13	.310	.450
Arozarena, Randy	L	.400	20	8	0	0	4	5	1	2	.478	1.000
Bats Right	R	.227	44	10	2	0	3	6	5	20	.340	.477
Arraez, Luis	L	.231	26	6	0	0	0	4	4	1	.333	.231
Bats Left	R	.349	86	30	9	0	0	9	4	10	.374	.453
Arroyo, Christian	L	.158	19	3	0	0	1	3	0	6	.158	.316
Bats Right	R	.290	31	9	1	0	2	5	4	5	.371	.516
Avila, Alex	L	.250	12	3	0	0	0	1	1	3	.400	.250
Bats Left	R	.162	37	6	2	0	1	1	10	19	.340	.297
Bader, Harrison	L	.360	25	9	3	1	2	4	0	4	.429	.800
Bats Right	R	.185	81	15	4	1	2	7	13	36	.309	.333
Baez, Javier	L	.218	55	12	4	0	2	7	2	16	.254	.400
Bats Right	R	.198	167	33	5	1	6	17	5	59	.233	.341
Barnes, Austin	L	.316	19	6	0	0	0	3	5	5	.409	.316
Bats Right	R	.224	67	15	3	0	1	9	10	19	.338	.313
Barnhart, Tucker	L	.053	19	1	1	0	0	2	3	7	.182	.105
Bats Left	R	.241	79	19	2	0	5	11	9	21	.318	.456
Bart, Joey	L	.185	27	5	3	0	0	2	0	12	.214	.296
Bats Right	R	.250	76	19	2	2	0	5	3	29	.313	.329
Beaty, Matt	L	.333	6	2	1	0	0	1	0	1	.429	.500
Bats Left	R	.205	44	9	0	0	2	4	2	13	.255	.341

Batter	vs	Avg	AB	H	2B	3B	HR	RBI	BB	SO	OBP	Slg
Bell, Josh	L	.180	50	9	0	0	2	6	8	17	.290	.300
Bats Both	R	.241	145	35	3	0	6	16	14	42	.311	.386
Bellinger, Cody	L	.216	74	16	2	0	3	8	9	19	.301	.365
Bats Left	R	.252	139	35	8	0	9	22	21	23	.350	.504
Belt, Brandon	L	.115	26	3	1	0	1	6	6	9	.281	.269
Bats Left	R	.350	123	43	12	1	8	24	24	27	.456	.659
Bemboom, Anthony	L	.111	18	2	0	0	1	3	2	7	.227	.278
Bats Left	R	.267	30	8	1	0	2	5	5	6	.389	.500
Benintendi, Andrew	L	.000	7	0	0	0	0	0	3	4	.364	.000
Bats Left	R	.125	32	4	1	0	0	1	8	13	.300	.156
Berti, Jon	L	.220	41	9	1	0	1	3	9	11	.360	.317
Bats Right	R	.278	79	22	4	0	1	11	14	26	.402	.367
Betts, Mookie	L	.200	55	11	1	0	0	2	9	15	.313	.218
Bats Right	R	.323	164	53	8	1	16	37	15	23	.385	.677
Bichette, Bo	L	.333	30	10	2	0	1	8	1	9	.355	.500
Bats Right	R	.290	93	27	7	1	4	15	4	18	.320	.516
Biggio, Cavan	L	.299	67	20	7	0	1	9	18	23	.460	.448
Bats Left	R	.229	153	35	9	0	7	19	23	38	.333	.425
Bishop, Braden	L	.235	17	4	2	0	0	2	1	7	.278	.353
Bats Right	R	.077	13	1	0	0	0	2	1	3	.200	.077
Blackmon, Charlie	L	.375	80	30	5	0	2	16	6	11	.414	.513
Bats Left	R	.262	141	37	7	1	4	26	13	33	.325	.411
Bogaerts, Xander	L	.375	64	24	2	0	4	8	5	12	.420	.594
Bats Right	R	.266	139	37	6	0	7	20	16	29	.340	.460
Bohm, Alec	L	.270	37	10	3	0	2	5	5	5	.349	.514
Bats Right	R	.358	123	44	8	0	2	18	11	31	.416	.472
Bonifacio, Jorge	L	.316	19	6	1	0	0	4	1	5	.381	.368
Bats Right	R	.194	67	13	2	0	2	13	4	21	.247	.313
Bote, David	L	.122	41	5	1	0	2	10	5	11	.234	.293
Bats Right	R	.238	84	20	2	1	5	19	12	29	.337	.464
Bradley Jr., Jackie	L	.288	59	17	4	0	3	5	10	14	.391	.508
Bats Left	R	.280	132	37	7	0	4	17	13	34	.351	.424
Brantley, Michael	L	.231	52	12	4	0	1	4	3	10	.273	.365
Bats Left	R	.331	118	39	11	0	4	18	14	18	.402	.525
Braun, Ryan	L	.233	43	10	0	0	2	7	4	9	.298	.372
Bats Right	R	.233	86	20	7	1	6	19	3	18	.272	.547
Bregman, Alex	L	.319	47	15	6	0	2	5	8	4	.411	.574
Bats Right	R	.208	106	22	6	1	4	17	16	22	.323	.396
Brinson, Lewis	L	.260	50	13	5	0	2	7	4	12	.315	.480
Bats Right	R	.196	56	11	1	0	1	5	4	18	.224	.268
Brosseau, Mike	L	.333	42	14	5	0	4	10	2	14	.383	.738
Bats Right	R	.273	44	12	0	1	1	2	6	17	.373	.386
Bruce, Jay	L	.111	18	2	1	0	0	2	0	9	.111	.167
Bats Left	R	.218	78	17	3	2	6	13	7	17	.282	.538
Bryant, Kris	L	.286	28	8	3	0	0	2	5	5	.429	.393
Bats Right	R	.184	103	19	2	1	4	9	7	35	.250	.340
Butera, Drew	L	.143	21	3	2	0	0	4	1	6	.174	.238
Bats Right	R	.167	18	3	0	0	0	2	1	5	.211	.167
Buxton, Byron	L	.250	28	7	1	0	2	6	1	7	.267	.500
Bats Right	R	.255	102	26	2	0	11	21	1	29	.267	.598
Cabrera, Asdrubal	L	.314	51	16	3	2	4	11	1	6	.315	.686
Bats Both	R	.216	139	30	6	1	4	20	18	34	.302	.360
Cabrera, Miguel	L	.400	35	14	2	0	2	8	6	6	.488	.629
Bats Right	R	.219	169	37	2	0	8	27	18	45	.295	.373
Calhoun, Kole	L	.229	48	11	2	0	4	11	7	17	.296	.521
Bats Left	R	.225	142	32	7	0	12	29	26	33	.351	.528
Calhoun, Willie	L	.368	19	7	0	0	0	4	1	2	.409	.368
Bats Right	R	.148	81	12	2	1	1	9	4	15	.186	.235
Camargo, Johan	L	.233	30	7	1	0	1	1	0	9	.258	.367
Bats Both	R	.189	90	17	7	0	3	8	6	26	.240	.367
Cameron, Daz	L	.143	7	1	0	1	0	0	0	4	.143	.429
Bats Right	R	.200	50	10	2	0	3	2	2	15	.231	.240
Candelario, Jeimer	L	.400	40	16	2	1	2	8	4	8	.455	.650
Bats Both	R	.269	145	39	9	2	5	21	16	41	.346	.462
Canha, Mark	L	.333	42	14	5	1	0	5	11	10	.482	.500
Bats Right	R	.221	149	33	7	1	5	28	26	44	.358	.383
Cano, Robinson	L	.264	53	14	4	0	4	9	3	8	.316	.566
Bats Left	R	.339	118	40	5	0	6	21	6	16	.368	.534
Caratini, Victor	L	.292	24	7	1	0	1	3	4	9	.433	.458
Bats Both	R	.228	92	21	6	0	0	13	8	22	.304	.293
Carlson, Dylan	L	.182	11	2	1	0	0	3	2	4	.286	.273
Bats Both	R	.202	99	20	6	1	3	13	6	31	.248	.374
Carpenter, Matt	L	.190	21	4	2	0	0	6	3	7	.320	.286
Bats Left	R	.185	119	22	4	0	4	18	20	41	.326	.319
Casali, Curt	L	.290	31	9	1	0	3	3	4	10	.389	.613
Bats Right	R	.178	45	8	2	0	3	5	10	19	.351	.422

Batters vs. Left-Handed and Right-Handed Pitchers

Batter	vs	Avg	AB	H	2B	3B	HR	RBI	BB	SO	OBP	Slg
Castellanos, Nick	L	.235	51	12	2	1	3	10	2	10	.278	.490
Bats Right	R	.222	167	37	9	1	11	24	17	59	.303	.485
Castro, Harold	L	.333	3	1	0	0	0	0	1	1	.500	.333
Bats Left	R	.348	46	16	4	0	0	3	4	10	.400	.435
Castro, Jason	L	.167	18	3	1	0	0	1	4	10	.318	.222
Bats Left	R	.194	62	12	8	0	2	8	8	23	.286	.419
Castro, Starlin	L	.500	2	1	2	1	0	1	1	3	.529	.750
Bats Right	R	.182	44	8	1	0	2	3	2	10	.217	.341
Castro, Willi	L	.391	23	9	1	0	1	3	2	5	.440	.565
Bats Both	R	.340	106	36	3	2	5	21	5	33	.368	.547
Cave, Jake	L	.188	32	6	1	0	1	3	1	15	.235	.313
Bats Left	R	.235	81	19	2	2	3	12	4	29	.303	.420
Cervelli, Francisco	L	.211	19	4	1	0	1	1	0	7	.211	.421
Bats Right	R	.265	34	9	1	0	2	6	8	7	.419	.471
Cespedes, Yoenis	L	.000	10	0	0	0	0	0	1	5	.167	.000
Bats Right	R	.238	21	5	1	0	2	4	1	10	.273	.571
Chapman, Matt	L	.190	21	4	1	0	1	2	2	5	.261	.381
Bats Right	R	.240	121	29	8	2	9	23	6	49	.279	.562
Chavis, Michael	L	.212	52	11	0	1	2	6	3	18	.246	.365
Bats Right	R	.213	94	20	5	1	3	13	5	32	.267	.383
Chirinos, Robinson	L	.259	27	7	2	0	1	4	4	5	.375	.444
Bats Right	R	.106	47	5	1	0	0	3	2	16	.140	.128
Chisholm, Jazz	L	.286	14	4	0	1	1	2	0	4	.286	.643
Bats Left	R	.119	42	5	1	0	1	4	5	15	.229	.214
Choi, Ji-Man	L	.118	17	2	0	0	1	2	1	8	.167	.294
Bats Left	R	.248	105	26	13	0	2	14	19	28	.354	.429
Choo, Shin-Soo	L	.222	36	8	1	0	1	4	1	7	.263	.333
Bats Left	R	.243	74	18	2	0	4	11	12	26	.348	.432
Colon, Christian	L	.200	10	2	1	0	0	0	1	1	.273	.300
Bats Right	R	.077	13	1	0	0	0	0	0	2	.077	.077
Conforto, Michael	L	.284	74	21	3	0	4	10	8	20	.384	.486
Bats Left	R	.344	128	44	9	0	5	21	16	37	.429	.531
Contreras, Willson	L	.186	43	8	3	0	0	4	4	14	.286	.256
Bats Right	R	.260	146	38	7	0	7	22	16	43	.375	.452
Cooper, Garrett	L	.350	40	14	5	0	4	14	3	8	.395	.775
Bats Right	R	.250	80	20	3	0	2	6	8	23	.333	.363
Cordero, Franchy	L	.000	6	0	0	0	0	0	3	1	.333	.000
Bats Left	R	.250	32	8	3	0	2	7	1	3	.273	.531
Correa, Carlos	L	.279	61	17	2	0	2	7	6	18	.353	.410
Bats Right	R	.257	140	36	7	0	3	18	10	31	.314	.371
Crawford, Brandon	L	.226	31	7	2	0	0	0	5	7	.351	.290
Bats Left	R	.262	141	37	10	0	8	28	10	40	.321	.504
Crawford, J.P.	L	.242	62	15	2	0	1	10	8	14	.338	.323
Bats Left	R	.261	142	37	5	2	1	14	15	25	.335	.345
Cron, C.J.	L	.154	13	2	1	0	1	2	0	5	.154	.462
Bats Right	R	.207	29	6	2	0	3	6	9	11	.410	.586
Cronenworth, Jake	L	.218	55	12	2	0	0	1	6	14	.295	.255
Bats Left	R	.316	117	37	13	3	4	19	12	16	.382	.581
Cruz, Nelson	L	.465	43	20	1	0	6	11	7	4	.549	.907
Bats Right	R	.254	142	36	5	0	10	22	18	54	.350	.500
Dahl, David	L	.156	32	5	0	0	0	1	1	10	.182	.156
Bats Left	R	.197	61	12	2	2	0	8	3	18	.242	.295
Dalbec, Bobby	L	.296	27	8	3	0	3	7	1	14	.321	.741
Bats Right	R	.245	53	13	0	0	5	9	9	25	.375	.528
d'Arnaud, Travis	L	.235	34	8	0	0	0	1	1	0	.270	.235
Bats Right	R	.344	131	45	8	0	9	31	14	39	.415	.611
Davidson, Matt	L	.214	28	6	1	0	3	10	3	9	.290	.571
Bats Right	R	.067	15	1	0	0	0	1	1	4	.125	.067
Davis, Chris	L	.000	5	0	0	0	0	0	2	2	.286	.000
Bats Left	R	.128	47	6	3	0	0	1	1	15	.146	.191
Davis, J.D.	L	.235	68	16	5	0	2	4	13	17	.373	.397
Bats Right	R	.254	122	31	4	0	4	15	18	39	.370	.385
Davis, Jonathan	L	.125	8	1	0	0	1	3	1	4	.200	.500
Bats Right	R	.316	19	6	2	0	0	3	2	7	.435	.421
Davis, Khris	L	.303	33	10	3	0	0	5	5	7	.415	.394
Bats Right	R	.135	52	7	2	0	2	5	5	19	.224	.288
DeJong, Paul	L	.125	24	3	0	0	0	1	4	8	.276	.125
Bats Right	R	.273	128	35	6	0	3	24	13	42	.331	.391
Delmonico, Nicky	L	-	0	0	0	0	0	0	0	0		
Bats Left	R	.150	20	3	0	0	0	3	2	2	.227	.150
Demeritte, Travis	L	.231	13	3	0	0	0	2	0	7	.286	.231
Bats Right	R	.125	16	2	1	0	0	2	3	7	.263	.188
DeShields, Delino	L	.222	27	6	1	1	0	3	1	7	.250	.333
Bats Right	R	.263	80	21	2	1	0	4	8	22	.330	.313
Devers, Rafael	L	.222	81	18	5	0	1	6	5	26	.292	.321
Bats Left	R	.285	151	43	11	1	10	37	8	41	.321	.570

Batter	vs	Avg	AB	H	2B	3B	HR	RBI	BB	SO	OBP	Slg
Diaz, Aledmys	L	.200	20	4	1	0	0	0	0	4	.200	.250
Bats Right	R	.263	38	10	4	0	3	6	1	8	.282	.605
Diaz, Elias	L	.231	26	6	1	0	1	5	2	4	.286	.385
Bats Right	R	.238	42	10	1	0	1	4	3	11	.289	.333
Diaz, Isan	L	.667	3	2	0	0	0	1	0	0	.667	.667
Bats Left	R	.105	19	2	0	0	0	0	0	7	.105	.105
Diaz, Lewin	L	.000	12	0	0	0	0	0	0	6	.000	.000
Bats Left	R	.222	27	6	2	0	0	3	2	6	.276	.296
Diaz, Yandy	L	.265	34	9	2	0	0	3	11	7	.444	.324
Bats Right	R	.325	80	26	1	0	2	8	12	10	.419	.413
Dickerson, Alex	L	.273	11	3	0	0	1	3	0	4	.333	.545
Bats Left	R	.300	140	42	10	1	9	24	16	26	.373	.579
Dickerson, Corey	L	.212	52	11	1	0	3	5	2	14	.241	.404
Bats Left	R	.275	142	39	4	1	4	12	13	21	.335	.401
Dietrich, Derek	L	.286	7	2	0	0	2	3	2	1	.444	1.143
Bats Left	R	.185	54	10	1	0	3	5	7	20	.333	.370
Donaldson, Josh	L	.067	15	1	0	0	1	1	6	5	.364	.267
Bats Right	R	.258	66	17	2	0	5	10	12	19	.375	.515
Dozier, Hunter	L	.250	24	6	3	0	0	1	5	9	.379	.375
Bats Right	R	.224	134	30	1	2	6	11	22	39	.338	.396
Drury, Brandon	L	.261	23	6	1	0	0	0	0	4	.261	.304
Bats Right	R	.043	23	1	0	0	0	1	2	5	.115	.043
Dubon, Mauricio	L	.341	44	15	0	0	2	7	5	9	.408	.477
Bats Right	R	.248	113	28	4	1	2	12	10	27	.310	.354
Duggar, Steven	L	.000	2	0	0	0	0	0	0	0	.000	.000
Bats Left	R	.188	32	6	2	0	0	3	1	11	.235	.250
Duvall, Adam	L	.277	47	13	5	0	3	7	2	13	.320	.574
Bats Right	R	.224	143	32	3	0	13	26	13	41	.296	.517
Dyson, Jarrod	L	.286	7	2	0	0	0	2	1	3	.375	.286
Bats Left	R	.167	54	9	0	0	3	3	3	10	.211	.167
Eaton, Adam	L	.103	39	4	0	0	1	3	4	8	.186	.179
Bats Left	R	.267	120	32	11	1	3	14	8	24	.318	.450
Edman, Tommy	L	.317	41	13	1	1	2	9	0	8	.317	.537
Bats Both	R	.233	163	38	6	0	3	17	16	40	.317	.325
Encarnacion, Edwin	L	.121	33	4	1	0	3	3	6	12	.275	.424
Bats Right	R	.167	126	21	4	0	7	16	10	42	.243	.365
Engel, Adam	L	.303	33	10	1	0	1	7	1	3	.343	.424
Bats Right	R	.291	55	16	4	1	2	5	2	16	.328	.509
Ervin, Phillip	L	.122	41	5	0	0	0	2	8	9	.280	.122
Bats Right	R	.182	33	6	3	0	0	2	6	13	.308	.273
Escobar, Eduardo	L	.213	61	13	3	0	1	4	3	8	.246	.311
Bats Both	R	.211	142	30	4	3	3	16	12	33	.280	.345
Espinal, Santiago	L	.324	34	11	3	0	0	2	0	7	.324	.412
Bats Right	R	.192	26	5	1	0	0	4	4	9	.290	.231
Estrada, Thairo	L	.286	21	6	0	0	1	2	0	7	.286	.429
Bats Right	R	.074	27	2	0	0	0	1	1	12	.194	.074
Evans, Phillip	L	.429	14	6	1	0	1	5	0	1	.429	.714
Bats Right	R	.320	25	8	1	0	0	4	5	6	.452	.360
Farmer, Kyle	L	.400	25	10	2	0	0	3	1	2	.423	.480
Bats Right	R	.179	39	7	1	0	0	1	4	11	.273	.205
Fisher, Derek	L	.400	5	2	0	0	0	2	1	2	.500	.400
Bats Left	R	.192	26	5	2	1	1	5	6	9	.333	.462
Fletcher, David	L	.348	69	24	7	0	1	8	8	5	.416	.493
Bats Right	R	.304	138	42	6	0	2	10	12	20	.355	.391
Flores, Wilmer	L	.274	62	17	3	0	7	17	4	11	.313	.661
Bats Right	R	.265	136	36	8	1	5	15	9	19	.315	.449
Flowers, Tyler	L	.118	17	2	1	0	0	2	3	12	.286	.176
Bats Right	R	.250	52	13	5	0	1	3	5	22	.339	.404
Ford, Mike	L	.000	8	0	0	0	0	0	1	2	.111	.000
Bats Left	R	.152	66	10	4	0	2	11	6	14	.240	.303
Forsythe, Logan	L	.214	14	3	1	0	1	1	1	6	.267	.500
Bats Right	R	.050	20	1	0	0	0	1	3	6	.174	.050
Fowler, Dexter	L	.118	17	2	0	0	0	1	1	5	.167	.118
Bats Both	R	.260	73	19	2	0	4	14	9	23	.349	.452
Fraley, Jake	L	.000	6	0	0	0	0	0	0	4	.143	.000
Bats Left	R	.200	20	4	1	1	0	0	2	7	.273	.350
France, Ty	L	.211	57	12	4	0	1	6	4	14	.297	.333
Bats Right	R	.369	84	31	5	1	3	17	7	23	.418	.560
Franco, Maikel	L	.318	44	14	3	0	1	7	4	8	.375	.455
Bats Right	R	.268	179	48	13	0	7	31	12	30	.308	.458
Frazier, Adam	L	.200	45	9	1	0	1	5	2	8	.250	.289
Bats Left	R	.238	164	39	6	0	6	18	15	27	.309	.384
Frazier, Clint	L	.273	33	9	2	0	2	6	3	9	.368	.515
Bats Right	R	.265	98	26	4	1	6	20	22	35	.402	.510
Frazier, Todd	L	.293	58	17	5	0	3	13	5	13	.359	.483
Bats Right	R	.202	99	20	4	1	2	6	6	29	.269	.323

Batters vs. Left-Handed and Right-Handed Pitchers

Batter	vs	Avg	AB	H	2B	3B	HR	RBI	BB	SO	OBP	Slg
Freeman, Freddie	L	.245	53	13	3	0	1	8	9	13	.355	.358
Bats Left	R	.373	161	60	20	1	12	45	36	24	.495	.733
Freeman, Mike	L	.500	2	1	0	0	0	0	0	0	.500	.500
Bats Left	R	.222	36	8	3	0	0	3	3	11	.293	.306
Fuentes, Josh	L	.258	31	8	2	0	2	10	1	16	.265	.516
Bats Right	R	.328	67	22	5	0	0	7	1	13	.348	.403
Gallagher, Cam	L	.200	5	1	1	0	0	0	1	1	.333	.400
Bats Right	R	.292	48	14	4	0	1	3	5	10	.358	.438
Gallo, Joey	L	.143	70	10	2	0	5	13	7	34	.241	.386
Bats Left	R	.203	123	25	6	0	5	13	22	45	.333	.374
Galvis, Freddy	L	.229	35	8	1	0	2	4	2	8	.270	.429
Bats Both	R	.217	106	23	4	0	5	12	11	22	.320	.396
Gamel, Ben	L	.238	21	5	2	0	0	0	3	8	.333	.333
Bats Left	R	.237	93	22	6	1	3	10	10	31	.311	.419
Garcia, Avisail	L	.291	55	16	6	0	1	9	11	16	.418	.455
Bats Right	R	.214	126	27	4	0	1	6	9	33	.293	.270
Garcia, Greg	L	.000	6	0	0	0	0	1	1	3	.125	.000
Bats Left	R	.222	54	12	3	0	0	10	6	15	.300	.278
Garcia, Jose	L	.300	20	6	0	0	0	2	0	3	.300	.300
Bats Right	R	.149	47	7	0	0	0	1	1	23	.167	.149
Garcia, Leury	L	.500	8	4	0	0	1	4	0	0	.500	.875
Bats Both	R	.235	51	12	1	0	2	4	4	9	.291	.373
Garcia, Luis	L	.143	35	5	0	0	0	1	0	13	.143	.143
Bats Left	R	.323	99	32	6	0	2	15	5	16	.356	.444
Gardner, Brett	L	.190	21	4	0	0	0		2	6	.261	.190
Bats Left	R	.229	109	25	5	1	5	15	24	29	.370	.431
Garlick, Kyle	L	.125	8	1	0	0	0	0	0	3	.125	.125
Bats Right	R	.143	14	2	1	0	0	3	0	4	.200	.214
Garneau, Dustin	L	.111	9	1	0	0	0		2	3	.273	.111
Bats Right	R	.172	29	5	0	1	1	4	4	12	.273	.345
Garver, Mitch	L	.304	23	7	0	0	1	1	3	7	.385	.435
Bats Right	R	.102	49	5	1	0	1	4	4	30	.182	.184
Gimenez, Andres	L	.261	23	6	0	0	1	1	2	6	.346	.391
Bats Left	R	.263	95	25	3	2	2	11	5	22	.330	.400
Goldschmidt, Paul	L	.286	28	8	2	0	2	6		9	.459	.571
Bats Right	R	.307	163	50	11	0	4	15	28	35	.409	.448
Gonzalez, Erik	L	.304	46	14	4	1	2	8	2	9	.333	.565
Bats Right	R	.200	135	27	9	0	1	12	6	42	.229	.289
Gonzalez, Marwin	L	.217	60	13	2	0	0	6	4	13	.269	.250
Bats Both	R	.209	115	24	2	0	5	16	13	28	.295	.357
Goodrum, Niko	L	.333	33	11	4	1	2	7	3	10	.378	.697
Bats Both	R	.144	125	18	3	0	3	13	15	59	.232	.240
Goodwin, Brian	L	.158	38	6	1	0	2	2	2	14	.220	.342
Bats Left	R	.236	106	25	8	1	4	20	15	40	.325	.443
Gordon, Alex	L	.214	28	6	0	0	0	1	1	5	.267	.214
Bats Left	R	.207	135	28	4	0	4	10	17	32	.305	.326
Gosselin, Phil	L	.278	54	15	3	0	2	9	8	14	.371	.444
Bats Right	R	.211	38	8	2	0	1	3	2	13	.250	.342
Grandal, Yasmani	L	.286	28	8	0	0	2	8	7	10	.405	.500
Bats Both	R	.218	133	29	7	0	6	19	23	48	.338	.406
Gregorius, Didi	L	.203	64	13	1	2	4	12	3	12	.243	.469
Bats Left	R	.318	151	48	9	0	6	28	12	16	.380	.497
Greiner, Grayson	L	.100	10	1	0	0	1	1	2	5	.308	.400
Bats Right	R	.122	41	5	2	0	2	7	1	15	.143	.317
Grichuk, Randal	L	.328	61	20	4	0	4	9	3	11	.359	.590
Bats Right	R	.252	155	39	5	0	8	26	10	38	.293	.439
Grisham, Trent	L	.267	60	16	1	1	2	5	5	21	.333	.417
Bats Left	R	.245	155	38	7	2	8	21	26	43	.359	.471
Grossman, Robbie	L	.100	20	2	0	1	0	1	4	6	.250	.200
Bats Both	R	.260	146	38	12	1	8	22	17	32	.357	.521
Guerrero Jr., Vladimir	L	.224	58	13	3	1	5	9	8	12	.318	.569
Bats Right	R	.276	163	45	10	1	4	24	12	26	.333	.423
Guillorme, Luis	L	.125	8	1	0	0	0	0	2	4	.300	.125
Bats Left	R	.367	49	18	6	0	0	9	8	13	.448	.490
Gurriel, Yuli	L	.290	62	18	5	0	4	8	2	5	.318	.565
Bats Right	R	.208	149	31	7	1	2	14	10	22	.256	.309
Gurriel Jr., Lourdes	L	.286	63	18	5	0	3	11	4	15	.324	.508
Bats Right	R	.317	145	46	9	0	8	22	10	33	.359	.545
Guzman, Ronald	L	.167	18	3	1	1	0	2	0	5	.211	.333
Bats Left	R	.267	60	16	0	0	4	7	7	19	.343	.467
Gyorko, Jedd	L	.267	45	12	2	0	5	10	11	13	.404	.644
Bats Right	R	.236	72	17	1	0	4	7	4	25	.282	.417
Haggerty, Sam	L	.333	18	6	2	0	1	4	2	6	.400	.611
Bats Both	R	.219	32	7	2	0	0	2	2	10	.265	.281
Hamilton, Billy	L	.091	11	1	0	0	1		1	5	.167	.364
Bats Both	R	.143	21	3	0	0	0	1	1	2	.174	.143
Hampson, Garrett	L	.212	66	14	0	1	1	5	4	22	.257	.288
Bats Right	R	.248	101	25	4	2	4	6	9	38	.306	.446
Happ, Ian	L	.250	48	12	1	0	1	2	10	18	.379	.333
Bats Both	R	.260	150	39	10	1	11	26	20	45	.355	.560
Harper, Bryce	L	.281	57	16	3	0	4	10	13	19	.423	.544
Bats Left	R	.263	133	35	6	2	9	23	36	24	.419	.541
Harrison, Josh	L	.278	36	10	2	0	2	7	1	5	.308	.500
Bats Right	R	.279	43	12	0	0	1	7	5	7	.385	.349
Harrison, Monte	L	.111	18	2	0	0	1	1	3	9	.238	.278
Bats Right	R	.207	29	6	1	0	0	2	1	17	.233	.241
Haseley, Adam	L	.400	10	4	1	0	0	2	0	1	.400	.500
Bats Left	R	.261	69	18	4	0	0	11	7	16	.342	.319
Hayes, Ke'Bryan	L	.500	22	11	4	0	1	3	0	3	.522	.818
Bats Right	R	.333	63	21	3	2	4	8	9	17	.417	.635
Hays, Austin	L	.250	28	7	2	0	1	2	2	5	.300	.429
Bats Right	R	.287	94	27	4	0	3	7	6	20	.337	.383
Hechavarria, Adeiny	L	.273	11	3	1	0	0	0	0	2	.273	.364
Bats Right	R	.250	48	12	2	0	0	2	4	10	.308	.292
Hedges, Austin	L	.130	23	3	1	0	0	1	3	9	.231	.174
Bats Right	R	.152	46	7	0	0	3	5	3	14	.231	.348
Heim, Jonah	L	.333	9	3	0	0	0	2	0	0	.333	.333
Bats Both	R	.172	29	5	0	0	0	3	3	3	.250	.172
Heineman, Scott	L	.154	26	4	1	0	1	4	0	5	.154	.308
Bats Right	R	.154	26	4	2	0	0	3	2	6	.214	.231
Heineman, Tyler	L	.286	7	2	0	0	0	1	3	1	.500	.286
Bats Both	R	.171	35	6	1	0	0	0	1	5	.237	.200
Hernandez, Cesar	L	.246	61	15	5	0	1	9	3	13	.303	.377
Bats Both	R	.297	172	51	15	0	2	11	21	44	.373	.419
Hernandez, Kike	L	.217	46	10	3	0	2	6	2	10	.260	.413
Bats Right	R	.237	93	22	5	1	3	14	4	21	.276	.409
Hernandez, Teoscar	L	.275	51	14	2	0	5	9	4	19	.327	.608
Bats Right	R	.295	139	41	5	0	11	25	10	44	.344	.568
Hernandez, Yadiel	L	.167	6	1	1	0	0	1	1	1	.286	.333
Bats Left	R	.200	20	4	2	0	1	5	0	11	.190	.450
Heyward, Jason	L	.167	36	6	2	0	1	6	5	10	.262	.306
Bats Left	R	.297	111	33	4	2	5	16	25	27	.432	.505
Hicks, Aaron	L	.244	45	11	2	0	2	7	9	7	.370	.422
Bats Both	R	.218	124	27	8	2	4	14	32	31	.382	.411
Higashioka, Kyle	L	.125	16	2	0	0	0	0	0	1	.125	.125
Bats Right	R	.313	32	10	1	0	4	10	0	10	.313	.719
Hilliard, Sam	L	.194	31	6	0	0	1	2	0	11	.194	.290
Bats Left	R	.216	74	16	2	2	5	8	9	31	.301	.500
Hiura, Keston	L	.241	54	13	0	0	2	6	6	23	.333	.352
Bats Right	R	.202	163	33	4	0	11	23	10	62	.284	.429
Hoerner, Nico	L	.257	35	9	1	0	0	3	3	5	.333	.286
Bats Right	R	.205	73	15	3	0	0	10	9	19	.302	.247
Holaday, Bryan	L	.083	12	1	0	0	0	0	0	3	.083	.083
Bats Right	R	.211	19	4	1	0	0	4	2	6	.286	.263
Holt, Brock	L	.357	14	5	3	0	0	0	0	5	.357	.571
Bats Left	R	.185	81	15	3	0	0	5	9	19	.272	.222
Hoskins, Rhys	L	.341	41	14	4	0	4	12	13	5	.509	.732
Bats Right	R	.209	110	23	5	0	6	14	16	38	.331	.418
Hosmer, Eric	L	.204	49	10	2	0	2	10	2	9	.245	.367
Bats Left	R	.330	94	31	4	0	7	26	7	19	.379	.596
Huff, Sam	L	.286	7	2	0	0	1	1	0	2	.286	.857
Bats Right	R	.375	24	9	2	0	2	3	2	9	.423	.708
Iglesias, Jose	L	.375	32	12	1	0	1	3	0	2	.394	.500
Bats Right	R	.373	110	41	16	0	2	21	3	15	.402	.573
Inciarte, Ender	L	.217	23	5	0	0	1	1	2	7	.280	.348
Bats Left	R	.183	93	17	2	1	0	9	10	18	.257	.226
Jansen, Danny	L	.103	39	4	1	0	1	6	5	12	.217	.205
Bats Right	R	.222	81	18	2	0	5	14	16	19	.357	.432
Jay, Jon	L	.000	6	0	0	0	0	0	1	0	.000	.000
Bats Left	R	.182	44	8	1	0	1	3	3	11	.240	.273
Jeffers, Ryan	L	.300	20	6	0	0	0	1	2	8	.417	.300
Bats Right	R	.257	35	9	0	0	3	6	3	11	.316	.514
Jimenez, Eloy	L	.289	45	13	0	0	4	9	1	13	.304	.556
Bats Right	R	.298	168	50	14	0	10	32	11	43	.339	.560
Jones, JaCoby	L	.286	21	6	3	0	2	6	1	7	.348	.714
Bats Right	R	.263	76	20	6	0	3	8	5	27	.329	.461
Jones, Taylor	L	.000	4	0	0	0	0	0	0	2	.000	.000
Bats Right	R	.235	17	4	1	0	1	3	1	5	.278	.471
Joyce, Matt	L	.154	13	2	0	0	0	1	0	2	.154	.154
Bats Left	R	.263	114	30	4	0	2	13	20	39	.370	.351

Batters vs. Left-Handed and Right-Handed Pitchers

Batter	vs	Avg	AB	H	2B	3B	HR	RBI	BB	SO	OBP	Slg
Judge, Aaron	L	.240	25	6	0	0	3	8	2	9	.321	.600
Bats Right	R	.263	76	20	3	0	6	14	8	23	.341	.539
Kelly, Carson	L	.130	46	6	1	0	2	5	3	11	.184	.283
Bats Right	R	.276	76	21	4	0	3	14	3	18	.313	.447
Kemp, Matt	L	.300	50	15	3	0	2	9	6	16	.375	.480
Bats Right	R	.194	67	13	0	0	4	12	9	25	.289	.373
Kemp, Tony	L	.000	7	0	0	0	0	0	0	1	.125	.000
Bats Left	R	.267	86	23	5	0	4	9	15	13	.381	.326
Kendrick, Howie	L	.200	25	5	0	0	2	5	1	3	.231	.440
Bats Right	R	.303	66	20	4	0	0	9	6	14	.351	.364
Kepler, Max	L	.128	47	6	2	0	0	4	5	13	.208	.170
Bats Left	R	.266	124	33	7	0	9	19	17	23	.364	.540
Kieboom, Carter	L	.343	35	12	1	0	0	5	4	12	.415	.371
Bats Right	R	.125	64	8	0	0	0	4	13	21	.309	.125
Kiermaier, Kevin	L	.158	19	3	1	0	0	5	2	6	.238	.211
Bats Left	R	.227	119	27	4	3	3	17	18	36	.333	.387
Kiner-Falefa, Isiah	L	.373	59	22	1	1	1	7	6	8	.424	.492
Bats Right	R	.243	152	37	2	2	2	3	8	24	.290	.322
Kingery, Scott	L	.121	33	4	0	0	0	0	4	12	.216	.121
Bats Right	R	.175	80	14	5	0	3	6	5	23	.233	.350
Kipnis, Jason	L	.091	22	2	2	0	0	0	8	5	.333	.182
Bats Left	R	.272	92	25	6	1	3	16	10	36	.343	.457
Kirk, Alejandro	L	.143	7	1	0	0	0	0	3	1	.143	.143
Bats Right	R	.471	17	8	2	0	1	3	1	1	.500	.765
Knapp, Andrew	L	.313	16	5	1	0	0	2	0	2	.313	.375
Bats Both	R	.268	56	15	3	1	2	13	15	17	.425	.464
Kratz, Erik	L	.364	11	4	2	0	0	1	0	3	.364	.545
Bats Right	R	.294	17	5	0	0	0	3	2	3	.368	.294
La Stella, Tommy	L	.216	51	11	3	0	0	3	6	3	.305	.275
Bats Left	R	.303	145	44	11	2	5	22	21	9	.393	.510
Lamb, Jake	L	.176	17	3	1	0	1	4	1	1	.300	.412
Bats Left	R	.197	71	14	4	0	2	6	7	24	.278	.338
Laureano, Ramon	L	.205	44	9	1	0	2	8	3	17	.286	.364
Bats Right	R	.216	139	30	7	1	4	17	21	41	.353	.367
LeMahieu, DJ	L	.400	40	16	4	1	0	4	4	2	.455	.550
Bats Right	R	.355	155	55	6	1	10	23	14	19	.413	.600
Leon, Sandy	L	.143	14	2	0	0	0	0	4	2	.333	.143
Bats Both	R	.135	52	7	1	0	2	4	10	19	.286	.269
Lewis, Kyle	L	.224	58	13	1	0	4	5	12	20	.357	.448
Bats Right	R	.277	148	41	2	0	7	23	22	51	.366	.432
Lin, Tzu-Wei	L	.000	6	0	0	0	0	0	1	3	.143	.000
Bats Left	R	.174	46	8	1	0	0	3	1	14	.188	.196
Lindor, Francisco	L	.293	58	17	5	0	0	4	4	3	.364	.379
Bats Both	R	.247	178	44	8	0	8	23	20	38	.325	.427
Locastro, Tim	L	.224	49	11	2	1	1	2	5	12	.309	.367
Bats Right	R	.450	20	9	2	0	1	5	3	2	.577	.700
Long Jr., Shed	L	.063	32	2	0	0	0	1	3	15	.143	.063
Bats Left	R	.212	85	18	5	0	3	8	8	22	.280	.376
Longoria, Evan	L	.308	52	16	2	0	3	8	3	9	.339	.519
Bats Right	R	.234	141	33	8	1	4	20	8	30	.281	.390
Lopes, Tim	L	.218	55	12	4	0	2	5	3	15	.271	.400
Bats Right	R	.250	88	22	8	0	0	10	3	19	.283	.341
Lopez, Nicky	L	.136	44	6	0	0	1	5	5	11	.240	.205
Bats Left	R	.224	125	28	8	0	0	8	13	30	.302	.288
Lowe, Brandon	L	.300	50	15	6	0	9	6	14	14	.417	.720
Bats Left	R	.259	143	37	6	2	8	28	19	44	.341	.497
Lowe, Nate	L	.133	15	2	0	0	1	2	2	12	.235	.133
Bats Left	R	.250	52	13	2	0	4	10	7	16	.310	.519
Luplow, Jordan	L	.270	37	10	3	0	1	4	4	7	.349	.432
Bats Right	R	.122	41	5	2	1	1	4	8	12	.265	.293
Lux, Gavin	L	.100	10	1	0	0	0	1	1	5	.182	.100
Bats Left	R	.189	53	10	2	0	3	7	5	14	.259	.396
Machado, Manny	L	.313	64	20	1	0	5	10	7	11	.380	.563
Bats Right	R	.300	160	48	11	1	11	37	19	26	.366	.588
Machin, Vimael	L	.143	7	1	1	0	0	0	5	1	.500	.286
Bats Left	R	.214	56	12	1	0	0	9	3	9	.254	.232
Madrigal, Nick	L	.227	22	5	0	0	0	2	0	0	.227	.227
Bats Right	R	.370	81	30	3	0	0	9	4	7	.414	.407
Maldonado, Martin	L	.279	43	12	2	0	2	12	8	14	.404	.465
Bats Right	R	.185	92	17	2	0	4	12	19	37	.324	.337
Margot, Manuel	L	.222	36	8	1	0	1	2	4	5	.300	.333
Bats Right	R	.284	109	31	8	0	0	9	9	20	.336	.358
Marisnick, Jake	L	.375	16	6	2	0	1	3	1	3	.412	.688
Bats Right	R	.294	17	5	1	0	1	2	0	7	.294	.529
Markakis, Nick	L	.375	16	6	1	0	0	2	2	3	.444	.438
Bats Left	R	.237	114	27	14	0	1	13	8	20	.293	.386

Batter	vs	Avg	AB	H	2B	3B	HR	RBI	BB	SO	OBP	Slg
Marmolejos, Jose	L	.167	24	4	0	0	1	2	2	8	.259	.292
Bats Left	R	.217	83	18	4	0	5	16	5	24	.261	.446
Marte, Ketel	L	.423	52	22	7	1	1	3	1	4	.444	.654
Bats Both	R	.233	129	30	7	0	1	14	6	17	.277	.310
Marte, Starling	L	.290	62	18	4	0	0	4	4	6	.353	.355
Bats Right	R	.277	166	46	10	1	6	23	8	35	.335	.458
Martinez, J.D.	L	.214	56	12	4	0	2	8	5	15	.286	.393
Bats Right	R	.213	155	33	12	0	5	19	17	44	.293	.387
Martinez, Jose	L	.174	46	8	4	0	1	4	4	17	.240	.283
Bats Right	R	.190	42	8	0	0	1	6	6	10	.292	.262
Mateo, Jorge	L	.176	17	3	2	0	0	2	1	8	.222	.294
Bats Right	R	.111	9	1	1	0	0	0	0	3	.111	.222
Mathias, Mark	L	.238	21	5	3	0	0	2	0	4	.238	.381
Bats Right	R	.333	15	5	0	0	0	2	0	3	.333	.333
Mathis, Jeff	L	.067	15	1	0	0	0	1	1	7	.118	.067
Bats Right	R	.191	47	9	1	1	3	8	4	17	.255	.447
Mathisen, Wyatt	L	.333	15	5	0	0	1	3	1	7	.375	.533
Bats Right	R	.083	12	1	0	0	1	2	4	5	.353	.333
Maybin, Cameron	L	.263	19	5	2	0	0	1	3	3	.364	.368
Bats Right	R	.243	74	18	6	1	1	6	4	22	.291	.392
Mayfield, Jack	L	.111	9	1	0	0	0	2	1	1	.200	.111
Bats Right	R	.212	33	7	1	0	0	1	1	13	.250	.242
Mazara, Nomar	L	.333	24	8	2	0	0	6	2	10	.385	.417
Bats Left	R	.205	112	23	4	0	1	9	8	34	.276	.268
McBroom, Ryan	L	.267	30	8	1	0	4	6	2	12	.313	.700
Bats Right	R	.235	51	12	2	0	2	4	2	18	.264	.392
McCann, James	L	.429	28	12	0	2	6	4	5	.528	.714
Bats Right	R	.232	69	16	1	0	5	9	4	25	.280	.464
McCutchen, Andrew	L	.283	60	17	4	0	4	11	10	14	.394	.500
Bats Right	R	.242	157	38	5	0	6	23	12	34	.294	.389
McGuire, Reese	L	.000	17	0	0	0	0	0	0	5	.000	.000
Bats Left	R	.125	24	3	0	0	1	1	0	6	.125	.250
McMahon, Ryan	L	.192	52	10	1	1	4	10	4	17	.263	.481
Bats Left	R	.225	120	27	5	0	5	16	14	49	.309	.392
McNeil, Jeff	L	.303	66	20	5	0	0	10	6	9	.368	.379
Bats Left	R	.316	117	37	9	0	4	13	14	15	.391	.496
Meadows, Austin	L	.143	35	5	1	0	0	6	4	15	.220	.171
Bats Left	R	.227	97	22	7	1	4	7	13	35	.324	.443
Mejia, Francisco	L	.083	12	1	1	0	0	0	0	2	.083	.167
Bats Both	R	.074	27	2	0	0	1	2	1	7	.167	.185
Mendick, Danny	L	.194	31	6	2	0	1	2	3	9	.265	.355
Bats Right	R	.263	76	20	2	1	2	4	3	16	.288	.395
Mercado, Oscar	L	.107	28	3	1	0	1	2	0	8	.103	.250
Bats Right	R	.138	58	8	0	0	0	4	5	19	.206	.138
Merrifield, Whit	L	.296	54	16	4	0	1	3	4	4	.345	.407
Bats Right	R	.278	194	54	8	0	8	27	8	29	.319	.443
Miller, Brad	L	.176	17	3	0	0	1	1	2	7	.300	.353
Bats Left	R	.240	125	30	8	1	6	24	23	39	.364	.464
Molina, Yadier	L	.192	26	5	1	0	2	5	0	3	.300	.462
Bats Right	R	.277	119	33	1	0	2	11	3	16	.304	.336
Moncada, Yoan	L	.222	36	8	1	0	1	3	9	7	.370	.333
Bats Both	R	.226	164	37	7	3	5	21	19	55	.308	.396
Mondesi, Adalberto	L	.321	53	17	4	2	4	10	2	11	.345	.698
Bats Both	R	.235	166	39	7	1	2	12	9	59	.278	.325
Moore, Dylan	L	.234	47	11	5	0	2	5	3	12	.294	.468
Bats Right	R	.267	90	24	4	0	6	12	11	31	.389	.511
Moran, Colin	L	.231	52	12	4	0	1	4	4	10	.286	.365
Bats Left	R	.254	126	32	6	0	9	19	15	38	.340	.516
Moreland, Mitch	L	.240	25	6	1	0	1	4	1	8	.296	.400
Bats Left	R	.270	111	30	8	0	9	25	14	24	.352	.586
Morrison, Logan	L	.000	3	0	0	0	0	0	0	1	.000	.000
Bats Left	R	.136	22	3	1	0	1	2	3	8	.240	.318
Mountcastle, Ryan	L	.267	30	8	2	0	0	2	3	7	.324	.333
Bats Right	R	.354	96	34	3	0	5	21	8	23	.406	.542
Moustakas, Mike	L	.214	42	9	3	0	1	7	4	10	.298	.357
Bats Left	R	.237	97	23	6	0	7	20	14	26	.345	.515
Mullins II, Cedric	L	.171	35	6	1	0	1	3	2	11	.216	.286
Bats Both	R	.305	105	32	3	3	2	9	6	26	.348	.448
Muncy, Max	L	.239	67	16	1	0	4	10	12	17	.363	.433
Bats Left	R	.169	136	23	3	0	8	17	27	43	.315	.368
Munoz, Yairo	L	.375	8	3	0	0	0	0	0	0	.375	.375
Bats Right	R	.324	37	12	5	0	1	4	0	9	.324	.541
Murphy, Daniel	L	.200	35	7	1	0	0	3	0	8	.200	.229
Bats Left	R	.250	88	22	2	0	3	13	7	13	.302	.375
Murphy, John Ryan	L	.429	7	3	0	0	0	1	0	3	.429	.429
Bats Right	R	.137	51	7	2	0	0	1	4	25	.200	.176

Batters vs. Left-Handed and Right-Handed Pitchers

Batter	vs	Avg	AB	H	2B	3B	HR	RBI	BB	SO	OBP	Slg
Murphy, Sean	L	.235	34	8	1	0	2	5	4	13	.316	.441
Bats Right	R	.232	82	19	4	0	5	9	20	24	.382	.463
Myers, Wil	L	.328	64	21	6	0	5	12	6	16	.386	.656
Bats Right	R	.269	134	36	8	2	10	28	12	40	.338	.582
Naquin, Tyler	L	.000	20	0	0	0	0	1	0	8	.045	.000
Bats Left	R	.257	113	29	8	1	4	19	5	32	.286	.451
Narvaez, Omar	L	.211	19	4	1	0	0	0	1	8	.250	.263
Bats Left	R	.169	89	15	3	0	2	10	15	31	.302	.270
Naylor, Josh	L	.375	8	3	0	0	1	3	1	1	.444	.750
Bats Left	R	.236	89	21	3	1	0	3	4	11	.277	.292
Newman, Kevin	L	.276	29	8	0	0	1	5	5	2	.389	.379
Bats Right	R	.213	127	27	5	0	0	5	7	19	.252	.252
Nido, Tomas	L	.500	8	4	1	0	1	4	1	3	.556	1.000
Bats Right	R	.188	16	3	0	0	1	2	1	3	.235	.375
Nimmo, Brandon	L	.196	51	10	2	1	1	2	5	14	.317	.333
Bats Right	R	.311	135	42	6	2	7	16	28	29	.436	.541
Nola, Austin	L	.192	52	10	2	1	1	4	5	11	.276	.327
Bats Right	R	.312	109	34	7	0	6	24	13	23	.389	.541
Nottingham, Jacob	L	.286	14	4	0	0	3	8	2	5	.412	.929
Bats Right	R	.147	34	5	1	0	1	5	3	15	.216	.265
Nunez, Renato	L	.220	41	9	3	0	1	5	4	10	.289	.366
Bats Right	R	.266	154	41	7	0	11	26	13	54	.333	.526
Odom, Joseph	L	.000	9	0	0	0	0	0	2	7	.182	.000
Bats Right	R	.167	30	5	0	0	0	2	2	13	.219	.167
Odor, Rougned	L	.104	48	5	1	0	2	7	2	16	.157	.250
Bats Left	R	.200	90	18	3	0	8	23	5	31	.237	.500
O'Hearn, Ryan	L	.333	12	4	2	0	0	2	0	4	.333	.500
Bats Left	R	.178	101	18	4	0	2	16	18	33	.300	.277
Ohtani, Shohei	L	.182	44	8	2	0	1	4	10	15	.333	.295
Bats Left	R	.193	109	21	4	0	6	20	12	35	.273	.394
Olivares, Edward	L	.171	35	6	2	0	1	1	2	7	.216	.314
Bats Right	R	.279	61	17	0	1	2	9	2	18	.297	.410
Olson, Matt	L	.208	53	11	1	0	3	10	6	22	.300	.396
Bats Left	R	.191	157	30	3	1	11	32	28	55	.314	.433
O'Neill, Tyler	L	.154	26	4	1	0	0	5	4	7	.267	.192
Bats Right	R	.177	113	20	4	0	7	14	11	36	.260	.398
Osuna, Jose	L	.292	24	7	2	0	1	4	2	2	.346	.500
Bats Right	R	.167	54	9	1	0	3	7	2	14	.196	.352
Owings, Chris	L	.250	20	5	0	0	1	1	1	6	.286	.400
Bats Right	R	.286	21	6	1	0	1	4	2	5	.348	.476
Ozuna, Marcell	L	.356	45	16	2	0	7	19	9	11	.463	.867
Bats Right	R	.333	183	61	12	0	11	37	29	49	.423	.579
Panik, Joe	L	.303	33	10	2	0	0	3	5	9	.410	.364
Bats Right	R	.195	87	17	4	0	1	4	15	18	.314	.276
Paredes, Isaac	L	.438	16	7	0	0	0	2	1	4	.471	.438
Bats Right	R	.179	84	15	4	0	1	4	7	20	.242	.262
Pederson, Joc	L	.333	9	3	0	0	0	0	1	2	.400	.333
Bats Left	R	.179	112	20	4	0	7	16	10	32	.276	.402
Pence, Hunter	L	.107	28	3	0	1	2	6	2	8	.167	.393
Bats Right	R	.083	24	2	0	0	0	0	1	7	.154	.083
Peralta, David	L	.261	46	12	0	0	1	7	3	11	.300	.326
Bats Left	R	.312	157	49	10	1	4	27	10	34	.351	.465
Peraza, Jose	L	.196	46	9	3	1	0	1	4	6	.260	.304
Bats Right	R	.246	65	16	5	0	1	7	1	12	.286	.369
Perez, Michael	L	.500	8	4	0	0	0	3	3	2	.636	.500
Bats Left	R	.132	76	10	3	0	1	10	4	25	.183	.211
Perez, Roberto	L	.154	26	4	2	0	0	2	2	11	.214	.231
Bats Right	R	.169	71	12	0	0	1	3	9	27	.280	.211
Perez, Salvador	L	.257	35	9	3	0	3	8	1	8	.297	.600
Bats Right	R	.357	115	41	9	0	8	24	2	28	.370	.643
Peterson, Jace	L	.000	2	0	0	0	0	1	2	0	.000	.000
Bats Left	R	.209	43	9	1	0	2	4	13	18	.393	.372
Pham, Tommy	L	.300	30	9	2	0	2	4	5	7	.400	.567
Bats Right	R	.177	79	14	0	0	1	8	10	20	.278	.215
Phillips, Brett	L	.429	7	3	0	0	0	1	1	1	.500	.429
Bats Left	R	.159	44	7	0	2	2	5	7	14	.275	.386
Pillar, Kevin	L	.342	76	26	6	0	4	15	5	15	.390	.579
Bats Right	R	.258	132	34	6	3	2	11	8	26	.305	.394
Pina, Manny	L	.211	19	4	1	0	0	1	2	4	.318	.263
Bats Right	R	.250	20	5	0	0	2	4	1	7	.348	.550
Pinder, Chad	L	.160	25	4	0	0	2	5	1	6	.192	.400
Bats Right	R	.290	31	9	3	0	0	3	4	7	.371	.387
Piscotty, Stephen	L	.229	48	11	2	0	0	4	2	12	.255	.271
Bats Right	R	.225	111	25	4	0	5	25	7	41	.277	.396
Plawecki, Kevin	L	.367	30	11	2	0	1	6	0	1	.367	.533
Bats Right	R	.327	52	17	3	1	0	11	5	13	.407	.423

Batter	vs	Avg	AB	H	2B	3B	HR	RBI	BB	SO	OBP	Slg
Polanco, Gregory	L	.139	36	5	1	0	1	4	5	16	.244	.250
Bats Left	R	.157	121	19	5	0	6	18	8	49	.205	.347
Polanco, Jorge	L	.345	55	19	3	0	1	7	1	5	.351	.455
Bats Both	R	.227	154	35	5	0	3	12	12	30	.287	.318
Pollock, A.J.	L	.345	55	19	5	0	7	15	3	9	.367	.818
Bats Right	R	.248	141	35	4	0	9	19	9	36	.293	.468
Profar, Jurickson	L	.294	68	20	1	0	3	9	4	11	.329	.441
Bats Both	R	.268	112	30	5	0	4	16	11	17	.352	.420
Pujols, Albert	L	.231	65	15	4	0	2	9	1	11	.242	.385
Bats Both	R	.218	87	19	4	0	4	16	8	14	.289	.402
Quinn, Roman	L	.206	34	7	1	1	2	4	2	8	.250	.471
Bats Both	R	.216	74	16	2	0	0	3	3	31	.266	.243
Ramirez, Jose	L	.386	57	22	7	0	8	14	9	9	.493	.930
Bats Both	R	.259	162	42	9	1	9	32	22	34	.353	.494
Ramos, Wilson	L	.275	40	11	2	0	1	3	6	7	.370	.400
Bats Right	R	.225	102	23	4	0	4	12	4	24	.266	.382
Ravelo, Rangel	L	.188	16	3	1	0	1	3	4	2	.350	.438
Bats Right	R	.158	19	3	0	0	0	3	0	4	.143	.158
Realmuto, J.T.	L	.386	44	17	3	0	2	9	7	12	.500	.591
Bats Right	R	.225	129	29	3	0	9	23	9	36	.291	.457
Reddick, Josh	L	.262	65	17	7	0	1	10	7	16	.333	.415
Bats Left	R	.236	123	29	4	1	3	13	13	26	.307	.358
Refsnyder, Rob	L	.235	17	4	1	0	0	1	2	5	.333	.294
Bats Right	R	.154	13	2	0	0	0	0	0	6	.154	.154
Rendon, Anthony	L	.288	59	17	5	0	4	12	14	8	.425	.576
Bats Right	R	.285	130	37	6	1	5	19	24	23	.415	.462
Renfroe, Hunter	L	.146	41	6	0	0	5	8	4	14	.294	.512
Bats Right	R	.160	81	13	5	0	3	14	6	23	.227	.333
Rengifo, Luis	L	.111	36	4	0	0	1	1	2	9	.158	.194
Bats Both	R	.185	54	10	1	0	0	2	12	17	.333	.204
Reyes, Franmil	L	.261	46	12	2	0	0	2	7	14	.352	.304
Bats Right	R	.279	165	46	8	0	9	32	17	55	.342	.491
Reyes, Victor	L	.342	38	13	1	0	0	3	1	6	.419	.368
Bats Both	R	.262	164	43	6	2	4	11	4	39	.288	.396
Reynolds, Bryan	L	.195	41	8	3	1	0	3	7	14	.313	.317
Bats Both	R	.188	144	27	3	1	7	16	14	43	.264	.368
Riddle, JT	L	.222	9	2	1	0	0	0	0	2	.222	.333
Bats Right	R	.138	58	8	1	0	1	1	2	11	.167	.207
Riley, Austin	L	.244	41	10	4	0	2	5	4	14	.304	.488
Bats Right	R	.238	147	35	3	1	6	22	12	35	.300	.395
Rios, Edwin	L	.313	16	5	1	0	3	4	2	4	.368	.938
Bats Left	R	.233	60	14	5	0	5	13	2	14	.281	.567
Rizzo, Anthony	L	.204	49	10	0	0	1	5	8	9	.350	.265
Bats Left	R	.227	154	35	6	0	10	19	20	29	.339	.461
Robert, Luis	L	.273	44	12	2	0	2	9	6	9	.353	.455
Bats Right	R	.222	158	35	6	0	9	22	14	64	.287	.430
Robertson, Daniel	L	.364	11	4	0	0	0	1	1	2	.417	.364
Bats Right	R	.300	10	3	0	0	0	1	2	4	.417	.300
Robles, Victor	L	.326	46	15	2	1	0	5	4	12	.404	.413
Bats Right	R	.180	122	22	3	0	3	10	5	41	.250	.279
Rodgers, Brendan	L	.111	9	1	1	0	0	0	0	4	.111	.222
Bats Right	R	.083	12	1	0	0	0	2	0	2	.083	.083
Rojas, Josh	L	.222	27	6	0	0	0	0	2	8	.276	.222
Bats Left	R	.147	34	5	0	0	0	2	5	8	.244	.147
Rojas, Miguel	L	.500	36	18	6	1	2	8	2	1	.538	.889
Bats Right	R	.225	89	20	4	0	2	12	14	17	.337	.337
Romine, Austin	L	.318	22	7	0	0	1	4	1	2	.348	.455
Bats Right	R	.222	108	24	5	0	3	13	3	45	.241	.296
Rosario, Amed	L	.316	57	18	1	1	1	9	3	5	.350	.421
Bats Right	R	.209	86	18	2	0	3	6	1	29	.218	.337
Rosario, Eddie	L	.236	55	13	2	0	0	8	2	8	.263	.273
Bats Left	R	.265	155	41	5	0	13	34	17	26	.333	.548
Ruf, Darin	L	.259	58	15	5	0	4	8	7	14	.338	.552
Bats Right	R	.310	29	9	1	0	1	10	6	9	.429	.448
Ruiz, Rio	L	.289	38	11	1	0	2	6	1	10	.308	.474
Bats Left	R	.204	147	30	10	0	7	26	16	36	.280	.415
Sanchez, Gary	L	.094	32	3	1	0	2	6	9	16	.293	.313
Bats Right	R	.161	124	20	3	0	8	18	9	48	.241	.379
Sanchez, Jesus	L	.000	7	0	0	0	0	0	0	5	.000	.000
Bats Left	R	.056	18	1	1	0	0	2	4	6	.227	.111
Sandoval, Pablo	L	.300	10	3	0	0	0	0	3	4	.500	.300
Bats Both	R	.203	74	15	1	0	1	6	5	15	.250	.257
Sano, Miguel	L	.159	44	7	2	0	2	3	3	23	.213	.341
Bats Right	R	.218	142	31	10	0	11	22	15	67	.297	.521
Santana, Carlos	L	.246	61	15	4	0	3	12	5	11	.303	.459
Bats Both	R	.179	145	26	3	0	5	18	42	32	.365	.303

Batters vs. Left-Handed and Right-Handed Pitchers

Batter	vs	Avg	AB	H	2B	3B	HR	RBI	BB	SO	OBP	Slg
Santana, Danny	L	.105	19	2	1	0	1	2	0	10	.100	.316
Bats Both	R	.167	36	6	3	0	0	5	7	14	.302	.250
Santana, Domingo	L	.056	18	1	0	0	0	3	7	19	.190	.056
Bats Right	R	.192	52	10	3	0	2	12	10	18	.333	.365
Santander, Anthony	L	.167	30	5	2	0	2	4	2	7	.219	.433
Bats Both	R	.285	123	35	11	1	9	28	8	18	.338	.610
Schoop, Jonathan	L	.281	32	9	1	1	1	6	0	9	.265	.469
Bats Right	R	.277	130	36	3	1	7	17	8	30	.338	.477
Schwarber, Kyle	L	.189	53	10	0	0	2	4	6	22	.295	.302
Bats Left	R	.188	138	26	6	0	9	20	24	44	.313	.428
Seager, Corey	L	.275	69	19	2	1	4	11	5	13	.320	.507
Bats Left	R	.322	143	46	10	0	11	30	12	24	.376	.622
Seager, Kyle	L	.185	65	12	3	0	3	11	7	14	.280	.369
Bats Left	R	.268	138	37	9	0	6	29	25	19	.387	.464
Segura, Jean	L	.273	55	15	2	0	3	10	7	13	.355	.473
Bats Right	R	.263	137	36	3	2	4	15	16	32	.344	.401
Semien, Marcus	L	.224	49	11	1	0	4	10	5	14	.296	.490
Bats Right	R	.222	162	36	8	1	3	13	20	36	.308	.340
Senzel, Nick	L	.074	27	2	1	0	1	2	2	4	.133	.222
Bats Right	R	.256	43	11	5	0	1	6	4	11	.319	.442
Severino, Pedro	L	.162	37	6	1	0	2	5	6	9	.279	.351
Bats Right	R	.276	123	34	4	1	3	16	10	31	.336	.398
Shaw, Travis	L	.295	44	13	5	0	3	2	8	3	.326	.409
Bats Left	R	.218	119	26	5	0	6	14	14	42	.299	.412
Sierra, Magneuris	L	.250	4	1	1	0	0	3	1	3	.429	.500
Bats Left	R	.250	40	10	2	1	0	4	4	6	.318	.350
Simmons, Andrelton	L	.270	37	10	2	0	0	4	2	8	.325	.324
Bats Right	R	.309	81	25	5	0	0	6	6	8	.356	.370
Sisco, Chance	L	.167	12	2	0	0	2	4	2	8	.333	.667
Bats Left	R	.221	86	19	4	0	2	6	15	33	.368	.337
Slater, Austin	L	.316	38	12	1	0	4	6	11	5	.469	.658
Bats Right	R	.255	47	12	1	1	1	5	7	17	.352	.383
Smith, Dominic	L	.283	53	15	6	0	2	14	8	14	.391	.509
Bats Left	R	.331	124	41	15	1	8	28	6	31	.370	.661
Smith, Kevan	L	.100	10	1	0	0	1	2	3	7	.357	.400
Bats Right	R	.333	21	7	3	0	0	6	2	4	.391	.476
Smith, Mallex	L	.000	4	0	0	0	0	0	0	2	.000	.000
Bats Left	R	.146	41	6	2	0	0	3	2	11	.186	.195
Smith, Pavin	L	.429	7	3	0	0	0	0	0	0	.429	.429
Bats Left	R	.233	30	7	0	1	1	4	5	8	.324	.400
Smith, Will	L	.294	34	10	5	0	0	4	6	6	.400	.441
Bats Right	R	.288	80	23	4	0	8	21	14	16	.402	.638
Smith Jr., Dwight	L	.250	8	2	1	0	0	1	1	3	.333	.375
Bats Left	R	.218	55	12	2	0	2	6	6	16	.302	.364
Smoak, Justin	L	.167	24	4	2	0	0	2	2	3	.231	.250
Bats Both	R	.179	95	17	5	0	5	13	8	39	.255	.389
Sogard, Eric	L	.182	11	2	0	0	0	2	3	3	.357	.182
Bats Left	R	.212	104	22	5	0	1	8	8	17	.272	.288
Solak, Nick	L	.313	67	21	3	0	0	10	4	14	.347	.358
Bats Right	R	.246	142	35	7	0	2	13	14	28	.317	.338
Solano, Donovan	L	.350	60	21	5	0	1	3	3	8	.381	.483
Bats Right	R	.315	130	41	10	1	2	26	7	31	.357	.454
Soler, Jorge	L	.263	19	5	3	0	0	4	1	6	.300	.421
Bats Right	R	.223	130	29	5	0	8	20	18	54	.329	.446
Soto, Juan	L	.360	50	18	6	0	5	15	5	8	.429	.780
Bats Left	R	.346	104	36	8	0	8	22	36	20	.514	.654
Souza Jr., Steven	L	.200	10	2	1	0	0	0	3	6	.385	.300
Bats Right	R	.118	17	2	1	0	1	3	1	6	.167	.353
Springer, George	L	.229	48	11	1	0	4	7	6	11	.309	.500
Bats Right	R	.277	141	39	5	2	10	25	18	27	.376	.553
Stallings, Jacob	L	.324	34	11	4	0	1	9	7	9	.439	.529
Bats Right	R	.220	91	20	3	0	2	9	8	31	.280	.319
Stanton, Giancarlo	L	.176	17	3	1	0	1	2	4	8	.333	.412
Bats Right	R	.271	59	16	6	0	3	9	11	19	.403	.525
Starling, Bubba	L	.083	24	2	0	0	0	1	3	10	.179	.083
Bats Right	R	.229	35	8	1	0	1	4	1	17	.250	.343
Stassi, Max	L	.295	44	13	1	0	5	12	6	7	.365	.659
Bats Right	R	.261	46	12	1	0	2	8	5	14	.340	.413
Stevenson, Andrew	L	.000	1	0	0	0	0	1	1	0	.500	.000
Bats Left	R	.375	40	15	7	1	2	11	4	11	.444	.750
Stewart, Christin	L	.222	9	2	1	0	0	1	0	3	.300	.333
Bats Left	R	.160	81	13	2	0	3	8	5	25	.216	.296
Stewart, D.J.	L	.125	16	2	0	0	1	1	2	8	.222	.313
Bats Left	R	.208	72	15	2	0	6	14	18	30	.380	.486
Story, Trevor	L	.328	64	21	1	1	5	9	12	13	.434	.609
Bats Right	R	.275	171	47	12	3	6	19	12	50	.322	.485

Batter	vs	Avg	AB	H	2B	3B	HR	RBI	BB	SO	OBP	Slg
Strange-Gordon, Dee	L	.077	26	2	1	0	0	0	0	6	.111	.115
Bats Left	R	.265	49	13	0	0	0	3	5	7	.345	.265
Straw, Myles	L	.033	30	1	0	0	0	0	0	8	.033	.033
Bats Right	R	.308	52	16	4	0	0	8	4	14	.357	.385
Suarez, Eugenio	L	.176	51	9	3	0	4	10	7	16	.283	.471
Bats Right	R	.211	147	31	5	0	11	28	23	51	.322	.469
Suzuki, Kurt	L	.345	29	10	3	0	1	8	2	3	.429	.552
Bats Right	R	.244	82	20	5	0	1	9	9	16	.319	.341
Swanson, Dansby	L	.186	43	8	3	0	0	4	4	14	.255	.256
Bats Right	R	.294	194	57	12	0	10	31	18	57	.364	.510
Tapia, Raimel	L	.364	55	20	4	1	0	8	2	11	.390	.473
Bats Left	R	.302	129	39	4	1	1	9	12	27	.361	.372
Tatis Jr., Fernando	L	.242	62	15	5	0	3	8	8	18	.333	.468
Bats Right	R	.290	162	47	6	2	14	37	19	43	.378	.611
Tauchman, Mike	L	.100	20	2	0	0	0	0	1	10	.143	.100
Bats Left	R	.280	75	21	6	0	0	14	13	16	.389	.360
Taveras, Leody	L	.282	39	11	3	0	1	6	6	14	.378	.436
Bats Both	R	.200	80	16	3	1	3	5	8	29	.273	.375
Taylor, Beau	L	.000	5	0	0	0	0	0	1	2	.167	.000
Bats Left	R	.063	16	1	0	0	0	2	1	7	.118	.063
Taylor, Chris	L	.200	50	10	2	0	2	9	10	16	.333	.360
Bats Right	R	.296	135	40	8	2	6	23	16	39	.379	.519
Taylor, Michael A.	L	.172	29	5	2	0	2	4	2	11	.250	.448
Bats Right	R	.206	63	13	4	0	3	12	4	16	.254	.413
Taylor, Tyrone	L	.250	16	4	2	0	1	2	2	3	.333	.375
Bats Right	R	.227	22	5	2	0	2	5	0	6	.261	.591
Tejeda, Anderson	L	.190	21	4	0	0	1	2	0	9	.190	.333
Bats Both	R	.278	54	15	4	1	2	6	2	21	.304	.500
Tellez, Rowdy	L	.333	27	9	3	0	4	2	7	7	.367	.444
Bats Left	R	.267	86	23	2	0	8	19	9	13	.340	.570
Thaiss, Matt	L	.400	5	2	0	0	1	1	1	2	.500	1.000
Bats Left	R	.063	16	1	0	0	0	0	3	8	.211	.063
Thames, Eric	L	.182	22	4	1	0	1	2	3	6	.280	.364
Bats Left	R	.208	101	21	4	0	2	10	11	36	.304	.307
Thomas, Lane	L	.125	8	1	0	0	0	0	0	3	.125	.125
Bats Right	R	.107	28	3	2	0	1	2	4	10	.219	.286
Toro, Abraham	L	.174	23	4	1	0	1	2	0	8	.269	.348
Bats Both	R	.141	64	9	1	0	2	7	3	15	.225	.250
Torrens, Luis	L	.207	29	6	2	0	1	2	3	7	.281	.379
Bats Right	R	.293	41	12	3	0	0	4	4	8	.356	.366
Torres, Gleyber	L	.235	34	8	2	0	1	5	5	6	.350	.382
Bats Right	R	.245	102	25	6	0	2	11	17	22	.358	.363
Trevino, Jose	L	.273	33	9	4	0	1	2	1	7	.314	.485
Bats Right	R	.233	43	10	4	0	1	7	2	8	.255	.395
Tromp, Chadwick	L	.321	28	9	1	0	2	5	0	7	.321	.571
Bats Right	R	.121	33	4	0	0	2	5	1	13	.139	.303
Trout, Mike	L	.245	53	13	1	0	3	10	8	17	.349	.434
Bats Right	R	.295	146	43	8	2	14	36	27	39	.404	.664
Tsutsugo, Yoshi	L	.243	37	9	1	0	2	4	5	16	.349	.432
Bats Left	R	.183	120	22	4	1	6	20	21	34	.303	.383
Tucker, Cole	L	.258	31	8	0	0	1	2	4	7	.343	.355
Bats Both	R	.205	78	16	3	0	0	6	1	24	.213	.244
Tucker, Kyle	L	.217	69	15	1	1	4	11	4	13	.260	.435
Bats Left	R	.293	140	41	11	5	5	31	14	33	.355	.550
Turner, Justin	L	.234	47	11	1	0	2	7	8	10	.362	.383
Bats Right	R	.340	103	35	8	1	2	16	10	16	.419	.495
Turner, Trea	L	.375	56	21	4	2	4	12	8	8	.453	.732
Bats Right	R	.322	177	57	11	2	8	29	14	28	.374	.542
Upton, Justin	L	.219	64	14	2	0	6	10	4	22	.265	.531
Bats Right	R	.193	83	16	3	0	3	12	7	21	.306	.337
Urias, Luis	L	.265	34	9	2	1	0	1	2	10	.324	.382
Bats Right	R	.227	75	17	2	0	0	10	8	22	.301	.253
Urias, Ramon	L	.429	7	3	1	0	0	1	1	1	.500	.571
Bats Right	R	.333	18	6	1	0	1	2	1	5	.368	.556
Urshela, Gio	L	.233	30	7	2	0	1	7	5	6	.378	.300
Bats Right	R	.314	121	38	9	0	6	29	11	19	.365	.537
Valaika, Pat	L	.279	43	12	1	0	4	4	5	12	.354	.581
Bats Right	R	.276	98	27	3	0	4	12	3	22	.297	.429
VanMeter, Josh	L	.182	11	2	0	0	0	0	2	6	.357	.273
Bats Left	R	.119	59	7	2	0	2	6	5	18	.200	.254
Vargas, Ildemaro	L	.107	28	3	0	0	1	1	2	7	.167	.214
Bats Both	R	.304	23	7	1	1	0	2	0	3	.292	.435
Varsho, Daulton	L	.143	35	5	1	0	0	4	1	12	.167	.171
Bats Left	R	.212	66	14	4	2	3	5	11	21	.342	.470
Vazquez, Christian	L	.236	55	13	4	0	4	13	6	14	.311	.473
Bats Right	R	.305	118	36	8	0	3	10	10	29	.359	.449

Batters vs. Left-Handed and Right-Handed Pitchers

Batter	vs	Avg	AB	H	2B	3B	HR	RBI	BB	SO	OBP	Slg
Velazquez, Andrew	L	.250	20	5	0	1	0	2	2	6	.318	.350
Bats Both	R	.116	43	5	1	0	0	1	8	17	.255	.140
Verdugo, Alex	L	.320	75	24	4	0	1	3	6	22	.378	.413
Bats Left	R	.302	126	38	12	0	5	12	11	23	.360	.516
Villar, Jonathan	L	.242	62	15	2	0	1	3	2	13	.266	.323
Bats Both	R	.228	123	28	3	0	1	12	17	41	.317	.276
Viloria, Meibrys	L	.500	4	2	0	0	0	0	1	2	.667	.500
Bats Left	R	.118	17	2	1	0	0	0	1	7	.167	.176
Vogelbach, Daniel	L	.083	12	1	0	0	0	2	2	5	.267	.083
Bats Left	R	.223	103	23	3	0	6	14	18	28	.339	.427
Vogt, Stephen	L	.111	9	1	0	0	0	0	2	2	.273	.111
Bats Left	R	.175	63	11	5	0	1	7	6	16	.243	.302
Voit, Luke	L	.229	48	11	0	0	6	12	5	12	.302	.604
Bats Right	R	.291	165	48	5	0	16	40	12	42	.348	.612
Votto, Joey	L	.178	45	8	0	0	2	2	13	13	.362	.311
Bats Left	R	.241	141	34	8	0	9	20	24	30	.352	.489
Wade, Tyler	L	.043	23	1	0	0	1	2	0	9	.080	.174
Bats Left	R	.215	65	14	3	0	2	8	12	13	.354	.354
Wade Jr., LaMonte	L	.000	4	0	0	0	0	0	0	1	.000	.000
Bats Left	R	.257	35	9	3	0	0	1	4	8	.350	.343
Walker, Christian	L	.232	56	13	3	1	2	7	7	12	.333	.429
Bats Right	R	.284	162	46	15	0	5	27	12	38	.333	.469
Walker, Neil	L	.000	8	0	0	0	0	0	0	2	.000	.000
Bats Both	R	.290	31	9	3	0	0	3	1	11	.303	.387
Wallach, Chad	L	.500	10	5	2	0	1	4	2	2	.583	1.000
Bats Right	R	.147	34	5	1	0	0	2	1	10	.171	.176
Walsh, Jared	L	.324	34	11	2	0	1	6	0	6	.306	.471
Bats Left	R	.277	65	18	2	2	8	20	5	9	.333	.738
Ward, Taylor	L	.256	39	10	2	1	0	3	1	13	.275	.359
Bats Right	R	.291	55	16	4	1	0	2	7	15	.371	.400
Wendle, Joey	L	.294	34	10	1	0	0	3	4	6	.368	.324
Bats Left	R	.284	134	38	8	2	4	14	6	29	.336	.463
White, Eli	L	.048	21	1	0	0	0	0	1	8	.091	.048
Bats Right	R	.296	27	8	2	0	0	3	2	8	.333	.370
White, Evan	L	.140	57	8	2	0	1	3	7	23	.234	.228
Bats Right	R	.192	125	24	5	0	7	23	11	61	.261	.400
Wieters, Matt	L	.143	7	1	0	0	0	2	0	1	.143	.143
Bats Both	R	.214	28	6	1	0	0	2	3	9	.333	.250
Winker, Jesse	L	.265	34	9	2	0	2	4	4	13	.390	.500
Bats Left	R	.252	115	29	5	0	10	19	24	33	.387	.557
Wolters, Tony	L	.158	19	3	0	0	0	1	3	8	.304	.158
Bats Left	R	.247	81	20	4	0	0	7	3	22	.274	.296
Wong, Kolten	L	.294	34	10	1	0	0	3	2	4	.333	.324
Bats Left	R	.259	147	38	3	2	1	13	18	26	.353	.327
Yastrzemski, Mike	L	.284	67	19	5	1	5	13	11	19	.385	.612
Bats Left	R	.304	125	38	9	3	5	22	19	36	.408	.544
Yelich, Christian	L	.293	58	17	5	0	5	8	14	21	.431	.638
Bats Left	R	.169	142	24	2	1	7	14	32	55	.326	.345
Young, Andy	L	.111	18	2	1	0	0	1	2	8	.273	.167
Bats Right	R	.375	8	3	1	0	1	3	3	2	.583	.875
Zimmer, Bradley	L	.167	6	1	0	0	0	1	0	2	.167	.167
Bats Left	R	.161	31	5	0	0	1	2	7	12	.386	.258
Zunino, Mike	L	.045	22	1	0	0	1	3	2	11	.160	.182
Bats Right	R	.189	53	10	4	0	3	7	4	26	.271	.434
AL	L	.242	-	-	-	-	-	-	-	-	.315	.411
	R	.243	-	-	-	-	-	-	-	-	.320	.415
NL	L	.249	-	-	-	-	-	-	-	-	.327	.424
	R	.246	-	-	-	-	-	-	-	-	.324	.420
MLB	L	.245	-	-	-	-	-	-	-	-	.321	.418
	R	.244	-	-	-	-	-	-	-	-	.322	.418

Pitchers vs. Left-Handed and Right-Handed Batters

Pitcher	vs	Avg	AB	H	2B	3B	HR	RBI	BB	SO	OBP	Slg
Abreu, Bryan	L	.000	7	0	0	0	0	0	2	3	.300	.000
Throws Right	R	.250	4	1	1	0	0	1	5	0	.700	.500
Adam, Jason	L	.172	29	5	2	0	1	7	4	9	.273	.345
Throws Right	R	.190	21	4	0	1	1	2	4	12	.320	.429
Adams, Chance	L	.350	20	7	2	0	0	3	0	3	.350	.450
Throws Right	R	.400	20	8	3	0	1	4	0	3	.400	.700
Akin, Keegan	L	.240	25	6	1	0	0	0	2	7	.296	.280
Throws Left	R	.269	78	21	7	0	3	12	8	28	.337	.474
Alcala, Jorge	L	.364	33	12	2	0	2	5	6	14	.462	.606
Throws Right	R	.170	53	9	0	0	1	4	2	13	.200	.226
Alcantara, Sandy	L	.268	71	19	7	0	3	10	11	20	.366	.493
Throws Right	R	.190	84	16	1	0	1	5	4	19	.236	.238
Alexander, Scott	L	.056	18	1	0	0	1	1	4	5	.227	.222
Throws Left	R	.333	24	8	0	0	1	5	5	4	.448	.458
Alexander, Tyler	L	.225	40	9	2	0	0	2	0	12	.244	.275
Throws Left	R	.306	98	30	3	1	8	15	9	22	.378	.602
Allard, Kolby	L	.263	38	10	0	1	3	9	4	11	.349	.553
Throws Left	R	.228	92	21	4	1	1	14	16	21	.339	.326
Allen, Logan	L	.111	9	1	0	0	0	0	1	2	.200	.111
Throws Left	R	.344	32	11	3	0	1	3	6	5	.462	.531
Almonte, Yency	L	.264	53	14	2	0	1	9	4	10	.322	.358
Throws Right	R	.220	50	11	3	1	1	6	2	13	.278	.380
Altavilla, Dan	L	.250	20	5	2	0	1	5	5	4	.400	.500
Throws Right	R	.228	57	13	5	0	2	9	7	20	.313	.421
Alvarado, Jose	L	.000	9	0	0	0	0	0	1	6	.250	.000
Throws Left	R	.333	27	9	2	0	2	7	5	7	.424	.630
Alvarez, Jose	L	.444	9	4	1	0	0	1	1	3	.500	.556
Throws Left	R	.200	15	3	1	0	0	0	2	3	.294	.267
Alzolay, Adbert	L	.219	32	7	2	0	0	4	7	13	.366	.281
Throws Right	R	.128	39	5	0	1	1	4	6	16	.239	.256
Anderson, Brett	L	.257	35	9	3	0	1	2	2	5	.316	.429
Throws Left	R	.273	150	41	9	2	5	19	8	27	.317	.460
Anderson, Chase	L	.328	61	20	5	0	5	15	4	16	.379	.656
Throws Right	R	.305	82	25	6	0	6	12	6	22	.352	.598
Anderson, Ian	L	.145	62	9	0	0	0	4	8	26	.254	.145
Throws Right	R	.200	60	12	4	0	1	7	6	15	.284	.317
Anderson, Nick	L	.154	26	4	0	0	1	3	1	12	.185	.269
Throws Right	R	.034	29	1	0	1	0	0	2	14	.097	.103
Anderson, Shaun	L	.143	21	3	0	0	1	4	1	8	.182	.286
Throws Right	R	.206	34	7	0	1	2	4	11	10	.400	.441
Anderson, Tyler	L	.309	68	21	3	2	2	16	4	13	.364	.500
Throws Left	R	.233	159	37	13	0	3	16	21	28	.324	.371
Andriese, Matt	L	.204	49	10	2	0	4	10	6	10	.291	.490
Throws Right	R	.169	65	11	1	1	1	10	5	23	.239	.262
Antone, Tejay	L	.210	62	13	2	0	3	6	10	18	.324	.387
Throws Right	R	.119	59	7	4	0	1	4	6	27	.209	.237
Armstrong, Shawn	L	.176	17	3	3	0	0	1	2	5	.263	.353
Throws Right	R	.167	36	6	1	0	1	4	1	9	.211	.278
Arrieta, Jake	L	.304	79	24	4	0	4	14	8	15	.367	.506
Throws Right	R	.293	92	27	5	0	2	8	8	17	.350	.413
Avilan, Luis	L	.176	17	3	0	0	0	3	1	7	.222	.176
Throws Left	R	.353	17	6	1	0	2	5	4	2	.476	.765
Bacus, Dakota	L	.250	12	3	0	0	0	0	3	1	.400	.250
Throws Right	R	.314	35	11	2	0	1	8	6	6	.405	.457
Baez, Michel	L	.300	10	3	1	0	0	3	0	4	.300	.400
Throws Right	R	.364	11	4	1	0	0	1	2	3	.462	.455
Baez, Pedro	L	.097	31	3	0	0	0	2	3	6	.176	.097
Throws Right	R	.219	32	7	2	0	2	4	4	7	.306	.469
Bailey, Brandon	L	.200	15	3	1	0	1	1	1	2	.250	.467
Throws Right	R	.273	11	3	1	0	0	0	2	2	.429	.364
Bailey, Homer	L	.308	13	4	1	0	0	0	3	3	.471	.385
Throws Right	R	.125	16	2	0	0	1	3	0	4	.125	.313
Banda, Anthony	L	.222	9	2	1	0	0	2	3	3	.417	.333
Throws Left	R	.400	20	8	3	1	1	7	2	1	.500	.800
Baragar, Caleb	L	.161	31	5	1	0	1	4	1	6	.182	.290
Throws Left	R	.240	50	12	5	0	2	6	4	13	.309	.460
Bard, Daniel	L	.265	49	13	1	0	2	5	8	16	.379	.408
Throws Right	R	.205	44	9	3	0	0	4	2	11	.271	.273
Bard, Luke	L	.250	8	2	0	0	1	1	0	3	.250	.625
Throws Right	R	.333	15	5	1	1	1	2	0	4	.333	.733
Barlow, Scott	L	.228	57	13	2	0	3	10	6	19	.323	.421
Throws Right	R	.250	56	14	3	0	1	6	3	20	.283	.357
Barnes, Jacob	L	.167	24	4	2	0	0	4	1	12	.192	.250
Throws Right	R	.333	45	15	3	0	1	6	3	12	.392	.467
Barnes, Matt	L	.167	36	6	0	0	0	1	9	18	.326	.167
Throws Right	R	.250	48	12	1	0	4	11	5	13	.345	.521
Barria, Jaime	L	.273	66	18	7	1	2	9	7	17	.347	.500
Throws Right	R	.164	55	9	4	0	1	4	2	10	.193	.291
Bashlor, Tyler	L	.294	17	5	3	0	1	3	2	4	.368	.647
Throws Right	R	.267	15	4	2	0	1	6	2	2	.421	.600
Bass, Anthony	L	.161	31	5	0	0	0	1	4	8	.257	.161
Throws Right	R	.203	59	12	4	0	2	10	5	13	.266	.373
Bassitt, Chris	L	.248	101	25	8	0	4	10	8	24	.309	.446
Throws Right	R	.223	139	31	7	0	2	8	9	31	.273	.317
Bauer, Trevor	L	.170	135	23	2	1	8	11	10	55	.233	.378
Throws Right	R	.146	123	18	2	2	1	4	7	45	.205	.220
Bednar, David	L	.313	16	5	2	0	1	3	1	2	.353	.625
Throws Right	R	.429	14	6	1	0	0	3	1	3	.467	.500
Bedrosian, Cam	L	.192	26	5	1	0	0	1	3	2	.267	.231
Throws Right	R	.200	25	5	2	0	0	0	3	9	.286	.280
Beeks, Jalen	L	.240	25	6	1	0	1	5	0	10	.240	.400
Throws Left	R	.294	51	15	4	0	0	3	4	16	.345	.373
Benjamin, Wes	L	.200	25	5	1	0	0	0	1	5	.231	.240
Throws Left	R	.288	66	19	2	0	4	9	6	16	.347	.500
Bergen, Travis	L	.143	14	2	1	0	1	3	6	4	.400	.429
Throws Left	R	.231	13	3	0	0	0	1	3	7	.375	.231
Berrios, Jose	L	.180	111	20	5	1	6	14	19	33	.303	.405
Throws Right	R	.287	129	37	4	0	2	12	7	35	.331	.364
Betances, Dellin	L	.375	16	6	1	0	0	3	4	3	.524	.438
Throws Right	R	.207	29	6	0	0	0	1	8	8	.395	.207
Biagini, Joe	L	.462	13	6	4	0	1	6	3	2	.563	1.000
Throws Right	R	.400	10	4	0	0	0	2	1	2	.455	.400
Bieber, Shane	L	.153	131	20	3	0	1	6	11	57	.218	.198
Throws Right	R	.181	144	26	3	0	6	9	10	65	.239	.326
Bielak, Brandon	L	.229	70	16	1	0	2	11	11	19	.333	.329
Throws Right	R	.397	58	23	7	0	7	12	6	7	.470	.879
Bleier, Richard	L	.158	38	6	2	0	0	2	1	10	.179	.211
Throws Left	R	.333	24	8	3	0	0	0	3	1	.429	.458
Bolanos, Ronald	L	.571	7	4	0	0	0	0	2	1	.700	.571
Throws Right	R	.400	10	4	0	0	2	6	1	1	.455	1.000
Borucki, Ryan	L	.125	32	4	1	0	0	4	7	11	.275	.156
Throws Left	R	.286	28	8	2	0	1	6	5	10	.394	.464
Boxberger, Brad	L	.192	26	5	1	0	1	2	3	5	.276	.346
Throws Right	R	.279	43	12	2	0	2	7	5	13	.360	.465
Boyd, Matthew	L	.135	37	5	1	0	1	4	2	11	.179	.243
Throws Left	R	.304	204	62	16	2	14	39	20	49	.377	.608
Brach, Brad	L	.250	12	3	0	0	0	1	6	2	.526	.250
Throws Right	R	.161	31	5	1	0	2	2	8	12	.333	.387
Bradley, Archie	L	.171	35	6	1	0	0	4	1	9	.216	.200
Throws Right	R	.324	34	11	3	0	1	5	2	9	.361	.500
Brasier, Ryan	L	.270	37	10	4	0	0	5	7	10	.378	.378
Throws Right	R	.230	61	14	3	0	2	7	4	20	.277	.377
Brault, Steven	L	.217	23	5	1	0	0	1	3	8	.357	.261
Throws Left	R	.190	126	24	1	0	2	14	19	30	.307	.246
Braymer, Ben	L	.300	10	3	0	0	0	3	2	2	.417	.300
Throws Left	R	.211	19	4	1	0	0	1	3	6	.318	.263
Brennan, Brandon	L	.222	9	2	1	0	1	1	2	2	.364	.667
Throws Right	R	.263	19	5	0	0	1	6	3	5	.364	.421
Brewer, Colten	L	.234	47	11	3	0	3	9	8	10	.345	.489
Throws Right	R	.333	60	20	4	0	3	5	6	15	.403	.550
Brice, Austin	L	.308	26	8	4	0	2	5	6	8	.455	.692
Throws Right	R	.196	46	9	3	0	1	7	7	17	.315	.326
Britton, Zack	L	.077	13	1	0	0	0	1	3	5	.250	.077
Throws Left	R	.196	56	11	4	0	0	4	4	11	.250	.268
Brogdon, Connor	L	.133	15	2	0	0	1	2	1	6	.188	.333
Throws Right	R	.125	24	3	1	0	2	7	4	11	.250	.417
Brubaker, JT	L	.287	101	29	9	0	2	11	13	25	.379	.436
Throws Right	R	.232	82	19	3	0	4	15	4	23	.270	.415
Bubic, Kris	L	.320	25	8	0	0	1	2	6	5	.452	.440
Throws Left	R	.254	173	44	8	1	7	25	16	44	.325	.434
Buchter, Ryan	L	.273	11	3	0	0	2	7	5	1	.500	.818
Throws Left	R	.167	12	2	1	0	0	0	1	7	.231	.250
Buehler, Walker	L	.176	74	13	2	0	3	8	5	25	.228	.324
Throws Right	R	.180	61	11	1	0	4	10	6	17	.265	.393
Bumgarner, Madison	L	.255	47	12	4	0	2	8	1	13	.300	.468
Throws Left	R	.285	123	35	8	0	11	19	12	17	.364	.618
Bummer, Aaron	L	.231	13	3	0	0	0	4	0	4	.231	.231
Throws Left	R	.100	20	2	0	0	0	0	5	10	.280	.100
Bundy, Dylan	L	.217	138	30	8	2	4	14	13	34	.294	.391
Throws Right	R	.196	107	21	6	0	1	9	4	38	.239	.280
Burdi, Zack	L	.188	16	3	0	0	0	2	2	5	.278	.188
Throws Right	R	.444	18	8	1	0	4	6	1	6	.474	1.167

Pitchers vs. Left-Handed and Right-Handed Batters

Pitcher	vs	Avg	AB	H	2B	3B	HR	RBI	BB	SO	OBP	Slg
Burnes, Corbin	L	.200	120	24	4	2	1	6	14	48	.289	.292
Throws Right	R	.140	93	13	2	0	1	6	10	40	.238	.194
Burrows, Beau	L	.154	13	2	1	0	0	0	1	1	.214	.231
Throws Right	R	.400	15	6	0	0	3	6	0	2	.438	1.000
Buttrey, Ty	L	.273	44	12	3	0	3	8	6	7	.353	.545
Throws Right	R	.291	55	16	4	1	1	9	3	11	.333	.455
Cabrera, Genesis	L	.069	29	2	0	0	0	0	7	13	.250	.069
Throws Left	R	.170	47	8	2	0	3	5	9	19	.350	.404
Cahill, Trevor	L	.111	45	5	2	0	1	4	5	14	.212	.222
Throws Right	R	.262	42	11	2	0	2	5	9	17	.396	.452
Canning, Griffin	L	.232	95	22	6	0	4	12	11	27	.306	.421
Throws Right	R	.278	115	32	5	2	4	14	12	29	.346	.461
Carrasco, Carlos	L	.224	125	28	6	0	4	10	19	41	.331	.368
Throws Right	R	.218	124	27	5	0	4	10	8	41	.269	.355
Carroll, Cody	L	.667	6	4	2	0	0	6	3	2	.778	1.000
Throws Right	R	.625	8	5	1	0	0	3	2	1	.667	.750
Castano, Daniel	L	.313	32	10	2	0	1	2	2	5	.353	.469
Throws Left	R	.244	82	20	3	1	2	7	9	7	.315	.378
Castellani, Ryan	L	.229	70	16	2	2	6	13	12	8	.353	.571
Throws Right	R	.241	87	21	3	0	6	10	14	17	.365	.483
Castellanos, Humberto	L	.200	15	3	0	0	1	4	3	4	.333	.400
Throws Right	R	.310	29	9	3	0	1	5	2	8	.394	.517
Castillo, Diego	L	.136	22	3	1	0	0	0	5	6	.321	.182
Throws Right	R	.164	55	9	2	0	3	6	6	17	.246	.364
Castillo, Luis	L	.244	135	33	12	1	4	18	17	41	.327	.437
Throws Right	R	.221	131	29	6	0	1	8	7	48	.266	.290
Castro, Miguel	L	.303	33	10	1	1	2	9	7	16	.425	.576
Throws Right	R	.265	68	18	3	0	2	8	6	22	.333	.397
Cease, Dylan	L	.256	125	32	9	0	7	14	20	20	.377	.496
Throws Right	R	.202	89	18	5	1	5	11	14	24	.311	.449
Cessa, Luis	L	.237	38	9	4	0	1	4	1	6	.256	.421
Throws Right	R	.234	47	11	2	1	1	8	6	11	.321	.383
Chacin, Jhoulys	L	.250	8	2	0	0	0	2	2	0	.400	.250
Throws Right	R	.308	13	4	1	0	1	5	1	3	.357	.615
Chafin, Andrew	L	.273	22	6	1	0	1	3	2	6	.333	.455
Throws Left	R	.278	18	5	2	0	1	1	3	7	.381	.556
Chapman, Aroldis	L	.077	13	1	0	0	0	0	2	7	.200	.077
Throws Left	R	.185	27	5	1	1	2	6	2	15	.267	.519
Chatwood, Tyler	L	.265	49	13	7	0	0	3	4	18	.321	.408
Throws Right	R	.333	27	9	1	0	2	7	5	7	.424	.593
Chavez, Jesse	L	.222	27	6	3	0	0	5	3	5	.294	.333
Throws Right	R	.359	39	14	0	0	6	13	4	8	.419	.821
Chirinos, Yonny	L	.250	24	6	1	0	0	0	1	7	.308	.292
Throws Right	R	.364	22	8	1	0	2	4	3	3	.462	.682
Cimber, Adam	L	.143	14	2	1	0	0	0	1	3	.200	.214
Throws Right	R	.355	31	11	1	1	1	8	1	2	.353	.548
Cishek, Steve	L	.194	31	6	3	0	0	4	6	13	.325	.290
Throws Right	R	.319	47	15	2	0	4	15	3	8	.396	.617
Cisnero, Jose	L	.184	38	7	1	0	0	2	7	11	.311	.211
Throws Right	R	.222	72	16	3	1	1	9	3	23	.282	.333
Civale, Aaron	L	.231	147	34	8	2	3	18	12	35	.286	.374
Throws Right	R	.333	144	48	9	1	8	19	4	34	.364	.576
Clarke, Taylor	L	.185	65	12	4	0	2	5	12	14	.308	.338
Throws Right	R	.240	96	23	5	0	6	17	9	26	.305	.479
Claudio, Alex	L	.212	33	7	2	0	1	4	1	9	.257	.364
Throws Left	R	.268	41	11	0	1	1	9	5	6	.348	.390
Clevinger, Mike	L	.250	80	20	4	0	3	6	9	22	.326	.413
Throws Right	R	.209	67	14	3	1	3	8	5	18	.264	.418
Clippard, Tyler	L	.213	47	10	1	0	0	2	2	11	.245	.234
Throws Right	R	.191	47	9	3	0	2	6	2	15	.224	.383
Cobb, Alex	L	.271	96	26	4	1	4	13	8	18	.327	.458
Throws Right	R	.236	110	26	4	0	4	13	10	20	.311	.382
Cody, Kyle	L	.133	30	4	1	0	0	0	3	10	.212	.167
Throws Right	R	.224	49	11	1	1	1	5	10	8	.356	.347
Cole, A.J.	L	.139	36	5	0	1	1	8	5	5	.244	.278
Throws Right	R	.292	48	14	3	0	2	7	4	15	.340	.479
Cole, Gerrit	L	.191	110	21	7	0	9	14	9	40	.264	.500
Throws Right	R	.201	159	32	7	0	5	11	8	54	.240	.340
Colome, Alex	L	.098	41	4	1	0	0	1	5	13	.213	.122
Throws Right	R	.231	39	9	3	0	0	1	3	3	.286	.308
Coonrod, Sam	L	.304	23	7	3	1	2	10	3	9	.370	.783
Throws Right	R	.270	37	10	2	0	0	4	4	6	.372	.324
Corbin, Patrick	L	.262	61	16	3	1	2	5	2	16	.286	.443
Throws Left	R	.321	215	69	13	1	8	26	16	44	.366	.502
Cordero, Jimmy	L	.426	54	23	3	1	2	6	6	9	.492	.630
Throws Right	R	.179	56	10	2	0	0	5	3	13	.242	.214

Pitcher	vs	Avg	AB	H	2B	3B	HR	RBI	BB	SO	OBP	Slg
Cortes, Nestor	L	.444	9	4	1	0	1	4	3	2	.615	.889
Throws Left	R	.308	26	8	1	0	5	11	3	6	.400	.923
Covey, Dylan	L	.300	20	6	2	0	0	4	1	2	.333	.400
Throws Right	R	.316	38	12	1	0	2	7	1	9	.333	.500
Crichton, Stefan	L	.185	27	5	1	0	0	2	6	5	.389	.222
Throws Right	R	.246	69	17	7	0	1	7	3	18	.288	.391
Crick, Kyle	L	.375	8	3	0	0	09	2	3	1	.545	.375
Throws Right	R	.235	17	4	1	0	0	4	1	6	.278	.294
Crismatt, Nabil	L	.286	14	4	2	0	1	1	1	3	.333	.643
Throws Right	R	.125	16	2	0	0	1	2	0	5	.125	.313
Crochet, Garrett	L	.143	7	1	0	0	0	0	0	3	.143	.143
Throws Left	R	.143	14	2	0	0	0	0	0	5	.200	.143
Crowe, Wil	L	.538	13	7	1	0	2	3	4	0	.647	1.077
Throws Right	R	.292	24	7	1	0	3	5	4	8	.414	.708
Cueto, Johnny	L	.265	117	31	9	1	3	13	17	28	.360	.436
Throws Right	R	.233	129	30	3	1	6	21	9	28	.291	.411
Curtiss, John	L	.184	38	7	1	0	0	1	0	11	.225	.211
Throws Right	R	.250	56	14	2	0	3	7	3	14	.288	.446
Darvish, Yu	L	.211	171	36	7	2	4	14	10	48	.262	.345
Throws Right	R	.211	109	23	5	0	1	2	4	45	.239	.284
Davies, Zach	L	.183	120	22	3	1	2	6	7	21	.228	.275
Throws Right	R	.244	135	33	5	0	7	15	12	42	.304	.437
Davis, Austin	L	.636	11	7	1	0	0	1	1	0	.667	.727
Throws Left	R	.211	19	4	0	0	1	5	1	5	.250	.368
Davis, Wade	L	.286	14	4	1	0	1	3	1	2	.333	.571
Throws Right	R	.625	8	5	0	1	2	6	2	1	.700	1.625
Dayton, Grant	L	.121	33	4	2	0	0	1	4	10	.216	.182
Throws Left	R	.257	70	18	2	0	4	11	7	22	.329	.457
De Jong, Chase	L	.400	20	8	0	0	2	7	3	7	.480	.700
Throws Right	R	.333	12	4	0	0	0	1	1	2	.385	.333
De Leon, Jose	L	.250	12	3	0	0	1	6	6	3	.500	.500
Throws Right	R	.250	12	3	0	0	0	3	5	7	.471	.250
deGrom, Jacob	L	.184	125	23	9	0	4	9	14	50	.264	.352
Throws Right	R	.195	123	24	3	0	3	10	4	54	.219	.293
Del Pozo, Miguel	L	.333	3	1	0	0	0	1	2	0	.600	.333
Throws Left	R	.429	14	6	2	0	0	8	6	2	.600	.571
DeSclafani, Anthony	L	.333	81	27	5	1	4	15	11	13	.417	.568
Throws Right	R	.255	55	14	3	0	3	11	5	12	.323	.473
Detwiler, Ross	L	.194	31	6	0	0	0	3	1	6	.242	.194
Throws Left	R	.295	44	13	4	0	2	8	4	9	.354	.523
Devenski, Chris	L	.125	8	1	0	0	0	2	1	4	.222	.125
Throws Right	R	.600	10	6	2	0	1	6	2	1	.667	1.100
Diaz, Edwin	L	.178	45	8	2	0	1	5	9	24	.327	.289
Throws Right	R	.204	49	10	1	0	1	7	5	26	.291	.286
Diaz, Jairo	L	.317	41	13	3	0	4	16	6	9	.396	.683
Throws Right	R	.409	44	18	6	0	0	7	8	8	.518	.545
Diehl, Phillip	L	.250	12	3	0	0	2	3	1	4	.308	.750
Throws Left	R	.333	12	4	2	0	0	4	0	0	.333	.500
Diekman, Jake	L	.185	27	5	0	0	1	2	7	9	.353	.296
Throws Left	R	.070	43	3	0	0	0	0	5	22	.184	.070
Dobnak, Randy	L	.296	81	24	4	0	2	8	7	10	.363	.420
Throws Right	R	.263	99	26	3	0	1	10	6	17	.318	.323
Dolis, Rafael	L	.162	37	6	2	0	1	6	10	17	.340	.297
Throws Right	R	.217	46	10	2	0	0	3	4	14	.294	.261
Doolittle, Sean	L	.214	14	3	1	0	1	2	1	5	.267	.500
Throws Left	R	.375	16	6	0	0	2	4	3	1	.450	.750
Drake, Oliver	L	.200	20	4	1	0	1	5	5	3	.360	.400
Throws Right	R	.176	17	3	1	0	1	3	1	4	.211	.412
Duffey, Tyler	L	.171	41	7	0	0	1	4	2	17	.227	.244
Throws Right	R	.136	44	6	4	0	1	2	4	14	.208	.295
Duffy, Danny	L	.219	32	7	0	0	1	1	2	9	.265	.313
Throws Left	R	.254	181	46	10	0	9	27	20	48	.329	.459
Dugger, Robert	L	.522	23	12	5	1	3	12	1	0	.542	1.217
Throws Right	R	.300	30	9	4	0	2	8	2	4	.344	.633
Dunn, Justin	L	.193	83	16	2	1	6	15	20	24	.358	.458
Throws Right	R	.185	81	15	2	0	4	8	11	14	.283	.358
Dunning, Dane	L	.246	61	15	3	0	2	9	8	16	.352	.393
Throws Right	R	.152	66	10	0	0	2	7	5	19	.211	.242
Eflin, Zach	L	.279	104	29	8	0	7	18	10	35	.348	.558
Throws Right	R	.250	124	31	10	0	1	9	5	35	.279	.355
Eibner, Brett	L	.500	8	4	1	0	1	3	0	0	.500	1.000
Throws Right	R	.333	9	3	0	0	1	3	4	4	.538	.667
Elledge, Seth	L	.316	19	6	4	0	2	6	5	7	.458	.842
Throws Right	R	.217	23	5	3	0	0	2	3	7	.333	.348
Eovaldi, Nathan	L	.191	94	18	4	2	3	6	5	29	.248	.372
Throws Right	R	.355	93	33	6	0	5	13	2	23	.381	.581

Pitchers vs. Left-Handed and Right-Handed Batters

Pitcher	vs	Avg	AB	H	2B	3B	HR	RBI	BB	SO	OBP	Slg
Erlin, Robbie	L	.424	33	14	4	0	4	13	3	6	.472	.909
Throws Left	R	.241	79	19	5	3	4	15	4	19	.291	.532
Eshelman, Thomas	L	.321	53	17	6	0	3	10	4	1	.368	.604
Throws Right	R	.218	78	17	5	0	4	7	5	15	.267	.436
Espino, Paolo	L	.333	9	3	1	0	0	2	1	2	.400	.444
Throws Right	R	.313	16	5	0	0	1	1	1	5	.353	.500
Estevez, Carlos	L	.313	48	15	5	1	3	9	3	13	.365	.646
Throws Right	R	.321	56	18	2	2	3	14	6	14	.406	.589
Fairbanks, Pete	L	.191	47	9	2	0	1	4	7	16	.309	.298
Throws Right	R	.259	54	14	0	0	1	4	7	23	.355	.315
Familia, Jeurys	L	.278	36	10	5	0	1	2	10	5	.435	.500
Throws Right	R	.161	62	10	2	0	1	6	9	18	.297	.242
Farmer, Buck	L	.289	45	13	0	0	2	4	4	5	.340	.422
Throws Right	R	.189	37	7	3	0	1	5	1	9	.211	.351
Farrell, Luke	L	.222	9	2	0	0	1	2	0	3	.300	.556
Throws Right	R	.273	11	3	2	0	0	3	5	5	.500	.455
Fedde, Erick	L	.188	80	15	1	0	3	6	10	8	.278	.313
Throws Right	R	.278	115	32	8	0	7	19	12	20	.359	.530
Ferguson, Caleb	L	.280	25	7	1	0	0	0	1	9	.308	.320
Throws Left	R	.191	47	9	1	0	4	9	2	18	.224	.468
Feyereisen, J.P.	L	.167	18	3	0	0	2	4	2	4	.273	.500
Throws Right	R	.091	11	1	0	0	1	3	3	3	.267	.364
Fiers, Mike	L	.244	119	29	5	0	5	15	11	24	.318	.412
Throws Right	R	.308	117	36	4	1	4	10	5	13	.344	.462
Finnegan, Kyle	L	.179	39	7	0	0	1	4	9	11	.333	.256
Throws Right	R	.259	54	14	2	0	1	9	4	16	.322	.352
Flaherty, Jack	L	.232	82	19	3	0	5	12	8	26	.312	.451
Throws Right	R	.209	67	14	1	0	1	8	8	23	.303	.269
Fleming, Josh	L	.270	37	10	0	0	2	5	0	8	.289	.432
Throws Left	R	.212	85	18	3	1	3	5	7	17	.272	.376
Fletcher, Aaron	L	.000	6	0	0	0	0	0	3	4	.455	.000
Throws Left	R	.500	14	7	1	0	1	4	4	3	.611	.786
Floro, Dylan	L	.188	32	6	0	1	0	6	1	5	.206	.250
Throws Right	R	.283	60	17	2	1	1	5	3	14	.313	.400
Font, Wilmer	L	.400	25	10	3	0	1	8	5	4	.500	.640
Throws Right	R	.367	49	18	2	0	1	8	4	11	.418	.469
Foster, Matt	L	.188	48	9	4	0	0	3	4	13	.250	.271
Throws Right	R	.137	51	7	1	0	2	5	5	18	.214	.275
Freeland, Kyle	L	.279	61	17	1	0	4	9	4	15	.323	.492
Throws Left	R	.278	216	60	15	0	5	21	19	31	.343	.417
Freeman, Sam	L	.091	11	1	0	0	0	0	5	5	.375	.091
Throws Left	R	.143	7	1	0	0	0	0	2	1	.333	.143
Fried, Max	L	.220	41	9	7	0	0	4	3	7	.292	.390
Throws Left	R	.209	158	33	9	1	2	8	16	43	.290	.316
Fry, Jace	L	.231	26	6	3	0	0	2	2	8	.286	.346
Throws Left	R	.222	45	10	0	0	3	5	10	16	.364	.422
Fry, Paul	L	.273	44	12	3	0	2	4	3	15	.333	.477
Throws Left	R	.227	44	10	1	0	1	3	6	14	.320	.318
Fulmer, Carson	L	.158	19	3	1	0	0	1	3	7	.273	.211
Throws Right	R	.250	20	5	2	0	1	4	2	4	.375	.500
Fulmer, Michael	L	.258	66	17	4	0	1	6	8	15	.347	.364
Throws Right	R	.519	54	28	1	0	7	18	4	5	.533	.926
Funkhouser, Kyle	L	.300	30	9	1	1	1	7	7	6	.421	.500
Throws Right	R	.333	39	13	2	0	2	5	4	6	.395	.538
Gallegos, Giovanny	L	.158	19	3	0	0	0	1	2	8	.238	.158
Throws Right	R	.176	34	6	1	0	1	5	2	13	.222	.294
Gallen, Zac	L	.215	121	26	4	0	3	8	12	31	.296	.322
Throws Right	R	.206	141	29	2	0	6	13	13	51	.273	.348
Gant, John	L	.176	17	3	0	0	0	2	3	4	.300	.176
Throws Right	R	.162	37	6	1	0	0	2	4	14	.244	.189
Garcia, Bryan	L	.225	40	9	1	0	0	3	5	5	.304	.250
Throws Right	R	.220	41	9	1	0	0	2	5	7	.319	.244
Garcia, Deivi	L	.226	62	14	2	0	1	5	4	11	.273	.306
Throws Right	R	.276	76	21	3	0	5	12	2	22	.304	.513
Garcia, Jarlin	L	.172	29	5	0	0	0	2	3	5	.286	.172
Throws Left	R	.188	32	6	2	0	0	3	4	9	.263	.250
Garcia, Luis	L	.389	18	7	1	0	1	7	3	5	.476	.611
Throws Right	R	.167	18	3	1	0	0		6	6	.375	.222
Garcia, Luis	L	.286	21	6	3	1	1	4	2	3	.360	.667
Throws Right	R	.048	21	1	0	0	0	0	3	6	.167	.048
Garcia, Rico	L	.200	10	2	0	0	1	3	0	1	.182	.500
Throws Right	R	.379	29	11	3	0	0	5	4	6	.455	.483
Garcia, Rony	L	.154	39	6	2	0	0	3	3	6	.214	.205
Throws Right	R	.396	48	19	3	0	7	21	6	8	.463	.896
Garcia, Yimi	L	.217	23	5	3	0	0	1	2	5	.280	.348
Throws Right	R	.125	32	4	0	0	0	2	3	14	.200	.125

Pitcher	vs	Avg	AB	H	2B	3B	HR	RBI	BB	SO	OBP	Slg
Garrett, Amir	L	.043	23	1	0	0	0	0	5	12	.214	.043
Throws Left	R	.231	39	9	0	0	4	8	2	14	.268	.538
Garrett, Braxton	L	.400	5	2	0	0	0	0	1	2	.500	.400
Throws Left	R	.250	24	6	1	0	3	5	4	6	.357	.667
Gausman, Kevin	L	.217	115	25	7	2	4	12	7	39	.260	.417
Throws Right	R	.225	111	25	3	0	4	12	9	40	.281	.360
Gerber, Joey	L	.278	18	5	2	0	0	7	4	2	.375	.389
Throws Right	R	.222	36	8	2	1	1	6	1	4	.263	.417
Gibaut, Ian	L	.192	26	5	1	0	1	5	4	6	.300	.346
Throws Right	R	.273	22	6	2	0	1	2	5	8	.429	.500
Gibson, Kyle	L	.265	113	30	3	1	7	21	12	18	.357	.496
Throws Right	R	.283	152	43	6	1	5	17	18	40	.366	.434
Gilmartin, Sean	L	.222	9	2	0	0	0	1	1	4	.300	.222
Throws Left	R	.455	11	5	0	0	2	3	3	1	.571	1.000
Ginkel, Kevin	L	.241	29	7	3	0	1	6	5	10	.353	.448
Throws Right	R	.378	37	14	0	1	2	6	8	8	.489	.595
Giolito, Lucas	L	.180	150	27	6	0	5	15	19	59	.276	.320
Throws Right	R	.190	105	20	2	0	3	11	9	38	.254	.295
Givens, Mychal	L	.172	29	5	1	0	3	3	2	7	.226	.517
Throws Right	R	.216	51	11	2	1	2	6	8	18	.339	.412
Glasnow, Tyler	L	.200	105	21	2	2	3	7	9	44	.263	.343
Throws Right	R	.200	110	22	4	0	8	19	13	47	.282	.455
Godley, Zack	L	.295	61	18	4	1	4	11	8	14	.380	.590
Throws Right	R	.375	64	24	3	0	5	10	6	14	.444	.656
Gomber, Austin	L	.192	26	5	1	0	1	4	5	3	.364	.346
Throws Left	R	.189	74	14	1	1	0	2	10	24	.279	.230
Gonsolin, Tony	L	.179	84	15	4	2	1	5	4	20	.225	.310
Throws Right	R	.207	82	17	2	0	1	6	3	26	.233	.268
Gonzales, Marco	L	.274	73	20	5	0	1	5	2	15	.321	.384
Throws Left	R	.202	193	39	8	0	7	20	5	49	.226	.352
Gonzalez, Chi Chi	L	.333	33	11	3	0	1	4	4	5	.421	.515
Throws Right	R	.256	43	11	2	1	2	8	6	11	.365	.488
Gonzalez, Gio	L	.278	36	10	1	0	1	4	7	10	.422	.389
Throws Left	R	.316	95	30	3	0	5	14	12	24	.393	.505
Gonzalez, Victor	L	.143	35	5	1	0	0	2	2	11	.211	.171
Throws Right	R	.205	39	8	1	0	0	2	0	12	.238	.231
Goody, Nick	L	.357	14	5	1	1	1	5	2	3	.438	.786
Throws Right	R	.281	32	9	2	1	2	6	6	10	.385	.594
Gott, Trevor	L	.350	20	7	2	1	3	4	2	4	.409	1.000
Throws Right	R	.214	28	6	1	0	4	9	4	9	.371	.679
Goudeau, Ashton	L	.308	13	4	0	0	1	3	0	1	.267	.538
Throws Right	R	.524	21	11	2	0	2	6	2	1	.583	.905
Graterol, Brusdar	L	.360	25	9	0	1	2	1	1	2	.385	.520
Throws Right	R	.164	55	9	0	0	2	2	2	11	.226	.182
Graveman, Kendall	L	.115	26	3	0	0	0	2	3	6	.200	.115
Throws Right	R	.286	42	12	3	2	2	9	5	9	.362	.595
Gray, Jon	L	.265	98	26	6	1	6	19	7	14	.327	.531
Throws Right	R	.306	62	19	4	1	0	10	4	8	.343	.403
Gray, Sonny	L	.202	119	24	6	1	2	11	16	37	.301	.319
Throws Right	R	.205	88	18	2	0	2	7	10	35	.293	.295
Green, Chad	L	.075	40	3	1	0	2	5	4	15	.159	.250
Throws Right	R	.200	50	10	0	0	3	6	4	17	.255	.380
Greene, Shane	L	.286	42	12	1	0	2	6	4	11	.354	.452
Throws Right	R	.185	54	10	3	0	0	3	5	10	.267	.241
Greinke, Zack	L	.206	131	27	5	1	1	12	6	45	.246	.282
Throws Right	R	.305	131	40	12	1	5	17	3	22	.319	.527
Grimm, Justin	L	.556	9	5	0	0	2	4	2	1	.636	1.222
Throws Right	R	.286	14	4	0	0	2	4	2	5	.375	.714
Grotz, Zac	L	.429	7	3	1	0	1	5	1	1	.500	1.000
Throws Right	R	.348	23	8	1	0	3	10	10	3	.579	.783
Gsellman, Robert	L	.385	26	10	2	0	2	8	3	4	.448	.692
Throws Right	R	.343	35	12	3	1	2	7	5	5	.429	.657
Guerra, Deolis	L	.077	13	1	1	0	0	1	1	3	.143	.154
Throws Right	R	.474	19	9	0	0	3	8	1	5	.545	.947
Guerra, Javy	L	.250	28	7	1	0	1	2	4	6	.344	.393
Throws Right	R	.343	35	12	2	0	1	6	3	7	.395	.486
Guerra, Javy	L	.520	25	13	2	0	1	10	2	5	.552	.720
Throws Right	R	.343	35	12	1	0	0	5	3	7	.395	.371
Guerra, Junior	L	.219	32	7	2	0	1	7	12	8	.444	.375
Throws Right	R	.196	51	10	3	0	0	6	3	13	.250	.255
Guilbeau, Taylor	L	.385	13	5	2	0	0	2	3	0	.500	.538
Throws Left	R	.176	17	3	1	0	0	1	3	3	.300	.235
Hader, Josh	L	.154	13	2	0	0	1	4	3	6	.313	.385
Throws Left	R	.115	52	6	2	0	2	4	7	25	.258	.269
Hahn, Jesse	L	.000	28	0	0	0	0	1	6	11	.176	.000
Throws Right	R	.143	28	4	1	0	0	2	2	8	.226	.179

Pitchers vs. Left-Handed and Right-Handed Batters

Pitcher	vs	Avg	AB	H	2B	3B	HR	RBI	BB	SO	OBP	Slg
Hale, David	L	.233	30	7	1	0	0	3	3	7	.303	.267
Throws Right	R	.390	41	16	6	0	2	6	1	7	.405	.683
Hall, Matt	L	.476	21	10	2	0	1	8	7	4	.607	.714
Throws Left	R	.318	22	7	2	0	1	8	3	5	.423	.545
Hamilton, Ian	L	.222	9	2	0	0	0	1	3	3	.417	.222
Throws Right	R	.333	6	2	0	0	0	0	2	1	.500	.333
Hand, Brad	L	.125	8	1	0	0	0	0	0	4	.222	.125
Throws Left	R	.174	69	12	5	1	0	5	4	25	.227	.275
Happ, J.A.	L	.204	49	10	0	0	2	5	3	11	.250	.327
Throws Left	R	.209	129	27	7	0	6	14	12	31	.282	.403
Harper, Ryne	L	.361	36	13	4	0	3	12	7	11	.465	.722
Throws Right	R	.250	64	16	3	0	2	9	2	14	.284	.391
Harris, Will	L	.343	35	12	2	0	1	5	2	10	.378	.486
Throws Right	R	.225	40	9	1	0	2	4	7	11	.340	.400
Hart, Kyle	L	.429	14	6	0	0	1	4	3	4	.500	.643
Throws Left	R	.429	42	18	4	0	3	14	7	9	.510	.738
Hartlieb, Geoff	L	.182	33	6	0	0	1	3	7	5	.341	.273
Throws Right	R	.222	45	10	3	0	0	3	12	14	.400	.289
Harvey, Hunter	L	.182	11	2	0	0	0	0	1	3	.250	.182
Throws Right	R	.273	22	6	0	0	2	5	1	3	.320	.545
Harvey, Matt	L	.471	34	16	3	0	3	10	3	4	.514	.824
Throws Right	R	.423	26	11	1	0	3	5	2	6	.464	.808
Hatch, Thomas	L	.200	40	8	1	1	1	6	4	13	.289	.350
Throws Right	R	.185	54	10	1	0	1	6	9	10	.313	.259
Heaney, Andrew	L	.268	82	22	4	0	1	10	7	24	.333	.354
Throws Left	R	.236	174	41	10	1	8	19	12	46	.291	.443
Hearn, Taylor	L	.261	23	6	0	0	2	8	4	10	.370	.522
Throws Left	R	.175	40	7	1	0	0	2	7	13	.306	.200
Heller, Ben	L	.231	13	3	1	0	1	3	2	4	.333	.538
Throws Right	R	.200	10	2	0	0	1	2	0	2	.333	.500
Helsley, Ryan	L	.222	18	4	1	0	1	3	3	4	.333	.444
Throws Right	R	.160	25	4	1	0	2	5	5	6	.323	.440
Hembree, Heath	L	.292	24	7	1	0	3	7	4	5	.414	.708
Throws Right	R	.345	55	19	4	1	6	13	4	15	.393	.782
Hendricks, Kyle	L	.209	158	33	5	0	5	9	4	40	.232	.335
Throws Right	R	.274	146	40	5	0	5	13	4	24	.291	.411
Hendriks, Liam	L	.200	35	7	1	0	1	2	2	19	.243	.314
Throws Right	R	.135	52	7	1	0	0	3	1	18	.148	.154
Herget, Jimmy	L	.087	23	2	1	0	1	5	10	6	.400	.261
Throws Right	R	.239	46	11	3	0	1	9	4	11	.294	.370
Hernandez, Carlos	L	.313	32	10	1	0	4	7	3	4	.371	.719
Throws Right	R	.321	28	9	2	0	2	3	9	4	.406	.393
Hernandez, Darwinzon	L	.143	7	1	0	0	0	0	2	5	.333	.143
Throws Left	R	.167	24	4	0	0	0	0	6	8	.355	.167
Hernandez, Elieser	L	.240	50	12	4	0	2	4	2	17	.283	.440
Throws Right	R	.184	49	9	1	0	3	5	3	17	.245	.388
Hernandez, Jonathan	L	.244	45	11	1	2	1	6	2	13	.314	.422
Throws Right	R	.200	65	13	1	0	1	7	6	18	.274	.262
Hess, David	L	.308	13	4	1	1	0	2	1	0	.357	.538
Throws Right	R	.353	17	6	2	0	1	3	1	1	.389	.647
Heuer, Codi	L	.130	46	6	2	0	0	2	6	14	.231	.174
Throws Right	R	.162	37	6	0	0	1	2	3	11	.225	.243
Hill, Cam	L	.176	34	6	2	0	2	6	3	7	.256	.412
Throws Right	R	.172	29	5	0	0	2	4	2	9	.242	.379
Hill, Rich	L	.176	17	3	0	0	0	4	2	7	.333	.176
Throws Left	R	.208	120	25	5	0	3	12	13	29	.289	.325
Hill, Tim	L	.225	40	9	2	0	1	6	3	10	.311	.350
Throws Left	R	.258	31	8	2	0	2	6	3	10	.324	.516
Hirano, Yoshihisa	L	.300	30	9	1	0	2	5	3	5	.364	.533
Throws Right	R	.391	23	9	2	0	0	4	5	6	.500	.478
Hoffman, Jeff	L	.378	45	17	2	1	1	10	4	9	.429	.533
Throws Right	R	.326	46	15	7	0	2	11	5	11	.400	.609
Holder, Jonathan	L	.350	40	14	3	0	0	7	6	7	.426	.425
Throws Right	R	.224	49	11	3	0	3	5	5	7	.296	.469
Holland, Derek	L	.161	31	5	1	0	0	4	1	7	.188	.194
Throws Left	R	.285	130	37	8	0	12	24	14	38	.367	.623
Holland, Greg	L	.179	56	10	3	0	0	7	2	15	.220	.232
Throws Right	R	.227	44	10	3	1	1	6	5	16	.327	.409
Houck, Tanner	L	.111	18	2	1	0	0	0	4	5	.273	.167
Throws Right	R	.114	35	4	0	0	1	1	5	16	.244	.200
Houser, Adrian	L	.336	125	42	6	1	7	26	17	21	.420	.568
Throws Right	R	.219	96	21	6	0	1	7	4	23	.272	.313
Howard, Sam	L	.259	27	7	2	0	1	4	5	12	.375	.444
Throws Left	R	.200	50	10	3	0	3	11	4	15	.293	.440
Howard, Spencer	L	.333	51	17	3	1	4	11	7	10	.407	.667
Throws Right	R	.265	49	13	0	0	2	5	3	13	.315	.388
Hoyt, James	L	.267	15	4	2	0	0	3	2	4	.353	.400
Throws Right	R	.135	37	5	2	0	1	4	6	16	.267	.270
Hudson, Dakota	L	.130	77	10	3	0	3	5	5	18	.193	.286
Throws Right	R	.241	58	14	1	0	2	7	10	13	.353	.362
Hudson, Daniel	L	.139	36	5	1	0	3	5	5	15	.262	.417
Throws Right	R	.244	41	10	2	0	3	10	6	13	.367	.512
Hughes, Jared	L	.297	37	11	3	0	2	6	7	5	.435	.541
Throws Right	R	.226	53	12	3	0	1	10	7	16	.349	.340
Hunter, Tommy	L	.295	44	13	4	1	1	7	3	9	.367	.500
Throws Right	R	.188	48	9	2	0	1	3	3	16	.250	.292
Iglesias, Raisel	L	.237	38	9	1	0	0	2	1	13	.275	.263
Throws Right	R	.156	45	7	2	0	1	6	4	18	.220	.267
Irvin, Cole	L	.800	5	4	1	0	0	1	1	1	.833	1.000
Throws Left	R	.438	16	7	0	1	1	5	0	4	.438	.750
Jackson, Luke	L	.375	48	18	3	0	0	10	8	5	.458	.438
Throws Right	R	.323	65	21	2	0	2	19	5	15	.370	.446
James, Josh	L	.286	28	8	2	0	1	5	8	6	.444	.464
Throws Right	R	.194	36	7	2	0	3	9	9	15	.383	.500
Jansen, Kenley	L	.159	44	7	2	0	1	4	3	21	.245	.273
Throws Right	R	.261	46	12	1	0	1	6	6	12	.358	.348
Javier, Cristian	L	.248	113	28	6	0	7	17	10	27	.304	.487
Throws Right	R	.101	79	8	0	0	4	4	8	27	.202	.253
Jeffress, Jeremy	L	.136	44	6	0	0	1	3	5	8	.255	.205
Throws Right	R	.138	29	4	1	0	0	3	7	9	.297	.172
Jimenez, Joe	L	.324	37	12	2	0	3	11	5	8	.409	.622
Throws Right	R	.255	51	13	3	0	4	12	1	14	.316	.549
Johnson, Pierce	L	.087	23	2	1	0	0	1	4	11	.222	.130
Throws Right	R	.277	47	13	2	0	2	7	5	16	.340	.447
Jones, Nate	L	.273	33	9	1	0	3	7	3	11	.368	.576
Throws Right	R	.364	44	16	3	0	2	9	3	12	.396	.568
Junis, Jakob	L	.354	65	23	3	0	5	11	2	10	.391	.631
Throws Right	R	.300	40	12	2	0	2	5	4	9	.356	.500
Jurado, Ariel	L	.455	11	5	1	0	0	1	0	0	.455	.545
Throws Right	R	.444	9	4	1	0	1	4	0	2	.444	.889
Kaminsky, Rob	L	.250	4	1	0	0	0	2	1	2	.333	.250
Throws Left	R	.167	12	2	0	0	0	3	1	1	.214	.167
Karinchak, James	L	.179	39	7	1	1	0	3	9	23	.327	.256
Throws Right	R	.143	49	7	0	0	1	6	7	30	.237	.204
Kay, Anthony	L	.341	41	14	4	1	1	7	5	8	.404	.561
Throws Left	R	.195	41	8	4	0	2	6	9	14	.333	.439
Keller, Brad	L	.214	117	25	0	0	2	9	15	19	.304	.265
Throws Right	R	.184	76	14	2	0	4	9	2	16	.213	.211
Keller, Mitch	L	.179	39	7	1	0	3	5	11	6	.373	.436
Throws Right	R	.069	29	2	1	0	1	1	7	10	.250	.207
Kelly, Joe	L	.235	17	4	2	0	0	2	0	4	.235	.353
Throws Right	R	.235	17	4	1	0	1	5	7	5	.440	.294
Kelly, Merrill	L	.173	52	9	2	0	2	5	2	12	.204	.327
Throws Right	R	.254	67	17	5	0	3	8	3	17	.296	.448
Kennedy, Ian	L	.259	27	7	0	0	4	8	3	6	.355	.704
Throws Right	R	.371	35	13	2	0	3	8	2	9	.405	.686
Kershaw, Clayton	L	.180	50	9	3	0	3	5	2	13	.208	.420
Throws Left	R	.199	161	32	7	1	5	10	6	49	.232	.348
Keuchel, Dallas	L	.171	41	7	0	0	0	3	4	8	.244	.171
Throws Left	R	.228	197	45	8	1	2	9	13	34	.276	.310
Kickham, Mike	L	.235	17	4	1	0	1	1	2	3	.316	.471
Throws Right	R	.370	46	17	3	0	5	11	3	14	.431	.761
Kikuchi, Yusei	L	.265	49	13	2	0	0	8	7	12	.351	.306
Throws Left	R	.228	123	28	9	1	3	16	13	35	.299	.390
Kilome, Franklyn	L	.286	21	6	1	0	2	8	6	5	.444	.619
Throws Right	R	.308	26	8	2	0	3	6	3	8	.400	.731
Kim, Kwang-hyun	L	.192	26	5	3	0	0	1	4	9	.300	.308
Throws Left	R	.198	116	23	6	0	3	7	8	15	.250	.328
Kimbrel, Craig	L	.207	29	6	1	1	2	4	5	13	.361	.517
Throws Right	R	.154	26	4	0	0	0	2	7	15	.333	.154
King, John	L	.333	15	5	0	0	0	1	2	3	.444	.333
Throws Left	R	.267	30	8	2	0	2	6	2	6	.333	.533
King, Michael	L	.255	47	12	4	0	3	8	9	13	.375	.532
Throws Right	R	.295	61	18	2	1	2	10	2	13	.338	.459
Kinley, Tyler	L	.111	45	5	1	0	1	8	4	15	.196	.200
Throws Right	R	.242	33	8	1	0	1	5	8	11	.409	.364
Kintzler, Brandon	L	.300	40	12	4	0	1	4	7	3	.396	.475
Throws Right	R	.184	49	9	1	0	2	5	4	11	.245	.327
Kittredge, Andrew	L	.250	8	2	0	0	0	1	0	2	.250	.250
Throws Right	R	.286	21	6	2	0	0	3	2	1	.348	.381
Kline, Branden	L	.200	5	1	1	0	0	4	3	1	.500	.400
Throws Right	R	.083	12	1	0	0	0	0	0	6	.083	.083

Pitchers vs. Left-Handed and Right-Handed Batters

Pitcher	vs	Avg	AB	H	2B	3B	HR	RBI	BB	SO	OBP	Slg
Knebel, Corey	L	.290	31	9	2	0	2	7	6	6	.405	.548
Throws Right	R	.261	23	6	1	0	2	5	2	9	.320	.565
Kolarek, Adam	L	.077	39	3	1	0	0	2	1	8	.100	.103
Throws Left	R	.286	28	8	0	0	1	4	3	5	.344	.393
Kremer, Dean	L	.152	33	5	2	1	0	2	6	10	.282	.273
Throws Right	R	.270	37	10	4	2	0	6	6	12	.364	.486
Kriske, Brooks	L	.333	9	3	0	0	1	3	4	3	.538	.667
Throws Right	R	.000	6	0	0	0	0	0	3	5	.333	.000
Kuhl, Chad	L	.196	92	18	5	0	4	10	17	26	.321	.380
Throws Right	R	.233	73	17	1	0	4	7	11	18	.349	.411
Lail, Brady	L	.200	30	6	0	0	2	3	3	5	.273	.400
Throws Right	R	.250	32	8	1	0	3	5	4	7	.368	.563
Lakins, Travis	L	.133	30	4	0	0	2	6	5	10	.250	.333
Throws Right	R	.300	70	21	7	0	0	10	8	15	.388	.400
Lamet, Dinelson	L	.133	135	18	2	0	3	7	13	51	.220	.215
Throws Right	R	.196	107	21	7	0	2	9	7	42	.256	.318
Lauer, Eric	L	.333	12	4	1	0	0	2	1	3	.429	.417
Throws Left	R	.351	37	13	4	0	2	14	8	9	.468	.622
LeBlanc, Wade	L	.188	16	3	1	0	0	2	5	2	.375	.250
Throws Left	R	.316	76	24	3	0	6	12	3	11	.342	.592
Leibrandt, Brandon	L	.118	17	2	0	0	0	3	3	3	.250	.118
Throws Left	R	.083	12	1	0	0	0	0	4	0	.313	.083
Leone, Dominic	L	.389	18	7	1	0	1	4	2	6	.450	.611
Throws Right	R	.292	24	7	2	0	2	5	3	10	.370	.625
Lester, Jon	L	.233	30	7	3	0	0	3	3	8	.303	.333
Throws Left	R	.266	214	57	10	1	11	27	14	34	.320	.477
Leyer, Robinson	L	.643	14	9	1	0	2	9	4	3	.722	1.143
Throws Right	R	.250	12	3	1	0	1	2	4	6	.438	.583
Lindblom, Josh	L	.284	95	27	6	2	6	17	11	24	.364	.579
Throws Right	R	.195	77	15	1	0	0	5	5	28	.262	.208
Littell, Zack	L	.273	11	3	0	0	1	1	2	0	.385	.545
Throws Right	R	.563	16	9	0	0	4	6	1	3	.611	1.313
Loaisiga, Jonathan	L	.257	35	9	3	0	0	2	2	9	.350	.343
Throws Right	R	.231	52	12	3	0	3	10	5	13	.310	.462
Lockett, Walker	L	.290	31	9	2	0	0	3	1	3	.333	.355
Throws Right	R	.333	36	12	2	0	2	9	3	8	.400	.556
Lopez, Jorge	L	.286	77	22	4	0	5	12	7	15	.341	.532
Throws Right	R	.308	78	24	1	0	2	16	5	13	.364	.397
Lopez, Pablo	L	.269	119	32	12	0	1	15	7	19	.318	.395
Throws Right	R	.184	98	18	1	0	3	11	11	40	.261	.286
Lopez, Reynaldo	L	.208	53	11	1	0	3	9	11	9	.344	.396
Throws Right	R	.333	51	17	4	0	6	11	4	15	.393	.765
Lopez, Yoan	L	.355	31	11	2	1	2	8	5	4	.444	.677
Throws Right	R	.213	47	10	4	0	2	6	4	12	.275	.426
Lorenzen, Michael	L	.250	68	17	2	0	0	9	7	16	.316	.279
Throws Right	R	.220	59	13	3	1	3	9	10	19	.343	.458
Loup, Aaron	L	.212	33	7	3	0	0	2	1	8	.278	.303
Throws Left	R	.192	52	10	3	0	3	9	3	14	.246	.423
Lucchesi, Joey	L	.400	10	4	1	0	0	2	0	3	.455	.500
Throws Left	R	.500	18	9	1	0	0	4	2	2	.524	.556
Lugo, Seth	L	.275	69	19	3	0	4	10	6	21	.333	.493
Throws Right	R	.273	77	21	4	1	4	11	4	26	.317	.506
Luzardo, Jesus	L	.260	50	13	5	0	1	7	2	14	.283	.420
Throws Left	R	.256	176	45	7	0	8	20	15	45	.325	.432
Lyles, Jordan	L	.292	113	33	6	0	4	18	14	16	.366	.442
Throws Right	R	.279	122	34	6	1	8	27	9	20	.328	.541
Lynn, Lance	L	.182	154	28	5	0	5	10	10	45	.235	.312
Throws Right	R	.229	157	36	10	1	8	21	15	44	.316	.459
Maeda, Kenta	L	.182	137	25	1	1	4	6	9	41	.233	.292
Throws Right	R	.149	101	15	3	0	5	11	1	39	.157	.327
Magill, Matt	L	.167	12	2	0	0	1	3	4	3	.333	.167
Throws Right	R	.259	27	7	0	0	3	5	3	7	.333	.593
Mahle, Tyler	L	.176	85	15	3	1	3	8	13	25	.297	.341
Throws Right	R	.218	87	19	3	2	3	13	8	35	.290	.402
Manaea, Sean	L	.250	52	13	2	1	3	9	1	11	.264	.500
Throws Left	R	.277	159	44	8	0	4	17	7	34	.308	.403
Margevicius, Nick	L	.205	44	9	2	0	2	4	3	11	.255	.386
Throws Left	R	.259	54	14	2	0	4	11	11	25	.325	.455
Marquez, German	L	.253	174	44	12	2	2	18	14	39	.307	.379
Throws Right	R	.239	142	34	4	1	4	19	11	34	.290	.366
Marshall, Evan	L	.119	42	5	1	0	0	5	5	15	.213	.143
Throws Right	R	.273	44	12	3	0	1	8	2	15	.304	.409
Martin, Brett	L	.176	17	3	0	0	1	2	5	2	.364	.353
Throws Left	R	.147	34	5	1	1	1	3	4	6	.231	.324
Martin, Chris	L	.107	28	3	1	0	0	0	2	11	.194	.143
Throws Right	R	.147	34	5	0	0	1	3	1	9	.171	.235
Martinez, Carlos	L	.310	42	13	2	0	2	7	7	8	.408	.500
Throws Right	R	.388	49	19	4	1	4	16	3	9	.407	.755
Maton, Phil	L	.267	45	12	1	0	1	4	3	18	.340	.356
Throws Right	R	.268	41	11	1	2	0	7	3	14	.348	.390
Matz, Steven	L	.333	27	9	3	0	1	7	3	9	.400	.556
Throws Left	R	.320	103	33	4	0	13	27	7	27	.360	.738
Matzek, Tyler	L	.190	42	8	1	0	1	4	2	18	.227	.286
Throws Left	R	.224	67	15	2	1	0	5	8	25	.325	.284
May, Dustin	L	.242	99	24	2	0	6	10	13	20	.333	.444
Throws Right	R	.198	106	21	2	0	3	7	3	24	.220	.302
May, Trevor	L	.200	45	9	0	0	3	7	6	21	.288	.400
Throws Right	R	.256	43	11	0	0	2	4	1	17	.273	.395
Mayers, Mike	L	.100	60	6	1	0	1	4	3	27	.143	.167
Throws Right	R	.235	51	12	3	0	1	11	6	16	.328	.353
Mazza, Chris	L	.294	51	15	2	0	2	9	6	10	.368	.451
Throws Right	R	.284	67	19	4	0	1	7	9	19	.380	.388
McCarthy, Kevin	L	.333	12	4	0	0	1	4	1	0	.385	.583
Throws Right	R	.429	14	6	0	0	0	1	1	2	.500	.429
McClain, Reggie	L	.375	8	3	2	0	0	2	0	0	.333	.625
Throws Right	R	.353	17	6	0	0	1	3	3	2	.450	.529
McCullers Jr., Lance	L	.190	105	20	11	2	2	12	9	34	.265	.390
Throws Right	R	.253	95	24	7	0	3	15	11	22	.349	.421
McFarland, T.J.	L	.289	38	11	4	0	3	5	3	7	.341	.447
Throws Left	R	.313	48	15	2	0	2	5	2	2	.353	.479
McGee, Jake	L	.304	23	7	2	0	1	2	1	5	.333	.522
Throws Left	R	.135	52	7	2	1	1	3	2	28	.167	.269
McGowin, Kyle	L	.100	10	1	0	0	0	0	2	6	.250	.100
Throws Right	R	.250	32	8	0	0	2	8	3	10	.314	.438
McKenzie, Triston	L	.222	54	12	4	0	3	6	14	21	.263	.463
Throws Right	R	.143	63	9	0	0	3	6	7	28	.229	.286
Means, John	L	.244	45	11	2	0	3	5	2	17	.277	.489
Throws Left	R	.210	119	25	0	0	9	17	5	25	.264	.437
Mears, Nick	L	.143	7	1	0	0	0	2	2	2	.333	.143
Throws Right	R	.273	11	3	1	0	1	4	5	5	.471	.636
Mejia, Humberto	L	.304	23	7	2	0	2	5	3	7	.385	.652
Throws Right	R	.316	19	6	2	0	1	3	4	4	.435	.579
Melancon, Mark	L	.333	36	12	1	0	0	3	4	3	.390	.361
Throws Right	R	.208	48	10	0	0	1	4	3	11	.283	.271
Mella, Keury	L	.200	10	2	1	0	0	0	1	3	.273	.300
Throws Right	R	.286	28	8	1	0	1	3	2	9	.323	.429
Menez, Conner	L	.188	16	3	1	0	0	1	2	5	.278	.250
Throws Left	R	.136	22	3	1	0	2	3	3	8	.269	.455
Mengden, Daniel	L	.250	28	7	2	0	1	2	7	7	.417	.429
Throws Right	R	.333	21	7	2	0	1	3	0	3	.318	.571
Merryweather, Julian	L	.111	18	2	0	0	0	0	2	9	.200	.111
Throws Right	R	.290	31	9	3	0	0	4	4	6	.371	.387
Middleton, Keynan	L	.235	17	4	0	0	0	2	3	5	.333	.235
Throws Right	R	.296	27	8	3	0	2	5	3	6	.344	.630
Miley, Wade	L	.067	15	1	0	0	0	0	1	3	.176	.067
Throws Left	R	.341	41	14	5	0	1	9	8	9	.460	.537
Miller, Andrew	L	.158	19	3	0	0	0	1	3	9	.273	.158
Throws Left	R	.214	28	6	1	0	0	3	2	5	.333	.250
Miller, Tyson	L	.111	9	1	0	0	1	2	1	0	.200	.444
Throws Right	R	.143	7	1	1	0	0	1	0	2	.300	.286
Mills, Alec	L	.275	138	38	8	0	10	22	12	22	.338	.551
Throws Right	R	.163	92	15	3	0	3	5	7	24	.228	.293
Milner, Hoby	L	.256	39	10	0	0	4	16	3	9	.326	.564
Throws Left	R	.231	13	3	1	0	1	2	3	4	.375	.538
Milone, Tommy	L	.256	39	10	1	2	3	7	2	10	.293	.615
Throws Left	R	.344	131	45	11	2	6	23	4	30	.367	.595
Minor, Mike	L	.230	61	14	2	0	1	3	4	10	.277	.311
Throws Left	R	.231	156	36	5	0	10	28	16	52	.305	.455
Minter, A.J.	L	.250	24	6	2	0	0	1	2	8	.308	.333
Throws Left	R	.176	51	9	2	1	1	4	7	16	.276	.314
Misiewicz, Anthony	L	.216	37	8	1	0	0	2	2	12	.256	.243
Throws Left	R	.308	39	12	5	0	2	7	4	13	.386	.590
Mize, Casey	L	.300	60	18	5	0	5	11	9	12	.417	.633
Throws Right	R	.200	55	11	0	0	2	9	4	14	.279	.309
Montas, Frankie	L	.350	100	35	8	1	6	22	15	25	.431	.630
Throws Right	R	.198	111	22	1	0	4	9	8	35	.256	.315
Montero, Rafael	L	.188	32	6	1	0	1	5	1	7	.212	.313
Throws Right	R	.194	31	6	3	1	1	6	5	12	.324	.452
Montgomery, Jordan	L	.229	48	11	4	0	0	1	3	12	.302	.313
Throws Left	R	.278	133	37	5	1	7	21	6	35	.309	.489
Montgomery, Mike	L	.000	3	0	0	0	0	0	0	2	.000	.000
Throws Left	R	.333	18	6	0	1	1	5	1	2	.350	.611

Pitchers vs. Left-Handed and Right-Handed Batters

Pitcher	vs	Avg	AB	H	2B	3B	HR	RBI	BB	SO	OBP	Slg
Moran, Brian	L	.333	9	3	2	0	0	3	4	3	.538	.556
Throws Left	R	.273	11	3	0	0	1	3	2	4	.385	.545
Morejon, Adrian	L	.294	34	10	2	0	3	5	0	9	.294	.618
Throws Left	R	.244	41	10	0	0	4	5	4	16	.311	.537
Morgan, Adam	L	.200	30	6	0	0	2	2	4	11	.294	.400
Throws Left	R	.364	22	8	3	0	1	5	2	5	.417	.636
Morton, Charlie	L	.242	62	15	2	1	3	11	7	21	.333	.452
Throws Right	R	.304	92	28	7	0	1	8	3	21	.337	.413
Mujica, Jose	L	.500	12	6	1	0	0	2	1	1	.538	.583
Throws Right	R	.444	9	4	1	0	2	9	1	0	.500	1.222
Murphy, Patrick	L	.375	8	3	0	1	0	1	2	3	.500	.625
Throws Right	R	.200	15	3	1	0	0	0	2	2	.200	.267
Musgrove, Joe	L	.183	82	15	4	1	3	9	12	31	.296	.366
Throws Right	R	.281	64	18	5	0	2	4	4	24	.324	.453
Neidert, Nick	L	.400	10	4	2	0	0	0	1	2	.455	.600
Throws Right	R	.273	22	6	1	0	1	4	1	2	.304	.455
Nelson, Nick	L	.270	37	10	2	0	2	5	6	7	.372	.486
Throws Right	R	.244	41	10	0	0	2	6	5	11	.319	.390
Neris, Hector	L	.275	40	11	0	0	0	8	12	14	.442	.275
Throws Right	R	.260	50	13	2	1	0	5	1	13	.275	.340
Neverauskas, Dovydas	L	.382	34	13	3	0	3	16	4	12	.447	.735
Throws Right	R	.244	45	11	2	0	2	5	6	11	.333	.422
Newberry, Jake	L	.267	30	8	1	0	0	3	7	9	.410	.300
Throws Right	R	.250	48	12	2	0	3	10	5	15	.327	.479
Newcomb, Sean	L	.381	21	8	1	0	2	6	0	3	.435	.714
Throws Left	R	.308	39	12	2	0	2	5	6	7	.404	.513
Newsome, Ljay	L	.379	29	11	4	0	2	5	1	3	.400	.724
Throws Right	R	.243	37	9	1	1	2	4	0	6	.263	.486
Nola, Aaron	L	.210	119	25	11	0	2	14	17	36	.312	.353
Throws Right	R	.201	144	29	1	0	7	13	6	60	.238	.354
Norris, Daniel	L	.154	26	4	1	0	1	4	2	11	.214	.308
Throws Left	R	.256	82	21	7	0	1	10	5	17	.299	.378
Nova, Ivan	L	.267	45	12	1	0	2	8	6	3	.353	.422
Throws Right	R	.294	34	10	3	0	2	8	3	6	.351	.559
O'Day, Darren	L	.100	10	1	0	0	0	1	2	3	.357	.100
Throws Right	R	.143	49	7	1	0	1	4	3	19	.208	.224
Odorizzi, Jake	L	.190	21	4	0	0	0	1	2	5	.261	.190
Throws Right	R	.353	34	12	3	0	4	8	1	7	.389	.794
Osich, Josh	L	.212	33	7	0	0	2	6	1	11	.257	.394
Throws Left	R	.304	46	14	1	0	4	5	4	13	.373	.587
Oswalt, Corey	L	.250	24	6	4	0	0	3	1	3	.280	.417
Throws Right	R	.286	28	8	3	0	3	7	1	8	.333	.714
Ottavino, Adam	L	.294	17	5	1	0	0	4	6	6	.458	.353
Throws Right	R	.263	57	15	4	0	2	12	3	19	.311	.439
Oviedo, Johan	L	.200	50	10	2	1	1	8	7	7	.305	.340
Throws Right	R	.311	45	14	4	0	2	9	3	9	.396	.533
Paddack, Chris	L	.270	122	33	4	2	8	18	8	26	.311	.533
Throws Right	R	.252	107	27	8	0	6	13	4	32	.292	.495
Pagan, Emilio	L	.205	39	8	0	1	2	5	5	13	.295	.410
Throws Right	R	.158	38	6	1	0	2	5	4	10	.233	.342
Paredes, Enoli	L	.143	42	6	0	1	0	2	3	8	.217	.190
Throws Right	R	.353	34	12	2	0	1	8	8	12	.465	.500
Parker, Blake	L	.258	31	8	2	1	0	5	6	12	.378	.387
Throws Right	R	.143	28	4	0	0	2	5	3	13	.219	.357
Patino, Luis	L	.188	32	6	1	0	1	3	4	10	.297	.313
Throws Right	R	.316	38	12	0	0	2	7	10	11	.458	.474
Paxton, James	L	.286	21	6	2	0	1	4	0	5	.318	.524
Throws Left	R	.283	60	17	4	1	3	11	7	21	.353	.533
Pazos, James	L	.333	9	3	1	0	2	3	2	1	.455	1.111
Throws Left	R	.500	14	7	2	0	1	5	3	0	.556	.857
Pearson, Nate	L	.313	32	10	1	0	4	8	7	5	.436	.719
Throws Right	R	.114	35	4	0	0	1	4	6	11	.238	.200
Pena, Felix	L	.225	40	9	1	0	0	4	5	8	.326	.250
Throws Right	R	.273	66	18	4	0	2	8	3	21	.304	.424
Peralta, Freddy	L	.186	59	11	3	0	0	6	9	27	.319	.237
Throws Right	R	.224	49	11	4	0	2	10	3	20	.269	.429
Peralta, Wandy	L	.171	41	7	0	1	1	5	5	12	.271	.293
Throws Left	R	.254	59	15	0	1	2	10	6	13	.333	.390
Perdomo, Luis	L	.100	30	3	1	0	0	1	7	9	.270	.133
Throws Right	R	.294	34	10	3	0	3	6	3	7	.351	.647
Perez, Cionel	L	.000	9	0	0	0	0	0	4	5	.308	.000
Throws Left	R	.412	17	7	0	0	0	1	2	3	.474	.412
Perez, Martin	L	.231	39	9	1	0	2	7	6	7	.362	.410
Throws Left	R	.242	190	46	15	0	6	23	22	39	.322	.416
Perez, Oliver	L	.185	27	5	1	0	0	4	1	4	.258	.222
Throws Left	R	.229	35	8	2	0	0	4	5	10	.341	.286
Peterson, David	L	.161	31	5	2	0	0	1	4	10	.278	.226
Throws Left	R	.211	147	31	7	0	5	18	20	30	.314	.361
Petit, Yusmeiro	L	.077	26	2	0	0	0	1	2	4	.143	.077
Throws Right	R	.304	56	17	2	0	3	8	3	13	.333	.500
Phelps, David	L	.190	42	8	0	0	3	8	2	21	.244	.405
Throws Right	R	.311	61	19	1	0	4	6	3	10	.350	.649
Phillips, Evan	L	.158	19	3	0	0	0	1	5	6	.360	.158
Throws Right	R	.297	37	11	0	0	1	7	5	14	.409	.378
Pineda, Michael	L	.308	52	16	4	0	0	5	5	14	.362	.385
Throws Right	R	.184	49	9	2	0	0	5	2	11	.226	.224
Pivetta, Nick	L	.333	27	9	1	1	2	5	3	6	.400	.667
Throws Right	R	.250	36	9	3	0	2	6	3	11	.317	.500
Plesac, Zach	L	.205	88	18	1	1	4	9	4	24	.239	.375
Throws Right	R	.180	111	20	4	0	4	5	2	33	.202	.324
Plutko, Adam	L	.239	46	11	4	0	0	2	3	4	.300	.326
Throws Right	R	.311	61	19	4	0	5	13	4	11	.354	.623
Pomeranz, Drew	L	.143	14	2	0	0	0	0	2	6	.250	.143
Throws Left	R	.146	48	7	0	0	1	5	8	23	.263	.208
Ponce, Cody	L	.212	33	7	2	1	3	3	4	6	.297	.606
Throws Right	R	.185	27	5	1	0	2	4	2	6	.241	.444
Ponce de Leon, Daniel	L	.175	63	11	0	1	3	5	10	22	.307	.349
Throws Right	R	.207	58	12	3	0	5	11	10	23	.324	.517
Poppen, Sean	L	.235	17	4	1	0	0	1	1	6	.278	.294
Throws Right	R	.357	14	5	0	1	0	2	3	4	.471	.500
Porcello, Rick	L	.278	108	30	6	1	6	15	7	23	.322	.361
Throws Right	R	.324	136	44	9	1	4	22	8	31	.370	.493
Pressly, Ryan	L	.227	44	10	3	1	1	7	3	16	.292	.409
Throws Right	R	.282	39	11	0	1	1	5	4	13	.349	.410
Quantrill, Cal	L	.204	54	11	1	0	0	2	5	18	.283	.222
Throws Right	R	.294	68	20	3	0	4	8	3	13	.342	.515
Quijada, Jose	L	.200	10	2	0	0	1	5	1	5	.333	.500
Throws Right	R	.667	6	4	0	0	0	2	1	1	.625	.667
Quintana, Jose	L	.364	11	4	1	0	1	1	0	6	.364	.727
Throws Left	R	.222	27	6	2	0	0	2	3	6	.300	.296
Rainey, Tanner	L	.107	28	3	2	0	1	4	1	9	.138	.286
Throws Right	R	.128	39	5	0	0	3	4	6	23	.261	.359
Raley, Brooks	L	.121	33	4	0	0	1	4	2	14	.194	.212
Throws Left	R	.225	40	9	4	0	2	8	4	13	.340	.475
Ramirez, Erasmo	L	.143	21	3	0	0	0		2	5	.217	.143
Throws Right	R	.179	28	5	1	0	1	1	2	4	.233	.321
Ramirez, Nick	L	.167	6	1	0	0	1	1	0	1	.286	.667
Throws Left	R	.206	34	7	0	0	2	6	4	10	.282	.382
Ramirez, Noe	L	.273	22	6	1	0	1	6	3	0	.360	.455
Throws Right	R	.173	52	9	2	0	1	6	6	14	.267	.269
Ramirez, Yohan	L	.222	27	6	1	0	3	5	8	10	.447	.593
Throws Right	R	.071	42	3	0	0	0	2	12	16	.286	.071
Rasmussen, Drew	L	.375	32	12	3	0	2	8	6	6	.474	.656
Throws Right	R	.167	30	5	0	0	1	4	3	15	.242	.267
Ray, Robbie	L	.207	58	12	1	0	3	8	6	21	.281	.379
Throws Left	R	.283	145	41	13	0	10	26	39	47	.433	.579
Rea, Colin	L	.172	29	5	1	0	0	3	0	7	.172	.207
Throws Right	R	.333	30	10	1	0	3	6	2	3	.364	.667
Reed, Cody	L	.300	10	3	0	0	0	1	4	3	.500	.300
Throws Left	R	.222	36	8	3	0	2	9	4	9	.317	.472
Reid-Foley, Sean	L	.000	7	0	0	0	0	1	3	5	.300	.000
Throws Right	R	.176	17	3	0	0	0	2	3	1	.300	.176
Reyes, Alex	L	.172	29	5	1	0	0	1	9	9	.368	.207
Throws Right	R	.214	42	9	2	0	1	7	5	18	.298	.333
Richards, Garrett	L	.296	98	29	4	0	5	15	11	22	.364	.490
Throws Right	R	.189	95	18	6	1	2	6	6	24	.252	.337
Richards, Trevor	L	.259	54	14	2	0	3	6	5	12	.317	.463
Throws Right	R	.361	83	30	6	0	3	11	6	15	.404	.542
Roark, Tanner	L	.218	87	19	1	2	4	12	15	25	.333	.414
Throws Right	R	.383	107	41	12	0	10	22	8	16	.432	.776
Robles, Hansel	L	.360	25	9	2	0	3	7	5	6	.467	.800
Throws Right	R	.238	42	10	3	0	1	7	5	14	.327	.381
Rodon, Carlos	L	.333	3	1	1	0	0	0	0	0	.500	.667
Throws Left	R	.286	28	8	4	0	1	8	3	6	.355	.536
Rodriguez, Dereck	L	.400	5	2	0	0	0	0	1	1	.500	.400
Throws Right	R	.500	16	8	0	0	2	5	1	1	.556	1.000
Rodriguez, Joely	L	.188	16	3	1	0	0	1	1	7	.235	.250
Throws Left	R	.167	30	5	2	0	0	2	4	10	.265	.233
Rodriguez, Nivaldo	L	.318	22	7	1	0	1	4	3	5	.400	.500
Throws Right	R	.471	17	8	1	0	2	5	3	5	.524	.882
Rodriguez, Richard	L	.140	43	6	0	0	0	4	3	20	.208	.279
Throws Right	R	.220	41	9	1	0	1	4	2	14	.273	.317

Pitchers vs. Left-Handed and Right-Handed Batters

Pitcher	vs	Avg	AB	H	2B	3B	HR	RBI	BB	SO	OBP	Slg
Roe, Chaz	L	.143	7	1	1	0	0	0	0	2	.250	.286
Throws Right	R	.333	27	9	3	0	0	6	3	7	.387	.444
Rogers, Taylor	L	.250	12	3	1	0	0	2	1	5	.308	.333
Throws Left	R	.311	74	23	7	0	2	13	3	19	.346	.486
Rogers, Trevor	L	.265	34	9	4	0	0	3	7	13	.395	.382
Throws Left	R	.291	79	23	6	0	5	17	6	26	.345	.557
Rogers, Tyler	L	.250	40	10	1	0	1	5	4	7	.375	.350
Throws Right	R	.292	72	21	2	1	1	14	2	20	.311	.389
Romano, Jordan	L	.083	24	2	1	0	1	1	1	14	.120	.250
Throws Right	R	.214	28	6	0	0	1	2	4	7	.313	.321
Romero, JoJo	L	.227	22	5	1	0	1	6	2	6	.346	.409
Throws Left	R	.400	20	8	2	0	0	3	0	4	.400	.500
Romo, Sergio	L	.219	32	7	2	0	0	4	4	9	.316	.281
Throws Right	R	.205	44	9	1	0	3	9	3	14	.286	.432
Rondon, Hector	L	.281	32	9	2	0	2	5	5	12	.395	.531
Throws Right	R	.308	52	16	4	2	4	13	6	11	.373	.692
Rosario, Randy	L	.400	5	2	0	0	0	3	2	1	.500	.400
Throws Left	R	.455	11	5	0	0	1	5	1	3	.538	.818
Rosenthal, Trevor	L	.119	42	5	2	0	0	1	5	22	.224	.167
Throws Right	R	.179	39	7	2	1	2	2	3	16	.238	.436
Rosso, Ramon	L	.389	18	7	3	0	1	5	2	2	.450	.722
Throws Right	R	.105	19	2	1	0	0	2	6	9	.346	.158
Ryan, Kyle	L	.240	25	6	1	0	3	6	4	2	.345	.640
Throws Left	R	.286	35	10	2	0	2	4	2	9	.324	.514
Ryu, Hyun-Jin	L	.220	50	11	2	0	1	3	1	11	.250	.320
Throws Left	R	.238	206	49	10	0	5	17	16	61	.293	.359
Sadler, Casey	L	.184	38	7	2	1	1	3	5	14	.279	.368
Throws Right	R	.229	35	8	1	0	2	6	7	7	.357	.429
Samardzija, Jeff	L	.226	31	7	1	0	2	4	4	3	.314	.452
Throws Right	R	.350	40	14	2	0	5	14	0	3	.381	.775
Sanchez, Anibal	L	.300	120	36	6	1	4	12	9	24	.354	.467
Throws Right	R	.327	104	34	7	1	7	20	9	19	.391	.615
Sanchez, Ricardo	L	.000	0	0	0	0	0	0	2	2	.375	.000
Throws Left	R	.333	15	5	2	0	1	6	3	2	.421	.667
Sanchez, Sixto	L	.232	69	16	2	0	6	4	8	20	.270	.261
Throws Right	R	.267	75	20	1	0	3	9	7	15	.345	.400
Sandoval, Patrick	L	.233	60	14	4	0	5	12	5	17	.292	.550
Throws Left	R	.264	87	23	4	0	5	10	7	16	.319	.483
Santana, Dennis	L	.143	21	3	1	0	1	1	3	6	.250	.333
Throws Right	R	.279	43	12	1	0	3	9	4	12	.367	.512
Santos, Antonio	L	.462	13	6	3	1	0	5	3	2	.611	.846
Throws Right	R	.500	16	8	1	0	3	5	2	2	.529	.688
Scherzer, Max	L	.314	137	43	8	1	5	15	12	40	.364	.496
Throws Right	R	.205	132	27	4	0	5	13	11	52	.271	.348
Schmidt, Clarke	L	.231	13	3	1	0	0	4	3	5	.412	.308
Throws Right	R	.308	13	4	1	0	0	3	2	2	.438	.385
Schreiber, John	L	.360	25	9	3	0	1	7	1	5	.385	.600
Throws Right	R	.256	39	10	3	0	1	8	3	9	.318	.410
Scott, Tanner	L	.154	39	6	0	0	1	3	8	13	.340	.231
Throws Left	R	.176	34	6	2	0	0	3	2	10	.222	.235
Scrubb, Andre	L	.211	38	8	1	0	1	3	6	12	.311	.316
Throws Right	R	.171	41	7	0	0	0	4	14	12	.375	.171
Selman, Sam	L	.100	30	3	0	0	1	2	3	14	.206	.200
Throws Left	R	.250	40	10	1	1	1	5	6	9	.362	.400
Senzatela, Antonio	L	.247	150	37	7	2	4	12	14	19	.321	.400
Throws Right	R	.264	129	34	3	1	5	16	4	22	.289	.419
Sewald, Paul	L	.444	9	4	2	0	1	5	1	1	.500	1.000
Throws Right	R	.400	20	8	0	0	6	3	3	1	.480	.400
Shafer, Justin	L	.600	10	6	1	1	1	4	0	1	.583	1.200
Throws Right	R	.143	14	2	0	0	1	1	4	4	.333	.357
Sharp, Sterling	L	.222	9	2	0	0	1	2	4	2	.462	.556
Throws Right	R	.357	14	5	2	1	0	3	1	1	.438	.643
Shaw, Bryan	L	.273	11	3	2	0	0	3	2	4	.385	.455
Throws Right	R	.526	19	10	1	2	1	11	4	0	.600	.947
Sheffield, Justus	L	.154	52	8	1	0	0	0	4	14	.228	.173
Throws Left	R	.284	155	44	4	0	2	17	16	34	.354	.348
Sherriff, Ryan	L	.154	13	2	0	0	0	0	0	1	.154	.154
Throws Left	R	.211	19	4	0	0	0	2	1	1	.286	.211
Shoemaker, Matt	L	.194	62	12	2	0	5	9	5	15	.254	.468
Throws Right	R	.233	43	10	1	0	3	6	4	11	.298	.465
Shreve, Chasen	L	.063	32	2	0	0	2	3	8	12	.250	.250
Throws Left	R	.263	57	15	4	0	2	11	4	22	.306	.439
Sims, Lucas	L	.106	47	5	1	0	3	8	4	24	.208	.319
Throws Right	R	.190	42	8	3	0	1	5	6	10	.320	.262
Singer, Brady	L	.217	129	28	4	1	4	16	16	32	.313	.357
Throws Right	R	.224	107	24	2	0	4	10	7	29	.267	.355

Pitcher	vs	Avg	AB	H	2B	3B	HR	RBI	BB	SO	OBP	Slg
Skubal, Tarik	L	.136	22	3	0	0	0	0	2	6	.208	.136
Throws Left	R	.258	97	25	4	0	9	18	9	31	.327	.577
Slegers, Aaron	L	.222	36	8	0	0	0	4	3	6	.282	.222
Throws Right	R	.175	57	10	1	0	1	5	2	13	.230	.246
Smeltzer, Devin	L	.385	13	5	0	0	0	2	1	1	.467	.385
Throws Left	R	.269	52	14	4	1	2	10	4	14	.321	.500
Smith, Burch	L	.231	13	3	0	0	0	0	1	5	.286	.231
Throws Right	R	.133	30	4	2	0	1	3	0	8	.133	.300
Smith, Caleb	L	.143	14	2	0	0	1	1	1	6	.200	.357
Throws Left	R	.118	34	4	0	0	2	3	11	9	.333	.294
Smith, Drew	L	.182	11	2	0	0	0	1	1	3	.250	.182
Throws Right	R	.250	16	4	1	0	2	7	1	4	.294	.688
Smith, Josh A.	L	.293	41	12	4	0	0	5	8	8	.400	.390
Throws Right	R	.328	64	21	6	0	3	20	3	10	.357	.563
Smith, Riley	L	.143	21	3	0	0	1	4	0	9	.143	.286
Throws Right	R	.279	43	12	2	0	0	1	5	9	.354	.326
Smith, Will	L	.200	20	4	0	0	2	2	1	6	.238	.500
Throws Left	R	.184	38	7	0	0	5	6	3	12	.244	.579
Smyly, Drew	L	.083	36	3	1	0	0	3	3	14	.154	.111
Throws Left	R	.262	65	17	3	0	2	6	6	28	.319	.400
Sneed, Cy	L	.357	28	10	2	0	2	6	10	6	.526	.643
Throws Right	R	.279	43	12	5	0	1	12	0	15	.279	.465
Snell, Blake	L	.217	46	10	2	0	3	4	1	20	.234	.457
Throws Left	R	.232	138	32	5	0	7	11	17	43	.316	.420
Sobotka, Chad	L	.500	6	3	1	0	0	4	0	1	.500	.667
Throws Right	R	.250	12	3	2	0	0	2	2	1	.357	.417
Soria, Joakim	L	.130	23	3	0	0	0	1	3	7	.231	.130
Throws Right	R	.250	60	15	3	0	1	6	7	17	.314	.350
Soroka, Mike	L	.308	26	8	1	0	0	3	2	3	.379	.346
Throws Right	R	.130	23	3	0	0	0	0	5	5	.286	.130
Soto, Gregory	L	.095	21	2	0	0	0	1	4	11	.296	.095
Throws Left	R	.226	62	14	2	0	2	5	9	18	.324	.355
Sparkman, Glenn	L	.571	7	4	1	0	0	3	1	0	.556	.714
Throws Right	R	.278	18	5	1	0	0	2	0	2	.278	.333
Speier, Gabe	L	.000	9	0	0	0	0	0	2	4	.182	.000
Throws Left	R	.529	17	9	2	0	1	2	2	2	.579	.824
Springs, Jeffrey	L	.316	38	12	2	0	2	11	3	11	.357	.526
Throws Left	R	.346	52	18	6	0	3	13	4	17	.404	.635
Stammen, Craig	L	.262	42	11	1	0	0	7	1	7	.311	.286
Throws Right	R	.291	55	16	3	0	2	10	3	13	.328	.455
Stanek, Ryne	L	.556	9	5	1	0	1	2	2	1	.636	1.000
Throws Right	R	.194	31	6	0	0	2	5	6	10	.324	.387
Stashak, Cody	L	.154	26	4	1	0	0	1	3	7	.241	.192
Throws Right	R	.250	28	7	3	0	2	4	0	10	.250	.571
Staumont, Josh	L	.268	41	11	1	0	1	3	10	16	.423	.366
Throws Right	R	.173	52	9	0	0	1	4	6	21	.283	.231
Stephenson, Robert	L	.263	19	5	0	0	4	4	1	5	.333	.895
Throws Right	R	.300	20	6	0	0	4	5	2	8	.364	.900
Stiever, Jonathan	L	.286	14	4	0	0	3	5	3	2	.412	.929
Throws Right	R	.273	11	3	0	0	1	2	1	1	.333	.545
Stock, Robert	L	.217	23	5	3	0	0	5	7	8	.400	.348
Throws Right	R	.407	27	11	1	0	0	6	3	6	.452	.444
Strahm, Matt	L	.116	43	5	0	0	2	3	1	10	.156	.256
Throws Left	R	.290	31	9	2	0	1	7	3	5	.421	.452
Strasburg, Stephen	L	.400	10	4	0	0	1	3	0	2	.400	.700
Throws Right	R	.333	12	4	1	0	0	3	1	0	.385	.417
Stratton, Chris	L	.204	54	11	3	0	1	7	6	17	.279	.315
Throws Right	R	.242	62	15	3	0	2	10	7	22	.314	.387
Stripling, Ross	L	.220	100	22	5	0	6	13	9	25	.284	.450
Throws Right	R	.343	99	34	5	1	7	21	9	15	.404	.626
Suarez, Andrew	L	.214	14	3	2	0	0	1	5	2	.421	.357
Throws Left	R	.273	22	6	1	0	1	4	1	3	.304	.455
Suarez, Jose	L	.750	4	3	1	0	0	3	2	0	.833	1.000
Throws Left	R	.538	13	7	1	0	1	4	3	2	.647	.846
Suarez, Ranger	L	.500	8	4	0	0	2	3	0	1	.600	.500
Throws Left	R	.462	13	6	2	0	1	5	2	1	.563	.846
Suero, Wander	L	.163	43	7	2	0	0	4	6	13	.280	.209
Throws Right	R	.289	45	13	3	0	1	10	4	15	.365	.422
Sulser, Cole	L	.143	42	6	3	0	0	6	6	11	.250	.214
Throws Right	R	.282	39	11	1	1	2	9	11	8	.440	.513
Suter, Brent	L	.250	40	10	2	0	2	4	0	11	.268	.450
Throws Left	R	.241	83	20	1	0	2	11	5	27	.284	.325
Swanson, Erik	L	.353	17	6	1	0	1	4	0	5	.333	.588
Throws Right	R	.333	15	5	1	0	2	4	2	4	.407	.800
Tanaka, Masahiro	L	.188	96	18	3	1	6	12	4	24	.228	.427
Throws Right	R	.330	91	30	5	0	3	8	4	20	.365	.484

476

Pitchers vs. Left-Handed and Right-Handed Batters

Pitcher	vs	Avg	AB	H	2B	3B	HR	RBI	BB	SO	OBP	Slg
Tarpley, Stephen	L	.316	19	6	2	0	0	3	2	7	.417	.421
Throws Left	R	.250	20	5	1	0	2	6	6	4	.444	.600
Tate, Dillon	L	.294	17	5	0	0	1	3	4	2	.435	.471
Throws Right	R	.105	38	4	1	0	0	2	1	12	.146	.132
Taylor, Blake	L	.171	35	6	0	0	1	3	5	7	.275	.257
Throws Left	R	.175	40	7	2	0	1	5	7	10	.298	.300
Taylor, Josh	L	.182	11	2	1	0	0	0	3	3	.400	.273
Throws Left	R	.263	19	5	1	0	2	7	2	4	.333	.632
Teheran, Julio	L	.284	67	19	2	1	9	18	11	9	.375	.746
Throws Right	R	.328	61	20	3	0	3	11	5	11	.391	.525
Tepera, Ryan	L	.188	32	6	1	0	1	6	6	13	.325	.313
Throws Right	R	.256	43	11	2	0	1	8	6	18	.347	.372
Thielbar, Caleb	L	.136	22	3	0	0	0	1	3	7	.240	.136
Throws Left	R	.216	51	11	2	0	0	2	6	15	.298	.255
Thompson, Ryan	L	.250	32	8	2	0	0	2	4	3	.333	.313
Throws Right	R	.284	74	21	2	0	4	8	4	20	.321	.473
Thornburg, Tyler	L	.235	17	4	1	0	0	1	3	6	.350	.294
Throws Right	R	.200	10	2	0	0	0	1	2	4	.333	.200
Thornton, Trent	L	.385	13	5	2	0	0	3	2	4	.438	.538
Throws Right	R	.625	16	10	1	0	0	2	1	2	.647	.688
Thorpe, Lewis	L	.444	9	4	0	0	2	4	0	3	.444	1.111
Throws Left	R	.345	58	20	4	0	2	9	10	7	.441	.517
Tomlin, Josh	L	.231	65	15	3	0	2	10	6	16	.292	.369
Throws Right	R	.287	87	25	5	0	4	13	2	20	.311	.483
Topa, Justin	L	.273	11	3	1	0	1	2	0	6	.273	.636
Throws Right	R	.211	19	4	1	0	0	1	0	6	.211	.263
Toussaint, Touki	L	.255	47	12	3	1	3	11	10	14	.407	.553
Throws Right	R	.294	51	15	1	0	4	12	6	16	.400	.549
Treinen, Blake	L	.233	30	7	2	0	0	2	5	9	.368	.300
Throws Right	R	.242	66	16	2	0	1	10	3	13	.275	.318
Triggs, Andrew	L	.105	19	2	0	0	0	0	4	5	.261	.105
Throws Right	R	.429	14	6	0	0	3	4	2	2	.500	1.071
Trivino, Lou	L	.235	34	8	2	0	2	8	3	11	.297	.471
Throws Right	R	.163	49	8	0	0	1	6	7	15	.268	.224
Tropeano, Nick	L	.067	15	1	1	0	0	1	2	4	.176	.133
Throws Right	R	.289	45	13	5	0	1	6	2	15	.333	.467
Turley, Nik	L	.227	22	5	2	0	1	6	7	8	.419	.455
Throws Left	R	.151	53	8	4	0	0	8	4	12	.230	.226
Turnbull, Spencer	L	.218	119	26	8	2	0	11	19	27	.331	.319
Throws Right	R	.236	89	21	5	0	2	12	10	24	.317	.360
Underwood Jr., Duane	L	.289	38	11	3	0	3	6	4	12	.364	.605
Throws Right	R	.333	42	14	3	0	2	10	2	15	.364	.548
Urena, Jose	L	.406	32	13	1	1	3	9	2	1	.457	.781
Throws Right	R	.158	57	9	1	0	1	5	11	14	.304	.228
Urias, Julio	L	.137	51	7	2	0	2	7	4	14	.196	.294
Throws Left	R	.247	154	38	5	0	3	12	14	31	.310	.338
Urquidy, Jose	L	.136	59	8	0	0	1	3	3	10	.190	.186
Throws Right	R	.292	48	14	1	0	3	5	5	7	.358	.500
Valdez, Cesar	L	.190	21	4	2	1	0	2	1	2	.217	.381
Throws Right	R	.107	28	3	0	0	0	1	2	10	.167	.107
Valdez, Framber	L	.243	70	17	1	2	0	8	5	26	.304	.314
Throws Left	R	.238	193	46	5	1	5	17	11	50	.288	.352
Valdez, Phillips	L	.175	40	7	3	0	0	3	10	12	.333	.250
Throws Right	R	.338	77	26	1	1	3	14	6	18	.407	.494
Velasquez, Vince	L	.315	54	17	3	0	2	5	10	16	.422	.481
Throws Right	R	.238	80	19	5	0	3	13	7	30	.322	.413
Verlander, Justin	L	.154	13	2	0	0	1	1	1	3	.214	.385
Throws Right	R	.143	7	1	0	0	1	1	0	4	.143	.571
Vesia, Alex	L	.400	10	4	0	0	1	1	3	1	.538	.700
Throws Left	R	.300	10	3	0	0	2	5	4	4	.500	.900
Vincent, Nick	L	.219	32	7	1	0	2	5	1	6	.265	.438
Throws Right	R	.302	53	16	5	0	3	8	5	11	.362	.566
Volquez, Edinson	L	.273	11	3	1	0	0	1	1	1	.333	.364
Throws Right	R	.250	12	3	0	0	0	0	1	2	.357	.250
Voth, Austin	L	.295	95	28	8	1	4	11	9	15	.356	.526
Throws Right	R	.269	108	29	7	0	10	22	9	29	.347	.611
Wacha, Michael	L	.275	69	19	3	1	3	9	5	20	.333	.478
Throws Right	R	.346	78	27	8	1	6	16	2	17	.370	.705
Waguespack, Jacob	L	.282	39	11	0	0	0	3	6	8	.391	.282
Throws Right	R	.410	39	16	4	0	2	17	3	8	.455	.667
Wainwright, Adam	L	.217	120	26	2	0	7	15	7	22		.408
Throws Right	R	.226	124	28	7	0	2	8	8	32	.284	.331
Walden, Marcus	L	.393	28	11	1	2	2	9	1	6	.414	.786
Throws Right	R	.353	34	12	2	1	3	11	8	4	.476	.735
Walker, Taijuan	L	.265	83	22	3	0	6	12	9	22	.351	.518
Throws Right	R	.178	118	21	4	0	2	7	10	28	.252	.263
Watson, Tony	L	.174	23	4	0	0	1	4	2	5	.259	.304
Throws Left	R	.200	45	9	1	0	2	4	1	10	.217	.356
Weaver, Luke	L	.320	103	33	5	0	7	20	11	26	.388	.573
Throws Right	R	.265	113	30	11	2	3	16	7	29	.308	.478
Webb, Jacob	L	.000	10	0	0	0	0	0	4	4	.286	.000
Throws Right	R	.280	25	7	1	0	0	1	1	6	.308	.320
Webb, Logan	L	.291	103	30	7	0	2	21	10	22	.368	.417
Throws Right	R	.284	109	31	9	1	2	12	14	24	.386	.440
Webb, Tyler	L	.100	30	3	0	0	0	1	4	8	.206	.100
Throws Left	R	.292	48	14	2	0	2	9	3	11	.327	.458
Weber, Ryan	L	.227	75	17	5	0	4	8	9	11	.326	.453
Throws Right	R	.297	91	27	6	0	4	14	5	16	.337	.495
Weems, Jordan	L	.273	22	6	1	0	0	3	3	9	.346	.318
Throws Right	R	.143	28	4	1	0	1	2	4	9	.250	.286
Wendelken, J.B.	L	.194	36	7	2	0	1	5	7	12	.326	.333
Throws Right	R	.175	57	10	1	0	1	8	4	19	.226	.246
Wheeler, Zack	L	.250	136	34	9	0	1	13	10	26	.311	.338
Throws Right	R	.258	128	33	7	0	2	10	6	27	.317	.359
Wick, Rowan	L	.290	31	9	2	0	0	7	5	7	.389	.355
Throws Right	R	.243	37	9	4	0	1	4	1	13	.263	.432
Widener, Taylor	L	.265	34	9	1	1	3	8	4	9	.359	.618
Throws Right	R	.128	39	5	1	0	2	3	8	13	.306	.308
Williams, Devin	L	.075	53	4	1	0	1	1	8	30	.197	.151
Throws Right	R	.111	36	4	0	1	0	1	1	23	.158	.167
Williams, Taylor	L	.214	28	6	2	0	0	5	3	11	.290	.286
Throws Right	R	.276	29	8	1	0	1	6	4	9	.417	.414
Williams, Trevor	L	.260	127	33	5	0	5	14	11	27	.329	.417
Throws Right	R	.344	96	33	5	0	10	24	10	22	.405	.708
Wilson, Bryse	L	.429	21	9	2	0	0	2	2	3	.478	.524
Throws Right	R	.214	42	9	0	1	2	4	7	12	.340	.405
Wilson, Justin	L	.115	26	3	0	0	1	2	2	7	.207	.231
Throws Left	R	.306	49	15	1	0	0	3	7	16	.393	.327
Winkler, Dan	L	.100	20	2	0	0	0		2	6	.357	.100
Throws Right	R	.209	43	9	0	0	3	4	4	12	.277	.419
Wisler, Matt	L	.121	33	4	1	0	0	5	8	11	.293	.152
Throws Right	R	.190	58	11	1	0	2	4	6	24	.288	.345
Wittgren, Nick	L	.178	45	8	3	0	1	6	3	13	.245	.311
Throws Right	R	.244	41	10	2	0	3	4	3	15	.354	.512
Wojciechowski, Asher	L	.293	75	22	6	0	5	12	8	17	.365	.573
Throws Right	R	.324	71	23	3	0	6	16	7	14	.370	.620
Wood, Alex	L	.300	20	6	2	0	0	0	1	6	.364	.400
Throws Left	R	.306	36	11	4	0	2	12	5	9	.419	.583
Woodford, Jake	L	.194	36	7	0	0	1	2	3	6	.256	.278
Throws Right	R	.302	43	13	1	0	6	12	2	10	.326	.744
Woodruff, Brandon	L	.194	170	33	6	1	6	17	9	54	.243	.347
Throws Right	R	.220	100	22	2	0	3	8	9	37	.295	.330
Workman, Brandon	L	.318	44	14	2	1	3	11	6	13	.400	.614
Throws Right	R	.386	44	17	3	0	1	7	7	10	.471	.523
Wright, Kyle	L	.288	73	21	5	0	4	11	14	14	.402	.521
Throws Right	R	.197	71	14	1	0	3	9	10	16	.296	.338
Yajure, Miguel	L	.200	10	2	0	0	1	1	3	4	.429	.500
Throws Right	R	.077	13	1	0	0	0	0	2	4	.200	.077
Yamaguchi, Shun	L	.238	42	10	2	2	3	12	6	9	.340	.595
Throws Right	R	.316	57	18	3	0	3	10	11	17	.429	.526
Yamamoto, Jordan	L	.500	22	11	3	1	4	13	3	7	.538	1.273
Throws Right	R	.432	37	16	2	0	4	10	4	6	.488	.811
Yarbrough, Ryan	L	.259	54	14	2	0	1	3	4	11	.333	.352
Throws Left	R	.255	157	40	8	0	4	19	8	33	.308	.382
Yardley, Eric	L	.243	37	9	2	0	0	6	4	10	.326	.297
Throws Right	R	.208	48	10	3	0	2	3	6	9	.296	.396
Yates, Kirby	L	.417	12	5	0	0	1	5	2	4	.467	.667
Throws Right	R	.250	8	2	0	0	0	0	2	4	.400	.250
Ynoa, Huascar	L	.226	31	7	1	0	0	5	10	4	.405	.258
Throws Right	R	.308	52	16	5	0	2	6	3	13	.362	.519
Young, Alex	L	.241	54	13	1	0	2	5	3	12	.302	.370
Throws Left	R	.292	130	38	12	2	9	21	9	27	.333	.623
Zeuch, T.J.	L	.400	10	4	2	0	0	0	2	0	.500	.600
Throws Right	R	.152	33	5	1	0	1	2	2	3	.200	.273
Zimmer, Kyle	L	.150	40	6	1	0	0	1	7	15	.277	.175
Throws Right	R	.200	40	8	6	0	0	1	3	11	.273	.350
Zimmermann, Bruce	L	.250	8	2	0	0	0	0	2	5	.400	.250
Throws Left	R	.211	19	4	0	0	2	4	0	2	.286	.526
Zimmermann, Jordan	L	.563	16	9	2	0	0	4	2	3	.611	.688
Throws Right	R	.200	10	2	0	0	0	0	2	0	.200	.200
Zuber, Tyler	L	.270	37	10	1	0	1	4	9	13	.417	.378
Throws Right	R	.128	39	5	0	0	3	7	11	17	.320	.359

Pitchers vs. Left-Handed and Right-Handed Batters

Pitcher	vs	Avg	AB	H	2B	3B	HR	RBI	BB	SO	OBP	Slg
AL	L	.232	-	-	-	-	-	-	-	-	.319	.392
	R	.253	-	-	-	-	-	-	-	-	.322	.432
NL	L	.239	-	-	-	-	-	-	-	-	.323	.412
	R	.249	-	-	-	-	-	-	-	-	.323	.425
MLB	L	.236	-	-	-	-	-	-	-	-	.321	.402
	R	.251	-	-	-	-	-	-	-	-	.323	.429

2020 Leaderboards

Brian Reiff

Often in this section we like to highlight the achievements of individual players. Mike Trout and Christian Yelich have both taken their turns in the spotlight in recent years, and it's hard to argue that neither was deserved.

This year, though, I wanted to place the attention back on the leaderboards themselves. Browsing through the following pages, there is an abundance of information sure to win you a couple of bar bets. (Note: If you're reading this in 2020, please stop going to bars, at least ones without outdoor seating. If you're reading this after 2020, how is it there? Is it nice?)

One of the favorites I noticed is the National League Games leaderboard. Generally, the top of the leaderboard will be a tie with everyone who played in every game of the season. Starling Marte, however, decided to break the rules, playing 61 games in this 60-game season thanks to a mid-season team change and consequently finding himself alone at the top.

More relevant might be the American League Caught Stealing Percentage leaderboard, which shows Roberto Pérez leading the league by catching nine of the 13 runners (69%) who tried to steal against him. On its own, it's impressive, but with added context it's even more so; since 2002 (when Baseball Info Solutions first started collecting data), no catcher has had a higher caught stealing percentage when facing at least five attempts.

Finally, on the final page of this section, you will find new leaderboards related to the Batter Game Scores that Bill recently devised. There are separate leaderboards for the best and worst batter game scores of the season in both the AL and NL (and you'll find their pitching game score counterparts on the previous pages). You can read about the details of the batter game score system in Bill's article at the beginning of this book as well as in the Glossary at the end.

2020 American League Batting Leaders

Batting Average
(minimum 186 PA)

LeMahieu, DJ	.364
Anderson, Tim	.322
Fletcher, David	.319
Abreu, Jose	.317
Verdugo, Alex	.308
Gurriel Jr., Lourdes	.308
Cruz, Nelson	.303
Bogaerts, Xander	.300
Brantley, Michael	.300
Candelario, Jeimer	.297

On Base Percentage
(minimum 186 PA)

LeMahieu, DJ	.421
Rendon, Anthony	.418
Cruz, Nelson	.397
Trout, Mike	.390
Canha, Mark	.387
Ramirez, Jose	.386
Hicks, Aaron	.379
Fletcher, David	.376
Biggio, Cavan	.375
Abreu, Jose	.370

Slugging Average
(minimum 186 PA)

Abreu, Jose	.617
Voit, Luke	.610
Ramirez, Jose	.607
Trout, Mike	.603
Cruz, Nelson	.595
LeMahieu, DJ	.590
Hernandez, Teoscar	.579
Jimenez, Eloy	.559
Lowe, Brandon	.554
Springer, George	.540

Home Runs

Voit, Luke	22
Abreu, Jose	19
Ramirez, Jose	17
Trout, Mike	17
Cruz, Nelson	16
Hernandez, Teoscar	16
Jimenez, Eloy	14
Lowe, Brandon	14
Olson, Matt	14
Springer, George	14

Games

Abreu, Jose	60
Franco, Maikel	60
Guerrero Jr., Vladimir	60
Lindor, Francisco	60
Merrifield, Whit	60
Olson, Matt	60
Santana, Carlos	60
Seager, Kyle	60
4 tied with	59

Plate Appearances

Lindor, Francisco	266
Biggio, Cavan	265
Merrifield, Whit	265
Abreu, Jose	262
Hernandez, Cesar	261
Santana, Carlos	255
Ramirez, Jose	254
Devers, Rafael	248
Seager, Kyle	248
Olson, Matt	245

At Bats

Merrifield, Whit	248
Abreu, Jose	240
Lindor, Francisco	236
Hernandez, Cesar	233
Devers, Rafael	232
Franco, Maikel	223
Guerrero Jr., Vladimir	221
Biggio, Cavan	220
3 tied with	219

Hits

Abreu, Jose	76
LeMahieu, DJ	71
Merrifield, Whit	70
Anderson, Tim	67
Fletcher, David	66
Hernandez, Cesar	66
Gurriel Jr., Lourdes	64
Ramirez, Jose	64
Jimenez, Eloy	63
3 tied with	62

Singles

Fletcher, David	50
Kiner-Falefa, Isiah	49
LeMahieu, DJ	49
Merrifield, Whit	49
Anderson, Tim	45
Alberto, Hanser	44
Solak, Nick	44
Hernandez, Cesar	43
Reyes, Victor	43
3 tied with	42

Doubles

Hernandez, Cesar	20
Iglesias, Jose	17
Biggio, Cavan	16
Devers, Rafael	16
Franco, Maikel	16
Martinez, J.D.	16
Ramirez, Jose	16
Verdugo, Alex	16
4 tied with	15

Triples

Tucker, Kyle	6
Candelario, Jeimer	3
Kiermaier, Kevin	3
Kiner-Falefa, Isiah	3
Moncada, Yoan	3
Mondesi, Adalberto	3
Mullins II, Cedric	3
23 tied with	2

Total Bases

Abreu, Jose	148
Ramirez, Jose	133
Voit, Luke	130
Trout, Mike	120
Jimenez, Eloy	119
LeMahieu, DJ	115
Devers, Rafael	112
Gurriel Jr., Lourdes	111
3 tied with	110

Runs Scored

Anderson, Tim	45
Ramirez, Jose	45
Abreu, Jose	43
Biggio, Cavan	41
LeMahieu, DJ	41
Trout, Mike	41
Voit, Luke	41
Grichuk, Randal	38
Merrifield, Whit	38
2 tied with	37

RBI

Abreu, Jose	60
Voit, Luke	52
Ramirez, Jose	46
Trout, Mike	46
Devers, Rafael	43
Olson, Matt	42
Rosario, Eddie	42
Tucker, Kyle	42
Jimenez, Eloy	41
Seager, Kyle	40

Walks

Santana, Carlos	47
Biggio, Cavan	41
Hicks, Aaron	41
Rendon, Anthony	38
Canha, Mark	37
Trout, Mike	35
Lewis, Kyle	34
Olson, Matt	34
Seager, Kyle	32
Ramirez, Jose	31

Strikeouts

Sano, Miguel	90
White, Evan	84
Gallo, Joey	79
Olson, Matt	77
Adames, Willy	74
Robert, Luis	73
Moncada, Yoan	72
Lewis, Kyle	71
Mondesi, Adalberto	70
2 tied with	69

2020 American League Batting Leaders

Intentional Walks

Cruz, Nelson	5
Trout, Mike	4
Martinez, J.D.	3
Santander, Anthony	3
Seager, Kyle	3
Tauchman, Mike	3
12 tied with	2

BA Bases Loaded
(minimum 4 PA)

Gonzalez, Marwin	1.000
Solak, Nick	1.000
Bonifacio, Jorge	.800
Gurriel, Yuli	.667
Tucker, Kyle	.667
Upton, Justin	.667
8 tied with	.600

Sacrifice Hits

DeShields, Delino	4
McGuire, Reese	4
Mullins II, Cedric	4
Velazquez, Andrew	4
Jansen, Danny	3
Lopez, Nicky	3
9 tied with	2

Sacrifice Flies

Seager, Kyle	6
Canha, Mark	5
Gurriel, Yuli	5
Reyes, Franmil	5
Franco, Maikel	4
Gonzalez, Marwin	4
Solak, Nick	4
Trout, Mike	4
Urshela, Gio	4
5 tied with	3

BA Close & Late
(minimum 19 PA)

Kemp, Tony	.467
Severino, Pedro	.440
Dozier, Hunter	.412
Canha, Mark	.391
Laureano, Ramon	.391
Mazara, Nomar	.389
Fletcher, David	.370
Naquin, Tyler	.350
Choi, Ji-Man	.333
Soler, Jorge	.333

Batting Average w/ RISP
(minimum 38 PA)

Iglesias, Jose	.421
Castro, Willi	.400
Fletcher, David	.400
Cabrera, Miguel	.390
O'Hearn, Ryan	.387
Hernandez, Cesar	.386
Maldonado, Martin	.375
LeMahieu, DJ	.364
Brantley, Michael	.359
Rosario, Eddie	.353

SLG vs. LHP
(minimum 47 PA)

Anderson, Tim	1.000
Ramirez, Jose	.930
Cruz, Nelson	.907
Brosseau, Mike	.738
Lowe, Brandon	.720
Mondesi, Adalberto	.698
Stassi, Max	.659
Hernandez, Teoscar	.608
Voit, Luke	.604
Adames, Willy	.596

SLG vs. RHP
(minimum 140 PA)

Trout, Mike	.664
Abreu, Jose	.633
Voit, Luke	.612
LeMahieu, DJ	.600
Devers, Rafael	.570
Hernandez, Teoscar	.568
Jimenez, Eloy	.560
Springer, George	.553
Tucker, Kyle	.550
Rosario, Eddie	.548

Leadoff Hitters OBP
(minimum 56 PA)

LeMahieu, DJ	.423
Biggio, Cavan	.390
Fletcher, David	.371
Verdugo, Alex	.362
La Stella, Tommy	.361
Springer, George	.358
Anderson, Tim	.357
Kepler, Max	.340
Meadows, Austin	.337
Hernandez, Cesar	.333

Cleanup Hitters SLG
(minimum 56 PA)

Abreu, Jose	.690
Chapman, Matt	.672
Hernandez, Teoscar	.644
Nunez, Renato	.587
Bogaerts, Xander	.566
Rendon, Anthony	.560
Stanton, Giancarlo	.533
Rosario, Eddie	.533
Candelario, Jeimer	.525
Canha, Mark	.522

BA vs. LHP
(minimum 47 PA)

Cruz, Nelson	.465
Anderson, Tim	.449
Ramirez, Jose	.386
Alberto, Hanser	.375
Bogaerts, Xander	.375
Kiner-Falefa, Isiah	.373
Fletcher, David	.348
Polanco, Jorge	.345
Brosseau, Mike	.333
Canha, Mark	.333

BA vs. RHP
(minimum 140 PA)

LeMahieu, DJ	.355
Abreu, Jose	.335
Gurriel Jr., Lourdes	.317
Fletcher, David	.304
La Stella, Tommy	.303
Jimenez, Eloy	.298
Hernandez, Cesar	.297
Hernandez, Teoscar	.295
Trout, Mike	.295
Tucker, Kyle	.293

Home BA
(minimum 93 PA)

LeMahieu, DJ	.423
Trout, Mike	.344
Mondesi, Adalberto	.330
Guerrero Jr., Vladimir	.323
Voit, Luke	.319
Ramirez, Jose	.317
Verdugo, Alex	.314
Hernandez, Cesar	.313
Jimenez, Eloy	.313
Franco, Maikel	.312

Away BA
(minimum 93 PA)

Gurriel Jr., Lourdes	.350
Fletcher, David	.343
Anderson, Tim	.333
Adames, Willy	.330
Merrifield, Whit	.328
Abreu, Jose	.328
Bogaerts, Xander	.327
Candelario, Jeimer	.327
Alberto, Hanser	.324
Reyes, Franmil	.312

OBP vs. LHP
(minimum 47 PA)

Cruz, Nelson	.549
Anderson, Tim	.509
Canha, Mark	.482
Ramirez, Jose	.478
Biggio, Cavan	.460
Rendon, Anthony	.425
Kiner-Falefa, Isiah	.424
Bogaerts, Xander	.420
Lowe, Brandon	.417
Fletcher, David	.416

OBP vs. RHP
(minimum 140 PA)

Rendon, Anthony	.415
LeMahieu, DJ	.413
Trout, Mike	.404
La Stella, Tommy	.393
Seager, Kyle	.387
Abreu, Jose	.385
Hicks, Aaron	.382
Springer, George	.376
Hernandez, Cesar	.373
Lewis, Kyle	.366

2020 American League Batting Leaders

Stolen Bases

Mondesi, Adalberto	24
Margot, Manuel	12
Merrifield, Whit	12
Moore, Dylan	12
Ramirez, Jose	10
Robert, Luis	9
8 tied with	8

Caught Stealing

Mondesi, Adalberto	8
Kiner-Falefa, Isiah	5
Lopez, Nicky	5
Moore, Dylan	5
Margot, Manuel	4
7 tied with	3

Highest SB Success Pct
(minimum 8 SBA)

Bogaerts, Xander	100.0
Taveras, Leody	100.0
Grossman, Robbie	88.9
Kiermaier, Kevin	88.9
Tucker, Kyle	88.9
Goodrum, Niko	87.5
Ohtani, Shohei	87.5
Solak, Nick	87.5
Robert, Luis	81.8
3 tied with	80.0

Lowest SB Success Pct
(minimum 8 SBA)

Kiner-Falefa, Isiah	61.5
Crawford, J.P.	66.7
Moore, Dylan	70.6
Choo, Shin-Soo	75.0
Lindor, Francisco	75.0
Margot, Manuel	75.0
Mondesi, Adalberto	75.0
Straw, Myles	75.0
Ramirez, Jose	76.9
Mullins II, Cedric	77.8

Steals of Third

Mondesi, Adalberto	6
Merrifield, Whit	4
Bogaerts, Xander	3
Hernandez, Teoscar	3
Wendle, Joey	3
6 tied with	2

Grounded Into DP

Abreu, Jose	10
Rendon, Anthony	10
Cruz, Nelson	8
Devers, Rafael	8
Lindor, Francisco	8
Schoop, Jonathan	8
Gurriel Jr., Lourdes	7
Laureano, Ramon	7
Polanco, Jorge	7
15 tied with	6

Grounded Into DP Pct
(minimum 19 GIDP Ops)

14 tied with	0.00

Hit By Pitch

Laureano, Ramon	12
Canha, Mark	10
Moore, Dylan	8
Seager, Kyle	7
Toro, Abraham	7
Upton, Justin	7
Sisco, Chance	6
8 tied with	5

Pitches Seen

Ramirez, Jose	1146
Santana, Carlos	1123
Lindor, Francisco	1118
Biggio, Cavan	1112
Hernandez, Cesar	1077
Canha, Mark	1063
Abreu, Jose	1027
Trout, Mike	1023
Olson, Matt	1002
Merrifield, Whit	996

At Bats Per Home Run
(minimum 186 PA)

Voit, Luke	9.7
Cruz, Nelson	11.6
Trout, Mike	11.7
Hernandez, Teoscar	11.9
Abreu, Jose	12.6
Ramirez, Jose	12.9
Springer, George	13.5
Lowe, Brandon	13.8
Sano, Miguel	14.3
Olson, Matt	15.0

Highest GB/FB Ratio
(minimum 186 PA)

Lopez, Nicky	2.88
Kiner-Falefa, Isiah	2.85
LeMahieu, DJ	2.68
Fletcher, David	2.63
Anderson, Tim	2.07
Guerrero Jr., Vladimir	1.96
Verdugo, Alex	1.91
Bradley Jr., Jackie	1.90
Jimenez, Eloy	1.82
Hernandez, Cesar	1.79

Lowest GB/FB Ratio
(minimum 186 PA)

Gallo, Joey	0.48
Trout, Mike	0.50
Ramirez, Jose	0.59
Semien, Marcus	0.71
Kepler, Max	0.71
Nunez, Renato	0.71
Seager, Kyle	0.73
Rosario, Eddie	0.76
Lowe, Brandon	0.76
Olson, Matt	0.79

Pitches Per Plate App
(minimum 186 PA)

Ramirez, Jose	4.51
Grandal, Yasmani	4.43
Santana, Carlos	4.40
Canha, Mark	4.37
Hicks, Aaron	4.35
Bogaerts, Xander	4.30
Moncada, Yoan	4.25
Trout, Mike	4.25
Sano, Miguel	4.24
Gallo, Joey	4.23

Pct Pitches Taken
(minimum 555 Pitches)

Grandal, Yasmani	66.0
Frazier, Clint	64.7
Diaz, Yandy	64.4
Bregman, Alex	63.9
Biggio, Cavan	63.7
Santana, Carlos	63.7
Trout, Mike	63.3
Fletcher, David	62.8
Gardner, Brett	62.6
Canha, Mark	62.0

Best BPS on OutZ
(minimum 186 PA)

Fletcher, David	.826
Brantley, Michael	.750
LeMahieu, DJ	.738
Merrifield, Whit	.709
Devers, Rafael	.643
Vazquez, Christian	.642
Rendon, Anthony	.622
Ramirez, Jose	.621
Anderson, Tim	.618
Grichuk, Randal	.614

Worst BPS on OutZ
(minimum 186 PA)

Dozier, Hunter	.197
Sano, Miguel	.204
Biggio, Cavan	.216
Lopez, Nicky	.218
Olson, Matt	.224
Moncada, Yoan	.273
Crawford, J.P.	.290
White, Evan	.293
Lewis, Kyle	.295
Hernandez, Teoscar	.312

2020 American League Batting Leaders

Best OPS vs Fastballs
(minimum 93 PA)

Cruz, Nelson	1.184
Hernandez, Teoscar	1.171
LeMahieu, DJ	1.095
Ramirez, Jose	1.089
Bradley Jr., Jackie	1.074
Voit, Luke	1.018
Jimenez, Eloy	.992
Candelario, Jeimer	.988
Nunez, Renato	.987
Abreu, Jose	.976

Best OPS vs Curveballs
(minimum 19 PA)

Trout, Mike	1.383
Vazquez, Christian	1.350
Abreu, Jose	1.314
Guerrero Jr., Vladimir	1.297
Verdugo, Alex	1.274
Martinez, J.D.	1.272
Merrifield, Whit	1.263
Semien, Marcus	1.215
La Stella, Tommy	1.139
Gurriel Jr., Lourdes	1.107

Best OPS vs Changeups
(minimum 19 PA)

Urshela, Gio	1.526
Rendon, Anthony	1.406
Wendle, Joey	1.339
Gurriel Jr., Lourdes	1.249
Rosario, Eddie	1.139
Castro, Willi	1.117
Abreu, Jose	1.099
Gardner, Brett	1.088
Cruz, Nelson	1.057
Adames, Willy	1.032

Best OPS vs Sliders
(minimum 32 PA)

Sisco, Chance	1.500
Walsh, Jared	1.382
Buxton, Byron	1.351
Santander, Anthony	1.333
Brantley, Michael	1.252
Nola, Austin	1.209
Kiermaier, Kevin	1.186
Devers, Rafael	1.131
McBroom, Ryan	1.114
Robert, Luis	1.096

OPS
(minimum 186 PA)

LeMahieu, DJ	1.011
Ramirez, Jose	.993
Trout, Mike	.993
Cruz, Nelson	.992
Abreu, Jose	.987
Voit, Luke	.948
Hernandez, Teoscar	.919
Lowe, Brandon	.916
Rendon, Anthony	.915
Springer, George	.899

OPS First Half
(minimum 260 PA)

OPS Second Half
(minimum 201 PA)

LeMahieu, DJ	1.011
Ramirez, Jose	.993
Trout, Mike	.993
Cruz, Nelson	.992
Abreu, Jose	.987
Voit, Luke	.948
Hernandez, Teoscar	.919
Lowe, Brandon	.916
Rendon, Anthony	.915
Springer, George	.899

OPS by Catchers
(minimum 93 PA)

Perez, Salvador	1.048
Nola, Austin	.942
McCann, James	.905
Grandal, Yasmani	.891
Stassi, Max	.877
Vazquez, Christian	.836
Murphy, Sean	.828
Maldonado, Martin	.727
Jansen, Danny	.676
Severino, Pedro	.675

OPS by First Basemen
(minimum 93 PA)

Walsh, Jared	1.000
Abreu, Jose	1.000
Voit, Luke	.966
Candelario, Jeimer	.913
Nunez, Renato	.811
Sano, Miguel	.773
Guerrero Jr., Vladimir	.752
Olson, Matt	.734
Dozier, Hunter	.707
Santana, Carlos	.699

OPS by Second Basemen
(minimum 93 PA)

LeMahieu, DJ	1.032
Lowe, Brandon	.965
La Stella, Tommy	.870
Schoop, Jonathan	.799
Hernandez, Cesar	.766
Biggio, Cavan	.752
Arraez, Luis	.746
Madrigal, Nick	.745
Mendick, Danny	.743
Alberto, Hanser	.703

OPS by Third Basemen
(minimum 93 PA)

Ramirez, Jose	.961
Diaz, Yandy	.927
Rendon, Anthony	.915
Urshela, Gio	.863
Donaldson, Josh	.855
Seager, Kyle	.807
Bregman, Alex	.806
Devers, Rafael	.800
Franco, Maikel	.783
Chapman, Matt	.779

OPS by Shortstops
(minimum 93 PA)

Castro, Willi	.899
Anderson, Tim	.886
Bogaerts, Xander	.875
Bichette, Bo	.847
Adames, Willy	.817
Fletcher, David	.741
Lindor, Francisco	.737
Torres, Gleyber	.713
Mondesi, Adalberto	.710
Simmons, Andrelton	.702

OPS by Left Fielders
(minimum 93 PA)

Gurriel Jr., Lourdes	.912
Jimenez, Eloy	.907
Mountcastle, Ryan	.877
Tucker, Kyle	.876
Rosario, Eddie	.757
Meadows, Austin	.753
Gardner, Brett	.745
Grossman, Robbie	.741
Upton, Justin	.730
Gordon, Alex	.613

OPS by Center Fielders
(minimum 93 PA)

Trout, Mike	.983
Buxton, Byron	.844
Jones, JaCoby	.835
Grichuk, Randal	.829
Springer, George	.825
Bradley Jr., Jackie	.814
Hicks, Aaron	.800
Lewis, Kyle	.800
Mullins II, Cedric	.752
Robert, Luis	.741

OPS by Right Fielders
(minimum 93 PA)

Santander, Anthony	.908
Judge, Aaron	.893
Frazier, Clint	.871
Verdugo, Alex	.865
Hernandez, Teoscar	.804
Kepler, Max	.795
Merrifield, Whit	.777
Reddick, Josh	.719
Gallo, Joey	.693
Renfroe, Hunter	.646

OPS by Designated Hitters
(minimum 47 PA)

Cruz, Nelson	.997
Tellez, Rowdy	.905
Stanton, Giancarlo	.887
Guerrero Jr., Vladimir	.878
Iglesias, Jose	.873
Nunez, Renato	.867
Reyes, Franmil	.800
Lopes, Tim	.800
Martinez, Jose	.793
Soler, Jorge	.791

2020 American League Batting Leaders

OPS Batting Left vs. LHP
(minimum 47 PA)

Lowe, Brandon	1.137
Biggio, Cavan	.908
Bradley Jr., Jackie	.900
Verdugo, Alex	.791
Reddick, Josh	.749
Olson, Matt	.696
Tucker, Kyle	.695
Crawford, J.P.	.661
Seager, Kyle	.649
Brantley, Michael	.638

OPS Batting Left vs. RHP
(minimum 140 PA)

Tucker, Kyle	.905
Kepler, Max	.904
La Stella, Tommy	.903
Devers, Rafael	.890
Rosario, Eddie	.882
Grossman, Robbie	.878
Seager, Kyle	.851
Ramirez, Jose	.847
Lowe, Brandon	.838
Candelario, Jeimer	.808

OPS Batting Right vs. LHP
(minimum 47 PA)

Anderson, Tim	1.509
Cruz, Nelson	1.456
Ramirez, Jose	1.407
Brosseau, Mike	1.121
Mondesi, Adalberto	1.044
Stassi, Max	1.024
Bogaerts, Xander	1.014
Rendon, Anthony	1.001
Adames, Willy	.992
Bregman, Alex	.985

OPS Batting Right vs. RHP
(minimum 140 PA)

Trout, Mike	1.069
Abreu, Jose	1.018
LeMahieu, DJ	1.013
Voit, Luke	.960
Springer, George	.929
Hernandez, Teoscar	.913
Gurriel Jr., Lourdes	.904
Jimenez, Eloy	.898
Rendon, Anthony	.877
Nunez, Renato	.859

OPS vs. LHP
(minimum 47 PA)

Anderson, Tim	1.509
Cruz, Nelson	1.456
Ramirez, Jose	1.407
Lowe, Brandon	1.137
Brosseau, Mike	1.121
Mondesi, Adalberto	1.044
Stassi, Max	1.024
Bogaerts, Xander	1.014
Rendon, Anthony	1.001
Adames, Willy	.992

OPS vs. RHP
(minimum 140 PA)

Trout, Mike	1.069
Abreu, Jose	1.018
LeMahieu, DJ	1.013
Voit, Luke	.960
Springer, George	.929
Hernandez, Teoscar	.913
Tucker, Kyle	.905
Gurriel Jr., Lourdes	.904
Kepler, Max	.904
La Stella, Tommy	.903

RC Per 27 Outs vs. LHP
(minimum 47 PA)

Anderson, Tim	16.3
Cruz, Nelson	15.0
Ramirez, Jose	12.3
Maldonado, Martin	10.2
Brosseau, Mike	9.8
Canha, Mark	9.5
Kiner-Falefa, Isiah	9.3
Lowe, Brandon	8.9
Biggio, Cavan	8.3
Fletcher, David	8.3

RC Per 27 Outs vs. RHP
(minimum 140 PA)

Trout, Mike	9.7
LeMahieu, DJ	8.8
Tucker, Kyle	8.4
Springer, George	7.9
Jimenez, Eloy	7.7
Voit, Luke	7.7
La Stella, Tommy	7.7
Abreu, Jose	7.4
Kepler, Max	7.3
Devers, Rafael	7.1

Highest RBI %
(minimum 186 PA)

Voit, Luke	47.23
Trout, Mike	46.46
Abreu, Jose	46.15
Lowe, Brandon	45.29
Jimenez, Eloy	44.66
Ramirez, Jose	44.49
Cabrera, Miguel	43.10
Tucker, Kyle	41.67
Rosario, Eddie	41.30
LeMahieu, DJ	40.91

Lowest RBI %
(minimum 186 PA)

Dozier, Hunter	19.77
Kiner-Falefa, Isiah	20.24
Lopez, Nicky	21.28
Reyes, Victor	23.61
Gurriel, Yuli	24.64
Mondesi, Adalberto	24.89
Altuve, Jose	25.53
Lindor, Francisco	25.89
Verdugo, Alex	26.74
Martinez, J.D.	28.60

Highest Strikeout per PA
(minimum 186 PA)

Sano, Miguel	.439
White, Evan	.416
Adames, Willy	.361
Gallo, Joey	.350
Robert, Luis	.322
Olson, Matt	.314
Moncada, Yoan	.312
Hernandez, Teoscar	.304
Mondesi, Adalberto	.300
Grandal, Yasmani	.299

Lowest Strikeout per PA
(minimum 186 PA)

La Stella, Tommy	.053
LeMahieu, DJ	.097
Fletcher, David	.109
Gurriel, Yuli	.117
Merrifield, Whit	.125
Alberto, Hanser	.130
Seager, Kyle	.133
Rendon, Anthony	.134
Kiner-Falefa, Isiah	.140
Rosario, Eddie	.147

Home Runs At Home

Voit, Luke	16
Trout, Mike	10
Olson, Matt	9
Rendon, Anthony	9
Abreu, Jose	8
Jimenez, Eloy	8
LeMahieu, DJ	8
Ramirez, Jose	8
Santander, Anthony	8
4 tied with	7

Home Runs Away

Abreu, Jose	11
Cruz, Nelson	10
Hernandez, Teoscar	10
Buxton, Byron	9
Ramirez, Jose	9
Gurriel Jr., Lourdes	8
Lowe, Brandon	8
Springer, George	8
5 tied with	7

Longest Avg Home Run
(min 10 over the wall)

Hernandez, Teoscar	418
Sano, Miguel	416
Cruz, Nelson	415
Trout, Mike	414
Springer, George	413
Perez, Salvador	413
Olson, Matt	413
Robert, Luis	412
Buxton, Byron	409
Lowe, Brandon	407

Shortest Avg Home Run
(min 10 over the wall)

Santander, Anthony	388
Grichuk, Randal	391
Nunez, Renato	392
Jimenez, Eloy	392
Rosario, Eddie	394
Ramirez, Jose	395
Voit, Luke	397
Gurriel Jr., Lourdes	402
Bogaerts, Xander	405
Lewis, Kyle	405

2020 American League Batting Leaders

Under Age 26: AB Per HR
(minimum 186 PA)

Jimenez, Eloy	15.2
Robert, Luis	18.4
Lewis, Kyle	18.7
Devers, Rafael	21.1
White, Evan	22.8
Adames, Willy	23.1
Tucker, Kyle	23.2
Reyes, Franmil	23.4
Guerrero Jr., Vladimir	24.6
Biggio, Cavan	27.5

Under Age 26: OPS
(minimum 186 PA)

Jimenez, Eloy	.891
Verdugo, Alex	.844
Tucker, Kyle	.837
Adames, Willy	.813
Biggio, Cavan	.807
Lewis, Kyle	.801
Reyes, Franmil	.795
Devers, Rafael	.793
Guerrero Jr., Vladimir	.791
Robert, Luis	.738

Under Age 26: RC/27 Outs
(minimum 186 PA)

Jimenez, Eloy	7.4
Tucker, Kyle	7.3
Biggio, Cavan	6.5
Adames, Willy	5.7
Verdugo, Alex	5.6
Reyes, Franmil	5.1
Lewis, Kyle	5.0
Devers, Rafael	4.9
Moncada, Yoan	4.9
Crawford, J.P.	4.8

Longest Home Run

Stanton, Giancarlo, 7/25	483
Hernandez, Teoscar, 8/12	466
Jimenez, Eloy, 8/21	466
Murphy, Sean, 9/11	464
Reyes, Franmil, 8/14	462
Correa, Carlos, 9/6	461
Hernandez, Teoscar, 8/14	459
Lowe, Brandon, 8/13	459
Stanton, Giancarlo, 7/23	459
Tellez, Rowdy, 8/12	459

Swing and Miss %
(minimum 555 Pitches Seen)

Sano, Miguel	41.9
Robert, Luis	40.1
Mondesi, Adalberto	39.3
Adames, Willy	38.3
Goodrum, Niko	38.0
Reyes, Franmil	37.8
Gallo, Joey	37.1
White, Evan	37.0
Chavis, Michael	36.7
Soler, Jorge	36.2

Highest First Swing %
(minimum 186 PA)

Robert, Luis	49.3
Voit, Luke	47.9
Altuve, Jose	42.4
Gurriel Jr., Lourdes	41.3
Mondesi, Adalberto	39.7
Jimenez, Eloy	38.7
Alberto, Hanser	38.2
Devers, Rafael	38.2
Tucker, Kyle	37.0
Martinez, J.D.	36.1

Lowest First Swing %
(minimum 186 PA)

Fletcher, David	8.8
Verdugo, Alex	12.3
La Stella, Tommy	13.6
Grandal, Yasmani	13.9
Trout, Mike	14.3
Bogaerts, Xander	14.7
Crawford, J.P.	14.8
Polanco, Jorge	15.9
Biggio, Cavan	17.4
Ramirez, Jose	17.8

Home RC Per 27 Outs
(minimum 93 PA)

LeMahieu, DJ	13.4
Trout, Mike	12.6
Ramirez, Jose	10.3
Voit, Luke	10.1
Jimenez, Eloy	9.4
Frazier, Clint	9.4
Guerrero Jr., Vladimir	8.0
Hicks, Aaron	7.6
Lewis, Kyle	7.5
Grichuk, Randal	7.5

Road RC Per 27 Outs
(minimum 93 PA)

Springer, George	9.9
Candelario, Jeimer	8.8
Merrifield, Whit	8.7
Abreu, Jose	8.4
Semien, Marcus	8.4
Tucker, Kyle	8.3
Adames, Willy	8.2
Canha, Mark	8.0
Reyes, Franmil	7.7
Grandal, Yasmani	7.5

Lead Changing RBI

Abreu, Jose	17
Lowe, Brandon	16
Seager, Kyle	16
Devers, Rafael	15
Guerrero Jr., Vladimir	14
Nunez, Renato	14
Trout, Mike	14
Tucker, Kyle	14
4 tied with	13

2020 National League Batting Leaders

Batting Average (minimum 186 PA)		On Base Percentage (minimum 186 PA)		Slugging Average (minimum 186 PA)		Home Runs	
Soto, Juan	.351	Soto, Juan	.490	Soto, Juan	.695	Ozuna, Marcell	18
Freeman, Freddie	.341	Freeman, Freddie	.462	Freeman, Freddie	.640	Tatis Jr., Fernando	17
Ozuna, Marcell	.338	Ozuna, Marcell	.431	Ozuna, Marcell	.636	Alonso, Pete	16
Turner, Trea	.335	Harper, Bryce	.420	Smith, Dominic	.616	Betts, Mookie	16
Solano, Donovan	.326	Goldschmidt, Paul	.417	Myers, Wil	.606	Calhoun, Kole	16
Conforto, Michael	.322	Conforto, Michael	.412	Turner, Trea	.588	Duvall, Adam	16
Tapia, Raimel	.321	Acuna Jr., Ronald	.406	Seager, Corey	.585	Machado, Manny	16
Smith, Dominic	.316	Nimmo, Brandon	.404	Acuna Jr., Ronald	.581	Pollock, A.J.	16
McNeil, Jeff	.311	Yastrzemski, Mike	.400	Machado, Manny	.580	3 tied with	15
Seager, Corey	.307	Turner, Trea	.394	Tatis Jr., Fernando	.571		

Games		Plate Appearances		At Bats		Hits	
Marte, Starling	61	Ozuna, Marcell	267	Swanson, Dansby	237	Turner, Trea	78
Castellanos, Nick	60	Swanson, Dansby	264	Story, Trevor	235	Ozuna, Marcell	77
Freeman, Freddie	60	Freeman, Freddie	262	Turner, Trea	233	Freeman, Freddie	73
Gregorius, Didi	60	Story, Trevor	259	Marte, Starling	228	Machado, Manny	68
Machado, Manny	60	Turner, Trea	259	Ozuna, Marcell	228	Story, Trevor	68
Ozuna, Marcell	60	Tatis Jr., Fernando	257	Machado, Manny	224	Blackmon, Charlie	67
Swanson, Dansby	60	Machado, Manny	254	Tatis Jr., Fernando	224	Conforto, Michael	65
10 tied with	59	Grisham, Trent	252	Baez, Javier	222	Seager, Corey	65
		Marte, Starling	250	Blackmon, Charlie	221	Swanson, Dansby	65
		Muncy, Max	248	Betts, Mookie	219	2 tied with	64

Singles		Doubles		Triples		Total Bases	
Blackmon, Charlie	48	Freeman, Freddie	23	Story, Trevor	4	Ozuna, Marcell	145
Tapia, Raimel	48	Smith, Dominic	21	Turner, Trea	4	Freeman, Freddie	137
Turner, Trea	47	Walker, Christian	18	Yastrzemski, Mike	4	Turner, Trea	137
Ozuna, Marcell	45	Cronenworth, Jake	15	Cabrera, Asdrubal	3	Machado, Manny	130
Peralta, David	45	Markakis, Nick	15	Cronenworth, Jake	3	Tatis Jr., Fernando	128
Conforto, Michael	44	Solano, Donovan	15	Escobar, Eduardo	3	Seager, Corey	124
Marte, Starling	43	Swanson, Dansby	15	Grisham, Trent	3	Betts, Mookie	123
Solano, Donovan	43	Turner, Trea	15	Hampson, Garrett	3	Story, Trevor	122
Wong, Kolten	41	7 tied with	14	Nimmo, Brandon	3	Myers, Wil	120
2 tied with	40			19 tied with	2	Pollock, A.J.	111

Runs Scored		RBI		Walks		Strikeouts	
Freeman, Freddie	51	Ozuna, Marcell	56	Harper, Bryce	49	Hiura, Keston	85
Tatis Jr., Fernando	50	Freeman, Freddie	53	Yelich, Christian	46	Yelich, Christian	76
Swanson, Dansby	49	Machado, Manny	47	Freeman, Freddie	45	Baez, Javier	75
Betts, Mookie	47	Tatis Jr., Fernando	45	Soto, Juan	41	Swanson, Dansby	71
Acuna Jr., Ronald	46	Blackmon, Charlie	42	Muncy, Max	39	Castellanos, Nick	69
Turner, Trea	46	Smith, Dominic	42	Acuna Jr., Ronald	38	Suarez, Eugenio	67
Machado, Manny	44	Seager, Corey	41	Ozuna, Marcell	38	Anderson, Brian	66
Grisham, Trent	42	Turner, Trea	41	Goldschmidt, Paul	37	McMahon, Ryan	66
Harper, Bryce	41	3 tied with	40	Votto, Joey	37	Schwarber, Kyle	66
Story, Trevor	41			Nimmo, Brandon	33	Polanco, Gregory	65

2020 National League Batting Leaders

Intentional Walks		BA Bases Loaded		Sacrifice Hits		Sacrifice Flies	
		(minimum 4 PA)					
Soto, Juan	12	Stallings, Jacob	1.000	Hedges, Austin	5	Blackmon, Charlie	5
Harper, Bryce	8	Fowler, Dexter	.800	Eaton, Adam	4	Aguilar, Jesus	4
Freeman, Freddie	7	Blackmon, Charlie	.750	Garcia, Greg	3	Arenado, Nolan	4
Alonso, Pete	4	Gonzalez, Erik	.750	Hampson, Garrett	3	Bell, Josh	4
Bell, Josh	4	Stevenson, Andrew	.750	Haseley, Adam	3	Cabrera, Asdrubal	4
Blackmon, Charlie	4	Carpenter, Matt	.667	7 tied with	2	Calhoun, Kole	4
Escobar, Eduardo	4	Hiura, Keston	.667			DeJong, Paul	4
Machado, Manny	4	Myers, Wil	.667			Machado, Manny	4
Rizzo, Anthony	4	Peralta, David	.667			11 tied with	3
3 tied with	3	Machado, Manny	.625				

BA Close & Late		Batting Average w/ RISP		SLG vs. LHP		SLG vs. RHP	
(minimum 19 PA)		(minimum 38 PA)		(minimum 47 PA)		(minimum 140 PA)	
Pham, Tommy	.529	Bohm, Alec	.452	Ozuna, Marcell	.867	Freeman, Freddie	.733
Nimmo, Brandon	.500	Betts, Mookie	.439	Pollock, A.J.	.818	Betts, Mookie	.677
Pillar, Kevin	.500	Freeman, Freddie	.423	Soto, Juan	.780	Belt, Brandon	.659
Swanson, Dansby	.500	Soto, Juan	.421	Turner, Trea	.732	Soto, Juan	.654
Pollock, A.J.	.467	Tatis Jr., Fernando	.400	Hoskins, Rhys	.732	Seager, Corey	.622
Bohm, Alec	.444	Anderson, Brian	.395	Cabrera, Asdrubal	.686	Acuna Jr., Ronald	.620
Peralta, David	.419	Wong, Kolten	.389	Flores, Wilmer	.661	Tatis Jr., Fernando	.611
Turner, Justin	.412	Machado, Manny	.381	Slater, Austin	.658	d'Arnaud, Travis	.611
Tatis Jr., Fernando	.400	Solano, Donovan	.380	Myers, Wil	.656	Machado, Manny	.588
Blackmon, Charlie	.393	Bote, David	.379	Marte, Ketel	.654	Myers, Wil	.582

Leadoff Hitters OBP		Cleanup Hitters SLG		BA vs. LHP		BA vs. RHP	
(minimum 56 PA)		(minimum 56 PA)		(minimum 47 PA)		(minimum 140 PA)	
Acuna Jr., Ronald	.406	Calhoun, Kole	.804	Marte, Ketel	.423	Freeman, Freddie	.373
Locastro, Tim	.403	Belt, Brandon	.743	Realmuto, J.T.	.386	Belt, Brandon	.350
Nimmo, Brandon	.401	Smith, Dominic	.655	Blackmon, Charlie	.375	Soto, Juan	.346
Turner, Trea	.400	Hosmer, Eric	.644	Turner, Trea	.375	Conforto, Michael	.344
Yastrzemski, Mike	.394	Ozuna, Marcell	.583	Tapia, Raimel	.364	d'Arnaud, Travis	.344
Betts, Mookie	.383	Schwarber, Kyle	.518	Soto, Juan	.360	Ozuna, Marcell	.333
Tatis Jr., Fernando	.373	Suarez, Eugenio	.510	Ozuna, Marcell	.356	Betts, Mookie	.323
Hampson, Garrett	.371	d'Arnaud, Travis	.508	Solano, Donovan	.350	Turner, Trea	.322
Tapia, Raimel	.370	Gyorko, Jedd	.500	Pollock, A.J.	.345	Seager, Corey	.322
Swanson, Dansby	.365	Realmuto, J.T.	.485	Hoskins, Rhys	.341	Gregorius, Didi	.318

Home BA		Away BA		OBP vs. LHP		OBP vs. RHP	
(minimum 93 PA)		(minimum 93 PA)		(minimum 47 PA)		(minimum 140 PA)	
Belt, Brandon	.383	Turner, Trea	.407	Hoskins, Rhys	.509	Soto, Juan	.514
Ozuna, Marcell	.364	Cano, Robinson	.373	Realmuto, J.T.	.500	Freeman, Freddie	.495
Machado, Manny	.353	Soto, Juan	.365	Slater, Austin	.469	Belt, Brandon	.456
Tapia, Raimel	.349	d'Arnaud, Travis	.356	Ozuna, Marcell	.463	Nimmo, Brandon	.436
Seager, Corey	.347	Smith, Dominic	.348	Turner, Trea	.453	Conforto, Michael	.429
Swanson, Dansby	.345	Freeman, Freddie	.345	Marte, Ketel	.444	Ozuna, Marcell	.423
Freeman, Freddie	.337	Bohm, Alec	.326	Story, Trevor	.434	Harper, Bryce	.419
4 tied with	.333	Conforto, Michael	.321	Yelich, Christian	.431	d'Arnaud, Travis	.415
		Ozuna, Marcell	.314	Soto, Juan	.429	Goldschmidt, Paul	.409
		Aguilar, Jesus	.313	Harper, Bryce	.423	Yastrzemski, Mike	.408

2020 National League Batting Leaders

Stolen Bases	
Story, Trevor	15
Quinn, Roman	12
Turner, Trea	12
Tatis Jr., Fernando	11
Betts, Mookie	10
Grisham, Trent	10
Marte, Starling	10
Berti, Jon	9
Villar, Jonathan	9
5 tied with	8

Caught Stealing	
Villar, Jonathan	5
Edman, Tommy	4
Turner, Trea	4
10 tied with	3

Highest SB Success Pct	
(minimum 8 SBA)	
Quinn, Roman	100.0
Grisham, Trent	90.9
Acuna Jr., Ronald	88.9
Gimenez, Andres	88.9
Slater, Austin	88.9
Profar, Jurickson	87.5
Betts, Mookie	83.3
Marte, Starling	83.3
Story, Trevor	83.3
Berti, Jon	81.8

Lowest SB Success Pct	
(minimum 8 SBA)	
Villar, Jonathan	64.3
Machado, Manny	66.7
Akiyama, Shogo	70.0
Hamilton, Billy	75.0
Soto, Juan	75.0
Turner, Trea	75.0
Tatis Jr., Fernando	78.6
Harper, Bryce	80.0
Tapia, Raimel	80.0
Berti, Jon	81.8

Steals of Third	
Grisham, Trent	3
Turner, Trea	3
Villar, Jonathan	3
Betts, Mookie	2
Hampson, Garrett	2
Harper, Bryce	2
Harrison, Monte	2
Robles, Victor	2
Tapia, Raimel	2
Tatis Jr., Fernando	2

Grounded Into DP	
Arcia, Orlando	10
Longoria, Evan	10
Machado, Manny	9
Moran, Colin	9
Baez, Javier	8
d'Arnaud, Travis	8
Davis, J.D.	8
Seager, Corey	8
4 tied with	7

Grounded Into DP Pct	
(minimum 19 GIDP Ops)	
Albies, Ozzie	0.00
Gimenez, Andres	0.00
Inciarte, Ender	0.00
Myers, Wil	0.00
Quinn, Roman	0.00
Robles, Victor	0.00
Swanson, Dansby	0.00
Carpenter, Matt	2.27
Profar, Jurickson	2.38
Grisham, Trent	2.44

Hit By Pitch	
Contreras, Willson	14
Hiura, Keston	11
Rizzo, Anthony	10
Marte, Starling	9
Robles, Victor	9
Conforto, Michael	7
Davis, J.D.	7
9 tied with	6

Pitches Seen	
Muncy, Max	1100
Yelich, Christian	1100
Ozuna, Marcell	1074
Swanson, Dansby	1060
Grisham, Trent	1048
Story, Trevor	1036
Turner, Trea	1033
Freeman, Freddie	1021
Suarez, Eugenio	999
Hiura, Keston	990

At Bats Per Home Run	
(minimum 186 PA)	
Acuna Jr., Ronald	11.4
Soto, Juan	11.8
Calhoun, Kole	11.9
Duvall, Adam	11.9
Pollock, A.J.	12.3
Ozuna, Marcell	12.7
Alonso, Pete	13.0
Tatis Jr., Fernando	13.2
Myers, Wil	13.2
Suarez, Eugenio	13.2

Highest GB/FB Ratio	
(minimum 186 PA)	
Tapia, Raimel	2.59
Davis, J.D.	2.38
Bell, Josh	2.17
Moran, Colin	1.97
Edman, Tommy	1.95
Marte, Starling	1.90
Soto, Juan	1.81
Garcia, Avisail	1.78
Ahmed, Nick	1.77
Wong, Kolten	1.72

Lowest GB/FB Ratio	
(minimum 186 PA)	
Duvall, Adam	0.54
Story, Trevor	0.62
Betts, Mookie	0.70
Suarez, Eugenio	0.74
Flores, Wilmer	0.76
Harper, Bryce	0.79
Arenado, Nolan	0.79
McCutchen, Andrew	0.80
Acuna Jr., Ronald	0.81
Gregorius, Didi	0.84

Pitches Per Plate App	
(minimum 186 PA)	
Yelich, Christian	4.45
Muncy, Max	4.44
McMahon, Ryan	4.36
Nimmo, Brandon	4.35
Acuna Jr., Ronald	4.34
Suarez, Eugenio	4.33
Schwarber, Kyle	4.26
Goldschmidt, Paul	4.23
Soto, Juan	4.22
Flores, Wilmer	4.19

Pct Pitches Taken	
(minimum 555 Pitches)	
Yelich, Christian	65.4
Berti, Jon	65.0
Soto, Juan	63.8
Votto, Joey	63.8
Muncy, Max	63.4
Heyward, Jason	63.0
Smith, Will	61.8
Grisham, Trent	61.7
Stallings, Jacob	61.2
Bote, David	60.9

Best BPS on OutZ	
(minimum 186 PA)	
Soto, Juan	.745
Machado, Manny	.692
McCutchen, Andrew	.680
Yastrzemski, Mike	.649
Marte, Ketel	.648
Cronenworth, Jake	.644
Freeman, Freddie	.642
Betts, Mookie	.635
Cabrera, Asdrubal	.614
Suarez, Eugenio	.612

Worst BPS on OutZ	
(minimum 186 PA)	
Calhoun, Kole	.182
Hiura, Keston	.233
Baez, Javier	.237
Anderson, Brian	.244
Riley, Austin	.254
McMahon, Ryan	.254
Votto, Joey	.266
Reynolds, Bryan	.277
Grisham, Trent	.313
Pollock, A.J.	.323

2020 National League Batting Leaders

Best OPS vs Fastballs
(minimum 93 PA)

Freeman, Freddie	1.292
Harper, Bryce	1.204
Ozuna, Marcell	1.177
Pollock, A.J.	1.167
Seager, Corey	1.043
d'Arnaud, Travis	1.032
Belt, Brandon	1.018
Turner, Trea	1.008
Machado, Manny	1.004
Goldschmidt, Paul	1.002

Best OPS vs Curveballs
(minimum 19 PA)

Seager, Corey	1.506
Smith, Dominic	1.424
Tatis Jr., Fernando	1.395
Dickerson, Corey	1.320
Walker, Christian	1.282
Escobar, Eduardo	1.213
Rizzo, Anthony	1.160
Winker, Jesse	1.147
Gregorius, Didi	1.096
Aguilar, Jesus	1.064

Best OPS vs Changeups
(minimum 19 PA)

Segura, Jean	1.474
Hosmer, Eric	1.355
Yastrzemski, Mike	1.305
Story, Trevor	1.224
Ozuna, Marcell	1.213
Myers, Wil	1.192
Cronenworth, Jake	1.179
Soto, Juan	1.177
Gamel, Ben	1.164
Suarez, Eugenio	1.095

Best OPS vs Sliders
(minimum 32 PA)

Calhoun, Kole	1.741
Nottingham, Jacob	1.591
Myers, Wil	1.471
Carlson, Dylan	1.467
Locastro, Tim	1.417
Hayes, Ke'Bryan	1.415
France, Ty	1.383
Belt, Brandon	1.336
Ruf, Darin	1.297
Soto, Juan	1.209

OPS
(minimum 186 PA)

Soto, Juan	1.185
Freeman, Freddie	1.102
Ozuna, Marcell	1.067
Smith, Dominic	.993
Acuna Jr., Ronald	.987
Turner, Trea	.982
Yastrzemski, Mike	.968
Harper, Bryce	.962
Myers, Wil	.959
Machado, Manny	.950

OPS First Half
(minimum 260 PA)

OPS Second Half
(minimum 201 PA)

Freeman, Freddie	1.102
Ozuna, Marcell	1.067
Acuna Jr., Ronald	.987
Turner, Trea	.982
Yastrzemski, Mike	.968
Harper, Bryce	.962
Myers, Wil	.959
Machado, Manny	.950
Seager, Corey	.943
Tatis Jr., Fernando	.937

OPS by Catchers
(minimum 93 PA)

d'Arnaud, Travis	.961
Smith, Will	.945
Realmuto, J.T.	.887
Suzuki, Kurt	.795
Gomes, Yan	.787
Ramos, Wilson	.714
Stallings, Jacob	.702
Kelly, Carson	.682
Barnhart, Tucker	.679
Barnes, Austin	.674

OPS by First Basemen
(minimum 93 PA)

Freeman, Freddie	1.130
Belt, Brandon	1.008
Hoskins, Rhys	.895
Goldschmidt, Paul	.882
Gyorko, Jedd	.872
Alonso, Pete	.870
Aguilar, Jesus	.859
Hosmer, Eric	.842
Cabrera, Asdrubal	.830
Bell, Josh	.830

OPS by Second Basemen
(minimum 93 PA)

Moustakas, Mike	.888
Cano, Robinson	.856
Kipnis, Jason	.835
Albies, Ozzie	.779
Solano, Donovan	.767
Cronenworth, Jake	.752
Segura, Jean	.722
McMahon, Ryan	.716
Hiura, Keston	.702
Marte, Ketel	.695

OPS by Third Basemen
(minimum 93 PA)

Hayes, Ke'Bryan	1.124
Machado, Manny	.941
Bohm, Alec	.913
Turner, Justin	.839
Anderson, Brian	.818
Suarez, Eugenio	.781
Riley, Austin	.747
Arenado, Nolan	.738
Longoria, Evan	.725
Davis, J.D.	.656

OPS by Shortstops
(minimum 93 PA)

Turner, Trea	.982
Seager, Corey	.923
Tatis Jr., Fernando	.916
Rojas, Miguel	.879
Story, Trevor	.874
Gregorius, Didi	.832
Swanson, Dansby	.809
Crawford, Brandon	.796
Galvis, Freddy	.763
Arcia, Orlando	.739

OPS by Left Fielders
(minimum 93 PA)

Soto, Juan	1.133
Dickerson, Alex	.977
McNeil, Jeff	.934
Profar, Jurickson	.883
Pollock, A.J.	.855
Tapia, Raimel	.818
McCutchen, Andrew	.815
Schwarber, Kyle	.786
Yelich, Christian	.764
Peralta, David	.758

OPS by Center Fielders
(minimum 93 PA)

Acuna Jr., Ronald	1.008
Yastrzemski, Mike	.987
Nimmo, Brandon	.934
Bellinger, Cody	.855
Dubon, Mauricio	.816
Grisham, Trent	.811
Happ, Ian	.808
Bader, Harrison	.786
Marte, Starling	.776
Garcia, Avisail	.636

OPS by Right Fielders
(minimum 93 PA)

Conforto, Michael	.949
Harper, Bryce	.946
Myers, Wil	.942
Yastrzemski, Mike	.919
Betts, Mookie	.907
Calhoun, Kole	.870
Heyward, Jason	.845
Blackmon, Charlie	.841
Castellanos, Nick	.794
Markakis, Nick	.790

OPS by Designated Hitters
(minimum 47 PA)

Ozuna, Marcell	1.155
Contreras, Willson	.992
Cano, Robinson	.965
Davis, J.D.	.961
Winker, Jesse	.906
Walker, Christian	.879
Vogelbach, Daniel	.857
Cooper, Garrett	.847
Miller, Brad	.801
Slater, Austin	.761

2020 National League Batting Leaders

OPS Batting Left vs. LHP (minimum 47 PA)	
Soto, Juan	1.209
Yelich, Christian	1.068
Yastrzemski, Mike	.997
Harper, Bryce	.966
Blackmon, Charlie	.926
Smith, Dominic	.900
Cano, Robinson	.882
Conforto, Michael	.870
Tapia, Raimel	.863
Seager, Corey	.827

OPS Batting Left vs. RHP (minimum 140 PA)	
Freeman, Freddie	1.228
Soto, Juan	1.168
Belt, Brandon	1.114
Seager, Corey	.998
Nimmo, Brandon	.977
Harper, Bryce	.960
Conforto, Michael	.960
Dickerson, Alex	.959
Yastrzemski, Mike	.952
Winker, Jesse	.944

OPS Batting Right vs. LHP (minimum 47 PA)	
Ozuna, Marcell	1.330
Hoskins, Rhys	1.241
Turner, Trea	1.185
Pollock, A.J.	1.185
Slater, Austin	1.127
Marte, Ketel	1.098
Realmuto, J.T.	1.091
Gyorko, Jedd	1.048
Story, Trevor	1.044
Myers, Wil	1.042

OPS Batting Right vs. RHP (minimum 140 PA)	
Betts, Mookie	1.061
d'Arnaud, Travis	1.026
Acuna Jr., Ronald	1.020
Ozuna, Marcell	1.002
Tatis Jr., Fernando	.989
Machado, Manny	.954
Myers, Wil	.920
Turner, Trea	.917
Taylor, Chris	.898
Swanson, Dansby	.874

OPS vs. LHP (minimum 47 PA)	
Ozuna, Marcell	1.330
Hoskins, Rhys	1.241
Soto, Juan	1.209
Pollock, A.J.	1.185
Turner, Trea	1.185
Slater, Austin	1.127
Marte, Ketel	1.098
Realmuto, J.T.	1.091
Yelich, Christian	1.068
Gyorko, Jedd	1.048

OPS vs. RHP (minimum 140 PA)	
Freeman, Freddie	1.228
Soto, Juan	1.168
Belt, Brandon	1.114
Betts, Mookie	1.061
d'Arnaud, Travis	1.026
Acuna Jr., Ronald	1.020
Ozuna, Marcell	1.002
Seager, Corey	.998
Tatis Jr., Fernando	.989
Nimmo, Brandon	.977

RC Per 27 Outs vs. LHP (minimum 47 PA)	
Ozuna, Marcell	17.0
Hoskins, Rhys	13.7
Slater, Austin	11.8
Marte, Ketel	11.5
Realmuto, J.T.	11.3
Turner, Trea	11.0
Soto, Juan	10.8
Tapia, Raimel	9.2
Blackmon, Charlie	9.0
Pollock, A.J.	8.9

RC Per 27 Outs vs. RHP (minimum 140 PA)	
Freeman, Freddie	15.5
Soto, Juan	13.8
Betts, Mookie	9.9
Belt, Brandon	9.3
Solano, Donovan	8.5
Yastrzemski, Mike	8.4
Tatis Jr., Fernando	8.3
Ozuna, Marcell	7.7
Conforto, Michael	7.6
Myers, Wil	7.5

Highest RBI % (minimum 186 PA)	
Soto, Juan	52.71
Freeman, Freddie	50.24
Myers, Wil	50.13
Tatis Jr., Fernando	48.60
Turner, Trea	46.17
Betts, Mookie	45.88
Yastrzemski, Mike	45.22
Ozuna, Marcell	45.05
Smith, Dominic	44.63
Taylor, Chris	44.32

Lowest RBI % (minimum 186 PA)	
Escobar, Eduardo	22.91
Dickerson, Corey	23.91
Davis, J.D.	25.17
Robles, Victor	25.21
Arcia, Orlando	25.87
Baez, Javier	26.49
Bell, Josh	27.19
Yelich, Christian	27.23
Garcia, Avisail	28.09
Nimmo, Brandon	28.89

Highest Strikeout per PA (minimum 186 PA)	
Hiura, Keston	.346
McMahon, Ryan	.342
Baez, Javier	.319
Yelich, Christian	.308
Acuna Jr., Ronald	.297
Schwarber, Kyle	.295
Suarez, Eugenio	.290
Anderson, Brian	.288
Castellanos, Nick	.285
Robles, Victor	.280

Lowest Strikeout per PA (minimum 186 PA)	
Arenado, Nolan	.100
Marte, Ketel	.108
McNeil, Jeff	.115
Gregorius, Didi	.118
Profar, Jurickson	.139
Turner, Trea	.139
Freeman, Freddie	.141
Soto, Juan	.143
Wong, Kolten	.144
Machado, Manny	.146

Home Runs At Home	
Machado, Manny	13
Betts, Mookie	11
Myers, Wil	11
Votto, Joey	10
Freeman, Freddie	9
Pollock, A.J.	9
6 tied with	8

Home Runs Away	
Ozuna, Marcell	10
Suarez, Eugenio	10
Alonso, Pete	9
Bellinger, Cody	9
Calhoun, Kole	9
Duvall, Adam	9
Soto, Juan	9
Tatis Jr., Fernando	9
Seager, Corey	8
8 tied with	7

Longest Avg Home Run (min 10 over the wall)	
Ozuna, Marcell	429
Soto, Juan	416
Story, Trevor	414
Acuna Jr., Ronald	414
Machado, Manny	413
Yelich, Christian	413
Seager, Corey	411
Tatis Jr., Fernando	410
Freeman, Freddie	409
Castellanos, Nick	409

Shortest Avg Home Run (min 10 over the wall)	
Flores, Wilmer	382
Rizzo, Anthony	386
Happ, Ian	387
Anderson, Brian	391
Winker, Jesse	393
Bellinger, Cody	394
Betts, Mookie	396
Realmuto, J.T.	396
Duvall, Adam	397
Votto, Joey	399

2020 National League Batting Leaders

Under Age 26: AB Per HR
(minimum 186 PA)

Acuna Jr., Ronald	11.4
Soto, Juan	11.8
Alonso, Pete	13.0
Tatis Jr., Fernando	13.2
Hiura, Keston	16.7
Smith, Dominic	17.7
Bellinger, Cody	17.8
McMahon, Ryan	19.1
Grisham, Trent	21.5
Riley, Austin	23.5

Under Age 26: OPS
(minimum 186 PA)

Soto, Juan	1.185
Smith, Dominic	.993
Acuna Jr., Ronald	.987
Tatis Jr., Fernando	.937
Alonso, Pete	.817
Grisham, Trent	.808
Bellinger, Cody	.789
Riley, Austin	.716
McMahon, Ryan	.714
Hiura, Keston	.707

Under Age 26: RC/27 Outs
(minimum 186 PA)

Soto, Juan	13.1
Acuna Jr., Ronald	7.6
Tatis Jr., Fernando	7.1
Smith, Dominic	7.1
Grisham, Trent	5.4
Bellinger, Cody	5.2
Alonso, Pete	4.8
McMahon, Ryan	4.3
Riley, Austin	4.1
Edman, Tommy	4.0

Longest Home Run

Acuna Jr., Ronald, 9/25	495
Dickerson, Alex, 9/1	480
Acuna Jr., Ronald, 8/26	473
Riley, Austin, 9/4	471
Harper, Bryce, 8/22	470
Ozuna, Marcell, 8/26	469
Kemp, Matt, 8/28	468
Ozuna, Marcell, 9/27	468
Soto, Juan, 8/12	466
Soto, Juan, 8/10	463

Swing and Miss %
(minimum 555 Pitches Seen)

Hiura, Keston	42.4
Polanco, Gregory	42.2
Baez, Javier	37.8
Happ, Ian	34.9
Garcia, Avisail	33.7
Miller, Brad	33.3
Castellanos, Nick	33.3
Contreras, Willson	33.1
Yelich, Christian	33.1
Anderson, Brian	33.0

Highest First Swing %
(minimum 186 PA)

McNeil, Jeff	50.2
Crawford, Brandon	47.1
Seager, Corey	46.3
Riley, Austin	45.6
Robles, Victor	40.9
Harper, Bryce	40.8
Garcia, Avisail	40.5
Freeman, Freddie	40.4
Machado, Manny	39.9
Baez, Javier	38.9

Lowest First Swing %
(minimum 186 PA)

Yelich, Christian	13.0
Cronenworth, Jake	14.0
McCutchen, Andrew	14.4
Aguilar, Jesus	14.6
Rizzo, Anthony	17.6
Longoria, Evan	18.4
Soto, Juan	18.6
Flores, Wilmer	20.3
Wong, Kolten	20.3
Marte, Ketel	20.6

Home RC Per 27 Outs
(minimum 93 PA)

Soto, Juan	14.4
Freeman, Freddie	13.5
Belt, Brandon	11.5
Acuna Jr., Ronald	10.1
Swanson, Dansby	10.1
Votto, Joey	9.6
Ozuna, Marcell	9.3
Betts, Mookie	8.7
Machado, Manny	8.7
Seager, Corey	8.6

Road RC Per 27 Outs
(minimum 93 PA)

Soto, Juan	11.6
Freeman, Freddie	10.2
Turner, Trea	10.1
Ozuna, Marcell	9.7
Smith, Dominic	9.6
Tatis Jr., Fernando	9.4
Cano, Robinson	8.9
Calhoun, Kole	8.3
Conforto, Michael	8.2
Myers, Wil	7.9

Lead Changing RBI

Marte, Starling	14
Smith, Dominic	14
Yastrzemski, Mike	14
Ozuna, Marcell	13
Seager, Corey	13
Tatis Jr., Fernando	13
Turner, Trea	13
Aguilar, Jesus	12
Harper, Bryce	12
Story, Trevor	12

2020 American League Pitching Leaders

Earned Run Average
(minimum 60 IP)

Bieber, Shane	1.63
Keuchel, Dallas	1.99
Bassitt, Chris	2.29
Ryu, Hyun-Jin	2.69
Maeda, Kenta	2.70
Cole, Gerrit	2.84
Carrasco, Carlos	2.91
Gonzales, Marco	3.10
Bundy, Dylan	3.29
Lynn, Lance	3.32

Winning Percentage
(minimum 6 Decisions)

Bieber, Shane	.889
Foster, Matt	.857
Maeda, Kenta	.857
Glasnow, Tyler	.833
Hernandez, Jonathan	.833
Gonzales, Marco	.778
Keuchel, Dallas	.750
Bassitt, Chris	.714
Javier, Cristian	.714
Ryu, Hyun-Jin	.714

Opponent Batting Average
(minimum 60 IP)

Bieber, Shane	.167
Maeda, Kenta	.168
Giolito, Lucas	.184
Cole, Gerrit	.197
Lynn, Lance	.206
Bundy, Dylan	.208
Keuchel, Dallas	.218
Singer, Brady	.220
Carrasco, Carlos	.221
Gonzales, Marco	.222

Baserunners Per 9 IP
(minimum 60 IP)

Maeda, Kenta	6.75
Bieber, Shane	7.91
Cole, Gerrit	8.88
Gonzales, Marco	9.04
Giolito, Lucas	9.58
Keuchel, Dallas	9.81
Bundy, Dylan	9.87
Lynn, Lance	10.18
Greinke, Zack	10.34
Ryu, Hyun-Jin	10.48

Games

Barlow, Scott	32
Cordero, Jimmy	30
Cisnero, Jose	29
Mayers, Mike	29
Holland, Greg	28
Buttrey, Ty	27
Fairbanks, Pete	27
Hernandez, Jonathan	27
Karinchak, James	27
Soto, Gregory	27

Games Started

Lynn, Lance	13
14 tied with	12

Complete Games

Cole, Gerrit	2
Boyd, Matthew	1
Bundy, Dylan	1
Civale, Aaron	1
Gibson, Kyle	1
Giolito, Lucas	1
Gonzales, Marco	1
Keller, Brad	1
Lynn, Lance	1
Minor, Mike	1

Shutouts

Cole, Gerrit	1
Gibson, Kyle	1
Giolito, Lucas	1
Keller, Brad	1
Minor, Mike	1

Wins

Bieber, Shane	8
Cole, Gerrit	7
Gonzales, Marco	7
8 tied with	6

Losses

Boyd, Matthew	7
Allard, Kolby	6
Bubic, Kris	6
Civale, Aaron	6
Gibson, Kyle	6
Lyles, Jordan	6
Minor, Mike	6
6 tied with	5

No Decisions

Fulmer, Michael	8
Anderson, Chase	6
Canning, Griffin	6
Greinke, Zack	6
Roark, Tanner	6
16 tied with	5

Wild Pitches

Glasnow, Tyler	7
Snell, Blake	7
Carrasco, Carlos	6
Fairbanks, Pete	6
Valdez, Framber	6
Williams, Taylor	6
7 tied with	5

Strikeouts

Bieber, Shane	122
Giolito, Lucas	97
Cole, Gerrit	94
Glasnow, Tyler	91
Lynn, Lance	89
Carrasco, Carlos	82
Maeda, Kenta	80
Valdez, Framber	76
Bundy, Dylan	72
Ryu, Hyun-Jin	72

Walks Allowed

Cease, Dylan	34
Dunn, Justin	31
Gibson, Kyle	30
Turnbull, Spencer	29
Giolito, Lucas	28
Perez, Martin	28
Carrasco, Carlos	27
Berrios, Jose	26
Lynn, Lance	25
5 tied with	23

Intentional Walks Allowed

Buttrey, Ty	3
Perez, Oliver	3
Soria, Joakim	3
11 tied with	2

Hit Batters

Yarbrough, Ryan	7
Gibson, Kyle	6
Lynn, Lance	6
Boyd, Matthew	5
Cease, Dylan	5
Jimenez, Joe	5
McCullers Jr., Lance	5
Mize, Casey	5
Valdez, Framber	5
Wittgren, Nick	5

2020 American League Pitching Leaders

Runs Allowed	
Lyles, Jordan	49
Boyd, Matthew	46
Gibson, Kyle	44
Civale, Aaron	39
Roark, Tanner	39
Minor, Mike	36
Heaney, Andrew	35
Montas, Frankie	35
Teheran, Julio	35
Lynn, Lance	34

Hits Allowed	
Civale, Aaron	82
Gibson, Kyle	73
Boyd, Matthew	67
Greinke, Zack	67
Lyles, Jordan	67
Fiers, Mike	65
Lynn, Lance	64
Heaney, Andrew	63
Valdez, Framber	63
2 tied with	60

Doubles Allowed	
McCullers Jr., Lance	18
Boyd, Matthew	17
Civale, Aaron	17
Greinke, Zack	17
Perez, Martin	16
Bassitt, Chris	15
Lynn, Lance	15
4 tied with	14

Home Runs Allowed	
Boyd, Matthew	15
Cole, Gerrit	14
Roark, Tanner	14
Lynn, Lance	13
Cease, Dylan	12
Gibson, Kyle	12
Lyles, Jordan	12
Means, John	12
Teheran, Julio	12
6 tied with	11

Run Support Per Nine IP	
(minimum 60 IP)	
Cole, Gerrit	7.64
Valdez, Framber	7.13
Maeda, Kenta	7.02
Bundy, Dylan	6.85
Keuchel, Dallas	6.25
Berrios, Jose	5.86
Gonzales, Marco	5.81
Boyd, Matthew	5.22
Ryu, Hyun-Jin	5.10
Bassitt, Chris	5.00

% Pitches In Strike Zone	
(minimum 60 IP)	
Heaney, Andrew	45.2
Bassitt, Chris	44.3
Valdez, Framber	44.1
Cole, Gerrit	42.9
Gonzales, Marco	42.8
Giolito, Lucas	42.8
Bundy, Dylan	42.4
Lynn, Lance	42.3
Singer, Brady	41.9
Civale, Aaron	40.1

Pitches Per Start	
(minimum 11 GS)	
Lynn, Lance	108.3
Bieber, Shane	103.2
Giolito, Lucas	101.2
Cole, Gerrit	100.3
Civale, Aaron	100.1
Gibson, Kyle	94.9
Ryu, Hyun-Jin	94.3
Berrios, Jose	91.8
Carrasco, Carlos	91.8
Boyd, Matthew	90.5

Pitches Per Batter	
(minimum 60 IP)	
Bassitt, Chris	3.63
Valdez, Framber	3.64
Keuchel, Dallas	3.74
Gibson, Kyle	3.78
Bundy, Dylan	3.81
Gonzales, Marco	3.82
Civale, Aaron	3.85
Greinke, Zack	3.88
Heaney, Andrew	3.89
Carrasco, Carlos	3.93

Quality Starts	
Bieber, Shane	10
Lynn, Lance	10
Carrasco, Carlos	9
Cole, Gerrit	8
Giolito, Lucas	8
Maeda, Kenta	8
Civale, Aaron	7
Ryu, Hyun-Jin	7
5 tied with	6

Batters Faced	
Lynn, Lance	344
Civale, Aaron	312
Gibson, Kyle	301
Bieber, Shane	297
Cole, Gerrit	288
Giolito, Lucas	288
Valdez, Framber	288
Carrasco, Carlos	280
Heaney, Andrew	279
Gonzales, Marco	277

Innings Pitched	
Lynn, Lance	84.0
Bieber, Shane	77.1
Civale, Aaron	74.0
Cole, Gerrit	73.0
Giolito, Lucas	72.1
Valdez, Framber	70.2
Gonzales, Marco	69.2
Carrasco, Carlos	68.0
Gibson, Kyle	67.1
2 tied with	67.0

Most Pitches in a Game	
Giolito, Lucas	119
Singer, Brady	119
Bieber, Shane	118
Heaney, Andrew	117
Lyles, Jordan	115
Maeda, Kenta	115
5 tied with	114

Stolen Bases Allowed	
Dunn, Justin	13
Turnbull, Spencer	11
Bundy, Dylan	10
Glasnow, Tyler	9
Fairbanks, Pete	7
Fiers, Mike	7
Walker, Taijuan	7
7 tied with	6

Caught Stealing Off	
Canning, Griffin	5
Alexander, Tyler	4
Bieber, Shane	3
Civale, Aaron	3
Gibson, Kyle	3
Snell, Blake	3
22 tied with	2

Stolen Base Pct Allowed	
(minimum 60 IP)	
Singer, Brady	0.0
Perez, Martin	33.3
Bieber, Shane	40.0
Boyd, Matthew	50.0
Carrasco, Carlos	50.0
Cole, Gerrit	50.0
Giolito, Lucas	50.0
Keuchel, Dallas	50.0
Ryu, Hyun-Jin	50.0
2 tied with	62.5

Pickoffs	
Alexander, Tyler	3
Berrios, Jose	2
Canning, Griffin	2
Detwiler, Ross	2
Fiers, Mike	2
Plesac, Zach	2
Sheffield, Justus	2
Singer, Brady	2
39 tied with	1

2020 American League Pitching Leaders

Strikeouts Per 9 IP
(minimum 60 IP)

Bieber, Shane	14.20
Giolito, Lucas	12.07
Cole, Gerrit	11.59
Carrasco, Carlos	10.85
Maeda, Kenta	10.80
Bundy, Dylan	9.87
Berrios, Jose	9.71
Valdez, Framber	9.68
Ryu, Hyun-Jin	9.67
Lynn, Lance	9.54

Opp On-Base Percentage
(minimum 60 IP)

Maeda, Kenta	.202
Bieber, Shane	.229
Cole, Gerrit	.250
Gonzales, Marco	.253
Giolito, Lucas	.267
Keuchel, Dallas	.271
Bundy, Dylan	.271
Lynn, Lance	.277
Greinke, Zack	.282
Ryu, Hyun-Jin	.285

Opp Slugging Average
(minimum 60 IP)

Bieber, Shane	.265
Keuchel, Dallas	.286
Maeda, Kenta	.307
Giolito, Lucas	.310
Valdez, Framber	.342
Bundy, Dylan	.343
Ryu, Hyun-Jin	.352
Singer, Brady	.356
Gonzales, Marco	.361
Carrasco, Carlos	.361

Opponent OPS
(minimum 60 IP)

Bieber, Shane	.494
Maeda, Kenta	.508
Keuchel, Dallas	.556
Giolito, Lucas	.577
Bundy, Dylan	.614
Gonzales, Marco	.614
Valdez, Framber	.635
Ryu, Hyun-Jin	.636
Singer, Brady	.649
Cole, Gerrit	.655

Home Runs Per Nine IP
(minimum 60 IP)

Keuchel, Dallas	0.28
Valdez, Framber	0.64
Bundy, Dylan	0.69
Greinke, Zack	0.81
Ryu, Hyun-Jin	0.81
Bieber, Shane	0.81
Bassitt, Chris	0.86
Giolito, Lucas	1.00
Gonzales, Marco	1.03
Carrasco, Carlos	1.06

Batting Average vs. LHB
(minimum 46 BF)

Colome, Alex	.098
Mayers, Mike	.100
Marshall, Evan	.119
Heuer, Codi	.130
Urquidy, Jose	.136
Paredes, Enoli	.143
Sulser, Cole	.143
Zimmer, Kyle	.150
Bieber, Shane	.153
2 tied with	.154

Batting Average vs. RHB
(minimum 225 BF)

Javier, Cristian	.101
Maeda, Kenta	.149
Walker, Taijuan	.178
Plesac, Zach	.180
Bieber, Shane	.181
Dunn, Justin	.185
Giolito, Lucas	.190
Bundy, Dylan	.196
Montas, Frankie	.198
Glasnow, Tyler	.200

Opp BA w/ RISP
(minimum 46 BF)

Weber, Ryan	.140
Lynn, Lance	.145
Berrios, Jose	.174
Carrasco, Carlos	.189
Keuchel, Dallas	.189
Giolito, Lucas	.196
Fiers, Mike	.196
Bundy, Dylan	.197
3 tied with	.200

OBP vs. Leadoff Hitter
(minimum 56 BF)

Bieber, Shane	.205
Bassitt, Chris	.227
Plesac, Zach	.232
Maeda, Kenta	.246
Keuchel, Dallas	.258
Greinke, Zack	.261
Gonzales, Marco	.268
Glasnow, Tyler	.271
Lynn, Lance	.282
Yarbrough, Ryan	.283

Strikeouts / Walks Ratio
(minimum 60 IP)

Gonzales, Marco	9.14
Maeda, Kenta	8.00
Greinke, Zack	7.44
Bieber, Shane	5.81
Cole, Gerrit	5.53
Valdez, Framber	4.75
Civale, Aaron	4.31
Bundy, Dylan	4.24
Ryu, Hyun-Jin	4.24
Heaney, Andrew	3.68

Highest GB/FB Ratio
(minimum 60 IP)

Valdez, Framber	3.08
Keuchel, Dallas	2.40
Gibson, Kyle	2.36
Ryu, Hyun-Jin	1.82
Singer, Brady	1.77
Bieber, Shane	1.61
Maeda, Kenta	1.60
Civale, Aaron	1.41
Carrasco, Carlos	1.32
Greinke, Zack	1.23

Lowest GB/FB Ratio
(minimum 60 IP)

Lynn, Lance	0.85
Cole, Gerrit	0.87
Boyd, Matthew	0.89
Gonzales, Marco	0.92
Heaney, Andrew	1.00
Perez, Martin	1.09
Giolito, Lucas	1.10
Berrios, Jose	1.13
Bundy, Dylan	1.13
Bassitt, Chris	1.16

Sacrifice Flies Allowed

Lyles, Jordan	5
Canning, Griffin	4
Duffy, Danny	4
Karinchak, James	4
Wojciechowski, Asher	4
8 tied with	3

Sacrifice Hits Allowed

Dolis, Rafael	2
Keuchel, Dallas	2
Loup, Aaron	2
Sneed, Cy	2
Sulser, Cole	2
Turnbull, Spencer	2
Yarbrough, Ryan	2
56 tied with	1

GIDP Induced

Cease, Dylan	10
Perez, Martin	10
Dobnak, Randy	9
Keller, Brad	9
Valdez, Framber	9
Civale, Aaron	8
Gibson, Kyle	8
Giolito, Lucas	8
Kikuchi, Yusei	8
2 tied with	7

GIDP Per Nine IP
(minimum 60 IP)

Perez, Martin	1.45
Valdez, Framber	1.15
Gibson, Kyle	1.07
Giolito, Lucas	1.00
Civale, Aaron	0.97
Ryu, Hyun-Jin	0.94
Boyd, Matthew	0.75
Keuchel, Dallas	0.71
Carrasco, Carlos	0.66
Bassitt, Chris	0.57

2020 American League Pitching Leaders

Saves

Hand, Brad	16
Hendriks, Liam	14
Colome, Alex	12
Pressly, Ryan	12
Barnes, Matt	9
Rogers, Taylor	9
Britton, Zack	8
Montero, Rafael	8
Bass, Anthony	7
Rosenthal, Trevor	7

Blown Saves

Barnes, Matt	4
Buttrey, Ty	4
Pressly, Ryan	4
Chavez, Jesse	3
Cole, A.J.	3
Karinchak, James	3
Ottavino, Adam	3
Pena, Felix	3
Sulser, Cole	3
22 tied with	2

Save Pct
(minimum 7 Save Ops)

Britton, Zack	100.0
Hand, Brad	100.0
Montero, Rafael	100.0
Hendriks, Liam	93.3
Colome, Alex	92.3
Rogers, Taylor	81.8
Bass, Anthony	77.8
Pressly, Ryan	75.0
Barnes, Matt	69.2
Sulser, Cole	62.5

Save Opportunities

Hand, Brad	16
Pressly, Ryan	16
Hendriks, Liam	15
Barnes, Matt	13
Colome, Alex	13
Rogers, Taylor	11
Bass, Anthony	9
Buttrey, Ty	9
3 tied with	8

Easy Saves

Hand, Brad	12
Hendriks, Liam	8
Rogers, Taylor	8
Barnes, Matt	7
Britton, Zack	7
Colome, Alex	7
Pressly, Ryan	7
Montero, Rafael	5
Romo, Sergio	5
2 tied with	4

Regular Saves

Bass, Anthony	6
Hendriks, Liam	6
Anderson, Nick	5
Buttrey, Ty	5
Pressly, Ryan	5
Colome, Alex	4
Hand, Brad	4
Rosenthal, Trevor	4
Sulser, Cole	4
2 tied with	3

Tough Saves

Beeks, Jalen	1
Cessa, Luis	1
Cole, A.J.	1
Colome, Alex	1
Dolis, Rafael	1
Lakins, Travis	1
Montero, Rafael	1
Newberry, Jake	1
Perez, Oliver	1
Soria, Joakim	1

Holds Adjusted Saves %
(minimum 7 Save Ops + Holds)

Anderson, Nick	100.0
Barlow, Scott	100.0
Britton, Zack	100.0
Hahn, Jesse	100.0
Hand, Brad	100.0
Holland, Greg	100.0
May, Trevor	100.0
Montero, Rafael	100.0
Rosenthal, Trevor	100.0
Staumont, Josh	100.0

Relief Wins

Fairbanks, Pete	6
Foster, Matt	6
Hernandez, Jonathan	5
17 tied with	3

Relief Losses

Sulser, Cole	5
Rogers, Taylor	4
Yamaguchi, Shun	4
14 tied with	3

Relief Games

Barlow, Scott	32
Cordero, Jimmy	30
Cisnero, Jose	29
Mayers, Mike	29
Holland, Greg	28
Buttrey, Ty	27
Hernandez, Jonathan	27
Karinchak, James	27
Soto, Gregory	27
4 tied with	26

Holds

Diekman, Jake	13
Duffey, Tyler	12
Brasier, Ryan	10
Romo, Sergio	10
Wittgren, Nick	10
6 tied with	8

Relief Innings

Hernandez, Jonathan	31.0
Andriese, Matt	30.1
Valdez, Phillips	30.1
Barlow, Scott	30.0
Mayers, Mike	30.0
Cisnero, Jose	29.2
Alexander, Tyler	28.2
Holland, Greg	28.1
Karinchak, James	27.0
2 tied with	26.2

Inherited Runners Scrd %
(minimum 12 IR)

Cisnero, Jose	5.9
Cordero, Jimmy	6.3
Anderson, Nick	7.1
Raley, Brooks	7.7
Scrubb, Andre	13.3
Brice, Austin	14.3
Armstrong, Shawn	15.4
Clippard, Tyler	15.4
Dolis, Rafael	16.7
Newberry, Jake	16.7

Relief Opp On Base Pct
(minimum 18 IP)

Hendriks, Liam	.187
Green, Chad	.212
Duffey, Tyler	.217
Andriese, Matt	.219
Curtiss, John	.222
Hand, Brad	.226
Heuer, Codi	.228
Mayers, Mike	.231
Colome, Alex	.247
4 tied with	.250

Relief Opp Slugging Avg
(minimum 18 IP)

Diekman, Jake	.157
Heuer, Codi	.205
Colome, Alex	.213
Hendriks, Liam	.218
Thielbar, Caleb	.219
Karinchak, James	.227
Britton, Zack	.232
Scott, Tanner	.233
Scrubb, Andre	.241
Garcia, Bryan	.247

2020 American League Pitching Leaders

Relief Opp BA Vs LHB
(minimum 19 AB)

Hahn, Jesse	.000
Green, Chad	.075
Petit, Yusmeiro	.077
Romano, Jordan	.083
Herget, Jimmy	.087
Soto, Gregory	.095
Colome, Alex	.098
Mayers, Mike	.100
Rosenthal, Trevor	.111
Marshall, Evan	.119

Relief Opp BA Vs RHB
(minimum 19 AB)

Anderson, Nick	.034
Diekman, Jake	.070
Ramirez, Yohan	.071
Bummer, Aaron	.100
Tate, Dillon	.105
Zeuch, T.J.	.105
Valdez, Cesar	.107
Givens, Mychal	.125
Zuber, Tyler	.128
Smith, Burch	.133

Relief Opp Batting Average
(minimum 18 IP)

Diekman, Jake	.114
Ramirez, Yohan	.130
Green, Chad	.144
Heuer, Codi	.145
Duffey, Tyler	.153
Castillo, Diego	.156
Karinchak, James	.159
Andriese, Matt	.160
Hendriks, Liam	.161
Mayers, Mike	.162

Relief Earned Run Average
(minimum 18 IP)

Diekman, Jake	0.42
Colome, Alex	0.81
Zimmer, Kyle	1.29
Scott, Tanner	1.31
Dolis, Rafael	1.50
Heuer, Codi	1.52
Castillo, Diego	1.66
Curtiss, John	1.66
Garcia, Bryan	1.66
Petit, Yusmeiro	1.66

Rel OBP 1st Batter Faced
(minimum 40 BF)

Duffey, Tyler	.000
Montero, Rafael	.063
Raley, Brooks	.063
Hendriks, Liam	.125
Wendelken, J.B.	.143
Hernandez, Jonathan	.148
Britton, Zack	.150
Anderson, Nick	.158
Holder, Jonathan	.167
Cisnero, Jose	.172

Rel Opp BA w/ Runners On
(minimum 18 IP)

Diekman, Jake	.061
Ramirez, Yohan	.073
Taylor, Blake	.105
Hendriks, Liam	.125
Scott, Tanner	.130
Green, Chad	.132
Castillo, Diego	.133
Zimmer, Kyle	.143
Soria, Joakim	.147
Colome, Alex	.152

Relief Opp BA w/ RISP
(minimum 18 IP)

Ramirez, Yohan	.000
Zimmer, Kyle	.053
Castillo, Diego	.059
Colome, Alex	.063
Scott, Tanner	.065
Alexander, Tyler	.071
May, Trevor	.100
Petit, Yusmeiro	.111
Soria, Joakim	.118
Thielbar, Caleb	.125

Fastest Avg Fastball-Relief
(minimum 18 IP)

Staumont, Josh	98.1
Hernandez, Jonathan	97.8
Heuer, Codi	97.6
Fairbanks, Pete	97.5
Soto, Gregory	97.3
Alcala, Jorge	97.0
Cordero, Jimmy	96.7
Scott, Tanner	96.5
May, Trevor	96.4
Nelson, Nick	96.4

Fastest Average Fastball
(minimum 60 IP)

Cole, Gerrit	96.7
Berrios, Jose	94.3
Bieber, Shane	94.2
Giolito, Lucas	94.0
Carrasco, Carlos	93.6
Lynn, Lance	93.5
Singer, Brady	93.4
Valdez, Framber	93.1
Bassitt, Chris	92.9
Gibson, Kyle	92.3

Slowest Average Fastball
(minimum 60 IP)

Greinke, Zack	87.1
Keuchel, Dallas	87.3
Gonzales, Marco	88.2
Ryu, Hyun-Jin	89.6
Bundy, Dylan	90.2
Maeda, Kenta	91.4
Heaney, Andrew	91.5
Boyd, Matthew	91.7
Civale, Aaron	91.8
Perez, Martin	92.1

Pitches 100+ Velocity

Crochet, Garrett	61
Staumont, Josh	58
Chapman, Aroldis	33
Rosenthal, Trevor	23
Tapia, Domingo	22
Castro, Miguel	17
Eovaldi, Nathan	13
Cease, Dylan	11
Glasnow, Tyler	10
2 tied with	7

Pitches 95+ Velocity

Cole, Gerrit	613
Glasnow, Tyler	569
Cease, Dylan	517
Montas, Frankie	473
Luzardo, Jesus	391
Staumont, Josh	341
Snell, Blake	331
Soto, Gregory	314
Cisnero, Jose	312
Lynn, Lance	289

Pitches Less Than 80 MPH

Boyd, Matthew	329
Hill, Rich	305
Yarbrough, Ryan	283
Keuchel, Dallas	278
Ryu, Hyun-Jin	278
Civale, Aaron	257
Milone, Tommy	256
Eshelman, Thomas	252
Romo, Sergio	248
Bubic, Kris	223

Lowest % Fastballs
(minimum 60 IP)

Maeda, Kenta	25.9
Civale, Aaron	31.4
Perez, Martin	33.1
Keuchel, Dallas	34.6
Ryu, Hyun-Jin	34.7
Bieber, Shane	37.5
Carrasco, Carlos	39.3
Bundy, Dylan	41.9
Gonzales, Marco	45.3
Greinke, Zack	45.7

Highest % Fastballs
(minimum 60 IP)

Lynn, Lance	67.8
Valdez, Framber	58.2
Heaney, Andrew	58.1
Singer, Brady	57.9
Bassitt, Chris	54.3
Cole, Gerrit	52.8
Boyd, Matthew	52.7
Berrios, Jose	51.5
Giolito, Lucas	50.6
Gibson, Kyle	49.4

Highest % Curveballs
(minimum 60 IP)

Valdez, Framber	33.5
Berrios, Jose	29.8
Bieber, Shane	26.3
Civale, Aaron	21.1
Cole, Gerrit	17.2
Gonzales, Marco	16.1
Greinke, Zack	15.7
Ryu, Hyun-Jin	13.2
Bundy, Dylan	11.7
Carrasco, Carlos	10.8

2020 American League Pitching Leaders

Highest % Changeups		Highest % Sliders		Balks		Strikeout/Hit Ratio	
(minimum 60 IP)		(minimum 60 IP)				(minimum 18 IP)	
Giolito, Lucas	33.7	Maeda, Kenta	39.9	Brasier, Ryan	2	Diekman, Jake	3.88
Maeda, Kenta	28.9	Singer, Brady	37.4	Javier, Cristian	2	Karinchak, James	3.79
Keuchel, Dallas	27.9	Bundy, Dylan	25.0	22 tied with	1	Ramirez, Yohan	2.89
Ryu, Hyun-Jin	27.8	Heaney, Andrew	24.8			Bieber, Shane	2.65
Carrasco, Carlos	27.0	Cole, Gerrit	24.4			Hendriks, Liam	2.64
Perez, Martin	25.6	Gibson, Kyle	24.3			Green, Chad	2.46
Greinke, Zack	22.6	Lynn, Lance	23.4			Mayers, Mike	2.39
Bundy, Dylan	21.3	Boyd, Matthew	22.7			Duffey, Tyler	2.38
Berrios, Jose	18.8	Carrasco, Carlos	22.6			Wisler, Matt	2.33
Gibson, Kyle	17.9	Greinke, Zack	16.0			Hand, Brad	2.23

Opp OPS vs Fastballs		Opp OPS vs Curveballs		Opp OPS vs Changeups		Opp OPS vs Sliders	
(minimum 251 BF)		(minimum 37 BF)		(minimum 37 BF)		(minimum 64 BF)	
Gonzales, Marco	.459	Bieber, Shane	.393	Plesac, Zach	.357	Snell, Blake	.163
Keller, Brad	.538	Karinchak, James	.433	Maeda, Kenta	.392	Plesac, Zach	.218
Dunn, Justin	.558	Hill, Rich	.469	Keuchel, Dallas	.424	Scott, Tanner	.329
Bieber, Shane	.562	Duffey, Tyler	.496	Valdez, Cesar	.434	Wendelken, J.B.	.336
Giolito, Lucas	.579	Berrios, Jose	.574	Foster, Matt	.475	Pineda, Michael	.344
Walker, Taijuan	.590	Greinke, Zack	.595	Clippard, Tyler	.487	Lyles, Jordan	.352
Minor, Mike	.602	Valdez, Framber	.597	Ryu, Hyun-Jin	.493	Ramirez, Yohan	.382
Happ, J.A.	.607	Scrubb, Andre	.616	Giolito, Lucas	.499	Hand, Brad	.392
Singer, Brady	.610	Lopez, Jorge	.699	Canning, Griffin	.506	Javier, Cristian	.392
Glasnow, Tyler	.646	Canning, Griffin	.713	Manaea, Sean	.539	Ray, Robbie	.443

Earned Runs

Boyd, Matthew	45
Lyles, Jordan	45
Gibson, Kyle	40
Civale, Aaron	39
Roark, Tanner	36
Minor, Mike	35
Teheran, Julio	35
Heaney, Andrew	33
Montas, Frankie	33
3 tied with	31

Hits Per Nine Innings

(minimum 60 IP)

Bieber, Shane	5.35
Maeda, Kenta	5.40
Giolito, Lucas	5.85
Cole, Gerrit	6.53
Lynn, Lance	6.86
Bundy, Dylan	6.99
Singer, Brady	7.27
Carrasco, Carlos	7.28
Keuchel, Dallas	7.39
Gonzales, Marco	7.62

2020 National League Pitching Leaders

Earned Run Average (minimum 60 IP)	
Bauer, Trevor	1.73
Darvish, Yu	2.01
Lamet, Dinelson	2.09
deGrom, Jacob	2.38
Davies, Zach	2.73
Gallen, Zac	2.75
Hendricks, Kyle	2.88
Wheeler, Zack	2.92
Woodruff, Brandon	3.05
Wainwright, Adam	3.15

Winning Percentage (minimum 6 Decisions)	
Fried, Max	1.000
Baragar, Caleb	.833
Kershaw, Clayton	.750
Peterson, David	.750
Darvish, Yu	.727
Bard, Daniel	.667
deGrom, Jacob	.667
Eflin, Zach	.667
Stammen, Craig	.667
Wheeler, Zack	.667

Opponent Batting Average (minimum 60 IP)	
Bauer, Trevor	.159
Lamet, Dinelson	.161
deGrom, Jacob	.190
Woodruff, Brandon	.204
Nola, Aaron	.205
Gallen, Zac	.210
Darvish, Yu	.211
Davies, Zach	.216
Wainwright, Adam	.221
Mills, Alec	.230

Baserunners Per 9 IP (minimum 60 IP)	
Bauer, Trevor	7.52
Lamet, Dinelson	8.22
deGrom, Jacob	8.60
Darvish, Yu	8.88
Hendricks, Kyle	9.07
Woodruff, Brandon	9.41
Davies, Zach	9.61
Wainwright, Adam	9.73
Nola, Aaron	9.97
Gallen, Zac	10.25

Games	
Rogers, Tyler	29
Greene, Shane	28
Jansen, Kenley	27
Stratton, Chris	27
Treinen, Blake	27
Crichton, Stefan	26
Diaz, Edwin	26
Estevez, Carlos	26
6 tied with	25

Games Started	
Freeland, Kyle	13
Marquez, German	13
Woodruff, Brandon	13
15 tied with	12

Complete Games	
Bauer, Trevor	2
Nola, Aaron	2
Wainwright, Adam	2
12 tied with	1

Shutouts	
Bauer, Trevor	2
Clevinger, Mike	1
Eflin, Zach	1
Hendricks, Kyle	1
Mills, Alec	1
Nola, Aaron	1

Wins	
Darvish, Yu	8
Davies, Zach	7
Fried, Max	7
Hendricks, Kyle	6
Kershaw, Clayton	6
Lopez, Pablo	6
Peterson, David	6
8 tied with	5

Losses	
Weaver, Luke	9
Williams, Trevor	8
Corbin, Patrick	7
Porcello, Rick	7
Castillo, Luis	6
Houser, Adrian	6
Marquez, German	6
9 tied with	5

No Decisions	
Freeland, Kyle	8
Lamet, Dinelson	8
Buehler, Walker	7
Cueto, Johnny	7
Gallen, Zac	7
May, Dustin	7
Urias, Julio	7
4 tied with	6

Wild Pitches	
Gray, Sonny	7
Ray, Robbie	6
Scherzer, Max	6
Burnes, Corbin	5
13 tied with	4

Strikeouts	
deGrom, Jacob	104
Bauer, Trevor	100
Nola, Aaron	96
Darvish, Yu	93
Lamet, Dinelson	93
Scherzer, Max	92
Woodruff, Brandon	91
Castillo, Luis	89
Burnes, Corbin	88
Gallen, Zac	82

Walks Allowed	
Ray, Robbie	31
Kuhl, Chad	28
Castellani, Ryan	26
Cueto, Johnny	26
Gray, Sonny	26
Anderson, Tyler	25
Gallen, Zac	25
Marquez, German	25
5 tied with	24

Intentional Walks Allowed	
Crichton, Stefan	4
Finnegan, Kyle	4
Kintzler, Brandon	3
Melancon, Mark	3
27 tied with	2

Hit Batters	
Webb, Logan	7
Wheeler, Zack	7
Bumgarner, Madison	6
Brault, Steven	5
Castellani, Ryan	5
Hughes, Jared	5
Oviedo, Johan	5
Strahm, Matt	5
Toussaint, Touki	5
13 tied with	4

2020 National League Pitching Leaders

Runs Allowed		Hits Allowed		Doubles Allowed		Home Runs Allowed	
Williams, Trevor	42	Corbin, Patrick	85	Castillo, Luis	18	Williams, Trevor	15
Cueto, Johnny	41	Marquez, German	78	Eflin, Zach	18	Matz, Steven	14
Houser, Adrian	41	Freeland, Kyle	77	Anderson, Tyler	16	Paddack, Chris	14
Marquez, German	41	Porcello, Rick	74	Corbin, Patrick	16	Voth, Austin	14
Porcello, Rick	41	Hendricks, Kyle	73	Freeland, Kyle	16	Bumgarner, Madison	13
Sanchez, Anibal	40	Senzatela, Antonio	71	Fried, Max	16	Mills, Alec	13
Weaver, Luke	39	Sanchez, Anibal	70	Marquez, German	16	Castellani, Ryan	12
Webb, Logan	38	Scherzer, Max	70	Weaver, Luke	16	Holland, Derek	12
Voth, Austin	36	Wheeler, Zack	67	Webb, Logan	16	Stripling, Ross	12
2 tied with	35	Williams, Trevor	66	Wheeler, Zack	16	3 tied with	11

Run Support Per Nine IP (minimum 60 IP)		% Pitches In Strike Zone (minimum 60 IP)		Pitches Per Start (minimum 11 GS)		Pitches Per Batter (minimum 60 IP)	
Davies, Zach	6.88	Darvish, Yu	47.0	Scherzer, Max	101.1	Wainwright, Adam	3.55
deGrom, Jacob	6.49	Hendricks, Kyle	45.4	Hendricks, Kyle	96.8	Marquez, German	3.56
Wheeler, Zack	6.47	Marquez, German	44.9	Castillo, Luis	96.1	Corbin, Patrick	3.62
Nola, Aaron	6.31	Lamet, Dinelson	42.9	Darvish, Yu	96.1	Hendricks, Kyle	3.69
Lester, Jon	6.05	Woodruff, Brandon	42.1	Nola, Aaron	95.7	Freeland, Kyle	3.70
Mills, Alec	5.49	Scherzer, Max	41.9	Cueto, Johnny	95.4	Wheeler, Zack	3.74
Lamet, Dinelson	5.22	Wainwright, Adam	41.1	Senzatela, Antonio	94.8	Mills, Alec	3.75
Scherzer, Max	4.95	Castillo, Luis	40.9	deGrom, Jacob	94.6	Senzatela, Antonio	3.75
Corbin, Patrick	4.80	Wheeler, Zack	40.4	Marquez, German	94.3	Lester, Jon	3.80
Senzatela, Antonio	4.66	Senzatela, Antonio	39.8	Woodruff, Brandon	93.2	Davies, Zach	3.82

Quality Starts		Batters Faced		Innings Pitched		Most Pitches in a Game	
Darvish, Yu	10	Marquez, German	344	Marquez, German	81.2	Wainwright, Adam	122
Bauer, Trevor	9	Hendricks, Kyle	315	Hendricks, Kyle	81.1	Scherzer, Max	119
Freeland, Kyle	9	Freeland, Kyle	304	Darvish, Yu	76.0	Scherzer, Max	119
Gallen, Zac	9	Senzatela, Antonio	303	Woodruff, Brandon	73.2	Wheeler, Zack	118
Hendricks, Kyle	9	Darvish, Yu	297	Senzatela, Antonio	73.1	Mills, Alec	114
Marquez, German	9	Corbin, Patrick	295	Bauer, Trevor	73.0	6 tied with	113
deGrom, Jacob	8	Scherzer, Max	295	Gallen, Zac	72.0		
4 tied with	7	Woodruff, Brandon	293	Nola, Aaron	71.1		
		Castillo, Luis	292	Wheeler, Zack	71.0		
		Gallen, Zac	291	Freeland, Kyle	70.2		

Stolen Bases Allowed		Caught Stealing Off		Stolen Base Pct Allowed (minimum 60 IP)		Pickoffs	
deGrom, Jacob	13	Houser, Adrian	5	Hendricks, Kyle	0.0	Anderson, Tyler	4
Sanchez, Anibal	11	Hendricks, Kyle	4	Wainwright, Adam	0.0	Fried, Max	4
Burnes, Corbin	9	Webb, Logan	4	Mills, Alec	33.3	Peralta, Wandy	3
Gallen, Zac	7	Clevinger, Mike	3	Castillo, Luis	50.0	Velasquez, Vince	3
Nola, Aaron	7	Lindblom, Josh	3	Lester, Jon	60.0	Clarke, Taylor	2
Scherzer, Max	7	Paddack, Chris	3	Corbin, Patrick	66.7	Corbin, Patrick	2
Smyly, Drew	7	21 tied with	2	Bauer, Trevor	75.0	Hendricks, Kyle	2
Webb, Logan	7			Woodruff, Brandon	75.0	Holland, Derek	2
6 tied with	6			Nola, Aaron	77.8	34 tied with	1
				Lamet, Dinelson	80.0		

2020 National League Pitching Leaders

Strikeouts Per 9 IP	
(minimum 60 IP)	
deGrom, Jacob	13.76
Bauer, Trevor	12.33
Scherzer, Max	12.30
Lamet, Dinelson	12.13
Nola, Aaron	12.11
Castillo, Luis	11.44
Woodruff, Brandon	11.12
Darvish, Yu	11.01
Gallen, Zac	10.25
Corbin, Patrick	8.22

Opp On-Base Percentage	
(minimum 60 IP)	
Bauer, Trevor	.219
Lamet, Dinelson	.236
deGrom, Jacob	.243
Darvish, Yu	.253
Hendricks, Kyle	.260
Woodruff, Brandon	.263
Davies, Zach	.269
Wainwright, Adam	.271
Nola, Aaron	.273
Gallen, Zac	.284

Opp Slugging Average	
(minimum 60 IP)	
Lamet, Dinelson	.260
Bauer, Trevor	.302
Darvish, Yu	.321
deGrom, Jacob	.323
Gallen, Zac	.336
Woodruff, Brandon	.341
Wheeler, Zack	.348
Nola, Aaron	.354
Davies, Zach	.361
Castillo, Luis	.365

Opponent OPS	
(minimum 60 IP)	
Lamet, Dinelson	.496
Bauer, Trevor	.522
deGrom, Jacob	.565
Darvish, Yu	.575
Woodruff, Brandon	.604
Gallen, Zac	.620
Nola, Aaron	.627
Davies, Zach	.630
Hendricks, Kyle	.632
Wainwright, Adam	.640

Home Runs Per Nine IP	
(minimum 60 IP)	
Wheeler, Zack	0.38
Darvish, Yu	0.59
Castillo, Luis	0.64
Lamet, Dinelson	0.65
Marquez, German	0.66
deGrom, Jacob	0.93
Woodruff, Brandon	1.10
Senzatela, Antonio	1.10
Hendricks, Kyle	1.11
Bauer, Trevor	1.11

Batting Average vs. LHB	
(minimum 46 BF)	
Williams, Devin	.075
Sims, Lucas	.106
Cahill, Trevor	.111
Kinley, Tyler	.111
Hudson, Dakota	.130
Lamet, Dinelson	.133
Jeffress, Jeremy	.136
Urias, Julio	.137
Rodriguez, Richard	.140
Anderson, Ian	.145

Batting Average vs. RHB	
(minimum 225 BF)	
Burnes, Corbin	.140
Bauer, Trevor	.146
Mills, Alec	.163
Lopez, Pablo	.184
Gomber, Austin	.189
Richards, Garrett	.189
Alcantara, Sandy	.190
Brault, Steven	.190
Lindblom, Josh	.195
deGrom, Jacob	.195

Opp BA w/ RISP	
(minimum 46 BF)	
Fried, Max	.119
Scherzer, Max	.143
Guerra, Junior	.152
Burnes, Corbin	.167
Peterson, David	.171
Gallen, Zac	.174
Anderson, Brett	.179
Darvish, Yu	.190
Senzatela, Antonio	.193
Lorenzen, Michael	.205

OBP vs. Leadoff Hitter	
(minimum 56 BF)	
Gray, Sonny	.186
Scherzer, Max	.214
deGrom, Jacob	.221
Gausman, Kevin	.222
Castillo, Luis	.236
Davies, Zach	.236
Fried, Max	.246
Bauer, Trevor	.250
Hendricks, Kyle	.250
Lopez, Pablo	.254

Strikeouts / Walks Ratio	
(minimum 60 IP)	
Hendricks, Kyle	8.00
Darvish, Yu	6.64
Bauer, Trevor	5.88
deGrom, Jacob	5.78
Woodruff, Brandon	5.06
Lamet, Dinelson	4.65
Nola, Aaron	4.17
Scherzer, Max	4.00
Castillo, Luis	3.71
Wainwright, Adam	3.60

Highest GB/FB Ratio	
(minimum 60 IP)	
Wheeler, Zack	2.95
Castillo, Luis	2.60
Freeland, Kyle	2.05
Marquez, German	1.94
Nola, Aaron	1.80
Senzatela, Antonio	1.74
Hendricks, Kyle	1.48
Mills, Alec	1.43
Corbin, Patrick	1.42
Darvish, Yu	1.40

Lowest GB/FB Ratio	
(minimum 60 IP)	
Bauer, Trevor	0.72
Scherzer, Max	0.83
Lamet, Dinelson	0.87
Davies, Zach	1.11
deGrom, Jacob	1.15
Cueto, Johnny	1.20
Wainwright, Adam	1.26
Lester, Jon	1.30
Woodruff, Brandon	1.38
Gallen, Zac	1.39

Sacrifice Flies Allowed	
Young, Alex	5
Jackson, Luke	4
Mahle, Tyler	4
9 tied with	3

Sacrifice Hits Allowed	
Diaz, Jairo	2
Guerra, Junior	2
Stammen, Craig	2
Stripling, Ross	2
Tarpley, Stephen	2
46 tied with	1

GIDP Induced	
Freeland, Kyle	14
Wheeler, Zack	13
Arrieta, Jake	9
Gallen, Zac	9
Senzatela, Antonio	9
Houser, Adrian	8
Marquez, German	8
Webb, Logan	8
6 tied with	7

GIDP Per Nine IP	
(minimum 60 IP)	
Freeland, Kyle	1.78
Wheeler, Zack	1.65
Gallen, Zac	1.13
Senzatela, Antonio	1.10
Corbin, Patrick	0.96
Marquez, German	0.88
Darvish, Yu	0.83
Wainwright, Adam	0.82
Hendricks, Kyle	0.77
Cueto, Johnny	0.71

2020 National League Pitching Leaders

Saves

Hader, Josh	13
Kintzler, Brandon	12
Jansen, Kenley	11
Melancon, Mark	11
Hudson, Daniel	10
Iglesias, Raisel	8
Jeffress, Jeremy	8
Bard, Daniel	6
Bradley, Archie	6
Diaz, Edwin	6

Blown Saves

Hudson, Daniel	5
Pagan, Emilio	5
Diaz, Edwin	3
Estevez, Carlos	3
Harris, Will	3
Neris, Hector	3
Rogers, Tyler	3
Turley, Nik	3
Workman, Brandon	3
29 tied with	2

Save Pct
(minimum 7 Save Ops)

Hader, Josh	86.7
Kintzler, Brandon	85.7
Jansen, Kenley	84.6
Melancon, Mark	84.6
Iglesias, Raisel	80.0
Jeffress, Jeremy	80.0
Diaz, Edwin	66.7
Hudson, Daniel	66.7
Neris, Hector	62.5
Workman, Brandon	62.5

Save Opportunities

Hader, Josh	15
Hudson, Daniel	15
Kintzler, Brandon	14
Jansen, Kenley	13
Melancon, Mark	13
Iglesias, Raisel	10
Jeffress, Jeremy	10
Diaz, Edwin	10
Neris, Hector	8
Workman, Brandon	8

Easy Saves

Jansen, Kenley	10
Hudson, Daniel	7
Hader, Josh	6
Kintzler, Brandon	6
Melancon, Mark	5
Iglesias, Raisel	4
Jeffress, Jeremy	4
Workman, Brandon	4
6 tied with	3

Regular Saves

Hader, Josh	6
Kintzler, Brandon	6
Melancon, Mark	6
Iglesias, Raisel	4
Bradley, Archie	3
Diaz, Edwin	3
Gallegos, Giovanny	3
Hudson, Daniel	3
Rodriguez, Richard	3
Wick, Rowan	3

Tough Saves

Jeffress, Jeremy	2
Bard, Daniel	1
Hader, Josh	1
Hoffman, Jeff	1
Kolarek, Adam	1
Neris, Hector	1
Pomeranz, Drew	1
Quantrill, Cal	1
Tarpley, Stephen	1
Vincent, Nick	1

Holds Adjusted Saves %
(minimum 7 Save Ops + Holds)

Baez, Pedro	100.0
Bard, Daniel	100.0
Greene, Shane	100.0
Rainey, Tanner	100.0
Watson, Tony	100.0
Wick, Rowan	100.0
Williams, Devin	100.0
Wilson, Justin	100.0
Pomeranz, Drew	92.9
Treinen, Blake	90.9

Relief Wins

Baragar, Caleb	5
Bard, Daniel	4
Cabrera, Genesis	4
Iglesias, Raisel	4
Jeffress, Jeremy	4
Matzek, Tyler	4
O'Day, Darren	4
Stammen, Craig	4
Williams, Devin	4
16 tied with	3

Relief Losses

Phelps, David	4
Workman, Brandon	4
11 tied with	3

Relief Games

Rogers, Tyler	29
Greene, Shane	28
Jansen, Kenley	27
Stratton, Chris	27
Treinen, Blake	27
Crichton, Stefan	26
Diaz, Edwin	26
Estevez, Carlos	26
6 tied with	25

Holds

Rogers, Tyler	10
Watson, Tony	10
Wilson, Justin	10
Greene, Shane	9
Pomeranz, Drew	9
Rainey, Tanner	9
Treinen, Blake	9
Williams, Devin	9
Hunter, Tommy	8
2 tied with	7

Relief Innings

Stratton, Chris	30.0
Matzek, Tyler	29.0
Rogers, Tyler	28.0
Almonte, Yency	27.2
Greene, Shane	27.2
Dayton, Grant	27.1
Peralta, Wandy	27.1
Williams, Devin	27.0
Familia, Jeurys	26.2
2 tied with	26.1

Inherited Runners Scrd %
(minimum 12 IR)

Morgan, Adam	7.7
Bleier, Richard	8.3
Harper, Ryne	10.5
Hartlieb, Geoff	11.1
Wilson, Justin	12.5
Minter, A.J.	13.3
Baragar, Caleb	13.6
Hunter, Tommy	14.3
Matzek, Tyler	16.7
Rainey, Tanner	16.7

Relief Opp On Base Pct
(minimum 18 IP)

Williams, Devin	.182
Antone, Tejay	.183
Kolarek, Adam	.208
Rainey, Tanner	.213
McGee, Jake	.218
Gonzalez, Victor	.224
Rodriguez, Richard	.239
Iglesias, Raisel	.244
Pomeranz, Drew	.260
Baragar, Caleb	.262

Relief Opp Slugging Avg
(minimum 18 IP)

Williams, Devin	.157
Jeffress, Jeremy	.192
Antone, Tejay	.194
Pomeranz, Drew	.194
Gonzalez, Victor	.200
Kolarek, Adam	.224
Iglesias, Raisel	.265
Kinley, Tyler	.269
Cabrera, Genesis	.276
Graterol, Brusdar	.278

2020 National League Pitching Leaders

Relief Opp BA Vs LHB (minimum 19 AB)		Relief Opp BA Vs RHB (minimum 19 AB)		Relief Opp Batting Average (minimum 18 IP)		Relief Earned Run Average (minimum 18 IP)	
Garrett, Amir	.043	Antone, Tejay	.081	Williams, Devin	.090	Williams, Devin	0.33
Shreve, Chasen	.063	Burnes, Corbin	.100	Antone, Tejay	.097	Minter, A.J.	0.83
Cabrera, Genesis	.069	Williams, Devin	.111	Rainey, Tanner	.119	Kolarek, Adam	0.95
Perdomo, Luis	.071	Hader, Josh	.115	Hader, Josh	.123	Gonzalez, Victor	1.40
Williams, Devin	.075	Brogdon, Connor	.125	Cabrera, Genesis	.132	Jeffress, Jeremy	1.54
Kolarek, Adam	.077	Garcia, Yimi	.125	Jeffress, Jeremy	.137	Yardley, Eric	1.54
Tomlin, Josh	.083	Rainey, Tanner	.128	Sims, Lucas	.146	Diaz, Edwin	1.75
Johnson, Pierce	.087	McGee, Jake	.135	Kolarek, Adam	.164	Antone, Tejay	1.89
Clarke, Taylor	.095	Hoyt, James	.135	Kinley, Tyler	.167	Webb, Tyler	2.08
Baez, Pedro	.097	Menez, Conner	.136	Clarke, Taylor	.169	Kintzler, Brandon	2.22

Rel OBP 1st Batter Faced (minimum 40 BF)		Rel Opp BA w/ Runners On (minimum 18 IP)		Relief Opp BA w/ RISP (minimum 18 IP)		Fastest Avg Fastball-Relief (minimum 18 IP)	
Williams, Devin	.045	Cabrera, Genesis	.024	Cabrera, Genesis	.000	Graterol, Brusdar	99.2
Garrett, Amir	.143	Williams, Devin	.071	Graterol, Brusdar	.067	Diaz, Edwin	97.8
Kolarek, Adam	.150	Pomeranz, Drew	.091	Williams, Devin	.067	Reyes, Alex	97.6
O'Day, Darren	.158	Rainey, Tanner	.107	Hartlieb, Geoff	.074	Bard, Daniel	97.1
Almonte, Yency	.167	Antone, Tejay	.115	Antone, Tejay	.083	Estevez, Carlos	96.9
Baez, Pedro	.167	Kintzler, Brandon	.119	Rainey, Tanner	.095	Treinen, Blake	96.9
Martin, Chris	.167	Hader, Josh	.120	Selman, Sam	.100	Lorenzen, Michael	96.8
Smith, Will	.167	Jeffress, Jeremy	.125	Minter, A.J.	.111	Familia, Jeurys	96.6
Harper, Ryne	.174	Gonzalez, Victor	.129	Baragar, Caleb	.125	Rainey, Tanner	96.6
2 tied with	.182	Graterol, Brusdar	.129	Kintzler, Brandon	.125	Williams, Devin	96.5

Fastest Average Fastball (minimum 60 IP)		Slowest Average Fastball (minimum 60 IP)		Pitches 100+ Velocity		Pitches 95+ Velocity	
deGrom, Jacob	98.6	Hendricks, Kyle	87.4	Graterol, Brusdar	95	Woodruff, Brandon	773
Castillo, Luis	97.5	Davies, Zach	88.6	deGrom, Jacob	86	Wheeler, Zack	700
Lamet, Dinelson	97.1	Lester, Jon	89.2	May, Dustin	39	Castillo, Luis	603
Wheeler, Zack	96.9	Wainwright, Adam	89.3	Sanchez, Sixto	35	May, Dustin	553
Woodruff, Brandon	96.5	Mills, Alec	90.0	Guerra, Javy	27	deGrom, Jacob	520
Marquez, German	95.7	Corbin, Patrick	90.2	Rosenthal, Trevor	23	Marquez, German	504
Darvish, Yu	95.5	Cueto, Johnny	91.3	Coonrod, Sam	21	Lamet, Dinelson	478
Scherzer, Max	94.7	Freeland, Kyle	91.9	Castro, Miguel	17	Alcantara, Sandy	383
Senzatela, Antonio	94.4	Nola, Aaron	92.4	Buehler, Walker	15	Buehler, Walker	377
Bauer, Trevor	93.5	Gallen, Zac	93.3	Diaz, Edwin	13	Burnes, Corbin	372

Pitches Less Than 80 MPH		Lowest % Fastballs (minimum 60 IP)		Highest % Fastballs (minimum 60 IP)		Highest % Curveballs (minimum 60 IP)	
Wainwright, Adam	357	Darvish, Yu	24.8	Wheeler, Zack	65.9	Wainwright, Adam	38.3
Hendricks, Kyle	315	Freeland, Kyle	33.5	Woodruff, Brandon	65.1	Nola, Aaron	26.7
Corbin, Patrick	278	Wainwright, Adam	36.9	Mills, Alec	59.0	Marquez, German	24.8
Milone, Tommy	256	Davies, Zach	38.5	Senzatela, Antonio	56.0	Freeland, Kyle	18.9
Davies, Zach	254	Gallen, Zac	39.3	Hendricks, Kyle	54.5	Gallen, Zac	17.2
Mills, Alec	253	Lester, Jon	42.1	Castillo, Luis	52.3	Hendricks, Kyle	16.6
Harper, Ryne	252	Cueto, Johnny	43.6	Marquez, German	52.3	Bauer, Trevor	15.7
Erlin, Robbie	248	deGrom, Jacob	44.9	Corbin, Patrick	52.1	Mills, Alec	15.0
Nola, Aaron	233	Nola, Aaron	46.0	Bauer, Trevor	47.8	Darvish, Yu	13.0
Lindblom, Josh	207	Scherzer, Max	46.0	Lamet, Dinelson	46.3	Lester, Jon	12.8

2020 National League Pitching Leaders

Highest % Changeups
(minimum 60 IP)

Davies, Zach	41.3
Castillo, Luis	30.0
Hendricks, Kyle	28.9
Nola, Aaron	27.4
Cueto, Johnny	27.0
Freeland, Kyle	24.0
Gallen, Zac	19.0
Woodruff, Brandon	17.6
deGrom, Jacob	16.9
Scherzer, Max	15.9

Highest % Sliders
(minimum 60 IP)

Lamet, Dinelson	53.4
Corbin, Patrick	40.2
deGrom, Jacob	35.6
Senzatela, Antonio	24.5
Freeland, Kyle	23.8
Scherzer, Max	19.0
Castillo, Luis	17.7
Marquez, German	17.2
Bauer, Trevor	16.4
Wheeler, Zack	15.9

Balks

Cueto, Johnny	2
Sanchez, Anibal	2
33 tied with	1

Strikeout/Hit Ratio
(minimum 18 IP)

Williams, Devin	6.63
Rainey, Tanner	4.00
Hader, Josh	3.88
Cabrera, Genesis	3.20
Diaz, Edwin	2.78
Sims, Lucas	2.62
Bauer, Trevor	2.44
Alzolay, Adbert	2.42
Burnes, Corbin	2.38
Lamet, Dinelson	2.38

Opp OPS vs Fastballs
(minimum 251 BF)

Gonsolin, Tony	.464
Hudson, Dakota	.467
Gallen, Zac	.503
Alcantara, Sandy	.523
Bauer, Trevor	.536
deGrom, Jacob	.536
Nola, Aaron	.572
Urias, Julio	.579
Peterson, David	.583
Lopez, Pablo	.589

Opp OPS vs Curveballs
(minimum 37 BF)

Marquez, German	.445
Urias, Julio	.447
Mills, Alec	.449
Gallen, Zac	.468
Wainwright, Adam	.498
Harper, Ryne	.518
Gray, Sonny	.547
Stripling, Ross	.594
Johnson, Pierce	.606
Fried, Max	.610

Opp OPS vs Changeups
(minimum 37 BF)

Williams, Devin	.146
Anderson, Ian	.350
Sanchez, Sixto	.386
Brault, Steven	.445
Peralta, Wandy	.454
Watson, Tony	.489
Cueto, Johnny	.532
Paddack, Chris	.534
Clarke, Taylor	.556
Nola, Aaron	.566

Opp OPS vs Sliders
(minimum 64 BF)

Gallegos, Giovanny	.228
Bauer, Trevor	.277
Burnes, Corbin	.291
Pagan, Emilio	.295
Hader, Josh	.307
Gonzalez, Victor	.323
Lamet, Dinelson	.330
Scherzer, Max	.374
Miller, Andrew	.379
Perdomo, Luis	.389

Earned Runs

Sanchez, Anibal	39
Cueto, Johnny	38
Weaver, Luke	38
Williams, Trevor	38
Porcello, Rick	37
Lester, Jon	35
Voth, Austin	35
Corbin, Patrick	34
Freeland, Kyle	34
Marquez, German	34

Hits Per Nine Innings
(minimum 60 IP)

Bauer, Trevor	5.05
Lamet, Dinelson	5.09
deGrom, Jacob	6.22
Woodruff, Brandon	6.72
Nola, Aaron	6.81
Gallen, Zac	6.88
Darvish, Yu	6.99
Davies, Zach	7.14
Wainwright, Adam	7.40
Mills, Alec	7.65

2020 American League Fielding Leaders

2B Pivot %
(minimum 36 G)

Hernandez, Cesar	0.769
Lopez, Nicky	0.765
Biggio, Cavan	0.762
Schoop, Jonathan	0.759
Odor, Rougned	0.750
Alberto, Hanser	0.731
Altuve, Jose	0.708
Lowe, Brandon	0.640
LeMahieu, DJ	0.619
Kemp, Tony	0.333

SS Pivot %
(minimum 36 G)

Correa, Carlos	0.719
Crawford, J.P.	0.667
Semien, Marcus	0.667
Mondesi, Adalberto	0.621
Anderson, Tim	0.611
Bogaerts, Xander	0.600
Adames, Willy	0.556
Torres, Gleyber	0.500
Polanco, Jorge	0.429
Lindor, Francisco	0.414

Highest Pct CS by Catchers
(minimum 600 INN or 50 SBA)

Perez, Roberto	69.2
Grandal, Yasmani	41.7
Maldonado, Martin	31.6
Perez, Michael	31.6
Murphy, Sean	28.6
Perez, Salvador	27.3
Sanchez, Gary	26.3
Severino, Pedro	25.0
Vazquez, Christian	25.0
McCann, James	20.0

Lowest Pct CS by Catchers
(minimum 600 INN or 50 SBA)

Romine, Austin	11.5
Stassi, Max	13.5
Jansen, Danny	16.7
McCann, James	20.0
Severino, Pedro	25.0
Vazquez, Christian	25.0
Sanchez, Gary	26.3
Perez, Salvador	27.3
Murphy, Sean	28.6
2 tied with	31.6

2B Double Play %
(minimum 36 G)

Lopez, Nicky	0.696
Hernandez, Cesar	0.681
Odor, Rougned	0.667
Schoop, Jonathan	0.667
Biggio, Cavan	0.647
Lowe, Brandon	0.621
Altuve, Jose	0.593
Alberto, Hanser	0.579
LeMahieu, DJ	0.515
Kemp, Tony	0.423

3B Double Play %
(minimum 36 G)

Franco, Maikel	0.571
Ramirez, Jose	0.526
Urshela, Gio	0.526
Ruiz, Rio	0.522
Moncada, Yoan	0.516
Shaw, Travis	0.467
Devers, Rafael	0.429
Seager, Kyle	0.400
Rendon, Anthony	0.368
Kiner-Falefa, Isiah	0.286

SS Double Play %
(minimum 36 G)

Crawford, J.P.	0.744
Correa, Carlos	0.667
Anderson, Tim	0.629
Lindor, Francisco	0.604
Mondesi, Adalberto	0.603
Adames, Willy	0.545
Bogaerts, Xander	0.531
Polanco, Jorge	0.471
Semien, Marcus	0.378
Torres, Gleyber	0.367

Errors

Devers, Rafael	14
Adames, Willy	9
Torres, Gleyber	9
Semien, Marcus	7
9 tied with	6

Fielding Errors

Anderson, Tim	5
Devers, Rafael	5
Ramirez, Jose	5
Sanchez, Gary	5
Semien, Marcus	5
11 tied with	4

Throwing Errors

Devers, Rafael	9
Adames, Willy	5
Castro, Willi	5
Ruiz, Rio	5
Torres, Gleyber	5
Chapman, Matt	4
Garneau, Dustin	4
LeMahieu, DJ	4
7 tied with	3

Range Factor for 2B
(minimum 36 games)

Lopez, Nicky	4.44
LeMahieu, DJ	4.42
Schoop, Jonathan	4.38
Alberto, Hanser	4.17
Altuve, Jose	4.11
Biggio, Cavan	4.09
Odor, Rougned	4.00
Hernandez, Cesar	3.68
Kemp, Tony	3.62
Lowe, Brandon	3.39

Range Factor for 3B
(minimum 36 games)

Seager, Kyle	3.08
Urshela, Gio	3.04
Ruiz, Rio	2.84
Shaw, Travis	2.75
Kiner-Falefa, Isiah	2.73
Moncada, Yoan	2.69
Franco, Maikel	2.44
Rendon, Anthony	2.39
Bregman, Alex	2.35
Devers, Rafael	2.16

Range Factor for SS
(minimum 36 games)

Crawford, J.P.	4.32
Mondesi, Adalberto	4.15
Semien, Marcus	4.11
Correa, Carlos	4.00
Bogaerts, Xander	3.88
Anderson, Tim	3.75
Adames, Willy	3.70
Lindor, Francisco	3.67
Torres, Gleyber	3.54
Polanco, Jorge	3.33

2020 National League Fielding Leaders

2B Pivot %
(minimum 36 G)

Wong, Kolten	0.720
Frazier, Adam	0.667
Marte, Ketel	0.640
Cronenworth, Jake	0.632
Solano, Donovan	0.577
Garcia, Luis	0.571
Hiura, Keston	0.529

SS Pivot %
(minimum 36 G)

Gonzalez, Erik	0.846
Rosario, Amed	0.778
Rojas, Miguel	0.765
Swanson, Dansby	0.733
Ahmed, Nick	0.692
DeJong, Paul	0.667
Story, Trevor	0.667
Baez, Javier	0.639
Tatis Jr., Fernando	0.621
Turner, Trea	0.600

Highest Pct CS by Catchers
(minimum 600 INN or 50 SBA)

Molina, Yadier	45.5
Barnhart, Tucker	36.4
Contreras, Willson	32.0
Stallings, Jacob	25.0
Narvaez, Omar	23.8
Realmuto, J.T.	21.1
Alfaro, Jorge	20.0
Smith, Will	19.0
Ramos, Wilson	15.2
Suzuki, Kurt	15.2

Lowest Pct CS by Catchers
(minimum 600 INN or 50 SBA)

Kelly, Carson	5.0
d'Arnaud, Travis	7.7
Gomes, Yan	10.0
Barnes, Austin	11.1
Bart, Joey	14.8
Wolters, Tony	15.0
Ramos, Wilson	15.2
Suzuki, Kurt	15.2
Smith, Will	19.0
Alfaro, Jorge	20.0

2B Double Play %
(minimum 36 G)

Wong, Kolten	0.659
Frazier, Adam	0.615
Cronenworth, Jake	0.613
Marte, Ketel	0.553
Garcia, Luis	0.519
Solano, Donovan	0.514
Hoerner, Nico	0.417
Hiura, Keston	0.414

3B Double Play %
(minimum 36 G)

Arenado, Nolan	0.500
Suarez, Eugenio	0.476
Escobar, Eduardo	0.464
Machado, Manny	0.417
Anderson, Brian	0.344
Riley, Austin	0.333
Longoria, Evan	0.290
Bohm, Alec	0.188

SS Double Play %
(minimum 36 G)

Swanson, Dansby	0.725
Rojas, Miguel	0.707
Gonzalez, Erik	0.690
Ahmed, Nick	0.674
DeJong, Paul	0.647
Story, Trevor	0.611
Rosario, Amed	0.588
Baez, Javier	0.582
Tatis Jr., Fernando	0.577
Gregorius, Didi	0.569

Errors

Solano, Donovan	11
McMahon, Ryan	10
Story, Trevor	10
Anderson, Brian	9
Turner, Trea	9
Baez, Javier	8
Crawford, Brandon	8
Escobar, Eduardo	8
Newman, Kevin	8
Seager, Corey	8

Fielding Errors

Solano, Donovan	9
Turner, Trea	6
Crawford, Brandon	5
Edman, Tommy	5
Escobar, Eduardo	5
Garcia, Luis	5
McMahon, Ryan	5
Story, Trevor	5
6 tied with	4

Throwing Errors

Anderson, Brian	6
Baez, Javier	6
McMahon, Ryan	5
Story, Trevor	5
Ahmed, Nick	4
Gregorius, Didi	4
Hiura, Keston	4
Newman, Kevin	4
Seager, Corey	4
21 tied with	3

Range Factor for 2B
(minimum 36 games)

Wong, Kolten	4.26
Marte, Ketel	4.20
Frazier, Adam	4.01
Hoerner, Nico	3.68
Cronenworth, Jake	3.65
Solano, Donovan	3.54
Hiura, Keston	3.30
Garcia, Luis	3.25

Range Factor for 3B
(minimum 36 games)

Arenado, Nolan	3.45
Riley, Austin	2.96
Anderson, Brian	2.95
Machado, Manny	2.89
Bohm, Alec	2.70
Longoria, Evan	2.64
Escobar, Eduardo	2.57
Suarez, Eugenio	2.32

Range Factor for SS
(minimum 36 games)

Rojas, Miguel	4.72
Baez, Javier	4.70
Story, Trevor	4.56
Crawford, Brandon	4.16
Gregorius, Didi	4.04
Swanson, Dansby	3.96
Seager, Corey	3.81
DeJong, Paul	3.71
Turner, Trea	3.70
Arcia, Orlando	3.65

2020 Active Career Batting Leaders

Batting Average (minimum 1000 PA)		On Base Percentage (minimum 1000 PA)		Slugging Average (minimum 1000 PA)		Home Runs	
McNeil, Jeff	.319	Votto, Joey	.419	Trout, Mike	.582	Pujols, Albert	662
Cabrera, Miguel	.313	Trout, Mike	.418	Judge, Aaron	.558	Cabrera, Miguel	487
Altuve, Jose	.311	Soto, Juan	.415	Soto, Juan	.557	Encarnacion, Edwin	424
LeMahieu, DJ	.305	Goldschmidt, Paul	.392	Bellinger, Cody	.547	Cruz, Nelson	417
Votto, Joey	.304	Cabrera, Miguel	.391	Pujols, Albert	.546	Braun, Ryan	352
Trout, Mike	.304	Nimmo, Brandon	.390	Stanton, Giancarlo	.546	Cano, Robinson	334
Blackmon, Charlie	.304	Judge, Aaron	.390	Arenado, Nolan	.541	Bruce, Jay	318
Cano, Robinson	.303	Harper, Bryce	.387	Cabrera, Miguel	.540	Stanton, Giancarlo	312
Posey, Buster	.302	McNeil, Jeff	.383	Acuna Jr., Ronald	.538	Upton, Justin	307
Betts, Mookie	.301	Freeman, Freddie	.383	Story, Trevor	.535	Longoria, Evan	304

Games		At Bats		Hits		Total Bases	
Pujols, Albert	2862	Pujols, Albert	10839	Pujols, Albert	3236	Pujols, Albert	5923
Cabrera, Miguel	2457	Cabrera, Miguel	9153	Cabrera, Miguel	2866	Cabrera, Miguel	4942
Cano, Robinson	2234	Cano, Robinson	8673	Cano, Robinson	2624	Cano, Robinson	4263
Markakis, Nick	2154	Markakis, Nick	8302	Markakis, Nick	2388	Braun, Ryan	3525
Molina, Yadier	2025	Molina, Yadier	7115	Molina, Yadier	2001	Markakis, Nick	3513
Encarnacion, Edwin	1960	Encarnacion, Edwin	7040	Braun, Ryan	1963	Encarnacion, Edwin	3494
Votto, Joey	1771	Braun, Ryan	6622	Votto, Joey	1908	Cruz, Nelson	3384
Braun, Ryan	1766	Longoria, Evan	6576	Encarnacion, Edwin	1832	Votto, Joey	3245
Gordon, Alex	1753	Pence, Hunter	6420	Kemp, Matt	1808	Longoria, Evan	3108
Kemp, Matt	1750	Zimmerman, Ryan	6399	Pedroia, Dustin	1805	Kemp, Matt	3081

Doubles		Triples		Runs Scored		RBI	
Pujols, Albert	669	Fowler, Dexter	82	Pujols, Albert	1843	Pujols, Albert	2100
Cabrera, Miguel	581	Gardner, Brett	69	Cabrera, Miguel	1457	Cabrera, Miguel	1729
Cano, Robinson	571	Pence, Hunter	55	Cano, Robinson	1257	Cano, Robinson	1302
Markakis, Nick	514	Strange-Gordon, Dee	54	Markakis, Nick	1119	Encarnacion, Edwin	1261
Votto, Joey	412	Braun, Ryan	49	Encarnacion, Edwin	1099	Braun, Ryan	1154
Braun, Ryan	408	Andrus, Elvis	48	Braun, Ryan	1080	Cruz, Nelson	1152
Zimmerman, Ryan	401	Blackmon, Charlie	48	Votto, Joey	1041	Markakis, Nick	1046
Pedroia, Dustin	394	McCutchen, Andrew	48	Upton, Justin	1009	Longoria, Evan	1043
Longoria, Evan	392	Trout, Mike	48	McCutchen, Andrew	974	Kemp, Matt	1031
Molina, Yadier	381	2 tied with	44	Choo, Shin-Soo	961	Zimmerman, Ryan	1015

Walks		Intentional Walks		Hit By Pitch		Strikeouts	
Pujols, Albert	1331	Pujols, Albert	312	Rizzo, Anthony	155	Davis, Chris	1852
Votto, Joey	1217	Cabrera, Miguel	235	Choo, Shin-Soo	152	Upton, Justin	1841
Cabrera, Miguel	1159	Votto, Joey	141	Dietrich, Derek	123	Cabrera, Miguel	1812
Santana, Carlos	991	Cano, Robinson	112	Gordon, Alex	121	Kemp, Matt	1641
Encarnacion, Edwin	903	Goldschmidt, Paul	105	Marte, Starling	120	Cruz, Nelson	1625
Markakis, Nick	891	Trout, Mike	104	Jay, Jon	110	Choo, Shin-Soo	1579
Choo, Shin-Soo	868	Harper, Bryce	89	Pujols, Albert	108	Bruce, Jay	1559
McCutchen, Andrew	845	Freeman, Freddie	87	Suzuki, Kurt	106	Gordon, Alex	1535
Trout, Mike	838	Longoria, Evan	81	Encarnacion, Edwin	105	Longoria, Evan	1472
Goldschmidt, Paul	770	Stanton, Giancarlo	80	Turner, Justin	93	Encarnacion, Edwin	1426

2020 Active Career Batting Leaders

Sacrifice Hits

Kershaw, Clayton	108
Andrus, Elvis	100
Cueto, Johnny	85
Teheran, Julio	67
Gardner, Brett	64
Hamels, Cole	64
Wainwright, Adam	60
Bailey, Homer	55
Jay, Jon	55
Strasburg, Stephen	55

Sacrifice Flies

Pujols, Albert	115
Longoria, Evan	89
Cabrera, Miguel	86
Markakis, Nick	73
Kemp, Matt	72
Molina, Yadier	71
Zimmerman, Ryan	67
Encarnacion, Edwin	66
Cano, Robinson	62
Suzuki, Kurt	62

Stolen Bases

Strange-Gordon, Dee	333
Andrus, Elvis	305
Hamilton, Billy	305
Gardner, Brett	270
Altuve, Jose	256
Dyson, Jarrod	256
Marte, Starling	249
Villar, Jonathan	218
Braun, Ryan	216
Trout, Mike	201

Seasons Played

Pujols, Albert	20
Cabrera, Miguel	18
Perez, Oliver	18
Greinke, Zack	17
Molina, Yadier	17
7 tied with	16

At Bats Per Home Run

(minimum 1000 AB)

Gallo, Joey	12.6
Judge, Aaron	12.8
Sanchez, Gary	13.5
Stanton, Giancarlo	13.9
Olson, Matt	14.4
Bellinger, Cody	14.7
Renfroe, Hunter	14.9
Schwarber, Kyle	14.9
Muncy, Max	14.9
Trout, Mike	15.0

Grounded Into DP

Pujols, Albert	399
Cabrera, Miguel	321
Cano, Robinson	284
Molina, Yadier	261
Markakis, Nick	214
Zimmerman, Ryan	203
Kendrick, Howie	193
Encarnacion, Edwin	185
Kemp, Matt	184
Longoria, Evan	183

Highest SB Success Pct

(minimum 100 SBA)

Dyson, Jarrod	85.3
Trout, Mike	84.5
Betts, Mookie	83.4
Turner, Trea	83.4
Yelich, Christian	83.1
Mondesi, Adalberto	81.9
Cain, Lorenzo	81.4
Hamilton, Billy	81.1
Pollock, A.J.	80.9
Gardner, Brett	80.8

Lowest SB Success Pct

(minimum 100 SBA)

Odor, Rougned	55.9
Bruce, Jay	61.9
Castro, Starlin	63.6
Molina, Yadier	64.1
Frazier, Todd	65.8
LeMahieu, DJ	66.9
Fowler, Dexter	68.5
Pence, Hunter	68.6
Hernandez, Cesar	69.6
Cruz, Nelson	70.4

Strikeouts / Walks Ratio

(minimum 1000 AB)

Pujols, Albert	.980
Pedroia, Dustin	1.048
Santana, Carlos	1.066
Bregman, Alex	1.110
La Stella, Tommy	1.112
Votto, Joey	1.113
Soto, Juan	1.136
Panik, Joe	1.172
Ramirez, Jose	1.217
Betts, Mookie	1.271

At Bats Per GIDP

(minimum 1000 AB)

Gallo, Joey	252.7
Moncada, Yoan	251.2
Kingery, Scott	170.5
Hamilton, Billy	157.7
Buxton, Byron	138.0
DeShields, Delino	137.0
Engel, Adam	130.6
Goodwin, Brian	126.1
Carpenter, Matt	119.9
Albies, Ozzie	115.3

OPS

(minimum 1000 PA)

Trout, Mike	1.000
Soto, Juan	.972
Judge, Aaron	.948
Votto, Joey	.937
Cabrera, Miguel	.931
Pujols, Albert	.924
Goldschmidt, Paul	.914
Bellinger, Cody	.911
Acuna Jr., Ronald	.909
Stanton, Giancarlo	.905

Secondary Average

(minimum 1000 PA)

Trout, Mike	.507
Soto, Juan	.487
Judge, Aaron	.486
Gallo, Joey	.468
Hoskins, Rhys	.448
Harper, Bryce	.442
Bellinger, Cody	.441
Acuna Jr., Ronald	.438
Muncy, Max	.436
Stanton, Giancarlo	.423

Highest Strikeout per PA

(minimum 1000 PA)

Gallo, Joey	.376
Sano, Miguel	.370
Zunino, Mike	.345
Alfaro, Jorge	.344
Davidson, Matt	.342
Davis, Chris	.329
Santana, Domingo	.319
Jones, JaCoby	.318
Hernandez, Teoscar	.316
2 tied with	.315

Lowest Strikeout per PA

(minimum 1000 PA)

Simmons, Andrelton	.090
Pedroia, Dustin	.097
Panik, Joe	.099
Fletcher, David	.103
Molina, Yadier	.103
Pujols, Albert	.105
La Stella, Tommy	.106
Brantley, Michael	.108
Gurriel, Yuli	.108
Altuve, Jose	.117

Plate Appearances

Pujols, Albert	12394
Cabrera, Miguel	10467
Cano, Robinson	9446
Markakis, Nick	9321
Encarnacion, Edwin	8126
Molina, Yadier	7811
Votto, Joey	7595
Longoria, Evan	7380
Braun, Ryan	7340
Gordon, Alex	7250

At Bats Per RBI

(minimum 1000 AB)

Soto, Juan	5.1
Pujols, Albert	5.2
Cabrera, Miguel	5.3
Aguilar, Jesus	5.3
Sanchez, Gary	5.4
Arenado, Nolan	5.4
Stanton, Giancarlo	5.4
Cruz, Nelson	5.6
Encarnacion, Edwin	5.6
Abreu, Jose	5.6

2020 Active Career Pitching Leaders

Earned Run Average		Winning Percentage		Opponent Batting Average		Baserunners Per 9 IP	
(minimum 750 IP)		(minimum 100 Decisions)		(minimum 750 IP)		(minimum 750 IP)	
Kershaw, Clayton	2.43	Kershaw, Clayton	.697	Clippard, Tyler	.197	Kershaw, Clayton	9.16
deGrom, Jacob	2.61	Strasburg, Stephen	.655	Kershaw, Clayton	.208	deGrom, Jacob	9.58
Ryu, Hyun-Jin	2.95	Scherzer, Max	.653	Sale, Chris	.218	Sale, Chris	9.85
Sale, Chris	3.03	Price, David	.652	Darvish, Yu	.218	Kluber, Corey	10.08
Hendricks, Kyle	3.12	Cole, Gerrit	.647	deGrom, Jacob	.219	Strasburg, Stephen	10.11
Clippard, Tyler	3.13	Verlander, Justin	.637	Strasburg, Stephen	.223	Clippard, Tyler	10.18
Kluber, Corey	3.16	Lester, Jon	.635	Hill, Rich	.223	Scherzer, Max	10.23
Strasburg, Stephen	3.19	Wainwright, Adam	.630	Scherzer, Max	.223	Hendricks, Kyle	10.30
Cole, Gerrit	3.19	Tanaka, Masahiro	.629	Verlander, Justin	.228	Cole, Gerrit	10.38
Bumgarner, Madison	3.20	Kluber, Corey	.628	Nola, Aaron	.230	Bumgarner, Madison	10.38

Games		Games Started		Complete Games		Shutouts	
Smith, Joe	782	Greinke, Zack	459	Verlander, Justin	26	Kershaw, Clayton	15
Clippard, Tyler	777	Verlander, Justin	454	Hernandez, Felix	25	Hernandez, Felix	11
Romo, Sergio	732	Lester, Jon	423	Kershaw, Clayton	25	Wainwright, Adam	10
Soria, Joakim	732	Hamels, Cole	422	Wainwright, Adam	24	Verlander, Justin	9
Perez, Oliver	690	Hernandez, Felix	418	Cueto, Johnny	17	Cueto, Johnny	8
Robertson, David	661	Scherzer, Max	368	Hamels, Cole	17	Holland, Derek	8
Jansen, Kenley	632	Kershaw, Clayton	354	Kluber, Corey	17	Hamels, Cole	7
Watson, Tony	627	Porcello, Rick	351	Price, David	17	Kluber, Corey	7
Shaw, Bryan	612	Gonzalez, Gio	328	Greinke, Zack	16	Sanchez, Anibal	7
Melancon, Mark	606	Sanchez, Anibal	327	Sale, Chris	16	Bumgarner, Madison	6

Wins		Losses		Innings Pitched		Batters Faced	
Verlander, Justin	226	Hernandez, Felix	136	Verlander, Justin	2988.0	Verlander, Justin	12214
Greinke, Zack	208	Verlander, Justin	129	Greinke, Zack	2939.0	Greinke, Zack	12002
Lester, Jon	193	Greinke, Zack	126	Hernandez, Felix	2729.2	Hernandez, Felix	11284
Kershaw, Clayton	175	Porcello, Rick	125	Hamels, Cole	2698.0	Hamels, Cole	11115
Scherzer, Max	175	Hamels, Cole	122	Lester, Jon	2598.2	Lester, Jon	10860
Hernandez, Felix	169	Liriano, Francisco	114	Scherzer, Max	2357.1	Scherzer, Max	9573
Wainwright, Adam	167	Sanchez, Anibal	113	Kershaw, Clayton	2333.0	Kershaw, Clayton	9179
Hamels, Cole	163	Lester, Jon	111	Wainwright, Adam	2169.1	Wainwright, Adam	9001
Porcello, Rick	150	Samardzija, Jeff	106	Porcello, Rick	2096.1	Porcello, Rick	8912
Price, David	150	Kennedy, Ian	105	Price, David	2029.2	Sanchez, Anibal	8315

Strikeouts		Walks Allowed		Hit Batters		Wild Pitches	
Verlander, Justin	3013	Verlander, Justin	851	Morton, Charlie	121	Hernandez, Felix	156
Scherzer, Max	2784	Lester, Jon	837	Cueto, Johnny	107	Liriano, Francisco	100
Greinke, Zack	2689	Liriano, Francisco	816	Hernandez, Felix	105	Cahill, Trevor	98
Hamels, Cole	2560	Gonzalez, Gio	815	Hamels, Cole	100	Greinke, Zack	89
Kershaw, Clayton	2526	Hernandez, Felix	805	Sale, Chris	98	Kershaw, Clayton	88
Hernandez, Felix	2524	Hamels, Cole	767	Verlander, Justin	98	Verlander, Justin	87
Lester, Jon	2397	Perez, Oliver	760	Lester, Jon	87	Gray, Sonny	79
Sale, Chris	2007	Volquez, Edinson	735	Perez, Oliver	87	Richards, Garrett	78
Price, David	1981	Greinke, Zack	676	Scherzer, Max	86	Volquez, Edinson	77
Gonzalez, Gio	1860	Sanchez, Anibal	653	Porcello, Rick	84	2 tied with	76

2020 Active Career Pitching Leaders

Saves			Save Pct			Home Runs Allowed			Strikeouts Per 9 IP	
			(minimum 50 Save Ops)						(minimum 750 IP)	
Kimbrel, Craig	348		Kimbrel, Craig	90.2		Hamels, Cole	310		Ray, Robbie	11.13
Jansen, Kenley	312		Britton, Zack	90.0		Verlander, Justin	310		Darvish, Yu	11.12
Chapman, Aroldis	276		Chapman, Aroldis	89.0		Greinke, Zack	298		Sale, Chris	11.08
Soria, Joakim	223		Jansen, Kenley	88.6		Lester, Jon	269		Miller, Andrew	10.66
Holland, Greg	212		Giles, Ken	88.5		Hernandez, Felix	264		Scherzer, Max	10.63
Melancon, Mark	205		Holland, Greg	88.3		Scherzer, Max	264		Strasburg, Stephen	10.58
Osuna, Roberto	155		Davis, Wade	88.0		Porcello, Rick	260		deGrom, Jacob	10.46
Britton, Zack	153		Iglesias, Raisel	86.9		Kennedy, Ian	253		Cole, Gerrit	10.15
Diaz, Edwin	141		Diaz, Edwin	86.5		Leake, Mike	238		Clippard, Tyler	9.95
Davis, Wade	139		Rosenthal, Trevor	86.3		Happ, J.A.	231		Paxton, James	9.90

Opp On-Base Percentage			Opp Slugging Average			Hits Per Nine Innings			Home Runs Per Nine IP	
(minimum 750 IP)			(minimum 750 IP)			(minimum 750 IP)			(minimum 750 IP)	
Kershaw, Clayton	.261		Kershaw, Clayton	.319		Clippard, Tyler	6.38		Kershaw, Clayton	0.70
deGrom, Jacob	.269		deGrom, Jacob	.334		Kershaw, Clayton	6.77		Ross, Tyson	0.73
Sale, Chris	.273		Sale, Chris	.351		deGrom, Jacob	7.24		Wainwright, Adam	0.73
Clippard, Tyler	.279		Strasburg, Stephen	.353		Sale, Chris	7.25		Martinez, Carlos	0.74
Strasburg, Stephen	.279		Clippard, Tyler	.353		Darvish, Yu	7.26		Morton, Charlie	0.76
Kluber, Corey	.280		Gray, Sonny	.356		Hill, Rich	7.40		deGrom, Jacob	0.78
Scherzer, Max	.282		Richards, Garrett	.360		Strasburg, Stephen	7.44		Richards, Garrett	0.79
Tanaka, Masahiro	.284		Miller, Andrew	.361		Scherzer, Max	7.46		Gonzalez, Gio	0.80
Bumgarner, Madison	.285		Martinez, Carlos	.361		Verlander, Justin	7.64		Stroman, Marcus	0.83
Petit, Yusmeiro	.285		Verlander, Justin	.365		2 tied with	7.72		Lynn, Lance	0.85

Strikeouts / Walks Ratio			Stolen Base Pct Allowed			GIDP Induced			GIDP Per Nine IP	
(minimum 750 IP)			(minimum 750 IP)						(minimum 750 IP)	
Sale, Chris	5.37		Cueto, Johnny	44.0		Hernandez, Felix	271		Chatwood, Tyler	1.36
Kluber, Corey	4.99		Miley, Wade	46.9		Lester, Jon	236		Perez, Martin	1.31
deGrom, Jacob	4.79		Greinke, Zack	50.6		Greinke, Zack	224		Gibson, Kyle	1.15
Tanaka, Masahiro	4.76		LeBlanc, Wade	51.6		Hamels, Cole	216		Keuchel, Dallas	1.09
Tomlin, Josh	4.72		Kershaw, Clayton	51.9		Wainwright, Adam	216		Stroman, Marcus	1.08
Strasburg, Stephen	4.49		Ryu, Hyun-Jin	53.8		Porcello, Rick	210		Martinez, Carlos	1.04
Pineda, Michael	4.44		Eovaldi, Nathan	54.5		Leake, Mike	189		Anderson, Brett	1.03
Scherzer, Max	4.34		Lynn, Lance	55.8		Liriano, Francisco	181		Nova, Ivan	1.00
Kershaw, Clayton	4.32		Wainwright, Adam	57.7		Keuchel, Dallas	166		Ross, Tyson	0.95
Cole, Gerrit	4.31		Wood, Alex	57.8		Kershaw, Clayton	162		Morton, Charlie	0.94

Complete Game %			Quality Start Pct			Walks Per 9 IP			Games Finished	
(minimum 100 GS)			(minimum 100 GS)			(minimum 750 IP)				
Kluber, Corey	0.08		deGrom, Jacob	74.3		Tomlin, Josh	1.31		Kimbrel, Craig	477
Wainwright, Adam	0.07		Kershaw, Clayton	73.4		Tanaka, Masahiro	1.78		Jansen, Kenley	467
Kershaw, Clayton	0.07		Sale, Chris	69.8		Zimmermann, Jordan	1.93		Chapman, Aroldis	419
Sale, Chris	0.07		Cole, Gerrit	68.1		Hendricks, Kyle	1.94		Soria, Joakim	407
Hernandez, Felix	0.06		Verlander, Justin	67.4		Kluber, Corey	1.96		Melancon, Mark	353
Verlander, Justin	0.06		Price, David	65.3		Leake, Mike	1.98		Holland, Greg	329
Carrasco, Carlos	0.06		Scherzer, Max	65.2		Ryu, Hyun-Jin	2.02		Cishek, Steve	291
Keuchel, Dallas	0.06		Kluber, Corey	64.2		Hunter, Tommy	2.02		Romo, Sergio	277
Cueto, Johnny	0.06		Bumgarner, Madison	64.1		Pineda, Michael	2.03		Robertson, David	276
Price, David	0.05		Greinke, Zack	63.6		Sale, Chris	2.07		Osuna, Roberto	247

2020 American League Bill James Leaders

Top Game Scores

Pitcher	Date	Opp	IP	H	R	ER	BB	SO	GS
Giolito, Lucas, CWS	8/25	Pit	9.0	0	0	0	1	13	99
Bieber, Shane, Cle	7/30	Min	8.0	3	0	0	0	13	89
Plesac, Zach, Cle	7/29	CWS	8.0	3	0	0	0	11	87
Maeda, Kenta, Min	8/18	Mil	8.0	1	1	1	2	12	86
Singer, Brady, KC	9/10	Cle	8.0	1	0	0	2	8	86
Bundy, Dylan, LAA	8/6	Sea	9.0	4	1	1	0	10	85
Gibson, Kyle, Tex	9/16	Hou	9.0	4	0	0	3	9	85
Carrasco, Carlos, Cle	9/20	Det	7.0	1	0	0	3	11	83
Giolito, Lucas, CWS	8/20	Det	7.0	3	0	0	1	13	83
Greinke, Zack, Hou	8/18	Col	8.0	3	0	0	0	7	83
Happ, J.A., NYY	9/19	Bos	8.0	4	0	0	0	9	83
Lynn, Lance, Tex	8/14	Col	9.0	2	2	1	0	6	83

Worst Game Scores

Pitcher	Date	Opp	IP	H	R	ER	BB	SO	GS
Montas, Frankie, Oak	8/18	Ari	1.2	6	9	9	4	1	4
Lopez, Jorge, Bal	9/25	Tor	2.0	9	8	8	1	1	6
Godley, Zack, Bos	8/12	TB	3.0	10	8	8	2	3	8
Cortes, Nestor, Sea	8/14	Hou	0.1	5	8	7	2	1	10
Lyles, Jordan, Tex	8/22	Sea	4.0	11	8	8	0	2	10
Lynn, Lance, Tex	9/24	Hou	5.2	12	10	9	2	5	10
Boyd, Matthew, Det	9/9	Mil	3.0	8	7	7	4	2	13
Civale, Aaron, Cle	9/26	Pit	4.0	10	8	8	0	4	14
Dobnak, Randy, Min	8/29	Det	4.1	12	6	6	2	1	14
Kremer, Dean, Bal	9/23	Bos	2.2	7	7	7	3	2	15

Runs Created

Ramirez, Jose	52
Abreu, Jose	49
Trout, Mike	49
LeMahieu, DJ	46
Voit, Luke	46
Jimenez, Eloy	44
Tucker, Kyle	44
Canha, Mark	43
Biggio, Cavan	42
Springer, George	42

Runs Created Per 27 Outs

LeMahieu, DJ	9.3
Trout, Mike	8.5
Ramirez, Jose	8.4
Voit, Luke	7.5
Springer, George	7.5
Brantley, Michael	7.4
Canha, Mark	7.4
Jimenez, Eloy	7.4
Tucker, Kyle	7.3
Abreu, Jose	7.3

Offensive Winning %

LeMahieu, DJ	.802
Canha, Mark	.781
Ramirez, Jose	.759
Trout, Mike	.748
Cruz, Nelson	.728
Voit, Luke	.724
Springer, George	.717
Lowe, Brandon	.716
Brantley, Michael	.716
Jimenez, Eloy	.714

Secondary Average

(minimum 186 PA)

Trout, Mike	.503
Ramirez, Jose	.502
Hicks, Aaron	.456
Lowe, Brandon	.430
Cruz, Nelson	.427
Grossman, Robbie	.416
Voit, Luke	.413
Rendon, Anthony	.413
Springer, George	.407
Biggio, Cavan	.395

Isolated Power

(minimum 186 PA)

Voit, Luke	.333
Trout, Mike	.322
Ramirez, Jose	.315
Abreu, Jose	.300
Cruz, Nelson	.292
Hernandez, Teoscar	.289
Lowe, Brandon	.285
Springer, George	.275
Sano, Miguel	.274
Jimenez, Eloy	.263

Power / Speed Number

(minimum 186 PA)

Ramirez, Jose	12.6
Merrifield, Whit	10.3
Robert, Luis	09.9
Mondesi, Adalberto	09.6
Bogaerts, Xander	09.3
Hernandez, Teoscar	08.7
Tucker, Kyle	08.5
Grossman, Robbie	08.0
Lewis, Kyle	06.9
2 tied with	06.9

Speed Scores

Smith, Mallex	8.77
Mondesi, Adalberto	8.73
Kiermaier, Kevin	8.02
Villar, Jonathan	7.70
Biggio, Cavan	7.35
Betts, Mookie	7.18
Merrifield, Whit	7.15
Gardner, Brett	7.15
Garcia, Leury	7.14
Moncada, Yoan	7.01

Cheap Wins

Fiers, Mike	3
Civale, Aaron	2
Dunn, Justin	2
Gonzales, Marco	2
16 tied with	1

Tough Losses

Bubic, Kris	3
Civale, Aaron	3
10 tied with	2

2020 National League Bill James Leaders

Top Game Scores

Pitcher	Date	Opp	IP	H	R	ER	BB	SO	GS
Hendricks, Kyle, ChC	7/24	Mil	9.0	3	0	0	0	9	90
Mills, Alec, ChC	9/13	Mil	9.0	0	0	0	3	5	89
Woodruff, Brandon, Mil	9/11	ChC	7.0	1	0	0	0	12	87
Woodruff, Brandon, Mil	9/26	StL	8.0	2	0	0	1	10	87
Burnes, Corbin, Mil	9/9	Det	7.0	1	0	0	0	11	86
Brault, Steven, Pit	9/17	StL	9.0	2	1	1	2	8	85
Hendricks, Kyle, ChC	9/18	Min	8.0	3	0	0	1	10	85
Nola, Aaron, Phi	9/1	Was	8.0	2	0	0	3	9	84
Anderson, Tyler, SF	8/22	Ari	9.0	3	1	0	0	4	83
Bauer, Trevor, Cin	9/9	ChC	7.2	3	0	0	0	10	83
Nola, Aaron, Phi	8/10	Atl	8.0	2	1	1	1	10	83

Worst Game Scores

Pitcher	Date	Opp	IP	H	R	ER	BB	SO	GS
DeSclafani, Anthony, Cin	8/13	Pit	2.0	9	9	9	2	1	1
Chatwood, Tyler, ChC	8/6	KC	2.1	11	8	8	0	4	7
Gray, Jon, Col	8/10	Ari	3.1	11	8	8	0	2	8
Newcomb, Sean, Atl	8/10	Phi	1.1	6	8	8	2	1	9
Holland, Derek, Pit	8/8	Det	5.0	13	9	9	1	6	10
Marquez, German, Col	8/20	Hou	5.0	10	10	10	2	5	10
Arrieta, Jake, Phi	8/30	Atl	1.1	6	7	7	3	0	11
Bumgarner, Madison, Ari	9/15	LAA	5.1	13	8	8	1	2	11
Flaherty, Jack, StL	9/15	Mil	3.0	8	9	9	2	6	11
Kuhl, Chad, Pit	9/13	KC	2.1	4	9	9	6	5	12
Rogers, Trevor, Mia	9/11	Phi	3.0	9	9	8	0	5	12

Runs Created

Freeman, Freddie	68
Ozuna, Marcell	58
Soto, Juan	53
Betts, Mookie	52
Turner, Trea	52
Tatis Jr., Fernando	48
Machado, Manny	46
Harper, Bryce	44
Myers, Wil	44
Yastrzemski, Mike	43

Runs Created Per 27 Outs

Soto, Juan	13.1
Freeman, Freddie	11.8
Ozuna, Marcell	9.5
Betts, Mookie	8.3
Turner, Trea	8.0
Yastrzemski, Mike	7.9
Myers, Wil	7.9
Acuna Jr., Ronald	7.6
Harper, Bryce	7.5
Tatis Jr., Fernando	7.1

Offensive Winning %

Soto, Juan	.899
Freeman, Freddie	.837
Betts, Mookie	.777
Ozuna, Marcell	.770
Turner, Trea	.766
Myers, Wil	.762
Yastrzemski, Mike	.759
Harper, Bryce	.731
Goldschmidt, Paul	.728
Tatis Jr., Fernando	.722

Secondary Average
(minimum 186 PA)

Soto, Juan	.649
Acuna Jr., Ronald	.619
Harper, Bryce	.574
Freeman, Freddie	.519
Yelich, Christian	.475
Ozuna, Marcell	.465
Tatis Jr., Fernando	.464
Calhoun, Kole	.453
Yastrzemski, Mike	.438
Suarez, Eugenio	.429

Isolated Power
(minimum 186 PA)

Soto, Juan	.344
Acuna Jr., Ronald	.331
Myers, Wil	.318
Calhoun, Kole	.300
Smith, Dominic	.299
Freeman, Freddie	.299
Ozuna, Marcell	.298
Duvall, Adam	.295
Tatis Jr., Fernando	.295
Pollock, A.J.	.291

Power / Speed Number
(minimum 186 PA)

Tatis Jr., Fernando	13.4
Story, Trevor	12.7
Betts, Mookie	12.3
Turner, Trea	12.0
Acuna Jr., Ronald	10.2
Grisham, Trent	10.0
Harper, Bryce	09.9
Machado, Manny	08.7
Soto, Juan	08.2
Bellinger, Cody	08.0

Speed Scores

Story, Trevor	7.77
Turner, Trea	7.71
Robles, Victor	7.69
Acuna Jr., Ronald	7.56
Tatis Jr., Fernando	7.53
Wong, Kolten	7.44
Marte, Starling	7.44
Albies, Ozzie	7.36
Eaton, Adam	7.24
Tapia, Raimel	7.08

Cheap Wins

Stripling, Ross	2
16 tied with	1

Tough Losses

Bauer, Trevor	3
Marquez, German	3
Weaver, Luke	3
Woodruff, Brandon	3
11 tied with	2

Additional Bill James Leaders

Top AL Batter Game Scores

Batter	Date	Opp	AB	R	H	HR	RBI	RC	GS
Abreu, Jose, CWS	9/12	Det	4	5	4	2	7	5.11	126
Cruz, Nelson, Min	7/26	CWS	5	4	4	2	7	5.14	121
Abreu, Jose, CWS	8/22	ChC	4	3	4	3	4	6.29	113
Higashioka, Kyle, NYY	9/16	Tor	4	3	3	3	5	4.77	103
Jansen, Danny, Tor	9/23	NYY	4	3	4	2	3	5.50	100
Trout, Mike, LAA	8/29	Sea	4	4	3	1	6	3.41	99
Tucker, Kyle, Hou	8/19	Col	5	3	4	1	4	4.80	98
Ramirez, Jose, Cle	9/17	Det	5	3	4	2	4	4.78	98
Voit, Luke, NYY	9/11	Bal	4	3	3	2	6	3.72	97
Ramirez, Jose, Cle	8/6	Cin	5	4	3	2	4	4.22	97
Devers, Rafael, Bos	8/30	Was	4	3	4	2	3	5.11	96
Chapman, Matt, Oak	8/10	LAA	5	3	3	2	6	3.61	96

Worst AL Batter Game Scores

Batter	Date	Opp	AB	R	H	SO	DP	RC	GS
Lindor, Francisco, Cle	8/19	Pit	5	0	0	3	2	-1.18	3
Madrigal, Nick, CWS	8/1	KC	5	0	0	1	2	-1.15	3
Ramirez, Jose, Cle	9/15	ChC	5	0	0	1	1	-1.14	4
Abreu, Jose, CWS	8/7	Cle	4	0	0	1	2	-1.08	4
Chirinos, Robinson, Tex	8/8	LAA	3	0	0	0	2	-0.99	5
Machin, Vimael, Oak	7/26	LAA	3	0	0	0	2	-0.99	5
Canha, Mark, Oak	8/7	Hou	6	0	0	2	0	-0.93	6
Devers, Rafael, Bos	9/22	Bal	5	0	0	4	1	-0.89	6
Santana, Carlos, Cle	8/29	StL	5	0	0	3	1	-0.87	6
Correa, Carlos, Hou	8/1	LAA	5	0	0	3	1	-0.87	6
Gurriel Jr., Lourdes, Tor	9/21	NYY	5	0	0	3	1	-0.87	6
Judge, Aaron, NYY	7/25	Was	5	0	0	2	1	-0.85	6

Top NL Batter Game Scores

Batter	Date	Opp	AB	R	H	HR	RBI	RC	GS
Dickerson, Alex, SF	9/1	Col	6	5	5	3	6	7.58	146
Duvall, Adam, Atl	9/9	Mia	4	5	3	3	9	5.75	142
Betts, Mookie, LAD	8/13	SD	4	4	4	3	5	6.29	123
Grisham, Trent, SD	8/22	Hou	5	3	4	3	6	5.53	115
Cabrera, Asdrubal, Was	8/10	NYM	4	3	4	2	5	5.89	114
Anderson, Brian, Mia	9/18	Was	4	3	3	3	7	4.77	113
Miller, Brad, StL	9/1	Cin	6	3	4	2	7	4.59	111
Ozuna, Marcell, Atl	9/1	Bos	5	3	3	3	6	4.53	105
Acuna Jr., Ronald, Atl	9/9	Mia	4	4	3	1	5	4.28	103
Suarez, Eugenio, Cin	9/5	Pit	4	3	3	3	5	4.77	103
Duvall, Adam, Atl	9/2	Bos	4	3	3	3	5	4.77	103
Belt, Brandon, SF	8/25	LAD	5	2	4	2	5	5.25	103

Worst NL Batter Game Scores

Batter	Date	Opp	AB	R	H	SO	DP	RC	GS
Dickerson, Alex, SF	8/28	Ari	4	0	0	0	2	-1.06	4
Bellinger, Cody, LAD	8/11	SD	4	0	0	0	2	-1.06	4
Kieboom, Carter, Was	8/25	Phi	4	0	0	0	2	-1.06	4
McMahon, Ryan, Col	9/25	Ari	3	0	0	0	2	-0.99	5
Grisham, Trent, SD	8/28	Col	6	0	0	2	0	-0.93	6
Moran, Colin, Pit	8/7	Det	6	0	0	2	1	-0.93	6
Castellanos, Nick, Cin	9/1	StL	2	0	0	0	2	-0.91	6
Adams, Matt, Atl	8/18	Was	5	0	0	4	1	-0.89	6
Freeman, Freddie, Atl	9/19	NYM	5	0	0	4	1	-0.89	6
Harper, Bryce, Phi	9/16	NYM	5	0	0	3	0	-0.87	6
Villar, Jonathan, Mia	8/8	NYM	5	0	0	2	1	-0.85	6
Calhoun, Kole, Ari	7/28	Tex	5	0	0	2	1	-0.85	6

AL Batters Win Shares

LeMahieu, DJ	12
Canha, Mark	11
Lowe, Brandon	11
Ramirez, Jose	11
Tucker, Kyle	11
Abreu, Jose	10
Biggio, Cavan	10
Seager, Kyle	10
Springer, George	10
Trout, Mike	10

NL Batters Win Shares

Freeman, Freddie	17
Soto, Juan	14
Betts, Mookie	13
Ozuna, Marcell	13
Turner, Trea	13
Anderson, Brian	12
Tatis Jr., Fernando	12
Machado, Manny	11
4 tied with	10

AL Pitchers Win Shares

Bieber, Shane	11
Keuchel, Dallas	7
Lynn, Lance	7
Maeda, Kenta	7
Bassitt, Chris	6
Carrasco, Carlos	6
Cole, Gerrit	6
Hand, Brad	6
Hendriks, Liam	6
Plesac, Zach	6

NL Pitchers Win Shares

Bauer, Trevor	10
Darvish, Yu	9
Burnes, Corbin	7
Gallen, Zac	7
Hendricks, Kyle	7
Lamet, Dinelson	7
Senzatela, Antonio	7
8 tied with	6

Career Batters Win Shares

Pujols, Albert	488
Cabrera, Miguel	411
Cano, Robinson	349
Votto, Joey	312
Trout, Mike	309
McCutchen, Andrew	283
Molina, Yadier	281
Braun, Ryan	280
Markakis, Nick	244
2 tied with	243

Career Pitchers Win Shares

Verlander, Justin	238
Greinke, Zack	227
Kershaw, Clayton	207
Hamels, Cole	189
Scherzer, Max	189
Hernandez, Felix	188
Lester, Jon	177
Wainwright, Adam	156
Price, David	144
Sale, Chris	144

AL Component ERA
(minimum 60 IP)

Maeda, Kenta	1.48
Bieber, Shane	1.61
Keuchel, Dallas	2.21
Giolito, Lucas	2.40
Bundy, Dylan	2.41
Gonzales, Marco	2.43
Cole, Gerrit	2.65
Ryu, Hyun-Jin	2.94
Valdez, Framber	2.94
Lynn, Lance	3.01

NL Component ERA
(minimum 60 IP)

Bauer, Trevor	1.59
Lamet, Dinelson	1.60
deGrom, Jacob	2.00
Darvish, Yu	2.03
Woodruff, Brandon	2.51
Hendricks, Kyle	2.62
Davies, Zach	2.71
Nola, Aaron	2.72
Wainwright, Adam	2.85
Gallen, Zac	2.91

Win Shares

Mark Simon

Everybody loves a good surprise.

Wait a second. That was the lede of this essay in last year's book. New author, same sentence. What's going on here?

The surprise is not that Freddie Freeman led the majors in Win Shares. That fact was a reasonable expectation coming into 2020, given Freeman's history and the Braves' expectation of success (though Freeman's preseason battle with COVID-19 raised concerns of how he would fare). If you wish to read about Freeman, check the Hall of Fame Value chapter, which takes a snapshot of his candidacy.

The surprise is in three players that were among the seven who finished tied atop the American League Win Shares leaderboard—Kyle Tucker of the Astros, Mark Canha of the Athletics, and Brandon Lowe of the Rays (less surprising were José Abreu, José Ramirez, DJ LeMahieu, and Shane Bieber).

Before the season started, if you had been asked to pick which Astros player would be highest on the Win Shares leaderboard, you probably would have ranked Alex Bregman and José Altuve some combination of 1-2, and you might have snuck Justin Verlander in there with them. Then you would have put George Springer, Carlos Correa, and Michael Brantley in some combination.

Bluntly put, Tucker would have been an afterthought. But he had an excellent season. Tucker basically matched the slashline numbers he put up in a 72-plate appearance cameo in 2019, slashing .268/.325/.512. He had 12 doubles, an MLB-best 6 triples, 9 home runs and 42 RBI. He also produced defensively, saving 5 runs between left field and right field. That the Astros got what they did from someone like Tucker basically allowed them to salvage their regular season and make the playoffs in a weak AL West.

Canha established himself as a good player this season, but certainly Matt Chapman, Matt Olson, and last year's surprise Win Shares leader, Marcus Semien, would have been ahead of him in any sort of Win Shares expectations.

But Canha delivered. Yes, he hit only .246 with 5 home runs, but his walk and hit by pitch totals pushed him to a .387 on-base percentage. Canha's versatility made him a classic Moneyball-type player for Oakland, which lost Chapman to injury and got underwhelming seasons from Olson and Semien. He started games at all three outfield spots and first base and saved one run in total.

Lowe was a good hitter in 2019 but ascended a level in 2020. He nearly matched his 2019 home run total and did match that season's walk total in 103 fewer plate appearances. His 14 home runs nearly doubled the next-closest player on the Rays. Lowe raised his OPS from .850 to .916, which ranked eighth in the AL.

Fair to say none of these three guys would be a surprise if they were on this list again in 2021.

That's a Winner

Speaking of winning, the game-winning RBI has not been seen on statistical ledgers for so long that many probably don't even know what it is. Simply put, it's the RBI that puts a team ahead in a game to stay (regardless of how close the score was).

The MLB leaders in game-winning RBI in 2020 were José Abreu, Kyle Tucker, Kyle Seager, Matt Olson, and Jesús Aguilar with 8 each. Nolan Arenado's 68 are the most in MLB over the last five seasons, eight more than Bryce Harper.

WIN SHARES BY YEAR

Player	<11	11	12	13	14	15	16	17	18	19	20	Career
Abreu, Jose					29	27	20	24	17	20	10	147
Acuna Jr., Ronald									19	28	9	56
Adames, Willy									8	15	9	32
Adams, Matt			1	12	15	3	9	11	8	6	0	65
Adrianza, Ehire				0	1	3	1	6	7	7	1	26
Aguilar, Jesus					0	1	0	9	19	7	8	44
Ahmed, Nick					1	8	3	4	15	17	6	54
Akiyama, Shogo											3	3
Alberto, Hanser							1	1	0	12	4	18
Albies, Ozzie								8	18	29	5	60
Alfaro, Jorge							0	5	12	10	4	31
Almonte, Yency									2	1	4	7
Almora Jr., Albert							5	11	13	3	1	33
Alonso, Pete										24	5	29
Altuve, Jose		2	17	11	30	27	36	35	23	17	2	200
Alvarez, Jose				0	0	5	3	3	7	6	1	25
Anderson, Brett	17	4	3	0	3	8	0	1	3	11	3	53
Anderson, Brian								2	27	13	12	54
Anderson, Chase					6	5	6	14	8	7	0	46
Anderson, Ian											3	3
Anderson, Nick										8	6	14
Anderson, Tim							10	7	13	19	7	56
Anderson, Tyler							8	5	8	0	3	24
Andrus, Elvis	37	18	23	15	13	21	26	25	7	17	1	203
Antone, Tejay											4	4
Arcia, Orlando							4	18	5	12	5	44
Arenado, Nolan				9	12	26	26	26	28	24	2	153
Arozarena, Randy										1	4	5
Arraez, Luis										14	7	21
Arrieta, Jake	5	5	0	3	12	27	16	11	8	6	2	95
Avila, Alex	10	27	15	6	14	6	2	13	3	6	1	103
Avilan, Luis			4	10	2	3	2	4	3	2	0	30
Bader, Harrison								2	13	9	4	28
Baez, Javier					2	1	14	15	24	19	3	78
Baez, Pedro					2	4	6	6	4	8	2	32
Bailey, Homer	12	5	12	11	8	0	0	1	0	10	1	60
Bard, Daniel	15	7	1	0							4	27
Barnes, Austin						1	1	13	3	3	3	24
Barnes, Matt					0	1	5	7	7	7	2	29
Barnhart, Tucker					1	4	12	14	9	9	5	54
Bass, Anthony		5	1	0	0	3		0	1	5	4	19
Bassitt, Chris					2	4	0		3	9	6	24
Bauer, Trevor			0	0	5	8	11	12	18	11	10	75
Bell, Josh							3	16	15	24	2	60
Bellinger, Cody								23	19	31	9	82
Belt, Brandon		5	17	24	5	20	24	12	14	15	7	143
Benintendi, Andrew							4	19	24	15	0	62
Berrios, Jose							0	10	12	13	4	39
Berti, Jon									0	7	6	13
Betances, Dellin	0			0	14	14	12	9	9	0	0	58
Betts, Mookie					8	23	29	26	36	25	13	160
Bichette, Bo										6	6	12
Bieber, Shane									7	19	11	37
Biggio, Cavan										14	10	24
Blackmon, Charlie		1	1	7	16	20	22	33	25	21	7	153
Bogaerts, Xander				1	7	22	19	16	27	25	6	123
Bohm, Alec											8	8
Bonifacio, Jorge								10	4	1	4	19
Bote, David									6	9	5	20
Boxberger, Brad			2	1	8	8	1	3	6	1	1	31
Boyd, Matthew					0	5	4	8	10	0		27
Brach, Brad	0	3	1	5	9	12	11	4	2	0		47
Bradley, Archie				0	6	12	7	9	4			38
Bradley Jr., Jackie			1	5	10	19	14	16	10	5		80
Brantley, Michael	8	11	18	21	31	21	1	10	16	21	9	167
Brault, Steven							0	2	3	4	3	12
Braun, Ryan	106	37	28	9	17	20	20	9	15	15	4	280
Bregman, Alex							10	23	36	31	6	106
Britton, Zack		6	3	1	17	15	19	6	5	9	4	85
Brosseau, Mike										4	5	9
Bruce, Jay	32	22	18	21	10	10	18	21	10	5	1	168
Bryant, Kris						30	32	26	15	23	3	129
Buehler, Walker								0	10	13	2	25

WIN SHARES BY YEAR

Player	<11	11	12	13	14	15	16	17	18	19	20	Career
Bumgarner, Madison	9	12	11	12	16	17	19	8	9	11	0	124
Bundy, Dylan		0					7	11	3	6	5	32
Burnes, Corbin									5	0	7	12
Buxton, Byron						2	5	14	1	11	5	38
Cabrera, Asdrubal	46	25	19	12	15	11	21	17	20	16	4	206
Cabrera, Genesis										0	3	3
Cabrera, Miguel	195	38	32	37	28	26	25	7	5	9	9	411
Cahill, Trevor	23	9	11	6	0	2	5	3	5	2	2	68
Cain, Lorenzo	6	0	7	12	19	27	13	24	25	11	1	145
Calhoun, Kole			0	8	20	21	19	17	8	14	7	114
Camargo, Johan								7	16	5	1	29
Candelario, Jeimer							0	4	11	4	9	28
Canha, Mark						12	0	1	12	19	11	55
Cano, Robinson	114	30	34	35	34	21	28	23	18	7	5	349
Caratini, Victor								1	2	7	4	14
Carpenter, Matt		0	9	35	27	30	21	20	28	11	3	184
Carrasco, Carlos	3	5		0	12	14	12	18	15	3	6	88
Casali, Curt					2	4	2	1	4	6	4	23
Castellanos, Nick				0	13	13	15	18	26	16	3	104
Castillo, Diego									5	7	4	16
Castillo, Luis								6	6	16	6	34
Castro, Jason	4		8	18	10	7	9	12	1	7	3	79
Castro, Starlin	12	25	23	7	20	13	15	13	18	11	1	158
Castro, Willi										1	9	10
Cave, Jake									10	5	3	18
Cease, Dylan										2	3	5
Cervelli, Francisco	10	4	0	3	7	17	9	6	19	3	3	81
Cespedes, Yoenis			24	14	18	27	19	10	6		0	118
Chacin, Jhoulys	10	12	4	15	2	2	5	10	12	0	0	72
Chapman, Aroldis	2	4	21	12	13	13	15	9	12	10	2	113
Chapman, Matt								11	25	25	5	66
Chatwood, Tyler			3	3	11	1		11	8	2	6	1	46
Chavez, Jesse	4	0	0	3	7	6	3	3	12	5	0	43
Chirinos, Robinson		1		0	11	4	6	10	13	11	0	56
Choi, Ji-Man							0	1	6	14	3	24
Choo, Shin-Soo	71	8	25	31	9	25	5	17	15	18	3	227
Cishek, Steve	1	6	10	14	10	3	11	6	10	8	1	80
Civale, Aaron										6	4	10
Clarke, Taylor										2	3	5
Claudio, Alex					1	1	5	12	5	4	1	29
Clevinger, Mike							2	11	17	14	4	48
Clippard, Tyler	16	13	11	10	10	9	7	3	7	6	3	95
Cobb, Alex			3	6	13	13	0	12	3	0	2	52
Cole, Gerrit				8	7	18	6	10	16	22	6	93
Colome, Alex				1	2	6	12	12	9	12	5	59
Conforto, Michael						8	6	20	21	20	8	83
Contreras, Willson							9	17	14	13	9	62
Cooper, Garrett								1	1	9	6	17
Corbin, Patrick			4	13		5	5	11	15	16	2	71
Correa, Carlos						18	26	26	12	13	6	101
Crawford, Brandon		5	13	11	22	20	21	13	18	13	6	142
Crawford, J.P.								2	5	10	8	25
Crichton, Stefan									0	2	4	6
Cron, C.J.					8	9	14	10	12	12	2	67
Cronenworth, Jake											7	7
Cruz, Nelson	49	16	17	16	22	26	21	24	22	22	8	243
Cueto, Johnny	25	12	21	5	22	12	19	6	4	0	2	128
Curtiss, John								0	0	0	4	4
Dahl, David							6		9	12	1	28
Dalbec, Bobby											3	3
d'Arnaud, Travis				1	8	11	3	10	1	15	6	55
Darvish, Yu			14	18	10		8	12	1	9	9	81
Davies, Zach						2	8	13	1	11	6	41
Davis, Chris	16	4	19	33	12	27	17	8	2	2	0	140
Davis, J.D.								1	1	14	4	20
Davis, Khris				6	12	11	15	20	23	8	0	95
Davis, Wade	10	6	7	2	15	19	11	12	12	0	0	94
deGrom, Jacob					11	15	11	11	20	21	6	95
DeJong, Paul								13	16	20	6	55
DeSclafani, Anthony						0	7	7	3	10	0	27
DeShields, Delino						16	2	10	6	10	3	47
Devenski, Chris							11	10	3	3	0	27
Devers, Rafael								7	9	24	6	46

WIN SHARES BY YEAR

Player	<11	11	12	13	14	15	16	17	18	19	20	Career
Diaz, Aledmys							18	4	12	7	1	42
Diaz, Edwin							8	10	18	3	4	43
Diaz, Yandy								3	3	7	5	18
Dickerson, Alex					0	8				6	5	19
Dickerson, Corey				4	15	8	9	18	16	10	3	83
Diekman, Jake			1	3	4	4	7	2	4	3	4	32
Dietrich, Derek				5	6	6	15	12	16	9	2	71
Dobnak, Randy										3	3	6
Dolis, Rafael		0	0	1							4	5
Donaldson, Josh	0	8	32	27	32	28	25	7	25	3		187
Doolittle, Sean			5	8	11	2	4	11	12	9	0	62
Dozier, Brian			4	19	19	24	24	26	15	11	0	142
Dozier, Hunter								0	1	16	3	20
Drury, Brandon						0	9	12	0	4	0	25
Dubon, Mauricio										3	4	7
Duffey, Tyler						5	0	3	0	6	4	18
Duffy, Danny		1	2	3	12	7	15	10	6	7	2	65
Duvall, Adam					0	2	16	12	5	4	4	43
Dyson, Jarrod	2	2	8	7	9	6	12	8	4	10	1	69
Eaton, Adam			2	5	20	24	24	5	12	16	4	112
Edman, Tommy										12	5	17
Eflin, Zach							0	0	6	9	3	18
Encarnacion, Edwin	62	11	31	22	19	24	19	18	14	18	0	238
Engel, Adam								4	4	4	3	15
Eovaldi, Nathan		2	3	5	4	9	6		5	1	3	38
Escobar, Eduardo		0	2	2	13	14	7	14	20	22	2	96
Fairbanks, Pete										1	3	4
Familia, Jeurys			0	0	9	15	16	2	9	1	2	54
Fiers, Mike		0	8	0	7	9	7	3	12	12	3	61
Flaherty, Jack								0	9	17	2	28
Fleming, Josh											4	4
Fletcher, David									8	18	7	33
Flores, Wilmer				2	7	16	9	8	11	8	5	66
Floro, Dylan							0	0	7	3	3	13
Flowers, Tyler	0	3	3	3	10	7	10	12	7	6	0	61
Foltynewicz, Mike					0	0	6	5	14	5	0	30
Forsythe, Logan		3	8	3	4	16	16	10	9	7	0	76
Foster, Matt											4	4
Fowler, Dexter	28	16	15	13	16	22	22	16	3	17	2	170
France, Ty										5	7	12
Franco, Maikel					1	13	17	6	13	7	8	65
Frazier, Adam							5	13	12	15	3	48
Frazier, Clint								3	0	9	6	18
Frazier, Todd		3	13	15	20	13	15	13	12	18	3	125
Freeland, Kyle								11	21	0	5	37
Freeman, Freddie	0	19	18	35	28	22	28	22	26	28	17	243
Fried, Max								1	2	12	5	20
Fuentes, Josh										0	3	3
Fulmer, Michael							14	10	4		0	28
Gallegos, Giovanny								0	1	9	3	13
Gallen, Zac										7	7	14
Gallo, Joey						2	0	16	13	11	6	48
Galvis, Freddy			3	4	2	15	16	18	14	12	4	88
Gamel, Ben							1	13	9	7	2	32
Garcia, Avisail			1	5	4	10	11	22	6	13	3	75
Garcia, Bryan										0	3	3
Garcia, Greg					0	2	7	6	3	11	1	30
Garcia, Jarlin								2	1	6	3	12
Garcia, Leury				2	1	1	1	8	9	8	2	32
Garcia, Luis											3	3
Garcia, Yimi					1	4	1		0	4	3	13
Gardner, Brett	29	16	2	22	19	19	17	19	13	17	5	178
Garrett, Amir								0	4	6	3	13
Garver, Mitch								1	11	18	1	31
Gausman, Kevin				1	6	5	12	9	9	1	4	47
Gibson, Kyle				0	8	12	4	7	13	7	2	53
Giles, Ken					7	11	6	12	5	11	0	52
Gimenez, Andres											3	3
Giolito, Lucas							0	4	1	15	5	25
Givens, Mychal						4	7	10	5	5	1	32
Glasnow, Tyler							1	1	4	8	4	18
Goins, Ryan				2	2	12	3	12	1	3	0	35
Goldschmidt, Paul		6	17	36	20	35	25	29	25	21	9	223

Player	<11	11	12	13	14	15	16	17	18	19	20	Career
Gomber, Austin										4	3	7
Gomes, Yan			2	14	18	5	4	12	9	8	2	74
Gonsolin, Tony										4	4	8
Gonzales, Marco					2	0		1	10	11	5	29
Gonzalez, Erik							0	2	3	1	3	9
Gonzalez, Gio	17	15	17	11	8	9	6	17	8	6	1	115
Gonzalez, Marwin			2	2	6	8	7	26	13	12	4	80
Gonzalez, Victor											3	3
Goodwin, Brian							1	6	6	10	3	26
Gordon, Alex	32	24	20	21	26	16	9	6	11	13	1	179
Grandal, Yasmani			11	4	12	15	19	12	17	24	7	121
Gray, Jon						1	9	10	7	12	1	40
Gray, Sonny				5	13	16	0	10	6	17	5	72
Green, Chad							2	9	9	4	3	27
Greene, Shane					4	0	3	9	5	11	3	35
Gregorius, Didi			0	10	9	17	16	18	21	11	9	111
Greinke, Zack	74	10	16	17	15	26	10	18	17	21	3	227
Grichuk, Randal					1	12	13	7	13	8	8	62
Grisham, Trent										3	7	10
Grossman, Robbie				7	10	0	10	10	13	11	7	68
Guerra, Junior						0	10	1	5	9	2	27
Guerrero Jr., Vlad										11	5	16
Guillorme, Luis									1	1	3	5
Gurriel, Yuli							2	18	19	20	2	61
Gurriel Jr., Lourdes									8	9	9	26
Gyorko, Jedd				12	11	11	12	15	13	1	3	78
Hader, Josh								6	14	16	4	40
Haggerty, Sam										0	3	3
Hahn, Jesse					5	5	0	2		0	4	16
Hamels, Cole	67	17	18	13	15	12	16	10	12	9	0	189
Hamilton, Billy				2	15	5	9	10	8	3	1	53
Hand, Brad		1	0	1	3	1	8	14	12	11	6	57
Happ, Ian								12	12	7	9	40
Happ, J.A.	23	1	5	3	7	10	18	10	14	6	4	101
Harper, Bryce			21	19	9	38	20	22	23	27	9	188
Harris, Will			0	5	1	9	11	5	5	10	1	47
Harrison, Josh		5	4	3	25	12	15	15	9	1	2	91
Harvey, Matt			5	14		14	2	0	5	0	0	40
Hayes, Ke'Bryan											5	5
Healy, Ryon							11	12	9	4	0	36
Heaney, Andrew					0	8	0	0	8	4	3	23
Hechavarria, Adeiny			3	5	13	13	9	9	5	8	1	66
Hendricks, Kyle					7	8	17	11	13	12	7	75
Hendriks, Liam		0	0	0	0	5	3	5	1	17	6	37
Hernandez, Cesar				3	1	12	24	18	22	16	7	103
Hernandez, Jonathan										1	4	5
Hernandez, Kike					5	9	2	9	13	12	4	54
Hernandez, Teoscar							2	3	11	12	7	35
Herrera, Kelvin		0	10	5	10	8	13	7	7	1	0	61
Heuer, Codi											4	4
Heyward, Jason	23	11	22	14	23	21	12	14	16	13	9	178
Hicks, Aaron				4	4	11	4	11	22	7	7	70
Hill, Rich	20	1	3	0	1	4	12	11	7	5	3	67
Hiura, Keston										12	4	16
Hoerner, Nico										3	3	6
Holland, Derek	5	14	8	13	4	2	4	0	10	0	0	60
Holland, Greg		0	9	11	18	15	7	12	5	4	5	86
Holt, Brock			3	1	12	14	6	2	11	8	1	58
Hoskins, Rhys								10	22	18	6	56
Hosmer, Eric		13	10	18	14	22	17	30	16	17	6	163
Hudson, Dakota									3	12	4	19
Hudson, Daniel	10	16	0		0	4	4	3	2	11	1	51
Hughes, Jared		0	6	1	6	7	4	7	11	5	1	48
Hunter, Tommy	18	3	4	10	8	4	3	8	6	1	2	67
Iglesias, Jose		0	1	13		12	13	11	15	12	8	85
Iglesias, Raisel						4	7	14	11	9	6	51
Inciarte, Ender					10	15	14	22	17	7	1	86
Jansen, Danny									3	9	3	15
Jansen, Kenley	6	6	15	16	11	12	17	19	10	10	4	126
Javier, Cristian											3	3
Jay, Jon	8	13	15	17	16	3	12	12	11	4	0	111
Jeffers, Ryan											3	3
Jeffress, Jeremy	1	1	0	1	3	7	10	4	16	2	6	51

Player	<11	11	12	13	14	15	16	17	18	19	20	Career
Jimenez, Eloy										12	9	21
Jones, JaCoby						0	1	5	4	3		13
Joseph, Caleb				7	12	2	8	4	1	0		34
Joyce, Matt	17	19	13	11	10	1	11	14	3	8	3	110
Judge, Aaron							0	29	19	16	4	68
Karinchak, James										1	4	5
Kela, Keone					8	2	6	8	4	0		28
Keller, Brad									12	9	5	26
Kelly, Carson							0	1	0	11	3	15
Kelly, Joe			5	9	5	6	2	7	5	3	1	43
Kelly, Merrill										8	3	11
Kemp, Matt	73	37	21	6	20	18	16	6	17	0	4	218
Kemp, Tony							1	1	9	5	3	19
Kendrick, Howie	64	18	16	13	27	18	11	10	2	12	1	192
Kennedy, Ian	13	20	11	2	9	4	14	3	4	10	0	90
Kepler, Max						0	8	12	13	19	6	58
Kershaw, Clayton	32	23	19	22	22	21	16	19	12	15	6	207
Keuchel, Dallas			0	3	16	22	6	13	11	7	7	85
Kiermaier, Kevin				0	9	19	13	13	7	11	6	78
Kim, Kwang-hyun											5	5
Kimbrel, Craig	4	17	18	17	16	11	9	19	14	0	1	126
Kiner-Falefa, Isiah									5	2	5	12
Kintzler, Brandon	0	1	2	8	4	0	7	11	4	7	3	47
Kipnis, Jason		6	24	27	10	22	19	9	17	13	5	152
Kluber, Corey		0	1	9	21	14	20	23	20	1	0	109
Knapp, Andrew								4	2	3	4	13
Knebel, Corey					0	4	2	17	8		0	31
Kolarek, Adam								0	3	6	3	12
La Stella, Tommy					9	3	4	5	2	8	7	38
Lagares, Juan				7	15	13	2	2	3	2	0	44
Lamb, Jake					1	9	16	17	4	4	3	54
Lamet, Dinelson								4		3	7	14
Laureano, Ramon									9	17	7	33
Leclerc, Jose							1	4	12	8	0	25
LeMahieu, DJ		0	6	8	9	14	22	20	19	33	11	142
Leon, Sandy			0	0	1	3	12	9	6	3	1	35
Lester, Jon	61	14	8	12	18	13	18	9	14	8	2	177
Lewis, Kyle										3	7	10
Lindor, Francisco						14	21	27	30	19	6	117
Locastro, Tim								0	0	7	3	10
Longoria, Evan	71	25	14	24	21	18	20	18	7	14	1	233
Lopez, Nicky										6	3	9
Lopez, Pablo									2	4	3	9
Lorenzen, Michael						2	4	6	7	12	3	34
Loup, Aaron			3	7	7	1	0	4	1	1	3	27
Lowe, Brandon									6	14	11	31
Lucroy, Jonathan	4	15	15	19	26	10	22	11	10	5	0	137
Lugo, Seth							6	3	8	12	2	31
Luzardo, Jesus										2	3	5
Lynn, Lance		2	11	7	16	12		11	6	18	7	90
Machado, Manny			7	20	12	27	28	19	28	18	11	170
Madrigal, Nick											4	4
Maeda, Kenta							11	7	5	10	7	40
Mahle, Tyler								1	3	2	4	10
Maldonado, Martin		0	7	3	4	5	7	11	11	6	7	61
Manaea, Sean							7	8	9	4	2	30
Margot, Manuel							1	13	10	9	4	37
Marisnick, Jake				2	5	9	3	6	5	7	1	37
Markakis, Nick	93	19	16	11	20	20	17	14	22	11	1	244
Marmolejos, Jose											3	3
Marquez, German							1	11	16	13	6	47
Marshall, Evan					5	0	0	0	0	6	3	14
Marte, Ketel						9	7	6	16	29	5	72
Marte, Starling			5	20	17	20	17	10	21	21	6	137
Martin, Chris					0	0			3	6	3	12
Martinez, Carlos				1	4	14	16	12	10	9	0	66
Martinez, J.D.		6	7	3	19	25	17	20	33	22	2	154
Martinez, Jose							1	10	20	8	2	41
Matz, Steven						4	9	0	4	8	0	25
May, Dustin										2	5	7
Maybin, Cameron	13	17	13	0	5	16	14	10	9	8	2	107
Mayers, Mike							0	0	2	0	4	6
Mazara, Nomar							16	16	10	10	3	55
McCann, James					0	10	9	10	6	16	5	56
McCullers Jr., Lance						8	6	5	7		2	28
McCutchen, Andrew	40	28	40	34	33	35	17	22	20	8	6	283
McGee, Jake	0	2	8	5	15	7	4	7	0	2	3	53
McKenzie, Triston											3	3
McMahon, Ryan								0	4	11	4	19
McNeil, Jeff									11	24	6	41
Meadows, Austin									5	23	2	30
Melancon, Mark	3	10	0	15	15	17	16	3	3	8	3	93
Mercer, Jordy			2	13	10	8	13	12	9	5	0	72
Merrifield, Whit							8	21	22	21	9	81
Miley, Wade		2	14	10	7	9	3	4	7	11	0	67
Miller, Andrew	4	2	4	2	9	13	19	11	3	4	2	73
Miller, Brad				10	11	15	15	6	5	6	5	73
Mills, Alec								0	1	3	3	7
Milone, Tommy		2	10	6	5	8	1	0	0	4	1	37
Minor, Mike	0	3	7	13	3			11	11	18	0	66
Minter, A.J.								1	9	0	3	13
Molina, Yadier	92	18	29	29	19	16	21	19	18	16	4	281
Moncada, Yoan							0	6	13	23	6	48
Mondesi, Adalberto							2	1	8	12	5	28
Montgomery, Mike						2	7	10	6	3	0	28
Moore, Dylan										5	5	10
Moran, Colin							0	1	13	14	2	30
Moreland, Mitch	6	8	9	10	3	16	10	12	12	8	5	99
Morrison, Logan	9	11	4	7	11	9	9	16	3	0	0	79
Morton, Charlie	4	8	0	6	4	2	1	10	13	18	2	68
Mountcastle, Ryan											5	5
Moustakas, Mike		4	14	5	9	21	1	15	19	19	5	112
Mullins II, Cedric									2	1	3	6
Muncy, Max						1	2		21	22	5	51
Murphy, Daniel	16	14	20	22	21	19	31	27	10	9	2	191
Murphy, Sean										2	5	7
Myers, Wil				14	6	9	19	19	10	10	10	97
Naquin, Tyler							13	0	5	8	2	28
Narvaez, Omar							3	7	10	14	4	38
Neris, Hector					0	2	11	11	3	13	2	42
Nicasio, Juan	4	2	4	3	3	5	10	0	0	2	0	33
Nimmo, Brandon							2	6	22	8	6	44
Nola, Aaron						4	3	12	22	14	4	59
Nola, Austin										7	8	15
Nottingham, Jacob									0	1	3	4
Nova, Ivan	2	11	5	13	0	2	8	8	6	9	0	64
Nunez, Eduardo	2	8	4	6	3	6	15	18	7	1	0	70
Nunez, Renato							0	1	5	11	4	21
O'Day, Darren	20	0	10	8	10	12	3	6	1	1	2	73
Odor, Rougned					11	16	18	8	13	13	3	82
Odorizzi, Jake			0	1	7	11	11	7	7	12	0	56
Ohtani, Shohei									20	12	1	33
Olson, Matt							0	9	19	21	8	57
O'Neill, Tyler									6	3	3	12
Osuna, Roberto						11	15	13	8	14	1	62
Ottavino, Adam	0	5	7	6	4	5	3	14	8	1		53
Owings, Chris				2	8	6	11	9	3	2	1	42
Ozuna, Marcell				8	19	10	15	29	19	14	13	127
Panik, Joe					10	17	13	15	6	11	3	75
Parker, Blake			0	4	0		1	10	7	5	1	28
Paxton, James				3	5	3	5	11	11	9	0	47
Peacock, Brad		2		2	2	0	1	12	5	6	0	30
Pederson, Joc					0	15	19	7	11	17	3	72
Pena, Felix							1	1	4	5	3	14
Pence, Hunter	75	24	18	25	26	7	15	13	3	12	0	218
Peralta, David					7	20	2	16	23	13	6	87
Peraza, Jose						0	7	5	14	5	1	32
Perez, Hernan			0	1	0	4	19	7	2	0		34
Perez, Martin			1	8	2	3	9	9	1	6	3	42
Perez, Oliver	42	3	4	5	2	2	2	5	4	3		72
Perez, Roberto					2	7	5	8	2	18	3	45
Perez, Salvador		7	10	23	17	18	18	16	13		7	129
Peterson, David											4	4
Peterson, Jace					1	14	9	3	4	2	2	35
Petit, Yusmeiro	7	0	2	4	3	2	10	8	10	3		49
Pham, Tommy					0	7	4	21	17	17	2	68

Player	<11	11	12	13	14	15	16	17	18	19	20	Career
Phegley, Josh				2	0	8	1	2	2	10	0	25
Phelps, David		7	3	4	3	12	4	3	2			38
Pillar, Kevin				1	1	15	15	9	11	16	5	73
Pina, Manny	0	0					2	12	8	5	2	29
Pinder, Chad							1	7	8	8	2	26
Pineda, Michael		10			8	7	6	5		9	2	47
Piscotty, Stephen						11	22	7	21	7	4	72
Plawecki, Kevin					7	3	4	5	4	4		27
Plesac, Zach										9	7	16
Polanco, Gregory				8	17	14	6	18	2	1		66
Polanco, Jorge				1	1	8	14	11	26	6		67
Pollock, A.J.			2	14	10	27	1	15	13	10	5	97
Pomeranz, Drew		1	4	0	5	5	12	15	0		4	50
Porcello, Rick	18	8	7	9	13	5	19	8	12	6	1	106
Pressly, Ryan				4	2	3	6	3	8	9	2	37
Profar, Jurickson			0	5			6	1	16	10	6	44
Pujols, Albert	347	26	25	10	19	18	17	7	8	10	1	488
Quantrill, Cal										3	3	6
Quintana, Jose			9	13	12	15	15	10	9	6	0	89
Ramirez, Erasmo			2	2	0	10	6	0	0		2	28
Ramirez, Jose				1	7	4	22	28	29	17	11	119
Ramos, AJ				0	5	8	14	11	6	0	0	44
Ramos, Wilson	3	13	3	8	10	11	24	6	19	15	1	113
Ray, Robbie					0	6	7	17	7	8	1	46
Realmuto, J.T.					1	10	19	19	25	22	6	102
Reddick, Josh	1	7	16	13	13	17	12	21	10	12	5	127
Rendon, Anthony				12	26	9	22	29	22	31	7	158
Renfroe, Hunter							2	9	12	11	2	36
Reyes, Franmil									8	13	4	25
Reyes, Victor								1	5	4		10
Reynolds, Bryan										19	3	22
Richards, Garrett		0	1	6	13	14	2	2	4	0	3	45
Riley, Austin										6	4	10
Rios, Edwin										2	3	5
Rivera, Rene	4	2		2	14	5	6	7	3	1	0	44
Rizzo, Anthony		0	12	14	28	32	29	25	22	25	5	192
Roark, Tanner				7	15	4	17	7	8	8	0	66
Robert, Luis											7	7
Robles, Hansel						3	6	3	3	15	0	30
Robles, Victor								1	2	15	3	21
Rodon, Carlos						9	8	3	6	1	0	27
Rodriguez, Richard								0	8	5	4	17
Rodriguez, Sean	12	10	8	4	6	2	13	2	2	3	0	62
Rogers, Taylor							4	7	8	13	2	34
Rojas, Miguel					1	4	3	8	13	12	10	51
Romano, Jordan										0	3	3
Romine, Austin		0		2	1	0	5	2	7	7	2	26
Romo, Sergio	16	9	11	9	8	5	4	4	7	11	3	87
Rondon, Hector				2	11	16	7	4	7	5	0	52
Rosario, Amed								2	14	19	1	36
Rosario, Eddie						12	5	14	16	17	8	72
Rosenthal, Trevor				2	7	11	14	1	7	0	5	47
Ruf, Darin				1	8	1	7	0			4	21
Ruiz, Rio							1	2	0	8	4	15
Rusin, Chris			0	3	0	4	6	11	1	0	0	25
Ryu, Hyun-Jin				13	9		0	7	7	18	5	59
Samardzija, Jeff	3	7	8	7	11	6	11	8	0	11	0	72
Sanchez, Anibal	27	10	10	17	8	5	1	1	10	11	0	100
Sanchez, Gary						0	11	16	8	15	2	52
Sanchez, Yolmer					1	7	3	14	15	15	1	56
Sandoval, Pablo	42	23	18	22	21	6	0	2	6	8	0	148
Sano, Miguel						16	11	14	4	17	4	66
Santana, Carlos	7	22	21	26	22	13	19	17	19	24	6	196
Santana, Danny					18	3	1	3	0	15	0	40
Santana, Domingo				0	6	7	21	4	11	1		50
Santander, Anthony								0	1	9	6	16
Schebler, Scott					1	7	9	8	1	0		26
Scherzer, Max	26	10	14	20	18	18	20	21	22	16	4	189
Schoop, Jonathan			0	6	9	18	26	8	9	6		82
Schwarber, Kyle						10	0	10	15	18	6	59
Seager, Corey						6	29	31	4	20	9	99
Seager, Kyle		3	24	23	28	17	30	20	14	11	10	180
Segura, Jean			4	21	13	12	23	16	24	15	6	134

Player	<11	11	12	13	14	15	16	17	18	19	20	Career
Semien, Marcus				2	7	10	21	11	21	36	8	116
Senzatela, Antonio								9	5	2	7	23
Severino, Pedro				0	2	0	4	0	4	6	4	16
Shaw, Bryan	3	4	7	8	7	7	7	7	0	5	0	48
Shaw, Travis					7	12	22	21	3	3		68
Sheffield, Justus									0	1	3	4
Shoemaker, Matt			1	11	5	9	4	1	3	1		35
Simmons, Andrelton		8	19	13	14	14	24	22	6	2		122
Sims, Lucas								1	0	3	4	8
Singer, Brady											3	3
Slater, Austin								3	4	7	4	18
Slegers, Aaron								0	0	0	3	3
Smith, Dominic								3	1	5	7	16
Smith, Mallex							6	6	18	8	0	38
Smith, Will			2	3	4	7	3		10	14	1	44
Smith, Will									10	7		17
Smoak, Justin	7	10	9	12	4	10	4	23	21	10	0	110
Smyly, Drew			6	10	10	5	4			3	2	40
Snell, Blake							5	6	22	6	4	43
Sogard, Eric	0	1	1	10	7	8		8	1	15	3	54
Solak, Nick										5	6	11
Solano, Donovan			8	9	10	1	1			10	7	46
Soler, Jorge					4	10	7	0	6	18	4	49
Soria, Joakim	57	7		2	6	10	5	6	8	5	3	109
Soto, Juan									15	24	14	53
Souza Jr., Steven					0	7	10	19	5			41
Springer, George					10	13	23	24	19	25	10	124
Stallings, Jacob							1	1	4	4	1	11
Stammen, Craig	6	2	9	7	4	1		7	10	9	1	56
Stanton, Giancarlo	13	19	19	15	31	14	12	29	18	3	2	175
Stassi, Max			0	1	1	0	0	9	1	4		16
Stevenson, Andrew								1	2	1	3	7
Stewart, D.J.									2	2	4	8
Story, Trevor							13	13	26	22	7	81
Strange-Gordon, Dee		6	3	2	22	26	7	18	11	10	0	105
Strasburg, Stephen	5	2	14	11	13	8	11	17	7	19	0	107
Strickland, Hunter					2	5	7	4	1	4	0	26
Strop, Pedro	0	3	10	5	6	8	5	7	12	4	0	60
Suarez, Eugenio					9	10	16	21	21	16	6	99
Suter, Brent							2	6	4	4	3	19
Suzuki, Kurt	51	8	10	6	14	8	7	12	10	11	2	139
Swanson, Dansby							4	10	15	15	10	54
Tanaka, Masahiro					12	10	18	8	11	7	3	69
Tapia, Raimel							1	3	1	7	6	18
Tatis Jr., Fernando										18	12	30
Taveras, Leody											3	3
Taylor, Chris					5	1	1	23	17	13	9	69
Taylor, Michael A.					1	14	4	14	5	0	1	39
Teheran, Julio		0	0	12	15	8	13	7	9	11	0	75
Tellez, Rowdy									5	6	5	16
Thames, Eric		7	3					15	9	13	1	48
Tomlin, Josh	4	9	0	0	2	6	10	6	0	6	2	45
Torres, Gleyber									19	28	3	50
Treinen, Blake					4	3	8	7	19	4	2	47
Trout, Mike		3	38	40	40	42	35	29	39	33	10	309
Tsutsugo, Yoshi											4	4
Tucker, Kyle									0	2	11	13
Turnbull, Spencer										6	3	9
Turner, Justin	0	15	4	3	18	18	25	24	19	20	8	154
Turner, Trea						0	17	17	25	19	13	91
Upton, Justin	42	26	16	21	21	21	14	22	17	4	1	205
Urias, Julio							5	0	0	9	4	18
Urshela, Gio						3		1	0	21	8	33
Valaika, Pat							0	5	1	1	3	10
Valdez, Framber									4	1	4	9
Vazquez, Christian					4		3	11	4	15	5	42
Verdugo, Alex								0	1	11	5	17
Verlander, Justin	77	27	23	14	8	8	20	17	20	23	1	238
Villar, Jonathan				3	5	4	24	8	15	19	2	80
Vincent, Nick			3	6	4	1	5	6	4	2	1	32
Vogelbach, Daniel							0	0	2	12	3	17
Vogt, Stephen			0	4	8	18	9	6		11	1	57
Voit, Luke								2	10	17	9	38

					WIN SHARES BY YEAR						
Player	<11	11	12	13	14	15	16	17	18	19	20	Career
Volquez, Edinson	23	0	6	0	11	13	5	3		0	0	61
Votto, Joey	79	33	27	30	8	33	33	33	22	11	3	312
Wacha, Michael				4	7	14	2	8	6	4	0	45
Wainwright, Adam	74		9	16	23	3	10	6	1	9	5	156
Walker, Christian					0	0		0	0	16	5	21
Walker, Neil	16	20	21	20	21	22	19	16	9	7	0	171
Walker, Taijuan				1	3	6	5	11	1	0	3	30
Walsh, Jared										1	4	5
Watson, Tony		3	5	8	11	12	9	7	9	3	3	70
Webb, Tyler								0	1	4	3	8
Wendle, Joey							2	1	19	5	7	34
Wheeler, Zack				5	8			1	11	12	5	42
White, Evan											4	4
Wieters, Matt	21	23	23	19	5	7	16	7	7	5	1	134
Williams, Devin										0	5	5
Wilson, Justin			0	8	2	7	5	10	4	6	2	44
Winker, Jesse								3	12	8	5	28
Wisler, Matt						3	4	0	1	1	4	13
Wittgren, Nick							5	2	2	8	3	20
Wolters, Tony							5	5	3	10	2	25
Wong, Kolten				1	10	18	9	14	12	24	8	96
Wood, Alex				4	13	8	2	15	6	0	0	48
Woodruff, Brandon								2	3	11	6	22
Workman, Brandon				2	0			3	5	15	1	26
Yarbrough, Ryan									9	9	3	21
Yardley, Eric										1	3	4
Yastrzemski, Mike										14	10	24
Yates, Kirby					2	0	1	4	12	14	0	33
Yelich, Christian				8	22	15	21	23	34	33	4	160
Zimmermann, Jordan	4	11	15	15	16	11	4	3	5	0	0	84
Zunino, Mike				2	11	5	8	14	7	5	2	54

Instant Replay

John Shirley

The current instant replay review system has been part of the game for a few years now. While there might still be some holdouts who believe otherwise, allowing umpires the ability to get a second look at split-second interactions that might alter a game's outcome is only benefiting the sport.

Instant replay reviews were up slightly in 2020, averaging 5.9 per every ten games compared to 5.7 per every ten games in 2019. The overturn rate was 43 percent, compared to 45 percent in 2019.

Last year in this book we wrote that fan interference could be a thing of the past due to the extension of netting down the lines. That prediction was technically correct, as there were zero fan interference reviews, but we will have to see how it plays out when there are actually fans back in the stands, hopefully next season.

On the team level, the Phillies continued to benefit from challenges, as they ranked first in net challenges overturned after coming in second in 2019. They finished with a net of eight, which was three more than any other team. This was nothing new for manager Joe Girardi, who has had 108 of his 151 (72 percent) challenges overturned during his managerial career, the best rate of any manager. The Red Sox were the best team in regards to challenge accuracy, winning 10 out of their 13 challenges.

For the second year in a row the Yankees issued the fewest challenges of any team, tying the Brewers with only nine challenges each.

2020 Instant Replay Summary

Replay Type	Total Replays	Overturned	Percent
Tag Play	202	73	36.1
Force Play	200	117	58.5
Hit By Pitch	28	12	42.9
Fair or Foul	22	3	13.6
Boundary Call (Home Run)	12	4	33.3
Trap or Catch	11	6	54.5
Rules Check	9	0	0.0
Stadium Boundary	7	4	57.1
Catcher's Interference	7	4	57.1
Home Plate Collision	6	0	0.0
Slide Interference	5	0	0.0
Record Keeping	3	2	66.7
Timing Play	3	0	0.0
Tag-Up Play	2	0	0.0
Missed Base	2	0	0.0
Passed Runner	1	0	0.0
Runner Placement	1	0	0.0

2020 Challenges

Team	Challenges	Overturned	Pct	Opponent Challenges	Opponent Overturned	Opponent Pct	Net
Philadelphia Phillies	24	13	54.2	13	6	46.2	7
Washington Nationals	12	8	66.7	11	3	27.3	5
Chicago Cubs	15	10	66.7	15	5	33.3	5
Colorado Rockies	13	7	53.8	13	3	23.1	4
Boston Red Sox	13	10	76.9	17	6	35.3	4
Cincinnati Reds	16	8	50.0	13	5	38.5	3
Cleveland Indians	20	9	45.0	15	6	40.0	3
Houston Astros	13	6	46.2	13	3	23.1	3
Miami Marlins	23	10	43.5	15	7	46.7	3
Minnesota Twins	28	9	32.1	10	6	60.0	3
Detroit Tigers	14	8	57.1	10	6	60.0	2
Arizona Diamondbacks	15	7	46.7	16	5	31.3	2
Tampa Bay Rays	20	7	35.0	14	5	35.7	2
St Louis Cardinals	11	7	63.6	10	6	60.0	1
San Francisco Giants	20	7	35.0	14	6	42.9	1
Los Angeles Angels	17	8	47.1	16	7	43.8	1
Kansas City Royals	10	7	70.0	13	7	53.8	0
Texas Rangers	14	7	50.0	15	7	46.7	0
Toronto Blue Jays	25	7	28.0	23	7	30.4	0
Oakland Athletics	15	5	33.3	12	6	50.0	-1
Seattle Mariners	10	3	30.0	11	5	45.5	-2
Los Angeles Dodgers	15	7	46.7	19	9	47.4	-2
Atlanta Braves	13	4	30.8	17	7	41.2	-3
Baltimore Orioles	18	6	33.3	17	9	52.9	-3
Chicago White Sox	11	8	72.7	27	11	40.7	-3
New York Yankees	9	5	55.6	20	9	45.0	-4
San Diego Padres	20	8	40.0	23	14	60.9	-6
Milwaukee Brewers	9	3	33.3	14	9	64.3	-6
Pittsburgh Pirates	12	2	16.7	19	10	52.6	-8
New York Mets	14	5	35.7	24	16	66.7	-11

2020 Projections Review

Bill James

This is the portion of the book in which we normally revisit the previous year's projections, brag about those we got pretty much right, weasel off the hook about those we got mostly wrong, and use some Andy-Reid-style misdirection plays to distract your attention from those that we got REALLY wrong. These are not predictions, exactly, because I am squeamish about using the word "prediction". Or "predict" or "predicted"...I don't use it. We try to encourage the readers to distinguish between predictions, which are attempts to say "this is what I think will happen", and projections, which is a way of saying "if we carry this data into the future, this is where it appears to be heading." OK, it's a subtle difference.

Anyway, we got almost everything wrong last year, but we have a *really* good excuse, so good that we don't even need to tell you what it is. Anyone who accurately predicted beforehand what would happen in 2020 should be locked in a storage container and shipped to Bora Bora before they can offer any more predictions.

That said, we did have a few predictions that, by a weird combination of offsetting errors, we got about right. In the comparisons below, all of the top lines are what the player actually did, and all of the second lines are what we had projected the player would do, which you can tell, actually, because all of the projections were for more than 60 games played:

Hitter	G	AB	R	H	D	T	HR	RBI	BB	SO	SB	Avg	Slg
Erik González	50	181	14	41	13	1	3	20	8	51	2	.227	.359
Erik González	82	180	19	41	8	2	3	16	8	55	3	.228	.344

We had projected that Erik González would go 41-for-180 with 3 homers, 8 walks and 3 stolen bases. In reality, he went 41-for-181 with 3 homers, 8 walks and 2 stolen bases. Eric González, if you are not up on these things, is a shortstop-third baseman for the Pittsburgh Pirates. Why we projected that he would hit .228 when his previous major league batting average was .260, I really don't know, but anyway, that wins the Blind Pig Award for 2020.

We also had not-too-bad projections for Brad Miller and Lewis Brinson:

Hitter	G	AB	R	H	D	T	HR	RBI	BB	SO	SB	Avg	Slg
Brad Miller	48	142	21	33	8	1	7	25	25	46	1	.232	.451
Brad Miller	87	214	28	49	10	2	11	30	25	69	2	.229	.449

Hitter	G	AB	R	H	D	T	HR	RBI	BB	SO	SB	Avg	Slg
Lewis Brinson	47	106	14	24	6	0	3	12	6	30	4	.226	.368
Lewis Brinson	63	136	14	28	6	1	4	15	10	47	2	.206	.353

And then we had a whole bunch of projections which were just absolutely terrible, but because it is 2020 the normal rules don't apply, so we don't have to tell you what those were.

We not only had a lot of bad projections last year, but we'll probably have a lot of bad projections for 2021, also—even assuming that a full slate of games is played. Minor leagues not playing in 2020, a certain number of players sitting out the 2020 season, projecting changes in player skills based on smaller sample sizes; it has to affect the accuracy of our projections for the 2021 season.

A couple of general points that seem related here. First, it is my opinion...which I have not validated by research...but it is my opinion that when there is a major interruption in the schedule, it is often related to a substantial changing of the guard in major league talent. In other words 1981 was a major schedule interruption. I think that if you compare 1980 and 1982, compare the lists of dominant players, you would find a somewhat larger-than-normal transition. I don't know if that is true or not.

The other thing I wanted to say was that, despite all of the troubles of the 2020 season, I really enjoyed the season. I don't mean that I enjoyed it more than a normal season; obviously when this is in the rear-view mirror, not many people are going to look back over the seasons and pick this one as a particularly good season. But I thought they made the best of it.

It was kind of a free play. In football, when the defense jumps off side, the offense has a free play, so the quarterback usually throws a deep pass, because you don't have to worry about the interception, and, if it happens to click, so much the better.

The powers that be treated 2020 like a free play. OK, this season is a mess; let's go deep and see what we can make happen. Let's throw everything against the wall and see what sticks.

And it worked, or at least it did for me. I didn't like ALL of the innovations, but I didn't hate any of them as much as I thought I would. It seemed to me that a lot my fellow sportswriters were just absurdly negative about the season. A lot of writers were convinced that there was no way baseball could get through this season, with the constant high risk of Covid-19 outbreaks. Well, that's OK; people are entitled to their own opinions, but writers continued to write that and say that even after it was really obvious that they **were** going to make the season work. I felt that a lot of writers were rooting for baseball's effort to stage a baseball season to fail. In the end, every game except two was played—two of the revised, 60-game effort. Good for the commissioner, and good for the players, for making it work despite the nattering nabobs of negativism. And I enjoyed the show.

2021 Hitter Projections

Hitter	Team	Age	G	AB	H	2B	3B	HR	R	RBI	RC	RC27	BB	SO	SB	CS	SB%	Avg	OBP	Slg	OPS
Abreu, Jose	CWS	34	157	619	168	36	2	32	86	110	96	5.5	41	147	1	1	.50	.271	.330	.491	.821
Acuna Jr., Ronald	Atl	23	144	556	155	30	3	37	109	90	112	7.1	76	172	26	7	.79	.279	.373	.543	.917
Adames, Willy	TB	25	147	530	129	26	3	16	72	58	65	4.2	55	173	6	4	.60	.243	.318	.394	.712
Adell, Jo	LAA	22	140	501	104	31	0	17	66	47	50	3.2	40	200	4	1	.80	.208	.273	.371	.644
Adrianza, Ehire	Min	31	92	198	49	11	1	3	25	19	22	3.9	19	46	2	1	.67	.247	.323	.359	.681
Aguilar, Jesus	Mia	31	135	415	105	20	0	18	53	68	58	4.9	45	108	0	0	.00	.253	.332	.431	.763
Ahmed, Nick	Ari	31	158	566	142	32	4	17	73	72	72	4.4	48	124	8	4	.67	.251	.313	.412	.724
Akiyama, Shogo	Cin	33	136	435	100	17	3	0	45	27	42	3.2	70	98	16	8	.67	.230	.344	.283	.627
Alberto, Hanser	Bal	28	137	534	146	25	2	9	61	53	59	3.9	15	66	5	3	.63	.273	.300	.378	.678
Albies, Ozzie	Atl	24	136	545	152	34	6	19	86	67	85	5.6	41	109	14	3	.82	.279	.334	.468	.802
Alfaro, Jorge	Mia	28	110	340	84	13	1	11	35	43	37	3.8	17	116	3	1	.75	.247	.301	.388	.689
Almora Jr., Albert	ChC	27	115	287	74	14	1	6	36	29	32	3.9	16	55	1	1	.50	.258	.299	.376	.676
Alonso, Pete	NYM	26	157	576	139	27	1	46	92	114	100	5.9	72	177	1	1	.67	.241	.344	.531	.875
Altuve, Jose	Hou	31	141	568	165	34	3	20	93	71	93	5.9	51	96	10	4	.71	.290	.355	.467	.822
Alvarez, Yordan	Hou	24	149	529	152	35	0	42	93	106	118	8.1	77	160	2	1	.67	.287	.382	.592	.974
Anderson, Brian	Mia	28	153	567	144	31	3	21	76	82	79	4.9	60	155	2	1	.67	.254	.341	.430	.771
Anderson, Tim	CWS	28	144	574	173	31	3	20	84	58	89	5.7	23	143	15	4	.79	.301	.333	.470	.803
Andrus, Elvis	Tex	32	128	455	126	25	3	11	60	52	62	4.8	32	73	16	6	.73	.277	.329	.418	.746
Andujar, Miguel	NYY	26	77	229	64	15	1	8	27	33	33	5.2	12	40	1	0	1.00	.279	.321	.459	.780
Aquino, Aristides	Cin	27	74	229	52	9	1	15	29	35	31	4.5	18	81	3	1	.75	.227	.292	.472	.764
Arcia, Orlando	Mil	26	146	448	108	21	2	13	48	48	51	3.9	35	98	7	3	.70	.241	.299	.384	.683
Arenado, Nolan	Col	30	147	547	169	36	3	38	90	109	121	8.3	56	91	2	2	.50	.309	.376	.594	.970
Arozarena, Randy	TB	26	109	360	93	21	2	16	59	46	55	5.3	37	104	12	3	.80	.258	.352	.461	.813
Arraez, Luis	Min	24	143	503	155	34	1	5	71	50	76	5.7	48	50	3	1	.75	.308	.370	.410	.779
Arroyo, Christian	Bos	26	101	313	79	19	1	10	38	42	39	4.3	22	74	1	1	.50	.252	.310	.415	.725
Avila, Alex	Min	34	65	156	32	7	0	5	17	16	18	3.9	32	68	0	0	.00	.205	.344	.346	.690
Bader, Harrison	StL	27	142	399	91	18	3	15	63	44	48	4.0	40	138	10	4	.71	.228	.317	.401	.718
Baez, Javier	ChC	28	151	571	146	33	4	28	85	88	79	4.8	29	174	11	4	.73	.256	.299	.475	.773
Barnes, Austin	LAD	31	95	255	57	13	1	6	35	27	29	3.7	33	68	5	1	.83	.224	.324	.353	.677
Barnhart, Tucker	Cin	30	121	370	90	19	1	10	36	43	45	4.2	44	90	1	1	.50	.243	.327	.381	.708
Bart, Joey	SF	24	152	462	94	18	5	8	63	44	35	2.5	23	176	0	0	.00	.203	.265	.316	.581
Bell, Josh	Pit	28	149	514	131	28	3	22	73	79	78	5.3	68	123	1	2	.33	.255	.345	.449	.795
Bellinger, Cody	LAD	25	158	582	163	32	3	43	102	106	125	7.7	86	133	15	3	.83	.280	.376	.567	.943
Belt, Brandon	SF	33	136	430	112	28	3	17	62	58	71	5.8	69	112	2	1	.67	.260	.367	.458	.825
Bemboom, Anthony	LAA	31	55	115	24	4	0	3	11	10	11	2.9	11	33	0	0	.00	.209	.283	.322	.605
Benintendi, Andrew	Bos	26	140	546	145	37	4	15	82	77	83	5.3	69	130	13	4	.76	.266	.353	.430	.784
Berti, Jon	Mia	31	111	400	96	15	4	6	60	37	45	3.8	47	111	20	6	.77	.240	.333	.343	.676
Betts, Mookie	LAD	28	153	602	176	42	4	33	117	91	123	7.4	76	101	21	4	.84	.292	.375	.540	.915
Bichette, Bo	Tor	23	147	603	163	42	6	22	86	83	91	5.3	44	149	22	7	.76	.270	.322	.469	.791
Biggio, Cavan	Tor	26	159	576	137	30	4	26	96	93	95	5.6	116	190	17	2	.89	.238	.371	.439	.810
Blackmon, Charlie	Col	34	156	618	189	36	7	28	110	83	116	7.0	52	125	5	3	.63	.306	.368	.523	.891
Bogaerts, Xander	Bos	28	151	593	169	41	2	23	96	96	102	6.2	63	119	12	2	.86	.285	.358	.477	.835
Bohm, Alec	Phi	24	152	544	143	26	1	19	79	81	76	4.9	60	124	3	2	.60	.263	.342	.419	.761
Bote, David	ChC	28	120	314	75	14	1	13	40	46	41	4.5	37	99	4	2	.67	.239	.331	.414	.745
Bradley Jr., Jackie	Bos	31	151	522	127	31	3	17	77	67	69	4.5	58	147	10	4	.71	.243	.331	.412	.742
Brantley, Michael	Hou	34	146	567	166	37	2	17	80	80	92	5.9	52	77	6	1	.86	.293	.356	.455	.811
Braun, Ryan	Mil	37	131	425	115	25	2	21	62	66	68	5.7	35	95	7	2	.78	.271	.333	.487	.820
Bregman, Alex	Hou	27	146	545	154	40	3	28	98	94	109	7.2	89	89	5	2	.71	.283	.392	.521	.913
Brinson, Lewis	Mia	27	115	312	66	13	3	9	33	34	30	3.1	21	103	6	1	.86	.212	.272	.359	.631
Brosseau, Mike	TB	27	94	254	65	15	1	13	36	41	38	5.2	22	73	3	1	.75	.256	.330	.476	.806
Bruce, Jay	Phi	34	82	209	50	11	1	12	26	34	30	4.8	19	54	1	1	.50	.239	.306	.474	.779
Bryant, Kris	ChC	29	141	529	139	32	3	26	94	76	89	5.9	72	149	3	2	.60	.263	.368	.482	.850
Buxton, Byron	Min	27	106	333	82	18	4	16	50	46	46	4.8	21	100	11	2	.85	.246	.297	.468	.765
Cabrera, Asdrubal	Was	35	130	429	114	26	2	17	58	63	64	5.3	41	94	1	0	1.00	.266	.334	.455	.789
Cabrera, Miguel	Det	38	120	377	105	17	0	14	43	53	58	5.6	45	88	1	0	1.00	.279	.358	.435	.794
Cain, Lorenzo	Mil	35	144	555	154	28	3	12	82	52	78	5.0	54	106	16	5	.76	.277	.348	.404	.752
Calhoun, Kole	Ari	33	145	502	124	24	2	26	77	72	75	5.2	60	134	3	1	.75	.247	.336	.458	.794
Calhoun, Willie	Tex	26	104	378	95	20	1	16	47	51	51	4.7	31	65	1	0	1.00	.251	.313	.437	.750
Camargo, Johan	Atl	27	106	309	80	19	1	9	39	40	39	4.4	22	74	1	1	.50	.259	.312	.414	.727
Cameron, Daz	Det	24	108	329	66	14	5	7	42	33	31	3.0	33	121	8	2	.80	.201	.287	.337	.625
Candelario, Jeimer	Det	27	123	409	101	24	3	15	54	54	57	4.8	47	114	2	1	.67	.247	.333	.430	.764
Canha, Mark	Oak	32	141	442	108	25	2	18	71	63	64	4.9	58	120	4	1	.80	.244	.353	.432	.785
Cano, Robinson	NYM	38	134	501	136	27	1	19	65	68	71	5.1	36	83	0	0	.00	.271	.327	.443	.770
Caratini, Victor	ChC	27	114	320	84	17	1	8	36	41	42	4.6	32	78	1	1	.50	.263	.341	.397	.738
Carlson, Dylan	StL	22	152	554	137	34	7	23	87	78	81	5.0	58	163	9	3	.75	.247	.324	.458	.783
Carpenter, Matt	StL	35	119	343	81	21	1	15	57	44	52	5.1	58	104	2	1	.67	.236	.356	.434	.791
Casali, Curt	Cin	32	85	208	48	9	0	9	23	29	26	4.2	25	63	2	1	.67	.231	.322	.404	.726
Castellanos, Nick	Cin	29	156	591	155	43	4	28	84	83	91	5.4	46	161	2	2	.50	.262	.322	.491	.813
Castro, Welington	Was	34	68	218	51	10	0	9	22	32	25	3.9	15	66	0	0	.00	.234	.289	.404	.693
Castro, Harold	Det	27	85	237	61	9	1	2	23	20	22	3.3	9	56	2	1	.67	.257	.287	.329	.617
Castro, Jason	SD	34	82	230	47	13	0	8	29	24	25	3.6	31	87	0	0	.00	.204	.304	.365	.669
Castro, Starlin	Was	31	135	518	143	28	2	16	63	65	70	4.8	29	102	2	1	.67	.276	.317	.431	.747
Castro, Willi	Det	24	125	442	116	22	5	13	60	57	58	4.6	29	131	6	2	.75	.262	.319	.423	.742
Cave, Jake	Min	28	110	312	77	16	3	10	43	38	38	4.2	23	106	2	1	.67	.247	.309	.413	.722
Chapman, Matt	Oak	28	140	537	128	33	3	31	80	81	82	5.2	59	167	1	1	.50	.238	.322	.484	.806
Chavis, Michael	Bos	25	127	444	101	19	2	20	59	65	53	4.0	35	157	5	1	.83	.227	.293	.414	.707
Chirinos, Robinson	NYM	37	84	223	45	10	0	9	28	28	23	3.4	26	78	0	0	.00	.202	.305	.368	.672
Chisholm, Jazz	Mia	23	151	513	109	16	5	31	74	75	67	4.3	58	208	14	4	.78	.212	.302	.444	.747
Choi, Ji-Man	TB	30	113	328	78	20	1	12	39	49	46	4.7	49	95	1	1	.50	.238	.342	.415	.757

526

2021 Hitter Projections

Hitter	Team	Age	G	AB	H	2B	3B	HR	R	RBI	RC	RC27	BB	SO	SB	CS	SB%	Avg	OBP	Slg	OPS
Choo, Shin-Soo	Tex	38	123	421	106	20	1	16	64	49	61	5.0	58	122	9	3	.75	.252	.356	.418	.774
Conforto, Michael	NYM	28	154	573	147	31	2	29	91	90	93	5.6	81	161	6	4	.60	.257	.360	.469	.830
Contreras, Willson	ChC	29	139	493	126	27	2	20	69	72	71	5.0	54	135	2	2	.50	.256	.348	.440	.788
Cooper, Garrett	Mia	30	101	322	86	18	1	11	39	45	45	5.0	27	87	0	0	.00	.267	.331	.432	.763
Cordero, Franchy	KC	26	112	389	99	16	7	15	51	47	54	4.8	31	132	10	3	.77	.254	.313	.447	.760
Correa, Carlos	Hou	26	138	510	137	30	2	22	73	86	82	5.7	61	128	1	0	1.00	.269	.351	.465	.816
Crawford, Brandon	SF	34	151	523	128	30	3	15	63	70	64	4.2	49	129	3	3	.50	.245	.317	.400	.716
Crawford, J.P.	Sea	26	143	526	122	24	4	9	68	54	58	3.7	66	119	10	5	.67	.232	.324	.344	.669
Cron, C.J.	Det	31	121	434	113	23	1	23	53	72	64	5.2	32	111	1	1	.50	.260	.326	.477	.803
Cronenworth, Jake	SD	27	151	545	148	30	5	11	83	61	76	5.0	55	108	11	2	.85	.272	.346	.406	.751
Cruz, Nelson	Min	40	146	542	145	24	1	36	84	99	96	6.3	63	156	0	0	.00	.268	.354	.515	.869
Culberson, Charlie	Atl	32	105	284	65	13	2	6	32	31	27	3.1	16	84	2	2	.50	.229	.275	.352	.627
Dahl, David	Col	27	79	229	61	13	3	8	33	31	32	5.0	15	67	3	1	.75	.266	.317	.454	.771
Dalbec, Bobby	Bos	26	153	535	121	21	1	37	74	92	81	5.1	69	176	2	0	1.00	.226	.330	.477	.807
d'Arnaud, Travis	Atl	32	111	396	103	20	1	16	50	65	56	4.9	35	102	1	0	1.00	.260	.326	.437	.763
Davis, Chris	Bal	35	47	98	19	4	0	5	12	13	11	3.5	12	40	0	0	.00	.194	.288	.388	.676
Davis, J.D.	NYM	28	142	479	124	26	1	20	63	67	70	5.1	52	136	2	1	.67	.259	.340	.443	.783
Davis, Khris	Oak	33	79	210	49	9	0	12	30	35	29	4.6	22	66	0	0	.00	.233	.315	.448	.763
DeJong, Paul	StL	27	146	541	132	29	1	25	77	80	73	4.6	49	159	4	2	.67	.244	.318	.440	.758
Demeritte, Travis	Det	26	105	320	69	17	2	13	47	41	38	3.9	35	126	3	1	.75	.216	.299	.403	.702
DeShields, Delino	Cle	28	109	321	75	14	2	3	46	24	33	3.4	37	91	16	5	.76	.234	.317	.318	.634
Desmond, Ian	Col	35	151	513	134	26	5	19	74	71	72	4.9	40	142	9	3	.75	.261	.320	.442	.762
Devers, Rafael	Bos	24	152	600	163	40	3	29	97	103	95	5.6	47	144	4	3	.57	.272	.329	.493	.822
Diaz, Aledmys	Hou	30	90	273	68	17	1	9	36	34	34	4.2	20	48	2	2	.50	.249	.307	.418	.725
Diaz, Elias	Col	30	94	269	72	14	1	5	29	34	32	4.3	18	53	0	0	.00	.268	.316	.383	.699
Diaz, Lewin	Mia	24	148	532	134	36	1	22	77	83	74	4.8	45	144	0	0	.00	.252	.315	.447	.762
Diaz, Yandy	TB	29	110	398	108	19	2	7	52	40	55	4.9	57	83	1	1	.50	.271	.365	.382	.747
Dickerson, Alex	SF	31	110	314	82	20	3	14	47	47	49	5.4	29	69	0	0	.00	.261	.335	.478	.813
Dickerson, Corey	Mia	32	122	414	109	26	3	15	51	53	57	4.8	26	86	2	1	.67	.263	.310	.449	.759
Dietrich, Derek	Tex	31	96	245	57	12	2	10	35	30	31	4.2	23	72	1	1	.50	.233	.338	.420	.758
Donaldson, Josh	Min	35	124	444	112	25	1	26	78	73	79	6.1	77	123	2	1	.67	.252	.370	.489	.859
Downs, Jeter	Bos	22	78	272	81	14	0	10	47	41	45	6.1	27	59	4	2	.67	.298	.370	.460	.829
Dozier, Hunter	KC	29	130	481	116	26	4	17	62	56	63	4.5	52	151	5	2	.71	.241	.318	.418	.736
Drury, Brandon	Tor	28	56	111	27	7	0	3	11	12	13	3.9	8	29	0	0	.00	.243	.300	.387	.687
Dubon, Mauricio	SF	26	145	476	125	22	2	12	61	48	58	4.2	33	98	9	5	.64	.263	.314	.393	.707
Duvall, Adam	Atl	32	123	375	90	19	2	24	54	66	55	5.0	31	111	1	1	.50	.240	.308	.493	.802
Dyson, Jarrod	CWS	36	69	135	31	4	1	2	20	10	14	3.3	13	27	9	2	.82	.230	.302	.319	.621
Eaton, Adam	Was	32	138	524	144	28	5	13	86	52	77	5.2	56	105	11	3	.79	.275	.357	.422	.779
Edman, Tommy	StL	26	138	498	138	24	6	11	73	52	68	4.8	36	108	11	4	.73	.277	.335	.416	.750
Encarnacion, Edwin	CWS	38	102	312	75	12	0	21	49	55	50	5.5	43	86	1	0	1.00	.240	.342	.481	.822
Engel, Adam	CWS	29	103	266	59	12	3	6	32	24	26	3.2	17	81	5	2	.71	.222	.284	.357	.641
Ervin, Phillip	Sea	28	87	185	43	9	2	5	23	21	22	4.0	20	52	4	1	.80	.232	.321	.384	.704
Escobar, Eduardo	Ari	32	151	574	148	31	6	23	73	84	81	4.9	46	124	3	2	.60	.258	.317	.453	.770
Espinal, Santiago	Tor	26	72	216	56	12	1	3	25	29	26	4.1	19	48	4	1	.80	.259	.322	.366	.688
Evans, Phillip	Pit	28	44	92	23	4	0	3	10	10	11	4.2	8	20	0	0	.00	.250	.317	.391	.708
Farmer, Kyle	Cin	30	108	271	68	16	1	5	26	30	30	3.8	17	66	2	1	.67	.251	.305	.373	.677
Fisher, Derek	Tor	27	132	478	105	20	3	21	69	65	61	4.2	65	182	10	4	.71	.220	.318	.406	.724
Fletcher, David	LAA	27	143	564	160	33	3	6	76	50	74	4.7	45	70	7	2	.78	.284	.340	.385	.725
Flores, Wilmer	SF	29	133	429	119	27	1	20	54	66	67	5.7	29	66	1	0	1.00	.277	.329	.485	.814
Flowers, Tyler	Atl	35	96	310	67	14	1	8	35	36	31	3.3	33	116	0	0	.00	.216	.314	.345	.659
Ford, Mike	NYY	28	55	101	25	6	0	6	14	16	16	5.6	13	23	0	0	.00	.248	.339	.485	.824
Forsythe, Logan	Mia	34	113	350	83	18	1	8	42	35	41	4.0	44	98	2	1	.67	.237	.329	.363	.692
Fowler, Dexter	StL	35	103	290	70	13	2	10	44	34	39	4.6	41	83	4	2	.67	.241	.343	.403	.747
France, Ty	Sea	26	147	527	140	30	2	22	74	83	75	5.0	38	130	1	2	.33	.266	.340	.455	.795
Franco, Maikel	KC	28	143	478	128	26	1	21	56	77	71	5.2	38	79	1	0	1.00	.268	.324	.458	.782
Frazier, Adam	Pit	29	144	477	130	27	4	10	63	49	64	4.7	40	76	3	3	.50	.273	.337	.409	.745
Frazier, Clint	NYY	26	105	356	83	21	2	15	52	46	47	4.5	38	114	4	1	.80	.233	.316	.430	.746
Frazier, Todd	NYM	35	122	393	89	18	1	17	52	52	48	4.1	40	103	2	1	.67	.226	.311	.407	.718
Freeman, Freddie	Atl	31	161	609	185	44	3	32	109	110	132	8.0	94	132	6	2	.75	.304	.404	.544	.947
Fuentes, Josh	Col	28	126	417	93	21	2	10	48	49	37	3.0	16	132	2	1	.67	.223	.257	.355	.612
Gallagher, Cam	KC	28	58	151	36	8	0	2	14	14	15	3.4	13	30	0	0	.00	.238	.307	.331	.638
Gallo, Joey	Tex	27	146	496	103	23	2	36	79	85	76	5.0	82	217	5	2	.71	.208	.327	.480	.807
Galvis, Freddy	Cin	31	148	541	131	26	4	16	63	61	63	3.9	36	131	5	2	.71	.242	.294	.390	.684
Gamel, Ben	Mil	29	117	299	75	16	3	6	42	31	37	4.2	30	86	2	1	.67	.251	.323	.385	.708
Garcia, Avisail	Mil	30	129	442	114	21	2	14	57	58	56	4.4	33	120	4	3	.57	.258	.321	.410	.730
Garcia, Greg	SD	31	75	108	25	5	1	1	14	10	11	3.5	16	24	1	1	.50	.231	.341	.324	.665
Garcia, Leury	CWS	30	114	381	100	16	3	7	50	36	42	3.9	18	91	8	3	.73	.262	.303	.375	.678
Garcia, Luis	Was	21	145	507	130	23	2	6	66	44	51	3.5	22	108	6	1	.86	.256	.289	.345	.634
Gardner, Brett	NYY	37	131	411	98	17	3	12	67	42	51	4.2	52	95	9	3	.75	.238	.330	.382	.712
Garneau, Dustin	Hou	33	52	109	23	5	0	4	12	12	11	3.4	10	35	0	0	.00	.211	.289	.367	.656
Garver, Mitch	Min	30	91	291	69	16	1	14	43	42	40	4.7	32	96	1	0	1.00	.237	.319	.443	.762
Gimenez, Andres	NYM	22	132	402	99	20	3	9	57	42	45	3.8	25	108	17	4	.81	.246	.313	.378	.691
Goldschmidt, Paul	StL	33	161	593	170	32	2	31	96	94	116	7.1	96	158	5	1	.83	.287	.390	.504	.895
Gomes, Yan	Was	33	113	412	97	22	1	15	48	54	48	4.0	31	110	2	0	1.00	.235	.300	.403	.703
Gonzalez, Erik	Pit	29	102	273	62	14	2	5	28	26	24	2.9	12	80	4	3	.57	.227	.262	.348	.610
Gonzalez, Marwin	Min	32	118	358	93	19	1	13	43	50	49	4.8	32	86	1	1	.50	.260	.327	.427	.755
Goodrum, Niko	Det	29	123	412	92	22	4	13	51	47	48	3.9	40	145	12	3	.80	.223	.295	.391	.686
Goodwin, Brian	Cin	30	130	373	86	21	2	14	49	46	46	4.2	36	127	8	2	.80	.231	.303	.410	.714
Gosselin, Phil	Phi	32	68	117	28	6	1	2	15	13	13	3.7	11	31	0	0	.00	.239	.310	.359	.669
Grandal, Yasmani	CWS	32	140	490	115	24	1	28	69	75	79	5.4	86	149	2	1	.67	.235	.352	.459	.812
Gregorius, Didi	Phi	31	142	536	142	26	3	22	76	84	74	4.8	34	80	5	3	.63	.265	.317	.448	.765

2021 Hitter Projections

PLAYER			BATTING												BASERUNNING			AVERAGES			
Hitter	Team	Age	G	AB	H	2B	3B	HR	R	RBI	RC	RC27	BB	SO	SB	CS	SB%	Avg	OBP	Slg	OPS
Grichuk, Randal	Tor	29	150	560	138	32	3	31	79	82	78	4.8	36	155	3	2	.60	.246	.298	.480	.778
Grisham, Trent	SD	24	159	561	138	25	5	25	85	78	88	5.3	88	115	16	4	.80	.246	.354	.442	.796
Grossman, Robbie	Oak	31	144	495	121	29	2	12	64	54	65	4.5	72	115	12	5	.71	.244	.346	.384	.730
Guerrero Jr., Vladimir	Tor	22	157	582	165	34	2	26	80	98	98	6.1	58	100	2	1	.67	.284	.353	.483	.836
Guillorme, Luis	NYM	26	81	217	56	10	0	2	26	20	25	4.0	29	46	3	1	.75	.258	.348	.332	.680
Gurriel Jr., Lourdes	Tor	27	131	479	128	28	1	23	64	79	69	5.1	27	120	5	3	.63	.267	.313	.474	.787
Gurriel, Yuli	Hou	37	144	540	147	35	2	18	72	79	74	4.9	29	71	2	1	.67	.272	.315	.444	.760
Guzman, Ronald	Tex	26	104	335	79	17	2	12	42	42	41	4.2	32	102	2	1	.67	.236	.310	.406	.716
Gyorko, Jedd	Mil	32	100	242	57	10	0	12	31	32	32	4.5	27	66	1	0	1.00	.236	.317	.426	.743
Hampson, Garrett	Col	26	115	326	80	14	4	9	42	25	41	4.3	28	97	13	2	.87	.245	.307	.396	.703
Haniger, Mitch	Sea	30	137	500	125	27	2	21	73	67	72	4.9	56	141	6	2	.75	.250	.336	.438	.774
Happ, Ian	ChC	26	132	438	114	26	2	24	64	64	75	6.0	61	153	5	3	.63	.260	.356	.493	.849
Harper, Bryce	Phi	28	159	570	152	34	2	38	107	107	121	7.4	121	158	15	5	.75	.267	.399	.533	.933
Harrison, Josh	Was	33	83	227	57	12	1	5	27	23	25	3.8	13	43	3	1	.75	.251	.309	.379	.688
Haseley, Adam	Phi	25	128	422	108	22	1	10	55	52	52	4.3	40	106	3	1	.75	.256	.333	.384	.717
Hayes, Ke'Bryan	Pit	24	146	519	137	34	5	15	72	59	76	5.2	55	132	9	2	.82	.264	.340	.435	.776
Hays, Austin	Bal	25	145	412	104	21	2	17	58	54	52	4.4	23	107	6	3	.67	.252	.300	.437	.737
Hechavarria, Adeiny	Atl	32	93	239	63	11	1	4	30	25	27	4.0	14	47	2	0	1.00	.264	.307	.368	.675
Hedges, Austin	Cle	28	78	172	36	7	0	7	18	22	17	3.2	12	54	1	0	1.00	.209	.269	.372	.641
Hernandez, Cesar	Cle	31	160	621	169	31	4	12	88	59	84	4.8	69	135	7	3	.70	.272	.350	.393	.743
Hernandez, Kike	LAD	29	136	405	100	22	2	17	58	55	55	4.7	39	94	2	1	.67	.247	.319	.437	.756
Hernandez, Teoscar	Tor	28	139	488	115	23	3	27	71	68	67	4.6	44	165	10	4	.71	.236	.303	.461	.764
Heyward, Jason	ChC	31	146	499	126	24	4	14	71	60	67	4.3	63	102	5	2	.71	.253	.341	.401	.742
Hicks, Aaron	NYY	31	134	478	115	24	3	20	79	64	72	5.1	80	118	8	3	.73	.241	.352	.429	.781
Higashioka, Kyle	NYY	31	70	211	48	10	0	11	24	33	25	4.0	15	60	0	0	.00	.227	.285	.431	.716
Hill, Derek	Det	25	73	212	42	8	1	5	33	19	17	2.6	16	87	4	2	.67	.198	.264	.316	.580
Hilliard, Sam	Col	27	113	373	76	15	4	17	49	44	41	3.5	34	156	10	3	.77	.204	.274	.402	.676
Hiura, Keston	Mil	24	150	540	136	28	2	33	75	79	81	5.2	42	187	9	4	.69	.252	.328	.494	.822
Hoerner, Nico	ChC	24	134	456	119	25	3	6	69	54	54	4.1	39	81	9	3	.75	.261	.329	.368	.697
Holt, Brock	Was	33	91	225	57	12	1	3	30	23	26	4.0	25	54	2	1	.67	.253	.336	.356	.692
Hoskins, Rhys	Phi	28	125	498	117	29	2	31	81	88	85	5.8	86	144	3	1	.75	.235	.359	.488	.847
Hosmer, Eric	SD	31	129	459	120	23	1	17	60	71	63	4.8	41	107	5	2	.71	.261	.325	.427	.752
Huff, Sam	Tex	23	92	313	74	16	0	13	51	44	37	4.0	22	108	0	0	.00	.236	.287	.412	.699
Iglesias, Jose	Bal	31	138	503	142	30	2	8	57	55	62	4.5	23	65	5	3	.63	.282	.323	.398	.720
Inciarte, Ender	Atl	30	121	398	106	18	3	5	57	34	47	4.1	35	68	13	6	.68	.266	.330	.364	.695
Jansen, Danny	Tor	26	110	341	80	18	1	15	44	48	47	4.6	43	77	1	0	1.00	.235	.334	.425	.759
Jay, Jon	Ari	36	51	120	32	5	1	1	15	9	13	3.9	8	24	1	0	1.00	.267	.328	.350	.678
Jeffers, Ryan	Min	24	90	271	69	10	0	18	35	35	42	5.4	23	78	0	0	.00	.255	.329	.491	.820
Jimenez, Eloy	CWS	24	148	555	157	30	2	34	76	97	96	6.3	36	144	0	0	.00	.283	.330	.528	.858
Jones, JaCoby	Det	29	113	370	84	19	3	11	48	38	40	3.6	28	128	6	2	.75	.227	.296	.384	.679
Jones, Nolan	Cle	23	143	508	110	24	3	29	98	72	75	4.9	85	169	4	0	1.00	.217	.334	.447	.781
Joyce, Matt	Mia	36	115	263	60	13	0	8	37	30	32	4.1	42	73	1	1	.50	.228	.337	.369	.705
Judge, Aaron	NYY	29	119	449	115	21	1	31	82	76	83	6.4	72	163	3	2	.60	.256	.365	.514	.879
Kelly, Carson	Ari	26	114	356	85	18	0	14	42	47	46	4.4	40	83	0	0	.00	.239	.323	.407	.730
Kemp, Matt	Col	36	80	193	55	10	0	10	27	34	32	6.0	14	53	1	0	1.00	.285	.333	.492	.826
Kemp, Tony	Oak	29	123	295	78	13	3	4	40	27	37	4.3	31	48	7	3	.70	.264	.342	.369	.712
Kendrick, Howie	Was	37	93	268	80	16	1	8	39	34	43	5.9	21	49	2	1	.67	.299	.356	.455	.811
Kepler, Max	Min	28	138	479	120	28	3	23	73	69	74	5.3	57	97	4	2	.67	.251	.336	.466	.802
Kieboom, Carter	Was	23	140	511	123	23	2	12	73	63	62	4.1	69	161	2	1	.67	.241	.345	.364	.709
Kiermaier, Kevin	TB	31	116	347	81	16	5	9	46	37	40	3.9	30	90	13	4	.76	.233	.302	.386	.688
Kiner-Falefa, Isiah	Tex	26	134	489	125	22	3	5	55	39	52	3.6	38	88	13	7	.65	.256	.320	.344	.663
Kingery, Scott	Phi	27	115	373	88	21	2	12	49	36	43	3.9	26	114	7	2	.78	.236	.293	.399	.692
Kipnis, Jason	ChC	34	100	291	70	17	2	9	35	35	37	4.3	30	71	3	1	.75	.241	.318	.405	.723
Kirilloff, Alex	Min	23	146	525	140	25	2	23	71	73	74	5.0	36	126	5	3	.63	.267	.321	.453	.774
Kirk, Alejandro	Tor	22	94	307	80	20	0	8	52	41	36	4.2	14	51	0	0	.00	.261	.293	.404	.697
Knapp, Andrew	Phi	29	98	239	55	12	1	5	27	26	27	3.8	32	79	0	0	.00	.230	.326	.351	.677
La Stella, Tommy	Oak	32	136	478	132	25	2	13	66	58	69	5.2	51	50	2	1	.67	.276	.352	.418	.770
Lamb, Jake	Oak	30	67	145	34	8	1	6	19	21	20	4.7	20	43	1	1	.50	.234	.335	.428	.763
Laureano, Ramon	Oak	26	145	484	123	28	3	20	76	64	71	5.1	48	148	9	2	.82	.254	.340	.448	.788
LeMahieu, DJ	NYY	32	147	594	181	31	3	16	96	72	96	6.0	53	90	6	3	.67	.305	.366	.448	.813
Leon, Sandy	Cle	32	51	95	19	4	0	2	9	9	8	2.7	9	28	0	0	.00	.200	.276	.305	.581
Lewis, Kyle	Sea	25	156	559	140	29	1	26	85	89	85	5.3	73	205	8	1	.89	.250	.338	.445	.784
Lindor, Francisco	Cle	27	158	640	182	41	3	30	102	85	112	6.3	61	108	18	5	.78	.284	.352	.498	.851
Locastro, Tim	Ari	28	103	261	67	15	2	5	44	20	31	4.1	19	55	9	3	.75	.257	.349	.387	.736
Long Jr., Shed	Sea	25	107	369	83	16	3	11	46	41	41	3.7	36	119	8	3	.73	.225	.297	.374	.671
Longoria, Evan	SF	35	136	470	122	27	2	18	57	64	64	4.8	34	105	2	1	.67	.260	.316	.440	.757
Lopes, Tim	Sea	27	66	138	34	8	1	2	15	14	16	3.9	11	33	5	1	.83	.246	.307	.362	.669
Lopez, Nicky	KC	26	135	459	115	19	3	4	54	36	47	3.5	42	76	4	4	.50	.251	.319	.331	.650
Lowe, Brandon	TB	26	151	547	139	31	3	34	84	101	92	5.9	61	179	7	1	.88	.254	.339	.508	.847
Lowe, Nate	TB	25	146	504	128	28	0	26	78	82	82	5.6	73	155	3	1	.75	.254	.354	.464	.818
Luplow, Jordan	Cle	27	83	216	53	13	1	10	33	29	32	5.1	27	57	2	1	.67	.245	.337	.454	.791
Lux, Gavin	LAD	23	155	581	162	31	6	29	99	80	103	6.4	67	170	8	3	.73	.279	.354	.503	.857
Machado, Manny	SD	28	161	617	170	33	2	37	90	99	110	6.4	67	117	10	4	.71	.276	.349	.515	.865
Madrigal, Nick	CWS	24	147	521	155	26	3	3	76	53	69	4.8	37	32	14	4	.78	.298	.352	.376	.728
Maldonado, Martin	Hou	34	122	377	77	16	0	12	44	40	35	3.1	37	116	1	1	.50	.204	.291	.342	.633
Mancini, Trey	Bal	29	145	551	149	29	3	25	77	73	85	5.5	47	142	1	1	.50	.270	.334	.470	.804
Margot, Manuel	TB	26	132	387	94	20	4	8	48	35	44	3.8	31	76	20	7	.74	.243	.302	.377	.680
Marisnick, Jake	NYM	30	100	245	53	12	1	9	38	28	25	3.3	16	84	5	2	.71	.216	.275	.384	.659
Markakis, Nick	Atl	37	122	422	117	28	1	6	53	53	57	4.9	46	68	1	1	.50	.277	.352	.391	.743
Marmolejos, Jose	Sea	28	69	199	50	10	1	7	23	27	25	4.4	15	55	0	0	.00	.251	.307	.417	.724
Marte, Ketel	Ari	27	145	555	162	34	8	16	77	65	90	5.9	46	84	6	2	.75	.292	.351	.468	.820

528

PLAYER			BATTING													BASERUNNING			AVERAGES			
Hitter	Team	Age	G	AB	H	2B	3B	HR	R	RBI	RC	RC27	BB	SO		SB	CS	SB%	Avg	OBP	Slg	OPS
Marte, Starling	Mia	32	155	605	169	34	5	18	91	75	85	5.0	33	118		23	7	.77	.279	.334	.441	.776
Martinez, J.D.	Bos	33	147	574	164	39	2	35	93	105	112	7.1	66	156		3	1	.75	.286	.363	.544	.907
Martinez, Jose	ChC	32	95	241	65	13	1	7	29	32	34	5.1	25	57		1	0	1.00	.270	.341	.419	.760
Mateo, Jorge	SD	26	101	333	69	14	6	5	38	32	28	2.7	18	115		11	3	.79	.207	.254	.330	.585
Mathis, Jeff	Tex	38	56	102	19	4	0	2	8	8	7	2.3	8	38		1	0	1.00	.186	.245	.284	.530
Mathisen, Wyatt	Ari	27	88	273	60	12	1	13	39	36	34	4.1	33	96		1	1	.50	.220	.330	.414	.744
Maybin, Cameron	ChC	34	100	269	67	14	1	6	37	28	33	4.2	30	71		9	3	.75	.249	.329	.375	.704
Mazara, Nomar	CWS	26	128	468	113	23	1	16	57	64	55	4.0	38	123		2	2	.50	.241	.307	.397	.704
McBroom, Ryan	KC	29	102	287	69	13	0	12	35	33	36	4.2	25	97		0	0	.00	.240	.310	.411	.721
McCann, James	CWS	31	113	390	93	17	1	14	44	48	44	3.8	27	117		2	2	.50	.238	.298	.395	.693
McCutchen, Andrew	Phi	34	131	470	118	24	2	20	72	65	70	5.1	66	115		7	4	.64	.251	.349	.438	.788
McMahon, Ryan	Col	26	137	420	100	21	2	21	54	64	58	4.7	43	144		2	1	.67	.238	.313	.448	.761
McNeil, Jeff	NYM	29	140	524	157	33	3	18	78	70	88	6.2	44	77		4	3	.57	.300	.369	.477	.847
Meadows, Austin	TB	26	129	426	105	26	4	19	63	58	61	4.9	41	113		8	3	.73	.246	.318	.460	.779
Mejia, Francisco	SD	25	59	125	31	7	1	4	14	15	15	4.2	8	30		0	0	.00	.248	.304	.416	.720
Mendick, Danny	CWS	27	71	182	42	8	0	5	21	19	20	3.6	18	45		3	1	.75	.231	.307	.357	.664
Mercado, Oscar	Cle	26	115	402	100	20	2	10	58	40	48	4.0	31	100		17	5	.77	.249	.311	.383	.694
Merrifield, Whit	KC	32	152	621	177	38	5	15	86	65	90	5.2	41	109		23	7	.77	.285	.335	.435	.770
Miller, Brad	StL	31	114	309	74	15	2	14	40	44	44	4.9	40	96		2	1	.67	.239	.332	.437	.769
Molina, Yadier	StL	38	112	403	109	20	1	11	41	53	51	4.5	23	63		3	1	.75	.270	.318	.407	.725
Moncada, Yoan	CWS	26	136	488	120	24	5	19	72	63	68	4.8	57	168		6	3	.67	.246	.328	.432	.761
Mondesi, Adalberto	KC	25	152	585	145	27	10	18	80	74	73	4.2	31	189		54	12	.82	.248	.288	.421	.709
Moniak, Mickey	Phi	23	146	540	119	34	8	11	68	67	56	3.4	43	180		7	3	.70	.220	.280	.374	.654
Moore, Dylan	Sea	28	123	418	88	20	2	14	52	45	42	3.2	39	125		18	9	.67	.211	.298	.368	.666
Moran, Colin	Pit	28	147	479	130	26	1	18	54	73	70	5.2	43	126		0	0	.00	.271	.337	.443	.779
Moreland, Mitch	SD	35	123	397	93	21	1	19	52	63	54	4.6	43	101		1	0	1.00	.234	.314	.436	.750
Mountcastle, Ryan	Bal	24	150	542	145	28	2	23	69	80	75	4.9	30	154		1	1	.50	.268	.311	.454	.765
Moustakas, Mike	Cin	32	144	529	132	30	1	30	69	82	80	5.2	50	108		3	1	.75	.250	.324	.480	.804
Mullins II, Cedric	Bal	26	129	427	101	19	5	11	62	38	50	3.9	35	101		17	3	.85	.237	.299	.382	.681
Muncy, Max	LAD	30	147	508	120	22	1	31	87	78	83	5.5	87	157		3	1	.75	.236	.355	.467	.822
Munoz, Yairo	Bos	26	85	217	56	11	1	5	26	24	25	4.0	12	52		7	3	.70	.258	.300	.387	.687
Murphy, Daniel	Col	36	116	342	102	24	2	12	48	57	58	6.2	25	53		1	0	1.00	.298	.350	.485	.835
Murphy, Sean	Oak	26	124	390	86	22	1	18	61	52	51	4.4	51	115		1	0	1.00	.221	.318	.421	.739
Murphy, Tom	Sea	30	79	246	48	12	1	10	24	29	22	2.9	16	97		1	1	.50	.195	.250	.374	.624
Myers, Wil	SD	30	143	470	118	29	2	25	68	69	74	5.4	52	151		10	3	.77	.251	.330	.481	.810
Naquin, Tyler	Cle	30	86	218	56	12	1	7	26	27	27	4.3	14	62		1	1	.50	.257	.308	.417	.725
Narvaez, Omar	Mil	29	107	296	74	12	0	9	35	30	38	4.4	37	74		0	0	.00	.250	.339	.382	.721
Naylor, Josh	Cle	24	127	419	114	23	1	13	55	54	60	5.1	42	79		3	2	.60	.272	.343	.425	.767
Newman, Kevin	Pit	27	113	365	98	18	2	5	45	34	43	4.1	25	54		6	3	.67	.268	.322	.370	.692
Nimmo, Brandon	NYM	28	137	468	115	24	5	15	72	50	68	5.0	78	134		5	3	.63	.246	.369	.415	.783
Nola, Austin	SD	31	103	320	80	18	1	8	38	41	40	4.3	32	74		1	0	1.00	.250	.328	.388	.715
Nottingham, Jacob	Mil	26	54	167	32	7	0	7	18	22	15	3.0	14	67		1	0	1.00	.192	.274	.359	.633
Nunez, Renato	Bal	27	145	529	123	25	1	29	66	77	69	4.4	43	156		1	0	1.00	.233	.299	.448	.747
Odor, Rougned	Tex	27	127	442	101	23	2	23	62	68	55	4.1	33	132		6	4	.60	.229	.291	.446	.737
O'Hearn, Ryan	KC	27	66	130	28	7	1	5	13	18	15	3.9	15	42		0	0	.00	.215	.301	.400	.701
Ohtani, Shohei	LAA	26	128	454	118	26	3	25	69	80	77	5.9	53	139		16	4	.80	.260	.340	.496	.835
Olivares, Edward	KC	25	133	466	114	21	2	14	58	59	55	4.0	35	123		12	2	.86	.245	.304	.388	.693
Olson, Matt	Oak	27	150	528	121	26	1	33	74	88	80	5.1	70	169		2	0	1.00	.229	.327	.470	.797
O'Neill, Tyler	StL	26	131	366	84	15	1	23	55	61	50	4.6	33	133		6	1	.86	.230	.299	.464	.763
Osuna, Jose	Pit	28	70	147	38	10	1	6	19	22	21	4.9	10	32		1	1	.50	.259	.310	.463	.773
Owings, Chris	Col	29	85	220	57	12	2	6	27	26	28	4.4	14	66		5	1	.83	.259	.309	.414	.723
Ozuna, Marcell	Atl	30	147	534	153	28	2	29	79	94	97	6.6	59	127		4	2	.67	.287	.360	.509	.869
Pache, Cristian	Atl	22	152	555	139	40	5	19	68	75	75	4.7	42	172		5	1	.83	.250	.307	.443	.750
Panik, Joe	Tor	30	114	331	88	19	2	6	42	32	43	4.6	34	45		2	1	.67	.266	.340	.390	.729
Paredes, Isaac	Det	22	118	399	106	20	0	9	45	48	52	4.6	42	75		2	0	1.00	.266	.343	.383	.727
Pederson, Joc	LAD	29	120	320	77	16	1	21	52	47	51	5.4	40	85		2	2	.50	.241	.338	.494	.832
Peralta, David	Ari	33	143	551	155	32	5	19	69	78	85	5.6	45	125		3	1	.75	.281	.341	.461	.802
Peraza, Jose	Bos	27	114	347	97	17	3	5	40	31	42	4.3	16	51		8	3	.73	.280	.322	.389	.712
Perez, Michael	TB	28	63	124	27	6	0	4	12	16	13	3.5	12	38		0	0	.00	.218	.292	.363	.655
Perez, Roberto	Cle	32	105	329	68	12	1	11	34	42	34	3.4	41	116		0	0	.00	.207	.300	.350	.650
Perez, Salvador	KC	31	116	466	125	27	0	25	53	72	66	5.0	16	103		2	1	.67	.268	.303	.487	.790
Peterson, Jace	Mil	31	85	207	47	11	2	5	26	23	25	4.0	28	55		5	2	.71	.227	.322	.372	.694
Pham, Tommy	SD	33	136	490	131	24	3	18	79	65	79	5.6	70	126		18	5	.78	.267	.366	.439	.804
Phillips, Brett	TB	27	72	136	25	4	2	4	17	14	13	3.1	18	58		6	1	.86	.184	.284	.331	.615
Pillar, Kevin	Col	32	151	556	163	37	4	17	78	70	84	5.5	26	96		12	4	.75	.293	.333	.466	.799
Pina, Manny	Mil	34	95	306	74	16	1	10	32	37	36	4.0	23	77		1	0	1.00	.242	.307	.399	.706
Pinder, Chad	Oak	29	113	319	79	17	1	12	40	39	39	4.3	21	90		0	0	.00	.248	.304	.420	.724
Piscotty, Stephen	Oak	30	102	313	79	19	1	11	40	43	42	4.6	28	82		4	2	.67	.252	.322	.425	.747
Plawecki, Kevin	Bos	30	62	192	47	11	1	4	20	25	22	3.9	16	40		1	1	.50	.245	.316	.375	.691
Polanco, Gregory	Pit	29	136	462	106	29	3	18	61	62	59	4.3	47	140		9	2	.82	.229	.303	.422	.725
Polanco, Jorge	Min	27	147	579	159	34	5	16	75	72	83	5.1	49	108		8	5	.62	.275	.334	.434	.768
Pollock, A.J.	LAD	33	138	511	141	30	3	30	78	72	88	6.1	39	115		8	2	.80	.276	.335	.523	.857
Posey, Buster	SF	34	115	408	116	24	1	9	50	51	60	5.3	43	62		2	1	.67	.284	.358	.414	.772
Profar, Jurickson	SD	28	140	452	114	26	2	16	62	57	63	4.8	48	77		10	2	.83	.252	.336	.425	.761
Pujols, Albert	LAA	41	124	422	106	17	0	17	44	65	53	4.3	31	65		1	0	1.00	.251	.305	.412	.718
Quinn, Roman	Phi	28	73	150	34	5	2	3	21	11	16	3.5	12	48		12	2	.86	.227	.293	.347	.639
Ramirez, Jose	Cle	28	153	581	162	43	4	32	97	95	113	6.9	73	92		24	6	.80	.279	.364	.532	.896
Ramos, Wilson	NYM	33	116	371	96	16	0	13	37	55	47	4.4	28	70		0	0	.00	.259	.314	.407	.721
Realmuto, J.T.	Phi	30	137	522	140	31	3	23	80	75	79	5.3	39	123		7	2	.78	.268	.330	.471	.801
Reddick, Josh	Hou	34	131	410	107	19	2	11	53	49	53	4.5	38	72		3	1	.75	.261	.324	.398	.721
Rendon, Anthony	LAA	31	150	570	166	42	2	27	97	100	112	7.2	84	99		3	1	.75	.291	.392	.514	.906

2021 Hitter Projections

PLAYER			BATTING											BASERUNNING			AVERAGES			
Hitter	Team	Age	G	AB	H	2B	3B	HR	R	RBI	RC	RC27	BB	SO	SB	CS	SB%	Avg	OBP	Slg	OPS
Renfroe, Hunter	TB	29	119	363	82	18	1	21	47	54	47	4.4	29	114	3	0	1.00	.226	.289	.455	.743
Rengifo, Luis	LAA	24	124	422	97	18	4	9	58	39	47	3.7	51	107	9	5	.64	.230	.320	.355	.676
Reyes, Franmil	Cle	25	155	541	136	25	1	31	78	90	82	5.3	57	175	1	1	.50	.251	.325	.473	.798
Reyes, Victor	Det	26	144	507	141	26	5	10	69	53	65	4.6	24	113	16	4	.80	.278	.313	.408	.722
Reynolds, Bryan	Pit	26	144	518	140	30	4	20	79	69	81	5.5	57	146	4	3	.57	.270	.348	.459	.808
Riddle, JT	Pit	29	50	95	23	5	1	2	11	10	10	3.5	5	22	1	1	.50	.242	.280	.379	.659
Riley, Austin	Atl	24	144	524	137	28	2	31	76	89	83	5.6	44	167	1	1	.50	.261	.326	.500	.826
Rios, Edwin	LAD	27	76	179	41	10	0	10	23	29	23	4.3	13	72	0	0	.00	.229	.292	.453	.745
Rizzo, Anthony	ChC	31	154	543	151	31	2	27	83	94	98	6.4	75	96	6	3	.67	.278	.388	.492	.880
Robert, Luis	CWS	23	151	526	130	27	5	30	93	84	77	5.0	40	173	19	6	.76	.247	.308	.489	.796
Robles, Victor	Was	24	150	519	130	29	3	13	76	56	62	4.0	36	138	17	6	.74	.250	.327	.393	.720
Rodgers, Brendan	Col	24	148	543	128	27	2	17	61	66	59	3.7	35	152	4	1	.80	.236	.294	.387	.681
Rogers, Jake	Det	26	73	237	45	9	1	11	33	36	24	3.3	27	97	1	0	1.00	.190	.286	.376	.662
Rojas, Miguel	Mia	32	138	479	130	25	2	7	53	50	58	4.2	36	67	9	5	.64	.271	.330	.376	.706
Romine, Austin	Det	32	97	294	70	14	0	7	31	38	29	3.3	15	82	1	1	.50	.238	.277	.357	.635
Rooker, Brent	Min	26	105	328	73	18	1	16	43	52	42	4.3	33	138	2	0	1.00	.223	.309	.430	.739
Rosario, Amed	NYM	25	145	514	138	23	6	11	66	56	62	4.2	26	114	12	6	.67	.268	.308	.401	.708
Rosario, Eddie	Min	29	151	589	162	31	3	29	88	93	90	5.4	34	108	6	3	.67	.275	.316	.486	.801
Ruf, Darin	SF	34	65	125	31	6	0	6	15	19	17	4.8	12	34	1	0	1.00	.248	.319	.440	.759
Ruiz, Keibert	LAD	22	97	312	84	11	0	9	33	36	39	4.5	24	35	0	0	.00	.269	.329	.391	.720
Ruiz, Rio	Bal	27	131	410	95	20	2	15	46	57	49	4.0	40	105	1	1	.50	.232	.302	.400	.702
Sanchez, Gary	NYY	28	111	351	81	16	0	25	51	60	52	5.0	36	113	0	0	.00	.231	.313	.490	.803
Sanchez, Yolmer	CWS	29	78	227	54	11	2	3	26	22	23	3.4	18	55	3	2	.60	.238	.300	.344	.643
Sandoval, Pablo	Atl	34	82	170	41	9	0	5	19	21	19	3.8	12	39	0	0	.00	.241	.295	.382	.677
Sano, Miguel	Min	28	134	476	106	24	1	33	75	81	72	5.0	61	207	0	0	.00	.223	.315	.485	.800
Santana, Carlos	Cle	35	156	549	136	29	2	25	87	82	89	5.6	101	108	2	1	.67	.248	.368	.444	.812
Santana, Danny	Tex	30	64	159	38	9	2	6	23	20	19	4.1	9	52	5	2	.71	.239	.284	.434	.718
Santana, Domingo	Cle	28	77	192	47	10	0	8	25	28	27	4.8	26	72	2	1	.67	.245	.341	.422	.763
Santander, Anthony	Bal	26	144	547	145	34	3	29	69	86	83	5.4	32	116	2	1	.67	.265	.312	.497	.809
Schoop, Jonathan	Det	29	135	489	131	25	1	23	67	69	68	4.9	23	122	1	1	.50	.268	.312	.464	.776
Schwarber, Kyle	ChC	28	137	416	97	19	1	26	65	64	66	5.3	64	135	2	1	.67	.233	.341	.471	.812
Seager, Corey	LAD	27	136	531	153	38	2	27	84	84	97	6.6	51	106	2	1	.67	.288	.355	.520	.875
Seager, Kyle	Sea	33	145	509	126	29	1	23	67	76	72	4.9	54	103	5	2	.71	.248	.329	.444	.773
Segura, Jean	Phi	31	152	591	165	31	4	14	85	62	80	4.8	39	98	10	4	.71	.279	.331	.416	.747
Semien, Marcus	Oak	30	156	623	161	36	4	22	94	76	91	5.1	70	130	10	4	.71	.258	.334	.435	.769
Senzel, Nick	Cin	26	112	370	97	22	3	14	52	45	54	5.0	33	99	11	5	.69	.262	.326	.451	.777
Severino, Pedro	Bal	27	117	371	87	15	1	12	36	42	41	3.7	31	89	2	1	.67	.235	.299	.377	.676
Shaw, Travis	Tor	31	132	427	98	22	1	20	53	58	57	4.5	51	123	2	0	1.00	.230	.316	.426	.742
Sierra, Magneuris	Mia	25	66	158	39	6	2	1	19	10	15	3.3	9	37	7	2	.78	.247	.292	.329	.621
Simmons, Andrelton	LAA	31	124	483	132	26	2	7	59	52	59	4.4	33	52	9	2	.82	.273	.324	.379	.703
Sisco, Chance	Bal	26	100	292	67	14	0	11	39	36	35	4.1	34	104	0	0	.00	.229	.332	.390	.723
Slater, Austin	SF	28	99	273	68	15	1	8	36	33	37	4.6	33	83	9	2	.82	.249	.341	.399	.740
Smith Jr., Dwight	Bal	28	69	164	39	8	1	4	19	19	18	3.8	15	39	2	1	.67	.238	.309	.372	.681
Smith, Dominic	NYM	26	147	515	128	32	2	20	66	76	68	4.6	42	134	1	1	.50	.249	.313	.435	.748
Smith, Mallex	Sea	28	70	187	46	8	3	2	25	15	21	3.8	16	47	14	4	.78	.246	.312	.353	.665
Smith, Pavin	Ari	25	150	536	147	29	3	15	78	82	80	5.3	62	103	3	1	.75	.274	.349	.424	.773
Smith, Will	LAD	26	99	331	78	17	1	22	52	64	53	5.5	44	97	1	0	1.00	.236	.336	.492	.828
Sogard, Eric	Mil	35	85	192	47	9	1	3	24	17	22	3.9	21	35	2	0	1.00	.245	.322	.349	.671
Solak, Nick	Tex	26	138	483	126	21	2	18	72	64	68	5.0	48	125	11	2	.85	.261	.338	.424	.762
Solano, Donovan	SF	33	114	354	97	21	1	5	37	40	42	4.2	18	72	0	0	.00	.274	.315	.381	.696
Soler, Jorge	KC	29	148	523	127	28	1	30	71	84	81	5.3	67	177	2	1	.67	.243	.338	.472	.810
Soto, Juan	Was	22	144	524	156	37	2	37	108	114	132	9.3	115	115	14	3	.82	.298	.427	.588	1.015
Springer, George	Hou	31	144	559	150	27	2	33	104	86	98	6.2	73	130	5	4	.56	.268	.362	.501	.863
Stallings, Jacob	Pit	31	106	340	81	21	0	8	41	41	37	3.7	26	91	0	0	.00	.238	.300	.371	.671
Stanton, Giancarlo	NYY	31	117	427	107	22	1	30	72	79	75	6.0	58	148	3	2	.60	.251	.347	.518	.865
Stassi, Max	LAA	30	83	211	45	8	0	9	24	27	23	3.6	22	68	0	0	.00	.213	.297	.379	.676
Stephenson, Tyler	Cin	24	103	321	80	17	0	12	48	50	43	4.6	35	87	0	0	.00	.249	.336	.414	.750
Stevenson, Andrew	Was	27	71	155	38	7	2	2	20	16	17	3.7	13	49	3	1	.75	.245	.308	.355	.663
Stewart, Christin	Det	27	101	226	51	11	1	10	25	31	28	4.2	24	70	0	0	.00	.226	.311	.416	.727
Stewart, D.J.	Bal	27	94	282	64	15	1	14	40	43	40	4.7	39	86	3	1	.75	.227	.333	.436	.770
Story, Trevor	Col	28	157	621	174	41	6	37	98	97	117	6.7	60	185	26	7	.79	.280	.348	.544	.893
Strange-Gordon, Dee	Sea	33	88	237	64	7	3	1	30	15	24	3.6	10	38	11	4	.73	.270	.305	.338	.643
Straw, Myles	Hou	26	63	111	28	4	1	0	17	8	12	3.7	12	27	7	1	.88	.252	.325	.306	.632
Suarez, Eugenio	Cin	29	156	571	144	26	2	37	83	96	96	5.8	72	175	4	2	.67	.252	.345	.499	.844
Suzuki, Kurt	Was	37	112	399	103	22	0	13	48	60	50	4.4	28	60	1	0	1.00	.258	.324	.411	.735
Swanson, Dansby	Atl	27	152	582	148	32	3	18	86	76	79	4.7	61	159	10	3	.77	.254	.331	.412	.744
Tapia, Raimel	Col	27	134	419	112	23	5	6	54	40	51	4.3	25	96	12	3	.80	.267	.312	.389	.701
Tatis Jr., Fernando	SD	22	159	595	172	28	7	43	119	104	124	7.5	63	182	25	7	.78	.289	.368	.576	.944
Tauchman, Mike	NYY	30	115	311	72	16	2	6	41	33	34	3.6	33	77	9	4	.69	.232	.309	.354	.663
Taveras, Leody	Tex	22	141	514	117	27	6	13	71	51	59	3.8	53	165	19	7	.73	.228	.300	.379	.679
Taylor, Chris	LAD	30	150	519	134	37	4	17	76	65	75	5.0	56	157	8	4	.67	.258	.336	.441	.777
Taylor, Michael A.	Was	30	72	135	31	8	1	5	17	17	16	4.0	11	48	4	1	.80	.230	.293	.415	.707
Taylor, Tyrone	Mil	27	72	174	40	7	1	5	18	16	18	3.4	11	38	2	1	.67	.230	.283	.368	.651
Tejeda, Anderson	Tex	23	142	482	103	17	5	24	47	57	49	3.3	15	187	25	6	.81	.214	.237	.419	.657
Tellez, Rowdy	Tor	26	108	344	84	20	0	17	43	51	48	4.8	33	90	1	1	.50	.244	.318	.451	.768
Thames, Eric	Was	34	102	243	58	13	1	13	32	37	35	5.1	32	86	2	1	.67	.239	.339	.461	.800
Toro, Abraham	Hou	24	132	457	123	31	4	16	70	72	70	5.4	47	116	4	3	.57	.269	.355	.460	.815
Torrens, Luis	Sea	25	66	219	52	13	0	5	22	25	23	3.9	23	53	0	0	.00	.237	.313	.365	.678
Torres, Gleyber	NYY	24	140	512	142	26	1	27	77	85	88	6.2	59	123	5	2	.71	.277	.358	.490	.848
Trevino, Jose	Tex	28	69	190	43	10	0	3	19	19	16	2.9	9	39	0	0	.00	.226	.265	.326	.591
Trout, Mike	LAA	29	149	543	159	30	4	44	115	105	139	9.4	118	144	11	2	.85	.293	.429	.606	1.035

2021 Hitter Projections

Hitter	Team	Age	G	AB	H	2B	3B	HR	R	RBI	RC	RC27	BB	SO	SB	CS	SB%	Avg	OBP	Slg	OPS
Tucker, Cole	Pit	24	55	100	23	4	1	2	14	9	10	3.4	9	28	2	1	.67	.230	.300	.350	.650
Tucker, Kyle	Hou	24	156	539	137	30	5	28	85	93	85	5.4	52	142	18	4	.82	.254	.326	.484	.810
Turner, Justin	LAD	36	136	501	147	31	1	21	79	72	88	6.5	55	90	3	1	.75	.293	.381	.485	.866
Turner, Trea	Was	28	153	621	181	36	7	23	103	75	108	6.3	55	126	35	7	.83	.291	.353	.483	.836
Upton, Justin	LAA	33	122	403	96	19	1	22	61	66	58	4.8	46	131	3	2	.60	.238	.325	.454	.779
Urias, Luis	Mil	24	114	353	84	17	3	7	48	33	41	3.9	41	96	4	2	.67	.238	.331	.363	.693
Urshela, Gio	NYY	29	123	412	109	23	1	11	52	52	52	4.5	27	77	1	0	1.00	.265	.316	.405	.721
Valaika, Pat	Bal	28	111	289	62	13	1	11	31	33	28	3.2	17	87	1	1	.50	.215	.258	.381	.639
VanMeter, Josh	Ari	26	61	115	29	7	1	4	15	14	16	4.9	12	31	3	1	.75	.252	.328	.435	.763
Vargas, Ildemaro	ChC	29	71	136	35	6	1	2	14	11	15	3.7	7	16	1	0	1.00	.257	.299	.360	.659
Varsho, Daulton	Ari	24	152	540	142	29	3	21	106	74	81	5.2	57	132	13	4	.76	.263	.344	.444	.789
Vazquez, Christian	Bos	30	125	451	118	25	1	13	56	54	57	4.4	33	100	7	4	.64	.262	.315	.408	.723
Verdugo, Alex	Bos	25	148	541	162	40	3	15	69	59	91	6.2	48	99	8	2	.80	.299	.361	.468	.829
Villar, Jonathan	Tor	30	135	450	112	21	2	12	61	45	56	4.2	44	133	28	8	.78	.249	.319	.384	.703
Vogelbach, Daniel	Mil	28	96	246	56	11	0	12	33	37	35	4.8	43	71	0	0	.00	.228	.345	.419	.764
Vogt, Stephen	Ari	36	66	137	33	8	1	5	15	18	18	4.3	13	32	1	1	.50	.241	.311	.423	.735
Voit, Luke	NYY	30	138	517	138	25	2	32	80	89	90	6.2	58	145	0	0	.00	.267	.351	.509	.860
Votto, Joey	Cin	37	143	488	133	28	2	21	76	64	89	6.5	94	111	2	0	1.00	.273	.395	.467	.862
Wade, Tyler	NYY	26	84	146	33	7	1	2	21	11	15	3.3	14	42	5	1	.83	.226	.302	.329	.631
Walker, Christian	Ari	30	153	536	131	30	2	23	75	73	72	4.6	50	155	4	2	.67	.244	.316	.437	.752
Wallach, Chad	Mia	29	58	154	31	7	0	4	16	15	14	2.9	15	51	0	0	.00	.201	.281	.325	.605
Walsh, Jared	LAA	27	83	235	58	13	1	17	35	43	39	5.7	23	80	0	0	.00	.247	.324	.528	.852
Ward, Taylor	LAA	27	91	266	65	14	1	9	39	29	36	4.7	35	84	5	1	.83	.244	.339	.406	.745
Waters, Drew	Atl	22	150	554	128	40	4	10	83	59	58	3.5	39	205	8	3	.73	.231	.285	.372	.657
Wendle, Joey	TB	31	133	452	113	26	4	8	57	44	50	3.8	25	100	12	4	.75	.250	.302	.378	.681
White, Evan	Sea	25	150	512	120	23	1	25	75	83	64	4.2	44	198	3	3	.50	.234	.300	.430	.730
Wieters, Matt	StL	35	65	178	41	8	0	5	17	22	19	3.6	16	43	0	0	.00	.230	.301	.360	.661
Winker, Jesse	Cin	27	140	456	120	25	1	19	61	59	72	5.5	65	102	2	2	.50	.263	.365	.447	.812
Wolters, Tony	Col	29	98	234	57	11	2	2	26	25	24	3.6	24	56	0	0	.00	.244	.324	.333	.658
Wong, Kolten	StL	30	148	480	128	25	4	9	63	53	64	4.6	48	85	13	4	.76	.267	.351	.392	.742
Yastrzemski, Mike	SF	30	150	537	131	31	6	21	82	74	75	4.8	59	163	4	3	.57	.244	.326	.441	.767
Yelich, Christian	Mil	29	147	532	149	31	3	30	96	85	105	7.1	81	148	16	3	.84	.280	.381	.519	.900
Zimmerman, Ryan	Was	36	74	244	64	14	1	12	32	41	37	5.4	21	56	0	0	.00	.262	.326	.475	.801
Zunino, Mike	TB	30	74	180	35	8	0	9	20	24	18	3.2	15	71	0	0	.00	.194	.271	.389	.660

2021 Pitcher Projections

Pitcher	Team	Age	G	GS	IP	H	HR	BB	SO	HB	W	L	Pct	Sv	BR/9	ERA
			HOW MUCH			WHAT HE WILL GIVE UP					THE RESULTS					
Adam, Jason	ChC	29	36	0	38	28	5	20	48	3	2	2	.500	0	12.1	3.76
Akin, Keegan	Bal	26	26	26	135	126	16	65	153	4	7	8	.467	0	13.0	4.14
Alcantara, Sandy	Mia	25	28	28	170	162	20	72	140	9	8	11	.421	0	12.9	4.39
Alexander, Scott	LAD	31	33	0	30	28	3	14	23	1	2	1	.667	0	12.9	4.37
Alexander, Tyler	Det	26	13	13	66	83	12	14	60	5	2	5	.286	0	13.9	5.05
Allard, Kolby	Tex	23	26	26	139	154	17	56	123	3	6	10	.375	0	13.8	4.67
Allen, Logan	Cle	24	13	13	68	70	9	29	61	4	3	4	.429	0	13.6	4.70
Almonte, Yency	Col	27	56	0	66	67	9	28	56	5	3	4	.429	0	13.6	4.78
Altavilla, Dan	SD	28	49	0	47	37	6	28	59	3	3	2	.600	0	13.0	4.04
Alvarez, Jose	Phi	32	37	0	31	32	3	10	27	1	2	2	.500	0	12.5	4.09
Alzolay, Adbert	ChC	26	21	21	111	97	14	58	134	5	7	6	.538	0	13.0	4.06
Anderson, Brett	Mil	33	28	28	151	164	17	40	93	5	8	9	.471	0	12.5	4.47
Anderson, Chase	Tor	33	24	24	120	119	24	39	107	6	6	7	.462	0	12.3	4.62
Anderson, Ian	Atl	23	25	25	126	108	14	65	154	4	8	6	.571	0	12.6	3.93
Anderson, Nick	TB	30	58	0	53	40	8	15	80	1	4	2	.667	18	9.5	2.99
Anderson, Shaun	SF	26	46	0	50	54	7	20	45	1	2	3	.400	0	13.5	4.68
Anderson, Tyler	SF	31	25	25	119	122	21	47	98	4	5	8	.385	0	13.1	4.81
Andriese, Matt	LAA	31	49	0	76	77	13	26	76	3	4	4	.500	0	12.6	4.44
Antone, Tejay	Cin	27	46	0	54	54	5	23	56	3	3	3	.500	0	13.3	4.33
Archer, Chris	Pit	32	19	19	101	104	15	39	114	4	5	6	.455	0	13.1	4.33
Armstrong, Shawn	Bal	30	46	0	51	49	7	20	54	3	3	3	.500	0	12.7	4.24
Arrieta, Jake	Phi	35	23	23	119	128	17	43	93	5	6	7	.462	0	13.3	4.73
Baez, Pedro	LAD	33	56	0	56	46	7	22	52	2	4	2	.667	7	11.3	3.96
Baragar, Caleb	SF	27	51	0	51	45	8	19	43	2	3	3	.500	0	11.6	4.27
Bard, Daniel	Col	36	56	0	58	56	7	34	61	8	3	4	.429	21	15.2	4.89
Barlow, Scott	KC	28	72	0	74	67	11	31	88	4	4	4	.500	0	12.4	4.08
Barnes, Jacob	LAA	31	42	0	44	44	6	19	47	1	3	2	.600	0	13.1	4.30
Barnes, Matt	Bos	31	69	0	67	54	7	36	97	3	5	3	.625	25	12.5	3.63
Barria, Jaime	LAA	24	25	25	131	137	24	38	113	5	7	7	.500	0	12.4	4.61
Bass, Anthony	Tor	33	69	0	72	67	8	24	60	1	4	4	.500	10	11.5	4.02
Bassitt, Chris	Oak	32	31	31	180	180	23	58	162	14	10	10	.500	0	12.6	4.33
Bauer, Trevor	Cin	30	31	31	194	152	25	66	243	12	13	9	.591	0	10.7	3.50
Bedrosian, Cam	LAA	29	43	0	47	42	5	18	44	1	3	2	.600	0	11.7	4.00
Benjamin, Wes	Tex	27	10	10	49	55	9	18	42	0	2	4	.333	0	13.4	4.87
Berrios, Jose	Min	27	32	32	187	172	23	58	188	10	12	9	.571	0	11.6	3.92
Betances, Dellin	NYM	33	38	0	33	23	2	22	47	4	2	2	.500	0	13.4	3.64
Bieber, Shane	Cle	26	33	33	211	173	24	43	271	4	16	8	.667	0	9.4	3.05
Bleier, Richard	Mia	34	60	0	54	54	3	10	31	3	3	3	.500	0	11.2	3.96
Borucki, Ryan	Tor	27	41	0	36	34	4	15	32	1	2	2	.500	0	12.5	4.16
Boxberger, Brad	Mia	33	47	0	38	35	5	21	42	1	2	2	.500	0	13.5	4.38
Boyd, Matthew	Det	30	32	32	177	175	33	56	188	9	8	12	.400	0	12.2	4.35
Brach, Brad	NYM	35	43	0	40	36	4	24	43	1	2	2	.500	0	13.7	4.28
Bradley, Archie	Cin	28	64	0	64	56	7	23	71	3	4	3	.571	5	11.5	3.74
Brasier, Ryan	Bos	33	65	0	66	60	8	23	71	3	4	3	.571	0	11.7	3.88
Brault, Steven	Pit	29	27	27	139	132	15	72	120	10	7	9	.438	0	13.9	4.60
Brewer, Colten	Bos	28	33	0	36	41	4	18	36	2	2	2	.500	0	15.3	4.88
Brice, Austin	Bos	29	51	0	51	50	8	22	53	5	3	3	.500	0	13.6	4.59
Britton, Zack	NYY	33	57	0	56	46	3	26	46	1	4	3	.571	0	11.7	3.84
Brubaker, JT	Pit	27	21	21	108	119	10	38	99	8	5	7	.417	0	13.8	4.46
Bubic, Kris	KC	23	28	28	147	156	27	62	146	6	6	10	.375	0	13.7	4.87
Buehler, Walker	LAD	26	28	28	157	129	18	43	181	6	12	5	.706	0	10.2	3.40
Bumgarner, Madison	Ari	31	28	28	150	156	27	39	130	9	8	9	.471	0	12.2	4.53
Bummer, Aaron	CWS	28	46	0	52	43	3	21	52	2	3	2	.600	0	11.4	3.62
Bundy, Dylan	LAA	28	30	30	182	168	33	57	190	8	11	9	.550	0	11.5	4.13
Burnes, Corbin	Mil	26	31	31	167	154	20	65	216	8	10	9	.526	0	12.2	3.76
Buttrey, Ty	LAA	28	74	0	74	77	8	27	75	4	4	4	.500	0	13.1	4.26
Cabrera, Edward	Mia	23	17	17	81	77	22	35	89	7	3	6	.333	0	13.2	5.06
Cabrera, Genesis	StL	24	42	0	53	50	8	27	59	3	3	3	.500	5	13.6	4.50
Cahill, Trevor	SF	33	33	11	74	71	12	35	72	4	4	5	.444	0	13.4	4.68
Canning, Griffin	LAA	25	29	29	151	135	17	55	155	7	10	7	.588	0	11.7	3.92
Carrasco, Carlos	Cle	34	28	28	158	144	21	44	182	6	10	7	.588	0	11.1	3.70
Castano, Daniel	Mia	26	24	24	117	141	8	36	75	2	5	8	.385	0	13.8	4.62
Castellani, Ryan	Col	25	17	17	86	98	16	46	62	8	3	6	.333	0	15.9	5.81
Castillo, Diego	TB	27	60	0	63	47	6	24	71	3	4	3	.571	6	10.6	3.45
Castillo, Luis	Cin	28	32	32	187	157	24	66	215	6	12	9	.571	0	11.0	3.67
Castro, Miguel	NYM	26	60	0	63	49	7	33	68	2	4	3	.571	0	12.0	3.88
Cease, Dylan	CWS	25	29	29	153	152	22	77	148	8	7	10	.412	0	13.9	4.71
Cessa, Luis	NYY	29	44	0	71	72	10	25	61	2	4	4	.500	0	12.5	4.44
Chafin, Andrew	ChC	31	52	0	36	35	4	16	43	1	2	2	.500	6	13.0	4.00
Chapman, Aroldis	NYY	33	52	0	50	32	4	22	78	3	4	2	.667	30	10.3	2.91
Chatwood, Tyler	ChC	31	14	14	72	67	8	45	69	4	4	4	.500	0	14.5	4.76
Chavez, Jesse	Tex	37	47	0	57	62	11	17	49	2	2	4	.333	0	12.8	4.74
Cimber, Adam	Cle	30	48	0	40	39	4	10	28	3	2	2	.500	0	11.7	4.22
Cishek, Steve	CWS	35	49	0	46	38	5	19	44	6	3	3	.500	0	12.3	4.07
Cisnero, Jose	Det	32	72	0	77	70	8	35	86	6	4	5	.444	0	13.0	4.06
Civale, Aaron	Cle	26	28	28	176	181	24	42	156	6	10	9	.526	0	11.7	4.14
Clarke, Taylor	Ari	28	32	15	120	116	18	47	101	4	6	7	.462	0	12.5	4.47
Clase, Emmanuel	Cle	23	36	0	42	41	3	10	41	1	3	2	.600	0	11.1	3.56
Claudio, Alex	Mil	29	64	0	57	58	5	17	41	3	3	3	.500	0	12.3	4.29

532

2021 Pitcher Projections

Pitcher	Team	Age	G	GS	IP	H	HR	BB	SO	HB	W	L	Pct	Sv	BR/9	ERA
Clevinger, Mike	SD	30	27	27	158	129	17	58	176	3	11	7	.611	0	10.8	3.58
Clippard, Tyler	Min	36	70	0	72	61	11	21	75	4	5	3	.625	0	10.8	3.85
Cobb, Alex	Bal	33	27	27	148	171	25	43	102	5	6	10	.375	0	13.3	4.99
Cody, Kyle	Tex	26	18	18	94	74	6	53	75	0	5	6	.455	0	12.2	4.05
Cole, A.J.	Tor	29	54	0	55	62	10	23	53	1	2	4	.333	0	14.1	5.08
Cole, Gerrit	NYY	30	33	33	210	163	30	55	277	5	16	8	.667	0	9.6	3.20
Colome, Alex	CWS	32	63	0	65	55	6	23	55	2	4	3	.571	30	11.1	3.86
Coonrod, Sam	SF	28	49	0	42	43	5	21	41	4	2	3	.400	0	14.6	4.82
Corbin, Patrick	Was	31	31	31	194	196	25	60	203	3	12	10	.545	0	12.0	3.99
Cordero, Jimmy	CWS	29	52	0	56	57	6	26	48	4	3	3	.500	0	14.0	4.66
Cortes, Nestor	Sea	26	23	0	31	29	5	12	31	1	1	2	.333	0	12.2	4.21
Crichton, Stefan	Ari	29	62	0	66	64	6	21	61	6	4	3	.571	18	12.4	4.06
Crick, Kyle	Pit	28	44	0	44	37	4	25	51	4	2	3	.400	0	13.5	4.11
Crowe, Wil	Was	26	19	19	89	100	15	39	77	3	4	6	.400	0	14.4	5.11
Cueto, Johnny	SF	35	25	25	134	135	20	50	114	7	6	8	.429	0	12.9	4.57
Curtiss, John	TB	28	32	5	50	44	6	23	54	2	3	3	.500	0	12.4	4.08
Darvish, Yu	ChC	34	32	32	189	160	28	55	226	9	12	9	.571	0	10.7	3.63
Davies, Zach	SD	28	32	32	187	188	25	60	142	5	11	10	.524	0	12.2	4.36
Dayton, Grant	Atl	33	39	0	58	55	14	20	69	2	3	3	.500	0	11.9	4.42
deGrom, Jacob	NYM	33	33	33	206	159	21	52	263	4	15	8	.652	0	9.4	3.03
DeSclafani, Anthony	Cin	31	27	27	147	157	31	49	132	5	7	9	.438	0	12.9	4.87
Detwiler, Ross	CWS	35	39	0	52	63	12	18	37	2	2	4	.333	0	14.4	5.72
Devenski, Chris	Hou	30	46	0	48	46	9	16	53	2	3	2	.600	0	12.0	4.22
Diaz, Edwin	NYM	27	70	0	69	46	9	28	119	5	5	2	.714	23	10.3	2.92
Diaz, Jairo	Col	30	54	0	55	63	7	26	54	4	3	3	.500	0	15.2	4.99
Diekman, Jake	Oak	34	63	0	61	44	4	35	81	7	4	3	.571	0	12.7	3.59
Dobnak, Randy	Min	26	26	26	136	131	10	34	98	9	8	7	.533	0	11.5	3.97
Dolis, Rafael	Tor	33	46	0	48	34	3	28	60	2	3	2	.600	18	12.0	3.53
Doolittle, Sean	Was	34	57	0	59	53	9	15	63	2	4	3	.571	12	10.7	3.82
Drake, Oliver	TB	34	38	0	42	36	5	16	47	1	3	2	.600	0	11.4	3.74
Duffey, Tyler	Min	30	65	0	70	62	10	20	85	3	5	3	.625	0	10.9	3.62
Duffy, Danny	KC	32	30	30	163	166	25	59	149	7	8	10	.444	0	12.8	4.50
Dunn, Justin	Sea	25	21	21	94	95	14	47	95	5	4	7	.364	0	14.1	4.79
Dunning, Dane	CWS	26	29	29	151	137	9	60	158	8	9	7	.563	0	12.2	3.76
Eflin, Zach	Phi	27	31	31	176	180	27	50	166	7	10	10	.500	0	12.1	4.25
Eovaldi, Nathan	Bos	31	26	26	139	147	22	37	139	7	8	7	.533	0	12.4	4.31
Eshelman, Thomas	Bal	27	28	9	87	111	16	22	57	2	3	6	.333	0	14.0	5.33
Estevez, Carlos	Col	28	71	0	71	80	13	25	78	3	4	4	.500	0	13.7	4.76
Fairbanks, Pete	TB	27	44	0	45	38	6	20	66	2	3	2	.600	0	12.0	3.65
Familia, Jeurys	NYM	31	69	0	72	67	6	44	70	4	4	4	.500	0	14.4	4.51
Farmer, Buck	Det	30	66	0	65	71	8	24	57	2	3	4	.429	0	13.4	4.57
Fedde, Erick	Was	28	20	20	106	122	16	42	75	4	5	7	.417	0	14.3	5.18
Fiers, Mike	Oak	36	30	30	175	182	32	51	122	10	8	11	.421	0	12.5	4.78
Finnegan, Kyle	Was	29	48	0	49	44	5	22	55	1	3	2	.600	0	12.3	3.90
Flaherty, Jack	StL	25	28	28	149	116	19	49	174	7	10	7	.588	0	10.4	3.50
Fleming, Josh	TB	25	30	19	138	150	20	32	102	5	7	8	.467	0	12.2	4.44
Floro, Dylan	LAD	30	61	0	61	63	7	17	50	1	4	3	.571	0	12.0	4.16
Foster, Matt	CWS	26	55	0	62	51	8	22	67	1	4	3	.571	0	10.7	3.68
Freeland, Kyle	Col	28	29	29	163	186	24	61	121	5	8	10	.444	0	13.9	5.00
Fried, Max	Atl	27	30	30	163	161	16	63	161	9	10	8	.556	0	12.9	4.15
Fry, Jace	CWS	27	56	0	56	47	6	34	68	2	3	3	.500	0	13.3	4.04
Fry, Paul	Bal	28	63	0	61	58	7	28	69	5	3	4	.429	0	13.4	4.28
Fulmer, Michael	Det	28	22	22	117	131	16	38	89	5	5	8	.385	0	13.4	4.77
Gallegos, Giovanny	StL	29	53	0	55	40	7	14	68	1	4	2	.667	18	9.0	3.08
Gallen, Zac	Ari	25	30	30	184	159	24	64	204	7	12	9	.571	0	11.3	3.78
Gant, John	StL	28	51	0	48	43	5	21	44	1	3	3	.500	0	12.2	4.09
Garcia, Bryan	Det	26	53	0	46	39	5	22	37	1	2	3	.400	30	12.1	4.27
Garcia, Deivi	NYY	22	26	26	137	137	20	56	160	11	8	7	.533	0	13.4	4.37
Garcia, Jarlin	SF	28	58	0	57	54	8	22	43	3	3	3	.500	0	12.5	4.43
Garcia, Yimi	Mia	30	46	0	49	43	10	12	52	4	3	3	.500	0	10.8	4.08
Garrett, Amir	Cin	29	60	0	53	48	9	26	64	2	3	3	.500	0	12.9	4.25
Gausman, Kevin	SF	30	32	32	169	162	25	54	185	5	9	9	.500	0	11.8	3.97
Gaviglio, Sam	Tor	31	23	0	34	36	6	10	28	1	2	2	.500	0	12.4	4.63
Gerber, Joey	Sea	24	47	0	47	52	5	15	36	4	2	3	.400	0	13.2	4.50
Gibson, Kyle	Tex	33	32	32	186	182	27	76	169	9	8	12	.400	0	12.9	4.50
Gilbert, Logan	Sea	24	24	24	124	108	9	47	137	10	7	7	.500	0	12.0	3.69
Ginkel, Kevin	Ari	27	48	0	44	35	6	20	57	0	3	2	.600	0	11.3	3.67
Giolito, Lucas	CWS	26	32	32	195	155	28	77	228	8	12	10	.545	0	11.1	3.74
Givens, Mychal	Col	31	60	0	63	53	9	25	73	3	4	3	.571	5	11.6	3.86
Glasnow, Tyler	TB	27	27	27	141	103	20	58	194	2	9	7	.563	0	10.4	3.36
Godley, Zack	Bos	31	25	14	80	87	11	35	72	5	4	5	.444	0	14.3	4.90
Gomber, Austin	StL	27	26	26	116	112	16	49	113	4	6	7	.462	0	12.8	4.35
Gonsolin, Tony	LAD	27	26	26	133	107	14	40	132	4	10	5	.667	0	10.2	3.55
Gonzales, Marco	Sea	29	31	31	193	193	24	42	157	8	10	12	.455	0	11.3	4.05
Gonzalez, Chi Chi	Col	29	13	13	70	77	12	32	54	4	3	5	.375	0	14.5	5.27
Gonzalez, Gio	CWS	35	29	13	91	91	12	41	83	2	5	5	.500	0	13.3	4.50
Gonzalez, Victor	LAD	25	54	0	58	54	6	14	58	4	4	2	.667	0	11.2	3.74
Gore, MacKenzie	SD	22	26	26	133	139	24	55	159	7	7	8	.467	0	13.6	4.60
Gott, Trevor	SF	28	42	0	37	36	6	16	36	2	2	2	.500	0	13.1	4.50
Graterol, Brusdar	LAD	22	56	0	53	42	4	16	43	5	4	2	.667	0	10.7	3.73
Graveman, Kendall	Sea	30	26	0	35	39	5	13	27	2	1	2	.333	0	13.9	4.89

2021 Pitcher Projections

Pitcher	Team	Age	G	GS	IP	H	HR	BB	SO	HB	W	L	Pct	Sv	BR/9	ERA
Gray, Jon	Col	29	26	26	141	160	22	47	125	4	7	8	.467	0	13.5	4.76
Gray, Sonny	Cin	31	30	30	171	142	19	71	192	7	11	8	.579	0	11.6	3.75
Green, Chad	NYY	30	60	0	65	54	8	18	85	2	5	3	.625	0	10.2	3.32
Greene, Shane	Atl	32	73	0	74	66	10	26	68	4	4	4	.500	5	11.7	4.08
Greinke, Zack	Hou	37	33	33	199	188	29	35	182	4	14	8	.636	0	10.3	3.80
Gsellman, Robert	NYM	27	48	0	58	64	8	23	47	4	3	4	.429	0	14.1	4.89
Guerra, Javy	Was	35	44	0	55	58	8	20	46	1	3	3	.500	0	12.9	4.59
Guerra, Junior	Ari	36	58	0	56	52	9	27	50	3	3	3	.500	0	13.2	4.58
Hader, Josh	Mil	27	59	0	62	41	11	25	101	3	4	3	.571	35	10.0	3.13
Hahn, Jesse	KC	31	50	0	51	47	3	25	49	2	3	3	.500	13	13.1	4.10
Hale, David	Phi	33	29	0	48	59	5	13	35	2	2	3	.400	0	13.9	4.79
Hamels, Cole	Atl	37	22	22	115	113	16	44	107	8	6	6	.500	0	12.9	4.43
Hand, Brad	Cle	31	61	0	61	47	7	18	82	6	4	2	.667	35	10.5	3.25
Happ, J.A.	NYY	38	26	26	147	143	25	45	129	4	8	8	.500	0	11.8	4.32
Harper, Ryne	Was	32	63	0	63	70	8	19	65	2	4	3	.571	0	13.0	4.29
Harris, Will	Was	36	61	0	55	51	6	17	59	1	3	3	.500	6	11.3	3.69
Hartlieb, Geoff	Pit	27	52	0	59	61	5	34	59	3	3	4	.429	0	14.9	4.66
Harvey, Hunter	Bal	26	46	0	51	59	13	19	52	4	2	4	.333	0	14.5	5.56
Hatch, Thomas	Tor	26	20	20	106	110	18	45	94	8	5	7	.417	0	13.8	4.92
Heaney, Andrew	LAA	30	31	31	178	176	33	51	191	8	11	9	.550	0	11.9	4.23
Hearn, Taylor	Tex	26	42	0	46	38	5	23	54	2	2	3	.400	0	12.3	3.88
Hembree, Heath	Phi	32	51	0	45	44	10	19	51	2	2	3	.400	0	13.0	4.70
Hendricks, Kyle	ChC	31	32	32	194	188	24	37	155	7	12	10	.545	0	10.8	3.93
Hendriks, Liam	Oak	32	71	0	77	60	6	19	104	1	6	3	.667	36	9.4	2.86
Herget, Jimmy	Tex	27	41	0	42	39	5	24	40	2	2	3	.400	0	13.9	4.61
Hernandez, Darwinzon	Bos	24	48	0	52	44	4	47	79	6	3	3	.500	0	16.8	4.59
Hernandez, Elieser	Mia	26	22	22	117	103	20	37	132	11	6	7	.462	0	11.6	4.03
Hernandez, Felix	Atl	35	16	16	81	91	14	30	65	7	4	5	.444	0	14.2	5.17
Hernandez, Jonathan	Tex	24	48	0	49	51	7	22	49	3	2	3	.400	0	14.0	4.69
Heuer, Codi	CWS	24	57	0	60	48	2	20	58	0	4	3	.571	0	10.2	3.30
Hicks, Jordan	StL	24	46	0	44	32	2	22	43	3	3	2	.600	0	11.7	3.65
Hill, Cam	Cle	27	34	0	36	33	8	14	36	2	2	2	.500	0	12.3	4.63
Hill, Rich	Min	41	18	18	90	82	14	34	87	5	5	5	.500	0	12.1	4.27
Hill, Tim	SD	31	63	0	53	51	5	17	53	4	3	3	.500	0	12.2	3.97
Hirano, Yoshihisa	Sea	37	42	0	41	40	6	18	40	2	2	3	.400	24	13.2	4.50
Hoffman, Jeff	Col	28	36	0	46	52	8	20	45	3	2	3	.400	0	14.7	5.09
Holder, Jonathan	NYY	28	40	0	50	51	7	17	46	1	3	3	.500	0	12.4	4.32
Holland, Derek	Pit	34	41	10	100	102	19	47	97	5	4	7	.364	0	13.9	5.00
Holland, Greg	KC	35	64	0	65	55	8	30	68	3	4	4	.500	15	12.2	4.07
Houck, Tanner	Bos	25	21	21	119	124	12	64	122	14	6	7	.462	0	15.3	4.84
Houser, Adrian	Mil	28	28	28	151	157	20	53	135	9	8	9	.471	0	13.1	4.47
Howard, Sam	Pit	28	52	0	51	47	7	21	54	3	3	3	.500	0	12.5	4.24
Howard, Spencer	Phi	24	25	25	133	121	17	50	143	6	8	7	.533	0	12.0	3.97
Hoyt, James	Mia	34	50	0	46	45	5	21	55	3	2	3	.400	0	13.5	4.21
Hudson, Daniel	Was	34	61	0	64	53	9	29	68	6	4	3	.571	18	12.4	4.18
Hughes, Jared	NYM	35	57	0	67	60	8	28	54	5	4	4	.500	0	12.5	4.33
Hunter, Tommy	Phi	34	48	0	52	49	6	12	49	3	3	3	.500	0	11.1	3.81
Iglesias, Raisel	Cin	31	63	0	66	56	9	21	81	2	4	3	.571	31	10.8	3.52
Jackson, Luke	Atl	29	58	0	75	80	7	34	82	3	4	4	.500	0	14.0	4.38
James, Josh	Hou	28	39	0	44	36	4	24	59	3	3	2	.600	0	12.9	3.83
Jansen, Kenley	LAD	33	70	0	67	54	10	18	84	4	5	2	.714	35	10.2	3.43
Javier, Cristian	Hou	24	26	26	148	105	18	63	176	5	11	6	.647	0	10.5	3.51
Jeffress, Jeremy	ChC	33	57	0	63	58	7	26	54	4	4	3	.571	26	12.6	4.31
Jimenez, Joe	Det	26	68	0	63	62	10	23	75	6	3	4	.429	0	13.0	4.23
Johnson, Pierce	SD	30	46	0	40	34	4	20	48	1	3	2	.600	0	12.4	3.88
Junis, Jakob	KC	28	24	24	127	141	24	35	114	9	6	8	.429	0	13.1	4.82
Karinchak, James	Cle	25	60	0	71	41	5	44	121	0	6	2	.750	0	10.8	2.82
Kay, Anthony	Tor	26	22	22	115	114	14	59	116	7	6	7	.462	0	14.1	4.62
Keller, Brad	KC	25	25	25	156	156	12	61	111	7	8	9	.471	0	12.9	4.35
Keller, Mitch	Pit	25	25	25	128	124	13	58	135	5	7	8	.467	0	13.1	4.19
Kelly, Joe	LAD	33	53	0	51	44	4	25	53	3	4	2	.667	0	12.7	3.95
Kelly, Merrill	Ari	32	19	19	101	103	19	29	87	2	5	6	.455	0	11.9	4.50
Kennedy, Ian	KC	36	48	0	47	50	9	16	45	1	2	3	.400	0	12.8	4.70
Kershaw, Clayton	LAD	33	29	29	173	149	27	34	177	2	13	6	.684	0	9.6	3.58
Keuchel, Dallas	CWS	33	30	30	178	183	19	54	129	5	10	10	.500	0	12.2	4.29
Kikuchi, Yusei	Sea	30	28	28	144	158	26	51	119	4	6	10	.375	0	13.3	4.91
Kim, Kwang-hyun	StL	32	28	28	147	125	16	47	90	0	9	8	.529	0	10.5	4.03
Kimbrel, Craig	ChC	33	57	0	56	35	8	28	90	4	4	2	.667	8	10.8	3.28
Kinley, Tyler	Col	30	60	0	60	55	7	37	63	3	3	3	.500	0	14.3	4.58
Kintzler, Brandon	Mia	36	64	0	64	62	6	21	44	3	3	4	.429	26	12.1	4.27
Kluber, Corey	Tex	35	21	21	118	100	14	27	128	3	7	6	.538	0	9.9	3.44
Knebel, Corey	Mil	29	35	0	37	29	5	19	50	1	2	2	.500	0	11.9	3.73
Kolarek, Adam	LAD	32	63	0	55	52	3	16	43	3	4	2	.667	7	11.6	3.88
Kopech, Michael	CWS	25	28	28	147	133	14	79	184	14	8	8	.500	0	13.8	4.13
Kremer, Dean	Bal	25	21	21	107	114	13	48	117	1	5	7	.417	0	13.7	4.42
Kuhl, Chad	Pit	28	21	21	105	102	15	53	98	4	5	7	.417	0	13.6	4.67
Lail, Brady	Sea	27	22	0	38	41	7	17	36	1	1	3	.250	0	14.0	4.98
Lakins, Travis	Bal	27	48	0	59	61	6	30	53	3	3	4	.429	0	14.3	4.66
Lamet, Dinelson	SD	28	29	29	174	127	23	65	230	10	12	7	.632	0	10.4	3.38
Lauer, Eric	Mil	26	16	16	78	82	11	31	74	4	4	5	.444	0	13.5	4.62
Leake, Mike	Ari	33	29	29	159	188	24	28	102	8	8	10	.444	0	12.7	4.73

2021 Pitcher Projections

Pitcher	Team	Age	G	GS	IP	H	HR	BB	SO	HB	W	L	Pct	Sv	BR/9	ERA
LeBlanc, Wade	Bal	36	11	11	52	62	11	14	36	1	2	4	.333	0	13.3	5.28
Leclerc, Jose	Tex	27	45	0	47	30	4	28	67	3	3	2	.600	0	11.7	3.40
Lester, Jon	ChC	37	32	32	181	204	28	58	148	6	9	11	.450	0	13.3	4.77
Lindblom, Josh	Mil	34	19	19	97	100	16	33	105	7	5	6	.455	0	13.0	4.46
Loaisiga, Jonathan	NYY	26	32	0	52	54	9	18	57	4	3	3	.500	0	13.2	4.50
Lockett, Walker	Sea	27	26	0	36	44	6	10	26	2	1	3	.250	0	14.0	5.13
Lopez, Jorge	Bal	28	17	17	88	101	16	31	72	6	3	6	.333	0	14.1	5.17
Lopez, Pablo	Mia	25	26	26	141	134	17	42	134	10	7	8	.467	0	11.9	4.04
Lopez, Reynaldo	CWS	27	25	25	112	110	19	44	99	5	6	7	.462	0	12.8	4.62
Lopez, Yoan	Ari	28	59	0	58	53	10	22	51	1	3	3	.500	0	11.8	4.36
Lorenzen, Michael	Cin	29	58	0	63	57	6	26	59	2	4	3	.571	0	12.1	4.06
Loup, Aaron	TB	33	46	0	50	47	5	15	48	3	3	3	.500	0	12.2	4.01
Lucchesi, Joey	SD	28	13	13	62	60	9	21	61	2	4	3	.571	0	12.0	4.15
Lugo, Seth	NYM	31	50	0	52	46	7	13	60	2	3	2	.600	4	10.6	3.58
Luzardo, Jesus	Oak	23	28	28	153	142	17	42	160	7	9	8	.529	0	11.2	3.74
Lyles, Jordan	Tex	30	27	27	145	155	29	57	122	4	6	11	.353	0	13.4	5.03
Lynn, Lance	Tex	34	33	33	204	185	27	72	214	11	10	12	.455	0	11.8	3.98
Maeda, Kenta	Min	33	31	31	179	153	27	50	197	5	12	8	.600	0	10.5	3.68
Magill, Matt	Sea	31	39	0	39	38	7	17	42	2	2	3	.400	0	13.2	4.62
Mahle, Tyler	Cin	26	28	28	146	137	22	53	155	8	8	8	.500	0	12.2	4.14
Manaea, Sean	Oak	29	27	27	144	135	18	33	124	6	8	8	.500	0	10.9	3.91
Margevicius, Nick	Sea	25	19	19	99	109	22	29	81	2	4	7	.364	0	12.7	4.96
Marquez, German	Col	26	32	32	199	205	30	54	197	6	12	10	.545	0	12.0	4.14
Marshall, Evan	CWS	31	65	0	65	60	6	24	68	1	4	3	.571	0	11.8	3.76
Martin, Brett	Tex	26	46	0	53	63	5	20	50	1	2	4	.333	0	14.3	4.67
Martin, Chris	Atl	35	54	0	53	50	7	7	57	2	4	2	.667	0	10.0	3.52
Martinez, Carlos	StL	29	46	0	50	48	6	21	49	3	3	3	.500	0	13.0	4.32
Maton, Phil	Cle	28	51	0	53	49	7	18	66	4	3	3	.500	0	12.1	3.86
Matz, Steven	NYM	30	23	23	118	122	24	40	116	5	6	7	.462	0	12.7	4.69
Matzek, Tyler	Atl	30	62	0	71	53	4	30	100	5	5	3	.625	0	11.2	3.15
May, Dustin	LAD	23	29	29	156	143	14	43	137	12	11	6	.647	0	11.4	3.88
May, Trevor	Min	31	66	0	69	57	11	27	91	2	5	3	.625	0	11.2	3.66
Mayers, Mike	LAA	29	59	0	65	62	10	23	72	2	4	3	.571	26	12.0	4.09
Mazza, Chris	Bos	31	21	11	68	77	7	25	54	5	4	4	.500	0	14.2	4.74
McCarthy, Kevin	KC	29	31	0	36	42	3	11	23	1	2	2	.500	0	13.5	4.63
McCullers Jr., Lance	Hou	27	21	21	110	96	9	40	114	8	8	5	.615	0	11.8	3.74
McFarland, T.J.	Oak	32	65	0	62	73	7	19	35	1	3	4	.429	0	13.5	4.87
McGee, Jake	LAD	34	64	0	58	52	10	15	65	2	4	2	.667	0	10.7	3.80
McKay, Brendan	TB	25	16	16	81	65	7	24	102	2	5	4	.556	0	10.1	3.18
McKenzie, Triston	Cle	23	24	24	127	95	18	38	146	5	9	6	.600	0	9.8	3.44
Means, John	Bal	28	28	28	137	139	22	32	115	6	7	9	.438	0	11.6	4.28
Melancon, Mark	Atl	36	66	0	68	76	5	20	55	3	4	4	.500	25	13.1	4.24
Mella, Keury	Ari	27	39	0	41	49	6	17	32	2	2	3	.400	0	14.9	5.27
Menez, Conner	SF	26	17	0	31	28	4	15	36	2	2	2	.500	0	13.1	4.21
Mengden, Daniel	Oak	28	8	8	44	43	6	14	34	1	2	3	.400	0	11.9	4.31
Mikolas, Miles	StL	32	26	26	141	148	18	25	106	8	8	8	.500	0	11.6	4.18
Miley, Wade	Cin	34	26	26	132	138	17	59	111	6	6	8	.429	0	13.8	4.77
Miller, Andrew	StL	36	63	0	66	51	7	28	83	10	4	3	.571	17	12.1	3.70
Mills, Alec	ChC	29	30	30	157	166	24	52	133	7	8	9	.471	0	12.9	4.59
Minor, Mike	Oak	33	32	32	186	167	27	57	178	6	11	10	.524	0	11.1	3.97
Minter, A.J.	Atl	27	52	0	52	51	4	23	60	1	3	3	.500	0	13.0	3.92
Misiewicz, Anthony	Sea	26	40	0	40	47	6	12	39	1	2	3	.400	0	13.5	4.62
Mize, Casey	Det	24	31	31	167	182	25	58	157	19	7	12	.368	0	14.0	4.80
Montas, Frankie	Oak	28	23	23	122	124	17	43	125	4	7	7	.500	0	12.6	4.24
Montero, Rafael	Tex	30	43	0	49	48	6	20	54	2	2	3	.400	22	12.9	4.13
Montgomery, Jordan	NYY	28	20	20	104	97	15	27	105	2	7	5	.583	0	10.9	3.85
Montgomery, Mike	KC	31	30	10	72	81	8	25	51	3	3	5	.375	0	13.6	4.76
Morejon, Adrian	SD	22	19	19	97	98	19	31	120	4	6	5	.545	0	12.3	4.27
Morton, Charlie	TB	37	27	27	139	120	13	45	157	11	8	7	.533	0	11.4	3.61
Musgrove, Joe	Pit	28	25	25	132	125	17	36	135	7	8	7	.533	0	11.5	3.91
Neidert, Nick	Mia	24	42	0	38	44	6	12	33	1	2	3	.400	0	13.5	4.86
Neris, Hector	Phi	32	68	0	65	57	9	27	83	4	4	3	.571	24	12.2	3.85
Neverauskas, Dovydas	Pit	28	35	0	41	44	6	22	48	1	2	3	.400	0	14.7	4.83
Newberry, Jake	KC	26	46	0	51	47	6	24	50	1	3	3	.500	0	12.7	4.16
Newsome, Ljay	Sea	24	13	13	67	70	10	10	47	2	3	4	.429	0	11.0	4.21
Nola, Aaron	Phi	28	33	33	194	160	23	65	226	7	13	9	.591	0	10.8	3.56
Norris, Daniel	Det	28	19	19	101	111	17	33	93	3	4	7	.364	0	13.1	4.68
Nova, Ivan	Det	34	18	18	101	121	18	25	61	4	4	8	.333	0	13.4	5.17
O'Day, Darren	Atl	38	40	0	35	26	4	11	44	4	2	1	.667	0	10.5	3.36
Odorizzi, Jake	Min	31	27	27	142	137	22	52	141	5	8	8	.500	0	12.3	4.25
Osich, Josh	ChC	32	53	0	61	67	10	21	61	2	3	4	.429	0	13.3	4.65
Osuna, Roberto	Hou	26	43	0	47	38	4	8	50	2	4	2	.667	0	9.2	3.19
Ottavino, Adam	NYY	35	69	0	56	42	6	31	73	3	4	3	.571	0	12.2	3.78
Paddack, Chris	SD	25	30	30	160	139	27	34	165	7	11	7	.611	0	10.1	3.74
Pagan, Emilio	SD	30	65	0	68	53	10	20	79	2	5	3	.625	0	9.9	3.47
Paredes, Enoli	Hou	25	42	0	40	31	2	20	46	3	3	2	.600	0	12.2	3.63
Parker, Blake	Phi	36	46	0	53	46	9	19	63	2	3	3	.500	0	11.4	3.88
Patino, Luis	SD	21	16	16	84	81	12	61	102	4	4	5	.444	0	15.6	4.99
Paxton, James	NYY	32	19	19	95	87	13	30	113	2	6	4	.600	0	11.3	3.71
Pearson, Nate	Tor	24	27	27	146	130	23	66	142	4	8	8	.500	0	12.3	4.29
Pena, Felix	LAA	31	53	0	57	55	9	20	58	4	3	3	.500	12	12.5	4.27

2021 Pitcher Projections

Pitcher	Team	Age	G	GS	IP	H	HR	BB	SO	HB	W	L	Pct	Sv	BR/9	ERA
Peralta, Freddy	Mil	25	42	0	82	65	9	38	116	4	5	4	.556	0	11.7	3.49
Peralta, Wandy	SF	29	59	0	64	67	8	29	52	3	3	4	.429	0	13.9	4.78
Perdomo, Luis	SD	28	38	0	64	67	8	24	52	2	4	4	.500	0	13.1	4.57
Perez, Martin	Bos	30	32	32	176	198	26	70	130	5	9	11	.450	0	14.0	5.01
Perez, Oliver	Cle	39	61	0	48	44	4	15	47	5	3	2	.600	0	12.0	3.84
Peterson, David	NYM	25	26	26	132	142	15	58	121	7	7	8	.467	0	14.1	4.67
Petit, Yusmeiro	Oak	36	75	0	69	62	9	13	57	0	4	3	.571	0	9.8	3.73
Phelps, David	Phi	34	62	0	58	52	11	22	72	2	3	3	.500	0	11.8	4.03
Phillips, Evan	Bal	26	33	0	36	34	4	21	45	4	2	2	.500	0	14.8	4.50
Pineda, Michael	Min	32	28	28	151	153	25	33	139	5	9	8	.529	0	11.4	4.13
Pivetta, Nick	Bos	28	18	18	95	100	15	36	98	3	5	5	.500	0	13.2	4.55
Plesac, Zach	Cle	26	25	25	165	136	20	37	153	5	11	7	.611	0	9.7	3.56
Plutko, Adam	Cle	29	16	16	82	87	16	24	59	2	4	5	.444	0	12.4	4.83
Pomeranz, Drew	SD	32	56	0	69	63	11	35	81	2	4	4	.500	0	13.0	4.30
Ponce de Leon, Daniel	StL	29	26	26	129	98	14	71	142	8	8	7	.533	0	12.3	3.99
Porcello, Rick	NYM	32	33	33	173	179	27	45	157	8	9	10	.474	0	12.1	4.29
Pressly, Ryan	Hou	32	59	0	56	45	7	17	72	2	4	2	.667	32	10.3	3.36
Price, David	LAD	35	28	28	159	145	21	48	175	7	11	6	.647	0	11.3	3.81
Puk, A.J.	Oak	26	24	24	136	131	14	58	182	6	8	7	.533	0	12.9	3.81
Quantrill, Cal	Cle	26	18	18	94	104	13	28	82	4	5	5	.500	0	13.0	4.50
Quintana, Jose	ChC	32	28	28	154	162	20	50	142	4	9	9	.500	0	12.6	4.33
Rainey, Tanner	Was	28	61	0	62	41	8	42	91	3	4	3	.571	0	12.5	3.77
Raley, Brooks	Hou	33	40	0	40	31	7	12	52	8	3	2	.600	0	11.5	3.88
Ramirez, Erasmo	NYM	31	32	0	46	46	9	15	35	2	2	3	.400	0	12.3	4.80
Ramirez, Nick	Det	31	29	0	53	52	7	22	47	1	2	3	.400	0	12.7	4.33
Ramirez, Noe	LAA	31	57	0	59	54	10	21	58	4	3	3	.500	0	12.1	4.28
Ramirez, Yohan	Sea	26	35	0	35	26	4	32	46	5	1	2	.333	12	16.2	4.76
Ramos, AJ	Col	34	35	0	35	37	6	24	33	1	1	2	.333	0	15.9	5.53
Ray, Robbie	Tor	29	31	31	159	145	32	89	203	6	8	10	.444	0	13.5	4.59
Reyes, Alex	StL	26	28	0	39	28	4	29	51	2	2	2	.500	5	13.6	3.96
Richards, Garrett	SD	33	28	28	149	141	21	58	141	4	9	8	.529	0	12.3	4.24
Richards, Trevor	TB	28	26	13	92	93	13	34	85	3	5	6	.455	0	12.7	4.36
Roark, Tanner	Tor	34	30	30	149	165	27	51	127	8	7	10	.412	0	13.5	4.95
Robertson, David	Phi	36	38	0	43	30	5	17	55	1	3	2	.600	6	10.0	3.22
Robles, Hansel	LAA	30	56	0	57	54	10	23	60	2	3	3	.500	0	12.5	4.34
Rodon, Carlos	CWS	28	17	17	88	81	11	40	85	6	5	5	.500	0	13.0	4.35
Rodriguez, Eduardo	Bos	28	25	25	137	128	16	50	146	5	9	7	.563	0	12.0	3.95
Rodriguez, Richard	Pit	31	68	0	68	58	10	21	79	4	4	4	.500	24	11.0	3.73
Roe, Chaz	TB	34	42	0	36	33	3	16	41	3	2	2	.500	0	13.0	3.91
Rogers, Taylor	Min	30	58	0	62	55	6	14	72	4	4	2	.667	25	10.6	3.41
Rogers, Trevor	Mia	23	21	21	103	112	18	47	134	6	4	7	.364	0	14.4	4.72
Rogers, Tyler	SF	30	64	0	64	59	4	23	55	6	3	4	.429	5	12.4	4.02
Romano, Jordan	Tor	28	48	0	48	44	7	18	54	4	3	3	.500	0	12.4	4.14
Romero, JoJo	Phi	24	47	0	57	65	8	24	50	3	3	4	.429	0	14.5	4.98
Romo, Sergio	Min	38	68	0	60	54	10	19	61	3	4	3	.571	10	11.4	4.08
Rondon, Hector	Ari	33	63	0	60	60	9	24	59	2	3	4	.429	0	12.9	4.43
Rosenthal, Trevor	SD	31	51	0	53	38	6	38	77	7	3	3	.500	7	14.1	4.08
Ross, Joe	Was	28	10	10	54	64	8	19	44	3	3	3	.500	0	14.3	5.08
Ryan, Kyle	ChC	29	58	0	52	53	8	25	44	2	2	3	.400	0	13.8	4.94
Ryu, Hyun-Jin	Tor	34	31	31	188	183	26	41	177	4	11	10	.524	0	10.9	3.90
Sadler, Casey	Sea	30	45	0	54	57	8	18	50	3	2	4	.333	0	13.0	4.50
Sale, Chris	Bos	32	17	17	94	74	10	22	133	7	7	3	.700	0	9.9	2.97
Samardzija, Jeff	SF	36	21	21	109	112	19	29	80	5	5	7	.417	0	12.1	4.54
Sanchez, Anibal	Was	37	30	30	164	180	30	56	137	6	8	10	.444	0	13.3	4.89
Sanchez, Sixto	Mia	22	27	27	140	142	13	36	125	6	7	8	.467	0	11.8	3.95
Sandoval, Patrick	LAA	24	12	12	62	65	9	26	65	1	3	3	.500	0	13.4	4.50
Scherzer, Max	Was	36	30	30	182	148	22	48	240	8	13	7	.650	0	10.1	3.20
Schreiber, John	Det	27	35	0	37	33	4	13	40	2	2	2	.500	0	11.7	3.85
Scott, Tanner	Bal	26	57	0	51	44	4	28	63	3	3	3	.500	0	13.2	3.92
Scrubb, Andre	Hou	26	36	0	42	36	2	28	45	1	3	2	.600	0	13.9	4.01
Selman, Sam	SF	30	51	0	43	28	2	20	55	3	3	2	.600	5	10.7	3.15
Senzatela, Antonio	Col	26	30	30	185	213	26	64	117	7	9	12	.429	0	13.8	5.04
Severino, Luis	NYY	27	18	18	97	83	10	25	114	3	7	4	.636	0	10.3	3.36
Sheffield, Justus	Sea	25	26	26	146	146	18	65	137	5	7	10	.412	0	13.3	4.44
Shoemaker, Matt	Tor	34	15	15	78	71	16	26	69	2	4	5	.444	0	11.4	4.40
Shreve, Chasen	NYM	30	55	0	61	49	9	30	75	2	4	3	.571	0	12.0	3.90
Sims, Lucas	Cin	27	49	0	64	55	11	29	77	5	4	4	.500	0	12.5	4.22
Singer, Brady	KC	24	30	30	164	157	21	56	155	8	9	9	.500	0	12.1	4.12
Skubal, Tarik	Det	24	26	26	133	110	23	54	186	6	7	8	.467	0	11.5	3.73
Slegers, Aaron	TB	28	21	0	53	60	10	14	38	3	2	4	.333	0	13.1	5.01
Smith, Caleb	Ari	29	27	27	150	130	28	67	162	6	8	8	.500	0	12.2	4.29
Smith, Josh A.	Mia	33	37	0	44	53	6	15	39	2	2	3	.400	0	14.3	4.91
Smith, Will	Atl	31	54	0	53	41	9	16	68	0	4	2	.667	0	9.7	3.37
Smyly, Drew	SF	32	17	17	90	91	21	41	111	1	4	6	.400	0	13.3	4.75
Sneed, Cy	Hou	28	38	0	45	48	6	17	42	1	3	2	.600	0	13.2	4.40
Snell, Blake	TB	28	27	27	122	99	15	46	150	1	8	6	.571	0	10.8	3.52
Soria, Joakim	Oak	37	64	0	65	56	5	22	70	2	4	3	.571	0	11.1	3.53
Soroka, Mike	Atl	23	21	21	121	118	10	32	99	5	8	6	.571	0	11.5	3.88
Soto, Gregory	Det	26	49	0	57	60	8	31	59	3	2	4	.333	0	14.8	4.90
Stammen, Craig	SD	37	69	0	73	72	9	17	65	3	4	4	.500	0	11.3	4.01
Stanek, Ryne	Mia	29	56	0	53	44	6	28	62	0	3	3	.500	0	12.2	3.88

536

2021 Pitcher Projections

Pitcher	Team	Age	G	GS	IP	H	HR	BB	SO	HB	W	L	Pct	Sv	BR/9	ERA
Staumont, Josh	KC	27	57	0	61	51	8	45	77	4	3	4	.429	0	14.8	4.50
Stephenson, Robert	Cin	28	36	0	39	32	7	19	45	1	2	2	.500	0	12.0	4.16
Strahm, Matt	SD	29	54	0	70	67	12	19	68	6	4	4	.500	0	11.8	4.25
Strasburg, Stephen	Was	32	27	27	167	144	19	47	188	8	11	7	.611	0	10.7	3.55
Stratton, Chris	Pit	30	63	0	79	88	11	33	76	1	4	5	.444	0	13.9	4.73
Stripling, Ross	Tor	31	31	21	122	133	21	33	110	2	6	7	.462	0	12.4	4.50
Stroman, Marcus	NYM	30	32	32	176	171	18	57	151	3	10	9	.526	0	11.8	4.03
Suarez, Andrew	SF	28	20	0	30	36	4	11	22	1	1	2	.333	0	14.4	5.10
Suarez, Jose	LAA	23	11	11	53	60	8	24	52	5	2	3	.400	0	15.1	5.18
Suarez, Ranger	Phi	25	23	0	32	36	3	11	24	2	2	2	.500	0	13.8	4.64
Suero, Wander	Was	29	68	0	71	66	5	26	77	5	4	3	.571	0	12.3	3.75
Sulser, Cole	Bal	31	40	0	49	49	5	24	54	1	2	3	.400	0	13.6	4.22
Suter, Brent	Mil	31	35	7	72	68	10	14	71	2	4	4	.500	0	10.5	3.72
Syndergaard, Noah	NYM	28	12	12	63	61	6	16	63	2	4	3	.571	0	11.3	3.74
Taillon, Jameson	Pit	29	16	16	88	88	9	24	79	3	5	5	.500	0	11.8	4.00
Tanaka, Masahiro	NYY	32	28	28	151	155	27	33	134	5	9	8	.529	0	11.5	4.26
Tarpley, Stephen	Mia	28	30	0	32	28	3	17	35	3	2	2	.500	0	13.5	4.23
Tate, Dillon	Bal	27	42	0	46	46	6	16	38	5	2	3	.400	0	13.1	4.50
Taylor, Josh	Bos	28	39	0	37	39	4	18	42	2	2	2	.500	0	14.4	4.50
Teheran, Julio	LAA	30	27	27	143	136	27	65	119	9	7	9	.438	0	13.2	4.88
Tepera, Ryan	ChC	33	45	0	46	38	6	21	52	3	3	2	.600	0	12.1	3.97
Thielbar, Caleb	Min	34	32	0	40	38	3	10	43	1	3	2	.600	0	11.0	3.40
Thompson, Ryan	TB	29	48	0	52	60	6	15	46	2	3	3	.500	0	13.3	4.42
Thornton, Trent	Tor	27	14	14	72	78	9	23	68	2	4	4	.500	0	12.9	4.38
Tomlin, Josh	Atl	36	48	10	104	122	22	15	79	3	5	6	.455	0	12.1	4.76
Topa, Justin	Mil	30	36	0	36	40	4	10	38	2	2	2	.500	0	13.0	4.13
Toussaint, Touki	Atl	25	11	11	58	56	7	35	66	7	3	3	.500	0	15.2	4.74
Treinen, Blake	LAD	32	69	0	67	61	6	26	66	3	5	3	.625	7	12.1	3.96
Trivino, Lou	Oak	29	55	0	62	55	5	27	63	2	4	3	.571	0	12.2	3.86
Tropeano, Nick	Pit	30	35	0	54	57	9	21	54	2	3	3	.500	0	13.3	4.67
Turley, Nik	Pit	31	48	0	43	38	4	20	43	4	2	3	.400	0	13.0	4.12
Turnbull, Spencer	Det	28	29	29	154	154	12	65	148	12	7	10	.412	0	13.5	4.24
Underwood Jr., Duane	ChC	26	45	0	47	51	6	20	48	2	2	3	.400	0	14.0	4.60
Urena, Jose	Mia	29	20	20	102	103	15	37	71	6	4	7	.364	0	12.9	4.68
Urias, Julio	LAD	24	28	28	145	120	13	53	133	4	11	6	.647	0	11.0	3.74
Urquidy, Jose	Hou	26	27	27	154	145	25	34	148	2	10	7	.588	0	10.6	3.88
Valdez, Cesar	Bal	36	55	0	59	60	7	14	46	2	3	4	.429	15	11.6	4.17
Valdez, Framber	Hou	27	27	27	165	157	16	64	182	12	11	7	.611	0	12.7	3.98
Valdez, Phillips	Bos	29	51	0	68	74	7	30	57	6	4	4	.500	0	14.6	4.83
Velasquez, Vince	Phi	29	21	21	110	108	19	47	125	7	6	6	.500	0	13.3	4.54
Vincent, Nick	Mia	34	47	0	51	51	6	12	45	3	3	3	.500	0	11.6	4.10
Voth, Austin	Was	29	25	25	121	133	22	43	109	6	6	8	.429	0	13.5	4.91
Wacha, Michael	NYM	29	24	24	125	131	21	46	116	4	6	8	.429	0	13.0	4.61
Wainwright, Adam	StL	39	28	28	175	183	22	59	144	7	9	10	.474	0	12.8	4.43
Walden, Marcus	Bos	32	53	0	50	56	4	23	43	3	3	3	.500	0	14.8	4.77
Walker, Taijuan	Tor	28	21	21	107	100	16	39	97	7	6	6	.500	0	12.3	4.30
Watson, Tony	SF	36	58	0	53	52	7	13	45	3	3	3	.500	15	11.5	4.12
Weaver, Luke	Ari	27	23	23	121	125	16	40	123	3	7	7	.500	0	12.5	4.17
Webb, Jacob	Atl	27	43	0	46	37	6	24	47	1	3	2	.600	0	12.1	4.07
Webb, Logan	SF	24	28	28	142	159	15	55	130	10	7	9	.438	0	14.2	4.69
Webb, Tyler	StL	30	62	0	62	56	7	22	56	2	4	3	.571	5	11.6	3.98
Weber, Ryan	Bos	30	39	10	97	116	12	28	67	6	5	6	.455	0	13.9	4.92
Weems, Jordan	Oak	28	32	0	35	35	3	22	41	1	2	2	.500	0	14.9	4.50
Wendelken, J.B.	Oak	28	44	0	55	47	7	22	64	1	3	3	.500	0	11.5	3.76
Wheeler, Zack	Phi	31	30	30	188	191	21	54	163	9	11	10	.524	0	12.2	4.14
Whitley, Forrest	Hou	23	24	0	134	130	23	90	186	9	7	8	.467	0	15.4	4.91
Wick, Rowan	ChC	28	51	0	50	42	4	22	55	2	3	2	.600	0	11.9	3.70
Widener, Taylor	Ari	26	23	0	40	40	6	16	45	2	2	2	.500	0	13.1	4.39
Williams, Devin	Mil	26	59	0	63	38	6	30	101	3	5	2	.714	0	10.1	2.86
Williams, Taylor	SD	29	30	0	31	30	3	15	34	2	2	2	.500	0	13.6	4.21
Williams, Trevor	Pit	29	29	29	156	162	23	54	125	8	7	10	.412	0	12.9	4.62
Wilson, Justin	NYM	33	61	0	54	46	5	28	64	2	3	3	.500	0	12.7	3.82
Winkler, Dan	ChC	31	37	0	39	33	5	21	39	3	2	2	.500	0	13.2	4.28
Wisler, Matt	Min	28	49	11	66	69	9	21	70	2	4	3	.571	0	12.5	4.16
Wittgren, Nick	Cle	30	66	0	66	65	11	19	70	4	4	4	.500	0	12.0	4.16
Wojciechowski, Asher	Bal	32	15	15	73	76	19	27	67	4	3	5	.375	0	13.2	5.18
Wood, Alex	LAD	30	13	13	62	62	8	18	58	4	4	3	.571	0	12.2	4.15
Woodford, Jake	StL	24	23	0	42	39	7	18	33	2	2	3	.400	0	12.6	4.72
Woodruff, Brandon	Mil	28	30	30	176	153	22	52	200	9	11	9	.550	0	10.9	3.64
Workman, Brandon	Phi	32	62	0	63	48	7	33	77	1	4	3	.571	0	11.7	3.68
Wright, Kyle	Atl	25	26	26	142	142	19	66	130	7	8	8	.500	0	13.6	4.63
Yarbrough, Ryan	TB	29	31	23	151	150	20	35	128	11	8	9	.471	0	11.7	4.14
Yardley, Eric	Mil	30	51	0	52	49	4	15	41	3	3	3	.500	0	11.6	3.99
Yates, Kirby	SD	34	47	0	51	38	6	16	78	4	4	2	.667	25	10.2	3.00
Young, Alex	Ari	27	20	20	106	113	16	39	92	4	5	6	.455	0	13.2	4.67
Zimmer, Kyle	KC	29	36	0	54	53	6	32	55	1	3	3	.500	0	14.3	4.67
Zimmermann, Jordan	Det	35	12	12	52	67	10	13	40	2	2	4	.333	0	14.2	5.28
Zuber, Tyler	KC	26	45	0	45	34	6	29	57	3	2	3	.400	0	13.2	4.13
Adam, Jason	ChC	29	36	0	38	28	5	20	48	3	2	2	.500	0	12.1	3.76

537

Career Targets

Bill James

Every few years we should check our systems to make sure that they actually work. It has been a few years since I have re-evaluated these systems, so I have run some studies on how well these career target systems that we use are actually working.

Starting with the "3000 hits" system. I guess I'll have to explain the system briefly. In theory, it's an extremely simple system. You just estimate (1) the number of hits per season that the player has proven that he can get (his established hit level) and (2) how many years he has remaining in his career. If the number of hits he gets per year times the number of years that he has left in his career is greater than the number of hits that he needs to get to 3,000, then he probably WILL get to 3,000. If it isn't, then he probably won't. That's really all there is to it, and it doesn't even matter very much how you estimate his Established Hit Level and his Years Remaining or how you put them together; there are different formulas that you can use and still get about the same result.

Of course, in evaluating the process that casual approach does not work; you have to use a particular method that gets a specific result, and the dragon is in the details. The Established Hit Level that we would use for post-2019 is 1 times hits in 2017, plus 2 times hits in 2018, plus 3 times hits in 2019, divided by six, so that if you had 100 hits in 2017, 150 in 2018, and 200 in 2019, your established hit level would be 166.7 (100 + 300 + 600) / 6. The "Years Remaining" is 42 – age, divided by two, so that if a player was 26 years old in 2019, he would have 8 years remaining, (42 - 26) / 2 = 8. If you were 26 years old and had an established hit level of 166.7, your expected remaining career hits would be 1,333. If you had 800 career hits now, you would need 2,200 more. You need far more hits than you are likely to get, so your chance of getting 3,000 career hits would not be good. We would then divide your expected remaining hits (1333) by your "need hits" (2200), which gives .606. If that number was 1.00, you'd be 50/50 to get there. Since you are at .606, your chance of reaching the goal would be just 11%. You CAN get there, but not at 167 hits per year for 8 years. You have to step it up to 180 hits a year and last 12 years, basically, and that is possible but it isn't likely.

My study found, I am happy to report, that that little system works REALLY well. It works really, REALLY well. It is almost impossible to imagine that it could work any better than it does, for the 3,000-hit standard, but I'll get to that in a minute. But, of course, there are always hard cases and exceptional cases, and this requires that we add a long list of "special case" rules, which are petty and annoying, but you have to do it. Among those petty and annoying special case rules are:

1) Shortened seasons. The 1994-1995 strike affects the calculation of the player's Established Hit Level not only for 1994 and 1995, but also for 1996 and 1997, since they are still within the three-year window which is used to establish his hit level. The 2020 pandemic will affect the calculations through 2022.

2) Not fully established players. Ichiro as a rookie in 2001 had 242 hits. His Established Hit Level based on 0, 0, and 242 would be 121. Obviously he has proven he can get more than 121 hits a season, so his Established Hit Level has to be overridden by a rule that says that your Established Hit Level cannot be less than 75% of your last season's hits.

3) Old guys who are still playing well. If a player is 41 years old but still playing regularly and still playing OK, you can't figure that he has only half a season left. You have to adjust his "Estimated Years Remaining" by a rule that says that, if a player has at least 400 plate appearances in a season, his Estimated Years Remaining cannot be less than 1.2.

4) Players who would show as having a greater than 100% chance of getting to 3,000 career hits. This very rarely happens; it only happens when a player is within a year or two of getting to 3,000 hits and it usually seems obvious that he is going to make it, but you can't say that a player has a 282% chance of getting 3,000 career hits, anyway. We modify the system to say that a player's chance of getting 3,000 hits cannot exceed .97 to the power (the number of years he is away from getting to 3,000).

5) Completely missed seasons. Until now, this really only applied to the World War II players, but now it will apply to some 2020 players. If a player completely skips a season, his last three seasons that he has played are treated as his last three seasons. For players who skip 2020, we will

figure their Established Hit Level (next year) based on 2018, 2019, and 2021.

So I took the data back to 1946 (which required that we study data back to 1940), and I figured every player's chance of getting 3,000 hits after every season. The question is, of those players who figure as having a 57% chance of getting 3,000 career hits, what percentage of them actually do get 3,000 hits? Of those who figure at 39%, what percentage actually do—or 85%? How well do the actual results match the expected percentages?

I invented this system, which was called "The Favorite Toy" until a couple of years ago, sometime in the mid-1970s. At that time no one had personal computers. We didn't have spreadsheets, we didn't have online batting records or sortable statistics. My ability to test the accuracy of the system was limited, because doing then what I have done here was essentially impossible. I just put together a system that seemed like it ought to work, not really expecting it to be highly accurate over a period of time. That's why I called it The Favorite Toy—to emphasize the fact that it was just something that I liked to play around with, rather than some serious thing which had been demonstrated to work. When I wrote about it in my annual books, I would always introduce it with an emphasis that there was no proof that this system actually works. At the moment that I became a nationally known figure, due to an article published in Sports Illustrated in 1981, I was photographed sitting on second base at Kauffman Stadium with the scoreboard reading "There is a 97% chance that some active player will break Lou Brock's career stolen base record." That was a prediction made because of The Favorite Toy. I can't tell you how many people told me I was wrong about that, for any of a hundred different reasons. But I wasn't wrong; I was right.

Given its primitive origins, I can now report that this system works fantastically well. There are several caveats and exceptions that I will note beginning in the next paragraph, but if you take a group of players that the system says have a 42% chance of getting 3,000 hits, 42% of them are going to get 3,000 hits. If you take a group of players who the system says have a 78% chance of getting 3,000 hits, 78% of them are going to get 3,000 hits. The system works; it works so well that, in my opinion, neither you nor I could develop a system that worked any better than that if we worked on it for a year. It is astonishingly close to perfect.

With these limitations and caveats:

1)   The system is astonishingly close to perfect in regard to the 3,000 hit goal.   With regard to home run targets—500 homers, 600 homers, 762 homers—it is not as accurate.

2)   With regard to 3,000 hits, the system loses some accuracy on estimates below 20%.   If the system says that a player has a 12% chance of getting 3,000 hits, it is actually more like 7%.

3)   For players before World War II, the system doesn't work at all.   It was a different game; a lot of guys would get around 200 hits a year in their late twenties and then retire at age 33.   There were a different set of career expectations then that cause the system to be not applicable to that era.

4)   There is a different way of looking at the "accuracy" issue which is not what I have tried to measure here, and, looking at the problem from that angle, you probably COULD develop a more accurate method. Maybe; I don't know.   I'll explain the alternative approach at the end of this article.

OK, let me get to the studies, and starting at the top of the chart.   I reviewed the predictions which would emanate from this system for every player for every season from 1946 to 2015; post-2015 data would not be useful because almost all of the players involved would still be active, so you don't know whether they are going to make it or not.   But from 1946 to 2015, and not counting predictions made for players who are still active, the system says that there were 58 players who had a 90% or greater chance of getting to 3,000 hits—not 58 DIFFERENT players, of course, but like Hank Aaron after the 1966 season (91%), Hank Aaron after the 1967 season (94%), Hank Aaron after the 1968 season (96%) and Hank Aaron after the 1969 season (99%).

Of the 58 players that our system says had a 90 to 99.999% chance of getting 3,000 hits, 53 did so, or 91%.   Our system expected it to be 54.6 (that is, the sum of the chances for all 58 players was 54.6), so our system was over-optimistic by some small number.   The five players that our system said had a

90% chance of getting 3,000 hits, but who did not do so, were Roberto Alomar (post-2002 and post-2003), Barry Bonds (post-2007) and Frank Robinson (post-1974 and 1975).

There are 20 players (1946-2015) who would be seen by our system as having an 80 to 89% chance of getting 3,000 hits, and the sum total of expected 3,000-hit-getters among them is 17.1. In fact, only 15 of them did get 3,000 hits, the five exceptions being Mel Ott, 1946, Frank Robinson, 1973, Vada Pinson, 1974, and Vladimir Guerrero and Johnny Damon, both 2011. Of course, dealing with small data sets, you are going to get nominal discrepancies between expectations and outcomes, no matter how good your system is. They only matter if the nominal discrepancies are systematic. I would regard the difference between 15 and 17.1 in this outcome as a nominal discrepancy of the type which is unavoidable.

In the years 1946 to 2015 there are 20 players who are regarded by the system as having a 70 to 79% chance of getting 3,000 hits (regarded in that way at some point in their careers.) The sum total of expected 3,000-hit players in that population is 14.9. The actual number who got 3,000 hits is 15.

The 60 to 69% cohort is the poorest performing group in the study, excepting the sub-20% groups. In the years 1946 to 2015 there are 24 players who as having a 60 to 69% chance of getting 3,000 hits, with a total expectation of 15.4 players. In fact, only 11 of them did get 3,000 hits, or 46%.

But in the 50 to 59% group, there are 28 players shown as having that range of chances, with a total expectation of 15.7 3,000 hit players. In fact, 18 of the 28 players (64%) did get 3,000 hits. If you combine the two groups to make 50 to 69%, there is an expectation that 31.1 players will get 3,000 hits. In fact, 29 players did, or 56%.

In the range of 40 to 49% there are 72 players with a sum expectation of 31.98 3,000-hit players. In fact, 33 of them did make 3,000 hits.

In the range of 30 to 39%, 150 players show with a total expectation of 50.8 3,000-hit careers. In fact, 54 of these players did get 3,000 hits, or 36%.

Between 1946 and 2015 there are 356 players who show as having a 20 to 29% chance of getting 3,000 hits, with a sum expectation for them of 84.9 successes (as always, not counting active players who are still working on it.)   In fact, 91 of these players did go on to get 3,000 hits, or 26%.

There is an issue with the accuracy of the system under 20%, and I'll detail that in a moment.   First, let me chart the accuracy of the system's predictions:

| Range | | Candidates | Expected | Actual | Actual |
From	To				Percentage
90%	99.999%	58	54.6	53	91%
80%	89%	20	17.1	15	75%
70%	79%	20	14.9	15	75%
60%	69%	24	15.4	11	46%
50%	59%	28	15.7	18	64%
40%	49%	72	32.0	33	46%
30%	39%	150	50.8	54	36%
20%	29%	356	84.9	91	26%
Total					
20%	99%	728	285.4	290	40%
10%	19%	679	94.5	59	9%
>0%	9%	537	36.8	24	4%

Below 20%, as noted, there is a problem, which is actually not difficult to diagnose.   Below 20% there are a large number of candidates shown—almost 20 a year—and some of those are legitimate, and some of them aren't. And it's really not hard to tell; you can just look at the list and say, "Eh; that guy's not going to make it."   I could easily write some formulas to sort it out and make the system more accurate in that range, and I suppose I should do that, but the formulas would be messy and complicated. I hate to mess with a system of such beautiful simplicity by hanging onto it a cluster of additional considerations which aren't really necessary through 80% of the system's range.

The normal progression toward 3,000 hits is that a player first appears on the chart at somewhere around 5 to 10%, as a young player, and then this just climbs and climbs and climbs; he goes from 7% to 9, from 9% to 12, from 12% to 13, to 16%, 18%, 21%, 26%, 28%, 34%, and then finally, 10 to 13 years into his career, he has a good year at an age when he might be expected to be in decline, and his chances jump by 20 points in a year.

Except, of course, that most players DON'T make it. Out of every four players who have a 25% chance to get 3,000 hits, one will keep increasing his chances until he gets there, and the other three will break down somewhere and head suddenly back toward zero.

The players who show with a 5 to 20% chance of getting 3,000 hits are of three groups: young players just passing through that range, established players who have stalled out in that area, and veteran players who are collapsing back through that range.   You know, intuitively, which ones have a legitimate chance, and it wouldn't REALLY be hard to make a set of formulas that would put that knowledge into the system. It's just a matter of doing it, steeling myself to mess with the essential simplicity of the old tool. I'm like an old gardener facing the fact that he needs to replace that hoe he has been using for the last 45 years.

With respect to the Home Run goals, now, the system is not as accurate, and here we have to talk about steroids or, if you prefer, PEDs. I stress that I am not trying to say that my simple little system would work except for the steroid era; it doesn't have a high degree of historical accuracy.   That's all; that's a fact, Jack. However, these two things are also facts:

1)   That covering the entire spectrum of 1946 to 2015, the system gives estimates which are significantly too high, so that the number of players who have reached the goal is significantly less than the number that we would have expected, but:

2)   All of the discrepancy—and more—is in the steroid era. If you excluded the projections from the steroid era, the system would actually be too conservative in its estimates, not too liberal. Other than the steroid era, the number of players who have gotten to 500 Home Runs has actually exceeded the number predicted by our method.

From 1946 to 2015 there have been exactly 100 players whose numbers say, by our system, that they have a 90% chance or more to hit 500 career homers. The sum of the expectations for that group is 94.6 500-homer players. The actual number who have hit 500 is 80.

However, in the years 1946 to 1997, there were 45 players who were estimated at 90 to 99.99%, and 44 of those did hit 500 home runs. The only one who did not was Dave Kingman.

From 1998 to 2015, however, there have been 55 players who have shown as 90% certain to hit 500 home runs, 36 of whom did, but 19 of whom did not. The ones who showed a 90% chance of hitting 500 home runs, but did not, were Jose Canseco (4 times, 1998-1999-2000-2001), Fred McGriff (4 times), Carlos Delgado (4 times), Adam Dunn (3 times), Jeff Bagwell (2 times), and Juan Gonzalez and Vladimir Guerrero (once each). I am not saying that all of those were steroid users, but some of them were. Steroids gave players "phony power", which (a) went away once the steroids were banned, but also (b) contributed in some cases—some PEDs—to injuries.

Our system shows 35 players who had an 80% chance to hit 500 homers, of whom only 22 did. Of the 13 who did not, however, 11 were from the steroid era. The only players who showed an 80% chance to hit 500 homers and did not, before 1996, were Duke Snider and Ralph Kiner, both of whom had back problems. We have 23 players who show as having a 70 to 79% chance at 500 homers, of whom only 8 made it. But of the 15 who did not, ten were steroid-era players.

This chart summarizes the data for our system's estimates of players with a chance to hit 500 homers, in the same form used before:

Range		Candidates	Expected	Actual	Actual Percentage
From	To				
90%	99.999%	100	95.0	80	80%
80%	89%	35	30.1	22	63%
70%	79%	23	17.5	8	35%
60%	69%	32	20.7	23	72%
50%	59%	54	29.7	19	35%
40%	49%	71	31.6	22	31%
30%	39%	133	46.1	44	33%
20%	29%	165	40.4	30	18%
10%	19%	273	39.7	24	9%
0%	9%	450	20.3	21	5%
Total		1336	371	293	22%

Overall, there is a 21% shortfall in actual versus expected results.

We could, then, re-assure you that our system has worked except for the PED era, so it will probably work going forward, but unfortunately, we can't. There are two reasons that we can't. One is that I lack confidence that PEDs are truly gone from the game at this time—speaking for myself, Bill James, not for anyone else. Whether you believe it or not, PEDs were truly under control from 2006 until about 2012. I see more and more signs now that people are figuring out how to beat the system. I could be wrong; let's hope that I am.

But even if that is not true, the problem is not as simple as PEDs. The game has changed. Up until 1995, almost everyone who hit 30 to 40 home runs on a regular basis was a really good player, and could expect to have a good long career because he was a really good player. Now, many of the people who hit 30 or 30+ home runs every year are not really good players. They are home-run hitting specialists, like Dave Kingman and Adam Dunn.

A specialist has a different career profile than an all-around player. Rickey Henderson and Tim Raines were great players with a mix of skills. Vince Coleman was a base stealing specialist. It's a different thing; it's got a different profile.

This is hard to explain, but the system we are using implicitly assumes that your ability in the specific area being measured is representative of your overall ability. If you hit 40 homers a year but have huge holes in your game, that's a different thing. The way that baseball is played today, the system may continue to overestimate players' chances to hit 500 or 600 home runs—or it may not; we really don't know. Until we know for sure whether it does or doesn't, there is not a lot we can do.

But we did do something. In this year's projection system, and for future years, we have changed the "Years Remaining" for home runs from (42 - Age) / 2 to (41 - Age) / 2. In other words, a 28-year hitter is assumed to have SEVEN years remaining in which to continue to collect hits, but only SIX AND A HALF years remaining in which to hit however many home runs he needs to hit.

We made this change in response to this research, but also, it just makes sense, anyway. As a player ages, the percentage of his hits which are home runs declines. I knew that anyway, but I just did a new study (details not reported) to confirm that this is true.   But that means that a player at any age post-peak has, in effect, more seasons of "hits remaining" than of "home runs remaining."   It just makes sense to recognize this in making the estimates.

Well, I promised to tell you at the end of the article how the system could be better than it is, in a way that this approach doesn't measure.   This study shows that when our system estimates that a player has a 35% chance to get 3,000 career hits, his chance of getting 3,000 career hits is actually 35%.   Over the years 1946 to 2015 there have been nine players who came in at 35%, four of whom did make it, and five of whom did not.   Four out of nine is pretty close to 35%, so the system is pretty good, in that sense.

Those nine players were Henry Aaron, 1958, Tony Gwynn, 1994, Rafael Palmeiro, 1999, and Alex Rodriguez, 2001, all of whom DID make 3,000 hits, and Curt Flood, 1969, Kirby Puckett, 1988, Ken Griffey Jr., 2000, Johnny Damon, 2012, and Michael Young, 2012, who did not.   (It is worth directing your attention to the fact that, at the moment he refused to report to Philadelphia, choosing instead to challenge the reserve clause, Curt Flood had a 35% chance to finish with 3,000 career hits.   That's what he gave up.   Flood was one year older than his teammate, the late Lou Brock, and was 446 career hits ahead of him at that time.   Brock did get to 3,000 hits.)   Anyway, the system is not bad, but suppose that our prediction system had said that Aaron, Gwynn, Palmeiro and A-Rod WOULD get to 3,000 hits, 100%, and that Flood, Puckett, Griffey, Damon and Young would NOT get to 3,000 hits, 0% chance.   That would be more accurate, wouldn't it?

So if our system said that Aaron, Gwynn, Palmeiro and A-Rod had higher numbers, and the other five had lower numbers, the system would, in fact, be more accurate, although it would not necessarily measure as being any more accurate in this type of analysis.   It would be more accurate because the gross error of all of the predictions would be lower, which is a different way to measure accuracy.

Thanks for reading, and thank you all for supporting my research over these last 45 years.

Bill James

Career Targets

762 Home Runs
% chance to break record

Trout, Mike	12%
Acuna Jr., Ronald	1%

2,298 RBI
% chance to break record

Freeman, Freddie	1%

2,296 Runs Scored
% chance to break record

Betts, Mookie	10%
Trout, Mike	6%
Acuna Jr., Ronald	6%
Soto, Juan	1%
Harper, Bryce	< 1%

4,257 Hits
% chance to break record

900 Home Runs
% chance to reach milestone

2,000 RBI
% chance to reach milestone

Pujols, Albert	done
Freeman, Freddie	15%
Trout, Mike	11%
Harper, Bryce	8%
Cabrera, Miguel	8%
Machado, Manny	7%
Devers, Rafael	7%
Soto, Juan	5%
Arenado, Nolan	3%
Bogaerts, Xander	1%

6,857 Total Bases
% chance to break record

Trout, Mike	1%
Machado, Manny	< 1%

4,000 Hits
% chance to reach milestone

800 Home Runs
% chance to reach milestone

Trout, Mike	7%

600 Home Runs
% chance to reach milestone

Pujols, Albert	done
Trout, Mike	33%
Machado, Manny	18%
Harper, Bryce	16%
Suarez, Eugenio	14%
Bellinger, Cody	12%
Acuna Jr., Ronald	10%
Alonso, Pete	7%
Soto, Juan	7%
Arenado, Nolan	6%

793 Doubles
% chance to break record

Freeman, Freddie	11%
Castellanos, Nick	8%
Devers, Rafael	8%
Bogaerts, Xander	4%
Lindor, Francisco	2%

Most Likely No-Hitter
% chance to reach milestone

Bieber, Shane	32%
Glasnow, Tyler	23%
deGrom, Jacob	20%
Burnes, Corbin	18%
Giolito, Lucas	17%
Lamet, Dinelson	17%
Bauer, Trevor	15%
Nola, Aaron	14%
Woodruff, Brandon	11%
Cole, Gerrit	10%

700 Home Runs
% chance to reach milestone

Trout, Mike	22%
Pujols, Albert	13%
Acuna Jr., Ronald	6%
Bellinger, Cody	5%
Machado, Manny	4%
Harper, Bryce	2%
Suarez, Eugenio	2%
Soto, Juan	< 1%

500 Home Runs
% chance to reach milestone

Pujols, Albert	done
Cabrera, Miguel	87%
Trout, Mike	48%
Encarnacion, Edwin	32%
Machado, Manny	29%
Harper, Bryce	29%
Suarez, Eugenio	28%
Arenado, Nolan	27%
Yelich, Christian	21%
Freeman, Freddie	21%

1,000 Stolen Bases
% chance to reach milestone

3,000 Hits

% chance to reach milestone

Pujols, Albert	done
Cabrera, Miguel	83%
Freeman, Freddie	26%
Cano, Robinson	26%
Machado, Manny	19%
Bogaerts, Xander	16%
Betts, Mookie	16%
Lindor, Francisco	14%
Trout, Mike	12%
Altuve, Jose	11%
Markakis, Nick	10%
LeMahieu, DJ	9%
Arenado, Nolan	9%
Devers, Rafael	8%
Hosmer, Eric	7%
Turner, Trea	7%
Castellanos, Nick	7%
Harper, Bryce	7%
Castro, Starlin	6%
Story, Trevor	6%
Albies, Ozzie	6%
Yelich, Christian	6%
Bellinger, Cody	5%
Soto, Juan	5%
Marte, Ketel	3%
Acuna Jr., Ronald	3%
Segura, Jean	3%
Anderson, Tim	2%
Ozuna, Marcell	2%
Ramirez, Jose	< 1%

The 300-Win Candidates

Mark Simon

As new generations of baseball fans come along, it's worthwhile to teach them the evolution of the game, understanding how what preceded them led to what they see now. And when you do so, you should teach them about the evolution of the 300-game winner.

There was a time when pitchers pitched every day, then every other day, then every fourth day, to now every fifth day. There was a time when pitchers regularly went nine innings, then seven, and now five is the new seven in many instances.

It's certainly possible that someone will win 300 games in the future, but we have to be realistic about the current group of baseball pitchers.

Justin Verlander entered 2020 with better than a 50-50 shot (pre-COVID). Now he'll likely be 39 before he pitches another regular season game, in need of 74 wins. Three more 20-win seasons wouldn't get him there.

Zack Greinke needs 92 wins heading into his age-37 season. Five seasons of 18 wins (his win total from 2019) leaves him two wins shy of 300.

Max Scherzer enters his age-36 season with 175 wins. That means six 20-win seasons wouldn't cut it.

Clayton Kershaw looked like vintage Kershaw for 10 starts in 2020, but it was only 10 starts. Kershaw has the same number of wins as Scherzer and is three years younger. But he hasn't made more than 27 starts in a season since 2015, and when you're chasing 300, you need to max out on win opportunities.

Kershaw could average 15 wins a season for eight seasons and still not hit that milestone. His chance of doing this is not even 1% per our measurements (Jon Lester, with 193 wins, is at 1%. He'll turn 37 in January).

If you're looking at someone in the 30-or-younger crowd, I suppose there's Gerrit Cole. But with 101 wins, he's ten 20-win seasons away. From the 25-and-youngers, there's Shane Bieber, who looked like the best Indians pitcher this side of Bob Feller in 2020. But Bieber's still got 266 wins to go. In other words, he's got to win the same number of games that Feller did in his entire career to get there.

Pitchers on Course For 300 Wins

Name	2020 Age	R/L	W	L	EWL	Momentum	Chance
Greinke, Zack	36	R	208	126	13.4	.768	16%
Scherzer, Max	35	R	175	93	14.1	.778	11%
Lester, Jon	36	L	193	111	11.2	.602	1%

EWL: Established Win Level

Milestone Whiffs

Though 300 wins is not within reach, 3,000 strikeouts is very much a reachable milestone. Max Scherzer could get there next season. He's at 2,784. Zack Greinke looks to be two years away at 2,689.

Cole Hamels is a question mark after missing almost all of 2020 due to injury. He's at 2,560. Clayton Kershaw is two to three years away at 2,526. Félix Hernández is at 2,524, but doesn't look to be a serious contender to reach 3,000.

Baseball Glossary

% Inherited Scored
The percentage of inherited baserunners a relief pitcher allows to score.

% Pitches Taken
The percentage of pitches that a batter does not swing at out of the total number of pitches thrown to him.

1st Batter Average
The Batting Average that a relief pitcher allows to the first batter he faces when he enters a game.

1st Batter OBP
The On-Base Percentage that a relief pitcher allows to the first batter he faces when he enters a game.

1st to 3rd (Baserunning)
"Moved" is the number of times a runner goes from 1st base to 3rd base on a SINGLE. "Chances" are the number of times a runner is on 1st base and a batter is credited with a SINGLE.

1st to Home (Baserunning)
"Moved" is the number of times a runner goes from 1st base to home on a DOUBLE. "Chances" are the number of times a runner is on 1st base and a batter is credited with a DOUBLE.

2nd to Home (Baserunning)
"Moved" is the number of times a runner goes from 2nd base to home on a SINGLE. "Chances" are the number of times a runner is on 2nd base and a batter is credited with a SINGLE.

Active Career Batting Leaders
A list of batting leaders among active (appearing in the most recent season) players. An active player is eligible when he meets the minimum requirements for the following categories:

> 1,000 At Bats—Batting Average, On-Base Percentage, Slugging Average, At
>   Bats Per HR, At Bats Per GDP, At Bats Per RBI, Strikeout-to-Walk Ratio
> 100 Stolen Base Attempts—Stolen Base Success Percentage

Active Career Pitching Leaders
A list of pitching leaders among active (appearing in the most recent season) players. An active player is eligible when he meets the minimum requirements for the following categories:

> 750 Innings Pitched—Earned Run Average, Opponent Batting Average, all "Per
>   9 Innings" categories, Strikeout-to-Walk Ratio
> 250 Games Started—Complete Game Frequency
> 100 Decisions—Win-Loss Percentage

ART
See PART System

BA w/ RISP
The Batting Average allowed by a pitcher while pitching with runners in scoring position.

Base Taken
A player is credited with a Base Taken whenever he moves up a base on a Wild Pitch, Passed Ball, Balk, Sacrifice Fly, or Defensive Indifference.

Batting Average
Hits divided by at bats.

Batting Average on Balls in Play (BABIP)
Hits in play divided by balls in play. Home runs are not counted as balls in play.

Batting Average Plus Slugging (BPS)
Batting Average plus Slugging Average. Used in Leaderboards on out-of-zone pitches (OutZ).

Blown Save
When a relief pitcher enters a game in a Save Situation (see definition for Save Situation) and allows the other team to score the tying or go-ahead run.

Bomb (Intentional Walk)
An Intentional Walk is counted as a "Bomb" if
1. The next batter, after the IBB, does not ground into a double play, and
2. Multiple runs are scored in the inning, after the intentional walk.

BR Gain (Baserunning)
BR Gain (or Loss if a negative number) is the total of all the types of extra baserunning advances minus the (triple) penalty for all the BR Outs compared with what would be expected based on the MLB averages.

BR Outs (Baserunning)
BR Outs include the sum of Outs Advancing, Doubled Offs, and when a runner is tagged out on the bases when another runner moves up on a Wild Pitch, Passed Ball, or scores on a Sacrifice Fly.

BS Win
A Blown Save Win is a "win" credited to a reliever who has blown a save opportunity.

Career Targets
This method, also called the Favorite Toy, is a way to estimate the probability that a player will achieve a specific career goal. In this example, 3,000 hits will be used. The four components of the formula are:

1. Needed Hits. This is the number of Hits (or any statistic) that a player needs to reach a desired goal.

2. Years Remaining. This is the estimated number of years remaining in the player's career. It is determined using the player's age (on June 30th of the previous year; after a given season ends, use the season when making the calculation). The formula is (42 - age) divided by two. This means a player who is 20 years old will have 11 remaining seasons, a player who is 25 years old will have 8.5 remaining seasons and a player who is 35 years old will have 3.5 remaining seasons. If the player is a catcher, then multiply his remaining seasons by .7. The only stipulation is that years remaining must always be greater than or equal to 1.5.

3. Established Hit Level. The Established Hit Level is a weighted average of the player's hits over the past three seasons. To calculate the Established Hit Level after a given season is complete, add (Hits from two years ago), (Hits from last year multiplied by two), and (Hits from this year multiplied by three), then divide by six. If the Established Hit Level is less than 75% of the most recent performance, then the Established Hit Level is equal to .75 times the most recent performance.

4. Projected Remaining Hits. This is calculated by multiplying Years Remaining by the Established Hit Level.

The probability of achieving the specified goal is found by dividing Projected Remaining Hits by Needed Hits, then subtracting .5. The maximum that any player has of achieving a goal is .85 raised to the power of (Need Hits / Established Hit Level). This prevents the possibility of a player reaching a goal from being higher than 100 percent, which is impossible.

Catcher Pickoffs (CPO, CPkof)
The number of baserunners throw out when a catcher throws to a base with a leading baserunner, and the runner is tagged out attempting to return to the base. Catcher pickoffs are not an official statistic and are not counted toward Caught Stealing totals.

Catcher's ERA
The ERA for a catcher is equal to the ERA of pitchers pitching while the catcher is playing behind the plate. It is calculated exactly like ERA for pitchers. Take the number of earned runs allowed while the catcher is playing, multiply it by 9 and then divide it by the total number of defensive innings that the catcher was behind the plate.

Cheap Win
A starting pitcher who wins the game with a game score under 50 gets credit for a cheap win. See Game Score.

Clean Outing
A Clean Outing is a game in which the reliever is not charged with a run (earned or otherwise) AND does not allow an inherited runner to score.

Cleanup Slugging Average
The Slugging Average of a batter when he bats in the cleanup spot, or fourth, in the batting order.

Close and Late
A situation in a game that is very similar to a Save Situation. The following requirements are necessary for a Close and Late game:
1. The game is in the seventh inning or later AND
2. The batting team is either leading by one run or tied OR
3. The tying run is on base, at bat, or on deck.

Component ERA (ERC)
A statistic that estimates what a pitcher's ERA should have been, based on his pitching performance. The ERC formula is calculated as follows:

1. Subtract the pitcher's Home Runs Allowed from his Hits Allowed.

2. Multiply Step 1 by 1.255.
3. Multiply his Home Runs Allowed by four.
4. Add Steps 2 and 3 together.
5. Multiply Step 4 by .89.
6. Add his Walks and Hit Batsmen.
7. Multiply Step 6 by .475.
8. Add Steps 5 and 7 together.

This yields the pitcher's total base estimate (PTB), which is:

$$PTB = 0.89 \times (1.255 \times (H - HR) + 4 \times HR) + 0.475 \times (BB + HB)$$

For those pitchers for whom there is intentional walk data, use this formula instead:

$$PTB = 0.89 \times (1.255 \times (H - HR) + 4 \times HR) + 0.56 \times (BB + HB - IBB)$$

9. Add Hits and Walks and Hit Batsmen.
10. Multiply Step 9 by PTB.
11. Divide Step 10 by Batters Facing Pitcher. If BFP data is unavailable, approximate it by multiplying Innings Pitched by 2.9, then adding Step 9.
12. Multiply Step 11 by 9.
13. Divide Step 12 by Innings Pitched.
14. Subtract .56 from Step 13.

This is the pitcher's ERC, which is:

$$\frac{(H + BB + HB) \times PTB}{BFP \times IP} \times 9 - 0.56$$

If the result after Step 13 is less than 2.24, adjust the formula as follows:

$$\frac{(H + BB + HB) \times PTB}{BFP \times IP} \times 9 \times 0.75$$

Consecutive Days
A count of how many times the pitcher was used after having pitched on the previous day or (in a few cases) in an earlier game on the same day.

Defensive Misplay
Any play which is not an error (or a passed ball) on which the fielder surrenders a base advance or the opportunity to make an out when a better play or a different play would have or might have gotten the out or prevented the advancement.

Defensive Runs Saved
Defensive Runs Saved (Runs Saved, for short) is the innovative metric introduced by John Dewan in *The Fielding Bible—Volume II* and modified in each subsequent volume. The Runs Saved value indicates how many runs a player saved or cost his team in the field compared to the average player at his position. A player of zero Runs Saved is about average; a positive number of runs saved indicates above-average

556

defense, below-average fielders post negative Runs Saved totals. There are eight components of Runs Saved:

PART Runs Saved (all positions; outfielders or players prior to 2013 use the Range and Positioning System)
Range and Positioning Runs Saved (non-catchers prior to 2013 and outfielders from 2013 forward.)
Adjusted Earned Runs Saved (Catchers)
Strike Zone Runs Saved (Catchers)
Stolen Base Runs Saved (Catchers, Pitchers)
Bunt Runs Saved (Corner Infielders, Pitchers, Catchers)
Double Play Runs Saved (Infielders)
Outfield Arm Runs Saved (Outfielders)
Good Play/Misplay Runs Saved (All Positions)

Double Play %

Successful Double Plays divided by the number of Double Play opportunities. This statistic includes both the fielder who started the play and the pivot man.

Double Play Opportunity

A fielder is considered to have a double play opportunity when a ground ball is hit with a runner on first base and less than 2 outs and that fielder is involved in the play. This is used to calculate Double Play % and Pivot %.

Doubled Off

A runner is Doubled Off when he is out for failing to get back to his base before he, or the base, is tagged after a ball hit in the air is caught.

Early Entry

A count of the number of times the reliever entered the game in the sixth inning or earlier.

Earned Run Average

The number of earned runs that a pitcher surrenders per nine innings that he pitches. It is calculated by multiplying the total earned runs allowed by nine and dividing by the total number of innings pitched.

Easy Save

This label is used to separate Saves by difficulty level (Easy or Tough). A Save is considered Easy if the relief pitcher enters the game, pitches one inning or less, and the first batter he faces does not at least represent the tying run.

Fielding Percentage

The percentage of plays a player makes in the field without making an error out of his total opportunities. Calculated by dividing (Putouts plus Assists) by (Putouts plus Assists plus Errors).

Games Finished

The relief pitcher who is in the game for each team when the game ends is credited with a Game Finished.

Game Score (Hitters)

To determine a hitter's Game Score:

Start with 15.

Add 10 times his Runs Created in the game (Runs Created for a single game is described in this Glossary).

Add 5 times his Runs Scored.

Add 5 times his RBI.

Game Score (Pitchers)

To determine the starting pitcher's Game Score:

Start with 50.

Add 1 point for each out recorded by the starting pitcher.

Add 2 points for each inning the pitcher completes after the fourth inning.

Add 1 point for each strikeout.

Subtract 2 points for each hit allowed.

Subtract 4 points for each earned run allowed.

Subtract 2 points for an unearned run.

Subtract 1 point for each walk.

GDP

Grounded into Double Play.

GDP Opportunity

This is a situation where the batter has a chance to ground into a double play. It occurs with at least a runner on first base and less than two outs.

Good Fielding Play

A Good Fielding Play is a play that is made when it is not clear whether or not the play can be made. It is a play that is made when, had the play not been made, no one would have faulted the fielder for not making it.

Ground / Fly Ratio (Grd/Fly, GB/FB)

Calculated for both batters and pitchers. For batters, it is the number of groundballs hit divided by the number of flyballs hit. For pitchers, it is exactly the same but uses the number of groundballs and flyballs allowed. Every fair batted ball is included except for bunts and line drives.

Hold

A relief pitcher is given a Hold anytime he enters the game in a Save Situation (see definition for Save Situation), records one out or more, and exits the game without giving up the lead. If the pitcher finishes the game, then he will only earn credit for a Save. He cannot receive credit for both a Hold and a Save.

Holds Adjusted Save Percentage (same as Save/Hold Percentage)

Holds plus Saves divided by Holds plus Saves Opportunities.

Inherited Runner

Any runner who was on base at the time a relief pitcher enters the game.

Isolated Power

Slugging Average minus Batting Average.

K/BB Ratio
Strikeouts divided by Walks.

Leadoff On-Base Percentage
The On-Base Percentage of a batter when he bats leadoff, or first, in the batting order.

Leverage Index
Leverage is the amount of swing in the possible change in win probability, compared to the average swing in all situations. The average swing value, by definition, is indexed to 1.00.

If the score of the game is 12-0 or 14-1 the possible changes in win probability will be very close to negligible. Whether the pitcher gives up a home run or gets a double play ball doesn't really change the outcome of the game. There won't be much swing in either direction for the probability of the win. But in the late innings of a close game, the change in win probability among the various events will have rather wild swings. With a runner on first, two outs, down by one, and in the bottom of the ninth, the game can hinge on one swing of the bat. A home run and an out will both end the game, but with different outcomes for the teams involved. The Leverage Index we use (LI) was developed at the website Tangotiger.net, and compiled at the website FanGraphs.com.

Long Outing
A Long Outing is one in which the starting pitcher throws more than 110 pitches. Prior to 2002, we used 120 pitches as the cutoff in the Manager's Record section.

Long Save
A Long Save is when the pitcher credited with a save pitches more than one inning.

Manufactured Runs
1. A run that scores without a hit, or a run on which the only hit(s) is/are infield hits, is always scored as a Manufactured Run.
2. A run which is driven in by a home run is never scored a Manufactured Run, under any circumstance.
3. A run which is driven in by a double or a triple is scored as a Manufactured Run only if *two* of the four bases result from advancing on one of these four acts: a sacrifice bunt, a stolen base, a hit and run, or a bunt single.
4. Otherwise, a run is considered to be a Manufactured Run if two of the four bases do not result from the runner being forced along by a walk, a hit batsman, or a safe hit reaching the outfield.
5. A forceout or fielder's choice which does not improve the position of the base runners should not be counted as contributing toward a Manufactured Run. Advancing on a forceout or a fielder's choice DOES count toward a manufactured run, if the play is one which improves the position of the baserunners.
6. A base "gained" on a double play does not count as a contribution to a Manufactured Run. A run scored on a double play is a Manufactured Run only if two of the OTHER bases are not attributable to forced advancement.

Net Gain
Net Gain is a statistic that measures baserunning production that includes all baserunning advancements on both hits and outs (BR Gain) and stolen bases (SB Gain).

Not Good Outcome (Intentional Walk)

A Not Good Outcome (NG) for an Intentional Walk occurs when one run scored in the inning after the intentional walk (and the next batter after the intentional walk did not ground into a double play).

Offensive Winning Percentage (OWP)

A player's Offensive Winning Percentage is the winning percentage of a hypothetical team which has an offense consisting of nine of that player, and pitching and defense which is average for the player's league. It is calculated by taking the square of RC/27 (see the definition for Runs Created per 27 Outs), dividing it by the sum of the square of RC/27 and the square of the average runs scored per game in the league.

On-Base Percentage

(Hits plus Walks plus Hit by Pitcher) divided by (At Bats plus Walks plus Hit by Pitcher plus Sacrifice Flies).

$$\frac{H + BB + HBP}{AB + BB + HBP + SF}$$

On-Base Plus Slugging (OPS)

On-Base Percentage plus Slugging Average

$$\frac{H + BB + HBP}{AB + BB + HBP + SF} + \frac{TB}{AB}$$

Opponent Batting Average

Hits Allowed divided by at-bats against a pitcher.

Opposition OPS

The OPS of the hitters facing the pitcher.

Out Advancing

A runner is out advancing when he is tagged out attempting to score from 2nd base on a single or from 1st base on a double, or attempting to go from 1st base to 3rd base on a single.

OutZ

Pitches outside the strike zone

Park Index

To calculate the park index for home runs in a given ballpark, we take the total home runs of both the home team and its opponents at the ballpark and compare it to the total home runs of the home team and its opponents in other games. We then divide each of those totals by the at-bats in the equivalent situations, so that if there are more at-bats in either situation, the index is not skewed. The result is then multiplied by 100 to yield the familiar form.

The park indices for doubles, triples, walks, strikeouts and home runs by lefties and righties are determined like home runs above—relative to at-bats. Indices of at-bats, runs, hits, errors and infield fielding errors (E-Infield) are calculated relative to games. The three batting average indices are calculated as is, since these are already relative to at-bats.

PART System (Positioning, Airballs, Range, and Throwing)
The PART System, introduced in *The Bill James Handbook 2020* and formalized in *The Fielding Bible–Volume V*, is a method for evaluating defensive play on batted balls, and is used in Defensive Runs Saved for infielders from 2013 forward.

The core of the system is similar to the Range and Positioning System, which is still used for DRS prior to 2013 and for outfielders from 2013 forward, in that it evaluates players through a system of credits and debits compared to the average fielder against similar batted balls.

The PART System evaluates players' positioning, range, and throwing based on how frequently they make plays compared to the average player as measured from different points in the play: before considering positioning, after considering positioning, and after the ball was fielded. Positioning Runs Saved, while measured in PART Runs Saved, is considered to be the team's responsibility, and is only included for the purposes of team totals. Individual infielder DRS consists of Air, Range and Throwing Runs Saved, along with the other components of DRS.

PCS (Pitchers' Caught Stealing)
The number of runners officially scored as Caught Stealing where the pitcher initiated the play. PCS plays are often referred to as pickoffs, but differ when the runner breaks towards the next base instead of returning to the base he was on. Pickoffs, which aren't an official statistic, involve the pitcher throwing to the base the runner was leading from, and the runner is out trying to return there.

Pitcher Pickoffs (PPO, PPkof)
The number of baserunners thrown out when a pitcher throws to a base with a leading baserunner, and the runner is tagged out attempting to return to the base. PPO is not an official statistic and does not count toward Caught Stealing totals.

Pivot %
Successful Double Plays turned by pivot man divided by the number of Double Play opportunities with that pivot man involved.

Plate Appearances
At Bats plus Total Walks plus Hit By Pitches plus Sacrifice Hits plus Sacrifice Flies plus Times Reached on Defensive Interference.

Platoon Advantage %
Platoon Advantage % is the percentage of players in the starting lineup who have the platoon advantage (i.e. bats right against a left-handed pitcher or bats left against a right-hander) against the starting pitcher; e.g. if the opposing starting pitcher is right handed and the batting team has six left-handed batters in its lineup, the platoon advantage for that game would be 67%.

Power/Speed Number
A single number that reflects a combination of power and speed. To calculate the Power/Speed Number, multiply Home Runs by Stolen Bases by two, and divide by the sum of Home Runs and Stolen Bases.

$$\frac{2 \times HR \times SB}{HR + SB}$$

Productive Out

An out made by the batter which advances at least one runner. See also Unproductive Out.

Quality Start

A game where the starting pitcher pitches for at least six innings and allows no more than three earned runs.

Quality Start Percentage

Quality Starts divided by Games Started (see the definition for Quality Start).

Quick Hooks

Used in the Manager's Record. For Quick Hooks and Slow Hooks a score is calculated for each game that is the sum of the number of Pitches plus 10 times the number of Runs Allowed. The bottom 25% of scores in the league are considered to be Quick Hooks.

Range and Positioning System

Formerly called the Plus/Minus System, the Range and Positioning System is a method for evaluating defensive play on batted balls, and is used in Defensive Runs Saved for non-catchers prior to 2013 and outfielders from 2013 forward.

It is made possible by a game scoring system in which each batted ball is rated for type (line drive, grounder, etc.), velocity within its type (based on hang time for flyballs and time to the infielder or through the infield on groundballs), and location on the field.

A player gets credit (a "plus" number) if he makes a play that at least one other player at his position missed during the season and he loses credit (a "minus" number") if he misses a play that at least one player made. The size of the credits are proportional to the percentage of times all players make the play.

All plays for each player at his position are summed to get his total Plays Saved for the season. A total of zero would be average and any other number would approximate how many plays more or less the player made than the average player at the position for the number of chances the player had to field batted balls.

Range Factor

The number of Successful Chances (Putouts plus Assists) times nine divided by the number of Defensive Innings Played.

RBI %

The percentage of all potential runs driven in by a certain hitter. Simply put, it's RBIs divided by RBI Opportunities. RBI Opportunities are defined as RBI plus a weighted total of baserunners who the hitter failed to drive in. Any plays where the batter reached safely and no outs were recorded aren't counted as missed opportunities. They are defined like so:

    1.00 for each runner on third base with less than 2 outs, plus
    .70 for each runner on third base with 2 outs, plus
    .70 for each runner on second base, plus
    .40 for each runner on first base, plus
    .10 for each bases-empty plate appearance.

Regular Saves

Any save which does not meet the definition either of an Easy Save or a Tough Save is a "Regular" Save.

R/P
See Range and Positioning System

Run Support Per 9 IP
The total number of runs scored by a pitcher's team while he is in the game multiplied by nine and divided by total Innings Pitched.

Runs Created
"Runs Created" is an estimate of the number of a team's runs which are created by each individual hitter. There are many different formulas for estimating runs created. . .did you want the one that involves swinging a dead cat in the cemetery under a full moon? Yeah, I don't blame you. . .worm-eaten persimmons are so hard to find in the modern world.

This is the one we use now; it is complicated enough. First, there is an "A" Factor in the formula, a "B" Factor, and a "C" factor. The "A" Factor, which represents the number of times the hitter is on base, is Hits, Plus Walks, Plus Hit Batsmen, Minus Caught Stealing, Minus Grounded Into Double Play. The "B" Factor, which represents the hitter's ability to advance other runners, is 1.125 times the player's Singles, plus 1.69 times his Doubles, plus 3.02 times his Triples, plus 3.73 times his Home Runs, plus .29 times his Walks and Hit Batsmen, not counting intentional walks, plus .492 times Sacrifice Hits, Sacrifice Flies and Stolen Bases, minus .04 times Strikeouts. The "C" Factor, which represents opportunities, is At Bats, Plus Walks, Plus Hit By Pitch, Plus Sacrifice Hits, Plus Sacrifice Flies.

Having made these initial calculations of the A, B and C factors, we then change the "A" factor to "A plus 2.4 times C".

We change the "B" factor to "B plus 3 times C".

We change the "C" factor to "9 times C".

Multiply A times B, divide by the new C ("9 times C"), and subtract .90 times by the original C.

This is our first, temporary estimate of the player's runs created. What we have done here is to ask these questions:

1. How many runs would a team probably score that consisted of eight "ordinary" type of hitters, plus this particular hitter?
2. How many of those runs would be created by the eight ordinary type of hitters?
3. What is the difference and thus, how many runs did our player create?

To estimate this, we have placed our player in the context of eight hitters with a .300 on base percentage (2.4 divided by 8) and a .375 advancement percentage (3 divided by 8). For each trip through the batting order, the eight ordinary-type hitters would produce 9/10 of a run (2.4 times 3, divided by 8). The "9" in the denominator is eight ordinary hitters plus our man. The "-.9" being subtracted at the end is the runs created by the "ordinary" hitters. In essence, we have placed the hitter in a neutral solution, measured the neutral solution without our hitter, measured it with our hitter, and then estimated the contribution of this hitter as being the difference between the two.

We're not quite done. After that, we adjust the player's runs created estimate for his performance in two "run-sensitive" situations. Suppose that a player whose overall batting average is .250, has batted 100 times with runners in scoring position, and has gone 30-for-100. That's five hits better than expected, 30 hits where we would have expected 25. His team will score an extra five runs because he has done that, and so we increase the player's runs created estimate by five runs. If the player has hit poorly with runners in scoring position, we decrease it by the shortfall in the same way.

Suppose that a player has batted 250 times with runners on base, 250 times with the bases empty, and that he has hit 20 home runs overall. We would expect him to have hit 10 with men on base, 10 with the bases empty, right?

Suppose that he didn't. Suppose that he hit 12 with the bases empty, 8 with men on base. His team would score two runs less than expected because he did this, and we would thus penalize him two runs for the shortfall.

This is our second runs created estimate: the player's runs created, adjusted for his batting performance in run sensitive situations.

Suppose, however, that we figure the runs created for all of the individuals on a team, and we add them up, and it doesn't match the runs actually scored by the team? What if the formulas say that the team should have scored 800 runs, but they actually scored 820?

Then obviously, the formulas missed. We're trying to measure the runs ACTUALLY created by each hitter as best we can, in the real world, not the theoretical impact of some combination of singles, doubles, triples and walks. If the actual number is different than the estimates, we have to adjust the estimates to fit the facts. In this case—820 runs scored with only 800 runs created— we would multiply each runs created estimate by 820/800, or 1.025. Then we round it off to an integer, and that's the player's estimated runs created.

Let go of that cat, Arthur. Heck, the moon isn't full for three weeks, anyway.

Runs Created (Single Game)
The single-game Runs Created Formula, like all Runs Created formulas, has an A Factor, a B Factor, and a C Factor.

The A factor, which is basically "Times On Base", is
H + BB + HBP - (IBB/3) - GDP - CS

In other words, intentional walks count as times on base, but they only count as 2/3 of a time on base, because the intentional walk generally occurs late in the inning. Nobody intentionally walks the leadoff hitter.

The B Factor, which is basically "Potential advancement of other runners", is:
TB + (BB + HBP - IBB) * .3 + (SH + SF + 1.6 * SB) * .4 - SO * .07

And the C factor, which is basically "Context", is just plate appearances:
AB + BB + HBP + SH + SF

But these are not put together simply as A * B / C, as some runs created formulas are, but rather are placed in a neutral context before they are evaluated. The formula is:

$(11.035 + \text{A Factor}) * (13 + \text{B Factor}) / (36 + \text{C Factor}) - 4 + (.0015 * (\text{C Factor} = 0))$

So let us say that a player goes 1 for 4 with the one hit being a single, but also has a strikeout in the game. Then his A factor would be 1.00, his B factor would be .93, and his C Factor would be 4. So his Runs Created in the game would be

$(12.035 * 13.93) / 40 - 4 + (0)$

Which is .191. Basically, we expect his team to score 4 runs in every game, PLUS however many he creates. The +.0015 if the C factor is zero is just a little nuisance thing. .0015 is 1 over 667; for some reason the formula is just that much off of zero if a player has no plate appearance (and no stolen base or caught stealing), which you don't need to worry about unless he has no plate appearances, in which case it looks weird to say that he created .0015 runs.

Or, to take a complicated one, let us suppose that a player in a game goes two-for-four, both singles, but let us suppose that in that game he also has two walks, one of them intentional and the other not, and that in that game he also has a stolen base, a caught stealing, and grounds into a double play. (That would be Paul Molitor on June 8, 1985). Then in runs created for the game would be:
A Factor = 1.67 (2 + 2 - .333 - 1 - 1)
B Factor = 2.94 (2 + .3 + (.16 * .4))
C Factor = 6
Runs Created = (12.705 * 15.94) / 42 - 4
Which works out to .821.

Add up the Runs Created in each game and it should match a player's season-level Runs Created as nearly as possible.

Runs Created per 27 Outs (RC/27)
This statistic estimates the number of runs per game that a team made up of nine of the same player would score. To calculate RC/27, multiply Runs Created by league outs per team game, divide the result by outs made by the player (the sum of at bats plus sacrifice hits plus sacrifice flies plus caught stealing plus grounded into double plays, minus hits). The formula written out is:

$$\frac{\frac{RC \times 3 \times LgIP}{2 \times LgG}}{AB - H + SH + SF + CS + GDP}$$

Runs Saved
See Defensive Runs Saved.

Save Opportunities
The sum of Saves and Blown Saves (see Save Situation).

Save/Hold Percentage (same as Holds Adjusted Saves Percentage)
The sum of Saves and Holds, divided by the sum of Saves, Holds, and Blown Saves.

For several years we figured "Save Percentage", which is simply Saves divided by Save Opportunities, and this stat had some currency in the game. But the Save Percentage severely discriminates against middle relievers, who have no real chance to be credited with the Save, since they will be taken out of the game and replaced by the Closer even if they throw 110 miles an hour and strike out everybody they see. Middle relievers typically have Save Percentages of zero, even if they pitch well. The Save/Hold Percentage is a much more realistic evaluation of a pitcher's success in Save situations.

Save Percentage

A pitcher's Saves divided by the total number of Save Situations he faces (see definition for Save Situation).

Save Situation

A relief pitcher is in a Save Situation when he enters the game with his team in the lead, has the opportunity to finish the game, is not the winning pitcher of record at the time, and meets any one of the three following conditions:

1.The pitcher's team is leading by no more than three runs and the pitcher has the chance to pitch for at least one inning,

OR

2.The pitcher enters the game with the potential tying run on base, at bat, or on deck,

OR

3. The pitcher pitches three or more effective innings regardless of the lead. The determination of a save in this situation is made by the official scorer.

It is not possible to have more than one save credited to a single team in a game.

SB Gain (Baserunning)

Stolen Base attempts must be successful greater than about two thirds of the time to have a positive result on the number of runs scored. SB gain is therefore the number of bases stolen minus two times the number of caught stealing (SB Gain = SB - 2CS). For example, a runner steals 30 bases and is caught stealing 7 times. His SB Gain would be 30 - 2 * 7 = +16. Another runner steals 10 bases and is caught stealing 6 times. His SB Gain (actually a loss) would be 10 - 2 * 6 = -2.

SB Success Percentage

Stolen Bases divided by the number of Stolen Base attempts (Stolen Bases plus Caught Stealing).

$$\frac{SB}{SB + CS}$$

Secondary Average

A number meant to reflect everything else except for batting average. A player will have a high Secondary Average if he hits for power, takes walks and steals bases. It is calculated with the following formula:

$$\frac{TB - H + BB + SB}{AB}$$

Similarity Score
A number which reflects the similarity between two different statistical lines, either for a player or for a team. A score of 1,000 means that the statistical lines are identical.

Slow Hooks
Used in the Manager's Record. For Quick Hooks and Slow Hooks a score is calculated for each game that is the sum of the number of Pitches plus 10 times the number of Runs Allowed. The top 25% of scores in the league are considered to be Slow Hooks.

Slugging Average
Total Bases divided by At Bats.

Slugging Average on Balls in Play (SlgBIP)
Total bases gained on balls in play divided by balls in play. Home runs are not counted as balls in play.

Speed Score
Speed score is an estimate of a player's running speed, based on six indicators of running speed found in his batting and fielding records. Those six indicators are stolen base success rate, the frequency of stolen base attempts, triples, grounding into double plays, runs scored as a percentage of times on base, and defensive position and range.

The full process of estimating Speed Scores is long and complex, and can be found on Bill James Online or by contacting Baseball Info Solutions.

Total Bases (TB)
Hits plus Doubles plus (2 times Triples) plus (3 times Home Runs).

$$H + 2B + (2 \times 3B) + (3 \times HR)$$

Tough Loss
A starting pitcher who loses the game with a game score (see definition for Game Score) over 50 gets credit for a tough loss.

Tough Save
This label is used to separate Saves by difficulty level (Easy or Tough). A Save is considered Tough if the relief pitcher enters the game with the tying run on base.

Total Chances (TC)
The number of plays in which a defensive player participated, determined as Assists + Putouts + Errors.

Unproductive Out
An out made by the batter with runners on base that fails to advance any baserunner or results in a weaker baserunner configuration than before. Excludes the third out of an inning. See also Productive Out.

Win Probability
The probability of a team winning the game determined at any time during the game based on the score, inning, outs and base situation.

Win Shares

Win Shares are a system devised by Bill James for valuing a player's overall contribution to his team over a season. This allows us to more effectively compare players across positions, even between pitchers and position players. The use of the word "shares" is important, because they are split up among players based on how many wins a team actually earns. For each win, a team has three Win Shares to allocate among its players. Those shares are then allocated according to how much each player contributed to the team's run scoring and prevention.

Winning Percentage

Wins divided by (Wins plus Losses).

Minor League Abbreviation Key

Abbreviation	Team	Level	League	MLB Affiliate	First Year	Last Year
Abrdn	Aberdeen IronBirds	A-	New York-Penn League	Baltimore Orioles	2016	2019
Akron	Akron RubberDucks	AA	Eastern League	Cleveland Indians	2016	2019
Albq	Albuquerque Isotopes	AAA	Pacific Coast League	Colorado Rockies	2016	2019
Altna	Altoona Curve	AA	Eastern League	Pittsburgh Pirates	2016	2019
Amrillo	Amarillo Sod Poodles	AA	Texas League	San Diego Padres	2019	2019
Angels	AZL Angels	R	Arizona League	Los Angeles Angels	2016	2019
Ark	Arkansas Travelers	AA	Texas League	Los Angeles Angels	2016	2016
Ark	Arkansas Travelers	AA	Texas League	Seattle Mariners	2017	2019
As	AZL Athletics	R	Arizona League	Oakland Athletics	2016	2018
AsGold	AZL Athletics Gold	R	Arizona League	Oakland Athletics	2019	2019
AsGrn	AZL Athletics Green	R	Arizona League	Oakland Athletics	2019	2019
Ashvll	Asheville Tourists	A	South Atlantic League	Colorado Rockies	2016	2019
Astros	GCL Astros	R	Gulf Coast League	Houston Astros	2016	2019
Auburn	Auburn Doubledays	A-	New York-Penn League	Washington Nationals	2016	2019
Augsta	Augusta GreenJackets	A	South Atlantic League	San Francisco Giants	2016	2019
B Jays	GCL Blue Jays	R	Gulf Coast League	Toronto Blue Jays	2016	2019
Batvia	Batavia Muckdogs	A-	New York-Penn League	Miami Marlins	2016	2019
Beloit	Beloit Snappers	A	Midwest League	Oakland Athletics	2016	2019
BG	Bowling Green Hot Rods	A	Midwest League	Tampa Bay Rays	2016	2019
Billings	Billings Mustangs	R+	Pioneer League	Cincinnati Reds	2016	2019
Biloxi	Biloxi Shuckers	AA	Southern League	Milwaukee Brewers	2016	2019
Bklyn	Brooklyn Cyclones	A-	New York-Penn League	New York Mets	2016	2019
Bkrsfld	Bakersfield Blaze	A+	California League	Seattle Mariners	2016	2016
Bluefld	Bluefield Blue Jays	R+	Appalachian League	Toronto Blue Jays	2016	2019
Bnghtn	Binghamton Mets	AA	Eastern League	New York Mets	2016	2016
Bnghtn	Binghamton Rumble Ponies	AA	Eastern League	New York Mets	2017	2019
Boise	Boise Hawks	A-	Northwest League	Colorado Rockies	2016	2019
Bowie	Bowie Baysox	AA	Eastern League	Baltimore Orioles	2016	2019
Bradtn	Bradenton Marauders	A+	Florida State League	Pittsburgh Pirates	2016	2019
Braves	GCL Braves	R	Gulf Coast League	Atlanta Braves	2016	2019
BrewersB	AZL Brewers Blue	R	Arizona League	Milwaukee Brewers	2019	2019
Brewrs	AZL Brewers	R	Arizona League	Milwaukee Brewers	2016	2018
BrewrsGold	AZL Brewers Gold	R	Arizona League	Milwaukee Brewers	2019	2019
Brham	Birmingham Barons	AA	Southern League	Chicago White Sox	2016	2019
Brstol	Bristol Pirates	R+	Appalachian League	Pittsburgh Pirates	2016	2019
BrvdCt	Brevard Co. Manatees	A+	Florida State League	Milwaukee Brewers	2016	2016
Buffalo	Buffalo Bisons	AAA	International League	Toronto Blue Jays	2016	2019
BuiesCk	Buies Creek Astros	A+	Carolina League	Houston Astros	2017	2018
Burlgtn	Burlington IA Bees	A	Midwest League	Los Angeles Angels	2016	2019
Burlgtn	Burlington NC Royals	R+	Appalachian League	Kansas City Royals	2016	2019
Cards	GCL Cardinals	R	Gulf Coast League	St Louis Cardinals	2016	2019
Carlina	Carolina Mudcats	A+	Carolina League	Atlanta Braves	2016	2016
Carlina	Carolina Mudcats	A+	Carolina League	Milwaukee Brewers	2017	2019
Charllt	Charlotte NC Knights	AAA	International League	Chicago White Sox	2016	2019
Charltt	Charlotte FL Stone Crabs	A+	Florida State League	Tampa Bay Rays	2016	2019
Chatt	Chattanooga Lookouts	AA	Southern League	Minnesota Twins	2016	2018
Chatt	Chattanooga Lookouts	AA	Southern League	Cincinnati Reds	2019	2019
Clinton	Clinton LumberKings	A	Midwest League	Seattle Mariners	2016	2018
Clinton	Clinton LumberKings	A	Midwest League	Miami Marlins	2019	2019
Clmbs	Columbus Clippers	AAA	International League	Cleveland Indians	2016	2019
Clrwtr	Clearwater Threshers	A+	Florida State League	Philadelphia Phillies	2016	2019
ColSpr	Colorado Spr. Sky Sox	AAA	Pacific Coast League	Milwaukee Brewers	2016	2018
Columb	Columbia Fireflies	A	South Atlantic League	New York Mets	2016	2019
Conn	Connecticut Tigers	A-	New York-Penn League	Detroit Tigers	2016	2019
CpChr	Corpus Christi Hooks	AA	Texas League	Houston Astros	2016	2019
Crpds	Cedar Rapids Kernels	A	Midwest League	Minnesota Twins	2016	2019
CtnSC	Charleston RiverDogs	A	South Atlantic League	New York Yankees	2016	2019
Cubs	AZL Cubs	R	Arizona League	Chicago Cubs	2016	2019
Cubs2	AZL Cubs2	R	Arizona League	Chicago Cubs	2018	2019
Danvle	Danville Braves	R+	Appalachian League	Atlanta Braves	2016	2019
Dayton	Dayton Dragons	A	Midwest League	Cincinnati Reds	2016	2019
Dbcks	AZL D-backs	R	Arizona League	Arizona Diamondbacks	2016	2019

Minor League Abbreviation Key

Abbreviation	Team	Level	League	MLB Affiliate	First Year	Last Year
Ddgrs	AZL Dodgers	R	Arizona League	Los Angeles Dodgers	2016	2018
Ddgrs	AZL Dodgers 1	R	Arizona League	Los Angeles Dodgers	2019	2019
Ddgrs2	AZL Dodgers 2	R	Arizona League	Los Angeles Dodgers	2019	2019
Dlmrva	Delmarva Shorebirds	A	South Atlantic League	Baltimore Orioles	2016	2019
Dnedin	Dunedin Blue Jays	A+	Florida State League	Toronto Blue Jays	2016	2019
Drham	Durham Bulls	AAA	International League	Tampa Bay Rays	2016	2019
DwnEast	Down East Wood Ducks	A+	Carolina League	Texas Rangers	2017	2019
Dytona	Daytona Tortugas	A+	Florida State League	Cincinnati Reds	2016	2019
Elizab	Elizabethton Twins	R+	Appalachian League	Minnesota Twins	2016	2019
ElPaso	El Paso Chihuahuas	AAA	Pacific Coast League	San Diego Padres	2016	2019
Erie	Erie SeaWolves	AA	Eastern League	Detroit Tigers	2016	2019
Eugene	Eugene Emeralds	A-	Northwest League	Chicago Cubs	2016	2019
Everett	Everett AquaSox	A-	Northwest League	Seattle Mariners	2016	2019
Faytvll	Fayetteville Woodpeckers	A+	Carolina League	Houston Astros	2019	2019
Florida	Florida Fire Frogs	A+	Florida State League	Atlanta Braves	2017	2019
Frdrck	Frederick Keys	A+	Carolina League	Baltimore Orioles	2016	2019
Fresno	Fresno Grizzlies	AAA	Pacific Coast League	Houston Astros	2016	2018
Fresno	Fresno Grizzlies	AAA	Pacific Coast League	Washington Nationals	2019	2019
Frisco	Frisco RoughRiders	AA	Texas League	Texas Rangers	2016	2019
FtMyrs	Fort Myers Miracle	A+	Florida State League	Minnesota Twins	2016	2019
FtWyn	Fort Wayne TinCaps	A	Midwest League	San Diego Padres	2016	2019
GdJunc	Grand Junction Rockies	R+	Pioneer League	Colorado Rockies	2016	2019
Giants	AZL Giants	R	Arizona League	San Francisco Giants	2016	2018
Giants Blk	AZL Giants Black	R	Arizona League	San Francisco Giants	2019	2019
Giants Orng	AZL Giants Orange	R	Arizona League	San Francisco Giants	2018	2019
Gr Falls	Great Falls Voyagers	R+	Pioneer League	Chicago White Sox	2016	2019
Grnsbr	Greensboro Grasshoppers	A	South Atlantic League	Miami Marlins	2016	2018
Grnsbr	Greensboro Grasshoppers	A	South Atlantic League	Pittsburgh Pirates	2019	2019
Grnvlle	Greeneville Astros	R+	Appalachian League	Houston Astros	2016	2019
Grnvlle	Greenville Drive	A	South Atlantic League	Boston Red Sox	2016	2019
Gt Lks	Great Lakes Loons	A	Midwest League	Los Angeles Dodgers	2016	2019
Gwnntt	Gwinnett Braves	AAA	International League	Atlanta Braves	2016	2017
Gwnntt	Gwinnett Stripers	AAA	International League	Atlanta Braves	2018	2019
Helena	Helena Brewers	R+	Pioneer League	Milwaukee Brewers	2016	2018
Hgrstn	Hagerstown Suns	A	South Atlantic League	Washington Nationals	2016	2019
Hi Dsrt	High Desert Mavericks	A+	California League	Texas Rangers	2016	2016
Hkry	Hickory Crawdads	A	South Atlantic League	Texas Rangers	2016	2019
Hlsbro	Hillsboro Hops	A-	Northwest League	Arizona Diamondbacks	2016	2019
Hrsbrg	Harrisburg Senators	AA	Eastern League	Washington Nationals	2016	2019
Hrtfrd	Hartford Yard Goats	AA	Eastern League	Colorado Rockies	2016	2019
HudVal	Hudson Valley Renegades	A-	New York-Penn League	Tampa Bay Rays	2016	2019
Idaho	Idaho Falls Chukars	R+	Pioneer League	Kansas City Royals	2016	2019
Indians	AZL Indians Blue	R	Arizona League	Cleveland Indians	2019	2019
Indians2	AZL Indians2	R	Arizona League	Cleveland Indians	2018	2018
IndiansR	AZL Indians Red	R	Arizona League	Cleveland Indians	2019	2019
Indns	AZL Indians	R	Arizona League	Cleveland Indians	2016	2018
Indy	Indianapolis Indians	AAA	International League	Pittsburgh Pirates	2016	2019
InldEm	Inland Empire 66ers	A+	California League	Los Angeles Angels	2016	2019
Iowa	Iowa Cubs	AAA	Pacific Coast League	Chicago Cubs	2016	2019
Jacksn	Jackson Generals	AA	Southern League	Seattle Mariners	2016	2016
Jacksn	Jackson Generals	AA	Southern League	Arizona Diamondbacks	2017	2019
Jaxnvl	Jacksonville Suns	AA	Southern League	Miami Marlins	2016	2016
Jaxnvl	Jacksonville Jumbo Shrimp	AA	Southern League	Miami Marlins	2017	2019
Jhscty	Johnson City Cardinals	R+	Appalachian League	St Louis Cardinals	2016	2019
Jupiter	Jupiter Hammerheads	A+	Florida State League	Miami Marlins	2016	2019
Kane	Kane County Cougars	A	Midwest League	Arizona Diamondbacks	2016	2019
Knapol	Kannapolis Intimidators	A	South Atlantic League	Chicago White Sox	2016	2019
Kngspt	Kingsport Mets	R+	Appalachian League	New York Mets	2016	2019
Lakwd	Lakewood BlueClaws	A	South Atlantic League	Philadelphia Phillies	2016	2019
Lancst	Lancaster JetHawks	A+	California League	Houston Astros	2016	2016
Lancst	Lancaster JetHawks	A+	California League	Colorado Rockies	2017	2019
Lk Cty	Lake County Captains	A	Midwest League	Cleveland Indians	2016	2019
Lk Els	Lake Elsinore Storm	A+	California League	San Diego Padres	2016	2019
Lkland	Lakeland Flying Tigers	A+	Florida State League	Detroit Tigers	2016	2019

Minor League Abbreviation Key

Abbreviation	Team	Level	League	MLB Affiliate	First Year	Last Year
Lnsng	Lansing Lugnuts	A	Midwest League	Toronto Blue Jays	2016	2019
Lowell	Lowell Spinners	A-	New York-Penn League	Boston Red Sox	2016	2019
LsVgs	Las Vegas 51s	AAA	Pacific Coast League	New York Mets	2016	2018
LsVgs	Las Vegas Aviators	AAA	Pacific Coast League	Oakland Athletics	2019	2019
Lsvlle	Louisville Bats	AAA	International League	Cincinnati Reds	2016	2019
LV	Lehigh Valley IronPigs	AAA	International League	Philadelphia Phillies	2016	2019
Lxngtn	Lexington Legends	A	South Atlantic League	Kansas City Royals	2016	2019
Lynbrg	Lynchburg Hillcats	A+	Carolina League	Cleveland Indians	2016	2019
Mdest	Modesto Nuts	A+	California League	Colorado Rockies	2016	2016
Mdest	Modesto Nuts	A+	California League	Seattle Mariners	2017	2019
Mdlnd	Midland RockHounds	AA	Texas League	Oakland Athletics	2016	2019
Memp	Memphis Redbirds	AAA	Pacific Coast League	St Louis Cardinals	2016	2019
Mets	GCL Mets	R	Gulf Coast League	New York Mets	2016	2019
MhVlly	Mahoning Valley Scrappers	A-	New York-Penn League	Cleveland Indians	2016	2019
Missi	Mississippi Braves	AA	Southern League	Atlanta Braves	2016	2019
Mobile	Mobile BayBears	AA	Southern League	Arizona Diamondbacks	2016	2016
Mobile	Mobile BayBears	AA	Southern League	Los Angeles Angels	2017	2019
Mont	Montgomery Biscuits	AA	Southern League	Tampa Bay Rays	2016	2019
Mrlns	GCL Marlins	R	Gulf Coast League	Miami Marlins	2016	2019
MrtlBh	Myrtle Beach Pelicans	A+	Carolina League	Chicago Cubs	2016	2019
Ms	AZL Mariners	R	Arizona League	Seattle Mariners	2016	2019
Msoula	Missoula Osprey	R+	Pioneer League	Arizona Diamondbacks	2016	2019
Nashv	Nashville Sounds	AAA	Pacific Coast League	Oakland Athletics	2016	2018
Nashv	Nashville Sounds	AAA	Pacific Coast League	Texas Rangers	2019	2019
Nats	GCL Nationals	R	Gulf Coast League	Washington Nationals	2016	2019
NewOr	New Orleans Zephyrs	AAA	Pacific Coast League	Miami Marlins	2016	2016
NewOr	New Orleans Baby Cakes	AAA	Pacific Coast League	Miami Marlins	2017	2019
Nham	New Hampshire Fisher Cats	AA	Eastern League	Toronto Blue Jays	2016	2019
Norfolk	Norfolk Tides	AAA	International League	Baltimore Orioles	2016	2019
NWArk	NW Arkansas Naturals	AA	Texas League	Kansas City Royals	2016	2019
Ogden	Ogden Raptors	R+	Pioneer League	Los Angeles Dodgers	2016	2019
OkCity	Oklahoma City Dodgers	AAA	Pacific Coast League	Los Angeles Dodgers	2016	2019
Omha	Omaha Storm Chasers	AAA	Pacific Coast League	Kansas City Royals	2016	2019
Orem	Orem Owlz	R+	Pioneer League	Los Angeles Angels	2016	2019
Orioles	GCL Orioles	R	Gulf Coast League	Baltimore Orioles	2016	2019
Padres	AZL Padres	R	Arizona League	San Diego Padres	2016	2019
Padres2	AZL Padres2	R	Arizona League	San Diego Padres	2017	2019
Peoria	Peoria Chiefs	A	Midwest League	St Louis Cardinals	2016	2019
Phillies	GCL Phillies	R	Gulf Coast League	Philadelphia Phillies	2016	2019
PhilliesW	GCL Phillies West	R	Gulf Coast League	Philadelphia Phillies	2016	2019
Pirates	GCL Pirates	R	Gulf Coast League	Pittsburgh Pirates	2016	2019
PlmBh	Palm Beach Cardinals	A+	Florida State League	St Louis Cardinals	2016	2019
Pnscla	Pensacola Blue Wahoos	AA	Southern League	Cincinnati Reds	2016	2018
Pnscla	Pensacola Blue Wahoos	AA	Southern League	Minnesota Twins	2019	2019
Portlnd	Portland ME Sea Dogs	AA	Eastern League	Boston Red Sox	2016	2019
Prnctn	Princeton Rays	R+	Appalachian League	Tampa Bay Rays	2016	2019
Ptomc	Potomac Nationals	A+	Carolina League	Washington Nationals	2016	2019
Pulski	Pulaski Yankees	R+	Appalachian League	New York Yankees	2016	2019
Pwtckt	Pawtucket Red Sox	AAA	International League	Boston Red Sox	2016	2019
QuadC	Quad Cities River Bandits	A	Midwest League	Houston Astros	2016	2019
Rays	GCL Rays	R	Gulf Coast League	Tampa Bay Rays	2016	2019
Rchmd	Richmond Flying Squirrels	AA	Eastern League	San Francisco Giants	2016	2019
RckyMt	Rocky Mountain Vibes	R+	Pioneer League	Milwaukee Brewers	2019	2019
Rcuca	Rancho Cucamonga Quakes	A+	California League	Los Angeles Dodgers	2016	2019
Rdng	Reading Fightin Phils	AA	Eastern League	Philadelphia Phillies	2016	2019
RdRck	Round Rock Express	AAA	Pacific Coast League	Texas Rangers	2016	2018
RdRck	Round Rock Express	AAA	Pacific Coast League	Houston Astros	2019	2019
Reds	AZL Reds	R	Arizona League	Cincinnati Reds	2016	2019
RedSx	GCL Red Sox	R	Gulf Coast League	Boston Red Sox	2016	2019
Reno	Reno Aces	AAA	Pacific Coast League	Arizona Diamondbacks	2016	2019
Rngrs	AZL Rangers	R	Arizona League	Texas Rangers	2016	2019
Roch	Rochester Red Wings	AAA	International League	Minnesota Twins	2016	2019
Rome	Rome Braves	A	South Atlantic League	Atlanta Braves	2016	2019
Royals	AZL Royals	R	Arizona League	Kansas City Royals	2016	2019

Minor League Abbreviation Key

Abbreviation	Team	Level	League	MLB Affiliate	First Year	Last Year
Salem	Salem Red Sox	A+	Carolina League	Boston Red Sox	2016	2019
Salt Lk	Salt Lake City Bees	AAA	Pacific Coast League	Los Angeles Angels	2016	2019
Sbend	South Bend Cubs	A	Midwest League	Chicago Cubs	2016	2019
Scrmto	Sacramento River Cats	AAA	Pacific Coast League	San Francisco Giants	2016	2019
SlKzr	Salem-Keizer Volcanoes	A-	Northwest League	San Francisco Giants	2016	2019
SnAnt	San Antonio Missions	AA	Texas League	San Diego Padres	2016	2018
SnAnt	San Antonio Missions	AAA	Pacific Coast League	Milwaukee Brewers	2019	2019
SnJos	San Jose Giants	A+	California League	San Francisco Giants	2016	2019
Spkane	Spokane Indians	A-	Northwest League	Texas Rangers	2016	2019
Sprgfld	Springfield Cardinals	AA	Texas League	St Louis Cardinals	2016	2019
Stcktn	Stockton Ports	A+	California League	Oakland Athletics	2016	2019
StCol	State College Spikes	A-	New York-Penn League	St Louis Cardinals	2016	2019
Stluci	St. Lucie Mets	A+	Florida State League	New York Mets	2016	2019
Stnlld	Staten Island Yankees	A-	New York-Penn League	New York Yankees	2016	2019
S-WB	Scranton WB RailRiders	AAA	International League	New York Yankees	2016	2019
Syrcse	Syracuse Chiefs	AAA	International League	Washington Nationals	2016	2018
Syrcse	Syracuse Mets	AAA	International League	New York Mets	2019	2019
Tacom	Tacoma Rainiers	AAA	Pacific Coast League	Seattle Mariners	2016	2019
Tampa	Tampa Yankees	A+	Florida State League	New York Yankees	2016	2017
Tampa	Tampa Tarpons	A+	Florida State League	New York Yankees	2018	2019
Tenn	Tennessee Smokies	AA	Southern League	Chicago Cubs	2016	2019
Tigers	GCL Tigers	R	Gulf Coast League	Detroit Tigers	2016	2019
TigersW	GCL Tigers West	R	Gulf Coast League	Detroit Tigers	2016	2019
Toledo	Toledo Mud Hens	AAA	International League	Detroit Tigers	2016	2019
TriCity	Tri-City NY ValleyCats	A-	New York-Penn League	Houston Astros	2016	2019
TriCity	Tri-City WA Dust Devils	A-	Northwest League	San Diego Padres	2016	2019
Trntn	Trenton Thunder	AA	Eastern League	New York Yankees	2016	2019
Tulsa	Tulsa Drillers	AA	Texas League	Los Angeles Dodgers	2016	2019
Twins	GCL Twins	R	Gulf Coast League	Minnesota Twins	2016	2019
Vancvr	Vancouver Canadians	A-	Northwest League	Toronto Blue Jays	2016	2019
Visalia	Visalia Rawhide	A+	California League	Arizona Diamondbacks	2016	2019
Vrmnt	Vermont Lake Monsters	A-	New York-Penn League	Oakland Athletics	2016	2019
Wilmg	Wilmington Blue Rocks	A+	Carolina League	Kansas City Royals	2016	2019
WinSa	Winston-Salem Dash	A+	Carolina League	Chicago White Sox	2016	2019
Wisc	Wisconsin Timber Rattlers	A	Midwest League	Milwaukee Brewers	2016	2019
Wmich	West Michigan Whitecaps	A	Midwest League	Detroit Tigers	2016	2019
Wmspt	Williamsport Crosscutters	A-	New York-Penn League	Philadelphia Phillies	2016	2019
Wsox	AZL White Sox	R	Arizona League	Chicago White Sox	2016	2019
WV	West Virginia Power	A	South Atlantic League	Pittsburgh Pirates	2016	2018
WV	West Virginia Power	A	South Atlantic League	Seattle Mariners	2019	2019
WV	West Virginia Black Bears	A-	New York-Penn League	Pittsburgh Pirates	2016	2019
Yanks1	GCL Yankees	R	Gulf Coast League	New York Yankees	2016	2019
Yanks2	GCL Yankees2	R	Gulf Coast League	New York Yankees	2016	2019

Baseball Info Solutions

Since the company's founding, analytics' place in sports has changed a lot, but Baseball Info Solutions (BIS) has remained true to its objective. The company's mission is to provide the most accurate, in-depth, and timely professional baseball, football, and basketball data, including cutting-edge research and analysis, striving to educate professional teams and the public about sports analytics. BIS is thrilled to work with the majority of teams in Major League Baseball as a part of that goal. It also operates as Sports Info Solutions, delivering NFL and NCAA FBS advanced data to broadcasters, NFL teams and directly to the public, as well as advanced NBA draft prospect data to NBA teams.

It all begins with the data collection operation. BIS's staff of operations analysts does excellent work in organizing the ever-expanding crew of highly trained video scouts, and together they record data from every Major League Baseball, Nippon Professional Baseball, and Korean Baseball Organization game, as well as many minor league games. That data covers everything from basic box score data to pitch locations, types, and velocities to batted ball hang times, defensive shifts, and much more. BIS collects a lot of data that cannot be found any place else. BIS video scouts log 10-12 hours on every game capturing the most in-depth information possible.

The data itself is valuable to many clients, but BIS's research and development department creates analytics and undertakes research projects with the data to help it reach its full potential utility. Their most well-known endeavor is the Defensive Runs Saved statistic, which estimates how many runs fielders save their teams because of a variety of skills such as range, throwing, prevention of stolen bases, pitch framing, many other factors. Recent R&D department innovations include applying ally collected infielder positioning data to make enhancements to DRS and the of a Synthetic Statcast tool.

an co-founded BIS in 2002, having already spent a couple of decades in the the forefront of the sabermetric movement. He got his start in the field as e Director of Project Scoresheet, which was a Bill James-led effort to oely collect baseball data. This led to the incorporation and development from a bedroom office to its sale to News Corp in 2000. Without those be the statistics and analytics that we all take for granted may not even

If
ope contact Baseball Info Solutions for data inquiries, potential job
al information, you can reach us at:
Bas
41 S
Copl
610-2
www.
www.s
m

Acknowledgments

The production of the 32nd edition of *The Bill James Handbook* was as unique as the 2020 baseball season, and while the counting stats didn't climb as high as usual this year, the number of things that had to be adjusted and accounted for were at all-time levels. On top of that, with a season that started on July 23 and the book due to the publisher by October 12, the book—like the season—had to be completed on a condensed timeline. Add to these facts that our office is still not open to full capacity and it's a wonder that this book will once again be on bookshelves by November 1. An extra special thank you goes out to all of those with a hand in the *Handbook*.

At the top of the list of people to thank is Bill James, without whom none of what we all get to do for a living would be possible. He has inspired all of us, and we are grateful for the opportunity to work with him and to continue to be enriched by his insight.

On the topic of allowing us to analyze sports for a living, we are all very appreciative of the primary owners of Baseball Info Solutions, Sue and John Dewan. During a tumultuous year, they each exerted considerable effort to provide constant assistance, including ensuring that the company did not layoff or furlough any full-time employees. Sue serves as our Director of Human Resources, while John is our CEO and final approver of everything that goes into the *Handbook*. They started BIS in 2002 along with Steve Moyer, who has since passed but whose contributions live on. John and Sue also serve on the Board of Directors of The Dewan Foundation, a non-profit that provides grants to people in poverty by supporting U.S. based charitable organizations that help the poorest of the poor help themselves.

The President of Baseball Info Solutions, Rob Dougherty, wears too many hats to enumerate in his role at the driver's seat of the organization. He leads our overall strategic vision and financial success, amongst other responsibilities, and he provided a steady hand as we weathered the storm that has been 2020. In terms of the book process, Rob oversees things from an executive level and works with our publisher to handle the business of the book.

Joe Rosales has done a truly extraordinary job as the point person for the production of *The Bill James Handbook*. If there were a statistic for book production that could take into account context akin to the way that DRS adjusts for play difficulty, it would show that Joe had an October that would make Reggie Jackson blush.

Along with Joe, there are a few individuals who went above-and-beyond to make this book possible. Jon Vrecsics leads the quality control process on every stat in the book, including all of the particularly bizarre-looking ones because of the shortened season, a massive undertaking. On the technical side, Will Creager and Brian Reiff not only did all the dirty work to put the book into the form that you see it in today, but they also had to code countless adjustments for all of the big and little things that made this season unique.

Our Operations Department is responsible for gathering the data that is at the very core of what we do. They deserve great thanks for both their incredible attention to detail and their ability to continually readjust to all of the schedule changes and other challenges that 2020 placed in front of us. They were the first ones back in our office (at half capacity) after the country reopened, and as always, they never missed a score, chart, audit, anomaly report, or any of the other countless steps that go into creating the most pristine data in existence.

The aforementioned Jon Vrecsics is our Director of Operations, leading a team that includes Dan Casey, Todd Radcliffe, Nathan Phares, Jason Paff, Michael Churchward, Josh Hofer, Ted Baarda, Cole Ratliff, Justin Stine, John Verros, Evan Butler, Ken Gaffney, and David Salway. A tip of the cap also goes out to Tim Kwilos, who was a tremendous help in a part-time role.

In case you are curious to learn more about football or basketball, you will be excited to learn that Baseball Info Solutions has expanded in recent years, and we now also go by the name Sports Info Solutions. Along those lines, that means that we now have Operations for those sports as well. Matt Manocherian has been instrumental in the success of that expansion as Vice President of Football and Research. He works with Dan Foehrenbach and Nathan Cooper to lead our Football Operation.

Our newly formed Basketball Operation is led by Jake Loos, who previously served as the Director of Analytics for the Phoenix Suns. His ground-breaking vision in NBA Draft analytics sets the basis for the company's newest expansion. His team includes Sergio Santamaria, Spencer Pearlman, Baxter Price, Brooks Bellman, Grant Aqui, Derek Murray, Max Carlin, Connor Ayubi and Christien Wright.

Senior Researcher and Strategic Advisor Joe Rosales leads all baseball-related research initiatives, while Matt Manocherian oversees the Research and Development Department. Their team includes the key staff responsible for the bulk of the content and analytics that you find in the book. Lindsay Zeck, Alex Vigderman, Mark Simon, John Shirley, and Bryce Rossler round out the current R&D team, and we'd also like to thank Andrew Kyne (now of the Cincinnati Reds), Nate Weller, and former intern Logan King (now of Vanderbilt Football) for their contributions over the past year. Check out SportsInfoSolutionsBlog.com for more baseball, football, and basketball research all year long!

The SIS Information Technology Department is the silent engine that enables all of this data collection and research to make it to our team clients and the public. Director of IT Patrick Coyle leads an incredibly talented team featuring Will Creager, Brian Reiff, Tim Paul, Zach Smith, Megan McGrail, Ruben Agosto, and Ronan Potts, and formerly featuring Craig Saboe and Brandyn Bechtel. They work tirelessly to develop new applications for internal and external use, and they service the myriad needs of our clients in all sports.

Corey March leads our Business Development initiatives along with Noah Gatsik and Kyle Rodemann. Carol Olsen manages our office and works closely with our HR Specialist, Melanie Pries. Carol and Melanie deserve a special shout-out for all of the work they have done on behalf of our employees through all the twists and turns of this year. Additionally, our Accountant/Bookkeeper Kelly Pohl works diligently to ensure that all of our finances are in line, with key assistance given as needed by Jason Trifilo.

We are especially grateful to all of our outstanding team of Video Scouts, this year more than ever. Their dedication and attention to detail provide the foundation of our business.

Senior Video Scouts are full-time employees who contribute to multiple operations within the company. They include: Jeff Dean, Segev Goldberg, Ben Hrkach, Nick Rabasco, John Todd, Dan Wallie, Stephen Marciello, Glen Mueller, Chad Tedder, Alec Mallon, and Jordan Edwards.

Our Video Scout Associates have spent multiple seasons with us, and they include: Brendon Baker, Christian Beyer, Colin Grant, Jeff Israel, Johnny Kraft, Corey Leaden, Joey Mahon, Chance Peacock, Francis Pinckney, Christopher Ranalli, Dominick Ricotta, Max Schell, Brandon Tew, and Joseph Wittreich.

Our Video Scouts are made up of: Alexander Arcidiacono, Nicholas Armetta, Christopher Ashley, Bryan Borruso, Graydon Bower, Dayquam Bridges, Riley Caldwell, Christian Chavez, Seamus Cole, Jai Correa, Nicholas Costanza, Alex Courtney, Trey Daubert, Patrick Deken, Andrew Delzotto, Evan Dennis, Vincent DiSilvio, Dylan Dobert, Christopher Dominguez, Nikolas Donadic, Brett Downey, Corey Eiferman, Aaron Furman, Louis Goedeker, Zach Harrison, Allen Ho, Noah Hole, Luke Iorio, Ben Jaffy, Harrison Jewell, Daniel Jimenez, Stephanie Johnson, Joseph Kircher, Payton Kuhnel, Trey Lake, Adam Lan, Andrew LeMaster, Alex Macias, Brooks Mattingly, Josiah McBride, Cullen Mersch, Sam Minier, Adam Modic, Spencer Moyer, Andrew Onder, Drew Onega, Christopher Pettit, Anthony Piraro, Brian Ransom, Steve Schwarz, Chandler Shumake, Adam Sinkoe, Matthew Skiba, Kevin Spiegel, Tanner Tenore, Blake Thomas, Will Topham, Darren Trainor, Patrick Vandergrift, Samson Waisanen, Justin Wasik, Daniel Worth, and Ethan Young.

Our partners at ACTA Publications include publisher Greg Pierce, cover designer Tom Wright, Fielding Bible logo designer Patricia Lynch, and customer service and fulfillment team Mary Rickey, Kathy Pierce, and Isz.

Thank you to our friends in the baseball industry who have helped us over the years. They include: Andy Andres, David Appelman, Scott Bush, Jim Callis, Dave Cameron, Chris Dial, Rylan Edwards, Tony Farwell, Sean Forman, Fred Fosnacht, Peter Gammons, Vince Genarro, Jason Grey, Ben Jedlovec, Brian Kenny, Peter Kreutzer, Michael Lehrer, Ben Lindbergh, Rob Mains, Gene McCaffrey, Rob MacKay, Bob Meyerhoff, Mike Murphy, Rob Neyer, Alex Patton, Mike Phillips, David Pinto, Joe Posnanski, Pat Quinn, Adam Richman, Hal Richman, Travis Sawchik, Brett Sayre, Peter Schoenke, Ron Shandler, Joe Sheehan, John Sickels, Chris Singleton, Dave Studenmund, Tom Tango, Rick Wilton, Don Zminda and Pete Zundel. We would also like to thank Steve Ruskowski for his assistance in stat-checking.

There are too many people to thank for making this book possible to fit them all in this section, but you know who you are, and we extend our sincerest gratitude for your help.

Most importantly, thank you to all of our readers. You inspire us and empower us to continue to dive deeper, and we're thrilled that you keep coming back to learn more about the game that we all love. Thank you for your continued support, and we're already excited to share what we learn with you next year.

NOTES

NOTES

NOTES

NOTES

More From

Like what you read? There are plenty of ways to get more of our content.

Blog:
SPORTSINFOSOLUTIONSBLOG.COM

SIS BASEBALL PODCAST
APPLE PODCASTS, SPOTIFY, ANCHOR, AND MORE

Twitter:
@SPORTSINFO_SIS

Instagram:
@SPORTSINFOSOLUTIONS

Newsletter:
WWW.STATOFTHEWEEK.COM